THE
ACTS AND MONUMENTS

OF

THE CHURCH;

CONTAINING THE HISTORY AND SUFFERINGS OF

THE MARTYRS:

WHEREIN IS SET FORTH AT LARGE THE WHOLE RACE AND COURSE OF THE
CHURCH, FROM THE PRIMITIVE AGE TO THESE LATER TIMES.

WITH

A PRELIMINARY DISSERTATION,

ON THE DIFFERENCE BETWEEN THE CHURCH OF ROME THAT NOW IS,
AND THE ANCIENT CHURCH OF ROME THAT THEN WAS.

BY JOHN FOXE.

WITH A MEMOIR OF THE AUTHOR, BY HIS SON.

A NEW EDITION,

WITH FIVE APPENDICES, CONTAINING
ACCOUNTS OF
THE MASSACRES IN FRANCE: THE DESTRUCTION OF THE SPANISH ARMADA:
THE IRISH REBELLION IN THE YEAR 1641: THE GUNPOWDER TREASON; AND A TRACT,
SHOWING THAT THE EXECUTIONS OF PAPISTS IN QUEEN ELIZABETH'S REIGN,
WERE FOR TREASON AND NOT FOR HERESY.

THE WHOLE CAREFULLY REVISED, CORRECTED, AND CONDENSED.

BY

THE REV. M. HOBART SEYMOUR, M.A.

LONDON:

PRINTED FOR SCOTT, WEBSTER, AND GEARY,
CHARTERHOUSE SQUARE.
1838.

LONDON:
PRINTED BY STEWART AND MURRAY,
OLD BAILEY.

Volume 1

JOHN FOXE.

EDITOR'S PREFACE.

THE energies—exhibited of late, by the emissaries of the Church of Rome, for the re-establishment of her influence in this country—have loudly demanded the re-publication of those works with which our forefathers withered her influence, and baffled her energies. There is no volume in the range of our literature, that has been more effective in maintaining the principles of the Reformation—that noblest of all achievements—than *the Acts and Monuments of Martyrs*, by Master John Foxe. It is this conviction which has induced the present edition of that admirable work.

When we speak of *the Church of Rome*, we speak of a religious, though a fatally erring community. But when we speak of *the Papacy*, we allude to an ecclesiastical system, which not only teaches such absurdities as Transubstantiation—such blasphemies as the Sacrifice of the Mass—such idolatry as the Worship of Saints—and such a novelty as her Creed, but also has elevated an Italian Bishop to the throne of an Italian Prince, who has territories, and broad domains, and numerous subjects of his own, and placed him in such a peculiar position, that he can bind, by solemn oaths, and demand allegiance from, a portion of the subjects of every other prince. This man—combining in himself the offices of *Priest* and *King*—has been raised to such a lofty pinnacle of secular authority, that he can control, punish, or reward a portion of the subjects of other Princes, so as to secure to himself the service and fealty of all those who, as members of the priesthood, possess either power or influence in other states. We must not regard this as a purely spiritual power, for those persons are bound by the most solemn oaths—not to defend the royalties of their liege sovereign, but—to defend, to the utmost of their power, the usurped or pretended royalties of this Italian Bishop, in the heart of every other state. It is a fearful, and a melancholy fact, that in our own fair England, palmy and beautiful England—the land of the brave, and the home of the free—there should be many hundreds of men, holding and wielding a certain influence in the land, who have been appointed by this foreign potentate, who ought to have no authority in this realm, and who have sworn—not to maintain the royalties of the sovereign of England, but—to maintain the royalties of this Italian Prince.*

As loyal subjects of the sovereign of England, and as liege subjects of the King of kings, we never can consent that this Italian Potentate should possess authority in this realm. We feel that the experience of this nation, and the history of the world have proved, that he exercises his authority to minister to his own ambition, and to the degradation of mankind, and that the ecclesiastical system of Rome is a mighty

---

* The Court of Rome has at present—A. D. 1838—above six hundred Missionary Priests in England.

A

confederacy against the civil liberties, and religious privileges of man. We likewise feel that the emissaries of this system have never been very scrupulous as to the means of accomplishing their ends. It may be the darkening of a nation's glory, as in the time of King John, of England. It may be the sundering of all the civil ties of man, as in the history of the German emperors. It may be the massacre of thousands, as in France, on the day of St. Bartholomew. It may be the tortures of an Inquisition, as in the atmosphere of Spain. It may be the most terrible persecution, as in the reign of Mary, of England. Any, and all means are alike welcome to accomplish the objects of that church, and there is at all times an ample agency, in the Bishops, and Priests— in the Monks and Friars of Rome. By such agency and such means the most potent Monarchs of Europe have been humbled; the most noble Princes of Christendom have been ruined; Emperors have been dethroned, and Kings trampled under foot; Nations have flowed with blood, and Kingdoms have been broken into dust—all to satiate the ambition of an Italian Priest, who, while professing to be meek and lowly, compelled imperial potentates to kiss his feet, and accept their crowns and kingdoms at his hands.

When we contemplate this system—though shorn of much of its power and splendor — concentrating its energies in connexion with all the peculiar doctrines and discipline of the Church of Rome, and endeavouring with all its powers to re-establish her influence in this country, it is high time for every lover of religious liberty, and every friend of civil freedom to make those efforts which seem best calculated to prevent so terrible a calamity.

The Church of Rome has never abandoned her claim to this country; and from the age of the Reformation to the present time, she has repeated her efforts to re-assert that claim with an untiring perseverance. We shall touch on the chief of those efforts which she has made from time to time in this country.

In the time of good King Edward VI. the Church of England was completely emancipated from the influence of these Italian ecclesiastics. The stately and venerable pile which had been marred by the hand of time, was restored to its primitive beauty. Its goodly pillars, that had been overgrown with the mould of years; and its noble arches, that had been overspread with many corruptions, were cleared of all that deformed them. The minions of Priestcraft, who had made it a den of thieves, and had driven their merchandize of men's souls within her porches, were removed and the Church of England returned to her original and apostolic purity. Had the life of this young and gentle Prince been spared, the religious freedom of England had been established beyond the possibility of danger. But it was the purpose of God to scourge this nation with a scourge of scorpions, so as to teach us to cherish an undying hatred of the whole system of Popery, that the memory of its horrors, and its cruelties, might live in the minds of our children, and our children's children, that so there might be cherished among us a high and unwavering resolve that it should never again be established in this country. Edward was taken to his rest, and Mary ascended the throne. We know not what feminine amiabilities she may have naturally possessed, but we do know that she surrendered herself into the hands of the Italian Priests, and they, to use the language of our Redeemer, "made her two-fold more the child of hell than themselves."

It was on the accession of this queen that the Papacy made its first effective efforts to re-establish its influence in this land; Mary, with more zeal than prudence, restored the reign of Popery. To that reign we are to look for a true portraiture of this Italian religion, when possessing influence in a Protestant nation. It is not by the unauthorised professions of modern members of that system, softened and attenuated for a purpose, that we are to look for a living exhibition of its character, but we are to read the records of those times, wherein the Papacy possessed the power of accomplishing its own purposes, and unfolding its own characteristics. If we desire to know the fierceness of the lion, or the ferocity of the tiger, we must view them, not with their teeth drawn, and their claws extracted, and confined within cages of iron, but as in their native wildness they range the forest, or crouch in the jungle. We must form our judgment of the nature of Popery, not from her present chained and fettered state, but from the tendencies she displayed when she possessed power and influence in the nation, and could without restraint accomplish her purposes.

The peculiar characteristic of the effort made in this reign to restore the dominion of the Papacy was PERSECUTION. Mary commenced her career with a fearful abandonment of moral principle. She pledged herself to the men of Norfolk and Suffolk, who had embraced the principles of the Reformation, that if they would assist in placing her upon the throne, she would never interfere with the Protestant principles of the nation. On this pledge she induced them to take arms in her cause, and they placed her triumphantly on the throne. Her whole reign was one continued act of perfidy to that pledge.* The system of persecution which she put in force, was the most awful exhibition of cruelty, and cold and deliberate blood-guiltiness, that the records of our race present to us. There may have been at other times, and in other lands, persecution as terrible and as bloody; but this continued through the whole five years of her reign. The loftiest in the land were its martyrs, and a woman was the perpetrator.

No rank, or virtue, or learning, gave exemption to the possessor—Cranmer, Ridley, Latimer, Hooper, Farrer,—all bishops of the church, were removed from their sees— degraded from their office—cast into prison, and finally martyred amidst the fires. Many hundreds of Christian souls were persecuted to the death.† Two persons were publicly appointed in every parish, to discover and inform against every Protestant who refused to conform to Popery. They were then apprehended, examined, and, if they still refused, martyred. Many thousands were thus compelled to fly their homes, their properties, and their country, to seek in foreign lands a welcome that was denied them in their father-land. Among these fugitives was MASTER JOHN FOXE, the justly celebrated Author of this justly celebrated Work, " The Acts and Monuments of Martyrs," wherein we have the only full and faithful narration of the cruelty of this persecution, in which men, women, children, without regard to age or sex, were indiscriminately martyred. Sometimes five, and sometimes ten were consumed in one fire, and on one occasion three women were burned at one stake, and—the blood runs cold while we write it—when one of them, under the pain of the flames, travailed with child, and one of the multitude, more humane than the rest, rescued the new-born babe, the authorities commanded it instantly to be burned with its mother! When such scenes were transacted under the authority of one who was herself a woman, we may well feel that there is an alchemy in Popery, that if it finds us angels can transform us into devils.

The death of this woman, whose only claim upon our respect is that, like one of old, she was " a king's daughter," stayed the work of persecution, and thus rendered ineffectual the first great effort of the Papacy to re-establish itself in this country. The accession of Elizabeth freed the Church of England from Italian influence, and settled it upon surer pillars, and more steadfast foundations than ever.

---

* One of the most interesting historical documents ever read, is the petition of these men of Norfolk, and Suffolk, to the Queen's Council, in the time of persecution. It will be found at page 913.

† Grindal, who lived during this period, says the number was 800; others estimate it at half that number.

The noble spirit of this Queen was such as became the monarch of this gallant nation, over whose destinies she presided. When, by that act of Popish perfidy—the massacre of St. Bartholomew—the streets of Paris flowed with the blood of her Protestant sons, the French ambassador appeared at the court of Elizabeth. He looked around for the splendour and chivalry of England. His cheek paled. The court of Elizabeth was arrayed in the deepest mourning!

Under her reign this country stood forth the friend and protector of the reformed religion both at home and abroad, and the grand antagonist of the Papal system. It was therefore scarcely to be expected that with an enemy so powerful, persevering, and unscrupulous as Popery, this country could be left in tranquillity. The second great effort for the re-establishment of the Church of Rome, unfolded a system of internal REBELLION and foreign INVASION.

Pope Pius was pleased in A.D. 1570, for the accomplishment of this effort, to issue his bull anathematising the Queen of England, and absolving all her subjects of their oaths of allegiance. "The nobles, subjects, and inhabitants of England," says this audacious manifesto, "who have in any way sworn to her, we declare to be absolved for ever from any such oath, and from all manner of duty, allegiance, and obedience, as we do by the authority of these presents absolve them, and do deprive the said Elizabeth of her pretended right to the kingdom, and all other things aforesaid. We command and interdict all nobles, subjects, people, and others aforesaid, that they presume not to obey her mandates, monitions, or laws. Those who shall act otherwise we bind under a similar sentence of anathema," &c.

This Italian Priest, not contented with thus anathematising the Queen of England, and blasphemously assuming to absolve the people of England from their allegiance, proceeded to two other measures that strikingly illustrate the character of the Papacy. He first sent certain Jesuits into Ireland with bulls, authorising them to raise the inhabitants of that island in rebellion against England. They unhappily accomplished his purpose there. He then took upon him to make over the realm of England, its crown, its revenues, and its dependencies as a gift to Philip of Spain. There too he succeeded in inducing that prince to equip the celebrated Armada, and prepare for an invasion of England.

Such were the means by which it was proposed to re-establish Popery in this land. Rebellion in Ireland—treason in England—a foreign invasion in both!

But, by the Providence of God, the rebellion in Ireland was crushed, the treason in England baffled, and the armada of Spain destroyed. We could mourn over the fate of that gallant armament, were we not acquainted with its object. The pomp of the chivalry of Spain, the flower of all her gallant youth were there. All that high hope could expect from noble daring, and all that the enthusiasm of superstition could achieve, might have been expected there. The voice of Papal infallibility had proclaimed it invincible. It walked the mighty ocean in its pride. It spread its fluttering wings for the shores of England. But an Angel of Heaven was moving over it unseen. The winds rushed in their fury above it. The waves swept in their madness beneath it. There were fearless hearts before them, and mighty arms to meet them. The chivalry of England manned her fleets, and the yeomanry of England lined her shores; and this "invincible armada," scattered on the deep, or stranded on our cliffs, strewed our shores with the mouldering bones of the youth of Spain.

Thus ended the second great effort to restore the influence of Rome in this country. Its characteristics were rebellion and invasion—suitable precursors of the next attempt of these Italian Priests.

The vigour of Elizabeth's government was felt even after her death. James I. received a kingdom, from which the more daring and dangerous spirits had been exiled for their treasons, or had gone into banishment to escape the vengeance of the laws. Those were members of the Church of Rome, and devotedly attached to the interests of the Papacy. They had religiously believed that the Papal authority could absolve subjects of their allegiance, and depose sovereigns from their thrones. They had held that heresy—the designation given to the reformed faith—was sufficient to lead to a forfeiture of all rights and privileges, and they therefore entered eagerly into every conspiracy that was deemed likely to re-establish the Papacy in its ancient influence in England.

These men resided chiefly in Flanders and Spain, where the members of the Order of Jesuits were in considerable numbers and activity; Garnet, Creswell, Baldwin, Parsons, and other celebrated Jesuits, soon obtained an ascendancy over these emigrants, and, with the deep subtlety, and unwavering courage of their order, implicated them in endless conspiracies. It is to the intrigues of this remarkable class of ecclesiastics, that we owe the GUNPOWDER-TREASON, which was discovered on the eve of its consummation. They bound each of the agents of this horrible treason, under an oath of secrecy, administered on receiving the Sacrament! The form of the oath was, " You shall swear by the blessed Trinity, and by the Sacrament you now propose to receive, never to disclose, directly or indirectly, by word or circumstance, the matter which shall be proposed to you, to keep secret, nor desist from the execution thereof, until the rest shall give you leave." There must be a frightful amount of human depravity, when a number of ecclesiastics could administer the Sacrament, and swear by the Trinity to go forward in this terrible conspiracy. It appears, likewise, that another Priest, named Gerrhard, gave absolution of the sin to each of the agents, preparatory to the accomplishment of their treason. Well might that celebrated lawyer, Coke, say, " I never yet knew a treason without a Romish Priest."

The whole design of this conspiracy was developed on the trial of the conspirators. The written confessions of Guy Fawkes and Thomas Winter, give ample details of the mode of accomplishment.* It was proposed to blow up, by gunpowder, the houses of Parliament, when, at the opening of the Session, the King, with the Royal Family, the Peers, and Members of the House of Commons, would be assembled together. By such a stroke, it was expected that they would destroy the heads of all the principal Protestant families in the kingdom. And then it was arranged to seize the infant daughter of the King, who was then in Warwickshire, and proclaim her Queen, to educate her a Papist, and themselves to govern the realm during her long minority.

Such were the objects of this conspiracy, and such the third great effort to re-establish the Papacy in England. The next was of a different character.

It was made in the time of James II. Four of the sovereigns of England had successively been Protestants; and when it might have been expected that all hope, or at least all efforts to restore the system of Popery had been crushed for ever, an avowed Papist ascended the throne in the person of James II., and gave new life to the hopes and energies of the emissaries of Rome. He was a man bigoted to his sect, and resolved to re-establish Popery on the ruins of Protestantism. His efforts to accomplish this object were different from all that had gone before. He proposed to encourage the growth of Popery,—not by persecution, as in the days of Mary; for the nation would not bear it,—but by all THE POWER OF THE CROWN, and the influence of the Court. He knew that in the then state of the nation it would not suit his purposes to make an

---

* These confessions, together with an account of the whole conspiracy, will be found in the Appendix to this Edition of the Acts and Monuments.

avowed assault upon its Protestantism, and he therefore adopted the more gradual and insinuating instrumentality of courtly favour and royal authority.

His reign, like that of Mary, was one continued act of perfidy to promises the most solemn. He had solemnly promised in Parliament, before he came to the throne, that he would cherish his religious principles between himself and his God, and never permit them to interfere with his government of the nation. He had solemnly promised, afterwards, on opening the first Parliament of his reign, in the speech delivered on that most public occasion, that he would never interfere with the religion of the Established Church. His whole reign was an illustration how pledges the most binding, and promises the most sacred, can all be violated, with a recklessness peculiar to the Church of Rome, whenever her interests are involved in the results. It is as easy to stay the planets in their course, as to find a moral tie, either of promises, or pledges, or oaths, that will bind the Church of Rome.

The extraordinary lengths to which this unhappy monarch was led by Father Petre, and those other Priests to whose guidance he so implicitly committed himself, awakened the dormant spirit of this nation. His measures respecting the Judges of the land, his proceedings among the Officers of the Army, his attempts against the Universities, his attack upon the Bishops, his claim of a dispensing power, his whole proceedings could not but compel the nation to look to its civil liberties, and its religious freedom; and to take measures for the preservation of the former against a Despot, and of the latter against a Papist.

The Revolution was the consequence, and thus, in the triumph of civil and religious liberty, ended the fourth great effort of the emissaries of Rome to re-establish Popery in England.

The principles involved in the Revolution were carried out during the reign of William III. The civil and religious institutions of the Country became inseparably blended, in our National Constitution. The Protestantism of the Church of England became amalgamated with the State, and it was designed that one should be as lasting as the other. Well nigh a century and a half has elapsed since that glorious event, and the experience of every added year only unfolds more manifestly the wisdom of those principles on which the Revolution was founded.

From that period the authority of the Church of Rome seemed annihilated in England. The perfect triumph of the principles of the Reformation at the time, and the steady attachment of the population of the Country to those principles, seem to have continued unabated until late years, in which a new method of procedure has been adopted by the emissaries of the Church of Rome, with the view of again extending the influence of the Papacy in this Country.

In the time of the unhappy James II. the emissaries of Rome sought to extend their influence through the despotic principles of the MONARCHY. But now they endeavour to promote the same result, through the growing strength of the DEMOCRACY. Such questions, as the principles of Monarchy on one hand, and Democracy on the other, are insignificant in their views, except so far as they can be made subservient to the interests of the Church of Rome; and, therefore, the emissaries of that Church are always prepared to ally themselves and their influence, with those principles that are most calculated at the time to subserve their purpose.

In this Country, they have allied themselves to the democratic party, upon the principle, that they will thereby render themselves, and their objects, more popular among the mass of the population, and at the same time secure to their cause that influence, which for some years past, has been on the ascendancy in this country. They have thereby obtained, already, not only a voice, but also a powerful influence in the Legislature, and an entrance to the Councils. And despite of promises, and even oaths, are eagerly seizing upon every opportunity by which they hope to cripple the energies of Protestantism, and to enhance the influence of Romanism.

At the same time that this process is carrying on in the Legislature, and in the Councils, there are other means employed with an unwearied diligence, and an unexampled expenditure of exertion and wealth, to advance the interests of the Papacy among the population. More than Six hundred Missionary Priests, of the Church of Rome, have been sent into this country. These missionaries, either settle themselves in certain localities, or move in various directions through the land, every where endeavouring to disseminate their peculiar principles, through the instrumentality of Sermons, Lectures, Tracts, &c. Their efforts have so far succeeded, as that during the last forty years they have increased the number of their chapels from about *thirty*, to above *five hundred*. A large number of Seminaries, or Colleges, have been formed with the view of securing the education of our youth. And many Nunneries and Monasteries have been established, so as to become centres for the propagation of the whole system of Popery. The success with which their measures of proselytism have been crowned, has been beyond their most sanguine expectations; and the ignorance of the population on one hand, and the political party to whom the emissaries of Rome have allied themselves, on the other hand, seem to promise still more ample success to their unwearied exertions. They hesitate no longer to avow their expectation, that this nation will return to the bosom of the Church of Rome.

This state of things is pregnant with the most disastrous consequences to the Protestantism of England, and demands the mightiest efforts that Christians and Protestants can make for the defence of our faith. They have a mighty adversary, against which they have to contend, in the Church of Rome; but they have a still mightier treasure to preserve, in the true religion established among us. It may truly be said of England, as of Israel, in the day of her blessedness, that she is a great and understanding nation, and that there is no nation that hath God so nigh, or to which he hath given such statutes and ordinances, that we might walk in them, and live in them, and be a delightsome land. We have, by the REFORMATION, *an English Service*, and *an open Bible*. We have, by the REVOLUTION, all the *religious liberty* that Christians can wish, and all the *civil liberty* that good subjects can desire.

Shall it be, that such matchless treasures shall be lost by our apathy? Shall it be, that by our indifference, we shall again be doomed to come under Italian influence, blighting our morals—withering our privileges—destroying our liberties—our homes ceasing to be happy; and our altars ceasing to be free? Shall it be, that the souls of our children, and our children's children, shall become the merchandize of Friars, and their morals become contaminated by the Priests of the Confessional? Shall their birthright of an open Bible, and an English Service, and a freedom to think and judge for themselves, be taken from them by our apathy, or neglect? It were better that the blast of death should sweep through the land, and as of old, leave the first-born dead in every house; and that the wail of the desolate, and the cry of the mourning should be heard on every wind, and echoed from every home, than that a calamity so disastrous as this, should befal our father land. Then, indeed, would the dark spirit of Popery be traced by the fall of our fanes and the ruin of our altars; and she would erect her throne amidst the fallen columns—the crumbling arches, and the mouldering aisles of the Temple of Protestantism. Then, indeed, would the glory of Britain—not the triumphs of her iron-hearted battalions on the battle-field, nor of her bannered masts upon the wave—not the treasure of her gold and silver and precious stones, nor the countless navies that waft to her shores the merchandize of the world—but her truest and her best, the Glory of her essential Protestantism be departed; and if ever such an eclipse shall darken it, then will "Ichabod" be written upon her ruins, and "The glory is departed," become the requiem of fallen England.

It is with the view of strengthening the religious principles of Protestantism, in the convictions of the People of England, and with the view of exhibiting fully and faithfully before their eyes, a living portraiture of the Papacy, that this FAMILY EDITION of *the Acts and Monuments of Martyrs*, has been published.

It is impossible for a mind, candid and unprejudiced, to peruse this work and to think otherwise of it, than that it was a noble production for its age, and an invaluable compilation for any age. MASTER JOHN FOXE, who was born in the same year that Luther commenced the Reformation, has collected together those scattered registries, and official documents, and original writings, respecting the Martyrs of Protestantism, which had been long since lost to the Church, were it not for his assiduity and zeal. He had access to Diocesan Registries, which are now lost for ever; excepting in those extracts which he has made from them. They give the official account of the articles charged against the Martyrs, and their answers to the same, in public courts. He had access to some documents, as Monitions, and Proclamations, which now are only to be found in the pages of this work; and which illustrate the spirit and tendencies of the times. He had access to many of the Martyrs themselves, and possessed their own original statements, written by their own hands, detailing the course of their previous sufferings, and the methods of their examination. These have all long since passed away for ever, except so far as they have been preserved in these *Acts and Monuments*. This is sufficient, of itself, to make the work an invaluable treasure; as an extensive compilation of evidences, and materials for the general historian; and especially for those who feel an interest in the confessions of those Martyrs of the Anglican Church, who were "slain for the word of God, and for the testimony which they held;" and whose blood proved such prolific seed for the Church of England. The greater portion of the work is a compilation of these original documents. He gives them to the world as such, and exhibits no trace of that vanity which has tempted so many to clothe original materials in more modern phraseology, so as to pass them current as their own; and sure we are, that the name of JOHN FOXE, will live green in the memory of our children, and our children's children, when his envious and malicious detractors shall have passed into oblivion.

The work proposes to give a general sketch of the history of the Christian Church— a more detailed account of the Church of England—an accurate portraiture of the rise, and progress, and genius, of the Church of Rome—and finally, the most full and ample account of the examinations, sufferings, and martyrdoms, of those holy men of God, who were the strength and ornament of the Protestantism of this land.

The edition which we now present to the public, possesses certain peculiarities which require to be noticed.

I. There is a large mass of official documents and forms, which, though interesting to the writers of history, possess no interest or value for the religious, or general reader. They seem to have been published by Foxe, more with the view of preserving them as records, than in the expectation that they would be perused by the general reader.

A large portion of these have been omitted from this edition.

II. There is a series of narrations, from time to time introduced by the author, connected with the superstitious credulity of the dark ages. Some of them are absurd, others are marvellous. And Foxe, while he inserts them, does not hesitate to express judgment on them, pronouncing them to be apocryphal.

These have been excluded from this edition, as calculated to injure, rather than promote the interests of religion.

III. There is also inserted in the original work, a variety of Latin quotations, a few from the Greek, and a number of letters and documents, also in the Latin language.

These have been removed from the present edition, as being calculated to encumber it unnecessarily.

IV. Owing to the state of society in the age in which this work was written, there was a coarseness of expression, and an absence of delicacy and propriety, in some of the narrations, which render it unfit for family perusal, in the present state of society, and which have aided much in consigning the work itself into oblivion.

All these narrations, and indelicacies, have been most carefully expunged from this edition.

V. There are many errors in the dates, embodied in the original work. Some of these are, perhaps, the result of those mistakes into which authors of that age were very likely to fall, in reference to more ancient history. Many of them are merely the mistakes of the printing press, accumulated through successive editions.

These have been carefully corrected in the present edition, so as to prevent the reader falling into error.

These particulars, present the peculiarities of this edition. The object has been, to present the Protestant population of this land, with A FAMILY EDITION —one that, in point of size and cheapness, would be accessible to all—one that could be perused without toiling through unnecessary and uninteresting documents—and especially one that could be read with interest, and advantage, in the family circle.

In endeavouring to accomplish these objects, every effort has been made to render this edition an available repository of all that was calculated to strengthen the religious principles of the Reformation, in the Protestants of England, and to supply them with as much as possible, that would arm them against the principles and the practices of the Church of Rome—thus making this edition consist of all the information that was valuable, in the original work, and all that was likely to be available in the controversy with Rome.

Those who desire an ecclesiastical history of England, will find it here. Those who seek for a detail of the iniquities of Popery, both abroad and at home, will not be disappointed. The Christian, who desires examples of faithfulness unto the death, will be amply recompensed in a perusal; and those who wish to obtain a practical knowledge of the controversy with Rome, will find it one of the most useful works in our language.

In order to render the work complete, an Appendix has been added, containing accounts of the massacre of St. Bartholomew—of the Spanish Armada—of the Gunpowder Treason—of the great Rebellion of Ireland, in 1641—all written by authors who wrote immediately after the events which they narrate. Also an account of the executions in the reign of Elizabeth, proving them to have been the punishment for treason, and not a persecution of Popery.

M. HOBART SEYMOUR.

LONDON, *January*, 1838.

THE LIFE

OF

MR. JOHN FOXE.

JOHN FOXE was born in Boston, in the county of Lincoln, A.D. 1517, his father and mother being of the commonalty of that town, of good reputation, and in respectable circumstances. While young, his father died, and his mother married again, which brought him under the care of his step-father, with whom he dwelt during his childhood. At an early age, he gave indications of love of learning, which his friends well approving of, sent him to study at Oxford. The first nurse of his more serious studies, was Brasen-nose College, where he was chamber-fellow with Doctor Nowell, so famous a man in this city afterwards, and dean of St. Paul's. It was therefore no marvel if their manners were so like in the course of their lives, whose education and nurture in youth was the same. The native excellence and soundness of his judgment, were well seconded by the fitness of the place; where the emulation of equals was frequent, and where each student's proficiency was narrowly sought into; neither was industry wanting, which as it seldom accompanies the greatest talents, so, where it is conjoined, is most available. When in a short space he had won the admiration of all, and the love of many, in reward of his learning and good behaviour he was chosen fellow of Magdalen College; which being accounted a principal honour in the university, and usually due to the students of that house, was seldom, and not unless in regard of singular deserts, bestowed upon any others. It appears he gave the first indications of an early wit, to the exercises of poetry, and wrote divers Latin comedies, in a copious and graceful style, but somewhat lofty, which fault of writing he left not altogether in his elder years, though age and experience did not a little mitigate it. But even then he began to give earnest of what he afterwards proved, for those first efforts of his youth were spent only in holy histories of the bible; nor followed he that course long. He betook himself to the study of divinity, with somewhat more fervency than circumspection, and discovered himself in favour of the Reformation, before he was known to them that maintained the cause, or were of ability to protect the maintainers of it; whence grew his first troubles. This was the time when Henry VIII, uncertain what course to take, being at variance with the pope, and not resolved in himself, thinking the affairs of the church, (then

grown to an infinite height of power and pride,) neither in all respects tolerable, nor that it was necessary wholly to alter them, while he desired to shew moderation in both, prevailed in neither, obscuring an act, than which none was of more glory since the world began, by an unprofitable indifference. Never before were the people in more distraction, or less security of their lives and estates, there being in the laws such contrarieties, as no man could tell what to take to with safety, or what to avoid. For although the pope's supremacy had been renounced, yet his doctrine was still retained. The first news of the abolishing of the pope's supremacy was as prosperous as it was welcome to the reformers; and many joined themselves to them out of love to the truth, being further assured of the king's intentions, by the punishment inflicted on some of the opposite party, and especially when the abbies were dissolved; nor was their hope a little increased, when they perceived the noblemen more or less to rise in the good opinion and favour of the king, in proportion as they most opposed the pope's pretensions. In the mean while the act of the Six Articles was still in force, and if any were found guilty of the breach, they were sure of punishment. So that as long as the king held the middle way between his own judgment, and the advice of his counsellors, feeding them with favours, upon which they could build no assurance, and pleasing himself in his own severity, fear and hope equally prevailed.

But when the protectors themselves, and pillars of the reformed religion, were taken away, the duke of Suffolk by untimely death, the lord Cromwell by the sword, the archbishop Cranmer and his friends borne down by those of the contrary side; and that neither in the laws, nor in the protection of the peers, there was any help remaining; then began all things rapidly to hasten back to their former abuses, and that with so much the more violence, because the conquest seemed a kind of revenge.

In the universities and schools there was yet no open change, or innovation; I know not whether through fear, or that they would not be followers.

This was the state of the church affairs, when Master Foxe began attentively to seek into the substance of the controversy, then in agitation. He found the contention to have been of great antiquity, and no age to have been free from some debate in the church. But those first quarrels were rather for dominion, and increase of territory; the Romans, endeavouring by subtle practices, and pretext of religion to retain under the jurisdiction of a high priest the ancient honour of their city, which by open force they could not defend. Then no sooner did any one shew himself to differ from them in point of faith, but the hastening of his punishment prevented any infection that might spread itself among others.

Thus by their cruelty, and the patience of princes, who suffered it, the greatest part of these dissensions were appeased. Afterwards, the pope grown bolder by good success, began to draw to himself all power and authority, nor contented to have weakened the estate of the Roman empire alone, now longed to be fingering the sceptres of other princes; and to compass his design, spared not to violate any human or divine right; meanwhile the clergy little impressed by the great damage done to religion, by men of immoral life and conversation being sometimes chosen to the papacy, by whose example the strictness of life, used by their forefathers, was drawn into scorn, and their poverty into disgrace. The industry of the priesthood languished, and on the contrary side ambition, riot, and avarice began to reign among them. Then at length were the practices of the churchmen brought to light, and their delusions laid open. It was then known why the ceremonies and rites in the church, had been brought to that excessive multitude, namely, that the number of the clergy might be increased to perform them. These of necessity were to be maintained; and to that end were such opinions broached, as seemed most likely to draw money from all places. Of the merit of works; of purgatory; of the power of absolution, and the pope's indulgences; all which being in themselves false, and soon subject to decay, were thought fit to be cemented together with that new and subtle invention of the pope's infallibility in matters of faith.

By this ingenious bond, and linking one opinion to another, the credulity of the christians was easily ensnared; all this while the new forged opinions yielding plentiful increase, and great sums of money, by a hundred devises were screwed out of the clergy and the common people, and came daily to the pope, and court of Rome.

I have often heard Master Foxe affirm, That the first matter which occasioned his search into the popish doctrine, was, that he saw divers things in their own natures, most repugnant to one another, thrust upon men to be both believed at one time; as that the same man might in matters of faith be superior, and yet in his life and manners inferior to all the world besides. Upon this beginning, his resolution and intended obedience to that church, was somewhat shaken, and by little and little there followed some dislike to the rest.

His first care was to look into both the ancient and modern history of the church; to learn what beginning it had; what growth and increase: by what arts it flourished, and by what errors it began to decline; to consider the causes of all those controversies which in the mean time had sprung up, and to weigh diligently of what moment they were, and what on either side was advanced which was sound or erroneous.

This he performed with such diligence of study, and in so short a time: that before the thirtieth year of his age, he had read over all that either the Greek or Latin fathers had left in their writings; the schoolmen in their disputations; the councils in their acts; or their consistory in their degrees; and had acquired no mean skill in the Hebrew language.

By report of some who were fellow-students with him, he used over and above his day's exercise, to bestow whole nights at his study, or not till it were very late to betake himself to rest. Near to the college was a grove, wherein for the pleasantness of the place, the students took delight to walk, and spend some idle hours for their recreation. This place, and the dead time of the night, had Master Foxe chosen, with solitude and darkness, to confirm his mind; which trembled at the guilt of a new imagination.

How many nights he watched in these solitary walks;

what combats and wrestlings he suffered within himself; how many heavy sighs, and sobs, and tears he poured forth in his prayers to Almighty God; I had rather omit in this discourse, than it should have the appearance of ostentation. But of necessity, it was to be remembered, because from hence sprang the first suspicion of his alienated affections. For no sooner was the fame spread abroad of his nightly retirements, but the more understanding sort out of their own wisdom, others according as they stood inclined towards him, were apt to interpret all to the worst sense. At length, those with whom he was intimate, being drawn into suspicion of him; there were some employed, who under pretence to admonish him, might observe his walks, and pry with more curiosity into his words and actions; and there wanted not others who comparing his customs formerly used, with the present course he now took, did with more bitterness aggravate the act. Why does he not come to church, so often as in former times he had been accustomed to? Why should he shun the company of his equals, and refuse to recreate himself after his wonted manner, unless he had felt in his mind some sudden alteration? nor if that alteration were for the better, would he conceal it.

Being thus reported of, surrounded with treacheries, and by every one accused, when the matter came to more severe scanning, and that he could neither hide his resolution longer, nor, being a man of plain dealing, thought fit to excuse himself by forging a lie,—by the judgment of the college he was convicted, condemned as a heretic, and removed from the house. Nevertheless his adversaries affirmed he was favourably dealt with by that sentence, and might have been examined for his life, if they had not rather used clemency towards him than extremity. But this wound raged worse than it was thought it would; his friends, upon the report of this accident, being sorely displeased, and especially his stepfather, who was now grown altogether implacable, either through a real hatred conceived against him for this cause, or pretending himself aggrieved, that he might now with more justice, at least with more security, withhold from Foxe his own father's estate. For he both knew it could not be safe for one publicly hated, and in danger of the law, to seek remedy by it; and that Foxe was by nature so ignorant in requiting injuries, that he would many times with much ado confess himself wronged, even then, when he had in his hands ability of revenge.

When he was thus forsaken by his own friends, and left naked of all human assistance, God's providence began to shew itself, procuring him a safe refuge in the house of a worshipful knight of Warwickshire, called Sir Thomas Lucy, to whom he was sent for, to instruct his children; in which house he afterwards married a wife, and there continued till the children arrived at mature years, and had now no longer need of a tutor. But the fear of the popish inquisitions hastened his departure thence; which now relying on the favour of the laws, were not contented to pursue public offences, but began also to break into the secrets of private families.

Often would Foxe, in the later days of his life, with much vehemence of mind, while conversing with his friends, detest the wretched condition of that departing, and say, That all other mischances he had pretty well endured; but in this case, the misery was so much the greater, because to have borne it patiently would have seemed unnatural; having brought his faithful consort, who entirely loved him, from her friends and kindred, whose grief and tears were with all officious piety to be comforted; it behoved him, therefore, either to find some speedy remedy, or, in assurance of his love, to weep with her. For in vain should he shew an example of his constancy, where she might rather suspect her grief unregarded, than his mind unconquered with so great calamities. He consulted, therefore, with himself what was best to be done; and of two ways only left, whereby he might free himself from further inconvenience, he, after long deliberating whether he might with most safety make choice of, either to go to his wife's father, or his stepfather by marriage of his mother.

His wife's father dwelt nearest, being a citizen of Coventry, nor yet bearing any hatred towards him, and more likely to be entreated for his daughter's sake. His stepfather was better known to him, but more suspected. At last he resolved to go first to his wife's father, and in the meanwhile by letters to try whether his stepfather would receive him or not. His stepfather's answer was, That it seemed to him a hard condition, to take one into his house whom he knew to be guilty, and condemned for a capital offence; neither was he ignorant what hazard he should undergo in so doing; nevertheless, that he would shew himself a kinsman, and for that cause neglect his own danger. If he would alter his mind, he might come, on condition to stay as long as himself desired; but if he could not be persuaded to that, he should content himself with the shorter stay, and not bring him and his mother into hazard of their fortunes, who were ready to do any thing for his sake.

Mr. Foxe's state was at that crisis that he thought no condition ought to be refused; besides, he was underhand advised by his mother to come, and not fear his stepfather's severity; for that perhaps it was needful to write as he did, but when occasion should offer, he would make recompence for his words with his actions. The truth is, he had better entertainment with both of them than he any way hoped for; but so his business required, that he should rely long upon neither; and therefore, by often going to and fro from the one to the other, which carried with it some shew of business, he both deceived their diligence who inquired after him, and effected that neither of them grew weary of his company.

But, however, he by this means kept himself concealed; yet certain it is, that no time of his life passed more unknown to posterity than that; whether while he did but little, which is scarce credible, or whether it more concerned them who knew what he did, that it should be withheld than published abroad. For his own part he always forbore, with particular care, to speak of that story; lest where he had deserved so much, he might, by extolling a small courtesy, seem rather to upbraid the slenderness of the requital, than to shew himself thankful by remembering it. Afterwards he took his journey towards London; but from what motive is uncertain, unless we may imagine the convenience of the place enticed him thither; which being full of all classes of people, both inhabitants and strangers from all places, afforded him a better opportunity, either to conceal himself or to make known his abilities, or to get acquaintance with those of like inclination.

By computation of times, I should think the chief cause of his going thither to have been, that about that time religion began at length a little to recover itself and gather strength, especially about the city; for he did not go to London till within a few years before king Henry departed this life; who, as I said before, though the kingdom were divided into factions, yet as long as his youth and strength remained, so ordered the matter, that, sometimes the power of each party being equalled, and sometimes one or other prevailing, by his authority both were retained in their obedience. But when he grew into years, perceiving his health every day impaired, and that his death could not be far off, he then began to consider with himself which side was most trusty, and which most to be doubted; and at what age he should expose his son to the raging hatred of the papists, who was yet, by reason of his youth, unfit to govern, and brought up in the discipline of a religion which they opposed.

He therefore, at last, resolved upon that which in reason seemed most wholesome, and in the end proved most fortunate; and having put the papist officers from their authority, by his will he appointed his son such tutors whose love to himself he had always found readiest, and by long trial of their fidelity thought likely to continue the same to his successor. This set the protestant religion again in safety, and the professors thereof, were thereby secured of their lives; yet

hence no public benefit or profit was afforded them: so that Foxe was still in as great want as before, having already spent all that either his friends had bestowed on him, or his own daily industry had acquired.

I should here forbear to speak of a marvellous accident, and great example of God's mercy, were not the matter so well known abroad, that it would be to no purpose for modesty's sake to be silent.

As Mr. Foxe one day sat in St. Paul's church, exhausted with long fasting, his countenance thin, and eyes hollow, after the ghastful manner of dying men, every one shunning a spectacle of so much horror, there came to him one whom he never remembered to have seen before, who, sitting by him and saluting him with much familiarity, thrust an untold sum of money into his hand, and bidding him be of good cheer; he added, that he knew not how great the misfortunes were which oppressed him, but suspected that it was no light calamity. He therefore requested him to accept in good part that small gift from his countryman, which common courtesy had forced him to offer; and he recommended him to go and nurse himself, and take all occasions to prolong his life; and in the mean time he informed him that within a few days his prospects would be improved, and a more certain condition of livelihood would be secured to him. Foxe could never learn who that man was, by whose seasonable bounty, in that extreme necessity, he had been relieved, though he earnestly endeavoured to find him out. Some who looked further into the event which followed that prophecy, believed that this man came not of his own accord, but was sent by some others, who very much desired Foxe's safety; and that it might perchance be through the servant's negligence, that he had suffered so much misery before any relief had been afforded. Certain it is, that within three days the issue seemed to make good the prediction, for there was a message sent from the duchess of Richmond, to invite him upon fair terms into her service. It had so fallen out, not long before, that the duke of Norfolk, the famous warrior and most renowned general of his time, together with his son, the earl of Surrey, a man as far as may be imagined, of sincere meaning and good understanding, was committed to custody in the Tower of London, for what crimes is uncertain. While they were in prison, the earl's children were sent to the aforesaid duchess, their aunt, to be brought up and educated: Thomas, who succeeded in the dukedom; Henry, who was afterwards earl of Northampton; and Jane, afterwards countess of Westmoreland.

To these young lords was Foxe appointed tutor, to instruct them both in manners and learning; in which charge he deceived not the expectation which the duchess, a woman of great wisdom, had of him. For the two sons grew to that height of proficiency in their behaviour and scholarship, that, building in their riper years upon this foundation, the elder, Thomas, seemed to deserve more than the kingdom could bestow upon him; and the younger, Henry, came to that happiness, that he was able to measure his fortunes, not by the opinion of others, but by his own enjoyment.

The young lady Jane profited so wondrously in the Greek and Latin tongues, that she might well stand in competition with the most learned men of that time, for the praise of elegancy in both kinds.

There he dwelt during those golden days of felicity, not seen for a long time before, in the last years of king Henry's reign, and through the five years' reign of king Edward the Sixth, (a young prince incomparably hopeful, who, by perfecting the work begun by his father, surpassed all the acts of his predecessors,) till the beginning of queen Mary's sovereignty; who, coming to the crown, and turning the stream of religion, all things again yielded to the papists' authority; whence, not long after, that cruel tempest proceeded, the noise whereof hath come also to the ears of our age; many who suffered in that common shipwreck, swimming out to these peaceful times, as to safe harbours of everlasting tranquillity.

Among these Foxe made one, at that time sheltered by the protection of the duke, his scholar; yet not without the observance of many, who for hatred or envy narrowly watched him, and secretly laid wait for him. Among these was Doctor Gardiner, bishop of Winchester, who both saw something in him which he greatly feared, and also disdained much that the heir of one of the chiefest families in the kingdom, and nearest joined to himself in friendship, should by his company be depraved.

Of this man, because he was Foxe's greatest enemy, it will not be from our purpose to speak something further, that both their natures may the better be known.

The bishop of Winchester was a man famous in his youth, for of his birth or parentage I have no certainty, one that stood in the midway between good and bad; and always as he grew older, growing worse. Industry, wit, and eloquence, nature had bestowed on him; his pride, craftiness, and desire of bearing sway, he learned of cardinal Wolsey.

Hence his abilities qualified him for any employment, which he managed with exceeding diligence, to gain new honours; and having obtained them, he then put on boldness instead of industry, flattery for obedience; and instead of fidelity, deceit and compliments, and such like frivolous fashions of the court. He was, in bearing those honours which his virtue won to him, cruel and proud: in regaining any that he lost, able to weary any man with submission and humility. For in his fortunes also appeared as great diversity, as in his conditions. Some while he was pleasing to king Henry, and high in his favour; having by his pen maintained the king's authority against the pope: afterwards, when his prevaricating therein was understood, he was slighted by the king, and that he might be the less able to do hurt, stripped of his dignity. Under Edward VI, he was not only neglected, but imprisoned, and underwent the reproach of a mean estate. At length, in queen Mary's reign, he was set at liberty, and being again restored to his former honours, he exercised not so much command as tyranny: till even sick with envy, that cardinal Pole out-shone him in dignity, and with height of honours overshadowed his glory, having often, but still in vain tried to cure his malady by a cardinalship, anger at length exasperating his disease, he pined away.

After this manner began, and ended that man, commended for many excellences of mind, while he led a private life; but in his honours unbridled, and of no moderation: well might one say, nature had made him a worthy man, and fortune corrupted him.

Now Foxe, although he was cherished in the bosom of a most loving duke; yet after he saw all sorts of men troubled for their religion's sake, some imprisoned, and others burnt; in brief nothing on all sides, but flight, slaughter, and gibbets; and that the bishop of Winchester was the principal incendiary of all this, who for private respects was already his enemy; he then began to fear what might become of him, and to think of some speedy way for his departure thence. As soon as the duke knew his intent, gently chiding his fearfulness, he used many words to persuade him to leave all thought of going away; affirming it neither agreeable to honour or modesty, for him to suffer his tutor, so well deserving at his hands, at any time of his life to be taken from him: but that it should then be done, was not beseeming for him that desired it. Let him but think with himself, how great a burthen of hatred his scholar must needs bear, among those who were ignorant, whether he forsook him of his own accord, or were forsaken by him: yet that he entreated not to be excused from any hatred, which might light upon him, if at least he might do it for Foxe's advantage: but in flying, what misery would be wanting? banishment, poverty, contempt, and among those which knew him not, the reproach of a runagate. That he acknowledged was less evil than death; but that it was not yet come to such extremity; neither would he suffer it should: that he had yet wealth, and favour, and friends, and the fortune of his house: if the mischance prevailed further, himself would partake of the danger, and make the destruction common: that he remembered, with what precepts he had fortified his younger years; neither had he with more attention hearkened to his in-

structions, than he would with constancy put them in practice; only let him be of good courage, and so avoid the violence of his enemies, as not to be weary of his friend's company: that this he spake, as hoping by his authority to prevail with him: but if that might not be obtained, he would then further him in the course he intended.

There was in the duke's speech the more credit, because it was known to proceed from the sincerity of his heart, and a most tender good will towards him: and Foxe now grew ashamed, not so much in that he had done in asking leave, as that he had believed his request might have been granted: but his modesty excused him: his answer being, that the same care befitted not the lord and his servant: that it was indeed for the duke's honour, to defend his tutor from any injury; but his own part, to have a care, lest for his safety, the duke might incur apparent danger, or perpetual trouble: neither that his fear wanted all excuse. For though he well knew the duke could not be drawn from his promise and good intentions towards him; yet was he not ignorant, that by some wile or other, he might be circumvented and deceived.

For even at that time was the bishop of Winchester very intimate with the duke, relying upon the ancient friendship he had always used to that family, by whose credit he had increased his dignity. Thither he often resorted, to present his service to the duke; and at several times desired of him, that he might see his old tutor. At first the duke denied his request, one while alleging his absence, another while that he was ill at ease; still after feigning several delays, to put him off, at length it chanced, that Foxe (not knowing the bishop was within the house) entered the room where the duke and he were in discourse; and seeing the bishop, with a shew of bashfulness withdrew himself. The bishop, asking who that was, the duke answered, "his physician, who was somewhat uncourtly, as being newly come from the university." "I like his countenance and aspect very well," replied the bishop, "and when occasion shall be, will make use of him." The duke straight understood that speech, as the messenger of some approaching danger; and now he himself thought it high time for Foxe no longer to remain within the same city, or within the same see, against the force of a crafty, and then open deceiver; but by all means, the bishop being sick, must be prevented. From that time he caused all things necessary for his flight, with the least noise that might be, to be provided; sending one of his servants before to Ipswich haven, to hire a bark, and make ready all things needful for the voyage: and because it seemed scarce safe for Foxe to stay in any city, or place of resort, he chose out the house of one of his servants, a farmer, where he might with convenience wait a fair wind to put to sea. Thither Foxe went as secretly as he could, taking his wife as companion in his travels, then pregnant, but resolved to go with him, nor yielding to the entreaty of those who persuaded her to the contrary; and as soon as it was told him, his company expected him, he made haste to the port, and went on board.

Scarce had they weighed anchor, when suddenly a boisterous wind arose from the contrary shore, and which caused the waves to rage with such violence, that the stoutest mariners began to tremble: then followed a dark night, with continual showers, and a great multitude of clouds gathered together into a thick storm of rain and hail, which both hindered the seamen's work, and took away all possibility to direct their course by the compass any longer. That night, with much ado, they lay at anchor, and as soon as the day appeared, when the tempest seemed not likely to cease, they began to cast about, and make back again to the shore: so that the tide a little favouring them, at length with much difficulty they arrived in the evening at the same haven again, from whence they had loosed the day before. In the mean while that Foxe had been at sea, a pursuivant from the bishop of Winchester had broke open the farmer's house, with a warrant to apprehend him, wherever he might be found, and bring him back a prisoner to the city; but understanding he was gone already, after he had pursued him even to the port, and there found that the ship he was embarked in was yet scarce out of sight, had returned back. Foxe, as soon as he came ashore, hearing by report of the people what had passed, although the news somewhat amazed him, yet, recollecting himself, presently took horse, and made as if he would have left the town; but the same night returning, he bargained with the master of the ship to set sail again with the first convenience of the winds; telling him that so his business required, nor did he much care what shore he landed at; only desiring him to go forward, and not doubt but that God would prosper so pious a work. Whether for reward or piety's sake, the pilot took upon him this venturous task, and performed it accordingly; for, loosing thence in the silence of the night, as soon as the tide turned, though the sea was rough and the weather blustering, within two days' time he landed Foxe and his company in safety at Newport-Haven, on the other side of the sea.

Whoever shall read this history, needeth not a more evident argument to force him to acknowledge either the certain course of providence or the uncertainty of all human forecast; when he may see the subtlest deliberations of the wisest heads oftentimes by errors come to no effect, often overthrown by sudden accidents, and now and then thwarted by contrary counsels; and that all this is done to teach men so to use their authority, as that the more power fortune hath conferred upon them, so much the less they should know they are able to do of themselves, and not despise those that are of meaner condition. For that God regardeth all men alike, having made them in nature equal, and distinguished them by degrees; not to puff up the one sort, or shame the other, but to exercise both their modesties, or his own justice, if they neglect their duty.

Foxe, when he had spent some days at Newport, in refreshing himself and his company, went to Antwerp, and from thence by easy journeys to Basil.

This city was at that time much spoken of, for the great friendship and courtesy showed to those of the English nation; for which cause many famous men, withdrawing themselves from the cruelty of the times, had escaped out of England thither. Of these, many were but of small fortune, who, some one way and some another, but the most part maintained their livelihood by reviewing and correcting the press: this place then surpassing all the cities of Germany for careful printing, and abounding with diligent and wealthy men in that profession, and preferring the industry of our men in that employment before any of their own countrymen.

To these men Foxe joined himself, and was so much the better liked, as, having been always inured to hardiness, and in his youth put to the trial of his patience, he had learned how to endure labour; and that which seemed the greatest misery to others—to suffer want, to sit up late, and keep hard diet—were to him but the sports of fortune. This perhaps may seem strange to many, who remember Foxe to have been all his life long but a slender-bodied man, and in his elder years somewhat sickly. But let no man compare his old age, worn out and eaten up with cares, and by the course of nature worn out, with the flourishing prime of his youth, which appears to have been most healthful: whether it be, that in those of indifferent size, an upright shape of the limbs and members may sufficiently serve for health, or that the mind, animated with desire of virtuous actions, being content with its own abilities to pursue those things it affecteth, needeth the less help from the body.

His industry may be from hence abundantly testified, that, being so full of employment at Basil, there, nevertheless, he began to write his History of the Acts and Monuments of the Church—a work by the title alone seeming beyond man's belief. At first it sufficed only to mark it out, and to draw the first lines or rudiments, or as it were to fasten the warp to the loom; the whole body of the history he added and interwove with it after he returned into his own country. First he wrote it in Latin, and sent the copy to Basil to be printed, where the work is still in great estimation, as also in divers other foreign nations, but among our own countrymen it

is hardly known; which shows that whilst we seek after and admire strangers, we, either through carelessness or envy, neglect our own countrymen. Shortly after, to gratify the unlearned, he wrote it in English.

In the meanwhile the reformed religion began again to flourish in England, and the papist faction much to decline, by the death of queen Mary—a woman, while she followed her own inclination, every way excellent, and well worthy so royal parentage; but while she denied not any thing to some wicked counsellors, she obtained not that praise she had otherwise deserved; and if she be not ill spoken of, it may be attributed to the unwillingness of the succeeding age, to speak very freely of princes.

The whole christian world immediately felt some benefit by this change of the English government.

The neighbouring nations, now disburdened of the exiled Englishmen, rejoiced as much for the good fortune of their guests, as for their own. But at home what could be devised to assure their safety, or relieve their distresses, which they did not sooner enjoy than presume to hope for? They who had forsaken their houses, were now called home. They who had suffered imprisonment, were now released. They who by loss of goods were decayed, were now by gifts repaired. They who had been thrust from places of honour, were now restored to their former dignities. The unjust laws which had been enacted were in the mean while abrogated, and wholesome laws established in their places. Their minds were at quiet. Their consciences at liberty; all degrees at peace among themselves, and every man's goods without danger. For in such sort did queen Elizabeth, even in the infancy of her reign, dispose the affairs of the commonwealth, that whatsoever the long and prosperous government of other princes doth hardly produce in many years, at her very first entrance all at once broke forth, beyond the people's wish, as if some deity had diffused itself, and poured forth felicity upon the world. Of which incomparable, and most glorious queen, to make mention upon any occasion, and not to supply some further digression, let it be accounted for a capital crime among all writers of history.

She was born of the lady Anne Boylen, whom king Henry VIII, after his divorce from his first marriage, took to wife. From her she received, as a princely dowry, a true zeal for religion. As she grew older in years, so she increased in manners, knowledge and beauty, which as well make as beseem a princess. So that both nature seemed to have boasted in her the master piece of her most absolute workmanship; and fortune to have raised her to as high a degree, as hope could ever aspire to.

It made her the more capable to bear so great a fortune, that she at first learned to obey; then to command, and to use that honour first to others, which was shortly after to be used by others to her; having in a private life had experience of the hatred, fatal to the successors of great empires, yet of a nobler spirit than to return the like upon those who were to succeed her. As soon as she came to the kingdom, her several virtues appeared at once in their brightest lustre; her mind descended not to an over-nice care of her body. The principles of her new sovereignty were, to acquaint herself with the public reasons of state; to seek fit men to bear part of her cares; to strengthen all parts of the kingdom with faithful ministers; to know the temper and abilities of those about her; and to search into the strength, councils and attempts of foreign princes; but all these qualities, if not well tempered, might have had, perhaps, no long continuance. Such therefore was her gravity, as nothing more pleasing. Such her severity, as nothing more gentle; and such her frugality, as nothing more bountiful. Only she knew no measure, in those excellencies, whose glory is founded, not in the even balancing of different virtues; but as it were in the throng of illustrious actions. So was the nobility of her birth heaped with desire of glory. Her religion was most sincere, and was seconded with zeal for a holy life. But when all these virtues brake forth into actions, what days of happiness we then enjoyed! What more cheerful, more secure or wealthy did England see, than that four and forty years of peace! For never did she voluntarily provoke any to war, and always preferred the justice of the quarrel before the victory. To the Irish war, honour, and shame to have lost a province, enforced her. To the French, piety, and pity of her neighbours' danger. To the Spanish, her own safety, and necessity comprehending in itself the force of all other causes, compelled her.

In the progress of this war we heard of, and saw that which, perchance, never happened in any before. For other nations, though they fought with mortal hatred against each other, yet were their battles restrained to some certain fields and places; but this war was so scattered over all places, and managed with such nobleness of courage on both sides, that through all seas and havens from east to west, the sun might still behold the English and Spanish navies fighting for their lives, honours, or estates. Never till then had that sea, which was accustomed to no other command but ours, frothed with strokes of foreign oars. Nor would a large volume contain the discourse, if I should relate the number and stateliness of ships, the strength of sea and land forces, the supply of ammunition, engines, weapons, guns, and provision of victuals belonging to that navy, which Philip the Second, king of Spain, with intention to raze out the English name, sent hither in the year 1588. Let this suffice, that never was any preparation by sea comparable to this fleet, made by any the most powerful princes or states, to be shewed in all the records of antiquity; yet that so huge and threatening armada, swelling with self-confidence, and a presumed hope of victory, was by the fortune of this invincible princess, even in a moment utterly defeated.

The navies met together, for number and strength unequal. But the manner of the fight was to the Spaniards' disadvantageous, because the English vessels being for bulk much less, and lower built before, could with more ease cast about for the wind, and immediately having discharged, retire to open sea; thereby deluding the sluggish and unwieldy ships of their enemies, and by levelling at the broadsides of the Spanish galleons, bestowing their shot with a more certain and successful aim. To this, our captains in the skill of sea-fight, and knowledge of the tides, far excelled the Spanish commanders, who now taught by the former day's experience, that they could no way, but in a set fight bear the English encounters, casting their anchors near Calais, there expected new forces out of Flanders, and by the goodness of their ordnance defended themselves. This laid them open to the English for the victory. For having filled some ships with tow, pitch, brimstone, and all sorts of combustible materials, and setting them on fire, with a favorable tide, they drove them directly upon the enemy; who were by this action so exceedingly terrified, that the whole fleet, cutting their cables as fast as they could, betook themselves instantly to flight. In which flight some of their ships were burnt, some sunk, some forced to run themselves on shore, some split upon the rocks, and some for haste falling foul on their fellows, and so torn and bruised, were taken by our soldiers. Those that escaped best, not daring to go back the same way they came thither, with long labour both by sea and land, returned at length into Spain, by the coasts of Scotland, and the islands of the Orkney, through those seas, which in no age had been sailed on, but by such as were very good at flying. Where so great virtues and victories met together in one person, of necessity envy would be an attendant, followed by hatred and treacheries; which could not, by this most innocent queen, be so avoided, but that her safety was through all her life daily endangered. Which maketh me the rather wonder, what rare doctrine of our adversaries this may be, for piety sake which they pretend, persecuting even virtue itself, whereas (not only in no heathen, but in none the most barbarous nation, which doth at all acknowledge any deity) it was never thought just to take revenge upon virtue, even in their enemies; unless it be so that the indulgence of the christian religion may be so far extended, that although we are commanded to forgive our enemies, either they must not be

virtuous, or they must not be forgiven. But evident enough it is, that in human affairs, the desires of men are often employed to one end, and the will of God to another. By him was queen Elizabeth protected always, from the injuries and wicked enterprizes of her enemies, and brought full of years to that honour, as to carry with her that glory unspotted to heaven, which she obtained on earth, envy now in vain carping at her after death, whose cause all posterity doth patronise.

Now let us return to our history.

Master Foxe, when by his friends he understood the happy news in England, that queen Elizabeth reigned, and that the state of religion was sure, and likely to continue, about the end of that year, in which this was in hand, came back to his country. So much time he had taken to bethink himself, lest (if by any inconstancy of the people they should grow weary of their present state) he should again be forced to seek his fortunes abroad; besides (his family being then increased with two children) he was obliged to stay, till money might from home be sent him, to bear his charges in travelling. But before he could get from thence, he was informed that some hard speeches had passed respecting him, as if through pride he had delayed to come, thereby seeking a shorter and more speedy way to preferment, as being due to him, when he should be sent for. This he knew to be a cast of their cunning, who themselves with all earnestness striving for honours, feared Master Foxe, as a man deserving, and likely to be preferred before them. Yet he thought it not worth his labour, to make any excuse for such a crime, as would of itself come to nothing; but equally despising injuries, and neglecting his own right, hid himself wholly in his study. As in our bodies it is commonly seen, that those men are more healthful, who use moderate diet and exercise, than those who exceed in either; so I suppose doth the case stand with our minds, that he, who if fortune hath given him no rule prescribeth none to himself, can hardly persist in the soundness of his duty; whereas he who useth modesty in his fortunes, is always more fresh and vigorous for any illustrious undertakings. For Master Foxe, being for his abilities famous, and supported (as I before shewed) with the friendship of great personages, might with ease have attained to whatever his desires had inclined him; but affecting neither riches nor authority, the wishes of happy men, (though his deserts were equal with any) yet was he well contented to keep the conscience of well-doing to himself, and that rewards should remain in the possession of others. This I neither admit, as wholly to his commendation, nor yet find fault with, as many have done. Let us at least favour good men so far, as to allow virtue, to choose what degree of fortune it chooses to shine in; or if we will needs restrain it within certain limits, let us do it to those who are good with hope of reward; as for them who are so for no design, if their glory overwhelm us not, we shall not need to fear their multitude.

I shall write of a life, bearing continually true and solid fruits, but not such whereon the reader's senses may surfeit; where neither the rare stratagems of war or peace shall be related, nor any such discourses as writers use, when they intend to captivate the ears of the hearers. I am to speak of a life passed over without noise, of modesty at home and abroad, of charity, contempt of the world, and thirst after heavenly things; of unwearied labours, and all actions so performed as might be exemplary or beneficial to others.

I have shewed before, that Foxe first applied himself to write the history of the church, whilst he was at Basil; and that the reason why he did not there finish it, was, that he might afterwards use the testimony of more witnesses. This work not a little vexed the minds of the papists. For well they saw that in vain they had shed so much blood, and to no effect been guilty of so great cruelty, if an account of these proceedings should be transmitted to succeeding ages: and that the work itself could not be taken out of men's hands, they well understood. There was therefore no other hope left, but by charging the author with falsehood, and feigning some cavils against him, so to lessen his credit and authority;

which, whilst Foxe endeavoured to remove, and take away from himself, he could not avoid it, but was obliged to pass the lawful bounds of a history, by a new collection of matters and testimonies. And let us but by this judge of the industry of our author, that he not only gathered together so many things, as the materials of his work, from all distances of time or places, and through all counties of the kingdom, collected the acts of both courts, and the records of matters judged, but also alone by a most distracted kind of diligence searched out, examined, freed even from moth-eating, and afterwards reduced into convenient order those things themselves, being partly as it were rusty, and eaten out by antiquity, partly by hatred or flattery of authors corrupted, and partly hid in the rugged and short form of old writing. I find by the author's own notes, that in the eleventh year after he began to write it, the work was finished; and it is very probable, that the work shall live, which was so long in being brought forth: neither in all that time used he the help of any servant about his writing or other business: so much doth industry employed to one purpose, and gathered into itself, afford more useful assistance, than being scattered, and the mind divided into many cares at once, though it hath never so many helping hands.

Foxe, when he had for many years left no time free from his study, either not at all, or not seasonably affording himself what nature required, was at length brought to that condition, that his natural liveliness and vigour being spent, neither his friends nor kindred could by sight remember him. By this means he first fell into that withered leanness of body, in which many afterwards saw him, never again returning to that pleasing and cheerful countenance which he had before; but when he would not be persuaded to lessen his accustomed labours, or to lay aside his study, or to recreate himself, which was the cause of the debility which had been produced, the signs thereof did likewise remain.

From this time Foxe began to be much spoken of, for a good historian; the other virtues of his mind, as they were less known abroad, so were overshadowed by that which was known. Shortly after, he began also to wax famous for other endowments, not only as a learned man, but as one for his friendliness useful, and helpful to others. But modesty will not allow me, by way of journal, to rehearse the voluntary pains he took upon him: however, it will not be amiss, in general, to say something of it; and to show how, either by good advice, comfortable persuasions, or a charitable hand, he either relieved the wants, or satisfied the desires of innumerable persons; whereupon no man's house was in those times thronged with more clients than his. There repaired to him both citizens and strangers, noblemen and common people of all degrees, and almost all for the same cause; to seek some relief for a wounded conscience. At length, some who were likewise sick in body, would needs be carried to him; but this, to stop rumours, he would not suffer to be done. For, because they were brought thither, they were by some reported to be cured.

Thus spending the day at home in such like duties, frequently preaching abroad, and going to visit those who were not able to come themselves to him, he both fulfilled that, which, by the courtesy of his own disposition, was enjoined him, and neglected not the performance of that duty, which the office of his ministry had imposed upon him. That little time which his friends, either called away by other occasions, or ashamed of being too tedious, had left free to his own disposal, he bestowed not in sleeping, or taking his pleasure, but in prayer and studying; when he engaged in either of these exercises, he always retired into some private apartment, or made use of the night's silence for secresy, unless by chance sometimes the vehement groans he mingled with his prayers, being heard by some that were near the place, gave notice how earnest he was in his devotions. For at no time of the night could any man come to find his labours ended; but often hath the next morning's light seen the last of his night's care concluded.

Now, although these things be true, ye well I know there are many who will find fault, that I have so slightly passed them over; and demand, why I produce not the matters themselves, as witnesses of his actions, or at least some particular example of each kind, that they may with more security give credit to the rest. But many things there are which hinder me from so doing.

First, that common civility forbiddeth us, to publish abroad that which the conscience of another hath committed to our secrecy; and a very ill example should he give, who should not rather by all means conceal, than make known to the world, the secrets of private houses, the jarrings of friends, and such private affairs in men's lives, whereof it may either shame, or repent them: next, that the matters themselves, which used to be attended to in the greatest privacy that might be, could by no means come to our knowledge; or, if by suspicion somewhat were gathered, and that I should instance in one or two particulars; yet what great assurance in the rest, could I draw from hence?

I will now bring the last argument, I know not whether I should say, of his ability or industry; that he, who so wholly had given himself to please his friends, that he had set apart no time, for his other occasions, yet wrote so much, as it might well have been believed, he had done nothing else.

I have here for their sakes, who may desire it, set down the titles of those books he wrote; which are these—Comœdiarum libri 2. Syllogisticon. Admonitio ad Parliamentum. De lapsis per errorem in Ecclesiam restituendis. Oliva Evangelica. De Christo gratis justificante. De Christo Crucifixo. Papa confutatus. Contra Osorium de Justitia. Meditationes supra Apocalypsim Rerum in Ecclesia gestarum Commentarii. The Acts and Monuments of the Church.

We are now come so far, as to be able from hence, to give the reader a full sight at once, of the rest of Foxe's life, which ought, I suppose, in like manner to please them, as we see those that travel, when they have been long tired with continual rugged ways and rough forests, and come at length into the plain and champaigne countries, are with the very change of soil not a little delighted and refreshed.

In this (as it were) sketch of his conditions, we shall first observe that which might well be thought the chiefest of his virtues; namely, a deliberate and resolved contempt of all things, which are in greatest esteem among men, and especially of pleasures: which disposition of his, whether inbred by nature, acquired by discipline, or infused by God, did of necessity give him great ability to perform with commendation whatever he chose to take in hand; there being nothing which can mislead the mind into errors, which would otherwise of itself hold the right way, but what proceedeth from some pleasure or other; lying in wait to entrap us in our journey. But so did Foxe hold play with these enemies, as one who desired not to save himself by flying, or shelter himself in some secret place of retirement; but by often skirmishing, and experience in the manner of fighting, to increase his own strength, and give to others an example of fortitude; using to say, That they did not great matter, who forsook business and employments in the world, lest they should suffer themselves to be allured and deceived by them. For, that the things were in themelves innocent, and then first of all grew hurtful, when they were overvalued and pursued with avaricious desire; which he that can beat back when it assaileth him, and striveth to break in upon him, is deservedly called temperate; but that he who was never in any temptation, may rather seem to have been good through want of occasion to be otherwise, than by his own virtue.

He never therefore declined the friendship of illustrious personages; not to gain honour to himself, but that thereby he saw his commendation would be more effectual, when he should desire favour on the behalf of others. The money, which sometimes rich men offered him, he accepted, returning it back to the poor. He likewise frequented the tables of his friends, not for his own pleasure, being of a spare diet; but from courtesy to keep them company, and lest any should imagine, he either feared or fled from the wrestling, and striving with voluptuous encounters, or that he thought himself, by being absent, better defended against the pleasures incident to eating and drinking, than by the guard of his own moderation. In a word, so did Mr. Foxe behave himself in those things which are accompanied by delights, that certain it is, none of those who were always in his company, can remember any speech or action of his, which might betray the least shew of a desire for them; and so far was he from thirsting after honour, riches, applause, or any outward good, that he would at no time suffer the care of his private estate to enter his mind, much less that it should by taking thought for his household affairs, be overcome or drawn aside: which either security of his, or as some called it, slothfulness in his own fortunes, I will hereafter declare whence it proceeded. In the mean time, whilst I consider the cause wherefore he thought all other things so contemptible, especially since that could not be imagined to arise from any obstinate disdainfulness, much less from a sluggishness of mind; I assure myself, it was only the love of God, wherewith his mind was so filled, and so much delighted, that he left no room, nor any affection free for other pleasures, of his own accord separating himself from the fashions of the world, of which he was not otherwise incapable; and devoting himself wholly to this care, like one who had found an invaluable treasure, he bent his eyes and mind upon this only, neither hoping nor expecting any thing besides, but resolved to make this the scope of all his wishes and desires: whereby (as in such a case must needs happen) it so fell out, that they who observed his mind so steadfastly fixed upon God, and that he both spoke and did many things beyond the opinions of an ordinarily good man, believed that he could not be void of some divine inspiration; and now some began, not as a good man to honour him, but as one sent from heaven, even to adore him, through the folly of mankind, madly doting upon any thing, whatsoever their own will hath set up to be worshipped.

It will not be out of the way to add in general what Foxe thought of the church of Rome, and the bishop thereof, as far as they may be gathered out of his speeches when, being of ripe years, he had strengthened his judgment with much experience.

The heads of his opinions were these:

That among the christian church the Roman had been in dignity always chief, and of most antiquity. That it retained this dignity and preference many ages after, by little and little, growing to greater authority, not by consent of the people, or by any right to that claim, but by reason of a certain inclination and custom among men, that where any chanced to excel others, they first began to be powerful among the rest, and at length to exercise command over them. That the greatest honour and authority it had was among these western kingdoms, which, as every one mostly loved the christian religion, so were they by the diligence and piety of the Romans most assisted; in this respect it had not ill deserved to be called the mother of those churches. That the occasion of so great an increase was, that the city of Rome, being of so ancient renown, and as it were by destiny appointed monarch of the world, in all ages abounding with men of great courage and virtue, being well peopled, wealthy, usefully seated, and always under the emperors' sight, easily afforded this convenience. That at the first the christians could no where meet together with less trouble, or be more plentifully provided for, or more safely concealed, or, when need was, die with more constancy; all which made posterity greatly to admire and honour them. That the church at first flourished rather in good discipline, and the approved holiness of the professors, than in abundance of riches, there being yet no looseness, no pride or ambition found in the manners of the clergy; and money, servants, lands, jewels, and such like goods, were altogether unknown to them; in short, all things were so restrained, either by modesty in using what they had, or contented in wanting what they had not, as that in Rome alone seemed to be the seat of the christian religion. All this was observed

with the greatest strictness in the times nearest to the church's infancy; but, in process of time, by little and little, it began to be neglected and corrupted, after the same manners as rivers, whose streams being small and clear near their head, the farther they proceed the larger is the channel, but with more troubled waters; till at length, by mixture with the sea, they become also unwholesome; and though in no one place can we perceive where they are any jot changed from their first purity; yet may we easily enough find a great difference, if we compare the extremes together. In the church it so fell out, that having brought all nations to the christian faith, after they once began to think it for the honour of the empire, that the priests should no longer (as they had formerly been accustomed) endure poverty, but live in a more sumptuous way, to which purpose the emperors granted many things to the churchmen, both as an ornament and reward to them; then also the priests began, first to be taken with the love of riches, then, by degrees, to grow wanton through abundance, and not to care what little pains they took; afterwards (as always the succeeding age adds to the vice of the former) they affected power also, which, when they had once obtained, and, by the emperor's gift, received the command of the church, they gave not over, till (having cast down the emperors, by whose bounty they had so prevailed) they both invaded the privileges of the empire, and now laid claim to both spiritual and temporal government; in the mean while, neglecting those rules of religion which their predecessors had prescribed them, neither themselves searching the scriptures, nor permitting others to do it; and esteeming the worship of God to consist rather in outward devotion and pomp of ceremonies, than in the obedience of faith. That by this means it came to pass, that the church of Rome (as all other immoderate empires) not only fell from that high degree it once held, but also subverted in itself the very substance and state of a church: nor that this ought to seem strange, if, as the most healthful bodies fall into sickness with most danger, so it happeneth, that the prime of all churches should have no mean, but either remain in the perfection of health, or become the most dangerous enemy to it; and that for this cause the pope now seemed to be antichrist. That notwithstanding the case was so plain, yet neither part ought to lend too much belief to arguments, nor be too earnest in hindering it, if by any moderation of men the matter might be brought to soundness and agreement. That it was not, perhaps, in our power to take from Rome her ancient honour, and the opinion of her religion so fixed already in the minds of men. That the church of Rome had fallen by her own covetousness, ambition, and prevarication; but that never any man had gone so far in sinning, as that repentance had not reached as far. That therefore it was fit to allow them, as a returning to repentance, so some convenient means to move them to it, and sufficient space to repent in. That it might be the author disliked them, because a German or Frenchman, and not an Italian of their own nation had told them of their errors. That there might one day among their own men be found some, by whose authority they should not be ashamed to amend their faults, and with more willingness part with their own power to procure the peace of the whole world. That there was at least this hope left, it might so fall out that they had no further erred in the articles of faith than that they would not suffer too much to be known. That the conditions of agreement would be, first, That the pope should forsake all those tenets, by which he gained such great sums of money; there being nothing whereto the people might with more difficulty be persuaded, than that Christ, the Saviour of the world, had instructed his church in the way of getting money, and setting the scriptures to sale. Next, that he should renounce all secular jurisdiction, and not suppose himself to have title, or any thing to do with the right of princes. That, on the other side, his opposers should not refuse, that some one man may have the principal place of counsel and government in the church affairs, as being a thing which would have many conveniences in it, when it might be done with security;

neither that the Romish church, because it had once fallen, ought to make against it ; nor that it had first flourished to prevail for it, herein to be preferred before any other ; but that all this was to be left to the discretion of a general council of the christians, which might be so equitable, as that neither the power or favour of any one should be able, either from the place of meeting, or the difference in number of voices, to promise itself any advantage to the injury of the rest. That, in the mean while, it would be of great moment to the hope and speediness of settling all controversies, if hereafter on both sides they would give such instructions, as might cause in each party a better hope and opinion of the other, especially that they ought to leave off that stubborn conceit, whereby each of them, presuming itself to be the only true church, supposeth the other excluded. For that it were not only wicked, but also highly to the dishonour of God, to think that he had so given his commandments to mankind as that they should be turned to the destruction of those that obey them ; which must of necessity come to pass, if when all men will not consent in the same opinion, they who understand most shall refuse to admit the rest ; was therefore the kingdom of heaven reserved only for the more understanding sort, and those that know most ? Where should then the fools of the world be ; where should little children be, whom Christ had set apart for himself ? How much better should we serve God by following that which was evident, than by interpreting that which was doubtful ? How much more probable were it, that God's mercy was so abundant, as when men were once agreed in point of general obedience, there should nothing else be laid to their charge ? For, that the force of obedience was before God so great, as thereby only all other inequalities might be made even ; but if all were not in equal condition, that certainly with God they were best esteemed who judged with the most modesty of others.

I will now speak of the friends of Mr. Foxe: among whom, I have already shewed with how great affection he was beloved by the duke of Norfolk, being by his bounty maintained in his lifetime, and after his death by the pension he bestowed on him, which his son, the right honourable the earl of Suffolk, to whom those revenues descended, out of his liberality continued.

His fortunes were increased by the lord William Cecil, then lord treasurer, a man beyond expression excellent, whom it as much availed queen Elizabeth to have for her minister, as it availed the kingdom to have Elizabeth for their queen; and without doubt most deserving, that in himself and in his posterity he should flourish in that kingdom, which he had by his wisdom and advice made most flourishing. He, of the queen's gift, obtained for Mr. Foxe the rectory of Shipton, upon no other inducement but his public merits, and when Mr. Foxe delayed, and after his manner entreated leave to excuse himself, the lord Cecil politically overcame his bashfulness by telling him, that he neither accepted that for an answer, nor had he deserved that the blame of Mr. Foxe's refusing the queen's gift should be laid upon him, as if he had been his hindrance.

To the earls of Bedford and of Warwick he was very acceptable.

He was very intimate with sir Francis Walsingham, secretary of state, a prudent and vigilant man, and one who deservedly was the first that advanced the power of the secretaryship.

The two brothers, sir Thomas Hennage and Master Michael Hennage, he sincerely loved, the first for the sweetness of his behaviour, the other for his solid learning and singular modesty of life, and though they were each of them, in their kind, most accomplished gentlemen, yet he was wont to say that sir Thomas Hennage had as much as was requisite in any way to become a complete courtier, but that Master Michael Hennage had both all his brother in himself, and that besides of his own which the court had not corrupted.

To sir Drew Drury he bare likewise a strong affection, as to a man of sincere intentions, and of great constancy in all fortunes, and perhaps, the only man in the court who continued his favour without loss of his freedom.

Among the prelates he principally reverenced Doctor Grindall, archbishop of Canterbury ; Doctor Elmar, bishop of London ; and Doctor Pilkington, bishop of Durham ; and Doctor Nowell, dean of St. Paul's, who were his partners in banishment at Basil.

Among the writers of his time he preferred, before the rest, Doctor Humphrey, Doctor Whiteaker, and Doctor Fulke, with whose learning he was greatly delighted, and esteemed it no small benefit to be again beloved by them.

But with none had he more familiar acquaintance than with Master John Crowly and Master Baldwine Collins, whose counsel he made use of in all his affairs, especially of Master Collins, concerning whom he was wont to say, That he knew not which had the greatest share in him, excellence of knowledge, or modesty of mind.

Among military men, sir Francis Drake was much delighted with his familiarity ; whom to commend near the times he lived in, were needless, but to commend him to posterity, according to his merits, many volumes would scarce suffice.

Among the citizens of London, he always found great good will ; especially with sir Thomas Gresham, sir Thomas Roe, Alderman Bacchus, Master Smith, Master Dale, and Master Sherington, who held him in great estimation, being part of them such as had borne the highest places of honour in the city, and part of them merchants of great substance.

I pass by many, who perhaps had as great a share in Master Foxe's friendship as any of these ; nor ought it to be accounted a fault, if I either knew not, or remembered not all : but this I ought not to omit, (as being the chief cause why I thought fit to mention the above-named worthy men) that these were they, from whom, I before said, Master Foxe received such large sums of money to divide among the poor : which, although they did it with so much privacy, as that they trusted not to messengers in delivering it, not regarding any outward praise, their well-doing might procure them, knowing the consciousness of it to be as much as they needed to desire. Yet it was not fitting for me in Foxe's history, to dissemble it, or to give any man occasion to suppose the truth was not opened by Foxe, though they themselves thought good to neglect the fruit of so great liberality, especially since it may abundantly serve for commendation of both him and them, that they should be known by their own actions, and he by none but his own.

He used always among his friends a pleasant kind of familiarity, wherewith he seasoned the gravity and severity of his other behaviour.

Being once asked at a friend's table, what dish he desired to be set up to him to begin his meal with, he answered, " the last ;" which word was pleasantly taken, as if he had meant some choicer dish, such as are usually brought for the second course ; whereas he rather signified the desire he had to see dinner ended, that he might depart home.

Going abroad, by chance, he met a woman that he knew, who, pulling a book from under her arm, and saying, " See you not that I am going to a sermon ;" Foxe replied, " But if you will be ruled by me, go home, rather, for to-day you will do but little good at church ;" and when she asked, " At what time therefore he would counsel her to go ?" " Then," answered he, " when you tell nobody before hand."

It happened at his own table that a gentleman there spake somewhat too freely against the earl of Leicester, which, when Foxe heard, he commanded a bowl filled with wine to be brought him, which being done : " This bowl," said he, " was given to me by the earl of Leicester," so stopping the gentleman in his intemperate speeches without reprehending him.

When a young man, a little too forward, had in presence of many, said, " That he could conceive no reason in the reading of old authors, why men should so greatly admire them." " No marvel indeed," replied Foxe, " for if you could conceive the reason, you would then admire them yourself."

I could mention many anecdotes of this kind, but that I will not exceed my intended limits too far.

At length having in such actions, and such behaviour spent out his age, being now full of years, and blessed with friends, ere he had quite passed through his seven-tieth year, (1587) he died, not through any known disease, but through much age.

Upon the report of his death the whole city lamented, honouring the small funeral which was made for him, with the concourse of a great multitude of people, and in no other fashion of mourning, than as if among so many, each man had buried his own father, or his own brother.

CHRONOLOGICAL TABLE OF CONTENTS.

BOOK I.

CONTAINING

THREE HUNDRED YEARS NEXT AFTER CHRIST, WITH THE TEN PERSECUTIONS OF THE PRIMITIVE CHURCH.

BOOK II.

CONTAINING

THE NEXT THREE HUNDRED YEARS, WITH SUCH THINGS SPECIALLY AS HAVE HAPPENED IN ENGLAND FROM THE TIME OF KING LUCIUS TO GREGORY, AND SO AFTER TO THE TIME OF KING EGBERT.

BOOK III.

CONTAINING

THE THREE HUNDRED YEARS FROM THE REIGN OF KING EGBERT TO THE TIME OF WILLIAM THE CONQUEROR.

BOOK IV.

CONTAINING

THE THREE HUNDRED YEARS FROM WILLIAM THE CONQUEROR TO THE TIME OF JOHN WICKLIFE.

BOOK V.

CONTAINING

THE LAST THREE HUNDRED YEARS FROM THE LOOSING OUT OF SATAN.

BOOK VI.

PERTAINING

TO THE LAST THREE HUNDRED YEARS FROM THE LOOSING OUT OF SATAN.

BOOK VII.

BEGINNING WITH

THE REIGN OF KING HENRY VIII.

BOOK VIII.

CONTAINING

THE HISTORY OF ENGLISH AFFAIRS APPERTAINING BOTH TO THE ECCLESIASTICAL AND CIVIL STATES.

BOOK IX.

CONTAINING

AN ACCOUNT OF THE ACTS AND EVENTS OF THE REIGN OF KING EDWARD THE SIXTH.

BOOK X.

CONTAINING

THE FIRST ENTERING OF QUEEN MARY TO THE CROWN, WITH THE ALTERATION
OF RELIGION IN THE REALM.

BOOK XI.

COMPRISING

THE HISTORY OF THOSE WHO SUFFERED MARTYRDOM AND PERSECUTION
IN THE TIME OF QUEEN MARY.

BOOK XII.

COMPRISING

THE PERSECUTIONS AGAINST THE FAITHFUL AND TRUE SERVANTS OF CHRIST, FROM THE BEGINNING OF JANUARY 1557, AND THE FIFTH YEAR OF QUEEN MARY.

APPENDIX I

THE MASSACRE OF THE PROTESTANTS IN FRANCE IN 1572. 998

APPENDIX II.

A BRIEF DISCOURSE TOUCHING THE GREAT PREPARATIONS MADE BY THE SPANIARDS, AND OTHER ROMAN CATHOLICS, FOR THAT INVINCIBLE NAVY, INTENDED FOR THE INVADING AND SURPRISING OF THE REALM OF ENGLAND, TOGETHER WITH THEIR UTTER OVERTHROW. 1013

APPENDIX III.

CONTAINING

A DISCOURSE TOUCHING THE MANNER OF THE DISCOVERY OF THE GUNPOWDER TREASON, WITH THE EXAMINATION OF SOME OF THE PRISONERS. . . 1018

APPENDIX IV.

THE HISTORY OF THE IRISH REBELLION IN THE YEAR 1641, WHEN THE PAPISTS ATTEMPTED TO EXTIRPATE THE PROTESTANTS IN THE KINGDOM OF IRELAND. BY SIR JOHN TEMPLE, KNT., MASTER OF THE ROLLS, AND ONE OF HIS MAJESTY'S MOST HONOURABLE PRIVY-COUNCIL AT THAT TIME IN IRELAND. . . 1035

APPENDIX V.

CONTAINING

THE EXECUTION OF JUSTICE IN ENGLAND, NOT FOR RELIGION, BUT FOR TREASON. 1067

THE

ACTS AND MONUMENTS,

BY

JOHN FOXE.

EDITED BY

REV. M. HOBART SEYMOUR, M.A.

THE AUTHOR'S PREFACE.

To the True and Faithful Congregation of Christ's Universal Church, with all and singular the Members thereof, wheresoever congregated or dispersed, throughout the Realm of England, a Protestation or Petition of the Author, wishing to the same abundance of all peace and tranquillity, with the speedy coming of Christ the Spouse, to make an end of all mortal misery.

Solomon, the peaceable prince of Israel, as we read in the First Book of Kings, after he had finished the building of the Lord's Temple, (which he had seven years in hand) made his petition to the Lord for all that should pray in the temple, or turn their face toward it; and his request was granted, the Lord answering him, as we read in ch. ix. 3. " I have heard thy prayer and have hallowed this house," &c. although the infinite Majesty of God is not to be confined within any material walls, yet it so pleased his goodness to respect this prayer of the king, that he not only promised to hear them who prayed there, but also filled the same with his own glory. For we read, " The priests could not stand to minister, because of the cloud, for the glory of the Lord had filled the house of the Lord," 1 Kings viii. 11.

Upon the like trust in God's gracious goodness, if I, a sinful wretch, not comparing my work with the building of that temple, but yet following the zeal of the builder, might either be so bold as to ask, or so happy as to speed, after my seven years' labour about this Ecclesiastical History, I would most humbly crave of Almighty God to bestow his blessing upon the same; that as the prayers of them who prayed in the outward temple were heard, so all true disposed minds which shall resort to the reading of this history, containing the acts of God's holy martyrs, and monuments of his church, may, by the example of their life, faith, and doctrine, receive some spiritual fruit to their souls, through the operation of his grace, that it may be to the advancement of his glory, and profit of his church, through Christ Jesus our Lord. Amen.

But as it happened in that temple of Solomon, that all who came thither came not to pray, but many to prate, some to gaze and hear news, some to talk and walk, some to buy and sell, some to carp and find fault, and some also at the last to destroy and pull down, as they did indeed; (for what is in this world so strong, but it will be impugned? what so perfect, but it will be abused? so true, that will not be contradicted? or so circumspectly done, but wranglers will find fault?) Even so in writing this history, I expect that amongst many well disposed readers, some wasp's-nest or other will be stirred up to buzz about my ears, so dangerous a thing is it now-a-days, to write or do any good, but either by flattering a man we must offend the godly, or by true speaking procure hatred of the wicked. Of such stinging wasps and buzzing drones I had sufficient trial in my former edition; who, if they had found in my book any just cause to find fault, or upon any true zeal of truth had proceeded against the untruths of my history, and

had brought just proofs for the same, I could right well abide it, for God forbid but that faults, wheresoever they be, should be detected and accused. And therefore, accusers in a commonwealth, after my mind, are of no small service.

But then such accusers must beware they do not act like the dog of whom Cicero in his oration speaks, which being set in the capitol to frighten away thieves by night, let the thieves alone, and barked at true men walking in the day. To bay and bark where true faults are, is not amiss. But to carp where no cause is; to spy straws in others, and leap over their own blocks; to swallow camels and to strain at gnats; to oppress truth with lies, and to set up lies for truth; to blaspheme the dear martyrs of Christ, and to canonize for saints those whom scripture would scarcely allow for good subjects; that is intolerable: such barking curs, if they were well served, would be made awhile to stoop: but with these brawling spirits I intend not at this time much to wrestle.

Wherefore, to leave them a while, till further leisure serve me to attend upon them, thus much I thought in the mean season, by way of protestation or petition, to write unto you, both in general and particular, the true members and faithful congregation of Christ's church, wherever either congregated together or dispersed through the whole realm of England, that for so much as all these adversaries seek, is to do what they can, by discrediting of this History with slanders and sinister surmises, to withdraw the readers from it: this, therefore, shall be in few words to warn and desire all well-minded lovers and partakers of Christ's gospel, not to suffer yourselves to be deceived with the boastings and hyperbolical speeches of those slandering tongues, whatever they have, or shall hereafter, exclaim against the same; but impartially deferring your judgment till truth be tried, that you will first *peruse*, and then *refuse;* measuring the untruths of this history, not by the scoring up of their hundreds and thousands of lies which they give out, but wisely weighing the purpose of their doings according as you find, and so to judge of the matter.

I allure neither one nor other to read my books; let every man do as he pleases. If any shall think his labour too much in reading this history, his choice is free, either to read this or any other work. But if the fruit thereof shall recompence the reader's trouble, then I would wish no man so light-eared as to be carried away by any sinister clamour of adversaries, who many times deprave good doings, not for the faults they find, but only find faults because they would deprave. As for me and my history, as my purpose was to profit all and displease none; so if skill in any part be wanting, yet hath my purpose been simple, and the cause no less urgent also, which moved me to take this enterprise in hand.

For first to see the simple flock of Christ, especially the unlearned sort, so miserably deluded, and all for ignorance of history, not knowing the course of times, and true descent of the church, it grieved me that that part of history had been so long unsupplied in this my country church of England. Again, considering the multitude of chronicles and history-writers, both in England and out of England, of whom the most part have been either monks or clients to the See of Rome, it grieved me to behold how partially they handled their stories. Whose diligent labour, although I cannot but commend, in committing many things to writing not unfruitful to be known, nor unpleasant to be read; yet I lamented to see that the principal points, which chiefly concerned the state of Christ's church, and were most necessary to be known by all christian people, were either altogether omitted in their monuments, or if any mention thereof were inserted, yet all things were drawn to the honour specially of the church of Rome, or else to the favour of their own sect of religion. Whereby the unlearned, hearing and reading in their writings no other church mentioned or magnified, but only that church which flourished in this world in riches and riot, were led, to think that no other church stood in all the earth but only the church of Rome.

In the number of this sort of writers, besides our monks of England (for every monastery almost had its chronicler) I might also recite both Italian and other authors, as Platina, Sabellicus, Nauclerus, Martin, Antony, Vincent, Onuphrius, Laziard, George Lilius, Polydore Virgil, with many more, who taking upon them to intermeddle with matters of the church, although they express some part of the truth in matters concerning the bishops and see of Rome, yet in suppressing another part they play with us, as Ananias and Sapphira did with their money, or as the painter Apelles did, who, painting the one half of Venus coming out of the sea, left the other half imperfect. So these writers, while they show us one half of the bishop of Rome, leave the other half of him imperfect, and utterly untold. For as they paint him on the one part glittering in wealth and glory, in showing what succession the popes had from the chair of St. Peter, when they first began, and how long they sat, what churches and what famous buildings they erected, how far their possessions reached, what laws they made, what councils they called, what honour they received of kings and emperors, what princes and countries they brought under their authority, with other like stratagems of great pomp and royalty; so on the other side, what vices these popes brought with them to their seat, what abominations they practised, what superstition they maintained, what idolatry they procured, what wicked doctrine they defended contrary to the express word of God, to what heresies they fell, into what division of sects they cut the unity of christian religion, how some practised by simony, some by necromancy and sorcery, some by poisoning, some indenting with the devil to come by their papacy, what hypocrisy was in their lives, what corruption in their doctrine, what wars they raised, what bloodshed they caused, what treachery they traversed against their lords and emperors, imprisoning some, betraying some to the templars and Saracens, in bringing others under their feet, also in beheading some, as they did with Frederick and Conradine, the heirs and offspring of the house of Frederick Barbarossa, A.D. 1269. Furthermore, how mightily Almighty God hath stood against them, how their wars never prospered against the Turks, how the godly and learned from time to time have ever opposed their errors, &c. Of these and a thousand other things not one word hath been said, but all kept as secret as in auricular confession.

When I considered this partial dealing and corrupt handling of historians, I thought nothing more wanting in the church than a full and complete history, which being faithfully collected out of all our monastic writers, and written monuments, should neither contain every vain written fable, for that would be too much; nor yet leave out any thing necessary, for that would be too little; but with a moderate discretion taking the best of every one, should both ease the labour of the reader from turning over such a number of writers, and should also open the plain truth of times lying long hid in the obscure darkness of antiquity. Whereby all studious readers, beholding as in a glass the stay, course, and alteration of religion, decay of doctrine, and the controversies of the church, might discern the better between antiquity and novelty. For if the things which are *first*, (after the rule of Tertullian) are to be preferred before those that are *later*, then is the reading of history very necessary in the church, to know what went before, and what followed after; and therefore, not without cause in old authors history is called the Witness of Times, the Light of Verity, the Life of Memory, Teacher of Life, and Shewer of Antiquity, &c. Without the knowledge of which, man's life is blind, and soon may fall into any kind of error, as by manifest experience we see in these desolate times of the church, when the bishops of Rome under colour of antiquity have turned truth into heresy, and brought such new-found devices of strange doctrine and religion, as in the former age of the church were never heard of, and which are now believed, all through ignorance of times, and for lack of true history.

For to say the truth, if times had been well searched, or if they who wrote histories had without partiality gone upright between God and Baal, halting on neither side, it might well have been found, that the most part of all this catholic corruption intruded into the church by the bishops of Rome, as transubstantiation, elevation and adoration of the sacrament, auricular confession, forced vows of priests not to marry, veneration of images, private and satisfactory masses, the order of Gregory's mass now used, the usurped authority and supreme power of the see of Rome, with all the rest of their ceremonies and weeds of superstition now overgrowing the church; all these (I say) to be new nothings lately coined in the mint of Rome, without any stamp of antiquity, as by reading of this History shall I trust sufficiently appear. Which history, therefore, I have here taken in hand, that as other writers heretofore have employed their labour to magnify the church of Rome, so in this history there might appear to all christian readers the image of both churches, as well of the one as of the other; especially of the poor, oppressed and persecuted church of Christ. Which persecuted church though it has been of long season trodden under foot by enemies, neglected in the world, not regarded in histories, and scarce visible or known to worldly eyes, yet has it been the only true church of God, wherein he has mightily wrought hitherto, in preserving the same in all extreme distresses, continually stirring up from time to time faithful ministers, who have always kept some sparks of his true doctrine and religion.

Now, forasmuch as the true church of God goeth not lightly alone, but is accompanied with some other church of the devil to deface and malign the same, it is necessary that the difference between them should be seen, and the descent of the right church described from the apostle's time, which hitherto has been lacking in most histories, partly for fear, because men durst not, partly for ignorance, because men could not discern rightly between the one and the other, who beholding the church of Rome so visible and glorious in the eyes of all the world, so shining in outward beauty, to bear such a port, to carry such a train and multitude, and to stand in such high authority, supposed the same to be the only right catholic mother: the other, because it was not so visibly known in the world, they thought, therefore, could not be the true church of Christ. Wherein they were much deceived: for, although the right church of God is not so invisible in the world that none can see it, yet neither is it so visible that every worldly eye may perceive it. For like as is the nature of truth, so is the proper condition of the true church, that commonly none see it, but such only as are the members and partakers of it. And therefore, they who require that God's holy church should be evident and visible to the whole world, seem to define the great synagogue of the world, rather than the true spiritual church of God.

In Christ's time, who would have thought but that the congregations and councils of the pharisees had been the right church? And yet Christ had another church in earth besides that; which, although it was not so manifest in the sight of the world, yet it was the only true church in the sight of God: to this church Christ referred, speaking of the temple, which he would raise again the third day. And yet, after that the Lord was risen, he shewed not himself to the world, but only to his elect, which were but few. The same church after that increased and multiplied mightily among the Jews, yet the Jews had not eyes to see God's church, but did persecute it, till at length all their whole nation was destroyed.

After the Jews, came the heathen emperors of Rome, who, having the whole power of the world in their hands, did all the world could do to extinguish the name and church of Christ; whose violence continued the space of three hundred years, all which time the true church of Christ was not great in the sight of the world, but rather was abhorred every where, and yet, notwithstanding, the same small flock, so despised in the world, the Lord highly regarded, and mightily preserved. For although many of the christians suffered death, yet was their death neither loss to them, nor detriment to the church; but the more they suffered, the more of their blood increased.

In the time of these emperors, God raised up in this realm of Britain, divers worthy preachers and witnesses, as Elnanus, Meduinus, Meltivianus, Amphibolus, Albanus, Aaron, Julius, and others, in whose time the doctrine of faith, without men's traditions, was sincerely preached. After their death and martyrdom it pleased the Lord to provide a general quietness to his church, whereby the number of his flock began more to increase.

In this age then followed in this land, Fastidius, Nivian, Patrick, Bacchiarius, Dubricius, Congellus, Kentigern, Helmotus, David, Daniel, Sampson, Elnodugus, Asaphus, Gildas, Henlanus, Elbodus, Dinothus, Samuel, Nivius, and many more, who governed the church of Britain by christian doctrine a long season; although the civil governors for the time were then dissolute and careless, (as Gildas very sharply lays to their charge), and so at length were subdued by the Saxons.

All this while, about the space of four hundred years, religion remained uncorrupt in Britain, and the word of Christ was truly preached, till, about the coming of Austin the monk, and his companions from Rome, many of the said British preachers were slain by the Saxons. After that Christian faith began to enter and spring among the Saxons, after a certain Romish sort, yet, notwithstanding somewhat more tolerable than were the times which followed, through the diligent industry of some godly teachers who then lived amongst them, as Aidanus, Finianus, Coleman, archbishop of York, Bede, John of Beverly, Alcuin, Noetus, Hucharius, Serlo, Achardus, Ealtedus, Alexander, Neckham, Negellus, Fenallus, Alfricus, Sygeferthus, and such others, who, though they erred in some few things, yet they are not so greatly to be complained of compared with the abuses that followed. For as yet, the error of transubstantiation and elevation, with auricular confession, had not crept in for a public doctrine in Christ's church, as by their own Saxon sermon made by Ælfric, and set out in this present history may appear. During which time, although the bishops of Rome were held in some reverence by the clergy, yet they had nothing as yet to do in making laws touching matters of the church of England; but that appertained only to the kings and governors of the land, as in this history will be seen.

And thus, although the church of Rome began then to decline from God, yet during all this time it remained in some reasonable order, till, at length, the bishops of Rome began to shoot up in the world, through the liberality of good princes, and, especially of Matilda, a noble duchess of Italy, who, at her death, made the pope heir of all her lands, and endowed his see with great revenues; then riches begat ambition, and ambition destroyed religion, so that all came to ruin. Out of this corruption sprang forth here in England (as did in other places) another Romish kind of monkery, worse than the other before, being much more drowned in superstition and ceremonies, which was during the tenth century. Of this swarm were Egbert, Aigelbert, Egwine, Boniface, Wilfred, Agathon, James, Romain, Cedda, Dunstan, Oswold, Athelwold, Althelwine, duke of Eastangles, Lanfranc, Anselme, and such other.

And yet in this time also, through God's providence, the church lacked not some of better knowledge and judgment, to weigh with the darkness of those days. For although King Edgar, with Edward, his base son, being seduced by Dunstan, Oswold, and other monks, was then a great author and favourer of superstition, erecting as many monasteries as were Sundays in the year; yet, notwithstanding, this continued not long, for soon after the death of Edgar came King Ethelred, and Queen Elfthred his mother, with Alferus, duke of Merceland, and other peers and nobles of the realm, who displaced the monks again, and restored the married priests to their old possessions and livings. Moreover, after that followed also the Danes, who overthrew those monkish foundations as fast as King Edgar had set them up before.

And thus, hitherto, stood the condition of the true church of Christ, although not without some opposition and difficulty, yet in some mediate state of the truth and verity, till the time of Pope Hildebrand, called Gregory VII., which was about the year 1080, and of Pope Innocent III., in the year 1215, by whom all was turned upside down, all order broken, discipline dissolved, true doctrine defaced, christian faith extinguished. Instead whereof, was set up preaching of men's decrees, dreams and idle traditions. And whereas before truth was free to be disputed amongst learned men, now liberty was turned into law, argument into authority. Whatsoever the bishop of Rome announced, that stood for an oracle to be received of all men, without opposition or contradiction; whatever was contrary thereto, was heresy, to be punished with faggot and flaming fire! Then the sincere faith of this English church, which held out so long, began to quail. Then was the clear sunshine of God's word overshadowed with mists and darkness, appearing like sackcloth to the people, who could neither understand what they read, nor yet were permitted to read what they could understand. In these miserable days, as the true visible church began now to shrink, and keep in for fear: so, up start a new sort of players, to furnish the stage, as school-doctors, canonists, and four orders of friars, besides other monastic sects and fraternities, of infinite variety, which have ever since kept such an influence in the church, that none almost durst stir, neither Cæsar, king, nor subject. What they defined stood; what they approved, was catholic; what they condemned was heresy; whomsoever they accused, few, indeed, could save. And thus these continued, or rather reigned in the church, the space of now four hundred years, and odd. During which time, although the true church of Christ durst not openly appear in the face of the world, being oppressed by tyranny, yet neither was it so invisible and unknown, but by the providence of the Lord, some remnant always remained, which not only shewed secret good affection to sincere doctrine, but also stood in open defence of truth against the disordered church of Rome.

In which catalogue, first to omit Bertram and Berengarius, who were before Pope Innocent III., a learned multitude of sufficient witnesses might here be produced, whose names are neither obscure, nor doctrine unknown: as Joachin, abbot of Calabria; Almeric, a learned bishop, who was judged an heretic, for holding against images in the time of the said Innocent; besides the martyrs of Alsatia, of whom we read an hundred to be burned by the said Innocent in one day, as writes Herman Mucius. Add likewise to these, the Waldenses, or Albigenses, which, to a great number, separated themselves from the church of Rome. To this number also belonged Reymund, earl of Tholouse, Marsilius Patavius, William de S. Amore, Simon Tornacensis, Arnold de Nova Villa, John Semeca, besides divers other preachers in Suevia, standing against the pope, (A. D. 1440); Laurence, of England, a master of Paris, (A. D. 1260); Peter John, a minorite, who was burned after his death, (A. D. 1290); Robert Gallus, a dominic friar, (A. D. 1291); Robert Grosthead, bishop of Lincoln, who was called the Hammer of the Romanists, (A. D. 1250); Lord Peter de

Cugnerlis, (A. D. 1329). To these we may add, more-over, William Ockam, Bongratius Bergomensis, Leopold, Andrew Laudensis, Ulric Hangenor, treasurer to the emperor; John de Ganduno, (A. D. 1330), mentioned in the extravagants, Andreas de Castro, Buridian, Euda, duke of Burgundy, who counselled the French king not to receive the new-found constitutions and extravagants of the pope into his realm, Dante Alligerius, an Italian, who wrote against the pope, monks, and friars, and against the donation of Constantine, (A. D. 1330.) Taulerus, a German preacher; Conrad Hager, imprisoned for preaching against the mass, (A. D. 1339); the author of the book called Pœnitentiarius Asini, compiled about the year 1343; Michael Cesenas, a gray friar; Peter de Corbaria, with John de Poliaco, mentioned in the extravagants, and condemned by the pope; John de Castilione, with Francis de Arcatara, who were burned about the year of our Lord, 1322; John Rochtaylada, otherwise called Haybalus, with another friar, martyred about the year 1346; Francis Petrarch, who called Rome the whore of Babylon, &c. (A. D. 1350); George Ariminensis, (A. D. 1350); John de Rupe Scissa, imprisoned for certain prophecies against the pope, (A. D. 1340); Gethard Ridder, who also wrote against monks and friars, a book called Lacrymæ Ecclesiæ, (A. D. 1350); Godfrid de Fontanis, William de Landuno; John, the monk; Richard Armachanus; Nicolas Orem, preacher, (A. D. 1364); Militzius, a Bohemian, who then preached that antichrist was come, and was excommunicated for the same, (A. D. 1366); James Misnensis; Matthew Parisiensis, a Bohemian born, and a writer against the pope, (A. D. 1370); John Montziger, rector of the university of Ulm, (A. D. 1384); Nilus, archbishop of Thessalonica; Henry de Jota; Henry de Hassia, &c. (A. D. 1371.)

I do but recite the principal writers and preachers in those days. How many thousands there were which never bowed their knees to Baal, is known to God alone. Of whom we find in the writings of one Brushius, that six and thirty citizens of Maguntia were burned, (A.D. 1390), who, following the doctrine of the Waldenses, affirmed the pope to be the great antichrist. Also Massæus records of one hundred and forty, which, in the province of Narbon, were put to the fire, for not receiving the decretals of Rome, besides them that suffered at Paris, to the number of four and twenty at one time, (A.D. 1210); and the next year after were four hundred burnt under the name of heretics; besides, also, a certain good hermit, an Englishman, of whom mention is made in John Bacon, (Dist. 2. Quæst. 1.), who was committed for disputing in Paul's church against certain sacraments of the church of Rome, A.D. 1306.

To descend now somewhat lower in drawing out the descent of the church. What a multitude was there of faithful witnesses in the time of John Wickliff, (A.D. 1379), as Ocliff, William Thorp, White, Purvey, Fatshal, Pain, Gower, Chaucer, Gascoin, William Swinderby, Walter Brute, Roger Dexter, William Santry, about the year 1400. John Badby, (A.D. 1410), Nicholas Tailer, Richard Wagstaff, Michael Scrivener, William Smith, John Henry, William Parchmenar, Roger Goldsmith, with an anchoress, called Matilda, in the city of Leicester, Lord Cobham, Sir Roger Acton knight, John Beverley preacher, John Husse, Jerome of Prague, a schoolmaster, with a number of faithful Bohemians, and Thaborites not to be told; to whom I might also add Laurence Valla, and John Picus, the learned Earl of Mirandula. But why do I stand upon recital of names, which are almost infinite?

Wherefore, if any one be so deceived as to think, that the doctrine of the church of Rome (as it now stands), is of such antiquity, and that it was never opposed before the time of Luther and Zuinglius, let him read these histories; or, if he thinks the said history not to be of sufficient credit to alter his persuasion, let him peruse the acts and statutes of parliament passed in this realm, and therein consider and confer the course of times. In the 5th Richard II. (A.D. 1382), he may read of a great number (which are there called evil

persons) going about from town to town in frieze gowns, preaching to the people, &c. Which preachers although the words of the statute do term them to be dissembling persons, preaching divers sermons containing heresies and notorious errors, to the emblemishment of christian faith, and of holy church, &c., as the words do there pretend; yet notwithstanding every true christian reader may conceive of those preachers to teach no other doctrine, than now they hear their own preachers in pulpits preach against the bishop of Rome, and the corrupt heresies of his church.

He may also read in the 2nd Henry IV. chap. 15, (A.D. 1402), of another like company of good preachers and faithful defenders of true doctrine against blind heresy and error, whom, although through the corruption of that time the words of the statute falsely term false and perverse preachers, under dissembled holiness, teaching in those days openly and privily new doctrines and heretical opinions, contrary to the faith and determination of holy church, &c., yet notwithstanding whoever reads histories, and confers the order and descent of times, shall understand these to be no false teachers, but faithful witnesses of the truth, not teaching any new doctrines contrary to the determination of holy church, but rather shall find that church to be unholy which they preached against, itself rather teaching heretical opinions, contrary both to antiquity and the verity of Christ's true catholic church.

In a letter from Henry Chichesly, Archbishop of Canterbury, to Pope Martin the Fifth, in the fifth year of his popedom, (A.D. 1422), we find mention is made of a like number of faithful favourers and followers of God's holy word, of whom he says "there are many here in England infected with the heresies of Wickliff and Husse, and without force of an army they cannot be suppressed," &c. Whereupon the pope sent two cardinals to the archbishop, to cause a tenth to be gathered of all spiritual and religious men, and the money to be laid in the apostolic chamber; and if that were not sufficient, the residue to be made up of chalices, candlesticks, and other implements of the church, &c.

Shall we need then any more witnesses to prove this matter, when you see, so many years ago, whole armies and multitudes thus standing against the pope? who, though they were then termed heretics and schismatics, yet in that which their enemies called heresy they served the living Lord within the ark of his true spiritual and visible church.

And where then is the frivolous boast of the papists, (who make so much of their painted sheath, and would needs bear us down), that this government of the church of Rome, which now is, has been of such an old standing, time out of mind, even from the primitive antiquity, and that there never was any other visible church here in earth for men to follow, besides the said only catholic mother-church of Rome? when, as we sufficiently proved before, by the continual descent of the church till this present time, that the church, after the doctrine which is now reformed, is no new begun matter; but even the old church, continued by the providence and promise of Christ still standing, which although it has been of late years repressed by the tyranny of Roman bishops more than before, yet notwithstanding it was never so oppressed, but God ever maintained in it the truth of his gospel, against the heresies and errors of the church of Rome, as is to be seen more at full in this history.

Let us now proceed further in deducing this descent of the church to the year 1501, when grievous afflictions and bloody persecutions began to ensue upon Christ's church for his gospel's sake, according as is described in this history, wherein is to be seen what christian blood has been spilt, what persecutions raised, what tyranny exercised, what torments devised, what treachery used against the poor flock and church of Christ; in such sort that since Christ's time greater has not been seen.

And now we come from that time, (A.D. 1501), to the year now present, (A.D. 1570). In which the full seventy years of the Babylonish captivity draws now well to an end. Or if we reckon from the beginning of Luther and his persecution, then lacketh yet sixteen years. Now, what the Lord will do with this wicked world, or what rest he will give to his church after these long sorrows,—he is our Father in Heaven, his will be done on earth as seemeth best to his divine Majesty.

In the mean time let us, for our parts, with all patient obedience, wait God's time, and glorify his holy Name, and edify one another with all humility. And if there cannot be an end of our disputing and contending one against another, yet let there be a moderation in it. And as it is the good will of our God, that Satan should be thus let loose amongst us for a short time; yet let us strive in the meanwhile what we can to amend the malice of the time with mutual humanity. They that are in error let them not disdain to learn; they who have greater talents of knowledge committed to them, let them instruct in simplicity them that be simple. No man lives in that commonwealth where nothing is amiss; but yet because God has so placed us Englishmen here in one commonwealth, also in one church, as in one ship together; let us not mangle or divide the ship, which being divided perishes; but let every man serve with diligence and discretion in his order, wherein he is called; let those that sit at the helm keep well the point of the needle, to know how and whither the ship goes; whatever weather betides, the needle, well touched with the stone of God's word, will never fail; let such as labour at the oars, start for no tempest, but do what they can to keep from the rocks; likewise let those who are in inferior stations take heed that they move no sedition nor disturbance against the rowers and mariners. No storm is so dangerous to a ship on the sea, as discord and disorder in a commonwealth; the countries, nations, kingdoms, empires, cities, towns, and houses, that have been dissolved by discord is so manifest in history, that I need not spend time in rehearsing examples. The God of peace, who hath power both of land and sea, reach forth his merciful hand to help them up that sink, to keep up them that stand, to still these winds and surging seas of discord and contention among us, that we, professing one Christ, may in one unity of doctrine gather ourselves into one ark of the true church together, where we, continuing steadfast in faith, may at the last be conducted safely to the joyful port of our desired landing-place, by his heavenly grace! To whom, both in heaven and earth, be all power and glory, with his Father and the Holy Spirit for ever. Amen.

THE UTILITY OF THIS HISTORY.

THE world being filled with such an infinite multitude of all kinds of books, I may seem, perhaps, to take a superfluous and needless matter in hand, at this present time, to write such volumes, especially of histories, considering that the world is so greatly pestered, not only with plenty thereof, but of all other treatises, that now books seem rather to lack readers, than readers to lack books. I doubt not but that many do both perceive, and lament the boldness of many in these days both in writing and printing this multitude of books; which, to say the truth, for my part I lament as much as any man; and I would therefore have no man think that I have attempted this enterprise unadvisedly or with rashness, but rather as one being not only doubtful, but also both bashful and fearful within myself for setting the same abroad. For I perceived how learned this age of ours is in reading of books, neither could I tell what the judgment of readers would be, to see so weak a being undertake such a weighty enterprise, not being sufficiently furnished with eloquence to do justice to so great a history, or sufficient to serve for the use of the studious, or the delight of the learned; and the more I perceived ability to be wanting in me, the less bold I felt to become a writer.

But again, on the other hand, when I weighed with myself what memorable acts have occurred in this later age of the church by the patient sufferings of the worthy martyrs, I thought it not to be neglected, that so many precious monuments worthy of being recorded and registered, should by my default be buried, under darkness and oblivion. I thought somewhat was to be said of them for their well deserving, and something also for the benefit which we have received by them. But above all things, nothing did so urge me forward as the consideration of the common utility which every man may plentifully receive by the reading of those monuments of martyrology; and as I have taken this history in hand chiefly for the use of the English church, I have written it in that tongue which the simple people could best understand.

Now if men commonly delight so much in other chronicles which treat only on matters of policy, and take pleasure in reading the variable events of worldly affairs, the stratagems of valiant captains, the terror of battle fields, the sacking of cities, the turmoils of realms and people; and if men think it such a great thing in a commonwealth to commit to history an account of these things, and bestow all their wit and eloquence in adorning the same, how much more meet is it for christians to preserve in remembrance the lives, acts, and doings, not of bloody warriors, but of the mild and constant martyrs of Christ, which serve not so much to delight the ear, as to improve the life, to show us examples of great profit, and to encourage men to all kind of christian godliness? And first, by reading thereof, we may see a lively testimony of God's mighty working in the life of man, contrary to the opinion of the atheists; for like as one said of Harpalus in times past, that his doings gave a lively testimony *against* God, because he being so wicked a man, escaped so long unpunished; so, contrariwise, in these men we have a much more assured and plain witness *of* God, in whose lives and deaths there appeared such manifest declarations of God's divine working, while in such sharpness of torments we behold in them such constant strength above man's reach, such readiness to answer, such patience in imprisonment, such godliness in forgiving, such cheerfulness and courage in suffering, besides the manifold sense and feeling of the Holy Ghost, which they so plentifully tasted in their afflictions, as in reading their letters we may evidently understand: and besides this, the mild deaths of the saints avail not a little to the establishing of a good conscience, to teach us the contempt of the world, and to bring us to the fear of God: moreover, they confirm faith, increase godliness, abate pride in prosperity, and open a hope of heavenly comfort in adversity. For what man reading the misery of these godly persons may not behold therein, as in a glass, his own case, whether he be godly or godless? For if God gave adversity unto good men, what may not the better sort expect, or the evil fear? And as by reading of profane histories we are made perhaps more skilful in warlike affairs; so by reading this we are made better in our livings, and besides, are better prepared for the like conflicts, (if by God's permission they shall happen hereafter) more wise by their doctrine, and more steadfast by their example.

To be brief, they declare to the world what true christian fortitude is, and what is the right way to conquer, which stands not in the power of man, but in the hope of the resurrection to come, and is now, I trust, at hand. In consideration whereof, methinks I have good cause to wish, that not only subjects, but also kings and princes, who commonly delight in heroic stories, would diligently peruse such monuments of martyrs, and keep them always in sight, not only to read, but to follow, and would paint them upon their walls, cups, rings, and gates. For doubtless such as these are more worthy of honour than an hundred Alexanders, Hectors, Scipios, and warlike Cæsars. And though the world judge preposterously of things, yet with God, the true Judge, not those that kill one another with a weapon are to be reputed, but rather they who being killed in God's cause do retain an invincible constancy against the threats of tyrants, and the violence of tormentors. Such as these are indeed the true conquerors of the world, by whom we learn true manhood, so many as fight under Christ, and not under the world. With this valiantness did that most mild Lamb, and invincible Lion of the tribe of Juda first of all go before us. Of whose unspeakable fortitude we hear this prophetical admiration, "Who is this, travelling in the greatness of his strength?" Is. lxiii. 1. Verily, it is the high Son of the high God, once conquered of the world, and yet conquering the world after the same manner he was conquered.

All his martyrs followed in the like course to whom the ancient church did attribute so much honour, as never king or emperor could purchase in this world, with all their images, pillars, triumphs, temples, and all their solemn feasts; in proof whereof we see with what admiration the memory of those good martyrs was received and kept among the ancient christians: whereby it is manifest in what estimation the martyrs were held in times past; with what gratulation, mirth, and general joy the afflictions of those godly men, dying in Christ's quarrel, were sometimes received and solemnized; and that not without good and reasonable cause; for the church did well consider how much she was beholden to them, by whose death she understood her treasures to increase. Now, then, if martyrs are to be compared with martyrs, I see no cause why the martyrs of our time deserve any less commendation, than the others in the primitive church; who assuredly are in no point inferior unto them, whether we view the number of them that suffered, or the greatness of their torments, or their constancy in dying, or consider the fruit that they brought to the amendment of posterity, and increase of the gospel. The primitive martyrs did water with their blood the truth that was newly springing up; so these later martyrs by their deaths restored it again, being so decayed and fallen down. *They* standing in the foreward of the battle, did receive the first encounter and violence of their enemies, and taught us by that means to overcome such tyranny; *these* with like courage again, like old beaten soldiers, did win the field in the rear of the battle. *They*, like famous husbandmen of the world, did sow the fields of the church, that first lay unmanured and waste; *these* with the richness of their blood did cause it to grow and fructify. Would to God the fruit might speedily be gathered into the barn, which now only remains to come!

Now, if we ascribe reputation to godly preachers (and worthily) who diligently preach the gospel of Christ, when they live notwithstanding, by the benefit of time, without all fear of persecution; how much more cause have we to praise and extol such men as stoutly spend their lives for the defence of the same? All these premises being duly considered, seeing we have found so famous martyrs in this our age, let us not fail in publishing and setting forth their doings, lest in that point we seem more unkind to them, than the writers of the primitive church were to theirs. And though we repute not their ashes, chains, and swords as relics; yet let us yield thus much unto their commemoration, to glorify the Lord in his saints, and imitate their death (as much as we may) with like constancy, or their lives at least with like innocency. They offered their bodies willingly to the rough handling of the tormentors; and is it so great a matter then for us to mortify our flesh, with all the members thereof? They neglected not only the riches and glory of the world for the love of Christ, but also their lives; and shall we then make so great a stir one against another for the transitory trifles of this world? They continued in patient suffering, when they had most wrong done to them, and when their very heart's blood gushed out of their bodies; and yet will we not forgive our poor brother, be the injury never so small, but are ready for every trifling offence to seek his destruction. They wishing well to all men, did of their own accord forgive their persecutors; and therefore ought we, who are now the posterity and children of the martyrs, not to degenerate from their steps, but being admonished, by their examples, if we cannot express their charity toward all men, yet at least to imitate the same to our power and strength. Let us give no cause of offence to any: and if any offence be given to us, let us overcome it with patience, forgiving and not revenging the same: and let us not only keep our hands from shedding of blood, but our tongues also from hurting the fame of others; besides, let us not shrink, if case so require, by martyrdom, or loss of life, according to their example, to yield up the same in the defence of the Lord's flock; which if men would do, there would be much less contention in the world than now is. And thus much touching the utility of this History.

PRELIMINARY DISSERTATION.

THE DIFFERENCE BETWEEN THE CHURCH OF ROME THAT NOW IS, AND THE ANCIENT CHURCH OF ROME THAT THEN WAS.

CHRIST our Saviour, in the gospel of St. Matt. xvi. 18, hearing the confession of Simon Peter, who acknowledged him to be the Son of God, and perceiving the secret hand of his Father therein, answered, and alluding to his name, called him a rock, upon which rock he would build his church so strong, that the gates of hell should not prevail against it, &c. In which words three things are to be noted. First, that Christ will have a church in this world. Secondly, that the church should be mightily opposed, not only by the world, but also by the utmost strength and powers of hell. And, thirdly, that the same church, notwithstanding the devil and all his malice, should continue. Which prophecy of Christ we see wonderfully verified, insomuch that the whole course of the church to this day, may seem nothing but a verifying of this prophecy. First, that Christ set up a church, needs no declaration. Secondly, what princes, kings, monarchs, governors, and rulers of this world, with their subjects publicly and privately, with all their strength and cunning, have bent themselves against this church. And, thirdly, how the church, notwithstanding all this, hath yet endured and held its own. It is wondrous to behold what storms and tempests it hath withstood; for the more evident declaration whereof I have written this history, intending by the favourable aid of Christ our Lord, not so much to delight the ears as to profit the hearts of the godly, in perusing antiquities of ancient times, to the end that the wonderful works of God, in this church, might appear to his glory. Also that the continuance and proceedings of the church from time to time, being set forth in these *Acts and Monuments*, may redound to the profit of the reader and edification of christian faith.

For the better accomplishing whereof, I have thought good, beginning from the time of the primitive church, and so continuing to these latter years, to run over the whole state and course of the church in general, dividing the whole of this history into five periods.

First, I will treat of the suffering time of the church, which continued from the apostles' age, about three hundred years.

Secondly, of the flourishing time of the church, which lasted other three hundred years.

Thirdly, of the declining time of the church, which comprehends other three hundred years; during which time although the church was much altered in ambition and pride, from the simple sincerity of the primitive time, yet in outward profession of doctrine and religion it was something tolerable, and had some face of a church; notwithstanding some corruption of doctrine, with superstition and hypocrisy, had even then crept in; yet in comparison of that which followed, it might seem as I have said, something sufferable.

Fourthly, followed the time of antichrist, and desolation of the church, containing the space of four hundred years; in which time both doctrine and sincerity of life were almost extinguished, namely, in the chief heads and rulers of this western church, through the means of the Roman bishops, especially counting from Gregory VII, called Hildebrand, Innocent III, and the friars, which crept in with him, till the time of John Wickliffe and John Husse, during four hundred years.

Fifthly, after this time of antichrist reigning by violence and tyranny, follows the reformation and purging of the church of God, wherein antichrist begins to be revealed, and to appear in his colour, and his doctrine to be detected, the number of his church decreasing, and the number of the true church increasing, which time has continued hitherto about the space of two hundred and eighty years, and how long it shall continue more, the Lord and Governor of all times only knoweth. In these five periods I suppose the whole course of the church may be comprised; which church being universal, and dispersed through all countries, I shall not be bound to any one nation more than another; yet notwithstanding, I have purposed principally to tarry upon such historical acts and records, as most appertain to England and Scotland.

And as the church of Rome, in all these ages, has challenged to itself the supreme title, and ringleading of the whole universal church on earth. In writing of the church of Christ, I cannot but partly also intermeddle with the acts and proceedings of the church of Rome; for so much as the doings and orderings of all other churches, as well here in England, as in other nations, have for this long time chiefly depended upon the same. Wherefore, as it is needful and requisite to have the doings and orderings of the said church made manifest to all christian congregations; so have I framed this history, according to that purpose. First, in a general description, briefly to declare the misguiding of that church, comparing the former primitive state of the church of Rome with these latter times of the same; which done, then in a more special way, to prosecute more at large all the particulars thereof, so far as shall seem profitable for the public instruction of all other christian churches. In which church of Rome four things seem to me chiefly to be considered. To wit, Title, Jurisdiction, Life, and Doctrine. Wherein I have here to declare, first, concerning the title or primacy of the church, how it first began, and upon what occasion. Secondly, concerning the jurisdiction and authority thereof, what it was, and how far it extended. Thirdly, touching the disorder of life and conversation, how inordinate it is. And, fourthly, the form of doctrine, how superstitious and idolatrous it has been of late; of which four, the first was prejudicial to all bishops; the second, derogatory to kings and emperors; the third detestable to all men; the fourth, injurious to Christ.

For first, the title and style of that church was such that it went beyond all other churches, being called " the Holy

Universal Mother Church, which could not err; and the bishop thereof, Holy Father the Pope, Bishop Universal, Prince of Priests, Supreme head of the Universal Church, and Vicar of Christ here in earth, which must not be judged, having all knowledge of scripture, and all laws contained within the chest of his breast."

Secondly, the jurisdiction of that bishop was such, that challenging to himself both the swords, that is, both the keys of the scripture, and the sceptre of the laity; he not only subdued all bishops under him, but also advanced himself above all kings and emperors, causing some of them to lie under his feet, some to hold his stirrup, kings to lead his horse by the bridle, some to kiss his feet, placing and displacing emperors, kings, dukes, and earls, whom and when he chose, taking upon him to transfer the empire at his pleasure, from Greece to France, from France to Germany, preferring and deposing whom he pleased, and confirming them which were elected. Also being emperor himself, when the throne was vacant, pretending authority or power to invest bishops, to give benefices, to spoil churches, to give authority to bind and loose, to call general councils, to judge over the same, to set up religions, to canonize saints, to take appeals, to bind consciences, to make laws, to dispense with the law and word of God, to deliver from purgatory, to command angels, &c.

Thirdly, what was the life and conversation of the court of Rome, will be seen in this history.

Fourthly, his doctrine in like manner was tedious to students, pernicious to men's consciences, injurious to Christ Jesus, and contrary to itself. In laws more divers, in volume more large, in diligence and study more applied to, in vantage and preferment more gainful than ever was the study and learning of the holy scripture of God.

These four points being well considered in this history, I trust it may minister to the christian reader, sufficient instruction to judge what is to be thought of this church of Rome.

But here it is to be noted, that all these deformities of vain title, of pretended jurisdiction, of heretical doctrine, of schismatical life, came not into the church of Rome all at one time, nor sprang with the beginning of the church, but with long working, and by little and little, and came not to full perfection till the time, partly of Pope Boniface III, partly of Pope Gregory VII, partly of Pope Innocent III, and finally of Pope Boniface VIII.; of which four popes, the first brought in the Title, (A.D. 607), which was never in such ample wise before publicly enacted, and received publicly in the said church of Rome, the second brought in Jurisdiction, (A.D. 1073); the third, which was Pope Innocent, (A.D. 1198), with his rabble of monks and friars, and with such other bishops as succeeded him, corrupted and obscured the sincerity of Christ's doctrine and manners, and, lastly, Pope Boniface VIII. (A.D. 1294); and after him Pope Clement V, (A.D. 1305), besides the jurisdiction advanced before by Pope Hildebrand, added moreover the temporal sword to be carried before them, and that the succession of no emperor should be sufficient and lawful, without the pope's admission, whereby the pope's power was brought to his full pride and perfection in the fourteenth century. And thus came up the corruption of the Romish church in continuance of years by degrees, and not altogether, nor at one time.

Wherefore, whoever shall have to do with any adversaries, about the antiquity or authority of the church of Rome, let him well consider when and how, the title, jurisdiction, and corruption of doctrine first began in the pope's see. And so he shall see, that the church of Rome, as it is now governed, never descended from the primitive age of the apostles. As the picture of the holy virgin, is not the holy virgin, and as a man painted on the wall is not a man; so it is to be said of the church of Rome, (the institution and doctrine of the church of Rome I mean), that although it has the name of the church apostolical, and brings forth a long genealogy of outward succession from the apostles, as the Pharisees did in Christ's time bringing their descent from Abraham their father;

yet all this is in name only, and not in effect or matter; for the definition of the apostolical church neither now agrees with this present church of Rome, nor yet the manner, form, and institution of the Romish church, as it now stands, had ever any succession from the primitive church. But as Christ said of the pharisees, that they were the children not of Abraham, but of the devil; so it may be answered, that this church of Rome now present, with this title, jurisdiction, and doctrine now used, cannot be fathered upon the apostles, nor Peter, nor Linus, but on another author, whom I will not here name.

And here comes in the argument of Pighius, Hosius, and Eccius, who, arguing for the antiquity and authority of the church of Rome, reason on this manner.

"That as an ordinary and a known church visible must be known continually on earth, from the time of the apostles, to which all other churches must have recourse;

And seeing there is no other church visible known to have endured from the apostles' time, but only the church of Rome;

They conclude, therefore, that the church of Rome is that church whereunto all other churches must have recourse," &c.

To which I answer that although the name of the church and outward succession of bishops have had their continuance from the time of the apostles, yet the definition and matter which makes a true apostolical church, neither is now in the church of Rome, nor yet the form and institution of the church now used in Rome, was ever from the apostles, which apostles were never authors or fathers of this title, jurisdiction, and doctrine now taught in Rome, but rather were ever enemies to the same.

Again, although the necessity of the church, enduring from the apostles, may and must be granted, yet the same necessity was not bound to any certain place or person, but only to faith; so that wherever, that is, in whatever church true faith was, there was the church of Christ. And because the true faith of Christ must needs ever remain on earth, therefore the church also must needs remain on earth. And God forbid that the true faith of Christ should only remain in one city in the world, and not in another as well. And therefore as this true and sincere faith of Christ is not given, to remain fixedly in one place or city alone; so neither is there any one church in the world so ordained and appointed of God, that all other churches should have their recourse unto it, for determination of their causes and controversies.

Now, as to the authorities of the fathers in commendation of the church of Rome, whoever will understand rightly their authorities must learn to make a distinction between the church of Rome, as it *was* and as it *is*; forasmuch as the church of Rome is not the same church now which it was then, and nothing agreeing to what it was then, save only in outward name and place, therefore, by this distinction, I answer the place of Ireneus, Cyprian, &c. commending the church of Rome as catholic and apostolical, and say that these speak of the church of Rome which then was, and said not untrue, calling it catholic and apostolical, for that the same church took their ordinary succession of bishops, joined with the ordinary doctrine and institution, from the apostles. But, speaking of the church of Rome which now is, we say the said places of the fathers are not true, neither appertain to the same; for they neither knew the church of Rome that now is, neither if they had, would they ever have judged any thing therein worthy such commendation.

Our adversaries yet more objecting against us, and labouring for the antiquity of the Romish church, for lack of other reasons, are driven to scanning the times and years. What? (say they) where was this church of yours before these fifty years? In answer, we demand what they mean by this which they call our church? If they mean the ordinance and institution of doctrine and sacraments now received by us, we affirm that our church was in existence when this church of theirs was not yet hatched out of the shell, nor had yet seen the light; that is, in the time of the apostles, in the primitive age, in the time of Gregory I., and the old Roman church, when as yet no universal pope was received publicly, but repelled in Rome: nor this fulness of plenary power yet known, nor this doctrine and abuse of sacraments yet heard of. In witness whereof we have the old acts and histories of ancient time to give testimony with us, wherein we have sufficient matter for us to declare the same form, usage, and institution of this our church as now reformed, not to be the beginning of any new church of our own, but to be the renewing of the old ancient church of Christ.

And where our adversaries charge us with the faith of our fathers and godfathers, wherein we were baptised, accusing us that we are revolted from them and their faith, wherein we were first christened: we answer, that we, being first baptized by our fathers and godfathers, in water, in the name of the Father, of the Son, and of the Holy Ghost, the same faith wherein we were christened then, we do retain: and because our godfathers were themselves also in the same faith, therefore they cannot say that we have forsaken the faith of our godfathers. As for other points of ecclesiastical uses, and circumstances considered, besides the principal substance of faith and baptism, if they held any thing which receded from the doctrine and rule of Christ, therein we now remove ourselves; not because we would differ from them, but because we would not with them remove from the rule of Christ's doctrine. Neither does our baptism bind us in all points to the opinions of them that baptized us, but to the faith of him in whose name we were baptized. For, as if a man were christened by a heretic, the baptism, notwithstanding, were good, although the baptizer were naught: so, if our godfathers or fathers, which christened us, were taught any thing not consonant to christian doctrine in all points, neither is our baptism worse for that, nor are we bound to follow them in all things, wherein they themselves did not follow the true church of Christ.

Wherefore, as it is false, that we have renounced the faith of our godfathers wherein we were baptized, so is it not true, that we are removed from the church of Rome; but rather I say, and will prove that the church of Rome has utterly departed from the church of Rome, according to my former distinction. Which thing the more evidently to declare, I will here compare the church of Rome with the church of Rome; and in a general description set forth the difference of both the churches, that is, of both the periods of the church of Rome: to the intent it may be seen whether we or they have most apostatised from the church of Rome. And here, first, I divide the church of Rome into two distinct periods of time; first, of those first six hundred years which were immediately after Christ; and, secondly, of the other six hundred years, which now have been in these our later days: and so, in comparing these two together, will search out what difference is between them. Of which two ages and states of the Roman church, the first I call the *primitive* church of Rome, the other I call the *later* church of Rome.

To begin with the order and qualities of life, I ask, where was this church of theirs in the time of the primitive church of Rome, with this pomp and pride, with this riches and superfluity, with this worldly splendour and name of cardinals, with this prancing dissoluteness, with this extortion, bribing, buying, and selling of spiritual dignities, these annates, reformations, procurations, exactions, and other practices for money, this avarice insatiable, ambition intolerable, fleshly filthiness most detestable, barbarousness and negligence in preaching, promise-breaking faithlessness, poisoning and supplanting one another, with such schisms and divisions in the elections and courts of Rome for these seven hundred years, with such extreme cruelty, malice, and tyranny in burning and persecuting their poor brethren to death?

It were too long to dwell particularly upon these things: and if a man should detail all the schisms in the church of Rome, to the number of eighteen, what a

volume would it require? Or if here should be recorded all that this see has burned and put to death, who would be able to number them? Or if all their schemes to get money should be described, who would be able to recite them all? Of which the principal are reckoned at least at fourteen or fifteen schemes.

I. For annates or vacancies of arch-bishoprics, bishoprics, abbacies, priories conventual, and other benefices elective.

II. For the holding of all spiritual livings whatever.

III. New annates for all the same again, as often as any one of all his spiritual livings be, or are fained to be, not orderly come by, whereby it has chanced. divers times, three or four annates to be paid for one benefice.

IV. For giving benefices before they fall, and many times giving to several persons for money's sake.

V. For resignations, which in many cases the pope challenges to be reserved to himself.

VI. For commendams.

VII. For compounding with such as be aosent from their charge.

VIII. For dispensations, so as to dispense with age, with order, with benefices incompatible; also for irregularity, for adultery, for times of marriage, for marrying in degrees forbidden, for gossips to marry, for which in France a thousand crowns were paid to Rome at one time, for dispensing with this canonical affinity of gossips; also dispensing for eating meats in times prohibited.

IX. For innumerable privileges, exemptions, graces; for not visiting, or visiting by a proctor; for confirmations of privileges; for transactions made upon favour of the pope; for exchanges of benefices, or making of pensions, with such like.

X. For mandates granted by the pope, to ordinaries, whereof every ordinary, if he have the collation or presentation often, may receive one mandate; if he have fifty, two mandates; and for every mandate there comes to the pope about twenty ducats. And yet so many are sold, as will come buyers to pay for them.

XI. For the pope's penitentiary; for absolution of cases reserved to the pope; for breaking of vows; for translation from one monastery to another, also from one order to another; for licence to enter into certain monasteries, to carry about altars, with many other things of like device.

XII. For giving and granting of pardons and indulgences, to be read not only in public temples, but also to be bought in private houses.

XIII. For making notaries, and prothonotaries, and other offices of the court of Rome.

XIV. For bulls and commissions of new foundations, or for changing the old; for reducing regular monasteries to a secular state, or for restoring them again into the old; and for other writs about matters in controversy, that ought to be decided by the ordinary.

XV. For giving the pall to archbishops.

By reason of all which devices (besides the annates) it has been accounted from the king's records in France, that in the time of Louis IX., the sum of two hundred thousand crowns, were paid out of France and transported to Rome. Which sum, since that time, has been doubled and trebled, besides annates and palls, which altogether, of late years, has been considered to make the total yearly sum going out of France to the pope's coffers, one hundred thousand crowns. Now, as to what has been drawn besides from other kingdoms and nations, let others conjecture.

Wherefore, if the gospel send us to the fruit to know the tree, what is to be thought of the church of Rome, with these fruits of life? Or, if we seek the church in length and number of years, where was then this church of Rome with these qualities, when the church of Rome was a *persecuted*, and not a *persecuting* church? And when the bishops thereof did not make martyrs, as they now do, but were made martyrs themselves, to the number of twenty-five, in order one after another? Or when the bishops thereof were elected, not by factious conspiring, not by money or friends making, as they now are, but by the free voices of the people and of the clergy, with the consent of the emperor, and not by a few conspiring cardinals, closed up in a corner, as they now are.

And yet if there were no other difference in the matter, but only corruption of life, all that, we would impute to the common frailty of man, and charge them no farther than we might charge ourselves. Now over and above this deformity of life, we have to charge them in greater points, more nearly touching the substantial ground of the church, as in their jurisdiction presumptuously usurped,—in their title falsely grounded,—and in their doctrine heretically corrupted. In all which three points this later church of Rome hath utterly separated itself from the nature of the ancient church of Rome, and they have erected to themselves a new church of their own making, usurping a jurisdiction never known before to their ancient predecessors. For although the church of Rome in the primitive time had its due authority, among other patriarchal churches, over such churches as were within its boundary : yet the plenitude of power, spiritual and temporal, in deposing and dispensing matters not belonging to the pope, in taking appeals, in giving elections, investing in benefices, in exempting himself from obedience and subjection to his ordinary magistrate, was never received in the old Roman church.

For although Victor, bishop of Rome, (A. D. 200), went to excommunicate the Eastern churches, for the observation of Easter day : yet neither did he proceed therein, nor was he permitted by Ireneus to do so. And although Boniface I., writing to the bishops of Carthage, required of them to send their appeals to Rome, alleging the decree of the Nicene council for his authority : the bishops and clergy of Carthage assembling in a general council (called the sixth council of Carthage) to the number of two hundred and seventeen bishops, after they had perused the decrees of the Nicene council, and found no such matter as Boniface alleged, made a decree, that none of that country should make any appeal to that see, &c. And what wonder if appeals were forbidden then to be made to Rome, when here in England the kings would not permit any to appeal to Rome, before the time of Henry II. ? And also in France the like prohibitions were expressly made by Louis IX., (A. D. 1268), which did forbid by a public instrument, all exactions of the pope's court within that realm. Also King Philip (A. D. 1296), not only restrained all sending of his subjects to Rome, but also, that no money, armour, or subsidy should be transported out of his kingdom. Also King Charles V., and his son Charles VI., punished as traitors certain persons for appealing to Rome. The like resistance was also made in France, against the pope's reservations, preventions, and other like practices in the days of Pope Martin V., also when King Henry VI. in England, and King Charles VII. in France, did both agree with the pope, in investing and in collation of benefices : yet notwithstanding the high court of parliament in France did not admit the same, but still maintained the old liberty and customs of the French church. Insomuch that when the duke of Bedford came with the king's letters patents to have the pope's procurations and reservations admitted, the court of parliament would not agree to the same, (A. D. 1425). In the days of King Charles VII., was set forth in France, *The Pragmatic sanction,* as they call it, against the annates, reservations, expectatives, and other proceedings of the popes, (A. D. 1438). Wherefore what wonder if this jurisdiction of the pope's court in excommunicating, taking appeals, and giving of benefices, was not used in the old church of Rome, when in these latter days it has been so much resisted.

And what should I say of the form of elections now used in the church of Rome, being quite changed from the manner of the old church of their predecessors ? For in those ancient days, when the church remained in the apostles only, and a few other disciples, the apostles then, with prayer and imposition of hands, elected bishops and ministers; as by the apostles James was made bishop of Jerusalem, Paul elected Titus to Crete, and Timothy to Ephesus. Also Peter ordained Linus and Clement in Rome, &c. After the time of the apostles, when the church began to multiply, the election of bishops and ministers stood in the clergy and the people, with the

consent of the chief magistrate, and so continued during all the time of the primitive church, till the time of Constantine, who (as write Platina and Sabellicus), published a law concerning the election of the Roman bishop, that he should be taken for a true bishop, whom the clergy and people of Rome did choose and elect, without waiting for any authority of the emperor of Constantinople, or the deputy of Italy : as the custom had ever been before that day. And here the bishops began first to extricate their elections and their necks, a little from the emperor's subjection. But there are many reasons, rather to think this constitution of Constantine forged and untrue: for it is taken out of the pope's library, a suspected place, and collected by the keeper of the pope's library, a suspected author, who carefully compiled whatever feigned or apocryphal writings he could find in the pope's chest of records, making any thing on his master's side.

And as in elections, so also in judiciary power, in deciding causes of faith and of discipline, the state of the church of Rome now has no conformity with the old Roman church. For then bishops debated all causes of faith only by the scriptures ; and other questions of discipline, they determined by the canons, not of the pope, but of such as were decreed by the ancient councils of the church. Whereas now, both the rule of scripture, and sanctions of the old councils are set aside, and all things for the most part, are decided by certain new and extravagant constitutions, compiled in the pope's canon law, and practised in his courts.

And whereas the old ordinance, as well of the common law, as of the sacred councils and institution of ancient fathers, have given to bishops, and other prelates, also to patrons, and doctors of ecclesiastical benefices, every one within his own precinct and dominion, also to cathedral churches and others, to have their free elections, disposing all ecclesiastical benefices whatever, after their own wills, as appeareth by the first general council of France, by the first general council of Nice, (cap. 6.), by the general council of Antioch, (cap. 9). And, likewise, beside these ancient decrees, in more later years, by Louis IX. of France, in his constitution, made and provided by full parliament against the pope's exactions, (A. D. 1228), in these words : " All exactions and oppressive burdens of money, which the court of Rome hath laid upon the church of our kingdom, (whereby our said kingdom hath been, hitherto, miserably impoverished) or hereafter shall impose or lay upon us, we utterly discharge and forbid to be levied or collected hereafter for any manner of cause, unless there come some reasonable, godly, and most urgent and inevitable necessity ; and that also, not to be done without the express and voluntary commandment of us, and of the church of the same our foresaid kingdom, &c." Now, contrary to these express decrees of general councils and constitutions, this later church of Rome, degenerating from all the steps of their elders, have taken upon them, for their own advantage, to intermeddle in disposing churches, colleges, monasteries, with the collations, exemptions, election, goods and lands to the same belonging, by reason whereof have come in these impropriations, first-fruits, and reservations of benefices, to the miserable despoiling of parishes, and great decay of Christian faith, which things among the old Roman elders were never known.

Likewise, advowsons and pluralities of benefices were things then as much unknown, as now they are pernicious to the church, taking away from the flock of Christ all free election of ministers.

All these inconveniences, as they first came and crept in by the pretended authority abused in this later church of Rome : so it cannot be denied, but the later church of Rome has taken and attributed to itself much more than either the limits of God's word do give, or stand with the example of the old Roman church, in these three things ; whereof, as mention has before been made, so I will briefly recapitulate the same.

The first is this, that whatever the scripture gives and refers, either to the whole church universally, or to every particular church severally, this church of Rome arrogates to itself, absolutely and only, both doing injury to other churches, and also abusing the scriptures of God. For although the scripture gives authority to bind and loose, it limits it neither to person or place, that is, neither to the city of Rome only, more than to other cities, nor to the see of Peter more than to other apostles, but gives it clearly to the church, so that wheresoever the true church of Christ is, there is annexed power to bind and loose, given and taken merely as from Christ, and not mediately by the pope.

The second point wherein this present church of Rome abuses jurisdiction, contrary to the scripture and steps of the old Roman church, is this, it extends her authority further and more amply, than either the warrant of the word, or example of time will give. For although the church of Rome has (as other particular churches have) authority to bind and absolve, yet it has no such authority to absolve subjects from their oath, subjection, and loyalty to their rulers and magistrates, to dispense with perjury, to denounce remission where no earnest repentance is seen before, to number remission by days and years, to dispense with things expressly forbidden in the word, or to restrain that which the word makes free, to burden consciences with constitutions of men, to excommunicate for worldly matters, as for breaking of parks, for not ringing of bells at the bishop's coming, for not bringing litter for their horse, for not paying their fees and rents, for withholding the church goods, for holding on their prince's side in princely cases, for not going at the pope's commandment, for not agreeing to the pope's election in another prince's kingdom, with other such things, more and more vain than these, &c. Again, although the scripture gives leave and authority to the bishop and church of Rome, to *minister* sacraments: yet it gives no authority to *make* sacraments, much less to *worship* sacraments. And though their authority serves to baptize *men*, yet it extends not to christen *bells*: neither have they authority by the word of God to add to the word of God, or take from the same, to set up unwritten tenets under pain of damnation, to make other articles of belief, to institute strange worship, otherwise than he hath prescribed, who hath told us how he would be worshipped, &c.

The third abuse of the pope's jurisdiction stands in this, that as in spiritual jurisdiction they have vehemently exceeded the bounds of scripture, so they have impudently intermeddled themselves in temporal jurisdiction, wherein they had nothing to do. Insomuch that they have transferred their empire, they have deposed emperors, kings, princes, rulers, and senators of Rome, and set up others, or the same again at their pleasure; they have proclaimed wars, and have warred themselves. And whereas emperors in ancient times, have dignified them with titles, have enlarged them with donations, and have given them confirmation, they, like ungrateful clients to such benefactors, have afterwards stamped upon their necks, have made them to hold their stirrups, some to hold the bridle of their horse, and have caused them to seek their confirmation at their hand; moreover, they have extorted into their own hands the power and jurisdiction of both the swords (spiritual and temporal power), especially since the time of Pope Gregory VII., surnamed Hildebrand; which Hildebrand deposing the emperor Henry IV., made him give attendance at his city gate. And after him, Pope Boniface VIII. shewed himself to the people, on the first day like a bishop, with his keys before him, and the next day in his imperial robes, and having a naked sword carried before him, like an emperor, (A. D. 1298.) And for so much as this inordinate jurisdiction has not only been used by them, but, also, to this day is maintained at Rome; let us therefore, now compare her to the old manner in times past, meaning the primitive age of the church of the Romans. Wherein the old bishops of Rome, as they were then subject to their emperor, so were other bishops of other nations in like manner subject every one to his own king and prince, acknowledging them for their lords, and were ordered by their authority, and obeyed their laws, and that not only in civil causes, but also ecclesiastical.

Thus was Gregory I. (the Great), subject to Maurice, and to Phocas, although a wicked emperor. So, also, both pope and people of Rome, took their laws of the emperors, and submitted to them, not only in the time of Honorius, an hundred years after Constantine the Great, but also in the time of Marcian, (A. D. 451), and to the time of Justinian and of Charlemagne. In all which period the imperial law did rule and bind in Rome, both in the days of Justinian, and one hundred and fifty years after; whereby it may appear false, that the city of Rome was given by Constantine to the bishop of Rome; for Pope Boniface I., writing to the emperor Honorius, calls Rome the emperor's city; and the emperor Lothaire appointed magistrates and laws in Rome. Moreover, that both the bishop of Rome, and all other ecclesiastical persons were in former times, and ought to be subject to their emperors and lawful magistrates, in causes as well spiritual as civil, by many evidences may appear, taken out both of God's law, and man's law. And first, by God's law, we have the example of godly King David, who numbered all the priests and levites, and disposed them into twenty-four orders or courses, appointing them continually to serve in the ministry, every one in his proper order and turn: which institution of the clergy also, good King Hezekiah afterwards renewed, of whom it is written: "He did that which was right in the sight of the Lord, according to all that David his father did: he removed the high places, and brake the images," &c. 2 Kings, xviii. 3, 4. The said Hezekiah also reduced the priests and levites into their orders as prescribed by David, to serve every one in his office of ministration, 2 Chron. xxxi. 2. And this order from David still continued till the time of Zacharias, at the coming of Christ, who was of the course of Abia, which was the eighth order of the priests appointed to serve in the tabernacle, Luke i. 5. To pass over other lighter offices, such as concerning the ordering of oblations in the temple, and the repairing of the house of the Lord, we find Solomon displacing Abiathar the high priest by his kingly power, and placing Zadok in his stead. 1 Kings, ii. 27. Also, his dedicating the temple of the Lord with all the people, and blessing all the congregation of Israel, 1 Kings, viii. 55. Judas Maccabeus also elected priests, such as, being without spot, had a zeal to the law of the Lord, to purge the temple, which the idolatrous Gentiles had before profaned, 1 Mac. iv. 42.

Also, King Alexander, writing to Jonathan, appointed him chief priest, 1 Mac. x. 20. Demetrius ordained Simon and Alchinus in the like office of priesthood. Jehoshaphat likewise, set judges in the whole land; so, also, in Jerusalem he appointed levites and priests, and the chief of the fathers of Israel, to have the hearing of causes, and to minister judgment over the people, 2 Chron. xix. 8. By these and many others, is to be seen, that kings and princes in the old time, had the dealing in ecclesiastical matters, as in calling the people to God's service, in cutting down groves, in destroying images, in gathering tithes into the house of the Lord, in dedicating the temple, in blessing the people, in casting down the brazen serpent, in correcting and deposing priests, in constituting the order and offices of priests, in commanding such things as pertained to the service and worship of God, and in punishing the contrary, &c. And in the New Testament, what means the example of Christ himself, both giving and teaching tribute to be given to Cæsar? to Cæsar, I say, and not to the high-priest. What mean his words to Pilate, not denying power to be given to him from above?

And again, declaring the kings of nations to have dominion over them, and commanding his disciples not to do so, giving us to understand the difference between the regulation of his spiritual kingdom, and of the kingdoms of this world, commanding all states to be subject under the rulers and magistrates, in whose regulation is dominion and subjection. Whereunto accords also the doctrine of St. Paul, where it is written: "Let every soul be subject unto the higher powers," Rom. xiii.; under whose obedience, neither pope, cardinal, patriarch, bishop, priest, friar nor monk, is excepted or exempted. In like agreement with the holy apostle St. Paul, joins also St. Peter: "Submit yourselves to every ordinance of man, whether it be the king, as supreme, or unto governors," &c. 1 Pet. ii. 13. Let any man now judge, whether the pope has not done open wrong to the emperor, in raising himself above the jurisdiction of his lawful prince and magistrate.

And as it is proved by God's law, that all ecclesiastical persons owe subjection to their lawful princes, in matters temporal as well as spiritual; so no less may it be inferred out of man's law, and the examples of the oldest fathers. The popes' decrees and canons are full of records, testifying how the ancient church of Rome, not only received, but also required of the emperors, laws and constitutions to be made, touching not only such causes, but also such persons, as were ecclesiastical. Boniface I. bishop of Rome, sent an humble supplication to the emperor, to provide some remedy against the ambitious contentions of the clergy concerning the bishoprick of Rome. Honorius, at his request, directed and established a law, that none should be made bishop of Rome through ambition, charging all ecclesiastical ministers to cease from ambition; appointing, moreover, that if two were elected together, neither of them should be taken, but the election to proceed to another, to be chosen by a full consent of voices.

To this I add, also, the law and constitution of the emperor Justinian, ratified and renewed afterwards in the council of Paris, where all bishops and priests are expressly forbidden to excommunicate any man, before his cause was known and proved to be such as the ancient canons of the church would have him to be excommunicated for. The same Justinian, moreover, in his laws and constitutions did dispose and ordain in church matters, so as to have a determinate number of churchmen, or clerks in churches, (Const. 3). Also, concerning monasteries and monks, (Const. 5). How bishops and priests should be ordained, (Const. 6). Concerning the removing of ecclesiastical persons from one church to another Also, that the holy mysteries should not be done in private houses; so that whoever should attempt the contrary, should be deprived, (Const. 57). Moreover, concerning clerks leaving their churches, (Const. 58). Also, concerning the order and manner of funerals, (Const. 59). And that bishops should not keep away from their flock, (Const. 67). And (Const. 123)., agreeable to the doctrine of St. Paul, he commands all bishops and priests to sound out their service, and to celebrate the mysteries, not in a secret manner, but with a loud voice, so that every thing which was said and done, might not only be heard, but also be understood of the faithful people, whereby it is to be gathered, that divine prayers and service was then in the vulgar tongue.

And as Justinian, and other emperors in those days, had the jurisdiction and government over spiritual matters and persons, so, also, the like examples may be brought of other kings in other countries, who had no less authority in their kingdoms, than the emperors had in their empire. As in France, Clovis summoned a council of thirty-three bishops, at which thirty-three canons were instituted concerning the government of the church. Charlemagne called five synods, one at Mentz, the second at Rome, the third at Rhemes, the fourth at Cabilone, the fifth at Arelate, where sundry ordinances were given to the clergy, about eight hundred and ten years after Christ. He also decreed, that only the canonical books of scripture, and none other, should be read in the church; which before had also been decreed (A. D. 417), in the third general council of Carthage.

Moreover, he instructs and informs the bishops and priests in the office of preaching, desiring them not to suffer any to preach to the people any new doctrine of their own invention, not agreeing with the word of God; and that they themselves will both preach such things as lead to eternal life, and also set others to do the same.

Also, the said kings and emperors forbade that any freeman or citizen should enter into the monastic life, without a license of the government having been obtained; for which they gave two reasons: first, that many not for mere devotion, but for idleness, and avoiding the king's wars, gave themselves to religion: for that many were craftily circumvented and deluded by subtle covet-

ous persons, who sought to get from them what property they had. They also forbade that any young children or boys should be shaven, or enter into any profession without the will of their parents; and that no young maiden should take the veil or profession of a nun, before she came to sufficient years of discretion, so as to discern and choose what she should follow.

Moreover, Louis the Pious, before mentioned, with his son Lothaire, among other ecclesiastical sanctions, ordained a godly law, for laymen to communicate the sacrament of the body and blood of the Lord; and they also enacted that no goods of the church should be alienated. Louis II., the son of Lothaire, who succeeded as emperor and king of France, about the year 848, caused Pope Leo IV. to be brought before him, on a charge of treason. The pope pleaded his cause at the bar, before the emperor, and was acquitted and released. Which declares that popes and bishops all that time were in subjection to their kings and emperors.

Moreover, Louis IX. (A. D. 1228) made a law against the pestiferous simony in the church; also for the maintenance of the liberty of the church of France, and established a law or decree, against the new inventions, reservations, preventions, and exactions of the court of Rome. Philip IV. (A. D. 1303) also set forth a law, wherein was forbidden any exaction of new tithes and first fruits, and other unaccustomed collections to be put upon the church of France. Charles V. (A. D. 1369) by a law commanded that no bishops or prelates, or their officials within his kingdom of France, should execute any censure of suspense, or excommunication, at the pope's commandment, over or upon the cities or towns, corporations, or commons of his realm. Charles VI. (A. D. 1388) provided by a law, that the fruits and rents of benefices, with other pensions, and bishops' goods that departed, should no more be exported by the cardinals and other officials and collectors of the pope unto Rome, but should be brought to the king, and so restored to them to whom they did rightly appertain.

The like may also be proved by the examples of our kings in England, as Offa, Egbert, Ethelwolf, Alfred, Edgar, Canute, Edward the Confessor, William the Conqueror, William Rufus, Henry I., Henry II., till the time of king John and after. Whose dealing as well in ecclesiastical cases as temporal, is sufficient to prove what injury the popes in these latter days have done unto the emperors, their lawful governors and magistrates; in usurping such power and jurisdiction over them, to whom properly they owe subjection, contrary to the steps and example of their ancestors, the old Roman bishops; although it is not to be denied, but that ecclesiastical ministers have their power also committed unto them, after their sort, in the Lord: yet it becomes every man to know his own place and standing, and to keep, wherein his own precinct doth confine him, and not rashly to break out into other men's walks. As it is not lawful for a civil magistrate to intermeddle with a bishop's or a preacher's function: so it was unseemingly and unorderly that Boniface VIII. should have had carried before him the temporal mace and naked sword of the emperor; or that any pope should bear a triple crown, or take upon him like a lord and king. Wherefore let every man consider the compass and limitation of his charge, and exceed no farther.

The third point wherein the church of Rome has departed, is in the style and title annexed to the bishop of that see. As where he is called pope, most holy father, vicar general, and vicar of Christ, successor of Peter, universal bishop, prince of priests, head of the church universal, head bishop of the world, the admiration of the world, neither God nor man, but a thing between both, &c., for all these terms are given to him in popish books. Although the name pope being a Greek name, which is as much as father, may seem more tolerable, as having been used in the old time among bishops; for so Austin was called of the council of Africa, Jerome, Boniface and others; also Cyprian, bishop of Carthage. But that this or any of these terms were so peculiarly applied to the bishop of Rome, that other bishops were excluded from the same, or that any one bishop above the rest had the name of Oecumenical, or universal, or head, to the derogation of other bishops, is to be found neither in histories of the old time, nor in any example of the primitive church. Before the council of Nice, it is evident that there was no respect paid to the church of Rome, but every church then was ruled by her own government, till the year 325. Then followed the council of Nice, where it was decreed, that throughout the whole church, which was now far spread over all the world, certain provinces or precincts, to the number of four, should be appointed, every one to have its head church, and chief bishop, who were called metropolitan or patriarch, and had the oversight of such churches as did lie about him. Among which patriarchs or metropolitans, the bishop of Rome had the first place, the bishop of Alexandria the second, the bishop of Antioch the third, and the bishop of Jerusalem was the fourth patriarch. Afterward, in the number of these patriarchs came in also the bishop of Constantinople in the room of the bishop of Antioch. So that these four or five metropolitans or patriarchs, had their peculiar circuits and precincts especially appointed, in such sort, as one of them should not deal within another's precinct, and also that there should be among them an equality of honour. Again, speaking of the said patriarchs or primates, we read in the second and third chapter of the council of Constantinople, that bishops should not invade the diocese of other bishops beyond their borders, nor confound together churches, &c. Moreover, the old doctors for the most and best part, do accord in one sentence, that all bishops placed wheresoever in the church of God, are of one merit, of like honour, and all equally successors together of the apostles. Also, he that is the author of the book called Dionysius Areopagita, calleth all the bishops of equal order, and of like honour, &c. All this while the bishop of Rome was a patriarch, and a metropolitan or bishop of the first see, but no oecumenical bishop, nor head of the universal church, nor any such matter. Insomuch, that he, with all other bishops, was debarred from that, by a plain decree of the council of Carthage, (Can. 39). "That the bishop of the first seat shall not be called the prince of priests, or the high priest, or any such thing."

And lest any here should take occasion of cavilling, to hear him called bishop of the first seat, here is to be expounded what is meant by the first seat, and why he was so called: not for any dignity of the person, either of him which succeeds, or of him whom he is said to succeed, but only of the place wherein he sits. This is plainly proved by the council of Chalcedon, cap. 28. Wherein is manifestly declared the cause why the see of Rome among all other patriarchal sees is numbered for the first see by the ancient fathers: for, saith the council, our forefathers did worthily attribute the chief degree of honour to the see of old Rome, because the principal reign or empire was in that city, &c. The same also is confirmed by Eusebius, declaring, that the excellency of the Roman empire did advance the popedom of the Roman bishop above other churches, &c. He says too, that the council of Nice gave this privilege to the bishop of Rome, that like as the king of the Romans is named emperor above all other kings, so the bishop of the same city of Rome should be called pope above other bishops, &c. By these places, (and many more), it appears, that though these titles of superiority had been attributed to the bishop of Rome, yet it remains certain, that the said bishop received that preferment by man's law, and not by the law of God.

As touching therefore these titles of pre-eminence, we shall set forth and declare what history doth say in this matter. First, we shall see what titles the bishop of Rome takes and challenges to himself, and what is the meaning of them. 2. When they first came in, whether in the primitive time or not, and by whom. 3. How they were first given to the Roman bishops; that is, whether of necessary duty, or voluntary devotion; and whether in respect of Peter, or in respect of the city, or else of the worthiness of the bishop which sat there. 4. And if the aforesaid names were then given by certain bishops, unto the bishop of Rome: whether all the said names were really given. 5. Or whether they were then received by all bishops of Rome, to whom they were given, or whether they were refused by some. 6. And finally, whether they ought to have been refused when given, or not.

And first to begin with the names and titles now claimed by and attributed to the bishop of Rome, that is, the Chief Priest of the World, the Prince of the Church, Bishop Apostolical, the universal Head of the Church, the Head and Bishop of the Universal Church, the Successor of Peter, most holy Pope, Vicar of God on Earth, neither God nor man, but a mixed thing between both; the Patriarch or Metropolitan of the Church of Rome, the Bishop of the first See, &c. Unto which titles or styles is annexed a triple crown, a triple cross, two cross keys, a naked sword, seven-fold seals, in token of the seven-fold gifts of the Holy Ghost, having the plenary fulness of power, as well of temporal as spiritual things in his hands: that all things are his, and that all such princes as have given him any thing, have given him but his own, having at his will and pleasure to preach indulgences, and the cross against princes: and that the emperor and certain other princes, ought to make to him confession of subjection at their coronation; having authority to depose, and that he has deposed emperors and the king of France: also to absolve the subjects from their allegiance to their princes: whom kings have served for foot-men to lead his horse, and the emperor to hold his stirrup; that he may and does give power to bishops upon the bodies of men, and has granted them to have prisons; without whose authority no general council has any force; and to whom appeals in all manner of causes may and ought to be made. That his decrees are equal with the decrees of the Nicene council, and are to be observed and taken in no less force than if they had been confirmed with the heavenly voice of St. Peter himself. That the bishop of Rome may dispense above the law, and of injustice make justice, in correcting and changing laws, for he has the fulness of power. And if the pope do lead with him innumerable souls by flocks into hell, yet no man must presume to rebuke his faults in this world. And, that it stands upon necessity of salvation to believe in the primacy of the see of Rome, and to be subject to the same, &c.

Now let us see whether these names and titles were ever attributed to any in the primitive time of the bishop of Rome. If our adversaries, being convicted by plain evidence of history, and example of time, will yield unto us (as they needs must) in part, and not in the whole; let us come then to the particulars, and see what part they will defend, and derive from the ancient custom of the primitive church, (that is, from the first six hundred years, after Christ). First in the Council of Nice, which was in the year 325, and in the sixth canon of the said council, we find it so decreed: that in every province or precinct some one church, and bishop was appointed to have the inspection and government of other churches about him, after the ancient custom, as the words of the council do purport: so that the bishop of Alexandria should have power of Libya and Pentapolis in Egypt, inasmuch as the bishop of the city of Rome has the like in the same manner. And so as also in Antioch and in other countries, let every church have its due honour, and consequently that the bishop of Jerusalem have his due honour, so that such order be kept, that the metropolitan cities be not defrauded of their dignity which to them is due and proper. In this council, and in the same sixth and seventh canons, the bishops of Alexandria, of Rome, and of Antioch are joined together in like manner of dignity, and there appears no difference of honour to be therein meant; also there immediately follows, that no bishop should be made without consent of their metropolitans, yea and that the city also of Jerusalem should be under its metropolitan, and that the metropolitan should have the full power to confirm every bishop made in his province.

After this followed the sixth council of Carthage, (A. D. 420,) at which were assembled two hundred and seventeen bishops, among whom were Augustine, Prosper, Orosius, and divers other famous persons. This council continued for the space of five years, at which there was great contention about the supremacy and jurisdiction of Rome. Zosimus, the Roman bishop, had received into the communion of the church without any examination, one that came to complain to him from Africa, named Apiarius, a priest whom the metropolitan with the council of Africa had worthily excommunicated. Upon this, Zosimus, after having received and shewed favour to Apiarius, who had appealed to him, sends to the council his messengers, with these requests: that Apiarius, whom he had absolved might be received of them again, and that it might be lawful for bishops or priests to appeal from the sentence of their metropolitans, and also of the council, to the see of Rome; that if any priest or deacon were wrongfully excommunicated by the bishops of their own province, it should be lawful for them to remove the hearing and judging of their cause to their neighbouring bishops; and that Urban their bishop, should either be excommunicated, or sent to Rome, unless he would correct those things that were to be corrected, &c. For the proof whereof, Zosimus alleged the words (as he pretended) of the Nicene council. The council of Carthage hearing this, and remembering no such thing in the council of Nice, and yet not suspecting the bishop of Rome, to dare wrongfully to falsify the words of that council, writes to Zosimus, declaring that they never read, in their common Latin copy of the Nicene council, any such canon, yet for quietness sake, they would observe the same until they might procure the original copies of that council to be sent to them from Constantinople, Alexandria, and from Antioch. In like effect afterward they wrote to Pope Boniface I., who succeeded Zosimus. And thirdly, also to Celestine, who shortly after succeeded Boniface.

In the meantime, this council sent to Atticus, patriarch of Constantinople, and to Cyril, patriarch of Alexandria, for the authentic copies in Greek of the Nicene council, which being sent unto them, and they finding in the true originals no such canon, as the bishop of Rome had falsely forged, they wrote a sharp letter to Celestine, bishop of Rome, in which they styling him "brother bishop," they declare to him, that they had perused all the copies of the council of Nice, and could find no such canon as he and his predecessors had falsely alleged, and reciting the sixth canon, declared that the decrees of the Nicene council had committed all and singular persons ecclesiastical, as well bishops as others, unto the charge of their metropolitans.

Wherefore they declared that it was not convenient to bring their matters over to Rome; neither was it to be found in the decrees of any council that any legates should be sent from Rome to them, to decide in their matters. And they therefore exhorted the bishop of Rome, not to introduce the swelling pride of the world into the church of Christ, which church sheweth and giveth the light of simplicity and of humility to such as love God, &c. In these letters, moreover, it is signified that Apiarius, whom the bishop of Rome had absolved and received to the communion of the church, was afterwards found culpable, and therefore the council proceeded against him, brought him to open confession of his faults, and so enjoined him due penance for his demerits, notwithstanding the absolution and inconsiderate clearing of the bishop of Rome before proceeding.

In short, out of this council of Carthage these points are to be gathered. First, that the bishops of Rome were glad to receive such as came to them for succour.

2. That their pride was increased thereby, thinking and seeking to have all under their subjection.

3. To the intent to allure others to seek them from their being ready to release and acquit this Apiarius as guiltless, although he was afterwards found culpable by his own confession.

4. How that contrary to the acts and doings of the Romish bishop, this council condemned him, whom the bishop of Rome had absolved, little respecting the proceedings of the Romish church.

5. How the bishops of old time, have been falsifiers of ancient councils and writings, whereby it may be suspected, that they who were not ashamed to falsify and corrupt the council of Nice, would not stick to abuse and falsify the decretal epistles and writings of particular bishops and doctors for their own advantage, as they have often done.

6. In this council, whereat Augustine was present, and where the president Aurelius was called Papa, the bishop of Rome was called expressly in their letters merely bishop of the city of Rome.

7. The dominion of this Roman patriarch, in this council of Carthage, was cut so short, that it was neither permitted to them of Africa to appeal over the sea to him, nor for him to send over his legates to them for ending their controversies. By which it may sufficiently appear, that the bishop of Rome in those days was not at all admitted to be the chief of all other bishops, nor the head of the universal church of Christ on earth, &c.

8. We hear in this council, causes or reasons given, why it is not necessary, nor yet convenient for all foreign causes to be brought to one universal head or judge.

9. Lastly, by the said council of Carthage, we hear a virtuous exhortation given to the bishop of Rome, that he would not induce the meek and humble church of Christ to fume and swell with the pride of the world, as has been described. In this, or in some other council of Carthage, it was moreover provided by express law, and also specified in the pope's decrees, that no bishop of the first seat, should be called the prince of priests, or the chief priest, or any such like thing.

Not long before this council, there was celebrated in Africa another council, at which also Augustine was present, where it was decreed under pain of excommunication, that no minister or bishop should appeal over the sea to the bishop of Rome. Whereby it may appear that the bishop of Rome at this time was not universally called by the term of oecumenical or universal bishop, but bishop of the first seat; so that if there were any preferment therein, it was in the reverence of the place, and not in the authority of the person.

These titles then, as Bishop, Metropolitan, the Bishop of the first See, Primate, Patriarch, Archbishop; that is to say, chief bishop, or head bishop to other bishops of his province, we deny not that they were in the old time applied, and might be applied to the bishop of Rome, like as the same were also applied to other patriarchs in other chief cities and provinces.

As touching the name likewise of the high priest, or high priesthood, neither do I deny that it has been found in old monuments and records of ancient times: but in such wise and sort as it has been common to bishops indifferently, and not singularly attributed to any one bishop or see.

And thus much as touching the name or title of high priest, or supreme bishop. Which title as I do not deny it to have been used in the manner and form aforesaid; so do I deny this title, as it is now used in Rome, to have been used, or usually received during all the primitive time of the church, that is, six hundred years after Christ; after the manner of that authority and glory, which in these days is used and is given to the same; until the time of Phocas, the wicked emperor, which was after the year 608. Which title as it is too glorious for any one bishop in the church of Christ to use: so is it not to be found in any of the approved and most ancient writers of the church; namely these, Cyprian, Basil, Fulgentius, Chrysostom, Jerome, Ambrose, Augustine, Tertullian: but rather written against by the same. And therefore not without cause it is written and testified of Erasmus, who speaking of the said name, denies plainly the same to be heard of among the old writers.

The same is also to be affirmed of other presumptuous titles of like ambition, as the Head of the Universal Church, the Vicar of Christ in earth, Prince of Priests, with such like: which all be new found terms, strange to the ears of the old primitive writers and councils, and not received openly and commonly before the time of Boniface III., and the Emperor Phocas.

Now remains the name of the pope, which being a word which signifies as much as father, was then used, not as proper only to the bishop of Rome, but common to all other bishops or personages of worthy excellency. But now this name is so restrained and abused, that not only is it appropriated to the bishop of Rome, but also distinguishes the authority and pre-eminence of that bishop alone from all other bishops, for which cause it is now worthily come into contempt and execration.

Although it cannot be denied, but some in the primitive time began privately to pretend to that proud and wicked title of universal bishop, as Menna, and especially John patriarch of Constantinople, who calling a council at Constantinople, went about to dignify his throne by the consent of the council, and the emperor of Constantinople, and obtained the same; as appears in the fifth general council of Constantinople, act the first, where both Menna and also John in the said council are titled "Universal Patriarchs." Concerning which title although it was then used in Constantinople through the sufferance of the emperors, being then willing to have their imperial city advanced; yet this title was not in the city of Rome. And in Constantinople it stood in force only by man's law. Neither the bishop of Rome, nor any of the Western churches did acknowledge, but rather did oppose the same: namely, Pelagius II., and Gregory I., both bishops at that time of Rome. Pelagius writing to all bishops says plainly in these words, "that no patriarch should take the name of universality at any time, because that if any be called universal, the name of patriarch is derogatory from all other. But let this be far from all faithful men, to will to take that thing to him, whereby the honour of his brethren is diminished. Wherefore the said Pelagius charges all such bishops, that none of them in their letters will name any patriarch to be universal." What can be more evident than these words of Pelagius, who was bishop of Rome next before Gregory? (A.D. 583). In like manner or more plainly, and more earnestly writes also Gregory, proving that no man ought to be called universal bishop. With sharp words and rebukes, detesting the same title, calling it new, foolish, proud, perverse, wicked, profane, and that to consent unto it, is as much as to deny the faith. He added further and saith, that whoever goes about to extol himself above other bishops, in so doing followeth the act of Satan, to whom it was not sufficient to be counted equal or like unto other angels. In his epistles how oft does he repeat and declare the same to be directly against the gospel, and ancient decrees of councils; affirming that none of his predecessors did ever usurp to himself that stile or title, and concludes that whoever doth so, declares himself to be a forerunner of antichrist, &c.

But Gregory, confirming the sentence of Pelagius, had no small conflicts about this title, both with the patriarch, and with the emperor of Constantinople. The history is thus; after John had been made a patriarch of Constantinople, by his flattery and hypocrisy, and had obtained of the emperor to be extolled above other bishops, with the name of universal patriarch, and that he would write to Gregory then bishop of Rome, for his consent concerning the same, Gregory abiding still in his constancy, did set himself stoutly against the antichristian title, and would give it no place. Gregory perceiving the Emperor Maurice to be displeased with him about the matter, writes to Constantina, the empress, arguing and declaring in his letters, that the presumption and pride of him to be universal patriarch, was both against the rule of the gospel, and decrees of the canons; namely, the sixth canon of the Nicene council, and the novelty of that new found title to declare nothing else, but that the time of antichrist was near. Upon this Maurice, the emperor, taking displeasure with him, calls home his soldiers from Italy, and incites the Lombards against the Romans, who, with their king, set upon the city of Rome, and besieged it for a whole year, Gregory, notwithstanding, still remaining in his former constancy. After these afflictions, Eulogius, patriarch of Alexandria, writes to Gregory, and in his letters, names him universal pope: which Gregory refuses, and answers as follows:

"Behold: in the preface of your epistle directed to me, ye have used a word of a proud name, calling me universal pope, which I pray your holiness you will cease hereafter to do, for that is derogated from you, whatsoever is attributed to another more than right and reason requireth. As for me I seek not mine advancement in words, but in manners: neither do I account that any honour wherein the honour of my brethren I see to be hindered: for my honour I take to be the honour of the universal church: my honour is the whole and perfect vigour of my brethren. Then am I honoured when to no man is denied the due honour which to him belongeth. For if your holiness call me universal pope, in so doing you deny yourself to be that, which ye affirm me to be, universal: but that God forbid. Let these words therefore go, which do nothing but puff up vanity, and wound charity, &c."

It were too long to insert here all such letters of his concerning this matter, but these shall appear more largely hereafter in the body of the history, when we come to the year and time of Gregory, which was well nigh six hundred years after Christ. In the mean time this is sufficient to declare, how the church of Rome with the form and manner of their title of universal supremacy now used and maintained, has utterly swerved from the ancient steps of the primitive church of Rome.

Now let us see what the adversary has to object again for the title of their universality, or rather singularity.

One objection of our adversaries is this; although (say they) no bishop of Rome was ever called, or would be called by the name of universal bishop, yet it follows not, therefore, that they are not, or ought not to be heads of the universal church. Their reason is this:

As St. Peter had the charge of the whole church committed unto him, although he were not called universal apostle:

So no more absurd it is for the pope to be called the head of the whole church, and to have the charge thereof, although he be not called universal bishop, &c.

Wherein is a double untruth to be noted: first, in that they pretend Peter to be the head, and to have the charge of the whole church: if we take here (charge or head) for dominion or mastership upon or above the church in all cases judiciary, both spiritual and temporal: for the words of the Scripture are plain, "Not as being lords over God's heritage, but being ensamples to the flock," 1 Pet. v. 3; and "But ye shall not be so, but he that is greatest among you let him be as the younger, and he that is chief as he that doth serve," Luke xxii. 26. Again, that the church is greater, or rather the head of Peter, it is clear, 1 Cor. iii. 22, "All things are yours, whether it be Paul, or Apollos, or Cephas, or the world, or death, or life, and you are Christ's, and Christ is God's," &c. In which words the dignity of the church no doubt is preferred above the apostles, and above Cephas also. Moreover, as the dignity of the wife is above the servant, so must needs the honour and worthiness of the church (being the spouse of Christ) surmount the state of Peter or other apostles, which be but servants to Christ and to the church. The same Lord that said to Peter, "Feed my sheep," said also to the other, "Go and preach this gospel to all nations." And he that said to Peter, "Whatsoever thou loosest," said also to the other, "Whatsoever ye remit in the earth." Moreover, if the matter go by preaching, Paul the apostle laboured more therein, than ever did Peter by his own confession, 1 Cor. xv. 10; also suffered more for the same, 2 Cor. xi. 23; neither was his doctrine less sound. Yea, and in one point he went before Peter, and was teacher and schoolmaster unto Peter, whereas Peter was by him justly corrected, Gal. ii. 11. Furthermore, teaching is not always nor in all things a point of mastership, but sometimes a point of service. As if a Frenchman should be put to an Englishman to teach him French, although he excels him in that kind of knowledge; yet it follows not, therefore, that he has fulness of power upon him, to appoint his diet, to rule his household, to prescribe his laws, to stint his lands, and such other. Wherefore seeing in travel of teaching, in pains of preaching, in gifts of tongues, in largeness of commission, in operation of miracles, in grace of vocation, in receiving the Holy Ghost, in vehemency of torments, and death for Christ's name, the other apostles were nothing inferior to Peter: why Peter then should claim any special prerogative above the rest, I under-

c

stand no cause. As, indeed, he never claimed any: but the patrons of the apostolical see do claim that for him, which he never claimed himself: neither if he were here, would he less abhor it with soul and conscience than we do now: and yet our abhorring now is not for any malice of person, or any vantage to ourselves, but only the vehemency of truth, and zeal to Christ and to his Church. Moreover, if these men would needs have Peter to be the curate and overseer of the whole universal church (which was too much for one man to take charge of) and to be prince of all other apostles, then would I fain learn of them, what means the right hand of fellowship between Peter, Paul, and Barnabas, mentioned Gal. ii. 9. What taking of hands is there between subjects and their prince, in way of fellowship? Or where fellowship is, what mastership is there? Or, again, what state of mastership is it like that Christ would give to Peter, who being indeed master of all, took such little mastership upon himself, and that not only in inward affection, but also in outward act? Although I am not ignorant that Peter in divers places of the gospel has his commendation, neither do I deny Peter to be worthy of the same. But yet these words of commendation give to him no state of superiority, or jurisdiction over all others, to have all under his subjection.

They produce another argument, proving, that the bishop of Rome was entitled the head of Christ's church, in the primitive time.

St. Peter, they argue, was called by the ancient fathers, head of Christ's church;—And as St. Peter was bishop of Rome:—Therefore, the bishop of Rome was called head of the church in the old ancient time.

How can they prove that St. Peter, although he were at Rome, and taught at Rome, and suffered at Rome, yet was bishop and proper ordinary of that city of Rome? As to the places of the fathers, to prove this, I answer concerning Orosius, Tertullian, Cyprian, Jerome, and Augustine, that where they speak of St. Peter's chair, or planting the faith at Rome, straightway the papist argues thereupon, that Peter was bishop of Rome. But that does not clearly follow. For the office of the apostles was to plant the faith in all places, and in every region, yet were they not bishops in every region. And as for the chair, as it is no difference essential that maketh a bishop (for so much as a doctor may have a chair, and yet be no bishop) so they cannot conclude by the chair of Peter, that St. Peter was bishop of Rome. All this proves no more, but that Peter was at Rome, and there taught the faith of Christ, as Paul did also, and peradventure in a chair likewise: yet we say not that Paul was therefore bishop of Rome, but that he was there as an apostle of Christ, whether he taught there standing on his feet, or sitting in a chair. In the Scripture commonly the chair signifies doctrine or judgment, as sitting also declares such as teach or

judge, whether they sit in the chair of Moses, or in the chair of pestilence. Planting likewise is a word apostolical, and signifies not the office of a bishop only. Wherefore it is no good argument to say that he sate, he taught, he planted at Rome, his chair and seat was at Rome, and that, therefore, he was bishop of Rome.

As for Abdias, Ado, Optatus, and others, I answer with this distinction of a bishop, which is to be taken either generally or specially. And first, generally, a bishop is he to whomsoever the public cure and charge of souls is committed, without any limitation of place. And so the name of bishop is co-incident with the office of apostle, or any public pastor, doctor, or curate, of the universal flock of Christ. And thus may Paul, Peter, or any other of the apostles be called bishops. So also is Christ himself by express word called bishop and pastor, 1 Peter ii. 25. And thus may Peter well be named a bishop. But this public and general charge universally over the whole, without limitation, ceased after Christ and the apostles. For then were bishops appointed by places and provinces, to have special oversight of some particular flock or province, and so to be resident and attendant only upon the same.

The other view of this name bishop, is to be taken after a more special sort, which is, when a person is assigned specially to some one certain place, city, or province, where he is bound to employ his office and charge, and no where else, according to the old canons of the apostles, and of the council of Nice. And this bishop differing from the other, bears the name of his city or diocese. And thus we deny that Peter the apostle was ever bishop elected, installed, or intituled to the city of Rome. And if Ado say that Peter was bishop of Rome five and twenty years, until the last year of Nero, that is easily refuted both by the scriptures and histories: for so we understand by the declaration of St. Paul, Gal. ii. 1. that fourteen years after his conversion, St. Paul had Peter by the hand at Jerusalem.

Moreover, Paul witnesses that the charge apostolical was committed to Peter over the circumcised, Gal. ii. 7. Also, St. Paul writing to the Romans, in his salutations to them in Rome, makes no mention of St. Peter, who, doubtless, should not have been forgotten, if he had then been in Rome.[1] Again, St. Peter dating his epistle from Babylon, was not then at Rome.[2]

Furthermore, histories record that Peter was at Pontus five years, then at Antioch seven years. How could he then be five-and-twenty years at Rome? Finally, where our adversary says, that St. Peter was there five-and-twenty years, until the last year of Nero; how can that stand, when St. Paul suffering under Nero was put to death the same day twelve month, that is, a whole year after Peter? But especially, how agrees this with Scripture, that Christ should make Peter an apostle universal to walk in all the world? " Go ye into

(1) Barrow, of whose celebrated " Treatise of the Pope's Supremacy," Archbishop Tillotson said, " He hath exhausted the subject and hath said enough to silence this controversy for ever," has thus expressed himself on this point.

" The discourses of those men, have evinced that it is hard to assign the time when Peter was at Rome, and that he could never long abide there. For,

" The time which old tradition assigneth of his going to Rome, is rejected by divers learned men, even of the Roman party.

" He was often in other places, sometimes at Jerusalem, sometimes at Antioch, sometimes at Babylon, sometimes at Corinth, sometimes, probably at each of those places unto which he directeth his catholic epistles. Among which, Epiphanius saith, that Peter did often visit Pontus and Bithynia.

" And that he seldom was at Rome, may well be collected from St. Paul's writings, for he, writing at different times, one epistle to Rome and divers epistles from Rome, as that to the Galatians— that to the Ephesians — that to the Phillipians — and that to the Colossians and the Second to Timothy, doth never mention him sending any salutation to him or from him.

" Particularly St. Peter was not there when St. Paul mentioning Tichicus, Onesimus, Aristarchus, Marcus and Justus, addeth, ' These alone my fellow-workers unto the kingdom of God, have been a comfort unto me,' Col. iv. 11.

" He was not there when St. Paul said, ' At my first defence no man stood with me, but all men forsook me.' 2 Tim. iv. 16.

" He was not there immediately before St. Paul's death, 'When the time of his departure was at hand,' when he telleth Timothy that ' All the brethren did salute him,' and naming divers of them omitteth Peter. 2 Tim. iv. 21.

" Which things being considered, it is not probable St. Peter would assume the Episcopal Chair at Rome, he being little capable to reside there, and for that other needful affairs would have forced him to leave so great a church destitute of their pastor.

" Had he done so, he must have given a bad example of non-residence, a practice that would have been very ill relished in the primitive church."

(2) It was during the life of our Author, John Fox, that the Rhemish Testament was published, and though he little thought that the Papists would identify Babylon with Rome, yet his "Acts and Monuments," were scarcely before the world, when the Rhemish Annotators—finding no evidence in the Scriptures to prove that Peter was ever at Rome — did actually fasten upon the dating of his first epistle from Babylon, and explain it as a mystic name for Rome!

Cartwright—who was a contemporary of Fox, and wrote his " Confutation of the Rhemists," &c. during the lifetime of our Martyrologist, thus writes:

" That Peter sat not at Rome is confirmed in that Peter writeth from Babylon, which to be Babylon in Chaldea, and not in Italy, this is an evident reason, for that this Babylon was a place of principal abode of the Jews, towards whom Peter's charge specially lay, Gal. ii. 7. Whereas at this time, the Jews were not suffered to make their abode in Rome, Acts, xviii. 9. Whereunto may be added that, writing to the dispersed Jews, and making rehearsal of divers countries wherein they were, he leaveth out Chaldea, which, considering the great numbers that remained there, still after the return into Judea out of Captivity, he would never have done, unless Chaldea were the place from whence he wrote his epistles."—Cartwright in loc. [ED.]

all the world," Mark xvi. 15.; and "ye shall be witnesses unto the uttermost part of the earth," Acts i. 8. And our papists would needs make him a sitting bishop, and locate him at Rome. How accord these—*apostle* and *bishop*—to *go* and to *sit*—to *all nations* and *at Rome*—together?

Now, the second untruth in the argument is, that because Peter was the head of the church, therefore, the pope must also be the head of the church, although he was not called universal bishop for a long time. But this we deny, yea, the matter denies itself by their own position; for the title of universal bishop was not received at Rome, but refused to the time of Gregory; then it must necessarily be granted that the bishops of Rome, before Gregory, had not the charge of the whole church, neither could be admitted, by that reason, to be heads of the church. For, as there can be no head but that which is universal to the whole body, so none can have charge of the whole, but he must needs be universal to all parts of that whereof he has the charge. Wherefore, if a bishop be he who has the charge of all souls in his diocese, then he whose charge extends to all churches, and who must render account for every christian soul within the whole world, to him cannot be denied the name of a universal bishop, having the office of a universal bishop. Or if he be not a universal bishop, he cannot then have the charge of the whole, that is, of all the churches of Christ. This word, universal, in the Greek writers, signifies that which we in our English tongue call catholic; yet I suppose our adversaries here will not take universal in that sense. For after that meaning, as we do not deny that the bishops of Rome may be universal bishops, so neither can they deny but other bishops may also be as universal, that is, as catholic as they. But such as more distinctly discuss this matter, define universal or catholic by three things, to wit, by time, place, and person. So that whatever extends itself to all times, all places, and all persons, that is properly universal or catholic. And contrariwise, what is to be called universal or catholic, reaches to all those three, comprehending all places, times, and persons, or else it is not to be called properly universal or catholic. And thus there are three things which most commonly we call catholic or universal; that is, the church which is called the catholic church; faith, which is called the catholic faith; a man whom also we call a catholic man, because these three extend themselves so, that no time, place, nor person is excluded. Which three conditions, if they altogether concur in the charge of the bishop of Rome, then is it a universal charge, and he a universal bishop; if not, then is his charge neither universal, nor he the head of the church, nor yet universal bishop. For how these three can be separated, I cannot see, except they prove it more evidently than they have done.

And thus much to the objection of our adversaries, arguing, that as St. Peter, not being called universal apostle, was yet the head of the universal church; so the pope, although he was not first called universal bishop, had, and might have the charge of the whole church, and was the universal head of the same.

Our adversaries, notwithstanding, do busy themselves to prove out of Theodoret, Ireneus, Ambrose, and Augustine; that the see of Rome, having the pre-eminence and principality, hath been honoured above all other churches; arguing that Ireneus, Ambrose, Augustine, and Theodoret affirm that the church of Rome is the chief of all other churches; and that therefore, the bishop and head of that church is chief and head over all bishops, and head over all other churches.

But this conclusion is to be denied, for the excellency of the church or place does not always argue the excellency of the minister or bishop, nor yet necessarily causes the same. For in matters of the church which are spiritual, all pre-eminence stands upon spiritual and inward gifts, as faith, piety, learning, and godly knowledge, zeal and fervency in the Holy Ghost, unity of doctrine, &c. which gifts many times may excel in a church where the minister or bishop is inferior to bishops or ministers of other churches. As the most famous school in a realm has not always the most famous schoolmaster, nor does it make him thereby more excellent in learning than all others. So if our adversaries do mean by this pre-eminence of the church of Rome, such inward gifts of doctrine, faith, unity, and peace of religion; then, I say, the excellency hereof does not argue the excellency of the bishop. But here our adversaries will reply again and say, that the pre-eminence of the church of Rome is not meant here so much by inward gifts and endowments belonging to a christian church, as by outward authority and dominion over other churches. Whereto is to be answered: what necessity is there? or where did our papists learn, to bring into the spiritual church of Christ, this outward form of civil policy? that, as the Roman emperors in times past governed over all the world, so the Roman bishop must have his monarchy upon the universal clergy, to make all other churches to stoop under his subjection? And where then are the words of our Saviour?—"But it shall not be so among you." If they say there must needs be distinction of degrees in the church, and superiority must be granted for the discipline of the church, for quieting of schisms, for setting orders, for commencing convocations and councils, &c. Against this superiority we stand not, and therefore we yield to our superior powers, kings, and princes, our due obedience, and to our lawful governors under God of both governments, ecclesiastical and temporal. Also in the ecclesiastical state, we take not away the distinction of degrees, such as are appointed by the primitive church, or by the scripture allowed, as patriarchs, archbishops, bishops, ministers, and deacons. In which degrees, as we grant diversity of office, so we admit diversity of dignity. For, as we give to the minister place above the deacon, to the bishop above the minister, to the archbishop above the bishop, so we see no cause of inequality, why one minister should be above another minister; one bishop in his degree above another bishop, to deal in his diocese; or one archbishop above another archbishop. And this is to keep an order duly and truly in the church.

Now here joins the question between us and the papists, whether the metropolitan church of Rome, with the archbishop of the same, ought to be preferred before other metropolitan churches and archbishops, through universal christendom, or not? To the answer whereof, if the voice of order might here be heard, it would say, give to things that be equal and similar, equal honour; to things unequal and dissimilar, unequal honour, &c. Wherefore, seeing the see of Rome is a patriarchal see, appointed by the primitive church, and the bishop thereof and archbishop limited within his own bordering churches, which the council of Nice calls suburban churches, as other archbishops be; he ought, therefore, to have the honour of an archbishop and such outward pre-eminence as is due to other archbishops. If he requires more, he breaks the rule of right order, he falls into presumption, and does wrong unto his equals; and they also do wrong unto themselves, who, feeding his ambition, give more to him than the rule of order requires. For so much as they yield to him more than is his right, so much they take from themselves. And this is the reason why both Gregory and Pelagius reprehend them, who gave to the archbishop of Constantinople that which now the bishop of Rome claims to himself, charging them with the breach of order in these words, "Lest that while any singular thing is given to one person, all other priests be deprived of their due honour." And Pelagius exhorts that no priest give to any archbishop the name of universal bishop, "Lest in so doing he take from himself his due honour, while he yields that which is not due to another." And also in the same epistle, "If he be called the chief universal patriarch, then is the name of patriarch derogated from others," &c. Wherefore, seeing the bishop of Rome is an archbishop, order requires that he should have the dignity which to archbishops is due; whatever is added more, is derogatory to the rest. And thus much concerning distinction of degrees, and order in giving to every degree his place and honour.

Wherefore, even if it be admitted that the pope sits and succeeds in the chair of Peter and also that he is the bishop of the greatest city in the world, yet it follows not that he should have rule and lordship over all other bishops and churches of the world. For, first, touching the succession of Peter, many things are to be considered:—

I. Whether Peter sat and had his chair in Rome or not?

II. Whether he sat there as an apostle, or as a bishop?

III. Whether the sitting in the outward seat of Peter makes successors of Peter?

IV. Whether he sits in the chair and seat of Peter who sits not in the doctrine of Peter?

V. Whether the succession of Peter makes rather an apostle than a bishop, and so we should call the pope the apostle of Rome, and not the bishop of Rome?

VI. Whether ecclesiastical functions ought to be esteemed by ordinary succession of place, or by God's secret calling and sending?

VII. Whether it stand by scripture, that any succession at all is appointed in Christ's church, or why more from Peter than from other apostles?

All which being well discussed, it would appear what little reason the pope has to take this state upon him, above all other churches. In the meantime this one argument may suffice, instead of many, for our adversaries to answer at their convenient leisure.

All the true successors of Peter sit in the chair of the doctrine of Peter, and other apostles uniformly,—but no popes of this latter church of Rome sit in the chair of St. Peter's and other apostles' doctrine uniformly,—and therefore no popes of this latter church of Rome are the true successors of Peter.

And when they have well perused this argument, and have well compared together the doctrine taught them by St. Peter, with the doctrine taught now by the popes, of justification of a christian-man, of the office of the law, of the strength and largeness of sin, of men's merits, of free-will, of works of supererogation, of setting up images, of seven sacraments, of auricular confession, of satisfaction, of sacrifice of the mass, of communicating under one kind, of elevating and adoring the sacramental elements, of Latin service, of invocation, of prohibition of meats and marriage, of vowing chastity, of sects and rules of divers religions, of indulgences and pardons: also of their doctrine now taught concerning magistrates, of the fulness of power of the see of Rome, with many other things like to these, then will I be glad to hear what they shall say.

And if they would prove by Ireneus, Ambrose, Augustine, and Theodore, the bishop of Rome to be the chief of all bishops, because the city whereof he is bishop, is the chief and principal above all other churches, it followeth no more than this:—

London is the chief city in all England; and therefore the bishop of London is the chiefest of all bishops in this realm.

Which argument were derogatory to the archbishops both of Canterbury and York.

Yea, to grant yet more to our adversaries, that these fathers in giving principality to Rome, referred to the succession from Peter, and not to the greatness of the city: yet their argument will fail if it be rightly considered; thus,

The apostolical see of Rome, having succession from Peter, with the bishops thereof, was chief of all other churches in the primitive time: therefore, the apostolical see of Rome, with the bishops thereof, having succession from Peter, ought now to be the chief of all other churches.

This might follow, if the times were like, or if succession which gave the cause of pre-eminence, were the same now, which it was then. But now the time and succession does not correspond, for then succession was as well in apostolical doctrine as in apostolical place. Now the succession of apostolical doctrine has long ceased in the apostolical see: and nothing remains but only place, which is the least matter of true spiritual and apostolical succession.

Besides these objections, our adversaries object against us examples of the primitive time of the church, testimonies of general councils, and opinions of ancient writers taken out of the book of councils, and epistles decretal, whereby their intent is to prove the foresaid terms (of the head of the church, ruler of the church, chief of all other priests) to be applied not only to Peter, but also to the bishop of Rome within the compass of the primitive time. To all which objections fully and exactly to answer in order, would require a whole volume by itself. In the meantime, leaving the rest to them, to whom it more properly appertains, I answer with this short distinction these and all such like places where St. Peter with his successors are called head of the church, chief of bishops, prince of the apostles, &c. In which places this word head, chief, and prince of the apostles, may be taken two manner of ways: to note either dominion or else commendation. For we read sometimes *head* and *chief*, to be words not of authority, but of excellency, whereby is declared the chief and worthiest among many, and not the possessor and governor of the whole. Like as in the person of man, the head is the principal part of the whole body, being endued with reason, and furnished with senses, by which the whole man is directed; so there is derived a metaphor, that to what man nature or condition has given the greatest excellency of gifts, he is called *head* or *chief*. And yet he has not always dominion or jurisdiction of the rest. So we call in our common speech those, the head or chief men of the parish, who for their riches, wisdom, or place, are most specially noted: after like phrase of speech we call the head man of the inquest, him that has first place: and yet neither of these have any dominion or jurisdiction over the rest. In a school the chief scholar in learning, is not therefore the master or governor of his fellows. Neither has Cicero any title to claim subjection of all other orators, because he is named the prince of eloquence; and though Homer may be also called prince of poets, yet poets owe not to Homer anything but fame and praise.

And what if Peter be called and counted as head and prince of the apostles, for his excellent faith, for his divine confession, and singular affection to the Lord Jesus: yet what right has he to challenge authority over the apostles, or the pope after him over all other bishops and the whole church of Christ, even though the pope should have the like excellency of Christ's faith which Peter had, as would to God he had.

And if our adversaries provoke us to the numbering of testimonies, and dividing the house (speaking of the writers and councils of the primitive age) for these testimonies alleged on their side, I could recite out of the witness of doctors, out of the examples of councils, and practices of emperors, no less than sixty voices, much more opposed to their assertion. But I refer it either to them that have more leisure at this time, or else omit it to another time, if the good pleasure of the Lord shall be to grant me further leisure in another book to treat thereof at large in such order, as shall appear sufficient to prove by the doctors, general councils, examples and histories that the bishops of Rome, during the first five hundred years after Christ, although for the greatness of the empire, they were somewhat more magnified than the others, and therefore were sought, and were flattered, and they did set forth themselves more than they should; yet by the common consent of the churches they were stopped of their purpose, so that by the consent of the most part, within that age, the bishops of Rome had not this state of title, jurisdiction and power which they now usurp, but were taken as archbishops of equal honour, of equal merit with other archbishops and rulers of the church. And if any preference was given to them above the rest, yet neither was it so given by all nor by the most part; secondly, neither was it so given by them for any such necessity of God's word, as did bind them thereto, nor yet so much for respect of Peter and his succession, as for certain other causes and respects, as may be gathered to the number of thirteen.

I. The greatness of the city and monarchy of Rome.

II. The authority of the emperor Constantine the great, the first of the emperors converted to the faith, and ruling in the same city, by whom the universal liberty of the church was first promoted; and the causes of the bishops then at variance, were committed partly to the bishop of Rome, partly to other bishops near by, to be decided, as appears by Eusebius. (lib. 10, cap. 5.)

III. The council of Nice, which confirmed the pre-eminence of that church to have the oversight of the churches bordering about it.

IV. The unquiet state of the Greek church, much troubled in those days with sects, factions, and dissensions.

V. When synods were called by other metropolitans; then if the bishops of Rome chanced to be absent, and their sentence, to be required, by the occasion thereof they began at length to take their sentence for a canon or rule ecclesiastical, and to refuse other synods, where their decree or sentence was not required.

VI. When any common matter was in hand at other places, whatever was done, the manner commonly was to write to the Roman bishop for his approbation for public unity and consent in Christ's church.

VII. Also sometimes the testimony of the Roman bishop was wont in those days also to be desired for admitting teachers and bishops in other churches.

VIII. Their sentence was not only required, but also often received by other bishops. And when bishops of other provinces were at any dissension among themselves, they of their own accord appealed to the bishop of Rome, desiring him to cite up both parties, and to have the hearing and deciding of the cause, as did Macarius and Hesychius send to Julius, then bishop of Rome, &c.

IX. Certain of the Arians returning from their Arianism, offered up and exhibited unto the bishops of Rome their evidences of repentance, and were received again, as Ursatius and Valens did to Julius. (Socrat. lib. 2, cap. 24.)

X. Gratian the emperor made a law that all men should retain that religion which Damasus, the bishop of Rome, and Peter, bishop of Alexandria, did hold. (Sozom. lib. 7, cap. 4.)

XI. If it happened that the bishop of Rome disallowed the ordering of any minister or ministers, the popes perceiving how diligent and ready they were to seek their favour, and to send up their messengers to Rome for their purgation, took thereby no little manner of exaltation. (Theodoret, lib. 5, cap. 23.)

XII. The bishops of Rome had also another artful practice, that in sending out their letters abroad they were ever harping on the greatness of their name, and of their apostolic see, and of the primacy of St. Peter, their predecessor, and prince of all the apostles, &c. And this they used to do in every letter, whensoever they wrote to any, as appeareth in all their letters decretal, namely, in the letters of Miltiades, Marcellus, and Marcus, &c.

XIII. If any of the Eastern church directed any writing to them, wherein any signification was contained of never so little reverence given unto them (as learned men commonly use for modesty's sake) that was taken by and by, and construed for plain subjection and due obedience.

Thus you have the first and original grounds, by means whereof the archbishops of the Romish see have achieved their great kingdom over Christ's church, first beginning the mystery of their iniquity by that which was modestly and voluntarily given them; afterward by use and custom claiming it ambitiously of duty and service; and, lastly, holding fast that which once they had got into their possession, so that now in no case can they abide the birds to call home their feathers again, which they so long have usurped.

And thus much concerning the life, jurisdiction, and title of the Roman bishops; in all which (as is declared) they, and not we, have fallen from the primitive church of Rome. To these I might also join the manner of government, wherein the Romish bishops have no less altered, both from the rule of scripture, and from the steps of the true church of Rome, which government as it has been, and ought to be only spiritual, yet has the bishop of Rome used it of late years no otherwise than an earthly king or prince has governed his realm and dominions, with riches, glory, power, terror, outward strength, force, prison, death, execution, laws, policies, promoting his friends to dignities, revenging his affections, punishing and correcting faults against his person more than other offences committed against God, using and abusing in all these things the word of God for his pretext and cloak to work his worldly purpose; whereas indeed, the word of God ministers no such power to spiritual persons, but such as is spiritual, according to the saying of the apostle: the weapons of our warfare, are not carnal, but spiritual; such as serve not against flesh and blood, nor against the weak person of man, but against Satan and the gates of hell.

Which weapons as they are all spiritual, so ought they, who have the dealing thereof, to be likewise spiritual, well furnished with all such gifts and graces of the Holy Ghost as are meet for the governance of his spiritual church; with wisdom and knowledge in the scripture to instruct the ignorant, with inward intelligence and foresight of the crafty operations of Satan, with power of the Spirit to resist the same, with practice and experience of temptations, to comfort such as be afflicted and oppressed of Satan, with heavenly discretion to discern spirits, and truth from untruth, with judgment and knowledge of tongues and learning to convict error, with zeal of God's glory, with fervency of prayer, with patience in persecution, with a mind contented with all cases and states incident, with tears and compassion on other men's griefs, with stoutness and courage against proud and stout oppressors, with humility towards the poor and miserable, with the counsel of the Lord Jesus by his Word and Spirit to direct him in all things, with strength against sin, with hatred of this world, with the gift of faith, power of the keys in spiritual causes, as to minister the word, the sacraments and excommunication when the word biddeth, that the spirit may be saved, and to reconcile again as cause requireth, &c. These and such like are the matters wherein consist the sinews and strength of the church, and for true governing the same. But contrary to these, the bishop and clergy of this later church of Rome, under the name and pretence of Christ and his word, have for a long time exercised nothing else but a worldly dominion, seeking indeed their own glory, not the glory of Christ; the riches of this world, not the lucre of souls; not feeding the flock, but filling the purse; revenging their own wrongs, but neglecting God's glory; striving against man only, and killing him, but not killing the vice nor confuting the error of man; strong against flesh and blood, but weak against the devil; stout against the simple, but meek against the mighty; briefly doing almost all things preposterously, more like to secular princes than spiritual pastors of Christ's flock, with outward forcement and fear of punishment, with prisoning, famishing, hanging, racking, drowning, beheading, slaying, murdering, and burning, and warring also: on the other side, with riches and treasures, with guard and strength of men, with court and cardinals, with pomp and pride about them, with their triple crown, with the naked sword, with their ordinary succession, with their laws and executions, their promotions and preferments, their biddings and commandings, threatenings and revengings, &c.

In fine, to compare, therefore, the images of a worldly kingdom, with this kingdom of the pope, there is no difference, save only that this kingdom of the pope, under hypocrisy, makes a face of the spiritual sword, which is the word of God; but in very deed doth all things with the temporal sword, that is, with outward force, differing not from civil and secular government in any respect or condition. For as in an earthly kingdom, first there is a prince or some chief magistrate sppointed, having dominion over his nobles and commons, containing all his subjects under his statutes and laws; with which laws notwithstanding he dispenses at his pleasure; under whom all other inferior magistrates have their order and place appointed to rule over the subjects, and yet to be subject under him; so if the state and form of the pope be well considered, we shall see it differs nothing from the same, but only in the names of the persons. In civil government, all subjection is referred to one head ruler, whose authority surmounts all the rest, and keeps them under obedience. In like manner, the government of the popish church is committed to one man, who, as chief steward, overseer, and ruler of Christ's household, in his absence hath supreme power over all churches, to direct all the affairs thereof. But here stands the difference, in civil policy he is called a king or prince; here he is called a pope.

The king has next unto him his dukes and earls; the pope's nobility stands in his cardinals and legates, who, though they be no dukes in name, yet in pomp and pride, will not only give check to them, but also mate to kings themselves, if they might be suffered, as did Theodore, Lanfranc, Anselm, Thomas à Becket, and so would Thomas Wolsey have done, had not the king given him a check betimes. In civil policy, next to dukes and earls, followeth the order of lords, barons, knights, esquires, gentlemen, with majors, sheriffs, constables, bailiffs, wardens, &c. The like race is to be seen also, although under other names, in the pope's policy; of primates, bishops, suffragans, provosts, deans, canons, vicars, archdeacons, priests, deacons, subdeacons, acolyths, exorcists, lectors, door-keepers, singsters, with other clerks. And in the other, under wardens comes the order of scavengers; so neither does the pope's monarchy lack his chanelrakers, to whom may well be compared that rabblement of abbots, provincials, priors, monks, and friars, with their convents and nunneries.

Moreover, from justices, judges, lawyers, sergeants, attorneys, which be necessary officers in the commonwealth, what differ the pope's inquisitors, canonists, doctors, and bachelors of the pope's law, commissaries, officials, proctors, promoters, with such others, which serve no less in the spiritual court, and in the consistory, than the other do in the temporal court. Now whoever wishes to compare the glory and magnificence of the one with the glory of the other; also the power of the one with the power of the other; and the riches of the one with the riches of the other; I suppose he shall see no great odds between them both, taking the pope's kingdom as it stood in his full ruff, and yet stands where churches are not reformed. As for subtilty and politic practice there is no man that is impartial that doubts, or that hath his eyes that sees not, that the pope's hierarchy, in holding up their state, far excelleth all the kingdoms of worldly princes.

Thus in comparing the pope's government with civil governments, as they disagree in little or nothing; so in comparing again the same with the order of scriptures, or with the government that was in the ancient church of Rome, we shall see no resemblance between them. As we read in the apostles' time, all the armour of Christ's ministers was spiritual and full of godly power against the spiritual enemies of our salvation, governing the church with peace, patience, humility, true knowledge of God, the sword of the Spirit, the shield of faith, the breastplate of righteousness, hearty charity, sincere faith, and a good conscience; so after the apostles in the time of Ambrose, by his own testimony it is to be understood, that the armour of churchmen was then prayers and tears; where now the armour of the pope's priesthood is nothing else but fire and sword, wherewith they keep all things under their subjection. And here comes the enormous and horrible abuse of excommunication, suspension, and interdict: for many things, for which the civil magistrate will not commit any citizen to the stocks, the pope's censure will not hesitate to commit a christian to the devil; not to speak of other usurped dealings and doings in maters that belong to the civil sword. As in punishing immorality and adultery, in administration and probates of testaments, in bearing civil office cardinals to be captains

in war, and rulers of regions; bishops to be presidents or chancellors; priests to be stewards in great men's houses, or masters of mints, or clerks of the market, or gardeners to gentlemen, &c. All which I here pass over, referring them to the consideration of such as have more leisure to mark the order of their doings, and so to judge of the same with impartiality, according to the rule of truth taught in God's word, and the public examples of the ancient church of Christ in the primitive time.

Thus having discoursed so much concerning the manner of life, title, jurisdiction, and government of the pope's see, (in all which points it is to be seen how this later church of Rome, has receded from the true ancient church of Rome), it now remains according to my promise, to proceed to the fourth and last point, which is Doctrine; wherein consists the chief matter that makes with us and against them, so that they are not to be reputed for true catholics, being altered so far; nor we other than heretics, if we should now join with them. For the proof of which let us examine the doctrine and rites of the church of Rome now used, and compare them with the teaching of the ancient catholics, that such simple souls as have been, and yet are seduced, by the false appearance and image of this pretended and bastardly church, perceiving what lies within it, may be warned in time, either to eschew the peril, if they are willing to be instructed, or, if not, to blame none but themselves for their own wilful destruction. And although I could here charge the new-fangled church of the pope with seven or eight heinous crimes, as blasphemy, idolatry, heresy, superstition, absurdity, vanity, cruelty, and contradiction, (in which it neither agrees with the old learning of their predecessors, nor yet with themselves in sundry points), yet I will, and dare boldly affirm, that in this doctrine of the pope now taught in the church of Rome, there is neither any consolation of conscience, nor salvation of man's soul. For seeing there is no life, nor soul's health but only in Christ, nor any promise of salvation or comfort made, but only by faith in the Son of God: what assurance can there be of perfect peace, life, or salvation, where that which only maketh all, is made least of, and other things which make least are the most esteemed? For to say the simple truth, what else is the whole course and body of the pope's law now set forth, but a doctrine of laws, a heap of ceremonies, teaching of traditions, a mediation of merits, a foundation of new religions? all which avail not one jot to the justification of our souls before the terrible judgment of God.

And, therefore, as it may be truly said that this doctrine of the pope is void of all true comfort and salvation; so likewise it seems that these, who addict themselves so devoutly to the pope's learning, were never earnestly afflicted in conscience, never humbled in spirit, nor broken in heart, never entered into any serious feeling of God's judgment, nor ever felt the strength of the law and of death. For if they had, they should soon have seen their own weakness, and been driven to Christ; then should they have seen what a horrible thing it is to appear before God the Father, or once to think on him, as Luther saith, without Christ. And, on the contrary side, then should they know what a glory, what a kingdom, what liberty and life it were to be in Christ Jesus by faith, holding their inheritance, not with the bondson of Hagar, but with the free son of Sarah; by promise, and not by the law; by grace, and not by works; by gift, and not by deserving; that God only might be praised, and not man.

And thus were the old Romans first taught, by St. Paul writing to the Romans. The same did Cornelius the Roman, and the first that was baptized of all the Gentiles, learn of St. Peter, when he received the Holy Ghost, not by the deeds of the law, but only by hearing the faith of Jesus preached. And in the same doctrine, the said church of the Romans continued many years, so long as they were in affliction. And in the same doctrine the bishop of Rome, with his Romans, now also should still remain, if they were such ancient catholics as they pretend, and would follow the old mother church of Rome, and hold the first liquor wherewith they were first seasoned. But the sweet freshness and scent of that liquor, and pleasant perfume, is now clean put out through other unsavory infusions of the pope's, so that hardly any taste or piece remaineth of all that primitive doctrine, which St. Paul and the other apostles first planted among the Gentiles. And what marvel if the Romans now in so long time have lost their first sap, seeing the church of the Galatians in the very time of St. Paul, their schoolmaster, as soon as he turned his back a little, were almost turned from the doctrine of faith, and had much ado to be recovered again.

Of this defection and falling away from the faith, St. Paul expressly foretells us in his epistles both to the Thessalonians, and also to Timothy, where he shews that a defection shall come, and that certain shall depart from the faith, attending to spirits of error, &c. 1 Tim. iv. 1, and to know what errors these shall be, the circumstance plainly leads us to understand in the same place, where the apostle speaks of seared consciences, forbidding men to marry, and to eat meats ordained of God to be taken with thanksgiving, for man's sustenance; most evidently, as with his finger, pointing out unto us the church of Rome, which not in these points only, but also in all other conditions is almost utterly revolted from the pure original sincerity of that doctrine, which St. Paul planted in the church of the Romans, and of all other Gentiles, and of which the following is a summary.

I. The doctrine of St. Paul describes all our justification freely and only to faith in Christ, as to the only means and cause whereby the merits of Christ's passion can be applied unto us, without any respect of work or works of the law whatever; Ephes. ii. 8, 9; and in this doctrine, the church of the Romans was first planted.

II. The same doctrine of St. Paul, cutting off and excluding all man's deserving, rests only upon God's promise, and upon grace, not man's merits: upon mercy, not man's labouring or running, Rom. ix. 16: upon election and calling, not man's willing, &c.

III. The same doctrine casting down the strength of man and his natural integrity, as they call it, concludes all flesh under sin, and makes the same destitute of the glory of God, Rom. iii. 9—23.

IV. It makes a difference between the law and the gospel, declaring the use and end of them to be different; the one to kill, the other to quicken; the one to condemn, the other to justify; the one to have an end, the other to be perpetual, &c.: Rom. v. 20.; vii. 4. Gal. iii. 10—13.

V. The same doctrine of St. Paul, as it shews a difference between the law and the gospel, so it makes no less difference between the righteousness of God and the righteousness of man, abhorring the one, that is, man's own righteousness, coming by the law and works; and embracing the other which God imputes freely and graciously to us for Christ his Son's sake, in whom we believe, Philip. iii. 9.: Rom. iv. 24.

VI. It wipes away all traditions, and constitutions of men, especially from binding of conscience, calling them beggarly elements of this world, Gal. iv. 9. Col. ii. 20—22.

VII. Likewise it rejects and wipes away all curious subtilties, and superfluous speculations, and knows nothing else but only Christ crucified, which is the only object to which our faith looks, 1 Cor. ii. 1, 2.

VIII. Furthermore, as the same doctrine of St. Paul defines all men to be transgressors by the disobedience of one Adam, though they never touched the apple, they coming of his stock by nature; so doth it prove all men to be justified by the obedience of one, even Christ, though they did not his obedience, they being likewise born of him by spiritual regeneration and faith, Rom. v. 17—19.

IX. And therefore as all men coming of Adam are condemned originally, before they grow up to commit any sin against the law; so all men regenerated by faith in Christ are saved originally before they begin to do any good work of charity, or any other good deed, Rom. v. 18, 19.

X. The doctrine of St. Paul, considering the high glory of a christian man's state in Christ Jesus by faith, first sets him in a perfect peace with Almighty God, Rom. v. 1. Secondly, exempts him from all condemnation, Rom. viii. 1. Thirdly, it matches him with angels; it equals him with saints and fellow-citizens of heaven; it numbers him with the household of God; and inherits him with Jesus Christ himself. Ephes. ii. 19. Fourthly, it adopts him from the state of a servant, to the state of a Son of God, crying, "Abba, Father:" Gal. iv. 6. Fifthly, it opens to him a bold access and entrance to the high Majesty and throne of grace, Ephes. ii. 18.; Heb. iv. 16. Sixthly, it subjects all things under him, as ministers, yea, the apostles themselves, in their highest office, death, life, things present, things to come, with the whole world besides, and assigns him no spiritual head, but only Christ, saying, "And you are Christ's, and Christ is God's," 1 Cor. iii. 23. Seventhly, it advances and sets him in a spiritual liberty or freedom, above all terrors of spirit, either of God's law, or man's law, above all dreadful fears of sin, damnation, malediction, rejection, death, hell, or purgatory; above all servile bondage of ceremonies, men's precepts, traditions, superstitions, vices, yokes, customs, or what else soever oppresseth and entangleth the spiritual freedom of a conscience, which Christ hath set at liberty; and requireth, moreover, that we walk and stand stout in that liberty whereto we are brought with the free son of Sarah, and not suffer ourselves any more to be clogged with any such servile bondage; that is to say, although we must be content to subject our bodies to all service, and to all men, yet must we not yield our spiritual consciences and souls as slaves and servants, to be subject to the fear or bondage of any thing in this world, for so much as we are made lords and princes over all things whatsoever that can harm, bind, or terrify us, Gal. iv. 9.

XI. The right vein of St. Paul's doctrine puts no difference nor observation in days and times, Gal. iv. 10: Col. ii. 16.

XII. It leaveth all meats to be indifferent, with thanksgiving, to serve the necessity of the body, and not the body to serve them, Col. ii. 16. 1 Tim. iv. 4.

XIII. It permits marriage without restraint or exception, lawful and also expedient for all men, having need thereof, 1 Cor. vii. 2. Heb. xiii. 4.

XIV. It admits no sacrifice for sin, but the sacrifice of Christ alone, and that done once for all with blood. For without blood there is no remission of sin, which is applied to us by faith only, and by nothing else, Heb. ix. 22.

XV. As touching the holy communion, by the first epistle of St. Paul to the Corinthians, xi. 23—26., we understand, that the use then amongst them was, to have the participation of the bread called the Lord's body, and of the cup called the Lord's blood, administered not at an altar, but at a plain board or table, the congregation there meeting together after the time of their supper, where not the minister alone did receive, and the other looked on; but the whole congregation together did communicate with reverence and thanksgiving, not lifting over the priest's head, nor worshipping, nor kneeling, nor knocking their breasts; but either sitting at the supper, or standing after the supper.

XVI. The apostle, besides the sacramental supper, makes mention of baptism, or washing of regeneration, although he himself baptized but few, 1 Cor. i. 14., of other sacraments he makes no mention.

XVII. By the same doctrine of St. Paul, no tongue is to be used in the congregation, which is not known, and doth not edify, 1 Cor. xiv. 2.

XVIII. The rule of St. Paul's doctrine subjects every creature under the obedience of kings and princes, and ordinary magistrates, ordained of God to have the sword and authority of public government, to order and dispose in all things not contrary to God, whatever pertaineth to the maintenance of the good, or to the correction of the evil; from whose jurisdiction there is no exemption of vocations or persons, whether they be ecclesiastical or political. And therefore to this office it appertains to preserve peace, to set things in lawful order, to preserve christian discipline in the church of Christ, to remove offences, to bridle the disobedient, to provide and procure wholesome and faithful teachers over the people, to maintain learning, and set up schools, to have oversight not only of the people, but also of all ecclesiastical ministers, to see every one to do his duty, and to remove or punish such as be negligent; also to call councils and synods, and to provide that the church goods be faithfully dispensed by the hands of true dealers, to the sustenance of the church, and of true teachers, and to the public necessity of the poor, &c. Rom. xiii. 1. 4. 6., Tit. iii. 1.

XIX. Furthermore, by St. Paul's doctrine, the ministers of Christ's church have their authority and armour likewise limited to them, which armour is only spiritual and not carnal, whereby they fight not against flesh and blood, but against the power of darkness, error, and sin; against the spiritual seduction and craftiness in heavenly things, against the works and proceedings of Satan the prince of this world, in comforting weak consciences against the terrors of the devil and desperation, and finally against every thought lifted up against Christ, to subdue every lofty thing to the subjection and power of Christ Jesus the Son of God. Eph. vi. 13—18.

Briefly to reduce the whole doctrine of St. Paul, it consists chiefly in these five points:

First, in setting forth the grace, great love and good will, and free promises of God the Father in Christ Jesus his Son to mankind, who so loved the world that he hath given his own Son for the redemption thereof, John iii. 16. Who gave his Son to die for us being his enemies, Rom. v. 8. Who hath quickened us being dead in sin, Ephes. ii. 1. Who so mercifully hath reconciled the world to himself by his Son, and also by his ambassadors desireth us to be reconciled unto him, 2 Cor. v. 20. Who hath given his own Son to be sin for us, 2 Cor. v. 21. To be accursed for us, Gal. iii. 13. Who by firm promise hath assured us of our inheritance, Rom. iv. 16. Who not by the works of righteousness that we have done, but of his own mercy hath saved us by the washing of regeneration, Tit. iii. 4.

The second point consists in preaching and expressing the glorious and triumphant majesty of Christ Jesus the Son of God, and the excellency of his glory; who being once dead in the infirmity of the flesh, rose again with power, and ascending up with majesty, hath led captivity captive, Eph. iv. 8., who sitteth and reigneth in glory on the right hand of God in heavenly things above all principalities and powers, and dominions, and above every name that is named, not only in this world, but also in the world to come, Ephes. i. 21. At whose name every knee is to bow both in heaven and in earth, and under the earth, and every tongue to confess our Lord Christ Jesus to the glory of God the Father, Phil. ii. 10. In whom and by whom all things are made both in heaven and in earth, things visible and invisible, whether they be thrones or dominions, or principalities, or powers, all are by him and for him created, and he is before all, and all things consist in him who is the head of his body the church, the beginning and first-born from the dead, in whom dwelleth all fullness, Col. i. 16. To whom the Father hath given all judgment, and judgeth no man himself any more, John v. 22. To whom the Father hath given all things to his hands, John xiii. 3. To whom the Father hath given power over all flesh, John xvii. 2. To whom all power is given in heaven and earth, Matt. xxviii. 18. In whom all the promises of God are yea and amen, 2 Cor. i. 20.

Thirdly, he declareth the virtue of his cross and passion, and what exceeding benefits proceed to us by the same. By whose blood we have redemption and remission of our sins, Ephes. i. 7. By whose stripes we are healed, Isa. liii. 5. By whose cross all things are made peace, both in heaven and in earth, Col. i. 20. By whose death we are reconciled, Rom. v. 10. Who hath destroyed death and brought life to light, 2 Tim. i. 10. Who by death hath destroyed him which had the power of death, that is, the devil, and hath delivered them which lived under fear of death all their life in bondage, Heb. ii. 14. By whose obedience we are made righteous, by whose righteousness we are justified to life, Rom. v. 18. By whose curse we are blessed, and delivered from the curse of the law, Gal. iii. 13. By whose blood we that once were far off, are made near unto God, Ephes. ii. 13. Who in one body hath reconciled both Jews and Gentiles unto God, Ephes. ii. 16. Who by his flesh hath taken away the division and separation between God and us, abolishing the law which was set against us in precepts and decrees, Ephes. ii. 15. Who is our peace, our advocate, and propitiation for the sins of the whole world, 1 John ii. 2. Who was made accursed, and sin for us, that we might be the righteousness of God in him, 2 Cor. v. 21. Who is made of God for us, our wisdom, and righteousness, and sanctification, and redemption, 1 Cor. i. 30. By whom we have boldness and entrance with all confidence through faith in him, Ephes. iii. 12. Who forgiveth all our sins, and hath torn in pieces the obligation or hand-writing, which was against us in the law of the commandments, and hath crucified it upon the cross, and utterly hath despatched and abolished the same, and hath spoiled principalities and powers, as in an open show of conquest, triumphing over them openly in himself, Col. ii. 14. Who justifieth the wicked by faith, Rom. iv. 1. In whom we are made full and complete, Col. ii. 10., &c.

The fourth branch is, to teach us and inform us, to whom these benefits of Christ's passion and victory appertain, and by what means they are applied to us; which means is only one, that is by faith in Christ Jesus, and no other thing. Which faith it pleases Almighty God to accept for righteousness. And this righteousness it is, which only stands before God, and none other, as we are plainly taught by the scriptures, and especially by the doctrine of St. Paul. Which righteousness thus rising from faith in Christ, St. Paul calls the righteousness of God, where he speaks of himself, utterly refusing the other righteousness which is of the law, that he might be found in him, not having his own righteousness which is of the law, but the righteousness of Christ, which is of faith, Phil. iii. 9. Again, the apostle writing of the Jews, who sought for righteousness and found it not; and also of the Gentiles, who sought not for it, and yet found it, shews the reason why: Because, says he, the one sought it by the works of the law, and not knowing the righteousness of God, and seeking to set up their own righteousness, did not submit themselves to the righteousness which is of God. The other, which were the Gentiles, and sought not for it, obtained righteousness, that righteousness which is of faith, &c., Rom. ix. 30. Also in another place of the same epistle, St. Paul writing of this righteousness which cometh of faith, calls it the righteousness of God, in these words: "whom God hath set forth for a propitiation by faith in his blood, to declare his righteousness for the remission of sins that are past, through the forbearance of God," Rom. iii. 25. By which righteousness it is evident that St. Paul means the righteousness of faith, which Almighty God now reveals and makes manifest by the preaching of the gospel. Wilt thou see yet more plainly this righteousness of God, how it is taken in St. Paul, for the righteousness of faith, and therefore is called the righteousness of God, because it is imputed only of God to faith, and not deserved of man? In the same epistle to the Romans and in the third chapter, his words are manifest: "the righteousness of God," says he, "is by faith of Jesus Christ, unto all, and upon all them that believe," &c., Rom. iii. 22.

Wherefore whosoever studies to be accepted with God, and to be found righteous in his sight, let him learn diligently by the doctrine of St. Paul to make a difference as far as from heaven to earth, between the righteousness of works, and the righteousness of faith: and bring no other means for his justification, or for the remission of his sins, but only faith apprehending the body or person of Christ Jesus crucified. For as there is no way into the house but by the door, so is there no coming to God but by Christ alone, which is by faith. And as the mortal body, without bodily sustenance of bread and drink, cannot but perish, so the spiritual soul of man hath no other refreshing but only by faith in the body and blood of Christ, whereby to be saved. With this faith the idolatrous Gentiles apprehended Jesus Christ, and received thereby righteousness. Cornelius, (the first baptized Roman), so soon as he heard Peter preach Christ, received straightway the Holy Ghost, Acts x. 44. Peter himself confessed, and for his confession had the keys of heaven, Matt. xvi. 19. Zaccheus received the person of Christ into his house, and withal received salvation both to him and his whole household, Luke xix. 9. What a sinner was Mary, who had in her no less than seven devils, and yet because she set her heart and affection upon that person, many sins were forgiven her, Luke vii. 47. The right hand thief, how far was he from all works of the law, and yet by faith he entered justified into Paradise the same day with Christ? Luke xxiii. 43. In like manner, although the poor publican came to the church with less holiness after the law, yet he went home to his house more justified than the pharisee with all his works, and all by reason of faith, Luke xviii. 14. The parable of the prodigal son which was lost, yet revived again; also of the lost piece of silver; and of the lost sheep which went astray and was found again; what do these declare, but that that which is lost by the law is to be recovered by faith and grace? Luke xv. 11. And how often do we read in the gospels: Thy faith hath saved thee, &c. Jesus seeing their faith, &c. He that believeth in me, I will raise him up at the last day, &c. Believe also in me, &c. He that believeth in me hath everlasting life, &c. Without me ye can do nothing, &c. He that is in me, &c. He that loveth me, &c. He that heareth me, &c. He that abideth in me, &c. He that receiveth me, &c. Unless ye eat my flesh, and drink my blood, &c. That they may receive forgiveness of sins by faith that is in me, &c. To him give all the prophets witness, that through his name, whosoever believeth in him shall receive remission of sins, &c. He that believeth and is baptized, &c. He that believeth on me, the works that I do shall he do also, and greater than these, &c. Luke xviii. 42. Matt. ix. 2. John vi. 40. John xiv. 1. John iii. 36. John lxv. 5. John xv. 4. John i. 12. John v. 53. Acts xxvi. 18. Acts x. 43. Mark xvi. 16. John xiv. 12.

And likewise in the writings of St. Paul, how often do we hear the name of Christ almost in every third or fourth line, where he still repeateth: In Christ Jesus,—by Christ Jesus,—through Jesus Christ our Lord, &c. Who believe in him, &c. All who believe in him, &c. Believing on him, in him, in his name, in the name of our Lord Jesus Christ, &c. Believe, saith St. Paul to the jailor, on the Lord Jesus Christ, and thou shalt be saved and thy house, &c., Acts xvi. 31.

Thus then thou seest, as the passion of Christ is the only efficient or personal cause immediate of our salvation; so is faith the only instrumental or mean cause that makes the merits of Christ available. For as the passion of Christ serves to none but such as do believe; so neither does faith (as it is only a bare quality or action in man's mind) itself justify, unless it be directed to the body of Christ crucified as to his object, of whom it receives all his virtue. And therefore, these two must always jointly concur together, faith, and Christ Jesus crucified. As for example, when the children of Israel were bid of Moses to look up to the brazen serpent; neither could the serpent have helped them, except they had looked up, nor yet their looking up have profited them, unless they had directed their eyes upon the serpent, as the only object for them to behold. So our faith directed to the body of Jesus our Saviour, is the only means whereby Christ's merits are applied to us, and we are justified before God, according to the doctrine of St. Paul, who, in express words defining to us what this faith is, and how it justifies, saith, "if thou shalt confess with thy mouth the Lord Jesus, and shalt believe in thy heart that God hath raised him from the dead, thou shalt be saved," &c. Rom. x. 9. Besides this, whatever action or quality there is in man, either hope, charity, or

any other kind of faith and believing, be it never so true, except it apprehend this object which is the body of Christ the Son of God, it serves not to justification. And that is the cause why we add this particle (only) to faith, and say that *only* faith in Christ justifies us, to exclude all other actions, qualities, gifts, or works of man, from the cause of justifying; for so much as there is no other knowledge nor gift given of God to man, be it never so excellent, that can stand before the judgment of God unto justification, or whereunto any promise of salvation is annexed; but only this faith looking up to the brazen serpent, that is, to the body of Christ Jesus crucified for us.

As for example, when the Turk says, that he believes in one living God that made heaven and earth, his belief therein is true, yet it justifies him not, because it lacks the right object, which is Christ. So when the Jew says, that he believes in one God maker of heaven and earth, and believes also the same God to be omnipotent, merciful, just, and true of promise, and that he has elected the seed of Abraham; true it is that he believes, and yet all this serves him not, because Christ the Son of God is not joined withal. And though the said Jew should be never so devout in his prayers, or charitable in alms, or precise in keeping the law, and believe never so steadfastly that he is elected to be saved; yet he is never the nearer to salvation for all this, so long as his faith is not grounded upon the head corner stone, which is the person and body of Jesus Christ the true Saviour. After like sort it may be said of the papist, when he saith, that he is baptized, and believes in the Father, the Son, and the Holy Ghost, three persons, and one God, and also confesses Jesus Christ to be the Son of God, which died for our sins, and rose again for our righteousness, &c., his belief therein is true, and indeed would save him, if he did stay his salvation in this faith, and upon Christ his Saviour only, according to the promise and grace of God, and go no further. But that he does not: for neither does he admit Christ only to be his perfect Saviour without the help of the patrons, heads, advocates, and mediators, nor yet permits his faith in Christ only to be the means of his justification, but sets up other by-means, as hope, charity, sacrifice of the mass, confession, penance, satisfaction, merits and pardons, supposing thereby to work his justification before God, contrary to the word of promise, to the gospel of grace, and to the doctrine of St. Paul.

And thus much of the true causes of our justification after the doctrine of St. Paul. Concerning which causes this distinction is to be added, that as touching the original causes of our salvation, which are various, some are external, and without us; some are internal, and within us. Of the external causes which are without us, the first and principal is the mercy and grace of God. On this followeth predestination and election. Then cometh vocation. The last and next cause to us is the death and bloodshed of Christ, whereby we are redeemed, and all these are external causes, because they are without us. Of internal causes that are in man through the gift of God, there is but one, and no more appointed in scripture, that is our faith in Christ, which is the gift of God in us. Besides this, there is no gift of God given to man, virtue, work, merit, nor any thing else, that is any part or cause of salvation, but only this gift of faith, to believe in Christ Jesus. And this is the cause why we hold that faith only justifies, meaning that amongst all the works, deeds, actions, labours and operations whatsoever, that man does or can do, there is nothing in man that works salvation, but only his faith given to him of God to believe in Christ his Son. And therefore in the epistle to the Romans, St. Paul reasoning of the glory of justifying, asks this question, how boasting of this glory is excluded; whether by the law of works? And concludes no; ascribing only the glory thereof to the law of faith, and consequently upon the same he infers, "we conclude that a man is justified by faith without the deeds of the law," Rom. iii. 28.

And how then can that be accounted any part of our justification, which St. Paul utterly debars and excludes? Of which the whole course of St. Paul's doctrine is full, where he still concludes; " It is the gift of God, not of works, lest any man should boast," &c. " Not by works of righteousness which we have done, but according to his mercy," &c. " Not according to our works, but according to his own purpose and grace which was given us," &c. " A man is not justified by works," &c. "To him that worketh not, but believeth on him that justifieth the ungodly, his faith is counted for righteousness," &c. Eph. ii. 8, 9.—Tit. iii. 5. 2 Tim. i. 9. Gal. ii. 16. Rom. iv. 5. By these plain declarations, what does he mean, but utterly to exclude all kind of man's merits, and works of the law, from the office and dignity of justifying? And, although he expresses not the word *only*; yet upon his exclusives, and negatives, this exceptive must needs be inferred. And thus much concerning faith in Christ proved to be the only mean, or instrumental, or conditional cause of our salvation, and no other besides the same alone, is taught by the doctrine of St. Paul to the ancient Romans.

The fifth branch. which I note in St. Paul's doctrine, is this : that after he has thus established us in the certainty of our salvation through faith in Christ, then he exhorts us vehemently to good works, shewing the true use and end of good works : which is, first, to shew our obedience and dutiful service unto God, who hath done so great things for us. Secondly, to relieve our neighbours with our charity and kindness, as God hath been kind to us, his enemies. Thirdly, to stir up others by our example to praise God, to embrace the same religion, and to do the like. For it is requisite, that as God has been so merciful to us, and gracious in eternal gifts, we should be merciful likewise in temporal things. And seeing it has pleased him of his Fatherly goodness to call us to so high a vocation, to give the blood of his Son for us, to forgive us all our sins, to deliver us from this present wicked world, to make us citizens of heaven, yea, his children, more than servants: little then can we do, and well may we think those benefits ill bestowed, if we forgive not our neighbours, and shew not something worthy of that holy calling wherewith he hath called us, in mortifying our worldly lusts here, and studying after heavenly things: and, finally, if we being provoked with such love and kindness, render not again some love for love, some kindness for kindness, seeking how to walk in the steps which he has prepared for us to walk in, serving him (so much as we may), in holiness and righteousness all the days of our life. And though our obedience shall always be imperfect, yet we should shew obedience, as loving children to such a loving father.

And this is the cause why St. Paul so vehemently and urgently calls upon us to do good works, not that works should justify, but that we being justified so mercifully and tenderly through the grace of God, should not abuse his grace in vain, but endeavour ourselves, to our uttermost, to render our service again to him, in such conversation of life as may most make to his glory, and the profit of our neighbour. And though the words of our Saviour seem, in some places, to attribute great rewards in heaven to our obedience and charity here in earth, that is of his own free grace and goodness so to impute small matters for great deserts, and it is not for us to claim any meed thereby, or thank at his hand, as by any worthiness of our doings; no more than the servant can, when he comes from the plough, and serving the cattle in the field, serves first his master at home, and waits upon his table : the master is not bound, (saith Christ) to thank his servant, because he did the things that were commanded him : " So likewise ye," saith he, " when ye shall have done all those things which are commanded you, say, We are unprofitable servants; we have done that which was our duty to do," Luke xvii. 10.

Again, here also is to be understood, that where such rewards are ascribed to men's deeds, it is not the worthiness of the deed itself, but the faith of the doer, which makes the work to be good in God's sight: for if an infidel should do the same work that the christian does, it were nothing but mere sin before God. In

that, therefore, the christian man's work is accepted, be it never so small (as to give a cup of cold water) the same is only for his faith sake that does it, and not for the work which is done. Whereby again we may learn how faith only justifies a man, and that three manner of ways :—

First, it justifies the person in making him accepted, and the child of God by regeneration, before he begin to do any good work.

Secondly, it justifies a man from sin, in procuring remission and forgiveness of the same.

Thirdly, it justifies the good deeds and works of man, not only in bringing forth good fruits, but also in making the same works to be good and acceptable in the sight of God, which otherwise were impure and execrable in his sight.

The office, therefore, of faith and works is different, and must not be confounded. Faith goes before, and regenerates a man, and justifies him in the sight of God, both in covering his ill deeds, and making his good deeds acceptable to God, climbing up to heaven, and there wrestling with God and his judgment for righteousness, for salvation, and for everlasting life. Works and charity follow faith, and are exercised here upon the earth, and have glory only before man, but not before God, in shewing forth obedience both to God and to man. Further than this our good works do not reach, nor have any thing to do in the judgment of God touching salvation. I speak of our good works (as St. Paul speaketh, Rom. vii.) as they are ours, and imperfect. For if our works could be perfect according to the perfection of the law, as Christ wrought them in the perfection of his flesh ; that is, if we could perfect them ; then, as it is said : " The man which doeth those things shall live by them," Rom. x. 5. But now seeing the weakness of our flesh cannot attain thereto, it follows that all glory of justifying is taken from works, and transferred only to faith.

And thus much concerning the principal contents of St. Paul's doctrine: wherein the church of the ancient Romans was first grounded and planted, and so continued, or at least did not much alter, during the primitive state of the church. Likewise, the same form of doctrine the later Romans should have maintained, and not have fallen away for any man's preaching, but should hold him accursed, yea if he were an apostle or angel from heaven, teaching any other doctrine than that which we have preached unto you, Gal. i. 8., for so were they warned before by the apostle St. Paul to do. And yet, notwithstanding all this forewarning and diligent instruction of this blessed apostle of the Gentiles, what a defection of faith is fallen among the Gentiles, especially among the Romans, whereof the said apostle also foretold them so long before, prophecying, that the day of the Lord shall not come, " except there come a falling away first, and that man of sin be revealed," &c. 2 Thess. ii. 3., meaning a departing and a falling from that faith which the Holy Ghost had then planted by his ministry among the Gentiles, as we see it now come to pass in the church of Rome. Which church is so gone from the faith that St. Paul taught, that if he were now alive, and saw these decrees and decretals of the bishop of Rome, these heaps of ceremonies and traditions, these mass-books, these festivals and legends, these processionals, hymns, and sequences, these beads and graduals, and the manner of their invocation, their canons, censures, and later councils, such swarms of superstitious monks and friars, such sects, and so many divers religions—the testament of St. Francis, the rule of St. Benedict, of St. Bridget, of St. Anthony, &c. the intricate subtleties and labyrinths of the schoolmen, the infinite cases and distinctions of the canonists, the sermons in churches, the assertions in schools, the glory of the pope, the pride of the clergy, the cruelty of persecuting prelates with their officials and promoters : he would say this were not a defection, but rather a plain destruction, and a ruin of faith ; neither that this were any true church of Christ, but a new found religion, or paganism rather, brought in under the shadow of christianity, wherein remains almost nothing else but the name only of Christ, and the outward form of his religion, the true vein and effect whereof is utterly decayed; as will soon appear to them who will examine all the parts of this new Romish religion.

For save only that they pretend the solemn form and words of the creed, and are baptized, confessing the name of the Father, the Son, and the Holy Ghost: as touching all other points, and true sincerity of the christian faith, which they outwardly profess, they are utterly degenerated from that which St. Paul, and the word of God first had taught them.

For, they confess the Father in word, but his will expressed in his word, they renounce; his grace they acknowledge not; his benefits and promises given unto us in his Son, they receive not; the vigor of his law they feel not; the terror of his judgments they fear not, and his commandments they observe by traditions and commandments of their own.

Likewise the name of Christ his Son, they confess in word, but in deed they deface and diminish his office; his glory they seek not, but under his name they seek their own glory; the power of his blood and passion they know, not, for they neither admit to be the head of his church alone, nor Saviour alone, nor to be our only patron and advocate, but place him with the Virgin Mary, and other patrons, so that almost every parish in Christendom has his peculiar patron, besides Christ.

In like manner, they confess the name of the Holy Ghost, but God himself knoweth how far they are from the comfort, knowledge, and taste of the Holy Ghost; as may well appear by their councils, by their expounding of scripture, by their superstitious ceremonies, by their outward worshippings, and idolatrous invocation to stocks and stones, and to dead creatures, by their scrupulous observation of days, times, places, numbers and gestures; and no less also by their doctrine, which defrauds the poor hearts of simple christians of their due consolation, joy and liberty in the Holy Ghost, keeping them still in a servile bondage, and a doubtful uncertainty of their salvation, contrary to the working of the Holy Spirit of God.

And thus the church of Rome, pretending only the name of Christ and of his religion, is so far altered from the truth of what it pretends, that under the name of Christ, it persecutes both Christ and his religion; working more harm to the church of Christ, than ever did the open tyrants and persecuting emperors among the heathen: not much unlike the old synagogue of the scribes and pharisees, who, under the name of God, crucified the Son of God, and under pretence of the law, fought against the gospel, and under the title of Abraham's children, persecuted the children of Abraham. And as they boasting so highly of the temple of the Lord, did, indeed, destroy the true temple of the Lord; just so, these pretended catholics in these days, after they have raised up a catholic church of their own, and have armed it with laws, and have gathered a multitude of priests, prelates, abbots, priors, monks, cardinals, and also of secular princes, to take their part; now, under the name of the catholic church, they persecute the true catholic church, and colouring their proceeding still with the name of the Lord, most cruelly put them to death, who die for the name of the Lord, condemning them for heretics, schismatics, and rebels, who deny no part of the creed which they themselves profess, and whom they cannot convince by any scripture; but who will not join with their errors and heresies, contrary to the honour of God, and truth of his word.

And lest any should think that our protest against the corrupt errors and manifold deformities of this later church of Rome proceeds more of rancour or affection, rather than grounded upon necessary causes and demonstration, my purpose is to take herein some little pains, and as I have collected, a little before, the contents of St. Paul's doctrine, wherewith the old church of Rome was first seasoned and acquainted, so now, in a like summary table, I will describe the particular branches and contents of the pope's doctrine, that all true christian readers, comparing the one with the other, may discern what great alteration there is between the church of Rome that now is, and the church of Rome that then was planted by the apostles in the primitive time. And to open to the simple reader some way whereby he may the better judge in such matters of doctrine, and not be deceived in discerning truth from error, we will first propound certain principles or general positions, as infallible rules or truths of the scripture, whereby all other doctrines and opinions of men being tried and examined, as with the touchstone, may the more easily be judged whether they be true or false, and whether they make against the scripture, or no.

The First Principle.

As sin and death came originally by the disobedience of one to all men of his generation by nature: so righteousness and life came originally by the obedience of one to all men regenerated of him by faith and baptism, Rom. v. 15.

The Second Principle.

The promise of God was freely given to our first parents without their deserving; that the seed of the woman should bruise the serpent's head, Gen. iii. 15.

The Third Principle.

Promise was given freely to Abraham before he deserved any thing, that in his seed all nations should be blessed, Gen. xii. 3.

The Fourth Principle.

We must neither add to, nor diminish from the word of God, Deut. iv. 2.

The Fifth Principle.

He that doth the works of the law shall live therein, Levit. xviii. 5. Gal. iii. 12.

The Sixth Principle.

Accursed is he which abideth not in every thing that is written in the book of the law, Deut. xxvii. 26. Gal. iii. 10.

The Seventh Principle.

God only is to be worshipped, Deut. vi. 13. Luke iv. 8.

The Eighth Principle.

All our righteousness are as filthy rags, Isaiah lxiv. 6.

The Ninth Principle.

In all my holy hill they shall not kill nor slay, saith the Lord, Isaiah xi. 9. lxv. 25.

The Tenth Principle.

God loveth mercy and obedience more than sacrifice, Hosea vi. 6. 1 Sam. xv. 22.

The Eleventh Principle.

The law worketh wrath, condemneth and openeth sin, Rom. iv. 15.; iii. 19, 20.

The Twelfth Principle.

Christ is the end of the law for righteousness to every one that believeth, Rom. x. 4.

The Thirteenth Principle.

Whosoever believeth and is baptized, shall be saved, Mark xvi. 16.

The Fourteenth Principle.

A man is justified by faith without works, freely by grace, not of ourselves, Gal. ii. 16; Ephes. ii. 9.

The Fifteenth Principle.

There is no remission of sins without shedding of blood, Heb. ix. 22.

The Sixteenth Principle.

Whatsoever is not of faith is sin, Rom. xiv. 23. Without faith it is impossible to please God, Heb. xi. 6.

The Seventeenth Principle.

One mediator between God and man, Christ Jesus, Tim. ii. 5. And he is the propitiation for our sins, 1 John ii. 2.

The Eighteenth Principle.

Whosoever seeketh to be justified by the law, is fallen from grace, Gal. v. 4.

The Nineteenth Principle.

In Christ all the promises of God are yea and amen, 2 Cor. i. 20.

The Twentieth Principle.

Let every soul be subject unto the higher powers, giving to Cesar that which is Cesar's, and to God that which is God's, Rom. xiii. 1; Mark xii. 17.

As no man can deny these principles and infallible rules of the scripture, so if they be granted, the doctrine of the pope's church must be found not to be catholic, but rather full of errors and heresies, as in the sequel remains more expressly and particularly by the grace of Christ to be proved. I now proceed to give a summary account of the errors, heresies, and absurdities, contained in the pope's doctrine, contrary to the rules of God's word, and the first institution of the church of Rome.

OF FAITH AND JUSTIFICATION.

FIRST, as to the only means and cause of our justification, whereby the merits of Christ's passion are applied to us and made ours, we saw before how St. Paul ascribes it only to faith; as appears by all his epistles, especially to the Romans. Where, excluding all kind of works, he ascribes all our salvation, justification, righteousness, reconciliation, and peace with God, only unto faith in Christ. Contrary to which doctrine, the pope and his church has set up divers and sundry other means of their own devising whereby the merits of Christ's passion (as they say) are applied to us and made ours, to the putting away of sins, and for our justification, such as hope, charity, sacrifice of the mass, auricular confession, satisfaction, merits of saints, and holy orders, the pope's pardons, &c. So that Christ's sacrifice, stripes, and suffering, by this teaching, does not heal us, though we believe never so well, unless we add also these works and merits above recited. Which if it be true, then that it is false which Isaiah the prophet doth promise, (chapter liii. 5.) "with his stripes we are healed," &c. This error and heresy of the church of Rome, though it seem at first sight to the natural reason of man to be but of small importance, yet if it be earnestly considered, it is in very deed the most pernicious heresy almost that ever crept into the church, upon which, as the foundation, all or the greater part of the errors, absurdities, and inconveniences of the pope's church are grounded. For this being once admitted, that a man is not justified by his faith in Christ alone, but that other means must be sought by our own working and merits to apply the merits of Christ's passion unto us, then there is neither any certainty left of our salvation, nor any end to setting up new means and merits of our own devising for remission of sins. Neither hath there been any heresy that either hath rebelled more presumptuously against the high majesty of God the Father, nor more perniciously injured the souls of the simple, than this doctrine.

First of all, it subverts the will and testament of God. For where almighty God of his mercy has given us his Son to die for us, and with him has given his full promise, that whosoever believeth on him, should be saved by faith, and assigns none other condition, either of the law, or of works, but only of faith, to be the means between his Son and us: these men take upon them to alter this testament that God hath set, and add other conditions, which the Lord in his word never appointed nor knew. To whom the words of Jerome may be well applied upon the epistle to the Galatians, " They make of the gospel of Christ the gospel of men, or rather the gospel of the devil," &c.

Secondly, whereas the christian reader in the gospel, reading of the great grace and sweet promises of God given to mankind in Christ his Son, might thereby take much comfort of soul, and be at rest and peace with the Lord his God: there comes the pestiferous doctrine of these heretics, wherewith they obscure this free grace of God, choke the sweet comforts of man in the Holy Ghost, oppress christian liberty, and bring us into spiritual bondage.

Thirdly, as in this their impious doctrine they shew themselves manifest enemies to God's grace: so are they no less injurious to christian men, whom they leave in a doubtful distrust of God's favour and of their salvation, contrary to the word and will of God, and right institution of the apostolic doctrine. And, whereas, they object to us that we rather leave men's conscience uncertain, forasmuch as, if life (say they) were not a due reward, it were uncertain: and now forsomuch as due debt is certain, and mercy or favour is uncertain, therefore (say they) we leaving men's consciences to the mercy of God, do leave them in a doubtful uncertainty of their salvation. To this I answer, that due debt, if it be proved by the law duly deserved, must be certain. But if the law shall prove it imperfect, or not due, then it is not certain, neither can there be any thing duly claimed. Now as touching mercy, so long as it remains secret in the prince's will, and not known to his subjects, so long it is uncertain. But when this mercy shall be openly published by proclamation, ratified by promise, conferred by will and testament, established in blood, and sealed with sacraments, then this mercy remains no more doubtful, but ought firmly to be believed of every true faithful subject. And, therefore, St. Paul, to establish our hearts in this assurance, and to answer to this doubt, in his epistle to the Romans, does teach us, saying, " Therefore it is of faith, that it might be by grace, to the end the promise might be sure to all the seed," Rom. iv. 16. Meaning, hereby, that works have nothing to do in this case of justifying, and stating the reason why: for then our salvation should stand in doubt, because in working we are never certain whether our deserts be perfect and sufficient in God's judgment or no: and, therefore, (saith St. Paul) to the intent our salvation should be out of all doubt and certain, it stands not of works in deserving, but of faith in apprehending, and of God's free grace in promising.

Fourthly, as in this their sinister doctrine they break this principle of christian religion, which saith that a man is justified by faith without works, so again it breaks another principle above rehearsed. For this rule being granted, that nothing is to be added to God's word, nor taken from it, then have these men done wickedly in adding (as they do) to God's word. For where the word of God limits to our justification no condition but faith, " Believe on the Lord Jesus Christ, and thou shalt be saved and thy house," &c. Acts xvi. 31, these add other conditions besides, and such as the word excludes, as hope, charity, the sacrifice of the mass, the work of the priest, auricular confession, satisfaction, meritorious deeds, &c. And thus much concerning the doctrine of faith and justification. Whereby it may appear to what horrible blindness and blasphemy the church of Rome is now fallen, where this kind of doctrine is not only suffered, but also publicly professed.

OF WORKS AND THE LAW.

As touching the doctrine of good works, and the law, what the teaching of St. Paul was to the Romans, we have seen before. Who, although he excludes good works from the office of justifying, yet he excludes them not from the practice and conversation of christian life, but most earnestly calls upon all faithful believers in Christ, to walk worthy their vocation, to lay down their old conversation, to give their members servants of righteousness, to offer their bodies up to God a lively sacrifice, &c. Whose teaching the reformed churches follow, as their sermons, their preachings, writings, exhortings, and lives bear record. Who, although they cannot say with Christ, " Which of you convinceth me of sin ?" yet they may say to the adversaries, whosoever of you is without fault, cast the first stone of reproach against us.

What the errors of the church of Rome are, touching this part of doctrine, remains to be stated. Their first error stands in this, that they, misunderstanding the nature of good works, do call good works, not such as properly are commanded by the law of God, but such as are agreeable to the pope's law; as building of abbeys and churches, giving to the high altar, founding of trentals, finding of chanteries, gilding of images, hearing of masses, going on pilgrimage, fighting for the holy cross, keeping of vows, entering into orders, fasting of vigils, creeping to the cross, praying to saints, &c.—all which are not only reputed for good works, but so preferred also before all other works, that to these is given pardon from the pope, double and triplefold, more than to any other good work of charity commanded in the law of Almighty God.

Another error also may be noted in the papists, touching the efficient or formal cause of good works. Although they all confess in their books, that " the grace of God truly given" is the chief and principal cause thereof, and works in us " the first justification" (as they call it) yet the good works after regeneration they refer to other subordinate causes, under God, as to free-will, or to " a habit of virtue," or " natural integrity," and nothing at all to faith, whereas faith only next under God is the root and fountain of well-doing: as in the fruits of a good tree, although the planter or the husbandman be the principal agent, and some cause also may be in the good ground; yet the immediate cause is the root that makes the tree fruitful. In like manner, the grace of God, in a soft and repentant mollified heart, plants the gift of faith: faith, as a good root, cannot lie dead or unoccupied, but springs forth, and makes both the tree fruitful, and the fruit good, which otherwise had no goodness in them, were it not for the goodness of the root from whence they spring; so St. Paul, although he had certain works in him, such as they were before his conversion, yet had he no good works before the grace of Christ had rooted faith in him: so Mary Magdalene the sinner, and Zaccheus the publican: so all the nations of the Gentiles began to bring forth fruit, and especially good fruit, when they began to be ingrafted in Christ, and to receive the root of his faith, whose fruits before that, were all damnable and unsavoury. As touching the cause therefore of good works, there is no other in man but faith, as it is the office of faith to justify us in heaven, so the nature of it is here in earth to work by love, as the root works by the sap. For as a man sees and feels by faith the love and grace of God toward him in Christ his Son, so he begins to love again both God and man, and to do for his neighbour as God hath done to him. And hereof properly springs the running fountain of all good works and deeds of charity.

Thirdly, as they err in the *cause* of good works, so do they err much more in the *end* of the law, and of good works; for where St. Paul teaches the law to be given to this use and end, to convict our transgressions, to prove us sinners, to shew and condemn our infirmity, and to drive us to Christ, they take and apply no other end to the law, but to make us perfect, to keep us from wrath, and to make us just before God! And likewise, where St. Paul proves all our good works to be imperfect, and utterly excludes them from justifying, they contrariwise teach, as though the end of good works were to merit remission of sins, to satisfy God, to deserve grace, to redeem souls from purgatory, and that by them the person of the regenerate man pleases God, and is made just before God. For so they teach most wickedly and horribly, saying, that Christ suffered for original sin, or sins going before baptism; but the actual sins, which follow after baptism, must be done away by men's merits. And so they assign to Christ the beginning of salvation, or obtaining the first grace (as they call it) but the perfection or consummation of grace they give to works and our own strength. Neither can they bear the doctrine, that we be justified freely by the mercy of God through faith only apprehending the merits of Christ. However, all papists do not agree in this error. For some make a distinction, and say, that we are justified by Christ principally; and by the dignity of our own deeds, less principally. Others hold that we are made righteous before God, not by our works that go before faith, but by our virtues that follow after. Some again do thus expound the saying of St. Paul, " We are justified by faith," that is, (say they) by faith preparing us, or setting us in a good way to be justified. Others expound it by faith conjoined together with other virtues; others thus, by faith, that is, being formed with charity, &c. Thus all these derogate from the benefit of Christ, and attribute unto works a great or the greatest part of our justification, directly against the true vein of St. Paul's doctrine, and first institution of the ancient church of Rome, and against all the principles of holy scripture.

Furthermore, as to the doctrine of the law and good works, they err in misunderstanding the nature of the law and works. For where St. Paul argues that the law is spiritual, and requires of us perfect obedience, which we being carnal, are never able to accomplish, they affirm otherwise, that the law requires only the outward obedience of man, and is contented therewith. And this obedience (they say) man is not only able to perform, but also to do more and greater things than the law requires. Whereof rise the works of supererogation. There are also (say they) certain works of the law, which pertain not to all men, but are counsels left for perfect men, as matter for them to merit by, and these they call " works of perfection, or works of supererogation," adding also unto these new devices, to serve God after their own traditions besides the word of God, as monastical vows, wilful poverty, difference of meats and garments, pilgrimage to relics and saints, worshipping of the dead, superstitious ceremonies, rosaries, &c. with such like; and these they call works of perfection, which they prefer before the others commanded in the law of God. Insomuch that in comparison of these, the other necessary duties commanded and commended by the word of God (as to bear office in the commonwealth, to live in the godly state of matrimony, to sustain the office of a servant in a house) are contemned, and accounted as profane in comparison of these.

OF SIN.

They teach not rightly of sin, nor after the institution of the apostles, and the ancient church of Rome, while they consider not the deepness and largeness of sin, supposing it still to be nothing else but the inward actions with consent of will, or the outward, such as are against will; whereas the strength of sin extends not only to these, but also comprehends the blindness and ignorance of the mind, lack of knowledge and true fear of God, the untowardness of man's mind to God-ward, the privy rebellion of the heart against the law of God, the undelighting will of man to God and his word. The sense of flesh St. Paul also calleth an enemy against God, and feels in himself, that is, in his flesh, nothing dwelling but sin.

As touching also original sin, wherein we are born, which is the destruction of original righteousness, and of God's image in us (remaining in us, and bringing forth in us wicked thoughts, affections, and motions of sin against the law of God, and never ceasing so long as man lives) this original sin the pope's doctrine doth not deny, but yet much extenuates it, and holds that this inward concupiscence, and these vicious affections, are not mortal nor damnable sins, and that this concupiscence in us is no depravation of the higher, but only of the lower parts of man, being a thing indifferent, and no less natural in us, than is the appetite to eat and drink, and that the same is left to remain in the saints after baptism, to be to them occasion of more meriting.

OF PENANCE OR REPENTANCE.

This later church of Rome has made a sacrament of penance, which they say consists of three parts, Contrition, Confession, and Satisfaction. Contrition (as they teach) may be had by strength of free-will, without the law and the Holy Ghost, through man's own action and endeavour: which contrition must be sufficient, and so it merits remission of sin. In confession they require a full rehearsal of all sins, whereby the priest knowing the crimes, may minister satisfaction accordingly: and this rehearsing of sins deserves remission. Satisfactions they call works not due, enjoined by the ghostly father: and this satisfaction (say they) takes away and changes eternal punishment into temporal pains, which pains also it mitigates. And again, these satisfactions may be taken away by the pope's indulgence, &c.

This unsavoury and heathenish doctrine of penance differs much from the true teaching of holy scripture. By the which teaching, repentance properly contains these three parts, contrition, faith, and new life. Contrition is called in scripture the sorrow of heart, rising upon the consideration of sin committed, and of the anger of God provoked, which sorrow drives a man to Christ for succour, whereupon rises faith. Faith brings afterward amendment or newness of life, which we call new obedience bringing forth fruits worthy of repentance.

DIFFERENCE BETWEEN THE LAW AND THE GOSPEL.

As there is nothing more necessary and comfortable for troubled consciences, than to be well instructed in the difference between the law and the gospel; so the church of Rome is much to blame because it confounds together those two, being in nature so divers and contrary one from another, as threatenings, with promises—things temporal, with things eternal—sorrowful things, with glad tidings—death, with life—bondage, with freedom, &c. Teaching the people that whatever the law saith, the gospel confirms; and whatever the gospel saith, the same is agreeable to the law, and so they make no difference between Moses and Christ; save only that Moses was the giver of the old law, Christ the giver of the new and a more perfect law. And thus they imagine the gospel to be nothing else but a new law given by Christ, binding to the promises thereof the condition of our doings and deservings, no otherwise than to the old law. And so they divide the whole law after this distinction into three parts, to wit, the law of nature, the law of Moses, and the law of Christ. And as for the gospel (they say) it is revealed for no other cause, but to shew to the world more perfect precepts and counsels than were in the old law; to the fulfilling whereof they attribute justification, and so leave the poor consciences of men in perpetual doubt, and induce other manifold errors; bringing the people into a false opinion of Christ, as though he were not a remedy against the law, but came as another Moses, to give a new law to the world.

Furthermore, as they make no difference between the nature of the law, and the nature of the gospel, confounding Moses and Christ together; so neither do they distinguish the time of the law, and the time of the gospel asunder. For where St. Paul brings in the law to be a schoolmaster, and limits his time unto Christ, and saith that Christ is the end of the law; that is, where the law ceases, there Christ begins, and where Christ begins there the law ends: they, on the other hand, make the law to have no end nor ceasing, but give to it immortal life and kingdom equal with Christ, so that Christ and the law together do reign over the soul and conscience of man. Which is untrue; for either Christ must give place and the law stand, or the law (the condemnation and malediction of the law I mean) must end, and Christ reign. For both these, Christ and the law, grace and malediction cannot reign and govern together. But Christ the Son of God, which once died, can die no more, but must reign for ever. Wherefore the law with its strength, sting and curse must needs cease and have an end. And this is what St. Paul, speaking of the triumph of Christ, saith, that he ascending up led captivity captive, and hath set man at liberty; not at liberty to live as flesh lusteth, neither hath freed him from the use and exercise of the law, but from the dominion and power of the law, so that "there is now no condemnation to them that are in Christ Jesus, which walk not after the flesh, &c." Rom. viii. 4. And in another place, St. Paul speaking of the same power and dominion of the law, saith that Christ "Blotting out the hand-writing of ordinances that was against us, which was contrary to us, and took it out of the way, nailing it to the cross," Col. ii. 14. So that as the kingdom of Christ first began upon the cross, even so upon the same cross, and at the same time, the kingdom of the law expired, and the malediction of the law was so crucified upon the cross, that it shall never rise again, to have any power against them that be in Christ Jesus. For like as if a woman be discharged from her first husband, being dead, and has married another man, the first husband has no more power over her, Rom. vii. 2; even so we now being espoused unto Christ our second husband, are discharged utterly from our first husband the law, and as St. Paul saith, (Rom. vi. 14.) are no more under the law, that is, under the dominion and malediction of the law, but under grace, that is, under perpetual remission of sins, committed not only before our baptism, but as well also after baptism, and during all our life long. For therein properly consists the grace of God, in not imputing sin to us, so often as the repenting sinner rising up by faith, flies unto Christ, and apprehends God's mercy and remission promised in him, according to the testimony both of the Psalm, "Blessed is the man to whom the Lord imputeth no sin," &c. and also of all the prophets, which (as St. Peter saith) "give witness that through his name, all that believe in him shall receive remission of their sins," &c. Acts x. 43. Which being so, as cannot be denied, then what need these private and extraordinary remissions to be brought into the church by ear-confession, by meritorious deeds, and by the pope's pardons? For if there be no condemnation but by the law, and if this law itself which was the first husband, be made captive, crucified, abolished, and departed, what condemnation then can there be to them that be in Christ Jesus, or by whom should it come? If there be no condemnation, but a free and general deliverance for all men, once gotten by the victory of Christ from the penalty of the law, what needs then any particular remission of sins at sundry times to be sought at the priest's hands or the pope's pardons? He that has a general pardon, needs no particular. If remedy for sin be general and perpetual, once gotten, for ever to all them that be in Christ Jesus, what needs any other remedy by auricular confession? If it be not general and perpetual, how then is it true that St. Paul saith, the law is crucified, and condemnation abolished? Or how stands redemption perpetual and general, if remission be not general? For what else is redemption, but remission of sin, or sins bought out? Or what else to kill the law, but to discharge us from condemnation for ever? He that delivers his friend for a time out of his enemy's hand does him good; but he that kills the enemy once out of the way, gives perpetual safety. So if remission of sins by Christ were for some sins, and not for all, the law then must needs live still. But now the killing and crucifying of the law imports full and absolute remission, and our safety to be perpetual. But here some will object; how is remission of sins certain and perpetual, seeing new offences being daily committed, do daily require new remission? I answer: although sins do daily grow, whereby we have need daily to desire God to "forgive our trespasses," &c. yet notwithstanding the cause of our remission stands ever one and perpetual, neither is it to be repeated any more, nor any other cause to be sought besides that alone. This cause is the body of Christ sacrificed once upon the cross for all sins that either have been or shall be committed. Besides this cause there is no other, neither confession nor man's pardons, that remits sins.

Furthermore, as the cause is one and ever perpetual, which worketh remission of sins to us; so is the promise of God ever one, once made, and stands perpetual, that offers it to the faith of the repenting sinner. And because the promise of God is always sure and cannot fail, which offers remission to all them that believe in Christ, being limited neither to time nor number, therefore we may boldly conclude, that whenever a repenting sinner believes, and by faith applies to himself the sacrifice of Christ, he has by God's own promise, remission of his sins, whether they were done before or after baptism.

And, moreover, as the promise of God offers remission to the repentant sinner, by no other means nor condition, but only one, that is, by faith in Christ; therefore excluding all other means and conditions of man's working, we say, that what repenting sinner soever believes in Christ, has already in himself (and needs not to seek to any priest) perpetual assurance of remission, not for this time or that time only, but for ever! For the promise saith not, he that believeth in Christ shall be pardoned this time, so he sin no more; neither does it say that the law is staid or the sentence reprieved, but saith plainly that the law, with her condemnation and sentence, is itself condemned and crucified, and shall never rise again to them that be in Christ Jesus, and promises without limitation, remission of sins, "To all that believe in his name," &c. Acts x. 43. And likewise in another place, the scripture speaking absolutely, saith, "Sin shall not have dominion over you," and addeth the reason why, saying, "Because ye are not under the law but under grace," Rom. vi. 14. Adding this lesson, not that sinners should sin more because they are under grace, but only that weak infirmities might be relieved, broken consciences comforted, and repenting sinners preserved from desperation, to the praise of God's glory. For as God forgives not sinners, because they should sin, so neither does infirmity of falling diminish the grace of Christ, but does rather illustrate the same, as it is written, "My strength is made perfect in weakness," 2 Cor. xii. 9. And again, "Where sin abounded, grace did much more abound," Rom. v. 20.

In remission of sins, therefore, these four things must concur together: first, the cause that works (which is the sacrifice of Christ's body); secondly, the promise that offers; thirdly, faith that apprehends and applies; fourthly, the repenting sinner that receives. And although sins do daily grow, which daily provoke us to crave remission; yet, as touching the cause that works remission of our daily sins, and the means which apply the said cause unto us, they remain always one and perpetual; besides which no other cause nor means is to be sought of man. So that to them that are repenting sinners, and in Christ Jesus, there is no law to condemn them, though they have deserved condemnation; but they are under a perpetual kingdom, and a heaven full of grace, and remission to cover their sins, and not to impute their iniquities, through the promise of God in Christ Jesus our Lord.

And therefore is the doctrine of them wicked and impious, first, who seek any other cause of remission, than only the blood of our Saviour; secondly, who assign any other means to apply the blood-shedding of Christ unto us, besides only faith; thirdly and especially, who so limit and restrain the eternal privilege of Christ's passion, as though it served only for sins done without and before faith, and that the rest committed after baptism, must be done away by confession, pardons, and satisfactory deeds. And all this rises because the true nature of the law and the gospel is not known, nor the difference rightly considered between the times of the one and of the other. Neither, again, do they make any distinction between the malediction of the law, and the use of the law. And therefore whensoever they hear us speak of the law (meaning the malediction of the law), to be abolished, thereupon they maliciously slander us, as though we spake against the good exercises of the law, and gave liberty to carnal men to live as they like. Whereof more shall be said (by the Lord's grace) as place and time shall hereafter require.

OF FREE-WILL.

Concerning free-will, as it may peradventure in some case be admitted, that men without grace may do some outward functions of the law, and keep some outward observances or traditions: so as to things spiritual and appertaining to salvation, the strength of man not regenerate by grace, is so infirm and impotent, that he can perform nothing, neither in doing well nor willing well. Who, after he be regenerated by grace, may work and do well, but yet there still remains a great imperfection of flesh, and a perpetual conflict between the flesh and the spirit. And thus was the original church of the ancient Romans first instructed. From which we may see how far this later church of Rome has degenerated, which holds and affirms, that men without grace may perform the obedience of the law, and prepare themselves to grace by working, so that those works may be meritorious, and of congruity obtain grace. Which grace once obtained, then men may, (say they) perfectly perform the full obedience of the law, and accomplish those spiritual actions and works which God requires, and so those works of condignity, deserve everlasting life. As

for the infirmity which still remains in our nature, that they do not regard nor once speak of.

OF INVOCATION AND ADORATION.

Besides these uncatholic and almost unchristian absurdities and departures from the apostolical faith, let us consider the manner of their invocation, not to God alone, as they should; but to dead men, saying that saints are to be called upon as mediators of intercession; and Christ as the mediator of salvation. And they affirm moreover, that Christ was a mediator only in the time of his passion. Which is repugnant to the words of St. Paul, writing to the old Romans, (chap. viii. 34,) where, speaking of the intercession of Christ, he says, "Who is on the right hand of God, who also maketh intercession for us," &c. And if Christ be a mediator of salvation, why need we then any other intercession of saints for our petitions? For salvation being once had, what can we require more? Or what more does he want to be obtained of the saints, who is sure to be saved only by Christ? And then in their devotions, why do they teach us thus to pray to the blessed Virgin: "Save all them that glorify thee," &c. if salvation belong only to Christ? unless they purposely study to seem contrary to themselves.

Hereto also pertains the worshipping of relics, and the false adoration of sacraments, that is, the outward signs of the things signified. Add to this also, the profanation of the Lord's Supper, contrary to the use for which it was ordained, in reserving it after the communion, in setting it to sale for money, and falsely persuading both themselves and others, that the priest merits both to himself that speaketh, and to him that heareth, only by the mere doing of the work, though the party that useth the same hath no devotion in him.

OF SACRAMENTS, BAPTISM, AND THE LORD'S SUPPER.

As touching the sacraments, their doctrine likewise is corrupt and erroneous.

First, they err falsely in the number; for where the institution of Christ ordains but two, they have added five other sacraments.

Secondly, they err in the use; for where the word has ordained those sacraments to excite our faith, and to give us admonitions of spiritual things, they contrariwise teach that the sacraments do not only stir up faith, but also that they avail and are effectual without faith, as is to be found in the writings of Thomas Aquinas, Scotus, and others.

Thirdly, in the operation and effect of the sacraments they fail, where, contrary to the mind of the scriptures they say, that they give grace, and not only do signify, but also contain and exhibit that which they signify, to wit, grace and salvation.

Fourthly, they err also in application, applying their sacraments both to the quick and the dead, to them also that be absent, to remission of sins, and releasing of pain, &c.

In the sacrament of baptism they are to be reproved, not only for adding to the simple words of Christ's institution divers other new found rites and fancies of men, but also where the use of the old church of Rome was only to baptize men, they baptize also bells, and apply the words of baptism to water, fire, candles, stocks and stones, &c.

But especially in the Supper of the Lord their doctrine most filthily swerves from the right mind of the scriptures, from all order, reason and fashion, and is most worthy to be exploded out of all christian churches. Touching the which sacrament, the first error is their idolatrous abuse by worshipping, adoring, censing, knocking, and kneeling unto it, in reserving also and carrying the same about in pomp and procession in towns and fields. Secondly, also in the substance thereof, their teaching is monstrous: they say there is no substance of bread and wine remaining, but only the real body and blood of Christ, putting no difference between *calling* and *making*: because Christ *called* bread his body, therefore, say they, he *made* it his body, and so of a wholesome sacrament, they make a perilous idol: and that which the old church of Rome did ever take to be a mystery, they turn into a blind mist of mere accidents to blear the people's eyes, making them believe they see that they see not; and not to see that which they see, and to worship a thing made, for their Maker, a creature for their Creator; and that which was threshed out of a wheaten sheaf, they set up in the church, and worship for a saviour; and when they have worshipped him, then they offer him to his father; and when they have offered him, then they eat him up, or else close him fast in a pit, where, if he corrupt and putrify before he be eaten, then they burn him to powder and ashes. And notwithstanding they know well by scriptures, that the body of Christ can never corrupt and putrify; yet for all this corruption will they needs make it the body of Christ, and burn all them which believe not that which is against true christian belief, Acts ii. 27.

OF MATRIMONY.

The order and rule which St. Paul set for marriage is manifest in his epistle to the Corinthians, where, as he prefers single life in such as have the gift of continence, before the married estate; so, again, in such as have not the gift, he prefers the married life before the other; willing every such one to have his wife, because of fornication. 1 Cor. vii. 2. Furthermore, how the apostle allows a bishop to be the husband of one wife, (so he exceeded not after the manner of the Jews, which were permitted to have many), and how vehemently he reproves them that restrain marriage, his Epistles to Timothy do record, 1 Tim. iii. 2, and iv. 3. Moreover, what degrees are permitted by the law of God to marry, is to be seen in Lev. xviii. Also how children ought not to marry without the consent of their parents, is apparent by manifest examples of the scriptures.

Contrary to these ordinances of the scripture, the new catholics of the pope's church repute and call marriage a state of imperfection, and prefer single life, be it never so impure, pretending that where the one replenishes the earth, the other fills heaven. Furthermore, as good as the third part of Christendom, (if it be no more), both men and women, they keep through compulsory vows from marriage, having no respect whether they have the gift or no. Such ministers and priests as are found to have wives, they not only remove out of place, but also pronounce sentence of death upon them, and account their children illegitimate. Again, as good as the third part of the year they exempt and suspend from liberty of marriage; they extend the degrees of forbidden marriage further than ever did the law of God, even to the fifth or sixth degree; which degree, notwithstanding they release again when they choose for money. Over and besides all this, they have added a new found prohibition of spiritual kindred, that is, that such as have been gossips, or godfathers and godmothers together in christening another man's child, must not marry together; and, finally, in this doctrine of matrimony, they gain and rake to themselves much money from the people, they augment horrible crimes, they nourish adultery, they fill the world with offences, and give great occasion of murdering infants.

OF MAGISTRATES AND CIVIL GOVERNMENT.

We have seen before what rules and lessons St. Paul gave to the old Romans concerning magistrates, to whose authority he would have all human creatures to be subject, and how they are the ministers of God, having the sword given unto them, wherewith they ought to repress false doctrine and idolatry, and maintain that which is true and right, Rom. xiii. 1. Now let us survey a little the pope's proceedings, and mark how far he transgresses in this, as he does in almost all other points, from true christianity.

1. The pope, with all his clergy, exempt themselves from all civil obedience.

2. They arrogate to themselves authority to ordain and constitute, without leave or knowledge of the magistrate.

3. Yea, they take upon them to depose and set up rulers and magistrates whom they choose.

OF PURGATORY.

The paradoxes, or, rather the fancies of the later church of Rome, concerning purgatory, are monstrous, neither old nor apostolical.

1. They say there is a purgatory, where souls burn in fire after this life.

2. The pain of purgatory differs nothing from the pains of hell, but only that it has an end; the pains of hell have none.

3. The painful suffering of this fire fretteth and purgeth away the sins before committed in the body.

4. The time of these pains endures in some longer, in some less, according as their sins deserve.

5. After which time of their pains being expired, then the mercy of God translates them to heavenly bliss, which the body of Christ has bought for them.

6. The pains of purgatory are so great, that if all the beggars in the world were seen on the one side, and but one soul in purgatory on the other side, the whole world would pity more that one, than all the others.

7. The whole time of punishment in this purgatory must continue so long, till the fire have clean fretted and purged away the rusty spots of every sinful soul there burning, unless there come some release.

8. The helps and releases that may shorten the time of their purgation are the pope's pardons and indulgences, sacrifice of the altar, dirges, and trentals, prayer, fasting, meritorious deeds out of the treasure-house of the church, alms and charitable deeds of the living, in satisfying God's justice for them, &c.

9. Lack of belief of purgatory brings to hell.

Many other false errors and great deformities, heresies, absurdities, vanities, and follies, besides their blasphemous railings, and contumelies, may be noted in the later church of Rome, wherein they have made manifest departure from the old faith of Rome, as in depriving the church of one kind of the sacrament, in taking from the people the knowledge and reading of God's word, in praying and speaking to the people, and administering sacraments in a tongue unknown, in mistaking the authority of the keys, in their unwritten tenets, in making the authority of the scripture insufficient, in untrue judgment of the church, and the wrong notes of the same, in the supremacy of the see of Rome, in their wrong opinions of antichrist.

But because these, with all other parts of doctrine, are more copiously, and at large, comprehended in other books, both in Latin and English, set forth in these our days; I shall not travel further herein, especially seeing the contrariety between the pope's church and the church of Christ, between the doctrine of the one, and the doctrine of the other, is so evident, that he is blind that sees it not, and has no hands almost that feels it not.

For, whereas the doctrine of Christ is altogether spiritual, consisting wholly in spirit and truth, and requires no outward thing to make a true christian man but only baptism, (which is the outward profession of faith), and receiving the Lord's Supper. Let us now examine the whole religion of this later church of Rome, and we shall find it, from top to toe, to consist in nothing else but altogether in outward and ceremonial exercises; as outward confession, absolution at the priest's hand, outward sacrifice of the mass, buying of pardons, purchasing of obits, worshipping of images and relics, pilgrimage to this place or that, building of churches, founding of monasteries, outward works of the law, outward gestures, garments, colours, choice of meats, difference of times and places, peculiar rites and observances, set prayers, and number of prayers prescribed, fasting of vigils, keeping of holidays, coming to church, hearing of service, extern succession of bishops, and of Peter's see, extern form and notes of the church, &c. So that by this religion to make a true christian and a good catholic, there is no working of the Holy Ghost required. As for example, to make this matter more plain let us here define a christian man after the pope's making, whereby we may see the better what is to be judged of the scope of his doctrine.

After the pope's catholic religion, a true christian man is thus defined ; first, to be baptized in the Latin tongue (where the godfathers profess they cannot tell what), then confirmed by the bishop ; the mother of the child to be purified, after he be grown in years, then to come to the church, to keep his fasting days, to fast in Lent, to come under the priest's blessing, that is, to be confessed of the priest, to do his penance, at Easter to take his rites, to hear mass and Divine service, to set up candles before images, to creep to the cross, to take holy bread and holy water, to go on procession, to carry his palms and candle, and to take ashes, to fast in the ember days, rogation days, and vigils, to keep the holidays, to pay his tithes and offering days, to go on pilgrimage, to buy pardons, to worship his Maker over the priest's head, to receive the pope for his supreme head, and to obey his laws, to have his beads, and to give to the high altar, to take orders if he will be a priest, to say his matins, to sing his mass, to lift up fair, to keep his vow, and not to marry, when he is sick to be absolved and anointed, and take the rites of the holy church, to be buried in the church-yard, to be rung for, to be sung for, to be buried in a friar's cowl, to find a soul-priest, &c.

All which points being observed, who can deny but this is a devout man, and a perfect christian catholic, and sure to be saved, as a true, faithful child of the holy mother church ?

Now look upon this definition, and tell me, good reader, what faith or spirit, or what working of the Holy Ghost is required in all this doctrine ? The grace of our Lord Jesus give the true light of his gospel to shine in our hearts. Amen.

ACTS AND MONUMENTS,

BOOK I.

CONTAINING

THREE HUNDRED YEARS NEXT AFTER CHRIST, WITH THE TEN PERSECUTIONS OF THE
PRIMITIVE CHURCH.

HAVING thus prepared the way, let us now (by the grace of Christ our Lord) enter into the matter : that as we have set forth the state as well of the primitive as of the later times of this church of Rome ; so now we may discourse of the Acts of every age by itself.

First, To declare of the suffering time of the church, which contains about three hundred years after Christ.

Secondly, The flourishing and growing time of the same, containing other three hundred years.

Thirdly, The declining time of the church, and of true religion, other three hundred years.

Fourthly, Of the time of antichrist, reigning and raging in the church.

Lastly, Of the reforming time of Christ's church, in these later three hundred years.

In treating of all which things, our chief purpose shall be, not so much to intermeddle with outward affairs of princes, or civil matters, as specially minding to prosecute such things as appertain to the state of the church ; as first, to treat of the establishing of christian faith, then of the persecutions of tyrants, the constancy and patience of God's saints, the conversion of christian realms to the faith of Christ, namely, of this realm of England and Scotland : to declare the maintenance of true doctrine, the false practice of prelates, the creeping in of superstition and hypocrisy, the manifold assaults, wars, and tumults of the princes of this world against the people of God. Wherein may appear the wonderful operation of Christ's mighty hand, ever working in his church, and never ceasing to defend the same against his enemies, according to the verity of his own word, promising to be with his church while the world shall stand.

In the treatment of all which things, two special points I chiefly commend to the reader, as most requisite and necessary for every christian man to observe and to note for his own experience and profit ; as first the disposition and nature of this world ; secondly, the nature and condition of the kingdom of Christ ; the vanity of the one, and establishment of the other ; the unprosperous and unquiet state of the one, ruled by man's violence and wisdom, and the happy success of the other, ever ruled by God's blessing and providence ; the wrath and revenging hand of God in the one, and his mercy upon the other. The world I call all such as be without or against Christ, either by ignorance, not knowing him, or by heathenish life, not following him, or by violence resisting him. On the other side, the kingdom of Christ in this world, I take to be all them which belong to the faith of Christ, and here take his part in this world against the world ; the number of whom, although it be much smaller than the other, and is always hated and molested of the world, yet it is the number which the Lord peculiarly doth bless and prosper, and ever will. And this number of Christ's subjects it is which we call the visible church here on earth. Which visible church, having in itself a difference of two sorts of people, so is it to be divided into two parts, of which the one stands of such as are of outward profession only, the other which by election inwardly, are joined to Christ : the first in words and lips seem to honour Christ, and are in the visible church only, but not in the church invisible, and partake the outward sacraments of Christ, but not the inward blessing of Christ. The other are both in the visible, and also in the invisible church of Christ, who, not only in words, and outward profession, but also in heart do truly serve and honour Christ, partaking not only of the sacraments, but also of the heavenly blessings and grace of Christ.

And many times it happens that between these two parts of this visible church there grows great variance and mortal persecution, insomuch that sometime the true church of Christ has no greater enemies than of her own profession, as happened not only in the time of Christ and his apostles, but also from time to time almost continually, and especially in these later days of the church, under the persecution of antichrist and his retinue.

At the first preaching of Christ, who should rather have known and received him, than the pharisees and scribes ? And yet, who persecuted and rejected him more than they ? What followed ? They in refusing Christ to be their king, and choosing rather to be subject to Cæsar, were by their own Cæsar destroyed. Whereby is to be learned, what a dangerous thing it is to refuse the gospel of God.

The like example of God's wrathful punishment is to be noted no less in the Romans also. For when Tiberius Cæsar, having heard by letters from Pontius Pilate, of the doings of Christ, of his miracles, resurrection and ascension into heaven, and how he was received by many as God, was himself moved with belief of the same, and proposed to the senate to have Christ adored as God: they refused him, because that contrary to the law of the Romans, he was consecrated (said they) God, before the senate of Rome had so decreed, (Tertul. Apol. cap. 5). Thus the vain senate, contented with the emperor to reign over them, and not contented with the meek King of Glory, the Son of God to be their king; were, like the Jews, scourged for their refusing, by the same power which they themselves did prefer. For as they preferred the emperor, and rejected Christ, so by the just permission of God, their own emperors were stirred up against them, so that the senators themselves were nearly all devoured, and the whole city most horribly afflicted for almost three hundred years. For the same Tiberius, who for a great part of his reign was a moderate prince, was afterwards a sharp and heavy tyrant, who neither favoured his own mother, nor spared his own nephews, nor the princes of the city, of whom, to the number of twenty, he left not more than two or three alive. Suetonius reports him to be so stern and tyrannical, that in his reign, many were unjustly accused, and condemned with their wives and children. In one day he records twenty persons drawn to execution. By him, also, through the just punishment of God, Pilate, under whom Christ was crucified, was accused at Rome, deposed, then banished, and at length did slay himself. Neither did Herod and Caiaphas long escape: and Agrippa also was cast into prison. In the reign of Tiberius, the Lord Jesus, the Son of God, in the four-and-thirtieth year of his age, through the malice of the Jews, suffered his blessed passion, for the conquering of sin, death, and Satan the prince of this world, and rose again the third day. After whose blessed passion and resurrection, this Tiberius lived six years, during which time no persecution was yet stirring against the Christians.

In the next year after the passion of our Saviour, or somewhat more, St. Paul was converted to the faith. Tiberius, having reigned three-and-twenty years, was succeeded by Caius Cæsar Caligula, (A. D. 37), Claudius Nero, (A. D. 41), and Domitius Nero, (A. D. 54); which three were likewise scourges to the senate and people of Rome. Caligula commanded himself to be worshipped as God, and temples to be erected in his name, and used to sit in the temple among the gods, requiring his images to be set up in all temples, and also in the temple at Jerusalem. His cruel displeasure was such towards the Romans, that he wished that all the people of Rome had but one neck, that he might destroy such a multitude. By Caligula, Herod, the murderer of John Baptist, and condemner of Christ, was condemned to perpetual banishment, where he died miserably. Caiaphas also, who wickedly sat in judgment upon Christ, was removed from the high priests' room, and Jonathan set in his place. The raging fierceness of this Caligula against the Romans would not so soon have ceased, had he not been cut off by the hands of a tribune and other officers, who slew him in the fourth year of his reign, (A. D. 41).

But that which Caligula had only conceived, the other two which came after, brought to pass; Claudius Nero reigned thirteen years with great cruelty, and then died by poison; but especially Domitius Nero, who succeeding Claudius, reigned fourteen years, with such fury and tyranny, that he slew the most part of the senators, and destroyed the whole order of knighthood in Rome. So prodigious a monster was he, more like a beast, yea a devil than a man, that he seemed to be born to the destruction of men. Such was his wretched cruelty, that he caused his mother, his brother-in-law, his sister, his wife, all his instructors, Seneca and Lucan, with many more of his own kindred and consanguinity to be put to death. Moreover, he commanded Rome to be set on fire in twelve places, and it continued six days and seven nights in burning, (A. D. 64), while he to see the example how Troy burned, sung the verses of Homer. And to avoid the infamy thereof, he laid the fault upon the christians, and caused them to be persecuted. And so this miserable emperor continued to reign fourteen years, till the senate proclaiming him a public enemy to mankind, condemned him to be drawn through the city and to be whipped to death. For fear whereof, he fled in the night to the country, where he was forced to slay himself. In the latter end of this Domitius Nero, Peter and Paul were put to death for the testimony and faith of Christ, (A. D. 67).

Thus we see, how the just scourge and indignation of God ever follows, where Christ Jesus is contemned, and not received; as may appear, both by the Romans who were thus consumed and plagued by their own emperors, by civil wars and other casualties. And also by the destruction of the Jews, who (A. D. 73,) were destroyed by Titus and Vespasian, to the number of eleven hundred thousand, besides them which Vespasian slew in subduing Galilee, and them also which were sold to vile slavery, to the number of seventeen thousand. Two thousand were brought with Titus in his triumph; of whom he gave part to be devoured of the wild beasts, and a part were most cruelly slain. All nations and realms may thus take example, what it is to reject the visitation of God's truth, and much more to persecute them which be sent of God for their salvation.

And as this vengeance of God hath thus been shewed upon both the Jews and the Romans, for their contempt of Christ, so neither the emperors themselves, for persecuting Christ in his members, escaped without their just reward. For among those emperors who put so many christian martyrs to death, few of them escaped either being slain themselves, or by some miserable end or other worthily punished. The slaughter of the three Neroes is declared before. After Nero, Domitius Galba within seven months was slain by Otho. And so did Otho afterward slay himself, being overcome by Vitellius. And was not Vitellius shortly after drawn through the city of Rome, and after he was tormented thrown into the Tiber? Titus, a good emperor, is thought to be poisoned by Domitian his brother. Domitian, after he had been a persecutor of the christians, was slain in his chamber, with the consent of his wife. Commodus was murdered. The like end was of Pertinax and Julian. After Severus died here in England, (and lieth at York), did not his son Caracal slay his brother Geta, and he slain after by Martial? Macrinus with his son Diadumenus were both slain by their own soldiers. Heliogabalus was slain by his own people, and drawn through the city and cast into the Tiber. Alexander Severus, that worthy and learned emperor, although in life and virtues he was unlike other emperors, yet experienced the like end, being slain with his godly mother Mammea, by Maximin. Maximin also after three years was himself slain by his soldiers. What should I speak of Maximus and Balbinus in like sort, both slain in Rome? Of Gordian, slain by Philip: of Philip, the first christened emperor, slain; of wicked Decius drowned, and his son slain the same time in battle; of Gallus, and Volusianus his son, emperors after Decius, both slain by Æmilianus, who within three months after, was himself slain. Valerianus was taken prisoner of the Persians, and there made a riding fool of by Sapores their king, who used him for a stool to leap upon his horse, while his son Galienus sleeping at Rome, either would not, or could not once proffer to avenge his father's ignominy. At length Galienus was killed by Aureolus. It were too long here to speak of Aurelian, another persecutor, slain of his secretary; of Tacitus and Florinus his brother, of whom the first was slain at Pontus; the other was murdered at Tarsis; Probus, although a good emperor, was yet destroyed by his soldiers. After whom Carus was slain by lightning. Next to Carus followed the impious and wicked persecutor Dioclesian, with his fellows, Maximin, Valerius, Maximinus, Maxentius, and Licinius, under whom all at one time the greatest and most grievous persecution was moved against the christians ten years together. Dioclesian and Maximian deposed themselves from the empire. Galerius the chief minister of the persecution, after his terrible persecutions, fell into a wonderful sickness, and so did swarm with worms, that being curable neither by surgery nor physic, he confessed that it happened for his cruelty towards the christians, and so called in his proclamations against them. Maximinus being tormented with pain in his bowels there died. Maxentius was drowned in the Tiber. Licinius, being overcome by Constantine the Great, was deposed, and afterward slain by his soldiers. But on the other side, after the time of Constantine, when the faith of Christ was received into the imperial seat, we read of no emperor after the like sort destroyed or molested, except it were Julian, or Basil, or Valens.

And thus have we briefly collected out of the chronicles the miserable state of the emperors of Rome, until the time of Christian Constantine, with the examples, no less terrible than manifest, of God's severe justice upon them, for their contemptuous refusing and persecuting the faith and name of Christ their Lord.

Moreover, if leisure would suffer me to come more near home, I could also infer the like examples of this our country of England, concerning the terrible plagues of God against the refusing or abusing the benefit of his truth. We read how God stirred up Gildas to preach to the old Britains, and to exhort them to repentance and amendment of life, and to warn them of plagues to come if they repented not. What availed it? Gildas was laughed to scorn, and taken for a false prophet, and a malicious preacher. What followed? God sent in their enemies on every side and destroyed them, and gave the land to other nations. Not many years past, God seeing idolatry, superstition, hypocrisy, and wicked living used in this realm, raised up that godly learned man John Wickliffe, to preach unto our fathers, and to exhort them to amend their lives, to forsake their papistry and idolatry, their hypocrisy and superstition, and to walk in the fear of God. His exhortations were not regarded, he with his sermons were despised, his books and himself after his death were burnt. What followed? They slew their king, and set up three wrong kings, under whom all the noble blood was slain, and half the commons, in fighting among themselves for the crown; and the cities and towns were decayed, and the land nearly brought to a wilderness, compared with what it was before. Since that time even of late years, God, again having pity of this realm of England, raised up his prophets; namely, William Tindall, Thomas Bilney, John Frith, Doctor Barnes, Jerome Garret, Anthony Person, with others, who earnestly laboured to call us to repentance, that the fierce wrath of God might be turned away from us. But how were they treated? They themselves were condemned and burnt as heretics, and their books condemned and burnt as heretical. "The time shall come, saith Christ, that whosoever killeth you, will think that he doth God service," John xvi. 1. If God has deferred his punishment, or forgiven us these our wicked deeds, as I trust he has, let us not therefore be proud and high minded, but most humbly thank Him for his tender mercies, and beware of the like ungodly proceedings hereafter. I need not speak of these our later times, which have been in King Henry's and King Edward's days, seeing the memory thereof is yet fresh and cannot be forgotten. But, of this I am sure, that God yet once again is come to this church of England, yea, and that more lovingly and beneficially than ever he did before. For in this visitation he has redressed many abuses, and cleansed his church of much ungodliness and superstition, and made it a glorious church. We now declare the persecutions raised up against the servants of Christ, within the space of three hundred years after Christ. Which persecutions in number are commonly counted to be ten, besides the persecutions by the Jews in Jerusalem against the apostles. In which, St. Stephen was put to death, with many others.

After the martyrdom of Stephen, James the apostle and brother of John suffered. Mention is made of James in the Acts, xii. 1. Where is declared, how Herod stretched forth his hand, to afflict certain of the church: among whom James was one, whom he slew with the sword. Of this James, Eusebius mentions, that when brought to the tribunal, he that brought him (and was the cause of his trouble) seeing him condemned, and that he would suffer death: as he went to the execution, being moved in heart and conscience, confessed himself a Christian.

And so they were led forth, and were beheaded together. (A. D. 36).

Dorotheus testifies, that Nicanor, one of the seven deacons, with two thousand others, who believed in Christ, suffered also the same day, when Stephen suffered.

Dorotheus witnesses also, that Simon, another of the deacons, was burned. Parmenas, also another of the deacons suffered.

Thomas preached to the Parthians, Medes, and Persians, also to the Germans, Hiraconies, Bactries, and Magies. He suffered in Calamina, being slain with a dart.

Simon Zelotes preached at Mauritania, and in Africa, and in Britain; he was crucified.

Judas, brother of James, preached to the Edessens, and all Misopotamia; he was slain in Berito.

Simon, brother to Jude and to James, all sons of Mary Cleophas, and of Alpheus, was bishop of Jerusalem after James, and was crucified in a city of Egypt.

Mark the evangelist, and first Bishop of Alexandria, preached the gospel in Egypt, and there, being drawn with ropes unto the fire, was burned.

Bartholomew is said also to have preached to the Indians, and to have translated the gospel of St. Matthew into their tongue, where he continued a great space, doing many miracles. At last in Albania, after divers persecutions, he was beaten down with staves, then crucified, and after being flayed, he was at length beheaded.

Andrew, the apostle and brother to Peter, preached to the Scythians, Saxons, &c. When Andrew, through his diligent preaching, had brought many to the faith of Christ; Egeas the governor, resorted thither, to constrain as many as believed Christ to be God, to do sacrifice to the idols. Andrew thinking good at the beginning to resist the wicked doings of Egeas, went to him, saying; that, "It behoved him to know his judge which dwelleth in heaven, and to worship him, and so in worshipping the true God, to revoke his mind from false gods and blind idols."

But he demanded of him, whether he was the same Andrew that overthrew the temple of the gods, and persuaded men of that sect, which the Romans had commanded to be abolished. Andrew plainly affirmed, that the princes of the Romans did not understand the truth, and that the Son of God, coming into the world for man's sake, had taught and declared how those idols, whom they so honoured as gods, were not only not gods, but also most cruel devils, enemies to mankind, teaching the people nothing else but that with which God is offended, and being offended turns away and regards them not.

The proconsul commanded Andrew not to teach and preach such things any more; or if he did, that he should be fastened to the cross. Andrew answered, he would not have preached the honour and glory of the cross, if he had feared the death of the cross. Whereupon sentence of condemnation was pronounced. Andrew seeing afar off the cross prepared, neither changed countenance nor colour, as the imbecility of mortal man is wont to do, neither did his blood shrink, neither did he fail in his speech, his body fainted not, neither was his mind molested, his understanding did not fail him, but out of the abundance of his heart his mouth did speak, and fervent charity did appear in his words; he said, "O cross, most welcome and long looked for; with a willing mind joyfully and desirously I come to thee, being the scholar of him which did hang on thee: because I have been always thy lover, and have coveted to embrace thee." So being crucified, he yielded up the ghost and fell asleep.

Matthew, named Levi, wrote his gospel to the Jews in the Hebrew tongue, as records Eusebius, (lib. 3. cap. 24. 39. lib. 5. cap. 8. cap. 10. Also Irenæus, lib. 3. cap. 1. Hieronymus in Cat. scrip. Eccl.) Concerning this apostle and evangelist, divers things are recorded, but in such sort, as may greatly be suspected to be some crafty forgery, for the establishment of later decretals, and Romish doctrine, as touching merits, consecration of nuns, the superstitious prescription of Lent-fast, not only in abstaining from all flesh meats, but also separating man and wife, during the time of Lent. Also, the strict prohibition not to taste any bodily sustenance, before receiving the Lord's Supper. In ordaining of mass, and that no nun must marry after the vow of her profession, with such other like.

It is recorded of Matthias, that after he had preached to the Jews, he was at length stoned and beheaded. (Joan. de Monte Regali.)

Philip, the apostle, after he had laboured much in preaching the word of salvation, suffered in Hierapolis, being crucified and stoned to death.

After Festus had sent the apostle Paul to Rome, and the Jews had lost their hope of performing their malicious vow against him, they fell upon James, the brother of our Lord, who was bishop at Jerusalem, and required him before all the people, to deny the faith of Christ; but he freely, and with great constancy before all the multitude, confessed Jesus to be the Son of God, our Saviour, and our Lord; whereupon they killed him.

Egesippus thus describes the manner of his death: When many of the chief persons believed in Christ, there was a tumult made of the scribes and pharisees; therefore they gathered together, and said to James, "We beseech thee restrain the people, for they believe in Jesus, as though he were the Christ; we pray thee persuade the people that they be not deceived; stand upon the pillar of the temple that thou mayst be seen from above, and that thy words may be heard by all the people." And thus the scribes and pharisees set James upon the battlements of the temple; and he said, with a great voice, "What do you ask me of Jesus the Son of Man, seeing that he sitteth on the right hand of God in heaven, and shall come in the clouds of heaven?" Many, persuaded of this, glorified God upon the witness of James, and said, "Hosannah in the highest to the Son of David!" Then the scribes and the pharisees said among themselves, "We have done evil, that we have caused such a testimony of Jesus, but let us go up, and let us take him, that they, being compelled with fear, may deny that faith." Therefore they went up, and threw down the just man, and they took him to smite him with stones, for he was not yet dead when he was cast down. But he, turning, fell down upon his knees, saying, "O Lord God, Father, I beseech thee to forgive them, for they know not what they do."

This James was so notable a man, that he was had in honour of all men, insomuch that the wise men of the Jews, shortly after his martyrdom, imputed the cause of the besieging of Jerusalem, and other calamities, to the violence and injury done to this man.

These things being thus declared as to the martyrdom of the apostles, and the persecution of the Jews, let us now, by the grace of Christ our Lord, narrate the persecutions raised by the Romans against the christians, till the coming of godly Constantine, which persecutions are reckoned, by most writers, to the number of ten.

It is marvellous to see and read the incredible numbers of christian innocents that were slain and tormented, some one way, some another, as Rabanus saith, "Some slain with the sword; some burnt with fire; some scourged with whips; some stabbed with forks: some fastened to the cross or gibbet; some drowned in the sea; some their skins pluckt off; some their tongues cut off; some stoned to death; some killed with cold; some starved with hunger; some their hands cut off, or otherwise dismembered." Whereof, Augustine also saith, "They were bound—imprisoned—killed—tortured —burned—butchered—cut in pieces," &c. Although these punishments were divers, yet the manner of constancy in all these martyrs was one. And notwithstanding these torments, and the cruelty of the tormentors, yet such was the number of these constant saints that suffered, or, rather such was the power of the Lord in his saints, that, as Jerome says, "there is no day in the whole year, to which the number of five thousand martyrs cannot be ascribed, except only the first day of January."

THE FIRST PERSECUTION.

The first of these ten persecutions was stirred up by the Emperor Nero Domitius, (A.D. 64). His rage was so fierce against the christians, as Eusebius records, that a man might then see cities full of the dead bodies of men and women cast out naked in the open streets. Likewise, Orosius writes of Nero, that he was the first in Rome to raise persecutions against the christians, and not only in Rome, but through all the provinces, thinking to destroy the whole name of christians.

In this persecution, the apostle Peter was condemned and crucified, as some write, at Rome; although others doubt it: concerning his life and history, because it is sufficiently described in the gospel, and in the Acts. I need not make any repetition of it. There are many who relate the cause and manner of his death, although they do not all precisely agree in the time. Jerome says that after he had been bishop of the church of Antioch, and had preached to the dispersed of them that believed, of the circumcision, in Pontus, Galatia, Cappadocia, Asia, and Bithynia, in the second year of the Emperor Claudius, (A.D. 44) he came to Rome to withstand Simon Magus, and there kept the priestly chair the space of five and twenty years, until the last year of Nero, by whom he was crucified, his head being down, and his feet upward, himself so requiring, because he was, he said, unworthy to be crucified after the same form and manner as the Lord was.[1]

---

(1) Foxe here has a marginal note; "This report seems neither to come from Jerome, nor to be true of Peter."

The manner in which later editions of 'The Fathers' have been corrupted, and the prodigious extent to which they were interpolated in the monastic libraries, before the discovery of printing, has rendered it a matter of exceeding difficulty to ascertain whether any statement be truly the genuine opinion of the father to whom it is ascribed. And in subsequent times the *Index expurgatorius* has erased so many important sentences, and sometimes whole paragraphs, that we cannot be certain of anything in those ancient writings. There is at this moment in the library of Trinity College, Dublin, a copy of Chrysostom's works, which had passed through the hands of one of the Inquisitors of the Index, and his pen has been drawn over every sentence that seemed to conflict with the peculiar views of the Roman church, and not unfrequently is the word *dele* and *deleatur* inserted in his handwriting in the margin.

Foxe seems to regard as an interpolation this passage in Jerome which describes Peter as being twenty-five years at Rome, but whether it be genuine or otherwise this much at least is certain, that it was both a moral and physical impossibility that the statement could be true in reference to that apostle, as will thus appear:

I. St. Paul was converted in the year 35; and three years afterwards he visited Jerusalem, where he found Peter, (Gal. i. 18.) this was about the year 38, so that at this time St. Peter was not at Rome.

II. In three years after this, we find St. Peter visiting the regions about Jerusalem, and justifying his proceedings before the apostles and brethren in that city, (Acts, xi. 2). This was about the year 41, so that at this time St Peter was not at Rome.

III. In about three years afterwards we find St. James beheaded (Acts, xii. 2), and immediately after we find St. Peter imprisoned at Jerusalem, (Acts, xii. 3). This was about the year 44. So that St. Peter could not have been at Rome at this period.

IV. St. Paul preached at Antioch in about the year 42, remaining there a whole year. He preached there again some years after, namely, about 46, and it is not improbable that it was during this visit that he had the contention with St Peter (Gal. ii. 11). So that Peter was not at that time at Rome.

V. The assembly of the apostles and elders at Jerusalem, to determine the question of the observance of the Jewish rites, or as the Papists call it, the Council of Jerusalem, was in the year 52. Now Peter was there and spoke at it, (Acts, xv. 7). So that he could not have been at Rome at this time.

VI. The Epistle of Paul to the Romans was written in the year 60, and it contains internal evidence that Peter was not at Rome at that period.

VII. There is no further mention made of St. Peter in the sacred history, but we find St. Paul at Rome for two whole years, (Acts, xxviii. 30). These were the years 64 and 65, as nearly as they can be computed. It is certain that Peter was not at Rome during those two years, for in the several epistles which St. Paul wrote during his residence there, he never mentions that apostle as being even at Rome, much less being bishop or pope of it, (See note, page 16).

VIII. The martyrdom of Peter was about the year 66, or 67 at the latest, so that his visit to Rome must have been after 65, and before 67; and this is the probable account of the matter. He *perhaps*, visited Rome at that time after Paul's imprisonment and preaching there. And he then, perhaps, was seized and martyred.

Thus Foxe is fully justified in saying that it cannot be true of Peter that he was 25 years at Rome. [ED.]

Paul the apostle, after his great and unspeakable labours in promoting the gospel of Christ, suffered also in this first persecution under Nero, and was beheaded.

Among his other manifold labours and travels in spreading the doctrine of Christ, he won Sergius Paulus, the proconsul of Cyprus, to the faith of Christ, whereupon he took his name, as some suppose, turned from Saulus to Paulus.

And because it is sufficiently comprehended in the Acts of the Apostles concerning the wonderful conversion, and conversation of this most worthy apostle, that which remains of the rest of his history, I will here briefly add how he was sent up in bonds to Rome, where, remaining two years together, he disputed daily against the Jews, proving Christ to be come. And here is to be noted, that after his first answer, or defence, he was discharged, and went to preach the gospel in the western parts, and about the coasts of Italy.

But afterwards being brought the second time before Nero, this worthy preacher and messenger of the Lord, in the same day in which Peter was crucified (although not in the same year, but in the next year following) was beheaded at Rome for the testimony of Christ.

THE SECOND PERSECUTION.

The first Roman persecution ceased under Vespasian, who gave some rest to the poor christians. After whose reign the second persecution was moved by the emperor Domitian, (about A. D. 94). Of whom Eusebius and Orosius write, that he beginning mildly, did afterwards so far outrage in intolerable pride, that he commanded himself to be worshipped as God, and that images of gold and silver in his honour should be set up in the capitol. The chief nobles of the senators, either upon envy, or for their goods, he caused to be put to death, some openly, and some he sent into banishment, there causing them to be slain privately.

And as his tyranny was unmeasurable, so the intemperance of his life was no less. He put to death all the nephews of Jude, called the Lord's brother, and caused all that could be found of the stock of David to be slain (as Vespasian also did before him) for fear, lest he were yet to come of the house of David, who should enjoy the kingdom. In the time of this persecutor, Simeon, bishop of Jerusalem, after other torments, was crucified.

In this persecution, John the apostle and evangelist, was exiled to Patmos. Of whom various memorable acts are reported in sundry chronicles. As how he was put in a vessel of boiling oil, by the proconsul of Ephesus. Also, how he raised up a widow and a certain young man from death to life. How he drank poison and it hurt him not, raising also to life two which had drank the same before. These, and such other miracles, although they may be true, yet, because they are no articles of our christian belief, I let them pass, and only content myself with that which I read in Eusebius, declaring of him, that in the second persecution, John was banished into Patmos for the testimony of the word, (A. D. 97). And after the death of Domitian, John was released, and came to Ephesus, (A. D. 100). Where he continued and governed the churches in Asia; where also he wrote his gospel, and so lived till the year after the passion of our Lord, threescore and eight, which was the year of his age, one hundred and twenty, (A. D. 101.)

And, as we now have in hand the story of John the evangelist, here comes in a great doubt and difficulty, such as has occupied all the catholic, subtile, illuminate, and seraphical doctors of the pope's catholic church, these five hundred years! The difficulty is this, as auricular confession has been, and is yet received in the pope's catholic church for an holy and necessary sacrament, extending universally to all christians; here ariseth a question, who was the Virgin Mary's confessor or ghostly father? But it is decreed and confessed, with full consent of all the catholics, to be St. John. Whosoever denies, or doubts of this, is straightways a heretic! This, then, so determined, arises another question or

doubt, that seeing our lady was without all original sin, and also actual or mortal sin, what need had she of any confessor? Or what should she confess to him? for if she had confessed any sin when she had none, then had she made herself a liar, and so had sinned indeed. Here, therefore, gentle reader, in this perplexity these our illuminate doctors stand in need of thine aid to help at a pinch. Albert, the great divine, denies not, but that she indeed, although most pure, yet confessed to her ghostly father, to keep the observance of the law, appointed for such as had that need, which she had not; and, therefore, (saith he) it was necessary that she should confess with her mouth. But then here it is to be asked, What did she say in her confession, when she had nothing to confess? To this Albert answers again, and tells us plainly what she said in her confession, which was this, That she had received that great grace, not of any worthiness of her own. And this was it that she said in her confession. (Albert. cap. 74. super Evang. Missus est, &c.)

Moreover, to help this case out of all doubt, comes in famous Thomas of Watring, and thus looses the knot, saying, that as Christ, although he did owe nothing to the law, yet notwithstanding received circumcision, to give to others example of humility and obedience; in like manner would our lady shew herself obedient to the observance of the law, although there was no cause why she had any need of it. And thus hast thou, gentle reader, this doubtful question moved and solved, to the intent I would reveal to thee some part of the deep divinity of our catholic masters that have ruled and governed the church in these their late popish days!

But I return again to this second persecution under Domitian, in which, besides these before mentioned, and other innumerable godly martyrs, suffering for the testimony of the Lord Jesus, Flavia, the daughter of one of the Roman consuls, with many others, was banished out of Rome for the testimony of Christ.

This Domitian feared the coming of Christ as Herod did, and therefore commanded them to be killed who were of the stock of David in Judea. There were remaining alive at that time certain of the Lord's kindred, which were the nephews of Jude, that was called the Lord's brother after the flesh. When the lieutenant of Judea had brought them to Domitian, the emperor demanded, Whether they were of the stock of David? Which, when they had granted, he asked again, what possessions and what substance they had? They answered, That they had no more between them in all but nine-and-thirty acres of ground, and that they got their living and sustained their families with the hard labours of their hands, shewing their hands to the emperor, being hard and rough, worn with labour, to witness that to be true which they had spoken. Then the emperor, inquiring of them concerning the kingdom of Christ, what manner of kingdom it was, how, and when it should appear? They answered, That his kingdom was no worldly thing, but a heavenly and angelical kingdom, and that it should appear in the consummation and end of the world, when he coming in glory, should judge the quick and the dead, and render to every one according to his deservings. Domitian, hearing this, let them go, and staid the persecution then moved against the christians.

By this story the cause may appear why the emperors so persecuted the christians, which causes were chiefly these:—First, Fear, for the emperors and senate, not knowing the nature of Christ's kingdom, feared lest it would subvert the empire, and therefore they sought by all possible means, by death and all kinds of torments, utterly to extinguish the christians. Secondly, Hatred, for the christians serving only the true living God, despised their false gods, spake against their idolatrous worshippings, and many times stopped the power of Satan, working in their idols.

Upon these and such causes, rose up those malicious slanders, false surmises, infamous lies, and slanderous accusations of the heathen idolaters against the christian servants of God, which incited the princes of this world the more to persecute them; for whatever crimes malice could invent, or rash suspicion could minister, were imputed to the christians ; and, whatever happened to the city or provinces of Rome, either famine, pestilence, earthquake, wars, wonders, unseasonableness of weather, or what other evils happened, it was imputed to the christians.

Also among these causes crept in some piece of covetousness, so that the wicked promoters and accusers, for lucre sake, and to seize the possessions of the christians, were the more ready to accuse them.

Thus hast thou, christian reader, first, the causes of these persecutions ; secondly, the cruel law of their condemnation ; thirdly, now hear what was the form of inquisition, which was (as is witnessed in the second apology of Justin) that they should swear to declare the truth, whether they were in very deed christians or not ; and if they confessed, then by the law the sentence of death proceeded.

Neither yet were these tyrants contented with death only. The kinds of death were various and horrible. Whatever the cruelty of man's invention could devise for the punishment of man's body, was practised against the christians. Crafty trains, outcries of enemies, imprisonment, stripes and scourgings, drawings, tearings, stonings, plates of iron laid unto them burning hot, deep dungeons, racks, strangling in prisons, the teeth of wild beasts, gridirons, gibbets and gallows, tossing upon the horns of bulls ; moreover, when they were thus killed, their bodies were laid in heaps, and dogs there left to keep them, that no man might come to bury them, neither would any prayer obtain for them to be interred and buried.

As it is impossible to comprehend the names and number of all the martyrs that suffered in these persecutions, so it is hard in such a variety of matter to keep a perfect order and course of years and times, especially as the authors themselves, whom we follow in this present work, do disagree both in the times, in the names, and also in the kind of martyrdom of them that suffered. As for example, where the common reading and opinion of the church, take Anacletus to succeed after Clement, next before Evaristus, as bishop of Rome ; Eusebius making no mention of Cletus, but of Anacletus, saith, That Evaristus succeeded next to Clement. Likewise, Ruffinus and Epiphanius, speaking nothing of Anacletus, make mention of Linus, and of Cletus, next before Clement, but say nothing of Anacletus ; whereby it may appear that Cletus and Anacletus were both one. Moreover, where Antoninus, Vincentius, Jacobus, Simoneta, Aloisius, with others, declare of Linus, Cletus, Clement, Anacletus, Evaristus, Alexander, bishops of Rome, that that they died martyrs ; Eusebius, in his ecclesiastical history, writing of them, makes no mention thereof.

And first, as touching Clement (whom Marianus Scotus calleth the first bishop of Rome after Peter) they say that he was sent out into banishment with two thousand christians : but Eusebius only says, that after he had governed the church of Rome nine years, the said Clement left the succession thereof to Evaristus.

Of which Evaristus, next bishop of Rome, thus we find in Irenæus, (lib. 3. cap. 3.) Peter and Paul (says he) committed the charge of that church to Linus ; after whom came Anacletus, then succeeded Clement, next to Clement followed Evaristus. Little or nothing remains of the acts and monuments either of this, or of other bishops of Rome in those days. Whereby it may appear that no great account was then made of Roman bishops, whose acts and deeds were then either so lightly reputed, or so slenderly committed to history. Notwithstanding, however, certain decretal epistles are remaining, or rather thrust upon us in their names, containing in them little substance of any doctrine, but altogether stuffed with laws, injunctions, and stately decrees, little to the purpose, and still less savouring of the time then present. Amongst which are also numbered the two epistles of this Evaristus : who, when he had given these orders, and had made six priests, two deacons, and five bishops for sundry places (says the history) he suffered martyrdom. But what kind of death, for what cause he suffered, what constancy he shewed, what was the order or conversation of

his life, is not touched, and that seems, therefore, the more to be doubted which our new histories say ; because the old ancient writers have no remembrance thereof, who otherwise would not have passed such things over in silence, if they had been true.

After him succeeded Alexander in the governance of that church, of whose time and death there is the like discrepancy among the writers.

They who write of the deeds and doings of this bishop, declare that he had converted a great part of the senators to the faith of Christ, amongst whom was Hermes, a great man in Rome.

And then (says the history) about the second year of Adrian, Aurelian the ruler took Alexander, with Hermes, his wife, children, and his whole household, to the number of one thousand two hundred and fifty, and threw them in prison. And not long after, Alexander with Euentius his deacon, and Hermes, and the rest, were burned in a furnace. Theodulus, another deacon of Alexander, seeing and rebuking the cruelty of the tyrant, suffered also the same martyrdom.

Quirinus also, the same time having first his tongue cut out, then his hands and feet, was beheaded and cast to the dogs.

Various miracles are reported of this Alexander, in the legends and lives of saints ; which as I deny not, but because I cannot avouch them by any grave testimony of ancient writers, therefore I dare not affirm them, but do refer them to the authors and patrons thereof, where they are found. Notwithstanding, whatever is to be thought of his miracles, this is to be affirmed and not doubted, that he was a godly and virtuous bishop.

THE THIRD PERSECUTION.

Between the second persecution and the third was but one year, under the Emperor Nerva, after whom succeeded Trajan ; and under him followed the third persecution, (A.D. 98). Trajan might seem, in comparison of others, a worthy and commendable prince, familiar with inferiors, and behaving himself towards his subjects, as he himself would have the prince to be to him, if he were a subject. He was noted to be a great observer of justice, but toward the christian religion he was impious and cruel, and caused the third persecution of the church. In which persecution, Pliny the second, a man learned and famous, seeing the lamentable slaughter of christians, and moved with pity, wrote to Trajan the following epistle :—

" It is my property and manner (my sovereign) to make relation to you of all those things wherein I doubt. For who can better either correct my slackness or instruct mine ignorance, than you ? I was never yet present myself at the examination and execution of these christians ; and therefore what punishment is to be administered, and how far, or how to proceed in such inquisitions, I am ignorant, not able to resolve in the matter whether any difference is to be had in age and person, whether the young and tender ought to be with like cruelty intreated as the elder and stronger, whether repentance may have any pardon, or whether it may profit him or not to deny, who has been a christian, whether the name only of christians, without other offences, or whether the offences joined with the name of a christian ought to be punished. In the meantime, as touching such christians as have been presented to me, I have kept this order. I have inquired the second and third time of them whether they were christians, menacing them with fear of punishment ; and such as did persevere, I commanded to execution. For thus I thought, that whatsoever their profession was, yet their stubbornness and obstinacy ought to be punished. Whether they were also of the same madness ; whom, because they were citizens of Rome, I thought to send them back again to the city. Afterward, in further process and handling of this matter, as the sect did further spread, so the more cases did ensue.

" There was a paper offered to me, bearing no name, wherein were contained the names of many which denied themselves to be christians, contented to do sacrifice with incense and wine to the gods, and to your image (which image I caused to be brought for that purpose) and to blaspheme Christ, whereto none such as were true christians indeed could be compelled : and those I did discharge and let go. Others confessed that they had been christians, but afterwards denied the same, &c. affirming to me the whole sum of that sect or error to consist in this, that they were wont at certain times appointed, to meet before day, and to sing certain hymns to one Christ their God, and to confederate among themselves, to abstain from all theft, murder, and adultery, to keep their faith, and to defraud no man : which done, then to depart for that time, and afterward to resort again to take meat in companies together both men and women one with another and yet without any act of evil.

" In the truth whereof to be further certified whether it were so or not, I caused two maidens to be laid on the rack, and to be examined with torments. But finding nothing in them, but immoderate superstition, I thought to cease further inquiry till I might be further advised from you ; for the matter seemed to me worthy and needful of advice, especially for the great number of those that were in danger of your statute. For very many there were of all ages and states, both men and women, and more are like hereafter to incur the same peril of condemnation. For that infection has crept not only into cities, but villages also and boroughs about. For as much as we see in many places that the temples of our gods, which were wont to be desolate, begin now to be frequented, and that they bring sacrifices from every part to be sold, which before very few were found willing to buy. It may easily be conjectured what multitudes of men may be amended, if space and time be given them, wherein they may be reclaimed."

To the above epistle the emperor returned the following answer :—

" The statute concerning christians ye have rightly executed. For no such general law can be enacted wherein all special cases particularly can be comprehended. Let them not be sought for, but if they are brought and convicted, then let them suffer execution : so notwithstanding, that whoever shall deny himself to be a christian, and do it unfeignedly in open audience, and do sacrifice to our gods, however he may have been suspected before, let him be released, upon promise of amendment. Such writings as have no names, suffice not to any just crime or accusation ; for that should give an evil precedent, neither does it agree with the example of our time."

Tertullian writing upon this letter of Trajan, thus says, " O sentence of a confused necessity ; he would not have them to be sought for as innocent men, and yet causes them to be punished as persons guilty !" Thus the rage of that persecution ceased for a time, although many men and cruel officers ceased not to afflict the christians in various provinces ; and especially if any occasion were given, or if any commotion were raised in the provinces abroad, the fault was laid upon the christians. As in Jerusalem, after the Emperor Trajan had sent down his command, that whoever could be found of the stock of David, should be put to death. Certain sectaries of the Jews accused Simeon, the bishop of Jerusalem, to have come of the stock of David, and that he was a christian. Of which accusers it happened also that some of them likewise were apprehended and taken as being of the stock of David, and so were justly put to execution themselves who had sought the destruction of others. The blessed bishop was scourged, during the space of many days together, though an hundred and twenty years of age. In his martyrdom he endured so constant, that both the consul and the multitude marvelled to see him at that age so constantly to suffer, and so at last being crucified, he finished his course in the Lord, for whom he suffered.

In this persecution Phocas, bishop of Pontus, also suffered, whom Trajan, because he would not do sacrifice to Neptune, cast into a hot lime-kiln, and afterward put into a scalding bath, where the constant godly martyr, for the testimony of Christ, ended his life, or rather entered into life.

In the same persecution suffered also Sulpitius and Servilian, whose wives having been converted by Sabina to the faith of Christ, were also martyred. Sabina was beheaded in the days of Adrian. Under whom also suffered Seraphia, a maiden of Antioch.

In this persecution, beside many others, Ignatius, the blessed martyr of Christ, who to this day is had in great reverence, also suffered. Ignatius was appointed to the bishopric of Antioch next in succession after Peter. Being sent from Syria to Rome, because he professed Christ, he was given to the wild beasts to be devoured. It is said of him, that when he passed through Asia, he strengthened and confirmed the churches through all the cities as he went, both with his exhortations and preaching of the word of God. And thus when he came to Smyrna, he wrote one epistle to the church of Ephesus, and another to the church of Magnesia : also another to the church of Trallis, in which he saith :—

" I, being exercised, and now well acquainted with their injuries, am taught every day more and more ; but hereby am I not yet justified. And would to God I were once come to the beasts, which are prepared for me, which also I wish with gaping mouths were ready to come upon me, whom also I will provoke that they without delay may devour me, and forbear me nothing at all, as those whom before they have not touched or hurt for fear ! And if they will not unless they be provoked, I will then enforce them against myself. Pardon me, I pray you. How beneficial it is to me, I know. Now begin I to be a scholar ; I esteem no visible things, nor yet invisible things, so that I may obtain Christ Jesus. Let the fire, the gallows, the devouring of wild beasts, the breaking of bones, the pulling asunder of my members, the bruising or pressing of my whole body, and the torments of the devil or hell itself come upon me, so that I may win Christ Jesus."

Besides this godly Ignatius, many thousands also were put to death in the same persecution, as appears by the letter of Pliny. Jerome mentions one Publius, bishop of Athens, who for the faith of Christ during this persecution, was martyred.

Next after this, Trajan succeeded the Emperor Adrian, (A. D. 118).

It is stated in the histories, that in the time of Adrian, Zenon, a nobleman of Rome, with ten thousand two hundred and three other persons were slain for Christ. Ten thousand were crucified in the Mount Ararat, crowned with crowns of thorn, and thrust into the sides with sharp darts, after the example of the Lord's passion.

There was one Eustachius, a captain, sent out to war against the barbarians. After he had by God's grace valiantly subdued his enemies, and was returning home with victory, Adrian for joy meeting him in his journey to bring him home with triumph, first would by the way do sacrifice to Apollo for the victory, requiring Eustachius to do the same. But Eustachius could by no means be forced thereto, and being brought to Rome, with his wife and children suffered martyrdom.

We read also of Faustinus and Jobita, who suffered with grievous torments. At the sight whereof, one Calocerius, seeing their great patience in so great torments, cried out with these words, " Verily, great is the God of the Christians." Which words being heard, he was forthwith apprehended, and being brought to the place of execution, was made partaker of their martyrdom.

Symphorissa, the wife of Getulus the martyr, with her seven children, is said about the same time to suffer ; who first was several times beaten and scourged, afterwards was hanged up by the hair of her head ; at last, having a huge stone fastened to her, was thrown headlong into the river ; and her seven children, in like manner, with various kinds of punishment martyred by the tyrant.

Sophia, with her three children : also Seraphia and

Sabina, also Anthia, and her son, who was bishop of Apulia; also Justus and Pastor suffered, (A. D. 130).

While Adrian was at Athens, he purposed to visit Elusina, and did so; where sacrificing to the Gentiles' gods, he gave free leave and liberty to persecute the christians. Whereupon Quadratus, a man of no less excellent zeal than of famous learning, being then bishop of Athens, did exhibit to the emperor a learned and excellent apology in defence of the christian religion; wherein he declared the christians, without any just cause to be so cruelly treated and persecuted. The like also did Aristides, another no less excellent philosopher in Athens, who, being noticed by the emperor for his singular learning and eloquence, and coming to his presence, there made before him an eloquent oration. Moreover he exhibited to the emperor a memorable apology for the christians, so full of learning and eloquence, that as Jerome said, it was a spectacle and admiration to all men in his time, that loved to see wit and learning. Besides these, there was also another named Serenus Granius, a man of great nobility, who wrote very pithy and grave letters to Adrian, shewing that it was consonant with no right nor reason, for the blood of innocents to be given to the rage and fury of the people, and to be condemned for no fault, only for the name and sect that they followed.

Thus the goodness of God being moved with the prayers and constant labour of these excellent men, so turned the heart of the emperor, that he, being better informed concerning the order and profession of the christians, became more favourable to them.

In the days of this Adrian, the Jews rebelled again, and spoiled the country of Palestine. Against whom the emperor sent Julius Severus, who overthrew in Judea fifty castles, and burnt and destroyed nine hundred and eighty villages and towns, and slew fifty thousand of the Jews with famine, sickness, sword, and fire; so that Judah was almost desolate. But at length Adrian, who was also named Ælius, repaired and enlarged the city of Jerusalem, which was called after his name, Æliopolis, or Ælia: he granted only to the Gentiles and to the christians to live in it, utterly forbidding the Jews to enter into the city.

After the death of Adrian, succeeded Antonius Pius, about the year 140, and reigned twenty and three years, who for his clemency and modest behaviour, had the name of Pius. His saying was, That he had rather save one citizen, than destroy a thousand of his adversaries. At the beginning of his reign, although there was no edict to persecute the christians, yet the rage of the heathen multitude did not cease to afflict the people of God, imputing and ascribing to the christians whatever misfortune happened contrary to their desires: moreover, inventing against them all false crimes whereof to accuse them. By reason of which, some were put to death; although, not by the consent of the emperor, who was so mild and gentle, that either he raised no persecution against the christians, or else he soon stayed the same being moved; as may well appear by his letter sent down to the countries of Asia, in which he writes these things of the christians:—

"This is their joy and desire, that when they are accused, they rather covet to die for their God than to live. Whereby they are victorious, and overcome you, giving rather their lives, than doing that which you require of them. And here it shall not be inconvenient to advertise you of the earthquakes which have and do happen among us, that when at the sight of them you tremble and are afraid, then you may compare your case with them. For they, upon a sure confidence of their God, are bold and fearless, much more than you; who in the time of this your ignorance, do both worship other gods, and neglect the religion of immortality, and such christians as worship him you drive out, and persecute unto death. Of these matters, many presidents of our provinces did write to our father of famous memory, heretofore. To whom he directed his answer, desiring them in no case to molest the christians, except they were found in some prejudicial trespass against the

empire. And to me also, many write, signifying their mind in like manner; to whom I have answered to the same effect and manner as my father did. Wherefore, if any hereafter shall offer any vexation or trouble, to such, having no other cause, but only for that they are christians, let him that is impeached be released, and discharged free, yea, although he be found to be such (that is, a christian), and let the accuser sustain the punishment," &c.

This godly edict of the emperor was proclaimed at Ephesus, in the public assembly of all Asia. By this means persecution began to be appeased, through the merciful providence of God, who would not have his church to be utterly overthrown.

THE FOURTH PERSECUTION.

After the decease of Antonius Pius, followed his son-in-law Marcus Aurelius Antonius, with Lucius Verus, his adopted brother, (A. D. 161). Marcus was a stern and severe man, in whose time a great number of christians suffered cruel torments and punishments, both in Asia and France. In the number of whom was Polycarp, the bishop of Smyrna, who, in the great rage of this persecution in Asia, was martyred. Of his end and martyrdom I thought it here not inexpedient to commit to history so much as Eusebius declares to be taken out of a certain epistle, written by those of his own church to the brethren of Pontus: the tenor of this epistle here followeth.

"The church which is at Smyrna, to the church which is at Philomilium, and to all the churches throughout Pontus, mercy to you, peace and the love of God our Father, and of our Lord Jesus Christ, be multiplied, Amen. We have written unto you, brethren, of those men which have suffered martyrdom, and of blessed Polycarp, who hath ended and appeased this persecution, as it were, by the shedding his own blood." And in the same epistle, before they enter into further matter of Polycarp, they discourse of other martyrs, describing what patience they shewed in suffering their torments; which was so admirable (says the epistle) that the lookers on were amazed, seeing and beholding how they were so scourged and whipped, that the inward veins and arteries appeared, yea even so much, that the very entrails of their bodies were seen, and after that, were set upon sharp shells taken out of the sea, and certain nails and thorns were put for the martyrs to walk upon, which were sharpened and pointed. Thus they suffered all kind of punishment and torment that might be devised: and lastly, were thrown to the wild beasts to be devoured.

Now we will return to Polycarp, of whom the aforesaid letter declares as follows. That in the beginning, when he heard of these things he was not at all afraid nor disquieted in mind, but purposed to have tarried still in the city, till being persuaded by the entreaty of them that were about him, he hid himself in a village not far from the city, and there abiding with a few more, did nothing, night or day, but abode in supplication, wherein he made his humble petition for the obtaining of peace unto all the churches throughout the world. It is further mentioned, that when they were hard at hand, who so narrowly sought for him, he was forced for the affection and love of his brethren to fly into another village, to which place notwithstanding within a little while after the pursuers came, and found him in the house, from whence he might have escaped if he would; but this he would not do, saying, "The will of God be done." Furthermore, when he knew that they were come, he came down and spake to them with a cheerful and pleasant countenance, so that it was a wonder to see them now beholding his comely age, and his grave and constant countenance, lamenting that they had so employed their labour, that so aged a man should be apprehended. To conclude, he commanded that straightway without any delay, the table should be laid for them, and persuaded them that they would eat and dine well, and required of them boldly, that he might have an hour's respite to pray. Which being granted, he arose and went to pray, and was so replenished with the grace of God, that they which were present, and hearing the prayers that he made, were astonished, and many were sorry that so godly an aged man should be put to death.

After he had made an end of his prayers, and the hour was come in which they ought to set forward; they set him on an ass, and brought him to the city. And there met him the Irenarch Herod and his father Nicetes, who causing him to come into the chariot where they sat, persuaded him, and said, " What hurt, I pray thee, shall come thereof, if thou say (by way of salvation) my lord Cæsar, and do sacrifice, and thus save thyself?" But he made no answer, till they forced him to speak; he then said, " I will not do as you counsel me." When they saw he could not be persuaded, they gave him very rough language, and purposely molested him, so that in going down from the chariot, he might hurt or break his legs. But he treating very light of the matter, as if he had felt no hurt, went merrily and diligently forward, making haste to the place appointed. The proconsul, when he was come, gave him counsel to deny his name, and said to him, " Be good to thyself, and favour thine old age; take thine oath, and I will discharge thee: defy Christ." Polycarp answered, " Eighty-six years have I been his servant, yet in all this time hath he not so much as once hurt me: how then may I speak evil of my King and sovereign Lord, who hath thus preserved me?" Hereupon the proconsul stood up; " I have," said he, " wild beasts to whom I will throw thee, unless thou take a better course." Whereunto Polycarp answered, " Let them come; we have determined with ourselves, that we will not turn us from the better way to the worse, but rather turn from things that be evil unto that which is good." " Again," said the proconsul, " I will tame thee with fire." Then said Polycarp, " You threaten me with fire, which shall burn for the space of an hour, and shall be within a little while after extinguished; but thou knowest not the fire of the judgment to come, and of everlasting punishment, which is reserved for the wicked and ungodly. But why make you all these delays? Give me what death ye list." These and many other such things being spoken by him, he was filled with joy and boldness, and his countenance appeared so full of grace and favour, that he was not only not troubled with those things which the proconsul spake to him, but contrarily, the proconsul himself began to be amazed, and sent for the crier, who in the middle of the stage was commanded to cry three times, " Polycarp hath confessed himself to be a christian;" which words of the crier were no sooner spoken, but the whole multitude desired that he would let loose the lion at Polycarp. To whom he made answer, " That he could not do so, because he had already his prey." Then they cried again all together with one voice, that he would burn Polycarp alive. And the pro-consul had no sooner spoken, but it was at once performed. For the multitude brought out of their shops, workhouses and barns, wood and other dry matter for that purpose.

And thus the pile being laid, and when he had now put off his garments and undone his girdle, straightway those instruments which are requisite to such a bonfire, were brought to him, and when they would have nailed him to the stake with iron hoops, he said, " Let me alone as I am, for he that hath given me strength to suffer and abide the fire, shall also give power, that without this your provision of nails, I shall abide, and not stir in the midst of this fire." Which when they heard, they did not nail him, but bound him. Therefore when his hands were bound behind him, he was sacrificed, saying, " O Father of thy well-beloved and blessed Son Jesus Christ, by whom we have attained the knowledge of thee, the God of angels and powers, and of every creature, and of all just men which live before thee, I give thee thanks that thou hast vouchsafed to grant me this day that I may have my part among the number of the martyrs in the cup of Christ, unto the resurrection of eternal life, both of body and soul, through the operation of thy Holy Spirit, among whom I

shall this day be received into thy sight for an acceptable sacrifice: and as thou hast prepared and revealed the same before this time, so thou hast accomplished the same, O thou most true God, which canst not lie. Wherefore I in like case for all things praise thee, and bless thee, and glorify thee by our everlasting bishop, Jesus Christ, to whom be glory evermore, amen."

The subtle adversary, when he saw the worthiness of his martyrdom, and that his conversation even from his younger years could not be reproved, and that he was adorned with the crown of martyrdom, and had now obtained that incomparable benefit, gave in charge that we should not take and divide his body, for fear lest the remnants of the dead corpse should be taken away, and so worshipped by the people. Whereupon some whispered Nicetes the father of Herod, and his brother Dalces, to admonish the proconsul, that in no case should he deliver his body, lest said he, they leave Christ, and begin to worship Polycarp. And this they spake, because the Jews had given them secret warning, and provoked them thereto; who also watched us, that we should not take him out of the fire; not being ignorant how that we meant at no time to forsake Christ, who gave his life for the salvation of the whole world, (as many I mean as are elected to salvation by him) neither yet that we could worship any other. For why? him we worship as the Son of God, but the martyrs we love as disciples of the Lord, (and that worthily), for their abundant love towards their king and master, of whom we also desire and wish to be companions, and to be made his disciples. When therefore the centurion saw and perceived the object of the Jews, the corpse being laid abroad, they burnt the same, as was their manner.

Thus good Polycarp, with twelve others that came from Philadelphia, suffered martyrdom at Smyrna; which Polycarp especially above the rest is had in memory, so that in all places among the Gentiles he is most esteemed.

He was a very aged man, who had served Christ eighty-six years since the first knowledge of him, and served also in the ministry about the space of seventy years: he was the scholar and hearer of John the evangelist, and was placed by John in Smyrna.

It is witnessed by Ireneus, that Polycarp came to Rome in the time of Anicetus bishop of Rome, about the year one hundred and fifty-seven, the cause of his coming hither appears to be about the controversy of Easter day: wherein the Asians and the Romans disagreed. And therefore Polycarp, in behalf of the brethren and church of Asia, took his long journey there to come and confer with Anicetus. Whereof, writes also Nicephorus, (lib. 4.) declaring, that Polycarp and Anicetus varied something in opinion and judgment about that matter, and that yet notwithstanding, both communicated friendly the one with the other, in so much that Anicetus in his church gave place to Polycarp to minister the communion and sacrament of the Lord's supper for honour sake. Which may be a notable testimony now to us, that the doctrine concerning the free use and liberty of ceremonies, was at that time retained in the church without any offence, or breach of christian peace in the church.

In this fourth persecution, besides Polycarp and others before mentioned, we read various others, who, at the same time, did suffer at Smyrna.

Metrodorus, a minister, was given to the fire, and consumed. Pionius, who, after much boldness of speech, as his apologies exhibited, and his sermons made to the people in the defence of christian faith, and after much relieving and comforting of such as were in prison, and otherwise discomforted, at last was put to cruel torments, then given to the fire, and so finished his blessed martyrdom.

And as these suffered in Asia, so in Rome suffered Felicitas with her seven children; of whom, her first and eldest son, after he was whipped and scourged with rods, was pressed to death with leaden weights; two had their brains beaten out; another was cast down headlong, and had his neck broken; the rest were beheaded.

Last of all, Felicitas the mother, was slain with the sword.

In this fourth persecution, suffered Justin, a man of learning and philosophy, and a great defender of the christian religion, who presented a book in defence of our doctrine to the Emperor Antoninus Pius, and to the Senate. After which he was crowned with the like martyrdom to those whom he had defended in his book.

Under the same Antoninus also suffered Ptolomy and Lucius for the confession of Christ, in Alexandrina.

Concordus, a minister of the city of Spolet, because he would not sacrifice to Jupiter, but did spit in the face of the idol, after divers and sundry punishments, at last was beheaded with the sword.

A little before, mention was made of Symphorosa, wife of Getulus, with her seven sons, whom the chronicle of Ado declares to be put to death, being fastened to seven stakes, and so racked up with a pully, and at last were thrust through, Crescens in the neck, Julianus in the breast, Nemesius in the heart, Primitivus in the stomach, Justinus cut in every joint of his body, Statteus run through with spears, Eugenius cut asunder from the breast to the lower parts, and then cast into a deep pit. After the martyrdom of whom, Symphorosa, the mother, did likewise suffer.

Under Marcus Antoninus, and in the same persecution, suffered the glorious and most constant martyrs of Lyons and Vienne, two cities in France, giving to Christ a glorious testimony, and to all christian men a spectacle, or example of singular constancy and fortitude in Christ our Saviour ; and as the history of them is written and set forth by their own churches, where they suffered, (Euseb. lib. 5. cap. 2). I thought good to give it in their own words, as in the following epistle to their brethren in Asia and Phrygia.

" The servants of Christ inhabiting the cities of Vienne and Lyons, to the brethren in Asia and Phrygia, having the same faith and hope of redemption with us: Peace, grace, and glory from God the Father, and from Jesus Christ our Lord.

" The greatness of this our tribulation, the furious rage of the Gentiles against us, and the torments which the blessed martyrs suffered, we can neither in words, nor yet in writing, set forth as they deserve. For the adversary in every place practised, and instructed his ministers how, in most spiteful manner, to set them against the servants of God ; so that not only in our houses, shops, and markets, were we restrained, but also universally commanded, that none should be seen in any place. But God hath always mercy in store, and took out of their hands such as were weak amongst us, and others he set up as firm and immoveable pillars, who, by suffering, were able to abide and valiantly to withstand the enemy, enduring all the punishment they could devise ; they fought this battle for Christ, esteeming their great troubles but as light ; thereby shewing that all that may be suffered in this present life, is not to be compared with the great glory which shall be shewed upon us after life. They patiently suffered railings, scourgings, drawings and halings, flinging of stones, imprisonings, and whatever the rage of the multitude is wont to use against their enemies ; then being led into the market-place, and there judged ; after their confession, made openly before the multitude, they were sent back again to prison. One Vetius Epagathus, one of the brethren, having within him the fervent zeal of love, and spirit of God, could not suffer that wicked judgment which was given upon the christians ; but being vehemently displeased, desired that the judge would hear the excuse which he was minded to make in behalf of the christians, in whom, said he, is no impiety found. The justice did not grant him his request, but only asked him, whether he himself was a christian or not ? And he immediately, with a loud and bold voice, answered and said, I am a christian. And thus he was received into the fellowship of the martyrs, and called the advocate of the christians.

By this man's example, the rest of the martyrs were the more animated with all courage of mind. Some there were unready and not so well prepared, and as yet weak, not well able to bear so great a conflict ; of whom there were ten that fainted, ministering to us much heaviness and lamentation, who by their example caused the rest, which were not yet apprehended, to be less willing thereto. With these also certain men-servants were apprehended, and they, fearing the torments which they saw the saints suffer, being also compelled thereto by means of the soldiers, charged against us that we kept the feastings of Thyestes, and of Œdipus, and many such other crimes, which are neither to be remembered, nor named of us, nor yet to be thought that any man would ever commit the like.

" These things being bruted abroad, every man began to shew cruelty against us, insomuch that those which before were more gentle, now vehemently disdained us, and waxed mad against us. And thus was fulfilled that which was spoken by Christ, saying, " The time will come, that whosoever killeth you, shall think that he doth God service." Then suffered the martyrs of God such bitter persecution as is passing to be told. Satan still shooting at this mark, to make them to utter some blasphemy by all possible means. Marvellous therefore was the rage both of the people and prince, especially against one Sanctus, who was deacon of the congregation of Vienne, and against Maturus, being but a little before baptized, but yet a worthy soldier of Christ, and also against Attalus, who was the foundation and pillar of that church, and also against Blandina. Blandina was so filled with strength and boldness, that they which had the tormenting of her from morning to night, gave over for very weariness, and were themselves overcome, confessing that they could do no more against her, and marvelled that she yet lived, having her body so torn and rent : and testified that any one of those torments alone, without any more, had been enough to have plucked the life from her body.

" Sanctus also, another of the martyrs, who in the midst of his torments, endured more pains than the nature of a man might bear with, abode in such constancy of mind, that he neither told them his name, nor what countryman he was, nor in what city brought up, neither whether he was a freeman or a servant : but every question that was asked him, he answered, ' I am a christian,' and this was all that he confessed both of his name, city, kindred, and all other things in the place of execution : whereupon both the governor and tormentors were the more vehemently bent against him : they clapped plates of brass red hot to the most tender parts of his body, yet he never shrunk, but was bold and constant in his confession, being strengthened and moistened with the fountain of lively water, flowing out of Christ's side. Truly his body was a sufficient witness what torments he suffered : for it was all drawn together and most pitifully wounded and scorched, so that it had lost the proper shape of a man, in whose suffering Christ obtained unspeakable glory, for he overcame his adversaries, and, to the instruction of others, declared that nothing else is terrible, or ought to be feared where the love of God is, and nothing grievous wherein the glory of Christ is manifested.

" Also Satan now thinking to have settled himself in the heart of one Biblias, being one of them who had denied Christ, and thinking to have caused her, being a weak and feeble woman in faith, to have damned her soul, in blaspheming the name of God, brought her to the place of execution ; but she, in the middle of her torments, returning to herself, and waking as it were out of her dead sleep by that temporal pain, called to her remembrance the pains of hell fire, and against all expectations answered the tormentors, saying, ' How should we christians eat young infants, (as ye report of us) for whom it is not lawful to eat the blood of any beast ?' Upon that, so soon as she had confessed herself to be a christian, she was martyred. Thus when Christ had ended those tyrannical torments, by the patience and suffering of the saints, the Devil yet invented other engines and instruments. For when the christians were cast into prison, they were shut up in dark and ugly dungeons, and were drawn by the feet in a rack or engine made for that purpose. Very many of them were strangled and killed in prisons, whom the Lord in this manner would have to enjoy everlasting life, and set forth his glory. And surely these good men were so pitifully tormented, that if they had had all the helps and medicines in the world, it was thought impossible for them to live, and to be restored. And thus they remaining in prison, destitute of all human help, were so strengthened of the Lord, and confirmed both in body and mind, that they comforted and stirred up the minds of the rest.

"Photinus, who was deacon to the bishop of Lyons, was about eighty-nine years old, and a very feeble man, yet he was of a lively courage and spirit when he was brought to the judgment-seat, although his body was feeble and weak, both because of his old age, and also through sickness, yet was his life preserved, that Christ might triumph and be glorified. Being demanded of the chief ruler, what was the christian man's God? He answered, If thou be worthy to know, thou shalt know. He being somewhat touched with these words, caused him to be beaten. Those that stood next him, did him all the spite and displeasure that they could, both with hand and foot, having no regard at all to his old age or white hairs. And they who were further off threw at him whatever came next to hand, and every man thought that he did very wickedly refrain who withheld his hand from doing the like. He was then thrown into prison, and within two days after died.

"Then Maturus and Attalus were brought together to the common scaffold, there in the face of the people to be cast to the beasts. They suffered the tearing of wild beasts, and whatever else the frantic people on every side cried for and willed. And above all the rest they brought an iron chair, in which their bodies being set, were fried and scorched, as on a gridiron fried on the coals. And yet for all that the tormentors ceased not, but waxed more fierce and mad against them, labouring to overcome the patience of the saints. Notwithstanding all this, they could not get out of Sanctus' mouth any other thing but the confession which at the beginning he declared. And thus these holy men, after they had long continued alive in most horrible conflict, were at length slain, being made all that whole day a spectacle to the world, in place and instead of the games and sights which were wont to be exhibited to the people.

"Now the emperor had written that all the confessors should be punished, and the others let go. The governor therefore caused all the holy martyrs to be brought to the sessions, that the assembled multitude might behold them, and he again examined them; as many of them as he thought had the Roman freedom he beheaded, the residue he gave to the beasts to be devoured. And truly Christ was much glorified by those who a little before had denied him, who now contrary to the expectation of the infidels confessed him even to the death. While they were being examined, one Alexander, standing somewhat near to the bar, by signs encouraged such as were examined to confess Christ; so that by his countenance sometimes rejoicing, and sometimes sorrowing, he was observed of the standers by. The people not taking in good part to see those who had recanted again to stick to their first confession, cried out against Alexander as one that was the cause of this matter. And when he was forced by the judge and demanded what religion he was of? he answered, 'I am a Christian.' He had no sooner spoken the word, but he was condemned to be devoured by the beasts.

"The blessed Blandina being the last that suffered, after she had, like a worthy mother, given exhortations unto her children, and sent them before as conquerors to their heavenly King, and had called to her remembrance all their battles and conflicts, so much rejoiced at her children's death, and so hastened her own, as though she had been bidden to a bridal, and not to be thrown to the wild beasts. After this her pitiful whipping, her delivery to the beasts, and her torments upon the grid-iron, at length she was put in a net, and thrown to the wild bull; and when she had been sufficiently gored and wounded with

the horns of the beast, and heeded nothing of all that chanced to her, for the great hope and consolation she had in Christ and heavenly things, was thus slain, insomuch that the very heathen men themselves confessed, that there was never woman put to death, that suffered so much as this woman did. Neither yet was their furious cruelty thus assuaged against the christians. For the cruel barbarous people, like wild beasts, knew not when the time was to make an end, but invented new and sundry torments every day against our bodies. Neither yet did it content them when they had put the christians to death. For those whom they strangled in their prisons, they threw to the dogs, setting keepers both day and night to watch them, that they should not be buried, and bringing forth the remnant of their bones and bodies, some half burned, some left of the wild beasts, and some all mangled, also bringing forth heads of others which were cut off, and committing them to the charge of the keepers to see them remain unburied.

"Thus were the bodies of the martyrs made a wondering stock, and lay six days in the open streets; at length they burned them, and threw their ashes into the river Rhone, so that there might appear no remnant of them upon the earth. And this they did, as if they had been able to have pulled God out of his seat, and to have hindered the regeneration of the saints, and taken from them the hope of the resurrection."

Such was the epistle of the brethren of France to those of Asia.

Among others that suffered under Antoninus, mention was made of Justin, who exhibited two apologies, in the defence of christian doctrine, the one to the senate, and the other to the emperor.

Of which apologies, the first he wrote to the senate; when with great liberty, he declared that he was of necessity compelled to write and utter his mind to them. For that in persecuting of the christians they highly offended God, and therefore they had need to be admonished. And writing to the lieutenant of the city, said, "That he put men to death and torments for no offence committed, but only for the confession of the name of Christ; which proceedings and judgments neither became the emperor, nor his son, nor the senate:" defending moreover in the apology, and clearing the christians of such crimes as were falsely laid and objected against them.

And likewise in his second apology writing to the emperor, with like gravity and free liberty, he declares to them how they had the name, being commonly reputed and taken as virtuous philosophers, maintainers of justice, lovers of learning; but whether they were so, their acts declared. As for him, neither for flattery, nor favour at their hands, was he constrained thus to write unto them; and in plain words he charges, the emperor as well as the senate with manifest wrong, for not granting the christians that which is not denied to all other malefactors, judging men to death, only for the hatred of the name. "Other men who are accused," said he, "are not condemned in judgment, before they are convicted: but on us, you take our name only for the crime, when indeed you ought to see justice done upon our accusers. And again, if a christian being accused only deny that name, you release him, not being able to charge him with any other offence: but if he stand to his name, you condemn him only for his confession; where indeed it were your duty rather to examine their manner of life, than what thing they confess or deny, and according to their demerits to see justice done."

I find that all his apologies stand upon most strong and firm proofs, denying, that the christians ought at the will and commandment of the emperor and the senate to do sacrifice to the idols: for which they being condemned, affirm, that they suffer open wrong; affirming moreover, that the true and only religion is the religion of the christians. Although Justin, did not so prevail with the emperor, as to cause him to love his religion, and become a christian, yet obtained thus much, that Antoninus writing to his officers in Asia, commanded them that those christians only who were found guilty of any trespass should suffer, and such as were not convicted, should not therefore for the name only be punished, because they were called christians.

Besides this Justin, there were at the same time in Asia, Apollinaris, bishop of Hieropolis, and Melito, bishop of Sardis, who exhibited learned and eloquent apologies in defence of Christ's religion, as Quadratus and Aristides above mentioned did to the emperor, whereby they moved him somewhat to stay the rage of his persecution. In like manner did this Apollinaris and Melito defend the cause of the christians. Of this Melito, Eusebius makes mention in his fourth book, and quotes certain parts of his apology in these words " The godly suffer persecution by occasion of certain proclamations and edicts proclaimed throughout Asia, for villanous sycophants, robbers, and spoilers of other men's goods, grounding themselves upon those proclamations, and taking occasion of them, rob openly night and day, and spoil those which do no harm. Which if it be done by your commandment, be it so; for a good prince will never command but good things, and so we will be contented to sustain the honour of this death. This only we most humbly beseech your majesty, that calling before you and examining the authors of this tumult and contention, your grace would justly judge whether we are worthy of cruel death, or quiet life. And then if it be not your pleasure, and that it proceedeth not by your commandment (which indeed against your barbarous enemies were too bad) the more a great deal we are petitioners to your highness, that hereafter you will vouchsafe to hear us, who are so vexed and oppressed with this kind of villanous robberies."

Thus much out of the apology of Melito, who in writing to Onesimus, gives us the benefit of knowing the true catalogue and the names of all the authentic books of the Old Testament, received in the time of the primitive church. Concerning the number and names whereof, Melito in his letter to Onesimus declares; how that returning into the parts where these things were done and preached, he there diligently inquired concerning the books of the Old Testament, the names whereof he subscribes, and sends to him as follows, the five books of Moses, (Genesis, Exodus, Leviticus, Numbers, Deuteronomy,) Joshua, the Judges, Ruth, four books of Kings, two books of Chronicles, the Psalms, Proverbs of Solomon, the book of Wisdom, the Preacher, the Song of Songs, Job, the prophets Isaiah, Jeremiah, Twelve Prophets in one book, Daniel, Ezekiel, Ezra. And thus much of this matter which I thought here to record, for it is not unprofitable for these later times to understand what in the first times was received and admitted as authentic, and what otherwise.

But to return to the apologies of Apollinarius and Melito, whether it was by the occasion of these apologies, or whether it was through the writing of Athenagoras, a philosopher, and a legate of the christians, is uncertain: but this is certain, that the persecution at that time was stayed.

After the death of Marcus Aurelius Antoninus, his son Lucius Antoninus Commodus succeeded, (A.D. 180,) who reigned thirteen years.

In the time of Commodus, although he was an incommodious prince to the senators of Rome, yet there was, notwithstanding, some rest from persecution through the whole church of Christ, by what occasion is not certain. Some think that it came through Marcia, the emperor's concubine, who favoured the christians; but however it came, the fury of the raging enemies was then somewhat mitigated, and peace was given by the grace of Christ unto the church throughout the whole world. At which time the doctrine of the gospel influenced the hearts of all sorts of people, and drew them to the true religion of God, insomuch that many, both rich and noble personages of Rome, with their whole families and households, joined themselves to the church of Christ.

The Emperor Commodus, upon one of his birth-days, having called the people of Rome together, clothed himself with great royalty, having his lion's skin upon him, and offered sacrifices to Hercules and Jupiter, causing it to be proclaimed through the city, that Her-

cules was the patron and defender of the city. There was the same time at Rome, Vincentius, Eusebius, Peregrinus, and Potentianus, learned men and instructors of the people, who, following the steps of the apostles, went about from place to place where the gospel was not yet preached, converting the Gentiles to the faith of Christ. These, hearing of the madness of the emperor, and of the people, began to reprove their idolatrous blindness, teaching in the villages and towns, all that heard them to believe upon the true and only God, and to come away from such worshipping of devils, and to give honour to God alone, who only is to be worshipped, exhorting them to repent and to be baptized. One Julius, a senator, hearing their preaching, was converted with others to the religion of Christ. But the emperor hearing thereof caused them to be apprehended, and to be compelled to sacrifice to Hercules, which when they stoutly refused, after divers grievous torments, they were at last pressed to death with leaden weights.

Julius being a senator of Rome, and now won by the preaching of these blessed men to the faith of Christ, did soon invite them and brought them home to his house, where being more fully instructed by them in the christian religion, he believed the gospel, and was baptized with all his family; he did not keep his faith close and secret, but with a marvellous and sincere zeal, openly professed it, wishing and praying that it might be given to him by God, not only to believe in Christ, but also to hazard his life for him. The emperor hearing that Julius had forsaken his old religion, and become a christian, forthwith sent for him, and said, " O Julius, what madness has possessed thee, that thou dost fall from the religion of thy forefathers, who acknowledged and worshipped their gods, and now dost embrace a new and fond kind of religion of the christians ?" Julius having now a good occasion to shew his faith, gave an account thereof to him, and affirmed that Hercules and Jupiter were false gods, and how the worshippers of them should perish with eternal damnation. The emperor hearing how he condemned and despised his gods, was very wrath, and committed him forthwith to the master of the soldiers, a very cruel and fierce man, charging him either to see Julius sacrifice to Hercules, or if he still refused, to slay him : and Julius continuing steadfast in the faith, was beaten to death with cudgels.

THE FIFTH PERSECUTION.

After the death of Commodus, Pertinax reigned but a few months, after whom succeeded Severus (A. D. 193), under whom the fifth persecution was raised against the christian saints : he reigned eighteen years, and for the first ten years was very favourable to the christians : afterward through sinister suggestions and malicious accusations of the malignant, he was so incensed against them, that he commanded by proclamations that the christians should be no more tolerated. Thus the rage of the emperor being inflamed against them, great persecution was stirred up on every side, whereby an infinite number of martyrs were slain about the year of our Lord 205, as Eusebius in his sixth book records. The crimes and false accusations objected against the christians are partly touched before; as sedition and rebellion against the emperor, sacrilege, murdering of infants, and eating raw flesh. It was also objected against them that they worshipped the head of an ass ; I find no certain cause whence this charge arose, except it were, perhaps, by the Jews. Also they were charged for worshipping the sun, because before the sun rose, they assembled together, singing their morning hymns unto the Lord, or else because they prayed towards the east : but they were specially accused, because they would not worship idolatrous gods.

The place where the force of this persecution most raged, was Africa. The number that suffered was innumerable. The first was Leonides, the father of Origen, who was beheaded. Origen being yet young, was fervently attached to the doctrine of Christ's faith, by the operation of God's heavenly providence, and partly also by the diligent education of his father who brought him up from his youth most studiously in all good lite-rature, but especially in the reading and exercise of the holy scripture, wherein he had such inward and mystical speculation, that many times he would ask his father questions of the meaning of this place or that place in the scripture, insomuch that his father would often un-cover his breast being asleep, and kiss it, giving thanks to God which had made him so happy a father of such a happy child. After the death of his father, all his goods having been confiscated to the emperor, Origen, with his poor mother, and six brethren were brought to such ex-treme poverty, that he sustained both himself and them by teaching a school : till at length, being weary of the profession, he transferred his study only to the know-ledge and seeking of divine scripture, and such other learning as conduced to the same.

They that write of the life of Origen, testify of him that he was of quick and sharp wit, very patient of labour, learned in various tongues, of a spare diet, of a strict life, and a great faster ; he was often in danger of being stoned of the multitude ; and sometimes by the provision of christian men had his house guarded about with soldiers, for the safety of those who daily resorted to hear his readings. Among others who resorted to him, and were his hearers, was Plutarch, who died a martyr ; and with him Serenus, his brother, who was burned ; Heraclides and Heron, who were both be-headed ; Serenus, who was also beheaded ; Rhais and Potamiena, who was tormented with pitch poured upon her, and martyred with her mother, Marcella, who died also in the fire.

Besides these that suffered in this persecution of Severus, one Andoclus, whom Polycarp had sent into France, because he had spread there the doctrine of Christ, was apprehended by Severus, and first beaten with staves and bats, and afterwards beheaded.

About the same time, Ireneus was martyred with a great multitude of others, for the confession and doc-trine of Christ. This Ireneus was a great writer, and great searcher of all kind of learning. After the mar-tyrdom of Photinus, he was appointed bishop of Lyons, where he continued about the space of twenty-three years. In the time of Ireneus the state of the church was much troubled, not only by outward persecution, but also by divers sects and errors then stirring, against which he diligently laboured and wrote much. The nature of this man, well agreeing with his name, was such, that he ever loved peace, and sought to set agree-ment when any controversy rose in the church. And therefore, when the question of keeping the Easter-day was renewed in the church between Victor, bishop of Rome, and the churches of Asia, and when Victor would have excommunicated them as schismatics, for disagree-ing from him therein, Ireneus, with other brethren of the French church, sorry to see such a contention among brethren for such a trifle, assembled themselves together in a council, and directing their letter with their common consent subscribed, sent unto Victor, entreating him to stay his purpose, and not to proceed in excommunicating his brethren for that matter. Al-though they themselves agreed with him in observing the Sunday Easter as he did ; yet with great reasons and arguments they exhorted him not to deal so rigor-ously with his other brethren, following the ancient custom of their country in that behalf. And besides this, he wrote divers other letters abroad concerning the same contention, declaring the excommunication of Victor to be of no force.

Not long after Ireneus, followed also Tertullian, a man expert both in Greek and Latin, having great gifts in disputing, and in eloquent writing, as his books de-clare, and as the commendation of all learned men testifies.

Such men God raised up from time to time, as pillars and stays for his poor church, as he did this Tertullian in these dangerous days of persecution. For when the christians were vexed with wrongs, and falsely accused by the Gentiles, Tertullian, taking their cause in hand, defended them against the persecutors, and against their slanderous accusations, declaring they were falsely belied and wrongfully persecuted, not for any desert of theirs, but only for the hatred of their name. And yet he proves in the same apology, that the religion of the christians was not impaired by persecution, but rather increased. "The more," (says he) "we are mown down of you, the more we rise up. The blood of chris-tians is seed. For what man, in beholding the painful torments, and the perfect patience of them, will not search and inquire what is the cause ? And when he has found it out, who will not agree to it ? And when he agrees to it, who will not desire to suffer for it ? Thus this sect will never die, but the more it is cut down, the more it grows. For every man seeing and wondering at the sufferance of the saints, is moved the more thereby to search the cause ; in searching, he finds it, and finding he follows it.

Thus Tertullian, in this time of persecution, defended the innocency of the christians against the blasphemy of the adversaries ; and moreover, for the instruction of the church, he compiled many works, some of which are extant, some are not to be found. Notwithstanding the great learning and many virtues of this worthy man, certain errors and blemishes are noted in his doctrine. This by the way will be sufficient to admonish the reader never to look for perfection in any man in this world ; however excellent he may be, some blemish or other joins itself with him.

And now, to return again to the order of bishops of Rome. After Eleutherius, succeeded Victor, (A. D. 185). This Victor was a great stirrer in the controversy of Easter-day, for which he would have proceeded in ex-communication against the churches of Asia, had not Ireneus, with the counsel of his brethren, repressed his violence. As to that controversy of Easter in those days of the primitive church, the original cause of it was this, as Eusebius, Socrates, Platina, and others record. It is certain that the apostles, being only attentive to the doctrine of salvation, gave no heed to the observation of days and times, nor did they bind the church to any ceremonies and rites, except those things mentioned in the Acts, (xv. 29), as things strangled and blood, which was ordained then of the Holy Ghost, not without a most urgent and necessary cause, touched partly in the history before. For when the murdering and blood of infants was commonly charged by the heathen persecu-tors against the christians, they had no other argument to help themselves, nor to refute the adversary, but only their own law, by which they were commanded to ab-stain, not only from all men's blood, but also from the blood of all common beasts. And, therefore, that law seems to be given by the Holy Ghost, and continued in the church so long as the cause, that is, the persecu-tions of the heathen Gentiles continued. Besides these, we read of no other ceremonies or rites, which the apos-tles greatly regarded, but they left such things free to the liberty of christians, every man to use his own discretion, for the using or not using thereof ; so that concerning all the ceremonial observations of days, times, places, meats, drinks, vestures, and such others, the diversity among men was not greatly noted, nor any uniformity greatly required.

The doctrine of christian liberty remained whole in the church till the time of Victor. Neither did the vio-lence of Victor take such effect, but that the doctrine of christian liberty was defended and maintained by means of Ireneus and others, and so continued in the church till after the council of Nice.

But to return to Victor again, we will shew what di-versity there was in observing the day of Easter. In the time of Pius, the question of Easter began first to be moved ; he decreed the observation of that day to be changed from the wonted manner of the fourteenth day of the moon, in the first month, to the next Sunday after. After him came Anicetus, Soter, and Eleuthe-rius, bishops of Rome, who also determined the same. Against these stood Melito, bishop of Sardis, Polycarp, and as some think, Egesippus, with other learned men of Asia. Which Polycarp being sent by the brethren of Asia, came to Rome, to confer with Anicetus in that matter ; and although after long debating, they could not agree. yet notwithstanding, they both communicated together with reverence, and separated in peace. And so the celebration of Easter-day remained as a thing indifferent in the church till the time of Victor, who, following after Anicetus and his fellows, and chiefly stirring in this matter, endeavoured by all means to draw, or, rather to subdue the churches of Asia to his opinions, thinking, moreover, to excommunicate all those bishops and the churches of Asia, as heretics and schismatics, who disagreed from the Roman order, had not Ireneus otherwise restrained him from so doing, (A. D. 191). Thus, then the uniformity of keeping that holy day first began to be required as a thing necessary, and all they accounted as heretics and schismatics, who dissented from the bishop and tradition of Rome.

With Victor, stood Theophilus, bishop of Cesarea, Narcissus of Jerusalem, Ireneus of Lyons, Palmas of Pontus, Banchillus of Corinth, the bishop of Ostroena, and others; all of whom condescended to have the celebration of Easter upon the Sunday, because they would differ from the Jews in all things as much as they might, and partly because the resurrection of the Lord fell on the same day.

On the contrary side there were divers bishops in Asia, of whom, the principal was Polycrates, bishop of Ephesus, who, being assembled with a great multitude of bishops and brethren of those parts, by the common assent of the rest, wrote to Victor, and to the church of Rome, declaring that they had ever from the beginning observed that day, according to the rule of scripture unchanged, neither adding nor altering any thing from the same; alleging, moreover, the examples of the apostles, and holy fathers their predecessors, as Philip, the apostle, with his three daughters at Hieropolis; also John the apostle and evangelist, at Ephesus, Polycarp at Smyrna, Thraseas, bishop and martyr at Eumenia; likewise of Sagaris, bishop and martyr at Laodicea; holy Papirius and Melito at Sardis. Besides these, seven bishops, also of his own kindred, and his own ancestors, all of whom observed the solemnity of Easter-day, after the same manner as we do now.

Victor, being not a little moved herewith, by letters again denounced against them (more bold upon authority than wise in his commission), violent excommunication, although by the wise handling of Ireneus and other learned men, the matter was staid, and Victor otherwise persuaded. What the persuasions of Ireneus were, partly appear in Eusebius (lib. 5. cap. 26), to this effect: That the variance and difference of ceremonies is no strange matter in the church of Christ, as this variety is not only in the day of Easter, but also in the manner of fasting, and in other usages among the christians; for some fast one day, some two days, some fast more. And this varying mode of fasting in the churches began not only in our time, but was among our fore-elders. And yet with all this diversity they were in unity among themselves, and so should we be; neither does this difference of ceremonies hinder, but rather commends the unity of faith. And he brings forth the examples of the fathers, of Telesphorus, Pius, Anicetus, Soter, Eleutherius, and such others, who neither observed the same usage themselves, nor prescribed it to others, and yet notwithstanding kept christian charity with such as came to communicate with them, not observing the same form of things which they observed, as appeared by Polycarp and Anicetus, who, although they agreed not in one uniform custom of rites, yet refused not to communicate together, the one giving reverence to the other. Thus, the controversy being taken up between Ireneus and Victor, the matter remained free to the time of the Nicene council.

After Victor, Zephirinus succeeded in the see of Rome, (about A. D. 203). To this Zephirinus two epistles are ascribed; but as of the epistles of other Roman bishops, so I say and verily suppose of this, that neither the style, nor the matter therein contained, nor the state of the time, warranted us to think of them otherwise than as forged letters; letters not written by these fathers, nor in those times, but crafty and wickedly packed in by some, who, to set up the primacy of Rome, have most pestilently abused the authority of these holy and ancient fathers, to deceive the simple church.

Severus, the persecutor, reigned eighteen years; and about the later time of his reign came with his army into Britain, where, after many conflicts with the Britons in the north, he cast up a ditch with a mighty wall made of earth and turfs, and strong stakes, to the length of one hundred and thirty-two miles from the one side of the sea to the other, beginning at the Tyne and reaching to the Scottish sea, which done, he removed to York, and there died, (A. D. 211), leaving his two sons Basianus, (surnamed Caracalla,) and Geta, joint emperors.

After Caracalla and Macrinus, Heliogabalus succeeded to the empire, who may rather be called a monster than a man, so prodigious was his life in all gluttony and filthiness. To let pass his sumptuous vestures which he would only wear of gold, and most costly silks; his shoes glistering with precious stones finely engraved, he never wore one garment twice, he was never two days served with one kind of meat; some days his company was served with the brains of ostriches, and another day with the tongues of popinjays and other sweet singing birds. When he was near the sea he never used fish; but in places far distant from the sea, all his house was served with most delicate fishes; at one supper he was served with seven thousand fishes, and five thousand fowls. He sacrificed young children, and preferred the most abandoned characters to the highest offices in the state, as public dancers, minstrels, charioteers, and such like; in one word, he was an enemy to all honesty and good order. And when he was foretold by his sorcerers and astronomers, that he should die a violent death, he provided ropes of silk to hang himself, swords of gold to kill himself, and strong poison in precious caskets to poison himself, if he should be forced thereto; moreover, he made a high tower, having the floor of boards covered with gold plate, and bordered with precious stones, from which tower he would throw himself down, if he should be pursued of his enemies. But, notwithstanding all his provision, he was slain of the soldiers, drawn through the city, and cast into the Tiber, after he had reigned two years and eight months, as witnesseth Eutropius; others say four years.

This Heliogabalus, having no issue, adopted as his son and heir Aurelius Alexander Severus, the son of Mammea, who began to reign A. D. 222, and continued thirteen years, who is much commended as being virtuous, wise, gentle, liberal, and hurtful to no man. Among his other virtues, it appears also that he was friendly and favourable to the christians.

And thus this good emperor continued the space of thirteen years; at length, at a commotion in Germany, he was slain with his mother Mammea. After him succeeded Maximinus, contrary to the mind of the senate, only appointed by the soldiers to be emperor. During the reign of Severus, although the church of Christ had not perfect peace, yet it had some tranquillity from persecution.

At this time were converted Tiburtius, and Valerianus, the husband of Cecilia, who both, being noblemen of Rome, remained constant in the faith unto the end and suffered martyrdom. Of this Cecilia it is written that after she had brought Valerian her husband, and Tiburtius his brother to the knowledge and faith of Christ, and with her exhortations had made them constant unto martyrdom, she was apprehended and brought to the idols to do sacrifice; which, when she abhorred to do, she was to be presented before the judge to have the condemnation of death. In the meantime, the serjeants and officers who were about her, beholding her comely beauty, and her prudent conversation, began with many persuasive words to solicit her to favour herself, and such excellent beauty, and not to cast herself away, &c. But she so replied to them with reasons and godly exhortations, that by the grace of Almighty God their hearts began to kindle, and at length to yield to that religion, which before they persecuted. She perceiving this, desired of the judge a little respite, which being granted, she sent for Urbanus, the bishop, home to her house, to establish and ground them in the faith of Christ; and so they, with divers others, were baptized, both men and women, to the number (as the history says) of four hundred persons, among whom was one Gordian, a nobleman. This done, this blessed martyr was brought before the judge, where she was condemned, and inclosed in a hot bath; but remaining there a whole day and night without any hurt, she was brought out again, and was beheaded.

Under the same Alexander Severus, various others are there said to have suffered martyrdom, as one Agapetus, of the age of fifteen years, who, being apprehended and condemned at Preneste in Italy, because he would not sacrifice to idols, was assailed with sundry torments:—first, scourged with whips, then hanged up by the feet, and after having hot water poured upon him, at last was cast to the wild beasts.

Also, with the same Agapetus is numbered Calepodius, a minister of Rome, whose body was first drawn through the city of Rome, and afterwards cast into the Tiber.

Then follows Pammachius, a senator of Rome, with his wife and children, and others, both men and women, to the number of forty-two. Also, another noble senator of Rome, named Simplicius, all which together, in one day, had their heads smitten off, and hanged up in divers gates of the city, for a terror of others, that none should profess the name of Christ.

Besides these suffered also Quiritius, a nobleman of Rome, who, with his mother Julia, and a great number more, were likewise put to death.

Also, Tiberius and Valerianus, citizens of Rome, and brethren, suffered the same time, being bruised and broken with bats, and afterwards beheaded.

Also, Martina, a christian maiden, who, after divers bitter punishments, being constant in her faith, suffered in like manner by the sword.

THE SIXTH PERSECUTION.

After the death of the Emperor Alexander Severus, who, with his mother Mammea (as is said) was murdered in Germany, followed Maximinus, chosen by the will of the soldiers, rather than by the authority of the senate, (A.D. 235.) who raised up the sixth persecution against the christians, especially against the teachers and leaders of the church, thinking thereby the sooner to vanquish the rest, if the captains were removed out of the way. In the time of this persecution, Origen wrote his book on martyrdom, which book, if it were extant, would give us some knowledge of such as suffered in this persecution, who are now unknown, and no doubt but they were a great number, and would have been still greater, had not the provident mercy of God shortened his days, and bridled his tyranny, for he reigned but three years. After him succeeded Gordian, (A.D. 238), a man no less studious for the utility of the commonwealth, than mild and gentle to the christians. This Gordian, after he had governed the empire of Rome with much peace and tranquillity for six years, was slain by Philip, the emperor after him.

In the days of these emperors above recited, was Pontianus, bishop of Rome, who succeeded next after Urban, (A.D. 230). He was banished under Maximinus, and died in the beginning of the reign of Gordian. In his decretal epistles, (which seem likewise to be forged), he appears very devout, after the example of other bishops, to uphold the dignity of priests, and of clergymen, saying, that God has them so familiar with him, that by them he accepts the offerings and oblations of others, he forgives their sins, and reconciles them unto him. Also, that they make the body of the Lord with their own mouth, and give it to others, &c. How this doctrine stands with the testament of God, and the glory of Christ, let the reader use his own judgment.

Other notable fathers also in the same time were raised up in the church, as Philetus, bishop of Antioch, and after him Zebenus, bishop of the same place.

To these also may be added Ammonius, the schoolmaster of Origen, and also the kinsman of Porphyry, the great enemy of Christ. As he left various books in defence of Christ's religion, so, also, he constantly persevered in the doctrine of Christ, which he had received in the beginning.

After the decease of Pontianus, bishop of Rome, succeeded Anterius, who, because he caused the acts and deaths of the martyrs to be written, was put to martyrdom himself, by Maximinus the judge. Next to this bishop was Fabian, of whom more is to be said hereafter.

Hippolytus also was a bishop and a martyr. He was a great writer, and left many works in the church. He lived about A.D. 230.

Prudentius, in his Peristephanon, making mention of great heaps of martyrs buried by threescore together, speaks also of Hippolytus, and says that he was drawn with wild horses through fields, dales, and bushes, and describes a pitiful story.

After the Emperor Gordian, the empire fell to Philip, (A.D. 244), who, with Philip his son, reigned about six years. This Philip, with his son, and all his family, was christened and converted by Fabian and Origen, who by letters exhorted him and Severa his wife, to be baptized, being the first of all the emperors that brought in christianity into the imperial seat. However, Pomponius Letus reports him to be a dissembling prince; this is certain, that for his christianity he was slain, with his son, by Decius, one of his captains.

THE SEVENTH PERSECUTION.

Philip being slain, Decius invaded the crown, (A.D. 249). By him a terrible persecution was moved against the christians. The occasion of his hatred and persecution against them was chiefly because the treasures of the emperor were committed to Fabian.

This Fabian, being a married man, (as Platina writes), was made bishop of Rome after Anterius, in which function he remained to the time of Decius; who, either because Philip had committed to him his treasures, or because of the hatred he bare to Philip, caused him to be put to death, sending out, moreover, his proclamation into all quarters, that all who professed the name of Christ should be slain.

To this Fabian, Origen wrote one of his works. This Origen (as was stated before) was bold and fervent in assisting, comforting, exhorting, and kissing the martyrs that were imprisoned and suffered for the name of Christ. To the danger of his own life he continued teaching, writing, confuting, exhorting, and expounding, about the space of fifty-two years, and sustained great persecutions, but especially under Decius, as Eusebius testifies, declaring that for the doctrine of Christ, he sustained bands and torments in his body, racking with bars of iron, dungeons, besides terrible threats of death and burning.

Epiphanius writes, that being urged to sacrifice to idols, and taking the boughs in his hand, wherewith the heathen were wont to honour their gods, he called upon the christians to carry them in honour of Christ; which fact, the church of Alexandria not approving, removed him from their communion: whereupon Origen, driven away with shame and sorrow out of Alexandria, went into Judea, where, being in Jerusalem among the congregation, and there requested of the priests and ministers (he being also a priest) to make some exhortation in the church, he refused a great while. At length, by importunate petition being constrained, he rose up, and turning the book, as though he would have expounded some place of the scripture, he only read this verse: "God saith unto the wicked, what hast thou to do to, to declare my statutes, or that thou shouldest take my covenant in thy mouth," Ps. l. 16. Which being read, he shut the book, and sat down weeping and wailing, the whole congregation also weeping and lamenting with him.

Nicephorus, and others who write of this persecution under Decius, declare the horribleness of it to be so great, and the martyrs who suffered so innumerable, that he says, it is as easy to number the sands of the sea, as to recite the particular names of those whom this persecution devoured. Although, therefore, it be hard here to insert all persons that died in this persecution, yet such as are most notable in history, I will briefly touch by the grace of him for whose cause they suffered.

Alexander was appointed bishop of Jerusalem, where he continued a very aged man, above forty years governor of that church, till the time of Decius, when being brought from Jerusalem to Cesarea into the judgment place, after a constant and evident confession of his faith made before the judge, he was committed to prison, and there finished his life.

Babylas, bishop of Antioch, also died in prison under Decius.

We read in Chrysostom, a noble and long history of one Babylas, a martyr, who about these times was put to death for not suffering a certain emperor to enter into the temple of the christians after a cruel murder committed, the history of which murder is this: There was a certain emperor, who upon conclusion of peace with a certain nation, had received for hostage or surety of peace, the son of the king, being - of young and tender age, on condition that he should not be molested by them, and that they should never be vexed by him. Upon this the king's son was delivered, not without great care and fear of the father, to the emperor, who, contrary to promise, caused him in a short time to be slain. This horrible fact being committed, the tyrant with all haste would enter into the temple of the christians, where Babylas being bishop or minister, withstood him that he should not approach that place. The emperor, not a little insensed, in great rage bade him forthwith to be laid in prison with as many irons as he could bear, and from thence shortly after to be brought forth to death and execution. Babylas, going boldly to his martyrdom, desired after his death to be buried with his irons and bands, and so he was.

In the city of Antioch, Vincentius speaks of forty young maidens who suffered martyrdom in the persecution of Decius.

In the country of Phrygia, Vincentius also speaks of one Peter, who was apprehended, and suffered bitter torments for Christ's name, under Optimus the proconsul; and in Troada likewise, of other martyrs that there suffered.

Also in Babylon, divers christian confessors were found by Decius, and led away into Spain, to be executed there.

In the country of Cappadocia, in like manner, Germanus, Theophilus, Cesarius, and Vitalus suffered martyrdom for Christ. Mention is also made of Polychronius, bishop of Babylon, and in Pamphilia, of Nestor, the bishop, that died martyrs.

At Perside, Olympiades and Maximus; in Tyrus, also a maiden named Anatolia, and Audax gave up their lives for the testimony of Christ's name.

Eusebius moreover in his sixth book recites out of the epistles of Dionysius Alexandrinus, many that suffered at Alexandria; which extracts from Dionysius, as they are cited in Eusebius, I thought good here for the ancientness of the author, to insert, in his own words, and in our language, as he wrote them to Fabius, bishop of Antioch, as follows:

"This persecution," says he, "began not with the proclamation set forth by the emperor, but began a whole year before, by the occasion and means of a wicked person, a soothsayer, and a follower of wicked arts; who, coming to our city here, stirred up the multitude of the heathen against us, and incited them to maintain their own old superstition; whereby, they obtaining full power to prosecute their wicked purpose, declared all their religion to consist in idolatrous worship of devils, and in our destruction. And first flying upon a certain priest of ours, named Metra, they apprehended him, and brought him forth to make him speak after their wicked blasphemy; which, when he would not do, they laid upon him with staves and clubs, and with sharp reeds pricked his face and eyes, and afterward bringing him out into the suburbs, there they stoned him to death. Then they took a faithful woman, called Quinta, and brought her to the temple of their idols, to compel her to worship with them: which, when she refused to do, and abhorred their idols, they bound her feet, and drew her through the whole street of the city upon the hard stones, and so dashing her against millstones, and scourging her with whips, brought her to the same place of the suburbs, as they did the other before, where she likewise ended her life. This done, in a great outrage, and with a multitude running together, they burst into the houses of the religious and godly christians, spoiling, sacking, and carrying away all that they could find of any value. Such things as were of less value, and of wood, they brought into the open market, and set them on fire. In the mean time, the brethren withdrew themselves, taking patiently and no less joyfully, the spoiling of their goods, than they did of whom St. Paul testifies, Heb. x. 32.

"Amongst the rest that were taken, there was a certain woman well stricken in years, named Apollinia, whom they brought forth, and dashing all her teeth out of her jaws, made a great fire before the city, threatening to cast her into the same, unless she would blaspheme with them and deny Christ; whereat she pausing a little, as one that would consider with herself, suddenly leaped into the midst of the fire, and there was burned.

"There was also one Serapion, whom they took in his own house, and after they had assailed him with sundry kinds of torments, and had broken almost all the joints of his body, they cast him down from an upper loft, and so he completed his martyrdom. Thus was there no way neither private nor public, left for us, neither by day nor by night to escape, all the people making an outcry against us, that unless we uttered words of blasphemy, we should be drawn to the fire and burned. And this outrageous tumult endured a certain space, but at length, as the Lord would, the miserable wretches fell at dissension among themselves, which turned the cruelty they exercised against us, upon their own heads. And so had we a little breathing time for a season, while the fury of the heathen people by this occasion assuaged.

"Shortly after this, word was brought to us that the state of the empire, which before was something favourable to us, was altered and changed against us, putting us in great fear. And soon followed, the edict of the emperor so terrible and cruel, that according to the forewarning of the Lord, the elect (if it had been possible) might have been thereby subverted. Upon that edict such fear came over us all, that there were many, especially of the richer sort, of whom some for fear, came running, some were led by the occasion of time, some were drawn by their neighbours being cited by name, to those impure and idolatrous sacrifices. Others came trembling and shaking, not as men who should sacrifice, but who should be sacrificed themselves, the multitude laughing them to scorn. Some again came boldly to the altars, declaring themselves never to have been of that profession, of whom it is said, that they shall hardly be saved. Of the rest, some followed one part, some another, some ran away, some were taken; of whom certain continued constant in bands and torments; others again after long imprisonments, before they should come before the judge, renounced their faith. Some also, after they suffered torments, yet after revolted. But others being as strong as blessed and valiant pillars of the Lord's, fortified with constancy agreeing to their faith, were made faithful martyrs of the kingdom of God.

"Of whom the first was Julian, a man diseased with the gout, and not able to walk, being carried by two men, the old man confessing the Lord with a perfect faith, was laid upon camels, and there scourged, at length cast into the fire, and with great constancy was so consumed.

"As these were going to their martyrdom, there was a certain soldier, who in their defence, took part against them that railed upon them. For which cause the people crying out against him, he also was apprehended, and being constant in his profession, was forthwith beheaded.

"Likewise one Macar, being admonished and exhorted of the judge to deny his faith, and not agreeing to his persuasions, was burned alive.

"After these suffered Epimachus, and one Alexander,

who being long detained in prison and in bands, after innumerable pains and torments with razors and scourges, were also cast into the burning fire with four women, who all there ended their martyrdom.

"Also Ammonarion, an holy maiden, whom the cruel judge had long and bitterly tormented, because she had assured him before, that no punishment should cause her to yield to his request, and constantly performing the same, she suffered likewise martyrdom with two other women, one of whom was an aged matron, named Mercuria, the other was called Dionysia, being a mother of many fair children, whom yet she loved not above the Lord. These, after they could not be overcome by any torments of the cruel judge, but he rather ashamed and confounded to be overcome by feeble women, at length being past feeling of all torments, were slain with the sword.

"Heron, Ater, and Isidorus, and with them Dioscorus, also a child of fifteen years, were crowned with the same crown of martyrdom. The judge began with the child, thinking him more easy to be won with words to entice him, than with torments to constrain him. But he persisted immoveable, giving place neither to persuasions nor punishment. The rest, after he had grievously tormented them, being constant in their profession, he committed to the fire. The judge, greatly marvelling at Dioscorus for his wise answers and grave constancy, dismissed him, sparing his age to a longer respite; which Dioscorus is yet with us at this present, waiting for a long trial.

"Nemesion was accused as a companion of thieves, but being acquitted before the centurion, was then accused of christianity, and for that cause was brought to the president; who most unrighteously tormenting and scourging him double, at length burned him to death among the thieves, making him a blessed martyr.

"There were standing before the tribunal seat, certain of the warriors or knights, whose names were Ammon, Zenon, Ptolomeus, Ingenuus, and with them a certain aged man called Theophilus; who, when a christian man was examined, seeing him for fear ready to decline and fall away, did almost burst for sorrow within themselves, making signs to him with their hands, to be constant. This being noted of all the standers by, they were ready to lay hold upon them; but they preventing this matter, pressed up of their own accord before to the bench of the judge, professing themselves to be christians. Insomuch that both the president with the benchers, were all astonished, the christians, who were judged, were more emboldened to suffer, and the judges thereby terrified. This done, they departed from the place, glad and rejoicing for the testimony that they had given of their faith. Many others besides, were in other cities and towns rent and torn asunder by the heathen, among whom I will speak of one as worthy of memory.

"Ischirion who was in the service of a certain nobleman, was commanded of his master to make sacrifice, and for not obeying, was therefore rebuked: after persisting in the same, he was grievously threatened with sharp and menacing words. At last his master, when he could not prevail against him, taking a stake or pike in his hands, ran him through the body and slew him.

"What shall I speak of the multitude of those, who wandering in deserts and mountains, were consumed with hunger, thirst, cold, sickness, thieves, or wild beasts, of whose blessed victory they who are yet alive, are witnesses? In the number of whom, one I will speak of, among others, named Cheremon, bishop of Nilus, an aged man: he with his wife, flying to the mountains of Arabia, never returned again, nor ever could be seen after. And though they were sought for diligently by their brethren, yet neither they nor their bodies were found: many others there were, who flying to the mountains of Arabia were taken by the Arabs: of whom some with much money could scarce be ransomed, some were never heard of yet to this present day," (Eusebius, lib. 6. cap. 41, 42., &c.)

Thus much out of the epistles of Dionysius.

Moreover, Dionysius in another place, writing to Germanus, of his own dangers and of others, sustained in this persecution, and before this persecution of Decius, thus speaks, "I behold before the sight of God, I lie not, and He knoweth, I lie not, how that I having no regard of mine own life, and not without the motion of God, did fly and avoid the danger of this persecution. Yea, and also before that this persecution of Decius did rage against us, Sabinus the same hour sent a farmer to seek me, at which time I remaining at home waited three days for his coming. These three days being past, upon the fourth day, the Lord God so willing and commanding me to fly, and also marvellously opening to me the way, I with my children and many other brethren went out together. And that this did not come of myself, but was the work of God's providence, the sequel of those things declared, wherein afterward I was not unprofitable peradventure to some," &c.

Bergomensis makes relation of many martyred under Decius, as Meniatus, who suffered at Florence; Agatha, a maiden of Sicily, who is said to have suffered many and bitter torments, with imprisonment, with beatings, with famine, with racking, being rolled also upon sharp shells and hot coals.

It is impossible to recite all that suffered in this persecution, when whole multitudes went into wildernesses and mountains, wandering without succour or comfort, some starved with hunger and cold, some consumed with sickness, some taken and carried away by barbarous thieves.

Mention is made of Triphon, a man of great holiness, and constancy in his suffering, who for his confession of Christ's name, was afflicted with divers and grievous torments, and at length put to death with the sword.

When Decius had erected a temple in the midst of the city of Ephesus, compelling all that were in the city to sacrifice to the idols: seven christians were found, who refusing the idolatrous worship, were accused to the emperor to be christians. Although they openly professed and did not deny that they were christians; because, they were soldiers in the emperor's service, respite was given them for a time to deliberate with themselves, till the return of the emperor, who was then going to war. In the mean time, the emperor being departed, they taking counsel together, went and hid themselves in some secret caves of the mount Celius. The emperor returning again, after great search had been made for them, hearing where they were, caused the mouth of the cave to be closed up with heaps of stones, that they, not able to get out, should be famished within. And thus were those good men martyred.

Agathon, of Alexandria, for rebuking of certain persons scornfully deriding the dead bodies of the christians, was cried out and railed on of the people, and afterward accused to the judge, and was condemned to lose his head.

Also Paulus and Andreas, whom the proconsul of Troada gave to the people; being scourged, and drawn out of the city, were trodden to death with the feet of the people.

Among others that suffered under this wicked Decius, there is mention made of one Justin, a priest, and of Nicostratus, a deacon, also Portius, a priest, who is reported to have been the converter of Philip, the emperor.

Abdon and Sennas, two noblemen, because they had buried the christians, were accused to Decius, and brought to Rome; where, being commanded to sacrifice to dead idols, they would not obey; and were given to the wild beasts to be devoured.

One Secundianus was accused to be a christian, which profession when he stoutly maintained, he was commanded to prison. As the soldiers were leading him to the gaol, Verianus and Marcellianus confessed themselves christians, and were apprehended, and being commanded to sacrifice, they did spit upon the idols, and so they were beaten with trunchions, and afterwards were hanged and tormented, having fire set to their sides.

To give the history of the lives and sufferings of all, who were martyred in this terrible persecution, were too long, and almost infinite: briefly therefore to rehearse the names of such as we find alleged out of a treatise of Bede, shall be at this time sufficient. Under Decius suffered Hippolitus and Concordia, Hiereneus and Abundus, Victoria, a maiden, being noble personages of Antioch; Bellias, bishop of the city of Apollonia, Leacus, Tirsus, and Gallinetus. Nazanzo, Triphon in the city of Egypt, called Tamas, Phileas bishop, Philocomus, with many others in Perside, Philcronius a bishop of Babylon; Thesiphon bishop of Pamphilia, Neffor bishop in Corduba, Parmenius a priest, with divers more. In the province called Colonia, Circensis, Marianus, and Jacobus. In Africa, Nemesianus, Felix, Rogatianus a priest, Felicissimus. At Rome, Jovinus, Basileus, also two maidens named Ruffina and Secunda, Tertullianus, Valerianus, Nemesius, Sempronianus and Olympius. In Spain, Teragon. At Verona, Zeno the bishop. At Cesarea, Marinus and Archemius. In the town of Milan, Privatus the bishop, Theodorus, surnamed Gregorius, bishop of Pontus.

Now that I have recorded sufficiently of them, who under this tempest of Decius gave their lives to martyrdom for the testimony of Christ: it remains that a few words also be spoken of such as for fear or frailty in this persecution did shrink and slide from the truth of their confession. In the number of whom, was Serapion, a very aged man. Of whom Dionysius Alexandrinus writes to Fabius, declaring that this Serapion was an old man, who lived amongst them a sincere and upright life for a long time, but at length fell. This Serapion often desired to be received again, but no man listened to him, for he had sacrificed before. Not long after this, he fell into sickness, when he remained three days dumb, and benumbed of all his senses. The fourth day, beginning to recover a little, he called to him his sister's son, and said, "How long, how long (my son) do you hold me here? Make haste, I pray you, that I may be absolved. Call some of the ministers to me:" and so, saying no more, he held his peace again as dumb and speechless. The boy ran (it was then night) to the minister, who, being sick, could not come with the messenger, but said, "As he always desired that such as lay dying, if they wished to be received and reconciled, and especially if they required it earnestly, should be admitted, whereby with the better hope and confidence they may depart hence:" therefore he gave to the boy a little of the eucharist, desiring him to crumble it into the cup, and so to drop it into the mouth of the old man. With this the boy returned, bringing with him the holy eucharist. As he was now near at hand, before he had entered in, Serapion, the old man speaking again, said, "Comest thou, my son?" The messenger answered, "The priest is sick, and cannot come; but do as he desires you, and let me go." And the boy mixed the eucharist, and dropt it in softly into the mouth of the old man, who, after he had tasted a little, immediately gave up the ghost.

Dionysius, in his epistles, also writing to Fabius, and lamenting the great terror of this persecution, declares how many worthy and notable christians, for fear and horror of the great tyranny thereof, did shew themselves feeble and weak men; of whom, some for dread, some of their own accord, others after great torments suffered, yet afterwards revolted from the constancy of their profession. Also St. Cyprian recites with great sorrow, and testifies how a great number at the first threatening of the adversary, neither being compelled nor thrown down with any violence of the enemy, but of their voluntary weakness fell down themselves. "Neither," says he, "tarrying while the judge should put incense in their hands, but before any stroke was stricken in the field, turned their backs, and played the cowards; not only coming to their sacrifices, but pretending to come without compulsion, bringing moreover their infants and children, either put into their hands, or taking them with them of their own accord, and exhorting moreover others to do the like after their example."

Upon the occasion of these and others, which were a great number that fell and renounced the faith in this persecution of Decius, first rose up the heresy of Novatus, who, in these days, made a great disturbance in the church, holding this opinion, that they, which once renounced the faith, and for fear of torments had offered incense to the idols, although they repented,

yet could not afterward be reconciled, nor admitted to the church of Christ. This Novatus being first priest under Cyprian at Carthage, afterward by stirring up discord and factions began to disturb the bishopric of Cyprian, to appoint there a deacon against the bishop's mind or knowledge, also to allure and separate certain of the brethren from the bishop, all which is declared by Cyprian, (lib. 2. epist. 8.) After this, Novatus going to Rome, kept there the like stir with Cornelius, as the same Cornelius testifies in Eusebius, (lib. 6. cap. 43.) setting himself up as bishop of Rome, against Cornelius, who was the lawful bishop. He allured to him, to be his adherents, three or four good men and holy confessors, who had suffered great torments for their confession, whose names were Maximus, Urbanus, Sidonius, and Celerinus. After this he enticed three simple bishops about the coasts of Italy, to repair to Rome, under the pretence to make an end of certain controversies then in hand; he then caused them to lay their hands upon him, and to make him bishop, which they did. Thus, there were two bishops together in one church of Rome, Novatus and Cornelius, which was unseemly, and contrary to the discipline of the church. And hereupon arises the true cause and meaning of St. Cyprian, writing in his epistles so much of one bishop, and of the unity to be kept in ecclesiastical government. And in like sort also Cornelius himself writes of one bishop, saying, "He knew not that there ought to be one bishop in a catholic church," &c. This by the way, (not out of the way I trust,) I have briefly touched, to detect and refute the cavilling of the papists, who falsely apply these passages of Cyprian and Cornelius to maintain the pope's supreme mastership alone, over the whole universal church of Christ in all places; when their meaning is otherwise, how that every one catholic church or diocese ought to have one bishop over it, not that the whole world ought to be subject to the dominion of him that is bishop of Rome.

Now, to return to the history again. Novatus being thus bishop, took not a little upon him, endeavouring by all means to defeat Cornelius, and to allure the people from him; insomuch that when Novatus came to the distributing of the offerings, and should give every man his part, he compelled the simple persons every man to swear that they would adhere to him, before they should receive of the benediction, and of the collects, or oblations, holding both their hands in his, and speaking these words unto them: "Swear to me by the body and blood of our Lord Jesus Christ, that thou wilt not leave me and go to Cornelius." He held their hands, till they, swearing unto him, instead of Amen, (to be said at the receiving of the bread), should answer, "I will not return to Cornelius." Where, note by the way, that the Latin book of Christoferson's translation, in this place, craftily leaves out the name of bread. This story being written in Eusebius, and also contained in Nicephorus, although not in the same order of words, yet in effect drawn out of him, declares in plain words in both authors, that the sacrament of the body of Christ is termed with the plain name of bread, after the consecration.

And thus much of Novatus, against whom, as Eusebius testifies, a synod was holden at Rome, of sixty bishops, in the time of Cornelius, under the reign of Decius, (A. D. 251), whereby it may be supposed that the heat of the persecution at that time was somewhat calmed.

After Fabian, next succeeded to the bishopric of Rome, Cornelius, whom Cyprian notes to be a worthy bishop, and much recommended for his great virtue, chosen to that office, not so much by his own consent, as by the full agreement both of the clergymen, and also of the people.

In this persecution of Decius, he demeaned himself very constantly, and faithfully, sustaining great conflicts with the adversaries. By the commandment of Decius he was banished, and afterwards sent his letters to Cyprian, bishop of Carthage, and Cyprian again to him. This coming to the ears of Decius, the emperor, he sends for Cornelius, asking him how he durst be so bold to shew such stubbornness, that he neither caring for the gods, nor fearing the displeasure of his princes, durst give and receive letters from others? against the common wealth. To whom Cornelius answering cleared himself, declaring to the emperor, that he had, indeed, written letters, and received answers concerning the praises and honouring of Christ, and the salvation of souls, but nothing as touching any matter of the commonwealth. Then Decius, moved with anger, commanded him to be beaten with scourging, and so to be brought to the Temple of Mars, either there to do sacrifice, or to suffer the extremity. But he, rather willing to die, than to commit such iniquity, prepared himself to martyrdom. And so commending the charge of the church unto Stephanus his archdeacon, he was brought to the way of Appius, where he ended his life in faithful martyrdom.

And thus much of the tyranny of this wicked Decius against God's saints. Now to touch also the power of God's vengeance and punishment against him. Like as we commonly see a vehement tempest not continue long, so it happened with this tyrannical tormentor, who, reigning but two years, was slain with his son in battle with the barbarians, as he had slain Philip and his son before, so was he, with his son, slain by the righteous judgment of God himself.

Neither did the just hand of God plague the emperor only, but also all the persecutors of his word throughout all provinces and dominions; amongst whom the Lord, immediately after the death of Decius, sent such a plague and pestilence, lasting for the space of ten years together, as is horrible to hear, and almost incredible to believe. And although the greatness of the plague touched also the christians somewhat, yet it scourged the heathen idolators much more, beside that the order of their behaviour in the one, and in the other was very different. For, as Dionysius records, the christians, through brotherly love and piety, did not refuse one to visit and comfort another, and to minister to him what need required, notwithstanding it was great danger to them, for there were many who, in closing up their eyes, in washing their bodies, and interring them in the ground, took the disease, and soon followed them to their graves. Yet all this stayed them not from doing their duty, and shewing mercy one to another; whereas the heathens contrarily being extremely visited by the hand of God, felt the plague, but considered not the striker, nor did they consider their neighbour, but every man, shifting for himself, cared not one for another, but such as were infected, they would cast out of doors half dead to be devoured of dogs and wild beasts, some they let die within their houses without all succour, some they suffered to lie unburied, for that no man durst come near them; and yet, notwithstanding their care not to come near the sick, the pestilence followed them whithersoever they went, and miserably consumed them.

The Emperor Gallus, who, with his son Volusianus, succeeded Decius, (A. D. 251) was somewhat quiet in the beginning of his reign, yet shortly after, following the steps of Decius, he set forth edicts in like manner for the persecution of christians, although in this edict we find no number of martyrs to have suffered, but this persecution was only in the banishment of bishops or guides of the flock. We do not read of other sufferings or executions, for the terrible pestilence following immediately, kept the barbarous heathen otherwise occupied. Cyprian, being now banished, yet had no less care of his flock and of the whole church, than if he had been present with them, and therefore never ceased in his epistles continually to exhort and call upon them to be constant in their profession and patient in their afflictions. Amongst others whom he comforted in his banishment, (although he was in that case to be comforted himself,) were certain that were condemned to labour in the mines, whose names were Nemesianus, Felix, Lucius, with other bishops, priests, and deacons, to whom he writes, " How it is no shame but a glory, not to be feared, but to be rejoiced at, to suffer banishment or other pains for Christ; and confirming them in the same, or rather commending them, signifies how worthily they show themselves to be as valiant captains of virtue, exciting

both by the confessions of their mouth, and by the suffering of their bodies, the hearts of the brethren to christian martyrdom, whose example was and is a great confirmation to many, both women and children to follow the like; as for punishment and suffering, it is (saith he) a thing not execrable to a christian; for a christian man's breast, whose hope doth wholly consist in the cross, dreadeth neither bat nor club; wounds and scars of the body are ornaments to a christian man, such as bring no shame nor dishonesty to the party, but rather prefer and free him with the Lord. And although in the mines where the metals are digged there are no beds for christian men's bodies to take their rest, yet they have their rest in Christ; and though their weary bones lie upon the cold ground, yet it is no pain to lie with Christ. Their feet have been fettered with bands and chains, but he is happily bound of man, whom the Lord Christ doth loose; happily doth he lie tied in the stocks, whose feet thereby are made swifter to run to heaven. Neither can any man tie a christian so fast, but he runneth so much the faster for his garland of life. They have no garments to save them from cold, but he that putteth on Christ is sufficiently clothed. Do their hungry bodies lack bread? ' But man liveth not by bread only, but by every word proceeding from the mouth of God.' Your deformity (saith he) shall be turned to honour, your mourning to joy, your pain to pleasure and infinite felicity. And if this do grieve you that you cannot now employ your sacrifices and oblations after your wonted manner, yet your daily sacrifice ceaseth not, which is a contrite and humble heart, as when you offer up daily your bodies a lively and a glorious sacrifice unto the Lord, which is the sacrifice that pleaseth God. And though your labour be great, yet is the reward greater, which is most certain to follow; for God beholding and looking down upon them that confess his name, in their willing mind approveth them, in their striving helpeth them, in their victory crowneth them, rewarding that in us which he hath performed, and crowning that in us which he hath perfected." With these and such like comfortable words he doth animate his brethren, admonishing them that they are now in a joyful journey, hasting apace to the mansions of the martyrs, there to enjoy after this darkness an eternal light and brightness greater than all their sufferings, according to the apostle's saying, ' The sufferings of this present time are not worthy to be compared with the glory which shall be revealed in us,' Romans viii. 18.

And with like words of sweet comfort and consolation, writing to Seagrius and Rogatianus, who were in prison and bonds for the testimony of truth, he encourages them to continue steadfast and patient in the way wherein they have begun to run; for that they have the Lord with them, their helper and defender, who promises to be with us to the world's end; and therefore he exhorts them to set before their eyes, in their death immortality, in their pain everlasting glory, of whom it is written, " Precious in the sight of the Lord are the death of his saints." Although before men they suffered torments, yet their hope is full of immortality, and being vexed in small things, they shall be well requited in great matters; " For the Lord hath tried them as gold in the fire." He admonishes them that it is appointed from the beginning of the world, that righteousness should suffer here in secular conflicts; for so just Abel was slain in the beginning of the world, and after him all just and good men, the prophets also and the apostles sent of the Lord himself; unto whom the Lord first gave an example in himself, teaching that there is no coming to his kingdom, but by that way which he entered himself, saying by these words, " He that loveth his life shall lose it." And again, " Fear ye not them that kill the body, but are not able to kill the soul." And St. Paul likewise, admonishing all them who would be partakers of the promises of the Lord, to follow the Lord, saith, " If we suffer we shall also reign with him."

At the same time, Lucius, bishop of Rome, was sent to banishment, who succeeded next after Cornelius, (about A. D. 253), although he did not long continue in this banishment, but returned home to his church.

After him next came Stephen, bishop of Rome.

After the reign of Gallus, and his son Volusianus, Emilianus, who slew them both by civil sedition, succeeded in their place, who reigned but three months, and was also slain. Next to whom Valerian, and his son Galienus, were advanced to the empire, (A. D. 253).

About the changing of these emperors the persecution which first began by Decius, and afterward slacked in the time of Gallus, was now extinguished for a time, partly for the great plague reigning in all places, partly by the change of the emperors, (although it was not very long): for Valerian, in the beginning of his reign, for three or four years, was very courteous and gentle to the people of God, and well accepted of the senate.

Neither was there any of all the emperors before him, even of those who openly professed Christ, that shewed themselves so loving and familiar toward the christians as he did. In so much that his whole court was filled with holy saints, and servants of Christ, and godly persons, so that his house might seem to be made a church of God. But, by the malice of Satan, through wicked counsel, these quiet days did not endure very long. For in process of time this Valerian being charmed or incensed by a certain Egyptian, a chief ruler of the heathen synagogue of the Egyptians, was so far infatuated and bewitched, that through the detestable provocations of that devilish Egyptian, he was wholly turned to abominable idols, and to execrable impiety, in sacrificing young infants, and quartering bodies, and dividing the entrails of new-born children; and so, proceeding in his fury, he moved the eighth persecution against the christians, whom the wicked Egyptian could not endure, (A. D. 257).

THE EIGHTH PERSECUTION.

The chief original cause of this persecution is partly signified before, namely through the influence of the wicked Egyptian: but as this was the outward and political cause, so St. Cyprian shews other causes. We (says he) must understand and confess that this oppression and calamity which has wasted for the most part our whole company, and daily consumes it, rises chiefly of our own wickedness and sins, while we walk not in the way of the Lord, nor observe his precepts left unto us for our institution. The Lord observed the will of his Father in all points, but we observe not the will of the Lord, having all our mind and study set upon lucre and possessions, given to pride, full of emulation and dissension, void of simplicity and faithful dealing, renouncing this world in word only, but nothing in deed, every man pleasing himself, and displeasing all others. And therefore are we thus scourged, and worthily: for what stripes and scourges do we not deserve, when the confessors themselves (such as have stood the trial of their confession) and such as ought to be an example to the rest of well-doing, do keep no discipline. And therefore because some such there be, proudly puffed up with this swelling and unmannerly boasting of their confession, these torments come, such as do not easily send us to the crown, except by the mercy of God: some, being taken away by quickness of death, do escape the tediousness of punishment. These things do we suffer for our sins and deserts.

Finally, in the end of the epistle, Cyprian adds, "the Lord vouchsafes to many of his servants to foreshew the restoring of his church, and the stable quiet of our health and safeguard; after rain fair weather, after darkness light, after stormy tempest peaceable calm, the fatherly help of his love, the wont and old glory of his divine Majesty, whereby both the blasphemy of the persecutor shall be repressed, and the repentance of such as have fallen be reformed, and the strong and stable confidence of them that stand shall rejoice and glory."

As to the crimes and accusations in this persecution laid to the charge of the christians, this was the principal: that they refused to do worship to idols and to the emperors; and that they professed the name of Christ: besides, all the calamities and evils that happened in the world, as wars famine, and pestilence, were imputed to the christians. Against all which accusations Cyprian eloquently defends the christians.

Cyprian was born in Carthage, and was an idolater and Gentile, given to the study and practice of the magical arts: of his conversion and baptism he himself in his first book and second epistle, writes an eloquent history. His conversion was through the grace of God, and the means of Cecilius, a priest, and through the occasion of hearing the history of the prophet Jonas. Immediatiely upon his conversion he distributed among the poor all his substance, and being ordained a priest, was not long after constituted bishop of the church of Carthage.

He was courteous and gentle, loving and full of patience, and yet strict and severe in his office, according as the cause required: he was most loving and kind toward his brethren, and took much pains in helping and relieving the martyrs.

Now a few words touching his exile and martyrdom. He himself states that he voluntarily absented himself, lest he should do more hurt than good to the church, by reason of his presence; and from the desolate places of his banishment, wherein he was oftentimes sought for, he writes to his brethren. But after he returned out of exile in the reign of Valerian, he was the second time banished by Paternus, the pro-consul of Africa. But when Paternus was dead, Galienus Marimus succeeded him, who, finding Cyprian in a garden, caused him to be apprehended, and to be brought before the idols to offer sacrifice, and on his refusing, the proconsul condemned him to have his head cut off; he patiently and willingly submitted his neck to the stroke of the sword. And so this blessed martyr ended this present life in the Lord, (A.D. 259).

Now to speak something of his works and books left behind him, although all that he wrote do not remain: some are missing, some again are not written in his own name: but such as be certainly his may be soon discerned by the style and sense. Such is the eloquence of his phrase, and gravity of his sentence, vigour of wit, power in persuasion, so differing from all others, that he cannot easily be imitated. Of which extant books, as the eloquence is worthily commended by the school of rhetoricians, so is the authority of no less reputation, not only in this age of the church, but also among the ancient fathers.

As we have set forth the commendation of this blessed martyr Cyprian, we must take heed that we do not incur the old and common danger, which the Papists are commonly accustomed to run into, whose fault is almost always to be immoderate and excessive in their proceedings, making too much of every thing. Thus in speaking of the Holy Sacraments, they make more of them than the nature of sacraments require; not using them, but abusing them, not referring or applying them, but adoring them, not taking them in their kind, for things godly, as they are, but taking them for God himself, turning religion into superstition, and the creature to the Creator, the sign to the thing signified, &c. To the church likewise and ceremonies of the church, to general councils, to the blessed virgin Mary mother of Christ, to the bishop of Rome, &c; they are not contented to attribute that which is sufficient, but they exceed the bounds of judgment and of verity, judging so of the church and general councils, as though they never could, or never did err in any jot. That the blessed mother of Christ was blessed among women, and a virgin full of grace, the scriptures and truth allow: but to say that she was born without original sin, or to make of her an advocate or mother of mercy, there they run further than truth will bear. The ceremonies were first ordained to serve only for the sake of order, to which they have at length attributed so much that they have set in them a great part of our religion, yea, and also of salvation. And what thing is there wherein the Papists have not exceeded?

Wherefore, to avoid this common error of the Papists, we must beware in commending the doctors and writers of the church, that truth and consideration go with our commendation. For though this cannot be denied, but that Cyprian, and other blessed martyrs were holy men;

yet notwithstanding, they were men, that is, such as might have, and had their falls and faults; men, I say, and not angels, nor gods; saved by God, not saviours of men, nor patrons of grace. And though they were also men of excellent learning, yet with their learning they had also their errors; and though their books be (as they ought to be) of great authority, yet they ought not to be equal with the scriptures. And although they said well in most things, yet it is not therefore enough that what they said must stand for a truth. That pre-eminence of authority only belongs to the word of God, and not to the pen of man. For men and doctors, be they never so famous, there is none that is free from fault. In Origen (although in his time the admiration of his learning was singular) yet how many things there are, which the church now does not hold. For examining him by the scriptures, where he said well, they admit him, where otherwise, they leave him. In Polycarp, the church has corrected and altered that which he held in celebrating Easter. Neither can holy and blessed Ignatius be defended in all his sayings; as where he makes the fasting upon the Sunday or the Sabbath day as great an offence, as to kill Christ himself: (Ignat. Epist. ad Philip.) contrary to this saying of St. Paul, "Let no man judge you in meat or in drink," Col. ii. 16. Ireneus held that man was not made perfect in the beginning. He seems also to defend free will in man, in spiritual things. He says that Christ suffered after he was fifty years old. Tertullian is noted to be a millinarian; also to have been a montanist. He held also with Justin, Cyprian and others, that the angels fell first for the love of women. He defends free will of man after the corruption of nature, inclining also to the error of them, which defend the possibility of keeping God's law. Justin also seems to have inclined to the error of the millinarians, also of the fall of certain angels by women, of free will of man, of possibility of keeping the law, and such others. Neither was Cyprian wholly exempt from error, he, contrary to the doctrine of the church, held with rebaptizing such as were before baptized of heretics. Of Augustine likewise, of Ambrose, Jerome, Chrysostom, the same may be said, that all of them had their peculiar faults and errors, whereof it were too long and out of our purpose to treat at present.

About this time suffered also Sixtus II., bishop of Rome, who, being accused of being a christian, was brought with his six deacons to the place of execution, where he, with Nemesius and the deacons, were beheaded and suffered martyrdom.

Now let us enter upon the history of that most constant and courageous martyr of Christ, St. Lawrence, whose words and works deserve to be as fresh and green in christian hearts, as is the flourishing laurel tree. This thirsty heart, longing after the water of life, was desirous to pass unto it through the strait door of bitter death, when he saw his vigilant shepherd, Sixtus, led as an harmless lamb, of harmful tyrants, to his death.

Let us draw near to the fire of martyred Lawrence, that our cold hearts may be warmed thereby. The merciless persecutor, understanding this virtuous Levite, not only to be a minister of the sacraments, but a distributor, also, of the church riches, promised to himself a double prey, by the apprehension of one poor soul. First with the rake of avarice to scrape to himself the treasure of poor christians: then, with the fiery fork of tyranny, so to toss and turmoil them, that they should wax weary of their profession. With furious face, and cruel countenance, the greedy wolf demanded where this deacon Lawrence had bestowed the substance of the church? Who craving three days' respite, promised to declare where the treasure might be had. In the mean time, he caused a good number of poor christians to be congregated: so when the day of his answer was come, the persecutor strictly charged him to stand to his promise. Then valiant Lawrence, stretching out his arms over the poor, said: "These are the precious treasure of the church, these are the treasure indeed, in whom the faith of Christ reigneth, in whom Jesus Christ hath his mansion-place. What more precious jewels can Christ have, than those in whom he hath promised to dwell? For so

it is written, 'I was hungry, and ye gave me to eat; I was thirsty, and ye gave me to drink; I was houseless, and ye lodged me.' And again; 'Look what ye have done to the least of these, the same have ye done to me.' Oh, what tongue is able to express the fury and madness of the tyrant's heart! How he stamped, he stared, he ramped, he fared, as one out of his wits. His eyes glowed like fire, his mouth foamed like a boar, his teeth grinned like a hell-hound. Now he might be called, not a reasonable man, but a roaring lion. "Kindle the fire," he cried, "spare no wood. Hath this villain deluded the emperor? away with him—away with him. Whip him with scourges, jerk him with rods, buffet him with fists, brand him with clubs. Does the traitor jest with the emperor? Pinch him with fiery tongs, gird him with burning plates; bring out the strongest chains, and the fire-forks, and the grated bed of iron; put it on the fire! bind the rebel hand and foot; and when the bed is hot, on with him! Roast him, broil him, toss him, turn him: on pain of our high displeasure do every man his office, O ye tormentors." The word was no sooner spoken, but all was done.

After many cruel handlings, this meek lamb was laid, I will not say on his fiery bed of iron, but on his soft bed of down. So mightily God wrought with his martyr Lawrence; so miraculously God tempered his element, the fire, that it was not a bed of consuming pain, but a pallet of nourishing rest to Lawrence. Not Lawrence, but the emperor, might seem to be tormented: the one broiling in the flesh, the other burning in the heart.

O rare and unaccustomed patience! O faith invincible! that not only not burnest, but by means unspeakable dost recreate, refresh, establish, and strengthen those that are burned, afflicted, and troubled. And why dost thou so mightily comfort the persecuted? Because, through thee they believe in God's infallible promises. By thee this glorious martyr overcomes his torments, vanquishes this tyrant, confounds his enemies, confirms the christians, sleeps in peace, and reigns in glory. The God of might and mercy grant us grace, by the life of Lawrence, to learn to live in Christ, and by his death to learn to die for Christ. Amen.

Such is the wisdom and providence of God, that the blood of his dear saints (like good seed) never falls in vain to the ground, but it brings some increase: so it pleased the Lord to work at the martyrdom of this holy Lawrence, that by the constant confession of this worthy and valiant deacon, a certain soldier of Rome, being converted to the same faith, desired forthwith to be baptized of him; for which he was called to the judge, scourged, and afterwards beheaded.

Under the same Valerian, Dionysius, bishop of Alexandria, suffered much affliction and banishment, with certain other brethren: of which he writes himself. Dionysius, with three of his deacons, came to Emilianus the president, who signified to them the clemency of his emperors, who had granted them pardon of life, so that they would worship the gods of the empire; trusting, as he said, that they would not show themselves ungrateful to the clemency of them which so gently did exhort them. To this Dionysius said: "We worship not many, nor divers gods, but only that one God, who is the Creator of all things, and hath committed to our lords, Valerian and Galien, the government of their empire, making to him our prayers incessantly, for their prosperous health and continuance." Then the president said: "And what hurt is it, if you both worship your God, what god soever he be, and these our gods also?" Dionysius answered, "We worship none other, but as we have said." Emilianus the president, said, "I see you are ungrateful men, and consider not the benignity of the emperor; wherefore you shall remain no longer in this city, but shall be sent out to the parts of Libya; neither shall it be lawful for you to collect your assemblies, or to resort, as ye are wont, to your burial places: And if any of you shall be found out of your places, where you are appointed, at your peril be it." Dionysius, speaking of himself, saith: "Although I was sick, yet he urged me so strictly to depart, that he would not give me one day's respite. And yet neither am I altogether absent from the society of the Lord's flock; I am absent in body, yet present in spirit; and a great congregation remained with me, as well of those brethren which followed me out of the city, as also of them which were remaining there out of Egypt. And there the Lord opened to me the door of his word: although at first I was persecuted and stoned among them, yet afterward a great number of them turned from their idols, and were converted to the Lord; and so the word was preached to them: which ministry, after we had accomplished there, the Lord removed us to another place. For Emilianus translated us to more sharp and stricter places of Libya."

Moreover, Dionysius, making mention in his epistle of them which were afflicted in this persecution of Valerian, says, "It were superfluous here to recite the names, peculiarly of all our brethren slain in this persecution; this is certain, that there were men, women, young men, maidens, old wives, soldiers, simple innocents, and of all sorts and ages of men; of whom some with scourgings and fire, some with the sword, obtained the victory, and got the crown. Some continued a great time, and yet have been reserved. In which number I am reserved hitherto, to some other time known unto the Lord, who saith, ' In the time accepted I have heard thee, and in the day of salvation I have helped thee,' &c. Neither does the president yet cease cruelly murdering such as are brought before him, tearing some with torments, imprisoning and keeping some in custody, commanding that no man should come to them, inquiring also who resorted unto them. Yet, notwithstanding, God comforts the afflicted with cheerfulness, and the daily resort of the brethren."

As touching Dionysius himself, the histories report, that he survived all these troubles and persecutions, by the providence of God, and lived to about the year A.D. 268, and so departed in peace in great age.

In Cesarea Palestine, suffered also at the same time, Priscus, Malchus and Alexander, which three dwelling in the country, and good men, seeing the valiant courage of the christians, so boldly to venture, so constantly to stand, and so patiently to suffer in this persecution, began to accuse their own cowardly negligence, to see others so zealous and valiant, and themselves so cold and faint-hearted: so, consulting and agreeing with themselves, they came to Cesarea, and declared what they were, and obtained the end they came for, being given to the wild beasts.

There suffered also in Africa, three constant maidens, Maxima, Donatilla, and Secunda, who had vinegar and gall given for their drink, then were tried with scourges, after that were tormented upon the gibbet, and rubbed with lime, then were scorched upon the fiery grid-iron, and at last were cast to the wild beasts.

In Simela, a city in Italy, one Pontius being apprehended, by the commandment of Claudius the president, was first hanged upon the rack, and was then cast to the wild beasts.

Zenon, bishop of Verona, is said also to have suffered martyrdom in the same persecution.

Fructuosus, bishop of Tarraconia, in Spain, with his two deacons, Augurius and Eulogius, suffered also martyrdom, being burned after six days' imprisonment in this persecution. The charge of the judge to the bishop was, "That he should worship the gods whom the emperor Galien worshipped." To whom Fructuosus, the bishop, answered, "Nay, I worship no dumb god of stocks and blocks, whom Galien worships, but I worship the lord and master of Galien, the Father and Creator of all times, and his only Son sent down to us, of whose flock I am here the pastor and shepherd." At this word, Emilianus answered again, "Nay, say not thou art, but say thou wast." And forthwith commanded them to be committed to the fire, where (as is said) their bands and manacles being loosed by the fire, they lifted up their hands to heaven, praising the living God, to the great admiration of them that stood by, praying also that the element might work his full force upon them, and speedily dispatch them.

And thus continued wicked Valerian in his tyranny against the saints of Christ. But as all the tyrants before, and oppressors of the christians had their deserved reward at the just hand of God, " which rendereth to every man according to his works;" so this cruel Valerian felt the just stroke of his hand, whose indignation he had provoked; for making his expedition against the Persians, he fell into the hands of his enemies, (A. D. 260), where he led his wretched age in a more wretched captivity. Insomuch, that Sapor, the king of the Persians, used him for his riding-block: for whensoever the king would mount his horse openly in the sight of the people, Valerian was brought forth instead of a block, for the king to tread upon his back in going to his horseback. And so continued this blockish butcherly emperor with shame and sport enough to his final end.

Eusebius, in a certain sermon, declares a cruel handling of him, affirming that he was slain, writing in these words: "and thou, Valerian, for so much as thou hast exercised the same cruelty in murdering of the subjects of God, therefore hast proved unto us the righteous judgment of God, in that thyself hast been bound in chains, and carried away for a captive slave with thy gorgeous purple, and thy imperial attire, and at length also, being commanded of Sapor, king of the Persians, to be slain and powdered with salt, hast set up unto all men a perpetual monument of thine own wretchedness," &c.

Galien succeeded his father Valerian, (A. D. 260), and being (as is thought) terrified by the example of his father, removed, at least moderated the persecution stirred up by the edicts of Valerian.

By which some peace was granted under Galien to the church of Christ; although there were some who suffered, of whom was one Marinus. This Marinus being a warrior and a nobleman in Cesarea, stood for the dignity of a certain order, which by right was next to fall upon him, had not the envious ambition of him, that should follow after him, supplanted him both of office and life; for he accused him of being a christian, and therefore said that he was not to be admitted unto their offices, which was against their religion. Whereupon, Achaius, then being judge, examined him of his faith; who finding him to be a christian indeed, and constantly to stand to his profession, gave him three hours to deliberate and advise with himself. There was at the same time in Cesarea, a bishop named Theotechnus, who perceiving him to stand in doubtful deliberation and perplexity, took him by the hand and brought him into the church of the christians, laying before him a sword and a book of the New Testament, and desired him to take his free choice which of them both he would prefer. The soldier immediately without delay, ran to the book of the gospel, taking that before the sword. And thus, he being animated by the bishop, presented himself boldly before the judge, by whose sentence he was beheaded, and died a martyr.

After the death of Galien, followed Claudius, a quiet emperor, (A.D. 268). This Claudius reigned but two years, after whom came his brother Quintilian, who reigned only seventeen days, and was succeeded by Aurelian (A.D. 270); under whom Orosius numbers the ninth persecution against the christians.

THE NINTH PERSECUTION.

Hitherto from the captivity of Valerian, the church was in some quietness till the death of Quintilian, as has been declared; after whom Aurelian possessed the crown; who in the beginning of his reign shewed himself a moderate and discreet prince. He was severe of nature, and rigorous in correcting, dissolute in manners; and as his beginning was not unfruitful to the commonwealth, so neither was he any great disturber of the christians, whom he not only tolerated in their religion, but also their councils. Notwithstanding in progress of time, through sinister motion and instigation of certain about him, his nature, somewhat inclinable to severity, was altered to a plain tyranny; which tyranny he first shewed, beginning with the death of his own sister's son. After that he proceeded either to move, or at least to purpose persecution against the christians : although that wicked purpose of the emperor the merciful working of God soon overthrew. For as the edict or proclamation should have been denounced for the persecuting of the christians, and the emperor was now ready to subscribe the edict with his hand, he was suddenly terrified with lightning, and so stopped from his wicked tyranny. Not long after he was slain, (A.D. 275). Thus Aurelian rather intended than moved persecution.

After Aurelian, the succession of the empire fell to Tacitus, who reigned only six months ; his brother Florianus succeeded him, who reigned two months ; and after him followed Marcus Aurelius, surnamed Probus, (A.D. 276.)

Mention is made before of Eusebius, whom God stirred up to visit and comfort the saints that were in prison and bonds, and to bury the bodies of the blessed martyrs, not without great peril of his own life, who afterwards was made bishop of Laodicea. But before he came to Laodicea to be bishop there, while he remained at Alexandria, the city was besieged by the Romans. In which siege half of the city held with the Romans, and the other half withstood them. In that part which went with the Roman captain was Eusebius : with the other half that resisted the Romans was Anatholius, governor of the school of Alexandria. This Anatholius, perceiving the citizens to be in miserable distress of famine and destruction, sends to Eusebius, who was then with the Romans, and certifies him of the lamentable penury and peril of the city, instructing him moreover what to do in the matter : Eusebius, understanding the case, repairs to the captain requesting this favour of him, that so many as would fly out of the city from their enemies, might be allowed to escape and pass freely, which was granted. As Eusebius was thus labouring with the captain, Anatholius, on the other side, laboured with the citizens, saying, I shall counsel you in this miserable lack of things to remove out of your city all the women, young children, and aged men, with such others as are feeble and impotent, and not suffer them to perish here with famine. The senate hearing this, and understanding moreover the grant of the Roman captain promising them their safety, consented to the proposal of Anatholius ; who taking especial care of those that belonged to the church, calls them together, and telling them what they should do, and what had been obtained for them, caused them to leave the city. At their coming out, Eusebius was ready to receive and refresh them, whereby not only they, but the whole city of Alexandria was preserved from destruction.

By this short history of Eusebius and Anatholius, the reader may partly understand what was the practice of the prelates in those days in the church, that they were then only employed in saving life, and succouring the people among whom they lived ; to which practice if we compare the practice of our later prelates of the church of Rome, I suppose no little difference will appear.

The Emperor Marcus Aurelius Probus was a wise and virtuous prince and no less valiant in martial affairs, than fortunate in the success of the same. During this time we read of no persecution stirring in the church, but much quietness as well in matters of religion as also in the commonwealth.

Carus, with his two sons, succeeded next after Probus in the empire, (A.D. 282).

All this time we read of no great persecution stirring in the church ; it was in quiet and tranquillity to the nineteenth year of Dioclesian, (A.D. 303) ; so that the peace of the church, which God gave to his people, seems to continue above forty-four years. During which time of peace and tranquillity, the church of the Lord did mightily increase and flourish, insomuch that amongst the emperors themselves there were many which not only bore good will and favour to them of our profession, but also committed unto them offices and governments over countries and nations. What need to speak of those who not only lived under the emperors in liberty, but also were familiar in the court with the princes themselves, entertained with great honour and special favour beyond the other servitors of the court ? As was Dorotheus, with his wife, children, and whole family, highly accepted and advanced in the palace of the emperor ; also Gorgonius in like manner with various others, who, for their doctrine and learning which they professed, were in great estimation with their princes. Bishops of cities and dioceses were also held in the same reverence by the presidents and rulers where they lived ; who not only suffered them to live in peace, but also had them in great regard so long as they kept themselves upright, and continued in God's favour. Who is able to number at that time the mighty and innumerable multitudes and congregations assembling together in every city, and the notable concourses of such as daily flocked to the common oratories to pray ? For which cause they, not being able to be contained in their old houses, had large churches built new from the foundation. Eusebius says the church of Christ grew and shot up daily more and more, spreading through all quarters, which neither the envy of men could infringe, nor any devil enchant, nor the crafty policy of man supplant, so long as the protection of God went with his people.

But as the common nature of all men, being of itself unruly and untoward, always seeks and desires prosperity, and yet can never use prosperity well ; always would have peace, and yet having peace, always abuses the same ; so likewise, it happened with these men, who through great liberty and prosperity, began to degenerate, and one to work against another, striving and contending amongst themselves, on every occasion ; bishops against bishops, and people against people, moving hatred and sedition one against another. And thus, whilst they were given only to the study of contentions, threatenings, emulations, mutual hatred and discord, every man seeking his own ambition, and persecuting one another ; then, I say, the Lord, according to the voice of Jeremiah, took away the beauty of the daughter of Sion, and the glory of Israel fell down from heaven ; neither did he remember the footstool of his feet in the day of his wrath. And the Lord overturned all the comely ornaments of Israel, and destroyed all her gorgeous buildings, and according to the saying of the psalm, subverted and extinguished the testament of his servant, and profaned his sanctuary in the destruction of his churches, and in laying waste the buildings thereof. He stroke down to the ground, and diminished her days, and over all this poured upon her confusion. All these things were fulfilled upon us, when we saw the temples razed from the top to the ground, and the sacred scriptures to be burnt in the open market-place, and the pastors of the church to hide themselves, some here, some there ; others taken prisoners with great shame, were mocked by their enemies, when also according to the saying of the prophet in another place, contempt was poured out upon the princes, and they caused to go out of the way, and not to keep the straight path.

THE TENTH PERSECUTION.

By reason whereof (the wrath of God being kindled against his church) the tenth and last persecution arose against the christians, so horrible and grievous, that it makes the pen almost to tremble to write it ; so tedious that never was any persecution before or since to be compared to it for the time it continued, lasting the space of ten years together. Although this persecution passed through the hands of different tyrants, yet it principally bears the name of Dioclesian, who succeeded to the empire next after Carus and his sons. (A. D. 284).

After being established in the empire, and seeing on every side many commotions rising up against him, which he was not well able himself to sustain, in the beginning of his reign he chose for his colleague, Maximian. Which two emperors, chose two other noblemen, Galerius and Constantius, whom they called Cesars. Of whom Galerius was sent into the east parts against the Persians. Constantius was sent over to this our country of England, where he took to wife Helena, the daughter of king Coill, a maiden excelling in beauty, and no less in learning, of whom was born Constantine the Great.

All this while no persecution was yet stirred by these four princes against the church of Christ, but they governed the commonwealth quietly and moderately; wherefore God prospered their doings and affairs, and gave them great victories. By reason of which victories, Dioclesian and Maximian puffed up in pride, ordained a solemn triumph at Rome, after which triumph Dioclesian gave commandment that he should be worshipped as God, saying, that he was brother to the sun and moon, and adorning his shoes with gold and precious stones, commanded the people to kiss his feet.

And not long after began the great and grievous persecution of the christians, moved by the outrageous cruelty of Dioclesian, who commanded all the churches of the christians to be spoiled and cast to the earth, and the books of the holy scripture to be burned.

Thus most violent proclamations were set forth, for the overthrowing of the christians' temples throughout all the Roman empire. And this was the first edict by Dioclesian. The next proclamation that came forth, was for the burning of the books of the holy scripture; which was done in the open market-place; then next to that were edicts given for the displacing of such as were magistrates, and that with great ignominy, and all others whoever bore any office, imprisoning such as were of the common sort, if they would not abjure christianity, and subscribe to the heathen religion.

Not long after, new edicts were sent forth, for their cruelty not inferior to the first; for the casting of the elders and bishops into prison, and then constraining them with sundry kinds of punishments to offer to their idols. Then followed a great persecution among the governors of the church, among whom many stood manfully, passing through many exceeding bitter torments, many of them being tormented and examined in various ways, some scourged all over their bodies with whips and scourges, some with racks and intolerable raisings of the flesh, were excruciated, some one way, some another way put to death. Some again were violently drawn to the impure sacrifice, and as though they had sacrificed, when indeed they did not, were let go. Some neither coming to their altars, nor touching any piece of their sacrifices, were yet said by them that stood by, to have sacrificed, and so suffering that false defamation of their enemies, went quietly away. Others were carried and cast away as dead men, being but half dead. Some they cast down upon the pavement, and trailing them a great space by the legs, made the people believe that they had sacrificed. Others there were which stoutly withstood them, affirming with a loud voice that they had done no such sacrifice. Some of whom said they were christians, and gloried in the profession of that name: some cried, saying, that they neither had, nor would ever be partakers of that idolatry; and those, being buffetted on the face and mouth with the hands of the soldiers, were made to hold their peace, and so thrust out with violence. And if the saints seemed never so little to do what their enemies would have them, they were made much of; although all this purpose of the adversary did not prevail against the holy and constant servants of Christ. Yet there were many of the weak sort, who for fear and infirmity fell and gave over, even at the first brunt.

At the first coming down of these edicts into Nicomedia, a christian nobleman, moved by the zeal of God, after the proclamation was set up, went and took it down, and openly tore it in pieces, not fearing the presence of the two emperors, then in the city. For which act he was put to a most bitter death, which death he endured even to the last gasp with great faith and constancy.

What number of martyrs, and what blood was shed throughout all cities and regions for the name of Christ, can hardly be told. At that time the bishop of Sidon was martyred. Sylvanus, the bishop of Gazensis, with nine and thirty others, were slain in the metal-mines of Phenicia. Pamphilus, the elder of Cesarea, being the glory of that congregation, died a most worthy martyr.

In Syria, all the chief teachers of the congregation were first committed to prison, a most heavy and cruel spectacle to behold; and also the bishops, elders, and deacons, who were all esteemed as men-killers, and perpetrators of most wicked facts. After that, we read of another whose name was Tirannion, who was made meat for the fishes of the sea, and of Zenobius, a good physician, who also was slain with brickbats in the same place.

Eusebius mentions others who were not tormented to death, but every day terrified without ceasing; others that were brought to the altars and commanded to do sacrifice, who would rather thrust their right hand into the fire, than touch the profane or wicked sacrifice; also some others, that before they were apprehended, would cast themselves down from steep places, lest being taken they should commit any thing against their profession. Also two fair maidens, with their mother, who had carefully brought them up, even from their infancy in all godliness, being long sought for, and at last found, and strictly kept by their keepers, threw themselves down headlong into a river; and two other young maidens being sisters, and of a worshipful stock, indued with many goodly virtues, who were cast by the persecutors into the sea. But Sylvanus, the bishop of Emissa, the notable martyr, together with certain others, was thrown to the wild beasts.

The christians in Mesopotamia were molested with many and various torments; they were hanged up by the feet, and their head downwards, and suffocated with the smoke of a small fire; and also in Cappadocia, where the martyrs had their legs broken.

So outrageous was the beginning of the persecution which the emperor made in Nicomedia, that he refrained not from the slaughter of the children of emperors, neither yet from the slaughter of the chief princes of his court, whom a little before he made as much of, as if they had been his own children. Among whom was Peter, who suffered various torments, being stripped naked, and lifted up, his whole body was so beaten with whips and torn, that a man might see the bare bones; and afterwards they mingled vinegar and salt together, and poured it upon the most tender parts of his body; and lastly, roasted him at a soft fire, as a man would roast flesh to eat; and so this victorious martyr ended his life. Dorotheus and Gorgonius being in a great authority under the emperor, after various torments, were strangled with a halter; both of whom being of the privy chamber, when they saw the grievous punishment of Peter, their household companion, exclaimed, "Wherefore, O emperor, do you punish in Peter that opinion which is in all us? Why is this which we all confess accounted an offence in him? We are of the same faith, religion, and judgment that he is of." Therefore he commanded them to be brought forth, and to be tormented with like pains as Peter was, and afterwards hanged. After whom Anthimus, the bishop of Nicomedia, after he had made a notable confession, bringing with him a great company of martyrs, was beheaded. These men being thus dispatched, the emperor vainly thought that he might cause the rest to do whatever he pleased. To this end came Lucianus, the elder of the congregation of Antioch, and was martyred after he had made his apology before the emperor. (Eusebius, lib. 8. cap. 13.)

Hermanus also, that monster, caused Serena, the wife of Dioclesian the emperor, to be martyred for the christian religion; so much did the rage of persecution utterly forget all natural affections. Other martyrs of Nicomedia, as Eulampius and Eulampia, Agape, Irene, Chionia, and Anastasia, were bound hand and foot to a post and burnt. About that time there assembled together in their temple many christian men to celebrate the nativity of Christ, some of every age and sort. Maximian, thinking this a very fit occasion to execute his tyranny upon the poor christians, gave orders to burn the temple; the doors being shut and fastened round about, they came with fire, but first commanded the cryer with a loud voice to cry, That whoever would save his life should come out of the temple, and do sacrifice upon the next altar of Jupiter they came to; and unless they would do this they should all be burnt with the temple. Then one stepping up in the temple, answered in the name of all the rest, with great courage and boldness of mind, that they were all christians, and believed that Christ was their only God and king, and that they would do sacrifice to him, with his Father, and the Holy Ghost; and that they were now all ready to be offered to him. With these words the fire was kindled and enveloped the temple, and some thousands of men, women, and children were burnt. There was a city in Phrygia, to which the emperor sent his edicts, that they should do sacrifice to the gods and worship idols; all the citizens, the mayor himself, the questor, and chief captain, confessed that they were all christians. The city, upon this, was besieged and set on fire, with all the people. In Melitina, a region of Armenia, the bishops and elders were cast in prison. In Arabrace, Eustratius was martyred. This man, beholding the constancy of the martyrs, thirsted with the desire of martyrdom, for he had privily learned the christian religion. Therefore he professed that he was a christian, openly execrating the madness and vanity of the wicked heathens. He therefore being carried away, was tied up, being first most bitterly beaten. After that he was parched with fire put into his bowels, and then basted with salt and vinegar, and lastly, so scorched and bemangled with sharp and cutting shells, that his whole body seemed to be all one continual wound. After this he was carried away to Sebastia, where, with his companion Orestes, he was burnt. But at Alexandria, especially, the christians and martyrs suffered most notable conflicts. In this persecution of Alexandria, the principal that then suffered were Peter the bishop of Alexandria, with the elders of the same, most worthy martyrs; as Faustus, Didius, and Ammonius; also, Phileas, Hesichius, Pachiminus, and Theodorus; all of whom were bishops of the churches within Egypt, and besides them many other distinguished men. The whole legion of christian soldiers, which lay at Thebes in Egypt, under the christian Captain Mauritius, when they would not obey the emperor's commandment, touching the worshiping of images, were decimated to death once, and then again, and at last, through the exhortation of Mauritius, died all together like constant martyrs. Likewise, at Antino, divers christian soldiers, notwithstanding they were seriously dissuaded, suffered death together, among whom were Ascla, Philemon, and Apollonius. And also in the other parts of Africa and Mauritania there was great persecution. Also in Sammium, of which place Chronicon makes mention, and Sicily, where there were seventy-nine martyrs slain for the profession of Christ.

Now let us come to Europe: at Nicopolis, the martyrs were most miserably and pitifully handled. Euphemia suffered in Chalcedon.

Agricola and Vitalis, at Bohemia. And at Aquileia, the emperor commanded every man to kill the christians. And among those martyrs were Felices and Fortunatus. In all places of Italy the persecution became great. In France, Rectionarus played the cruel hellhound, of whose great cruelty against the christians many histories are full. And at Massilia, Maximian set forth his decree, that either they should all do sacrifice unto the heathen gods, or else be all slain with various kinds of torments. Therefore many martyrs died there for the glory of Christ.

In many places of Spain, there was great persecution, as at Emerita, where Eulalia suffered; and Adula, where Vincentius, Sabina, and Christina also suffered. At Toletum. Leucadia the virgin, suffered; at Cesarea Augusta, eighteen were put to death, besides a great number of other martyrs who suffered under Decian, the governor, who afflicted with persecution all the coasts of Spain. Rectionarus made such persecution at Trevers that the blood of the christian men that were slain ran like small brooks, and coloured great and main rivers. Neither yet did this suffice him, but from thence he sent certain horsemen with his letters, commanding them to ride into every place, and charge all such as had taken and apprehended any christians, that they should immediately put them to death.

Bede says, that this persecution reached even to the Britains. And the chronicle of Martinus, and the "Nosegay of Time" declare, that all the christians in Britain were utterly destroyed. The kinds of death and punishment were so great and horrible, as no man is able to express. In the beginning, the emperor threatened them with bonds and imprisonment; but within a while, when he began to work the matter in good earnest, he devised innumerable sorts of torments and punishments, as whippings, and scourgings, rackings, horrible scrapings, sword, fire, and shipboats, wherein a great number being put were sunk and drowned in the bottom of the sea. Also hanging them upon crosses, binding them to the bodies of dead trees, with their heads downward, hanging them by the middles upon gallows till they died for hunger; throwing them alive to such kind of wild beasts as would devour them; as lions, bears, leopards, and wild bulls. Pricking and thrusting them with bodkins and talons of beasts till they were almost dead; lifting them up on high with their heads downward, with other sorts of punishments most tragical, or rather tyrannical and pitiful to describe. As first, the binding of them to trees, and to the boughs thereof; the pulling and tearing asunder of their members and joints, being tied to the boughs and arms of trees. The mangling of them with axes, the choaking of them with smoke by small fires, the dismembring of their hands, ears and feet, with other joints; the holy martyrs of Alexandria suffered scorching and broiling with coals, not unto death, but every day renewed. With such kind of torments the martyrs at Antioch were afflicted. But in Pontus, other horrible punishments, and fearful to be heard, did the martyrs of Christ suffer; some of whom had sharp bodkins thrust in their finger ends under their nails; some were sprinkled with boiling lead, having their most necessary members cut from them; others suffering most intolerable, and undurable torments and pains.

Phileas, the bishop of the Thumitans, a man singularly well learned, hath described, in his epistle to the Thumitans, which epistle is to be found in Eusebius, (lib. viii. cap. 10), how great the persecution which reigned in Alexandria was, and with how many and sundry kinds of new devised punishments the martyrs were afflicted, of which we will here briefly recite a part. "Because every man might torment the holy martyrs as they pleased, some beat them with cudgels, some with rods, some with whips, some with thongs, and some with cords; and this example of beating was executed with much cruelty. For some of them having their hands bound behind their backs, were lifted up upon timber logs, and with certain instruments their members and joints were stretched forth, whereupon their whole bodies hanging were subject to the will of the tormentors, who were commanded to afflict them with all manner of torments, and not on their sides only (as homicides were) but all over their bodies, thighs, and legs, they scratched them with the talons and claws of wild beasts. Others were seen to hang by one hand upon the engine, whereby they might feel the more grievous pulling out of the rest of their joints and members. Others were bound to pillars with their faces turned to the wall, having no support under their feet, and were violently drawn down with the weight of their bodies. And this they suffered, not only during the time of their examination, and while the sheriff had to do with them, but also the whole day long. And whilst the judge went thus from one to another, he appointed certain officers to attend upon those he left, that they might not be let down, until either through the intolerableness of the pain, or by the extremity of the cold, they were near the point of death. And, further, they were commanded that they should not shew one spark of mercy or compassion upon us, but so extremely and furiously did they deal with us, as though our souls and bodies should have died together."

Thus wrote Phileas to the church where he was bishop, before he received the sentence of death, being yet in bonds; and in the same he exhorts his brethren constantly to persist after his death, in the truth of Christ.

But as all their torments were marvellous and notable for their horribleness, and most grievous and sharp, yet, notwithstanding, these martyrs were neither dismayed nor overcome, but rather confirmed and strengthened, so cheerfully and joyfully they sustained whatever was put upon them. Eusebius says, that he himself beheld the great persecution that was done in Thebaide; insomuch that the very swords of the hangmen and persecutors being blunt with the great and often slaughter, they, themselves, for weariness sat down to rest, and others were obliged to take their places. And yet, notwithstanding all this, the murdered christians shewed the marvellous readiness, willingness, and divine fortitude with which they were endowed; with courage, joy, and smiling, receiving the sentence of death pronounced upon them, and sung even unto the last gasp, hymns and psalms to God.

Some there were, also, that were overcome with fear and threatenings, and by their own infirmities, and went back, among whom Socrates names Miletius; and Athanasius, in his second apology, names the bishop of Licus. Of the fall of Marcellinus, the bishop of Rome, I will speak afterwards; for he being persuaded by others, and especially of the Emperor Dioclesian himself, did sacrifice to the idols, whereupon he was excommunicated. The number of the martyrs increased daily, sometimes ten, sometimes twenty were slain at once; sometimes thirty, and oftentimes threescore, and sometimes a hundred in one day, men, women, and children, by divers kinds of death. Also Damasus, Beda, Orosius, Honorius, and others do witness, that there were slain in this persecution by the names of martyrs, within the space of thirty days, seventeen thousand persons, besides a great number that were condemned to the metal mines and quarries with like cruelty.

At Alexandria, Peter the bishop, with three hundred others were slain with axes; Gereon was beheaded at Colonia Agrippina, with three hundred of his fellows; Mauritius, the captain of the christian soldiers, with his fellows, six thousand six hundred and sixty-six. Victor, in the city of Troy, now called Xanthus, with his fellows, three hundred and threescore were slain. Reginus recites the names of many other martyrs, to the number of one hundred and twenty.

And as mention has been made of Mauritius and Victor, I thought good here to insert a more particular account of them taken out of Ado, and other historians, as follows:

"Mauritius came out of Syria into France and Italy, being captain of the band of the Theban soldiers, to the number of six thousand six hundred and sixty, being sent for by Maximian, to go against the rebellious Bangandes; but rather, as it should seem, by the reason of the tyrant, who thought he might better in these quarters use his tyranny upon the christians, than in the eastern part. These Thebans, with Mauritius the captain, after they had entered into Rome, were confirmed in the faith by Marcellus the blessed bishop, promising by oath that they would rather be slain of their enemies, than forsake that faith which they had received. At that time the Cesareans were encamped not far from the town called Ottodor, where Maximian offered sacrifice to his devils, and called all the soldiers both of the east and west to the same, strictly charging them by the altars of his gods, that they would fight against those rebels the Bangandes, and persecute the christian enemies of the emperor's gods; which commandment was shewed to the Theban host, who were also encamped about the river Rhone; but they would in no wise come to Ottodor, for every man agreed rather to die in that place than either to sacrifice to the gods, or bear armour against the christians. The emperor being very wroth with them, commanded every tenth man of that whole band to be put to the sword, to which they committed their necks with great joy. To which notable and great strength of faith, Mauritius himself was a great encourager, who exhorted and animated his soldiers both to fortitude and constancy. Who, being called to the emperor, answered him thus, 'We are, O emperor! your soldiers, but yet also, to speak freely, the servants of God. We owe to thee service of war, to him innocency. Of thee we receive for our labour wages; of him the beginning of life. But in this we may in no wise obey thee, O emperor! to deny God our author and Lord, and not only ours, but your Lord likewise. If we be not so extremely forced that we offend him, doubtless, as we have hitherto done, we will yet obey you; but we will rather obey him than you. We offer here our hands against any other enemies; but to defile our hands with the blood of innocents, that we may not do. These right hands of ours have skill to fight against the wicked and true enemies; but to spoil and murder the godly and citizens, they have no skill at all. We have in remembrance how we took armour in hand, for the defence of the citizens, and not against them. We fought always for justice sake, piety, and for the health of innocents. These have been always the rewards of our perils and labour. We have fought in the quarrel of faith, which in no wise we can keep to you, if we do not shew the same to our God. We first sware upon the sacraments of our God, then afterward to the king; and do you think the second will avail us, if we break the first? By us you would plague the christians to do which feat we are only commanded by you. We are here ready to confess God the author of all things, and believe in his son Jesus Christ our Lord. We see before our eyes our fellows, and the partakers of our labours put to the sword, and we sprinkled with their blood. We have not bewailed nor mourned the death of our blessed companions, but rather have been glad, and have rejoiced thereat, for that they have been counted worthy to suffer for the Lord their God. The extreme necessity of death cannot move us against your majesty, neither yet any desperation, O emperor, which is wont in venturous affairs to do much, shall arm us against you. Behold here we cast down our weapons, and resist not, for that we had rather to be killed, than kill; and die guiltless, than live guilty. Whatsoever more ye will command, appoint, and enjoin us, we are here ready to suffer, yea, both fire and sword, and whatsoever other torments. We confess ourselves to be christians, we cannot persecute christians, nor will do sacrifice to your devilish idols.'

"With which answer, the emperor, being much displeased, commanded the second time the tenth man of those that were left to be murdered. That cruelty also being accomplished, at length, when the christian soldiers would in no wise condescend to his mind, he set upon them with his whole host, both footmen and horsemen, and charged them to kill them all; they making no resistance, but throwing down their armour, yielded their lives to the persecutors, and offered to them their naked bodies, and were thus slain.

"Victor was not of that band; but being an old soldier, was dismissed for his age; he coming suddenly upon them as they were banqueting and making merry with the spoils of the holy martyrs, was bidden to sit down with them; who asking the cause of their great rejoicing, and understanding the truth thereof, detested the guests, and refused to eat with them. And then it being demanded of him whether he were a christian or no? he openly confessed that he was a christian, and ever would be. Upon which they rushed upon him, and killed him, and made him partner of the like martyrdom and honour.

Dioclesian and Maximinian, seeing the number of the christians rather increase than diminish, notwithstanding all the cruelty that they could show, were now out of all hope of rooting them out; and loathing the shedding of more blood, they at last ceased of their own accord to put any more christians to death. But yet they tormented great multitudes, thrusting out their right eyes, and maiming their left legs with a searing-iron, condemned them to the mines, not so much for the use of their labour, as for the desire of afflicting them.

When Dioclesian and Maximinian had reigned together emperors twenty-one years, they abdicated the throne, Dioclesian at Nicomedia, and Maximinian at Midiolan, both of them led a private life. (A.D. 305.)

In the beginning of this persecution, you heard how Dioclesian, being made emperor, took to him Maximinian. Also how these two governing as emperors together, chose two others as Cesars under them, namely, Galerius Maximinus, and Constantius the father of Constantine the Great. So Dioclesian and Maximinian being now displaced, the Imperial Dominion remained with Constantius and Galerius Maximinus which two divided the whole monarchy between them. Maximinus governing the eastern countries, and Constantius the western parts. Galerius Maximinus appointed Maximius and Severus to be the two Cesars. And these were the emperors and Cesars who, succeeding after Dioclesian and Maximinian, continued that persecution which Dioclesian and Maximinian began, save only that Constantius, with his son Constantine was no great doer therein, but rather a maintainer and supporter of the christians. Which Constantius was a prince very excellent, civil, meek, gentle, liberal, and desirous to do good unto those who had any private authority under him. To these virtues he added yet a more worthy ornament, that is, devotion, love, and affection towards the word of God, which caused great peace and tranquillity, in all his provinces. He neither levied any wars contrary to piety and christian religion, neither did he destroy the churches, but commanded that the christians should be preserved and defended.

Galerius Maximinus, joint-emperor with Constantius, was so great an idolater, that he built up temples in every city, and repaired those that were fallen in decay. And he chose out the most worthy of his political magistrates to be the idols' priests, and ordained that they should execute their office with great authority and dignity, and also with warlike pomp. But he was much opposed to christian piety and religion, and in the eastern churches exercised cruel persecution.

He was at length revoked from his cruelty by the just judgment and punishment of God. For he was suddenly seized with a most extraordinary and desperate disease, which, beginning outwardly in his flesh, from thence proceeded to the inward parts of his body. The physicians not being able to cure him, he was at length put in remembrance that this disease was sent from God, and began to think of the wickedness that he had done against the saints of God, and so coming again to himself, first confessed to God all his offences, and then forthwith commanded all men to cease from the persecutions of the christians. Requiring moreover that they should set up his imperial proclamations for the restoring of their temples, and that the christians in their assemblies should devoutly pray to their God for the emperor. Then was the persecution stayed, and the imperial proclamations were set up in every city, containing the countermand of those things which were before decreed against the christians.

The governors therefore of every province, released all such prisoners as were condemned to the mines, and to perpetual imprisonment for their faith. This seemed to them as unlooked for, and as light to travellers in a dark night. They gathered themselves together in every city, they called their synods and councils, and marvelled much at the sudden change and alteration. The infidels themselves extolled the only and true God of the christians. The christians received again all their former liberties; and such as fell away before in the time of persecution, repented themselves, and after having done penance, they returned again to the church. Now the christians rejoiced in every city, praising God with hymns and psalms. This was a marvellous sudden alteration of the church, from a most unhappy state into a better: but the tyrant Maximinus scarcely suffered this peace to continue six months unviolated; for he took from the christians all liberty to assemble and congregate in churchyards.

And the emperor by-and-bye commanded to be published throughout every city, and to be hung in the midst of every city (which was never done before) the edicts against the christians, graven in tables of brass. And the children in the schools, with great noise and clapping of hands, did every day resound the blasphemies of Pilate unto Jesus, and whatever other things were devised of the magistrates, after a most despiteful manner.

Thus came it to pass, that at length the persecution was a great as ever, and the magistrates of every province were very severe against the christians; some they condemned to death, and some to exile. Among whom they condemned three christians at Emisa, in Phenicia, with whom Sylvanus the bishop, a very old man, being forty years in the ecclesiastical function, was condemned to death. At Nicomedia, Lucianus, the elder of Antioch, being brought thither, after he had exhibited to the emperor his apology concerning the doctrine of the christians, was cast into prison, and after put to death. At Alexandria, Peter, a most worthy bishop, was beheaded, with whom many other Egyptian bishops also died. Quirinus, the bishop of Scescanus, having a hand-mill tied about his neck, was thrown headlong from the bridge into the flood, and there a long while floated above the water, and when he opened his mouth to speak to the lookers on, that they should not be dismayed by his punishment, he was drowned. At Rome died Marcellus, the bishop, as saith Platina; also Timotheus the elder, with many other bishops and priests, were martyred. To conclude, many in sundry places everywhere were martyred, whose names the book intituled Fasciculus Temporum declareth; as Victorianus, Symphorianus, Castorius with his wife, Castulus, Cesarius, Mennas, Nobilis, Dorotheus, Gorgonius, Petrus, and other innumerable martyrs; Erasmus, Bonifacius, Juliana, Cosmas, Damianus, Basilinus, with seven others. Dorothea, Theophilus, Theodosia, Vitalis, Agricola, Acha, Philemon, Hireneus, Januarius, Festus, Desiderius, Gregorius, Spoletanus, Agapes, Chionia, Hirenea, Theodora, and two hundred threescore and ten other martyrs. Florianus, Primus and Felicianus, Vitus, and Modestus, Crescentia, Albinius, Rogatianus, Donatianus, Pancratius, Catharina, Margareta, Lucia the virgin, and Antheus the king, with many thousand martyrs more. Simplicius, Faustinus, Beatrix, Panthaleon, Georgius, Justius, Leocandia, Anthonia, and other more (to an infinite number) suffered martyrdom in this persecution, whose names God hath written in the book of life. Also Felix, Victor, with his parents, Lucia the widow, Gemenianus, with threescore and nineteen others. Sabinus, Anastasia, Chrysogonus, Felix and Audactus, Adrianus, Natholia, Eugenia. Agnes also, when she was but thirteen years old, was martyred. Eusebius, in his eighth book, and fifteenth chapter, mentions these kinds of torments and punishments inflicted on the christians; "Fire, wild beasts, the sword, crucifyings, the bottom of the sea, the cutting and burning of members, the thrusting out of eyes, dismembering of the whole body, hunger, imprisonment, and whatsoever other cruelty the magistrates could devise." All which notwithstanding, the godly ones manfully endured, rather than do sacrifice as they were bid, to the idols. Neither yet could the christians live safely in the wilderness, but were fetched even from thence to death and torments, insomuch that this was a more grievous persecution under Maximinus the Tyrant, than was the former cruel persecution under Maximinian the Prince.

And as you have heard that the cruel edict of Maximinus proclaimed against the christians, was graven in brass which he thought should perpetually endure to the abolishing of Christ and his religion: now mark the great handywork of God, which immediately fell upon the same; for there soon followed a most unseasonable drought, with famine and pestilence among the people. By which famine and pestilence the people were greatly consumed; great numbers died in the cities, but many more in the country and villages, so that most part of the husbandmen and countrymen died with the famine and pestilence. There were many who, bringing out their best treasure, were glad to give it for any kind of sustenance, were it never so little; others, selling away their possessions, came to extreme poverty and beggary; some eating grass, and other unwholesome herbs, were obliged to fill themselves with such food as did hurt and poison their bodies. Also, a number of women in the cities, being brought to extreme misery, were constrained to depart from the city, and to beg through the country. Some others being weak and faint, wandering up and down, and not able to stand for feebleness, fell down in the middle of the streets, and holding up their hands, most pitifully cried for some scraps or fragments of bread to be given them, and being at the last gasp, ready to give up the ghost, and not able to utter any other words, yet cried out that they were hungry. The market-place, streets, lanes, and alleys lay full of dead and naked bodies, being cast out and unburied, to the pitiful and grievous beholding of them that saw them, wherefore many were eaten of dogs.

In like manner, the pestilence spreading through all houses and ranks of men, destroyed many, especially those, who, having plenty of victuals, escaped the famine. Thus, the rich princes, the presidents, and magistrates, being the more apt to receive the infection, by reason of their plenty, were quickly cut off. The miserable multitude being consumed with famine and with pestilence, all places were full of mourning, neither was there any thing else seen, but wailing and weeping in every corner; so that what with famine and pestilence, death in a short time brake up and consumed whole households, two or three dead bodies being carried out together from one house to one funeral.

These were the rewards of the vain boasts of Maximinus and his edicts, which he published in all towns and cities against us, when it was evident to all men how diligent and charitable the christians were to them in all this their miserable extremity. For they only in all this time of distress, shewed compassion upon them, travelling every day, some in curing the sick, and some in burying the dead, who were forsaken by their own kindred. Some of the christians calling and gathering the multitude together, who were in danger of famine, distributed bread to them, whereby they gave occasion to all men to glorify the God of the christians, and to confess them to be the true worshippers of God, as appeared by their works. By the means hereof, the great God and defender of the christians, who before had shewed his anger and indignation against all men, for their wrongful afflicting of us, opened again to us the comfortable light of his Providence, so that peace fell upon us, as light unto them that sit in darkness, to the great admiration of all men, who easily perceive God himself to be a perpetual director of our doings, who many times chastens his people with calamities for a time to exercise them, but after sufficient correction, again shews himself merciful and favourable to them who with faith call upon him.

Thus, at that time was fulfilled most plainly and evidently the true promise of Christ to his church, that the gates of hell shall not prevail against his church builded upon his faith, as may sufficiently appear by these ten persecutions above described; in which, as no man can deny, but that Satan and his malignant world assayed the uttermost of their power and might to overthrow the church of Jesus; so all men must needs grant, that read these histories, that when Satan and the gates of hell had done their worst, yet they did not prevail against this mount of Sion, nor ever shall. For else what was to be thought, when so many emperors and tyrants together, Dioclesian, Maximinian, Galerius, Severus, Maxentius, Licinius, with their captains and officers, were let loose, like so many lions, upon a scattered and unarmed flock of sheep, intending nothing else but the utter subversion of all christianity, and especially also

when laws were set up in brass against the christians, as a thing perpetually to stand; what was here to be looked for, but a final desolation of the name and religion of christians? But what followed, you have partly heard, and more is to be marked in the history following.

Maxentius, son of Maximinian, having been declared emperor at Rome, (A. D. 306,) by his grievous tyranny and unspeakable wickedness, oppressed the citizens and senators, who sent their complaints to Constantine, desiring him to help and release their country and city of Rome. Constantine, understanding their miserable and pitiful state, first sent letters to Maxentius, desiring and exhorting him to restrain his corrupt doings, and great cruelty. But when no letters nor exhortations would prevail, at length, pitying the woful case of the Romans, he gathered together his army in Britain and France, therewith to repress the violent rage of the tyrant Maxentius. Thus, Constantine, sufficiently furnished with strength of men, but especially with strength of God, began his journey towards Italy, which was about the last year of the persecution, (A. D. 312). Maxentius, understanding of the coming of Constantine, and trusting more to his devilish art of magic, than to the good will of his subjects, durst not shew himself out of the city, nor encounter him in the open field, but with secret garrisons laid in wait for him by the way; with whom Constantine had many skirmishes, and by the power of the Lord vanquished them, and put them to flight. Notwithstanding Constantine was in great dread of Maxentius as he approached Rome, being in great doubt and perplexity in himself, and revolving many things in his mind, as he drew towards the city, he looked up to heaven, and in the south part, about the going down of the sun, he saw a great brightness in heaven, appearing in the form of a cross, with certain stars of equal size, giving this inscription: IN HOC VINCE, that is, In this overcome. (Eusebius de vita Constant. lib. 2. Niceph. lib. 7. cap. 29. Eutrop. lib. 11. Sozom. lib. 1. cap. 3. Socrat. lib. 1. cap. 2. Urspergensis, Chronic. Paul. Diacon. lib. 11). This miraculous vision Eusebius Pamphilius declares to be true in his first book, (the Life of Constantine), and testifies that he had heard Constantine himself often report, and also swear this to be true and certain, which he saw with his own eyes in heaven, and also his soldiers about him. At the sight of which, he was greatly astonished, and consulted with his men upon the meaning of it. The same night Christ appeared to him in his sleep, with the sign of the same cross which he had seen in the heavens, bidding him inscribe his banners with that figure, and carry it before him in the wars, and so he should have the victory.[1]

Here it is to be noted, that this sign of the cross, and these letters added, *in hoc vince*, was given to him by God, not to induce any superstitious worship of the cross, as though the cross itself had any power or strength in it, to obtain victory, but only to be an admonition to him, to seek and aspire to the knowledge and faith of him, who was crucified upon the cross for the salvation of him, and of all the world, and so to set forth the glory of his name, as came to pass afterwards. This by the way. Now to return to the history.

The day following, after this night's vision, Constantine caused a cross to be made of gold and precious stone, and to be borne before him instead of his standard, and so with much hope of victory, and great confidence, as one armed from heaven, he advanced against his enemy. Maxen-

---

(1) The truth of this narrative is very far from being established so as to justify an author in admitting it without some qualification. It is now most generally regarded as a fiction, which was built upon some dream of the emperor. Mosheim thus notices it:

"It is easy indeed, to refute the opinion of those who look upon this prodigy as a cunning fiction, invented by the emperor to animate his troops in the ensuing battle, or who consider the narration as wholly fabulous. The sentiment also of those who imagine that this pretended cross was no more than a natural phenomenon in a solar halo, is perhaps more ingenious than solid and convincing; nor, in the third place, do we think it sufficiently proved that the Divine Power interposed here to confirm the wavering faith of Constantine, by a stupendous miracle. The only hypothesis then which remains, is, that we consider this

famous cross as a vision presented to the emperor in a dream." Mosheim, c. iv. p. 1.

Eusebius gives the narration on the sole authority of Constantine, who imagined that he had seen this cross,; it was natural that in the troubled sleep of the emperor, on the eve of so eventful a battle, his dreams should be vivid, and their impression strong; but it is remarkable that Eusebius gives no evidence from the thousands of persons in the army who must have seen it, if it were really a miraculous display of the Divine Power, neither Sozomen nor Ruffin, who wrote so soon after, make any mention of it. And it has been thought that Eusebius, bearing the emperor, narrating his dream, mistook him as narrating a fact, for Constantine always stated that he was influenced by a dream in making use of the sign of the cross in his army. [ED.]

tius, being constrained by force to come, he advances out of the city, sends all his army to join with him in the field beyond the river Tiber, where he was put to such a flight, and driven to such exigence, that in retiring back with haste to get into the city, he was overturned by the fall of his horse into the bottom of the river, and being unable to get out from the weight of his armour, he, with a great part of his men, were drowned.

We read in history of many victories and great conquests, yet we never read, and never shall, of any victory so wholesome, so desirable, so opportune to mankind, as this was, which made an end of so much bloodshed, and obtained liberty and life to the posterity of so many generations. For although some persecution was yet stirring in the east by Maximinus, and Licinius, who had been appointed Cæsar in room of Severus, yet in Rome, and in all the west, no martyr died after this heavenly victory. And also in the east Constantine so vanquished the tyrants, and so established the peace of the church, that for the space of a thousand years after that, we read of no open persecution against the christians, until the time of John Wickliffe, when the bishops of Rome began to persecute the true members of Christ, as shall appear in further process of this history. So happy and glorious was this victory of Constantine, sirnamed the Great. For joy and gladness of which the citizens who had sent for him, brought him into the city of Rome with great triumph, where he with the cross was most honourably received, and the triumph celebrated for the space of seven days together, having his image set up in the Market-place, holding in his right hand the sign of the cross, with this inscription: "With this saving sign, the true token of fortitude, I have rescued and delivered our city from the yoke of the tyrant." (Euseb. lib. 9. cap. 9.)

By this victory of Constantine, no little tranquillity came to the church of Christ. Although in the east the storm was not yet altogether quieted, yet here in Europe great tranquillity followed, and continued in the church without any open slaughter for a thousand years (to the time of John Wickliffe and the Waldenses, as is before mentioned) by the means of the godly beginning of good Constantine, who, with his fellow, Licinius, being now established in their dominion, set forth their general proclamation or edict, that no man should be constrained to any religion, but that all men should have liberty, that the christians might continue in their profession without any danger, and whosoever pleased might freely join them. Which thing was very well received and highly approved by the Romans, and all wise men.

The copy of the imperial constitution of Constantine *and* Licinius, *for the establishing of the free worshipping of God after the christian religion.*

"Not long ago we, considering with ourselves, that liberty and freedom of religion ought not in any case to be prohibited, but that free leave ought to be given to every man to do therein according to his will and mind. We have given commandment to all men to qualify matters of religion as they themselves thought good, and that also the christians should keep the opinions and faith of their religion; but because many and sundry opinions spring and increase through the liberty granted by our first license, we thought good to add thereunto, and to make plain those things whereby perchance some in time to come, may be hindered from their religious observance. When, therefore, by prosperous success, I, Constantine Augustus, and I, Licinius Augustus, came to Mediolanum, and there sat in council upon such things as served for the utility and profit of the commonwealth; these things amongst others we thought would be beneficial to all men; before all other things we purposed to establish those things wherein the true reverence and worship of God is comprehended; that is, to give to the christians free choice to follow what religion they think good, and whereby the same sincerity and celestial grace which is in every place received, may also be embraced and accepted of all our loving subjects. According, therefore, unto this our pleasure

upon good advisement and sound judgment we have decreed, that no man be denied to choose and follow the christian observance or religion, but that this liberty be given to every man, that he may apply his mind to what religion he thinketh meet himself, whereby God may perform upon us all his accustomed care and goodness. To the intent therefore you might know that this is our pleasure, we thought it necessary to write this unto you, whereby all these errors and opinions which are contained in our former letters sent to you in behalf of the christians, and which seem very indiscreet and contrary to our clemency, may be made frustrate and annihilated. Now, therefore, we firmly and freely will and command that every man have free liberty to observe the christian religion, and that without any grief or molestation he may be suffered to do the same. These things have we thought good to signify unto you by plain words, that we have given to the christians free and absolute power to keep and use their religion. And as this liberty is absolutely given by us unto them, to use and exercise their former observance, if any be disposed, it is manifest that the same helpeth much to establish the public tranquillity of our time, every man to have liberty to use and choose what kind of worshipping he pleases himself. And this is done of us for the intent, that we would have no man forced to one religion more than another. And this thing also amongst others we have provided for the christians, that they may again have possession of the places in which they have been accustomed to make their assemblies; so that if any have bought or purchased the same either of us, or of any other, we command the same places without either money or other recompense, forthwith and without delay, to be restored to the christians. And if any man have obtained the same by gift from us, and shall require any recompense to be made to them in that behalf, then let the christians repair to the president (being the judge appointed for that place) that consideration may be had of those men by our benignity; all which things we will and command, that you see freely given and restored to the society of the christians, without any delay. And because the christians themselves are understood to have had not only those places wherein they were accustomed to resort together, but certain other peculiar places also, not being private to any one man, but belonging to their church and society; you shall see also all those to be restored unto the christians, that is to say, to every fellowship and company of them, according to the decree whereof we have made mention, provided that the order we have taken in the mean time be observed, that if any (taking no recompense) shall restore the same lands and possessions, they shall not mistrust, but be sure to be saved harmless by us. In all these things it shall be your part to employ your diligence in the behalf of the aforesaid company of the christians, whereby this our commandment may speedily be accomplished, and also in this case by our clemency the common and public peace may be preserved. For undoubtedly by this means, as we have said before, the good-will and favour of God towards us (whereof in many cases we have had good experience) shall always continue with us. And to the intent that this our constitution may be notified to all men, it shall be requisite that the copy of these our letters be set up in all places, that men may read and know the same, lest any should be ignorant thereof."

By this history I doubt not but that the reader considers and beholds the marvellous working of God's mighty power; to see so many emperors at one time confederate together against the Lord and Christ his anointed, who having the subjection of the whole world under their dominion, exerted their whole might to extirpate the name of Christ, and of christians. Wherein if the power of man could have prevailed, what could they not do? or what could they do more than they did? If policy or devices could have served, what policy was there lacking? If torments or pains of death could have helped, what cruelty of torment could be invented by man, which was not attempted? If laws, edicts, proclamations, written not only in tables, but engraven in brass, could have stood, all this was practised against the weak christians. And yet, notwithstanding, to see how no counsel can stand against the Lord, observe how all these be gone, and yet Christ and his church still stand. Only Maximinus now in the eastern parts remained, who bore a deadly hatred against the christians, to whom Constantine and Licinius caused this constitution of theirs to be delivered. At the sight of which, although he was somewhat appalled, and defeated of his purpose; yet as he saw himself too weak to resist the authority of Constantine and Licinius, the superior princes, he dissembled, as though he himself had desired the quiet of the christians; but shortly after, making war, and fighting a battle with Licinius, he lost the victory, and coming home again, he took great indignation against the priests and prophets of his gods, whom before that time he had great regard to and honoured; and depending upon whose answers and enchantments, he began his war against Licinius. But after he perceived himself to be deceived by them, as by wicked enchanters and deceivers, and such as had betrayed his safety and person, he put them to death. And he shortly after, oppressed with a mortal disease, glorified the God of the christians, and made a most absolute law for their safety and preservation.

Thus the Lord makes his enemies, be they never so stern and stout, at length to stoop, and their hearts to confess him, as this Maximinus did, who not long after ended his life, leaving no more tyrants alive to trouble the church, except Licinius.

This Licinius being a Dane born, and first made Cæsar by Galerius, as is above specified, was afterwards joined with Constantine in the government of the empire, and in setting forth the edicts, which we have before described, although all this seems to have been done by him with a dissembling mind. For so he is described in all histories, to be a man passing all others in desire of insatiable riches, hasty, stubborn, and furious. He was such an enemy to learning, that he named the same a poison and a common pestilence, and especially the knowledge of the laws. He thought no vice worse became a prince than learning, because he himself was unlearned.

There was between him and Constantine in the beginning great familiarity, and such agreement, that Constantine gave to him his sister Constantia in matrimony. Neither would any man have thought him to have been of any other religion than Constantine was of, he seemed in all things to agree so well with him. He made a decree with Constantine in the behalf of the christians, as we have shewed. Such was Licinius in the beginning; but afterwards he began to conspire against the person of Constantine, but finding he could not prevail in his conspiracies he began vehemently to hate him, and not only to reject the christian religion, but also to hate the same. He said he would become an enemy to the christians, because in their assemblies and meetings they prayed not for him, but for Constantine. Therefore first by little and little, and that secretly, he went about to wrong and hurt the christians, and banished them his court. Then he commanded that all those who were knights of the honourable order should be deprived, unless they would do sacrifice to devils. The same persecution he afterward stretched from his court into all his provinces.

The flattering officers that were under him, thinking by this means to please him, slew many bishops, and without any cause put them to death, as though they had been homicides and heinous offenders; they cut their bodies into small pieces in the manner of a butcher, and threw them into the sea to feed the fishes. What shall we say of the exiles and confiscations of good and virtuous men? For he took by violence every man's substance, and cared not by what means he came by it; threatening them with death, unless they would give it up. He banished those who had committed no evil. He commanded that many honourable men should be put out of the way; and gave their daughters to his followers. Which cruel outrage caused many godly men to forsake their houses,

of their own accord; and flee to the woods, fields, desert places, and mountains, which were the only habitations and resting-places of the poor and miserable christians. Of those worthy men and famous martyrs, who in this persecution found the way to heaven, was Theodorus, who first being hanged upon the cross, had nails thrust into his arm-pits, and after that, his head stricken off. Also another Theodorus, the bishop of Tyre; Basil also, the bishop of Amasenus; Nicholas the bishop of Mirorus, Gregory of Armenia; after that Paul of Neocesarea, who had both his hands cut off with a searing iron. Besides these in the city of Sebastia, there were forty worthy men, and christian soldiers in the cold time of winter drowned in a horse-pond. The wives of those forty good men were carried to Heraclea a city in Thracia, and there, with a certain deacon whose name was Amones, were, after innumerable torments, slain with the sword. Licinius was determined to have overrun all the christians, to which neither will, nor opportunity were wanted. But God brought Constantine into those parts to oppose him.

Divers battles were fought between them, the first in Hungary, where Licinius was overthrown; then he fled into Macedonia, and repairing his army was again discomfited. Finally, being vanquished both by sea and land, he, lastly, at Nicomedia yielded himself to Constantine, and was commanded to live a private life in Thesalia, where at length he was slain by the soldiers.

Thus you have heard the end and conclusion of all the seven tyrants who were the authors and workers of this tenth and last persecution against the true people of God. The chief captain and promoter of which persecution, was Dioclesian, who died at Salona, as some say, by his own poison, (A. D. 313). The next was Maximinian, who, (as is said) was hanged by Constantine at Marseilles, (A. D. 310). Then died Galerius, plagued with an horrible disease sent of God, (A. D. 311). Severus was slain by Maximinian, father of Maxentius, the wicked tyrant, (A. D. 307), who was overcome and vanquished of Constantine, (A. D. 312). Maximinus, the sixth tyrant, not long after, who being overcome by Licinius, died (A. D. 313). Lastly, this Licinius was overcome by Constantine, and slain, (A. D. 323). Only Constantius, the father of Constantine, being a good and a godly emperor, died in the third year of the persecution, (A. D. 306), and was buried at York.

It now remains, after having described these persecutors, to gather up the names and stories of certain particular martyrs, who are worthy of special memory, for the singular constancy and fortitude shewed in their sufferings and cruel torments; it is impossible to include the names of all who suffered in this tenth persecution; but the most notable we here insert, for the edification of other christians.

When Dioclesian and Maximinian, the pagan emperors, had directed their letters with all severity for the persecuting of the christians, Alban, being then an infidel, received into his house a certain clerk, flying from the persecutor's hands, whom when Alban beheld, continually both day and night to persevere in watching and prayer, he began to imitate the example of his faith and virtuous life; whereupon being instructed, he became a christian. The wicked prince was informed that this good man and confessor of Christ, was harboured in Alban's house, whereupon he gave charge to the soldiers to make diligent search as soon as they came to the house of Alban, he by-and-bye putting on the apparel which his guest usually wore, offered himself in the stead of the other, to the soldiers, who binding him, brought him forthwith to the judge. It happened that when Alban was brought to the judge, they found the judge at the altars, offering sacrifice unto devils, who, as soon as he saw Alban, was in a great rage that he should presume to give himself a prisoner for his guest whom he harboured, and he commanded him to be brought before the images of the devils whom he worshipped, saying, "Because thou hadst rather hide and convey away a rebel, than deliver him to the officers (as a contemner of our gods) that he should not suffer punishment and merit of his blasphemy, the punishment he should have had, thou shalt suffer for him, if I perceive thee any whit to revolt from our manner of worshipping." But blessed Alban, who of his own accord had bewrayed that he was a christian, feared not at all the menaces of the prince, but being armed with the spiritual armour, openly pronounced that he would not obey his commandment. Then said the judge, "Of what stock or kindred art thou come?" Alban answered, "What is that to you? Of what stock soever I came of, if you desire to hear the verity of my religion, I call you to witness that I am a christian." Then the judge answered with fury, "If thou wilt enjoy the felicity of this present life, do sacrifice to these mighty gods." Alban replied, "These sacrifices which ye offer unto devils, can neither help them that offer them, neither yet can they accomplish the desires and prayers of their suppliants; but rather shall they who offer sacrifice to these idols, receive for their meed everlasting pains of hell fire." The judge, when he heard these words, was passing angry, and commanded the tormentors to whip this holy confessor of God, endeavouring to overcome the constancy of his heart with stripes. And when he was cruelly beaten, he yet suffered the same patiently, nay, joyfully, for the Lord's sake. Then, when the judge saw that he would not with torments be overcome, nor be seduced from the worship of the christian religion, he commanded him to be beheaded.

The rest of this story that follows in the narration of Bede, as of drying up the river, as Alban went to the place of his execution; then of making a well-spring in the top of the hill, and of the falling out of the eyes of him that did behead him, (with such other prodigious miracles mentioned in history) they seem more legend-like than truth-like.

The like estimation I have of the long history, wherein is written at large a fabulous discourse of all the doings and miracles of St. Alban.

But among all evidences sufficient to disprove these legends of Alban, nothing makes more against, than the very story itself: as where he brings in the head of the holy martyr to speak to the people after it was smitten off from the body. Also, where he brings in the angels going up and coming down in a pillar of fire, and singing all the night long. Also, in the river which Alban made dry, such as were drowned before in the bottom were found alive. With other such like monkish miracles, and gross fables, wherewith these abbey monks were wont, in times past, to deceive the church of God, and to beguile the whole world for their own advantage. Notwithstanding I write not this to any derogation of the blessed and faithful martyr of God, who was the first that I did ever find in this realm to suffer martyrdom for the testimony of Christ. And worthy no doubt of all commendation, especially of us here in this land; whose christian faith in the Lord, and charity towards his neighbour, I pray God we may all follow. As also I wish, moreover, that the stories both of him, and of all other christian martyrs, might have been delivered to us simple as they were, without the admixture of all these abbey-like additions of monkish miracles, wherewith they were wont to paint out the glory of such saints the most, by whose offerings they were accustomed to receive most advantage.

The Clerk mentioned in this story, whom Alban received into his house, flying into Wales, was brought back again, and martyred, with cruel torments.

The time of martyrdom of this blessed Alban and the other, seems to be about the second or third year of the tenth persecution, under Dioclesian, before the coming of Constantius to his government. Where, by the way is to be noted, that this realm of Britain was never touched with any other of the nine persecutions, before this tenth persecution of Dioclesian and Maximinian. In which persecution our histories record, that all christianity was almost destroyed in the whole island, the churches subverted, all books of the scripture burned, many of the faithful, both men and women were slain; among whom, the first and chief (as has been said) was Alban. And thus much touching the martyrs of Britain. Now from England to return again to other countries,

where this persecution raged more vehemently, we will add (the Lord willing) the histories of others, that beginning with Romanus, the notable and admirable soldier and true servant of Christ, whose history is set forth in Prudentius as follows; so lamentably described by him, that it will be hard for any man with dry cheeks to hear it.

"Pitiless Galerius with his grand captain Asclepiades, violently invaded the city of Antioch, intending by force of arms to drive all christians utterly to renounce their pure religion. The christians, as God would, were at that time congregated together, to whom Romanus hastily ran, declaring that the wolves were at hand which would devour the christian flock; 'But fear not,' said he, 'neither let this imminent peril disturb you, my brethren.' It was brought to pass, by the great grace of God working in Romanus, that old men and matrons, fathers and mothers, young men and maidens, were all of one will and mind, most ready to shed their blood in defence of their christian profession. Word was brought to the captain, that the band of armed soldiers was not able to wrest the staff of faith out of the hand of the armed congregation, and all because that one Romanus did so mightily encourage them, that they hesitated not to offer their naked throats, wishing gloriously to die for the name of Christ. 'Seek out that rebel, (quoth the captain) and bring him to me, that he may answer for the whole sect.' He was apprehended, and being bound as a sheep appointed to the slaughter-house, was presented to the emperor, who, with wrathful countenance beholding him, said, 'What? Art thou the author of this sedition? Art thou the cause why so many shall lose their lives? By the gods I swear thou shalt smart for it, and first in thy flesh shalt thou suffer the pains, whereunto thou hast encouraged the hearts of thy fellows.' Romanus answered, 'O, emperor, I joyfully embrace thy sentence, I refuse not to be sacrificed for my brethren, and that by as cruel means as thou mayst invent; and, whereas, thy soldiers were repelled from the christian congregation, that was, because it was not fit for idolaters and worshippers of devils, to enter the holy house of God, and to pollute the place of true prayer.' Then Asclepiades, wholly inflamed with this stout answer, commanded him to be trussed up, and his bowels drawn out. The executioners themselves, more pitiful in heart than the captain, said, 'Not so, sir, this man is of noble parentage, it is unlawful to put a nobleman to so ignoble a death.' 'Scourge him then with whips (quoth the captain) with knaps of lead at the ends.' Instead of tears, sighs, and groans, Romanus sung psalms all the time of his whipping, requiring them not to favour him for nobility sake; 'Not the blood of my progenitors (said he) but christian profession makes me noble.' Then with great power of spirit he inveighed against the captain, laughing to scorn the false gods of the heathen, with the idolatrous worshipping of them, affirming the god of the christians to be the true God that created heaven and earth, before whose judgment-seat all nations shall appear. But the wholesome words of the martyr were as oil to the fire of the captain's fury. The more the martyr spake, the madder he was, insomuch that he commanded the martyr's sides to be lanced with knives, until the bones appeared white again. 'I am sorry, O captain (quoth the martyr) not that my flesh shall be thus cut and mangled, but for thy cause am I sorrowful, who, being corrupted with damnable errors, seducest others.' The second time he preached at large the living God, and the Lord Jesus Christ his well beloved Son, and eternal life through faith in his blood; expressing therewith the abomination of idolatry, with a vehement exhortation to worship and adore the living God. At these words Asclepiades commanded the tormentors to strike Romanus on the mouth, that his teeth being stricken out, his pronunciation at least might be impaired. The commandment was obeyed, his face buffeted, his eye-lids torn with their nails, his cheeks scotched with knives, the skin of his beard was plucked by little and little from the flesh; finally, his seemly face was wholly defaced. The meek martyr said, 'I thank thee, O captain, that thou hast opened unto me many mouths, wherein I may preach my Lord and Saviour Christ. Look how many wounds I have, so many mouths I have lauding and praising God." The captain, astonished with this singular constancy, commanded them to cease from the tortures. He threatened cruel fire, reviled the noble martyr, and blasphemed God, saying, "They crucified Christ is but a yesterday's god, the gods of the Gentiles are of most antiquity."

"Here again, Romanus made a long oration of the eternity of Christ, of his human nature, of the death, and satisfaction of Christ for all mankind. Which done, he said, 'Give me a child, O captain, but seven years of age, which age is free from malice and other vices, wherewith ripe age is commonly infected, and thou shalt hear what he will say.' His request was granted. A pretty boy was called out of the multitude, and set before him. 'Tell me, my babe," quoth the martyr, "whether thou think it reason, that we worship one Christ, and in Christ one Father, or else that we worship many gods?" Unto whom the babe answered, "That certainly, whatever it be that man affirm to be God, must needs be one; and as this one is Christ, of necessity Christ must be the true God; for that there be many Gods, we children cannot believe." The captain much astonished at this, said, "Thou young villain and traitor, where, and of whom learnedst thou this lesson?" "Of my mother," quoth the child, "with whose milk I sucked in this lesson, that I must believe in Christ." The mother was called, and she gladly appeared. The captain commanded the child to be horsed up and scourged. The pitiful beholders of this pitiless act, could not refrain from tears: the joyful and glad mother alone stood with dry cheeks: yea, she rebuked her sweet babe for craving a draught of cold water, she charged him to thirst after the cup that the infants of Bethlehem once drank of, forgetting their mother's milk; she willhim to remember little Isaac, who beholding the sword therewith, and the altar whereon he should be sacrificed, willingly offered his tender neck to his father's sword. While this counsel was giving, the butcherly tormentor plucked the skin from the crown of his head, hair and all. The mother cried "Suffer it, my child, anon thou shalt pass to him, that will adorn thy naked head with a crown of eternal glory." The child thus counselled, and encouraged, received the stripes with a smiling countenance. The captain perceiving the child invincible, and himself vanquished, committed the blessed babe to the stinking prison, commanding the torments of Romanus to be renewed and increased, as the chief author of this evil.

"Thus was Romanus brought forth again to new stripes, the punishments to be renewed and received upon his old sores, in so much as the bare bones appeared, the flesh all torn away.

"Yea, no longer could the tyrant forbear, but he must needs draw nearer to the sentence of death. "Is it painful to thee, (said he) to tarry so long alive? A flaming fire shall be prepared for thee by-and-by, wherein thou and that boy, thy fellow of rebellion shall be consumed into ashes. Romanus and the babe were led to the place of execution. As they laid hands on Romanus, he looked back, saying, "I appeal from this thy tyranny, O unjust judge, unto the righteous throne of Christ that upright judge; not because I fear thy cruel torments and merciless handlings, but that thy judgments may be known to be cruel and bloody." Now when they were come to the place, the tormentors required the child of the mother, for she had taken it up in her arms; and she only kissing it, delivered the babe; "Farewell," she said, "my sweet child." And as the hangman applied his sword, to the babe's neck, she sang on this manner:

All land and praise with heart and voice,
O Lord we yield to thee;
To whom the death of all thy saints,
We know most dear to be.

"The innocent's head being cut off, the mother wrapped it up in her garment, and laid it on her breast. On the other side a mighty fire was made, whereinto Romanus was cast. His sorrowful life and pains being ended, he now enjoys quiet rest in the Lord, with perpetual hope

of his miserable body to be restored again, with his soul, into a better life.

"Gordius was a citizen of Cesarea, a worthy soldier, and captain of a hundred men. In the time of extreme persecution, he refused any longer to execute his charge, and willingly chose exile, and lived many years in the desert a religious and solitary life. But on a certain day when a solemn feast of Mars was celebrated in the city of Cesarea, and many people were assembled in the theatre to behold the games, he left the desert, and got up into the chief place of the theatre, and with a loud voice uttered this saying of the apostle, "Behold I was found of them that sought me not, and I was manifest to them that asked not for me." At this noise, the multitude looked about to see who it was that made such exclamation. As soon as it was known to be Gordius, the crier commanded silence, and he was brought to the sheriff, who was present, and ordained the games. When he was asked the question who he was, from whence, and for what purpose he came thither, he telling the whole truth, answered; "I am come to publish, that I set nothing by your decrees against the christian religion, but that I profess Jesus Christ to be my hope and safety." The sheriff was greatly moved with these words, and poured all his displeasure upon Gordius, commanding the executioners to bring out the scourges. Gordius answered, "That it would be an hinderance and damage to him, if he could not suffer and endure divers torments and punishments for Christ's cause. The sheriff being more offended with his boldness, commanded him to feel as many kind of torments as there were. With all which, Gordius, notwithstanding, could not be mastered or overcome; but lifting up his eyes unto heaven, singeth this saying out of the Psalms. "The Lord is my helper, I will not fear what man can do to me:" and also this saying, "I will fear no evil, because thou Lord art with me."

"When the sheriff saw that he could win but little by torment, he tried by gentleness and enticing words, to turn the stout and valiant mind of Gordius. He promised him if he would deny Christ, he would make him a captain, and give him riches, treasure, and whatever he desired. But it was all in vain. The magistrate thoroughly angry prepared to condemn him; and caused him to be taken out of the city to be burnt. Great multitudes went out of the city, to see him put to execution, some take him in their arms, and lovingly kiss him, persuading him to save himself, and that with tears. To whom Gordius answered, "Weep not, I pray you, for me, but rather for the enemies of God, who always make war against the christians; weep, I say, for them who prepare for us a fire, purchasing hell fire for themselves in the day of vengeance; and cease, I pray you, to molest and disquiet my settled mind: for truly, I am ready for the name of Christ to suffer and endure a thousand deaths if need were. Some others came unto him, who persuaded him to deny Christ with his mouth, and to keep his conscience to himself. "My tongue," saith he, "which by the goodness of God I have, cannot be brought to deny the author and giver of the same; for with the heart we believe unto righteousness, and with the tongue we confess unto salvation." He spake many more such words; but especially persuading the beholders to suffer death, and desire martyrdom. After all which, with a cheerful and glad countenance, never changing so much as his colour, he willingly gave himself to be burnt."

Not much unlike the history of Gordius is the history also of Menas an Egyptian, who was likewise a soldier, in this persecution of Dioclesian, he forsook all, and went into the desert, where for a long time he gave himself to abstinence, watching, and meditation of the scriptures. At length returning again to the city Octis, there in the open theatre, he with a loud voice openly proclaimed himself to be a christian, and upon this was brought to Pyrrhus the president; who demanded of him his faith, when he made this answer, "It is right that I should confess God, in whom is light and no darkness, forsomuch as Paul teaches that with the heart we believe to righteousness, and with the mouth confession is made unto salvation." After this the innocent martyr

F

was most painfully pinched and tortured with sundry punishments. In all which notwithstanding he shewed a constant heart, and invincible faith, having in the midst of his torments these words in his mouth: "There is nothing in my mind that can be compared to the kingdom of heaven: neither is all the world, if it were weighed in a balance, to be compared with the price of one soul; who is able to separate us from the love of Jesus Christ our Lord? Shall affliction or anguish? I have thus learned of my Lord and my king, not to fear them which kill the body and have no power to kill the soul, but to fear him rather, who hath power to destroy both body and soul in hell fire." To make the story short, after he had suffered manifold torments, at last the sentence of death was pronounced upon him, which was that he should be beheaded. Menas being then led to the place of execution, said, "I give thee thanks my Lord and God, who hast accepted me as a partaker of thy precious death, and hast not given me to be devoured of my fierce enemies, but hast made me to remain constant in thy pure faith unto this my latter end." And so this blessed soldier fighting valiantly under the banner of Christ, lost his head, and won his soul.

Basil, in a certain sermon concerning forty martyrs, mentions this story, not unworthy to be recorded. There came into a certain place, the emperor's marshal or officer, with the edict which the emperor had issued against the christians, that whoever confessed Christ, should after many torments suffer death. And first they privily suborned certain to detect and accuse the christians whom they had found out, or had laid wait for. Upon this, the sword, the gibbet, the wheel, and the whips were brought forth; at the terrible sight of which, the hearts of the beholders shook and trembled. Some fled for fear, some stood in doubt what to do; some were so terrified at beholding these engines, and tormenting instruments, that they denied their faith. But some began to suffer, and for a time did abide the conflict and agony of martyrdom, but vanquished at length, by the intolerable pain of their torments, made shipwreck of their consciences, and lost the glory of their confession. Among others, there were at that time forty young soldiers, who, after the marshal had shown the emperor's edict, and required of all men obedience to the same, freely and boldly confessed themselves to be christians, and declared to him their names. The marshal, somewhat amazed at their boldness of speech, stands in doubt what was best to do. Yet forthwith he tries to win them with fair words, advising them to consider their youth, and that they should not change a sweet and pleasant life, for a cruel and untimely death: after that he promised them money and honourable offices in the emperor's name. But they little esteeming all these things, brake forth into a long and bold oration, affirming that they neither desired life, dignity, nor money, but only the celestial kingdom of Christ, saying further, that they are ready for the love and faith they have in God, to endure the affliction of the wheel, the cross and the fire. The rude marshal being herewith offended, devised a new kind of punishment. He had seen in the middle of the city a certain great pond, which lay exposed to the cold northern wind, for it was in the winter time; he caused them all to be put into this pond, and kept there all that night; but they comforting one another, received this their appointed punishment with cheerfulness, and said, as they were putting off their clothes, "We put off not our clothes, but we put off the old man, which is corrupt according to the deceitful lust. We give thee thanks, O Lord, that with this our apparel we may also put off by thy grace, the sinful man; for by means of the serpent we once put him on, and by the means of Jesus Christ we now put him off." When they had thus said, they were brought naked into the place where they felt most vehement cold; insomuch that their bodies became stiff therewith. As soon as it was day, they were brought to the fire, in which they were consumed, and their ashes thrown into the flood.

In this fellowship and company of martyrs, we cannot leave out, or forget the history of Cyrus. This Cyrus was a physician born in Alexandria, who, flying into Egypt in the persecution of Dioclesian and Maximinian, led a solitary life in Arabia, being much spoken of for his learning. After a certain time one John, born in the city of Edessa, joined himself to Cyrus, leaving the soldier's life, which before that time he had exercised. But while the persecution raged in a city in Egypt, called Canope, a certain godly christian woman, called Athanasia, and her three daughters, Theoctiste, Theodota, and Eudoxia, with whom Cyrus was well acquainted, were cast into prison for the confession of their faith: he, fearing their weakness, accompanied with his brother John, came and visited them for their better confirmation, at which time, Lirianus was chief captain and lieutenant of Egypt, of whose wickedness and cruelty, especially against females, Athanasius makes mention in his apologies, and in his epistles. This Cyrus, therefore, and John, being accused and apprehended, as those by whose persuasions the daughters of Athanasia despised the gods and the emperor's religion, and could not be brought to do sacrifice, were, after the publication of their constant confession, put to death by the sword. Athanasia also, and her three daughters, being condemned to death.

There was a lieutenant-general of Dioclesian named Sebastian, born in France, who, by his exhortations, encouraged many martyrs of Christ to constancy, and kept them in the faith. He being, therefore, accused to the emperor, was commanded to be apprehended, and brought into the open field, where he was thrust through the body with innumerable arrows by his own soldiers. Other martyrs suffered with Sebastian, among whom were Nicostratus, with Zoe his wife; Tranquillinus, with Martia his wife; Traglinus, Claudius, Castor, Tibertius, Castellus, Marcus, and Marcellinus, with many others.

In a certain exhortation of Ambrose, he commends the martyrdoms of Agricola and Vitalis, who suffered also in the same persecution. This Vitalis was servant to Agricola, who both had determined to give their lives with other martyrs, for the name of Christ. Vitalis, being sent before by his master, to offer himself to martyrdom, fell first into the hands of persecutors, who laboured by all means to cause him to deny Christ; which, when he would in no case do, but stoutly persisted in the confession of his faith, they began to exercise him with all kind of torments, so unmercifully, that there was no whole skin left on all his body. So Vitalis, in the midst of the agony and painful torments, in a short prayer commended himself to God, and gave up his life. After him, the tormentors set upon Agricola, his master, whose virtuous manners being singularly well liked, and known to the enemies, his suffering was the longer deferred. But Agricola not abiding the long delay, and driving off, and provoking the adversaries to be quicker, was, at length, fastened to the cross, and so finished his martyrdom, which he so long desired.

No less worthy of commemoration is the lamentable martyrdom of Vincentius. This Vincentius was a Spanish priest, a godly and virtuous man, who at this time suffered martyrdom at Valence, under Dacian, the president. Bergomensis gives an account of his martyrdom, taken out of a certain sermon of St. Augustine, as follows: "Our heart conceived not a vain and fruitless sight, (as it were in beholding of lamentable tragedies), but certainly a great and marvellous sight, and with singular pleasure received it, when the painful passion of victorious Vincentius was read to us. Is there any so heavy hearted that will not be moved in the contemplation of this immoveable martyr, so manly, or, rather so godly, fighting against the craft and subtilty of that Serpent, against the tyranny of Dacian, against the horrors of death, and by the mighty Spirit of his God, conquering all? But let us in few words rehearse the number of his torments, though the pains thereof cannot be expressed in many words. First, Dacian caused the martyr to be laid upon the rack, and all the joints of his body distended, until they cracked again. This being done in the most extreme and cruel manner, all the members of his painful body were grievously pierced with deadly wounds. Thirdly, they tore his flesh with iron combs sharply filed. And in order that the tormentors might not omit any cruelty on the meek and mild martyr's flesh, they themselves also were scourged at the president's commandment. And lest his pains might seem too easy, they laid his body, being all out of joint, on an iron grate, and tearing it with iron hooks, they seared it with fiery plates, sprinkling him with burning salt. Last of all, this mighty martyr was cast into a dungeon, the floor of which was thickly spread with the sharpest shells that could be got, his feet being then fast locked in the stocks, he was left alone without any worldly comfort; but the Lord his God was with him, the Holy Spirit of God (whose office is to comfort the godly afflicted), filled his heart with joy and gladness. Hast thou prepared a terrible rack, (O, cruel tyrant! O, devouring lion!) for the martyr's bed? the Lord shall make that bed soft and sweet unto him. Dost thou rack his bones and joints all asunder? His bones, his joints, his hairs, are all numbered. Dost thou torment his flesh with mortal wounds? the Lord shall pour abundantly into all his sores of his oil of gladness. Thy scraping combs, thy sharp fleshhooks, thy hot searing irons, thy parched salt, thy noisome prison, thy cutting shells, thy pinching stocks, shall all work together for good, to this patient martyr. All shall work contrary to thy expectation, he shall reap great joy into the barn of his soul, out of this mighty harvest of pains that thou hast brought him into. Yea, thou shalt find him Vincentius indeed, that is, a vanquisher, a triumpher, a conqueror, subduing thy madness by his meekness, thy tyranny by his patience, thy manifold tortures by the manifold graces of God, wherewith he is plentifully enriched."

In this catalogue of holy martyrs, that suffered in this tenth persecution, there are very many more mentioned in various authors, beside them whom we have hitherto comprehended, as Philoromus, a man of noble birth, and great possessions in Alexandria, who, being persuaded by his friends to favour himself, to consider his wife and children, not only rejected their counsels, but also was not moved by the threats and torments of the judge, but kept the confession of Christ inviolate unto death, and was beheaded.

Of like dignity also was Procopius in Palestine, who, after his conversion, brake his images of silver and gold, and distributed the same to the poor, and after all kind of torments, racking, cording, tearing his flesh, goring stabbing, and firing, at length had his head also smitten off.

To these may be added also Georgius, a young man of Cappadocia, who, stoutly inveighing against the impious idolatry of the emperors, was apprehended and cast into prison, then torn with hooked irons, burnt with hot lime, stretched with cords, after that his hands and feet with other members of his body being cut off, at last had his head cut off with a sword.

With these aforenamed, add also Sergius and Bacchius, Panthaleon, a physician in Nicomedia, Theodorus of the city of Amasia, Faustus a martyr of Egypt, Gereon, with three hundred and eighteen fellow martyrs, who suffered about Celeur. Hermogenes, the president of Athens, who being converted by the constancy of one Menas, and Eugraphus in their torments, suffered also for the like faith; also Samonas Gurias and Abibus. Hieron also, with certain of his confessors, under Maximinus, Judes and Domuas, who suffered with many other martyrs, above mentioned, at Nicomedia. Evelasius and Maximinus, the emperor's officers, whom Fausta, the maiden, converted in her torments. Also Thirsus, Lucius, Callinicius, Apollŏnius, Philemon, Asilas, Leonides, with Arrianus, president of Thebaide. Cyprian, likewise, a citizen of Antioch, who, after he had continued a long time a filthy magician, or sorcerer, at length was converted and made a deacon, then a priest, and at last the bishop of Antioch. This Cyprian, with Justina, a maiden, suffered among the martyrs. Also Glicerios at Nicomedia, Felix a minister, Fortunatus, Achilleus, deacons in the city of Valent. Arthemius of Rome,

Ciriacus, deacon to Marcellus, the bishop, Carpophorus, priest, at Thuscia, with Abundus, his deacon. Also Claudius Sirinus Antoninus, who suffered with Marcellinus, the bishop. Cucusatus, in the city of Barcinona. Felix, bishop of Apulia, with Adauctus, and Januarius his priest, Fortunatus and Septimus his readers, who suffered in the city Venusina, under Dioclesian.

No less admirable and wonderful was the constancy also of women, who in the same persecution, gave their bodies to the tormentors, and their lives for the testimony of Christ, with no less boldness of spirit, than the men themselves. Of whom we will narrate some examples, such as seem most notable, beginning with Eulalia.

There is a city in Portugal called Emerita, wherein dwelt, and was brought up, a maiden born of noble parentage, whose name was Eulalia. Emerita was a rich and celebrated city, yet was it more adorned and celebrated by the martyrdom, blood, and sepulchre of this blessed Eulalia. She had refused great and honourable offers in marriage as one not delighting in courtly dalliance, neither yet taking pleasure in purple and gorgeous apparel, or costly ornaments; but forsaking and despising all these pompous allurements, she shewed herself most earnest in preparing her journey to her hoped inheritance, and heavenly patronage. As she was modest and discreet in behaviour, so was she also witty and sharp in answering her enemies. But when the furious rage of persecution forced her to join herself with God's children in the household of faith, and when the christians were commanded to offer incense and sacrifice to devils or idol gods, then the blessed spirit of Eulalia began to kindle, and being of a prompt and ready wit, and pouring out her heart before God, provoked thereby the force and rage of her enemies against her. But the godly care of her parents, fearing lest the willing mind of this damsel, so ready to die for Christ, might be the cause of her own death, hid her and kept her close at their house in the country, being a great way out of the city. She yet disliking that quiet life, and not wishing any delay, softly steals out of the doors in the night; and leaving the common road, passed through the thorny and briary places; and although the silent night was dark and dreadful, yet she had with her, the Lord and giver of light. And as the children of Israel coming out of Egypt, had by the mighty power of God, a cloudy pillar for their guide in the day, and a flame of fire in the night, so had this godly maiden, travelling in this dark night, when flying and forsaking the place where filthy idolatry abounded; she was not oppressed with the dreadful darkness of the night.

In the morning, with a bold courage she goes to the tribunal, and in the midst of them all with a loud voice crying out, said, " I pray you what a shame is it for you thus to destroy and kill men's souls, and to throw their bodies alive against the rocks, and cause them to deny the omnipotent God? Would you know (O you unfortunate) what I am? Behold, I am one of the christians, an enemy to your devilish sacrifices, I spurn your idols under my feet, I confess God omnipotent with my heart and mouth. Isis, Apollo and Venus, what are they? Maximinus himself, what is he? The one a thing of nought, for that they be the works of men's hands; the other but a castaway, because he worships them. Therefore, they are both frivolous; Maximinus is a lord of substance, and yet he himself falls down before a stone, and vows the honour of his dignity to those that are much inferior to his vassals. Why then does he oppress so tyrannically, more worthy and courageous spirits than himself? He must needs be a good guide and an upright judge, who feedeth upon innocent blood, doth rent and tear the bodies of godly men, and what is more, hath his delight in destroying and subverting the faith. " Go to therefore, burn, cut, and mangle these earthly members. It is an easy matter to break a brittle substance, but the inward mind thou shalt not hurt." Then the judge in a great rage, said, " Hangman, take her, and pull her out by the hair of her head, and torment her to the uttermost, let her feel the power of our country's gods, and let her know what the imperial government of a prince is. But yet, O thou sturdy girl, fain would I have thee (if it were possible) before thou die, to revoke this thy wickedness. Behold what pleasures thou mayest enjoy by the honourable house thou camest of, thy fallen house and progeny follows thee to death with lamentable tears, and the nobility of thy kindred makes doleful lamentation for thee. What meanest thou? Wilt thou kill thyself so young a flower, and so near these honourable marriages and great dowries thou mayest enjoy? Does not the glistering and golden pomp of a bridal move thee? Does not the piety of thine ancestors touch thee? Who is not grieved by thy rashness and weakness? Behold here the furniture ready prepared for thy terrible death; either thou shalt be beheaded with this sword, or else with these wild beasts shalt thou be pulled in pieces, or else being cast into the fiery flames, thou shalt be consumed to ashes. What great matter is it for thee, I pray thee, to escape all this? If thou wilt but take and put with thy fingers a little salt and incense into the censers, thou shalt be delivered from all these punishments." To this Eulalia made no answer, but throws down the idols, and spurns with her feet the incense prepared for the censers. Then without further delay, the executioners took her, and pulled one joint from another, and with the talons of wild beasts tore her sides to the hard bones; she all this while singing and praising God in this wise: "Behold, O Lord, I will not forget thee; what a pleasure is it for them, O Christ, that remember thy triumphant victories, to attain unto these high dignities! and she still calls upon that holy name, all stained and imbrued with her own blood." This she sang with a bold spirit, neither lamenting nor yet weeping, but being glad and cheerful, abandoning from her mind all heaviness and grief, when as out of a warm fountain, her mangled members bathed her white and fair skin with fresh blood. Then they proceed to the last and final torment, which was not only the goring and wounding of her mangled body with the iron grate and hurdle, and terrible harrowing of her flesh, but burned her on every side with flaming torches; when the cracking flame reaching the crown of her head consumed her; so she rested in peace.

As you have now heard the christian life, and constant death of Eulalia, worthy of praise and commendation, so no less worthy was the blessed Agnes, that constant damsel and martyr of God, who as she was of honourable parents in Rome, so she lies there honourably buried. She was very young when she was first dedicated to Christ, and boldly resisted the edicts of the emperor; and would not through idolatry deny or forsake the holy faith. She willingly offered her body to hard and painful torments, not refusing to suffer whatever it should be, yea though it were death itself. She was therefore ordered to be beheaded. And when she saw a sturdy and cruel fellow stand behind her, and approaching near to her with a naked sword in his hand, "I am now glad," said she, "and rejoice that thou art come. I will willingly receive into my bosom the length of this sword, that thus married unto Christ my spouse, I may surmount and escape all the darkness of this world. O eternal governor, vouchsafe to open the gates of heaven, once shut up against all the inhabitants of the earth, and receive, O Christ, my soul that seeks thee!" Thus speaking, and kneeling upon her knees, she prays to Christ in heaven, that her neck might be the readier for the sword. The executioner then with his bloody hand finished her hope, and at one stroke cut off her head, and by such short and swift death prevented her feeling the pain of it.

I have oftentimes before complained, that the histories of saints have been mixed up with many false additions, and fabulous inventions of men, who either of a superstitious devotion, or of a subtle practice, have so mangled their histories and lives, that very few remain simple and uncorrupt. This I especially find in the history of good Katherine, whom I have now in hand; although I do not doubt that there was great holiness in her life, excellency in her knowledge, constancy in her death, yet that all things be true that are told of her, I do not affirm, neither am I bound to think so. Of the many strange fictions of her some seem incredible, some impudent.

As where Petrus de Natalibus writing of her conversion declares, how that Katharine sleeping before a certain picture or table of the crucifix, Christ with his mother Mary appeared unto her; and when Mary had offered her unto Christ to be his wife, he first refused her for her blackness! The next time she being baptized, Mary appearing again, offered her to marry with Christ, who then being pleased, was espoused to him and married, having a golden ring the same time put on her finger in her sleep! Bergomensis writes, that because in the sight of the people she openly resisted the emperor Maxentius to his face, and rebuked him for his cruelty, she was committed to prison. The same night an angel came to her, comforting her and exhorting her to be strong and constant unto the martyrdom, for she was accepted in the sight of God, and that the Lord would be with her, and that he would give her a mouth and wisdom which her enemies should not withstand; with many other things which I here omit. I also omit concerning the fifty philosophers, whom she convicted in disputation, and converted to our religion, and who died martyrs for the same. At length, after she had endured the rack, and the four sharp cutting wheels, she was beheaded, and so finished her martyrdom.

Among the works of Basil, a certain oration is extant concerning Julitta the martyr, who came to her martyrdom by this occasion. A certain avaricious and greedy person of great authority, violently took from her all her goods, lands, chattels, and servants, contrary to all equity and right. She complained to the judges; a day was appointed when the cause should be heard. The spoiled woman, and the spoiling extortioner stood forth together: the woman declared her cause, the man, frowningly, beheld her face. When she had proved that the goods were her own, and that he had dealt wrongfully with her, the wicked extortioner, preferring vile worldly substance to the rightful claims of a christian body, affirmed her action to be of no force, because she was an outlaw in not observing the emperor's gods. His allegation was allowed as good. Whereupon incense and fire were prepared for her to worship the gods, and unless she would do this, neither the emperor's protection, laws, or judgment, should be extended to her, nor should she enjoy life in that commonwealth. When this handmaid of the Lord heard these words, she said, "Farewell life, welcome death; farewell riches, welcome poverty. All that I have, if it were a thousand times more, I would rather lose, than speak one wicked and blasphemous word against God my Creator. I yield thee, O my God, most hearty thanks for this gift of grace, that I can contemn and despise this frail and transitory world, esteeming christian profession above all treasures." After this, when any question was demanded, her answer was, "I am the servant of Jesus Christ." Her kindred and acquaintance flocking to her, advised her to change her mind; but that she refused, with detestation of their idolatry. Forthwith the judge condemned her to the fire, and the joyful martyr embraced the sentence as a most sweet and delectable thing. She prepares herself for the flames, in countenance, gesture and words, declaring the joy of her heart, and then embracing the fire, she sweetly slept in the Lord.

Beside these, divers godly women have been faithful martyrs. Barbara, a noble woman in Thuscia, after miserable imprisonment, sharp cords, and burning flames put to her sides, was at last beheaded. Fausta, a maiden, suffered under Maximinus: by her Euelasius, a ruler of the emperor's palace, and Maximinus, the president, were both converted, and also suffered martyrdom. Juliana, a maiden of singular beauty, in Nicomedia, after divers agonies, suffered likewise under Maximinus. Anasia, a maiden of Thessalonica, also suffered under Maximinus. Justina, who suffered with Cyprian bishop of Antioch. Tecla, Lucia, and Agatha, were also martyrs; all of whom glorified the Lord Christ with their constant martyrdom, in this tenth and last persecution of Dioclesian.

During the time of this persecution, the following bishops of Rome succeeded each other; Caius, who succeeded Sixtus, Marcellinus, Marcellus, (whom Eusebius does not mention) Eusebius, and Miltiades; all of whom died martyrs in the tempest of this persecution. After the martyrdom of Caius, Marcellinus was ordained bishop: he being brought by Dioclesian to the idols, first yielded to their idolatry, and was seen to sacrifice; but having been excommunicated by the christians, he fell into such repentance, that he returned again to Dioclesian, and standing to his former confession, and publicly condemning the idolatry of the heathen, he recovered the crown of martyrdom, suffering with Claudius, Cyrinus, and Antoninus.

Marcellus, likewise, was urged by Maxentius to renounce his bishopric and religion, and to sacrifice with them to idols, and when he refused, he was beaten with sticks and expelled the city. Having entered the house of Lucina, a widow, he assembled the congregation, which, when it came to the ears of Maxentius the tyrant, he turned the house of Lucina into a stable, and made Marcellus the keeper of the beasts; who died from the effects of this cruel treatment.

Among the decretal epistles, in the book of general councils, there is a long account of the judgment and condemnation of Marcellinus, which patrons of popery in these days take great hold of to prove the supremacy of the pope to be above all general councils, and that he ought not to be subject to the condemnation of any one. The bishops of this council of Sinuesse, did condemn Marcellinus, for the words of the council are plain. "They subscribed to his condemnation, and condemned him to be expelled out of the city." Moreover, the forty-two witnesses against Marcellinus were brought in by the same council, and the verdict of the witnesses was demanded and received. What does all this declare, but that the bishop of Rome was called there, and did appear before the judgment-seat of the council, and there stood subject to their sentence and authority, by the which he was expelled from the city. For he being urged of them to condemn himself, did so; prostrating himself, and weeping before them. Whereupon they immediately proceeded to the sentence against him, condemning and pronouncing him to be expelled the city. Now, whether by this may be gathered that the bishops of Rome ought not to be cited, accused, and condemned by any person or persons, let the impartial reader simply judge.

And thus have been given the histories and names of those blessed saints who suffered in the time of the persecution, from the nineteenth year of Dioclesian to the seventh and last year of Maxentius, with the deaths also and punishments of those tormentors and cruel tyrants, who were the captains of the same persecution. And here ended (blessed be Christ) these persecutions in the western churches of Europe, so far as the dominion of Constantine chiefly extended. Yet in Asia, under Licinius, persecution did not cease for four years after.

In Persia, about this time, under the king Sapor, many valiant and constant martyrs suffered, Acindimus, Pegasius, Anempodistus, Epidephorus, Simeon archbishop of Selucia, Ctesiphon another bishop of Persia, with other ministers and religious men of that region, to the number of one hundred and twenty-eight. The idolatrous magicians in Persia, taking council together against the christians, accused Simeon and Ctesiphon to Sapor the king, of being favourable to the Roman emperor, and of betraying to him what was done in Persia. Whereupon Sapor was greatly irritated against the christians, oppressing them with taxes and tributes, utterly impoverishing them and killing all their priests with the sword. After that he calls for Simeon the archbishop, who there before the king declared himself a valiant captain of Christ's church. For when Sapor had commanded him to be led to suffer torments, he neither shrunk for any fear, nor asked for any pardon; whereat the king partly wondering and partly offended, asked, "Why he did not kneel down as he was wont to do before?" Simeon answered to this, "Before this time I was not brought unto you in bonds to betray the true God, as I am now; and so long I refused not to perform that which the order and custom of the realm required of me; but now it is not lawful for me so to do, for now I come to stand in defence of our religion and true doctrine."

When Simeon had thus answered, the king persisting in his purpose, offered to him the choice either to worship with him after his manner (promising to him many great gifts, if he would do so) or if he would not, threatened destruction to him and to all the other christians within his land. But Simeon, neither allured with his promises, nor terrified with his threatenings, continued constant in his purpose, so that he could neither be seduced to idolatrous worship, nor to betray the truth of his religion. For which he was committed into bonds, and commanded to be kept until the king's pleasure should be known.

It happened as he was going to prison, that there was sitting at the king's gate a certain eunuch, an old tutor or school-master of the king's, named Usthazares, who had been once a christian, and afterward falling from his profession, joined with the heathenish multitude in their idolatry. This Usthazares sitting at the door of the king's palace, and seeing Simeon passing by to prison, rose up and reverenced the bishop. Simeon again, with sharp words (as time would permit) rebuked him, and in great anger cried out against him, who being once a christian, had cowardly revolted from his profession, and returned to the heathenish idolatry. Hearing these words, the eunuch forthwith burst into tears, and laying aside his courtly apparel, which was sumptuous and costly, he put on a black suit as the token of mourning, sitting before the court gates, and weeping, he said, "Woe is me, with what hope, with what face shall I look hereafter for my God, who have now denied him, when as this Simeon my familiar acquaintance, thus passing by me, so much disdains me, that he refuses with one gentle word to salute me?"

These words being brought to the ears of the king procured against him no little indignation. Whereupon Sapor the king sending for him, first with gentle words and courtly promises, began to speak to him, asking him, 'What cause he had to mourn so, and whether there was any thing in his house which was denied him, or which he had not at his own will and asking?' Whereunto Usthazares answering again, said, "That there was nothing in that earthly house which was lacking to him, or which he desired. Yea would to God," (said he) "O king, any other grief or calamity in all the world, whatsoever it were, had happened to me rather than this, for which I do most justly mourn! For this grieves me, that I am this day alive, who should rather have died long since, than see this sun, which for your pleasure, I appeared to worship against my heart and mind; for which cause I am doubly worthy of death: First, for that I have denied Christ; secondly, because I did dissemble with you." Sapor being astonished at the sudden alteration of this man, and doubting whether to be angry with the enchanters or with him; whether to treat him with gentleness or with rigour, at length commanded Usthazares his ancient servant and first tutor to be beheaded. As he was going to the place of execution, he desired of the executioners a little to stay, that he might send a message to the king, which was this, that for all the old and faithful service he had done to his father and to him, he would now requite him with this one office, to cause a public crier to proclaim the following words, "That Usthazares was beheaded, not for any treachery or crime committed against the king or the realm, but only because he was a christian, and would not at the king's pleasure deny his God." And so according to his request, it was performed and granted. Usthazares desired the cause of his death to be published, because his shrinking back from Christ had been a great occasion to many christians to do the like; so now the same, hearing that Usthazares died for no other cause than the religion of Christ, they might learn by his example to be fervent and constant in their profession. And thus the blessed eunuch did consummate his martyrdom. Of which Simeon hearing in prison, was very joyful, and gave God thanks; who the following day, being brought forth before the king, and still refusing at the king's request, to worship visible creatures, was likewise by the commandment of the king beheaded, with a great number more, who the same day suffered to the number of an hundred and more; all which were put to death before Simeon, he standing by and exhorting them with comfortable words; admonishing them to stand firm and steadfast in the Lord; preaching and teaching them concerning death, resurrection, and true piety; and proving by the scriptures that which he had said to be true, declaring moreover, that it was true life indeed so to die, and that it was death indeed to deny or betray God for fear of punishment: and added further, that there was no man alive but must needs die. "For as much as it is appointed all men here to have an end. But those things which follow hereafter are eternal, which shall not come to all men after one sort. But as the condition and trade of life differ in different men, and are not in all men like, so the time shall come, when all men in a moment shall receive according to their doings in this present life immortal rewards: such as have here done well, life and glory; such as have done evil, perpetual punishment." With these words of comfortable exhortation, the holy martyrs willingly yielded up their lives to death. After whom at last followed Simeon, with two other priests or ministers of his church: Abedecalaas and Ananias, which also with him were partakers of the same martyrdom.

At the suffering of those above mentioned, it happened that Pusices, one of the king's officers, and overseers of his artificers, was there present, who seeing Ananias being an aged old father, somewhat to shake and tremble at the sight of them that suffered, "O father," said he, "a little moment shut thine eyes and be strong, and shortly thou shalt see the sight of God.' Upon these words, Pusices was immediately apprehended, and brought to the king; he there confessed himself to be a christian, and because he was very bold and hardy before the king in this cause of Christ's faith, was most cruelly handled in the execution of his martyrdom. For they made a hole in the upper part of his neck to thrust in their hand, and plucked his tongue out of his mouth, and so he was put to death. At which time also the daughter of Pusices, a godly maiden, was apprehended and put to death.

The following year, upon the same day, when the christians celebrated the remembrance of the Lord's passion, which we call Good Friday before Easter, Sapor the king issued a cruel and sharp edict throughout all his land, condemning to death all who confessed themselves to be christians. So that an innumerable multitude of christians, through the wicked procuring of the malignant magicians, suffered death by the sword, both in the city and the towns. Some being sought for, and some offering themselves willingly, lest they should seem by their silence to deny Christ. Thus all the christians that could be found were slain, and many also of the king's own court and household. Amongst whom was Azades an eunuch, one whom the king loved and favoured. After the king understood that Azades was put to death, being very sorry for him, he commanded that no christians should be slain except those who were the doctors and teachers of the christian religion.

In the same time it happened that the queen fell into a severe disease; upon which the cruel Jews, with the wicked magicians, falsely accused Trabula, the sister of Simeon the martyr, with another sister also of hers, of having wrought privy charms to hurt the queen, for the revenging of the death of Simeon. This accusation being believed, innocent Trabula, with her sister, were condemned and cut asunder with a saw, whose quarters being hung upon stakes, the queen passed between them, thinking thereby to be delivered of her sickness.

Now as the king had commanded that no christians should be put to death, but only such as were the teachers and leaders of the flock, the magicians left no means untried to set forward the matter. Whereby great affliction and persecution arose among the bishops and teachers of the church.

Miserable, and almost innumerable were the slaughters under the reign of this Sapor, of bishops, ministers, deacons, monks, nuns, and other ecclesiastical persons, who cleaved to the doctrine of Christ, and suffered for the same. The names of the bishops, besides the other multitude taken in the persecution are, Barbasimes, Paulus, Gaddiabes, Sabinus, Mareas, Mocius, Johannes,

Hormisdas, Papas, Jacobus, Romas, Maares, Agas, Bochres, Abdas, Abiesus, Joannes, Abramius, Agdelas, Sabores, Isaac, Dausas, Bicor also with Maureanda his fellow bishop, and the rest of his churches under him, to the number of two hundred and fifty persons. It is not possible for any history to comprehend the whole multitude of those that suffered in this persecution, the manner of their apprehension, the cruelness of their torments, how and in what places they suffered. The number of them that can be reckoned comes to the sum of sixteen thousand men and women.

The rumour of this miserable affliction of the christians in the kingdom of Persia, coming to the ears of the Emperor Constantine, put him in great heaviness, not knowing how to help in the matter, which indeed was very difficult for him to do. At the same time it happened that certain ambassadors were at Rome from Sapor, king of Persia; to whom Constantine readily granted all their requests, thinking thereby to obtain the more friendship at their king's hands, and that at his request he would be good to the christians; he wrote, therefore, to Sapor in their behalf, and sent his epistle by the ambassadors:

Declaring to him he should stand much beholden to him, if at his request he would give some quiet and rest to the christians, in whose religion there was nothing which he could justly blame. "For," said he, "in their sacrifices they kill nothing, and shed no blood, but only offer up unbloody sacrifices, in making their prayers unto God; they delight not in bloodshedding; but only in the soul that loves virtue, and follows that doctrine and knowledge which is agreeing to true piety. And, therefore, such men as learn so to believe and to worship God, are more to be commended." Moreover, he assures him he would find God more merciful to him, if he would embrace the godly piety and truth of the christians, &c. And in the end of the epistle Constantine adds these words:—"What joy—what gladness would it be to my heart, to hear that the state also of the Persians flourishes, as I wish it to do, by your encouraging the christians? So that both you with them, and they with you, in long prosperity may enjoy as much felicity together as your hearts would desire, and in so doing no doubt ye shall. For so shall you have God, who is the Author and Creator of all this universal world, merciful and gracious to you. These men, therefore, I commend to you upon your kingly honour, and upon your clemency and piety wherewith you are endued, I commit them to you, desiring you to receive them according to your humanity and benignity, and convenient to your estate; in so doing you will now both procure to yourself grace through your faith, and also will grant to me great pleasure and a benefit worthy of thanks."

This letter, written by Constantine to King Sapor, shews what care this godly prince had for them that believed in Christ, not only in his own monarchy, but also in all places of the world.

Under the Emperor Julian the apostate, many suffered martyrdom by the idolaters. Of the lamentable tragedy of Marcus Arethusius the bishop, Sozomen, and also Theodoret, thus write—

"This man, at the commandment of Constantine, pulled down a certain temple dedicated to idols, and, instead thereof, built up a church where the christians might congregate. The Arethusians remembering the little good will that Julian bare unto him, accused him as a traitor and enemy to him. At the first, according as the scripture teacheth, he prepared himself to flee; but when he perceived that there were certain of his kinsmen or friends apprehended in his stead, returning of his own accord, he offered himself to those that thirsted for his blood. When they had got him in their possession, as men neither pitying his old age and worn years, nor abashed at the virtuous conversation of a man so distinguished, both by his life and doctrine, they first stript him naked, and pitifully beat him; then they cast him into a foul filthy sink, and then bringing him out, they caused boys to pierce him with sharp sticks. Lastly, they put him in a basket, and anointing him with honey and broth, they hung him up in the heat of the Sun, as meat for wasps and flies. And all this they did to him to force him either to build the temple again, or else to give so much money as should pay for its building; but as he purposed with himself to suffer and abide their grievous torments, so he refused to do what they demanded. At length, taking him to be but a poor man, and not able to pay such a sum of money, they promised to forgive him one-half, if he would pay the other. But he hanging in the basket pitifully wounded with the sharpened sticks, and bitten by the wasps, not only concealed his pain, but also derided those wicked ones, and called them base, low, and worldly people, and declared himself to be exalted and set on high. When at length they demanded of him but a small sum of money, he answered thus; ' It is as great wickedness to give one penny in a case of impiety, as to bestow the whole.' Thus they not being able to prevail against him, let him down, and leaving him, went their way, so that every man might learn at his mouth the example of true piety and faithfulness.''

Although the treating of these persecutions of Persia somewhat stray out of the order of time and place, yet, as these holy martyrs also gave so faithful a testimony of the Lord Jesus with their blood, I thought it improper to pass over them without some testimony. And here these persecutions of the primitive church ended.

It may perhaps astonish some, while reading the history of these terrible persecutions, that God the Almighty director of all things, should suffer his own faithful servants, believing in his only begotten son Jesus, to be so cruelly and wrongfully tormented and put to death, and that during so many years together. To which astonishment I have nothing to answer, but to say in the words of Jerome, "We ought not to be astonished to see the wicked prevail against the holy; for, as in the beginning of the world, we see that Abel the just was killed by wicked Cain, and that the sons of Israel were afflicted by the Egyptians, so even the Lord himself was crucified by the Jews, Barrabas the thief being let go. Time would not suffice me to recite how the godly suffer in this world while the wicked flourish and prevail; whatever be the cause this is sufficient for us, and may be to all men, that we are sure these afflictions and persecutions of God's people in this world come not by any chance or blind fortune, but by the appointment and forewarning of God. For so in the old law, by the affliction of the children of Israel, he prefigured these persecutions of the christians. So by the words of Christ's own mouth in the gospel he forewarned his church of these troubles, neither did he suffer these great afflictions to fall upon his servants, before he had warned them sufficiently by special revelation in the Apocalypse of John his servant; in which he declared to his church, not only what troubles were coming, where, and by whom they should come, but also in plain numbers, if the words of the prophecy be well understood, assigns the true time, how long the persecutions should continue, and when they should cease. For as there is no doubt, but by the beast with seven heads, bearing the whore of Babylon, drunken with the blood of saints, is signified the city of Rome. So in my judgment the forty-two months (in the thirteenth of the Apocalypse) is to be expounded by taking every month for a sabbath of years; that is, reckoning a month for seven years, so that forty and two such sabbaths of years, make up the number of years between the time of Christ's death and the last year of the persecution of Maxentius, when Constantine, fighting under the banner of Christ, overcame him, and made an end of all persecution within the monarchy of Rome.[1] The number of these years amounted to two hundred ninety and four,

to which, if the other six years of persecution under Licinius in Asia be added, it fills up full three hundred years. And so long continued the persecution of Christ's people, under the heathen tyrants and emperors, of the monarchy of Rome, according to the number of the forty and two months specified in the thirteenth of the Apocalypse. For the better explanation of which, because the matter being of no small importance, greatly appertains to the public utility of the church; and lest any should suspect me of following any private interpretation of mine own, I thought good to communicate to the reader what has been imparted unto me, in the opening of these mystical numbers in this aforesaid book of the Revelation as follows:

While I was engaged in these histories, and considered the exceeding rage of these persecutions, the intolerable torments of the blessed saints, so cruelly racked, torn, and plucked in pieces with all kinds of tortures that could be devised, more bitter than death itself; I could not without great sorrow of mind, behold their grievous afflictions, or write of their bloody sufferings; and the hotter the persecutions grew, the more my sympathy with them increased; not only pitying their woful case, but almost reasoning with God, thus foolishly thinking why God of his goodness should suffer his children and servants to be so vehemently tormented and afflicted? If mortal things were governed by heavenly Providence (as must needs be granted), why did the wicked thus flourish, and the godly suffer? If sinners deserved punishment, they alone were not sinners, and why was their death above all others so sharp and bitter? At least, why should the Lord suffer the vehemency of these horrible persecutions to endure so long, shewing no certain determined end of their tribulations, whereby they knowing the appointed determination of Almighty God with more consolation might endure the same? As the Israelites in the captivity of Babylon had seventy years limited unto them; and under Pharaoh they were promised a deliverance; and also under the Syrian tyrants threescore and two weeks were assigned to them. But in these persecutions I could find no end determined for their deliverance. Whereupon much marvelling with myself, I searched the Book of Revelation to see whether any thing might be there found; and although I perceived the beast there described to signify the empire of Rome, which had power to overcome the saints; yet concerning the time and continuance of these persecutions under the beast, I found nothing to satisfy my doubt. For although I read there of forty-two months, of a time, times, and half a time, of one thousand two hundred and threescore days; yet all this by computation coming but to three years and a half, came nothing near the long continuance of these persecutions, which lasted three hundred years. Thus being vexed in spirit, about the reckoning of these numbers and years; it so happened upon a Sunday in the morning, I lying in my bed, and musing about these numbers, suddenly it occurred to my mind, to count these months by sabbaths, as the weeks of Daniel are counted by sabbaths. Whereupon I began to reckon the forty-two months by sabbaths; first of months, that would not serve; then by sabbaths of years, wherein I began to feel some probable understanding. Yet not satisfied herewith, in order to make the matter more sure, I repaired to certain merchants of mine acquaintance, of whom one is departed a true faithful servant of the Lord, the other two are yet alive, and witnesses hereof. To whom the number of these aforesaid forty-two months being propounded and examined by sabbaths of years, the whole sum was found to amount to two hundred and ninety-four years, the full time of these persecutions, neither more nor less.

Now this one clasp being opened, the other numbers that follow are plain and manifest to the intelligent

---

(1) That our author has not succeeded in so elucidating this remarkable portion of scripture, as to free it from the numberless difficulties that envelope it, is no more than must be said of every other commentator who has undertaken the exposition of unfulfilled prophecy.

He has however miscalculated the dates of his first period of 300 years — for from the crucifixion of our Lord to the defeat of Maxentius by Constantine, (A. D. 312,) was a period of only 279 years, which added to the 6 years of persecution under Licinius, would be only 285 years, instead of the precise 300. [ED.]

reader. For where mention is made of three years and a half, of one time, two times and half a time, also of one thousand two hundred and threescore days, all these come to one reckoning and signify forty and two months, by which months, as is said, is signified the whole time of these primitive persecutions, as here in order may appear.

THE MYSTICAL NUMBERS IN THE APOCALYPSE OPENED.

First, where mention is made (Revelation xi. 3), that the two prophets shall prophesy 1260 days; and also that the woman flying into the desert, shall there be fed 1260 days: (Rev. xii. 6.) who knoweth not that 1260 days make three years and a half? that is, forty-two months.

Secondly, where we read (chap. xi. 8.) the bodies of the two aforesaid prophets shall lie in the streets of the great city unburied the space of three days and a half, and after the said three days and a half they shall revive again, &c., let the hours of these three days and a half (which be 42), be reckoned every day for a sabbath of years, or else every day for a month, and they come to forty-two months.

Thirdly, where it is said (Rev. xii. 14.) that the woman had two wings given her to fly unto the desert for a time, times and half a time: give for one time one year, or one day; for two times, two years or two days; for half a time, half a year, or half a day; and so it is manifest, that these three years and a half amount to forty-two months.

Fourthly, account these forty-two months aforesaid, which the beast had power to make (Revelations xi), by sabbath of years; that is, seven years for a month, or every month for seven years, and it amounteth to two hundred and ninety-four years.

And so we just have the years, days, times, and months of these aforesaid persecutions under the beast, neither shorter nor longer, reckoning from the death of John Baptist under Herod, to the end of Maxentius, and of Licinius, the two last great persecutors, the one in the West, the other in the East, who were both vanquished by godly Constantine. And so peace was given to the church, although not in such ample wise, but that many tumults and troubles afterward ensued, yet they lasted not long: and the chief brunt of these Roman persecutions which the Holy Ghost especially considered above all other in this his Revelation thus ended in the time of Constantine. Then was the great dragon, the devil, to wit, the fierce rage and power of his malicious persecuting, chained for a thousand years after this, so that he could not prevail, but the power and glory of the gospel gradually increasing and spreading with great joy and liberty, so prevailed that at length it got the upper hand and replenished the whole earth, rightly verifying therein the water of Ezekiel, which issuing out of the right side of the altar, the further it ran, the deeper it grew, till at length it replenished the whole ocean, and healed all the fishes therein. So also the course of the gospel proceeding of small and hard beginnings still kept his stream: the more it was stopped, the swifter it ran: by blood it feeded, by death it quickened, by cutting it multiplied, through violence it sprung; till at last out of thraldom and oppression burst forth into perfect liberty, and flourished in all prosperity. Would that the christians could have used this liberty wisely and moderately, and not abused it, forgetting their former estate to their own pride, pomp, and worldly ease, as it afterwards came to pass, of which more is to be said (the Lord willing) in the proper place and time.

And thus much touching the prophetical numbers in the Apocalypse. In which the eternal wisdom and high providence of Almighty God is to be magnified, so disposing and governing his church, that no adversity or perturbation happens at any time to it, which his wisdom does not fore-see and pre-ordain; neither doth he pre-ordain or determine anything which he does not most truly perform, both fore-seeing the beginning of such persecutions, and determining the end of them, how long to continue, and when to cease.

Thus much by the way I have mentioned, lest any should be surprised to read of the church being so long and for so many years under such miserable and extreme afflictions, wherein neither chance nor fortune, nor disposition of man, has had any place, but only the forecounsel and determination of the Lord governing and disposing the same, who not only suffered them, and foresaw those persecutions before they occurred, but also appointed the times and years how long they should last, and when they should have an end, as by the forty-two months in the eleventh and twelfth chapters of Revelations has beeen declared. Which months, containing two hundred ninety and four years (if they be rightly gathered), make the full time between the first year of the persecution of Christ under the Jews and Herod, till the last year of persecution under Licinius; which was from the nativity of Christ, in the year 324. After which year according to the preordinate council of God, when his severity had been sufficiently declared upon his own house, it pleased him to shew mercy again, and to bind up Satan the old serpent, according to the twentieth chapter of the Revelation, for the space of a thousand years; that is, from the time of Licinius to the time of John Wickliffe and John Husse. During all which time, although certain conflicts and tumults have been among christian bishops themselves in the church, yet no universal murdering persecution was stirring before the preaching of Wickliffe, Husse, and such others, as in the further process of this history (Christ willing and aiding us) shall appear.

Thus having discoursed at length of these horrible persecutions and heavy afflictions of the christian martyrs; now by the grace of God, coming out of this red sea of bloody persecution, leaving Pharoah and his host behind, let us sing gloriously to the worthy name of our God, who through the blood of the Lamb after long and tedious afflictions, at length has visited his people with comfort, has chained Satan, has sent his meek Moses (gentle Constantine I mean), by whom it has pleased the Lord to work deliverance to his captive people, to set his servants at liberty, to turn their mourning into joy, to magnify the church of his son, to destroy the idols of all the world, to grant life and liberty (and would God also not so much riches) unto them who before were the abjects of all the world, and all by the means of godly Constantine, the meek and most christian emperor, of whose divine victories against so many tyrants and emperors, persecutors of Christ's people, and lastly, against Licinius, (A. D. 324), of whose other noble acts and prowesses, of whose blessed virtues and his happy birth and progeny, we have partly comprehended before, and part now remains to be declared.

This Constantine was the son of Constantius, the emperor, a good and virtuous child of a good and virtuous father, born in Britain (as says Eutropius), whose mother was named Helena, daughter of King Coilus; although Ambrose, in his funeral oration on the death of Theodosius says, she was an innholder's daughter. He was a most bountiful and gracious prince, having a desire to encourage learning, and often used to read and study himself. He had wonderful success and prosperity in all things he took in hand, the reason of which was truly supposed to be because he was so great a favourer of the christian faith. When he had once embraced this faith he ever after most devoutly and religiously reverenced it, and commanded by special proclamation, that every man should profess the same religion throughout all the Roman empire. The worshipping of idols (whereto he was addicted by the allurement of Fausta, his wife, so that he did sacrifice to them) after the discomfiture of Maxentius in battle, he utterly abjured; but he deferred his baptism to his old age, because he had determined a journey into Persia, and thought to have been baptized in Jordan. (Euseb. lib. 4. De vita Constantini.)

As to his natural disposition and wit, he was very eloquent, a good philosopher, and sharp and ingenious in disputation. He was accustomed to say that an emperor ought to refuse no labour for the utility of the commonwealth ; yea, and to adventure the mangling of his body for the remedy thereof.

He first entered into the empire by the mercy of God, who after long waves of doleful persecution would restore to his church peace and tranquillity, (A. D. 311,) as Eusebius accounts in his chronicle. The church enjoyed great peace and tranquillity under the reign of this good emperor, who took great pains in the preservation thereof. First, before he had subdued Licinius, he set forth many edicts for the restitution of the goods of the church, for bringing back the christians out of exile, for quieting the dissensions of the doctors or bishops of the church, for the setting of them free from public charges, and such like even as his Constitutions declare, in which is contained this prayer of the good Constantine :—

" To thee therefore now I pray : Oh most mighty God, that thou wilt vouchsafe to be merciful, and pardon all the eastern parts, and the inhabitants of the same, being oppressed with calamity : and that by me thy servant thou wilt of thy goodness help and relieve the same. And these things crave I not rashly at thy hands, O Lord, most mighty and holiest God of all. For I being persuaded by the only oracles, have both begun and also finished wholesome and profitable things : and further, by the bearing and shewing of thine ensign, have overcome a mighty and strong host ; and when any necessity of the commonwealth committed to my charge requires, (following those signs and tokens of thy virtues) I boldly go forth and fight against mine enemies : and for this cause I have sacrificed my soul unto thee, purified and cleansed both with thy love and fear. Yea, truly, thy name do I sincerely love, and thy power do I reverence, which by many tokens and wonders hast shewed and confirmed thereby my belief and faith. Therefore will I do my endeavour, and bend myself thereunto, that I may rebuild thy most holy house, which those wicked and ungodly emperors have laid waste ; thy people do I desire to bring and establish in firm peace and tranquillity, and that for the public utility of all the inhabitants of the earth. Those which yet err, and are out of the way, enjoy the benefit of peace and quietness, with and amongst the number of the faithful : for I trust the restitution of the like society and participation may be a means to bring them also that err into the perfect way of truth. Let no man therefore be grievous one unto another, but what every man thinketh best, that let him do : for such as are wise, ought thoroughly to be persuaded, that they only mean to live holily, and as they should do, whom the Spirit of God moveth to take their delight and recreation in reading in his holy will : and if others wilfully will go out of the way, cleaving to the synagogues of false doctrine, they may at their own peril. As for us, we have the most worthy house or church of God's truth, which he according to his own goodness and nature hath given us. And this also we wish unto them, that with like participation and common consent, they may feel with us the same delectation of mind. For this our religion is neither new, nor newly invented, but it is as old as we believe the creation of the world to be, and which God hath commanded to be celebrated with such worship as pleased him : but all living men are liars, and are deceived with divers and sundry allusions. Thou, O God, for Christ thy Son's sake, suffer not this wickedness again to root : thou hast set up a clear burning light, that thereby as many as thou hast chosen may come unto thee, these thy miracles approve the same. It is thy power that keepeth us in innocency and fidelity. The sun and the moon run their appointed course. Neither yet in ranging-wise do the stars wander to what place of the world they choose themselves. The days, years, months, and times keep their appointed turns. The earth abideth firm and unmoveable at thy word : and the wind at the time (by thee directed) stormeth and bloweth. The streaming watery floods ebb in time according as they flow. The raging sea abideth within her bounded limits : and for that the ocean stretcheth out herself in equal length and breadth with the whole earth, this must be wrought with some marvellous workmanship of thine own

hand. Which thing, unless it were at thy will made and disposed : without all doubt so great difference and partition between, would ere this time have brought utter ruin and destruction both to the life of man, and to all that belongeth to man beside. Which for that they have such great and huge conflicts amongst themselves, as also the invisible spirits have ; we give thee thanks, O Lord most mighty, God of all gods, that all mankind hath not been destroyed thereby. Surely even as greatly as thy benignity and gentleness is manifested by divers and sundry benefits bestowed upon us, so much also is the same set forth and declared in the discipline of thy eternal word, to those that be heavenly wise, and apply themselves to the attainment of sincere and true virtue. But if any such there be that little regard, or have but small respect unto the consideration thereof, let them not blame or lay a fault in others that do the same : for that physic whereby health is obtained, is manifestly offered unto all men. Now therefore let no man go about to subvert that, which experience itself doth shew (of necessity) to be pure and good. Let us therefore altogether use the participation of this benefit bestowed upon us ; that is to say, the benefit of peace and tranquillity, setting apart all controversy. And let no man hurt or be prejudicial to his fellow for that thing wherein he thinketh himself to have done well. If by that, which any man knoweth and hath experience of, he thinketh he may profit his neighbour, let him do the same ; if not, let him give over and remit it till another time ; for there is a great diversity betwixt the willing and voluntary embracing of religion, and that when a man is thereunto enforced and compelled."

Such was the goodness of this emperor Constantine, or rather such was the providence of Almighty God toward his church in stirring him up, that all his care was how to benefit and enlarge the same. Neither was it enough for him to deliver the church and people of God from outward vexation of foreign tyrants and persecutors. His godly care was no less excited in quieting the inward dissensions and disturbance of the church, among the christian bishops themselves. Nor did his vigilance less extend to erecting, restoring, and enriching the churches of God in all cities, and in providing for the ministers of the same.

In writing to Miltiades bishop of Rome, and to Marcus, he declares in his letters, how Cecilianus bishop of Carthage had been accused to him by divers of his colleagues and fellow bishops. Wherefore his will is, that the said Cecilianus with ten bishops his accusers, with ten other his defendants should repair to him at Rome ; where with the assistance of the aforesaid Miltiades, Rheticus, Maternus, Marinus, and of their other fellow colleagues, the cause of Cecilianus might be heard and rightly examined, so that all schism and division might be cut off from among them, wherein the fervent desire of Constantine to peace and unity may well appear.

Upon the like cause also, he writes to Chrestus bishop of Syracuse ; being so desirous to nourish peace and concord in the church, that he offers to him, with his under ministers and three servants, his free carriage to come up to him to the council of other bishops, for the agreeing of certain matters belonging to the church.

To the provinces likewise of Palestine and the parts about, he directs his edict in the behalf of the christians, for the releasing of such as were in captivity, and for the restoring again of them which had sustained any loss in the former persecution, and for the refreshing of such as had been oppressed with any ignominy or molestation for their confession sake ; declaring in the said edict how that his whole body, life and soul, and whatsoever is in him, he owes to God and to the service of him, &c.

Moreover, he writes another letter to Eusebius, for the edifying of new christian churches, and restoring of them which had been wasted before by foreign enemies. And after he had collected the synod of Nice for the study of peace and unity of the church, he writes upon the same to Alexander and Arius. In which his letters he most lamentably uttered the great grief of his heart, to see and hear of their contention and division, whereby the peace and common harmony of the church was broken, the synod provoked and resisted, the holy people of the Lord divided into parts and tumults, contrary to the office of good and circumspect men, whose duty were rather to nourish concord, and to seek tranquillity. Declaring moreover in the said epistle, the first origin and occasion of their contentious dissension to rise upon vain and trifling terms, vile causes and light questions, and pieces of questions; about such matters as are neither to be moved, nor being moved, to be answered to, more curious to be searched, and perilous to be expressed, than necessary to be inquired. Wherefore by all means he entreats them and persuades them, not only with reasons, but also with tears and sighing sobs, that they would again restore peace to the church, and quietness to the rest of his life (which otherwise would not be sweet unto him) and that they would return again to the communion of the reverend council. Thus much I thought summarily to comprehend, whereby the divine disposition and singular gentle nature of this meek and religious Constantine, might more plainly appear to all princes, for them to learn by his example what zeal they ought to bear toward the church of Christ, how gently they ought to govern it, and how to be beneficial to it.

Many other edicts and epistles written to other places and parties, are expressed at large in the second book of Eusebius's "Life of Constantine," wherein the zealous care and princely beneficence of this noble emperor toward the church of Christ may appear; a brief recapitulation of which here follows. (Sozo. lib. i. cap. 8, 9.)

First, he commanded all them to be set free, who for the confession of Christ had been condemned to banishment, or to the mines, or to any public or private labour. Such as were put to any infamy or shame among the multitude, he ordered to be discharged from all such ignominy. Soldiers which before were deprived either of their place, or their wages, had liberty given them either to serve again in their place, or to live quietly at home. Whatever honour, place, or dignity had been taken away from any man, he commanded to be restored to them again. And that the goods and possessions of them that had suffered death for Christ, however they were alienated, should return to their heirs or next of kin, or for lack of them should be given to the church. He commanded, moreover, that christians only should bear office; he charged and restrained the heathens, that they should neither sacrifice nor exercise any more divinations and ceremonies of the Gentiles, nor set up any images, nor keep any feasts of the heathen idolaters. He corrected moreover and abolished all such unlawful manners and usages in the cities as might be hurtful to the church.

Among the Romans was an old law, that such as had no children, should be amerced of half their goods. Also, that such as being above the years of twenty-five were unmarried, should not be numbered in the same privileges with them that were married, neither should be heirs to them, to whom notwithstanding they were next in kin. These laws, because they seemed unreasonable, he abrogated and took away. There was also another law among the Romans, that they which made their wills being sick, had certain prescribed words appointed to them to use, which unless they followed, their wills stood of no effect. This law also Constantine repealed, permitting every man in making his testament to use what words or what witnesses he would. Likewise among the Romans he restrained and took away the cruel and bloody spectacles and sights, where men were wont to kill one another with swords. Where no churches were, there he commanded new to be made; where any were decayed, he commanded them to be repaired; where any were too little, he caused them to be enlarged, giving to the same, great gifts and revenues, not only out of the public tributes and taxes, but also out of his own private treasures. When any bishops required any council to be had, he satisfied their petitions; and whatever they established in their councils and synods, that was godly and honest, he was ready to confirm.

He inscribed the armour of his soldiers with the sign of the cross, that they might learn the sooner to forget their old superstitious idolatry. Moreover, like a worthy emperor, he prescribed a certain form of prayer, instead of a catechism for every man to have, that he might learn how to pray, and to invoke God. Which form of prayer is recited in the fourth book of Eusebius's "Life of Constantine," as follows:

"We acknowledge thee to be our only God, we confess thee to be our King, we invoke and call upon thee our only Helper, by thee we obtain our victories, by thee we vanquish and subdue our enemies, to thee we attribute whatsoever present benefits we enjoy, and by thee we hope for good things to come: unto thee we direct all our prayers and petitions, most humbly beseeching thee to preserve Constantine our emperor and his noble children in long life, and to give them victory over all their enemies, through Christ our Lord: Amen."

In his own palace he set up an house for prayer and preaching, and used to pray and sing with his people. Also in his wars he went not without his tabernacle appointed for the same purpose. The Sunday he commanded to be kept holy by all men, and free from all judiciary causes, from markets, fairs, and all manual labours, husbandry only excepted: especially charging that no Images or monuments of Idolatry should be set up.

He gave men of the clergy and of the ministry in all places special privileges and immunities, so that if any were brought before the civil magistrates, and wished to appeal to the sentence of his bishop, it should be lawful for him to do so, and that the sentence of the bishop should stand in as great force as if the magistrate or the emperor himself had pronounced it.

But here it is to be observed, that the clerks and ministers then newly coming out of persecution, were in those days neither so great in number, nor in order of life of like disposition to these now living in our days.

Constantine also had no less care and provision for the maintenance of schools pertaining to the church, and for the encouragement of the arts and liberal sciences, especially of divinity: not only furnishing them with stipends and subsidies, but also defending them with large privileges and exemptions.

Besides this, so far did his godly zeal and princely care and provision extend to the church of Christ, that he provided books and volumes of scripture, to be plainly written and copied out, to remain in the public churches for the use of posterity. Whereupon writing to Eusebius bishop of Nicomedia, in a special letter, (Euseb. De vita Constant. lib. iv.) he desires him with all diligence to procure fifty volumes of parchment well bound and compacted, wherein he should cause to be written out of the scripture in a fair legible hand, such things as he thought necessary and profitable for the instruction of the church, and allows him for that business two public ministers, &c.

In perusing and writing this history, and in considering the christian zeal of this emperor, I wish that either this our art of printing, and plenty of books, had been in his days, or that the same heroic heart towards the christian religion, which was in this excellent monarch, might something appear in inferior princes reigning in these our printing-days.

The liberal hand of this emperor born to do all men good, was no less also open and ready towards the need and poverty of such, as either by loss of parents, or other occasions, were not able to help themselves: for whom he commanded, a due supply both of corn and raiment to be ministered out of his own coffers, to the necessary relief of the poor men, women, children, orphans, and widows. (Euseb. de vita Constant. lib. 4.)

Here it will be requisite to say something of the donation of Constantine, whereupon, as their chief anchorhold, the bishops of Rome ground their supreme dominion and right over all the political government of the western parts, and the spiritual government of all the other sees and parts of the world. Many arguments might here be adduced, if leisure from other matters would suffer me to prove that Constantine never gave this donation, and that the history thereof is false, and a forgery.

First, No ancient history, nor yet doctor, makes any mention thereof.

Nauclerus reports it to be affirmed in the history of Isidorus. But in the old copies of Isidorus, no such thing is to be found.

Gratian, the compiler of the decrees, recites that decree, not upon any ancient authority, but only under the title of Palea.

Gelasius is said to give some testimony thereof, (Dist. 15. Sancta Romana), but the clause of the said distinction touching that matter, is not extant in the ancient books.

Otho Phrysingensis, who was about the time of Gratian, after he has declared the opinion of the favourers of the papacy, affirming this donation to be given by Constantine to Pope Sylvester, also mentions the opinion of them that favour the empire, affirming the contrary.

How could Constantine have yielded up to Sylvester all the political dominions over the west, when the said Constantine at his death, dividing the empire to his three sons, gave the western part of the empire to one, the eastern part to the second, the middle part to the third?

Is it likely that Theodosius after them, being a just and a religious prince, would or could have occupied the city of Rome, if it had not been his right, but had belonged to the pope?—and so did many other emperors after him.

The phrase of this decree, being compared with the phrase and stile of Constantine, in his other edicts and letters above specified, does not agree with them.

Seeing the papists themselves confess that the decree of this donation was written in Greek, how agrees that with the truth, when it was written, not to the Grecians, but to the Romans; and also Constantine himself, not understanding the Greek tongue, was obliged to use the Latin, in the council of Nice?

The contents of this donation (whoever was the forger thereof), betrays itself: for if it be true which there is confessed, that he was baptized at Rome, by Sylvester, and the fourth day after his baptism this patrimony was given, (which was before his battle against Maximinus, or Licinius, (A. D. 317), as Nicephorus recordeth) how then accords this with that which follows in the donation, for him to have jurisdiction given over the other four principal sees of Antioch, Alexandria, Constantinople, and Jerusalem? when as the city of Constantinople was not yet begun before the death of Maximinus, or Licinius, and was not finished before the eight-and-twentieth year of the reign of Constantine, (A. D. 339), or if it be true, (as Jerome counted, it was finished the three-and-twentieth year of his reign, which was A.D. 334, long after this donation, by their own account.

Furthermore, where in the said Constitution it is said that Constantine was baptized at Rome by Pope Sylvester, and thereby was purged of leprosy, the fable thereof agrees not with the truth of history, (Eusebius, lib. 4. de vita Constantina. Hieronymus in Chron. Ruffin. lib. 2. cap. 11. Socrates, lib. 1. cap. 39. Theod. lib. 1. cap. 31. Sozomenus, lib. 2. cap. 34.) For all the historians agree that he was baptized, not at Rome, but at Nicomedia; and that moreover, as by their testimony

appears, not by Sylvester, but oy Eusebius, bishop of Nicomedia, not before his battle against Maximinus, or Licinius, but in the thirty-first year of his reign, a little before his death.

Again, whereas Constantine in this donation appointed him to have the principality over the other four patriarchal sees, that makes Constantine contrary to himself, who in the council of Nice, afterwards agreed with other bishops, that all the four patriarchal sees should have equal jurisdiction, every one over his own territory and precinct.

Briefly to conclude: whoever desires to be more abundantly satisfied touching this matter, let him read the books of Marsilius Patavinus, intitled, Defensor pacis, (A. D. 1324); of Laurentius Valla, (A. D. 1440); of Antoninus archbishop of Florence, who, in his history plainly denies that this donation is to be found in the old books of the decrees. Of Cusanus Cardinalis, lib. 3. cap. 2., writing to the council of Basil, (A. D. 1460); of Æneas Silvius In dialogo; of Hier. Paulus Cattalanus, (A. D. 1496); of Raphæl Wolateranus, (A. D. 1550); of Lutherus, (A. D. 1537), &c. All which, by many and evident proofs, dispute and prove this donation not to proceed from Constantine, but to be a thing untruly pretended, or rather, a fable imagined, or else to be the deed of Pepin or Charles, or some such other, if it were ever the deed of any.

And thus I have briefly collected the narration of the noble acts, and heavenly virtues of this most famous Emperor Constantine the Great; a singular spectacle for all christian princes to behold and imitate, and worthy of perpetual memory in all congregations of christian saints: whose fervent zeal and piety to all congregations, and to all the servants of Christ, was notable; but especially the affection and reverence of his heart toward them who had suffered for the confession of Christ in the persecutions before, is to be admired; he had them principally in veneration, insomuch that he embraced and kissed their wounds and stripes. And if any bishops, or any other ministers brought to him any complaints one against another, (as they often did) he would take their bills of complaint and burn them before their faces; so studious and zealous was his mind to have them agree, whose discord caused more grief to him than it did to themselves. To commit to history all the virtuous acts, and memorable doings of this divine and renowned emperor, would be matter enough of itself to fill a great volume; therefore we must be content with the above brief account, as it is impossible to say enough of him, I shall not pursue his history any further.

And here is an end of the lamentable persecutions of the primitive church, during the space of three hundred years from the passion of our Saviour Christ, till the coming of Constantine; by whom, as by the elect instrument of God, it has pleased his Almighty Majesty, by his determinate purpose, to give rest after long trouble to his church, according to that which St. Cyprian declares before to be revealed by God to his church: that after darkness and stormy tempest, should come peaceable, calm, and stable quietness, meaning this time of Constantine. At which time it so pleased the Almighty, that the murdering malice of Satan should at length be restrained, and he chained up for a thousand years, through his great mercy in Christ, to whom, therefore, be thanks and praise, now and for ever. Amen.

END OF THE FIRST BOOK.

ACTS AND MONUMENTS,

BOOK II.

CONTAINING

THE NEXT THREE HUNDRED YEARS, WITH SUCH THINGS SPECIALLY AS HAVE
HAPPENED IN ENGLAND, FROM THE TIME OF KING LUCIUS, TO GREGORY,
AND SO AFTER TO THE TIME OF KING EGBERT.

By these persecutions it may be understood that the fury of Satan, and rage of men, have done what they could to extinguish the name and religion of christians; for all that either death could do, or torments could work, or the gates of hell could devise, was to the utmost attempted. And yet, notwithstanding, all the fury and malice of Satan, all the wisdom of the world, and strength of men, doing, devising, and practising, what they could, the religion of Christ has had the upper hand, which I wish to be greatly noted, and diligently pondered, in considering these histories, which I trust will not be found unworthy the reading.

Now, I propose, in this second book, to leave for a time the treating of these general affairs of the universal church, and to pursue such domestic histories as more nearly concern England and Scotland, beginning with King Lucius, with whom the christian faith first began in this realm, as is the opinion of some writers. And as here may and does rise a great controversy in these popish days, concerning the origin and planting of the faith in this realm, it will not be greatly out of our purpose to stay and say somewhat on this question, Whether the church of England first received the faith from Rome or not? which, although I were to grant, yet being granted, it little avails the purpose of those who would so have it. For even if England first received the christian faith and religion from Rome, in the time of Eleutherius their bishop, (A.D. 180), and also in the time of Austin, whom Gregory sent hither, (A.D. 600), yet it follows not that we must therefore still fetch our religion from thence as from the chief fountain of all godliness. And, as they are not able to prove this, so neither have I any cause to grant the other, that is, that our christian faith was first derived from Rome, which I may prove by six or seven good conjectural reasons. The first I take on the testimony of our countryman, Gildas, who, in his history, plainly affirms that Britain received the gospel in the time of the Emperor Tiberius, under whom Christ suffered. (Lib. de victoria Aurelii Ambrosi). And says, moreover, that Joseph of Arimathea, after the dispersion of the Jews, was sent by Philip the apostle from France to Britain, about the year 63, and remained in this land all his life, and so with his companions laid the first foundation of christian faith among the British people, whereupon other preachers and teachers coming afterward, confirmed the same and increased it.

The second reason is from Tertullian, who, living near the time of this Eleutherius, in his book (Contra Judæos) declares plainly the same thing, where, testifying how the gospel was dispersed abroad, by the preaching of the apostles, and reckoning up the Medes, Persians, Parthians, and dwellers in Mesopotamia, Judea, Cappadocia, Pontus, Asia, Phrygia, Egypt, Pamphilia, and many other nations, at length comes to the coast of the Moors, the borders of Spain, and the nations of France; and there, amongst others, recites also the parts of Britain, which the Romans could never attain to, and reports the same now to be subject to Christ; and also reckons up the places of Sarmatia, of the Danes, the Germans, the Scythians, with many other provinces and isles unknown to him, in all which places (he says) the name of Christ reigns, which now begins to be common. Note here how, among other believing nations, he mentions also the wildest parts of Britain, and these in his time were christianised. Therefore Pope Eleutherius was not the first who sent the christian faith into this realm, but the gospel was brought here before his time, either by Joseph of Arimathea, as some chronicles record, or by some of the apostles, or of their disciples, who preached Christ before Eleutherius wrote to Lucius.

My third proof I take from Origen, who calls this island "Christian Britain," (Hom. 4. in Ezechielem). Whereby it appears that the faith of Christ was spread in England before the days of Eleutherius.

For my fourth proof I take the testimony of Bede, who affirms, that in his time, and almost a thousand years after Christ, Easter was kept in Britain after the manner of the eastern church. Whence it is to be collected, that the first preachers in this land came from the eastern part of the world, rather than from Rome.

Fifthly, I may allege the words of Nicephorus, (lib. ii. cap. 40), where he says that Simon Zelotes spread the gospel of Christ to the western ocean, and brought it to the isles of Britain.

Sixthly, may be here added also the words of Peter

abbott of Clugny, who writing to Bernard, affirms that the Scots in his time celebrated Easter, not after the Roman manner, but after the Greek. And as the Britons were not under the Roman order in the time of this abbot, neither were they nor would they be under the Roman legate in the time of Gregory, nor would admit any supremacy of the bishop of Rome.

For the seventh argument, moreover, I make my proof by the plain words of Eleutherius, by whose epistle, written to King Lucius, we may understand that Lucius had received the faith of Christ in this land, before the king sent to Eleutherius for the Roman laws; for so the express words of the letter manifestly purport, as hereafter shall be seen. From all which proofs it is more than probable that the Britons were taught first by the Grecians of the eastern church, rather than by the Romans.

Perhaps Eleutherius might help either to convert the king, or else to increase the faith then newly sprung up among the people, but that he was the first cannot be proved. And if we grant he was, as indeed the greater part of our English histories confess; yet what do they obtain thereby, for to conclude this matter in few words, if the christian faith was first derived from Rome by this nation through Eleutherius, then let them but grant to us the same faith which was then taught at Rome, and from thence derived here by Eleutherius, and we will desire no more; for then there was neither any universal pope above all churches and councils (which did not occur before the time of Boniface, which was four hundred years after), nor any mention or use of the mass, the history whereof shall hereafter be seen. Neither was there any propitiatory sacrifice for souls in purgatory, but simply the communion was frequented at christian tables, where oblations and gifts were offered to God as well by the people as by the priests. Neither was there any transubstantiation heard of for a thousand years after. Neither were there then any images of departed saints set up in churches; for a great number of the saints worshipped in our time were not then born, nor the churches where they were worshipped built, but occurred long after, especially in the time of the Empress Irene, (A. D. 781), and the Emperor Constans. Neither were relics or pilgrimages then in use. The marriage of priests was then as lawful (and no less received) than at present, neither was it condemned before the days of Hildebrand, almost a thousand years afterward. Their service was then in the vulgar tongue, as Jerome witnesses; the sacraments ministered in both kinds as well to laymen as to priests, as Cyprian testifies. Yea, and worldly men who would not communicate at Easter, Whitsuntide, and Christmas, were not then counted for catholics, as the pope's own distinction testifies. At funerals priests did not then flock together, selling trentals and dirges for sweeping of purgatory; but a funeral concion alone was used, with psalms of praises and halleluiahs sounding on high, which shook the gilded ceilings of the temple, as Nazianzen, Ambrose, Jerome, &c. witness.

In the supper of the Lord, and in baptism, no such ceremonies were used, as have been introduced of late: both Augustine and Paulinus then baptized in rivers, not in hallowed fonts, as Fabian witnesses. Neither the ordinary of Sarum, of York, of Bangor, with the daily matins and even-song; nor the orders of monks and friars were then dreamed of for almost a thousand years after. So that, as I said before, if the papists would needs derive the faith and religion of this realm from Rome, then let them carry us back whence they found us, that is, let them suffer us to stand content with that faith and religion which was then taught and brought from Rome by Eleutherius (as now we differ in nothing from the same) and we desire no better. And if they will not, then let the reader judge where the fault is, in us, or them, which neither themselves will persist in the antiquity of the Romish religion which they so much boast of, neither will they permit us to do so.

And thus much by the way to answer the aforesaid objection, whereby we may now more readily return to the order and course of the history. Therefore, grant-ing to them what they so earnestly contend for, that the christian faith and religion of this realm was brought from Rome, first by Eleutherius and afterward by Austin; the chronicles thus write of the matter.

About the year 180, King Lucius, son of Coilus, king of the Britons, hearing of the miracles and wonders done by the christians at that time, directed letters to Eleutherius, bishop of Rome, desiring to receive the christian faith from him, although there is great difference in authors about the computation of the time. The good bishop hearing the request of the king, sends him certain preachers called Fagan and Damian, who converted the king and people of Britain, and baptized them with the baptism and sacrament of Christ's faith. They overthrew the temples of the idols, and converted the people from their many gods to serve one living God. Thus true religion increasing, superstition decayed, with all other rites of idolatry. There were then in Britain twenty-eight head priests who they called flamines, and three arch-priests who were called archflamines, having the oversight of their manners, and as judges over the rest. These twenty-eight flamines they turned to twenty-eight bishops, and the three archflamines to three archbishops. After this King Lucius sent again to Eleutherius for the Roman laws, unto whom Eleutherius writes as follows :—

" Ye require us to send you the Roman laws and the emperors, which you may practise and put in force within your realm. The Roman laws and the emperors we may ever reprove, but the law of God we may not. Ye have received of late through God's mercy in the realm of Britain, the law and faith of Christ; ye have with you within the realm, both the parts of the scriptures. Out of them by God's grace, with the council of your realm take ye a law, and by that law (through God's sufferance) rule your kingdom of Britain. For you are God's vicar in your kingdom, according to the saying of the psalm, ' O God, give thy judgment to the King, and thy righteousness to the King's son,' &c. He said not, the judgment and righteousness of the emperor, but thy judgment and justice; that is to say, of God. The King's sons are the christian people of the realm, which are under your government, and live and continue in peace within your kingdom, as the gospel saith, ' Like as the hen gathereth her chickens under her wings,' so doth the king his people. The people and folk of the realm of Britain are yours: whom, if they be divided, ye ought to gather in concord and peace, to call them to the faith and law of Christ, and to the holy church, to cherish and maintain them, to rule and govern them, and to defend them always from such as would do them wrong, from malicious men and enemies. A king hath his name for ruling, and not for having a realm. You shall be a king while you rule well; but if you do otherwise, the name of a king shall not remain with you, and you shall lose it, which God forbid. The Almighty God grant you so to rule the realm of Britain, that you may reign with him for ever, whose vicar you be in the realm."

After this manner was the christian faith either first brought in, or else confirmed in this realm, not with any cross or procession, but only by the simple preaching of Fagan and Damian, through whose ministry this island was reduced to the faith and law of the Lord, according as was prophesied by Isaiah, as well of this as of other islands, where he saith, " He shall not fail nor be discouraged, till he have set judgment in the earth, and the isles shall wait for his law."—Isaiah, xlii. 4. The faith thus received continued and flourished for the space of two hundred and sixty-one years, till the coming of the Saxons, who then were Pagans.

But although Lucius, through the merciful providence of God was then converted and the gospel almost generally received in the land, yet the state thereof, as well of the religion as of the commonwealth, could not be quiet, for the emperors and nobles of Rome were infidels, and enemies to the same; but especially because Lucius the christian king died without issue. For thereby such trouble and variance occurred among the Britons, that they not only brought upon them the idolatrous Romans, and at length the Saxons, but also entangled themselves in much misery and desolation. For sometimes the idolatrous Romans, sometimes the Britons reigned and ruled as violence and victory would serve; one king murdering another, till at length the Saxons came and dispossessed them both, as shall hereafter be seen.

Thus the commonwealth was miserably rent and divided into two sorts of people, differing not so much in country as in religion; for when the Romans reigned, the people were governed by the infidels; when the Britons ruled, they were governed by christians. Thus how little quietness was or could be in the church in so unquiet and doubtful days, may easily be considered.

Notwithstanding all these heathen rulers of the Romans, which governed here, yet (God be praised) we read of no persecution during all the ten above mentioned, that touched the christian Britons, before the last persecution of Dioclesian. This persecution, was the first of many that followed in the church and realm of England. The rage of Dioclesian (as it was through all the churches in the world,) was fierce and vehement in Britain, and all our English chronicles testify that christianity was destroyed almost throughout the land, churches were subverted, the scriptures burned, and many of the faithful, both men and women were slain.

Now concerning the government of the kings of Britain, although I have little or nothing to note which greatly appertains to the matter of this ecclesiastical history, yet this is not to be passed over. First, that Constantine the great and worthy emperor, comes in the order of these kings, who was not only a Briton born, by his mother Helena, being the daughter of King Coilus, but also by help of the British army (under the power of God) which Constantine took with him from Britain to Rome, he obtained the peace and tranquillity to the universal church of Christ: in consequence of his taking with him three legions of chosen and able British soldiers, the strength of this land was not a little impaired and endangered.

After him Maximian, took with him all the remaining able and fighting men, in order to subdue France.

Thus poor Britain being left naked and destitute on every side, as a maimed body without might and strength, was left open to her enemies, unable to succour herself without the help of foreign friends; to whom the Britons were then constrained to fly, especially to the Romans, to whom they sent this message. " The groans of Britain —the barbarians drive us into the sea—the sea drives us back to the barbarians. Thus we have before us two kinds of death, we must be either butchered or drowned!" As the realm of Britain almost from the beginning was never without civil war, at length came wicked Vortigern, who cruelly causing his prince to be murdered, ambitiously invaded the crown; and sent over for the aid of the Saxons, who were then infidels; and not only that, but also married with an infidel, the daughter of Hengist, called Rowena. Whereupon Vortigern not long after was with like treachery dispossessed of his kingdom, and the people of Britain driven out of their country, after the Saxons, under Hengist and his chiefs, had slain their chief nobles and barons.

These Saxons coming in daily, filled the land with their multitudes, so that the Britons at length were neither able to hold what they had, nor to recover what they had lost; leaving an example to all ages and countries, of what it is to let foreign nations into their dominion, but especially what it is for princes to join in marriage with infidels, as this Vortigern did with Hengist's daughter, who was the mother of all this mischief; and gave to the Saxons, not only strength, but also occasion and courage to attempt what they did. The British lords and nobility being offended therewith, deposed their king, and enthroned his son Vortimer in his room. Vortimer, being a brave prince, the Saxons were repulsed, and driven again into Germany, where they stayed till the death of Vortimer, whom Rowena, daughter of Hengist, caused traiterously to be poisoned. Then Vortigern being restored to his kingdom, through the entreaty of his wife Rowena, sent into Germany for Hengist, who

came in with a navy of three hundred well appointed ships. The nobles of Britain hearing this, prepared themselves on the other side in all force, to resist them. But Hengist, through his daughter Rowena, influenced the king, and excused himself, saying, that he brought not the multitude to work any violence either against him, or against his country, and that he commits both himself and his people to him, to appoint how few or how many of them he would permit to remain within his land, and the rest were to return. And so it pleased the king to appoint day and place where they might meet and talk together of the matter, both he and his followers would stand to such order as the king with his council should appoint. With these fair words, the king and his nobles, well contented, assigned both day and place, which was in the town of Amesbury, where he meant to talk with them; adding this condition, that each party should come without any weapon. Hengist agreed, but gave privy commandment to his followers that each man should secretly carry in his hose a long knife, and a watch-word also was agreed on, which, when they heard, they were to draw their knives, and every Saxon kill the Briton with whom he talked. The British lords being slain, the Saxons took Vortigern the king, and bound him; for whose ransom they required the cities of London, York, Lincoln, Winchester, with other the most strong holds in the land to be delivered to them; which being granted, they begin to make spoil and havock of the nation, destroying the citizens, pulling down churches, killing the priests, burning the books of the holy scripture, and leaving nothing undone that tyranny could work, which was about A.D. 462. The king, seeing this miserable slaughter of the people, fled to Wales.

Aurelius Ambrosius, and Uter Pendragon, King Constans' brothers, whom Vortigern caused to be killed, were then in Little Britain. To them the Britons sent word, desiring their aid. Aurelius goes over to satisfy their desire, and being crowned as their king, seeks out wicked Vortigern, the cause of all this trouble, and the murderer of his brother Constans. And finding him in a strong tower in Wales, where he had immured himself, set his castle on fire, and thus Vortigern was burned to death. That done, he moved his power against the Saxons, with whom and with Elle, captain of the South Saxons, (who then was newly come over) he had several conflicts.

After the death of Aurelius, who was poisoned by order of Pascentius, the son of Vortigern, (who suborned a man in the garb of a monk, to pass himself for a physician, and to poison him); his brother Uter, surnamed Pendragon, succeeded to the throne, about A.D. 497, who fighting against Octa and Cosa, took them and brought them to London; but they breaking out of prison, returned into Germany for more aid. In the mean time, there was daily intercourse of the Saxons, from Saxony, with whom the Britons had many conflicts, sometimes winning, sometimes losing. Not long after Octa and Cosa returned again, and joined the other Saxons against the Britons. From this time the state of Britain began to decay more and more, while the idolatrous Saxons prevailed in numbers and strength against the christian Britons; oppressing the people, throwing down the churches and monasteries, murdering the prelates, and sparing neither age nor person, but wasting christianity almost through the whole realm. To these miseries it happened, moreover, that Uter their king was ill, and could not stir, but being grieved for the lamentable destruction of his people, he caused his bed to be brought into the camp, where God gave him the victory, Octa and Cosa being slain. Shortly after, Uter died of poison, put (as it is said) into a fountain whereof the king used to drink, about A.D. 516.

About this time the West Saxons came so violently upon the Britons, that they of the western part of the realm were not able to resist them. After this the merciful providence of Almighty God raised up for them King Arthur, the son of Uter, who was then crowned after him, and reigned victoriously. The old British histories ascribe to Arthur twelve great victories against the Saxons, which gave the Britons some peace during life, and that of certain of his successors. [After

Arthur, the next king of the Britons was Constantine. After him Aurelius Conanus. Then Vortiporinus; after whom followed Malgo. And after him the last king of the Britons was Carecius, all of whom were continually engaged in civil war, execrable to God and man, and being chased out by the Britons themselves, the land came into the possession of the Saxons, (A. D. 568), by whom all the clergy of the Britons were utterly driven out; insomuch that Theonus archbishop of London, and Theodosius archbishop of York, seeing their churches wasted, and parishes dispersed, left their sees in Britain, and fled into Cambria, which is now called Wales.

The race of the Saxon kings who thus expelled the British, divided their land into seven kingdoms; many of whom delighted in war and bloodshed, while few were sincere or good. But none escaped either being slain in war, or murdered in peace, or else being constrained to become a monk.

Now although the example of those kings who became monks (in number seven or eight), is rare and strange, and much commended by the historians of the time; I cannot assent to their commendation, first, in altering their estate from kings to monks, if they did it to find more ease, and less trouble, I see not how that excuse stands with the office of a good man, to change his public vocation for a private convenience. If fear of danger drove them thereto, what praise or commendation do they deserve in so doing? Let the monkish histories judge what they like, methinks that just so much praise as they deserve in providing for their own safety, just so much they deserve again to be discommended for forsaking the commonwealth. If they did it (as most likely they did) for holiness sake, thinking in that kind of life to serve and please God better, or to merit more toward their salvation than in the estate of a king, they were greatly deceived; not knowing that the salvation which comes of God is to be esteemed, not by man's merits, or by any perfection of life, or by any difference of vocation, but only by the free grace of the gospel, which freely justifies all them that faithfully believe in Christ Jesus. But here it will be said again, perhaps in the solitary life of a monk, there are fewer occasions of evils than in kings' courts, wherefore that life conduces more to holiness, and is more to be preferred than the other. To this I answer, to avoid the occasion of evil is good where strength lacks to resist, but otherwise, where duty and charge constrain, there to avoid the occasions of evil, where they ought rather to be resisted, declares rather a weakness of the man than deserves any praise.

These things thus premised, it remains to enter on such things as in the time of these kings happened in the church; first putting the reader in mind of the former three or four persecutions within the realm, and which happened before the coming of Austin into England.

The first was under Dioclesian, and that not only in England, but generally throughout all the Roman monarchy, as is above specified. In this persecution Alban, Julius, Aaron, with many more christian Britons were martyred for Christ's name.

The second persecution was by the invasion of the Huns and the Picts, who made miserable havock of Christ's saints, spoiling and wasting churches, without mercy either to women or children.

The third persecution was under Hengist and the Saxons; who likewise destroyed and wasted the christian congregations within the land, like raging wolves flying upon the sheep, and spilling the blood of christians, till Aurelius Ambrosius came, and restored again the destroyed churches.

The fourth destruction of the christian faith and religion was by Gurmund, a Pagan king of the Africans, who joining in league with the Saxons, wrought much grievance to the christians of the land; and this persecution remained to the time of Ethelbert the king of Kent. (A. D. 589.)

In the reign of this Ethelbert, who was the fifth king of Kent, the faith of Christ was first received among the Saxons by means of Gregory, bishop of Rome, in the following manner, as collected from the old histories:

First then, the christian faith received by King Lucius. indured in Britain till this time above 400 years, when by Gurmund (as is said) fighting with the Saxons against the Britons, it was nearly extinct in all the land, during the space of about forty-four years. So that the first springing of Christ's gospel in this land was in A.D. 180. The coming of Austin was in A. D. 596. In which year Austin being sent from Gregory, came into England. The cause of Gregory sending him hither was this:

In the days of Pelagius bishop of Rome, Gregory chancing to see certain beautiful children in the marketplace of Rome, brought out of England to be sold, demanded from whence they were? and understanding they were heathens from England, he lamented the case of the land whose inhabitants being so beautiful and angelic[1] were subject to the prince of darkness. And asking moreover out of what province they were, it was answered, out of Deira, a part of North-saxons. Then he, alluding to the name of *Deira*, "These people," said he, "are to be delivered '*De Dei ira*,'" that is, "from God's wrath." Moreover, understanding the king's name of that province to be *Alle*, alluding likewise to his name, "There," saith he, "ought *Allelujah* to be sung to the living God." Whereupon he being moved, and desirous to go and help the conversion of that country, sent Austin thither, with other preachers to the number of forty. And he directed letters to Austin, and to his fellows, exhorting them to go forward boldly to the Lord's work, as by the following epistle appears:

"Gregory the servant of God's servants, to the servants of the Lord. Forasmuch as it is better not to take good things in hand, than after they be begun to think to revolt back from the same again, therefore now you may not nor cannot, dear children, turn back, but with all fervent study and labour must needs go forward in that good business, which through the help of God you have well begun. Neither let the labour of your journey, nor the slanderous tongues of men appal you, but with all instance and fervency proceed and accomplish the thing which the Lord hath ordained you to take in hand; knowing that your great labour shall be recompensed with a reward of greater glory hereafter. Therefore as we send here Austin to you again, whom also we have ordained to be your governor, so do you humbly obey him in all things, knowing that it shall be profitable for your souls, whatsoever at his admonition ye shall do. Almighty God with his grace defend you, and grant me to see in the eternal country the fruit of your labour; that although I cannot labour as I would with you, yet I may be found partaker of your retribution, for that my will is good to labour in the same fellowship with you together. The Lord God keep you safe, most dear and well-beloved children. Dated the tenth before the Kalends of August, in the reign of our sovereign lord Maurice most virtuous emperor, the fourteenth of his empire."

Thus they being emboldened and comforted through the good words of Gregory, went on their journey till they came to the Isle of Thanet. Near the landing-place was then the palace of the king, not far from Sandwich. The king then reigning in Kent was Ethelbert, who had married a christian Frenchwoman, named Bertha, whom he had received of her parents upon this condition, that he should permit her to retain her bishop, called Lebard, and to enjoy the freedom of her faith, by means whereof he was sooner induced to embrace the doctrine of Christ. Austin being arrived, sent forth certain messengers to the king, signifying that such a one was come from Rome, bringing with him glad tidings to him and all his people of life and salvation eternally to reign in heaven, with the only true and

(1) He asked of what nation were those beautiful children. He was told they were *Anglici* (English), on hearing which, he said they should rather be called *Angelici* (Angelic). [ED.]

living God for ever, if he would as willingly hearken as he was gladly come to preach and teach it to him.

The king who had heard of this religion before by his wife, within a few days comes to the place where Austin was, to speak with him. Austin, as the histories affirm, erected a banner of the crucifix (such was the grossness of that time), and preached to him the word of God. The king answering said, "The words are very fair that you preach and promise; nevertheless, because it is new to me, I cannot soon start away from my country's laws wherewith I have been so long inured, and assent to you. Yet as ye are come (as ye say) so far for my sake, you shall not be molested by me, but shall be treated well, having all things ministered to you necessary for your support. Besides this, neither do we debar you, but grant you free leave to preach to our subjects, to convert whom ye may to the faith of your religion."

When they had received this comfort of the king, they went with procession to the city of Canterbury, singing Allelujah with the litany. The words of the litany were, "We beseech thee, O Lord, in all thy mercies, that thy fury and anger may cease from this city, and from thy holy house, for we have sinned, Allelujah." The king having given them a mansion for their abode, they continued there preaching and baptizing such as they had converted in the old church of St. Martin (where the queen was wont to resort), to the time that the king himself was converted to Christ. At length, when the king had well considered the honest conversation of their life, and moved with the miracles wrought through God's hands by them, he heard them more gladly; and lastly, by their wholesome exhortations and example of godly life, he was converted and christened. After the king was thus converted, innumerable others were daily joined to the church of Christ; whom the king did specially embrace, but compelled none; for so he had learned, that the faith and service of Christ ought to be voluntary, and not compulsory. Then he gave Austin a place for the bishop's see at Christ's Church, and built the abbey of St. Peter and Paul in the east side of the city, where afterwards Austin and all the kings of Kent were buried, and that place is now called St. Austin.

At this time Austin sailed to France, to be consecrated archbishop by the command of Gregory: who, hearing of Austin's success, sends to the church of England more coadjutors and helpers, as Melitus, Justus, Paulinus, and Ruffianus, with books and such other matters as he thought necessary for the English church. He sends also to Austin a Pall with letters, wherein he appoints the two metropolitan sees, the one to be at London, the other at York. But he grants to Austin during his life, to be the only archbishop: and after his time, then to return to the two sees of London and York, as is contained in the following epistle of Gregory, to Austin.

"To the reverend and virtuous brother Augustine, his fellow bishop, Gregory the servant of the servants of God. Although it is most certain, that unspeakable rewards of the heavenly king be laid up for all such as labour in the word of the Almighty God: yet it shall be requisite for us to reward the same also with our benefits, to the end they may be more encouraged to go forward in their spiritual work. And now, as the new church of Englishmen is brought to the grace of Almighty God, through his mighty help, and your labour, therefore we have granted to you the use of the pall, only to be used at the solemnity of your mass; so that it shall be lawful for you to ordain twelve bishops, such as shall be subject to your province. So that hereafter the bishop of the city of London shall always be ordained and consecrated by his own proper synod; and so to receive the pall of honour from the holy and apostolic see, wherein I here (by the permission of God) do serve. And as touching the city of York, we will send also a bishop thither, whom you may think meet to ordain. So that if that city with other places bordering thereby, shall receive the word of God, he shall have power likewise to ordain twelve bishops, and have the honour of a metroplitan; to whom also, if God spare my life, I intend by the favour of God,

to send a pall: this provided, that notwithstanding he shall be subject to your brotherly appointment. But after your decease, the same metropolitan, so to be over the bishops whom he ordereth, that he be in no wise subject to the metropolitan of London after you. And hereafter, betwixt these two metropolitans of London and York, let there be had such distinction of honour, that he shall have the priority, which shall be first ordained. With the common counsel, and affection of heart, let them go both together, disposing with one accord such things as are to be done for the zeal of Christ. Let them consider and deliberate together prudently, and what they deliberate wisely, let them accomplish with concord, not jarring or swerving one from the other. But as for your part, you shall be endued with authority, not only over those bishops that you constitute, and over the other constituted by the bishop of York; but also you shall have all other priests of whole Britain, subject unto our Lord Jesus Christ: to the end that through your preaching and holiness of life, they may learn both to believe rightly, and to live purely, and so in directing their life, both by the rule of true faith and virtuous manners, they may attain, when God shall call them, the fruition and kingdom of heaven. God preserve you in health, reverend brother. The tenth before the kalends of July, in the reign of our Lord Maurice most virtuous emperor."

Besides this, Gregory sends another letter to Melitus concerning his judgment, what is to be done with the idolatrous temples and fanes of the English newly converted, which fanes he thinks best not to pull down, but to convert the use thereof, and so let them stand. And likewise of their sacrifices, and killing of oxen, how the same ought to be ordered, and how to be altered.

He directed another epistle to king Ethelbert, in which epistle first he praises God, then commends the goodness of the king, by whom it pleased God to work such goodness of the people. Secondly, exhorts him to continue in the profession of Christ's faith, and to be fervent and zealous in converting the multitude; in destroying the temples and works of idolatry, in ruling and governing the people in all holiness and godly conversation. Lastly, comforting him with the promises of life and reward to come, with the Lord that reigneth and liveth for ever.

Melitus, of whom mention is made before, was sent specially to the East Saxons in the province of Essex, where he was made bishop of London, under Sigebert, king of Essex; Sigebert, together with his uncle Ethelbert first built the church and minster of St. Paul in London, and appointed it to Melitus for the bishop's see. Austin, with this Melitus and Justus, assembled and gathered together the bishops and doctors of Britain in a place, which taking the name of Austin, was called Austin's Oak. In this assembly he charged the bishops, that they should preach with him the word of God, and also that they should among themselves reform certain rites and usages in their church, specially for keeping of Easter, baptizing after the manner of Rome, and such other like. To this the Scots and Britons would not agree, refusing to leave the custom which they so long time had continued, without the assent of all who used the same.

Then Austin gathered another synod, to the which came seven bishops of Britain, with the wisest men of that famous abbey of Bangor. But first they took counsel of a certain wise and holy man amongst them what to do; and whether they should be obedient to Austin or not. And he said, "If he be the servant of God, agree unto him." "But how shall we know that?" said they. To whom he answered again, "If he be meek and humble of heart, by that know that he is the servant of God." To this they said again, "And how shall we know him to be humble and meek of heart?" "By this" (quoth he) "seeing you are the greater number, if he at your coming into your synod rise up, and courteously receive you, perceive him to be an humble and a meek man; but if he shall contemn and despise you (being as ye are), the greater part despise you him again." Thus the British bishops entered into the council, Austin after the Romish manner keeping his chair, would not remove. Whereat being not little offended, after some heat of words, in disdain and great displeasure departed thence. To whom then Austin spake, and said, "That if they would not take peace with their brethren, they should receive war with their enemies ; and if they disdained to preach with them the way of life to the English nation, they should suffer by their hands the revenge of death. Which not long after so came to pass by the means of Ethelfride, king of Northumberland, who being yet a pagan, and stirred with fierce fury against the Britons, came with a great army against them. There was at the same time at Bangor in Wales an exceeding great monastery, containing upwards of two thousand monks, who all lived by the sweat of their brow, and labour of their own hands, having one for their ruler, named Dino. Out of this monastery came the monks of Chester, to pray for the good success of Brocmaile, fighting for them against the Saxons. They continued three days in fasting and prayer. When Ethelfride, seeing them so attentive to their prayers, demanded the cause of their coming thither in such a company, and when he perceived it, " Then," saith he, " Although they bear no weapon, yet they fight against us, and with their prayers and preachings they persecute us." Whereupon after Brocmaile was overcome, the king commanded his men to turn their weapons against the unarmed monks, of whom he slew, or rather martyred, eleven hundred, only fifty persons of that number did escape, the rest were all slain. The authors that write of this lamentable murder, declare how the saying of Austin was here verified upon the Britons, who because they would not join peace with their friends, he said should be destroyed by their enemies. Of both these parties the reader may judge what he pleases ; I think both were to be blamed, And as I cannot but accuse the one, so I cannot defend the other. First, Austin in this matter can in no wise be excused; who being a monk before, and therefore a scholar and professor of humanity, shewed so little humility in this assembly, to seven bishops and an archbishop, coming at his commandment to the council, that he would not rise up at their coming in. Much less would his pharisaical solemnity have girded himself, and washed his brethren's feet after their journey, as Christ our great Master did to his disciples ; seeing his lordship was so high, or so heavy, or so proud, that he could not find in his heart to give them a little moving of his body, to declare a brotherly and an humble heart. Again, the Britons were as much or more to blame, who so much neglected their spiritual duty, in revenging their temporal injury, that they refused to join their helping labour, to turn the idolatrous Saxons to the way of life and salvation, in which respect all private cases ought to give place, and be forgotten. For which cause, although lamentable to us, yet no great marvel, if the stroke of God's punishment did light upon them according to the words of Austin, as is before declared. But especially the cruel king was most of all to blame so furiously to fly upon them, who had neither weapon to resist him, nor yet any will to harm him.

About this time Gregory, bishop of Rome died, of whom it is said, that of the number of all the bishops before him in the primitive time, he was the worst ; of all that came after him, he was the best. About which time also died in Wales, David, first archbishop of Kaerlon, who then translated the see from thence to Menevia, and therefore is called " David of Wales." Not longer after this also, the aforesaid Austin died in England, after he had sat there fifteen or sixteen years.

As touching the acts and deeds of Gregory, above mentioned, how he withstood the ambitious pride of John patriarch of Constantinople, who wished to be the universal priest, and only chief bishop of all others, declaring him to be no less than the forerunner of antichrist, who would assume that name and title upon him. How, and with what reasons, he answered the letters of the emperor Maurice in that matter, sufficient relation is made in the beginning of this history. This Gregory, among many other things began and brought in this title among the Roman bishops, to be called " the servant of the servants of God ;" putting them in remembrance thereby, both of their humbleness and

also of their duty in the church of Christ. Moreover, as concerning his act for the single life of priests first begun, and then broken again ; also concerning the order of Gregory's mass book to be received in all churches : hereof who wishes to read more, shall find the same when we come to the time of Pope Adrian the first.

After the death of Gregory came Sabinian, who, as he was a malicious detractor of Gregory, and of his works, so he continued not long, scarce the space of two years. After whom succeeded Boniface III., who, although he reigned but one year, yet in that one year did more hurt than Gregory with so much labour, and in so many years, could do good. For that which Gregory kept out, he brought in, obtaining of Phocas, the wicked emperor, for him and his successors after him, that the see of Rome should have the pre-eminence above all other churches, and that the bishop of Rome should be the universal head of all churches of Christ in Christendom, alleging this frivolous reason, that St. Peter had and left to his successors in Rome, the keys of binding and loosing, &c. And thus Rome began first to take a head above all other churches, by means of Boniface III., who, as he lacked no boldness nor ambition to seek it, so neither lacked he an emperor fit and meet to give such a gift. This emperor's name was Phocas, a man of such wickedness and ambition (most like to his own bishop Boniface) that in order to gain the empire, he murdered his own master the Emperor Maurice and his children. Thus coming to be emperor, after this detestable villany, and thinking to establish his empire with the friendship and favour of his people, and especially with the bishop of Rome, he quickly condescended to all his petitions, and so granted him (as it is said) to be what he wished, the universal and head bishop over all christian churches. But as blood commonly requires blood again, so it came to pass on Phocas. For as he had cruelly slain the lord and emperor Maurice before, so he in like manner had his hands and feet cut off by Heraclius, the emperor, who succeeded him, and was cast into the sea. And thus wicked Phocas, who gave the supremacy to Rome, lost his own. But Rome would not so soon loose this supremacy once given, as the giver lost his life. For ever since, from that day it has held, defended, and maintained the same still, and does yet to this present day, by all force and policy possible. And thus much concerning Boniface, whom by the words of Gregory, we may well call the fore-runner of antichrist.

Mention was made a little before of Ethelbert, king of Kent, and also of Ethelfrid, king of North Saxony. This Ethelbert having under his subjection all the other Saxon kings unto the Humber, after he had first himself received the christian faith by the preaching of Austin, caused it to be received by others. When he had reigned the course of fifty and six years, he changed this mortal life about A. D. 616. Some histories say he was slain in a fight between him and Ethelfrid, king of the North Saxons.

In the mean time Ethelfrid, after the cruel murder of the monks of Bangor, escaped not long, for after he had reigned four-and-twenty years he was slain in the field by Edwin, who succeeded in Northumberland after him.

This Edwin not being the son of Ethelfrid, but of Alla, was first a panim or idolater, but was afterwards converted, and was the first christened king in Northumberland.

Quicelinus, with Kinegilsus, his brother, kings of the West Saxons, conspiring the death of Edwin, king of Northumberland, sent upon an Easter-day, a sword-man privily to slay him. This sword-man or cutthroat, came to a city beside the water of Derwent, in Derbyshire, there to wait his time ; and having found the king smally accompanied, attempted to run him through with a poisoned sword. But one Lilla, the king's trusty servant, not having a shield or any other weapon to defend his master, started between the king and the sword, and was stricken through the body and died, thus saving the king, who, however, was wounded with the same stroke. The assassin having wounded another knight, was at last taken, and confessed by whom he was sent to work that treason. The second knight that was wounded, died, and the king lay sick a long time ere he was healed.

In this time there was such peace in the kingdom of Edwin after his conversion, that a woman laden with gold, might have gone from the one side of the sea to the other, and no man molest her. Moreover, by the highway sides, through all his kingdom he caused a dish or bowl of brass to be chained by every well or spring, to take up water for refreshing such as went by the way, which bowls of brass remained there safe, and no man touched them during all the life of Edwin. Such was then the tender care and study of christian princes, for the refreshing of their subjects.

This Edwin who first brought the faith into the north parts, continuing after his baptism six years, was at length slain in battle by Cedwella, king of the Britons.

After the decease of Edwin and his son Offrick, reigned Ofricus and Eaufridus, the one in Deira, the other in Bernicia.

After whom, succeeded the second son of Ethelfrid, named Oswald. Of this Oswald much praise and commendation is written for his zeal in Christ's religion, and pity towards the poor, with other great virtues. Being well and virtuously disposed to the setting forth of Christ's faith and doctrine, he sent into Scotland for a certain bishop called Aidan, a famous preacher, to preach to his people. The king, when he was in Scotland, had learned the Scottish tongue: wherefore as this Aidan preached in his Scottish tongue to the Saxons, the king himself interpreted what he said; he disdained not to preach and expound to his nobles and subjects in the English tongue.

Towards the poor and needy, his pity and tenderness was such, notwithstanding his princely calling, that as he was sitting with Aidan at meat, and was served after the manner of kings in silver; there comes to him one of the servitors, bringing him word that there was a great multitude of poor people sitting in the street, who desired some alms of the king. He hearing this, commanded not only the meat prepared for his table to be carried unto them, but also taking a silver platter which stood before him, brake it in pieces and sent it amongst them, and so relieved his poor subjects, not only with the meat of his table, but with the dishes also.

After Oswald had reigned nine years, he was slain by wicked Penda, king of the Mercians; which Penda at length, after all his tyranny, was overcome, and slain by Oswy, brother to Oswald.

Oswy succeeded Oswald, and with him was joined Oswine his cousin. This Oswine was gentle and liberal to his people, and no less devout toward God. He once had given to Aidan, the bishop, a princely horse, with the trappings and all that appertained to it, that he should not travel so much on foot. Aidan, as he was riding upon his kingly horse, meets by the way a poor man, asking his charity. Aidan having nothing else to give him, lighted down, and gave to him his horse with all the trappings as he was. The king hearing this, and not being pleased, as he was entering to dinner with Aidan, said, "What meant you, father bishop, to give away my horse I gave you, to the beggar? had I not other horses in my stable that might have served him well enough, but you must give away that which was picked out for you amongst the chiefest?" To whom the bishop answered again, rebuking the king, saying, "What are these words, O king! that you speak? why set you more price by a horse, which is but the foal of a horse, than you do by him which is the Son of Mary, yea, which is the Son of God?" He said but this, when the king forthwith ungirding his sword from about him (as he was then newly come in from hunting), falls down at the feet of the bishop, desiring him to forgive him that, and he would never again speak a word to him for any treasure he should afterwards give away of his.

Oswine having been slain by the king of Bernicia,

Oswy, with his son Egfrid, reigned in Northumberland, in whose time the question of Easter, and of shaving, and other ecclesiastical matters being moved, it was determined, that a convocation should be held in the abbey, called Sternhalt, and this question determined. To which place came the kings, Oswy and Egfrid, Bishop Colman, with his clergy of Scotland, Agilbert, with Agathon and Wilfrid priests. James and Roman were on their sides, Hilda the abbess, with her company, was on the Scottish part, and the Bishop Cedda, was appointed prolocutor for both parties, King Oswy began first with an oration, declaring that it was necessary for such as served one God, to live in one uniform order. This said, he commanded his Bishop Colman to declare what was the rite and custom that he used. Then Colman said, "The Easter which I observe, I received of my ancestors that sent me hither a bishop, which all our forefathers, being men of God, celebrated in like manner; and lest it should be contemned or despised of any man, it is manifestly apparent to be the very same which the holy evangelist St. John, (a disciple especially beloved of the Lord), did customarily use in all churches and congregations where he had authority," When Colman had spoken many things to this effect, the king commanded Agilbert to declare his opinion, and to shew the order that he used, from whence it came, and by what authority he observed the same. Agilbert requested the king that his scholar Wilfrid, a priest, might speak for him, inasmuch as they both, with the rest of his clergy, were of one opinion herein, and that Wilfrid could utter his mind better, and more plainly in the English tongue, than he himself could. Then Wilfrid, at the king's commandment, said, "The Easter which we keep, we have seen at Rome, where the holy apostles, Peter and Paul, did live and teach, did suffer, and were buried. The same also is used in Italy and in France; in which countries we have travelled for learning, and have noted it to be celebrated of them all. In Asia also and in Africa, in Egypt and in Greece, and finally in all the world, the same manner of Easter is observed that we use, save only by these here present, with their accomplices, the Picts and Britons." To whom Colman replied, saying, "I marvel you will call this order foolish, that so great an apostle as was worthy to lie on the Lord's breast, did use, whom all the world well knows to have lived most wisely." And Wilfrid answered, "God forbid that I should reprove St. John of his folly, who kept the rites of Moses's law, according to the letter (the church being yet Jewish in many points), and the apostles not as yet able to rescind all the observations of the law before ordained. As for example, they could not reject images invented of the devil, the which all men that believe on Christ, ought of necessity to forsake and detest, lest they should be an offence to those Jews that were amongst the Gentiles. For this cause did St. Paul circumcise Timothy, for this cause did he sacrifice in the temple, and did shave his head with Aquila and Priscilla at Corinth; all which things were done to no other purpose, than to avoid the offending the Jews. Hereupon also said James to Paul, "Thou seest, brother, how many thousand Jews do believe, and all these are zealous of the law. Yet seeing the gospel is so manifestly preached in the world, it is not lawful for the faithful to be circumcised, neither to offer sacrifice of carnal things to God." Therefore John, according to the custom of the law, the fourteenth day of the first month at evening, did begin the celebration of the feast of Easter, not respecting whether it were celebrated on the Sabbath. But Peter, when he preached at Rome, remembering that the Lord did arise from death on the first day after the Sabbath, giving thereby a hope to the world of the resurrection, thought good to institute Easter on that day, and not after the use and precepts of the law, on the fourteenth day of the first month; even so, John looking for the moon at night, if it did arise, and the next day after were Sunday, which then was called the Sabbath, then did he celebrate the Easter in the evening, like as we use to do even at this day. But if Sunday were not the next day after the fourteenth day, but fell on the sixteenth day, or seventeenth, or on any other day unto the one and twentieth, he tarried always for it, and did begin the holy solemnity of Easter on the evening next before the Sabbath. And so it came to pass, that Easter was always kept on the Sunday, and was not celebrated but from the fifteenth day to the one and twentieth; neither does this tradition of the apostle break the law, but fulfil the same. In which it is to be noted, that Easter was instituted from the fourteenth day of the first month at evening, to the one and twentieth day of the same month at evening; which manner all St. John's successors in Asia followed after his death and the catholic church throughout the whole world. And that this is the true Easter, was not newly decreed, but confirmed by the council of Nice. Whereupon it is manifest that you (Colman) do neither follow the example of St. John, as ye think, nor of St. Peter, whose tradition you do willingly resist, nor of the church, nor yet of the gospel, in the celebration of Easter. For St. John, observing Easter according to the precepts of the law, kept it not on the first day after the Sabbath; but you precisely keep it on the first day after the Sabbath. Peter did celebrate Easter from the fifteenth day of the moon to the one and twentieth day, but you keep Easter from the fourteenth unto the twentieth day; so that you begin Easter oftentimes the thirteenth day at night, of which manner neither the law nor the gospel makes any mention. But our Lord in the fourteenth day, either did eat the old passover at night, or else did celebrate the sacraments of the New Testament, in the remembrance of his death and passion. You do also utterly reject from the celebration of Easter, the one and twentieth day, which the law has chiefly willed to be observed; and therefore, as I said, in the keeping of Easter, you neither agree with St. John nor with St. Peter, nor with the law, nor yet with the gospel." Then Colman again answered to these things, saying, "Did then Anatholius, a godly man, and one much commended in ecclesiastical history, write against the law and the gospel, who writes that the Easter was to be kept from the fourteenth day unto the twentieth? Or shall we think that Columba, our reverend father, and his successors, being men of God, who observed the Easter after this manner, did it against the holy scripture? Whereas some of them were men of much godliness and virtue, as was declared by their wonderful miracles. And I hereby (nothing doubting of their holiness) do endeavour to follow their life, order, and discipline." Then, said Wilfrid "It is certain that Anatholius was both a godly man, and worthy of great commendation; but what have you to do with him, seeing you observe not his order? For he following the true rule in keeping his Easter, observes the circle of nineteen years; the which either you know not, or if you do, you condemn the common order observed in the universal church of Christ. And moreover, the said Anatholius so counts the fourteenth day, in the observation of Easter, as he confesses the same to be the fifteenth day at night, after the manner of the Egyptians, and likewise notes the twentieth day, to be in the feast of Easter, the one and twentieth in the evening; that you know not this distinction, may appear by this, that you keep the Easter, on the thirteenth day before the full moon. I can answer you touching your father Columba and his successors, whose order you say you follow, moved thereto by their miracles, on this wise, that the Lord will answer to many that shall say in the day of judgment, that in his name they have prophesied and cast out devils, and have done many miracles, &c. that he never knew them. But God forbid that I should say so of your fathers, because it is much better to believe well of those we know not, than ill. Whereupon I deny not but they were the servants of God, and holy men, which loved the Lord of a good intent, though of a rude simplicity. And I think that the order which they used in the Easter, did not much hurt them, so long as they had none amongst them that could shew them the right observation of the same for them to follow. For I think, if the truth had been declared to them, they would as well have received it in this matter as they did

in others. But you and your fellows, if you refuse the order of the Apostolical see, or rather of the universal church, which is confirmed by the holy scripture; without all doubt you do sin. And though your forefathers were holy men, what is their fewness, being but a corner of an island, to be preferred before the universal church of Jesus Christ, dispersed throughout the whole world? And if Columba your father, (and ours also, being of Christ Jesus), were mighty in miracles, is he therefore to be preferred before the prince of the holy apostles? To whom the Lord said, 'Thou art Peter, and upon this rock will I build my church, and the gates of hell shall not prevail against it, and I will give thee the keys of the kingdom of heaven.'"

Wilfred having thus ended his argument, the king said to Colman, "Is it true that the Lord spake these things to St. Peter?" And Colman answered "Yea." Then said the king, "Can you declare any thing that the Lord gave to Colman?" Colman answered, "No." Then quoth the king, "Do both of you agree and consent in this matter without any controversy, that these words were principally spoken to Peter, and that the Lord gave him the keys of the kingdom of heaven?" And they both answered "Yea." Then concluded the king, on this wise, "For so much as St. Peter is the door-keeper of heaven, I will not gainsay him; but as far as I am able, I will obey his orders in every point, lest when I come to the gates of heaven, he shut them against me."

Upon this simple and rude reason of the king, the multitude soon consented, and with them also Cedda was contented to give over, only Colman the Scot, being then archbishop of York, left the realm in displeasure. And thus much concerning this matter of Easter.

About this time Theodore was sent from Italy into England, by Vitalian the pope, to be archbishop of Canterbury, and with him other monks of Italy, to set up here in England Latin service, masses, ceremonies, litanies, with other Romish ware, &c. This Theodore being made archbishop and metropolitan of Canterbury, began to act as if he was king, placing and displacing the bishops at his pleasure. As for Cedda and Wilfrid archbishops of York, he thrust them both out, under the pretence that they were not lawfully consecrated, notwithstanding they were sufficiently authorised by their kings.

In the time of this Theodore, and by the means of him, a provincial synod was holden at Thetford, mentioned in Bede; the principal contents whereof were these:

First. That Easter-day should be uniformly kept and observed through the whole realm, upon one certain day, namely, the first full moon after the fourteenth day of the first month.

Secondly. That no bishop should intermeddle within the diocese of another.

Thirdly. That monasteries consecrated unto God should be exempt and free from the jurisdiction of the bishops.

Fourthly. That the monks should not stray from one place (that is) from one monastery to another, without the license of their abbot; also to keep the same obedience which they promised at their first entering.

Fifthly. That no clergyman should forsake his own bishop, and be received in any other place, without letters commendatory of his own bishop.

Sixthly. That foreign bishops and clergymen coming into the realm, should be content only with the benefit of such hospitality, as should be offered them; neither should intermeddle any further within the precinct of any bishop, without his special permission.

Seventhly. That provincial synods should be held within the realm at least once a year.

Eighthly. That no bishop should prefer himself before another, but must observe the time and order of his consecration.

Ninthly. That the number of bishops should be augmented, as the number of people increases.

And Tenthly. That no marriage should be admitted, but that which was lawful; neither any man to put away his wife for any cause, except only for fornication, after the rule of the gospel.

In the year following was the sixth general council at Constantinople, whereat this Theodore was also present under Pope Agatho : where marriage was permitted to Greek priests, and forbidden to the Latin. In this council, the Latin mass was first openly said by John Portuensis, the pope's legate, before the patriarch and princes at Constantinople, in the temple of St. Sophia.

King Iva or Inas, who reigned in West Saxony, after Cadwallader, the last king of Britain, began his reign about A. D. 689., and reigned with great valiantness over the West Saxons for thirty seven years.

About the sixth year of the reign of this Iva, we find mention of one whom they call St. Cuthlake a confessor, who about the four-and-twentieth year of his age, renouncing the pomp of the world, professed himself a monk. Why this Cuthlake should be sainted for his doings, I see no great cause ; as I cannot think the fabulous miracles reported of him to be true ; as where the vulgar people are made to believe that he inclosed the devil in a boiling pot, and caused wicked spirits to erect up houses, with such other fables and lying miracles. Among which lying miracles also may be reckoned that which the stories mention to be done of one Brithwald, or Drithelme, who, being dead a long season, was restored to life again, and told many wonders of strange things that he had seen, causing thereby great alms and deeds of charity to be done by the people !

About the sixteenth year of Iva, Ethelred, king of Mercia, after he had there reigned thirty years, was made a monk, and afterwards abbot of Bardney.

And about the eighteenth year of the reign of Iva, died the worthy and learned Bishop Adelme, first abbot of Malmesbury, afterwards bishop of Shirborne ; there was learning and virtue in him above the rest, at that time (next after Bede), as the great number of books and epistles, with poems by him set forth, will declare. Although concerning the miracles ascribed to him ; as, first, in causing an infant of nine days old to speak at Rome, to declare Pope Sergius, who was then suspected the father of the said child ; also in hanging his casule upon the sunbeams ; also, in making whole the altar-stone of marble brought from Rome ; also in drawing a length one of the timber pieces which went to the building of the temple in Malmesbury ; also in saving the mariners at Dover, &c. These, and such other miracles, which are attributed to him, I cannot but think to be monkish devices, forged upon their patrons to maintain the dignity of their houses.

Moreover, about the twenty-fifth year of Iva, St. John of Beverley, who was then bishop of York, died, and was buried at the porch of the minster of Deirwood, or Beverley. In which porch it is recorded in monkish chronicles, that as John was praying in the porch of St. Michael in York, the Holy Ghost, in the similitude of a dove, sat before him upon the altar in brightness shining above the sun. This brightness being seen of others, first comes one of his deacons running into the porch, who beholding the bishop there standing in his prayers, and all the place filled with the Holy Ghost, was stricken with the light thereof, having all his face burnt, as it were, with hot burning fire ! Notwithstanding the bishop by-and-bye cured the face of his deacon again, charging them (as the story says) not to publish what he had seen, during his life-time, &c. Which tale seems as true as what we read about the same time done by St. Egwine, who, when he had fettered both his feet in irons, for certain sins done in his youth, and had fast locked them, and cast the key thereof into the sea, afterward a fish brought the key again into the ship, as he was sailing homeward from Rome !

But to leave these monkish fictions, and return to the right course again of the history. In the time of this Iva, the right observing of Easter-day first began among the Picts and the Britons. In the observance of which day, three things are necessary to be observed : first, the full moon of the first month, that is of the month of March. Secondly, the dominical letter. Thirdly, the equinoctial day, which equinoctial was wont to be counted in the eastern church, and especially among the Egyptians, to be about the seventeenth day of March.

So that the full moon on the equinoctial day, or after the equinoctial day being observed, the next dominical day following that full moon, is to be taken for Easter-day. Wherein are diligently to be noted two things first, the fulness of the moon must be perfectly full, so that it be the beginning of the third week of the moon, which is the fourteenth or fifteenth day of the moon. Secondly, it is to be noted, that the perfect fulness of the moon, beginning the third week, must happen either in the very evening of the equinoctial day, or after the equinoctial day : for else if it happen either on the equinoctial day before the evening, or before the equinoctial day, then it belongs to the last month of the last year, and not to the first month of the first year, and so serves not to be observed.

This rite and usage in keeping Easter-day being received in the Latin church, began now to take place among the Picts and Britons, through the exertions of Elbert the holy monk. as they term him, and of Colfrid, abbot of Sirwin in Northumberland. who wrote to Narcanus, or Naiton, the king of Picts, concerning the same : who also among other things, writes of the shaven crowns of priests, saying, that it was as necessary for the vow of a monk, or the degree of a priest, to have a shaven crown for restraint of their lust. as for any christian man to bless him against spirits, when they come upon him. The copy of which letter, as it is in Bede, I have here annexed, not for any great reason contained therein, but only to amuse the reader, that he may see the fond ignorance of that monkish age : the letter thus proceeds.

OF THE SHAVING OF PRIESTS.

"Concerning the shaving of priests, (whereof you wrote to me) I exhort you that it be decently observed, according to the christian faith. We are not ignorant that the apostles were not all shaven after one manner, neither does the catholic church at this day agree in one uniform manner of shaving, as they do in faith, hope, and charity. Let us consider the former time of the patriarchs, and we shall find that Job (an example of patience) even in the very point of his afflictions, did shave his head : and he proves also, that in the time of his prosperity, he used to let his hair grow. And Joseph, an excellent doctor, and executor of chastity, humility, piety, and other virtues, when he was delivered out of prison and servitude, was shaven : whereby it appears, that whilst he abode in prison he was unshaven. Behold both these, being men of God, used an order in the habit of body, one contrary to the other, whose consciences notwithstanding within did well agree in the like grace of virtues. But to speak truly and freely, the difference of shaving hurts not such as have a pure faith in the Lord, and sincere charity towards their neighbour; especially as there was never any controversy amongst the catholic fathers about the diversity thereof, as there has been about the difference of the celebration of Easter and of faith. But of all these shavings that we find, either in the church, or elsewhere, there is none in mine opinion so much to be followed and embraced, as that which he used on his head, to whom the Lord said, 'Thou art Peter, and upon this rock I will build my church, and the gates of hell shall not prevail against it, and I will give thee the keys of the kingdom of heaven.' And contrariwise, there is no shaving so much to be abhorred and detested, as that which he used, to whom the same St. Peter said, 'Thy money perish with thee, because thou thoughtest the gift of God could be purchased with money—thou hast neither part nor lot in the matter.' Neither ought we to be shaven on the crown only, because St. Peter was so shaven, but because Peter was so shaven in remembrance of the Lord's passion : therefore, we that desire by the same passion, to be saved, must wear the sign of the same passion with him upon the top of our head, which is the highest part of our body. For as every church, that is made a church by the death of the Saviour, is used to bear the sign of the holy cross in the front, that it may the better by the power of that banner, be kept from the invasions of evil spirits; and by the often admonition thereof is taught to crucify the flesh with the affections and lusts: in like manner it behoves such as have the vows of monks, and degrees of the clergy, to bind themselves with a stricter bit for the Lord's sake. And as the Lord bare a crown of thorns on his head in his passion, whereby he took and carried away from us the thorns and pricks of our sins: so must every one of us, by shaving our heads, patiently bear, and willingly suffer the mocks and scorns of the world for his sake, that we may receive the crown of eternal life, which God hath promised to them that love him, and shall, by shaving their corporal crowns, bear the adversity, and condemn the prosperity of this world. But the shaving which Simon Magus used, what faithful man doth not detest, together with his magical art? which at the first appearance has a show of a shaven crown, but if you mark his neck, you shall find it curtailed in such wise, as you will say, it is rather meet to be used of the Simonists, than of the Christians. And such (by foolish men) are thought worthy of the glory of the eternal crown! whereas, indeed, for their ill living, they are worthy not only to be deprived of the same, but also of eternal salvation. I speak not this against them that use this kind of shaving, and live catholicly in faith and good works, but surely I believe there are divers of them very holy and godly men; amongst which is Adamnan, the abbot and worthy priest of the Columbians: who when he came ambassador from his country to King Alfrid, desired greatly to see our monastery; where he displayed a wonderful wisdom, humility, and religion, both in his manners and words. Amongst other talk, I asked him, Why he that did believe to come to the crown of life that should never have an end, did use contrary to his belief, a defined image of a crown on his head? And if you seek (quoth I) the fellowship of St. Peter, why do you use the fashion of his crown whom St. Peter did accurse, and not of his rather with whom you desire to live eternally? Adamnan answered saying, 'You know right well, brother, though I use Simon's manner of shaving, after the custom of my country, yet do I detest, and with all my heart abhor his infidelity. I desire, notwithstanding, to imitate the footsteps of the holy apostle, as far forth as my power will extend.' Then said I, 'I believe it is so: but then it is apparent you imitate those things which the apostle Peter did, from the bottom of your heart, if you use the same upon your face that you know he did: for I suppose your wisdom understandeth that it is right decent to differ in the trimming your face, or shaving, from his, whom in your heart you abhor. And contrariwise, as you desire to imitate the doings of him whom you desire to have a Mediator between God and you, so it is meet you imitate the manner of his apparel and shaving.' Thus much said I to Adamnan, who seemed then well to like our churches: insomuch that he returned into Scotland, and reformed many of his churches there after our celebration, although he could not do so amongst the monks, with whom he had special authority. He endeavoured also to have reformed their manner of shaving if he had been able. And now, O king, I exhort your majesty to labour together with your people, over whom the King of kings, and Lord of lords hath made you governor, to imitate likewise in all these points, the catholic and apostolical churches. So shall it come to pass, that in the end of this your temporal kingdom, the most blessed prince of the apostles shall open you the gates of the heavenly kingdom, together with the elect of God. The grace of the Eternal King preserve you, most dearly beloved son in Christ, long time to reign over us, to the great tranquillity of us all."

When this letter was read before King Naiton, with other of his learned men, and diligently translated into his proper language, he seemed to rejoice very much at the exhortation, insomuch that, rising up from among his noblemen, he kneeled on the ground, and gave God thanks that he had deserved to receive so worthy a present out of England, and so caused it forthwith by public proclamation to be written out, learned, and observed throughout all the provinces of the Picts, defacing

the errors that had been used there for the space of 704 years. For all the ministers of the altar, and all monks were shaven on the crown, and all the people rejoiced for the new discipline of the most blessed prince of the apostle St. Peter, which they had received. (Beda, lib. 5. cap. 21.)

By this monkish letter above prefixed, void of all scripture, of all proofs and truth of history, the reader may note how this vain tradition of shaven crowns has come in, and upon how light and trifling an occasion: which in very deed was none other but the dreaming fictions of monks of that time, falsely grounded upon the example of Peter, when by no old monument of any ancient record, can they ever prove either Peter or Simon Magus to have been shaven. In the letter also is to be noted, how the Scottish clergy at that season, did wear no such priestly crowns as our English churchmen then did.

But to cut off this matter of shaving, more worthy to be laughed at, than to be recorded, let us now return to King Iva, who, by the importunate persuasion and subtle policy of his wife Ethelburga, was allured to go to Rome, there to be made a monk. Ethelburga, after she had a long time laboured to persuade him to leave the world, and could not bring about her purpose, at one time, when the king and she had rested in a fair palace richly hanged, and were departed on the morrow, she caused the palace to be filled with all kinds of dirt and filth, and hogs and vile beasts to be turned in, as well in the chambers as in the other parts of the house; and in their own chamber a sow was laid with her young pigs. And when she knew that this palace was thus deformed, she besought the king to visit it. And when she had brought him there, she said to him, "I pray you, my lord, behold now this house, where are now the rich clothes of gold and silk, and other apparel, that we left here the other day? And where are the delicacies and pleasant servitors, and costly dishes, that you and I lately were served with? Are not all these passed and gone? My lord, in like manner shall we vanish away. And our bodies, which are now delicately kept, shall fall and turn into the filth of the earth. Wherefore bear in mind my words that I have often shewed and told you, and use your diligence to purchase that palace that shall ever endure in joy without changing."

By means of these words, the queen turned the king's mind, so that shortly after he resigned his kingdom to Ethelard his nephew, and took on him the habit of a poor man, and setting apart all the pomp and pride of this wicked world, associated himself in the fellowship of poor men, and travelled to Rome, with great devotion, when he had been King of the West Saxons thirty-seven years. After whose departing, Ethelburga his wife, went to Barking, where, in the nunnery of Barking, she continued, and ended the rest of her life, when she had been abbess of the place a certain time. Malmesbury also testifies that this Iva was the first king that granted a penny for every fire-house through his dominion, to be paid to the court of Rome, which afterward was called Rome-shot, or Peter-pence, and long after was paid in many places of England.

And as I must here mention Bede, a man of venerable memory, and as I see writers do not agree, some saying that he was not an Englishman; I thought to report so much of him, as I find by his own words testified of himself in his ecclesiastical history of England.

Bede declares that he was born in the territory of the monastery of Peter and Paul, where he was, at the age of seven years, committed to the tuition of Benedict, and of Celfrid, abbots of the monastery. In which monastery, continuing from that time forth, all his long life, he gave himself and all his whole study to the holy scripture. Whatever time or leisure he had from his daily service in the church, he spent either in learning, or teaching, or writing something. About the nineteenth year of his age, he was made deacon, the thirtieth year of his age he was made priest. From which time, to the age of fifty-nine years, he occupied himself in interpreting the works of the ancient fathers for his own use, and the necessity of others; and in writing treatises; which came in all to the number of thirty-seven volumes, which he digested into seventy-eight books.

Some say that he went to Rome, either there to defend his books as consonant to catholic doctrine, or, else if they should be found faulty, to amend and correct the same, as he should be commanded. Although the reporter of his life dare not certainly affirm that he was ever at Rome; yet that he was invited and called to come thither, is manifest in histories, and also the epistle of Pope Sergius sufficiently proves; declaring moreover in what estimation Bede was held, as well in the court of Rome, as in other places.

So notable and famous was the learning of Bede, that the church of Rome stood in need of his help, and also required the same about the discussing of certain controversies appertaining to learning. Moreover, the whole Latin church at that time gave him the mastery in judgment and knowledge of the holy scriptures. In all his explanations, his chiefest scope and purpose was always simply to instruct and inform his reader, without any curiousness of style, in the sincere love of God and his neighbour. As touching the holiness and integrity of his life, it is not to be doubted. For how could he attend to any vicious idleness, or have any leisure for the same, who in reading and digesting so many volumes, consumed all his time and thoughts in writing upon the scriptures? for so he testifies of himself in the third book of Samuel, saying in these words, "If my Treatise and Expositions," saith he, "bring with them no utility to the readers thereof; yet to myself they conduce not a little thus, that while all my study and cogitation was set upon them, I had little mind in the meanwhile for the slippery inticements and vain cogitations of this world." Thus in this labour of study he continued till the age of sixty-two years: at length, drawing to his latter end, being sick seven weeks together, besides other occupyings of his mind, and other studies which he did not intermit; he translated also the gospel of St. John into English. At length, with great comfort of spirit, he departed this life, pronouncing many comfortable sayings to them that stood about him.

Celulfus, king of Northumberland, after he had reigned eight years, was made a monk in the abbey of Farne. After whom succeeded Egbert his cousin, brother to Egbert (the same time being bishop of York). Egbert erected a noble library in York, whose example I wish other bishops now would follow.

About the reign of this Egbert, Cuthbert was archbishop of Canterbury, who collected a great synod of bishops and prelates in the month of September (A. D. 747.) near to the place called Clonesho. In which synod these decrees were enacted.

First. That bishops should be more diligent in seeing to their office, and in admonishing the people of their faults.

2. That they should live in a peaceable mind together, notwithstanding they were in place dissevered asunder.

3. That every bishop should go about all the parishes of his diocese once a year.

4. That the bishops, every one in his diocese should admonish their abbots and monks to live regularly: and that prelates should not oppress their inferiors, but love them.

5. That they should teach the monasteries which the secular men had invaded, and could not then be taken from them, to live regularly.

6. That none should be admitted to orders, before his life should be examined.

7. That in monasteries the reading of holy scripture should be more frequented.

8. That priests should be no disposers of secular business.

9. That they should take no money for baptizing infants.

10. That they should both learn and teach the Lord's Prayer and Creed in the English tongue.

11. That all should join together in their ministry after one uniform rite and manner.

12. That in a modest voice they should sing in the church.

13. That all holy and festival days should be celebrated at one time together.

14. That the Sabbath day be reverently observed and kept.

15. That the seven canonical hours be observed every day.

16. That the rogation days, both the greater and lesser, should not be omitted.

17. That the feast of St. Gregory and St. Austin our patron, should not be omitted.

18. That the fast of the four times should be kept and observed.

19. That monks and nuns should go regularly apparelled.

20. That bishops should see these decrees not to be neglected.

21. That the churchmen should not give themselves to drunkenness.

22. That the communion should not be neglected by the churchmen.

23. That the same also should be observed by laymen, as time required.

24. That laymen should be first well tried before they entered into monkery.

25. That alms be not neglected.

26. That bishops should see these decrees to be notified to the people.

27. They disputed of the profit of alms.

28. They disputed of the profit of singing psalms.

29. That the congregation should be constituted, after the ability of their goods.

30. That monks should not dwell among laymen.

31. That public prayer should be made for kings and princes.

These decrees and ordinances being thus concluded among the bishops, Cuthbert the archbishop, sends the copy thereof to Boniface, which Boniface, otherwise named Winfrid, an Englishman born, was then archbishop of Mentz, and afterwards made a martyr, as the popish stories term him.

This Boniface wrote a letter to Ethelbald, king of Merceland, who was also present in the same synod.

I thought this letter not unworthy to be noticed here, not so much for the author's sake, as for some good matter, that peradventure may be found in it.

For in this letter is to be seen and noted, first, the corruption and great disorder of life, which always from time to time has been found in these religious houses of nuns, whose professed vow of compulsory chastity has never yet been good to the church, nor profitable to the commonwealth, and least of all to themselves.

Secondly, No less are they also to be reprehended who maintained these superstitious orders of unprofitable nuns and of other religions. In the number of whom was this Boniface, otherwise called Winfrid, who, although in this letter he does justly reprehend the vicious enormities both of secular and of religious persons, yet he himself is not without the same or greater reprehension, for he gave the occasion thereof in maintaining such superstitious orders of nuns and other religions, and restraining the same from lawful marriage. For we find of him in histories that he was a great setter-up and upholder of such blind superstition, and of all popery. From this Boniface proceeded that detestable doctrine which now stands in the pope's registered decrees, (Dist. 40. cap. Si Papa), which in a certain epistle of his is this, that in case the pope were of the most abominable living, and forgetful or negligent of himself and of the whole of christianity, so that he led innumerable souls with him to hell, yet no man ought to rebuke him in so doing, for he has power to judge all men, and ought to be judged again by no man.

About this time it was that Gregory III. first brought into the mass-canon the clause for relics, the memorial, the offering, and sacrifice for the dead: like as Zachary brought in the priests' vesture and ornaments, and as Constantine also was the first pope that gave his feet to be kissed by the emperors. But to turn again into the course of our English history.

In the latter part of the reign of Offa, king of Mercia, Ethelbert a learned and godly prince, came to the court of Offa, to sue for the marriage of his daughter, but the queen conceiving a false suspicion, that Ethelbert with his company had come under the pretence of marriage, to work some violence against her husband, persuaded king Offa to seize him and to strike off his head. And thus the innocent king was wrongfully murdered about the year A.D. 793. Offa understanding afterwards the innocence of this king, and the heinous cruelty of his act, gave the tenth part of his goods to the holy church; and on the church of Hereford he bestowed great lands. He built the abbey of St. Albans, with certain other monasteries. And afterwards he went to Rome for his penance, where he gave to the church of St. Peter a penny through every house in his dominion, which was called commonly Rome-shot or Peter-pence, paid to the church of St. Peter; and there at length was transformed from a king to a monk, about A.D. 794.

A little before, in speaking of certain bishops of Rome, mention was made of Pope Constantine I., Gregory II., Pope Gregory III., and of Pope Zachary, who deposed Childerick, and set up Pepin the French king, &c. Next after this Zachary followed Pope Stephan II., to whom Pepin, to gratify again the see of Rome for this their benefit, gave and contributed to the said see of Rome, the Exarchate or princedom of Ravenna, the kingdom of the Lombards, and many other great possessions of Italy, with all the cities thereto adjoining the borders of Venice. And this donation of Pepin, no doubt, if the truth were rightly tried, should be found to be the same, which hitherto falsely has been thought to be the donation of the emperor Constantine.

Next to Stephan succeeded Paul I, who following his predecessors, thundered out great excommunications against Constantine the emperor of Constantinople, for abrogating and plucking down the images set up in temples. Notwithstanding this, Constantine neglecting the Pope's vain curses, persevered in his blessed purpose, in destroying idolatry till the end of his life. Then came to be pope, Constantine II., a layman, and brother to Desiderius the king of Lombardy; for which cause he was shortly deposed, and thrust into a monastery, having his eyes put out.

In whose stead succeeded Stephan III., who ordained that no layman should be pope: condemning, moreover, the seventh council of Constantinople for heretical, because in that council the worshipping of images was reproved and condemned. Contrary to the which council, this pope not only maintained the filthy idolatry of images in christian temples, but also advanced their veneration, commanding them most heathenishly to be incensed.

Then in this race of popes, after Stephan III., comes Adrian I., who likewise following the steps of his fathers the popes, added and attributed to the veneration of images more than all the others had done before, writing a book on the adoration and utility proceeding of them; holding moreover a synod at Rome against Felix, and all others that spake against the setting up of such stocks and images. And as Paul I. before him made much of the body of Petronilia, St. Peter's daughter, so this Adrian clothed the body of St. Peter all in silver, and covered the altar of St. Paul with a pall of gold. This Pope Adrian ratified the order of St. Gregory's mass, above the order of St. Ambrose's mass: for to his time, (which was about A.D. 780,) the liturgy of St. Ambrose was more used in the Italian churches. The history whereof because it is registered in Durandus, Nauclerus, and Jacobus de Voragine, I here insert, that the reader may understand the time when this usual mass of the Papists began first to be universal and uniform, and generally to be received in churches. Jacobus de Voragine, in the life of Pope Gregory I., thus speaks concerning this matter.

" In time past (saith he) when the service which Ambrose made, was more used in churches, than the service which Gregory had appointed, the bishop of Rome, then called Adrian, gathered a council together, in which it was ordained that Gregory's service should be observed and kept universally. Which determination of the council the Emperor Charles diligently put in execution, visiting various provinces, and informed all the clergy, partly with threatenings, and partly with punishments to receive that order. And as to the books of Ambrose's service, he burnt them to ashes in all places, and threw into prison many priests that would not consent and agree to the matter. Blessed Eugenius the bishop coming unto the council, found that it was dissolved three days before his coming. Notwithstanding, through his wisdom, he so persuaded the lord pope that he called again all the prelates that had been present at the council, and were now departed for the space of three days. Therefore when the council was gathered again, all the fathers did consent and agree in this, that both the mass-books of Ambrose and Gregory should be laid upon the altar of blessed St. Peter the apostle, and the church doors diligently shut, and most warily sealed up with the signets of many and divers bishops. Again, that they should all the whole night give themselves to prayer, that the Lord might reveal, open, and shew unto them by some evident sign or token, which of these two services he would have used in the temples. Thus doing in all points as they had determined, in the morning they opened the church doors, and found both the missals or mass-books open upon the altar; or rather (as some say) they found Gregory's mass-book utterly plucked asunder, one piece from another, and scattered over all the church. As touching Ambrose's book, they only found it open upon the altar in the very same place where they before laid it. This miracle pope Adrian, like a wise expounder of dreams, interpreted thus, that as the leaves were torn and blown abroad all the church over, so should Gregory's book be used throughout the world. Whereupon they thought themselves sufficiently instructed and taught of God, that the service which Gregory had made, ought to be set abroad and used throughout the world, and that Ambrose's service should only be observed and kept in his own church of Mediolanum, where he was bishop."

Thus the reader has heard the full and whole narration of this mystical miracle, with the pope's exposition upon the same. Concerning which miracle, I need not admonish the reader to smell out the blind practices of these night-crows, to blind the world with forged inventions instead of true stories. Although to grant the miracle to be most true, yet as to the exposition thereof, another man beside the pope might interpret this great miracle, thus, that God was angry with Gregory's book, and therefore rent it in pieces, and scattered it abroad; and the other as good, lay sound, untouched, and at least to be preferred. Yet, whatever is to be thought of this miracle with the exposition, thus the matter fell out that Gregory's service only had the place, and yet has to this day in the greatest part of Europe, the service of Ambrose being excluded. And thus much touching the great act of Pope Adrian for the setting up of the mass. By the relation whereof the reader, at least, may understand how commonly in christian nations abroad, as yet no uniform order of any missal or mass-book was received.

Now from the popes to return again to the emperors, as Pepin, the father of Charles the Great, called Charlemagne, had given to the papal see all the princedom of Ravenna, with other donations and revenues and lands in Italy; so this Charlemagne, following his father's devotion, confirmed the same, adding moreover the city and dominion of Venice, Istria, the dukedom Forojuleinse, the dukedom Spoletanum, and Beneventanum, and other possessions, to the patrimony of St. Peter, making him the prince of Rome and Italy. The pope, again to recompense his kindness, made him to be entitled " most christian king," moreover ordained him only for emperor of Rome. For these causes Charlemagne bare no little affection to Adrian above all other popes.

Partly also, for that Carloman his elder brother being dead, his wife called Bertha, with her two children, came to Adrian, to have them confirmed in their father's kingdom, whereto the pope, to shew a pleasure to Charlemagne, would not agree: but gave the mother with her two children, and Desiderius the Lombard king, with his whole kingdom, his wife and children, into the hands of Charlemagne, who led them with him captive into France, and there kept them in servitude during their life.

Thus Charlemagne being proclaimed emperor of Rome, through Adrian and Pope Leo III. who succeeded next after him, the empire was translated from the Grecians to the French, (about A. D. 801), where it continued above one hundred years, till the coming of Conrad and his nephew Otho, who were Germans; and so has continued after them among the Germans to this present time. This Charlemagne built many monasteries, he was beneficial to the churchmen, also merciful to the poor, valiant and triumphant in his undertakings, and skilful in all languages; he held a council at Frankfort where was condemned the council of Nice and Irene, for setting up and worshipping images, &c.

Concerning which council of Nice, and the things there concluded and enacted (that no man may think the detesting of images to be any new thing now begun) thus I find it recorded in an ancient history of Roger Hovedon; his words are these, "In A. D. 792, Charles, the French king, sent a book containing the acts of a certain synod, to Britain, directed to him from Constantinople. In which book (lamentable to be told) many things inconvenient and contrary to the true faith are to be found; especially for that by the common consent of almost all the learned bishops of the Eastern church, being above three hundred, it was there agreed that images should be worshipped; which thing the church of God hath always abhorred. Against which book Alcuine wrote an epistle, substantially grounded on the authority of holy scripture, which epistle with the book Alcuine in the name and person of our bishops and princes, did present to the French king."

And thus by the way of Romish matters: now to return again to the Northumberland kings, where we left at Egbert, which Egbert (as is before declared) succeeded Celulphus, after he was made monk. And likewise the said Egbert also following the devotion of his uncle Celulphus, and Kenred before him, was likewise shorn a monk, after he had reigned twenty years in Northumberland; leaving his son Osulphus to succeed.

After the reign of King Egbert such trouble and perturbation was in the dominion of Northumberland, with slaying, and expelling and deposing their kings one after another, that after the murdering of Ethelbert, none durst take the government upon him, seeing the great danger. Insomuch that the kingdom did lie void and waste the space of three-and-thirty years together; after which this kingdom of Northumberland, with the kingdoms also of the other Saxons besides, came altogether into the hands of Egbert, king of the West Saxons, and his progeny; which monarchy began A. D. 827.

In the mean time, Irene, empress of the Greeks, was busy at Constantinople: she, first through the means of Pope Adrian, took up the body of Constantine, emperor of Constantinople, her own husband's father. And when she had burned the same, she caused the ashes to be cast into the sea, because he disannulled images. Afterwards reigning with her son Constantine VI., son to Leo IV. (whom also we declared to be excommunicated for taking away images), being at dissension with him, she caused him to be taken to prison. He afterward through the influence of friends was restored to his empire, and at last she caused him, although her own son, to be cast into prison, and his eyes to be put out, so that within a short time he died. After this Irene, with the advice of Therasius, bishop of Constantinople, held a council at Nice, where it was decreed that images should be again restored to the church; which council was repealed by another council held at Frankfort by Charlemagne. At length she was deposed

by Nicephorus (who reigned after) and was expelled the empire, and ended her life in much penury and misery.

Hitherto I have brought down the confused and turbulent reigns of the seven Saxon kings, who after the expulsion of the Britons, ruled and reigned in sundry quarters of this land together, to the time of Egbert king of the West Saxons, by whom it pleased God to begin to reduce and unite all these scattered kingdoms, into one monarchical form of dominion. Wherefore, as in Egbert, begins another alteration of the Commonwealth, here in this land among the Saxons: so my purpose is (the Lord willing) with the same Egbert, to begin my third book, after first making a brief recapitulation of such things as in this second book are to be noted, especially touching the monasteries built, the kings who entered the monastic life and profession, also the queens and queens' daughters, who at the same time professed solitary life in the monasteries, which they or their ancestors had erected.

We have hitherto set forth and declared concerning these seven kingdoms: first, the names and lineal descent of the kings: then what were the doings and acts of the same, how first being pagans, they were converted to the christian faith; what things happened in their time in the church, how many of them were made monks; how devout they were then to the holy church and to the churchmen, and especially to the church of Rome. But the churchmen then were very different in life to what they afterwards declared themselves to be. Through which devotion of these kings, first came in the Peter-pence or Rome-shots in this realm, as first by Iva, then by Offa, and afterwards brought in and ratified through the whole realm by Adelwulph. It is also to be noted, that by the kings and queens of the Saxons, the greatest abbeys and nunneries, in this realm, were first began and built, as partly by the following names of some of them is to be seen.

First, the church or minster of St. Paul in London, was founded by Ethelbert, king of Kent, and Sigebert, king of Essex, (about A. D. 604).

The first cross and altar within this realm, was set up in the north parts in Hevenfield, upon the occasion of Oswald, king of Northumberland, fighting against Cadwalla, where he in the same place set up the sign of the cross, kneeling and praying there for victory, A. D. 635. (Polychron. lib. 5. cap. 12.)

The church of Winchester was first began, and founded by Kinegilsus, king of the Mercians, having nine miles about it: afterwards finished by his son Kenwalcus, where Wine was first English bishop, A. D. 636. (Guliel. Malms. lib. de gestis pont. Ang.)

The church of Lincoln first founded by Paulinus a bishop, (A. D. 629.)

The church of Westminster, began first by a certain citizen of London, through the instigation of Ethelbert king of Kent, which before was an isle of thorns, (A. D. 614).

The common schools first erected at Cambridge, by Sigebert king of Eastangles, (A. D. 636).

The abbey of Knovisburgh built by Furceus the Hermit, (A. D. 637).

The monastery of Mamlesbury by one Meldulphus a Scot, to (about A. D. 640), afterwards enlarged by Agilbert bishop of Winchester.

The monastery in Glocester, first built by Ofricus king of Mercia, as Cestrensis says; but as William Malmesbury writes by Ulferus and Ethelred, brethren to Kineburga abbess of the same house, (A. D. 679).

The monastery of Melrose, by the flood of Tweed, by Aidanus a Scottish bishop.

The nunnery of Heorenton by Hevi, who was the first nun in Northumberland, (Beda. lib. 4. cap. 1.)

The monastery of Hetesey by Oswy king of Northumberland, who also with his daughter Elfrid gave possessions for twelve monasteries in the parts of Northumberland, (A. D. 656).

The monastery of St. Martin in Dover, built by Whithred king of Kent.

The abbey of Lestingy by Ceadda (whom we call St.

Ced) through the grant of Oswald, son to St. Oswald king of Northumberland, (A. D. 651).

The monastery of Whitby, called otherwise Stenhalt, by Hilda, daughter to the nephew of Edwin king of Northumberland, (A. D. 657).

Another monastery called Hacanos, not far from the same place, built by Hilda the same year.

The abbey of Abbington, built by Sissa king of Southsex, (A. D. 666).

An abbey in the east side of Lincoln, called Joanno, by St. Botulph, A. D. 654. (Polych. lib. 5. cap. 16).

The monastery in Ely, founded by Etheldred or Etheldrida daughter of Anna king of Eastangles, and the wife of Elfride king of Northumberland, (A. D. 674).

The monastery of Chertsey in Southery, founded by Erkenwald bishop of London, (A. D. 674), thrown down by the Danes, after re-built by King Edgar.

The nunnery of Berking, built by the said Erkenwaldus bishop of London about the same time.

The abbey of Peterborough, called otherwise Modehamsted, founded by King Ethelwald, king of the Mercians, (A. D. 675).

Bardney abbey by Ethelred king of the Mercians, (A. D. 700).

Glastonbury by Iva king of the West Saxons, and after repaired and enriched by King Edgar, (A. D. 701).

Ramsey in the time of King Edgar, by one Ailwinus a nobleman, (A. D. 973). King Edgar built in his time forty monasteries, who reigned A. D. 901.

The nunnery of Winburne built by Cuthberga sister to Ingilsus, King Iva's brother, A. D. 717.

The monastery of Sealsey by the Isle of Wight, by Wilfridus bishop of York, (A. D. 678).

The monastery of Wincombe by Kenulphus king of the Mercians, (A. D. 737).

St. Albans built by Offa king of the Mercians, (A. D. 755).

The abbey of Evesham by Edwin, bishop, (A. D. 691).

Ripon in the north by Wilfrid, bishop, (A. D. 709).

The abbey of Echlinghey, by King Alfred, (A. D. 891).

The nunnery of Shaftsbury by Alfred, the same year.

Thus we see what monasteries began to be founded by the Saxon kings, newly converted to the christian faith, within the space of two hundred years; who, as they seemed to have a certain zeal and devotion to God, according to the leading and teaching that then was: so it seems to me, there were two things to be wished in these kings: first, that they who began to erect these monasteries of monks and nuns, to live solely and singly by themselves, had foreseen what danger, and what absurd enormities might and did ensue, both publicly to the church of Christ, and privately to their own souls: secondly, that to this their zeal and devotion had been joined like knowledge and doctrine in Christ's gospel, especially in the article of our free justification by the faith of Jesus Christ; because of the lack whereof, as well the builders and founders, as they that were professed in the same, seem both to have ran the wrong way, and to have been deceived. For although there was in them a devotion and zeal of mind, that thought well in this their doing, which I will not here reprehend: yet the end and cause of their deeds and buildings cannot be excused, being contrary to the rule of Christ's gospel; for so much as they did these things seeking thereby merit with God, and for the remedy of their souls, and remission of their sins, as may appear testified in their own records.

By the contents of which may well be understood how great the ignorance and blindness of these men was; who, lacking no zeal, only lacking knowledge to rule it withall; seeking their salvation not by Christ only, but by their own deservings and meritorious deeds. Which I recite not here to any infamy or reprehension of them; but rather to put us in mind how much we at this present time are bound to God for the true sincerity of his truth, hidden so long before from our ancestors, and opened now unto us by the good will of our God, in his

Son Christ Jesus. Lamenting this only by the way, to see them to have such works, and to lack our faith, and us to have the right faith, and to lack their works. And this blind ignorance of that age, was the cause not only why these kings built so many monasteries, but also why so many of them, forsaking their orderly vocation of princely government, gave themselves over to the monastic profession, or rather wilful superstition. Concerning the names and number of which kings that were professed monks, is sufficiently declared before; the names of whom we shewed to be seven or eight, within these two hundred years. Such was then the superstitious devotion of kings and princes, and no less also to be noted in queens' and kings' daughters, with other noble women of the same age and time; the names of whom it were too long here to recite. As Hilda daughter to the nephew of Edwin king of Northumberland, abbess of Ely. Erchengoda, with her sister Ermenilda, daughters of Ercombertus king of Kent, which Erchengoda was professed in St. Bridget's order in France. Edelberga wife and queen to King Edwin of Northumberland, and daughter of King Anna, who was also made a nun in the same house of St. Bridget. Etheldreda, whom we term St. Eldred, wife to King Ecfride of Northumberland, who was professed a nun at Helings. Werburga was the daughter of Ulferus King of Mercians, and made nun at Ely. Kenreda, sister of King Ulferus and Kineswida her sister, were both nuns professed. Sexburga daughter of King Anna, king of Mercians, and wife of Ercombert king of Kent, was abbess at Ely. Elfrida daughter of Oswy king of Northumberland was abbess of Whitney; Mildreda, Milburga, and Milguida, all three daughters of Merwardus, king of West Mercians, entered the profession and vow of devoted nuns. Kineburga, wife of Alfride king of Northumberland, and sister to Ofricus king of Mercians, and daughter of King Penda, was professed abbess of the monastery in Glocester. Elfieda daughter of Oswy king, and wife of Peda, son of King Penda, likewise enclosed herself in the same profession and vow. Likewise Alfritha wife to King Edgar, and Editha, daughter to the said Edgar, with Wolfride her mother, &c., all which holy nuns with divers more, the Romish catholics have canonized for saints, and put the most part of them in their calendar, only because of the vow which they solemnly professed. Concerning which I will say, that although they kept it never so perfectly, yet it is not that which maketh saints before God, but only the blood of Christ Jesus, and a true faith in him.

It likewise remains, that as we have declared the devotion of these noble women, who professing monastic life, cast off all worldly dignity and delights; so we should also treat of such noblemen, who among the Saxon kings in like zeal of devotion, have given over themselves from the world (as they thought) to the contemplative life of the monkish profession. The names of whom are these nine.

1. Kinigils, king of the West Saxons.
2. Iva, king of the West Saxons.
3. Ceolulf, king of Northumberland.
4. Edbert, king of Northumberland.
5. Ethelred, king of Mercia.
6. Kenred, king of Mercia.
7. Offa, king of the East Saxons.
8. Sebbi, king of the East Saxons.
9. Sigebert, king of East Angles.

What is to be thought of these kings and their doings, the reader has seen before.

By these histories it is apparent what changes, what perturbations, and what alterations of state have been in this realm of Britain, first from British kings to Roman; then to British again; afterward to Saxon. First, to seven reigning together, then to one, &c. And this alteration not only happened in the civil government, but also followed in the ecclesiastical state. For as in the Britons' time the metropolitan see was in London, so in the Saxons' time, after the coming of Austin, it was removed to Canterbury; the catalogue and order of which metropolitans, from the time of Austin to Egbert, is thus described in the history of Malmesbury.

The names and order of the archbishops of Canterbury from Austin to the time of King Egbert, of whom the first seven were Italians or other foreigners.

1. Austin.
2. Laurentius.
3. Melitus.
4. Justus.
5. Honorius.
6. Deusdedit.
7. Theodorus.
8. Berctualdus.
9. Tacuinus.
10. Nothelmus.
11. Cutbertus.
12. Berguinus.
13. Lambrightus, or Lambertus.
14. Ethelardus.
15. Ulfredus.
16. Feolegeldus.
17. Celnothus.

During the course of these seventeen archbishops of Canterbury, there were thirty-four popes in Rome, of whom we have partly declared.

And thus much touching the time of the seven kingdoms of the Saxons, ruling together in England, from the reign of Hengist unto Egbert, the first monarch of the whole land, after the expulsion of the Britons.

It now remains (by the grace of Christ) in the next book, to give the history of such kings as principally reigning alone had this realm in their possession, from the time of Egbert king of the West Saxons, to the coming of William the Conqueror, the Norman; comprehending therein the rest of the next three hundred years, with the acts and state of religion in the church during that space; wherein may appear the declining time of the church, and of true religion, preparing the way to antichrist, which followed not long after.

THE END OF THE SECOND BOOK.

ACTS AND MONUMENTS.

BOOK III.

CONTAINING

THE THREE HUNDRED YEARS, FROM THE REIGN OF KING EGBERT TO THE TIME OF
WILLIAM THE CONQUEROR.

It now remains, as I before described, the descent and diversity of the seven kings, all reigning and ruling together in this land: so to prosecute in like order the lineal succession of them, which, after Egbert, king of the West Saxons, governed and ruled solely, until the conquest of William the Norman; and first, of King Egbert:

In the reign of Brightric, about A. D. 795, there was a noble personage called Egbert, who was feared by Brightric, because he was of kingly blood, and was by force and conspiracy chased out of Britain into France, till the death of Brightric. After hearing whereof, Egbert came back to his country, where he obtained the government of the kingdom of the West Saxons.

Bernulph, king of Mercia, with other kings, had this Egbert in much derision, making scoffing jests at him; all which he sustained for a time. But when he was more established in his kingdom, he assembled his knights, and gave battle to Bernulph, and won the field; which done, he made war upon the Kentish Saxons, and obtained the victory. He also subdued Northumberland, and caused the kings of these three kingdoms to live under him as tributaries. After these and other victories, he called a council of his lords at Winchester, where by their advices he was crowned king and chief lord over this land, which before that day was called Britain; but then he sent out into all the land his commandments and commissions, charging straightly, that from that day forward, the Saxons should be called Angles, and the land Anglia.

About the thirtieth year of the reign of Egbert, the Danes, who a little before had made horrible destruction in Northumberland, and especially in the isle of Lindefarne, where they spoiled the churches, and murdered the ministers, with men, women, and children, after a cruel manner, entered now the second time with a great host into this land, and spoiled the isle of Sheppy in Kent: Egbert assembled his people, and met with them at Charmouth. But he did not succeed so well in that conflict as he had done before, but with his knights was compelled to forsake the field. Notwithstanding, in the next battle, Egbert, with a small force, overthrew a great multitude of them, and so drove them back. The

next year the Danes returned again, and after this they were continually abiding in one part or other of the realm of England, till the time of Hardecanute. And although they were often driven out of the land, and chased from one country to another, yet they always gathered new strength and power, and abode still in the land.

Egbert, when he had ruled the West Saxons, and the greater part of England, thirty-seven years, died, and was buried at Winchester, leaving his kingdom to his son Ethelwolf, who first was bishop of Winchester, and afterwards, upon necessity, was made king.

Ethelwolf had entered into the order of sub-deacon, and, as some say, was made bishop of Winchester; but afterwards, being the only son of Egbert, was made king through the dispensation of the pope. This Ethelwolf (as being himself once in that order) was always good and devout to holy church and religious orders, insomuch that he gave to them the tithe of all his goods and lands in West Saxony, with liberty and freedom from all servage and civil charges.

Whence, it may appear, how and when the churches of England began first to be endued with temporalities and lands; and enlarged with privileges and exemptions.

Ethelwolf, having done these things in his realm, went to Rome with Alfred his youngest son, and committed him to the bringing up of Pope Leo IV.; and he gave and granted to Rome a penny to be paid for every fire-house through his whole land, as King Iva in his dominion had done before. He also gave and granted, towards maintaining the light of St. Peter, 100 marks, to be paid annually; to the light of St. Paul, 100 marks; for the use of the pope also another 100.

Ethelwolf had always about him two bishops, whose counsel he was most ruled by, Swithin bishop of Winchester, and Adelstan bishop of Sherborne. One was more skilful in temporal and civil affairs, touching the king's wars, and filling of his coffers. The other (which was Swithin) was of a contrary disposition, wholly inclined to spiritual meditation, and to minister spiritual counsel to the king: he had been schoolmaster to the king before. And herein appeared one good feature in this king's nature, among his other virtues, not only in following the precepts of his old schoolmaster, but also that, like a kind and thankful pupil, he so reverenced him, that he made him bishop of Winchester.

From the time of Pope Adrian I. unto Pope Adrian II. the emperors had some hand in the election (at least in the confirmation) of the Roman pope; but several of these popes began to endeavour to bring their purpose about. Yet all their devices could take no full effect, before Adrian III. So that the emperors all this while had some authority in choosing the popes, and in assembling general councils. Wherefore, by the commandment of the Emperor Lewis, in the time of Gregory IV., a general synod was commenced at Aquisgrane, where it was decreed by Gregory and his assistants: first, that every church should have sufficient of its own proper lands and revenues to keep the priests thereof, that none should lack or go about a begging. Also, that none of the clergy, of what order or degree soever he be, should use any vesture of any precious or scarlet colour. Neither should wear rings on their fingers, unless it be when prelates be at mass, or give their consecrations. Also, that prelates should not keep too great houses or families, nor keep many horses, use dice, or be guilty of immoral conduct; and that the monks should not exceed in gluttony or riot. Also, that none of the clergy being either anointed or shaven, should use either gold or silver in their shoes, slippers, or girdles, like to Heliogabalus. By this it may be conjectured, what pomp and pride in those days was crept into the clergy. Moreover, by Pope Gregory IV., the feast of All Saints was first brought into the church.

After this pope, came Sergius II., who first brought in the altering of the pope's names, because he was named before "Swines-snout;" he also ordained the Agnus to be sung thrice at the mass, and the host to be divided into three parts.

After him was Pope Leo IV. By this pope it was first enacted in a council, that no bishop should be condemned under threescore and twelve witnesses, according as ye see by the witnesses, was practised at the condemnation of Stephen Gardiner.

Also contrary to the law of Gregory IV., his predecessor, this pope ordained the cross (all set with gold and precious stones), to be carried before him, like a pope.

And here next comes in the whore of Babylon, (Rev. xix. 2.), rightly in her true colours, by the permission of God, and manifestly to appear to the whole world; and that not only after the spiritual sense, but after the very letter. For after this Leo above mentioned, the cardinals proceeding to their ordinary election (after a solemn mass of the Holy Ghost, to the perpetual shame of them, and of that see), instead of a man pope, elected a woman, called Joan VIII., to minister sacraments, to say masses, to give orders, to constitute deacons, priests, and bishops; to promote prelates, to make abbots, to consecrate churches and altars, to have the reign and rule of emperors and kings. This woman's proper name was Gilberta, who went with an English monk out of the Abbey of Fulda, in man's apparel, to Athens, and through her wit and learning was promoted to the popedom, where she sat two years and six months.[1] At last openly in the face of a general procession, she gave birth to a child, and so died, and was succeeded by Benedict III., who first ordained the dirge to be said for the dead.

After him came Pope Nicholas I., who enlarged the pope's decrees with many constitutions, equalling the authority of them with the writings of the apostles. He ordained that no secular prince, nor the emperor himself, should be present at their councils, unless in matters concerning the faith; to the end that such as they judged to be heretics, they should execute and murder. Also, that no laymen should sit in judgment upon the clergymen, or reason upon the pope's power. Also, that no christian magistrate should have any power upon any prelate, alleging that a prelate is called God. Also, that all church service should be in Latin, yet allowing the Sclavonians and Polonians to retain still their vulgar language. Sequences in the mass were by him first allowed. By this pope priests began to be debarred from marrying; whereof Huldrike, bishop of Ausburgh, (a learned and a holy man), sending a letter to the pope, gravely and learnedly refutes and declaims against his indiscreet proceedings touching that matter; which letter I judged meet for the instruction of the reader, and worthy to be inserted here, as follows:—

"*A learned epistle of Huldrike, Bishop of Ausburgh, sent to Pope Nicholas I., proving by substantial proofs, that priests ought not to be restrained from marriage.*

"Huldrike, bishop only by name, unto the reverend father Nicholas, the vigilant provisor of the holy church of Rome, with due commendation sendeth love as a son, and fear as a servant. Understanding, reverend father, your decrees which you sent to me concerning the single life of the clergy, to be far from all discretion, I was troubled partly with fear, and partly with heaviness. With fear, because, as it is said, the sentence of the pastor, whether it be just or unjust, is to be feared. For I was afraid lest the weak hearers of the scripture (which scarcely obey the just sentence of their pastor, much more despising this unjust decree) through the onerous transgression of their pastor, should shew themselves disobedient. I was troubled with heaviness, and with compassion, because I doubted how the members of the body should do, their head being so greatly out of frame. For what can be more grievous, or more to be lamented, touching the state of the church, than for you, being the bishop of the principal see, to whom appertaineth the government of the whole church, to swerve never so little out of the right way? Certainly in this you have not a little erred, in that you have gone about to constrain your clergy to singleness of life, through your imperious tyranny, whom rather you ought to stir up to the honourable estate of marriage. For is not this to be counted a violence and tyranny in the judgment of all wise men, when a man is compelled by your decrees to do that which is against the institution of the gospel and the proceeding of the Holy Ghost? Seeing then there be so many holy examples both of the Old and New Testament, teaching us, as you know, due information; I desire your patience not to think it grievous for me to bring a few here out of many.

"First, in the old law, the Lord permitteth marriage unto the priests, which afterward in the new law we do not read to be restrained, but in the gospel thus he saith, 'There be some eunuchs which have made themselves eunuchs for the kingdom of heaven's sake. He that is able receive it, let him receive it,' Matt. xix. 12. Wherefore, the apostle saith, 'Concerning virgins, I have no commandment of the Lord, yet I give my judgment,' 1 Cor. vii. 25. Which counsel also all men do not take, as in the commandment of the Lord before, but many

---

(1) This extraordinary event has naturally been disputed by the modern advocates of the church of Rome. The election and session of a woman, who is incapable of orders, in the seat of the pontiff, is such a sundering of the links of apostolic succession in the papal chair, and such an impeachment of the orders of some in that church, that it were passing strange if every effort that talent, learning, and ingenuity could devise, were not made to obliterate such a fact from the page of history.

There is however this broad, plain, and unquestionable fact, which requires an answer more cogent than any it has yet received, namely, that for *five hundred years* after the time of Pope Joan, it was acknowledged as an historical event of as great notoriety as any other connected with the papal chair, and that it

was never called in question till the church of Rome began to feel the necessity of defending herself against those who openly opposed her assumed authority. Marianus Scotus, who lived very near the time of Pope Joan, mentions her as "Joanna, Muller," and adds that she was pope for two years, five months and five days, and all the historians for some centuries — although all were members of the church of Rome — in like manner acknowledge the facts, and even since the reformation a large number of Romish divines — among whom are some of their best learned men — have admitted it.

Thus much at all events is certain. If this matter be an invention or falsehood, it rests not on protestants — but on romanists themselves. [ED.]

there be, false dissemblers and flatterers, going about to please men, and not God, whom we see under a false pretence of holiness to fall into horrible wickedness. And, therefore, lest through the infection of this wicked pestilence, the state of the church should too much go to ruin, he said, 'Let every man have his own wife;' touching which saying, our false hypocrites falsely do lie and feign, as though it only pertained to the laity, and not to them. And yet they themselves, seeming to be set in the most holy order, are not afraid to do outrage in all manner of wickedness.

"These men have not rightly understood the scripture; for the saying of the apostle, 'Let every man have his own wife,' doth except none in very deed, but him only which hath the gift of continency. Wherefore, O, reverend father! it shall be your part to cause and oversee, that whosoever hath made a vow of celibacy, and afterward would forsake it, should either be compelled to keep his vow, or else by lawful authority should be deposed from his order.

"And to bring this to pass, you should not only have me, but also all other of my order, to be helpers unto you. But that you may understand, that such which know not what a vow doth mean, are not to be violently compelled thereunto: hear what the apostle saith to Timothy; a bishop, saith he, 'Must be blameless, the husband of one wife,' 1 Tim. iii. 2. Which sentence lest you should turn and apply only to the church; mark what he inferreth after. 'If a man know not how to rule his own house, how shall he take care of the church of God;' and 'Let the deacon be the husband of one wife, ruling their children and own houses well,' 1 Tim. iii. 5—12. And this wife, how she is wont to be blessed by the priest, you understand sufficiently, I suppose, by the decrees of holy Sylvester the pope.

"To these and such other holy sentences of the scripture agreeth also, he that is the writer of the rule of the clergy, writing after this manner, of the clerks, 'Let them have one wife.' Whereby it is to be gathered, that the bishop and deacon are noted infamous and reprehensible, if they be divided with more women than one; otherwise, if they do forsake one under pretence of religion, they, as well the bishop as the deacon, are here condemned by the canonical sentence, which says, 'Let no bishop or priest forsake his own wife, under the colour and pretence of religion. If he do forsake her, let him be excommunicate. And if he so continue, let him be dragged.' St. Augustine also, (a man of discreet holiness), says in these words, 'There is no offence so great or grievous, but it is to avoid a greater evil.'

"Furthermore, we read in the second book of the Tripartite history, that when the council of Nice, going about to establish the same decree, would enact that bishops, priests, and deacons, after their consecration, either should utterly forsake their own wives, or else should be deposed; then Paphnutius, (one of those holy martyrs, whose right eye the Emperor Maximus had put out, and houghed their left legs), rising up amongst them, withstood their purposed decree; confessing marriage to be honourable, and so persuaded the council from making that law, declaring what evil might come of it. And thus much did Paphnutius (being unmarried himself), declare to them. And the whole council commending his sentence, agreed thereto, and left the matter freely without compulsion, to the will of every man, to do therein as he thought.

"Notwithstanding there be some which take St. Gregory for their defence in this matter, whose temerity I laugh at, and ignorance I lament; for they know not, being ignorantly deceived, how dangerous the decree of this heresy was, (being made of St. Gregory), who afterwards revoked the same, with much repentance.

"Peradventure if these men had read with me what happened through this decree, I think they would not be so rash in their doing and judging; fearing at least the Lord's commandment, 'Judge not that you be not judged.' And St. Paul saith, 'Who art thou that judgest another man's servant? To his own master he standeth or falleth, yea, he shall be holden up, for God is able to make him stand.' Therefore let your holiness cease to compel and enforce those whom you ought only to admonish, lest through your own private commandment (which God forbid) you be found contrary as well to the Old Testament as to the New. For as St. Augustine saith to Donatus, 'This is only what we do fear in your justice, lest (not for the consideration of christian lenity, but for the grievousness and greatness of transgressions committed), you be thought to use violence in executing punishment of that, which only we do desire you (by Christ) not to do. For transgressions are so to be punished, that the life of the transgressors may repent.' Also another saying of St. Augustine we would have you to remember, which is this, 'Let nothing be done through the greediness of hurting, but all things through the charity of profiting; neither let any thing be done cruelly, nothing ungently.' Also by the same Augustine it is written, 'In the fear and name of Christ I exhort you, who have not the goods of this world, be not greedy to have them. Such as have them, presume not too much upon them. For, I say, to have them is no damnation, but if you presume upon them, that is damnation; if for the having of them you shall seem great in your own sight, or if you do forget the common condition of man through the excellency of any thing you have. Use, therefore, therein due discretion, tempered with moderation, the which cup of discretion is drawn out of the fountain of the apostolic preaching, which said, 'Art thou bound unto a wife? Seek not to be loosed. Art thou loosed from a wife? Seek not a wife,' 1 Cor. vii. 27. Where, also it follows 'It remaineth, that they who have wives be as though they had none, and they that use this world as not abusing it.'

"Concerning the widow, he saith, 'She is at liberty to be married to whom she will, only in the Lord,' 1 Cor. vii. 39. To marry in the Lord, is nothing else but to attempt nothing in contracting of matrimony, which the Lord doth forbid. Jeremy also saith, 'Trust ye not in the lying words, saying, The Temple of the Lord, The Temple of the Lord, The Temple of the Lord, are these,' Jer. vii. 4. The which saying of Jeremy, Jerome expounding, saith thus, 'This may agree also, and be applied to such nuns as boast of their vow, and know not how the apostle defineth the virgin, that she should be holy in body, and also in spirit. For what availeth the purity of the body, if the mind inwardly be unholy? Or if it have not the other virtues, which the prophetical sermon doth describe?' The which virtues, for so much as we see partly to be in you, and because we are not ignorant, that this discretion, although neglected in this part, yet in the other actions of your life is kept honestly of you, we do not despair, but you will also soon amend the little lack which is behind. And therefore with as much gravity as we can, we cease not to call upon you, to correct and amend this your negligence. For although, according to our common calling, a bishop is greater than a priest, and Augustine was less than Jerome; notwithstanding the good correction proceeding from the lesser to the greater, was not to be refused or disdained, especially when he which is corrected is found to strive against the truth to please men. For as St. Augustine saith, writing to Boniface, 'The disputations of all men, be they never so catholic or approved persons, ought not to be had instead of the canonical scriptures.' So that we may disapprove or refuse (saving the honour and reverence which is due unto them) any thing that is in their writings, if any thing there be found contrary to truth. And what can be found more contrary to the truth than this? When as the truth itself, speaking of abstaining from marriage, saith, 'He that can receive it, let him receive it,' which saying, these men (moved, I know not by what) do turn and say, 'He that cannot receive it, let him be accursed.' And what can be more foolish amongst men, than when any bishop or archdeacon run themselves headlong into all kind of sin, and yet say, that the marriage of priests is an abomination; and, as void of all compassion and true righteousness do not desire or admonish their clerks, as their fellow-servants to abstain from marriage, but command them, and enforce them as servants, violently to abstain. Unto the which imperious commandment of theirs, or counsel, (whether you will call it), they add also this foolish and wicked suggestion, saying, ' That it is better to sin privately than openly in the sight of men to be bound to one wife.' Which truly they would not say, if they were either *of* him, or *in* him, who saith, ' Woe to you, pharisees, which do all things to be seen of men.' And so the psalmist, ' Because they please men, they are confounded, for the Lord hath despised them,' Ps. liii. 5. These be the men who ought to teach us that we should rather be ashamed to sin privily in the sight of Him to whom all things be open, than seem in the sight of men to be holy. These men, therefore, although through their sinful wickedness, they deserve no counsel of godliness to be given them; yet we, not forgetting our humanity, cease not to give them counsel by the authority of God's word, which seeketh all men's salvation, desiring them by the bowels of charity, and saying with the words of scripture, ' Thou hypocrite, first cast out the beam out of thine own eye, and then thou shalt see clearly to cast out the mote of thy brother's eye.

" Moreover, we desire them to attend, to what the Lord saith of the woman taken in adultery. ' He that is without sin among you, let him first cast a stone at her.' As though he would say, ' If Moses bid you, I also bid you. But yet I require you that be the competent ministers and executors of the law, take heed what you add thereunto; take heed also (I pray you) what you are yourselves; for if (as the scripture saith) thou shalt well consider thyself, thou wilt never defame another.'

" Moreover, it is signified unto us also, that there be some of them, who (when they ought like unto good shepherds to give their lives for the Lord's flock) yet are they puffed up with such pride, that without all reason they presume to rend and tear the Lord's flock with whippings and beatings, whose unreasonable doings St. Gregory bewailing, thus saith, ' What shall become of the sheep when the pastors themselves be wolves?' But who is overcome, but he which exerciseth cruelty? Or who shall judge the persecutor, but he which gave patiently his back to stripes? And this is the fruit which cometh to the church by such persecutors, also which cometh to the clergy by such despiteful handling of their bishops, or rather infidels. For why may you not call them infidels, of whom St. Paul thus speaketh, and writeth to Timothy? ' That, in the latter days some shall depart from the faith, giving heed to seducing spirits and doctrines of devils: speaking lies in hypocrisy, having their consciences seared with an hot iron, forbidding to marry, and commanding to abstain from meats, &c., 1 Tim. iv. 1. These be they which bring into the church God this heresy (as blind guides leading the blind) that it might be fulfilled which the Psalm speaketh of, as foreseeing the errors of such men, and accursing them after this manner, ' Let their eyes be darkened, that they may not see, and bow down their back always,' Rom. xi. 10. For so much then (O apostolical Sir) as no man which knoweth you, is ignorant, that if you through the light of your discretion had understood and seen what poisoned pestilence might have come into the church through the sentence of this your decree, you would never have consented to the suggestions of certain wicked persons. Wherefore we counsel you by the fidelity of our due subjection, that with all diligence you would put away so great slander from the church of God: and through your discreet discipline, you will remove this pharisaical doctrine from the flock of God: do not separate the holy people, and the kingly priesthood from her spouse which is Christ, through an unrecoverable divorcement: seeing that no man without holiness shall see our Lord, who with the Father and the Holy Ghost liveth and reigneth for ever. Amen."

By this epistle of bishop Hulderick, it is easy to conceive what was then the opinion of learned men concerning the marriage of ministers.

After this Pope Nicholas succeeded Adrian II., John VIII., Martin II. After these came Adrian III., and Stephan VI. By this Adrian it was first decreed, That no emperor after that time should intermeddle or have any thing to do in the election of the pope. And thus the emperors began first to decay, and the papacy to swell and rise.

Now to return where we left King Ethelwolf. About the latter end of his reign, the Danes who before had invaded the realm, in the time of King Egbert, made their re-entry again, with three and thirty ships arriving about Hampshire.

Concerning the occasion given by the Englishmen which moved the Danes first to invade the realm, I find in certain histories two causes most specially assigned. The first was given by the means of Osbright, reigning under-king of the West Saxons. This Osbright had treated with violence the wife of one of his nobles, called Bruer, whereupon Bruer consulting with his friends, first went to the king resigning into his hands all the service and possessions which he held of him : he then took shipping and sailed into Denmark. There making his complaint to Codrinus the king, he desired his aid in revenging the villany of Osbright against him and his wife. Codrinus hearing this, and glad to have some just quarrel to enter that land, levied an army with all speed, and preparing all things necessary for the same, sends an innumerable multitude of Danes into England; who first arriving at Holderness, they burnt up the country, and killed without mercy, both men, women, and children, whom they could lay hands upon. Then marching towards York, entered into battle with Osbright, where he with most part of his army was slain. And so the Danes took possession of the city of York. The second cause assigned by some historians, for the invasion of the Danes is as follows :

A certain Danish nobleman, called Lothbroke, entering with his hawk into a skiff or small boat alone, was driven by a tempest with his hawk to the coast of Norfolk, where being found and detained, he was presented to the king. The king understanding his parentage, and seeing his case, entertained him in his court accordingly, and every day perceiving more and more his great dexterity in hunting and hawking, bare special favour to him. Insomuch that the king's falconer, or master of his game, bearing privy envy against him, as they were hunting together in a wood murdered him, and threw him into a bush. This Lothbroke, being murdered, in two or three days began to be missed in the king's house : of whom no tidings could be heard ; but a spaniel dog of his, which continuing in the wood with the corpse of his master, at various times came and fawned upon the king : and that so long that at length they followed the trace of the hound, and were brought to the place where Lothbroke lay. Whereupon inquisition being made, at length by certain evidence, it was known how he was murdered by the king's huntsman. Who being convicted, was put into the same boat, alone and without any tackling, to drive by sea, either to be saved by the weather or to be drowned in the deep. And as it chanced that Lothbroke was driven from Denmark to Norfolk, so it happened that from Norfolk the murderer was carried into Denmark, where the boat of Lothbroke being well known, hands were laid upon him, and inquisition made of the party. In his torments, to save himself, he uttered an untruth of King Edmund, saying, " That the king had put Lothbroke to death in the county of Norfolk." Whereupon the Danes being very angry, appointed an army, and sent great multitudes into England to revenge that fact.

In the mean time, King Ethelwolf, when he had chased the Danes, from place to place, causing them to take to the sea, departed himself both from land and life : leaving behind him four sons, who reigned every one in his order, after the decease of his father.

King Ethelbald the eldest son of Ethelwolf, succeeding his father in the province of West Saxony, and Ethelbright in the province of Kent, reigned both together the term of five years, one with the other. After these two succeeded Ethelred, the third son, who in his time was so incumbered with the Danes, bursting in on every side, especially about York, that in one year he stood in nine battles against them.

About the latter time of the reign of this Ethelred, which was about (A. D. 870), certain of the Danes being possessed of the northern country, took shipping from thence, and landed in Norfolk, and came to Thetford. Edmund, then under-king of that province, assembled an host and gave them battle.

The king put to the worse, fled to the castle of Framingham, where being on every side compassed by his enemies, he yielded himself to their persecution. And when he would not deny Christ, they most cruelly bound him to a tree, and caused him to be shot to death ; and lastly, caused his head to be smitten from his body, and cast into the thick bushes.

Tidings soon after were brought to king Ethelred, of the landing of Osrike king of Denmark, who with the assistance of the other Danes had gathered a great host, and were encamped upon Ashdon. To this battle king Ethelred, with his brother Alured, called Alfred, hasted to withstand the Danes, the king staying a little behind to offer up prayer to God, Alfred who was come before entered already into the whole fight with the Danes, who stuck together with huge violence. Afterwards, through the grace of God, and their godly manhood, the king coming with his fresh soldiers, so discomfited the Danes that day that in flying away not only they lost the victory, but many of them their lives. Their king Osrike, and five of their dukes being slain.

After this the Danes yet re-assembled their people, and gathered a new host; so that within fifteen days they met at Basingstoke, and there gave battle to the king, and had the better. Then the king again gathered his men at the town of Merton, and he gave them a sharp battle, but the Danes had the honour of the field, and king Ethelred was there wounded.

After these two battles thus won by the Danes, they spread over a great circuit of ground, and destroyed man and child that would not yield to them. The churches and temples they turned to the use of stables, and other vile occupations.

Thus the king being beset with enemies on every side, seeing the land so miserably oppressed by the Danes, his knights and soldiers consumed, his own land of the West Saxons in such desolation, he being also wounded himself, rather wished to die honestly than to reign in such trouble and sorrow. And not long after deceased being succeeded by his brother

KING ALURED, OTHERWISE CALLED ALFRED.

Among the Saxon kings I find none to be compared to Alfred, for great and singular qualities, worthy of high renown and commendation ; whether we behold in him the valiant acts and manifold trials which he sustained against his enemies in wars, during almost all his reign, for the public preservation of his people ; or whether we consider in him his godly and excellent virtues, joined with a public and tender care, and a zealous study for the common peace and tranquillity of the public weal; appearing as well in his prudent laws as also by the virtuous institution of his life, or whether we respect his notable knowledge of good letters, with a fervent love and princely desire to set forth the same through all his realm, before his time both rude and barbarous. All which heroic properties, joined together in one prince, as it is a rare thing, and seldom seen in princes now-a-days ; so I thought the same more to be noted and exemplified in this good king. Wherefore, to discourse in order of these things, we will first treat of his acts and painful trials sustained in defence of the public realm, against the raging tyranny of the Danes.

King Alfred, the first of all the English kings, taking his crown and unction at Rome of Pope Leo, in the beginning of his reign, perceived his lords and people much wasted and decayed, by reason of the great wars of Ethelred against the Danes, yet as well as he could, he gathered his people, and in the second month that he was made king he met with the Danes beside Wilton, where he gave them battle. But being far over-matched through the multitude of the enemy, he was put there to the worse ; although not without a great slaughter of the Pagan army. The next year the Danes left those parts, and drew to Lindsey, robbing and spoiling the towns and villages as they went, and holding the common people under their bondage. Afterwards joining with the three other kings of the Danes, they grew in mighty force and strength, till the fourth year of King Alfred. In which year Alfred's men had a conflict on the sea with six of the Danes' ships, of which they took one, and the others fled away. The army of the three Danish kings returned again to West Saxony, and entered the castle of Wareham ; where Alfred with a sufficient force was ready to assault them. But the Danes seeing his strength, durst not attempt it with him. In the meantime they were constrained to treat for truce ; leaving sufficient pledges in the king's hand, and promising moreover upon their oath to leave the country of the West Saxons. The king upon the surety let them go. But they falsely breaking their league, privily in the night brake out, taking their journey toward Exeter. In which voyage they lost six score of their small ships by a tempest. Then king Alfred followed after the horsemen of the Danes, but could not overtake them before they came to Exeter, where he took of them pledges and fair promises of peace, and so returned. Notwithstanding the number of the Pagans daily increased, in so much that if in one day thirty thousand of them were slain, shortly after they increased double as many again.

The next year, the Danes having all the rule of the north part of England, from the river Thames, disdained that Alfred should bear any dominion on the other side of the Thames southward. Whereupon the three kings, with all the forces and strength they could make, marched with such a multitude, that the king with his people was not able to resist them ; and of the people which inhabited there, some fled over the sea, some remained with the king, and many submitted themselves to the Danes. Thus Alfred being overset with a multitude of enemies, and forsaken by his people, having neither land to hold, nor hope to recover that which he had lost, withdrew himself with a few of his nobles, into a certain wood country in Somersetshire called Etheling, where he had little to live on but such as he and his people might procure by hunting and fishing. This Etheling stands in a great marsh or moor, so that there is no access unto it without ship or boat, and has in it a great wood called Selwood, and in the middle a little plain about two acres of ground, in which isle is venison, and other wild beasts, with fowls and fishes. In this wood king Alfred at his first coming spied a certain cottage of a poor swineherd, keeping swine in the wood, by whom the king then unknown was entertained and cherished with such poor fare as he and his wife could make him. For which king Alfred afterwards set the poor swineherd to learning, and made him bishop of Winchester.

Notwithstanding the king in process of time was strengthened and comforted, through the providence of God, respecting the miserable ruin of the English. First, the brother of King Halden the Dane coming in with three and thirty ships, landed about Devonshire; where by chance being resisted by a bushment of King Alfred's men (who for their safeguard their lay in garrison) were slain to the number of 1300 men, and their ensign called the Raven was taken. Both Inguar and Hubba were slain among the other Danes. After this King Alfred being better cheered shewed himself more at large, so that the men of Wiltshire, Somersetshire, and Hampshire daily resorted to him, till he was strongly accompanied.

Then the king undertook a bold and dangerous adventure ; for, apparelling himself in the habit of a minstrel, (as he was very skilful in all Saxon poems), with his instrument of music he entered into the camp of the Danes, lying then at Eddendun ; and while playing his interludes and songs, he espied all their sloth and idleness, and heard much of their counsel. Shortly after he fell upon the Danes suddenly in the night and slew a great multitude of them, and chased them from that coast, insomuch that through his strong and valiant assaults he clearly voided the country of them between that and Selwood. His subjects soon hearing of his valiant victories and manful deeds, drew to him daily out of all coasts. Who through the help of God held the Danes so short, that he won from them Winchester and other towns.

At length he forced them to seek for peace, which was concluded upon certain covenants, whereof one and the principal was, that Gutrum their king should be christened. The other was, that such as would not be christened should depart the country.

About the fifteenth year of the reign of Alfred, the Danes returning from France to England, landed in Kent, and so came to Rochester and besieged that city; and there lay so long that they built a tower of timber against the gates of the city. But by the strength of the citizens that tower was destroyed, and the city defended, till King Alfred came and rescued them. Whereby the Danes were so distressed, and so near trapped, that for fear they left their horses behind them, and fled to their ships by night. But the king, when he was aware thereof, sent after them and took sixteen of their ships, and slew many of the Danes. This done, the king returned to London, and repaired that city, and made it habitable, which before was decayed and enfeebled by the assaults of the Danes.

About the one-and-twentieth year of his reign, the Danes again landed in four places of this land; in the east, in the north, and in two places in the west.

When King Alfred ascertained that the Danes were landed, he went forth against them from where he was in East Anglia, and he pursued so sharply, that he drove them out from those parts. They then landed in Kent, whither the king, with his people, in like manner drave them out. After this, the Danes took shipping, and sailed into North Wales, and there robbed and spoiled the Britons.

The fourth host of the Danes, the same year, came to Chester, which at length they won: but then the country adjoining pressed so sore upon them, and besieged them so long, keeping them within the city, that at last the Danes, wearied with the long siege, were compelled to eat their own horses for hunger. Alfred, in the meanwhile, with his host marched thitherward. Then the Danes, leaving their strong-holds and castles, furnished with men and victuals, again took shipping, and so set their course that they landed in Sussex, and came to the port of Lewes, and from thence toward London, and builded a tower or castle twenty miles from London. But the Londoners hearing thereof, sent out a certain number of men of arms, who, with the assistance of them of that country, put the Danes from that tower, and after beat it down to the ground. Soon after the king came down thither, and to prevent the dangers that might ensue, commanded the river of Lea to be divided in three streams; so that where a ship might sail in times before, there a little boat might scarcely row. From thence the Danes leaving their ships and wives, were forced to fly that country, and took their way again toward Wales, to the river of Severn; where, upon the borders thereof they builded them a castle, there resting themselves for a time, whom the king soon pursued with his army. The year following, the Danes divided their host, part went to Northumberland, some to Norfolk, part sailed to France, others came to Westsax, where they had conflicts with the English, both by land, and upon the sea; some of whom were slain, many perished by shipwreck, others were taken and hanged, and thirty of their ships were taken.

Not long after this, Alfred, when he had reigned nine-and-twenty years and six months, quitted this mortal life. And thus much, we write, touching the painful labours and trials of this good king; which he no less valiantly achieved, than patiently sustained for the defence of his realm and subjects.

Now if there be any who desires to see and follow the virtuous and godly disposition of this king, both touching the institution of his own life, and also concerning his careful government of the commonwealth, thus the histories record:—That when young, perceiving himself disposed to dissoluteness and vice, he did not, as many young princes and kings' sons in the world now do, that is, give themselves to all kind of license, and dissolute sensuality, but, wishing to avoid the temptation, he besought God that he would send to him some continual sickness, whereby he might be kept from any dissolute habits, and be more profitable to the public business of the commonwealth, and more apt to serve God in his calling.

The bountiful goodness joined with prudence in this man, in the ordering and disposing his riches and rents, is not unworthy to be recited; he divided his goods into two equal parts, the one he appropriated to secular uses, the other to spiritual or ecclesiastical. Of which two principal parts, the first he divided into three portions, the first to the support of his house and family; the second upon the workmen and builders of his new works, whereof he had great delight and cunning; the third upon strangers. Likewise the other half for spiritual uses, he divided into four portions, one to the relieving of the poor, another to the monasteries, the third portion to the schools of Oxford, for the maintaining of good letters; the fourth he sent to foreign churches without the realm.

He was most sparing and frugal of time, as of a thing in this earth most precious. He so divided the day and night in three parts (if he were not hindered by wars and other great business) that he spent eight hours in study and learning, eight hours in prayer and alms-deeds, and eight hours in his natural rest, sustenance of his body, and the needs of the realm.

How careful he was of the commonwealth, and for the maintenance of public tranquillity, his laws set forth and devised by him may declare. Wherein especially was provided by him for the extirpating and abolishing of all thieves out of the realm. Whereby the realm was brought into such tranquillity, or rather perfection, that in every cross or turning way through his dominion he caused to be set up a golden brooch, at least of silver gilded, and none were found so hardy as to take it down either by day or night. He diligently searched out the doings of his officers, and especially of his judges, so that if he knew any of them to err, either through covetousness or unskilfulness, he removed them from their office.

And thus much concerning the valiant acts and noble virtues of this worthy prince; whereunto although there were no other ornaments besides, yet they alone were sufficient to set forth a prince worthy of excellent commendation. Now, besides these other qualities and gifts of God's grace in him, there remains another part of no little praise and commendation, which is his learning and knowledge of good letters, whereof he was not only excellently expert himself, but also a worthy maintainer of the same through all his dominions; where there was no grammar or other sciences practised; through the industry of the king, schools began to be erected, and studies to flourish. Although among the Britons, in the town of Chester, both grammar and philosophy, with other tongues, was then taught. After that some other writers record that in the time of Egbert, king of Kent, this island began to flourish with philosophy. About which time some also think that the university of Grantchester, near to that which now is called Cambridge, began to be founded by Bede. Before these times, it is thought that there were two schools or universities within the realm, the one Greek at the town of Greglade, which afterward was called Kirkelade; the other for Latin, which place was then called Latinlade, afterward Lethelade near to Oxford.

But however it chanced that the knowledge and study of good letters being once planted in this realm, afterward went to decay; yet King Alfred deserves no little praise for restoring or rather increasing the same. But this we may see, what it is to have a prince learned himself, who, feeling and tasting the price and value of science and knowledge, is thereby not only the more apt to rule, but also to instruct and frame his subjects, from a rude barbarity, to a more civil life, although it was somewhat late before he learned, yet such was the docility of his nature that, being a child, he had the Saxon poems (such as were used then in his own tongue) by heart and memory. Afterwards, with years he grew up in much perfection of learning and knowledge, which is the more to be marvelled at, for he was twelve years of age before he knew any letter. At which time his mother having by chance a book in her hand, which he wished to have, promised to give it to him if he would learn it. Upon which he, through his desire to possess the book, soon learned the letters, his master being Pleimundus, afterwards bishop of Canterbury. And so he daily grew more and more in knowledge, that at length he translated a great part of the Latin library into English. Of which books, translated by him, was Orosius, Gregory's Pastoral, the History of Bede, Boetius on the Consolation of Philosophy. He also wrote a book in his own tongue, which he called a Hand Book. Besides the history of Bede translated into the Saxon tongue, he also himself compiled a history in the same speech, called The History of Alfred, &c. And as he was himself excellently well learned, so he likewise inflamed all his countrymen with the love of letters. Also his nobles he allured to the embracing of good letters, so that they set all their sons to schools ; or if they had no sons, yet they caused their servants to be taught. He began, moreover, to translate the Psalter in English, and had almost finished the same, when death prevented him.

Moreover, among other learned men who were about King Alfred, histories make mention of John Scot, (a godly divine, and a learned philosopher). This John is described to be of a sharp wit, of great eloquence, and well expert in the Greek tongue, of a pleasant and merry nature, as appears by many of his doings and answers. He left his own country of Scotland, by reason of the great tumults of war, and went to France, where he was worthily entertained, and for his learning was held in great estimation by Charles the Bald, the French king ; so that he was commonly and familiarly about the king. One day, the king sitting at meat, and seeing something (belike in this John Scot) which seemed not very courtly, merrily asked of him what difference there was betwixt a Scot and a *sot ?* to which the Scot sitting over against the king, somewhat lower, replied again suddenly, rather than advisedly (yet merrily) saying, *the table only ;* importing thereby himself to be the Scot, and so calling the king a *sot* by craft. Which word, how other princes would have taken, I know not, but this Charles, for the great reverence he bear to his learning, turned it but to a laughter among his nobles, and so let it pass.

Another time, the same king being at dinner, was served with a certain dish of fish, wherein were two great fishes and a little one. After the king had taken thereof his repast, he sent the fish down to John Scot, to distribute to the other two clerks sitting with him, who were two tall and mighty persons, he himself being but a little man. John, taking the fish, takes and carves to himself the two great ones ; the little fish he reaches to the other two. The king perceiving his division thus made, reprehended it. Then John, whose manner was ever to find out some honest matter to delight the king, answered, proving his division to stand just and equal : for here, (said he) are two great, and a little, pointing to the two great fishes and himself ; and likewise here again is a little one and two great, pointing to the little fish, and the two great persons. I pray you (said he) what odds is there, or what distribution can be more equal ? Whereat the king with his nobles being much delighted, laughed merrily.

The same John Scot moreover compiled a book, in which is contained the resolution of many profitable questions ; but he is thought to follow the Greek church rather than the Latin, and for the same was counted of some to be an heretic ; because there be some things in that book which in all points accord not with the Romish religion. Wherefore the pope, writing to King Charles, complains that a certain man called John, a Scottish man, had translated the book of Dionysius the Areopagite, of the names of God, and of the heavenly orders, from Greek into Latin. Which book, according to the custom of the church, ought first to have been approved by our judgment ; namely, seeing the said John (although he is said to be a man of great learning and science) in time past has been noted to have been a man not of upright or sound doctrine, in certain points, &c. For this cause Scot, being constrained to remove from France, came to

England, allured by the letters of King Alfred, by whom he was entertained with great favour, and continued a long time about the king ; till at length (whether before or after the death of the king it is uncertain) he went to Malmesbury, where he taught certain scholars a few years, by which scholars at last he was most impiously murdered and slain with their penknives, and so died.

King Alfred having these helps of learned men about him, and no less learned also himself, passed his time to the great utility and profit of his subjects. Alfred had two sons, Edward and Ethelward, and three daughters, Elfleda, Ethelgora, and Ethelguida. Edward, his eldest son, succeeded him in the kingdom ; the second son, Ethelward, died before his father : Ethelgora, his middle daughter, was made a nun, the other two were married, the one in Merceland, the other to the Earl of Flanders. Thus King Alfred, the valiant, virtuous, and learned prince, after he had thus christianly governed the realm, the term of nine-and-twenty years and six months, departed this life, 5th November, (A. D. 901), and lies buried at Winchester. Of whom I find, moreover, this thing greatly noted and commended in history, and not here to be forgotten, for the rare example thereof, that wherever he was, or whithersoever he went, he always bore about him a little book containing the Psalms of David, and certain other orisons of his own collecting. Whereupon he was continually reading or praying, whenever he had any leisure.

As to the course and proceedings of the Romish bishops, I last mentioned Pope Stephen VI. After his time there was much broil in the election of the bishops of Rome, one contending against another ; so that in the space of nine years, there were nine bishops ! the first was Formosus, who succeeded Stephen VI., being made pope against the mind of certain in Rome, who preferred Sergius. This Formosus had offended Pope John VIII., by reason whereof, for fear of the pope, he left his bishopric. And because, being sent for by the pope, he would not return, he was excommunicated. At length coming to make his satisfaction to the pope, he was degraded from a bishop into a secular man's habit, swearing to the pope that he would no more re-enter into the city of Rome, nor claim his bishopric again, subscribing moreover with his own hand, to continue from that time in the state of a secular person. But then Pope Martin, (the next pope after John), released Formosus of his oath, and restored him again to his bishopric ; whereby Formosus entered not only into Rome again, but also shortly after obtained the papacy. Thus, he being placed in the popedom, there arose a great doubt or controversy among the divines about his consecration, whether it was lawful or not ; some holding against him, that as he was solemnly deposed, degraded, unpriested, and also sworn not to reassume the ecclesiastical state, therefore he ought to be taken no otherwise than for a secular man. Others alleged again, that whatever Formosus was, yet for the dignity of the order, and for the credit of those whom he ordained, all his consecration ought to stand in force, especially as Formosus was afterwards received and absolved by Pope Martin from his perjury and degradation, &c. In the mean time, Formosus sends to King Arnulphus for aid against his adversaries ; when then marching toward Rome, was there resisted by the Romans from entering. But Arnulphus obtaining the city of Rome, rescues Pope Formosus, and beheads his adversaries ; the pope to gratify him in return, blesses and crowns him as emperor. Thus Formosus sitting about the space of four or five years, followed his predecessors ; after whose time (as I said) within the space of nine years were nine bishops as follows. But in the mean time concerning this Formosus, I would gladly ask, and more gladly learn of some impartial good catholic person, who being a papist, not in obstinacy, but in simple error, would answer his conscience—whether he thinks the holy order of priesthood, which he takes for one of the seven sacraments, to be an indelible character or not ? If it be not indelible, that is, if it be such a thing as may be put off, why then does the pope's doctrine pretend it to be indelible, and unremoveable ? or if it be indeed as they teach and affirm, of an indelible character, why then did Pope John, or could Pope John annihilate and evacuate one of his seven pope-holy-sacraments, making of a priest a non-priest, or layman, uncharactering his own order which is (as he says) a character which in nowise may be blotted out or removed? Again, however Pope John is to be judged in this matter, as either well or not well; this I would know, whether he did well in dispriesting and discharacterising Formosus for such private offences? If he did, how then stands his doing with his own doctrine which teaches the contrary? If he did not well, how then stands his doctrine with his doings, which teaches that the pope with his synod of cardinals cannot err? Moreover, if this Pope John did not err in his disordaining Formosus, how then did Martin his successor not err in repealing the act of his predecessor? or how did not Pope Formosus err himself, who being unpriested by Pope John without reiterating the character or order of priesthood, took upon him to be pope, and made acts and laws in the church? Again, if Formosus, when he was pope, did not err, how then did Pope Stephen, his successor, afterwards not err, who annihilated the consecration, and all other acts of Formosus as erroneous? Or, again, if we say that this Stephan with his synod of cardinals did right, then how could it be that Pope Theodore, and Pope John IX. who came after Stephen, did not err, who approving of the consecration of Formosus, did condemn and burn the synodical acts of Stephen and his cardinals, who before had condemned Formosus?

After Formosus had governed the see of Rome five years, Boniface VI. succeeded, who continued but five-and-twenty days. Then came Stephen VII. who so hated the name of his predecessor Formosus, that he abrogated and dissolved his decrees, and taking up his body after it was buried, cut two fingers off his right hand, and commanded them to be cast into the Tiber, and then buried the body in a private or lay-man's sepulchre!

After Stephen had sat in the chair of pestilence one year, Pope Romanus succeeded, and sat three months, repealing the acts decreed by Stephen against Formosus. Next to him came Theodore II., who, taking part with Formosus against Stephen, reigned but twenty days. Than sat Pope John IX., who to confirm the cause of Formosus more surely, held a synod at Ravenna of seventy-four bishops, with the French king, and his archbishops present at it. At this council were ratified all the decrees and doings of Formosus, and the contrary acts of the synod of Stephen VII. were burned. This pope continued not quite two years, after whom succeeded Benedict IV., who kept the chair three years. After whom Leo V., within forty days of his papacy, was taken and cast into prison by one Christopher, his own chaplain. Which Christopher, being pope about the space of seven months, was likewise himself driven from his papal throne by Sergius III., as he had done to his master before. And thus within the space of nine years, nine popes had succeeded one after another. Then Sergius after he had thrust down Pope Christopher, and shorn him and put him as a monk into a monastery, occupied the room seven years. This Sergius, a rude man and unlearned, very proud and cruel, had before been put back from the popedom by Formosus above mentioned. Therefore to revenge himself on Formosus, he caused the body of Formosus, where it was buried, to be taken up; and afterwards sitting in the papal see (as in his pontificalibus) first degraded him, then commanded his head to be smitten off, with the other three fingers that were left, and then commanded his body to be thrown into the Tiber, deposing likewise all such as by Formosus had before been consecrated and invested. This body of Formosus, thus thrown into the Tiber, was afterward (as our writers say) found and taken up by certain fishers, and so brought into St. Peter's temple. At the presence whereof (as they say) certain images standing by, bowed themselves down, and reverenced the same! But such deceivable miracles of stocks and images, in monkish temples are no news to us, especially here in England, where we have been so inured with the like and so many, that such wily practices cannot be invisible, to us, though this crown-shorn generation think themselves to dance in a net. But the truth is, while they think to deceive the simple, these wily beguilers most of all deceive themselves, as they will find, except they repent. By this Pope Sergius first came up the custom of bearing about candles on Candlemas-day, for the purifying of the blessed Virgin; as if the sacred conception of Jesus the Son of God, were to be purified as a thing impure, and that with candle light.

After Sergius was Pope Anastasius. After Anastasius had sat two years, followed Pope Lando, the father (as some historians think) of Pope John, which John is said to have been set up by Theodora, an infamous woman of Rome, either against Lando, or after Lando to succeed in his room. Luithprand, mentions this Theodora and Pope John X., and says, "that Theodora had a daughter named Marozia, which Marozia had a son by Pope Sergius, who afterward was Pope John XI. The same Marozia afterwards married Guido, marquis of Tuscia, through the means of which Guido and his friends at Rome, she had this Pope John X. smothered with a pillow after he had reigned thirteen years, that so John XI., her son, might succeed after him. But because the clergy and people of Rome did not agree to his election, therefore Pope Leo was set up. Thus Pope John, the son of Sergius, and Marozia being rejected, Pope Leo reigned seven months. After him Pope Stephen two years, who being poisoned, then was Pope John XI., the son of Sergius and Marozia set up again in the papacy, where he reigned near the space of five years. Of the wickedness of this Marozia, how she married two brothers, one after the death of the other, and how she governed all Rome, and the whole church at that time I let pass. After John XI., followed Pope Leo, who reigned three years and four months. Pope Stephen IX., three years and four months. Pope Martin three years and six months; after him Pope Agapetus eight years and six months. About whose time, or a little before, first began the order of monks, called, "The monks of Cluny," &c. But now to leave off these monstrous matters of Rome, we return again to our country of England, where we left off.

KING EDWARD THE ELDER.

After the reign of Alfred, his son Edward succeeded. This Edward began his reign, (A. D. 901.) and governed right valiantly and nobly twenty-seven years. In knowledge of good letters and learning he was not to be compared to his father, otherwise in princely renown, in the civil government, and such like martial prowess, he was nothing inferior, but rather excelled him; through whose valiant acts first the princedom of Wales and the kingdom of Scotland, with Constantine king thereof, were subdued to him. He added moreover to his dominion, the country of East Anglia, that is Norfolk, Suffolk, and Essex. All Merceland also he recovered, and Northumberland out of the hands of the Danes. In all his wars he never lightly went without victory. The subjects of his provinces and dominions were so inured and hardened in continual practice and feats of war, that when they heard of enemies coming (never tarrying for any bidding from the king or from his dukes) straightways they encountered with them, always excelling their adversaries both in numbers and the knowledge of the art of war.

About the twelfth year of his reign, the Danes repenting them of their covenants, and minding to break the same, assembled an host, and met with the king in Staffordshire, at a place called Totenhall, and soon after at Wodenfield, at which two places, the king slew two kings, two earls, and many-thousands of Danes that occupied the country of Northumberland.

Thus the importunate rage of the Danes being assuaged, King Edward having now some leisure given from wars to other studies, gave his mind to the building or repairing of cities, towns, and castles, that had been razed, shattered, and broken by the Danes.

As touching the laws and statutes of this Edward, as also of his father Alfred, I omit here to record them on account of their length: yet notwithstanding I think good to note that in the days of these ancient kings of

England, the authority both of conferring bishoprics and spiritual promotions, and also of prescribing laws as well to the churchmen, as to the laity, and of ordering and intermeddling in matters merely spiritual, was then in the hands of the kings ruling in the land, and not only in the hand of the pope, as appears by the laws of Alfred.

Whence it may appear, how the government and direction of the church in those days depended not upon the pope of Rome, but upon the king who governed the land. To this also the example of King Edward's time gives testimony; for Edward with Pleimundus, archbishop of Canterbury, and other bishops in a synod assembled, assigned and elected seven bishops in seven metropolitan churches of the realm, in which election the king's authority seemed then alone to be sufficient, &c.

KING ETHELSTAN, OR ADELESTON.

Ethelstan succeeded, after the death of Edward his father, (A. D. 928)., and was crowned at Kingston. He was a prince of worthy memory, valiant and wise in all his acts, nothing inferior to his father. In like worldly renown of civil government, joined with much prosperous success, in reducing this realm under the subjection of one monarchy. For he both expelled the Danes, subdued the Scots, and quieted the Welshmen.

Among the victorious and noble acts of this king, one blot is written of him, wherein he is as much worthy to be reprehended, as in the others to be commended; that is, the innocent death and murder of his brother Edwin. The occasion thereof was this. The said Ethelstan being born of Egwina, the wife to Edward before he was married to her, and fearing his next brother Edwin, who was rightly born, especially being stirred thereto through the sinister suggestion of his butler, felt such dislike to Edwin his brother, that he caused him to be set in an old rotten boat in the broad sea, without any tackling or other provision. Where the young and tender prince being dismayed with the rage of winds and of the floods, and now weary of his life, cast himself overboard into the sea, and so was drowned. The king, afterwards coming to the remembrance of himself, was stricken with great repentance the space of seven years together, and at length was revenged of him that was the accuser of his brother. This accuser was the king's cup bearer, who (as God the righteous judge of all things would have it) upon a certain solemn feast, bearing the cup to the king, chanced in the middle of the floor to stumble with one foot, helping and recovering himself with the other, saying in these words, " Thus one brother helps another." These words being thus spoken in the hearing of the king, so moved his mind, that forthwith he commanded the false accuser of his brother, to be had out to execution. Whose just recompense I would wish to be a warning to all men, what it is to sow discord between brother and brother.

King Ethelstan (besides his seven years lamentation for this act) built the two monasteries of Midleton and of Michlenes for his brother's sake, or (as the histories say) for his soul. Whereby it may appear what was the cause in those days of building monasteries, to wit, for releasing the sins both of them departed, and them alive: which cause, how it stands with the grace and verity of Christ's gospel, and of his passion, let the christian reader try and examine with himself. This cruel act of the king towards Edwin, caused him afterward to be more tender and careful towards his other brethren and sisters left in his hands unmarried. Which sisters, he bestowed in great marriages; one to the king of Northumberland; another he gave unto Lewis king of Aquitain; the third to Otho, who was the first emperor of the Germans.

The fourth of his sisters being of singular beauty, Hugo the French king required to be given to him, sending to King Ethelstan precious and sumptuous presents, such as were not before seen in England. Among which presents and gifts, besides the rare odours of sundry favours, and fine spices; and besides the precious and costly gems, besides also many beautiful coursers and palfries richly trapped; especially of one jewel

which was a certain vessel finely and subtilly made of the precious onyx stone, so radiantly wrought, that in it appeared the lively corn growing, and men's images walking, &c. Besides these, there was sent also the sword of Constantine the Great, with the name of the possessor, written in golden letters, where in the haft of the same all beaten in gold, was one of the iron nails wherewith our Saviour was nailed on the cross. Among them, moreover, was the spear (as is reported) wherewith the side of our Saviour was opened, with a portion likewise of the holy cross inclosed in crystal, also a part of the crown of thorns in like manner inclosed, &c. Of the truth of all which relics I am not much disposed to say all I suspect.

Ethelstan prescribed certain constitutions also, touching tithes, where he proclaimed as follows: " I, Ethelstan King, charge and command all my officers through my whole realm, to give tithes unto God of my proper goods, as well in living cattle, as in the corn and fruits of the ground, and that my bishops likewise of their proper goods, and mine aldermen, and my officers and headmen shall do the same. Also this I will, that my bishops and other headmen do declare the same to such as be under their subjection, and that to be accomplished at the term of St. John the Baptist. Let us remember what Jacob said unto the Lord, " Of all that thou shalt give me I will surely give a tenth unto thee." Gen. xxviii. 22.

And thus much briefly concerning the history of King Ethelstan, who reigned about the space of sixteen years. And because he died without issue, therefore his brother Edmund succeeded after him (A. D. 940), who reigned six years.

KING EDMUND.

Edmund, the son of Edward, and brother of Ethelstan, was twenty years of age when he began his reign; he had two sons, Edwin and Edgar, who both reigned after him. This Edmund continued his reign six years and a half. By him the Danes, Scots, Normans, and all foreign enemies were expelled out of the land, and then the king set his mind to redressing and maintaining the state of the church, all which then stood in building of monasteries, and furnishing of churches, either with new possessions or restoring the old which were taken away before. In the time of Edmund, I find this written in an old history, " In the time of this king, there was a scattering or dispersion made of the monks out of the monastery of Evesham, and canons substituted in their place, through the doing of Athelm and Ulric, laymen, and of Osulfus bishop," &c.

Here, as concerning this matter between monks and others of the clergy, first it is to be understood, that in the realm of England, before the time of Dunstan, the bishops' sees and cathedral churches were not filled with monks, but with priests and canons, called then clerks or clergy. After this a difference begins to rise between these two parties in strictness of life, and in habit; so that they who lived after a strict rule were called monks, and professed chastity, that is, to live a single life (for so chastity was defined in those blind days) as though holy matrimony were no chastity. The other sort who were not monks but priests or clergy, lived more free from those monkish rules and observances, and were then commonly (or at least lawfully) married, and in their life and habit came nearer to the secular state of other christians. By reason whereof there was great disdain and emulation among them, so that in many cathedral churches, where priests were before, there monks were put in; and sometimes where monks had intruded, there priests and canons were again placed, and the monks thrust out; whereof more shall appear hereafter (by the grace of Christ) when we come to the life of Dunstan. In the mean time, to satisfy the reader, who would know of the first coming of monks into this realm and church of England, this is to be noted.

About this time of King Edmund, or shortly after, when strictness of life joined with superstition, was had in veneration, and counted for great holiness; men, either to win fame with men, or merits with God, gave themselves to lead a strict life, thinking thereby (the stranger their conversation was, and the further from the common trade of vulgar people) to be the more perfect towards God and man. There was at that time a monastery in France named Floriake, after the order of Benedict: from which monastery sprung a great part of our English monks, who being there professed, and afterward returning into England, congregated men daily to their profession. And so, partly for strangeness of their rule, partly for outward holiness of life, partly for the opinion of holiness that many had of them, they were in great admiration, not only with the rude sort, but with kings and princes, who founded their houses, maintained their rules, and enlarged them with possessions. Among the monks was one Oswald, first a monk of Floriake, then bishop of Worcester and York, a great patron and setter up of monkery. Of this Oswald, bishop of York, and Dunstan, bishop of Canterbury, and Ethelwald, bishop of Winchester, and how they filled divers monasteries and cathedral churches with monks, and how they discharged married priests and canons out of their houses, to plant monks in their cells, more shall be spoken hereafter.

In the time of this king, Dunstan was not yet archbishop of Canterbury, but only abbot of Glastonbury, of whom many fabulous narrations pass among the writers, whereof this is one of the first. When Edgar was born, Dunstan being abbot of Glastonbury (as the monkish fables dream) heard a voice in the air of certain angels singing after this tenor and saying, Now peace cometh to the church of England in the time of this child, and of our Dunstan, &c. This I mention that the christian reader might the better ponder with himself the impudent and abominable fictions of this Romish generation. Of the same mint also they have forged, how at another time the said Dunstan heard the angels sing, which is as true as that the harp, hanging in a woman's house, played by itself the tune of an anthem. What would not these deceivers pretend in matters something likely, who in things so absurd are not ashamed to lie and to forge so impudently and also so manifestly? Through the instigation of this Dunstan, King Edmund built and furnished the monastery of Glastonbury, and made Dunstan abbot of it.

By the laws of King Edmund (ordained and set forth, as well for the redress of church matters, as also of civil government) it may appear that the state both of temporal and spiritual causes appertained then to the king's right (notwithstanding the false pretended usurpation of the bishop of Rome) as by these laws are to be seen: where he, by the advice of his lords and bishops did enact and determine concerning the pure life of ecclesiastical ministers, and such as were in the orders of the church, with the penalties also for those who transgressed the same.

Also for tithes to be paid for every christian man, and for the church fees, and alms fees, &c.

Concerning professed women, whom we call nuns, &c.

For every bishop to see his churches repaired of his own proper charge; and boldly to inform the king, whether the houses of God were well maintained, &c.

For flying into the church for sanctuary, &c.

Concerning cases and determinations on matrimonial questions, &c.

All which constitutions declare what interest kings took in those days in ecclesiastical matters as well as others, within their dominion, and not only in disposing the ordinances and rites, such as appertained to the institution of the church, but also in placing and setting bishops in their sees, &c.

In the time of this Edmund, Ulstan was archbishop of York, and Odo archbishop of Canterbury.

This Odo continued bishop the space of twenty years. After whom Elsinus was elected and ordained by the king to succeed through favour and money; but in going to Rome for the pope's pall, in his journey over the Alps he died through the cold. Whereupon Dunstan succeeded. Before this king Edmund died, and was buried by Dunstan at Glastonbury.

He was succeeded by his brother Edrid, (A.D. 948,) who governed as protector until Edwin the eldest son of Edmund came of age.

KING EDWIN.

Edwin, sometimes called Edwy, began his reign A.D. 955, being crowned at Kingston by Odo the archbishop of Canterbury. Of this Edwin it is reported that the first day of his coronation, while sitting with his lords, he suddenly left them for the company of a certain lady, whom he retained, (it not being known whether she was his wife), to the great displeasure of his lords, and especially of the clergy. Dunstan was yet but abbot of Glastonbury, who following the king, brought him back, and accused him to Odo the archbishop, by whom the king was suspended out of the church. By reason whereof the king being displeased with Dunstan, banished him. About the same time the order of Benedict monks, or black monks, (as they were called), began to multiply and increase in England, so that where other priests and canons had been, there monks were set in, and the secular priests (as they then were called, or canons) put out. But king Edwin for the displeasure he bare to Dunstan, so vexed all the orders of monks that in Malmesbury, Glastonbury, and other places, he thrust out the monks, and set in secular priests in their stead.

Notwithstanding, it was not long before these priests and canons were again removed, and the monks restored in their stead, both in the aforesaid houses, and in many other cathedral churches, besides.

In fine, king Edwin being hated by all his subjects, was removed from his kingly honour, and his brother Edgar received in his stead.

KING EDGAR.

Edgar, the second son of Edmund, being of the age of sixteen years, began his reign A.D. 959, but was not crowned till fourteen years after; the causes whereof hereunder follow to be declared. In the beginning of his reign he called home Dunstan, whom king Edwin had exiled. Then was Dunstan, who was abbot of Glastonbury, made bishop of Worcester, and then of London. Not long after, this Odo the archbishop of Canterbury deceased, after he had governed that church above twenty years. After whom Brithilinus bishop of Winchester, was first elected; but because he was thought not sufficient Dunstan, was ordained archbishop, and the other sent home again to his old church. Where, note by the way, how in those days the donation and assigning of ecclesiastical dignities remained in the king's hand; only they brought their pall from Rome as a token of the pope's confirmation. So Dunstan being by the king made archbishop, took his journey to Rome for his pall of Pope John XIII. Dunstan obtaining his pall, shortly after his return from Rome, intreats king Edgar that Oswald might be promoted to be bishop of Worcester, which was granted to him. And not long after, through means of Dunstan, Ethelwold was also made bishop of Winchester.

The monks began first to swarm in the churches of England, that is, in the days of this Edgar, by the means of these three bishops, Dunstan, Ethelwold, and Oswald. Although Dunstan was the chief ringleader, yet Ethelwold being now bishop of Winchester, and Oswald bishop of Worcester were not much behind. By the instigation and counsel of these three, King Edgar is recorded to have built either new out of the ground, or to have re-edified more than forty decayed monasteries. In setting up and building which Ethelwold was a great founder under the king. Moreover, through the influence of this Dunstan and his fellows, King Edgar in many great houses and cathedral churches, where prebendaries and priests were before, displaced the priests and set in monks.

After the king was thus persuaded to advance monkery, Oswald bishop of Worcester, and also made archbishop of York, having his see in the cathedral church of St. Peter, began with fair persuasions to try the minds of the canons and priests, whether they would be content to change their profession, and be made monks or no; when he saw it would not take effect, he practised this policy with them: Near to the church of St Peter, within the churchyard, he erected another church of our lady, which he filled with monks, there he continually frequented, and was always there to be seen, by reason of which the other church was left naked and desolate, and all the people gathered where the bishop was. The priests seeing themselves so neglected both by the bishop and the people, were driven either to relinquish the house, or else become monks. Ethelwold also drove out the canons and priests from the new monastery in Winchester, and in Oxford, and in Mildune, with other places, the secular priests with their wives were expelled to give place to monks. The cause whereof is thus pretended in certain writers: the priests and clerks were thought negligent in their church service, and set vicars in their stead, while they lived in pleasure, and mis-spent the patrimony of the church. Then king Edgar gave to the vicars the same land which before belonged to the prebendaries; who also not long after shewed themselves as negligent as the others. Wherefore king Edgar, by the consent of Pope John XIII., removed the priests and ordained monks there.

As we have entered upon the mention of monks and nuns, and of their profession so greatly commended in our monkish histories, lest perhaps the reader may be deceived in hearing the name of monks to be such an ancient thing in christian life (even from the primitive church after the apostles' time) therefore to prevent all error herein, it shall not be unprofitable to say somewhat concerning the original institution of monks, what they were who in the old time were called monks, in what the monks in the primitive time did differ from the monks of the middle time, and from the monks of this later age; moreover, in what all these three differ from priests (as we call them) and from the clergy. Wherefore to answer to the superstitious scruple of such as allege the antiquity of the name of monks; I grant the name and order to be of old continuance, from the time of three hundred years after Christ. Several old authors write of them, as Augustine, Jerome, Basil, (who was himself one of the first instituters and commenders of that superstition), Chrysostom, Nazianzen, Evagrius, Sozomen, Dionysius, and others. In the number of these monks (who then were divided into hermits or anchorites, and coenobites) were Antony, Paul, John, with divers other recluses. Cassian makes mention of a certain monastery in Thebes, wherein were above five thousand monks, under the government of one abbot. And here also in England, mention is made before of Bangor, wherein were two thousand and two hundred monks under one man's ruling, (A. D. 596). Whereby it appears that monks were then, and two hundred years before, in the primitive church. But these monks were such as either by persecution were driven into solitary and desert places; or else such as not constrained by any, but by their own voluntary devotion (joined with some superstition) withdrew themselves from all company. And all these were then nothing else but laymen; of whom there were two sorts, one of the vulgar and common people, who were only partakers of the sacraments; the other, following a monastic life, were called monks, (being nothing but laymen) leading a more severe and stricter life than the others.[1]

Monks in the former age of the church, although they lived a solitary life, yet were only laymen, differing from priests, and differing from the other monks who succeeded them in the middle age of the church, in three points: first, they were bound to no prescribed form, either of diet or apparel, or any thing else. Secondly, they remained in the order of laymen (only being of a stricter life than the rest) and had nothing to do in matters ecclesiastical. Thirdly, the monks of that age (although the most part of them lived single) yet some of them were married; and certainly none of them were forbidden or restrained from marriage. Of such as were married, speaks Athanasius *in Epistola ad Dracontium*, who says that he knew both monks and bishops married men, and fathers of children, &c.

And yet the monks of the old time, though they were better than those that followed; yet superstition began to creep among them into the church, through the crafty subtilty of Satan, and all for the ignorance of our free justification by faith in Jesus Christ. Examples declare the vain and prodigious superstition of these men; two or three shall suffice for many, which I here insert, that the mind of the godly reader may the better consider and understand, how shortly after the time of Christ and his apostles, the doctrine of christian justification began to be forgotten, true religion turned to superstition, and the price of Christ's passion obscured through the vain opinion of men's merits, &c. A certain abbot named Moses thus testifies of himself in the collations of Cassian, that he so afflicted himself with fasting and watching, that sometimes for two or three days together, he not only felt no appetite to eat, but also had no remembrance of any meat at all, and by reason thereof, was driven also from sleep. So that he was obliged to pray to God for a little refreshing sleep to be given him some part of the night. In the same author mention is made of a certain old man a hermit, who because he had conceived in himself such a purpose never to eat meat, without he had some guest or stranger with him, was sometimes constrained to abstain five days together until Sunday, when he came to the church, and brought some stranger or other home with him.

Two other examples I will add out of Cassian, to shew how the subtilty of Satan, through superstition and false colour of holiness, blinds the miserable eyes of such as rather attend to men's traditions than the word of God. A certain abbot named John, in the desert wilderness of Scythia, sent two novices with figs to one that was sick, eighteen miles off from the church. It chanced these two young novices, missing the way, wandered so long in the wild forest or wilderness, and could not find the cell, that for emptiness and weariness they waxed faint and tired; and yet rather would they die than taste the figs committed to them to carry, and so they did; for shortly after they were found dead, their figs lying whole by them.

Another story he also recites of two monastical brethren, who making their progress in the desert of Thebes, purposed to take no sustenance but such as the Lord himself should minister to them. It happened as they were wandering in the desert, and fainting almost for want, certain Mazises, a kind of people by nature fierce and cruel, notwithstanding being suddenly altered into a new nature of humanity, came forth, and of their own accord offered bread to them; which bread the one thankfully received as sent of God; the other, as counting it sent of man, and not of God, refused it, and so perished.

I might also add the story of Mucius, who, to shew his obedience, did not stick, at the commandment of his abbot, to cast his son into the water, not knowing whether any were ready to rescue him from drowning; so far were the monks in those days drowned in superstition. What is this, but for man's traditions and commandments to transgress the commandments of God, which saith, "Thou shalt do no murder; thou shalt not tempt the Lord thy God?" What man is so blind, that sees not by these and many other examples, what pernicious superstition begun by reason of this monkery, almost from the beginning, to creep into the church? Whereat I cannot marvel enough, seeing that that age of the church had so many learned doctors, who not only approved and followed these monastical sects, but also themselves were authors and instituters of the same. Among whom may be reckoned Basil and Nazianzen,

(1) August. lib. de moribus ecclesiæ, cap. 13. Item, lib. de operibus Monachorum. Item, Epistola ad Aurelium. Also by Hierome ad Heliodorum. Also the same appeareth likewise by the fourth canon of the council of Chalcedon, where it is provided, "ne monachi se ecclesiasticis negotiis immisceant;" that is, "that monks should not intermeddle with matters of the church," &c. Et Leo Epistola, 62, vetat monachos et laicos, "etsi scientiæ nomine glorientur, admitti ad officium docendi et concionandi."

who with immoderate austerity so reduced themselves, that when they were called to the office of bishops, they were not able to bear the labour thereof.

After these monks followed other monks of the middle age of the church; who, increasing both in multitude and in superstition, began by little and little to leave their desolate dens in the vast wilderness and approach nearer to great towns; where they had solemn monasteries founded by kings and queens, and kings' daughters. I note, that the most part of these monasteries were first erected upon some great murder, either by war in the field, or privately committed at home, as will appear to those that read the books I have mentioned. But to return to our monks again, who, as I said, first began to creep from the cold field into warm towns and cloisters, from towns then into cities, and at length from their close cells and cities into cathedral churches, where, they not only abounded in wealth and riches (especially these monks of our later time) but much more in superstition and pharisaical hypocrisy, being yoked and tied in all their doings, to certain prescribed rules, and formal observances; in watching, in sleeping, in eating, in rising, in praying, in walking, in talking, in looking, in tasting, in touching, in handling, in their gestures, in their vestures, every man apparelled not as the proper condition of others would require, nor as the season of the year did serve, but as the rules and order of every sect enforced them. The number of which sects was infinite; some after Basil's rule, went in white; some after Benedicts' rule in black; some of Cluny; some after Jerome's rule, leather girdled, and coped above their white coat; some Gregorians copper coloured; some grey monks; some Grandimontenses, wearing a coat of mails upon their bare bodies, with a black cloak thereon; some Cistercians, who had white rochets on a black coat; some Celestines, all in blue, both cloak, cowl, and cap; some charter monks, wearing haircloth next their bodies; some Flagellants, going bare-foot in long white linen shirts, with an open place in the back, where they beat themselves with scourges on the bare skin every day before the people's eyes, till the blood ran down, saying, that it was revealed to them by an angel, that in so scourging themselves, within thirty days and twelve hours, they should be made so pure from sin, as they were when they first received baptism; some starred monks; some Jesuites, with a white girdle and russet cowl. But who can reckon the innumerable sects and disguised orders of their fraternities? Some holding of St. Benedict, some of St. Jerome, some of St. Basil, some of St. Bernard, some of St. Bridget, some of St. Bruno, some of St. Lewis, as though it were not enough for christians to hold of Christ only. So subject were they to servile rules, that no part of christian liberty remained among them; so drowned and sunk in superstition, that they had not only lost Christ's religion, but also almost the sense and nature of men. For where men naturally are and ought to be ruled by the discreet government of reason in all outward doings, wherein one rule can serve for all men; the circumstance of time, place, person and business being so sundry and divers; on the contrary among these, no reason, but only the knock of a bell ruled all their doings; their rising, their sleeping, their praying, their eating, their coming in, their going out, their talking, their silence, and altogether like insensible people, either not having reason to rule themselves, or else as persons ungrateful to God, neither enjoying the benefit of reason created in them, nor yet using the grace of Christ's liberty, whereunto he redeemed them.

Thus the reader sees what the monks were in the primitive time of the church, and what were the monks of the middle age, and of these our later days of the church. Whereto join this, that where the monks of elder time were mere laymen and no spiritual ministers: afterwards Boniface III. made a decree, (A. D. 606), that monks might use the office of preaching, of christening, of hearing confessions, and also of absolving people from their sins, &c. So then monks, who in the beginning were but laymen, and no spiritual ministers, forbidden by the general council of Chalcedon to inter-

meddle with matters ecclesiastical; afterwards in process of time, did so much encroach upon the office of spiritual ministers, that at length the priests were discharged out of their cathedral churches, and monks set in their places; because that monks in those days, leading a stricter life, and professing celibacy, had a greater countenance of holiness among the people than the priests, who then in the days of King Edgar had wives (at least so many as would) no law forbidding them to the contrary, till the time of Hildebrand, called Gregory VII.

And thus much by the way, as to the order and profession of monks. Now to turn again to the matter of King Edgar. Such provinces and lordships, as were not yet come under the king's subjection, he united to his dominion, and so made one perfect monarchy of the whole realm of England, with all the islands and borders about the same. Such as were wicked, he kept under, he repressed them that were rebels, the godly he maintained, he was devout to God, and beloved of his subjects, whom he governed in much peace and quietness. And as he was a great seeker of peace, so God did bless him with much abundance of peace and rest from all wars. He was a great maintainer of religion and learning, not forgetting herein the footsteps of King Alfred his predecessor.

It is reported of this Edgar, by divers authors, that about the thirteenth year of his reign, he being at Chester, eight kings, to wit, petty kings, came and did homage to him. All which kings, after they had given their fidelity to Edgar, the next day (for a pomp or royalty), he entered with them into the river Dee, where he, sitting in a boat, took the helm, and caused these eight kings, every person taking an oar in his hand, to row him up and down the river, to and from the church of St. John to his palace again, in token that he was master and lord of so many provinces.

And thus ye have heard, touching the commendation of King Edgar, such reports as the old monkish writers bestow upon him, as the great patron of their monkish religion, who had built so many monasteries for them, as were Sundays in the year.

Now, on the other side, what vices were in him, let us likewise consider, according as we find in the said authors described, which most wrote to his advancement. One vice is noted to be cruelty, as well upon others, as upon a certain earl, called Ethelwold. The story is this; Ordgar, Duke of Devonshire, had a certain daughter named Elfrida, whose beauty being highly commended to the king, he sent this Ethelwold, (whom he especially trusted), to the party, to see and to bring him word again, and if her beauty were such as was reported, he desired him also to negociate a marriage between them. Ethelwold finding the party, and seeing her beauty nothing inferior to her fame, and thinking to serve himself, gave a false account to the king. Whereupon the king changed his mind, and in the end Ethelwold himself married the maiden.

Not long after the king hearing how he was deceived, set a fair face upon the matter before Ethelwold, and merrily jesting with him, told him he would come and see his wife, and indeed appointed the day when he would be there. Ethelwold perceiving this matter to go hardly with him, made haste to his wife, declaring to her the coming of the king, and also opening the whole order of the matter how he had done; desiring her on her love for him, as she would save his life, to disfigure herself with such garments and attire as the king might not discover her beauty. Elfrida hearing this, contrary to the request of her husband and the promise of a wife, against the king's coming trimmed herself at the glass, and decked herself in her best array. When the king beheld her, he was not so much delighted with her, as in hatred with her husband, who had so deceived him. Whereupon the king shortly after, making as though he would go to hunt in the forest of Harwood, sent for Ethelwold to come to him under the pretence of hunting, and there ran him through and slew him.

And besides the vices objected to King Edgar in our monkish writers, I also observe another, which was blind superstition and idolatrous monkery brought into the church of Christ, with the wrongful expelling of lawful married priests out of their houses. Whereupon what inconveniences ensued after in this realm, especially in the House of the Lord, I leave to the consideration of them which have heard of the detestable enormities of those religious votaries; the occasion whereof first and chiefly began in this Edgar, through the instigation of Dunstan and his fellows, who after they had inveigled the king, and had brought him to their purpose, caused him to call a council of the clergy, where it was enacted, that the canons of divers cathedral churches, parsons, vicars, priests, and deacons, with their wives and children, either should give over that kind of life, or else give room to monks, &c.

And thus much concerning the history of King Edgar, and of such things as happened in his time in the church. When he had reigned the space of sixteen years, he died, and was buried at Glastonbury, leaving after him two base born children, Editha and Edward, and one lawful son, named Ethelred.

King Edgar is noted in all histories to have lived a riotous and debauched kind of life; in consequence of his having taken a nun named Elfied into his house; he was kept back from his coronation by Dunstan archbishop of Canterbury, the space of seven years; and so the king beginning his reign in the sixteenth year of his age, (A. D. 959), was crowned (A. D. 974). Concerning the coronation and the presumptuous behaviour of Dunstan against the king, and his penance enjoined by Dunstan; you shall hear both Osbern, Malmesbury, and other authors speak in their own words as follow:

"After Dunstan had understood the king's offence perpetrated with the professed nun, and that it was blazed amongst the people, he came with great ire and passion of mind to the king, who, seeing the archbishop coming, arose from his regal seat towards him, to take him by the hand, and to give him place. But Dunstan refused to take him by the hand, and with stern countenance bending his brows, spake to this effect to the king. 'You that have not feared to corrupt a virgin dedicated to Christ, presume you to touch the consecrated hands of a bishop? You have defiled the spouse of your Maker, and think you by flattering service to pacify the friend of the bridegroom? No, Sir, his friend will not I be, who has Christ as his enemy,' &c. The king terrified with these thundering words of Dunstan, and touched with inward repentance of his sin, fell down weeping at the feet of Dunstan, who, after he had raised him from the ground, began to utter the horribleness of his act; and finding the king ready to receive whatever satisfaction he would lay upon him, enjoined him this penance for seven years' space, as follows:—

"That he should wear no crown all that time; that he should fast twice in the week; he should distribute his treasure, left to him of his ancestors, liberally to the poor, he should build a monastery of nuns at Shaftsbury, that as he had robbed God of one devoted maiden through his transgression, so he should restore to him many again in times to come. Moreover he should expel clerks of evil life, (meaning such priests as had wives and children, out of churches, and place convents of monks in their room," &c.

It follows then in the story of Osbern, that when the seven years of the king's penance were expired, Dunstan calling together all the peers of the realm, with the bishops, abbots, and other ecclesiastical degrees of the clergy, in the public sight of all the multitude, set the crown upon the king's head at Bath, which was the one-and-thirtieth year of his age, and the thirteenth year of his reign; so that he reigned only but three years crowned king. All the other years Dunstan probably ruled the land as he pleased.

Among his other laws, this king ordained that the Sunday should be solemnized from nine o'clock on Saturday evening till Monday morning. He also made a certain oration to the clergy, not unworthy to be read, as follows:[1]

THE ORATION OF KING EDGAR TO THE CLERGY.

"Because God hath shewed his great mercy to work with us; it is meet (most reverend fathers,) that with worthy works we should answer his innumerable benefits. For we possess not the land by our own sword, and our own arm hath not saved us: but his right hand and his holy arm, because he hath been delighted in us. Therefore it is meet that we should submit both ourselves and our souls to him, that hath subjected all these things under our government; and we ought stoutly to labour, that they, whom he hath made subject to us, might be subject to his laws. It belongs to me to rule the lay-people with the law of equity, to do just judgment between a man and his neighbour, to punish church-robbers, to hold under rebels, to deliver the helpless from the hand of the stronger, the needy also and the poor from them that rob them. It belongs also to my care to provide necessary things for the ministers of the churches, for the flocks of the monks, for the company of nuns, and to provide for their peace and quiet. The examining of all whose manners belongeth unto us; whether they live purely, if they behave themselves honestly toward them that be without, whether they be diligent at God's service, if they be earnest to teach the people, if they be sober in eating and drinking, if they keep measure in apparel, and if they be discreet in judgment. If ye had regarded these things with a trial of them (O reverend fathers, by your leaves I speak) such horrible and abominable things of the clerks should not have come unto our ears. I omit to speak how their crown is not broad, nor their rounding convenient: the wantonness of your life, the pride of your gesture, the filthiness of your words do declare the evil of the inward man.

"Furthermore, what negligence is in God's service, whence they will scarce be present at the holy Vigils? And when they come to mass, they seem rather to be gathered to play and laugh than to sing. I will tell that, which good men will be sorry for, and the evil laugh at. I will speak with sorrow (if so be I may express it) how they are riotous' in banquetings, in chambering, drunkenness and riotings that now clerks' houses may be thought to be convents of players. There is dice, there is dancing and singing, there is watching to midnight, with crying and shouting. Thus the goods of kings, the alms of princes, yea (and what is more) the price of that precious blood is not esteemed. Have our fathers then spent their treasure for this purpose? Have the king's coffers decayed by taking away many revenues for this cause? Hath the king's liberality given lands and possessions to Christ's churches for this intent, that clerks' dancers and singers should be decked with the same? that riotous feasts might be dressed? that hounds and hawks and such other toys might be gotten? The soldiers cry out for these things, the people grudge, minstrels sing, and dance, and yet ye regard it not, ye spare it, ye dissemble it. Where is the sword of Levi, and the zeal of Simeon, which killed the Sichemites and the circumcised, who bare the figure of them that defile Christ's church with filthy deeds, because they abused Jacob's daughter? Where is Moses' spirit, which spared not his own kinsfolk that worshipped the head of the calf? Where is Phineas the priest's dagger, which pacified God's anger by holy zeal, when he killed him that sinned with the Midianite? Where is Peter's spirit, by whose power covetousness is destroyed, and simoniacal heresy is condemned? Be earnest ye priests, be earnest to follow the ways of the Lord, and the righteousness of our God. It is time to act against them that have broken the law of God. I have Constantine's sword, and ye have Peter's sword in your hands; let us join right hands,

---

(1) Foxe had placed this oration at the end of the present book, with this observation— "A certain oration of King Edgar's which should have been placed before, chanced in the meantime to come to my hands, not unworthy to be read: I thought by the way, in the end of this book, to insert the same, (although out of order) yet I judge it better out of order, than out of the book." It is here inserted in its proper place. [ED.]

let us couple sword to sword, that the lepers may be cast out of the temples, that the holy place of the Lord may be purged, and the sons of Levi may minister in his temple, who said to his father and mother, I know you not; and to his brother, I know you not. Go to, diligently, I pray you, lest we repent to have done that we have done, and to have given that we gave, if we shall see that to be spent not in God's service, but on the riotousness of wicked men, through vile and corrupt liberty of life, for lack of chastisement. Let the relics of holy saints, which they despise, and the holy altars before which they play the madmen, move you. Let the great devotion of our ancestors move you, whose alms the madness of the clerks doth abuse. My great grandfather (as ye know) gave the tenth part of all his lands to churches and abbeys. My great-great grandfather, Alfred, of holy memory, thought it not meet to spare his treasures, his goods, nor costs, nor rents, that he might enrich the church. Your fatherhood is not ignorant how great things my grandfather the elder Edward gave to the churches. It becometh you to remember with what gifts my father and his brothers did enrich Christ's altars. O father of fathers, Dunstan! behold (I pray thee) the eyes of my father looking on thee, from that bright place of heaven : hearken to his complaining words sounding in thine ears, thus pitifully lamenting, O Father Dunstan! thou, thou (I say) gavest me counsel to build abbeys and churches, thou wast my helper and fellow-worker in all things : I chose thee as a shepherd and bishop of my soul, and a keeper of my manners. When did I not obey thee? What treasures did I prefer in respect of thy counsels? What possessions did I not despise, if thou badest me? If thou thoughtest meet to give any thing to the poor, I was ready. If thou thoughtest meet to give any thing to churches, I deferred not. If thou complainedst that monks or clerks wanted any thing I supplied. Thou saidst that alms lasted for ever, and that there was none more fruitful than that which was given to abbeys or churches. For with that both God's servants are sustained, and that which remaineth is given to the poor. O, worthy alms! O, worthy price of the soul! O, wholesome remedy for our sins, which now doth stink in the sweet furrs of priests' lemmans, wherewith they adorn their ears, and deck their fingers, apparelling their delicate bodies with silk and purple! O, father! is this the fruit of my alms? is this the effect of my desire, and of thy promise? What wilt thou answer to this complaint of my fathers? I know, I know: when thou didst see a thief, thou runnedst not with him, neither hast thou put thy portion with adulterers. Thou hast rebuked, thou hast exhorted, thou hast blamed them; but words have been despised; now we must come to stripes of correction. Thou hast here with thee the worshipful father, Edward bishop of Winchester. Thou hast the reverend prelate, Oswald bishop of Worcester. I commit this business to you, that both by bishoply correction, and the king's authority, the filthy livers may be cast out of the churches and they that live orderly may be brought in," &c.

In this oration of King Edgar above prefixed, three things are chiefly to be noted and considered by them that have judgment to mark and understand, to wit, The religious zeal and devotion of kings, both in giving to the church, and also in correcting the manners of churchmen. Secondly, the dissolute behaviour of the clergy, then abusing the great donations and patrimonies of princes bestowed upon them. Thirdly, the blind ignorance and superstition of that time in both states, as well ecclesiastical as temporal, in esteeming Christ's religion chiefly to consist in giving to churches, and in maintaining of monkery; being falsely persuaded that the remission of their sins, and the remedy of their souls therein, did lie in building monasteries, erecting churches and cloisters, and in placing monks in the same, and such other alms-deeds, and works of devotion. Wherein appears how ignorant they of that time were of the true doctrine of Christ's faith, and of the free grace of the gospel, which promises life, remedy, and justification, not by any devout merits of ours nor by any works

either of the law of God, or of the inventions of man, but only and freely by our faith in Christ Jesus the Son of God, in whom only consist all the promises of God. Amen.

KING EDWARD, CALLED THE MARTYR.

After the death of King Edgar no small trouble arose among the lords and bishops concerning the succession of the crown; the principal cause whereof rose upon this occasion: Immediately after the decease of the king, Alferus, duke of Mercia, and many other nobles who held with Ethelred, the only right heir and lawful son of Edgar, disliking the placing and intruding of monks into churches, and the thrusting out of the secular priests, with their wives and children out of their ancient possessions, expelled the abbots and monks, and brought in again the priests with their wives. Against whom certain other there were on the contrary part that made resistance, as Ethelwin duke of East Angles, Elfwold his brother, and the Earl Brithnoth, saying, That they would never suffer the religious monks to be expelled and driven out of the realm, who held up all religion in the land; and thereupon levied an army to defend the monasteries by force.

In this hurly-burly amongst the lords, about the placing of monks, and putting out of priests, rose also the contention about the crown, who should be their king; the bishops, and such lords as favoured the monks, seeking to advance such a king as they knew would incline to their side; so that the lords thus divided, some of them would have Edward, and some Ethelred, the lawful son. Then Dunstan archbishop of Canterbury, and Oswald archbishop of York, with their fellow bishops, abbots, and other lords and dukes assembled in a council together. In which council Dunstan coming in with his cross in his hand, and bringing Edward before the lords, so persuaded them that in the end Edward was elected, consecrated, and anointed for their king.

After Dunstan and his fellows had thus set up Edward for their king, they supposed all to be sure on their side, and that they had established the kingdom of monkery for ever, through the help of the young king, and the duke of East Angles, and certain other nobles whom they had drawn to their part. However this matter passed not so well with them as they hoped, for shortly after the coronation of the young king, Alferus, duke of Mercia, stoutly standing on the other side, drove out the monks from the cathedral churches, and restored the priests with their wives. The words of the very author are these, " Alferus, duke of Mercia, with other great men more, drove out the monks from the great monasteries whom King Edgar had there set in before, and restored again the priests with their wives." (Hist. Jornal in vita Edgari.)

Whereby it evidently appears that priests in those days were married, and had their lawful wives.

The duke and nobles of England expelled the monks out of the monasteries after the death of King Edgar; whereof let us hear what the abbey of Crowland records. " The monks being expelled out of certain monasteries, the clerks were again brought in, who distributed the manors or farms of the said monasteries to the dukes and lords of the land, that they being obliged to them, should defend them against the monks. And so were the monks of Evesham thrust out, and the secular clerks placed, and the lands of the church given to the lords; with whom the queen, the king's stepmother holding the same time, took part also with the said clerks against the king. On the contrary part stood the king and the holy bishops, taking part with the monks. Howbeit the lords and peers of the realm, staying upon the favour and power of the queen triumphed over the monks," &c.

Thus, as there was much ado through all quarters of the realm among the lords, so arose no less contention between the priests and monks. The priests complaining to the king and Dunstan, said for themselves that it was uncomely, uncharitable, yea and unnatural, to put out an old known dweller for a new unknown; and that God was not pleased that that should be taken from the ancient possessor which by God was given him. The monks on the other side said for their part, that Christ allowed neither the old dweller, nor the new comer, nor yet looked upon the person, but that whoever would take the cross of penance upon him, and follow Christ in virtuous living, should be his disciple.

These and such other were the allegations of the monks. But whether a monk's cowl, or a wifeless life make a sufficient title to enter into other men's possessions or no, I refer to the judgment of the godly. The troublous cares in marriage, the necessary provision for house-keeping, the virtuous bringing up of children, the daily helping of poverty, and bearing of public charges, with other manifest perturbations and encumbrances daily incident to matrimony, might rather appear to wise men to come nearer to the cross of penance, than the easy and loitering idleness of monkery. In the end, upon this controversy a council of bishops, and other of the clergy was held, where the greater part both of the nobles and commons, judged the priests to have suffered great wrong, and sought by all means possible to bring them again to their old possession and dignities.

Not long after, King Edward, whom the writers describe to be a virtuous and a meek prince, very pitiful and beneficial to the poor, about the fourth year of his reign, came once from hunting in the forest alone, without the company of his servants to the place in the west country, where Alfrith his mother, with her son Ethelred lived. When the queen-mother was warned of his coming, she calls a servant who was of special trust, shewing him how and what to do for the accomplishing of her wicked purpose. Which thing so done, she made towards the king, and received him with all courtesy, desiring him to tarry that night, but he in like courtesy excused himself, and desired to see his brother, and to drink upon his horse sitting.

Now, while the cup was at his mouth, the servant of the queen struck him in the body with a long two-edged dagger. After which the king struck the horse with the spurs, and galloped towards the place where he supposed to meet with his company, but he bled so much, that he fell from his horse with faintness, one foot being caught in the stirrup, by which he was drawn by his horse over fields and lands till he came to a place named Corf-gate, where he was found dead.

In the order and course of the Roman bishops, mention was made last of Agapetus II., after whom next succeeded Pope John XII.[1] This pope is noted to be very wicked and infamous, with abominable vices; an adulterer, gamester, an extortioner, perjurer, a fighter, a murderer, cruel and tyrannous. Of his cardinals, some he put out their eyes, from some he cut off their tongues, some their fingers, some their noses, &c. In a general council before the Emperor Otho I., these objections were articled against him, "That he never said his service; that in saying his mass he did not communicate; that he ordained deacons in a stable; that playing at dice he called for the devil to help; that for money he made boys bishops; that he committed adultery; that he put out the eyes of the Bishop Benedict; that he caused houses to be set on fire; that he brake open houses; that he drank to the devil; that he never crossed himself," &c. For which causes he was deposed by the consent of the emperor with the prelates, and Pope Leo VIII. was substituted in his place. But after his departing, Pope John was restored again to his place, and Leo was deposed. At length about the tenth year of the popedom of this John, he being found without the city with another man's wife, was so wounded by her husband, that within eight days after he died.

After him the Romans elected Pope Benedict V.,

without the consent of the emperor; whereupon the said Otho, the emperor, being not a little displeased for displacing of Leo VIII., whom he had before promoted, and for the choosing also of Benedict V., came with his army, and laid siege to Rome, and so set up Pope Leo VIII. again. Leo, to gratify his benefactor, in return crowned Otho for emperor, and intitled him to be called Augustus. Also the power which Charlemagne had given before to the clergy and people of Rome, this Leo granted to the emperor and his successors; that is, touching the election of the bishop of Rome. The emperor again restored to the see of Rome all such donations and possessions which either Constantine (as they falsely pretend) or which Charlemagne took from the Lombards, and gave to them.

After Pope Leo, succeeded Pope John XIII. Peter, the head captain of the city, with two consuls, twelve aldermen, and divers other nobles, gathering their power together, laid hands upon him in the church of Lateran, and put the pope in prison eleven months. The emperor hearing this, with all speed returned with his army to Rome; who after execution done upon the authors and chief doers of that act, committed Peter to the pope's sentence, he caused him first to be stripped naked, then his beard being shaven, to be hanged by the hair a whole day together, after that to be set upon an ass (his face turned backward, and his hands bound under the ass's tail), and so to be led through the city, that all men might see him; that done, to be scourged with rods, and so banished the city. Thus ye see how the holy father followeth the injunction of the gospel, "Love your enemies." From this pope proceeded first the christening of bells, (A.D. 971).

After him followed Pope Benedict VI., who in like manner was apprehended by Cinthius, a captain of Rome, and cast in prison, where he was strangled, or as some say, famished to death.

Then came Pope Donus II., after Boniface VII. was pope, who likewise seeing the citizens of Rome conspire against him, was constrained to hide himself, and seeing no place there for him to tarry, took the treasure of St. Peter's church, and so privily stole to Constantinople. In whose stead the Romans set up one Pope John. Not long after Boniface returning again from Constantinople, by his money and treasure procured a garrison or company to take his part: this Pope John was taken, his eyes put out, and so thrown into prison, where he was, as some say, famished; some say he was slain by Ferrucius. Neither did Boniface reign many days after, but suddenly died; whose carcass after his death was drawn by the feet through the streets of Rome after a most despiteful manner, the people shrieking and exclaiming against him, (A.D. 976).

Next pope after him was Benedict VII., by the consent of the Emperor Otho II. and reigned nine years.

After Benedict succeeded Pope John XIV., and died the eighth month of his papacy; next to whom came John XV., and after him Gregory V. (A.D. 995). This Gregory was a German, and therefore the more disliked by the clergy and people of Rome. Whereupon, Crescentius, with the people and clergy, conspiring against Gregory, set up John XVI. Gregory went in all haste to the emperor, who set forward with his army to Italy, got the city, and there took both Crescentius the consul, and John the pope. John first having his eyes put out, was deprived after of his life. Crescentius the consul was set upon a vile horse, having his nose and ears cut off, and so was led through the city, his face being turned to the horse's tail, and afterward having his members cut off, was hanged upon a gibbet.

Pope Gregory thus being restored, reigned four years in his papacy.

---

(1) The reader must bear in mind that Foxe introduces Pope Joan with the designation the VIIth., [see page 90] and therefore he arranges all the succeeding Johns under numbers proportionably higher in the numeral line of succession. Again, during the pontificate of Boniface VII., there was another John, whom Foxe reckons as the XVth, and who was elected, after the election, and deposed before the death of this Boniface VII.: and who, therefore, is generally omitted in the line of succession in the papal chair. These occasion much difficulty to the general reader, as confusing the designations of the many popes of this name; therefore the designation of Joan as the VIIIth, and of the Pope John in the time of Boniface, as the XVth, are omitted in this edition, and the others styled in the usual way. [Ed.]

KING ETHELRED II. SOMETIMES CALLED EGELRED AND ELRED.

King Edward being murdered, as before said, the crown fell next to Ethelred. This Ethelred had a long reign given him of God, which endured the term of eight-and-thirty years, but very unfortunate and full of great miseries; and he himself seems a prince not of the greatest courage to govern a commonwealth. Our English histories writing of him, report of his reign, that in the beginning it was ungracious, wretched in the middle, and hateful in the latter end.

About the eleventh year (some say the ninth year) of this king's reign Dunstan died.

Not long after the death of Dunstan, the Danes again entered England, in many and different places of the land; so that the king scarcely knew to which coast he should go first to withstand his enemies. But [in the end, he was compelled to appease them with great sums of money: and when that money was spent, they fell to robbing the people, and assailing the land, not only about Northumberland, but also besieged the city of London at last. But being from thence repelled by the manhood of the Londoners, they strayed to other countries adjoining, burning and killing wherever they went; so that for lack of a good head or governor, many things in the land perished. For the king gave himself to vice and taxing his subjects, and disinheriting men of their possessions, and caused them to redeem the same again with great sums of money; for he paid great tributes to the Danes yearly, which was called dane-gilt. Which tributes so increased, that from the first tribute of ten thousand pounds, it was brought at last in process of five or six years, to forty thousand pounds.

To this sorrow, moreover, was joined hunger and penury among the commons, insomuch that every one of them was constrained to pluck and steal from others. So that what for the pillage of the Danes, and what by inward thieves and bribers, this land was brought into great affliction.

The Danes thus prevailing more and more over the English grew in such pride and presumption, that when they caused the husbandmen to ear and sow the land, and to do all other vile labour belonging to the house, they would sit at home at their pleasure. And when the husbandman came home, he could scarcely have of his own, as his servants had; so that the Dane had all at his will, and fill, faring of the best; when the owner scarcely had his fill of the worst. Thus the common people being so oppressed by them, were in such fear and dread, that not only were they constrained to suffer them in their doings, but also glad to please them.

And thus hitherto we have brought this history to A. D. 1000. In this year, Ethelred, through the counsel of his familiars about him, in the one-and-twentieth year of his reign, began a matter which was the occasion of a new plague to the Saxons, for the king this year married Emma the daughter of Richard duke of Normandy. By reason of which marriage King Ethelred was not a little inhanced in his own mind; and sent secret and strict commissions to the rulers of every town in England, that upon St. Brices' day at an hour appointed, the Danes should be suddenly slain. And so it was performed.

Soon after tidings came into Denmark of the murder of those Danes, Swanus king of Denmark with a great host and navy, landed in Cornwall; and took Exeter, and beat down the walls. From thence proceeding further into the land, they came to Wilton and Shereborne, where they cruelly spoiled the country, and slew the people. But Swanus hearing that the king was coming to him took to his ships. And as soon as he heard of any host of Englishmen coming toward him, then he took shipping again. So that when the king's army sought to meet him in one coast, then would he suddenly land in another. And thus they wearied the English, and in conclusion brought them into extreme and unspeakable misery; insomuch, that the king was

fain to take peace with them, and gave to King Swanus 30,000*l.*

After this, Swanus hearing of the increase of his people in England, broke his covenants not to molest the English, and with a great army and navy, landed in Northumberland and proclaimed himself king. Where after much vexation when he had subdued the people, and caused the earl with the rulers of the country to swear to him fealty; he passed the river of Trent, and subduing the people there, forced them to give him pledges or hostages; which hostages he committed with his navy, unto his son Canute to keep, while he went further into the land; and so with a great host came to Mercia, killing and slaying. Then he took by strength Winchester and Oxford, and did there what he liked. That done, he came toward London, and hearing the king was there, passed by the river Thames, and came into Kent, and there besieged Canterbury, where he was resisted for the space of twenty days. At length by the treason of a deacon called Almaric he won it, and took the goods of the people, and fired the city, and decimated the monks of St. Augustine's abbey (that is, they slew nine out of every ten by cruel torment, and the tenth they kept alive as their slave). So they slew there of monks to the number of nine hundred persons; of other men, women and children, they slew above eight thousand. And finally, when they had kept the bishop Elphegus in prison the space of seven months, because he would not give them 3000*l.*; after many villanies done to him, they brought him to Greenwich, and there stoned him to death.

King Ethelred in the mean time, fearing the end of this persecution, sent his wife Emma, with his two sons Alfred and Edward, to the Duke of Normandy, with whom also he sent the bishop of London. The Danes proceeded still in their fury and rage, and when they had won a great part of West Saxony, they returned again to London. Whereof the Londoners hearing, sent unto them certain great gifts and pledges. At last the king about the five-and-thirtieth year of his reign, was chased unto the Isle of Wight, and with a secret company he spent there a great part of the winter; and finally, without cattle or comfort, sailed to Normandy to his wife. Shortly after Swanus died suddenly.

When King Ethelred heard of the death of Swanus, he returned to England. Canute, being unprovided, fled to Sandwich, and there cutting off the noses and hands of the hostages whom his father left with him, sailed into Denmark; the next year he returned again with a great navy, and landed in the south country. The eldest son of King Ethelred, called Edmund Ironside, made provision to meet him. At this time King Ethelred being at London, was taken with great sickness, and there died, after he had reigned thirty and six years; leaving his said eldest son Edmund Ironside, and Elfred, and Edward. This Ethelred, although he was miserably assailed and vexed by his enemies, yet with his council he gave forth many wholesome laws.

EDMUND IRONSIDE A SAXON, AND CANUTE A DANE, KINGS TOGETHER IN ENGLAND.

After the death of Ethelred variance fell between the Englishmen for the election of their king. For the citizens of London, with certain other lords, named Edmund the eldest son of Ethelred, (a young man of lusty and valiant courage), in martial adventures both hardy and wise, who could very well endure all pains; wherefore he was surnamed Ironside. But more of the lords favoured Canute, the son of Swanus, especially the abbots, bishops, and other spiritual men, who before had sworn to his father. By means whereof, between these two martial princes many great battles were fought, first in Dorsetshire, where Canute was compelled to fly the field. And after that they fought another battle in Worcestershire, so hard fought that none could tell who had the better; but either for weariness or for lack of day, they departed one from the other, and on the next morning fought again; but then Canute was compelled to forsake the field. After this they met in Mercia, and there fought again; where Edmund had the worse. Thus there were many great conflicts between these two princes. But upon a season, when the hosts were ready to join, and a certain time of truce was taken before the battle, a knight of the party of Edmund stood up upon a high place, and said these words: "We die daily and none has the victory: and when the knights be dead on either part, then the dukes compelled by need shall agree, or else they must fight alone. And is this kingdom not sufficient for two men, which sometimes sufficed seven? But if the covetousness of lordship in these two be so great, that neither can be content to take a part and live with the other, nor the one under the other, then let them fight alone that will be lords alone. If all men continue to fight, at the last all men shall be slain, and none left to be under their lordship, nor able to defend the king that shall be against strange enemies and nations."

These words were so well approved of both by the hosts and princes, that both were content to try the quarrel between the two princes only. Then the place and time was appointed, where they both met in sight of the two armies. And when they had assailed each other with swords and sharp strokes, first by the motion of Canute (as some write) suddenly they both agreed, and kissed each other to the comfort of both hosts. And shortly after they agreed upon the partition of the land; and after that during their lives they loved as brethren. Soon after a son of wicked duke Edric espied when King Edmund was unarmed, and with a spear (some say with a long knife) thrust him through, whereof Edmund shortly died, after he had reigned two years. He left behind him two sons, Edmund and Edward, whom Edric the wicked duke, after the death of their father, took from their mother (not knowing yet of the death of Edmund her husband) and presented them to king Canute. Thus Canute, after the death of Edmund Ironside, was king of the whole realm of England.

When Canute was established in the kingdom, he called a parliament at London, where this question was proposed to the bishops, barons, and lords of the parliament, whether in the composition made between Edmund and Canute, any provision was made for the children of Edmund, for any partition of the land. The lords flattering the foreign king, and speaking against their own minds, as also against their native country, said there was not. Affirming moreover with an oath (for the king's pleasure) that they to the uttermost of their powers, would put off the blood of Edmund in all that they might. By reason of which answer and promise, they thought to have purchased great favour with the king. But by the just retribution of God it chanced far otherwise. For many of them he distrusted and disdained ever after, so that some he exiled, and a great many he beheaded. Among whom was wicked Edric the traitor. For as the king was in his palace, Edric coming to him, began to reckon up his benefits and labours in forsaking and betraying Ethelred, then in slaying King Edmund his son, with many such other deeds more, which for his sake he had done. "Well," said the king, "thou hast here rightly judged thyself, and thou shalt die deservedly for slaying thy natural prince, and my sworn brother." And so he commanded him to be bound immediately hand and foot, and to be thrown into the Thames.

Thus the Danes being settled in England, began by little and little to become christians. Canute went to Rome, and returning again to England, governed that land the space of twenty years, leaving after him two sons, Harold and Hardicanute.

Harold (called Harefoot, for his swiftness), began his reign over England, A.D. 1036: he reigned but four years.

Hardicanute was next king of England, and when he had reigned two years he was suddenly stricken dumb, and fell down to the ground, and within eight days after died without issue of his body. He was the last Danish king that reigned in England.

The earls and barons, after his death, assembled in council, and determined that no Dane should ever be king of England, for the despite that they had done to Englishmen. For evermore before, if the Englishmen and the Danes had happened to meet upon a bridge, the Englishmen were obliged to stand still till the Dane had passed. And moreover, if the Englishmen had not bowed down their heads to do reverence to the Danes, they would have been beaten. For which despites and villanies they were driven out of the land after the death of Hardicanute, and they never came again.

The earls and barons, by their common consent and council, sent unto Normandy for these two brethren, Alfred and Edward; intending to crown Alfred the elder brother, and to make him king of England. And to this the earls and barons made their oath: but the earl Godwin of West Sax, falsely and treacherously, thought to slay these two brethren as soon as they came into England, that he might make Harold his son king: which son he had by his wife, Hardicanute's daughter.

When Alfred had heard these messengers, and perceived their tidings, he thanked God, and in all haste came to England, arriving at Southampton. There Godwin the false traitor (having knowledge of his coming) welcomed and received him with joy, pretending to lead him to London, where the barons waited to make him king, and so they passed forth together toward London. But when they came to Guilddown, the traitor commanded his men to slay all that were in Alfred's company, which came with him from Normandy; and after that, to take Alfred, and to lead him into the Isle of Ely where they should put out both his eyes; so they slew all the company that were there, to the number of twelve gentlemen, which came with Alfred from Normandy; and after that they took Alfred, and in the Isle of Ely they cruelly murdered him. And so this innocent Alfred, being the right heir of the crown, died through the treason of wicked Godwin. When the lords of England heard thereof, and how Alfred, that should have been their king, was put to death through the false traitor Godwin they were very wroth, and swore between God and them that he should die a worse death, and would immediately have put him to death, but that the traitor fled thence into Denmark, and there continued more than four years, and lost all his lands in England.

And thus much of Canute, and of his sons Harold and Hardicanute.

Of this Canute, it is reported that he following the superstition of Achelnot, archbishop of Canterbury, went on a pilgrimage to Rome, and there founded an hospital for English pilgrims. He gave the pope precious gifts, and burdened the land with a yearly tribute, called the "Rome-shot." He shrined the body of Berinus, and gave great lands and ornaments to the cathedral church of Winchester; he built St. Benedict's in Norfolk, which before was an hermitage. Also St. Edmunsbury, which King Athlestan before ordained for a college of priests, he turned to an abbey of monks of St. Benedict's order.

Henry, archdeacon of Huntington, makes mention of this Canute, as does also Polydore. That after his coming from Rome, he was walking upon a time by the port of Southampton, but Polydore saith and Fabian affirmeth the same, that it was by the Thames side of London, when his flatterers coming about him, began to exalt him with high words, calling him a king of all kings (most mighty) who had under his subjection both the people, the land, and also the sea: Canute revolving this matter in his mind (either for pride of his heart exalted, or to try and refute their flattering words) commanded his chair of state to be brought to the sea-side, at the time it should begin to flow: (Polydore saith that no seat was brought, but that he sat upon his garments, being folded together under him), he there charged and commanded the floods arising and coming towards his feet, that they should touch neither him nor his clothes. But the water keeping its ordinary course came nearer and nearer; first to his feet, and so growing higher, began to wash over him. Wherewith the king abashed, and partly also afraid, started back, and looking to his lords; "Lo," said he, "ye call me such a mighty king, and yet I cannot command this little water to stay at my word, but it is ready to drown me. Wherefore all earthly kings may know, that all their powers are vain, and that none is worthy to have the name of a king, but he alone which hath all things subject to the power and authority of his word, which is the Lord of heaven and earth, the Creator of all things, the Father of Christ our Lord, who with him for ever is to be glorified: Him let us worship and extol for our King for ever." After this (as histories witness) he never suffered the crown to come upon his head but went to Winchester, or (as some say) to Canterbury; but both those may be true; for his going to Canterbury, was to acknowledge that there was a Lord much higher and of more power than he himself was, and therewithal to render up his crown for ever.

Here is also to be noted in this Canute, that although he acted in the beginning of his reign upon King Edgar's laws, yet in process of time, he set forth peculiar laws of his own. Among which, there are several that concern ecclesiastical causes. Whereby it may appear, that the government of spiritual matters did not depend then on the bishop of Rome: but appertained to the lawful authority of the temporal prince, no less than matters and causes temporal.

And here being an end of the Danish kings, we return to the English kings, whose right line comes in again as follows

KING EDWARD, CALLED THE CONFESSOR.

The next election and right of the crown appertained to Edward the younger son of King Ethelred and Emma, a true Englishman: who had now been long banished in Normandy: he was a man of gentle and soft spirit, more appliable to other men's council, than able to trust to his own; so averse to all war and bloodshed, that being in his banishment he wished rather to continue all his life long in that private estate, than by war or bloodshed to aspire to any kingdom. This Edward came over, accompanied with a few Normans, and was crowned, (A. D. 1043). After he had thus taken upon him the government of the realm, he guided the same with much wisdom and justice, the space of nearly four-and-twenty years; from whom issued (as out of a fountain) much godliness, mercy, pity, and liberty toward the poor, gentleness and justice toward all men, and in all honest life he gave a virtuous example to his people.

In the time of this Edward, Emma his mother was accused, of being familiar with Alwin, the bishop of Winchester: upon which accusation he took from her many of her jewels, and caused her to be kept more strictly in the abbey of Warwel, and the bishop he committed to the examination of the clergy. Polydore says they were both in prison at Winchester, where she sorrowing the defame both of herself and the bishop, and trusting upon her conscience, desires justice, offering herself ready to abide any lawful trial, yea, although it were with the sharpest.

Then many of the bishops petitioned the king for them both, and would have obtained their wish, had not Robert then archbishop of Canterbury stopped the suit. Who, being not well pleased with their labour, said to them; "My brethren, how dare you defend this woman? She has defamed her own son the king, and degraded herself with the bishop. And if it be so, that the woman will purge the priest, who shall then purge the woman, that is accused to be consenting to the death of her son Alfred, and who procured venom to the poisoning of her son Edward? But let her be tried in this way, whether she be guilty or guiltless; if she will go barefooted for herself four steps, and for the bishop five, upon nine red hot plough-shares; then if she escape harmless, he shall be acquitted by this challenge, and she also."

To this she consented, and the day was appointed; at which day the king, and a great part of his nobles were present, except only Robert the archbishop. This Robert had been a monk of a house in Normandy, and an helper of the king in his exile, and so came over and was made first bishop of London, afterwards archbishop of Canterbury. Then she was led blindfold unto the place between two men, where the irons lay burning hot, and passed the nine shares unhurt. "At last," says she: "Good Lord, when shall I come to the place of my purgation?" When they

then opened her eyes, and she saw she was past the pain, she kneeled down giving God thanks.

Then the king repented, (says the history,) and restored to her what he had taken from her, and asked her forgiveness.

About this time, William Duke of Normandy, came with a goodly company into England to see King Edward, and was honourably received: and the king at his return enriched him with many great gifts, and there (as some write) promised him, that if he died without issue, the said William should succeed him in the kingdom of England.

This virtuous and blessed King Edward, after he had reigned twenty-three years and seven months, died, and was buried in the monastery of Westminster, which he had greatly augmented and repaired.

KING HAROLD II.

Harold, the son of Earl Godwin, and last king of the Saxons, succeeded, although many of the nobles went with Edgar Adeling, the next heir after Edmund Ironside: yet he contemning the young age of Edgar, and forgetting also his promise which he had made to Duke William, that he would marry his daughter and keep the kingdom for him, took upon him to be king of England, (A. D. 1066).

Immediately on which, William, duke of Normandy, sent an ambassage to Harold, king of England, reminding him of the covenants that were agreed between them: which was, to have kept the land to his use after the death of Edward. But because the daughter of Duke William (that was promised to Harold) was dead, Harold thought himself thereby discharged.

Upon this answer, Duke William having in the meanwhile that the messengers went and came, gathered his knights, and prepared his navy, and having obtained the consent of the lords of his land to aid and assist him in his journey: sends to Rome to Pope Alexander, concerning his title and voyage into England, the pope confirms him, and sent to him a banner, desiring him to bear it in the ship, in which himself should sail. Thus Duke William took shipping at the haven of St. Valery, where he tarried a long time for a convenient wind: at last the wind came about, and they took shipping with a great company, and landed at Hastings in Sussex.

There were three causes which induced Duke William to enter this land to subdue Harold. One was, that it was given to him by King Edward his nephew. The second was, to take vengeance for the cruel murder of his nephew Alfred, and of the Normans, which deed he ascribed chiefly to Harold. The third was, to revenge the wrong done to Robert archbishop of Canterbury, who was exiled by means of Harold.

Thus, while Harold was in the north, Duke William made so great speed, that he came to London before the king; out of which he was kept till he made good surety, that he and his people should pass through the city without tarrying: which promise he well observing, passed the bridge, and went over to Sussex, whence he sent a monk to Harold, and proffered him three ways. First, to render to him the possession of the land, and so to take it again of him under tribute, reigning under him; secondly, to abide and stand to the pope's arbitration; or, thirdly, to defend this quarrel in his own person against the duke, and they two only to try the matter by dint of sword, without any other blood-shedding.

But Harold refused all these offers, saying, "It should be tried by dint of swords, and not by one sword:" and so gathered his people and joined battle with the Normans, in the place where afterwards was builded the abbey of Battel in Sussex. In the beginning of which fight, the Englishmen kept them in good array and were likely to vanquish the Normans: wherefore, Duke William caused his men to give back, as though they fled, whereby the Englishmen followed fast, and broke their array. Then the Normans, fiercely giving a charge upon them, in conclusion obtained the victory through the just providence of God. Where King Harold, who before had murdered Alfred the true heir of the crown, with his company of Normans so cruelly, was now wounded of the Normans in the left eye with an arrow, and thereof died: although Gerard says he fled away to Chester, and lived after that a monk in the monastery of St. James.

This Duke William and King Edward were cousins by the father's side. For Richard the first of that name, which was the third duke of Normandy after Rollo, was father to Duke Richard the second of that name, and brother to Emma mother to King Edward. Which Duke Richard the second was father to duke Robert, this Duke William's father.

Although the church of Christ and state of religion, first founded and grounded by Christ and his apostles, did not continually remain in the primitive perfection, wherein it was first instituted; but in process of time began from better to worse, to decrease and decline into much superstition and inconveniency; partly through the coming in of Mahomet, partly through the increase of wealth and riches, partly through the decrease of knowledge and diligence in such as should be the guides of Christ's flock: yet the infection and corruption of that time (though it were great) did not so abound in such excessive measure as afterwards in later times now following, that is, about a thousand years after Christ, whereof we have to treat. About which time and year came Sylvester II., who succeeded after Gregory V., and occupied the see of Rome about A. D. 1000.

After Sylvester, succeeded John XVII., by whom was brought in the feast of All Souls (A. D. 1004), through the means and instigation of one Odilo, abbot of Cluny, to be celebrated next after the feast of All Saints. This monk Odilo, thinking that purgatory should be in the Mount Etna, dreamed upon a time, in the country of Sicily, that he by his masses had delivered divers souls from thence: saying moreover, "that he did hear the voices and lamentations of devils, crying out for that the souls were taken from them by the masses and dirges!" Not long after, came John XVIII. and Sergius IV. After whom succeeded Benedict VIII., then John XIX., who brought in the fast of the eve of John Baptist and St. Lawrence. After him followed Pope Benedict IX., who was fain to sell his seat to his successor, Gregory VI., for £1500. At which time were three popes together in Rome, reigning and raging one against another; Benedict IX., Sylvester III, and Gregory VI. For which cause the emperor coming to Rome, displaced the three monsters, placing Clement II., in the papal chair, and thereupon enacting that there should be no bishop of Rome henceforth chosen, but by the consent and confirmation of the emperor. Which constitution, though it was both agreeable, and also necessary for the public tranquillity of that city, yet the Cardinals would not suffer it long to stand, but did impugn it afterward by subtile practice and open violence. In the time of this Clement, the Romans made an oath to the emperors concerning the election of the bishops, to intermeddle no further therein, but as the consent of the emperor should approve. However the emperor departing into Germany, by and by they forgot their oath, and within nine months after poisoned the bishop. Which act some impute to Stephen, his successor, called Damasus II. Some impute it to Brazutus, who (as histories record) within thirteen years poisoned six popes; that is, Clement II., Damasus II., Leo IX., Victor II., Stephen IX., Nicholas II.

Thus Clement being poisoned, after him succeeded Damasus II., neither by consent of the people, nor elected by the emperor, but by force and invasion, who also within twenty-three days being poisoned, (A. D. 1049.) much contention and striving began in Rome about the papal seat; whereupon the Romans through the counsel of the Cardinal sent to the emperor, desiring him to give them a bishop: and so he did, whose name was Bruno, afterward called Leo IX. This Bruno being a simple man, and easy to be led with evil counsel, coming from the emperor towards Rome in his pontifical apparel like a pope; there meet him by the way, the abbot of Cluny, and Hildebrand, a monk, who seeing him so in his pontifical robes, began to rate him, laying to his charge that he would so take his authority of the emperor, and not rather of the clergy of Rome,

and the people thereof, as his predecessors were wont to do: and so counselled him to lay down that apparel, and to enter in with his own habit, till he had his election by them. Bruno following their counsel, and confessing his fault before the clergy of Rome, obtained their favour, and so was nominated Leo IX., whereby Hildebrand was made a cardinal. Under this Pope Leo, two councils were held; one at Versailles, where the doctrine of Berengarius against the real presence in the sacrament was first condemned (although Berengarius yet recanted not, which nevertheless was done after in the council of Lateran, under Nicholas II., A. D. 1060). The other was held at Moguntia, where amongst many other decrees it was enacted, That priests should be excluded and debarred utterly from marriage.

After the death of Leo, whom Brazutus poisoned the first year of his popedom, Theophylactus strove to be pope; but Hildebrand, to defeat him, went to the emperor, who assigned another bishop, called Victor II. This Victor holding a council at Florence, deposed divers bishops and priests for simony and fornication; for simony, in that they took their dignities of secular men for money; for fornication, in that, contrary to their canon, they were married, &c. The second year of his papacy, and little more, this pope also followed his predecessors, being poisoned by Brazutus, through the procurement of Hildebrand and his master.

Here now the church and clergy of Rome began to wring out of the emperor's hand the election of the pope; electing Stephen IX. for pope, contrary to their oath, and to the emperor's assignment. This Stephen was not ashamed to accuse the Emperor Henry of heresy, for minishing the authority of the Roman see. So this was their heresy at that time, not to maintain the ambitious proceedings of the Romish prelate. And they called it simony, to take and enjoy any spiritual living at a secular man's hand.

In the mean time, Stephen the pope, tasting of Brazutus' cup, fell sick. Hildebrand, hearing that, returned home with all speed. So being come to Rome, he assembleth all the companies and orders of the clergy together, making them to swear that they should admit none to be bishop but he who shall be appointed by the public consent of them all together. This being done, Hildebrand, takes his journey into Florence, to fetch the bishop of Florence to install him bishop; the clergy swearing unto him that no bishop should be ordained before his return again. But the people of Rome, not suffering the election to stand so long, after the death of Stephen, elected one of their own city, called Benedict X. Hildebrand hearing of this, was not a little offended; wherefore returning to Rome with one Garhard, bishop of Florence, he caused the clergy to proceed to a new election, saying, That Benedict was not lawfully called, but came in by force and bribing. But the clergy not daring to attempt any new election at Rome, went to Sene, and there elected this Garhard, whom Hildebrand brought with him. So there were two popes in Rome together: but Garhard, named Nicholas II., holding a council at Sutrium, through the help of Duke Godfrid and Guibert, and other bishops about Italy, caused the other pope to be deposed. Benedict understanding them to be set against him through the means of Hildebrand, unpoped himself, and went to Velitras; living there more quietly than he would have done at Rome.

Nicholas being thus set up without the mind either of the emperor or of the people of Rome, after his fellow pope was driven away, brake up the Synod of Sutrium, and came to Rome, where he assembled another council, called the Council of Lateran. In which council first was promulgated the terrible sentence of excommunication mentioned in the decrees. The effect whereof is this: first, that he after a subtile practice undermines the emperor's jurisdiction, and transfers to a few cardinals, and certain catholic persons, the full authority of choosing the pope. Secondly, against all such as do creep into the seat of Peter by money or favour, without the full consent of the cardinals, he thunders with terrible blasts of excommunication, accursing them and their children with devils, as wicked persons, to the anger of

Almighty God, giving also authority and power to cardinals, with the clergy and laity, to depose all such persons, and call a general council, wherever they will against them.

In the council of Lateran, under Pope Nicholas II. Berengarius, an arch-deacon, was driven to the recantation of his doctrine, denying the real substance of Christ's holy body and blood to be in the sacrament, otherwise than sacramentally and in mystery.

In the same council also was hatched and invented the new found device and term of transubstantiation.

It were too long here to declare the confederation betwixt this Nicholas and Robert Guiscard, whom this pope (contrary to all right and good law, displacing the right heir) made duke of Apulia, Calabria, Sicily, and captain-general of St. Peter's lands: that through his force of arms and violence he might the better subdue all such as should rebel against him. Now, let all men, which be godly and wise, judge and understand how this stands with the doctrine of Christ, the example of Peter, or the spirit of a christian bishop, by outward arms and violence to conquer christian men and countries, under the obedience of a bishop's see. Thus Pope Nicholas II., by might and force continued three years and a half. But at length he met with Brazutus' cup, and so died.

At the beginning of this, Nicholas, or somewhat before, (about A. D. 1057). Henry IV., after the decease of Henry III. was made emperor, being but a child, and reigned fifty years: but not without great molestation and much disquietness, and all through the ungracious wickedness of Hildebrand, as hereafter (the Lord so permitting) shall be declared.

Here by the way comes to be noted an example, whereby all princes may learn and understand how the pope is to be handled, whoever looks to have any goodness at his hand. If a man stand in fear of his curse, he shall be made his slave; but if he be despised of you, you shall have him as you like. For the pope's curse may well be likened to Domitian's thunder: If a man give ear to the noise and crack, it seems a terrible thing; but if you consider the causes and effect thereof, it is most vain and ridiculous.

In the reign of this Nicholas, (A. D. 1060), Aldred bishop of Worcester, was appointed archbishop of York, who, coming to Rome with Tostius, Earl of Northumberland, for his pall, could not obtain it, but was deprived of all dignity. Whereupon returning again to Rome with Tostius, he there made his complaint, but would not be heard, till Tostius, a man of stout courage, taking the matter in hand, told the pope to his face, "That his curse was not to be feared in far countries when the pope's own neighbours, yea, and the most vile vagabonds derided and despised it at home." Wherefore he required the pope, either to restore Aldred again to his goods, or else it should be known that they were lost, through his means and subtilty. And that the king of England hearing this would debar him of St. Peter's tribute, thinking it shameful treatment to him and his realm, if Aldred should come from Rome both deprived of dignity, and spoiled also of his goods. The pope being thus persuaded by the argument of his purse, was content to send home Aldred with his pall, according to his request.

After the death of Nicholas, the Lombards being oppressed before by Pope Nicholas, and brought under fear, were the more desirous, and thought it good to have a bishop of their company, and so elected the bishop of Parmen, called Cadolus, to be pope: sending to the emperor, and desiring his favour and support therein, for the election of the pope (they said) most properly appertained unto him.

The emperor, well pleased and content, gave them his voice and support. But Hildebrand, a stout maintainer of popish liberties against good emperors, hearing this, sets up by a contrary faction another bishop, Anselm, after called Alexander II. Cadolus, thus elected by the emperor and the cardinals, sets forward to Rome with a sufficient army and strength of men.

Alexander, also, no less prepared, there received him with another army, where they had a great conflict, and many slain on both sides. But Cadolus, as he had the better cause, so he had the worse fortune. The emperor seeing this hurly-burley, to take up the matter, sent thither his ambassador Otho archbishop of Cullen: who, coming to Rome, sharply chides the pope for taking so upon him without the leave or knowledge of the emperor, declaring how the election of that see ought chiefly to appertain to the right of the emperor, as it had done for the most part in the time of his predecessors before. But Hildebrand all set on wickedness and ambition, and also puffed up not a little with his late victories, not suffering the ambassador to tell to the end, interrupted him in the middle of his tale; affirming that if they should stand to law and custom, the liberty of that election should rather belong to the clergy than to the emperor. To make short, Otho the ambassador agreeing more with the clergy than with the emperor, was content to be persuaded, and only required this in the emperor's name, that a council should be held, to decide the matter, whereat the emperor should be present himself; which was agreed. In the which council being held at Mantua, Alexander was declared pope, the other had his pardon granted. In this council, amongst many other considerations, it was concluded concerning priests, That they should have no wives: priests' children not to be secluded from holy orders: no benefices to be bought for money: halleluiah to be suspended in time of lent out of the church, &c. This also was decreed (which made most for Hildebrand's purpose) that no spiritual man, whatsover he be, should enter into any church, by a secular person, and that the pope should be elected only by the cardinals, &c. Cardinal Benno writes of Alexander, that after he perceived the frauds of Hildebrand, and of the emperor's enemies, and understanding that he was set up and enthroned only for a purpose; being at his mass, as he was preaching to the people, told them he would not sit in the place, unless he had the license of the emperor. Which when Hildebrand heard, he was stricken in such a fury, that he could scarcely keep his hands off him, while mass was doing. After the mass was finished, by force of soldiers and strength of men, he had him into a chamber, and there struck Pope Alexander with his fists, rating and rebuking him because he would seek for favour of the emperor.—Thus Alexander being kept in custody, and being stinted to a certain allowance, as about five groats a-day, Hildebrand engrossed all the whole revenues of the church to himself. At length Alexander, under the miserable indurance of Hildebrand, died after eleven years and-a-half, of his popedom. And thus much of Romish matters.

Now returning again to the history of our own country, we enter upon the reign of William the Conqueror, the next king following in England. But first, as at the end of the former book, we will give the order of the archbishops of Canterbury; beginning with Ethelred, who succeeded after Celnoth, the last mentioned.

The names and order of the archbishops of Canterbury, from the time of King Egbert to William Conqueror.

18. Ethelred.
19. Pleimund.
20. Athelm.
21. Ulfelm.
22. Odo.
23. Elfius, or Elfinus.
24. Dunstan.
25. Ethelgar.
26. Elfric.
27. Siric.
28. Elphege.
29. Livinge.
30. Egenold.
31. Edsius.
32. Robert.
33. Stigand.
34. Lanfranc.

ACTS AND MONUMENTS.

BOOK IV.

CONTAINING

THE THREE HUNDRED YEARS, FROM WILLIAM THE CONQUEROR, TO THE TIME OF
JOHN WICKLIFFE;

WHEREIN IS DESCRIBED THE PROUD AND MIS-ORDERED REIGN OF ANTICHRIST, BEGINNING TO STIR IN
THE CHURCH OF CHRIST.

WILLIAM, duke of Normandy, surnamed the Conqueror, base son of Robert, the sixth duke of Normandy, and nephew to King Edward, after the victory against Harold, was received as king over the realm of England, not so much by assent, as for fear and necessity; for the Londoners had promised their assistance to Edgar Etheling. But being weakened and wasted so greatly in former battles, and the duke coming so fast upon them, and fearing that they could not make their party good, they submitted themselves. William was crowned upon Christmas-day, (A. D. 1066), by the hands of Aldred, archbishop of York; for at that time Stigand archbishop of Canterbury was absent, or else durst not, or would not come into the presence of the king.

This king reigned over England twenty-one years and ten months, with great severity towards the English, burthening them with tributes and exactions; requiring for every hide of ground containing twenty acres, six shillings. Some parts of the land rebelled, and especially the city of Exeter. But at last William overcame them, and punished them. On account of that and other severities of William, several of the Lords departed into Scotland; wherefore he kept the other lords that tarried the stricter, and exalted the Normans, giving them the chief possessions of the land. And as he obtained the kingdom by the sword, he changed the whole state of the government, and ordained new laws at his own pleasure, profitable to himself, but grievous and hurtful to the people; abolishing the laws of King Edward, though he was sworn to observe and maintain them.

William endeavoured to establish a form of government both in the church and commonwealth answerable to his own mind: however he allowed the clergy a kind of jurisdiction of bringing persons before them and of exercising such ecclesiastical discipline as that age and time did use.

Besides this, William, as he was a warrior, delighting in forts and bulwarks, built four strong castles; two at York, one at Nottingham, and another at Lincoln, which garrisons he furnished with Normans.

About the third year of his reign, Harold and Canute, sons of Swanus, king of Denmark, entered into the north country. The Normans within York, fearing that the Englishmen would aid the Danes, fired the suburbs of the town. And the flame was so great and the wind so strong that it took to the city, and burnt a great part of it with the minster of St. Peter, where no doubt many worthy works and monuments of books were consumed. The Danes by the favour of some of the citizens entered the city, and slew more than three thousand of the Normans. But not long after King William chased them out, and drove them to their ships, and was so displeased with the inhabitants of that country, that he destroyed the land from York to Durham, so that nine years after the province lay waste, and the inhabitants kept in such penury by the war of the king; that (as our English history relates) they eat rats, cats, and dogs, with other vermin.

Also in the fourth year of the reign of this king, Malcolm king of Scots entered into Northumberland, and destroyed the country, and slew there many of the people, both men, women, and children, in a lamentable way, and took some prisoners. But within two years after, King William made such war upon the Scots, that he forced Malcolm their king to do him homage.

And thus much concerning the outward calamities of this realm under this foreign conqueror, which is now the fifth time that the land has been scourged by the hand of God. First, by the Romans, then by the Scots and Picts, afterwards by the Saxons; and then by the Danes. And yet the indignation of God ceased not, but stirred up the Normans against them, who conquered and altered the whole realm; so, that besides the innovation of the laws, coins, and possessions, there was scarcely an English bishop in any church of England, but only Normans and foreigners placed through all their dioceses. To such a misery was this land then brought, that not only of all the English nobility not one house was standing, but also it was thought reproachful to be called an Englishman.

In the fourth year of this king, a solemn council of the clergy of England was held at Winchester. At which council were present two cardinals sent from Pope Alexander II. In this council, the king being present, several bishops, abbots, and priors were deposed, (by the means of the king) without any cause, that his Normans might be promoted to the rule of the church, as he had promoted his knights to the rule of the temporality. Among whom also Stigand archbishop of Canterbury was deprived of his dignity, and kept in Winchester as a prisoner during his life. This Stigand is noted for a man so covetous and sparing, that when he would take nothing of his own, and swore that he had not a penny, yet by a key fastened about his neck, great treasure of his was found hid under the ground.

At the same time, Thomas, a Norman, was preferred to the archbishopric of York, and Lanfranc, an Italian, was made archbishop of Canterbury.

After this, Lanfranc and Thomas came to Rome, with Remigius Bishop of Dorchester for their palls, as the manner was; without which no archbishop nor bishop could be confirmed, although their election were never so lawful. This pall must be asked no where but of the pope or his assigns, and that within three months, which was no small gain to the Romish see. For although at the beginning the pall was given without money, according to the decree, (Dist. 100), or for little; yet in process of years it grew to such excess, that where the bishoprick of Mentz was wont to give to Rome only ten thousand florins, afterwards he could not obtain it without twenty thousand. And from thence it exceeded to five and twenty thousand, and at length to seven and twenty thousand florins; which sum James archbishop of Mentz was obliged to pay a little before the council of Basil, so that at his death (which was four years after), he said that his death did not so much grieve him as to remember that his poor subjects would be constrained to pay so terrible a fine for the pope's pall. Now by this; the enormous sum which comes to the pope in the whole of Germany, containing in it above fifty bishopricks, may be easily conjectured.

Lanfranc coming to Rome with the other two bishops, for the fame of his learning obtained of Alexander two palls, one of honour, the other of love. He obtained for the other two bishops also their confirmation. At the time while they were there the controversy began first to be moved (or rather renewed) for the primacy between the two metropolitans, that is, between the archbishop of Canterbury and the archbishop of York, which of them should have the pre-eminence. For Canterbury challenged to himself the prerogative and primacy over all Britain and Ireland; this contention continued a long time between these two churches, and was often renewed in the days of several kings after this; as in the reign of Henry I., between Thurstin of York and Radulph of Canterbury. And again, in the seven and twentieth year of the same king, at his second coronation. For Radulph would not suffer the first coronation to stand, because it was done by the bishop of York, without his consent. Also in the reign of Henry II., where pope Alexander made a decretal letter between these two Metropolitans, for bearing the cross, (A.D. 1159.) Also another time, in the reign of the said king, betwixt Richard of Canterbury, and Roger of York. Again, about the year of our Lord 1170, when Thomas Becket hearing that the king was crowned by Roger bishop of York, complained greviously to Pope Alexander III. Also another time, (A. D. 1176), betwixt Richard and Roger, which of them should sit on the right hand of Cardinal Hugo, in his council in London. Moreover, in the beginning of the reign of King Richard, (A. D. 1190), betwixt Baldwin of Canterbury, and Godfrid of York, &c.

Now to proceed in the history of this: after this question was brought to the pope's presence, he (not disposed to decide the matter) sent them home to England, there to have their cause determined. Upon which (A.D. 1070), they brought the matter before the king and the clergy at Windsor. Lanfranc first alleging for himself, how that from the time of Austin to the time of Bede, (which was about a hundred and forty years) the bishop of Canterbury had ever the primacy

over the whole land of Britain and Ireland; how he kept his councils several times within the precincts of York; how he called and cited the bishops of York thereto; of whom, some he constituted, some he excommunicated, and some he removed; besides also he alleged various privileges granted by princes and prelates to the primacy of that see, &c.

To this Thomas archbishop of York replied, and first beginning with the original of the Britons' church, declared in order of time how the Britons, the first possessors of this kingdom of Britain, which endured from Brutus and Cadwallader, 2076 years, under an hundred and two kings, at length received the christian faith in the year 162, in the time of Lucius their king, Eleutherius, bishop of Rome, having sent the preachers Fagan and Damian to them,[1] at which time after their conversion, they assigned and ordained in the realm eight and twenty bishops, with two archbishops, Theonus, the archbishop of London, and Theodosius archbishop of York. Under those bishops and archbishops the church of Britain was governed after their conversion, almost three hundred years, till at length the Saxons, being then infidels, with Hengist their king, subduing the Britons by fraudulent murder invaded their land, which was about A.D. 449. After this the Britons being driven into Cambria (which we now call Wales), the Saxons over-running the land, divided themselves into seven kingdoms. And so being Infidels and Pagans, continued till the time that Gregory bishop of Rome sent Austin to preach to them; which Austin coming first to Dover, being then the head city of Kent, called in Latin, Dorobernia, and there planting himself, converted first the king of Kent, called Ethelbert, who had then subdued certain other kings unto the Humber. By reason of which Austin was made archbishop of Dover, by the appointment of Gregory, who sent him certain palls with his letter from Rome, as is before mentioned.[2] Which letter being recited, then Thomas declares how the meaning of Gregory in this letter was, to reduce the new church of the Saxons to the order that was among the Britons; that is, to be under two metropolitans, one of London, the other of York. Notwithstanding, he gives to Austin this prerogative during his life time, to have authority and jurisdiction, not only over his twelve bishops, but over all other bishops and priests in England. And after his decease then these two metropolitans, London and York, were to oversee the whole clergy, as in times past amongst the Britons; whom he joins together after the death of Austin, to constitute bishops, and to oversee the church. And that he so means London to be equal with York, appears by four arguments: First, that he ordains London to be consecrated by no bishop, but by his own synod. Secondly, he ordains no distinction of honour to be betwixt London and York, but only according as each one of them is elder in time. Thirdly, he places these two equally together in common council, and with one agreement to consent together in doing such things as they shall consult upon in the zeal of Christ Jesus; and that in such sort that one should not dissent from the other. What means this, but that they should govern together? Fourthly, where he writes that the bishop of York should not be subject to the bishop of London; what means this, but that the bishop of London should be equivalent with the metropolitan of York, or rather superior unto him?

And thus he expounded the meaning of Gregory in the letter. Lanfranc again answers, "That he was not the bishop of London, and that the question pertained not to London." Thomas replies, "That this privilege was granted by Gregory to Austin alone, to have all other bishops subject to him; but after his decease there should be equality of honour betwixt London and York, without distinction of priority; except only the priority of time. And although Austin translated the see from London to Kent; yet Gregory, if his mind had been to give the same prerogative to the successors of

(1) Some allege 162 instead of 180, for the introduction of the christian faith. It appears this Thomas alleged the former date. [Ed.]

(2) See page 78.

Austin (which he gave to him) would expressly have uttered it in the words of his epistle, writing thus to Austin: 'That which I give to thee, Austin, I give also and grant to all thy successors after thee.' But as he makes here no mention of his successors, it appears thereby, that it was not his mind so to do."

To this Lanfranc argued again: "If this authority had been given to Austin alone, and not to his successors, it had been but a small gift, proceeding from the apostolic see, to his special and familiar friend; especially seeing also that Austin in all his life did constitute no bishop of York, neither was there any such bishop to be subject to him. Again, we have privileges from the apostolic see, which confirm this dignity in the successors of Austin, in the same see of Dover. Moreover, all Englishmen think it both right and reason to fetch the direction of well living from that place, where first they took the sparkle of right believing. Further, whereas you say that Gregory might have confirmed with plain words the same thing to the successors of Austin, which he gave to him; all that I grant; yet, this is not prejudicial to the see of Canterbury. For, if you know your logic, that which is true in the whole is also true in the part, and what is true in the more, is also true in the less. Now the church of Rome is as the whole, to whom all other churches are as parts thereof. The church of Rome is greater than all churches; that which is wrought in it ought to work in the less churches also; so that the authority of every chief head of the church ought to stand also in them that succeed; unless there be any precise exception made by name. Wherefore like as the Lord said to all bishops of Rome the same thing which he said to Peter, so Gregory in like manner said to all the successors of Austin, that which he said to Dunstan. So thus I conclude, as the bishop of Canterbury is subject to Rome, because he had his faith from thence; so York ought to be in subjection to Canterbury, which sent the first preachers thither. Now whereas you allege that Gregory desired Austin to be resident at London, that is utterly uncertain. For how is it to be thought that such a disciple would do contrary to the mind of such a master? But grant (as you say) that Austin removed to London, what is that to me, who am not bishop of London? Notwithstanding all this controversy ceasing betwixt us, if it shall please you to come to some peaceable composition with me (all contention set apart) you shall find me not out of the way, so far as reason and equity shall extend."

With these reasons of Lanfranc, Thomas gave over, condescending that his province should begin at the Humber. Whereupon it was then decreed that York from that time should be subject to Canterbury, in all matters appertaining to the rites and government of the catholic church; so that wherever within England the archbishop of Canterbury would hold his council, the archbishop of York should resort thither with his bishops, and be obedient to his canonical decrees.

Provided that when the archbishop of Canterbury should decease, York should repair to Dover, there to consecrate with others the bishops that should be elect. And if York should decease, his successor should resort to Canterbury, or else where the bishop of Canterbury should appoint, there to receive his consecration, making his profession there, with an oath of canonical obedience. Thomas being content withal, Lanfranc, the Italian, triumphed with no small joy, and put the matter forthwith in writing, that the memory of it might remain to his successors. But yet that decree did not stand long; for shortly after the same scar, so superficially cured, burst out again; so that in the reign of king Henry I., (A. D. 1121) Thurstin, archbishop of York, could not be compelled to swear to the archbishop of Canterbury; and yet by letters of Calixtus II., was consecrated without any profession made to the said bishop, with much more matter of contention, to recite all which were too long. But this I thought to commit to history, that men might see the lamentable decay of true christianity amongst the christian bishops, who, enflamed with glorious ambition, so contended for honour, that without the force of the law no modesty could take place.

About A. D. 1016, the bishopric of Lindaffarne, otherwise named Holyland, was translated to Durham; so likewise in the days of this Lanfranc, archbishop of Canterbury (A. D. 1076), several bishops' sees were altered and removed from townships to greater cities. As the bishopric of Selese was removed to Chichester; that of Cornwal to Exeter; from Wells to Bath; from Sherborne to Salisbury; from Dorchester to Lincoln; from Litchfield to Chester; which bishopric of Chester, Robert being then bishop, was removed from Chester to Coventry. Likewise after that in the reign of William Rufus (A. D. 1095), Herbert, bishop of Thetford, from thence removed the see to Norwich, &c.

As concerning Dover and Canterbury, whether the see was likewise translated from the town of Dover to the city of Canterbury in the time of Theodore; or whether in the old time Canterbury had the name of Dorobernia (as the letter of Lanfranc to Pope Alexander above mentioned pretends), I find it not expressly defined in histories; save that I read by the words of William, being yet duke of Normandy, charging Harold to make a well of water for the king's use in the castle of Dorobernia, that Dorobernia was then taken for that which we now call Dover; but whether Dorobernia and the city of Canterbury are both one or different is not important. Notwithstanding I read this in the epistle of Pope Boniface to King Ethelbert, as also to Justin, archbishop: also in the epistle of Pope Honorius to Bishop Honorius: also of Pope Vitalian to Theodore: of Pope Sergius to King Ethelred, Alfred and Adulphus, and to the bishops of England: Likewise of Pope Gregory III. to the bishops of England: Also of Pope Leo to Athelard, archbishop of Canterbury: of Formosus to the bishops of England, and of Pope John to Dunstan; that the names of Dorobernia and of Canterbury are indifferently taken for one matter.

In this time, (and by the management of this Lanfranc), in the ninth year of William I., a council was held at London, where these were the principal things concluded:

1. For the order of sitting, that the archbishop of York should sit on the right hand, and the bishop of London on the left hand, or in the absence of York, London should have the right, and Winchester the left hand of the archbishop of Canterbury sitting in council.

2. That bishops should translate their sees from villages into cities, whereupon those sees above named were translated.

3. That monks should have nothing as private possessions; and if any so had, he dying unconfessed should not be buried in the churchyard.

4. That no clerk or monk of any other diocese should be admitted to orders, or retained without letters commendatory or testimonial.

5. That none should speak in the council, except bishops and abbots, without leave of the arch-metropolitans.

6. That none should marry within the seventh degree, with any either of his own kindred, or of his wife's.

7. That none should either buy or sell any office within the church.

8. That no sorcery or any divination should be used or permitted in holy church.

9. That no bishop nor abbot, nor any of the clergy, should be at the judgment of any man's death or dismembering, neither should be any favourer of the judicants.

Moreover in the days of this Lanfranc, many good bishops of the realm began to take part with the priests against the monks, in displacing these out of their churches, and to restore the married priests again; so that Walkelm, bishop of Winchester had placed above forty canons instead of monks in his diocese; but this godly enterprise was stopped by Lanfranc.

After the death of Pope Alexander above mentioned, next followed Hildebrand, sirnamed Gregory VII. This Hildebrand, as he was a sorcerer, so was he the first and principal cause of all this trouble that is now and has been since his time in the church; through his example all this ambition, boldness, and pride entered into the church of Rome, and has ever since continued. For before Hildebrand came to Rome working his feats there, setting up and displacing what bishops he chose, corrupting them with pernicious counsel, and setting them against emperors, under pretence of chastity destroying matrimony, and under the title of liberty breaking peace, and resisting authority; before this (I say) the church of Rome was in some order, and the bishops quietly governed under christian emperors, and also were defended by the same; as Marcellus, Miltiades, and Sylvester, were under obedience to Constantine, (A.D. 340); Siricius to Theodosius, (A.D. 388); Gregory to Maurice, (A.D. 600); Adrian and Leo to Charlemagne, (A.D. 801); Paschal and Valentius to Lewis the Pious, (A.D. 830); Sergius II. to Lothaire, (A.D. 840); Benedict III. and John VIII. to Lewis, son of Lothaire, (A.D. 856). But against this obedience and subjection Hildebrand first began to spurn, and by his example taught all other bishops to do the same.

At length they brought to pass that it should be lawful for a few cardinals (contrary to ancient ordinances and decretal statutes) to choose what pope they liked, without any consent of the emperor at all. And, whereas, before it stood in the emperor's gift to give and to grant bishoprics, archbishoprics, benefices, and other ecclesiastical preferments within their own limits, to whom they chose; now the popes, through much wrestling, wars, and contention, have extorted all that into their own hands; yea, have plucked in all the riches and power of the whole world: and not content with that, have usurped and prevailed so much above emperors, that, as before, no pope might be chosen without the confirmation of the emperor: so now no emperor may be elected without the confirmation of the pope, taking upon them more than princes to place or displace emperors at their pleasure for every light cause; to put down or set up when and whom they pleased; as Frederic I., for holding the left stirrup of the pope's saddle, was persecuted almost to excommunication, which cause moves me to use more diligence here, in setting out the history, acts, and doings of this Hildebrand, from whom, as their first patron and founder, sprang all this ambition and contention about the liberties and dominion of the Roman church.

And first, how this Hildebrand had behaved himself, before he was pope, I have partly declared. For though he was not yet pope in name, yet he was then pope indeed, and ruled the popes and all their doings as he liked. What devices he had attempted ever since his first coming to the court of Rome, to magnify and maintain false liberty against true authority; what practice he wrought by councils, what factions and conspiracies he made, in stirring up popes against emperors, striving for superiority; and what wars followed, I have also expressed. Now let us see further the worthy virtues of this princely prelate, after he came to be pope, as they are described in the histories of several writers.

THE TRAGICAL HISTORY OF GREGORY THE SEVENTH, OTHERWISE NAMED HILDEBRAND.

Hitherto the bishops of Rome have been elected by the voices and suffrages of all sorts and degrees, as well of the priests and the clergy, as of the nobility, people, and senate, all assembling together. And this election I find in force, if ratified by the Roman emperors, who had authority to call and assemble all these, as well as bishops to councils, as the case required. Under the authority and jurisdiction of these emperors in Germany, France, Italy, and through the whole dominion of Rome, all patriarchs, bishops, masters of churches and monasteries were subject by the decree of councils, according to the old custom of our ancestors. The holy and ancient fathers, (as Christ with his disciples and apostles both taught and did) honoured and esteemed their emperors as the supreme potentate next

under God on earth, set up, ordained, elected, and crowned of God, above all other mortal men, and so counted them, and called them their lords. To them they yielded tribute, and paid their subsidies, and also prayed every day for their life. Such as rebelled against them they regarded as rebels, and resisters against God's ordinance and christian piety. The name of the emperor was of great majesty, and received as given from God. Then these fathers of the church never intermeddled nor entangled themselves with political affairs of the commonwealth, much less did they occupy themselves in martial arms, and feats of chivalry: all their contention with other christians was only in poverty and modesty, who should be poorest and most modest among them. And the more humbleness appeared in any, the higher opinion they conceived of him. They took the sharp and two-edged sword given to the church of Christ, to save and not to kill; to quicken and not to destroy; and they called it the sword of the Spirit, which is the word of God, the life and the light of men, who revokes from death to life, making of men gods; of mortal, immortal. They were far from thrusting out any prince or king (though he were never so far out of the way, yea, an Arian) from his kingdom, or to curse him, or to release his subjects from their oath and their allegiance, to change and translate kingdoms, to subvert empires, to pollute themselves with christian blood, or to war with their christian brethren for rule and principality. This was not their spirit and manner then, but rather they loved and obeyed their princes. Again, princes loved them also like fathers and fellow-princes with them of the souls of men.

Now this Gregory VII., otherwise named Hildebrand, was the first of all others who, contemning the authority of the emperor, invaded the see of Rome, vaunting himself as having both the ecclesiastical and temporal sword committed to him by Christ, and that fulness of power was in his hand to bind and loose at his will. Thus he presumed to grasp both governments, to challenge all the whole dominion, both of the eastern and western churches, yea, and all power to himself alone, admitting none as equal, much less superior, to him, derogating from others, and arrogating to himself their due right and honour, set at nought Cesars, kings, and emperors. Bishops and prelates as his underlings he kept in awe, suspending and cursing, and cutting off their heads, stirring up strife and wars, sowing discord, making factions, releasing oaths, defeating fidelity and due allegiance of subjects to their princes. Yea, and if he had offended or injured the emperor himself, yet notwithstanding he ought to be feared, as he himself glories in an epistle, as one that could not err, and had received of Christ our Saviour, and of Peter, authority to bind and unbind at his will and pleasure. Priests then in those days had wives openly and lawfully (no law forbidding to the contrary) as appears by the deed and writings of their chapter-seals and donations, which were given to temples and monasteries, wherein their wives also are cited with them for witness, and were called presbyterissæ. Also, as for bishops, prelates, parsons of churches, governors of the clergy, masters of monasteries, and religious houses; all these were then in those times in the emperor's appointment, to assign to whom he would. Now these two things Gregory could not endure, for which two causes only was all his striving from his first beginning to abolish the marriage of priests, and to translate the imperial authority to the clergy. To this scope only tended all his labour, as appeared before in the council of Lateran, under Pope Nicholas, and also in the council of Mantua, under Alexander, making their marriage heresy, and the other to be simony. And that which previously he went about by others, now he practises by himself, to condemn ministers that were married as Nicholaitans, and to receive any spiritual charge of secular persons as simony, directing his letters to Henry the emperor, to dukes, princes, potentates, and tetrarchs; namely to Berchtold, to Rodulph of Swevia, to Whelpo, Adalberon, and to their wives: also, to bishops, archbishops, priests, and to all the people; in which letters he denounces them to be no priests who were married, forbidding men to salute them, to talk, to eat, to company with them, to pay them tithes, or to obey them if they would not be obedient to him. Among others, he directed special letters to Otho bishop of Constance concerning this matter. But Otho perceiving the ungodly and unreasonable pretence of Hildebrand, would never separate them that were married from their wives, nor yet forbid them to marry who were unmarried. The following is the letter of Hildebrand sent to the bishop of Constance against priests' marriages :—

" Gregory, bishop, servant of servants of God, to the clergy and laity, both more and less, within the diocese of Constance, salvation and benediction. We have directed to our brother Otho, your bishop, our letters exhortatory ; wherein we enjoined him, according to the necessity of our duty, by the apostolical authority, that he should utterly abolish out of his church the heresy of simony, and also should cause to be preached with all diligence the chastity of priests. But he, neither moved with reverence of St. Peter's precept, nor yet with the regard of his duty, neglected to do these things, whereto we so fatherly have exhorted him, incurring thereby a double offence, not only of disobedience, but also of rebellion, in that he has gone and done clean contrary to our commandment (yea, rather the commandment of blessed St. Peter), so that he hath permitted his clergy, not only such as had wives, not to put them away, but also such as had none, to take them. Whereupon we being truly informed, and grieved therewith, have directed to him another letter, declaring the motion of our displeasure and indignation. In which letters also we have cited him up to our council at Rome, there to appear and give account of his disobedience in the audience of the whole synod. And now, therefore, we thought it best to signify this to you (our dear children) whereby in this behalf we might the better provide for your health and salvation. For if your bishop shall continue so obstinately to repugn and resist our commandment, he is not meet to sit over you. Wherefore, these shall be command you, and all them that be obedient to God, and to blessed St. Peter, by our apostolical authority, that if this your bishop shall persist in his obstinacy, you that be his subjects hereafter give to him no service nor obedience. For the which we here discharge you before God and your souls. For if your bishop shall act contrary to the decrees and apostolical injunctions, we, through the apostolical authority of St. Peter, discharge and absolve you from the band of your allegiance to him. So that if you be sworn to him, so long as he is a rebel against God and the apostolic seat, we loose you from the peril of your oath, that you shall not need to fear therein any danger," &c.

In the council held at Rome, Hildebrand, with other bishops of Rome, did then enact, among many others, these three things especially, First, That no priest hereafter should marry. Secondly, That all such as were married should be divorced. Thirdly, That none hereafter should be admitted to the order of priesthood, but should swear perpetual celibacy, &c. This council of Rome being ended, forthwith the act of Hildebrand, concerning the single life of priests, was proclaimed and published in all places, and strict commandment given to bishops to execute the same. The following is the copy of his bull sent into Italy and Germany :—

" Gregory the pope, otherwise Hildebrand, the servant of the servants of God, sends the apostle's blessing to all within the kingdoms of Italy and Germany, that shew true obedience to St. Peter. If there be any priests, deacons, and subdeacons, that still will remain in the sin of marriage, we forbid them the church's entrance, by the omnipotent power of God, and by the authority of St. Peter, till in time they amend and repent. But if they persevere in their sin, we charge that none of you presume to hear their service ; for their blessing is turned into cursing, and their prayer into sin, as the Lord doth testify to us by his prophets, ' I will turn your blessing,' " &c.

The bishops of France being called upon daily by the pope's letters, were compelled to obey the decree of the council ; but the rest of the clergy manfully and stoutly withstanding the pope's decree and their bishops, would not agree, and said that the council did manifestly oppose the word of God, and that the pope did take from priests that which both God and nature had given them ; and therefore was a heretic and author of a wicked doctrine, who ruled not by the Spirit of God, but by Satan ; that the decree and act set forth was directly against the word of God and the saying of Christ, " All men receive not this saying." Against the sound doctrine of St. Paul, writing these words, " Concerning virgins I have no commandment of the Lord," &c. 1 Cor. vii. 25. Again, " Let them marry," 1 Cor. vii. 9. And that it was against the canons both of the apostles, and of the Nicene council. Moreover, that it was against the course of nature, that men being separated from their wives, should be compelled to live as angels ; and that, therefore, the bishop opened a pernicious window to immorality and vice. In short, they concluded, That they had rather give up their benefices than forsake their lawful wives. And, finally, if married priests could not please them, they ought to call down angels from heaven to serve the churches. But Hildebrand, nothing moved, either with honest reason, or with the authority of holy scripture, or with the determination of the Nicene council, or any thing else, follows up this matter, calls upon the bishops still, accuses them of negligence, and threatens them with excommunication, unless they cause the priests to obey his decree. Whereupon a great number of bishops, for fear of the pope's tyranny, laboured the matter with their priests, by all means possible to bereave them of their accustomed matrimony.

Among others, the archbishop of Mentz, perceiving this might produce no little trouble, talks with his clergy gently, admonishes them of the pope's mind and decree, and gives them half a year's respite to deliberate upon the matter ; exhorting them diligently to shew themselves obedient to the pope and to him. The time of deliberation expired, the archbishop assembles his clergy at Erpsford, and there requires them either to abjure all matrimony or to renounce their benefices. The clergy defend themselves against the decree with scripture, with reason, with the acts of general councils, with examples of ancestors, by strong arguments, declaring the pope's decree inconsistent, and that it ought not to take effect. But the archbishop said he was compelled by the pope, and could not but execute that which was enjoined him.

The clergy seeing that no reason, nor prayer, nor disputation would serve, consulted among themselves what was best to be done ; some gave counsel not to return to the synod, some thought it good to return and thrust out the archbishop from his see, and to punish him with death, that by his example others might be warned never to attempt it again to the prejudice of the church, and the rightful liberty of ministers. After this was signified to the archbishop by certain spies, he, to prevent the matter, sends to the priests as they were coming out, certain messengers, bidding them be of good hope, and they should have what would content their minds. So being thus persuaded, they come again to the council. The bishop promises he would do what he could, to change the mind of the bishop of Rome, desiring them in the mean time to continue as they had done in their ministry. The next year Hildebrand the soldier of Satan sends his legate to the archbishop of Mentz, and assembled a council, in which the archbishop again proposes the matter, commanding all the clergy, under pain of the pope's curse, either to renounce their wives or their livings. The clergy defended their cause again with great constancy. But when no defence would avail, but all went by tyranny, it burst at last to an uproar and tumult, where the legate and the archbishop hardly escaped with their lives, and so the council broke up. By this schism and tumult the churches afterwards, in choosing their priests, would not send them to the bishops (the enemies and suppressors of matrimony) to be confirmed and inducted, but elected them within themselves, and so put them in their office without all leave or knowledge of the bishops, who then agreed and were determined to admit no priests, but such as would take an oath never to marry. And thus first came up the oath and profession of single priesthood. Notwithstanding, if other nations had followed in like manner, the constancy and concord of those German ministers, the devilish decree of this Hildebrand (or rather hell-brand) had been frustrated. But the greediness of livings in weak priests made them yield up their liberty to wicked tyranny. And thus much for the prohibition of matrimony.

Now let us proceed to the contention between Hildebrand and the emperor. But it will not be amiss first to say a little of the character of this pope, as we find it described in the epistles of Benno a cardinal, written to other cardinals of Rome. This Cardinal Benno lived at the same time with Hildebrand.

He is thus described in one epistle of Benno to his brother cardinals as follows :—

" We have made mention before of some colleges of the church of Rome which refused to hold communion with him; as Leo, Benno, Ugobald, John; all cardinals: Peter, chancellor and cardinal, being all instituted before the time of this Hildebrand. These three also, though consecrated by him, Natro, Innocent, and Leo, forsook him, cursing the detestable errors which he held. Also Theodine, whom he constituted arch-deacon, and other cardinals more, John, surnamed Primicerius, Peter Oblationarius, with all that belonged to them, saving one man only. And now when this Hildebrand saw that the bishops also would forsake him, he called to him the laymen, and made them his privy councillors, thinking thereby to separate the bishops, so that they should have no conference with the cardinals. Then he called the bishops together, and being guarded with bands of laymen, he forced the bishops partly through fear, and partly through his menacing words, to swear that they would never oppose what he wished to have done, and that they would never defend the king's quarrel, and that they would never favour nor obey any pope who might be instituted in his stead.

" As soon as Pope Alexander was dead, who died somewhat before night, the same day, contrary to the canons, Hildebrand was chosen pope by the laymen. But the cardinals did not subscribe to his election. For the canons prescribed (under an anathema or curse) that none should be chosen pope before the third day after the burial of his predecessor. But Hildebrand removed the cardinals from being members of the council. And then, contrary to the minds of the cardinals, and to the regular order of pronouncing judgment by the canons, he rashly excommunicated the emperor, although he had not been in any synod solemnly accused before. The sentence of which excommunication none of the cardinals would subscribe.

" The emperor was wont oftentimes to go to St. Mary's church to pray. Hildebrand, when he knew all the doings of the emperor, caused the place where the emperor was accustomed either standing or prostrate on his face to pray, to be marked, and he hired an assassin to gather and lay together a heap of great stones directly over the place in the vault of the church, where the emperor would stand, that in throwing them down upon his head, he might slay the emperor. As the assassin hasted, and was busy removing to the place a stone of great weight, it broke the plank on which it lay, and as the assassin was also standing on it, they fell together from the roof to the pavement of the church, by which he was killed. After the Romans had learned the matter, they fastened a rope to one of the feet of the assassin, and caused him to be drawn through the streets of the city three days together as an example to others.

" In the Easter week, when the clergy and the people were assembled at St. Peter's church to hear mass, after the gospel, Hildebrand went into the pulpit as he was in his pontifical attire, and in the presence of the bishops, cardinals, senate, and people of Rome openly preached, that the emperor should die before the feast of St. Peter next ensuing: or at least, that he should be so hurled from his kingdom, that he should not be able to gather together above six knights. This he preached to the bishops and cardinals, and all that were present, crying out of the pulpit in these words, ' Never accept me for pope any more, but pluck me from the altar, if this prophesy be not fulfilled by the day appointed.' About the same time he sought by murderers to kill the emperor, but God preserved him.

" When the time was expired that Hildebrand had named, and when neither was the king dead, nor the power of the empire impaired : he subtilely turned his words, saying, ' that he meant them not of the body of the king, but of his soul.' "

It were too long and tedious here to recite all the detestable doings, and diabolical practices of Hildebrand, of which there is a long narration in the epistles of the cardinal Benno to the other cardinals, to which the reader may refer, who has either leisure to read or mind to understand more of the abominable parts and devilish acts of this pope.

Now let us proceed to set forth the vexation which the virtuous and godly emperor sustained by that ungodly pontiff.

When Henry VI. was encumbered with civil dissension in Germany, the time seemed to Hildebrand very opportune to work out his objects : his study from the beginning was to advance the Romish seat above all other bishops, and also to press down the authority of the temporal princes, under the spiritual men of the church. The emperor busied in his wars, had no leisure to attend to councils. But the pope proceeds to assemble his council ; and threatens even to excommunicate the emperor, and depose him from his royal kingdom, unless he would renounce the right of presenting to benefices, and do penance. The council being ended, Guibert, archbishop of Ravenna persuaded one Centius to take the emperor's part against the pope, and he watching his time, in the temple of St. Mary, upon Christmas day in the morning, takes the pope and puts him fast in a strong tower. The next day the people of Rome hearing this, proceed to help the bishop, whom they loosed out of prison, and then they besieged the house of Centius, and pulled it down to the ground; his family having their noses cut off, were cast out of the city ; Centius himself escaping, fled to the emperor. The emperor being moved with the arrogant presumption of the proud prelate, called a council at Worms. In which council all the bishops not only of Saxony, but of all the empire of Germany, agreed and concluded upon deposing Hildebrand, and that no obedience hereafter should be given to him. This being determined in the council, Roland was sent to Rome with the sentence, who in the name of the council, commanded the pope to resign his seat, and charged the cardinals to resort to the emperor for a new election of another pope. The following was the sentence of the council of Worms against Pope Hildebrand :

" Forsomuch as thy first ingress and coming in hath been so spotted with so many perjuries, and also the church of God brought into no little danger through thine abuse and new fangleness ; moreover, because thou hast defamed thine own life and conversation, with so much and great dishonesty, that we see no little peril or slander to rise thereof ; therefore the obedience, which yet we never promised thee, hereafter we utterly renounce, and never intend to give thee. And as thou hast never taken us yet for bishops (as thou hast openly reported of us) so neither will we hereafter take thee to be apostolic."

The pope touched with this sentence, first condemns it in his council of Lateran with an excommunication. Secondly, deprives Sigifrid archbishop of Mentz of his dignities and ecclesiastical livings, with all other bishops, abbots, and priests, as many as took the emperor's part. Thirdly, accuses Henry the emperor himself, depriving him of his kingdom, and releasing all his subjects of their oath of allegiance in the following sentence excommunicatory, against Henry the emperor by Pope Hildebrand.

" O blessed St. Peter, prince of the apostles, bow down thine ears I beseech thee, and hear me thy servant, whom thou hast brought up even from mine infancy, and hast delivered me until this day from the hands of the wicked, who hate and persecute me, because of my faith in thee. Thou art my witness, and also the blessed mother of Jesus Christ, and thy brother St. Paul, fellow partner of thy martyrdom, how that I entered this function not willingly, but enforced against my will; not that I take it so as a robbery, lawfully to ascend into this seat, but because that I had rather pass over my life like a pilgrim or private person, than for any fame or glory to climb up to it; I do acknowledge (and that worthily) all this to come of thy grace, and not of my merits, that this charge over christian people, and this power of binding and loosing is committed to me. Wherefore, trusting upon this assurance for the dignity and tuition of holy church in the name of God omnipotent, the Father, the Son, and the Holy Ghost, I do here depose Henry, the son of Henry, once the emperor, from his imperial seat, and princely government, who hath so boldly and presumptuously laid hands upon the church. And furthermore, all such as heretofore have sworn to be his subjects, I release them of their oath, whereby all subjects are bound to the allegiance of their princes. For it is meet and convenient that he should be void of dignity, who seeks to diminish the majesty of thy church. Moreover, for that he has contemned my admonitions, tending to his health and the wealth of his people; and has separated himself from the fellowship of the church (which he, through his seditions, studies to destroy) therefore I bind him by virtue of excommunication, trusting and knowing most certainly, that thou art Peter (in the rock of whom as in the true foundation) Christ our king has built his church."

The emperor, thus assaulted with the pope's censure, sends his letters through all nations to clear himself, declaring how wrongfully he was condemned. The princes of Germany partly fearing the pope, and partly rejoicing that an excuse was given to rebel against the emperor, assembled and consulted together, and so concluded to elect another emperor, unless he would submit and obtain pardon from the pope.

Here we may see the lamentable affections of the Germans in those days, thus to forsake such a valiant emperor, and to regard so much a vile bishop. But this was the ignorance and rudeness of the world then, for lack of better knowledge. The emperor, seeing the chief princes ready to forsake him, promises them with an oath, that if the pope would repair to Germany, he would ask forgiveness.

Upon this the bishop of Treves was sent to Rome, to intreat the pope to come into Germany. The pope was content and entered into Germany, thinking to come to Augsburgh; but he retired in fear to Canusium.

Henry (immediately coming out of Spires with his empress and his young son) resorts to Canusium. All his peers and nobles had left him for fear of the Pope's curse, neither did any accompany him. Wherefore the emperor, being not a little troubled (laying apart his regal ornaments) came barefooted with his empress and child to the gate of the city, where from morning to night (all the day fasting) he most humbly desired absolution. Thus he continued three days together; at length an answer came, that the pope's majesty had yet no leisure to speak with him. The emperor patiently and humbly waits without the walls, with no little grievance and pain; for it was a sharp winter, and all freezing with cold. At length it was granted, through the entreaty of Matilda the pope's favorite, and of Arelaus earl of Sebaudia, and the abbot of Cluny, that he should be admitted to the pope's presence. On the fourth day being admitted, he yields to the pope his crown, with all other imperial ornaments, and confessed himself unworthy of the empire, if ever he should do against the pope hereafter, as he had done before, desiring for that time to be absolved and forgiven. The pope answered, he would neither forgive him, nor release the bond of his excommunication,

but upon certain conditions. First, to promise that he should be content to stand to his arbitration, and to take such penance as he shall enjoin him; also that he shall be ready to appear, in whatever place or time the pope shall appoint him. Moreover, that he, being content to accept the pope as judge of his cause, shall answer to all objections and accusations laid against him, and that he shall never seek any revenge in return. Also that he shall submit to the pope's mind and pleasure, whether he shall have his kingdom restored or not. Finally, that before his trial, he shall neither use his kingly ornaments, sceptres or crown, nor usurp authority to govern, nor to exact any oath of allegiance from his subjects, &c. These things being promised to the bishop by an oath, and put in writing, the emperor is released from his excommunication.

The pope with his cardinals vaunted and triumphed with no little pride, that they had so quailed the emperor, and brought him on his knees to ask forgiveness. Yet, mistrusting themselves, and what might befall them if fortune should turn, and God give the emperor a more quiet kingdom; they study and consult privily how to displace Henry from his kingdom. They determined to offer the empire to Rodulph, a man of great nobility among the chief states of Germany. To bring this purpose the better to pass, legates were sent down from the pope, who should persuade all France, that Henry was rightfully excommunicated, and that they should give to the bishop of Rome their consent in choosing Rodulph to the empire.

While this conspiracy was in hand Henry was absent. In the meantime Rodulph was elected emperor. Upon this comes the bishop of Strasburgh to the emperor, certifying him what was done. He mustered his men with expedition, and marched forward to defend his right, and attempted battle against Rodulph. A great slaughter took place on both sides, but the victory was certain on neither part; so that both the captains yet challenged the empire. Their armies being refreshed, they soon had another conflict, but victory was again doubtful. Thus both the captains being wearied in wars, the Romish beast, the bishop, who was the cause of all, sends his legates to call together a council in Germany, where it should be determined to whom the empire should belong.

But the emperor would not permit the legates to hold any council within Germany unless they would first depose Rodulph. The pope hearing this, and seeing his purpose was so thwarted by the emperor, draws out another excommunication against him, and again deprives him of his kingdom.

The Second Excommunication of Hildebrand against the Emperor.

" Blessed St. Peter, prince of the apostles, and thou St. Paul also, the teacher of the Gentiles, give ear unto me, I beseech you a little, and gently hear me, for you are the disciples and lovers of truth. The things that I shall say are true. This matter I take in hand for truth's sake, that my brethren (whose salvation I seek) may the more obsequiously obey me, and better understand, how that I trusting upon your defence (next to Christ, and his mother the immaculate Virgin) resist the wicked, and am ready to help the faithful. I did not enter this seat of mine own accord, but much against my will and with tears, for that I accounted myself unworthy to occupy so high a throne. And this I say, not that I have chosen you, but you have chosen me, and have laid this great burthen upon our shoulders. And now, whereas by this your assignment, I have ascended up this hill, crying to the people and shewing them their faults, and to the children of the church their iniquities; the members of Satan have risen up against me, and have laid hands together to seek my blood. For the kings of the earth have risen up against me, and the princes of this world, with whom also have conspired certain of the clergy against the Lord and against us his anointed, saying, " Let us break their bonds asunder, and cast their cords away from us." This have they done against me, to bring me either to death or to banishment. In the number of whom is Henry, whom they call king, the son of Henry the emperor, who has lifted up so proudly his horns against the church of God, making conspiracy with divers other bishops, Italians, French, and Germans. Against the pride of whom hitherto your authority has prevailed; who rather being broken than amended, coming to me in Cisalpina, made humble suit to me for pardon and absolution. I, thinking there was true repentance in him, received him again to favour, and did restore him to the communion only, from which he was excommunicated, but to his kingdom (from which in the synod of Rome he was worthily expelled) I did not restore him, nor to the rents and fruits thereof, (that he might return to the faith again) that I granted not to him. And that I did for this purpose, that if he should defer to agree with certain of his neighbours whom he has always vexed, and to restore again the goods both of the church and otherwise, then he might be compelled by the censures of the church, and force of arms thereto. Whereby divers and sundry bishops and princes of Germany (such as he had long troubled) being helped by this opportunity, elected Rodulph their duke to be king in place of Henry, whom they for his transgressions had removed and dispatched from his empire. But Rodulph, first in this matter using a princely modesty and integrity, sent up his messengers to me, declaring how he was constrained to take that regal government upon him, although he was not so desirous thereof, but that he would rather show himself obedient to us, than to the other that offered him the kingdom; and whatever our arbitration should be therein, he would be under obedience both to God and to us. And for more assurance of his obedience he hath sent his own children hither for pledges. Upon this Henry began to be angry, and first intreated us to restrain and inhibit Rodulph, through the pain of our curse, from the usurpation of his kingdom. I answered I would see which of them had the best right and title thereto, and so send our legates thither to know the whole state of the matter; and thereon I would decide between them which of them had the true right. But Henry would not suffer our legates to come to take up the matter, and slew many both secular men and clergy, spoiling and profaning churches; and so by this means hath endangered himself in the bonds of excommunication. I therefore, trusting in the judgment and mercy of God, and in the support of the blessed virgin, also upon your authority, do lay the sentence of curse upon the said Henry and all his adherents; and here again I take his regal government from him, charging and forbidding all christian men that have been sworn to him, whom I discharge here of their oath, that hereafter they obey him in nothing, but that they take Rodulph as their king, who is elected by many princes of the province. For it is right and convenient, that as Henry for his pride and stubbornness is deprived of his dignity and possession; so Rodulph being acceptable to all men for his virtue and devotion, be exalted to the imperial throne and dominion.

"Therefore, O you blessed princes of the apostles, grant this, and confirm with your authority what I have said, so that all men may understand, if you have power to bind and loose in heaven, you have also power in earth to give and take away empires, kingdoms, principalities, and whatever here on earth belongs to mortal men. For if you have power to judge in such matters as appertain to God: what then should we think you have of these inferior and profane things? And if it be in your power to judge the angels, ruling over proud princes, what then shall it beseem you to do upon their servants? Therefore let the kings understand by this example, and all other princes of the world, what you are able to do in heaven, and what you are with God; that thereby they may fear to contemn the commandment of holy church. And now do you exercise this judgment quickly upon Henry, whereby all men may see this son of iniquity fall from his kingdom, not by any chance, but by your provision and only work. Notwithstanding this I would crave of you, that he, being brought to repentance through your intercession, yet in the day of judgment may find favour and grace with the Lord."

After this, Henry and Rodulph, to try the matter by the sword, contended together in battle, where Henry, by the favour of God, contrary to the judgment of Hildebrand, had the victory. Rodulph being severely wounded in the conflict, was taken out of the army, and carried to Hyperbolis, where he commanded the bishops and chief movers of his conspiracy to be brought before him. When they came, he lifted up his right hand in which he had received his deadly wound, and said, "This is the hand which gave the oath and sacrament of fidelity to Henry my prince, and which through your instigation so often has fought against him and fought in vain; now go and perform your first oath and allegiance to your king; for I must go to my fathers," and so he died. Thus the pope gave battle, but God gave the victory.

Henry, after his enemy was thus subdued, forgot not the injuries received from Hildebrand, by whom he was twice excommunicated, and expelled from his kingdom. Therefore he calls a council of the bishops of Italy, Lombardy, and Germany, at Brixia, (A.D. 1083), where he cleared himself, and then accused Hildebrand of various crimes, as an usurper, perjured, a necromancer, a sower of discord; complaining moreover of wrongs and injuries done by the bishop and church of Rome; his father, who was emperor before him, had installed many bishops by his assignment, without the election of any other: and now this pope, contrary to his oath and promise, thrust himself in without the will and knowledge of him who was the emperor and chief magistrate. For, in the time of his father Henry III., this Hildebrand with others, bound themselves with an oath, that so long as the emperor and his son should live, they should neither themselves presume, nor suffer any other to aspire to the papal seat, without the assent and approbation of the emperors; which now this Hildebrand, contrary to his oath, had done. Wherefore the council, with one agreement, condemned this Hildebrand that he should be deposed, and passed the following sentence against him.

"Because it is known that this bishop was not elected of God, but has intruded himself by fraud and money—who has subverted all ecclesiastical order—who has disturbed the government of the christian empire—menacing death of body and soul against our catholic and peaceable king—who has set up and maintained a perjured king—sowing discord where concord was—causing debate amongst friends—slanders and offences amongst brethren—divorce and separation among the married, (for he took away the marriage of priests)—and finally disquieting the peaceable state of all quiet life: Therefore we here, in the name and by the authority of God, congregated together, with the legates and nineteen bishops, on this day of Pentecost, at Mentz, do proceed in canonical judgment against Hildebrand, a most wicked man, preaching sacrilege and burning, maintaining perjury and murders, calling in question the catholic faith of the body and blood of the Lord, a follower of divination and dreams, a manifest necromancer, a sorcerer, and infected with an evil and heathen spirit, and therefore departed from the true faith, and we judge him to be deposed and expelled, and unless he, hearing this, shall yield and depart the seat, to be perpetually condemned."

This being enacted and sent to Rome, they elected Guibert, archbishop of Ravenna in the place of Hildebrand, to govern the church of Rome, under the title of Clement III. But when Hildebrand neither would give over his hold, nor give place to Clement, the emperor gathering an army came to Rome to depose him, and to place Clement. But Hildebrand sending to Matilda, who possessed great power and authority in Italy, required her, in remission of all her sins, to withstand Henry, and so she did. But Henry prevailed, and came to Rome, where he besieged the city all the Lent, and after Easter got it, the Romans being compelled to open the gates to him; so, coming to the temple of St. Peter, he there places Clement in his papacy. Hildebrand straight flies into Adrian's tower with his adherents, where, being beset round about, he sends for Robert Guiscard his friend, a Norman. In the meantime, while Robert collects his power, the abbot of Cluny, conferring with Gregory, exhorts him to crown Henry as emperor in Lateran. Which if he would do, the other promises to induce Henry to depart with his army into Germany: the people of Rome did likewise move him unto this. Gregory answered, " That he was content so to do, but upon condition that the emperor would submit himself to ask pardon to amend his fault and to promise obedience. The emperor not agreeing to those conditions, went to Senas, taking Clement the new pope with him.

After the return of the emperor, Robert Guiscard, approaching with his soldiers, burst in at one of the gates, and spoiled the city. And not long after, delivered Hildebrand out of his enemy's hands, and carried him away to Campania; where he not long after died in exile.

Antony writes, that Hildebrand, as he lay dying, called to him one of his chief cardinals, bewailing to him his fault, and the disorder of his spiritual ministry, in stirring up discord, war, and dissension, whereupon he desired the cardinal to go to the emperor, and desire of him forgiveness, absolving from the danger of excommunication both him and all his partakers both quick and dead.

Thus the reader has the full history of Pope Gregory VII. called Hildebrand; which I have laid out more at large, because from this pope sprang all the occasions of mischief, of pomp, pride, presumption, and tyranny, which since that time has reigned in the cathedral church of the Romish clergy. For here came first the subjection of the temporal authority under the spiritual jurisdiction; and emperors, who before were their masters, now are made their underlings. Also here came in the suppression of priests' marriage. Here came in moreover the authority of both the swords spiritual and secular into spiritual men's hands. So that christian magistrates could do nothing in election, in giving bishopricks or benefices, in calling councils, in hearing and correcting the excesses of the clergy, but the pope alone must do all. And finally, here came in the first example to persecute emperors and kings with rebellion and excommunication.

Now we may return to the history of England. About the death of Pope Hildebrand, or not long after, followed the death of King William the Conqueror, in the year, 1087, after he had reigned in England the space of one-and-twenty years and ten months.

By the life and acts of this king it may appear true, as histories report of him that he was wise, but guileful; rich, but covetous; a fair speaker, but a great dissembler; glorious in victory, and strong in arms, but rigorous in oppressing those whom he overcame, and passing all others in laying taxation. Insomuch that he caused to be enrolled and numbered in his treasury every hide of land, and the owner thereof, what fruit and revenues were derived of every lordship, every township, castle, village, field, river, and wood, within the realm of England; how many parish churches, how many living cattle there were, what and how much every baron in the realm could spend, what fees were belonging to them, what wages were taken, &c. The tenor and contents of all which yet remains in rolls.

The king had such pleasure in hunting, and in parks, that in the county of Southampton, for the space of thirty miles, he cast down churches and townships, and there made the new forest; loving his deer so dearly, as though he had been a father to them, making sharp laws for the increasing thereof, under pain of losing both the eyes. So hard was he to Englishmen, and so favourable to his own country, that there was no English bishop remaining, but only Wolstan of Winchester, who being commanded by the king and Lanfranc to resign up his staff, partly for inability, partly for lack of the French tongue, refused otherwise to resign it, but only to him that gave it, and so went to the tomb of King Edward, where he thought to resign it, but was permitted to enjoy it still.

Among his other conditions, this is noted, that he was so given to peace and quiet, that any maiden laden with gold or silver, might pass through the whole realm without harm or resistance. This William in his time built two monasteries, one in England, at Battle in Sussex, where he won the field against Harold, called the Abbey of Battle; another besides, named Barmondsey, in his own country of Normandy.

A little above, mention was made of the bishop's see of Sherborne, translated from thence to Salisbury. The first bishop of Salisbury was Hirman, a Norman, who first began the new church and minster of Salisbury. After whom succeeded Osmund, who finished the work, and endowed the house with great revenues, and much good singing. This Osmund first began the ordinary which was called " *Secundum usum Sarum*," (A. D. 1076). The occasion whereof was this, as I find in an old story book, entitled " *Eulogium*." A great contention chanced at Glastonbury, between Thurstan the abbot, and his convent, in the days of William the Conqueror. The cause of this contention was, that Thurstan contemning their choir service, then called the use of St. Gregory, compelled his monks to the use of one William, a monk of Fiscam in Normandy. Whereupon came strife and contentions among them, first in words, then from words to blows, after blows then to armour. The abbot, with his armed guard, fell upon the monks, and drove them to the steps of the high altar, where two were slain, and eight wounded with arrows, swords, and pikes. The monks then driven to such a straight and narrow shift, were compelled to defend themselves with forms and candlesticks, with which they wounded some of the soldiers. One monk (an aged man), instead of his shield took an image of the crucifix in his arms for his defence, which image was wounded in the breast by one of the bowmen, whereby the monk was saved. My story adds that the striker immediately fell mad, which seems some monkish addition. This matter being brought before the king, the abbot was sent again to Cadonum, and the monks, by the command of the king, were scattered in far countries. Thus Osmund, bishop of Salisbury, devised that ordinary, which is called " the use of Sarum," and was afterward received in a manner through England, Ireland, and Wales.

WILLIAM RUFUS.

William Rufus, the second son of William the Conqueror, began his reign (A. D. 1087), and reigned thirteen years, being crowned at Westminster by Lanfranc. After his coronation, he released out of prison, at the request of his father, several English lords, who had been in custody. It happened that, at the death of William the Conqueror, Robert, his eldest son, was absent in Germany, who hearing of the death of his father, and how William his younger brother had taken upon him the kingdom, was greatly incensed: he laid his dukedom to pledge to his brother Henry, and gathered an army, and landed at Hampton. But William Rufus sent to him fair and gentle words, promising him subjection, as to the more worthy and elder brother, only requiring that as he was in possession, he might enjoy it during his life, paying to him yearly three thousand marks, with condition that whichever of them outlived the other should enjoy the kingdom. The occasion of this variance between these brothers brought a great dissension between the Norman lords and bishops, both in England and in Normandy. But Duke Robert, by the advice of his council, was content to consent to all that was desired, and returned shortly after into Normandy.

This Rufus was so disliked by the Normans, that between him and his lords there was frequently dissension. All the Normans took part against him, so that he was forced of necessity to draw to him the Englishmen. Again, he was so covetous and so immeasurable in his taxes and takings, in selling benefices, abbeys, and bishoprics, that he was hated by all Englishmen.

King William was an exceeding plunderer of church goods, after he had given the bishopric of Lincoln to his chancellor, Robert Blevet, he then began to cavil, avowing that the see of Lincoln belonged to the see of York, till the bishop of Lincoln had pleased him with a great sum of money, viz., five thousand marks.

And as nothing could come in those days without money, so Herbert Losinga, by paying to the king a piece of money, was made Bishop of Thetford, as he had paid a little before to be made abbot of Ramsay. He removed his see from Thetford to the city of Norwich, and there elected the cathedral church with the cloister, where he furnished the monks with sufficient living and rents of his own charges, besides the bishop's lands. Afterwards, repenting of his open and manifest simony, he went to Rome, where he resigned into the pope's hands his bishopric, but so that immediately he received it back again.

We heard a little before of the death of Pope Hildebrand, after whose time the emperors began to lose their authority in the pope's election, and in giving of benefices. For next after this Hildebrand came Pope Victor III., through the influence of Matilda, and the Duke of Normandy, with the faction and retinue of Hildebrand, who likewise shewed himself stout against the emperor. But God restrained his power. For Victor being poisoned, as some say, in his chalice, sat but one year and a half. However, the example of Hildebrand continued still in those that followed him. And as the kings of Israel followed for the most part the steps of Jeroboam, till the time of their desolation; so the popes followed the steps and proceedings of this Hildebrand, their spiritual Jeroboam, in maintaining false worship, and chiefly in upholding the dignity of that see, against all rightful authority, and the lawful kingdom of Sion.

Next to Victor sat Urban II., by whom the acts of Hildebrand were confirmed, and also new decrees enacted against Henry the emperor. In this time were two popes together at Rome, Urban II. and Clement III., whom the emperor set up. Under Pope Urban II. came in the white monks of the Cistercian order. In this order the monks lived by the labour of their hands; they payed no tithes nor offerings, they wore no fur nor lining, they wore red shoes, white cowls, and black coats, all shorn, save a little circle round their heads; they only eat flesh in their journeys.

This Urban held several councils; one at Rome, where he excommunicated all such lay persons as gave investiture of any ecclesiastical benefice; also all such of the clergy as degraded themselves to be the underlings or servants to lay persons for ecclesiastical benefices.

He held another council at Cleremont in France, where among other things, the bishop made an oration to the lords there present, concerning the recovering the Holy Land from the Turks and Saracens. The cause of which first sprang by one Peter, a monk or hermit, who being in Jerusalem, and seeing the great misery of the christians under the pagans, declared it to Pope Urban II., and was a great advocate for the crusade to all christian princes. By which, after the oration of Pope Urban II., 30,000 men (taking on them the sign of the cross), made preparation for that voyage. Their chiefs were Godfrey, duke of Loraine, with his two brothers, Eustace and Baldwin; the bishop of Pody; Bohemond, duke of Puell, and his nephew Tancred; Raymond, earl of St. Egidius; Robert, earl of Flanders, and Hugh le Grand, brother of Philip the French king. To whom also was joined Robert Curthoise, duke of Normandy, with other noblemen, together with Peter the hermit, who was the chief cause of the undertaking.

At that time many of the noblemen laid their lands and lordships to mortgage, to assist in this crusade; as Godfrey, duke of Loraine, who sold the dukedom of Bologne, to the bishop of Eburone for a great sum of money. Also Robert Curthoise, duke of Normandy, pledged his dukedom to his brother William, king of England, for ten thousand pounds.

Thus the christians, who passed first over the Bosphorus, under the guidance of Peter the hermit (a man more devout than expert in guiding an army), being entrapped by their enemies, were slain and murdered in great numbers.

When the nobles and the whole army met together at Constantinople, (where Alexius was emperor), passing over by the Hellespont on their way to Jerusalem, they took the cities of Nice, Eraclea, Tarsis, and subdued the country of Cicilia.

Antioch was besieged, and in the ninth month of the siege it yielded to the christians by one Pyrrhus; about which time were fought many strong battles, or the great slaughter and desolation of the Saracens, and not without the loss of many christian men. The government of this city was committed to Bohemond, duke of Puell, whose martial knighthood was frequently proved in the time of the siege.

And not long after, Corbona master of the Persian chivalry, was vanquished and slain, with an hundred thousand infidels. In which discomfiture 15,000 camels were taken.

On the nine-and-thirtieth day of the siege, Jerusalem was conquered by the christians, and Robert, duke of Normandy, was elected king of it. However, he refused it, hearing of the death of William Rufus, king of England, wherefore he never succeeded well in all his affairs afterwards. Then Godfrey, captain of the christian army, was proclaimed the first king of Jerusalem. At the taking of the city, such was the murder of men, that blood was congealed in the streets the thickness of a foot. Then after Godfrey, reigned Baldwin his brother; after him Baldwin II., his nephew. Then Gaufride, duke of Gaunt, and after him Gaufride his son, by whom many great battles were fought against the Saracens, and all the country thereabout subdued, save Ascalon, &c. And thus much touching the voyage to the Holy Land. Now to our own land again.

About this time (as Matthew Paris writes) the king of England did not much favour the See of Rome, because of the impudent and unsatiable exactions which they required; nor would he suffer any of his subjects to go to Rome.

By Pope Urban II. it was decreed, that no bishop should be made, but under the name and title of some certain place.

That mattins and hours of the day should be said every day.

Also that every Saturday there should be said the mass of our lady, and all the Jews' sabbath turned to the service of our lady.

That all such of the clergy as had wives should be deprived of their order.

That it should be lawful for subjects to break their oath of allegiance with all such as were excommunicated by the pope.

In the year 1093, the king gave the archbishopric of Canterbury to Anselm, abbot of Beck in Normandy.

This Anselm was an Italian, born and brought up in the abbey of Beck in Normandy, where he was so strict a follower of virtue, that (as the story records) he wished rather to be without sin in hell, than with sin in heaven. Which saying and wish of his, if it were his, may seem to proceed out of a mind neither speaking orderly according to the phrase and understanding of the scripture, nor yet sufficiently acquainted with the justification of a christian man.

Of this Anselm it is reported, that he was so unwilling to take the archbishopric, that the king had much ado to thrust it upon him; and he was so desirous to have him take it, that the city of Canterbury, which previously was held by Lanfranc, only at the king's good will and pleasure, he now gave absolutely to Anselm, (A.D. 1093). But as desirous as the king then was to place Anselm there, so much did he repent it afterwards, seeking all possible means to defeat him if he could. Such strife and contention rose between them for certain matters, the ground and occasion whereof first was this:

After Anselm had thus been elected to the see of Canterbury, before he was fully consecrated, the king communed with him that such lands and possessions of the church of Canterbury as the king had given and granted to his friends since the death of Lanfranc, they might still enjoy as their own lawful possessions. But to this Anselm would not agree. At which the king, conceiving great displeasure against him, stopped his consecration, till in process of time the king, forced by the daily complaints and desires of his people, for want of an archbishop to moderate the church, was constrained to admit him. Thus Anselm, taking his consecration, and doing his homage to the king, went to his see of Canterbury, and not long after the king sailed over to Normandy.

About this time there were two striving in Rome for the popedom, as is before touched, Urban and Guibert, different realms consenting, some to the one, some to the other. England, taking part with the king, rather inclined to Guibert, called Clement III.; but Anselm went with Urban. After the king returned from Normandy, the archbishop comes to him, and asks leave to go to Rome, to obtain his pall of Urban. When he could not at first obtain leave, he appeals from the king to the pope. The king being justly displeased, charges the archbishop with breach of his fealty, contrary to his promise made, that without his licence he should not appeal either to Urban, or to any other pope. Anselm answers again, that it was to be referred to some greater council, where it is to be disputed, whether this be breach of a man's allegiance to an earthly prince, if he appeal to the vicar of St. Peter. And here much arguing and contending was on both sides. The king's reason proceeds thus : "The custom, saith he, from my father's time, has been in England, that no person should appeal to the pope without the king's licence. He that breaks the customs of the realm, violates the power and crown of the kingdom ; and he that violates and takes away my crown is a traitor and enemy against me," &c. To this Anselm replied again,—"The Lord, saith he, easily discusses this question, briefly teaching what fidelity and allegiance we ought to give to the vicar of St. Peter, where he saith, ' Thou art Peter, and upon this rock will I build my church, and to thee will I give the keys of the kingdom of heaven, and whatsoever thou shalt bind in earth, shall be bound in heaven ; and whatsoever thou shalt loose in earth, shall be loosed in heaven,' &c. Again, to them all in general, he saith, ' He that heareth you, heareth me ; and whoso despiseth you, despiseth me.' And in another place, ' He that toucheth you, toucheth the apple of mine eye.' On the other side, what duty we owe to the king, he shews also. ' Give,' saith he, ' to the emperor, what belongeth to the emperor, and to God, that which to God belongeth.' Wherefore, in such things as belong to God, I will yield, and must yield by good right and duty, my obedience to the vicar of St. Peter ; and in such things as belong again to earthly dignities of my prince, in those I will not deny my faithful help and counsel so far as they can extend."

Thus you have the arguments of this prelate against his prince, to which perhaps was joined also some piece of a stubborn heart. But in this conclusion none of his fellow bishops durst take his part, but were all against him ; namely, William, bishop of Durham, to whom Anselm thus protests, saying, "Whoever he were that would presume to prove it any breach of allegiance or fealty to his sovereign, if he appealed to the vicar of St. Peter, he was ready to answer at all times to the contrary." The bishop of Durham answered again,— "That he who would not be ruled by reason, must be constrained with force." &c. The king, having on his part the agreement of the bishops, thought to deprive the archbishop of his pastoral see, and to expel him out of the realm. But he could not perform this ; for Anselm, as he was ready to depart the realm, said, whenever he went, he would take his office and authority with him, though he took nothing else. Whereupon that matter was deferred till a longer time. In the meanwhile, the king had sent privately two messengers to Pope Urban, to intreat him to send his pall to the king, for him to give it where he chose ; which messengers by this time were returned again, bringing with them from Rome Galtar, bishop of Alban, the pope's legate, with the pall to be given to Anselm. This legate, first landing at Dover, came privately (unknown to Anselm) to the king, declaring and promising, that if Urban was received pope in England, whatever the king required to be obtained, he, by his privilege from

the apostolical see, would ratify and confirm, save only that when the king required of the legate that Anselm might be removed, the legate thereto would not agree, saying, "That that was impossible for such a man as he, being lawfully called, to be expelled without manifest cause." In conclusion, although he could not obtain his request of the legate, yet the legate so managed with the king, that Urban was proclaimed lawful pope throughout all the realm.

Then certain bishops were sent to Anselm, to influence his mind, declaring what charges and pains the king had been at in his behalf, to procure the pall for him from Rome, which otherwise would have stood him in great expenses, and that all this the king had done for his sake ; therefore it was but good reason and proper that he, to gratify the king, should yield somewhat to his request in return. But with all this Anselm, the stout archbishop, would not be moved. Therefore the king, seeing no other remedy, was compelled to grant to him the full right of his archbishopric. And so on the appointed day, when the pall was to be brought to Canterbury, (being carried with all solemnity in a silver box), the archbishop, with a great concourse of people, came forth barefoot with his priestly vestments, to meet it. And so being brought in, it was laid upon the altar, while Anselm, spreading over his shoulders his popish vestments, proceeded to his popish mass.

Thus agreement being made between the king and the bishop, so long as it would hold ; it happened the year following, that the king entered with his army into Wales, to subdue such as rebelled against him there. After victory the king, returning home with triumph, found Anselm was coming to congratulate him on his success. But the king prevented him by messengers, laying to the bishop's charge both the small number and the evil service of his soldiers sent to him at his need. At hearing this, all the hopes of Anselm were dashed to the ground, for he had thought to have obtained and done many great matters with the king, touching the state of the church. But here all turned contrary to his expectation, so that he was charged, against the next court of parliament, to make his answer. But he avoided that by appealing to Rome. So he made his suit and interest with the king for licence to go to the pope. The king answered, "That he should not go, neither was there any cause for him to do so : for that both he knew him to be of so sound a life, that he had done no such offence, whereof he needed to crave absolution at Rome, neither was there any such lack of science and knowledge, that he needed to borrow any counsel there ; insomuch, saith the king, I dare say Pope Urban rather has to give place to the wisdom of Anselm, than Anselm to have need of Urban. Wherefore as he has no cause to go, so I charge him to tarry. And if he continue in his stubbornness still, I shall assuredly seize upon his possessions, and convert his archbishopric into my coffers, because he transgresses and breaks fidelity and obedience, promising before to observe all the customs of my kingdom. Neither is it the fashion in this realm, that any of my nobles should go to Rome without my sending. And therefore let him swear to me, that he will never for any grievance appeal hereafter to the see of Rome, or else let him leave my realm."

Anselm thinking best not to reply by any message, but by word of mouth, comes himself personally to the king, and places himself on the right hand of the prince, where he made his reply to the message sent to him by the king. "Whereas you say I ought not to go to Rome, either in regard of any trespass, or for abundance of counsel and knowledge in me (although I grant neither of them to be true), yet what the truth is therein, I refer it to the judgment of God. And whereas ye say that I promised to keep and observe your customs ; that I grant, but with a condition, so far to keep them, and to observe such of them as were consonant to the laws of God, and ruled with right and equity. Moreover, whereas ye charge me with breach of my fidelity and allegiance, for that, contrary to your customs I appeal to the apostolic see (my reverence and duty to your sovereignty reserved) ; if another person would say it, it would be untrue. For the fidelity and obedience that I owe to thee, O king! I have it of the faith and fidelity of God, whose vicar St. Peter is, to whose seat I do appeal. Further, whereas ye require me to swear, that I shall for no cause hereafter at any time appeal to Rome, I pronounce openly that a christian prince has no right to require such an oath of his archbishop; for if I should forswear St. Peter, I should deny Christ. And when I shall at any time deny Christ, then shall I be content and ready to stand to the satisfaction of my transgression to you, for asking licence to go to Rome. And peradventure when I am gone, the goods of the church shall not so serve your temporal desires and commodities as ye ween for." At these words of the bishop the king and his nobles were not a little incensed. And declared again, "That in his promise of observing the king's customs, there was neither condition, nor any clause put in, either of God or right," &c.

At length the king, after many threatening words, told him he should carry nothing out of the realm with him. "Well," said the bishop; "if I may neither have my horse nor garments with me, then will I walk on foot;" and so he prepared to set out on his journey, (all the other bishops forsaking him), of whom none would take his part; but if he came to them for counsel, they said he was wise enough, and needed not their counsel, as being one who for his prudence knew best what was to be done, as also for his holiness, was willing and able to follow what he knew. As for them, they neither durst nor would stand against the king their lord, whose favour they could not be without, for the peril that might happen both to themselves and their kindred.

Anselm coming to Rome, made his complaint to Pope Urban of the king; and the pope, writing to the king in behalf of Anselm, his letters and commands were despised. In the meantime, while the pope's letters were sent to the king, and Anselm was bid to wait about the pope for an answer back, till perceiving at length how little the king regarded the pope's letters, he began to be weary of waiting, and desired the pope that he might be discharged from his archiepiscopal office. To this the pope would not consent, but added, "As touching these matters we shall sufficiently provide at the next council to be holden at Bayonne, where I require you to be present.

When the time of the council was come, Anselm among others was called for, who, first sitting outside the bishops, was afterwards placed at the right foot of the pope, whence the same place was appointed to the successors of the see of Canterbury, in every general council by the decree of Pope Urban, to sit at the right foot of the pope. In this council there was great stir and much reasoning against the Grecians, concerning the matter and order of the proceeding of the Holy Ghost. Where is to be noted, that the Greek church has for a long time dissented from the Latin church in many points, to the number of twenty, or twenty-nine Articles, as I have them collected out of the register of the church of Hereford, of which some are as follow:

Wherein the Greek church differeth from the Latin.

1. They are not under the obedience of the church of Rome, because that the church of Constantinople is not subject but equal to the same.
2. They hold that the bishop of the apostolic see of Rome has not greater power than the four patriarchs. And whatever the pope does beside their knowledge, or without their approbation, it is of no value.
3. They say whatever has been done or concluded, since the second general council, is of no authority; because from that time they account the Latins to be in error, and excluded out of the holy church.
4. They hold the eucharist consecrated by the church of Rome not to be the very body of Christ. Also where the Romish church consecrates in unleavened bread, they consecrate in bread leavened.
5. They say that the Romish church errs in the words of baptism, for saying, " I baptize thee;" when

they should say, "Let this creature of God be baptized," &c.
6. They hold moreover that there is no purgatory, and that the suffrages of the church do not avail the dead, either to lessen the pain of them that be destined to hell, or to increase the glory of them that be ordained to salvation.
7. They hold that the souls out of the bodies departed (whether they have done good or evil) have not their perfect pain nor glory, but are reserved in a certain place till the day of judgment.
8. They condemn the church of Rome for mixing cold water in their sacrifice.
9. They condemn the church of Rome, for that women as well as priests anoint children (when they baptize them) on both shoulders.
10. They call our bread *panagia.*
11. They blame the church of Rome for celebrating their mass on other days besides Sundays, and certain other feasts appointed.
12. Also in this the Greek church varies from the Latin; for they have neither cream nor oil, nor sacrament of confirmation.
13. Neither do they use extreme unction, or anointing after the manner of the Roman church, expounding the place of St. James of the spiritual infirmity, and not corporal.
14. They enjoin no satisfaction for penance, but only that they shew themselves to the priests, anointing them with simple oil in token of remission of sins.
15. Only on Maunday Thursday they consecrate for the sick, keeping it for the whole year after, thinking it to be more holy on that day consecrated than upon any other. Neither do they fast any Saturday through the whole year, but only on Easter-eve.
16. They give but only five orders, as of clerks, subdeacons, deacons, priests and bishops; whereas the Roman church gives nine orders after the nine orders of angels.
17. Moreover the Grecians in their orders make no vow of celibacy, alleging for them the fifth canon of Nice, requiring that priest or deacon will not forsake his wife for honesty sake.
18. Every year the Grecians use upon certain days to excommunicate the church of Rome, and all the Latins as heretics.
19. Among the Grecians they are excommunicated that beat or strike a priest. Neither do their religious men live in such priestly celibacy as the Roman priests do.
20. Their emperor amongst them ordains patriarchs, bishops, and other of the clergy, and deposes the same at his pleasure; also he gives benefices to whom he chooses, and retains the fruits of the same benefices as pleases him.
21. They blame the Latin church because they eat no flesh, eggs, and cheese on Fridays, and do eat flesh on Saturdays.
22. They hold against the Latin men for celebrating without the consecrated church, either in the house or in the field; and fasting on the Sabbath day; also for suffering dogs and other beasts to enter into the church.
23. The Grecians use not to kneel in all their devotions, yea not to the body of Christ, but one day in the whole year; saying and affirming that the Latins are goats and beasts, for they are always prostrating themselves upon the ground in their prayers.
24. The Grecians moreover permit not the Latins to celebrate upon their altars. And if it chance any Latin priest celebrates upon their altar, they wash the altar in token of abomination and false sacrifice. And they diligently observe that whenever they do celebrate, they do but one liturgy or mass upon one altar or table that day.
25. They dissent from the church of Rome touching the order and manner of the proceeding of the Holy Ghost.

These articles, wherein is declared the difference between the east and west church, of the Grecians and Romans, as I found them articled and collected in an ancient and authentic register of the church of Hereford, so I thought here to insert them, and leave them to the consideration of the reader. Other four articles more in the same register are there expressed concerning simony and usury, not forbidden with them; and touching also their emperor; and how they teach their children to hurt or damnify the Latin priests in all manner of ways. Which articles, because they seem not truly collected out of their teachings, or else not greatly pertinent to the doctrine of religion; I pass them over, and return to our history again.

When some of these questions were moved in the council to be discussed, namely concerning the assertion of the proceeding of the Holy Ghost, and concerning leavened bread in the ministration of the Lord's supper, Anselm was called for, who in the handling and treating of the articles so bestirred him in that council, that he well pleased the pope and them about him.

Then in the history it follows, after long debating and discussing of these matters in the council, when they had published their judgment on them, and the pope had blasted out his thundering excommunications against the Grecians, and all that took their part: at length the complaints and accusation against the king of England were brought in. Upon this, Pope Urban with his adherents was ready to proceed in excommunication against the king. But Anselm kneeling before the pope, after he had first accused his king, afterwards obtained for him longer time to be given for further trial.

Thus the council breaking up, the pope returning again to Rome, directs his letters to the king, commanding him that Anselm should be reinvested in his archbishopric, and all other possessions there pertaining. To this the king sends answer by messengers; who coming to the pope, declared in the king's behalf, that the king their master did not a little marvel what induced him to command Anselm to be reinvested in his archbishopric; seeing he before told him plainly, that if he went out of England without his leave, he would deprive him of it. "Well," said the pope, "have you no other matter against Anselm but only this?" "No," quoth they. "And have ye taken all this travel," said the pope "to come hither so far to tell me this, that the primate of your country is dispossessed, because he has appealed to the apostolical see and judgment? Therefore if you love your lord, speed home and tell him, if he will not be excommunicated, that he quickly reinvest Anselm again to all that he had before. And lest I have you be hanged for your labour, look to your time, and see that you bring me answer again from him to this city, against the next council the third week after Easter." The messenger or speaker being somewhat astonished at the hearing of this tragical answer, and thinking yet to work something for his king and master, came secretly to the pope, saying that he would confer a certain mystery from his king privately with his holiness. What mystery that was, or what there passed from the king to the pope and the court of Rome, my author does not shew; but so cunningly that mystery was handled, that with a full consent both of the pope and all the court of Rome, a longer day was given, from Easter to Michaelmas, and the pope's choleric heat so assuaged, that when the council came (which was held at St. Peter's church at Rome) although great complaints were denounced against the king; yet such favour was found that he suffered no harm. Only the sentence of excommunication was there pronounced against such lay persons as gave investiture of churches, and them that were so invested. Also against them that consecrate such, or who gave themselves in subjection to lay men for ecclesiastical livings, as is before touched.

This council being finished, the archbishop seeing the unstedfastness of the pope (which but pleased him but little) took his journey to Lyons, where he continued his abode a long time, till the death first of pope Urban, then afterwards of the king.

Of this King William many things are differently recorded, some to his commendation, and some to his blame; whereof this is one, which some will ascribe to hardiness, but I rather ascribe to rashness in him. As the king once was in his sport of hunting, suddenly word came to him that Cenourona (a city in Normandy) was besieged. The king without tarrying or advice took the straight way toward the sea-side, sending to his lords that they should follow after. They advised him to stay till his people were assembled, but he would not be stayed, saying that such as loved him (he knew) would follow him shortly, and so went and took ship. The shipmaster seeing the weather so dark and cloudy was afraid, and counselled the king to tarry till the wind would change, and the weather be more favourable. But the king persisting, commanded him to make all speed he could for his life, saying, "That he never heard that any king yet was ever drowned." And so he passed the sea in safety, and came to Normandy.

In the thirteenth year of his reign King William, (having at the same time in his hand three bishoprics, Canterbury, Winchester, and Sarum; also twelve abbeys in farm), was wounded to death, as he was in his sport of hunting in the New Forest, by the glancing of an arrow, shot by a knight named Walter Tyrrel, and was carried speechless to Westminster, and there buried. His life was such, that it is hard for a history that should tell the truth, to say whether he was more to be commended or reproved. Among other vices, there is especially to be rebuked in him unmeasurable and unreasonable covetousness; so that he coveted to be every man's heir. This one example of liberal and princely nature I find in him; that upon a time when a certain abbot of a place was dead, there came to his court two monks of the same house, who had gathered much money, and used influence with the king, and severally made large offers to be promoted to that dignity. There was also a third monk of the same place, who of meekness and humility followed the other two, in order that upon him whom the king would admit for abbot, he should give attendance, and as his chaplain return with him. The king called before him the two monks severally, of whom the one outbid the other. As the king cast his eye aside, he espied a third monk standing by, supposing that his coming had been also for the same matter. Then the king calling him, asked what he would do, whether he would give more than his brethren had offered, to be appointed abbot. He answered the king, and said, that he neither had nor would (if he could) offer money for it by any such unlawful means.

When the king had well pondered this third Monk's answer, he said that he was best worthy to be the abbot, and to have the rule of so holy a charge; and so he gave him that benefice without taking any money.

Urban bishop of Rome, who (as is said) succeeded after Victor, ruled the church of Rome about the space of twelve years; and amongst his other acts he excommunicated the emperor Henry IV., as a man not very devoted to the see of Rome. But yet he was a worthy and victorious prince, in whom also some vice perchance might be noted, yet none such for which any prelate or minster of Christ ought to excite his subjects to rebel against public authority appointed of God. This Emperor Henry IV. was excommunicated by four popes severally; by Hildebrand, by Victor, by Urban, and by Paschal. Which excommunication wrought so in the ignorant and blind hearts of the people, that many (as well the nobles as of the multitude, contrary to their sworn allegiance) rebelliously conspired against the king and emperor.

KING HENRY THE FIRST.

Henry, the first of that name, the third son of William the Conqueror, succeeding his brother Rufus, began his reign in England, (A. D. 1100)., for his knowledge and science in the seven liberal arts, he was sirnamed Clerk or Beauclerk. In him it may well appear how knowledge and learning greatly conduce to the government and administration of any realm or country. At the beginning he reformed the state and condition of the clergy, released the grievous payments introduced against King Edward's laws, with amendments thereof; he reformed the old and untrue measures, and made a measure after the length of his arm; he greatly abhorred excess of meats and drinks; he reformed many abuses; and used to vanquish more by counsel than by sword.

In the second year of his reign, Robert his elder brother, duke of Normandy, being occupied in the christian wars against the Turks, and being elected king of Jerusalem, hearing of the death of Rufus, refused the kingdom thereof. Thus returning to Normandy, he made there his preparation, and came over to England with a great army to challenge the crown; but by mediation of the lords, it was agreed upon that Robert should have yearly during his life three thousand marks, as was likewise promised him before by King Rufus his brother; and whichever of them overlived the other, should be the other's heir. In process of time there was variance again between King Henry and Robert; and at length Robert in the wars was taken prisoner and brought over to England, and was put into the castle of Cardiff in Wales, where he continued a prisoner as long as he lived.

It has been already stated how Anselm went to the pope; after the death of King William he was sent for again by King Henry, and returned, and was at the council of the king at Westminster, where the king, in the presence of the lords, as well as temporal as spiritual, ordained and invested two bishops, Roger bishop of Salisbury, and Roger bishop of Hereford.

After this council, Herbert bishop of Norwich had much ado with the priests of his diocess; for they would neither leave their wives, nor yet give over their benefices as had been decreed in the council. Whereupon he wrote to Anselm the archbishop for advice. Anselm required him to persuade the people of Norfolk and Suffolk; that as they professed christianity, they should subdue them as rebels against the church, and utterly drive both them and their wives out of the country, placing monks in ther rooms.

Gerard the archbishop of York had also much trouble in depriving the priests of his province of their wives, which with all his excommunications and thunderings, he could hardly bring about.

About the end of the third year of the reign of this king, which was A. D. 1103., a variance arose between King Henry and Anselm, the occasion of which was this: you heard a little before how Henry had, of his own authority invested two bishops, one Roger, who was chancellor, bishop of Salisbury; and another bishop of Hereford. Besides these he invested others also, and several other things he took upon him in the ecclesiastical state, which he might lawfully do, God's word allowing the same; but because he was restrained by the bishop of Rome, and forbidden to do so, this Anselm was so enraged that he would neither consent to it, nor yet confirm them, nor communicate nor talk friendly with them, whom the king had instituted and invested; but opprobriously called them abortives, or children of destruction, disdainfully rebuking the gentle king as a defiler of religion, and polluter of their holy ceremonies. With this uncomely outrage the king was much displeased, and required Gerard the archbishop of York to consecrate them: who without delay did so, saving that one William Gifford, to whom the king had given the bishopric of Winchester, refused to take his consecration by the hands of the bishop of York. For which cause the king deprived him both of bishopric and goods, and banished him the realm.

Moreover, the king required of Anselm, to do homage, after the manner of his ancestors. Also it was asked, whether he would join with the king in giving investitures, as Lanfranc his predecessor had done. Anselm answered that he would not do homage to the king; alleging the pope's excommunication, who, in his council of Rome a little before, had given forth open sentence of excommunication upon all such lay persons (whatever they were) that should from henceforth confer or give any spiritual promotions: also upon them that received such promotions at their hands, and those who consecrated any such receivers. Moreover he pronounced all them accursed who for benefices or other ecclesiastical promotions should subject themselves under the homage or service of any great man, king, prince, duke, or earl of the laity. For (the pope said) it was unseemly and a thing very execrable, that the hands which were converted into so high a working, as was granted to no angel (that is, to create Jesus Christ in the mass, even him who created all, and to offer up the same before the sight of the Father for the salvation of the whole world) should be brought to such a slavery, as to be subject to those filthy hands, which are polluted with robberies, and bloodshed, &c. Anselm alleging this decree of Pope Urban, refused to do homage, fearing (as he said) the pope's excommunication.

In the mean time, while there was long disputation on both sides for investing, the nobles of the realm contended, that investings did belong to the king's dignity; wherefore the king calling for Anselm again, required him either to do homage to him or else to leave his kingdom. To whom Anselm replying again, required the pope's letters to be brought forth, and the matter to be decided according to the tenor thereof. For now the messengers were returned from Rome, with the pope's answer; altogether agreeing with Anselm. Then said the king; "What have I to do with pope's letters? I will not forego the liberties of my kingdom for any pope." Thus the contention continued between them. Then other ambassadors were sent again to the pope, that he would something qualify and moderate (or rather abolish) the sternness of the Roman decree before-mentioned. On the part of Anselm were sent two monks, Baldwin and Alexander. On the king's behalf were sent two bishops, Robert bishop of Lichfield, and Herbert bishop of Norwich.

After the ambassadors (thus sent on both sides to Rome) had pleaded their causes; the pope glad to gratify the king (yet loath to grant his request, being against his own profit, and therefore more inclining to Anselm's side) sent his letters to Anselm, signifying that he would not repeal the statutes of his holy fathers for one man's pleasure: charging him moreover, not only not to yield in the cause of investing, but constantly to adhere to the decree of Pope Urban, &c. Besides this letter to Anselm, he directed also another to the king himself: which letter, the king suppressed and did not shew, only declaring by word of mouth, what the ambassadors had said unto him from the pope. Which was, that he permitted unto him the licence of investing, upon condition that in other things he would execute the office of a good prince, &c. The contention still continuing, it was agreed by the king and his nobles, that Anselm should go himself to Rome. And much entreaty was made that he would take that journey in hand, in his own person, to present himself to the pope, for the peace of the church and of his country. And so at length by persuasion, he went to Rome and spake with the pope. He was followed also by the king's ambassador, William Warlwast, new elect bishop of Exeter. There it was decreed, that the bishops who were invested by the king, should be excommunicated. The absolution and satisfaction of whom was left to Anselm, the king only, who had invested them, being excepted.

Thus Anselm, leaving Rome, took his journey toward England. But the ambassador, pretending to go to St. Nicholas, remained behind, to see whether he could win the pope's mind to the king's purpose. Which when he saw he could not do, he overtakes Anselm by the way, at Placentia, and told him the king's pleasure. "The king," said he, "gives to you in charge and commandment, that if you will come to England, and there behave yourself to him, as your predecessor did to his father, you should be received and retained in the realm accordingly: if not — you are wise enough to know what I mean, and what will follow." And so with these words, parting from him, he returned again to the king: and Anselm remained at Lyons a year and a half, and wrote to the king as follows:

"*To his Reverend Lord, Henry, King of England, Anselm, Archbishop of Canterbury, faithful Service, with Prayers.*

"Although you understand by William Warlwast what we have done at Rome; yet I shall shortly shew you that which belongs to me. When I came to Rome

I declared the cause wherefore I came to the lord pope. He answered that he would not swerve from the statutes of his predecessors. Furthermore, he commanded me that I should have no fellowship with those who received investings of churches at your hands, after the knowledge of this prohibition, unless they would do penance, and forsake what they had received, without hope of recovery; also that I should not communicate with the other bishops that had consecrated such men, unless they would present themselves to the judgment of the apostolic see. The aforesaid William can be a witness of all these things if he will. This William, when we departed asunder (reckoning up in your behalf, the love and liberality which you had always towards me) warned me as your archbishop, that I should shew myself such an one, that if I would come into England, I might be with you as my predecessor was with your father, and you might treat me with the same honour and liberty that your father treated my predecessor. By which I understand, that unless I should shew myself such a one, you would not have me come into England. For your love and liberality I thank you: but that I should be with you as my predecessor was with your father, I cannot do it. For I dare not do homage to you, nor communicate with those who take investings of churches at your hands: because of this inhibition made, I myself hearing it. Wherefore I desire you to send me your pleasure herein if it please you, whether I may return into England (as I said) with your peace and power of mine office."

In the meanwhile there was great debate, and many messengers sent to and fro between the king, the archbishop, and the pope, but nothing was done: for the pope would not agree to the king, neither would the king condescend to the archbishop. At last the archbishop, seeing he could by no means prevail against the king, thought to revenge himself by excommunication, and so went about the same. The king, hearing of this by the Countess Adela his sister, desires her to come to him into Normandy, and bring Anselm with her: whereupon (through the means of the countess) the king and Anselm were reconciled, and the archbishop was restored to his former possessions again. Only his return was deferred, because he would not communicate with those whom the king had invested. So the king took his passage over into England, and Anselm abode at the abbey of Becke.

In the meantime complaints were daily brought from England to Anselm, against the priests and canons, who, in his absence, contrary to the late council holden at London, received their wives unto their houses again, and were permitted so to do by the king, they paying him certain money for the same. Anselm, the sore enemy against lawful marriage, grieved therewith, addressed his letters to the king, requiring him to refrain from taking any more of such exactions, declaring, moreover, and affirming, that the offences of all such ecclesiastical ministers must be corrected by the bishops, and not by laymen.

It was not long after that the king, as he had promised, went again to Normandy, and meeting with Anselm at the abbey of Becke, he agreed with him in all such points as the archbishop required. As first, that all his churches, which before were made tributary to King William, now should remain free from all tribute; that he should require nothing of the said churches or provinces in the time of the seat being vacant. Moreover, concerning such priests and ministers as had given money to the king for liberty to keep their wives, it was agreed that they should cease from all ecclesiastical functions for the space of three years.

Thus Anselm, the stout champion of popery and superstition, after he had gained this victory over the king, for which he had so long fought, sailed into England with joy and triumph, having obtained all his popish requests. Where first he flies like a lion upon the married priests, contrary to the word of God, divorces and punishes, by man's authority, those whom the Eternal and Almighty God had coupled. Next, he looks to those who held any church by farm under the king. Against simony, likewise, and against those that married within the seventh degree, he proceeds with his full pontifical authority.

Shortly after, as King Henry had finished his war in Normandy, he returned again with victory into England, about the sixth year of his reign, Anselm archbishop of Canterbury (by the permission of the king) assembled a great council of the clergy and prelates of England at Westminster in London. In which (by the bishop of Rome's authority) he so wrought with the king, that at length (though not without great difficulty) it was newly confirmed and enacted, that no temporal man after that day should make investiture with cross or with ring, or with pastoral hook. In this council various injunctions were given forth to priests and deacons. And, as we are here mentioning the synodal acts concluded in the time of this Anselm, I here place them all together, taking them from Malmesbury and other authors.

The first thing decreed by this Anselm, in his synodal councils, was touching the fault of simony, whereby many bishops and abbots (as is before mentioned) were at the same time deposed: and laymen were forbidden to confer any ecclesiastical promotion.

Also, it was decreed, that no bishop should bear any office in secular men's business or meetings: and that such should not go apparelled as the laymen did, but should have their vestures decent and meet for religious persons. And that in all places they should never go without some to bear witness of their conversation.

That no archdeaconries should be let out to farm.

That no archdeacon should be under the degree of a deacon.

That no archdeacon, priest, deacon, sub-deacon, colligener, nor canon, should from that time marry, nor yet keep his wife, if he had been married to one before.

That every sub-deacon, being under the degree of a canon, marrying a wife after the profession of celibacy, should be subject to the same rule.

That any priest who did not put away his wife, should be reputed unlawful, and that he should say no mass, and if he said mass, he should not be heard.

That none should be admitted to orders from that time forward, from the degree of a sub-deacon, unless he professed celibacy.

That priests' sons should not claim the benefices of their fathers by heritage, as the custom had always been before.

That no spiritual person should sit in any secular office, as to be procurators or judges of blood.

That priests should not resort to taverns or banquets, nor sit drinking by the fireside.

That the garments of priests should be of one colour, and that their shoes should be decent.

Besides all these synodal acts, with others which we omit, given out by Anselm, he also directed other new injunctions to the priests.

That they and their wives should never meet in one house, neither yet have dwelling in their territories.

That the priests, deacons, and sub-deacons, should keep no female in their house, unless they were of their next kin.

That such as had separated themselves from the society of their wives, and yet for some cause had to communicate with them, might do so, if it were out of doors, and before two or three witnesses.

That if any of them should be accused by two or three witnesses, and could not clear himself again by six able men of his own order if he be a priest; or, if he be a deacon, by four; or, if he be a sub-deacon, by two; then he should be judged a transgressor of the statutes, deprived of his benefice, and be made infamous, or be put to open reproach of all men.

That any who rebelled, and in contempt of this new statute still held his wife, and presumed to say mass, upon the eighth day after (if he made not due satisfaction) should be solemnly excommunicated.

That all archdeacons and deacons should be straitly sworn not to wink or dissemble at their meetings, nor to bear with them for money. And if they would not be sworn to this, then to lose their offices without recovery.

That such priests, as forsaking their wives were willing to serve still and remain in their holy order, first must cease forty days from their ministration, setting vicars to serve for them in the mean time, and taking such penance upon them, as should be enjoined by their bishop.

Thus you have heard of the life and doings of Anselm, how superstitious he was in his religion, how stubborn against his prince, what occasion of war and discord he ministered by his complaints (if they had been taken); what zeal without right knowledge, what fervency without cause he pretended, what pains without profit he took. Who, if he had bestowed that time and labour in preaching Christ at home to his flock, which he took in going to Rome to complain of his country, in my mind he had been better occupied. Moreover, you have heard what violent and tyrannical injunctions he set forth concerning investing and other things; but especially against the lawful and godly marriage of priests: what a vehement adversary he was in this matter, may appear by these extracts from letters, which we here annex as follows:—

A LETTER OF ANSELM.

Anselm, Archbishop; to his Brethren and Dearest Sons the Lord Prior and others at Canterbury.

" As concerning priests, of whom the king commanded that they should have both their churches and their wives as they had in the time of his father, and of Lanfranc archbishop: both because the king hath revested and reseized the whole archbishopric, and because so cursed a marriage was forbidden in a council in the time of his father and of the said archbishop: I boldly command by the authority which I have by my archbishopric, not only within my archbishopric but also throughout England, that all priests who keep wives, shall be deprived of their churches and ecclesiastical benefices."

A LETTER OF POPE PASCHAL TO ANSELM.

Paschal, Bishop, Servant of God's Servants; to his Reverend Brother Anselm, Archbishop of Canterbury, greeting and apostolical blessing.

" We believe your brother-hood is not ignorant what is decreed in the Romish church concerning priests' children. But because there is so great multitude of such within the realm of England, that almost the greater and better part of the clerks are reckoned to be on this side: therefore we commit this dispensation to your care. For we grant these to be promoted to holy offices by reason of the need at this time, and for the profit of the church (such as learning and life shall commend among you) so that yet notwithstanding the prejudice of the ecclesiastical decree be taken heed to hereafter," &c.

ANOTHER LETTER OF ANSELM.

Anselm, Archbishop; to the Rev. Gudulph, Bishop; and to Arnulph Prior; and to William, Archdeacon of Canterbury; and to all in his Diocese, greeting.

" William, our archdeacon, hath written unto me, that some priests that be under his custody (taking again their wives that were forbidden) have fallen into the error from the which they were drawn by wholesome counsel and commandment. When the archdeacon would amend this thing, they utterly despised with wicked pride his warning and worthy commandment to be received. Then he, calling together many religious men and obedient priests, worthily excommunicated the proud and disobedient, who despised the curse, and were not afraid to defile the holy ministry, as much as lay in them," &c.

And thus much concerning Anselm archbishop of Canterbury; whose stout example gave no little courage

to Thurstin and Becket his successors, and others that followed after, to do the like against their kings and princes, as hereafter by the grace of Christ shall appear.

About the same time and year when King Henry began to reign, Pope Paschal entered his papacy, succeeding after Urban, (about A. D. 1100), nothing swerving from the steps of Hildebrand his superior. About the same time, (A. D. 1101), the bishop of Florence began to teach and to preach of antichrist then to be born and to be manifest, as Sabellicus testifies: whereupon, Paschal, assembling a council, put to silence the said bishop, and condemned his books. In this council at Trecas, priests that were married were condemned for Nicolaitans.

Concerning the excommunication and other troubles that Hildebrand wrought against the Emperor Henry IV. it is declared sufficiently before. This excommunication Paschal renewed against Henry. And not only that, but also convening the princes of Germany to a general assembly, set up the emperor's own son against him, causing the bishops of Mentz, of Cologne, and of Worms to deprive him of his imperial crown, and to place his son Henry V. in his father's kingdom. So coming to the place at Hilgeshem, first they required his diadem, his purple, his ring, and other ornaments pertaining to the crown, from him. The emperor demanded the cause, being then excommunicate and void of friends. They pretended, for selling bishoprics, abbacies, and other ecclesiastical dignities for money: also alleging the pope's pleasure and other princes. Then he inquired first of the bishop of Mentz (and likewise of the other two, whom he had preferred to their bishoprics before) asking them in order, if he had received one penny of them for promoting them to their dignities. This they could not deny to be so, " Well " (saith he) " and do you requite me again with this treatment?" and with many other words of exhortation he admonished them to remember their oath and allegiance to their prince. But the perjured prelates, neither reverencing his majesty, nor moved with his benefits, nor regarding their fidelity, ceased not for all this, but first plucked from him (sitting in his throne) his imperial crown, then disvestured him, taking from him his purple and his sceptre. The good emperor, being left desolate and in confusion, said to them: " Let God see and judge." Thus leaving him, they went to his son to confirm him in his kingdom, and caused him to drive his father out. In the end, being utterly dispossessed of his kingdom, he was brought to that distress, that coming to Spire, he begged of the bishop there, whom he had done much for before, to have a prebend in the church: and as he had some skill in his book, he desired to serve in our lady's quire, yet he could not obtain so much at his hand, who swore by our lady, he should have nothing there. Thus the woeful emperor came to Leodium, and there died for sorrow, after he had reigned fifty years.

After the decease of this emperor, his son Henry V. reigned the space of twenty years. Who, coming to Rome to receive the crown of the pope, could not obtain it, before he would fully assent to have this ratified, that no emperor should have any thing to do with the election of the Roman bishops or with other bishoprics. Soon after, however, the emperor prevailing against the pope, compelled him to agree to restore to him his right in the election of the pope and other bishops: but as soon as the emperor was returned again to Germany, forthwith the pope, calling a synod, not only revoked all that he had agreed to before, but also excommunicated Henry as he had done his father before.

The emperor seeing no end of these conflicts (unless he would yield to the pope) was obliged to give over, and forego his privilege, agreeing not to meddle with matters pertaining to the pope's election, nor with investing, nor such other things belonging to the church and churchmen. And thus the peace between them was concluded, and proclaimed to the no small rejoicing of both the armies, then lying by Worms, near the river Rhine.

After the death of Paschal (A. D. 1118), succeeded

Pope Gelasius, chosen by the cardinals, but without the consent of the emperor, whereupon rose no little variance in Rome. And at length another pope was set up by the emperor called Gregory, and Gelasius driven away into France, and there died. After whom came Calixtus II., chosen likewise by a few cardinals, without the voice of the emperor, who, coming up to Rome to enjoy his seat, first sent his legate into Germany to excommunicate the Emperor Henry; who then, having divers conflicts with his fellow Pope Gregory, at length drove him out of Rome.

In conclusion, the emperor being overcome, and fearing the dangerous thunderbolt of his curse, was obliged to condescend to the unreasonable conditions of the pope. First, to ratify his election, although the other pope was yet alive. Secondly, that he should resign up his right and title in matters pertaining to the election of the pope, and investiture of bishops.

This being done and granted, and the writings set up in the church of Lateran, as a triumph over the emperor, the pope went after Gregory his rival pope, who was then in a town called Sutrium; which being besieged and taken, Gregory also was taken. Calixtus the pope setting him upon a camel, (his face to the camel's tail), brought him so through the streets of Rome, holding the tail in his hand instead of a bridle; and afterwards being shorn, he was thrust into a monastery.

The same Calixtus, holding a general council at Rheims, decreed that priests, deacons, and sub-deacons should put away their wives; and whoever was found to keep his wife should be deprived of benefice, and all other ecclesiastical livings.

After the death of Anselm, (A.D. 1109), the church of Canterbury stood empty five years; and the goods of the church went to the king's use. And when he was prayed to appoint a pastor, his answer was, that as his father and brother had been accustomed to set the best tried and approved men in that see, that he might do the same, he took the more time. And so he delayed the time, while he filled his coffers with the riches of that benefice.

After this (A.D. 1115), Rodulph, bishop of Rochester, (an Englishman) was promoted to be archbishop of Canterbury, and Thurstin, the king's chaplain, was elected archbishop of York. Who being content to receive his benediction or consecration of the see of Canterbury, yet, because he refused to make his profession of obedience to the same see, was deprived by the king of his dignity.

Then Thurstin (by the instigation of certain of his clerks at York) took his journey to Rome; who there making his complaint to Paschal, brought with him a letter from the pope to the king, where among other words was contained as follows:

"We hear and understand, that the archbishop elect of the church of York (a discreet and industrious man) is sequestered from the church of York, which stands against both divine justice and the institution of holy fathers. Our purpose is, that neither the church of Canterbury should be impaired, nor again that the church of York should suffer any prejudice, but that the same constitution which was by blessed Gregory (the apostle of the English nation) set and decreed between those two churches, should remain still in force and effect inviolate. Wherefore, as touching the foresaid elect archbishop, let him be received again by all means, as is right and meet unto his church. And if there be any question between the foresaid churches, let it be handled and decided in your presence, both the two parties being there present."

Upon the occasion of this letter, a solemn assembly was appointed at Salisbury, about the hearing of this controversy. The variance between these two prelates still increased more and more. Rodulph archbishop of Canterbury in no case would yield or condescend to give imposition of hands to him, unless he would make his profession of obedience. Thurstin again said, he would willingly receive and embrace his benediction; but as to the profession of his subjection, that he would not agree unto. Then the king signified to Thurstin, that without his subjection and obedience professed to the archbishop of Canterbury, he should not enjoy the archbishoprick of York. Thurstin upon this renounced his archbishoprick, promising moreover to make no more claim unto it, nor to molest them that should enjoy it.

Shortly after this, it happened that pope Paschal died: after whom, as is above rehearsed, succeeded pope Gelasius, who lived not more than a year, and died in France. The cardinals (who then followed Pope Gelasius to Cluny) created another pope of their own choosing, whom they called Calixtus II. The other cardinals who were at Rome chose another pope called Gregory. About these two rival popes there was much stir in the christian world. As this Calixtus was remaining in France, and there calling a general council at Rheims, Thurstin the archbishop of York desired licence of the king to go to the council, purposing there to open the cause of his church; first promising to the king that he should there attempt nothing that should be prejudicial to the church of Canterbury. In the meantime the king had sent secret word to the pope, by Rodulph and other proctors, that he should in no case consecrate Thurstin. Yet, notwithstanding the faithful promise of the pope made to the king, the pope was inclined to consecrate him, and gave him the pall; and required of the king that he would license Thurstin to return with favour into his realm. But the king utterly refused, unless he would profess subjection to the church of Canterbury, as his predecessors had done before; and excused himself by his oath which he had before made. To this the pope answered that he, by his apostolical authority, would easily dispense with him for his promise or oath. Then the king said that he would consult his council, and send an answer; which answer was this, "That, for the love and request of the pope, he was content that Thurstin should re-enter his realm, and quietly enjoy his prelateship, upon this condition, that he would profess his subjection to the church of Canterbury."

The year following after that, (which was A.D. 1120), Pope Calixtus directs his letters for Thurstin to the king, and to Rodulph archbishop of Canterbury. In which epistle, by his full power apostolical, he interdicts both the church of Canterbury and the church of York, with all the parish churches within the same cities, from the burial of the dead, also from all divine service, excepting only baptizing of children, and absolution of them that are dying; unless, within a month after the receipt of the same, Thurstin (without any exaction of subjection) were received and admitted to the see of York, and that the king also should be excommunicated except he would consent to the same. Whereupon, for fear of the pope's curse, Thurstin was immediately sent for and reconciled to the king, and was placed quietly in his archiepiscopal see of York.

It followed not long after (within two years) that Rodulph archbishop of Canterbury died, in whose see succeeded after him William de Turbine. About which time (in the twenty-seventh year of the king's reign, or a little before), the king called a council at London, where the spirituality of England consented to the punishment of married priests. By reason of which the priests, paying a certain fine to the king, were suffered to retain their wives still, whereby the king gathered no small sum of money, (Rog. Hoved. Guliel. Gisburnesis.)

It was before stated that Matilda or Maud, daughter of king Henry, was married to the emperor Henry V.; and after his decease she returned about this time with the imperial crown to her father in Normandy, bringing with her the hand of St. James! For the joy of obtaining this relic, the king built the abbey of Reading, where the hand was deposited. This Matilda was received by the council as next heir to the king, her father, in possession of the English crown, for lack of issue male. And soon after she was sent over to Normandy, to marry Geoffrey Plantagenet Earl of Anjou, of whom came Henry II., who was king of England after Stephen.

After Calixtus, succeeded Pope Honorius II.; notwithstanding that the cardinals had elected another, yet he by the means of certain citizens obtained the papacy, (A.D. 1125). About the second year of his induction there was a certain legate of his called John Cremensis sent to England. This legate coming with the pope's letters, after he had refreshed himself in the bishops' houses, and amongst the abbots, at length resorted to London, where he assembled the whole clergy together, inquired concerning priests' wives, and made thereupon a statute in the said synod of London after this tenor: "To priests, deacons, subdeacons, and canons, we do utterly inhibit by authority apostolical, all manner of society and conversation with all kind of women, except only their mother, sister, or aunt, or such whereof can rise no suspicion. And whoever shall be found to violate this decree, being convicted thereof, shall sustain thereby the loss of all that he hath by his order." But see how God works against such ungodly proceedings. It happened that the same cardinal was found to be guilty of gross vice, although he had so strictly given out his precepts the day before, to the no little slander and shame (as Matthew Paris writes) of the whole clergy.

After Honorius succeeded Pope Innocent II, (A.D. 1130.) But as it was with his predecessors before him, that at every change of popes there came new troubles, and very commonly when a pope was elected, some other was set up as a rival against him, (there being sometimes two and sometimes three popes together), so likewise it happened with this Innocent; for after he was chosen, the Romans elected another pope, named Anacletus. Between these two popes there was much trouble, and great conflicts.

About the time of these things, (A.D. 1135,) king Henry being in Normandy, as some say, by a fall from his horse, as others say, by a surfeit in eating lampreys, fell sick and died, after he had reigned five-and-thirty years and odd months; leaving for his heirs his daughter the empress Matilda, with her young son Henry, to succeed after him; to whom all the prelates and nobility of the realm were sworn. But contrary to their oath made to her, in the presence of her father, William the archbishop of Canterbury, and the nobles of the realm, crowned Stephen earl of Boulogne, and sister's son to king Henry, upon St. Stephen's day in Christmas week.

KING STEPHEN.

Thus, when king Stephen, contrary to his oath, had taken upon him the crown, he swore before the lords at Oxford, that he would not hold the benefices that were vacant, and that he would remit the danegilt, with many other things, which afterwards he little performed. As he dreaded the coming of the empress, he gave licence to his lords, every one to build upon his own ground strong castles or fortresses. All his reign he was annoyed with wars, especially with David king of the Scots, with whom, however, he at length made peace. But yet the Scottish king would pay him no homage: although Henry, the son to king David, did homage to king Stephen. But he repenting thereof, entered into Northumberland with a great army, and burnt and slew the people in a most cruel manner, neither sparing man, woman, or child. The children they tossed upon spear points, and laying the priests upon the altars, they mangled and cut them all to pieces, after a most terrible manner. But by the valour of the English lords and soldiers, and through the means of Thurstin, archbishop of York, they were met and defeated, a great number of them being slain, and David their king constrained to give his son Henry as hostage for surety of peace. In the mean time, king Stephen was occupied in the South countries, besieging various castles of bishops and other lords, and took them by force, and fortified them with his knights and servants, to withstand the empress, of whose coming he was ever afraid.

About the sixth year of his reign, the empress came into England out of Normandy, and by the aid of Robert, Earl of Gloucester, and Ranulph of Chester, made war upon king Stephen. In the end the king's party was chased, and himself taken prisoner; and sent to Bristol, there to be kept in close confinement.

After this battle the queen, King Stephen's wife, made great entreaty to the empress and her council, to have

the king released and put in to some monastery, but could not obtain it. Also the Londoners made great suit to the empress, to have Saint Edward's laws again, and not the laws of her father, which were more strict and strange to them than the other. When they could not obtain this request of her and her council, the citizens of London, being discontented, would have taken the empress: but she fled privately from London to Oxford: then the Kentish-men and Londoners, taking the king's part, joined battle against the empress; where Robert, earl of Gloucester, and base brother to the empress, was taken, and so by exchange, both the King and the Earl Robert were released from prison. Then Stephen without delay, gathering a strong army, pursued Matilda or Maud, with her partisans, besieging them in the castle of Oxford. In the siege there fell a great snow, and the frost was so hard, that a man heavily-burthened might pass over the water: upon this the empress, arranged with her friends and retinue clothed in white sheets, and issuing out by a postern-gate, went upon the ice over the Thames, and so escaped to Wallingford. After this, the king gained the castle, and when he found not the empress he was much displeased. He pursued the empress and her company so hard, that at last he caused them to fly the realm, which was the sixth year of his reign.

The second year after this, which was the eighth of his reign, there was a parliament at London, to which all the bishops of the realm resorted, and there denounced the king as accursed, and all those with him that did any hurt to the church, or to any minister of it: upon this the king began somewhat to amend his proceedings for a time, but afterwards was as bad as before. The empress being compelled to fly the realm, returned again to Normandy to Geoffrey Plantagenet her husband: who, after he had valiantly won and defended the duchy of Normandy against King Stephen, ended his life, leaving his son Henry to succeed in that dukedom. In the meanwhile, Robert earl of Gloucester, and the earl of Chester, had several conflicts with the king, so that at a battle at Wilton the king was nearly taken, but yet escaped.

Soon after this Henry, duke of Normandy, with a great army entered England, and won the castle of Malmesbury, the tower of London, and afterward the town of Nottingham, the castles of Wallingford, with other holds and castles. Between him and the king many battles were fought. During which time, Eustace the king's son died. Upon this occasion, the king caused Theobald archbishop of Canterbury to mediate with the Duke for peace, which was concluded upon this condition, that Stephen, during his lifetime, should hold the kingdom, and Henry in the meantime be proclaimed heir-apparent in the chief cities throughout the realm. These things being concluded, duke Henry returned to Normandy, and the same year king Stephen, as some say for sorrow, ended his life, after he had reigned nineteen years.

As Theobald succeeded after William archbishop of Canterbury, so in York, after Thurstin, succeeded William, who was called St. William of York, and was poisoned in his chalice by his chaplains.

Matthew Paris writes how Stephen king of England, reserved to himself the right and authority of bestowing spiritual livings, and investing prelates.

At this time also, the Emperor Lotharius began to do the same in recovering again the right and privilege taken away from Henry his predecessor; had not Bernard given him contrary counsel.

At this time came into the church the manner of cursing with bell, book and candle, devised in the Council of London, held by William, bishop of Winchester under Celestine II. who succeeded Innocent II. (A.D. 1143).

KING HENRY THE SECOND.

Henry II. the son of Geoffrey Plantagenet, and the Empress Maud, daughter of King Henry I. began his reign after King Stephen, (A.D. 1154), and continued five-and-thirty years. The first year of his reign he subdued Ireland; and not long after, Thomas Becket was made Lord Chancellor of England. He went into the north, where he subdued William king of Scotland, who at that time held a great part of Northumberland, and joined Scotland to his own kingdom, from the South Ocean to the North Isles of Orcades. Also he put under his dominion the kingdom of Wales. So that by his great manhood and policy, the dominion of England was increased with the addition of Scotland, Ireland, the Orcades, Brittany, Poictou, and Guienne. Also he had in his rule Normandy, Gascoyn, Anjou, and Chinon ; also Auvergne and the city of Tholouse : besides these (by the title of his wife Eleanor, daughter to the Earl of Poictou) he obtained the Mount Pyrame in Spain : so that we read of none of his progenitors, who had so many countries under his dominion.

Now the time requires us to proceed to the history of Frederick I. (called Barbarossa) successor to Conrad in the empire, who marched into Italy, to subdue certain rebels there. The Pope hearing this, came with his clergy to meet him, in hopes to obtain his assistance against his enemies. The emperor, on seeing the bishop, alighted from his horse to receive him, holding the stirrup to the prelate on the left side, when he should have held it on the right, at which the pope shewed himself somewhat annoyed. The emperor smiling, excused himself, that he was never accustomed to hold stirrups ; and as it was done only of good will, and of no duty, it was little matter which side of the horse he held. The next day, to make amends to the bishop, the emperor sent for him, and received him holding the right stirrup, and so all the matter was settled.

After this, as they were come in and sat together, Adrian, the pope, began to declare unto him, how his ancestors before him, such as sought unto the See of Rome for the crown, were wont always to leave behind them some special token or monument of their benevolence for the obtaining thereof. Wherefore he required some benefit to proceed likewise from him to the church of Rome, in restoring again the country of Apulia to the church of Rome ; which if he would do, he for his part would do what appertained to him to perform : meaning in giving him the crown, for at that time the popes had brought the emperors to seek their crown at their hand.

Frederick with his princes perceiving that, unless he would of his own proper costs and charges recover Apulia out of Duke William's hands, he could not secure the crown, promised all that the pope required, and so the next day after was crowned.

This done, the emperor returned into Germany, while Adrian, not liking to be idle, gives forth his excommunication against William, duke of Apulia. Besides, not content with this, he sends also to Emmanuel, Emperor of Constantinople, inciting him to war against William. The duke perceiving this, sends to the pope for peace, promising to restore to him whatever he wished.

But the pope, through the malignant counsel of his cardinals, would grant no peace, thinking to get more by war. The duke, seeing nothing but war, prepared himself with all expedition, and he arrived at Apulia, and there put the Emperor Emmanuel to flight. Then he proceeded to the city of Bonaventure, where the pope with his cardinals were looking for victory. He so besieged and pressed the city, that the pope with his cardinals were glad to treat for peace, which they refused before. The duke granted peace upon certain conditions, viz. that he should not invade such possessions as belonged to Rome, and that the pope should make him king of both Sicilies.

The emperor, Frederick Barbarossa, all this while sitting quietly at home, began to consider with himself how the pope had extorted from the emperors his predecessors, the investiture of prelates ; how he had sickened and taxed all nations by his legates, and also had been the sower of seditions through all his empire ; he began therefore to require of all the bishops of Germany homage, and an oath of allegiance ; commanding also the pope's legates, if they came into Germany, without his sending for, not to be received. Charging moreover all his subjects that none of them should appeal to Rome. Besides this, in his letters he set and prefixed his name before the pope's name : whereupon the pope, being not a little offended, directed his letters to the Emperor Frederick after this tenor, as follows :

"Adrian bishop, servant of the servants of God, to Frederick emperor, health and apostolical benediction. The law of God as it promises to them that honour father and mother long life, so it threatens the sentence of death to them that curse father and mother. We are taught by the word of truth, that every one who exalteth himself shall be brought low. Wherefore, my well-beloved son in the Lord, we marvel not a little at your wisdom, in that you seem not to show that reverence to blessed St. Peter, and to the holy church of Rome, which you ought to shew. For why ? In your letters sent to us, you place your own name before ours, wherein you incur the note of insolency, yea, rather of arrogancy. Why should I here recite to you the oath of your fidelity, which you sware to blessed St. Peter and to us, and how you observe and keep the same ? Seeing you so require homage and allegiance of them that be gods, and all the sons of the high God, and presume to join their holy lands with yours, working contrary to us : seeing you also exclude, not only out of your churches, but also out of your cities, our cardinals, whom we direct as legates from our side : what shall I say then to you ? Amend, therefore I advise you, amend ; for while you go about to obtain of us your consecration and crown, and to get those things you have not, I fear much your honour will lose the things you have. Thus fare ye well."

The Answer of Frederick the Emperor to the Pope.

"Frederick by the grace of God, Roman Emperor, ever Augustus, to Adrian Bishop of the Roman church, and to all such as be willing to cleave to those things which Jesus began to do and to teach, greeting. The law of justice gives to every person accordingly that which is his. Neither do we derogate from our parents, of whom according as we have received this our dignity of the imperial crown and governance ; so in the same kingdom of ours, we do render their due and true honour to them again. And for so much as duty in all sorts of men is to be sought out, let us see first in the time of Constantine (Sylvester then being bishop of Rome) what patrimony or regality he had of his own, due to him that he might claim. Did not Constantine of his liberal benevolence give liberty and restore peace to the church ? And whatever regality of patrimony the see of your papacy has, was it not by the donation of princes given to them ? Revolve and turn over the ancient chronicles, (if either you have not read or neglected what we do affirm) where it is to be found. Of them which are gods by adoption, and hold our lordships of us, why may we not justly require their homage, and their sworn allegiance, when he which is both your master and ours (taking nothing of any king or any man, but giving all goodness to all men) paid toll and tribute for him and Peter unto Cæsar ? giving you example to do the like. And therefore he saith to you and all men, 'Learn of me, for I am meek and lowly,' &c. Wherefore either render again your lordships and patrimonies which ye hold of us ; or else if ye find them so sweet to you, then give that which is due to God unto God ; and that which is due to Cæsar, unto Cæsar. As for your cardinals, we shut them out both of churches and cities, because we see they are not preachers but prowlers ; not makers of peace, but rakers for money ; not pillars and upholders of the church, but the insatiable taxers of the world, and collectors of money and gold. When we shall see them otherwise (such as the church requires them to be) as members and makers of peace, shining forth like lights to the people, assisting poor and weak men's causes in the way of equity, &c., then shall they find us forward and ready to relieve them with salaries, and all things necessary. And where you bring such questions as these to secular men (little conducing to religion) you incur thereby no little note and blemish of your humility, which is keeper of all virtues, and of your meekness. Therefore let your fatherhood beware and take heed, lest in moving such matters as seem to us unseemly for you, ye give thereby offence to such as depend on your word (giving ear to your mouth as it were to an evening shower) : for we cannot but tell you of what we hear ;

K

seeing now the detestable beast of pride creeps into the seat of Peter, providing always as much as we may (by God's grace) for the peace of the church. Fare ye well."

Upon this Adrian the pope directs a bull against Frederick, excommunicating him with public and solemn ceremonies, and then conspiring with William Duke of Apulia, he sought all manner of ways to infest the emperor, and to set all men against him, especially the clergy. The pope understanding the intent of the emperor, and how loth he was to come under subjection to his see, devised by all crafty ways to bring it to pass; and sent some sharp letters to him, and yet not so sharp as proud and disdainful. Wherein the first salutation by his legates was this: "Our most blessed father the pope greeteth you, and the universal company of the cardinals, he as your father, they as your brethren." Meaning that the emperor should understand himself to be subject and underling to the pope, no less than the cardinals were. The emperor with his princes, perceiving, on perusing the letters, at what the pope by his legates was aiming, could not brook such intolerable presumption, whereupon there was much contention between the legates and the princes. "And of whom then," say the legates, "does the emperor receive the empire, if not from the pope?" With this the German princes were so much offended that, had not the emperor stopped them with some difficulty, they would have used violence against the legates. But the emperor not permitting that, commanded the legates away, charging them to make no turn by the way, but to depart straight home. And he, to certify to the whole state of the empire the truth of the matter, directs forth these letters that follow:

The Emperor's Letter sent through all his empire.

"For so much as the providence of God (whereof dependeth all power, both in heaven and earth) hath committed to us, his anointed, this our empire to be governed, and the peace of his churches by our imperial arms to be protected, we cannot but lament and complain to you with great sorrow of heart, seeing such causes of dissension the root and fountain of evils, and the infection of pestiferous corruption thus to rise from the holy church, imprinted with the seal of peace and love of Christ.

"By reason whereof, (except God turn it away) we fear the whole body of the church is like to be polluted, the unity thereof to be broken, and schism and division to be betwixt the spiritual and temporal government. For we being of late at Bisunze, and there intreating busily of matters pertaining as well to the honour of our empire, as to the wealth of the churches, there came ambassadors of the see apostolical, declaring that they brought a legacy to our majesty of great importance, redounding to the no small commodity of our honour and empire.

"Who then, the first day of their coming, being brought to our presence, and received of us (as the manner is) with honour accordingly, audience was given them to hear what they had to say. They forthwith bursting out of the mammon of iniquity, haughty pride, stoutness and arrogancy, out of the execrable presumption of their swelling heart, delivered their message with letter apostolical, whereof the tenor was this: 'That we should always have before our eyes, how that our sovereign lord the pope gave us the imperial crown, and that it doth not repent him, if so be we have received greater benefits at his hand.' And this was the effect of that so sweet and fatherly legation, which should nourish peace both of the church and of the empire, to unite them fast together in the band of love.

"And at the hearing of this so false, untrue, and most vain-glorious presumption of so proud a message, not only the emperor's majesty conceived indignation, but, also all the princes (there present) were moved with such anger and rage thereat, that if our presence and request had not stayed them, they would not have held their hands from these wicked priests, or else

would have proceeded with sentence of death against them.

"Furthermore, because a great number of other letters (partly written already, partly with seals ready signed, for letters to be written according as they should think good to the churches of Germany) were found about them, whereby to work their conceived intent of iniquity here in our churches, to spoil the altars, to carry away the jewels of the church, and to tear off the limbs and plates of golden crosses, &c. To the intent their avaricious meaning should have no further power to reign, we gave them commandment to depart the same way they came. And now seeing our reign and empire stands upon the election of princes from God alone, who in the passion of his Son subdued the world to be governed with two swords; and again, seeing Peter the apostle hath so instructed the world with this doctrine, 'Fear God, honour your king;' therefore, whoso sayeth that we have and possess our imperial kingdom by the benefit of the lord pope, is contrary both to the ordinance of God, and to the doctrine of Peter, and also shall be reproved for a liar.

"Therefore as our endeavour has been heretofore to help and to deliver the servile captivity of churches out of the hand and from the yoke of such Egyptians, and to maintain the right of their liberties and dignities, we desire you all with your compassion to lament with us this slanderous ignominy, cast upon us and our kingdom, trusting that your faithful good will, which has been ever trusty to the honour of this empire (never yet blemished from the first beginning of this city, and of religion) will provide that it shall have no hurt through the strange novelty and presumptuous pride of such. Which thing rather than it should come to pass, know you this for certain; I had rather incur the danger of death, than suffer such confusion to happen in our days."

This letter of the emperor fretted the pope not a little, who wrote again to the bishops of Germany, accusing the emperor, and requiring them to work against him what they could.

This pope continued not very long, the space only of four years and odd months.

Although this Adrian was bad enough, yet the next was much worse. Alexander III. was not elected alone, for the emperor with nine cardinals set up another pope, named Victor IV. Between these two popes rose a great discord that long continued. So that the emperor, being required to take up the matter, sent for them both to appear before him, that in hearing them both he might judge their cause better. Victor came, but Alexander refused to appear. Whereupon the emperor, with a full consent of his bishops and clergy ratified the election of Victor. Alexander flying into France accursed them both, sending his letters through all Christendom against them, as men to be avoided and cast out of all christian company. Also at Rome, by flattery and money he got on his side the greatest part of the city. After this, Alexander coming from France to Sicily, and from thence to Rome, was there received with much favour, through the help of Philip the French king.

The emperor, hearing of this, marched with great force into Italy. Coming at length to Rome, he required the citizens that the cause betwixt the two popes might be decided, and that he who had the best right might be taken. Alexander mistrusting his part, and doubting the will of the citizens, fled to Venice.

The emperor sent his son Otho, with men and ships against Venice, charging him not to attempt any thing before his coming. The young man more hardy than circumspect, joined battle with the Venetians, was overcome, and taken prisoner.

The father, to help the captivity and misery of his son, was compelled to submit himself to the pope, and to treat for peace. So the emperor coming to Venice (at St. Mark's church, where the bishop was, there to get his absolution) was obliged to kneel down at the pope's feet.

The proud pope, setting his foot upon the emperor's neck, said this verse of the psalm, "Thou shalt tread upon the adder and the serpent, the lion and the dragon shalt thou tread under thy feet." The emperor answered, "Not to thee but to Peter." The pope again, "Both to me and to Peter." The emperor, fearing to give any occasion for further quarrelling, held his peace, and so was absolved, and peace made between them. The conditions were: first, that he should receive Alexander as the true pope, and secondly, that he should restore to the church of Rome all that he had taken away. And thus the emperor, obtaining his son's release, departed.

Here, as I noted in various writers a great diversity and variety concerning this matter, of whom some say that the emperor encamped in Palestine before he came to Venice, some say after, so I marvel to see in Volateran (so great a favourer of the pope) such a contradiction, who in his two-and-twentieth book saith, that Otho the emperor's son was taken in this conflict, which was the cause of the peace between his father and the pope. And in his three-and-twentieth book again saith, that the emperor himself was taken prisoner in the same battle; and so afterwards (peace concluded) took his journey to Asia and Palestine. This pope, in the time of his papacy (which continued one and twenty years) kept sundry councils both in Turin and at Lateran, where he confirmed the wicked proceedings of Hildebrand, and his other predecessors; as to bind all orders of the clergy to the vow of celibacy.

Now, as Thomas Becket lived in the time of this Pope Alexander, let us narrate somewhat of him, so far as shall seem worthy of knowing: to the end that the truth being sifted from all flattery and lies of such popish writers as write his history, men may the better judge both of him, and his cause.

THE LIFE AND HISTORY OF THOMAS BECKET, ARCH-BISHOP OF CANTERBURY.

If it be the cause that makes a martyr, I do not see why we should esteem Thomas Becket a martyr, more than any other whom the prince's sword punishes for their crimes. To die for the church I grant is a glorious matter. But the church (as it is a spiritual and not a temporal church) stands upon a heavenly foundation, as upon faith, religion, true doctrine, sincere discipline, obedience to God's commandments; and not upon things pertaining to this world, as possessions, liberties, exemptions, privileges, dignities, patrimonies, and superiorities. If these be given to the church, I pray God church-men may use them well; but if they be not given, the church cannot claim them; or if they be taken away, such a measure is in the prince's power. To contend with princes about it does not in my mind make a martyr, but rather a rebel. Therefore as I suppose Thomas Becket to be far from the title of a martyr, yet would I have wished the law rather to have found out his fault, than the swords of men to have smitten him, without command of either prince, or of the law to do so. It would have been the better way, for the laws to have executed their justice upon him; and certainly it had been the safest way for the king, and also thereby his death had been without all suspicion of martyrdom, neither had there been that shrining and sainting of him that followed. If the emperors had dealt according to the law with the popes who contended against them, when they had taken them prisoners, that is, if they had used the law of the sword against them, and chopped off the heads of one or two, according to their traitorous rebellions, they had broken the neck of much of that disturbance, which long after troubled the church. But, because the emperors having the sword, and the truth on their side, would not use their sword; but standing in awe of the pope's vain curse, and reverencing his seat for St. Peter's sake, durst not lay hands upon him, though he were never so abominable and traitorous a malefactor; the popes, perceiving that, took so much upon them, not as the scripture would give, but as the superstitious fear of emperors and kings would suffer them to take.

Now to the history, if that be true which is set forth by those four, who took upon them to narrate the life of Thomas Becket, it appears, that he was a man of a stout, severe and inflexible temper. Whatever opinion he had once conceived, from that he would in nowise be removed, or very hardly. Threatenings and flattering were to him both alike; following no man's counsel so much as his own. He had more natural than cultivated talents, although he was somewhat skilled in the civil law; he had a good memory, and was well trained in courtly and worldly matters. Besides this, he was of a chaste and strict life, if the histories be true; although in the first part of his life (being yet archdeacon of Canterbury, and after lord chancellor) he was very civil, courtly, pleasant, much given both to hunting and hawking, according to the guise of the court; and he was highly favoured by his prince, who not only had thus promoted him, but also had committed his son and heir to his instruction and government. But in this his first beginning he was not so well beloved, but that afterward he was much hated, both by the king, and also by the greater part of his subjects, save only certain monks and priests, and such as were persuaded by them, who magnified him not a little for upholding the liberties of the church; that is, the licentious life and excesses of church-men. He was full of devotion, but without any true religion; zealous, but without knowledge. And therefore as he was stiff and stubborn of nature, so (a blind conscience being joined with all) it turned to plain rebellion. So superstitious was he to the obedience of the pope, that he forgot his obedience to his natural and most beneficent king: and in maintaining so contentiously the constitutions and decrees of men, he neglected the commandments of God. But here he is most of all to be reprehended, that he not only (contrary to the king's knowledge) sought to convey himself out of the realm, when holding so high place and calling, but also set matter of discord between the pope and his king, and also between the French king and him, contrary to all propriety, good order, natural subjection, and true christianity. Upon which followed no little disquiet to the king, and damage to the realm.

His first preferment was to the church of Branfield, which he had by the gift of St. Alban. After that, he entered into the service of the archbishop of Canterbury, by whom he was then preferred to be his archdeacon; in process of time the king made him lord chancellor, and he then left playing the archdeacon, and began to play the chancellor. He fashioned his proceedings like the king's both in weighty matters and trifles; he would hunt with him, and watched the time when the king dined and slept. He began to love the merry jestings of the court, to delight himself with the great applause of men, and praise of the people. And that I may pass over his household-stuff, he had his bridle of silver, and the bosses of his bridle were worth a great treasure. At his table and in other expenses he surpassed any earl. He acted also the good soldier under the king in Gascony, and both won and kept towns: in the four-and-fortieth year of his age, he was made priest, and the next day, consecrated bishop.

As touching the priesthood of this man, I find histories to vary in themselves: for if he were beneficed, and chaplain to Theobald, and afterwards archdeacon (as some say) it is not likely, but that he was priest before, and not (as most English histories say) made priest in one day, and archbishop the next.

The chief cause of the variance that sprung up between the king and this Thomas Becket, was this, a canon having reviled the king's justices, the king was offended, the archbishop, to pacify the king, commanded the canon to be whipped and deprived of his benefices for certain years. But the king was not content with this gentle punishment, because it rather increased their boldness, and therefore he called the archbishop, bishops, and all the clergy, to assemble at Westminster. When they were assembled, the king commanded that such wicked clerks should have no privilege of their clergy, but be delivered to the jailors; and this he said their own canons and laws had decreed. The archbishop, counselling with his bishops and learned men, desired heartily the king's gentleness, that under Christ our new king, and under the new law of Christ he would bring in no new kind of punishment into this realm against the old decrees of the holy

K 2

fathers; and he frequently said, "That he neither ought nor could suffer it." The king being angered at this, alleges the old laws and customs of his grandfather, observed and agreed upon by archbishops, bishops, prelates, and other privileged persons, inquiring likewise of the archbishop whether he would agree to the same. To which laws and customs Thomas partly granted, and partly would not grant. The copy of the which said laws are contained in the number of eight-and-twenty or nine-and-twenty, whereof I thought here to recite some not unworthy to be known.

The Copy of the old Laws and Customs whereunto Thomas Becket did agree.

" 1. That no order should be given to husbandmen's children and bondmen's children, without the assent or testimonial of the lords of the country where they were born and brought up: and if their sons become clerks, they shall not receive the order of priesthood without licence of their lords.

" 2. That if a man of holy church hold any lay fee in his hand, he shall do therefore the king the service that belongeth thereto, as upon juries, assize of lands and judgments, saving only at execution doing of death.

" 3. That if any man were the king's traitor, and had taken to the church, it should be lawful for the king and his officers to take him out.

" 4. That if any felon's goods were brought to holy church, there should none such keep there; for every felon's goods be the king's.

" 5. That no land should be given to the church, or to any house of religion, without the king's licence."

These Articles following, Thomas agreed not unto.

" 1. If there were any striving for church-goods, between a clerk and a layman, the plea should be done in the king's court.

" 2. That neither bishop nor clerk should go out of the land without the king's licence, and then he should swear that he would procure no hurt against the king, nor any of his.

" 3. If any man were denounced accursed, and were come again to amendment, the king would not that he should be sworn, but only find sureties to stand to that, that holy church should award.

" 4. That no man, that held of the king in chief, or in service, should be accursed without the king's licence.

" 5. That all the bishoprics and abbeys that were vacant, should be in the king's hands, until such time that he should choose a prelate thereto, and he should be chosen out of the king's chapels; and first before he were confirmed, he should do his homage to the king.

" 6. If any plea were brought to the consistory, they should appeal from thence to the archdeacon, and from thence to the bishop's court, and from the bishop's court to the archbishop's, and from thence to the king, and no further. So that in conclusion, the complaints of holy church must come before the king, and not the pope.

" 7. That debts, that were owing through troth plight, should not be pleaded in spiritual, but in temporal courts.

" 8. That the Peter-pence, which were gathered to the pope, should be taken to the king.

" 9. If any clerk were taken for felony and so proved, he should be first degraded, and then through judgment be hanged, or if he were a traitor, be drawn."

Other Laws and Constitutions made at Clarendon in Normandy, and sent to England, whereunto Becket and the Pope would not agree, he being then fled out of the realm.

" 1. If any person shall be found to bring from the pope, or from the archbishop of Canterbury, any writing containing any interdict or curse against the realm of England, the same man to be apprehended without delay for a traitor, and execution to be done upon the same.

" 2. That no monk nor any clerk shall be permitted to pass over into England without a passport from the king or his justices: who so doth the contrary, to be attached and imprisoned.

" 3. No man to be so bold as to appeal to the pope, or to the archbishop of Canterbury out of England.

" 4. That no decree or commandment, proceeding from the authority of the pope, or the bishop of Canterbury, be received into England, under pain of taking and imprisoning.

" 5. In general, to forbid any man to carry over any commandment or precept, either of clerk or layman, to the pope, or to the archbishop of Canterbury, under pain of imprisonment.

" 6. If any bishop, clerk, abbot, or layman shall do contrary to this inhibition, or will keep the sentence of interdicting, the same to be thrust out of the land, with all their kindred, and to leave all their goods behind them.

" 7. All the possessions, goods, and chattels of such as favour the pope or the archbishop of Canterbury, to be seized and confiscate for the king.

" 8. All such of the clergy as be out of the realm, and derive their rents and profits out of the land, to be summoned and warned home through every shire within three months to repair home, or else their rents and goods to return to the king.

" 9. That St. Peter's-pence should be no more paid to the apostolical see, but to be reserved diligently in the king's coffers, and there to be at his commandment.

" 10. That the bishops of Salisbury and Norwich be at the king's mercy, and be summoned by the sheriff, and beadles, that they before the king's justices do right to the king and his justices, because (contrary to the statutes of Clarendon) by commandment they interdicted the land of Earl Hugh, and published the same in their diocese without licence of the king's justices."

By these and such other laws and decrees it may appear, that the abolishing of the pope's authority is no new thing in the realm of England. This only difference is, that the pope being driven out then, could not be kept out so long as he is now. The cause is, that the time was not yet come that antichrist should be so fully revealed; nor was his wickedness then so fully ripe as in our time. We will now return to

The Communication and Controversy between the King and Thomas Becket, with his Clergy.

The king assembling his nobles and clergy, required the punishment of some delinquent clergymen; but Thomas Becket not assenting, the king demanded whether he would consent, that the customs set forth in the realm (meaning the first part of those decrees above specified) should be observed. To which the archbishop, consulting together with his brethren, answered, That he was content, adding this, *Salvo ordine suo;* that is, *Saving his order.* And in like manner all the other bishops answered with the same addition, *Salvo ordine suo.* Hilarius, bishop of Chichester, alone agreed to observe them *bona fide.* The king was greatly offended at this exception or saving clause; and turning to the archbishop and prelates, said, " That he was not well content with that clause of theirs, *Salvo ordine suo,* which was captious and deceitful, having some venom lurking under it; and therefore required an absolute agreement, without any exception, to the king's ordinances." To this the archbishop answered again, " That they had sworn to him their fidelity, both life, body, and earthly honour, *Salvo ordine suo;* and that in the same earthly honour also those ordinances were comprehended, and to the observing of them they would bind themselves after no other form, but as they had sworn before." The king with this was very angry, and all his nobility not a little. As for the other bishops, there was no doubt but they would easily have changed their minds, had not the boldness of the archbishop made them more constant than otherwise they would have been. The day being well spent, the king departed in great anger, giving no salutation to the bishops. The day following, the king took from the archbishop all the honours and lordships he had given him before in the time that he was chancellor; which shewed the great displeasure of the king against him and the clergy. Not long after this, the king removing from London (unknown to the bishops) sailed over to Normandy, whither the bishop of London resorted to crave the king's favour, and gave him counsel how to gain over some of the other bishops. And the greater part of the bishops were by this means reconciled again to the king; the archbishop, with a few others, only remained still in their obstinacy. The king, to try every means, when he saw no fears nor threats could change him, tried him with gentleness; but it would not serve. Many of the nobles laboured between them to influence Becket, but it would not be. The archbishop of York, with other bishops and abbots, especially the bishop of Chester, did the same. Besides this, his own household daily called upon him, but no one could persuade him. At length learning what danger might happen not only to himself, but to the other clergy from the king's displeasure, and considering the love and kindness of the king towards him in time past, he was content to give way to the king's wishes, and came to Oxford to him, and reconciled himself. The king being somewhat softened by this, received him with a more cheerful countenance, but yet not so familiarly as before, saying, " That he would have his ordinances and proceedings after the prescribed form, confirmed in the public audience and open sight of all his bishops and all his nobles." After this, the king at Clarendon called there all his peers and prelates before him, requiring to have all performed, which they had promised, in consenting to the observing of his grandfather's ordinances and proceedings. The archbishop now drew back from his promise, but at last he was induced to assent. First came to him the bishops of Salisbury and of Norwich, weeping and lamenting to the archbishop, desiring him to have some compassion of them, and to cease this opposition to the king, lest it should exasperate the king's displeasure, and cause himself to be imprisoned, and the whole clergy endangered. Besides these two bishops, there went to him two noble peers of the realm, influencing him to relent and yield to the king's wishes : or if not, that they should be forced to use such violence, as would not be consistent with the king's fame, and much less with his quietness; but yet the obstinacy of the man would not give over. After this came to him two rulers of the temple, called templars, with their company, lamenting and bewailing the great danger which they declared was hanging over his head: yet neither with their tears, nor with their kneelings would he be persuaded. At length came the last message from the king, signifying with express words, and also with tears, what he might expect, if he would not give over.

By this message, either terrified or persuaded, he at last submitted. The king immediately assembling the states, the archbishop, before all others, promises the king obedience and submission, and that *cum bona fide,* leaving out his former addition, *Salvo ordine:* instead of which he promised *in verbo veritatis,* to observe and keep the king's customs, and swear to the same. After him the other bishops took the same oath; upon which the king commanded certain instruments obligatory to be drawn, of which the king should have one, the archbishop of Canterbury another, the archbishop of York the third, requiring the latter prelate also to set to his hand and seal. He, though he was ready to do so, yet desired a little delay that he (being but newly come to his bishopric) might better peruse the customs and ordinances of the king. This request, as it seemed but reasonable, was easily granted.

Alanus, one of the four writers of the life of this Thomas Becket, records, that the archbishop in his journey to Winchester, began greatly to repent of what he had done through the instigation chiefly of his cross-bearer, who earnestly expostulated with him for yielding to the king's request, against the privilege and liberties of the church, polluting not only his fame and conscience, but also giving a pernicious example to those that should come after. To make the matter short, the archbishop was touched with such repentance, that keeping himself from all company, lamenting with tears, with fasting, and afflicting himself with much penance, he suspended himself from all Divine service, and would not be comforted, till he was absolved by the pope, who, compassionating the tears of his dear chicken, directed to him letters by the same messenger which Thomas had sent to him. In which letters he not only absolved him, but also with words of great consolation encouraged him to be determined in the affair which he took in hand. The copy of which consolatory letter here follows :—

" Alexander bishop, &c. Your brotherhood is not ignorant that it has been advertised us, how that upon the occasion of a certain transgression or excess of yours, you have determined to cease henceforth from saying of mass, and to abstain from the consecration of the body and blood of the Lord; which determination, how dangerous it is (especially in such a personage) and also what inconvenience may rise from it, I wish you advisedly to consider, and discreetly to ponder. Your wisdom ought not to forget what difference there is between those who advisedly and willingly offend, and those who through ignorance and for necessity sake offend. For, as you read, so much the greater is wilful sin, as the same not being voluntary is a lesser sin. Therefore if you remember yourself to have done any thing that your own conscience accuses you of, whatever it be, we counsel you (as a prudent and wise prelate) to acknowlege it. Which done, the merciful and pitiful God, who has more respect to the heart of the doer than to the thing done, will remit and forgive you the same according to his accustomed great mercy. And we, trusting in the merits of the blessed apostles St. Peter and St. Paul, do absolve you from the offence committed, and by the authority apostolical we release you to your fraternity, counselling you and commanding you, that henceforth you abstain not (for this cause) from the celebration of the mass."

This letter, with others of the same kind, the pope then wrote to him, animating and comforting him in this quarrel, which so nearly pertained to the pope's profit. By which, Becket took no small courage and consolation. In the meantime, the king hearing how he now refused to set his seal to those sanctions which he yielded to before, felt no small displeasure against him, so that threatening him, he began to call him to account, and to burthen him with payments, that all men could perceive that the king was against him. The archbishop thought to escape out of the realm, and went in the night (with two or three stealing with him out of his house), to take shipping privately. Now among other of the king's ordinances and laws, this was one, " That none of the prelacy or nobility, without the king's licence, or of his justices, should depart out of the realm. So Becket twice attempted to take shipping to flee to the see of Rome; but the weather not being favourable, he was driven home again, and for that time frustrated in his purpose. After his flight began to be known, the king's officers came to Canterbury to seize upon his goods in the king's behalf. But the night before their coming, Becket had returned, and was found at home, so they did not proceed in their purpose.

Upon this, the archbishop (understanding the king's displeasure against him, and that the seas would not serve him), made haste to the court, which was then at Woodstock. The king received him, but not so familiarly as he used, taunting him jestingly and merrily, as though one realm were not large enough to hold them both. Becket, although he was permitted to go and come at his pleasure to the court, he could not obtain the favour that he wanted. The archbishop of York laboured to make peace between them; but the king would not be reconciled unless Becket would subscribe to his laws. The king, considering his regal authority, thought it too much that any subject should stand against him. And the archbishop, emboldened by the authority of the pope, thought himself strong enough against the king and all his realm. So that the archbishop would not yield, but by virtue of his apostolical authority gave censure upon these laws and constitutions of the king, condemning some, and approving others. Besides this, there came also Rotrodus archbishop of Rothomage (sent from the pope) to make peace between the king and Canterbury: to which the king was content, provided the pope would agree to ratify his ordinances. But when that could not be obtained at the pope's hands, then the king being stopped by Becket's apostolic legacy, (being legatus a latere) sent to the pope, to obtain of him, that the same authority of the apostolic legacy might be conferred on the archbishop of York: but the pope refused. However, the pope was willing that the king himself should be legate; at which the king felt great indignation (as Hoveden writes), so that he sent back the pope's letters.

The pope being perplexed, began after the old practice of popish prelacy, to play with both hands: privily conspiring with the one, and openly dissembling with the other. First he granted to the king's ambassadors their request, to have the legate removed, and to place the archbishop of York in that office; and then to protect the cause of Thomas Becket. He adds a promise, that Becket should receive no harm or damage thereby. Thus the pope craftily managing the matter between them both, writes to the king openly, and secretly directs another letter to Becket: the contents whereof here follow.

Alexander the pope, to Thomas Archbishop of Canterbury.

" Although we, condescending to the king's request, have granted the gift of our legacy after his mind from you: yet let not your mind thereby be discomforted, nor brought into sighs of despair. For before we had granted that, or gave our consent thereunto, the king's ambassadors firmly promised in the word of truth (ready also to be sworn upon the same, if I would so have required) that their letters also which he had obtained, should not be delivered to the archbishop of York without our knowledge and consent therein. This is certain, and so persuade yourself boldly without any scruple, doubt or mistrust. that it was never my mind or purpose, nor ever shall be (God willing) to subdue you or your church under the obedience of any person, to be subject to any, save only to the bishop of Rome. And therefore we warn you and charge you, that if you shall perceive the king to deliver these foresaid letters, which we trust he will not attempt without our knowledge to do; forthwith by some trusty messengers or by your letters you will give us knowledge thereof: whereby we may provide upon the same both for your person, your church, and also your city committed to you, to be clearly exempt by our authority apostolical, from all power and jurisdiction of any legacy."

The king, after he had received the letters from the pope, began to put forth more strength to his purposed proceedings, against the archbishop, beginning with inferiors of the clergy, such as were offenders against his laws: as felons, robbers, quarrellers, breakers of peace, and especially such as had committed homicide and murders, whereof more than a hundred at that time were proved upon the clergy, (Guliel. Neuburgensis, de gestis Anglorum, lib. 2. cap 16.) urging and constraining them to be arraigned after the order of the temporal law, and justice to be administered to them according to their deserts: as, first, to be deprived, and so be committed to the secular hands. This seemed to Becket to derogate from the liberties of holy church, that the secular power should pass in criminal causes, or sit in judgment against any ecclesiastical person. This law of exemption, the clergy had forged out of Anacletus, and Euaristus, by whose falsely alleged and pretended authority, they have deduced this constitution from the apostles, giving immunity to all ecclesiastical persons to be free from secular jurisdiction! Becket, therefore, like a valiant champion (fighting for his liberties, and having

the pope on his side) would not permit his clerks to be examined and deprived for their crimes, unless before ecclesiastical judges, and no secular judge to proceed against them: but that after their deprivation, if they should incur the like offence again, then the temporal judge might proceed against them. This obstinate and stubborn rebellion of the archbishop stirred up much anger and vexation in the king, and not only in him but also in the nobles and the greater part of the bishops, so that he was almost alone a wonder to all the realm.

The king's wrath daily increasing more and more against him, he caused him to be cited to appear by a certain day at the town of Northampton, there to make answer to such things as should be laid to his charge. So when the day was come (all the peers and nobles, with the prelates of the realm upon the king's proclamation being assembled in the castle of Northampton) great fault was found with the archbishop for that he (though personally cited to appear) did not come himself, but sent another in his stead. The cause why he came not, Hoveden assigns to be this: the king had placed his horse and horse-men in the archbishop's lodging; he being offended at this, sent word that he would not appear, unless his lodging were cleared of the king's horsemen, &c. Upon which, by the public sentence as well of all the nobles, as of the bishops, all his moveables were adjudged to be confiscated for the king, unless the king's clemency would remit the penalty.

The next day the king laid an action against him in behalf of his marshal, for certain injuries done to him, and required of the archbishop the repaying of certain money, lent to him when chancellor, amounting to five hundred marks. This money the archbishop denied not that he had received from the king, but he said it was by way and title of a gift, though he could bring no proof thereof. The king required him to give security for the payment: the archbishop was so called upon, that either he should be accountable to the king for the money; or else he should incur present danger, the king being so bent against him. And being brought to such a strait, and destitute of his own suffragans, he could not have escaped, had not five persons of their own accord stepped in, being bound for him, every man for one hundred marks each. And this was concluded upon the second day.

The morrow after, which was the third day of the council, as the archbishop was sitting below in a conclave with his fellow bishops about him, consulting together, the doors being fast locked on them, as the king had commanded, it was propounded to him in the behalf of the king, that he had divers bishopricks, and abbaricks in his hand which were vacant, with the fruits and revenues thereof due to the king for certain years, of which he had rendered as yet no account to the king: wherefore it was demanded of him to bring in a full and clear reckoning of the same.

Thus, while the bishops and prelates were in council, advising and deliberating what was to be done, at length it came to voices, every man to say his mind, and to give sentence what was the best course for their archbishop to take. First began Henry bishop of Winchester, who took part with Becket so much as he durst for fear of the king, he said, " He remembered that the archbishop, first being archdeacon, and then lord chancellor, when he was promoted to the church of Canterbury, was discharged from all bonds and reckonings of the temporal court, as all the other bishops could not but remember and witness."

Next spake Gilbert, bishop of London, exhorting the archbishop, that he should call to mind from whence the king took him, and set him up; what, and how great things he had done for him; also that he should consider the dangers and perils of the time, and what ruin he might bring upon the whole church (and upon them all there present) if he resisted the king's mind in the things he required. And if it were to render up his archbishoprick, although it were ten times better than it is, yet he should not hesitate in the matter. To this the archbishop answering, " Well, well," said he, " I perceive well enough, my Lord, whither you tend." Then spake Winchester, " This form of counsel," saith he, " seems to me very pernicious to the catholic church, tending to our subversion, and to the confusion of us all. For if our archbishop and primate of all England do lean to this example, that every bishop should give over his authority and the charge of the flock committed to him, at the command and threat of the prince, to what state shall the church be brought, but that all shall be confounded at his pleasure and arbitrament, and nothing shall remain certain by any order of law, and as the priest is, so shall the people be?"

Hilary, the bishop of Chichester replies to this saying, "If it were not that the urgency and the great danger of the times did otherwise require and force us, I would think this counsel here given were good to be followed. But now seeing the authority of our canon fails, and cannot serve us, I judge it not best to go so strictly to work, but so to moderate our proceedings, that dispensation with sufferance may win that which severe correction may destroy. Wherefore my counsel and reason is, to give place to the king's purpose for a time, lest by over hasty proceeding, we exceed so far, that both it may redound to our shame, and also we cannot rid ourselves out again when we would."

Much to the same end spake Robert the bishop of Lincoln, "Seeing," saith he, "it is manifest that the life and blood of this man is sought, one of these two must needs be chosen; that either he must part with his archbishoprick, or else with his life. Now what profit he shall take in this matter of his bishoprick, his life being lost, I do not greatly see."

Next followed Bartholomew bishop of Exeter with his advice, who inclining his council to the state of the time, affirmed how the days were evil and perilous; and if they could escape the violence of that raging tempest by bearing and relenting, it were not to be refused. But that, he said, could not be, except strictness should give place to moderation; and the state of the times required no less, especially as that persecution was not general, but personal and particular; and he thought it more holy and convenient, for one head to run into some danger, than the whole of the church of England be exposed to inevitable inconvenience.

The answer of Roger bishop of Worcester advised neither the one, nor the other: he said that he would give answer on neither part; "for if I should say that the pastoral function and cure of souls ought to be relinquished at the king's will or threatening, then my mouth shall speak against my conscience to the condemnation of my own head. And if I shall give again contrary counsel to resist the king's sentence, they are here who will hear it, and report it to his grace, and so I shall be in danger to be thrust out of the synagogue, and accounted amongst the public rebels to be condemned with them: wherefore neither do I say this, nor counsel that."

Against these voices and censures of the bishops, Becket the archbishop replies, expostulating and checking them with rebukeful words, "I perceive (said he) and understand you go about to maintain and cherish but your own cowardliness under the colourable shadow of sufferance, and under pretence of dissembling softness to choak the liberty of Christ's church. Who hath thus bewitched you, O insatiable bishops? What mean ye? Why do ye so, under the impudent title of forbearing, bear a double heart, and cloak your manifest iniquity? What call ye this bearing with the times, to the detriment of the church of Christ? Let terms serve the matter. Why pervert you that which is good with untrue terms? For that ye say we must bear with the malice of time, I grant with you: but yet we must not heap sin to sin. Is not God able to help the state and condition of his church, without the sinful dissimulation of the teachers of the church? Certainly God is disposed to try you. And tell me when should the governors of the church put themselves to dangers for the church, in time of tranquillity, or in time of distress? And now then (the church lying in so great distress and vexation) why should not the good pastor put himself into peril for it? For neither do I think it a greater act or merit for the ancient bishops of the old time, to lay the foundation of the church then with their blood, than now for us to shed our blood for the liberties of the same. And to tell you plain, I think it not safe for you to swerve from an example which you have received of your holy elders."

On the next day following, because it was Sunday, nothing was done. So the day after, the archbishop was cited to appear before the King. But the night before he was taken with a disease, so he kept his bed that day, and was not able to rise. The morrow after, some that were about him, fearing that some danger would happen to him, gave him counsel in the morning to have a mass in honour of the holy martyr St. Stephen, to keep him from the hands of the enemies that day. When the morrow was come (being Tuesday) there came to him the bishops and prelates, counselling and persuading him covertly by insinuation, (for they durst not openly) that he would submit himself with all his goods (as also his archbishoprick) to the will of the king, if peradventure his indignation by that means might assuage. Adding, that unless he would do so, perjury would be laid against him: for that he being under the oath of fidelity to keep the king's laws and ordinances, would not now observe them. To this Becket the archbishop answered again, "Brethren, ye see and perceive well how the world is set against me, and how the enemy rises and seeks my confusion. And although these things are dolorous and lamentable, yet the thing that grieves me most of all, is this, the sons of mine own mother are pricks and thorns against me. And although I do hold my peace, yet the posterity will know and report how cowardly you have turned your backs, and have left your archbishop and metropolitan alone in his conflict, and how you have sat in judgment against me (although guiltless of crime) now two days together, and not only in the civil and spiritual court, but also in the temporal court, are ready to do the same. But in general, this I charge and command (on the virtue of pure obedience, and in peril of your order) that ye be present personally in judgment against me. And that ye shall not fail so to do, I here appeal to our mother (the refuge of all such as be oppressed) the church of Rome: and if any secular men shall lay hands upon me (as it is rumoured they will) I straitly enjoin and charge you in the same virtue of obedience, that you exercise your censure ecclesiastical upon them, as it becomes you to do for a father and an archbishop. And this I do you to understand, that though the world rage, and the enemy be fierce and the body trembles (for the flesh is weak), yet God so favouring me, I will neither cowardly shrink, nor yet vilely forsake my flock committed to my charge," &c.

But the bishop of London, contrary to this commandment of the archbishop, did forthwith appeal from him. And thus the bishops departed from him to the Court, save only two, Henry of Winchester, and Joceline of Salisbury, who returned with him secretly to his chamber, and comforted him. This done, the archbishop, (who yesterday was so sore sick that he could not stir out of his bed) now addresses him to his mass of St. Stephen with all solemnity, as though it had been an high festival day, with his metropolitan pall, which was not used but upon the holy days, &c.

The mass being ended, the archbishop (putting off his pall, his mitre, and other robes) proceeded to the king's court. But yet not trusting to the strength of his mass, to make the matter more sure, he takes also the sacrament privately about him, thinking himself sufficiently defended thereby against all evils. In going to the king's chamber (there to wait the king's coming) as he entered the door, he takes from Alexander his crozier, the cross, with the cross-staff, in the sight of all that stood by, and carries it in himself, the other bishops following him, and saying he did otherwise than became him. Amongst others, Robert bishop of Hereford offered himself to bear his cross, rather than he should so do, for that it was not comely; but the archbishop would not suffer him. Then said the bishop of London to him, "If the king shall see you come armed into his chamber, perchance he will draw out his sword against you, which is stronger than yours, and then what shall this profit you?" The archbishop answered again, "If the king's sword do cut carnally, yet my sword cuts spiritually and strikes down to hell. But you, my lord, as you have played the fool in this matter, so you will not yet leave off your folly for any thing I can see;" and so he came into the chamber. The king hearing of his coming, and of his manner, tarried not long. First, the crier called the prelates and all the lords of the temporalty together. That being done (and every one placed in his seat according to his degree) the king begins with a great complaint against the archbishop for his manner of entering into the court, "not as a subject into a king's court, but as a traitor, shewing himself in such sort as has not been seen before in any christian king's court, professing christian faith." To this all there present gave witness with the king, affirming him always to be a vain and proud man, and that the shame of his act did not only redound against the prince himself, but also against his whole realm. They said, too, that this had so happened to the king, because that he had done so much for such a man, advancing him so highly. And so all together with one cry, called him traitor on every side, as one that refused to give earthly honour to the king, in keeping (as he had sworn) his laws and ordinances, at whose hands also he had received such honour and great perferments : and therefore he was well worthy (said they) to be handled like a perjured traitor and rebel. Whereupon there was great doubt and fear what would befal him. The archbishop of York, coming down to his men, said he could not abide to see what the archbishop of Canterbury was like to suffer. Likewise, the tipstaves, and other ministers of the assembly, coming down with an outcry against him, crossed themselves at seeing his haughty stubbornness, and the business that was about him. Some there were of his disciples sitting at his feet, comforting him softly, and bidding him to lay his curse upon them. Others bidding him not to curse, but to pray and forgive them ; and if he lost his life in the quarrel of the church and the liberty thereof, he should be happy. In the meantime comes Bartholomew bishop of Exeter, desiring him to have regard and compassion of himself, and also of them, or else they were all likely to suffer ; for (said he) "there comes out a precept from the king that he shall be taken, and suffer for an open rebel, whoever takes your part. It is said, too, that Joceline bishop of Salisbury, and William bishop of Norwich, are to be brought to the place of execution, for their resisting and making intercession for the bishop of Canterbury." When he had thus said, the archbishop, looking upon the said bishop of Exeter, "Avoid hence from me," saith he, "thou understandest not, neither dost savour those things that be of God."

The bishops and prelates then going aside by themselves from the other nobles, the king permitting them to do so, took council together what was to be done. Here the matter stood in a doubtful perplexity, for they must either incur the dangerous indignation of the king, or else with the nobles they must proceed in condemnation against the archbishop for resisting the king's sanctions. In this strict necessity they at length agreed upon this, that they with common assent should cite the archbishop to the see of Rome upon perjury: and that they should oblige and bind themselves to the king with a sure promise, to work their diligence in deposing the archbishop ; upon this condition that the king should promise their safety, and discharge them from the peril of the judgment which was against them. So all the bishops, obliging themselves thus to the king, went to the archbishop, one speaking for the rest, (which was Hilary bishop of Chichester,) in these words, "Once you have been our archbishop, and so long we were bound to your obedience ; but now forasmuch as you, once swearing your fidelity to the king, do resist him, neglecting his injunctions and ordinances, concerning and appertaining to his civil honour and dignity ; we here pronounce you perjured, neither are we bound to give obedience to an archbishop thus being perjured ; but, putting ourselves and all ours in the pope's protection, we do cite you up to his presence." And they assigned him his day and time to appear. The archbishop upon this sends to Rome in all haste to the pope, informing

him by letters of the whole matter, how, and wherefore, and by whom he was cited.

The archbishop being thus cited up to Rome, still sat with his cross in the court, neither giving place to the king's request, nor abashed with the clamour of the whole court against him, calling him traitor on every side ; at length the king, by certain earls and barons, sent command to him that he should without delay come and render a full account of all he had received, as the profits and revenues of the realm during the time he was chancellor, and specially for the 30,000 marks, for the which he was accountable to the king. The archbishop answered, "The king knew how often he had made his reckoning of those things which were now required of him ; and that Henry, his son and heir of his realm, with all his barons, and also Richard Lucy, chief justice of England told him, that he was free and clear before God and holy church from all receipts and reckonings, and from all secular exactions on the king's behalf. And that he, taking thus his discharge at their hands, entered into his office ; and therefore he would make no other account besides this." When this word was brought to the king, he required his barons to put the law in force against him ; and they sentenced him to be apprehended and laid in prison. This done, the king sends the earl of Cornwall and Devonshire, and the earl of Leicester, to declare to him his judgment. The archbishop answered, "Hear, my son, and good earl, what I say to you : how much more precious the soul is than the body, so much more ought you to obey me in the Lord, rather than your earthly king. Neither does any law or reason permit the children to judge or condemn their father. Wherefore, to avoid both the judgment of the king, of you, and all others, I put myself wholly to the arbitration of the pope, under God alone, to be judged by him, and by no other ; to whose presence I do appeal here before you all ; committing the ordering of the church of Canterbury, my dignity, with all other things appertaining to the same, under the protection of God and him. And as for you, my brethren and fellow bishops, who rather obey man than God, you also I call and cite to the audience and judgment of the pope, and depart henceforth from you, as from the enemies of the catholic church, and of the authority of the apostolic see."

While the barons returned with this answer to the king, the archbishop, passing through the throng, takes his palfry, holding his cross in one hand, and his bridle in the other, the courtiers following after, and crying, "Traitor ! traitor ! tarry, and hear thy judgment." But he passed on. While the king was at supper, he prepares his journey secretly to escape away ; and changing his garment and his name, went first to Lincoln, and from thence to Sandwich, where he took ship and sailed into Flanders, and from thence journeyed into France, as Hoveden writes. However Alanus, differing something in the order of his flight says, "that he departed not that night ; but at supper-time there came to him the bishops of London and Chichester, declaring to him that if he would surrender to the king his two manors of Otford and Wingham, there was hope to recover the king's favour, and to have all forgiven. But when the archbishop would not agree, as those manors belonged to the church of Canterbury, the king hearing thereof took great displeasure, so that the next day Becket was fain to send to the king for leave to depart the realm. The king answered, "That he would pause till the next day, and then he should have an answer." But Becket not waiting for his answer, conveyed himself away secretly to Lewis the French king. But before he came to the king, Gilbert the bishop of London, and William, the earl of Arundel, were sent from the king of England to France, requiring the French king, on the part of the king of England, not to receive nor retain in his dominion the archbishop of Canterbury.

The French king, understanding the matter, and thinking thereby to have some advantage against the king of England, not only harbours this Becket, but also writing to the pope, intreats him to support the cause of the archbishop. The king sent another embassage to Pope Alexander. The ambassadors sent on this message were Roger archbishop of York, Gilbert bishop of London, Henry bishop of Winchester, Hilary bishop of Chichester, Bartholomew bishop of Exeter; with other doctors and clerks; also William Earl of Arundel, with other lords and barons, who coming to the pope's court were friendly received by some of the cardinals. Among the cardinals there arose some dissension about the matter. Some judging that the bishop of Canterbury in defence of the liberties of the church was to be maintained. Some thinking again, that he (being a disturber of peace and unity) was rather to be bridled for his presumption, than to be fostered and encouraged. But the pope wholly inclined to Becket. Wherefore the day following, the pope sitting in consistory with his cardinals, the ambassadors were called for the hearing of Becket's matter; and first begins the bishop of London; next, the archbishop of York; then Exeter; and the other bishops, every one in their order. Their orations were not well received by the pope, and some of them were disliked. The earl of Arundel perceiving that, began after this manner:

"Although it is unknown to me, who am both unlettered and ignorant, what it is that these bishops here have said, nor am I so able to express my mind in that tongue as they have done; yet being sent and charged thereto by my prince, neither can nor ought I but to declare (as well as I may) what is the cause of our sending hither: not indeed to contend or strive with any person, nor to offer any injury or harm to any man, especially in this place, and in the presence here of such an one to whose beck and authority all the world stoops and yields. But for this time is our legation hither directed, to present here before you, and in the presence of the whole church of Rome, the devotion and love of our king and master, which he ever has had, and yet has still towards you. And that the same might the better appear to your excellency, he has assigned and appointed to this legation, not the least, but the greatest, not the worst, but the best and chiefest of all his subjects; both archbishops, bishops, earls, barons, with other potentates more, of such worthiness and parentage, that if he could have found greater in all his realm, he would have sent them, both for the reverence of your person, and of the holy church of Rome. Over and beside this, I might add more (which your holiness has sufficiently tried and proved already) the true and hearty fidelity of this our king and sovereign toward you (in his first entrance to his kingdom) wholly submitting himself, with all that is his besides, to your will and pleasure. And truly, to testify of his majesty how he is disposed to the unity of the catholic faith: we believe there is none more faithful to Christ than he, nor more devout to God, nor yet more moderate in keeping the unity of peace whereto he is called. And as I may be bold to protest this for our king and master, so neither do I affirm the archbishop of Canterbury to be a man destitute or unfurnished with gifts and qualities in his calling, but to be a man both sage and discreet in such things as appertain to him, save only that he seems to some more quick and sharp than needs. This blot alone if it were not, and if the breach between our king and him had not so happened, both the authorities together (the temporal and spiritual) might quietly have flourished one with the other in much peace and concord, both under a prince so worthy, and a pastor so virtuous. Wherefore, the case so standing as it does, our message hither, and our supplication to your vigilant prudence is, that (through your favour and wisdom) the neck of this dissension may be broken, and that reformation of unity and love (by some good means) may be sought."

This oration of his, although it was liked for its softness and moderation, yet it did not persuade the Romish bishop to condescend to their request; which was, to have two legates or arbitraters to be sent into England, to examine the controversy between the king and the archbishop. But the pope would not grant their petition; as it would be prejudicial and tending to the oppression of the archbishop. And therefore he desired them to wait his coming; otherwise being absent, he would not in any case proceed against him. But they, alleging that their appointed time was expired, said, "That they could not wait for the coming of Becket, but must return back with their cause frustrated, and without the pope's blessing to the king." Within four days after, Becket comes to the pope's court, where prostrating himself at his feet, he brought out of his bosom a scroll containing the customs and ordinances of the king. The pope receiving the scroll, and reading it in the open hearing of his cardinals, condemned and accursed the most part of the decrees of the king which he called "his grandfather's ordinances." Besides this, the pope blamed Becket, for having so much yielded at the beginning: yet, because he was repentant, he was content to absolve him for the same, and that the rather, because of his great troubles, which for the liberties of holy church he had sustained, and so with great favour dismissed him for that day.

The next day, Alexander the pope assembling his cardinals together in his secret chamber, archbishop Becket appears before them, making this oration to the pope and his popelings, which here I thought to set out in our English tongue, that posterity hereafter may understand either the vain superstition or vile slavery of the churchmen in those days, who being not content with their own natural prince and king given them by God, must seek further to the pope.

The Oration of Becket resigning his bishoprick to the Pope.

"Fathers and lords, I ought not to lie in any place, much less before God and in your presence here. Wherefore, with much sighing and sorrow of heart, I grant and confess, that these troubles of the church of England were raised through my miserable fault. For I entered into the fold of Christ, but not by the door of Christ; for that the canonical election did not call me lawfully thereunto, but terror of public power drove me in. And although against my will I took this burden upon me, yet not the will of God, but man's pleasure placed me in that office. And therefore no wonder all things have gone contrary and backward with me. And as for the resigning it again, if I had so done, and given up to their hands the privilege of my episcopal authority, which I had granted to me at the command of the king (as my fellow bishops did urgently call upon me to do), then had I left a pernicious and dangerous example to the whole catholic church. Therefore I thought good to defer that to your presence. And now acknowledging my ingress not to be canonical, and therefore fearing it to have the worse end; and again pondering my strength and ability as not sufficient for such a charge) lest I should be found to hold that office to the ruin of the flock to whom I was appointed an unworthy pastor, I here render up to your fatherly hands the archbishopric of Canterbury, &c." And so putting off his ring from his finger, and offering it to the pope, he desired a bishop to be provided for the church of Canterbury: seeing he thought not himself meet to fulfil the same, and so (with tears, as the history saith) he ended his oration.

This done, the archbishop was bid to stand aside, and the pope conferred with his cardinals about the resignation of Becket, what was best to be done. Some thought it best to take the opportunity offered, thinking that thereby the king's wrath might easily be assuaged, if the church of Canterbury were assigned to some other person, and Becket otherwise provided for. Others again thought otherwise, whose reason was, "If he (who for the liberties of the church had ventured not only his goods, dignity, and authority, but also his life) should now at the king's pleasure be deprived, it might be a precedent hereafter to others; and so it might redound not only to the weakening of the Catholic church, but also to the derogation of the pope's authority. Briefly, this sentence at length prevailed; and so Becket receives his pastoral office from the pope's hand again, with commendation and much favour. But as he could not well be placed in England, in the mean while the pope sends him with a monk's habit into the abbey of Pontigny in France, where he remained two years, from thence he removed to Senon, where he abode five years. So the time of his exile continued seven years in all.

Upon this, the king being certified by his ambassadors of the pope's answer, how his favour inclined more to Becket than to him, was moved (and very naturally) with displeasure; and upon sailing from England unto Normandy, he directed certain injunctions against the pope and the archbishop of Canterbury.

These and other injunctions Becket partly specifies in a letter, writing to a friend of his in this manner.

"Thomas archbishop of Canterbury, to his well-beloved friend, &c. Be it known to your brotherly goodness that we, with all ours here (by God's grace) are safe and in good health. Having a good hope and trust in your faithful friendship, I charge you, and require you, that either by the bringer hereof, or by some other (whom ye know faithful and trusty to our church of Canterbury, and to us) you write with all speed what is done. As to the king's decrees here set out, they are these: 'That all havens and ports should be diligently kept, that no letters of the pope's interdict or curse be brought in. And if any monks bring them in, they shall have their feet cut off; if he be a priest or clerk, he shall be mutilated; if he be a layman, he shall be hanged; if he be a leper he shall be burned. And if any bishop, for fear of the pope's interdict, will depart, let him have nothing else besides his staff only in his hand. Also the king's will is, that all scholars and students beyond the seas shall repair home, or else lose their benefices. And if they shall remain still, they shall lose the liberty of ever returning. Further, if any such priests shall be found who for the pope's suspension or interdict will refuse to officiate, they shall be mutilated. In short, all such priests as shew themselves rebels to the king, let them be deprived of their benefices," &c.

Besides these and such like injunctions, it was also set forth by the king's proclamation, (A. D. 1166.) That all manner of persons, both men and women, whoever were found of the kindred of Thomas Becket, should be exiled, without taking any part of their goods with them, and sent to him where he was, which was no little vexation to Becket to behold them. Moreover, as he was then living with Gwarine, abbot of Pontigny, to whom the pope had commended him. The king wrote to the abbot, required him not to retain the archbishop of Canterbury in his house; for if he did, he would drive out of his realm all the monks of his order. Upon which Becket was forced to remove, and went to Lewis the French king, by whom he was placed at Senon, and there remained for the space of five years.

In the meantime the pope writes to King Henry, to exhort and charge him to shew favour to Thomas Becket; where, in the course of the epistle, are these words: "Therefore we do desire, admonish, and exhort your honour by these our apostolical writings, and also enjoin you upon the remission of your sins, in the behalf of Almighty God, and of St. Peter, prince of the apostles, by our authority, that you will receive again the aforesaid archbishop into your favour and grace, for the honour of God, his church, and of your own realm," &c.

Thus have we heard the pope's intreating letter. Now here is another letter sent to the king, wherein he menaces him.

"*Bishop Alexander, servant of the servants of God, to King Henry, king of England, health and blessing apostolical.*

"How fatherly and gently we have oft-times entreated and exhorted both by legates, and letters, your princely honour, to be reconciled again with our reverend brother Thomas, archbishop of Canterbury, so that he and his may be restored again to their churches and other possessions to them appertaining, your wisdom is not ignorant, seeing it is notified and spread almost throughout all Christendom. Forsomuch, therefore, as hitherto

we could not prevail with you, neither move nor stir your mind with fair and gentle words, it laments us not a little, to be so frustrated and deceived in the hope and expectation which we had conceived of you. Especially seeing we love you so dearly, as our own dearly beloved son in the Lord, and understand so great a jeopardy to hang over you.

"But forsomuch as it is written, 'Cry out and cease not, lift up thy voice like a trumpet, and declare to my people their wickedness, and to the house of Jacob their sins.' Also forsomuch as it is in Solomon commanded, 'That the sluggish person should be stoned with the dung of oxen,' we have thought good, therefore, not to forbear or support your stubbornness any longer against justice and salvation: neither that the mouth of the archbishop should be stopped from henceforth any more; but that he may freely prosecute the charge of his office and duty, and revenge with the sword of ecclesiastical discipline, the injuries both of himself, and of his church committed to his charge.

"And here I have sent unto you two legates, Peter de ponte Dei, and Bernard de Corilio, to admonish you of the same. But if ye will neither be advised by us, nor give ear to them in obeying, it is to be feared, doubtless, lest such things as they shall declare to you from us in our behalf may happen and fall upon you. Dated at Benevent, the ninth day before the kalends of June."

To answer these letters again, there was another writing drawn out and directed to the pope, made by some of the clergy, as it seems; but not without consent of the king, as may appear by the title, inveighing against, and disproving the misbehaviour of the archbishop. The tenor whereof here follows, and begins:

An answer to the Pope.

"Time now requires more to seek help than to make complaints. For the holy mother church (our sins deserving the same), lies in a dangerous state of great decay, which is like to ensue, unless the present mercy of the Lord support her.

"Such is the wickedness now of schismatics, that the father of fathers, Pope Alexander (for the defence of his faith, and for the love of righteousness) is banished out of his country; not able to keep free residence in his own proper see, by reason of the hardened heart of Frederick the Pharaoh.

"The church also of Canterbury is miserably impaired and blemished, as well in the spiritual as in the temporal estate; much like to the ship in the sea, being destitute of her guide, tossed in the floods, and wrestling with the winds, while the pastor being absent from his province, dare not there remain through the power of the king; who, being over wise, (to the jeopardy of himself, his church, and us also), hath brought and entangled us likewise with himself in the same partaking of his punishments and labours, not considering how we ought to forbear, and not to resist superior powers. And also he shews himself unkind to us, who with all our affections bear with him the burthen of his afflictions, not ceasing yet to persecute us who stand in the same condemnation with him. For, betwixt him and our sovereign prince, the king of England, arose a certain matter of contention, whereupon they were both agreed, that a day should be appointed, to have the controversy discussed by equity and justice.

"The day being come, the king commanded all the archbishops, bishops, and other prelates of the church to be called in a solemn assembly; so that the greater and more general this council was, the more manifest the detection of this stubborn malice should appear and be seen.

"At the day therefore above mentioned, this troubler of the realm and of the church, presents himself in the sight of our catholic king; and not trusting the quality and condition of his cause, arms himself with the armour of the cross, as one who should be brought to the presence of a tyrant. By reason of which the king's majesty being somewhat aggrieved (yet because he would be delivered from all suspicion) commits the matter to the hearing of the bishops. This done, it rests in the bishops to decide and cease this contention, and to set agreement between them, removing all occasion of dissension. Which thing they going about, this archbishop comes in, forbidding, and commanding that no man should proceed in any sentence upon him before the king.

"This being signified to the king, his mind was grievously provoked to anger; whose anger, notwithstanding, had been easily assuaged, if the other would have submitted himself, and acknowledged his default. But he adding stubbornness to his trespass, through the greatness of his excess was the author of his own punishment, which now by the civil law he bears, and yet shames to crave pardon for his deserts at the king's hand; whose anger he fears not to stir up, in such a troublesome time of the persecution of the church, augmenting and increasing thereby the persecution which the church now lies under. Much better it had been for him to have tempered himself with the bridle of moderation, in the highest estate of his dignity, lest in exceeding too far in straining the strict points of things by overmuch presumption, peradventure through his presumption, being not in mean and tolerable things, he might fall from higher. And if the detriment of the church would not move him; yet the great benefits and preferments of riches and honours ought to persuade him not to be so stubborn against the king. But here peradventure his friend and our adversary will object, that his bearing and submitting to the king in this behalf were prejudicial against the authority of the apostolical see. Although he did not, or might not understand, that although the dignity of the church should suffer a little detriment in that judgment; yet he might, and ought to have dissembled, for the time, to obtain peace to the church. He will object again, alleging the name of father, that it sounds like a point of arrogancy, for children to proceed in judgment of condemnation against the father, which thing is not convenient. But he must understand again, that it was necessary that the obedience and humility of the children should temper the pride of the father, lest afterward the hatred of the father might redound upon the children. Wherefore by these premises your father may understand that the action of this our adversary ought to fall down, as void, and of none effect, who only under the influence of malice has proceeded thus against us, having no just cause nor reason to stand upon.

"And forsomuch as the care and charge of all churches (as ye know) lies upon us, it stands upon us to provide concerning the state of the church of Canterbury, by our diligence and circumspection: so that the church of Canterbury, by the excesses of its pastor, be not driven to ruin or decay."

By this epistle it may appear that Becket (being absent from England) went about to work some trouble against some of the clergy and the laity, in excommunicating such as he took to be his evil willers.

Now to understand further what his working was, or who they were whom he excommunicated, this letter, sent to William bishop of Norwich, shall declare.

A Letter of Becket to the Bishop of Norwich.

"He binds himself to the penalty of the crime, whoever receiving power and authority of God, uses and exercises not the same with due severity, in punishing vice: but winking and dissembling, ministers boldness to wicked doers, maintaining them in their sin. For the blood of the wicked is required at the hand of the priest, who is negligent or dissembles. And as the scripture saith, 'Thorns and brambles grow in the hands of the idle drunkard.' Wherefore, lest (through our too much sufferance and dissembling) the transgressions of manifest evil-doers should also be laid to our charge, and redound to the destruction of the church through our guilty silence; we therefore following the authority of the pope's commandment, have laid our sentence of curse and excommunication upon the Earl Hugo: commanding you throughout all your diocese publicly to denounce the said earl as accursed, so that,

according to the discipline of the church, he be sequestered from the fellowship of all faithful people. Also, it is not unknown to your brotherhood, how long we have born with the transgressions of the bishop of London; who, amongst other acts, I would to God were not a great doer, and favourer of this schism, and subverter of the rites and liberties of holy church. Wherefore we, being supported with the authority of the apostolic see, have also excommunicated him. Besides, also the bishop of Salisbury, because of his disobedience and contempt: and others likewise, upon divers and sundry causes, whose names here follow subscribed:—Hugo Bernard's son, Rodulph de Brock, Robert de Brock a clerk, Hugo de St. Clare, and Letardus a clerk of Norfolk, Nigellus of Scacavil, and Richard Chaplin, William of Hasting, and the friar who possesses my church of Monchot. We therefore charge and command you by the authority apostolical and ours, and on the virtue of your obedience, and on the peril of salvation, and of your order; that ye cause these openly to be proclaimed excommunicate, throughout all your diocese, and to command all the faithful to avoid their company. Fare ye well in the Lord. Let not your heart be troubled, nor fear: for we stand sure through the assistance of the apostolic see, God being our support against the shifts of the malignant sort, and against all their appeals. Furthermore, all such as have been solemnly cited by us shall sustain the like sentence of excommunication, if God will, on ascension-day: unless they shall otherwise agree with me. That is, to wit, Geoffrey archdeacon of Canterbury, and Robert his vicar, Rice of Wilcester, Richard de Lucy, William Giffard, Adam of Cherings, with others: who, either at the command of the king, or upon their own temerity, have invaded the goods and possessions either appertaining to us, or to our clerks about us. With these also we do excommunicate all such as are known, either with aid or council, to have incensed or set forward the proceeding of our king against the liberties of the church, and exiling of the innocents. And such also as are known to impeach or hinder by any manner of way the messengers (sent either from the pope, or from us) for the necessities of the church. Fare you well again, and ever."

Hitherto the reader has seen divers and sundry letters of Thomas Becket, whereby we may collect a sufficient history of his doings and demeanor, though nothing else were said further of him, concerning his lusty and haughty spirit, about that which beseemed either his degree or cause which he took in hand. And here perhaps I may seem to tarry too long in the history of this one man, having to write of so many others better than he, yet for the weaker sort, who have counted him, and yet do count him for a saint, having in themselves little understanding to judge or discern in the causes of men, I thought to add this letter more, wherein he complains of his king to a foreign power; doing all in his power to stir up for his own cause mortal war to the destruction of many. For suppose wrong had been offered him by his prince, was it not enough for him to fly? What cause had he, for his own private revenge, to set potentates in public discord? Now, having no just cause, but rather offering injury in a false quarrel, so to complain of his prince; what is to be said of this, let every man judge who sees this letter.

An Epistle of Thomas Archbishop of Canterbury to Pope Alexander.

"To our most loved father and lord, Alexander, by the grace of God bishop, Thomas the humble minister and servant of the church of Canterbury due and reverend obedience. Long enough and too long most loving father have I forborne, still looking after the amendment of the king of England, but no fruit have I reaped of this my long patience: nay rather, whilst unwisely I do thus forbear, I augment and procure the detriment and diminishing of mine authority, as also of the church of God: for oftentimes have I by devout and religious messengers invited him to make condign satisfaction, as also by my letters (the copies whereof I have sent you) intimated and pronounced God's severity and vengeance against him, unless he repent and amend. But he, notwithstanding that, grows from evil to worse, oppressing and crushing the church and sanctuary of God; persecuting both me and those who take part with me: so that with fearful and threatening words his purpose is to terrify such, as (for God's cause and mine own) seek any way to relieve and help me. He wrote also letters to the abbot of the Cistercian order, That as he valued the abbacy of his order (which he said was in his power) he should not receive me into the fellowship thereof, nor do any thing else for me. Why should I use many words? So much has the rigour and severity as well of the king as of his officers, under our patience and sufferance, shewed itself; that if a great number of men, yea, and that of the most religious sort, should shew to you the matter as it is indeed, I partly doubt whether your holiness would give credit to them or not. With heaviness of mind therefore considering these things, and beholding as well the peril of the king as of ourself, I have publicly condemned not only those pernicious customs, but all those perversities and wicked doings whereby the church of England is disturbed and brought to confusion; as also the writing whereby they were confirmed; excommunicating generally as well the observers and exacters thereof, as also the inventers and patrons of the same, with their favourers, counsellors, and coadjutors whatever, either of the clergy or laity, absolving also our bishops from their oath, whereby they were so strictly enjoined to the observation of the same. These are the articles which in that writing I have principally condemned, first, That it is inhibited to appeal to the see apostolical for any cause, but by the king's licence. That a bishop may not punish any man for perjury, or for breaking of his troth. That a bishop may not excommunicate any man that holds of the king in capite, or else interdict either their lands or offices without the king's licence. That clerks and religious men may be taken from us to secular judgment. That the king or any other judge may hear and decide the causes of the church and tithes. That it shall not be lawful for any archbishop or bishop to go out of the realm, and to come at the pope's call without the king's licence; and divers others such as these. I have also excommunicated John of Oxford, who has communicated with that schismatic and excommunicate person (Reginald Coloniensis) who also, contrary to the commandment of the lord pope and ours, hath usurped the deanery of the church of Salisbury, and has (to renew his schism) taken an oath in the emperor's court. Also I have denounced and excommunicated Richard of Worcester, because he is fallen into the same damnable heresy, and communicated with that famous schismatic of Cologne; devising and foregoing all mischief possible, with the schismatics and Flemings, to the destruction of the church of God, and especially of the church of Rome, by composition made between the king of England and them. Also Richard de Lucy, and Jocelin de Baliol, who have assisted the favourers of the king's tyranny and workers of their heresies. Also Rodulph de Brock, and Hugo de St. Clare, and Thomas the son of Bernard, who have usurped the possessions and goods of the church of Canterbury without our licence and consent. We have also excommunicated all those, who without our licence stretch out their hands to the possessions and goods of the church of Canterbury. The king himself we have not yet excommunicated personally, still waiting for his amendment: whom (notwithstanding) we will not defer to excommunicate, unless he quickly amend, and be warned by what he has done. And therefore that the authority of the see apostolic, and the liberty of the church of God, which in these parts are almost utterly lost, may be by some means restored, it is meet and very necessary that what we have herein done should be ratified by your holiness, and confirmed by your letters. Thus I wish your holiness long to prosper and flourish."

By this epistle, he that wishes to understand the doings of Becket, may partly judge what is to be thought of them. Although in some part they may be imputed either to ignorance of mind, or blindness of zeal, or human frailty; yet in this point, so vilely to complain of his natural prince, he can by no wise be defended. But such was the blindness of the prelates in those days, who measured and esteemed the dignity and liberties of Christ's church by nothing but by the goods and possessions flowing and abounding in the clergy; and thought no greater point of religion to be in the church, than to maintain the same. For which cause they most abominably abused christian discipline and the excommunication of the church. And what wonder if the acts and doings of this archbishop seem now to us in these days both fond and strange: when the suffragans of his own church and clergy, writing to him, could not but reprehend him, as may be seen in this their epistle.

An effectual and pithy Letter, full of reason and persuasion, sent from all the Suffragans of the Church of Canterbury to Thomas Becket their Archbishop.

" Such troubles and perturbations as happened through the strangeness of your departure out of the realm, we hoped by your humility and prudence should have been reduced again (God's grace working withal) into a peaceable tranquillity. And it was no little joy to us, to hear so of you in those parts where you are conversant, how humbly you there behaved yourself, nothing vaunting yourself against your prince and king, and that you attempt no risings or wrestlings against his kingdom, but that you bear with much patience the burthen of poverty, and gave yourself to reading and prayer, and to redeem the loss of your time spent, with fasting, watchings, and tears; and so, being occupied with spiritual studies, to tend and rise up to the perfection of virtue, &c. But now, through the secret relation of some, we hear (what we are sorry for) that you have sent to him a threatening letter, wherein there is no salutation premised. In which also ye pretend no intreating nor prayers for the obtaining of favour, nor use any friendly manner in declaring what you write, but menacing with much austerity, threaten to interdict him, and to cut him from the society of the church. Which thing if you shall accomplish with like severity, as in words ye threaten to do, you shall not only put us out of all hope of any peace, but also put us in fear of hatred and discord without measure, and without all redress amongst us. But wisdom will consider before the end of things, labouring and endeavouring to finish that which she wisely begins. Therefore your discretion shall do well diligently to forecast and consider whereto ye tend; what end may ensue thereof, and whereabout ye go. Certainly we, for our parts, hearing what we do hear, are discouraged from what we hoped for, who, previously having some good comfort of tranquillity to come, are cast from hope to despair: so that while one is drawn thus against another, there is scarcely any hope or place left to make entreaty or supplication. Wherefore, writing to your fatherhood, we exhort and counsel you by way of charity, That you add not trouble to trouble, nor heap injury upon injury: but that you so behave yourself, that all menaces set aside, you rather give yourself to patience and humility, and to yield your cause to the clemency of God, and to the mercy of your prince; and in so doing you shall heap coals of charity upon the heads of many. Thus charity shall be kindled, and that which menacings cannot do (by God's help and good men's counsel) peradventure pity and godliness shall obtain. It were better to sustain poverty with praise, than in great promotions to be a common note to all men. It is right well known unto all men, how kind the king has been to you, from what baseness to what dignity he has advanced you, and also into his own familiarity has so much preferred you, that from the northern ocean to the Pyrinean mountains, he has subdued all things to your authority: in so much that they were among all others accounted for fortunate men, whoever could find any favour with you.

" And, furthermore, lest your estimation should be over matched by any nobility, he (against the mind of his mother, and of his realm) has placed and ratified you substantially in ecclesiastical dignity, and advanced you to this honour wherein ye stand: trusting through your help and counsel to reign more safely and prosperously. Now, if he shall find disquietness, wherein he trusted to have quietness, what shall all men say or think of you? What recompence or retribution shall this be thought to be for so many and great benefits received? Therefore (if it shall please you) ye shall do well to favour and spare your fame and estimation, and to overcome your lord and sovereign with humility and charity. Whereto if our advice cannot move you; yet the love and fidelity you bear to the bishop and holy church of Rome ought to incline you not to attempt any such thing, whereby the troubles of the church our mother may increase, or whereby her sorrow may be augmented in the loss of them, whose disobedience she now bewails: for what if it so happen through provocation, that the king (whom all his subjects and kingdoms obey) should relinquish the pope, which God forbid, and should deny all obedience to him, as he denies to the king help or aid against you? what inconvenience would grow thereof? And think you, he hath not great instigations, supplications, gifts, and many fair promises so to do? Yet he (notwithstanding) abides firm hitherto in the rock, despising with a valiant mind all that the world can offer. This one thing we fear, lest his mind (whom no worldly offers can assail, no glory, riches, nor treasure can overturn) only through indignation of unkindness be subverted. Which thing if it chance to happen through you, then may you sit down and sing the song of the Lamentation of Jeremiah, and weep your full.

" Consider therefore, if it please you, and foresee well with yourself, this purpose of yours, if it proceed, how hurtful and perilous it will be; not only to the pope, and to the holy church of Rome, but also to yourself most especially. But some peradventure about you, of haughty and high minded stoutness, more stout than wise, will not suffer you to take this way, but will give you contrary counsel, rather to prove and declare what you are able to do against your lord and prince, and to practice against him and all his utmost of your power and authority, which power and authority of yours, to him that offends is fearful; and to him that will not amend, terrible. Such counsel as this, some peradventure will whisper in your ear. But to these again, we say this, and answer for our king, whom notwithstanding we do not affirm to be without fault; but yet we speak confidently and protest in his behalf, that he is always ready to amend and make satisfaction.

" The king, appointed as the Lord's anointed, provides for the peace of his subjects all that he is able: and therefore to the intent that he may preserve this peace in his churches and among his subjects committed to him, he wills and requires such ordinances as are due to the kings, and were exhibited before time to them to be exhibited to him also. Wherein if there has any contradiction sprung between him and us, he being admonished from the pope by the reverend bishops of London and Hereford, burst not out into any defiance, but meekly and humbly answered, that wherein soever the church or any ecclesiastical person can shew himself grieved he would therein stand to the judgment of the church of his kingdom. Which also he is ready no less to perform, thinking nothing more sweet unto him than to be admonished of his fault, if he have offended the Lord, and to reform the same; and not only to reform and amend his fault, but also to satisfy it to the utmost, if the law shall so require him. Wherefore, seeing he is so willing to recompense and satisfy the judgment of the church in all things appertaining to the church; refusing no order that shall be taken, but in all things submitting his neck to the yoke of Christ: with what right, by what canon, or reason can you interdict him, or use excommunication against him? It is a thing laudable and a virtue of great commendation in wise men, wisely to go with judgment and reason, and not to be carried with puffs of hasty violence. Whereupon this is the only and common petition of us all, that your fa-

therly care will diligently provide for your flock and sheep committed to you, so that they miscarry not, or run to any ruin through any inconsiderate or too much heady counsel in you: but rather that through your softness and sufferance, they may obtain life, peace and security. It doth move us all, what we hear of late to be done by you against the bishop of Salisbury, and the dean of the same church, prosperously, as some men suppose; against whom you have given out the sentence of excommunication and condemnation, before there was any question of their crime; following therein, as seems, more the heat of hastiness than the path of righteousness. This is a new order of judgment, unheard of yet to this day in our laws and canons, first to condemn a man, and after to inquire of the fact committed. Which order lest you should hereafter attempt to exercise in like manner against our sovereign and king, or against us and our churches, and parishes committed to us, to the detriment of the pope, and the holy church of Rome, and to the no little confusion of us all; therefore we lay here against you, for ourselves, the remedy of appeal. And, as before, openly in the public face of the church with lively voice we appealed to the Pope for certain perils that might have happened: so now again in writing we appeal to the same, assigning as the term of our appeal the day of the Lord's ascension. Most humbly and reverently beseeching your goodness, that you, taking a better way with you in this matter, will let your cause fall, sparing herein both the labours and charges, as well of yourself, as ours also. And thus we wish you right well to fare, reverend in the Lord."

The Letter of Matilda the Empress, and Mother of the King, to Thomas Becket.

" My Lord the Pope commanded me, and upon the forgiveness of my sins enjoined me, that I should be a mediator and means of peace and concord between my son and you, by reconciling of yourself to him, whereunto (as you know) you requested me. Wherefore the earnester and with more affection (as well for the divine honour as for holy church) I took the enterprise upon me. But this by the way, I assure you, that the king, his barons, and council, take it grievously, that you, whom he entirely loved, honoured and made chiefest in all this realm to the intent to have more comfort and better trust in you, should thus (as the report is) rebel, and stir his people against him. Yea and further, that as much as in you lies, you went about to disinherit him, and deprive him of his crown. Upon the occasion whereof, I sent to you our trusty and familiar servant Lawrence archdeacon, by whom I pray you that I may understand your mind herein, and good will toward my son, and how you mean to behave yourself (if my prayer and petition may be heard by him in your behalf) toward his Grace. But this one thing I assure you of, that unless it be through your great humility and moderation, evidently appearing in you, you cannot obtain the favour of the king. Herein what you mean to do, I pray you send me word by your proper letters and messengers."

But to proceed further in the order of the history. After these letters sent to and fro, (A. D. 1169), which was the fifteenth year of the reign of King Henry II. the king doubting and fearing with himself, that the archbishop would proceed in his excommunication against his person, made his appeal to the presence of the pope, requiring to have certain legates sent down from Rome, to take up the matter between the archbishop and him; requiring moreover that they might also be absolved that were interdicted. Whereupon two cardinals, being sent from Alexander the Pope with letters to the king, came to Normandy: where they appointed the archbishop to meet them before the king upon St. Martin's day. But the archbishop, neither agreeing with the day nor the place, delayed his coming till the eighth day after, neither would go any further than to Grisortium, where the two cardinals and archbishop, with other bishops meeting together, had a treaty of peace and reconciliation, but it came to no conclusion.

The contents of which treaty or action, because it is sufficiently contained in the cardinal's letters, who were called William and Otho, written to the pope, it requires no further labour, than to give the letter itself, as follows.

The copy of the Epistle written and sent by two Cardinals to the Pope, concerning the matter of the Archbishop Becket.

"William and Otho, cardinals of the church of Rome to Alexander the Pope, &c. Coming to the land of the king of England, we found the controversy betwixt him and the archbishop of Canterbury more sharp and vehement than we would. For the king, and the greater part of them about him, said, that the archbishop had stirred up the French king, grievously against him; and also the earl of Flanders his kinsman (who bare no displeasure to him before) he made his open adversary, ready to war against him, as is by divers evidences most certain. Thus when we came to Cadomus, into the king's presence, we gave the letters of your fatherhood to his hands, which after that he had received and considered (bringing forth other letters received from you before, something different and altering from these which he received of us) he was moved with no little indignation; saying, that after our departure from you, the archbishop had received of you other contrary letters, by the virtue whereof he was exempted from our judgment, so that he should not be compelled to answer us. Moreover, the king affirmed to us, and so did the bishops there present, testify the same, that concerning the old and ancient customs of his progenitors (whereof complaint was made to you) all that for the most part was false and untrue which was intimated to you; offering further to us, that if there were any such customs or laws in his time, that seemed prejudicial or disagreeable to the statutes of the church, he would willingly be content to revoke and disannul the same. Whereupon we with other archbishops, bishops and abbots of the land hearing the king so reasonable, laboured by all the means we might, that the king should not utterly break from us, but rather should incline to us to have the matter brought before us between him and the forenamed archbishop. By reason whereof, we directed our chaplains with letters to the archbishop, appointing him both time and place where he might safely meet with us in the feast of St. Martin. Nevertheless he, pretending certain excuses, made delays, putting off the time from the day of St. Martin to the eighth day following, which stirred the king's heart more than is to be thought.

"Thus although we offered to the archbishop safe conduct, yet when he refused to meet us in the borders of the king, we, to satisfy his mind, condescended to meet him within the land of the French king, in the place where he himself appointed, because there should be no hinderance in us, whereby to stop his profit. After we had entered communication, we began to exhort him, all that we could, to submit and humble himself to his sovereign and king, who had heaped him with such benefits and dignities. He, being thus moved and exhorted by us, departed aside to consult with his council upon the matter. At length after counsel taken, he comes again, answering in this manner: that he would submit and humble himself to the king, "Saving the honour of God, and liberty of the church, saving also the honesty of his person, and possessions of churches: and moreover, saving the justice of him and of all his in all things," &c. After which communication, we moved and required him more urgently, that he would come to the specialties. Likewise we demanded of him, if he would stand and submit himself to our letters, if the king and the bishops were contented to do so. To which he said, "That he had received from you a commandment, not to answer until he and all his were restored fully to all their possessions; and then he would proceed in the matter, according as he should receive commandment from the see apostolical.

"Thus we breaking off communication, seeing that he neither would stand to judgment, nor come to conformity, thought to make relation thereof to the king, and so did: declaring that which he had expressed to us; yet not uttering all, but keeping back a great part of that which we had heard and seen. Which when the king and his nobles had understanding of, he affirmed to us again that he therein was cleared so much the more, for that the archbishop would not stand to their judgment, nor abide their trial. After much heaviness and lamentation of the king, the archbishop, bishops, and abbots of the realm requiring of us, whether we had any such power, by virtue of our commission, to withstand him and proceed against him; and perceiving that our authority would not serve thereto, and fearing lest the archbishop, refusing all order of judgment, would work again disquietness to some noble personages of the realm: and seeing our authority could not extend so far as to help them against him, they holding consultation among themselves agreed with one consent, to make their appeal to your audience, prefixing accordingly the term of their appeal."

By this epistle of these two cardinals sent to the pope, may sufficiently appear all the discourse and manner of that assembly concerning the confidence between the cardinals and the archbishop. When William, who was the more eloquent of the two cardinals, had reasoned long with him as concerning the peace of the church: which Becket said he preferred above all things. "Well then," said the cardinal, "seeing all this contention between the king and you rises upon certain laws and customs to be abrogated, and that you regard the peace of the church so much: then what say you? Will you renounce your bishoprick, and the king will renounce his customs? The peace of the church now lies in your hands, either to retain or to let go; what say you?" To whom he answereth again, "That the proportion was not like. For I," saith he, "(saving the honour of my church and my person) cannot renounce my bishopric. On the other hand, it becomes the king for his soul's health and honour to renounce these his ordinances and customs." Which thing he thus proved; because the pope had condemned those customs, and he likewise with the church of Rome had done the same, &c.

After the cardinals were returned, the French king seeing the king of England disquieted and solicitous to have peace (or at least pretending to set an agreement between them) brought the matter to a communication among them. In which communication the French king made himself as umpire between them. The king of England, hearing that the archbishop would commit himself to his arbitration, was the more willing to admit his presence. Whereupon, many being there present, the archbishop, prostrating himself at the king's feet, declared to him kneeling upon his knees, that he would commit the whole cause, whereof the dissension rose between them, unto his own arbitration; adding (as he did before) "Saving the honour of God." The king (as is said before) being greatly offended at this word, hearing and seeing the stiffness of the man sticking so much to this word, was highly displeased, rebuking him with many grievous words, as a man proud and stubborn, and also charging him with sundry and great benefits bestowed upon him, as a person ungrateful, and forgetting what he had so gently done and bestowed upon him.

And speaking to the French king there present: "See, sir, if it please you," saith the king of England, "whatsoever displeases this man, he calls it contrary to the honour of God. And so by this means he will vindicate and challenge to himself both what is his and what is mine also. And yet as I will not do anything contrary or prejudicial to God's honour, this I offer him: there have been kings in England before, both of greater and less puissance than I am; likewise there have been bishops of Canterbury many both great and holy men: what the greatest and most holy of all his predecessors before him has done to the least of my progenitors and predecessors, let him do the same to me and I am content." They that stood by, hearing these words of the king, cried all with one voice, "The king hath debased himself enough to the bishop." The archbishop made no answer, but kept silence, "What," saith the French king to him, "my lord archbishop, will you be better than those holy men? Will ye be greater than Peter? What stand you doubting? Here now you have peace and quietness placed in your own hands, if ye will take it." To this the archbishop answered again. "Truth it is," saith he, "my predecessors were both much better and greater than I, and every one of them for his time, although he did not extirpate all, yet did pluck up and correct somewhat which seemed adverse and repugnant to God's honour. For if they had taken all together away, no such occasion then had been left for any man to raise up this fiery trial now against us; that we, being so proved with them, might also be crowned with them, being likewise partakers of praise and reward, as we are of their labour and travel. And though some of them have been slack, or exceeded in their duty, we are not bound in that to follow their example. When Peter denied Christ, we rebuke him; but when he resisted the rage of Nero, therein we commend him. And therefore because he could not find in his conscience to consent to what he ought in no wise to dissemble, neither did he; by reason thereof he lost his life. By such like oppressions the church has always grown. Our fore-fathers and predecessors, because they would not dissemble the name and honour of Christ, therefore they suffered. And shall I, to have the favour of one man, suffer the honour of Christ to be suppressed?" The nobles standing by, hearing him thus speak, were greatly grieved with him, noting in him both arrogancy and wilfulness, in perturbing and refusing such an honest offer of agreement. But specially one amongst the rest was most grieved, who there openly protested, that seeing the archbishop so refused the counsel and the request of both of the kingdoms, he was not worthy to have the help of either of them; but as the kingdom of England had rejected him, so the realm of France should not receive him.

Alan, Herbert, and another of his chaplains that committed to history the doings of Becket, record (whether truly or no I cannot say), that the French king sending for him, as one much sorrowing and lamenting the words that he had spoken, at the coming of Becket did prostrate himself at his feet, confessing his fault, in giving counsel to him in such a cause (pertaining to the honour of God) to relent therein and to yield to the pleasure of man: wherefore, declaring his repentance, he desired to be absolved thereof. So that after this, the French king and Becket were great friends together; insomuch that King Henry sending to the king to intreat him, and desire him that he would not support nor maintain his enemy within his realm, the French king utterly denied the king's request, taking part rather with the archbishop than with him.

Besides these quarrels and grudges betwixt the king and the archbishop above mentioned, there followed yet another, which was this: shortly after this communication between the king and Becket, the king of England returning again from Normandy into England (A. D. 1170, and the sixteenth year of his reign), kept his court of parliament at Westminster; in which parliament he (through the assent both of the clergy and the lords temporal) caused his son Henry to be crowned king. Which coronation was done by the hands of Robert archbishop of York, with the assistance of other bishops administering to the same, as Gilbert of London, Jocelin of Salisbury, Hugo of Durham, and Walter of Rochester. By reason of which Becket of Canterbury, being neither mentioned nor called for, took no little displeasure; and so did Louis the French king, hearing that Margaret his daughter was not crowned with her husband: whereupon gathering a great army, he forthwith marched into Normandy. But the matter was soon composed by the king of England, who sending his son to him in Normandy, there entreated and concluded peace with him, promising that his son should be crowned again, and then his daughter should be crowned also. But the archbishop not ceasing his displeasure and emulation, sent to the pope, complaining of these four bishops, especially of the archbishop of York; who durst be so bold in his absence, and without his licence, to crown the king, being a matter proper and peculiar to his jurisdiction. At this request, the pope sent down the sentence of excommunication against the

bishop of London. The other three bishops with the archbishop of York he suspended.

This being done, the archbishop of York with the other bishops resorted to the king with a grievous complaint, declaring how miserably their case stood, and what they had sustained for fulfilling his commandment. The king, hearing this, was highly moved, as no marvel was. But what remedy? The time of the ruin of the pope was not yet come; and what prince then could withstand the injurious violence of that Romish potentate?

In the mean time the French king with his clergy and courtiers lost no occasion to excite and solicit Alexander the pope against the king of England to excommunicate him also: thinking to have some advantage against the realm. Nor was the king ignorant of this, which made him more ready for reconciliation. At length came down from the pope two legates, the archbishop of Rothomage and the bishop of Navern, with the direction and full commission either to drive the king to be reconciled, or to be interdicted by the pope's censures out of the church. The king understanding himself to be in greater straits than he could avoid, at length through the mediation of the French king and of other prelates and great princes, was content to yield to peace and reconciliation with the archbishop, whom he both received to his favour, and also permitted and granted him free return to his church again. Concerning his possessions and lands of the church of Canterbury, although Becket made great labour there for, yet the king (being then in Normandy) would not grant him them, before he should repair to England to see how he would there agree with his subjects.

Thus a sort of peace being concluded between the king and him, the archbishop, after six years banishment, returned to England, where he was right joyfully received by the church of Canterbury; although by Henry the young king, he was not so greatly welcomed. So that coming up to London to the king, he was sent back to Canterbury, and there bid to keep his house. Roger Hoveden makes mention in his chronicle, that the archbishop (upon Christmas-day) excommunicated Robert de Brock for cutting off the tail of a certain horse of his the day before. In the mean time the four bishops before mentioned, whom the archbishop excommunicated, sent to him, humbly desiring to be released of their censure. To whom when the archbishop would not grant clearly and simply without cautions and exceptions, they went over to the king, declaring to him and complaining of their miserable state and uncourteous handling by the archbishop. Whereupon the king conceived great sorrow in his mind, and displeasure toward the party. Insomuch that he lamented to them about him, (amongst so many that he had done for) there was none that would revenge him of his enemy. By occasion of which words, certain that were about the king (to the number of four) hearing him thus complain and lament, addressed themselves in great heat of haste to satisfy the grieved mind and quarrel of their prince: who within four days after Christmas-day, sailing over into England, came to Canterbury, where Becket was commanded to keep. After certain consultations among themselves, they pressed at length into the palace where the archbishop was setting with his company about him: first to try him with words, to see whether he would relent to the king's mind, and come to some conformity. They brought to him, they said, commandment from the king, and bid him choose whether he had rather openly there in presence, or secretly receive it. Then the company being desired to leave, as he sat alone, they said, "You are commanded from the king beyond the sea, to repair to the king's son here, and to do your duty to him, swearing to him your fidelity for your barony and other things, and to amend those things wherein you have trespassed against him." Whereupon the archbishop refusing to swear, and perceiving their intent, called in his company again, and in multiplying of words to and fro, at length they came to the bishops who were excommunicate for the coronation of the king, whom they commanded in the king's name he should absolve and set free again. The archbishop answered, "That he neither suspended nor excommunicated them, but the pope; wherefore, if that were the matter that grieved them, they should resort to the pope, he had nothing to do with the matter."

Then said Reginald one of the four; "although you in your own person did not excommunicate them, yet through your instigation it was done." To whom the archbishop said again, "and if the pope (said he) tendering the injuries done to me and my church, wrought this revenge for me, I confess it offends me nothing." "Thus then (said they) it appears well by your own words, that it pleases you right well (in contempt and contumely of the king's majesty) to sequestrate his bishops from their ministry, who at the commandment of the king did service in the coronation of his son. And seeing you have so presumed thus to stand against the exaltation of this our sovereign, our new king, it seems likely that you aspired to take his crown from him, and to be exalted king yourself." "I aspire not (said he) to the crown and name of the king, but rather if I had four crowns (to give him more), I would set them all upon him; such good will I do bear him, that only his father the king excepted, there is none, whose honour I more tender and love. And as concerning the sequestrating of those bishops, this I give you to understand, that nothing was done in that behalf without the knowledge and assent of the king himself; to whom when I had made my complaint at the feast of Mary Magdalene, of the wrong and injury done to me and my church therein; he gave me his good leave to obtain at the pope's hand such remedy as I could, promising moreover his help to me in the same." "What is this," quoth they, "that thou sayest? Makest thou the king a traitor, and a betrayer of the king his own son? that when he had commanded the bishops to crown his son, he would give thee leave afterward to suspend them for so doing? Certainly, it had been better for you not to have accused so the king of this treachery." The archbishop said to Reginald, that he was there present at that time, and heard it himself. But that he denied, and swore it was not so. "And think you (said they) that we the king's subjects will or ought to suffer this?" And so approaching near him, they said he had spoken enough against his own head; whereupon followed great exclamation and many threatening words. Then said the archbishop, "I have since my coming over sustained many injuries and rebukes, concerning both myself, my men, my cattle, my wines, and all other goods; notwithstanding the king, writing over to his son, required him that I should live in safety and peace, and now, beside all others, you come hither to threaten me." To this Reginald answering again, said, "If there be any that works you any injury otherwise than is right, the law is open, why do you not complain?" "To whom, (said Becket,) should I complain?" "To the young king," said they. Then said Becket, "I have complained enough if that would help, and have sought for remedy at the king's hands, so long as I could be suffered to come to his speech; but now seeing that I am stopt from that neither can find redress of so great vexations and injuries as I have and do daily sustain, nor can have the benefit of the law or reason; such right and law, as an archbishop may have, that will I exercise and will be hindered for no man." At these words one of them, bursting out in exclamation, cried, "He threatens, he threatens. What? will he interdict the whole realm and us altogether?" "Nay, that he shall not, (saith another,) he has interdicted too many already." And drawing more near to him, they protested and denounced him to have spoken words to the jeopardy of his own head. And so departing in great fury and with many high words, they rushed out of the doors; but returning to the monks, charged them in the king's name, to keep him forthcoming, that he should not escape away. "What," quoth the archbishop, "think ye, I will flee away? Nay, neither for the king, nor any man alive, will I stir one foot from you." "No, (say they,) thou shalt not leave, though thou wouldst." And so they departed, the archbishop following them out of the chamber door, crying after them, "Here, here, here shall you find me," laying his hand upon his crown.

The names of these four soldiers above mentioned were these, Reginald Bereson, Hugh Mortevil, William Thracy, and Richard Brito, who going to put on their armour, returned the same day, but finding the hall door of the palace of Canterbury shut against them, they went to an inward back door leading into the orchard; there they broke a window, and opened the door, and so got into the palace. The monks (it being about even-song time) had got the archbishop into the church, who being persuaded by them, caused his cross to be borne before him, and through the cloister, by a door which was broken up for him, he proceeded into the choir. The armed men following after, at length came to the church-door, which door the monks would have shut against them; but, as the history says, the archbishop would not suffer them. So they approaching into the church, and the archbishop meeting them upon the stairs, there he was slain; every one of the four soldiers striking him with his sword into the head, who afterward flying into the north, at length, with much ado, obtained their pardon of the pope by the king's procurement, and as some histories record, went to Jerusalem.

Thus you have the life and death of Thomas Becket, what judgment we should form respecting him, let his own actions and conduct declare. And although the Scripture ought to be the only rule for us to judge all things by, yet if any one shall require further testimony to satisfy the mind, we have the judgments of certain men, in years and times almost as ancient as himself respecting his conduct.

And first to begin with the testimony of one of his own religion and church, and also not far from his own time, who in writing of his martyrdom and miracles, gives to us the judgment and opinion of others concerning his promotion and behaviour. The Chronicle being written in Latin, is here translated for the English reader: "Many there are who as to his promotion regard it not as canonical. For it was effected rather by the influence of the king (thinking him a man ready and useful to him) than by the assent either of the clergy or of the people. It is remarked in him as presumption and want of discretion, that when scarce worthy to take the oar in hand, he would take upon him to sit at the helm and guide the ship of the church, where the crew being in gesture and vesture religious, is wont to have their prelate of the same profession. Whereas he scarcely bearing the habit of a clergyman, and going in his changes and soft apparel, is more conversant among the delicate rufflers in the court, rather savouring of worldly things, not refusing to climb up to the high preferment of such an holy dignity, but rather willingly and of his own accord aspiring to it. Moses we read did otherwise, he being the friend of God and sent by him to conduct his people Israel out of Egypt, trembled at the message, and said, who am I, Lord, that I should go to Pharoah, and bring thy people Israel out of Egypt, &c."

And although scarcely any testimony is to be taken of that age (being all blinded and corrupted with superstition), yet let us hear what Neubergensis an ancient historian says, who being a contemporary and continuing his history to the time of King Richard I. has these words, writing of Thomas Becket.

"Whereas many are wont, in those whom they love or praise (judging them more by affection than prudence) to allow and approve whatever they do, yet if I might judge this reverend man, verily I do not think his doings and action praiseworthy or allowable, for so much as they were unprofitable and only stirred up the anger of the king, whereupon afterward sprung many and great mischiefs, although what he did might have proceeded from a laudable zeal."

To this matter also refer the words of Cesarius the monk, about the eight and fortieth year after the death of Thomas Becket, (A.D. 1220), his words are to this effect:—

"There was a question moved among the masters of the university of Paris, whether that Thomas Becket was saved or damned? To this question Roger, a Norman, answered, that he was worthy of death and damnation, because he was so obstinate against God's minister, his king. On the other hand, Peter Cantor, a Parisian, disputed, saying and affirming, that his miracles were great signs and tokens of salvation, and also of great holiness in that man; affirming, moreover, that the cause of the church allowed and confirmed his martyrdom, for which church he died," &c.

And thus have ye the judgment and censure of the school of Paris touching this question, for the sainting of Thomas Becket. In which judgment as the greatest argument rests in the miracles said to have been wrought by him after his death; let us, therefore, pause a little, and examine these miracles. In this examination we shall find one of these two things to be true, either that if the miracles were true, they were wrought not by God, but by a contrary spirit, of whom Christ our Lord gives us warning in his gospel, saying, "There shall arise false Christs and false prophets, and shall shew great signs and wonders, insomuch that if it were possible, they shall deceive the very elect," Matt. xxiv. 24. 2 Thes. ii. 9. Rev. xiii. 14.; or else we shall find that no such miracles were ever wrought at all, but were feigned and forged by idle monks, and by nuns and friars, for the exaltation of their churches, and the profit of their purses: this, indeed, seems rather to be the truth, as may appear by the miracles themselves, set forth by one of his own monks, and of his own time. This monk, in five solemn books, has included all the revelations, virtues, and miracles of the archbishop; which books I have seen and perused: in them is contained the whole sum of all his miracles, to the number of two hundred and seventy; and they are far beyond all truth and reason; some are ridiculous, some monstrous, and vain, and absurd, some blasphemous, and some so impudent, that not only they deserve no credit, (altogether savouring of mere forgery), but also for very shame would abash a modest pen to write them. Now if miracles serve for convincing infidels, what necessity was there, in a christian realm that has the word of God, for God to work such miracles after the death of a man who never wrought any miracle in all his life? Then if we consider the object of these miracles, to what purpose do they tend, but only to bring men to Canterbury, with their vows and offerings to enrich the Convent?

Beside the number of these miracles, which is said to be so great, that they lose all credit, what disease is there belonging to man or woman, in the curing of which some miracle has not been wrought by this wonderworker, as fevers, the gout, tooth-ache, palsy, consumption, falling sickness, leprosy, head-ache, broken arms, maimed legs, swelling throats, the raising up the dead who have been two days departed, with numberless others.

To recite all these prodigious revelations and fantastical miracles, falsely imagined and ascribed to this archbishop, were nothing else but to write a legend of lies, and to occupy the people with trifles. And because it pertains rather to the idle profession of such dreaming monks and cloisterers, that have nothing else to maintain their religion with; I will not take their profession out of their hands. Wherefore, to omit all such vain and lying apparitions and miracles, as how this angry saint (three days after his death) appeared by vision at the altar in his Pontifical robes, commanding the choir not to sing, but to say this office of his mass, *Exurge, quare obdormis, Domine, &c.* To omit also the blasphemous lie, how in another vision the archbishop said, "That his blood did cry out of the earth to God, more than the blood of righteous Abel." Also in another vision that appeared to a monk, how this saint Thomas had his place in heaven appointed with the apostles, above Stephen, Lawrence, Vincent, and all other martyrs; for which this reason is given that St. Stephen, Lawrence, and others, suffered only for their own cause; but that this Thomas Becket suffered for the universal church. Also, how it was shewn to a young man twelve years before the death of this Becket, that among the apostles and martyrs in heaven there was a vacant place left for a certain priest of England, which was credibly supposed to be this Thomas Becket. Also, how a certain knight's son, being two days dead,

was revived again so soon as he had the water of Canterbury put into his mouth, and had four pieces of silver offered by his parents, in Canterbury, in the child's behalf. All these, I say, with such others, I omit, giving only this one story, or another that follows, which shall suffice to express the vanity and impudent forgery of all the rest.

There is a miracle of a countryman of Bedfordshire, whose name was Eilward; in his drunkenness, bursting into another man's house, who was his debtor, he took out of his house a whetstone, and a pair of hedging gloves. The other party seeing this value not sufficient for his condemnation, entered an action of felony against him for other things besides, as for stealing his wimble, his axe, his net, and other cloths. Whereupon Eilward being condemned, was judged to have both his eyes put out. Which punishment by the malice of his adversary being executed upon him, he, lying in great danger of death by bleeding, was counselled to make his prayer to this Thomas of Canterbury. Which done, saith the miracle, there appeared one to him by night, in white apparel, bidding him to watch and pray, and put his trust in God and our lady, and holy St. Thomas Becket. In conclusion, the miracle thus fell out. The next day at evening, the man, rubbing his eyelids, began to feel his eyes restored again; first, in a little, after in a greater measure, so that one was of a grey colour, the other was of black. This one miracle I thought here to express, that by this one thou mightest judge of all the rest of his miracles. Wherefore, as I said, if the holy sainting of Thomas Becket stands upon nothing but his miracles, what credit is to be given thereto? and upon what a weak ground his shrine has stood so long, by this may easily be seen. Another fable as notable as this we read in the story of Gervasius. That Thomas Becket appearing to a certain priest, named Thomas, declared to him that he had so brought to pass, that all the names of the monks of the church of Canterbury, with the names of the priests and clerks, and with the families belonging to that city and church of Canterbury, were written in the book of life!

But whatever is to be thought of his miracles, or however the testimony of the school of Paris, or of these ancient times, went with him or against him, certain it is, that this anthem, lately written and used in his praise, is blasphemous, and derogates from the praise of him to whom only all praise and honour is due.

> By the blood of Thomas,
>   Which he for thee did spend,
> Grant us, Christ, to climb,
>   Where Thomas did ascend.

After the death of Thomas Becket, the king, fearing the pope's wrath and curse, sent the archbishop of Rothomage, with other bishops and archdeacons, to the pope with his excuse, which the pope would in nowise hear. And after other messengers were sent, it was shewn to them that on Good Friday, the pope was used to absolve or to curse, and that it was rumoured that the king of England, with his bishops, would be cursed, and his land interdicted, and that they should be put into prison. After this, certain of the cardinals shewed the pope, that the messengers had power to swear to the pope, that the king would obey his punishment and penance. So that on the same day the pope cursed the perpetrators, and all that either aided or harboured them.

The king's ambassadors could find no grace or favour for a long time at the pope's hands. At length it was agreed, that two cardinals should be sent down to inquire into the matter concerning those that were consenting to Becket's death. The king, perceiving what was preparing at Rome, and being yet uncertain what the design of the pope and coming down of the cardinals would tend to, applied himself with a great army to invade Ireland, giving it in charge and commandment, that no bearer of any brief or letter should come into England, or pass out of the realm, without special licence and assurance, that he would bring nothing that should be prejudicial to the realm.

L

This being ordained, the king, with four hundred great ships, takes his voyage to Ireland, where he subdued in a short time the whole land, which at that time was governed under several kings, to the number of five; of whom four submitted themselves to King Henry, the fifth only refused to submit, keeping in the woods and marshes.

While the king was thus occupied in Ireland, the two cardinals that were sent from the pope, Theodine and Albert, were come to Normandy. The year following, the king went to meet them, (October, A. D. 1172). The king, returning out of Ireland, by Wales, into England, and from thence to Normandy, there cleared himself of the charge, before the pope's legates, as to the death of Becket, to which he swore he was neither aiding nor consenting, but only that he spoke severely against him, because his knights would not avenge him against Thomas; for which cause this penance was enjoined him under his oath.

First, that he should send so much money into the Holy Land, as would supply two hundred knights or soldiers for the defence of that land.

Also, that from Christmas-day next following, he should set forth in his own person to fight for the Holy Land, for the space of three years together, unless he should be otherwise dispensed with by the pope.

Also, that if he would make his journey into Spain, he should there fight against the Saracens, and as long as he should abide there, so long he might take in prolonging his journeys to Jerusalem.

Also, that he should not hinder, nor cause to be hindered by him, any appeal made to the pope of Rome.

Also, that neither he nor his son should depart or dissever from Pope Alexander, or from his catholic successors, so long as they should count him or his son for catholic kings.

Also, that the goods and possessions taken from the church of Canterbury should be restored, as they stood the year before Thomas Becket departed the realm; and that free liberty should be granted to all such as were outlawed for Becket's cause to return again.

Also, that the customs and decrees established by him against the church, should be extinct and repealed, (such only except that concerned his own person, &c.), besides other secret fastings and alms enjoined him.

All these conditions the king with his son agreed to, debasing himself in such submission before the two cardinals, that they took no little glory from it, using this verse of the Psalm : "He looketh on the earth, and it trembleth, He toucheth the hills, and they smoke," Psalm civ. 32. It is mentioned, too, that a little after, the king returning out of Normandy to England, came first to Canterbury, (A.D.1174) and as he came within sight of Becket's church, lighting off his horse, and putting off his shoes he went barefoot to the tomb, the steps of which were found bloody, through the roughness of the stones. And not only that, but he received the further penance of the discipline of the rod, by every monk of the cloister. By which great degradation of the king, if it were true, we may see the blind and lamentable superstition and ignorance of those days.

The next year (A. D. 1175), a convocation of bishops was held at Westminster by Richard archbishop of Canterbury. In which all the bishops and abbots of the province of Canterbury and of York being present, determined (as it had done a little before in the days of King Henry I. A. D. 1113) about the obedience that York should pay to Canterbury; that is, whether the archbishop of York might bear his cross in the diocese of Canterbury or not, of which somewhat was mentioned before in this history. Upon these and other such matters rose such controversy between these two sees, that the one appealed the other to the presence of the bishop of Rome.

In these and such like causes, how much better had it been if the supremacy had remained more near at home in the king's hands. By which not only much labour and travelling had been saved, but also the great and wasteful expenses at Rome might with much more fruit and profits have been spent among their cures and flocks committed to them.

We have stated already among the acts and doings of Pope Alexander III., how he had brought the emperor's head under his foot in St. Mark's church at Venice, when the peace was there concluded, and a composition made between the pope and the Emperor Frederick. This pacification Roger Hoveden, and Walter Gisburn, refer to about this time, (A. D. 1177), bringing in two letters sent from the said pope to Richard archbishop of Canterbury, and to Roger archbishop of York, and to Hugh bishop of Durham. Out of which letters, so much as serves to our present purpose, I have here inserted.

The Letter of Pope Alexander.

"Alexander servant of the servants of God, to his reverend brethren Roger archbishop of York, and Hugh bishop of Durham, greeting and apostolical blessing. The obsequiousness and service of your kind devotion, which hitherto you are known to have given both devoutly and laudably to us and to the church, requires that we should describe to you, as to our special friends, the prosperous success of the church, and to let you know, as spiritual children of the church, what has happened to the same. For it is meet, convenient, and also honest, that you, whom we have had so firm and sure in our devotion, should now be cherished and made joyous in the prosperity of us and of the church."

And about the end of the epistle it follows thus :

"The next day, which was the feast of St. James, the emperor so requesting us, we came to the church of St. Mark, to celebrate there our solemn mass; where (as we were coming in the way) the emperor met us without the church, and placing us on his right hand, he brought us so into the church. After the mass was done, placing us again on his right hand, he brought us to the church door. And moreover, when we would mount our palfry he held our stirrup, exhibiting to us such honour and reverence, as his progenitors were wont to exhibit to our predecessors. Wherefore these shall serve to excite your diligence and zeal towards us, that you may rejoice with us and the church in these our prosperous successes, and also that you may open the same source of peace to other devout children of the church: that such as are touched with the zeal of the house of the Lord, may be thankful and rejoice in the Lord for the great peace which he hath given. Given at Venice, the 26th of July."

This year the contention revived again between the two archbishops of York and Canterbury, the occasion whereof was this; the manner and practice of the pope is, when he begins to want money, to send some cardinal abroad to gather in his harvest. So there came this year into England a cardinal from Rome, called Hugo, who would needs keep a council at Westminster. To this council resorted a great concourse of bishops, abbots, priors, doctors, and others of the clergy. As every one was there placed in his order, and according to his rank, first comes the archbishop of York, who to anticipate the other archbishop, came something sooner, and placed himself on the right hand of the cardinal, the archbishop of Canterbury following shortly after, and seeing the first place occupied, refuses to take the second; complaining of the archbishop of York, as having prejudiced his see. So while the one would not rise, and the other would not sit down, there arose no small contention between them. The archbishop of Canterbury claimed the upper seat by the pre-eminence of his church. On the other hand, the archbishop of York alleged the old decree of Gregory. By which this order was appointed between the two metropolitans of Canterbury and York, that which ever of them should be first in election, should have the pre-eminence in dignity before the other. Thus contending to and fro, they waxed so warm in words, that at last they turned to blows. How strong the archbishop of York was in reason and argument, I cannot tell; but the archbishop of Canterbury was stronger at the arm's end; whose servants being more in number and like valiant men, not suffering their master to take up with such a trick, so succeeded against York, as he sat on the right hand of the cardinal, that they plucked him down from the hand to the foot of the cardinal upon the ground, treading and trampling upon him with their feet, so that it was a marvel he escaped with life. His robes were all rent and torn from his back.

But what did the noble Roman cardinal? Standing up in the midst, and seeing the house in such a broil, he committed himself to flight. The next day the archbishop of York brings to the cardinal his robes, to bear witness what injury and violence he had sustained; appealing and citing up the archbishop of Canterbury to the bishop of Rome. And thus the holy council was dissolved the same day it was begun.

Under the reign of this King Henry II, the dominion and crown of England extended so far as had not been seen in this realm before him; histories record him as possessing under his rule and jurisdiction, first, Scotland, to whom William king of Scots, with all the lords temporal and spiritual, did homage both for them and for their successors (the seal whereof remains in the king's treasury) as also Ireland, England, Normandy, Aquitaine, Gaunt, &c., to the mountains of the Pyrennees, being also protector of France; to whom Philip the French king yielded both himself and his realm wholly to his government, (A. D. 1181). He was offered also to be made king of Jerusalem, by the patriarch and master of the hospital there; who, being distressed by the Soldan, brought him the keys of the city, desiring his aid against the infidels; which offer he refused, alleging the great charge which he had at home, and the rebellion of his sons, which might happen in his absence.

The wisdom, discretion, manhood, and riches of this prince was so spread abroad and renowned in all quarters, that messages came from Emmanuel emperor of Constantinople, Frederick emperor of Rome, and William archbishop of Treves in Germany, the duke of Saxony, and from the earl of Flanders, and also from the French king, to ask counsel and determination in difficult questions from this King Henry, as one most wise, and schooled in all wisdom and justice, so as to solve their questions and doubts. Alphonso king of Castile, and Sancius king of Navarre being in strife for certain castles and other possessions, submitted them (of their free accord, and by their oath) to abide the award of this King Henry: who made his award and pleased them both; by this it is to be supposed, that this king, to whom other princes so resorted, as to their arbitrer and judge, was not given either to sloth or vicious living. From which it may appear that the acts of this prince were not so vicious as some monkish writers describe.

Among many other memorable things in this king, one is that he reigned five-and-thirty years, and having such wars with his enemies, yet he never put upon his subjects any tribute or tax. And yet his treasury after his death amounted to above nine hundred thousand pounds, besides jewels, precious stones, and household furniture.

But as there is no felicity or wealth in this mortal world so perfect, as not to be darkened with some cloud of adversity; so it happened to this king, that among his other princely successors, this affliction followed him, that his sons rebelled and stood in arms against him, taking the part of the French king against their father.

At the coronation of his son Henry, whom the father joined with him as king, he being both father and king, notwithstanding, set down as if he was only an attendant, the first dish to his son, renouncing the name of a king. The archbishop of York, sitting on the right hand of the young king, said, "Sir, ye have great cause this day to joy, for there is no prince in the world that hath such an attendant this day," &c. And the young king disdaining his words, said, "My father is not dishonoured in doing this, for I am a king and a queen's son, and he is not so." And not only this, but afterwards he even persecuted his father; and so in his youth when he had reigned but a few years he died; teaching us what is the reward of breaking the commandment of God.

After him likewise his son Richard (who was called Richard Cœur de Lion) rebelled against his father, and also John his youngest son did not much degenerate from the steps of his brethren. Insomuch that this

Richard, taking part against his father, brought him to such distress of body and mind, that for sorrow of heart he fell into an ague, and within four days departed, (A.D. 1189) after he had reigned five-and-thirty years.

And thus much concerning the reign of Henry II., and the death of Thomas Becket; whose death happened in the days of Pope Alexander III.; which pope usurping the keys of the ecclesiastical government one-and-twenty years (or as Gisburn writes, three and-twenty years) governed the church with much tumult.

This pope, among many other acts, had certain councils, some in France, some at Rome, in Lateran; by whom it was decreed, that no archbishop should receive the pall, unless he should first swear to obey the pope. Concerning the solemnity of which pall, for the order and manner of giving and taking the same with obedience to the pope, as it is contained in their own words, I thought it good to set it forth.

The form and manner how and by what words the pope is wont to give the pall unto the Archbishop.

"To the honour of Almighty God, and of blessed Mary the virgin, and of blessed St. Peter and Paul, and of our lord Pope N., and of the holy church of Rome, and also of the church of N., committed to your charge, we give to you the pall taken from the body of St. Peter, as a fulness of the pontifical office, which you may wear within your own church upon certain days which are expressed in the privileges of the said church, granted by the see apostolic."

In like manner proceedeth the oath of every bishop swearing obedience to the pope as follows:

" I, N., bishop of N., from this hour henceforth, will be faithful and obedient to blessed St. Peter, and to the holy apostolic church of Rome, and to my lord N. the pope. I shall be in no council, nor help either with my consent or deed, whereby either of them, or any member of them may be impaired, or whereby they may be taken with any evil taking. The council which they shall commit to me either by themselves, or by messenger, or by their letters wittingly or willingly I shall utter to none to their hinderance and damage. To the retaining and maintaining the papacy of Rome, and the regalities of St. Peter, I shall be an aider (so mine order be saved) against all persons, the legate of the apostolic see, both in going and coming, I shall honourably treat and help in all necessities. Being called to a Synod I shall be ready to come, unless I be hindered, by some lawful and canonical impeachment. The palace of the apostles every third year I shall visit either by myself or my messenger, except otherwise being licensed by the see apostolic. All such possessions as belong to the table and diet of my bishoprick, I shall neither sell, nor give, nor lay to mortgage, nor lease out, nor remove away by any manner of means without the consent and knowledge of the bishop of Rome; so God help me and the holy gospels of God."

In the reign of King Henry, (about A.D. 1178), I find in Roger Hoveden and others, that in the city of Toulouse there was a great multitude of men and women whom the pope's commissioners prosecuted and condemned as heretics; some of them were scourged naked, some were chased away, and some were compelled to abjure. Concerning their opinions I can give no certain account, because I find the papists so often falsifying things in their accusations, and untruly collecting men's words, not as they meant them, but wresting and depraving men's assertions in such a way as pleased themselves. But I find that one of the commissioners or inquisitors (Henry the abbot), in a letter, wrote thus of one of them, that, "After a new opinion he affirmed that the holy bread of eternal life, consecrated by the ministry of h e priest, was not the body of the Lord," &c.

In the time of this Pope Alexander commenced the doctrine and name of those who were called, "Poor men of Lyons," who, from Waldus or Waldo, a chief senator in Lyons, were named "Waldenses," (about A.D., 1160, or as Laziard writes A.D. 1170.)

Not long before this time lived Gratian, master of the

decrees, and Peter Lombard, master of the sentences, both arch-pillars of all papistry; after whom followed two others as bad or worse than they, Francis and Dominic, maintaining blind hypocrisy not less than the others maintained proud prelacy. As these laboured one way by superstition and worldly advancement to corrupt the simplicity of the christian religion, so it pleased Christ on the contrary, working against them, to raise up the Waldenses against the pride and hypocrisy of the others.

Thus we never see any great corruption in the church, but some sparks of the true and clear light of the gospel by God's providence remains; whatever doctors Austin, Reinerius, Sylvius, Cranzius, with others in their popish histories, write of them, defaming them and accusing them as disobedient to orders, rebels to the catholic church, and contemners of the Virgin Mary; yet they that judge impartial judgment, rather trusting truth than wavering with the times, in weighing their articles, shall find it otherwise; and that they maintained nothing but the same doctrine which is now defended in the church.

The history of the Waldenses concerning their original and doctrine, with their persecutions.

The first origin of these Waldenses was one Waldus, (or Waldo), a man of great substance in the city of Lyons. About the year 1160 some of the best and chief inhabitants of the city of Lyons, walking in a certain place after their old accustomed manner, especially in the summer time, conferred and consulted together on various matters, either to pass away the time, or to debate their measures. Among them it chanced that one fell down suddenly dead; this Waldus was among them at the time. He, looking on the matter more earnestly than the others, and terrified with so awful an example, and God's Holy Spirit working within him, was stricken with a deep and inward repentance. Upon this followed a great change, with a careful study to reform his former life. So that first he began to minister large alms of his goods to such as were in need. Secondly, to instruct himself and his family with the true knowledge of God's word. Thirdly, to admonish all that resorted to him on any occasion, to repentance and virtuous amendment of life. Partly through his extensive charities to the poor, partly through his diligent teaching and wholesome admonitions, more of the people daily frequented about him; and when he saw them ready and diligent to learn, he began to give out to them certain easy portions of the scripture, which he had translated himself into the French tongue; for as he was wealthy in riches, so he was also not unlearned in languages.

Although Laziard, Volateran, with others, describe him as utterly unlearned, and charge him with ignorance, yet by others that have seen his works yet remaining in old parchment monuments, it appears he was both able to declare and translate the books of scripture, and also to collect the comments of the learned upon them.

But whatever he was, whether lettered or unlettered, the bishops and prelates seeing him thus intermeddle with the scriptures, and have such resort about him, although it was only in his own house and in private conference, could not abide that the scriptures should be explained by any other than themselves, and yet they would not take the pains to explain it themselves. So they threatened to excommunicate him if he did not cease to do so. Waldus seeing his proceedings to be godly, and their malice stirred up without just or godly cause, neglected the threatenings and frettings of the wicked, and said, "that God must be obeyed rather than man." To be brief, the more diligent he was in setting forth the true doctrine of Christ against the errors of antichrist, the more maliciously their fierceness increased. So that when they saw their excommunication despised, they ceased not to persecute him with

prison, with sword, and banishment, till at length they had driven both Waldus and all the favourers of his true preaching out of the city.

Whereupon came first their name, that they were called Waldenses, or the poor men of Lyons, not because they would have all things common among them, or that they, professing any wilful poverty, would imitate to live as the apostles did (as Eneas Sylvius falsely belied them), but because, being thrust out both of country and of goods, they were compelled to live poorly whether they would or not.

And thus much touching the first occasion and beginning of these men, and of the restoring and maintaining of the true doctrine of Christ's gospel, against the proud proceedings of popish errors. Now, concerning their articles, which I find in order and in number to be these:—

I. Only the holy scripture is to be believed in matters pertaining to salvation, and no man's writing, or man besides.

II. All things necessary to salvation are contained in holy scripture, and nothing is to be admitted in religion, but only what is commanded in the word of God.

III. There is one only Mediator; other saints are in no wise to be made mediators, or to be invoked.

IV. There is no purgatory, but all men are justified by Christ to life, or without Christ are condemned; and besides these two there is not any third or fourth place.

V. That all masses, namely, such as are sung for the dead, are wicked and ought to be abolished.

VI. All men's traditions are to be rejected, at least not to be reputed as necessary to salvation, and therefore this singing and superfluous chanting in the chancel should be ceased; constrained and prefixed fasts bound to days and times, difference of meats, such variety of degrees and orders of priests, friars, monks, and nuns, superfluous holy days, so many sundry benedictions and hallowing of creatures, vows, pilgrimages, with all the rites and ceremonies brought in by man, ought to be abolished.

VII. The supremacy of the pope usurping above all churches, and especially above all realms and governments, and his usurping the jurisdiction of both the swords, is to be denied; and no degree of orders is to be received in the church, but priests, deacons, and bishops.

VIII. The communion under both kinds is necessary to all people, according to the institution of Christ.

IX. The church of Rome is the very Babylon spoken of in the Apocalypse; and the pope the fountain of all error, and the very antichrist.

X. The pope's pardons and indulgences they reject.[1]

XI. The marriage of priests and of ecclesiastical persons, is godly, and also necessary in the church.

XII. Such as hear the word of God, and have a right faith, are the right church of Christ. And to this church the keys of the church are given, to drive away wolves, and to institute true pastors, and to preach the word, and to minister the sacraments.[2]

These are the principal articles of the Waldenses, although there are some who add more to them; some again divide these into more parts.

The Waldenses, at length exiled, were dispersed in many and various places, many remained long in Bohemia, who, writing to their king, Uladislaus, to clear themselves against the slanderous accusations of Dr. Austin, gave their confession together with an apology of their christian profession; defending with strong and learned arguments the same defence and confession which is now received in most reformed churches concerning grace, faith, charity, hope, repentance, and works of mercy.

As for purgatory, they say that Thomas Aquinas is the creator of it.

Concerning the supper of the Lord, their faith was,

---

(1) This article seems to be given of them in Bohemia not long after, for indulgences came not in before Boniface VIII.

(2) Some ancient authors add another article—viz. "They receive and approve of two sacraments only, Baptism and the Communion." [ED.]

that it was ordained to be eaten, not to be shewed and worshipped; for a memorial, not for a sacrifice; to serve for the present ministration, and not for reservation; to be received at the table, not to be carried out of the doors; according to the ancient use of the primitive church, when they used to communicate sitting. And this they prove both by an old chronicle called Chronica Gestorum, as also by ancient Origen upon the third book of Moses, bringing in his words, which are these, proving that this sacramental bread ought not to be reserved:—" Whoever receives this bread of the supper of Christ upon the second or third day after, his soul shall not be blessed, but polluted. Therefore because the Gibeonites brought old bread to the children of Israel, it was enjoined them to carry wood and water," &c.

Dr. Austin, disputing against them about this matter of the holy eucharist, urges them with this question, whether it be the same Christ present in the sacrament which is present at the right hand of the Father? If it be not the same Christ, how is it true in the scripture, " One faith, one Lord Jesus Christ?" If it be the same Christ, then how is he not to be honoured and worshipped here as well as there?

To this the Waldenses answer and grant that Christ is one and the same with his natural body, in the sacrament which he is at the right hand of his Father, but not after the same existence of his body. For the existence of his body in heaven is personal and local, to be apprehended by the faith and spirit of men. In the sacrament the existence of the body is not personal or local, to be apprehended or received of our bodies, after a personal or corporeal manner, but after a sacramental manner; that is, where our bodies receive the sign, and our spirit the thing signified. Moreover, in heaven the existence of his body is complete with the full proportion and quantity wherewith he ascended. Here, the existence of his complete body, with the full proportion, measure, and stature, does not, and cannot stand in the sacrament.

That answer being made to the captious proposition of Dr. Austin, the Waldenses (retorting the like question to him) demand of him to answer them: Whether it be all one Christ substantially and naturally, which sits in heaven, and which is under the forms of bread and wine, and in the receivers of the sacrament? If he grant it to be so; then they bid him say, seeing Christ is as well in the sacrament as in heaven, and as well in the receiver as in the sacrament, and all one Christ in substance and nature; why then is not the same Christ to be worshipped as well in the breast of the receiver, as under the forms of bread and wine in the sacrament; seeing he is there after a more perfect manner in man, than in the sacrament? for in the sacrament he is but for a time, and not for the sacrament's sake, but for the man's sake: in man he is not for the sacrament's sake, but for his own; and that not for a season, but for ever, as it is written, " He that eateth this bread shall live for ever," &c.

Besides this, seeing transubstantiation is the passing of one substance into another; they question again with him, whether, the forms of bread and wine remaining, the substance be changed into the whole person of our Lord Christ Jesus; that is, into his body, soul, and divinity, or not into the whole Christ? If he grant the whole; then say they, that is impossible (concerning the divinity) both to nature and to our faith, that any creature can be changed into the Creator. If he say, the bread is changed into the body and soul of Christ, not to his divinity, then he separates the natures in Christ. If he say, into the body alone, and not the soul, then he separates the natures of the true manhood, &c. and so it cannot be the same Christ that was betrayed for us; for that he had both body and soul. To conclude, to what part soever he would answer, this doctrine of transubstantiation could not be defended without great inconveniences.

Besides this, Eneas Sylvius, writing of their doctrine and assertions (perchance as he found them, perchance making worse of them than they taught or meant) reports of them after this manner:

" The bishop of Rome is equal with other bishops. Among priests there is to be no difference of degree. No priest is to be reputed for any dignity of his order, but for the worthiness of his life.

"The souls of men departed enter either into pain everlasting, or everlasting joy. There is no fire of purgatory. To pray for the dead is vain, and a thing only invented for the lucre of priests.

" The images of God (as of the Trinity) and of saints should be abolished. The hallowing of water and palm are a mere ridicule. The religion of begging friars is an invention of the devil. Priests should not engross riches in this world, but rather follow poverty, being content with their tithes, and men's devotion. The preaching of the word should be free to all men called thereto.

" No deadly sin is to be tolerated, for the sake of a greater convenience. The confirmation which bishops exercise with oil, and extreme unction, are not to be counted among the sacraments of the church. Auricular confession is but a childish thing; it is enough for every man to confess himself in his chamber to God. Baptism ought to be administered only with pure water, without any mixture of hallowed oil. The temple of the Lord is the wide world. The majesty of God is not restrained within the walls of temples, monasteries, and chapels, so as that his grace should be found in one place more than in another.

" Priests' apparel, ornaments of the high altar, vestments, corporals, chalices, patins, and other church-plate, are of no use. It makes no matter in what place the priest consecrates or ministers to them who require it. It is sufficient to use only the sacramental words without other superfluous ceremonies.

" The suffrages of saints, reigning with Christ in heaven, are prayed for in vain; they being unable to help us. In saying or singing the hours and matins of the day the time is lost. A man ought to cease from his labour no day, but only upon the Sunday.

" The feasts and festivals of saints ought to be rejected. Such fasts as are compulsory, and enjoined by the church, have no merit in them."

The doctrines of the Waldenses being thus specified by Eneas Sylvius, who afterwards was pope, I thought it well to give them in English, that as they are the less to be doubted, being described by the pen of this pope, so we may the better know what their opinions were, and also understand how this doctrine, now preached and taught in the protestant church, is no new doctrine, inasmuch as we here see it both taught and persecuted almost 400 years ago. And as I have spoken hitherto sufficiently concerning their doctrine: so now we will briefly somewhat touch of the order of their life and conversation, as we find it registered in a certain old book of inquisition.

" The manner of the Waldenses is this, kneeling upon their knees, and leaning on some bank or stay, they continue in their prayers with silence so long as a man may say the Lord's prayer thirty or forty times. And this they do every day with great reverence, among themselves, and such as are of their own religion, and no strangers with them, both before and after dinner; likewise before and after supper; also when they go to bed, and in the morning when they rise, and at certain other times also, as well in the day as in the night. They use no other prayer but the Lord's prayer, and that without any ' Hail, Mary,' or the creed, which they affirm not to be by Christ, but only by the church of Rome. Although they use the seven articles of faith concerning the divinity, and seven articles concerning the humanity, and the ten commandments, and seven works of mercy, which they have compiled together in a compendious book.

" Before they go to meat they ask a blessing, and that the Lord Christ may have mercy upon them, and they say the Lord's prayer. Which being said, then the elder among them begins thus in their own tongue:—
" God who blessed the five barley loaves, and two fishes

in the desert before his disciples, bless this table, and what is set upon it, or shall be set upon it: In the name of the Father, of the Son, and of the Holy Ghost, Amen." And likewise again, when they rise from meat, the senior gives thanks, saying the words of the Apocalypse, " Blessing, and worship, and wisdom, and thanksgiving, honour, virtue, and strength to God alone for ever and ever, Amen." And adds, moreover, "God reward them in their bosoms, and be beneficial to all them that be beneficial to us, and bless us. And may the God who has given us bodily food grant us his spiritual life; and may God be with us, and we always with him." To which they answer again, " Amen." And thus saying grace, they hold their hands upward, looking up to heaven. After their meat and grace said, they teach and exhort amongst themselves, conferring together upon their doctrine," &c.

In their doctrine and teaching they were so diligent and painful, that Reinerius, a writer about their time, and a violent enemy against them, in a long process, wherein he describes their doctrine and teaching, testifies that he heard of one who knew the party, that a certain heretic, as he calls him, merely to turn a person away from our (Roman) faith, and to bring him to that of the Waldenses, swam in the night, and in the winter time, over the river Ibis, to come to him, and to teach him. So perfect were they in the scriptures, that Reinerius says, he heard and saw an unlettered countryman who could recite the whole book of Job word by word, without book, and others who had the whole New Testament perfectly by heart.

And although some of them rather strangely than unskilfully expounded the words, " Sui non receperunt eum," John i. 11. ; " swine received him not ;" yet they were not so ignorant and devoid of learning, nor yet so few in number, but that they greatly spread; so that Reinerius has these words: " There was none durst stop them for the power and multitude of their favourers. I have often been at their inquisition and examination, and there were numbered forty churches infected with their heresy, insomuch that in one parish of Cammach, were ten open schools of them," &c.

And Reinerius, when he had said all he could in slandering and impugning them, yet is driven to confess this, where he distinguishes their sect from every other sect. " This sect of the Lyonists has a great shew of holiness, they live justly before men, and believe all things well of God, and hold all the articles contained in the creed; only they blaspheme the Romish church, and hate it," &c.

Now to say a little about their persecutions: After they were driven out of Lyons, they were scattered into various places (the Providence of God so permitting it,) that the sound of their doctrine might be heard abroad in the world. Some went to Bohemia, many fled into the provinces of France, some into Lombardy, others into other places, &c. But as the cross commonly follows the true and sincere preaching of God's word, so neither could these be suffered to live or remain at rest. There are yet to be seen the consultations of lawyers, archbishops, and bishops of France, which yet remain in writing, for the extirpation of these Waldenses, written above three hundred years ago; by which it appears that there was a great number of them in France.

Besides, there was a council held in Toulouse about three hundred and fifty-five years ago, (A. D. 1229,) against these Waldenses, who were condemned in another council at Rome before that.

What great persecutions were raised up against them in France by the pope's commissioners before alluded to, appears by their writings; I will recite some of their words, which towards the end are these :—" Who is such a stranger that he knows not the condemnation of the heretical Waldenses decreed, so many years ago, so famous, so public, followed up with so great labours, expenses, and travel of the faithful, and sealed with so many deaths of these infidels, so solemnly condemned and openly punished ?" By this we may see persecution to be no new thing in the church of Christ, when antichrist so long before (even three hundred years ago)

began to rage against these Waldenses. In Bohemia likewise afterwards, under the name of Taborites (as Sylvius records) they suffered no little trouble. But never was persecution stirred up against them, or against any other people more terrible than in these later years in France by the French king (A. D. 1545), the lamentable story is described in Sleidan, and hereafter in the course of this book, when we come to the proper period it shall be narrated (by the grace of Christ) more at large. In this persecution it is stated that in one town, Cabriera, there were slain eight hundred persons at once, without respect of women or children of any age; of whom forty women, and most of them great with child, thrust into a barn, and the windows being kept with pikes, and fire being applied to them, were all consumed. Besides, in a cave not far from the town Mussium, five-and-twenty persons, were at the same time destroyed with smoke and fire. At Merindolum (when all the rest had fled away) one young man, being found, was tied to an olive-tree, and most cruelly destroyed with torments. There was much more persecution, as shall appear hereafter in the history translated out of Sleidan.

There is also an old document of process, wherein it appears that four hundred and forty-three were brought to examination in Pomerania, Marchia, and places thereabouts, (about A. D. 1391).

And thus much touching the origin, doctrine, and lamentable persecutions of the Waldenses, who, as is declared, first began about the time of this King Henry II. It now remains in the order of time to narrate, such other incidents as occurred under the reign of this king, not unworthy to be observed.

There was a great war in Palestine, when the city of Jerusalem, with the cross and king of the city, and others of the temple, were taken by the Saracens, and most part of the christians there were either slain or taken. There was cruel murder and slaughter by the Turk, who caused all the chief of the christians to be brought forth and beheaded before his face, so that Pope Urban III. died for sorrow, and Gregory VIII., next pope after him, lived not two months. Then, in the days of Pope Clement III., sorrow was growing daily for the loss of Palestine, and destruction of the christians. King Henry of England, and Philip the French king, the duke of Burgundy, the earl of Flanders, the earl of Campania, with other christian princes with a general consent upon St. George's day, took the mark of the cross upon them, promising together to take their voyage into the Holy Land. At which time the histories say, the king of England received first the red cross, the French king took the white cross, the earl of Flanders took the green cross; and so likewise other princes took various colours, so as to be known every one by his proper cross. But King Henry (after the three years were expired, in which he promised to perform his voyage) sent to the pope for further delay of his promise, offering to erect three monasteries instead.

Almaric, king of Jerusalem, destroyed Babylon (A. D. 1170), so that it was never after to this day restored, but lies waste and desolate; wherein was fulfilled that which in the prophets was threatened against Babylon. This Almaric had a son named Baldwin, and a daughter called Sibylla.

Sibylla was first married to one Willerm, marquis of Mount Ferrat, by whom she had a son called also Baldwin. After him she was married to another husband named Guido de Liziniaco, earl of Joppa and of Ascalon. After the death of Baldwin, and the next heir, his crown by descent fell to Sibylla the wife of Guido. The peers and nobles, joining together in council, offered Sibylla as the lawful heir to the crown, that she should be their queen, with this condition, that she should separate, by solemn divorce, from her husband Guido; but she refused the kingdom offered to her on that condition, till at last the magistrates, with the nobles in general, granted to her, and by their oaths confirmed it, that whoever she would choose as her husband, they would all obey as their king. Guido her husband, among the rest, humbly requested her that the kingdom might not, for his account, or for his private loss, be destitute of government. At length, with tears consenting to their entreaty, she was solemnly crowned their queen, and received their allegiance by their oath. Upon this, Guido, without any hope of wife and kingdom, departed home quietly to his own place. Then the queen, assembling her states and prelates together, conferred with them about choosing a king, according to what they had promised, and sworn to her, that they would obey him as their king whom she would name to be her husband. Thus, while they were all in great expectation, waiting every man to see whom she would nominate, the queen with a loud voice said to Guido that stood among them, "Guido, my lord, I choose thee for my husband, and, yielding myself and my kingdom unto you, openly I proclaim you to be the king." At these words all the assembly, being amazed, wondered that one simple woman had beguiled so many wise men. And she was worthy, no doubt, to be commended and extolled for her singular virtue, both of faithfulness and prudence: so managing the matter, that she obtained to her husband the kingdom, and retained to herself her husband, whom she so faithfully loved.

As I have hitherto described the public acts of King Henry, so now I mean to say something of his private condition. He was of mean stature, eloquent, and learned, manly and bold in chivalry, fearful of the mutability and chance of war, more lamenting the death of his soldiers when dead, than loving them when alive. No one was more courteous and liberal for obtaining his purpose; in peace and tranquillity none was more rough; stubborn against the stubborn; sometimes merciful to those whom he had vanquished; strict to his household servants, but liberal to strangers; publicly of public things liberal, sparing of his own; whoever he once took a displeasure against he hardly or never would receive again to favour; somewhat lavish of his tongue, a willing breaker of his promise, a lover of his ease, but an oppressor of his nobility; a severe avenger and promoter of justice, variable of word, and crafty in his talk, a nourisher of discord amongst his children; moreover the papists, bearing him (for Thomas Becket's quarrel, and such like, as may be gathered) no good will, term him an adversary of the faith.

He died in the five-and-thirtieth year of his reign, in the castle of Chinon in Normandy.

KING RICHARD.

King Richard, the eldest son of Henry II., succeeded his father (A. D. 1189); at which time Pope Clement sat at Rome, succeeding Gregory, who died a little before with sorrow for the loss of the holy cross.

During the time of his coronation it happened, that, although the king, the day before his coronation, by public edict, had commanded the Jews and their wives not to presume either to enter the church or palace, during the solemnization of his coronation, amongst his nobles and barons, yet, while the king was at dinner, the chief of the Jews, with several others, entered the court gates. A christian man, being offended, struck one of them, and bade him stand further from the court gate, as the king had given commandment. Others following the example, and displeased against the Jews, offered them similar insult. Others, also, supposing that the king had so commanded, fell upon all the Jews that stood outside the court gate: and first they beat them; but afterwards they took up stones and such other things as they could get, and threw at them from the court gates, some of them they wounded, some they slew, and some they left for dead.

There was among the Jews, one who was called the blessed Jew of York, who was so severely wounded, that for fear of his life, he said he would become a christian, and was baptized; by which he escaped death, and the persecutors' hands. In the meanwhile, there was a great rumour spread throughout all the city of London, that the king had commanded to destroy all the Jews. Upon

which, the citizens, and innumerable people, being assembled to see the king's coronation, armed themselves and came together. The Jews thus being for the most part slain, the rest fled into their houses, where, for a time, they were defended; but at length their houses were set on fire, and they destroyed within them.

These things being declared to the king while he was with his nobles and barons at dinner, he sends immediately Ranulfe de Glanville, the lord high steward of England, with other noblemen to accompany him, that they might stay and refrain these excesses of the Londoners; but all was in vain; for in so great a tumult, there was none that either regarded what the nobility said, or reverenced their persons, but, rather with stern looks and threatening words, advised them to depart, and that quickly. They, thinking it best to do so, departed; the tumult and insurrection continuing till the next day. At which time the king, sending certain of his officers into the city, gave them in command to apprehend and present such as were the chief of the malefactors. Three were condemned to be hanged; one, because he had robbed a christian's house in the tumult; and the other two because they fired the houses to the great danger of the city. After this, the king sent for the man that from a Jew was converted to christianity, and in the presence of those that saw where he was baptized, the king asked him whether he was become a christian or not? He, answering the king, said "No; but to the intent he might escape death, he promised to do whatever the christians would have him." Then the king asked the archbishop of Canterbury (other archbishops and bishops being present) what were best to be done with him? Who, unadvisedly answering, said, "If he will not be a man of God, let him be a man of the devil," and so he returned again to Judaism.

Then the king sent his writs to the sheriffs of every county, to inquire for the authors of this outrage. Of whom three were hanged; and several were imprisoned. So great was then the hatred of Englishmen against the Jews, that as soon as they began to be removed from the court, the Londoners fell upon them, set their houses on fire, and spoiled their goods. The country again, following the example of the Londoners, did the same. And thus the year which the Jews took to be their jubilee, was to them a year of confusion. In the city of York, the Jews obtaining a certain castle for their preservation, and afterward not being willing to restore it to the christians again, when they saw no other remedy, but to be vanquished by force, first offered money for their lives; when that would not be taken, by the counsel of an old Jew among them, every one, with a sharp razor, cut another's throat, whereby a thousand and five hundred of them were destroyed.

King Richard, after the death of his father, coming to remembrance of himself, and of his rebellion against his father, sought for absolution; and, in satisfaction for the same, agreed with Philip the French King, to take his voyage with him for the recovery of Christ's patrimony, as they call the Holy Land.

After this, King Richard, preparing to set all things in an order before his going, committed the whole government of the realm, principally to William, bishop of Ely, his chancellor, and to Hugh, bishop of Durham, whom he appointed the chief justice of all England in his absence, sending also to Pope Clement, in behalf of William, bishop of Ely, that he might be made the pope's legate through all England and Scotland, which also was obtained. Thus the bishop, being advanced to high authority, provides out of every city in England, two palfries, and two sumpters, and also out of every abbey, one palfry, and one sumpter, for the king's service in Palestine.

These things being set in order, the king, according to his appointment, sailed into France, where the French king and he conferring together, prorogued their voyage till after midsummer. In the meantime, the king occupied himself in redressing and establishing such things as were requisite. He appointed the captains and constables over his navy, and set laws to be observed in his voyage upon the seas, but especially his care was to make unity and concord between parties that were at variance, and to reconcile them.

After King Richard had composed such things as were to be redressed within the realm, he advanced forward his journey, and came to Touraine, to meet with Philip the French king; and so after that went to Vezelay; where the French king and he joining together, for the continuance of their journey, assured themselves by solemn oath, swearing fidelity one to the other; the form of whose oath was this: "That either of them should defend and maintain the honour of the other, and bear true fidelity unto him of life, members, and worldly honour; and that neither of them should fail one the other in their affairs; but the French king should aid the king of England in defending his land and dominions, as he would himself defend his own city of Paris, if it were besieged; and that King Richard of England likewise should aid the French king in defending his land and dominions, no otherwise than he would defend his own city of Rouen if it were besieged," &c.

But how slenderly this oath held these two kings, and by whose chief occasion it first fell asunder, the sequel of the history (the Lord willing) shall declare.

The laws and ordinances appointed by King Richard for his navy were these:

1. That whoever killed any person on shipboard, should be tied with him that was slain, and thrown into the sea.

2. And if he killed him on the land, he should in like manner be tied with the party slain, and be buried with him in the earth.

3. He that shall be convicted by lawful witness to draw out his knife or weapon, to the intent to strike any man, or that hath stricken any to the drawing of blood, shall lose his hand.

4. Also, he that strikes any person with his hand, without effusion of blood, shall be plunged three times in the sea.

5. Whoso speaks any opprobrious or contumelious words in reviling or cursing one another, for so often as he hath so reviled, shall pay so many ounces of silver.

6. A thief or felon that has stolen, being lawfully convicted, shall have his head shorn, and boiling pitch poured upon his head, and feathers or down strewed upon the same, whereby he may be known; and so at the first landing-place they shall come to, there to be cast up, &c.

King Richard sending his navy by the Spanish seas, and by the straits of Gibraltar, to meet him at Marseilles, went himself to Vezelay, to the French king. The two kings from thence went to Lyons, where the bridge over the Rhone gave way with the press of people, and many, both men and women, were drowned. The two kings were then constrained to separate for the rest of their journey, arranging to meet in Sicily; and so Philip took his way to Genoa, and King Richard to Marseilles, where he remained eight days, appointing his navy to meet him there. From thence crossing over to Genoa, where the French king was, he passed forward by the coast of Italy, and entered the Tiber not far from Rome, where meeting with Ottoman, the cardinal and bishop of Hostia, he complained greatly of the filthy simony of the pope and the pope's court, for receiving seven hundred marks for consecrating the bishop Cenomanensis; also a thousand and five hundred marks from William the bishop of Ely for his office as legate; and likewise an infinite sum of money from the bishop of Bordeaux, for acquitting him when he should have been deposed for a certain crime laid to his charge by his clergy, &c.

The seventh day of August King Richard departed from Marseilles, and the three-and-twentieth of September arrived at Messina, with such a noise of trumpets and shawms, with such a rout and show, that it was to the great wonder and terror both of the Frenchmen and all others that heard and beheld the sight.

The French king had come to the town of Messina before the sixteenth day of the month of September, and had taken the palace of Tancred, king of Sicily, for his lodgings. King Richard after his arrival, soon went to him; and when the two kings had conversed together,

immediately the same day the French king took shipping to sail to the land of Jerusalem. But after he was out of the haven, the wind rising against him, he returned to Messina. The last day of September, Richard passed over the flood of Delfar, and there gained a strong hold called De la Bagmare, or Le Bamre, and placing therein a sufficient garrison, he returned to Messina. The second of October he won another stronghold, and he deposited there all his store and provision, which came from England or other places.

The citizens of Messina, seeing that the king of England had won the castle and island in De la Bagmare, and also the church of the Griffons, and doubting lest the King would extend his power further to invade their city, and if he could, all the Isle of Sicily, began to stir against the king's army, and to shut the Englishmen out of the gates, and keep their walls against them. The Englishmen seeing that, made to the gates, and by force would have broken them open, so that the king riding among them with his staff, and breaking some of their heads, could not assuage their fierceness; such was the rage of the Englishmen against the citizens of Messina.

The fourth day of the month of October, the archbishop of Messina came to King Richard, with two other archbishops, also with the French king, and other earls, barons, and bishops, to treat for peace. As they were consulting, and had almost concluded upon the peace, the citizens of Messina issued out of the town, some went up upon the mountains, some with open force invaded the mansion or lodging of Hugh Brun an English captain. The noise of this coming to the ears of the king, he, suddenly breaking off the conference with the French king and the rest, departed, and coming to his men, commanded them forthwith to arm themselves; who then, with some of his soldiers, making up to the top of a mountain, there put the citizens to flight, chasing them down the mountain, to the very gates of the city; some of the king's servants pursued them within the city, where five valiant soldiers, and twenty of the king's servants were slain, the French king looking on, and not once desiring to rescue them, contrary to his oath and league with the king of England. For the French king with his men, being there present, rode in the midst of them safely and without harm to and fro, and might well have assisted the king's party, if he wished.

This being known to the English army, how their comrades were slain, and the Frenchmen permitted in the city, and that they were excluded, and the gates barred against them, being also stopped from buying of food and other things; they with great indignation, gathered themselves in arms, burst open the gates, and scaled the walls, and so, winning the city, set up their flags, with the English arms upon the walls. When the French king saw this he was offended; requiring the king of England that the arms of France might also be set up and joined with his; but King Richard would not agree; but to satisfy his mind, he consented to take down his arms, and commit the custody of the city to the Hospitale and Templars of Jerusalem, till the time that Tancred king of Sicily and he, should agree together upon the conditions.

In this mean time, as these two kings of France and England were thus wintering at Messina, the emperor, Frederick I. (on whose neck Pope Alexander trod in the church of Venice, saying the verse of the psalm, "Thou shalt tread on the serpents and the adders,") and his son Conrad, with a mighty army of Germans and others, were coming likewise to the siege of Acre; where the emperor, falling off his horse into a river, was drowned. Conrad, his son, taking the command of his army, came to the siege of Acre, in which siege he also died. In consequence of the coming of this multitude of Germans, there was a dearth in the camp, which lasted two months, so that a loaf of bread, which before the coming of the German army was sold for one penny, was afterward sold for three pounds, by reason of this many christian soldiers perished through famine. The chief food which the princes had to feed upon was horse-flesh. This famine being so miserable, some good bishops who were in the camp, namely, Hubert bishop of Salisbury, with certain others, making a general collection through the whole camp for the poor, made such a provision that in this penury of all things, no man was so destitute and needy, but he had somewhat for his relief; till within a few days after by the merciful providence of God, who is the feeder of all creatures, ships came to them with abundance of corn, wine, and oil.

The siege of this town of Acre lasted a long time, and as it was ably assailed by the christians, so it was strongly defended by the Saracens, especially by the help of wildfire, which the Latins call *Greek fire*, so that there was great slaughter on both sides.

The next year following (A. D. 1191), King Richard sent over his gallies to Naples, there to meet his mother Elenor, and Berengaria the daughter of Sancius king of Navarre, whom he purposed to marry. In the meantime King Richard shewed himself exceeding bountiful and liberal to all. To the French king he gave several ships; upon others he bestowed rich rewards; and of his goods and treasure he distributed largely to his soldiers and servants about him. It was reported that he distributed more in one month, than any of his predecessors did in a whole year; by which he obtained great love and favour, which not only redounded to the advancement of his fame, but also to his great advantage and profit, as the sequel proved.

To proceed then in the progress of King Richard, leaving the city of Messina, he went to Catana, where Tancred king of Sicily then lay, where he was honourably received, and remained with King Tancred three days and three nights. On the fourth day, when he was departing, Tancred offered him many rich presents in gold and silver, and precious silks; of which King Richard would receive nothing, but one little ring, as a token of his good will. For which King Richard again gave him a rich sword. At length, when King Richard should take his leave, King Tancred would not so let him part, but would give him four great ships, and fifteen gallies; and he himself would accompany him the space of two days journey to a place called Tavernium.

Then the next morning when they should take their leave, Tancred declared to him the message which the French king a little before had sent to him by the duke of Burgundy, which was this: " That the king of England was a false traitor, and would never keep the peace that was between them. And if Tancred would war against him, or attack him secretly by night, he would assist him with all his power, and join with him to the destruction of him and all his army," &c. Richard the king protested that he was no traitor, nor ever was; and as to the peace begun between them, it should never be broken through him ; nor could he believe that the French king, being his good lord and his sworn partner in that voyage, would utter any such words by him. When Tancred heard this, he brings forth the letters of the French king sent to him by the duke of Burgundy; affirming, that if the duke of Burgundy would deny the bringing of the letters, he was ready to meet him by any of his dukes. King Richard receiving the letters, and musing not a little upon them, returns to Messina. From that time King Richard being angered against King Philip, never shewed him any gentle countenance peace and amity, as he was wont before.

Soon after this, King Philip sailed for Acre, and the next month King Richard sailed with an hundred and fifty great ships, and three-and-fifty great gallies well manned and appointed, also towards Acre; on Good Friday there rose a mighty tempest, which scattered all his navy. The king with a few ships, was driven to the isle of Crete. The ship that carried the king's sister queen of Sicilia, and Berengaria the king of Navarre's daughter, with two other ships, were driven to the isle of Cyprus. The king making great moan for the ship of his sister, and Berengaria his intended wife, and not knowing where they were, after the tempest was blown over, sent his gallies diligently to search for the ship wherein his sister was, and the maiden whom he was to marry; at length they were found safe and well at the port of Limisso in the isle of Cyprus. Though the two ships, which were in their company in the same haven, were lost. The king of Cyprus was then Isakius (called also the emperor of the Griffons) who took and imprisoned all Englishmen, who were cast by shipwreck upon his land ; and would not suffer the ship wherein the two ladies were to enter within the port.

The tidings of this being brought to King Richard, he in his great wrath, gathering his gallies and ships together, landed in Cyprus, where he first in gentle terms signifies to King Isakius, how he with his Englishmen, coming as strangers to the support of the Holy Land, where by distress of weather, driven upon his borders, and therefore with all humble petition besought him in God's behalf, and for reverence of the holy cross, to release such prisoners of his as he had in captivity, and to restore again the goods of them who were drowned, and which he detained in his hands, to be employed for the benefit of their souls, &c. And this the king, once, twice, and thrice requested of Isakius. But he, answering proudly, sent the king word, that he would neither let the captives go, nor return the goods of those who were drowned, &c.

When King Richard heard how little Isakius made of his humble and honest petition, and how nothing there could be got without force; he soon gives command through all his army, to put themselves in armour, and to follow him, to revenge the injuries received from that proud and cruel king of Cyprus; desiring them to put their trust in God, and not to doubt but the Lord would stand with them, and give them the full victory. Isakius in the mean time, stood guarding the sea coasts, where the Englishmen should arrive, with swords, bills, and lances, and such other weapons as they had, setting boards, stools, and chests before them instead of a wall. However, but few of them were in armour, and for the most part inexpert, and unskilful in the feats of war. Then King Richard with his soldiers, issuing out of their ships, first set his bowmen forward, who with their shot made a way for others to follow. The Englishmen, thus gaining the land, pressed so fiercely upon the Griffons, that after long fighting, and many blows, Isakius was put to flight; King Richard valiantly pursued, and slew many, and several he took alive, and had nearly taken the king, had not the night come on and parted the battle. And thus King Richard returning with much spoil and great victory to the port town of Limisso, which the townsmen had abandoned for fear, found there great abundance of corn, wine, oil, and provisions.

The same day, Joan the king's sister, and Berengaria the maiden entered the port and town of Limisso, with fifty great ships, and fourteen galliots ; so that the whole navy, there meeting together, were two hundred and fifty four tall ships, and above threescore galliots. Then Isakius, seeing no way to escape by sea, pitched his tents five miles off, swearing that the third day he would give battle to King Richard. But Richard set upon the tents of the Griffons early, while they were unwares and asleep, and made a great slaughter of them, so that Isakius was compelled to run away naked, leaving his tents and pavilions to the Englishmen, full of horses and rich treasure, also with the imperial standard, the lower part of which with a costly streamer was covered and wrought all with gold. King Richard then returning with victory and triumph to his sister and Berengaria, shortly after, married Berengaria, in the isle of Cyprus.

Is akius being afterwards taken and sent in chains of silver and gold to Tripoli, and all things being set in order touching the possession of the isle of Cyprus, the keeping of it he committed to Radulph, son of Godfrey, lord chamberlain. King Richard departed from the isle of Cyprus, with his ships and gallies towards the siege of Acre ; and on his voyage he met with a great bark, fraught with soldiers and men of war, to the number of one thousand and five hundred; who pretending to be Frenchmen, and shewing their flag with French arms, were really Saracens in disguise, secretly sent with wildfire, and barrels of unknown serpents, to the defence of the town of Acre. King Richard at length perceiving this, soon set upon them, and vanquished them, the most of them were drowned, and some were taken alive. The next day, King Richard came to Acre : soon after his coming, the Pagans within the city seeing their walls undermined, and towers overthrown, were driven to escape with life and limb, to surrender the city to the two kings. Another great help to the christians in winning the city was this : in the city of Acre there was a secret christian among the Saracens, who in the time of the siege, used to cast over the walls, into the camp of the christians, certain letters written in Hebrew, Greek, and Latin, in which he disclosed to the christians, from time to time, the doings and counsels of their enemies, advertising them how, and by what way they should work, and what to beware of ; and always his letters began thus : " In the name of the Father, and of the Son, and of the Holy Ghost." By this, the christians were much advantaged in their proceedings. But it was a source of great heaviness to them, that he would never tell his name, nor when the city was got, could they ever understand who he was.

To make of a long siege a short narration, upon the twelfth day of July (A. D. 1191), the princes and captains of the Pagans, upon agreement came to the tent of the Templars, to commune with the two kings touching peace and giving up of their city.

The twentieth day of July, King Richard, speaking with the French king, desired him that they two with their armies would bind themselves by oath to remain there still in the land of Jerusalem the space of three years, for the winning and recovering again of those countries. But he said he would swear no such oath. So about the beginning of the month of August, Philip the French king, went from Acre to Tyre ; although King Richard and all the princes of the christian army with great intreaty desired him to tarry ; shewing what a shame it were for him to come so far, and now to leave undone that for which he came. After his departure the Pagans refused to keep their covenants ; they would neither restore the holy cross, nor the money, nor the captives, as they had pledged ; sending word to King Richard, that if he beheaded the hostages left with him at Acre, they would chop off the heads of such captives of the christians as were in their hands. Shortly after this, the Saladin, sending great gifts to King Richard, requested the time limited, viz., forty days for beheading the captives might be prolonged ; but the king refused to take his gifts, and to grant his request. Whereupon the Saladin caused all the christian captives within his possession forthwith to be beheaded, which was the eighteenth day of August. But yet, King Richard would not anticipate the time before prescribed for the execution of his prisoners, being the twentieth of August. Upon which day he caused the prisoners of the Saracens, openly in the sight of the Saladin army, to lose their heads : the number came to two thousand five hundred, save only that certain of the principal of them he reserved for purposes, and considerations, especially to make exchange for the holy cross, and some of the christian captives.

After this, King Richard purposed to besiege the city of Joppa ; where, by the way between Acre and Joppa, Saladin with a great multitude of his Saracens came fiercely against the king's rear : but through God's merciful grace, the king's warriors acquitted them so well, that the Saladin was put to flight (whom the christians pursued the space of three miles), and lost the same day many of his nobles and captives, so that the Saladin had not been put to such confusion for forty years before. From thence King Richard went to Joppa, and then to Ascalon, where he found first the city of Joppa forsaken by the Saracens, who durst not abide the king's coming. And Ascalon, the Saladin threw down to the ground, and forsook the holy land of Syria ; through all which the king had free passage without resistance, neither durst the Saracen prince encounter after that with King Richard.

Many other valiant and famous acts were achieved by him and the French king, and more would have been accomplished, had not those two kings, falling into discord, separated themselves. Philip, the French king, returned home within a short time, and soon invaded Normandy, urging John, the brother of King Richard, to seize the kingdom of England in his brother's absence ;

who then made league with the French king, and did homage to him. Richard being then in Syria, and hearing of this, made a peace with the Turks for three years. And not long after (in the spring following) King Richard returned also. In his return he was driven, by distress of weather, about the parts of Istria, in a town called Synaca, and was there taken by Leopold, duke of the same country, and sold to the Emperor Henry, for 60,000 marks.

King Richard, being thus shipwrecked, and traitorously taken and sold to the emperor by the Duke of Austria, was there kept in custody a year and three months. In some histories, it is affirmed that King Richard, returning out of Asia, came to Italy with prosperous winds, where he desired of the pope to be absolved from an oath made against his will, and could not obtain the absolution. And so setting out from thence towards England, passing by the country of Conrad, the marquis, whose death was falsely imputed by the French king to the king of England, was there traitorously taken, as is before said, by Leopold, duke of Austria. Although in another history I find the matter more credibly set forth, which saith, " That King Richard slew the brother of this Leopold, playing with him at chess in the French king's court. And Leopold, taking his advantage, was the more cruel against him, and delivered him, as is said, to the emperor ; in whose custody he was detained during the time above mentioned, a year and three months. The French king, in the meantime, raised war in Normandy ; and Earl John, the king's brother, invaded England ; but the barons and bishops of the land mightily withstood him, and besieged him in the castle of Windsor, where they took from him all the castles and forts, which he had got before. Thus the earl, seeing no hope of prevailing in England, and suspecting the deliverance of the king his brother, went to France, and stayed with the French king. At length it was agreed and concluded with the emperor, that King Richard should be released for a hundred thousand pounds. That sum of money was here gathered, and made in England, of chalices, crosses, shrines, candlesticks, and other church plate, also with public contribution of friaries, abbies, and other subjects of the realm. Part of this sum was immediately paid, and for the residue, hostages and pledges were taken, which was about the fifth year of his reign. And then it was obtained of the pope, that priests might celebrate with chalices of pewter and tin, and so it was granted and continued long after.

Thus King Richard being ransomed, was restored again and repaired into England. At his return Earl John his brother, coming to him with humble submission, desired to be pardoned for his transgressions. King Richard answered, " I would to God that this your misconduct as it dies in oblivion with me, so it may remain in remembrance with you," and so he gently forgave him. And after he had recovered his holds and castles, he caused himself to be crowned again. Which done, he went with his forces against the French king, and drove him out of Normandy. And after that, he went against the Welshmen, and subdued them.

The year following, (A.D. 1197,) Philip the French king brake the truce made between him and King Richard ; and the king was compelled to sail over again to Normandy to withstand the malice of his enemy. About which time, my history records of one called Fulco by some ; some say he was the archbishop of Rouen, called Walter. This Fulco being then in England, and coming to the king's presence, said to him with great courage and boldness ; " Thou hast, O mighty king, three daughters very vicious and of evil disposition ; take good heed of them, and at once provide for them good husbands ; lest, by untimely bestowing them in marriage, thou shalt not only incur great loss and injury, but also utter ruin and destruction to thyself." The king in a rage said, " Thou lying and mocking hypocrite, thou knowest not where thou art, or what thou sayest ; I think thou art mad, or not well in thy wits ; for I have never had a daughter, as all the world knows, and therefore thou open liar get thee out of our presence." Fulco answered, " No, and like your grace,

I lie not, but say truth : for you have three daughters which continually frequent your court, and wholly possess your person, and such three naughty ones as never before was heard of . I mean, mischievous *pride*, greedy *covetousness*, and filthy *luxury ;* and therefore again I say, O king, beware of them, and at once provide marriages for them, lest in not so doing, thou utterly undo both thyself and all the whole realm.''

The king took his words in good part, with correction of himself, and confession of the same. Whereupon immediately, he called his lords and barons before him, to whom he declared the conversation of Fulco, who had desired him to beware of his three daughters, *pride, avarice,* and *luxury,* with advice to marry them immediately, lest further inconvenience should ensue both to him and to the whole realm : "His good counsel (my lords) I intend to follow, not doubting of all your consent thereto. Wherefore here before you all, I give my daughter swelling *pride* to wife to the proud Templars ; my greedy daughter *avarice* to the covetous order of the Cistercian monks ; and last of all, my filthy daughter *luxury* to the riotous prelates of the church, whom I think to be very meet men for her ; and so severally well agreeing to all their natures, that the like matches in this our realm are not to be found for them.'' And thus much concerning Fulco.

Not long after this, a certain noble personage found a great treasure both of gold and silver hid in the ground, a great part of which he sent to King Richard, as chief lord and prince over the whole country. Which the king refused ; saying, he would have all or none, for that he was the principal chieftain over the land. But the finder would not condescend to that. Therefore the king laid siege to a castle of his, called Galuz, thinking the treasure to lie there. But the keepers and warders of the castle, seeing themselves not sufficient to withstand the king, offered to him the castle, desiring to depart with life and armour. To this the king would in no wise grant, but bid them to re-enter the castle again, and to defend it in all the forcible wise they could. It so befel, that as the king with the duke of Brabant went about the castle, viewing the places thereof ; a soldier within, named Bertrand Cordoun struck the king with an arrow in the arm, and the iron remaining and festering in the wound, the king within nine days after died ; who, because he was not content with the half of the treasure that another man found, lost all his own treasure that he had. The king, being thus wounded, caused the man that struck him to be brought to him, and asked him the cause why he so wounded him ? Who answered him (as the history says), that he thought to kill rather than to be killed ; and what punishment soever he should sustain, he was content, so that he might kill him who had before killed his father and brothers. The king, hearing his words, freely forgave him and caused an hundred shillings to be given him. Although (as the history adds) after the death of the king, the duke of Brabant, caused him after great torments, to be hanged. The history of Gisburn says, that the killer of King Richard coming to the French king, thinking to have a great reward, was commanded to be drawn asunder with horses, and his quarters to be hanged up.

Another history affirms, and Gisburn partly testifies the same, that a little before the death of King Richard, three abbots of the order Cistercian came to him, to whom he was confessed ; and when he saw them somewhat stay at his absolution, he added these words : that he did willingly commit his body to be eaten of worms, and his soul to the fire of purgatory, there to be tormented till the judgment, in the hope of God's mercy.

KING JOHN.

After the death of King Richard, called Cœur de Lion, his brother John, earl of Morton began his reign, A. D. 1199. The archbishop put the crown on his head, and swore him to defend and to maintain the church. And unless he resolved in his mind to do so, the archbishop charged him not to presume to take on him this dignity. And on St. John Baptist's day next following, King John sailed into Normandy and came to Rouen, where he was royally received, and a truce concluded between him and

the French king for a time. And there came to him the earl of Flanders, and all other lords of France that were of King Richard's band and friendship, and were sworn unto him.

Not long after this, Philip the French king made Arthur a knight, and received his homage for Normandy, Brittany, and all other his possessions beyond the sea, and promised him assistance against King John. After this, King John and the French king conferred with their lords about one hour's space ; and the French king asked so much land for himself and Knight Arthur, that King John would grant him none, and so he departed in wrath.

The same year a legate came into France, and commanded the king on pain of an interdict, to release one Peter out of prison, who was elected to a bishoprick ; and he was accordingly released.

And after that the legate came into England, and commanded King John, also under pain of an interdict, to deliver the archbishop whom he had kept as prisoner two years ; which the king refused to do, till he had paid him six thousand marks ; because he took him in armour in battle against him, and sware him upon his deliverance, that he should never wear armour against any Christian man.

This time a divorce was made between King John and his wife, daughter of the Earl of Gloucester, because they were in the third degree of kindred. And afterwards by the advice of the French king, King John wedded Isabel, daughter of the Earl of Angouleme ; and then Arthur of Brittany did homage to King John for Brittany and other lands.

At this time there was a contention between King John and Geffrey the archbishop of York ; first, because he would not suffer and permit the sheriff of York, to proceed in such affairs as he had to do for the king within his diocese. Secondly, because he also excommunicated the sheriff. Thirdly, because he would not sail with him into Normandy, to make the marriage between Louis the French king's son, and his niece, &c.

In the year 1202, Philip the French king, required that King John should part with all his lands in Normandy and Pictavia to Arthur his nephew, or else he would war against him ; when King John refused, the next day the French king with Arthur attacked his towns and castles in Normandy, and put him to much trouble ; but he received, however, such a repulse at the Englishmen's hands, that they, pursuing the Frenchmen in their flight, so followed them that they not only took Arthur prisoner, with many others, but gave such an overthrow, that none was left to bear tidings home.

This Arthur was nephew to King John, and son to Geffrey, who was the elder brother to John. For King Henry II. had eight children ; one William, who died in childhood ; the second, Henry who died also while his father was yet alive ; the third, Geffrey, earl of Brittany, who likewise died in his father's days, leaving behind him two children, Arthur and Brecca ; the fourth, Richard Cœur de Lion, king ; the fifth, John, now reigning ; and three daughters besides.

Arthur being thus taken, was brought before the king, and having been exhorted with many gentle words to leave the French king, and to incline to his uncle, answered boldly and with great indignation ; demanding the kingdom of England, with all the other dominions thereto belonging, as the lawful heir of the crown. By this he provoked the king's displeasure against him and was sent to the tower of Rouen, where at length (whether by leaping into the ditch, thinking to make his escape, or whether by some other secret hand, or by what chance else it is not yet agreed upon in history) he finished his life. King John was under great suspicion ; whether justly or unjustly, the Lord knows.

The year following, John lost all his holds and possessions in Normandy, through the power of the French king.

After these losses, came other troubles upon him, with as great or greater enemies, that is, with the pope and his popelings in the affair of the archbishop of Canterbury.

In A. D. 1205, Hubert the archbishop of Canterbury died. Before his body was yet committed to the earth, the younger sort of the monks gathered themselves together at midnight, and elected their superior Reginald, and without the king's license, or even knowledge, placed him in the metropolitan seat. And lest the king should make the election void, they charged him by virtue of his oath to keep all secret, and to reveal nothing till he came to the pope; but he, contrary to his oath, so soon as he came into Flanders, opened abroad all the matter. The next day the elder monks sent to the king, desiring him of his gracious license canonically to choose their archbishop. The king most gently and favourably granted their petition, desiring that for his sake they would shew favour to John Gray, then bishop of Norwich, as indeed they did, electing him to that See of the primacy. As the authority of kings and princes was then but small in their own dominions, without the pope's consent and confirmation; he also sent to Rome to have the election ratified by the pope. The suffragans of Canterbury then being not a little offended at these two elections sent speedily to Rome to have them both stopped; for they had not been consulted about them. And from them grew a most prodigious tumult.

In this year the clergy grew so unruly, that they neglected their charge, and incensed the king's displeasure so much against them, that he took order about the goods of such as were faulty.

A Letter of King John, touching the Lands and Goods of such Clergymen as refuse to celebrate Divine Service.

"The king to all clerical and lay persons within the bishoprick of Lincoln, greeting: know ye that from Monday next before the feast of Easter, we have committed to William of Cornhill, archdeacon of Huntington, and to Joseline of Canvil, all the lands and goods of the abbots and priors, and of all the spiritual persons; and also of all clerks within the bishoprick of Lincoln, who will not from that time celebrate divine service. And we command you, that from thence you assist them as our bailiffs; and believe them in those things which they shall tell you privately on our behalf. Witness ourself at Clarendon the 18th day of March, in the 9th year of our reign."

But to proceed in this troublesome election: the next year, the suffragans of the province of Canterbury on one side, and the monks of Canterbury on the other, came before the pope with their brawling matter. First, the monks, presenting Reginald their superior, desired that their election might be confirmed. The suffragans likewise complained that the monks should presume to choose the archbishop without their consent, and therefore desired the first election to be annulled. The pope, deciding the matter, pronounced with the monks; charging the suffragans and bishops to meddle no more with that election, but to let the monks alone. The monks of Canterbury, now having the whole election in their own hands, fell out among themselves. The younger sort who had chosen Reginald their superior, wished that election to stand. The elder sort of monks replied that the first election was done by stealth and by night, and by the younger part; also without the counsel of the other monks. Besides, it was done without the king's license and appointment, and without due solemnity.

When they had multiplied talk on both sides a long time, and could not agree upon one person, Pope Innocent condemned both their elections, commanding them to choose Stephen Langton, then cardinal of St. Chrysogon, for their archbishop. The monks then answered, that they durst not so do without consent of their king. The pope in a passion, taking the words out of their mouths, said to them, "We desire you to know that we have full power and authority over the church of Canterbury, and are not wont to tarry for the consent of princes, therefore we command you, on pain of our great curse, that ye choose him only whom we have appointed."

The monks at these words abashed and terrified, though they much murmured in their hearts, yet consented, and thus Stephen Langton was made archbishop of Canterbury.

Upon this occasion King John conceived an exceeding displeasure against the clergy and monks of Canterbury for doing so many things against his prerogative. Without his license they elected their archbishop, and set aside the bishop of Norwich, whom he had appointed. They wasted a great part of his treasure, and to bring all to the devil, they made Stephen Langton their high metropolitan; so that in his anger he banished them out of the land to the number of sixty-four.

The king then sends messengers to the pope with his letters, wherein he sharply remonstrates with the pope, because he so uncourteously refused the election of the bishop of Norwich, and set up Stephen Langton, consecrating him archbishop of Canterbury; and among other things he adds, that he will stand for his liberties, if need be, unto death; and he thus concludes, saying, "That if he be not heard in this his request, he will so provide for the sees that there shall be no such gadding and coursing any more over to Rome, suffering the riches of the land no more to be transported there. And seeing he has of his own, archbishops, bishops, and other prelates of the church, sufficiently provided and instructed in all kinds of knowledge, he shall not require to seek for judgment and justice abroad.

When these came to the pope, he directs letters in return to the king in this form:

"Innocent, pope, servant of the servants of God, to our well-beloved son in Christ, the king of England, health and apostolical blessing. Whereas we have written to you heretofore, exhorting and intreating you after an humble, diligent, and gentle way; you have written to us in reply after a threatening and upbraiding manner; both spitefully and frowardly. And whereas we have borne with you and given way to you above what our right and duty required; you for your part have given to us not so much as by right and duty you are bound to do. And though your devotion, as you say, has been to us very necessary, yet consider again that ours also is not a little opportune and expedient for you. And whereas we have not shewed at any time the like honour to any prince as we have to you; you again have so much derogated from our honour, as no prince else hath presumed to do besides you alone; pretending certain frivolous causes and occasions," &c.

Then alluding at length to the election of Langton, he thus proceeds: "Wherefore be it known to your discretion or kingly prudence, that as this election of Stephen Langton has proceeded without fraud or deceit upon a person meet for the same; therefore we will for no man's pleasure, neither may we without danger of fame and of conscience defer or protract any longer the consummation of the said election. Wherefore, my well-beloved son, seeing we have had respect to your honour, above what our right and duty required, study to honour us so much as your duty requires again, so that you may the more plentifully deserve favour both at God's hand and ours; lest that by doing the contrary you bring yourself into such a sea of troubles as you shall afterwards scarce free yourself of again. For know this for a certainty, that in the end it must needs fall out that he shall have the better, to whom every knee of 'things in heaven, and things in earth, and things under the earth' doth bow, whose place I serve in earth, though I be unworthy. Therefore set not yourself to obey their persuasions, who always desire your unquietness, that they may fish the better in the troubled water; but commit yourself to our pleasure, which undoubtedly shall turn to your praise, glory, and honour."

After this letter was sent, there proceeded not long after a charge and commandment into England to certain bishops, requiring them by apostolic authority that if the king would not receive the prior of Canterbury and his monks they should interdict him throughout all his realm. For the executing of this four bishops were appointed by the pope's bulls, namely, William, bishop of London; Eustace, bishop of Ely; Walter, bishop of Winchester; and Giles, bishop of Hereford. These bishops went to the king, and shewed their commission from the pope, and wished him to consent; but the king refused, and would by no means grant their request. They went on the morrow after the Annunciation of the Virgin, and pronounced the general interdict throughout all England, so that the church doors were shut up with keys and other fastenings, and with walls, &c.

Now when the king heard of this, he began to be moved against them, and took all the possessions of the four bishops into his hands, appointing certain men to keep the livings of the clergy throughout the realm, and that they should enjoy no part thereof. Which being done, the bishops cursed all them that kept, or should meddle with church goods.

After a time certain prelates, on the king's part, made an arrangement with them, and when the form of agreement was concluded, it was engrossed in two indentures; and the four bishops set their seals to one part, and the other part the bishops, earls, and abbots carried to the king. When the king saw the arrangement he liked it well, only he would not agree to make restitution of the church goods. So he sent to the four bishops again that they should put out that point of restitution. But they answered stoutly that they would not put out one word. Then the king sent word to the archbishop, by the four bishops, that he should come to Canterbury to speak with him. When the archbishop Stephen came to Canterbury, the king sent his treasurer the bishop of Winchester to him, to persuade him to put out of the indentures the clause of restitution; but he refusing to alter a word of it, angered the king so that immediately it was proclaimed throughout England at the king's command that all those that had any church livings, and went over sea should come back to England by a certain day, or else lose their livings for ever. And further in that proclamation, he charged all sheriffs within the realm, to inquire if any bishops, abbots, priors, or any other churchman (from that day forward) received any command that came from the pope, and that they should take his or their body and bring it before him: and also that they should take into their hands, for the king's use, all the church lands that were given to any man by the Archbishop Stephen, or by the priors of Canterbury, from the time of the election of the archbishop; and he further charged that all the woods, that were the archbishop's, should be cut down and sold.

When tidings came to the pope that the king had acted thus, he was moved with fiery wrath, and sent to the king two legates (Pandulph and Durant), to warn him in the pope's name that he should cease his doings to the holy church, and amend the wrong he had done to the archbishop of Canterbury, to the priors and the monks of Canterbury, and to all the clergy of England. And further, that he should restore the goods again that he had taken against their will, or else they should curse the king by name; and for this purpose, the pope gave them his bulls and letters patent. These two legates, coming into England, came to the king, and informed him of the pope's pleasure.

Then the king answered, "All that ye have said I would gladly do, and all things else that you would ordain; but as to the archbishop, I shall tell you as it lies in my heart. Let the archbishop leave his bishoprick, and if the pope shall then intreat for him, perhaps I may give him some other bishoprick in England, and upon this condition I will receive and admit him."

Then said Pandulph to the king, "Holy church was wont never to degrade an archbishop without reasonable cause; but she was ever wont to correct princes that were disobedient to her."

"What? How now?" said the king, "do ye threaten me?"

"Nay," said Pandulph, "but you have now openly told us as it stands in your heart; and now we will tell you what is the pope's will. He has wholly interdicted and cursed you, for the wrongs you have done to the church and to the clergy. And for so much as ye continue in your malice, and will come to no amendment, you are to understand, that from this time forward the sentences against you have force and strength. And all those that have had intercourse with you before this time, whether that they be earls, barons, knights, or any other, we absolve them safely from their sins up to this day; but from this time forward we accurse them openly, and specially by this our sentence, that hold intercourse with you. And we absolve, moreover, earls,

barons, knights, and all other manner of men, of their homages, services, and fealties. Also, Sir King," said Pandulph, "all the kings, princes, and the great dukes of Christendom, have requested the pope to give license to them to cross themselves, and to war against thee, as upon God's great enemy, and win thy land, and to appoint for king whom the pope pleases. And we here now absolve of their sins all those that will rise against thee here in thine own land."

Then the king, hearing this, answered, "What further shame may ye do to me than this?"

Pandulph again: "We say to you, by the word of God, that neither you, nor any heir that you have, after this day shall be crowned."

So the king said, "By him that is Almighty God, if I had known of this thing before ye came into this land, and that ye had brought me such news, I would have made you stay away these twelve months out of my realms."

Then answered Pandulph, "Full well we thought, at our first coming, that you would have been obedient to God and to holy church, and have fulfilled the pope's commandment, which we have shewed and pronounced to you. And now you say, that if you had known the cause of our coming, you would have made us stay away a whole year; you might as well say, that you would have taken a whole year's respite without the pope's leave; but, though we were to suffer death for it, we shall not shrink from telling all the pope's message and will, that he gave us in charge."

In another chronicle I find the words between the king and Pandulph somewhat otherwise described, as if the king had threatened him with hanging, if he had foreknown of his coming. Pandulph answered, that he looked for nothing else at his hands, but to suffer for the church's rights. Whereupon the king, being mightily incensed, departed. The king, being then at Northampton, desired the sheriffs and bailiffs to bring forth all the prisoners there, that such as had deserved it should be put to death, to the intent (as some think) to make Pandulph afraid. Among them was a certain clergyman, who, for counterfeiting the king's coin, was condemned to be hanged, drawn, and quartered; and was commanded by the king, thereby to anger Pandulph, to be hanged higher than the rest. Pandulph hearing of this, though he began to fear lest he should be hanged himself, yet went with courage to the church to bring out book, bell, and candle, charging that no man, under pain of cursing, should lay hands upon the clergyman. Upon this the king and the cardinal parted in no little anger; and Pandulph went to Rome, and reported to the pope and the cardinals what had been done.

Then the pope summoned all the bishops, abbots, and clergy of England, to repair to Rome, to consult what was to be done. In which council it was decreed, that John king of England should be accursed, with all such as held with him. However, it was not yet permitted that the people should assume the cross to fight against him, because as yet he had shed no blood. But afterwards the pope, seeing that King John would not stoop under his subjection, sent to the French king, that upon remission of all his sins, and those of all that would accompany him, he should invade the realm of England.

Pope Innocent again commanded, on pain of his great curse, that no man should obey King John: he forbid all persons to eat and drink with him, or talk with him, to commune or counsel with him; yea, he forbid his own familiar household to do him any kind of service, either at bed, or at board, in church, in hall, or in stable. Neither was the pope content with this, but gave sentence definitive that King John should be put from his regal seat and deposed, and another put in his room. And for the speedy execution of this sentence he appointed the French king Philip, promising to give him full remission of all his sins, and the clear possession of all the realm of England, to him and his heirs, if he either killed him or expelled him.

The next year the French king began his attempt, being well manned with bishops, monks, prelates, priests, and their servants. But, behold the work of God, the English navy took three hundred of the French king's ships, well laden with wheat, wine, meal, flesh, armour, and such materials for the war; and burnt one hundred within the harbour, taking the spoils with them. In the meantime the priests within England had provided them a false prophet, called Peter Wakefield of Poiz, who was an idle wanderer and talking fellow. They made this Peter prophesy lies, rumouring his prophesies abroad, to bring the king out of all credit with his people. This knavish fellow prophesied of King John, that he should reign no longer than Ascension-day (A.D. 1213), and this, he said, he had by revelation. Then it was demanded of him whether John would be slain, or expelled, or resign the crown? He answered, that he could not tell; but of this he was sure, that neither he, nor any of his stock, or lineage, should reign after that day. The king, hearing of this, laughed much at it. "Tush, (said he,) it is but an idiot knave, and one out of his wits." But when this foolish prophet had escaped the king's displeasure, he used to talk more than enough; so that they who loved the king apprehended him as a malefactor, and he was thrown into prison without the king knowing it.

Soon after, the fame of this prophet went all over the realm, and his name was known every where, specially because he was imprisoned for the matter. From thence old gossips' tales went abroad, new tales were invented, fables were added to fables, and lies grew upon lies, so that every day new slanders were raised against the king, rumours arose, blasphemies were spread, the enemies rejoiced, and treasons were maintained by the priests.

When the Ascension-day was come, which was prophesied of before, King John commanded his regal tent to be spread abroad in the open field, passing that day with his noble council and men of honour, in the greatest solemnity that he ever did before, solacing himself with musical instruments and songs, and always in sight among his trusty friends. When that day was past in all prosperity and mirth, his enemies turned all to an allegorical understanding, to make the prophesy good, and said, "he is no longer king, for the pope reigns, and not he." Then was the king persuaded by his council, that this false prophet had troubled the realm, perverted the hearts of the people, and excited the commons against him. The king, therefore, commanded that he should be hanged and drawn like a traitor.

Then the popish prelates, monks, canons, priests, &c., began to practise with Pope Innocent and the French king abroad, besides the treasons which they wrought within the realm, and they blinded the nobility and commons by their confessionals. The king thus surrounded with enemies, and knowing the conspiracies that were working against him, as well by the pope, as by Philip the French king, and being aware that his lords and barons were rebelliously incited against him, and seeing the pope's curses and interdicts against such as took his part, and his absolutions and dispensations for all those that would rebel against him, commanding them to detain from him such homage, service, duties, debts, and all other allegiance that godly subjects owe and are bound to yield and give to their liege lord and prince. The king, I say, in the thirteenth year of his reign, seeing all this, and that the French king began an invasion upon his realm, sent ambassadors to the pope, the fountain of all this mischief, promising to do whatever the pope should command him in the reformation of himself, and restitution of all wrongs done to holy church.

Then the pope sent again into England his legate Pandulph, with others, and the king waited their coming at Canterbury; where, the thirteenth day of May, the king received them, making an oath, that of and for all things wherein he stood accursed, he would make ample restitution and satisfaction. All the lords and barons of England (so many as were there with the king) sware in like manner, that if the king would not accomplish in every thing the oath which he had taken, they would compel him to hold and confirm the same.

Then the king submitted himself to the court of Rome, and resigned his dominions and realms of England and Ireland for himself and for his heirs for ever. With this condition, that the king and his heirs should take again these two dominions of the pope to farm, paying yearly to the court of Rome one thousand marks of silver. Then the king took the crown from his head, and kneeling upon his knees, in the presence of all his lords and barons of England, he gave it to Pandulph, saying, "Here I resign the crown of the realm of England to the hands of the pope, Innocent III., and place myself wholly at his mercy." Then Pandulph took the crown, and kept it five days as a possession and seizin-taking of these two realms of England and Ireland, confirming also all things promised by his charter obligatory, as follows:—

The Copy of the Letter Obligatory that King John made to the Pope, concerning the yielding up of the Crown and Realm of England into the Pope's hands, for a certain sum of money yearly to be paid

"To all christian people throughout the world, John, by the grace of God, king of England, greeting: be it known unto you all, that as we have grieved and offended God, and our mother church of Rome, and as we have need of the mercy of our Lord Jesus Christ, and we can offer nothing so worthy, or make so competent satisfaction to God and to holy church, as with our realms of England and of Ireland, then, by the grace of the Holy Ghost, we desire to humble ourselves, for the love of him that humbled himself to the death upon the cross. And through counsel of the nobles, earls, and barons, we offer and freely grant to God, and to the apostles St. Peter and Paul, and to our mother church of Rome, and to our holy father Pope Innocent III., and to all the popes that come after him, all the realm, patronages of churches of England and of Ireland, with all the appurtenances, for remission of sins, and help and health of our kings' souls, and of all christian souls. So that from this time afterward, we will receive and hold of our mother church of Rome, as in farm, doing fealty to our holy father the pope, Innocent III., and to all the popes that come after him, in the manner above said. And in the presence of the wise Pandulph, the pope's legate, we make liege homage, as if it were in the pope's presence; and thereto we bind us, and all that come after us, and our heirs for ever, without any gainsaying to the pope. And in token of this, we will confirm, and ordain, that he be our special renter of the aforesaid realms, saving St. Peter-pence, in all things. To the mother church of Rome, paying by the year 1000 marks of silver, at two periods of the year, for all customs that we should do for the said realms, that is to say, at Michaelmas, and at Easter; that is, for England 700 marks, and 300 marks for Ireland, saving to us and to our heirs, our justices and our other franchises. And all these things, we will that they be firm and stable without end, and to that obligation, we and all our successors, and our heirs in this manner are bound, that if we or any of our heirs through any presumption fail in any of these things, and he being warned and not amending, he shall then lose the aforesaid realms for ever; and this charter of obligation and our warrant for ever, shall be firm and stable without gainsaying. We shall from this day afterward be true to God, and to the mother church of Rome, and to thee, Innocent III., and to all that come after thee, and the realms of England and of Ireland we shall maintain against all manner of men, by our power through God's help."

Upon this obligation, the king was discharged the second day of July, from that tyrannical interdict, under which he continued five years and three months. But before the release, he was thus miserably compelled to give over both his crown and sceptre to that antichrist of Rome, for the space of five days, and as his client, vassal, feudary, and tenant, to receive it again of him at the hands of another cardinal, being bound both for himself and for his successors, to pay yearly (for acknowledgment thereof) 1000 marks for England and Ireland.

In (A.D. 1215), as witnesses, Paulus Æmilius,

and other histories, Pope Innocent III. held a general synod at Rome, called the council of Lateran. The chief causes of that council were these : In the days of this Innocent, heresy, as he calls the truth of God, or the doctrine that rebukes sin, began to spread forth its branches, so that many princes were excommunicated, as Otho the emperor, John the king of England, Peter king of Arragon, Raimund the earl of Toulouse, Aquitain, Sataloni, and others. Therefore this council was proclaimed, and prelates from all nations called to it. And the pope gave out that his intent was only to have the church universally reformed, and the Holy Land recovered from the Turks. But all this was craft and falsehood, as the sequel proved. For his purpose was to subdue all princes, and to make himself rich and wealthy. For there he made this antichristian act, and established it by public decree, that the pope should have from thenceforth the correction of all christian princes, and that no emperor should be admitted, except he were sworn before, and were also crowned by him. He ordained, too, that whoever should speak evil of the pope, should be punished in hell with eternal damnation : (*Conradus, Urspergensis, Hieronymus, Marius.*)

In this council transubstantiation was first invented and brought in ; of which John Scot, sirnamed Duns, makes mention in his fourth book, writing in these words : " The words of the scripture might be expounded more easily, and more plainly, without transubstantiation. But the church did choose this sense, which is more hard ; being moved thereto, as it seems, chiefly because about the sacraments men ought to hold as the holy church of Rome holds," &c.

Now let us return to King John again, and mark how the priests and their adherents were plagued for their treatment of his majesty's will. In the council of Lateran, Stephen Langton, archbishop of Canterbury, was excommunicated, with all those bishops, prelates, priests, barons, and commons, who had been with him in the former rebellion. And when the archbishop had made suit to be absolved, the pope answered with great indignation,—" I swear by St. Peter, thou shalt not so soon at my hand obtain the benefit of absolution." With the barons of England, the pope had been so deeply offended and angered a little before, that he rent and destroyed the great charter of the liberties of England, and by sentence condemned it for ever ; and cursed all the other rebels, with book, bell, and candle.

About the same time were such treasons and conspiracies wrought by the bishops, priests, and monks throughout all the realm, that the king knew not where to find trusty friends ; he was compelled to travel from place to place, but not without a great army of men, looking every day when his barons and their confederates would cruelly set upon him. For the space of three months he remained in the Isle of Wight, abroad in the air to quiet himself for a time from all tumults, and led there a solitary life among rivers and watermen. He rather coveted to die than to live, being so traitorously handled by his bishops and barons, and not knowing how to be avenged. Therefore, he took upon him the cross, or voyages against the Turks, for the recovery of Jerusalem. Influenced rather by the doubts which he had of his people, than by any devotion ; and he said to his familiar servants, " Since I submitted myself and my lands (England and Ireland) to the church of Rome, nothing ever prospered with me, but all hath gone against me."

In this year (A. D. 1216,) died Pope Innocent III. After whom succeeded Cintius, called Honorius III., a man of very great age : yet he lived in the papacy ten years and a half, and more.

In the same year, as King John was come to Swinstead abbey, not far from Lincoln, he rested there two days : where (as most writers testify) he was most traitorously poisoned by a monk of that abbey.

Among other peculiar traits belonging to this king, there was one which is not to be reprehended, but rather commended in him : for being above the superstition which kings at that time were commonly subject to, he regarded not the popish mass ; I find testified of him,

that on a time in his hunting, coming where a very fat stag was cut up and opened, the king beholding the fatness and the liking of the stag : " See," saith he, " how easily and happily he has lived, and yet for all that he never heard a mass."

It is recorded in the chronicle of William Caxton, that the Monk Simon being much offended with the king, cast in his wicked heart how he most speedily might bring him to his end. And first of all he took counsel with his abbot, shewing him the whole affair, and what he designed to do. He alleged the prophesy of Caiaphas, " It is expedient for us that one man die for the people, and that the whole nation perish not," John, xi. 50. " I am well contented," saith he, " to lose my life, and so become a martyr, that I may utterly destroy this tyrant." The abbot wept for gladness, and much commended his fervent zeal. The monk then being absolved by his abbot beforehand for doing this act, conveyed poison into a cup of wine, and with a smiling and flattering countenance said to the king, " If it please your princely majesty, here is such a cup of wine as ye never drank better in all your life time ; I trust this wassail shall make all England glad :" and with that he drank a great draught of it himself, the king pledging him. The monk died, and had continually from thenceforth three monks to sing mass for his soul, confirmed by their general chapter ! What became of King John, ye shall now learn. I would ye did mark well the wholesome proceedings of these holy votaries, how virtuously they obey their king, whom God hath appointed, and how religiously they bestow their confessions, absolutions, and masses !

The king within a short space after (feeling great pain in his body) asked for Simon the monk ; and answer was made that he was dead. " Then God have mercy upon me," said he, " I suspected as much, after he had said that all England should thereof be glad." With that he commanded his chariot to be prepared, for he was not able to ride. So he went from thence to Sleaford castle, and from thence to Newark on Trent, and there within less than three days he died. Upon his death-bed he much repented of his former life, and forgave all them that had done him injury ; desiring that his elder son Henry might be admonished by his example, and learn by his misfortunes to be natural, favourable, gentle, and loving to his people. His soldiers both Englishmen and strangers were still about him, and followed his body in their armour, till they came to the cathedral church of Worcester, and there he was honourably buried by Silvester the bishop, between St. Oswald and St. Wolstan, two bishops of that church. He died A. D. 1216, the nineteenth day of October, after he had reigned in such calamity, eighteen years and six months and odd days.

Many opinions are among the chroniclers of the death of King John. Some of them write that he died of sorrow and heaviness of heart, as Polydore : some of surfeiting in the night, as Radulph Niger : some of a bloody flux, as Roger Hoveden : some of a burning ague ; some of cold sweat, some of eating apples, some of eating pears, some of plums, &c.

Thus you see what variety is among the writers concerning the death of this King John. Of which writers, although the most of them agree in this, that he was poisoned by the monk, yet Matthew Paris writes thus, " That going to Lincolnshire, and there hearing of the loss of his carriage and of his treasures upon the washes, he fell into great heaviness of mind ; insomuch that he fell thereby into a burning fever, at the abbey of Swinsted. This ague he also increased through evil surfeiting and improper diet, by eating of peaches and drinking of new ciser, or as we call it cider. Thus being sick, he was carried from thence to the castle of Sleaford, and from thence to the castle of Newark ; where calling for his son Henry, he gave to him the succession of his crown and kingdom, writing to all his lords and nobles to receive him for their king ; and shortly after, upon St. Lucy's eve, he departed this life, being buried at Worcester," &c.

In the reign of this King John, the citizens of London first obtained of the king to choose yearly a mayor. In whose time also the bridge of London was first built of stone, which before was of wood.

KING HENRY THE THIRD.

After King John had reigned seventeen years, he died. He left behind him four sons and three daughters; first, Henry, the second Richard earl of Cornwall, the third William of Valentia, the fourth Guido Disenaie: he had also another son, who afterwards was made bishop. Of his daughters, the first was Isabel, married to the emperor Frederick, the second Elenor, married to William earl marshal, the third to Mountford the earl of Leicester, &c. Another history says, that he had but two daughters, Isabel and Elenor, or as another calls her Joan, who was after queen of Scotland.

Henry the eldest son was then nine years of age, when the majority of the barons of England adhered to Lewis the French king's son, whom they had previously invited to come to England, proposing, in their opposition to King John, then under the pope's curse, to elect this Lewis as their king, and had sworn to him their allegiance. Then William, earl marshal, a nobleman, of great authority, and a grave and sound counsellor, in a friendly and quiet way called together several earls and barons, and taking this Henry the young prince, he sets him before them, using these words, "Behold, right honourable and well beloved, although we have persecuted the father of this young prince for his evil demeanour, and worthily; yet this young child whom here ye see before you, as he is in years tender, so is he pure and innocent from these his father's doings: wherefore in as much as every man is charged only with the burthen of his own works and transgressions, neither shall the child (as the scripture teacheth us) bear the iniquity of his father: we ought therefore of duty and conscience to pardon this young and tender prince, and take compassion of his age. And now for so much as he is the king's eldest son, and must be our sovereign and king and successor of this kingdom; come and let us appoint him our king and governor, and let us remove from us Lewis the French king's son, for it is a shame to our nation, and let us cast off the yoke of our servitude from our shoulders." To these words the earl of Gloucester answered; "And by what reason or right," said he, "can we so do, seeing we have called him hither, and have sworn to him our fealty?"

The earl marshal again said, "Good right and reason we have, and ought of duty to do no less; for contrary to our mind and calling he has abused our affiance and fealties. It is true we invited him, and meant to prefer him to be our chieftain and governor; but he has contemned and despised us: and if we shall so suffer him, he will subvert and overthrow both us and our nation, and so shall we remain a spectacle of shame to all men, and as outcasts of all the world."

At these words they all cried with one voice, "Be it so, Henry shall be our king." And so the day was appointed for his coronation. Notwithstanding this, Lewis did not forego his claim, but laid siege to the castle of Dover. When he could not succeed there he took the castle of Berkhamstead, and also the castle of Hertford, doing much harm in the countries, in spoiling and robbing the people where he went: so that the lords and commons, who held with the king, assembled together to drive Lewis out of the land, and gave battle to him; in conclusion Lewis lost the field and fled to London, which was in the hands of his friends, causing the gates to be shut, and waiting there for more succour out of France. In the meantime, Eustace, a French lord, came with a grand army and a hundred ships to assist Lewis; but before they arrived, they were encountered upon the seas by Richard, King John's natural son; who having no more than eighteen ships to keep the cinque ports, set eagerly upon them, and through God's grace overcame them, and he smote off the head of Eustace: the rest of the French lords to the number of ten, he brought ashore with him, where he imprisoned them in the castle of Dover, and slew almost all their men, and sunk their ships in the sea, so that only fifteen ships escaped. Lewis hearing this loss of his ships and men, proposed terms, and left the kingdom.

The life and acts of Pope Innocent III. are partly de-

scribed before; how he intruded Stephen Langton against the king's will into the archbishoprick of Canterbury, stirring up sixty-four monks of the church of Canterbury privily to work against the king. How he excommunicated the king as a public enemy of the church, putting him and his whole kingdom under interdict, for the space of five years and three months, and at length deposed and deprived him of his sceptre, keeping it in his own hands for five days. How he absolved his subjects from their due obedience and subjection to him. How he gave away his kingdoms and his possessions to Lewis the French king's son, commanding Lewis to spoil him both of lands and life. Whereupon the king, being forsaken of his nobles, prelates, and commons, was forced against his will to submit and swear obedience to the pope, paying a yearly tribute of one thousand marks a year, for receiving his kingdom again, whereby both he and his successors after him were vassals to the pope. These were the apostolical acts of this holy vicar of Jesus Christ in the realm of England! Moreover, he condemned Almeric, a learned man and a bishop, as an heretic, for teaching and holding against images. This pope brought first into the church the paying of private tithes. He ordained the receiving the communion once a year at Easter. To the papal decretals he added the decree, which declares every human creature to be subject to the pope. Also the reservation of the sacrament, and the going with the bell and light before the sacrament, was appointed by him. In the council of Lateran he also ordained that the canon of the mass should be received with equal authority, as though it had proceeded from the apostles themselves. And it was he, in this council, who first formally established transubstantiation as the doctrine of the church of Rome.

In this council of Lateran there were present sixty-one archbishops and primates, four hundred bishops, twelve abbots, eight hundred priors and conventuals, besides other ambassadors and legates, doctors and lawyers innumeble, &c.

In the history of Herman Mutius, we read how in A. D. 1212, in this pope's time several noblemen, and others in the country of Alsatia, held contrary to the tradition of the Romish popes, that every day was free for eating flesh, if done in moderation. They held also that it was wicked to restrain priests and ministers from their wives, for which opinions, this pope Innocent and his bishops, caused an hundred of them in one day to be burned and martyred!

In the days of this Pope Innocent, began the two orders of friars, one called "The Preachers' Order, and Black Friars of St. Dominic;" the other called "The Minorites of St. Francis."

The preachers of the black friars order began with one Dominic, a Spaniard, about the parts of Toulouse, who after he had laboured ten years in preaching against the Albigenses, and such others as held doctrines contrary to the church of Rome, afterward came to the council of Lateran, and desired of Innocent, to have his order of preaching friars confirmed, which the pope a great while refused to grant: at length he had a dream, that the church of Lateran was ready to fall; and that this Dominic, with his shoulders propped up the church, and so preserved the building from falling, &c. And right well this dream may seem verified, for the friars have been always the chief pillars and upholders of the pope's church. Upon this the pope, waking out of his dream, called Dominic to him, and granted his petition: and so came up this order of the dominicans!

The order of the minors or minorite friars, was descended from one Francis, an Italian, who, hearing how Christ sent forth his disciples to preach, thought to imitate the same in himself and his disciples, and so left off his shoes, and had but one coat, and that of coarse cloth. Instead of a latchet to his shoe, and of a girdle, he took about him a hempen cord, and so he apparelled his disciples, teaching them to fulfil, for so he speaks, the perfection of the gospel, to embrace poverty, and to walk in the way of holy simplicity. He left in writing, to his disciples and followers, his rule, which he called "The Rule of the Gospel." As if the gospel of Christ were not a sufficient rule to all christian men, but it must take its perfection from Francis! This Francis, as he was superstitious in all things; so by way of penitential deception he covered his body in the winter season with ice and snow! These Franciscan or begging friars, although all under one rule of St. Francis, yet are divided into many orders: some go on treen shoes or pattins, some barefooted, some are called *Regular Franciscans* or *Observants*, some *Minors* or *Minorites*, others *Minimi*, others *Gospelers*, others *De Caputio*. They all differ in many things, but agree in superstition and hypocrisy. As we have here entered into the matter of these two orders of friars, I thought a little to digress from our history, in reciting the whole catalogue or rabblement of monks, friars, and nuns of all sects, rules, and orders, set up and confirmed by the pope. The names are as follow:

THE RABBLEMENT OF RELIGIOUS ORDERS.[1]

	A.D.
Augustinians, the first order.	
Ambrosians, two sorts	409
Antony's Hermits	324
Austin's Hermits	498
Austin's Observants	490
Armenians.	
Ammonites and Moabites.	
Basilin's Order	384
Benedict's Order	524
Bernardus' Order	1120
Barefooted Friars	1222
Bridget's Order	1370
Beghearts or White Spirits	1399
Brethren of Jerusalem	1103
Brethren of St. John de Civitate, Black Friars	1220
Brethren of Wilful Poverty.	
Cluny, Order of	913
Canons of St. Augustine	1080
Charter-house Order	1086
Cistercian Order	1098
Cross-bearers, or Crossed Friars	1216
Carmelites, or White Friars	1212
Clare's Order	1225
Celestine's Order	1297
Camaldulensi's Order	950
Cross-starred Brethren.	
Constantinopolitan Order.	
Cross-bearers.	
Chapter-Monks.	
Dutch Order	2216
Dominican Black Friars	1220
Franciscans	1224
Grandmontain Order	1076
Gregory's Order	594
George's Order	1407
Gulielmites (Williamites)	1246
Gerundinensis Order.	
Galilei, or Galileans.	
Hermits.	
Helen's Brethren. Humiliati	1166
Hospital Brethren.	
Holy Ghost Order.	
Jerome's Orders, two sorts	1412
John's Hermits.	
Justin's Order	1432
John's Order, Joannites	380
Otherwise Knights of Rhodes	1308
Injesuati	1365
Jerome's Hermits	490
Joseph's Order.	
Janu's Order.	
James' Brethren Order.	
James' Brethren with the Sword.	
Indian's Order.	

	A.D.
Katharine of Sienna Order	1455
Keyedmonks, Knights of Rhodes.	
Lazarites of Mary Magdalene's, our Lady Brethren	1034
Lords of Hungary.	
Minorites, who are divided into	
Conventuals. De Caputio.	
Observants. De Evangelio.	
Reformed. Amedet.	
Collectane. Clarini and others.	
Minors or Minorites	1224
Mary's Servants	1304
Monks of Mount Olivet	1046
Marovinies.	
Minorites.	
Monachi and Monachæ.	
Morbonei and Meresti.	
Menelaish and Jasonish Sect.	
New Canons of St. Austin	1430
Nestorini.	
Nalheart Brethren.	
New Order of our Lady.	
Nazareans.	
Paul's Hermits	345
Præmonstre Order	1119
Preacher-Order or Black Friars.	
Peter the Apostle's Order	1409
Purgatorean Brethren.	
Rechabites.	
Sarrabites.	
Sambonites	1199
Scourgers, the first Sect	1266
Soldiers of Jesus Christ	1323
Scopenits or St. Salvator's Order	1367
Specularii, or the Glass Order.	
St. Sepulchre's Order.	
Sheer Order.	
Swerd's Order.	
Starred Monks.	
Starred Friars.	
Sclavonian Order.	
Scourgers, the second Sect, called Ninevites.	
Stool Brethren.	
Scottish Brethren Order.	
Sicarii.	
St. Sophia's Order.	
Templar Lords	1110
Templar Knights	1120
The Valley of Jehoshaphat's Order.	
Vallis Umbrosa	1400
Waldenses Sect.	
Wentzelaus Order.	
Wilhelmer Order.	
White Monks of Mount Olivet	1406
Zelote's Order.	

The reader sees what orders and what sects of religion have been set up by the pope, the catalogue and number of them all, so far as we could search them out. The number of which rabblement of monkish persons came to one hundred and one.

Now as I have reckoned up the names and varieties of these prodigious sects, I will add the words of Hildegardis, a celebrated nun in 1146, against the Romish prelates, and especially against the friars. This Hildegardis is held among the papists themselves as a great prophetess, and therefore let us hear her opinion about these men, long before the Reformation.

" In those days shall arise a senseless people, proud, greedy, without faith, and subtle, who shall eat the sins of the people, holding a certain order of foolish devotion

---

(1) This list is very far from satisfactory. The various orders of monks and nuns were far more numerous than are here given: Emillianne specifies half as many more, while he omits some that are here specified by Foxe. "The Lords of Hungary," or Teutonic Knights, "The Templars," &c. as here inserted, are a very small portion of the military orders. It is not easy to explain the insertion of such names as Galileans — Rechabites — Waldenses, &c. They seem to have been taken without correction from some list which confounded sects and orders without distinction — an error very natural to writers before the Reformation, and not unfrequently committed. [ED.]

under the feigned cloak of being "mendicants," preferring themselves above all others by their feigned devotion, arrogant in understanding, and pretending holiness, walking without shamefacedness or the fear of God, in inventing many new mischiefs strong and stout. But this order shall be accursed of all wise men and faithful christians. They shall cease from all labour, and give themselves over unto idleness, choosing rather to live through flattery and begging. Moreover, they shall together study how they may perversely resist the teachers of the truth, and slay them together with the noblemen; how to seduce and deceive the nobility, for the necessity of their living and pleasures of this world: for the devil will graft in them four principal vices, that is to say, flattery, envy, hypocrisy, and slander. Flattery, that they may have large gifts given them; envy, when they see gifts given to others, and not to them; hypocrisy, that by false dissimulation they may please men. Backbiting, that they may extol and commend themselves, and backbite others, for the praise of men, and seducing of the simple. Also they shall instantly preach, but without the devotion, or after the example of the martyrs, and shall speak evil of the secular princes, taking away the sacraments of the church from the true pastors, receiving alms of the poor, diseased, and miserable, and also associating themselves with the common people; instructing women how they shall deceive their husbands and friends by their flattery and deceitful words, and to rob their husbands to give to them, for they will take all these stolen and evil-gotten goods and say, ' Give it to us, and we will pray for you;' so that they being curious to hide other men's faults, do utterly forget their own. And alas, they will receive all things of rovers, pickers, spoilers, thieves, and robbers, of sacrilegious persons, usurers, and adulterers, heretics, schismatics, apostates, noblemen, perjurers, merchants, false judges, soldiers, tyrants, princes, of such as live contrary to the law, and of many perverse and wicked men, following the persuasion of the devil, the sweetness of sin, a delicate and transitory life, and fulness even unto eternal damnation.

"All these things shall manifestly appear in them to all people, and they (day by day) shall wax more wicked and hard-hearted: and when their wickedness and deceits shall be found out, then shall their gifts cease, and then shall they go about their houses hungry, and as mad dogs looking down upon the earth, and drawing in their necks as doves, that they might be satisfied with bread. Then shall the people cry out upon them, ' Woe be unto you, ye miserable children of sorrow, the world has seduced you, and the devil hath bridled your mouths, your flesh is frail, and your hearts without savour, your minds have been unsteadfast, and your eyes delighted in much vanity and folly, your dainty appetites desire delicate meats, your feet are swift to run into mischief. Remember when you were apparently blessed, yet envious; poor in sight, but rich; simple to see to, but mighty flatterers, unfaithful betrayers, perverse detractors, holy hypocrites, subverters of the truth, righteous overmuch, proud, unshamefaced, and unsteadfast teachers, delicate martyrs, confessors for gain; meek, but slanderers; religious, but covetous; humble, but proud; pitiful, but hard-hearted liars; pleasant flatterers; persecutors, oppressors of the poor, bringing in new sects newly invented of yourselves; thought merciful, but found wicked; lovers of the world, sellers of pardons, spoilers of benefices, unprofitable orators, seditious conspirators, drunkards, desirers of honours, maintainers of mischief, robbers of the world, unsatiable preachers, men-pleasers, seducers, and sowers of discord. You have builded up on high, and when you could ascend no higher, then did you fall even as Simon Magus, whom God overthrew, and did strike with a cruel plague; so you likewise through your false doctrine, naughtiness, lies, detractions, and wickedness are come to ruin. And the people shall say unto them, ' Go, ye teachers of wickedness, subverters of the truth, brethren of the Shunamite, fathers of heresies, false apostles, which have feigned yourselves to follow the life of the apostles, and yet have not followed it in any part: ye sons of iniquity, you will not follow the knowledge of your ways, for pride and presumption hath deceived you, and insatiable covetousness hath subverted your erroneous hearts. And when you would ascend higher than was meet or comely for you, by the just judgment of God, you are fallen back into perpetual opprobrium and shame."

About the same time that these Franciscans and Dominican friars began, then sprang up also the Cross-Bearers, or Crutched Friars. Innocent III. raised an army, signed with a cross on the breast, to fight against the Albigenses, whom the pope accounted for heretics in the neighbourhood of Toulouse. What these Albigenses were cannot be well gathered from the old popish histories; for if any held, taught, or maintained anything against the pope or his papal pride, or withstood and gainsayed his traditions, rites, and religions, &c., the historians of that time do so deprave and misrepresent them that they paint them forth as worse than Turks and infidels. And it was that, I suppose, which caused the popish historians to write of them as they did. I find in some records that the opinions of the Albigenses were sound enough, holding and professing nothing else but only against the wanton wealth, pride and tyranny of the prelates, and denying the pope's authority to have ground in the scriptures; neither could they bear with the ceremonies and traditions, images, pardons, purgatory of the Romish church, calling them (as some say) blasphemous occupyings, &c. Of these Albingenses there were slain and burned a great multitude by the means of the pope, one Simon and others.

As mention is here made of these superstitious sects of friars, and such other mendicant orders, it might seem not out of place, as I have done with Hildegardis before, so now to annex also another ancient treatise compiled by Geoffery Chaucer, by the way of a dialogue or questions, moved in the person of a certain uplandish and simple ploughman of the country. The author intitled it "Jack Upland," and shews in it to all the world the blind ignorance and discord of these irreligious monks; whereby it may be seen that it is no new thing, but that their blasphemous doings have been detected by various good men in old time.

A Treatise of Geoffrey Chaucer, intitled Jack Upland.

I, Jack Upland make my moan to God, and to all that are true in Christ, that antichrist and his disciples (by colour of holiness) walking and deceiving Christ's church by many false figures, where through, (by antichrist and his) many vertues been transposed to vices.

But the felliest folk that ever antichrist found, been last brought into the church and in a wonder wise, for they been of divers sects of antichrist, sown of divers countries and kindreds. And all men known well, that they be not obedient to bishops, ne leegemen to kings: neither they tillen, ne sowen, weeden, ne repen, wood, corn, ne grass, neither nothing that man should help; but only themselves their lives to sustain. An these men han all manner power of God as they seein in heaven and in yearth, to sell heaven and hell to whom that them liketh, and these wretches weet never were to been themselfs.

And therefore (Freer) in thine orders and rules been grounded on Goddis law, tell thou me, Jack Upland, that I ask of thee, and if thou be or thinkest to be on Christ's side keep thy paciens.

Saint Paul teacheth, that all our deeds should be doo in charity, and else it is nought worth, but displeasing to God and harme to our own souls. And for that freers challenge to be greatest clerks of the church, and next following Christ in living. Men should for charity ax them some questions, and pray them to ground their answers in reason and holy writ, for else their answer would nought be worth, be it florished never so fair: and as mee think men might skilfully ask thus of a freer.

1. Freer, how many orders be in earth, and which is the perfectest order? Of what order art thou? Who made thine order? What is thy rule? Is there any perfecter rule than Christ himself made? If Christ's rule be most perfect, why rulest thou thee not thereafter?

Without more why, shall a freer be more punished if he break the rule that his patron made, than if he break the hests that God himself made?

2. Approoveth Christ any more religions then one, that St. James speaketh of? If he approoveth no more, why hast thou left his rule and takest another? Why is a freer apostate that leaveth his order and taketh another sect, sith there is but one religion of Christ?

3. Why be you wedded faster to your habits then a man is to his wife? For a man may leave his wife for a year or two as many men done: and if you leave your habit a quarter of a year, ye should be holden apostate.

4. Maketh your habit you men of religion or no? If it do, then ever as it weareth, your religion weareth, and after that your habit is better, your religion is better, and when you have liggen it beside, then lig ye your religion beside you, and bin apostates: why bie you so pretious clothes? sith no man seeketh such but for vain glory, as St. Gregory saith.

What betokeneth your great hood, your scalpery, your knotted girdle, and your wide cope?

5. Why use ye all one colour, more then other christian men doo? What betokeneth that ye been clothed all in one manner of clothing?

If ye say, it betokeneth love and charity, certes then ye be oft hypocrits, when any of you hateth another, and in that that ye wooll be said holy by your clothing.

Why may not a freer wear clothing of another sect of friers, sith holiness stondeth not in the cloths?

6. Why hold ye silence in one house, more then another, sith men ought over all to speak the good and leave the evil?

Why eat you flesh in one house more than another, if your rule and your order be perfect, and the patron that made it?

7. Why get you your dispensations to have it more easie? Certes, either it seemeth that ye be unperfect, or he that made it so hard, that ye may not hold it, and siker, if ye hold not the rule of your patrons, ye be not then her freers, and so ye lie upon your selves.

8. Why make you as dead men when ye be professed, and yet ye be not dead, but more quick beggers then ye were before? And it seemeth evil a dead man to go about and beg.

9. Why will yee not suffer your novises hear your councils in your chapter-house ere that they have been professed, if your councels been true and after God's law?

10. Why make ye you so costly houses to dwell in? sith Christ did not so, and dead men should have but graves, as falleth it to dead men, and yet ye have more courts than many lords of England: For ye now wenden through the realm, and each night will lig in your own courts, and so mow but few right lords do.

11. Why heire you to ferm your limitors, giving therefore ecth year a certain rent, and will not suffer one in another's limitation, right as yee were your selves lords of countries?

Why be ye not under your bishops' visitations, and leege men to our king?

Why axe ye no letters of bretherheds of other men prayers, as ye desire that other men should axe letters of you?

If your letters be good, why grant ye them not generally to all manner of men for the more charity?

12. Mow ye make any man more perfect brether for your prayers then God hath by our believe? by our baptism and his own grant? If ye mow, certes then ye be above God.

Why make ye men believe that your golden trental song of you, to take therefore ten shillings, or at least five shillings, wool bring souls out of hell, or out of purgatory? If this be sooth, certes ye might bring all souls out of pain, and that woel ye nought, and then ye be out of charity.

13. Why make ye men believe that he that is buried in your habit shall never come in hell, and ye weet not of yourself whether ye shall to hell or no? and if this were sooth, ye should sell your high houses to make many habits for to save many men's souls.

14. Why steal ye men's children for to make hem of your sect, sith that theft is against God's hests, and sith your sect is not perfect? ye know not whether the rule, that ye bind him to, be best for him or worst.

15. Why underneme ye not your brethren for their trespass after the law of the gospel, sith that underneming is the best that may be? But ye put them in prison oft when they do after God's law, and by St. Augustine's rule, If any do amiss and would not amend him, ye should put him from you.

16. Why covet ye shrifts and burying of other men's parishens, and none other sacrament that falleth to christian folk?

Why bussy ye not to hear to shrift of poor folk as well as of rich lords and ladies, sith they mow have more plenty of shrift fathers than poor folk mow.

Why say ye not the gospel in houses of bedred men, as ye do in rich men's that mow go to church and hear the gospel?

Why covet you not to bury poor folk among you? sith that they bin most holy (as ye saine that ye been for your poverty?)

17. Why will ye not be at hir dirges as ye have bin at rich men's? sith God praiseth him more then he doth other men.

What is thy prayer worth? sith thou wilt take therefore, for all chapmen ye need be most wise for dread of simony.

What cause hast thou that thou wilt not preach the gospel, as God saith that thou shouldest? sith it is the best lore and also our believe.

Why be ye evil apaid that secular priests should preach the gospel? sith God himself hath bodden hem.

18. Why hate ye the gospel to be preached, sith ye be so much hold thereto? For ye win more by year with in principio, then with all the rules that ever your patrons made, and in this minstrels bin better then ye, for they contrarien not to the mirths that they maken, but ye contrarien the gospel both in word and deed.

19. Freer, when thou receivest a penny for to say a mass, whether sellest thou God's body for that penny, or thy prayer, or else thy travel? If thou sayest thou wolt not travel for to say the mass, but for the penny, that certes if this be sooth, then thou lovest too little meed for thy soul: and if thou sellest God's body, other thy prayer, then it is very simony, and art become a chapman worse then Judas that sold it for thirty pence.

20. Why writest thou her names in thy tables that yeveth thee money? sith God knoweth all things: for it seemeth by thy writing that God would not reward him, but thou writest in thy tables, God would els forgotten it.

Why bearest thou God in hand and slanderest him that he begged for his meat? sith he was Lord over all, for then had he bin unwise to have begged, and have no need thereto.

Freer, after what law rulest thou thee? where findest thou in God's law that thou shouldest thus beg?

21. What manner men needeth for to beg?

For whom oweth such men to beg?

Why beggest thou so for thy brethren?

If thou sayst, for they have need, then thou dost it for the more perfection, or els for the least, or els for the mean. If it be the most perfection of all, then should all thy brethren do so, and then no man needed to beg but for himself, for so should no man beg but him needed. And if it be the least perfection, why lovest thou then other men more then thyself? For so thou art not well in charity, sith thou shouldest seek the more perfection after thy power, living thyself most after God. And thus leaving that imperfection thou shouldest not so beg for them. And if it be a good mean thus to beg as thou doest, then should no man do so, but they bin in this good mean, and yet such a mean granted to you may never be grounded on God's law; for then both lerid and leaud that bin in mean degree of this world, should go about and beg as ye do. And if all should do so, certes well nigh all the world should go about and beg as ye done, and so should there be ten beggers against one yever.

M 2

Why procurest thou men to yeve thee their alms, and sayest it is so needful, and thou wilt not thyself win thee that meed?

22. Why wilt not thou beg for poor bedred men that bin poorer then any of your sect? That liggon and mow not go about to help himselfes, sith we be all brethren in God, and that bretherhed passeth any other that ye or any man could make, and where most need were, there were most perfection, either els ye hold them not your pure brethren, but worse, but then ye be unperfect in your begging?

Why make ye so many masters among you? sith it is against the teaching of Christ and his apostles?

23. Whose been all your rich courts that ye han, and all your rich jewels? sith ye saine that ye han nought ne in proper ne in common. If ye saine they been the popes, why gether ye then of poor men and lords so much out of the king's hand to make your pope rich? And sith ye saine that it is great perfection to have nought in proper ne in common, why be ye so fast about to make the pope that is your father rich, and put on him imperfection? sithen ye saine that your goods been all his, and he should by reason be the most perfect man, it seemeth openlich that ye been cursed children so to slander your father and make him imperfect. And if ye saine that the goods be yours, then do ye aienst your rule, and if it be not aienst your rule, then might ye have both plough and cart, and labour as other good men done, and not so to beg by losengery, and idle as ye doone. If ye say that it is more perfection to beg, then to travel or to worch with your hand, why preach ye not openly and teach all men to do so? sith it is the best and most perfect life to the help of their souls, as ye make children to beg that might have been rich heirs.

Why make ye not your feasts to poor men and yeveth him yefts, as ye done to the rich? sith poor man han more need then the rich.

What betokeneth that ye go twain and twain together? If ye be out of charity, ye accord not in soul.

Why beg ye and take salaries thereto more then other priests? sith he that most taketh, most charge hath.

24. Why hold ye not St. Francis' rule and his testament? sith Francis saith, that God shewed him this living and this rule: and certes if it were God's will, the pope might not fordo it; or else Francis was a lier that said on this wise. And but this testament that he made accord with God's will, or else erred he as a lier that were out of charity: and as the law saith, he is accursed that letteth the rightful last will of a dead man. And this testament is the last will of Francis that is a dead man; it seemeth therefore that all his freers been cursed.

25. Why will you not touch no coined money with the cross, ne with the king's head, as ye done other jewels both of gold and silver? Certes if ye despise the cross or the king's head, then ye be worthy to be despised of God and the king; and sith you will receive money in your hearts, and not with your hands, and it seemeth that ye hold more holiness in your hands then in your hearts, and then be false to God.

26. Why have ye exempt you from our king's laws and visiting of our bishops more then other christen men that liven in this realm, if ye be not guilt of traitory to our realm, or trespassers to our bishops? But ye will have the king's laws for the trespass do to you, and ye will have power of other bishops more then other priests, and also have leave to prison your brethren, as lords in your courts, more then other folks han that been the king's leege men.

27. Why shall some sect of your freers pay ech a year a certain to her general provincial or minister, or else to her sovereigns? but if he steal a certain number of children (as some men saine) and certain if this been sooth, then ye be constrained upon a certain pain to doe theft against God's commandment, *Non furtum facies*.

28. Why be ye so hardy to grant by letters of fraternity to men and women, that they shall have part and merit of all your good deeds, and ye weeten never whether God be apaid with your deeds because of your

sin? Also ye witten never whether that man or woman be in state to be saved or damned, then shall he have no merit in heaven for his own deeds ne for none other man's. And all were it so, that he should have part of your good deeds: yet should he have no more then God would give him after that he were worthy, and so much shall each man have of God's yeft without your limitation. But if ye will say that ye been God's fellows, and that he may not do without your assent, then be ye blasphemers to God.

29. What betokeneth that ye have ordained, that when such one as ye have made your brother or sister, and hath a letter of your seal, that letter mought be brought in your holy chapter and there be read, or else ye will not pray for him. And but ye willen pray especially for all other that were not made your brethren or sistren, then were we not in right charity, for that ought to be commen, and namely in ghostly things.

30. Freer, What charity is this, to overcharge the people by mighty begging under colour of preaching or praying, or masses singing? sith holy writ biddeth not thus, but even the contrary: for all such ghostly deeds should be done freely, as God yeveth them freely?

31. Freer, What charity is this to beguile children or the commen to discretion, and bind hem to your orders that bin not grounded in God's law against her friends will? sithen by this folly bin many apostates both in will and deed, and many bin apostates in her will during all her life, that would gladly be discharged if they wist how, and so many bin apostates that shoulden in other states have bin true men.

32. Freer, What charity is this, to make so many freers in every country to the charge of the people? sith parsons and vicars alone, yea secular priests alone, yea monks and canons alone, with bishops above them were inough to the church to do the priest's office. And to add more then inough is a foul error, and great charge to the people, and this openly against God's will that ordained all things to be done in weight, number, and measure. And Christ himself was apaid with twelve apostles and a few disciples, to preach and to do priest's office to all the whole world, then was it better done then is now at this time by a thousand dele. And right so as four fingers with a thumb in a man's hand helpeth a man to worch, and double number of fingers in one hand should let him more, and so the more number that there were passing the measure of God's ordinance, the more were a man letted to worch: right so (as it seemeth) it is of these new orders that bin added to the church without ground of holy write and God's ordinance.

33. Freer, What charity is this, to the people to lye, and say that ye follow Christ in poverty more than other men done? and yet in curious and costly housing, and fine and precious clothing, and delicious and liking feeding, and in treasure and jewels, and rich ornaments, freers passen lords and other rich worldly men, and soonest they should bring her cause about (be it never so costly) though God's law be put back.

34. Freer, What charity is this, to gather up the books of holy write, and put hem in treasory, and so emprison them from secular priests and curates, and by this cautel let hem to preach the gospel freely to the people without worldly meed, and also to defame good priests of heresie, and lien on hem openly for to let hem to shew God's law by the holy gospel to the christian people?

35. Freer, What charity is this, to fain so much holiness in your bodily clothing (that you clepe your habit) that many blind fools desiren to die therein more than in another? and also that a freer, that leaveth his habit late founden of men, may not be assoiled till he take again, but is apostate as ye sain, and cursed of God and man both? The freer believeth truth, and patience, chastity, meekness and sobriety, yet for the more part of his life he may soon be assoiled of his prior, and if he bring home to his house much good by the year (be it never so falsely begged and pilled of the poor and needy people in countries about) he shall behold a noble freer. O Lord, whether this be charity?

36. Freer, What charity is this, to prease upon a rich man, and to intice him to be buried among you from his parish-church, and to such rich men give letters of fraternity confirmed by your general seal, and thereby to bear him in hand that he shall have part of all your masses, mattens, preachings, fastings, wakings, and all other good deeds done by your brethren of your order (both whilst he liveth, and after that he is dead) and yet ye witten never whether your deeds be acceptable to God, ne whether that man that hath that letter be able by good living to receive any part of your deeds, and yet a poor man (that ye wite well or supposen in certen to have no good of) ye ne given no such letters, though he be a better man to God than such a rich man: nevertheless, this poor man doth not retch thereof. For as men supposen such letters and many other that freers behotten to men, be full false deceits of freers, out of all reason, and God's law and christian men's faith.

37. Freer, What charity is this, to be confessors of lords and ladies, and to other mighty men, and not amend hem in her living? but rather as it seemeth, to be the bolder to pill her poor tenants, and to live in riot, and there to dwell in your office of confessor for winning of worldly goods, and to be hold great by colour of such ghostly offices? this seemeth rather pride of freers, than charity of God.

38. Freer, What charity is this, to sain that who so liveth after your order, liveth more perfectly, and next followeth the state of apostles in poverty and pennance, and yet the wisest and greatest clerks of you wend or send, or procure to the court of Rome to be made cardinals or bishops of the pope's chaplains, and to be assoiled of the vow of poverty and obedience to your ministers, in the which (as ye sain) standeth more perfection and merit of your orders, and thus ye farren as pharisees that sain one and do another to the contrary.

Why name ye more the patron of your order in your *confiteor* when ye begin mass, then other saints, apostles, or martyrs, that holy church hold more glorious then hem, and clepe hem your patrons and your avowries?

Freer, Whether was St. Francis in making of his rule that he set thine order in, a fool and a lyar, or else wise and true? If ye sain that he was not a fool, but wise; ne a lyar but true: why shew you contrary by your doing, when by your suggestion to the pope ye said, That your rule that Francis made was so hard that ye mow not live to hold it without declaration and dispensation of the pope, and so by your deed? Ne let your patron be a fool that made a rule so hard that no man may well keep, and eke your deed proveth him a lyar, where he saith in his rule, "That he took and learned it of the Holy Ghost." For how might ye for shame pray the pope undo that the Holy Ghost bit, as when ye prayed him to dispence with the hardness of your order?

Freer, Which of the four orders of freers is best to a man that knoweth not which is the best, but would fain enter into the best, and none other? If thou sayest that thine is the best, then saiest thou that none of the other is as good as thine, and in this each freer in the three other orders wooll say that thou lyest, for in the self manner each other freer wooll say that his order is best. And thus to each of the four orders bin the other three contrary in this point: in the which if any say sooth, that is one alone, for there may but one be the best of four. So followeth it that if each of these orders answered to this question as thou dost, three were false, and but one true, and yet no man should wite who that were. And thus it seemeth, that the most part of freers bin or should be lyers in this point, and they should answer thereto. If you say that another order of the freers is better than thine, or as good; why took ye not rather thereto as to the better, when thou mightst have chose at the beginning? And eke why shouldst thou be an apostate to leave thine order and take thee to that is better, and so why goest thou not from thine order in that?

Freer, Is there any perfecter rule of religion than Christ God's Son gave in his gospel to his brethren?

Or then that religion that St. James in his epistle maketh mention of? If you say yes, then puttest thou on Christ (that is the wisdome of God the Father) unkunning, unpower, or evil will: for then he could not make his rule so good as another did his. And so he had unkunning, that he might not so make his rule so good as another man might, and so were he unmighty, and not God, as he would not make his rule so perfect as another did his, and so he had bin evil willed, namely to himself.

For if he might and could, and would have made a rule perfect without default, and did not, he was not God's Son Almighty. For if any other rule be perfecter than Christ's, then must Christ's rule lack of that perfection by as much as the other weren more perfecter, and so were default, and Christ had failed in making of his rule: but to put any default or failing in God is blasphemy. If thou say that Christ's rule, and that religion which St. James maketh mention of, is perfectest; why holdest thou not thilk rule without more? And why clepest thou the rather of St. Francis or St. Dominick's rule, or religion, or order, than of Christ's rule, or Christ's order?

Freer, Canst thou assign any default in Christ's rule of the gospel (with the which he taught all men sikerly to be saved) if they kept it to her ending? If thou say it was too hard, then sayst thou Christ lyed; for he said of his rule, "My yoke is soft, and my burthen light." If thou say Christ's rule was too light, that may be assigned for no default, for the better it may be kept. If thou sayest that there is no default in Christ's rule of the gospel, sith Christ himself saith "It is light and easie;" what need was it to patrons of freers to add more thereto? and so to make an harder religion to save freers, than was the religion of Christ's apostles and his disciples helden and were saved by. But if they woulden that her freers saten above the apostles in heaven for the harder religion that they keepen here, so would they sitten in heaven above Christ himself, for their more and strict observations, then so should they be better than Christ himself with mischance.

Go now forth and frain your clerks, and ground ye you in God's law, and gif Jack an answer, and when ye han assoiled me that I have said sadly in truth, I shall soil thee of thine orders, and save thee to heaven.

If freers kun not or mow not excuse hem of these questions asked of hem, it seemeth that they be horrible guilty against God, and her even christian; for which guilts and defaults it were worthy that the order that they call their order were fordone. And it is wonder that men sustain hem or suffer her live in such manner. For holy write biddeth, "That thou do well to the meek, and give not to the wicked, but forbed to give hem bread, least they be made thereby mightier through you."

After these digressions, we may now return to the course of our history again.

After England had been subjected by King John, and made tributary to the pope, it is incredible how the unsatiable avarice of the Romans oppressed and wrung the commons and all estates of the realm, especially beneficed men, and such as had any thing of the church; who were brought into such slavery and penury, that when the king durst not remedy their wrongs by himself; yet by his advice, Simon Montfort, and the Earl of Leicester, with other noblemen, thought to bridle and restrain the insatiable ravening of these greedy wolves. They devised a letter, giving command to the ecclesiastics, and to such as had churches to farm, that henceforth they should not pay the Romans such farms and rents any more, as follows:

"*A complaint of the nobles of England against the intolerable covetousness of the Pope and Prelates of Rome.*

"To such and such a bishop, and such a chapter; all the university and company of them, that had rather die than be confounded by the Romans, wishes health. How the Romans and their legates have hitherto behaved' themselves toward you and other ecclesiastical persons of this realm of England is not unknown to your discretion, in disposing and giving away the benefices of the realm after their own fancies, to the intolerable prejudice and grievance both of you, and all other Englishmen. For, whereas the collation of benefices should and does properly belong to you and your fellow-bishops (ecclesiastical persons), they, thundering against you the sentence of excommunication, ordain that you should not bestow them upon any person of this realm, until in every diocese and cathedral church within the realm, five Romans, such as the pope shall name, be provided for, to the value of every man an hundred pounds a-year. Besides these, many other grievances the Romanists do inflict on the laity and nobles of the realm, for the patronages and alms bestowed by them and their ancestors, for the support of the poor of the realm, and also for the clergy and ecclesiastical persons of the realm touching their livings and benefices. And yet the Romans, not contented with these, do also take from the clergy of this realm the benefices which they have to bestow them on men of their own country, &c.

"Wherefore, we considering the rigorous austerity of these aforesaid Romans, who once coming in but as strangers here, now take upon them not only to judge, but also to condemn us, laying upon us insupportable burthens, whereunto they will not put one of their own fingers to move; and laying our heads together upon a general and full advice had among ourselves concerning the same, have thought good, although very late, to withstand them, rather than be subject to their intolerable oppressions, and greater slavery hereafter to be looked for. For which cause we straitly charge and command you (as your friends going about to deliver you, the church, the king, and the kingdom from that miserable yoke of servitude) that you do not intermeddle, or take any part concerning such exactions or rents to be required or given to the said Romans. Letting you to understand for truth, that in case you shall (which God forbid) be found culpable herein, not only your goods and possessions shall be in danger of burning, but you also in your persons shall incur the same peril and punishment as shall the Romish oppressors themselves. Thus fare ye well."

In the reign of this Henry III., cardinal Otho was sent from the pope with letters to the king, as other letters also were sent to other places for exactions of money.

The king, opening the letters, and perceiving the contents, answered, "That he alone could say nothing in the matter which concerned all the clergy and commons of the whole realm." Not long after a council was called at Westminster (A.D. 1226), where the letters being opened, the form was this: "We require to be given to us, first, of all cathedral churches, two prebends, one for the bishops' part, the other for the chapter; and likewise of monasteries where are divers portions, one for the abbot, another for the convent; of the convent so much as appertains to one monk, the portion of the goods being proportionally divided; of the abbot likewise as much," &c.

When those proposals of the legate were propounded in the assembly on the pope's behalf, answer was made that the matter concerned especially the king; but in general it touched all the archbishops, with their suffragans, the bishops, and all the prelates of the realm. Wherefore, seeing the king, by reason of his sickness, was absent, and the archbishop of Canterbury, with other bishops, also were not there, therefore in their absence they had nothing to say in the matter, neither could they do so without prejudice of those that were absent. And so the assembly broke up.

Not long after, Cardinal Otho, coming again from Rome, called another council at London, and caused all prelates, archbishops, bishops, abbots, priors, and others of the clergy, to be summoned to the council, to be held in the church of St. Paul's, at London. The pretence of which council was for the redress of matters concerning benefices and religion; but the chief and principal object was to hunt for money; for putting them in fear and in hope, some to lose, some to obtain spiritual promotions at his hand, he thought some gain would rise thereby, and so it did. For, in the meantime, precious gifts were offered him in palfries, in rich plate and jewels, in costly and sumptuous garments, richly furred; in coin, in victuals, and such like things of value, well worthy of acceptance. Wherein one endeavoured to go beyond another in munificence.

The time of the council drawing nigh, the cardinal commanded at the west end of St. Paul's church an high and solemn throne to be prepared, rising up with a glorious scaffold upon substantial stages strongly built, and of great height. Thus, on the day assigned, the archbishops, bishops, abbots, and others of the prelacy, assembled both far and near throughout all England, wearied and vexed with the winter's journey, bringing their letters procuratory. Being assembled together, the cardinal was about to begin his sermon, when there broke out a great dispute between the two archbishops of Canterbury and York, about sitting at the right hand and left hand of the glorious cardinal, for which the one appealed against the other. The cardinal, to pacify the strife between them, brought forth a bull of the pope; in the midst of this bull was pictured the figure of the cross. On the right side of the cross stood the image of St. Paul, and on the left side St. Peter. "Lo!" said the cardinal, holding open the bull with the cross; "here you see St. Peter on the left hand of the cross, and St. Paul on the right, and yet there is between these two no contention, for both are of equal glory. And yet St. Peter, for the prerogative of his keys, and for the pre-eminence of his apostleship and cathedral dignity, seems most worthy to be placed on the right side. But yet because St. Paul believed on Christ when he saw him not, therefore has he the right hand of the cross; for, 'blessed be they,' saith Christ, 'which see not, and yet have believed.'" And from that time forth the archbishop of Canterbury enjoyed the right hand, and the archbishop of York the left.

The cause why the pope was so greedy and needy of money, was this; he had mortal hatred and waged continual battle against the good emperor Frederick II. who had married Isabel, the sister of King Henry. And therefore because the pope's war could not be sustained without charges, it made the pope the more importunate to take money in all places, but especially in England; so that he shamed not to require the fifth part of every ecclesiastical man's living, as Matthew Paris writes. And he bargained with the citizens of Rome that if they would join with him in vanquishing Frederick, he would grant to them, that all the benefices in England, which should be vacant should be bestowed at their own will to their children and kinsfolks! Upon which it follows thus in the forenamed history. "The pope sent commandment to the archbishop of Canterbury and four other bishops, that provision should be made for three hundred Romans in the chief and best benefices in all England at the next vacancies, so that the archbishop and bishops should be suspended in the meantime from all collation or gift of benefices, until the foresaid three hundred were provided for."

At length the bishops, abbots, and archdeacons came to the king, lamentably complaining of the exactions of the pope, desiring the king, that seeing the matter touched not themselves alone, but the whole church, and seeing the valuation of churches was better known to their archdeacons than to themselves, therefore there might be a general calling and conference on the matter. In the octaves of St. John the Baptist, the day and place was assigned where they should confer; at which day and place the prelates of England, assembling together, durst not give any direct denial of that contribution, but after a modest way insinuated certain exceptions against it.

[Not long after followed a general council at Lyons, (A.D. 1245) called by pope Innocent IV. in which the English nation exhibited the following articles of their grievances.

I. The kingdom of England is grieved that the pope,

being not content with his Peter-pence, requires and extorts from the clergy great exactions, without the consent of the king, and against the customs of the realm.

II. The church and kingdom of England is grieved, that the patrons of the same cannot present as they were wont, to their churches because of the pope's letters ; but the churches are given to Romans, who know neither the realm nor the language, both to the great peril of souls and robbing away the money out of the realm.

III. It is grieved, because the pope having agreed by his letters, that in requiring pensions and provisions in the realm of England he would require only twelve benefices, now contrary to his agreement and letter, many more benefices and provisions are given away by him.

IV. The realm is grieved and complains that in the benefices in England, one Italian succeeds another, the Englishmen being not only excluded, but also compelled for determining of their matters, to seek to Rome, contrary both to the customs of the realm, and also to the privileges granted by the pope's predecessors to the king and kingdom of England.

V. The fifth grievance is for the frequent recourse of that infamous legate, by whom both faith and fidelity, the ancient customs of the realm, the authorities of old grants, statutes, laws, and privileges, are annulled and abrogated, whereby an infinite number in England are grievously afflicted and oppressed.

VI. The realm is also grieved in general taxings, collections and assessments made without the king's consent, the appeal and contradiction of the king's proctors to the contrary notwithstanding.

VII. The realm complains and is grieved, that in the benefices given to Italians, neither the old ordinances, nor relief of the poor, nor hospitality, nor any preaching of God's word, nor care of men's souls, nor service in the church, nor yet the walls of the churches are kept up and maintained, as the manner and custom of the realm requires.

Over and above these grievances, there came also from the pope other letters, charging and commanding the prelates of England to find at their own costs and charges for one whole year, some ten armed soldiers, some five, some fifteen, to be ready at the pope's command wherever he should appoint.

After these and other grievances and enormities of Rome, the states of England, consulting together, direct their letters to the pope, for the reformation of them. First the abbots and priors, then the bishops and suffragans, afterward the nobles and barons, last of all the king himself.]

At length the ambassadors who were at Rome came home, bringing word that the pope, hearing what was done in the council of Westminster, and by the king, was greatly displeased with him and the realm, denouncing the king and his people as half schismatics. The king was marvellously incensed at this, and commanded by general proclamation through all his realm, that no man should hereafter consent to any tax or subsidy of money for the court of Rome. But afterwards the king, for fear of the pope, and partly through the persuasions of the bishop of Worcester and other prelates, gave over.

At this time it is told of the legate Otho that as he left no place unsought, where any advantage might be got: so among others he came to Oxford, where he was received with great honour ; the scholars presenting him honourably with such dishes and rewards as they had, thinking to gratify the cardinal after the best manner. This being done before dinner, and the dinner ended, they came reverently to see and welcome him, supposing that they also should be entertained with like courtesy. As they came to the gate, the porter (an Italian) asks what they wanted. They said they came to see the lord legate. But the porter holding the door half open, with proud and insolent language thrust them out, and would not suffer them to enter. The scholars seeing that, by force thrust open the gate and came in ; and when the Romans who were within would have repelled them with their fists, and such staves as they had in their hands, they fell to much heaving and pushing, and many blows were given on both sides. In the meantime, while some

of the scholars ran home for their weapons, there chanced a poor scholar (an Irishman) to stand at the gate waiting for his alms. When the master-cook saw him at the gate, he took hot scalding water and cast it in his face. One of the scholars, a Welshman, that came with his bow and shafts, seeing this, let fly an arrow, and shot this master of cooks clean through the body, and slew him at once. When the cook fell dead, there was a mighty uproar and a great clamour throughout all the house. The cardinal, hearing the tumult and great noise about him, like a valiant Roman runs as fast as he could into the steeple, and there locks the doors fast, where he remained till midnight. The scholars in the meanwhile, not yet pacified, sought all about for the legate, exclaiming and crying out, " Where is that usurer, that simonist, that pilferer and taxer of our livings, that prowler and extortioner of our money, who perverts our king, and subverts his kingdom, enriching himself with our spoils ?" &c. All this the cardinal heard and held his peace : when the night approaching had broken up the field, the cardinal coming out of his fort, and taking his horse in the silence of night was privately conveyed over the river to the king.

Mention was made a little before of the Albigenses living about the city of Toulouse. These Albigenses, because they began to discover the pope, and to control the inordinate proceedings and discipline of the see of Rome, the pope therefore accounting them as a heretical people, excited Lewis, the young French king, through the instance of Philip his father, to lay siege against Toulouse to eradicate and extinguish these Albigenses. Whereupon Lewis reared a mighty army to beset the city. But after he had long wearied himself and his men, there fell upon the French host such famine and pestilence both of men and horses, besides the other daily slaughter of the soldiers, that Lewis was forced to retire and return to France. In the slaughter, besides many others, Earl Simon de Montfort, general of the army, to whom the lands of the earl of Toulouse were given by the pope, was slain.

In the year 1226, died Pope Honorius III., a great adversary against the Emperor Frederick, after whom succeeded Gregory IX. In which year also died Lewis, the perjured French king, at the siege of Avignon, whom the pope now the second or third time had set up to fight against Reymond the good earl of Toulouse, and the Albigenses of that country, the origin whereof was this. In the days of Philip the French king, this Reymond (earl of Toulouse) was disdained by the pope for holding with the Albigenses, and, therefore, by the instigation of the pope, the lands of the earl were taken from him and given to Simon Montfort ; but when Earl Reymond would not be removed from the right of his possessions, then the pope set Philip to make war against him. Whereupon Lewis (his son) was sent, as above declared, to besiege the city of Toulouse ; but being repulsed, returned home, after he had lost the most part of his army by pestilence and other calamity. And thus continued the good earl still in quiet possession till this present time (A.D. 1226), when the pope, not forgetting his old malice against the earl, and no less inflamed with insatiable avarice, directed his legate Romanus to France for two purposes ; one to extirpate the earl, the other to enlarge his own revenues. Thus the legate begins to summon a council, requiring the French king, with the archbishops, bishops, and clergy of France, to appear before him at Bitures. The council being set, and the pope's letters read, there appears before them Reymond earl of Toulouse on the one part, and Simon Montfort on the other part. Simon demanded the lands and possessions of Reymond, which the pope and Philip the French king had given to him and to his father before, confirmed by the donation of the pope and of the king. Adding, moreover, that the Earl Reymond was deprived and disinherited in the general council at Rome for the heresy, which is called the heresy of the Albigenses.

To this the Earl Reymond answered, offering himself ready to all duty and office both towards the French king and to the church of Rome, whatever duly appertained to him. And as to the heresy with which he was there charged, he not only there offered himself in that council before the legate, but most humbly entreated of him, that he would take the pains to come into every city within his precinct, to inquire of every person there the articles of his belief; and if he found any person or persons holding that which was not catholic, he would see the same corrected and amended according to the censure of holy church to the uttermost. Or if he should find any city rebelling against him, he, to the uttermost of his might, with the inhabitants, would compel them to do satisfaction. And, as to himself, if he had committed or erred in anything, he offered there full satisfaction to God and the church, as became any faithful christian man to do, &c. But all this the legate despised, neither could the catholic earl there find any grace, unless he would give up his heritage, both for himself and for his heirs for ever.

After much altercation on both sides about the matter, the legate required every archbishop to call aside his suffragans, to deliberate with them upon the case, and to give in writing what was concluded. Which being done accordingly, the legate denounced excommunication against all such as revealed any part of that which was there concluded, before the pope and the king had intelligence of it.

In the meantime certain preaching friars were directed by the legate, throughout all France. to incite and stir up the French to assume the cross, and to war against the earl and the people of Toulouse, whom they accounted for heretics. He ceased not to prosecute the pope's fury against him and his subjects, stirring up the king and the French, under pain of excommunication, to war against them. Lewis being thus forced by the legate, answered, that he for his own safety would not achieve that expedition, or venture against the earl, unless the pope would first write to the king of England, commanding him, that, during the time of that expedition, he should invade and molest no piece of his lands and possessions. All this being done and accomplished, the French king and the legate, crossing themselves to the field, appointed a day for the French army to meet together at Lyons, under pain of the pope's excommunication, and with horse and armour to set upon the Toulossians.

When the day was come, the French king marched forward with a mighty host, after whom also came the legate, with his bishops and prelates. The number of fighting-men in his army, besides the victuallers and waggoners, were fifty thousand men. The legate openly excommunicated the earl of Toulouse, and all that took his part, and interdicted his whole land. Thus the king came marching forward, till he came into the province of Toulouse, and the first city of the earls which he came to there was Avignon, which city they thought first to have besieged, and so in order to have destroyed and wasted the whole province belonging to the earl. And first the king demanded of them to have his passage through the city, pretending peace, as desiring only to pass through. The citizens, consulting with themselves what was to be done, gave answer, "That they mistrusted their coming, and supposed that in deceit they required entrance into their city, and for no necessity of their journey."

The king being much offended at this, swore an oath, that he would not depart till he had taken the city, and immediately he began to make assaults. The citizens manfully defended themselves, and casting stone for stone, and shooting shot for shot, slew and wounded many of the French. Thus when they had long besieged the city, and could not win it, at length provisions began to fail in the French camp, and many of the French army died for hunger; for the earl of Toulouse, as a wise man of war, hearing before of their coming, took into the town all the provision that was abroad, and left nothing without to serve for their defence and succour. He ploughed up the fields, that there should be no pasture to serve their horses; he put out of the town all the old people and young children, lest they who kept the town should want provisions, and before their coming sent them far away, so that within the town they had plenty, and

without they died for famine. And, besides, in seeking about for their forage, many fell into the hands of them that kept the city, who secretly lay in wait for them abroad, and slew many of them; besides a great number of cattle and horses died for want of forage, and poor soldiers, that had no great store of money, died for want of victuals. By which mortality a pestilence broke out among them, so that the king himself, and also the legate, were greatly dismayed, thinking it to be no little disgrace, as well to the realm of France, as also to Rome, that they should depart and break up their siege : and the soldiers also thought that it was much better for them to end their lives by battle, than to starve and die like dogs. Wherefore, with one consent, they determined to give a new assault at the bridge that goes over the river Rhone into the town; to which place they came in such number, that either by the weakness of the bridge, or the subtilty of the soldiers that kept the town, the bridge broke, and three thousand of them, with bridge and all, fell armed into the violent stream, and were drowned. There was nothing then but joy and gladness among the citizens, and much lamentation and heaviness among the others; and shortly after the citizens (when they saw a convenient time) came suddenly upon them, and slew two thousand of them, and returned to the town again with safety. Lewis the king, to avoid the pestilence that was in the camp, went into an abbey not far off, where he shortly after died; of whose death there are various opinions, some saying, that he was poisoned; some, that he died of dysentery.

The legate thought to keep his death secret till the town should be surrendered; for he thought himself disgraced for ever, if he should depart before the town was taken; so he considered how by falsehood he might betray them, and he sent certain heralds, to desire them that they should consult among themselves upon articles of peace, and bring the same to the French camp; they faithfully promised the safe conduct of the messengers, both in coming and going; and when they had given their pledges, the messengers from the citizens talked with the legate, who promised them, if they would deliver up their city, they should have their lives, goods, and possessions in as ample a manner as they now enjoyed them. But the citizens and soldiers refused, and after much talk on both sides, the legate requested them, that he and his prelates might come into their city to examine what faith and belief they were of, and that he neither sought nor meant any other thing, but their own safety as well of body as of soul, which he faithfully sware to. "For," saith he, "the report of your great infidelity has come to the lord pope's ear, and therefore he desired us to truly certify thereof." The citizens, not mistrusting his oath and promise, granted entrance to him and the clergy. But the soldiers of the camp, as was privately arranged by the legate, made themselves ready; so that at the entrance of the prelates in at the gate, disregarding their oath and fidelity, the soldiers were ready, and suddenly, with violence, rushing in, slew the porter and warders, and at length won the city and destroyed it. Thus when they had taken this noble city by falsehood and policy, they carried the king's corpse to Paris, where they buried it. Of the whole number of the French soldiers who were destroyed in this siege by famine, pestilence, and drowning, are recounted more than two-and-twenty thousand.

In the former part of this history it has been stated how the church and commons of England were miserably afflicted by the intolerable oppression of the pope, who, through his violent extortion, had procured the best benefices to be given to his Romans, and the chief fruits of them to be reserved to his own coffers. You heard before what complaints had been made, but yet no redress could be had. Such was the insatiable avarice of these Roman exactors, prowling and taking wherever they came, with their provisions and exactions out of measure, and never satisfied. And these importunate exactions and contributions of these Italian harpies, besides the Peter-pence, besides the common tribute, increased daily more and more, to the great grievance of the realm, so that the wealth of this land was almost sucked out, and transferred to the court of Rome. The king was not ignorant of this, but he could not help the matter. Therefore it was devised by some of the nobles, (A. D. 1231), that certain letters, under the pretended authority of the king, should be sent abroad, commanding that such corn and grain, with other revenues, as were taken up for the pope, should be stayed and forthcoming by a certain day appointed in the letters.

At that time, (about A. D. 1232), there was at St. Albans a great consistory of abbots, priors, archdeacons, with several both of the nobility and clergy. At the breaking up of which consistory, there was a certain clerk, whose name was Cincius, a Roman, carried away by the soldiers ; and one John, archdeacon of Norwich, a Florentine, hardly escaping, got to London, where he hid himself. Cincius, after being kept five weeks, when they had well emptied his bags, was safely sent again without any more injury to London.

Not long after this, the barns of a beneficed man, a Roman, being full of corn, were broke up by a like company of armed soldiers, and the corn brought out to be sold and given away to the poor people.

The same year, about Easter, all the barns in England which were in the hands of any Roman or Italian, were likewise wasted, and the corn sold to the best advantage for the poor commoners ; of which, great alms were distributed, and many times money, also with corn together was scattered for the poor people to gather up. Neither was there any that would or durst stand against them. As for the Romans and Italians themselves, they were struck with such fear, that they hid themselves in monasteries and cells, not daring to complain of their injuries, but held it better to lose their goods, than to lose their lives. The authors and workers of this feat were to the number of fourscore armed soldiers, of whom the principal captain was one naming himself William Withers, surnamed Twing.

This coming to the pope's knowledge, he sends his letters immediately to the king, with sharp threats and imperious commands, charging him for suffering such villany within his realm, straightly enjoining him, under pain of excommunication, to search out the perpetrators with all diligence, and so punish them that all others might take example by them.

Thus, after inquisition made of all parties, and witnesses sworn and examined, many were found culpable in the matter, some that were actors, some that were consenters, of whom some were bishops and chaplains to the king, some archdeacons and deans, with soldiers and laymen. Among them was the Robert Twing above mentioned, a comely young man, and a tall soldier, who, of his own accord, with five other servitors, whom he took with him abroad to work that feat, came to the king, openly protesting himself to be the author of that deed, and said he did it for hatred of the pope and the Romans, because that by the sentence of the bishop of Rome, and fraudulent circumvention of the Italians, he was bereaved of the patronage of his benefice, having no more to give but that one ; wherefore to be revenged of that injury, he enterprised that which was done, preferring rather to be justly excommunicated for a season, than to be spoiled of his benefice for ever. Then the king, and other executors of the pope's commandment, gave him counsel, that seeing he had so incurred the danger of the pope's sentence, he should offer himself to the pope to be absolved of him again, and there make his declaration to him, that he justly and canonically was possessed of that church. The king, moreover, sent with him his letters testimonial to the pope, urgently desiring the pope that he might be heard with favour. At this request, Pope Gregory both released him of the sentence, and restored to him his patronage, writing to the archbishop of York, that he might again enjoy the right of his benefice, in as ample a manner as he did before it was taken from him.

Variance between Pope Gregory IX. and the Romans.

At this time dissension and variance began in Rome, between the pope and the citizens. The citizens claimed by old custom and law, that the bishop of Rome might not excommunicate any citizen of the city, nor suspend the city with any interdict for any manner of excess.

To this the pope answered, " That although he was less than God, yet he was greater than any man : and therefore, greater than any citizen, yea also, greater than king or emperor." And as he is their spiritual father, he both ought, and lawfully may chastise his children when they offend, as being subject to him in the faith of Christ.

The citizens alleged again for themselves that the authorities of the city, and the senators received from the church of Rome a yearly tribute, which the bishops of Rome were bound to pay to them, both by new and also ancient laws. Of which yearly tribute they have been ever in possession before this Pope Gregory IX.

To this the pope answered, that although the church of Rome in time of persecution, for defence and peace, was wont to respect the rulers of the city with gentle rewards, yet that ought not now to be taken for a custom ; for that custom only ought to stand, which consists not upon examples, but upon right and reason.

By these and such other controversies rising between the pope and the Romans, such dissension was kindled, that the pope with the cardinals, leaving the city of Rome removed to Perusium, there to remain and to plant themselves ; but the Romans overthrew several of his houses in the city, for which he excommunicated them. The Romans then flying to the emperor, desired his aid and succour ; but he, to please the pope, gathering an army, went rather against the Romans. Then the pope's army, whose captains were the earl of Toulouse, (to purchase the pope's favour,) and Peter the bishop of Winchester, whom the pope had sent for, partly for his treasure, partly for his skill in feats of war, and the emperor's army, joined together, and going about the city of Rome, cast down the castles or mansions belonging to the citizens round about the suburbs, to the number of eighteen, and destroyed all their vines and vineyards about the city. The Romans not a little enraged, brake out of the city with more heat than order, to the number of one hundred thousand, to destroy Viterbium the pope's city with sword and fire. But the multitude being in disorder, and out of battle-array, and unprepared for contingencies, fell into the hands of their enemies, who were in wait for them, and destroyed a great number ; so that on both sides there were slain to the number of thirty thousand ; but the greater portion was of the citizens. And this dissension thus begun, was not soon ended, but continued long after.

By these and such other histories, who sees not how far the church of Rome has degenerated from the true image of the right church of Christ ? which by the rule and example of the gospel, ought to be a daughter of peace, not a mother of debate, not a revenger of herself, nor a seeker of wars ; but a forgiver of injuries, humbly and patiently referring all revenge to the Lord ; not a raker for riches, but a winner of souls ; not contending for worldly mastership, but humbling themselves as servants ; and not vicars of the Lord, but jointly like brethren serving together, bishops with bishops, ministers with ministers, deacons with deacons ; and not as masters separating themselves by superiority one from another ; but briefly communicating together in doctrine and counsel, one particular church with another ; not as a mother, one over another, but rather as a sister church one with another, seeking together the glory of Christ, and not their own. And such was the church of Rome first in the old ancient beginning of her primitive state, especially while the cross of persecution yet kept the bishops and ministers in humility of heart, and fervent calling upon the Lord for help ; so that happy was that christian then, who with liberty of conscience might only hold his life, how barely soever he lived. And as for the pride and pomp of the world, as striving for patrimonies, buying of bishopricks, gaping for benefices, so far was this off from them, that then they had little leisure, and less desire so much as once to think of them. Neither did the bishops of Rome then fight to be consuls of the city, but sought how to bring the consuls to Christ, being glad if the consuls would permit them to dwell with them in the city. Neither did they then presume so high, as to bring the emperors' necks under their girdles, but were glad to save their own necks in any corner from the sword of the emperors. Then they lacked outward peace, but they abounded with inward consolation. God's holy Spirit mightily working in their hearts. Then was one catholic unity of truth and doctrine amongst all churches against errors and sects. Neither did the east and west, nor distance of place divide the church; but both the eastern church and western church, the Greeks and Latins made all one church. And although there were then five patriarchal sees appointed for order sake, differing in regions, and peradventure also, in some rites one from another; yet all these consenting together in one unity of catholic doctrine, having one God, one Christ, one Spirit, one faith, one baptism, one head, and linked together in one bond of charity, and in one equality of honour, they made altogether one body, one church, one communion, called one Catholic Universal and Apostolic Church. And so long as this knot of charity and equality did join them in one unity together, so long the church of Christ flourished and increased, one ready to help and harbour another, in time of distress, as Agapetus and Vigilius flying to Constantinople, were there aided by the patriarch, &c. So that all this while, neither foreign enemy, neither Saracen, nor Soldan, nor Sultan, nor Calipha, nor Corasmine, nor Turk, had any power greatly to harm it.

But through the malice of the enemy, this catholic unity did not long continue, and all by reason of the bishop of Rome, who, not contented to be like his brethren, began to extend himself, and to claim superiority above the other four patriarchal sees, and all other churches in the world. And thus as equality amongst christian bishops was by pride oppressed, so unity began by little and little to be dissolved, and the Lord's vesture, which the soldiers left whole, began to be divided. Which vesture of christian unity, although now it has for a long time been rent asunder by the occasion aforesaid, yet notwithstanding in some part it held together in some mean agreement, under subjection to the see of Rome, till the time of this Pope Gregory IX. (A. D. 1230), at which time this rupture and schism of the church brake out into a plain division, utterly dissevering the eastern church from the western church, upon this occasion.

There was a certain archbishop elected to an archbishoprick among the Grecians; who, coming to Rome to be confirmed, could not be admitted unless he promised a great sum of money. Which when he refused to do, and detested the execrable simony of the court of Rome, he repaired home again to his own country unconfirmed, declaring there to the whole nobility of that land, how the case stood. There were others also, who having come lately from Rome, and having there experienced the same or worse treatment came in and gave testimony to the truth of his saying. Upon which, all the churches of the Grecians, hearing this, departed utterly from the church of Rome, in the days of this Pope Gregory IX.

By the occasion of this separation of the Grecians from Pope Gregory, it happened shortly after, (A. D. 1237) that Germanus, patriarch of Constantinople, wrote to the pope, humbly desiring him to study and seek some means of unity, that the seamless coat of the Lord Jesus thus lamentably rent, not with the hands of soldiers, but by the discord of prelates, might be healed again; offering this besides, that if he would take the pains to do so, he for his part, notwithstanding his old age and feeble body, would not refuse to meet him in the mid-way, that the truth on both sides being debated by the scriptures, the wrong may be reduced, the slander stopped, and unity reformed between them.

This request of the patriarch, as it was both godly and reasonable, so it was the pope's part again with like humility to have yielded and agreed to it, and to have been glad with all his might to help forward the reformation of christian unity in the church of Christ, and so to have shewed himself the son of peace: but the proud bishop of Rome, more like the son of discord and dissension, standing still upon his majesty, refused, and wrote answer to his letters, with great disdain, seeking nothing

else, but how to advance his see above all other churches; and not only that, but shortly after sent forth his preaching friars, to move all christians to take the sign of the cross, and to fight against the Grecians no less than against the Turks and Saracens: so that in the isle of Cyprus many good men and martyrs were slain for the same, as by the letters of Germanus patriarch of Constantinople is to be seen.

Shortly after, pope Gregory prepared to send men-of-war signed with the cross, to fight against the Grecians; upon which the archbishop of Antioch, with Germanus, solemnly excommunicated the pope, after he first had excommunicated them. In the meantime by the tenor of the letters of the patriarch sent to the pope and to the cardinals, it is evident to all men,

First, that the whole universal church of Christ from the east to the west, in ancient times, were altogether united in one consent of doctrine, and linked together in brotherly charity, one church brotherly helping another, both with temporal aid and spiritual counsel, as case required. Neither was there any one mother-church above other churches, but the whole universal church was the mother-church and spouse of the Lord to every faithful believer. Under the universal church in general were comprehended all other particular churches in particular, as sister churches together, not one greater than another, but all in like equality, as God gave his gifts so serving one another, ever holding together the unity of faith and sisterly love. And so long was it and rightly might it be called "the catholic church," having in it true unity, universality and free consent. Unity in doctrine, universality in communicating and joining together of voices, consent in spirit and judgment. For whatever was taught at Rome touching faith and salvation, was no other than that which was taught at Antioch, Syria, &c.

Secondly, how in process of time, through occasion of the tyranny and violent oppression of the bishops of Rome, this ring of equality being broken, all flew in pieces, the eastern church from the western, the Greeks from the Latins, and that which was one before, now was made two; unity turned to division, universality to singularity, and free consent to dissension.

Thirdly, here is also to be noted after this piteous breach of equality, how many and what great nations departed from the communion of the church of Rome, and especially about this time, (A. D. 1230) so that both before and after that time many councils were held, and many things concluded in the western church, to which one-half of Christendom in the east never agreed; and on the other hand, many councils were holden with them, which in the Latin church were not received. So that the church now as she lost the benefit of universal consent, so also she lost the name catholic. Upon which this question is to be asked, that when the council of Lateran, under pope Innocent III. ordained the doctrine of transubstantiation, and auricular confession here in the western church, without the free consent of the eastern church, whether that doctrine is to be accounted catholic or not?

Fourthly, in the departing of these churches from the bishop of Rome, there is also to be noted that the churches of the Greeks, although they separated themselves from the church of Rome, and that justly, yet they still kept their unity with their God, and still received the true and sincere doctrine of faith, ready to discuss and try the truth of their religion by the scriptures. Wherefore the church of Rome has done them open wrong, for, when the Greeks offered so gently to try and to be tried by the truth of God's word, she not only would stand to no trial, nor abide any conference, but even excommunicated as heretics, those who appear to have been more orthodox christians than they themselves.

Fifthly, these things being so, then we have to conclude that the church of Rome falsely pretends itself catholic, for if the name of catholic must needs import an universal consent of the whole, how can that be catholic where the consent of so many famous and true christian churches has been wanting; and further, where the consent that has been among themselves, has rather been a constrained than any true or free consent? As is easy to be proved; for let the fires and faggots cease, let kings and princes leave off pressing their subjects with the pope's obedience; let the scripture and the bishops alone, every one in his own diocese, to govern their flock after the rule of God's word, and how few are there in this western world, that would not do the same that these Grecians, Ethiopians, and Syrians, have done before us.

When I consider the acts of this Gregory, and then the conduct of the Greek church, I cannot but commend their wisdom, and judge their state happy and blessed, in shaking off from their necks the miserable yoke of the pope's tyranny; and on the other side, considering with myself the wretched thraldom of these our churches here in the western part of the world under the bishop of Rome, I cannot tell whether more to marvel at or to lament their pitiful state, who were brought into such oppression and slavery under him, that they could neither abide him, nor yet dare to cast him off. So intolerable were his exactions, so terrible was his tyranny, his suspensions and excommunications like to a mad man's dagger, drawn at every trifle, that no christian patience could suffer it, nor nation abide it. Again, so deep did he sit in their consciences, they falsely believing him to have the authority of St. Peter, that for conscience sake neither king nor emperor durst withstand him, much less poor subjects. And although his takings and spoilings, in this realm of England, were such that neither the laity nor spiritualty could bear; yet was there no remedy, they must bear them, or else the pope's sentence was upon them, to curse them as black as pitch.

In reading the histories of these times, any good heart would lament and rue, to see the miserable captivity of the people which they suffered under this thraldom of the bishop of Rome.

A brief Table or Declaration of the Pope's unreasonable gatherings, exactions, and oppressions in the realm of England.

And first to begin with the elections of the bishops, abbots, deans, and priors within this realm, it cannot be told what mass of money grew to the popes by them in this king's time, for no election happened either of archbishop, bishop, abbot, or any dignity, but when the convent or chapter had chosen one, the king would set up another. By which when the other appealed to Rome, no small rivers of English money went flowing to the pope's sea. And although the election went never so clear, yet the new elect must needs respect the Holy Father with some gentle reward.

A contention happened between the king and the monks of Winchester, about the election of William Rale, whom the monks had chosen, but the king refused, and therefore sent to Rome, with no small sum of money to evacuate the election of William Rale; commanding also that the gates of Winchester should be shut against him; and that no man should be so hardy as to receive him into the house. Upon this William being excluded, after he had laid his curse upon the whole city of Winchester, repaired to Rome, where for eight hundred marks promised to the pope, his bishopric (spite of the king) was confirmed, (Ex. Mat. Paris, fol. 164 and 240.)

After the death of Stephen Langton archbishop of Canterbury, the monks had elected Walter, a monk of Canterbury. But the king to stop that election, sent to the pope to annul it. Perceiving at first how hard and unwilling the pope and cardinals were thereto, and considering how all things might be bought for money, rather than the king should fail of his purpose, his proctors promised on the king's behalf to the pope, a tenth part of all, the moveables in the realm of England and of Ireland. At the contemplation of which money the pope soon began to pick quarrels with Walter, for not answering rightly to his questions about Christ's descending to hell, making of Christ's body on the altar, the weeping of Rachel for her children, she being dead before; about the sentence of excommunication, and certain causes of matrimony. He was therefore put back, and the king's man preferred, which cost the whole realm of England and Ireland the tenth part of their moveable goods. (Ex. Mat. Paris, fol. 71.)

There was the like dissension also between the king and the convent of Durham, for not choosing Master Lucas the king's chaplain, whom the king offered to be their bishop, when much money was bestowed on both sides, the pope defeating them both, admitted neither Master William, nor Master Lucas, but ordained the bishop of Sarum to be their bishop, (A.D. 1228.)

Between the monks of Coventry, and the canons of Lichfield there arose another quarrel, which of them should have the superior voice in choosing their bishop. In which suit after much money bestowed in the court of Rome, the pope to requite each for their money gave this order that each by course should have the choosing of the bishop. (A.D. 1228.)

What business arose likewise between Edmund archbishop of Canterbury, and the monks of Rochester, about the election of Richard Wendour, to be their bishop? And what was the end? First, the archbishop was obliged to travel himself to the pope, and so did the convent also send their proctors. Who being better monied, weighed down the cause, so that the good archbishop was condemned by the pope in a thousand marks, of which the greatest part (no doubt) redounded to the pope's coffers. (A.D. 1238.)

After the returning of Edmund archbishop of Canterbury from Rome, the monks of Canterbury had elected their prior without his assent; for which he excommunicated the monks, and evacuated their election. Not long after this, the pope's exactors went about to extort from the churchmen the fifth part of their goods to the service of the pope, who was fighting then against the emperor. This cruel exaction being a great while resisted by the prelates and clergy, at length the archbishop, thinking thereby to get the victory against the monks, was contented to grant the exaction, adding moreover of his own, for an overplus, eight hundred marks; whereupon the rest of the clergy were obliged to follow after, and contribute to the pope's exactors. (A.D. 1240.)

In the church of Lincoln there arose a contention between Robert Grosthead then bishop, and the canons of the cathedral church about their visitation, whether the bishop should visit them, or the dean; the bishop and the chapter, both went to Rome, and there after they had well wasted their purses, they received at length their answer, but paid full sweetly for it. (A.D. 1239.)

Robert Grosthead bishop of Lincoln having a great anxiety to bring the privileged orders of religious houses within his precinct, under his subjection and discipline, went to Rome, and there with great labour and much money procured of the pope a mandate, whereby all such religious orders were commanded to be under his power and obedience. Not long after the monks (who could soon weigh down the bishop with money) sent to the pope, and with their golden eloquence so persuaded him, and stirred his affections, that they soon purchased to themselves freedom from their ordinary bishop. Robert Grosthead having intelligence of this, again went up to Rome, and there complaining to the pope, declared how he was disappointed and confounded in his purpose, contrary to the promises and assurance made to him before. Pope Innocent looking with a stern countenance, made this answer, "Brother what is that to thee? Thou hast delivered and discharged thine own soul. It hath pleased us to shew favour to them. Is thine eye ill, because I am good?" And thus was the bishop sent away, murmuring with himself, yet not so softly, but that the pope heard him say these words: "O money, money! what canst not thou do in the court of Rome?" Wherewith the pope being somewhat pinched, gave this answer, "O ye Englishmen, Englishmen! of all men most wretched, for all your seeking is how ye may consume and devour one another," &c. (A.D. 1250).

It happened also the same year that Robert Grosthead excommunicated and deprived one Ranulph, a beneficed person in his diocese, being accused of immorality, who after the term of forty days, refusing to submit himself, the bishop wrote to the sheriff of Rutland to apprehend him as contumacious. The sheriff, because he deferred or refused to do so (bearing favour to the party,) and being therefore solemnly excommunicated by the bishop, uttered his complaint to the king. The king taking great displeasure with the bishop for excommunicating his sheriff, and not first making his complaint to him, sends forthwith to pope Innocent, a substantial messenger, by virtue of whose words the pope, easy to be intreated, sends down a proviso to the abbot of Westminster, charging that no prelate nor bishop in the realm of England, should molest or enter action against any of the king's bailiffs or officers, in such matters as to the king's jurisdiction appertained. And thus was the strife ended, not without some help and heap of English money; so that no wind of any controversy stirred here in England, were it never so small, but it blew some profit for the pope's advantage.

I come now likewise to touch briefly of some of the pope's dispensations, provisions, exactions, contributions and extortions in England in this king's days; for to tell of all, it is not one book would contain it.

Simon Montfort, earl of Leicester, had married Elenor the king's sister, who had taken the mantle and ring. Wherefore the king, and his brother Richard, earl of Exeter, were greatly offended with the marriage; which the Earl Simon seeing, took a large sum of money, and posting over to Rome, after he had talked a few words in Pope Innocent's ear, the marriage was good enough; and letters were sent to Otho the pope's legate here, to give sentence solemnly with the earl. Notwithstanding which the Dominican friars, and others of the religious fraternity, withstood the sentence of the pope stoutly, saying, that the pope's holiness was deceived, and souls were in danger; that Christ was jealous over his wife; and that it could not be any wise possible that a woman who had vowed marriage with Christ, could afterward marry with any other, &c. (A. D. 1238).

As there was nothing so hard in the wide world, with which the pope would not dispense for money; so by the dispensations much mischief was wrought abroad. For the people trusting upon the pope's dispensation, little regarded what they did, what they promised, or what they sware. As well appeared by this King Henry III.; who being a great exactor of the poor commons, and thinking to win the people to his devotion, most faithfully promised them once or twice, and thereto bound himself with a solemn oath, both before the clergy and laity, to grant to them the old liberties and customs as well of Magna Charta, as Charta de Foresta, perpetually to be observed. Whereupon a fifteenth was granted to the king. But after the payment was sure, the king, confident of the pope's dispensation for a little money to discharge him of his oath and covenant, went from what he had promised and sworn before.

In like manner the king another time, being in need of money, signed himself with the cross, pretending and swearing deeply in the face of the whole parliament, that he would himself personally fight in the Holy Land against the Saracens. But as soon as the money was taken, small care was had for performance of his oath; for the pope for a hundred pounds or two, would quickly discharge him thereof.

Out of the same corrupt spring of these popish dispensations, have proceeded also many other foul absurdities. For there were many young men in those days who enjoyed benefices, and yet were no priests, and when by the procurement of Robert Grosthead, bishop of Lincoln, these young men should be forced, whether they would or not, to enter orders, they laying their purses together, sent to Rome, and obtained of the pope a dispensation to remain still as they were, that is, to have the fruits of benefices to keep them at school or at the university, and yet themselves neither ministers to take charge, nor yielding any service for their profits taken. Besides innumerable heaps of enormities more, proceeding from the pope's dispensations, as dispensing one man to have several bishoprics, to engross pluralities of benefices, to make children parsons, to legitimatize natural children, with such other like; the particulars whereof for brevity sake, I omit to further opportunity.

The intolerable oppression of the Realm of England by the Pope's exactions and contributions, and other sleights used in the time of King Henry III.

Although these emoluments, thus rising daily to the pope's purse by simony and bribery, by elections and dispensations, might seem sufficient to satisfy his greedy appetite; yet so insatiable was the avarice of that see, that he not yet contented, sent continually some legate or other into this realm. With all violence exacting and extorting continual provisions, contributions, and sums of money to be levied out of cells, abbeys, priories, fruits of benefices, and bishoprics, and also laymen's purses, to the miserable impoverishing both of the clergy and temporality.

First, after Pandulph, Cardinal Otho was sent into this realm. Great preparation was made for receiving him; many rich and precious gifts in scarlet, in plate, in jewels, in money and palfries, were given him. The king also himself went as far as the sea-side to receive him, bowing down his head in low courtesy to the cardinal's knees. To whom also the bishop of Winchester for his part gave towards keeping of his house, fifty fat oxen, a hundred semes of wheat, and eight great vessels of pure wine. This legate at his first coming, began first to bestow such benefices, as he found vacant, upon them whom he brought with him, without respect whether they were meet or unmeet.

After this the pope hearing how the nobles and commons of the realm began to dislike the cardinal for his excessive procurations and exactions, sent for him home; but as the king stood in fear of his nobles, and thought to have some support from the cardinal against all occurrences, he entreated him to stay while he wrote to the pope to obtain further licence for him to tarry; and so he did, not without some English money you may be sure.

In the mean time, Otho, thinking to lose no time, but to gather also some crumbs in Scotland, made as though he would set things in order there, and so comes to the king of Scots, who was then in York with King Henry, to have leave to enter. The king thus made answer, that he never to his remembrance saw any pope's legate in his land, neither was there any need (God be praised) for such to be sent for. Matters there were well enough, and needed no help of his. And as he could never learn, either in the days of his father, or any of his predecessors, that any such entrance was granted to any legate; so he for his part would not now begin. "But yet as I hear (said he) that you are a good man, this I tell you beforehand, that if you will adventure in, do it warily, and take care of yourself, lest it happen to you otherwise than I would wish; for they are a savage and unruly people, given much to murder, and shedding blood, whom I myself am scarce able to bridle; so that if they fall upon you, I shall not be able to help you. How they also invaded me, and sought to expel me from my kingdom, you heard of late. And therefore I warn you beforehand, take heed in time what you think best to do." After the cardinal heard the king speak these words, he drew in his horns, and durst proceed no further, but kept still by the side of King Henry. Shortly after, however, coming to the borders of Scotland, he there called the bishops to him, and when he had well filled his bags, came back again.

Not long after licence came from Pope Gregory to his legate Otho, for his longer abode here, with new authority also to proceed in the pope's affairs. Who first shewing to the bishops and the clergy his letters of longer tarrying, required of them, as no man (said he) wars of his own charges, to be supported with new procurations; which was to have of every able church four marks; and where one church was not able to reach thereto, that other churches should join withal to make up the money. Notwithstanding the bishops a great while stood in the denial thereof.

Besides, he assembled together all the black monks of

St. Benedict's order, giving to them strict orders, which shortly after (for money) he released them from.

Moreover, collation of benefices being taken out of the hands of the patrons, were given to light and vile runnagates, coming from Italy and other places, such as the pope and his legate pleased to give them to, to the great prejudice of the ancient liberty and right of the true patrons. Upon this the earls, and barons, and nobles of the realm, addressed letters unto Pope Gregory by Sir Robert Twing, knight, for redress of such wrongs and injuries; who otherwise should be forced (they said) to invoke the succour of their king, who was both able, and no less willing, according to his duty, they trusted, to reform such enormities, and to defend the liberties of his realm. The tenor of whose writing is to be read in Matthew Paris. (fol. 128, a).

Not long after, (A. D. 1240), came a new precept from Pope Gregory, by Peter Rubeus the pope's nuncio, that all beneficed clergy, as well in England as in France, should pay to the pope the fifth part of their revenues. Upon this, when the clergy made their complaint to the king, seeking to be relieved by him, the king answered that he neither would, nor durst stand against the pope, and so without any hope of assistance sent them away. Then were the archbishops, bishops, abbots, and prelates of the church commanded to assemble together at Reading, there to hear the pope's pleasure concerning the payment of this fifth part, where in the end, thus the matter concluded; that the prelates desired a further time to be given them to advise upon the matter; and for that season the assembly brake up. Notwithstanding at last, after many excuses made by the clergy; first, "That because the money was gathered to fight against the emperor, they ought not to contribute their money, contrary to the liberties of the church. Also, forsomuch as they had paid a tenth not long before to the pope, upon condition that no more such payments should be required of them, much less now the fifth part should be exacted of them, because an action twice done, makes a custom. Also seeing they had oftentimes to repair to the court of Rome, if they should give this money against the emperor, it would turn to their danger coming through his land. Also, seeing their king had many enemies, against whom they must needs relieve the king with their money, they could not do so if the realm were thus impoverished," &c. They were, however. compelled at length to conform to the pope's good pleasure, through the example given by Edmund, archbishop of Canterbury, who, to obtain his purpose against the monks of Canterbury (with whom he was then in strife) began first to yield to the legates, eight hundred marks for his part, whereby the rest also were obliged to follow after.

The same year the pope agreed with the people of Rome, that if they would aid him against the Emperor Frederick, whatever benefices were vacant in England should be bestowed upon their children. Whereupon commandment was sent to Edmund, archbishop, and to the bishops of Lincoln and Sarum, that all the collations of benefices within the realm should be suspended, till provision were made for three hundred children of the citizens of Rome to be first served!

This done, then Peter Rubeus the pope's nuncio, and Ruffin went into Scotland, from whence they brought with them three thousand pounds to the pope's use about Allhallows the same year. At which time also, cometh another harpy from the pope to England, named Mumelius, bringing with him three-and-twenty Romans here into the realm to be beneficed. Thus, what by the king on the one side, and what by the Cardinal Otho, Peter Rubeus, Ruffin, and Mumelius on the other side, poor England was in a wretched case.

Another pretty practice of the pope to prowl for money was this: Peter Rubeus, coming into religious houses, and into their chapters, caused them to contribute to the pope's holiness, by the example of this bishop and that abbot, pretending that he and he, of their own voluntary devotion, had given so much and so much, and so seduced them. Also the pope craftily suborned certain friars, authorized with full indulgence,

that whoever had vowed to fight in the Holy Land, and was disposed to be released of his vow, needed not to repair to Rome for absolution, but paying so much money as his charges would come to going thither, he resorting to the friars, might be absolved at home.

This passed A. D. 1240. Now all these troubles laid together, were enough to vex the meekest prince in the world; the king had also much ado with the prelates and clergy, who were always tampering with his title, especially in their assemblies and councils : he sent Geoffry Langley to the archbishop of York, and to other bishops purposed to meet at Oxford, to appeal for him, lest, in the council there called, they should presume to ordain any thing against his crown and dignity. This was done A. D. 1241. In which year also came a command apostolical to the house of Peterborough, that they must grant the pope some benefice, the fruits of which were worth at least a hundred pounds, and if it were more it should be the better welcome; so that they should be as the farmers, and he to receive the profits. In fine, the convent excused themselves by the abbot being then not at home. The abbot, when he came home, excused himself by the king being the patron and founder of the house. The king being grieved with the unreasonable ravening of these Romanists, utterly forbade any such example to be given.

In the time of the council of Lyons, Pope Innocent IV. (as the instrument whereby the realm of England stood tributary to the pope, was thought to be burned in the pope's chamber a little before), brought forth either the same, or another chart like it, to which he straitly charged and commanded every English bishop present at the council, to set his hand and seal. Which unreasonable demand of the pope, although it went sore against the hearts of the bishops, yet (see in what miserable subjection the pope had all the bishops under him) none of them durst but accomplish the pope's request, both to their own shame, and to the prejudice of the public freedom of the realm. Which act, when the king and the nobility understood, they were mightily and worthily offended therewith, (A. D. 1245).

When Cardinal Otho was sent for by Pope Gregory in all haste to come to the general council, two others remained here in his room, whose names were Peter Rubeus, and Peter de Supino. Of whom the one, bearing himself for the pope's kinsman, brought out his bills and bulls under the pope's authority, to such an abbot, or to such a prior, or to such and such a bishop, and so extorted from them a great quantity of gold and silver. The other, namely, Peter de Supino, sailed to Ireland, from whence he brought with him a thousand and five hundred marks to the pope's use, (A. D. 1241). All which money, however, fell into the hands of Frederick the emperor, who caused it to be restored, as near as he could, to them of whom it was taken.

After these came Master Martin, from the new Pope Innocent IV. (A. D. 1244), armed with full power, to suspend all prelates in England from giving benefices, till the pope's kinsmen were first preferred. Neither would he take the fruits of any benefice, unless it were above the value of thirty marks. At his first coming, he required prelates, and especially religious houses to furnish him with horses and palfries, such as were convenient for the pope's special chaplain and legate to sit upon; also with plate, raiment, provision for his kitchen and cellar, &c., and such as denied, or excused, he suspended, as the abbot of Malmesbury, and the prior of Merton. All prebends that were void he sought out and reserved for the pope, among which was the golden prebend of Sarum, belonging to the chancellor of the choir, whom he preferred to the bishopric at Bath, and so seized upon the prebend being void, against the wills both of the bishop and the chapter. He brought with him blanks in paper and parchment, signed in the pope's chamber with his stamp and seal, wherein he might afterward write to whom, and what he would. He, moreover, required of the king, in the pope's behalf, to help his holiness with a contribution to be taxed amongst his clergy, at least 10,000 marks. And to the end that the pope might win the king sooner to his devotion, he writes to the nobles and commons of the realm, that they should not fail, upon pain of his great curse, to grant such subsidy of money to the support of the king, as he then demanded of them, but they stood stiff in not granting to him.

While the insatiable avarice of the pope thus made no end in gathering riches and goods together in England; the nobles and barons, with the community as well of the clergy as the laity, weighing the miserable state of the realm, and especially of the church, who now neither had liberty left to choose their own ministers, nor yet could enjoy their own livings, laid their heads together, and so exhibited an earnest intimation to the king, beseeching him to consider the pitiful affliction of his subjects under the pope's extortion, living in more thraldom than the people of Israel under Pharaoh. Whereupon the king beginning at last to look up, and to consider the injuries and wrongs received in this realm through the avarice of the court of Rome, directs to Pope Innocent IV. this letter, in tenor as follows:

The king's letter to Pope Innocent IV.

" To the most holy father in Christ, and lord Innocent IV., by the grace of God, chief bishop, Henry, by the same grace, king of England, &c. Greeting and kissings of his blessed feet. The more devout and obsequious the son shews himself in obeying the father's will, the more favour and support he deserves to find at his father's hands again. This therefore I write because both we and our realm have ever and in all things been hitherto at the devotion and commandment of your fatherhood; and although in some certain affairs of ours and of our kingdom, we have found your fatherly favour and grace some times propitious to us, yet in some things again, as in provisions given and granted to your clerks of foreign nations, both we and our kingdom have felt no small detriment. By reason of which provisions, the church of England is so sore charged and burthened, that not only the patrons of churches to whom the donations thereof do appertain, are defrauded of their right, but also many other good works of charity thereby do decay, for that such benefices, which have been mercifully bestowed upon religious houses, to their sustenance are now wasted and consumed by your provisions.

" Wherefore as your apostolic see ought to be favourable to all that are petitioners to the same, so that no person be wronged in that which is his right, we thought therefore to be suitors to your fatherhood, most humbly beseeching your holiness, that you will desist and cease for a time from such provisions. In the meantime, it may please your fatherhood, we beseech you, that our laws and liberties (which you may rightly repute none other but your own), you will receive to your tuition, to be conserved whole and sound, nor to suffer the same by any sinister suggestion in your court to be violated and infringed. Neither let your holiness be any whit moved therefore with us, if in some such cases as these be, we do or shall hereafter resist the tenor of your commandments; for so much as the complaints of such, which daily call upon us, do necessarily inforce us thereto, who ought, by the charge of this our office, and kingly dignity committed to us of Almighty God, to foresee that no man in that which is their right be injured, but truly to minister justice to every one, in that which duly to him appertains." This letter was sent the eight-and-twentieth year of the king's reign. (Ex Parisiensi, fol. 172.)

A man would think that this so gentle and obedient letter of the king to the pope would have wrought some good effect in the apostolical breast. But how little all this prevailed to stop his insatiable greediness and intolerable extortions and oppressions, the sequel well declares. Shortly after, the pope sent Master Martin with blanks, being bulled for contribution of ten thousand marks, in all haste to be paid also, even immediately upon the receiving of this letter. And the pope, after all this great submission of the king, and so manifold benefits and payments yearly out of his realm was not ashamed

to take of David, prince of North Wales, five hundred marks a-year, to set him against the king of England, and exempted him from his fealty and obedience due to his own liege lord and king, to whom both he and all other Welchmen had sworn their subjection before. (Matth. Parisiensi, fol. 172.)

Neither did Master Martin in the meanwhile slip his business, in making up his market for the pope's money of ten thousand marks, but still was calling upon the prelates and clergy, who, first excusing themselves by the absence of the king and the archbishop of Canterbury, afterward being called again by new letters, made their answer by the dean of St. Paul's their prolocutor :—

That the poverty of the realm would not suffer them to consent thereto.

That, whereas they had given before a contribution to Cardinal Otho, for paying of the pope's debts, and knew the money to be employed to no such end as it was demanded, for they had now more cause to doubt. lest this contribution in his hands, which was a much more inferior messenger than the cardinal, would come to the same, or a worse effect.

That, if they should now agree to a new contribution, they feared lest it would grow to a custom, seeing that one action, twice done, makes a custom.

That, forsomuch as a general council is shortly looked for, where every prelate of the realm must needs bestow both his travel and expenses, and also his present to the pope, if the prelates now should be bound to this tax, they were not able to abide this burthen.

That, seeing it is alleged, that the mother church of Rome is so far in debt, it were reason and right, that the mother so oppressed should be sustained of all her devout children meeting together in the general council; whereas by helps of many, more relief might come than by one nation alone.

And, last of all, they alleged, that for fear of the emperor and his threatenings, they durst not consent to the contribution.

While these things were thus in talk between the pope's priests and the clergy of England, comes in John Mariscal and other messengers from the king, commanding in the king's name, that no bishop that held his baronage of the king, should infeft his lay fee to the court of Rome, which they ought only to him, &c.

Not long after this, (in A. D. 1245), the whole nobility of the realm, by general consent, and not without the king's knowledge also, caused all the ports by the seaside to be watched, that no messenger with the pope's letters and bulls from Rome should be permitted to enter the realm; some were taken at Dover and there stayed. But, notwithstanding, when complaint was brought to the king by Martin, the pope's legate, there was no remedy, but the king must needs cause these letters to be restored again, and executed to the full effect.

Then the king, upon advice, caused a view to be taken through every shire in England, to what sum the whole revenues of the Romans and Italians amounted, which, by the pope's authority, went out of England; the whole sum whereof was found to be yearly sixty thousand marks, to which sum the revenues of the whole crown of England did not extend! (Ex Matt. Parisiensi, fol. 185. a.)

The nobles then understanding the miserable oppression of the realm, being assembled together at Dunstable for certain causes, sent one Fulco, in the name of the whole nobility, to Martin, the pope's legate, with this message; that he immediately upon the same warning should prepare himself to be gone out of the realm, under pain of being cut to pieces. At which message, the legate being sore aghast, went straight to the king, to know whether his consent was to the same or not. Of whom when he found little better comfort, he took his leave of the king, who bade him adieu in the devil's name, says Matthew Paris, and thus was the realm rid of Master Martin, (A. D. 1245.)

As soon as Pope Innocent had intelligence hereof, by the complaint of his legate, he was in a mighty rage.

And, remembering how the French king, and the king of Arragon, not long before had denied him entrance into their land, and being therefore in displeasure with them likewise, he began in great anger to knit his brows, and said, "It is best that we fall in agreement with our prince, whereby we may the sooner bring under these little petty kings; and so the great dragon being pacified, these little serpents we shall handle at our own pleasure as we please."

After this, immediately then followed the general council of Lyons, to which council the lords and states of the realm, with the consent of the commonalty, sent two bills, one containing a general supplication to the pope and the council, the other with the articles of such grievances as they desired to be redressed, whereof relation is made sufficiently before. The other bill of the supplication, because it is not before expressed, I thought here to exhibit for two causes; first, that men in these days may see the pitiful blindness of those ignorant days, wherein our English nation here did so blindly humble themselves and stand to the pope's courtesy, whom rather they should have shaken off, as the Grecians did. Secondly, that the pride of the pope might the better appear in his colours, who so disdainfully rejected the humble suit of our lords and nobles, when they had much more cause, rather to disdain and to stamp him under their feet. The tenor of the supplication was this:

The copy of the supplication written in the names of all the nobles and commons of England, to Pope Innocent IV., in the general council at Lyons, (A. D. 1245.)

"To the reverend father in Christ, Pope Innocent, chief bishop, the nobles, with the whole commonalty of the realm of England, sendeth commendation with kissing of his blessed feet.

"Our mother, the church of Rome, we love with all our hearts, as our duty is, and covet the increase of her honour with so much affection as we may, as to whom we ought always to fly for refuge, whereby the grief lying upon the child, may find comfort at the mother's hand. Which succour the mother is bound so much the rather to impart to her child, how much more kind and beneficial she finds him in relieving her necessity. Neither is it unknown to our mother how beneficial and bountiful a giver the realm of England has been now of long time for the more amplifying of her exaltation, as appeared by your yearly subsidy, which we term by the name of Peter-pence. Now the said church, not contented with this yearly subsidy, has sent divers legates for other contributions, at divers and sundry times to be taxed and levied out of the same realm; all which contributions and taxes notwithstanding have been lovingly and liberally granted.

"Furthermore, neither is it unknown to your fatherhood, how our forefathers, like good catholics, both loving and fearing their Maker, for the soul's health, as well of themselves, as of their progenitors and successors also, have founded monasteries, and have largely endowed the same, both with their own proper lands, and also patronages of benefices, whereby such religious persons professing the first and chiefest perfection of holy religion in their monasteries, might with more peace and tranquillity occupy themselves devoutly in God's service, as to the order appertained; and also the clerks presented by them into their benefices, might sustain the other exterior labours for them in that second order of religion, and so discharge and defend them from all hazards, so that the said religious monasteries cannot be defrauded of those their patronages and collations of benefices, but the same must touch us also very near, and work intolerable griefs unto our hearts.

"And now see, we beseech you, which is lamentable to behold what injuries we sustain by you and your predecessors, who, not considering those our subsidies and contributions above remembered, do suffer also your Italians and foreigners, which are out of number, to be possessed of our churches and benefices in England, pertaining to the right and patronage of those monasteries aforesaid, which foreigners, neither defending the said religious persons, whom they ought to see to, nor yet having the language, whereby they may instruct the flock, take no regard of their souls, but utterly leave them to wild wolves to be devoured. Wherefore it may truly be said of them, that they are no good shepherds, whereas they neither know their sheep, nor do the sheep know the voice of their shepherds, neither do they keep any hospitality, but only take up the rents of those benefices, carrying them out of the realm, wherewith our brethren, our nephews, and our kinsfolks might be sustained, who could and would dwell upon them, and employ such exercises of mercy and hospitality as their duty required. Whereof a great number now for mere necessity are laymen, and obliged to fly out of the realm.

"And now to the intent more fully to certify you of the truth, ye shall understand that the said Italians and strangers receiving of yearly rents out of England, not so little as sixty thousand marks by year, besides other avails and excises deducted, do reap in the said our kingdom of England more emoluments of mere rents, than doth the king himself, being both tutor of the church, and governor of the land.

"Furthermore, whereas at the first creation of your papacy we were in good hope, and yet are, that by means of your fatherly goodness we should enjoy our franchises, and free collation of our benefices and donatives, to be reduced again to the former state, now comes another grievance which we cannot but signify unto you, pressing us above measure, which we receive by Master Martin, who, entering late into our land without leave of our king, with greater power than ever was seen before in any legate, although he bears not the state and shew of a legate, yet he has doubled the doings of a legate, charging us every day with new mandates, and so most extremely has oppressed us; first, in bestowing and giving away our benefices, if any were above thirty marks, as soon as they were vacant, to Italian persons.

"Secondly, after the decease of the said Italians, unknowing to the patrons, he has intruded other Italians therein, whereby the true patrons have been spoiled and defrauded of their right.

"Thirdly, the said Master Martin yet also ceases not to assign and confer such benefices still to the like persons; and some he reserves to the donation of the apostolical see; and extorts, moreover, from religious houses immoderate pensions, excommunicating and interdicting whoever dare withstand him.

"Wherefore, forasmuch as the said Master Martin has so far extended his jurisdiction, to the great perturbation of the whole realm, and no less derogation to our king's privilege, to whom it has been fully granted by the see apostolic, that no legate should have to do in his land, but such as he by special letters did send for: with most humble devotion we beseech you, that as a good father will always be ready to support his child, so your fatherhood will reach forth your hand of compassion to relieve us your humble children from these grievous oppressions.

"And although our lord and king, being a catholic prince, and wholly given to his devotions and service of Christ Jesus our Lord, so that he respects not the health of his own body, will fear and reverence the see apostolic, and, as a devout son of the church of Rome, desires nothing more than to advance the estate and honour of the same; yet we who labour in his affairs, bearing the heat and burden of the day, and whose duty, together with him, is to tender the preservation of the public wealth, neither can patiently suffer such oppressions, so detestable to God and man, and grievances intolerable, neither by God's grace will suffer them, through the means of your godly remedy, which we well hope and trust of you speedily to obtain. And thus may it please your fatherhood, we beseech you to accept this our supplication, who in so doing shall worthily deserve of all the lords and nobles, with the whole commonalty of the realm of England, condign and special thanks accordingly." A. D. 1245. (Ex Mat. Paris. fol. 188.)

This supplication being sent by the hands of Sir R. Bigot, knight, W. de Powick, esq., and Henry de la Mare, with other knights and gentlemen, after it was there opened and read, Pope Innocent, first keeping silence, delayed to make answer, making haste to proceed in his detestable excommunication and curse against the good emperor Frederick; which curse being done, and the English ambassadors waiting still for their answer, the pope told them flatly they should not have their request fulfilled. Whereat the Englishmen, departing in great anger, sware with terrible oaths, that they would never more suffer any tribute, or fruits of any benefices, whereof the noblemen were patrons, to be paid to that insatiable and greedy court of Rome, worthy to be detested in all worlds.

The pope hearing these words, although making then no answer, thought to watch his time, and did so. During the council, he caused every bishop of England to put his hand and seal to the obligation made by King John for the pope's tribute; threatening, moreover, and saying, that if he had once brought down the emperor Frederick, he would bridle the insolent pride of England.

But here by occasion of this council at Lyons, that the reader may see upon what slippery uncertainty and variableness the state of the king depended, it is material here to introduce the form of a letter sent by Henry III. to the prelates of his land, before they were transported over the sea to Lyons; wherein may be gathered, that the king suspected they would be pushing and heaving at his royalty, and therefore directed these letters to them, otherwise to prepare their affections: the tenor whereof follows:—

A Letter of Charge to the Prelates of England, purposed to assemble in the Council at Lyons, that they should ordain nothing to their King's prejudice.

"The king to the archbishops, bishops, and to all other prelates of his land of England, appointed to meet at a council at Lyons, greeting: you are (as you know) bound to us by oath, whereby you ought to keep all the fealty that you can to us in all things, concerning our royal dignity and crown. Wherefore we command you upon the fealty and allegiance wherein you are firmly bound to us, enjoining that you do your uttermost endeavour, as well to get as to keep, and also to defend the right of us and our kingdom. And that neither to the prejudice of us, or of the same kingdom, nor yet against us or our rights, which our predecessors and we by ancient and approved custom have used, you presume to procure or attempt anything in your council at Lyons; nor that you give assent to any that shall procure or ordain ought in this case, upon your oath aforesaid, and the loss of your temporalities, which you hold of us. Wherefore in this behalf so behave yourselves, that for your good dealing and virtue of thankfulness, we may rather specially commend you, than for the contrary by you attempted (which God forbid) we reprove your unthankfulness, and reserve vengeance for you in due time. Witness myself, &c., the nine-and-twentieth year of our reign."

In the same way he wrote to the archbishops and bishops, &c. of Ireland and Gascony.

In the beginning of the year following (A.D. 1246), Pope Innocent came to Cluny, where a secret meeting was then appointed between the pope and Lewis the French king (who was then preparing his voyage to Jerusalem). The pope sought all means to persuade the French king, in revenge of his injury, to war against the weak and feeble king of England, as he called him, either to drive him utterly from his kingdom, or else to damnify him, whereby he should be constrained, whether he would or no, to stoop to the pope's will and obedience, wherein he also would assist him with all the authority he could. Nevertheless, the French king would not agree to this.

Straight upon this followed then the exaction of Boniface archbishop of Canterbury, that he had bought of the pope; which was to have the first year's fruits of all benefices and spiritual livings in England for the space of seven years together, until the sum should come to ten thousand marks. At this the king at first was greatly grieved. But in conclusion, he was obliged at last to agree with the archbishop, and so the money was gathered.

Over and besides all other exactions wherewith the pope miserably oppressed the church of England, this also is not to be passed over in silence, how the pope, sending down his letters from the see apostolic, charged and commanded the prelates to find him some ten, some five, and some fifteen able men, well furnished with horse and armor for one whole year, to fight in the pope's wars. And lest the king should have knowledge of it, it was enjoined them, under pain of excommunication, that they should reveal it to none, but to keep it in secret only to themselves.

When Pope Innocent IV. had knowledge of certain rich clerks leaving great substance of money, who died intestate, as of one Robert Hailes, archdeacon of Lincoln, who died leaving thousands of marks and much plate behind him, all which, because no will was made, came to temporal men's hands: also of Almarike, archdeacon of Bedford, being found worth a great substance when he died; and likewise of another, John Hotosp, archdeacon of Northampton, who died suddenly intestate, leaving behind him five thousand marks, and thirty standing pieces of plate, with other infinite jewels besides; he sent forth a statute to be proclaimed in England, that whatsoever ecclesiastical person henceforth should decease in England intestate, that is, without making his will, all his goods should redound to the pope's use.

The pope, not yet satisfied with all this, addresses new letters to the bishop of Winchester, and to William bishop of Norwich, for gathering up among the clergy, and religious houses in England, six thousand marks for the holy mother church, without any excuse or delay, by virtue of obedience. Which, being greatly grudged by the clergy, when it came to the king's ear, he directed contrary letters to all the prelates, and every one of them, commanding them, upon forfeiting their temporalities to the king, that no such subsidy-money should be gathered or transported out of the realm. But the pope again hearing of this, in great anger writes to the prelates of England, that this collection of money, upon pain of excommunication and suspension, should be provided, and brought to the new Temple in London, by the feast of the Assumption next ensuing.

And as he perceived the king to go about to oppose his proceedings, taking thereat great disdain, he was about to interdict the whole land. To whom then one of his cardinals, called John Anglicus, an Englishman born, speaking for the realm of England, desired his fatherhood for God's cause to mitigate his moody ire, and with the bridle of temperance to assuage the passion of his mind: "Which," said he, "to tell you plain, is here stirred up too much without cause. Your fatherhood may consider that these days be evil. First, the Holy Land lies in great perils to be lost. All the Greek church is departed from us. Frederick the emperor is against us, the mightiest prince this day in all Christendom. Both you and we, who are the peers of the church, are banished from the papal see, thrust out of Rome, yea, excluded out of all Italy. Hungary, with all coasts bordering about it, looketh for nothing but utter subversion by the Tartars. Germany is wasted and afflicted with inward wars and tumults. Spain is fierce and cruel against us, even to the cutting out of the bishops' tongues. France is so impoverished by us that it is brought to beggary, which also conspires against us. Miserable England, being so often plagued by our manifold injuries, even much like to Balaam's ass, beaten and bounced with spurs and staves, begins at length to speak and complain of her intolerable griefs and burthens, being so wearied and damnified, that she may seem past all recovery; and we, after the manner of Ishmael, hating of men, provoke all men to hate us."

For all these words of John Anglicus his cardinal, the

pope's passion could not yet be appeased, but forthwith he sends commandment with full authority to the bishop of Worcester, that in case the king would not speedily cease his rebellion against his apostolical proceedings he would interdict his land. So that in conclusion, the king, for all his stout enterprise, was obliged to relent at last, and the pope had his money, (A. D. 1246).

What man having eyes is so blind who sees not these execrable dealings of the pope to be such, as would cause any nation in the world to do as the wise Grecians did, and perpetually to renounce the pope, and well to consider the usurped authority of that see not to be of God? But such was the rude dulness then of miserable England, for lack of learning and godly knowledge, that they feeling what burdens were laid upon them, yet would play still the ass of Balaam, or else the horse of Æsop, which receiving the bridle once in his mouth, could afterward neither abide his own misery, nor yet recover liberty. And so it fared with England under the pope's thraldom.

And so it follows in the history of Matthew Paris, how the pope taking more courage by his former abused boldness, and perceiving what a tame ass he had to ride upon, ceased not thus, but directed a new precept the same year (A.D. 1246), to the prelates of England, commanding by the authority apostolic, that all beneficed men in the realm of England, who were resident upon their benefices, should yield to the pope the third part of their goods, and they who were not resident should give the one-half of their goods, and that for the space of three years together, with terrible threatenings to all them that should resist; and ever with this clause withal, *non obstante*, which was like a key that opened all locks. Which sum, cast together, was found to amount to sixty thousand pounds, which sum of money could scarce be found in all England to pay for King Richard's ransom. (Paris. fol. 207.) The execution of this precept was committed to the bishop of London, who conferring about the matter with his brethren in the church of St. Paul's, as they were busily consulting together, and bewailing the insupportable burden of this contribution, which was impossible for them to sustain, suddenly comes in certain messengers from the king, Sir John Lexinton, knight, and Master Lawrence Martin, the king's chaplain, straightly in the king's name forbidding them in any case to consent to this contribution, which would be greatly to the prejudice and desolation of the whole realm.

And thus much hitherto of these matters, to the intent that all who read these histories, and see the doings of this western bishop, may consider what just cause the Grecians had to separate from his subjection, and communion. For what christian communion can be held with him who so contrary to Christ and his gospel seeks for worldly dominion, so cruelly persecutes his brethren, so given to avarice, so greedy in getting, so injurious in oppressing, so insatiable in his exactions, so malicious in revenging, stirring up wars, depriving kings, deposing emperors, playing the monarch in the church of Christ, so erroneous in doctrine, so abominable in abusing excommunication, so false in promise, so corrupt in life, so void of God's fear: and briefly, so far from all the qualifications of a true evangelical bishop? For what seems he to care for the souls of men, who sets boys and outlandish Italians in the benefices: and further appoints one Italian to succeed another, who neither knew the language of the flock, nor could bear to see their faces? And who can blame the Grecians then for dissevering themselves from such an oppressor against Christ?

If this realm had followed their wise example, as it might, our predecessors had been rid of an infinite number of troubles, injuries, oppressions, wars, commotions, long journeys and charges, besides the saving of innumerable thousands of pounds, which this bishop of Rome full falsely had raked and transported out of this realm. But as I must not exceed the bounds of my history, my purpose being not to stand upon declamations, nor to dilate on common places, I will pass this over, leaving the judgment of it to the further examination of the reader. For if I wished to prosecute this argument so far as the matter would lead me, and truth perhaps require me to say, I might not only say, but could well prove the pope and court of Rome to be the fountain and principal cause, not only of much misery here in England, but of all the public calamities and notorious mischiefs which have happened these many years through all these western parts of Christendom, and especially of the lamentable ruin of the church, which not only we, but the Grecians also this day do suffer by the Turks and Saracens. As whoever well considers by reading of histories, and views the doings and acts passed by the bishop of Rome, shall see good cause to think with me. Only one narrative touching this argument, I am disposed to set before the readers, it happened about this present time of King Henry's reign (A. D. 1244.)

It happened that Lewis the French king, son to Queen Blanch, fell very sick, lying in a trance for some days, in such a way that few thought he would have lived, and some said he was gone already. Among others, there was with him his mother, who sorrowing bitterly for her son, and given somewhat to superstition, went and brought forth a piece of the holy cross, with the crown and the spear; and blessing him with them, laid the crown and spear to his body, making a vow in the person of her son, that if the Lord would visit him with health, and release him of that infirmity, he should be crossed or marked with the cross, to visit the holy sepulchre, and solemnly to render thanks in the land which Christ had sanctified with his blood. Thus as she, with the bishop of Paris, and others there present were praying, the king, who was supposed by some to be dead, began with a sigh to move his arms and legs, and stretching himself began to speak, giving thanks to God, who from on high had visited him, and called him from the danger of death. As the king's mother with others took this as great a miracle wrought by the virtue of the holy cross: so the king amending more and more, as soon as he was well recovered, received solemnly the badge of the cross.

After this there was great preparation and much ado in France toward the setting forth to the Holy Land. For after the king first began to be crossed, the greater part of the nobles of France with several archbishops and bishops, with earls, and barons, and gentlemen to a mighty number, received also the cross upon their sleeves. A. D. 1246. (Ex Matt. Parisiensi, fol. 204. 6.)

The next year, the French king yet persevering in his purposed journey, Lady Blanch his mother, and the bishop of Paris his brother, with the lords of his council, and other nobles, and his special friends advised him with great persuasions to alter his mind as to that adventurous and dangerous journey, for his vow, they said, was unadvisedly made, and in time of his sickness, when his mind was not perfectly established: and what dangers might happen at home was uncertain; the king of England being on the one side, the emperor on the other side, and the Pictavians in the midst, so fugitive and unstable: and as to his vow, the pope would dispense with it, considering the necessity of his realm, and the weakness of his body.

To this the king answered, "As you say, that it was in feebleness of my senses I took this vow upon me: lo, as you wish me, I lay down the cross that I took." And putting his hand to his shoulder, he tare off the badges of the cross, saying to the bishop, "Here I resign to you the cross wherewith I was signed." At the sight of this there was no small rejoicing among all that were present. The king then, altering his countenance and his speech, thus spake to them: "My friends, whatever I was in my sickness, now I thank God I am of perfect sense, and sound reason, and now I require my cross again to be restored unto me:" saying moreover, "That he would eat no food until he were recognized again with the same cross, as he was before." At this all present were astonished, supposing that God had some great matter to work, and so moved no more questions to him.

Upon this drew nigh the feast of John Baptist, which was the time appointed for setting forth. And being in readiness, the king in a few days after was entering his journey: but yet one thing was wanting. The king, perceiving the mortal variance between the pope and good Frederick the emperor, thought best before his going to have that matter appeased, by which his way might be safer through the emperor's countries, and also be less danger at home after his departure; and therefore, he first went to Lyons, where the pope was, partly to take his leave; but especially to make reconcilement between the emperor and the pope.

Here it may be noted by the way, that with the good emperor there was no difficulty or hindrance. He rather sought all means how to compass the pope's favour, and never could obtain it: so that before he was excommunicated in the council of Lyons, he not only answered sufficiently by his attorney, discharging himself against whatever crimes or objections could be brought against him; but so far humbled himself to the pope and the council, that for all detriments, damages, losses, or wrongs done on his part, what amends soever the pope could or would require, he would recompence it to the uttermost. This the pope would not take.

He then offered, that if the pope could not abide his remaining in his own dominions and empire, he would go and fight against the Saracens and Turks, never to return into Europe again, offering there to recover the lands and kingdoms, that at any time belonged to Christendom, provided that the pope would be contented that Henry his son, who was nephew to King Henry here in England, should be emperor after him. Neither would this be admitted by the pope.

Then he offered for the security of his promise, to put in the French king and the king of England to be his sureties, or else for trial of his cause to stand to their award and arbitration. Neither would that be granted.

At last he desired, that he might come himself and answer before the council. But the proud pope in no case would abide that, saying, "That he did not yet find himself so ready and meet for martyrdom, to have him to come to the council; for if he did, he would depart himself," &c.

Such was the obstinate rancor and devilish malice of Pope Innocent and his predecessor, against that valiant emperor and against the Grecians; what disturbance and mischief it wrought to the whole church, what strength it gave to the Saracens and Tartars, how it impaired christian concord, and weakened all christian lands, not only the army of the French King found shortly after, but Christendom even to this day may and does feel and rue it. Nor can there in history be found any greater cause that made the Turks so strong, to get so much ground over Christendom as they have, than the pestilent working of this pope, in deposing and excommunicating this worthy emperor.

In the mean time, when the French king coming thus to the pope at Lyons to intreat for the emperor, could find no favour, he took his leave, and with great heaviness departed, setting forward on his journey.

About the beginning of October, the French took Damietta, being the principal fort or hold of the Saracens in Egypt (A.D. 1249.) After winning Damietta, the Saracens, being terrified at the loss, offered to the christians great ground and possessions more than ever belonged to Christendom before, on condition that they might have Damietta restored to them again. But the pride of the earl of Artois, the king's brother, would not accept the offers of the Saracens, but required both Damietta and Alexandria, the chief metropolitan city of all Egypt, to be surrendered. The Saracens, seeing the pride and greediness of the Frenchmen, would not abide that: which turned afterwards to the great loss of the christians.

At length after long conferences between them, the Soldan proposed to them to resign to him the city of Damietta, with every thing which they found in it, and that they should have in return all the country about Jerusalem, with all the captive christians, restored to them. The christians, said he, ought to be contented with this, and to seek no more, but only to possess the land of Jerusalem; which being granted to them, they ought not encroach into lands and kingdoms, whereto they had no right. This form of peace well pleased the meaner sort of the poor soldiers, and many of the council and nobility; but the proud earl of Artois, the king's brother, would not assent to it, but still required the city of Alexandria to be yielded to him, which the Egyptians would by no means agree to.

From that time the French army, being surrounded by sea and by land, began every day more and more to be distressed for provisions and with famine, being driven to that misery, that they were obliged to eat their own horses in Lent time, which should have served them unto other uses. Neither could any christian power, nor Frederick, being deposed by the pope, send them any succour. The more misery the christians were in, the more fiercely the Saracens pressed upon them on every side, detesting their froward wilfulness. Many of the christian soldiers deserted, and not able to abide the affliction, privately went over to the Saracens, who gladly received and relieved them, and some were permitted still to keep their faith, some marrying wives among them, and for hope of honour apostatized. The Soldan, being perfectly informed by these fugitives of every thing in the king's army, sent to him in derision, asking where were all his mattocks, forks, and rakes, scythes, ploughs, and harrows, which he brought over with him, or why he did not occupy them, but let them lie by him to rust and canker? All this and much more the king with his Frenchmen were obliged to bear with.

The French king, with his army, seeing himself distressed, and that nothing was done against the Soldan of Egypt, after he had fortified the city of Damietta, with an able garrison, and left it with the duke of Burgundy, he removed his camp from thence to go eastward. In his army followed William Longspath, who came from England to fight in the Holy Land, accompanied with a picked number of English warriors: but such was the hatred of the French against this William Longspath and the English, that they could not abide them, but flouted them in an insulting manner, calling them "English tails," insomuch that the good king himself had much ado to keep peace between them.

The original cause of this grudge between them began thus: there was, not far from Alexandria in Egypt, a strong fort or castle, filled with noble ladies, and rich treasure of the Saracens: this stronghold it happened that William Longspath, with his company of English soldiers, got possession of, more by good luck and politic dexterity, than by open force of arms, by which he and his followers were greatly enriched. When the French had knowledge of this, they began to conceive a heartburning against the English soldiers, and could not speak well of them after that. It happened again, not long after, that William Longspath had intelligence of a company of rich Saracen merchants going to a fair about the parts of Alexandria, with their camels, asses, and mules, richly laden with silks, precious jewels, spices, gold and silver, with cart-loads of other wares, besides victuals and other furniture, of which the soldiers then stood in great need. Having secret knowledge of this, he gathered all the English, and so by night falling upon the merchants, some he slew, some he took, and some he put to flight. The carts with the drivers and with the oxen, and the camels, asses, and mules, with the whole carriage and provisions he took and brought with him, losing in all the skirmish but one soldier, and eight of his servitors.

This being known in the camp, forth came the French, who all this while loitered in their pavilions, and meeting the carriages by the way, took all the spoils wholly to themselves, rating Longspath and the English, for adventuring and issuing out of the camp without leave or knowledge of their general, contrary to the discipline of war. William Longspath said, he had done nothing but he would answer to it, that his purpose was to have the spoil divided to the whole army: when this would not serve, being grieved in mind at being spoiled in so cowardly a way, of that for which he had so adventurously travelled, he went to the king to complain. But when no reason nor complaint would serve, owing to the proud earl of Artois disliking him, he bid the king farewell, and said he would serve him no longer. And so William Longspath, with his followers, breaking from the French host, went to Acre. Upon their departure the earl of Artois said, "Now is the army of the

French well rid of these tailed people." Which words, spoken in great despite, were evil taken by many good men that heard him.

The king, setting forward from Damietta, directed his journey towards Cairo. The Soldan in the meantime hearing of the coming of the French host, in great hopes of conquering all, sent to the king, offering to the christians the quiet and full possession of the Holy Land, with all the kingdom of Jerusalem, and more; besides other infinite treasure of gold and silver, or what else might please them, only upon this condition, they would restore again Damietta, with the captives there, and so would join together in mutual peace and amity. Also they should have all their christian captives delivered home, and so both countries should freely pass one to another with their wares and traffic, such as they chose to adventure. It was also firmly asserted that the Soldan, with most of his nobles, were willing to leave the filthy law of Mahomet, and receive the faith of Christ, so that they might quietly enjoy their lands and possessions. Then great quietness had no doubt pervaded in all Christendom, with the end of bloodshed and misery, had it not been for the pope and his legate, who (having command from the pope, that if any such offers should come, he should not take them) in no wise would receive the conditions offered, (Paris. fol. 233).

After this every thing was prepared on both sides for war. The king comes to the great river Nile, thinking to pass over upon a bridge of boats. On the other side the Soldan pitched himself to oppose his passage. In the mean time there occurred a certain festival among the Saracens, in which the Soldan was absent, leaving his tents by the water side. This was observed by a Saracen lately converted to Christ, serving with Earl Robert the king's brother, who pointed out a shallow ford in the river, where they might more easily pass over; the earl and the master of the Templars, with a great force of about the third part of the army, passed over the river, followed by William Longspath with his band of English soldiers. Being joined together on the other side of the water, they encountered the Saracens remaining in the tents, and put them to flight. After this victory the French earl, elated with pride and triumph, as if he had conquered the whole earth, would needs press forward, dividing himself from the main host, thinking to win the spurs alone. Some sage men among the Templars advised him not to do so, but rather to return and take their whole strength with them, and that so they would be more sure against all deceits and dangers. The practice of that people (they said) they knew well, and had had more experience of than he: alleging also, their wearied bodies, their tired horses, their famished soldiers, and the insufficiency of their number, which was not able to withstand the multitude of the enemies: with other such like words of persuasion. When the proud earl heard them, being inflamed with no less arrogancy than ignorance, he reviled them, called them cowardly dastards and betrayers of the whole country, objecting to them the common report, which said, That the land of the holy cross might be won to Christendom, were it not for the rebellious Templars, with the Hospitallers and their fellows, &c.

To these contumelious rebukes the master of the Templars answered for himself and for his companions, bidding the earl display his ensign whenever he would, and wherever he dared, they were quite as ready to follow him, as he to go before them. Then began William Longspath the worthy knight to speak, desiring the earl to give ear to those men of experience, who had better knowledge of those countries and people than he had, commending their counsel to be discreet and wholesome, and so turning to the master of the temple he began with gentle words to soften and appease him. The knight had not half ended his talk, when the earl, taking the words out of his mouth, began to fume and swear, crying out of these cowardly Englishmen with tails. "What a pure army (said he) should we have here, if these tails, and tailed people were purged from it?" with other like words of great villany and much hatred. The English knight answered "Well, Earl Robert!

wheresoever you dare set your foot, my step shall go as far as yours; and I believe, we go this day where you shall not dare to come near the tail of my horse." In the event it proved true.

Now, seeing Earl Robert would needs set forward to get all the glory to himself, he attacked a place called Mansor. Then immediately comes the Soldan with all his main power; he seeing the christian army to be divided, and the brother separated from the brother, had that which he had long wished for, and so enclosing them round about so that none should escape, he fell on them and there was a cruel fight. Then the earl began to repent of his rashness, but it was too late: then seeing William Longspath the English knight gallantly fighting in the chief brunt of the enemies, cried to him in a most cowardly way to fly, seeing God (said he) fights against us. The knight answered "God forbid that my father's son should run away from the face of a Saracen." The earl then turning his horse fled away, thinking to escape by the swiftness of his horse, and so taking the river of Thafnis, pressed down with his armour, he sunk and was drowned. Thus the earl being gone, the French began to despair and scatter. Then William Longspath, bearing all the force of the enemy, stood against them as long as he could, wounding and slaying many a Saracen, until at length his horse being killed, and his legs maimed, he could no longer stand, yet as he was down, he mangled their feet and legs, and did the Saracens much sorrow, till at last, after many blows and wounds, being stoned by the Saracens, he yielded his life. After his death the Saracens setting upon the rest of the army, whom they had compassed on every side, destroyed them all, so that scarce one man escaped alive, saving two Templars, one Hospitaller, and one poor soldier, who brought tidings of it to the king.

These things being known in the French camp to the king and his soldiers, there was no little sorrow and heaviness on every side, with great fear and doubt in themselves what was best to do. At last, when they saw no remedy, but they must stand manfully to revenge the blood of their brethren, then the king with his host passed over the Nile, and coming to the place where the battle had been, there they beheld their fellows and brethren, pitifully lying with their heads and hands cut off. For the Saracens for the reward before promised by the Soldan or Sultan, to them that could bring the head or hand of any christian, had mangled the christians, leaving their bodies to the wild beasts. Thus as they were sorrowing and lamenting the rueful case of their christian fellows, suddenly appears the coming of the Soldan, with a multitude of innumerable thousands. Against them the Frenchmen soon prepare themselves to encounter, and so the battle being struck up, the armies began to join. But alack for pity, what could the French do, their number was so lessened, their hearts wounded with fear and sorrow, their bodies consumed with penury and famine, their horses for feebleness not able to serve them? In conclusion, the Frenchmen were overthrown, slain, and dispatched; and seeing there was no flying, happy was he that first could yield himself. In which miserable conflict, the king with his two brethren, and a few that clave unto him, were taken captives, to the confusion of all christian realms, and presented to the Soldan. All the rest were put to the sword, or else stood to the mercy of the Saracens, whether to be slain or to remain in woful captivity. And this was the end of that sorrowful battle, wherein almost all the nobility of France was slain, and there was scarcely one man in the multitude who escaped free, but was either slain, or taken prisoner.

The Soldan, after taking of the French king, deceitfully disguising an army of Saracens to the number of the French army, with the arms and ensigns of them that were slain, made toward Damietta, where the duke of Burgundy, with the French queen, and Otho, the pope's legate, and other bishops, and their garrisons were remaining, supposing under the shew of Frenchmen to be let in; but the captains mistrusting their hasty coming, and doubting their visages, not like to the Frenchmen, shut the gates against them.

As the Soldan missed his purpose, he thought by advice of his council, to use the king's life for his own advantage in recovering the city of Damietta, as in the end it came to pass. For, although the king at the first was greatly unwilling, and had rather die than surrender Damietta again to the Saracens, yet the conclusion fell out, that the king was put to his ransom, and the city of Damietta was also resigned, which city being twice won, and twice lost by the christians, the Soldan or Soladine afterward caused it utterly to be razed down to the ground. The ransom of the king, upon condition that the Soldan should see him safely conducted to Acre, came to 60,000 marks. The number of French and others who died in that war by water and by land, came to 80,000 persons.

And thus you have the brief narration of this lamentable pilgrimage of Lewis the French king, all occasioned by the pope and Otho his legate; by whose sinister means and pestilent pride, not only the lives of so many christians were then lost, but also the loss of other cities and christian regions bordering in the same quarters, is to be ascribed; for by the occasion of all this, the hearts of the Saracens on the one side were so encouraged, and the courage of the christians on the other side so much discomfited, that in a short time after, both the dominion of Antioch, and of Acre, with all other possessions belonging to the christians, were lost, to the great diminishing of Christ's church.

Another reason, too, why the ruin of this French army is deservedly imputed to the pope, is this; for, when Lewis the French king perceiving what a necessary friend and helper Frederick the emperor might be to him against the Saracens, and therefore was an earnest suitor for him to the pope, to have him released; yet neither he, nor the king of England, by any means could obtain it. Through which, not only the French king's army went to wreck, but also such a fire of mischief was kindled against Christendom, as yet to this day cannot be quenched. For the Saracens, and after them the Turks, got such a hand over Christendom, as to this day we all have great cause to rue and lament.

The chief and greatest cause of all which, was, that the emperor who could have done the most, was deposed by the pope's tyranny, by which all those churches in Asia were left desolate. As to the Emperor Frederick, whom we have frequently mentioned before, as his history is strange, his acts wonderous, and his conflicts tragical, which he sustained against four or five popes one after another, I thought it well to set it forth, that the reader may know what is to be thought of this see of Rome, which had wrought such abominable mischief in the world, as in the sequel of the history following, may be seen.

The whole tragical history of the Emperor Frederick II., translated out of the Latin book of Nicholas Cisnerus, (from A.D. 1193, to A.D. 1250.)

Frederick II. was of the noblest lineage, being grandson to Frederick Barbarossa, and son to the Emperor Henry VI., and Constantia, daughter of the king of Sicily.

The Emperor Henry VI., when he died, which was shortly after the birth of Frederick II., committed the protection of him to Constantia his wife, to Philip his brother, governor of Etruria, and to the bishop of Rome, then Innocent III.

Constantia, not long after the death of Henry her husband, being sickly and growing into age, resigned, and willed by her testament the safety both of her son Frederick, and also of his dominions, to the protection and government of Innocent III.

This Pope Innocent, as soon as he had the protection of the young emperor, became, instead of a patron and protector to him and his dominions, both an enemy and conspirator. The examples are many; he persuaded Sibylla, the wife of Tancred (whom Henry put from the kingdom of Sicily), to recover the same again. Whereupon Walter, who was married to the daughter of this Tancred, by the instigation, counsel, and aid of the French king, with the pope, invaded Campania and Apulia. At which time also, the same worthy protector, Innocent III., sent his legates with letters of excommunication against all that would not take Walter for their king.

Again, when the princes, electors, and other nobles, had promised by their oath to Henry, that they would make Frederick his son emperor after his decease, the pope absolved them all from the oath which they had taken and given for the election of Frederick. He then went about to procure that Otho, the son of Henry Leo, should be made emperor. He deprived all such bishops as he knew to be favourable to Philip, who ruled the empire during the minority of his nephew Frederick. But Philip, whose cause was better, and whose skill in martial affairs was greater, and who was stronger in power, after many and great conflicts, and the fearful disturbance and desolation of the whole empire, by God's help, defeated the other. All which calamities and mischiefs, Conrad Lichtenau, living at that time, in his annals, most pitifully complains of, and accuses the bishop of Rome and his adherents to be the chief authors and devisers of this great and lamentable mischief.

Thus you may see how it was by the counsel and consent of Pope Innocent, and by his instigation, besides his secret conspiracies, that this good Frederick and his dominions were hurt and damaged.

At this time Frederick was come to the age of twenty years; by the provision of Constantia his mother, he was so well instructed in letters, and so accomplished with other arts and virtues, that at these years there appeared and shone in him excellent gifts both of wisdom and knowledge.

He was excellently well versed in the Latin and Greek languages, although at that time learning began to decay, and barbarousness to increase. He had also the German tongue, the Italian tongue, and the Saracen tongue. He daily exercised and put in practice those virtues which nature had planted in him, as piety, wisdom, justice, and fortitude; so that he might well be compared and accounted among the worthiest and most renowned emperors his predecessors.

When Frederick had gathered his armies, he was crowned; and after that, he set the empire at rest, and in order, and appeased the whole of Germany. And then with all his nobles and princes he returned to Rome, and by Pope Honorius III. was with great solemnity consecrated and called Augustus. Which Honorius succeeded Innocent in the papal see.

After the consecration of Frederick was with great solemnity finished, he departed from Rome, to set in order and settle the cities and great towns of Italy, for the better tranquillity of himself, and the safety of his subjects, where he heard of some that began to raise and make new factions against him. Among whom were Thomas and Richard, the brothers of Innocent III., who held some castles from him by force. These castles he besieged and beat down. Richard he took and sent as a prisoner into Sicilia; but Thomas escaped to Rome; there also repaired certain bishops and others that were conspirators against Frederick, and were by this bishop of Rome maintained and defended. Frederick began to expostulate with the pope, who, on the other side, was so chafed and vexed, that immediately, without further delay, he thunders out against Frederick his curses and excommunications.

Thomas Fazel declares the detestation or defiance that broke out between them in a different manner. There were, says he, among those who were found traitors to the emperor, certain bishops, who flying to the pope, requested his aid: upon which the pope sent his legates to the emperor, and requested him, that he would admit and receive to favour those bishops whom he had banished and put from their offices, and that he would not intermeddle with any ecclesiastical charge wherewith he had nothing to do: and said further, that the correction and punishment of such matters pertained to the bishop of Rome, and not to him. And, moreover, that the oversight of those churches in that kingdom, from the which he had expelled the bishops, pertained and belonged to the pope.

To this Frederick replied, "That forsomuch as now

four hundred years and more (from the time of Charlemagne) all emperors and kings in their dominions might lawfully commit to meet and fit men for the same, such ecclesiastical functions and charges as were within their territories and kingdoms; that he also looked to have the like privilege and authority, which his predecessors had before him." And being chafed and moved with these demands of the pope, he breaks forth and says, "How long will the bishop of Rome abuse my patience? When will his covetous heart be satisfied? Whereunto will his ambitious desire grow?" With such words, repeating certain injuries and conspiracies, both against him and his dominions, plotted as well by Honorius as by Innocent. "What man, (says he,) can suffer and bear this incredible boldness and intolerable insolency of so proud a bishop? Go," says he, to the legates, "and tell Honorius, that I will hazard both the seigniory of my empire, and crown of my kingdom, rather than suffer him thus to diminish the authority of our majesty."

Whilst Frederick was in Sicilia, his wife Constantia died. In the mean time the christians, with a great navy sailed into Egypt, and took the city Heliopolis, commonly called Damietta, being in good hope to have driven the Soldan out of Egypt, they experienced a great and marvelous overthrow by the water of the Nile (which then overflowed their camp), and they were obliged to agree to a truce with the Soldan for some years, and to deliver up the city again. Upon this, John surnamed Brennus, king of Jerusalem, arrived in Italy, and prayed aid of the emperor, in whom he had great hopes of finding a remedy of these calamities; thence he went to Rome to the pope, describing to him the great discomfiture, as also the present peril and calamity that they were in. By his means, the emperor was reconciled again to the pope, and promised, that, he would prepare an army for the recovery of Jerusalem, and go there himself. In the mean time Honorius, to whom he was lately reconciled, purposed to have made against him some great and secret attempt, had he not been prevented by death.

After him succeeded Gregory IX., who was as great an enemy of Frederick. This Gregory was scarcely settled in his papacy, when he threatened the emperor with excommunication, unless he would proceed into Asia according to his promise; the reason why the pope so hastened the journey of Frederick, you shall hear hereafter. For he could not well bring to pass, what he had devised in his mischievous mind, unless the emperor were farther from him. However, Frederick it should seem smelling a rat, or mistrusting somewhat, as well he might, alleged different excuses for delay.

Fazell, a Sicilian writer, says, that the special cause of the emperor's stay was, the oath of truce and peace during certain years, which was made between the Saracens and christians, and which time was not yet expired.

The same also writes of King John of Jerusalem, that when his daughter was brought to Rome, the emperor and the pope were reconciled together. And being called up to Rome to celebrate the marriage of the emperor with Joel, the daughter of John, Pope Gregory (as the manner of those proud prelates is) offered his right foot to the emperor to kiss. But the emperor, not stooping so low, scarcely with his lip touched the upper part of his knee, and would not kiss his foot; which the pope took in very evil part, and was marvellously offended. But no opportunity that time served to revenge his malice, so he dissembled for that time, thinking to recompence it at the full, as time would serve.

After this, the emperor hearing how the christians were oppressed by the Soldan in Syria, and that there came a great army against the christian princes, he made the more haste, and was with more desire encouraged to set forward on his journey into Asia.

With all his power, he made speedy preparation for the wars: he rigged and manned a puissant navy; he had the most picked men and the best soldiers that were in every country, and made warlike provision for every thing pertaining to such a voyage and expedition. Great bands assembled and mustered both of German soldiers and others, and appointed under their captains, they set forth and marched to Brundusium, where lying a long time, and waiting for the emperor, who was delayed by sickness, a great pestilence broke out among them, through the great heat of that country; and many a soldier there lost his life; among them died Thuringus, one of their generals. The emperor when he had somewhat recovered his health, launched with all his navy, and set forward to Brundusium. And when he came to the straits of Peloponnesus and Crete, he suddenly fell sick, his diseases returning upon him again, and so sending before all or the most part of his bands and ships into Palestine, and promising to follow them so soon as he might recover and get never so little health; he himself with a few ships returned to Brundusium, and from thence for want of health, went into Apulia.

When tidings hereof came to the pope's ear, he sent out his thundering curses and excommunications against the emperor. The pretended cause of this, I find noted and mentioned by his own letters, how that when Frederick had robbed and taken from Brundusium, prince of Thuring, his horses, his money, and other rich furniture of his house at the time of his death, he sailed into Italy; not to make war against the Turk, but to convey his prey away from Brundusius; and so neglecting his oath and promise which he had made, and feigning himself to be sick, came home again: and by that his default Damietta was lost, and the host of the christians sore afflicted. Then Frederick, to repel and refute the slander, sends the bishop of Brundis and other legates to Rome; but the pope would not suffer them to come to his presence, nor yet to the councils of the cardinals, to make his vindication. Wherefore the emperor, to purge himself of the crimes which the pope so falsely accused him of, both to all christian kings, and especially to the princes of Germany, and all the nobles of the empire, writes his letters that those things are both false and feigned and invented by the pope's own head; and he shews, how that his ambassadors with his vindication were not suffered to come into the pope's presence.

"Amongst other catholic princes," says Matthew Paris, "he also wrote his letters to the king of England, embossed with gold; declaring in the same, that the bishop of Rome was so inflamed with the fire of avarice and manifest covetousness, that he was not contented with the goods of the church which were innumerable, but also that he shamed not to bring princes, kings, and emperors to be subjects and contributors to him, and so to disinherit them, and put them from their kingly dignities: and that the king of England himself had good experiment thereof, whose father, King John, they held so long excommunicated, till they had brought both him and his dominions under servitude, and to pay tribute to him. Behold the manners and conditions of our Roman bishops! behold the snares wherewith these prelates seek to entangle men; to wipe their noses of their money, to make their children bondmen, to disquiet such as seek to live in peace, being clothed with sheeps' clothing, when indeed they be but ravening wolves, sending their legates hither and thither to excommunicate and suspend; as having power to punish whom they please, not sowing the seed, that is, the word of God, to fructify, but that they may bribe and tax men's persons, and reap that which they never sowed. Thus it comes to pass, that they spoil the holy churches and houses of God, which should be the refuge for the poor, and the mansion houses of saints, which our devout and simple parents built for that purpose, and ordained for the relief of poor men and pilgrims, and for the sustenance of such as were well disposed and religious. But these degenerate varlets, whom letters have only made both mad and malapert, strive and gape to be both kings and emperors.

"Doubtless the primitive church was built and laid in poverty and simplicity of life, and then, as a fruitful mother she begat those her holy children, whom the catalogue of saints now makes mention of; and verily no other foundation can be laid by any other church, than that which is laid by Jesus Christ. But this church as it swims and wallows in all superfluity of riches, and builds and raises the frame in all superfluous wealth and glory; so is it to be feared lest the walls thereof fall to decay, and when the walls be down, utter ruin and subversion follow after," &c.

But now, that Frederick might in very deed stop the mouth of the cruel pope, who persisted still in his excommunication against him, when he had prepared all things for the war, and had levied a great army, he departed, and came by sea to Cyprus with his army.

From Cyprus the emperor sailed to Joppa, which he fortified; but it came to pass, that in short space they wanted provisions, and were afflicted with famine. Then they made their humble supplication to God, and the great tempest and foul weather ceased, whereby, the seas being now calm, they had provisions and all other necessary things brought to them. Immediately the emperor and his army, as also the inhabitants of Joppa, were greatly refreshed and animated; and, on the other side, their enemies being disappointed of their purpose, were greatly discouraged, so that the king of Egypt, who with a great army had encamped within one day's journey of Joppa, thinking to have besieged it, was now contented to treat for peace. Whereupon ambassadors were sent with the emperor's demands, and the Saracens immediately granted them, so that a peace for ten years was concluded, and was confirmed by solemn oath on the behalf of both princes, according to their several usages and manner: the form and condition of which articles of peace briefly collected, are these:—

"First, That Frederick the emperor should be crowned and anointed king of Jerusalem, according to the manner of the kings of Jerusalem before him.

"Secondly, That all the lands and possessions which were situated between Jerusalem and Ptolemais, and the greatest part of Palestine, and the cities of Tyre and Sidon, which were in Syria, and all other territories which Baldwin IV. at any time had and did occupy there, should be delivered unto him, only certain castles being reserved.

"Thirdly, That he might fortify and build what fortresses and castles, cities and towns, he thought good in all Syria and Palestine.

"Fourthly, That all the prisoners which were in the Saracens' hands, should be ransomed freely and sent home. And again, that the Saracens might have leave without armour to come into the temple, where the Lord's sepulchre is, to pray; and that they should still hold and keep Chratum and the king's mount."

As Frederick thought the conclusion of this peace to be both necessary, and also profitable for all christians, and as he had got as much thereby, as if the wars had continued, he sent his legates with letters to all christian kings, princes, and potentates, as also to the bishop of Rome, declaring the circumstance and success of his journey and wars, as you have partly heard; requiring them that they also would praise and give God thanks for his good success and profitable peace concluded. And he desired the pope, that as he had now accomplished his promise, and there was no cause why he should be displeased with him, he might be reconciled and obtain his favour.

In the meantime the emperor with all his army marched to Jerusalem, where, upon Easter-day (A.D. 1229,) he was with great triumph, and to the joy of all his nobles, and also the magistrates of that kingdom, solemnly crowned king.

After this he rebuilt the city and the walls, which were beaten down by the Saracens; he supplied it with munition, he built up the churches and temples that were in ruins, he fortified Nazareth and Joppa with strong garrisons, provisions, and all other necessary things.

Now see and behold, I pray you, whilst Frederick was thus occupied, what practices the pope was about in Italy; not any whit careful in the affairs of the christian commonwealth, but studying and labouring what mischief he might work against the emperor. First, he caused the soldiers, whom the emperor sent for out of Germany to the maintenance of the holy wars, to be stopped as they passed through Italy, preventing their journey, and spoiling them of all such provision as they had. And not only this, but he sent secretly letters into Asia to the patriarch of Jerusalem, and the sol-

diers that kept the temple and the hospital, enticing and inciting them to rebel against the emperor; and, furthermore, he dissuaded the princes of the Saracens, that they should make no league nor truce with Frederick, nor deliver up to him the crown and kingdom of Jerusalem. Which letters, as they were manifest testimonies of his treachery and treason towards him, whom God had instituted and made his liege lord and sovereign, and mightiest potentate upon the earth; so it was his will that he should come to the knowledge thereof, and that those letters should fall into his hands, that he kept those letters for the more certain testimony of all this, he protests in his last epistle to the christian princes.

When the pope had thus conspired against Frederick, and had betrayed him, as far as he could, to the public enemy of all christians, the Turk, he could not dissemble this his mischievous treasons, nor content himself with it, but he must needs devise and practise another. For he incited John, father-in-law to Frederick, to make war against him, and caused the subjects of the empire to withdraw their allegiance from him, as also the inhabitants of Picenum and of Lombardy; and thus joining themselves together they sought further assistance of the French king, by which they gained great power. That done, they divided their force in two armies, invading with one the empire, and with the other the territories belonging to the inheritance of Frederick.

But when the pope saw, that fortune neither favoured his designs, nor served his longings, he was as a man bereft of his wits, and especially at these tidings of the prosperous success of the emperor against the Saracens. He tore and threw all his letters on the ground, and with all insulting language rebuked and reviled the legates for the emperor their master's sake.

These injuries of the pope against Frederick, are great and most wicked treasons. But still his cruel and tyrannical mind was not contented, but it went so far as is scarce credible, for he not only set variance between Frederick and his son Henry, but also caused the son to become an enemy to the father. And this was the drift of all his policy, that at one instant in different and many places far one from another, war might be made against the emperor.

When the emperor understood what commotion the pope kept up in all his dominions in his absence, thinking to prevent the pope's purpose, and also to confirm the friendship of those whom in his absence he found his trusty subjects; he left Asia, and with all speed came to Calabria. During the time of his being there, he assembled his forces, and made all the preparation he could. From thence he went to Berletta, where the duke of Spoletanum, with all his garrisons came to him; and thence he came into Apulia; and within a short time, by God's help, recovered again all his dominions there. And then, going into Campania, he won as many towns and holds as the pope had there, even almost to Rome. And now although the emperor had got this entrance upon the pope's dominions, whereby he might have revenged himself of all the injuries done to him; yet he preferred nothing before the christian and public tranquillity, for the love of which, restraining his wrath, he sends his legates to treat for peace. Furthermore, to treat for this peace, and decide all controversies, he sent to the pope eight or ten of the noblest and chiefest about him, princes and dukes of the empire.

But yet so great was the insolence and pride of the pope, that by no gentleness or kindness could he be brought to promote the profitable concord of the church and christian commonwealth. O, worthy head, that challenges all authority to himself in the church of Christ, and for his own wilful revenge, cares nothing for the health and advantage of all Christendom! The next year a peace was concluded between them, by the help of Leopold of Austria. The pope absolving the emperor of his excommunication, took therefore of him 120,000 ounces of gold, restoring the titles both of his empire, and also of his kingdoms.

Although Frederick concluded with the pope this peace unprofitable for himself, yet he performed those things that were agreed upon faithfully. But the pope, who thought it but a trifle to break his promise, would not stand to the conditions of the peace. For, to pass over other things, he neither restored, as he promised, the customs of the land of Sicily, nor yet the city Castellana. Yet Frederick, for the quietness and advantage of the commonwealth, bore and suffered these small injuries, and studied in all that he could, as well by liberal gifts as otherwise, to make the pope a trusty friend.

Whilst these things were done in Italy and Sicily, great rebellions were moved in Germany against the emperor, by his sons Henry Cæsar, and Frederick of Austria. For Henry being now shaken off from his lord pope, by reason of the peace between his father and the pope, began now to make an open claim to the empire.

When intelligence of these things was brought to the emperor, he sent his legates, and commanded that both the Cæsar his son, and other princes of Germany, who had assembled their armies, should break up and disperse. And as he saw his son made so apparent rebellion against him, and fearing greater insurrections in Germany, he thought it good to prevent the same with all expedition. So he determined to go in all haste to Germany with his army, from whence he had now been absent fourteen years. The pope promised the emperor that he would write letters in his behalf to all the princes of Germany, but persuaded him to the utmost of his power, that he should in no case go into Germany himself. For why? his conscience accused him that he had written to the nobles in Germany, even from the beginning of his papacy, that they should not suffer the emperor, nor any of his heirs, to enjoy the empire; and had stirred them all up to rebel against him; and had moved Henry the emperor's son, by his bribes and fair promises to conspire against his father. And to conclude, he was the author and procurer of the conspiracy which the Lombards then made against him, and fearing lest these things should come now to the emperor's ear, he was greatly troubled. But the emperor not thinking it good at so important a time to be absent, went speedily into Germany. And assembling there a council, Henry Cæsar his son, after his conspiracy was manifestly detected, whereof the pope was chief author, was by judgment and sentence of seventy princes, condemned of high treason; and being commanded by his father to be bound, was brought to Apulia, where, not long after, he died in prison. Furthermore, by public commandment he renounced his son Frederick of Austria, and caused him to be proclaimed an enemy to the public weal. And when he saw that that punishment did not cause him to remember himself, and acknowledge his misconduct, the emperor, with a great army, took from him all Austria and Styria, and brought them again under his own obedience and fidelity.

Then when he had set Germany in quietness, he left there his son Conrad Cæsar, and returned to Italy, to punish such as had conspired against him, whose treasons were all detected at the condemnation of his son, chiefly set on by the pope. The pope understanding that the emperor marched towards Italy, pretended himself reconciled, and a friend to Frederick, yet was he notwithstanding a most secret and dangerous enemy. He advised the rebellious to join together, and to fortify strongly their cities with garrisons, that they should send for aid to their friends, and that with all the force they were able, they should prepare for the war.

And he sent his ambassadors to the emperor, to whom, under the pretence of promoting a peace, he had given a secret commandment that they should interdict him and his army, so soon as he came within the borders of Italy.

The emperor then prosecuted his purpose, and marched into Italy, where he brought under his subjection those cities that rebelled against him. And then he set upon the great host of the confederators, of whom he took one thousand prisoners, and also their general, and slew several captains, and took all their ensigns.

The pope now somewhat dismayed at this overthrow of his confederates, began to fear the emperor; and whereas before, he wrought secretly and by others, now he goes to work with might and main to subdue and deprive the emperor. And although the emperor saw and perceived what hate and mortal malice he bare towards him; yet, that there should be no fault found in him for the breach of the peace, he sent four legates to the bishop of Rome, who should answer and refute those criminating charges which he laid to him.

The bishop, when he understood the ambassadors to be not far from Rome, thought that in hearing the excuse and reasonable answer of the emperor, perhaps he might be provoked to desist from his purpose, so he refused to speak with them, and at the day appointed pronounced the sentence of proscription against him, depriving him of all his dignities, honours, titles, prerogatives, kingdoms and whole empire. And calling the Venetian and Genoese legates, he made a peace between them, and covenanted with them, that at their charges they should rig and man five-and-thirty galleys, which should spoil and burn all along the sea-coasts of the kingdoms and dominions of Frederick.

But when the pope saw the good will and fidelity which the good duke of Venice bare to the emperor, and saw also what aid the emperor had from him, and that he was not likely to win him to his purpose; then he had recourse again to his old crafty practices and subtilties. And he devised to put forth an edict at Rome to the universal church and people; wherein he declares the causes why he curses and gives the emperor to the devil of hell, and has dejected him from all his princely dignity. He in the same edict accuses him of many and great crimes, that are detestable even to name. And, besides that, he restrains his sovereign lord and emperor of the appeal, which every private man by law may have. He accuses him of treason, perjury, cruelty, sacrilege, killing of his kindred, and all impiety; he accuses him for an heretic, a schismatic, and a miscreant: and to be brief, what mischief soever the pope can devise, with that he charges and burthens the emperor. The pope issued two other mandates, in which he commanded all bishops, prelates, and other of the clergy, that they should solemnly recite the same in their churches instead of their sermon, that by his decree he had excommunicated Frederick out of the fellowship of christian men, put him from the government of the empire, and that he had released all his subjects of their allegiance and fidelity towards him. And charges them, and all other christian men, under pain of cursing and damnation, that they neither succour the emperor, nor yet so much as wish him well.

Among the other noblemen of Germany at that time, was Otho, a prince of great honour, riches, and estimation. This prince, the pope both with fair promises and rewards, enticed from the emperor. Otho again caused three other princes and dukes to revolt from the emperor to the pope. To whom came also Frederick of Austria, his son; who was easily won to the pope.

The emperor was at Patavium when this news was brought to him. Therefore he commanded Peter of Venice his secretary, upon Easter day, to make a narration to the people of his great and liberal munificence to the bishops and church of Rome, and again, of the injuries of them toward him in recompence thereof; of his innocence also in that, of which the pope had accused him, and of the unseemliness of such an act or deed, of the right use of the ecclesiastical censure, and of the errors and abuse of the church of Rome. By which oration of his, he so removed the cloud of blind superstition from many men's hearts, and the conceived opinion of holiness of the church of Rome, and its bishops, and their usurped power, and subtle persuasion, that they plainly saw the vices of the church of Rome, and of the bishops of that see, as also their fraudulent deceits, and flagitious doings, most vehemently lamenting and complaining of the same.

The emperor also, by his letters and legates, gives intelligence to all christian kings, to the princes of his own empire, to the college of cardinals, and people of Rome; as well of the pretended crimes wherewith he was charged, as also of the cruelty of the bishop of Rome against him. The copy of which letter or epistle is as follows:—

The Emperor to the Prelates of the World.

" In the beginning and creation of the world, the inestimable foreknowledge and providence of God (who asketh counsel of none) created in the firmament of heaven two lights, a greater and a less; the greater he created to rule the day, and the less to rule the night: which two so perform their proper offices and duties in the zodiac, that although oftentimes the one be in an oblique aspect to the other, yet the one is not an enemy to the other; but rather the superior communicates his light to the inferior. Even so the same eternal foreknowledge hath appointed upon the earth two authorities, that is to say, priesthood and kingly power; the one for knowledge and wisdom, the other for defence; that man which is made of two parts, might have two reins to govern and bridle him withal, that thereby peace and love might dwell upon the face of the earth. But alas, the bishop of Rome sitting in the chair of perverse doctrine or pestilence, that pharisee anointed with the oil of iniquity above the rest of his consorts in this our time, who for his abominable pride is fallen from heaven, endeavours with his power to destroy and to undo all, and thinks, I believe, to star himself again there, from whence he fell. His purpose is to darken and to shadow the light of our unspotted life, whilst that, altering the verity into lies, his papal letters, stuffed with all untruths, are sent into sundry parts of the world; of his own corrupt humour, and upon no reasonable cause, blemishing the sincerity of our religion. The lord pope has compared us to the beast rising out of the sea, full of names of blasphemy, and spotted like a leopard. But we say, that he is that monstrous beast of whom it is said, and of whom we thus read: 'And there went out another horse that was red, and power was given to him that sat thereon to take peace from the earth, and that they should kill one another,' Rev. vi. 4. For since the time of his promotion he has not been the father of mercy, but of discord; a diligent steward of desolation, instead of consolation, and has enticed all the world to commit offence. And to take the words in a right sense and interpretation, he is that great dragon that has deceived the whole world; he is that antichrist, of whom he has called us the forerunner; he is that other Balaam hired for money to curse us; the prince of darkness, who has abused the prophets. This is the angel leaping out of the sea, having his vials filled with bitterness, that he may hurt both the sea and the land; the counterfeit vicar of Christ, that sets forth his own imaginations. He says, that we do not rightly believe in the christian faith, and that the world is deceived with three manner of deceivers, which to name, God forbid we should open our mouth; seeing that we openly confess only Jesus Christ our Lord and Saviour to be the everlasting Son of God, coequal with his Father and the Holy Ghost, begotten before all worlds, and in process of time sent down upon the earth for the salvation of mankind; conceived by the Holy Ghost; who was born of the glorious Virgin Mary, and after that suffered and died, as touching the flesh; and by his godhead the third day he raised from death that other nature which he assumed in the womb of his mother. But we have learned that the body of Mahomet hangs in the air, and his soul is buried in hell: whose works are damnable and contrary to the law of the Most High. We affirm also, that Moses was the faithful servant of God and a true teacher of the law; and that he talked with God in Mount Sinai. By whom also God wrought miracles in Egypt, and delivered the law written to the Israelites, and that afterwards with the elect he was called to glory. In these and other things our enemy and envier of our state, causing our mother the church to accuse her son, has written against us venomous and lying slanders, and sent the same to the whole world. If he had rightly understood the apostle's meaning, he would not have preferred his violent will, which bears such sway with him, before reason; neither would he have sent out his mandates at the suggestion of those who call light darkness, and evil good; who suspect honey to be gall, for the great good opinion they had conceived of that holy place, which indeed is both weak and infirm, and converts all truth into falsehood, and affirms that to be which is not.

"Truly my opinion, so impartial on every side, ought not in any case to be infringed and turned from the faith to such enemies of so corrupt a conscience. Wherefore we are greatly forced to marvel not a little, which thing also doth much disquiet us to see; that you, who are the pillars and assistants in the office of righteous dealing, the senators of Peter's city, and the principal beams in God's building, have not remedied the disturbances of so fierce a judge; as do the planets of heaven in their kind, which to mitigate the passing swift course of the great orb or sphere of heaven, draw a contrary way by their opposite movings. In very deed our imperial felicity has been, almost from the beginning, spurned against, and envied by the papal see and dignity: as Simonides being demanded why he had no more enemies and enviers of his state, answered: 'Because I have had no good success in any thing that ever I took in hand.' And whereas we have had prosperous success in all our enterprises (the Lord's name be blessed therefore), especially in the overthrow, of late, of our rebellious enemies, the Lombards, to whom in their quarrel he promised life and absolution, with remission of their sins, and this our success is the cause why this apostolical bishop mourns and laments. And now, not by your counsels, I suppose, he labours to oppose this our felicity, but out of his own power of binding and loosing, of which he glories so much. But presently where power and ability wants redress, there abuse takes place. We see in him who was so mighty a king, and the worthiest prince among all the prophets, a desire and craving of the restitution of God's Holy Spirit, when he had polluted the dignity of his office. But the proverb is, 'As things indissoluble are not to be loosed, so things that cannot be bound, are not to be bound.' Which thing is manifestly proved in him. For why, the scriptures of God instruct men how to live, they mortify our souls which are immortal, and quicken the same which are dead for want of life. And doubtless he is able to humble and bring down those that are unworthy of dignity, as much as he pleases, and when he pleases. Doubtless if the bishop of Rome were a true bishop indeed, innocent, unpolluted, and not associated with wicked livers and evil men, his life should prove him to be so. He would not then be an offerer of dissentious sacrifice, but a peaceable offerer of love and charity, and would cense, not with the incense of grief and hatred, but with the sweet smelling incense of concord and unity, neither yet would make of a sanctified office an execrable abuse. If he were such a bishop as he ought to be, he would not wrest or abuse the preaching the word into the fruit and gain of his own dissension, neither should we be accused as such an enemy of our mother the true church, as is laid unto her Son's charge by such a bishop. Which true and mother church we honour with all reverence, and embrace, being so beautified and adorned with God's holy sacraments. Some singular persons notwithstanding, feigning themselves to be our brethren by that mother, and who yet are not, such, I say, as are subject and slaves to corruptible things (putting them from amongst us) we utterly reject: especially because injuries done by them are not merely transitory and belonging to this life, wherewith our majesty is so molested, vexed, and grieved. Wherefore we cannot so easily mitigate our mood, neither ought we in very deed do to so, and therefore are we forced the more to take the greater revenge of them. You therefore that are men of grave and deliberate counsel, having the excellent gift (as from God) of wisdom and understanding; oppose that roaring enemy of ours in these his proceedings, whose beginnings are so wicked and detestable, wisely comparing things past, with those to come. Otherwise you that are under our subjection, as well of our empire as other our dominions, shall feel and perceive (both of my chief enemy and persecutor, as also of the princes that are his favourers and adherents) what revenge by sword Frederick Augustus shall take upon them, God so permitting."

The bishops and prelates, with one consent supporting the emperor, and contemning the pope's mandates and writs, and also the curses and threatenings of Albert his legate, accused, reproved, and greatly blamed his temerity, and also the tyranny which he usurped against the churches of Germany, and especially against the good emperor; that without his consent he durst be so bold as to meddle in churches committed to the emperor's government against the old and ancient customs; and that he had excommunicated the emperor without just cause; that he had condemned the emperor's faithful subjects as enemies to the church, for standing with their liege and sovereign prince (which allegiance without horrible iniquity they might not violate), and so had sought to disquiet them likewise in their charges and administrations; and had also in that quarrel given such defiance to the emperor. They accused and condemned Albert for a most impudent impostor, and for a most pestiferous botch and sore of the christian commonwealth, and they give him to the devil as a ruinous enemy, as well of the church as of his own natural country, and further think him worthy to have his reward with the rest of the pope's pursuivants, being one of the most wicked inventors and devisers of mischief that were in all Germany. This done, they informed the emperor of it by their letters; and, further, they advertised all the princes of Germany (especially those which were of the pope's faction or rebellion, and were the favourers of Albert), that they should take heed and beware in any case of his subtle deceits and pernicious deceivable allurements, and that they should not assist the pope against the emperor.

While these things were thus in working in Germany, Frederick came to Etruria, and after he had allayed certain insurrections there, from thence to Pisa, where he was received and welcomed with great amity and honour. This city was always faithful to the emperors of Germany.

Frederick then getting on his side the Lucenses, the Volaterans, the Genenses, the Aretines, and several cities besides in Etruria, came to Viterbium, which took part with him.

When the pope understood that Frederick was come to Viterbium he was very heavy, for he feared he would come to Rome, the good-will of which city the pope much mistrusted. He, therefore, caused a supplication to be drawn, pourtraying the heads of Peter and Paul, and with a sharp and contumelious oration he much defaced the emperor, promising everlasting life and the badge of the cross to as many as would arm themselves and fight against the emperor, as against the most wicked enemy of God and the church. Now when the emperor, marching somewhat near to the gates of Rome, beheld those whom the pope had, with his goodly spectacle of St. Peter and St. Paul, and with his alluring oration, stirred up against him, and marked with the badge of the cross, coming forth in battle against him; disdaining to be accounted for the enemy of the church, when he had been so beneficial to it, he made a fierce charge upon them, and soon put them to flight, and as many as he took (cutting off that badge from them) he caused to be hanged.

After this, when the emperor had greatly afflicted by battle such as conspired with the pope against him, he marched to vanquish the rest of his enemies in Italy, and besieged Asculinum. There understanding what the pope's assistants had done with the princes electors, and other princes of Germany, he wrote his letters to them. In which, first he shewed how that those contumelies and spiteful words, which the pope blustered out against him, are lighted upon himself; and how the bishops of Rome not only seek to bring emperors, kings, and princes under their obedience, but also seek to be honoured as gods, and say that they cannot err, nor yet be subject or bound to any religion. And further, as princes they command (under pain of cursing) that men believe every thing they say, how great a lie soever it be. Insomuch that by this covetousness of his, all things go backward, and the whole commonwealth is subverted, neither can any enemy be found more hurtful or perilous to the church of God than he. He wrote to them further, that he, seeing their good wills and practices towards him, would, with all the power and ability that God had given him, endeavour that he who in the likeness of

the shepherd of the flock, and the servant of Christ, and chief prelate in the church, shews himself so very a wolf, persecutor and tyrant, may be removed from that place, and that a true and careful shepherd of God's flock may be appointed in the church. Wherefore he exhorts them, if they desire the safety and preservation of the whole state of the commonwealth and empire, that they be furtherers of his purpose and proceedings, lest otherwise they also should happen to fall into the same snare of servitude with the bishop of Rome.

When the pope, as is said before, would not hear the emperor's legates that came to treat for peace, he called to a council at Rome, all such prelates out of Italy, France and England, as he thought to favour him and his proceedings, that thereby, as his last shift and only refuge, he by their help might deprive Frederick of his empire, as an utter enemy to God and to the church. All which things Frederick having knowledge of, determined to prevent their passage to Rome, as well by sea as by land. So that all the passages by land being now stopped and prevented, he commanded his son Henry with certain galleys to go and keep the coasts of Sardinia, and from thence to go to Pisa, and with the Pisans to rig out a navy to meet with such as should come to aid the pope at Rome. The pope's champions understanding they could not safely repair to Rome by land, procured galleys and ships out of Genoa to the number of forty sail for their defence; thinking that if they should happen to meet with any of the emperor's ships or galleys, they should be able to make their part good, and give them the repulse. Encius in like manner and Huglinus (being captain and admiral of the Pisan navy for the emperor) launched forth to sea with forty ships and galleys; and met with the Genoese ships, and fiercely began to grapple with them and board them, in which fight at length three of the Genoese ships were sunk, with all the riches and treasure in them. In these, three legates of the popes, were taken, of whom were two cardinals, all cruel enemies against the emperor, and many other prelates more; besides a great number of legates and procurators of cities, with an infinite number of monks and priests, besides six thousand soldiers, with others.

Pandolph Colonutius, in describing the circumstances of the great loss and misfortune of these champions of the pope by sea, declares that besides the great spoil and booty, they also found many writings and letters against Frederick, which much helped them in the defence of those causes, wherein they had laboured against him.

News hereof was brought to the emperor not long after, who immediately led his army towards Rome; and in the way he reconciled the city of Pisa to the cause. But Fanum, because the townsmen shut their gates and would not suffer the emperor to come in, he took by force and destroyed. The emperor, seeing that neither by petition to the pope, nor yet by lawful excuse, could he do any good with him, thought, by his sudden coming there, and the fear of the imminent peril, he might be brought to leave off his pertinacity. And although the emperor was too strong for the pope, yet, because he regarded nothing more than the public tranquillity of the empire, and that he might then take the Tartar wars in hand, he refused not to treat for peace, as if he had been both in force and fortune much his inferior.

While this ruffle was betwixt the emperor and the pope, the emperor of the Tartars' son, invaded the borders next adjoining to him, and there won Roxolanum, Bodolium, Mudanum, with many other cities, towns, and villages, destroying, wasting and burning the countries all about, killing and slaying man, woman, and child, sparing none of any sex or age. At this sudden invasion, the people being in such fear and perplexity, having no city, no refuge, nor aid to stand in defence for them, were obliged to leave all that they had, and disperse themselves into woods, and fly into marshes and mountains, or wherever any succour offered itself to them.

The emperor thought it very requisite, that this mischief should be remedied and prevented with all speed; but his great enemy the pope, was the only hinderance. For when he saw and perceived that he himself could do no good, and only laboured in vain in seeking peace with the pope, he gave commandment to Boiemus and Boius, to intreat and persuade with him. And (considering the imminent peril likely to ensue, by reason of such civil dissension, to the whole state of Christendom) that he would take up and conclude a peace, and mitigate somewhat his fierce and wrathful mood; and when he saw further, that neither by that means of intreaty nor any other, the pope would desist from his stubborn and malicious purpose, he wrote to the king of Hungary, that he was right sorry and greatly lamented their miserable state, and that he much desired to relieve the need and necessity that he and all the rest stood in. But that he could not redress the same, nor be any assistance to him, because as the bishop of Rome refused all treaty of peace, he could not without great peril to himself depart out of Italy, lest by the pope's mischievous imaginations, he should be in peril of losing all at home. This was the loving zeal and affection of the pope and his adherents in this time of calamity towards the christian state and commonwealth; that he had rather bend his force and revenge his malice upon the good and christian emperor, than either he himself withstand, or suffer and permit, by any profitable peace, that this most bloody and cruel Tartar should be restrained from so great a havock, spoil and slaughter of christian men; and yet forsooth these men will seem to have the greatest regard of all others to the christian preservation, and think to have the supremacy given therein! What else is this, but manifest mockery and deceiving of the people.

When Frederick saw there was no other remedy, and that he laboured in vain to have peace with the pope, he prosecuted this war to the uttermost; and when he had got Tudertum, he destroyed the towns of Geminum and Narvia, and gave the spoil to his soldiers; he gently received the surrender of Siburnium, and wasted all the country about Rome. The pope, dismayed and troubled, and seeing that things prospered not so well with him and against the emperor as he wished, died for very anger.

In the stead of Gregory, succeeded Celestine IV., who, the eighteenth day after he was created pope, also died.

When the cardinals were all assembled, they made Sinibald pope, whom they called Innocent IV. Of which election, when Frederick was informed, he was well pleased; and as he had in all this troublous time been his friend, he hoped that the christian commonwealth would now have been brought to much peace and concord.

The legates of Frederick also, with the assistance of Baldwin, the emperor of Constantinople, laboured very diligently for the conclusion of the promise of peace. And to be brief, every man was in good hope, and looked for no less. But the matter fell out far otherwise, and contrary to all their expectation. For the pope was secretly set on and encouraged by the cardinals and others against Frederick. And while the emperor's legates waited for the answer, Rainerus, the cardinal, went secretly to Viterbium with a number of soldiers, and took the town.

The emperor, hearing of this, mustered his bands, and with a sufficient force entered the pope's territory to recover Viterbium. From thence he sent ambassadors to Rome, and with them also the emperor of Constantinople, and the earl of Toulouse, who he thought were able to do much with the pope in the prosecuting of this peace. But when the legates perceived no conclusion of peace was purposed, they began to despair of the matter; and so sent word to the emperor. The emperor yet doubted not, but if he might himself speak with the pope, he should, upon reasonable conditions, accord with him; so by his legates and letters, he desired him to appoint a place where the emperor might resort to him. The pope seemed to be contented, and appointed a day at Fescennia, where they would talk together; and the pope promised that he would be there before him, and wait the emperor's coming. But the pope had made a confederacy with the French king against Frederick; and when he knew the three galleys previously hired to be ready, he secretly in the night took ship, and came to

Genoa, and from thence to Lyons in France, where, calling a council, he, with a loud voice summoned Frederick, and appointing him a day, commanded him there personally to plead his cause.

And although his sudden departing out of Italy, made plain demonstration of no conclusion of a peace; yet the most modest emperor, using the innocency and uprightness of his cause, and as one most desirous of peace and christian concord, sent the patriarch of Antioch, the bishop of Panormia and Thadeus Suessanus, the president of his court, a most skilful and prudent civilian, to the council of Lyons, who signified to them that the emperor would be there for the defence of his own cause; and, as the day was very short, required a more convenient time for him to repair there. The emperor also sent to intreat that he would prorogue the day of hearing, till he might conveniently travel thither. But the pope would not give so much as three days' space, in which time the ambassadors assured them of the emperor's presence. When the day was come, the pope, with his confederates, against God's law, against christian doctrine, against both the precept of the law of nature and reason, against the rule of equity, against the constitutions of emperors, and also the decrees of the empire, without any observation of the law, or granting dilatory days, without proof of any crime, or his cause suffered to be pleaded or heard what might be answered therein, taking upon him to be both adversary and judge, condemned the emperor in his absence. What more wicked sentence was ever pronounced? What more cruel act, considering the person, could be committed? Or, what thing more brutish could have been imagined or devised?

When the emperor heard of this cruel and tyrannical sentence of the pope, passed and pronounced against him he thought good by his letters, to let all christian princes and potentates understand, as well what injurious and manifold displeasure he had sustained by the four preceding popes in their times, as also the cruelty and tyranny of this pope, in pronouncing the sentence of judgment and condemnation against him passing the bounds both of justice, equity, and reason.

This policy the pope used to disturb Germany, and the whole empire; and utterly to destroy and subvert the same. And thus, Germany was divided, some taking part with Frederick the emperor; some with those that should by the pope's appointment be the electors of the new emperor, and thus was the public peace and quiet broken, and all together in tumult.

By these civil wars, Germany suffered no little calamity; in every place was manslaughter and murder, the country spoiled, the towns and villages set on fire and burnt, the churches and temples, wherein the husbandmen had put their goods and substance, violated and robbed; houses were pulled down, the goods divided, and every man's cattle driven away. To conclude, in this turmoil and contention of deposing and choosing another emperor, in this faction of princes, and this liberty of wearing armour; in this licence of hurting and sinning, the impudent boldness of private soldiers, and especially of such as were the horsemen, then counted the better sort of soldiers, was so great, and their unbridled and unsatiable desire in robbing, spoiling and taking of booties, catching and snatching all that came to hand, so much, that nothing could be sure and in safety that any good man enjoyed.

Otho Boius, however, kept his promise and faith which he had pledged before to the emperor Frederick and Conrad his son. Whereupon Philip Javavensis, Albert and others calling a council at Mildorsus by the pope's commandment, sent for Otho, to whom they opened the pope's pleasure and commandment. To all which when he had heard, Otho answered, "I cannot marvel at some of you enough, that, when heretofore you persuaded me to leave and forsake the part I took with the bishop of Rome, whom you yourselves affirmed to be Antichrist and that I should take part with the emperor, you yourselves will not keep your fidelity and promise made to those good princes." And he said, that " he perceived in them a great inconstancy and levity, both in their words and deeds, who now call that wicked, unjust and violent wrong, that but lately they thought equal, just and right." He said further, " that they were overcome with pleasures, corrupted with superfluity, won with bribes, gaping for honour and estimation ; and that they neither regarded honesty, godliness, nor their duty and office ; but studied how to make dissension and commotions, and longed after war and bloody battle."

He said further, that for his part he would obey God and his prince, to whom he had sworn fidelity ; and that he nought esteemed the feigned holiness and detestable practices of such prelates. He said he believed in Christ, and would trust to his mercy ; and that he believed how those whom they cursed and gave to the devil, were in the greatest favour with God. However, those prelates took in good part this expostulation of his, and seemed to bear Otho no malice or grudge for what he had said, but to be desirous of peace and unity ; yet not long after Otho was cursed as black as all the rest, and counted as bad as the worst.

Albert the pope's champion now bethought him of a mischievous device against Conrad Cæsar the emperor's son. Albert with certain of his confederates, by means of Ulric a chief officer of the monks, came in the dead time of the night into the chamber, where the Cæsar with a few others about him was lying down ; and falling upon them, they took some, and slew others ; and finding no other body in the chamber or lodging, they thought that Cæsar had been slain among the rest. But he hearing the noise, forsook his bed, and hid himself under a bench, and so escaped their hands. The next day he outlawed or proscribed the bishop and his companions, and also the monk's bailiff for treason, and seized upon all the goods of the house. But at the suit of the guiltless monks he released all to them again, taking by way of fine one hundred pounds. Ulric lost his office, and Albert, to escape punishment, took the habit of a monk. Conrad Hochenfolseus, who was the murderer of these men, though he escaped the punishment of man's hand, yet the vengeance of God for the fact he escaped not. For as he was riding in the day time abroad, he was suddenly stricken with a thunderbolt and died.

During all this busy and contentious time, it may well be gathered, that Frederick was not still, but had his hands full suppressing these rebellious Popish tumults, and having done strict execution on those that had conspired against his person, he came to Cremona and took with him the wisest, most virtuous, and best learned men that there were, thinking with them to have gone himself to Lyons to the pope, and there to have communication with him as well concerning the sentence, as also about the conclusion of some peace, if by any means he might. And when all things were prepared and ready, he took the journey in hand. When within three days' journey of Lyons, he was certified that Parma was taken by the outlaws of sundry factions of the pope ; when he understood this and that the pope was the chief actor, he saw manifestly it would little prevail to attempt any further the thing he went about, and then at length when he saw no other remedy, putting from him all hope of peace, he prepared himself to the wars with all his force and might. Thus altering his purpose and journey, he took the straightest way into Lombardy, and with an army of sixty thousand men he besieged Parma. In the beginning all things prospered well with Frederick, and had good success ; for he sharply repelled the charges of them that defended the city of Parma. And further, Robert Castilion, who was the emperor's lieutenant in Picenum near to Auximum, discomfited the pope's army, and slew of them more than four thousand, and took many such as were of the confederate cities prisoners. But this good success and prosperous fortune lasted not long. For when Frederick to recreate himself (as he seldom had his health) rode about the fields with some of his horsemen to hawk and hunt, many of the soldiers wandered and ranged unarmed about the fields. The soldiers in Parma, having this opportunity, entered with all force and speed possible the emperor's camp, which not being strongly fenced, nor having gates to shut against them, was a thing easy enough to do. When they had killed and slain a great number of the emperor's soldiers, and had burnt and destroyed the camp, they came again to Parma.

After this also, Richard in another conflict in Picenum, discomfited the pope's soldiers, and slew their captain Hugolinus, besides two thousand others slain and taken prisoners. When Frederick had now again gathered, and new mustered his bands at Dominum, he marched forth to Cremona ; and notwithstanding that there he understood of the good success and victory that Encius had at Rhegium, yet he perceived the defection of the most part of Lombardy from him, and he determined to take his journey into Apulia, and when he had there levied a strong and sufficient army, he purposed to make his speedy return again into Lombardy.

When news was brought him thither, that Encius his son (coming to aid the Mutinenses against the Bononians) was taken prisoner two miles from Mutina ; and that in his absence, the pope's captains, with their bands and garrisons, went throughout all Lombardy, Emilia, Flamminia, and Etruria, to stir and procure the cities to revolt from the obedience of the emperor, and working the same partly by subtle policies, and partly by force and sinister means to bring them to his purpose : he determined, with all the force and power he might by any means procure, to begin afresh, and prosecute this war to the utmost. Nor was it to be doubted but that he would have wrought some marvellous exploit and great attempt, but that he was prevented by unlooked-for death. When he fell into this ague, which led to his death, he made and ordained his testament. And when to Conrad and his other children he had given and appointed the great and innumerable mass of money which he had collected and levied for the maintenance of his wars, and godly purpose (as it is called) and also had given all his kingdoms and dominions (to every one according to their ages and years) he departed this wretched and miserable world.

Pandolph writes, that Frederick was very willing to die, and, as they made certain report to him who were present at his death, that his mind was altogether set and bent on heavenly joy and felicity. He died in A. D. 1250, the 13th of December, in the seven-and-fiftieth year of his age, and seven-and-thirtieth year of his reign.

This Frederick had not his equal in martial affairs, and in warlike policies none could be compared to him among all the princes of that age : he was a wise and skilful soldier, a great endurer of painful labours, most bold in greatest perils, prudent in foresight, industrious in all his doings, prompt and nimble about what he took in hand, and in adversity most stout and courageous. But as in this corruption of nature, there are few that attain perfection, neither yet is there any prince of such government and godly institution both in life and doctrine as is required of them : so neither was this Frederick without his fault and human frailty, for the writers impute to him some faults wherewith he was stained and spotted.

As you have heard of the iniquity and raging pride of the popish church against the lawful emperor ; so now you shall hear how God begins to resist and withstand the corruption of that church, by stirring up certain faithful teachers in sundry countries ; as in Suevia, (about A. D. 1240), where many preachers, mentioned in Urspergensis, and also in Crantzius, (lib. viii. cap. 16 and 18), preached against the pope. These preachers (as Crantzius saith) ringing the bells, and calling together the barons in Hallis of Suevia, preached that the pope was a heretic, and that his bishops and prelates were simoniacs and heretics ; and that the inferior priests and prelates had no authority to bind and loose, but were all deceivers. That no pope, bishop, or priest could restrain men from their duty of serving and worshipping God ; and therefore such cities or countries, as were then under the pope's curse, might lawfully resort to the receiving of sacraments as well as before. That friars, Dominican, and Franciscan, subverted the church with their preaching. And that the indulgence of the pope was of no value. And thus much I thought here to recite, whereby it may appear how the resisting of the pope's usurped power and corrupt doctrine is no new thing in these days in the church of Christ.

And not long after rose up Arnold De Nova Villa, a Spaniard, and a man famously learned and a great writer, (A. D. 1250), whom the pope condemned among heretics for holding and writing against the corrupt errors of the popish church. His teaching was, that Satan had seduced the world from the truth of Christ Jesus. That the faith (which then christian men were commonly taught) was such a faith as the devils had; meaning belike (as we now affirm) that the papists do teach only the historical faith, that christian people (meaning the most part) are led by the pope unto hell. That all monks and nuns are void of charity and damned; that masses are not to be celebrated; and that they ought not to sacrifice for the dead.

And as this Arnold was condemned, so also at the same time John Semeca, the gloss-writer of the pope's decrees, and provost of Halberstat was excommunicated and deprived of his provostship, for resisting Pope Clement IV. in gathering his exactions in Germany; and therefore he appealed from the pope to a general council, and had many great favourers on his side, till at last both the pope and he died.

Then followed the worthy and valiant champion of Christ, and adversary of antichrist William de St. Amore, a master of Paris, and chief ruler of that university. This William in his time had no small ado writing against the friars, and their hypocrisy, condemning their whole order. All the testimonies of scripture that make against antichrist, he applied against the clergy of prelates, and the popish spirituality. He compiled many worthy works, wherein, although he uttered nothing but truth, yet he was by antichrist condemned for a heretic, exiled, and his books burnt.

In the days of this William there was a most detestable and blasphemous book set forth by the friars, which they called "The Everlasting Gospel," or "The Gospel of the Holy Ghost." In which book many abominable errors of the friars were contained, so that the gospel of Jesus Christ was utterly defaced, which, this book said, was not to be compared with this Everlasting Gospel, no more than the shell is to be compared with the kernel, than darkness to light, &c. Moreover, that the gospel of Christ shall be preached no longer than fifty years, and then that this "Everlasting Gospel" should rule the church, &c. Also, that whatever was in the whole bible, was likewise contained in this new gospel. At length this friars' gospel was accused to the pope, and six persons were chosen to peruse and judge of the book, among whom this William was one, who mightily impeached this pestiferous and devilish book. These six, after perusing the book, were sent to Rome. The friars likewise sent their messenger, where they were refuted, and the book condemned; but the pope commanded the book to be condemned not publicly, but privately, wishing to preserve the estimation of the religious orders, as of his own chief champions.

Among the others of that age, who withstood the bishop of Rome and his antichristian errors, was one Lawrence an Englishman, and master of Paris; another was Peter John, a minorite. Lawrence was about the year A. D. 1260; in his teaching, preaching, and writing, he stoutly defended William de St. Amore against the friars. Other things also he wrote, wherein by various proofs and testimonies he argued, that antichrist was not far off to come.

The other, Peter John, was about the year A.D. 1290. He taught and maintained many things against the pope, proving that he was antichrist, and that the synagogue of Rome was Babylon.

To these is to be added Robert Gallus, who being born of a noble parentage, for devotion sake was made a dominican friar about the year A.D. 1290. This man calls the pope an idol, who having eyes sees not, neither desires to see the abominations of his people, nor the excessive enormity of their licentiousness, but only to see to the heaping up of his own treasure.

It is time that we return to our own country again. Wherein following the course of time, we will now add the bishop of Lincoln, named Robert Grosthead, a man famously learned in Latin, Greek, and Hebrew, and in all liberal sciences; his works and sermons are yet extant. He was a man of excellent wisdom, of profound doctrine, and an example of all virtue. He set forth many books concerning philosophy. Afterward being doctor in divinity, he drew out several treatises out of the Hebrew glosses, and translated divers works out of the Greek. Many other works and volumes besides were written by Grosthead.

This godly and learned bishop, after many conflicts sustained against the bishop of Rome, at length, after great labour and trouble of life, finished his course A.D. 1253. Of his decease Matthew Paris thus writes, (fol. 278) "Out of the prison and banishment of this world (which he never loved) was taken the holy bishop of Lincoln, Robert; who was an open reprover of the pope and of the king, a rebuker of the prelates, a corrector of the monks, a director of the priests, an instructor of the clerks, a favourer of scholars, a preacher to the people, a persecutor of the incontinent, a diligent searcher of the scripture, a mallet against the Romans, and a contemner of their doings, &c. What a mallet he was to the Romans in the sequel shall better appear.

Pope Innocent had a certain cousin or nephew (so popes were wont to call their sons) named Frederick, being yet young and under years, whom Innocent would needs prefer to be a canon or prebendary in the church of Lincoln, in the time of Robert bishop of that church; and he directed letters to certain here in England for the execution thereof.

It is no great wonder if this godly bishop Robert Grosthead was offended with these letters; he deserves a double commendation, in that he was so firm and constant in standing against the pope, according as his answer to the pope appears, wherein he denounces the pope's attempt to appoint one who would not be a true pastor, saying, among other things:—

"This would be a great apostasy, corruption, and abuse of the seat and fulness of power, and an utter separation from the glorious throne of our Lord Jesus Christ, and a near approach to the two principal princes of darkness, sitting in the chair of pestilence, prepared for the pains of hell (i. e. Lucifer and antichrist). Neither can any man, who is faithful to the see, obey with sincere and unspotted conscience such precepts and commandments, or other such attempts, even though proceeding from the high order of angels themselves, but rather ought with all their strength to withstand and rebel against them. Wherefore, my reverend lord, I, like an obedient child, upon my bounden duty of obedience and fidelity which I owe to the holy and apostolic see, and partly for love of unity in the body of Christ, do not obey but withstand and utterly rebel against these things contained in the letter, and which especially urge and tend to the aforesaid wickedness, so abominable to the Lord Jesus Christ, so repugnant to the holiness of the holy apostolic see, and so contrary to the unity of the catholic faith."

Then it follows, in the history both of Matthew Paris, and of Florilegus, in these words:—

"That when this epistle came to the knowledge of the pope, he, fuming and fretting with anger and indignation, answered with a fierce look and proud mind, saying, What old doting frantic wretch is this, so boldly and rashly to judge of my doings? By St. Peter and Paul, were it not but that we are restrained by our own clemency and good nature, we would hurl him down to such confusion, that we would make him, a fable, a gazing-stock, an example and wonderment to all the world. For is not the king of England our vassal? and, to say more, our errand-boy or page, who may at our pleasure and beck both hamper him, imprison him, and put him to utter shame? When the pope in his great fury and rage had uttered this among his brethren the cardinals, they were scarce able to appease his furious violence."

Not long after this, this reverend and godly Robert, bishop of Lincoln, fell grievously sick, and within a few days departed. In the time of his sickness he called to him a certain friar of the preaching order, a man expert and cunning both in physic and divinity, partly to receive of him some comfort of his body, and partly to confer with him in spiritual matters. Thus upon a certain day, the bishop reciting the doings of the pope, rebuked and reprehended severely the preaching friars, and the other order also of the minors. The vehemency of his disease more and more increasing, and because the nights were somewhat longer, the third night before his departure, the bishop, feeling his infirmity to grow, directed certain of his clergy to be called to him, that he might be refreshed with some conference or communication with them. To them the bishop mourning and lamenting in his mind for the loss of souls, reproved such detestable enormities of the court of Rome, as, all kinds of avarice, the usury, the simony, the extortion, all kinds of filthiness, gluttony, and their sumptuous apparel in that court; afterwards he went about to prosecute more, how the court of Rome, like a gulf, never satisfied, ever gaping so wide, that the flood of Jordan might run into his mouth, aspired how to possess himself of the goods of them that die intestate, and of legacies bequeathed without form of law; and in order the more licentiously to bring this to pass, they used to join the king, as partaker with them in their spoils, extortions, and robbing. "Neither," saith he, "shall the church be delivered from the servitude of Egypt, but by violence and force, and with the bloody sword." "And although," saith he, "these be yet but light matters, yet shortly more great and grievous things than these shall be seen."

And in the end of this which he scarcely could utter without sighing, sobbing, and weeping, his tongue and breath began to fail, and so his voice being stopped, he made an end of both his speech and life. (Matth. Paris.)

Ye have heard it often complained of, how the pope violently encroached upon the church of England, in giving benefices and prebends to his Italians and strangers, to the great damage and ruin of Christ's flock. This injury could by no lawful and gentle means be reformed; so about this time it began to be somewhat bridled by means of another kind. In the reign of this king, the bishop of London, named Fulco, had given a certain prebend, in the church of St. Paul, to one Rustand, the pope's messenger here in England, who, dying shortly after, the pope immediately conferred the prebend on one of his specials, a stranger as the other was. About the same instant, it befel that the bishop of London also died, by which the vacant bishopric fell into the king's hands, who, hearing of the death of Rustand, gave the prebendship to one John Crakehale, who, with all solemnity, took his installation, not knowing as yet that it was already bestowed by the pope on another. Not long after, this being noised at Rome, forthwith comes down a proctor, with the pope's letters, to receive collation to the benefice, wherein John Crakehale had been already installed by the king's donation. This matter coming before Boniface archbishop of Canterbury, he, inquiring and searching which donation was the first, and finding it was the pope's grant, gave sentence with him against the king; so that in conclusion, the Roman clerk had the advantage of the benefice, although the other had long enjoyed the possession. Thus the pope's man being preferred, and the Englishman excluded, after the party had been invested and stalled, he, thinking himself in sure possession, attempted to enter the chapter-house, but was not permitted, whereupon the pope's clerk, giving place to force and number, went to the archbishop to complain. This being known, certain monks pursued him, and one in the thickness of the throng, who was never after known, suddenly rushed upon him, and cut off his head. This heinous murder being famed abroad, a strict inquiry was made, but the murderer could not be known; and although great suspicion was laid upon Crakehale, the king's chaplain, yet no proof could be brought against him. But most men thought, that this bloody act was done by certain ruffians about the city or the court, who disdained that Romans should be so enriched with Englishmen's livings. And therefore because they saw the church and realm of England in such subjection, and so much trodden down by the Romans and the pope's messengers, they thought by such means to prevent them from coming so much into this land.

Besides many other matters, I pass over the conflict,—not between the frogs and the mice which Homer writes of,—but the mighty pitched field, fought A.D. 1259, between the young students and scholars of the university of Oxford, having no other occasion, but the difference of the country where they were born. For the northerns, joining with the Welch, to try their manhood against the southerns, fell on them with their ensigns and warlike array, so that in the end several on both sides were slain. This heavy and bloody conflict increased among them, and the end was that the northern lads with the Welch had the victory. After fury and fiery fierceness had done what it could, the victors thinking partly of what they had done, partly how it would be taken by the higher powers, and fearing punishment, took counsel together, and offered to king Henry four thousand marks, to Edward his son three hundred, and to the queen two hundred, to be released of all punishment. But the king answered that he set a higher value on the life of one true subject than on all they offered, and would not receive the money. The king, however, being then occupied in great affairs and wars, and partly involved in discord at home with his nobles, had no leisure to attend to the correction of these university men. (Matth. Paris.)

This that follows concerning the commotion between the king and the nobles, is lamentable, and contains much fruitful example, both for princes and subjects, to see what mischief grows in the commonwealth, where the prince regards not offending his subjects, and where the subjects forget the office of christian patience in suffering their princes' injuries; therefore, I thought it not unprofitable to occupy the reader a little in perusing this lamentable matter.

King Henry married Elenor, daughter of the earl of Provence, by which a great door was opened for foreigners, not only to enter the land, but also to fill the court; to them the king seemed more to incline his favour, advancing them to greater preferment than his own English lords, which was no little grievance to them. The king, too, by Isabel his mother, who was a foreigner, had several brothers, whom he supported with great livings and possessions, and large pensions, which was another heart-sore and hinderance to his nobles. Over and besides which, there were unreasonable collections of money from time to time, levied by the king, as well on the spirituality, as on the laity. By reason of all which collections, the commonwealth of the realm was utterly stripped, to the great impoverishment of the English.

In the year 1260, a great number of aliens resorted to England, and had the management of all principal matters of the realm under the king, which not a little troubled the nobility of England. So that Simon Montfort earl of Leicester, offering to stand to death for the liberties of the realm, conferred with other lords and barons upon the matter, who, then coming to the king with an humble sort of petition, declared how all his realm, and his own affairs were altogether disposed by the hands and after the wills of strangers, neither profitable to him, nor to the public weal; for his treasures being wasted and himself in great debt, he was not able to satisfy the provision of his own house. And now therefore, said they, if your highness will please to be informed by our advice, and to commit your house to the guiding and government of your own faithful and natural subjects, we will take upon us to discharge your whole debt within one year, out of our own proper goods and revenues, so as that we within five years may repay ourselves again.

To these words so lovingly declared,—so humbly pretended,—so heartily and freely offered, the king so willingly condescended, assigning to them both day and place where to confer and to deliberate further upon the matter, which should be at Oxford the fifteenth day after Easter. At which day and place all the states and lords, with the bishops of the realm, were summoned to appear. Where an oath was taken, first by the king himself, then by the lords, that what decrees or laws should in the said assembly be provided to the profit of the king and of the realm, the same should universally be kept and observed to the honour of God, and utility of his church, and wealth of the realm. Besides these lords and the king, there were also nine bishops, who swearing to the same, excommunicated all such as should withstand the provisions there made ; the king holding a burning taper in his hand, and the lords openly protesting to rise with all their force against all that shall stand against the same.

In this assembly it was enacted that all strangers and aliens of what state or condition soever, should forthwith leave the realm on pain of death. Various other provisions were ordained and established at the same time, that if any held of the king in whole or in part, and should die (while his heir was under age,) the wardship of the heir should belong to the king.

Moreover, it was there decreed, that the wool of England should be wrought only within the realm, neither should it be transported out to foreigners.

That no man should wear any cloth, but which was wrought and made within the realm.

That garments too sumptuous should not be brought in nor worn.

That all excessive and prodigal expenses, wasted upon pleasure and superfluity, should be avoided by all persons.

Many other laws and decrees were ordained in this assembly, which continued the space of fifteen days.

After the promulgation of the laws many things displeased the king, and he began to repent of his oath. But because he could not at that present otherwise choose, he dissembled for a season. Within a year following, (A.D. 1261), the king sent to the pope, praying both for himself and his son Edward to be released of their oath made at Oxford. This absolution being easily obtained (or rather bought at the pope's hands) the king stepping back from all that was before concluded, calls another parliament at Oxford, where before the lords and nobles he declared, how in the late council of Oxford they had agreed on certain measures for the common utility of the realm of the king, as they pretended, for the increasing of his treasure, and diminishing his debt ; and thereupon bound themselves with an oath, causing also himself and his son Edward to be bound to the same. But now that they, contrary to their covenant made, sought not so much the profit of him and of the realm, as their own, taking him not as their lord, but going about to bring him under their subjection ; and that moreover his treasure greatly decreasing, his debts increasing, and his princely liberality cut short and trodden under foot, they should not marvel, if he henceforth would be no more ruled by their counsel, but would provide himself with some other remedy. And moreover, as to the oath wherewith he and his son stood bound to them, he had sent already to Rome, and had obtained absolution and dispensation of the same, both for him, and his son Edward, and for all others that would take his part. And therefore he required of them to be restored again to that state and condition he had enjoyed in times past.

To this the nobility gave answer on the other side, in the number of whom was Simon Montfort earl of Leicester, Richard Clare earl of Gloucester, with many more ; whose answer to the king was, " that the provisions made at the council at Oxford, to which they were sworn, they would hold, defend and maintain to their lives' end." All this while, the pope's absolution for the king, although it was granted and obtained at Rome, yet was not brought down in solemn writing.

At length, the writing of the king's absolution being brought from Rome, the king soon commanded it to be published throughout the realm, and sends to the French king and other strangers for help ; moreover he seized all his castles into his own hand, rejecting the counsel of the lords, to whose custody they were before committed ; also removing the former officers, as justices, the chancellor, with others placed before by the lords, he appointed new ones in their stead.

After this followed the year 1263, in which the barons of England, confederating themselves together, for maintaining the statutes and laws of Oxford, and partly moved with their old dislike conceived against the foreigners, joined all their forces, and attacked the foreigners who were about the king. Their goods and

manors they wasted and spoiled, whether they were persons ecclesiastical or temporal. By reason of this it came to pass, that a great number of foreigners especially monks, and rich priests, were urged to such extremity, that they were glad to flee the land.

In the mean time, the king keeping then in the Tower, and seeing the greatest part of his nobles and commons with the Londoners set against him, agreed to the peace of the barons, and was contented to assent again to the ordinances and provisions of Oxford ; although the queen, by all means possible, went about to persuade the king not to assent thereto ; so that as she was endeavouring to pass by barge from the Tower to Windsor, the Londoners standing on the bridge with their exclamations, cursing and throwing of stones and dirt at her, interrupted her course, forcing her to return to the Tower again.

When this contention was referred to the French king, and he decided against the barons, it wrought in their hearts great indignation, and they hastened home to defend themselves with all their strength and power. The king called his council together at Oxford, whence he excluded the university of students for a season ; and hearing that the barons were assembled in a great number at Northampton, went there with his host, and with his banners displayed. The king commanded the barons that were therein, to yield the city to him, or he would immediately destroy them. But they boldly, and with one mind answered, That they would not obey the king's will, but would rather defend themselves and the city, if need were, even to the death. Which the noblemen of the king's part hearing, sent word again, that at least they should come to the wall of the city to speak to the king, if by any means peace might be made. And they, suspecting no deceit, came to the wall. But in the mean time, while matters were reasoned and treated of, the Lord Philip Basset, with mattocks and other instruments, undermined the wall of the city ; and the wall fell down, and there was made a great plain, so that there might have gone together forty horsemen abreast. And of this subtlety the foreign monks were thought to be the workers, because they made way and entrance for them that came in. But when they that passed by saw this, and the king's banners were erected ready to enter in, there was a great howling made, and the noise of the people came to the ears of the barons, and they made speed to resist them, but it was all in vain, because they were already prevented by a great company of their enemies. But the clerks of the university of Oxford, (which university by the barons' commandment was translated thither) did the king's men more hurt than the barons, with their slings, long bows, and crossbows, for they had a banner by themselves, that was set up on high against the king. The king being greatly moved, sware at his entering in, that they should all be hanged. Which when they heard, many of them shaved their crowns, and they that were able ran away as fast as they could. And when the king entered the city, many fled in their armour into the castle, others left their horse and armour, and ran into the churches, and a few were slain, and those were of the common people ; but there was not much bloodshed, because all things were done as upon the sudden. When the city was at length set in quiet, the king commanded his oath to be executed upon the clerks. But his counsellors said to him, " This be far from thee, O king, for the sons of thy nobles, and of other great men of thy kingdom, were there gathered together into the university ; whom if thou wouldst cause to be hanged or slain, even they that now take thy part would rise up against thee, not suffering, to the utmost of their powers, the blood of their sons and kinsfolk to be shed." And so the king was pacified, and his wrath against the clerks was appeased.

The king then went to Rochester, and raising the siege, proceeded to Tunbridge, and thence he continued his journey to Winchester, where he received to peace the seamen of the haven towns. And three days after, he came to the town of Lewes, and was received into the abbey, and his son Edward into the castle.

The barons now drew near to the king ; for they were

not far distant from Lewes : and the king's troops being without provision for their horses, it was commanded them to go out and seek for hay : when they were attacked by their enemies, and most of them killed. Then the barons, coming to the full plain, descended there, and girding and trimming their horses, put on their armour. And there the Earl Simon created the earl of Glocester, and Robert de Vere, and many other new knights. Which being done, he divided and distinguished his host into four several divisions, and he appointed noblemen to guide and govern every division. In the meantime the king's host came forth, preparing themselves to the field in three divisions, of which Edward the king's son led the first. The most part of the king's army were but young men, for the king thought not that his barons had come so nigh. Their armies being on both sides set in array and order, they exhorted one another on either party to fight valiantly : and after they buckled together, the battle was great, and many horsemen were overthrown even in a moment. But by and by Edward the king's son with his band, as a fierce young gentleman and valiant knight, fell upon his enemies with such force, that he compelled them to recoil back a great way, so that the hindmost (thinking by reason of their giving back, that the foremost were slain) ran many of them away. Straightway the Londoners, knowing not how the battle went, took to their heels : Edward pursued them with his band, killing them for the space of two or three miles; for he hated them because they had rebelled against his father, and disgraced his mother when she was in her barge upon the Thames, as is before mentioned.

Whilst Prince Edward was thus in chase of the Londoners, the main division of the barons set upon the king's main division, of which the king of Almain the brother of King Henry had the leading, who was soon discomfited, and he with his son Henry and other captains taken prisoners, the reserve where the king himself fought was immediately attacked, and he seeing his knights and soldiers on every side about him beaten down and slain, and his soldiers forsaking the field, retired into the abbey, and shutting up the gates, caused them to be strongly guarded with soldiers. The barons thus getting the field, after a long fight, and many men on both sides slain, entered the town of Lewes.

In the mean time, when Prince Edward returning from the chase of the Londoners, came to the place where the bloody battle had been fought, and saw the great discomfiture and overthrow, which in his absence, had happened with great slaughter, his heart was much dismayed, and his countenance altered. Yet comforting and encouraging his knights and soldiers, of whom he had a valiant company, he marched in battle array toward the town; against whom came the barons again with all their power. And thus was begun between them a fresh field and new battle, and many men slain on both sides. But at length the earl de Warenia, with the king's two brothers, forsook the field and fled : after whom went more than seven hundred chosen soldiers, who were of their house and family, who the same day came to Pevensy, and there took shipping over the sea. Also Hugh Bigot, with several others, fled, and left the valiant prince fighting in the field : upon which he retreated to the town. And when he found not the king at the castle, he went from thence to the abbey where he was. In the meantime the town was divided into parts, some fighting, some spoiling, some getting booties. But when within a while the barons had assembled some company, they gave an assault upon the castle, thinking to have rescued John Gifford and others, whom the king's soldiers had taken prisoners and put therein. But the soldiers within manfully defended it, and in throwing out balls of wild-fire for the defence of it, they fired part of the town. Then the barons retired and left the castle, and purposed to have set upon the abbey where the king and Prince Edward his son was, which also was set on fire by the assault given to the castle; but yet it was shortly recovered and quenched. Then Edward the king's son, perceiving the bold enterprize of the barons, prepared with the courageous knights and soldiers, who yet remained within the abbey, to have issued out, and to have given a new charge upon them. But the barons, perceiving that, sent to the king messengers to intreat a truce for that day, and on the morrow to talk and conclude of a further peace between them, when Prince Edward was given as hostage for the king and his party, and Henry, son of the king of Almain, for his father.

In this year also, Boniface, archbishop of Canterbury, a foreigner, having been some years beyond the seas in disgrace with the king of England, upon occasion of some misdemeanour, the king being of a relenting nature, and bearing much with clergymen's insolencies, consulted with his nobles about the return of Boniface into England.

After much ado, we read that Boniface returned, and becoming more holy towards his death, he went with other bishops to the king, requesting him, that being mindful of the decay of his kingdom, by ecclesiastical livings bestowed upon foreigners, he would hereafter prefer learned and godly men of his own nation. The king answered that he would willingly do it. "Wherefore I think it meet that you, who are yourself a foreigner and unlearned, and also my brother Ethelmer, bishop of Winchester, whom I have preferred to such dignities only for kindred's sake, should first give examples to others, and forsake your churches, and I will provide other learned men to serve in them." Which answer of the king so pierced this Boniface, that he always after lived a wearisome life in England. Wherefore, perceiving himself to be disliked of the king and the people, he desired to return into his country. And thereupon first felling and selling the woods, letting out the archbishopric, taking great fines of his tenants, and making a great mass of money of the clergy of his province, he went with the curse of all men unto Savoy, and soon after died.

After the death of Pope Urban, succeeded Pope Clement IV. (A.D. 1265.) Clement, (as affirmeth Nic. Trivet), was first a married man, and had wife and children, and was solicitor and counsellor to the French king; then after the death of his wife, was bishop; and afterwards archbishop of Narbon; and at last made cardinal; and being sent as legate by Pope Urban, was in his absence elected pope by the cardinals.

Now, after all the tumults and broils of the king and his barons, to the vexation of the whole land, it was thought meet and necessary that all parties at variance should be reconciled. Whereupon peace was made between them.

The king now was at leisure to reform the abuses of the church; and as he considered that non-residence being a blame worthy abuse, required reformation, he wrote his mind to the bishop of Hereford for the redress of the same ; his letter, because it is memorable, and the matter contained in it is applicable to non-residents of our time, we have here inserted it.

A Letter of King Henry III. to the Bishop of Hereford concerning Non-residence.

The king to the bishop of Hereford sendeth greeting : Pastors or shepherds are set over flocks, that by exercising themselves in watching over them day and night, they may know their own cattle by their look, bring the hunger-starved sheep into the meadows of fruitfulness, and the straying ones into one fold by the word of salvation, and the rod of correction ; and to do their endeavour, that indissoluble unity may be kept. But some there are who damnably despising this doctrine, and not knowing how to discern their own cattle from others, take away the milk and the wool, not caring how the Lord's flock may be nourished ; they catch up the temporal goods, and who perishes in their parish with famishment, or miscarries in manners, they regard not ; which men deserve not to be called pastors, but rather hirelings. And even we in these days, when removing ourselves into the borders of Wales, to take order for the disposing of the garrisons of our realm, have found this default in your church of Hereford ; we report it with grief ; for we have found there a church destitute of a pastor's comfort, as having neither bishop nor official, vicar nor dean, that may exercise any spiritual function and duty in the same. But the church itself, which in time past was wont to flow in delight, (and had canons that attended upon service day and night, and that ought to exercise the works of charity, they forsaking the church, and leading their lives in countries far hence,) hath put off her stole or robe of pleasure, and fallen to the ground, bewailing her widow-hood, and there is none among all her friends and lovers that will comfort her. Verily while we beheld this, and considered diligently, pity did move our bowels, and the sword of compassion did inwardly wound our heart very sore, that we could no longer dissemble so great an injury done to our mother the church, nor pass the same over uncorrected.

"Wherefore we command and straitly charge you, that all occasions set aside, you endeavour to remove yourselves with all possible speed unto your church, and there per-sonally execute the pastoral charge committed unto you in the same. Otherwise we will you to know for cer-tainty that if you have not a care to do this, we will wholly take into our own hands all the temporal goods, and whatsoever else does belong unto the barony of the same church, which goods, it is certain our progenitors of godly devotion have bestowed thereupon for spiritual exercise sake. And such goods and duties as we have commanded hitherto to be gathered and safely kept and turned to the profit and commodity of the same church, the cause now ceasing we will seize upon ; and suffer no longer that he shall reap temporal things, who fears not unreverently to withdraw and keep back spiritual things, whereunto by office and duty he is bound ; or that he shall receive any profits who refuses to undergo and bear the burthens of the same. Witness the king at Hereford, the first of June, in the forty-eighth year of our reign."

But leaving these affairs of the church, and church-men, we will now enter into other troubles of the tempo-ral state. You heard before of a pacification concluded between the king and his barons, when Prince Edward was given as hostage (A.D. 1264.) But it came to pass among the lords and barons, that no such firm recon-ciliation was made as was likely to last long. For in the year 1265, the sons of the Earl Simon did that which much displeased the earl of Gloucester : inso-much that he challenged Henry, the eldest son of the Earl Simon Montfort : this affair, however, was settled without fighting, but afterwards the earl of Gloucester sent to the Lord Roger Mortimer, who always took the king's part, desiring that they two might talk together about the interests of the king. When they met, the earl of Gloucester shewed him all that he purposed to do, and lamenting that he had so offended the king, said he would now make amends, and would deliver Prince Ed-ward, so they sent secretly to Robert the brother of the earl of Gloucester, who was near about the Earl Simon, and made him consent with them. And to work this more circumspectly, Roger Mortimer sent to Edward, the king's son, a horse excelling all others in fleetness, to which he might safely trust, when he saw conveni-ent opportunity. After which things thus contrived, Prince Edward desired leave of the Earl Simon to prove his courser against such time as he should ride at the tilt. As soon as he had got leave, and that with gallop-ing and ranging the field, he had wearied several of their horses : at the last, getting up upon that fleet horse which was sent for that purpose, and spying a servant on horse-back coming toward him with two swords, he turned about to his keeper, and to others that were with him, saying, "My loving lords, thus long have I kept your company, and have been in your custody ; and now not purposing to use your company any longer, I commit you to God." And quickly turning his horse about, put to the spurs, and away he went. The others pricked after apace, but could not overtake him. When the prince's escape was publicly known, much people came to him out of every quarter, with great joy. Among whom the first was the earl of Gloucester, and the other soldiers of the king, and within a short space he had a great and a mighty host.

Which when the Earl Simon understood, he much doubted and mistrusted himself ; and sending into Wales, he got from thence a great many men, and augmented his force as strongly as he could from every part of England. He sent also Simon his son to the noblemen of the northern parts, that with all possible speed he might bring them with him ; who with a great com-pany came with him, and staid a while at Kenilworth, and there pitched their tents. And when this was de-clared to Edward, he prepared himself in the night, to go to the place where Simon and his company had pitched. In the morning they were very early in arming themselves, and met some of their enemies straggling loosely, and thinking to have gone a foraging ; whom they took, and with their fresh horses new horsed their sol-diers that had their horses tired with long travel. And so marching forward, came very early in the morning upon their enemies, whom for the most part they found sleeping ; and laying lustily about them, they slew seve-ral ; some they took, the rest they put to flight, and fifteen of their chiefest ensigns they took, with many other rich spoils.

But when Edward heard that Earl Simon was coming to-ward Kenilworth, to join with his son's battle, he march-ed forward to meet him the third day after at Evesham. Edward caused his own standards and ensigns to be taken down, and young Simon's, which he had taken, to be displayed ; so that the Earl Simon thinking them to have been his son's army, and not knowing of his overthrow, was deceived, till his scout the better to descry them, went up to the abbey steeple, where he could plainly dis-cern them and all their standards ; for by this time they had mounted the hill, thinking to have that advantage, when they should give their charge, and they had also dis-played again his own standards. Then he cried aloud to the Earl Simon, and said, "We are all but dead men ; for it is not your son, as you suppose, that comes, but it is Edward the king's son that comes from one part, and the earl of Gloucester from another part, and Roger Morti-mer from the third part." Then said the earl, "The Lord be merciful to our souls, forsomuch as our bodies and lives are now in their hands ;" commanding that every man should make himself ready to God, and to fight out the field, for that it was their wills to die for their laws, and in a just quarrel. And such as would depart, he gave leave to go their ways, that they should be no discouragement to the rest.

Then came to him his eldest son Henry, and comforted him, desiring him to have no despair, nor yet mistrust in the good success of this victory, with other such cheerful words. "No, my son," says he, "I despair not ; but yet, it is thy presumption, and the pride of the rest of thy brethren that has brought me to this end you see ; not-withstanding, yet I trust I shall die to God, and in a righteous quarrel." After words of comfort given to all his host, and the oration made as is the manner, they all armed themselves. The king also (whom the earl always kept with him) he armed in an armour of his own : and then dividing their battles, they marched towards their enemies. But before they joined, the Welshmen ran away, and thinking to escape over the river Dee, some were drowned, and some slain. Then when the battle joined and they fought hand to hand, in a short time many of the earl's party fell and were slain ; the king himself being struck at, cried with a loud voice to them, saying, "Kill me not, I am Henry your king :" by which words, the Lord Adam Monthaut knew him, and saved him. Also Prince Edward his son, hearing his cry, came and delivered him to the guard and care of certain knights. In the mean time the Earl Simon was hard beset and beaten, and slain before Edward the prince came at him. But before he fell, when he fought for his life, and his son Henry, and other noblemen on his part were about him, he brake out into these words to his enemies, say-ing, "What ! is there no mercy and compassion with you ?" Who again answered, "What compassion should there be shewed to traitors ?" Then said he, "The Lord be merciful to our souls, our bodies are in your hands." And so soon as these words were spoken, they mangled his body, and cut off his head, which head Roger Mortimer sent to his wife. And not far off from him also was slain Henry his eldest son.

After this great slaughter and overthrow there was a parliament summoned at Winchester by the earl of Gloucester, and others. Here it is to be remembered, that although the king was in the camp of the earl of Leicester, being then in custody, and his son Edward with the earl of Gloucester, yet the king was on that side against his will, and therefore in the parliament the king was restored to his kingly dignity, which was before that time under the custody of the barons.

Soon after, a general voyage being proclaimed to war against the Turks, and a subsidy being collected in England for the same, Prince Edward, with others, were appointed to take their voyage, and were now on their journey.

After some stay in Sicily, Prince Edward took shipping again, and soon after Easter arrived at Acre, and went ashore, taking with him a thousand of the best and most expert soldiers, and tarried there a whole month, refreshing both his men and horses, and that in this space he might learn the secrets of the land. After this he took with him six or seven thousand soldiers, and marched forward twenty miles from Acre, and took Nazareth; and slew all those that he found there, and afterwards returned again to Acre; but their enemies following after them, thought to have attacked them unawares. The prince perceiving this, again charged, and slew many of them, and put the rest to flight.

When the fame of Prince Edward thus grew among his enemies, and they began to fear him, they devised among themselves how by some policy they might circumvent and betray him. Whereupon the great prince and admiral of Joppa sent to him, pretending, with great hypocrisy, to become a christian, and that he would draw with him a great number besides, provided they might be honourably entertained and treated by the christians. This pleased the prince well, and induced him to finish the thing, he had begun so well, by writing again; he also sent by the same messenger, and wrote back to him several times about the matter, by which no distrust should arise. When this messenger came the fifth time, and was searched by the prince's servants, according to custom, to see what weapon and armour he had about him, as also his purse; and when not so much as a knife could be found about him, he was brought up into the prince's chamber, and after doing homage, he pulled out certain letters, which he delivered to the prince from his lord, as he had done before; at which time the prince was laid bareheaded upon his bed in his jerkin, for the great heat of the weather.

When the prince had read the letters, it appeared by them, that upon the Saturday next following the prince of Joppa would be there ready to accomplish all that he had written and promised. The report of this news by the prince to those standing by pleased them well, and they drew somewhat back to consult about it among themselves. In the meantime the messenger kneeling and making his obeisance to the prince (questioning further with him) put his hand to the belt, as though he would have pulled out some secret letters, and suddenly he pulled out an envenomed knife, thinking to have stricken him therewith as he lay there on the bed; but the prince lifting up his hand to defend his body from the blow, received a great wound in the arm: and the assassin being about to fetch another stroke at him, the prince with his foot gave him such a kick that he felled him to the ground. With that the prince got him by the hand, and wrested the knife from him with such violence, that he hurt himself with it in the forehead, but immediately thrust the traitorous messenger through and slew him. The prince's servants being in the next chamber not far off, hearing the bustling, came running in with great haste, and finding the messenger lying dead on the floor, one of them took up a stool and beat out his brains; at which the prince was angry, because he struck a dead man, and one that was killed before. The rumour of this attack being so strange, soon went throughout all the court, and from thence among the common people, so that they were very heavy and greatly discouraged. The captain of the temple also came to the prince, and brought him a costly and precious drink against poison, lest the venom of the knife should penetrate the blood; and in a blaming way said to him, "Did I not shew your grace before of the deceit and subtilty of this people? Notwithstanding," saith he, "let your grace take a good heart, you shall not die of this wound, my life for yours." But the surgeons and physicians were immediately sent for, and the prince's wound was dressed, and within a few days after it began to putrefy, and the flesh to look dead and black; whereupon they that were about the prince began to be very sad and heavy: which he perceiving, said to them, "Why do you whisper thus among yourselves? What see you in me, can I not be healed? Tell me the truth, be ye not afraid." Whereupon one said to him, "Your grace, you may be healed, we mistrust it not; but yet it will be very painful for you to suffer."—"May suffering," said he again, "restore health?"—"Yea," saith the other, "on pain of losing my head."—"Then," said the prince, "I commit myself to you, do with me what you think good." Then said one of the physicians, "Is there any of your nobles in whom your grace reposes special trust?" To whom the prince answered, "Yea," naming certain of the noblemen that stood about him. Then said the physician to the two whom the prince first named, the Lord Edmund, and the Lord John Voisie, "And do you also faithfully love your lord and prince?" Who answered both, "Yea, undoubtedly." Then saith he, "Take you away this gentlewoman and lady (meaning his wife) and let her not see her lord and husband until such a time as I tell you." Whereupon they took her out of the prince's presence, crying out and wringing her hands. Then said they unto her, "Be ye contented, good lady and madam; it is better that one woman should weep a little while, than that all the realm of England should weep a great season." Then upon the morrow they cut out all the dead envenomed flesh out of the prince's arm, and said to him, "How cheers your grace? We promise you within these fifteen days you shall shew yourself abroad (if God permit) upon your horseback, whole and well as ever you were." And according to the promise he made the prince so it came to pass, to the no little comfort and admiration of all his subjects. When the great Soldan heard of it, and that the prince was yet alive, he would scarcely believe the same; and sending to him three of his nobles and princes, he excused himself by them, calling his gods to witness, that the same was done neither by him, nor with his consent. Which princes and messengers standing aloof from the king's son, worshipping him, fell flat upon the ground. "You," saith the prince, "do reverence me, but yet you love me not." Nevertheless he treated them honourably, and sent them away in peace.

Thus when Prince Edward had been eighteen months in Acre, he took shipping, returning homeward, and came to Rome, where he was honourably entertained by the pope; from thence he came into France, where his fame and noble prowess was much celebrated among the common people, and envied by the nobility, especially by the Earl de Chalons, who sent him and required him that he might break a staff with him at a tilt in his country. As the prince would not diminish his honour and fame by declining the challenge (although he might have well alleged sufficient excuse), he willingly consented; whereupon it was proclaimed, that Prince Edward by such a day, with those that were with him, had challenged all comers at the tilt and barriers. Then great assemblies were made in the country all about, and several horsemen as well as footmen had sworn among themselves, and conspired against the Englishmen, selling their horses and armour aforehand, and drinking one to another in good success of the spoil of them whom they would take as their prisoners. Prince Edward in the meantime sent into England for certain earls and barons to come to him. When the day appointed was arrived, the prince had with him more than one thousand horsemen, who were knights, besides his footmen, but yet there were as many more on the other side both in horsemen and footmen. When the parties met the French footmen, who had before conspired, began both to spoil, rifle, and kill the Englishmen, who resisted and defended themselves both with bows and slings; slew many of the Frenchmen, and drove them to the gates of their city; the others they chased over a river, where many of them were drowned. In the meantime the Earl de Chalons, with fifty of his knights who followed him, came forth and joined battle with a like number of the prince's followers, and a long time together they tried it with their swords, laying one at another. At the last the earl perceiving himself not able to match with Prince Edward at the arm's end, closed with him, and taking him about the neck, held him with his arms very tight. "What mean you, my lord," said the prince, "think you to have my horse?"—"Yea, marry," said the earl, "I mean to have both thee and thy horse." Hereat Prince Edward, being indignant, lifted up himself, and gave him such a blow, that therewith he, forsaking his horse, hung still about the prince's neck, till he shook him off to the ground, and the prince, being somewhat in a heat, left the grounds to take the air, thereby to refresh himself. But when he saw the injury of the French towards his men, and how they had slain many of them, he said to them, that they used rather the exercise of battle, than of tourney. "Spare ye not, therefore," said he, "from henceforth, any of them all, but give them again as good as they give you." Then they began to kill each other freely on their part, and let their swords work.

And when by this time the English footmen were again returned, and saw the conflicts of the horsemen, and that many of the Englishmen were overthrown; they put themselves amidst the grounds; and some stabbing the horses, some cutting asunder the girths of the Frenchmen's saddles, they overthrew the riders. Then when the Earl De Chalons was horsed again by some of his men and had come among the throng, Prince Edward also rushed in among the thickest, and coupled again with him, and cried to him that he should yield himself as vanquished; but he would not do so, notwithstanding when his strength began to fail him, he was obliged to yield himself to a simple knight, according as Prince Edward bade him, and all the rest of his horsemen and knights fled and saved themselves. However, many of them were slain in that place, and the Englishmen returned having the victory. But when after this they expected to be quiet and at rest, the citizens attacked them unawares by two and by three at once, and killed some of them as they went in the streets. When the prince heard this, he sent for the mayor and burgesses, commanding them to see this matter redressed, and that immediately: for otherwise, by his knighthood he assured them, that upon the morrow he would fire the city, and make it level with the ground. Upon which they went, and set watchmen in many places to keep peace, by which means the prince and his men were in safety and quiet. Thus in this pastime of tourneying, much blood was spilt.

From thence the prince came to Paris, and was honourably entertained by the French king, and after certain days, he went from thence into Gascony, where he stayed till he heard of the death of the king his father.

KING EDWARD THE FIRST.

Edward the eldest son of Henry III., as soon as he heard of his father's death, returned from Gascony home to his country, and was crowned (A.D. 1274.) He then laid down his crown, saying he would no more put it on, before he had gathered together all the lands appertaining to the same. Of the gentle nature of this courageous prince, sufficient proof is given by this one example; at one time he being engaged in his sport of hawking, happened sharply to rebuke the negligence of one of his gentlemen, for what fault I cannot tell, about his hawk; the gentleman being on the other side of the river, hearing his menacing words said, "he was glad that the river was between them." The courageous blood of this prince being moved with this answer, he leaped straight into the flood, which was a swift stream and of a dangerous deepness, and no less hard in getting out: notwithstanding,

either forgetting his own life, or neglecting the present danger, and having a good horse, he ventured his own death, to have the death of his man. At length, with much difficulty recovering the bank, with his sword drawn he pursued his provoker, who having not so good an horse, and seeing himself in danger of being overtaken, reined in his horse, and returning back bareheaded to the prince, submitted his neck under his hand to strike. The prince, whose courage and passion could not be quenched by the water of the whole river, so cooled at the little submission of this man that the quarrel fell, his anger ceased, and his sword was put up without any stroke given. And so both returned to the hunting good friends again.

As Edward urged his claim to Scotland as well as England, and pursued it by force of arms, and as the Scots, &c., saw they could not make their party good, they sent privily to pope Boniface for his aid and counsel, who immediately sent down his precept to the king, that he should cease to disquiet or molest the Scots, for that they were a people exempt from his jurisdiction and properly pertaining to the papal chair. The king briefly made answer, swearing with an oath, that he would to his uttermost keep and defend that which was his right, evidently known as it was to all the world. Thus the Scots bearing themselves bold upon the pope's message, and also confederating themselves with the Frenchmen, passed over that year. The next year (which was the 29th of the king), Pope Boniface directs his letters again to the king, wherein he claims the kingdom of Scotland to be the property of the church of Rome, and not subject to the king of England. And therefore it was against God, against justice, and also prejudicial to the church of Rome, for him to have or to hold any dominion over the same; adding furthermore, that the kingdom of Scotland first was converted by the relics of the blessed apostle St. Peter, through the divine operation of God, to the unity of the catholic faith!

The king, after he had received these letters of the pope, assembled a parliament at Lincoln: by the advice of which he addressed letters in reply to the pope, wherein first in all reverend manner he desires him not to give a light ear to the sinister suggestions of false reports, and imaginers of mischief. Then he declares out of old records and histories from the first time of the Britons, that the realm of Scotland had always from time to time been one with England, beginning first with Brutus in the time of Eli and Samuel the prophet, which Brutus, coming from Troy to this isle, called then Albion, after called by him Britannia, had three sons; Locrinus, to whom he gave that part of the land, called then of him Loegria, now Anglia; Albanactus his second son, to whom he gave Albania, now called Scotia, and his third son Camber, to whom he gave Cambria, now called Wales, &c.—The letter then continued:

"And thus much concerning the first division of this isle, as in ancient histories is found recorded. In which matter, passing over the death of King Humber, the acts of Dunwald king of this realm, the division of Belyn and Brenne, the victories of King Arthur, we will resort (saith the king) to more near times, testified and witnessed by sufficient authors, as Marian Scot, William Malmesbury, Roger Abyndon, Henry Huntington, Radulph de Bizoto and others; all of whom make special declaration, and give manifest evidence of the execution of this our right (saith he) and title of superiority ever continued and preserved hitherto.

"And first to begin with King Edward before the conquest, son to Alfred king of England, about A.D. 900, it is plain and manifest, that he had the king of Scots under his dominion and obedience. And here is to be noted, that this matter was so notorious and manifest, that Marian the Scot, writing that history in those days, grants, confesses and testifies the same; and this dominion continued in that state twenty-three years. At which time, Athelstane succeeded to the crown of England, and having by battle conquered Scotland, he made one Constantine king of that party, to rule and govern the country of Scotland under him, adding this princely word, that it was more honour to him to make a king, than to be a king.

"Twenty-four years after that, (which was A.D. 947) Eldred the king our progenitor, Athelstane's brother, received homage of Irise, then king of Scots.

"Thirty years after that, (which was A.D. 977), King Edgar our predecessor received homage of Kynald king of Scots. Here was a little trouble in England by the death of St. Edward king and martyr, destroyed by the deceit of his mother-in-law, but yet within memory.

"Forty years after the homage done by Kynald to King Edgar, (that is to say, A.D. 1017,) Malcoline the king of Scots did homage to Canute our predecessor. After this homage done, the Scots shewed some piece of their natural disposition, whereupon (by war made by our progenitor St. Edward the Confessor, thirty-and-nine years after that homage done, (that is to say, A.D. 1056) Malcoline king of Scots was vanquished, and the realm of Scotland given to Malcoline his son by our said progenitor St. Edward, unto whom the said Malcoline made homage and fealty.

"Within fifty years after that, William the Conqueror entered this realm, whereof he accounted no perfect conquest until he had likewise subdued the Scots; and therefore in the same year (A.D. 1068), the said Malcoline king of Scots did homage to the said William the Conqueror as his superior, by conquest king of England.

"Twenty-five years after that, (which was A.D. 1093) the said Malcoline did homage and fealty to William Rufus, son to the said William the Conqueror, and yet after that, he was for his offences and demerits deposed, and his son substituted in his place: who likewise failed in his duty. Edgar brother to the last Malcoline, and son to the first, was ordained king of Scotland by the said William Rufus, who did his homage and fealty accordingly.

"Seven years after that, (which was in A.D. 1100), the said Edgar, king of the Scots, did homage to Henry I. our progenitor.

"Thirty-seven years after that, David king of Scots did homage to Matilda the empress, as daughter and heir to Henry I. Wherefore being after required by Stephen, then obtaining possession of the realm, to make his homage: he refused so to do, because he had before made it to Matilda, and thereupon forbare. After David's death, which followed shortly after, the son of the said David made homage to King Stephen.

"Fourteen years after that (which was in A.D. 1150), William king of Scots, and David his brother, with all the nobles of Scotland, made homage to the son of Henry II., with a reservation of their duty to Henry II. his father.

"Twenty-five years after that (which was in A.D. 1175), William king of Scotland, after much rebellion and resistance, according to their natural inclination (king Henry II. then being in Normandy) acknowledged finally his error, and made his peace and composition, confirmed with his great seal, and the seals of the nobility of Scotland, making therewith his homage and fealty.

"Within fifteen years after that (which was in A.D. 1190), the said William king of Scots came to our city of Canterbury, and there did homage to our noble progenitor King Richard I.

"Fourteen years after that, the said William did homage to our progenitor King John, upon a hill besides Lincoln, making his oath upon the cross of Hubert, then archbishop of Canterbury, being there present, and a marvellous multitude assembled for that purpose.

"Twenty-six years after that (which was in A.D. 1230), Alexander king of Scots married Margaret the daughter of our progenitor Henry III. at our city of York, in the feast of Christmas. At which time the said Alexander did his homage to our said progenitor, who reigned in this realm fifty-six years. And therefore between the homage made by the said Alexander king of Scotland, and the homage done by Alexander, son to the said king of Scots, to us at our coronation at Westminster, there was about fifty years. At which time, the said Alexander king of Scots repaired to the said feast of our coronation, and there did he his duty as is aforesaid."

In the year 1303, William Wallace in his rebellion, gathered great multitudes of the Scots to withstand the king, till at length he was taken, and sent up to London, and there executed. After which the king held his parliament at Westminster. Shortly after, Robert Bruce, forgetting his oath to the king, within a year or two after this, by the counsel of the abbot of Stone, and the bishop of St. Andrews, sent to Pope Clement V. for a dispensation of his oath; insinuating to him, that King Edward vexed and grieved the realm of Scotland wrongfully. Whereupon the pope wrote to the king to leave off such doings. Notwithstanding which inhibition of the pope, the king prosecuting his own right, gathered his men, and set off to Scotland, where joining battle with Sir Robert and all his army of Scotland in a plain, near to St. John's Town, he put him to flight, and so chased the Scots, that there were slain of them to the number of seven thousand. In which victory, such bishops and abbots as were taken he sent to the pope; the temporal lords and other Scots he sent to London. Sir Robert Bruce after this discomfiture, when he had thus lost both the field and his chief friends, fled into Norway. When this noble Edward had thus subdued the Scots, he yielded thanks to God for his victory, and returned to London, which was the thirty-fifth and last year of his reign.

Now touching the variance and dissension between Philip the French king, and Pope Boniface VIII. After the bishoprick of Rome had been vacant through the dissension of the cardinals, for the space of two years and three months; at length Pope Celestine was chosen successor to Pope Nicholas IV. Celestine in his first consistory began to reform the clergy, by which he procured to himself such hatred among his clergy, that this Boniface, speaking through a reed in his chamber wall at midnight, warned him, as it had been a voice from heaven, that he should give over his papacy, as being a burthen greater than he could wield.

This Pope Celestine after he had sat six months, was induced by the treachery and falsehood of this Boniface, to resign his bishoprick, partly on account of the voice spoken of before, partly from fear; being told of certain persons craftily suborned in his chamber, that, if he did not resign, he should lose his life.

This Pope Boniface succeeding after Celestine, behaved himself so imperiously, that he put down princes, and excommunicated such kings as did not take their confirmation at his hand: many of his cardinals he drove away for fear, some of them he deposed as schismatics and spoiled of all their substance. Philip the French king he excommunicated, for not suffering his money to go out of the realm; and therefore cursed both him and his to the fourth generation. Albert the emperor, not once or twice, but thrice sought at his hands to be confirmed, and yet was rejected. This pope first ordained the jubilee in Rome, in the solemnizing whereof, the first day he shewed himself in his pontifical robes, and gave free remission of sins to as many as came to Rome out of all the parts of the world. The second day (being arrayed with imperial ensigns) he commanded a naked sword to be carried before him, and said with a loud voice, "Lo, here the power and authority of both the swords!"

These things thus premised of Pope Boniface, now I will come to the occasion of the strife between him and the French king. In A.D. 1301, the bishop of Oppanuham, being accused of a conspiracy against the French king, was brought up to his court, and so committed to prison. The pope hearing this, sends word to the king by his legate to set him at liberty. The French king, not daring to the contrary, released the bishop; but at the same time, he dismissed both the bishop and the legate, commanding them to leave his realm. Upon this Pope Boniface revoked all the graces and privileges granted either by him or his predecessors to the kingdom of France; and not long after he thundered out the sentence of his curse against him. Moreover, he cited all the prelates, all divines, and lawyers both civil and canon, to appear personally before him at Rome, at a certain day. Against this citation the king provided and commanded by proclamation, that no person should export out of the realm either gold, or silver, or any ware or merchandise, upon pain of forfeiting all their goods, and their bodies at the king's pleasure : providing at the same time, that the roads and harbours or seaports, should be diligently kept, that none might pass unsearched. Besides which, the king defeated the pope in giving and bestowing prebends, and benefices, and other ecclesiastial livings, contrary to the pope's profit. For which cause, the pope wrote to the king in form and effect as follows.

" Boniface, bishop, and servant to God's servants, to his beloved son Philip, by the grace of God, king of France, greeting and apostolical blessing.

" Boniface, the servant of God's servants. Fear God, and observe his commandments. We will thee to understand, that thou art subject to us both in spiritual things, and temporal ; and that no gift of benefices or prebends belongs to thee ; and if thou have the keeping of any being vacant, that thou reserve the profits of them to the successors. But if thou have given any, we judge the gift to be void, and revoke how far soever thou hast gone forward. And whosoever believes otherwise, we judge them heretics."

To this letter of the pope, King Philip made answer as follows :

Philip, by the grace of God king of France, to Boniface not in deeds behaving himself for pope, little friendship or none.

" To Boniface, bearing himself for chief bishop, little health or none. Let thy foolishness know, that in temporal things we are subject to no man, and that the gifts of prebends and benefices, made and to be made by us, were and shall be good, both in time past and to come. And that we will defend manfully the possessors of the said benefices, and we think them that believe or think otherwise, fools and madmen. Given at Paris the Wednesday after Candlemas, 1301."

After these and other writings passing to and fro, between the French king and the pope, within a year and a half after, the king summoned a parliament, sending down his letters to his sheriffs and other officers, to summon the prelates and barons of the realm to the court of parliament.

A declaration of master William Nagareta, made against Pope Boniface the Eighth, with his appellation also made at Paris, before the king and his council in the church of Paris.

In the name of God, amen. In the year of our Lord, 1303, the 12th day of March, and the ninth year of the popedom of the most holy father the Lord Boniface VIII., by God's providence pope, and in the presence of us common notaries, and witnesses under written, the nobleman master William Nagareta, (or de Nogaret), knight, a worshipful professor of the laws, standing before the most excellent prince the lord Philip, by the grace of God most noble king of France, spake with lively words, and gave in writings these things that follow:

" There have been false prophets among the people, as there have been also false teachers among you. St. Peter, the glorious prince of the apostles, speaking to us by the Spirit, told us things to come; that likewise as there were false prophets aforetimes, so there should come among you false teachers, bringing in sects of destruction; by the which the way of truth shall be defaced; and covetously they shall make merchandise of you with feigned words; such masters follow the way of Balaam, the son of Bosor, who loved the reward of wickedness, and had his bridled ass to correct his madness, which speaking in a man's voice, did stop the foolishness of the prophet. All which things as they are shewn to us by the greatest patriarch himself; your eyes see them fulfilled this day

according to the letter. For there sits in St. Peter's chair the master of lies, causing himself to be called 'Boniface,' that is 'a well doer,' when he is notable in all kind of evil doing, and so he has taken to himself a false name ; and where he is not a true ruler and master, he calls himself the lord, judge, and master of all men. And coming in contrary to the common order appointed by the holy fathers, and also contrary to the rules of reason, and so not entering in at the door into the Lord's sheepfold, he is not a shepherd nor even a hireling, but rather a thief and robber. For he (the true husband of the Romish church yet living) deceived him that was delighted in simplicity, and enticed him with feigned flatterings and gifts to let him have his spouse to be his wife, against truth, which cries, ' Those whom God hath joined together, let no man put asunder;' and at length laying violent hands upon him, persuading him falsely that which the deceiver said was come from the Holy Spirit, was not ashamed to join to himself with wicked practice that holy church, which is mistress of all churches, calling himself her husband, whereas he cannot be so; for Celestine, the true Romish bishop, agreed not to the divorce, being deceived by so great subtilty ; nothing is so contrary to agreeing as, error and deceit, as man's laws bear witness, therefore I need not speak of his violence. But because the Spirit inspires whom he will, and he that is led by the Spirit, is not under the law; the holy universal church of God, not knowing the crafts of that deceiver, stumbling and doubting whether it came from the holy ghost that Celestine should leave off his government, and the sins of the people deserving it, for fear of a schism suffered the foresaid deceiver: although, according to the doctrine of our Lord, ' By his fruits he might be known,' whether he came to the said government by the holy ghost or otherwise: his fruits (as it is plainly here written beneath) are now manifest to all men, by which it is apparent to the world, that he came not in by God, but other ways; and so came not in by the sheepfold. His fruits are most wicked, and his end is death; and therefore it is necessary that so evil a tree, according to the Lord's saying, ' should be cut down and cast into the fire. This cannot avail to his excuse, which is made by some men, that is, that the cardinals agreed upon him again, after the death of Celestine the pope, seeing he could not be her husband, whom it is manifest he defiled by adultery, when her first husband was yet living, and she being worthy to have the promise of marriage kept to her ; therefore, because that which is done against the Lord turns to the wrong of all men; and especially in so great a mischief, I, like a bridled ass, by the power of the Lord, and not by the voice of a perfect man, being not able to bear so great a burthen, take in hand to rebuke the madness of the said false prophet Balaam, who at the instance of King Balak, that is, of the Prince of Devils, whom he serves, is ready to curse the people blessed of the Lord. I beseech you, most excellent prince, and Lord Philip, by the grace of God, king of France, that like as the angel of God in time past met the prophet Balaam in the way, with a drawn sword, as he was going to curse God's people ; so you, who are unwilling to execute fierce justice, and are therefore like the angel of the Lord, and minister of power and office, would meet with a naked sword this said wicked man, who is far worse than Balaam, that he perform not that evil which he intends to the people.

" 1. I propound that the foresaid man, who names himself Boniface, is no pope, but wrongfully keeps the seat which he has to the great damage of all the souls of God's holy church. I say also, that his entering was faulty in many ways, and he entered not in at the door, but otherways, and therefore is to be judged a thief and a robber.

" 2. I propound also, that the said Boniface is a manifest heretic, and utterly cut off from the body of the holy church, because of many kinds of heresies, which are to be declared in convenient time and place.

" 3. I propound also, that the said Boniface is an horrible simoniac, and such a one as has not been since the beginning of the world : and the mischief of this sin in him is notorious to all the world, (which thing is manifest to all that will plainly understand) insomuch that he, being openly slandered, said openly, that he could not commit simony.

"4. I propound also, that the said Boniface, being wrapt in many manifest and heinous sins, is so hardened in them, that he is utterly impossible to be corrected; and lies in dungeon of mischief so deep, that he cannot be suffered any longer, without the overthrow of the church. His mouth is full of cursing, his feet are swift to shed blood. He utterly tears in pieces the churches, which he ought to cherish; wickedly wasting the goods of the poor, and making much of wicked men that give him rewards; persecuting the righteous, and not gathering but scattering among the people, bringing in new sects of destruction that have not been heard of; blaspheming the way of truth, and by robbery thinking himself equal to the Lord Jesus Christ who is blessed for ever. And he being most covetous thirsts for gold, covets gold, and by some device gets gold of every people; and utterly disregarding the worshipping of God, with feigned words, sometimes by flattering, sometimes by threatening, sometimes by false teaching, and all to get money withal, he makes merchandise of us all; envying all things but his own; loving no man, nourishing war, persecuting and hating the peace of his subjects. He is rooted in all unspeakable sins; contrarying and striving against all the ways and doctrines of the Lord. He is truly the abomination of the people, which Daniel the Lord's prophet described.

"Therefore I answer, that laws, weapons, and all the elements ought to rise against him, who thus overthrows the state of the church; for whose sins God plagues the whole world. And finally nothing remains to him, being so unsatiable, to satisfy him withal, but only the unsatiable mouth of hell, and the fire that cannot be quenched, continuing for ever. Therefore seeing that in a general council it so becomes, and I see this wicked man to be damned, who offends both God and all men: I ask and require as instantly as I can, and I beseech you, my lord and king aforesaid, that you would declare thus much to the prelates, doctors, people and princes, your brethren in Christ, and chiefly to the cardinals and all prelates, and call a council. In the which (when the aforesaid wicked man is condemned) by the worshipful cardinals, the church may be provided with a shepherd: and for that council I offer myself ready lawfully to pursue the aforesaid things. And whereas the said man, being in the highest dignity, in the mean time cannot be suspended of his superior; therefore he ought to be taken, suspended indeed for the things aforesaid, seeing his state is called into judgment, by the means aforesaid.

"I beseech and require the said cardinals by you, and I presently require them and the church of God, that this wicked man being put in prison, the church of Rome may be provided with a vicar, who may minister those things that shall appertain, until the church of God be provided with a bishop, utterly to take away all occasion of a schism. And lest the said wicked man should let and hinder the prosecuting thereof, I require these things of you, my lord king, affirming you to be bound to do this for many causes. First, for the faith's sake. Secondly, for your kingly dignity, to whose office it belongs to root out such wicked men. Thirdly, for your oath sake, which you made for the defence of the churches of your realm, which the aforesaid ravener utterly tears in pieces. Fourthly, because you are the patron of the churches, and therefore you are not bound only to the defence of them, but to the calling for again of their goods, which this aforesaid man has wasted. Fifthly, following the footsteps of your ancestors, you ought to deliver your mother, the Romish church, from so wicked a band wherein by oppression she is tied and bound. I require that a public instrument may be made of these requests by the notaries here present, under the witness of the worshipful men that be here present. These things were done and spoken as is aforesaid, at Paris, in the king's house of Lupara."

After this protestation of Master Nagareta, immedi-

ately ensued the appeal of the king, pronounced and published against Boniface, recapitulating and amplifying the same charges as are in the appeal of Nagareta.

Then King Philip made his appeal to a general council, in form as follows:

"We, Philip, by the grace of God, hearing and understanding the objections propounded by our beloved faithful knight, William of Nagareta, against Boniface, now having the government of the Romish church: although we would gladly cover with our own cloak, the filthy parts of such a father; yet for the love of the catholic faith, and great devotion that we bear to the holy Romish and universal church our mother, and all faithful men. and spouse of Christ, following the steps of our ancestors, who hesitated not to shed their own blood for the increase and defence of the church's liberty, and the faith; and desiring to provide for the purity of the faith and state of the church; as also to avoid the hurt of the general slander, not being able any longer to pass over these things with winking and dissembling, and my conscience driving to the same; seeing this estimate and opinion of this Boniface in these matters is not rashly conceived by us, but vehemently and plainly increased by the many and continual complaints of credible men, and fearing, moreover, the destruction of the faith, both of us and of all other subjects, and especially of kings and princes of the world, who ought to reprove negligence, who acknowledge that we have received power given us from the Lord, to the promoting and increasing of it; we agree to your request in this behalf, and to the calling and assembling a council for the glory of God (saving the honour and reverence that is due to the holy Romish church in all things) whereby the truth may appear in the premises, and all error avoided: that the state of the universal church, and all christianity, and the matters of faith, and the holy land may be provided for, and the slanders and jeopardies hanging over us may be withstood; we are ready, and offer ourselves gladly, as much as in us lies, to bestow our labours and diligent pains thereabout; earnestly requiring and beseeching in the merciful bowels of Jesus Christ, you archbishops and other prelates here present, as children of the church and pillars of faith, called of the Lord to the promoting, increase and preserving thereof, to care for the same, that with all diligence you would give heed, as becomes you, and that you would effectually labour by all ways and fit means, to the calling and assembling of this council, in which we intend to be personally present. And lest the said Boniface, who has boldly and wrongfully many times threatened to proceed against us, stopping and hindering our purposes and intent, lest any of his works of darkness (if there be any) should come to light, directly or indirectly hindering the calling and gathering of this council; or lest any state being in the same realm that will indeed proceed against us, or our state, churches, prelates, barons, and other faithful vassals, our subjects, our lands, or our realm, and the state of the realm, by abusing any spiritual sword, in excommunicating, suspending, or other ways, by any means: for us and our well-willers, and them that will follow us, we provoke and appeal in writing to the aforesaid general council (which we instantly desire to be called) and to one lawful chief bishop that shall be, or to any other to whom we should appeal; and yet not going from the appeal made by William of Nagareta, to whom we adhered then, and also yet adhere: requiring earnestly a witness of our appeal by you prelates and notaries, expressly to renew such provocation and appeal, when and before whom it shall be thought meet to you."

Then the archbishops, bishops, abbots, and priors, make their appeal in like manner with the king to a general council.

These things being done, then followed the year 1304. In the which year, a garrison of soldiers, sent partly by the French king, partly by the cardinals of Columna, came to the gates of Arvagium, where the pope hid himself. The captains of which army were one Schaira, brother to those cardinals, and another, William de Longareto, high steward to the French king, who, invading the pope's town, and finding the gates open, gave assault to the pope's frontier, where the pope, with his nephew, a marquess, and three other cardinals were immured. The townsmen, seeing all their intent and strength to be bent against the pope, caused the common bell to be rung, and so assembling themselves in a common council, ordained Adolphus, one of the chiefest rulers of the town, for their captain, who, unknown to them, was a great adversary to the pope. This Adolphus joined with the French company against the pope, and beset his palace on every side. And first, setting upon the palaces of the three cardinals, who were then chief about the pope, they rifled and spoiled all their goods. The cardinals by a back door hardly escaped their hands; but the pope's palace, through the strength of the marquess, was somewhat better defended. At length the pope, perceiving himself not able to make his party good, desired truce with Schaira, which was granted from one till nine. During which time of truce, the pope privily sends to the townsmen of Arvagium, desiring them to save his life, which, if they would do, he promised so to enrich them, that they should all have cause never to forget or repent their kindness bestowed on him. To this they made answer, excusing themselves, that it lay not in their ability to do him any good, for that the whole power of the town was with the captain. Then the pope, all destitute and desolate, sends to Schaira, beseeching him to draw out in articles wherein he had wronged him, and he would make him amends to the uttermost. Schaira to this makes a plain answer, signifying to him again, "That he should in no wise escape with his life, except upon these three conditions. First, to restore again the two cardinals of Columna his brethren, whom he had before deprived, with all other of their stock and kindred. Secondly, that after their restitution, he should renounce his papacy. Thirdly, that his body should remain in his power and custody." These articles seemed to the pope so hard, that in no case would he agree to them. When the truce expired, the captains and soldiers, setting themselves against the bishop, first fired the gates of the palace, whereby the army, having a full entrance, fell to rifle and spoil the house. The marquess upon hoping to save his life, and the life of his children, yielded himself to the hands of Schaira, and the other captain, which, when the pope heard, he wept and made great lamentation. After this breaking through the windows and doors, they burst in to the pope, whom they treated with words and threats accordingly. Upon this he was put to his choice, whether he would presently leave his life, or give over his papacy. But he said that he would never while he lived renounce his popedom. Then Schaira was ready to slay him, but he was prevented by some that were about him. The soldiers, who ranged in the meantime through all the corners of the pope's house, loaded themselves with all the immense treasure of gold, silver, plate, and ornaments that were collected there. Thus Boniface, bereaved of all his goods, remained in their custody three days, during which time, they set him on a wild unbroken colt, his face turned to the horse's tail, and caused the horse to gallop, so that the pope was almost breathless: they kept him so without meat, that he was nearly famished to death. After the third day, the Arvagians and people of the town, mustering themselves together, to the number of ten thousand, secretly burst into the house where the pope was kept, and slaying the keepers, delivered the pope by a strong hand. Being then brought into the middle of the town, he gave thanks with weeping tears to the people for saving his life, promising, moreover, (forsomuch as he was out of all his goods, having neither bread nor drink to put in his mouth), God's blessing and his, to all them that now would relieve him with any thing, either to eat or drink. And here now see what poverty and affliction can work in a man; the pope, before in all his pomp and most ruffling wealth, was never so proud, but now he was as humble and lowly, that every poor simple man might

have a bold and free access to his person. To make the story short, the pope, in that great distress of famine, was not so greedy of the people's victuals, as they were greedy of his blessing. The women and people of the town came so thick, some with bread, some with wine, some with water, some with meat, some with one thing, some with another, that the pope's chamber was too little to receive the offering; insomuch, that when there lacked cups to receive the wine, they poured it down on the chamber floor, not regarding the loss of wine to win the pope's holy blessing. Thus Pope Boniface, being refreshed by the town of Arvagium, took his journey from thence, accompanied with a great multitude of soldiers, and came to Rome, where, shortly after, partly from fear, partly from famine, partly from sorrow for the loss of so inestimable a treasure, he died.

Now, after this matter between the French king and Pope Boniface, let us proceed in our English history. About this time, in the days of King Edward, the church of Rome began daily more and more to rise up, and swell so high in pride and worldly dominion, that no king could do scarcely any thing, but as pleased the pope, who ruled all in all countries, but chiefly here in England. When the king and the church of Canterbury in their election had chosen one Robert Burnhil, bishop of Bath, to be archbishop of Canterbury, Pope Boniface, of his own presumptuous authority, ruling the matter after his own pleasure, frustrated their election, and thrust in another, named John Peckham; for among others, this had always been one practice of the court of Rome, ever to have the archbishop of their own appointing, or such an one as they might be sure of on their side, to weigh against the king. To this John Peckham, Pope Boniface directed a solemn bull from Rome, as also to all quarters of the universal church. In which bull it was decreed, directly against the rule of scripture and christian obedience, "That no church nor ecclesiastical person should henceforth yield to his king or temporal magistrate, either any giving or lending, or promising of tribute or subsidy, or portion whatsoever of the goods and possessions belonging to him, but should be clearly exempted and discharged from all taxation in the behalf of the prince and his affairs." This decree manifestly rebelled against the ordinance of God, and the apostolical canon of St. Peter, and all other examples of holy scripture. For as there is no word in the scripture that excludes spiritual men more than temporal from obedience and subjection to princes; so if the prince was to be too rigorous in his exacting, or cruel in oppression, that is no cause for the clergy to be exempt, but they rather should bear the common burthen of obedience, and pray to God to turn and move the prince's mind.

This bull being directed from Rome to the archbishop of Canterbury, and likewise through the whole church, under the pope's authority; it happened not long after that the king held his parliament at St. Edmundsbury, where was granted to him by all cities and boroughs an eighth, and by the commons a twelfth of their goods. Only the clergy, by virtue of this bull, stoutly refused to pay any thing to the king. This answer not pleasing the king, he desired them to deliberate better with themselves upon the matter, and after mature advice to give him answer against the next parliament, which should be held the next Hilary term at London.

In conclusion, when the parliament met, the clergy persisted still in the denial of their subsidy, alleging the pope's bull for their warrant and discharge. Whereupon the king excluded them from under his protection and the safeguard of his laws. And as concerning the archbishop of Canterbury above mentioned, because he was found more stubborn than the rest, and was the inciter to the others; he seized upon all his goods, and caused an inventory of the same to be enrolled in the exchequer. Several of the other bishops relented soon after to the king, and contributed the fifth of their goods unto him, and were received again to favour.

After the death of John Peckham, archbishop of Canterbury, succeeded Robert Winchelsey; with whom also the king had similar variance. And as this king was troubled in his time with both the archbishops, John Peckham, and also Robert Winchelsey; so it happened to all other kings for the most part, from the time of Lanfranc (that is, from Pope Hildebrand) that every king in his time had some trouble or other with that see. As William Rufus, and Henry I. were troubled with Anselm; Henry II. with Thomas Becket; King Richard and all England, with William, bishop of Ely, the pope's legate; King John, with Stephen Langton; King Henry III. with Edmund, archbishop, called St. Edmund; likewise this King Edward I., with John Peckham and Robert Winchelsey. And so other kings after him, with some prelate or other.

After Pope Boniface succeeded Benedict XI. and then Pope Clement V., who translated the pope's court to Avignon in France, where it remained for seventy-four years after. At the coronation of this Clement, was present Philip, king of France; Charles his son; and Duke John, duke of Brittany, with a great number of other men of state and nobility. At which coronation, in the middle of the pomp and procession, a great wall break down and fell upon them: by the fall of which, Duke John, with twelve others, were slain; King Philip, hurt and wounded; the pope struck from his horse, and lost out from his mitre upon his head, a carbuncle, esteemed to the value of 6000 florins. By this Clement it was ordained, that the emperor, though he might be called king of the Romans before, yet he might not enjoy the title and right of the emperor, until he was confirmed by him. And that the emperor's seat being vacant, the pope should reign as emperor, till a new emperor was chosen. By him the order of the Templars (who at that time were too abominable) was put down at the council of Vienna. He also ordained and confirmed the feast of Corpus Christi, assigning indulgences to such as heard the service. And as Pope Boniface before heaped up the book of decretals, called Sextus Decretalium, so this Clement compiled the seventh book of the decretals, called of the same Clement, The Clementines. In the time of this pope, the Emperor Henry VI. was poisoned in receiving the sacrament, by a false dissembling monk called Bernard, that feigned himself to be his familiar friend; which was thought to be done not without the consent of the pope's legate. The emperor, perceiving himself poisoned, warned him to flee and escape away; for the Germans would surely have slain him; although he escaped himself, yet many of his order were slain with fire and sword.

This Pope Clement V. had well provided against the empire of Rome to bring it under his girdle, insomuch that, without the pope's benediction, no emperor might take the state upon him, and now he proceeded to intermeddle with the empire of Constantinople; where he first exercised his tyranny and power of excommunication against the emperor Andronicus Paleologus, (A. D. 1306), declaring him to be a schismatic and heretic, because he neither would nor durst suffer the Greeks to make their appeal from the Greek church to the pope, nor would acknowledge him for his superior. From this it may appear, that the Greek church did not admit the pope's superiority as yet, nor indeed at any time before, except about the time of Pope Innocent III. (A. D. 1202), when Baldwin, earl of Flanders, joined with the Venetians, and went against the Greeks, to place Alexius in the empire of Constantinople, upon condition (as writes Platina) of subduing the Greek church under the church of Rome. Alexius being restored, and shortly after slain, the empire came to the Frenchmen, with whom it remained the space of fifty-eight years, till the coming of Michael Paleologus, who restored the empire to its pristine state. After this, Michael, emperor of Constantinople, being called up to a council at Lyons by Pope Gregory X., about the controversy of the procession of the Holy Ghost and obedience to the church of Rome, submitted himself and the Greeks to the subjection of Rome, and he thereby procured to himself such grudge and hatred among the Greek monks and priests, that after his death they denied him the due honour and place of burial. The

son of this Michael Paleologus was Andronicus above mentioned: who was constrained by the Greeks not to admit any appeal to the bishop of Rome, and was therefore accursed by the pope's censures for a heretic. Whereby it appears, that the Greeks, recovering their state again, refused all subjection at this time unto the church of Rome, which was A. D. 1307. After this Clement V. followed Pope John XXII. with whom Lewis the emperor had much trouble. After whom next in course succeeded Pope Benedict XII. Now to return to the English history in the year 1307, which was the thirty-fourth of the reign of this king, the king kept a parliament at Carlisle, where great complaints were brought in by the nobles of the realm, concerning the manifold and intolerable oppressions of churches and monasteries, and exactions of money by the pope's legate, William Testa. The pope sent this legate into England with his bulls, in which he reserved the first fruits of all churches vacant at any time, within the realm of England, Scotland, Wales, and Ireland, and also the fruits of abbies and priories, &c. The king, with his nobles, seeing the inconvenience and injury of this to the whole realm, in the parliament held at Carlisle, withstood the legate, commanding him by the assent of the earls and barons, that henceforth he should abstain from all such exactions. And as concerning his lord the pope, the king wrote, declaring and admonishing the pope, that he should not exact the first fruits of the churches and abbeys, founded by his predecessors and the noble men of the land, for the honour and maintenance of God's service, for alms and hospitality.

During this parliament, as men were talking of the pope's oppressions, there suddenly fell down among them a certain paper, with this superscription.

An Epistle of Cassiodorus to the Church of England, concerning the Abuses of the Romish Church.

" To the noble church of England, serving in clay and brick, as the Jews did in time past under the tyranny of the Egyptians; Peter the son of Cassiodorus a catholic soldier, and devout champion of Christ, sends greeting, and wishing it to cast off the yoke of bondage, and to receive the reward of liberty.

" To whom shall I compare thee, or to whom shall I liken thee, O daughter of Jerusalem? To whom shall I match thee, O daughter of Sion? Great is thy troubled state, like to the sea. Thou sittest alone without comfort all the day long, thou art confounded and consumed with heaviness. Thou art given up into the hands of him from whence thou canst not rise without the help of one to lift thee up: for the scribes and pharisees sitting upon the chair of Moses, the enemies of the Romans are as thy heads and rulers: enlarging their guarded phylacteries, and seeking to be enriched with the marrow of thy bones, laying heavy burdens, and not able to be borne upon thy shoulders, and on thy ministers, and they set thee under tribute, (who of old time hast been free) beyond all honesty or measure. But marvel not thereat, for thy mother, which is the lady of people, like a widow having married and coupled herself to her subjects, has appointed him to be thy father: that is to say, the bishop of Rome, who shews no point of any fatherly love towards thee. He magnifies and extends to the utmost his authority over thee, and by experience he declares himself to be the husband of thy mother. He remembers oft with himself the prophetical saying of the prophet, and well digested the same in the inward part of his breast: ' Take to thee a great book, and write therein quickly with the pen of a man;' ' take the spoil, rob quickly.' But is this it which the apostle says that he was appointed for, where he writes thus? ' Every bishop, taken from among men, is appointed for men in those things that belong to the Lord:' not to spoil, nor to lay on them yearly taxes, nor to kill men, but ' to offer gifts and sacrifices for sins,' and to sorrow with them that be ignorant and do err. And so we read of Peter the fisherman (whose successor he boasts himself to be) that after the resurrection of Christ, he returned with the other apostles, to the office of fishing: who when he could take nothing on the left-side of the ship, at the bidding of Christ turned to the right-side, and drew to land a net full of fishes. Wherefore the profitable ministry of the church is to be exercised on the right side, by which the devil is overcome, and plenty of souls are gained and won to Christ. But certainly the labour on the left side of the ship is far otherwise: for in it the faith stumbles, heaviness bears rule, when that which is desired by seeking, is not found. For who is so foolish as to think that he can at one time serve both God and man? satisfy his own will, or stick to the revelations of flesh and blood, and offer worthy gifts to Christ? And doubtless that shepherd who watches not for the edifying of the flock, prepares another way for 'the roaring lion seeking whom he may devour.' And now behold, I say, O daughter, the deeds of him that is called thy Father, are such as have not been heard of before: he drives away the good shepherds from the sheepfold, and places in their stead bishops, to rule, but not to profit (his nephews, cousins, and parents) some that know no letters, and others dumb and deaf, who understand not the plain voice of the sheep, not curing their wounds, who are hurt by the wolves: but like hirelings, plucking off the fleeces, and reaping that which other men have sown, whose hands moreover are always ready in their baskets and pouches, but their backs are turned from their burthens. By which it is manifest, that the priesthood is clean changed in these days,—the service of God decayed, —alms diminished and brought to nought,—the whole devotion of kings, princes and christians, is banished. May not this be thought wonderful in the eyes of all men; that whereas Christ commands tribute to be paid to kings for him and for Peter, this bishop now goes about by dominion of his style, to subdue to him both realms, and princes of realms (against his will, whose vicar he saith he is, and who refused the realms and judgments of the world) which this bishop contrarywise challenges, claiming all that which he in his style writes to be his? Alas! O daughter, what doth he yet more against thee? Mark, he draws from thee whatever pleases him, and yet is not content, to have the tenth part only of thy goods from thee; except he have also the first fruits of the benefices of the ministers, whereby he may get a new patrimony, as well for himself as for his kindred, contrary to the godly wills of the first founders. Over and besides all this, he introduces other execrable taxes and stipends for his legates and messengers, whom he sends into England; who not only take away the feeding and clothing of thee and thine, but also like dogs tear in pieces your flesh and skins. May not this prince be compared to King Nebuchadnezar, who destroyed the temple of the Lord, and carried away the golden and silver vessels thereof? The very same does this man also; he robbed the ministers of God's house, and left them destitute of due help.—In like manner does he: truly they are better who are killed with the sword, than they who are pined with hunger; for they are dead immediately, but these are wasted with the barrenness of the earth. O daughter, all they that pass by, let them have pity and compassion on thee, for there is no sorrow like thy sorrow. For now thy face is blacker than coals, through much sorrow and weeping, and thou art no more known in the streets: thy foresaid ruler has placed thee in darkness, and has given thee wormwood and gall to drink. O Lord, hear the sorrow and sighing of thy people, behold, Lord, and descend, for the heart of this man is more hardened than the heart of Pharaoh. For he will not suffer the people to depart, except only by the strength of thy hand. For he not only scourges them miserably upon the earth, but also after their death, he intends, to ingross the goods of all christians under the name and title of dying intestate, or making no will. Therefore, let the chivalry of England well remember, how the Frenchmen in times past, directing their greedy eyes on the realm of England, laboured with all their power how to bring the same under their subjection. But it is to be feared, lest the new devices and practice of this new enemy supply that which hitherto has been lacking in

them. For in diminishing the treasure of the realm, and spoiling the church goods, the realm shall be brought into such inability, that it shall not be able to help itself against the enemy. Therefore, O daughter, and you the ministers thereof, suffer not yourselves to be led any more into such miserable bondage. It is better for the wealth of thee and thine, that the christian king and the powers of the realm, who have clothed thee with great benefits, and you also who are clothed with their benefits, do labour with all your power how to resist the devices, conspiracies, arrogance, presumption, and pride of the foresaid person: who not for any zeal of God, but for the inriching of his parents, and for his own kindred (exalting himself like an eagle) by these and such other exactions goes about, after another kind of extortion, to scrape up and devour all the money and treasure of England. Now, lest the dissembled simplicity of the realm in this behalf do bring utter subversion, and afterward be compelled to seek remedy when it is too late: I beseech the Lord God of Hosts to turn away the veil from the heart of that man, and to give him a contrite and an humble mind, in such sort as he may acknowledge the ways of the true God, whereby he may be brought out of darkness, and be forced to relinquish his old sinister attempts; and that the vineyard, which the Lord's hand has planted, may be replenished continually with the preachers of the word. Let the words of the Lord, prophesied by the mouth of Jeremy, stir up your minds to withstand and resist the subtle practices of this man, by which words the Lord speaks: 'O thou pastor which hast scattered my people, and hast cast them out of their habitations, behold I will come and visit upon thee, and upon the malice of thy studies: neither shall there be any of thy seed which shall sit upon the seat of David, neither which shall have power any more in Judah. So that thy nest shall become barren, and utterly subverted, like Sodom and Gomorrah.' "'And if he being terrified by these words, do not leave off from this which he beginneth, and does not make restitution of those which he has received, then let all and singular persons sing for him being hardened, to him that seeth all things,' the 108 Psal. For as truly as favour, grace, and benevolence, remits, and neglects many things; so again the gentle benignity of man, being too much oppressed and grieved, seeking to be delivered and freed from the same, strives and searches to have the truth known, and casts off that yoke by all means possible that grieves him," &c.

In the year 1307, King Edward, marching toward Scotland, fell sick, which sickness increased so upon him, that he despaired of life: wherefore calling before him his earls and barons, he caused them to be sworn that they should crown his son Edward. That being done, he called his son Edward, informing and advising him with wholesome precepts; and he charged him also, as he valued his blessing, with several matters. First, That he should be courteous, gentle, upright in judgment, fair spoken to all men, constant in deed and in word, familiar with the good; and especially to be merciful to the miserable. He gave him also charge not to be too hasty in taking his crown before he had revenged his father's injuries against the Scots; but that he should remain in those parts to take with him his father's bones, after being well boiled from the flesh; and so being inclosed in some fit vessel, should carry them with him till he conquered all the Scots, saying, that so long as he had his father's bones with him, none should overcome him. He desired and required him to love his brothers Thomas and Edmund; also to cherish and be tender to his mother Margaret the queen. He, also, strictly charged him upon his blessing (as he would avoid his curse) that he should in no case call to him again, or send for Peter Gaveston, which Peter Gaveston the king had before banished from the realm, for his naughty and wicked intimacy with his son Edward, and for his leading him astray with evil counsel. For which he banished both Peter Gaveston utterly out of the realm, and also put Edward his son into prison; and, therefore, he strictly charged his son not to send for this Gaveston, or to have him about him. And, finally, because he had conceived in himself a vow to have returned in his own person to the Holy Land, (which from his many wars with the Scots he could not perform), therefore he had prepared thirty-two thousand pounds of silver, for sending some soldiers with his heart to the Holy Land; which he required his son to see accomplished, so that the money, under his curse and malediction, should not be employed to other uses. But these injunctions and precepts the disobedient son did not observe after the decease of his father, but leaving off the war with the Scots, he hasted with all speed to his coronation. Also contrary to the mind of his nobles, and against the precept of his father, he sent for Peter Gaveston, and prodigally bestowed upon him all that treasure which his father had bequeathed to the Holy Land. He was moreover a proud despiser of his peers and nobles, and therefore reigned unfortunately.

KING EDWARD THE SECOND.

Edward II. was born at Carnarvon, in Wales, and after the death of his father, entered the government, A.D. 1307, but was not crowned before the year following (A.D. 1308,) by reason of the absence of Robert Winchelsey, who was banished by King Edward I. Whereupon the king wrote to the pope for the restitution of the archbishop, for by an ancient law of the realm the coronation of the king could not proceed without the archbishop of Canterbury. This Edward, as he was personable in body and outward shape, so in conditions and evil dispositions he was much deformed; being unsteadfast in his word, and lightly disclosing secrets of great counsel; also refusing the company of his lords and men of honour, he associated with villains and vile personages, given moreover to drinking, and such vices as usually ensue on drunkenness. And as of his own nature he was disposed to such vices, so he was made much worse by the counsel and familiarity of certain evil disposed persons, as Peter, or Pierce Gaveston, and the two Spensers, and others, following whose wanton counsel he gave himself to riot and debauchery; not ordering his government with gravity, discretion, or justice, which caused great variance between him and his nobles, so that he shortly became odious to them, and in the end was deprived of his kingdom. In the first year of his reign he took to wife Isabel, daughter of Philip king of France, with whom, the year after, he was crowned at Westminster by the bishop of Winchester, as Robert Winchelsey, archbishop of Canterbury, was not yet returned home. The barons and lords first made request to the king to put Peter Gaveston from him, or else they would not consent to his coronation; whereupon he was forced to grant them at the next parliament to have their requests accomplished, and so he was crowned. In the meantime this Peter or Pierce, emboldened by the king's favour, continued triumphing and setting at light all the other states and nobles of the realm, so that he ruled both the king and the realm, and all things went as he wished, neither had the king any delight or kept company with any, but with him; with him only he told all his mind, and conferred all his counsels. This seemed strange to the lords and earls, and inflamed them so much against this Peter Gaveston, that through the exciting of the nobles, the bishops of the land proceeded in excommunication against him unless he departed the land.

At length the parliament met (A.D. 1310), and articles were drawn by the nobles to be exhibited to the king, which articles were the same as contained in Magna Charta, and de Foresta, with such other articles as his father had charged him with before; to wit, that he should remove from him and his court all aliens and perverse counsellors, and that all the matters of the commonwealth should be debated by the common council of the lords both temporal and spiritual; and that he should stir no war out of England in any other foreign realm, without the common assent of the same, &c. The king perceiving their intent to be, as it was indeed, to separate Peter Gaveston from his company, and seeing no other remedy but he must yield and grant

his consent, agreed that Gaveston should be banished to Ireland; and so the parliament breaking up, the lords returned home well pleased.

In the history of King Edward I. mention was made of Pope Clement V., who succeeded Benedict; also of the suppression of the Templars, which happened in this year by means of the French king. He burned in the city of Paris this year fifty-four Templars, with the grand master of the order, and induced Pope Clement to call a council at Vienna, where the whole order of Templars was condemned, and shortly after, with the consent of all christian kings, totally suppressed in one day. After this the French king thought to make his son king of Jerusalem, and to transfer to him all the lands of the Templars. But Clement the pope would not agree, and transferred all their lands to the order of Hospitallers, for the great sum of money given for the same. The cause of these impious Templars being suppressed, was on account of their abominable and filthy practices, which are better not told, if those things be true which some authors write.

Another matter of similar abomination I may here mention, touching a certain nunnery in France called Provines, within which, at the cleansing of a fish-pond, many bones of young children were found, and the bodies also of some infants not yet decomposed. On account of this, several of the nuns of this nunnery, to the number of twenty-seven, were brought to Paris, and there imprisoned.

In the same council also it was decreed by Clement V., that all religious orders who were then exempt should be subject to the common laws as others were. But the Cistercian monks with money and great gifts redeemed their privileges and exemptions of the pope. These Cistercians succeeded better than the Minorites of the Franciscans in their suit. Of which Franciscans, when certain of them had offered to the pope forty thousand florins of gold, besides silver, if he would dispense with their having lands and possessions against their rule. The pope asked them where was that money? They answered, in the merchants' hands. So the space of three days was given them to produce the merchants. Then the pope absolved the merchants of their bond made to the friars, and commanded all that money to be employed to his own use; declaring to the friars that he would not infringe or violate the rule of St. Francis lately canonized, neither ought he to do it for any money. And thus these rich friars, although they called themselves "the begging friars," and "the mendicant order," lost both their money and their indulgence.

This Pope Clement V. excommunicated the Venetians for aiding and preferring Azoda to the state of Ferrara; and wrote his letters throughout all Europe, condemning them as enemies of the church, and giving their goods as a lawful prey to all men, which caused them to sustain great harm. But Francis Dandulus, a nobleman of Venice, being ambassador from the Venetians to Clement, in order to obtain their absolution and the safety of their city and country, and to pacify the pope's fury, so humbled himself before this proud prelate, that he suffered a chain of iron to be tied about his neck, and lay down flat before his table, to catch the bones and fragments that fell from it, as if he had been a dog, till the pope's fury was assuaged; so that afterwards in reproach (because he so humbled himself for the behalf and helping of his country), he was by some called a dog. But the city of Venice showed themselves not ungrateful to Dandulus for his gentle good will thus shown to his country; for as he had abased himself in the vile and ignominious condition of a dog for his country's sake, so they extolled him with as much glory when he returned home, decking and adorning him after the best array, with the chief princely ornaments of the city, to make him amends for his former reproach.

Let us proceed to the next year (A.D. 1311). In which year Peter Gaveston, who had wandered the countries about, and could find no safe resting place, secretly returning into England, presented himself to the king. The king for joy ran to meet him, and embracing him, not only retained him, but also for his sake undid all such acts as had been enacted in the parliament. The queen and the whole court seeing this doting of the king, were exceeding sorrowful. After this return of Gaveston was noised among the commons, the peers, and nobles of the realm were not a little stirred, consulting with themselves what was best to be done. At last they determined that Thomas, earl of Lancaster should be elected among them the chieftain, and chief doer in this business; to whom all other earls, barons, and prelates also consented, except only Walter bishop of Coventry, whom Robert the archbishop, therefore, afterwards excommunicated. The earl of Lancaster, by the assent of the rest, sent to the king, (who was then at York) humble petitions in the name as well of the whole nobility as of the commons, desiring his grace to give Gaveston over to them, or else, according to the ordinance of the realm, that he might be banished; but the tyrannous king, who set more value on the love of one stranger than on his whole realm besides, would neither hearken to their counsel, nor give place to their supplications, but in all hasty fury removed from York to Newcastle, where he remained till near midsummer.

In the meantime the barons had gathered an host of sufficient and able soldiers, and came towards Newcastle, not intending any molestation against the king, but only the execution of the laws upon the wicked Gaveston. The king not having men to resist their power, removed to Tynemouth, and thence to the castle of Scarborough, where leaving Peter Gaveston to the safe keeping of his men, himself journeyed toward Warwick. The lords hearing where Peter was, bent thither all their power; so that at length Gaveston seeing no remedy but he must needs come into their hands, yielded, and submitted himself, requiring no other condition, but only that he might talk but a few words to the king in their presence.

It chanced that Guy, the earl of Warwick, came to the place where Gaveston was in custody, and taking him out of the hands of his keepers, he carried him to the castle of Warwick, where they would have put him to death; but doubting and fearing the king's displeasure, they stayed a little. When one of the company (a man of sage and wise counsel, as mine author writes) standing up among them, gravely declared the nature of the man, the wickedness of his own condition, the realm so greatly endamaged by him, the nobles despised and rejected, the intolerable pride and ambition of the man, the ruin of things like to ensue by him, and the great charges and expenses they had been at in so long pursuing and catching him; and now being gotten and in their hands, he exhorted them to use and take the occasion now present.

Briefly he so persuaded the hearers, that forthwith Gaveston was brought out and beheaded. And thus he that had called the earl of Warwick the black dog of Ardeine, was thus worried by the dog.

After this, great disturbance began to rise between the king and the lords; who having their forces lying about Dunstable, sent message to the king at London, to have their former acts confirmed. Gilbert, earl of Glocester, the king's nephew, (who neither held against the king, nor yet against the nobles), with the bishops and prelates of the realm, went between both parties with great diligence to make unity. At which time also came two cardinals from Rome, with letters from the pope. The nobles answered to the message of the cardinals, then at St. Albans; that as to themselves, they should be at all times welcome, but as touching their letters (forasmuch as they were unlettered men, and only brought up in war and feats of arms) therefore they cared not for seeing the same. Then message was sent again, requiring that they would at least speak with the pope's legates, who purposely came for the intent to set quiet and unity in the realm. They answered again, that they had bishops both godly and learned, by whose counsel only they would be led, and not by any strangers, who knew not the true cause of their commotion. And therefore they said explicitly, that they would have no

foreigners or aliens to be doers in their business and affairs pertaining to the realm. Yet notwithstanding, through the mediation of the archbishop, and of the earl of Glocester, the matter at length was so taken up, that the barons agreed to restore to the king or to his attorney of St. Albans, all the treasure, horses, and jewels of Gaveston which were taken at Newcastle, so that their requests should be granted. And so the matter at that time was settled.

Shortly after this, Isabel the queen was delivered of a fair child at Windsor. At the birth there was great rejoicing through all the land, and especially the king so much joyed, that he began daily more and more to forget the sorrow and remembrance of Gaveston's death, and was after that more agreeable to the will of his nobles.

In the mean time the Scots began to be busy, and to rebel through the means of Robert Bruce; who being chased out of Scotland by King Edward I., as is before mentioned, went into Norway, but was now returned again into Scotland, where he so influenced the lords there, that in a short time he was made king of the realm, and warred so strongly upon them that took the king's part, that he won from them many castles and strongholds, and invaded the borders of England. The king hearing this, assembled a great army, and enters the realm of Scotland by sea. Against whom Robert Bruce with his Scots fought a strong battle at Estrivelin; in the end, the Englishmen were discomfited.

The Scots after this, exalted with pride and fierceness, invaded the realm of England, killing and destroying man, woman, and child; they came winning and wasting the north parts as far as to York. Besides this, there was such dearth of victuals, and penury of all things so oppressed the whole land, such murrain of sheep and oxen; that men were compelled to eat horse-flesh, dogs, cats, mice, and whatever else they could get. Moreover, such a price of corn followed, that the king hardly had bread for the sustenance of his own household. Moreover, there were some that stole children and eat them, and many died for the lack of victuals. And yet all this amended not the king of his evil living.

The cause and origin of this great dearth, was partly the wars and dissension between the English and the Scots, whereby a great part of the land was wasted. But the chiefest cause was the intemperate season of the year, which contrary to the common course, was so moist with abundance of rain, that the grain laid in the earth could have no ripening by the heat of the sun, nor grow to any nourishment. They that had any thing to eat could not be satisfied, but soon were as hungry again. They that had nothing were driven to steal and rob; the rich were constrained to abandon and diminish their households; the poor died from famine. And not so much the want of provisions, which could not be gotten, as the unwholesomeness of the same when it was taken, so consumed the people, that the living were not sufficient to bury the dead. For the corruption of the meats, by reason of the unseasonableness of the ground, was so infectious that many died of hot fevers, many of the pestilence, and other diseases. And not only the bodies of men were infected, but also the beasts, by the putrifaction of the herbs and grass, fell into so great a murrain, that the eating of flesh was suspected and thought contagious. A quarter of corn and salt, from the month of June to September grew from thirty shillings unto forty shillings. The flesh of horses was then precious to the poor. Many were driven to steal fat dogs, and to eat them. Some were said in secret corners to eat their own children. Some would steal other men's children to kill them and eat them privily. The prisoners and thieves that were in prison, for hunger fell upon such as were newly brought in to them, and tearing them in pieces eat them half alive. Briefly, this extreme penury had extinguished and consumed (as it was thought) the greatest part of the people of the land, had not the king by the advice of the Londoners given forth command through all his land, that no corn should at that time be turned to the making of drink. Such a Lord is God, thus able to do where he is disposed to strike. And yet we miserable creatures in our wealth and abundance will not cease daily to provoke his terrible majesty.

Soon after this two legates came from Rome, sent by Pope John XXII., under pretence of setting agreement between England and Scotland; who for their charges and expenses, required of every spiritual person four pence in every mark. But all their labour availed nothing; for the legates as they were in the north parts with their whole family and train, were robbed and despoiled of their horses, treasure, apparel, and what else they had, and being severely handled, retired back again to Durham, where they staid waiting for an answer from the Scots. But when neither the pope's legacy nor his curse could obtain any place with the Scots, the legates returned to London, where they first excommunicated and cursed as black as soot all those arrogant and presumptuous robbers of Northumberland. Secondly, for supplying the losses which they had received, they exacted of the clergy eightpence in every mark to be paid to them. But the clergy would not agree, seeing it was their own covetousness (as they said) that made them venture farther than they needed. Whereof the king being advertised, and taking part with his clergy, directed his letters to the legates in form as follows:

" The king to Master Rigand of Asserio, canon of Aurelia, greeting: we have taken notice of the clamours and lamentable petitions of the subjects of our realm, perceiving by the same that you practise many and sundry inconveniences very strange, never heretofore accustomed, nor heard of in this our realm, as well against the clergy and ecclesiastical persons, as against the laity, even to the utter oppression and impoverishing of many of our liege people, which if it should be winked at (as God forbid) may in process of time be occasion of greater perils; whereat we are (not without cause) moved, and not a little grieved: we command you therefore, that from henceforth you practise not, or presume in any case to attempt any thing within this our realm, either against our clergy or laity, that may any way tend to the prejudice of our royal person, or of our crown and regal dignity. Witness the king at Windsor, the sixth day of February, in the eleventh year of his reign."

In the same year the king wrote to the same effect to the archbishop of Canterbury, to the archbishop of York, and to every other bishop through England. By which letters the greedy legates being restrained of their ravening purpose, taking what they could get, and settling a peace (such as it was) between the king and the earl of Lancaster, were obliged to depart.

Besides the restraint above mentioned for strange impositions, there followed the same year the king's prohibition for the gathering of Peter-pence, directed to the legate, the tenor whereof follows.

A Prohibition of Peter-pence.

" The king to Master Rigand of Asserio, canon of Aurelia, greeting. We are given to understand that you demand and purpose to levy the Peter-penny within our realm, otherwise than the said Peter-penny hath been heretofore accustomed to be levied in the time of any of our progenitors, exercising herein grievous censures ecclesiastical, to the great annoyance and damnifying of the subjects of our realm: for present remedy whereof, our loving subjects have made their humble supplication to us. And forasmuch as the said Peter-penny hath been hitherto accustomed to be gathered and levied upon lands and tenements within our realm, after a due manner and form: we, not willing that any such unaccustomed impositions shall, in anywise be made upon the lands and tenements of any our subjects within our dominions, prohibit you, upon grievous penalty, straitly charging that in nowise you presume to exact, gather, or levy the said Peter-penny in any other form or manner than has been heretofore accustomed to be gathered and levied in the time of our progenitors, or since the beginning of our reign until further order be taken in our

high court of parliament, by the advice of the nobles and peers of our realm, such as may well be taken without prejudice of our crown, and damage of our subjects. Witness the king at Westminster, the first day of March."

To the same effect, letters were directed to the archbishops, deans, archdeacons, and the rest of the clergy.

Touching the first original of which Peter-pence, though mention is made already in the life of King Offa, and others: yet to make a brief recapitulation of the matter, according to the rolls it thus follows: " It is thus found recorded in ancient chronicles touching the Peter-pence of St. Peter, (A.D. 187), Offa, king of Mercia, travelled up to Rome in the time of Pope Adrian I., to obtain the canonizing of St. Alban. And having performed his vow, visiting the college of English students which then flourished in Rome, he gave to the maintenance of the scholars of England, students in Rome, one penny out of every tenement within this realm that had land belonging to the same, amounting to the yearly value of thirty pence."

In the meantime the lords and nobles of England, detesting the outrageous pride of the two Spensers, whereby they wrought daily both great dishonour to the king, and hinderance to the commonwealth, conspired against them. These Spensers being favoured by the king, were as haughty and proud as Peter Gaveston was, and having much influence over the king, they were greatly hated both by the nobles and commons, who now gathering their forces together, made a request to the king, that he should remove the Spensers from his person. For which there was a parliament called in London, and the barons came together with a great company. At this parliament both the Spensers were banished the land for the term of their lives: and they took shipping at Dover, and so left the land. But it was not long after, before the king sent for them again, and set them in high authority. Wherefore, the barons again intending to reform this mischief, assembled their forces; but the king, making much haste, gathered his people as soon, and as he was stronger than they, he pursued them so in divers places, that the barons not fully joined together, were in the end chased so closely, that Thomas, earl of Lancaster, was taken and put to death, with the rest of the nobility, to the number of two-and-twenty of the greatest men, and chiefest captains of this realm.

After the ruin of these noble personages, the king, as though he had gained a great conquest, began to triumph not a little with the Spensers, trusting and committing all to their counsel; insomuch, that both the queen and the other nobles were but little regarded.

Polydore Virgil, among other histories of our English nation which he intermeddles with, prosecuting also the acts and life of this present king, and coming to write of the queen's going over into France, infers much variety and difference of authors concerning the cause thereof. The precise truth of the matter is as follows:

The king of England had been frequently cited to the court of France, to do homage for the dukedom of Aquitaine, and other lands which the king held of France, when the king of England refused, the French king began to enter all such possessions as the king held in France; upon which there were great contention and conflicts on both sides. At length in this year, a parliament was called in London; where it was at last determined that certain should be sent over to make agreement between the two kings. For the better forwarding of which agreement, it was thought good that Queen Isabel, sister to Charles, the French king, should be sent over. Where is to be noted first, that the queen's lands, and possessions and castles, upon the breach between the French king and the king of England, a little before, were seized into the king's hands, and the queen put to her pension, &c. Thus the queen being sent over, with a few to attend upon her, only Sir John Cromwel, baron, and four knights, took their passage into France: by whose mediation it was there concluded that the king of England (if he would not himself come to do his homage) should give to his son Edward, the dukedom of Aquitaine, and the earldom of Pontigne, and so he should come to make his homage to the king, and to possess the same. Upon this, deliberation was taken in the council of England. But the two Spensers, fearing either to take the voyage with the king, or else to remain behind without the king, so appointed, that Prince Edward was sent, which proved afterwards their utter desolation. For all things being quieted and ordered according to the agreement in France, King Edward, of England, sends for his wife and his son again out of France. But she sending home most part of her family, refused to return herself; for what cause is not fully certain. The king seeing this, gives forth in proclamation, and limits a certain day to the queen and his son to return ; or else to be proclaimed traitors to the king, and to the realm. Notwithstanding, the queen persisting in her purpose, refused to return, unless the other nobles who were fled might be permitted also to return safely with her. The king immediately caused them both to be proclaimed traitors.

Here then began great hatred between king and king, and between the king and the queen much preparation of war. Then the king, (by the counsel of the Spensers) sent privily to procure the death of the queen and of his son, through the means of the earl of Richmond, the queen's familiar friend. But that was prevented and utterly frustrated. The queen, however, doubting what corruption might do in the court of France, removed from thence, and was received, with Edward, joyously and honourably in the court or country of the earl of Henawde, or Heinault, where a marriage was concluded between Edward her son, and the earl's daughter. When this was noised in England, several men of honour and name came over to the queen. And soon after the earl of Heinault prepared a body of five hundred men of arms to send over with the young prince and his mother to England. The fame of this spread shortly through the realm. The king made all provision to have the havens and ports securely kept, to resist the landing of his enemies. On the other side the queen, with no less preparation, provided all things necessary to her expedition. When she saw her time, she hastened to the sea-coast with Prince Edward, Lord Edmund, earl of Kent, the king's brother, Sir Roger Mortimer, the Lord Wygmore, and other exiles of England, accompanied also by the band of Heinaulters, of whom Sir John Heinault, the earl's brother, was a captain, having with her of Englishmen and strangers, the number of two thousand seven hundred and fifty-seven soldiers : she took shipping, and had the wind so favourable, that they landed in England, near Harwich, in Suffolk. After her landing, the Earl Marshal, and the earl of Leicester, joined her, with other barons, knights, and bishops also ; namely, the bishops of Lincoln, Hereford, Durham, and Ely. The archbishop of Canterbury, though he came not himself, yet sent his aid, and money. Thus the queen, well furnished with both men and provisions, sets forward toward London ; so that the further she came, the more her number daily increased, and the king's power on the other hand decreased ; so that not one almost in all the realm could be hired with any wages to fight on the king's behalf against the queen, neither did the queen's army hurt any man or child, either in goods or any thing else, by the way.

At the arriving of the queen, the king was in London, who first would not believe it to be true. Afterward he fortified the tower of London with men and provisions, committing the charge of it to John Eltham, his younger son. And leaving Walter Stapleton, bishop of Exeter, behind him to rule the city of London, he himself hearing daily the great recourse of the people that drew to the queen, fled with a small company westward toward Wales. But before his departing from London, he caused a proclamation to be made, wherein all persons were charged upon forfeiture of life and goods, every man with all his power to rise and invade the rebels and destroy them all, only the life of the queen, his son, and his brother, reserved. Also that no man should help, rescue, or relieve the rebels, with goods, victuals, or otherwise. It was also proclaimed, that whoever would bring to the king the head and body of Sir Roger Mortimer, either dead or alive, should have out of the king's coffers, a thousand pounds.

On the other hand, the queen sets forth another proclamation, wherein it was forbidden to take or spoil violently any man's goods against the will of the owner, under pain of losing his finger, if it were three-pence: of his hand, if it were sixpence : of his head, if it were twelve-pence. Moreover, whoever would bring to the queen the head of Hugh Spenser the younger, should receive for so doing of the queen, two thousand pounds. This done, the queen sends her letters to the city of London for aid and succour to subdue the oppressor of the realm.

These letters being published and perused, the bishop of Exeter, to whom was committed the rule of the city, sent to the mayor for the keys of the gates, using so sharp words in the king's name, that variance began to kindle between him and the citizens ; so that the commons in their rage took the bishop and beheaded him and two of his household at the Standard in Cheapside. Then the king, with Hugh Spenser, and Sir Robert Baldock, chancellor, and the earl of Arundel, went into Wales. And the queen so pursued them, that they took Sir Hugh Spenser the father, who being drawn and torn, they at last hanged up at Bristol in iron chains. As the king was thus flying, the queen caused to be proclaimed through her army, that the king should come and appear, and so receive his kingdom again, if he would be comfortable to his liege subjects: and when he did not appear, Prince Edward his son was proclaimed high keeper of the realm.

In the meantime, Henry earl of Lancaster, brother to the good Earl Thomas who was beheaded, also Lord William Souch, and Master Uphowel were sent by the queen into Wales to pursue the king; and there they took him and sent him to the castle of Kenilworth : and took Hugh Spenser the son, and Sir Robert Baldock, chancellor, and Sir John Earl of Arundel, and brought them all to the town of Hereford. And, soon after, Hugh Spenser the son, was drawn and hanged on a gallows fifty feet high, and then beheaded and quartered, whose quarters were sent into four quarters of the realm. Sir John of Arundel was beheaded, Sir Robert Baldock was put into Newgate at London, where shortly after he pined away and died among the thieves. This done, a parliament was assembled at London, from whence message was sent to the king, that if he would resign up his crown, his son should have it after him : if not, another should take it to whom the lot would give it. Whereupon the king, being constrained to yield up his crown to his son, was kept in prison ; where he is said to have felt great repentance.

It is thought by some writers, that the year following, by means of Sir Roger Mortimer, the king while in prison, was miserably slain : he was buried at Gloucester, after he had reigned nineteen years.

In the time and reign of this king, the college of Cambridge, called Michael House, was founded and built by Sir Henry Stanton, knight, for the use and increase of learning.

About the same time also was Nicolas de Lyra, who wrote the ordinary Gloss of the Bible. Also William Ocham, a worthy divine, and of a right sincere judgment, as the times then would either give or suffer.

Among those who fell into trouble with this king during his contention with his barons, was one Adam, bishop of Hereford : who being impeached of treason with others, was arrested in the parliament. Many things there were laid against him, for taking part with them that rose against the king, with other matters and heinous rebukes, &c. Whereto the bishop a great while answered nothing.

At length the bishop claiming the liberties and privileges of the church, answered to the king in this form : " I, an humble minister and member of the holy church of God, and bishop consecrate (although unworthy) cannot, and ought not to answer to these high matters without authority of the archbishop of Canterbury, my direct judge, next under the high bishop of Rome, whose suffragan I am, and the consent likewise of the other my fellow bishops." After which, the archbishop and other bishops with him were ready to make humble intercession for him to the king, and did so. But when the king would not be won nor turned with any supplication; the bishop, together with the archbishop and the clergy, coming with their crosses, took him away, challenging him for the church, without making any more answer; charging, moreover, none to presume to lay any further hands upon him, under the censures of the church and excommunication. The king, moved with this boldness and stoutness of the clergy, commanded notwithstanding, to proceed in judgment, and the jury of twelve men to go upon the inquiry of his cause: who finding and pronouncing the bishop to be guilty, the king immediately caused all his goods and possessions to be confiscated unto himself: moreover, he made his plate and all his household provision to be thrown out of his house into the street; but yet he remained still under the protection and defence of the archbishop.

This archbishop was Walter Winchelsey, after whom succeeded Simon Mepham in the same see of Canterbury, A. D. 1327. (Ex Thom. Walsingham).

After Pope Clement V., by whose decease the Romish see stood vacant two years and three months, Pope John XXII., a Cistercian monk, was next elected, who sat in that papacy eighteen years. He was stout and inflexible, given so much to the heaping of riches, that he proclaimed them heretics, who taught that Christ and his apostles had no possessions of their own in this world. At this time was emperor Lewis of Bavaria, a worthy man; who had no less contention with this pope, and others that followed him, than had Frederick, before mentioned in the time of King Henry III. This contention continued the space of four-and-twenty years. The cause and first origin of this tragical conflict, rose upon the constitution of Clement V. predecessor to this pope; by whom it was ordained, that the emperors might be called kings of the Romans, but might not enjoy the title or right of the empire, to be nominated emperors, without their confirmation by the pope. Wherefore, because this emperor used the imperial dignity in Italy, before he was authorised by the pope, the pope therefore excommunicated the emperor. And, notwithstanding, the emperor several times proffered himself to make treaty of peace and concord, yet the pope would not bend. The writings of both parties are yet extant, wherein the bishop makes his boast, that he had full power to create and depose kings and emperors at his pleasure. In the same time were several learned men, who, seeing the matter, greatly condemned the bishops of Rome's doings; among whom was William Ocham, whose treatises were afterwards condemned by the pope, for writing against the temporal jurisdiction of their see. And another named Marsilius, who wrote the book intitled 'Defensor Pacis,' which was given into the hands of the emperor, wherein the controversy of the pope's unlawful jurisdiction in things temporal is largely disputed, and the usurped authority of that see set forth to the utmost. It is found in some writers, that a great cause of this variance was that one of the emperor's secretaries, unknown to the emperor, in some of his letters had likened the papal see to the beast rising out of the sea in the Apocalypse. At length, when the emperor, after much suit made to the pope at Avignon, could not obtain his coronation; coming to Rome, he was there received with great honour, where he and his wife were both crowned by the full consent of all the lords and cardinals. Not long after which, the pope died at Avignon in France. After him succeeded Benedict XII., and reigned seven years, who confirmed and prosecuted the censures and cursings that John his predecessor had published against the Emperor Lewis. Moreover, he deprived him of his imperial crown, and also of his dukedom of Bavaria.

After whom followed Pope Clement VI., a man of the most furious and cruel disposition. Renewing the former excommunications of his predecessors, he caused his letters to be set upon church doors, wherein he threatened and denounced most terrible thunderbolts against the Emperor Lewis, unless within three days he should satisfy God and the church, and renounce the imperial possession of the crown. The emperor upon this comes to Frankfort, and there ready to stand in all things to the ordinance of the pope, sends his orators to the court of Rome, to intreat the pope's favour and good will towards him. To which messengers the pope answered that he would never pardon the emperor, before he gave over and confessed his errors and heresies, and resigning up his empire to his hands, would submit himself, his children, and all his goods to the will and pleasure of the bishop, declaring that he should not receive again any part of the same, but upon his good grace, as his will should be to restore them.

The pope also sent to the emperor certain written conditions for him to sign. The princes and electors, seeing the conditions, some of which sounded to the malicious defacing and destruction of the empire, abhorring the wickedness thereof, desired the emperor to stand to the defence of the imperial dominion, as he had begun, promising that their assistance and aid to the utmost should not be wanting. Upon that, other orators were sent to Pope Clement from the princes, desiring him to abstain from such articles conceived against the state and majesty of the empire. The pope surmising all this to spring from the Emperor Lewis, to the utter subversion of him and all his posterity, on Maunday-Thursday issued out most black curses against him, renewing all the former processes of his predecessor against him, as against both an heretic and a schismatic; commanding, moreover, the princes electors to proceed in choosing a new emperor. Upon which, the archbishop of Cologne, the duke of Saxony, and some other electors, being bribed by the king of Bohemia, elected his son Charles emperor. In the meantime, what sorrow there was among the princes and citizens of Germany, and what complaints were made against Pope Clement, and those electors, cannot be expressed. For as they were all together at Spires in a general assembly, so there was none among them all, that allowed the election of Charles, or that cared for the pope's process, promising all to adhere and continue faithful subjects to Lewis their lawful emperor. But Lewis, remembering his oath made before to the pope, voluntarily and willingly gave over his imperial dignity, and went to Burgravia, where, shortly after, through the procurement of Pope Clement, poison was given him to drink; and there the good and gentle emperor, wickedly persecuted and murdered of the pope, fell down dead, whom I may well recount among the innocent and blessed martyrs of Christ. For if the cause being righteous makes a martyr, what papist can justly disprove his cause or faith? If persecution joined thereto causes martyrdom, what martyr could be more persecuted than he who having three popes like three bull dogs upon him, at length was devoured by them.

This Pope Clement first reduced the year of jubilee to every fiftieth year, which before was kept but on the hundreth year. And so he being absent to Avignon (which he then purchased with his money to the see of Rome) caused it to be celebrated at Rome, (A.D. 1350.) In which year there were numbered, of pilgrims going in and coming out every day at Rome, to the calculation of five thousand. The bull of Pope Clement, given out in this present year of jubilee, proceeds in these words:—

"What person or persons soever, for devotion sake, shall take their pilgrimage to the holy city, the same day when he sets forth out of his house, he may choose to him what confessor or confessors, either in the way, or where else he chooses; to which confessors we grant, by our authority, plenary power to absolve all cases papal, as fully as if we were in our proper person there present. Also, we grant that whoever being truly confessed, shall chance to die by the way, he shall be quit and absolved of all his sins. Moreover, we command the angels of Paradise to take his soul out of his body, being absolved, and to carry it into the glory of Paradise, &c."

And in another bull, he says, "We will that no pain of hell shall touch him; granting, moreover to all persons, signed with the holy cross, power, and authority to deliver and release three or four souls, whom they themselves please, out of the pains of purgatory," &c.

KING EDWARD III.

After the imprisonment of King Edward II., as is above expressed, Edward his son was crowned king of England, being about fifteen years of age, and reigned the space of fifty years. He was a prince of great temperance, very expert in feats of arms, and no less fortunate in all his wars than his father was unfortunate before him; he was worthily commended for his liberality and clemency; and, briefly, in all princely virtues he was famous and excellent. Concerning the memorable acts of this prince, both in war and in peace, as how he subdued the Scots, had great victories by the sea, how he conquered France, (A.D. 1332), won Calais, (A.D. 1348), and took the French king prisoner, and how the French arms were first brought in by him, and joined with the English arms; also, how the Order of the Garter was first invented and ordained by him, (A.D. 1356.) How he in his parliament at Nottingham, decreed that all such in Flanders, or elsewhere, that had skill in making cloth, might peaceably inhabit the land, and be welcome. (For three years before that it was enacted, that no wool should be transported over the sea, which was to bridle the pride of the Flemings, who then loved better the sacks of wool, than the nation of Englishmen.) All these, with other noble acts of this worthy prince, although they are fully treated of in other chronicles; yet according to the order I have begun (saying somewhat of each king's reign, although not pertinent to our ecclesiastical history), I have here mentioned them, making haste to other matters, shortly and compendiously abridging them out of many and various authors.

The coronation of King Edward III. and all the pomp thereof was no sooner ended, than Robert Bruce king of Scotland, understanding the state and government of the realm to be (as it was indeed) in the queen, the young king, the earl of Kent and sir Roger Mortimer, and that the lords and barons, as he was informed, did scarcely well agree amongst themselves, thought this a fit time for his purpose, to make invasion. Whereupon, about the feast of Easter he sent his ambassadors with heralds and letters of defiance to the young King Edward III., the queen and the council; declaring, that his purpose was with fire and sword to enter and invade the realm of England, &c.

The king and queen made speedy preparation for this expedition: the noblemen provided themselves with all things necessary; the English captains and soldiers (their bands thoroughly furnished) were ready at their appointed time and place. After this, the king set forward his army towards Durham, and encamped himself near about the same, he also sent the lord Vifford and the lord Mounbrey to Carlisle with a sufficient company to keep that entrance; and also the lord marshal of England to keep the town of Newcastle with a sufficient company to defend the same, and the country adjoining.

But the Scots privily passed the river between the two towns into England, few being aware of it till the great fires which the Scots had kindled and made in England, betrayed them: who came burning and destroying the country all about as far as Stanhope-park. This being declared to the king, he commanded his army with all speed to march towards them; but the Scots, understanding the superior force of the king always kept the advantage of the hills, retiring in the night from one to another: that without great advantage on the one side, and hazard to the other, the king could not set upon them.

Thus the Scots keeping the advantage of the hills, in the day time, and in the night time retiring till they came to another hill, came near the bank of that river where they first passed over, and there they made a shew to offer battle to the king upon the morrow. Whereupon the king being busied in putting his men and divisions in readiness to fight the next morning, being almost wearied in pursuing the Scots from place to place: the Scots in the meantime crossed over the river, and escaped the danger of the king. It would have availed the king very little to have made pursuit after them, as the wily Scots knew full well. For the joy whereof, the Lord William Douglas, one of the Scot's generals, with two hundred horses, gave alarm in the king's camp; and came so near that he cut certain of the lines of the king's tent in sunder with his sword, and retired to his company without great loss of any of his men. A truce of four years was soon after concluded between them.

After the truce of four years, the king prepared another army against Scotland, and wasted the land, burnt, destroyed, and took towns and castles with small resistance or none; and during the space of six months together did what he pleased in that land, without any battle offered to him. For the king of Scots was but a child, not above fifteen years of age, and wanted good captains that should have defended the realm.

Then Sir Robert de Artois, a nobleman of France, descended of the blood royal, being in England with the king, often put him in mind of his good and rightful title to the crown of France. King Edward was not unwilling to hear of this, but took delight often in reasoning and debating the matter with him. But yet, he thought it not good to make any attempt without advised and cautious counsel; therefore, calling together certain of his council, he sought their deliberate advice touching the matter. In fine, it was thought good by them, that the king should send certain ambassadors over to the earl of Heinault, whose daughter he had married, as well to hear his advice and counsel herein; as also to learn what friends and aid, by him and his means, might be procured. The king appointed for this ambassage the bishop of Lincoln with two baronets, and two doctors; who in a short space returned to the king with this answer, that not only the earl's council and advice should be at the service of the king of England, but also the whole country of Heinault. And further, that he would procure for the king greater aid, as the duke of Brabant his cousin-germain, and a puissant prince, the duke of Guerles, the archbishop of Cologne, the marquess of Juliers, &c., who were all good men of war, and able to make ten thousand fighting men. This answer well pleased the king, and made him very joyous. But this counsel of the king, secret as it was, came to the French king's ears: whereupon he stayed the voyage of the cross which he had then in hand, sending forth countermands to stay the same, till he knew further the purpose of the king of England.

The king hereupon himself takes shipping, and when he had consulted with all the lords of the empire in this matter, and understood their fidelity, he repaired to the emperor, at whose hands he was well entertained, and honourably received. Philip hearing this, prepared his army, and rigged his navy, that so soon as the king should enter into the dominion of France, they also might enter into England, requiring like for like.

The king of England, after the feast of St. John Baptist, according to his purpose, prepared all things ready to such an expedition, conducting his army, and gathering a greater force in the empire, as was promised, using the emperor's authority therein, as his lieutenant-general, although at the charge altogether of the king of England. The French king, as soon as King Edward had landed his army at Machelen in Flanders, sent certain ships lying ready, and waiting for such opportunity to the coast of England; which, upon a Sunday, whilst the townsmen were at the church, little looking for any such matter, entered the haven of Southampton, took the town and spoiled the same, shamefully ill-treated the women, burnt, killed, took captives, and carried away rich spoils to their ships, and so again departed into France. Further, as the king of England had allied himself with the noblemen of the empire, and had the friendly favour of the emperor, so the French king made league and alliance with David the king of Scots, and forthwith sent garrisons and bands into Scotland to keep play with the Englishmen. King Edward, departing from Machelen, set forward his host toward Heinault till they came to Cambray, and besieged it with 40,000 men, while another company went to St.

Quintin. But neither there, nor at Cambray, nor elsewhere, was any thing remarkable achieved. But the summer being well spent, and the king of England prevailing little in the siege of Cambray, being strong in situation, and well defended with men and ammunition, he brake up the siege, and marched further into the heart of France. And afterwards (without any battle either given or taken) he returned with his army to Gaunt.

The winter then drew on, and the king thought best for a season to return to England with his army, giving over the wars till the next spring. When he came to London, he was told of the great spoil the Frenchmen had made at Southampton: he answered, "That within one year he doubted not but they should be well paid and recompensed." In the spring the king again prepared his army, and rigged his navy, purposing to land in Flanders. But the archbishop of Canterbury, then lord chancellor, having understood that the French forces were upon the sea, watching for the king, gave him information of it, desiring him to go more strongly or else not to venture. But the king not crediting the archbishop, and being angry with him, said, "That he would go forward:" whereupon the bishop resigned the chancellorship, and removed himself from his council: then the king consulting farther with the Lord Morley his admiral, and others, furnished himself with a greater force, and embarked; so that a few days before midsummer, he was upon the sea with a great fleet. The French king, to stop his passage, had ready a great navy, well near to the number of twenty score sail, before the town of Sluse; and had made the Christopher of England (which the Frenchmen had captured at Southampton) their admiral's ship; betwixt which two navies there was a long and terrible fight. But in the end, the victory, by God's grace, fell to the king of England, (in which fight he himself was personally engaged). So that of the number of thirty thousand Frenchmen, few or none escaped alive, and two hundred sail of ships were taken, in one of which were found four hundred dead bodies.

This victory being achieved, and the fame thereof spreading abroad in England, it was not believed, till letters came from the king to Prince Edward his son, then at Waltham, directed to the bishops and prelates of the realm: the effect of which letters here follows:—

"The bountiful benignity of God's great clemency poured upon us of late, for your true certainty and rejoicing, we thought good to intimate to you. It is not unknown (we suppose) to you, and to our other faithful subjects, who also have been partakers with us of the same, with what storms of boisterous wars of late we have been tossed and shaken, as in the great ocean. But although the rising surges of the sea are marvellous, yet more marvellous is the Lord above, who, turning the tempest into a calm, in so great dangers, so mercifully has respected us. For whereas we of late ordained our passage upon urgent causes into Flanders; the Lord Philip de Valois, our bitter enemy, understanding thereof, laid against us a mighty navy of ships, intending thereby either to take us, or at least to stop our voyage. Which voyage, if it had been staid, had been the cutting off of all the great enterprises by us intended and taken in hand; and, moreover, we ourselves had been brought to a great confusion. But the God of mercies, seeing us so distressed in such perils and dangers, hath graciously, and beyond man's expectation, sent to us great succour and strength of fighting soldiers, and a prosperous wind after our own desires. By the means and help of which, we set out of the haven into the seas, where we soon perceived our enemies well appointed and prepared with a main multitude to set upon us, upon midsummer-day last past. Against whom, notwithstanding, Christ our Lord and Saviour hath rendered to us the victory, through a strong and vehement conflict. In which conflict, a mighty number of our enemies were destroyed, and well near all their whole navy was taken; with some loss also of our part, but nothing in comparison to theirs. By reason of which we doubt not but our passage by the seas hereafter shall be more quiet and safe for our subjects, and also many other advantages shall ensue, as we have good cause to hope well of the same. For which cause we, devoutly considering the heavenly grace so mercifully wrought upon us, do render most humble thanks and praise to Christ our Lord and Saviour, beseeching him, that as he hath been and always is, ready to anticipate our necessities in time of opportunity, so he will continue his helping hand ever towards us, and so to direct us here temporally, that we may reign and joy with him in heaven eternally. And in like sort we require your charity, that you also with us rising up to the praise of God alone, who hath begun so favourably to work with us to our goodness, in your prayers and divine service do instantly recommend us to the Lord, while we are travelling here in these foreign countries, studying not only to recover our right here in France, but also to advance the whole catholic church of Christ, and to rule our people in justice. And also that ye call upon the clergy and people, every one through his diocese, to do the same, invocating the name of our Saviour, that of his mercy he will give to us his humble servant a docible heart, so to judge and rule hereupon rightly, doing that which he hath commanded, that at length we may attain to that which he hath promised, &c." Which letter was written to the bishops and prelates, A.D. 1340.

After this victory the king passing into Flanders, came to Gaunt in Brabant, where he had left the queen, who joyfully received him, being a little before delivered of her fourth son, whose name was John, commonly called John of Gaunt, who was earl of Richmond and duke of Lancaster. At Villenorth the king assembled his council, whereat the noblemen of Flanders, Brabant, and Heinault, joining together in most firm league, the one to help and defend the other, with the king of England, against the French king, purposing and determining from thence to march toward Tournay to besiege it. The French king, understanding their counsel, fortified and victualled the same before their coming thither. Furthermore to stop King Edward, he sent with King David of Scotland a great army, to make invasion in England, thereby the sooner to cause the king to remove his siege.

This David (with the aid of the Scots and Frenchmen) so much succeeded, that they recovered almost all Scotland. Then they invaded England, and came with their army, wasting and burning the country before them, till they came as far as Durham, and then returned again into Scotland, where they recovered all their holds again, saving the town of Berwick. Edinburgh they took by a stratagem or subtile device practised by Douglas, and others: who apparelling themselves in poor men's habits, as victuallers with corn and provender, and other things, demanded of the porter early in the morning whether they had need thereof? Who nothing mistrusting, opened the outward gate, where they should tarry till the captain rose: and perceiving the porter to have the keys of the inward gate, they threw down their sacks in the outward gate, that it might not be shut again, and slew the porter, taking from him the keys of the town. Then they blew their horns as a warning to their bands, who laid not far off: and they coming quickly, and finding the gates ready opened, entered upon the sudden, and killed as many as resisted them, and so obtained the city of Edinburgh.

At the same time the French king gathered together an army, purposing to raise the siege of Tournay: and among others sent for the king of Scots, who came to him with a great force, besides other noblemen of France: so that the French king had a great army, and thought himself able enough to raise the siege. But for all this, he durst not yet approach the king of England so near, as to give him battle, but kept himself with his army aloof, in a sure place for his better defence. And although the king of England wasted, burnt, spoiled, and destroyed the country, twenty miles about Tournay, and took many strong towns and holds, and slew above three hundred men of arms, and killed of noblemen, the Lord of Duskune, of Mauris-leou, of Rely, of Chastillion, of Melly, of Fenis, of Hamelar, Mountfaucon, and other barons, to the number of fourteen; and also slew and killed above one hundred and thirty knights, being all men of great possessions and prowess, and took other small cities and towns to the number of three hundred : yet for all this, the French king, durst neither rescue his towns, nor relieve his own men: but of his great army he lost (which is to be marvelled at, being in the midst of his own country) by famine and other inconveniencies, and for want of water, more than twenty thousand men without fighting any battle. Whereupon at the entreaty of Philip by his ambassadors to the king, and by the mediation of the Lady Jane, sister to Philip, and mother to the earl of Heinault, whose daughter king Edward had married ; a truce for one year was concluded.

As soon as this truce was finished, King Edward brake up his camp, removing his siege from Tournay, and came again to Gaunt. From whence (very early in the morning) he with a small company took shipping, and came by sea to the tower of London, very few or none having been aware of it. And being greatly displeased with some of his council and high officers (for through their default he was constrained against his will, not having money to maintain his wars, to condescend to the truce) he commanded the Lord John Stonehore chief justice of England, and Sir John Poultney, with divers others, to be apprehended and brought to him to the Tower. And the next morning he sent for the bishop of Chichester, and the Lord Wake, the lord treasurer, and others that were in authority and office, and commanded them all to be kept as prisoners in the Tower, the bishop only excepted.

The history treating of this matter reports, that the king had at this time under him evil substitutes, and covetous officers: who attending more to their own gain than to the public honour and commodity of the realm, left the king destitute and naked of money. With which crime also John Stratford then archbishop of Canterbury was suspected.

About the year A. D. 1341, there were sent from the pope two cardinals to treat with King Edward for three years truce more, to be concluded with the French king, besides the former truce taken before for one year, and all by the pope's means. For here is to be understood, that it was not for the pope's purpose to have the king of England to reign over so many countries.

The next year, which was A. D. 1342, the emperor, who before had shewed great courtesy to King Edward in his first voyage, insomuch that he made him his vicar or vicegerent-general, and offered him also aid against the French king; now (either turned by inconstancy, or seduced by the pope) writes to him contrary letters, wherein he revokes the vicegerentship granted to him, and befriends the French king.

In the mean time Pope Benedict XII. died ; after whom succeeded Pope Clement VI. Of whom it is reported, that he was very liberal and bountiful to his cardinals, enriching them with goods and possessions not of his own however, but with the ecclesiastical dignities and preferments of the church of England. But the king being offended therewith, made void and frustrated all those provisions of the pope ; charging and commanding that no person whatever should busy himself with any such provisions, under pain of imprisonment and losing his life, (A. D. 1344.)

Pope Clement began to make new provisons for two of his cardinals of the benefices and churches that should be next vacant, besides bishopricks and abbotships, to the extent of two thousand marks. And the proctors of the cardinals were sent down for them. But the king and nobility of the realm not suffering such proceedings under pain of imprisonment, caused the proctors forthwith to leave the realm, and the nobles and commons shortly after wrote a fruitful epistle to the pope, for the liberties and maintenance of the English church, which the pope and the cardinals were not able to answer. The argument of which letter, is as follows :

The letter of the king of England, and the nobles of the same, to the pope, against the reservations and provisions which he had in England.

" To the most holy father in God, Lord Clement, by the grace of God, of the holy church of Rome, and of the universal church, chief and high bishop ; his humble and devout children, the princes, dukes, earls, barons, knights, citizens, burgesses, and all the commonalty of the realm of England, assembled at the parliament holden at Westminster the fifteenth day of May last past ; send devout kissings of his holy feet, with all humble reverence and humility. Most holy father, the holy discretion, government and equity, which appears to be in you, and ought of duty to be so, (being so high and holy a prelate, and head of the holy church), by whom the holy universal church and people of God ought to be as by the sun-beams enlightened, gives us good hope and likelihood, that the just petitions (to the honour of Jesus Christ and holy church, and your holiness also) by us declared, shall be by you graciously heard and considered ; and that all errors and other iniquities should be quite taken away and removed ; instead whereof, fruitful exploits and necessary remedies (by the grace of the Holy Spirit which you in so high an estate have received) may be by you likewise graciously ordained and disposed. Wherefore most holy father we all (upon great deliberation and common assent) come unto your holiness, shewing and declaring that the noble kings of England, our progenitors, our ancestors, and we, according to the grace of the Holy Spirit to them and us given, every one according to his devotion, have established, founded, and endowed within the realm of England, churches, cathedrals, colleges, abbeys, priories, and other houses of religion ; and to the prelates and governors of the same places have given lands, possessions, patrimonies, franchises, advowsons, and patronages of dignities, revenues, offices, churches, with many other benefices ; whereby the service of God and the faith of Christ might have been honoured and had in reverence, that the hospitals and alms-houses that are made, with all the churches and edifices, might be honestly kept and maintained, and that devout prayers might in those places be made for the founders, and the poor parishioners aided and comforted. And such only ought to have the cure thereof, as are able to hear confessions ; and in their own natural tongue are otherwise meet to inform and teach their parishioners. And forsomuch as (most holy father) you cannot well come to the notice of divers such errors and defaults, neither yet understand the conditions of the places, being so far off, unless your holiness be informed and advertised ; we having the perfect intelligence and understanding of the said errors and defaults of the places, within the realm, have thought meet to signify the same unto your holiness : that divers reservations, provisions, and collations by your predecessors apostolic of Rome, and by you, most holy father, in your time, have been granted, and that more largely than they have been accustomed to be, to divers persons as well as strangers, and of sundry nations, as to some such as are our enemies having no understanding at all of the tongue and condition of them, of whom they have the government and cure. Whereby a great number of souls are in peril, — a great many of their parishioners in danger, — the service of God destroyed, — the alms and devotion of all men diminished, — the hospitals perished, — the churches with their appurtenances decayed, — charity withdrawn, — the good and honest persons of our realm unadvanced, — the charge and government of souls not regarded, — the devotion of the people restrained, — many poor scholars unpreferred, — and the treasure of the realm carried out against the minds and intents of the founders. All which errors, defaults and slanders, most holy father, we neither can nor ought to suffer or endure. We therefore most humbly require your holiness, that the slanders, errors and defaults, which we have declared to you, may be through your great discretion considered ; and that it may please you that such reservations, provisions, and collations may be utterly annulled, that from henceforth the same be no more used among us; and to take such order and remedy therein, that the benefices, edifices, rights, with their appurtenances, may be to the honour of God, occupied, defended, and governed by our own countrymen. And that it may further please your holiness by your letters to signify to us, without delay, what your pleasure is touching this our lawful request; that we may do our endeavour with diligence herein for the remedy, correction, and amendment of those enormities above specified. In witness whereof, unto these letters patent we have set our seals. Given in the full parliament at Westminster, the eighteenth day of May, A. D. 1343.''

The king shortly after sent over his proctors, the Earl of Lancaster and Derby, Hugh Spenser, Lord Ralph Stafford, with the bishop of Exeter, and others, to the pope's court, to discuss and plead about the right of his title before the pope. To whom Pope Clement VI., not long after sent down this message; how that Lewis, Duke of Bavaria the emperor, whom the pope had before deposed, had submitted himself to him in all things; and therefore deserved at his hands the benefit of absolution; and how the pope had conferred and restored to him justly and graciously the empire, which he before held unjustly, &c. Which message when the king heard, being moved to anger, he answered again, saying, "That if the pope also agreed and compounded with the French king, he was ready to fight with them both."

Within this year, pence, half-pence, and farthings, began to be coined in the Tower. And the next year following, (which was A. D. 1344), the castle of Windsor (where the king was born) began to be repaired; and in which the house called the round table was situate, the diameter whereof, from the one side to the other, contained two hundred feet: to the expenses of which house there was allowed weekly an hundred pounds for the maintaining of the king's chivalry, till at length by the occasion of the French wars, it came down to nine pounds a week.

During the same year the clergy of England granted to the king tenths for three years; for which the king in recompence granted to them his charter, containing these privileges: that no archbishop nor bishop should be arraigned before his justices, if the said clergyman do submit and claim his right as a clergyman, professing himself to be a member of holy church; who doing so, shall not be bound to come before the justices. And if it shall be laid to their charge that they have married two wives, or have married a widow, the justices shall have no power to proceed against them. But the cause shall be reserved to the spiritual court, &c.

About this present time at the setting up of the round table, the king made Prince Edward, his eldest son, the first Prince of Wales. All this while the truce continued between the two kings. Although it is thought that the French king made many attempts to infringe it. Whereupon Henry Earl of Lancaster, with six hundred men at arms, and as many archers, was sent over to Gascony, the year after, (A. D. 1345), who there so valiantly behaved himself, that he subdued fifty-five townships to the king, he took twenty-three noblemen prisoners, encountering with the French at Allebroke. So courteously and liberally he dealt with the soldiers, that it was a joy to them, and a preferment to fight under him. His manner was in winning any town, to reserve little or nothing to himself, but to divide the whole spoil to his soldiers. One example in the author (whom I follow) is mentioned; how the earl at the winning of the town of Briers, where he had granted to every soldier for his booty the house with all its contents, which he should obtain by victory; among his other soldiers was one who took a certain house which contained the mint and coined money for that country; when the soldier had found it, in breaking up a house where the gross metal was not yet perfectly wrought, he came to the earl, declaring to him the treasure, to know what was his pleasure therein. To whom the earl answered, "That the house was his, and whatever he found therein.'' Afterward the soldier, finding a whole mint of pure

silver ready coined, again informed the earl, as he thought such treasure too great for his portion; the earl again answering, declared that "He had once given him the whole house, and what he had once given, he would not call back again, as children use to play.'' And therefore bade him enjoy that which was granted to him; and if the money were thrice as much, it should be his own. Which story, whether it was true or otherwise in those days, I have not to affirm. But, if in these our covetous, wretched days now present, any author should report the like act to be practised, I would hardly believe it to be true.

As the Earl of Lancaster was thus occupied in Gascony, the Scots were as busy in England, wasting and spoiling without mercy; who were thought to be set on by the French king. And therefore he was judged both by that, and by other ways to have broken the covenants of truce between him and the king of England.

Wherefore the next year (A. D. 1346) King Edward first sending his letters to the court of Rome, and therein complaining to the pope of Philip, how he transgressed and broke the truce between them; about the month of July made his voyage into Normandy, in such a secret way, that no man well knew whither he designed to go. First he entered the town of Hogs, and from thence proceeded to Cardoyne. Where, about the twenty-seventh of July, by the river of Cardoyne, he fought a great battle with the Normans and other Frenchmen, who to stop his passage, defended the bridge. At the battle there were taken of the lords of France, the Earl of Ewe, the Earl of Tankerville; and of knights with other men of arms, to the number of one hundred; of footmen six hundred; and the town and suburbs beaten down to the hard walls. And all that could be borne away, was transported to the ships.

A little before, mention was made how the French king began first to infringe the truce, and how the Earl of Lancaster on that account, was sent unto Gascony. It appears that the French king (contrary to the form of truce taken at Vanes) had seized some of the nobles of England, and had brought them to Paris to be imprisoned and put to death; besides other slaughters and spoilings made in Brittany, Gascony, and other places. King Edward therefore seeing the truce broken on the French king's part, A. D. 1345, the fourteenth of the month of June, published and sent abroad his letters of defiance.

Now concerning the campaign of the king, with his achievements from the winning of Codane or Cardoyne, to the town of Poissy, all is sufficiently described by one of the king's chaplains and his confessor; who being a Dominican Friar, and accompanying the king through all his journey, writes as follows:

"We have great cause to praise and laud the God of Heaven, and to confess his holy name, who has wrought mercy to us. For after the conflict at Codane, in which many were slain, and the city taken and sacked even to the bare walls, the city of Baia immediately yielded, fearing lest their counsels had been betrayed. After this the lord our king directed his progress toward Rouen. And while at the town of Lexon, there came certain cardinals to him, greatly exhorting him to peace. The cardinals being courteously entertained by the king from reverence to the pope's see, it was answered them; that the king being desirous of peace, had tried by all reasonable ways and means how to maintain it, and therefore had offered conditions of peace to the no small prejudice of his own cause. And he is yet ready to admit any reasonable offer of peace. With this answer the cardinals going to the French king, to persuade him in like manner, returned to King Edward again, offering to him in the French king's name, the dukedom of Aquitaine, besides the hope also of obtaining more, if treaty of peace might be obtained. But for so much as that did not content the king, and as the cardinals did not find the French king so tractable and desirous of peace as they looked for, they returned, leaving the matter as they found it. So the king hastening forward, subdued the country and the great towns, without any resistance of the inhabitants, who all fled and ran away. Such fear God struck into them, that it seemed as if they had lost their hearts. As the king had gotten many towns and villages, so he also subdued many strong castles, and that with little difficulty. His enemy being at the same time at Rouen had reared a great army, yet he ever kept on the other side of the river Seine, breaking down all the bridges that we should not come over to him. And although the country round about was spoiled, sacked, and consumed with fire for a circuit of twenty miles ; yet the French king, being distant scarcely the space of one mile from us, either would not, or else dared not (when he might easily have passed over the river) make any defence of his country and people. And so our king journeying forward, came to Pusiake or Poissy, where the French king had also broken down the bridge, and kept on the other side of the river."

After coming to Poissy, this chaplain and confessor to the king, named Michael Northburgh, describes the king's progress, and the acts of the English from the town of Poissy, to his coming to Calais as follows :—

A Letter of William Northburgh the King's Confessor, describing the King's Progress into France.

"Salutations premised, we give you to understand, that our sovereign lord the king came to the town of Poissy, the day before the assumption of our lady, where was a bridge over the Seine, broken down by the enemy, but the king waited there, till the bridge was again made. And while the bridge was repairing, there came a great number of men-at-arms, and other soldiers, to hinder the works. But the earl of Northampton issued out against them and slew more than one thousand ; the rest fled away, thanks be to God. At another time our men passed the water, although with much difficulty, and slew a great number of the common soldiers about the city of Paris, and adjoining country ; so that our people now made other good bridges, God be thanked, without any great loss or damage to us. On the morrow after the assumption of our lady, the king passed the river Seine and marched toward Poissy, a town of great defence and strongly immured, and a very strong castle within it. When our vanguard was passed the town, our rear-guard gave an assault and captured it, there were slain more than three hundred men-at-arms of our enemies. The next day, the Earl of Suffolk and Sir Hugh Spenser marched forth upon the commons of the country assembled and well armed, and discomfited them, and slew more than two hundred, and took six hundred gentlemen prisoners, beside others. After that, the king marched toward Grand Villers, and while he was encamped there, the vanguard was descried by the men-of-arms of the king of Bohemia ; whereupon our men issued out in great haste, and joined battle with them, but were forced to retire. But thanks be unto God, the earl of Northampton issued out, and rescued the horsemen with other soldiers ; so that few or none of them were either taken or slain, (except only Thomas Talbot,) but had the enemy in chase within two leagues of Amiens, of whom we took eight, and slew twelve of their best men-at-arms ; the rest being well horsed, reached the town of Amiens. After this, the king of England marched toward Pountife upon Bartholomew day, and came to the water of Somme where the French king had laid five hundred men-at-arms, and three thousand footmen, purposing to have stopped our passage, but thanks be to God, the king of England and his host entered the water of Somme, without the loss of any of our men. After that he encountered with the enemy, and slew more than two thousand of them ; the rest fled to Abbeville, in which chase there were taken many knights, squires, and men-at-arms. The same day Sir Hugh Spenser took the town of Croylay, where he and his soldiers slew four hundred men-at-arms, and kept the town, where they found great store of victuals. The same night the king of England encamped in the forest of Cressy upon the same water, for the French king's host came on the other side of the town near to our passage ; and so marched toward Abbeville. And upon the Friday following, the king being still encamped in the forest, our

scouts descried the French king, marching toward us in four great divisions. And having then information of our enemies, a little before the evening we drew to the plain field, and set our forces in array ; and immediately the fight began, it was sore, cruel, and long, for our enemies behaved themselves right nobly. But thanks be given to God, the victory fell on our side, and our adversary was discomfited with all his host, and put to flight : there was slain the king of Bohemia, the duke of Lorrain, the earl of Dabeson, the earl of Flanders, the earl of Blois, the earl of Arcot, with his two sons, the earl of Damerler, the earl of Navers, and his brother, the lord of Tronard, the archbishop of Meymes, the archbishop of Saundes, the high prior of France, the earl of Savoy, the lord of Morles, the lord de Guis, seignior de St. Novant, seigniour de Rosinburgh, with six earls of Germany and other earls, barons, knights and squires, whose names are unknown. Philip (the French king) himself, with another marquess, who was called Lord Elector among the Romans, escaped from the battle. The number of the men-at-arms found dead in the field, besides the common soldiers and footmen, were one thousand five hundred and forty-two. And all that night the king of England with his host, remained armed in the field where the battle was fought. On the next morrow before the sun rose, there marched toward us another great army, mighty and strong. But the earl of Northampton, and the earl of Norfolk issued out against them in three divisions ; and after a long and terrible fight, they discomfited them by God's great help and grace (for otherwise it could never have been) where they took of knights and squires a great number, and slew above two thousand, pursuing the chase three leagues from the place where the battle was fought. The same night the king encamped again in the forest of Cressy, and on the morrow marched toward Boulogne, and by the way took the town of Staples ; and from thence he marched toward Calais, which he intends to besiege. And therefore our sovereign lord the king commands you, to send to the siege, convenient supplies of victuals. For after the time of our departing from Chaam, we have travelled through the country, with great peril and danger of our people, but yet always had plenty of victuals, thanks be to God. But now as the case stands, we need your help to be refreshed with victuals. Thus fare you well. Written at the siege before the town of Calais the 14th day of September."

After the siege and winning of Poissy, the third day of September A.D. 1346, the king through the midst of France, directed his course to Calais, and besieged it ; which siege he continued from the 3rd of September, till the 3rd of August next ensuing, upon which day it was surrendered and subdued to the crown of England.

After thus winning Calais, King Edward, remaining in the town, was in consultation concerning his proceeding further into France. But by means of the cardinals, a truce for a time was accepted, and instruments made that certain noblemen as well for the French king, as for the king of England, should come to the pope, there to debate upon the articles. To which King Edward, for peace sake, was not much opposed (A. D. 1347).

In A.D. 1350, the town of Calais was, by the treason of the keeper of the castle, almost betrayed and won from the Englishmen. And within the same year Philip the French king died. After whom King John his son, succeeded to the crown.

About A.D. 1354, concord and agreement began to come well forward, and instruments were drawn upon the same between the two kings. But the matter being brought up to Pope Innocent VI., partly by the quarrelling of the Frenchmen, partly by the winking of the pope, who ever held with the French side, the conditions were repealed, which were these : that to the king of England all the dukedom of Aquitaine with other lands there, should be restored without homage to the French king. And that King Edward again should surrender to him all his right and title, which he had in France ; whereupon rose the occasion of great war and tumult which followed after between the two realms.

It followed after this, (A. D. 1355,) that King Edward hearing of the death of Philip the French king, and that King John his son, had granted the dukedom of Aquitaine to Charles his eldest son and dauphin of Vienna, sent over Prince Edward with the earls of Warwick, of Salisbury, of Oxford, and with them a sufficient number of able soldiers into Aquitaine. Where he being willingly received by some, he subdued the rest, partly by force of sword, partly by their submitting themselves to his protection.

Not long after this, in the same year, word was brought to King Edward, that John, the French king, was ready to meet him at St. Omers, there to give him battle, so he gathered his forces, and set over to Calais with his two sons, Lionel earl of Wilton, and John of Gaunt earl of Richmond, with Henry duke of Lancaster, &c. When Edward was come to St. Omers, the French king with a mighty army, heard of his coming, but the nearer he approached to them, the further they retired back; wasting and destroying behind them, so that the English army in pursuing them, might find no provisions. By which, King Edward following him for the space of nine or ten days to Hadem (when he could find neither his enemy to fight, nor provisions for his army) returned to Calais. King Edward, seeing the shrinking of his enemy, crossed the seas into England, where he recovered again the town of Berwick, which the Scots before by subtlety had gotten.

The same year, when King Edward had recovered Berwick, and subdued Scotland, Prince Edward being in Gascony, made toward the French king. The victorious prince made way with his sword, and after much slaughter of the French, and many prisoners taken, he at length came up with the French king at Poictiers, and with scarcely two thousand men, overthrew the French with seven thousand men of arms and more. In which conflict, the French king himself, and Philip his son, with Lord James of Bourbon, the archbishop of Senon, eleven earls, and twenty-two lords were taken. Of other warriors and men of arms two thousand. Some affirm, that in this conflict there were slain two dukes, of lords and noblemen twenty-four, of men of arms two thousand and two; of other soldiers about eight thousand. The common report is, that more Frenchmen were there taken prisoners, than the whole English army which took them. This noble victory gotten by the grace of God, excited no little admiration among all men.

It were too long, and little pertaining to the purpose of this history, to comprehend in order all the doings of this king, with the circumstances of his victories, of the bringing in of the French king into England, of his abode there, of the ransom levied on him, and of David the Scotish king; of which, the one was rated at one million of pounds, the other at an hundred thousand marks, to be paid in ten years.

Thus having treated of all martial affairs and warlike exploits in the reign of this king between him and the realms of France and Scotland: now, to return to our ecclesiastical matters, it follows to notify the troubles and contentions growing between the king and the pope, and other ecclesiastical persons in matters touching the church, taken out of the records in the Tower. In the fourth year of his reign, the king wrote to the archbishop of Canterbury to this effect: that whereas King Edward I. his grandfather, gave to his chaplain, the dignity of treasurer of York, (the archbishoprick of York being then vacant and in the king's hands,) in the quiet possession of which the chaplain continued, until the pope would have displaced him, and promoted a cardinal of Rome to that dignity, the king therefore straitly charges the archbishop of York not to suffer any matter to pass, that may be prejudicial to the donation of his grandfather, upon pain of his highness's displeasure.

The like precepts were also directed to these bishops following: to the bishop of Lincoln, bishop of Worcester, bishop of Sarum, archdeacon of Richmond, archdeacon of Lincoln, the prior of Lewen, the prior of Lenton, to Master Rich of Bentworth, to Master Iherico de Concore, to the pope's nuncio, to Master Guido of Calma. And he wrote letters to the pope consisting of three parts. First, in the declaration and defence of his right

and title to the donation and gift of all manner of temporalties, of offices, prebends, benefices and dignities ecclesiastical, held of him *in capite*, as in the right of his crown of England. Secondly, in expostulating with the pope for intruding himself into the ancient right of the crown of England, intermeddling with such collations, contrary to right and reason, and the example of all his predecessors. Thirdly, intreating him that he would henceforth abstain and desist from molesting the realm with such novelties and strange usurpations; and so much the more, because in the parliament lately held at Westminster, it was agreed by the universal assent of all the estates of the realm, that the king should stand to the defence of all such rights and jurisdictions as to his regal dignity and crown any way appertained.

The tenth year of his reign he wrote also to the pope to this effect: that whereas the prior and chapter of Norwich nominated a clerk to be bishop of Norwich, and sent him to Rome for his investiture, without the king's knowledge; therefore the pope would withdraw his consent, and not intermeddle in the matter appertaining to the king's peculiar jurisdiction and prerogative.

After this, in the sixteenth year of this king, it happened that the pope sent over legates to hear and determine matters appertaining to the right of patronages of benefices; the king perceiving this to tend to the no small derogation of his right, and the liberties of his subjects, writes to the said legates, admonishing and requiring them not to proceed therein, nor attempt any thing unadvisedly, otherwise than might stand with the lawful ordinances and customs of the laws of his realm, and the freedom and liberties of his subjects.

The year following, which was the seventeenth of his reign, he wrote another letter to the pope, against his provisions and reservations of benefices.

The year following, another letter likewise was sent by the king to the pope, upon occasion taken of the church of Norwich, requiring him to cease his reservations and provisions of the bishoprics within the realm, and to leave the elections thereof free to the chapters of such cathedral churches, according to the ancient grants and ordinances of his noble progenitors.

Proceeding now to the nineteenth year of this king's reign, there came to the king certain legates from Rome, complaining of certain statutes passed in his parliament, tending to the prejudice of the church of Rome, and the pope's primacy, viz., that if abbots, priors, or any other ecclesiastical patrons of benefices should not present to to the benefices within a certain time, the lapse should come to the ordinary or chapter thereof, or if they did not present, then to the archbishop, if the archbishop likewise did fail to present, then the gift to pertain not to the lord pope, but to the king and his heirs. Another complaint also was this, that if archbishops should be slow in giving such benefices as properly pertained to their own patronage in due time, then the collation thereof likewise should appertain to the king and his heirs. Another complaint was, that if the pope should make void any elections in the church of England for any defect found therein, and so had placed some honest and discreet persons in the same, that then the king and his heirs was not bound to render the temporalties to the parties placed by the pope's provision. Whereupon, the pope being not a little aggrieved, the king wrote to him, certifying that he was misinformed, denying that there was any such statute made in that parliament. And further, as touching all other things, he would confer with his prelates and nobles, and would return answer by his legates.

In the twentieth year of his reign, another letter was written to the pope by the king, the effect whereof was this: "That in respect of his great charges sustained in his wars, he had by the counsel of his nobles, taken into his own hands the fruits and profits of all his benefices in England."

To proceed in the order of years, in the twenty-sixth year of this king, one Nicholas Heath, clerk, a busy-headed body, and a troubler of the realm, had procured some bishops, and others of the king's council to be cited up to the court of Rome, there to answer such complaints as he had made against them. Whereupon commandment was given by the king to all the ports of the realm for the restraint of all passengers out, and for searching and arresting all persons bringing in any bulls or other process from Rome, tending to the derogation of the dignity of the crown, or molestation of the subjects.

The same year the king wrote also to the pope's legate resident in England, requiring him to cease from exacting divers sums of money of the clergy, in the name of first fruits of benefices.

The thirty-eighth year of his reign an ordinance was made by the king and his council, and proclaimed in all port towns within the realm,—"That good and diligent search should be made, that no person whatsoever coming from the court of Rome, &c., do bring into the realm with him any bull, instrument, letters patent, or other process that may be prejudicial to the king, or any of his subjects; or that any person, passing out of this realm toward the court of Rome, do carry with him any instrument or process that may redound to the prejudice of the king or his subjects; and that all persons passing to the said court of Rome, with the king's special license, do, notwithstanding, promise and find surety to the lord chancellor, that they shall not in any wise attempt or pursue any matter to the prejudice of the king or his subjects, under pain to be put out of the king's protection, and to forfeit his body, goods, and chattels, according to the statute made in the twenty-seventh year of his reign."

And thus much concerning the letters and writings of the king, with such other domestic matters and troubles as passed between him and the pope, taken out of the public records of the realm, whereby I thought to give the reader to understand the horrible abuses, the intolerable pride, and the insatiable avarice of that bishop, more like a proud Lucifer than a pastor of the church of Christ, in abusing the king, and oppressing his subjects with immeasurable exactions; and not only exercising his tyranny in this realm, but raging also against other princes, both far and near, amongst whom he did not spare, even the emperor himself. In the history of the Emperor Lewis, whom the pope excommunicated upon Maunday Thursday, and the same day placed another emperor in his room, mention was made of certain learned men, who took the emperor's part against the pope. In number of whom was Marsilius of Padua, William Ockam, John of Ganduno, Leopold, Andrew Landensis, Ulric Hangenor, treasurer of the emperor, Dante, Aligerius, &c. Of whom Marsilius compiled a worthy work entitled ' Defensor Pacis,' written in the emperor's behalf against the pope. Wherein (both godly and learnedly disputing against the pope) he proves all bishops and priests to be equal, and that the pope has no superiority above other bishops, much less above the emperor. That the word of God ought to be the only chief judge in deciding and determining causes ecclesiastical; that not only spiritual persons, but laymen also being godly and learned, ought to be admitted unto general councils; that the clergy and the pope ought to be subject to magistrates; that the church is the university of the faithful, and that the foundation and head of the church is Christ, and that he never appointed any vicar or pope over his universal church; that bishops ought to be chosen every one by their own church and clergy; that the marriage of priests may lawfully be permitted; that St. Peter was never at Rome; that the clergy and synagogue of the pope is a den of thieves; that the doctrine of the pope is not to be followed, because it leads to destruction; and that the corrupt manners of the christians do spring and flow out of the wickedness of the spiritualty. He disputes moreover in another work of free justification by grace, and extenuated merits, saying that they are no efficient causes of our salvation, that this is to say, that works are no cause of our justification, but yet our justification goes not without them. For which doctrine, most sound and catholic, he was condemned by the pope, A.D. 1324, (by the pope's decree *Extravagant. cap. Licet inter doctrinam.*) Concerning which man and his doc-

trine, I thought good to commit thus much to history, to the intent men may see that they which charge this doctrine now taught in the church, with the note of novelty or newness, are ignorant of the histories of past times.

In the same number and catalogue comes also Ockam, (A.D. 1326), and who wrote likewise in defence of the emperor against the pope; and also in defence of Michael, general of the Grayfriars, whom the pope had excommunicated and cursed for a heretic. Several treatises were set forth by Ockam, of which some are extant and in print, some are extinct and suppressed. Some again are not published under the name of the author, as the dialogue between the soldier and the clerk, wherein it is to be conjectured, what books and works this Ockam had collected against the pope. Of this Ockam, John Sleidan in his history makes mention, to his great commendation; his words are these: " William Ockam, in the time of the Emperor Lewis IV., flourished about A.D. 1326, who, among other things, wrote of the authority of the bishop of Rome. In which book he handles these eight questions very copiously : whether both the administrations of the bishop's office, and of the emperor's, may be in one man? Secondly, whether the emperor takes his power and authority only from God, or else from the pope? Thirdly, whether the pope and church of Rome have power by Christ to set and place kings and emperors, and to commit to them their jurisdiction? Fourthly, whether the emperor being elected, has full authority upon his election, to administer his empire? Fifthly, whether other kings besides the emperor and the king of the Romans, in that they are consecrated by priests, receive of them any part of their power? Sixthly, whether the kings in any case be subject to their consecrators? Seventhly, whether if the kings should admit any new sacrifice, or should take to themselves the diadem without any further consecration, they should thereby lose their kingly right, and title? Eighthly, whether the seven princes electors give as much to the election of the emperor, as succession rightfully gives to other kings? Upon these questions he disputes and argues with many arguments and various reasons on both sides, at length he decides the matter on the part of the civil magistrate; and by occasion thereof enters into the mention of the pope's " Decrees extravagant," declaring how little force or regard is to be given thereto."

Trithemius makes mention of one Gregory of Arimini, a learned and a famous and right godly man, who, not much differing from the age of this Ockam, (about A.D. 1350), disputed in the same doctrine of grace and free will as we do now, and dissented therein from the papists and sophisters, counting them worse than Pelagians.

And what should I speak of the duke of Bungundy, named Eudo, who, at the same time (A.D. 1350), persuaded the French king not to receive in his land the new found constitutions, decretal and extravagant, nor to suffer them within his realm, whose sage counsel then given, yet remains among the French king's records?

Dante, an Italian writer, a Florentine, lived in the time of Lewis the emperor, (about A.D. 1300), and took part with Marsilius against three sorts of men, who he said were enemies to the truth, that is, the pope; secondly, the order of monks and friars, who count themselves the children of the church, when they are the children of the devil their father; thirdly, the doctors of decrees and decretals. Certain of his writings are still extant, wherein he proves the pope not to be above the emperor, nor to have any right or jurisdiction in the empire. He proves the donation of Constantine to be a forged and a feigned thing, for which he was thought by many to be an heretic. He complains very much, that the preaching of God's word was omitted, and instead of it, the vain fables of monks and friars were preached and believed by the people, and so the flock of Christ was fed not with the food of the gospel, but with wind. " The pope," saith he, " of a pastor is made a wolf, to waste the church of Christ, and to procure with his clergy, not the word of God to be preached, but his own decrees." In his canticle of purgatory, he declares the pope to be the whore of Babylon.

Here may be added the saying out of the book of Jornand, imprinted with Dante; that, forsomuch as antichrist comes not before the destruction of the empire, therefore such as strive to have the empire extinct, are in so doing rorerunners and messengers of antichrist. "Therefore let the Romans," saith he, "and their bishops beware, lest their sins and wickedness so deserving, by the just judgment of God, the priesthood be taken from them. Furthermore, let all the prelates and princes of Germany take heed," &c.

And because our adversaries who object to us the newness of our doctrine shall see and perceive the course and form of this religion now received, not to have been either such a new thing now, or a thing so strange in times past; I will add to these above recited, Master Taulerus, a preacher of Argentine in Germany, (A. D. 1350), who, contrary to the pope's proceedings, taught openly against all human merits, and against invocations of saints, and preached sincerely of our free justification by grace, referring all man's trust only to the mercy of God, and was an enemy to all superstition.

With whom also may be joined Francis Petrarch, a writer of the same age, who, in his works and Italian verses, speaking of Rome, calls it "The whore of Babylon,—the school and mother of error,—the temple of heresy,—the nest of treachery, growing and increasing by the oppressing of others;" and saith further, that she extols herself against her founders, that is, the emperors who first set her up, and did so enrich her, and seems plainly to affirm, that the pope was antichrist, declaring that no greater evil could happen to any man, than to be made pope. This Francis Petrarch was about A. D. 1350.

About the year, (A. D. 1340), in the city of Herbipoli, was one named Master Conrad Hager, who, (as appears by the old bulls and registers of Otho, bishop of the city), is there recorded to have maintained and taught for the space of twenty-four years together, that the mass was no sacrifice; and that it profits not any man, either quick or dead, and that the money given by the dying for masses, are very robberies and sacrileges of priests. He said too, that if he had a store full of gold and silver, he would not give one farthing for any mass. For this doctrine, this good preacher was condemned, and inclosed in prison; but what afterward became of him was never heard.

There is among other old and ancient records of antiquity, belonging to this time, a certain monument in verses poetically compiled, but not without a certain moral, intitled, "Pœnitentiarius Asini," i. e. The Asses' Confessor; bearing the date and year A. D. 1343. In this treatise are brought forth the wolf, the fox, and the ass, coming to confess, and doing penance. First, the wolf confesses to the fox, who easily absolves him from all his faults, and also excuses him in them. In like manner the wolf, hearing the fox's confession, showed to him the like favour in return. After this comes the ass to confession, whose fault was this: that he being hungry took a straw out from the sheaf of a man that went on a pilgrimage to Rome. The ass, repenting of this act, and thinking it not so heinous as the faults of the others, hoped the more for his absolution. But what followed? After the silly ass had uttered his crime in auricular confession, immediately the discipline of the law was executed upon him with severity. neither was he judged worthy of any absolution, but was apprehended upon the same, slain, and devoured. Whoever was the author of this fabulous tale, he had a moral in it; for by the wolf was meant the pope; but the fox represented the prelates, courtesans, priests, and the rest of the spiritualty. By the spiritualty the pope is soon absolved, as, in return, by the ass the pope soon absolves them in like manner. By the ass is meant the poor laity, upon whose back the strict censure of the law is executed; especially when the German emperors come under the pope's inquisition, to be examined by his discipline, there is no absolution or pardon to be found, but in all haste he must be deposed, as in these histories may partly appear before.

Not long after this, (about A. D. 1350), Gerhard Riddler wrote against the monks and friars a book, intitled, "Lacryma Ecclesiæ," wherein he disputes against the order of the begging friars; proving that kind of life to be far from christian perfection, as being against charity to live upon others, when a man may live by his own labour; and affirms them to be hypocrites, filthy livers, and such as for man's favour, and for lucre sake, do mix with true divinity, fables, apocryphas, and dreams of vanity. Also that, under pretence of long prayer, they devour widows' houses, and with their confessions, sermons, and burials, trouble the church of Christ. And therefore he persuaded the prelates to bridle and keep short the inordinate license and abuses of these monastical persons, &c.

As yet I have made no mention of Michael Sesenas, provincial of the Gray Friars, nor Peter de Corbaria, of whom Antonine writes and says they were condemned in the "Extravagant" of Pope John, with one John de Poliaco. Their opinions, says Antonine, were these,—That Peter the apostle was no more the head of the church than the other apostles; and that Christ left no vicar behind him, or head of his church; and that the pope has no authority to correct and punish, to institute or depose the emperor; also, that all priests, of what degree soever, are of equal authority, power, and jurisdiction, by the institution of Christ: but by the institution of the emperor, the pope may be superior, who, by the same emperor also, may be revoked again. Also, that neither the pope, nor yet the church, may punish any man with bodily restraint or compulsion; unless they receive the license of the emperor. This Michael, master of the Gray Friars, wrote against the tyranny, pride, and primacy of the pope, accusing him to be antichrist, and the church of Rome to be the whore of Babylon, drunk with the blood of saints. He said there were two churches, one of the wicked, which was flourishing, wherein reigned the pope; the other of the godly, which was afflicted. Also, that the truth was almost utterly extinct; and for this cause he was deprived of his dignity, and condemned by the pope. Notwithstanding, he stood constant in his assertions. This Michael was about A. D. 1322. And he left behind him many favourers and followers of his doctrine, of whom a great part were slain by the pope: some were condemned, as William Ockam; some were burned, as John de Castilione, and Francis de Arcatara.

Much about this time the nuns of St. Bridget's order began first. About this time also was built the Queen's College, in Oxford, by Queen Philippa, of England, wife to King Edward III. (about A. D. 1360.)

And here to make an end of this Fourth Book; it now remains to prosecute the race of the archbishops of Canterbury, contained in this Fourth Book, beginning, where we before left off, (page 108), at Lanfranc.

A Table of the Archbishops of Canterbury, contained in the Fourth Book.

34. Lanfranc.
35. Anselm.
36. Radulph.
37. William Curboil.
38. Theobald.
39. Thomas Becket.
40. Richard.
41. Baldwin.
42. Hubert.
43. Stephen Langton.
44. Richard Magnus.
45. Edmund, of Abingdon.
46. Boniface.
47. Robert Kilwarby.
48. John Peckham.
49. Robert Winchelsey.
50. Walter Reynald.
51. John Stratford.
52. John Offord.
53. Thomas Braidwarden.
54. Simon Islip.

ACTS AND MONUMENTS.

BOOK V.

CONTAINING

THE LAST THREE HUNDRED YEARS, FROM THE LOOSING OUT OF SATAN.

THUS having discoursed in these former books the order and course of years, from the first tying up of Satan to A. D. 1360, I have a little overpassed the limit of time in the scripture, appointed for the loosing out of him again. For so it is written by St. John, (Rev. xx. 3), that after a thousand years, Satan, the old dragon, shall be let loose again for a season, &c.

For the better explanation of which mystery, let us first consider the context of the scripture : afterwards let us examine by history, and course of times, the meaning of the same. And first, to recite the words of scripture, the text of the prophesy is this, (Rev. xx. 1.)

"And I saw an angel come down from heaven, having the key of the bottomless pit, and a great chain in his hand. And he laid hold on the dragon, that old serpent, which is the devil and Satan, and bound him a thousand years, and cast him into the bottomless pit, and shut him up, and set a seal upon him, that he should deceive the nations no more till the thousand years should be fulfilled : and after that he must be loosed a little season. And I saw thrones, and they sat upon them, and judgment was given unto them ; and I saw the souls of them that were beheaded for the witness of Jesus," &c.

By these words of the Revelation, here recited, three special times are to be noted.

First, Satan's being abroad to deceive the world.

Secondly, The binding of him.

Thirdly, The loosing of him again, after a thousand years, for a season.

Concerning the interpretation of which times, I see the common opinion of many to be deceived by ignorance of histories, and state of things done in the church ; they supposing that the chaining up of Satan for a thousand years, spoken of in the Revelation, was meant from the birth of Christ our Lord. Wherein I grant that spiritually, the strength and dominion of Satan, in accusing and condemning us for sin, was cast down at the passion and by the passion of Christ our Saviour, and locked up, not only for a thousand years, but for ever. Although, as to the malicious hatred and fury of that serpent, against the outward bodies of Christ's poor saints, (which is the heel of Christ) to afflict and torment the church outwardly ; that I judge to be meant in the Revelation of St. John, not to be restrained till the ceasing of those terrible persecutions of the primitive church, when it pleased God to pity the sorrowful affliction of his poor flock, being so long under persecution, the space of three

hundred years, and so to assuage their griefs and torments : which is meant by the binding up of Satan, the worker of all those mischiefs : understanding thereby that as the devil, the prince of this world, has now, by the death of Christ the Son of God, lost all his power and interest against the soul of man, he should turn his furious rage and malice, which he had to Christ, against the people of Christ, (which is meant by the heel of the seed, Gen. iii. 15.) in tormenting their outward bodies. Which yet should not be for for ever, but for a determinate time, as it should please the Lord to bridle the malice, and snaffle the power of the old serpent, and give rest to his church for the term of a thousand years. Which time being expired, the serpent shall be suffered loose again for a certain or a small time.

And I am led by three reasons thus to expound this prophetical passage of scripture :

The first is, that the binding up of Satan, and closing him in the bottomless pit by the angel, imports as much as that he was at liberty, raging and doing mischief before. And certainly, those terrible and horrible persecutions of the primitive time universally through the whole world, during the space of three hundred years of the church, do declare no less. Wherein it is to be thought and supposed, that Satan all that time, was not fastened and closed up.

The second reason, moving me to think that the closing up of Satan was after the ten persecutions of the primitive church, is taken out of the twelfth chapter of Revelations ; where we read, that after the woman, (meaning the church) had travailed of her man-child ; the old dragon, the devil, the same time being cast down from heaven, drawing the third part of the stars with him, stood before the woman with great anger, and persecuted her (that is, the church of God), with a whole flood of water, (that is, with abundance of all kinds of torments), and from thence went moreover to fight against the residue of her seed, and stood upon the sands of the sea ; whereby it appears that he was not as yet locked up.

The third reason I collect out of the thirteenth chapter of Revelation ; where it is written of the beast, signifying the imperial monarchy of Rome, that he had power to make war forty and two months. By which months is meant, no doubt, the time that the dragon, and the persecuting emperors, should have in afflicting the saints of the primitive church. The computation of which forty-two months (counting every month for a sabbath of years ; that is, for seven years, after the order of scripture) rises to the sum (counting from the passion of the Lord Christ) of three hundred years, lacking six, when Maxentius, the last persecutor in Rome, fighting against Constantine, was drowned with his soldiers, like as Pharaoh, persecuting the children of Israel, was drowned in the Red Sea ; to the which forty-two months, or sabbaths of years, if we add the other six years wherein Licinius persecuted in the East, ye shall find just three hundred years, as is specified before in the First Book.[1]

After which forty and two months being expired, it is manifest that the fury of Satan, that is, his violent malice and power over the saints of Christ, was diminished and universally restrained through the whole world.

Thus then the matter standing evident, that Satan after three hundred years, counting from the passion of Christ, began to be chained up, when the persecution of the primitive church began to cease : now let us see how long this binding up of Satan should continue, which was promised in the book of the Revelation to be a thousand years. Which thousand years, if ye add to the forty-two months of years, that is, to two hundred and ninety-four years ; they make one thousand two hundred and ninety-four years after the passion of the Lord. To these, moreover, add the thirty years of the age of Christ, and it comes to A. D. 1324, which was the year of the letting out of Satan, according to the prophecy.

These things thus premising for the loosing out of Satan, according to the prophecy in the Revelations, now let us enter (Christ willing) to the declaration of these later times which followed after the letting out of Satan into the world. Describing the wonderous troubles and cruel tyranny stirred up by him against Christ's church ; also the valiant resistance of the church of Christ against him and antichrist, as in these our books here following may appear.

The argument of which books consists in two parts : First, to treat of the raging fury of Satan now loosed, and of antichrist, against the saints of Christ fighting and labouring for the maintenance of truth, and the reformation of the church. Secondly : To declare the decay and ruin of antichrist, through the power of the word of God, being at length, either in a great part of the world overthrown ; or at least universally in the whole world detected.

Thus then to begin with the year 1360, wherein I have a little transgressed the limits of the first loosing of Satan : we are come now to the time wherein the Lord, after long darkness, begins some reformation of his church, by the diligent industry of his faithful and learned servants, of whom several we have already touched in the former book, as having withstood the corrupt errors, and intolerable enormities of the Bishop of Rome.

Now to these (the Lord willing) we will add such other holy martyrs and confessors, as followed after in the course of years with like zeal and strength of God's word, and also with like danger of their lives, gave the like resistance against the enemy of Christ's religion, and suffered at his hands the like persecutions. First, beginning with that godly man, whosoever he was, the author of the book, entitled, The Prayer and Complaint of the Ploughman, written about this present time, as follows :—

An old ancient Writing, intituled, The Prayer and Complaint of the Ploughman.[2]

"Ah Lord, thou forgave sometime Peter his sins, and also Mary Magdalen, and many other sinful men without shriving to priests, and taking penance of priests for their sins. And, Lord, thou art as mighty now as thou were that time, but gif any man have bynomen thee thy might. And we lewd men beleven, that there is no man of so great power, and gif any man maketh himself of so great power, he heighteth himself above God. And St. Paul speaketh of one that sitteth in the temple of God, and heighten him above God ; and gif any such be, he is a false Christ.

"But hereto seyn priests, that when Christ made clean leprous men, he bade them go and shew them to priests. And therefore they seyn that it is a commandment of Christ, that a man should shewen his sin to priests. For as they seyn, lepre in the old law betokenneth sin in this new law. A, Lord God, whether thine apostles knew not thy meaning as well as men done now ? And gif they hadden yknow that thou haddest commanded men to shriven them to priests, and they ne taught not that commandment to the people, me thinketh they hadden ben to blame. But I trow they knewen well that it was none of thy commandments, ne needful to heal of man's soul. And as me thinketh, the law of lepre is nothing to the purpose of shriving : for priests in the old law hadden certain points and tokens to know whether a man were leprous or not : and gif they were leprous, they hadden power to putten them away from other clean men, for to that they weren clean ; and then they hadden power to receiven him among his brethren, and offeren for him a sacrifice to God.

"This is nothing to the purpose of shriving. For there is but one priest, that is Christ, that may know in certain the lepre of the soul. Ne no priest may make the soul clean of her sin, but Christ that is priest after Melchisedec's order : ne no priest here beneath may ywit for certain whether a man be clean of his sin, or clean assoiled, but gif God tell it him by revelation. Ne God ordained not that his priests should set men a penance for their sin, after the quantity of the sin, but this is man's ordinance, and it may well be that there commeth good thereof. But I wot well that God is much unworshipped thereby. For men trust more in his absolutions, and in his years of grace, than in Christ's absolutions, and thereby is the people much appaired. For now the sorrow a man should make for his sin, is put away by this shrift : and a man is more bold to do sin for trust of this shrift, and of this bodilich penance.

"Another mischief is, that the people is ybrought into this belief, that one priest hath a great power to assoylen a man of his sin and clennere, than another priest hath.

"Another mischief is this, that some priest may assoylen them both of sin and pain : and in this they taken them a power that Christ granted no man in earth, ne he ne used it dought on earth himself.

"Another mischief is, that these priests sellen forgiveness of men's sins and absolutions for mony ; and this is an heresie accursed that is ycleped simony : and all thilk priests that axeth price for granting of spiritual grace, beth by holy laws deprived of their priesthood, and thilke that assenteth to this heresie. And be they ware ; for Helyse the prophet took no mony of Naaman, when he was made clean of his lepre ; but Giesi his servant ; and therefore the lepre of Naaman abode with him and with his heirs evermore after.

"But, Lord God, he that sitteth in thy stede hath undo thy law of mercy and love ; Lord, thou biddest loven enemies as our self ; and shewest in the gospel there as the Samaritan had mercy on the Jew. And thou biddest us also prayen for them that cursen us, and that defamen us, and pursuen us to death. And so Lord thou diddest, and thine apostles also. But he that clepeth himself thy vicar on earth, and head of thy church, he hath undone thy law of love and mercy. For gif we speaken of loving our enemies, he teacheth us to fight with our enemies, that Christ hath forboden. He curseth and desireth vengeance to them that so doth to him. Gif any man pursueth him, he curseth him,

---

(1) See note page 69. [ED.]
(2) The old language and spelling of this treatise called " The Ploughman's Lament," renders it in a great degree unintelligible to the general reader. It is of considerable length, and we have retained only a portion of it, that the reader may be enabled to judge of its nature. [ED.]

that it is a sorrow a christen man to hearen the cursings that they maken, and blasphemies in such cursing. Of what thing that I know, I may bear true witness.

"But gif we speak of loving of our brethren, this is undone by him that saith he is God's vicar in earth. For Christ in the gospel biddeth us, that we shoulder clepen us no father upon earth: but clepen God our father, to maken us love perfitlich together. And he clepeth himself Father of fathers, and maketh many religions, and to everich a father. But whether is love and charity encreased by these fathers and by their religions, or else ymade less? For a frier ne loveth not a monk, ne a secular man neither, nor yet one frier another that is not of the order, and it is againward.

"But, Lord, in the old law the tithings of the lewd people ne were not due to priests, but to that other childer of Levi that serveden thee in the temple, and the priest hadden their part of sacrifices, and the first bygeten beasts and other things as the law telleth. And, Lord, St. Paul thy servant saith, that the order of the priesthood of Aaron ceased in Christ's coming and the law of that priesthood. For Christ was end of sacrifices yoffered upon the cross to the Father of heaven, to bring man out of sin, and become himself a priest of Melchisedek's order. For he was both king and priest, without beginning and end; and both the priesthood of Aaron, and also the law of that priesthood ben ychanged in the coming of Christ. And S. Paul saith it is reproved, for it brought no man to perfection. For blood of goats, ne of other beasts ne might done away sin, for to that Christ shad his blood.

"Ah Lord Jesus; whether thou ordenest an order of priests to offren in the auter thy flesh and thy blood to bringen men out of sin, and also out of pein? And whether thou geve them alonelich a power to eat thy flesh and thy blood, and whether none other man may eat thy flesh and thy blood withouten leve of priests? Lord, we beleven, that thy flesh is very meat, and thy blood very drink; and who eateth thy flesh, and drinketh thy blood, dwelleth in thee, and thou in him, and who that eateth this bread shall live without end. But Lord thine disciples said; this is a word; but thou answerest them and saidest; when ye seeth man soon stiven up there he was rather, the Spirit is that maketh you live, the words that ych have spoken to you ben spirit and life. Lord, yblessed mote thou be, for in this word thou teachest us that he that keepeth thy words, and doth after them, eateth thy flesh, and drinketh thy blood, and hath an everlasting life in thee. And for we shoulden have mind of this living, thou gavest us the sacrament of thy flesh and blood, in form of bread and wine at thy supper, before that thou shouldest suffer thy death, and took bread in thine hand, and saidest; 'Take ye this, and eat it, for it is my body:' and thou tookest wine, and blessedst it, and said; 'This is the blood of a new and an everlasting Testament, that shall be shed for many men in forgiveness of sins: as oft as ye do this, do ye this in mind of me.'

"Ah Lord, thou ne bede not thine disciples maken this a sacrifice, to bring men out of peines, gif a priest offred thy body in the altar; but thou bed them go and fullen all the folk in the name of the Father, and the Son, and the Holy Ghost, in forgiveness of their sins; and teach ye them to keep those that ych have commanded you. And Lord, thine disciples ne ordained not priests principallich to make thy body in sacrament, but for to teach the people, and good husbandmen that well govern their households, both wives and children, and their meiny, they ordeined to be priests to teachen other men the law of Christ, both in word, in dede, and they lived ein as true Christian men, every day they eaten Christ's body, and drinken his blood, to the sustenance of living of their souls, and other whiles they token of the sacrament of his body in form of bread and wine, in mind of our Lord Jesus Christ.

"But all this is turned upsedown: for now whoso will liven as thou taughtest, he shall been holden a fool. And gif he speak thy teaching, he shall ben holden an heretick, and accursed. Lord, have no longer wonder hereof, for so they seiden to thee when thou were here

sometime. And therefore we moten take in patience their words of blasphemy as thou diddest thy self, or else we were to blame. And trulich Lord I trow, that if thou were now in the world, and taughtest as thou diddest sometime, thou shouldest ben done to death. For thy teaching is damned for heresie of wise men of the world, and then moten thy needs ben hereticks that teachen thy lore, and all they also that travalien to live thereafter.

"Lord in the gospel thou sayest, that true heriers of God ne herieth him not in that hill beside Samaria, ne in Hierusalem neither, but true heriers of God herieth him in spirit and in truth. And Lord God, what herying is it to bilden thee a church of dead stones, and robben thy quick churches of their bodilich livelood? Lord God, what herying is it, to cloth mawmets of stocks and of stones in silver and in gold, and in other good colours? And Lord I see thine image gone in cold and in hete, in clothes all to broken, without shone and bosen, an hungred and athrust. Lord what herying is it to teende tapers and torches before blind mawmets that mowen not seyen? And hide thee that art our light and our lantern towards heaven, and put thee under a bushel, that for darkness we ne may not seen our way toward bliss? Lord what herying is it to kneel tofore mawmets that mow not yheren, and worshepen them with prayers, and maken thine quick images kneel before them, and asken of them absolutions and blessings, and worshepen them as gods, and putten thy quick images in thraldom and in travail evermore as beasts, in cold and in hete, and in feeble fare to finden them in liken of the world? Lord what herying is it to fetch deed mens bones out of the ground, there as they shoulden kindelich rotten, and shrinen them in gold and silver; and sufferen the quick bones of thine images to rot in prison for default of clothings? And suffren also thy quick images to perish for default of sustenance, and rooten in the hoorehouse in abominable lechery? Some become thieves and robbers, and manquellers, that mighten ben yholpen with the gold and silver that hongeth about deed mens bones, and other blind mawmets of stocks and stones.

"Lord, here been great abominations that thou shewdist to Ezechiel thy prophet, that priests done in thy temple, and yet they clepen that thine herying. But leve Lord, methinketh that they loven thee little that thus defoulen thy quick images, and worshepen blind mawmets.

"And Lord, another great mischief there is now in the world, an hunger that Amos thy prophet speaketh of, that there shall comen an hunger in the earth, not of bread, ne thrust of drink, but of hearing of God's words. And thy sheep woulden be refreshed, but their shepheards taken of thy sheep their livelode, as tythings, &c. And liven themselves thereby where them liketh.

"O Lord deliver the sheep out of the ward of these shepherds, those hired men, that stonden more to keep their riches that they robben of thy sheep, than they stonden in keeping of thy sheep.

"O Lord when thou come to Jerusalem, sometime thou drove out of the temple sellers of beasts and of other chaffare, and saidst, Mine house should ben cleped an house of prayers, but they maden a den of thieves of it. O Lord thou art the temple in whom we should praien thy Father of heaven. And Salomon's temple, that was ybelded at Jerusalem, was a figure of this temple. But Lord, he that clepeth himself thy vicar upon earth, and saith that he occupieth thy place here on earth, is become a chapman in thy temple, and hath his chapmen walking in divers countries to sellen his chaffare, and to maken him rich. And he saith, Thou gave him so great a power aboven all other men, that whatever he bindeth other unbindeth in earth, thou bindest other unbindest the same in heaven. And so of great power he selleth other men forgiveness of their sin. And for much money he will assoilen a man so clean of his sin, that he behoteth men of the bliss of heaven withouten any pain after that they be dead, that given him much money.

Bishopricks and chirches, and such other chaffares he selleth also for money, and maketh himself rich. And thus he beguiled the puple.

"O Lord Jesus here is much untruth, and mischief, and matter of sorrow. Lord thou saidest sometime, that thou wouldest be with thy servants unto the end of the world. And thou saidest also, there as tweine or three ben ygraded togedder in thy name, that thou art in the middle of them. A Lord, then it was no need to thee to maken lief-teenant, sith thou wolte be evermore amongst thy servants.

"Lord, thou axedst of thy disciples, who they trowed that thou were. And Peter answered and said, 'That thou art Christ God's Son.' And thou saidst to Peter, ' Thou art yblessed Simon Barjona, for flesh and blood ne showed not this to thee, but my Father that is in heaven.' And I say to thee, ' That thou art Peter, and upon this stone ych would bilde my church, and the gates of hell he shullen not availen agens it.

"And to thee ych wole geve the keys of heaven, and what ever thou bindest upon earth shall be bound in heaven, and what ever thou unbindest on earth, shall be unbounden in heaven.' This power also was granten unto the other disciples, as well as to Peter, as the gospel openlich telleth. In this place men seggen that thou granted to Peter's successor, the selve power that thou gave to Peter. And therefore the bishop of Rome, that saith he is Peter's successor, taketh this power to him to binden and unbinden in earth what him liketh. But Lord, ych have much wonder how he may for shame clepen himself Peter's successor : for Peter knowledged that thou were Christ and God, and kept the hests of thy law ; but these han forsaken the hests of thy law, and hath ymaken a law contrary to thine hests of thy law. And so he maketh himself a false Christ, and a false god in earth. And I trow thou gave him no power to undo thy law. And so in taking this power upon him, maketh him a false Christ and antichrist.

"For who may be more agens Christ, than he that in his words maketh himself Christ's vicar in earth ; and in his werkes undoth the ordinance of Christ, and maketh men believen that it is needful to the heal of men's souls, to believen that he is Christ's vicar in earth ? And what ever he bindeth in earth, is ybounden in heaven, and under this colour he undoth Christ's law, and maketh men always to keepen his law and hests.

"And thus man may yseen that he is against Christ, and therefore he is antichrist that maketh men worshippen him as a god on earth, as the proud King Nabugodonosor did sometime, that was king of Babylon. And therefore we lewde men that knowen not God but thee Jesus Christ, believen in thee that art our God, and our King, and our Christ, and thy laws ; and forsaken antichrist, and Nabugodonosor that is a false god, and a false Christ, and his laws being contrary to thy preaching.

"And Lord strength thou us against our enemies. For they ben about to maken us forsaken thee and thy law, other else to putten us to death.

"O Lord, onlich in thee is our trust to help us in this mischief, for thy great goodness that is withouten end.

"Lord thou ne taughtest not thy disciples to assoilen men of their sin, and setten them a penance for their sin, in fasting, ne in praying, ne other almous deed ; ne thyself, ne thy disciples, useden no such power here on earth. For Lord, thou forgive men her sins, and bede him sin no more. And thy disciples fulleden men in thy name, in forgiveness of her sins. Nor they took no such power upon them as our priests dare now. And Lord, thou ne assoiledst no man both of his sin and of his pain, that was due for his sin, ne thou grantedst no man such power here on earth.

"And Lord, me thinketh that gif there was a purgatory, and any earthlich man had power to deliver sinful men from the peines of purgatory, he should, and he were in charity, saven everich man that were in the way of salvation from thilke peines, sith they make them greater than any bodilich peines of this world. Also gif the bishop of Rome had such a power, he himself shuld never comen in purgatory, ne in hell. And sith we see well that he ne hath no power to keepen himself, ne other men nother out of these bodilich peines of the world,

and he may go to hell for his sin as another man may : I ne believe not, that he hath so great power to assoylen men of their sin as he taketh upon him aboven all other men. And I trow that in this he higheth himself above God.

"As touching the selling of bishopricks, and parsonages, I trow it be a point of falsehed. For agenst God's ordinance he robbeth poor men of a portion of their sustenance, and selleth it, other giveth it, to find proud men in idleness that don the lewd puple little profit, but much harme, as we told before. Thus ben thy commandments of truth, of meekness, and of poorness undone by him, that clepeth himself thy vicar here upon earth."

I doubt not, gentle reader, but in reading this godly treatise above prefixed, the matter is manifest and plain of itself without any further explication, what is to be thought and judged of this vicar of Christ, and successor of Peter, whom we call the bishop of Rome : whose life here is seen not only to be disordered in all points, swerving from the steps and example of Christ the prince and bishop of our souls, but also whose laws and doctrines are so repugnant and contrary to the precepts and rule of the gospel, that there is scarcely any similarity between them : as in the perusing of this complaining prayer, may be understood. Wherefore having no need to stand in any further expressing of this matter, but leaving it to the consideration and discretion of the reader, I will (Christ willing) proceed toward the time of John Wickliffe and his fellows, taking, in the order of years as I go, such things by the way, as both happened before the time of Wickliffe, and also may the better prepare the mind of the reader, to the entering of that history. Where first I think it not inconvenient to insert a prophetical parable, written about this time, or not much before, which the author morally applies to the bishop of Rome. To what author this moral is to be ascribed, I can not certainly affirm. In the meantime, as I have found it in Latin expressed, because it paints out the pope so rightly in his feathers and colours ; so I thought the thing was not to be omitted, and therefore took this present place, as most fit (although peradventure missing the order of years a little) to insert the same. The effect of which parable is as follows :

In the time of Pope Innocent VI., when friar John de Rupescissa was kept at Avignon in prison, Froysard heard in the pope's court this parable recited by this friar, to the cardinal Hostiensis, and cardinal Auxercensis.

"When on a certain time a bird was brought into the world all bare and without feathers, the other birds hearing thereof, came to visit her : and as they saw her to be a marvellous fair and beautiful bird, they counselled together how they might best do her good, as without feathers she might neither fly, nor live conveniently. They all wished her to live for her excellent form and beauty's sake, insomuch that among them all there was not one, that would not grant some part of her own feathers to deck this bird withal : yea, and the more trim they saw her to be, the more feathers still they gave to her, so that by these means she was passing well penned and feathered, and began to fly. The other birds that had thus adorned her with goodly feathers, beholding her flying abroad, were marvellously delighted therewith. In the end, this bird seeing herself so gorgeously feathered, and of all the rest to be had in honour, began to wax proud and haughty. Insomuch that she had no regard at all to them, by whom she was advanced : yea, she punged them with her beak, plucked them by the skin and feathers, and in all places hurted them. Whereupon the birds sitting in council again, called the matter in question, demanding one of another what was best to be done touching this unkind bird, whom they lovingly with their own feathers had decked and adorned ; affirming that they gave not their feathers, to the intent that she, thereby puffed up with pride, should contemptuously despise them all. The peacock therefore answers first, 'Truly,' says he, ' as she is bravely set forth with my painted feathers, I will again take them from her.' Then says the falcon, 'And I also will have mine again.' This sentence at length took place among them all, so that every one plucked from her those feathers which before they had given, each taking their own again. Now this proud bird, seeing herself thus dealt with, began forthwith to abate her haughty spirit, and humbly to submit herself openly, confessing and acknowledging, that of herself she had nothing; but that her feathers, her honour and other ornaments was their gift: she came into the world all naked and bare, they clad her with comely feathers, and therefore of right they may receive them again. Wherefore most humbly she desires pardon, promising to amend all that is past, neither would she at any time hereafter commit anything whereby through pride she might lose her feathers again. The gentle birds, that before had given their feathers, seeing her so humble and lowly, being moved with pity, restored again the feathers which lately they had taken away, adding withal this admonition, 'We will gladly,' say they, 'behold thee flying among us, so long as thou wilt use thine office with humbleness of mind, which is the chiefest comeliness of all the rest: but know this thou for certainty, that if at any time hereafter thou extol thyself in pride, we will straightways deprive thee of thy feathers, and reduce thee to thy former state wherein we found thee.' Even so, oh you cardinals," said this friar, "shall it happen to you: for the emperors of the Romans and Germans, and other christian kings, potentates, and princes of the earth, have bestowed upon you goods, lands, and riches, that should serve God, but you have poured it out, and consumed it upon pride, and all kind of wickedness, riot, and wantonness."

THE HISTORY OF ARMACHANUS.

In the catalogue of these learned and zealous defenders of Christ against antichrist above rehearsed, whom the Lord about this time began to raise up for the reanimation of his church, I cannot omit to write something of the reverend prelate, and famous clerk, Richard Armachanus, primate and archbishop of Ireland: a man for his life and learning so memorable that they had none almost his better. His name was Richard Fizraf. Such was the capacity and dexterity of this man, that being commended to King Edward III., he was promoted by him, first, to be archdeacon of Lichfield, then to be the commissary of the university of Oxford; at length to be archbishop of Armagh in Ireland. He had cause to come to London at the time when there was contention between the friars and clergy about preaching and hearing confessions, &c. Whereupon, this Armachanus, being requested to preach, made seven or eight sermons; wherein he propounded nine conclusions against the friars, for which he was cited by the friars to appear before this Pope Innocent VI., and so he went, and before the face of the pope valiantly defended, both in preaching and in writing, the same conclusions, and therein stood constantly to the death, as John Wickliffe well testifies. William Botonerus testifying of him in like manner, says, "That Armachanus first reproved begging-friars for hearing the confessions of professed nuns, without licence of their superiors, and also of married women without knowledge of their husbands. What dangers and troubles he sustained by his persecutors, and how miraculously the Lord delivered him from their hands, and in what peril of thieves and searchers he was, and yet the Lord delivered him; yea, and in what dangers he was of the king's officers, who coming with the king's letters, laid all the havens for him; and how the Lord Jesus delivered him, and gave him to triumph over all his enemies: how the Lord also taught him and brought him to the study of the scriptures of God. All this, with much more, he himself expresses in a certain prayer or confession made to Christ Jesus our Lord, in which he describes almost the whole history of his own life.

Thus the troubles of this good man, and how he was cited up by the friars to the pope, you have partly heard. Now his reasons and arguments wherewith he defended his cause in the pope's presence, are to be declared.

In the time of Innocent III., and the Lateran council, (A. D. 1215), lived Dominic, the author and founder of the preaching friars; who laboured at Pope Innocent for the confirmation of his order, but did not obtain it in the life time of that pope.

The year after this council Pope Innocent died, (A. D. 1216), after whom came Honorius III., who confirmed the order of the friar Dominic, and gave to him and his friars authority to preach, and to hear confessions, with other privileges. Dominic lived five years after the confirmation of his order, and died, A. D. 1221. About which year the order of the Franciscan friars began also to breed, and to spread in the world.

After this Honorius, next followed Pope Gregory IX., about A. D. 1228, who also promoted the order of Dominic.

This Gregory died about A. D. 1241, after whom came Celestine IV., and sat but eighteen days; then came Innocent IV., and sat eleven years and six months. Who, although he began first to favour the friars, yet afterward he debarred them of their liberties and privileges, and gave out precepts and excommunications against friars. And not long after was dispatched and made away with.

Innocent being thus removed out of the way, about A. D. 1254, succeeded Pope Alexander IV., a great maintainer of the friars, and sat seven years. He revoked and repealed the acts and writings of Pope Innocent his predecessor against the friars; the divines and students of Paris being not contented with this, stirred up four principal doctors. These four compiled a book against the begging order of friars, both Dominicans and Franciscans, entitled De Periculis Ecclesiæ, containing fourteen chapters, the fourteenth has thirty-nine articles against the friars. Besides these thirty-nine articles, are seven other articles, under the name of the students of Paris against the friars.

Besides these articles, certain conclusions were also propounded in the schools of Paris at the same time, solemnly to be disputed and defended against the friars: which were these:

First, That the begging friars were not in the state of salvation.

Secondly, That they were bound to labour with their hands, who could, and not to beg.

Thirdly, That they ought not to exercise the office of preaching, or to hear the confessions of them that will come to them.

All these articles and conclusions, with the book set forth by these Parisians, this Pope Alexander IV. condemned to be abolished and burned, writing his precepts to the French king, and also the university of Paris, in favour of the friars; commanding the friars to be restored to all their privileges and liberties.

Not long after Pope Alexander IV., followed Clement IV., (A. D. 1265), and sat three years: who also gave privileges to the friars.

Some time after this Clement came Pope Martin IV., (A. D. 1281), who renewed again the canon, in behalf of the curates against the friars.

Pope Boniface VIII. began to sit A. D. 1294, and sat eight years and nine months. Who taking side with the friars, gave them another privilege. In which privilege he licensed the friars, that without license of vicars of churches they shall first present themselves to the prelates to be admitted; by whom if they be refused the second time, then they, upon special authority of this pope, shall be privileged, without either bishop or curate, to preach, to bury, and to hear confessions.

By this Pope Boniface, a certain Dominican friar was made cardinal, named Nicolas Bocasin, of Tervisa, and after the death of Boniface he was made pope, (A. D. 1303), surnamed Pope Benedict XI., who made another constitution, revoking that of Boniface.

Again, after Benedict XI., followed Pope Clement V., (A. D. 1305), and sat nine years. Who, in his general council held at Vienna, revoked the constitution of Benedict his predecessor, and renewed the former decree of Boniface; which constitution, moreover, was confirmed afterward by Pope John XXII., (A. D. 1316).

Upon this variable diversity of the popes (one dissenting and repugning from another) rose among the divines and schoolmen in universities great matter of contention, as well in the university of Paris, as the university of Oxford about the begging friars, some holding one way, some another way.

The matter of contention about the friars stood in four points: first, preaching without licence of curates. Secondly, in hearing confession. Thirdly, in burying. Fourthly, in begging and taking of the people.

Popes that maintained the Friars.

Honorius III.	Clement IV.
Gregory IX.	Boniface VIII.
Alexander IV.	Clement V.

Popes that maintained Curates.

Innocent III.	Martin IV.
Innocent IV.	Benedict XI.

These considerations being premised, for the opening of this present cause of Armachanus against the idle beggarly sects of friars; it now remains, that we collect and open his reasons and arguments uttered in the consistory, and in the audience of the pope himself, wherewith he maintains the true doctrine and cause of the church against the pestiferous canker creeping in by these friars after subtle ways of hypocrisy, to corrupt the sincere simplicity of Christ's holy faith and perfect testament. Which reasons and arguments of his, I thought good and expedient for the utility of the church more amply and largely to discourse and prosecute, for I note in the sects, institutions, and doctrine of these friars, subtle poison to lurk, more pernicious and hurtful to the religion of Christ and souls of christians, than all men peradventure do consider.

Thus Armachanus, joining with the clergy of England, disputed and contended with the friars here of England, (A.D. 1358) about a double matter. Whereof the one was concerning confession and other escheats which the friars encroached in parish churches against the curates, and public pastors of churches. The other was concerning wilful beggary and poverty, which the friars then took upon them, not upon any necessity, being otherwise strong enough to work for their living, but only upon a wilful and affected profession. For which cause the friars appealed him up to the court of Rome. The occasion of which thus arose.

It happened that Armachanus, upon certain business coming up to London, found there certain doctors disputing and contending about the begging of Christ our Saviour. Whereupon he, being greatly urged and requested, made seven or eight sermons, wherein he uttered nine conclusions: whereof the first and principal conclusion was, touching the matter of the friars' privileges in hearing confessions. His conclusions were these:

First, That if a doubt or question be moved for hearing confessions, which of two places is rather to be chosen; the parish church is to be preferred before the church of the friars.

Secondly, being demanded; which is to be taken (to hear the confession of the parishioners, the parson or curate, or the friar) it is to be said, rather the parson or the curate.

Thirdly, that our Lord Jesus Christ in his human conversation was always poor, but that he loved not poverty, nor did covet to be poor.

Fourthly, that our Lord Jesus Christ did never beg, wilfully professing to be poor.

Fifthly, that our Lord Jesus Christ did never teach wilfully to beg, or to profess wilful beggary.

The sixth conclusion was, that Christ our Lord held the contrary, that men ought not wilfully or purposely, without necessity to beg.

Seventhly, that it is neither wisdom nor holiness, for any man to take upon him wilful beggary, perpetually to be observed.

The eighth, that it is not agreeing to the rule of the observants, or friars' minorites, to observe wilful poverty.

The last conclusion was, touching the bull of pope Alexander IV., which condemned the libel of the masters of Paris: that the same bull touched none of these seven last conclusions.

Upon these nine conclusions premised, Armachanus being cited, and brought up to the presence of the pope, began to prove the same.

I. Beginning with the first conclusion; that the parish church was a place more fit and convenient for the confessions or burials of the parishioners to be used, than any other exempt church or place of the friars. Which he proved by three causes; first, for the more sureness or certainty to the conscience of the parishioners confessed. Secondly, for the more utility and profit of him. Thirdly, for the less incommodity ensuing by confessions taken in parish churches, than in friars' churches.

As touching the first, for the more assuredness and certainty, he argued that as the sacraments of the church are to be frequented and used in no other place, but only in that, which by God himself is assigned and commanded, and seeing that elect place in the law, i. e. the temple represents the parish churches; and that the friars' church is not the place prescribed of God, but only permitted by bishops of Rome; he concluded therefore, that parish churches were more sure for confessions and burials than the places of the friars.

By another reason also he confirmed the same, for the parish church stands free from the pope's interdict, and the churches of the friars do not, but are under suspicion and doubt of the pope's interdict And further, he proved that it had fewer inconveniences, for every man to resort to his parish church than to the friars.

II. Now to the second conclusion, touching the person of the friar, and of the ordinary curate. If the question be, which of these two is to be preferred in the office of ecclesiastical administration; the opinion of Armachanus was, that the ordinary curate was better than the extraordinary friar.

He argued that it is more safe and sure for the parishioners to resort to their ordinary or parish priest; because the person of the lawful ordinary or priest, is expressly commanded by God, where the person of the friar is not, and therefore is forbid. Also, because the parishioner may more trust to his ordinary curate; as one who is more bound and obliged to be careful for him, than any other extraordinary person. And because in the person of the ordinary curate, commonly there is no doubt of any interdict to bind him; whereas in the friars there is good matter to doubt, whether he stand bound under the pope's censure of excommunication or not, and that for divers causes. As where it is decreed, that all such religious men are excommunicated *de facto*, whoever absolve any, against whom the sentence of excommunication has been denounced by the statute provincial, or synodal; as it is commonly said, that the friars are accustomed to do, in loosing them whom the censure of prelates or their officials have bound. Armachanus brings example of this in his own diocese: "For I (said he) in mine own diocese of Armagh have as good as two thousand under me, who, by the censure of excommunication every year denounced against wilful murderers, common thieves, burners of men's houses, and such like malefactors, stand accursed: of all which number notwithstanding, there are scarcely fourteen who come to me, or to any about me for their absolution. And yet all they receive the sacraments as others do, and all because they are absolved, or because they feign themselves absolved by none other than by friars; who in so doing are proved to be under the danger of excommunication, both the friars, and also the parishioners, if they knowing thereof do consent to their error."

Moreover, that it is the more sure way for the parishioners to resort to their appointed curates, than to the friars, he argues thus: that the parish priest or curate, being better acquainted with his own parishioner than is a stranger, he can better judge of the nature and disposition of his disease, and minister to him due physic of penance for the same, and also will be more careful in curing him.

About this matter Armachanus learnedly and worthily discourses, proving how pernicious these orders of friars are to the whole state of the church, and what mischief comes by the privileges of certain popes, who have privileged them to intermeddle in the office and function of ecclesiastical ministers, to preach and to take alms and tithes of the people, and impropriations from the church. To prosecute in order his reasons and arguments, as he has left them in writing, would make a large book. Yet because it will not be unfruitful both for the time present, and for posterity, to know the manifold detriments and inconveniences received through these friars, and to know what great benefit God has done for us in unburdening the church of this monstrous generation, I have briefly, therefore, contracted certain of his reasons, such as seemed most worthy of noting.

And first, alleging the authority of Innocent IV., he sets forth four inconveniences rising by the friars, which are these :—Contempt of the people against their ordinaries ; decreasing of devotion ; taking away of shame from the people by confessing to the friars ; detaining of oblations, such as the people are wont to give at their confessions and burials, and which by right belong to the parish churches.

Also, by the privileges of the popes, granted to the friars, many other great enormities do arise. As first, because thereby the true shepherds do not know the faces of their flock.

And, by the occasion of these privileges given to the friars, great contention, and sometimes blows rise between the friars and secular curates, about titles, impropriations, and other avails.

Also, by the occasion of these privileges many young men, as well in universities as in their fathers' houses, are allured craftily by the friars their confessors to enter their orders ; from whence afterward they cannot get out though they would, to the great grief of their parents, and no less repentance to the young men themselves. Armachanus states a case of a certain Englishman with him in Rome, who having a son at the university of Oxford, who was enticed by the friars to enter into their order, could by no means after release him ; but when his father and his mother would come to him, they could not be suffered to speak with him, but under the friars' custody. Whereas the scripture commands plainly, that whoso stealeth any man and selleth him (being thereof convicted) shall be put to death. Exod. xxi. 16. The father was compelled to come to Rome to seek remedy for his son.

And no less inconvenience and danger also by the friars rises to the clergy ; for laymen, seeing their children thus stolen from them in the universities by the friars, refuse to send them to their studies, willing rather to keep them at home to their occupation, or to follow the plough, than so to be circumvented and defeated of their sons at the university, as by daily experience manifestly appears. For whereas in my time (saith Armachanus) there were in the university of Oxford thirty thousand students, now are there not to be found six thousand. The occasion of which so great decay is to be ascribed to no other cause but to this circumvention only of the friars above mentioned.

Over and besides this, another inconvenience as great, or greater, Armachanus inferred to proceed by the friars through the decay of doctrine, and knowledge in all manner of faculties, and liberal sciences, which thus he declared :—For that these begging friars through their privileges obtained of the popes to preach, to hear confessions, and to bury ; and through their charters of impropriations, did grow thereby to such great riches and possessions by their begging, craving, catching, and intermeddling with church matters, that no book could stir of any science, either of divinity, law, or physic, but they were both able and ready to buy it up. So that every convent having a great library full stuffed and furnished with all sorts of books, and there being so many convents within the realm, and in every convent so many friars increasing daily more and more, it came to pass that very few books or none at all remain for other students. Which by his own experience he thus testifies, saying :—That he himself sent forth to the university four of his own priests or chaplains, who sending him word again, that they could neither find the bible, nor any other good profitable book of divinity meet for their study, therefore were minded to return home to their country, and one of them, he was sure, was returned by this time.

Furthermore, as he has proved hitherto the friars to be hurtful both to the laity, and to the clergy, so proceeding farther, he proves them to be hurtful also to themselves ; and that in three points, as incurring the vice of disobedience against God, and against their own rule, the vice of avarice, and the vice of pride. The proving of all which points he prosecuted in a long discourse.

As concerning the vice of avarice, it may be proved upon them (says Armachanus) ; for seeing so many charges belong to the office of a secular parish priest, as to minister the sacrament at Easter, to visit the sick with extreme unction, to baptize children, to wed, with such other, wherein stands as great devotion ; how then happens it that these friars, making no labour for these, only procure privileges to preach in churches, to hear confessions, and to bury from parish churches, but because there is lucre and gain in these, and none in the other.

Which also may appear by this, for if it were for mere devotion only, that they procure license to bury from parish churches, and to preach, why then have they procured license to take offerings, oblations, and legacies for their funerals ? And, for their preaching, why have they annexed also license to require and take of the people necessaries for their labour, unless only avarice is the cause thereof ?

Likewise for hearing of confession, when all good men have enough to know their own faults, and nothing list to hear the faults of others, it may be supposed that they would never have been so desirous of procuring that privilege, were it not that these friars did feel some sweetness and gain to hang upon the same.

Also, where the rule of Friar Francis forbids them to company with any woman, to enter into monasteries to be godfathers and gossips to men and women, how comes it that they, contrary to their rule, enter into the secret chambers of queens, and other women, and are made to know the most secret counsels of their doings, but that avarice and advantage have so blinded their eyes, and stirred their hearts.

III. His third conclusion was, that the Lord Christ in his human conversation was always poor, not because he loved or desired poverty for itself, &c. Wherein this is to be noted, that Armachanus differed not from the friars in this, that Christ was poor, and that he loved poverty ; but herein stood the difference, in the manner of loving, that is, whether he loved poverty for itself, or not.

IV. The fourth conclusion was, that Christ our Lord and Saviour did never beg wilfully. Which he proves by sundry reasons.

First, for that Christ in so doing should break the law, which saith, Thou shalt not covet thy neighbour's house, his wife, his servant, his maid, his ox, his ass, or anything that is his. Exod. xx. The danger of which commandment he that begs voluntarily must needs incur.

2. If Christ had begged voluntarily, he should have committed sin against another commandment, which says, " There shall be no beggar, nor needy person among you," &c. Deut. vi.

3. Christ in so doing should have transgressed the emperor's law, for the emperor's law said there shall no able-bodied beggar be suffered in the city.

4. If Christ had been a wilful beggar, he had broken the law of loving his neighbour ; whom he had vexed, having no need. For whoever without need asks or craves of his neighbour, does but vex him, in such a way as he would not be vexed himself. Which Christ would never do.

5. If Christ had begged wilfully, he had moved slander thereby to his own gospel, which he with miracles confirmed; for then they that saw his miracle in feeding five thousand in the wilderness, would have thought much with themselves how that miracle had been wrought, if he who fed others, either could not, or would not feed himself.

6. If Christ had begged wilfully, then he had done that which himself condemns by Paul, for so we read, 1 Tim. vi. 5, that Paul condemns them, who esteem piety to be gain and lucre. Which all they do, who under the colour of piety, hunt or seek for gain, when otherwise they need not.

7. If Christ had begged wilfully, he had offended in declaring an untruth in so doing; for he that knows in his mind that he needs not indeed that thing which he asks of another, declares in himself an untruth, as one who in word pretends to be otherwise than he is in very deed; which Christ without doubt never did, nor would ever do.

8. If Christ had begged wilfully, that is, having no true need thereto, then had he appeared either to be an hypocrite, seeming to be what he was not, and to lack when he did not; or else to be a true beggar in very deed, not able to suffice his necessity. For he is a true beggar in deed, who being constrained by mere necessity is forced to ask of others, that which he is not able to give to himself. But neither of these two agrees to Christ.

9. If Christ had begged wilfully, then why did Peter rebuke the mother of Clement his disciple, finding her to stand among the beggars, whom he thought to be strong enough to labour with her hands for her living, if she in so doing had followed the example of Christ?

10. If Christ had begged wilfully: and if the friars do rightly define perfection of the gospel by wilful poverty: then was Clement, St. Peter's successor, to blame, who laboured so much to remove away beggary and poverty from among all them that were converted to the faith of Christ, and is specially for the same commended of the church.

11. Again, why did Clement, writing to James bishop of Jerusalem, command so much to obey the doctrine and examples of the apostles· who as he shews in that epistle, had no beggar or needy person among them, if christian perfection (as by the friars' philosophy) stands in wilful beggary?

12. If Christ the high priest had begged wilfully, then did the holy church err wittingly, which ordained that none without sufficient title of living and clothing, should be admitted to holy orders. And moreover, when it is said in the canonical decrees, that the bishop or clerk that begs, brings shame upon the whole order of the clergy.

13. If Christ had wilfully begged, then the examples of wilful poverty had pertained to the perfection of christian life, which is contrary to the old law, which commands the priests to have possessions and tithes to keep them from beggary.

14. If Christ did wilfully beg, then beggary were a point of christian perfection. And so the church of God should err, in admitting such patrimonies and donations given to the church, and so in taking from the prelates their perfection.

15. Again, what will these friars who put their perfection in begging, say to Melchisedec, who without begging or wilful poverty, was the high priest of God, and king of Salem, and prefigured the order and priesthood of Christ?

16. And if beggary be such a perfection of the gospel (as the friars say) how comes it, that the Holy Ghost given to the apostles, which should lead them into all truth, told them no word of this beggarly perfection, neither is there any word mentioned thereof throughout the whole testament of God?

17. Moreover, where the prophet saith, "I never saw the righteous forsaken, nor his seed begging their bread;" how stands this with the righteousness of Christ, which was most perfectly righteous, if he should be forsaken, or his seed go beg their bread? And then how agrees this with the abominable doctrines of Franciscan friars, who put their perfection in wilful begging?

18. Finally, do we not read that Christ sent his disciples to preach without scrip or wallet, and bid them salute no man by the way? Meaning that they should beg nothing of any man. Did not the same Christ also labour with his hands under Joseph? St. Paul likewise, did he not labour with his hands, rather than he would burden the church of the Corinthians? And where now is the doctrine of the friars, which puts the state of perfection in wilful begging?

V. The fifth conclusion of Armachanus against the friars, was this, that Christ never taught any man wilfully to beg, which he proved thus: it is written Acts i. "Christ began to do and to teach." If Christ therefore, who did never wilfully beg himself, had taught men to do otherwise; then his doing and teaching had not agreed together.

And if Christ, who never begged himself wilfully, had taught men this doctrine of wilful begging contrary to his own doing; he had given suspicion of his doctrine.

Moreover, in so teaching, he had taught contrary to the emperor's just law, which expressly forbids the same.

VI. The sixth conclusion of Armachanus against the friars was, that our Lord Jesus Christ teaches us, that we should not beg wilfully, which he proves by Luke xiv. 13, 2 Thes. iii. 8—10; Prov. vi. 9, and xxxi. 13. &c.

VII. The seventh conclusion of Armachanus is, that no wise nor true holy man can take upon him wilful poverty to be observed always, which he proves by Prov. xxx. 8, by its being a temptation, and so against the Lord's prayer.

VIII. The eighth conclusion of this matter, that it is not agreeing to the rule of the friars observant, to observe wilful beggary. Which may be proved, for that friar Francis, both in his rule and in his testament left to his Franciscans, does plainly prefer labour before begging.

IX. The ninth and last conclusion is, that the bull of Pope Alexander IV., which condemns the book of the masters of Paris, impugns none of these conclusions premised.

Notes to be observed in this oration of Armachanus.

By this oration of Armachanus the learned prelate, thus made before Pope Innocent and his cardinals, many things there are for the utility of the church worthy to be observed. First, what troubles and vexations came to the church of Christ by these friars. Also what persecution follows by the means of them against so many learned men and true servants of Christ. Further, what opposition and contrariety was among the popes and how they could not agree among themselves about the friars. Fourthly, what pestiferous doctrine subverting well nigh the testament of Jesus Christ. Fifthly, what decay of ministers in Christ's church. Sixthly, what robbing and circumventing of men's children. Seventhly, what decay of universities, as appeared by Oxford. Eighthly, what damage to learning and lack of books to students came by these friars. Ninthly, to what pride, under colour of feigned humility, to what riches, under dissembled poverty they grew. Insomuch that at length through their subtle and most dangerous hypocrisy they crept up to be lords, archbishops, cardinals, and at last also chancellors of realms, yea, and of most secret counsel with kings and queens.

But enough of this oration of Armachanus. What success it had with the pope, is not certain. By his own life it appears that the Lord so wrought that his enemies did not triumph. Yet he was seven or eight years in banishment for the same matter.

I credibly hear of certain old Irish Bibles translated long since into the Irish tongue; which, if it be true, it is not unlikely the doing of this Armachanus. And thus much of this learned prelate and archbishop of Ireland, a man worthy for his christian zeal of immortal commendation.

After the death of Innocent VI. next was poped in the see of Rome Pope Urban V, who, by the father's side was an Englishman.

This pope maintained and kindled great wars in Italy, sending Egidius his cardinal and legate, and after him Arduinus a Burgundian, his legate and abbot, with great force and much money against several cities in Italy by whose means the towns and cities which had before broken from the bishop of Rome were oppressed, als Barnabes and Galeaceus, princes of Milan, vanquished By whose example others being afraid, submitted themselves to the church of Rome. And thus that wicked church arrived to her great possessions, which her patrons would needs father upon Constantine the godly emperor

In the time of this Pope Urban V., and in the second year of his reign, about the beginning of the year 1364, I find a certain sermon of one Nicholas Orem, made before the pope and his cardinals on Christmas-even. In which sermon the learned man worthily rebukes the prelates and priests of his time, declaring their destruction not to be far off, by certain signs taken of their wicked and corrupt life. All the sayings of the prophets, spoken against the wicked priests of the Jews, he aptly applies against the clergy of his time, comparing the church then present to the spiritual strumpet spoken of in the sixteenth chapter of the prophet Ezekiel. And proves in conclusion the clergy of the church then to be so much worse than the old synagogue of the Jews, by how much it is worse to sell the church and sacraments, than to suffer doves to be sold in the church. With no less judgment also and learning he answers to the old and false objections of the papists, who, although never so wicked, yet think themselves the church which the Lord cannot forsake.

In the fifth year of this Pope Urban, began the order of the Jesuits. And to this time, which was about A. D. 1367, the offices here in England, as the lord chancellor, lord treasurer, and of the privy seal, were wont to be in the hands of the clergy. But about this year, through the motion of the lords in the parliament, and partly for hatred of the clergy, all the offices were removed from the clergy to the lords temporal.

After the death of Pope Urban, succeeded Pope Gregory XI. who brought again the papacy out of France to Rome, after having been absent the space of seventy years he was influenced as Sabellicus records by the answer of a bishop, whom the pope asked, why he was so long absent from his charge and church, saying that, "it was not the part of a good pastor, to keep him from his flock so long" The bishop answering said, "And you yourself, being the chief bishop, who may and ought to be an example to us all why are you so long from the place where your church is" The pope sought all means after that to remove his court out of France again to Rome, and he did so.

The king of England, holding a parliament in the third year of this pope, sent his ambassadors to him, desiring that from henceforth he would abstain from his reservations of benefices used in the court of England; and that spiritual men, promoted within this realm to bishoprics, might freely conduct their elections within the realm, and be confirmed by their metropolitans, according to the ancient custom of the realm Wherefore, upon these, and such other matters, where the king and the realm thought themselves aggrieved, he desired of the pope to provide some remedy, &c The pope returned answer to the king, requiring to be certified of the king's mind concerning the same. But what answer it was, is not in history expressed save that the year following, which was 1374, there was a treating at Burges upon certain of the articles between the king and the pope, which hung two years in suspense; and so at length it was agreed, that the pope should no more use his reservations of benefices in England, and the king should no more confer and give benefices upon the writ, *Quare impedit, &c.* But as to the freedom of elec-

tions to be confirmed by the metropolitan, nothing was touched.

The king by the consent of the lords and commons, in the twenty fifth year of his reign, enacted a statute in accordance with a statute made in the thirtieth year of his grandfather Edward I., wherein an act was passed against the ravenous pillage of the pope, through provisions, reservations, and collations, &c but not put in execution by which provisions, the state of the realm decreased more and more, the king's royalty and prerogative was greatly obscured and diminished, innumerable treasure of the realm transported aliens and strangers placed in the best and fattest bishopricks, abbeys, and benefices within the realm, and such, as either for their offices in Rome, as cardinalships &c. could not be resident here, or if resident, yet were better away, for infinite causes The king not only revived the statute made by Edward I, but also enlarged the same. Adding very strait and sharp penalties against the offenders, as exemption out of the king's protection, loss of all their lands, goods, and other possessions and their bodies to be imprisoned at the king's pleasure and further, whoever was lawfully convicted, or for want of appearance by process, was within the lapse of this statute of præmunire for so was the name thereof), should suffer all and every such molestations and injuries, as men exempted from the protection of the king. So that whoever had killed such men, had been in no more danger of law, than for killing any outlaw, or one not worthy to live in a commonweal. Like unprofitable members they were then, yea, in that time of ignorance, esteemed in England who would offer themselves to the wilful slavery and servile obedience of the pope although in these days, yea and that amongst no small fools, it is counted more than evangelical holiness. He that wishes to peruse the statute, and would see every branch and article thereof at large discussed and handled, with the penalties, let him read the statute of provision and *præmunire*, made in the twenty-fifth year of this king's days. And let him read in the statutes made in the parliaments holden the twenty-seventh and thirty-eighth years of his reign; and under the same title of provision and *præmunire*, he shall find the pope's primacy and jurisdiction within this realm more nearly touched, and much of his papal power restrained insomuch that whoever, for any cause or controversy in law, either spiritual or temporal the same being determinable in any of the king's courts as all matters were whether they were personal or real citations, or other, should either appeal or consent to any appeal to be made out of the realm to the pope or see of Rome, should incur the penalty and danger of *præmunire*. Divers other matters wherein the pope is restrained of his usurped power, authority, and jurisdiction within this realm of England, are expressed in the titles and statutes, and at large set forth, whoever list to peruse the same, which for brevity's sake I omit, hasting to other matters.

About this time (being A. D. 1370, lived holy Bridget, whom the church of Rome has canonized not only for a saint, but also for a prophetess; who, notwithstanding, in her book of revelations, which has been oftentimes printed, was a great rebuker of the pope, and of the filth of his clergy, calling him a murderer of souls, a spiller and a pilferer of the flock of Christ, more abominable than the Jews, more cruel than Judas, more unjust than Pilate, worse than Lucifer himself. The see of the pope she prophesies shall be thrown down into the deep like a millstone, and that his assistant shall burn with brimstone, affirming that the prelates, bishops, and priests are the cause why the doctrine of Christ is neglected, and almost extinguished. And that the clergy have turned the ten commandments of God into two words, to wit, "Give money" It were long and tedious to declare all that she writes against them, let this suffice for all Bridget affirms in her revelations, that when the Holy Virgin said to her Son, "how Rome was a fruitful and fertile field;" "yea," said he, 'but of weeds only, and cockle," &c.

To this Bridget I will join also Catherine of Sienne,

an holy nun, who lived much about the same time, (A. D. 1379). This Catherine was wont much to complain of the corrupt state of the church, namely, of the prelates of the court of Rome, and of the pope, warning them of the great schism, which then followed in the church of Rome, and endured to the council of Constance. (A. D. 1414.)

Besides these, the Lord, who never ceases to work in his church, stirred up against the malignant church of Rome, the spirits of divers good and godly teachers, as Matthew Paris, a Bohemian born, who, about A.D. 1370, wrote a large book of antichrist, and proves him to be already come, and notes the pope to be the same. In this book he greatly inveighs against the wickedness and filthiness of the clergy, and against the neglecting of their duty in governing the church. The locusts mentioned in the Apocalypse, he says, are the hypocrites reigning in the church. The works of antichrist, he says, are these, the fables and inventions of men reigning in the church, the images and feigned relics that are worshipped every where. That men worship every one his own saint and saviour beside Christ, so that every man and city almost has his peculiar Christ. He taught and affirmed moreover, that godliness and true worship of God are not bound to place, persons, or times, to be heard more in this place than in another, at this time more than at another, &c. He argues also against the cloisterers, who leaving the only and true Saviour, set up to themselves their Francises, their Dominics, and such other, and have them for their saviours, glorifying and triumphing in them, and feigning many forged lies about them. He was greatly and much offended with monks and friars, for neglecting, or rather burying the word of Christ, and, instead of him, celebrating and setting up their own rules and canons, affirming him to be hurtful to true godliness ; that priests, monks, and nuns, should account themselves spiritual, and all others to be lay and secular, attributing only to themselves the opinion of holiness, and contemning other men. He further writes, that antichrist had seduced all universities and colleges of learned men, so that they teach no sincere doctrine, neither give any light to the christians with their teaching. Finally, he forewarns that it will come to pass, that God yet once again will raise up godly teachers, who, being fervent in the spirit and zeal of Elias, shall disclose and refute the errors of antichrist, and antichrist himself, openly to the whole world.

About the same time, or shortly after, (A. D. 1384), we read also of John of Mountziger, rector of the university of Ulme, who openly in the schools in his oration propounded that the body of Christ was not God, and therefore not to be worshipped as God with that kind of worship called Latreia, as the sophisters term it, meaning thereby that the sacrament was not to be adored, which afterward he also defended in writing ; affirming also, that Christ in his resurrection took to him again all his blood which he had shed in his passion ; meaning thereby to infer, that the blood of Christ, which, in many places is worshipped, neither can be called the blood of Christ, neither ought to be worshipped.

Nilus was archbishop of Thessalonica, and lived much about this time. He wrote a long work against the Latins, that is, against such as took part and held with the church of Rome. His first book, being written in Greek, was afterward translated into Latin, and lately now into English, in this our time. In the first chapter of this book, he lays all the blame and fault of the dissension and schism between the eastern and the western churches, upon the pope. He affirmed that the pope only would command what he pleased, were it never so contrary to all the ancient canons ; that he would hear and follow no man's advice ; that he would not permit any free councils to be assembled, &c. And that therefore it was not possible that the controversies between the Greek church and Latin church should be decided.

In the second chapter of this book he makes a very learned disputation. For first, he declares that the pope, not at all by God's commandment, but only by human law, has any dignity, more than other bishops,

which dignity, the councils, the fathers, the emperors, have granted to him. Neither did they grant it for any consideration, than that the city then had the empire of all the whole world, and not at all because Peter was ever there, or not there.

Secondly, he declares that the primacy is not so great as he and his sycophants usurp to themselves. Also he refutes the chiefest propositions of the papists one after another. He declares that the pope has no more dominion than other patriarchs, and that the pope may err as well as other mortal men ; and that he is subject both to laws and councils, as well as other bishops. That it belonged not to him, but to the emperor, to call general councils ; and that in ecclesiastical causes he could establish and ordain no more than all other bishops might. And, lastly, that he gets no more by Peter's succession than that he is a bishop, as all other bishops after the apostles are, &c.

I cannot leave out the memory of James Misuensis, who also wrote of the coming of antichrist. He mentions a certain learned man, whose name was Militzius, who was a famous and worthy preacher in Prague. He lived about A.D. 1366, long before Huss, and before Wickliffe also. In his writings he declares how the same good man Militzius was by the Holy Spirit of God incited, and moved to search out of the holy scriptures the manner and coming of antichrist ; and found that now in his time he was already come. And James says that Militzius was constrained to go up to Rome, and there publicly to preach ; and that afterwards he affirmed the same before the inquisitor—that the same mighty and great antichrist, which the scriptures made mention of, was already come.

He affirmed also, that the church, by the negligence of the pastors, should become desolate, and that iniquity should abound. Also, he said that there were in the church of Christ idols, which should destroy Jerusalem, and make the temple desolate, but were cloaked by hypocrisy. Further, that there are many who deny Christ, for they keep silence against their conscience ; neither do they hear Christ, whom all the world should know, and confess his truth before men.

There is also a bull of Pope Gregory XI. to the archbishop of Prague, wherein he is commanded to excommunicate and persecute Militzius and his hearers. The same bull declares that he was once a canon of Prague, but that afterwards he renounced his canonship, and began to preach, because he preached that antichrist was already come, and he was, by John, archbishop of Prague, put in prison. He had his company or congregation to whom he preached, and among them were certain converted women who had forsaken their evil life, and did live godly and well ; he was accustomed in his sermons to prefer these before all the blessed nuns that never offended. He taught also openly, that in the pope, cardinals, bishops, prelates, priests, and other religious men, was no truth, and that they taught not the way of truth, but that only he, and such as held with him, taught the true way of salvation.

About the year 1371, lived Henry de Jota, whom Gerson much commends, and also his companion Henry de Hassia, a learned and famous man. In an epistle of this Henry de Hassia, which he wrote to the Bishop of Normacia, the author greatly accuses the spiritual men of every order, yea, and the most holy of all others, the pope himself, of many and great vices. He said that the ecclesiastical governors in the primitive church were compared to the sun shining in the daytime ; and the political governors to the moon shining in the night. But the spiritual men, he said that now are, do neither shine in the day-time, nor yet in the night-time, but rather with their darkness do obscure both the day and the night, that is, with their filthy living, ignorance, and impiety. He cites also out of the prophecy of Hildegardis, these words : "Therefore doth the devil in himself speak of you priests ; dainty banquets and feasts, wherein is all voluptuousness, do I find amongst these men ; insomuch that mine eyes, mine ears, my body, and my veins be even filled with the froth of them." "Lastly," saith he, "they every day more and more, as Lucifer did, seek to climb higher and higher, till every day with him more and more, they fall deeper and deeper."

About the year 1390, there were burned at Bringa thirty-six citizens of Mentz, for the doctrine of the Waldenses, as Brussius affirms, which opinion was not contrary to what they held before, wherein they affirmed the pope to be that great antichrist which should come; unless peradventure the pope seemed then to be more evidently convicted of antichristianity, than at any other time.

For the like cause many others beside these are to be found in histories, who sustained similar persecutions by the pope, if leisure would serve to peruse all that might be searched. As where Masseus records of some to the number of a hundred and forty, who, in the province of Narbonne, chose rather to suffer every grievous punishment by fire, than to receive the decretals of the Romish church, contrary to the truth of the scripture.

What should I here speak of the twenty-four who suffered at Paris, (A. D. 1210)? Also in the same author is testified that (A. D. 1211) there were four hundred, under the name of heretics, burned, eighty beheaded, Prince Americus hanged, and the lady of the castle stoned to death.

Moreover, in the chronicles of Hoveden, and of other writers, are recited a great number, who, in France, were burned for heretics.

We will now, Christ willing, proceed upon no light reports of feeble credit, nor upon any fabulous legends without authority, but upon the true and substantial copies of the public records of the realm, remaining yet to be seen under the king's most sure and faithful custody. Out of which records such matter appears against the popish church of Rome, and against his usurped authority, such open standing and crying against that see, and that not privily, but even in open parliament, in the days of this King Edward III., that neither will the Romish people of this our age easily think it true when they see it, neither yet shall they be able to deny it.

King Edward III., in the sixth year of his reign, hearing that Edward Bailiol had proclaimed himself King of Scotland, required counsel of the whole state. And for this he summoned a parliament of all estates to meet at York about the beginning of December, where the king was already come, waiting for the coming of such as were summoned. But none of all the clergy came, except the archbishop of York, the bishop of Lincoln, and of Carlisle, and abbots of Bath and Selby. So that there came not the archbishop of Canterbury, nor any other of his province, and all because there was a dispute whether Canterbury or York should carry the cross.

It follows also in the records that the commons find great default at provisions coming from Rome, whereby foreigners were enabled to enjoy ecclesiastical dignities within this realm, and shew inconveniences ensuing thereby, namely, the decay of daily alms,—the transporting of the treasure to nourish the king's enemies, —the discovering of the secrets of the realm, and the disabling and impoverishing of the clergy within this realm.

They also shew how the pope had most covertly granted to two new cardinals within this realm above ten thousand marks of yearly taxes. They therefore required the king and nobles to find some remedy, for that they never could, or would any longer bear those strange oppressions, or else to help them to expel out of this realm the pope's power by force.

Hereupon, the king, lords, and commons, sent for the act made at Carlisle, in the thirty-fifth year of King Edward I., upon the like complaint, thereby forbidding that any thing should be attempted or brought into the realm, which should tend to the blemishing of the king's prerogative, or to the prejudice of his lords or commons. And so at this time the statute called the act of provision, was made common by consent, which generally forbids the bringing in of any bulls, or such trinkets from the court of Rome, or the using, enjoying, or allowing of any such bill, process, instrument, or such ware.

Also, It was propounded in the parliament, in the eighteenth year of Edward III., that if any bishop elect shall refuse to take any such bishoprics, otherwise than by the pope's bull; that then such shall not enter nor enjoy his temporalties without special license.

Also, that the king shall dispose of all such benefices and dignities of such foreigners, his enemies, as remain in the country of his enemies, and employ the profits to the defence of the realm.

Moreover it was propounded, that commissioners be sent to all the king's ports, to apprehend all such persons as shall bring in any such instrument from Rome, and to bring them forthwith before the council to answer thereto.

Propounded, furthermore, that the deanery of York, which is to be recovered by judgment in the king's court, may be bestowed upon some able man within the realm, who will maintain the same against him (meaning the cardinal, who holds the same by provision from Rome, being the enemy to the king and to the realm), and that the profits may be employed to the defence of the realm.

To all which petitions the king's answer was made in the form following:—" It is agreed by the king, earls, barons, justices, and otherwise men of the realm, that the petitions aforesaid be made in sufficient form of law, according to the petitions aforesaid."

To pass further, in the twentieth year of the king's reign in the parliament holden the same year, it was propounded, That all foreign monks should leave the realm by the day of St. Michael, and that their livings should be disposed to young English scholars. The livings of these the king took to his hands.

Also, that the king may take the profits of all other foreigners' livings, as cardinals and others, during their lives. The profits of which were also to be in the king's hands.

That such foreigners enemies, as are advanced to livings here in England (being in their own countries, shoemakers, tailors, or chamberlains to cardinals), should depart before Michaelmas, and their livings be disposed to poor English scholars. The livings also of these remained in the king's hands.

The commons refused to pay any payment to any cardinals, lying in France, to treat of war or peace, which was granted on the king's part as reasonable.

Also propounded and fully agreed, that the yearly advance of two thousand marks (granted by the pope to two cardinals, out of the provinces of Canterbury and York) should be restrained.

Likewise enacted, that no Englishman should take anything in farm of any foreign monk, or buy any of their goods, or be of their counsel, on pain of perpetual imprisonment.

Enacted further, that no person should bring into the realm, to any bishop or other, any bull, or any other letters from Rome, or from any alien, unless he shew the same to the chancellor or warden of the cinque ports, upon loss of all his goods.

Finally, in the end of the parliament the bishops were commanded, before the next convocation, to certify to the chancery the names of all such foreigners, of their benefices, and the values of the same.

The parliament of the twenty-fifth year was begun the 6th day of February, in which, beside other matters, it was propounded that remedy might be had against the pope's reservation, by which the pope received the first fruits of all ecclesiastical dignities: a greater consumption to the realm than all the king's wars.

Also that the same remedy might be had against such as in the court of Rome presume to undo any judgment given in the king's court, as if they had power to undo the laws of the realm.

Whereto it was answered, that there was sufficient remedy provided by law.

In the parliament holden at Westminster, the thirty-eighth year of Edward III., it was required by the king's own mouth, and declared to the whole estates, how daily citation and false suggestions were made to the pope, for matters determinable in his courts within the realm, and for procuring provisions to ecclesiastical dignities, to the great defacing of the ancient laws—to the spoiling of his crown—to the daily conveying away of the treasure—to the wasting of ecclesiastical livings —to the withdrawing of divine service, alms, hospitality, and other acceptable works, and to the daily increase of all mischiefs: wherefore, in person by his own mouth the king required the whole estate to provide due remedy.

In the fortieth year of the reign of King Edward III., another parliament was called at Westminster (A. D. 1366), the bishop of Ely being lord chancellor and speaker, who, in the second day of the assembly in the presence of the king, lords, and commons, declared, how the day before they generally understood the cause of this their assembly, and now should more particularly understand the same; specially how that the king understood that the pope (for the homage which King John made to the see of Rome for the realms of England and Ireland, and for the tribute by him granted), meant by process to cite the king to Rome to answer thereto. Wherein the king required their advice, what were best for him to do if any such thing were attempted. The bishops by themselves required a respite till the next day to answer. So did the lords and commons every one of them by themselves.

The next day the whole estates re-assembled together, and by common consent enacted in effect following, viz. forasmuch as neither King John, nor any other king, could bring his realm and people under such thraldom and subjection, but by the common assent of parliament, which was not done, therefore John acted against his oath at his coronation. If, therefore, the pope should attempt anything against the king, by process, or other matter, that the king, with all his subjects should with all their force and power resist the same.

Here, moreover, is not to be omitted, how in the present parliament the universities of Oxford and Cambridge on the one side, and the friars of the four mendicant orders in the universities on the other side, made long complaints, the one against the other to the king in parliament, and in the end submitted themselves to the king's order.

After which, the king upon full digesting of the whole matter (by assent of parliament) ordered, that the chancellor and scholars, as well as the friars of those orders in the universities, should in all graces and other school exercises use each other in friendly wise, without any rumour as before. That none of those orders should receive any scholars into their orders under the age of eighteen years. That the friars should take no advantage, or procure bulls, or other process from Rome, against the universities, or proceed therein. And that the king should have power to redress all controversies between them from thenceforth, and the offenders to be punished at the pleasure of the king, and of the Council.

In process of these acts and rolls of parliament, it follows, that in the fiftieth year of the reign of King Edward III. (A. D. 1376), another great parliament was assembled at Westminster, where a long bill was put up against the usurpations of the pope, as being the cause of all the plagues, murrains, famine, and poverty of the realm, so as there was not left one-third of the number of persons, or other commodity within the realm that there lately was.

2. That the taxes paid to the pope of Rome for ecclesiastical dignities, amount to five-fold as much as the tax of all profits which belong to the king, by the year, out of his whole realm; and that for some one bishopric or other dignity, the pope, by means of translations and deaths, has three, four, or five several taxes.

3. That the brokers of that sinful city promote for money many caitiffs (being altogether unlearned and unworthy), to a thousand marks living a year, where the learned and worthy can hardly obtain twenty marks, whereby learning decays.

4. That foreigners (enemies to this land) who never saw nor care not to see their parishioners, have those livings, whereby they despise God's service, and convey away the treasure, and are worse than Jews or Saracens.

5. Also it was put in the bill to be considered, that the laws of the church would have such livings to be bestowed for charity only, without praying or paying.

6. That reason would that livings given of devotion should be bestowed in hospitality.

7. That God had committed his sheep to the pope, to be pastured, and not to be shorn or shaven.

8. That lay patrons, perceiving the covetousness and simony of the pope, do thereby learn to sell their benefices to beasts, none otherwise than Christ was sold to the Jews.

9. That there is no prince in Christendom so rich, that has the fourth part of the treasure, which the pope most sinfully has out of this realm for churches.

10. Over and besides in the bill, repeating again the tender zeal for the honour of the church, were declared and particularly named all the plagues which have justly fallen upon this realm, for suffering the church to be so defaced, with a declaration that it will daily increase without redress.

11. Whereupon with much persuasion this was desired, to help to re-edify the same; and the rather because this was the year of jubilee, the fiftieth year of the king's reign, the year of joy and gladness, than which there could be no greater.

12. The means how to begin this was to write two letters to the pope, the one in Latin under the king's seal, the other in French under the seals of the nobles, importing their particularities, and requiring redress; of which letter of the lords the effect may be seen in a like letter mentioned before.

13. And for a further accomplishment hereof, to enact, that no money be carried out of the realm by letter of Lombardy or otherwise, on pain of forfeiture and imprisonment, and to enact the articles hereafter ensuing.

14. The king had heretofore by statute provided sufficient remedy, and otherwise pursued the same with the holy father the pope, and so minded to do from time to time, until he had obtained as well for the matters before, as for the articles ensuing, being in a manner all one.

15. That the pope's collector and other strangers the king's enemies, and only lieger spies for English dignities and disclosing of the secrets of the realm, may be touched.

16. That the same collector being also receiver of the pope's pence, keeps a house in London, with clerks and officers, as if it were one of the king's solemn courts, transporting yearly to the pope twenty thousand marks, and most commonly more.

17. That cardinals and other foreigners remaining at Rome, whereof one cardinal is dean of York, another of Salisbury, another of Lincoln, another archdeacon of Canterbury, another archdeacon of Durham, another archdeacon of Suffolk, another archdeacon of York, another prebendary of Thame and Nassington, another prebendary of Bucks in the church of York, have some of the best dignities of England, and have sent over to them yearly twenty thousand marks, over and above that which English brokers lying here have.

18. That the pope (to ransom the Frenchmen the king's enemies, who defend Lombardy from him), does always at his pleasure levy a subsidy of the whole clergy of England.

19. That the pope for the greater gain makes several translations of all the bishoprics and other dignities within the realm.

20. That the pope's collector has this year taken to his use the first fruits of all benefices, by collation or provision.

21. To renew all the statutes against provisors from Rome, since the pope reserves all the benefices of the world for his own proper gifts, and has this year created twelve new cardinals, so as now there are thirty, where was wont to be but twelve, and all those cardinals, except two or three, are the king's enemies.

22. That the pope in time will give the temporal

manors of those dignities to the king s enemies, since he so daily usurps upon the realm, and the king's regalities.

23. That all houses and corporations of religion, who to the time of the king's reign had free election of their heads, the pope has encroached the same to himself.

24. That in all legacies from the pope, the English clergy bear the charge of the legates, and all for the goodness of our money.

25. And so it appears, that if the money of the realm were as plentiful as ever it was, the collectors, with the proctors of cardinals, would soon convey the same away.

26. For remedy hereof it may be provided, that no such collector or proctor do remain in England, on pain of life and member. And that no Englishman, on the like pain, become any such collector or proctor, or remain at Rome.

27. For better information hereof, and namely touching the pope's collector, because the whole clergy being obedient to him, dare not displease him, it were good that Sir John Strensale, parson of St. Botolph's in Holborn, may be sent to come before the lords and commons of this parliament, who being straightly charged can declare much more, because he served the collector five years.

And thus much of this bill touching the pope's matters, whereby it may appear that it was not for nothing that the Italians and other foreigners, used to call Englishmen good asses, for they bare all burdens that were laid upon them.

In these rolls and records of parliament in this king's time several other things are to be noted worthy of being marked, and not to be suppressed in silence. Wherein the reader may learn and understand that the state of the king's jurisdiction here within this realm, was not straightened in those days (although the pope then seemed to be in his chief ruff) as was seen afterwards in other kings' days, as may appear in the parliament of the fifteenth year of this King Edward III., and in the twenty-fourth article of the parliament, where it is to be read, that the king's officers and temporal justices did then both punish usurers, and impeached the officers of the church for bribery, and for taking money for temporal pain, probate of wills, solemnity of marriage, &c. notwithstanding all the pretended liberties of the popish church to the contrary.

This is moreover to be added to the commendation of this king, how in the volumes of the acts and rolls of the king it appears, that King Edward III. sent John Wickliff, then reader of divinity lectures in Oxford, with other lords and ambassadors, over to Italy, to treat with the pope's legates concerning affairs betwixt the king and the pope with full commission; the tenor whereof here follows:—

"The king to all and singular to whom these presents shall come, greeting. Know ye, that we reposing assured confidence in the fidelity and wisdom of the reverend father John bishop of Bangor, and other our loving and faithful subjects, Master John Wickliff, reader of the divinity lecture, Master John Gunter, dean of Segobyen, and Master Simon Moulton, doctor of law, Sir William Burton Knight, Master John Belknap, and Master John Honnington, have directed them as our ambassadors and special commissioners to the parts beyond the seas. Giving to our ambassadors and commissioners, to six or five of them, of whom I desire that the bishop shall be one, full power and authority, with commandment special, to treat and consult mildly and charitably with the legates and ambassadors of the lord pope touching certain affairs. Whereupon of late we sent heretofore the bishop, and William Ughtred, monk of Durham, and Master John Shepy to the see apostolical; and hereof to make full relation of all things done and passed in the said assembly, that all such things which may tend to the honour of holy church, and the advancement of our crown and this our realm, may, by the assistance of God, and wisdom of the see apostolical, be brought to good effect, and accomplished accordingly. Witness ourselves, &c. at

London, dated the twenty-sixth day of July, in the forty-eighth year of our reign."

It may be seen by this letter what good will the king then bare to Wickliff, and what little regard he had for the sinful see of Rome. We will now proceed to the history of this valiant soldier of Christ.

JOHN WICKLIFF.

After all those before recited, by whom it pleased the Lord to work against the bishop of Rome, and to weaken the pernicious superstition of the friars; it now remains to enter into the history of John Wickliff, our countryman, and others of his time and country, whom the Lord by the power of his Spirit raised up here in England, to detect more fully and amply the poison of the pope's doctrine, and the false religion set up by the friars. In his opinions some blemishes perhaps may be observed, yet they are such blemishes as rather shew him to be a man that might err, than one who could directly fight against Christ our Saviour, as the popes and friars did. And from the primitive ages of the church what learned man has been so perfect, so absolutely sure, that no opinion of his has ever been erroneous; and yet these articles of his would be seen to be neither so many in number, nor yet so gross in themselves as his enemies give them out to be, if his books which they destroyed were remaining to be compared with those articles which they have wrested to the worst.

This much is certain, and cannot be denied, but that he, being the public reader of divinity to the university of Oxford, was for the rude time wherein he lived, famously reputed for a great clergyman, a deep scholar, and no less expert in all kind of philosophy, which not only appears by his famous and learned writings, but also by the confession of Walden his most cruel and bitter enemy, who, in a letter written to Pope Martin V., says, "That he was wonderfully astonished at his most strong arguments with the places of authority which he had gathered, with the vehemency and force of his reasons," &c. It appears that Wickliff flourished about A. D. 1371, in the reign of Edward III.; for thus we find in the chronicles of Caxton: "In the year of our Lord 1371, Edward III., king of England, in his parliament was against the pope's clergy: he willingly hearkened, and gave ear to the voices and tales of heretics, with some of his council; conceiving and following sinister opinions against the clergy; for which he tasted and suffered afterward much adversity and trouble. And not long after, in the year of our Lord 1372, he wrote to the bishop of Rome, that he should not by any means intermeddle any more within his kingdom, as to the reservation or distribution of benefices, and that all such bishops as were under his dominion, should enjoy their former and ancient liberty, and be confirmed by their metropolitans, as has been accustomed in times past," &c. This is without all doubt, that when the world was in a most desperate and vile state, and lamentable darkness and ignorance of God's truth overshadowed the whole earth, this man stepped out like a valiant champion.

Thus does Almighty God continually succour and help us, when all things else are in despair, being always, according to the Psalm, "a help in time of need." This was never more apparent than in these later days and extreme age of the church, when the whole state, not only of worldly things, but also of religion, was depraved and corrupted. The state of religion amongst the divines was in a deep lethargy, and past all the help and remedy of man. Only the name of Christ remained among the christians; his true and lively doctrine was as far unknown to most men, as his name was common to all men. As to faith,—consolation,—the end and use of the law,—the office of Christ,—our impotency and weakness,—the Holy Ghost,—the greatness and strength of sin,—true works—grace, and free justification by faith,—the liberty of a christian man; of all these things wherein consists the sum of our profession, there was no mention, and scarcely a word spoken. Scripture, learning, and divinity, was known but to a few, and that in the schools only, and there also it was almost all turned into sophistry. Instead of the epistles of Peter and Paul, men occupied their time in studying Aquinas and Scotus, and Lombards, the Master of Sentences. The world leaving and forsaking God's spiritual word and doctrine, was altogether led and blinded with outward ceremonies and human traditions. In these was all the hope of obtaining salvation fully fixed, so that scarcely any thing else was taught in the churches.

The people were taught to worship nothing but what they saw, and saw almost nothing which they did not worship.

The whole world was filled and overwhelmed with error and darkness. And no great wonder, for the simple and unlearned people, being far from all knowledge of the holy scripture, thought it sufficient for them to know only these things which were delivered to them by their pastors and shepherds, and they on the other hand taught nothing else, but such things as came forth from the court of Rome, of which the greater part tended to the profit of their order, more than to the glory of Christ.

The christian faith was nothing then, but that every man should know that Christ once suffered, that is to say, that all men should know and understand that which the devils themselves also knew. Hypocrisy was counted for wonderful holiness. Men were so given to outward forms, that even they who professed the knowledge of the scriptures, scarcely understood, or knew any thing but these forms. And this appeared, not only in the common sort of doctors and teachers, but also in the very heads and captains of the church, whose whole religion and holiness consisted in the observing of days, meats, and garments, and such circumstances, as of place, time, person, &c. From this there sprang so many fashions of vestures and garments, so many differences of colours and meats, so many pilgrimages to several places, as if St. James at Compostella could do that, which Christ could not do at Canterbury; or else, that God was not of the same power and strength in every place, or could not be found, unless by running hither and thither in the pilgrimages. &c. Thus the holiness of the whole year was transported and put off to the lent season. No country or land was counted holy, but only Palestine. Such was the blindness of that time, that men did strive and fight for the cross at Jerusalem, as if it had been for the chief and only strength of our faith. It is a wonder to read the monuments of the former times, to see and understand what great troubles and calamities this cross had caused in almost every christian commonwealth. For the Romish champions never ceased, by writing, admonishing, and counselling, yea, and by quarrelling, to move and stir up princes to mind war and battle, even as though the faith and belief of the gospel were of no power, or little effect without that wooden cross.

In these troublous times, and horrible darkness of ignorance, when there seemed to be no spark of pure doctrine remaining, this Wickliff sprang up by God's providence, through whom the Lord purposed to awaken the world, which was overwhelmed in the deep streams of human traditions.

Wickliff, after he had a long time professed divinity in the university of Oxford, and perceiving the true doctrine of Christ's gospel to be defiled with the inventions of bishops, orders of monks, and dark errors, and after long deliberating with himself, with many secret sighs, and bewailing the general ignorance of the world, could no longer bear it, he at last determined to remedy such things as he saw to be out of the way. But as he saw that this could not be attempted without great trouble, and that these things, which had been so long time rooted and grafted in men's minds, could not be suddenly plucked up, he thought that it should be done by little and little. Wherefore he first assailed his adversaries in logical and metaphysical questions, disputing with them of the first form and fashion of things, of the increase of time, and of the intelligible substance of a creature, with other such things of no great importance,

but yet it helped him not a little in preparing to dispute about greater matters.

From these beginnings the way was opened to greater matters, so that at the length he came to touch the matters of the sacraments, and other abuses of the church. Touching which things this holy man took great pains, protesting openly in the schools, that it was his chief and principal purpose to call back the church from her idolatry to some better amendment, especially in the matter of the sacrament of the body and blood of Christ; but this sore point could not be touched without the great grief and pain of the whole world. For first of all, the whole body of monks and begging friars were set into a rage and madness, and even as hornets with their sharp stings assailed this good man on every side. After them the priests, and then after them the archbishop took the matter in hand, depriving him of his benefice which he had in Oxford; but being somewhat befriended and supported by the king, he continued and bare up against the malice of the friars, and of the archbishop, till about A.D. 1377. I must now digress a little to make some mention of John of Gaunt duke of Lancaster, who was his special supporter and friend.

When King Edward III. had reigned now about fifty-one years, and was of great age, and in such feebleness, that he was unable to govern the affairs of the realm, a parliament being called the year before his death, it was resolved by the knights and burgesses, that twelve sage and discreet lords and peers should be placed as guardians about the king, to have the doing and disposing under him of matters pertaining to the government.

These twelve governors by parliament being appointed to have the tuition of the king, and to attend the public affairs of the realm, remained for a certain time about him, till afterwards, being again removed, all the government of the realm, next under the king, was committed to the duke of Lancaster the king's son. For as yet Richard, the son of Prince Edward, lately deceased, was very young and under age.

This duke of Lancaster had in his heart for a long time conceived a displeasure against the popish clergy, whether for corrupt and impure doctrine joined with abominable excess of life, or for what other cause, is not precisely known.

The duke sent for John Wickliff, who was then the divinity reader in Oxford, and had commenced several disputations contrary to the form and teaching of the pope's church in many things, and had been deprived of his benefice. The opinions which he began to put forth in Oxford, in his lectures and sermons, were these :—That the pope had no more power than others to excommunicate any man—that even if it be given by any person to the pope to excommunicate, yet to absolve the same is as much in the power of another priest as in the pope. He affirmed, that neither the king nor any temporal lord could give any perpetuity to the church, or to any ecclesiastical person; for that when such ecclesiastical persons sinned, and continued in the same, the temporal powers ought to take away from them what before had been bestowed upon them, which he proved to have been practised here in England by William Rufus. Which (said he) if he did it lawfully, why may not the same also be practised now? If he did it unlawfully, then does the church err unlawfully in praying for him.

Besides these his opinions and assertions, with others which are hereafter to be mentioned in order, he began also to touch the matter of the sacrament, proving that in the sacrament the accidents of bread remained not without the substance, both by the holy scriptures, and also by the authority of the doctors, but specially by such as were most ancient. As for the later writers he utterly rejected them, saying, that the simple and plain truth appears in the scriptures, to which all human traditions whatever must be referred, and specially such as are set forth and published now of late years. This was the cause why he refused the later writers of decretals, leaning only to the scriptures and ancient doctors, affirming out of them, that in the sacrament of the body which is celebrated with bread, the accidents are not present without the substance; that is to say, that the body of Christ is not present without the bread, as the common sort of priests in those days did dream.

Although through the favour and support of the duke of Lancaster, and Lord Henry Percy, he persisted hitherto, and was protected against the violence and cruelty of his enemies, at last, about A. D. 1376, the bishops still urging and inciting their archbishop Simon Sudbury, who had already deprived him, and afterwards prohibited him, had obtained by process and order of citation to have him brought before them, both space and time for him to appear was assigned to him after their usual form.

The duke having intelligence that Wickliff was to appear before the bishops, and fearing that he was too weak against such a multitude, called to him out of the orders of friars, four bachelors of divinity, one out of every order, to join them with Wickliff, for the greater security. When the day was come assigned to Wickliff to appear, which day was Thursday the 19th of February, John Wickliff went accompanied with the four friars, and the duke of Lancaster, and Lord Henry Percy, lord marshal of England—the Lord Percy going before them to make room and way where Wickliff should come.

As Wickliff, thus sufficiently guarded, was coming to the place where the bishops sat, they animated and exhorted him not to fear or shrink before the bishops, who were all unlearned as compared with him. With these words, and with the assistance of the nobles, Wickliff approached to the church of St. Paul in London, where a great concourse of people was gathered to hear what should be said and done. Such was the throng of the multitude, that the lords (notwithstanding all the authority of the high marshal) with great difficulty could get through. The bishop of London seeing the stir that the lord marshal kept in the church among the people, speaking to the Lord Percy, said, " That if he had known before what authority he would have assumed in the church, he would have stopped him from coming there." At which words the duke, not a little angered, answered, " That he would keep such authority there, whether the bishop liked it or not."

At last they pierced through and came to our Lady's chapel, where the dukes and barons were sitting with the archbishops and other bishops. John Wickliff, according to the custom, stood before them, to learn what should be laid to his charge. The Lord Percy kindly bid him to sit down ; but the bishop of London in anger said, " he should not sit there. Neither was it fitting," said he, " that he, who was cited before his ordinary, should sit during the time of his answer." On these words a fire began to kindle between them, so that they began to rate and revile one another.

Then the duke, taking Lord Percy's part, answered the bishop with hasty words. The bishop far excelled him in this railing art of scolding ; so the duke fell to threatening the bishop, that he would bring down the pride not only of him, but also of all the prelacy of England ; and softly whispering in the ear of the person next him, said, that he would rather pluck the bishop by the hair of his head out of the church, than he would take this at his hand. This was not spoken so secretly, but that the Londoners overheard him. Upon which they cried out in rage, that they would not suffer their bishop to be abused so contemptuously, but would lose their lives rather than allow him to be drawn out by the hair. Thus that council, being broken up with scolding and brawling for that day, was dissolved before nine o'clock.

Upon the 21st of June (A.D. 1377,) the worthy and victorious prince King Edward III died after he had reigned fifty one years. A prince not more aged in years than renowned for many heroic virtues, but chiefly remarkable and applauded for his singular meekness and clemency towards his subjects and inferiors, ruling them by gentleness and mercy, without rigour or severity. Among other noble and royal ornaments of his nature, he is described as a " father to the orphan, compassionate to the afflicted,—mourning with the miserable,—relieving the oppressed,—and a friend to all that wanted a helper in time of need " &c. But above all other

things in this prince in my mind deserving to be commemorated, is, that above all other kings of this realm, to the time of King Henry VIII., he was the greatest bridler of the pope's usurped power, and outrageous oppressions: during all the time of this king, the pope could never entirely succeed in this realm, and John Wickliff was maintained with favour and sufficient support.

KING RICHARD THE SECOND.

After King Edward succeeded his grandson, Richard II, at the age of eleven years : who was crowned at Westminster A.D. 1377, and who, following his father's steps, was no great opponent to the doctrine of Wickliff : although at the beginning, partly through the iniquity of the times, and partly through the pope's letters, he could not do all he wished in his behalf. The bishops now seeing the aged king taken away, during whose old age all the government depended upon the Duke of Lancaster ; and now again seeing the duke, with the Lord Percy, remain in their private houses without intermeddling, they thought now was the time to gain some advantage against Wickliff ; who had some degree of rest and quietness under the protection of the duke and lord Marshal. It is already stated how when he was brought before the bishops, by the means of the duke and lord Henry Percy, the council was interrupted, and brake up, by which Wickliff at that time escaped without any further trouble. These articles were at that time collected out of his sermons.

That the Holy Eucharist, after the consecration, is not the very body of Christ, but figuratively.

That the church of Rome is not the head of all churches : and that Peter had not any more power given by Christ, than any other Apostle had.

That the pope of Rome has no more in the keys of the church, than has any other person in the order of priesthood.

That the lords temporal may lawfully and deservedly take away their temporalties from the church-men who persevere in offending.

That if any temporal lord know the church to be so offending, he is bound, under pain of damnation, to take the temporalties from the same.

That all the Gospel is a *rule* sufficient of itself to rule the life of every christian man here, without any other rule.

That all other rules, under whose observances various monastic persons are governed, add no more perfection to the Gospel, than does the white colour to the wall.

That neither the pope, nor any other prelate of the church, ought to have prisons wherein to punish transgressors.

Besides these articles, various other conclusions were afterward gathered out of his writings and preachings, which the bishops sent to pope Gregory at Rome : where being perused, they were condemned for heretical and erroneous by three-and-twenty cardinals.

The next year following, (A.D. 1378), being the first year of King Richard II. Pope Gregory sent the following bull by means of one master Edmund Stafford, directed to the university of Oxford, rebuking them sharply, imperiously, and like a pope, for suffering so long the doctrine of John Wickliff to take root, and not plucking it up with the crooked sickle of their catholic doctrine.

Gregory the Bishop, the servant of God's servants, to his well-beloved Sons, the Chancellor and University of Oxford, in the Diocese of Lincoln, Greeting and Apostolical Benediction.

We are compelled not only to marvel, but also to lament, that you, considering the apostolical see has given to your University of Oxford so great favour and privilege, and also that you flow as in a large sea in the knowledge of the holy scriptures, and ought to be champions and defenders of the ancient and catholic faith (without which there is no salvation) by your great negligence and sloth will suffer wild cockle, not only to grow up among the pure wheat of the flourishing field of your university, but also to wax strong and choke the corn. Neither have ye any care (as we are informed) to extirpate and pluck the same up by the roots, to the great blemishing of your renowned name,—the peril of your souls,—the contempt of the church of Rome,—and to the great decay of the ancient faith. And further (which grieves us) the increase of that filthy weed was more sharply rebuked and judged of in Rome, than in England where it sprang. Wherefore let there be means sought by the help of the faithful, to root out the same. Grievously it is come to our ears, that one John Wickliff, parson of Lutterworth in Lincoln diocese, a professor of Divinity (would God he were not rather a master of errors) is run into a kind of detestable wickedness, not only and openly publishing, but also vomiting out of the filthy dungeons of his breast, diverse professions, false and erroneous conclusions, and most wicked and damnable heresies. Whereby he might defile the faithful sort, and bring them from the right path headlong into the way of perdition, overthrow the state of the church, and utterly subvert the secular policy. Of which his mischievous heresies some seem to agree (only certain names and terms changed) with the perverse opinions, and unlearned doctrine of Marsilius of Padua, and of John Gandune, of unworthy memory, whose books were utterly abolished in the realm of England, by our predecessor of happy memory John XXII., which kingdom does not only flourish in power, and abundance of faculties, but is much more glorious and shining in pureness of faith; accustomed always to bring forth men excellently learned in the true knowledge of the holy scriptures, ripe in gravity of manners, men notable in devotion, and defenders of the catholic faith. Wherefore we will and command you by your writing apostolical in the name of your obedience, and upon pain of privation of our favour, indulgences and privileges granted unto you and your university from the said see apostolical; that hereafter ye suffer not those pestilent heresies, and those subtle and false conclusions and propositions, misconstruing the right sense of faith and good works (howsoever they term it, or what curious implication of words soever they use) any longer to be disputed of, or brought in question; lest if it be not withstood at the first, and plucked up by the roots, it might perhaps be too late hereafter to prepare medicines when a greater number is infected with the contagion. And further, that ye apprehend immediately, or cause to be apprehended the said John Wickliff, and deliver him to be detained in the safe custody of our well-beloved brethren, the archbishop of Canterbury, and the bishop of London, or either of them. And if you shall find any gainsayers, corrupted with the said doctrine (which God forbid) in your university within your jurisdiction, that shall obstinately stand in the said errors: that then in like manner ye apprehend them, and commit them to safe custody, and otherwise to do in this case as it shall appertain unto you: so as by your careful proceedings herein, your negligence past concerning the premises may now fully be supplied and recompensed with present diligence. Whereby you shall not only purchase unto you the favour and benevolence of the see apostolical, but also great reward and merit of Almighty God.

Given at Rome at St. Mary's the Greater, xi. Kalend of June, and in the 7th year of our consecration.

The pope also sent letters of similar purport to the University of Oxford and to the bishops, and even to the King Richard.

The bishops being again assembled, and Wickliff being brought before them, they proceeded to examine him, when a certain personage of the prince's court, and yet of no very noble birth, named Lewes Clifford, entering in among the bishops, commanded that they should not proceed with any final sentence against John Wickliff. At these words they all were so amazed, that they became speechless. And thus by the unforeseen providence of God, John Wickliff escaped the second time out of the bishops' hands.

At the time of his examination, John Wickliff exhibited to the bishops in writing the following protestation, with a declaration of his mind, upon the following articles.

The Protestation of John Wickliff.

" First I protest (as I have often before done) that I do mind and intend with my whole heart (by the grace of God) to be a true christian, and as long as breath shall remain in me, to profess and defend the law of Christ. And if it shall happen that through ignorance or otherwise I shall fail therein: I desire of my Lord God pardon and forgiveness. And now again as before also, I do revoke and retract; most humbly submitting myself under the correction of our holy mother the church. And forsomuch as the sentence of my faith, which I have holden in the schools and elsewhere, is reported even by children, and moreover is carried by children to Rome: therefore lest my dear beloved brethren should take any offence by me, I will set forth in writing the sentence and articles, for which I am now accused and impeached: which also even to the death I will defend, as I believe all christians ought to do, and specially the bishop of Rome and all other priests and ministers of the church. For I do understand the conclusions after the sense and manner of speaking of the scriptures and holy doctors, which I am ready to expound: and if they shall be found contrary to the faith, I am ready to revoke, and speedily to call them back again.''

This protest was accompanied by an exposition of the articles exhibited against him.

The next year, which was 1382, by the command of William archbishop of Canterbury, there was a convocation held at London, at which John Wickliff was also commanded to be present. But whether he appeared personally or not, I find it not certainly affirmed.

Of the articles attributed to John Wickliff, there were ten which were condemned by the friars as heretical, the rest as erroneous, and are as follow. It may be supposed, that some of them were made worse by their sinister collecting, than he meant them in his own works and writings.

The Articles of John Wickliff, condemned as Heretical.

1. The substance of material bread and wine remains, in the sacrament of the altar after the consecration.

2. The accidents do not remain without the subject in the same sacrament, after the consecration.

3. That Christ is not in the sacrament of the altar truly and really, in his proper and corporal person.

4. That if a bishop or a priest be in deadly sin, he cannot ordain, consecrate, or baptize.

5. That if a man be duly and truly contrite and penitent, all exterior and outward confession is but superfluous and unprofitable.

6. That it is not found or established by the gospel, that Christ did make or ordain mass.

7. If the pope be a reprobate and evil man, and consequently a member of the devil; he has no power given to him over faithful christians, except it be given him by the emperor.

8. That since the time of Urban VI., there is none to be received for the pope, but every man is to live after manner of the Greeks, under his own law.

9. That it is against the scripture, that ecclesiastical ministers should have any temporal possessions.

The other Articles of John Wickliff, condemned as erroneous.

10. That no prelate ought to excommunicate any man except he knew him first to be excommunicate of God.

11. That he, who so excommunicates any man, is thereby himself either an heretic or excommunicated.

12. That a prelate or bishop excommunicating any of the clergy, who has appealed to the king or the council, is thereby himself a traitor to the king and realm.

13. That all such who leave off preaching or hearing the word of God or preaching of the gospel for fear of excommunication, are already excommunicated, and in the day of judgment shall be counted as traitors to God.

14. That it is lawful for any man, either deacon or priest, to preach the word of God without the authority or licence of the apostolic see or any other of his catholics.

15. That so long as a man is in deadly sin, he is neither bishop nor prelate in the church of God.

16. Also that the temporal lords may, according to their own will and discretion, take away the temporal goods of the churchmen whenever they offend.

17. That tithes are pure alms, and that the parishioners may, for offence of their curates, detain and keep them back, and bestow them upon others, at their own will and pleasures.

18. Also, that all special prayers applied to any private or particular person, by any prelate or religious man, do no more profit the same person, than general or universal prayers do profit others, under similar circumstances.

19. Moreover, if any man enters into any private religion, whatever it be, he is thereby made the more unapt and unable to observe and keep the commandments of God.

20. That holy men, who have instituted private religions, whatever they be (as well such as have possessions, as also the order of begging friars having no possessions) in so doing, have grievously offended.

21. That religious men, (i. e. monks,) being in their private religions, are not of the christian religion.

22. That friars are bound to get their living by the labour of their hands, and not by begging.

23. That whoever gives any alms to friars, or to any of the mendicant orders, is accursed, or in danger thereof.

While the archbishop and suffragans, with the other doctors of divinity and lawyers, with a great company of babbling friars and monastics were gathered together to consult as to John Wickliff's books, at the Gray Friars in London, upon St. Dunstan's day after dinner, about two o'clock, the very hour that they should go forward with their business, a wonderful and terrible earthquake fell throughout all England. Several of the suffragan bishops being frightened, thought it good to leave off from their purpose. But the archbishop confirmed and strengthened their hearts and minds, which were daunted with fear, to proceed in their attempted enterprise. Then discoursing upon Wickliff's articles, not according to the sacred canons of the holy scripture, but according to their own traditions, they pronounced and gave sentence, that some of them were simply and plainly heretical, others half erroneous, others irreligious, and some seditious, and not consonant to the church of Rome.

Whereupon the lord archbishop of Canterbury, wishing to check such heresies and errors, delivered to the chancellor, his letters patent to be executed as follow:

"William by the grace of God archbishop of Canterbury, primate of all England, and legate of the apostolical see, To our well beloved son in Christ the chancellor of the university of Oxford, within the diocess of Lincoln, greeting, grace, and benediction. The prelates of the church, about the Lord's flock committed to their charge, ought to be so much more vigilant as that they see the wolf, clothed in sheep's attire, fraudulently go about to worry and scatter the sheep. Doubtless, the common fame and report is come unto our ears, &c. We will therefore and command, straitly enjoining you, that in the church of our blessed lady in Oxford, upon those days in the which customarily the sermon is made, as also in the schools of the university upon those days when the lectures are read, ye publish and cause by others to be published to the clergy and people, as well in their vulgar tongue, as in the Latin tongue, manifestly and plainly without any curious implication, that the same heretical and erroneous conclusions, so repugnant to the determination of holy church, as is aforesaid, have been and are condemned; which conclusions we also declare by these our letters to be utterly condemned. And that furthermore you forbid, and canonically admonish and cause to be admonished, as we by the tenour of these presents do forbid and admonish you, once, twice, thrice,

and that peremptorily, that none hereafter hold, teach, and preach, or defend the heresies and errors above said, or any of them, either in school or out of school by any sophistical cavilling or otherwise: or that any admit to preach, hear or hearken unto John Wickliff, Nicholas Herford, Philip Reppington, canon regular, or John Ashton, or Lawrence Redman, who are vehemently and notoriously suspected of heresy, or any other whatever, so suspected or defamed; or that either privately or publicly they either aid or favour them or any of them, but that immediately they shun and avoid the same as a serpent which puts forth most pestiferous poison. And furthermore we suspend the said suspected persons from all scholastical act, till such time as they shall purge themselves before us in that behalf: and that you denounce the same publicly by us to have been and be suspended; and that ye diligently and faithfully inquire after all their favourers, and cause to be inquired throughout all the halls of the university. And that when you shall have intelligence of their names and persons, that ye compel all and every one of them to abjure their outrages by ecclesiastical censures and other pains canonical, under pain of the greater curse, which against all and singular the rebellious in this behalf, and disobeying our admonitions, we pronounce: so that their fault, deceit, and offence in this behalf deserve the same (the said admonition of ours being first sent) which in this behalf we esteem and allow canonical, that then and again according to the effect of these our letters, &c. The absolution of all and singular such, which shall incur the sentence of this instrument by us sent forth (which God forbid) we specially reserve unto ourselves: exhorting you the chancellor by the sprinkling of the blood of Jesus Christ, that to the utmost of your power hereafter you do your endeavour, that the clergy and people being subject to you, if there be any who have strayed from the catholic faith by such errors, may be brought home again to the praise and honour of his name that was crucified, and to the preservation of the true faith. And further our will is, that whatever you shall do in the premises, in manner and form of our process in this behalf it be had and done: and that you for your part, when you shall be required thereto, plainly and distinctly do certify us by your letters patents, having the tenour hereof."

The conclusions and articles mentioned in this letter are above prefixed. Of which some were condemned for heretical, some for erroneous.

After this, the archbishop directed his letters of admonition to Robert Rigge commissary of Oxford, for repressing this doctrine: which notwithstanding, both then, and yet to this day (God be praised) remains.

The Examination of Nicholas Herford, Philip Reppington, and John Ashton.

Some days afterwards, on June 18th 1382, in the chamber of the preaching-friars afore mentioned, before the archbishop in the presence of divers doctors and bachelors of divinity, and many lawyers both canon and civil, whose names are under written, appeared Nicholas Herford, Philip Reppington, and John Ashton, bachelors of divinity. Who after oath taken to give judgment upon the conclusions aforesaid, were examined severally, each by himself, before the archbishop. Who there required day and place to deliberate upon the conclusions, and to give their answer to the same in writing.

Two days afterwards, when the answers were returned, the lord archbishop of Canterbury demanded of all the doctors what their judgment was touching the answers that were made upon such conclusions. All which doctors severally said, "That all the answers given to the first, second, third, and sixth conclusions, were insufficient, heretical and subtle; and that all the answers made, especially to the ninth, tenth, and last conclusions, were insufficient, erroneous, and perverse." Whereupon the lord archbishop of Canterbury, considering the answers to be heretical, subtle, erroneous, and perverse, accordingly as the doctors had weighed and considered, admonished Nicholas and Philip; assigning to them eight days' space, that is to say, until the twenty-seventh day of the month, and that then they should appear before the said lord archbishop of Canterbury, to hear his decree that should be made in that behalf. This done, the archbishop of Canterbury admonished and cited John Ashton, under the tenor of these words following:

"In the name of God, we, William, by God's permission, archbishop of Canterbury, primate of all England, legate of the see apostolical, and through all our province of Canterbury, chief inquisitor of all heretical pravity, do monish and cite thee, John Ashton, master of arts, and student in divinity, appearing before us, judicially to say and speak the plain verity touching these conclusions, to which we refer thee, and to which we have caused thee to swear, laying thy hand upon a book," &c.

After this citation, John Ashton was examined before the bishops, and his answers not proving satisfactory to them, they determined against him, and then the archbishop proceeded thus:

"And thou John Ashton, admonished and commanded by us, as is aforesaid, after thine oath taken, without any reasonable cause, or any other license, neither wouldst thou, nor yet wilt, but refusedst, and yet dost contemptuously, to answer to such conclusions before us; judicially according to our admonition and commandment aforesaid; we do hold all such conclusions to be by thee confessed, and thee the aforesaid John, with all thy aforesaid conclusions, convicted. And, therefore, we do pronounce, and declare by giving sentence that thou John Ashton, concerning those conclusions, which by us, with good deliberation of divers prelates, our suffragans, and also divers and sundry professors of divinity, and other wise men and learned in the law, according to the canonical sanctions, being condemned and declared for a heretic, and heretical hast been, and still art a heretic, and thy conclusions heretical. And as touching thy other conclusions, by us heretofore counted erroneous, and for erroneous condemned, we do pronounce and declare sententially by these our writings, that both thou hast erred, and dost err."

On the appointed day, the archbishop, with the doctors, being assembled in the chief house of his church at Canterbury, before the hour of nine, expected Nicholas, Philip, and also Thomas Hilman, calling them and looking after them; nevertheless they appeared not before two o'clock the same day. At which hour the archbishop of Canterbury examined Thomas Hilman, who then and there judicially appeared, what his opinion was touching the aforesaid conclusions, who, somewhat stammering at them and their meaning, at last to all the conclusions then read and expounded to him, thus answered, "I suppose and judge all and singular those conclusions lately condemned by my lord of Canterbury to be heretical and erroneous, even as the same my lord of Canterbury, and other doctors of divinity, of the canon and civil law, by common consent and counsel have supposed and thought. And the same (being for heresies and errors, as before is said condemned) I do, as much as in me is, condemn, protesting that I will hold and affirm the contrary of those conclusions, and in the same faith live and die." Then the archbishop of Canterbury, sitting as tribunal or judge, pronouncing Nicholas and Philip, guilty of contumacy and disobedience, for not appearing in court, excommunicated them for their contumacy, as follows:—

The denouncing of the excommunication against Nicholas Herford and Philip Reppington.

"William, by God's permission, archbishop of Canterbury, &c. To our beloved Son in Christ, whoever he be, that this instant Sunday shall preach at St. Paul's cross in London, salutation, grace, and blessing. Forasmuch as we appointed a certain day and place to Master Nicholas Herford, and Master Philip Reppington, canon regular of the monastery of our lady of Leicester, being doctors of divinity, and suspected of heretical pravity (after certain answers not fully made,

but impertinent and nothing to the purpose, as also heretical and erroneous) in divers places of our province commonly, generally, and publicly taught and preached, and that therefore they should judicially appear before us, to do and receive peremptorily in that behalf whatever the quality of that business should move us to: and that we have for their contumacy in not appearing before us at that day and place, adjudged as right therein required. We, by these presents, command and commit to you, firmly enjoining you, when all the multitude of people shall be gathered together to hear your sermon, that in the day and place appointed you publicly and solemnly denounce the aforesaid Nicholas and Philip, holding up a cross, and lighting up a candle, and then throwing down the same upon the ground, to have been so and in such manner excommunicated, and still continuing so.

"Fare ye well. In our manor house at Lambeth, the thirteenth day of July, the year of our Lord 1382, and first year of our translation."

The archbishop sent also another letter to Master Rigge, commissary of Oxford, straightly enjoining and charging him, not only to denounce the sentence of excommunication, and to give out public citation against them, but also to make diligent search and inquisition through all Oxford for them, to have them apprehended and sent up to him, personally before him to appear at a certain day prescribed for the same. Whereby it may appear how busy this bishop was in disquieting and persecuting these poor men, whom he should have nourished and cherished as his brethren.

The archbishop not contented with this, solicits the king to join the power of his temporal sword, for he well perceived that as yet the popish clergy had not sufficient authority, by any public law or statute of this land, to proceed unto death against any person in question of religion, but only by the usurped tyranny and example of the court of Rome. Where note, gentle reader, for thy better understanding, the practice of the Romish prelates in seeking the king's help to further their bloody purpose against the good saints of God. The king being but young, and not arrived at years of ripe judgment, was seduced by the archbishop to give his private assent to an ordinance, which was indeed the very first law to be found against religion and the professors thereof, bearing the name of an act made in the parliament held at Westminster, in the fifth year of Richard II. Where among other statutes then published, and yet remaining in the printed books of statutes, this supposed statute is to be found, (cap. 5. & ultimo).

"Forasmuch as it is openly known that there be divers evil persons within the realm, going from county to county, and from town to town, in certain habits under dissimulation of great holiness, and without the licence of the ordinaries of the places, or other sufficient authority, preaching daily not only in churches and churchyards, but also in markets, fairs, and other open places where a great congregation of people is, divers sermons containing heresies and notorious errors, to the great blemishing of the christian faith, and destruction of the laws, and of the estate of holy church, to the great peril of the souls of the people, and of all the realm of England, as more plainly is found, and sufficiently proved before the reverend father in God the archbishop of Canterbury, and the bishops and other prelates, masters of divinity, and doctors of canon and of civil law, and a great part of the clergy of the said realm, specially assembled for this great cause; which persons do also preach divers matters of slander, to ingender discord and dissension betwixt divers estates of the said realm, as well spiritual as temporal, in exciting the people to the great peril of all the realm: which preachers being cited or summoned before the ordinaries of the places, there to answer to that whereof they are impeached, they will not obey the summons and commands, and care not for the admonitions nor censures of the holy church, but expressly despise them; and moreover, by their subtle and ingenious words, draw the people to hear their sermons, and maintain them in their errors by strong hand, and by great routs: it is ordained and assented in this present parliament, that the king's commissions be made and directed to the sheriffs, and other ministers of our sovereign lord the king, or other persons sufficiently learned, and according to the certificates of the prelates to be made in chancery from time to time, to arrest all such preachers, and also their favourers, maintainers and abetters, and to hold them in arrest and strong prison, till they justify themselves according to the law and reason of holy church. And the king wills and commands, that the chancellor make such commissions at all times, that he by the prelates, or any of them shall be certified and thereof required as is aforesaid."

An Examination of the aforesaid supposed Statute, and of the invalidity thereof.

As this supposed statute, was the principal ground whereupon proceeded all the persecution of that time; it is therefore not impertinent to examine the same more particularly, whereby it shall appear, that as it was fraudulently and unduly devised by the prelates only, so was it in like manner most injuriously and disorderly executed by them. For immediately upon the publishing of this law, without further warrant either from the king or his council, commissions under the great seal of England were made in this form, "Richard by the Grace of God," &c. "Witness myself at Westminster the 26th day of June, in the sixth year of our reign." Without more words of warrant under-written, such as in like cases are both usual and requisite, viz: "per ipsum regem:" "per regem et concilium:" "per breve de privato sigillo." All or any which words being utterly wanting in this place, as may be seen in the king's records of that time; it must therefore be done either by warrant of this statute, or else without any warrant at all. Whereupon it is to be noted, that whereas the statute appointed the commissions to be directed to the sheriff, or other ministers of the king, or to other persons sufficiently learned, for the arresting of such persons; the commissions are directed to the archbishop and his suffragans, being as it appears parties in the case, authorizing them further without either the words, or reasonable meaning of the statute, to imprison them in their own houses, or where else they pleased.

Besides also, what manner of law this was, by whom devised, and by what authority the same was first made and established, judge by that which follows, viz.

In the utas of St. Michael next following, at a parliament summoned and holden at Westminster, the sixth year of the king, among sundry petitions made to the king by his commons, to which he assented, there is one in this form. Article 52.

" That whereas a statute was made the last parliament in these words,—'It is ordained in this present parliament that commissions from the king be directed to the sheriffs, and other ministers of the king, or to other persons sufficiently skilful, and according to the certificates of the prelates thereof, to be made to the chancery from time to time, to arrest all such preachers, and their favorers, maintainers and abetters: and to detain them in strong prison, until they justify themselves according to reason, and law of holy church: and the king wills and commands, that the chancellor make such commissions at all times as he shall be by the prelates or any of them certified and thereof required, as is aforesaid,'—the which was never agreed nor granted by the commons; but whatever was moved therein, was without their assent. That the said statute be therefore disannulled. For it is not in any wise their meaning, that either themselves or such as shall succeed them, shall be further justified or bound by the prelates, than were their ancestors in former times," whereunto is answered, "Il plaist al, Roy. I." the king is pleased.

Hereby notwithstanding the former unjust law was repealed, and the fraud of the framers thereof sufficiently discovered: yet such means were taken by the prelates, that this act of repeal was never published, nor ever since printed with the rest of the statutes of that parliament: so that the repeal being concealed, similar commissions and other process were made from

time to time, by virtue of the statute, as well during all the reign of this king, as ever since against the professors of religion.

The young king was further induced by the importunity of the archbishop, to send special letters to the vice chancellor and proctors of the university of Oxford, in which he straightly and sharply enjoins them to make a general inquisition through the whole university, for John Wickliff, Nicholas Herford, Philip Reppington, John Ashton, and such others; and also for all whom they know or judge to be suspected of that doctrine, or to be maintainers, receivers, and defenders of the parties, or their opinions; to the intent that they being so apprehended, may be within seven days of their admonition expelled the university, and cited before the archbishop of Canterbury, moreover commanding the vice-chancellor and proctors with their assistants, that if any person or persons in any house, hall, or college, or in any other place shall be found to have any of the books or treatises compiled by John Wickliff, Nicholas Herford, &c. they will cause the said person or persons, to be arrested and attached, and their books to be seized and presented within one month, without correction, corruption, or alteration, to the archbishop upon their faith and allegiance, as they would avoid the forfeiture of all privileges of the university, &c.

The vice-chancellor at this time in Oxford was Master Robert Rigge. The two proctors were John Huntman and Walter Dish; who, as far as they durst, favoured the cause of John Wickliff, so that when some public sermons at the feast of the Ascension, and of Corpus Christi were to be preached in the cloister of Saint Frideswide (now called Christ's church) before the people, by the vice-chancellor and the proctors: they committed it to Philip Reppington and Nicholas Herford, so that Herford should preach on the Ascension-day, and Reppington upon Corpus Christi day. Herford was observed to defend John Wickliff openly as a faithful, good, and innocent man; at which there were great outcries among the friars. This Herford, after he had long favoured and maintained Wickliff's part, grew in suspicion among the enemies of truth. For as soon as he began somewhat liberally and freely to utter anything, which tended to the defence of Wickliff, by and bye the Carmelites, and all the orders of religion were on his watch, and laid not a few heresies to his charge; which they had strained here and there out of his sermons. After this the feast of Corpus Christi drew near: upon which day it was expected that Reppington would preach. This man was a canon of Leicester, who protested openly, that in all moral matters he would defend Wickliff. But as to the sacrament he would as yet hold his peace, until such time as the Lord should otherwise illuminate the hearts and minds of the clergy.

Now the day of Corpus Christi approaching near, when the friars understood that this man would preach, they arranged with the archbishop of Canterbury, that the same day, a little before Philip should preach, Wickliff's conclusions, which were privately condemned, should be openly defamed in the presence of the whole university.

These things being thus done, Philip Reppington at the hour appointed, proceeded to his sermon. In which among many other things, he was reported to have uttered these sayings, or to this effect:

" That the popes or bishops ought not to be exalted above temporal lords.

" That in moral matters he would defend Master Wickliff as a true catholic doctor.

" That the duke of Lancaster was very earnestly affected and minded in this matter, and wished that all such should be received under his protection," besides many things more which touched the praise and defence of Wickliff.

And finally, in concluding his sermon, he dismissed the people with this sentence,—" I will in the speculative doctrine, as pertaining to the sacrament of the altar, keep silence and hold my peace, until such time as God otherwise shall instruct and illuminate the hearts of the clergy."

When the sermon was done, Reppington entered into St. Frideswide's church, accompanied with many of his friends, who, as their enemies surmised, were privately armed under their garments against danger. Friar Stokes, the Carmelite, who was the chief champion against Wickliff, suspecting all this to be against him, kept within the sanctuary of the church. The vice-chancellor and Reppington, friendly saluting one another in the church porch, sent away the people, and so every man departed home to his own house. There was not a little joy through the whole university for that sermon; but in the meantime, the unquiet and busy Carmelite slipt not his matter. For by his letters he declared the whole matter to the archbishop, exaggerating the dangers he was in, and desiring his help and aid, omitting nothing to move and stir up the archbishop's mind, who of his own nature was ready enough to prosecute the matter. The vice-chancellor being afterward accused for contempt of the archbishop's letters, when he perceived and saw that no excuse would prevail to avoid that danger, humbling himself upon his knees, he desired pardon, which, when he had obtained, by the help of the bishop of Winchester, he was sent away again with certain commands, and suspensions of heretics. Then began the hatred on both sides to appear and develope itself, and all men were offended at these friars and monks, to whom they imputed whatever trouble or mischief was raised up, as to the authors and causers of the same.

Nicholas Herford, and Philip Reppington, being privily warned by the vice-chancellor, conveyed themselves out of sight, and fled to the duke of Lancaster; but the duke, whether for fear, or for what cause I cannot say, in the end forsook his poor and miserable clients.

Being repulsed by the duke, and destitute of his support, whether they were sent, or, of their own accord went to the archbishop, is uncertain; but Reppington was reconciled again to the archbishop, and admitted to the university. And so was also John Ashton. Of Nicholas Herford all this while I find no special relation.

In the meantime, about the twenty-third day of September, (A. D. 1382), the king sent his mandate to the archbishop for collecting a subsidy, and to have a convocation of the clergy summoned against the next parliament, which should begin the eighteenth day of November. All which being done, the parliament was assembled at Oxford the eighteenth day of November, where the convocation was kept in the monastery of Frideswide. The archbishop, with other bishops, sitting there in their pontifical robes, declared two causes of their present assembly, one to repress heresies, which began afresh in the realm; the other to aid and support the king with some necessary subsidy of money.

The convocation being continued the next day, the archbishop, with the other prelates, assembling themselves as before, the archbishop, after the usual solemnity, desired the proctors of the clergy, appointed for every diocess, to consult among themselves, in some convenient place, what they thought touching the redress of matters, and to be notified and declared to him and to his brethren, &c.

Further, forsomuch (saith he) as it is so noised through all the realm, that there were certain in the university of Oxford who held and maintained conclusions heretical and erroneous, condemned by him, and by other lawyers and doctors of divinity; he therefore assigned the bishops of Sarum, Hereford, and Rochester, with William Rugge, then vice-chancellor of the university of Oxford, (for probably Robert Rigge was then displaced,) as also William Berton, and John Middleton, doctors, giving them his full authority with cursing and banning to compel them to search, and to inquire with all diligence and possible ways over all and singular whatsoever, either doctors, bachelors, or scholars of the university, who did hold, teach, maintain, and defend, in schools, or out of schools, the conclusions mentioned before.

On which day, in the presence of the prelates and the clergy in the chapter-house of St. Frideswide, came in Philip Reppington, who there adjured those conclusions and assertions, in this form of words:

"In the name of God, Amen. I, Philip Reppington, canon of the house of Leicester, acknowledging one catholic and apostolic faith, do curse and also abjure all heresy, namely, these heresies and errors under written, condemned and reproved by the canonical decrees, and by you, most reverend father, touching which hitherto I have been defamed; condemning, moreover, and reproving both them and the authors of them, and do confess the same to be catholically condemned. And I swear also by these holy evangelists, which here I hold in my hand, and do promise, never by any persuasions of men, nor by any way hereafter, to defend or hold as true, any of the said conclusions underwritten; but do and will stand and adhere in all things, to the determination of the holy catholic church, and to yours, in this behalf. Over and besides, all such as stand contrary to this faith, I do pronounce them with their doctrine and followers worthy of everlasting curse. And if I myself shall presume at any time to hold or preach any thing contrary to the premises, I shall be content to abide the severity of the canons. Subscribed with mine own hand, and of mine own accord, Philip Reppington."

And thus he was discharged, and afterward was made bishop of Lincoln, and became at length the most bitter and extreme persecutor of this side, of all the other bishops within the realm.

After the abjuration of this Reppington, immediately was brought in John Ashton, who, appearing before the archbishop and the prelates, did in like form of words abjure as Reppington had before done.

Of this John Ashton we read, that afterward, by Thomas Arundel, archbishop of Canterbury, he was cited and condemned; but whether he died in prison, or was burned, we have no certainty.

As to Nicholas Herford, he did not appear during the time of this convocation, and therefore was excommunicated; against which he appealed from the archbishop to the king and council. The archbishop would not admit it, but caused him to be apprehended and put in prison. He escaped out of prison, returning again to his former exercise and preaching as he did before, though in as covert and secret a manner as he could. Upon which the archbishop, thundering out his bolts of excommunication against him, sends to all pastors and ministers, commanding them in all churches, and on all festival days, to proclaim the excommunication against him to all men.

Not contented with this, he addressed his letter to the king, requiring the aid of his temporal sword. See and note, reader, the seraphical charity of these priestly prelates towards the poor redeemed flock of Christ.

The letter of the Archbishop to the King.

"To the most excellent prince in Christ, &c. William, &c., greeting, in him by whom kings do reign, and princes bear rule. Unto your kingly highness by the tenor of these presents we intimate, that one Master Nicholas Herford, doctor of divinity, for his manifest contumacy and offence in not appearing before us being called at the day and place assigned, is therefore included in the sentence of the greater curse, publicly by our ordinary authority; and in the same sentence has continued now forty days, and yet still continues with obdurate heart, wickedly contemning the keys of the church, both to the great peril of his soul, and to the pernicious example of others. Forsomuch, therefore, as the holy mother, the church, cannot proceed any further in this matter, we humbly desire your kingly majesty to direct out your letters for the apprehending of the said excommunicate, according to the custom of this realm of England, wholesomely observed and kept hitherto; to the intent that such, whom the fear of God doth not restrain from evil, the discipline of the secular arm may bridle and pluck back from offending. Your princely highness, the Lord continue. From Lambeth, the fifteenth of January."

And thus far concerning Nicholas Herford, and the others. But all this while what became of John Wickliff is not certainly known;—it appears that he was banished and driven to exile. In the meantime it is not to be doubted, but he was alive during all this while, as may appear by his letter which he about this time wrote to Pope Urban VI.

The Epistle of John Wickliff sent to Pope Urban VI., A. D. 1382.

"Verily I do rejoice to open and declare to every man the faith which I hold, and specially to the bishop of Rome, which faith as I suppose it to be sound and true, he will most willingly confirm, or, if it be erroneous, amend.

"First, I suppose that the gospel of Christ is the whole body of God's law; and that Christ, who gave that same law himself, I believe to be a very man, and in that point, to exceed the law of the gospel, and all other parts of the scripture. Again, I do give and hold the bishop of Rome, forsomuch as he is the vicar of Christ here in earth, to be bound most of all other men to that law of the gospel. For the greatness amongst Christ's disciples did not consist in worldly dignity or honours, but in the near and exact following of Christ in his life and manners; whereupon I do gather out of the heart of the law of the Lord, that Christ for the time of his pilgrimage here was a most poor man, abjecting and casting off all worldly rule and honour, as appears by the gospel of St. Matthew, the eighth chapter, and second of the Corinthians, in the eighth chapter.

"Hereby I do fully gather, that no faithful man ought to follow, either the pope himself, or any of the holy men, but in such points as he has followed the Lord Jesus Christ. For Peter and the sons of Zebedee, by desiring worldly honour, contrary to the following of Christ's steps, did offend, and therefore in those errors they are not to be followed.

"Hereof I do gather, as a counsel, that the pope ought to leave unto the secular power all temporal dominion and rule, and thereunto effectually to move and exhort his whole clergy; for so did Christ, and especially by his apostles. Wherefore, if I have erred in any of these points, I will most humbly submit myself unto correction, even by death, if necessity so require; and if I could labour according to my will or desire in mine own person, I would surely present myself before the bishop of Rome; but the Lord has otherwise visited me to the contrary, and has taught me rather to obey God than men. Forsomuch then as God has given to our pope just and true evangelical instinctions, we ought to pray that those motions be not extinguished by any subtle or crafty device. And that the pope and cardinals be not moved to do any thing contrary to the law of the Lord. Wherefore let us pray to our God, that he will so stir up our Pope Urban the sixth, as he began, that he, with his clergy, may follow the Lord Jesus Christ in life and manners; and that they may teach the people effectually, and that they likewise may faithfully follow them in the same. And let us especially pray, that our pope may be preserved from all malign and evil counsel, which we do know that evil and envious men of his household would give him. And seeing the Lord will not suffer us to be tempted above our power, much less then will he require of any creature to do that thing which they are not able; forsomuch as that is the plain condition and manner of antichrist."

Thus much wrote John Wickliff to Pope Urban. But this pope was so hot in his wars against Clement, the French pope, his rival, that he had no leisure, and less will to attend to Wickliff. By which schism God provided for poor Wickliff some rest and quietness.

Concerning which schismatical wars of these popes, it will not be irrelevant to digress a little, so as to say something of the tragical doings of these two holy popes, striving for the triple crown, that the christian reader may see what difference there is between the popes, and Christ with his apostles. For though in the gospel it is written, that certain of the disciples did strive which should be the greater; yet we do not read that one of them ever took weapons against the other; and it appears too that for so striving as they did they were sharply rebuked by our Saviour Christ.

About the beginning of the year 1383, Pope Urban, studying how to conquer his rival pope, took to himself the sword of Romulus, instead of the keys of Peter, and set upon him with open war. And devising with himself whom he might best choose for his chief champion; he thought none more fitted for such affairs than Henry Spencer, then bishop of Norwich, a young and stout prelate, more fitting for the charge of a camp, than for the peaceable church of Christ. To this bishop of Norwich the pope had sent his bulls about this time, to confer the cross on whoever would go with him into France, to destroy the antipope. In which bulls these privileges were granted.

1. That the bishop of Norwich may use his sword against the antipope, and all his adherents, favourers, and counsellors, and with violence put them to death.

2. That he has full power to inquire after all schismatics, and to put them in prison, and to confiscate all their goods, moveable and immoveable.

3. That he has power and authority to deprive all laymen that are schismatics of all manner of secular offices whatever, and to give their offices to other fit and convenient persons.

4. That he may deprive all such clergy, and declare them to be schismatics, and to give and bestow their benefices either with cure or without cure, their dignities, parsonages or offices, to other persons more meet for the same.

5. He has power and authority over lay persons that are exempt, and clergy both secular and regular, yea, although they be friars mendicants, or masters and professors of other houses or hospitals of St. John's of Jerusalem, or St. Mary's of Flanders, or professors of what order soever.

6. He has power to dispense with any secular clergy soever, being beneficed either with cure or without cure, and also with such as have dignities, parsonages, or offices, being regulars either exempt or not exempt, that every one of them may be absent with him from their dignities and benefices, &c., under the standard of the cross, without license of any of their prelates being required, and yet to receive and take the entire income of their benefices, as though they had been personally resident upon the same.

7. There is granted to all that pass the seas in this quarrel, either at their own expenses, or at the expenses of any other, full remission of their sins; and as large privileges are granted to all those that go over the sea with him, as to any that pay their money, or go to fight for the Holy Land.

8. Also all such as with their proper goods and substance shall give sufficient stipend to able soldiers, mustered at the discretion of the foresaid lord bishop, or by his deputy, although themselves be not personally at this business, yet shall they have like remission and indulgence, as they who have been personally with him in this expedition.

9. All they are partakers of this remission, who give any part of their goods to the said bishop to fight against the said schismatics.

10. If any shall chance to die in the journey who are soldiers under the standard of the cross, or else before the quarrel are killed by some means, they shall fully and wholly receive the said grace, and shall be partakers of the remission and indulgence.

11. He has power to excommunicate, suspend, and interdict what persons soever be rebellious or disturbers of him in the execution of his power and authority committed to him, of what dignity, state, degree, pre-eminence, order, place, or condition soever they shall be; whether they shall be either of regal, queenly, or imperial

dignity, or of what dignity soever, either ecclesiastical or civil.

●12. He has power and authority to compel and enforce any religious person soever, and to appoint them, and send them over sea, if it seem good to him, yea, although they be professors of the friars mendicants, for the execution of the premises.

The Pope's Absolution pronounced by the Bishop.

"By the authority apostolical to me in this behalf committed, we absolve thee A. B. from all thy sins confessed with thy mouth, and being contrite with thy heart, and whereof thou wouldst be confessed if they came into thy memory; and we grant to thee plenary remission of all manner of sins, and we promise to thee thy part of the reward of all just men, and of everlasting salvation. And as many privileges as are granted to them that go to fight for the Holy Land, we grant to thee; and of all the prayers and benefits of the church, the universal synod, as also of the holy catholic church, we make thee partaker."

This courageous, or, rather outrageous bishop, armed thus with the pope's authority, and prompt with his privileges, came to the parliament, where there was great consultation and contention, and almost no less schism, about the voyage of this popish bishop in the parliament, than was between the popes themselves. In which parliament, there were many who thought it not safe to commit the king's people and subjects to an unskilful priest. So great was the diversity of judgments in that behalf, that the voyage of the bishop was protracted to the Saturday before Passion Sunday. After which Sunday the parties agreed that the bishop should set forward in his voyage, having given to him the fifteenth which was granted to the king in the parliament before. Which things thus concluded in the parliament, this warlike bishop preparing all things in readiness, set forward in this journey. And forthwith entered the seas, and went to Calais, where, waiting a few days for the rest of his army, he then took his journey to the town of Gravelines, which he besieged so desperately, without any preparation of engines of war, or counsel, that he seemed rather to fly upon them, than to invade them. At length, through the superstition of our men, trusting to the pope's absolution, they entered the town with their bishop, where, at his command, they destroyed both man, woman, and child, and left not one alive!

From Gravelines this warlike bishop set forward to Dunkirk, where not long after, the French meeting with him, he joined with them in battle; in which battle (if the story be true) twelve thousand of the French were slain in the chase, and of our men seven only were missing. It would require a long treatise here to relate all things done in these popish wars. Also it would be no less ridiculous to view and behold the glorious temerity of this new upstart captain. As when the bishop coming from Dunkirk to the siege of Ypres, a great number of Englishmen were lost there, and much money consumed, and yet nothing done, to the great shame and ignominy of the bishop. Again, after the siege of Ypres, the bishop proceeding with a small force to fight with the French king's camp, contrary to the counsel of his captains, was feign to break company with them, whereby part of the army went to Burburgh, and the bishop with his part returned to Gravelines, both which towns shortly after were besieged by the French army. In fine, when the bishop could keep Gravelines no longer, he crossed the seas, and came home again as wise as he went. And thus making an end of this pontifical war, we will return from whence we digressed, to the history of John Wickliff.

Which John Wickliff returning again within a short space, either from his banishment, or from some other place where he was secretly kept, repaired to his parish of Lutterworth, where he was parson; and there, quietly departing this mortal life, slept in peace in the Lord, in the beginning of the year 1384, upon Silvester's day

Here may be seen the great providence of the Lord in this man, as in several others whom the Lord so long preserved amidst the fury of so many enemies from all their hands, even to his old age. For it appears by Thomas Walden, that he was a very aged man before he departed. Such a Lord is our God, that whom he will have kept, nothing can hurt.

This Wickliff had written several works, which in the year A. D. 1410 were burnt at Oxford. And not only in England, but in Bohemia likewise, the books of Wickliff were consumed by the archbishop of Prague, who made diligent inquisition for them, and burned them; the number of volumes which he is said to have burned, most excellently written, and richly adorned with bosses of gold, and rich coverings (as Eneas Silvius writes) were about two hundred.

We will now add the testimonial of the University of Oxford concerning Wickliff.

The public testimony given out by the University of Oxford, touching the commendation of the great learning and good life of John Wickliff.

"Unto all and singular the children of our holy mother the church, to whom this present letter shall come, the vice-chancellor of the university of Oxford, with the whole congregation of the masters, with perpetual health in the Lord. Forsomuch as it is not commonly seen, that the acts and monuments of valiant men, nor the praise and merits of good men should be passed over and hidden in perpetual silence, but that true report and fame should continually spread abroad the same in strange and far distant places, both for the witness of the same, and example of others; forsomuch also as the provident discretion of man's nature, being recompensed with cruelty, hath devised and ordained this buckler and defence against such as do blaspheme and slander other men's doings, that whensoever witness by word of mouth cannot be present, the pen by writing may supply the same.

"Hereupon it followeth, that the special good will and care which we bear unto John Wickliff, sometime child of this our university, and professor of divinity, moving and stirring our minds (as his manners and conditions required no less) with one mind, voice and testimony, we do witness, all his conditions and doings throughout his whole life to have been most sincere and commendable; whose honest manners and conditions, profoundness of learning, and most redolent renown and fame, we desire the more earnestly to be notified and known unto all the faithful, for that we understand the maturity and ripeness of his conversation, his diligent labours and troubles to tend to the praise of God, the help and safeguard of others, and the profit of the church.

"Wherefore we signify unto you by these presents, that his conversation (even from his youth upward, unto the time of his death) was so praise-worthy and honest, that never at any time was there any note or spot of suspicion noised of him. But in his answering, reading, preaching and determining, he behaved himself laudably, and as a stout and valiant champion of the faith; vanquishing by the force of the scriptures, all such, who by their wilful beggary, blasphemed and slandered Christ's religion; neither was this doctor convicted of any heresy, neither burned of our prelates after his burial. God forbid, that our prelates should have condemned a man of such honesty for an heretic; who, amongst all the rest of the university, had written in logic, philosophy, divinity, morality, and the speculative arts, without an equal. The knowledge of which all and singular things we do desire to testify and deliver forth, to the intent that the fame and renown of this said doctor may be the more evident and had in reputation amongst them unto whose hands these present letters testimonial shall come.

"In witness whereof, we have caused these our letters testimonial to be sealed with our common seal. Dated at Oxford in our congregation-house, the 1st day of October, in the year of our Lord 1406."

Now as we have declared the testimony of the university of Oxford, concerning the praise of John Wickliff;

it follows likewise that we set forth the censures and judgments of his enemies, blinded with malicious hatred and corrupt affections against him, especially of the pope's council gathered at Constance, proceeding first in condemning his books, then his articles, and afterward burning his bones. The copy of which sentence given against him by that council here follows.

The sentence given by the Council of Constance, in condemning the Doctrine, and five and forty Articles of John Wickliff.

" The most holy and sacred council of Constance, making and representing the catholic church, for the extirpation of this present schism,[1] and of all other errors and heresies, springing and growing under the shadow and pretence of the same, and for the reformation and amendment of the church, being lawfully congregate and gathered together in the Holy Ghost, for the perpetual memory of the time to come.

" We are taught by the acts and histories of the holy fathers, that the catholic faith, without which, as the holy apostle St. Paul saith, it is impossible to please God, hath been always defended by the faithful and spiritual soldiers of the church, by the shield of faith, against the false worshippers of the same faith, or rather perverse impugners; who through their proud curiosity will seem to know more, and to be wiser than they ought to be, and for the desire of the glory of the world have gone about oftentimes to overthrow the same. These kinds of wars and battles have been prefigured to us before in those carnal wars of the Israelites against the idolatrous people. For in those spiritual wars the holy catholic church through the virtue and power of faith, being illustrated with the beams of the heavenly light, by the Providence of God, and being helped by the help and defence of the saints and holy men, hath always continued immaculate, (and the darkness and errors, as her most cruel enemies being put to flight), she hath most gloriously triumphed over all. But in these our days the old and unclean enemy hath raised up new contentions and strifes, that the elect of this world might be known, whose prince and captain in time past was one John Wickliff, a false christian, who, during his lifetime, taught and sowed very obstinately many articles contrary and against the christian religion and the catholic faith. And the same John Wickliff wrote certain books which he called a Dialogue, and a Trialogue, besides many other treatises and works which he both wrote and taught, in which he wrote the aforesaid, and many other damnable and execrable articles, which books for the publication and advancement of his perverse doctrine, he set forth openly for every man to read; whereby, besides many offences, great hurt and damage of soul has ensued in divers regions and countries, but especially in the kingdom of England and Bohemia. Against whom the masters and doctors of the universities of Oxford and Prague, rising up in the truth and verity of God, according to the order of schools, within a while after did reprove and condemn the said articles. Moreover, the most reverend fathers the archbishops and bishops, for that time present, of Canterbury, York, and Prague, legates of the apostolic see, in the kingdoms of England and Bohemia, did condemn the books of the said Wickliff to be burnt. And the said archbishop of Prague, commissary of the apostolic see, did likewise in this behalf determine and judge. And moreover he forbid that any of those books which remained unburned should be hereafter any more read. And, again, those things being brought to the knowledge and understanding of the apostolic see, and in the general council, the bishop of Rome, in his last council, condemned the said books, treatises, and volumes, commanding them to be openly burned. Most straightly forbidding that any men who should bear the name of Christ should be so hardy either to keep, read, or expound any of the said books or treatises, volumes or works, or by any means to use or occupy them, or else to allege them openly or privily, but to their reproof and infamy. And to the intent that this most dangerous and filthy doctrine should be utterly wiped away out of the church, he gave commandment throughout all places, that the ordinaries should diligently inquire and seek out by the apostolic authority and ecclesiastical censure, for all such books, treatises, volumes, and works. And the same so being found, to burn and consume them with fire; providing withal, that if there be any found who will not obey the same, should process be made against them, as against the favourers and maintainers of heresies. And this most holy synod hath caused the said forty-five articles to be examined, and oftentimes perused by many most reverend fathers of the church of Rome, cardinals, bishops, abbots, masters of divinity, and doctors of both laws, besides a great number of other learned men; which articles being so examined, it was found (as in truth it was no less) that many, yea, and a great number of them be notoriously reproved and condemned by the holy fathers for heretical; others not to be catholic, but erroneous; some full of offence and blasphemy; certain of them offensive to godly ears, and many of them to be rashful and seditious. It is found also that his books do contain many articles of like effect and quality, and that they do induce and bring into the church unsound and unwholesome doctrine contrary to the faith and ordinance of the church. Wherefore in the name of our Lord Jesus Christ, this sacred synod, ratifying and approving the sentences and judgments of the archbishops and council of Rome, do by their decree and ordinance perpetually for evermore condemn and reprove the said articles, and every one of them, his books which he intituled his Dialogue and Trialogue, and all other books of the same author, volumes, treatises and works, by what name soever they be intitled or called, the which we will here to be sufficiently expressed and named. Also we forbid the reading, learning, exposition, or alleging of any of the said books unto all faithful christians, except so far as shall tend to the reproof of the same; forbidding all and singular catholic persons, under the pain of curse, that from henceforth they be not so hardy openly to preach, teach, or hold, or by any means to allege the said articles, or any of them, except, as aforesaid, that it do tend to the reproof of them; commanding all those books, treatises, works, and volumes aforesaid, to be openly burned, as it was decreed in the synod at Rome, as it is afore expressed. For the execution whereof duly to be observed and done, the said sacred synod doth straightly charge and command the ordinaries of the place diligently to attend and look unto the matter, according as it appertaineth unto every man's duty by the canonical laws and ordinances.''

The Decree of the Council of Constance, touching the taking up of the Body and Bones of John Wickliff, to be burned forty-one years after he was buried in his own Parish at Lutterworth.

" Forsomuch as by the authority of the sentence and decree of the council of Rome, and by the commandment of the church, and the apostolical see, after due delays being given, they proceeded to the condemnation of the said John Wickliff, and his memory, having first made proclamation, and given commandment to call forth whosoever would defend the said Wickliff, or his memory, if there were any such (but there did none appear, which would either defend him or his memory.) And moreover witnesses being examined, by commissioners appointed by Pope John and his council, upon the impenitency and final obstinacy and stubbornness of the said John Wickliff (reserving that which is to be reserved, as in such business the order of the law requireth) and his impenitency and obstinacy even unto his end, being suffici-

---

[1] The schism here alluded to was that of the popedom. There being at that time no less than *three* rival popes. Benedict XIII., Gregory XII., John XXIII. The Council of Constance was convened A. D. 1414, to suppress this schism. The first was deposed. the two latter resigned; and the cardinals elected Otto de Colonna, under the title of Martin V. [ED.]

ently proved by evident signs and tokens, and also by lawful witnesses, and credit lawfully given thereto. Wherefore at the instance of the steward of the treasury, proclamation being made to hear and understand the sentence against this day, the sacred synod declares, determines, and gives sentence, that the said John Wickliff was a notorious obstinate heretic, and that he died in his heresy, and they curse and condemn both him and his memory.

" This synod also decrees and ordains, that the body and bones of the said John Wickliff, if it might be discerned and known from the bodies of other faithful people, should be taken out of the ground, and thrown away far from the burial of any church, according to the canon laws and decrees. Which determination and sentence definitive being read and pronounced, the lord president, and the aforesaid presidents of the four nations, being demanded and asked whether it did please them or no? They all answered (first Hostiensis the president, and after him the other presidents of the nations) that it pleased them very well, and so they allowed and confirmed all the premises, &c."

What Heraclitus would not laugh, or what Democritus would not weep, to see these sage and reverend Catoes occupy their heads about taking up a poor man's body, who had been dead and buried for the space of forty one years? and yet perhaps they were not able to find his right bones, but took up some other body, and so of a catholic made an heretic! Yet herein Wickliff had some cause to give them thanks, that they at least spared him so long till he was dead, and gave him so long respite after his death, forty-one years to rest in his sepulchre before they ungraved him, and turned him from earth to ashes; which ashes they also took and threw into the river. And so he was resolved into three elements, earth, fire, and water, thinking thereby utterly to extinguish and abolish both the name and doctrine of Wickliff for ever. Not much unlike the example of the old Pharisees, who when they had brought the Lord to the grave, thought to make him sure never to rise again. But these and all other must know, that as there is no counsel against the Lord; so there is no keeping down of the truth, but it will spring and come out of dust and ashes, as appeared right well in this man. For though they digged up his body, burnt his bones, and drowned his ashes; yet the word of God, and the truth of his doctrine, with the fruit and success thereof, they could not burn; which yet to this day, for the most part of his articles, do remain; notwithstanding the transitory body and bones of the man were thus consumed and dispersed.

These things thus finished and accomplished, which pertain to the history and time of Wickliff; let us now by the support of the Lord proceed to write of the rest, who either in his time or after his time, springing out of the same university, and raised up (as one might say) out of his ashes, were partakers of the same persecution. Of whom speaks Thomas Walden, where he says, that after Wickliff many suffered most cruel death, and many more did forsake the realm.

In the number of whom was William Swinderby, Walter Brute, John Purvey, Richard White, William Thorpe, Raynold Peacock bishop of St. Asaph, and afterward of Chichester.

To this catalogue also pertains Laurence Redman master of arts, David Sautre, divine, John Aschwarby vicar, as they call him, of St. Mary's church at Oxford, William James an excellent young man, well learned, Thomas Brightwell, and William Hawlam a civilian, Rafe Grenhurst, John Scut, and Philip Norice; who being excommunicated by Pope Eugenius IV., in the year 1446, appealed to a general council.

Peter Paine also, who flying from Oxford unto Bohemia, stoutly contended against the sophisters, as administering both kinds in the sacrament of the last supper. Also the Lord Cobham, &c., with others, whose names are named in the king's writ, sent to the sheriff of Northampton, which writ of the king follows in this tenor: " Forsomuch as John Attyate of Chepingwarden, John Warryner, Robert Brewood, &c., being receivers and

favourers of heretics, and especially of John Woodward priest, publicly defamed and condemned of heresy, will not be justified by the censures of the church, as the reverend father John bishop of Lincoln hath certified us: we therefore desiring to withstand all defenders and favorers of such heresies, do will and command as well the forenamed, as namely the aforesaid John Woodward to be apprehended, straightly charging the same to be imprisoned by their bodies, or otherwise punished as shall seem good to the justices, until they and every of them shall submit themselves to the obedience of the aforesaid bishop in that behalf accordingly. Whereof fail you not under pain of an hundred pounds. Witness ourselves: given at our manor of Langley the 8th day of March, the twelfth year of our reign."

To these above rehearsed, and other favorers of Wickliff, within this our country of England, we may add also the Bohemians; for the propagation of the doctrine of Wickliff in that country took root, coming from England to Bohemia by the following occasion.

There happened that at that time a certain student of the country of Bohemia was at Oxford, one of a wealthy house, and also of a noble stock; who returning home from the university of Oxford to the university of Prague, carried with him certain books of Wickliff. It happened at the same time that a certain nobleman in the city of Prague had founded and built a great church of Matthias and Mattheus, (which church was called Bethelem), giving to it great lands, and finding in it two preachers every day, to preach both holy-day and working-day to the people. Of which two preachers, John Huss was one, a man of great knowledge, of a pregnant wit, and most highly esteemed among them for his worthy life. Thus John Huss having familiarity with this young man, in reading and perusing these books of Wickliff, derived such pleasure and profit in reading them, that he not only began to defend the author openly in the schools, but also in his sermons, commending him for a good man, an holy man, and heavenly man, wishing himself, when he should die, to be there placed, where the soul of Wickliff should be.

And thus much briefly concerning the favorers and adherents of John Wickliff in general. Now particularly and in order let us (by Christ's grace) narrate the histories and persecutions of the parties aforenamed, beginning with the valiant champions William Swinderby and Walter Brute.

The History of William Swinderby.

In the year 1389, William Swinderby priest, within the diocess of Lincoln, being accused and seized for certain opinions, was presented before John bishop of Lincoln, after the form and order of the pope's law, according to their usual rite; his accusers were friar Frisby an Observant, friar Hincely an Augustinian, and Thomas Blaxton a Dominican.

The articles or conclusions were exhibited against him by the friars in the bishop of Lincoln's court. Which articles although he never preached, taught, or at any time defended, as appears in the process; yet the friars with their witnesses standing against him, declared him to be convicted; bringing dry wood with them to the town to burn him, and would not leave him, before they made him promise and swear for fear of death, never to hold them, teach them, nor preach them privily, or openly; and that he should go to certain churches to revoke the conclusions, which he never affirmed. Which he obediently accomplished, with this form of revocation, which they bound him to.

The Revocation of William Swinderby.

" I, William Swinderby, priest, although unworthy of the diocese of Lincoln, acknowledging one true catholic and apostolic faith of the holy church of Rome, do abjure all heresy and error opposed to the determination of the holy mother church, whereof I have been hitherto defamed, namely, the conclusions and articles above prefixed, and every one of them judicially objected to me, by the commissary of the reverend father in Christ

Lord John, by the grace of God bishop of Lincoln; and do revoke the same, and every one of them, some as heretical, some as erroneous and false, and do affirm and believe them to be so, and hereafter will never teach, preach, or affirm publicly or privily the same. Neither will I make any sermon within the diocese of Lincoln, without first asking and obtaining the license of the aforesaid reverend father and lord, the bishop of Lincoln. Contrary to the which if I shall presume hereafter to say or do, to hold or preach, I shall be content to abide the severity of the canon, as I have judicially by the necessity of the law, sworn, and do swear," &c.

Thus you see the conclusions and articles of this good man, falsely objected to him by the malicious and lying friars; and also the retraction to which they compelled him; by which it may be conjectured, what credit is to be given to the articles and conclusions which these cavilling friars, wresting all things to the worst, have objected and imputed to Wickliff and all others like him, whom they so falsely defame, so slanderously belie, and so maliciously persecute. After these things in the diocese of Lincoln, Swinderby removed to the diocese of Hereford; where he was as much or more molested by the friars again, and by John Tresnant bishop of Hereford, as by the process set out at large in their own registers may appear.

Here follow the informations laid before John Tresnant, bishop of Hereford, against William Swinderby in the cause of heretical pravity, as the popish heretics call it.

"Reverend father and high lord, Lord John, by God's sufferance bishop of Hereford: it is lamentably declared unto your reverend fatherhood on the behalf of Christ's faithful people, your devout children of your diocese of Hereford, that notwithstanding the unbelief of very many Lollards, who have too long sprung up in your diocese, there is newly come a certain child of wickedness, named William Swinderby; who by his horrible persuasions, and mischievous endeavours, and also by his public preaching and private teaching, perverts the whole ecclesiastical state, and stirs up, with all his power, schism between the clergy and the people. And that your reverend fatherhood may be the more fully informed, who and what manner of man the same William Swinderby is; there are proposed and exhibited here to your fatherhood, on behalf of the faithful people of Christ, against the same William Swinderby, cases and articles. Which if he shall deny, then shall these cases and articles be most evidently proved against him by witnesses worthy of belief, and by other lawful proof and evidences, to the end that your fatherhood may do and ordain therein, as to your pastoral office belongeth.

1. William Swinderby, pretending himself a priest, was openly and publicly convicted of certain articles and conclusions being erroneous, schismatical, and heretical, preached by him at several places and times, before a multitude of faithful christian people. And the same articles and conclusions he by force of law revoked and abjured, some as heretical, and some as erroneous and false, avouching and believing them for such as that from thenceforth he would never preach, teach, or affirm openly or privily any of the same conclusions: and if by preaching or avouching he should presume to do the contrary; that then he should be subject to the severity of the canons, according as he took corporal oath, judicially upon the holy gospels.

2. Also the conclusions, which by him were first openly taught and preached, and afterward abjured and revoked, are contained in the process of the bishop of Lincoln, written word by word. And for the cases and articles, they were exhibited by the faithful christian people against the said William Swinderby, together with the conclusions, and are hereafter written: of which cases and articles the tenor here follows:

3. The said William, contrary to the revocation and abjuration, not converted to repentance, but perverted from ill to worse, and given up to a reprobate mind, came into your diocese, where he running about in sundry places, has presumed to preach, or rather to pervert and to teach of his own rashness, many heretical, erroneous, blasphemous, and other slanderous things contrary and repugnant to the sacred canons, and the determination of the holy catholic church. What those things were, at what place and what time, shall hereafter more particularly be declared.

4. The same William, notwithstanding your commandments and admonitions sealed with your seal, and directed to all the curates of your diocese, ordaining among other things that no person of what state, degree, or condition soever, should presume to preach or to teach, or expound the holy scripture to the people, either in hallowed or profane places within your diocese, without sufficient authority, under any manner of pretence, as in the same your letters of admonition and of inhibition, is more largely contained; which letters the same William received into his hands, and read word by word in the town of Monmouth of your diocese, in the year 1390, so that these your letters came to the true and undoubted knowledge of the same William; yet notwithstanding, he has presumed in various places and times to preach within your diocese, after and against your commandment aforesaid.

5. The same William in his preaching to the people, on Monday the first of August, 1390, in the parish of Whitney in your diocese, held and affirmed, that no prelate of the world, of what estate, pre-eminence or degree soever he were, having cure and charge of souls, being in deadly sin, and hearing the confession of any could do anything in giving him absolution: as being one who neither looses him from his sin, nor, in correcting or excommunicating him from his demerits, binds him by his sentence, unless the prelate shall himself be free from deadly sin, as St. Peter was, to whom our Lord gave power to bind and loose.

6. The same William in many places said and affirmed, in the presence of many faithful christian people, that after the sacramental words uttered by the priest when he intends to consecrate, the very body of Christ is not made in the sacrament of the altar.

7. That accidents cannot be in the sacrament of the altar without a subject; and that there remains material bread there to such as are communicants of the body of Christ, in the same sacrament.

8. That a priest, being in deadly sin, cannot by the strength of the sacramental words make the body of Christ, or bring to perfection any other sacrament of the church, nor minister it to the members of the church.

9. That all priests are of equal power in all things, although some of them in this world are of higher and greater honour, degree, or pre-eminence.

10. That only contrition puts away sin, if so be that a man shall be duly contrite; and that all auricular and outward confession is superfluous, and not requisite of necessity to salvation.

11. Inferior curates have their power of binding and loosing not immediately from the pope or bishop, but immediately from Christ: and therefore neither pope nor bishop can revoke to themselves such kind of power, at their will and pleasure.

12. That the pope cannot grant annual and yearly pardons; because there may not be so many years to the day of judgment, as are in the pope's bulls or pardons contained. By which it follows that these pardons are not of such value as they pretend.

13. It is not in the pope's power to grant to any penitent person remission of the punishment of the fault.

14. That person that gives alms to any, who in his judgment is not in want, commits sin in so giving it.

15. That it is not in the power of any prelate, of what order soever he be, privately to give letters for the benefit of his order, neither does such benefit profit to the salvation of the soul, them to whom they be granted.

16. That the same William, unmindful of his own

salvation, hath many and oftentimes come into a certain desert wood, called Dervallwood, of your diocess, and there in a certain chapel not consecrated, or rather in a profane cottage, has in contempt of the keys, presumed of his own rashness to celebrate, nay rather to profane.

17. The same William has also presumed to do such things in a certain profane chapel, situated in the park of Newton nigh to the town of Leintwarden, of your diocess."

The Citation.

"John, by God's permission, bishop of Hereford, to his dear sons our dean of Leamster, to the parsons of of Croft, Almady, and Whitney, and also to the vicars of Kingston, Ladersley, Wiggemore, and Monmouth Clifford, and of St. John's altar in our cathedral church of Hereford, and to the rest of the deans, parsons, vicars, chaplains, parish priests, and to others whosoever in any place are appointed through our city and diocess of Hereford, sendeth greeting, grace and benediction.

"We bid and command, charging you straightly, in the virtue of holy obedience, that you cite or cause to be cited peremptorily (and under the pain of excommunication) William Swinderby, pretending himself to be a priest, that he appear before us, or our commissaries on the twentieth day of this present month of July, at North Lodebury, within our diocess, with the continuance of the days following in other places also to be assigned unto him if it be expedient, till such things as have been, and shall be laid against him, be fully discussed, to answer more at large to certain positions and articles, touching the catholic faith, and the holy mother church's determination that have been exhibited and ministered unto the said William. And to see and hear also many things that have openly in judgment before us, and a great number of faithful christians, by him been even in writing confessed, to be condemned as heretical, false, schismatical, and erroneous. And to see and hear positions and articles denied by the said William, to be proved by faithful witnesses, and other lawful trials against the said William. And to receive for his false, heretical, erroneous, and schismatical doctrine, that which justice shall appoint, or else to shew causes why the premises should not be done.

"And if the said William conceals himself, or cannot be cited in his proper person; we will that in your churches, when most people shall then come together to divine service, you openly with a loud voice, and that may be understood, cause the said William peremptorily to be cited unto the premises, certifying the said William, that whether he shall appear the day and place appointed or no, we notwithstanding will proceed unto the premises against the said William, according to the canonical decrees, by form of law, in the absence or contumacy of the said William notwithstanding. We will, moreover, if the said William shall appear at the said day and place, as is aforesaid, before us, friendly hear him, and honestly, and favourably, as far as we may with God's leave, deal with him; granting free license to come and go for his natural liberty without any hurt either in body or goods. And see that you fully certify us of the things that you or any of you shall do about the execution of this our commandment, and that by your letters patent signed with your seal authentic, giving also faithfully to the said William, or to his lawful proctor, if he require it, a copy of this our present commandment.

"Given at our house of Whitburne, under our seal, the fifth day of the month of July, in the year of our Lord 1391."

William Swinderby either explained or defended the various conclusions objected against him, and concluded in the following words, which we insert in the ancient style in which they were written:

"The fifth article telleth of forgiveness of sins, and is this; that very contrition withouten charity and grace, do away all sins before done of that man that is verily contrite; and all true confession made by mouth outwardly to a wise priest and a good, profiteth much to a man, and it is needful and helping, that men shew their life to such, trusting fully to God's mercy, that he forgiveth the sin.

"And hereto I say, that there been two remissions of sin, one that belongeth only to God, and that remission is the cleansing of the soul from sin, and the other remission, a certifying that one man certifieth another, that sins been forgiven of God, if he be sorry with all his heart for them, and is in full will to leave them for ever; and this manner of forgiveness longeth to priests. Of the first manner of forgiveness David saith, ' And I said, I will confess my unrighteousness unto the Lord, and thou forgavest me my misdeed.' And Zechary, saith, ' And thou, O child, shalt be called the prophet of the highest, &c. To give knowledge of salvation unto his people for the remission of their sins, by the bowels of God's mercy.' And John Baptist, ' Behold the Lamb of God that taketh away the sins of the world.' And St. John the Evangelist saith in his epistle, ' If we confess our sins, he is faithful and just to forgive us our sins, and cleanse us from all our iniquity.' And it followeth, ' If any man sin, we have an advocate with the Father, even Jesus Christ, and he it is that is the propitiation for our sins.' And of the other remission of sins, Christ speaketh in the gospel, and saith, ' Whose sins ye forgive they shall be forgiven.' And man's forgiveness availeth little, but if God forgive our sins through his grace.

"The sixth conclusion toucheth indulgences and pardons that the pope granteth in his bulls, and men callen it an absolution *a pœna et culpa*.

"Of this manner of speech I cannot find in the gospel, ne in no place of holy writ, ne I have not read that Christ used this manner of remission, ne none of his apostles. But as me seemeth, if the pope had such a power, sithen the pains after a man's death had been much greater than any bodily pains of the world; me thinketh he should of charity keep men out of such pains, and then men needed not to find so many vicious priests, after their life, to bring their souls out of purgatory. Another thing me thinketh, that sith the pope's power ne may not keep us in this world from bodily pains, as from cold, from hunger, from dread, from sorrow and other such pains, how should his power help us from spiritual pains, when we been dead? But for that no man cometh after his death to tell us the sooth of what pain they been, men mow tell thereof what him lust. St. John saith in his Apocalyps, that he saw under the altar the souls of them which were slain for the word of God, and for the testimony which they had. And they did cry with a loud voice, saying, ' How long, Lord holy and true, dost not thou revenge our blood of them which dwell on the earth?' And white stoles were given to every of them to rest awhile, till the number of their fellow servants and brethren should be fulfilled, which also remained to be slain as they were, &c. Here seemeth it, that these souls were not assoiled *a pœna*, that is, from pain; for their desire is not fulfilled. And they were bidden abide awhile, and that is a pain. And if martyrs were not assoiled from pain, it is hard for any man to say, that he assoileth other men *a pœna*. Also good men's souls have not but spiritual bliss, and they want bodily bliss until their resurrection in the day of doom. And after they desired to have that bliss, and abiden it, and that is pain to them. And I cannot see that the pope hath power to bring him from this pain. But if any man can shew me that he hath such a power granted in the troth of holy writ, I will gladly leefen it.

"The seventh point speaketh of the pope, and is this; sith it is only due to God, as I have said before, to geve and to grant plenar remission from pain and from blame; that whatsoever he be, pope or other, that presumptuously mistaketh upon him the power that is only due to God, in that, inasmuch as in him is, he maketh himself even with Christ, and blasphemeth God as Lucifer did, when he said, *Ascendam, et ero similis altissimo*, that is, I will ascend, and be like the highest, &c.

"For that I say, if the pope hold men of arms in maintaining of his temporal lordship, to avenge him on them that gilten and offenden him, and geveth remission to fight and to sley them, that contrarien him, as men sayden he did by the bishop of Norwich, not putting his sword in his sheath, as God commanded to Peter, he is antichrist. For he doth the contrary of the commandment of Jesus Christ, that bad Peter forgiven to his brother seventy sithe seven sithe. Well, I find in the gospel, that when Christ sent his disciples to Samaria, the Samaritans would not receive them. And some of them bidden Christ, that he should make fire come down from heaven to destroy the city. And he blamed them and said, ' Ye know not of what spirit ye are ; the Son of Man is not come down to destroy, but to save the lives and souls of men,' &c. If Christ then come to save men, and not to slay them ; who that doth the reverse hereof is against Christ, and then he is antichrist. Christ bade Peter put his sword into his sheath, and said, ' All which take the sword, shall perish with the sword.' And I cannot find that Peter drew out his sword after that time, but suffered as Christ said, ' When thou shalt wax old, another shall gird thee, and lead thee whether thou wilt not.' And, therefore, said Peter, ' Christ suffered for us, leaving us example that we should follow his steps.' And Paul saith, ' Not defending yourselves, but give place to anger, leave revenging to me and I shall reward them,' &c. And therefore it seemeth to me, that it is much against Christ's lore, that his vicar should be a fighter ; sithen that he mote be a shepherd, that should go before his sheep, and let them come after him, and not with swords to drive them away from him. For as Christ saith, ' A good shepherd shall put his life for his sheep.' And zif all that Christ had two swords, when that he was taken of the Jews, he said himself it was for that the scriptures moten zif be fulfilled, ' He was reputed among the wicked ;' and not figure two swords that men sayen the pope hath to govern with the church. And when I see such doings of the pope, and many other that accorden not with Christ's lore, ne his living ; and when I read divers scriptures of holy writ, I am foul astonied whether they shoulden be understood of him, or of any other. And I pray you for God's love tell me the sooth. Christ saith, ' Many shall come in my name, saying, I am Christ, and shall seduce many,' &c. Christ (I wot well) is as much to say, as he that is anointed, and two anointings there were in the law, one of kings, another of priests. And Christ was both king and priest, and so the pope saith that he is. And if all that have been emperors of Rome, and other heathen kings have been antichrists, they come not in Christ's name. But whoso cometh in Christ's name, and feigneth himself Christ's friend, and he be privily his enemy, he may lightly beguile many. St. Paul saith, before there cometh a defection first and the son of perdition shall be revealed, which is the adversary, and is extolled above all that is named God, or which is worshipped, so that he shall sit in the temple of God, shewing himself as God. And it followeth in the same place; and now ye know what holdeth till he be revealed in his time, for he worketh already the mystery of iniquity. Only he that holdeth, let him hold till he come abroad, and then that wicked one shall be revealed, whom the Lord Jesus shall slay with the spirit of his mouth, &c. And St. John saith in the Apocalyps, ' I saw another beast ascending out of the earth, and two horns like to the Lamb. He spake like the dragon, and had the power of the first beast.' Many such authorities astonied me oft sithes ; and therefore I pray you, for the love of God, to tell me what they mean.''

After two sittings in July, and two in August, the last of which was on the sixteenth of August, 1391, they proceed to sentence, October the third.—

" The name of Christ being invoked, we, John, by the permission of God, bishop of Hereford, sitting in tribunal seat, having God before our eyes, weighing and considering the articles by the aforesaid faithful christians put up against the said Swinderby, pretending himself to be priest, with his answers upon the same, Actis et Actitatis before us in the cause of heretical perversity, with ma-

ture deliberation had before in his behalf, with masters and doctors of divinity, and also of other faculties, with their counsel and consent, do pronounce, decree, and declare the said William to have been and to be a heretic, schismatic, and a false informer of the people, and such as is to be avoided of faithful christians. Wherefore we admonish, under the pain of the law, all and singular christians, of what sex, state, condition, or pre-eminence soever, that neither they nor any of them within our diocese, or any other, do believe, receive, defend, or favour the said William, till he shall deserve fully to be reconciled to the bosom again of holy church.''

Of the process, answers, and condemnation of this worthy priest, and true servant of Christ, William Swinderby, you have heard. What afterwards became upon him I have not been able to ascertain ; whether he died in prison, or whether he escaped their hands, or whether he was burned, there is no certain relation made. This remains out of doubt, that during the life of King Richard II. no great harm was done to him, which was until the year 1401, when King Richard being wrongfully deposed, Henry IV. seized the kingdom of England. About the beginning of his reign we read of a certain parliament held at London, in which it was decreed, that whoever shewed themselves favourers of Wickliff, who at that time were called Lollards, they should be apprehended, and if they obstinately persevered in that doctrine they should be delivered over to the bishop of the diocess, and from him committed to the secular magistrate. This law (says the history) brought a certain priest to punishment the same year, who was burned in Smithfield in the presence of a great number. But it does not appear what was the priest's name. Notwithstanding, by divers conjectures it appears to me that his name was Swinderby, who was forced to recant before the bishop of Lincoln. This is plain for all men to judge that if he were burned, then the bishops, friars, and priests, who were the causes thereof, have a great thing to answer to the Lord, when he shall come to judge the quick and the dead.

The history of Walter Brute.

After the history of William Swinderby, I thought good and convenient to add the acts and doings of Walter Brute, his joint fellow and companion, being a lay-man, and learned ; brought up as it seems in the university of Oxford, being there also a graduate. The treating of whose history, as it is something long, so therein will appear many things worthy to be read and considered.

First, the mighty operation of God's Spirit in him, his ripe knowledge, modest simplicity, his valiant constancy, his learned treatises, and many conflicts sustained against God's enemies. On the contrary part in his adversaries may appear might against right, man's authority against plain verity ; against whom they, having nothing directly to allege, proceed in condemnation against one whom they are not able to confute. The chief occasion, that seemed to stir up the heart and zeal of this Walter against the pope, was the impudent pardons and indulgences of Pope Urban, granted to Henry Spencer bishop of Norwich, to fight against Pope Clement, mentioned before. Secondly, the wrongful condemnation of the articles and conclusions of William Swinderby ; the whole order whereof, in the process here following, more plainly may appear.

The process of John, bishop of Hereford, against Walter Brute a learned lay-man, of the diocess of Hereford, touching the cause of Heresy.

" In the name of God, amen. To all manner of faithful christian people, that shall see and hear this our present process, John by the sufferance of God bishop of Hereford sends greeting and continual charity, in the Lord.

We would that you all should know, that of late by many faithful christian people, and specially zealous followers of the catholic faith, we were lamentably informed by way of complaint; that a certain son of ours, named Walter Brute, a learned lay person, of our diocess, has under a cloaked shew of holiness damnably seduced the people; and, setting behind him the fear of God, seduces them as much as he can from day to day, informing and teaching openly and privily as well the nobles as the commons, in certain conclusions, heretical, schismatical, and erroneous, and heretofore condemned. And they have also exhibited against the same Walter, the articles underwritten, in manner and form as followeth.

Articles exhibited and denounced to the bishop, against Walter Brute.

" ' Reverend father and lord, we the faithful people of Christ, and zealous lovers of the catholic faith, and also your humble and devout children, do minister and exhibit to your reverend fatherhood the articles underwritten, touching the catholic faith, contrary and against malicious persons, and detractors of the same faith, and the determinations of holy mother church, and namely, against the child of Belial, one Walter Brute, a false teacher and seducer amongst the people : humbly beseeching, that you would vouchsafe to have regard to the correction of the enormities underwritten, according to the canonical constitutions, even as to your pastoral office doth belong.

1. We do give and exhibit and intend to prove that the same Walter Brute, being unmindful of his salvation, has been by many and divers faithful christian people frequently accused of the cursedness of heresy; as by the swift report, slander, and rumour of the people, proceeding before the most reverend father and lord, lord William, archbishop of Canterbury, and also before the reverend father and lord, lord John, late bishop of Hereford, your predecessor, and now bishop of St. Asaph, hath been testified, and also hath been many and divers times cited to answer to articles avouched, and openly and publicly taught by him against the catholic faith. But he in this matter of heretical cursedness (so grievously and shamefully spoken of) has never purged his innocency; but lurkingly, and running into corners, has many years laboured to advance things erroneous, and schismatical, and also heretical, and to imprint them in the hearts of faithful people.

2. The aforesaid Walter Brute has openly, publicly, and notoriously avouched; and commonly said and taught, and stubbornly affirmed; that every christian man (yea and woman) being without sin, may make the body of Christ so well as the priest.

3. The same Walter has notoriously, openly and publicly avouched and taught, that in the sacrament of the altar there is not the very body, but a sign and a memorial only.

4. The aforesaid Walter has said commonly, and avouched, and also has laboured to inform men and companies, that no man is bound to give tithes, nor oblations; and if any man will needs give, he may give his tithes and oblations to whom he will, excluding thereby their curates.

5. That such as preach and prefer crosses, and pardons (granted by the high bishop to them that helped the purpose of the reverend father lord Henry, by the grace of God bishop of Norwich, when he took his journey to fight for the holy father the pope) are schismatics and heretics, and that the pope cannot grant such manner of pardons.

6. The said Walter has often said, and commonly avouched, that the pope is antichrist, and a seducer of the people, and utterly against the law and life of Christ.

7. Whereas of late your reverence proceeded in form of law against William Swinderby; and that the said William Swinderby had given his answers in writing, containing errors, schisms and heresies, even as you with the mature counsel of masters and doctors in divinity,

and other faculties have determined and given sentence, and have pronounced the same William Swinderby to be an heretic and a schismatic, and an erroneous teacher of the people : nevertheless, the aforenamed Walter has openly, publicly, and notoriously said, avouched and stubbornly affirmed, that the said William's answers are good, righteous, and not able to be convinced, in that they contain no error, and that your sentence, given against the said William, is evil, false, and unjust; and that your assistants have wickedly, naughtily, perversely, and unjustly condemned the answers aforesaid.'

"Now thereupon immediately those same faithful christian people have instantly required, that we would vouchsafe that other articles given by the same faithful christians against William Swinderby, together with the writings and answers of the same William, should be admitted against Walter Brute. Which things being done, the same faithful christian people, and especially Sir Walter Pride, the penitentiary of our cathedral church of Hereford, personally appearing before us, sitting in our judgment seat in the parish church of Whiteborne of our diocess brought forth and exhibited two public instruments against the same Walter Brute, in the case of cursed heresy aforesaid.

"At last, Walter Brute did present to us divers scrolls of paper, written with his own proper hand, for his answers to the same articles and conclusions above written; which scrolls were as follows :—

" ' In the name of the Father, and of the Son, and the Holy Ghost, Amen. I, Walter Brute, sinner, layman, husbandman, and a christian (having my offspring of the Britons, both by my father's and mother's side) of the Britons, have been accused to the bishop of Hereford, that I did err in many matters concerning the catholic christian faith; by whom I am required that I should write an answer in Latin to all those matters. Whose desire I will satisfy to my power, protesting first of all, before God and before all the world; that like as it is not my mind, through God's grace, to refuse the known truth, for any reward, greater or smaller, yea, be it never so big, nor yet for the fear of any temporal punishment; even so it is not my mind to maintain any erroneous doctrine for any personal advantage. And if any man, of what state, sect, or condition soever he be, will shew me that I err in my writings or sayings, by the authority of the sacred scripture, or by probable reason grounded on the sacred scripture, I will humbly and gladly receive his information. But as for the bare words of any teacher (Christ only excepted) I will not simply believe, except he shall be able to stablish them by the truth of experience, or of the scripture : because that, in the holy apostles elected by Christ, there has been found error by the testimony of the holy scripture, because that Paul himself confesses that he rebuked Peter, for that he was worthy to be rebuked, Gal. ii. 14. There have been errors found in the holy doctors, that have been before us, as they themselves confess of themselves. And oftentimes it happens, that there is error found in the teachers in our age : who are of contrary opinions among themselves, and some of them do sometimes determine one thing for truth, and others do condemn the self same thing to be heresy and error. Which protestation premised, I will here place two suppositions or cases for a ground and a foundation of all things that I shall say, out of which I would gather two probable conclusions established upon the same, and upon the sacred scripture. By which conclusions, when they shall be declared after my manner and fashion, it shall plainly appear what my opinion and judgment is concerning all matters that I am accused of. But because I am ignorant and unlearned, I will get me under the mighty defences of the Lord : O Lord, I will remember thine only righteousness.

" ' God the Father Almighty uncreate, the maker of heaven and earth, hath sent his Son (that was everlastingly begotten) into this world, that he should be incarnate for the salvation and redemption of mankind, who was conceived by the Holy Ghost, everlastingly pro-

R

ceeding from the Father and the Son, and was born of Mary the virgin, to the end that we might be born anew. He suffered passion under Pontius Pilate for our sins, laying down his life for us, that we should lay down our life for our brethren. He was crucified, that we should be crucified to the world, and the world to us. He was dead, that he might redeem us from death, by purchasing for us forgiveness of sins. He was buried, that we being buried together with him into death by baptism, and being dead to sins, should live to righteousness. He descended into hell, thereby delivering man from thraldom, and from the bondage of the devil, and restoring him to his inheritance which he lost by sin. The third day he rose from the dead, through the glory of the Father, that we also should walk in newness of life. He ascended up to the heavens, to which nobody has ascended, saving he that descended from heaven, even the Son of Man which is in heaven. He sitteth at the right hand of God the Father Almighty, until his enemies be made his footstool. He being in very deed so much better than the angels, as he hath obtained by inheritance a more excellent name than they. From whence he shall come to judge the quick and the dead, according to their works, because the Father hath given all judgment to the Son. In whose terrible judgment we shall rise again, and shall all of us stand before this judgment seat, and receive joy as well bodily as spiritually, for ever to endure, if we be of the sheep placed at the right hand; or else punishment both of body and soul, if we shall be found amongst goats, placed on the left hand, &c.

" 'Jesus Christ the Son of God, very God and very man, a king for ever, by establishing an everlasting kingdom (breaking to powder all the kingdoms, of the world,) Daniel ii. 44. A priest for ever after the order of Melchisedec, whereby also he is able evermore to save such as come unto God by him, and always liveth to make intercession for us, Heb. vii. 25. He offering one sacrifice for our sins, hath made perfect for ever by one oblation those that be sanctified, Heb. x. 14. Being the wisdom that cannot be deceived, and the truth that cannot be uttered, he has in this world taught the will of God his Father, which will he has in work fulfilled, to the intent that he might faithfully instruct us, and has given the law of charity to be observed by his faithful people, which he has written in the hearts and minds of the faithful with the finger of God, where is the Spirit of God, searching the inward secrets of the Godhead. Wherefore, his doctrine must be observed above all other doctrines, whether they be of angels or of men, because that he could not, and would not err' in his teaching. But in men's doctrine there chances oftentimes to be error; and therefore we must forsake their doctrines, if covertly or expressly they are repugnant to the doctrine of Christ. Men's doctrines being made for the people's profit, must be allowed and observed, so that they be grounded upon Christ's doctrine, or at least be not repugnant to his words.

" 'If the high bishop of Rome calling himself the servant of the servants of God, and the chief vicar of Christ in this world, makes and maintains any laws contrary to the gospel of Jesus Christ; then is he of those that have come in Christ's name, saying, I am Christ, and have deceived many, by the testimony of our Saviour in Matt. xxiv. 23. And the idol of desolation sitting in the temple of God and taking away from him the continual sacrifice for a time, times, and half a time, which idol must be revealed to the christian people by the testimony of Daniel. Whereof Christ speaketh in the gospel; when ye shall see the abomination of desolation that was told of by Daniel the prophet, standing in the holy place; let him that readeth understand, he is the pestiferous mountain infecting the whole universal earth, Jer. li. 25. And not the head of Christ's body. For the person ancient in years, and honourable in reverence, he is the head, and the prophet teaching lies, he is the tail, Is. ix. 15. And he is that wicked and sinful captain of Israel, whose foreappointed day of iniquity is come in time of iniquity, who shall take away the diadem and take away the crown, Ez. xxi. 26. To

whom it was said; Forasmuch as thy heart was exalted, and didst say, I am a God, and sittest in the seat of God, in the heart of the sea, seeing thou art a man and not God, and hast given thine heart, as if it were the heart of God; therefore behold I will bring upon thee the most strong and mighty strangers of the nations, and they shall draw their swords upon the beauty of thy wisdom, and shall defile the commandments, and kill thee, and pull thee out, and thou shalt die in the destruction of the slain. And it followeth, In the multitude of thine iniquities, and of the iniquities of thy merchandize, thou hast defiled thy sanctification. I will therefore bring forth a fire, from the midst of the whole earth, and will make thee as ashes upon earth. Thou art become nothing, and never shalt thou be any more, Ez. xxviii. Furthermore, he is the idle shepherd forsaking his flock, having a sword on his arm, and another sword on his right eye, Zech. xi. 17. And sitting in the temple of God, he doth advance himself above all things that is called God, or whatsoever is worshipped, 2 Thess. ii. 4. And in the defection or falling away shall the man of sin be revealed, whom the Lord Jesus shall slay with the breath of his mouth. For every kingdom divided in itself shall be brought to desolation. He is also besides, The beast ascending up out of the earth, having two horns like unto a lamb, but he speaketh like a dragon, and as the cruel beast ascending up out of the sea, whose power shall continue forty-two months. He worketh the things that he hath given to the image of the beast. And he compelled small and great, rich and poor, free men and bond slaves, to worship the beast, and to take his mark in their forehead or their hands, Rev. xiii. 16. And thus, by the testimony of all these places, is he the chief antichrist upon the earth, and must be slain with the sword of God's word, and cast with the dragon, the cruel beast and the false prophet that hath seduced the earth, into the lake of fire and brimstone to be tormented world without end.

" 'If the city of Rome do allow his traditions, and do disallow Christ's holy commandments, and Christ's doctrine, that it may confirm his traditions; then is she 'Babylon the great,' or the 'daughter of Babylon,' and the 'great whore sitting upon many waters,' with whom the kings of the earth have committed fornication, and the inhabitants of the earth are become drunken with the wine of her fornication. With whose spiritual whoredom, enchantments, witchcrafts, and Simon Magus merchandises, the whole world is infected and seduced; saying in her heart, 'I sit as queen, and am not a widow, neither shall I see sorrow and mourning.' Yet is she ignorant that within a little while shall come the day of her destruction and ruin by the testimony of God, Rev. chap. xvii. Because that from the time of the continual sacrifice being taken away, and the abomination of desolation placed, there be passed one thousand two hundred and ninety days by the testimony of Daniel, and the chronicles added do agree to the same. And the holy city also hath been trodden under foot of the heathen, for forty-two months, and the woman was nourished up in the wilderness (unto which she fled for fear of the face of the serpent) during one thousand two hundred and sixty days, or else for a time, times, and half a time, which is all one. All these things be manifest by the testimony of the book of Revelations, and the chronicles thereto agreeing. And as concerning the fall of Babylon aforesaid, it is manifest in the Revelations, where it is said, 'In one day shall her plagues come, death, lamentation, and famine, and she shall be burned with fire. For, strong is the Lord, which shall judge her.' And again, 'Babylon that great city is fallen, which hath made all nations to drink of the wine of her fornication.' And, thirdly, 'One mighty angel took up a mill-stone, that was a very great one, and did cast it into the sea, saying, With violence shall that great city Babylon be overthrown, and shall no more be found. For her merchants were the princes of the earth, and with her witchcraft all nations have gone astray, and in her is there found the blood of the saints and prophets.' And of her destruction Isaiah speaketh in the thirteenth chapter, ' And Babylon, that glorious city, being so noble amongst kingdoms in the pride of the Chaldeans, it shall be that like as the Lord did overturn Sodom and Gomorrah upside down, it shall never more be inhabited, nor have the foundation laid in no age, from generation to generation.' Jeremiah saith, ' Your mother that hath borne you is brought to very great confusion, and made even with the ground.' And again, ' The Lord hath devised and done as he hath spoken against the inhabiters of Babylon; which dwell richly in their treasures upon many waters, thine end is come.' And, thirdly, ' Drought shall fall upon her waters, and they shall begin to dry: for it is a land of graven images, and ·boasteth in her prodigious wonders : it shall never more be inhabited, neither be builded up in no age nor generation. Verily even as God hath subverted Sodom and Gomorrah with her calves.

" ' Pardon me (I beseech you) though I be not plentiful in pleasant words. For if I should run after the course of this wicked world, and should please men, I should not be Christ's servant. And because I am a poor man, and neither have nor can have notaries hired to testify of these my writings ; I call upon Christ to be my witness, who knows the inward secrets of my heart, that I am ready to declare the things that I have written to the profit of all christian people, and to the hurt of no man living, and am ready to be reformed if any man will shew me where I have erred ; being ready also (miserable sinner though I be) to suffer for the confession of the name of Christ, and of his doctrine, as much as shall please him by his grace and love to assist me a miserable sinner. In witness of all these things I have to this writing set the seal of our Lord and Saviour Jesus Christ: which I beseech him to imprint upon my forehead, and to take from me all manner of mark of antichrist. Amen.' "

These two suppositions (as they are termed in the schools) written by Walter Brute, and exhibited to the bishop, although they contained matter sufficient either to satisfy the bishop if he had been disposed to learn, or else to have provoked him to reply again, if his knowledge therein had been better than his : yet could neither of them work any effect in him. But he receiving and perusing them when he could neither confute that which was said, nor would reply or answer by learning, to that which was truth, said, " That this his writing was too short and obscure, and therefore required him to write upon the same again more plainly and more at large." Whereupon the said Master Walter satisfying the bishop's request (and ready to give to every one an account of his faith) in a more ample treatise renews his matter before declared. Of this treatise we give the following extracts :—

" Reverend father, forsomuch as it seems to you that my motion in my two suppositions or cases, and in my two conclusions, is too short and somewhat dark : I will gladly now satisfy your desire, according to my small learning, by declaring the same conclusions. In opening whereof, it shall plainly appear, what I do judge in all matters that I am accused of to your reverence ; desiring you first of all that your discretion would not believe that I do enterprize of any presumption to handle the secrets of the scriptures, which the holy and just, and wise doctors have left unexpounded. It is not unknown to many, that I am in all points far inferior to them, whose holiness of life and profoundness in knowledge is always allowed. But as for mine ignorance, and multitude of sins, they are to myself and others sufficiently known: wherefore I judge not myself worthy to unloose or to carry their shoes after them. Do you therefore no otherwise deem of me, than I do of mine own self. But if you shall find any goodness in my writings, ascribe it to God only: who, according to the multitude of his mercy, doth sometimes reveal those things to idiots and sinners, which are hidden from the holy and wise, according to this saying, ' I thank thee,

O Father, for that thou hast hidden these things from the wise and prudent, and hast revealed them unto babes : even so, O Father, for so it seemeth good in thy sight.' And in another place, ' For judgment am I come into this world, that they which see not, might perceive ; and that they which see, might be made blind.' And Paul says, ' That God hath chosen the weak things of the world, to confound the mighty ;' that no man shall glory in himself, but that all men should give the glory to God.

" He that hath the key of David, who openeth and no man shutteth, shutteth and no man openeth, does (when and how long it pleases him) hide the mysteries, and the secrets of the scriptures from the wise, prudent, and righteous ; and at his pleasure reveals them to sinners, and lay persons, and simple souls, that he may have the honour and glory in all things. Wherefore, as I have before said, if you shall find any good things in my writings, ascribe the same to God alone. If you shall find otherwise, think ye the same to be written in ignorance, and not in malice. And if any doubt of error be shewn me in all my writings, I will humbly allow your information and fatherly correction.

" In the first conclusion of mine answer, I have conditionally put it, who is that antichrist lying concealed in the hid scriptures of the prophets : I will pass on the declaration of that conclusion, bringing to light those things which lay hid in darkness, because nothing is hid which shall not be disclosed, and nothing covered which shall not be known. And therefore the thing which was said in the darkness, let us say in the light ; and the thing which we have heard in the ear, let us preach upon the house-tops. I, therefore say, that if the high bishop of Rome, calling himself the servant of God, and the chief vicar of Christ in this world, makes and justifies many laws contrary to the gospel of Jesus Christ: then is he the chief of many, who coming in the name of Christ, have said, I am Christ, who have deceived many ; which is the first part of the first conclusion, and is manifest. For Christ is called of the Hebrews the very same that we call anointed. And among them there was a double sort of anointing by the law, the one of kings, and the other of priests. And as well were the kings, as the priests, called in the law, Christs. The kings, as in the psalm, The kings of the earth stood up, and the princes took counsel together, against the Lord, and against his Christ, or anointed. And in the books of the Kings very often are the kings called Christs. And our Saviour was Christ, or anointed king, because he was a king for evermore upon the throne of David, as the scripture very often witnesses. The priests also were called anointed, as where it is written, Touch not my Christs ; that is, mine anointed ones, and do my prophets no harm. And so was our Saviour Christ, ' a priest for ever, according to the order of Melchisedec.'

" Seeing then that the bishops of Rome do say that they are the high priests ; they say also therein that they are kings, because they say that they have the spiritual sword pertaining to their priesthood, and the temporal sword which agrees to a king's state. So it is plain, that really, and in very deed, they say, that they are Christs, although they are not expressly called Christs. Now that they come in the name of Christ is manifest, because they say that they are his vicars in this world, ordained of Christ for the government of the christian church. Therefore, seeing they say, that really and in very deed they are Christs, and the chief friends of Christ ; if they make and justify many laws contrary to the gospel of Jesus Christ, then is it plain that they themselves in earth are antichrists, because there is no worse plague and pestilence than a familiar enemy. And if in secret they be against Christ, and yet in open appearance they say that they are his friends, they are so much the more meet to seduce and deceive the christion people, because that a manifest enemy will have much trouble to deceive a man, because men trust him not: but a hidden enemy, pretending outward friendship, may easily seduce."

" Paul to the Romans declareth in a godly discourse,

and to the Galatians likewise, 'That none shall be justified by the works of the law, but by grace in the faith of Jesus Christ.' As for the morals and ceremonies of the law, as circumcision, sacrifices for offences, and for sins, first-fruits, tenths, vows, divers sorts of washings, the sprinkling of blood, the sprinkling of ashes, abstaining from unclean meats, which are ordained for the sanctifying and cleansing of the people from sin, no nor yet the prayers of the priests, neither the preachings of the prophets could cleanse a man from his sin. For death reigned even from Adam to Moses, and sin from Moses to Christ, as Paul declareth to the Romans in the fifth chapter. But Christ, willing to have mercy and not sacrifice, being a priest for ever after the order of Melchisedec, and an high priest of good things to come, did neither by the blood of goats or calves, but by his own blood, enter in once into the holy place, when an everlasting redemption is found: neither did Jesus enter into the holy places that were made with hands, which are the examples of true things, but unto the very heaven, that now he may appear before the face of God for us. Nor yet he did so, that he should offer up himself oftentimes, as the high bishop entered into the holy place every year with strange blood, (for otherwise he must needs have suffered oftentimes since the beginning of the world), but now, in the latter end of the world, hath he once appeared by his own sacrifice, for the destruction of sin. And like as it is decreed for men once to die, and after that cometh judgment; even so was Christ once offered up to consume away the sins of many. The second time shall he appear without sin to the salvation of such as look for him. For the law having a shadow of good things to come, and not the very image or substance itself of the things, can never by those sacrifices which they offer (of one selfsame sort continually year by year) make them perfect that come unto her. Otherwise, men would leave off offering, because that those worshippers being once cleansed, should have no more prick of conscience for sin afterwards. But in them is there remembrance made of sins every year. For it is impossible, that by the blood of goats and bulls sins should be taken away. Wherefore he entering into the world doth say, As for sacrifice and offering thou wouldst not have, but a body hast thou framed unto me. And sacrifices for sin have not pleased thee: then said I, behold I come; in the head, or principal part of the book it is written of me, that I should do thy will O God. Wherefore he said before, that sacrifices, oblations, and burnt-offerings, and that for sin thou wouldest not have: neither were those things pleasant to thee which are offered according to the law: then said I, behold I come, that I may do thy will, O God: he taketh away the first that he may establish that that followed. In which will we are sanctified and made holy by the offering up of the body of Jesus Christ once. And verily every priest is ready every day ministering, and oftentimes offering the self-same sacrifices, which never can take away sins. But this man, offering one sacrifice for sins, doth for ever and ever sit at God's right hand, looking for the rest to come, till that his enemies be placed to be his footstool. For with one offering hath he for ever made perfect those that be sanctified. By which things it plainly appeareth, that Christ by once offering hath cleansed from their sins, they who could not be cleansed from the same by all the ceremonies of the law, and so did fulfil that which the priesthood of the law could not. Wherefore the moral and judicial law, he fulfilled by the law of charity, and by grace; and the ceremonial, by one offering up of his body on the altar of the cross. And so it is plain that Christ fulfilled the whole law.

"They say that the bishop of Rome (who is the chief priest and judge among them) hath full power and authority to remit sins. Whereupon they say, that he is able fully and wholly, to absolve a man *a pena et culpa*, so that if a man at the time of his death, had this remission, he should straightway fly to heaven without any pain of purgatory. The other bishops (as they say) have not so great authority. The priests constituted under every bishop, have power, say they, to absolve the sins of them that are confessed, but not all kind of sins; because there are some grievous sins reserved to the absolution of the bishops; and some again, to the absolution only of the chief and high bishop. They say also, that it behoves the offenders, for the necessity of their soul's health, to call to their remembrance their offences, and to declare them with all the circumstances to the priest in auricular confession, supplying the place of God, after the manner of a judge; and afterward humbly to fulfil the penance enjoined by the priest, except the penance so enjoined, or any part thereof, be released by the superior power. All these things (say they) are manifestly determined. And although these things have not expressly their foundation in the plain and manifest doctrine of Christ, nor any of the apostles; yet the authors of the decrees and decretals concerning this matter, have grounded the same upon divers places of the scriptures, as in the words of Christ in the gospel of St. Matthew the sixteenth chapter, whereupon they ground the pope's power judicial to surmount the powers of other priests, as where Christ said unto his disciples, 'Whom do men say that I am? And they answered, Some say that thou art John Baptist, some Elias, and some Jeremias, or one of the prophets. He said, But whom say ye that I am? Simon Peter, answered, and said, Thou art the Christ, the Son of the living God. And Jesus answered and said unto him, Blessed art thou Simon Bar-Jona; for flesh and blood hath not revealed this unto thee; but my Father which is in heaven. And I say unto thee, that thou art Peter, and upon this rock will I build my church, and the gates of hell shall not prevail against it. And to thee will I give the keys of the kingdom of heaven. And whatsoever thou shalt bind upon earth, shall also be bound in heaven; and whatsoever thou shalt loose upon earth, shall be loosed also in heaven.'

"Out of this text of Christ, divers expositors have drawn divers errors. As first when Christ said, 'And I say unto thee, that thou art Peter, and upon this rock will I build my church;' some affirm, that Christ meant he would build his church upon Peter. This exposition is ascribed to Pope Leo; the error whereof is manifestly known. For the church of Christ is not builded upon Peter, but upon the rock of Peter's confession, for he said, 'Thou art the Christ the Son of the living God.' And again when Christ said singularly to Peter, ' I will give unto thee the keys of the kingdom of heaven, and whatsoever thou shalt bind,' &c. By this saying they affirm, that Christ gave to Peter specially, as chief of the rest of the apostles, a larger power to bind and to loose, than he did to the rest of the apostles and disciples. And because Peter answered for himself and all the apostles, not only confessing the faith which he had chiefly above the rest, but also the faith which the rest of the apostles had even as himself, by the revelation of the heavenly Father; it appears that as the faith of all the apostles was declared by the answer of one, so by this that Christ said, 'Whatsoever thou shalt bind,' &c., is given unto the rest of the apostles, the same power and equality to bind and to loose, as unto Peter. Which Christ himself declares in the gospel of St. Matthew, the eighteenth chapter, in these words, ' Verily I say unto you, what things soever you shall bind upon earth, shall be bound in heaven; and whatsoever you shall loose upon earth, shall be also loosed in heaven.' And further he adds, 'And again I say unto you, that if two of you shall agree upon earth, touching anything ye shall ask, it shall be given unto you of my Father which is in heaven. For where two or three be gathered together in my name, I am there in the midst of them.' And in John, the twentieth chapter, he saith generally to them, 'Receive ye the Holy Ghost. Whose-soever sins ye remit, they are remitted unto them; and whose-soever sins you retain, they are retained.'

By this it appears, that the power to bind and to loose is not specially granted to Peter, as chief and head of the rest, and that by him the rest had their power to bind and to loose; for the head of the body of the church is one, which is Christ, and the head of Christ is

God. Peter and the rest of the apostles are the good members of the body of Christ; receiving power and virtue from Christ, whereby they confirm and glue together the other members (as well the strong and noble, as the weak and unable) to a perfect composition and seemliness of the body of Christ: that all honour from all parts and members may be given to Christ as head and chief, by whom as head all the members are governed. And therefore Paul says, 1 Cor. iii. 4., 'For while one saith, I am of Paul; and another I am of Apollos; are ye not carnal? Who then is Paul, and who is Apollos, but ministers by whom ye believed, even as the Lord gave to every man? I have planted, Apollos watered; but God gave the increase. So then neither is he that planteth any thing, neither he that watereth; but God that giveth the increase.' And to the Galatians he says (ii. 6—10.) 'But of those who seemed to be somewhat, whatsoever they were, it maketh no matter to me: God accepteth no man's person: for they who seemed to be somewhat in conference added nothing to me: but contrariwise, when they saw that the Gospel of the uncircumcision was committed unto me, as the Gospel of the circumcision was unto Peter; (for he that wrought effectually in Peter to the apostleship of the circumcision, the same was mighty in me toward the Gentiles:) and when James, Cephas, and John, who seemed to be pillars, perceived the grace that was given unto me, they gave to me and Barnabas the right hands of fellowship; that we should go unto the heathen, and they unto the circumcision. Only they would that we should remember the poor; the same which I also was forward to do.' Hereby it appears that Paul had not his authority of Peter to convert the Gentiles, to baptize them, and to remit their sins, but of him who said unto him, 'Saul Saul, why persecutest thou me? It is hard for thee to kick against the pricks." Here is Paul of the head of the church, and not of Peter: by which head they say, that all the members are sustained and made lively.

" The third error which the authors of the canons conceive in the text, ' Unto thee will I give the keys,' &c. is this, they say that in this sentence which was said to Peter of the authority to bind and to loose, was meant that as Christ gave to Peter above all the rest of the apostles a special, and as it were an excellent power above all the apostles; even so, say they, he gave power to the bishops of Rome (whom they call Peter's chief successors) the same special power and authority, exceeding the power of all other bishops of the world.

" The first part of this parallel and comparison, doth appear manifestly by the premises to be erroneous; wherein is plainly shewed that the other apostles had equal power with Peter to bind and loose. Wherefore consequently it follows that the second part of the parallel, grounded upon the same text is also erroneous. But if the first part of the parallel were truth, as it is not, yet the second part must needs be an error, wherein is said, that the bishops of Rome are Peter's chief successors. For although there is but one catholic christian church, of all the faithful sort converted; yet the first part of the church, and the first converted, was of the Jews, the second of the Greeks, and the third part was of the Romans or Latins. Whereof the first part was most perfectly converted to the faith, for they faithfully observed the perfection of charity, as appeareth in the acts of the apostles, by the multitude of the believers. They were of one heart, and one soul, neither called they any thing that they possessed their own, but all was common among them.

" Paul, in his epistle to the Romans, says, the gospel is ' salvation to every one that believeth, to the Jew first, and also to the Greek.' The Greeks were after the Jews the next converted, and after them the Romans, taking their information of the Greeks, as appears by the chronicles, although indeed some Romans were converted to the faith, by Peter and Paul. And as Christ said thrice to Peter, feed my sheep, so Peter ruled these three churches, as the chronicles witness. But first he reformed the church of the Jews in Jerusalem and Judea, as appears by the testimony of the acts of the apostles. For it is manifest how Peter standing up amongst his brethren. spake unto them concerning the election of an apostle in the place of Judas the traitor, alleging places to them out of the scripture, that another should take upon him his apostleship. And so by lot was Matthias constituted in the place of Judas. After that the Holy Ghost was come upon the apostles, and that they spake with the tongues of all men, the hearers were astonished at the miracle. And some mocked them, saying, these men are full of new wine; but Peter stood up and spake to them, saying, that it was fulfilled in them that was prophesied by Joel the prophet. And he preached unto the people Christ, whom they in their ignorance had put to death. To whom was a Saviour promised by the testimony of the prophets. And when they heard the words of Peter, they were pricked at the heart, saying unto him and the rest of the apostles, what shall we then do? And Peter said unto them, Repent, and let every one of you be baptized in the name of Jesus Christ for the remission of your sins, and ye shall receive the Holy Ghost. And there were joined unto them the same day about three thousand souls. And by Acts iii. 4, 5, it appears that Peter above the rest did those things which belonged to the ministry of the apostleship, as well in preaching as in answering. Whereupon some chronicles say, that Peter governed the church of the Jews at Jerusalem, four years before he governed Antioch. And by the testimony of Paul to the Galatians, the gospel of the uncircumcision is committed to Paul, even as the circumcision to Peter. And he that wrought with Peter in the apostleship of circumcision, wrought with Paul amongst the Gentiles. Whereby it appears that the church of the Jews was committed to the government of Peter. And in the process of the acts of the apostles it appears, that Peter believed that the faith of Christ was not to be preached to those Gentiles, who always lived in uncleanness of idolatry. But when Peter was at Joppa, Cornelius a Gentile sent to him that he would come and shew him the way of life; but Peter (a little before the coming of the messengers of Cornelius) being in his chamber, after he had prayed, fell in a trance, and saw heaven opened, and a certain vessel descending even as a great sheet, let down by four corners from heaven to earth. In which were all manner of four-footed beasts, serpents of the earth, and fowls of the air. And a voice spake unto him, saying, Arise Peter, kill and eat; and Peter said, Not so, Lord, because I have never eaten any common or unclean thing. This was done thrice. And Peter descended (not knowing what the vision did signify) and found the messengers of Cornelius.

" As concerning the judicial authority of the clergy, many things are written in the canons of decrees, greatly to be marvelled at, and far from the truth of the scripture. The authors of the canons say, that Christ gave unto the priests judicial power over sinners that confessed their sins unto them. And this they ground upon the text of Christ: ' I will give unto thee the keys of the kingdom of heaven, and whatsoever thou loosest,' &c. And these keys of the kingdom of heaven, they call the knowledge to discern, and the power to judge, which they say only belongeth to the priests, except in case of necessity; then they say a lay-man may absolve a man from sin. And as touching absolution, they say there are three things to be required on the sinner's part: first, hearty contrition, whereby the sinner ought to bewail their offending of God through sins; the second is, auricular confession, whereby the sinner ought to shew unto the priest his sins, and the circumstances of them; the third is satisfaction through penance enjoined to him by the priest for his sins committed. And of his part that gives absolution there are two things (say they) to be required: that is to say, knowledge to discern one sin from another, whereby he ought to make a difference of sins, and appoint a convenient penance, according to the quantity of the sins. The second is, authority to judge, whereby he ought to enjoin penance to the offender. And further, they say, that he that is confessed ought with all humility to submit himself to this authority, and wholly and voluntarily to do these penances which are commanded him by the priest, except the penance be released by a superior power; for all priests (as they say) have not equal authority to absolve sins. The chief priest whom they call Peter's successor, has power fully and wholly to absolve. But the inferior priests have power, some more, some less: the more as they are near him in dignity, the less as they are farther from the degree of his dignity. All this is declared by process in the decrees, but not by the express doctrine of Christ, or any of his apostles. For although Christ absolved men from their sins, I do not find that he did it after the manner of a judge, but of a Saviour. For Christ saith, 'God sent not his Son into the world to condemn the world, but that the world through him might be saved,' John iii. 17. Whereupon he spake unto him whom he healed of the palsy, 'Son, be of good cheer; thy sins be forgiven thee.' And to the woman taken in adultery, Christ said, 'Woman, where are thine accusers? hath no man condemned thee?' Who said, 'No man, Lord.' To whom then Jesus thus said, 'Neither will I condemn thee, go and sin no more.'

"By which words and deeds of Christ, and many other places of the scripture, it appears he was not as a judge at his first coming, to punish sinners according to their offences; but that day shall come hereafter, wherein he shall judge all men according to their works, as in Matt. xxv., where he saith, 'When the Son of Man shall come in his glory, and all his angels with him; then shall he sit upon the throne of his glory, and all nations shall be gathered before him, and he shall separate them one from another, as a shepherd divideth the sheep from the goats,' &c. Neither shall he judge alone, but his saints also with him. For he saith, 'You that have followed me in the regeneration, when the Son of man shall sit in the throne of his glory, shall sit upon twelve thrones, judging the twelve tribes of Israel.' If then Christ came not as a judge, why do the priests say that they supply the room of Christ on earth, to judge sinners according to the quantity of their offences? And yet not only this, but it is more to be wondered at, how the bishop of Rome dares to take upon him to be a judge before the day of judgment, and to prevent the time, judging some to be saints in heaven, and to be honoured of men, and some again to be tormented in hell eternally with the devils! Would to God these men would weigh the saying of St. Paul, 1 Cor. vi. 5. 'Judge nothing before the time the Lord come, who both will bring to light the hidden things of darkness, and make manifest the councils of the hearts, and then every one shall have praise of God.' Let the bishop of Rome take heed, lest that in Ezekiel be spoken him, 'Because thy heart is lifted up, and thou hast said I am a God, I sit in the seat of God, and in the midst of the seas, yet thou art a man, and not God.' It is manifest that the remission of sins principally belongs to God, who through grace washes away our sins. For it is said, 'The Lamb of God taketh away the sins of the world.' And to christians it belongs as the ministers of God. For in the twentieth chapter of John, Christ saith, 'Receive unto you the Holy Ghost: whose sins you remit, they are remitted unto them; and whose sins you shall retain, they are retained.' Seeing therefore that all christians that are baptized in the name of the Father, and of the Son, and of the Holy Ghost, receive the Holy Ghost; it appears that they have power given to them of Christ, to remit sins ministerially. Has not every christian authority to baptize? and in the baptism all the sins of the baptized are remitted. Ergo, they that do baptize do remit sins.

"Who is he therefore who so rashly takes upon him to judge the infants begotten of faithful parents, dying without baptism, to be tormented with eternal fire? Now let us consider the three things which the canons of decrees affirm to be requisite for the remission of the sins of those that sin after baptism, that is to say, contrition of heart, auricular confession, and satisfaction of the deed through penance enjoined by the priest for the sins committed. I cannot find in any place in the gospel where Christ commanded that this kind of confession should be done unto the priest; nor can I find that Christ assigned any penance to sinners for their sins, but that he desired them to sin no more. If a sinner confess that he has offended God through sin, and sorrows heartily for his offences, minding hereafter to sin no more, then is he truly repentant for his sin, and then he is converted unto the Lord. If he shall then humbly, and with good hope, crave mercy from God, and remission of his sins: who is he that can prevent God from absolving that sinner from his sin? And as God absolves a sinner from his sins, so has Christ absolved many, although they confessed not their sins to the priests, and although they received not due penance for their sins. And if Christ could after that manner once absolve sinners; how is he become now not able to absolve? Except some man will say that he is above Christ, and that his power is diminished by the ordinances of his own laws. How were sinners absolved by God in the time of the apostles, and always heretofore, to the time that these canons were made? I speak not these things as though confession to priests were wicked, but that it is not of necessity requisite to salvation. I believe verily that the confession of sins to good priests, and likewise to other faithful christians, is good, as witnesseth St. James the apostle: 'Confess your sins one to another, and pray one for another, that ye may be healed; for the effectual fervent prayer of a righteous man availeth much.' This kind of confession is good, profitable, and expedient; for if God peradventure hears not a man's own prayer, he is helped with the intercession of others. Yet nevertheless the prayers of the priests seem too much to be extolled in the decrees, where they treat of penitence, saying as is ascribed to Pope Leo (multiplex misericordia Dei, &c.), that it is ordained by the Providence of God's divine will, that the mercy of God cannot be obtained but by the prayer of the priests, &c. The prayer of a good priest much avails a sinner, confessing his faults to him. The counsel of a discreet priest is very profitable for a sinner, to give the sinner counsel to beware of sin hereafter, and to instruct him.

"After this manner I esteem confession to priests very expedient and profitable to a sinner. But to confess sins to the priest as to a judge, and to receive of him corporal penance for a satisfaction to God for his sins committed; I see not how this can be founded upon the truth of scripture. For before the coming of Christ, no man was sufficient or able to make satisfaction to God for his sins, although he suffered never so much penance for his sins. And therefore it was needful that he that was without sin, should be punished for sins, as witnesses Isaiah liii. 4. where he saith, 'He hath borne our griefs and carried our sorrows.' And again, 'He was wounded for our transgressions, and bruised for our iniquities.' And again, 'The Lord laid on him the iniquity of us all.' And again, 'For the transgression of my people was he stricken.' If therefore Christ through his passion has made satisfaction for our sins, whereas we ourselves were unable to do it: then through him have we grace and remission of sins. How can we say now that we are sufficient to make satisfaction to God by any penance enjoined to us by man's authority, seeing that our sins are more grievous after baptism, than they were before the coming of Christ? Therefore as in baptism the pain of Christ in his passion was a full satisfaction for our sins; even so is it also after baptism, if we confess that we have offended, and be heartily sorry for our sins, and mind not to sin again afterwards.

"Hereupon John writeth in his first epistle, ch. i. 'If we say we have no sin, we deceive ourselves, and the truth is not in us. If we confess our sins, God is faithful and just, to forgive us our sins, and cleanse us from all unrighteousness. If we say we have not sinned we make him a liar, and his word is not in us. My little children, these things I write unto you that ye sin not; but if any man sin, we have an advocate with the Father, Jesus Christ the righteous, and he is the propitiation for our sins, and not for ours only, but also for the sins of the whole world.' Therefore we ought to confess ourselves chiefly to God even from the heart, for that he chiefly remits sins, without whose absolution little avails the absolution of man. This kind of confession is profitable and good. The authors of the canons say, that although auricular confession made to the priest, be not expressly taught by Christ, yet say they it is taught in that saying which Christ said to the diseased of the leprosy, whom he commanded, 'Go your ways and shew yourselves unto the priests:' because they say the law of cleansing lepers, which was given by Moses, signified the confessions of sins to the priest. And whereas Christ commanded the lepers to shew themselves to the priests, they say, that Christ meant that those that were unclean with the leprosy of sin, should shew their sins to the priests by auricular confession. I marvel much at the authors of the canons; for even from the beginning of their decrees to the end, they ground their sayings upon the old law, which was the law of sin, and death, and not (as witnesses Paul) upon the words of Christ, which are spirit and life. Christ saith, 'The words which I speak unto you, they are the spirit, and they are life.' They ground their sayings in the shadow of the law, and not in the light of Christ, for every evil doer hateth the light, and cometh not unto it, lest his deeds should be reproved; but he that doth the truth cometh into the light, that his works may be made manifest, that they are wrought in God, John iii. 20.

" Now let us pass to the words that Christ spake to the leper; the leper said, 'Lord, if thou wilt, thou canst make me clean. And Jesus stretching forth his hand touched him, saying, I will, be thou clean; and straightways he was cleansed of his leprosy. And Jesus said unto him, See thou tell no man, but go and shew thyself to the priests, and offer the gifts that Moses commanded for a testimony unto them.' This gospel witnesses plainly, that the leper was cleansed only by Christ, and not by the priests, neither did Christ command the leper to shew himself to the priests, for any help of cleansing that he should receive of the priests; but to fulfil the law of Moses, in offering a sacrifice for his cleansing, and for a testimony to the priests, who always of envy accused Christ as a transgressor of the law. For if Christ after he had cleansed the leprosy, had licensed him to communicate with others that were clean, before he had shewed himself cleansed to the priests, then might the priests have accused Christ as a transgressor of the law; because it was a precept of the law, that the leper after he was cleansed, should shew himself to the priests. And they had signs in the book of the law, whereby they might judge whether he were truly cleansed or not. And if he were cleansed, then would the priests offer a gift for his cleansing: and if he were not cleansed, then would they separate him from the company of others that were clean. Seeing every figure ought to be assimilated unto the thing that is figured, I pray you then what agreement is there between the cleansing of lepers by the law, and the confession of sins? By the law the priest knew whether the man were leprous better than he that had the leprosy. In confession the priest knew not the sins of him that confessed, but by his own confession. In the law the priest did not cleanse the leprous. How now therefore ought the priests to cleanse sinners from their sin, and that without them they cannot be cleansed? In the law the priest had certain signs, by the which he could certainly know whether a man were cleansed from his leprosy or not. In confession the priest is not certain of the cleansing of sins, because he is ignorant of his contrition. He knows not also whether he will not sin any more; without which contrition and resolving to sin no more, God has not absolved any sinner. And if God has not absolved a man, without doubt then is he not made clean. And how then is confession figured under the law? Doubtless so it seems to me (under the correction of them that can judge better in the matter) that this law bears rather a figure of excommunication, and reconciliation of him that hath been obstinate in his sin, and is reconciled again. For so it appears by the process of the gospel, that when as the sinner doth not amend for the private correction of his brother, nor for the correction of two or three, neither yet for the public correction of the whole church; then is he to be counted as an heathen man and publican, and as a certain leper to be voided out of the company of all men. Which sinner, notwithstanding, if he shall yet repent, is then to be reconciled, because he is then cleansed from his obstinacy.

" But he who pretends himself to be the chief vicar of Christ, and the high priest, saith that he has power to absolve a pœna et culpa. I do not find how it is founded in the scripture, but of his own authority he enjoins to sinners penance for their sins. And grant that he may absolve them from their sins, yet from the pain (which they call a pœna) he does not simply absolve, as in his indulgences he promises. But if he were charitable, and had such power as he pretends, he would suffer none to lie in purgatory for sin, forsomuch as that pain far exceeds all other pain which we suffer here. What man is there, but if he sees his brother tormented in this world, will not help him and deliver him? Much more ought the pope then to deliver out of pains of purgatory, as well rich as poor alike. And if he sell to the rich his indulgences, doublewise, yea triplewise he seduces them. First, in promising them to deliver them out of the pain from whence he does not, and cannot deliver them, and so makes them falsely to believe that which they ought not to believe. Secondly, he deceives them of their money, which he takes for his indulgences. Thirdly, he seduces them in this, that he promising to deliver them from pain, induces them into grievous punishment indeed, for the heresy of simony, which both of them commit. and therefore are worthy both of great pain to fall upon them ; for so we read that Jesus cast out buyers and sellers out of his temple. Also Peter said unto Simon the first author of this heresy, ' Thy money,' said he, ' perish with thee, because thou thoughtest the gift of God could be purchased for money.' Moreover, whereas Christ saith, ' Freely you have received, freely give.' And whereas on the contrary the pope sells that thing which he has taken, what doubt is there, but that he grievously deserves to be punished, both he that sells and he that buys, for the crime of simony which they commit? Over and besides, by many reasons and authorities of the scripture it may be proved, that he does not absolve a man contrite for his sins, although he absolves him from the guilt.

" But this surprises me, that in his indulgences he promises to absolve men from all manner of deadly sins, and yet cannot absolve a man from debt; for as the debt which we owe to God is of much greater importance than the debt of our brother, if he be able to remit the debt due to God, much more it should seem that he is able to forgive the debt of our brother.

" Another thing there is that I wonder at: the pope shows himself more strict in absolving a priest for not saying, or negligently saying his matins, than for transgressing the commandment of God; considering that the transgression of the commandment of God is much more grievous than the breach of man's commandment.

" For these and many other errors concurring in this matter of the pope's absolutions, blessed be God, and honour be to him for the remission of our sins. And let us firmly believe and know, that he does and will absolve us from our sins, if we be sorry from the bottom of our hearts that we have offended him, having a good purpose and will to offend him no more. And let us be bold to resort to good and discreet priests, who with wholesome discretion and sound counsel can instruct us how to avoid the corruption of sin hereafter; and which, because they are better than we, may pray to God for us; whereby we may both obtain sooner the remission of our sins past, and also may learn better how to avoid the danger of sin to come." (Ex Registro Latino Episc. Hereford.)

And thus much concerning the judgment and doctrine of this Walter for Christian patience, charity, and mercy, which as they are true and infallible notes and marks of true Christianity, so Walter Brute, making comparison herein between Christ and the pope, goes about purposely to declare and manifest, whereby all men may see what contrariety there is between the rule of Christ's teaching, and the proceedings of the pope, between the example and life of the one, and the example of the other. Of which two, as one is altogether given to peace, so is the other on the contrary side as much disposed to war, murder, and bloodshed, as is easy to be seen. Whoso looks not upon the outward shows and pretended words of these Romish popes, but advises and considers their inward practices and secret works, shall easily perceive under the mask of peace what discord and debate they work, who bearing outwardly the meek horns of the lamb mentioned in the Revelations, do bear within the bowels of a wolf, full of cruelty, murder, and bloodshed; which if any do think to be spoken of me contumeliously, would God that man could prove as well the same to be spoken of me not truly. But truth it is, I speak it sincerely, without affection of blind partiality, according to the truth of histories both old and new. Thus under the phrase ' In the name of God, Amen,' how unmercifully does the pope condemn his brother! and while he pretended it was not lawful for him to kill any man; what thousands of men has he killed ? And likewise in this sentence, ' in the bowels of Jesus Christ,' pretending as though he would be a mediator to the magistrate for the party, yet indeed will he be sure to excommunicate the magistrate if he execute not the sentence given, who are the true heretics the Lord when he comes shall judge. But grant them to be heretics whom he condemns as heretics, yet what bowels of mercy are here, where there is nothing but burning, fagotting, drowning, prisoning, chaining, famishing, racking, hanging, tormenting, threatening, reviling, cursing, and oppressing, and no instructing, nor yet impartial hearing of them, what they can say ? The like cruelty also may appear in their wars, if we consider how Pope Urban V., besides the racking and murdering of seven or eight cardinals, set up Henry Spencer, bishop of Norwich, to fight against the French pope. Innocent IV. was in war himself against the Apulians. Likewise Alexander IV., his successor, stirred up the son of King Henry III. to fight against the son of the emperor, Frederick II., for Apulia. Boniface VIII. moved Albert (who stood to be emperor) to drive Philip the French king out of his realm. Gregory IX. excited Lewis the French king three sundry times to mortal war against the Earl Reymond and the city of Toulouse, and Avignon where Lewis the French king died. Honorius III. by strength of war many ways resisted Frederick II. and set out thirty-five gallies against the coasts of the emperor's dominions. The same pope also besieged Ferrara, to pass over the war at Ticinum, with many other battles and conflicts of popes against the Romans, Venetians, and divers other nations. Innocent III. set up Philip the French king to war against King John. What stir Pope Gregory VII., otherwise named Hildebrand, kept against the Emperor Henry IV. is not unknown. And who is able to recite all the wars, battles, and fields, fought by the stirring-up of the pope? These, with many other like examples, considered, caused this Walter Brute to write in this matter, making yet no universal proposition, but that christian magistrates in case of necessity might make resistance in defence of public right. Now he proceeds further to the matter of the sacrament.

" Touching the matter (saith he) of the sacrament of the body and blood of our Lord Jesus Christ, divers men have divers opinions, as the learned do know. As concerning my judgment upon the same, I firmly believe whatever the Lord Jesus taught implicitly or expressly to his disciples, and faithful people to be believed. For he is, as I believe and know, the true bread of God which descended from heaven, and giveth life to the world, of which bread whosoever eateth shall live for ever; as it is in the sixth of John declared. Before the coming of Christ in the flesh, although men did live in body, yet in spirit they did not live, because all men were then under sin, whose souls thereby were dead, from the which death no man by the law, nor with the law, was justified: ' For by the works of the law shall no flesh be justified.' Gal. ii. 16. And again in the same epistle, chap. iii. 11. ' But that no man is justified by the law in the sight of God it is evident : for the just shall live by faith; the law is not of faith; but the man that doeth them shall live in them.' And again in the same chapter, ver. 21, ' If the law had been given, which might have justified, then our righteousness had come by the law. But the scripture hath concluded all under sin, that the promise might be sure by the faith of Jesus Christ to all believers. Moreover, before that faith came, they were kept and concluded all under the law, until the coming of that faith which was to be revealed. For the law was our schoolmaster to bring us to Christ, that we should be justified by faith.' Also the said Paul, Rom. v. 20. saith, ' The law entered that the offence might abound. But where sin abounded, grace did much more abound; that as sin hath reigned unto death, so might grace reign through righteousness unto eternal life, by Jesus Christ our Lord.' Whereby it is manifest that by the faith which we have in Christ, believing him to be the true Son of God which came down from heaven to redeem us from sin, we are justified from sin, and so live by him which is the true bread and meat of the soul. And the bread which Christ gave is his flesh, given for the life of the world. For he being God, came down from heaven, and being truly carnal man, did suffer in the flesh for our sins, which in his divinity he could not suffer. Wherefore like as we believe by our faith that he is true God, so must we also believe that he is a true man, and then do we eat the bread of heaven, and the flesh of Christ. And if we believe that he did voluntarily shed his blood for our redemption, then do we drink his blood.

" And thus except we eat the flesh of the Son of man, and shall drink his blood, we have not eternal life in us, because the flesh of Christ is meat indeed, and his blood is drink indeed; and whosoever eateth the flesh of Christ, and drinketh his blood, abideth in Christ, and Christ in him. John vi. And as in this world the souls of the faithful live, and are refreshed spiritually with this heavenly bread, and with the flesh and blood of Christ; so in the world to come, the same shall live eternally in heaven, refreshed with the deity of Jesus Christ. And in the memory of this refreshment, present in this world, and in the world to come, Christ hath given to us (for eternal blessedness) the sacrament of his body and blood in the substance of bread and wine, as it appears in Matt. xxvi. ' As they were eating, Jesus took bread and blessed it, brake it, and gave it unto his disciples, and said, Take, eat, this is my body: And he took the cup, and gave thanks, and gave it them, saying, Drink ye all of this, this is my blood of the New Testament which is shed for many for the remission of sins.' And Luke in his gospel, chap. xxii. of this matter thus writeth, ' And he took bread, and gave thanks, and brake it, and gave it unto them, saying, This is my body which is given for you, do this in remembrance of me. Likewise also the cup after supper, saying, This cup is the New Testament in my blood, which is shed for you.' That Christ said, this is my body, in showing to them the bread, I firmly believe, and know that it is true: for Christ (forasmuch as he is God) is the very truth itself, and by consequence all that he saith is true. And I believe that the very same was his body, in such wise as he willed it to be his body; for in that he is Almighty, he hath done whatsoever pleased him. And as in Cana of Galilee he changed the water into wine really, so that after the transubstantiation it was wine and not water, so when he said, this is my body, if he would have had the bread really to be transubstantiated into his very body, so that after this changing it should have been his natural body, and not bread as it was before, I know that it must needs have been so; but I find not in the scripture that his will was to have any such real transubstantiation or mutation.

" And as the Lord God Omnipotent, in his perfection essential being the Son of God, exceeds the most pure creature, and yet when it pleased him he took upon him our nature, remaining really God as he was before, and was really made man; so that after this assuming of our substance, he was really very God, and very man; even so, if he would, when he said, this is my body, he could make this to be his body really, the bread still really remaining as it was before. Wherefore he that could make one man to be very God, and very man, could, if he would, make one thing to be really very bread, and his very body. But I do not find it expressed in the scripture, that he wished any such identity or conjunction to be made. And as Christ said, 'I am the true bread,' not changing his essence or being in the essence or substance of bread, but was the same Christ which he was before really, and yet bread by a similitude or figurative speech; so if he would, it might be, when he said, this is my body, that this should really have been the bread as it was before, and sacramentally or memorially to be his body. And this seems to me most nearly to agree to the meaning of Christ, forasmuch as he said, 'Do this in remembrance of me.' Then forasmuch as in the supper it is manifest that Christ gave to his disciples the bread of his body which he brake, to eat with their mouths; in which bread he gave himself also to them, as one in whom they should believe (as to be the food of the soul) and that by faith they should believe him to be their Saviour who took his body, wherein also he wished it to be manifest that he would redeem them from death; so was the bread eaten with the disciples' mouths, that he, being the true bread of the soul, might be in spirit received and eaten spiritually by their faith which believed in him.

"The bread which in the disciples' mouths was chewed, from the mouth passed to the stomach. For, as Christ saith, 'Whatsoever cometh to the mouth, goeth into the belly, and is cast out into the draught.' But that true and very bread of the soul was eaten of the spirit of the disciples, and by faith entered their minds, and abode in their hearts through love. And so the bread broken seemeth unto me to be really the meat of the body, and the bread which it was before, but sacramentally to be the body of Christ; as Paul, 1 Cor. x. 'The bread which we break, is it not the communion of the body of Christ?' So the bread which we break is the communion of the Lord's body. And it is manifest that the heavenly bread is not broken, neither yet is subject to such breaking; therefore Paul calls the material bread which is broken, the body of Christ which the faithful are partakers of. The bread, therefore, changes not its essence, but is bread really, and is the body of Christ sacramentally. Even as Christ is the very vine, abiding really and figuratively the vine: so the temple of Jerusalem was really the material temple, and figuratively it was the body of Christ; because he said, 'Destroy this temple, and in three days I will build it again.' And this spake he of the temple of his body; whereas others understood it to be the material temple, as appeared by their answer. For, said they, 'Forty and seven years was this temple in building, and wilt thou raise it up in three days?'

"The writers of this time and age affirm, that if by the negligence of the priest, the sacrament be so negligently left, that a mouse, or any other beast or vermin eat the same; then let they say, that the sacrament returneth again into the nature and substance of bread.[1] Whereby they must needs confess, that a miracle is as well wrought by the negligence of the priest, as there was made by the consecration of the priest in making the sacrament. For either by the eating of the mouse the body of Christ is transubstantiated into the nature of bread, which is a transubstantiation supernatural; or else this bread is produced by creation out of nothing; and therefore either of these operations is miraculous. Now, considering the varying opinions of the doctors,

and the absurdities which follow, I believe with Paul, that the bread which we break, is the communion of the body of Christ: and as Christ saith, that the bread is the body of Christ for a memorial and remembrance of him. And in such sort as Christ willed the same to be his body, in the same manner and sort do I believe it to be his body.

"But whether we can make the body of Christ, and minister it to the people: or whether priests are divided from the lay people by their knowledge, pre-eminence, and sanctity of life, or else by external signs only. Also, whether the signs of tonsure and other external signs of holiness in priests, are signs of antichrist, or else taught by our Lord Jesus Christ; it remains for me next to speak. And first of the three kinds of the priests. I remember that I have read, the first of them to be Aaronical, legal, and temporal; the second to be eternal and regal according to the order of Melchisedec; the third to be christian. The first of these ceased at the coming of Christ; for St. Paul to the Hebrews saith, The priesthood of Aaron was translated to the priesthood of the order of Melchisedec. The legal sort of priests of Aaron, were separated from the rest of the people by kindred, office, and inheritance. By kindred, for the children of Aaron only were priests. By office, for it only pertained to them to offer sacrifice for the sins of the people, and to instruct the people in the precepts and ceremonies of the law. By inheritance, because the Lord was their portion of inheritance; neither had they any other inheritance amongst their brethren, but those things which were offered to the Lord, as the first-fruits, parts of the sacrifices, and vows; except places for their houses for them and theirs, as appears by Moses' law. The priesthood of Christ much differed from this priesthood, as Paul witnesses to the Hebrews.

"First in kindred, because that our Lord and Saviour Jesus Christ, came of the stock and tribe of Judah; of which tribe none had to do with the altar, and in which tribe nothing at all was spoken of the priests of Moses.

"Secondly, Others were made priests without their oath taken: but he, by an oath, by him which said, 'The Lord sware and will not repent, thou art a priest for ever, after the order of Melchisedec.'

"Thirdly, by duration, for many of them were made priests but during the term of their lives: but he, because he remaineth for ever, hath an eternal priesthood. Wherefore he is able to save us for ever, having by himself access unto God, who ever liveth to make intercession for us.

"The law made also such men priests as had infirmities; but 'Sermo,' (that is the word, which according to the law is the eternal Son and perfect) by an oath.

"The priesthood of Christ also differed from the priesthood of Aaron and the law, in the matter of the sacrifice, and in the place of sacrificing. In the matter of their sacrifices, because they used in their sacrifices strange bodies for their sacrifices, and shed strange blood for the expiation of sins: but he offering himself to God his Father for us, shed his own blood for the remission of our sins. In the place of sacrificing, because that they did offer their sacrifice in the tabernacle, or temple: but Christ suffering death without the gates of the city, offered himself upon the altar of the cross to God his Father, and thence shed his precious blood. In his supping chamber also he blessed the bread, and consecrated the same for his body, and the wine which was in the cup he also consecrated for his blood; delivering the same to his apostles to be done for a commemoration and remembrance of his incarnation and passion. Neither did Jesus enter into the sanctu-

---

(1) The following is still part and parcel of the Rubric or Canon of the Missal:—"If the host when consecrated shall disappear, either by some *accident*, as by the *wind*, or by a *miracle*, or taken away by a *mouse* or any *animal*, and *cannot be found*, then let another be consecrated!" Such is the rule of the Missal, or Mass-Book: and thus, after teaching that the host is Jesus Christ, it supposes the gross absurdity of his disappearing by an

accident — by *wind* — eaten up by a *mouse* or other *animal!* There is nothing in Egyptian idolatry more absurd than this, for it supposes God not able to take care of himself.

They have lately become so ashamed of this, that in the later editions of the Missal they have surreptitiously omitted all mention of the mouse, though they retain the rest of the rule. [ED.]

ary made with man's hands, which be examples and figures of true things, but he entered into heaven itself, that he might appear before the majesty of God for us. Neither doth he offer himself oftentimes, as the chief priest in the sanctuary did with strange blood, (for then should he oftentimes have suffered from the beginning) but now once for all, in the latter end of the world, to destroy sin by his peace-offering hath he appeared. And even as it is decreed, that man once shall die, and then cometh the judgment; so Christ hath been once offered, to take away the sins of many. The second time he shall appear without sin, to those that look for him, to their salvation. For the law having a shadow of good things to come, can never by the image itself of things, (which every year without ceasing they offer by such sacrifices) make those perfect that come thereunto: for otherwise that offering should have ceased: because that such worshippers, being once cleansed from their sins, should have no more conscience of sin. But in these, commemoration is made every year of sin; for it is impossible that by the blood of goats and calves, sins should be purged and taken away. Therefore Christ coming into the world said; sacrifice and oblation thou wouldst not have, but a body hast thou given me; peace-offerings for sins have not pleased thee: then said I, behold I come: in the volume of the book it is written of me, that I should do thy will, O God: saying as above; because thou wouldst have no sacrifices nor burnt offerings for sin, neither dost thou take pleasure in those things that are offered according to the law. Then said I, Behold I come, that I may do thy will, O God. He taketh away the first to establish that which followeth. In which will we are sanctified by the oblation of the body of Jesus Christ once for all. And every priest is ready daily ministering, and oftentimes offering like sacrifices, which can never take away sins. But this Jesus, offering one sacrifice for sin, sitteth for evermore on the right hand of God, expecting the time till his enemies be made his footstool. For by his own only oblation, hath he perfected for evermore those that are sanctified. All these places have I recited which Paul writeth, for the better understanding and declaration of those things I mean to speak. By all which it appears manifestly, how the priesthood of Christ differs from the legal priesthood of Aaron: and by the same it also appears, how the same differs from all other christian priesthood, that imitates Christ. For the properties of the priesthood of Christ, above recited, are found in no other priest, but in Christ alone. Of the third priesthood, that is, the christian priesthood, Christ by his express words, speaks but little, to make any difference between the priest and the rest of the people, nor does he use the name of 'sacerdos' or 'presbyter,' in the gospel. But some he calls disciples, some apostles, whom he sent to baptize and to preach, and in his name to do miracles. He calls them the salt of the earth, in which name wisdom is meant; and he calls them the light of the world, by which good living is signified. For he saith, 'Let your light so shine before men, that they may see your good works, and glorify your Father which is in heaven.' And Paul, speaking of the priests to Timothy and Titus, seems not to me to make any difference between the priests and the other people, but that he would have them to surpass others in knowledge and perfection of life.

"But the fourth priesthood is the Roman priesthood, brought in by the church of Rome; which church makes a distinction between the clergy and the lay-people: and after that the clergy is divided into sundry degrees, as appears in the decretals. This distinction of the clergy from the laity, with the tonsure of clerks, began in the time of Anacletus, as it appears in the chronicles. The decrees of the clergy were afterward invented and distinguished by their officers, and there was no ascension to the degree of the priesthood but by inferior orders and degrees. But in the primitive church it was not so: for immediately after the conversion of some of them to faith and baptism received; they were made priests and bishops; as appears by Anianus, who was a tailor or shoemaker, whom Marcas made to be a bishop. And of many others it was

in like case done, according to the traditions of the church of Rome. Priests are ordained to offer sacrifices, to make supplication and prayers, and to bless and sanctify. The oblation of the priesthood only to priests (as they say) is congruent: whose duties are upon the altar to offer for the sins of the people the Lord's body, which is consecrated of bread. Of which saying I have great marvel, considering St. Paul's words to the Hebrews before recited. If Christ, offering for our sins one oblation for evermore, sits at the right hand of God, and with that one oblation has perfected for evermore those that are sanctified. If Christ evermore sitteth at the right hand of God, to make intercession for us, what need he to leave here any sacrifice for our sins to be daily offered by the priests? I do not find in the scriptures of God, nor of the apostles, that the body of Christ ought to be made a sacrifice for sin; but only as a sacrament and commemoration of the sacrifice passed, which Christ offered upon the altar of the cross for our sins. For it is an absurdity to say that Christ is now every day really offered as a sacrifice upon the altar by the priests; for then the priests should really crucify him upon the altar, which is a thing to be believed by no christian. But even as in his supper, he delivered his body and his blood to his disciples, in memorial of his body that should be crucified on the morrow for our sins: so after his ascension, his apostles used the same (when they brake bread in every house) for a sacrament, and not for a sacrifice, of the body and blood of our Lord Jesus Christ. And by this means were they put in remembrance of the great love of Christ, who so entirely loved us, that he willingly suffered the death for us, and for the remission of our sins. And thus did they offer themselves to God by love, being ready to suffer death for the confession of his name, and for the saving health of his brethren, fulfilling the new commandment of Christ, which said to them, 'A new commandment do I give unto you, that you love one another, as I have loved you.' But when love began to wax cold, or rather to be frozen for cold, through the anguish and anxiety of persecution for the name of Christ, then priests did use the flesh and blood of Christ, instead of a sacrifice. And because many of them feared death, some of them fled into solitary places, not daring to give themselves a sacrifice by death unto God through the confession of his name, and saving health of their brethren: some others worshipped idols, fearing death, as did also the chief bishop of Rome, and many others in different parts of the world. And thus it came to pass, that that which was ordained and constituted for a memorial of the one and only sacrifice, was altered (for want of love) into the reality of the sacrifice itself."

After these things thus discussed, he enters upon another brief treatise concerning women and laymen; whether in defect of the clergy, they may exercise the action of prayer, and administration of sacraments belonging to priests, where he declares the custom received in the pope's church for women to baptize, which, saith he, cannot be without remission of sins; wherefore seeing that women have power by the pope to remit sin, and to baptize, why may not they as well be admitted to minister the Lord's supper, in like cases of necessity? Wherein also he makes relation of Pope Joan the Eighth, a woman pope, proposing certain questions concerning her. All which, for brevity, I omit, proceeding to the ministration of prayer, and blessing of sanctification, appropriate to the office of priests, as follows.

"Furthermore, as touching the function and office of praying and blessing, whereto priests seem to be ordained (to omit here the question whether women may pray in churches, in lack of other meet persons) it remaineth now also to prosecute. Christ, being desired of his disciples to teach them to pray, gave them the common prayer both to men and women, to which prayer in my estimation, no other is to be compared. For in that, first, the whole honour due unto the Deity is comprehended. Secondly, whatsoever is necessary for us, both for the time present, or past, or for time to come, is there desired and prayed for. He informs us besides to pray secretly, and also briefly: secretly to enter into our close chamber, and there in secret he wills us to pray unto his Father. And saith moreover, ' When ye pray, use not vain repetitions, as the heathen do, for they think they will be heard for their much speaking. Be ye not therefore like to them.' By which doctrine he calls us away from the errors of the heathen gentiles; from whom proceed these superstitious manner of arts, (or rather of ignorances) as necromancy, the art of divination, and other species of conjuration, not unknown to them that are learned: for these necromancers believe one place to be of greater virtue than another; there to be heard sooner than in another. Like as Balaam, being hired to curse the people of God by his art of soothsaying or charming, when he could not accomplish his purpose in one place, he removed to another; but he in the end was deceived of his desire. For he, intending first to curse them, was not able to curse them whom the Lord blessed, so that his curse could not hurt any of all that people. After like sort, the necromancers turn their face to the East, as to a place more apt for their prayers. Also the necromancers believe that the virtue of the words of the prayer, and the curiosity thereof, causes them to bring to effect that which they seek after; which is also another point of infidelity, used much of charmers, sorcerers, enchanters, soothsayers, and such like. Out of the same art (I fear) proceedeth the practice of exorcising, whereby devils and spirits be conjured to do that whereunto they are inforced by the exorcist. Also whereby other creatures likewise are exorcised or conjured, so that by the virtue of their exorcism they may have their power and strength exceeding all natural operation.

"In the church of Rome many such exorcisms and conjurations are practised, and are called of them benedictions, or hallowings. But here I ask of these exorcisers, whether they believe the things and creatures so exorcised and hallowed, have that operation and efficacy given them which they pretend? If they so believe, every child may see that they are deceived. For holy water being of them exorcised or conjured, hath no such power in it, neither can have, which they in their exorcism do command. For there they enjoin and command, that wheresoever that water is sprinkled, all vexation or infestation of the unclean spirit should avoid, and not that no pestilent spirit there should abide, &c. But it is most plain that no water, be it never so holy, can have any such power so to do, as it is commanded, to wit, to be an universal remedy to expel all diseases.

"I would ask this of these exorcists; whether in their commanding, they do conjure or adjure the things conjured to be of an higher virtue and operation, than their own nature gives; or else whether they in their prayers desire of God, that he will infuse into them that virtue, which they require? If they in their commanding do so believe, then do they believe that they have that power in them to which the inferior power of the thing exorcised must obey, in receiving that which is commanded. And so doing they are much more deceived, forasmuch as they see themselves, that they who are so authorised to the office of exorcising, say to the devil being conjured, 'Go, and he goeth not; and to another, Come, and he cometh not;' and many things else they command the inferior spirit their subject to do, and he does it not. So in like case, when they pray to God to make the water to be of such virtue, that it may be to them health of mind and body, and that it may be able to expel every unclean spirit, and to chase away all manner of distemper and pestilence of the air (being an unreasonable petition asked, and displeasing to God) it is to be feared lest their benediction, their hallowing and blessing is changed into cursing, according to that saying that follows: ' and now, O ye priests, this commandment is for you; If ye will not hear, and if ye will not lay it to heart, to give glory to my name, saith the Lord of Hosts, I will send a curse upon you, and I will curse your blessings.' Mal. ii. 1, 2.

How many things are blessed, or hallowed in the church, that in hallowing thereof displease God, and are accursed? And therefore according to the saying of St. James, ' they ask and receive not, because they ask amiss, that they may consume it on their lusts.' Let a man behold the blessing or hallowing of their fire, water, incense, wax, bread, wine, the church, the altar, the churchyard, ashes, bells, copes, palms, oil, candles, salt, the hallowing of the ring, the bed, the staff, and of many such like things; and I believe that a man shall find out many errors of the heathen magicians, witches, soothsayers and charmers. And notwithstanding the ancient magicians in their books command those that are conjurors, that they in any wise live devoutly (for otherwise, as they say, the spirits will not obey their commandments, and conjurations) yet the Roman conjurors impute it to the virtue of the holy words, because it is they that work, and not the holiness of the conjurors: how comes it to pass that they say, the things consecrated by a cursed and vicious priest, should have as great virtue in pronouncing (as they say) the holy and mystical words, as if they were pronounced by a priest never so holy? But I marvel that they say so, reading this saying in the acts of the apostles: because the charmers pronouncing the name of Jesus (that is above all names) would have healed those that were possessed with devils, and said; ' We adjure you by Jesus, whom Paul preacheth.' And the possessed with devils answered, ' Jesus I know, and Paul I know, but who are ye?' And he beat the exorcists.

"And now considering this and many such like things, I marvel wherefore the vicious priests do sell their prayers and blessings dearer (as also their masses and trentals of masses) than those that be devout laymen, and holy women: who with all their heart desire to flee from vice, and take hold of virtue. Forasmuch as God in divers places of the scripture doth promise that he will not hear sinners and wicked persons. Neither should he seem to be just, if he should sooner hear the prayers of his enemies, than of his faithful friends. How, I pray you, shall a sinful priest deliver another man from sin by his prayers, or else from the punishment of sin, when he is not able to deliver himself by his prayer from sin? What then doth God so much accept in the mass of a vicious priest, that for his mass, his prayer or oblation, he might deliver any man either from sin, or from the pain due for sin? No, but because Christ once offered himself for our sins, and now sitteth on the right hand of God the Father, always shewing unto him what and how great things he hath suffered for us. And every priest always makes mention in his mass of this oblation. Neither do we this that we might bring the same oblation into the remembrance of God, because that he always in his presence sees the same; but that we should have in remembrance this so great love of God, that he would give his own Son to die for our sins, that he might cleanse and purify us from all our sins. What, doth it please God, that the remembrance of so great love is made by a priest, who loves sin more than God? Or how can any prayer of such a priest please God, in what holy place soever he be, or what holy vestments soever he put on, or what holy prayers soever he makes? And whereas Christ and his apostles do command the preaching of the word of God; the priests be now more bound to celebrate the mass, and more straightly bound to say the canonical hours; whereat I cannot but greatly marvel. For why? To obey the precepts of men more than the commandments of God, is in effect to honour man as God, and to bestow the sacrifice upon man which is due unto God, and this is also spiritual fornication. How therefore are priests bound at the commandment of man to leave the preaching of the word of God, at whose commandment they are not bound to leave the celebration of the mass, or singing of matins? Therefore, priests ought not at the commandment of any man to leave the preaching of the word of God, which they are bound both by divine and apostolical precepts.

"Do priests therefore sin or not, who bargain for money to pray for the soul of any dead man? It is well known that Jesus did whip those that were buyers and sellers out of the temple, saying; ' My house shall be called the house of prayer, but you have made it a den of thieves.' Truly he cast out such merchants from out of the church, because of their sins. Whereupon Jerome upon this text saith ; Let the priest be diligent and take good heed in this church, that they turn not the house of God into a den of thieves. He doubtless is a thief who seeks gain by religion, and by a shew of holiness studies to find occasion of merchandise. Peter the apostle said to Simon Magus, ' Thy money perish with thee, because thou hast thought that the gifts of God may be bought for money.' Therefore the spiritual gifts of God ought not to be sold.

"Verily, prayer is the spiritual gift of God, as is also the preaching of the word of God, or the laying on of hands, or the administration of other the sacraments. Christ, sending forth his disciples to preach, said unto them ; ' Heal ye the sick, cast out devils, raise the dead, freely ye have received, freely give.' If the priest have power to deliver souls in purgatory from grievous pains, without doubt he has received that power freely from God. How therefore can he sell his act, unless he resist the commandments of God, of whom he has received that authority ? This truly cannot be done without sin, as it is against the commandment of God. How plainly spake Christ to the pharisees and priests, saying ; ' Woe unto you scribes and pharisees, hypocrites, because ye devour widows' houses, and for a pretence make long prayers, therefore shall ye receive greater damnation.' Wherein I pray you do our pharisees and priests differ from them ? Do not our priests devour widows' houses and possessions, that by their long prayers they might deliver the souls of their husbands from the grievous pains of purgatory ? How many lordships I pray you have been bestowed upon the monastic men and women to pray for the dead, that they might deliver those dead men from the pain (as they said) that they suffer in purgatory, grievously tormented and vexed ? If their prayers and speaking of holy words shall not be able to deliver themselves from pain, unless they have good works ; how shall other men be delivered from pain by their prayers, who while they lived, gave themselves over to sin ? Yea, peradventure those lordships or lands, which they gave to the priests to pray for them, they themselves have gotten by might from other faithful men, unjustly, and violently : and the canons do say, that sin is not forgiven, till the thing taken away wrongfully be restored : how then shall they be able (who unjustly possess such lordships or lands) to deliver them by their prayers from pain, who have given to them these lordships or lands, seeing God from the beginning has hated all extortion in his burnt sacrifices ? ' Not every one that saith unto me, Lord, Lord, shall enter into the kingdom of Heaven : but he that doeth the will of my Father which is in Heaven.' And again, ' not the hearers of the law, but the doers of the law shall be justified.'

"If therefore the words of him that prays do not deliver himself from sin, nor from the pain of sin, how do they deliver other men from sin or from the pain of sin, when no man prays more earnestly for another man, than for himself ? Therefore many are deceived in buying or selling of prayers, as in the buying of pardons, that they might be delivered from pain ; when commonly they pay dearer for the prayers of the proud and vicious prelates, than for the prayers of devout women and devout men of the lay people. But out of doubt, God does not regard the person of him that prays, nor the place in which he prays, nor his apparel, nor the curiousness of his prayer, but the humility and godly affection of him that prays. Did not the pharisee and the publican go up into the temple to pray ? The publican's prayer for his humility and godly affection is heard. But the pharisee's prayer for his pride and arrogancy is contemned. Consider that neither the person, nor the place, nor the state, nor the curiousness of his prayer helps the pharisee : because the publican not thinking himself worthy to lift up his eyes to Heaven, for the multitude of his sins (saying, O God, be merciful unto me a sinner) is justified in his humility, and his prayer is heard. But the pharisee boasting in his righteousness is despised, because God thrusts down the proud, and exalteth the

humble and those that be meek. The rich glutton also that was clothed with purple and fine linen, and fared sumptuously every day, prayed unto Abraham, and is not heard, but it is buried in pains and torments of Hell fire. But Lazarus, who lay begging at his gate, (being full of sores) is placed in the bosom of Abraham. Behold that neither the richness of his apparel, nor the deliciousness of his banquets, nor the gorgeousness of his estate, neither the abundance of his riches, helps any thing to prefer the prayers or petitions of the rich glutton, nor yet diminish his torments, because that mighty men in their mightiness shall suffer torments mightily. How dare any man by composition demand or receive any thing of another man for his prayers ? If he believe that he can by his prayer deliver his brother from grievous pain, he is bound by charity to relieve his brother with his prayers although he be not hired : but if he will not pray unless he be hired, then has he no love at all. What therefore helps the prayer of him who abides not in charity ? Therefore let him first take compassion on himself by prayer, that he may come into charity, and then he shall be the better able to help others. If he believe not, or if he stands in doubt whether he shall be able to deliver his brother by his prayer, wherefore does he make with him an assured bargain, and take his money, and yet knows not whether he shall relieve him ever a whit the more, or not, from his pain ? I fear lest the words of the prophet are fulfilled, saying, From the least to the most, all men apply themselves to covetousness ; and from the prophet to the priest, all work deceitfully. For the poor priests excuse themselves concerning this selling of their prayers, saying, the young cock learns to crow from the old cock. For, he saith, that the pope himself, in stalling of bishops and abbots, takes the first-fruits : in the placing or bestowing of benefices he always taketh somewhat, especially if the benefices be great. And he selleth pardons or bulls, and to speak more plain, he takes money for them. Bishops in giving orders, in hallowing churches and churchyards, do take money : in ecclesiastical correction they take money for the mitigation of penance : in the grievous offences of convicted persons, money is required, and caused to be paid. Abbots, monks, and other religious men that have possession, will receive no man into their fraternity, or make them partakers of their spiritual suffrages, unless he bestow somewhat upon them, or promise them somewhat. Curates and vicars having sufficient livings by the tithes of their parishioners, yet in dirges and years' minds, in hearing confessions, in weddings and buryings, require and have money. The friars also of the four orders of beggars, who think themselves to be the most perfect men of the church, take money for their prayers, confessions, and buryings of the dead ; and when they preach, they believe that they shall have either money or some other thing worth money. Wherefore then are the poor priests blamed ? ought not they to be held excused, although they take money for their prayers by composition ? Truly (me thinketh) that this excuse by other men's sins does not excuse them, forasmuch as to heap one mischief upon another's head, is no sufficient discharge. I would to God all the buyers and sellers of spiritual suffrages would with the eyes of their heart behold the ruin of the great city, and the fall of Babylon, and that which they shall say after that fall. Does not the prophet say, ' And the merchants of the earth shall weep and mourn for her, for no man buyeth their merchandise, any more, the merchandise of gold and silver, and precious stone, and of pearl, and fine linen, and purple and silk.' Rev. xviii. 1. And again, he saith ; ' The merchants of these things which were made rich by her, shall stand afar off for the fear of her torment, weeping and wailing, and saying, alas ! alas ! that great city, that was clothed in fine linen and purple and scarlet, and decked with gold and precious stones and pearls, for in one hour so great riches are come to nought.' Rev. xviii. 15. And again ; ' And they cast dust upon their heads, and cried out, weeping and wailing, and saying ; alas ! alas ! that great city, wherein were made rich all that had ships in the sea, by reason of her costliness !, for in one hour is she made desolate.' Rev. xviii. 19.

"This Babylon, this great city, is the city of Rome.

Because the angel which shewed to St. John the destruction of the mighty harlot sitting upon many waters, with whom the kings of the earth have committed fornication, and all they which dwell upon the earth, are made drunk with the wine of her fornication, said unto him, 'And the woman which thou sawest, is the great city that reigneth over the kings,' &c. And indeed in the days of St. John the whole world was subject to the temporal empire of the city of Rome, and afterwards it was subject to the spiritual empire or dominion of the same. But touching the temporal government of the city of Rome, it is fallen already: and so the other also, for the multitude of her spiritual fornication, shall fall. The emperors of the city gave themselves to idolatry, and would have men honour them as gods, and put all those to death that refused such idolatry, and by the cruelty of their torments all infidels got the upper hand.

"Hereupon by the image of Nabuchadnezzar, the empire of the Romans is likened to iron, which beats together, and has the mastery of all metals. And in the vision of Daniel, wherein he saw the four winds of heaven to fight in the main sea ; and four very great beasts coming out of the sea ; the kingdom of the Romans is likened to the fourth terrible and marvellous beast, which had great iron teeth ; eating and destroying, and treading the rest under his feet : and this beast had ten horns, and as Daniel saith, he shall speak words against the most high, and shall tear with his teeth the saints of the most high : and he shall think that he may be able to change times and laws, and they shall be delivered into his power, until a time, times, and half-a time. In the Revelations, St. John saw a beast coming out of the sea, having seven heads and ten horns, and power was given to him to continue forty-two months. So long time endured the empire of the Romans; that is to say, from the beginning of Julius Cesar, which was the first emperor of the Romans, unto the end of Fredericus, which was the last emperor of the Romans. Under this empire Christ suffered, and other martyrs also suffered for his name's sake. And here is fallen Rome as Babylon (which is all one) according to the manner of speaking in the Revelation, as touching the temporal power of governing. And thus shall she fall also touching the spiritual power of governing, for the multitude of iniquities and spiritual fornication, and merchandise that are committed by her in the church.

"The feet of the image which Nebuchadnezzar saw, betoken the empire of Rome, and part of them were of iron, and part of clay and earth. The part that was of iron fell, and the power thereof vanished away, because the power thereof was at an end after certain months. That part of clay and earth yet endures, but it shall vanish away by the testimony of the prophets: whereupon St. John says in the Revelation ; after that, he saw the part made of iron rising out of the sea, to which each people, tribe, and tongue submitted themselves. And he saw another beast coming out of the earth, which had two horns, like to the horns of a lamb, and he spake like a dragon, and he vanquished the first beast in his sight.

This beast as seems to me, betokens the clay and earthen part of the feet and image, because he came out of the earth. For that by earthly help he is made the high and chief priest of the Romans in the church of Christ, and so from below he ascended on high. But Christ descended from heaven, because he who was God, and author of every creature, became man ; and he that was Lord of Lords, was made in the shape of a servant. And although in the heavens the company of angels minister unto him, he himself ministered or served in earth, that he might teach us humility, by which a man ascends into heaven, even as by pride a man goes down into the bottomless pit. This beast has two horns most like a lamb, because he challenges to himself both the priestly and kingly power above all other here in earth. The Lamb, that is, Christ, is king for ever upon the kingly seat of David, and he is a priest for ever after the order of Melchisedec ; but his kingdom is not of this world : but the kingdom of this beast is of this world, because those that be under him fight for him. And as Jesus is Christ two manner of ways, because that 'Christ' is as much as to say

'anointed'; he verily was anointed king and anointed priest: so this beast saith, that he is chief king and priest. Wherefore does he call himself Christ? Because that Christ, knowing that afore, said, 'Many shall come in my name, saying, I am Christ, and shall deceive many.' And thus because he is both king and priest, he challenges to himself the double sword, that is, the temporal sword and spiritual sword. The temporal sword is in his right hand, and his spiritual sword is in his right eye, by the testimony of Zechariah. But he speaks subtilly like a dragon, because that by the testimony of Christ he shall deceive many, as the book of Revelations witnesses. He did great wonders that he might make more fire to come from heaven to the earth in the sight of men, that he might deceive those that dwell upon the earth, because of the wonders, that are permitted him to do in the sight of the beast, and he overcame the first beast which ascended out of the sea. For that beast challenged to himself authority of government of the whole world. He has put to death and tormented those that resist his commandments, and would be honoured as a god upon the earth. The bishop of Rome says that the whole world ought to be in subjection to him ; those that are disobedient to his commandments he puts in prison, and to death if he can : if he cannot, he excommunicates them, and commands them to be cast into the devil's dungeon. But he has no power over the body, much less has he power over the soul. And truly his excommunication, or the excommunication of any priest under him, shall at that time little hurt him that is excommunicated, so that the person of him that is excommunicated be not first excommunicated of God through sin.

"This one thing is certain, that none in the church ought to sell spiritual merchandize (of which things we have spoken before) unless he have the mark of the beast. My counsel is, let the buyer beware of those marks; because that after the fall of Babylon, 'If any man worship the beast and his image, and receive his mark in his forehead or in his hand, the same shall drink of the wine of the wrath of God, which is poured out without mixture into the cup of his indignation, and he shall be tormented in fire and brimstone in the sight of the holy angels, and in the sight of the Lamb : and the smoke of their torments ascendeth up for ever and ever : and they have no rest day nor night, who worship the beast and his image, and whosoever receiveth the mark of his name.' The beast doubtless recompenses his friends with his small reward ; that is, with great temporal gifts and benefices; with a mean reward, that is, with great spiritual gifts, in authority of blessing, loosing, binding, praying, and exercising other spiritual works; and with his greatest reward, which after that they be dead, makes them to be honoured in earth among the saints. The number of his name, according to the opinion of some men, is, Dux Cleri, the 'captain of the clergy,' because by that name he is named, and makes his name known, and that name is 666. Rev. xiii. 18.

"This is my opinion of the beast ascending out of the earth, and shall be until such time as I shall be of the same beast better instructed. And although this beast signifies the Roman bishops ; yet the other cruel beast ascending out of the sea, signifies the Roman emperors. And although the dragon being a cruel beast, and the false prophet giving the mark, must be thrown into the lake of fire and brimstone to be tormented for ever ; I would have no man to judge, but I leave such things altogether to the final judgment of Christ to be determined. But Martin the Pope's confessor, who makes the chronicle of the emperors and the popes, recites many errors of the popes, more horrible and abominable than of the emperors. For he speaks of the idolatrous, heretical, simoniacal popes, and popes that were murderers, that used necromancy and witchcraft, that were evil livers, and defiled with all kind of vice. But I have partly declared how the pope's law is contrary to Christ's law, and how he saith, 'That he is the chief vicar of Christ in earth ;' and in his deeds is contrary to Christ, and forsakes both his doctrine and life. I cannot see who else may be so well antichrist, and a seducer of the people. For there is not a greater pestilence than a familiar enemy.

"As concerning idols, and the worshipping of them, I think of them, as Moses, Solomon, Isaiah, Jeremiah, and the rest of the prophets did, who speak against the making of images, as also the worshipping of images. And faithful David, full of the Spirit of God, saith, 'Let all them be confounded that worship images, and that rejoice in idols.' And again he saith, 'Let them be made like unto them that make them, and all such as put their trust in them' Wherefore I pray God that this evil come not upon me, which is the curse of God pronounced by David the prophet. Nor will I be, by God's grace, either a maker, or a worshipper of images."

After all the aforesaid things were exhibited and given by Walter Brute, to the bishop of Hereford; he further appointed to Walter, the 3d day of October, at Hereford, to hear his opinion. Which third day now at hand, being Friday, (A. D. 1393)., Walter Brute appeared before him, sitting in commission in the cathedral church of Hereford, about six o'clock; having for his assistants in the same place, divers prelates and abbots, and twenty bachelors of divinity, whereof twelve were monks, and two doctors of the law. Amongst these was Nicholas Hereford accompanied with many other prelates and worshipful men, and wise graduates in sundry faculties, charged Walter about his writings, and the contents therein: they were earnest in picking out of those writings his heresies, and in shewing his schisms, sundry errors, and other things. Now, after that they continued all that day, and the two days following in their informations and examinations; Walter Brute submitted himself to the church, as appears in a scroll written in the English tongue, as follows:

"I, Walter Brute, submit myself principally to the gospel of Jesus Christ, and to the determination of holy Kirk, and to the general councils of holy Kirk. And to the sentence and determination of the four doctors of holy writ; that is, Augustine, Ambrose, Jerome, and Gregory. And I meekly submit me to your correction, as a subject ought to his bishop."

Which scroll Walter Brute read with a loud and intelligible voice, at the cross in the church-yard on Monday, the sixth day of October, before the sermon, in presence of the bishop of Hereford and others, as also barons, knights, and noblemen, and clergy, and also a great multitude of people. After which Thomas Crawlay made a sermon, and took for his text the words of the apostle to the Romans, xi. 20.

Out of these declarations and writings of Walter Brute, the bishops, with the monks and doctors above rehearsed, gathered certain articles, to the number of thirty-seven, which they sent to the university of Cambridge to be confuted, to two learned men, Master Colwill and Master Newton, bachelors of divinity. Masters Colwill and Newton both laboured in the matter, to the utmost of their cunning, in replying to the said thirty-seven articles.

Besides them also, William Woodford a friar (who wrote likewise against the articles of Wickliff) labouring in the same cause, made a solemn and a long treatise, compiling the articles of Brute, to the number of nine-and-twenty.

I do not find what afterwards became of this Walter Brute: but it is probable that he for this time escaped. I here add certain writings and documents connected with his history.

The bull of Pope Boniface IX., against the Lollards.

"Boniface, bishop, servant of the servants of God, to the reverend brother, John, bishop of Hereford, sendeth greeting, and apostolical benediction. We mean to write unto our well-beloved son in Christ (Richard, the renowned king of England) in form inclosed within these presents. Therefore we will and command your brotherhood, that as much as ye may ye study and endeavour yourself to exhort and induce the same king to do those things which we have written unto him as it is said

before. And notwithstanding that now many a day you ought to have done it of yourself, and not to look that we should persuade you to that effect by us written; you may proceed as well by our authority, as by your own, forasmuch as it was given you before; that hereafter we may know effectually by your diligence, what zeal your devotion beareth unto the catholic faith, and to the conserving of the ecclesiastical honour, and also to the execution of your pastoral office.

"Given at Rome at St. Peter's, the 15th kalends of October, the sixth year of our bishop-like dignity."

The bull to the renowned prince, Richard, by the grace of God, king of England and of France, which was inclosed in the above, and there mentioned.

"To our well beloved son in Christ, Richard, the noble king of England, we send greeting, &c. It grieveth us from the bottom of our hearts, and our holy mother the church in all places through Christendom lamenteth. We understand that there be certain heresies sprung, and do without any condign restraint range at their own liberty, to the seducing of the faithful people, and do every day with overmuch liberty enlarge their undiscreet bounds. But how much the more carefully we labour for the preservation both of you and your famous kingdom, and also the purity of the faith, and do with much more ardent desire long that the prosperous state of the same should be preserved and enlarged; the sting of greater sorrow so much the more penetrates and molests us, as we see (alas the while!) in our time, and under the regal presidence of your most christian government, a certain crafty and hare-brain sect of false christians grow and increase in your kingdom, who call themselves the poor men of the treasury of Christ and his disciples, and whom the common people by a more sound name call Lollards, (as a man would say, 'withered darnel'), according as their sins require; and perceive that they may wax strong, and as it were prevail against the diocesans of some places, and other governors, as they meet together, not courageously addressing themselves against them as they ought to do (whereof chiefly and not undeservedly I give them admonition) for that they take thereby the more bolder presumption and courage among the unlearned people. And forasmuch as those whom we cannot call men, but the damnable shadows or ghosts of men, do rise up against the sound faith, and holy universal church of Rome; and that very many of them being indifferently learned, which little learning (to the confusion and eternal damnation of some of them) they got sitting upon their mother's lap the said church of Rome, do rise up or inveigh against the determination of the holy fathers, with too much presumptuous boldness, to the subversion of the whole ecclesiastical order and estate; and have not been afraid, nor are yet afraid, publicly to preach very many erroneous, detestable, and heretical articles, because they are not put to silence, reproved, driven out, rooted out, or otherwise punished by any that has authority and the fear and love of God. And also they are not afraid openly to write the same articles, and so being written to deliver them to your kingly parliament, and obstinately to affirm the same. The venemous and disdainful recital of which articles, upon good advise, at this present we pass over, lest the sufferance of such sensuality might chance to renew the wound that reason may heal. Yet notwithstanding, lest so great and contagious an evil should escape unpunished, and that without deserved vexation; and also that it might not get more heart, and wax more strong, we therefore (according to our office and duty, where there is such negligence and sluggishness of our prelates who are present where this thing is) do commit and give in commandment to our reverend brethren the archbishops of Canterbury and York by our letters; that they stand up in the power of God against this pestilent and contagious sect, and that they promptly persecute the same in form of law; root out and destroy those, that advisedly and obstinately refuse to withdraw their foot from the same stumbling-block, any restraint to the contrary notwithstanding. But because the assistance, counsel, favour, and aid of your kingly estate and highness are requisite to the execution of the premises; we require, exhort. and beseech the same your princely highness by the bowels of the mercy of Jesus Christ, by his holy faith, by your own salvation, by the benefit that to all men is common, and by the prosperity assured to every man and woman, that not only your kingly severity may readily shew, and cause to be shewed to our archbishops and their commissaries, convenient aid and favour, as otherwise also to cause them to be assisted; but that also you will enjoin your magistrates and justices of assize and peace, more straightly, that of their own good wills they execute the authority committed to them, with all severity against such damned men, according as they are bound by the office which they are put in trust with; against those, I mean, which have determined obstinately to defile themselves in their malice and sins, to expel, banish, and imprison, and there to keep them, till condign sentence shall pronounce them worthy to suffer punishment. For your kingly wisdom sees that such as they not only deceive poor simple souls (or at the least do what they can to deceive them) but also bring their bodies to destruction, and further prepare confusion and ruinous fall to their temporal lords. Go too, therefore, my sweet son, and endeavour yourself to work so in this matter, as undoubtedly we trust you will: that as this firebrand (burning and flaming overmuch) began under your presidence or government: so under your severe judgment and virtuous diligence, might, favour, and aid, there may not remain one spark hid under the ashes, but that it be utterly extinguished, and speedily put out.

"Given at our palace of St. Peter's at Rome, the 15th of the kalends of October, in the sixth year of our pontificality."

The king's commission.

"Richard, by the grace of God, king of England, and of France, and lord of Ireland, to all those unto whom these present letters shall come, greeting. Know ye, that whereas lately at the instance of the reverend father, William, archbishop of Canterbury, metropolitan of all England, and legate of the apostolical see, we for the redress and amendment of all those who would obstinately preach or maintain, publicly or privily, any conclusions of the holy scripture, repugnant to the determination of our holy mother the church, and notoriously redounding to the subversion of the catholic faith, or containing any heresy or error, within the province or bishoprick of Canterbury, have by our special letters patent. in the zeal of the faith, given authority and licence unto the foresaid archbishop, and to all and singular his suffragans, to arrest all and every of them that will preach or maintain any such conclusions, wherever they may be found, and to commit them either to their own prisons, or any other at their own pleasure, and to keep them in the same, until they repent them of the errors and depravities of those heresies, or till by us or by our council it should be otherwise determined, that is to say, to every one of them and their ministers throughout their cities and diocese. And now the reverend father in God, John, bishop of Hereford, hath for a certainty informed us, that although the same bishop hath according to justice convinced a certain fellow, named William Swinderby, pretending himself to be chaplain, and one Stephen Bell, a learned man, and hath pronounced them heretics, and excommunicate, and false informers among the common people, and hath declared the same by the definitive sentence of the aforesaid bishop, they have presumed to affirm and preach openly, in divers places within the diocese of Hereford, many conclusions or naughty opinions notoriously redounding to the subversion of the catholic sound faith, and tranquillity of our kingdom: the same bishop, notwithstanding, neither by the ecclesiastical censures, neither by the force and strength of our commission, was able to revoke the foresaid William and Stephen, nor yet to bridle the malice and indurate contumacy of them; for that they, after that they were convicted of such heretical pravity by the same bishop (to the intent they might delude his judgment and justice) conveyed themselves into

the borders of Wales, with such as were their favourers and accomplices, keeping themselves hid, to whom the force of our letters does in nowise extend. Whereupon the said bishop has made supplication to us, that we will vouchsafe to provide a sufficient remedy in that behalf. We, therefore, who always, by the help of Almighty God, are defenders of the faith, willing to withstand such presumptuous and perverse enterprises by the most safe way and means, give and commit full power and authority to the aforesaid bishop, and to his ministers, by the tenor of these presents, to arrest or take, or cause to be arrested or taken, the aforesaid William and Stephen, in any place within the city and diocese of Hereford, and our dominion of Wales, with all the speed that may be, and to commit them either to our prison, or else to the prison of the same bishop, or any other prison at their pleasure, if such need be, and there to keep them safe. And afterwards, unless they will obey the commandments of the church, with diligence to bring them before us and our council, or else cause them to be brought, that we may determine for their further punishment, as we shall think it requisite and convenient to be done by the advice of our council, for the defence and preservation of the catholic faith. And that the aforesaid William and Stephen, being succoured by the aid of their favourers, should not be able to fly or escape to their accustomed starting holes, and that the sharpness of their pains so aggravated, may give them sufficient cause to return to the lap again of their holy mother, the church; we straightly charge and command all and singular our sheriffs, bailiffs, barons, and all other our officers in the city and diocese of Hereford, and in any other places being within our dominion of Wales, by the tenor of these presents, that from time to time (where they think it most meet) they cause it openly to be proclaimed in our name, that none of what state, degree, pre-eminence, kind, or other condition he shall be, do cherish openly or secretly the aforesaid William and Stephen, until the time that they repent them of their heresies and errors, and shall be reconciled unto the holy church of God; neither that any person or persons, be believers, favourers, or receivers, defenders, or in any case wittingly instructors of the said William or Stephen, or any other of the residue of the heretics that are to be convinced, upon the forfeiture of all that ever they have. And that also they giving their attendance be obedient and answerable to the aforesaid bishop and his deputies in this behalf, for the execution of the premises; and that they certify us and our council distinctly and plainly, from time to time, of the names of all and singular persons, who shall be found culpable in this behalf, under their seals. In witness whereof we have caused these our letters patent to be made.

"Witness ourself at Westminster, the ninth day of March, in the fifteenth year of our reign.

Farrington."

Another letter of the King against Walter Brute.

"Richard, by the grace of God king of England, and of France, and Lord of Ireland, to his beloved and faithful John Chaundos, knight; John Eynfore, knight; Renold de la Bere, knight; Walter Deveros, knight; Thomas de la Bare, knight; William Lucy, knight; Leonard Hakeluke, knight; and to the mayor of the city of Hereford, to Thomas Oldcastle, Richard Nash, Roger Wygmore, Thomas Waylwayne, John Skydmore, John Up-Harry, Henry Morton, and to the sheriff of Hereford, sendeth salutations.

"Forasmuch as it is advertised us, that one Walter Brute, and other such children of iniquity, have damnably holden, affirmed, and preached, certain articles and conclusions, being notoriously repugnant against the holy scripture (of the which some of them as heresies, and the rest as errors are finally by the church condemned), and that in divers places within the diocese of Hereford, and parts near adjoining, both privately, openly, and obstinately, which thing we perceive not only to redound to the subversion, in a manner, of the catholic faith, which as well we as other catholic princes ought of duty to maintain, but also to forewarn us of the subversion of our faithful diocesans; and that the said bishop, upon the good deliberation and advice of a great number of doctors in divinity, and other learned and skilful men in the scriptures, of special devotion, according to his bounden duty, purposed to begin and make divers and sundry processes by law to be sent unto the aforesaid Walter and his accomplices to appear personally before him and other the doctors aforesaid in the cathedral church of Hereford, the morrow after the translation of St. Thomas of Hereford next ensuing, and to proceed in the same place against the same Walter, in the aforesaid articles and conclusions, for the amendment of his soul; and that they now afresh (because that the said Walter and others of their retinue, cleaving and confederating with him, might not suffer condign pains according to their demerits) endeavour themselves to make void and frustrate the said godly purpose of the same bishop, in such correction and execution as should have been done, and with force do resist, and prevent the same with all the power they may, to the great contempt of us and of our crown, and to the breaking and hurting of our peace, and pernicious example of others: we do appoint you, and every one of you, immediately as soon as this our commission shall be delivered unto you, in our behalf and name, to make open proclamation in the diocese and parts aforesaid, where ye shall think it most meet and convenient: that no man be so hardy henceforth, of what state or condition soever he shall be, within the diocese and parts aforesaid, upon pain of forfeiture of all that ever he hath, to make or levy any conventicles, assemblies, or confederacies, by any colour, or that they presume to attempt or procure any other thing, whereby our peace may be hurt or broken, or that the same bishops and doctors aforesaid may be by any means molested or hindered in the execution of such correction as is to be done, according to the canonical sanctions, and to arrest all those whom ye shall find, or take offending in this behalf, or that keep themselves in any such conventicles; and that they, being committed to prison, be there kept, till you shall have other commandment from us and from our council for their deliverance; and that ye distinctly and plainly certify us, and our said council, of all your doing in this behalf under your seals, or else the seals of some of you. And therefore we straightly charge and command you, and every one of you, that ye diligently attend upon the premises, and that in your deeds ye execute the same with all diligence and careful endeavour in the form and manner aforesaid. And further we give straight charge and commandment to all and singular sheriffs, majors, bailiffs, constables, and other our faithful subjects, by the tenor of these presents, that they attend upon you, counsel and aid you and every one of you, as is meet and convenient in the doing and execution of the premises. In witness whereof, we have caused these our letters patents to be made. Witness myself at Westminster, the twenty-second day of September, in the seventeenth year of our reign.

"By the same king and council."

Thus King Richard, by the setting on of William Courtney, archbishop of Canterbury, and his fellows, taking part with the pope and Romish prelates, became strict and hard against the poor christians of the other side who followed Wickliff. Yet during the life of this king I find none expressly by name that suffered burning. Some, however, there were, who, by the archbishop and other bishops, had been condemned, and some also abjured, and did penance as well in other places, as chiefly about the town of Leicester, as is declared in the archbishop's register and records as follows:

"At the time the said archbishop William Courtney was in his visitation at the town of Leicester, certain there were accused and detected to him, by the monks and other priests in the said town. The names of which persons there detected were Roger Dexter, Nicholas Taylor, Richard Wagstaff, Michael Scrivener, William Smith, John Henry, William Parchmentar, and Roger Goldsmith, inhabitants of the town of Leicester. These, with others, were denounced to the archbishop for

holding the opinion of the sacrament of the altar, of auricular confession, and other sacraments, contrary to that which the church of Rome preaches and observes. All which parties above named, and many others whose names are not known, held these heresies and errors here underwritten, and are of the church of Rome condemned.

"1. That in the sacrament of the altar, after the words of consecration, there remains the body of Christ with the material bread.

"2. That images ought not to be worshipped in any case, and that no man ought to set any candle before them.

"3. That no cross ought to be worshipped.

"4. The masses and mattens ought not with an high and loud voice to be said in the church.

"5. That no curate or priest, taken in any crime, can consecrate, hear confessions, or minister any of the sacraments of the church.

"6. That the pope and all prelates of the church cannot bind any man with the sentence of excommunication, unless they know him to be first excommunicated of God.

"7. That no prelate of the church can grant any pardons.

"8. That every layman may in every place preach and teach the gospel.

"9. That it is sin to give any alms or charity to the friars, preachers, Minorites, Augustinians, or Carmelites.

"10. That no oblation ought to be used at the funerals of the dead.

"11. That it is not necessary to make confession of our sins to the priest.

"12. That every good man, although he be unlearned, is a priest."

These articles they taught, preached, and affirmed manifestly in the town of Leicester, and other places adjoining. Whereupon the said archbishop admonished the said Roger and Nicholas, with the rest, on the next day to make answer unto him in the said monastery to the aforesaid articles. But the aforesaid Roger and Nicholas, with the rest, hid themselves out of the way, and appeared not. Whereupon the archbishop upon All-hallow day, being the first day of November, celebrating the high mass at the high altar, in the said monastery, being attired in his pontifical robes, denounced the said parties with all their adherents, favourers, and counsellors, excommunicate and accursed, who either held, taught, or maintained the aforesaid heretical and erroneous conclusions, and that in solemn wise, by ringing the bells, lighting the candles, and putting out the same again, and throwing them down to the ground, with other circumstances thereunto belonging. Upon the morrow after, being All-Souls day, he sent for all the curates and some laymen of the town of Leicester, to inquire more diligently of the verity of such matter as they knew, and were able to say against any persons whatever concerning the aforesaid articles, as also against the parties before named and specified upon their oaths, denouncing every one of them severally by their names to be excommunicated and accursed; and caused them also to be excommunicated in divers parish churches in Leicester. And further the said archbishop interdicted the whole town of Leicester, and all the churches in the same, so long as any of the aforesaid excommunicate persons should remain, or be within the same, and till all the Lollards of the town should return and amend from such heresies and errors, obtaining at the said archbishop's hands the benefit of absolution.

At length it was declared and shewed to the said archbishop, that there was a certain anchoress, whose name was Matilda, enclosed within the church-yard of St. Peter's church of the town of Leicester, infected with the pestiferous contagion of the aforesaid heretics and Lollards: whereupon, after the said archbishop had examined the aforesaid Matilda, touching the aforesaid conclusions, heresies, and errors, and found her not to answer plainly and directly to the same, but sophistically and subtlely; he peremptorily gave and assigned unto her a day, personally to appear before him in the monastery of St. James at Northampton, more fully to answer to the said articles, heresies, and errors, which was the sixth day of the said month of November ; commanding the abbot of the monastery of Pratis, that the door of the recluse, in which the said Matilda was, should be opened, and that till his return he should cause her to be put in safe custody. That done, he sent forth his mandate against the Lollards, under this form :—

" William, by the permission of God, &c. To his well-beloved sons, the mayor and bailiffs of the town of Leicester diocese, greeting. We have lately received the king's letters, graciously granted us for the defence of the catholic faith, in these words following : Richard, by the grace of God, king of England and of France, &c. We, on the behalf of our holy mother, the church, by the king's authority aforesaid, do require you, that you cause the same Richard, William, Roger, and the rest, to be arrested, and sent unto us ; that they with their pernicious doctrine do not infect the people of God, &c. Given under our seal," &c.

By another instrument also in the same register mention is made of one Margaret Caily, a nun, who, forsaking her order, was by the said archbishop constrained, against her will, again to enter the same, as by this instrument here-under ensuing may appear.

" William, by the grace of God, &c. To our reverend brother of God, John, by the grace of God, bishop of Ely, greeting, &c. In the visitation of our diocese of Lincoln according to our office amongst other enormities worthy reformation, we found one sheep strayed out of our fold, and entangled amongst the briars ; to wit, Margaret Caily, nun professed, in the monastery of St. Radegond, within your diocese, who, casting off the habit of her religion, was found in secular attire, many years being an apostate, and leading a dissolute life. And lest her blood should be required at our hands, we have caused her to be taken and brought unto you, being her pastor ; and straightly enjoining you, by these presents we do command, that you admit the same Margaret again into her aforesaid monastery (although returned against her will), or else into some other place, where for her soul's health you shall think most convenient ; and that from henceforth she be safely kept, as in the straight examination of the same you will yield an account. Given under our seal," &c.

By sundry other instruments also in the same register I find, that Matilda, the anchoress, upon the straight examination and handling of the archbishop, before whom she was peremptorily enjoined to appear, and till that day of appearance taken out of the recluse, and committed to safe custody, as you heard, retracted and recanted her aforesaid articles and opinions. For which she being enjoined forty days' penance, was again admitted into her recluse in Leicester.

Also, by another letter of the archbishop to the dean of the cathedral church of our lady of Leicester, I find that of the number of those eight persons before recited, whom the archbishop himself at high mass, in his pontifical robes so solemnly cursed with book, bell, and candle : after process against them, or else in the meantime they being apprehended and taken, two of them recanted their opinions ; to wit, William Smith and Roger Dexter. But in the meantime Alice, the wife of Roger Dexter, abjured the same. However, whether they presented themselves willingly, or else were brought against their wills (as most like it was) hard penance was enjoined them before they were absolved. The words of the instrument are as follows :—

" Seeing our holy mother the church denies not her lap to any penitent child returning to her unity, but rather proffers to them the same : we therefore receive again William, Roger, and Alice, to grace. And further have caused them to abjure all and singular the foresaid articles and opinions, before they received of us the benefit of absolution, and were loosed from the sentence of excommunication, wherein they were snarled, enjoining to them penance, according to the quantity of the crime, in form as follows , that is to say, that the Sunday next after their returning to their proper goods, they, the said William, Roger, and Alice, holding every of them an image of the crucifix in their hands, and in their left hands every one of them a taper of wax, weighing half a pound weight, in their shirts (having none other apparel upon them) do go before the cross three times, during the procession of the cathedral church of our lady of Leicester ; that is to say, in the beginning of the procession, in the middle of the procession, and in the latter end of the procession ; to the honour of him that was crucified, in the memorial of his passion, and to the honour of the Virgin his mother ; who also devoutly bowing their knees and kneeling, shall kiss the same crucifix, so held in their hands. And so with the same procession they entering again into the church, shall stand during all the time of the holy mass, before the image of the cross, with their tapers and crosses in their hands. And when the mass is ended, the said William, Roger, and Alice, shall offer to him that celebrated that day the mass. Then upon the Saturday next ensuing, the said William, Roger, and Alice, shall in the full and public market, within the town of Leicester, stand in like manner in their shirts, without any more clothes upon their bodies, holding the foresaid crosses in their right hands ; which crosses they shall devoutly kiss three times, (during the market) reverently kneeling upon their knees ; that is, in the beginning of the market, in the middle of the market, and in the end of the market. And the said William (because he somewhat understands the Latin tongue) shall say this anthem, with the collect, " Holy Catherine," &c. ; and the foresaid Roger and Alice, being unlearned, shall say devoutly a Pater Noster, and an Ave Maria. And, thirdly, the Sunday next immediately after the same, the said William, Roger, and Alice, in their parish church of the said town of Leicester shall stand and do, as upon the Sunday before they stood and did in the cathedral church of our lady aforesaid in all things. Which done, the foresaid William, Roger, and Alice, after mass, shall offer to the priest or chaplain that celebrated the same, with all humility and reverence the wax tapers, which they shall carry in their hands. And because of the cold weather that now is, lest the foresaid penitents might peradventure take some bodily hurt standing so long naked (being mindful to moderate partly our rigour) we give leave, that after their entrance into the churches above said, whilst they shall be in hearing the foresaid masses, they may put on necessary garments to keep them from cold, so that their heads and feet notwithstanding be bare and uncovered. We therefore will and command you, together and apart, that you pronounce the said William, Roger, and Alice to be absolved and restored again to the unity of our holy mother the church, and that you call them forth to do their penance in manner and form aforesaid. Given at Dorchester the 17th day of November, in the year 1389, and the ninth year of our translation."

To the above narration we will adjoin the history of Peter Pateshul, an Augustinian friar, who, obtaining by the pope's privilege (through the means of Walter Dis, confessor to the duke of Lancaster) liberty to change his coat and order, and hearing the doctrine of John Wickliff, and others of the same kind, began at length to preach openly, and expose the vices of his order, in such a way that all men wondered to hear the horrible recital. This being brought to the ears of his order, they to the number of twelve (coming out of their houses to the place where he was preaching) thought to have withstood him by force. Among whom one especially for the zeal of his religion, stood up openly, during his preaching, and contradicted what he said, as he was preaching in the church of St. Christopher in London. When the faithful Londoners saw this, taking grief hereat, they were very angry against the friar, thrusting him with his other brethren out of the church, whom they not only had beaten and sore wounded, but also followed them home to their house, intending to have destroyed their mansion with fire also; and would have so done, had not one of the sheriffs of London, with two of the friars of the house, well known and reported amongst the Londoners, with gentle words mitigated their rage and violence. After this, Peter Pateshul thus disturbed, was desired by the Londoners (forsomuch as he could not well preach amongst them) to put in writing what he had said, and other things besides that he knew about the friars. He at their request writing the same, accused the friars of murder committed against several of their brethren. And to make the matter more apparent and credible, he declared the names of them that were murdered, with the names also of their tormentors: and named moreover time and place, where and when they were murdered, and where they were buried. He affirmed further that they were guilty of other horrible sins, and were traitors both to the king and the realm; with many other crimes, which mine author for tediousness leaves off to recite. And for the more confutation of the friars, the Londoners caused the accounts to be openly set up at St. Paul's church-door in London, which was there read, and they were copied by many. This was done A. D. 1387, and in the tenth year of King Richard II.

Thus it may appear how the gospel of Christ, preached by John Wickliff and others, began to spread and fructify abroad in London, and other places of the realm: and more would have done no doubt, had not William Courtney the archbishop, and other prelates with the king, set them so forcibly with might and main to withstand the course thereof. However, as is said before, I find none who were put to death during the reign of this King Richard II. Whereby it appears of this king, that although he cannot utterly be excused for molesting the godly and innocent preachers of that time, (as by his briefs and letters afore mentioned may appear) yet was he not so cruel against them, as others that came after him: and that which he did, seemed to proceed by the instigation of the pope and other bishops, rather than by the consent of his parliament, or advice of his council about him, or else by his own nature. But however the doings of this king are to be excused, or not, it is undoubted, that Queen Anne his wife, most rightly deserves singular commendation; who at the same time, living with the king, had the gospels of Christ in English, with the writings of four doctors upon the same. This Anne was a Bohemian born, and sister to Wenceslaus, king of Bohemia: she was married to King Richard about the fifth (some say the sixth) year of his reign, and continued with him the space of eleven years. By the occasion whereof it may seem not improbable, that the Bohemians coming in with her, or resorting into this realm after her, perused and received here the books of John Wickliff, which afterward they conveyed into Bohemia.

The said virtuous Queen Anne, after she had lived with King Richard about eleven years, in the seventeenth year of his reign changed this mortal life, and was buried at Westminster. At whose funeral Thomas Arundel, then archbishop of York, and Lord Chancellor, made the sermon. In which sermon (as remains in the library of Worcester) he, treating of the commendation of her, said these words, That it was more joy of her than of any woman that ever he knew; for notwithstanding that she was born an alien, she had in English all the four gospels, with the doctors upon them: affirming, moreover, and testifying, that she had sent the same to him to examine; and he said they were good and true. And, further, with many words of praise he greatly commended her, in that she being so great a lady, and also a foreigner, would humbly study such virtuous books. And in that sermon he blamed sharply the negligence of the prelates and other men. Insomuch that some said, he would on the morrow give up the office of chancellor, and forsake the world, and fulfil his pastoral office, for what he had seen and read in those books; and then it had been the best sermon that ever they heard. In which sermon of Thomas Arundel, three points are to be considered: first, the laudable custom of those old times, to have the scrip-

ture and doctors in our vulgar English tongue. Secondly, the virtuous exercise and example of this godly lady, who had these books not for a shew hanging at her girdle; but also seemed by this sermon to be a studious reader of the same. The third thing to be noted is, what fruit the archbishop declared also himself to have received at the hearing and reading of the same books in the English tongue. However, the same Thomas Arundel, after this sermon and promise made, became the most cruel enemy that might be against English books, and the authors thereof, as follows afterwards in his history.

For shortly after the death of Queen Anne, in the same year (the king being then in Ireland) this Thomas Arundel, archbishop of York, and Robert Braybrocke the bishop of London, (whether sent by the archbishop of Canterbury and the clergy, or whether going of their own accord) crossed the seas to Ireland, to desire the king with all speed to return and help the faith and church of Christ, against such as holding Wickliff's doctrine, went about (as they said) to subvert all their proceedings, and to destroy the canonical sanctions of their holy mother church. At this complaint the king hearing the one party speak, and not hearing the other, was so incensed, that immediately leaving all his affairs incomplete, he hastened his return to England. In the beginning of the following year, (which was A. D. 1395,) a parliament was called at Westminster. In which certain articles or conclusions were put up by those of the gospel's side, to the number of twelve. Which conclusions were fastened upon the church-door of St. Paul in London, and also at Westminster: the copy of which conclusions, with the words and contents thereof here follow:—

The Book of Conclusions or Reformations, exhibited to the Parliament at London, and set up at the door of St. Paul's, and other places, in the eighteenth year of the reign of King Richard II., and in the year 1395.

THE first conclusion: When the church of England began first to dote in temporalities after her stepmother the great church of Rome, and the churches were authorised by appropriations; then faith, hope, and charity began in divers places to vanish and fly away from our church, for pride with her most lamentable and dolorus genealogy of mortal and deadly sins, challenged that place by title of heritage. And this conclusion is general, and approved by experience, custom, and manner, as ye shall after hear.

The second conclusion: That our usual priesthood, which took its original at Rome, and is feigned to be a power higher than angels, is not that priesthood which Christ ordained to his disciples. This conclusion is thus proved, Forsomuch as the Romish priesthood is done with signs and pontifical rites and ceremonies, and benedictions, of no force and effect, neither having any ground in scripture, forsomuch as the bishop's ordinal and the New Testament do not at all agree; neither do we see that the Holy Ghost gives any good gift through any such signs or ceremonies; because he, together with all noble and good gifts, cannot co-exist in any person with deadly sin. It is a lamentable and dolorous mockery to wise men, to see the bishops mock and play with the Holy Ghost in the giving of their orders.

The third conclusion.[1]

The fourth conclusion that most harms the innocent people, is this: That the feigned miracle of the sacrament of bread induces all men, except it be a very few, to idolatry: for they think that the body which shall never be out of heaven, is by the virtue of the priest's words essentially included in the little bread, which they shew to the people. But would to God they would believe that which the evangelical doctor[2] teaches us in his trialogue, "That the bread of the altar is the body of Christ accidentally:" forsomuch as we suppose that by

---

(1) This conclusion which reflects on the vices of the Romish priests, is omitted, being of too gross a nature for insertion in this edition. [ED].
(2) Wickliff.

that means every faithful man and woman in the law of God may make the sacrament of that bread without any such miracle. The corollary of this conclusion is, That as the body of Christ be endowed with eternal joy, the service of Corpus Christi, made by friar Thomas, is not true, but painted full of false miracles.

The fifth conclusion is this: That the exorcisms and hallowings, consecrations, and blessings over the wine, bread, wax, water, oil, salt, incense, the altar-stone, and about the church walls, over the vestiment, chalice, mitre, cross, and pilgrim-staves, are the very practices of necromancy, rather than of sacred divinity. This conclusion is thus proved: because that by such exorcisms the creatures are honoured as of more force and power than of their own proper nature; for we do not see any alteration or change in any creature so exorcised, except it be by false faith, which is the principal point of the devilish art: The corollary of this is, that if the book of exorcisation or conjuring of holy water, which is sprinkled in the church, were altogether faithful and true; we think certainly that holy water used in the church, were the best medicine for all kind of sickness and sores; daily experience teaches us the contrary.

The sixth conclusion is, that a king and bishop both in one person, a prelate and justice in temporal causes, a curate and officer in worldly office makes every kingdom out of good order. This conclusion is manifest, because the temporalty and the spiritualty are two parts of the holy universal church; and therefore he who addicts himself to the one part, let him not intermeddle with the other, for no man can serve two masters. The corollary of this conclusion is, that we the proctors of God in this case do sue to the parliament, that it may be enacted, that all the clergy (as well of the highest degree as of the lowest) should be fully excused from any temporal office, and occupy themselves with their own charge, and not with others.

The seventh conclusion, what we mightily affirm is, that spiritual prayers made in the church for the souls of the dead (preferring any one by name more than another) is a false foundation of alms, whereupon all the houses of alms in England are falsely founded. This conclusion is proved by two reasons: the one is, that a meritorious prayer (of any force or effect) ought to be a work proceeding from mere charity: and perfect charity excepts no person, because thou shalt love thy neighbour as thyself. Whereby it appears that the benefit of any temporal gift, bestowed and given to priests, and houses of alms, is the principal cause of any special prayers, which is not far different from simony. The other reason is, that every special prayer, made for men condemned to eternal punishment, is very displeasing to God. And although it be doubtful, yet it is very probable to faithful christians that the founders of every such house of alms, for their wicked endowing the same, are for the most part passed by "the broad-way." The corollary is, that every prayer of force and effect, proceeding from perfect charity, would comprehend generally all such as God would have saved. The merchandize of special prayers now used for the dead makes mendicant possessioners and other hireling priests, who otherwise were strong enough to work and to serve the whole realm, and maintains them in idleness, to the great charge of the realm, because it was proved in a certain book which the king has, that a hundred houses of alms are sufficient for the whole realm. And thereby might peradventure greater increase and profit come to the temporalty.

The eighth conclusion, needful to tell to the beguiled people is, that pilgrimages, prayers, and oblations made to blind crosses or roods, or to deaf images made either of wood or stone, are very near a kin to idolatry, and far different from alms. And although these things which are forbidden, are the book of errors to the common people; yet the usual and common image of the Trinity is most especially abominable. This conclusion God himself openly manifests, commanding alms to be given to the poor and needy, for he is the image of God in a more perfect similitude and likeness than any block or stone. For God did not say, let us make a block or stone unto our likeness and image, but let us make man; the supreme and highest honour, which the clergy call 'Latria,' pertains only to the godhead, and the inferior honour which the clergy call 'Dulia,' pertains to men and angels, and to no other inferior creature. The corollary is, that the service of the cross, celebrated twice every year in our church is full of idolatry; for if rood, tree, nails, and spear ought so profoundly to be honoured and worshipped, then were Judas' lips (if any man could get them) a marvellous goodly relic! But, thou pilgrim, we pray thee tell us when thou dost offer to the bones of the saints, and holy men which are laid up in any place, whether thou relievest the holy man who is already in joy, or the alms house which is so well endowed, whereas the saints are canonized (the Lord knows how) and to speak more plain, every faithful christian may well suppose that the strokes of that same man, whom they call St. Thomas, were no cause of martyrdom.

The ninth conclusion, that keeps the people down, is, that auricular confession, which is said to be so necessary for salvation, and the feigned power of absolution, exalts and sets up the pride of priests, and gives them opportunity of other secret talks, which we will not at this time talk of; for as both lords and ladies do witness, that for fear of their confessors they dare not speak the truth; and in time of confession is good opportunity ministered of wooing, or to play the villain, or to make other secret arrangements to deadly sin. They affirm and say, that they are commissaries sent of God to judge and discern of all manner of sin, to pardon and cleanse whatever pleases them. They say also, that they have the keys of heaven and hell, and that they can excommunicate, curse, and bless, bind and loose at their own will and pleasure; so that for a small reward, or for twelve pence, they will sell the blessing of heaven by charter and clause of warranty, sealed by their common seal. This conclusion is so common in use, that it needs not any proof. The corollary is, that the pope of Rome who feigned himself to be the profound treasurer of the whole church, having that same worthy jewel, the treasure of the passion of Christ, in his own keeping and custody, together with the merits of all the saints in heaven, by which he gives feigned indulgences and pardons, is a treasurer out of charity, who pretends he may deliver all captives in purgatory at his pleasure. But here every faithful christian may easily perceive that there is much falsehood hid in our church.

The tenth conclusion is, that manslaughter (either by war or by any pretended law of justice for any temporal cause or spiritual revelation) is expressly contrary to the New Testament, which is the law of grace, full of mercy. This conclusion is evidently proved by the examples of the preaching of Christ here in earth, who chiefly teaches every man to love his enemies, and have compassion upon them, and not to kill and murder them. The reason is this, that for the most part when men do fight, after the first stroke, charity is broken; and whoever dies without charity goes the right way to hell. And we know, that none of the clergy can deliver any from the punishment of death for one deadly sin, and not for another; but the law of mercy, which is the New Testament, forbids all manner of murder. For in the gospel it is spoken to our forefathers, "Thou shalt not kill." The corollary is, it is a robbing of the people, when lords purchase indulgences and pardon for such as help their armies to kill and murder the christian people in foreign countries, for temporal gain; as we see certain soldiers who run among the heathen people, to get themselves fame and renown by the murder and slaughter of men. Much more do they deserve evil thanks at the hands of the king of peace, forsomuch as by humility and peace, our faith is multiplied and increased; for murderers and manslayers Christ hates and menaces, "He that killeth with the sword shall perish with the sword."

The eleventh conclusion.[1]

---

(1) This conclusion reflects on the morals of nunneries, and though most true, it is also omitted for the same reason as the third.—[ED.]

s 2

The twelfth conclusion is, that the multitude of arts not necessary (used in this our church) causes much sin and offence in waste, curiosity, and disguising in curious apparel; experience and reason partly shew the same, for nature, with a few arts, is sufficient for man's use and necessity.

This is the whole tenor of our ambassage, which Christ hath commanded us to prosecute at this time, most fit and convenient for many causes. And although these matters are here only briefly noted and touched: yet they are more at large declared in another book, with many others beside in our own proper tongue, which we wish should be common to all christian people. Wherefore we earnestly desire and beseech God for his great goodness sake, that he will wholly reform our church (now altogether out of frame) to the perfection of her first beginning and original. (Ex Archivis Regiis.)

After these conclusions were thus proposed in the parliament, the king not long after returned home from Dublin into England, toward the latter end of the parliament. At his return he called certain of his nobles to him, Richard Stury, Lewis Clifford, Thomas Latimer, John Mountacute, &c., whom he sharply rebuked, and terribly threatened, for he heard they were favourers of that side; charging them straightly never to hold, maintain, nor favour any more those opinions and conclusions. And he took an oath of Richard Stury, that he should never from that day favour or defend any such opinions; which oath being taken, the king then answered, And I swear (saith he) again to thee, if thou dost ever break thine oath, thou shalt die for it a shameful death, &c.

All this while William Courtenay archbishop of Canterbury was yet alive, who was a great stirrer in these matters. But yet Pope Urban the great master of the catholic sect was dead and buried six years before. After whom succeeded in the schismatical see of Rome, Pope Boniface IX., who nothing inferior to his predecessor in all kind of cruelties, left no diligence untried to set forward what Urban had begun, in suppressing those that were setting forth the light of the gospel: and he had written several times to King Richard, as well for the repealing of the acts of parliament against his provisions, 'Quare impedit,' and 'Premunire facies:' as also that he should assist the prelates of England in the cause of God (as he pretended) against those, whom he falsely suggested to be Lollards and traitors to the church, to the king, and the realm, &c. Thus the courteous pope with the cruel slander of his malicious tongue sought to work his poison against those whom he could not reach with his sword; which letter he wrote to the king, A. D. 1396, the year before the death of William Courtenay Archbishop of Canterbury. After whom succeeded in that see, Thomas Arundel, brother to the earl of Arundel, being first bishop of Ely, afterwards archbishop of York, and lord chancellor of England, and at last made archbishop of Canterbury, about A. D. 1397. The next year following, which was A. D. 1398, and the ninth year of the pope, I find in certain records of the bishop of Durham, a letter of King Richard II., written to Pope Boniface, rebuking the schism in the popedom, which I judged worthy of being seen here, and therefore annex the same, as follows:—

To the most holy father in Christ, and Lord, Lord Boniface IX., by the grace of God, high pope of the most holy Romish and universal church, his humble and devout son Richard, by the grace of God, king of England, and France, lord of Ireland, greeting and desiring to help the miseries of the afflicted church, and kissing of those his blessed feet.

" Who will give my head water, and mine eyes streaming tears, that I may bewail the decay, and manifold troubles of our mother, which have chanced to her by her own children in the distress of this present schism and division? For the sheep have forgotten the proper voice of their shepherds, and hirelings have thrust in themselves to feed the Lord's flock, who are clothed with the apparel of the true shepherd, challenging the name of honour and dignity, resembling so the true shepherd, that the poor sheep can scarce know whom they ought to follow, or what pastor as a stranger they ought to flee, and whom they should shun as an hireling. Wherefore we are afraid lest the holy standard of the Lord be forsaken of his host, and so that city, being full of riches, become solitary and desolate, and lest the land or people which was wont to say (flourishing in her prosperities) I sat as a queen, and am not a widow, be destitute of the presence of her husband, and as it were so bewitched that she shall not be able to discern his face, and so wrapped in amazement, that she shall not know where to turn her, that she might more easily find him, and that she shall with weeping speak that saying of the spouse, 'I sought him whom my soul loveth, I sought him and found him not.' For now we are compelled so to wander, that if any man say, behold here is Christ, or there, we may not believe him so saying; and so many shepherds have destroyed the Lord's vineyard, and made his pleasant portion a vast wilderness.

This multitude of shepherds is become very burdenous to the Lord's flock. For when two strive to be chief, the state of both their dignities stands in doubt, and in so doing they give occasion to all the faithful of Christ, for a schism and division of the church. And although both parties go about to subdue to their power the whole church militant, yet contrary to both their purpose, by working this way, there begins to rise now a division in the body of the church, as when the division of the living innocent body was asked, when the two women did strive before Solomon; like as the ten tribes of Israel followed Jeroboam the intruder, and were withdrawn from the kingdom for Solomon's sin: even so of old time the desire of ruling has drawn the great power of the world from the unity of the church. Let yourselves remember, we beseech you, how that all Greece fell from the obedience of the Romish church in the time of the faction of the primarch of Constantinople; and how Mahomet with his fellows, by occasion of supremacy in ecclesiastical dignity, deceived a great part of Christians, and withdrew them from the empire and ruling of Christ. And how in these days, where the same supremacy has withdrawn itself from the obedience of it, insomuch that now in very few realms the candle that burns before the Lord remains, and that for his servant David's sake. And although now few countries remain professing the obedience of Christ's true vicar: yet peradventure if every man were left to his own liberty, he would doubt of the preferring of your dignity, or what is worse, would utterly refuse it by such doubtful evidence alleged on both sides; and this is the subtle craft of the crooked serpent, that is to say, under the pretence of unity to procure schisms, as the spider of a wholesome flower gathers poison, and Judas learned of peace to make war. Wherefore it is believed by wise men, that except this pestilent schism be withstood by and by, the keys of the church will be despised, and they shall bind the conscience but of a few: and when either none dare be bold to correct this fault, or to reform things contrary to God's law, so by this means at length temporal lords will take away the liberties of the church, and peradventure the Romans will come and take away their place, people, and lands: they will spoil their possessions, and bring the men of the church into bondage, and they shall be contemned, reviled, and despised, because the obedience of the people, and devotions towards them will almost be taken away, when the greater part of the church, left to their own liberty, shall wax prouder than they are wont, leaving a wicked example to them that see it. For when they see the prelates study more for covetousness than they were wont, to hoard up money, to oppress the subjects, in their punishings to seek for gain, to confound laws, to stir up strife, to suppress truth, to vex poor subjects with wrong corrections, intemperate in meat and drink, past shame in feastings: what marvel is it if the people despise them as the foulest forsakers of God's law? but all these things do follow if the church should be left long in this doubtfulness of a schism, and then should that old saying be verified ; ' In those days there was no king in Israel, but every one did that which was right in his own eyes.' Micah did see the people of the Lord scattered in the mountains, as they had been sheep without a shepherd : for when the shepherd is smitten, the sheep of the flock shall be scattered, the great stroke of the shepherd is the diminishing of his jurisdiction, by which the subjects are drawn from his obedience. When Jason had the office of the highest priest, he changed the ordinance of God, and brought in the customs of the heathen, the priests leaving the service of the holy altar, and applying themselves to wrestling, and other exercises of the Grecians, and despising those things that belonged to the priests, did labour with all their might to learn such things of the Grecians ; and by that means the place, people, and holy anointing of priests, which in times past were had in great reverence of kings, were trodden under foot of all men, and robbed by the king's power, and profaned by being thrust in for money. Therefore let the highest vicar of Christ look to this with a diligent eye, and let him be the follower of him by whom he has got authority above others.

" If you mark well, most holy father, you shall find that Christ rebuked sharply two brethren, coveting the seat of honour : he taught them not to play the lords over the people, but the more grace they were filled with, to be so much more humble than others, and more lowly to serve their brethren. To him that asked his coat, to give the cloak, to him that smote him on the one cheek, to turn the other to him. For the sake of the sheep that are given to his keeping, he must forsake all earthly things, and shed his own blood, yea, and if need required, to die. These things, I say, are those that adorn the highest bishop, if they be in him,—not his white horse, not his imperial crown, because he among all men is most bound to all the sheep of Christ. For the fear of God therefore, and for the love of the flock which ye guide, consider these things diligently, and do them wisely, and suffer us no longer to waver betwixt two : although not for your own cause, to whom peradventure the fulness of your own power is known ; yet in pitying our weakness, if thou be he, tell us openly, and shew thyself to the world, that all we may follow one. Be not to us a bloody bishop, lest by your occasion, man's blood be shed ; lest hell swallow a number of souls, and lest the name of Christ be evil spoken of by infidels, through such a worthy personage. But peradventure ye will say, our right is manifest enough, and we will not put it to other men's decision. If this answer should be admitted, the schism will continue still : seeing neither part is willing to agree to the other, and where the world is as it were equally divided between them, neither part can be compelled to give place to the other without much bloodshed. The incarnation of Christ, and his resurrection, was well enough known to himself and his disciples ; yet he asked of his Father to be made known to the world. He made also the gospel to be written, and the doctrine of the apostles, and sent his apostles into all the world, to do the office of preaching, that the same thing might be known to all men. The aforesaid reason is the subtlety of Mahomet, who knowing himself guilty of his sect, utterly forbad disputations. If ye have so full trust of your right, put it to the examination of worthy persons in a general council, to which it belongs by right to define such doubts, or else commit it to able persons, and give them full power to determine all things concerning that matter, or at least, by both parties forsaking the office, leave the church of God free, speedily to provide a new shepherd.

" We find kings have forsaken their temporal kingdoms only for devotion, and have taken the apparel of monk's profession. Therefore let Christ's vicar, (being a professor of most high holiness) be ashamed to continue in his seat, of honour to the offence of all people, and to the prejudice and hurt of the Romish church, and the devotion of it, and cutting away kingdoms from it.

" But if you say, it is not requisite that the cause of God's church should be called in controversy, and therefore we cannot so easily go from it, seeing our conscience forbids us.

" To this we answer, if it be the cause of God and the church, let the general council judge of it : but if it be a personal cause (as almost all the world probably thinks) if ye were the followers of Christ, ye would rather choose a temporal death, than to suffer such a schism and division. I say not, to the hurt of so many, but to the endless destruction of souls, to the offence of the whole world, and to an everlasting shame of the apostolical dignity. Did not Clement, named, or (that I may more truly speak) ordained of St. Peter to the apostolic dignity, and to be bishop, resign his right, that his deed might be taken of his successors for an example ? Also Pope Siricius gave over his popedom to be a comfort of the eleven thousand virgins. Therefore much more ought you (if need require) give over your popedom, that you might gather together the children of God who are scattered abroad. For as it is thought a glorious thing to defend the common right, even to bloodshed, so it is sometimes necessary for a man to wink at his own cause, and to forsake it for a greater profit, and by that means better to procure peace. Should not he be thought a devil, and Christ's enemy who would agree to an election of himself for the apostolical dignity and popedom, if it should be to the destruction of christians, division of the church, the offence and loss of all faithful people ? If such mischief should be known to all the world by God's revelation, to come to pass by such a person receiving the popedom and apostolical dignity : then by the like reason why should he not be judged of all men an apostate, and forsaker of his faith, who chooses dignity, or worldly honour, rather than the unity of the church ? Christ died that he might gather together the children of God, which are scattered abroad : but such an enemy of God and the church wishes his subjects bodily to die in battle, and the greater part of the world to perish in soul, rather than forsake his popedom. If the fear of God, the desire of the heavenly kingdom, and the earnest love of the unity of the church move your heart, shew indeed that your works may bear witness to the truth. Clement and Siricius, most holy popes, not only are not reproved, but rather are reverenced by all men, because they gave over their right for profitable causes, and for the same cause all the church of holy men shew forth their praise. Likewise, your name should live for ever and ever, if ye would do the like for a necessary cause, that is to say, for the unity of God's church. Give no heed to the unmeasurable cry of them that say, that the right choosing of popes is lost, except ye defend your part manfully : but be afraid, lest such stirrers up of mischief look for their own advantage or honour, that is to say, that under your wing they might be promoted to riches and honour. After this sort Ahithophel was joined with Absalom in persecuting his own father, and falsely usurping his kingdom.

" Furthermore, there should be no jeopardy to that election, because both parties stick stifly to the old fashion of election, and both of them covet the preeminence of the Romish church, counselling all christians to obey them. And although, through their resignation, the fashion of choosing the pope should be changed for a time, that might be borne, rather than to suffer any longer this division in God's church. For that fashion in choosing is not so necessarily required to the state of a pope, but that the successor of the apostle might come in at the door by another fashion of election, and that canonical enough. And this we are taught manifestly by examples of the fathers ; for Peter the apostle appointed after him Clement, and that not by falsely usurping the power. And it was thought that that fashion of appointing popes was lawful to the time of Pope Hilary, who first decreed that no pope should appoint his successor.

" Afterwards the election of the pope went by the clergy and people of Rome, and the consent of the emperor's council, as appears in the election of the blessed

Gregory. But Pope Martin, with the consent of the holy synod, granted Charles the power to choose the pope. But of late Nicholas II. was the first whom Martin makes mention of in his councils, as chosen by the cardinals. But all the bishops of Lombardy (for the most part) withstood this election, and chose Cadulus to be pope, saying, That the pope ought not to be chosen but within the precinct of Italy. Wherefore we think it not a safe way so earnestly to stick to the traditions of men, in the fashion of choosing the pope, and so often to change, lest we be thought to break God's traditions concerning the unity of the church. Yea rather, it were better yet to ordain a new fashion of his election, and meeter for him as it has been before. But all things concerning the same election might be kept safe, if God's honour were looked for before your own, and the peace of the church were uprightly sought: for such a dishonouring should be most honour to you, and that giving place should be the getting of a greater dignity, and the willing deposing of your honour should obtain you the entry of everlasting honour, and should procure the love of the whole world toward you, and you should deserve to be exalted continually, as David was in humbling himself. O how monstrous a sight, and how foul a monster is a man's body disfigured with two heads! So if it were possible, the spouse of Christ should be made so monstrous, if she were ruled with two such heads: but that is not possible, she is ever altogether fair, in whom no spot is found; therefore we must cast away that rotten member and thruster in of his second head. We cannot suffer any longer so great a wickedness in God's house, that we should suffer God's coat, that is without seam, by any means to be torn by the hands of two, that violently draw it in sunder. For if these two should be suffered to reign together, they would between them so tear in pieces that coat of the Lord, that scarce one piece would hang to another. They pass the wickedness of the soldiers that crucified Christ: for they, willing to have the coat whole, said, 'Let us not rend it, but let us cast lots for it, whose it shall be.' But these two popes suffering their right and title to be tried by no lot nor way (although not in words yet in deeds) they pronounce this sentence, 'It shall neither be thine nor mine, but let it be divided;' for they choose rather as it appears, to be lords, (though it be but in a little part, and that to the confusion of the unity of the church) than, in leaving that lording, to seek for the peace of the church. We do not affirm this, but we shew almost the whole judgment of the world. We looked for amendment of this intolerable confusion during the time that these two inventors of this mischief lived. But we looked for peace, and behold trouble: for neither in their lives nor in their deaths have they procured any comfort, but rather dying as it were in a doubt betwixt two ways, left to their successors matter of continual contention. But now for the space of seven years, we desired and looked that they should bear good grapes, and they bring forth wild grapes, in this matter we fall into a deep despair. But inasmuch as we hear the comfort of the Lord, who promised that miserably he would destroy those wicked men, and let his vineyard to other husbandmen who will bring him fruit at their appointed times, and hath promised faithfully that he will help his spouse in her need to the end of the world: we, leaning on the sure hope of this promise, and in hope believing against hope, by God's grace will put our helping hands to the easing of this misery, when a convenient time shall serve, as much as our kingly power is able, and although our wit does not perceive how these things may be amended, yet we being encouraged to this by the hope of God's promise, will do our endeavour: like as Abraham believed that even if his son were slain by sacrifice, that the multitude of his seed should increase to the number of the stars, according to God's promise. Now, therefore, the times draw near to make an end of this schism, lest a third election of a schismatic against the apostle's successor, make a custom of the thing, and so the pope of Avignon shall be besides the Romish pope, and he shall say with his partakers, as the patriarch of Constantinople said unto Christ's vicar, when he for-

sook him, 'The Lord be with thee, for the Lord is with us:' and this is much to be feared of all christian men: for that Pharisee begins now to be called the pope of Avignon among the people. But, perhaps, it would be thought by some men that it belongs not to secular princes to bridle outrages of the pope. To whom we answer, that naturally the members put themselves in jeopardy to save the head, and the parts labour to save the whole. Christ so decked his spouse, that her sides should cleave together, and should uphold themselves, and by course of time and occasion of things they should correct one another, and cleave together in harmony. Did not Moses put down Aaron, because he was unfaithful? Solomon put down Abiathar, who came by lineal descent from Anathoth, and removed his priesthood from his kindred to the stock of Eleazar, in the person of Zadok, who had his beginning from Eli the priest? Emperor Otho deposed Pope John XII. because he was immoral. The Emperor Henry put down Gratian, because he used simony in buying and selling spiritual livings. And Otho deposed Pope Benedict I. because he thrust himself in. Therefore, by like reason, why may not kings and princes bridle the Romish pope in default of the church; if the quality of his fault require it, or the necessity of the church compel to help the church oppressed by tyranny? In old time schisms, which rose about making the pope, were determined by the power of secular princes, as the schism betwixt Symmachus and Laurence was ended in a council before Theodric, king of Italy. The Emperor Henry, when two strove to be pope, deposed them both, and received the third being chosen at Rome to be pope, that is to say, Clement II., who crowned him with the imperial crown. And the Romans promised him that from thenceforth they would promote none to be pope without his consent. Alexander also overcame four popes, schismatics, all of whom the Emperor Frederick corrected.

"Thus look on the register of popes and their deeds, and ye shall find that schisms most commonly have been decided by the power of secular princes, the schismatics cast out, and sometimes new popes made, and sometimes the old ones cast out of their dignities, and restored to their old dignities again. If it were not lawful for secular princes to bridle the outrages of such a pope lawfully made, and afterwards becoming a tyrant; in such a case, he might oppress the church; he might change Christendom into heathens, and make the labour of Christ crucified to be in vain: or else truly, God would not have provided for his spouse in earth by all means as much as is possible by service of men to withstand dangers. Therefore we counsel you, with such a loving affection as becomes children, that ye consider in your heart well, lest in working by this means ye prepare a way to antichrist through your desire to bear rule, and so by this means as we fear, the one of these two things shall happen: either ye shall cause all the princes of the world to rise against you to bring in a true follower of Christ to have the state of the apostolical dignity, or what is worse, the whole world despising the ruling of one shepherd, shall leave the Romish church desolate. But God keep this from the world, that the desire of honour of two men should bring such a desolation into the church of God: for then, that departing away, which the apostle prophesied, should come before the coming of antichrist were at hand: which should be the last disposition of the world, to receive antichrist with honour. Consider, therefore, the state of your most excellent holiness, how ye received the power from God to the building of the church, and not to the destruction of it; that Christ has given you wine and oil to heal the wounded; and has appointed you his vicar in these things which pertain to gentleness, and has given us these things which serve to rigour. For we bear not the sword without a cause to the punishment of evil-doers, which power ordained of God we have received, ourselves being witness: beseeching you to receive our counsel effectually, that in doing thus, the waters may return to the places from whence they came, and so the waters may begin to be made sweet with salt: lest the axe swim on the water, and the wood sink, and lest the fruitful olive degenerate into a wild olive, and the leprosy of Naaman cleave continually to the house of Gehazi, and lest the pope and the Pharisees crucify Christ again. Christ, the spouse of the church, which was wont to bring the chief bishop into the holiest place, increase your holiness, or rather restore it being lost."

This epistle of King Richard II., written to Pope Boniface IX. in the time of the schism, (A.D. 1397,) as it contained much good matter of wholesome counsel to be followed, so how little it wrought with the pope the sequel afterwards declared. For the schism continued long after, in which neither of the popes would give over their hold.

We come now to the 22d year of King Richard's reign, which is A.D. 1399. In which year happened the strange and lamentable deposing of King Richard from his kingly sceptre, the cause of which was briefly as follows.

Several acts on the part of the king led to the estrangement of the people, and certain of the nobles appeared in arms against him. As this was going on in England, the report reached the king's ears, who was then in Ireland, he therefore left the business he had in Ireland, and returning, landed at Milford Haven, not daring, as it seemed, to come to London.

Henry duke of Hereford having returned from France, and taken up arms against the king, had now landed in the north, and was joined by the earl of Northumberland, lord Henry Percy, and Henry his son, the earl of Westmorland, lord Radulph Nevil, and other lords, with a great number of men, so that the multitude rose to sixty thousand able soldiers. Who first making toward the castle of Bristol, where the members of the council who held with the king, had shut themselves in, and having gained the castle they took the chief of them prisoners, namely; John Bushy, Henry Grene, William Scrope and William Bagot; of whom three were immediately beheaded, but Bagot escaped and fled away to Ireland.

The king lying about Wales, destitute and desolate, without comfort or counsel, neither durst come to London, nor would any man come to him; and perceiving that the commons, had a great force against him, and would rather die, than give over what they had begun, and being compassed on every side with miseries, he moved from place to place, the duke still following him; till at length, at the castle of Conway, the king desired to talk with Thomas Arundel archbishop, and the earl of Northumberland; to whom he declared, that he would resign his crown, on condition that an honourable living might be provided for him, and life promised to eight persons, such as he would name. Which being granted and ratified, but not performed, he came to the castle of Flint, where he was brought the same night by the duke of Lancaster and his army to Chester, and thence conveyed secretly to the Tower, there to be kept till the next parliament. As he came near to London, several evil disposed men of the city gathered themselves, thinking to have slain him, for the great cruelty he had used toward the city; but by the mayor and rulers of the city, the madness of the people was checked. Not long after the duke followed, and the parliament assembled. In which parliament the earl of Northumberland, with many other earls and lords were sent to the king in the Tower, to receive his full resignation, according to his promise. This done, certain accusations and articles were laid against the king. And the next year after he was removed to Pomfret castle, and there starved to death.

KING HENRY THE FOURTH.

And thus King Richard being deposed from his rightful crown, the duke of Lancaster was led by Thomas Arundel the archbishop to the royal seat; who there standing up, and crossing himself on the forehead and the breast, spake as follows:

' " In the name of God, Amen. I, Henry of Lancaster, claim the realm of England and the Crown, with all the appurtenances, as descended by right line of the blood, coming from that good Lord King Henry III. And through the right that God of his grace has sent to me, with the help of my kin and of my friends to recover the same, which was in danger of ruin by default of good government, and due justice," &c.

After which words the archbishop, asking the assent of the people, took the duke by the hand, and placed him on the throne, and shortly after he was crowned by the archbishop, king of England.

The next year, a parliament was held at Westminster; in which parliament one Sir William Sautre, a good man and a faithful priest, inflamed with zeal for true religion, required that he might be heard for the advantage of the whole realm. But the matter being suspected by the bishops, they obtained that the matter should be referred to the convocation; where William Sautre being brought before the bishops and notaries, the convocation was deferred to the Saturday next ensuing.

When Saturday was come, that is to say, the 12th day of February, A.D. 1400, Thomas Arundel archbishop of Canterbury, in the presence of his provincial council, being assembled in the chapter-house, objected against one Sir William Sautre, personally then and there appearing by the command of the archbishop of Canterbury; that the said Sir William had once renounced and abjured before the bishop of Norwich, divers and sundry conclusions heretical and erroneous; and that after such abjuration, he publicly and privately held, taught and preached the same conclusions, or such like, contrary to the catholic faith, and to the great peril, and pernicious example of others. And after this he caused such conclusions, held and preached, by Sir William, then and there to be read to the archbishop, in a certain scroll written, in tenor of words as follows:

" Sir William Sautre, otherwise called Chatris, parish priest of the church St. Scithe the Virgin in London, publicly and privately doth hold these conclusions under written.

1. That he will not worship the cross on which Christ suffered, but only Christ that suffered on the cross.

2. That he would sooner worship a temporal king than the wooden cross.

3. That he would rather worship the bodies of the saints, than the very cross of Christ on which he hung, if it were before him.

4. That he would rather worship a man truly contrite than the cross of Christ.

5. That he is bound rather to worship a man that is predestinate than an angel of God.

6. That if any man would visit the monuments of Peter and Paul, or go on pilgrimage to the tomb of St. Thomas à Becket, or anywhere else, for obtaining of any temporal benefit, he is not bound to keep his vow, but he may distribute the expenses of his vow upon the alms of the poor.

7. That every priest and deacon is more bound to preach the word of God than to say the canonical hours.

8. That after the pronouncing of the sacramental words of the body of Christ, the bread remains of the same nature that it was before, neither does it cease to be bread."

To which conclusions, or articles, the archbishop of Canterbury required Sir William to answer. And he then asked for a copy, and required a competent time to answer. On which the archbishop appointed the following Thursday to make answer. When the day was come the convocation was adjourned until the morrow. When the morrow came, Sir William Sautre, in the chapter-house, before the bishop and his provincial council, exhibited a certain scroll, containing the answers to the articles or conclusions given to him, and said that he delivered the same to the archbishop as his answer in that behalf, which answer was as follows:—

" I, William Sautre, unworthy priest, say and answer, that I will not, and intend not to worship the cross whereon Christ was crucified, but only Christ that suffered upon the cross; so understand me, that I will not worship the material cross, or the gross corporeal matter: yet notwithstanding I will worship the same as a sign, token, and memorial of the passion of Christ. And that I will rather worship a temporal king, than the wooden cross, and the material substance. And that I will rather worship the bodies of saints than the very cross of Christ whereon he hung, with this addition, even if the very same cross were before me, as touching the material substance. And also that I will rather worship a man truly confessed and penitent, than the cross on which Christ hung, as touching the material substance.

"And that also I am bound, and will rather worship him whom I know to be predestinate, truly confessed and contrite, than an angel of God; for that the one is a man of the same nature with the humanity of Christ, and so is not a blessed angel. Notwithstanding I will worship both of them, according as the will of God is I should.

"Also, that if any man has made a vow to visit the shrines of the apostles Peter and Paul, or to go on pilgrimage unto St. Thomas's tomb, or anywhere else, to obtain any temporal benefit or advantage, he is not bound simply to keep his vow upon the necessity of salvation; but he may give the expenses of his vow in alms amongst the poor, by the prudent counsel of his superior, as I suppose.

"And also I say, that every deacon and priest is more bound to preach the word of God, than to say the canonical hours, according to the primitive order of the church.

"Also, touching the sacrament of the altar, I say, that after the pronouncing of the sacramental words of the body of Christ, there ceases not to be very bread simply, but remains bread, holy, true, and the bread of life; and I believe the said sacrament to be the very body of Christ, after the pronouncing of the sacramental words."

When all these answers were publicly read, the archbishop inquired of Sir William whether he had abjured the heresies and errors objected against him, or else had revoked and renounced the conclusions or articles, or not? To which he answered and affirmed that he had not. And then the archbishop examined Sir William Sautre, especially upon the sacrament of the altar.

First, whether in the sacrament of the altar, after the pronouncing of the sacramental words, remains very material bread or not? To which interrogation Sir William somewhat waveringly answered, that he knew not. He said, however, that there was very bread, because it was the bread of life which came down from heaven.

After that the archbishop demanded of him, whether in the sacrament after the sacramental words, rightly pronounced of the priests, the same bread remains which did before the words pronounced, or not? And to this question William answered as before, saying, that there was bread, holy, true, and the bread of life.

After that, the archbishop asked him, whether the same material bread before consecration, by the sacramental words of the priest rightly pronounced, be transubstantiated from the nature of bread into the very body of Christ? Sir William said, that he knew not what that meant.

And then the archbishop assigned Sir William time to deliberate, and more fully to make his answer, till the next day, and continued this convocation then and there till the morrow. Which morrow, to wit, the 19th day of February, being come, the archbishop of Canterbury, before his provincial council then and there assembled, especially examined Sir William Sautre upon the sacrament of the altar, as before; and Sir William again answered as before.

Then the archbishop demanded, whether he would stand to the determination of the holy church or not, which affirms, that in the sacrament of the altar, after the words of consecration being rightly pronounced of the priest, the same bread, which before in nature was

bread, ceases any more to be bread? To this interrogation Sir William said, that he would stand to the determination of the church, where such determination was not contrary to the will of God.

He then demanded of him again, what his judgment was concerning the sacrament of the altar? who said and affirmed, that after the words of consecration, by the priest duly pronounced, remained very bread, and the same bread which was before the words spoken. Wherefore the said archbishop of Canterbury, by the counsel and assent of the whole convocation then and there present, gave sentence against Sir William Sautre (being personally present, and refusing to revoke his heresies, that is to say, his true doctrine, but constantly defending the same) under the tenour of words as follows:—

"In the name of God, Amen. We, Thomas, by the grace of God archbishop of Canterbury, primate of England, and legate of the see apostolical, by the authority of God Almighty, and blessed St. Peter and Paul, and of holy church, and by our own authority, sitting for tribunal or chief judge, having God alone before our eyes, by the counsel and consent of the whole clergy our fellow brethren and suffragans, assistants to us in this present provincial council, by this our sentence definitive do pronounce, decree, and declare by these presents, thee, William Sautre, otherwise called Chatris, parish priest pretended, personally appearing before us, in and upon the crime of heresy, judicially and lawfully convicted, as an heretic, and as an heretic to be punished."

The bishop of Norwich, according to the commandment of the said archbishop of Canterbury, presented to William Sautre a certain process, inclosed and sealed with his seal, giving the names of credible witnesses sealed with their seals, the tenour whereof follows thus:—

"That upon the last day of April, A.D. 1399, Sir William Sautre, parish priest of the church of St. Margaret in the town of Lynn, appeared before the bishop of Norwich, and there publicly affirmed and held the conclusions before specified.

"And afterwards, to wit, the 19th day of May, Sir William revoked and renounced all his conclusions, abjuring and correcting all such heresies and errors, taking his oath upon a book before the bishop of Norwich, that from that time forward he would never preach, affirm, nor hold, privily nor openly, the conclusions; and that he would pronounce, according to the appointment of the bishop, the aforesaid conclusions to be erroneous and heresies, in the parish churches of Lynn and Tilney, and in other places at the assignment of the said bishop."

This being done, the archbishop of Canterbury, in the convocation of his prelates and clergy, and such like men, caused the process of the bishop of Norwich to be read openly and publicly to Sir William Sautre. And after that demanded and objected against the said Sir William, that after he had before the said bishop of Norwich revoked and abjured divers errors and heresies, he affirmed, that in the same sacrament of the altar, after the consecration made by the priest, as he taught, there remained material bread; which heresy, amongst others as errors also, he abjured before the foresaid bishop of Norwich. Hereto William answered smiling, or in mocking wise, saying, and denying that he knew of the premises. Then finally it was demanded of Sir William, why he ought not to be pronounced as a man fallen into heresy, and why they should not further proceed to this degradation according to the canonical sanctions: to which he answered nothing, neither could he allege any cause to the contrary.

Whereupon the archbishop of Canterbury by the counsel and assent of the whole council, and especially by the counsel and assent of the reverend fathers and bishops, as also priors, deans, archdeacons, and other worshipful doctors and clerks then and there present in the council, fully determined to proceed to the degradation, and actual deposing of William Sautre, as relapsed into heresy and as incorrigible, according to the sentence in writing, as follows.

"In the name of God, Amen. We Thomas, by the grace of God archbishop of Canterbury, legate of the see apostolical, and metropolitan of all England, do find and declare, that thou William Sautre, otherwise called Chatris, priest, by us with the counsel and assent as all and singular our fellow brethren and whole clergy, by this our sentence definitive declared in writing, hast been for heresy convicted and condemned, and art (being again fallen into heresy) to be deposed and degraded by these presents."

Upon the 26th of February, the archbishop of Canterbury sat in the bishop's seat of the foresaid church of St. Paul in London, and solemnly apparelled in his pontifical attire, with six other bishops, commanded and caused Sir William Sautre, apparelled in priestly vestments, to be brought before him. That done, he declared and expounded in English to all the clergy and people assembled there in great multitude; that all process was finished against Sir William Sautre. Which thing finished, he recited and read the above-mentioned sentence of relapse against Sir William. And as he saw William nothing abashed, he proceeded to his degradation and actual deposition in form as follows.

"In the name of the Father, and the Son, and of the Holy Ghost. We Thomas by God's permission archbishop of Canterbury, primate of all England, and legate of the apostolic see, do denounce thee William Sautre, otherwise called Chatris, a pretended chaplain, in the habit and apparel of a priest, as an heretic, and re-fallen into heresy, by this our sentence, by counsel, assent, and authority to be condemned: and by conclusion of all our fellow brethren, fellow bishops, prelates, council provincial, and of the whole clergy, do degrade and deprive thee of thy priestly order. And in sign of degradation and actual deposition from thy priestly dignity, for thine incorrigibility and want of amendment, we take from thee the paten and chalice, and do deprive thee of all power and authority of celebrating the mass, and also we pull from thy back the casule, and take from thee the vestment, and deprive thee of all manner of priestly honour.

"Also, we Thomas archbishop by authority, counsel, and assent, which upon the foresaid William we have, being a pretended deacon, in the habit and apparel of a deacon, having the New Testament in thy hands, being an heretic, and twice fallen, condemned by sentence as is aforesaid, do degrade and put thee from the order of a deacon. And in token of this thy degradation and actual deposition, we take from thee the book of the New Testament, and the stole, and do deprive thee of all authority in reading of the gospel, and of all and all manner of dignity of a deacon.

"Also, we Thomas archbishop, by authority, counsel, and assent, which over thee the foresaid William we have, being a pretended sub-deacon, in the habit and vestment of a sub-deacon, an heretic, and twice fallen condemned by sentence, as is aforesaid, do degrade and put thee from the order of a sub-deacon; and in token of this thy degradation and actual deposition, we take from thee the surplice and maniple, and do deprive thee of all manner of sub-deaconical dignity.

"Also we Thomas archbishop aforesaid, by counsel assent, and authority which we have over thee, the foresaid William, a pretended acolyte, wearing the habit of an acolyte, and heretic, twice fallen, by our sentence condemned, do degrade and put from thee all order of an acolyte; and in sign and token of this thy degradation, and actual deposition, we take from thee the candlestick and taper, and also urceolum, and do deprive thee of all and all manner of dignity of an acolyte.

"Also we Thomas archbishop, by assent, counsel, and authority, which upon thee the foresaid William we have, a pretended exorcist, in the habit of an exorcist or holy-water clerk, being an heretic, twice fallen, and by our sentence as is aforesaid, condemned, do degrade and depose thee from the order of an exorcist; and in token of this thy degradation and actual deposition, we take from thee the book of conjurations, and do deprive thee of all and singular dignity of an exorcist.

"Also, we Thomas archbishop, by assent, counsel, and authority, as is abovesaid, do degrade and depose thee the aforesaid William, a pretended reader, clothed in the habit of a reader, an heretic, twice fallen, and by our sentence as is aforesaid, condemned from the order of a reader; and in token of this thy degradation and actual deposition, we take from thee the book of the divine lections (that is, the book of the church legend) and do deprive thee of all and singular manner of dignity of such a reader.

"Also, we Thomas archbishop of Canterbury aforesaid, by authority, counsel and assent, the which we have, as is aforesaid, do degrade and put thee the foresaid William Sautre, a pretended sexton, in the habit of a sexton, and wearing a surplice, being an heretic twice fallen, by our sentence definitive condemned, as aforesaid from the order of a sexton; and in token of this thy degradation and actual deposition, for the causes aforesaid, we take from thee the keys of the church-door, and thy surplice, and do deprive thee of all and singular manner of commodities of a door-keeper.

"And also, by the authority of omnipotent God the Father, the Son, and Holy Ghost, and by the authority, counsel, and assent, of our whole council provincial above written, we do degrade thee, and depose thee, being here personally present before us, from orders, benefices, privileges and habit in the church; and for thy pertinency incorrigible we do degrade thee before the secular court of the high constable and marshal of England, being personally present; and do depose thee from all and singular clerkly honours and dignities whatsoever, by these writings. Also, in token of thy degradation and deposition, here actually we have caused thy crown and ecclesiastical tonsure in our presence to be rased away, and utterly to be abolished, like to the form of a secular layman; and here we do put upon the head of thee the aforesaid William the cap of a lay secular person; beseeching the court aforesaid, that they will receive favorably the said William to them thus recommitted."

Thus William Sautre the servant of Christ being utterly thrust out of the pope's kingdom, and metamorphosed from a clerk to a secular layman, was committed to the secular power. Which so done, the bishops, not yet contented, cease not to call upon the king, to cause him to be brought forth to speedy execution. Whereupon the king, too ready to gratify the clergy, and to retain their favours, directs out a terrible decree against William Sautre, and sent it to the major and sheriffs of London to be put in execution; as follows:

The Decree of the King against William Sautre.

"The decree of our sovereign lord the king and his council in the parliament, against a certain new sprung up heretic. To the major and sheriffs of London, &c. Whereas the reverend father Thomas archbishop of Canterbury, primate of all England, and legate of the apostolic see, by the assent, consent, and counsel of other bishops, and his brethren suffragans, and also of all the whole clergy within his province or diocese, gathered together in his provincial council, the due order of the law being observed in all points in this behalf, hath pronounced and declared, by his definitive sentence, William Sautre sometime chaplain fallen again into his most damnable heresy, the which before time the said William had abjured, thereupon to be a most manifest heretic, and therefore hath decreed that he should be degraded, and hath for the same cause really degraded him from all prerogative and privilege of the clergy, decreeing to leave him to the secular power; and hath really so left him, according to the laws and canonical sanctions set forth in this behalf, and also that our holy mother the church hath no farther to do in the premises: we therefore being zealous in religion, and reverend lovers of the catholic faith, willing and minding to maintain and defend the holy church, and the laws and the liberties of the same, to root out all such errors and heresies out of our kingdom of England, and with condign punishment to correct and punish all heretics or such as be convicted; provided always that both according to the law of God and man, and the canonical institutions in this behalf accustomed, such heretics convicted and condemned in form aforesaid ought to be burned with fire: we command you, as straightly as we may, or can, firmly enjoining you that you do cause the said William, being in your custody, in some public or open place within the liberties of your city aforesaid (the cause aforesaid being published unto the people) to be put into the fire, and there in the same fire really to be burned, to the great horror of his offence, and the manifest example of other christians. Fail not in the execution thereof, upon the peril that will fall thereupon."

Thus it may appear how kings and princes have been blinded and abused by the false prelates of the church, insomuch that they have been their slaves and butchers, to slay Christ's poor innocent members. See therefore what danger it is for princes not to have knowledge and understanding themselves, but to be led by other men's eyes, and specially trusting to such guides, who through hypocrisy deceive them, and through cruelty devour the people.

As King Henry IV., who was the deposer of King Richard, was the first of all English kings that began the unmerciful burning of Christ's saints for standing against the pope: so was this William Sautre, the true and faithful martyr of Christ, the first of all them in Wickliff's time, who I find to be burned in the reign of this king, which was A. D. 1400.

After the martyrdom of this godly man, the rest of the same company began to conceal themselves for fear of the king, who was altogether bent to hold with the pope's prelacy. Such was the reign of this prince, that he was ever terrible to the godly, immeasurable in his actions, and really beloved by very few men; but princes never lack flatterers about them. Neither was the time of his reign quiet, but full of trouble, of blood and misery. Such was their desire of King Richard again in the reign of this king, that he was many years after rumoured to be alive (by those who desired that to be true which they knew to be false) for which several were executed. For the space of six or seven years together, scarcely a year passed without some conspiracy against the king.

Many of the nobles joined in these rebellions, and many of them were beheaded, or otherwise slain, but still the rebellions continued.

This civil rebellion of so many nobles and others, against the king, declared what hostile feelings the people then bore towards this King Henry. Among whom I cannot omit here the archbishop of York named Richard Scrope, who with the Lord Mowbray, marshal of England, gathered a great company in the north country against the king, to whom also was joined the forces of Lord Bardolf, and Henry Percy earl of Northumberland. And to stir up the people more willingly to take their parts, they collected certain articles against the said king, to the number of ten, and fastened them upon the doors of the churches and monasteries, to be read of all men in English. Which articles, as they contain a great part of the doings between King Henry and King Richard, I thought, for the better opening of the matter to insert the same, in such form as I found them:

Articles set upon the Church Doors against King Henry the Fourth.

"In the name of God, Amen. Before the Lord Jesus Christ, judge of the quick and dead, &c. We A. B. C. D. &c., not long since became bound by oath upon the sacred evangelical book, to our sovereign lord Richard, late king of England and France, in the presence of many prelates, potentates and nobility of the realm; that we, so long as we lived, should bear true allegiance and fide-

lity toward him and his heirs succeeding him in the kingdom by just title, right, and line, according to the statutes and custom of this realm of England. By virtue whereof we are bound to see that no vices, or heinous offences arising in the commonwealth, take effect, and we ought to give ourselves and our goods to withstand the same, without fear of the sword or death, upon pain of perjury, which pain is everlasting damnation. Wherefore we seeing and perceiving divers horrible crimes, and great enormities daily without ceasing committed by the children of the Devil and Satan's soldiers against the supremacy of the church of Rome, the liberty of the church of England, and the laws of the realm, against the person of King Richard and his heirs, against the prelates, noblemen, religion, and commonalty, and finally against the whole public weal of the realm of England, to the great offence of the majesty of Almighty God, and to the provocation of his just wrath and vengeance toward the realm and people. And fearing also the destruction both of the church of Rome and England, and the ruin of our country to be at hand, having before our eyes the justice and the kingdom of God, calling always on the name of Jesus, having an assured confidence in his clemency, mercy and power; have here taken certain articles, subscribed in the following form to be propounded, tried, and heard before the just judge, Jesus Christ, and the whole world, to his honour, the delivery of the church, the clergy, and commonalty, and to the utility and profit of the public weal. But if (which God forbid) by force, fear, or violence of wicked persons we shall be cast in prison, or by violent death prevented, so as in this world we shall not be able to prove the articles as we would wish, then do we appeal to the high celestial judge, that he may judge and discern the same, in the day of his supreme judgment.

"I. We depose, say, except, and intend to prove against the Lord Henry Darby, son of the Lord John of Gaunt, late duke of Lancaster, and commonly called king of England (himself pretending the same, although without all right and title thereunto) and against his adherents, favours, and accomplices; that they ever have been, are, and will be traitors, invaders, and destroyers of God's church in Rome, England, Wales, and Ireland, and of our sovereign lord Richard late king of England, his heirs, his kingdom, and commonwealth, as shall hereafter manifestly appear.

"II. We depose, &c. against the said Lord Henry, for that he had conceived, devised, and conspired certain heinous crimes and traitorous offences against his sovereign lord Richard's state and dignity, as manifestly appeared in the contention between the said Lord Henry, and the Lord Thomas duke of Norfolk begun at Coventry, but not finished thoroughly. Afterwards he was sent into exile by sentence of the King Richard, by the agreement of his father the Lord John duke of Lancaster, by the voice of many of the lords temporal, and nobility of the realm, and also by his own consent; there to remain for a certain time appointed unto him by the said lords, and withal he was bound by oath not to return into England before he had obtained favour and grace of the king. Not long after, when the king was departed into Ireland for reformation of that country appertaining to the crown of England, but as then rebelling against the same; the said Lord Henry in the meantime contrary to his oath and fidelity, and long before the time limited unto him was expired, with all his favourers and invaders secretly entered into the realm, swearing and protesting before the face of the people, that his coming into the realm in the absence of the king was for no other cause, but that he might in humble sort with the love and favour of the king, and all the lords spiritual and temporal, have and enjoy his lawful inheritance descending unto him of right after the death of his father: which thing as it pleased all men, so they cried, 'Blessed is he that cometh in the name of the Lord.' But how this blessing afterwards turned into cursing, shall appear in that which followed: and also ye shall understand his horrible and wicked conspiracy against his sovereign lord King Richard, and divers other lords as well spiritual as temporal; besides that his manifest perjury shall well be known, and that he remains not only foresworn and perjured, but also excommunicate, for he conspired against his sovereign lord our king. Wherefore we pronounce him by these presents as well perjured as excommunicate.

"III. We depose, &c. against the Lord Henry, that he, immediately after his entry into England, by crafty and subtle policy caused to be proclaimed openly throughout the realm, that no tenths of the clergy, fifteenths of the people, sealing up of cloth, diminution of wool, impost of wine, nor other extortions or exactions whatsoever, should hereafter be required or exacted; hoping by this means to purchase unto him the voice and favour of the prelates spiritual, the lords temporal, the merchants, and commonalty of the whole realm. After this he took by force the king's castles and fortresses, spoiled and devoured his goods wheresoever he found them, crying, Havock! Havock! The king's majesty's subjects as well spiritual as temporal, he spoiled and robbed, some he took captive and imprisoned them, and some he slew and put to miserable death, whereof many were bishops, prelates, priests, and religious men. Whereby it is manifest, that the said Lord Henry is not only perjured, in promising and swearing that there should be hereafter no more exactions, payments, or extortions within the realm, but also excommunicate for the violence and injury done to prelates and priests. Wherefore by these presents we pronounce him, as before, as well perjured as excommunicate.

"IV. We depose, &c. against the said Lord Henry, That he hearing of the king's return from Ireland into Wales, rose up against his sovereign lord the king with many thousands of armed men, marching forward with all his power towards the castle of Flint in Wales, where he took the king and held him prisoner, and so led him captive as a traitor unto Leicester: from whence he took his journey towards London, misusing the king by the way, both he and his, with many injuries and opprobrious contumelies and scoffs. And in the end committed him to the Tower of London, and held a parliament, the king being absent and in prison: wherein for fear of death he compelled the king to yield and resign to him all his right and title of the kingdom and crown of England. After which resignation being made, the said Lord Henry standing up in the parliament house, stoutly and proudly before them all, said and affirmed, that the kingdom of England and crown of the same, with all thereunto belonging, did pertain to him at that present, as of very right, and to no other; for that the said King Richard by his own deed was deprived for ever of all the right, title, and interest that ever he had, hath, or may have in the same. And thus at length by right and wrong he exalted himself unto the throne of the kingdom: since which time, our commonwealth never flourished nor prospered, but has been altogether void of virtue, for the spirituality is oppressed, exercise and war-like practices have not been maintained, charity is waxed cold, and covetousness and misery have taken place, and finally mercy is taken away and vengeance supplies the room. Whereby it doth appear (as before is said,) that the said lord Henry is not only perjured and false by usurping the kingdom and dominion belonging to another, but also excommunicate for the apprehending, unjust imprisoning, and depriving his sovereign lord the king of his royal crown and dignity. Wherefore, as in the articles before, we pronounce the said Lord Henry to be excommunicate.

"V. We depose, &c. against the said Lord Henry, that he the same Lord Henry with the rest of his favourers and accomplices, heaping mischief upon mischief, have committed and brought to pass a most wicked and mischievous fact, yea, such as has not been heard of at any time before. For after that they had taken and imprisoned the king, and deposed him by open injury against all human nature; yet, not content with this, they brought him to Pomfret castle, and there imprisoned him, where fifteen days and nights they vexed him with continual hunger, thirst, and cold, and finally bereft him of life with such a kind of death as never before that time was known in England, but by God's Providence it is come to light. Who ever heard of such a deed, or who ever saw the like of him? Wherefore, O England! arise, stand up, avenge the cause, the death and injury of thy king and prince: which if thou do not, take this for certain, that the right-

eous God will destroy thee by strange invasions and foreign power, and avenge himself on thee for this so horrible an act. Whereby doth appear not only his perjury, but also his excommunication most execrable; so that, as before, we pronounce the said Henry not only perjured, but also excommunicate.

"VI. We depose, &c. against the said Lord Henry, that after he had attained to the crown and sceptre of the kingdom, he caused forthwith to be apprehended divers lords spiritual, bishops, abbots, priors, and religious men of all orders, whom he arrested, imprisoned, and bound, and against all order brought them before the secular judges to be examined; nor sparing the bishops whose bodies were anointed with sacred oil, nor priests nor religious men, but commanded them to be condemned, hanged, and beheaded by the temporal law and judgment, notwithstanding the privilege of the church and holy orders, which he ought to have reverenced and worshipped, if he had been a true and lawful king: for the first and chief oath in the coronation of a lawful king is, to defend and keep inviolate the liberties and rights of the church, and not to deliver any priest or religious man into the hands of the secular power, except for heresy only, and that after his degradation, according to the order of the church. He has done contrary unto all this; so that it is manifest by this article as before in the rest, that he is both perjured and excommunicate.

"VII. We depose, &c. against the said Lord Henry, that he not only caused to be put to death the lords spiritual and other religious men, but also divers of the lords temporal and nobility of the realm, and chiefly those that studied for the preservation of the commonwealth, not ceasing as yet to continue his mischievous enterprise, if by God's Providence it be not prevented, and that with speed: amongst all other of the nobility, these first he put to death; the earl of Salisbury, the earl of Huntington, the earl of Gloucester, the Lord Roger Clarendon the king's brother, with several other knights and esquires, and afterwards, the Lord Thomas Percy earl of Worcester, and the Lord Henry Percy son and heir to the earl of Northumberland; which Lord Henry he not only slew, but to the utmost of his power again and again he endeavoured to have him slain. For after he was once put to death, and delivered to the lord of Furnile to be buried (who committed his body to holy sepulture, with as much honor as might be, commending his soul to Almighty God with the suffrages of blessed mass and other prayers) the said Lord Henry, most like a cruel beast still thirsting for his blood, caused his body to be exhumed and brought forth again, and to be placed between two millstones in the town of Shrewsbury, there to be kept with armed men; and afterwards to be beheaded and quartered, commanding his head and quarters to be carried into divers cities of the kingdom. Wherefore, for so detestable an act never heard of in any age before, we pronounce him, as in the former articles, excommunicate.

"VIII. We depose, &c. against the said Lord Henry, that after his attaining to the crown he willingly ratified, allowed, and approved a most wicked statute set forth and renewed in the parliament holden at Winchester. The which statute is directly against the church of Rome, and the power, and principality thereof given by our Lord Jesus Christ unto blessed St. Peter and his successors bishops of Rome; unto whom belongs by full authority the free disposing of all spiritual promotions as well superior as inferior: which wicked statute is the cause of many mischiefs, viz. of simony, perjury, adultery, disorder, and disobedience; for many bishops, abbots, priors, and prelates (we will not say by virtue, but rather by error of this statute) have bestowed the benefices vacant upon young men, rude and unworthy persons, who have bargained with them for the same, so that scarcely one prelate is found that has not convenanted with the party promoted for the half yearly, or, at the least, the third part of the said benefice so bestowed. And by this means the said statute is the destruction of the right of St. Peter, the church of Rome and England, the clergy and universities, the whole commonwealth, and maintenance of wars, &c.

"IX. We say and depose, &c. against the said Lord

Henry, that after he had tyrannously taken upon him the government of the realm, England never flourished since, nor prospered, by reason of his continual exactions of money, and yearly oppressions of the clergy and commonalty : neither is it known how this money so extorted is bestowed, when neither his soldiers, nor his gentlemen are paid as yet their wages and fees for their charges, and wonderful toil and labour, neither yet are the poor country people satisfied for the victuals taken of them : and nevertheless the miserable clergy, and more miserable commonalty, are forced still to pay by menaces and sharp threatenings.   Notwithstanding he sware, when he first usurped the crown, that hereafter there should be no such exactions nor vexations, neither of the clergy nor laity. Wherefore, as before, we pronounce him perjured, &c.

"X. In the tenth and last article we depose, say, and openly protest by these presents, for ourselves, and all our assistants in the cause of the church of Rome and England, and in the cause of King Richard, his heirs, the clergy and commonalty of the whole realm ; that our intention neither is, was, nor shall be, in word or deed to offend any state either of the prelates spiritual, lords temporal, or commons of the realm ; but rather, foreseeing the perdition and destruction of this realm to approach, we have here brought before you certain articles concerning the destruction of the same, to be circumspectly considered by the whole assembly, as well of the lords spiritual as temporal, and the faithful commons of England : beseeching you all in the bowels of Jesus Christ the righteous judge, and for the merits of our blessed lady the mother of God, and of St. George our defender, under whose displayed banner we wish to live and die, and under pain of damnation, that ye will be favourable to us, and to our causes which are three in number.   Whereof the first is, that we exalt unto the kingdom the true and lawful heir, and crown him in the kingly throne with the diadem of England.   And secondly, that we recall the Welshmen, the Irishmen, and all other our enemies to perpetual peace and amity.   Thirdly, and finally, that we deliver and make free our native country from all exactions, extortions, and unjust payment ; beseeching our Lord Jesus Christ to grant his blessing, the remission of their sins, and life everlasting to all that assist us to their power in this godly and meritorious work ; and to all those that are against us we threaten the curse of Almighty God, by the authority committed unto us by Christ and his holy church, and by these presents we pronounce them excommunicate."

These articles being seen and read, a great concourse of people daily resorted more and more to the archbishop. The Earl of Westmoreland hearing of this, mustered his soldiers with all the force he was able to make, and went against the archbishop ; but seeing his party too weak to encounter with him, he used policy, and under colour of friendship, he laboured to seek out the causes of that great stir. The archbishop shewed him the articles, which, when the earl had read, he seemed highly to commend the purpose and doings of the bishop ; promising that he would help in that quarrel to the utmost of his power. The archbishop, easily persuaded, was content, although much against the counsel of the earl marshal, and came to hold further conference. The articles being opened, published, and read, the earl of Westmoreland pretended to like them, and exhorted the archbishop that he would discharge the needless multitude of his soldiers, and dismiss them home to their works and business, and they would together drink and join hands in the sight of the whole company. Thus they shaking hands together, the archbishop sends away his soldiers in peace, not knowing himself to be circumvented, until he was arrested by the hands of the earl of Westmoreland ; and shortly after, the king coming with his army to York, he was there beheaded ; and with him also Lord Thomas Mowbray, marshal, with divers others. After whose slaughter, the king proceeds farther to pursue the earl of Northumberland, and Lord Thomas Bardolph. At length, within two years after, fighting against the king, they were slain in the field, (A.D. 1408.)

The king, after the shedding of so much blood, seeing himself so disliked by his subjects, thought to keep in with the clergy, and with the bishop of Rome. And therefore he was compelled in all things to serve their humour, as appeared as well in condemning William Sautre, as also in others whom we have now to treat of. In the number of whom comes now John Badby, who, by the cruelty of Thomas Arundel, archbishop, and other prelates, was brought to his condemnation in this king's reign, (A.D. 1409), as appears by their own registers.

JOHN BADBY, ARTIFICER.

In A. D. 1409, March 1st, the following examination of John Badby, a layman, was made upon the crime of heresy, before Thomas Arundel, archbishop of Canterbury, and the archbishop of York, bishops of London, of Winchester, of Oxford, of Norwich, of Salisbury, of Bath, of Bangor, and a great number of other lords both spiritual and temporal. Master Morgan read the articles of his opinions to the hearers, as follows :

"In the name of God, Amen. Be it manifest to all men by this present public instrument, that in the year after the incarnation of our Lord, according to the course and computation of the church of England, in the year 1409, John Badby, a layman, of the diocese of Worcester, appearing personally before the reverend father in Christ and Lord, Lord Thomas, by the grace of God bishop of Worcester, was detected of heresy, having heretically taught, and openly maintained, that the sacrament of the body of Christ, consecrated by the priest upon the altar, is not the true body of Christ by the virtue of the words of the sacrament. But that after the sacramental words spoken by the priests to make the body of Christ, the material bread remains upon the altar as in the beginning, neither is it turned into the very body of Christ after the sacramental words spoken of the priests. Which John Badby being examined, and diligently demanded by the reverend father, did answer that it was impossible that any priest should make the body of Christ, and that he believed firmly that no priest could make the body of Christ by such words sacramentally spoken in such sort. And also he said expressly that he would never while he lived believe that any priest could make the body of Christ sacramentally, unless that first he saw manifestly the like body of Christ to be handled in the hands of the priest upon the altar, in his corporal form. And, furthermore, he said that John Raker of Bristol had as much power and authority to make the like body of Christ, as any priest had. Moreover, he said that when Christ sat at supper with his disciples, he had not his body in his hand, to the intent to distribute it to his disciples ; and he said expressly, that he did not this thing. And he also spake many other words teaching and defending the heresy, both grievous, and also out of order, and horrible to the ears of the hearers, sounding against the catholic faith.

"Upon which occasion the reverend father admonished and requested John Badby oftentimes and very instantly to charity ; forsomuch as he would willingly that he should have forsaken such heresy and opinion holden, taught, and maintained by him, in such sort against the sacrament, to renounce, and utterly abjure them, and to believe other things which the holy mother church doth believe. And he informed the said John on that behalf, both gently, and yet laudably. Yet the said John Badby, although he were admonished and requested both often and instantly by the said reverend father, said and answered expressly, that he would never believe otherwise than he had before said, taught, and answered. Whereupon, the aforesaid reverend father, bishop of Worcester, seeing, understanding, and perceiving John Badby to maintain and fortify the heresy, being stubborn, and proceeding in the same stubbornness, pronounced the said John to be before this time convicted of such an heresy, and that he hath been and is an heretic, and in the end declared it in these words :

"In the name of God, Amen. We, Thomas, bishop of Worcester, do accuse thee, John Badby, being a layman, of our diocese, of and upon the crime of heresy, being oftentimes confessed and convicted before us sitting for chief judge, that thou hast taught, and openly affirmed, as hitherto thou dost teach, boldly affirm, and defend; that the sacrament of the body of Christ, consecrated upon the altar by the priest, is not the true body of Christ; but after the sacramental words, to make the body of Christ, by virtue of the said sacramental words pronounced, to have been in the crime of heresy: and we do pronounce thee both to have been and to be an heretic, and do declare it finally by these writings."

When these things were thus finished, and all the conclusions were read in the vulgar tongue, the archbishop demanded of him, whether he would renounce and forsake his opinions and such conclusions or not, and adhere to the doctrine of Christ and the catholic faith? He answered, that according to what he had said before, he would adhere and stand to those words which before he had made answer unto. Then the archbishop oftentimes required him by the bowels of Jesus Christ, that he would forsake those opinions and conclusions, and that henceforth he would cleave to the christian faith, which, in the audience of all the lords and others that were present, he expressly denied and refused.

After all this, when the archbishop of Canterbury and the bishop of London had consulted, to what safe keeping John Badby might be committed; it was concluded that he should be put into a certain chamber, or safe house within the mansion of the friars preachers; and then the archbishop of Canterbury said that he himself would keep the key thereof in the meantime. And when the day was expired, being the fifteenth day of March, and that the archbishop of Canterbury, with his fellow brethren and suffragans, were assembled in the church of St. Paul in London; the archbishop of Canterbury, taking the episcopal seat, called unto him the archbishop of York, and the following bishops: Richard of London; Henry of Winchester; Robert of Chichester; Alexander of Norwich; and the noble Prince Edmund; the duke of York; Ralph, earl of Westmoreland; Thomas Beaufort, knight; lord chancellor of England; and the Lord Beamond, with other noble men, as well spiritual as temporal, that stood and sat by, to whom it would be long to name: Before whom John Badby was called personally to answer to the articles. The articles were read by the official of the court of Canterbury, and by the archbishop (in the vulgar tongue) expounded publicly and expressly; and as he had before spoken and deposed, he still held and defended his opinions, and said that while he lived, he would never retract the same. And, furthermore, he said especially to be noted, that the lord duke of York, personally there present, and every man else for the time being, is of more estimation and reputation, than the sacrament of the altar, by the priest in due form consecrated. And whilst they were thus in his examination, the archbishop considering and weighing that he would in nowise be altered, and seeing moreover his countenance stout, and heart confirmed, so that he began to persuade others as it appeared: these things considered, the archprelate, when he saw that it was not in his power either by exhortations, reasons, or arguments, to bring John Badby from his constant truth to his catholic faith (executing and doing the office of his great master) proceeded to confirm and ratify the former sentence given by the bishop of Worcester against John Badby, pronouncing him for an open and public heretic. And thus they delivered him to the secular power; and desired the temporal lords then and there present, that they would not put John Badby to death for that his offence, nor deliver him to be punished or put to death in the presence of all the lords.

These things thus done and concluded by the bishops in the forenoon: in the afternoon, the king's writ was not far behind. John Badby, still persevering in his constancy unto the death, was brought into Smithfield, and there being put in an empty barrel, was bound with iron chains fastened to a stake having dry wood put about him.

And as he was thus standing in the barrel, it happened that the prince, the king's eldest son, was present; who, shewing some part of the good Samaritan, began to endeavour to save the life of him, whom the hypocritical Levites and pharisees sought to put to death. He admonished and counselled him, that he should speedily withdraw himself out of these dangerous labyrinths of opinions, adding oftentimes threatenings, which might have daunted any man's courage.

In the mean time the prior of St. Bartholomew's, in Smithfield, brought with all solemnity the sacrament of God's body, with twelve torches borne before, and so shewed the sacrament to the poor man at the stake. And then they demanding of him how he believed in it, he answered, That he knew well it was hallowed bread, and not God's body. And then was the barrel put over him, and fire put to him. And when he felt the fire, he cried, mercy, calling upon the Lord, and so the prince immediately commanded to take away the barrel, and quench the fire. The prince's commandment being obeyed, he asked him if he would forsake heresy and take to the faith of holy church? which, if he would do, he should have goods enough, promising also a yearly stipend out of the king's treasury.

But this valiant champion of Christ, neglecting the prince's fair words, refused the offer of worldly promises, being no doubt more vehemently inflamed with the Spirit of God, than with any earthly desire. Wherefore, when he continued unmoveable in his former mind, the prince commanded him straight to be put again into the barrel, and that he should not afterward look for any grace or favour. But as he could be allured by no rewards, even so was he nothing at all abashed at their torments, but, as a valiant champion of Christ, he persevered invincible to the end. Not without a great and most cruel battle, but with much greater triumph of victory; the Spirit of Christ having always the upper hand in his members, notwithstanding the fury, rage, and power of the whole world.

This godly martyr, John Badby, having thus perfected his testimony and martyrdom in fire, the persecuting bishops not yet contented, and thinking themselves as yet either not strong enough, or else not sharp enough against the poor innocent flock of Christ, to make all things sure and substantial on their side, so that this doctrine of the gospel now springing should be suppressed for ever, laid their conspiring heads together; and having now a king for their own purpose, ready to serve their turn, the bishops and clergy of the realm exhibited a bill to the king's majesty; subtilely declaring, what quietness had been maintained within this realm by his most noble progenitors, who always defended the ancient rites and customs of the church, and enriched the same with large gifts, to the honour of God and the realm: and contrariwise, what trouble and disquietness was now risen by wicked and perverse men, teaching and preaching openly and privily a certain new, wicked, and heretical kind of doctrine, contrary to the catholic faith and determination of holy church. The king, always oppressed with blind ignorance, by the crafty means and subtle pretences of the clergy, granted in the parliament (by consent of the nobility assembled) a statute to be observed, called *ex-officio*, as follows:—

The Statute Ex-Officio.

"That is to say, That no man within this realm, or other the king's majesty's dominions, presume to take upon him to preach privily or openly, without special license first obtained of the ordinary of the same place (curates in their own parish churches, and persons heretofore privileged, and others admitted by the canon law, only excepted). Nor that any hereafter do preach, maintain, teach, inform openly or in secret, or make or write any book contrary to the catholic faith, and determination of the holy church. Nor that any hereafter make any conventicles or assemblies, or keep and exercise any manner of schools touching this sect, wicked doctrine and opinion. And further, That no man hereafter shall by any means favour any such preacher, any such maker of unlawful assemblies, or any such bookmaker or writer ; and, finally, any such teacher, informer, or stirrer up of the people. And that all and singular persons having any of the said books, writings, or schedules, containing the said wicked doctrines and opinions, shall within forty days after this present proclamation and statute, really and effectually deliver, or cause to be delivered, all and singular the said books and writings unto the ordinary of the same place. And if it shall happen that any person or persons, of what kind, state or condition soever he or they be, to do or attempt any manner of thing contrary to this present proclamation and statute, or not to deliver the same books in form aforesaid : That then the ordinary of the same place in his own diocese, by authority of the said proclamation and statute shall cause to be arrested and detained under safe custody the said person or persons in this case defamed and evidently suspected, or any of them, until he or they so offending have by order of law purged him or themselves as touching the articles laid to his or their charge in this behalf ; or until he or they have denied and recanted (according to the laws ecclesiastical) the said wicked sect, preachings, teachings, and heretical and erroneous opinions. And that the said ordinary by himself or his commissaries proceed openly and judicially to all the effect of law against the said persons so arrested and remaining under safe custody, and that he end and determine the matter within three months after the said arrest (all delays and excuses set apart) according to the order and custom of the canon law. And if any person, in any cause abovementioned, shall be lawfully convicted before the ordinary of the diocese or his commissaries ; that then the said ordinary may lawfully cause the said person so convicted (according to the manner and quality of his offence, to be laid in any of his own prisons, and there to be kept so long as in his discretion shall be thought expedient.

" And further, The said ordinary (except in cases by the which according to the canon law the party offending ought to be delivered unto the secular power) shall charge the said person with such a fine of money to be paid unto the king's majesty, as he shall think competent for the manner and quality of his offence. And the said diocesan shall be bound to give notice of the said fine, into the king's majest'sy exchequer, by his letters patent under his seal ; to the intent that the said fine may be levied to the king's majesty's use of the goods of the person so convicted.

" And further, If any person within this realm and other the king's majesty's dominions, shall be convicted before the ordinary of the place, or his commissaries, of the said wicked preachings, doctrines, opinions, schools, and heretical and erroneous informations, or any of them ; and will refuse to abjure and recant the said wicked sect, preachings, teachings, opinions, schools, and informations ; or if, after his abjuration once made, the relapse be pronounced against him by the diocesan of the place, or his commissaries (for so by the canon law he ought to be left to the secular power, upon credit given to the ordinary or his commissaries) that then the sheriff of the same county, the mayor, sheriffs, or sheriff, or the mayor, or bailiffs of the same city, village, or borough of the same county, and nearest inhabiting to the said ordinary, or his said commissaries, shall personally be present, as often as they shall be required, to confer with the said ordinary or his commissaries in giving sentence against the said persons offending, or any of them : and, after the said sentence so pronounced, shall take unto them the said persons so offending, and any of them, and cause them openly to be burned in the sight of all the people ; to the intent that this kind of punishment may be a terror unto others, that the like wicked doctrines and heretical opinions, or authors and favourers thereof be no more maintained within this realm and dominions, to the great hurt (which God forbid) of christian religion, and decrees of holy church. In all which and singular the premises, concerning the statute aforesaid, let the sheriff, mayors, and bailiffs of the said counties, cities, villages, and boroughs be attendant, aiding and favouring the said ordinaries and their commissaries."

By this bloody statute so severely and sharply enacted against these simple men, the reader may well consider the nature and condition of this present world, how it has been set and bent ever from the beginning, by all might, counsel, and ways possible to strive against the ways of God, and to overthrow that which he will have set up. And although the world may see by infinite histories and examples, that it is but in vain to strive against him ; yet such is the nature of this world (all set in malignity) that it will not cease still to be like itself.

After this was issued the terrible constitution of the archbishop of Canterbury against the followers of God's truth, full of cruelty and persecution unto blood, but which is too long for insertion here.

Who would have thought by these laws and constitutions, but that the name and memory of this persecuted sort should utterly have been rooted up, and never could have stood ? And yet such be the works of the Lord, passing all men's admiration, that notwithstanding all this, so far was the number and courage of these good men from being vanquished, that rather they multiplied daily and increased. For so I find in registers recorded, that these foresaid persons, whom the king and the catholic fathers did so greatly detest for heretics, were in divers counties of this realm increased, especially at London, in Lincolnshire, in Norfolk, in Herefordshire, in Shrewsbury, in Calais, and other quarters. However there were some that did shrink, many did revolt and renounce, for danger of the law. Among whom was John Purvey, who recanted at Paul's Cross, of whom more follows (the Lord willing) to be said in the year 1421. Also John Edward, priest of the diocese of Lincoln, who revoked in the Greenyard at Norwich ; Richard Herbert, and Emmot Willy, of London ; also John Becket, who recanted at London ; John Seynons, of Lincolnshire, who was caused to revoke at Canterbury.

WILLIAM THORPE.

Thus much being signified briefly, touching those who have been forced in the time of this king, to open abjuration. Next comes the history of Master William Thorpe, a valiant warrior, under the triumphant banner of Christ, with the process of his examinations before Thomas Arundel, archbishop of Canterbury, written by Thorpe, and recorded by his own pen, at the request of his friends. In his examination (A.D. 1407) thou shalt have, good reader, both to learn and to marvel. To learn, in that thou shalt hear truth discoursed and discussed, with the contrary reasons of the adversary dissolved. To marvel, for thou shalt behold here in this man the marvellous force and strength of the Lord's might, spirit, and grace, working and fighting in his soldiers, and also speaking in their mouths, according to the word of his promise. Master Thorpe, in his preface to the account of his examination, says, that he was moved to write it, not only by the desire of his friends, but also that other christian people might profit by seeing truth opposed to error, and that they might be prepared to forsake all the things of this life, not knowing how soon they may be called to a like trial.

The Examination of William Thorpe, penned with his own hand.

" Be it known to all men, that read or hear this writing, that on the Sunday next after the feast of St. Peter, that we call Lammas (A. D. 1407), I, William Thorpe, being in prison in the castle of Saltwood, was brought before Thomas Arundel, archbishop of Canterbury, and chancellor then of England. And when I came to him he stood in a great chamber, and many people about him; and when he saw me he went into a closet, bidding all secular men that followed him to leave him soon, so that no man was left in that closet but the archbishop himself, and a physician that was called Masveren, parson of St. Dunstan's in London, and two other persons unknown to me, who were ministers of the law. By and by the archbishop said to me, 'William, I know well that thou hast this twenty winters or more travelled in the north country, and in divers other countries of England, sowing false doctrine, labouring with untrue teaching to infect and poison all this land. But through the grace of God thou art now withstood and brought into my ward, so that I shall now sequester thee from thine evil purpose, and prevent thee from poisoning the sheep of my province. Nevertheless, St. Paul saith, If it may be, as much as in us lies, we ought to live peaceably with all men. Therefore, William, if thou wilt now meekly and of good heart without any feigning, kneel down and lay thy hand upon a book and kiss it, promising faithfully as I shall here charge thee, that thou wilt submit thee to my correction, and stand to mine ordinance, and fulfil it duly by all thy skill and power, thou shalt yet find me gracious to thee.' Then said I to the archbishop, 'Sir, since ye deem me an heretic, and out of the faith, will you give me here audience to tell you my belief?' And he said, 'Yea, tell on.' And I said, 'I believe that there is but one God Almighty, and in this Godhead, and of this Godhead are three Persons, that is, the Father, the Son, and the Holy Ghost. And I believe that all these three Persons are equal in power and in knowledge, and in might, full of grace of all goodness. For whatsoever that the Father doth, or can, or will do, that thing also the Son doth, and can, and will do; and in all their power, knowledge, and will, the Holy Ghost is equal to the Father, and to the Son.

"'Besides this, I believe, that through the counsel of this most blessed Trinity, in the time before appointed for the salvation of mankind, the second person of this Trinity was ordained to take the form of man, that is, the nature of man. And I believe, that this second person, our Lord Jesus Christ, was miraculously conceived through the Holy Ghost in the womb of the blessed Virgin Mary. And I believe that in due time Christ was born of this most blessed virgin.

"'And I believe, that Christ our Saviour was circumcised in the eighth day after his birth, in fulfilling of the law, and his name was called Jesus, which was so called of the angel, before that he was conceived in the womb of Mary his mother.

"'And I believe that Christ, as he was about thirty years old, was baptized in the Jordan by John the baptist; and the Holy Ghost descended like a dove upon him, and a voice was heard from heaven, saying, 'Thou art my beloved Son, in whom I am well pleased.'

"'And I believe that Christ was moved then by the Holy Ghost to go into the desert, and there he fasted forty days and forty nights without bodily meat and drink. And I believe that by and by after this fasting, when the manhood of God hungered, the devil came to him, and tempted him in gluttony, in vain glory, and in coveting; but in all those temptations Christ confuted the devil, and withstood him. And then without tarrying Jesus began to preach, and to say to the people, 'Repent, for the kingdom of heaven is at hand.'

"'I believe that Christ lived here most holily, and taught the will of his Father most truly. And I believe that he suffered most wrongfully the greatest reproofs and despisings.

"'And after this, when Christ would make an end here of this temporal life, I believe that in the day next before he was to suffer passion, he ordained the sacrament of his flesh and his blood in form of bread and of wine; that is, his own precious body, and gave it to his apostles to eat; commanding them, and by them all their after-comers, that they should do it in this form that he shewed to them, use themselves, and teach and administer to other men and women this most worshipful and holiest sacrament, in remembrance of his holiest

living, and of his most true preaching, and of his willing and patient suffering of the most painful passion.

"'And I believe that this Christ our Saviour, after that he had ordained this most worthy sacrament of his own precious body, went forth willingly against his enemies, and he suffered them most patiently to lay their hands most violently upon him, and to bind him, and to lead him forth as a thief, and to scorn him and buffet him, and to defile him with their spittings. Besides this, I believe that Christ suffered most meekly and patiently his enemies to extract with sharp scourges the blood that was between his skin and his flesh; yea, without resisting, Christ suffered the cruel Jews to crown him with sharp thorns, and to strike him with a reed. And after, Christ suffered wicked Jews to draw him out upon the cross, and to nail him thereupon; and so Christ shed out willingly for man's blood the blood that was in the veins. And then Christ gave willingly his spirit into the hands or power of his Father, and so, as he would, and when he would, Christ died willingly for man's sake upon the cross. And notwithstanding that Christ was wilfully, painfully, and most shamefully put to death, as to the world, there was left blood and water in his heart, as before ordained, that he would shed out this blood and this water for man's salvation; and therefore he suffered the Jews to make a blind knight to thrust him in the heart with a spear, and this blood and water that was in his heart, Christ would shed out for man's love. And after this, I believe that Christ was taken down from the cross and buried. And I believe that on the third day by the power of his Godhead Christ rose again from death to life. And the fortieth day thereafter, I believe that Christ ascended up into heaven, and that he there sitteth on the right hand of the Father Almighty. And the fiftieth day after his ascension he sent to his apostles the Holy Ghost, that he had promised them before; and I believe that Christ shall come and judge all mankind, some to everlasting peace, and some to everlasting pains.

"'And as I believe in the Father, and in the Son, that they are one God Almighty, so I believe in the Holy Ghost that he is also with them the same God Almighty.

"'And I believe an holy church, that is, all they that have been, and that now are, and always to the end of the world shall be, a people who shall endeavour to know and to keep the commandments of God, dreading over all things to offend God, and loving and seeking to please him: and I believe, that all they that have had, and yet have, and all they that yet shall have the aforesaid virtues, surely standing in the belief of God, hoping steadfastly in his merciful doings, continuing to their end in perfect charity, willingly, patiently, and gladly suffering persecutions, by the example of Christ chiefly, and his apostles, all these have their names written in the book of life.

"'Therefore I believe, that the gathering together of this people, living now here in this life, is the holy church of God, fighting here on earth against the devil, the prosperity of the world, and their own lusts. Wherefore, seeing that all the gathering together of this church, and every part thereof, neither covets, nor wills, nor loves, nor seeks any thing but to eschew the offence of God, and to do his pleasing will; meekly, gladly, and willingly, with all mine heart, I submit myself unto this holy church of Christ, to be ever ready and obedient to the ordinance of it, and of every member thereof, after my knowledge and power by the help of God. Therefore I acknowledge now, and evermore shall, if God will, that with all my heart, and with all my might, I will submit me only to the rule and governance of them, whom after my knowledge I may perceive to be members of the holy church. Wherefore these articles of belief and all other (both of the old law, and of the new, which after the commandment of God any man ought to believe) I believe verily in my soul, as a sinful deadly wretch, of my knowledge and power, ought to believe: praying the Lord God for his holy name to increase my belief, and to help my unbelief.

"'And because to the praising of God's name, I desire above all things to be a faithful member of holy church,

I make this protestation before you all four that are now here present, desiring that all men and women who are now absent knew the same: that is, whatsoever before this time I have said or done, or whatever I shall do or say at any time hereafter, I believe, that all the old law, and new law, given and ordained by the council of the three persons of the Trinity, were given and written for the salvation of mankind. And I believe, that these laws are sufficient for man's salvation. And I believe every article of these laws, to the intent that these articles ordained and commanded by these three persons of the most blessed Trinity are to be believed.

"'And therefore to the rule and the ordinance of these laws of God, meekly, gladly, and willingly, I submit me with all mine heart; that whoever can or will by authority of God's law, or by open reason, tell me that I have erred or now err, or in any time hereafter shall err in any article of belief (from which misfortune God keep me by his goodness) I submit to be reconciled, and to be ready and obedient to those laws of God, and to every article of them. For by authority specially of these laws I will, through the grace of God, be united charitably to these laws. Yea, sir, and besides this; I believe and admit all the sentences, authorities and reasons of the saints and doctors according to the holy scripture, and declaring it truly.

"'I submit me willingly and meekly to be ever obedient, after my knowledge and power, to all these saints and doctors, as they are obedient in work and in word to God and to his law, and further not (to my knowledge) for any earthly power, dignity or state, through the help of God. But sir, I pray you tell me, if after your bidding I shall lay my hand upon the book, is it to the intent to swear thereby?' And the archbishop said to me, 'Yea wherefore else?' And I said to him: 'Sir, a book is nothing else but a thing coupled together of divers creatures, and to swear by any creature, both God's law and man's law is against it.

"'But sir, this thing I say here to you before these your clerks, with my protestation, that how, where, when, and to whom men are bound to swear or to obey in any wise after God's law, and saints, and true doctors, according with God's law; I will through God's grace be ever ready thereto, with all my skill and power. But I pray you sir, for the charity of God, that ye will before I swear, tell me how or to whom I shall submit me: and shew me that whereof ye will correct me, and what is the ordinance that ye will thus oblige me to fulfil.'

"And the archbishop said to me: 'I require that thou swear to me, that thou wilt forsake all the opinions which the sect of Lollards hold; so that, neither privily nor openly, wilt thou hold any opinion which I shall rehearse to thee. And that thou wilt not favour any man or woman, young or old, that holds these opinions; but after thy knowledge and power thou shalt exert thyself to withstand all such disturbers of holy church in every diocese that thou comest into, and them that will not leave their false and damnable opinions, thou wilt put them up, publishing them and their names, and make them known to the bishop of the diocese, or to the bishop's ministers. And besides this I will that thou preach no more until I know by good witness and true, that thy conversation be such, that thy heart and thy mouth accord truly in one, contradicting all the secular learning that thou hast taught here before.'

"And I hearing these words, thought in my heart that this was an unlawful demand; and I deemed myself accursed of God, if I consented to it. And because I stood still and spake not, the archbishop said to me: 'Answer one way or the other;' and I said, 'Sir, if I consented to swear to you thus as ye require, I should become an appealer, or every bishop's spy in all England. For if I should thus put up and publish the names of men and women, I should herein deceive many persons: yea, sir, by the doom of my conscience, I should be the cause of the death both of men and women, yea, both bodily and spiritually. But I find in no place in holy scripture, that this office of common informer and spy with which ye would now infeoff me, accords to any priest of Christ's sect, nor to any other

christian man: if I should do as you require, full many men and women would (as they might full truly) say that I had falsely and cowardly forsaken the truth, and slandered shamefully the word of God. For if I consented to your will for any fear of man, or of worldly consideration, I deem in my conscience, that I were worthy to be cursed of God and also of all his saints; from which misfortune keep me and all christian people, Almighty God, now and for ever for his holy name.' And then the archbishop said to me : 'Oh, thine heart is full hardened, as was the heart of Pharaoh, and the devil hath overcome thee, and perverted thee, and he hath so blinded thee, that thou hast no grace to know the truth, nor the measure of mercy that I have offered to thee. Therefore, as I perceive now by thy foolish answer, thou hast no will to leave thine old errors. But I say to thee, either quickly consent to mine ordinance, and submit to my decrees, or by St. Thomas thou shalt be degraded, and follow thy companion to Smithfield.' And at this saying I stood still and spake not, but I thought in mine heart, that God did to me great grace, if he would of his great mercy bring me to such an end. And in mine heart I was nothing afraid with this menacing of the archbishop. And I considered two things in him. One, that he was not yet sorrowful that he had caused William Sautre wrongfully to be burnt; and as I considered that the archbishop thirsted yet after more shedding of innocent blood, I was moved in my mind, to hold him neither for prelate nor for priest of God: and because mine inward man was thus altogether departed from the archbishop, methought I should not have any dread of him. But I was right heavy and sorrowful, because there were no secular men present to hear: but in my heart I prayed the Lord God to comfort me and strengthen me: I prayed God for his goodness to give me then and always grace to speak with a meek and a quiet spirit: and whatever I should speak, that I might have true authorities of the scriptures or open reason for it. As I stood thus still and spake nothing, one of the archbishop's clerks said to me, 'What thing musest thou? Do as my lord hath commanded thee.'

"And yet I stood still and answered him not; and then soon after the archbishop said to me, 'Art thou not yet determined whether thou wilt do as I have said to thee?' And I said then to him, 'Sir, my father and my mother spent much money about my learning, to have made me a priest to God. But when I came to years of discretion, I had no will to be priest, and therefore my friends were very harsh towards me, and then methought their grudging against me was so painful, that I purposed to have left their company. They spake to me oftentimes very grievous words, and menaced me in divers manners. And thus they were a long time busy about me, ere I consented to be a priest. At last, I prayed them that they would give me licence to go to wise priests, and of virtuous conversation, to have their counsel, and to know of them the office and charge of priesthood. My father and my mother consented gladly, and gave me their blessing and leave, and also money to spend in this journey. And so I went to those priests whom I heard to be of best name, and of most holy living, and best learned, and most wise of heavenly wisdom; and so I communed with them to the time that I perceived by their virtuous and continual occupations, that their honest and charitable works passed their fame which I had heard before of them.'

"And the archbishop said,—'I say to thee, who are these holy and wise men, of whom thou hast taken thine information?'

"'And I said, sir, Master John Wickliff was held by many men the greatest clerk that they knew then living, and he was named an able, a good, and an innocent man in his living; and therefore great men communed often with him, and they loved so his learning, that they wrote it, and endeavoured to rule themselves after it. Therefore, sir, this learning of Master John Wickliff is yet held by many men and women, the learning most in accordance with the living and teaching of Christ and his apostles, and most openly shewing and declaring how the church of Christ has been and yet should be ruled and governed. Therefore it is that so many men and women desire his learning, and purpose through God's grace to conform their lives like to this learning of Wickliff. Master John Ashton taught and writ accordingly, and full zealously, where, and when, and to whom he might, and he used it himself right perfectly to his life's end. And also Philip of Rampington, while he was a canon of Leicester, Nicholas Herford, Davey Gotray of Pakring, monk of Byland, and a master of divinity, and John Purvey, and many others who were held right wise men and prudent, taught and writ busily this learning, and conformed to it. And with all these men I was very familiar, and communed with them long time and often, and before all other men I chose willingly to be informed of them and by them, and especially of Wickliff himself, as of the most virtuous and godly wise man that I ever heard of or knew. And therefore of him especially, and of these men I took the learning that I have taught; and purpose to live thereafter (if God will) to my life's end.'

"And the archbishop said, 'That learning, that thou callest truth and soothfastness, is open slander to holy church, as is proved by holy church. For although Wickliff was a great clerk, and though many held him to be a perfect liver; yet his doctrine is not approved of holy church, but many sentences of his learning are damned as they well deserve. But as to Philip of Rampington, he neither holds now, nor will hold what he then taught, when he was a canon of Leicester. For no bishop in this land pursues now more sharply those that hold those doctrines than he.'

"And I said, 'Sir, many men and women wonder at him, and speak of him much to his shame, and hold him as a cursed enemy of the truth.'

"And the archbishop said to me, 'Wherefore dost thou delay me with such fables, wilt thou submit thee to me or no?'

"And I said; 'Sir, I tell you at one word; I dare not for fear of God submit me to you, according to the sentence ye have read to me.'

"And thus as if he had been wroth, he said to one of his clerks; 'Fetch hither quickly the certificate that came to me from Shrewsbury under the bailiff's seal witnessing the errors and heresies, which this fellow has venomously sown there.'

"Then the clerk hastily took out, and laid forth on a table, some rolls and writings, among which there was a little one, which the clerk delivered to the archbishop. And by and by the archbishop read this roll containing this sentence:

"'The third Sunday after Easter, the year of our Lord 1407, William Thorpe came unto the town of Shrewsbury, and through leave granted unto him to preach, he said openly in St. Chad's church, in his sermon, that the sacrament of the altar, after the consecration, was material bread. And that images should in nowise be worshipped. And that men should not go on pilgrimages. And that priests have no title to tithes. And that it is not lawful to swear in any wise.'

"And when the archbishop had read thus this roll, he rolled it up again, and said to me; 'Is this wholesome teaching to be among the people?'

"And said; 'Sir, I am both ashamed on their behalf, and sorrowful for them that have certified you these things thus untruly; for I never preached, nor taught thus privily or openly.'

"And the archbishop said to me, 'I will give credence to these worshipful men who have written to me, and witnessed under their seals among them. Though now thou deniest this, thinkest thou that I will give credence to thee? Thou hast troubled the worshipful commonalty of Shrewsbury, so that the bailiffs and commonalty of that town have written to me, praying me that am archbishop of Canterbury, primate and chancellor of England, that I will vouchsafe to grant them, that if thou shalt be made (as thou art worthy) to suffer for thine heresies, that thou may suffer openly there among them; so that all they whom thou and such others have there perverted, may through fear of thy deed be reconciled again to the unity of holy church. And also they that stand in true faith of holy church, may be more established therein.'

"But certainly neither the prayer of the men of Shrewsbury, nor the menacing of the archbishop made me afraid, but my heart greatly rejoiced. I thank God for the grace that I then thought, and yet think shall come to all the church of God in this matter, by the special mercy of the Lord. And as having no dread of the malice of tyrants, by trusting steadfastly in the help of the Lord. I said to the archbishop,—'Sir, if the truth of God's word might now be accepted as it should be, I doubt not to prove by likely evidence, that they that are feigned to be out of the faith of holy church in Shrewsbury, and in other places also, are in the true faith of holy church. For as their words sound, and their works shew to man's judgment (dreading and loving faithfully God) their desire, their will, their love, and their business, are most set to dread to offend God, and to love, and please him in true and faithful keeping of his commandments. And again, they that are said to be in the faith of holy church in Shrewsbury and in other places, by open evidence of their proud, envious, malicious, covetous, and other foul words and works, neither know, nor have will to know, truly and effectually the right faith of holy church.

"And where, sir, ye say that I have troubled the commonalty of Shrewsbury, and many other men and women with my teaching: if it thus be, it is not to be wondered at, since all the commonalty of the city of Jerusalem was troubled by Christ's own person, that was very God and man, and the most prudent preacher that ever was or shall be. And also all the synagogue of Nazareth was moved against Christ, and so filled with ire towards him for his preaching, that the men of the synagogue rose up and cast Christ out of their city, and led him up to the top of a mountain to cast him down headlong.

"And the archbishop said to me, 'It followeth of these thy words, that thou and such other thinkest, that ye do right well to preach and teach as ye do, without authority of any bishop. For you presume that the Lord hath chosen you only to preach, as faithful disciples and special followers of Christ.'

"And I said, 'Sir, by authority of God's law, and also of saints and doctors I am learned to deem, that it is every priest's office and duty to preach busily, freely, and truly the word of God.'

"And the archbishop said to me, 'Fellow, why makest thou such vain reasons to me? Asks not St. Paul, How should priests preach except they be sent? But I never sent thee to preach. For thy venomous doctrine is known throughout England, that no bishop will admit thee to preach. Why then wilt thou presume to preach, since thou art not sent, nor licensed of thy superior to preach? St. Paul saith, that subjects ought to obey their sovereigns, and not only good and virtuous, but also tyrants that are vicious.'

"And I said, 'Samuel the prophet said to Saul, the wicked king, that God was more pleased with the obedience of his commandments, than with any sacrifice of beasts. But David saith, and St. Paul, and St. Gregory say together, that not only they that do evil, are worthy of death and damnation, but also they that consent to evil doers. And, sir, the law of the holy church teaches in the decree, that no servant to his lord, nor child to the father or mother, nor wife to her husband, nor monk to his abbot ought to obey, except in lawful things.'

"And the archbishop said to the three clerks that stood before him, 'Sirs, this is the business of this fellow, and such others, to pick out such sharp sentences of holy scripture and doctors, to maintain their sect, against the ordinance of holy church. And therefore, it is that thou wishest to have again the psalter that I had taken from thee at Canterbury, to recite sharp verses against us. But thou shalt never have that psalter, nor any other book, till I know that thy heart and thy mouth agree fully to be governed by holy church.'

"And I said, 'Sir, all my will and power is, and ever
T

shall be (I trust to God) to be governed by holy church.'

"And the archbishop asked me, 'What was holy church?'

"And I said, 'Sir, I told you before what was holy church. But since ye ask me this question again, I call Christ and his saints, holy church.'

"And the archbishop said to me, 'I know well that Christ and his saints are holy church in heaven, but what is holy church in earth?'

"And I said, 'Sir, holy church has two parts. The first and principal part has overcome perfectly all the wretchedness of this life, and reigns joyfully in heaven with Christ. And the other part is here yet in earth, busily and continually fighting day and night against the temptations of the devil; forsaking and hating the prosperity of this world, despising and withstanding their fleshly lusts, who only are the pilgrims of Christ, wandering towards heaven by steadfast faith, and grounded hope, and by perfect charity. For these heavenly pilgrims may not, nor will not be hindered of their good purpose by reason of any doctors disagreeing from holy scripture, nor by the floods of any temporal tribulation, nor by the wind of any pride, of boast, or of menacing of any creature: for they are all fast grounded upon the sure rock, Christ, hearing his word, and loving it, exercising them faithfully and continually in all their wits to do thereafter.'

"And the archbishop said to his clerks, 'See ye not how his heart is hardened, and how he has travelled with the devil, bringing in such sentences to maintain his errors and heresies. Certainly, he will occupy us here all day, if we suffer him.'

"One of the clerks answered, 'Sir, he said just now, that this certificate that came to you from Shrewsbury, is untruly forged against him. Therefore, sir, question him now in the points which are certified against him, and we shall hear his answers of his own mouth, and witness them.'

"And the archbishop took the certificate in his hand, and looked thereon a while, and then he said to me:

"'Lo, here it is certified by worthy and faithful men of Shrewsbury, that thou didst preach there openly, that the sacrament of the altar was material bread after the consecration; what sayest thou? Was this truly preached?'

"And I said, 'Sir, I tell you truly that I touched nothing there of the sacrament of the altar, but in this wise as I will, with God's grace, tell you here. As I stood there in the pulpit, busying me to teach the commandment of God, a sacred bell began ringing, and therefore many people turned away hastily, and with noise ran towards it; and I seeing this, said to them thus, 'Good men, ye were better to stand here still, and to hear God's word. For the virtue of the most holy sacrament of the altar stands much more in the faith that you ought to have in your soul, than in the outward sight of it, and therefore ye were better to stand still quietly to hear God's word, because that through the hearing of it, men come to true belief. And I am certain I spake not more than this of the worthy sacrament of the altar.'

"And the archbishop said to me, 'I believe thee not whatsoever thou sayest, since so worshipful men have witnessed thus against thee. But since thou deniest what thou saidst thus, what sayest thou now? After the consecration, does there remain in the host, material bread or no?'

"And I said, 'Sir, I know in no place in holy scripture, where this term material bread is written: and therefore sir, when I speak of this matter, I use not to speak of material bread.'

"Then the archbishop said to me, 'How teachest thou men to believe in this sacrament?'

"And I said, 'Sir, as I believe myself, so I teach other men.'

"He said, 'Tell out plainly thy belief thereof.'

"And I said with my protestation, 'Sir, I believe that the night before Christ Jesus suffered for mankind, he took bread in his holy hands, lifting up his eyes, and

giving thanks to God his Father, blessed this bread, and brake it, and gave it to his disciples, saying to them, take and eat of this all you, this is my body. And that this is, and ought to be, all men's belief, Matthew, Mark, Luke, and Paul witness. Other belief, sir, I have none, nor will have, nor teach: for I believe that this is sufficient in this matter. For in this belief, with God's grace, I purpose to live and die, knowledging as I believe and teach other men to believe, that the holy sacrament of the altar is the sacrament of Christ's flesh and blood in the form of bread and wine.'

"And I said, 'Sir, by clear evidence, a thousand years after the incarnation of Christ, the determination, which I have here before you rehearsed, was accepted of holy church as sufficient to the salvation of all them that would believe it faithfully.'

"And the archbishop said to me, 'Well, well, thou shalt say otherwise before that I leave thee. But what say you to this second point that is recorded against thee by worthy men of Shrewsbury, saying, that thou preachedst there, that images ought not to be worshipped in anywise?'

"And I said, 'Sir, I preached never thus, nor through God's grace will I at any time consent to think, or to say thus. For lo, the Lord witnesseth by Moses, that the things which he had made were very good; and so they were, and are and shall be good and worshipful in their kind, and therefore to the end for which God made them, they are all praiseworthy and worshipful, and especially man, who was made after the image and likeness of God, is worshipful in his kind. And also I say, wood, tin, gold, silver, or any other matter that images are made of, are worshipful in their kind, and to the end that God made them for. But the carving, casting, and painting of an imagery ought not to be worshipped in form, nor in the likeness of man's craft.'

"Then the archbishop said to me, 'I grant that no body ought to worship any images for themselves; but a crucifix ought to be worshipped for the passion of Christ that is painted therein, and thus the images of the blessed Trinity, and of the Virgin Mary, Christ's Mother, and other images of saints ought to be worshipped. For as earthly kings and lords who send their letters sealed with their arms, or with their private signet to those that are with them, are worshipped by these men. For when these men receive their lord's letters, in which they see and know the wills of the lords, they doff their caps to these letters. Why not then, since in images made with man's hands, we may read and know many things of God, and of his saints, shall we not worship their images?'

"And I said 'That these worldly usages of temporal laws that ye speak now of, may be done without sin. But this is no similitude to worship images, made by man's hand, since Moses, David, Solomon, Baruch, and other saints in the bible forbid so plainly the worshipping of such images.'

"Then the archbishop said to me, 'In the old law before Christ took human nature, there was no likeness of any person of the Trinity; but now since Christ became man, it is lawful to have images to shew his manhood, yea, though many men held it an error to paint the Trinity; I say, it is well done to make and to paint the Trinity in images. For it is a great moving of devotion to men, to have and behold the Trinity and other images of saints carved, cast, and painted. For beyond the sea are the best painters that ever I saw. And sirs, I tell you, this is their manner, and it is a good manner: when an image-maker shall carve, cast in mould, or paint any images, he shall go to a priest, and confess himself as clean, as if he should then die; and take penance, and make some certain vow of fasting or of praying, or of pilgrimages, praying the priest specially to pray for him, that he may have grace to make a fair and devout image.'

"And I said, 'Sir, I doubt not if these painters that ye speak of, or any other painters, understood truly the text of Moses, of David, of the Wise Man, of Baruch, and of other saints and doctors, these painters should be moved to confess to God with inward sorrow of heart, taking upon them penance for the sinful and vain craft of painting, carving, or casting; promising God faithfully never to do so again.'

"Then the archbishop said unto me, 'I hold thee a vicious priest and accursed, and all they sect; for all priests of holy church, and all images that move men to devotion, thou and such others go about to destroy. Would it be a right thing to come into the church, and see no image in it?'

"And I said, 'Sir, they that come to the church, to pray devoutly to the Lord God, may in their inward parts be the more fervent, that all their outward senses be closed from all outward seeing and hearing, and from all disturbance and lettings. And since Christ blessed them that saw him not bodily, and have believed faithfully in him; it is sufficient to all men to believe in God, though they never see images made with man's hand after any person of the Trinity, or of any other saint.'

"And the archbishop said to me with a fervent spirit, 'I say to thee, that it is right well done to make and to have an image of the Trinity; yea, what sayest thou? Is it not a stirring thing to behold such an image?'

"And I said, 'Sir, ye said just now that in the old law, before Christ took mankind, no likeness of any person of the Trinity was shewed to men: wherefore, sir, ye said it was not then lawful to have images, but now ye say, since Christ is become man, it is lawful to have an image of the Trinity, and also of other saints. But sir, this would I learn of you: since the Father of heaven, yea and every person of Trinity was without beginning, God Almighty; and many holy prophets, were martyred violently in the old law, and also many men and women then died confessors; why was it not then as lawful and necessary as now, to have an image of the Father of heaven, and to have other images of martyrs, prophets, and holy confessors, to move men to devotion, as ye say that images now do?'

"And the archbishop said, 'The synagogue of the Jews had not authority to do those things as the church of Christ has now.'

"And I said, 'Sir, St. Gregory was a great man, and of great dignity, and he commended greatly a bishop, and he forbade utterly the images made with man's hand to be worshipped.'

"And the archbishop said, 'Ungracious fellow, thou savourest no more truth than an hound. Since at the rood at the north door at London, at our lady at Walsingham, and many other places in England, are many great and admirable miracles done; should not the images of such holy saints and places, to the reverence of God, and of our lady, and other saints, be more worshipped than other places and images, where no miracles are done?'

"And I said, 'Sir, there is no such virtue in any imagery, that any image should be worshipped; wherefore I am certain that there is no miracle done of God in any place in earth, in order that any images made with man's hand should be worshipped. And therefore, sir, as I preached openly at Shrewsbury and other places, I say now here before you, that nobody should trust that there is any virtue in images made with man's hand; and therefore nobody should vow to them, nor seek them, nor kneel to them, nor bow to them, nor pray to them, nor offer any thing to them, nor kiss them, nor offer incense to them. For even the most worthy of such images, the brazen serpent (by Moses made, at God's bidding) the good King Hezekiah destroyed worthily and thankfully, and all because it was worshipped. Therefore sir, if men take good heed to the writing and the learning of St. Augustine, of St. Gregory, and of St. John Chrysostome, and of other saints and doctors, how they spake and wrote of miracles, that shall now be done in the latest end of the world: it is to be feared that for the unfaithfulness of men and women, the devil hath great power to work many of the miracles that now are done in such places. For

both men and women delight now more to hear and know miracles, than they do to know God's word, or to hear it effectually.'

"And the archbishop said, 'As holy church hath suffered the images of the Trinity, and all other images to be painted and shewed; it is enough to them that are members of holy church. But since thou art a rotten member, cut away from holy church, thou savourest not the ordinance thereof. But since the day passes, we leave this matter.'

"And then he said to me, 'What sayest thou to the third point that is certified against thee, preaching openly in Shrewsbury, that pilgrimage is not lawful? And over this thou saidst that those men and women that go on pilgrimages to Canterbury, to Beverley, to Karlington, to Walsingham, and to any other such places, are accursed and made foolish, spending their goods for nothing.'

"And I said, 'Sir, I am accused to you that I taught that no pilgrimage is lawful. But I never said thus. For I know that there are true pilgrimages and lawful, and acceptable to God: and therefore, sir, however mine enemies have certified you of me, I told at Shrewsbury of two manner of pilgrimages.'

"And the archbishop said to me, 'Whom callest thou true pilgrims?'

"And I said, 'Sir, with my protestation I call them true pilgrims travelling toward the bliss of heaven, who in the state, degree, or order that God calls them to, do busy them faithfully to occupy all their mind bodily and spiritually, to know truly, and to keep faithfully the biddings of God, hating and fleeing all the seven deadly sins, and every branch of them; ruling themselves virtuously, doing discreetly, willingly, and gladly, all the works of mercy, seeking the gifts of the Holy Ghost, disposing themselves to receive them in their souls and to hold the right blessings of Christ. And then they shall be moved with the good Spirit of God, to examine their conscience often and diligently, that neither wilfully nor wittingly they err in any article of belief, having continually (as frailty will suffer) all their business, to dread and to fly the offence of God, to love him over all, and to seek ever to do his pleasant will. Of these pilgrimages I said, whatever good thought they at any time think, whatever virtuous word they speak, and whatever fruitful work they accomplish; every such thought, word, and work is a step numbered of God toward him into heaven. These pilgrims of God delight when they hear of saints or of virtuous men and women, how they willingly forsook the prosperity of this life, how they withstood the suggestion of the devil, how they restrained their fleshly lusts, how discreet they were in their penance doing, how patient they were in all their adversities, how prudent they were in counselling men and women, moving them to hate all sins, and to fly them, and to love all virtues, and to draw to them, imagining how Christ, and his followers by this example, suffered scorns and slanders, and how patiently they took the wrongful menacing of tyrants: how homely they were, and serviceable to poor men to relieve and comfort them bodily and spiritually, and how devout they were in prayers, how fervent they were in heavenly desires, and how they absented themselves from spectacles of vain sayings and hearings, and how constant they were to prevent and destroy all vices, and how laborious and joyful they were to sow and to plant virtues? These heavenly conditions, true pilgrims have, or endeavour to have, whose pilgrimage God accepteth.'

"And again I said, 'As their works shew, the most part of men and women, that now go on pilgrimages, have not these conditions, nor love to have them. For as I well know, since I have full often tried, examine whoever will, twenty of these pilgrims, and he shall not find three men or women that know surely a commandment of God, nor can say their Paternoster and Ave Maria, nor their creed readily in any manner of language. And as I have learned and also know somewhat by experience of these same pilgrims, telling the cause why many men and women go hither and thither now on pilgrimage, it is more for the health of their bodies, than of their souls : more to have riches and prosperity of this world, than to be enriched with virtues in their souls : more to have here worldly and fleshly friendship, than to have friendship of God and of his saints in heaven ; for whatsoever thing man or woman does, the friendship of God, or of any other saint, cannot be had, without keeping of God's commandments. Further with my protestation, I say now, as I said in Shrewsbury, though they that have fleshly wills, travel far their bodies, and spend much money, to seek and to visit the bones or images (as they say they do) of this saint or of that ; such pilgrimage going is neither praiseable nor thankful to God nor to any saint of God, since in effect all such pilgrims despise God and all his commandments and saints. For the commandments of God they will neither know, nor keep, nor conform them to the example of Christ and of his saints. Wherefore, sir, I have preached and taught openly, and so I purpose all my life time to do with God's help, saying, that such fond people waste blamefully God's goods in their vain pilgrimages. Also, sir, I know that when several men and women go thus after their own wills, and fixing on the same pilgrimage ; they will arrange beforehand to have with them both men and women that can sing wanton songs, and other pilgrims will have with them bagpipes : so that every town that they come through, what with the noise of their singing, and with the sound of their piping, and with the tangling of their Canterbury bells, and with the barking of dogs after them, they make more noise than if the king came there with all his clarions and minstrels.'

" And the archbishop said to me, ' Thou seest not far enough in this matter, for thou considerest not the great labour of pilgrims, therefore thou blamest a thing that is praiseworthy. I say, that it is right well done, that pilgrims have with them both singers and also pipers ; that when one of them that goes barefoot strikes his toe upon a stone, and hurts himself sorely, and makes him to bleed, it is well done that he or his fellow begin then a song, or else take out of his bosom a bagpipe, to drive away with such mirth the hurt of his fellow. For with such solace the labour and weariness of pilgrims is lightly and merrily borne out.'

" And I said, ' Sir, St. Paul teaches men to weep with them that weep.'

" And the archbishop said, ' What janglest thou against men's devotion ? Whatever thou or such other say, I say that the pilgrimage that now is used, is to them that do it a praiseworthy and a good mean to come to grace.'

" And (as if he had been displeased with my answer) he said to his clerks, ' What think ye that this idiot will speak there, where he has no dread ; since he speaks thus here in my presence ? Well, well, by God thou shalt be ordained for.' And then he spake to me angrily.

" Then the archbishop said, ' Well, well. By God, the king doth not his duty, unless he suffer thee to be condemned.'

" And then another clerk said to me, ' Why counsellest thou a man of my lord's, that he should not confess himself to man, but only to God ?'

" And with this question I was abashed ; and then I knew that I was betrayed by a man that came to me in prison, communing with me in this matter of confession. And certainly, by his words I thought that this man came to me of full fervent and charitable will ; but now I know he came to tempt me and to accuse me ; God forgive him, if such was his will. And with all my heart when I had thought thus, I said to this clerk, ' sir, I pray you that you would fetch this man hither ; and all the words, as near as I can, repeat them, which I spake to him in the prison, I will rehearse here before you all, and before him.'

" And the archbishop said then to me, ' They who are now here will repeat them. How saidst thou to him ?'

" And I said, ' Sir, that man came and asked me in divers things, and after his asking, I answered him.

And as he shewed to me by his words, how he was sorry of his living in court, and right heavy for his own vicious living, and also for the viciousness of other men, and specially of priests' evil living ; and therefore he said to me with a sorrowful heart (as I imagined) that he purposed within a short time to leave the court and to apply himself to know God's law, and to conform all his life after it. And when he had said to me these words and others, which I would rehearse if he were present, he prayed me to hear his confession. And I said to him, sir, wherefore come ye to me, to be confessed of me ? Ye know well that the archbishop holds me here, as one unworthy either to give or to take any sacrament of holy church.

" And he said to me, ' Brother, I know well, and so do many others, that you and such others are wrongfully vexed, and therefore I commune with you the more gladly.' And I said to him, certainly I know well, that many men of this court, and specially the priests of this household will be full evil against both you and me, if they were aware that ye were confessed of me. And he said, ' that he cared not, for he had little affection for them.' And as methought, he spake these words and many others, of a good will and of a high desire, to have known and done the pleasant will of God. And I said to him, as I say to you now here, sir, I counsel you to absent you from all evil company, and to draw you to them that love and busy them to know and to keep the precepts of God ; and then the good Spirit of God will move you to occupy all your wits in gathering together of all your sins, as far as he can bethink you, shaming greatly of them, and sorrowing heartily for them : yea, sir, the Holy Ghost will then put in your heart a good will and a fervent desire to take and to hold a good purpose, to hate ever and to fly all occasion of sin ; and so then wisdom shall come to you from above, lightening (with divers beams of grace and of heavenly desire) all your wits, informing you how ye shall trust steadfastly in the mercy of the Lord, acknowledging to him only all your vicious living, praying to him devoutly for charitable counsel and continuance, hoping without doubt, that if ye continue thus, busying you faithfully to know and to keep his biddings, he will (for he only may) forgive you all your sins. And this man said to me, ' Though God forgive men their sins, yet it behoveth men to be absolved of priests, and to do the penance that they enjoin them.' And I said to him, ' Sir, it is all one to absolve men of their sins, and to forgive men their sins. Wherefore, since it pertains only to God to forgive sin ; it suffices to counsel men and women to leave their sin, and to comfort them that do thus, to hope in the mercy of God. And again, priests ought to tell sharply to sinners, that if they will not make an end of their sin, but continue in sins, all such deserve pain without any end. And therefore priests should ever busy themselves to live well and holily, and to teach the people busily and truly the word of God, shewing to all in open preaching, and in privy counselling, ' That the Lord God only forgiveth sin.' And, therefore, those priests that take upon them to absolve men of their sins, blaspheme God ; since it pertains only to the Lord to absolve men of all their sins. For, no doubt, for a thousand years after that Christ was man, no priest of Christ durst take upon him to teach the people, either privily or openly, that they must come to be absolved by them as priests now do. But by authority of Christ's word priests used to bind indurate, customary sinners to everlasting pains, who would never have busied themselves faithfully to know the biddings of God, nor to keep them. And sir, accordingly to this sentence, upon Mid-lent Sunday (two years ago) I heard a monk of Feversham, (called Morden,) preach at Canterbury at the cross within Christchurch abbey, saying thus of confession : ' Since the Lord God is more ready to forgive sin than the devil is or may be powerful to move any body to sin, then whoever will shame and sorrow heartily for their sins, knowledging them faithfully to God, amending them after their power and cunning, without counsel of any other body than of God and of himself (through the grace of

God) all such men and women may find sufficient means to come to God's mercy, and so to be clean absolved of all their sins.' This sentence I said, sir, to this man of yours, and the words as near as I can guess.'

" And the archbishop said, ' Holy church approveth not this learning.'

" And I said, ' Sir, holy church, of which Christ is head in heaven and in earth, must needs approve this sentence. For lo, hereby all men and women may, if they will, be sufficiently taught to know and keep the commandments of God, and to hate and to fly continually all occasion of sin, and to love and to seek virtues zealously, and to believe in God steadfastly; and to trust in his mercy steadfastly, and so to come to perfect love, and continue therein persevering. And more the Lord asketh not of any man in this life. And certainly, since Jesus Christ died upon the cross, to make men free; men of the church are too bold and too ready to make men captives, binding them under the pain of endless curses, to do many observances and ordinances, which neither the living nor teaching of Christ nor of his apostles approve.

" And a clerk said then to me, ' Thou shewest plainly here thy deceit, which thou hast learned of them that travelled to sow the tares among the wheat. But I counsel thee to go away clean from this learning, and submit thee to my Lord, and thou shalt find him yet to be gracious to thee.'

" Then a clerk said to the archbishop, ' Sir, it is late in the day, and ye have far to ride to-night; therefore make an end with him, for he will make none: but the more, sir, that ye busy you to draw him toward you, the more contumacious he is made.'

" And then Malveren said to me, ' William, kneel down, and pray my lord's grace, and leave all thy fancies, and become a child of holy church.'

" And I said, ' Sir, I have prayed the archbishop often, and yet I pray him for the love of Christ, that he will cease his indignation against me: and that he will suffer me to do mine office of priesthood, as I am charged of God to do it. For I desire nought else but to serve my God to his pleasing in the state that I stand in.'

" And the archbishop said to me, ' If of good heart thou wilt submit thee now here meekly, to be ruled from this time forth by my counsel, obeying meekly and willingly my ordinance, thou shalt find it most profitable and best to thee to do thus. Therefore delay thou me no longer, do this I have said to thee now here shortly, or deny it utterly.'

" And I said, ' Sir, as I have before rehearsed, I will be ready gladly to obey Christ the head of the holy church, and the learnings and biddings, and counsels of every pleasing member of him.'

" Then the archbishop, striking with his hand fiercely upon a table, spake to me with a great spirit, saying, ' By Jesus, but if thou leave not such additions, obliging thyself without any exception to submit to mine ordinance (before I go out of this place) I shall make thee as sure as any thief that is in prison; advise thee now what thou wilt do.' And then as if he had been angered, he went from the table where he stood, to a window.

" And then Malveren and another clerk came nearer me, and spake to me many words pleasantly; and another time they menaced me, and counselled me to submit, or else, they said, I should not escape punishment; for they said I should be degraded, cursed, and burned, and then damned. But now they said, ' Thou mayst eschew all these mischiefs, if thou wilt submit thee willingly and meekly to this worthy prelate, that hath cure of thy soul. And for the pity of Christ bethink thee, how great clerks the bishop of Lincoln, Herford and Purvey were, and yet are. Who also have forsaken and revoked all the learning and opinions that thou and such others hold. Wherefore since each of them is much wiser than thou art, we counsel thee for the best; that by the example of these four clerks, thou follow them, submitting thyself as they did.'

" And I said to the clerks, that thus counselled me to follow these men; ' Sirs, if these men, had forsaken benefices of temporal profit, and of worldly worship, so that they had absented them, and eschewed from all occasions of covetousness and of fleshly lust, and had taken upon them simple living, and wilful poverty; they had given good example to me and to many other, to have followed them. But now, since all these four men have slanderously and shamefully done the contrary, consenting to receive, and to hold temporal benefices, living now more worldly and more fleshly than they did before, conforming them to the manners of this world: I forsake them herein, and in all their doings. For I purpose, with the help of God to flee these men, teaching and counselling whomsoever I may, to flee and to eschew the way that they have chosen. Wherefore sirs, I pray you that you busy not to move me to follow these men in revoking and forsaking the truth.'

" Then the archbishop said to his clerks, ' Busy you no longer about him, for he, and other such as he is, are confederate together, that they will not swear to be obedient, and to submit them to the prelates of holy church. For now since I stood here, his fellow also sent me word that he will not swear, and that this fellow counselled him that he should not swear to me. But blessed be God, he shalt not have his purpose of him. For he has forsaken all thy learning, submitting him to be ready and obedient to the ordinance of holy church, and weeps bitterly, and curses thee heartily for the venomous teaching which thou hadst shewed to him.

" ' And for thy false counsel to thy fellow thou hast great cause to be right sorry. For a long time thou hast busied thee in perverting whomever thou mightest. Therefore as many deaths thou art worthy of, as thou hast given evil counsels. And therefore, by Jesus, thou shalt go thither, where Nicholas Herford and Thomas Purvey were harboured. And I undertake, ere this day eight days, thou shalt be right glad to do whatever I bid thee. And I shall try, if I can make thee there as sorrowful as thou wast glad at my last going out of England. By St. Thomas, I shall turn thy joy into sorrow.'

" And I said, ' Sir, no body can prove lawfully that I ever joyed at the manner of your going out of this land. But sir, to say the truth, I was joyful when ye were gone; for the bishop of London, in whose prison ye left me, found in me no cause to hold me longer in his prison, but at the request of my friends, he delivered me to them, asking of me no submission.'

" Then the archbishop said to me, ' Why I went out of England is unknown to thee: but be this thing well known to thee, that God has called me again, and brought me into this land, to destroy thee and the false sect that thou art of: as, by God, I shall pursue you so narrowly, that I shall not leave a slip of you in this land.'

" And I said to the archbishop, ' Sir, the holy prophet Jeremiah said to the false prophet, When the word of the prophet shall come to pass, then shall the prophet be known that the Lord hath truly sent him.' Jer. xxviii. 9.

" And the archbishop (as if he had not been pleased with my saying) turned him awayward hither and thither, and said, ' By God, I shall set upon thy shins a pair of pearls, that thou shalt be glad to change thy voice.'

" These and many more words were spoken to me, menacing me and all others of the same sect with punishment and destruction to the utmost.

" And then the archbishop called to him a clerk, and conferred with him; and that clerk went forth, and soon he brought in the constable of Saltwood castle, and the archbishop conferred a good while with him; and then the constable went forth, and then came in divers seculars, and they scorned me on every side, and menaced me greatly, and some counselled the archbishop to burn me by and by, and some other counselled him to drown me in the sea, for it is near hand there.

" And a clerk standing beside me, there kneeled down to the archbishop, praying him, that he would deliver me to him to say matins with him, and he would undertake, that within three days I should not resist anything that were commanded me to do of my prelate.

" And the archbishop said that he would settle for me himself.

" And then came again the constable and spake privily to the archbishop; and the archbishop commanded the constable to lead me forth with him, and he did so. And when we were gone forth we were sent for again. And when I came in again before the archbishop, a clerk bade me kneel down and ask grace, and submit myself, and I should find it for the best.

"And I said then to the archbishop, 'Sir, as I have said to you several times to-day, I will willingly and humbly obey and submit to God and to his law, and to every member of holy church, as far as I can perceive that these members accord with their head Christ, and will teach me, rule me, or chastise me by authority, specially of God's law.'

"And the archbishop said, 'I knew well he would not without such additions submit.'

"And then I was rebuked, scorned, and menaced on every side; and yet after this divers persons cried upon me to kneel down and submit me; but I stood still, and spake no word. And then there was spoken of me, and to me, many words, and I stood and heard them menace, curse, and scorn me, but I said nothing.

"Then awhile after the archbishop said to me, 'Wilt thou not submit thee to the ordinance of holy church?'

"And I said, 'Sir, I will full gladly submit me, as I have showed you before.'

"And then the archbishop bade the constable to have me forth thence in haste.

"And so then I was led forth, and brought into a foul prison, where I never was before. But thanked be God, when all men were gone forth then from me, and had barred fast the prison-door after them, I, by myself, busied me to think on God, and to thank him for his goodness. And I was then greatly comforted, not only because I was then delivered for a time from the sight, from the hearing, from the presence, from the scorning, and from the menacing of mine enemies; but much more I rejoiced in the Lord, because that through his grace he so kept me, both among the flattering and among the menacing of mine adversaries, that without heaviness and anguish of my conscience I passed away from them. For as a tree laid upon another tree, overthwart or crosswise, so was the archbishop and his three clerks always contrary to me, and I to them.

"Now good God for thine holy name, and to the praising of thy most blessed name, make us one together, if it be thy will. And that it may thus be, let all who read or hear this writing, pray heartily to the Lord God, that he for his great goodness, that cannot be with tongue expressed, grant to us, and to all other who in the same wise, and for the cause specially, or for any other cause are separated, may be knit and made one in true faith, in steadfast hope, and in perfect charity. Amen."

What was the end of this good man, and blessed servant of God, William Thorpe, I find as yet specified in no history. It is thought that the archbishop, Thomas Arundel, being so hard an adversary against those men, would not let him go. Much less is it to be supposed, that he would ever retract his sentence and opinion, which he so valiantly maintained before the bishop, neither does it seem that he had any such recanting spirit. Again, neither is it found, that he was burned, wherefore it remains most like to be true, that he being committed to some straight prison (according as the archbishop in his examination threatened him), there (as Thorpe himself confesses) was so straightly kept, that either he was secretly made away, or else died by sickness.

The like end also I find to happen to John Ashton, another good follower of Wickliff, who for the same doctrine of the sacrament was condemned by the bishops, and because he would not recant he was committed to perpetual prison, wherein the good man continued till his death. (A.D. 1382.)

JOHN PURVEY.

In the examination of William Thorpe, mention is made of John Purvey, of whom we said something

before, promising to treat more particularly afterwards. Of this Purvey, Thomas Walden writes thus :—"John Purvey," saith he, "was the library of Lollards, and glossary upon Wickliff. He said that the worshipping of Abraham was but a salutation; and that this John Purvey, with Herford a doctor of divinity, were grievously tormented and punished in the prison of Saltwood, and at the length recanted at Paul's Cross at London, Thomas Arundel being then archbishop of Canterbury. Afterwards he was again imprisoned under Henry Chichely, archbishop of Canterbury, A.D. 1421." Thus much writes Walden. As touching the sacrament of the last supper, the sacrament of penance, the sacrament of orders, the power of the keys, the preaching of the gospel, of marriages, of vows, of possessions, of the punishing and correcting of the clergy, of the laws and decrees of the church, of the state and condition of the pope and the clergy; of all these generally he left several treatises, gravely and exactly written.

The articles which he taught, and afterward was forced to recant at Paul's Cross, were these :

I. That in the sacrament of the altar, after the consecration, there is not, neither can be any accident without the subject; but there verily remains the same substance, and the very visible and corruptible bread, and likewise the very same wine which before the consecration were set upon the altar to be consecrated by the priest; as when a pagan or infidel is baptized, he is spiritually converted into a member of Christ through grace, and yet remains the very same man which he before was in his proper nature and substance.

II. Auricular confession, or private penance, is a certain whispering, destroying the liberty of the gospel, and newly brought in by the pope and the clergy, to entangle the consciences of men in sin, and to draw their souls into Hell.

III. Every layman being holy and predestinate unto everlasting life, is a true priest before God.

IV. That many prelates and other of the clergy live wickedly, contrary to the doctrine and example of Christ and his apostles. Therefore they who so live, have not the keys either of the kingdom of Heaven, or yet of Hell; neither ought any christian to esteem the incensure any more than as a thing of no force. Yea, although the pope should peradventure, interdict the realm, yet could he not hurt, but rather profit us, forsomuch as thereby we should be dismissed from the observance of his laws, and from saying service according to the custom of the church.

V. If any man make an oath or vow, to keep perpetual celibacy, or do anything else whereto God has not appointed him, giving him grace to perform his purpose; the same vow or oath is unreasonable and indiscreet, neither can any prelate compel him to keep the same, except he will do contrary to God's ordinance. But he ought to commit him to the governance of the Holy Ghost and of his own conscience; forsomuch as every man, who will not fulfil his vow or oath, cannot do it for that cause.

VI. Whoever takes upon him the office of priesthood, although he have not the charge of souls committed unto him, according to the custom of the church, not only may, but ought to preach the gospel freely to the people; otherwise he is a thief, excommunicated of God, and of the holy church.

VII. That Pope Innocent III. and six hundred bishops, and a thousand other prelates, with all the rest of the clergy, who together with the pope agreed and determined, that in the sacrament of the altar, after the conversion of the bread and wine into the body and blood of Christ, the accidents of the said bread and wine do remain there without any proper subject of the same; who also ordained, that all christians ought to confess their sins once a year to a proper priest, and to receive the reverend sacrament at Easter, and made certain other laws at the same time: all they, saith he, in so doing, were fools and blockheads, heretics, blasphemers, and seducers of christian people. Wherefore we ought not to believe the determinations of them, or of their successors, neither ought we to obey their laws or ordinances, except they are plainly grounded upon the holy scripture, or upon some reason which cannot be impugned.

Other Articles drawn out of Purvey's Books more at large by Richard Levingham.

"As to the sacrament of thanksgiving, he saith, That that chapter of repentance and remission, (*omnis utriusque sexus*,) wherein it is ordained, that every faithful man ought once every year at the least, that is to say at Easter, to receive the sacrament of the Eucharist, is a beastly thing, heretical and blasphemous.

"That Innocent III., was the head of anti-christ, who after the letting loose of Satan, invented a new article of our faith, and a certain feigned doctrine touching the sacrament of the altar, that is to say, that the sacrament of the altar is an accident without a substance, or else an heap of accidents without a substance. But Christ and his apostles do teach manifestly, that the sacrament of the altar is bread and the body of Christ together, after the manner that he spake. And in that he calleth it bread, he would have the people to understand, as they ought with reason, that it is very and substantial bread, and no false nor feigned bread.

"And although Innocent, that anti-christ, doth allege that in the council at Lyons, where this matter was decided, were six hundred bishops with him, and one thousand prelates, who agreed in this determination; All those notwithstanding, he calls fools, according to that saying of Eccles. i. ' Of fools there are an infinite number.' And so in like manner he calleth them false christs and false prophets, of whom Christ speaketh in the 24th of Matthew, ' Many false christs and false prophets shall arise, and deceive many.' And therefore every christian man ought to believe firmly, that the sacrament of the altar is very bread indeed, and no false nor feigned bread. And although it be very bread indeed, yet notwithstanding, it is the very body of Christ in that way which he spake, and called it his body ; and so it is very bread, and the very body of Christ. And as Christ concerning his humanity was both visible and passible, and by his divinity was invisible and impassible : so likewise this sacrament in that it is very bread, may be seen with the corporal eye, and may also abide corruption. But although a man may see that sacrament, yet notwithstanding cannot the body of Christ in that sacrament be seen with the corporal eye, although it be the body of Christ in that manner he spake it ; for that notwithstanding, the body of Christ is now incorruptible in Heaven. So the sacrament of the cup is very wine, and the very blood of Christ, according as his manner of speaking was. Also Innocent III., with a great multitude of his secular priests, made a certain new determination, that the sacrament of the altar is an accident without a substance, whereas neither Jesus Christ, nor any of his apostles taught this faith (but openly and manifestly to the contrary, neither yet the holy doctors, for the space of a thousand years and more, taught this faith openly.

"Therefore when anti-christ or any of his shavelings doth ask of thee that art a simple christian, whether that this sacrament be the very body of Christ or not? affirm thou it manifestly to be so. And if he ask of thee whether it be material bread, or what other bread else ? say thou, that it is such bread as Christ understood and meant by his proper word ; and such bread as the Holy Ghost meant in St. Paul, when he called that to be very bread which he brake ; and wade thou no further therein. If he ask thee how this bread is the body of Christ? say thou, as Christ understood the same to be his body, which is both omnipotent and true, and in whom is no untruth ; say thou also as the holy doctors do say, ' That the terrestrial matter or substance may be converted into Christ, as the pagan or infidel may be baptized, and hereby spiritually be converted, and be a member of Christ, and so after a certain manner become Christ, and yet the same man remain still in his proper nature. For so doth St. Augustine grant, that a sinner forsaking his sin, and being made one spirit with God by faith, grace and charity, may be converted into God, and be after a manner God, as both David and St. John do testify, and yet be

the same person in substance and nature, and in soul and virtue be altered and changed. But yet men of more knowledge and reason may more plainly prove the falsity of antichrist both in this matter and in others, by the gift of the Holy Ghost working in them. Notwithstanding, if men will humbly hold and keep the manifest and apparent words of the holy scripture, and the plain sense and meaning of the Holy Ghost, and proceed no further, but humbly commit to the Spirit of God, that which passes their understanding ; then may they safely offer themselves to death, as true martyrs of Jesus Christ.

"As to the sacrament of penance ; that chapter (*omnis utriusque sexus*) by which a certain new-found auricular confession was ordained, is full of hypocrisy, heresy, covetousness, pride, and blasphemy, he reproves that chapter *verbatim*. Also he says that the penance and pains limited by the canons are unreasonable and unjust, for their austerity and rigour. And further shews how Innocent III. brought in a new-found confession, whereby the priests oppress the laymen compelling them to confess themselves to blind and ignorant priests, in whom there is nothing else but pride and coveteousness, holding those in contempt who are learned and wise. Also that the decretal of Innocent III., touching the auricular or vocal confession, was brought in and invented to entangle men's consciences with sin, and to draw them down to hell. And further, that such manner of confession destroys the evangelical liberty, and prevents men from inquiring after, and retaining the wise counsel and doctrine of such as are good priests, who would willingly teach the people the right way to heaven. For which abuse all christian men, and specially all Englishmen ought to exclaim against such wicked laws.

"As to the authority of the keys and censures, no christian man ought to esteem Satan (whom men call the pope) and his unjust censures, more than the hissing of a serpent, or the blast of Lucifer. Also, that no man ought to trust or put confidence in the false indulgences of covetous priests, which indulgences do draw away the hope, which men ought to repose in God, to a sort of sinful men, and do rob the poor of such alms as are given to them. Such priests are manifest betrayers of Christ and of the whole church, and are Satan's own stewards to beguile christian souls by their hypocrisy and feigned pardons. Also, forasmuch as those prelates and clergymen live so execrable a life, contrary to the gospel of Christ and examples of his apostles, and teach not truly the gospel, but only lies and the traditions of sinful wicked men ; it appears most manifestly, that they have not the keys of the kingdom of heaven, but rather the keys of hell. And they may be well assured, that God never gave to them authority to make and establish so many ceremonies and traditions contrary to the liberty of the gospel, and blocks in christian men's ways, that they can neither know nor observe his gospel in liberty of conscience, and so attain a ready way to heaven.

"As touching the preaching of the gospel, ' whosoever receiveth or taketh upon him the office of a priest, or of a bishop, and dischargeth not the same by the example of his good conversation and faithful preaching of the gospel, is a thief, excommunicate of God and of holy church.' And further, ' If the curates preach not the word of God, they shall be damned, and if they know not how to preach, they ought to resign their benefices.' So that those prelates who preach not the gospel of Christ (although they could excuse themselves from the doing of any other evil) are dead in themselves, are anti-christs, and satans, transfigured into angels of light, and betrayers of Christ's people.

"Now as to the correction of the clergy. By the law of God, and by reason, the king and all other christians may punish Italy, and all the false priests and clerks within the same, and reduce them to the humble ordinance of Jesus Christ. Also that the law of Sylvester the pope is contrary to the law of Christ ; and that proud and ambitious Sylvester by his law so defended two cardinals which were not to be defended by the law of Christ, that by no means they might be convicted, although they were both vicious and evil. And although Christ sustained and suffered the judgment of unjust temporal judges, our mitred prelates in these days so magnify themselves beyond Christ and his apostles, that they refuse such judgments. Also that those decretals of accusations which prohibit that any clerks should be brought before a secular judge to receive judgment, contain both heresy, blasphemy, and error, and bring great gain and commodity to antichrist's coffers.

"Furthermore, that all christian kings and lords ought to exclaim against the pope, and those that be his favourers, and banish them out of their lands, till such time as they will obey God and his gospel, kings, and other ministers of God's justice. Also that bishops and their favourers, that say it appertains not to kings and secular lords (but unto them and their officials) to punish adultery and fornication, do fall into manifest treason against the king, and heresy against the scripture. Also that it appertains to the king to have the order both of priests and bishops, as these kings Solomon and Jehoshaphat had.

"Furthermore that chapter (*Nullus judicium de foro competenti*), by which secular judges are forbidden, without the bishop's commandment, to condemn any clerk to death, is manifestly against the holy scripture, declaring that kings have power over clerks and priests, to punish them for their deserved crimes. Also that the decree of Boniface, made against the prosecutors, strikers, and imprisoners of cardinals, is contrary both to the holy scripture, and to all reason. Also that by the law of God and reason, a secular lord may lawfully take a cardinal and put him in prison for committing the crime of open simony, adultery, and manifest blasphemy. Also that the chapter (*Si Papa, Dist.* 40.), which saith that the pope ought to be judged of none, unless he be *Devius a fide*, is contrary to the gospel, which saith, If thy brother sin against thee, correct him. Also whereas St. Gregory and St. Augustine called themselves the servants of God's servants, this proud bishop of Rome, which will not be judged by his subjects (which be in very deed his lords, if they be just and good men) destroys the order of God's law, and all humility, and extols himself above God and his apostles. Also that christian kings ought not only to judge this proud bishop of Rome, but also to depose him by the example that Cestrensis, (lib. 6. cap. 8.) declares of Otho the emperor, who deposed John XII., and instituted Leo in his place. And further he makes an exhortation to the princes to judge the church of Rome, which he calleth the great and cursed whore, of which St. John writes in Rev. xvii.

"Lastly, touching the laws and determinations of the church; christians have reasonable excuses and causes to repel the statutes of the pope and of his shavelings, which are not expressly grounded on the holy scripture, or else upon reason inevitable. Also that simple men do reverently receive the sentences of the doctors, and other laws, so far forth as they are expressly grounded upon the holy scripture or good reason. Also that whereas the pope's laws, and laws of his ministers and clerks are contrary to themselves, and have not their foundation either upon scripture, or yet upon reason, simple men ought to bid them farewell. Also that that proud priest of Rome, with all his rabble, might easily err in the faith; and yet the christian faith be preserved whole and safe in the faithful members of Christ, which are his true church; while the pope and all his rabblement cannot prove that they be any part of his church. Also that the pope with all his favourers, may as well be deceived by a lying spirit, as was Ahab and all his prophets; and that one true prophet, as was Michaiah, may have the truth shewed to him. Also that all good christians ought to cast from them the pope's laws, saying, let us break their bands in sunder, and let us cast from our necks those heavy yokes of theirs. Also that where these prelates do burn one good book for one error perhaps contained in the same, they ought to burn all the books of the canon-law, for the manifold heresies contained in them."

And thus much out of a certain old written book in parchment, which book containing divers ancient records

of the university, seems to belong sometime to the library of the university, bearing the year of the compiling thereof, A. D. 1396. If this date be correct, then it was written before Purvey recanted before Thomas Arundel, archbishop, at Saltwood, where he was imprisoned.

Here is to be considered, at least to be admonished, that all this while the schism in the church of Rome did yet continue, and so endured till the council of Constance, which was in whole, the space of twenty and nine years. The origin whereof (as was said before) first began at Urban V., which Urban being dead, (A. D. 1389), next followed Pope Boniface IX., who sat fourteen years. He, in selling his pardons, was so impudent and so past shame, that he brought the keys of Peter (as saith Platina) into contempt. After him succeeded Innocent VII. and sat two years: who being dead, the cardinals consulting together, and seeing the enormity and inconvenience growing upon this schism in their church of Rome (minding to provide some remedy after the best device they could) in their conclave where they were assembled for a new election for the pope, took this order, promising among themselves with solemn vow made to God, to Mary the Blessed Virgin, to Peter and Paul, and to all the blessed company of saints; that if any of them, within the college or without the college, should be called to the high place of apostolical pre-eminence; he should immediately renounce the jurisdiction and title of his popedom, when the rival pope, for the time being, would in like manner, renounce his place and title, and his cardinals in the like manner condescend to the other cardinals of Rome. So that both these two colleges of cardinals agreeing together, one chief bishop was to be chosen and taken out of them both, to be made the true pope. Provided, moreover, that none should seek any release or absolution from the promise, vow and bond once passed among them; all which things every one subscribed with his hand. These things thus prefixed and ratified, they proceeded to the election. In which was chosen Gregory XII., who the same day of his election, in the presence of all the cardinals, confirmed the vow, sacrament, and promise made, subscribing the same with his hand, in form as follows: "And I, Gregory, this day being the last of November, A. D. 1407, chosen and elected for bishop of Rome, do swear, vow, and promise, and confirm all the premises above contained," &c. This being done, shortly after he was crowned, being of the age of eighty years. As the time thus passed, the people and cardinals were in great expectation, waiting when the pope, according to his oath, would give over, with the other pope also. And not long after, the matter began indeed between the two popes to be attempted, by letters from one to another; assigning both day and place, where and when they should meet together; but yet nothing followed.

This so passing on, there was great murmuring among the cardinals, to see their holy perjured father so neglect his oath and vow. Insomuch that at length, several of them forsook the pope, as being perjured (as no less he was) sending moreover to kings and princes of other lands, for their counsel and assistance, to appease the schism. Among the rest, Cardinal Bituriensis was sent to the king of England; who published propositions and conclusions (remaining in the registers of Thomas Arundel), proving that the pope ought to be subject to laws and councils. Then King Henry (moved to write to Gregory the pope) directs his letter, A. D. 1409.

The Letter of King Henry the Fourth to Pope Gregory the Twelfth.

"Most blessed father, if the discreet providence of the apostolical see would call to mind with what great perils the universal world has been damnified hitherto, under pretence of this present schism; and especially would consider, what slaughter of christian people, to the number of two hundred thousand (as they say) hath been through the occasion of war raised up in divers quarters of the world; and now of late, to the number of thirty thousand soldiers, who have been slain through the dissension moved about the bishoprick of Leodium, between two set up, one by the authority of one pope, the other by the authority of the other pope, fighting in camp for the title of that bishopric; certainly, ye would lament in spirit and be sore grieved in mind for the same. So that with good conscience ye would rather relinquish the honour of the apostolic see, than suffer such horrible bloodshed to ensue, under the cloke of dissimulation, following herein the example of the true mother in the book of Kings: who pleading before Solomon for the right of her child, rather would part from the child, than the child should be parted by the sword. And although it may be vehemently suspected by the new creation of nine cardinals by you lately made, contrary to your oath (as other men say), that you but little heed or care for ceasing the schism; yet far be it from the hearing and noting of the world, that your circumspect seat should ever be noted and distained with such an inconstancy of mind; whereby the last error may be worst than the first."

And to the cardinals likewise, the said king directed another letter with these contents here following:

King Henry the Fourth to the Cardinals.

"We, desiring to shew what zeal we have had and have, to the reformation of peace of the church, by the consent of the states of the realm, have directed to the bishop of Rome our letters, after the tenour of the copy herewith in these presents inclosed to be executed effectually: wherefore we seriously beseech your reverend college, that if it chance the said Gregory to be present at the council of Pisa, and to render up his popedom, according to your desire, and his own oath, you then so ordain for his state totally, that chiefly God may be pleased thereby, and that both the said Gregory, and also we who entirely love his honour and advantage, may have cause to give you worthily condign thanks for the same."

This being done in the year A.D. 1409, afterwards in the year next following, A.D. 1410, the cardinals of both the popes, to wit, of Gregory and Benedict, by common advice assembled together at the city of Pisa, for the reformation of unity and peace in the church. To which assembly, a great multitude of prelates and bishops being come, a new pope was chosen, named Alexander V. But to this election neither Gregory nor Benedict would fully agree. Whereby there were three popes together in the Roman church (that is, to understand) not three crowns upon one pope's head, but three heads in one popish church together! This Alexander, being newly made pope, scarcely had well warmed his triple crown, but straight gives out full remission, not of a few, but all manner of sins whatever, to all that conferred anything to the monastery of St. Bartholomew by Smithfield, resorting to the said church any of these days following; to wit, on Maundy Thursday, Good Friday, Easter even, the feast of the Annunciation, from the first even-song to the later. But this pope, who was so liberal in giving remission of many years to other, was not able to give one year of life to himself, for within the same year he died. In whose stead came in Pope John XXIII.

In the time of this Alexander great stir began in the country of Bohemia, by the occasion of the books of John Wickliff, which then coming to the hands of John Huss, and of others, both men and women, especially of the lay sort, and artificers, began there to do much good, so that many of them, not only men, but women also, partly by the reading of their books translated into their language, partly by the setting forward of John Huss, a remarkably learned man, and a singular preacher at that time in the university of Prague, were in a short time so ripe in judgment, and prompt in the scriptures, that they began to move questions, yea and to reason with the priests, touching matters of the holy scriptures.

By reason of this, complaint was brought to Pope Alexander, who soon caused John Huss to be cited to Rome. But when he came not at the pope's citation, then Pope Alexander addressed his letters to the archbishop of Swinco. Wherein he straightly charged him to prohibit and forbid, by the authority apostolical, all manner of preachings or sermons to be made to the people, except only in cathedral churches or colleges, or parish churches, or in monasteries, or else in their churchyards; and that the articles of Wickliff should, in no case by any person, of what state, condition, or degree, be suffered to be held, taught, or defended, either privily or openly. Commanding, moreover, and charging the archbishop, that with four bachelors of divinity, and two doctors of the canon law, he would proceed upon the same, and so provide that no person in churches, schools, or any other place, should teach, defend, or approve any of the aforesaid articles. So that whosoever should attempt the contrary, should be accounted an heretic, and unless he shall revoke solemnly and publicly the said articles, and shall for ever abjure the books in which the articles are contained, so that they may be utterly abolished out from the eyes of the faithful, he should be apprehended and imprisoned, without appeal, the help also of the secular arm being called in, if need shall require, &c. These were the contents of this mighty and fierce bull of Pope Alexander.

Against which bull John Huss, justly complaining, objecteth many things, as appears in his book, entitled *De Ecclesia*, cap. 18, where he declares this mandate of the pope to stand directly against the doings and sayings both of Christ and of his apostles; considering how Christ himself preached to the people, both in the sea, in the desert, in fields, in houses, in synagogues, in villages; and the apostles also in all places did the same, the Lord mightily working with them. He declared, moreover, the mandate or bull of the pope to redound to the great detriment of the church, in binding the word of God, that it might not have free course; also to be prejudicial to chapels newly erected for the word to be preached in them. Wherefore (saith he) from this commandment or mandate of Pope Alexander I appeal unto Alexander, being better informed and advised. And as I was prosecuting my appeal, the lord pope (saith John Huss) immediately died.

Then the archbishop of Swinco, to whom this present bull was directed, when he saw the process, bulls, and mandates of the bishop of Rome to be thus despised by John Huss and his fellows, and having no hope of redress in Winceslaus the king, who seemed to neglect the matter, went to Hungary, to complain to Sigismund king of Hungary, and brother to Winceslaus. But this archbishop, as soon as he arrived in Hungary (by the just judgment of God) died, as the history saith, for sorrow. Whereby a little more liberty and quiet was given by the Lord to his gospel, beginning to take root among the Bohemians. This tranquillity, however, did not continue long without trouble and persecution, nor could it in those furious days and reign of antichrist. For after this Alexander, Pope John XXIII. succeeded. Who, likewise playing his part in this tragedy, bent all his might and main to disturb the Bohemians, as (Christ willing) shall be declared hereafter in the course of our history.

Thus the poor christians, like the simple Israelites under the tyranny of Pharaoh, were oppressed in every place, but especially here in England, because the English king, unlike Winceslaus, entirely held with the pope and his prelates against the gospellers.

By reason of which the kingdom of the pope and his members began to be so strong in this realm, that none durst stir or move against them. The bishops having the king so entirely on their side, armed, moreover, with laws, statutes, punishments, sword, fire, and faggot, reigned and ruled as they pleased, as kings and princes within themselves. So strong were they that no human force was able to stand against them: so exalted in pride, and puffed up in glory, that they thought all things to be subject to their reverend majesties. Whatever they set forth or decreed, it must by all men be received and obeyed.

And such was their superstitious blindness and curious vanity, that whatever toy came once in their fancy, it was at once determined and established for a law to be observed by all men, were it never so frivolous or superstitious; as well appears by Thomas Arundel, archbishop of Canterbury and others, who having now a little leisure from slaying and killing the innocent people, martyrs and confessors of the Lord, and having now brought their enemies (as they thought) under their feet; began to set up themselves, and to invent some new custom, as the habit is of the pope's church, ever to intrude into the church of God some ceremony or custom of their own making, whereby the church of Christ has been hitherto exceedingly pestered. So likewise this Thomas Arundel, thinking the church not yet sufficiently filled with ceremonies and vain traditions of men, brought in a new-found gaud, commonly called "The tolling of Aves," in honour of our lady, with certain Aves to be said, and days of pardon to be given for the same. For the ratification of which, under the pretence of the king's request, he directed the following mandate to the bishop of London, well filled with words of idolatry, as by reading it will plainly appear.

A Mandate of Thomas Arundel, directed to the Bishop of London, to warn men to say certain Prayers at the tolling of the Aves, or ringing of the Curfew.

"Thomas, &c. To the right reverend brother, the Lord Robert, by the grace of God, bishop of London, greeting, &c. While we lift our eyes round about us, and behold attentively with circumspect consideration, how the most high Word that was in the beginning with God, chose to him a holy and immaculate virgin of the kingly stock, in whose womb he took true flesh by inspiral inspiration, that the merciful goodness of the Son of God, that was uncreate, might abolish the sentence of condemnation, which all the posterity of mankind, that was created, had by sin incurred: amongst other labours in the vine of the Lord of Sabbaoth, we sung to God our Saviour with great joy, thinking, that though all the people of the christian religion did extol with voices of praise so worthy a virgin, by whom we received the beginnings of our redemption, by whom the holy day first shined to us, which gave us hope of salvation; and although all the same people were drawn to reverence her, who being a happy virgin, conceived the Son of God, the King of heaven, the Redeemer and Saviour of all nations, ministering light to the people that were miserably drowned in the darkness of death: we truly, as the servants of her own inheritance, and such as are written of, to be of her peculiar dower, as we are by every man's confession acknowledged to be, we, I say, ought more watchfully than any others to shew our devotion in praising her. Who being hitherto merciful to us, willed that our power, being as it were spread abroad every where through all the coasts of the world, should with a victorious arm be feared among all foreign nations; that our power, being on all sides so defended with the buckler of her protection, did subdue unto our victorious standards, and make subject unto us, nations both near at hand and far off.

"Likewise our happy estate, all the time that we have passed since the beginning of our lives, may be well attributed only to the help of her medicine; to whom also we may worthily ascribe now of late in these our times, under the mighty government of our most christian king, our deliverance from the ravening wolves, and the mouths of cruel beasts, who had prepared against our banquets a mess of meat mingled full of gall, and who hated us unjustly, secretly lying in wait for us, in recompence of the good will that we shewed to them. Wherefore, that she being on high sitting before the throne of the heavenly Majesty, the defendress and patroness of us all, being magnified with all men's praises, may more plentifully exhibit to us the sons of adoption the breasts of her grace, in all those things that we shall have to do; at the request of the special devotion of our Lord the king himself, we command your brotherhood, straightly enjoining you, that you command the subjects of your city and diocese, and of all other suffragans, to worship our Lady Mary the mother of God, and our patroness and protectress, evermore in all adversity, with such like kind of prayer and accustomed manner of ringing, as the devotion of Christ's faithful people is wont to worship her at the ringing of *cour le feu*. And when before day in the morning ye shall cause them to ring, that with like manner of prayer and ringing she may be every where honoured devoutly by our and your suffragans, and their subjects as well regular as secular, in your and their monasteries and collegiate-churches: that we so humbly calling upon the mercy of the heavenly Father, the right hand of the heavenly piety may mercifully come to the help, the protection and defence of the same our lord the king, who for the happy remedy of quietness, and for our succour from tempestuous floods, is ready to apply his hands to work, and his eyes with all his whole desire to watching. We therefore desiring more earnestly to stir up the minds of all faithful people to so devout an exercise of God, &c.; we grant by these presents, to all and every man, &c. that shall say the Lord's Prayer and the Salutation of the Angel five times at the morning-peal with a devout mind, *toties quoties* forty days' pardon by these presents.

"Given under our seal in our manor of Lambeth the 10th day of February." (*Ex Regist. Thomas Arundel*).

By this frivolous and barbarous constitution, with many other of the same kind, heaped into the church by the papists, appear the proper natures and condition of this generation, whose priests were more solicitous about worldly honour than christian humility.

As, for example, what can be more suitable for a true ecclesiastical pastor, than humility of heart and spirit, according to the example of the Head Bishop himself? So what greater shew of arrogancy and pride could there be, than in this Thomas Arundel, archbishop of Canterbury? who, passing by the High-street of London, did not only look and wait for the ringing of the bells, in honour of his coming, but took great offence, and suspended all such churches in London (not only from the use of the steeple and bells, but also from the organs) as did not receive his coming with the ringing of bells, according as appears by his own registers, where is the following commission addressed to his own somner.

A Commission directed to the Somner, to suspend certain Churches of London, because they rung not their Bells at the presence of my Lord the Archbishop of Canterbury.

"Thomas, by the permission of God, &c. To our well-beloved Thomas Wilton, our somner sworn, health, grace, and blessing. The comeliness of our holy church of Canterbury, over which we bear rule, deserveth and requireth, that while we pass through the province of the same (having our cross carried before us) every parish church in their turns ought and are bounden, in token of special reverence that they bear to us, to ring their bells. Notwithstanding which, on Tuesday last, when we, between eight and nine of the clock before dinner, passed openly on foot as it were through the midst of the city of London, with our cross carried before us; several churches, whose names are here beneath noted, shewed towards us willingly (though they certainly knew of our coming) unreverence rather than reverence, and the duty that they owe to our church of Canterbury, ringing not at all at our coming. Wherefore, we being willing to revenge this injury, for the honour of our spouse, as we are bounden, command you, that by our authority you put all those churches under our inditement, suspending God's holy organs and instruments in the same. Which we also suspend by the tenor of these presents, till the ministers of the aforesaid churches be able hereafter to attain of us the benefit of more plentiful grace. Given," &c.

What reason was there in this, why this archbishop

should thus look for the ringing of the bells, or why he should be thus displeased with not ringing, I do not see. Perhaps his mind in the mean time was greatly occupied with some great subject, as a sense of God's fear, with repentance and remembrance of his sins, with zealous care and solicitude for his flock, with the earnest meditation of the passion and life of our Saviour, who in this world was so despised: or else was set upon some grave study, while he waited for the ringing of the bells, which were wont to be so noisome to all students. And why were not the trumpeters also punished as well, because they did not sound before his person? But though the bells did not clatter in the steeples, why should the body of the church be suspended? At least, the poor organs (methinks) suffered some wrong in being put to silence in the quire, because the bells rang not in the tower.

To show the glorious pomp of these prince-like prelates, in these blind days of popish religion, I add another example not much unlike, nor differing much in time, concerning certain poor men cited up, and enjoined strict penance by, William Courtney, predecessor of Thomas Arundel, for bringing litter to his horse, not in carts as they should do, but in little sacks, in a secret manner under their cloaks or coats. For which heinous and horrible sin the archbishop, sitting in his tribunal seat, called and cited before him the persons (*pro litera*, i. e. for litter, after his own Latin), and after their submission enjoined them penance. Which penance here follows out of the said archbishop's registers.

"Ignorance, the mother of error, hath so blinded and deceived certain persons, to wit, Hugh Pennie, John Forstall, John Boy, John Wanderton, William Hayward, and John White, tenants of the lord of Wengham, that against the coming of the archbishop to his palace of Canterbury, on Palm Sunday evening, A.D. 1390, where they being warned by the bailiff to convey and carry hay, straw, and other litter, to the palace, as they were bound by the tenour of their lands, which they hold of the see of Canterbury; refusing and disdaining to do their service, as they were accustomed, brought their straw and other litter, not in carts and waggons openly and sufficiently, but by piecemeal, and closely in bags or sacks, in contempt of their lord and derogation of the right and title of the see of Canterbury. Whereupon they being cited and presented before the archbishop, sitting in judgment at his manor of Statewood, yielded and submitted themselves to his lordship's pleasure, humbly craving pardon of their trespass. Then the aforesaid archbishop absolved the above-named Hugh Pennie, &c., they swearing to obey the laws and ordinances of holy church, and to do the punishment that should be appointed them for their deserts; that is, that they going leisurely before the procession, every one of them should carry openly on his shoulder his bag stuffed with hay and straw, so that the hay and straw should appear hanging out, the mouths of the sacks being open."

To proceed now in the reign of this king, and to treat something of his parliaments as we have done of others. First, we will begin with the parliament held in the first year of his reign.

As our papists will not believe the contrary, but that the jurisdiction of their father the pope has ever extended throughout all the world, as well here in England as in other places, therefore speaking of the parliaments holden in this king's days concerning this matter, I refer them to the parliament of King Henry in his first year, and to the twenty-seventh article. Where they may read in the tenth objection laid against King Richard, in plain words, how that as the crown of this realm of England, and the jurisdiction belonging to the same; as also the whole realm itself, at all times lately past, has been at such liberty, and enjoyed such prerogative, that neither the pope, nor any other out of the same kingdom, ought to intrude himself nor intermeddle therein, it was therefore objected to King

Richard II. that he procured the letters apostolical from the pope, to confirm and corroborate certain statutes, which seemed then to the parliament to tend against the crown and regal dignity, as also against the statutes and liberties of this our realm of England. (Act Parl. An. 1. Reg. Hen. 4. Act 27.)

Further, in the second year of the said king, it was required in the parliament that all such persons as shall be arrested under the statute made against the Lollards, in the second year of Henry IV. may be bailed, and freely make their purgation, that they be arrested by none other than by the sheriffs, or such officers.

In the eighth year, moreover, of this king's reign it was propounded in parliament, that all such persons as shall procure, or sue in the court of Rome any process touching any benefice, collation, or presentation of the same, shall incur the pain of the statute of provisors, made in the thirteenth year of Richard II., whereunto the king granted, that the statutes heretofore provided should be observed.

In the same parliament there was presented a petition, that the king might enjoy half the profits of every parson's benefice who is not resident thereon. The king answered, that the ordinaries should do their duties therein, or else he would provide further remedy to stay their pluralities.

In the same parliament it was required, that none do sue to the court of Rome for any benefice, but only to the king's courts.

Besides, in the parliament held the eleventh year of this king, the commons of the land put up a bill to the king to take the temporal lands out from spiritual men's hands or possession. The effect of which bill was, that the temporalities disorderly wasted by men of the church, might suffice to find to the king fifteen earls, fifteen hundred knights, six thousand two hundred esquires, and a hundred houses of alms to the relief of the poor people; and over all these aforesaid charges, the king might put yearly in his coffers twenty thousand pounds.

Provided, that every earl should have of yearly rent three thousand marks; and every knight a hundred marks and four plough-lands; every esquire forty marks by year, with two plough-lands; and every house of alms a hundred marks, with oversight of two true seculars to every house, and also with provision that every township should keep all their own poor people, which could not labour for their living; with a condition that if more fell in a town than the town might maintain, then the said almshouses should relieve such townships.

To which bill no answer was made, but that the king would deliberate and advise on the matter.

These things thus narrated, touching such acts and matters as occurred in the lifetime of this king, next follows the thirteenth year of his reign. In which year the king, after he had sent a little before a company of captains and soldiers to aid the duke of Burgundy in France (among whom was the Lord Cobham), keeping his Christmas at Eltham, fell grievously sick. From thence he was conveyed to London, where he began to call a parliament. In the meantime the infirmity of the king increasing more and more, he was taken and brought to a bed in a beautiful chamber at Westminster. And as he lay in his bed, he asked what they called the chamber he was in; and they answered Jerusalem. And then he said it was his prophesy, that he should die in Jerusalem. And so disposing himself toward his end in his chamber, he died on the twentieth of March, A.D. 1413.

KING HENRY V.

After the death of Henry IV., his son Henry V. began to reign. Henry was born at Monmouth in Wales, of whose other virtues, and great victories in France, I shall not much intermeddle, especially as the memory of his prowess, being sufficiently described in other writers, may both content the reader, and unburden my labour, especially as these later troubles of the church offer me so much, that little leisure will be left to intermeddle with secular matters.

After the coronation of this new king, which was on the ninth day of April, called then Passion Sunday, which was an exceeding stormy day, and so tempestuous, that many wondered at the omen : not long after a parliament began to be called, and held at Westminster, (A. D. 1413.) At which time Thomas Arundel, the archbishop of Canterbury, collected in St. Paul's church at London, an universal synod of all the bishops and clergy of England.

The Trouble and Persecution of Lord Cobham.

The chief and principal cause of the assembling of this synod, as the chronicle of St. Albans reports, was to repress the growing and spreading of the gospel, and especially to withstand the noble and worthy Lord Cobham, who was then noted to be a principal favourer, receiver, and maintainer of them, whom the bishop misnamed to be Lollards, especially in the dioceses of London, Rochester, and Hereford, setting those up to preach whom the bishops had not licensed, and sending them about to preach, which was against the provincial constitutions, holding also and teaching opinions of the sacraments, of images, of pilgrimage, of the keys and church of Rome, contrary and repugnant to the received determination of the Romish church, &c.

In the meantime, as the commotion was in debate concerning the good Lord Cobham, there resorted to them the twelve inquisitors of heresies (whom they had appointed at Oxford the year before, to search out heretics,) with all Wickliff's books, who brought two hundred and forty-six conclusions, which they had collected as heresies out of the books.

The articles being brought in, they proceeded in their communication, concluding that it was not possible for them to make whole Christ's coat without seam, unless certain great men were taken out of the way, who seemed to be the chief maintainers of the said disciples of Wickliff. Among whom this noble knight Sir John Oldcastle, the Lord Cobham, was complained of by the general proctors to be the principal. They accused him first for a mighty maintainer of suspected preachers in the dioceses of London, Rochester, and Hereford, contrary to the minds of the ordinaries. They not only affirmed him to have sent there the preachers, but also to have assisted them there by force of arms, notwithstanding their synodal constitution made to the contrary. Last of all, they accused him that he was far otherwise in belief of the sacrament of the altar, of penance, of pilgrimage, of image worshipping, and of the ecclesiastical power, than the holy church of Rome had taught many years before.

In the end it was concluded among them, that without any further delay, process should be awarded out against him, as against a most pernicious heretic.

Some of them who were of more crafty experience than the others, thought it best not to have the matter so rashly handled ; but considering Lord Cobham was a man of great birth, and in favour at that time with the king, their counsel was to know first the king's mind. This counsel was well accepted, and the archbishop, with his other bishops, and a great part of the clergy, went directly to the king, and laid most grievous complaints against Lord Cobham, to his great infamy and blemish, being a right godly man. The king gently heard those blood-thirsty prelates, and far otherwise than became his princely dignity : notwithstanding, requiring, and desiring them, that in respect of his noble stock and knighthood, they should deal favourably with him. And that they would, if it were possible, without rigor or extreme handling, reduce him again to the church's unity. He promised them also, that if they were contented to take some deliberation, he himself would seriously commune the matter with him.

Soon after the king sent for Lord Cobham ; and when he was come, he called him secretly, admonishing him to submit himself to his mother, the holy church, and as an obedient child to acknowledge himself culpable. The christian knight made this answer : " You, most worthy prince, I am always prompt and willing to obey, forsomuch as I know you are a christian king, and the appointed minster of God, bearing the sword to the punishment of evil doers, and for the praise of them that do well. Unto you (next to my eternal God) I owe my whole obedience, and submit thereunto, as I have ever done, all that I have, either of fortune or nature, ready at all times to fulfil whatsoever ye shall in the Lord command me. But as touching the pope and his spirituality, I owe them neither suit nor service, forsomuch as I know him by the scriptures to be the great antichrist, the son of perdition, the open adversary of God, and the abomination standing in the holy place." When the king had heard this, he would talk no longer with him, but left him.

And as the archbishop resorted again to him for an answer, he gave him his full authority to cite him, examine him, and punish him according to their devilish decree, which they called the laws of holy church. Then the archbishop, by the counsel of his other bishops and clergy, appointed to call before him Sir John Oldcastle, the Lord Cobham, and to cause him personally to appear, to answer to such articles as they should lay against him.

This most constant servant of the Lord, and worthy knight, Sir John Oldcastle, beholding the fury of antichrist thus kindled against him, perceiving himself also compassed on every side with deadly dangers, took paper and pen in hand, and wrote a christian confession of his faith, both signing and sealing it with his own hand. Wherein he also answered to the four chief articles that the archbishop laid against him. That done, he took the copy with him, and went therewith to the king, trusting to find mercy and favour at his hand. This confession of his was none other than the common belief or sum of the church's faith, called The Apostles' Creed, then used by all christian men, with a brief declaration upon the same, as follows :—

The Christian Belief of the Lord Cobham.

" I believe in God the Father Almighty, maker of heaven and earth : and in Jesus Christ his only Son our Lord, who was conceived by the Holy Ghost, born of the virgin Mary, suffered under Pontius Pilate, was crucified, dead and buried, He descended into hell, the third day He rose again from the dead, He ascended into heaven, and sitteth on the right hand of God the Father Almighty ; and from thence shall come to judge the quick and the dead. I believe in the Holy Ghost, the holy catholic church, the communion of saints, the forgiveness of sins, the resurrection of the body, and the life everlasting. Amen.

" And for a more large declaration (said he) of this my faith in the catholic church, I steadfastly believe, that there is but one God Almighty, in and of whose Godhead are these three persons, the Father, the Son, and the Holy Ghost, and that those three persons are the self-same God Almighty. I believe also, that the second person in this most blessed Trinity, in most convenient time appointed thereunto before, took flesh and blood of the most blessed virgin Mary, for the safeguard and redemption of the universal kind of man, which was before lost in Adam's offence.

" Moreover I believe, that the same Jesus Christ our Lord, thus being both God and man, is the only head of the whole christian church, and that all those that have been or shall be saved, are members of this most holy church. And this holy church I think to be divided into three sorts of companies.

" The first sort are now in heaven, and they are the departed saints. These as they were here conversant, conformed always their lives to the most holy laws and pure examples of Christ, renouncing Satan, the world, and the flesh and all their lusts and evils.

" The second sort are in purgatory (if any such place be in the scriptures) abiding the mercy of God, and a full deliverance of pain.

" The third sort are here upon the earth, and are called the church militant. For day and night they contend against the crafty assaults of the devil, the flattering prosperities of this world, and the rebellious lusts of the flesh.

"This last company by the just ordinance of God is also divided into three several estates, that is to say, into the priesthood, the knighthood, and the commons. Among whom the will of God is, that the one should aid the other, but not destroy the other. The priests first of all, secluded from all worldliness, should conform their lives to the examples of Christ and the apostles. They should be occupied in preaching and teaching the scriptures purely, and in giving wholesome examples of good living to the other two degrees of men. They should be more modest also, more loving, gentle, and lowly in spirit, than any sort of people.

"In the knighthood are all they who bear the sword by law of office; these should defend God's laws, and see that the gospel is purely taught, conforming their lives to the same, and excluding all false preachers; yea these ought rather to hazard their lives, than to suffer such wicked decrees as either blemish the eternal testament of God, or prevent the free passage thereof, whereby heresies and schisms might spring in the church. For they arise principally from erroneous constitutions, first creeping craftily in under hypocritical lies, for advantage. They ought also to preserve God's people from oppressors, tyrants, and thieves, and to see the clergy supported so long as they teach purely, pray rightly, and administer the sacraments freely. And if they see them do otherwise, they are bound by the law or office to compel them to change their doings; and to see all things performed according to God's prescribed ordinance.

"The last fellowship of this church, are the common people; whose duty is to bear their good minds and true obedience to the aforesaid ministers of God, their kings, civil governors and priests. The right office of these, is for every man justly to occupy his faculty, be it merchandise, handicraft or cultivating the ground. And so one of them be as an helper to another, following always the just commandments of the Lord God.

"Over and besides all this, I most faithfully believe, that the sacraments of Christ's church are necessary to all christian believers; so that they be truly ministered according to Christ's first institution and ordinance. And as I am maliciously and most falsely accused of misbelief in the sacrament of the altar, to the hurtful slander of many; I signify here to all men, that this is my faith concerning it. I believe in that sacrament Christ's very body and blood are contained, under the similitude of bread and wine, yea the same body that was conceived of the Holy Ghost, born of the Virgin Mary, crucified on the cross, died and was buried, arose the third day from the death; and is now glorified in heaven. I also believe the universal law of God to be most true and perfect, and they who do not follow it in their faith and works (at one time or another) can never be saved. Whereas he that seeks it in faith, accepts it, learns it, delights therein, and performs it in love, shall taste the felicity of everlasting innocency.

"Finally, this is my faith also, that God will ask no more of a christian believer in this life, but only to obey the precepts of that most blessed law. If any prelate of church require more, or any other kind of obedience, than this; he contemns Christ, exalting himself above God, and so becomes an open antichrist. All the premises I believe particularly, and generally all that God has left in his holy scripture, that I should believe; instantly desiring you my liege lord and most worthy king, that this confession of mine may be justly examined by the most godly wise, and learned men of your realm. And if it be found in all points agreeing to the truth, then let it be allowed; and I acknowledged as none other than a true christian. If it be proved otherwise, then let it be utterly condemned; provided always, that I be taught a better belief by the word of God; and I shall most reverently at all times obey it."

This brief confession of his faith the Lord Cobham took to the court, offering it with all meekness to the king to read it over. The king would not receive it, but commanded it to be delivered to them that should be his judges. Then he desired in the king's presence, that an hundred knights and esquires might be suffered to come in upon his purgation, who he knew would clear him of all heresies. Moreover, he offered himself, after the law of arms, to fight for life or death with any man living, christian or heathen, in the quarrel of his faith, the king and the lords of his council excepted. Finally, with all gentleness he protested before all that were present, that he would refuse no manner of correction that should after the laws of God be ministered to him, but that he would at all times with all meekness obey it. Notwithstanding all this the king suffered him to be summoned personally in his own privy chamber. There was nothing allowed that the Lord Cobham had required. But as he would not be sworn to submit himself to the church, and take what penance the archbishop would enjoin him; he was arrested again at the king's commandment, and led to the Tower of London.

As the day of examination was come, which was the 23d day of September, Thomas Arundel the archbishop, sitting in Caiaphas' room in the chapter-house of St. Paul's, with Richard Clifford bishop of London, and Henry Bolingbrook bishop of Winchester; Sir Robert Morely, knight and lieutenant of the Tower, brought Lord Cobham before them, to whom the archbishop thus spoke.

"Sir John, in the last general convocation of the clergy of this our province, you were detected of certain heresies, and by sufficient witnesses found culpable. Whereupon you were cited by form of spiritual law, and would in no case appear. In conclusion, upon your rebellious contumacy, you were both privately and openly excommunicated. Notwithstanding we neither shewed ourselves unready to have given you absolution (nor yet do to this hour) would ye have meekly asked it." To this the Lord Cobham seemed, as if he had not heard it, having his mind otherwise occupied, and so desired no absolution. But said, "He would gladly before him and his brethren make rehearsal of that faith which he held and intended always to stand to, if it would please them to license him thereto." And then he took out of his bosom a certain writing, concerning the articles whereof he was accused, and read it before them, giving it the archbishop as he concluded it.

Then the archbishop counselled with the other two bishops and with the doctors, what was to be done in this matter; commanding him to stand aside for the time. In conclusion by their common assent the archbishop thus addressed him; "Come hither, Sir John: in this your writing many good things are contained, and right catholic also, we deny it not: but you must consider that this day was appointed you to answer to other points concerning articles of which no mention is made in this your writing. And therefore you must declare to us your mind more plainly: "Whether you hold, affirm and believe that in the sacrament of the altar, after the consecration rightly done by a priest, material bread remains, or not? Moreover, whether you do hold, affirm, and believe, that as concerning the sacrament of penance, every christian man is necessarily bound to confess his sins to a priest ordained by the church or not?"

After certain other communications, this was the answer of the good Lord Cobham. "That he would not declare his mind, nor yet answer to these articles in any other way, than was expressly contained in his writing." Then said the archbishop to him; "Sir John, beware what ye do. For if you answer not clearly to those things that are here objected against you, the law of the holy church is, That compelled once by a judge we may openly proclaim you an heretic." To whom he gave this answer: "Do as ye shall think best, for I am determined." Whatever he or the other bishops asked him, he bade them refer to his bill; for by it he would stand to the very death. He would not give them any other answer that day; at which the bishops and prelates were much amazed and disquieted.

The day following, the archbishop sent to him into the Tower, this foolish and blasphemous writing, made by him and by his unlearned clergy.

The Determination of the Archbishop and Clergy.

"The faith and determination of the holy church touching the blissful sacrament of the altar, is this; That after the sacramental words are once spoken by a priest in his mass, the material bread, that was before bread, is turned into Christ's very body. And the material wine, that was before wine, is turned into Christ's very blood. And so there remains in the sacrament of the altar, from thenceforth, no material bread, nor material wine, which were there before the sacramental words were spoken; how believe ye this article?

"Holy church has determined that every christian man, living here bodily upon the earth, ought to confess to a priest ordained by the church, if he may come to him. How feel ye this article?

"Christ ordained St. Peter the apostle to be his vicar here in earth, whose see is the holy church of Rome; and he granted, that the same power which he gave to Peter should succeed to all Peter's successors, whom we now call popes of Rome; by whose power in particular churches, are ordained prelates, as archbishops, bishops, parsons, curates, and other degrees; whom christian men ought to obey after the laws of the church of Rome. This is the determination of holy church. How feel ye this article?

"Holy church has determined, that it is meritorious to a christian man to go on pilgrimage to holy places; and there especially to worship holy relics and images of saints, apostles, and martyrs, confessors, and all other saints beside, approved by the church of Rome. How feel ye this article?"

When Lord Cobham had read over this most wretched writing, he marvelled greatly at their mad ignorance. But he considered again, that God had given them over, for their unbelief's sake, into most deep errors and blindness of soul. He perceived by this, that their utmost malice was resolved against him, however he should answer. And therefore he put his life into the hands of God, desiring only his Spirit to assist him in his next answer. When the twenty-fifth day of September was come, Thomas Arundel, the archbishop of Canterbury, commanded his judicial seat to be removed from the chapter-house of St. Paul's, to the dominic friars within Ludgate, at London. And as he was there set with Richard, bishop of London; Henry, the bishop of Winchester; and Bennet, the bishop of Bangor: he called in unto him his council of his officers, with other doctors and friars. All these, with a great many more of priests, monks, canons, friars, parish clerks, bell-ringers, and pardoners, disdained Lord Cobham, with innumerable mocks and scorns, reckoning him to be an horrible heretic, and a man accursed before God.

Soon the archbishop called for a mass book, and caused all the prelates and doctors to swear that every man should faithfully do his office and duty that day. And that neither for favour nor fear, love nor hate, of the one party nor the other, should any thing be witnessed, spoken, or done, but according to the truth, as they would answer before God and all the world at the day of doom. Then were the two notaries sworn also to witness and to write the process that should be uttered by both parties, and to say their minds (if they otherwise knew) before they should register it. And all this dissimulation was but to colour their mischiefs, before the ignorant multitude.

After all this, Sir Robert Morley, knight, and lieutenant of the Tower, came before them, and brought with him the good Lord Cobham, leaving him there among them, as a lamb among wolves, to his examination and answer.

Then the archbisiop said to him, "Lord Cobham, you are aware of the words and process which we had on Saturday last in the chapter-house of St. Paul's. I said to you then, that you were accursed for your contumacy and disobedience to the holy church."

Then Lord Cobham, with a cheerful countenance, answered: "God said by his holy prophet, 'I will curse your blessings,'" Mal. ii. 2.

The archbishop continued. "Sir, at that time I gently offered to have absolved you if you would have asked it. And I still do the same if you will humbly desire it in due form and manner as holy church has ordained."

Then said the Lord Cobham; "Nay, I will not; for I never yet trespassed against you; and therefore I will not do it." And with that he kneeled down on the pavement, holding up his hands towards heaven, and said: "I confess myself here unto thee, my eternal living God, that in my frail youth I offended thee, O Lord, most grievously in pride, wrath, gluttony, and covetousness. Many men have I hurt in mine anger, and done many other horrible sins: good Lord, I ask thee mercy." And then weeping, he stood up again and said with a loud voice; "Lo! good people, lo! for the breaking of God's law, and his great commandments, they never yet cursed me; but for their own laws and traditions they most cruelly handle both me and other men. And therefore both they and their laws, by the promise of God, shall be utterly destroyed."

At this the archbishop and his company were not a little hurt. However, he took courage, and examined the Lord Cobham of his christian belief.

To which the Lord Cobham made this godly answer: "I believe fully and faithfully in the universal laws of God. I believe that all is true which is contained in the holy sacred scriptures of the bible. Finally, I believe all that my Lord God would I should believe." Then the archbishop demanded an answer to the bill which he and the clergy had sent to him to the Tower the day before, concerning the four articles whereof he was accused, especially concerning the sacrament of the altar, how he believed therein.

The Lord Cobham said, "That with that bill he had nothing to do. But this was his belief concerning the sacrament. That his Lord and Saviour Jesus Christ, sitting at his last supper with his most dear disciples, the night before he suffered took bread in his hand; and giving thanks to his Eternal Father, blessed it, brake it, and so gave it to them, saying, 'Take, and eat this, for this is my body which is given for you: do this in remembrance of me.' This, (said he) do I believe, for this faith am I taught in the gospel of Matthew, in Mark, and Luke, and also in the first epistle of St. Paul to the Corinthians."

Then the archbishop asked if he believed that it were bread after the consecration or sacramental words spoken over it.

Then Lord Cobham said; "I believe that in the sacrament of the altar is Christ's very body in form of bread, the same that was born of the Virgin Mary, crucified on the cross, dead, and buried, and that the third day arose from death to life, which now is glorified in heaven."

Then said one of the doctors of the law: "After the sacramental words be uttered, there remains no bread, but only the body of Christ."

The Lord Cobham said then to one Master John Whitehead: "You said once to me in the castle of Gowling, that the sacred Host was not Christ's body. But I held then against you, and proved that therein was his body, though the seculars and friars could not therein agree, but held each one against the other in that opinion. These were my words then, if ye remember it."

Then a set of them shouted together, and cried with great noise: "We all say that it is God's body."

And many of them asked him, in great anger, whether it were material bread after the consecration or not?

Then the Lord Cobham looked earnestly upon the archbishop, and said: "I believe surely that it is Christ's body in form of bread: Sir, believe not you thus?"

And the archbishop said,—"Yes, do I."

Then the doctors asked him whether it were only Christ's body after the consecration of a priest, and no bread, or not?

And he said to them: "It is both Christ's body and bread: I shall prove it thus: for like as Christ's dwelling here upon the earth had in him both godhead and manhood, and had the invisible godhead covered under that manhood, which was only visible and seen in him: so in the sacrament of the altar is Christ's very body and bread also, as I believe the bread is the thing that we see with our eyes, the body of Christ (which is his flesh and his blood) is thereunder hid, and not seen but in faith."

Then they smiled one upon another, that the people should judge him taken in a great heresy. And many of them said: "It is a foul heresy."

Then the archbishop asked what bread it was? And the doctors also inquired of him whether it were material or not?

Lord Cobham answered: "The scriptures make no mention of this word material, and therefore my faith hath nothing to do therewith. But this I say and believe, that it is Christ's body and bread. Therefore I say now again as I said before, as our Lord Jesus Christ is very God, and very man, so in the most blessed sacrament of the altar is Christ's very body and bread."

Then said they all with one voice: "It is an heresy."

One of the bishops stood up and said: "It is a manifest heresy, to say that it is bread after the sacramental words be once spoken."

Lord Cobham said: "St. Paul the apostle was, I am sure, as wise as you are now, and more godly learned, and he called it bread, writing to the Corinthians, 'The bread which we break,' saith he, 'is it not the communion of the body of Christ?' Lo, he called it bread and not Christ's body, but a means whereby we receive Christ's body."

Then they asked him if he believed not in the determination of the church?

And he said unto them,—"No; for it is no God. In all our creed the word in is but thrice mentioned concerning belief: In God the Father, in God the Son, in God the Holy Ghost, three persons and one God. The birth, the death, the burial, the resurrection and ascent of Christ, hath no in for belief, but only in him. Neither yet hath the church the sacraments, the forgiveness of sin, the later resurrection, nor yet the life everlasting, nor any other in than in the Holy God."

Then said one of the lawyers: "But what is your belief concerning holy church?"

The Lord Cobham answered: "My belief is that all the scriptures of the sacred Bible are true. All that is grounded upon them I believe. But in your lordly laws and idle determinations I have no belief. For ye are no part of Christ's holy church, as your open deeds do shew: but ye are very antichrists, obstinately set against his holy law and will. The laws that ye have made are nothing to his glory, but only for your vain glory and abominable covetousness."

This, they said, was an exceeding heresy, not to believe the determination of holy church.

Then said the archbishop: "Can you tell me who is of the church?"

Then Lord Cobham answered: "Yes; truly I can. Christ saith, 'That like as the evil tree is known by its fruit, so is a false prophet by his works.'"

Then said Doctor Walden unto him: "Ye make here no difference of judgments: rash judgment and right judgment, all is one with you. So swift judges always are the learned scholars of Wickliff!"

To whom the Lord Cobham answered. "Preposterous are your judgments evermore. For as the prophet Isaiah saith: 'Ye call evil good and good evil;' and therefore the same prophet concludes; 'That your ways are not God's ways, nor God's ways your ways.' And as for the virtuous man Wickliff, whose judgments ye so highly disdain, I shall say here of my part, both before God and man, that before I knew that despised doctrine of his, I never abstained from sin. But since I learned therein to fear my Lord God, it has, I trust, been otherwise with me: I could never find so much grace in all your glorious instructions."

Then said Doctor Walden yet again unto him. "It were not well with me if I had no grace to amend my life, till I heard the devil preach."

The Lord Cobham said: "Your fathers, the old Pharisees, ascribed Christ's miracles to Beelzebub, and his doctrine to the devil. And you as their natural children have still the self-same judgment concerning his faithful followers. They that rebuke your vicious living must needs be heretics!" Then said he to them all: "To judge you as you are, we need go no further than to your own acts. Where do you find in all God's law, that ye should thus sit in judgment on any christian man, or give sentence upon any other man unto death, as ye do here daily? you have no ground in all the scripture so lordly to take it upon you, but in Annas and Caiaphas, who thus sat upon Christ, and upon his apostles after his ascension. Of them only have ye taken it to judge Christ's members as ye do, and neither of Peter nor John."

Then said some of the lawyers: "Yes, forsooth, sir, for Christ judged Judas."

The Lord Cobham said: "No; Christ judged him not, but he judged himself, and thereupon went forth and so did hang himself: since his venom was shed into the church ye never followed Christ."

Then the archbishop asked him, what he meant by the venom of Judas?

The Lord Cobham said, "Your possessions and lordships. Before that time all the bishops of Rome were martyrs in a manner. And since that time we read of very few. But since that time, one has put down another, one has poisoned another, one has cursed another, and one has slain another, and done much more mischief besides, as all the chronicles tell. And let all men consider this well, That Christ was meek and merciful; the pope is proud and a tyrant; Christ was poor and forgave, the pope is rich and a malicious manslayer, as his daily acts do prove him. Rome is the very nest of antichrist, and out of that nest come all his disciples. Of whom prelates, priests, and monks, are the body, these friars are the tail."

Then said he unto them all, "Christ saith in his gospel, 'Woe unto you, scribes and pharisees, hypocrites! for ye shut up the kingdom of heaven against men: for ye neither go in yourselves, neither suffer ye them that are entering to go in;' but ye stop up the ways thereunto with your own traditions, and therefore are ye the household of antichrist; ye will not permit God's verity to have passage, nor yet to be taught of his true ministers, fearing to have your wickedness reproved. But by such flatterers as uphold you in your mischiefs, you suffer the common people most miserably to be seduced."

Then said the archbishop, "By our lady, sir, there shall none such preach within my diocese nor yet in my jurisdiction, as either make division or dissension among the poor commons."

The Lord Cobham said, "Both Christ and his apostles were accused of sedition making, yet were they most peaceable men. But Daniel and Christ prophesied, that such a troublous time should come, as hath not been yet since the world's beginning. And this prophecy is partly fulfilled in your days and doings; for many have ye slain already, and more will ye slay hereafter, if God fulfil not his promise."

Then a doctor of law, called Master John Kemp, plucked out of his bosom a copy of the bill which they had sent him into the Tower, thinking thereby to make shorter work with him. For they were so amazed with his answers (not all unlike to them who disputed with Stephen) that they knew not well how to occupy the time, their wits and sophistry so failed them that day.

"My Lord Cobham," said this doctor, "we must briefly know your mind concerning these four points here following. The first of them is this; (and then he read from the bill.) The faith and determination of holy church touching the blessed sacrament of the altar is this, That after the sacramental words be once spoken of a priest in his mass, the material bread, that was before bread, is turned into Christ's very body, and the material wine is turned into Christ's blood. And so there remaineth in the sacrament of the altar from thenceforth no material bread nor material wine, which were there before the sacramental words were spoken: sir, believe you not this?"

The Lord Cobham said, "This is not my belief. But my faith is, that in the worshipful sacrament of the altar is Christ's very body in form of bread."

Then said the archbishop, "Sir John, ye must say otherwise."

The Lord Cobham said, "Nay, that I will not, if God be upon my side (as I trust he is) but that there is Christ's body in form of bread, as the common belief is."

Then the doctor read again.

"The second point is this; holy church hath determined, that every christian man, living here bodily upon earth, ought to be confessed to a priest ordained by the church, if he may come to him. Sir, what say you to this?"

The Lord Cobham answered and said, "A diseased or sore wounded man hath need to have a wise surgeon. Most necessary were it therefore to be first confessed unto God, who only knoweth our diseases, and can help us. I deny not in this the going to a priest, if he be a man of good life and learning; for the laws of God are to be inquired of the priest, who is godly learned. But if he be an idiot, or a man of vicious living, that is my curate, I ought rather to fly from him than to seek to him."

Then the doctor read again.

"The third point is this; Christ ordained St. Peter the apostle to be his vicar here in earth, whose see is the church of Rome. And he granted that the same power which he gave unto Peter should succeed unto all Peter's successors, whom we call now popes of Rome. By whose special power in particular churches, be ordained prelates and archbishops, parsons, curates, and other degrees more, whom christian men ought to obey after the laws of the church of Rome. This is the determination of holy church. Sir, believe ye not this?"

To this he answered and said, "He that followeth Peter most nearly in pure living, is next unto him in succession. But your lordly order esteemeth not greatly the lowly behaviour of poor Peter whatsoever ye prate of him. Neither care ye greatly for the humble manners of them that succeeded him till the time of Silvester, which for the more part were martyrs, as I told you before."

One of the other doctors asked him; "Then what do ye say of the pope?"

The Lord Cobham answered, "As I said before, so I say again; That he and you together make whole the great antichrist. Of whom he is the great head, you bishops, priests, prelates, and monks, are the body, and the begging friars are the tail, for they cover the filthiness of you both with their subtle sophistry: neither will I in conscience obey any of you all, till I see you with Peter follow Christ in conversation."

Then the doctor read again.

"The fourth point is this; holy church hath determined, that it is meritorious to a christian man, to go on pilgrimage to holy places, and there specially to worship the holy relics and images of saints, apostles, martyrs, confessors, and all other saints besides, approved by the church of Rome. Sir, what say you to this?"

He answered, "I owe them no service by any commandment of God. It were best ye swept them far from cobwebs and dust, and so laid them, or else bury them, far in the ground, as ye do other aged people who are God's images.

"It is a wonderful thing that saints, now being dead, should become so covetous and needy, and thereupon so bitterly beg, who all their life time hated all covetousness and begging."

"Why, sir," said one of the clerks, "will ye not worship good images?"

"What worship should I give to them?" said the Lord Cobham.

Then said friar Palmer to him, "Sir, will ye worship the cross of Christ, that he died upon?"

"Where is it?" said the Lord Cobham.

The friar said, "I put you the case, sir, that it were here even now before you."

The Lord Cobham answered, "This is a wise man, to put me an earnest question of a thing, and yet he himself knows not where the thing itself is. Yet once again I ask you, what worship I should do to it."

A clerk said unto him, "Such worship as Paul speaks of, and that is this; 'God forbid that I should glory, save in the cross of Jesus Christ.'"

Then said the Lord Cobham, and spread his arms abroad; "This is the very cross, yea, and so much better than your cross of wood, in that it was created of God, yet will not I seek to have it worshipped."

Then said the bishop of London, "Sir, ye know well that he died on a material cross."

The Lord Cobham said, "Yea, and I know also, that our salvation came not in by that material cross, but alone by him who died thereon. And well I know, that holy St. Paul rejoiced in none other cross, but in Christ's passion and death only, and in his own sufferings of like persecution with him, for the self-same truth that he had suffered for before."

Another clerk asked him, "Will ye then do no honour to the holy cross?"

He answered him, "Yes, if it were mine own, I would lay him up honestly, and see unto him that he should take no more scathe abroad, nor be robbed of his goods, as he is now a-days."

Then said the archbishop unto him, "Sir John, much time have we spent here about you, and all in vain so far as I can see. We must now be at this short point with you, for the day passeth away: ye must either submit yourself to the ordinance of holy church, or else throw yourself into most deep danger. See to it in time, for it will be else too late."

The Lord Cobham said, "I know not to what purpose I should otherwise submit me. Much more have you offended me, than ever I offended you, in this troubling me before this multitude."

Then said the archbishop again unto him, "We once again require you to remember yourself well, and to have none other manner of opinion in these matters, than the universal faith and belief of the holy church of Rome is. And so like an obedient child return again to the unity of your mother. See to it, I say, in time, for yet ye may have remedy, whereas soon it will be too late."

The Lord Cobham said expressly before them all; "I will none otherwise believe in these points than that I have told you here before. Do with me what you will."

Finally, then the archbishop said; "Well, then I see none other but that we must needs do the law; we must proceed forth to the sentence definitive, and both judge you and condemn you for a heretic."

And with that the archbishop stood up and read a bill of his condemnation as follows:—

The Sentence of Condemnation against Lord Cobham.

"In the name of God, so be it, We, Thomas, by the sufferance of God, archbishop of Canterbury, metropolitan and primate of all England, and legate from the apostolic see of Rome, will this to be known unto all men. In a certain cause of heresy, and upon divers articles, whereupon Sir John Oldcastle, knight, Lord Cobham, after a diligent inquisition made for the same, was detected, accused, and presented before us in our last convocation of all our province of Canterbury, holden in the cathedral church of Paul's at London, at the lawful denouncement and request of our universal clergy of the said convocation, we proceeded against him according to the law (God to witness) with all the favour possible. And following Christ's example in all that we might, 'who willeth not the death of a sinner, but rather that he might be converted and live ;' we took upon us to correct him, and sought all other ways possible to bring him again to the church's unity, declaring unto him what the holy and universal church of Rome hath said, holden, determined, and taught in that behalf. And though we found him in the catholic faith far wide, and so stiff-necked, that he would not confess his error, nor purge himself, nor yet repent him thereof; we yet pitying him of fatherly compassion, and entirely desiring the health of his soul, appointed him a competent time of deliberation, to see if he would repent and seek to be reformed : but since that time we have found him worse and worse. Considering, therefore, that he is not corrigible, we are driven to the very extremity of the law, and with great heaviness of heart we now proceed to the publication of the sentence definitive, against him."

Then he brought forth another bill, containing the sentence, and that he read also as follows :—

" We take Christ to witness, that we seek nothing else, in this our enterprise, but only his glory. Forasmuch as we have found by divers acts done, brought forth and exhibited, by sundry evidences, signs, and tokens, and also by many most manifest proofs, the said Sir John Oldcastle knight, Lord Cobham, not only to be an evident heretic in his own person, but also a mighty maintainer of other heretics against the faith and religion of the holy and universal church of Rome ; namely, about the two sacraments (of the altar, and of penance) besides the pope's power and pilgrimages ; and that he, as the child of iniquity and darkness, hath so hardened his heart, that he will in no case attend to the voice of his pastor ; neither will he be allured by straight admonishments, nor yet be brought in by favourable words : the worthiness of the cause first weighed on the one side, and his unworthiness again considered on the other side, his faults also aggravated or made double through his damnable obstinacy (we being loath that he which is naught should be worse, and so with his contagiousness infect the multitude) by the sage counsel and assent of the very discreet fathers, our honourable brethren and lord bishops here present, Richard of London, Henry of Winchester, and Bennet of Bangor, and of other great learned and wise men here, both doctors of divinity, and of the laws canon and civil, secular and religious, with divers other expert men assisting us : we sententially and definitively by this present writing judge, declare and condemn the said Sir John Oldcastle knight, Lord Cobham, for a most pernicious detestable heretic, convicted upon the same, and refusing utterly to obey the church again, committing him here from henceforth as a condemned heretic, to the secular jurisdiction, power, and judgment, to do him thereupon to death. Furthermore, we excommunicate and denounce accursed, not only this heretic here present, but so many else besides, as shall hereafter in favour of his error either receive him or defend him, counsel him or help him, or any other way maintain him ; as very favourers, receivers, defenders, counsellers, aiders, and maintainers of condemned heretics.

" And that these premises may be the better known of all faithful christian men, we commit it here unto your charges, and give you straight commandment thereupon by this writing also, that ye cause this condemnation and definitive sentence of excommunication concerning both this heretic and his favourers, to be published throughout all dioceses, in cities, towns, and villages, by your curates and parish priests, at such times as they shall have most recourse of people. And see that it be done after this sort: as the people are thus gathered devoutly together, let the curate every where go into the pulpit, and there open, declare, and expound this excess in the mother tongue, in an audible and intelligible voice, that it may be perceived of all men : and that upon the fear of this declaration also the

people may fall from their evil opinions conceived now of late by seditious preachers. Moreover, we will, that after we have delivered unto each one of you bishops, which are here present, a copy hereof, that ye cause the same to be written out again into divers copies, and to be sent unto the other bishops and prelates, of our whole province, that they may also see the contents thereof solemnly published within their dioceses and cures. Finally, We will that both you and they signify again unto us seriously and distinctly by your writings as the matter is, without feigned colour, in every point performed ; the day whereon ye received this process, the time when it was of us executed, and after what sort it was done in every condition, according to the tenor hereof, that we may know it to be justly the same."

After the archbishop had thus read the condemnation before the whole multitude, the Lord Cobham said with a most cheerful countenance, " Though ye judge my body, which is but a wretched thing, yet am I certain and sure that ye can do no harm to my soul, no more than could Satan unto the soul of Job. He that created that, will of his infinite mercy and promise save it. I have therein no manner of doubt. And as concerning these articles before rehearsed I will stand to them even to the very death, by the grace of my eternal God."

And therewith he turned him unto the people, casting his hands abroad, and saying with a very loud voice, " Good christian people, for God's love be well aware of these men, for they will else beguile you, and lead you blindfold into hell with themselves. For Christ saith plainly unto you, If the blind lead the blind, both shall fall into the ditch."

After this, he fell down upon his knees, and thus before them all prayed for his enemies, holding both his hands and his eyes towards heaven, and saying, " Lord God eternal, I beseech thee of thy great mercy sake to forgive my persecutors, if it be thy blessed will." And then he was delivered to Sir Robert Morley, and led forth again to the Tower of London, and thus there was an end of that day's work.

While the Lord Cobham was thus in the Tower, he sent out privily to his friends, and they at his request wrote the following letter, causing it to be set up in divers quarters of London, that the people should not believe the slanders and lies that his enemies, the bishops' servants and priests, had made on him abroad.

" Forasmuch as Sir John Oldcastle, knight, and Lord Cobham, is untruly convicted and imprisoned, falsely reported and slandered among the common people by his adversaries, that he thinks and speaks of the sacraments of the church, and especially of the blessed sacrament of the altar, otherwise than was written in the confession of his belief, which was written and taken to the clergy, and so set up in several open places of the city of London, be it known here to all the world, that he never since varied from it, but this is plainly his belief, that all the sacraments of the church are profitable and expedient to all that shall be saved, taking them after the intent that Christ and his true church has ordained. Furthermore he believes, that the blessed sacrament of the altar is verily and truly Christ's body in form of bread."

After this, the bishops and priests were in great discredit both with the nobility and commons ; partly because they had so cruelly handled the good Lord Cobham, and partly because his opinion, as they thought, was right concerning the sacrament. The prelates feared this would become a further inconvenience to them ; they consulted, and consented to take a different course from what they had done before. They caused it to be spread abroad by their servants and friends, that Lord Cobham had submitted himself to holy church, utterly changing his opinion concerning the sacrament. And they counterfeited an abjuration in his name, that the people should take no hold of his opinion by anything they had heard of him before, and so should stand the more in awe of them, considering that he was so great a man, and yet was subdued by them.

This, say they, is the abjuration of Sir John Oldcastle, knight, sometime the Lord Cobham :—

An Abjuration counterfeited by the Bishops.

" In the name of God, Amen. I, John Oldcastle, denounced, detected, and convicted of and upon various articles, savouring both of heresy and error, before the reverend father in Christ and my good lord, Thomas, by the permission of God, lord archbishop of Canterbury, and my lawful and rightful judge in that behalf, expressly grant and confess, that as concerning the estate and power of the most holy father the pope of Rome, of his archbishops, his bishops, and his other prelates, the degrees of the church, and the holy sacraments of the same, specially of the sacraments of the altar, of penance, and other observances besides of our mother holy church, as pilgrimages and pardons ; I affirm, (I say) before the said reverend father archbishop and elsewhere, that I being evilly seduced by divers seditious preachers, have grievously erred, and heretically persisted, blasphemously answered, and obstinately rebelled ; and therefore I am by the said reverend father, before the reverend fathers in Christ also, the bishops of London, Winchester, and Bangor, lawfully condemned for an heretic.

" Yet, nevertheless, I now remembering myself, and desiring by this mean to avoid that temporal pain which I am worthy to suffer as an heretic, at the assignation of my most excellent Christian prince and liege lord, King Henry V., now by the grace of God most worthy king both of England and of France ; minding also to prefer the wholesome determination, sentence, and doctrine of the holy universal church of Rome, before the unwholesome opinions of myself, my teachers, and my followers, I freely, willingly, deliberately, and thoroughly confess, grant, and affirm, that the most holy fathers in Christ, St. Peter the apostle, and his successors bishops of Rome, specially now at this time, my most blessed Lord Pope John, by the permission of God, the three and twentieth pope of that name, who now holdeth Peter's seat (and each of them in their succession) hath full strength and power to be Christ's vicar in earth, and the head of the church militant , and that by the strength of his office he hath full authority and power to rule and govern, bind and loose, save and destroy, accurse and absolve all other Christian men.

" And agreeably still unto this I confess, grant, and affirm all other archbishops, bishops, and prelates in their provinces, dioceses, and parishes (appointed by the said pope of Rome to assist him in his doings or business), by his decrees, canons, or virtue of his office, to have had in times past, to have now at this time, and that they ought to have in time to come, authority and power to rule and govern, bind and loose, accurse and absolve the subjects or people of their aforesaid provinces, dioceses, and parishes, and that their said subjects or people ought of right in all things to obey them. Furthermore, I confess, grant, and affirm, that the said spiritual fathers, as our most holy father the pope, archbishops, bishops, and prelates, have had, have now, and ought to have hereafter, authority and power for the state, order, and governance of their subjects or people, to make laws, decrees, statutes, and constitutions, yea, and to publish, command, and compel their said subjects and people to the observation of them.

" Moreover, I confess, grant, and affirm, that all these aforesaid laws, decrees, statutes, and constitutions, made, published, and commanded according to the form of the spiritual law, all christian people, and every man in himself is straightly bound to observe, and meekly to obey, according to the diversity of the aforesaid powers, as the laws, statutes, canons, and constitutions of our most holy father the pope, incorporated in his decrees, decretals, clementines, codes, charts, rescripts, sextiles, and extravagants over all the world ; and as the provincial statutes of archbishops in their provinces, the synodal acts of bishops in their dioceses,

and the commendable rules and customs of prelates in their colleges, and curates in their parishes, all christian people are both bound to observe, and also most meekly to obey. Over and besides all this, I, John Oldcastle, utterly forsaking and renouncing all the aforesaid errors and heresies, and all other errors and heresies like them, lay my hand here upon this book, or holy gospel of God, and swear, that I will never more from henceforth hold these heresies, nor yet any other like them wittingly. Neither will I give counsel, aid, help, or favour at any time, to them that shall hold, teach, affirm, and maintain the same, as God shall help me, and these holy evangelists.

" And that I will from henceforth faithfully obey and inviolably observe all the holy laws, statutes, canons, and constitutions, of all the popes of Rome, archbishops, bishops, and prelates, which are contained and determined in their holy decrees, decretals, clementines, codes, charts, rescripts, sextiles, sums, papal extravagants, statutes provincial, acts synodal, and other ordinary rules and customs constituted by them, or that shall chance hereafter directly to be determined or made. To these, and all such other, will I myself with all power possible apply. Besides all this, the penance which it shall please my said reverend father the lord archbishop of Canterbury hereafter to enjoin me for my sins, I will meekly obey and faithfully fulfil. Finally, all my seducers and false teachers, and all other beside, whom I shall hereafter know suspected of heresy or errors, I shall effectually present, send or cause to be presented unto my said reverend father lord archbishop, or to them who have his authority, so soon as I can conveniently do it, and see that they be corrected to my utmost power."

This abjuration never came to the hands of the Lord Cobham, neither was it compiled by them for that purpose, but only to blear the eyes of the unlearned multitude for a time.

After Lord Cobham had remained in the Tower a certain time, he escaped one night, it is not known by what means, and fled into Wales, where he continued four years.

Sir Roger Acton also was apprehended, condemned and put to death or martyrdom three years and more before the Lord Cobham died. Likewise master John Brown, and John Beverley, the preacher, suffered with him the same kind of death (as some say) in the field of St. Giles, with others, to the number of thirty-six, if the story be true. Which was in the month of January, A.D. 1414, after the computation of our English histories.

These men, as is said, suffered before Lord Cobham about three years. Some say they were hanged and burnt in St. Giles' field; others that only some of them were hanged and burnt. Polydore, speaking only of their burning, makes no mention of hanging. An English Chronicle records of Sir Roger Acton, that his sentence before the justice was to be drawn through London to Tyburn, and there to be hanged. And when certain days were past (saith the author) a trumpeter of the king's called Thomas Cliff, got grant of the king to take him down, and to bury him.

After the decease or martyrdom of these, who were executed in the month of January, A. D. 1414, in the next month, and in the same year, God took away the great enemy of his word, and rebel to his king, Thomas Arundel archbishop of Canterbury : whose death following after the execution of these good men, by the marvellous stroke of God so suddenly, may seem somewhat to declare their innocency, and that he was also some great procurer of their death, in that God would not suffer him longer to live, striking him immediately with death. But as I did the other before, so this also I refer to the secret judgment of the Lord, who once shall judge all secrets openly.

Henry Chichesly succeeded next in the see of Canterbury, A. D. 1414, and sat five-and-twenty years. Following the steps of his predecessor, he shewed himself no small adversary against the favourers of the truth. In his time there was much trouble and great affliction in the church. For as the preaching and teaching of the word multiplied and spread abroad daily more and more, so on the contrary side, more vigilant care and straight inquisition increased against the people of God, by reason of which many suffered, and were burned; some for fear fled the country : many were brought for examination, and by infirmity constrained to abjure.

As true piety and sincere preaching of Christ's word began at this time to decay ; so idle monkery and vain superstition in place thereof began to increase. For about the same year the king began the foundation of two monasteries, one of the one side of Thames, of Friars Observants, the other on the other side of Thames called Sheen and Zion, dedicated to charter-house-monks, with certain Bridget-nuns or recluses, to the number of sixty, dwelling within the precincts, so that the whole number of these with priests, monks, deacons, and nuns, should equal the number of twelve apostles, and seventy-two disciples. The order of these was according to the description of St. Paul the apostle, Col. i. 24, " Eat not, taste not, touch not," &c. was to eat no flesh, to wear no linen, to touch no money, &c.

About Michaelmas, the same year, the king began his parliament at Leicester. In which parliament the commons put up their bill again, which they had put up before in the eleventh year of Henry IV. that temporalties, disorderly wasted by the men of the church, might be converted and employed to the use of the king, of his earls and knights, and to the relief of the poor people, as is before recited. In fear of which bill lest the king would give thereto any audience (as testifies Robert Fabian and other writers) the prelates put the king in mind to claim his right in France. Whereupon Henry Chichesly archbishop of Canterbury made a long and solemn oration before the king to persuade him to the same, offering to the king in the behalf of the clergy great and noble sums. By which (saith Fabian) the bill was again put off, and the king set his mind for the recovery of the same.

I will now return to other matters of the church.

The History of the Bohemians.

I declared a little before how by the occasion of Queen Anne, who was a Bohemian, and married to King Richard II., the Bohemians coming thereby to the knowledge of Wickliff's books here in England, began first to taste and favour Christ's gospel, till at length by the preaching of John Huss, they increased more and more in knowledge. Insomuch that Pope Alexander V. hearing of it, directs his bull to the archbishop of Swinco, requiring him to look to the matter, and to provide that no person in churches, schools, or other places, should maintain that doctrine, citing also John Huss to appear before him. John Huss in answer, declared that the mandate or bull of the pope was opposed to the manifest examples and doings both of Christ and of his apostles, and prejudicial to the liberty of the gospel, in binding the word of God so as not to have free course. And therefore from this mandate of the pope he appealed to the same pope better advised. But while he was prosecuting his appeal, Pope Alexander died, as is aforesaid.

After him succeeded Pope John XXIII., who sought by all means possible to suppress the Bohemians, beginning to work his malice upon John Huss their preacher, who preaching at Prague, seemed willing to teach the gospel of Christ, rather than the traditions of bishops, and was therefore accused to the pope as a heretic. The bishop committed the whole matter to Cardinal de Columna ; who, when he had heard the accusation, appointed a day to John Huss, that he should appear in the court of Rome : which thing once done, Wenceslaus king of the Romans, and of Bohemia, at the request of his wife Sophia, and of the whole nobility of Bohemia, as also at the earnest suit and desire of the town and university of Prague, sent his ambassadors to Rome, to desire the bishop to deliver John Huss from that sentence and judgment : and that if the bishop suspected the kingdom of Bohemia to be infected with any heretical or false doctrine, he should send his ambassadors, who might correct and amend the same, if there were any error or fault in them. And that all

this should be done at the costs and charges of the king of Bohemia ; and to promise in his name that he would aid and assist the bishop's legates with all his power and authority, to punish all such as should be taken or found in any erroneous doctrine. John Huss, also, before his appointed day, sent his proctors to the court of Rome, and with most firm and strong reasons proved his innocency. But when the Cardinal de Columna, (to whose will and judgment the whole matter was committed) would not admit any defence or excuse, John Huss' proctors appealed to the high bishop : yet notwithstanding this last refuge did not so prevail with Cardinal de Columna, but that he openly excommunicated John Huss as an obstinate heretic, because he came not at his appointed day to Rome.

However, as his proctors had appealed to the high bishop, they had other judges appointed, as Cardinal Aquileianus and Cardinal Venetus, with others. The judges, after they had deferred the matter for the space of one year and a half, at last returned to the sentence and judgment of Cardinal de Columna, and confirming it, commanded John Huss' proctors that they should leave off defending him any more, for they would suffer it no longer. Upon which, when his proctors would not cease their urgent suit, some of them were cast into prison, and grievously punished, the others leaving their business undone, returned into Bohemia.

The Bohemians, however, little cared for all this, but continuing still, as they grew more in knowledge, so the less they regarded the pope, complaining daily against him and the archbishop for stopping the word of God, and the gospel of Christ to be preached, saying, " That by their indulgences and other practices of the court of Rome, and of the bishop's consistory, they sought their own profit, and not the glory of Jesus Christ; that they took from the sheep of Christ the wool and milk, and did not feed them, either with the word of God, or with good examples. Teaching moreover and affirming, that the commandments of the pope and prelates are not to be obeyed, but so far as they follow the doctrine and life of Christ and of his apostles ; and that laymen ought to judge the works of prelates, as Paul judged the works of Peter in correcting him, Gal. ii. Furthermore, they had amongst them certain notes and observations, whereby they might discern how far and wherein they might obey their prelates ; they derided also and scorned the pope's jurisdiction, because of the schism that was then in the church, when there were three popes together, one striving against another for the papacy.

After the death of the Archbishop Swinco, one Conrad was appointed by the pope as chief general, this Conrad conferring with the divines and doctors of the university of Prague, required their advice and counsel, what way they should best take to assuage the dissension and discord between the clergy and the people. So a council was devised and holden, where it was decided after this manner.

" 1. That all doctors and masters of the university of Prague should be assembled in the court of the archbishop, and in his presence, that every doctor and master should swear, not to hold or maintain any of the forty-five articles of John Wickliff before condemned.

" 2. Concerning the seven sacraments of the church, the keys and censures of the church, the manners, rites, ceremonies, customs, and liberties of the church, concerning also the worshipping of reliques and indulgences, the orders and religions of the church, that every one shall swear that he holds, believes, and maintains, and will maintain, as does the church of Rome, and no otherwise, of the which church of Rome the pope is the head, and the college of cardinals is the body : who are the true and manifest successors of blessed St. Peter prince of the apostles, and of the college of the other apostles of Christ.

" 3. That every one shall swear, that in every catholic matter, belonging to the church, he will stand to the determination of the apostolical see, and that he will obey the prelates in all manner of things, wheresoever the thing, which is purely good, is not forbidden ; or that which is mere ill, is not commanded ; but is mean and indifferent between both. Which mean or indifferent thing, yet notwithstanding by circumstances of time, place or person, may be either good or evil.

"4. That every one shall swear and confess by his oath, that the opinions of Wickliff and others, touching the seven sacraments of the church, and other things above notified, being contrary to the church of Rome are false.

"5. That an oath be required of them all, that none of them shall hold, defend, or maintain any of the forty-five articles of John Wickliff aforesaid, or in any other matter catholic, and especially of the seven sacraments and other articles above specified, but only as the church of Rome does, and no otherwise.

"6. That every ordinary in his diocese shall cause the premises, contained in the first, second, third, and fourth articles, to be published in his synods, and by his preachers to the people in the kingdom of Bohemia.

"7. If any clerk, student, or layman shall withstand any of the premises, that the ordinary have authority, if he be convicted thereof, to correct him according to the old laws and canons, and that no man shall defend such a one by any means; for none but the ordinary has power to correct such a man, because the archbishop is chancellor both of the kingdom and university of Prague.

"8. That the songs lately forbidden, being odious, slanderous, and offensive to others' fame, be not sung either in streets, taverns, or any other place.

"9. That Master John Huss shall not preach so long as he shall have no absolution of the court, nor shall hinder the preaching in Prague by his presence; that by this, his obedience in the apostolical see may be known.

"10. That this council appears to be good and reasonable for the putting away of ill report and dissension that is in the kingdom of Bohemia.

"11. If Master John Huss with his accomplices will perform this, which is contained in the four former articles, then we will be ready to say as they would wish us and have us, whenever need shall require, that we do agree with them in matter of faith: otherwise if they will not so do, we in giving this testimony, should lie greatly unto our lord the king and the whole world. And moreover, we will be content to write for them to the court of Rome, and do the best we can for them."

This counsel and devise being considered amongst the heads of the university of Prague, the aforesaid administrator named Conrad, presented it to the king and to the barons of the realm, and also to the senate of Prague. As soon as information of it came to John Huss and his adherents, they likewise drew out other articles in manner and form of a council as follows:

"For the honour of God and the true preaching of his gospel, for the health of the people, and to avoid the sinister and false infamy of the kingdom of Bohemia, and of the marquis of Moravia, and of the city and university of Prague, and for the reforming of peace and unity between the clergy and the scholars of the university:

"1. Let the right and just decree of the princes, and of the king's council, be held in force, which between the Lord Archbishop Swinco on the one party, and between the rector and Master John Huss on the other party, was made, proclaimed, sealed, and solemnly on both parts received and allowed in the court of our sovereign lord the king.

"2. That the kingdom of Bohemia remain in its former rites, liberties, and common customs, as other kingdoms and lands; that is, in all approbations, condemnations, and other acts concerning the holy mother universal church.

"3. That Master John Huss (against whom the aforesaid Lord Swinco could object no crime before the council) may be present in the congregation of the clergy, and there whoever will object to him either heresy or error, let him object, binding himself to suffer the like pain, if he do not prove it.

"4. If no man will set himself on the contrary part against him, then let the command be made by our sovereign lord the king through all his cities, and likewise let it be ordained and proclaimed through all vil-

lages and towns, that Master John Huss is ready to render account of his faith, and therefore if any will object to him any heresy or error, let him write his name in the chancery of the lord archbishop, and bring forth his proofs openly before both the parties.

"5. If none such shall be found to object, or who will write his name, then let him be called for, who rumoured in the pope's court, that in the kingdom of Bohemia, in the city of Prague, and in the marquisdom of Moravia there were many whose hearts are infected with heresy and error, that they may prove who they are, and if they are not able to prove it, let them be punished.

"6. That commands be directed to doctors of divinity and of the canon law, and to the chapter of cathedral churches, and that it be required of them all and of every one particularly, that they will bring forth his name, if they know any such to be an heretic or erroneous, and if they deny to know any such, then let them make recognition thereof, before the public notary, confirming the same with their seals.

"7. These things thus done and premised, then that our sovereign lord the king, and also that the archbishop will give commandment under pain, that no man shall call one another heretic or erroneous, unless he will stand to the proof of that heresy or error.

"8. That our sovereign lord the king, with the consent of his barons, will then levy a subsidy, or collect of the clergy, and direct an honest ambassy to the pope's court, with which ambassadors let those persons go at their own proper charges or expenses for their purgation, who have caused this kingdom to be falsely and grievously defamed in the apostolic court.

"9. In the mean time for the presence of Master John Huss, no interdict ought to be made, as it was made of late contrary to the order and determination of our holy mother church."

As this matter was thus in altercation between the two parties, the one objecting, the other answering, it happened by the occasion of Ladislaus king of Naples, who had besieged the pope's towns and territories, that Pope John raising up war against Ladislaus, give full remission of sins to all them which would war on his side to defend the church. When this bull of the pope's indulgence was come to Prague, and there published, the King Wenceslaus, who then favoured that pope, gave command that no man should attempt anything against the pope's indulgences. But Huss with his followers, not able to abide the impiety of those pardons, began to speak against them; of which company were three certain artificers, who, hearing the priest preaching these indulgences, openly spoke against them, and called the pope antichrist, who would set up the cross to fight against his fellow christians. For this they were brought before the senate, and committed to prison; but the people joining together in arms, came to the magistrates, requiring them to be let loose. The magistrates with gentle words and fair promises satisfied the people, so that every man returning home to his own house, the tumult was assuaged; but the captains being in prison were there beheaded, whose names were John, Martin, and Stascon. The death and martyrdom of these three being known to the people, they took the bodies of them that were slain, and with great solemnity brought them to the church of Bethlehem. And so their bodies were sumptuously interred in the church of Bethlehem, John Huss, preaching at the funeral, much commending them for their constancy, and blessing God the Father of our Lord Jesus Christ, who had hid the way of his truth from the prudent of this world, and had revealed it to the simple lay people and inferior priests, who chose rather to please God than men.

Thus the city of Prague was divided. The prelates with the greatest part of the clergy, and most of the barons, who had anything to lose, did hold with the pope, especially Steven Paletz, being the chiefest doer on that side. On the contrary part the commons with part of the clergy and students of the university, went with John Huss. Wenceslaus the king, fearing lest this would grow to a tumult, being moved by the doctors, and prelates, and council of his barons, thought best to remove John Huss out of the city, who had been excommunicated before by the pope. And further to end this dissension in the church, he committed the matter to the doctors and the clergy. They, consulting together among themselves, set forth a decree, ratified and confirmed by the sentence of the king, containing the sum of eighteen articles, for the maintenance of the pope and of the see of Rome, against the doctrine of Wickliff and John Huss. John Huss, thus departing out of Prague, went to his country, where, being protected by the lord of the soil, he continued preaching there, to whom resorted a great concourse of people, neither yet was he so expelled out of Prague, but that sometimes he resorted to his church at Bethlehem, and there also preached unto the people.

Against the decree of the doctors John Huss, with his company, replied, and answered to their articles with contrary articles, as follow :—

The Objections of John Huss, and of his party against the Decree of the Doctors.

" 1. The foundation of the doctors, upon which they found all their writings and counsels, is false, which foundation is, that part of the clergy in the kingdom of Bohemia is pestilent and erroneous, and holds falsely of the sacraments.

" 2. The doctors hereby do defame the kingdom of Bohemia, and do raise up new discords.

" 3. Let them show, therefore, those persons of the clergy, whom they call pestilent, and so let them verify their report, binding themselves to suffer the like pain if they be not able to prove it.

" 4. It is false what they say of the pope and his cardinals as the true and manifest successors of Peter and of the apostles, and that no other successors of Peter and of the apostles can be found upon the earth besides them, when no man knows whether he is worthy of hatred or of favour, and all bishops and priests are successors of Peter and of the apostles.

" 5. Not the pope, but Christ only is the head; and not the cardinals, but all Christ's faithful people are the body of the catholic church, as all holy scripture and decrees of the holy fathers testify and affirm.

" 6. And as touching the pope, if he be a reprobate, it is plain that he is no head,—no, nor member even of the holy church of God, but of the devil, and of his synagogue.

" 7. The clergy of the gospellers agreeing with the saying of St. Austin which they allege, and according to the sanctions of the fathers, and determinations of the holy mother church, say and affirm laudably, that the condemnation and prohibition of the forty-five articles is unlawful, and unjust, and rashly done; and that not only because the doctors, but also all bishops and archbishops, in such great causes, namely, touching faith, as these articles do, have no authority at all.

" 8. The second cause of the discord, which they allege, also is most false; seeing the faith of all Christendom, concerning the church of Rome, is divided in three parts by reason of three popes, which now together do reign; and the fourth part is neutral. Neither is it true, that we ought to stand in all things to the determination of the pope, and of the cardinals, but so far as they agree with the holy scripture of the Old and New Testament.

" 9. In the fourth article they run into dotage, and are contrary to themselves; because they dotishly reprehended the gospellers, who, in all their doings, receive the holy scripture (which is the law of God, the way of truth and life) for their judge and measure; and afterward they themselves allege the scripture, Deut. xvii. where all judges, both popes and cardinals, are taught to judge and discern between leper and leper, and in every ecclesiastical cause, only after the rule of God's law. And so are they contrary to their second article, wherein they say, that in every catholic matter we must run to the pope, which is contrary to the foolish condemnation of the articles aforesaid.

" 10. Consequently, like idiots, they most falsely allege for their purpose the canon, under the name and authority of Jerome, where they do apply the words of Jerome most impertinently to the pope of Rome, which he writes to St. Austin, calling him a most blessed pope.

" 11. By which place of Jerome it is manifest that the first article of those doctors is false. For by these words it appears that other besides the bishop of Rome and his cardinals are called blessed popes, holding the faith and seat of Peter, and are successors of the apostles, as was Austin and other holy bishops.

" 12. It follows moreover, that the church of Rome is not that place where the Lord appointed the principal see of his whole church; for Christ, who was the head priest of all, first sat in Jerusalem, and Peter sat first in Antioch, and afterwards in Rome. Also other popes sat some in Bononia, some at Perusium, some at Avignon.

" 13. The prelates are falsifiers of the holy scriptures and canons, and therefore are worthy to be punished, who affirm and say, that we must obey the pope in all things, because it is known that many popes have erred, and one pope was also a woman; to whom not only it was not lawful to give obedience, but also unlawful to communicate with them.

" 14. Their sixth, seventh, eighth, ninth, tenth, and eleventh articles are grounded upon untrue and false persuasions, and therefore are to be rejected and detested, seeing they induce not to peace and verity, but to dissension and falsity.

" 15. It is manifest also to the laity, that this dissension among the clergy rises for no other cause, but only for the preaching of the gospel, which reprehends such simoniacs and heretics in the church of God as haunt the court of Rome, spreading out their branches abroad into all the world, who deserved to be removed and extirpated, not only by the clergy gospellers, but also by the secular power. And so these three vices, to wit, simony, luxury, and avarice (which is idolatry), are the causes of all this dissension among the clergy in the kingdom of Bohemia. These three vices being removed, peace and unity would soon be restored in the clergy.

" 16. Moreover, their last article is too gross, and not only is without all law, but also without all colour of law; whereas they fondly and childishly argue thus, that the processes made against Master John Huss ought to be obeyed, because forsooth the common sort of the clergy of Prague have received them. By the same reason they may argue also, that we must obey the devil, for our first parents Adam and Eve obeyed him. Also our ancestors before us were pagans, wherefore we must obey them, and be pagans also.

" 17. But let this frivolous opinion go: this is certain truth, that the processes made against Master John Huss, are by law null and void; for they were obtained, drawn, wrought, and executed contrary to the commission of the pope, against the determination of the holy mother church.

" 18. Finally, whoever wittingly and obstinately defends and executes the said process made, are all to be counted as blasphemers, excommunicate, and heretics.''

To these objections of John Huss the doctors again answered in a long tedious process; the scope of which principally tended to defend the principality of the pope, and to maintain his obedience above all other potentates in the world, affirming and contending, that although Christ is the head alone of the whole multitude of them that are sleeping in purgatory, and which are labouring in the church militant, and which are resting in heaven, yet this hinders not, but the pope is head of the church here militant, that is, of all the faithful, which here in this world live under his office, &c.

Thus then Master John Huss being driven out of Prague by these doctors, and moreover being so excommunicated that no mass must be said where he was present, the people began mightily to grudge and to cry out against the prelates and other popish priests, who were the workers thereof, accusing them to be simoniacs, covetous, immoral, adulterers, proud; sparing not to lay open their vices to their great ignominy and shame, and greatly crying for a reformation amongst the clergy.

The king seeing the inclination of the people, and being not ignorant of the wickedness of the clergy, began, under pretence of reforming the church, to require greater exactions upon such priests and men of the clergy as were known and accused to be wicked livers. Upon which they that favoured John Huss, taking the occasion, complained of all, accused many, and spared none, whoever they knew to be of the popish faction, or enemies to John Huss. By reason of which the popish clergy were brought, such as were faulty into great distress, and such as were not faulty, into great fear, so that they were glad to fall in, at least not to fall out, with the protestants, being afraid to displease them. By this means Master Huss began to take some more liberty, and to preach in his church at Bethlehem; by the same means the people also received some comfort, and the king much gain and money.

And thus the popish clergy, while they went about to persecute John Huss, were entrapped themselves in great tribulation, and afflicted on every side, so that women and children were against them; and by the means with which they thought to entangle him, they were overthrown themselves.

As there was a council held at Rome four years before, against the articles and books of John Wickliff, it will not be impertinent nor out of purpose to repeat a certain merry history, and worthy otherwise to be noted, written by Nicholas Clemangis, of a certain spirit which ruled the popish councils; his words are these:—

" The pope called a council at Rome about four years before, at the earnest suit of several men, and a mass of the Holy Ghost being said at the opening of the council (according to the accustomed manner), the council being set, and Pope John sitting highest in a chair prepared for him for that purpose, behold, an ugly and dreadful owl, or as the common proverb is, the evil sign of some mischance of death, flew to and fro, with her evil favoured voice, and standing upon the middle beam of the church, cast her staring eyes upon the pope. The whole company began to marvel, to see the night-crow, which is wont to abide no light, how he should in the mid-day come in the face of such a multitude, and judged (not without cause) that it was an ill-favoured token. For behold, said they (whispering one in another's ear) the spirit appears in the shape of an owl. And as they stood beholding one another, and advising the pope, scarcely could they keep their countenance from laughter. John himself, upon whom the owl steadfastly looked, blushing at the matter, began to sweat, and to fret, and fume with himself, and not finding by what other means he might solve the matter, being so confused, dissolved the council, and rose up and departed. After that there followed another session, in which the owl again, after the manner aforesaid although, as I believe, not called, was present, looking steadfastly upon the bishop. He beholding it come again, was more ashamed than he was before, saying he could no longer abide the sight of her, and commanded that she should be driven away with bats and shoutings; but she being afraid neither with their noise, neither at anything else, would not go away, until with the strokes of the sticks, which were thrown down at her, she fell down dead before them all."

The Council of Constance.

Here is to be noted, that during all this time of Pope John, there were three popes together for twenty-nine years, on account of which a general council was held at Constance, (A. D. 1414,) called by the emperor Sigismund, and Pope John XXIII., for healing the schism between the three popes striving for the popedom. The first was John whom the Italians set up. The second was Gregory, whom the French set up. The third was Benedict, whom the Spaniards set up. In this conflict every one defended his own pope, to the great disturbance of the christian nations. This council continued four years, and in it all matters were decided mostly by four nations, viz. the English, German, French, and Italian. Out of which four nations there were appointed four presidents, to determine the matters of the council. The names of which presidents were these: John the patriarch of Antioch for France, Anthony, archbishop of Reigen for Italy, Nicholas, archbishop of Geneva for Germany, and Nicholas bishop of Bath for England. First, this John XXIII. resigned his papacy, the emperor giving him thanks kissed his feet. This John afterward repenting that he had done so, sought means to flee; so changing his garments, he fled by night with a small company. The emperor pursuing, took him, and being thus deposed, he was carried to the castle of Manheim, where he was kept prisoner for the space of three years.

This Pope John was deposed by the decree of the council, more than three-and-forty most grievous and heinous crimes being objected and proved against him; as that he had hired a physician to poison Alexander his predecessor; that he was an heretic, a simoniac, a liar, an hypocrite, a murderer, a dice-player, an adulterer, and finally, what crime is it that he was not infected with?

And now to return to the council, first we will declare the order of their sessions, with the things therein concluded, in general; then we will (Christ willing) treat of such matters as pertain to the history of the Bohemians, and John Huss, and Jerome of Prague, who in the same ungodly council were condemned and burned.

This council therefore of Constance, which was summoned by the emperor Sigismund, and Pope John XXIII. (A. D. 1414), assembled about the latter end of the year. Which beginning, as the manner is, with a mass of the Holy Ghost, as they were singing according to their custom their hymn, "Come Holy Spirit," &c., there was at the same time a certain paper set up in the church, wherein were contained these words following: "We (i. e. The Spirit) are otherwise occupied at this time, so we cannot come to you." The council continued for the space of four years, and had five-and-forty sessions, wherein many things were concluded, which altogether were too long to be recited in this place; as the deposition of three several popes. Yet I mind to make some brief recapitulation of the principal matters.

In the first session chiefly was concluded,

1. That this council was lawfully assembled.

2. That the departure of the pope should be no hindrance, but the council might proceed.

3. This council should not be dissolved before the church were reformed, as well in the superiors as inferiors.

In the fourth session, this was first concluded; that a synod assembled in the Holy Ghost, making a general council, representing the whole catholic church here militant, has power from Christ immediately, to which power every person, of what state or dignity soever he be, yea, the pope himself, ought to be obedient in all such things as concern the general reformation of the church, as well in the heads, as in the members.

Also the pope should not translate the court of Rome, and the officers of the court, from the city of Constance. And that all his censures, doings and workings, to the prejudice of this council, should be of no effect.

In the fifth session the same articles were repeated and concluded again.

In the sixth session commissioners were appointed out of the four nations for the hearing of John Huss.

The memory of John Wickliff was condemned, and the sentence, given in the council held at Rome upon the condemnation and burning of Wickliff's books, was confirmed.

In the same session, citation was sent out against Jerome of Prague.

In the seventh session nothing was handled, but that the tenor of the citation against Pope John was recited.

In the eighth session, the sentence and condemnation of John Wickliff and his forty-five articles was recited, and sentence given against his memory, and bones to be burned.

In the ninth session the matter and cause of Pope

John was again treated, and commissioners appointed to inquire upon his cause, and judges for the same.

In the tenth session suspension was given out and read against the pope.

In the eleventh and twelfth sessions notaries were assigned and definitive sentence given against the pope: where also it was decreed that none of them, that sought for the papacy, should be chosen pope.

In the thirteenth session was decreed, that no priest, under pain of excommunication, shall communicate unto the people under both kinds of bread and wine.

In the fourteenth session came in the resignation of Pope Gregory XII., which was one of the three before mentioned, striving for the papacy, with certain other articles concerning the election of the bishop of Rome.

Then ensues the fifteenth session, in the which silence was commanded under pain of excommunication and the great curse, that no person or persons high or low, of what estate or degree soever he were, emperor, king, cardinal, or other, should disturb the said session with any manner of noise, either by hand, foot, or voice. This being done, the sentence and condemnation against John Huss was read and published.

In the sixteenth session ambassadors were assigned by the council to go into Arragon to Benedict XIII. to treat with him for the resignation of his papacy, as the other two had done before.

In the seventeenth session the emperor took upon him a journey to the king of Arragon, to treat with Pope Benedict. An excommunication denounced against all such as should go about to impeach the emperor's journey, about that matter, &c.

In the eighteenth session it was there also decreed, that such letters and bulls, as were written in the name of that council, should be received with no less credit and authority than the bulls proceeding from the see apostolical, and that the falsifiers of the same should incur no less penalty, than the falsifiers of the other. Legates also and ambassadors were sent into Italy.

In the nineteenth session Jerome of Prague was accused of heresy, and cast into prison by the council, and constrained to abjure.

It was decreed also, that notwithstanding the safe conduct given by the emperor and kings, &c., inquiry may be made against any man for heresy by a sufficient judge, and process to be made according to the law.

In the twentieth session there was nothing important.

In the year 1416, was the twenty-first session, beginning after their manner with a mass of the Holy Ghost, with procession and such other rites, in the time of which mass, James, bishop of Londy made a sermon, and Jerome of Prague being present, stood up, replying against the foresaid James and his sermon, whereupon Jerome was delivered to the secular power, and burned.

From the twenty-second to the thirty-first sessions there was nothing of particular importance.

In the thirty-second and thirty-third sessions the accusation of Pope Benedict was renewed, and his obstinacy accused, and witnesses brought in; at which the Emperor Sigismund was present.

In the thirty-fourth session the cause of the pope was heard, and process given out against him.

In the thirty-sixth session a citation was made and read against the pope, containing his deprivation, and the sentence against him. And whereas this pope had thundered out his curses, deprivations, and excommunications against them, the synod did annihilate all his doings.

The thirty-seventh session renewed again the accusation of the aforesaid pope, and the sentence definitive against him was published.

The thirty-eighth session referred to the king of Arragon.

Thus Pope Benedict being deposed and excommunicated, in the next sessions following they addressed themselves to the election of a new pope, beginning first in the thirty-ninth session, to give out decrees concerning general councils, and provision for the avoiding of such like schisms hereafter. Decreeing every tenth year to have a general council, after the two councils that should follow immediately after this; of which, the one should be kept within five years then next following, and the second within seven years after that.

In the same session was drawn out a form touching such things as the pope should profess and bind himself to observe at the time of his election, of which form the order and tenor is this:

"I, N. elected for pope, profess with heart and mouth unto Almighty God, whose church I take upon me to govern by his help, and to blessed St. Peter, the prince of the apostles, so long as I shall endure in this frail and brittle life, firmly to believe and hold the holy catholic faith after traditions of the apostles, of general councils, and of other holy fathers, and, namely, of the eight general councils; Nicene the first, the second of Constantinople, Ephesine the third, Chalcedon the fourth, the fifth and sixth of them in Constantinople, the seventh of Nice, the eighth of Constantinople. And also of the general councils of Lateran, Lyons, and Vienna, willing to observe the same faith inviolate even to the uttermost, and to preach and defend the same, even to the spending of my life and blood; and also by all means possible to prosecute and observe the rite of the sacraments canonically delivered to the catholic church. And this my profession and confession, by my commandment being written out by the notary of the arches of the holy church of Rome, I have subscribed with mine own hand, and sincerely with a pure mind and devout conscience I offer it unto the Almighty God upon such an altar, &c. In the presence of such witness, &c. Given," &c.

In the fortieth session, certain decrees were read, as to reformations to be made through the whole church by the pope, with the council, before this synod should break up.

Also, that they should proceed to the election of the bishop of Rome, notwithstanding the absence of those cardinals who were with Pope Benedict in Spain. This done, the order and manner was decreed for the election of the pope.

In the next session, which was forty-one, the constitution of Clement VI. was read, concerning the order and diet of the cardinals then in the conclave about the choosing of the pope, and oaths were ministered to the cardinals and other electors, binding them to observe and keep all such things as they should be bound to, during the time of the election.

1. That they should enter into the conclave within ten days after the fortieth session, which was this present day after sun-set.

2. That every cardinal should have but two servitors attending upon him, at the most, either of the laity or clergy, as they chose themselves.

3. That they should remain together in the conclave, without any wall between them, or any other cover, save only bare curtains, if any were disposed to sleep.

4. That the conclave should be so shut up, and the entry to the privy chamber be kept so straightly, that none of them should come in or out, nor any have recourse to them to talk with them privily or openly.

5. That no man should send to them either messenger or writings.

6. That a competent window should be assigned unto them to receive in their victuals, but that no person might come in thereat.

7. That no day after their first ingress into the conclave, beside bread, wine, and water, they should have any more dishes but one of one only kind, either of flesh or fish, eggs, pottage, made of fish or flesh, not after the daintiest sort, beside sallads, cheese, fruit, and conserves, whereof there shall be no principal mess made but for sauce and taste.

8. That not one should be compelled to go into the conclave; but if they did all refuse to go in, then they should be compelled.

9. That such as would go out might; but if they would all go out before the pope were elected, they should be compelled to go in again, except such whom infirmity excused; but without the excuse of infirmity, if any went out, he should no more be admitted, except they went all out together.

10. That such as went out by reason of infirmity, to be absent, and return before the election be determined, may be admitted again into the conclave in the same state wherein they shall find the election to stand.

Further, and besides, the keepers of the conclave should also be sworn to see all these premises observed and kept without fraud or guile, and that they should not straighten the cardinals and other electors above the order here taken.

These things thus prepared and set in order, the patriarch of Constantinople, with the cardinals and other archbishops, bishops, abbots, priors, deans, archdeacons, doctors, with other electors, entering into the conclave upon Monday, on Thursday after they had hatched out a pope, being St. Martin's even, whereupon they named him Martin. This Martin thus being elected, was straightway brought in by the emperor and the council into the church of Constance, and there enthroned for pope, with great solemnity and triumph. The twenty-first day of the said month, this Martin, according to their accustomed pomp, was honourably brought in to be crowned with sumptuous procession from the high church of Constance, to the monastery of St. Austin; the emperor on foot leading his horse by the bridle on the right hand, and the marquess of Brandenburgh prince elector likewise leading his horse on the left hand, the pope himself riding in the midst upon his palfrey.

And thus being brought to the monastery, and round about again from thence to the high church of Constance, he was there crowned with all magnificence.

In the forty-third session, certain other decrees and statutes were made by Pope Martin in the synod, annulling all the acts and proceedings of the other popes before, during the time of the schism from the time of Gregory II. As in matters concerning exemptions, unions, fruits, and profits of the church; benefices, simony, dispensations, tithes, and burthens of the church. Also concerning the apparel of the clergy, and such other things.

Now to finish our tedious rehearsal of this synod, the Cardinal Umbald, by the commandment of the pope and the council, with a high and loud voice pronounced these words: "Lord, depart in peace;" whereunto the standers by answered, "Amen."

The number of the foreigners resorting to this council, both spiritual and temporal, was sixty thousand five hundred, whereof the number of archbishops, and bishops, was three hundred and forty-six.

Abbots and doctors, five hundred and sixty-four.

Secular men (princes, dukes, earls, knights, esquires), sixteen thousand.

Besides women belonging to the same council, four hundred and fifty.

Barbers, six hundred.

Minstrels, cooks, and jesters, three hundred and twenty.

So that the whole multitude which were viewed to be in the town of Constance, between Easter and Whitsuntide, were numbered to be sixty thousand five hundred strangers and foreigners at that council.

Here is to be noted, that in this council of Constance nothing was decreed or enacted worthy of memory, but this only, that the pope's authority is under the council, and that the council ought to judge the pope.

And as touching the communion in both kinds, although the council did not deny, but that it was used by Christ and his apostles; yet notwithstanding it was decreed by the council to the contrary.

Hitherto we have comprehended the order and discourse of this council, with the acts and sessions concerning the same; which council, although it was principally thought to be assembled, for quieting of the schism between the three popes, yet notwithstanding a great part thereof was for the affair of the Bohemians, and especially for John Huss. For, before the council began, the Emperor Sigismund sent certain gentlemen of his own household, to bring John Huss to the council, under his safe conduct. The meaning of which was, that John Huss should purge and clear himself of the blame which they had laid against him; and for the better assurance, the Emperor not only promised him safe conduct, that

he might come freely to Constance, but also that he should return again into Bohemia, without fraud or interruption; he promised also to receive him under his protection, and under safeguard of the whole empire.

The safe Conduct given to John Huss.

"Sigismund, by the grace of God, king of the Romans, of Hungary and Denmark, Croatia, &c. To all princes as well ecclesiastical as secular, dukes, marquesses, and earls, barons, captains, borough masters, judges, and governors, officers of towns, burgesses, and villages, and unto all rulers of the commonalty, and generally to all the subjects of our empire, to whom these letters shall come, grace and all goodness.

"We charge and command you all, that you respect John Huss, who is departed out of Bohemia, to come to the general council, which shall be celebrated and held very shortly at the town of Constance. Which John Huss we have received under our protection and safeguard of the whole empire, desiring you that you will cheerfully receive him when he shall come towards you, and that you treat and handle him gently, shewing him favour and good will, and shew him pleasure in all things, as touching the forwardness, ease, and assurance of his journey, as well by land as by water.

"Moreover, we will, that he and all his company, with his carriage and necessaries, shall pass throughout all places, passages, ports, bridges, lands, governances, lordships, liberties, cities, towns, boroughs, castles, and villages, and all other your dominions, without paying of any manner of imposition or tribute, or any other manner of toll whatever. We will, also, that you suffer to pass, rest, tarry, and to sojourn at liberty, without doing unto him any manner of impeachment, or vexation, or trouble; and that if need shall so require, you do provide a faithful company to conduct him withal, for the honour and reverence which you owe unto our imperial majesty. Given at Spire the eighteenth of October, in the year of our Lord God, 1414."

By this it may appear, that this safe conduct was granted not in the time of the council by the bishop, but before the council by the emperor, who was, or ought to be the principal ordainer and director of the council under God. Now whether the bishops did well in breaking this promise of the emperor, I will defer to such time as may be more convenient to the full examination thereof.

John Huss seeing so many fair promises, and the assurance which the emperor had given, sent answer that he would come to the council. But before he departed out of the realm of Bohemia, and especially out of the town of Prague, he wrote certain letters, and caused them to be fastened upon the gates of the cathedral churches and parish churches, cloisters and abbeys: the copy whereof here follows:

"Master John Huss, bachelor of divinity, will appear before the most reverend father, the Lord Conrad, archbishop of Prague, and legate of the apostolic seat, in their next convocation of all their prelates and clergy of the kingdom of Bohemia, being ready always to satisfy all men which shall require him to give a reason of his faith and hope that he holds, and to hear and see all such as will lay to his charge, either any stubbornness of error or heresy, that they should write in their names there, as is required both by God's law and man's. And if so be that they could not lawfully prove any stubbornness of error or heresy against him, that then they should suffer the like punishment that he should have had, to whom all together he will answer at the next general council of Constance, before the archbishop and the prelates, and according to the decrees and canons of the holy father, shew forth his innocency in the name of Christ. Dated the Sunday next after the feast of St. Bartholomew."

After this, as all the barons of Bohemia were assembled in the abbey of St. James, about the affairs of the realm, the archbishop of Prague was also present. There John Huss presented petitions, by which he most humbly desired the barons that they would shew him that favour towards the archbishop, that if the archbishop suspected him of any error or heresy, he should declare it openly, and that he was ready to endure and suffer correction for the same at his hands. And if he had found or perceived no such thing in him, that he would then give him a testimonial thereof. The archbishop confessed openly, before all the assembly of barons, that he knew not that John Huss was culpable or faulty in any crime or offence.

About the ides of October, A.D. 1414, John Huss, being accompanied with two noble gentlemen, Wancelat of Duba, and John of Clum, departed from Prague, and took his journey towards Constance.

In all cities as he passed by, and principally when he was departed out of Bohemia, and entered into Germany, a great number of people did come unto him, and he was very gently received and entertained through all the towns of Germany, and especially by the citizens and burgesses, and oftentimes by the curates. And if it happened that there were any information before of his coming, the streets were always full of people desirous to see and gratify him; and especially at Nuremberg, where certain merchants certified the citizens of his coming. There were many curates who came to him, desiring that they might talk with him secretly: to whom he answered, That he loved much rather to pronounce and shew forth his mind and opinion openly before all men, for he would keep nothing hidden. So, after dinner, till it was night, he spake before the priests and senators, and other citizens, so that they all had him in great estimation and reverence.

The twentieth day after that he departed out of the town of Prague, which was the 3d day of November, he came unto Constance, and lodged at an honest matron's house, being a widow named Faith, in St. Galles Street.

The morrow after his arrival, Master John de Clum, and Master Henry Latzemboge, went to the pope, and certified him that John Huss was come, under the emperor's safe conduct; desiring also that he on his part would grant John Huss liberty to remain in Constance, without any trouble, vexation, or interruption. To whom the pope answered, That even if John Huss had killed his brother, yet he might go about, as much as in him lay, that no outrage or hurt should be done to him during his abode in the town of Constance.

The 26th day after the said Huss was come to Constance, during all which time he was occupied in reading, writing, and familiar talk with his friends; the cardinals sent two bishops; to wit, the bishops of Augusta, and of Trent, to the place where John Huss lodged, to report to him that they were sent by the pope and his cardinals, to advertise him that he should come to render some account of his doctrine before them, as he had oftentimes desired, and that they were ready to hear him.

John Huss answered, "I am not come for any such intent, as to defend my cause before the pope and his cardinals, protesting that I never desired any such thing, but I would willingly appear before the whole assembly of the council, and there answer for my defence openly, without any fear or doubt, unto all such things as shall be demanded or required of me. Notwithstanding," said he, "forasmuch as you require me so to do, I will not refuse to go with you before the cardinals. And if it happen that they evil entreat or handle me; yet nevertheless I trust in my Lord Jesus, that he will so comfort and strengthen me, that I shall desire much rather to die for his glory's sake, than to deny the verity and truth which I have learned by his holy scriptures." Wherefore, it came to pass, that the bishops being instant upon him, and not shewing any outward appearance that they bore any malice or hatred against him in their hearts, John Huss took his horse which he had at his lodging, and went to the court of the pope and the cardinals.

When he was come, and had saluted the cardinals, they began to speak to him in this sort: "We have heard many reports of you, which, if they be true, are in no case to be suffered: for men say, that you have taught great and manifest errors against the doctrine of the true church; and that you have sowed your errors abroad through all the realm of Bohemia for a long time; wherefore we have caused you to be called before us, that we might understand and know how the matter stands."

John Huss answered in few words, "Reverend fathers, you shall understand that I am thus minded, that I should rather choose to die, than I should be found culpable of one only error, much less of many and great errors. For this cause I am the more willingly come to the general council, to shew myself ready even with all my heart to receive correction, if any man can prove any errors in me." The cardinals answered him again, That his sayings pleased them very well, and upon that they went away, leaving John Huss, with Master John de Clum, under the guard and keeping of the armed men.

In the mean time, they suborned and furnished out a certain divine, a Franciscan friar, a subtle and crafty man, and a malicious hypocrite, to question John Huss, who was compassed round about with armed men. This man drawing near in his monkish gesture, said, "Reverend master, I a simple and ignorant man, am come to you to learn; for I have heard many strange and contrary things against the catholic faith ascribed to you. Wherefore I do desire you, even for the love which you bear to the truth, and to all good and godly men, that you would teach me, most simple and miserable man, some certainty and truth. And first, men say, that you hold opinion that after the consecration and pronunciation of the words in the sacrament of the altar, there remains only material bread." John Huss answered, "That it was falsely attributed and imputed unto him." Then said he, "I pray you, is not this your opinion?" "No verily," said John Huss, "I do not so think of it." When the monk asked this question the third time, Master John de Clum being moved somewhat with him, said, "Why art thou so importunate upon him? Verily, if any man had affirmed or denied any thing to me even once, I would have believed him. And thou, although he hath shewed thee his mind so often, yet ceasest not to trouble him." Then said the monk, "Gentle master, I pray you pardon me an ignorant and simple friar; surely I did it of a good mind and intent, being willing and desirous to learn." This friar put another question unto him, protesting his simplicity and ignorance, what manner of unity of the Godhead and manhood was in the person of Christ? When John Huss had heard this question, he turning himself to Master John de Clum, in the Bohemian language said, "Truly this friar is not simple as he pretends, for he hath propounded to me a very hard question." And afterward turning himself to the friar, he said to him, "Brother, you say that you are simple, but as I have heard you, I perceive very well that you are double and crafty, and not simple." "It is not so," said the friar. "Well," said John Huss, "I will cause you to understand that it is so. For as to the simplicity of a man, it is required in things that concern civility and manners that the spirit, the understanding, the heart, the words, and the mouth, should agree together: and I do not perceive that this is in you. There is in your mouth a certain semblance of simplicity, which would very well declare you to be an idiot and simple, but your deeds shew plainly and evidently a great subtlety and craft in you, with a great quickness and liveliness of wit, to propose to me so hard and difficult a question. Notwithstanding, I will not fear to shew you my mind in this question." And when he had made an end, the monk gave him great thanks for his gentleness, and so departed. After that, the pope's garrison which were about John Huss, told him, that this friar was called master Didace, who was esteemed and counted the greatest and most subtle divine in all Lombardy. "Oh," said John Huss, "if I had known that before, I would have handled him after another fashion; but I would to God they were all such, then through the help and aid of the holy scriptures I would fear none of them." In this manner Huss and master John de Clum, were left under the keeping of these men-at-arms, until four o'clock in the afternoon. After which time the cardinals assembled again in the pope's court, to devise and take counsel what they should do with John Huss.

A little before night, they sent the provost of the Roman court to master John de Clum, to shew him that he might return to his lodging; but as for John Huss, they had otherwise provided for him. When master John de Clum heard this news, he was wonderfully displeased, as through their crafts, subtleties, and glossing words, they had so drawn this good man into their snares, whereupon he went to the pope, declaring to him all that was done; most humbly beseeching him, that he would call to remembrance the promise which he had made unto him and master Henry Latzemboge, and that he would not so lightly falsify and break his faith and promise. The pope answered, that all these things were done without his consent or commandment, and said further to master Clum apart, "What reason is it that you should impute this deed unto me, seeing that you know well enough that I myself am in the hands of these cardinals and bishops?"

So the said master Clum returned very pensive and sorrowful; he complained very sore, both privately and openly, of the injury and outrage that the pope had done, but all profited nothing. After this, John Huss was led by the officers to the charter-house of the great church of Constance, where he was kept prisoner for the space of eight days; from thence he was carried to the Jacobines, hard by the river of the Rhine, and was shut up in the prison of the abbey.

After he had been inclosed there a certain time, he fell sore sick of an ague, by means of the stench of the place, and became so weak, that they despaired of his life. And for fear lest this good man should die in prison, as others are wont to do, the pope sent to him certain of his physicians to cure and help him. In the midst of his sickness, his accusers made importunate suit to the principals of the council, that John Huss might be condemned; and presented to the pope these articles here under-written:

Articles presented against John Huss.

"First, he errs about the sacrament of the church, and specially about the sacrament of the body of Christ, forsomuch as he hath openly preached, that it ought to be ministered openly unto the people under both kinds, that is to say, the body and blood. This article is evident, forsomuch as his disciples at this instant in Prague do minister the same in both kinds. Moreover it is affirmed by several, that he has taught both in the schools and in the church, or at the least that he holds this opinion, that after the words of consecration pronounced upon the altar, there remains still material bread in the sacrament. This article shall be known by his examination.

"Secondly, he errs as to the ministers of the church, forsomuch as he saith, that they cannot consecrate or minister the sacraments when they are in mortal sin. This article shall likewise be known by his examination. Notwithstanding, all that which is here contained may be gathered by his writings on the church, which if he deny, let there then be some divines and others appointed, to peruse and look over his writings. Moreover he saith, that other men beside priests may minister the sacrament. This article is evident, forsomuch as his disciples do the same at Prague, who of themselves do violently take the sacrament out of the treasury, and communicate among themselves, when the holy communion is denied unto them. By this and other things also it is sufficiently evident, that he has taught that every man, being without mortal sin, has the power of orders or priesthood, forsomuch as such only as have taken orders ought to minister the sacrament to themselves. And because he proceedeth from small matters unto great and weightier, it does consequently appear and follow, that those which be in the state of grace can bind and loose.

"Thirdly, he errs as to the church, and specially because he does not allow and admit that the church signifies the pope, cardinals, archbishops, and the clergy underneath them; but saith, that this signification was drawn out from the school-men, and is in no case to be held or allowed. This article is manifest by his treatise upon the church.

"Moreover, he errs concerning the church, in that he saith, that the church ought not to have any temporal possessions. And that the temporal lords may take them away from the church and the clergy without any offence. This error is evident, forsomuch as through his doctrine and enticements many churches in the kingdom of Bohemia, and in the city of Prague, are already spoiled and robbed of a great part of their temporalities and goods. He saith also that Constantine and other secular princes erred by enriching and endowing churches and monasteries. This article is manifest by that which goes next before.

"Fourthly, he errs as touching the church, in that he saith, that all priests are of like power, and therefore affirms, that the reservations of the pope's casualties, the ordering of bishops, and the consecration of the priests, were invented only for covetousness. This article somewhat appears by those foregoing, but by his examination shall be more evident.

"Fifthly, he errs concerning the church, in that he saith, that the church being in sin, has no power of the keys, when the pope, cardinals, and all other of the priests and clergy are in deadly sin; which he saith is possible enough. This also appears in his treatise upon the church in his first error as touching the ministers of the church.

"Sixthly, he errs touching the church, forasmuch as through contempt he does not fear excommunication. This notoriously appears by his own doings, that he contemned and despised the apostolic and ordinary censure, and in all the apostolic excommunications and injunctions he has borne himself upon the divine commandments, and in contempt of the keys, to the setting out of his hypocrisy, he has said mass all the way between this and the city of Prague, and thereby has profaned the process and authority of the church.

"Seventhly, he errs again as touching the church, because he keeps not the institutions and investitures thereof, but holds opinion that every man has authority to invest and appoint any man to the cure of souls. This is evident by his own doings, forsomuch as many in the kingdom of Bohemia, by their defenders and favourers, or rather by himself, were appointed and put into parish churches, which they have long ruled and kept, not being appointed by the apostolic see, neither yet by the ordinary of the city of Prague.

"Eighthly, he errs as touching the church, in that he holds opinion, that a man, being once ordained a priest or deacon, cannot be forbidden or kept back from the office of preaching. This is likewise manifest by his own doings, forasmuch as he himself could never be hindered from preaching, neither by the apostolic see, neither yet by the archbishop of Prague.

"And to the intent that John Huss, who is clothed in sheep's clothing, and inwardly a ravening wolf, may be the better known by his fruits, for the better information of you most reverend fathers: I say, that from the first time that he took in hand, or went about to sow such errors and heresies, which afterward he did indeed, he understanding and perceiving himself to be withstood and gainsayed by the Germans, who were in the university of Prague, forsomuch as he could conclude nothing, because they had three voices, and he on his part had but one only voice; he went about and brought to pass, and that by the secular power, that the Germans should have but one voice, and he and his parts three voices: which thing, when the Germans once perceived, rather than they would lose or forsake any part of their right which they had in voices, or be in danger in their persons, which would then have ensued upon it, to save themselves, they wholly with one consent agreed together to depart out of Prague; and by this means this solemn and famous university of Prague was made desolate, that had brought forth so many notable men in divers sciences. Behold this his first fruits which divided that so famous university, forsomuch as grapes are not gathered of thorns, neither figs of brambles.

"Moreover, when there were questions moved amongst the divines of the university of Prague upon the forty-five articles of John Wickliff, and that they had called a convocation, and all the divines of Bohemia, (for the Germans were already departed), they concluded that every one of those articles were either heretical, seditious, or erroneous. He alone held the contrary opinion, that none of those articles were either heretical, seditious, or erroneous, as afterward he did dispute, hold, and teach, in the common schools of Prague, whereby it is evidently enough foreseen, that he holds and affirms those articles of Wickliff, which are not only condemned in England, but also by the whole church, because they were first invented and set forth by the members of antichrist.

"Moreover, he being complained of to the archbishop of Prague, that he preached and set forth certain articles which were heretical, false, and seditious, he was forbidden by the said archbishop to preach any more, who proceeded against him, according to the canonical sanctions, the which process is confirmed by the apostolic see, and published as well in the court of Rome, as without; which John Huss and his adherents have divers and manifold ways violated and profaned. And whoever did speak against him, they were deprived of their benefices, and others placed in, who have ruled and do yet rule the said churches, and the flocks pertaining to the same, not having any cure or charge of the souls committed unto them, neither by the apostolic see, neither yet by the ordinary of the place.

"Also all those, as well priests as laymen, in the city of Prague and kingdom of Bohemia, who have spoken against the doctrine of Huss, and the profanation of the process aforesaid, or at the least not allowed the same, have suffered most mortal hatred and persecutions, and yet to this day do suffer. But at this present it is dissembled until the end of the process against John Huss. Wherefore if he be now let go again, without doubt they shall suffer great persecution both in body and goods, and throughout all the realm of Bohemia, house shall be against house, and this mischief will creep, yea suddenly spring up throughout all Germany, and innumerable souls shall be infected, so that there shall be such persecution of the clergy and faithful, as has not been since the time of the emperor Constantine to this present day; for he ceases not to move and stir up the laity against the clergy and faithful christians. And when any of the clergy would draw him away, or call him from his heresy, and for that cause forbid him to preach, that he does not teach any heresies: then says he that the clergy do that of envy and malice, because he rebukes their vices and faults; that is to say, their simony, and pride, and covetousness.

"Moreover, he stirs up the secular princes against the prelates of churches, monasteries, and universities, and generally against the whole clergy. Going about by this means, he preaches and teaches that prelates and other men of the church ought not to have any temporal goods or possessions, but only to live upon alms. And by this means he has done already very much hurt, and annoyed divers and many prelates, clerks, and churches in the kingdom of Bohemia, and city of Prague, forsomuch as thereby they are already spoiled and robbed of their possessions. Yea, he teaches also that it is lawful for the lay-people without sin to withhold and keep back the tithes and oblations, or to give the church goods to any other minister; all the secular princes are greatly inclined hereunto, but especially the laity, who follow every man his own will.

"He has generally with him all those heretics who do but very smally regard the ecclesiastical censures, and hate the authority of the Roman church, yea do utterly detest and abhor the same; which thing will more and more increase, except it be effectually and manfully withstood; and if he do by any means escape from the council, he and his favourers will say that his doctrine is just and true, and that it is allowed by the authority of the universal sacred council, and that all his adversaries are wicked and naughty men, so that he would do more mischief, than ever any heretic did since the time of Constantine the Great.

"Wherefore, most holy fathers, provide and take heed to yourselves, and to the whole flock amongst whom the Holy Ghost hath placed you, to rule the church of Christ, which he hath purchased with his own blood; and whilst the disease is new and fresh, help and remedy it, as well touching him who doth so infect and trouble the church of God, as also concerning the occasions, through the which he hath presumed, and might do the same, because the prelates do abuse the ecclesiastical censures, and they as well as those that are under them, do not keep and observe the order of the church which is appointed them by God, whereby it comes to pass, that whilst they themselves do walk the broken and unknown paths, their flock falls headlong into the ditch.

"Wherefore, let our sovereign lord the pope, and this most sacred council, ordain and depute commissioners, who may examine the said John Huss upon all before-written, and other things in the presence of them which know the matter. Let there be also certain doctors and masters appointed to read over and peruse his books which he hath written, whereof some are here present, that the church may be speedily purged and cleansed from these errors."

Upon this accusation, they ordained and appointed three commissioners or judges, that is to say, the patriarch of Constantinople, and the bishop of Castile, and the bishop of Lybuss,—which prelates being thus deputed, heard the accusation and the witness which was brought in by certain priests of Prague, confirmed by their oaths, and afterward recited the accusation to Huss in the prison, at such time as his ague was fervent and extreme upon him.

Upon this, John Huss required to have an advocate to answer for him; which was utterly denied him.

Thus John Huss remained in the prison of the convent of the Franciscans, until the Wednesday before Palm Sunday; and in the meantime to employ his time, he wrote certain books, concerning the ten commandments, of the love and knowledge of God, of matrimony, of penance, of the three enemies of mankind, of the prayer of our Lord, and of the supper of our Lord.

The same day Pope John XXIII. changed his apparel, and conveyed himself secretly out of Constance, fearing the judgment by which afterward he was deprived of his papal dignity, for the most execrable and abominable doings. This was the cause that John Huss was transported and carried unto another prison: for the pope's servants, who had the charge and keeping of John Huss, understanding that their master was fled and gone, delivered up the keys of the prison unto the Emperor Sigismund, and to the cardinals, and followed their master the pope. Then by the consent of the whole council, John Huss was put into the hands of the bishop of Constance, who sent him to a castle on the other side of the river of the Rhine, not very far from Constance, where he was shut up in a tower with fetters on his legs, that he could scarce walk in the day time, and at night he was fastened up to a rack against the wall hard by his bed.

In the meantime, certain noblemen and gentlemen of Poland and Bohemia did all their endeavour to procure his deliverance, having respect to the good renown of all the realm, which was wonderfully defamed and slandered by certain naughty persons. The matter was grown unto this point, that all they who were in the town of Constance, that seemed to bear any favour unto John Huss, were made as mocking stocks, and derided of all men, yea, even of the slaves and base people. Wherefore they took counsel and concluded together to present their request in writing to the whole council, or at the least to the four nations of Germany, Italy,

France, and England; this request was presented the 14th day of May, A. D. 1415: the tenour here ensues.

The first Schedule or Bill, which the Nobles of Bohemia delivered up to the Council for the deliverance of John Huss, the 14th day of May, A. D. 1415.

" Most reverend fathers and lords, the nobles and lords of Bohemia and Poland here present, by this their present writing do shew and declare unto your fatherly reverences, how that the most noble king and lord, the Lord Sigismund, king of the Romans, always Augustus, king of Hungary, Croatia, Dalmatia, &c. hearing of the great dissension that was in the kingdom of Bohemia, as heir, king, and lord successor, willing to foresee and provide for his own honour, sent these noblemen, Master Wenceslate de Duba, and John de Clum here present, that they would bring and assure Master John Huss under the king's name and safe conduct. So that he would come to the sacred general council of Constance, under the safe conduct of the said king, and the protection of the sacred empire, openly given and granted unto the said Master John Huss, that he might purge himself and the kingdom of Bohemia, from the slander that was raised upon them, and there to make an open declaration of his faith to every man that would lay any thing to his charge. The which the said nobles, with the forenamed Master John Huss, have performed and done, according to the king's commandment.

" When the said Master John Huss was freely of his own accord come unto Constance, under the said safe conduct, he was grievously imprisoned before he was heard, and at this present time is tormented both with fetters, and also with hunger and thirst. Although that in times past at the council holden at Pisa in the year of our Lord 1410, the heretics who were condemned, were suffered to remain there at liberty, and to depart home freely; notwithstanding this, Master John Huss, neither being convicted nor condemned, no not so much as once heard, is taken and imprisoned, when as neither king nor any prince elector, neither any ambassador of any university was yet come or present. And albeit the lord the king, together with the nobles and lords here present, most instantly required and desired, that as touching his safe conduct they would foresee and have respect to his honour, and that the said Master John Huss might be openly heard, forsomuch as he would render and shew a reason of his faith; and if he were found and convicted obstinately to affirm or maintain any thing against the truth of holy scripture, that then he ought to correct and amend the same, according to the instruction and determination of the council; yet could he never obtain this. But the said Master John Huss, notwithstanding all this, is most grievously oppressed with fetters and irons, and so weakened with thin and slender diet, that it is to be feared, lest that his power and strength being hereby consumed and wasted, he should be put in danger of his wit or reason.

" And although the lords of Bohemia here present are greatly slandered, because they, seeing the said Master John Huss so to be tormented and troubled, contrary to the king's safe conduct, have not by their letters put the king in mind of his safe conduct, that the said lord and king should not any more suffer any such matters, forsomuch as they tend to the contempt and disregard of the kingdom of Bohemia, which, from the first original and beginning, since it received the catholic faith, never departed or went away from the obedience of the holy church of Rome; yet, notwithstanding, they have suffered and borne all these things patiently hitherto, lest by any means occasion of trouble or vexation of this sacred council might arise or spring thereof.

" Wherefore, most reverend fathers and lords, the nobles and lords before named, do wholly and most earnestly desire and require your reverences here present, that both for the honour of the safe conduct of our said lord the king, and also for the preservation and increase of the worthy fame and renown, both of the kingdom of Bohemia, and your own also, you will make

a short end about the affairs of Master John Huss; forsomuch as by the means of his straight handling he is in great danger by any longer delay; even as they do most specially trust upon the most upright consciences and judgments of your fatherly reverences. But forasmuch as, most reverend fathers and lords, it is now come to the knowledge and understanding of the nobles and lords of Bohemia here present, how that certain backbiters and slanderers of the most famous kingdom of Bohemia aforesaid, have declared and told unto your reverences, how that the sacrament of the most precious blood of our Lord is carried up and down through Bohemia in vessels not consecrate or hallowed, and that coblers do now hear confessions, and minister the most blessed body of our Lord unto others. The nobles therefore of Bohemia here present, require and desire you, that you will give no credit unto false promoters and tale tellers, for that, as most wicked and naughty slanderers and backbiters of that kingdom aforesaid, they do report and tell untruths; requiring also your reverences, that such slanderous persons of the kingdom aforesaid may be named and known. And the lord the king, together with your reverences, shall well perceive and see that the lords of Bohemia will go about in such a manner to repel and put away the false and frivolous slanders of these naughty persons, that they shall be ashamed to appear hereafter before the lord the king and your reverences."

When the noblemen of Bohemia for a long time could obtain no answer to this, and a second supplication which they had already put up, they determined the last day of May, by another supplication to the principals of the council, to intreat that John Huss might be delivered out of prison, and defend his own cause openly, in which among other things they pray—

" Wherefore, most reverend fathers, his enemies, through the extreme hatred which they bear to him, have picked and taken out by piecemeal, certain articles out of the books of Master John Huss, rejecting and not looking upon the allegations and reasons, have compounded and made thereof certain false and feigned articles against him to this end, that all charity and love being set apart, they might the better overthrow him, and bring him unto death, *contrary to the safe conduct*, upon good and just occasion openly assigned, and given to the said Master John Huss, by the most noble prince the Lord Sigismund, king of the Romans, and of Hungary, for his just defence against all the frivolous accusations and assaults of the enemies, not only of the said Master John Huss, but also of the famous kingdom of Bohemia, and for the quiet appeasing of all such tumults and rumours rising and springing in the said kingdom of Bohemia, or elsewhere; the avoiding of which most perilous uproars, the said king of the Romans, doth greatly desire and wish, as the right heir and successor of the said kingdom.

" Wherefore it may please your fatherly reverences to command the said Master John Huss, neither convicted nor condemned, to be taken and brought out of his bonds and chains, in the which he is now most grievously detained and kept, and to put him into the hands of some reverend lord bishops, or commissioners, appointed, or to be appointed by this present council; that the said Master John Huss may somewhat be relieved, and recover again his health, and be the more diligently and commodiously examined by the commissioners. And for the more assurance, the barons and nobles aforesaid of the kingdom of Bohemia, will provide most sure and good sureties, the which will not break their fidelity and faith for any thing in the world. Which also shall promise in this behalf, that he shall not flee or depart out of their hands, until such time as the matter be fully determined by the said commissioners. In the execution of the which premises, we have determined to provide and foresee unto the fame and honour of the said kingdom of Bohemia, and also to the safe conduct of the most worthy prince, the king of the Romans, lest that the enemies and detractors of the honour and fame of the kingdom aforesaid, might not a little slander and reprove the said lords, pretending and shewing forth hereafter, that they had made unreasonable or unlawful requests; for the withstanding of which mischief we require your fatherly reverences, that you will decree, and most graciously consent, that this our petition and supplication may be drawn out again by your notary, and reduced into a public form and order."

The same day the said barons and lords presented a supplication to the emperor, embodying the foregoing supplication, and concluding thus:

"Wherefore we most humbly require and desire your princely majesty, that both for the love of justice, and also of the fame and renown of that most famous kingdom of Bohemia, whereof we acknowledge you undoubtedly the true lord, heir, and successor; and also foreseeing unto *the liberty of your safe conduct*, that you will with your favourable countenance, beholding these most reasonable and just supplications which we have put up to the lords aforesaid, put to your helping hand toward the said most reverend fathers and lords, that they will effectually hear us, in this our most just petition, which we have offered up to them, as is aforesaid, lest that the enemies of the renown and honour of the famous kingdom of Bohemia, and such be our slanderers also, hereafter may detract and slander us, that we should make unreasonable and unlawful requests unto the said reverend fathers and lords; and therefore we required and desired of them, that it would please them to decree by setting to their public hand and seal, to authorise our said publication. Likewise, we do most heartily require your highness, that you would vouchsafe in like manner, to give us your testimony of the premises."

But what answer the emperor made hereto, we could never understand or know, but by the process of the matter a man may easily judge, that this good emperor was brought, through the obstinate mischief of the cardinals and bishops, to break and falsify his promise and faith which he had made and promised; and this was their reason, that no defence could or might be given either by safe conduct, or by any other means to him, who was suspected or judged to be an heretic. But by the epistles and letters of John Huss, a man may easily judge what the king's mind was. Now we will proceed to the history.

The fifth day of June, the cardinals, bishops, and the rest of the priests, all that were in Constance, assembled to a great number, at the convent of the Franciscans in Constance, and there it was commanded, that before John Huss should be brought forth, in his absence they should rehearse the witnesses and articles which they had slanderously gathered out of his books. By chance there was then present a certain notary, named Mladoniewitz, who bare great love and amity to Huss, who, as soon as he perceived that the bishops and cardinals were already determined and appointed to condemn the said articles in the absence of John Huss, went with all speed to Master Wencelate de Duba, and John de Clum, and told them all the matter, who immediately made report of it to the emperor, who, understanding their object, sent to signify to them that nothing should be resolved or done in the case of John Huss, before they should send him all such articles as were laid against the said John Huss, which were either false or heretical, and he would do so much, that the said articles should be examined by good and learned men. Then according to the emperor's will, the judgment of the principals of the council was suspended, until such time as John Huss were present.

In the meantime, these gentlemen, master of Duba and of Clum, gave to the two princes, whom the emperor had sent, certain small treatises which John Huss had made, out of which they had drawn certain articles to present to them who rule the council, under this condition, that they would render them again, when they should demand them. The intent and meaning of these barons was, that by this means the adversaries of John Huss might the more easily be reproved, who, of a

naughty and corrupt conscience, had picked out corrupt sentences out of the books of John Huss. The books were delivered to the cardinals and bishops; and then John Huss was brought forth, and the princes who were sent by the emperor, departed. After they shewed the books to John Huss, and he confessed openly before the whole assembly that he had wrote them, and that he was ready, if there were any fault in them, to amend the same.

Now hearken a little to the holy proceedings of these reverend fathers, for here happened a strange and shameful matter. With much ado they had scarcely read one article, and brought forth a few witnesses upon the same against him, but as he was about to open his mouth to answer, all this mad herd or flock began so to cry out upon him, that he was not able to speak one word. The noise and trouble was so great and so vehement, that a man might well have called it an uproar or noise of wild beasts, and not of men; much less was it to be judged a congregation of men gathered together to judge and determine so grave and weighty matters. And if it happened that the noise and cry did ever so little cease, that he might answer any thing at all, out of the holy scriptures or ecclesiastical doctors, by and by he would hear such replies as were nothing to the purpose.

Besides all this, some did outrage in words against him, and others spitefully mocked him, so that seeing himself overwhelmed with these rude and barbarous noises and cries, and that it profited nothing to speak, he determined finally with himself to hold his peace and keep silence. From that time forward, all the whole rout of his adversaries thought that they had won the battle of him, and cried out all together "Now he is dumb, now he is dumb; this is a certain sign and token, that he doth consent and agree unto these his errors." Finally, the matter came to this point, that certain of the most moderate and honest among them, seeing this disorder, determined to proceed no further, but that all should be deferred and put off until another time. Through their advice, the prelates and others departed from the council for the present, and appointed to meet there again on the morrow to proceed in judgment.

The next day, which was the seventh of June, on which day the sun was almost wholly eclipsed, somewhat after, about seven of the clock, this same flock assembled again in the cloister of the friars minors, and by their appointment John Huss was brought before them, accompanied with a great number of armed men. Thither went also the emperor, whom the gentlemen, master of Duba and Clum, and the notary named Peter, which were great friends of the said Huss, did follow to see what the end would be. When they were come thither, they heard that in the accusation of Michael de Causis, they read these words following: as John Huss hath taught the people divers and many errors both in the chapel of Bethlehem, and also in many other places of the city of Prague, of the which errors some of them he hath drawn out of Wickliff's books, and the rest he has forged and invented of his own head, and maintains the same very obstinately.

First, that after the consecration and pronunciation of the words in the supper of the Lord, there remains material bread. To this John Huss, taking a solemn oath, answered that he never spake any such word; but thus much he did grant, that at what time the archbishop of Prague forbade him to use any more that term or word bread, he could not allow the bishop's command, as Christ, in the sixth chapter of John, oftentimes names himself the bread of life, which came down from heaven, to give life unto the whole world. But as touching material bread, he never spake any thing at all.

Then they returned again unto the witnesses, who every man for himself affirmed with an oath that which he had said. Amongst whom John Protyway, when he should confirm his testimony, added that John Huss said that St. Gregory was but a rhymer, when he alleged his authority against him. To whom John Huss answered, that in this point they did him great injury, as he always esteemed and reputed St. Gregory for a most holy doctor of the church.

Then was there read a certain article of accusation, in which it was alleged, that John Huss had taught, and obstinately defended certain erroneous articles of Wickliff's in Bohemia. Whereunto Huss answered, that he never taught any errors of John Wickliff's, or of any other man's. But to confirm their article, there was alleged, that John Huss did withstand the condemnation of Wickliff's articles. He answered that he durst not agree thereto, for offending his conscience, and especially for these articles, that Silvester the pope and Constantine did err in bestowing those great gifts and rewards upon the church. Also, that the pope or priest, being in mortal sin, cannot consecrate nor baptize. "This article," said he, "I have thus determined, as if I should say, that he unworthily consecrates or baptizes, when he is in deadly sin, and that he is an unworthy minister of the sacraments of God." Here his accusers, with their witnesses, were earnest and instant that the article of Wickliff was written in the very same words of the treatise of John Huss. "Verily," said John Huss; "I fear not to submit myself, even under the danger of death, if you shall not find it so as I have said." When the book was brought forth, they found it written as John Huss had said.

Then was there rehearsed another article of his accusation in this manner:—That John Huss to confirm the heresy which he had taught the common and simple people out of Wickliff's books, said openly these words, that at what time a great number of monks and friars, and other learned men were gathered together in England, in a certain church, to dispute against John Wickliff, and could by no means vanquish him, suddenly the church door was broken open with lightning, so that with much ado Wickliff's enemies hardly escaped without hurt. He added, moreover, that he wished his soul to be in the same place where John Wickliff's soul was. Whereunto John Huss answered, "That a dozen years before that any books of divinity of John Wickliff's were in Bohemia, he saw certain works of philosophy of his, which, he said, did marvellously delight and please him. And when he understood the good and godly life of Wickliff, he spake these words, I trust, said he, that Wickliff is saved; and although I doubt whether he be damned or no, yet with a good hope I wish that my soul were in the same place where John Wickliff's is." Then again did all the company jest and laugh at him.

It is also in his accusation, that John Huss did counsel the people, according to the example of Moses, to resist with the sword against all such as did gainsay his doctrine. And the next day after he had preached the same, there were found openly in divers places certain intimations, that every man, being armed with his sword about him, should stoutly proceed, and that brother should not spare brother, neither one neighbour another. John Huss answered, that "All these things were falsely laid unto his charge by his adversaries; for he at all times when he preached, did diligently admonish and warn the people, that they should all arm themselves to defend the truth of the gospel, according to the saying of the apostle, 'with the helmet and sword of salvation;' and that he never spake of any material sword, but of that which is the word of God. And as touching intimations, or Moses' sword, he never had anything to do withal."

When all the articles were in this way gone through, John Huss was committed to the custody of the bishop of Reggeo, under whom Jerome of Prague was also prisoner. But before he was led away, the cardinal of Cambray calling him back again in the presence of the emperor, said, "John Huss, I have heard you say, that if you had not been willing of your own mind to come to Constance, neither the emperor himself, neither the king of Bohemia, could have compelled you to do it." John Huss answered, "Under your license, most reverend father, I never used any such kind of talk or words. But this I did say, that there was in Bohemia a great number of gentlemen and noblemen, who did

favour and love me, who also might easily have kept me in some sure and secret place, that I should not have been constrained to come into this town of Constance, neither at the will of the emperor, neither of the king of Bohemia." With that the cardinal of Cambray, even for very anger, began to change his colour, and despitefully said, "Do you not see the unshamefacedness of the man here?" And as they were murmuring, and whispering on all parts, the Lord John de Clum, ratifying and confirming that which John Huss had spoken, said, "That John Huss had spoken very well; for on my part," said he, "who, in comparison of a great many others, am but of small force in the realm of Bohemia, yet if I would have taken it in hand, I could have defended him easily by the space of one year, even against all the force and power of both these great and mighty kings. How much better might they have done it who are of more force or puissance than I am, and have stronger castles and places than I have?" After that the Lord de Clum had spoken, the cardinal of Cambray said, "Let us leave this talk. And I tell you, John Huss, and counsel you, that you submit yourself to the sentence and mind of the council, as you did promise in the prison; and if you will do so, it shall be greatly both for your profit and honour."

And the emperor himself began to tell him the same tale, saying, "Although there be some who say, that the fifteenth day after you were committed to prison, you obtained of us our letters of safe conduct, notwithstanding I can well prove by the witness of many princes and noblemen, that the safe conduct was obtained and gotten of us by my Lords de Duba and de Clum, before you were departed out of Prague, under whose guard we have sent for you, to the end that none should do you any outrage or hurt, but that you should have full liberty to speak freely before all the council, and to answer as touching your faith and doctrine; and as you see, my lords the cardinals and bishops have so dealt with you, that we do very well perceive their good-will towards you, for the which we have great cause to thank them. And forasmuch, as divers have told us, that WE MAY NOT, OR OUGHT NOT, OF RIGHT TO DEFEND ANY MAN WHO IS AN HERETIC, OR SUSPECT OF HERESY; therefore now we give you even the same counsel which the cardinal of Cambray hath given you already, that you be not obstinate to maintain any opinion, but that you do submit yourself under such obedience as you owe unto the authority of the holy council, in all things that shall be laid against you, and confirmed by credible witnesses, which thing, if you do according to our counsel, we will give order that for the love of us, of our brother, and the whole realm of Bohemia, the council shall suffer you to depart in peace, with an easy and tolerable penance and satisfaction, which if you refuse to do, the presidents of the council shall have sufficient authority to proceed against you. And for our part be ye well assured, that we will sooner prepare and make the fire with our own hands, to burn you withal, than we will endure or suffer any longer that you shall maintain or use this stiffness of opinions, which you have hitherto maintained and used. Wherefore our advice and counsel is, that you submit yourself wholly unto the judgment of the council." John Huss answered, "O most noble emperor, I render unto your highness most immortal thanks for your letters of safe conduct." Upon this Lord John de Clum did break him of his purpose, and admonished him that he did not excuse himself of the blame of obstinacy.

Then said John Huss, "O most gentle Lord, I do take God to my witness, that I was never minded obstinately to maintain any opinion, and that for this same intent and purpose I came hither of mine own good will, that if any man could lay before me any better or more holy doctrine than mine, that then I would change mine opinion without any further doubt." After he had spoken and said these things, he was sent away with the serjeants.

The morrow after, which was the eighth day of June, the very same company which was assembled the day before, assembled now again at the convent of the Franciscars; and in this assembly were also John Huss' friends, Lord de Duba, Lord de Clum, and Peter the notary. Thither was John Huss also brought, and in his presence there were read about thirty-nine articles, which they said, were drawn out of his books. Huss acknowledged all those that were faithfully and truly collected and gathered, to be his, of which sort there were but very few; the residue were counterfeited and forged by his adversaries, for they could find no such thing in the books, out of the which they said they had drawn and gathered them.

These were the same articles in a manner which were shewed before in the prison to John Huss, and are rehearsed here in another order: although there were some more articles added to them, and others corrected and enlarged, mention is made in them of his appeal, which is as follows:—

The Appeal of John Huss from the Pope to Christ.

"Forasmuch as the most mighty Lord, one in essence, three in person, is both the chief and first, and also the last, and utmost refuge of all those who are oppressed, and that he is the God who defendeth verity and truth throughout all generations, doing justice to such as be wronged, being ready and at hand to all those which call upon him in verity and truth, unbinding those that are bound, and fulfilling the desires of all those who honour and fear him; defending and keeping all those that love him, and utterly destroying and bringing to ruin the stiff-necked and impenitent sinner, and that the Lord Jesus Christ very God and man, being in great anguish, compassed in with the priests, scribes, and pharisees, wicked judges and witnesses, willing by the most bitter and ignominious death to redeem the children of God, chosen before the foundation of the world, from everlasting damnation; hath left behind him this godly example for a memory unto them who should come after him, to the intent they should commit all their causes into the hands of God, who can do all things, and knoweth and seeth all things, saying in this manner: O Lord, behold my affliction, for my enemy hath prepared himself against me, and thou art my protector and defender. O Lord, thou hast given me understanding, and I have acknowledged thee, thou hast opened unto me all their enterprises; and for my own part, I have been as a meek lamb which is led unto sacrifice, and have not resisted against them. They have wrought their enterprises upon me, saying, Let us put wood in his bread, and let us banish him out of the land of the living, that his name be no more spoken of, nor had in memory. But thou, O Lord of Hosts, who judgest justly, and seest the devices and imaginations of their hearts, hasten thee to take vengeance upon them, for I have manifested my cause unto thee, forsomuch as the number of those which trouble me is great, and have counselled together, saying, the Lord hath forsaken him, pursue him and catch him. O Lord my God, behold their doings, for thou art my patience; deliver me from mine enemies, for thou art my God; do not separate thyself far from me, for tribulation is at hand, and there is no man which will succour. My God, my God, look down upon me, wherefore hast thou forsaken me? So many dogs have compassed me in, and the company of the wicked have besieged me round about, for they have spoken against me with deceitful tongues, and have compassed me in with words full of despite, and have enforced me without cause. Instead of love towards me they have slandered me, and have recompensed me with evil for good, and in place of charity they have conceived hatred against me.

"Wherefore, behold, I staying myself upon this most holy and fruitful example of my Saviour and Redeemer, do appeal before God for this my grief and hard oppression, from this most wicked sentence and judgment, and the excommunication determined by the bishops, scribes, pharisees, and judges, who sit in Moses's seat, and resign my cause wholly unto him; even as the holy patriarch of Constantinople, John Chrysostom, appealed twice from the council of the bishops and clergy; and Andrew, bishop of Prague, and Robert, bishop of Lin-

coln, appealed to the sovereign and most just Judge, who is not defiled with cruelty, neither can he be corrupted with gifts and rewards, neither yet be deceived by false witness. Also I desire greatly that all the faithful servants of Jesus Christ, and especially the princes, barons, knights, esquires, and all other who inhabit our country of Bohemia, should understand and know these things, and have compassion upon me, who am so grievously oppressed by the excommunication which is out against me, and which was obtained and gotten by the instigation and procurement of Michael de Causis my great enemy, and by the consent and furtherance of the canons of the cathedral church of Prague, and given and granted out by Peter of St. Angelo, dean of the church of Rome, and cardinal, and also ordained judge by Pope John XXIII., who hath continued almost these two years, and would give no audience unto my advocates and procurators, which they ought not to deny, (no not to a Jew or Pagan, or to any heretic whatsoever he were) neither yet would he receive any reasonable excuse, for that I did not appear personally, neither would he accept the testimonials of the whole university of Prague with the seal hanging at it, or the witness of the sworn notaries, and such as were called unto witness. By this all men may evidently perceive that I have not incurred any fault or crime of contumacy or disobedience, forsomuch as that I did not appear in the court of Rome, was not for any contempt, but for reasonable causes.

"And moreover, forsomuch as they had laid ambushments for me on every side by ways where I should pass, and also because the perils and dangers of others have made me the more circumspect and advised; and forsomuch as my proctors were willing and contented to bind themselves even to abide the punishment of the fire to answer to all such as would oppose or lay any thing against me in the court of Rome; as also because they did imprison my lawful procurator in the said court, without any cause, demerit, or fault, as I suppose. Forsomuch then as the order and disposition of all ancient laws as well divine of the old and new testament, as also of the canon laws, is this, that the judges should resort unto the place where the crime or fault is committed or done, and there to inquire of all such crimes as shall be objected and laid against him which is accused or slandered, and that of such men as by conversation have some knowledge or understanding of the party so accused (who may not be the evil willers or enemies of him which is so accused or slandered; but must be men of an honest conversation, no common quarrel pickers or accusers, but fervent lovers of the law of God;) and finally, that there should be a fit and meet place appointed, whither as the accused party might without danger or peril, resort or come, and that the judge and witnesses should not be enemies unto him that is accused. And also forsomuch as it is manifest, that all these conditions were wanting and lacking, as touching my appearance for the safeguard of my life, I am excused before God from the frivolous pretended obstinacy and excommunication. Whereupon I, John Huss, do present and offer this my appeal unto my Lord Jesus Christ, my just Judge, who knoweth and defendeth, and justly judgeth every man's just and true cause."

Articles formerly contained or picked out of the Treatise of John Huss of Prague, which he entitled " Of the Church," following in this part or behalf the errors, as they term them, of John Wickliff, with the judgment against them.

The first article. "No reprobate is true pope, lord, or prelate." The error is in the faith, and behaviour, and manners, being many times before condemned, as well against the poor men of Lyons, as also against the Waldenses and Pikards. The affirmation of which errors is temerarious, seditious, offensive and pernicious, and tending to the subversion of all human policy and government, forasmuch as no man knows whether he be worthy of love or hatred, for all men offend in many points, and thereby should all rule and dominion be made uncertain and unstable, if it should be founded upon predestination and charity; neither should the commandment of Peter have been good, who desires all servants to be obedient unto their masters and lords, although they be wicked.

The second article. "That no man who is in deadly sin, whereby he is no member of Christ, but of the devil, is true pope, prelate, or lord." The error of this is like to the first.

The third article. "No reprobate or person in deadly sin, sits in the apostolic seat of Peter, neither has any apostolical power over the christian people." This error is also like to the first.

The fourth article. "No reprobates are of the church, nor any who do not follow the life of Christ." This error is against the common opinion of the doctors, concerning the church.

The fifth article. "They only are of the church, and sit in Peter's seat, and have apostolic power who follow Christ and his apostles in their life and living." The error hereof is in faith and manners, as in the first article, but containing more arrogancy and rashness.

The sixth article. "That every man who lives uprightly, according to the rule of Christ, may and ought openly to preach and teach, although he be not sent, yea, although he be forbidden or excommunicated by any prelate or bishop, even as he might or ought to give alms; for his good life in living together with his learning, sufficiently sends him." This is a rash and temerarious error, offensive, and tending to the confusion of the whole ecclesiastical hierarchy.

The seventh article. "That the pope of Rome being contrary to Christ, is not the universal bishop, neither has the church of Rome any supremacy over other churches, except peradventure it be given to him of Cæsar, and not of Christ." An error lately and plainly reproved.

The eighth article. "That the pope ought not to be called most holy, neither that his feet are holy and blessed, or that they ought to be kissed." This error is temerarious, irreverently, and offensively published.

The ninth article. "That according unto the doctrine of Christ, heretics, be they never so obstinate or stubborn, ought not to be put to death, neither to be accursed or excommunicated." This is the error of the Donatists, temerariously, and not without great offence affirmed against the laws of the ecclesiastical discipline, as St. Augustine proves.

The tenth article. "That subjects and the common people, may and ought publicly and openly to detect and reprove the vices of their superiors and rulers, as having power given them of Christ, and example of St. Paul so to do." This error is pernicious, full of offence, inducing all rebellion, disobedience and sedition.

The eleventh article. "That Christ only is head of the church, and not the pope." It is an error according to the common interpretation of the doctors, if all the reason of the supremacy, and of being head, be secluded and taken away from the pope.

The twelfth article. "That the only church, which comprehends the predestinate and good livers, is the universal church, whereto subjects owe obedience. And this is consequent to the former article." The error is contained as in the former articles.

The thirteenth article. "That tithes and oblations given to the church, are public and common alms." This error is offensive, and contrary to the determination of the apostle, 1 Cor. ix.

The fourteenth article. "That the clergy living wickedly, ought to be reproved and corrected by the lay-people, by the taking away of their tithes and other temporal profits." A most pernicious error and offensive, inducing the secular people to perpetrate sacrilege, subverting the ecclesiastical liberty.

The fifteenth article. "That the blessings of such as are reprobate or evil livers of the clergy, are maledictions and cursings before God, according to the saying, I will curse your blessings." This error was reproved by St. Augustine, against St. Cyprian and his followers,

neither is the master of the sentences allowed of the masters in that point when he seems to favour this article.

The sixteenth article. "That in these days, and in long time before, there has been no true pope, no true church or faith, which is called the Romish church, whereunto a man ought to obey, but that it both was, and is the synagogue of antichrist and Satan." The error in this article is in this point, that it is derived, and takes its foundation upon the former articles.

The seventeenth article. "That all gift of money given to the ministers of the church, for the ministration of any spiritual matter, makes such ministers in that case users of simony." This error is seditious and temerarious, forasmuch as something may be given to the clergy, under the title of sustentation or maintaining the minister, without the selling or buying of any spiritual thing.

The eighteenth article. "That whoever is excommunicate of the pope, if he appeal to Christ, he is preserved that he need not fear the excommunication, but may utterly contemn and despise the same." This error is temerarious and full of arrogancy.

The nineteenth article. "That every deed done without charity, is sin." This error was reproved and revoked before this time at Paris, specially if it be understood of deadly sin; for it is not necessary that he who lacketh grace, should continually sin and offend anew, although he be continually in sin.

This following, the masters of Paris, by their whole voice and consent, did add and join to these nineteen articles, as their reason and determination.

"We affirm, that these articles aforesaid are notoriously heretical, and that they are judicially condemned for such, and diligently to be rooted out with their most seditious doctrines, lest they do infect others. For although they seem to have a zeal against the vices of the prelates and the clergy, which (the more is the pity and grief) do but too much abound, yet it is not according to learning; for a sober and discreet zeal suffers and laments those sins and offences, which one sees in the house of God, that he cannot amend or take away; for vices cannot be rooted out and taken away by other vices and errors, forasmuch as devils are not cast out through Beelzebub, but by the power of God, which is the Holy Ghost, who wills, that in correction the measure and mean of prudence be always kept, according to the saying, Mark who, what, where and why, by what means and when, prelates and bishops are bound, under grievous and express penalties of the law, diligently and vigilantly to bear themselves against the foresaid errors, and such other like, and the maintainers of them; for let it be always understood and noted, that the error which is not resisted is allowed, neither is there any doubt of privy affinity or society of him, who is slow to withstand a manifest mischief.

"These things are intermeddled by the way under correction, as by way of doctrine.

(Signed) "JOHN GERSON,
"Chancellor of Paris, unworthily."

These things thus declared, a man may easily understand, that John Huss was not accused for holding any opinion contrary to the articles of our faith, but because he did stoutly preach and teach against the kingdom of antichrist for the glory of Christ, and the restoring of the church.

Now to return unto the history: when the articles, which I have before rehearsed, were all read over, the cardinal of Cambray, calling to John Huss, said, "Thou hast heard what grievous and horrible crimes are laid against thee, and what number of them they are; and now it is thy part to devise with thyself what thou wilt do. Two ways are proposed and set before thee by the council, of which one thou must of necessity enter into.

"First, that thou do humbly and meekly submit thyself unto the judgment and sentence of the council, that whatever shall be there determined, by their common voice and judgment, thou wilt patiently bear and suffer. Which thing if thou wilt do, we of our part, both for the honour of the most gentle emperor here present, and also for the honour of his brother the king of Bohemia, and for thy own safeguard and preservation, will treat and handle thee with as great humanity, love and gentleness, as we may. But if as yet thou art determined to defend any of those articles which we have propounded to thee, and dost desire or require to be further heard thereupon, we will not deny thee power and license thereto ; but this thou shalt well understand, that there are such men, so clear in understanding and knowledge, and having so firm and strong reasons and arguments against thy articles, that I fear it will be to thy great hurt, detriment and peril, if thou shouldst any longer will or desire to defend the same. This I do speak and say to thee, to counsel and admonish thee, and not as a judge."

Many others of the cardinals, every man for himself, did exhort and persuade John Huss in the same way ; to whom, with a lowly countenance he answered, "Most reverend fathers, I have often said, that I came hither of mine own free will, not to defend any thing, but if in any thing I should seem to have conceived a perverse or evil opinion, that I would meekly and patiently be content to be reformed and taught. Whereupon I desire that I may have yet further liberty to declare my mind. Whereof, except I shall allege most firm and strong reasons, I will willingly submit myself."

Then said the cardinal of Cambray, " Forasmuch then as thou dost submit thyself to the information and grace of this council, this is decreed by all almost three-score doctors.

" First of all, thou shalt humbly and meekly confess thyself to have erred in these articles which are alleged and brought against thee.

" Moreover, thou shalt promise by an oath, that from henceforth thou shalt not teach, hold or maintain any of these articles. And last of all, that thou shalt openly recant all these articles."

Upon which sentence, when many others had spoken their minds, at length John Huss said, " I once again do say, that I am ready to submit myself to the information of the council ; but this I most humbly require and desire you all, even for his sake, who is the God of us all, that I be not compelled or forced to do the thing which my conscience rejects or strives against, or which I cannot do without danger of eternal damnation, that is, that I should make revocation by oath to all the articles which are alleged against me. For I remember, that I have read in the book of universalities, that to abjure, is to renounce an error which a man has before held. And forsomuch as many of these articles are said to be mine, which were never in my mind or thought to hold or teach, how should I then renounce them by an oath ? But as touching those articles which are mine indeed, if there be any man who can teach me contrariwise to them, I will willingly perform that which you desire."

Then said the emperor, " Why mayest not thou without danger also renounce all those articles which thou sayest are falsely alleged against thee by the witnesses ? For I verily would nothing at all doubt to abjure all errors, neither does it follow that therefore by and by I have professed any error." To whom John Huss answered : "Most noble emperor, this word, to abjure, signifies much more than your majesty here gives it." Then said the cardinal of Florence, " John Huss, you shall have a form of abjuration, which shall be gentle, and tolerable enough, written and delivered to you, and then you will easily and soon determine with yourself, whether you will do it or no." Then the emperor, repeating again the words of the cardinal of Cambray, said, " Thou hast heard that there are two ways laid before thee : first that thou shouldst openly renounce those thy errors, which are now condemned, and subscribe unto the judgment of the council, whereby thou shouldst try and find their grace and favour. But if thou proceed to defend thy opinions, the council shall have sufficient power,

whereby according to their laws and ordinances, they may decree and determine upon thee." To whom John Huss answered, " I refuse nothing, most noble emperor, whatsoever the council shall decree or determine upon me. Only this one thing I except, that I do not offend God or my conscience, or say that I have professed those errors which was never in my mind or thought to profess. But I desire you all, if it may be possible, that you will grant me further liberty to declare my mind and opinion, that I may answer as much as shall suffice, as touching those things which are objected against me, and specially concerning ecclesiastical offices, and the state of the ministry."

Here a certain very old bishop of Pole put in his verdict. He said, " The laws are evident as touching heretics, with what punishment they ought to be punished." But John Huss constantly answered as before, insomuch that they said he was obstinate and stubborn. Then a certain well fed priest, and gaily apparelled, cried out unto the presidents of the council, saying, " He ought by no means to be admitted to recantation, for he hath written unto his friends. that although he do swear with his tongue, yet he will keep his mind unsworn without oath ; wherefore he is not to be trusted." Unto this slander John Huss answered, as is said in the last article, affirming that he was not guilty of any error.

In the meantime there was exhibited to the council a certain article, wherein John Huss was accused, that he had slanderously interpreted a certain sentence of the pope's ; which he denied that he did, saying, that he never saw it but in prison, when the article was shewn him by the commissioners.

Then was there another article read, in the which was contained, that three men were beheaded at Prague, because that through Wickliff's doctrine and teaching they were contumelious and slanderous against the pope's letters : and that they were by the same Huss, with the whole pomp of the scholars, and with a public convocation or congregation, carried out to be buried, and by a public sermon placed among the number of saints.

Then said John Huss, that it was false, that the corpses were by him conveyed with any such pomp into their sepulchre or burial.

Other charges of the same kind were made and denied again, and then there was great silence kept for a while. Then Paletz, who had conducted the process against John Huss, rising up, as having now finished his accusation, said, " I take God to my witness before the emperor's majesty here present, and the most reverend fathers, cardinals, and bishops, that in this accusation of John Huss, I have not used any hatred or evil will ; but that I might satisfy the oath which I took when I was made doctor that I would be a most cruel and sharp enemy of all manner of errors, for the profit of the holy catholic church." Michael de Causis did also the like. "And I," said John Huss, " do commit all these things unto the Heavenly Judge, which shall justly judge the cause or quarrels of both parties." Then said the cardinal of Cambray, " I cannot a little commend and praise the humanity and gentleness of Master Paletz, which he hath used in drawing out the articles against Master John Huss. For as we have heard, there are many things contained in his book much worse, and more detestable."

When he had spoken these words, the bishop of Reggeo, unto whom John Huss was committed, commanded that the said John Huss should be carried again safely unto prison. Then John de Clum following him, did not a little encourage and comfort him. No tongue can express what courage and stomach he received by the short talk which he had with him ; when in so great a broil and grievous hatred, he saw himself in a manner forsaken of all men. After John Huss was carried away, the emperor began to exhort the presidents of the council in this manner, saying,

" You have heard the manifold and grievous crimes which are laid against John Huss, which are not only proved by manifest and strong witnesses, but also confessed by him ; of which, every one of them by my judgment and advice, have deserved, and are worthy of death. Therefore, except he do recant them all, I judge and think meet that he be punished with fire. And although he do that which he is willed and commanded to do, notwithstanding I do counsel you, that he be forbid the office of preaching and teaching, and also that he return no more into the kingdom of Bohemia. For if he be admitted again to teach and preach, and especially in the kingdom of Bohemia, he will not observe and keep that which he is commanded, but hoping upon the favour and goodwill of such as be his adherents and favourers there, he will return again unto his former purpose and intent, and then, besides these errors, he will also sow new errors amongst the people, so the last error shall be worse than the first.

"Moreover, I judge and think it good, that his articles which are condemned, should be sent to my brother the king of Bohemia, and afterward to Pole, and other provinces, where men's minds are replenished with his doctrine, with this commandment, that whosoever do hold or keep the same, should by the common aid both of the ecclesiastical and civil power, be punished. So at the length shall remedy be found for this mischief, if the boughs, together with the root, be utterly rooted and pulled up: and if the bishops, and other prelates, who here in this place have laboured for the extirpating of this heresy, be commended by the whole voices of the council to the king and princes, under whose dominion they are. Last of all, if there be any found here at Constance, who are familiars unto John Huss, they also ought to be punished with such severity and punishment as is due unto them, and especially his scholar, Jerome of Prague." Then said the rest, "When the master is once punished, we hope we shall find the scholar much more tractable and gentle."

After they had spoken these words, they departed out of the cloister, where they were assembled and gathered together. The day before his condemnation, which was the sixth of July, the Emperor Sigismund sent to him four bishops, accompanied by Master Wincelate de Duba, and John de Clum, that they should learn and understand of him what he intended to do. When he was brought out of prison to them, John de Clum began first to speak unto him, saying—

"Master John Huss, I am a man unlearned, neither am I able to counsel or advise you, being a man of learning and understanding: notwithstanding I do require you, if you know yourself guilty of any of those errors, which are objected and laid against you before the council, that you will not be ashamed to alter and change your mind to the will and pleasure of the council; if contrariwise, I will be no author to you, that you should do any thing contrary, or against your conscience, but rather to suffer and endure any kind of punishment, than to deny that which you have known to be the truth." To whom John Huss, with lamentable tears, said; "Verily, as before I have oftentimes done, I do take the most High God for my witness, that I am ready with my heart and mind, if the council can instruct or teach me any better by the holy scripture, and I will be ready with all my whole heart to alter and change my purpose." Then one of the bishops which sat by, said unto him, that he would never be so arrogant or proud, that he would prefer his own mind or opinion before the judgment of the whole council. To whom John Huss answered, "Neither do I otherwise mind or intend. For if he which is the meanest or least in all this council can convict me of error, I will with an humble heart and mind perform, and do whatever the council shall require of me." "Mark," said the bishops, "how obstinately he perseveres in his errors." And when they had thus talked, they commanded the keepers to carry him again to prison, and so they returned again unto the emperor with their commission.

The next day after, which was Saturday, and the sixth day of July, there was a general session held by the princes and lords, both of the ecclesiastical and temporal estates, in the head church of the city of Constance, the Emperor Sigismund being president, in his imperial robes and habit; in the midst whereof there was made a certain high place, being square like a table, and close by it there was a desk of wood, upon the which the garments and vestments pertaining to priesthood were laid for this purpose, that before John Huss should be delivered over to the civil power, he should be openly deprived and spoiled of his priestly ornaments. When John Huss was brought thither, he fell down upon his knees before the same high place, and prayed a long time. In the mean while the bishop of Londy went up into the pulpit, and made this sermon following.

The Sermon of the Bishop of Londy, before the Sentence was given upon John Huss.

"In the name of the Father, the Son, and of the Holy Ghost. Trusting by humble invocation upon the divine help and aid, most noble prince, and most christian emperor, and you, most excellent fathers, and reverend lords, bishops and prelates, also most excellent doctors and masters, famous and noble dukes, and high counts, honourable nobles and barons, and all other men worthy of remembrance; that the intent and purpose of my mind may the more plainly and evidently appear unto this most sacred congregation: I am first of all determined to treat or speak of that which is read in the epistle on the next Sunday, in the sixth chapter to the Romans; that is to say, ' Let the body of sin be destroyed,' &c.

"It appeareth by the authority of Aristotle, in his book entitled *De Cœlo et Mundo*, how wicked, dangerous, and foolish a matter it seemeth to be, not to withstand perverse and wicked beginnings. For he saith, that a small error in the beginning, is very great in the end. It is very damnable and dangerous to have erred, but more hard to be corrected or amended. Whereupon that worthy doctor St. Jerome, in his book upon the exposition of the catholic faith, teaches how necessary a thing it is that heretics and heresies should be suppressed, even in the first beginning of them, saying thus, the rotten and dead flesh is to be cut off from the body, lest that the whole body do perish and putrify. For a scabbed sheep is to be put out of the fold, lest that the whole flock be infected; and a little fire is to be quenched, lest the whole house be consumed and burned. Arius was first a spark in Alexandria, who, because he was not quenched at the first, he presumed, and went about with his wicked and perverse imaginations, and phantastical inventions, to spot and defile the catholic faith, which is founded and established by Christ, defended with the victorious triumphs of so many martyrs, and illuminated and set forth with the excellent doctrines and writings of so many men. Such, therefore, must be resisted; such heretics must of necessity be suppressed and condemned.

"Wherefore I have truly propounded, as touching the punishment of every such obstinate heretic, that the body of sin is to be destroyed. Whereupon it is to be considered according to the holy traditions of the fathers, that some sins are adverse and contrary unto another. Others are annexed or conjoined together; others are, as it were, branches and members of others; and some are, as it were, the roots and heads of others. Amongst all which, those are to be counted the more detestable, out of which the most and worst have their original and beginning. Wherefore, although all sins and offences are to be abhorred of us; yet those are especially to be eschewed, which are the head and root of the rest. For by how much the perverseness of them is of more force and power to hurt, with so much the more speed and circumspection ought they to be rooted out and extinguished, with apt preservatives and remedies. Forsomuch, then, as amongst all sins, none doth appear to be more inveterate than the mischief of this most execrable schism, therefore have I right well propounded, ' That the body of sin should be destroyed.' For by the long continuance of this schism, great and most cruel destruction is sprung up amongst the faithful, and hath long continued ; abominable divisions of heresies are grown ; threatenings are increased and multiplied ; the confusion of the whole clergy is grown thereupon, and the opprobriums and slanders of the christian people, are abundantly sprung up and increased : and truly it is no marvel, forsomuch as that most detestable and execrable schism, is, as it were, a body and heap of dissolution of the true faith of God : for what can be good or holy in that place, where such a pestiferous schism hath reigned so long a time ? For as St. Bernard saith, ' Like as in the unity and concord of the faithful, there is the habitation and dwelling of the Lord ; so likewise in the schism and dissipation of the christians, there is made the habitation and dwelling of the devil. Is not schism and division the original of all subversion, the den of heresies, and the nourisher of all offences ? For the knot of unity and peace being once troubled and broken, there is free passage made for all strife and debate. Covetousness is uttered in others for lucre sake ; lust and will is set at liberty, and all means opened unto slaughter ; all right and equity is banished, the ecclesiastical power is injured, and the calamity of this schism bringeth in all kind of bondage, sword and violence doth rule, the laity have the dominion, concord and unity are banished, and all prescribed rules of religion utterly contemned and set at naught.'

"Consider, most gentle lords, during this most pestiferous schism, how many heresies have appeared and shewed themselves, how many heretics have escaped unpunished ; how many churches have been spoiled and pulled down, how many cities have been oppressed, and regions brought to ruin ? What confusion hath there happened in the clergy ? What and how great destruction hath been amongst the christian people ? I pray you mark how the church of God, the spouse of Christ, and the Mother of all the faithful, is contemned and despised. For who doth reverence the keys of the church ? who feareth the censures or laws ? or who is it that doth defend the liberties thereof ? but rather who is it that doth not offend the same, or who doth not invade it, or else who is he that dare not violently lay hands upon the patrimony or heritage of Jesus Christ ? The goods of the clergy, and of the poor, and the relief of pilgrims and strangers, gotten together by the blood of our Saviour, and of many martyrs, are spoiled and taken away : behold, the abomination of desolation brought upon the church of God, the destruction of the faith, and the confusion of the christian people, to the ruin of the Lord's flock or fold, and all the whole company of our most holy Saviour and Redeemer. This loss is more great or grievous than any which could happen unto the martyrs of Christ, and this persecution much more cruel than the persecution of any tyrant, for they did but only punish the bodies, but in this schism and division the souls are tormented. There the blood of men was only shed ; but in this case the true faith is subverted and overthrown. That persecution was salvation unto many ; but this schism is destruction unto all men. When the tyrants raged, then the faith did increase ; but by this division it is utterly decayed. During their cruelty and madness the primitive church increased ; but through this schism it is confounded and overthrown. Tyrants did ignorantly offend ; but in this schism many do wittingly and willingly even of obstinacy offend. There came in heretics, users of simony, and hypocrites, to the great detriment and deceit of the church ; under those tyrants the merits of the just were increased.

"But during this schism, mischief and wickedness are augmented : for in this most cursed and execrable division, truth is made an enemy to all Christians, faith is not regarded, love and charity hated, hope is lost, justice overthrown, no kind of courage or valiantness, but only unto mischief : modesty and temperance cloaked, wisdom turned into deceit, humility feigned, equity and truth falsified, patience utterly fled, conscience small, all wickedness intended, devotion counted folly, gentleness abject and cast away, religion despised,

obedience not regarded, and all manner of life reproachful and abominable. With how great and grievous sorrows is the church of God replenished and filled, whilst tyrants do oppress it, heretics invade it, users of simony do spoil and rob it, and schismatics go about utterly to subvert it ? O most miserable and wretched christian people, whom now by the space of forty years, with such indurate and continual schism they have tormented, and almost brought to ruin ! O the little bark and ship of Christ, which hath so long time wandered and strayed now in the midst of the whirlpools, and by and by sticketh fast in the rocks, tossed to and fro with most grievous and tempestuous storms ! O miserable and wretched boat of Peter, if the most Holy Father would suffer thee to sink or drown, into what dangers and perils have the wicked pirates brought thee ? Amongst what rocks have they placed thee ? O most godly and loving christians, what faithful devout man is there, who beholding and seeing the great ruin and decay of the church, would not be provoked unto tears ? What good conscience is there that can refrain weeping, because that contention and strife is poured upon the ecclesiastical rulers, which have made us to err in the way, because they have not found, or rather would not find the way of unity and concord, whereupon so many heresies and so great confusion is sprung up, and grown in the flock of Peter and the fold of the Lord.

"Many princes, kings, and prelates, have greatly laboured and worked for the rooting out hereof ; but yet could they never bring to pass or finish that most wholesome and necessary work. Wherefore, most christian king, this most glorious and triumphant victory hath tarried only for thee, the crown and glory thereof shall be thine for ever, and this most happy victory shall be continually celebrated to thy great honour and praise, that thou hast restored again the church which was so spoiled, that thou hast removed and put away all inveterate and overgrown schisms and divisions, that thou hast trodden down users of simony, and rooted out all heretics. Dost thou not behold and see how great, perpetual, and famous renown and glory it will be unto thee ? For what can be more just, what more holy, what better, what more to be desired ; or, finally, what can be more acceptable, than to root out this wicked and abominable schism, to restore the church again unto her ancient liberty, to extinguish and put away all simony, and to condemn and destroy all errors and heresies from amongst the flock of the faithful ? Nothing, truly, can be better, nothing more holy, nothing more profitable for the whole world ; and, finally, nothing more acceptable unto God. For the performance of which most holy and godly work thou wast elect and chosen of God ; thou wast first deputed and chosen in heaven before thou wast elect and chosen upon earth. Thou wast first appointed by the celestial and heavenly Prince, before the electors of the empire did elect or choose thee, and specially, that by the imperial force and power thou shouldest condemn and destroy those errors and heresies which we have presently in hand to be condemned and subverted. To the performance of this most holy work God hath given unto thee the knowledge and understanding of his divine truth and verity, power of princely majesty, and the just judgment of equity and righteousness, as the Most High himself doth say, I have given thee understanding and wisdom, to speak and utter my words, and have set thee to rule over nations and kingdoms, that thou shouldest help the people, pluck down and destroy iniquity, and by exercising of justice thou shouldest, I say, destroy all errors and heresies, and specially this obstinate heretic here present, through whose wickedness and mischief many places of the world are infected with most pestilent and heretical poison, and by this means and occasion almost utterly subverted and destroyed. This most holy and godly labour, O most noble prince ! was reserved only for thee, upon thee it doth only lie, unto whom the rule and ministration of justice is given. Wherefore thou hast established thy praise and renown, even by the mouths of infants and sucking babes, for thy praises shall be celebrated for evermore, that thou hast

x 2

destroyed and overthrown such and so great enemies of the faith. The which that thou mayest prosperously and happily perform and bring to pass, our Lord Jesus vouchsafe to grant thee his grace and help, who is blessed for ever and ever. Amen."

When this sermon was thus ended, the proctor of the council rising up, named Henry de Piro, required that the process of the cause against John Huss might be continued, and that they might proceed unto the definitive sentence. Then a certain bishop, who was appointed one of the judges, declared the process of the cause, which was pleaded long since in the court of Rome, and elsewhere, between John Huss and the prelates of Prague.

At the last he repeated those articles which we have before mentioned, amongst which he rehearsed also one article, that John Huss should teach the two natures of the Godhead and manhood to be one Christ. John Huss went about briefly with a word or two to answer every of them; but as often as he was about to speak the cardinal of Cambray commanded him to hold his peace, saying, "Hereafter you shall answer all together, if you will." Then said John Huss, "How can I at once answer all these things which are alleged against me, when I cannot remember them all?" Then said the cardinal of Florence, "We have heard thee sufficiently." But when John Huss for all that would not hold his peace, they sent the officers that they should force him thereunto. Then he began to intreat, pray, and beseech them, that they would hear him, that such as were present might not credit or believe those things to be true which were reported of him. But when all this could nothing prevail, he, kneeling down upon his knees, committed the whole matter unto God, and the Lord Jesus Christ, for at their hands he believed easily he would obtain that which he desired.

When the articles abovesaid were ended, last of all there was added a notable blasphemy, which they all imputed to John Huss, that is, that he said there should be a fourth person in divinity, and that a certain doctor did hear him speak of the same. When John Huss desired that the doctor might be named, the bishop that alleged the article said that it was not needful to name him. Then said John Huss, "O miserable and wretched man that I am, who am forced and compelled to bear such a blasphemy and slander."

Afterwards the article was repeated, how that he had appealed to Christ, and that appeal was called heretical. Whereto John Huss answered, "O Lord Jesus Christ, whose word is openly condemned here in this council, unto thee again I do appeal, who when thou wast evil intreated of thine enemies didst appeal unto God thy Father, committing thy cause unto a most just Judge, that by thy example we also being oppressed with manifest wrongs and injuries should flee unto thee." Last of all the article was rehearsed, as touching the contempt of the excommunication by John Huss. Whereto he answered as before, that he was excused by his advocates in the court of Rome, wherefore he did not appear when he was cited; and also that it may be proved by the acts, that the excommunication was not ratified; and finally, to the intent he might clear himself of obstinacy, he was for that cause come unto Constance under the emperor's safe conduct. When he had spoken these words, one of them, who was appointed judge, read the definitive sentence against him, which follows thus word for word:—

The Sentence or Judgment of the Council of Constance against John Huss.

"The most holy and sacred general council of Constance, being congregated and gathered together, representing the catholic church, for a perpetual memory of the thing, as the verity and truth did witness, ' An evil tree bringeth forth evil fruit;' hereupon it cometh, that the man of most damnable memory, John Wickliff, through his pestiferous doctrine, not through Jesus Christ by the gospel, as the holy fathers in times past have begotten faithful children, but contrary to the wholesome faith of Jesus Christ, as a most venomous root, hath begotten many pestilent and wicked children whom he hath left behind him, successors and followers of his perverse and wicked doctrine, against whom this sacred synod of Constance is forced to rise up, as against bastards and unlawful children, and with diligent care, with the sharp knife of the ecclesiastical authority, to cut up their errors out of the Lord's field, as most hurtful brambles and briars, lest they should grow to the hurt and detriment of others.

"Forsomuch then as in the holy general council, lately celebrated and holden at Rome, it was decreed, that the doctrine of John Wickliff, of most damnable memory, should be condemned, and that his books which contained the same doctrine should be burned as heretical, and this decree was approved and confirmed by the sacred authority of the whole council, nevertheless, one John Huss here personally present in this sacred council, not the disciple of Christ, but of John Wickliff, an arch heretic, after, and contrary or against the condemnation and decree hath taught, preached, and affirmed the articles of Wickliff, which were condemned by the church of God, and in times past by certain most reverend fathers in Christ, lords, archbishops, and bishops, of divers kingdoms and realms, masters of divinity of divers universities; especially resisting in his open sermons, and also with his adherents and accomplices in the schools, the condemnation of the said articles of Wickliff's, oftentimes published in the said university of Prague, and hath declared him the said Wickliff, for the favour and commendation of his doctrine before the whole multitude of the clergy and people, to be a catholic man, and a true evangelical doctor. He hath also published and affirmed certain and many of his articles worthily condemned, to be catholic, the which are notoriously contained in the books of the said John Huss.

"Wherefore, after diligent deliberation and full information first had upon the premises by the reverend fathers and lords in Christ of the holy church of Rome, cardinals, patriarchs, archbishops, bishops, and other prelates, doctors of divinity, and of both laws, in great number assembled and gathered together, this most sacred and holy council of Constance, declareth and determineth the articles abovesaid (the which, after due conference had, are found in his books written with his own hand, the which also the said John Huss in open audience, before this holy council, hath confessed to be in his books), not to be catholic, neither worthy to be taught, but that many of them are erroneous, some of them wicked, others offensive to godly ears, many of them temerarious and seditious, and the greater part of them notoriously heretical, and even now of late by the holy fathers and general councils reproved and condemned. And forsomuch as the said articles are expressly contained in the books of the said John Huss, therefore this said sacred council doth condemn and reprove all those books which he wrote, in what form or phrase soever they be, or whether they be translated by others, and doth determine and decree, that they all shall be solemnly and openly burned in the presence of the clergy and people of the city of Constance, and elsewhere; adding moreover for the premises, that all his doctrine is worthy to be despised and eschewed of all faithful christians. And to the intent that this most pernicious and wicked doctrine may be utterly excluded and shut out of the church, this sacred synod doth straightly command, that diligent inquisition be made by the ordinaries of the places by the ecclesiastical censure, for such treatises and works, and that such as are found be consumed and burned with fire. And if there be any found, who shall contemn or despise this sentence or decree, this sacred synod ordaineth and decreeth, that the ordinaries of the places, and the inquisitors of heresies, shall proceed against every such person as they suspect of heresy.

"Wherefore, after due inquisition made against the said John Huss, and full information had by the commissaries and doctors of both laws, and also by the sayings of the witnesses which were worthy of credit, and many other things openly read before the said John Huss, and before the fathers and prelates of this sacred council (by the which allegations of the witnesses, it appeareth, that the said John Huss hath taught many evil and offensive, seditious and perilous heresies, and hath preached the same for a long time), this most sacred and holy synod, lawfully congregated and gathered together in the Holy Ghost, (the name of Christ being invoked and called upon) by this their sentence which here is set forth in writing, determineth, pronounceth, declareth, and decreeth, that John Huss was and is a true and manifest heretic, and that he hath preached openly errors and heresies lately condemned by the church of God, and many seditious, temerarious, and offensive things, to no small offence of the Divine Majesty, and of the universal church, and detriment of the catholic faith and church, neglecting and despising the keys of the church, and ecclesiastical censures. In the which error he has continued with a mind altogether indurate and hardened by the space of many years, much offending the faithful christians by his obstinacy and stubbornness, in his having made his appeal unto the Lord Jesus Christ as the most high Judge, omitting and leaving all ecclesiastical means. In the which appeal he allegeth many false, injurious, and offensive matters, in contempt of the apostolic see, and the ecclesiastical censures and keys.

"Whereupon, both for the premises and many other things, the said synod pronounceth John Huss to be an heretic, and judgeth him by these presents to be condemned and judged as an heretic, and reproveth the said appeal as injurious, offensive, and done in derision unto the ecclesiastical jurisdiction, and judgeth the said Huss not only to have seduced the christian people by his writings and preachings, and especially in the kingdom of Bohemia, neither to have been a true preacher of the gospel of Christ unto the said people, according to the exposition of the holy doctors; but also to have been a seducer of them, and also an obstinate and stiffnecked person, yea, and such an one as doth not desire to return again to the lap of our holy mother the church, neither to abjure the errors and heresies which he hath openly preached and defended. Wherefore this most sacred council decreeth and declareth, that the said John Huss shall be publicly deposed and degraded from his priestly orders and dignity, &c."

Whilst these things were thus read, John Huss, although he was forbidden to speak, notwithstanding did often interrupt them, and especially when he was reproved of obstinacy, he said, with a loud voice: "I was never obstinate, but as always heretofore, even so now again I desire to be taught by the holy scriptures, and I do profess myself to be so desirous of the truth, that if I might by one only word subvert the errors of all heretics, I would not refuse to enter into what peril or danger soever it were." When his books were condemned, he said: "Wherefore have you condemded those books, when you have not proved by any one article that they are contrary to the scriptures or articles of faith? And, moreover, what injury is this that you do to me, that you have condemned these books written in the Bohemian tongue, which you never saw, neither yet read?" And oftentimes looking up unto heaven he prayed.

When the sentence and judgment was ended, kneeling down upon his knees, he said: "Lord Jesus Christ, forgive mine enemies, by whom thou knowest that I am falsely accused, and that they have used false witness and slanders against me: forgive them, I say, for thy great mercy's sake." This his prayer and oration the greater part, and especially the chief of the priests derided and mocked.

At last, the seven bishops who were chosen out to degrade him of his priesthood commanded him to put on the garments pertaining unto priesthood, which, when he had done, he came to the putting on of the albe, he called to his remembrance the purple vesture which Herod put on Jesus Christ to mock him withal. So

likewise in all other things he comforted himself by the example of Christ. When he had now put on all his priestly vestures, the bishops exhorted him that he should yet alter and change his mind, and provide for his honour and safety; then he (according as the manner of the ceremony is) going up to the top of the scaffold, being full of tears, spake to the people in this sort:

"These lords and bishops do exhort and counsel me, that I should here confess before you all that I have erred; to do which thing, if it were such as might be done with the infamy and reproach of man only, they might peradventure easily persuade me thereto; but now truly I am in the sight of the Lord my God, without whose great displeasure and the hurt of mine own conscience, I can by no means do that which they require of me. For I do well know, that I never taught any of those things which they have falsely alleged against me, but I have always preached, taught, written, and thought contrary thereto. With what countenance then should I behold the heavens? With what face should I look upon them whom I have taught, whereof there is a great number, if through me it should come to pass that those things, which they have hitherto known to be most certain and sure, should now be made uncertain? Should I by this my example astonish or trouble so many souls, so many consciences, indued with the most firm and certain knowledge of the scriptures and gospel of our Lord Jesus Christ and his most pure doctrine, armed against all the assaults of Satan? I will never do it, neither commit any such kind of offence, that I should seem more to esteem this vile carcase appointed unto death, than their health and salvation."

At this most godly word he was forced again to hear, by the sentence of the bishops, that he did obstinately and maliciously persevere in his pernicious and wicked errors.

Then he was commanded to come down to the execution of his judgment, and in his coming down, one of the seven bishops before rehearsed, first took away from him the chalice which he held in his hand, saying: "O, cursed Judas, why hast thou forsaken the council and ways of peace, and hast counselled with the Jews? We take away from thee this chalice of thy salvation." But John Huss received this curse in this manner: "But I trust unto God the Father omnipotent, and my Lord Jesus Christ, for whose sake I do suffer these things, that he will not take away the chalice of his redemption, but I have a steadfast and firm hope that this day I shall drink thereof in his kingdom." Then followed the other bishops in order, who every one of them took away the vestments from him which they had put on, each one of them giving him their curse. Whereunto John Huss answered: "That he did willingly embrace and bear those blasphemies for the name of our Lord Jesus Christ." At the last they came to the erasing of his shaven crown. But before the bishops would go in hand with it, there was a great contention between them, with what instrument it should be done, with a razor or with a pair of shears.

In the mean time, John Huss, turning himself toward the emperor, said: "I marvel that forsomuch as they be all of like cruel mind and spirit, yet they cannot agree upon their kind of cruelty." Notwithstanding, at last they agreed to cut off the skin of the crown of his head with a pair of shears. And when they had done that, they added these words: "Now hath the church taken away all her ornaments and privileges from him. Now there resteth nothing else, but that he be delivered over unto the secular power." But before they did that, there yet remained another reproach. For they caused to be made a certain crown of paper, almost a cubit deep, in the which were painted three devils of wonderful ugly shape, and this title set over their heads, "ARCH-HERETIC," which, when he saw, he said: "My Lord Jesus Christ for my sake did wear a crown of thorns, why should not I then for his sake again wear this light crown, be it never so ignominious? Truly I will do it, and that willingly." When it was set upon his head, the bishop said: "Now we commit thy soul to the devil." "But I," said John Huss, lifting his eyes up towards the heavens, "do commit my spirit into thy hands, O Lord Jesus Christ, unto thee I commend my spirit which thou hast redeemed." These contumelies thus ended, the bishops turning themselves towards the emperor, said: "This most sacred synod of Constance leaveth now John Huss, who has no more any office in the church of God, to the civil judgment and power." Then the emperor commanded Lewis, duke of Bavaria, who stood before him in his robes, holding the golden apple with the cross in his hand, that he should receive John Huss from the bishops, and deliver him to them who should do the execution. As he was led by them to the place of execution, before the church doors he saw his books burning, whereat he smiled and laughed. And all men that passed by he exhorted, not to think that he should die for any error or heresy, but only for the hatred and ill will of his adversaries, who had charged him with most false and unjust crimes. Nearly the whole city followed him in armour.

The place appointed for the execution was before the gate Gotlebian, between the gardens and gates of the suburbs. When John Huss was come thither, kneeling down upon his knees, and lifting his eyes up unto heaven, he prayed, and said certain Psalms, and especially the thirty-first and fiftieth Psalms. And they who stood hard by, heard him oftentimes in his prayer, with a lively and cheerful countenance, repeat this verse: "Into thy hands, O Lord, I commend my spirit," &c. Which thing when the lay people beheld who stood next to him, they said: "What he hath done before we know not, but now we see and hear that he doth speak and pray very devoutly and godly." Others wished that he had a confessor. There was a certain priest by, sitting on horseback, in a green gown, drawn about with red silk, who said: "He ought not to be heard, because he is an heretic." Yet, notwithstanding, while he was in prison, he was both confessed, and also absolved by a certain doctor, a monk, as Huss himself witnesses in an epistle which he wrote to his friends out of prison. Thus Christ reigns unknown to the world, even in the midst of his enemies. In the meantime, while he prayed, as he bowed his neck backward to look upward unto heaven, the crown of paper fell off from his head upon the ground. Then one of the soldiers, taking it up again, said, "Let us put it again upon his head, that he may be burned with his masters, the devils, whom he has served."

When by the commandment of the tormentors he was risen up from his prayer, with a loud voice, he said: "Lord Jesus Christ assist and help me, that with a constant and patient mind, by thy most gracious help, I may bear and suffer this cruel and ignominious death, whereunto I am condemned for the preaching of thy most holy gospel and word." Then, as before, he declared the cause of his death to the people. In the meantime the hangman stripped him of his garments, and turning his hands behind his back, tied him fast to the stake with ropes that were made wet. And whereas by chance he was turned towards the east, certain cried out that he should not look towards the east, for he was an heretic; so he was turned towards the west. Then was his neck tied with a chain to the stake, which chain, when he beheld, smiling, he said, "That he would willingly receive the same chain for Jesus Christ's sake, who, he knew, was bound with a far worse chain." Under his feet they set two fagots, mixing straw with them, and so likewise from the feet up to the chin he was enclosed in round about with wood. But before the wood was set on fire, Lewis, duke of Bavaria, with another gentleman, who was the son of Clement, came and exhorted John Huss, that he would yet be mindful of his safety, and renounce his errors. To whom he said: "What errors should I renounce, when I know myself guilty of none? For as for those things which are falsely alleged against me, I know that I never did so much as once think them, much less preach them. For this was the principal end and purpose of my doctrine, that I might teach all men repentance and the remission

of sins, according to the verity of the gospel of Jesus Christ, and the exposition of the holy doctors; wherefore with a cheerful mind and courage I am here ready to suffer death." When he had spoken these words, they left him, and shaking hands together, they departed.

Then was the fire kindled, and John Huss began to sing with a loud voice, "Jesus Christ the Son of the living God have mercy upon me." And when he began to say the same the third time, the wind drove the flame so upon his face, that it choaked him. Yet notwithstanding he moved a while after, by the space that a man might almost say the Lord's Prayer three times. When all the wood was burned and consumed, the upper part of the body was left hanging in the chain, so they threw down stake and all, and making a new fire, burned it, the head being first cut in small pieces, that it might the sooner be consumed unto ashes. The heart, which was found amongst the bowels, being well beaten with staves and clubs, was at last pricked upon a sharp stick, and roasted at a fire apart until it was consumed. Then, with great diligence gathering the ashes together, they cast them into the river Rhone, that the least remnant of the ashes of that man should not be left upon the earth, whose memory notwithstanding cannot be abolished out of the minds of the godly, neither by fire, neither by water, neither by any kind of torment.

I know very well that these things are very slenderly written by me as touching the labours of this most holy martyr, John Huss, with whom the labours of Hercules are not to be compared. For that ancient Hercules slew a few monsters; but this our Hercules with a most stout and valiant courage, hath subdued even the world itself, the mother of all monsters and cruel beasts. This history were worthy some other kind of more curious handling; but forsomuch as I cannot otherwise perform it myself, I have endeavoured according to the very truth, as the thing was indeed, to commend the same unto all godly minds: neither have I heard it reported by others, but I myself was present at the doing of all these things, and as I was able, I have put them in writing, that by this my labour and endeavour, howsoever it were, I might preserve the memory of this holy man and excellent doctor of the evangelical truth.

What was the name of this author which wrote this history it is not expressed. Cochleus, in his second book "Contra Hussitas," supposeth his name to be Johannes Pizibram, a Bohemian.

This godly servant and martyr of Christ was condemned by the cruel council, and burned at Constance, A. D. 1415, about the month of July.

How grievously this death of John Huss was taken among the nobles of Bohemia and of Moravia, hereafter (Christ willing) shall appear by their letters which they sent to the council, and by the letters of Sigismund, the king of the Romans. Wherein he labours, all that can, to purge and excuse himself of Huss's death. Although he was not altogether free from that cruel act, and innocent from that blood; yet notwithstanding he pretends in words so to wipe away that blot from him, that the greatest part of the crime seems to rest upon the bloody prelates of that council.

But it appears that the emperor, partly ashamed and sorry, would gladly have cleared himself thereof, and with Pilate have washed his hands; yet he could not so clear himself, but that a great portion of that murder remained on him, as may appear by his last words spoken in the council to John Huss, whereof John Huss in his epistles complains, writing to his friends in Bohemia in his thirty-third epistle, as follows:—

"I desire you again, for the love of God, that the lords of Bohemia joining together, will desire the king for a final audience to be given to me. Forsomuch as he alone said to me in the council, that they should give me audience shortly, and that I should answer for myself briefly in writing: it will be to his great confusion, if he shall not perform that which he hath spoken. But I fear that word of his will be as firm and sure, as the other was concerning my safe conduct granted by him.

There were some in Bohemia, who desired me to beware of his safe conduct. And other said, he will surely give you to your enemies. And the lord Mikest Dwaky told me before Master Jessenitz, saying, 'Master, know it for certain, you shall be condemned.' And this I suppose he spake, knowing before the intention of the king. I hoped that he had been well affected toward the law of God and the truth, and had therein good understanding; now I conceive that he is not very skilful, nor so prudently circumspect in himself. He condemned me before even mine enemies did. Who, if it had pleased him, might have kept the moderation of Pilate the Gentile, who said, 'I find no cause in this man;' or at least, if he had said but thus, 'Behold, I have given him his safe conduct safely to return:' And if he will not abide the decision of the council, I will send him home to the king of Bohemia with your sentence and attestations, that he with his clergy may judge him.'"

John Huss, while in prison, wrote several treatises, as, "of the commandments;" "of the Lord's prayer;" "of mortal sin;" "of matrimony;" "of the knowledge and love of God;" "of the three enemies of mankind, the world, and flesh, and the devil;" "of penance;" "of the sacrament of the body and blood of the Lord;" "of the sufficiency of the law of God to rule the church," &c. He wrote also many epistles and letters to the lords, and to his friends of Bohemia. Some of his letters I thought here to insert, that the reader may have some taste, and take some profit of the christian writings and doings of this blessed man; first beginning with the letter of the Lord de Clum, concerning the safe conduct of John Huss.

A Letter of the Lord John de Clum, concerning the safe conduct of John Huss.

"To all and singular that shall see and hear these presents, I John de Clum do it to understand, how Master John Huss, bachelor of divinity, under the safe conduct and protection of the renowned prince and Lord Sigismund of the Romans, ever Augustus, and king of Hungary, &c. my gracious lord, and under the protection, defence, and safe-guard of the holy empire of Rome, having the letters patent of the said my lord, king of the Romans, &c.; came unto Constance to render a full account of his faith in public audience to all that would require the same. This the said Master John Huss, in this imperial city of Constance, under the safe conduct of the said my lord king of the Romans, hath been and yet is detained. And although the pope, with the cardinals, have been seriously required by solemn ambassadors of the said my lord king of the Romans, in the king's name and behalf, that the said Master John Huss should be set at liberty, and be restored unto me, yet, notwithstanding, they have and yet do refuse hitherto to set him at liberty, to the great contempt and derogation of the safe conduct of the king, and of the safeguard and protection of the empire, or imperial majesty. Wherefore I, John aforesaid, in the name of the king, do here publish and make it known, that the apprehending, and detaining of the said Master John Huss, was done wholly against the will of the forenamed king of the Romans my lord, seeing it is done in the contempt of the safe conduct of his subjects, and of the protection of the empire, because that the said my lord was then absent, far from Constance; and if he had been there present, would never have permitted the same. And when he shall come, it is to be doubted of no man, but that he, for this great injury and contempt of this safe conduct done to him and to the empire, will grievously be molested for the same.
"Given at Constance, in the day of the Nativity of the Lord, 1414.

An Epistle of John Huss unto the People of Prague.

"Grace and peace from our Lord Jesus Christ, that you being delivered from sin may walk in his grace, and may grow in all modesty and virtue, and after this may enjoy eternal life.
"Dearly beloved, I beseech you who walk after the law of God, that you cast not away the care of the salvation of your souls, when you hearing the word of God are forewarned wisely to understand that you be not deceived by false apostles; who do not reprehend the sins of men, but rather extenuate and diminish them: who flatter the priests, and do not shew to the people their offences; who magnify themselves, boast their own works, and marvellously extol their own worthiness, but follow not Christ in his humility, in poverty, in the cross, and other manifold afflictions. Of whom our merciful Saviour did warn us before, saying, 'False christs and false prophets shall rise, and shall deceive many.' And when he had forewarned his well-beloved disciples, he said unto them, 'Beware of false prophets, which come to you in sheep's clothing, but inwardly are ravening wolves: ye shall know them by their fruits.' And true it is, that the faithful of Christ have much need diligently to beware and take heed to themselves. For, as our Saviour himself says, 'The elect also, if it were possible, shall be brought into error.' Wherefore, my well-beloved, be circumspect and watchful, that ye be not circumvented with the crafty trains of the devil. And the more circumspect ye ought to be, for antichrist labours the more to trouble you. The last judgment is near at hand: death shall swallow up many, but to the elect children of God the kingdom of God draweth near, because for them he gave his own body. Fear not death, love together one another, persevere in understanding the good will of God without ceasing. Let the terrible and horrible day of judgment be always before your eyes, that you sin not; and also the joy of eternal life, whereunto you must endeavour. Furthermore, let the passion of our Saviour be never out of your minds; that you may bear with him, and for him gladly, whatever shall be laid upon you. For if you shall consider well in your minds his cross and afflictions, nothing shall be grievous unto you, and you shall patiently give place to tribulations, cursings, rebukes, stripes, and imprisonment, and shall not doubt to give your lives moreover for his holy truth, if need require. Know ye, well-beloved, that antichrist being stirred up against you, devises various persecutions. And many he has not hurt, no not the least hair of their heads, as by mine own example I can testify, although he has been vehemently incensed against me. Wherefore, I desire you all, with your prayers to make intercession for me to the Lord, to give me understanding, sufferance, patience, and constancy, that I never swerve from his divine verity. He hath brought me now to Constance. In all my journey, openly and manifestly, I have not feared to utter my name as becomes the servant of God. In no place have I kept myself secret, nor used any dissimulation. But never did I find in any place more pestilent and manifest enemies than at Constance. Which enemies neither should I have had there, had it not been for certain of our own Bohemians, hypocrites, and deceivers, who, for benefits received, and stirred up with covetousness, with boasting and bragging, have persuaded the people that I went about to seduce them out of the right way: but I am in good hope, that through the mercy of our God, and by your prayers, I shall persist strongly in the immutable verity of God unto the last breath. Finally, I would not have you ignorant, that whereas every one here is put in his office, I only as an outcast am neglected, &c. I commend you to the merciful Lord Jesus Christ, our true God, and the Son of the immaculate Virgin Mary, who hath redeemed us by his most bitter death, without all merits, from eternal pains, from the thraldom of the devil, and from sin.
"From Constance the year of our Lord, 1415."

Another Letter of John Huss to his Benefactors.

"My gracious benefactors and defenders of the truth, I exhort you by the bowels of Jesus Christ, that now ye setting aside the vanities of this present world, will give your service to the Eternal King, Christ the Lord. Trust not in princes, nor in the sons of men, in whom there is no help. For the sons of men are dissemblers and deceitful. To-day they are, to-morrow they perish, but God remaineth for ever. Who hath his servants, not for any need he hath of them, but for their own profit: unto whom he performs that which he promises, and fulfils that which he purposes to give. He casts off no faithful servant from him: for he saith, 'Where I am, there also shall my servant be.' And the Lord maketh every servant of his to be the lord of all his possession, giving himself unto him, and with himself, all things; that without tediousness, fear, and without defect he may possess all things, rejoicing with all saints in joy infinite. O! happy is that servant, whom, when the Lord shall come, he shall find watching. Happy is the servant which shall receive that King of Glory with joy. Wherefore, well beloved lords and benefactors, serve you that King in fear; who shall bring you, as I trust, by his grace, at this present time to Bohemia, in health, and hereafter to eternal life of glory. Fare you well, for I think that this is the last letter that I shall write to you; who, to-morrow, as I suppose, shall be purged in hope of Jesus Christ, through bitter death for my sins. The things that happened to me this night I am not able to write. Sigismund has done all things with me deceitfully, God forgive him, and only for your sakes. You also heard the sentence which he awarded against me. I pray you have no suspicion of faithful Vitus."

Another Epistle of John Huss, wherein he declares why God suffereth not his People to perish.

" The Lord God be with you. Many causes there were, my dear friends, well-beloved in God, which moved me to think that those letters were the last, which before I sent to you, looking that same time for instant death. But now understanding the same to be deferred, I take it for great comfort to me, that I have some leisure more to talk with you by letters. And therefore I write again to you, to declare and testify at least my gratitude and mindful duty toward you. And, as touching death, God doth know why he doth defer it both to me, and to my well-beloved brother, Master Jerome, who I trust will die holily and without blame; and do know also that he doeth and suffereth now more valiantly than I myself, a wretched sinner. God hath given us a long time, that we might call to memory our sins the better, and repent for the same more fervently. He hath granted us time, that our long and great temptation should put away our grievous sins, and bring the more consolation. He hath given us time, wherein we should remember the horrible rebukes of our merciful King and Lord Jesus, and should ponder his cruel death, and so more patiently might learn to bear our afflictions. And, moreover, that we might keep in remembrance, how that the joys of the life to come are not given after the joys of this world immediately, but through many tribulations the saints have entered into the kingdom of heaven. For some of them have been cut and chopped all to pieces, some have had their eyes bored through, some been boiled, some roasted, some flayed alive, some buried alive, stoned, crucified, ground betwixt millstones, drawn hither and thither unto execution, drowned in waters, strangled and hanged, torn in pieces, vexed with rebukes before their death, kept in prisons, and afflicted in bonds. And who is able to recite all the torments and sufferings of the holy saints, which they suffered under the Old and New Testament for the verity of God; namely, those which have at any time rebuked the malice of the priests, or have preached against their wickedness? And it will be a marvel if any man now also shall escape unpunished, whoever dare boldly resist the wickedness and perversity, especially of those priests, who can abide no correction. And I am glad that they are compelled now to read my books, in which their malice is somewhat described; and I know they have read the same more exactly and willingly, than they have read the holy gospel, seeking therein to find out errors.

" Given at Constance upon Thursday, the 28th day of June, A. D. 1415."

Another Letter of John Huss, wherein he confirmeth the Bohemians, and describeth the wickedness of the Council.

" John Huss, in hope the servant of God, to all the faithful in Bohemia, which love the Lord, greeting, through the grace of God. It cometh in my mind, wherein I must needs admonish you, that are the faithful and beloved of the Lord, how that the council of Constance being full of pride, avarice, and all abomination, has condemned my books written in the Bohemian tongue, for heretical, which books they never saw, nor ever heard. And if they had heard them, yet they could not understand the same, being some Italians, some Frenchmen, some Britons, some Spaniards, Germans, with other people of other nations; unless, peradventure, John, bishop of Litomysl, understood them, who was present in that council, and certain other Bohemians, and priests which are against me, and labour all they may how to deprave both the verity of God, and the honesty of our country of Bohemia; which I judge in the hope of God, to be a godly land, right well given to the true knowledge of the faith, for it so greatly desires the word of God, and honest manners. And if you were here at Constance, you would see the grievous abomination of this council, which they call so holy, and infallible. Of which council I have heard it reported, that the city of Constance cannot in thirty years be purged of those abominations committed in that council. And almost all are offended with that council, being sore grieved to behold such execrable things perpetrated in the same.

" When I stood first to answer before mine adversaries, seeing all things there done with no order, and hearing them also outrageously crying out, I said plainly to them, that I looked for more honest behaviour, and better order and discipline in that council. Then the chief cardinal answered, ' Sayest thou so? But in the Tower thou spakest more modestly.' To whom said I, ' In the Tower no man cried out against me, whereas now all do rage against me.' My faithful and beloved in Christ, be not afraid with their sentence in condemning my books. They shall be scattered hither and thither abroad, like light butterflies, and their statutes shall endure as spider-webs. They went about to shake my constancy from the verity of Christ; but they could not overcome the virtue of God in me. They would not reason from scripture against me, as divers honourable lords can witness with me, who being ready to suffer contumely for the truth of God, took my part stoutly; namely, Lord Wenceslate de Duba, and Lord John de Clum: for they were let in by King Sigismund into the council. And when I said, that I was desirous to be instructed if I did in any thing err, then they heard the chief cardinal answer again, ' Because thou wouldest be informed, there is no remedy but that thou must first revoke thy doctrine according to the determination of fifty bachelors of divinity appointed.' O high instruction!

" After like manner St. Katherine also should have denied and revoked the verity of God, and faith in Christ, because the fifty masters likewise withstood her: which, notwithstanding, that good virgin would never do, standing in her faith unto death: but she did win those her masters unto Christ, when as I cannot win these my masters by any means. These things I thought good to write to you, that you might know how they have overcome me, with no grounded scripture, nor with any reason: but only did assay with terrors and deceits to persuade me to revoke and to abjure. But our merciful God, whose law I have magnified, was and is with me, and I trust, so will continue, and will keep me in his grace unto death.

" Written at Constance, after the feast of John Baptist, in prison and in bonds, daily looking for death; although for the secret judgments of God, I dare not say, whether this be my last epistle: for now also Almighty God is able to deliver me."

Another Letter of John Huss, wherein he comforteth his Friends, and willeth them not to be troubled for the condemning of his Books; and also declareth the wickedness of the Clergy.

"Master John Huss, in hope the servant of God, to all the faithful which love him and his statutes, wisheth the truth and grace of God.

"Beloved, I thought it needful to warn that you should not fear or be discouraged, because the adversaries have decreed that my books should be burnt. Remember how the Israelites burned the preachings of the prophet Jeremiah, and yet they could not avoid the things that were prophesied of in them. For after they were burnt, the Lord commanded to write the same prophecy again, and that larger, which was also done. For Jeremiah, sitting in prison spake, and Baruch, who was ready at his hand, wrote. This is written either in the thirty-fifth or forty-fifth chapter of the vision of Jeremiah. It is also written in the books of the Maccabees, 'That the wicked did burn the law of God, and killed them that had the same.' Again, under the New Testament, they burned the saints, with the books of the law of God. The cardinals condemned and committed to fire certain of St. Gregory's books, and had burnt them all if they had not been preserved by God through the means of Peter, Gregory's minister. Having these things before your eyes, take heed lest through fear you omit to read my books, and deliver them to the adversaries to be burnt. Remember the saying of our merciful Saviour, by which he forewarned us, Matt. xxiv. 'There shall be,' saith he, 'before the day of judgment, great tribulation, such as was not from the beginning of the world until this day, no, nor yet shall be: so that even the elect of God should be deceived, if it were possible. But for their sakes those days shall be shortened.' When you remember these things, beloved, be not afraid, for I trust in God that that school of antichrist shall be afraid of you, and suffer you to be in quiet, neither shall the council of Constance extend to Bohemia. For I think, that many of them who are of the council, will die before they shall get from you my books. And they shall depart from the council, and be scattered abroad, throughout the parts of the world, like storks, and then they shall know when winter cometh, what they did in summer. Consider that they have judged their head, the pope, worthy of death, for many horrible acts that he hath done. Go to now; answer to this, you preachers, who preach that the pope is the god of the earth; that he may, as the lawyers say, make sale of the holy things; that he is the head of the whole holy church, in verity well governing the same; that he is the heart of the church in quickening the same spiritually: that he is the well-spring from which floweth all virtue and goodness: that he is the sun of the holy church: that he is the safe refuge to which every christian man ought to fly for succour. Behold now, that head is cut off with the sword, now the god of the earth is bound, now his sins are declared openly; now that well-spring is dried up, that sun darkened, that heart is plucked out and thrown away, lest that any man should seek succour thereat. The council hath condemned that head, and that for this offence, because he took money for indulgences, bishopricks, and other such like.

"I would that in that council God had said, 'He that amongst you is without sin, let him give the sentence against Pope John;' then surely they had gone all out of the council-house, one after another. Why did they bow the knee to him always, before this his fall, kiss his feet, and call him the most holy father, seeing they saw apparently before, that he was an heretic, that he was a killer, that he was a wicked sinner, all which things now they have found in him? Why did the cardinals choose him to be pope, knowing before that he had killed the holy father? Why suffered they him to meddle with holy things, in bearing the office of the popedom? for to this end they are his counsellors, that they should admonish him of that which is right. Are not they them-selves as guilty of these faults as he? seeing that they accounted these things vices in him, and were partakers of some of them themselves? Why durst no man lay ought to his charge, before he had fled from Constance, but as soon as the secular power, by the sufferance of God, laid hold upon him, then, and never before, they conspired all together that he should not live any longer? Surely, even at this day is the malice, the abomination and filthiness of antichrist revealed in the pope, and others of this council.

"Now the faithful servants of God may understand what our Saviour Christ meant by this saying, 'When you shall see the abomination of desolation, which is spoken of by Daniel, &c. whoso can understand it,' &c. Surely, these be great abominations, pride, covetousness, simony, sitting in a solitary place; that is to say, in a dignity void of goodness, of humility, and other virtues; as we do now clearly see in those that are constituted in any office and dignity. O how acceptable a thing should it be (if time would suffer me) to disclose their wicked acts, which are now apparent that the faithful servants of God might know them? I trust in God that he will send after me those that shall be more valiant; and there are alive at this day, those who shall make more manifest the malice of antichrist, and shall give their lives to the death for the truth of our Lord Jesus Christ, who shall give both to you and me the joys of life everlasting.

"This epistle was written upon St. John Baptist's day, in prison and in cold irons, I having this meditation with myself, that John was beheaded in his prison and bonds, for the word of God."

Another Letter of John Huss.

"John Huss, in hope the servant of God, to all the faithful at Bohemia which love the Lord, wisheth to stand and die in the grace of God, and at last to attain unto eternal life.

"Ye that bear rule over others, and be rich, and ye also that be poor, well-beloved and faithful in God, I beseech you, and admonish you all, that ye will be obedient unto God, make much of his word, and gladly hearing the same, will humbly perform that which ye hear. I beseech you stick fast to the verity of God's word, which I have written and preached unto you out of his law, and the sermons of his saints. Also I desire you if any man either in public sermon or in private talk heard of me any thing, or have read any thing written by me which is against the verity of God, that ye do not follow the same. Albeit I do not find my conscience guilty that I ever have spoken or written any such thing amongst you.

"I desire you, moreover, if any man, at any time have noted any levity either in my talk or in my conditions, that ye do not follow the same, but pray to God for me, to pardon me that sin of lightness. I pray you that ye will love your priests and ministers which be of honest behaviour, to prefer and honour them before others; namely, such priests as travel in the word of God. I pray you take heed to yourselves, and beware of malicious and deceitful men, and especially of these wicked priests of whom our Saviour doth speak, that they are under sheep's clothing, and inwardly are ravening wolves. I pray such as be rulers and superiors, to behave themselves gently towards their poor inferiors, and to rule them justly. I beseech the citizens that they will walk every man in his degree and vocation, with an upright conscience. The artificers also, I beseech that they will exercise their occupations diligently, and use them with the fear of God. I beseech the servants that they will serve their masters faithfully. And likewise the schoolmasters I beseech, that they living honestly, will bring up their scholars virtuously, and teach them faithfully, first to learn to fear God; then for the glory of God and the public utility of the commonwealth, and their own health, and not for avarice or for worldly honour, to employ their minds to honest arts. I beseech the students of the university, and all schools, in all honest things to obey their masters, and to follow them, and that with all diligence they will study to be profitable both to the setting forth of the glory of God, and to the soul's health, as well of themselves, as of other men. Together I beseech and pray you all, that you will yield most hearty thanks to the right honourable lords, the Lord Wenceslaus de Duba, Lord John de Clum, Lord Henry Lumlovio, Lord Vilem Zagecio, Lord Nicholas, and other lords of Bohemia, of Moravia, and Polonie; that their diligence towards me may be grateful to all good men; because that they, like valiant champions of God's truth, have oftentimes set themselves against the whole council for my deliverance, contending and standing against the same to the uttermost of their power; but especially Lord Wenceslaus de Duba, and Lord John de Clum. Whatsoever they shall report unto you, give credit unto them; for they were in the council when I there answered many. They know who they were of Bohemia, and how many false and slanderous things they brought in against me, and that council cried out against me, and how I also answered to all things whereof I was demanded. I beseech you also that ye will pray for the king of the Romans, and for your king, and for his wife, your queen, that God of his mercy would abide with them and with you, both now and henceforth in everlasting life. Amen.

"This epistle I have written to you out of prison and in bonds, looking the next day after the writing hereof, for the sentence of the council upon my death; having a full trust that he will not leave me, neither suffer me to deny his truth, and to revoke the errors, which false witnesses maliciously have devised against me. How mercifully the Lord God hath dealt with me, and was with me in marvellous temptations, ye shall know when hereafter by the help of Christ we shall all meet together in the joy of the world to come. As concerning Master Jerome, my dearly beloved brother and fellow, I hear no other but that he is remaining in straight bonds, looking for death as I do; and that for the faith which he valiantly maintained amongst the Bohemians, our cruel enemies of Bohemia have given us into the power and hands of other enemies, and into bonds. I beseech you pray to God for them.

"Moreover, I beseech you, namely of Prague, that ye will love the temple of Bethlehem, and provide so long as God shall permit, that the word of God may be preached in the same. For, because of that place, the devil is angry, and against the same place he hath stirred up priests and canons, perceiving that in that place his kingdom should be disturbed and diminished. I trust in God that he will keep that holy church so long as it shall please him, and in the same shall give greater increase of his word by other, than he hath done by me a weak vessel. I beseech you also, that ye will love one another, and withholding no man from the hearing of God's word, ye will provide and take care that good men be not oppressed by any force and violence. Written at Constance, the year of our Lord 1415."

Another right godly letter of John Huss to a certain priest, admonishing him of his office, and exhorting him to be faithful; worthy to be read of all Ministers.

"The peace of our Lord Jesus Christ, &c. My dear brother be diligent in preaching the gospel, and do the work of a good evangelist; neglect not your vocation; labour like a blessed soldier of Christ. First, live godly and holily. Secondly, teach faithfully and truly. Thirdly, be an example to others in well doing, that you be not reprehended in your sayings: correct vice and set forth virtue. To evil livers threaten eternal punishment; but to those that be faithful and godly, set forth the comforts of eternal joy. Preach continually, but be short and fruitful, prudently understanding, and discreetly dispensing the holy scriptures. Never affirm or maintain those things that be uncertain and doubtful, lest that your adversaries take hold upon you, which rejoice in depraving their brethren, whereby they may bring the ministers of God into contempt. Exhort men to the confession of their faith, and to the communion of both kinds both of the body and blood of Christ, whereby such as do repent earnestly of their sins, may the more often come to the holy communion. And I warn you that you enter into no taverns with guests, and be not a common company-keeper. For the more a preacher keeps him from the company of men, the more he is regarded. However, deny not yet your help and diligence, wheresoever you may profit other. Against fleshly lust preach continually all that ever you can; for that is the raging beast, which devoureth men, for whom the flesh of Christ did suffer. Finally, howsoever you do, fear God and keep his precepts; so shall you walk wisely, and shall not perish; so shall you subdue the flesh, contemn the world, and overcome the devil; so shall you put on God, find life, and confirm others, and shall crown yourself with the crown of glory, the which the just Judge shall give you. Amen."

This letter of John Huss containeth a confession of the infirmity of man's flesh, how weak it is, and repugnant against the spirit. Wherein he also exhorteth to persevere constantly in the truth.

"Health be to you from Jesus Christ, &c. My dear friend, know that Paletz came to me to persuade me that I should not fear the shame of abjuration, but to consider the good which thereof will come. To whom I said that the shame of condemnation and burning is greater than to abjure.

"Almighty God shall confirm the hearts of his faithful, whom he hath chosen before the foundation of the world, that they may receive the eternal crown of glory. And let antichrist rage as much as he will, yet he shall not prevail against Christ, who shall destroy him with the spirit of his mouth, as the apostle saith; and then shall the creature be delivered out of the bondage of corruption, into the liberty of the glory of the sons of God, as saith the apostle in the words following. 'We also within ourselves do groan, waiting for the adoption, to wit, the redemption of our body.'

"I am greatly comforted in those words of our Saviour, 'Happy are you when men shall hate you, and shall separate you, and shall rebuke you, and shall cast out your name as evil, for the Son of man's sake: rejoice and be glad, for behold, great is your reward in heaven,' Luke vi. O worthy, yea, O most worthy consolation, which not to understand, but to practise in time of tribulation, is a hard lesson.

"This rule St. James, with the other apostles, did well understand, when he saith, 'Count it exceeding joy, my brethren, when ye shall fall into divers temptations, knowing that the trial of your faith worketh patience: let patience have her perfect work.' For certainly it is a great matter for a man to rejoice in trouble, and to take it for joy to be in divers temptations. A light matter it is to speak it and to expound it; but a great matter to fulfil it. For why? our most patient and most valiant champion himself, knowing that he should rise again the third day, overcoming his enemies by his death, and redeeming from damnation his elect, after his last supper, was troubled in spirit, and said, 'My soul is exceeding sorrowful, even unto death.' Of whom also the gospel saith, 'That he began to fear, to be sorrowful and very heavy.' Who being then in an agony, was confirmed of the angel, and his sweat was like drops of blood falling upon the ground. And yet he notwithstanding, being so troubled, said to his disciples, 'Let not your hearts be troubled, neither fear the cruelty of them that persecute you, for you shall have me with you always, that you may overcome the tyranny of your persecutors.' Whereupon those his soldiers, looking upon the Prince and King of Glory, sustained great conflicts. They passed through fire and water, and were saved, and received the crown of the Lord God, of which St. James in his canonical epistle, saith, 'Blessed is the man who suffereth temptation, for when he shall be proved, he shall receive the crown of life, which God hath promised to them that love him.' Of this crown I trust steadfastly the Lord will make me a partaker also with you, which be the fervent sealers of the truth, and with all them which steadfastly and constantly do love the Lord Jesus Christ, who suffered for us, leaving to us an example that we should follow his steps. 'It behoved him to suffer,' as he saith, and us also it behoveth to suffer, that the members may suffer together with the head. For he saith, 'If any man will come after me, let him deny himself, and take up his cross, and follow me.'

"O most merciful Christ! draw us weak creatures after thee, for except thou should draw us, we are not able to follow thee. Give us a strong spirit, that it may be ready, and although the flesh be feeble, yet let thy grace go before us, go with us, and follow us; for without thee we can do nothing, and much less enter into a cruel death for thy sake. Give us that prompt and ready spirit, a bold heart, an upright faith, a firm hope, and perfect charity, that we may give our lives patiently and joyfully for thy name's sake. Amen.

"Written in prison in bonds on the vigil of St. John the Baptist, who being in prison and in bonds for the rebuking of wickedness, was beheaded."

By the life, acts, and letters of John Huss hitherto rehearsed, it is evident and plain, that he was condemned not for any error of doctrine, for he neither denied their popish transubstantiation, neither spake against the authority of the church of Rome, if it were well governed, nor yet the seven sacraments, but said mass, himself, and in almost all their popish opinions was a papist with them; but only through evil will was accused by his malicious adversaries, because he spake against the pomp, pride, and avarice, and other wicked enormities of the pope, cardinals, and prelates of the church, and because he could not abide the high dignities and livings of the church, and thought the doings of the pope to be antichrist like. For this cause he procured so many enemies and false witnesses against him, who, straining and picking matter out of his books and writings, having no one just article of doctrine to lay unto him, yet they made him an heretic, whether he would or no, and brought him to his condemnation.

The tragical and lamentable history of the famous learned man and godly martyr of Christ, Master Jerome of Prague, burned at Constance for like cause and quarrel as Master John Huss was, A. D. 1416.

These things being discoursed, touching the life, acts, and constant martyrdom of Master John Huss, with part also of his letters, whose death was on the sixth of July, (A.D. 1415), it now remains to describe the like tragedy and cruel handling of his christian companion Master Jerome of Prague, who, grievously sorrowing for the slanderous reproach and defamation of his country of Bohemia, and also hearing of the manifest injuries done to that man of worthy memory, Master John Huss, freely and of his own accord came to Constance the fourth day of April, (A. D. 1415), and there perceiving that John Huss was denied to be heard, and that watch and wait was laid for him on every side, departed to Iberling, until the next day, which city was a mile from Constance, and from thence he wrote his letters to Sigismund, king of Hungary, and his barons, and also to the council, most earnestly requiring that the king and the council would give him a safe conduct freely to come and go, and that he would then come in open audience to answer to every man, if there were any of the council that would lay any crime to him, as by the tenor of his intimation shall more at large appear.

When the king of Hungary was required thereto, being in the house of the lord cardinal of Cambray, he refused to give Master Jerome any safe conduct, excusing himself for the evil speed he had with the safe conduct of John Huss before, and alleging also certain other causes. The deputies also of the four nations of the council being moved thereto by the lords of the king of Bohemia, answered: "We will give him a safe conduct to come, but not to depart." Whose answers, when they were reported to Master Jerome, he the next day after wrote certain intimations according to the tenor under written, which he sent to Constance to be set upon the gates of the city, and upon the gates of the churches and monasteries, and of the houses of the cardinals, and other nobles and prelates. The tenor whereof here follows word for word in this manner :—

"To the most noble prince and lord, the Lord Sigismund, by the grace of God, king of the Romans, always Augustus, and of Hungary, &c., I Jerome of Prague, master of arts of the general universities of Paris, Cologne, Heidelberg, and Prague, by these my present letters do notify to the king, together with the whole reverend council, and as much as in me lieth, do all men to understand and know, that because of the crafty slanderers, backbiters, and accusers, I am ready freely, and of mine own will, to come to Constance, there to declare openly before the council, the purity and sincerity of my true faith, and mine innocency, and not secretly in corners before any private or particular person. Wherefore, if there be any of my slanderers, of what nation or estate soever they be, who will object against me any crime of error or heresy; let them come forth openly before me in the presence of the whole council, and in their own names object against me, and I will be ready, as I have written, to answer openly and publicly before the whole council, of mine innocency, and to declare the purity and sincerity of my true faith. And if so be that I shall be found culpable in error or heresy, then I will not refuse openly to suffer such punishment as shall be meet and worthy for an erroneous person, or an heretic.

"Wherefore I most humbly beseech my lord the king, and the whole sacred council, that I may have to this end and purpose aforesaid, safe and sure access. And if it happen that I offering such equity and right as I do, before any fault be proved against me, be arrested, imprisoned, or have any violence done unto me; that then it may be manifest to the whole world, that this general council does not proceed according to equity and justice, if they would by any means put me back from this profound and straight justice, being come hither freely of mine own mind and accord, which thing I suppose to be far from so sacred and holy council of wise men."

When he could not get any safe conduct, then the nobles, lords, and knights, especially of the Bohemian nation, present in Constance, gave to Master Jerome their letters patents, confirmed with their seals for a testimony and witness of the premises. With which letters Master Jerome returned again unto Bohemia; but by the treason and conspiracy of his enemies he was taken in Hirsaw by the officers of Duke John, and brought back to the presence of the duke. In the meantime such as were the setters forward of the council against Master John Huss, and Master Jerome, that is to say, Michael de Causis, and Master Paletz, and other their accomplices, required that Master Jerome should be cited by reason of his intimations, and certain days after a citation was set upon the gates and porches of the city and churches.

After Sigismund, king of Hungary, with the rest of the council, understood that Master Jerome was taken, they were earnestly requiring that he should be brought before them to the council. The Duke John, after he had received letters of the king and the council, brought Master Jerome bound to Constance, whom his brother, Duke Lewis, led through the city to the cloisters of the friars minors in Constance, where the chief priests and elders of the people, Scribes and Pharisees, were gathered together, attending and waiting for his coming. Master Jerome carried a great hand-bolt of iron with a long chain in his hand; and as he passed, the chain made a great ratling and noise, and for the more confusion and despite towards him, they led him by the same chain after Duke Lewis, holding and stretching out the same a great way from him, with which chain they also kept him bound in the cloister. When he was brought into the cloister, they read before him the letter of Duke John unto the council, containing in effect how that the duke had sent Master Jerome, who by chance was fallen into his hands, because he heard an evil report of him, that he was suspected of heresies of Wickliff, that the council might take order for him, whose part it was to correct and punish such as did err and stray from the truth, besides many other flattering tales which were written in the said letter for the praise of the council. After this they read the citation which was given out by the council against Master Jerome. Then certain of the bishops said to him: "Jerome, why didst thou fly and run away, and not appear when thou wast cited?" He answered: "Because I could not have any safe conduct, neither from you, neither from the king, as it appears by these letters patents of the barons, which you have, neither by my open intimations could I obtain any safe conduct. Wherefore I, perceiving many of my grievous and heavy friends to be here present in the council, would not myself be the occasion of my perils and dangers; but if I had known or had any understanding of this citation, without all doubt, although I had been in Bohemia, I would have returned again." Then all the whole rabble rising up, alleged various accusations against him with a great noise and tumult. When the rest held their peace, then spake Master Gerson, the chancellor of Paris: "Jerome, when thou wast at Paris thou thoughtest thyself by means of thy eloquence to be an angel, and didst trouble the whole university, alleging openly in the schools many erroneous conclusions with their corollaries, and especially in the question *de universalibus et de Idæis*, with many other very offensive questions." To whom Master Jerome said: "I answer to you, Master Gerson; those matters which I did put forth there in the schools at Paris, in which also I answered the arguments of the Masters, I did put them forth philosophically, and as a philosopher, and master of the university; and if I have put forth any questions which I ought not to have put forth, teach me that they are erroneous, and I will most humbly be informed, and amend them."

While he was yet speaking, another, rising up, said: "When thou wast also at Cologne, in thy position which thou didst there determine, thou didst propound many erroneous matters." Then said Master Jerome unto him: "Shew me first one error which I propounded." Wherewithal he being in a manner atonished, said: "I do not remember them now at the first, but hereafter they shall be objected against you."

And by and by a third man rising up, said: "When you were also at Heidelberg, you propounded many erroneous matters as touching the trinity, and there painted out a certain shield or escutcheon comparing the trinity of persons in the divinity to water, snow, and ice, and such like." Unto whom Master Jerome answered: "Those things that I wrote or painted there, the same will I also speak, write, and paint here; and teach me that they be erroneous, and I will most humbly revoke and recant the same."

Then certain cried out: "Let him be burned, let him be burned." To whom he answered: "If my death do delight or please you, in the name of God let it be so."

Then said the archbishop of Saltzburg: "Not so, Master Jerome, forsomuch as it is written, I will not the death of a sinner, but rather that he be converted and live."

When these and many other tumults and cries were passed, whereby they most disorderly and outrageously witnessed against him, they delivered him bound to the officers of the city of Constance, to be carried to prison for that night: and so every one of them returned to their lodgings.

In meantime, one of the friends of Master John Huss, looking out at a window of the cloister, said unto him: "Master Jerome." Then said he: "You are welcome, my dear brother." Then said Peter to him: "Be constant and fear not to suffer death for the truth sake, of which, when you were in times past at liberty, you did preach so much and so well." Jerome answered: "Truly brother I do not fear death, and as we know that we have spoken much thereof in times past; let us now see what may be known or done in effect." By and by his keepers coming to the window, threatening him with blows, put away Peter from the window of the cloister.

Then came there one Vitus to Master Jerome, and said: "Master, how do you do?" He answered,

"Truly brother, I do very well." Then his keepers coming about him laid hold of Vitus, saying: "This is also one of the number," and kept him. When it drew towards evening, the archbishop of Riegen sent his servants, who led away Master Jerome, being strongly bound with chains, both by the hands and by the neck, and kept him so for some hours. When night drew on, they carried him to a tower of the city, where, tying him fast to a great block, and his feet in the stocks, his hands also being made fast, they left him; the block was so high, that he could by no means sit upon it, so that his head must hang downward. They carried also Vitus to the archbishop of Riegen, who demanded of him, "Why he durst be so bold to talk with such a man, being a reprobate of all men, and an heretic;" and when he could find no cause of imprisonment in him, and that he said he was Master John de Clum's friend (taking an oath and promise of him, that he should not go about to endamage the council by reason of that imprisonment and captivity) he so dismissed him.

Master Jerome, unknown to his friends whither he was carried, lay in the tower two days and two nights, relieved only with bread and water. Then one of his keepers, coming to Master Peter, declared to him how Master Jerome lay hard by in bonds and chains, and how he was fed. Then Master Peter desired that he might have leave given him to give him meat, because he would procure the same for him. The keeper of the prison, granting his request, carried meat to him. Within eleven days after, so hanging by the heels, he used so small repast, that he fell sore sick even to death. When living in that captivity and prison, he desired to have a confessor; the council denied that he should have any, until such time as by great importunity he obtained one; his friends being then present in the prison and tower, wherein he lay by the space of one year, lacking but seven days.

After they had put John Huss to death, then about the feast of the nativity of the Virgin Mary, they brought forth Master Jerome, whom they had kept so long in chains; and threatening him with death, being instant upon him, they forced him to abjure and recant, and consent to the death of Master John Huss, that he was justly and truly condemned and put to death by them. He, for fear of death, and hoping thereby to escape out of their hands, according to their will and pleasure, and according to the tenor which was exhibited to him, did make abjuration, and that in the cathedral church and open session, the draught whereof penned to him by the papists, here ensues:

The abjuration of Master Jerome of Prague.

"I, Jerome of Prague, master of arts, acknowledging the catholic church, and the apostolic faith, do accurse and renounce all heresies, and especially that whereof I have hitherto been infamed, and that which in times past John Huss and John Wickliff have holden and taught in their works, treatises, and sermons, made unto the people and clergy; for the which cause the said Wickliff and Huss, together with the said doctrines and errors, are condemned by this synod of Constance as heretics, and all the said doctrine sententially condemned, and especially in certain articles expressed in the sentences and judgments given against them by this sacred council.

"Also I do accord and agree unto the holy church of Rome, the apostolic seat in this sacred council, and with my mouth and heart do profess in all things, and touching all things, and especially as touching the keys, sacraments, orders, and offices, and ecclesiastical censures, of pardons, relics of saints, ecclesiastical liberty, also ceremonies, and all other things pertaining unto the christian religion, as the church of Rome, the apostolic see, and this sacred council do profess: and especially that many of the said articles are notoriously heretical, and lately reproved by the holy fathers, some of them blasphemous, some others erroneous; some offensive unto godly ears, and many of them temerarious and seditious. And such also were counted the articles lately condemned by the sacred council, and it was inhibited and forbidden to all and singular catholic men hereafter to preach, teach, or presume to hold or maintain any of the said articles, under pain of being accursed.

"And I the said Jerome, forsomuch as I have laboured by scholastical arts to persuade the opinion, *de universalibus realibus*, and that one substance of the common kind should signify many things subject under the same, and every one of them, as St. Ambrose, Jerome, Augustine, do affirm, and likewise others; for the teaching hereof by a plain example I described as it were a certain triangle, form, or figure, the which I called the shield of faith.

"Therefore utterly to exclude and take away the erroneous and wicked understanding thereof, the which peradventure some men may gather thereby, I do say, affirm, and declare that I never made the said figure, neither named it the shield of faith to that intent or purpose, that I would extol or prefer the opinion of universalities above or before the contrary opinion, in such sort, as though that were the shield of faith, and that without the affirmation thereof the catholic faith could not be defended or maintained, when as I myself would not obstinately stick thereunto. But this I said, because I had put example in the description of the triangle or form, that one divine essence consisted in three subjects or persons in themselves distinct, that is to say, the Father, the Son, and the Holy Ghost. The article of the which Trinity is the chief shield of faith, and foundation of the catholic truth.

"Furthermore, that it may be evident unto all men what the causes were for which I was reputed and thought to stick to, and favour sometime John Huss, I signify unto all men by these presents, that when I heard him oftentimes both in his sermons, and also in the schools, I believed that he was a very good man, neither that he did in any point gainsay the traditions of our holy mother the church, or holy doctors; insomuch as when I was lately in this city, and the articles which I affirmed were shewed unto me, which were also condemned by the sacred council, at the first sight of them I did not believe that they were his, at the least not in that form. But when as I had further understood, by certain famous doctors and masters of divinity, that they were his articles, I required for my further information and satisfaction to have the books of his own handwriting shewed unto me, wherein it was said these articles were contained, which books when they were showed unto me written with his own hand, which I did know as well as mine own, I found all, and every one of those articles therein written in like form as they are condemned. Wherefore I do worthily judge and think him and his doctrine, with his adherents, to be condemned and reproved by the sacred council as heretical and without reason. All which the premises, with a pure mind and conscience, I do here pronounce and speak, being now fully and sufficiently informed of the foresaid sentences and judgments, given by the sacred council against the doctrines of the said John Wickliff, and John Huss, and against their own persons, unto the which judgment, as a devout catholic in all things, I do most humbly consent and agree.

"Also I the foresaid Jerome, who before the reverend fathers the lords cardinals, and reverend lords, prelates, and doctors, and other worshipful persons of this sacred council in this same place, did heretofore freely and willingly declare and expound mine intent and purpose amongst other things, speaking of the church, did divide the same into three parts. And as I perceived afterwards, it was understood by some that I would affirm, that in the triumphant church there was faith, whereas I do firmly believe that there is the blessed sight and beholding of God, excluding all dark understanding and knowledge, and now also I say, affirm, and declare, that it was never my intent and purpose to prove that there should be faith, speaking of faith as faith is commonly defined, but knowledge far exceeding faith. And generally whatsoever I said, either there, or at any time before, I do refer, and most humbly submit myself unto the determination of this sacred council of Constance.

"Moreover, I do swear both by the Holy Trinity,

and also by the most holy gospel, that I will for evermore remain and persevere without all doubt in the truth of the catholic church; and all such as by their doctrine and teaching shall impugn this faith, I judge them worthy together with their doctrines of eternal curse. And if I by myself at any time (which God forbid I should) do presume to preach or teach contrary thereunto, I will submit myself unto the severity of the canons, and be bound unto eternal pain and punishment. Whereupon I do deliver up this my confession and tenour of my profession willingly before this sacred general council, and have subscribed and written all these things with mine own hand."

After all this they caused him to be carried again to the same prison, but not so straightly chained and bound as he was before, notwithstanding kept every day with soldiers and armed men; and when his enemies understood and knew by the words and talk of Master Jerome, and by other certain tokens, that he made the same abjuration and recantation, not of a sincere and pure mind, but only to escape their hands, they put up new accusations against Master Jerome, and drew the same into articles, being very instant and earnest that he should answer thereunto; and as his judges, and certain cardinals, as the cardinal of Cambray, the cardinal de Ursinis, the cardinal of Aquilegia, and of Florence, considering the malice of the enemies of Master Jerome, saw the great injury that was done to him, they laboured before the whole council for his delivery.

It happened upon a certain day, as they were labouring in the council for the delivery of the said Master Jerome, that his enemies with all force and power resisted against it, crying out that he should in no case be dismissed. Then started up one called Doctor Naso, who said unto the cardinals, "We marvel much of you, most reverend fathers, that your reverences will make intercession for such a wicked heretic, for whose sake we in Bohemia, with the whole clergy, have suffered much trouble and mischief, and peradventure your fatherhoods shall suffer; and I greatly fear, lest that you have received some rewards either of the king of Bohemia, or of these heretics." When the cardinals were thus rebuked, they discharged themselves of Master Jerome's cause and matter.

Then his enemies obtained to have other judges appointed, as the patriarch of Constantinople, and a German doctor, as they did know that the patriarch was a grievous enemy to Master Jerome, because he being before appointed judge by the council, had condemned John Huss to death.

But Master Jerome would not answer them in prison, requiring to have open audience, because he would there finally declare to them his mind, neither would he by any means consent to those private judges. Whereupon the presidents of the council, thinking that Master Jerome would renew his recantation before the audience, and confirm the same, did grant him open audience.

In the year A.D. 1416, the twenty-fifth day of May, Master Jerome was brought to open audience before the whole council, in the great cathedral church of Constance, where the commissioners of the council laid against him a hundred and seven articles, to the intent that he should not escape the snare of death, which they provided and laid for him. He answered to more than forty articles most subtlely objected against him; denying that he held or maintained any such articles as were either hurtful or false, and affirming that those witnesses had deposed them against him falsely and slanderously, as his most cruel and mortal enemies. In the same session they had not yet proceeded to death, because that the noon-time drew so fast on, that he could not answer to the articles. Wherefore, for lack of time sufficient to answer to the residue of the articles, there was another time appointed, at which time again early in the morning he was brought to the cathedral church to answer to all the residue of the articles.

In all which articles, as well those which he had answered before, as in the residue, he cleared himself very learnedly, refuting his adversaries in such a way that they were themselves astonished at his oration, and the refutation of their testimonies against him, and with shame enough were put to silence. As when one of them had demanded of him what he thought of the sacrament of the altar, he answered, " Before consecration," said he, " it is bread and wine; after the consecration it is the true body and blood of Christ," adding more words according to their catholic faith. Then another rising up, " Jerome," said he, " there goes a great rumour of thee, that thou dost hold bread to remain upon the altar." To whom he pleasantly answered, saying, " That he believed bread to be at the baker's." At which words one of the Dominican friars rose angrily, and said, " What! dost thou deny, that which no man doubts?" His peevish sauciness Jerome with these words did well repress, " Hold thy peace, thou monk, thou hypocrite!" And thus the monk being nipped in the head, sat down dumb. After whom started up another, who with a loud voice cried out, " I swear, by my conscience, that to be true which thou dost deny." To whom Jerome replied, " Thus to swear by your conscience is the next way to deceive." Another there was, a spiteful and a bitter enemy of his, whom he called by no other name than dog, or ass. After he had thus refuted them one after another, that they could find no crime against him, neither in this matter, nor in any other, they were all driven to keep silence.

Then the witnesses were called, who coming gave testimony to the articles before produced. By reason whereof the innocent cause of Jerome was oppressed, and began to be concluded in the council. Then Jerome rising up began to speak, " Forsomuch," said he, " as you have heard mine adversaries so diligently, it is convenient that you should also now hear me speak for myself." Whereupon, with much difficulty, at last audience was given in the council for him to say his mind. Which being granted, he continued from morning to noon, treating of many matters, with great learning and eloquence. Who first beginning with his prayer to God, besought him to give him spirit, ability, and utterance, which might both tend to the profit and salvation of his own soul; and then began his oration as follows:—

" I know," said he " reverend lords, that there have been many excellent men, who have suffered much otherwise than they have deserved, being oppressed with false witnesses, and condemned with wrong judgments." And so beginning with Socrates, he declared how he was unjustly condemned of his countrymen, neither would he escape when he might; taking from us the fear of two things, which seem most bitter to men, to wit, imprisonment and death. Then he inferred the captivity of Plato, the banishment of Anaxagoras, and the torments of Zeno. Moreover, he brought in the wrongful condemnation of many Gentiles, as the banishment of Rupilius, reciting also the unworthy death of Boetius, and of others whom Boetius himself writes of.

From thence he came to the examples of the Hebrews, and first began with Moses the deliverer of the people, and the lawgiver, how he was oftentimes slandered of his people as being a seducer and contemner of the people. Joseph also for envy was sold of his brethren, and for false suspicion of crime was cast into bonds. Besides these, were Isaiah, Daniel, and almost all the prophets, who as contemners of God, and seditious persons, were oppressed with wrongful condemnation. From thence he proceeded to the judgment of Susanna, and of divers other besides, who being good and holy, were yet unjustly cast away with wrongful sentence. At length he came to John Baptist, and so in long process he descended to our Saviour, declaring how it was evident to all men, by what false witnesses both he and John Baptist were condemned. Moreover, how Stephen was slain by the college of the priests, and how all the apostles were condemned to death, not as good men, but as seditious stirrers up of the people, and contemners of the gods, and evil doers. It is unjust, said he, to be unjustly condemned one priest by another, and yet he proved that the same so happened most unjustly in that council of priests. These things did he discourse at large, with marvellous eloquence, and with singular admiration of all that heard him.

And forasmuch as all the whole sum of the cause did rest only in the witnesses, by many reasons he proved that no credit was to be given to them, especially seeing they spake all things of no truth, but only of hatred, malice, and envy. And so prosecuting the matter, so lively and expressly he opened to them the causes of their hatred, that he had almost persuaded them. In so lively and likely a way was their hatred detected, that almost no credit was given to their testimonies, save only for the cause and quarrel wherein they stood touching the pope's doctrine. All men's minds were moved and bending to mercy toward him; for he told them how that he of his own accord came up to the council, and to purge himself he did open to them all his life and doings, being full of virtue and godliness. This was (said he) the old manner of ancient and learned men, and most holy elders, that in matters of faith, they differed many times in arguments, not to destroy the faith, but to find out the truth. So did Augustine and Jerome dissent one from the other, and yet without any suspicion of heresy.

All this while the pope's holy council waited, still expecting when he would begin to excuse himself, and retract those things which were objected against him, and to crave pardon of the council; but he persisting still in his constant oration, did acknowledge no error, nor gave any signification of retractation.

At last entering to the praise and commendation of Master John Huss, he affirmed that he was a good, just, and holy man, and much unworthy that death which he suffered. He knew him from his youth upward to be neither immoral, a drunkard, nor any evil or vicious person, but a chaste and sober man, and a just and true preacher of the holy gospel; and whatever things Master John Huss and Wickliff had holden or written, specially against the abuse and pomp of the clergy, he would affirm even to the death, that they were holy and blessed men, and that in all points of the catholic faith he believes as the holy catholic church holds or believes. And finally, he concluded, that all such articles as John Wickliff and John Huss had written and put forth against the enormities, pomp, and disorder of the prelates, he would firmly and steadfastly, without recantation, hold and defend even to the death. And last of all he added, that all the sins that he had ever committed, did not so much gnaw and trouble his conscience, as did that only sin which he had committed in that most pestiferous act, when in his recantation he had unjustly spoken against that good and holy man and his doctrine, and specially in consenting to his wicked condemnation, concluding that he did utterly revoke and deny that wicked recantation which he made in that most cursed place, and that he did it through weakness of heart and fear of death. And, moreover, that whatever he had spoken against that blessed man, he had altogether lied upon him, and that he repented with his whole heart that he ever did it.

At the hearing hereof the hearts of the hearers were not a little sorry. For they wished and desired greatly that such a singular man should be saved, if otherwise their blind superstition would have suffered it. But he continued still in his opinion, seeming to desire rather death than life. And persisting in the praise of John Huss, he added moreover, that he never maintained any doctrine against the state of the church, but only spake against the abuses of the clergy, against the pride, pomp, and excess of the prelates. For as the patrimonies of the churches were first given for the poor, then for hospitality, and thirdly to the reparations of the churches; it was a grief to that good man (said he) to see the same mispent and cast away upon great feastings, and keeping of horses and dogs, upon gorgeous apparel, and such other things unbeseeming the christian religion. And herein he shewed himself marvellous eloquent; yea, never more.

And when his oration was interrupted many times by

several of them, carping at his sentences as he was in speaking, yet was there none of all those that interrupted him who escaped unscathed, but he brought them all to confusion, and put them to silence. When any noise began, he ceased to speak, and after began again, proceeding in his oration, and desiring them to give him leave a while to speak, whom they hereafter should hear no more, nor was his mind ever dashed at all these noises and tumults.

And this was marvellous to behold in him, notwithstanding he continued in prison three hundred and forty days, having neither book, nor almost light to read by, yet how admirably his memory served him; declaring how all those pains of his straight handling did not so much grieve him, as he did wonder rather to see their unkind humanity towards him.

When he had spoken these and many things as touching the praise of John Wickliff and John Huss, they who sat in the council whispered together, saying, by these his words it appears that he is resolved with himself. Then was he again carried into prison, and grievously fettered by the hands, arms, and feet, with great chains and fetters of iron.

The Saturday next before the ascension-day, early in the morning, he was brought with a great number of armed men to the cathedral church before the open congregation, to have his judgment given him. There they exhorted him that those things which he had before spoken in the open audience, as is aforesaid touching the praise and commendation of master John Wickliff, and master John Huss, confirming and establishing their doctrine, he would yet recant: but he marvellous stoutly without all fear spake against them, and among other things said to them, "I take God to my witness, and I protest here before you all, that I do believe and hold the articles of the faith, as the holy catholic church does hold and believe the same; but for this cause shall I now be condemned, because I will not consent with you to the condemnation of those most holy and blessed men, whom you have most wickedly condemned for certain articles, detesting and abhorring your wicked and abominable life." Then he confessed there before them all his belief, and uttered many things very profoundly and eloquently, insomuch that all men there present could not sufficiently commend and praise his great eloquence and excellent learning, and by no means could they induce or persuade him to recant.

Then a certain bishop, named the Bishop of Londy, made a certain sermon against Master Jerome, persuading them to condemn him.

After the bishop had ended the sermon, Master Jerome said again unto them, "You will condemn me wickedly and unjustly. But I after my death will leave a remorse in your conscience, and a nail in your hearts. And here I cite you to answer unto me before the most high and just Judge, within a hundred years."

No pen can sufficiently write, or note those things which he most eloquently, profoundly, and philosophically had spoken in the said audience, neither can any tongue sufficiently declare the same; wherefore I have but only touched here the superficial matter of his talk, partly and not wholly noting the same. Finally, when they could by no means persuade him to recant the premises, immediately even in his presence, the sentence and judgment of his condemnation was given against him, and read before him.

Sentence.

"In the name of God, Amen. Christ our God, and our Saviour being the true vine, whose Father is the husbandman, taught his disciples, and all other faithful men, saying, 'If any man abide not in me, let him be cast out as a bough or branch, and let him wither and dry,' &c. The doctrine and precepts of which most excellent doctor and master, this most sacred synod of Constance executing and following in the cause of inquisition against heretics, being moved by this sacred synod, through report, public fame, and open infamation, proceeding against Jerome of Prague, master of arts, lay-man. By the acts and processes of whose cause it appeareth that the said Master Jerome hath holden, maintained, and taught divers articles heretical and erroneous, lately reproved and condemned by the holy fathers, some being very blasphemous, other some offending godly ears, and many temerarious and seditious, which have been affirmed, maintained, preached and taught by the men of the most damnable memory, John Wickliff and John Huss, the which are also written in many of their works and books. Which articles of doctrine and books of the said John Huss, and John Wickliff, together with their memory, and the person of the said John Huss, were by the said sacred synod condemned of heresy. Which sentence of condemnation this Jerome afterwards during the time of inquisition, acknowledged in the said sacred synod, and approved the true catholic and apostolic faith, thereunto consenting, accursing all heresy, especially that whereof he was infamed, and confessed himself to be infamed, and that which in times past John Huss and John Wickliff maintained and taught in their works, sermons, and books, for which the said Wickliff and Huss, together with their doctrine and errors, were by the said sacred synod condemned as heretical. The condemnation of all which premises he did openly profess and allow, and did swear that he would persevere and continue in the verity of that faith. And if that he should presume at any time to hold opinion, or preach contrary thereunto, that he would submit himself to the trial and truth of the canons, and be bound to perpetual punishment. And this his profession written with his own hand, he delivered up unto the holy council. Not many days after his said profession and abjuration, as a dog returning unto his vomit, to the intent he might openly vomit up the most pestilent poison which had long lurked and lain hid in his breast, he required and desired that he might be openly heard before the council. The which being granted unto him, he affirmed, said, and professed before the whole synod, being publicly gathered together, that he had wickedly consented and agreed to the sentence and judgment of the condemnation of the said Wickliff and Huss, and that he had most shamefully lied in approving and allowing the said sentence, neither was he ashamed to confess that he had lied; yea, he did also revoke and recant his confession, approbation, and protestation, which he had made upon their condemnation, affirming that he never at any time had read any errors or heresy in the books and treatises of the said Wickliff and Huss. Although he had before confessed it, and it is evidently proved, that he did diligently study, read, and preach their books, wherein it is manifest that there are contained many errors and heresies. Also the said Master Jerome did profess as touching the sacrament of the altar and the transubstantiation of the bread into the body of Christ, that he doth hold and believe as the church doth hold and believe, saying also that he doth give more credit unto St. Augustine, and the other doctors of the church, than unto Wickliff and Huss. It appeareth moreover, by the premises, that the said Jerome is an adherent and maintainer of the said Wickliff and Huss, and their errors, and both is, and has been a favourer of them. Wherefore the said sacred synod determineth the said Master Jerome as a rotten and withered branch, not growing upon the vine, to be cut off and cast out. The said synod also pronounceth, declareth and condemneth him as an heretic and drowned in all kind of heresies, excommunicate and accursed, leaving him unto the sentence and judgment of the secular judge, to receive just and due punishment, according to the quality of so great an offence; the sacred synod notwithstanding, entreating that the said judge would moderate his sentence of judgment without peril of death."

Which sentence so given before his face, being ended, a great and long mitre of paper was brought unto him, painted about with red devils, which when he beheld and saw, throwing away his hood upon the ground amongst the prelates, he took the mitre and put it upon his head, saying, "Our Lord Jesus Christ, when he should suffer death for me most wretched sinner, did wear a crown of thorns upon his head; and I for his sake instead of that crown, will willingly wear this mitre and cap." Afterwards he was laid hold of by the secular power.

After that he was led out of the said church to the place of execution; when he was going out of the church, with a cheerful countenance and loud voice lifting his eyes up unto heaven, he began to sing, "I believe in one God," &c., as it is accustomed to be sung in the church. Afterward as he passed along, he sung some canticles of the church; which being ended, in the entering out of the gate of the city, as men go to Gothlehem, he sung this hymn, *Felix namque*. After that he came to the place of execution where Master John Huss before had innocently suffered death, and kneeling down before an image which was like to the picture of Master John Huss, which was there prepared to burn Master Jerome, he made a certain devout prayer.

While he was thus praying, the tormentors took him up, and lifting him up from the ground, spoiled him of all his garments, and left him naked, and afterwards girded him about the loins with a linen cloth, and bound him fast with cords and chains of iron, to the image which was made fast unto the earth; and so standing upon the ground, when as they began to lay the wood about him, he sung *Salve festa dies*. And when the hymn was ended, he sung again with a loud voice, "I believe in one God," unto the end. That being ended, he said unto the people in the German tongue, in effect as follows. "Dearly beloved children, even as I have now sung, so do I believe, and none otherwise. And this creed is my whole faith, notwithstanding now I die for this cause, because I would not consent and agree to the council, and with them affirm and hold that Master John Huss was by them holily and justly condemned; for I did know well enough that he was a true preacher of the gospel of Jesus Christ."

After that he was compassed in with the wood up to the crown of the head, they cast all his garments upon the wood also, and with a fire-brand they set it on fire; which being once fired, he began to sing with a loud voice, "Into thy hands, O Lord, I commend my spirit." When that was ended, and that he began vehemently to burn, he said in the vulgar Bohemian tongue, "O Lord God, Father Almighty have mercy upon me, and be merciful unto mine offences, for thou knowest how sincerely I have loved thy truth." Then his voice by the vehemency of the fire was choked and stopped, that it was no longer heard, but he moved continually his mouth and lips, as though he had still prayed or spoken within himself.

When his whole body with his beard was so burned round about, that there appeared through the great burning upon his body certain great blisters as big as an egg, yet he continually very strongly and stoutly moved, and shaked his head and mouth, by the space almost of one quarter of an hour. So burning in the fire, he lived with great pain and martyrdom, while one might easily have gone from St. Clement's over the bridge to our lady church. After he was thus dead in the fire, by and by they brought his bedding, his straw bed, his boots, his hood, and all other things that he had in the prison, and burned them all to ashes in the same fire. Which ashes, after that the fire was out, they diligently gathered together, and carried them in a cart, and cast them into the river Rhone, which ran hard by the city.

That man who was the true reporter hereof, and which testified to us the acts and doings about the condemnation of Master Jerome, and sent the same to us to Prague in writing, thus concludes. "All these things," said he, "I did behold, see, and hear to be done in this form and manner. And if any man do tell you the contrary, do not credit him; for all those things which happened unto him when he came toward Constance, and also at his first coming unto Constance of his own free will, and afterward when he was brought bound unto Constance, as is aforesaid, I myself did see and perfectly behold, and for a perpetual memory thereof to be had

for ever, I have directed the same unto you, not lying or falsifying any point thereof, as he which is the Searcher of all men's hearts can bear me witness, willing rather to sustain the charge of ignorance and rudeness of style, to bear witness to the truth, than I would by any means be compelled by tickling, or flattering the ears of the hearers with feigned and cloaked speech, to swerve or go aside from the truth."

Thus end the tragical histories of Master John Huss, and Master Jerome of Prague, faithfully gathered and collected by a certain Bohemian, being a present eye-witness and beholder of the same, written and compiled first in Latin, and sent by the said Bohemian into his country of Bohemia, and again translated out of the Latin with like fidelity into our English tongue.

In the mean time, while Master Jerome was in this trouble, and before the council, the nobles and lords of Bohemia and of Moravia directed their letters to this barbarous council of popish murderers: in tenor and form of words as followeth.

The Letter of the fifty-four Nobles of Moravia, written unto the Council of Constance in the defence of Master John Huss and Jerome of Prague.

"To the right reverend fathers and lords in Christ, the lords cardinals, patriarchs, primates, archbishops, bishops, ambassadors, doctors, and masters, and to the whole council of Constance, We, the nobles, lords, knights, and esquires, of the famous marquisdom of Moravia, wish the desire of all goodness, and the observation of the commandments of our Lord Jesus Christ.

"Forsomuch as every man, both by the law of nature and also by God's law, is commanded to do that unto another man, which he would have done unto himself, and is forbidden to do that thing unto another, which he would not have done unto himself, as our Saviour saith, 'All things whatsoever ye would that men should do to you, do ye even so to them: for this is the law and the prophets.' Yea, the law is fulfilled in this one point, 'Thou shalt love thy neighbour as thyself:' We, therefore, (God being our author), having respect as much as in us lieth unto the said law of God, and the love of our neighbour, did before send our letters unto Constance for our dearly beloved friend of good memory, Master John Huss, bachelor of divinity, and preacher of the gospel. Whom of late in the council of Constance (we know not with what spirit being led) you have condemned as an obstinate heretic; neither having confessed any thing, neither being lawfully convicted as was expedient; having no errors or heresies declared or laid against him, but only at the sinister, false, and importune accusations, suggestions, and instigations of his mortal enemies, and the traitors of our kingdom and marquisdom of Moravia. And being thus unmercifully condemned, you have slain him with most shameful and cruel death, to the perpetual shame and infamy of our most christian kingdom of Bohemia, and the famous marquisdom of Moravia (as we have written unto Constance, unto the most noble prince and lord, the Lord Sigismund, king of the Romans, and of Hungary, the heir and successor of our kingdom) which was also read and published in your congregations, which we will here also have enrolled; and have burned him, as it is reported, in reproach and contempt of us.

"Wherefore, we have thought good even now to direct our letters patent to your reverences now present in the behalf of Master John Huss, openly professing and protesting, both with heart and mouth, that he, the said Master John Huss, was a just, good, and catholic man, and for a long season worthily commended and allowed in our kingdom for his life and conversation. He also preached and taught us and our subjects the law of the gospel, and of the holy prophets, and the books of the Old and New Testament, according to the exposition of the holy doctors approved by the church, and left many monuments in writing, most constantly detesting and abhorring all errors and heresies, continually admonishing both us and all faithful christians to do the like, diligently exhorting all men as much as in him lay, by his words, writings, and labours, unto quietness and concord; so that using all the diligence that we might, we never heard or could understand, that Master John Huss had preached, taught, or by any means affirmed any error or heresy in his sermons, or that by any manner of means he had offended us, or our subjects, either by word or deed, but that he always led a quiet and a godly life in Christ, exhorting all men diligently, both by his word and works, as much as he might, to observe and keep the law of the gospel, and the institutions of the holy fathers, after the preaching of our holy mother the church, and to the edifying of men's souls. Neither did these premises which you had so perpetrated to the reproach both of us and our kingdom and marquisdom, suffice and content you, but that also without all mercy and pity you have apprehended, imprisoned, and condemned, and even now, peradventure, like as you did Master John Huss, you have most cruelly murdered the worshipful man, Master Jerome of Prague, a man abounding in eloquence, master of the seven liberal arts, and a famous philosopher, not being seen, heard, examined, neither convicted, but only at the sinister and false accusations of his and our accusers and betrayers.

" Furthermore, it is come to our knowledge and understanding (which we do not without great grief rehearse) as we may also evidently gather by your writings, how that certain detractors, odious both to God and men, privy enviers and betrayers, have wickedly and grievously, although falsely and traitorously, accused us, our kingdom and marquisdom aforesaid, before you in your council, that in the said kingdom of Bohemia, and marquisdom of Moravia, divers errors are sprung up, which have grievously and manifoldly infected both our hearts, and also the hearts of many faithful men; insomuch that without a speedy stop or stay of correction, the said kingdom and marquisdom, together with the faithful christians therein, should incur an irreparable loss and ruin of their souls.

" These cruel and pernicious injuries which are laid to us, and to our said kingdom and marquisdom, although most falsely and slanderously, how may we suffer? Forsomuch as through the grace of God (when in a manner all other kingdoms of the world have oftentimes wavered, making schisms and antipopes) our most gracious kingdom of Bohemia, and most noble marquisdom of Moravia, since the time they did receive the catholic faith of our Lord Jesus Christ, have always without reproof stuck constantly to the church of Rome, and have sincerely done their true obedience. Also with how great costs and charges, and great labour, with what worship and due reverence they have reverenced the holy mother the church and her pastors, by their princes and faithful subjects, is more manifest than the day-light to the whole world; and yourselves, if you will confess the truth, can witness the same also.

" Wherefore, that we, according to the mind of the apostle, may procure honest and good things, not only before God, but before men also, and lest by neglecting the famous renown of the kingdom and marquisdom, we be found cruel toward our neighbours; having a steadfast hope, a pure and sincere conscience and intent, and a certain true faith in Christ Jesus our Lord, by the tenour of these we signify and declare unto your fatherhoods, and to all faithful christians, openly professing both with heart and mouth, that whatsoever man, of what estate, pre-eminence, dignity, condition, degree, or religion, soever he be, who hath said, or affirmed, either doth say or affirm, that in the said kingdom of Bohemia, and marquisdom of Moravia, heresies have sprung up which have infected us and other faithful christians, as is aforesaid (the only person of our most noble prince and lord, Sigismund, king of Romans, and of Hungary, &c. our Lord and heir successor, being set apart, whom we trust and believe, not to be guilty in the premises) all and every such man (as is aforesaid) doth lie falsely upon his head, as a wicked and naughty

traitor and betrayer of the said kingdom and marquisdom, and most traitorous to us, and most pernicious heretic, the son of all malice and wickedness, yea, and of the devil himself, who is a liar, and the father of all lies.

" Notwithstanding, we for this present committing the foresaid injuries unto God, unto whom vengeance pertaineth, who will also abundantly reward the workers of iniquity, will prosecute them more amply before him, whom God shall appoint in the apostolic see, to govern his holy church, as the only and undoubted pastor. Unto whom, God willing, we exhibiting our due reverence and obedience as faithful children, in those things which are lawful, honest, and agreeable to reason and the law of God, will make our request and petition, that speedy remedy may be provided for us, our said kingdom and marquisdom upon the premises, according to the law of our Lord Jesus Christ, and the institutions of the holy fathers. The premises, notwithstanding, we setting apart all fear and men's ordinances provided to the contrary, will maintain and defend the law of our Lord Jesus Christ, and the devout, humble, and constant preachers thereof, even to the shedding of our blood.

" Dated at Sternberg, in A. D. 1415, upon St. Wenceslaus' day, martyr of our Lord Jesus Christ.''

Round about these letters there were fifty-four seals hanging, and the names of those noblemen subscribed, whose seals they were.

After these things, concerning the history of John Huss and Jerome of Prague, the order of time calls me back to other matters here of our own country, which passed in the mean time with us in England. Which things being finished, we will (Christ willing) afterward return to the troubles and conflicts of the Bohemians, with other things besides, pertaining to the later end of the council of Constance, and election of Pope Martin.

Ye heard before, how after the death of Thomas Arundel, archbishop of Canterbury, succeeded Henry Chichesley, (A. D. 1414,) and sat twenty-five years. In whose time was much trouble and great affliction of good men here in England; of whom many were compelled to abjure, some were burned, several were driven to exile. Whereof, partly now to treat, as we find them in registers and histories recorded, we will first begin with John Claydon of London, and Richard Turming. The history of which John Claydon in the registers is thus declared.

The History of John Claydon, Currier; and of Richard Turming, Baker.

The 17th of August, 1415, did personally appear John Claydon, currier of London (arrested by the mayor of the city for the suspicion of heresy) before Henry, archbishop of Canterbury, in St. Paul's church; which John (it being objected to him by the archbishop, that in the city of London, and other places of the province of Canterbury, he was suspected by divers godly and learned men of heresy, and to be contrary to the catholic faith and determination of the church) did openly confess, and denied not, but that he had been for the space of twenty years suspected both about the city of London, and also in the province of Canterbury, and especially by the common sort, of the opinions of the Lollards and heresy, and to be contrary to the catholic faith and determination of the church of Rome, and defamed of the same all the time aforesaid.

Insomuch, that in the time of Master Robert Braybrook, bishop of London, deceased, he was for the space of two years, committed to the prison of Conway for the foresaid defamation and suspicion, and for the same cause also he was in prison in the Fleet for three years. Out of which prison he (in the reign of King Henry IV.) was brought before the Lord John Scarle, then chancellor to the king, and there did abjure all heresy and error. And the said John Claydon being asked of the said archbishop whether he did abjure the

Y

heresy of which he was suspected before any other? did confess, that in a convocation at London, in St. Paul's church, before Thomas Arundel, late archbishop, deceased, he did abjure all such doctrine, which they called heresy and error, contrary to the catholic faith and determination of the church, and that he had not only left such articles and opinions, wherein he was defamed, but also did abstain from all company that were suspected of such opinions, so that he should neither give aid, help, counsel, nor favour unto them.

And, moreover, the said John was asked by the said archbishop, whether he had ever since his abjuration had in his house or in his keeping, any books written in English. Whereunto he confessed, that he would not deny, but that he had in his house, and in his keeping, many English books; for he was arrested by the mayor of the city of London for such books as he had, which books (as he thought) were in the mayor's keeping. Upon the which the mayor did openly confess, that he had such books in his keeping, which in his judgment were the worst, and the most perverse that ever he did read or see, and one book that was well bound in red leather, of parchment, written in a good English hand; and among the other books found with the said John Claydon, the mayor gave up the said book before the archbishop. Whereupon the said John Claydon, being asked of the archbishop if he knew that book, did openly confess that he knew it very well, because he caused it to be written of his own costs and charges, for he spent much money thereupon since his abjuration. Then was he asked who wrote it. He did answer, one called John Grime.

And further, being required what the said John Grime was, he answered, he could not tell. Again, being demanded whether he did ever read the same book, he did confess, that he could not read, but he had heard the fourth part thereof read of one John Fullar. And being asked, whether he thought the contents of that book to be catholic, profitable, good and true? He answered, that many things which he had heard in the same book, were both profitable, good, and healthful to his soul; and as he said he had great affection to the said book, for a sermon preached at Horslydown, that was written in the said book. And being further asked, whether, since the time of his said abjuration, he did commune with one Richard Turming, of the city aforesaid; he did answer, yea: for the said Richard Turming did come often unto his house to have communication with him. And being asked whether he knew the said Richard to be suspected and defamed of heresy, he did answer again, that he knew well that the said Richard was suspected and defamed by many men and women in the city of London, as one whom they thought to be an heretic.

Which confession being made, he did cause the said books to be delivered to Master Robert Gilbert, doctor of divinity, to William Lindewood, doctor of both laws, and other clerks to be examined, and in the mean time, David Beard, Alexander Philip, and Balthasar Mero, were taken for witnesses against him, and were committed to be examined to Master John Escourt, general examiner of Canterbury. This done, the archbishop continued his session till Monday next, in the same place. Which Monday being come, which was the twentieth of the said month, the said Master Escourt openly and publicly exhibited the witnesses, being openly read before the archbishop, and other bishops; which being read, then after that were read divers treatises, found in the house of the said John Claydon: out of the which being examined, various points were gathered and noted for heresies and errors, and especially out of the book aforesaid, which book John Claydon confessed by his own costs to be written and bound, which book was intitled "The Lanthorn of Light."

For the articles contained in this and other books, the archbishop, with other bishops, and learned men, communing together, first condemned the books as heretical, and burned them in the fire: and then, because they thought John Claydon to be forsworn and fallen into heresy, the archbishop proceeded to his definitive

sentence against him, he personally appearing before him in judgment, (his confessions being read and deposed against him) after this manner:

"In the name of God, Amen. We, Henry, by the grace of God, archbishop of Canterbury, primate of all England, and legate of the apostolical see, in a certain cause of heretical pravity, and of relapse into the same, whereupon John Claydon, layman of the province of Canterbury, was detected, accused and denounced, and in the said our province of Canterbury publicly defamed, (as by public fame and common report notoriously to us hath been known), first, sitting in judgment-seat, and observing all things lawfully required in this behalf, do proceed to the pronouncing of the sentence, definitive in form as followeth. The name of Christ being invoked and only set before our eyes, forasmuch as by the acts and things enacted, produced, exhibited and confessed before us; also by divers signs and evidences, we have found the said John Claydon to have been, and to be publicly and notoriously relapsed again into his former heresy, heretofore by him abjured; according to the merits and deserts of the said cause, being of us diligently searched, weighed, and pondered before, to the intent that the said John Claydon shall not infect others with his scab, by the consent and assent of our reverend brethren, Richard, bishop of London, John, bishop of Coventry and Lichfield, and Stephen, bishop of St. David's, and of other doctors, as well of divinity as of both laws and also of other discreet and learned men assisting us in this behalf, we do judge, pronounce, and declare the said John Claydon to be relapsed again into his heresy, which he before did abjure, finally and definitively appointing him to be left unto the secular judgment, and so do leave him by these presents."

Thus John Claydon, receiving his judgment and condemnation of the archbishop, was committed to the secular power, and by them was committed to the fire at Smithfield, where meekly he was made a burnt offering unto the Lord, A.D. 1415.

Robert Fabian, and other chronologers who follow him, add also, that Richard Turming, baker, of whom mention is made before, in the examination of John Claydon, was likewise at the same time burned with him in Smithfield. But in the register I find no sentence of condemnation given against the said Turming, neither yet in the history of St. Albans, is there any such mention of his burning made, but only of the burning of John Claydon aforesaid; wherefore the judgment hereof I leave free to the reader. Notwithstanding, concerning the said Turming this is certain, that he was accused to the bishops, and, no doubt, was in their hands and bands. What afterwards was done with him, I refer it to the authors.

The next year after the burning of these two aforesaid, and also of John Huss, being burnt at Constance, which was A.D. 1416, the prelates of England seeing the daily increase of the gospel, and fearing the ruin of their papal kingdom, were busily occupied with all their counsel and diligence to maintain the same. Wherefore, to make their state and kingdom sure, by statutes, laws, constitutions, and terror of punishment, as Thomas Arundel, and other prelates had done before, so Henry Chichesley, archbishop of Canterbury, in his convocation at London, makes another constitution (as though there had not enough been made before) against the poor Lollards; the copy and tenor whereof he sendeth abroad to the bishop of London, and to other his suffragans, by them to be put in straight execution, as follows:

"Henry, by the grace of God archbishop of Canterbury, primate of all England, and legate of the chief seat: to our reverend brother in the Lord, Richard, by the grace of God bishop of London, health and brotherly love, with continual increase. Lately in our last convocation in St. Paul's church in London, being kept by you and other our brethren and clergy of our province, we do remember to have made this order underwritten, by your consents : when as among many other our cares, this ought to be chief, that by some means we may take those heretics, who like foxes, lurk and hide themselves in the Lord's vineyard ; and that the dust of negligence may be utterly shaken from our feet, and from the feet of our fellow brethren ; in this the said convocation of the prelates and clergy, we have ordained, that our fellow brethren, our suffragans and archdeacons of our province of Canterbury, by themselves, their officials or commissaries in their jurisdictions, and every one of their charges in their country, twice every year at the least, do diligently inquire for such persons as are suspected of heresy ; and that in every such their archdeaconries in every parish, wherein is reported any heretics to inhabit, they cause three or more of the honestest men, and best reported of, to take their oath upon the holy evangelists, that if they shall know or understand any frequenting either in privy conventicles, or else differing in life or manners, from the common conversation of other catholic men, or else that hold any either heresies or errors, or else that have any suspected books in the English tongue, or that do receive any such persons suspected of heresies and errors into their houses, or that be favourers of them that are inhabitants in any such place, or conversant with them, or else have any recourse unto them ; they make certificates of those persons in writing, with all the circumstances wherewith they are suspected, to the said our suffragans or archdeacons, or to their commissaries, so soon, and with as much speed as possibly they can ; and that the said archdeacon, and every of their commissaries aforesaid, do declare the names of all such persons denounced, together with all the circumstances of them, the diocese and places, and secretly under their seals do send over unto us the same : and that the same diocesans effectually direct forth lawful process against them, as the quality of the cause requireth, and that with all diligence they discern, define and execute the same.

" And if perhaps they leave not such persons convicted unto the secular court, yet notwithstanding let them commit them unto the perpetual or temporal prisons, as the quality of the cause shall require, until the next convocation of the prelates and clergy of our province of Canterbury, there personally to remain ; and that in the same prisons they cause them to be kept according as the law requires ; and that of all and singular the things aforesaid, that is, what inquisition they have made, and what they have found, and how in the process they have behaved themselves, and what persons so convicted they have caused to be put in safe keeping, with what diligence or negligence of the commissaries aforesaid, with all and all manner of other circumstances premised, and thereunto in anywise appertaining, and especially of the abjurations, if in the meantime they shall chance to abjure any heresies, that then in the next convocation of the prelates and clergy under the form aforesaid, they cause the same distinctly and openly to be certified to us and our successors ; and that they deliver effectually to the official of our court, the same process to remain with them, or else in the register of our court of Canterbury, so that every one, to whom such things appertain, for the further execution of the same process, may have recourse unto the same official with all effect.

" We therefore command, that as touching the constitution brought unto your city and diocesan, you cause the same in convenient place and time to be published, and that in all points you both observe the same yourselves, and cause it also of others to be diligently observed ; commanding, furthermore, all and singular our fellow brethren and suffragans, that they in likewise cause the same to be published throughout all their cities and dioceses, and both diligently observe the same themselves, and also cause all others to do the same ; and what thing soever you shall do in the premises, that you certify us betwixt this and the feast of St. Peter *ad vincula* next coming, that you duly certify us of these things by your letters patent, containing the same effect, sealed with your seals. Dated at our house in London, the first day of July, A. D. 1416."

During the time of this convocation, two priests were presented and brought before the bishops, defamed for heretics, one named John Barton, to whom it was objected by Philip, bishop of Lincoln, that he had been excommunicated about six or seven years before, upon articles concerning religion, and yet neither would appear when cited, nor would seek to be reconciled again to the church. Which things being so proved against him, he was committed to the custody of Philip, bishop of Lincoln, and to be holden in prison, till he should hear further what should be done.

The other was Robert Chapel, otherwise named Holbech, chaplain sometimes to the Lord Cobham ; to whom likewise it was objected, that he being under the sentence of excommunication about three or four years, yet notwithstanding continued saying mass, and preaching, and sought not to be reconciled ; Chapel denying that he knew of any such excommunication given out against him. Then was the copy of his excommunication first made by the bishop of Rochester, afterward denounced by the bishop of London at St. Paul's cross, brought and read before him ; and that being done, the session brake up for that time, which was about the latter end of May, A. D. 1416.

The twelfth day of the month of July next following, Chapel appeared again before the archbishop and the prelates ; and confessing and submitting himself, he desired pardon. The bishop of Rochester putting in his hands the decree of the canon law, made him abjure all his former articles and opinions as heretical and schismatical, never to hold the same again, according to the contents of the canon. Upon which, Robert Chapel being absolved by the authority of the archbishop, (save only that he should not intermeddle with saying mass before he had been dispensed from the pope himself for irregularity), was enjoined by the archbishop himself for his penance, to stand at St. Paul's, and to publish these articles following unto the people, instead of his confession given him to be read.

" 1. I confess that bishops, priests, and other ecclesiastical persons, having no other possession to the contrary, may lawfully have, receive, and retain lands and possessions temporal, to dispense and dispose the same and the rents thereof, to the behoof of themselves, or of their church where they dwell, according as seemeth good to them.

" 2. I confess that it were very unlawful, yea, rather unjust, that temporal men upon any occasion soever, should take away temporal lands and possessions from the church, either universal or particular, to which they are given, the consideration of the abuse of mortal prelates, priests, or other ministers in the church conversant (which are mixt together good with bad) abusing the same, to the contrary notwithstanding.

" 3. I confess that pilgrimages to the relics of saints, and to holy places, are not prohibited, nor to be contemned of any catholic, but are available to remission of sins, and approved of holy fathers, and worthy to be commended.

" 4. I confess that to worship the images of Christ or of any other saints, being set up in the church or in any other place, is not forbidden ; neither does it conduce to idolatry, being so used as the holy fathers do will them to be worshipped ; but rather such images do profit much to the health of christians, because they do put us in remembrance of the merits of those saints whom they represent, and the sight of them doth move and stir up the people to prayers and devotion.

" 5. I confess that auricular confession used in the church is necessary for a sinner to the salvation of his soul, and necessary to be done of such a priest, as is ordained by the church to hear the confession of the sinner, and to enjoin him penance for the same ; without which confession (if it may be had) there is no remission of sins to him that is in mortal sin.

" 6. I confess and firmly do hold, that although the priest be in mortal sin, yet he may make the body of

2

Christ, and minister other sacraments and sacramentals, which nevertheless are profitable to all the faithful, whoever receives them in faith and devotion of the church.

"7. I confess that bishops in their own dioceses may forbid, decree, or ordain upon reasonable causes, that priests should not, without their special license, preach the word of God, and that those that do against the same, should suffer the ecclesiastical censures.

"8. I confess that private religions, as well of monks, canons, and others, as also of the begging friars, being allowed by the church of Rome, are profitable to the universal church, and in no means contrary to God's law, but rather founded and authorised thereof.

"9. I promise and swear upon these holy evangelists, which I hold here in my hands, that I will henceforth never hold, affirm, nor by any means teach any thing contrary unto the premises either openly or privately."

After the setting out of the constitution aforesaid, in the days of Henry Chichesley, archbishop of Canterbury, great inquisition followed in England, and many good men, whose hearts began to be won to the gospel, were brought to much vexation, and caused outwardly to abjure.

Thus, while Christ had the inward hearts of men; yet the catholic antichrist would needs possess their outward bodies, and make them sing after his song. In the number of those who were compelled to abjure, besides the other aforesaid, was also John Taylor of the parish of St. Michael's at Quern; William James, master of arts and physician, who had long remained in prison, and at length, after abjuration, was licensed with his keeper to practice his physic.

Also John Dwarf, so named for his low stature, who was sent by the duke of Bedford to the aforesaid Chichesley, and other bishops, to be examined before them or the convocation; there he at length revolting from his doctrine, recanted and did penance.

In like manner John Jourdelay of Lincolnshire, well commended in the registers for his learning, accused by the priests of Lincoln for a certain book, which he, contrary to the former decree of the bishops, concealed, and did not exhibit to them, was therefore forced to abjure. After whom was brought likewise before the bishops one Katharine Dertford, a spinster, who being accused and examined upon these three articles concerning the sacrament of the pope's altar, adoration of images, and of pilgrimage, answered, that she was not able, being unlearned, to answer to such high matters, neither had she any further skill, but only her creed and ten commandments; and so was she committed to the vicar general of the bishop of Winchester, (for she was of the same diocese), to be kept, and further to be examined of the same.

At the same sitting was also brought before the archbishop and his fellow bishops, by the lieutenant of the Tower, the parson of Heggeley in Lincolnshire, named Master Robert, who being long kept in the Tower, at length by the king's writ, was brought and examined the same time upon the like articles, to wit, touching the sacrament of their altar, pilgrimage, adoration of images, and whether it was lawful for spiritual men to enjoy temporal lordships, &c. To which articles he answered (saith the register) doubly and mockingly, save only in the sacrament he seemed something more conformable, although not yet fully to their content. Wherefore, being committed to the custody and examination of Richard, bishop of Lincoln, in the end he was also induced to submit himself.

The same likewise did William Henry of Tenterden, being suspected and arrested for keeping company with them whom the bishops called Lollards, and for having suspected books.

Besides these, many others there were who in the same convocation were assembled and revoked their opinions, as John Galle, a priest of London, for having a book in English, intituled "A Book of the New Law." Richard Monk, vicar of Chesham in Lincolnshire, who submitted himself likewise. In this race and number

followed moreover Bartholomew Cornmonger, Nicholas Hoper, servant to the Lord Cobham; Thomas Granter, with others, mentioned in the register.

Among the rest who were at this time troubled for their faith, was one Radulph Mungin, priest, who for the same doctrine was arrested and sent by the lord chancellor of England to the archbishop, and by him committed to David Price, vicar-general to the bishop of London; where, after he had endured four months in prison, he was presented to the convocation, against whom divers articles were objected.

But for the better explaining of the matter, first here is to be noted, that touching the time of this convocation provincial, Pope Martin had sent down to the clergy of England, for a subsidy to be gathered of the church, to maintain the pope's war against the Lollards (so the papists did term them) of Bohemia. Also another subsidy was demanded to persecute one Peter Clerk, master of arts of Oxford, who, flying out of England, was at the council of Basil, disputing on the Bohemians' side. And thirdly, another subsidy was also required to persecute William Russel, warden of the Gray Friars in London, who the same time was fled from England to Rome, to maintain his opinion before the pope, and there escaped out of prison, &c. of whom we shall treat more largely hereafter (Christ willing). In the meantime mark here the petty shifts of the pope to hook in the English money, by all manner of pretences possible.

Thus Ralph Mungin, appearing before the bishops in the convocation, it was objected against him, first, that he affirmed and held, that it was not lawful for any christian to fight and make war against the heretics of Bohemia.

Also, it was objected to him that he did hold and say that it was not lawful for any man to have property of goods, but that they should be common, which he expressly denied that ever he so said or affirmed. Whereby we have to observe how the crafty malice of these adversaries use falsely to collect and surmise of men, what they never spake, to oppress them wrongfully whom by plain truth they cannot expugn.

Moreover they objected against him, that he kept company with Master Clerk, and also that he dispersed in the city of London certain books of John Wickliff, and of Peter Clerk, namely the book 'Trialogus,' and the gospel of John Wickliff, &c. He was charged, moreover, to have spoken against the pope's indulgences, affirming that the pope had no more power to give indulgences than he had.

Upon these and other such articles objected, Mungin being asked if he would revoke, answered, "That it seemed to him not just or meet so to do, who did not know himself guilty of any heresy." Thus he being respited for the time, was committed to prison till the next sitting, who then being called afterward before the bishops, after long inquisition and straight examination made, also depositions brought in against him so much as they could search out, he notwithstanding still denied as before to recant. Wherefore the aforesaid Henry, the archbishop, proceeding to his sentence definitive, condemned him to perpetual imprisonment.

After this followed the recantation of Richard Monk, and Thomas Granter. Also of Edmund Frith who was before butler to Sir John Oldcastle.

Besides these, many are recorded in the register, who for their faith and religion were greatly vexed and troubled, especially in the diocese of Kent, in the towns of Romney, Tenterden, Woodchurch, Cranbrook, Staplehurst, Benenden, Halden, Rolvenden, and others, where whole households, both man and wife, were driven to forsake their houses and towns for danger of persecution; as sufficiently appears in the process of the archbishop Chichesley against those persons, and in the certificate of Burbath his official, wherein are named the following persons:

1. W. White, priest.
2. Thomas Grenested, priest.
3. Bartholomew Cornmonger.
4. John Wadnon.
5. Joan his wife.

6. Thomas Everden.
7. William Everden.
8. Stephen Robin.
9. W. Chiveling.
10. John Tame.
11. John Fowlin.
12. William Somer.
13. Marian his wife.
14. John Abraham.
15. Robert Munden.
16. Laurence Coke.

These being cited up together by the bishop, would not appear. Upon which great inquisition being made for them by his officers, they were constrained to fly their houses and towns, and shift for themselves as secretly as they could.

Concerning Sir John Oldcastle the Lord Cobham, his first apprehension with his whole history and life, has been sufficiently expressed before, and how being committed to the Tower, and condemned falsely of heresy, he escaped afterwards out of the Tower, and was in Wales about the space of four years. In which time, a great sum of money was promised by proclamation by the king, to him that could take Sir John Oldcastle, either alive or dead. About the end of which four years the Lord Powis, whether for love and greediness of the money, or whether for hatred of the true and sincere doctrine of Christ, seeking all manner of ways how to play the part of Judas, at length obtained his bloody purpose, and brought the Lord Cobham bound up to London; which was about A.D. 1417, and about the month of December. At which time there was a parliament assembled in London. The records of which parliament do thus say: "That on Tuesday the fourteenth day of December, and the nine-and-twentieth day of the said parliament, Sir John Oldcastle of Cowling, in the county of Kent, knight, being outlawed (as is before mentioned) in the king's bench, and excommunicated before by the archbishop of Canterbury for heresy, was brought before the lords, and having heard his said convictions, answered not thereto in his excuse. Upon which record and process it was adjudged that he should be taken as a traitor to the king and the realm; that he should be carried to the Tower of London, and from thence down through London, unto the new gallows in St. Giles without Temple Bar, and there to be hanged and burned hanging."

Thus, after long process, they condemned him again for heresy and treason, by force of the aforenamed act; he rendering thanks unto God, that he had so appointed him to suffer for his name's sake.

And, upon the day appointed, he was brought out of the Tower with his arms bound behind him, having a very cheerful countenance. Then was he laid upon a hurdle, as though he had been a most heinous traitor to the crown, and so drawn forth into St. Giles's-fields, where they had set up a new pair of gallows. As he was coming to the place of execution, and was taken from the burdle, he fell down devoutly upon his knees, desiring Almighty God to forgive his enemies. Then he stood up and beheld the multitude, exhorting them, in most godly manner, to follow the laws of God written in the scriptures, and, in any wise, to beware of such teachers as they see contrary to Christ in their conversation and living; with many other special counsels. Then was he hanged up there by the middle, in chains of iron, and so consumed alive in the fire, praising the name of God, so long as his life lasted. In the end he commended his soul into the hand of God, and so departed hence most christianly, his body being resolved into ashes. And this was done A.D. 1418, which was the fifth year of the reign of King Henry V.; the people there present, shewing great sorrow. How the priests that time fared, blasphemed, and accursed, requiring the people not to pray for him, but to judge him damned in hell because he departed not in the obedience of their pope, it were too long to write.

This terrible kind of death, with gallows, chains, and fire, appears not very precious in the eyes of men that be carnal, no more than did the death of Christ, when he was hanged up among thieves. "The righteous seemeth to die," saith the wise man, "in the sight of them which are unwise, and their end is taken for very destruction. Ungodly souls think their lives very madness, and their passage hence without all honour; but, though they suffer pains before men," saith he, "yet is their expectation full of immortality. They are accounted for the children of God, and have their portion among the saints. As gold in the furnace doth God try his elect, and as a most pleasant burnt offering, receiveth he them to rest." The more hard the passage be, the more glorious shall they appear in the latter resurrection. Not that the afflictions of this life are worthy of such a glory, but that it is God's heavenly pleasure so to reward them. Never are the judgments and ways of men like unto the judgments and ways of God, but contrary evermore, unless they be taught of him. "In the latter time," saith the Lord unto Daniel, "shall many be chosen, proved, and purified by fire; yet shall the ungodly live wickedly still, and have no understanding that is of faith." By an angel from heaven was John earnestly commanded to write that "blessed are the dead that die in the Lord." "Right dear," saith David, "in the sight of God, is the death of his servants."

Thus rested this valiant christian knight, Sir John Oldcastle, under the altar of God, which is Jesus Christ, among that godly company, who, in the kingdom of patience, suffered great tribulation with the death of their bodies, for his faithful word and testimony, abiding there with them, He, fulfilling of their whole number and the full restoration of his elect. The which he grant, in effect, who is one God eternal! Amen.

Thus have you heard the whole matter concerning the martyrdom of the good Lord Cobham, as we have gathered it partly out of the collections of John Bale and others.

Moreover, in the records above mentioned, it follows how in the parliament, after the martyrdom of this valiant knight, a motion was made, that the Lord Powis might be thanked and rewarded, according to the proclamation made for his great pains taken in the apprehension of "Sir John Oldcastle, knight, heretic." Thus stand the words of the record. Where two things are to be noted: first, how Sir John here in the record is called not traitor, but heretic only. Secondly, mark how this brother of Judas here craveth his reward for betraying the innocent blood. Wherein it is not to be doubted, but that his light fee, and "what will you give me?" in this world, will have an heavy reward hereafter in the world to come, unless he repented.

And now from our English matters, to return again to the history of the Bohemians, from whence we have a little digressed. When the news of the barbarous cruelty exercised at Constance against John Huss and Jerome of Prague, were noised in Bohemia, the nobles and gentlemen of Moravia and Bohemia, such as favoured the cause of John Huss, gathering themselves together in the zeal of Christ; first sent their letter to the council; expostulating with them for the injury done to those godly men, as is before expressed. For which letter they were all cited up to the council. To this letter Sigismund the emperor makes answer in the name of the whole council; first, excusing himself of John Huss's death, which, he said, was against his safe conduct, and against his will: insomuch that he rose in anger from the council, and departed out of Constance, as is before remembered. Secondly, he requires them to be quiet, and to conform themselves peaceably to the order of the catholic church of Rome, &c.

Also the council hearing or fearing some stir to rise among the Bohemians, did make several laws and articles whereby to bridle them.

The Bohemians, however, notwithstanding these cruel articles, contemning the vain devices of these prelates and fathers of the council, ceased not to proceed in their league and purpose, joining themselves more strongly together.

In the meantime it happened, that during this council

of Constance, after the deposing of Pope John, and spoiling of his goods, which came to seventy five thousand pounds of gold and silver, as is reported in the history of St. Alban's; Pope Martin, upon the day of St. Martin, was elected to the pontifical chair. Concerning his election great preparation was made before by the council, so that beside the cardinals, five other bishops of every nation should enter into the conclave, who there together should be kept with thin diet, till they had chosen a pope. At last, when they were together, they agreed upon this man, and not tarrying for opening the door, like mad men, for haste they broke open a hole in the wall, crying out, " We have Pope Martin !" The emperor hearing thereof, came with similar haste, and falling down kissed the new pope's feet. Then they all went to the church together, and sung Te Deum.

The next day, this Martin was made priest (for before, he was only a cardinal deacon) and the day after was consecrated bishop, and sang his first mass, whereat one hundred and forty mitred bishops were present. After this, the new holy pope ordained a general procession, where a certain clerk was appointed to stand with flax and fire, who, setting the flax on fire, thus said, " Behold, holy father, thus the glory of this world passeth away." Which done, the same day the holy father was brought up to a high scaffold (saith the history) I will not say to a high mountain, where was offered to him all the glory of the world, &c. there to be crowned for a triple king. This done, the same day after dinner, the new crowned pope was with great triumph brought through the midst of the city of Constance, where all the bishops and abbots followed wearing their mitres. The pope's horse was all in scarlet trappings down to the ground. The cardinal's horses were all in white silk; the emperor on the right side, and prince elector on the left, (playing both the pope's footmen) went on foot, leading the pope's horse by the bridle.

As this pageant, with the great giant, thus proceeded, and came to the market place, there the Jews (according to the manner) offered to him their law and ceremonies. Which the pope receiving, cast behind him saying, " Let old things pass away, all things are become new," &c. This was A. D. 1417. (Ex Hist. St. Alb. ex paralip. Ursperg.)

Thus the pope, being now confirmed in his kingdom, first begins to write his letters to the Bohemians, wherein partly he moves them to catholic obedience, partly he dissembles with them, pretending that if it were not for the emperor's request, he would enter process against them. Thirdly, and finally, he threatens to attempt the utmost against them, and with all force to invade them, as well with the apostolic, as with the secular arm, if they still persisted, as they began. However, these new threats of the new bishop did not move the constant hearts of the Bohemians, whom the inward zeal of Christ's word had before inflamed. And although it had been to be wished such bloodshed and wars had not followed; yet, to say the truth, how could these men greatly blame them herein, whom their bloody tyranny had before provoked so unjustly, if now with their glossing letters they could not so easily appease them again?

Wherefore, these Bohemians, partly for the love of John Huss and Jerome their countrymen; partly for the hatred of the malignant papistry, assembling together, first agreed to celebrate a solemn memorial of the death of John Huss and Jerome, decreeing the same to be held and celebrated yearly. And, afterward, by means of their friends, they obtained certain churches of the king, wherein they might freely preach and minister the sacraments to the congregation. This done, they suppressed several monasteries, pharisaical temples, and idolatrous fanes, beginning first with the great monastery of the Blackfriars, eight miles from Prague, driving away the wicked and vicious priests and monks out of

them, or compelling them to a better order. And thus their number more and more increasing under the safe conduct of a certain nobleman, named Nicholas, they went again to the king, requiring to have more and ampler churches granted to them. The king seemed at the first willingly and gently to give ear to Nicholas intreating for the people, and commanded them to come again the next day.

When the people were departed, the king turning himself to the nobleman Nicholas, who tarried still behind, said, " Thou hast begun a web to put me out of my kingdom, but I will make a rope of it, wherewithal I will hang thee." Whereupon he immediately departed out of the king's presence, and the king himself went into the castle of Vissegrade, and soon after, into a new castle, which he himself had built five stones' cast from thence, and sent ambassadors to his brother to require aid.

These protestants[1] being assembled in the town of Prague, holding their meetings, the king sent his chamberlain with three hundred horsemen to fall upon them; but he fearing for his life, fled. When the news was brought to the king, all that were about him being amazed, utterly detested the act: but the king's cupbearer standing by, said, " I knew before, that these things would thus come to pass." Whom the king taking hold of in a rage, threw down before his feet, and with his dagger would have slain him; but being prevented by such as were about him, with much persuasion he pardoned him his life. Immediately the king being taken with a palsy, fell sick, and within eighteen days after, when he had marked the names of such whom he had appointed to be put to death, and was incessantly calling for aid of his brother, and his other friends, he departed this life before the princes whom he had sent to, were come, when he had reigned five-and-fifty years, and was about the age of seven-and-fifty years.

The History of Zisca.

Immediately after the death of Wenceslaus, there arose a certain nobleman named Zisca, born at Trosnovia, who, from his youth upward, was brought up in the king's court, and had lost one of his eyes in a battle, where he had valiantly conducted himself. This man being grieved for the death of John Huss, and Jerome of Prague, and minding to revenge the injuries which the council had done, greatly to the dishonour of the kingdom of Bohemia, gathered together a number of men of war, and pulled down the monasteries and idolatrous temples, pulling down and breaking in pieces the images and idols, driving away the priests and monks, who he said were kept in their cloisters, like swine in their styes, to be fatted. After this, his army being increased, having gathered together about forty thousand men, he attempted to take the castle of Vissegrade, which was but slenderly defended. From thence Zisca went speedily unto Pelzina, where he knew he had many friends of his faction, and took the town into his power, fortifying it very strongly, and those who tarried behind, took the castle of Vissegrade.

Then the Queen Sophia sent letters and messengers to the Emperor Sigismund and other nobles, requiring aid and help: but the emperor made preparation against the Turk, who had then lately won certain castles of him. Upon which the queen, seeing all aid so far off, together with Zenko Warterberge, gathered a host with the king's treasure, and fortified the castle of Prague, and the lesser city which joins to the castle, making gates and towers of wood upon the bridge, that the protestants should have no passage that way. Then it happened that at the Isle of St. Benedict, one Peter Steremberge fought an equal or indifferent battle with them.

In the meantime, the number of the protestants being increased in Prague, they fought for the bridge. In which battle many were slain on both parts, but at length the Hussites won the bridge and the lower part of lesser Prague, the queen's party flying into the upper part, where they, turning again, fiercely renewed the battle, and fought continually day and night for the space of five days. Many were slain on both sides, and goodly buildings were destroyed, and the council house, which was in a low place, was utterly defaced and burned.

During the time of this troublous estate, the ambassadors of the Emperor Sigismund were come, who, taking upon them the rule and government of the realm, made a truce with the city of Prague on this condition, that the castle of Vissegrade being surrendered, it should be lawful for them to send ambassadors to the Emperor Sigismund to treat as to their estate, and that Zisca should surrender Pilzina and Piesta with the other forts which he had taken. These conditions thus agreed upon and received, all the foreign protestants departed out of the city, and the senate of the city began to govern again according to their accustomed manner, and all things were quieted. However, the papists, who were gone out of the town, durst not return, but still looked for the emperor, by whose presence they thought they should have been safe. But this their hope was frustrated by means of certain letters which were sent from the emperor, that he would shortly come and rule the kingdom, even after the same manner as his father Charles had done before him. Upon which, the protestants understood that their sect and religion should be utterly banished.

About Christmas, the Emperor Sigismund came to Brunna, a city of Moravia, and there he pardoned the citizens of Prague, on condition that they would let down the chains and bars of the city, and receive his rulers and magistrates. The whole city obeyed, and the magistrates, lifting up their hands to heaven, rejoiced at the coming of the new king. But the emperor turned another way, and went to Uratislavia, the head city of Silesia, where a little before the commonalty of the city had slain, in an insurrection, the magistrates, which his brother Wenceslaus had set in authority; the leaders of which he beheaded. When the news of this was reported at Prague, the citizens being terrified by the example of the Uratislavians, distrusting their pardon, rebelled, and having influenced Cencho to join them, who had the government of the castle of Prague, they sent letters into all the realm, that no man should suffer the emperor to enter, as he was an enemy to Bohemia, and sought nothing else but to destroy the kingdom: he had also bound the ancient city of the Prutenians under order, by pledges, and put the marquess of Brandenburg from the Bohemian crown: and had not only suffered John Huss and Jerome of Prague to be burned at the council of Constance, but also procured the same, and with all his endeavours impugned the doctrine and faith which they taught and followed. While these things were thus done, Zisca, having given over Pelzina by arrangement, was twice assaulted by his enemies, but through skill he was always victor. The places where they fought were rough and unknown, his enemies were on horseback, and his soldiers on foot, neither could there be any battle fought but on foot. Whereupon, when his enemies were alighted from their horses, Zisca commanded the women who usually followed the host, to cast their kerchiefs upon the ground, in which the horsemen being entangled by their spurs, were slain before they could unloose their feet.

After this, he went unto Ausca, a town situate upon the river Lucinitius, out of which town, Procopius and Ulricius, two brethren papists, had cast out many protestants. This town Zisca took by force of arms the first night of Lent, and set it on fire. He also took the castle of Litius, which was a mile off, where Ulric was fled, and put Ulric and all his family to the sword, saving one only.

Then, as he had no walled or fenced town to inhabit, he chose a certain place upon the river, which was fenced by nature, about eight miles from the city of Ausca. This place he compassed with walls, and commanded every man to build houses, where they had pitched their tents, and named this city Tabor, and the inhabitants, his companions, Taborites, because their city was builded upon the top of some hill or mount. This city, though it was fenced with high rocks and cliffs, yet was compassed with a wall and ramparts, and the river of Lucinitius fences a great part of the town; the rest is compassed in with a great brook, which, running straight into the river Lucinitius, is stopped by a great rock, and driven back towards the right hand all the length of the city, and at the further end it joineth with the great river. The way unto it by land is scarce thirty feet broad, for it is almost an island. In this place there was a deep ditch cast, and a triple wall made, of such thickness, that it could not be broken with any engine. The wall was full of towers and forts set in their convenient and meet places. Zisca was the first that built the castle, and those that came after him fortified it, every man according to his own device. At that time the Taborites had no horsemen among them, until such time as Nicholas, master of the mint (whom the emperor had sent into Bohemia with a thousand horsemen to set things in order, and to withstand the Taborites, lodging all night in a village named Vogize) was surprised by Zisca coming upon him suddenly in the night, taking away all his horse and armour, and setting fire to the village. Then Zisca taught his soldiers to mount on horseback, to leap, to run, to turn, and to cast a ring, so that after this he never led an army without his wings of horsemen.

In the meantime, Sigismund, the emperor, gathering together the nobles of Silesia, entered Bohemia, and went into Grecium, and thence, with a great army, to Cuthna, alluring Cencho with many great and large promises to surrender the castle of Prague, and there placed him to annoy the town. This Cencho, inflamed with double treason, returned home. The citizens of Prague sent for Zisca, who speeding himself thither with the Taborites, received the city under his government. In the Bohemian's host there were but only two barons, Hilco Crusina of Lituburge; and Hilco Waldestene; with a few other nobles; all the rest were of the common people. They went first to subdue the castle, which was by nature very strongly fenced, and could not be won by any other means than with famine: whereupon all the passages were stopped, that no victuals should be carried in. But the emperor opened the passages by dint of sword, and when he had given to the besieged all things necessary, and sent for aid out of the empire, he determined shortly after to besiege the city. There were in the emperor's camp the duke of Saxony; the marquess of Brandenburg; and his son-in-law, Albert of Austria. The city was assaulted for the space of six weeks. The Emperor Sigismund was crowned in the metropolitan house in the castle; Conrad, the archbishop, solemnizing the ceremonies of the coronation. The city was straightway besieged. In the meantime the captains, Rosenses and Chragery, who had taken the tents of the Taborites, being overcome in battle by Nicholas Huss, whom Zisca had sent with part of his force, for that purpose, were driven out of their tents, and Grecium, the queen's city, was also taken.

There is also above the town of Prague a high hill, which is called Videchon. On this hill had Zisca strongly planted a garrison, that his enemies should not possess it, with whom the marquis of Misnia skirmishing, lost a great part of his soldiers. For when the Misnians had got the top of the hill, being driven back into a corner, which was broken and steep, and fiercely set upon, when they could no longer withstand the violent force of their enemies, some of them were slain, and some falling headlong from the hill, were destroyed. Upon which the Emperor Sigismund raising his siege, departed to Cuthna, and Zisca with his company departed to Tabor, and subdued many places; among which he subverted a town pertaining to the captain of Vissegrade. During this time the castle of Vissegrade was strongly besieged, where, when other victuals failed, they were compelled to eat horse-flesh. Last of all, unless the emperor aided them, by a certain day, they promised to yield it up, but on this condition, that if the emperor came, they within the castle should be no more molested.

The emperor was present before the day, but being ignorant of the truce taken, entering into a strait underneath the castle, was suddenly set upon by the soldiers of Prague, where he had a great overthrow, and so leaving his purpose unperformed, returned back again. There were slain in that conflict fourteen noblemen of the Moravians, and of the Hungarians, and others a great number. The castle was delivered up to them. While these things were in doing, Zisca took Boslaus, a captain, who was surnamed Cigneus, by force, in a very strong town of his, and brought him to his religion. Who, a few years after, leading the protestant army in Austria, was wounded before Rhetium, and died. There were in the territory of Pelzina many monasteries, of which Zisca pulled down and burned five. And as the monastery of St. Clare was the strongest, there he pitched himself.

There also came the emperor with his army: but when Zisca brought forth his forces against him, he most cowardly fled, and not long after, he departed and left Bohemia. Then Zisca went with his army to Pelzina; but as he saw the city so fenced, that he was in doubt of winning it, he went to Committavia, a famous city, which he took by force, burning all the priests in it.

Afterwards, when as he lay before the town of Raby, and strongly besieged it, he was struck with an arrow in the eye, having only that one before to see with. From thence he was carried to Prague by physicians, where he was cured of his wound, and his life saved, although he lost his sight, and yet he would not forsake his army, but still took the charge of them.

After this the garrisons of Prague went to Verona, where there was a great garrison of the emperors, and took it by force, many being slain on both sides. They also took the town of Broda, in Germany, and slew the garrison, and afterward took Cuthna, and many other cities, by composition. Further, when they led their army unto a town called Pons, which is inhabited by the Misnians, the Saxons meeting them by the way, because they durst not join battle, they returned back. After all this, the emperor appointed the princes electors a day, that they should with their army invade the west part of Bohemia, and he, with an host of Hungarians, would enter the east part. There came to his aid the archbishop of Mentz, the county palatine of Rhein, the dukes of Saxony, the marquis of Brandenburg, and many other bishops out of Almaine; all the rest sent their aids. They encamped before the town of Sozius, a strong and well fenced place, which they could by no means subdue. The country was spoiled and wasted round about, and the siege continued until the feast of St. Galle. Then it was broken up, because the emperor was not come at his day appointed: but he having gathered together a great army of the Hungarians, and West Moravians, about Christmas entered into Bohemia; and took certain towns by force, and Cuthna was yielded unto him. But when Zisca (although he was blind) came towards him, and set upon him, he being afraid, and many of his nobles slain, fled. But first he burned Cuthna, which the Taborites, by means of the silver mines, called the Pouch of Antichrist. Zisca, pursuing the emperor a day's journey, got great and rich spoil, and taking the town of Broda by force, set it on fire, which afterward almost by the space of fourteen years, remained uninhabited. The emperor passed by a bridge over the river of Iglaria. And Piso, a Florentine, who had brought fifteen thousand horsemen out of Hungary to these wars, passed over the ice; which by the multitude and number of his horsemen being broke, drowned and destroyed a great number. Zisca having obtained this victory, would not suffer any image or idol to be in the churches, neither thought it tolerable that priests should minister with copes or vestments: for which cause he was much the more envied amongst the states of Bohemia. And the consuls of Prague, being grieved at the insolency of John Premonstratensis, called him and nine others of his adherents, whom they supposed to be the principals of this faction, into the council-house, as though they would confer with them as touching the commonwealth: and when they were come in, they slew them, and afterward departed home every man to his own house, thinking the city had been quiet, as though nothing had been done. But their servants not being circumspect enough, washing down the court or yard, washed out also the blood of those that were slain through the sinks or channels; which being once seen, the people understood what was done. By and by there was a tumult; the council-house was straightway overthrown, and eleven of the principal citizens who were thought to be the authors of it, were slain, and many houses plundered.

About the same time, the castle of Purgel, wherein the emperor had left a small garrison (whither also many papists with their wives and children were fled) was, through negligence, burned, and those who escaped out of the fire went unto Pelzina. After this, many of the Bohemian captains, and the senate of Prague, sent ambassadors to Vitold, duke of Lithuania, and made him their king. This did Zisca and his adherents gainsay. This Vitold sent Sigismund Coributus with two thousand horsemen into Bohemia, who was honourably received by the inhabitants of Prague. At his coming, they determined to lay siege to a castle situate upon a hill, which was called Charles' Stone.

Here Sigismund had left for a garrison four centurions of soldiers. The tents were pitched in three places. The siege continued six months, and the assault never ceased day and night. Five great slings threw continually great stones over the walls, and about two thousand vessels, tubs, or baskets, filled with dead carcases, and other excrements, were cast in amongst those which were besieged: which thing did so infect them with stench, that their teeth did either fall out, or were all loose. Notwithstanding they bare it out with stout courage, and continued their fight until the winter.

In the mean time, Frederick the Elder, prince of Brandenburg, entering into Bohemia with a great army, caused them of Prague to raise the siege. And Vitold, at the request of Uladislaus, king of Poland, which had talked with the emperor on the borders of Hungary, called Coributus, his uncle, with his whole army, out of Bohemia. Whereupon the emperor, supposing that the protestants, being destitute of foreign aid, would the sooner do his commandment: but he was far deceived therein; for they, leading their armies out of Bohemia, subdued the borderers thereupon adjoining. It is also reported that Zisca went into Austria, and when the husbandmen of the country had carried away a great number of their cattle by water into an isle of the river called Danube, and by chance had left certain calves and swine in their villages behind them: Zisca drove them to the river side, and kept them there so long, beating them, and causing them to roar out and cry, until the cattle feeding in the island, hearing the lowing and grunting of the cattle on the other side the water, for the desire of their like, did swim over the river; by the means whereof he got and drove away a great booty.

About the same time the Emperor Sigismund gave unto his son-in-law, Albert, duke of Austria, the country of Moravia, because it should not want a ruler. At the same time also, Eric, king of Denmark, and Peter Infant, brother to the king of Portugal, and father of James, cardinal of St. Eustace, came to the emperor, being both very expert men in the affairs of war, which did augment the emperor's host with their aid and power. Whereupon they straightway pitched their camp before Lutemperge, a town of Moravia, and continued the siege by the space of three months. There was at that time a certain knight at Prague, surnamed Aqua, which was very rich, and of great authority. This man, forsomuch as he had no child of his own, adopted his sister's son, named Procopius; whom when he was of mean nature and age, he carried with him into France, Spain, and Italy, and unto Jerusalem, and at his return caused him to be made priest. This man, when the gospel began to flourish in Bohemia, took part with Zisca; and as he was strong and valiant, and also painful, he was greatly esteemed.

This Procopius for his valiant acts was afterwards called Procopius Magnus, and had committed unto him the whole charge of the province of Moravia, and the defence of the Lutemperges, who receiving a great power by force, carried victuals into the town which was besieged, and so frustrated the emperor's siege. The emperor before this, had delivered to the marquises of Misnia the bridge and town of Ausca, upon the river Elbe, that they should fortify them with their garrisons. Whereupon Zisca besieged Ausca; and Frederick, the marquis of Misnia, with his brother the landgrave of Turing, gathering together a great army out of Saxonia, Turing, Misnia, and both the Lusaces, determined to rescue and aid those which were besieged.

There was a great battle fought before the city, and the victory was long uncertain, but at last it fell on the protestants' part. There were slain in the battle, the burgraves of Misnia or Chyrpogenses, the barons of Glychen, and many other nobles, besides nine thousand common soldiers, and the town of Ausca was taken and utterly razed.

At last, dissension rising between Zisca and them of Prague, they of Prague prepared an army against him, wherewith he perceiving himself overmatched, fled to the river Elbe, and was almost taken, but that he had passage through the town of Poggiebras; but they of Prague, pursuing the tail of the battle, slew many of his Taborites. At length they came to certain hills, where Zisca going into the valley, knowing the passes of the place, that his enemies could not spread their army, he commanded his standard to stand still, and exhorting and encouraging his soldiers, he gave them battle.

This battle was very fierce and cruel; but Zisca having the upper hand, slew three thousand of them of Prague, and put the rest to flight, and took the city of Cuthna by force (which they of Prague had repaired) and set it on fire: then with all speed he went with his army to besiege Prague, and encamped within a bowshot of the town. There were many both in the city, and also in his host, who grudged sore at that siege; some accusing Zisca, others them of Prague. There were great tumults in the camp, the soldiers saying that it was not reasonable that the city should be suppressed, which was both the head of the kingdom, and did not dissent from them in opinion, saying, that the Bohemians' power would soon decay, if their enemies should know that they were divided within themselves: also that they had sufficient wars against the emperor, and that it was but a foolish device to move wars amongst themselves. This talk came to the ear of Zisca, who, calling together his army, standing upon a place to be heard, spake in these words:

"Brethren, be ye not aggrieved against me, neither accuse him who hath sought your health and safety. The victories which ye have obtained under my conduct are yet fresh in memory, neither have I brought you at any time to any place, from whence you have not come victors. You are become famous and rich, and I for your sake have lost my sight, and dwell in darkness. Nothing have I gotten by all these fortunate battles, but only a vain name. For you have I fought, and for you have I vanquished; neither do I repent me of my toil; neither is my blindness grievous to me, but only that I cannot provide for you according to my accustomed manner: neither do I persecute them of Prague for mine own cause, for it is your blood that they thirst and seek for, and not for mine. It were but small pleasure for them to destroy me, being now an old man and blind, it is your valiantness and stout courage which they fear. Either you or they must perish, who while they seem to lie in wait for me, seek after your lives. You must rather fear civil wars than foreign, and civil sedition ought first to be avoided. We will subdue Prague, and banish the seditious citizens before the emperor shall have any news of this sedition. And then

having but a few of his faction left, we may with the less fear look for it, better than if these doubtful citizens of Prague were still in our camp. But because ye shall accuse me no more, I give you free liberty to do what you will. If it please you to suffer them of Prague to live in quietness, I will not be against it, so that there be no treason wrought. If you determine to have war, I am also ready. Look which part you will incline to; Zisca will be your aid and helper."

When he had spoken these words, the soldiers' minds were changed, and wholly determined to make war, so that they ran by and by to take up their armour and weapons, to run to the walls, to provoke their enemies to fight for the gates of the city. Zisca, in the mean time, prepared all things ready for the assault. There is near Pelzina, a certain village named Rochezana. In this place, there was a child born of poor and base parentage, whose name was John; he came to Prague, and got his living there by begging, and learned grammar and logic. When he came to man's estate, he became the schoolmaster of a nobleman's child; and as he was of an excellent wit, and ready tongue, he was received into the college of the poor: and last of all, being made priest, he began to preach the word of God to the citizens of Prague, and was named John of Rochezana, by the name of the town where he was born. The man grew to be of great name and authority in the town of Prague. Upon which, when as Zisca besieged Prague, he by the consent of the citizens, went out into the camp, and reconciled Zisca again to the city.

When the emperor perceived that all things came to pass according to Zisca's will and mind, and that upon him alone the whole state of Bohemia depended, he sought privy means to reconcile and get Zisca into his favour, promising him the government of the whole kingdom, the guiding of all his hosts and armies, and great yearly revenues, if he would proclaim him king, and cause the cities to be sworn to him. Upon which conditions, when Zisca, for the performance of the covenants, went to the emperor, during his journey at the castle of Priscovia, he was struck with sickness, and died.

It is reported, that when he was asked, while sick, in what place he would be buried; he commanded the skin to be pulled off from his carcase, and the flesh to be cast to the fowls and beasts, and that a drum should be made of his skin, which they should use in their battles; affirming, that as soon as their enemies should hear the sound of that drum, they would not abide, but take their flight. The Taborites, despising all other images, yet set up the picture of Zisca over the gates of the city.

The Epitaph of John Zisca, the valiant Captain of the Bohemians.

"I, John Zisca, not inferior to an emperor, or captain in warlike skill, a severe punisher of the pride and avarice of the clergy, and a defender of my country, do lie here. That which Appius Claudius, by giving good counsel, and M. Furius Camillus by valiantness, did for the Romans, the same, I being blind, have done for my Bohemians. I never slacked opportunity of battle, neither did fortune at any time fail me. I, being blind, did foresee all opportunity of well ordering or doing my business. Eleven times in joining battle I went victor out of the field. I seemed to have worthily defended the cause of the miserable and hungry against the delicate, fat, and gluttonous priests, and for that cause to have received help at the hands of God. If their envy had not promoted it, without doubt I had deserved to be numbered amongst the most famous men. Notwithstanding my bones lie here in this hallowed place, even in despite of the pope.

Signed "John Zisca, a Bohemian, enemy to all wicked and covetous priests, but with a godly zeal."

And thus have you the acts and doings of this worthy Zisca, and other Bohemians, which for the more credit we have drawn out of Æneas Sylvius, only his railing terms we have here suppressed.

All this while the emperor, with the whole power of the Germans, were not so busy on the one side, but Martin the pope was much occupied on the other side, who about the same time directed down a terrible bull, full of all poison, to all bishops and archbishops, against all such as took any part or side with Wickliff, John Huss, Jerome, or with their doctrine and opinions. The copy of which bull, which I found in an old written monument, I wish the reader thoroughly to peruse, wherein he shall see the pope to pour out at once all his poison.

The Bull of Pope Martin directed forth against the Followers of John Wickliff of England, of John Huss of Bohemia, and Jerome of Prague.

" Martin, bishop, the servant of God's servants, to our reverend brethren the archbishops of Salzeburg, Gueznen, and Prague, and to the bishops of Olumzen, Luthomuslen, Bambergen, Misnen, Patavien, Uratisla-vien, Ratisponen, Cracovian, Posnamen, and Nitrien, and also to our beloved children the inquisitors appointed of the prelates above recited, or where else soever, unto whom these present letters shall come, greeting, and apostolical benediction. Amongst all other pastoral cares wherewith we are oppressed, this chiefly and specially does enforce us, that heretics with their false doctrine and errors, being utterly expelled from amongst the company of christian men, and rooted out (so far as God will make us able to do), the right and catholic faith may remain sound and undefiled ; and that all christian people, immoveable and inviolate, may stand and abide in the sincerity of the same faith, the whole veil of security being removed. But lately in divers places of the world, but especially in Bohemia, and the dukedom of Moravia, and in the straits adjoining thereunto, certain arch-heretics have risen and sprung up, not against one only, but against divers and sundry documents of the catholic faith, being land-lopers, schismatics, and seditious persons, fraught with devilish pride, and wolfish madness, deceived by the subtlety of Satan, and from one evil vanity brought to a worse. Who although they rose up and sprang in divers parts of the world, yet agreed they all in one, having their tails as it were knit together, to wit, John Wickliff of England, John Huss of Bohemia, and Jerome of Prague, of damnable memory, who draw with them no small number to miserable ruin and infidelity. For when as those and such like pestiferous persons did in the beginning of their poisoned doctrine obstinately sow and spread abroad perverse and false opinions, the prelates who had the government and the execution of the judicial power, like dumb dogs not able to bark, neither yet revenging speedily with the apostle all such disobedience, nor regarding to cast out of the Lord's house (as they were enjoined by the canons) those subtle and pestilent arch-heretics, and their wolfish fury and cruelty, with all expedition, but suffering their false and pernicious doctrine negligently, by their over-long delays, to grow and wax strong ; a great multitude of people, instead of true doctrine, received those things, which they did long falsely, perniciously, and damnably sow among them, and giving credit unto them, fell from the right faith, and are entangled (the more pity) in the foul errors of paganism.

" Insomuch, that these arch-heretics, and such as spring of them, have infected the catholic flock of Christ in divers climates of the world, and parts bordering upon the same, and have caused them to putrify in the filthy dunghill of their lies. Wherefore the general synod of Constance was compelled with St. Augustine to exclaim against so great and ruinous a plague of faithful men, and of the sound and true faith itself, saying, ' What shall the sovereign medicine of the church do, with motherly love seeking the health of her sheep, chafing as it were, amongst a company of men frantic, and having the disease of the lethargy ? What, shall she desist and leave off her good purpose ? No, not so. But rather let her, if there be no remedy, be sharp to both these sorts, which are the grievous enemies of her

body. For the physician is sharp unto the man distracted and raging in his frenzy, and yet he is a father to his own rude and unmannerly son, in binding the one, in beating the other, by shewing therein his great love unto them both. But if they be negligent, and suffer them to perish,' saith St. Augustine, ' this mansuetude is rather to be supposed false cruelty.'

" And therefore the foresaid synod, to the glory of Almighty God, and preservation of his catholic faith, and augmenting of christian religion, and for the salvation of men's souls, hath corporally rejected and cast forth of the household of God, the foresaid John Wickliff, John Huss, and Jerome, who amongst other things did believe, preach, teach, and maintain, of the sacrament of the altar, and other sacraments of the church, and articles of the faith, contrary to that the holy church of Rome believeth, holdeth, preacheth, and teacheth, and have presumed obstinately to preach, teach, hold, and believe many other things, to the damnation of themselves and of others ; and the said synod hath separated the same, as obstinate and malapert heretics from the communion of the faithful people, and hath declared them to be spiritually thrown forth. And many other things both wholesome and profitable hath the same council, as touching the premises, established and decreed, whereby they, which by the means of those arch-heretics, and by their false doctrine, have spiritually departed from the Lord's house, may by the canonical rules be reduced to the straight path of truth and verity.

" And moreover (as we to our great grief do hear) not only in the kingdom of Bohemia, and dukedom of Moravia, and other places above recited, but also in certain parts and provinces near adjoining and bordering upon the same, there be many other of the sectaries and followers of the foresaid arch-heretics and heretical opinions ; casting behind their back as well the fear of God as the shame of the world, neither receiving fruit of conversion and repentance by the miserable destruction of the foresaid John Huss and Jerome, but as men drowned in the dungeon of their sins, cease not to blaspheme the Lord God, taking his name in vain (whose minds the father of lies hath damnably blinded), and do read and study the foresaid books or works, containing heresies and errors, being lately by the foresaid synod condemned to be burned ; also to the peril of themselves and many other simple men, and against the statutes, decrees, and ordinances in the synod aforesaid, and the canonical sanctions, do presume to preach and teach the same, to the great peril of souls, and derogation of the catholic faith, and slander of many others besides, we therefore considering, that error, where it is not resisted, seemeth to be allowed and liked, and having a desire to resist such evil and pernicious errors, and utterly root them out from amongst the company of faithful christians, especially from the afore-recited places of Bohemia, Moravia, and other straits and islands joining and bordering upon the same, lest they should stretch out and enlarge their limits, we will and command your discretions by our letters apostolical, the holy council of Constance approving and allowing the same, that you that are archbishops, bishops, and other of the clergy, and every one of you by himself, or by any other or others, being grave and fit persons to have spiritual jurisdiction, do see that all and singular persons, of what dignity, office, pre-eminence, state, or condition soever they be, and by what name soever they are known, which shall presume otherwise to teach, preach, or observe, touching the most high and excellent, the most wholesome and superadmirable sacrament of the blood of our Lord Jesus Christ, or else of the sacrament of baptism, confession of sins, penance for sins, and extreme unction, or else of any other sacraments of the church, and the articles of the faith, than that which the right holy and universal church of Rome doth hold, teach, preach, and observe ; or else that shall presume obstinately by any ways or means, privily or openly, to hold, believe, and teach the articles, books, or doctrine of the foresaid arch-heretics, John Wickliff, John Huss, and Jerome of Prague, being by the foresaid synod of Constance with their authors (as is said) damned and condemned, or dare presume publicly or privily to allow or commend in anywise the death and end of the said arch-heretics, or of any other their receivers, aiders, and favourers, in the favour or support of the foresaid errors, as also their believers and adherents; that then as before, you see and cause them, and every of them to be most severely punished, and that you judge and give sentence upon them as heretics, and that as arrant heretics you leave them to the secular court or power. Let the receivers also and favourers and defenders of such most pestiferous persons, notwithstanding they neither believe, favour, nor have devotion towards their errors, but haply shall receive or entertain such pestiferous persons because of earthly affection or friendly love, besides the punishment due unto them by both laws, over and above the same punishment by competent judges, be so afflicted, for such heinous acts of theirs, and with so severe pain and punishment excruciated, that the same may be to others in like case offending, an example of terror; that, at the least, those whom the fear of God by no means may revoke from such evil doing, yet the severity of this our discipline may force and constrain.

"As touching the third sort, which shall be any manner of ways infected with this damnable sect, and shall after competent admonition repent and amend themselves of such errors and sects aforesaid, and will return again into the lap and unity of our holy mother the church, and fully acknowledge and confess the catholic faith, towards them let the severity of justice, as the quality of the fact shall require, be somewhat tempered with a taste of mercy.

"And furthermore we will and command, that by this our authority apostolical ye exhort and admonish all the professors of the catholic faith, as emperors, kings, dukes, princes, marquises, earls, barons, knights, and other magistrates, rectors, consuls, proconsuls, shires, countries, and universities of the kingdoms, provinces, cities, towns, castles, villages, their lands and other places, and all other executing temporal jurisdiction, according to the form and exigence of the law, that they expel out of their kingdoms, provinces, cities, towns, castles, villages and lands, and other places, all and all manner of such heretics, according to the effect and tenor of the council of Lateran, beginning *Sicut ait Ecclesia, &c.*, that those whom publicly and manifestly by the evidence of their deeds shall be known to be such as like sick and scabbed sheep infect the Lord's flock, they expel and banish till such time as from us, or you, or else other ecclesiastical judges or inquisitors, holding the faith and communion of the holy church of Rome, they shall receive other order and countermand; and that they suffer no such within their shires and circuits to preach or to keep either house or family, either yet to use any handicraft or occupations, or other trades of merchandise, or else to solace themselves any ways, or frequent the company of christian men.

"And furthermore, if such public and known heretics shall chance to die (although not so denounced by the church), yet in this so great a crime let him and them have no christian burial, and let no offerings or oblations be made for them nor received. His goods and substance also from the time of his death, according to the canonical sanctions being confiscate, let no such enjoy them to whom they appertain, till that by the ecclesiastical judges, having power and authority in this behalf, sentence upon that his or their crime of heresy be declared, and promulgated; and let such owners as be found suspected or noted with any such suspicion of heresy, before a competent and ecclesiastical judge, according to the consideration and exigence of that suspicion, and according to the quality of the person, by the arbitrement of such a judge, shew and declare his proper and own innocency with devotion, as beseemeth in that behalf. And if in his purgation, being canonically interdicted, he do fail, or be not able canonically to make his purgation, or that he refuse to take his oath by damnable obstinacy to make such purgation; then let him be condemned as an heretic. But such as through

negligence or through slothfulness shall omit to shew their said innocency, and to make such purgation, let him be excommunicate, and so long put out from the company of christian men, till that they shall make condign satisfaction; so that if by the space of one whole year they shall remain in such excommunication, then let them as heretics be condemned.

"And further, if any shall be found culpable in any point of the aforesaid pestiferous doctrine of the arch-heretics aforesaid, or in any article thereof, whether it be by the report of the seditious, or else well-disposed; let them yet be punished according to the report of the canons. If only through infamy and suspicion of the aforesaid articles, or any of them, any man shall be suspected, and in his purgation canonical for this thing being interdicted, shall fail; let him be accounted as a man convicted, and as a convicted person by the canons let him be punished.

"And furthermore, we invocating and putting in execution the canon of our predecessor of happy memory, Pope Boniface VIII., which beginneth thus, *Ut inquisitionis negotium, &c.* In exhorting-wise require, and also command all temporal potentates, lords and judges before recited, by whatsoever dignities, offices and names they are known, that as they desire to be had, esteemed, and counted for the faithful members and children of the church, and do rejoice in the name of Christ, so likewise for defence of the same faith, they will obey, attend, give their aid and favourable help to you that are archbishops, bishops, and ecclesiastical men, inquisitors of all heretical pravity, and other judges and ecclesiastical persons by you hereunto, as aforesaid, appointed (holding the faith and communion of our holy mother the church) for the searching out, taking, and safe custody of all the aforesaid heretics, their believers, their favourers, their receivers, and their defenders, whensoever they shall be thereunto required.

"And that they bring and cause to be brought (all delay set apart) the aforesaid pestiferous persons so seeking to destroy others with them, into such safe keeping and prisons, as by you the archbishops, bishops, clergy and inquisitors aforesaid, are to be appointed, or else unto such other place or places, as either you or they shall command within any of their dominions, governments and rectories, where they by catholic men, that is, by you the archbishops, bishops, the clergy and inquisitors, or any other that shall be by you appointed, or are already appointed by any of you, may be holden and kept in safe keeping, putting them in fetters, shackles, bolts, and manacles of iron, under most straight custody for escaping away, till such time as all that business, which belongeth unto them, be by the judgment of the church finished and determined, and that of such heresy, by a competent ecclesiastical judge (which firmly holdeth the faith and communion of the aforesaid holy church of Rome) they be condemned.

"The residue let the aforesaid temporal lords, rectors, judges, or other their officers and pursuivants take amongst them with condign deaths, without any delay to punish. But fearing lest to the prejudice and slander of the aforesaid catholic faith and religion, through the pretext of ignorance, any man herein should be circumvented, or that any subtle and crafty men should under the veil of frivolous excuse, cloke and dissemble in this matter; and that as touching the convincing or apprehending of the aforesaid heretics, their receivers and defenders, favourers, believers, and adherents; and also of such as are suspected of heresy, and with such like perverse doctrine in any wise spotted, we might give more perfect instruction; therefore, as well to the kingdom of Bohemia, and parts near adjoining to the same, as all other where this superstitious doctrine began to spread, we have thought it good to send the articles hereunder written concerning the sect of those arch-heretics, for the better direction of the aforesaid catholic faith.

"Touching which articles, by virtue of holy obedience, we charge and command you and all other archbishops and bishops, all manner of commissaries and inquisitors, that every one of them within the diocese and limits of their jurisdiction; and also in the foresaid kingdom and dukedom, and places near adjoining, although the same places be beyond the same their jurisdiction, in the favour of the catholic faith, do give most diligent and vigilant care about the extirpation and correction of those errors, arch-heresies, and most pestiferous sect aforesaid; and also that they compel all defamed persons and suspected of so pestiferous a contagion, whether it be under the penalty of the crime confessed, or of excommunication, suspension, or interdict, or any other formidable pain canonical or legal, when and wheresoever it shall seem good unto them, and as the quality of the act requireth, by an oath corporally taken, either upon the holy Evangelists, or upon the relics of saints, or upon the image of the crucifix, according to the observances of certain places, and according to the interrogatories, to make convenient answer to every article therein written. For we intend against all and singular archbishops, bishops, ecclesiastical persons, or inquisitors which shall show themselves negligent and remiss in the extirpation of the leaven of this heretical pravity, and purging their territories, dioceses, and places to them appointed, of such evil and wicked men, to proceed and cause to be proceeded unto the deprivation and deposition of their pontifical dignities, and shall substitute such other in their places, which can and may be able to confound the said heretical pravity, and proceed to further pains against such by the laws limited, and to others yet more grievous, (if need require) we ourselves will proceed and cause to be proceeded, according as the party, his act, and filthiness of his crime committed, shall deserve. The tenor of those articles whereof we have made mention in this our own writing is in words as follow :—

The Articles of John Huss to be inquired upon.

1. There is one only universal church, which is the university of the predestinate, as shall after be declared.

2. The universal church is only one; and there is one university of those that are predestinate.

3. Paul was never a member of the devil, although he did certain acts like unto the acts of the church malignant.

4. The reprobate are not parts of the church, for that no part of the same finally falleth from her, because that the charity of predestination, which bindeth the same church together, never faileth.

5. The two natures (that is) the Divinity and the humanity, be one Christ.

6. The reprobate, although he be sometime in grace according to present justice, yet is he never a part of the holy church; and the predestinate is ever a member of the church, although sometime he fall from grace *adventitia*, but not from grace of predestination; ever taking the church for the convocation of the predestinate, whether they be in grace or not, according to present justice. And after this sort the church is an article of our belief.

7. Peter is not, nor never was the head of the holy catholic church.

8. Priests living viciously do defile the authority of priesthood, and so, as unfaithful children, do unfaithfully believe of the seven sacraments, of the keys of the church, of offices, of censures, of ceremonies, of the worshipping of relics, indulgences, orders, and other holy things of the church.

9. The papal dignity came and grew from the emperor; and his government and institution sprang from the emperor's government.

10. No man can reasonably affirm either of himself or other, that he is the head of any particular church, or that the bishop of Rome is head of the church of Rome.

11. A man ought not to believe that he who is bishop of Rome is the head of every particular church, unless God have predestinated him.

12. None is the vicar of Christ, or else of Peter, unless he follow him in manners and conditions, seeing that there is no other following more pertinent, nor otherwise apt to receive of God this power procuratory.

For unto the office of a vicegerent of Christ is required the conformity of manners, and the authority of the institutor.

13. The pope is not the manifest and true successor of Peter the prince of apostles, if he live in manners contrary to Peter; and if he hunt after avarice, then is he the vicar of Judas Iscariot. And likewise the cardinals be not the true and manifest successors of the college of the other apostles of Christ, unless they live according to the manner of the apostles, keeping the commandments and councils of our Lord Jesus Christ.

14. The doctors alleging that a man, who will not be amended by ecclesiastical censures, is to be delivered to the secular powers, do follow in this point the bishops, scribes and pharisees, that delivered Christ to the secular power, saying, it is not lawful for us to kill any man, because he would not obey them in all things; and that such be greater homicides than Pilate.

15. The ecclesiastical obedience is such an obedience as the priests of the church have found out, besides the express authority of the scripture. The immediate division of human works, is, that they be either virtuous or vicious: and if a man be vicious and doeth any thing, then he does it viciously; and if he be virtuous, and doeth any thing, then he does it virtuously. For like as vice, which is called a great offence or mortal sin, doth stain all the doings of a vicious man, so virtue doth quicken all the doings of a virtuous man.

16. A priest of God living after his law, and having a knowledge of the Scripture, and a desire to edify the people, ought to preach, notwithstanding any excommunication pretended of the pope. And further, if the pope, or any other magistrate, doth forbid a priest so disposed to preach, he ought not to be obedient unto him. For every one who taketh upon himself the order of priesthood, receiveth in charge the office of a preacher; and of that burden ought he well to discharge himself, any excommunication against him pretended in any wise notwithstanding.

17. By the censures ecclesiastical, as of excommunication, suspending and interdict, the clergy to their own advancement cause the lay people to aid them; they multiply their avarice, they defend their malice, and prepare the way to antichrist. And it is an evident sign that such censures proceed from antichrist, which in their process they call fulminations; that is, their thunderbolts wherewith the clergy principally proceedeth against those that declare the wickedness of antichrist, who so greatly for his own commodity hath abused them.

18. If the pope be evil, especially if he be a reprobate, then is he with Judas a very devil, a thief, and the son of perdition, and is not the head of the holy church militant, nor any member of the same.

19. The grace of predestination is the band wherewith the body of the church and every member of the same is indissolubly joined to their head Christ.

20. The pope or prelate that is evil and reprobate, is a pastor in name, and not in deed, yea he is a thief and a robber in very deed.

21. The pope ought not to be called the most holy one for his office sake, for then ought the king to be called by his office the most holy one; and the hangman, with other such officers also, were to be called holy; yea, the devil himself ought to be called holy, for as much as he is God's officer.

22. If the pope live contrary to Christ, although he climb up by the right and lawful election, according to the common custom of men; yet notwithstanding, should he otherwise climb than by Christ; yea, though we admit that he should enter by the election principally made by God. For Judas Iscariot was lawfully elect of God Christ Jesus to his bishoprick, and yet came not he the same way he ought to do unto the sheepfold.

23. The condemnation of the forty-five articles of John Wickliff made by the doctors is unreasonable, wicked, and nought, and the cause by them alleged is feigned—that is, that none of them are catholic, but every one of them heretical, erroneous, or slanderous.

24. Not for that the electors or the most part of them

have consented together with lively voice, according to the custom of men upon the person of any, therefore that person is lawfully elect, or therefore is the true and manifest successor and vicar of Peter the Apostle, or of any other the apostles in the ecclesiastical office. Wherefore, whether the electors have either well or evil made their election, it behoveth us to believe the same by the works of him that is elected. For in that that every one that worketh more meritoriously to the profit of the church, he hath so much the more authority from God.

25. There is not so much as one spark of appearance, that there ought to be one head, ruling and governing the church in spiritual causes, which should always be conversant in the church militant; for Christ without any such monstrous heads, by his true disciples dispersed through the whole world, could better a great deal rule his church.

26. The apostles and faithful priests of God have right worthily, in all things necessary to salvation, governed the church before the pope's office took place, and so might they do again, by like possibility until Christ came to judgment, if the office should fail.

Let every one that is suspected in the foresaid articles, or else otherwise found with the assertion of them, be examined in manner and form as followeth :—

1. Whether he knew John Wickliff of England, John Huss of Bohemia, and Jerome of Prague, or any of them, and how he came by the knowledge of them; whether that during the lives of them, or any of them, they had been conversant with them, or found any friendship at their hands?

2. Whether he knowing them, or any of them, to be excommunicate, did willingly participate with them; esteeming and affirming the same their participation to be no sin?

3. Whether that after their deaths, he ever prayed for them, or any of them, openly or privily, doing any work of mercy for them, affirming them to be either saints, or else to be saved?

4. Whether he thought them, or any of them to be saints, or whether that ever he spake such words, and whether ever he did exhibit any worship to them as to saints?

5. Whether he believe, hold, and affirm, that every general council, as also the council of Constance, represents the universal church?

6. Whether he believes that that which the holy council of Constance, representing the universal church, hath and doth allow in the favour of the faith, and salvation of souls, is to be approved and allowed of all the faithful christians; and that whatsoever the same council hath condemned and doth condemn to be contrary both to faith and to all good men, is to be believed, holden, and affirmed for condemned, or not?

7. Whether he believes that the condemnations of John Huss, John Wickliff, and Jerome of Prague, made as well upon their persons as their books and doctrine, by the holy general council of Constance be rightly and justly made, and of every good Catholic man are so to be holden or affirmed or not?

8. Whether he believe, hold, and affirm, that John Wickliff of England, John Huss of Bohemia, and Jerome of Prague, were heretics or not, and for heretics to be nominated and preached, yea or not; and whether their books and doctrines were and be perverse or not; for the which, together with their pertinancy, they were condemned by the holy sacred council of Constance for heretics?

9. Whether he have in his custody any treatises, small works, epistles, or other writings in what language or tongue soever, set forth and translated by any of these heretics, John Wickliff, John Huss, and Jerome, or any other of their false disciples and followers, that he may deliver them to the ordinaries of that place, or his commissary, or to the inquisitors upon his oath? And if he say that he hath no such writing about him, but that

they are in some other place, that then you swear him to bring the same before his ordinary, or other aforenamed, within a certain time to him prefixed.

10. Whether he knows any that has the treatises, works, epistles, or any other writings of the aforesaid John Wickliff, John Huss, and Jerome, in whatever tongue they are made or translated, and that he detect and manifest the same, for the purgation of their faith and execution of justice.

11. Especially let the learned be examined, whether he believes that the sentence of the holy council of Constance upon the forty-five articles of John Wickliff, and the thirty articles of John Huss be not Catholic; which saith that some of them are notorious and heretical, some erroneous, others blasphemous, some slanderous, some rash and seditious, some offensive to godly ears?

12. Whether he believes and affirms that in no case it is lawful for a man to swear?

13. Whether he believes that at the commandment of a judge or any other it is lawful to take an oath to tell the truth in any convenient cause, although it be but purging of infamy or not?

14. Whether he believes that perjury wittingly committed, upon what cause soever, whether it be for the safeguard of his own life, or of any other man's life, (yea although it be in the cause and defence of the faith), be a sin or not?

15. Whether a man contemning purposely the rites of the church, and the ceremonies of exorcism, of catechism, and the consecration of the water of baptism be in deadly sin or not?

16. Whether he believe, that after the consecration of the priest, in the sacrament of the altar, under the figure of bread and wine be no material bread and wine; but in all points the same very Christ which was crucified upon the cross, and sitteth upon the right hand of the father?

17. Whether he believe, that after the consecration made by the priest, under the only form of bread, and besides the form of wine, be the very flesh of Christ and his blood, his soul and his deity, and so whole Christ as he is; and in likewise, whether under the form of wine, without the form of bread, be the very flesh of Christ and his very blood, his soul and deity, and so whole Christ, and the same body absolutely under every one of those kinds severally?

18. Whether he doth believe, that the custom of administering to the lay people under the form of bread only, observed of the universal church, and allowed by the only council of Constance, be to be used, and not without the authority of the church at men's pleasures to be altered, and that they that obstinately affirm the contrary to this are to be punished as heretics, or not?

19. Whether he believe that those which contemn the receiving of the sacraments of confirmation, or extreme unction; or else the solemnization of matrimony, commit deadly sin or not?

20. Whether he believe that a christian man, over and besides the contrition of heart, being licensed of a convenient priest, is bound to confess himself only to a priest, and not to any layman, be he never so devout or good, upon the necessity of salvation?

21. Whether he believe, that in cases before put, a priest may absolve a sinner confessing himself, and being contrite, from all sins, and enjoin him penance for the same?

22. Whether he believe, that an evil priest, with due manner and form, with the intention of doing, does verily consecrate, verily absolve, verily baptize, and verily dispose all other sacraments even as the church does?

23. Whether he believe that St. Peter was the vicar of Christ, having power to bind and loose upon the earth?

24. Whether he believe that the pope being canonically elect, which for the time shall be, by that name expressly be the successor of Peter or not, having supreme authority in the church of God?

25. Whether he believe, that the authority or jurisdiction of the pope, an archbishop or a bishop, in binding

or loosing, be more than the authority of a simple priest or not, although he have charge of souls?

26. Whether he believe, that the pope may, upon a just and good cause give indulgences and remission of sins to all christian men, being verily contrite and confessed, especially to those that go on pilgrimage to holy places and good deeds?

27. Whether he believe, that by such grant the pilgrims that visit those churches, and give them any thing, may obtain remission of sins or not?

28. Whether he believe that all bishops may grant unto their subjects, according as the holy canons do limit, such indulgences, or not?

29. Whether he believe and affirm, that it is lawful for faithful christians to worship images and the relics of saints, or not?

30. Whether he believe that those religions, which the church hath allowed, were lawfully and reasonably brought in of the holy fathers, or not?

31. Whether he believe that the pope, or any other prelate for the time being, or their vicars, may excommunicate their subject ecclesiastical or secular for disobedience or contumacy, so that such an one is to be held and taken for excommunicated, or not?

32. Whether he believe, that for the disobedience and contumacy of persons excommunicated, increasing, the prelates or their vicars in spiritual things have power to aggravate and to reaggravate, to put upon men the interdict, and to call for the secular arm; and that the same secular arm or power ought to be obedient to the censures, by their inferiors called for?

33. Whether he believe that the pope and other prelates, or else their vicars, have power in spiritual things to excommunicate priests and laymen that are stubborn and disobedient, from their office, benefice, or entrance into the church, and from the administration of the sacraments of the church, also to suspend them?

34. Whether he believe that it is lawful for ecclesiastical persons, without committing sin, to have any possessions and temporal goods; and whether he believe that it is not lawful for laymen to take away the same from them by their authority: but rather that such takers away and encroachers upon ecclesiastical goods are to be punished as committers of sacrilege, yea, although such ecclesiastical persons live naughtily that have such goods?

45. Whether any such taking away or encroaching upon any priest rashly or violently made, although the priest be an evil liver, be sacrilege, or not?

36. Whether he believe that it is lawful for the laity whether men or women, to preach the word of God, or not?

37. Whether he believe that it is lawful to all priests freely to preach the word of God wherever, whenever, and to whoever it shall please them, although they be not sent at all?

38. Whether he believe that all mortal sins, and especially such as be manifest and public, are to be corrected and to be extirpated, or not?

" Furthermore, we will, command, and decree, that if any by secret information, by you or any other to be received, shall be found either infamed or suspected of any kind of the pestiferous sect, heresy, and doctrine of the most pestilent men, John Wickliff, John Huss, and Jerome of Prague, the arch-heretics aforesaid, or of favouring, receiving, or defending the aforesaid damned men whilst they lived on the earth, their false followers and disciples, or any that believeth their errors, or any that after their death pray for them or any of them, or that nominateth them to be amongst the number of catholic men, or that defendeth them to be placed amongst the number of the saints, either by their preaching, worshipping, or other ways, wherein they deserve to be suspected; that then they by you or some of you may be cited personally to appear before you or some of you, without either proctor or doctor to answer for them, an oath being openly taken by them as is aforesaid, to speak the plain and mere verity of the articles above written, and every of them, or other opportune, as

case and circumstance shall require, according to your discretion, as you or any of you shall see expedient to proceed against them, or any of them, according to these presents, or otherwise canonically, as you shall think good.

" Also that you do publish solemnly, and cause to be published these present letters, omitting the articles and interrogatories herein contained, in the cities and other places of your diocese, where conveniently you may, under our authority, and there to denounce and cause to be denounced all and singular such heretics, with their abettors and favourers of their heresies and errors; of what sex or kind soever, that do hold and defend the said errors, or do participate any manner of way with heretics, privily or openly; of what state, dignity, or condition soever he or they be, patriarch, archbishop, king, queen, duke, or of what other dignity either ecclesiastical or secular he be; also with their advocates and procurators whosoever, which are believers, followers, favourers, defenders, or receivers of such heretics, or suspected to be believers, followers, favourers, defenders, or receivers of them, to be excommunicate every Sunday and festival day, in the presence of the people.

" Furthermore, that you diligently cause to be inquired, by the said our authority, upon all and singular such persons both men and women, that maintain, approve, defend, and teach such errors, or that be favourers, receivers and defenders of them, whether exempt or not exempt, of what dignity, state, pre-eminence, degree, order, or condition soever. And such as you shall find in the said your inquisition, either by their own confession, or by any other means to be defamed, or otherwise infected with the spot of such heresy or error, you through the sentence of excommunication, suspension, interdict, and privation of their dignities, parsonages, offices, or other benefices of the church, and fees which they hold of any church, monastery, and other ecclesiastical places, also of honours and secular dignities and degrees of sciences, or other faculties, as also by other pains and censures of the church, or by any ways and means whatsoever that shall seem to you expedient, by taking and imprisoning their bodies, and other corporal punishments wherewith heretics are punished, or are wont, and are commanded by canonical sanctions to be used; and if they be clerks, by degradation, do correct and punish, and cause them to be corrected and punished with all diligence.

" Furthermore, that you do rise up stoutly and courageously against such heretics, and the goods as well of them, as of the laymen, according to the canonical sanction made against heretics and their followers, under which we will and command them and their partakers to be subject. And also such persons as shall be infamed of the heresies or errors aforesaid, or any of the premises, shall be bound to purge themselves at your arbitration; but the others, who either by witnesses, or by their own confessions, or other allegations or probations, shall be convicted of the aforesaid heresies or articles, or of any the premises, they shall be compelled to revoke and abjure publicly and solemnly the said articles and errors, and to suffer condign penance and punishment, yea, even to perpetual imprisonment (if need be) for the same.

" And to the intent that they shall not nourish any kind of heresies hereafter, either in word, deed or gesture, or shall induce other either in word or deed, privily or openly, directly or indirectly to believe the same, they shall be forced to put in sufficient surety. Who, if it so chance that they will not publicly and solemnly renounce and abjure their articles and errors, and take at your hands condign penance, though it be to perpetual or temporal punishment according to your discretion, neither will be contented to put in sufficient surety that they will not hereafter hold or nourish these errors and heresies, neither will induce other by word or deed privily or openly, directly or indirectly, or by any other manner of colour to believe the same, that then you all proceed against them, according to the quality of their errors and demerits; yea, and if you see it so expedient, as against heretics, and as infected with heresy, by our authority, according to the canonical sanctions summarily, and simply and plainly, *Sine strepitu et figura judicii*, and of office, all appellation or appellations whatsoever ceasing, and that you punish the same, according to the sanctions and traditions canonical, yea if need be, in leaving and committing them to the secular power; and against such as be superiors or learned doctors, laying the censures of ecclesiastical excommunication, all appellation set aside, also invocating, if need shall require, aid of the secular arm; the constitution as well of our predecessor Pope Boniface VIII. of blessed memory, wherein is decreed that no man without his city or diocese (except in certain cases) or in places being one day's journey distant from thence where he inhabiteth, shall be called into judgment, and that no man do presume to depute judges from the see apostolic, without the city and diocese where they are deputed to proceed against any; and do presume to commit their authority to any other person or persons, or to fetch and remove any man beyond one day's journey from out his diocese where he dwelleth, or at most two days' journey, if it be in a general council; as also all other constitutions of any bishop of Rome, touching as well judges delegate, as persons not be called to judgment beyond a certain number; or else any other edict, indulgence, privilege, or exemption general or special, granted from the apostolic see, for any person or persons not to be interdicted, suspended, or excommunicated, or cited up to judgment without the compass of certain limits, or else whatsoever thing otherwise may hinder, stop, or impeach your jurisdiction, power, and free proceeding herein by any means to the contrary notwithstanding. Given at Constance the first year of our popedom."

This bloody and abominable commission of Pope Martin, which I have copied out of a certain old monument, remaining in the hands of Master Hackluyt, student in the Temple, seems to be directed and given out to the public destruction of all faithful christian men, about the latter end and breaking up of the council of Constance, (A. D. 1418.) By the which the prudent reader may note and consider, what labour, what policy, what counsel, and what laws have been set, what ways have been taken, what severity has been shewed, how men's power, wit, and authority of the whole world have conspired together from time to time, continually by all manner of means to subvert and supplant the word and way of the Lord; and yet notwithstanding man has not prevailed, but all his force and devised polices hath been overthrown, dispatched, and with the counsel of Ahithophel and Ammon, have been brought to nought, and contrary to the fury of the world, the gospel of Christ has still increased. Neither yet for all this will the pope cease to spurn and rebel still against the kingdom of Christ and his gospel, against which neither he, nor yet the gates of hell shall ever prevail. The Lord of hosts be merciful to his poor persecuted flock! Amen.

Against this pestilent bull and inquisition of Pope Martin the great antichrist, I thought good here to annex another contrary writing of the Bohemians, bearing the name and subscription of Procopius, Conrad, and other captains of the Bohemians; which seems to have been written not long after the death of Zisca, against the pestiferous see of Rome, the tenor whereof here followeth.

A fruitful and Christian Exhortation of the Bohemians to kings and princes, to stir them up to the zeal of the Gospel.

"May the Almighty God the Father, by his well-beloved Son Jesus Christ, and by his Holy Spirit, open the understanding both of you and of all christians, and lighten your hearts with the light of his doctrine of righteousness, and make you to continue therein surely established to the end. This we desire of you for your salvation, all ye honourable, wise, and honest noblemen, and all the commonalty, yea rich and poor, hear and consider with diligent heed the words of this present letter, which is sent unto you from the country of the Bohemians. It is manifest and well known to you and many other cities, kings, princes, and lords, that now for a certain number of years there hath been great discord betwixt us and you; and there have been some which have moved you by letters, and provoked you to make war against us, and to destroy us. And as well on your part as ours many men, as well noble as unnoble, have foolishly lost their lives. Yet never hitherto have ye in any part understood our faith by our own confession, neither whether we be able to prove the same out of the scriptures, or not; and yet in the mean time kings, princes, lords, and cities, have sustained great damage. And hereof we greatly marvel that you do so much trust and believe the pope and his priests, which give you drink full of poison, and such comfort as no man can understand, in that they say that they will give you forgiveness of all your sins, and great grace and pardon, to this end that you should war upon us and destroy us; whereas their graces and pardons are none other than great lies, and a great seducing of the body and soul of all them that believe them, and put their trust in them. This we would prove to them, and convince them by the holy scripture; and we would suffer, that whoever is desirous to hear, the same should hear it. For the pope and all his priests herein deal with you as the devil would have done with our Lord Jesus Christ. Of whom Luke writes in his fourth chapter, that he brought him upon an high hill, and shewed unto him in the twinkling of an eye, all the kingdoms that are in the compass of the earth, and said unto him, 'I will give thee,' &c. So the devil deceiveth the pope, and all the priests, with the riches of the world, and worldly power; and they think they can give grace and pardon when they will; and they themselves shall never find favour before Almighty God, except they repent and make amends, because of their great deceiving of Christendom. And how can they give that to others, which they themselves have not? So did the devil, who was rich in promising, and poor in giving. And like as the devil is not ashamed to tell a lie, so all they are not ashamed to speak that which shall never be found true, nor be proved by the holy scriptures, because for no cause they stir up kings, princes, lords, and citizens, to make war against us, not to the end that the christian faith should thereby be defended, but because they fear that their secret vices and heresies shall be disclosed and made manifest. For if they had a true cause, and a godly love to the christian faith, they would then take the books of the holy scripture, and would come to us, and confute us with the weapons of God's word, and that is our chief desire. For so did the apostles of our Lord Jesus Christ, who came to the Pagans and Jews, and brought them from their infidelity to the true faith of our Lord Jesus Christ; and this they did in the spirit of meekness, as the apostle Paul writes in the sixth chapter of the Galatians, 'Brethren, if any man be grieved,' &c. So ought they also to do, if they perceived that they were just and we unjust. And if we would not abide instruction, then they might take to them kings, princes, lords, and imperial cities, and resist us according to the commandments of the holy scripture. But this is the subtle defence of all the bishops and priests, that they say that Master Huss and Jerome, which were burnt at Constance, were confuted by the holy father the pope, and by the whole council. For ye must understand that they were not overcome by the Holy Ghost, but unjustly, with wrongful violence, which God may yet hereafter grievously punish in all them that gave their counsel and aid thereto. And they say it ought not to be suffered, that we should be heard in confessing our faith. How may that be proved by the holy scripture, since Christ heard the devil, as it is written in the fourth chapter of Matthew? And they are not better than Christ, nor we worse than the devil. If they be just and have the truth with them (as they say they have) and we be unrighteous, why do they fear, since the truth ought not to be afraid of falsehood, as Esdras writeth in his second book, the third chapter? Zorobabel declareth that truth is of all things the most mighty, and overcometh all things. For Christ is the truth, John xiv. 'I am the way, the truth,' &c. And the devil is the father of lies, John viii. 'He is a liar from the beginning, and never abode in the truth, and there is no truth in him.' Therefore, if the pope and his priests have the truth, let them overcome us with the word of God. But if they have lies, then they cannot long abide in their presumption. Wherefore, we exhort and beseech all the imperial cities, all kings, princes, noblemen, rich and poor, for God's sake, and for his righteousness, that one of them write hereof to another, and that there may be some means made, how we may commune with you safely and friendly, at some such place as shall be fit both for you and us, and bring with you your bishops and teachers, and let them and our teachers fight together with the word of God, and let us hear them, and let not the one overcome the other by violence or false subtlety, but only by the word of God. And if your bishops and teachers have better proofs of their faith out of the holy scripture than we, and our faith be found untrue, we will receive penance and satisfaction, according to the gospel. But if your bishops and teachers be overcome of ours by the holy scripture, then do ye repent and hearken to us, and hold with us. And if your bishops and teachers will cease from their spiritual pride, and repent and make satisfaction ; then we will help you according to our power, and will compel them, either to join with us, or else we will expel them out of Christendom. And if your bishops and teachers will say that it is not lawful for laymen to hear such reasoning, or to be present at it ; that you may understand to tend to no other end, but that they fear they should be overcome and put to shame in the sight of you. For if they knew that they should overcome therein, out of doubt they would desire that every man should hear it, and thereby their glory should become the greater, and their fame and praises should be increased upon the earth. And if your bishops and teachers counsel you to come to no hearing with us, then do it whether they will or no, and suffer not yourselves at any time to be so foolishly seduced with their foolish pardons, but tarry at home in your houses with your wives and children. And let the pope of Rome come to us with all his cardinals and bishops, and with all his priests, with his own person and power, to war with us, and let themselves deserve the absolution of sins, grace and pardon, which they preach to you (for they have great need of forgiveness of sins, grace, and pardon,) and by the grace of God, we will give them pardon enough as they shall need. But their subtle excuse is this, they say that it belongs not to priests to fight with bodily weapons : and true it is that it belongs not to them ; but it belongs as little to them to stir up, to counsel, and to fortify others thereto. For Paul saith in the first chapter of the Romans, and in the fifth of the Galatians, 'That all that do such things are worthy of everlasting death.'

"And if ye will not determine to do any other thing than to fight against us, then will we take the Lord to our help and his truth, and we will defend it to the death, and we will not be afraid for the excommunication or curse of the pope, or his cardinals, or of the bishops, because we know that the pope is not God, as he maketh himself, that he can curse and excommunicate when he will, or bless when he will ; who has now these many years cursed and excommunicated us, and yet notwithstanding, God and his gracious blessing hath been our help. But peradventure ye will say, that though we see that bishops and priests be evil and wicked, yet we cannot do without them ; for who should baptize our children, who should hear confessions, and minister the holy sacraments ? and then also we should be within the excommunication of the pope, and of his bishops. Well-beloved, ye need to take no care for these matters. The excommunicating of the pope hurts you nothing. Fear ye the excommunicating of God, and the Lord will provide for those things well enough. If ye would banish evil bishops and priests, ye should have good priests who should baptize your children, hear confessions, and minister the holy mysteries, because when the devil is banished, then place is made for the Holy Ghost : so when ill bishops and priests shall be banished, then place shall be made for good priests and bishops. Also, your bishops and priests say, that we are miscreants and heretics, and that we believe not on purgatory, upon the Virgin Mary, nor upon the saints ; wherein they say ill, for we will prove by the holy scripture, that we know better by God's grace how we ought to believe upon purgatory, and upon Mary the mother of our Lord, and upon his well-beloved saints, than they can tell us. Also they say, that we will not be obedient unto the pope. Truly when he shall become holy and just, then we know well that we ought to be obedient to him in all things, and not before. They say also, that we destroy God's holy service, in that we destroy monasteries, banishing thence the wicked monks and nuns. Truly we did it, thinking once that they were holy, that they did the reverend service of God ; but after that we well perceived and considered their life and works, then we perceived that they were false lowly hypocrites, and wicked builders on high, and sellers of pardons and masses for the dead, and such as devoured in themselves the sins of the people. And whereas they said that they rise at midnight when other men sleep, and pray for the sins of the people : forasmuch as their selling of their prayers and masses for the dead for gifts, is no better than hypocrisy and heresy ; therefore, if we do speak against them and destroy their monasteries, we do not therein destroy the service of God, but rather the service of the devil, and the schools of heretics. And if ye knew them as we know them, ye would as diligently destroy them as we do. For Christ our Lord did not ordain any such order, and therefore it must needs come to pass that shortly it shall be destroyed, as our Lord said in the gospel of St. Matthew, chap. xv. Every plant which my Father hath not planted, shall be rooted up."

[Here are added sixteen articles against the Romish priests, which we omit.]

(Signed) Procopius, Smahors, Conrad, Samssmolich ; captains of Bohemia.

Now to return to the wars of the Bohemians again. After Zisca was dead, there was great fear, sorrow, and lamentation in the army, the soldiers accusing fortune which gave over such an invincible captain to be overcome with death. Immediately there was a division in the host, the one part choosing Procopius Magnus to be their captain, the other part saying, that there was none could be found worthy to succeed Zisca, whereupon they choosing out certain to serve the wars, named themselves orphans.

Thus the Taborites being divided into two armies, the one part retained their old and accustomed name, and the other, by reason of the death of their captain, named themselves orphans. And although often there was dissension between them, yet whenever any foreign power came towards them, they joined their powers together in one camp, and defended themselves. They seldom went to any fenced towns, except it were to buy necessaries, but lived with their wives and children in their camp and tents. They had amongst them many cars, which they used as a bulwark ; for whenever they went unto battle, they made two wings of them, which closed in the footmen. The wings of the horsemen were on the outside, and when they saw their time to join battle, the waggon-men which led the wings, going forth to the emperor's standard, and compassing in such part of their enemies as they would, did close themselves in together, whereby the enemies being enclosed, so that they could not be rescued, they were partly by the footmen, and partly by the men that were in the cars, with their darts, slain. The horsemen fought without the fortification ; and if it happened that they were oppressed, or put to flight, by and by the cars opening themselves, received them as it were into a fenced city ; and by this means they got many victories, forsomuch as their enemies were ignorant of their policies.

These two armies went forth, the one into Silesia, and the other into Moravia, and returned again with great prey, before their enemies knew of their coming. After this they besieged the town of Swietla in Austria, where the Taborites and the Orphans during two nights, continually assaulted the walls without ceasing; but Albert, duke of Austria, coming with his host to aid the citizens, they fought for the space of almost four hours, the valiantest warriors being slain on both parts. At length the battle was broken off, and the Taborites lost their cars, and Albert was put out of his camp and tents. Within a while after, Procopius Magnus came again and enclosed the city of Rhetium in Austria with a notable siege. They of Prague were in his army, and Boslaus Cygneus, of whom we spake before, was slain there with a dart, and the city of Rhetium was taken by force, sacked and burnt. The burgrave of Malderburg, lord of the town, was also taken and carried unto Prague, where also he died in prison.

These things being done, the emperor sent for the nobles of Bohemia, who went to him to a town of Hungary, called Posonium, in the borders of Austria, upon the banks of the river Danube; but they would not enter into the town, but remained without the town in their tents; whither, the emperor going out unto them, communed much with them, as touching his right and title, and the recovering of his father's kingdom, promising if there were any cause, which did alienate the Bohemians' minds from him, that he would take away all the occasion thereof: they made answer, that he had made war upon them without cause, and that he had suffered their countrymen, contrary to his promise, to be burnt at Constance not being heard, and the kingdom to be contumeliously interdicted, and the nobles of Bohemia to be condemned by the church of Rome as heretics; and that he should think the force and power of the Bohemians not to be so small, but that they would provide for their own honour. Whereto the emperor answered very gently, and offered them a general council, wherein they might declare their innocency, if they would submit themselves to the judgment of the universal church; but the Bohemians who were become valiant victors in arms, would not be overcome with words; and so nothing being finally concluded, the emperor returned home.

Then Pope Martin, perceiving the gospel to increase daily more and more, sent the cardinal of Winchester, an Englishman, born of a noble house, into Germany, to move them to war against the Bohemians. The emperor also assisted him.

There were three armies provided. In the first army were the dukes of Saxony, and the lower cities. The second army, which was gathered of the Franconians, was under the conduct of the marquis of Brandenburg. The third army was led by Otho, the archbishop of Treves, whom the Rhenenses, the Bavarians, and the imperial cities of Swevia followed. These armies entering into Bohemia in three several parts, after they were passed the wood, joined together and pitched before Misna. This town a certain learned and eloquent protestant, named Prichicho, the night before had won from the papists; wherefore the army was determined first to recover that city, before they would go any further. But when news came to the host, how the protestants had gathered an army, and came with all speed towards them, they fled before they saw their enemies, and went to Tacovia, leaving behind them their warlike engines with a great prey. The cardinal was not yet come to the camp, but meeting them in their flight at Tacovia, he marvelled at the cowardly flight of so many noble and valiant men, desiring them that they would turn again to their enemies, which, he said, were far weaker than they. Which thing, when he had long laboured about in vain, he was fain to be a companion with them in their flight. They were scarcely entered the wood, when the Bohemians coming upon them, set upon the rearward. Then was their flight much more disordered and fearful than before, neither did they leave flying before the Bohemians left following. Then all impediment or hindrance being taken away, they vanquished Tacovia; and having obtained great store of warlike engines, they destroyed Misna. And when they would have returned home by Franconia, they had great sums of money sent unto them, that they should not waste

or destroy the countries of Bamberg and Noremberg; whereby the host of the Bohemians was greatly enriched.

Sigismund, the emperor, having news of these things, went straight unto Noremberg, and gathered there fresh aid and help. Also Pope Martin sent Julian, the cardinal of St. Angelo, into Germany, with his ambassage, to make war against the Bohemians, and that he should in the council of Basil, which would now shortly draw on, be president in the pope's name. He, entering into Germany, went straight to Noremberg to the emperor, where many of the nobles of Germany were assembled.

There was a new expedition decreed against the Bohemians, against the eighth of the kalends of July, and Frederick, marquis of Brandenburg, appointed general of that war, who should follow the cardinal. He entered into Bohemia by the way that leadeth unto Thopa, and Albert, prince of Austria, was appointed to bring his army through Moravia.

In this expedition were Albert and Christopher of Bavaria, and Frederick, dukes of Saxony, John and Albert princes of Brandenburg, with their father, who was general of those wars. Also the bishops of Hyperbolis, Bamberge, and Eysten. Also the company of the Swevians, which they called the company of St. George, and the magistrates of the imperial cities, the bishop of Mentz, Treves, and Cologne, sent their aids, and with them the chieftains of their provinces. It is said that the number of their horsemen were above forty thousand, but their footmen were not full so many, for the Germans for the most part fight their battles on horseback.

Also Rhenatus, prince of Lorraine, promised to come to these wars; but being hindered by his civil wars, forsomuch as he went about to vanquish the earl of Vandome, he could not keep his promise, and the county palatine of Rheine, who did aid and succour the earl of Vandome, could not go against the Bohemians. The cardinal, staying for them, deferred his journey until the kalends of August. In the meantime Albert, leading his army out of Austria, understanding that the cardinal was not present at the day appointed, and seeing himself unable to encounter with the Bohemian power, he returned back again. After this the cardinal entered into Bohemia with a huge army, and destroyed many of the protestants' towns, killing men, women, and children, sparing neither old nor young; notwithstanding this, his tyranny was exercised in the uttermost borders of Bohemia, for his captains feared to enter far into the land. The Bohemians, as soon as they had heard that their enemy was come, made ready and gathered their host with all speed, and laid siege to a tower called Stiltiverge, and brought it under subjection.

In the meantime there fell such a marvellous sudden fear amongst the papists throughout the whole camp, that they began most shamefully to run away before any enemy came in sight. The cardinal Julian, marvelling at this most sudden fear, and what should move so great an army to flee, went about to the captains, exhorting them to put on armour, to order their battles, and courageously to abide their enemies, saying they did not fight for the glory of their kingdom, or for the possession of lands, but for their lives, honour, and religion of Christ, and for the salvation of souls. How ignominious a thing is it (said he) for the Germans to flee in battle, whose courage and valiantness all the world doth extol? It were much better to die, than to give place to any enemies before they were seen; for they can by no means live in safety within the walls, who give place unto their enemy in the field; for it is the weapon that defends a man and not the walls, and except they would even presently defend their liberty with the sword, they should shortly be in greater bondage, more miserable than any death. But this exhortation was all in vain, for fear had put away all boldness; for the ensigns were snatched up, and as though there had been no captain in the host, every man run headlong away. No man regarded any commandment, neither once took his leave of his captain, but casting away their armour with speedy flight, they ran away, as though their enemy had been at their

z

backs. The cardinal also, although it were against his will, was forced to do the like.

Thus the protestants, by the fear of their enemies, made the more bold and courageous, pursued them through the woods, and had a great prey and spoil of them. Notwithstanding, Albert, when he heard that the cardinal was entered into Bohemia, with all speed came again out of Austria with his army, and besieged the strong town of Prezorabia ; but when he understood how the cardinal was fled, he left off his purpose, and returned through Moravia, which was not yet subject to him, and destroyed above fifty towns with fire and sword, took many of their cities by force, and spoiled them, committing great murder and slaughter, and so afflicted them that they took upon them his yoke, and promised to be subject and obedient to him under this condition, that as touching religion he would be bound to do that which the council of Basil should determine.

Then was there an ambassage sent out of Bohemia unto Basil, where Sigismund held the council, who, during the time of the wars had kept himself at Noremberg. When he should take his journey unto Rome to be crowned emperor, he wrote letters unto the nobles of Bohemia, wherein was contained, how that he was a Bohemian born, and how he was not more attached to any nation than to his own, and that he went to Rome for none other cause but to be crowned, which honour should also be a renown to the Bohemians, to advance whom had been always his especial care.

Also, how that through his endeavour the council was begun at Basil, exhorting all such as were desirous to be heard as touching religion, that they should come thither, and that they would not maintain any quarrel contrary to the holy mother the church ; that the council would lovingly and gently hear their reasons ; that they should only endeavour themselves to agree with the synod as touching religion, and reserve and keep a quiet and peaceable kingdom for him, against his return : neither should the Bohemians think to refuse his government, whose brother, father, and uncle had reigned over them, and that he would reign over them, after no other mean or sort than other christian kings used to do.

The council of Basil also wrote their letter to the Bohemians, that they should send their ambassadors who should shew a reason of their faith, promising safe conduct to go and come, and free liberty to speak what they would. The Bohemians on this point, were of two opinions ; for the protestants, and almost all the common people said, it was not good to go, alleging the examples of John Huss, and Jerome of Prague, who going unto Constance, under the safe conduct of the emperor, were there openly burned. But the nobility, following the mind of Maynard. prince of the new house, said, that they ought to go to the council, and that they are not to be suffered who had invented those new and strange opinions of faith, and new kind of religion, except they would render account of their doings and sayings before the universal church, and defend those things which they had openly taught before learned men. This opinion prevailed, and an ambassage of three hundred horse was sent to Basil. The chief whereof were William Cosca, a valiant knight, and Procopius, surnamed Magnus, a man of worthy fame for his manifold victories, John Rochezana, preacher of Prague, Nicholas Galecus, minister of the Taborites, and one Peter, an Englishman, of excellent, prompt and pregnant wit. The people came in great numbers out of the town, and many out of the synod and council, attending before the gates to see the coming of this valiant and famous people ; others gathered together, in great numbers into the streets where they should pass through. The matrons, maids, and children filled the windows and houses to behold and see, and to marvel at their strange kind of apparel, and stout courageous countenances, saying, that it was not untrue which was reported of them : notwithstanding all men beheld Procopius, saying, this is he who has overthrown the papists in so many battles, who has subverted so many towns and slain so many

men, whom both his enemies, and also his own soldiers do fear and reverence ; also, that he was a bold, valiant, and invincible captain, who could not be overcome with any terror, labour, or travail.

These Bohemian ambassadors were gently received. The next day after, Cardinal Julian, sending for them to the council-house, made a gentle, long, and eloquent oration to them, exhorting them to unity and peace, saying, that the church was the spouse of our Saviour Christ, and the mother of all faithful, that it hath the keys of binding and losing, and also that it is white and fair, without spot or wrinkle, and cannot err in those points that are necessary to salvation, and that he who contemns the same church is to be counted as a profane heathen and publican, neither can this church be represented better by any means than in this council. He exhorts them also to receive the decrees of the council, and to give no less credit to the council than to the gospel, by whose authority the scriptures themselves are received and allowed. Also that the Bohemians, who call themselves the children of the church, ought to hear the voice of their mother, who is never unmindful of her children ; how that now of late they have lived apart from their mother ; although (said he) that is no new or strange thing, for there have been many in times past who have forsaken their mother, and yet seeking after salvation have returned to her again ; that in the time of Noah's flood, as many as were without the ark perished ; that the Lord's passover was to be eaten in one house ; that there is no salvation to be sought for out of the church, and that this is the garden and famous fountain of water, whereof whosoever shall drink, shall not thirst everlastingly ; that the Bohemians have done as they ought, in that they have sought the fountains of this water at the council, and have determined now at length to give ear unto their mother. Now all hatred ought to cease, all armour and weapon to be laid apart, and all occasion of war utterly to be rejected. For the fathers would lovingly and gently hear whatever they would say in their own cause or quarrel, requiring only that they would willingly receive and embrace the good counsels and determinations of the sacred synod ; whereto not only the Bohemians, but also all other faithful christians, ought to consent and agree, if they will be partakers of eternal life.

This oration of the cardinal was heard and very well approved by the fathers. Whereto the Bohemians answered in a few words, that they neither had contemned the church nor the council ; that the sentence given at Constance, against those who were unheard, doth diminish nothing of the christian religion ; that the authority of the fathers hath always remained amongst them inviolate ; and that whatever the Bohemians have taught, was confirmed by the scriptures and gospel ; and that they are now come to manifest their innocency before the whole church, and to require open audience, where the laity may also be present. Their request was granted them ; and being further demanded in what points they did disagree from the church of Rome, they propounded four articles.

First. They affirmed, that all such as would be saved, ought of necessity to receive the communion of the last supper under both kinds of bread and wine.

The second article. They affirmed all civil rule and dominion to be forbidden to the clergy by the law of God.

The third article. That the preaching of the word of God is free for all men, and in all places.

The fourth article. As touching open crimes and offences which are in nowise to be suffered for the avoiding of greater evil.

These were the only propositions which they propounded before the council in the name of the whole realm. Then another ambassador affirmed, that he had heard of the Bohemians very many things offensive to christian ears, amongst which this was one point, that they had preached that the invention of the order of begging friars was diabolical.

Then Procopius, rising up, said, " Nor is it untrue ; for if neither Moses, neither before him the patriarchs, neither after him the prophets, neither in the new law Christ and his apostles did institute the order of begging friars, who does doubt but that it was an invention of the devil, and a work of darkness?"

This answer of Procopius was derided by them all. And cardinal Julian went about to prove, that not only the decrees of the patriarchs and prophets, and those things which Christ and his apostles had instituted, were of God, but also that all such decrees as the church should ordain, being guided through the Holy Ghost, be the works of God. Although, as he said, the order of begging friars might seem to be taken out of some part of the gospel.

The Bohemians chose out four divines who shoud declare their articles to be taken out of the scriptures. Likewise on the contrary part there were four appointed by the council. This disputation continued fifty days, where many things were alleged on either part, whereof, as place shall serve, more hereafter (by the grace of Christ) shall be said, when we come to the time of that council.

In the meantime, while the Bohemians were thus in long conflicts with Sigismund the emperor and the pope, fighting for their religion, to whom, notwithstanding all the fulness of the pope's power was bent against them, God of his goodness had given such noble victories, as is above expressed, and ever did prosper them so long as they could agree among themselves; as these things (I say) were doing in Bohemia, King Henry V. of England, fighting likewise in France, although for no like matter of religion, fell sick at Blois and died, after he had reigned nine years, five months, three weeks, and odd days from his coronation. This king in life, and in all his doings, was so devout and serviceable to the pope and his chaplains, that he was called by many the prince of priests, he left behind him a son being yet an infant, nine months and fifteen days of age, whom he had by Queen Katharine, daughter to the French king, who was married to him about two or three years before. The name of which prince, succeeding after his father, was Henry VI., left under the government and protection of his uncle, named Humphrey, duke of Gloucester.

The names of the Archbishops of Canterbury contained in this Fifth Book.

54. Simon Islepe.
56. Simon Langham.
57. William Witlesey.
58. Simon Sudbury.
59. William Courtney.
60. Thomas Arundel.
61. Henry Chichesley.

THE END OF THE FIFTH BOOK

ACTS AND MONUMENTS.

BOOK VI.

PERTAINING TO

THE LAST THREE HUNDRED YEARS, FROM THE LOOSING OUT OF SATAN.

A PREFACE TO THE READER.

ACCORDING to the five different periods and states of the church, so have I divided hitherto the order of this present church history into five principal parts, every part containing three hundred years. So that now coming to the last three hundred years, that is, to the last times of the church, counting from the time of Wickliff: forasmuch as in the compass of the said last three hundred years are contained great troubles and perturbations of the church, with the marvellous reformation of the same through the wonderous operation of the Almighty; all which things cannot be comprehended in one book; I have therefore disposed the later three hundred years into several books, beginning now with the sixth book, at the reign of King Henry VI. In which book, beside the many and grievous persecutions raised up by antichrist, herein is also to be observed, that whereas it has of long time been received and thought of the common people, that this religion now generally used, has sprung up and risen but of late, even by the space (as many do think) of twenty or thirty years, it may now manifestly appear, not only by the acts and monuments heretofore passed, but also by the histories hereafter following, how this profession of Christ's religion has been spread abroad in England, of old and ancient time, not only for the space of these two hundred late years, from the time of Wickliff, but has continually from time to time sparkled abroad, although the flames thereof have never so perfectly burst out, as they have done within these hundred years and more; as by these histories here collected and gathered out of registers, especially of the diocese of Norwich, shall manifestly appear; wherein may be seen what men, and how many both men and women within the diocese of Norwich there have been, who have defended the same doctrine which now is received by us in the church. Which persons, although then they were not so strongly armed in their cause and quarrel as of late years they have been, yet were they warriors in Christ's church, and fought to their power in the same cause. And although they gave back through tyranny, yet judge thou the best, good reader, and refer the cause thereof to God, who reveals all things according to his determinate will and appointed time.

This young prince being under the age of one year, after the death of his father, succeeded to the throne and kingdom of England, (A. D. 1422), and in the eighth year was crowned at Westminster; and the second year after was crowned also at Paris, Henry, bishop of Winchester, cardinal, being present at them both, he reigned thirty-eight years, and then was deposed by Edward IV. as hereafter (Christ willing) shall be declared in his time. In the first year of his reign was burned the constant witness-bearer of Christ's doctrine, William Tailor, a priest, under Henry Chichesley, archbishop of Canterbury. Of this William Tailor I read, that in the days of Thomas Arundel he was first apprehended, and abjured. Afterwards in the days of Henry Chichesley, about A.D. 1421, which was a year before his burning, William Tailor appeared again in the convocation before the archbishop, being brought by the bishop of Worcester, being complained of as having taught at Bristol, these articles following:

First, That whoever hangs any scripture about his neck, takes away the honour due only to God, and gives it to the devil.

Secondly, That no human person is to be worshipped, but only God is to be adored.

Thirdly, that the saints are not to be worshipped nor invoked.

Upon these articles William Tailor being examined, denied that he did preach or hold them in way of defending them, but only did commune and talk upon the same, especially upon the second and third articles, only in way of reasoning, and for argument sake. And to justify his opinion to be true in what he held, he brought out of his bosom a paper, wherein were contained certain articles, with the testimonies of the doctors alleged, and exhibited the same to the archbishop. Who then being bid to stand aside, the archbishop consulting together with the bishops and other prelates what was to be done in the matter delivered the writings to Master John Castle, and John Rikinghale, the two vice-chancellors of Oxford, and Cambridge, and to John Langdon, monk of Canterbury, who, advising with themselves, and with other divines, about the articles and allegations, on the Monday following presented the articles of William Tailor to the archbishops and prelates. as erroneous and heretical. Upon which, William Tailor being called before them, in conclusion was contented to revoke the same, and for his penance was by them condemned to perpetual prison.

Notwithstanding, through favour, they were contented that he should be released from his incarceration, in case he would put in sufficient surety in the king's chancery, and swear that he shall never hold nor favour such opinions hereafter. And thus William Tailor, appointed to appear the next Wednesday at Lambeth, before the archbishop, to take his absolution from his long excommunication during the time from Thomas Arundel, appeared again before him, where he, laying aside his cloak, his cap, and stripped to his doublet, kneeled at the feet of the archbishop, who, then standing up, and having a rod in his hand, began the psalm *Miserere, &c.* His chaplains answering the second verse. After that was said, the collect, *Deus cui proprium, &c.* with certain other prayers. And so taking an oath of him, the archbishop committed him to the custody of the bishop of Worcester, to whom power and authority was permitted to release him upon those conditions. And thus was William Tailor for that time absolved, being enjoined notwithstanding to appear at the next convocation, whenever it should be, before the archbishop or his successor that should follow him.

In the meantime, while William Tailor was thus in the custody of the bishop of Worcester, there passed certain writings between him and one Thomas Smith, priest at Bristol, in the which writings William Tailor replied against Thomas, concerning the question of worshipping of saints. Upon the occasion of which reply, being brought to the hands of the bishop of Worcester, William Tailor began a new to be troubled, and was brought again before the public convocation of the clergy by the said bishop of Worcester, to answer unto his writings. This was the eleventh day of February, A. D. 1422. To which convocation William being presented, his writings were read to him; which he would not, nor could not, deny to be of his own hand-writing.

The tenor and effect of whose writing only tended to prove, that every petition and prayer for any supernatural gift ought to be directed to God alone, and to no creature. Although in his writing he did not utterly deny that it was lawful in any respect to pray to saints (and brings for the same Thomas Aquinas) but only in respect of that worship, which is called *latria;* and he seems little or nothing to differ from the superstition of the papists. And yet the writing, being delivered by the archbishop to the four orders of friars of London to be examined, was found erroneous and heretical in these points :—

1. That every prayer, which is a petition of some supernatural gift or free gift, is to be directed only to God.

2. That prayer is to be directed to God alone.

3. To pray to any creature is to commit idolatry.

4. Also, another opinion there was, much like to the other, to make up the fourth ;—hereupon came down a writ from the king, directed to the lord mayor and sheriffs of London, *De hæretico comburendo,*" i. e. "the writ for burning a heretic," dated the first day of March, the first year of his reign. Upon which, William Tailor, condemned as a relapse, was first degraded, and then sentenced to be burned, and so was committed to the secular power, then being brought to Smithfield, the first day of March, with christian constancy, after long imprisonment, he there consummated his martyrdom, (A. D. 1422.)

The manner of his degrading was all one with the degrading of John Huss before, for the papists use but one form for all men. First, Degrading them from priesthood, by taking from them the chalice and patine. From deaconship, by taking from them the gospel-book and tunicle. From sub-deaconship, by taking from them the epistle-book and tunicle. From acoluteship, by taking from them the cruet and candlestick. From an exorcist, by taking away the book of exorcisms or gradual. From the sextonship, by taking away the church-door-key and surplice. And likewise from benedict, in taking away the surplice, and first tonsure, &c. All which they in due order accomplished upon this godly martyr, before his burning.

John Florence, a Turner.

John Florence, a turner, dwelling in Shelton, in the diocese of Norwich, was attached, because he held and taught these heresies here underwritten (as they called them) contrary to the determination of the church of Rome.

That the pope and cardinals have no power to make or constitute any laws.

That there is no day to be kept holy, but only the Sunday which God has hallowed.

That images are not to be worshipped, neither that the people ought to set up any lights before them in the churches, neither to go on pilgrimage, neither to offer for the dead.

That curates should not take the tithes of their parishioners, but that such tithes should be divided amongst the poor parishioners.

That all such as swear by their life or power, shall be damned, except they repent.

On the second of August, in the year 1424, John Florence personally appeared before William Bernam, chancellor to William, bishop of Norwich, where, being threatened by the judge, he acknowledged that he had erred, and submitted himself to the correction of the church, and abjured, taking an oath that from that time forward he would not hold, teach, preach or willingly defend any error or heresy contrary to the determination of the church of Rome, neither maintain, help, or aid any that shall teach or hold any such errors or heresies, either privily or publicly ; and for his offence he was enjoined this penance following :—

That for three Sundays, in a solemn procession in the cathedral church of Norwich, he should be disciplined, *i. e.* have a rod or scourge laid on him before all the people. The same also should be done around his parish-church of Shelton, three other several Sundays, he being bareheaded, bare-footed, and bare-necked, after the manner of a public penitent, his body being covered with a canvass shirt, and canvass breeches, carrying in his hand a taper of a pound weight; and that done he was dismissed.

Richard Belward of Ersham.

Richard Belward of Ersham, in the diocese of Norwich, was accused of holding and teaching these errors and opinions here under-written, contrary to the determination of the church of Rome.

That ecclesiastical ministers have no power to excommunicate. And that if a bishop excommunicate any man, God absolves him.

That he held the erroneous opinions that Sir John Oldcastle held when he was in prison, and affirmed that Sir John Oldcastle was a true catholic man, and falsely condemned and put to death without reasonable cause.

That such as go on pilgrimage, offering to images made of wood and stone, are excommunicated, because they ought to offer to the living, and not to the dead ; and that the curates sell God upon Easter-day, when they receive offerings of such as communicate, before they minister the sacrament to them.

That he counselled women, that they should not offer in the church for the dead.

That the saints who are in heaven ought in no case to be prayed to, but God only.

The fifth day of July (A. D. 1424), Richard Belward was brought before John, bishop of Norwich, when articles were objected against him, which he there denied; therefore the bishop appointed him another day; upon which he appeared again before the bishop, and brought with him nine of his neighbours to purge him upon those articles, and there did solemnly purge himself. And afterwards, the bishop commanded him to swear upon the evangelists, That from that day forward he should not wittingly preach, teach, or defend any error or heresy, contrary to the church of Rome; neither aid, assist, favour, or maintain, privily or openly, any manner of person or persons, that should hold or maintain the said errors or heresies.

In like manner John Goddesel, of Dichingham, was accused upon the same articles, and brought before the bishop, where he denying them, purged himself by his neighbours, as Richard Belward before had done, being sworn also in like manner as he was, and so was dismissed and set at liberty, until the year 1428, when he was again apprehended, accused, and abjured, as shall be more at large declared in the history when we come to that year. Sir Hugh Pie also, chaplain of Ludney, in the diocese of Norwich, was likewise accused and brought before the bishop of Norwich the fifth day of July, (A.D. 1424,) for holding these opinions following:—

That the people ought not to go on pilgrimage.

That the people ought not to give alms, but only to such as beg at their doors.

That the image of the cross and other images are not to be worshipped. And that the said Hugh had cast the cross of Bromehold into the fire to be burned, which he took from one John Welgate, of Ludney. Which articles being objected against him, he utterly denied; whereupon he had a day appointed to purge himself by the witness of three laymen and three priests. That so done, he was sworn as the other before, and so dismissed.

After this, (A.D. 1428,) King Henry VI. sent down most cruel letters of commission unto John Exeter and Jacolet Germain, keeper of the castle of Colchester, for the apprehending of Sir William White, priest; and others, suspected of heresies, the tenour whereof here ensues.

The Copy of the King's Letters directed to John Exeter and Jacolet Germain, keeper of the Castle of Colchester, for the apprehending of Sir William White, priest; and other (as they called them) Lollards.

" Henry, by the grace of God, king of England and of France, lord of Ireland, to his well-beloved John Exeter, and Jacolet Germain, keeper of the castle of Colchester, health:

" Ye shall understand that we, fully trusting unto your fidelity and circumspections, have appointed you jointly and severally to take and arrest William White, priest; and Thomas, late chaplain of Setling, in the county of Norfolk; and William Northampton, priest; and all others, whatsoever they be, that are suspected of heresy or Lollardy, wheresoever they may be found, within the liberties or without; and straightway being so taken, to send them unto our next gaol or prison,'until such time as we shall have taken other order for their delivery: and therefore we straightly command you, that ye diligently attend about the premises, and fulfil the same in form aforesaid. Also we charge and command all and singular justices of peace, mayors, sheriffs, bailiffs, constables, and all other our faithful officers, by the tenour of these presents, That they do assist, aid, and counsel you and every of you, in the execution of the premises, as it shall be comely for them. In witness whereof we have caused these our letters patent to be made.

" Witness myself at Westminster, the sixth of July, the sixth of our reign."

By virtue of which commission we find in old monuments, that within a short time after, John Exeter, who was appointed one of the commissioners, attached six persons in the town of Bungay, in the diocese of Norwich, and committed them to be sent within ten days following, under safe custody, unto the castle of Norwich.

Besides these, we also find in the said old monuments within the diocese of Norfolk and Suffolk, specially in the towns of Beccles, Ersham, and Ludney, a great number both of men and women to have been vexed and cast into prison, and after their abjuration brought to open shame in churches and markets, by the bishop of the diocese, called William, and his chancellor William Bernham, John Exeter being the registrar; so that within the space of three or four years, that is, from the year 1428 to the year 1431, about the number of one hundred and twenty men and women were examined, and sustained great vexation for the profession of the christian faith, of whom some were only taken upon suspicion, for eating meats prohibited upon vigil days, who, upon their purgation made, escaped more easily away, and with less punishment.

Others were more cruelly handled, and some of them were put to death and burned, among whom we do specially find mention made of these three:—

Father Abraham of Colchester.
William White, priest.
John Waddon, priest.

A great number of good men and women, seventy-eight in all, were forced to abjure, sustaining such cruel penance as the bishop and his chancellor pleased to lay upon them.

These soldiers of Christ, being much beaten with the cares and troubles of those days, although they were constrained to relent and abjure, that is, to protest otherwise with their tongues than their hearts did think, partly through correction, and partly through infirmity (being as yet but new trained soldiers in God's field), yet for the good-will they bare to the truth, although with their tongues they durst not express it, we have thought good to mention them here; for this cause, either to stop the mouths of malignant adversaries, or to answer to their ignorance, who following rather blind prejudice, than the true knowledge of history, for lack of knowledge, blame what they know not, accusing the true doctrine of the word of God as a novelty, and carping at the teachers thereof as new made brethren. Who should understand by these histories, how this doctrine of the grace of God, lacking no antiquity, has from time to time continually sought to burst out, and in some places has prevailed, although in most places, through tyranny and the malice of men, Christ's proceedings have been suppressed and kept under from rising, so much as men's power and strength joined with craft and subtlety could labour to keep it down; as here by these good men of Norfolk and Suffolk may well appear. For if the knowledge and the goodness of those men had had the same liberty of time, with the help of the same authority, as we have now, and had not been restrained through the iniquity of the times and the tyranny of prelates, it had well appeared how old this doctrine would have been, which now they contemn and reject for its newness: neither needed Bonner to have asked of Thomas Hawks, and such others, where their church was forty years ago, inasmuch as for forty years ago, and more, within the country of Norfolk and Suffolk, was then found such plenty of persons of the same profession and the like doctrine which we now profess. And thus much for the number of these persons.

Now as touching their articles which they maintained and defended:

Concerning the articles, many of them either were falsely objected against them, or not truly reported, according to the common manner of these adversaries. The notaries reported them erroneously, either mistaking that which they said, or misunderstanding that which they meant, especially in these two articles concerning baptism and paying of tithes. For, when speaking against the ceremonial and superfluous traditions then used in baptism, as salt, oil, spittle, taper, light, chrisomes, exorcising of the water, with such other, they accounted them as no material thing in the holy institution of baptism, the notaries slanderously depraving this assertion, to make it more odious to the ears of the people, so gave out the article, as if they held that the sacrament of baptism used in the church by water is but a light matter and of small effect.

Again, in speaking against women christening new-born infants in private houses, against the opinion of such as think children damned who depart before they come to their baptism, they are falsely reported, as if they said, that christian people are sufficiently baptized in the blood of Christ, and need no water, and that infants are sufficiently baptized, if their parents be baptized before them.

Moreover they thought, or said, perhaps, that in certain cases tithes might be withheld from wicked priests sometimes, and be conferred to better uses to the benefits of the poor : therefore they are falsely slandered, as saying and affirming, that no tithes were to be given to the ministers and curates of the churches.

And likewise for matrimony, wherein they are reported to hold and affirm, as if it consisted only in the mutual consent betwixt the man and the woman, needing no other solemnizing in the public church, and all because they denied it to be a sacrament. Other articles were objected against them, as these which hereafter follow :—

That auricular confession is not to be made to a priest, but to God only ; because no priest has any power to absolve a sinner from his sin.

That no priest has power to make the body of Christ in the sacrament of the altar ; but that, after the sacramental words, there remains pure material bread as before.

That every true christian man is a priest to God.

That no man is bound under pain of damnation to observe Lent, or any other days prohibited by the church of Rome.

That the pope is antichrist, and his prelates the disciples of antichrist; and the pope has no power to bind and loose upon earth.

That it is lawful for every christian to do any bodily work (sin only except) upon holy days.

That it is lawful for priests to have wives.

That excommunications and ecclesiastical censures given out by the prelates, are not to be regarded.

It is not lawful to swear in private cases.

That men ought not to go on pilgrimages.

That there is no honour to be given to the images of the crucifix, of our lady, or any other saint.

That the holy water, hallowed in the church by the priest, is not holier or of more virtue than other running or well-water, because the Lord blessed all waters in their first creation.

That the death of Thomas Becket was neither holy nor meritorious.

That the relics, as dead men's bones, ought not to be worshipped or digged out of their graves, or set up in shrines.

That prayers made in all places are acceptable unto God.

That men ought not to pray to any saint, but only to God.

That the bells and ringing in the church was ordained for no other purpose, but to fill the priests' purses.

That it is no sin to withstand the ecclesiastical precepts.

That the catholic church is only the congregation of elect.

These were the articles which were generally objected against them all, wherein they did so agree in one uniform faith, that whatever one held, all the others maintained and held the same. By which their consent and doctrine it appears, that they all received it of some one instructor, who was William White, who being a scholar and follower of John Wickliff, resorted afterwards into this country of Norfolk, and there instructed these men in the light of the gospel. Now it remains to speak of their troubles, how they were handled, beginning with William White.

William White, Priest.

This William White, being a follower of John Wickliff, and a priest, not after the common sort of priests, but rather reputed amongst the number of them, of whom the wise man speaketh, " He was as the morning star in the midst of a cloud," &c. This man was well-learned, upright, and a well-spoken priest. He gave over his priesthood and benefice, and took him a godly young woman to his wife, notwithstanding he did not therefore cease from his former office and duty, but continually laboured to the glory and praise of the spouse of Christ, by reading, writing, preaching. The principal points of his doctrine were these, which he was forced to recant at Canterbury.

That men should seek for the forgiveness of their sins only at the hands of God.

That the wicked living of the pope, and his holiness, is nothing else but a devilish estate and heavy yoke of antichrist, and therefore he is an enemy unto Christ's truth.

That men ought not to worship images, or other idolatrous paintings.

That men ought not to worship the holy men which are dead.

That the Romish church is the fig-tree which the Lord Christ hath accursed, because it hath brought forth no fruit of the true belief.

That such as wear cowls, or be anointed or shorn, are the lance-knights and soldiers of Lucifer ; and that they all, because their lamps are not burning, shall be shut out when the Lord shall come.

Upon which articles he being attached at Canterbury under the archbishop Henry Chichesley, (A. D. 1424,) there for a certain space, stoutly and manfully witnessed the truth which he had preached ; but as there he lost his courage and strength, so afterwards he became again much stouter and stronger in Jesus Christ, and confessed his own error and offence. For after this, going into Norfolk with his wife, and there occupying himself busily in teaching and converting the people to the true doctrine of Christ, at the last, by the means of the king's letters sent down for that intent and purpose, he was apprehended and brought before William, bishop of Norwich, by whom he was convicted and condemned of thirty articles, and there was burned in Norwich, in the month of September, A.D. 1424.

This William White and his wife lived much with one Thomas Moon of Ludney. This man was of so devout and holy life, that all the people had him in great reverence, and desired him to pray for them ; so that one Margaret Wright confessed, that if any saints were to be prayed to, she would rather pray to him than any other. When he was come to the stake, thinking to open his mouth to speak to the people, to exhort and confirm them in the truth, one of the bishop's servants struck him on the mouth, to force him to keep silence. And thus this good man, receiving the crown of martyrdom, ended this mortal life to the great sorrow and grief of all the good men of Norfolk. His wife, following her husband's footsteps according to her power, teaching and sowing abroad the same doctrine, confirmed many men in God's truth : she suffered much trouble and punishment the same year at the hands of the bishop.

About the same time also was burned Father Abraham of Colchester, and John Waddon, priest, for the like articles.

Concerning them which abjured, how and by whom they were examined, what depositions came in against them, and what was the order and manner of the penance enjoined them, here it might be set out at large ; but for avoiding of prolixity, it shall be sufficient briefly to touch certain of the principals, whereby the better understanding may be given to the reader, after what manner and order all the other were entreated.

First, amongst those who were arrested and forced to abjure (A. D. 1428), were Thomas Pie, and John Mendham, who, being convicted upon the articles before-mentioned, were enjoined penance in their own parish church, as by tne bishop's letter directed to the dean of Rhodenhall, and the parish priest of Aldborough, more at large appears.

The copy of the Bishop of Norwich's Letter.

William, by the sufferance of God, bishop of Norwich, to our well-beloved sons in Christ, the dean of Rhodenhall of our diocese, and to the parish priest of the parish church of Aldborough of the same our diocese, health, grace, and benediction. Forasmuch as we, according to our office, lawfully proceeding to the correction and amendment of the souls of Thomas Pie and John Mendham of Aldborough, of the diocese aforesaid, because they have held, believed and affirmed divers and many errors and heresies, contrary to the determination of the holy church of Rome, and the universal church and catholic faith, have enjoined the said Thomas and John, appearing before us personally, and confessing before us judicially that they have holden, believed, and affirmed divers and many errors and heresies, this penance hereunder written, for their offences to be done and fulfilled in manner, form, and time hereunder written, according as justice doth require, that is to say, six whippings, or disciplinings about the parish church of Aldborough aforesaid, before a solemn procession six several Sundays, and three disciplinings about the market-place of Herelstone, of our said diocese, three principal market days, bare neck, head, legs, and feet, their bodies being covered only with their shirts and breeches, each of them carrying a taper in his hand of a pound weight, as well round about the church, as about the market-place, in each of the aforesaid appointed days; which tapers, the last Sunday after the penance finished, we will that the said John and Thomas do humbly and devoutly offer unto the high altar of the parish church of Aldborough, at the time of the offertory of the high mass the same day, and that either of them, going about the market-place aforesaid, shall make four several pauses and stays, and at every of those same pauses humbly and devoutly receive at your hands three disciplinings. Therefore we straightly charge and command you, and either of you, jointly and severally by virtue of your obedience, that every Sunday and market-day, after the receipt of our present commandment, you do effectually admonish and bring forth the said Thomas Pie and John Mendham to begin and accomplish their said penance, and so successfully to finish the same in manner and form afore-appointed. But if they will not obey your monitions, or, rather our commandments, in this behalf, and begin and finish their said penance effectually, you, or one of you, shall cite them peremptorily, that they, or either of them, appear before us, or our commissary, in the chapel of our palace at Norwich, the twelfth day after the citation so made, if it be a court day, or else the next court day following, to declare if they, or any of them, have any cause why they should not be excommunicated for their manifest offence in this behalf committed, according to the form and order of law, and further to receive such punishment as justice shall provide in that behalf. And what you have done in the premises, whether the said Thomas and John have obeyed your admonitions, and performed the same penance or no, we will that you, or one of you, which have received our said commandment for the execution thereof, do distinctly certify us between this and the last day of November next coming. Dated at our palace of Norwich, under our commissary's seal, the eighth day of October, A.D. 1428."

This, gentle reader, was for the most part, the order of their whole penance: however some were more cruelly handled; and after their penance they were banished out of the diocese, and others more straightly used by longer imprisonment, whereof we will briefly rehearse one or two for example.

John Beverly, alias Battild.

John Beverly alias Battild, a labourer, was attached by the vicar of Southcreke, the parish priest of Waterden, and a lawyer, and so delivered unto Master William Barnham the bishop's commissary, who sent him to the castle of Norwich there to be kept in irons: afterward being brought before the commissary, and having nothing proved against him, he took an oath, that every year afterward he should confess his sins once a year to his curate, and receive the sacrament at Easter, as other christians did; and for his offence was enjoined that the Friday and Saturday next after he should fast on bread and water, and upon the Saturday to be whipped from the palace of Norwich, going round about by Tomblands, and by St. Michael's church, by Cottlerew, and about the market, having in his hand a wax candle of twopence, to offer to the image of the Trinity after he had done his penance. And forsomuch as he confessed that he had eaten flesh upon Easter-day, and was not shriven in all Lent, nor received upon Easter-day, the judge enjoined him that he should fast Tuesday, Wednesday, and Friday in Whitsun-week, having but one meal a day of fish and other white meats, and after this penance he should depart out of the diocese, and never come there any more.

John Skilley of Flixon, Miller.

John Skilley of Flixon, miller, being apprehended and brought before the bishop of Norwich, the fourteenth day of March, A.D. 1428, for holding and maintaining the articles above-written, was thereupon convicted and forced to abjure; and after this abjuration solemnly made, he had a most sharp sentence of penance pronounced against him; that forsomuch as he was convicted by his own confession, for holding and maintaining the articles before-written, and for receiving certain good and godly men into his house, as Sir William White, priest, and John Wadden, whom they called famous, notorious, and damnable heretics, and had now abjured the same, being first absolved from the sentence of excommunication which he had incurred by means of his opinions, he was enjoined for penance seven years' imprisonment in the monastery of Langly, in the diocese of Norwich. And as in times past he used upon the Fridays to eat flesh, he was enjoined to fast on bread and water every Friday, for the space of that seven years to come; and that for the space of two years next immediately after the seven years expired, every Wednesday in the beginning of Lent, and every Maundy Thursday, he should appear before the bishop, or his successor, or commissary for the time being, in the cathedral church of Norwich, together with the other penitents, to do open penance for his offences.

Besides these there were others of the same company, who in the same year were forced to similar abjuration and penance. And so to proceed to the next year following, which was A.D. 1429, there ensues a great number in the same register, who were examined, and did penance also to the number of sixteen or seventeen. In the number of whom was John Baker, otherwise called Usher Tonstal, who for having a book with the Lord's Prayer, the Ave and Creed in English, and for certain other articles of fasting, confession, and invocation, contrary to the determination of the Romish church, after much vexation, was caused to abjure and sustain such penance, as others before him had done.

The History of Margery Backster.

Another was Margery Backster, against whom one Joan, wife of Cliffland, was brought in by the bishop, and compelled to depose.

First, that the said Margery Backster did inform this deponent, that she should in no case swear, saying to her in English: "Dame, beware of the bee, for every bee will sting, and therefore take heed you swear not, neither by God, neither by our lady, neither by any other saint; and if ye do contrary, the bee will sting your tongue and venom your soul."

Also, this deponent being demanded by Margery, what she did every day at church; she answered, "That she kneeled down and said five Pater Nosters, in worship of the crucifix, and as many Ave Maries in worship of our lady." Whom Margery rebuked, saying, "You do evil to kneel or pray to such images in the churches, for God dwelleth not in such churches, neither shall come down out of heaven, and will give you no more reward for such prayer, than a candle lighted, and set under the cover of the font, will give light by night to those which are in the church." Saying, moreover, in English; "Ignorant workmen hew and form such crosses and images, and after that, ignorant painters gloss them with colours. And if you desire so much to see the true cross of Christ, I will shew it you at home in your own house." Which this deponent being desirous to see, Margery, stretching out her arms abroad, said to this deponent, "This is the true cross of Christ, and this cross thou oughtest and mayest every day behold and worship in thine own house, and therefore it is but vain to run to the church to worship dead crosses and images."

Also, this deponent being asked by Margery how she believed touching the sacrament of the altar, said, "That she believed the sacrament of the altar, after the consecration, to be the very body of Christ in form of bread." To whom Margery said, "Your belief is wrong; for if every such sacrament were God, and the very body of Christ, there would be an infinite number of gods, because that a thousand priests and more do every day make a thousand such gods, and afterwards eat them. And therefore know for certainty, that by the grace of God it shall never be my God, because it is falsely and deceitfully ordained by the priests in the church, to induce the simple people to idolatry; for it is only material bread."

Moreover Margery said to this deponent, "That Thomas of Canterbury, whom the people called St. Thomas, was a false traitor, and damned in hell, because he injuriously endowed the churches with possessions, and raised up many heresies in the church, which seduce the simple people; and therefore if God be blessed, Thomas is accursed; and those false priests that say that he suffered his death patiently before the altar, do lie; for as a cowardly traitor he was slain in the church door, as he was flying away."

Moreover, this deponent saith, that Margery told her that the cursed pope, cardinals, archbishop, and bishops, and especially the bishop of Norwich and others that support and maintain heresies and idolatry, reigning and ruling over the people, shall shortly have the very same or worse mischief fall upon them, than that cursed man Thomas of Canterbury had. For they falsely and cursedly deceive the people, to extort money from the simple folk to sustain their pride, riot and idleness. And know assuredly that the vengeance of God will speedily come upon them, who have most cruelly slain the children of God, father Abraham, and William White, a true preacher of the law of God, and John Wadden, with many other godly men; which vengeance had come upon the said Caiaphas, the bishop of Norwich and his ministers, who are members of the devil, before this time, if the pope had not sent over these false pardons to those parties, which the said Caiaphas had falsely obtained, to induce the people to make procession for the state of them and of the church. Which pardons brought the simple people to cursed idolatry.

Also Margery said to this deponent, that every faithful man and woman is not bound to fast in Lent, or other days appointed for fasting by the church, and that every man may lawfully eat flesh and all other meats upon those days and times: and that it were better to eat the fragments left upon Thursday at night on the fasting days, than to go to the market to bring themselves in debt to buy fish: and that Pope Silvester made the Lent.

Also Margery said to this deponent, that William White was falsely condemned for an heretic, and that he was a good and holy man, and that he desired her to follow him to the place of execution, where she saw that when he would have opened his mouth to speak to the people to instruct them, but a devil, one of Bishop Caiaphas's servants, struck him on the lips, and stopped his mouth, that he could in no case declare the will of God.

This deponent saith, that Margery taught her that she should not go on pilgrimage, neither to our lady of Walsingham, nor to any other saint or place.

Also this deponent saith, that Margery desired her that she and Joan her maid would come secretly in the night to her chamber, and there she should hear her husband read the law of Christ to them; which law was written in a book that her husband was wont to read to her by night, and that her husband is well learned in the christian verity.

That Margery said to this deponent, that the people worshipped devils which fell from heaven with Lucifer, which devils in their fall to the earth, entered into the images which stand in the churches, and have long lurked and dwelled in them; so that the people, worshipping those images commit idolatry.

She said also to this deponent, that holy bread and holy water were but trifles of no effect or force, and that the bells are to be cast out of the church, and that they are excommunicated which first ordained them.

Moreover, that she should not be burned, although she were convicted of Lollardy, for that she had a charter of salvation in her body.

Also the said deponent saith, that Agnes Berthem her servant, being sent to the house of the said Margery the Saturday after Ash-Wednesday, the said Margery not being within, found a brass pot standing over the fire, with a piece of bacon and oatmeal seething in it, as the said Agnes reported to this deponent.

There were also, besides this deponent, others sworn and examined against the said Margery, as John Grimley and Agnes Berthem, servants to William Clifland, who altogether confirmed the former depositions.

Thus much we have thought good to note as concerning Margery Backster. But what became of her after this her accusation, because we find no mention made in the registers, we are not able to declare.

The same year also were the like depositions made by one William Wright against divers good men, as here followeth.

First, this deponent saith, that William Taylor told John Piry of Ludney, in the house of John Bungay of Beghton, in the presence of John Bungay, Robert Grigges, wright of Martham, and John Usher, that all the good men of Martham who were favourers and helpers to that good man William White, are evil troubled now-a-days, and that William White was a good and holy doctor; and that the best doctor after him was William Everden, who wrought with William Taylor of Ludney, for the space of one month, and that the first Sunday of the month, William Everden did sit all day upon the table at work, saying to William Taylor, that he would not go to church to shew himself a scribe or a pharisee; and the second Sunday he put on gentleman's apparel, and went to Norwich to hearken how the bishop and his ministers used the poor christians there in prison.

Also the said William Wright deposed, that William Taylor of Ludney was one of the sect, and went to London with Sir Hugh Pie, and had conversation oftentimes with Sir William White, having often conference upon the Lollards' doctrine.

Also that Anise, wife of Thomas Moon, is of the same sect, and favoured them, and receives them often, and also the daughter of Thomas Moon is partly of the same sect, and can read English.

Also that Richard Fletcher of Beckles is a most perfect doctor in that sect, and can very well and perfectly expound the holy scriptures, and has a book of the new law in English, which was Sir Hugh Pie's first.

Also that Nicholas Belward, son of John Belward, dwelling in the parish of Southelem, is one of the same sect, and has a new testament which he bought at London for four marks and forty pence, and taught the said William Wright and Margery his wife, and wrought with them continually by the space of one year, and studied diligently upon the New Testament.

That Thomas Gremner, turner, of Dychingham, is perfect in that sect and law.

John Clark the younger, of Bergh, had the bedding and apparel of William Everden in his custody, after the return of William White from Bergh, and is of the same sect.

Also William Bate, tailor, of Sething, and his wife, and his son, who can read English very well, are of the same sect.

Also William Skirving of Sething, received Joan the wife of William White into his house, being brought thither by William Everden, after their departure from Martham.

Also William Osbourn of Sething, John Reve, glover, and Bawdwin Cooper of Beckles, are of the same sect.

Also John Pert, late servant of Thomas Moon, is of the same sect, and can read well, and did read in the presence of William White, and was the first that brought Sir Hugh Pie into the company of the Lollards, who assembled oftentimes together at the house of Thomas Moon, and there conferred upon their doctrine.

Also Sir Hugh Pie bequeathed to Alice, servant to William White, a New Testament, which they then called the book of the new law, and was in the custody of Oswald Godfrey of Colchester.

John Perker, mercer, of a village by Ipswich, is a famous doctor of that sect. Also he said, that father Abraham of Colchester is a good man.

Also the said William Wright deposes, that it is read in the prophesies amongst the Lollards, that the sect of the Lollards shall be in a manner destroyed; notwithstanding at length the Lollards shall prevail and have the victory against all their enemies.

Also he said that Tucke knows all of that sect in Suffolk, Norfolk, and Essex.

Besides these, there were many others the same year, whose names being before expressed in the table of Norfolk men, here for brevity's sake we omit to treat of, passing over to the next year, which was 1430. [Ex Regist. Norw.]

John Burrel, servant to Thomas Moon of Ludney, in the diocese of Norwich, was apprehended and arrested for heresy, the ninth day of September, in this year (A.D. 1430,) and examined by Mr. William Bernham, the bishop's commissary, upon the articles before mentioned, and others.

That the catholic church is the soul of every good christian man.

That no man is bound to fast in Lent or other fasting days appointed by the church, for they were not appointed by God, but ordained by the priests; and that every man may eat flesh or fish upon the same days indifferently, according to his own will, and every Friday is a free day to eat both flesh and fish indifferently.

That pilgrimage ought not to be made, but only to the poor.

That it is not lawful to swear, but in case of life and death.

That masses and prayers for the dead are but vain; for the souls of the dead are either in heaven or hell: and there is none other place of purgatory but this world. Upon which articles he being convicted, was forced to abjure, and suffered a similar penance as the others before had done.

Thomas Moon of Ludney was apprehended and attached for suspicion of heresy, against whom were objected by the bishop the articles before written, but especially this article, that he had familiarity and communication with several heretics, and had received, comforted, supported, and maintained several of them, as Sir William White, Sir Hugh Pie, Thomas Pet, and William Callis, priests, with many more; upon which articles he being convicted before the bishop was forced to abjure, and received the penance, in like manner as before.

In like manner, Robert Grigges of Martham was brought before the bishop the seventeenth day of February, in the year aforesaid, for holding and affirming the aforesaid articles, but especially these hereafter following.

That the sacrament of confirmation, ministered by the bishop did avail nothing to salvation.

That it was no sin to withstand the ordinances of the church of Rome.

That holy bread and holy water were but trifles, and that the bread and water were the worse for the conjurations and characters which the priests made over them.

Upon which articles he being convicted, was forced to abjure, and received penance in manner and form as the others had done before him.

The like also (though somewhat more sharp) happened unto John Finch of Colchester, the twentieth day of September, who although he was of the diocese of London, being suspected of heresy, was attached in Ipswich in the diocese of Norwich, and brought before the bishop there, before whom he being convicted of the articles, as all the others before him, was enjoined penance, three disciplinings in solemn procession about the cathedral church of Norwich, three several Sundays, and three disciplinings about the market-place of Norwich, three principal market-days, his head and neck and feet being bare, and his body covered only with a short shirt or vesture, having in his hand a taper of wax of a pound weight, which, the next Sunday after his penance, he should offer to the Trinity; and that for the space of three years after, every Ash-Wednesday and Maunday-Thursday, he should appear in the cathedral church at Norwich, before the bishop or his vicegerent, to do open penance amongst the other penitentiaries for his offences.

About the same time, even the same year, 1430, shortly after the solemn coronation of King Henry VI., a certain man named Richard Hoveden, a wool-winder, and citizen of London, received the crown of martyrdom. Which man when he could by no persuasions be withdrawn or plucked back from the opinions of Wickliff, he was by the rulers of the church condemned for heresy: and as Fabian writes, burned hard by the Tower of London.

Nicolas, Canon of Eye.

Now to proceed in our account of the persecution of Norfolk and Suffolk, we find that in the year 1431, Nicolas, canon of Eye, was brought before the bishop of Norwich for suspicion of heresy, with witnesses sworn to depose against him, which witnesses appointed one William Christopher to speak, and he deposed as follows:

First, that on Easter-day, when all the parishioners went about the church of Eye solemnly in procession, as the manner was, this Nicolas Canon, as it were, mocking and deriding the other parishioners, went about the church the contrary way, and met the procession.

This article he confessed, and affirmed that he thought he did well in so doing.

Again, Nicolas asked of Master John Colman, of Eye, this question, "Master Colman, what think you of the sacrament of the altar?" Colman answered, "I think that the sacrament of the altar is very God, and very man, the very flesh and very blood of our Lord Jesus Christ under the form of bread and wine." To whom Nicolas in derision said, "Truly, if the sacrament of the altar be very God and very man, and the very body and blood of our Lord Jesus Christ, then very God and very man may be put in a small space; as when it is in the priest's mouth. And why may not we laymen as well eat flesh upon Fridays, and all other prohibited days, as the priest to eat the flesh and drink the blood of our Lord every day indifferently?" Nicolas thought he had spoken well in that matter.

Also, that on Corpus Christi day, at the elevation of high mass, when all the parishioners and strangers kneeled down, holding up their hands, and doing reverence to the sacrament, Nicolas went behind a pillar of the church, and turning his face from the high altar, mocked them that did reverence to the sacrament.

This article he also acknowledging affirmed that he believeth himself to do well in so doing.

Also, when his mother would have him to lift up his right hand, and cross himself from the crafts and assaults of the devil, when he deferred doing so, his mother took up his right hand, and crossed him, saying, "In the name of the Father, Son, and Holy Ghost. Amen;" and then Nicolas immediately deriding his mother's blessing, took up his right hand of his own accord, and blessed himself otherwise. This article Nicolas acknowledged to be true.

Also, that upon Allhallows-day, in the time of elevation of high mass, when many of the parishioners of Eye lighted many torches, and carried them up to the high altar, kneeling down there in reverence and honour of the sacrament, Nicolas carrying a torch went up to the high altar, and standing behind the priest's back, saying mass, at the time of the elevation stood upright upon his feet, turning his back to the priest, and his face toward the people, and would do no reverence to the sacrament. This article he acknowledged, affirming, that he thought he had done well in that behalf. All which articles the bishop's commissary caused to be copied out, word for word, and sent to Master William Worsted, prior of the cathedral church of Norwich, and to other doctors of divinity, that they might deliberate upon them, and shew their minds between that and Thursday next following. Upon which Thursday, Nicolas was again examined upon two other articles, that he doubted whether in the sacrament of the altar were the very body of Christ or no. This article he confessed before the commissary to be true.

Also, that he believed that a man ought not to confess his sins to a priest. This article he also confessed that he doubted upon.

Now remains to declare what these doctors concluded upon the articles; whose answer was this.

First of all, as to the first article, they said that the article in the terms as it was propounded, is not simply an heresy, but an error.

Also, as to the second article, the doctors agree as in the first.

Also, as to the third article, they affirm that it is an heresy.

To the fourth article, they answered as to the first and second.

Also, the doctors affirm the fifth article to be an heresy.

Also, as to the sixth article, the doctors conclude, that if the said Nicolas, being of perfect mind and remembrance, did doubt whether the sacrament of the altar were the very perfect body of Christ or no, then the article is simply an heresy.

Upon this, the commissary declared and pronounced Nicolas to be an heretic, and forced him to abjure; and enjoined Nicolas penance for his offences, three disciplinings about the cloister of the cathedral church of Norwich, before a solemn procession, bare-headed and barefoot, carrying a taper of half-a-pound in his hand.

Thomas Bagley, priest.

I find in Fabian's chronicles, that in the same year (A. D. 1431), Thomas Bagley, a priest, vicar of Monenden, beside Malden, being a valiant disciple, and adherent of Wickliff, was condemned by the bishops of heresy at London, about the midst of Lent, and was degraded and burned in Smithfield.

Paul Craw, a Bohemian.

The same year also, was Paul Craw, a Bohemian, taken at St. Andrews, by the bishop Henry, and delivered over to the secular power to be burnt, for holding opinions contrary to the church of Rome, touching the sacrament of the Lord's Supper, the worshipping of saints, auricular confession, with other of Wickliff's opinions.

The History of Thomas Rhedon, a Frenchman, and a Carmelite Friar, burnt in Italy for the profession of Christ.

We have before declared how this cruel storm of persecution, which first began in England after it had long raged here against many good and godly men, brake out and passed into Bohemia, and after a short time, increasing by little and little, invaded Scotland, and now, with greater force and violence, this furious devouring flame entered Italy, and suffered not any part of the world to be free from the murder and slaughter of good and godly men. It happened about his time that one Thomas Rhedon, a Carmelite friar, came with the Venetian ambassadors into Italy. This man, although he was a Carmelite, yet understood the word of God, judging that God ought not to be worshipped neither in that mount, nor at Jerusalem only, but in spirit and truth. This man being a true Carmelite, prepared himself to go into Italy, trusting that he should find there, some by whose good life he might be edified and instructed. For where ought more abundance of virtue to be, than in that place which is counted to be the fountain of all religion? And how could it otherwise be, but that where so great holiness is professed, where all men's eyes are bent as upon a stage, where St. Peter's seat is, and which is thought to be the ruler and governor of all the church, all things should flourish and abound worthy of so great a place? This holy man, having these things before his eyes, forsook his own country, and went to Rome, conceiving a firm and sure hope that by the example of so many notable and worthy men, he should greatly profit in godliness and learning: but the success of the matter utterly frustrated his hope, for all things were clean contrary. Whatever he saw was nothing else but mere dissimulation and hypocrisy. Instead of heavenly gifts, there reigned among them the pomp and pride of the world: in place of godliness, riot: instead of learning and study, slothfulness and superstition. Tyranny and haughtiness of mind had possessed the place of apostolic simplicity: that now there remained no more any place or liberty for a man to learn that which he knew not, or to teach that which he perfectly understood. Finally, all things were reversed—all things happened contrary to his expectation. But nothing so much offended this good man's mind, as the intolerable ambition and pompous pride in them, whom an example of humility should especially commend and praise to the whole world. And, although he saw nothing which accorded with the rule of the apostles, yet these things so much passed all measure and patience, that he could by no means refrain his tongue in so much abuse and corruption of the church, seeing such ambitious pride in their buildings, apparel, in their palaces, in their dainty fare, in their great trains of servants, in their horse and armour, and finally in all things. Which things, so far as they differed from the prescribed rule of the gospel, so much the more was this good man forced to speak; although he well understood how little he should prevail by speaking: for if admonition would profit any thing at all, the books of Wickliff, and others were not wanting. The famous testimonies of John Huss, and of Jerome of Prague, and their blood shed for the same, was yet present before their eyes: at whose most effectual exhortations, they were so little corrected and amended, that they seemed twice more cruel than they were before. Yet all this could not terrify this good man. So by this means, he who came to be a scholar to others, was now forced to be their teacher: and he who determined to follow other men's lives and manners, had now, on the other hand, set before them his life to be marked and followed. For he lived so among them, that his life might be a rule to them all, and so taught, as he might also be their schoolmaster. For even as Paul had foreshewn to such as desired to live godly in Christ, that they should suffer persecution, such reward happened to this man. He gave to them the fruit of godliness, which they should follow: they again set upon his head the diadem of martyrdom. He shewed them the way of salvation; and they for the benefit of life, rewarded him with death: and whereas no rewards had been worthy of his great labours and troubles, they with most extreme ignominy persecuted him even unto the fire. For when by continual preaching he had gotten great envy and hatred, the rulers began to consult together by what means they might circumvent this man's life. Here they had recourse to their accustomed remedies: for it was a peculiar and continual custom among the prelates of the church, that if any man did displease them, or that his talk was not according to their mind, or by any means hurtful, or a hindrance to their lucre and gain, by and by they frame out articles of some heresy, which they charge him withal. And like as every living thing has his peculiar and proper weapon to defend himself from harm, as nature hath armed the boar with his tusks, the hedgehog with his prickles, as the lion is feared for his claws, the dog for his biting, the bull fights with his horns, neither doth the ass lack his hoofs to strike withal; even so this is the only armour of the bishops, to strangle a man with heresy, if he once go about to mutter against their will and ambition; which thing may be easily perceived and seen in this most holy man, beside a great number of others. Who when he began to wax grievous unto them, and could no longer be suffered, what did they do? Straightways flew to their old devices, and as they had done with Huss, and Jerome of Prague, even so they went about to practise against this man. They overwhelm him with suspicion, they seek to entangle him with questions, they examine him in judgment, they compile articles against him, and lay heresy to his charge, they condemn him as an heretic, and being so condemned, they destroy and kill him! This was their godliness: this was the peaceable order of those Carmelites. Whose religion was to wear no sword nor shield, yet they bore in their hearts malice, rancour, vengeance, poison, craft, and deceit, sharper than any sword. With how great care and policy is it provided by law, that none of these clergymen should fight with sword in the streets? when in judgment and accusations there is no murderer who has more ready vengeance, or that does more vilely esteem his brother's soul than they. They shed no blood themselves, they strike not, nor kill, but they deliver them over to others to be slain! What difference is there I pray you, but that they are the authors, and the other are but the ministers of the cruel act? they kill no man as murderers do. How then? Although not after the same sort, yet they do it by other means.

The articles which they falsely gathered against this man, are affirmed by some to be these:—

That the church lacks reformation, and that it shall be punished and reformed.

That infidels, Jews, Turks, and Moors, shall be converted to Christ in the latter days.

That abominations are used at Rome.

That the unjust excommunication of the pope is not to be feared; and those which do not observe the same, do not sin or offend.

But yet there lacked a minister for these articles; however he could not long be wanting at Rome, where all things are to be sold, even men's souls. For this office and ministry there was no man thought more meet than William of Rouen, cardinal of St. Martin's in the mount, vice-chancellor of the court of Rome. Eugenius at that time was pope, who had a little before succeeded Pope Martin above mentioned. Before which Eugenius, this godly Rhedon the Frenchman was brought, and from thence sent unto prison. And again after his imprisonment, and divers and sundry grievous torments, he was brought before the judges. The wolf sat in judgment, the lamb was accused. Why? Because he had troubled the spring. But here need not many words. This good Thomas not being able to resist the malice of these mighty potentates, had offended enough, and was easily convicted and condemned to be burned, but not before he was deprived of all such degrees of priesthood as he had taken.

After the death of Pope Martin, who reigned fourteen years, Eugenius IV. succeeded, about the year A.D. 1431. Of whom Antonius thus writes, that he was much given to wars, as his conflicts and fighting with the Romans may declare; also the battles between the Venetians and the Florentines.

This pope began first to celebrate the council of Basil, which council Martin his predecessor had before intended to assemble, according to the direction of the council of Constance. Eugenius, however, perceiving afterward that this council of Basil would not favour him and his doings, and fearing some injury, afterwards laboured by all subtle practice to dissolve and interrupt the council, and to translate it first from Basil to Ferrara, then to Florence, nearer to his own see of Rome. Concerning which council of Basil, as we have begun here to make mention, it will be no great digression to discourse something more at large, so much as shall seem sufficient or necessary to be known.

THE ORDER AND MANNER OF THE COUNCIL OF BASIL,

With the principal matters concluded therein, briefly collected and abridged here in this present book.

In the thirty-ninth session of the council of Constance, it was decreed and provided concerning such general councils as should hereafter follow:—That the first that should ensue, should be assembled the fifth year after the council of Constance: that the second should be held the seventh year after that, and so all others to follow successively every tenth year. Wherefore, according to this decree, there followed a general council five years after the council of Constance, celebrated and held at Siene, under Pope Martin, A.D. 1424, but it soon broke up. After which council, the term of seven years being expired, another council was held at Basil, A.D. 1431, which council is noted to have been the most troublesome, and to have endured longer than any other council before celebrated and held in the church. This council continued almost the space of seventeen years, wherein it was concluded, as in the council of Constance, that the general councils were above the pope, and both of these two councils attributed to the general council the chief authority in decreeing, and determining, which is the reason that the opposite party derogate so much from the authority of this council.

When Pope Martin V. had appointed Julian cardinal and deacon of St. Angelo, his legate, to celebrate and hold a general council at Basil, for the reformation of the church, and rooting out of heresies, within a short space afterwards Pope Martin died. Eugenius IV. succeeded, and confirmed to Cardinal Julian the same authority which his predecessor had given him. To this council of Basil came the Emperor Sigismund, who during his life, with his presence and authority, protected and defended the synod. After the emperor's death, Pope Eugenius altering his mind and purpose, wished to remove the council to Bononia, and thus check the council of Basil. And first he held an opposition council at Ferrara, and afterwards at Florence. For, after the death of the Emperor Sigismund, there were no princes nor noblemen that had any care or regard for the council. Eugenius cited Cardinal Julian, and the fathers of the council, to Bononia, under a great penalty. They again cited the pope, that either he should come himself to the council, or send ambassadors under the like penalty. For this cause the ambassadors of Albert king of the Romans, and of the other princes of Germany, assembled together first at Nuremburg; and when they could determine nothing there, they assembled again at Frankfort to appease the dissension between the council and the pope: for it was thought that the electors of the empire could best assemble and meet in that place: in the meantime the emperor's ambassadors, and the ambassadors of the electors went to Basil, and having conference with the ambassadors of the other princes who were there, they earnestly exhorted the fathers of the council, that they would embrace the unity which they would offer. The request of the princes was, that the fathers would transport the council, and go unto another place; which was the very thing Pope Eugenius seemed always to seek and desire, that he might either divide the fathers of the council, or take away their liberty.

This sacred synod however, thought good neither to deny the princes' request, nor to grant what Pope Eugenius required. During this doubt, the emperor's ambassadors, the bishops of Patavia and Augusta, appointed a noble and valiant baron called Conrad Weinsperge, by the king's command to be protector and defender of the council and the fathers. By which the enemies perceived the emperor to be alienated from the pope, and the fathers of the council understood his good-will towards them, as he would not have sent them a protector if he had not judged it a lawful council; neither would he have judged it a council in Basil, if he had given credit to Pope Eugenius. But owing to a great pestilence which began to spread there, the assembly that should have been held at Frankfort was transported unto Mentz.

The assembly was very famous, for there were present the archbishops of Mentz, Cologne, and Treves, electors of the sacred empire, and all the ambassadors of the other electors. The archbishop of Cologne was the chief favourer of the council in this assembly, who with all his labour and diligence went about to bring the matter unto a good end. Rabanus, the archbishop of Treves, shewed himself somewhat more rough. The sacred synod also thought good to send their ambassadors, and appointed the patriarch of Aquileia, the bishop of Vicene, and the bishop of Argen; divines, John Segovius, and Thomas de Corcellis, with others. There was no man there present who would name himself the ambassador of Eugenius, although there were many of his favourers and friends, both from the council, and also out of Florence, who although they had sworn to the contrary, yet favoured Eugenius more than the council. But the chief Hercules of all the Eugenians was Nicolas Cusan, a man singularly well learned, and of great experience. After several consultations, the electors of the empire, and the ambassadors of the other princes of Germany, gave command throughout their whole nation and country, that the decrees of the council of Basil should be received and observed.

Whilst these things were thus debated at Mentz, there sprang a certain very doubtful question among the divines who remained at Basil, whether Eugenius might be called an heretic, who had so rebelliously contemned the commandments of the church. They gathered themselves together, disputing long among themselves, some affirming, and others holding the negative part. Upon this there arose three several opinions, some affirming that he was an heretic; others, not only an heretic, but also a relapse. The third sort would neither grant him to be an heretic nor a relapse. Among these divines, the chief and principal both in learning and authority, was the bishop of Ebrun, ambassador of the king of Castile, and a certain Scottish abbot, who, as two most valiant champions, subdued all their enemies, so that all the rest either consented to their arguments, or gave place to them, and so their determination took place, and Eugenius was pronounced both an heretic and relapse. Eight conclusions were there determined and allowed amongst the divines, which they called verities, a copy of which they published throughout all Christendom.

When the ambassadors of the council were returned from Mentz, by the commandment of the deputies, all the masters, and doctors, and clergy were called together, with all the other prelates, into the chapter of the great church, there openly to dispute and discuss Eugenius' heresy. This disputation continued six days, both forenoon and afternoon, among whom Cardinal Lewis, archbishop of Arelata, was appointed judge and arbiter, who, besides many other notable virtues, was both valiant and constant. Nicholas Amici, who was also a protector of the faith, a famous man among the divines of Paris, demanded of every man what their opinion was. John Deinlefist, public notary, wrote every man's sentence and judgment. The conclusions of the divines, which were the ground and foundation of their disputation, were these here following:—

1. It is a verity of the catholic faith, that the sacred general council hath power over the pope, or any other prelate.

2. The pope cannot by his own authority, either dissolve, transport, or prorogue the general council being lawfully congregated, without the whole consent of the council, and this is of like verity.

3. He who doth obstinately resist these verities, is to be counted an heretic.

4. Pope Eugenius IV. hath resisted these verities, when at the first, by the fulness of his apostolic power, he attempted to dissolve or to transport the council of Basil.

5. Eugenius being admonished by the sacred council, did recant the errors repugnant to these verities.

6. The dissolution or translation of the council, attempted the second time by Eugenius, is against the aforesaid verities, and containeth an inexcusable error touching the faith.

7. Eugenius, in going about to dissolve and transport the council again, is fallen into his before revoked errors.

8. Eugenius being warned by the syond that he should revoke the dissolution or translation the second time attempted, after that his contumacy was declared, persevering in his rebellion, and erecting a council at Ferraria, shewed himself thereby obstinate.

These were the conclusions which were read in the chapterhouse before the fathers of the council. Upon which, when they were desired to speak their minds, they all in a manner confirmed and allowed them. Archbishop Panormitan, however, disputed much against them. Also the bishop of Burgen, the king of Arragon's almoner. Yet they did not oppose the first three conclusions, but only those in which Pope Eugenius was touched. This Panormitan, as he was subtle, so did he subtlely dispute against the late conclusions, endeavouring himself to declare that Eugenius was not relapsed, and he had great contention with the bishop of Argens, John Segovius, and Francis de Fuxe, divines.

The oration of Panormitan was more praised than allowed of men. Yet it wrought this effect, that afterwards this word "relapse" was taken out of the conclusions, and the word "prolapse" put in. Neither durst Panormitan himself altogether excuse Eugenius of heresy, but defended more the first dissolution than the second, yet he departed not without answer, for John Segovius, an expert divine, rising up, answered him reverently, as was comely for such a prelate.

Segovius could scarcely finish his oration without interruption; for Panormitan, often interrupting him, went to confute now this, and now that reason. Whereupon the bishop of Argens rising up, a man not only eloquent, but also of a stout courage, assailed Panormitan in his reasons and arguments, and put him from his purpose; yet they proceeded so far, that they did not abstain from opprobrious taunts.

When the bishop of Argens chanced to say that the bishop of Rome ought to be the minister of the church, Panormitan could not suffer that: insomuch that he so forgot himself, and his knowledge (which otherwise was great) so failed him, that he was not ashamed to say that the pope was lord over the church. Segovius answered, " Mark (saith he) O Panormitan, what thou sayest; for this is the most honourable title of the bishop of Rome, wherein he calleth himself the ' servant of the servants of God.' Which is gathered upon this point, when as Christ said unto his disciples, when they demanded of him which of them was the greatest, you know he answered them, ' The princes of the Gentiles have rule and dominion over them, but amongst you it is not so,' &c. Wherein he utterly prohibits lordship and dominion; and Peter, who was the first vicar of Christ, said, ' Feed the flock of Christ which is committed unto you, providing for them not by compulsion, but willingly;' and immediately after he said, ' not as lords over God's heritage.' For if Christ, the Son of God, came not to be ministered unto, but to minister and to serve, how then can his vicar have any dominion, or be called lord, as you Panormitan will affirm? the disciple is not above his Master, nor the servant above his Lord. And the Lord himself saith,

' Neither be ye called masters: for one is your Master, even Christ. But he that is greatest among you shall be your servant.'" Panormitan, being somewhat disquieted with this answer, the council brake up and departed.

The next day there was a general congregation, and they returned all again to the chapterhouse after dinner, where the archbishop of Lyons, the king's orator, being required to speak his mind, after he had proved Eugenius to be a heretic, he bitterly complained of those that had preferred such a man unto the papacy, and so moved all their hearts who were present, that they altogether with him bewailed the calamities of the universal church.

Then the bishop of Burgen, the ambassador of Spain, divided the conclusions into two parts; some he called general, and others personal, disputing very excellently as to the three first conclusions, affirming, that he did in no point doubt of them, but only, that the addition, which made mention of the faith, seemed to be doubtful to him. But upon this point he stayed much, to prove that the council was above the pope. Which, after he had sufficiently proved, both by God's law and man's law, he taught it also by physical reason, alleging Aristotle for witness. He said, " That in every well ordered kingdom it ought especially to be desired, that the whole realm should be of more authority than the king; which, if it happened otherwise, it should not be called a kingdom but a tyranny: so likewise he thinks of the church, that it ought to be of more authority than the prince thereof; that is to say, the pope." His oration he uttered so eloquently, learned, and truly, that all men depended on him, and desired to have him continue his oration.

But when he entered into the other conclusions, he seemed to have forgotten himself, and to be no more the same man that he was; for neither was there the same eloquence in his words, neither gravity in oration, or cheerfulness of countenance; so that if he could have seen himself, he would peradventure greatly have marvelled at himself. Every man might well see and perceive then the power and force of the truth, which ministered matter to him, so long as he spake in the defence thereof. But when he began once to speak against her, she took away even his natural eloquence from him.

After this there were long and heated debates about the authority of councils, and about Pope Eugenius, and about the sessions of the council, and certain conclusions which were proposed, these discussions continued for many days; and it happened in them, even as in warlike affairs; for, as there, such as are most valiant and strong, and do most worthy feats, obtain most fame, as in the battle of Troy, Achilles, and Hector were the heroes: so in these spiritual wars and contentions, those who most excel in learning and eloquence, and do more than others, should be most renowned and named: for, on the one part, Panormitan was prince and captain; on the other, Arelatensis: and when all was finally determined, the protector also desired the sacred council, that none should be suffered to bring any weapon to the session which was to be held next day, as he was ready to enforce the safe conduct of the emperor; and, together with the senate of the city, to prohibit all quarrels that would lead to injury.

When the sixteenth day of May was come, all they whom the session pleased, assembled. The ambassadors also of the princes were come together into the quire of the church, to attempt further what they could do; and sending the bishop of Lubeck and Concense, and the dean of Turnon, an excellent learned man, they offered themselves to be present at the session, if the deposing of Pope Eugenius would be deferred four months. Who, when they had received a gentle answer of Arelatensis and the other principals, returning again to the ambassadors, they would only have the first conclusion decreed, and thereupon sent again to Arelatensis: answer was made, " That the chief force did consist in the two other conclusions, and that the council would specially determine upon them. If the ambassadors would not be present, they should understand, that the concord was broken by them, who would not observe what they had offered." With which answer they departed, and the session began to be celebrated. There was no prelate of Aragon present at it, neither out of Spain, nor out of Italy, only the bishop of Grossetane, and the abbot of Dona, who, for their constancy and steadfast good will toward the universal church, could not be changed from their purpose: but of doctors and other inferiors, there were a great number of Aragons, and almost all the inferiors of Spain and Italy (for the inferiors feared not the princes, as the bishops did) and then the worthy stoutness of the Aragons and Castilians appeared in the inferior sort, who would not shrink away in the necessity of the church. Of the two other nations there were only present twenty bishops. The rest lurked in their lodgings, professing the faith in their hearts, but not in their mouths. Arelatensis seeing beforehand what would come to pass, caused prayers to be made, and after prayers to Almighty God, with tears and lamentation, that he would send them his Holy Spirit to aid and assist them, they were greatly comforted and encouraged. This congregation was famous, and although there were not many bishops present, yet all the seats were filled with the bishops, proctors, archdeacons, presidents, priors, priests, and doctors of both laws, which were about the number of four hundred or more : amongst whom there was no noise, no chiding, no opprobrious words or contention, but one exhorted another to the profession of the faith, and there appeared a full and whole consent of them all to defend the church. The bishop of Massilia, a nobleman, read the decree, which was attentively hearkened to, and not one word interrupted. When it was ended, " Te Deum laudamus" was sung with great joy and gladness, and so the session dissolved, which was in number the thirty-third session, and amongst all the preceding ones the most quiet and peaceable.

The day following, being the 22d of May, the prince's ambassadors, against all men's expectation, came to the general congregation, by so doing, at the least giving their assent to the session before passed. In celebrating which, if the fathers had erred, it had not been lawful for the princes and ambassadors to have held the council with those fathers. But it was thought that they were touched with remorse of conscience, and even now detested and abhorred what they had done ; as it was not hidden to the ambassadors of the empire and France. For the bishop of Lubeck said, " That the cause of his absence was, that he was appointed by the emperor's commandment to treat for a peace: wherefore it was not comely for him to be present at any business, whereby he should be vexed or troubled, with whom the peace should be treated." Notwithstanding, he did much commend the session before held, and believed the decree therein promulgated to be most good and holy, and the verities therein contained to be undoubted; and said, " That he would stick thereto both now and ever, even to the death." But the bishop of Tournon, a man both learned and eloquent, speaking for him and his fellows, said, " That he heard how they were evil spoken of, in that they had not honoured their king in that most sacred session, whom it becomes specially to exalt and defend the faith; who also for that cause above all other kings was named *most christian*, notwithstanding," he said, " that they had a lawful excuse, in that it was convenient that they, who were sent to treat peace, should do nothing whereby their ambassage should be stopped or hindered."

After the bishop of Tournon had made an end, Cardinal Arelatensis gave thanks unto God, who had so defended his church, and after great storms and clouds had sent fair and clear weather; and commending the good will of the emperor and the king of France toward the church, he also praised the bishops of Lubeck, and Tournon, for that often in the council, and also of late at Mentz, they had defended the authority of the council. But especially he commended their present doings, that they had openly confessed the truth, and had not separated themselves from the faith of the church.

Afterward, entering into the declaration of the matter, he said, that he was at Pisa and at Constance, and never saw a more quiet or devout session than this; affirming that this decree was most necessary, to repress the ambition of the bishops of Rome, who exalting themselves above the universal church, thought it lawful to do all things after their own pleasure, and also affirming that no one man should transport the council from one place to another, as Eugenius attempted to do, now to Bononia, now to Florentia, then again to Bononia, after to Ferrara, and after that again to Florentia; and that hereafter the bishops should withdraw their minds from the carefulness of temporal goods; and therefore by how much this session was most holy and necessary, by so much more the assent of the ambassadors was most laudable and acceptable to all the fathers. These words thus spoken, he rose up, and the congregation was dissolved.

Now after Pope Eugenius was deposed from the bishopric of Rome, the principal fathers of the council, being called together in the chapter-house of the great church, consulted together, whether it were expedient that a new bishop should be created at once, or deferred for a time. Such as thought good that the election should be done with speed, shewed how dangerous a thing it was for such a congregation to be without a head; also what a pestiferous sickness was in all the city, which not only consumed young men and children, but also men of middle age, and old men in like manner; and that this plague came first by strangers to the poor of the city, and so infected the rich, and now was come to the fathers of the council; exaggerating and making the thing worse than it was. The other party which thought that there should be a delay, said, that the council wanted no head, for Christ was the head thereof; neither did lack a ruler, for it was governed by the presidents and other officers; and that no mention should be made of any pestilence in such case, seeing that to stout and strong men, death is not to be feared, neither can any thing daunt or fear them who contend for the christian faith. The matter being thus discussed amongst them, (although there were as many minds as there were men), yet it seemed to them all, that it was most profitable to choose the bishop by and by, but most honest to defer it.

Hereupon John Segovius, a man of excellent learning, said, "Most reverend fathers, I am drawn by various reasons, to this side and to that. But as I weigh the matter more deeply in my mind, this is my opinion, that to come to a speedy election seems good, to speak after man's judgment; but to delay it for two months, to speak after God's judgment, seems much better. I judge that not only the words, but also the meaning of our decree, ought to be observed. Wherefore, if ye will give any credit to me, follow rather dangerous honesty, than secure utility; although indeed utility cannot be discerned from honesty." This opinion of delay took place among the fathers, and they determined to stay for the space of two months.

In the mean time messengers were sent unto the princes, to declare the deposition of Eugenius by the synod, and publish it abroad.

During this time, the corrupt air was not at all purged, but the mortality daily increasing, many died and were sick. Whereupon a sudden fear came upon the fathers. Nor were they sufficiently advised what they ought to do; for they thought it not to be without danger, either to depart or tarry. However they thought it good to tarry, that since they had overcome famine, and the assaults of their enemies on earth, they would not seem to shrink for the persecution of any plague. When the dog-days were come, and that all herbs withered with heat, the pestilence daily increased more and more, that it is incredible how many died. It was horrible to see the corpses hourly carried through the streets, when on every side there was weeping, wailing and sighing. There was no house void of mourning; no mirth or laughter in any place, but matrons bewailing their husbands, and the husbands their wives. Men and women went through the streets, and durst not speak one to another. Some tarried at home, and others that went abroad, had perfumes to smell, to preserve them against the plague.

The common people died without number; and as in the cold autumn the leaves of the trees do fall, even so did the youths of the city consume and fall away. The violence of the disease was such, that you might have met a man merry in the street now, and within ten hours heard that he had been buried. The number of the dead corpses was such also, that they lacked place to bury them in; insomuch that all the church-yards were digged up, and filled with dead corpses, and great holes made in the parish churches, where a great number of corpses being thrust in together, they covered them over with earth. For which cause the fathers were so afraid, that there appeared no blood in their faces; and especially the sudden death of Lewis the prothonotary made all men afraid, for he was a strong man, and flourishing in age, and singularly learned in both laws, whom the same envious and raging sickness took away in a few hours. By and by, after died Lewis the patriarch of Aquileia, a man of great age, and brought up always in troubles and adversity, neither could he see the day of the pope's election which he had long wished for. However, he took partly a consolation, in that he had seen Eugenius deposed before his death. This man's death was regretted by all the fathers; for now they said, that two pillars of the council were decayed and overthrown, meaning the prothonotary and the patriarch, whereof the one by the law, and the other with his deeds, defended the verity of the council.

Likewise a great number of the registers and doctors died; and of such as fell into that disease, few or none escaped. One among all the rest, Æneas Sylvius, being stricken with this disease, by God's help escaped. This man lay three days even at the point of death, all men being in despair of him; notwithstanding it pleased God to grant him longer life. When the pestilence was most fervent and hot, and that daily there died about one hundred, there was great entreaty made to Cardinal Arelatensis, that he would go to some other town or village near hand; for these were the words of all his friends and household, "What do you, most reverend father? At the least avoid this wane of the moon and save yourself; who being safe, all we shall also be safe; if you die, we all perish. If the plague oppress you, unto whom shall we fly? Who shall rule us? Or who shall be the guide of this most faithful flock? The infection hath already invaded your chamber. Your secretary and chamberlain are already dead. Consider the great danger, and save both yourself and us." But neither the entreaty of his household, neither the corpses of those which were dead could move him, he being willing rather to preserve the council with peril of his life, than to save his life with peril of the council; for he knew, that if he should depart, few would have tarried behind, and that deceit would have been wrought in his absence.

Wherefore, as in war the soldiers fear no danger, when they see their captain in the midst of their enemies: so the fathers of the council were ashamed to fly from this pestilence, seeing their president to remain with them in the midst of all dangers. Which utterly subverted the opinion of them, who babbled abroad, that the fathers tarried in Basil, to seek their own profit and not the verity of the faith; for there is no commodity upon earth which men would change for their lives; for all such as serve the world, prefer it before all other things. But these our fathers, shewing themselves an invincible wall for the house of God, overcoming all difficulties, which this most cruel and pestiferous year brought upon them, at length all desire of life also being set apart, they overcame all dangers, and did not hesitate with most constant minds to defend the verity of the council, even to this present.

The time of the decree being passed, after the deposition of the pope, it seemed good to the fathers, to proceed to the election of another bishop. And first of all, they nominated those that together with the cardinals, should elect the pope. The first and principal of the electors, was the Cardinal Arelatensis, a man of invincible constancy, and incomparable wisdom; to whose virtue may justly be ascribed whatever was done in the council; for without him, the prelates had not persevered in their purpose, neither could the shadow of any prince have so defended them. This man came not to the election by any favour or denomination, but by his own proper right. The rest of the electors were chosen out of the Italian, French, German, and Spanish nations, and their cells and chambers appointed to them by lots, without respect of dignity or person, and as the lots fell, so were they placed; whereby it chanced a doctor to have the highest place, and a bishop the last.

The next day after there was a session held; Marcus a famous divine, made an oration to the electors; he reckoned up the manifold crimes of Pope Eugenius, who was deposed. He endeavoured to persuade the electors to choose such a man, as should in all points be contrary to Eugenius, and eschew all his vices; that as he, through his manifold reproaches, was hurtful to all men, so he who should be chosen, should shew himself acceptable to all men.

There was so great a number of people gathered together to behold this matter, that neither in the church, nor in the streets, could any man pass. There was present, John earl of Dierstein, who supplied the place of the emperor's protector; also the senators of the city, with many other noblemen, to behold the same. The citizens were without in arms, to take care that there should be no uproar. The electors received the communion together, and afterwards they received their oath; and the Cardinal Arelatensis, opening the book of decrees, read the form of the oath in the audience of all men, and first of all, he taking the oath himself, began in this manner:

"Most reverend fathers, I promise, swear, and vow before my Lord Jesus Christ (whose most blessed body I unworthy sinner have received, unto whom in the last judgment, I shall give an account of all my deeds) that in this business of election, whereto now by the will of the council we are sent, I will seek nothing else, but only the salvation of the christian people, and the profit of the universal church. This shall be my whole care and study, that the authority of the general councils be not contemned, that the catholic faith be not impugned, and that the fathers who remain in the council be not oppressed. This will I seek for: this shall be my care; to this, with all my whole force and power, will I bend myself; neither will I respect any thing in this point, either for mine own cause, or for any friend, but only God, and the profit of the church. With this mind and intent, and with this heart, will I take mine oath before the council."

His words were lively and fearful. After him all the other electors in their order, did swear and take their oath: then they went with great solemnity unto the conclave, where they remained seven days. The manner of their election was in this sort. Before the cardinals' seat was set a desk, whereupon there stood a bason of silver, into the which bason all the electors did cast their schedules; which the cardinal receiving, read one by one, and four other of the electors wrote as he read them.

The tenor of the schedules was in this manner: "I George, bishop of Vicenza, do choose such a man, or such a man for bishop of Rome," and peradventure named one or two; every one of the electors subscribed his name to the schedule, that he might thereby know his own, and say nay, if it were contrary to that which was spoken; whereby all deceit was utterly excluded. The first scrutiny thus ended, it was found that there were many named to the papacy; yet none had sufficient voices, for that day there were seventeen of different nations nominated. Notwithstanding, Amedeus duke of Savoy, a man of singular virtue, surmounted them all; for in the first scrutiny he had the voice of sixteen electors, which judged him worthy to govern the church.

After this, there was a diligent inquisition had in the council touching those who were named of the electors, and as every man's opinion served him, he either praised or discommended those who were nominated. But there was such report made of Amedeus, that in the next scrutiny, which was held in the nones of November, Amedeus had twenty-one voices, and in the third and fourth scrutiny, twenty-one voices. And as there was none found in all the scrutiny to have two parts, all the other schedules were burnt. And as there lacked but only one voice to the election of the high bishop, they fell to prayer, desiring God that he would vouchsafe to direct their minds to an unity and concord, worthily to elect and choose him who should take the charge over the flock of God. As Amedius seemed to be nearer unto the papacy than all others, there was great communication had among them, touching his life and disposition. Some said that a layman ought not so suddenly to be chosen; for it would seem a strange thing, for a secular prince to be called to the bishopric of Rome; which would also too much derogate from the ecclesiastical state, as though there were none therein meet or worthy for that dignity. Others said, That a man who was married and had children, was unmeet for such a charge. Others again affirmed, that the bishop of Rome ought to be a doctor of law, and an excellent learned man.

When these words were spoken, others rising up, spake far otherwise; that although Amedeus was no doctor, yet was he learned and wise, as all his whole youth he had bestowed in learning and study, and had sought not the name, but even the ground of learning. Then said another, "If ye be desirous to be instructed further of this prince's life, I pray you give ear to me, who know him thoroughly. Truly this man from his youth upward, and even from his young and tender years, has lived more religiously than secularly, being always obedient to his parents and masters, and being always indued with the fear of God, never given to any vanity or wantonness; neither has there at any time been any child of the house of Savoy, in whom has appeared greater wit or towardness; whereby all those who did behold and know this man, judged and foresaw some great matter in him; neither were they deceived. For if ye desire to know his rule and government, what and how noble it has been; first, know ye this, that this man has reigned since his father's decease, about forty years.

"During whose time, justice, the lady and queen of all other virtues, has always flourished: for he, hearing his subjects himself, would never suffer the poor to be oppressed, or the weak to be deceived. He was the defender of the fatherless, the advocate of the widows, and protector of the poor. There was no rapine or robbery in all his territory. The poor and rich lived all under one law, neither was he burthenous to his subjects, or importune against strangers throughout all his country; there were no grievous exactions of money throughout all his dominion. He thought himself rich enough, if the inhabitants of his dominions did abound and were rich; knowing that it was the point of a good shepherd to shear his sheep, and not to devour them. In this also was his chief study and care, that his subjects might live in peace, and such as bordered upon him, might have no occasion of grudge.

"By which policies he did not only quietly govern his father's dominions, but also augmented the same by others, who willingly submitted themselves unto him. He never made war upon any, but resisting against such as made war upon him, he studied rather to make peace than to seek any revenge, desiring rather to overcome his enemies with benefits, than with the sword. He married only one wife, who was a noble maiden, and of singular beauty and virtue. He would have all his family to live virtuously, and throughout all his house, honesty and integrity of manners was observed. When his wife had departed this life, and he perceived his duchy to be established, and that it would come without any controversy to his posterity, he declared his mind, which was always religious, and dedicated to God, and shewed what will and affection he had long borne in his heart. For he contemning the pomp and state of this world, calling to him his dear friends, departed and went into a wilderness; where building a goodly abbey, he addicted himself wholly to the service of God, and taking his cross upon him, followed Christ. In which place he being conversant by the space of many years, shewed forth great examples of holiness, wearing no other garments but such as could withstand the cold, neither using any kind of dainty fare, but only to resist hunger, watching and praying the most part of the night. Wherefore this prince is not newly come to the church (as some suppose) but being a christain, born of progenitors, who have been christians a thousand years and more, doth now serve God in a monastery.

"But as to that which is spoken concerning a wife, I do not regard it; when not he only who has had a wife, but he also who has a wife may be elected and chosen pope. For why do the doctors dispute, whether a married man chosen pope, ought to continue to live with his wife, but only because a married man might be received and chosen? For as you know well enough, there were many popes that had wives; and Peter also was not without a wife. But what do we stand about this? For peradventure, it had been better that more priests had been married; for many would be saved through marriage, who are now damned through their single life. But hereof we will speak in another place. I pray you, choose this man. He will augment the faith, he will reform manners, and preserve the authority of the church. Have ye not heard these troubles of the church to have been before spoken of, and that the time now present should be an end of all troubles? Have ye not heard that about this time there should a pope be chosen which should comfort Zion, and set all things in peace? And who, I pray you, should he be that could fulfil these things except we choose this man? Believe me, these sayings must be fulfilled, and I trust that God will move your minds thereto. Notwithstanding, do whatever you shall think most good and holy."

When he had spoken these words, the greatest number of the electors seemed to consent to him, and his words took such effect, that in the next scrutiny the matter was finished and ended, and when the scrutiny was opened, it was found that Amedeus, the most devout duke of Savoy, according to the decree of the council, was chosen pope. Wherefore suddenly, there was great joy and gladness among them, and all men highly commended their doings. Then the Cardinal Arelatensis published the name of the elect bishop. After this all the prelates in their pontifical robes and mitres, and all the clergy of the city coming unto the conclave, the electors being likewise adorned, they brought him to the great church, where after great thanks given to God, and the election again declared to the people, a hymn being sung for joy, the congregation was dissolved.

This Amedeus was a man of reverend age, of comely stature, of grave and discreet behaviour; also before married. Who thus being elected pope about November, was called Felix V., and was crowned in the city of Basil, in the month of July. There was present at his coronation, Lewis, duke of Savoy; Philip, Earl Gebenensis; Lewis, marquis of Salutz; the marquis of Rotelen; Conrad of Winsperg, chamberlain of the empire; the earl of Dierstein; the ambassadors of the cities of Strasburgh, Berne, Friburgh, Solatorn, with a great multitude of others beside, to the number of fifty thousand persons. At this coronation, the pope's two sons served and ministered to their father. Lewis, cardinal of Hostia, set on his head the pontifical diadem, which was esteemed at thirty thousand crowns. It were too long here to recite the whole order and solemnity of the procession of the pope's riding about the city. First proceeded the pope under his canopy of cloth of gold, having on his head a triple crown, and blessing the people as he went. By him went the marquis of Rotelen and Conrad of Winsperg, leading his horse by the bridle. The procession finished, they went to dinner, which lasted four full hours, being excessively sumptuous; where the pope's two sons were butlers to his cup; the marquis of Salutz was the steward, &c.

Of this Felix, Volaterane in his third book thus writes, that he being asked by certain of the ambassadors, if he had any dogs or hounds, to shew them; he desired them the next day to repair unto him, and he would

shew them such as he had. When the ambassadors, according to the appointment were come, he shewed to them a great number of poor people and beggars sitting at his tables at meat, declaring that those were his hounds, which he every day used to feed, hunting with them (he trusted) for the glory of heaven to come.

And thus you have heard the state of this council hitherto, which council endured a long season, the space of seventeen years.

About the sixth year of the council, Sigismund the emperor died, leaving but one daughter to succeed him in his kingdoms, whom he had married to Albert, the second duke of Austria, who first succeeded in the kingdoms of Hungary and Bohemia, a sore adversary to the Bohemians, and afterwards was made emperor, A. D. 1438, and reigned emperor but two years, leaving his wife, who was Sigismund's daughter, great with child. After which Albert, his brother Frederick, the third duke of Austria, succeeded in the empire, &c.

And having thus far proceeded in the matters of this council, until the election of Amedeus, called pope Felix V., before we prosecute the rest, order requires to intermix the matters concluded between this council and the Bohemians.

The Bohemians then were invited to Basil, where the council was appointed; and having, after much delay, and some treaty, procured a safe conduct from the council, from the princes, and from the city of Basil, they appeared by their ambassadors, and addressed the council.

Then Rochezanus made an oration, requiring to have a day appointed when they should be heard, which was appointed the sixteenth day of the same month. Upon which day John Rochezanus, having made his preface, began to propound the first article, touching the communion to be ministered under both kinds, and disputed upon the same for the space of three days always before noon. Then Wenceslaus, the Taborite, disputed upon the second article, touching the correction and punishing of sin, for the space of two days. After whom Ulderic, priest of the Orphans, propounded and disputed upon the third article, for the space of two days, touching the free preaching of the word of God.

Last of all, Peter Pain, an Englishman, disputed three days upon the fourth article, touching the civil dominion of the clergy, and afterward gave copies of their disputations in writing to the council, with hearty thanks that they were heard. The three last did somewhat inveigh against the council for condemning John Huss and John Wickliff for their doctrine. Whereupon John de Ragusso, a divine, rising up, desired that he might have leave to answer in his own name, to the first article of the Bohemians. The council consented, so that for the space of eight days in the forenoon, he disputed thereupon. But before he began to answer, John, the Abbot of Sistertia, made an oration to the Bohemians, that they should submit themselves to the determination of the holy church, which this council represents. This matter did not a little offend the Bohemians. John Ragusinus, a divine, after scholars' fashion, in his answer spake often of heresies and heretics. Procopius could not suffer it, but rising up with an angry spirit, complained openly to the council of this injury. "This our countryman, (saith he,) does us great injury, calling us oftentimes heretics." Ragusinus answered: "As I am your countryman both by tongue and nation, I do the more desire to reduce you again unto the church." It came almost to this point, that through this offence the Bohemians would depart from Basil, and could scarcely be appeased. Certain of the Bohemians would not hear Ragusinus finish his disputation.

After him a famous divine, one Egidius Carlerius, dean of the church of Cambray, answered to the second article, for the space of four days. To the third article answered one Henry, three days together. Last of all, one John Polomarius answered to the fourth article, likewise for the space of three days, so that the long time which they used in disputations seemed tedious to the Bohemians. Notwithstanding this answer, the Bohemians still defended their articles, and especially the

A A

first, insomuch as John Rochezanus did strongly impugn Ragusinus's answer, for the space of six days. But as one disputation bred another, and it was perceived how that by this means no concord could be made; the Prince William, duke of Bavaria, protector of the council, attempted another remedy, that all disputations being set aside, the matter should be friendly debated.

There were certain appointed on either part to treat upon the concord, who coming together the eleventh day of March, those who were appointed for the council, were demanded to say their minds. "It seemed good," said they, "if these men would be united unto us, and be made one body with us, that this body might then accord, and declare and determine all manner of diversities of opinions and sects, what is to be believed or done in them."

The Bohemians, when they had a while paused, said, "This way seems not apt enough, except first of all the four articles were exactly discussed, so that either we should agree with them, or they with us: for otherwise it would be but a frivolous matter, if they being now united, again disagree in the deciding of the articles." Here answer was made to the Bohemians, "That if they were rightly united, and the aid of the Holy Ghost called for, they would not err in the deciding of the matter, as every christian ought to believe that determination, which, if they would do, it would breed a most firm and strong concord and amity on either part." But this answer satisfied them not, so that the other three rose up, and disputed against the answers which were given. At that time Cardinal Julian, president of the council, made this oration unto the Bohemian ambassadors.

"This sacred synod," said he, "has now for the space of ten days patiently heard the propositions of your four articles." And afterward he annexed, "You have propounded," saith he, "four articles, but we understand that, beside these four, you have many other strange doctrines, wherein ye dissent from us. Wherefore it is necessary, if a perfect unity and fraternity shall follow between us, that all these things be declared in the council, to the end that by the grace of the Holy Ghost, which is the author of peace and truth, due provision may be made therein. Wherefore we desire you, that you will certify us upon these and certain other points, what you do believe, or what credit you give to them. But we do not require, that you should now declare your reasons, but it shall satisfy us, if you will answer unto every article by this word: 'We believe or believe not.' Which if you will do (as we trust you will) then we shall perceive that you desire that we should conceive a good estimation of you. If there be any thing whereof you would be certified by us, ask it boldly, and we will give you an answer out of hand; for we are ready, according to the doctrine of St. Peter, to render account unto every man which shall require it, touching the faith which we hold." Hereto the Bohemian ambassadors answered in few words, "That they came only to propound those four articles, not in their own name, but in the name of the whole kingdom of Bohemia," and spake no more. Whereupon William, the noble protector of the council, calling upon four men on either part, treated touching the pacifying the matter, by whose advice the council decreed to send a famous ambassage with the Bohemian ambassadors, to Prague, where the people should assemble upon Sunday. But they would not receive these conditions of peace which were offered, but made haste to depart. Whereupon on the fourteenth day of April, there were ten chosen out of the council, to go with the Bohemian ambassadors unto Prague.

After the coming of those ambassadors, much contention began to rise between the parties. First began John Rochezanus, who speaking in the public person of the commonalty, laboured to commend and prefer the four verities of the Bohemians before propounded; charging also the prelates and priests for their slanderous and undeserved contumelies wherewith they did defame the noble kingdom of Bohemia, complaining also that they would not receive those christian verities, left and

allowed by their king, Wenceslaus, now departed. Wherefore he required them in the behalf of the whole nation, that they would leave off hereafter to oppress them in such sort, that they would restore to them again their Joseph's vesture, that is, the ornament of their good fame and name, whereof their brethren, their enemies, had spoiled them, &c.

To this Polomar makes answer again, with a long and curious oration, exhorting them to peace and unity of the church, which, if they would embrace, all other obstacles and impediments (said he) should be soon removed, promising also, that this their vesture of honour and fame should be amply restored again; and afterward, if there were any doubtful matters, they might and should be the better discussed.

But all this pleased not the Bohemians, unless they might first have a declaration of their four articles, which, if they might obtain, they promised then to embrace peace and concord. Which peace (said they) began first to be broken by themselves, in that the council of Constance, by their unjust condemnation, burned John Huss, and Jerome of Prague; and also by their cruel bulls and censures, raised up first excommunication, then war against the whole kingdom of Bohemia.

When the ambassadors saw the matter could not otherwise be settled, they required to have those articles delivered to them in a certain form, which they sent to the council by three Bohemian ambassadors.

Afterward the council sent a declaration into Bohemia, to be published by the ambassadors, which were commanded to report unto the Bohemians, in the name of the council, that if they would receive the declaration of those three articles, and the unity of the church, there should be a means found whereby the matter touching the fourth article, of the communion under both kinds, should be passed with peace and quietness.

After the Bohemians had taken deliberation, they said, "That they would give no answer before they understood what should be offered them as touching the communion." Wherefore, it was necessary to declare the matter, as it was written in form following:—

"In the name of God and our Saviour Jesus Christ, upon the sacrament of whose most blessed last supper we shall treat, that he who hath instituted this most blessed sacrament of unity and peace, will vouchsafe to work this effect in us, and to make us that we may be one in the Lord Jesus our Head, and that he will subvert all the subtleties of the devil, who, through his envious craftiness hath made the sacrament of peace and unity, an occasion of war and discord; that, while christians do contend, touching the manner of communicating, they be not deprived of the fruit of communion. This was thought good above all things to be premised, that the general custom of the church, which your fathers and you also in times past have observed, hath a long time had and still useth, that they who do not consecrate, communicate only under the kind of bread. Which custom being lawfully brought in by the church and holy fathers, and now a long time observed, it is not lawful to reject, or to change at your will and pleasure, without the authority of the church. Therefore, to change the custom of the church, and to take in hand to communicate unto the people under both kinds, without the authority of holy church, is altogether unlawful. For holy church, upon reasonable occasions, may grant liberty unto the people to communicate under both kinds. And every communion, which, being attempted without the authority and license of the church, should be unlawful; when it is done with the authority of holy church, shall be lawful, if other things prevent it not; because, as the apostle saith, 'He that eateth and drinketh unworthily, eateth and drinketh his own damnation.'

"Moreover, doctors do say, that the custom of communicating to the people, only under the kind of bread, was reasonably introduced by the church and holy fathers, for reasonable causes, specially for the avoiding of two perils:—of error and irreverence. Of error, as to think that the one part of Christ's body were in the bread, and the other part in the cup, which were a great error. Of irreverence, as many things may happen, as well on the part of the minister, as on the part of the receiver: as it is said, that it happened when a certain priest carried the sacrament of the cup unto a sick man, when he should have ministered, he found nothing in the cup, being all spilt by the way, with many other such like chances. We have heard, moreover, that it hath often happened that the sacrament consecrated in the cup has not been sufficient for the number of communicants, whereby a new consecration must be made, which is not agreeable to the doctrine of the holy fathers, and also that oftentimes they minister wine unconsecrated for consecrated wine, which is a great peril. By this means, when it shall be brought to pass, that if you will effectually receive the unity and peace of the church in all other things besides the use of the communion under both kinds, conforming yourselves to the faith and order of the universal church, you that have that use and custom shall communicate still by the authority of the church under both kinds, and this article shall be discussed fully in the sacred council, where you shall see what as touching this article, is to be holden as a universal verity, and is to be done for the profit and salvation of the christian people, and all things being thus thoroughly handed, then if you persevere in your desire, and that your ambassadors do require it, the sacred council will grant licence in the Lord to your ministers, to communicate to the people under both kinds, that is to say, to such as be of lawful years and discretion, and shall reverently and devoutly require the same; this always observed, that the ministers shall say to those who shall communicate, that they ought firmly to believe, ' not the flesh only to be contained under the form of bread, and the blood only under the wine, but under each kind to be whole and perfect Christ.'"

Thus, hitherto we have declared the decree of the council. As to the other questions, a concord and unity was concluded and confirmed by setting to their hands. The Bohemians promised to receive the peace and unity of the church, and the declaration of the three articles. This was done in the year 1438.

At the last the concord was confirmed by writing with their seals at Inglavia, a city of Moravia, the fifth day of July, in the presence of the emperor.

Certain petitions which the Bohemians put up last of all in the sacred council of Basil, A. D. 1438, in the month of November.

"To the most reverend fathers in Christ, and our most gracious lords: we the ambassadors of the kingdom of Bohemia do most humbly and heartily require you that for the perpetual preservation of peace and concord, and for the firm preservation of all things contained in the composition, you will vouchsafe of your clemency to give and grant unto us all and singular our requests here underwritten, with effectual execution of the same.

"First, and above all things we desire and require you, for the extirpation of divers dissensions and controversies which will undoubtedly follow amongst our people under the diversity of the communion, and for the abolishing of infinite evils which we are not able to express as we have conceived them, that you will gently vouchsafe of your goodness and liberality to give, grant, and command, unto our kingdom of Bohemia, and marquisdom of Moravia, one uniform order of the communion unto all men, under both kinds, that is to say, unto the archbishop of Prague, the bishop of Luthonus, Olmutz, and other prelates of the kingdom and marquisdom, having charge of souls, and to their vicars, and also to their flocks and subjects, and that according to those things which are contained in the bull of the ambassadors, and in the compositions made in the name of the whole council, written in the chapter, *pro firmitate,* where it is thus said, 'And all other things shall be done, which shall be meet and necessary for the preservation of the peace and unity.' For this done, by your

benefit the whole kingdom shall be comforted above measure, and established in brotherly love; whereby an uniform subjection and obedience shall be perpetually attributed unto the holy church.

"Also, we require and desire (as before) that for the avoiding of all suspicion and doubtfulness of many, who suppose that the sacred council has granted the communion under both kinds to us but for a time, as neither profitable nor wholesome, but as the writing of divorcement; that you will vouchsafe, wholesomely and speedily to provide for our safety, and with your grant in this behalf, and with the bulls in your letters, to confirm that chapter, together with the other pertaining to the office of your ambassadors.

"Also, we beseech you (as before) that for the confirmation of obedience, and for the discipline of all the clergy, and for the final defence and observation of all things determined and agreed upon, and for the good order in spiritualties, ye will vouchsafe effectually to provide for us a good and lawful pastor, archbishops and bishops, who shall seem to us most meet and acceptable for our kingdom, to execute those offices and duties.

"Also, we require you that your fatherly reverences will vouchsafe, for the defence of the worthy fame of the kingdom and marquisdom, to declare and shew our innocency, in that they have communicated, do, and hereafter shall communicate under both kinds; to give out, ordain, and direct the letters of the sacred council, in manner and form most apt and meet for such declaration, to all princes, as well secular as spiritual, cities and commonalties, according to the compositions, and as the lords the ambassadors are bound to us to do.

"Also, we desire you that in the discussing of the matter for the communion under both kinds, and of the commandment given to all faithful, ye will not proceed otherwise than according to the Concordatum agreed upon in Egra: that is to say, according to the law of God, the order of Christ, and his apostles, the general councils, and the minds of the holy doctors, truly grounded upon the law of God.

"Also, we desire that your fatherly reverences, considering the great affection of our people, will give us the desired liberty to communicate to the younger sort the sacrament of the supper. For if this use of communicating should be taken away, which our kingdom being godly, moved by the writings of most great and holy doctors, and brought in by example, has received as catholic, and exercised now a long time; verily it would raise up an intolerable offence among the people, and their minds would be grievously vexed and troubled.

"Also, we require you (as before) that for like causes your fatherly reverences would vouchsafe to permit, at the least the gospels, epistles, and creed, to be sung and read in the church in our vulgar tongue, before the people, to move them to devotion; for in our language it has been used of old in the church, and likewise in our kingdom.

"Also, we require you in the name of the said kingdom, and of the famous university of Prague, that your fatherly reverences would vouchsafe to shew such diligence and care toward the desired reformation of that university, that according to the manner and form of other universities reformed by the church, prebends and collations of certain benefices of cathedral and parish churches may be annexed and incorporated into the said university, that thereby it may be increased and preferred.

"Also, we desire you (as before) as heartily as we may, and also (saving always your fatherly reverences) require you, and by the former compositions we most instantly admonish you, that with your whole minds and endeavours, and with all care and study, your reverences will watch and seek for that long desired and most necessary reformation of the church and christian religion, and effectually labour for the rooting out of all public evils, as well in the head, as in the members, as you have often promised to do in our kingdom, in the compositions, and as our fourth article, touching the avoiding of all public evils, exacts and requires."

There were certain answers provided by the council to these petitions of the Bohemians, which were not delivered to them, but kept back, for what purpose and intent we know not. Wherefore because we thought them not greatly necessary for this place, and also to avoid prolixity, we have judged it meet to omit them. Thus have ye heard compendiously the chief and principal matters treated of and done in this famous council of Basil.

Concerning the authority of this general council of Basil, what is to be thought of it, may be learned by all good men by the acts and fruits of it. Neither was it doubted by any man in the beginning, so long as the pope agreed and consented to it. But after the pope began to draw back, many others followed, especially of the richer sort of prelates, who had anything to lose. In the number of those inconstant prelates was Cardinal Julian, the first collector of this council, and vicar-general of the pope, as by his fervent and vehement letter, written to Pope Eugenius in defence of this council appears. In it he most earnestly expostulates with Pope Eugenius, for seeking to dissolve the council, and declares many causes, why he should rather rejoice, and give God thanks for the godly proceedings and joyful agreement between the council and the Bohemians, and so exhorts him with many persuasions to resort to the council himself, and not to seek its dissolution.

In like manner Æneas Sylvius also, with his own hand-writing, not only gave testimony to the authority of this council, but also bestowed his labour and pains in setting forth the whole history of it. Notwithstanding Sylvius afterward being made pope, with his new honour, altered and changed his old opinion. His epistle, touching the commendation of the council, because it is but short, I thought here, for satisfying the reader's mind, to insert :—

An Epistle of Æneas Sylvius to the Rector of the University of Cologne.

" To a christian man, which will be a true christian indeed, nothing ought to be more desired, than that the sincerity and pureness of faith, given to us of Christ by our forefathers, be kept of all men immaculate. And if at any time anything be wrought or attempted against the true doctrine of the gospel, the people ought with one consent to provide lawful remedy, and every man to bring with him some water to quench the general fire ; neither must we fear how we be hated or envied, so we bring the truth. We must resist every man to his face, whether he be Paul or Peter, if he walk not directly to the truth of the gospel. Which thing I am glad, and so are we all, to hear that your university has done in this council of Basil. For a certain treatise of yours is brought here to us, wherein you reprehend the rudeness, or rather the rashness of such, as deny the bishop of Rome, and the consistory of his judgment, to be subject to the general council ; and that the supreme tribunal seat of judgment stands in the church, and in no one bishop. Such men as deny this, you so confound with lively reasons and truth of the scriptures, that they are neither able to slide away like slippery eels, neither to cavil or bring any objection against you."

The deposed Pope Eugenius, not acknowledging the acts of deposition, called a council at Florence, and in the meantime prevailed on the French king to make war on the council of Basil. The dauphin was defeated, but the council was at last dissolved.

As these things were doing at Basil, Pope Eugenius brought to pass in his convocation at Florence, that the emperor and the patriarch of Constantinople, with the rest of the Greeks there present, were persuaded to receive the sentence of the church of Rome, concerning the proceeding of the Holy Ghost ; also to receive the communion in unleavened bread, to admit purgatory, and to yield themselves to the authority of the Romish bishop. To which, however, the churches of Greece would in no wise assent at their coming home, so that

with a public anathema they condemned all those legates who had consented to these articles, that none of them should be buried in christian burial. (A.D. 1439.)

And thus endeth the history, both of the council of Basil and of the council of Florence, also of the emperor Sigismund, and of the schism between Pope Eugenius and Pope Felix, (who was induced to resign the popedom to the successor of Eugenius,) and also of the Bohemians. The Bohemians, notwithstanding all these troubles and tumults, did right well, and were strong enough against all their enemies, till at length through discord, partly between the two preachers of the old and new city of Prague, partly also through the discord of the messengers and captains taking sides one against the other, they made their enemies strong, and enfeebled themselves. However they so defended the cause of their religion, not by sword, but by argument and disputation, that the bishop of Rome could never, nor yet to this day remove the Taborites and city of Prague from the communion of both kinds, nor could ever cause them to keep the conditions, which in the beginning of the council were enjoined their priests to observe.

During this business beyond the sea, our bishops here in England were not unoccupied. Whether it be the nature of the country, or the great livings and wealthy promotions of the clergy that influences them, it is certain that in England there is more burning and slaying for religion, and for all other matters more bloodshed among us, than in any other land or nation in Christendom besides. After the burning of Richard Hoveden, of Nicholas Canon, and of Thomas Bagley, priest, above recorded, whom the bishops condemned to death (A.D. 1431), not long after, about A.D. 1439, which was the seventeenth of the reign of King Henry VI., they had another poor man, named Richard Wiche, priest, who was first degraded, then burnt at Tower-hill for heresy.

After the burning of this man, a convocation was called by Henry, archbishop of Canterbury, wherein was propounded among the clergy, to consult what way were best for the removing away the law of *Premuniri facias;* for so were the hearts then of the temporalty set against the ecclesiastical sort, that where any vantage might be given them by the law, they did spare nothing ; by reason of which the churchmen at that time were greatly molested by the law of *Premuniri*, and by the king's writs, and other indictments. By long consultation and good advisement, at last this way was taken, that a petition or supplication should be drawn and presented to the king, for the abolishing of the law of *Premuniri facias,* and also for the restraining of other briefs, writs, and indictments, which seemed then to lie heavy upon the clergy. This bill or supplication being contrived and exhibited by the archbishops of Canterbury and of York to the king, when he was standing in need of a subsidy to be collected of the clergy ; this answer was given to their supplication, on the king's behalf ; that forsomuch as the time of Christmas drew near, whereby he had as yet no sufficient leisure to advise upon the matter, he would take therein a farther pause. In the meantime, as one tendering their quiet, he would send to all his officers and ministers within his realm, that no such brief of *Premuniri* should pass against them, or any of them, from the said time of Christmas, till the next parliament, A.D. 1439.

The Invention of Printing.

In following the course of years, we find this year of our Lord, 1450, to be famous and memorable, for the divine and miraculous inventing of printing. Nauclerius, and Wymselingus following him, refer the invention to A. D. 1440. Others refer it to A.D. 1446, and 1450. The first inventor is thought to be a German, dwelling first in Strasburg, afterwards citizen of Mentz, named John Faustus, a goldsmith. The occasion of this invention was by engraving the letters of the alphabet in metal, then laying black ink upon the metal, it gave the form of letters in paper. The man being industrious and active, thought to proceed further, and to try whether it would frame as well in words, and in whole sentences, as it did in letters : and when he perceived it did so, he acquainted one John Guttemberg, and Peter Schafferd, binding them by their oath to keep silence for a season. After ten years, John Guttemberg, co-partner with Faustus, began then first to broach the matter at Strasburg. The art, being yet but rude, in process of time was advanced by various men of inventive genius, adding more and more to the perfection of it. In the number of whom, John Mentel, John Pruss, Adolphus Ruschius, were great helpers. Ulricus Han, in Latin called Gallus, first brought it to Rome.

However, whatever man was the instrument, without all doubt God himself was the ordainer and disposer thereof, no otherwise, than he was of the gift of tongues, and that for a similar purpose. And well may this gift of printing be resembled to the gift of tongues ; for as God then spake with many tongues, and yet all that would not turn the Jews ; so now, when the Holy Ghost speaks to the adversaries in innumerable sorts of books, yet they will not be converted, nor turn to the gospel.

Now to consider to what end and purpose the Lord hath given this gift of printing to the earth, and to what great utility and necessity it serves, is not hard to judge.

And first, touching the time of this invention being given to man, this is to be observed, that when the bishop of Rome, with all the whole and full consent of the cardinals, patriarchs, archbishops, bishops, abbots, priors, lawyers, doctors, provosts, deans, archdeacons, assembled together in the council of Constance, had condemned poor John Huss, and Jerome of Prague to death for heresy, though they were no heretics, and after they had subdued the Bohemians and all the whole world under the supreme authority of the Romish see ; and had made all christian people obedient and vassals, having, as one would say, all the world at their will, so that the matter now was past, not only the power of all men, but the hope also of any man to be recovered : in this very time so dangerous and desperate, where man's power could do no more, then the blessed wisdom and omnipotent power of the Lord began to work for his church, not with sword and target to subdue his exalted adversary, but with printing, writing, and reading to convince darkness by light, error by truth, ignorance by learning. So that by this means of printing, the secret operation of God has heaped upon that proud kingdom a double confusion. For, whereas the bishop of Rome had burned John Huss before, and Jerome of Prague, who neither denied his transubstantiation, nor his supremacy, nor yet his popish mass, but said mass, and heard mass themselves, neither spake against his purgatory, nor any other great matter of his popish doctrine, but only exclaimed against his excessive and pompous pride, his unchristian or rather antichristian abomination of life : thus while he could not abide his wickedness of life to be touched, but made it heresy, or, at least matter of death, whatever was spoken against his detestable conversation and manners, God of his secret judgment, seeing time to help his church, has found a way by this art of printing, not only to confound his life and conversation, which before he could not abide to be touched, but also to cast down the foundation of his standing, that is, to examine, confute, and detect his most detestable doctrine, laws, and institutions in such sort, that though his life were never so pure, yet his doctrine standing as it does, no man is so blind but he may see, that either the pope is antichrist, or else that antichrist is near cousin to the pope ; and all this does and will hereafter more and more appear by printing.

The reason whereof is this : Hereby tongues are known, knowledge grows, judgment increases, books are dispersed, the scripture is seen, the doctors are read, histories opened, times compared, truth discerned, falsehood detected, and all, as I said, through the benefit of printing. Wherefore, I suppose, that either the pope must abolish printing, or he must seek a new world to reign over ; for else, as this world stands, printing doubtless will abolish him. But the pope, and all his college of cardinals, must understand this, that through the light of printing the world begins now to have eyes to see, and heads to judge : he cannot walk so invisible in a net, but he will be spied. And although through might he stopped the mouth of John Huss before, and of Jerome, that they might not preach, thinking to make his kingdom sure ; yet, instead of John Huss and others, God hath opened the press to preach, whose voice the pope is never able to stop with all the puissance of his triple crown. By this printing, as by the gift of tongues, and as by the singular organ of the Holy Ghost, the doctrine of the gospel sounds to all nations and countries under heaven, and what God reveals to one man, is dispersed to many, and what is known in one nation is opened to all.

The first and best were for the bishop of Rome, by the benefit of printing, to learn and know the truth. If he will not, let him well understand that printing is not set up for nought. To strive against the stream will not avail. What the pope has lost, since printing and the press began to preach, let him cast his counters. First, when Erasmus wrote, and Frobenius printed, what a blow thereby was given to all friars and monks in the world ? And who sees not that the pen of Luther following after Erasmus, and set forward by printing, has set the triple crown so awry on the pope's head, that it is like never to be set straight again ?

Briefly, if there were no demonstration to lead, yet by this one argument of printing, the bishop of Rome might understand the counsel and purpose of the Lord to work against him, having provided such a way in earth, that almost as many printing presses as there be in the world, so many bulwarks there are against the high castle of St. Angelo, so that either the pope must abolish knowledge and printing, or printing at length will root him out. As nothing made the pope strong in time past but lack of knowledge and ignorance of simple christians : so contrariwise, now nothing debilitates and shakes the high spire of his papacy so much as reading, preaching, knowledge and judgment, that is to say, the fruit of printing ; whereof some experience we see already, and more is likely (by the Lord's blessing) to follow. For although, through outward force and violent cruelty tongues dare not speak, yet the hearts of men daily, no doubt, are instructed through the benefit of printing. And though the pope hath now by cruelty, and in times past by ignorance, had all under his possession ; yet neither must he think, that violence will always continue, neither must he hope for that now which he had then. In former days books were scarce, and of such excessive price, that few could attain to the buying, and still fewer to the reading and studying of them, which books now by the means of this art, are made accessible to all men. Ye heard before how Nicholas Belward bought a New Testament in those days for four marks and forty pence, whereas now the same price will well serve forty persons with so many books !

Moreover, it was before noted and declared by the testimony of Armachanus, how for defect of books and good authors, both universities were decayed and good men kept in ignorance, while begging friars, scraping all the wealth from other priests, heaped up all books that could be gotten, into their own libraries, where either they did not diligently apply them, or else did not rightly use them, or at least kept them from such as more fruitfully would have perused them. Wherefore Almighty God of his merciful Providence, seeing both what lacked in the church, and how also to remedy the same, for the advancement of his glory, gave the understanding of this excellent art or science of printing, whereby three singular benefits at one time came to the world. First, the price of all books is diminished. Secondly, the speedy help of reading furthered. And thirdly, the plenty of all good authors enlarged.

By reason of which, as printing of books ministered matter of reading, so reading brought learning, learning shewed light, by the brightness of which blind ignorance was suppressed, error detected, and finally God's glory with truth of his word advanced.

The lamentable losing of Constantinople.

A. D. 1453, Constantinus Paleologus, being emperor of Constantinople, on the twenty-ninth day of May, the great city of Constantinople was taken by the Turk Mahomet, after a siege of fifty-four days, which siege began in the beginning of April. Within the city, beside the citizens, there were only six thousand rescuers of the Greeks; and three thousand of the Venetians and Genoese. Against these Mahomet brought an army of four hundred thousand, collected out of the countries and places adjoining near about, as out of Grecia, Illyrica, Wallachia, Dardanis, Triballis, Bulgaria, out of Bithynia, Galatia, Lydia, Sicily, and such other, which places had the name yet of Christians. Thus one neighbour for lucre's sake helped to destroy another.

The city was compassed by the Turks both by the sea and land. Mahomet, the Turk, divided his army into three sundry parts, which in three parts of the city so beat the walls and brake them down, that they attempted by the breaches thereof to enter the city. But the valiantness of the christians therein won much commendation, whose duke was called John Justinian of Genoa. But as the assaults were great, and the number of the christian soldiers daily decreased, fighting both at the walls and at the haven against such a multitude of the Turks, they were not able long to hold out. Beside the armies which lay battering at the walls, the Turk had upon the sea his navy of two hundred and fifty sail, lying upon the haven of the city, reaching from the one side of the haven's mouth to the other, as if a bridge should be made from the one bank to the other. Which haven by the citizens was barred with iron chains, whereby the Turks were kept out a certain space. Against which navy there were seven ships of Genoa within the haven, and three of Crete, and certain of Chios, which stood against them. Also the soldiers issuing out of the city, as occasion would serve, did manfully withstand them, and with wild-fire set their ships on fire, that a certain space they could serve to no use. At length the chains being broken, and a way made, the Turk's navy entered the haven, and assaulted the city, whereby the Turk began to conceive great hope, and was in forwardness to obtain the city. The assault and skirmish then waxing more hot, Mahomet the tyrant stood by upon a hill, with his warriors about him, crying and howling out to them to scale the walls and enter the town, otherwise, if any recoiled, he threatened to kill them, and so he did. Wherefore a great number of his soldiers, in their repulse and retreat, were slain by the Turk's men, being sent by his commandment to slay them, and so they were justly served, and well paid their hire.

Although this was some comfort to the christians to see and behold out of the city the Turk's retinue so consumed, yet that hope lasted not long. Shortly after by the rage of war, it happened that one Justinian, the duke above-named, was wounded; who, notwithstanding that he was earnestly desired by Paleologus the emperor, not to leave the tower which he had to keep, seeing his wound was not deadly dangerous; yet could he not be entreated to tarry, but left his standing and his fort undefended, setting none in his place to guard the same. And so this doughty duke hurt more with his false heart than with force of weapon, gave over and fled to Chio, where shortly after for sorrow, rather than for soreness of his wound, he died. Many of his soldiers, seeing their captain flee, followed after, leaving their fort utterly destitute without defence. The Turks, understanding that vantage, soon burst into the city. The Emperor Paleologus, seeing no other way but to fly, making toward the gate, either was slain, or else trodden down with the multitude. In the which gate, eight hundred dead men's bodies were found and taken up.

The city of Constantinople thus being got, the Turks sacking and ranging about the streets, houses, and corners, did put to the sword most unmercifully whomsoever they found, both aged and young, matrons, maidens, children, and infants, sparing none; the noble matrons and maidens were horribly insulted; the goods of the city, the treasuries in houses, the ornaments in churches were all sacked and spoiled; the pictures of Christ opprobriously handled in hatred of Christ. The spoil and havock of the city lasted three days together, while the barbarous soldiers murdered and rifled what they liked.

These things being done, and the tumult ceased, after three days Mahomet the Turk entered the city, and first calling for the heads and ancients of the city, such as he found alive he commanded to be mangled and cut in pieces. It is also (saith my author) reported, that in the feasts of the Turks, all such as were of the king's stock, after other barbarities, were hewn and cut in pieces for their sport.

And this was the end of that princely and famous city of Constantinople, beginning first by a Constantine, and ending also with a Constantine, which for its princely royalty was named and ever honoured, from the time of the first Constantine, equally with the city of Rome, and called also by the name thereof New Rome, and also continued the space of 1123 years. I pray God that Old Rome may learn of New Rome, to take heed and beware betime.

This terrible destruction of the city of Constantinople, the queen of cities, I thought here to describe, not so much to set forth the barbarous cruelty of these filthy and merciless murderers; as specially for this, that we being admonished by the doleful ruin and misery of these our fellow christians, may call to mind the deserved plagues and miseries which seem to hang no less over our own heads, and thereby may learn betime to invoke and call more earnestly upon the name of our terrible and merciful God, that he for his Son's sake will keep us, and preserve his church among us, and mitigate those plagues and sorrows, which we no less have deserved, than these above minded have done before us. Christ grant it, Amen.

The history of Reynold Peacock bishop of Chichester, afflicted and imprisoned for the gospel of Christ.

After the death of Henry Chichesley before mentioned, next succeeded John Stafford, (A. D. 1445), who continued eight years. After him came John Kemp, (A. D. 1453), who sat but three years. Then succeeded Thomas Burschere. In the time of which archbishop, Reynold Peacock, bishop of Chichester, was afflicted by the pope's prelate for his faith and profession of the gospel. This man (saith Hall) began to move questions not privately, but openly in the universities, concerning the Annates, Peter-pence, and other jurisdictions, and authorities pertaining to the see of Rome, and not only put forth the questions, but declared his mind and opinion in the same; wherefore he was for this cause abjured at Paul's Cross." This bishop, first of St. Asaph, then of Chichester, so long as Duke Humfrey lived, (by whom he was promoted and much made of) was quiet and safe, and also bold to dispute and to write his mind, and wrote several books and treatises. But after that good duke was made away, this good man was open to his enemies, and matter soon found against him. Being complained of, and accused to the archbishop, letters were directed down from the archbishop, to cite all men to appear that could say any thing against him.

This citation being thus issued, the bishop came before the judges and bishops to Lambeth, where Thomas the archbishop, with his doctors and lawyers, were gathered together in the archbishop's court. The duke of Buckingham was present, accompanied with the bishops of Rochester, and of Lincoln. What were the opinions and articles objected against him, shall be specified in his revocation. In his answering for himself, in such a company of the pope's friends, although he could not prevail; yet stoutly defending himself, he declared many things worthy great commendation of learning, if learning could have prevailed against power. But they on the contrary part, with all labour and diligence exerted themselves, either to reduce him, or else to confound him. Briefly, no stone was left unturned, no ways unproved, either by fair means to entreat him, or by terrible menaces to terrify his mind, till at length, he being vanquished and overcome by the bishops, began to faint, and gave over. Whereupon, by and by, a recantation was put unto him by the bishops, which he should declare before the people. The copy of which recantation here follows:

" In the name of God, Amen. Before you the most reverend father in Christ and Lord, the Lord Thomas, by the grace of God, archbishop of Canterbury, primate of all England and legate of the apostolic see, I Reynold Peacock, unworthy bishop of Chichester, do purely, willingly, simply, and absolutely confess and acknowledge, that I in times past, that is to say, by the space of these twenty years last past and more, have otherwise conceived, holden, taught and written, as touching the sacraments, and the articles of the faith, than the holy church of Rome, and universal church; and also that I have made, written, published, and set forth many and divers pernicious doctrines, books, works, writings, heresies, contrary and against the true catholic and apostolic faith, containing in them errors contrary to the catholic faith, and especially these errors and heresies hereunder written.

1. First of all, that we are not bound, by the necessity of faith, to believe that our Lord Jesus Christ after his death descended into hell.

2. That it is not necessary to salvation to believe in the holy catholic church.

3. That it is not necessary to salvation to believe the communion of saints.

4. That it is not necessary to salvation to affirm the body material in the sacrament.

5. That the universal church may err in matters which pertain unto faith.

6. That it is not necessary unto salvation to believe that which every general council doth universally ordain, approve, or determine, should necessarily for the help of our faith, and the salvation of souls, be approved and holden of all faithful christians.

" Wherefore I, Reynold Peacock, wretched sinner, who have long walked in darkness, and now by the merciful disposition and ordinance of God, am reduced and brought again unto the light and way of truth, and restored to the unity of our holy mother the church, renounce and forsake all errors and heresies aforesaid."

It is probable that this bishop repented afterward of his recantation; which may easily be supposed, because he was committed again to prison and detained captive, where it is uncertain whether he was oppressed with privy and secret tyranny, and there obtained the crown of martyrdom, or no.

From the persecutions and burnings in England we will now digress a little, to speak of foreign matters of the church of Rome.

Pope Nicholas, to get and gather great sums of money, appointed a jubilee A. D. 1450, at which time there resorted a greater number of people to Rome, than had at any time before been seen. At which time we read in the history of Platina, that to have happened, which I thought here not unworthy to be noted for the example of the thing. As there was a great concourse of people resorting to the mount Vatican to behold the image of our Saviour, which they had there to shew to the pilgrims, the people being thick going to and fro between the mount and the city, by chance a certain mule of the cardinals of St. Mark, came by the way, by which the people not being able to avoid the way, one or two falling upon the mule, there was such a throng upon that occasion on the bridge, that to the number of two hundred bodies of men, and three horses were there strangled, and on each side of the bridge many-besides fell over into the water, and were drowned.

In the time of this pope one Matthew Palmerius wrote a book On Angels, for defending which he was condemned by the pope, and burned at Corna.

After him succeeded Calixtus III., who among divers other things ordained, both at noon and evening the bell to toll the Aves, as it was used in the popish time, to help the soldiers that fought against the Turks; for which cause also he ordained the feast of the transfiguration of the Lord, solemnizing it with like pardons and indulgencies, as was Corpus Christi day.

Also this pope, proceeding contrary to the councils of Constance and Basil, decreed that no man should appeal from the pope to any council. By whom also St. Edmund of Canterbury, with divers others, were made saints.

Next after this Calixtus succeeded Pius II., otherwise called Æneas Sylvius, who wrote the two books of commentaries upon the council of Basil before mentioned. This Æneas, at the time of the writing of those books, seemed to be a man of tolerable judgment and doctrine, from which he afterward, being pope, seemed to decline and swerve, seeking by all means possible how to deface and abolish the books which he had written.

Sentences attributed unto this Pius.

" The divine nature of God may rather be comprehended by faith than by disputation.

" Christian faith is to be considered, not by what reason it is proved, but from whom it proceeds.

" Neither can a covetous man be satisfied with money, nor a learned man with knowledge.

" Learning ought to be to poor men instead of silver, to noblemen instead of gold, and to princes instead of precious stones.

" An artificial oration moves fools, but not wise men.

" Suitors in the law are as birds; the court is the bait; the judges are the nets; and the lawyers are the fowlers.

" Men are to be given to dignities, and not dignities to men.

" The office of a bishop is heavy, but it is blessed to him that doth well bear it.

" A bishop without learning may be likened to an ass.

" An evil physician destroyeth bodies, but an unlearned priest destroyeth souls.

" Marriage was taken from priests not without great reason; but with much greater reason it ought to be restored again."

The like sentence to this he utters in his second book of the council of Basil, saying, " Peradventure it were not the worst, that the most part of priests had their wives; for many should be saved in priestly marriage, which now in unmarried priesthood are damned." The same Pius also, as Celius reports, dissolved certain orders of nuns, of the orders of St. Bridget and St. Clare, bidding them to depart out, that they should no more disgrace the profession of religion.

This Pius, if he had brought so much piety and godliness as he brought learning unto his popedom, had excelled many popes that went before him.

Before his elevation he preferred general councils before the pope, now being pope, he decreed that no man should appeal from the high bishop of Rome to any general council. And likewise for priests' marriage, whereas, before he thought it best to have their wives restored, yet afterward he altered his mind.

After this Pius II. succeeded Paul II., a pope wholly set upon his own gratification and ambition, and not so much void of all learning, as the hater of learned men.

After this Paul came Sixtus IV. This pope, amongst his other acts, reduced the year of jubilee from the fiftieth to the twenty-fifth. He also instituted the feast of the Conception, and the presentation of Mary and of Anna her mother, and Joseph. Also he canonized Bonaventure and St. Francis for saints. By this Sixtus also were beads brought in, and instituted to make our lady's Psalter. This pope made two-and-thirty cardinals in his time.

Next after this Sixtus came Innocent, as rude, and as far from all learning, as his predecessor was before him. Amongst the noble acts of this pope this was one, that in the town of Polus apud Equicolos, he caused eight men and six women, with the lord of the place, to be apprehended and taken, and judged for heretics, because they said none of them was the vicar of Christ who come after Peter, but they only who followed the poverty of Christ. Also he condemned of heresy, George the king of Bohemia, and deprived him of his dignity and also of his kingdom, and procured his whole stock to be utterly rejected and put down, giving his kingdom to Matthias king of Pannonia.

Now, from the popes let us descend to other estates, beginning with our troubles here at home, pertaining to the overthrow of King Henry VI. and his seat. Here is to be remembered, how, after the death of the duke of Glocester, mischiefs came in by heaps upon the king and his realm. For, after the giving away of Anjou and Maine to the Frenchmen, by the unfortunate marriage of Queen Margaret above mentioned, the Frenchmen, perceiving now by the death of the duke of Glocester, the stay and pillar of this commonwealth to be decayed, and seeing, moreover, the hearts of the nobility amongst themselves to be divided, lost no time, having such an open way into Normandy, and in a short time they recovered the same, and also got Gascony, so that no more now remained to England of all the parts beyond the sea, but only Calais. Neither yet did the calamity of the realm only rest in this: for the king now having lost his friendly uncle, as the stay and staff of his age, who had brought him up so faithfully from his youth, was now thereby the more open to his enemies, and they more emboldened to set upon him; as appeared first by Jack Cade the Kentish captain, who, encamping first on Blackheath, afterward aspired to London, and had the spoil thereof, the king being driven into Warwickshire (A.D. 1450.) Not long after the suppression of Cade's insurrection, the duke of York, accompanied by three earls, set upon the king near to St. Alban's, where the king was taken captive, and the duke of York was by parliament declared protector in the same year 1455. After this followed long division and mortal war between the two houses of Lancaster and York, continuing many years. At length, in the year 1460, the duke of York was slain in battle by the queen near to the town of Wakefield, and with him also his son, the earl of Rutland. The queen, also, shortly after, discomfited the earl of Warwick, and the duke of Norfolk, to whom the keeping of the king had been committed by the duke of York, and so the queen again delivered her husband.

After these victories, the northern men, advancing not a little in pride and courage, began to take upon them great attempts, not only to spoil and rob churches, and religious houses, and villages, but also fully intending, partly by themselves, partly by the inducement of their lords and captains, to sack, waste, and utterly to subvert the city of London, and to take the spoil thereof; and no doubt (saith my history) would have proceeded in their conceived greedy intent, had not the opportune favour of God provided a speedy remedy. For as these mischiefs were in brewing, suddenly the noble Prince Edward came to London with a mighty army, on the twenty-seventh of February, (1461,) he was the son and heir to the duke of York above mentioned, and was accompanied by the earl of Warwick, and divers more. King Henry, in the meantime, with his victory, went up to York; when Edward being at London, caused there to be proclaimed certain articles concerning his title to the crown of England, on the second of March; and then on the fourth, accompanied with the lords spiritual and temporal, and with much concourse of people, he rode to Westminster-hall, and there, by the full consent, as well of the lords, as also by the voice of all the commons, took his possession of the crown, and was called King Edward IV.

These things thus accomplished at London, the king proceeded northward against Henry, when, with his army he had passed over the river of Trent, and was come near to Ferrybridge, where the army of King Henry was not far off, upon Palm Sunday, between Ferrybridge and Tadcaster, both the armies of the southern and northern

men joined together in battle. And although at the beginning, some horsemen of King Edward's side turned their backs, yet the courageous prince, with his captains, little discouraged, fiercely and manfully set on their adversaries. The battle was so cruelly fought on both sides, that in the conflict there were slain to the number, as is reported, beside men of name, thirty-six thousand of the poor commons. Notwithstanding, the conquest fell on King Edward's part, so that King Henry having lost all, was forced to fly into Scotland, where he gave up to the Scots the town of Berwick, after he had reigned eight-and-thirty years and a half.

KING EDWARD THE FOURTH.

King Edward, after his conquest and victory achieved against King Henry, returned again to London, where, upon the vigil of St. Peter and Paul, (A.D. 1461,) being on Sunday, he was crowned king of England, and reigned twenty-two years.

When it was proposed that the king should marry, several alliances were suggested; and first, the Lady Margaret, sister to James IV. king of Scots, was thought of; afterward the Lady Elizabeth, sister to Henry king of Castile, but she being under age, the earl of Warwick turned to the French king Lewis XI., to obtain Lady Bona, daughter of the duke of Savoy, and sister to the French queen, and obtained consent. Meanwhile the king was pleased with Elizabeth Grey, widow of Sir John Grey, knight, slain before in the battle of St. Albans, daughter to the duchess of Bedford, and Lord Rivers, and first endeavoured to have her as his mistress. But she being unworthy (as she said) to be the wife of such an high personage, and thinking herself to be too good to be his mistress, so won the king's heart, that before the return of the earl of Warwick, he married her; at which marriage only the duchess of Bedford, two gentlewomen, the priest and clerk, were present. Upon this so hasty and unlucky marriage ensued no little trouble to the king, much bloodshed to the realm, undoing almost to all her kindred, and finally confusion to King Edward's two sons, which both were declared afterward to be illegitimate, and also deprived of their lives. For the earl of Warwick, who had been the faithful friend and chief maintainer before of the king, at the hearing of this marriage, was so angry, that he ever afterwards endeavoured to work displeasure to the king. And although for a time he dissembled his wrathful mood, till he might find a time convenient, and a world to set forward his purpose, at last finding occasion serving to his mind, he made known his purpose to his two brethren, to wit, the Lord Mountecute, or Montague, and the archbishop of York, conspiring with them how to bring it about. Then he also thought to find out the mind of the duke of Clarence, King Edward's brother, and he likewise obtained him on his side, giving him his daughter in marriage.

This matter being thus prepared against the king, the first flame of his conspiracy began to appear in the north country; where the northern men in a short space gathering themselves in an open rebellion, and finding captains of their wicked purpose, came down from York toward London. Against whom was appointed by the king, William Lord Herbert earl of Pembroke, with the Lord Stafford, and certain other captains to encounter. The Yorkshiremen giving the overthrow first to the Lord Stafford, then to the earl of Pembroke, and his company of Welshmen at Banbury Field, at last joining together with the army of the earl of Warwick, and the duke of Clarence, in the dead of the night secretly stealing on the king's field at Wolney by Warwick, killed the watch, and took the king prisoner, who first being in the castle of Warwick, then was conveyed by night to Middleham castle in Yorkshire, under the custody of the archbishop of York, where he having loose keeping, and liberty to go on hunting, meeting with Sir William Stanley, Sir Thomas of Borough, and other friends, was too good for his keepers, and escaped the hands of his enemies and so came to York, where he was well received; from thence to Lancaster, where he met with the Lord Hasting his chamberlain, well accompanied, by whose help he came safe to London.

After this tumult, when reconciliation could not come to perfect peace and unity, although much labour was made by the nobility, the earl of Warwick raises up a new war in Lincolnshire, the captain whereof was Sir Robert Wells, knight, who shortly after, being taken in battle with his father and Sir Thomas Duncock, they were beheaded, the rest casting away their coats ran away and fled, giving the name of the field called Losecoat Field. The earl of Warwick, after this, put out of comfort and hope to prevail at home, fled out of England, A.D. 1470, first to Calais, then to Lewis the French king, accompanied by the duke of Clarence. The fame of the earl of Warwick, and of his famous acts, was at that time in great admiration above measure, and so highly favoured, that both in England and in France all men were glad to behold his person. Wherefore the coming of this earl, and of the duke of Clarence, was not a little grateful to the French king, and no less opportune to Queen Margaret, King Henry's wife, and Prince Edward her son, who also came to the French court to meet and confer together touching their affairs; where a league was concluded between them, and moreover a marriage between Edward prince of Wales, and Anne the second daughter of the earl of Warwick was wrought. Thus all things falling luckily upon the earl's part, beside the large offers and great promises made by the French king, that he would do his best to set forward their purpose, the earl having also intelligence by letters, that the hearts almost of all men went with him, and longed sore for his presence, so that there now lacked only haste to return with all speed possible; he, with the duke of Clarence, well fortified with the French navy, set forward towards England; for so was it before decreed between them, that they two should prove the first venture, and then Queen Margaret, with Prince Edward her son, should follow after. The arrival of the earl was no sooner heard of at Dartmouth in Devonshire, but great concourse of people by thousands went to him from all quarters to receive and welcome him; who immediately made proclamation in the name of King Henry VI., charging all men, able to bear armour, to prepare themselves to fight against Edward duke of York, usurper of the crown. There lacked no friends, strength of men, furniture, nor policy convenient for such a matter.

When King Edward (who was passing the time in hunting, in hawking, in all pleasure and dalliance), had knowledge what great resort of multitudes incessantly repaired more and more daily about the earl and the duke, he began now to provide for remedy when it was too late. Who trusting too much to his friends, and fortune before, did now right well perceive what a variable and inconstant thing the people is, and especially the people of England, whose nature is never to be content long with the present state, but always delighting in news, seek new variety of changes, either envying that which standeth, or else pitying that which is fallen. Which inconstant mutability of the light people, changing with the wind, and wavering with the reed, did well appear in the course of this king's story. For he, through the favour of the people, when he was down, was exalted; now being exalted by them, was forsaken: in which this is to be noted by all princes, that as there is nothing in this mutable world firm and stable, so there is no trust nor assurance to be made, but only in the favour of God, and in the promises of his word, only in Christ his Son, whose kingdom alone shall never end, and never change.

While these things were passing on in England, King Edward, accompanied by the duke of Gloucester his brother, and the Lord Hastings, who had married the earl of Warwick's sister, and yet was ever true to the king; and the Lord Scales, brother to the queen, sent abroad to all his friends for able soldiers to withstand his enemies. When he could obtain but little assistance, the king departed into Lincolnshire, where, perceiving his enemies daily increasing, and all the country in disturb-

ance, making fires, and singing songs, crying, " King Henry, King Henry! a Warwick, a Warwick!" and hearing that his enemies the Lancastrians were within half a day's journey of him, he was advised to fly over the sea to the duke of Burgundy, who not long before had married King Edward's sister.

Charles, duke of Burgundy, at hearing of the condition of King Edward his brother-in-law, was greatly amazed and perplexed, doubting what he should do. For being then at war with the French king, he could not well provoke the English nation against him, nor could he, without great shame, leave King Edward in that necessity. So he demeaned himself through fair speech, pretending to the Englishmen to join part with the house of Lancaster, being himself partly descended of the same family by his grandmother's side; so that he was his own friend openly, and the king's friend covertly, pretending what he did not, and doing what he pretended not.

When tidings were spread in England of King Edward's flying, innumerable people resorted to the earl of Warwick, to take his part against King Edward, and a few only of his constant friends took sanctuary. Among whom was Elizabeth his wife, who, in despair almost of all comfort, took sanctuary at Westminster, where in great penury she was delivered of a fair son called Edward, who was baptized without any pomp, like any poor woman's child, the godfathers being the abbot and prior of Westminster, the godmother was the lady Scroope.

To make the story short, the earl of Warwick having now brought all things to his wishes, upon the 12th of Oct. rode to the Tower, which was then delivered to him, and there took King Henry out of the ward, and placed him in the king's lodging. The 25th of the same month, the duke of Clarence, accompanied by the earls of Warwick, Shrewsbury, and the Lord Stanley, with a great company, brought him in a long gown of blue velvet through the high streets of London, first to Paul's church, then to the bishop's palace of London, and there he resumed again the royal crown, (A.D. 1470.) After this followed a parliament, in which King Edward with all his partakers were judged traitors. King Edward made urgent and successful suit to Duke Charles his brother, to rescue him with such forces as he could give him; for he was fully resolved to protract the time no longer.

The duke secretly gave to him 50,000 florins, and further caused four great ships to be appointed for him in a haven in Zealand, where it was free for all men to come. Also the duke had hired for him fourteen ships of the Easterlings well appointed, taking security from them to serve him faithfully till he were landed in England, and fifteen days after.

Thus King Edward with only two thousand men of war, took his voyage into England, and landed at Ravenspur in Yorkshire. Dissembling his purpose, he pretended not to claim the crown and kingdom, but only to claim the duchy of York, which was his own title, and caused the same to be published. This being notified to the people, that he desired no more than only his just patrimony and lineal inheritance, they began to be moved with mercy and compassion towards him, either to favour him or not to resist him; and so journeying toward York, he came to Beverley. He then proceeded to York without resistance, where he required of the citizens to be admitted into their city. They durst not grant it to him, but on the contrary sent him word to approach no nearer, as he loved his own safety. The desolate king was here driven to a narrow strait, he could not retire, for in the opinion of the country it would be the loss of his cause; neither could he advance, for the present danger of the city. So using policy as before, with loving words and gentle speech, he desired the messengers to declare to the citizens, that his coming was not to demand the realm of England, but only the duchy of York, his old inheritance; and therefore had determined to set forward, neither with army nor weapon. The messengers were no sooner within the gates, than he was there as soon.

The citizens hearing his courteous answer, and that he

intended nothing to the prejudice of the king, nor of the realm, were somewhat softened toward him, and began to parley with him from the walls, desiring him to withdraw his soldiers to some other place, and that they should be the more ready to aid him, at least he should have no damage by them.

However, he again used such lowly language, and delivered so fair speech to them, treating them so courteously, and saluting the aldermen by their names, requiring at their hands no more but only his own town, whereof he had the name and title, that at length the citizens, after long talk and debating upon the matter, partly also enticed with fair and large promises, agreed that if he would swear to be true to King Henry, and gentle in entertaining his citizens, they would receive him into the city.

This being concluded, the next morning at the entering of the gate, a priest was ready to say mass, in the which after the receiving of the sacrament, the king received a solemn oath to observe the two articles afore agreed. By which he obtained the city of York. Where, in short time forgetting his oath, he set garrisons of armed soldiers. King Edward, being soon more fully furnished at all points, by the accession of his friends, came to the town of Leicester, and there hearing that the earl of Warwick, with the earl of Oxford were at Warwick, with a great army, he marched his army, hoping to give battle to the earl. The duke of Clarence in the meantime, had levied a great host and was coming toward the earl of Warwick. But when the earl saw the duke delay the time, he began to suspect that he was altered to his brother's party. When the armies of the two brothers, King Edward and the duke of Clarence, were in sight of the other, Richard, duke of Glocester, brother to them both, as arbiter between them, first rode to the one, then to the other. Whether all this was for appearances, is uncertain. But hereby both the brothers, laying all army and weapons aside, first lovingly and familiarly communed; after that, brotherly and naturally joined together. And that fraternal amity was ratified by proclamation, and thereby put out of all suspicion.

Then it was agreed between the three brothers to attempt the earl of Warwick, if he likewise would be reconciled; but he crying out shame upon the duke of Clarence, stood in utter defiance. From thence King Edward so strongly supported, and daily increasing, takes his way to London. Where after it was known that the duke of Clarence had joined him, much fear fell upon the Londoners, as to what was best to be done. So the citizens consulting with themselves, having no walls to defend them, thought best to take that way which seemed to them most sure and safe, and therefore they concluded to take part with King Edward. This was no sooner known abroad, than the commonalty ran out by heaps to meet King Edward, and to salute him as their king. The duke of Somerset, with others of King Henry's council, hearing of this, and wondering at the sudden change in the world, fled away and left King Henry alone.

The earl had now passed a great part of his journey to London, when hearing the news how affairs were changed, and that King Henry was a prisoner in the Tower, was not a little appalled; so he stayed with his army at St. Albans, to see what course to take. And then removed to Barnet, ten miles from St. Albans.

Against him King Edward set forth with a strong army of picked and able persons, with artillery and every requisite; bringing with him also his prisoner King Henry. On Easter even he came to Barnet, and there he entrenched himself. In the morning upon Easterday the battle began, and fiercely continued almost till noon, with murder on each side, till both parts were almost weary with fighting and murdering. King Edward then, with a great body of fresh soldiers set upon his wearied enemies. Where the earl's men, encouraged with words of their captain, stoutly fought, but they being already wounded and wearied, could not long hold out. The earl, rushing into the midst of his enemies, ventured so far, that he could not be rescued; where he

was stricken down and slain, (April 14, 1471.) The Marquis Mountecute thinking to succour his brother, whom he saw to be in great jeopardy, was likewise overthrown and slain. After Richard Nevil, earl of Warwick, and his brother were gone, the rest fled, and many were taken.

In the same year, and about the same time, upon the Ascension-even, king Henry, being prisoner in the Tower, departed, after he had reigned in all thirty-eight years and six months. Polydore, and Hall following him, affirm that he was slain with a dagger, by Richard, duke of Gloucester, for the more quiet and safeguard of his brother King Edward.

Polydore, after he had described the virtues of this king, records, that King Henry VII. afterward removed his corpse from Chertsey, where he was buried, to Windsor, and adds, that certain miracles were wrought by him. For which cause King Henry VII. saith he, laboured with Pope Julius, to have him canonised for a saint, but the death of the king prevented the matter proceeding. Edward Hall, writing of this matter, adds, declaring the cause why King Henry's sainting was not completed, to be this: that the fees for canonizing of a king were so great at Rome, (more than of bishop or prelate) that the king thought it better to keep the money in his chests, than to buy so dear, and pay so much for a new holy-day of St. Henry in the Calendar.

During the time of these doings, about A. D. 1465, there was in England a Carmelite friar, who preached at St. Paul's, in London, that our Lord Jesus Christ, while here in this world, was in poverty, and did beg. To this doctrine, the provincial of that order seemed also to incline, defending it both in his reading and preaching, with other doctors and brethren of the same order; also certain of the Jacobites. On the contrary side, many doctors and also lawyers, both in their public lectures and preaching, withstood their assertion, as most pestiferous in the church. Such a bitter contention was among them, that the defendant part was driven for a while to keep silence. This question of the begging-friars, whether Christ did beg or no, went so far, that at length it came to the ears of Pope Paul II., who was no beggar ye may be sure. After the fame of this doctrine, mounting over the Alps, came flying to the court of Rome, A. D. 1465, it brought with it such an evil smell to the fine noses there, that there was no need to bid them to stir, for begging to them was worse than high heresy. Wherefore the holy father, Pope Paul II., to repress the sparkles of this doctrine, which otherwise, perhaps, might have set his whole kitchen on fire, takes the matter in hand, and directs his bull into England, insinuating to the prelates here, that this heresy, which pestiferously affirms that Christ did openly beg, was condemned of old time by the bishops of Rome, and his councils, and that the same ought to be declared in all places for a damned doctrine, and worthy to be trodden down under all men's feet, &c.

As to the rest of the affairs of this king, (who had vanquished in nine battles, himself being present) how afterward he, through the incitement of Charles, duke of Burgundy, his brother-in-law, ventured into France with a puissant army, and how the duke failed him in his promise; also how peace between these two kings was at length concluded in a solemn meeting of both kings together (which meeting is notified in histories, by a white dove sitting the same day of meeting upon the top of King Edward's tent) also of the marriage promised between the young dauphin and Elizabeth, King Edward's eldest daughter, but afterwards broken off on the French king's part; moreover, as touching the death of the duke of Burgundy, slain in war, and of his daughter Mary, niece to King Edward, spoiled of her lands and possessions wrongfully by Lewis, the French king, and married after to Maximilian; furthermore, as touching the expedition of King Edward into Scotland, by reason of King James breaking promise in marrying with Cicely, the second daughter of King Edward, and of driving out his brother, and how the matter was composed there, and of the recovery again of Berwick; of these, I say, and such other things more, partly because they are described sufficiently in our common English histories, partly also because they are matters not greatly pertaining to the church, I omit to speak, making of them a supersedeas. Two things I find here, among many other, specially to be remembered,

The first is, concerning a godly and constant servant of Christ, named John Goose, who in the time of this king, was unjustly condemned and burnt at the Tower-hill, A. D. 1473, in the month of August. Thus had England also its John Huss, (Huss signifies a goose) as well as Bohemia. Wherein this is to be noted, that since the time of King Richard II., there is no reign of any king in which some good man or other has not suffered the pains of fire for the religion and true testimony of Christ Jesus. Of this John Goose, or John Huss, I find it recorded, that being delivered to one of the sheriffs, to see him burnt in the afternoon; the sheriff, like a charitable man, brought him home to his house, and there exhorted him to deny his alleged errors. But the godly man, after long exhortation, desired the sheriff to be content, for he was satisfied in his conscience. However, this he desired of the sheriff, for God's sake to give him some meat, saying, that he was very sore hungered. Then the sheriff commanded him meat; whereof he took, and did eat, as if he had been in no manner of danger, and said to such as stood about him, "I eat now a good and competent dinner, for I shall pass a little sharp shower ere I go to supper." And when he had dined, he gave thanks, and required that he might shortly be led to the place where he should yield up his spirit unto God.

The second thing herein to be noted, is the death of George, duke of Clarence, the king's second brother; of whom relation was made before, how he assisted King Edward his brother, against the earl of Warwick, at Barnet Field, and helped him to the crown; and now, after all these benefits, was at length thus requited, that (for what cause it is uncertain) he was apprehended and cast into the Tower, where he being adjudged for a traitor, was privily drowned in a butt of malmsey. What the true cause was of his death it cannot certainly be affirmed.

Now having long tarried at home in describing the tumults and troubles within our own land, we will proceed more at large, to consider the afflictions and perturbations of other parties and places also of Christ's church, as well here in Europe, under the pope, as in the eastern parts under the Turk, first beginning our history from the time of Sigismund, which Sigismund, as it is above recorded, was so engaged in the council of Constance against John Huss, and Jerome of Prague. This emperor ever had evil luck fighting against the Turks. Twice he warred against them, and in both the battles was discomfited and put to flight; once, about the city of Mysia, fighting against Bajazet, the Great Turk, A. D. 1395, the second time fighting against Celebinus, the son of Bajazet, about the town called Columbacium. But especially after the council of Constance, wherein were condemned and burned these two godly martyrs, more unprosperous results followed him fighting against his own subjects, the Bohemians, A. D. 1420, by whom he was repulsed in so many battles, to his great dishonour, during all the life of Zisca, and of Procopius, as is before more at large expressed; he was so beaten by the Turks, and at home by his own people, that he never encountered the Turks afterwards. Then followed the council of Basil, after the beginning of which this Sigismund, who was emperor, king of Hungary, and king of Bohemia, died in Moravia, A. D. 1437.

THE EMPEROR ALBERT.

This Sigismund left behind him only one daughter, Elizabeth, who was married to Albert, duke of Austria, by which he was advanced to the empire, and so was both duke of Austria, emperor, king of Hungary, and also king of Bohemia. This Albert, being an enemy and a disquieter to the Bohemians, and especially to the good men of Tabor, as he was preparing and setting forth against the Turks, died in the second year of his reign, A. D. 1439, leaving his wife great with child; who being

then in Hungary, and believing that she should bear a daughter, called to her the princes and the chieftains of the realms, declaring to them that she was but a woman, and insufficient to the government of such a state; and moreover, how she thought herself to be with child of a daughter; and therefore required them to provide among them such a prince and governor, (reserving the right of the kingdom to herself) as were fit and able under her, to have the management of the empire committed to. The Turk, in the mean while, being elevated and encouraged with his victories against Sigismund, began more fiercely to invade Hungary, and those parts of Christendom. Wherefore the Hungarians, making the more haste, consulted among themselves to make Duke Uladislaus, brother to Casimir, king of Poland, their king.

But while this was in progress between the Hungarians and Uladislaus, in the mean space Elizabeth brought forth a son called Ladislaus, who being the lawful heir of the kingdom, the queen called back again her former word, minding to reserve the kingdom for her son, being the true heir, and therefore refused marriage with Uladislaus, which she had before designed. But Uladislaus joining with a great part of the Hungarians, persisting still in the condition before granted, would not give over; by which great contention and division kindling among the people of Hungary, Amurath, the Great Turk, taking his advantage of their discord, and partly elated with pride at his former success against Sigismund, with his whole main and force invaded the realm of Hungary; where Huniades, sirnamed Vainoda, prince of Transilvania, joining with the new king Uladislaus, both together set against the Turk, A. D. 1444, and there Uladislaus, the new king of Hungary, the fourth year of his kingdom, was slain. Elizabeth, with her son, fled in the meanwhile to Frederic the emperor. Of Huniades Vainoda, the noble captain, and of his acts, and also of Ladislaus (Christ willing) more shall be said hereafter, in his time and place.

FREDERIC III., EMPEROR.

After the decease of Albert, Frederic III., duke of Austria, succeeded in the empire, A. D. 1440. By whom it was procured (as we have before signified) that Pope Felix, elected by the council of Basil, resigned his popedom to Pope Nicholas V.; upon this condition, that Pope Nicholas should ratify the acts decreed in the council of Basil. In the days of this emperor much war and dissension raged almost through all christian realms, in Austria, Hungary, Poland, in France, in Burgundy, and also here in England, between King Henry VI. and King Edward IV., so that it might have been easy for the Turk to have overrun all the christian realms in Europe, had not the providence of our merciful Lord otherwise provided to keep Amurath the Turk occupied in other civil wars at home in the meanwhile. To this Frederic came Elizabeth, with Ladislaus her son, by whom he was nourished and entertained a certain space, till at length, after the death of Uladislaus, king of Hungary, the men of Austria, through the instigation of Ulric Eizingerus, and of Ulric, earl of Cilicia, rising in arms, required Frederic the emperor, either to give them their young king, or else to stand to his own defence.

When Frederic heard this, he would neither render a sudden answer, neither would he abide any longer delay; and so the matter going to war, the new city was besieged, where many were slain, and much harm done. At length the emperor's part being the weaker, the emperor, through the intervention of certain nobles of Germany, restored Ladislaus to their hands, who being yet under age, committed his three kingdoms to three governors. John Huniades, the worthy captain abovementioned, had the ruling of Hungary; George Pogiebracius had Bohemia; and Ulric, the earl of Cilicia, had Austria. Which Ulric, having the chief custody of the king, had the greatest authority; a man as full of ambition and tyranny, as he was hated almost by all the Austrians, and shortly after, by means of Eizingerus, was excluded also from the king and the court, but afterward restored again, and Eizingerus thrust out. Such is the unstable condition of those who are in place about princes.

Not long after, Ladislaus, the young king, went to Bohemia to be crowned there, where George Pogiebracius had the government. But Ladislaus during all the time of his being there, though being much requested, yet would neither enter into the churches, nor hear the service of those who followed the doctrine of Huss. So that when a certain priest, in the high tower of Prague, was appointed and addressed, after the manner of priests, to say service before the king, being known to hold with John Huss and Rochezana, the king disdaining him, commanded him to give place and depart, or else he would send him headlong from the rock of the tower ; and so the good minister repulsed by the king, departed. Also, another time, Ladislaus seeing the sacrament carried by a minister of that side, whom they called then Hussites, would pay no reverence to it.

At length the abode of the king, although it was not very long, yet seemed to the godly-disposed to be longer than they wished ; and that was not unknown to the king, which made him make the more haste away ; but before he departed, he thought first to visit the noble city Uratislavia, in Silesia ; in which city Ladislaus being there in the high church at service, many great princes were about him ; among whom was also George Pogiebracius, who then stood nearest to the king, to whom one Chilian, playing the parasite about the king, (as the fashion is of such as feign themselves fools, to make other men as very fools as they) spake as follows : "With what countenance you behold this our service I see right well, but your heart I do not see. Say, then, doth not the order of this our religion seem unto you decent and comely ? Do you not see how many and how great princes, yea, the king himself, follow one order and uniformity ? And why do you then follow rather your preacher Rochezana than these ? Do you think a few Bohemians more wise than all the church of Christ besides ? Why then do you not forsake that rude and rustic people, and join to these nobles, as you are a nobleman yourself ?"

To whom thus Pogiebracius sagely answered, " If you speak these words of yourself, you are not the man whom you feign yourself to be ; and so I answer to you not as to a fool. But if you speak this by the suggestion of others, then must I satisfy them. Hear, therefore : As to the ceremonies of the church, every man has a conscience of his own to follow. As for us, we use such ceremonies, as we trust please God : neither is it for our choice to believe what we will ourselves. The mind of man, being persuaded with great reasons, is captivated whether he will or no ; and as nature is instructed and taught, so is she drawn, in some one way, and in some another. As for myself, I am fully persuaded in the religion of my preachers. If I should follow thy religion, I might perchance deceive men, going contrary to mine own conscience, but I cannot deceive God, who seeth the hearts of all ; neither shall it become me to frame myself to thy disposition. That which is meet for a jester, is not likewise convenient for a nobleman. And these words either take to thyself as spoken to thee, if thou be a wise man, or else I refer them to those who set thee on work."

After the king was returned from the Bohemians again to Austria, the Hungarians likewise made their petitions to the king, that he would come to them. The governor of Hungary was John Huniades, whose victorious acts against the Turks are famous. Against this Huniades, wicked Ulric, earl of Cicilia, did all he could with the king to bring him to destruction, and therefore caused the king to send for him to Vienna, and there privily to work his death. But Huniades having intelligence, offers himself in Hungary, to serve his prince to all affairs. Out of the land where he was, it was neither best, said he, for the king, nor safest for himself to come. The earl being so disappointed, came down with certain nobles of the court to the borders of Hungary, thinking either to apprehend him and bring him to Vienna, or there to dispatch him. Huniades, said he,

would commune with him in the open fields, but within the town he should not be brought. After that another train also was laid for him, that under pretence of the king's safe conduct, he should meet the king in the broad fields of Vienna. But Huniades, suspecting deceit, came indeed to the place appointed, where he neither seeing the king to come, nor the earl to have any safe conduct for him, was moved, (and not without cause) against the earl, declaring how it was in his power there to slay him, who went about to seek his blood, but for his reverence to the king he would spare him, and let him go.

Not long after this, the Turk, with a great army of fighting men, to the number of one hundred and fifteen thousand, arrived in Hungary, where he laid siege to the city Alba. But through the merciful hand of God, John Huniades, and Capistranus, a certain Minorite, with a small garrison of christian soldiers, gave him the repulse, and put him to flight, with all his mighty host. Huniades shortly after this victory, died ; of whose death when the king and the earl were informed, they came the more boldly into Hungary, where being received by Ladislaus Huniades' son into the town of Alba, there viewed the place where the Turks before had pitched their tents. When this Ladislaus heard that the king was coming first toward the town, he obediently opened to him the gates. He prevented four thousand armed soldiers from entering the city.

In the mean time, while the king was resident in the city, the earl, with other nobles, sat in council, requiring Ladislaus also to resort to them ; who first doubting with himself what he might do, at length put on secret armour, and came to them. Whether the earl first began with him, or he with the earl, is not known. The opinion of some is, that Ulric first called him traitor, for shutting the gates against the king's soldiers. However the occasion began, this is undoubted, that Ulric, taking his sword from his page, struck at his head. To break the blow, some putting up their hands had their fingers cut off. The Hungarians, hearing a noise and tumult within the chamber, brake it open, and there instantly slew Ulric the earl, wounding and cutting him almost all to pieces. The king hearing thereof, although he was not a little discontented at it in his mind ; yet seeing there was then no other remedy, dissembled his grief for a time.

From thence the king took his journey again to Buda, accompanied with Ladislaus ; passing by the town where the wife of Huniades was mourning for the death of her husband, he seemed with many fair words to comfort her, and after he had there sufficiently refreshed himself, with such pretence of dissembled love, and feigned favour, that they were without all suspicion and fear, he set forward from thence in his journey, taking with him the two sons of Huniades, Ladislaus and Matthias, who were right ready to wait upon him. The king being come to Buda, (whether of his own head, or by sinister counsel set on) when he had them at a vantage, caused them both to be seized. And first, Ladislaus, the elder son, was brought forth to the place of execution, there to be beheaded, where he meekly suffered, being charged with no other crime but this, published by the voice of the cryer, saying, "Thus are they to be chastened who are rebels against their lord." Peucer, writing of his death, adds, that after the hangman had struck three blows at his neck, yet Ladislaus, having his hands bound behind him, after the third stroke, rose upright upon his feet, and looking up to heaven, called upon the Lord, and protested his innocency in that behalf ; and so laying down his neck again, at the fourth blow was dispatched. Matthias, the other brother, was led captive with the king into Austria. The rest of the captives brake the prison, and escaped.

It was not long after this act of cruelty, the king being about the age of twenty-two years, that talk was made of the king's marriage with Magdalen, daughter to the French king. The place of the marriage was appointed at Prague, where was great preparation for the matter. At the first entrance of the king into the city of Prague, Rochezana, with a company of ministers, such as were favourers of John Huss, and of sincere religion, came with all solemnity to receive the king, making there his oration to congratulate the king's most joyful and prosperous access into his own realm and country of Bohemia. After he had ended his oration, the king would scarcely open his mouth to give thanks to him, or any cheerful countenance to his company, but fiercely seemed to frown upon them. In the next pageant after these came forth the priests of the high minister, after the most popish manner, meeting him with procession, and with the sacrament of the altar. For as a panacea among physicians serves for all diseases, so the sacrament of the pope's altar serves for all pomps and pageants. First it must lie upon the altar, then it must be held up with hands, then it must hang in the pix, it must serve for the living, it must also help the dead, it must visit the sick, it must walk about the churchyard, it must go about the streets, it must be carried about the fields to make the grass to grow, it must be had to the battle, it must ride on horseback before the pope. And finally it must welcome kings into cities. These catholic fathers do seem somewhat to forget themselves. For if the pope, being inferior to the sacrament of the altar, sit still, while the kings come and kiss his feet, what reason is it that the sacrament of the altar, which is above the pope, should meet kings by the way, and welcome them to the town? But this by the way of parenthesis. Let us now continue the text.

When this catholic king, Ladislaus, who had shewed himself before so stout and stern against Rochezana and his company, had seen these catholic priests with their procession, and especially with their blessed sacrament, to come with all reverence and much devotion he lighted down from his horse, he embraced the cross and kissed it, and with cheerful countenance saluted the priests in order. All this while his young wife was not yet come out of France, but legates were sent in the most sumptuous way to conduct her. Other legates also were sent at the same time to the Emperor Frederick for conclusion of peace. The third legacy was directed likewise to Pope Calixtus about religion, how to reduce the Bohemians to the church of Rome. The author of this history (which was Pope Pius himself) declares further the opinion of some to be, that King Ladislaus the same time had intended to make a final end and destruction of all that sect in Bohemia, who held with the doctrine of John Huss and Jerome, by the assembly and concourse of the catholic princes, and popish prelates, who were appointed there to meet together at that marriage in Prague. For there were to have been first the Emperor Frederick, Elizabeth the king's mother, and his sisters Elizabeth and Anna, the princes of Saxony, Bajoria, Silesia, Franconia, the Palatine, and other princes of the Rhine. Many also of the lords of France, besides the pope's cardinals, legates, prelates, and other potentates of the pope's church, who if they had assembled altogether in Bohemia, no doubt but some great mischief had been wrought there against the Hussites; but when man has purposed, yet God disposes as pleaseth him.

And, therefore, it is truly writtten by Æneas Sylvius, in the same place, saying, " De regimine civitatum, de mutatione regnorum, de orbis imperio, minimum est quod homines possint (tum vero de religionis constitutione multo minus) magna magnus disponit Deus." That is, in the government of cities, in alteration of kingdoms, in ruling and governing the world, it is less than nothing that man can do; it is the high God that ruleth high things. Whereunto then I may well add this moreover, and say, that if the governance of worldly kingdoms standeth not in man's power, but in the disposition of God, much less is it then that man's power can do in the ordering and governing of religion. Example whereof in this purposed device of princes doth evidently appear. For as this great preparation and solemnity of marriage was in progress, and the princes ready to set it forth, with a little turn of God's holy hand, all these great purposes were suddenly turned and dashed. For in the midst of this business, about the twenty-first day of November, A.D. 1461, this great adversary of Christ's people, King Ladislaus, king of Bohemia, of Hungary, and prince of Austria sickened,

and within six and thirty hours died. As it came not without the just judgment of God, revenging the innocent blood of Ladislaus Huniades' son, so by the opportune death of this king the poor churches of Bohemia were graciously delivered. And this was the end of Ladislaus, one of the mightiest princes at that time in all Europe, in whom three mighty kingdoms were conjoined and combined together, Austria, Hungary, and Bohemia.

After the death of Ladislaus, the kingdom of Bohemia fell to George Pogiebracius, whom Pope Innocent VIII. excommunicated and deposed for his religion.

The kingdom of Hungary was given to Matthias, son of Huniades, who was in captivity (as is said) under King Ladislaus, and would have been put to death after his brother had not the king been overtaken by death.

The noble acts of John Huniades, and of this Matthias his son, were not only great stays to Hungary, but almost to all Christendom, in repelling the Turk. For beside the other victories of John Huniades the father, this Matthias his son succeeding no less in valiantness than in the name of his father, so recovered Sirmium, and the confines of Illyrica, from the hand of the Turks, and so vanquished their power, that both Mahomet and also Bajazet his son were forced to seek for truce.

Matthias, conducting his army into Bosnia, recovered again Jaitza, the principal town of that kingdom from the Turks' possession, and if other christian princes had joined their help withal, he would have proceeded farther into Thrace. But behold here the malicious subtlety of Satan, working by the pope; for while Matthias was thus occupied in this expedition against the Turks, wherein he should have been set forward and aided by christian princes and bishops, the bishop of Rome wickedly and sinfully ministers matter of civil discord between him and Pogiebracius, in removing him from the right of his kingdom, and transferring it to Matthias; by which not only the tide of victory against the Turks was stopped, but also great war and bloodshed followed in christian realms, as well between this Matthias and Pogiebracius, with his two sons Victorinus and Henry, as also between Casimir Uladislaus, and Matthias warring about Uratislavia, till at length the matter was taken up by the princes of Germany.

Notwithstanding all the execrable excommunication of the pope against Pogiebracius, a great part of Bohemia would not be removed from the obedience of their king, whom the pope had cursed and deposed; yet Matthias took from him Moravia, and a great portion of Silesia, and adjoined it to his kingdom of Hungary, A.D. 1474.

Where this by the way is to be noted, that the religion in Bohemia, planted by John Huss, could not be extinguished or suppressed with all the power of four mighty princes, Vinceslaus, Sigismund, Albert, and Ladislaus, although with the popes they did all they possibly could; but still the Lord maintained the same, as we see by this Pogiebracius, king of Bohemia, whom the pope could not remove out of the kingdom of Bohemia.

This Matthias, beside his other memorable acts of chivalry, is no less also commended for his singular knowledge and love of learning and of learned men, whom he with great salaries brought into Pannonia, where by the means of good letters, and supplies of learned men, he reduced in a short time the barbarous rudeness of that country into a flourishing commonwealth. Moreover, he there erected such a library, and replenished it with all kinds of authors, sciences, and histories, which he caused to be translated out of Greek into Latin, that its equal is not to be found next to Italy, in all Europe beside.

Immediately after this there was contention and war in every part of Europe; almost no angle or portion of all Christendom (whether we consider the church, or civil government) was free from discord, tumults, and dissensions. This cankered worm of ambition so mightily creeps, and every where prevails in these later ends of the world, that it suffers neither rest in commonwealths, nor peace in the church, nor scarcely any spark of charity to remain in the life of men. And what marvel then, if the Lord seeing us so far to degenerate, not only from his precepts and counsels, but almost from the sense and bond of nature, that brother with brother, uncle with nephew, blood with blood, cannot agree, in striving, killing, and fighting, for worldly dominions, do send these cruel Turks upon us, to scourge and devour us? of whose bloody tyranny and daily spilling of christian blood hereafter (by the grace of Christ) we will discourse more at large, when we come to the peculiar consideration of the Turkish histories. In the meantime this shall be for us to note and observe, not so much the scourge how grievous it is; but rather to behold the causes which bring the whip upon us, which is our own miserable ambition and wretched wars among ourselves.

And yet if this christian peace and love, left and commended so heartily unto us by the mouth of the Son of God, being now banished out of christian realms, and civil governance, might at last find some refuge in the church, or take sanctuary among men professing nothing but religion, and we should have less cause to mourn. Now, however, we see little peace and amity among civil potentates; so we find less in the spiritual sort of them, who chiefly take upon them the administration of Christ's church. So that it may well be doubted whether the scourge of the Turk, or the civil sword of princes have slain more in the fields, or the pope's keys have burnt more in towns and cities. And although such as are professed to the church do not fight with sword and target for dominions and revenues, as warlike princes do; yet this ambition, pride and avarice, appears in them nothing inferior to other worldly potentates; especially if we behold the doings and insatiable desires of the court of Rome. Great arguments and proof hereof are neither hard to be found, nor far to be sought; what realm almost through all Christendom has not only seen with their eyes, but have felt in their purses the intolerable ambition and insatiable avarice of that devouring church, and also have complained of the grievance, but never could obtain redress! What exactions and extortions have been here in England out of bishopricks, monasteries, benefices, deaneries, archdeaconries, and all other offices of the church, to fill the pope's coffers! and when they had done all, yet every year brought almost some new invention from Rome to fetch in our English money; and if all the floods in England (yea in all Europe) run into the see of Rome, yet were that ocean never able to be satisfied.

In France likewise what floods of money were swallowed up into this see of Rome! It was openly complained of in the council of Basil, as is testified by Henry Token, canon and ambassador of the archbishop of Maidenburg, that in the council of Basil, A. D. 1436, the archbishop of Lyons declared that in the time of Pope Martin, there came out of France to the court of Rome, nine millions of gold, which was gathered by the bishops and prelates, besides those which could not be counted of the inferior clergy, who daily without number ran to the court of Rome, carrying with them all their whole substance. The archbishop of Tours said also at Basil, A. D. 1439, that three millions of gold came to Rome in his time, within the space of fourteen years, from the prelates and prelacies, besides the inferior clergy who daily ran to that court.

And what made Pope Pius II. labour so earnestly to Lewis XI. the French king, that he should promise to abolish and utterly extinguish the constitution established at the council of Bourges, by King Charles VII. his predecessor, called the Pragmatic Sanction; but only the ambition of that see, which had no measure, and their avarice which had no end? The story is this: King Charles VII. willing to obey and follow the council of Basil, summoned a parliament at Bourges; where by the full consent of all the states in France, both spiritual and temporal, a certain constitution was decreed and published, called the Pragmatic Sanction; wherein was comprehended briefly the pith and effect of all the canons and decrees concluded in the council of Basil. Which constitution King Charles commanded through all his realm to be observed inviolably and ratified for

the honour and increase of christian religion for ever. This was A. D. 1438.

It followed that after the decease of Charles, succeeded King Lewis XI. who had promised before, while he was dauphin, to Pope Pius, that if he ever came to the crown, the pragmatic sanction should be abolished. Pius hearing of his being crowned, sent to him John Balveus, a cardinal, with his letters patent, desiring him to be mindful of his promise. The king, either willing, or else pretending a will to perform, and accomplish what he had promised, directed the pope's letters patent, with the cardinal, to the council of Paris, requiring them to consult upon the cause.

Thus the matter being brought and proposed in the parliament, the king's attorney named John Romane, a man well spoken, singularly witted, and well reasoned, stepping forth, with great eloquence, and no less boldness, proved the sanction to be profitable, holy, and necessary for the wealth of the realm, and in no case to be abolished. To whose sentence the university of Paris adjoining their consent, appealed from the attempts of the pope to the next general council. The cardinal understanding this, was not a little indignant at it, fretting and fuming, and threatening many terrible things against them; but notwithstanding all his threatening words, he returned again to the king, not having obtained his purpose, A. D. 1438.

Thus the pope's purpose in France was disappointed, which also in Germany had come to the like effect, if Frederick the emperor had there done his part toward the Germans; they, bewailing their miserable estate, went with humble suit to persuade the emperor, that he should no longer be under the subjection of the popes of Rome, unless they first obtained certain things as touching the charter of appeals; declaring their state to be far worse than the French or Italians. The nobles and commonalty of Germany intreat with most weighty reasons, to have the emperor's aid and help as he was bound to them by an oath; alleging also the great dishonour and ignominy in that they alone had not the use of their own laws, declaring how the French nation had not made their suit to their king in vain against the exactions of popes. The emperor being moved, and partly overcome by their persuasions, promised that he would provide no less for them, than the king of France had done for the French, and to make decrees in that behalf. But the grave authority of Æneas Sylvius, as Platina writes in the history of Pius II. brake off the matter; who by his subtle and pestiferous persuasions, so bewitched the emperor, that he, contemning the equal, just and necessary requests of his subjects, chose Æneas to be his ambassador to Calixtus, the newly chosen pope, to swear to him in his name, and to promise the absolute obedience of all Germany.

And here ceasing with the history of Frederick, we will now proceed to the reign of Maximilian, his son.

I must not pass over such christians as were condemned, and suffered the pains of fire for the testimony of Christ and his truth. Of whom one was John, a pastor or a neat-herd; who was a keeper of cattle: the other was John de Wesalia, although not burned, yet persecuted near to death, under the reign of this emperor, Frederick III.

And first, touching this John the neat-herd, thus writes Munster, that the bishop of Herbipolis condemned and burned for an heretick one John, who was a keeper of cattle at a town called Nicholas Hausen in Franconia, because he taught and held that the life of the clergy was ignominious and abominable before God.

The other was doctor John de Wesalia, who was complained of to Dietherus the archbishop of Mentz, by the Thomists, upon cetain articles and opinions gathered out of his books. Wherefore Dietherus directs commissions to the universities of Heidelburgh and Cologne, to take the matter in examination; who called this Doctor de Wesalia before them, making him to swear that he should present and give up all his treatises, works and writings, whatever he had made or preached; that being done, they divided his books among themselves, severally, every man to find out what heresies and errors they could. His articles and opinions are these :

"That all men be saved freely, and through mere grace by faith in Christ. Free will to be nothing. That we should only believe the word of God, and not the gloss of any man, or the fathers. That the word of God is to be expounded by the collating one place with another. That prelates have no authority to make laws, nor to expound the scriptures, by any peculiar right given to them more than to another. That men's traditions, as fastings, pardons, feasts, long prayers, pilgrimages, and such like, are to be rejected. Extreme unction and confirmation to be reproved ; confession and satisfaction to be reprehended. The primacy of the pope also he affirmed to be nothing."

Certain other articles also were gathered out of his books by his adversaries, but in such sort, that they may seem rather to follow their own malicious gathering, than the true intention of his mind.

Thus when Wesalia was commanded to appear, there was the archbishop, the inquisitor, the doctors of Cologne, and the doctors of Heidelburgh, with the masters of the same, and the rector of the university of Mentz, the dean of faculties, bachelors of divinity, and many other masters of the same university, canons, doctors, with the bishop's chancellor, and his counsellors, besides many religious prelates, scholars, with a doctor of Frankfort, the somner and beadles, who all met together in the great hall of the minorites, for the examination of this John de Wesalia.

Friar Elton, the inquisitor, first sits in the highest place, then after him, others according to their degree. In the beginning of the examination, first the inquisitor begins with these words, " Most reverend fathers and honourable doctors, &c. Our reverend father and prince elector has caused this present convocation to be called, to hear the examination of Master John de Wesalia, in certain suspected articles concerning the catholic faith. But something I will say before, that may do him good, and desire that two or three of them that favour him, or some other, will rise up and give him counsel to forsake and leave his errors, to acknowledge himself, and to ask pardon ; which, if he will do, he shall have pardon ; if he will not, we will proceed against him without pardon." And thus Wesalia being cited, and brought in the midst betwixt two minorites, being very aged, and having a staff in his hand, was set before the inquisitor. Beginning to answer for himself with a long protestation, he was not suffered to go on with his oration, but was cut off, and required briefly to make an end, and to tell them in a few words, whether he would stand to his opinions, or to the determination of the church. To this he answered, that he never spake any thing against the determination of the church, but said, " That he had written several treatises, in which, if he had erred, or were found to say otherwise than well, he was contented to revoke and call back the same, and do all things that were requisite." Then said the inquisitor, " Do you ask then pardon ?" The other answered, " Why should I ask pardon, when I know no crime or error committed ?" The inquisitor said, " Well, we will call you to the remembrance thereof, and proceed to the examination."

In the mean time, others called upon him instantly to ask pardon. Then said Wesalia, " I ask pardon." Notwithstanding which, the inquisitor proceeded to the examination, reading there two instruments, declaring that he had authority from the apostolic see ; after this, he cited John to appear to his examination. Thirdly, he commanded him under pain of disobedience, in the virtue of the Holy Ghost, and under pain of excommunication of the greater curse (from which no man could absolve him, but only the pope, or the inquisitor, except only at the point of death) to tell plainly the truth upon such things as should be demanded of him concerning his faith, without doubts and sophistication of words. And so being demanded first whether he believed upon his oath, that he was bound to tell the truth, although it were against himself or any other ; to this he answered, " I know it." Then the inquisitor bid him say, " I believe it." To which he answered again, " What need I say that I *believe* the thing which I *know* ?" There the inquisitor, something stirred with the matter, cried with a loud voice, " Master John, Master John, Master John, say I believe, say I believe ;" then he answered, " I believe."

Many other interrogatories were ministered unto him, whereof some were vain, some false.

Being demanded whether he was a favourer of the Bohemians, he said, he was not. Also, being demanded concerning the sacrament of the holy body and blood of our Lord, whether he thought Christ there to be contained really, or only spiritually, and whether he believed that in the sacrament, the substance of bread remained, or only the form of it ; to this he answered, not denying but the body of Christ was there really contained, and also that with the body of Christ the substance of bread remained.

After this, he was demanded his opinion concerning religious persons, as monks and nuns, whether he thought them to be bound to the vow of chastity, or to the keeping of any other vow, and whether he said to the friars Minorites any such word in effect, " I cannot save you in this your state and order." This he confessed that he had said, " how that not your religion saveth you, but the grace of God," &c. not denying but they might be saved.

Being required whether he believed, or had written, that there is no mortal sin, but which is expressed to be mortal in the canon of the holy Bible ; to this he answered, " that he did so believe as he hath written, till he was better informed." Likewise, being required what he thought of the vicar of Christ in earth, he answered, " That he believed that Christ left no vicar in earth ;" for the confirmation of which he alleged and said, " That Christ ascending up to heaven, said, ' Behold I am with you,' &c. In which words he plainly declared, that he would substitute under him no vicar here in earth ;" and said, moreover, " if a vicar signified any man who in the absence of the principal hath to do the works of the principal, then Christ hath no vicar here in earth."

In like manner, concerning indulgences and pardons, they demanded of him, whether they had any efficacy, and what he thought of them ; he answered " That he had written a certain treatise of that matter, and what he had written in that treatise he would persist therein, which was thus, ' That he believed that the treasure-box of the merits of saints could not be distributed by the pope to others, because that treasure is not left here in earth, for so it is written in the book of Revelations, ' their works follow them ;' and that their merits could not be applied to other men, for the satisfaction of their pain due unto them ; and therefore that the pope and other prelates, cannot distribute that treasure to men."

Also, being demanded what he thought of the hallowing and blessing of altars, chalices, vestments, wax-candles, palms, herbs, holy-water, and other divine things, &c. He answered, " That they had no spiritual virtue and power in them to drive away devils, and that holy-water has no more efficacy than other water not hallowed, as concerning remission of venial sins, and driving away devils, and other effects, which the school doctors attribute to it."

He believed, " That God may give grace to a man, having the use of reason, without all motion of free will." Also, he thought, " that St. Paul, in his conversion, did nothing of his own free will for his conversion." He believed, moreover, " That God may give such grace to a man having the use of reason, not doing that which is in him."

He affirmed, " That nothing is to be believed which is not contained in the canon of the Bible."

Also, " That the elect are saved only by the grace of God."

This examination being ended, and the articles condemned by the inquisitor and his assistants, then he said after this manner. " As you do with me, if Christ himself were here, he might be condemned as a heretic." After this they sent several to him to have communication with him, and to persuade him; at length, within three or four days after, he was content to yield to them, and to submit himself to their holy mother church, and the information of the doctors.

Although this aged and feeble old man, by weakness was constrained to give over to the Romish clergy, by outward profession of his mouth, yet, notwithstanding, his opinions and doctrine declared his inward heart, of what judgment he was, if fear of present death had not forced him to say otherwise than he thought.

In the year 1484, in the Emperor Maximilian's time, died Pope Sixtus IV., who was rather a monster of nature than a prelate of the church. Of him Platina writes, that he unjustly vexed all Italy with war and dissension and openly countenanced and encouraged gross vice and immorality.

Of the said pope it is recorded, that he was a special patron and tutor to all begging friars, granting them to have and enjoy revenues in this world, and in the world to come everlasting life. Among which friars there was one named Alanus de Rupe, a black friar, who made the rosary of our lady's psalter.

Concerning the institution of this rosary, there was a book set forth (about A. D. 1480). In the beginning whereof is declared, " That the blessed virgin entered into the cell of this Alanus, and espoused him to herself as her husband." For the truth of which story Alanus did swear deeply, cursing himself, if it were not even as he had made relation !

But leaving here Pope Sixtus with his vices, let us now proceed to the history of Maximilian, keeping also the order of our kings here in England. For a little before the reign of Maximilian, King Edward IV. died, (A. D. 1483), after he had reigned twenty-two years.

KING EDWARD V.

This King Edward left behind him by his wife Elizabeth, two sons, Edward and Richard, and two daughters, Elizabeth and Cecilia. Which two sons Edward and Richard, as they were under age, and not ripe to govern, a consultation was called among the peers, to debate whether the aforesaid young prince and king, should be under the government of his mother, or else that Richard, duke of Glocester, brother to King Edward IV., and uncle to the child, should be governor of the king, and protector of the realm. There was then among other noble peers of the realm, the duke of Buckingham, a man of great authority, who had married King Edward's wife's sister. Because the duke being so near allied to the king, had been unkindly, as he thought, treated by the king, having no advancement by him, nor any great friendship shewed to him, he took part with Richard, duke of Glocester, both against the queen and her children, to make the duke the chief governor and protector. Which being brought to pass, by the aid, assistance, and working of the duke of Buckingham, the queen took sanctuary with her younger son; the elder brother, who was the king, remaining in the custody of the duke of Glocester, his uncle, who, being now in a good towardness to obtain that which he had long looked for, sought all the means, and soon compassed the matter, by false colour of dissembled words, by perjury, and the labour of friends, namely of the duke of Buckingham, and the cardinal archbishop of Canterbury, that the other brother also should be committed to his care. Thus the ambitious protector and unnatural uncle, having the possession of his two nephews, and innocent babes, thought himself almost up the wheel where he would climb, although he could not walk in such mists and clouds, but his purposes began to be seen, which caused him more secretly to remove from him all suspicion, and to blind the people's eyes. But before he could accomplish his execrable enterprise, there were some whom he thought must first be rid out of the way, namely the Lord Hastings, and the Lord Stanley, who as they were sitting together in council within the Tower, the protector suddenly

rushed in among them, and after a few words there communed, he suddenly hasted out again, his mind being full of mischief and fury, and within the space of an hour he returned again into the chamber, with a stern countenance and a frowning look, and so sat down in his place. Shortly afterwards he charged them as traitors, and had them both arrested without any cause whatever.

The Lord Hastings was commanded to speed and confess his sins apace, for before dinner the protector sware by St. Paul that he should die; and so without further judgment, his head was struck off.

After this tyrannous murder, the mischievous protector aspiring still to the crown, to set his devices forward, first through gifts and fair promises, suborned Doctor Shaw, a famous preacher then in London, at St. Paul's Cross, to insinuate to the people, that neither King Edward with his sons, nor the duke of Clarence, were the lawful children of the duke of York, but that they were the children of the duchess their mother, by some other person, and that he alone was the true and only lawful heir of the duke of York. Moreover, to declare and to signify to the audience that King Edward was never lawfully married to the queen, but his wife before was dame Elizabeth Lucy, and that so the two children of King Edward were illegitimate, and therefore the title of the crown most rightly pertained to the lord protector. Thus this false flatterer, and loud lying preacher, to serve the protector's humour, was not ashamed most impudently to abuse that holy place, that reverend auditory, and the sacred word of God, whereupon such disdain of the people followed him, that for shame of the people crying out against him, in a few days after he pined away.

When this sermon would take no effect with the people, the protector, unmercifully drowned in ambition, rested not thus, but within a few days after excited the duke of Buckingham, first to break the matter in private talk to the mayor and certain heads of the city picked out for the purpose; that done, to come to the Guildhall, to move the people by all flattering and lying persuasions to the same, which shameless Shaw before had preached at St. Paul's Cross. Which the duke, with all diligence and helps of eloquence, being a man both learned and well spoken, endeavoured to accomplish, making to the people a long and artificial oration, supposing no less, but that the people, allured by his crafty insinuations, would cry, King Richard, King Richard ! But there was no King Richard in their mouths, less in their hearts. Whereupon the duke looking to the lord mayor, and asking what this silence meant, contrary to the promise of the one, and the expectation of the other, it was then answered of the mayor, that the people peradventure understood him not; wherefore the duke, reiterating his narration in other words, declared again what he had done before. Likewise the third time he repeated his oration again and again. Then the commons who before stood mute, being now in amaze, seeing this opportunity, began to mutter softly among themselves, but yet no king Richard could sound in their lips, save only that in the nether end of the hall, certain of the duke's servants, with one Nashfield, and other belonging to the protector, thrusting into the hall among the press, began suddenly to cry King Richard, King Richard ! throwing up their caps, whereat the citizens turning back their heads, marvelled not a little, but said nothing.

The duke and lord mayor taking this for sufficient testimony, came to the protector, who was then at Baynard's castle. Where the matter being arranged before, was now so contrived, that humble petition was made in the name of the whole commons, to the protector, that he, although it was utterly against his will to take it, yet would of his humility stoop so low as to receive the heavy kingdom of England upon his shoulders. At this their tender request and suit of the lords and commons made, the mild duke, seeing no other remedy, was contented at length to yield, although sore against his will (ye must so imagine), and to submit himself so low, as of a protector to be made king; not much herein unlike to our prelates in the popish church, who when they have before well compounded for the pope's bulls, yet must they for manner sake make courtesy, and thrice deny that for which they so long before have gaped, and so sweetly have paid for.

KING RICHARD III. USURPER.

And thus Richard duke of Glocester took upon him to be made and proclaimed king of England, in the month of June, A.D. 1483.

The triumph and solemnity of his usurped coronation being finished, this unquiet tyrant yet could not think himself safe, so long as young Edward the right king and his brother were alive; wherefore the next enterprize which he did set upon was this, how to rid those innocent babes out of the way, that he might reign king alone.

In the meantime, while all this ruffling was in hand, what dread and sorrow the tender hearts of these fatherless and friendless children were in, what little joy of themselves, what small joy of life they had, it is not so hard as grievous for tender hearts to understand. As the younger brother lingered in thought and heaviness, so the prince, who was eleven years old, was so out of heart, and so fraught with fear, that he never tied his points, nor enjoyed good day, till the traitorous impiety of their cruel uncle had delivered them of their wretchedness. After King Edward their uncle had first attempted to compass his devilish device by Robert Brakenbury, constable of the Tower, and could not win him to such a cruel act, then he got one James Tyril, and with him John Dighton, and Miles Forrest, to perpetrate this heinous murder. Dighton and Forrest, about midnight entering into the princes' chamber, so wrapped and entangled them amongst the clothes, keeping down the feather-bed and pillows hard to their mouths, that within a while they smothered and stifled them in their bed.

And thus these two young princes ended their lives, through the wretched cruelty of these tormentors, who, for their detestable and bloody murder, escaped not long unpunished by the just hand of God. For first Miles Forrest miserably rotted away by piece meal. John Dighton lived at Calais long after, so disdained and hated, that he was pointed at by all men, and died there in great misery. Sir James Tyril was beheaded at Tower Hill for treason. Also King Richard himself, within a year and half after, was slain in the field, hacked and hewed by his enemies' hands.

Furthermore, the justice of God's hand let not the duke of Buckingham escape free; for within less than a year after God so wrought, that he was beheaded for treason by the king, whom he so unjustly before had advanced.

Doctor Morton, bishop of Ely, had devised bringing Henry, earl of Richmond, to England, and marrying him to Elizabeth, King Edward's daughter, thereby joining the two houses of York and Lancaster together. This device was first broken to the duke of Buckingham, which soon after cost him his life. But that bishop, more crafty to save himself, fled into Britany; the device however once being broached, was so plausible and took such effect, that a message was sent over the sea to Henry, earl of Richmond, by his mother, and by the queen, mother to the Lady Elizabeth, that if he would make his return, and promise to marry with the Lady Elizabeth, King Edward's daughter, he should be received.

Embracing this offer, the earl of Richmond takes the seas at Harfleur, in the month of August, (A.D. 1485), accompanied only with two thousand men, and a small number of ships, arrived at Milford Haven, in Wales, and first came to Dale, then to Harford West, where he was joyfully received, and also by the coming in of Arnold Butler, and the Pembroke men, was increased in power. From thence he removing by Cardigan to Shrewsbury, and then to Newport, and so to Stafford, from thence to Lichfield, his army still more and more augmented. As a great flood, by coming in of many small rivers, gathers more abundance of water; so to this earl, many noble captains and men of power joined themselves, as Richard Griffith, John Morgan, Rice ap Thomas; then Sir George Talbot, with the young earl of Shrewsbury, his ward; Sir William Stanley; Sir Thomas Burchier; and Sir Walter Hungerford, knights. At last the earl, hearing of the king's coming, conducted his whole army to Tamworth.

King Richard, hearing of the arrival of the Earl Henry in the parts of Wales with so small a force, gave little or no regard to it. But understanding that he was come to Lichfield, without resistance or incumbrance, he was sore moved, cursing and crying out against them who had so deceived him, and in all speed sent for John duke of Norfolk, Henry earl of Northumberland, Thomas earl of Surrey, with other friends of special trust. Robert Brakenbury also, lieutenant of the Tower, was sent for, with Sir Thomas Burchier, and Sir Walter Hungerford, with certain other knights and esquires, whom he partly misdoubted. Thus, King Richard, well fortified and accompanied, leaving nothing undone that diligence could require, set forward toward his enemies. The earl by this time was come to Tamworth, to whom secretly in the evening, resorted Sir John Savage, Sir Bryan Sanford, Sir Simon Digby, and many others, forsaking the part of King Richard, whom all good men hated, as he indeed deserved. The king, having perfect knowledge of the earl being encamped at Tamworth, embattled himself in a place near a village called Bosworth, not far from Leicester, determining there to encounter his adversaries. Here the matter lay in great doubt and suspense concerning the Lord Stanley, (who was the earl's father-in-law, and had married his mother) to whose part he would incline. For although his heart went (no doubt) with the earl, and he had secret conference with him the night before, yet because of his son and heir, George Lord Strange, being then in the hands of King Richard, lest the king should attempt any thing against him, he durst not be seen openly to go that way where in heart he favoured, and therefore, closely kept himself between both, till the push came that his help might be of signal service.

The number of the earl's party was not more than one half of the side of King Richard. When the time and place was appointed, where the two battles should encounter and join together, sore stripes and great blows were given on both sides, and many slain. If number and multitude might govern the success of battle, King Richard had double the earl. But it is God, not man, that giveth victory, by what means it seemeth best to his divine providence. In what order, and by what occasion this field was won and lost, the certain intelligence we possess not, only the history of Polydore Virgil, whom Sir Thomas More follows word for word. In which history it appears, that as these two armies were coupling together, King Richard understanding by his spies where the earl of Richmond was, and how he was but slenderly accompanied, and seeing him approach more near to him, rather carried with courage, than ruled with reason, set spurs to his horse, and ranging out of the compass of his ranks, pressed toward the earl, and set upon him so sharply, that first he killed Sir William Brandon, the earl's standard-bearer, father to the Lord Charles Brandon, duke of Suffolk, then after overthrew Sir John Cheinie, thinking likewise to oppress the earl. But as the Lord by his secret providence disposeth the event of all things, as the earl with his men about him, being overmatched, began to despair of victory, suddenly and opportunely came Sir William Stanley, with three thousand well-appointed able men, whereby King Richard's men were driven back, and he himself, cruelly fighting in the thick of his enemies, was slain, and brought to his confusion and death, which he worthily deserved.

In the meantime, the earl of Oxford, who had the guiding of the forward, discomfited the forefront of King Richard's host, and put them to flight, in which chase many were slain, of noblemen especially above others, John duke of Norfolk, Lord Ferrers, Sir Richard Radcliff, and Robert Brankenbury, lieutenant of the Tower. &c. Lord Thomas Haward, earl of Surrey, there submitted himself, and although he was not received at first to grace, but remained long in the Tower, yet at length, for his fidelity, he was delivered and advanced to his recovered honour and dignity again.

This King Richard had but one son, who, shortly after the cruel murder of King Edward's sons, was taken with sickness and died.

Moreover, as to the Lord Stanley, thus reports the history, that King Richard being in Bosworth field, sent for Lord Stanley by a pursuivant, to advance with his company, otherwise he sware by Christ's passion, that he would strike off his son's head before dinner. The Lord Stanley sent word again, that if he did, he had more sons alive. The king immediately commanded the Lord Strange to be beheaded; at the very time when both the armies were within sight, and were ready to join together. Wherefore the king's councillors, pondering the time and the case, persuaded the king that it was now time to fight, and not to do execution, advising him to delay the matter till the battle was ended. And so (as God would) King Richard breaking his oath, or rather keeping his oath, for he himself was slain before dinner, the Lord Strange was committed to be kept prisoner within the king's tent; who then, after the victory was gotten, was sought out and brought to his joyful father. And thus you have the tragical life and end of this wretched King Richard.

Henry, the earl of Richmond, after hearty thanks given to Almighty God for his glorious victory, proceeded to the town of Leicester, where the crown was brought to him by the Lord Strange, and put on the earl's head.

In the meantime the dead corpse of King Richard was shamefully carried to the town of Leicester, being naked and despoiled to the skin; and being trussed behind a pursuivant of arms, was carried like a hog or a dog, having his head and arms hanging on the one side of the horse, and the legs on the other side, all sprinkled with mire and blood. And thus ended the usurped reign of King Richard, who reigned two years and two months.

KING HENRY THE SEVENTH.

When King Henry, by the providence of God, had obtained this triumphant victory and diadem of the realm, first sending for Edward Plantagenet, earl of Warwick, son to George duke of Clarence, and committing him to safe custody within the Tower, from Leicester he removed to London, and not long after, according to his oath and promise made before, he espoused the young Lady Elizabeth, heir of the house of York; whereby both the houses of York and Lancaster were joined together, to the no little rejoicing of all English hearts, and no less quiet unto the realm, which was A. D. 1485. This king reigned twenty-three years and eight months, and being a prince of great policy, justice, and temperance, kept his realm in good tolerable rule and order. And here, interrupting a little the course of our English matters, we will now (the Lord willing) enter the history above promised, of Maximilian the emperor, and matters of the empire, especially such as pertain to the church.

MAXIMILIAN THE EMPEROR.

So happy was the education of this emperor in good letters, so expert he was in languages and sciences, but especially such was his dexterity and promptness in the Latin tongues, that he, imitating the example of Julius Cæsar, did write and comprehend in Latin histories his own acts and feats. Moreover, as he was learned himself, so he was a singular patron and advancer of learned students, as may well appear by the erecting and setting up the university of Wittenburgh. By this emperor

many in those days were excited to embrace as well other liberal arts, as also the searching out of old histories, by which several persons were induced to exercise their diligence in collecting and explaining matters pertaining to the knowledge of history, as well of ancient as also of later times, as Cuspinianus, Nauclerus, Conradus, Peutingerus, Manlius, and others.

Here now it began to appear, what great benefit was conferred on the world by the art and faculty of printing. Through means of which the church and commonwealth of Christ began now to be replenished with learned men.

Among the many learned men of this time, must be numbered Weselus Groningensis, otherwise named Basilius. He was so notable and worthy a man, that the people called him " The Light of the World."

Concerning his doctrine, he reprehended the opinion of the papists, as touching repentance, which they divided into three parts, of which three parts, satisfaction and confession he disallowed. Likewise purgatory and supererogation of works and pardons he disproved, both at Rome and at Paris. He spake against the pope's indulgences, by occasion of which several of the pope's court, being persuaded by him, began to speak more freely against the matter, than he himself had done.

The abuses of masses, and praying for the dead he disallowed; and likewise the supremacy of the pope he utterly rejected, denying utterly that any supreme head or governor ought to be in the world over all other; affirming also, and saying many times, " That the pope had no authority to do any thing by commandment, but by truth, that is, so far as truth goes with him, so far his sentence to stand; neither that he ought to prevail by commanding, but only by teaching, as every true christian bishop may prevail over another." Also in some places in his writings he denies not, " but that pope's and their spiritual prelates, proceeding against Christ's doctrine, are plain antichrists.

Also, Weselus witnesses, that the fathers who were before Albert and Thomas, did resist and withstand the pope's indulgences, calling them in their writings, plain idolatry, mere fraud and error; adding moreover, that unless the severity of some good divines had withstood these pardons and indulgences of the pope, innumerable errors had overflown the church.

By this it may be seen and noted, how, by the grace of God and gift of printing, first came forth learning, and by learning came light to judge and discern the errors of the pope from the truth of God's word.

About the very same time, when the gospel began thus to branch and spring in Germany, the host of Christ's church began also to muster and to multiply here in England. For not long after the death of this Weselus, A.D. 1494, and in the ninth year of the reign of Henry VII., on the twenty-eighth of April, a very old woman named Joan Boughton, widow, and mother to the Lady Young, was burned, which lady was also suspected to be of that opinion which her mother was. Her mother was fourscore years of age or more, and held eight of Wickliff's opinions (which opinions my author does not shew) for which she was burnt in Smithfield. Our author says she was a disciple of Wickliff, whom she accounted for a saint, and held so fast and firmly eight of his ten opinions, that all the doctors of London could not turn her from one of them; and when it was told her that she should be burnt for her obstinacy and false belief, she set nothing by their menacing words, but defied them; for she said she was so beloved of God, and his holy angels, that she cared not for the fire, and in the midst thereof she cried to God to take her soul into his holy hands. The night following that on which she was burnt, the most part of her ashes were taken away by such as had a love to the doctrine that she died for.

Shortly after the martyrdom of this godly aged mother, on the seventeenth of January, A.D. 1497, being Sunday, two men, the one called Richard Milderale, and the other James Sturdy, performed the penance of carrying fagots before the procession of St. Paul's, and afterwards stood before the preacher in the time of his sermon. And upon the Sunday following two other men stood at Paul's Cross all the sermon time; the one garnished with painted and written papers, the other having a fagot on his neck. After that in Lent season, upon Passion Sunday, one Hugh Glover bore a fagot before the procession of St. Paul's, and after with the fagot stood before the preacher all the sermon time at Paul's Cross. And on the Sunday next following four men stood, and did their open penance at Paul's Cross in the sermon time, and many of their books were burnt before them at the cross.

The next year following, which was in the beginning of May, A.D. 1498, the king then being at Canterbury, a priest was burnt, who was so strong in his opinion that all the clerks and doctors then there being could not remove him from his faith. Whereof the king being informed, he caused the priest to be brought before his presence, who by his persuasion caused him to revoke, but still he was burnt immediately.

In the same year above mentioned, which was A.D. 1498, after the beheading of Edward Plantagenet, earl of Warwick, and son to the duke of Clarence, the king and queen being removed to Calais, a certain godly man and a constant martyr of Christ, named Babram, in Norfolk, was burnt in the month of July.

About which year likewise, or in the year next following, the twentieth day of July, was an old man burnt in Smithfield.

In the year 1499, the martyrdom and burning of Jerome Savanarola took place, a man no less godly in heart than constant in his profession. Who being a monk in Italy, and singularly well learned, preached against the evil living of the spiritualty, and especially of his own order, complaining against them as the springs and authors of all mischiefs and wickedness. Whereupon, by the help of certain learned men, he began to seek reformation in his own order. The pope perceiving this, and fearing that Jerome, who was now in great reputation among all men, should diminish or overthrow his authority, he ordained his vicar or provincial to see reformation of these matters, which vicar with great superstition began to reform things; but Jerome always withstood him, whereupon he was complained of to the pope, and because contrary to the pope's commandment he withstood his vicar, he was accursed. But for all that Jerome left not off preaching, but threatened Italy with the wrath and indignation of God, and prophesied to them, that the land should be overthrown for the pride and wickedness of the people, and for the untruth, hypocrisy, and falsehood of the clergy, which God would not leave unrevenged, as it afterwards came to pass, when King Charles came into Italy and to Rome, and so straightly beset Pope Alexander, that he was forced to make composition with the king.

Now as Jerome would not leave off preaching, he was commanded to appear before the pope, to give account of his new learning (for so then they called the truth of the gospel), but he made his excuse that he could not come. Then he was again forbidden by the pope to preach, and his learning pronounced and condemned as pernicious, false, and seditious.

This Jerome, as a man worldly wise, foreseeing the great perils and dangers that might come unto him, for fear left off preaching; but when the people, who sore hungered and longed for God's word, were urgent on him that he would preach again, he began again to preach A.D. 1496, in the city of Florence; and although many counselled him that he should not do so without the pope's commandment, yet he did not regard it, but went forward freely of his own good-will. When the pope and his shavelings heard news of this they were grievously incensed and inflamed against him, and now again cursed him, as an obstinate and stiff-necked heretic. But for all that, Jerome proceeded in teaching and instructing the people, saying that men ought not to regard such curses, which are against the true doctrine and the common advantage, whereby the people

should be taught and amended, Christ's kingdom enlarged, and the kingdom of the devil utterly overthrown.

In all his preaching he desired to teach no other thing than only the pure and simple word of God, making often protestation that all men should certify him if they had heard him teach or preach anything contrary thereto, for upon his own conscience he knew not that he had taught anything but the pure word of God. What his doctrine was all men may easily judge by his books that he has written.

After this (A.D. 1498,) he was taken and brought out of St. Mark's cloister, and two other friars with him, named Dominic and Sylvester, who favoured his learning, and was carried into prison, where he wrote a godly meditation upon that most comfortable thirty-first Psalm: "In thee, O Lord, do I put my trust, let me never be ashamed: deliver me in thy righteousness." Wherein he doth excellently describe and set forth the continual strife between the flesh and the spirit.

After this the pope's legates came to Florence, and called forth these three good men, threatening them marvellously; but they continued still constant. Then came the chief counsellors of the city, with the pope's commissioners, who had gathered out certain articles against these men, whereupon they were condemned to death; the tenour of which articles hereafter ensue:—

1. The first article was as touching our free justification through faith in Christ.

2. That the communion ought to be ministered under both kinds.

3. That the indulgences and pardons of the pope were of no effect.

4. For preaching against the filthy and wicked living of the cardinals and clergy.

5. For denying the pope's supremacy.

6. Also that he had affirmed that the keys were not given to Peter alone, but unto the universal church.

7. Also, that the pope did neither follow the life nor doctrine of Christ, for that he attributed more to his own pardons and traditions, than to Christ's merits, and therefore he was antichrist.

8. Also, that the pope's excommunications are not to be feared, and that he who doth fear or flee them is excommunicated of God.

9. That auricular confession is not necessary.

10. That he had moved the citizens to uproar and sedition.

11. That he had neglected and condemned the pope's citation.

12. That he had shamefully spoken against and slandered the pope.

13. That he had taken Christ to witness of his naughtiness and heresy.

14. Also, that Italy must be cleansed through God's scourge, for the manifold wickedness of the princes and clergy.

These and such other articles were laid against them and read before them. Then they demanded of Jerome and his companions, whether they would recant and give over their opinions. They answered, that through God's help they would steadfastly continue in the manifest truth, and not depart from the same. Then were they degraded one after another by the bishop of Vasion, and so delivered over to the secular rulers of Florence, with commandment to carry them forth, and handle them as obstinate and stiff-necked heretics.

Thus was this worthy witness of Christ, with the other two, first hanged up openly in the market-place, and afterward burnt to ashes, and the ashes gathered up, and cast into the river of Arum, the 24th of May, A.D. 1499. This Savanarola suffered under Pope Alexander VI.

Now to return to the order of popes, where we left off with Innocent VIII. After Innocent succeeded Pope Alexander VI. In Alexander, among other horrible things, this is to be noted, that when Gemes, brother to Bajazet the great Turk, was committed by the Rhodians to the safe custody, first of Pope Innocent, then of Alexander VI., (for whose keeping, the pope received every year forty thousand crowns); yet, when Pope Alexander was compelled to send Gemes to Charles VIII., the French king, as a pledge, he, being hired by the Turk, caused Gemes to be poisoned at Terracina.

Moreover, it appears that this Alexander taking displeasure with Charles the French king, about the winning of Naples, sent to Bajazet the Turk, to fight against Charles.

Munsterus declaring the history of Gemes something otherwise, saith that he was first committed by the Rhodians to the French king. And when Alexander the pope, through his fraudulent flattery, got him out of the hands of the French king into his own, then by his means Gemes afterward was poisoned, as is before expressed.

To these poisoning acts of the pope, let us also add his malicious wickedness, with like fury exercised upon Antonius Mancinellus, a man of excellent learning, because he wrote an eloquent oration against his wicked manners and filthy life, with other vices; he therefore commanded both his hands and his tongue to be cut off, playing with him, as M. Antonius the tyrant before did with M. Cicero, for writing against his horrible life. At length, as one poison requires another, this poisoning pope, as he was sitting with his cardinals, and other rich senators of Rome at dinner, his servants unawares brought to him a wrong bottle, by which he was poisoned, and some of his cardinals who were about him.

In the time of this Pope Alexander also it happened, that the angel, which stood in the high top of the pope's church, was beaten down with terrible thunder. After this pope, succeeded Pius III., (A. D. 1503.) After whom came Julius II., a man so far passing all other in iniquity, that Wigelius, and such other of his own friends, are compelled to say of him, "that he was more given to war and battle, than to Christ." Concerning the madness of this man, it is most certainly known, that when he was going to war, he cast the keys of St. Peter into the river Tiber, saying, that as the keys of St. Peter would not serve him to his purpose, he would betake himself to the sword of St. Paul.

Of this Julius it is certainly reported, that partly with his wars, and partly with his cursings, in the space of seven years, as good as two hundred thousand christians were destroyed. First, he besieged Ravenna against the Venetians, then Servia, Imolia, Faventia, Forolivium, Bononia, and other cities, which he got out of princes' hands, not without much bloodshed. The chronicles of John Sleidan make mention, that when this Julius was made pope, he took an oath, promising to have a council within two years; but when he had no leisure, being occupied with his wars in Italy among the Venetians, and with the French king, and in Ferraria, and in other countries, nine of his cardinals departing from him, came into Milan, and there appointed a council at the city of Pisa; among whom, the chief were Bernard, Cruceius, William Prenestinus, Francis, Constantine, with others; to whom also were added, the proctors of Maximilian the emperor, and of Charles the French king. So the council was appointed (A. D. 1511) to begin in the kalends of September. The cause why they called this council was, that the pope having broken his oath, gave no hope of having any council; and also because there were other crimes of which they had to accuse. Their purpose was to remove him out of his seat, which he had procured through bribes and ambition. Julius hearing this, commands, under great penalties, that no man should obey them, and himself calls another council against the next year, to be begun the nineteenth day of April. The French king understanding that Pope Julius had joined with the Venetians, to take their part against him, assembled a council at Turin, in the month of September; in which council these questions were proposed.

Whether it was lawful for the pope to wage war against any prince without cause?

Whether any prince in defending himself, might invade his adversary, and deny his obedience?

To which questions it was answered, that the bishop ought not to invade, and also that it was lawful for the

king to defend himself. Moreover, that the pragmatical sanction was to be observed through the realm of France, and that excommunications ought not to be feared, if they were found to be unjust. After this the king sent to Julius the answer of his council, requiring him either to agree to peace, or to appoint a general council somewhere else, where this matter might be more fully decided. Julius would do neither of these, but forthwith accursed Charles, the French king, with all his kingdom. At length at Ravenna, in a great battle, he was overcome by the French king, and at last, after much slaughter, and great bloodshed, and mortal war, this pope died the twenty-first day of February, A. D. 1513.

If it were not that I am afraid of filling this volume with foreign histories, when I have professed chiefly to treat of Acts and Monuments done here at home, I would add after these popes something also of the Turks' history, of their rise and cruel persecution of the saints of God, to the great peril of Christendom; yet there are certain causes which necessarily require their wicked proceedings, their cruel tyranny, and bloody victories, the ruin and subversion of so many christian churches, with the horrible murders and captivity of infinite christians, to be made known, as well to this our country of England, as also to other nations.

The great victories of the Turks, and the want of success of our men fighting against them, may admonish and teach us, following the example of the old Israelites, how to seek for greater strength to encounter with these enemies of Christ than hitherto we have done. First, we must consider that the whole power of Satan, the prince of this world, goes with the Turks, to resist which no strength of man's arm is sufficient, but only the name, spirit, and power of our Lord Jesus the Son of God going with us in our battles, as among the old Israelites the ark of God's covenant and promise went with them also fighting against the enemies of God. For so are we taught in the scripture, that we christian men have no strength but in Christ only. Whether we war against the devil, or against the Turk, it is true what the scripture saith, "without me you can do nothing." There is no power to stand against the devil, or to conquer the world, unless our faith only, to which all the promises of God (touching salvation) are annexed, beyond which promises we must not go, for the word must be our rule. He that presumes beyond the promises in the word expressed, goes not, but wanders, he cannot tell whither. Neither must we appoint God how to save the world, but must take that way which he hath appointed. Let us not set God to school, nor comprehend his Holy Spirit within our knowledge. He that made us without our counsel, did also redeem us as pleased him. If he be merciful, let us be thankful. And if his mercies surmount our capacity, let us therefore not resist but search his word, and thereto apply our will, which if we will do, all our contentions will be soon at a point. Let us, therefore, search the will of our God in his word; and if he wills his salvation to stand free to all nations, why do we make merchandise thereof? If he has graciously offered his waters to us, without money, or money's worth, let us not hedge in the plenteous springs of his grace so freely given us.

And if God has determined his own Son to stand alone, let us not presume to mix with his majesty any of our trumpery. He that brings St. George or St. Dennis as patrons to the field to fight against the Turk, leaves Christ (no doubt) at home. Now how we have fought these many years against the Turk, though history keeps silence, yet the success declares. We fight against a persecutor, being no less persecutors ourselves. We wrestle against a bloody tyrant, and our hands are as full of blood as his. He kills Christ's people with the sword, and we burn them with fire. He observing the works of the law, seeks his justification by the same, the like also do we. But neither he nor we seek our justification as we should, that is, only by faith in the Son of God.

And what marvel then, our doctrine being almost as corrupt as his, and our conversation worse, if Christ fight not with us, fighting against the Turk ? The Turk hath prevailed so mightily, not because Christ is weak, but because Christians are wicked, and their doctrine impure. Our temples are polluted with images, and our hearts with idolatry ; our priests sin before God in adultery, being restrained from lawful matrimony. The name of God is in our mouths, but his fear is not in our hearts. We war against the Turk with our works, masses, traditions, and ceremonies, but we fight not against him with Christ, and with the power of his glory, which if we did the field were won.

I do believe, that when the church of Christ with the sacraments thereof shall be so reformed, that Christ alone shall be received to be our justifier, all other religions, merits, traditions, images, patrons and advocates set apart, the sword of the christians, with the strength of Christ, shall soon vanquish the Turks' pride and fury. But of this I will treat more largely in the process of this history.

As to the time when this sect of Mahomet first began, history does not fully consent, but it is generally reckoned from his flight from Mecca, (A. D. 622), which they call the Hegyra, and in the eleventh year of Heraclius the emperor of Constantinople.

In this all writers agree, that this damnable Mahomet was born in the country of Arabia, bordering on the east part of Judea, (A.D. 571.) His father was an Arabian of the tribe of Koreish, and his mother was an Ishmaelite, which Ishmaelites being a people of Arabia, were called the Hagarens, which term Mahomet afterwards turned to the name of Saracens. Of this wretched Mahomet mention was made before, where we shewed, how he making himself the highest prophet of all other, yet denies not Christ to be an holy prophet, and next to him, and Moses also to be another. Moreover, he denies not Mary the mother of Christ to be a virgin, and to have conceived Christ by the Holy Ghost : affirming further, that Christ in his own person was not crucified, but another called Judas for him. He greatly commends John the son of Zachary for a chaste man, when he himself permits a man to have four wives, and as many concubines as he is able to find, and saith that whereas Christ and other prophets had the gift given them to work miracles, he was sent by force of the sword, to compel men to his religion.

The prodigious vanities, lies, and blasphemies contained in his law, called The Alkoran, are rather to be laughed at than recited.

It is thought that Sergius, a Nestorian, assisted Mahomet, in contriving this Alkoran, and so it appears by the scope, which especially tends to this end, to take the divinity from the person of Christ, whom he grants notwithstanding to be a most holy man, and also that he is received up to God, and shall come again to kill antichrist, &c.

Moreover, this ridiculous Alkoran is so intermingled with mixtures of the Christian, Jewish, and the Gentile laws, giving such liberty to all the lusts of the flesh, setting up circumcision, abstaining from swine's flesh, and Jewish washings, and so much stands upon father Abraham, that it is supposed by some that this filthy Alkoran was set out in the days of Mahomet, but that certain Jews had some handling also in the matter, and put it out after his death.

After Mahomet had thus seduced the people, teaching them that he came not by miracles, but by the sword to give his law, and that they who will not obey it must either be put to death, or else pay tribute (for so are the words of the Alkoran) ; and after he had gathered the strength of the Arabians about him, which Arabians had then occasion to rebel against the emperor, because their stipends were not paid them by the emperor's officers, he began to range with force and violence in parts of Syria, and subdued Mecca, then Damascus, and further increasing in power he entered Egypt, and subdued the same. From thence he turned against the Persians. Chosroes, the king of Persia, encountered him with a powerful army, and overthrew the Saracens, and

put Mahomet to flight. Of these Persians came the Turks, who afterward joining with the Saracens, maintained them against the christians.

After the death of this beast, (A. D. 632), who, as some say, was poisoned in his house, he was succeeded by his father-in-law, Abubeker, who took upon him the government of their followers, and got the city Gaza, and besieged also Jerusalem. He reigned two years at Damascus.

After him followed Omar, who conquered a great part of Syria, Egypt, and Persia.

The fourth king of the Saracens, after Mahomet, was Otman, then followed Ali the son-in-law of Mahomet, and after him Mahuvias, or Moawiyah, who, after a siege of seven years, obtained the christian city of Cesarea ; also overcame the Persians, and subdued that country to his law.

Thus the wicked Saracens, in the space of thirty years, subdued Arabia, got Palestine, Phœnicia, Syria, Egypt, and Persia.

Not long after Heraclius, emperor of Constantinople, succeeded Constans his nephew, who, in the sixteenth year of his empire, fighting unluckily against the Saracens in Lycia, was overthrown by Mahuvias, A.D. 657. The Saracens after this victory spoiled all Rhodes.

These cursed Saracens, in these great victories and conquests, were not without domestic sedition and divisions, yet the princes of the Saracens, then called Sultans, had in their possession the government of Syria, Egypt, Africa, and of a great part of Asia, about four hundred years, till at length the Saracen king who ruled in Persia, fighting against the Saracen of Babylon, sought aid of the Turks to fight with him against the sultan of Babylon. The Turks by little and little surprised the sultan of Persia, and not long after usurped the kingdom of Persia ; and this is the first beginning of the Turkish dominion.

These Turks, after they had thus overcome many countries and provinces, and made their power large and mighty both in Asia and Europe, began to divide their kingdoms and countries among themselves. But when they could not agree, but with deadly war contended for the bounds of those kingdoms and dominions, four of the principal families conquering and subduing all the rest, parted the whole empire among themselves. And yet they also were not contented, but fell to such cruel hatred, contention, war, and slaughter (no doubt by the just judgment of God against his blasphemous enemies), that there was no end of it, until the remnant of the ancient Turks was utterly rooted out.

These four families, with their captains and armies, about A.D. 1330, went raging throughout all Asia and Europe, and every one of them conquered some part of the countries where they passed.

The causes of these great invasions and victories, were the dissension and discord, falsehood, idleness, unconstancy, greedy avarice, lack of truth and fidelity among christian men of all states and degrees, both high and low. For by the wilful defection and backsliding of the christians, the Turkish power exceedingly increased, in that many desiring the licentious life and liberty of war and allured with the prosperous success of things, forsook the church of God, and made themselves bondslaves to Mahomet and his devilish sect, both because liberty is delightful to all men, and partly also because as fortune favours, so commonly the wills of men incline. And again, such as are profane and without the fear of God (of whom there is an infinite number in the church) in all ages are wont commonly to judge of religion, according to the success of realms and kingdoms. For many, not only for the variety of opinions, but also for the diversity of events and fortune among men, have inquired, and do inquire whether there is any church of God distinct from other nations, what it is, and where it is ; especially as the greatest part of men, both in the old time when the four monarchies flourished, was ignorant of this doctrine, which is peculiar to the church alone, and now also the barbarity of Mahomet prevails and reigns in the most part of the world. And how stands this with man's reason, that a small number, both miserable and also feeble and broken with many battles, should be regarded and loved of God, and the other flourishing in all wealth, prosperity, victory, authority, and power, should be rejected and despised of God, seeing there is no power and authority, but by the ordinance of God? Although therefore the power of the Turks has been, for these two hundred years, of greater force than any other monarchy of the world besides, yet is there no imperial dignity to be regarded in that Turkish tyranny, but among those nations only, where the heavenly doctrine of the gospel is preached, and other disciplines necessary for the church of God, and the common life of man maintained and regarded, where the laws of God, and other honest and civil ordinances agreeable to the same, flourish and reign; where lawful judgment is exercised; where virtue is honoured and rewarded; where sin and wickedness is punished; where honest families are maintained and defended.

These things are not regarded among the Turks, the enemies of the Son of God, and all lawful empires, because they dissolve and reject all godly societies, honest discipline, good laws, politics, righteous judgment, the ordinance of matrimony, and godly families. For what has the empire of the Turks been hitherto, but most deadly, cruel, and perpetual war, to work all mischief, destruction, and desolation? To subvert good laws, cities, kingdoms, policies, and to enlarge their cruel power and dominion? The stay and strength whereof is not love and favour proceeding of virtue and justice, as in lawful and well governed empires; but fear, violence, oppression, swarms and infinite thousands of barbarous and most wicked people, ministers of Satan's malice and fury. Which kind of dominion and tyranny has been condemned by the voice of God many years ago; the testimonies whereof the Lord would have to remain in the church, lest the godly, being moved with the power and success thereof, should fall away and forsake the Son of God.

Wherefore, let us not seek for any imperial state in that barbarity; but let us be thankful, and acknowledge the great benefit of God, that he hath reserved to us certain remnants of the Roman empire; and let us call upon him daily with hearty petitions and groans, and with zeal and love to the house of God, that this Turkish power joined with the malice of Satan against the Son of God, prevail not against the poor congregations and little remnant of his church, as it has hitherto done against those strong and noble christian kingdoms and churches, where now we see the Turkish tyranny to reign, and Satan to have taken full possession. Whose state was once far better than ours is now, and more likely to continue without such horrible overthrows and desolation. O that we might foresee a little the great danger that hangs over our heads! For though the Turk seems to be far off, yet do we nourish within our breasts at home, that which may soon cause us to feel his cruel hand and worse, if worse may be; to overrun us; to lay our land waste; to scatter us among the infidels, the enemies and blasphemers of the Son of God.

Now, although these four families above-mentioned long continued together in bloody wars, deadly hatred, yet one of them passed the rest in all cruelty and tyranny, and subduing the other three families, took upon him the government alone, and so became the first monarch, or emperor, that reigned amongst them, called Ottoman, of whom all that reigned after him were called Ottomans, who succeeding in the order of his line, have occupied the same dominion and seat of the Turks, from A.D. 1300, to this present time, to the number of twelve, of which twelve, in such order as they lived and reigned, I intend (Christ so permitting) severally and compendiously shortly to treat, briefly abstracting, out of prolix and tedious writers, such particulars as for us christians shall be briefly requisite to be known.

THE TWELVE GREAT EMPERORS OF THE TURKS.

I. OTTOMAN.—This man was at first of poor estate,

and obscure among the common sort of men, coming of a base progeny, and of rustic parents; but through his valiantness and activity in war, he got him a great name among the Turks. For he being a man of fierce courage, refusing no labour, delighting in war, and gathering together by great subtlety a multitude of common soldiers, began to make war, and by conquest and victories to advance himself and his family. First, he began to rob and spoil with a great band of rovers, and afterward he attempted to set upon all men. Neither did he vex and destroy the christians only, but set upon his own nation also, and sought all occasion to subdue them wholly to him. For now the princes and captains of the Turks, inflamed with ambition and desire of rule, began to fall out and contend among themselves, insomuch that they fell to domestic war, with all the power they could.

Ottoman considering this occasion very fit and meet to accomplish that which he had long sought for, gathered to him all such as he thought given to robbing and spoiling, and set them upon mischief, and in a short time he began to grow in authority, and set upon certain towns, as he saw opportunity. Of which towns some he took by force, some by surrender, others he spoiled and overthrew to terrify the rest, thus laying the first foundation of his rising. In the meantime, the discord which was among the christians was no small advantage to this Ottoman, by occasion whereof, he within ten years' space subdued Bithynia, and all the provinces about Pontus; also Natolia, which comprehends all the dominion of the Greeks within Asia; Ancyra, a city in Phrygia; Synope, a city in Galatia; and Sebastia, a city in Cappadocia: and thus still prevailing, he increased in a short time to a mighty power, either through the secret judgment of God against that nation, or else because God would have them so far and so cruelly to prevail, for the punishment of the sins of other nations.

This Ottoman, after he had reigned twenty-eight years, died A.D. 1328, leaving behind him three sons, of whom Orchanes, being the youngest, killed his two brethren, whilst they were at variance between themselves.

II. ORCHANES after he had slain his two brethren, took the government of the Turks after his father, who, after he had drawn to him the hearts of the multitude, such as had their dispositions set upon the licentious life of war, applied his power further to enlarge his father's dominion, winning and subduing Mysia, Lydia, Lycaonia, Phrygia, and Caria; all which countries, being within the compass of Asia, to the seaside of Hellespont, and the Euxine sea, he added to the Turkish empire. Also he won Prusa, which was the metropolitan city of Bithynia, which then he made the chief seat of the Turks' empire. Besides these, he conquered Nice, and got Nicomedia; all which were before christian cities and regions. And yet all this could not make the christian princes in Greece to cease their civil wars, and to join and accord among themselves. By reason of which the Turk's aid was sent for out of Asia to help our christians one to kill another, and at length to get all those parts of Europe from them both. Orchanes, after these victories, when he had reigned two-and-thirty years, was struck, some say, with a dart in the shoulder, at the siege of Prusa. The opinion of others is, that fighting against the Tartarians, where he lost a great part of his army, he was there also slain himself, (A.D. 1359.)

III. AMURATH.—The Greek writers inform us that Orchanes had two sons, Soliman and Amurath; but Soliman, who was very distinguished, died shortly before his father. After him followed Amurath, who, after Asia was subdued by his predecessors, sought by all means and ways how to proceed further, and to invade Europe. To whose ambitious purpose the domestic wars of the christians gave most prosperous occasion, which occasion is thus declared. Certain discord fell between the princes of Greece, and John Paleologus emperor of Constantinople. Whereupon

Paleologus, as he was not able to make his party good with the Grecians, most unwisely sent for Amurath to help him, who, being glad to have such an occasion offered, which he so long had sought, sent to aid him twelve thousand Turks into Thrace ; but first he used all the delays he could of crafty policy, to the intent that the Greeks should waste their strength and power upon themselves, by which he might be more able afterward to set upon them, and to accomplish his conceived desire.

The Turks thus being called into Europe, by the christians, whether they tasting the sweetness of the soil, induced Amurath their emperor to make invasion, or whether Amurath of his own head thought good to use the time, in A.D. 1363, he came himself over into Europe with sixty thousand Turks, falling upon the Greeks, being wasted and spent with their long wars and battles before. The pretence of the devilish Turk was, to aid and assist the emperor Paleologus, whether he would or no, and to subdue as had fallen from him.

Thus the Turks' army being conveyed over by the Grecian sea, called the Hellespont, first got Calipolis, with other towns and cities bordering about the sea, and there planting themselves, and preparing ships of their own for transporting their munitions out of Asia, advanced their power further into Thrace, and there won Philippolis, then got Adrianople, which was not far from Constantinople, and there Amurath made his chief seat. Then began Paleologus, the emperor, at length to bewail his offer and covenant made with Amurath. When the Turks had thus conquered a great part of Thrace, they extended forth their army to Mysia, which they soon subdued ; from thence proceeding and conquering the Bessos and Triballos, they entered into Servia and Bulgaria, where they joining battle with the prince of Servia, and with other dukes of Dalmatia and Epirus, won the field, and defeated them, where the prince being taken, and committed to prison, ended his life. This prince had a certain faithful client or servant, who to revenge his master's death, with a bold courage, although seeing death before his eyes, yet ventured his life so far, that he came to the tyrant and thrust him through with his dagger. This Amurath reigned thirty years, and was slain A.D. 1389.

IV. BAJAZET.—The power of the Turks began to increase in Europe, when Bajazet, the first of that name, after the death of his father, entered on the possession of the Turkish kingdom. This Bajazet had two brethren, Soliman and Sauces : Sauces had his eyes put out by his father, for striving for the kingdom. Soliman was slain of his brother. Thus Bajazet, beginning his kingdom with the murder of his brother, brought his imperial seat from Prusa, a city of Bithynia, to Adrianople, intending, with himself to subdue both Asia and Europe to his own power. First he set upon the Servians and Bulgarians, thinking to revenge his father's death, where he gave the overthrow to all the nobility of the Servians and Bulgarians, and put all those parts under his subjection, to the borders of the Illyrians. All Thrace he brought likewise under his yoke, only Constantinople and Pera excepted. That done, he invaded the rest of Grecia, prevailing against the countries of Thessaly, Macedonia, Phocia, and Attica, spoiling and burning as he passed without any resistance ; and so, returning with innumerable spoil of the christians to Adrianople, laid siege to Constantinople for the space of eight years, and would have taken it, but that Paleologus, being brought to extremity, was driven to crave aid of the French, and of Sigismund the emperor, who, being accompanied with a sufficient power of French and Germans, came down to Hungary, and towards Servia, against the Turk. Bajazet hearing of their coming, raised his siege from Constantinople, and with sixty thousand horsemen came to Nicopolis, where he encountering with them, overthrew all the christian army, and took John, the captain of the French, prisoner, (A. D. 1392.) Sigismund, who before in the council of Constance had burned John Huss, and

Jerome of Prague, hardly escaped by flying. Bajazet, after the victory, carried away duke John, with five others in bands, into Prusa, where before his face he caused all the other christian prisoners to be cut in pieces. Afterward John, being ransomed with two hundred thousand crowns, was delivered up. Some authors refer this history to the time of Calepinus.

Bajazet, the cruel tyrant, after this victory, and the tyranny shewed upon the christians, returned again to the siege of Constantinople, fully determined to conquer and subdue the same, which he would have no doubt accomplished, but that the providence of God had found such a means, that Tamerlane, king of Parthia, with a hundred thousand horsemen, and swarms of footmen, like a violent flood overrunning Asia, and pressing upon Syria and Sebastia, had taken Orthobule, the son of Bajazet prisoner, and afterwards slew him, exercising the like cruelty upon his prisoners, as Bajazet had done before upon the christians, insomuch that he spared neither sex nor age of the Turkish multitude, of whom he caused twelve thousand at one time to be overridden and trodden down under his horses' feet. By this, Bajazet, the tyrant, was forced to raise the siege of Constantinople, and to return with his army into Asia, where, near the hill called Stella, he pitched his tent to encounter Tamerlane.

The fight between these two was long and great on both sides, (A. D. 1402,) and the second year after the slaughter of our christians at Nicopolis in Pannonia ; but the victory of this battle fell to Tamerlane at length. In which battle, as Munster writes, two hundred thousand Turks were slain. Among whom Bajazet, the tyrant, having his horse slain under him, was taken prisoner ; and to make a spectacle of his wretched fortune, he was bound in golden fetters, and so being enclosed in an iron cage (whom before all Greece could not hold) was led about and shewn through all Asia, to be scorned and laughed at : and, moreover, was used instead of a footstool to Tamerlane, or a block, as often as he mounted upon his horse. Some add also that he was made like a dog to feed under Tamerlane's table. The tyranny of this Bajazet against the christians, as it was not much unlike to the cruelty of Valerian, the Roman emperor, so neither was the example of his punishment much different, for as Sapor, king of the Persians, did then with Valerian in the time of the eighth persecution of the primitive church, so likewise was Bajazet the persecutor worthily handled by Tamerlane, king of the Parthians, as is above mentioned.

Tamerlane, after this conquest, passed with his army into Mesopotamia, into Egypt, and into Syria, where he victoriously subduing the cities and munitions of the Turks, at length also conquered Damascus. In his sieges his manner was, the first day to go all in white attire, the second day in red, and the third day in black, signifying thereby mercy the first day to them that yielded ; the second day the sword ; the third day fire and ashes. At last, after having gotten great victories, and spoils of the Turks, he returned to his own country, and there died, (A. D. 1405.)

In writing of this Tamerlane, it is recorded that he had in his army eight hundred thousand men : and that he overcame the Parthians, Scythians, Iberians, Albans, Persians, Medes, and conquered all Mesopotamia ; and after he had also subdued Armenia, passing over the river Euphrates he invaded all Asia Minor, conquering and subduing from the river Tanais to the Nile in Egypt, and was called the terror of the world. He left behind him two sons, who, falling into discord for their possessions, lost all again that their father had got.

In the mean time Bajazet, in the second year of his captivity, died, (A.D. 1403) leaving behind him four sons : Isa, the eldest, Musa, Soliman, and Mahomet, who disputed with the second the right of succession to the remainder of his empire. This civil war ended in the triumph of Mahomet, and in the death of his brothers. In these discords and divisions among the Turks, an occasion was given to the christians to have recovered again of the Turks that which they had lost, if they had not been either negligent, or in their own private wars otherwise occupied with themselves.

V. SOLIMAN CALEPINUS.

—Calepinus or Chelebi, was the second son of Bajazet. This Calepinus, encouraged by the sloth and negligence of the princes of Europe, and by the discord of the Greeks among themselves and other nations, near about them, long troubled and vexed the Bulgarians, Servians, and Macedonians, even to the time of Sigismund. Which Sigismund seeing that Bajazet was now overcome and taken of Tamerlane, and the power of the Turks weakened in Europe, and having such occasion offered him, as it were from heaven, to destroy and utterly to root out, not only out of Asia, but also out of all Europe, that barbarous nation, and cruel enemies to the name and religion of Christ; and also to revenge the great slaughter and discomfiture of his army, when fighting before with Bajazet at Nicopolis a city in Mysia; with great power made war against Calepinus at Columbatium a town in Servia, as is also before mentioned, but as unluckily and with as little success as he did before against Bajazet his father. For in that battle were slain of the christians to the number of twenty thousand, and the rest utterly discomfited, the king himself escaping so hardly, that he entered not again into his kingdom for the space of eighteen months after. After this, Soliman was overcome by his brother Musa, in the civil contention which was still raging among the brothers, and was killed (A.D. 1409), after having reigned nearly eight years.

VI. MUSA CHELEBI.

—After the captivity of Bajazet above mentioned, histories vary. The Greek writers, making no mention at all of Calepinus, only mention the sons of Bajazet generally, and of the contention among them, until the time of Mahomet. The Latin histories, writing of the children of Bajazet and of their succession, do not agree, some affirming that Bajazet had only two sons, others that he had more. After the death of Soliman, Musa was saluted emperor by the European army, but shortly after was attacked by his brother Mahomet, and killed in battle, after he had reigned about eight years.[1]

VII. MAHOMET.

—This Mahomet, the last of the sons of Bajazet, secured to himself alone the kingdom, or tyranny rather of the murdering Turks (A.D. 1413). He afflicted the christians with sore wars within Europe, especially the country called Wallachia, lying not far from the river Danube, between Hungary and Thrace. From thence he removed into Asia, where he recovered divers parts in Galatia, Pontus, Cappadocia, Cilicia, which before Tamerlane had alienated from the Turks. This Mahomet planted his chief imperial seat in Adrianople not far from Constantinople, within the country of Thrace. In some writers the conflict between Sigismund and the great Turk, wherein the christians were so discomfited, is referred rather to this Mahomet, than to Calepinus; of which conflict mention is above made in the history of Sigismund. This Mahomet reigned, after the death of Musa, eight years, and died A.D. 1421.

VIII. AMURATH

the Second, was the son of Mahomet; he proved a wretched tyrant, and was permitted as a scourge of God, to correct the sins of the christians. Soon after Amurath began his reign, a person sprung up calling himself Mustapha, the son of Bajazet; but it would seem he was an impostor, as the real Mustapha was supposed to have been killed in battle before the death of Bajazet. However the Greeks supported this man, and set him up with sufficient materials and supplies of war, to fight against Amurath. But in conclusion he not being able to make his party good, came into the hands of his enemy, and had his neck broke with a bow-string, after the manner of the Turkish execution.

The Greeks, then terrified with this sinister adversity, required truce of the Turk; but when that would not be granted, they set up another Mustapha, who, likewise being armed by the Greeks, got the city of Nice in Bithynia, from Amurath. Although it was not long before he was overcome in the same city, and brought to Amurath; who caused him likewise to taste of the same death, as the other Mustapha had done before. Amurath being now out of all fear and doubt of brethren and kinsfolk to rise against him, collected all his power against the Greeks; and first ranging throughout Thrace, where many cities surrendered to them, which before belonged to the emperor of Constantinople, from thence he set forward to the noble and famous city of Thessalonica, being then under the liege and protection of the Venetians. After Thessalonica was subdued, Phocis with all the country about Athens, Bœtia likewise, Ætolia, Acarnania, with all the region beyond Peloponnesus, to the coast of Corinth, were brought in bondage and slavery unto the Turk.

In Epirus, and in that quarter that adjoins Macedonia named Albania, one John Castriot then reigned; who, perceiving himself too weak to match with the Turk's power, made with the Turk this convention, that he should have Croya, a famous city in Greece, and also gave to him his three sons for hostages, to wit, Constantine, Reposius, and George.

In this George there appeared such noble courage, such vigour of mind, and strength of body, that the Turk caused him more freely to be instructed after the Turkish religion and manner in his own court; where being trained up, he so excelled as well in feats of activity, as in strength of body, that he excelled all his companions, so that he was named Scanderbeg, which means as much as Alexander the Great.

After this Alexander was grown up to mature ripeness of age, and was well trained up in feats of war, he was sent out by the Turk to war against Caraman of Cilicia, the Turk's enemy. In which expedition he sped himself most manfully, fighting hand to hand, first with a footman of Scythia, then with an horseman of Persia, being challenged by them both to encounter, first with the one, after with the other; whom he so valiantly overthrew, that he won great renown with the Turk: insomuch that he, trusting to the Turk's favour, when he heard of the decease of his father, durst ask of the Turk the grant of his father's dominion to be given to him. Which request, although Amurath the Turk did not deny him; yet notwithstanding, he perceiving the matter to be dallied out with fair words, by subtle means and policy slipped out of the Turk's court, and came to Epirus his own inheritance, where first by forged letters he recovered Croya. The other cities voluntarily yielded themselves to him; then gathering to him the people of Epirus and Macedonia (who though not many in number, yet with good willing minds they stuck to him) he so manfully and valiantly behaved himself, that against all the power both of Amurath, and also of Mahomet, he maintained his own, repelled their violence, and put to flight their armies many years together. But to return again to the course of Amurath's victories, after he had prevailed against the eastern parts of Europe and Greece, and had treated thus for the dominion of Epirus, he invaded Illyricum, (now called Sclavonia) containing in it Dalmatia, Croatia, Istria, and Liburnia; which countries he spoiled and wasted, and then continued his course to Albania and Bosnia. In which regions, when he had subdued a great part, and had led away an innumerable multitude of captives, he moved further to Wallachia and Servia, hoping to conquer all Pannonia.

There reigned at the same time in Servia, a certain prince named George Despota, who made great suit to the Turk for truce and peace, promising to give him his

---

(1) The period from the death of Bajazet to the accession of Mahomet is usually styled "The Interregnum," the kingdom being divided by the contention of the brothers, but it was again united under Mahomet.—[ED.]

daughter in marriage; for by the Turks' law they marry as many wives as they please. It was not long after Amurath had married the daughter of Despota, that he, contrary to his league and promise, made war upon Despota his father-in-law, and expelled him out of his kingdom, taking from him divers cities, as Scopia, Novomonte, Sophia, and all Mysia. George himself fled into Hungary, leaving behind him his son to defend the town of Sinderonia. Amurath understanding of the flight of Despota his father-in-law, compassed the city of Sinderonia with a strong siege, which when he had taken he took his wife's brother, the son of Despota, and without all regard of mercy and affinity, after the barbarous tyranny of the Turks, put out his eyes, with a bason red hot set before his eyes, and after that led him about with him in derision and in despite of his cowardly father.

Servia being thus won, Amurath, thinking to go further into Hungary, besieged the city called Belgrade, and no doubt would have also destroyed it, had not the Providence of God found means, that partly through slaughter of his men, partly for lack of victuals and other forage, he was compelled to raise his siege and retire.

In the mean time John Huniades (of whom mention was made before) had got great victories against the Turkish power, and had recovered part of Servia, and all Moldavia; against whom Amurath the Turk, with a mighty army, moved into Pannonia. But Huniades with the power and aid of Ladislaus king of Poland, (and more especially by the power of the Lord) did soon weaken the power of the Turk, and gave him the overthrow, recovering to the christians the greatest part of Servia and Bulgaria.

In this battle Huniades had five conflicts with the Turks upon one day, and with five victories put them to the worse, and toward night did so discomfit and overthrow the great captain of Amurath, called Bassa, the duke of Anatolia, (which is otherwise named Asia Minor) that he slew of the Turks that day to the number of thirty thousand. Amurath, although he was not a little discouraged thereat, yet dissembling his fear, with stout countenance sent for Carambeius his principal stay and captain, with a new army brought out of Asia to assist him in his wars. This Carambeius, having arrived in the downs of Transylvania, Ladislaus the king of Poland (the Lord so working) through the industry of John Huniades, so received and with such celerity overcame him, that all his stout and sturdy army either was slain downright, or else put to flight, Carambeius the captain being himself taken prisoner in the same field.

These victories of Huniades struck no little terror to Amurath, so that for distress of mind he was ready to destroy himself (as some write) but being confirmed by Helibeus Bassa his counsellor, he kept himself within the straits of Mount Rhodope. Who then hearing that Caramannus invaded the country of Bithynia and Pontus in Asia, was glad to make truce with Ladislaus and Huniades upon such conditions as they pleased to make themselves; which conditions were these, that Amurath should depart from all the region of Servia, and should remove from thence all his garrisons; also he should restore George Despota, prince of Servia, to his possession, and set his children free, whom he had in captivity, and restore them to their inheritance. And that he should make no more claim nor title to the country of Moldavia above mentioned, nor to that part of Bulgaria which he had lost; and that he should desist hereafter from all wrongs and injuries against the christians. Upon these conditions the Turk being agreed, truce was concluded on both parts for ten years, and confirmed with a solemn oath between them.

This done, Amurath the tyrant addresseth himself toward Asia, to resist the invasion of Caramannus. At which time Pope Eugenius so soon as he heard the Turk to be returned into Asia, sent Julian Cæsarian his cardinal to Ladislaus, with full dispensation and absolution to break his oath and league with the Turk, promising moreover great hope and aid, if he would go in arms stoutly against the tyrant.

Where by the way is to be noted, that as there is no truth of promise in that pestilent see of Rome, neither was there ever any war prospered, which was taken in hand by the pope's council; so was there never any council of the pope that brought with it more detriment to christianity, than this. But the pope belike thought that as he might lawfully break promise with John Huss, and with other christians, so also he need not to observe any league or truce taken with the Turk: but it turned much otherwise than the pope imagined, as is to be seen by the sequel. For Ladislaus, being thus excited by the unadvised and sinister instigation of Pope Eugenius, contrary to the truce established a little before, set out with his army, and proceeding to Wallachia and Bulgaria, came to Varna, where he fell sick.

It was not long, but the Turk, having intelligence of this, left his wars in Asia, and made haste into Europe, passing over by the straits near to Callipolis, where all the Italian navy was looking on, but whether on purpose, or whether for cowardliness, they would not stir one oar to stop the passage of the Turkish army. When Amurath was come to Adrianople in Thrace, using such celerity as no man looked for, within eight days he was in Bulgaria, and there encamped himself against Ladislaus. The day of battle being set, the armies joined on both sides. Huniades was himself present, but all the matter was ruled by Julian the cardinal, and the pope's clergy. The fight continued three days and three nights together, with great courage and much bloodshed on each side; so that the field was covered with lakes of blood. It seemed at the first to incline to the christians, by breaking the first ranks of the Turks. But the priests and prelates who were at the field (who had been more fit to have been in the church) seeing the Turks to begin to fly, unskilfully left their array to pursue the enemy, so that they leaving the other posts of the christians naked, gave great advantage to the Turks with their darts and shot to disturb the christian ranks. By which occasion Amurath, enclosing the christians with his army round about, obtained the victory. In which field, Ladislaus, the young king of Poland, having his horse killed under him, was struck down and slain. The pope's bishops flying to save themselves, fell into the marshes, and were there destroyed, sustaining a death worthy of their filthy falsehood and untruth. Julian the cardinal, who, with the pope, was the chief doer in breaking the league, was found dead in the way, full of wounds, and spoiled to naked skin. Of the rest of the army that escaped by flying, part was drowned in the marshes, some perished miserably for hunger, some for cold, watching and wandering in the woods. Huniades hardly escaped the danger, by the merciful providence of God, being reserved to the further profit of Christendom. This battle of Amurath against the christians was fought at Varna, A. D. 1444.

This John Huniades, the worthy warrior, was born in Wallachia, being earl of Bistice, of all captains that ever went against the Turks he was most famous and singular, prudent and discreet in council, expert and politic in war, prompt of hand, circumspect before he attempted, quick in expedition: in whom was wanted almost no good property requisite in a warlike captain. Against two most mighty and fierce tyrants, Amurath and Mahomet, through the Lord's might, he defended all Pannonia, and therefore was called the thunderbolt and terror of the Turks. As Achilles was to the Grecians, so was he set up of God to be as a wall or bulwark of all Europe against the cruel Turks and enemies of Christ and of his christians. Neither was there any king or prince that ever achieved such noble victories, either so many in number, or so profitable for the public utility of all Europe, as did he, and that not only in the days of this Amurath, but also of Mahomet his successor, as hereafter remains further to be seen.

Amurath, by reason of this victorious overthrow of the christians, being filled with no small pride, directed his journey immediately toward the Greeks, where Castriot was, otherwise called Scanderbeg.

And first coming to Peloponnesus, and breaking down the wall about the straits of Corinth, encountered the brother of the emperor of Constantinople, whom, with his sudden coming, he oppressed, with all the Greeks' army, ere they were provided. Paleologus, the emperor, after that, built up the wall again, but at the Turk's bidding, he was compelled to undo it again: which wall afterwards the Venetians repaired. After the demolition of the wall, Amurath entering into Peloponnesus, took several towns and cities, and made all the parts of Thessaly and Achaia tributaries.

In the following year, the Turk bent all his force against the country of Epirus, which the noble and victorious Scanderbeg valiantly defended against all the power of Amurath; so that he discomfited and vanquished seven of the most expert dukes of the Ottoman emperor, one after another, with all their armies of most picked and chosen soldiers, and expelled them utterly out of all Epirus.

After this discomfiture, the saying is, that Amurath gave himself to a religious order, living a contemplative life with certain other priests, in the forests of Bithynia, renouncing the government of his realm to the hands of Haly, one of the princes (for the reader must understand, that the Turks also be not without their sundry sects of religion, no more than we christians are without our friars and monks.)

While Amurath was cloistered in his monkish religion, John Huniades, in the kingdom of Hungary; and Castriot Scanderbeg in Greece, kept a great stir against the Turks. By reason of which Amurath was taken again from his monkish vow and profession, and brought again into the field: for Huniades had rescued the whole country of Hungaria, and had repulsed all the army of the Turks far from Servia. And although the peevish practice of George, prince of Servia, had oftentimes disclosed his councils unto the Turks, whereby twice he was brought in danger, yet, notwithstanding, (through the Lord's gracious protection) he was preserved and delivered by the said George unto the Hungarians again, and after that manfully vanquished the Turks, so that they had no resting place about those parts of Servia and Bulgaria, so long as he lived.

Castriot Scanderbeg so foiled the Turk, and kept Amurath so short, that, coming from Epirus in the straits, he was so entangled by Castriot, that he was forced to give battle. In which battle he was so vanquished, and most part of his army slain, that, for grief and sorrow, falling into a raving sickness, he was transported out of his pavilion to Adrianople, and there in fury and madness died, after he had reigned thirty years, which was about the year 1451.

This Amurath first established the order of the Janizaries, who were the male children of such christians as he conquered and took captive; whom he forced to renounce the faith of Christ, wherein they were baptized, and brought them up in Mahomet's law, and exercised them in the same feats of war as he did his own people, and after they came to man's estate, he named them Janizaries (that is to say) soldiers of a strange country, and made them guard his person. They wear on their head, instead of a helmet, a white attire made of the coarsest sort of wool, and in so many folds about their head that it cannot be pierced with a sword. It hangs down on the back with a tail, and before, on the forehead, it is garnished with gold and silver. They formerly used bows and lances in the field, but now they use sabres and fire-arms as our cavalry do.

At the first institution there were but eight thousand, but now there are twice as many. This, of all bondage and servitude that the christians suffer under the Turks, is most intolerable, and greatly to be lamented by all true christians. For what can godly minds behold more to their grief, than to see their children pulled from the faith of Christ wherein they were baptized, and by whose blood they should eternally be saved, and to be instructed and nourished with the blasphemous doctrine of Mahomet, and so be professed enemies of Christ and his church, to make war against heaven, and to perish everlastingly? And, finally, what a lamentable thing is it, to see and behold our own children born of our own bodies, to become our mortal and cruel enemies, and to cut our throats with their own hands! This servitude of mind is far greater than death itself: which, if our princes would well consider, it would cause them the rather to agree, and bend their whole force and power against this cruel enemy.

IX. MAHOMET the Second.—Amurath left behind him three sons,—Mahomet, born of the daughter of Despota, being twenty years of age; the second son, called Turcines; the third, named Calepinus. This Turcines, being an infant, and but eighteen months old, was strangled at the commandment of the Turk, by his servant Moses, himself being there present and beholding the horrible murder. And when Moses, the executioner of the murder had desired him not to pollute his hands with the blood of his brother, he answered, that it was the manner of all the Ottoman Turks, that all the other brethren being destroyed, none should be left alive but one to govern the empire. Wherefore, Moses was commanded by the tyrant, there presently, and in his sight, to kill the infant. This horrible fact, when the mother of the child understood, she cried out, and almost mad for sorrow, cursed the tyrant to his face. But he, to mitigate the rage of his mother, at her request, being desirous to be revenged upon the executioner of her son's death, delivered Moses bound into her hands, who then, in the presence of the tyrant, thrust him to the heart with a knife, and opening his side, took out his liver, and threw it to the dogs to be devoured.

The third son, called Calepinus, who was but six months old, and who had been commended, by his father Amurath, to the custody of Halibassa, one of his nobles, who, to gratify and please the tyrant, betrayed the infant, and brought him to him, and he, at the tyrant's commandment, was strangled. Some affirm, that instead of Calepinus another child was offered to the tyrant, and that Calepinus was conveyed to Constantinople, and after the taking of Constantinople was carried to Venice, and then to Rome to Pope Calixtus, where he was baptized, and afterward came into Germany to Frederic the emperor, and there was honourably entertained, and kept in Austria during his life. Where note, how the merciful providence of God can fetch out of the devil's mouth. And note, moreover, Halibassa, the betrayer of the infant, how he escaped not. For Mahomet, understanding him to be a man of great substance and riches, through forging of false crimes, with great torments, put him to death to have his riches; for this tyrant was given to insatiable avarice. Thus this bloody Mahomet began his reign with horrible murder, after the example of other cursed tyrants his predecessors.

Although this Mahomet came of a christian mother, being the daughter of Despota, prince of Servia, and by her was brought up and instructed from his childhood in the precepts of christian religion and manners, yet, he soon forgetting all, gave himself to Mahomet's religion, and yet so, that he being addicted to neither religion, became an atheist, believing and worshipping no God at all, but only the goddess of good fortune, mocking the minds and judgments of men, who believe that God, by his providence, governs and regards the state of human things on earth.

After this Mahomet having heard of the victories and conquests of his predecessors, and having understood how Bajazet lay eight years about Constantinople, and could not win it; he dispraising Bajazet, and disdaining that so long time should be spent about the siege and yet no victory gotten, bent all his study and device how to subdue the same. But first, having a privy hatred against the city of Athens, and having his hands lately imbrued with the blood of his brethren, this murdering Mahomet first of all takes his voyage to subvert and destroy that famous school of all good learning and discipline. Against which city he so furiously raged for the hatred of good letters, that he thought he ought not to suffer the foundation thereof to stand, because that city was a good nurse and fosterer of good arts and sciences; wherefore he commanded the city to be razed and utterly subverted; and wherever any monuments or books could be found, he caused them to be cast into dirty sinks, and the filthiest places of the city, or put to the most vile uses that could be devised, for extirpating and abolishing all good literature; and if he understood that any lamented the loss, and ruin of that noble place, those he grievously punished and put to death.

Thus the famous and ancient school of Athens being destroyed, he turned his army into Thrace, where in all haste he, gathering his power both by sea and land, with a mighty multitude compassed the city of Constantinople, and began to lay his siege against it, in the year 1453; and in the four-and-fiftieth day of the siege it was taken, sacked, and the Emperor Constantine slain. As touching the cruelty and fierceness of the Turks in getting of this city, and what slaughter there was of men, and women, and children, what calamity and misery was there to be seen, as sufficient relation, with a full description, hath been made before, it would be superfluous now to repeat the same. This only is not to be omitted touching the principal causes of the overthrow of this city; whereof the first was the filthy avarice of those citizens, who, hiding their treasures in the ground, would not employ the same to the necessary defence of their city. For so I find it in history, that when the Turk, after the taking of the city, had found not so much treasure as he looked for, suspecting with himself (as the truth was) the treasures and riches to be hidden under the ground, commanded the earth to be dug up, and the foundations of the houses to be searched: where he then found treasures incredible. "What (quoth he) how could it be that this place could ever lack ammunition and fortification, which did flow and abound with such great riches, and plenty of all things?" The second cause was the absence of the navy of the Venetians, which, if they had been ready in time, might have been a safeguard against the invasion of the enemies.

Joannes Ramus, writing of the destruction of this city, amongst other matters makes relation of the image of the crucifix, being there in the high temple of Sophia; which image the Turk took, and writing this superscription upon the head of it, "This is the God of the christians," gave it to his soldiers to be scorned, and commanding the image, with a trumpet, to be carried through all his army, made every man to spit at it most contumeliously. Wherein the reader by the way may note, what occasion of slander and offence we christians give to the barbarous infidels by this our ungodly superstition, in having images in our temples, contrary to the express commandment of God in his word. For if St. Paul, writing to the Corinthians, saith, "We know Christ now no more after the flesh;" how much less then is Christ to be known by us in blind stocks and images set up in our temples, serving for no other purpose, but for the infidels to laugh both us and our God to scorn, and to provoke God's vengeance?

To make the history short, such was the cruelty of these Turks in winning the city, that when Mahomet had given license to the soldiers three days together, to spoil, to kill, and to do whatever they pleased, there was no corner in all Constantinople, which did not either flow with christian blood, or else was the scene of abomination and cruelty. Of which citizens, some they murdered, some they roasted upon spits, some they flayed off their skin, hanging them up to consume with famine, others they put salt into their wounds, the more terribly to torment them, so that one contended with another, who could devise most strange kinds of new torments and punishments, exercising such cruelty, that the place where the city was before, seemed now to be no city, but a slaughter-house or shambles of christian men's bodies. Among the dead bodies, the body also of Constantine the emperor was found; whose head, being brought to Mahomet, he commanded it to be carried upon a spear through the whole city, for a public spectacle and derision to all the Turkish army. And because he would diminish the number of the captives, who seemed to him to be very great, he never rose from

his table, but he put every day some of the nobles to death, in order to fill his cruel mind with blood, as his body was filled with wine; which he used to do so long as any of the nobles of that city were left alive. And of the other sort also, as histories credibly report, there passed no day in which he did not slay more than three hundred persons, the rest he gave to his soldiers to kill, and to do with them what they would. It is here to be noted, that as Constantine, the son of Helena, was the first emperor of Constantinople, so Constantine, the son also of Helena, was the last emperor.

Not far from the city of Constantinople, there was another little city, called Pera, and once called Galata, situated by the sea-side, who, hearing of the miserable destruction of Constantinople, and seeing the city flaming with fire, sent certain of the chief men with speed to Mahomet, declaring to them, that they neither had sent any help to the city of Constantinople, neither yet wrought any injury to any of his army; wherefore they desired and prayed him, that as they would gladly yield unto him, so he would be favourable to them, and spare them, and not to punish the guiltless with the guilty. Mahomet, although he was not ignorant that for fear, rather than of any good-will, they submitted themselves, and that they would rather resist him if they had been able, yet received for that time the submission of the messengers: but sending with them his ambassadors into the city, he commanded also his army to follow withal, and to enter with him into the city, which, although it was greatly suspected and disliked by the citizens, yet they durst not otherwise do but suffer them to enter; which being done, the ambassador gave a sign to the soldiers, every man to do whatever he was bidden; of whom, some ran to the walls, some to the temples and churches, some to the streets and houses of the city, plucking all things down to the ground, sacking and ranging with no less fury and abomination than they had done at Constantinople before, saving only that they abstained from murder: but the same day, letters came from Mahomet to the ambassador, that he would spare none, but destroy and murder all that were in the city; which message, because it seemed to the ambassador to be too cruel, as they had yielded themselves, he stayed his hand a little until night came. In the mean time, drunken Mahomet, coming something to himself, (whom drunkenness had before overcome) sent his second letters to revoke the first. Where again is to be noted the merciful providence of God towards his people in their deserved plagues, by staying the hands, and bridling the fury many times of their enemies, when otherwise the case seems to be past all remedy.

Mahomet thus being in himself not a little advanced and elevated by the winning of Constantinople, which he had now made the imperial seat of the Turkish dominion, on the third year following set out to the siege of Belgrade, a city of Hungary, lying near the banks of the Danube, thinking to have the like success there, as he had in the winning of Constantinople, although through the Lord's disposing, it fell out much otherwise. Within the city of Belgrade, at the time of the siege, was John Huniades, the valiant captain, of whom mention has been made before; who with a sufficient strength of picked soldiers, although in number nothing equal to the Turk's army, valiantly defended the city with great courage, and no less success. In which siege great diligence was bestowed, and many of the Turks slain. Among whom also Mahomet himself, being wounded under the left arm, was carried out of the field half dead, and the rest so put to flight, that of the Turks were destroyed to the number, or not much under the number of forty thousand, besides the loss of all their ordnance, which the Turks, in haste of their flight, were forced to leave behind them.

Jerome Zieglerus, writing of the siege of this Belgrade, adds, that when Mahomet was at the siege, seeing the town so small and weak of itself, that it could not be won with all his great multitude, commanded all his brazen pieces to be laid, to batter down the walls and towers of the town: so that the christians within the walls were vehemently distressed: for the siege continued both night and day without intermission. Among the rest of the christians who defended the town, was a certain Bohemian much worthy of commendation, who being upon the walls, and seeing that a Turk with a banner or ensign of the Turks had got up, by the sight whereof the whole town was in danger to be conquered and taken, runs to the Turk, and clasping him about the middle, speaking to John Capistranus standing below, asking him whether it were any danger of damnation to him, if he, of his voluntary mind, did cast himself with that dog (so he termed him) down headlong from the wall, to be slain with him; what would become of his soul, and whether he might be saved or not? To whom when the other had answered, that he should be saved without doubt, he forthwith tumbles himself with the Turk down off the wall, where by his death, he saved at the same time the life of all the city. Mahomet being so wounded, and in despair of winning the city, was carried, as he heard, out of the field; who at length coming again to himself, partly for fear, and partly for shame, was ready to kill himself. And thus was the town of Belgrade at that time rescued through God's providence, by the means of John Huniades and this Bohemian.

This siege of Belgrade began A. D. 1456, and endured six-and-forty days. At which siege were two hundred thousand Turks; of whom forty thousand were slain, where the victory fell to the christians through the prosperous success given of God to John Huniades. Which Huniades, not long after the victory, through the labour and fatigue in defending the town, was taken with a sore sickness, and died; to whose valiant prowess and singular courage, histories give great praise and commendation.

Mahomet after this done in Europe, returned into Asia to war with Usumcassanes, a Persian, with whom he had three battles; the first was about the river Euphrates, where the Turk lost ten thousand men, and was put to the worse. In the second field likewise, he was discomfited. The third battle at Arsenga, where through the terrible noise of the brazen pieces, the Persian horses disturbed the camp, and so was Usumcassanes overcome.

From thence the Turk reduced again his power against the christians, and first subdued unto him Synope, and all Paphlagonia; also the kingdom of Trebizond, which he besieging both by land and water, won from the christians, and sent David the king with his two sons, and Calus his uncle, to Constantinople, where they were miserably and cruelly put to death, and all the family of the Comneni, which were of the king's family, were destroyed by the Turk; which was about A. D. 1461, at which time this mischievous Mahomet was first saluted emperor.

Not long after he got from the Grecians, Corinth and Mitylene, not without great slaughter of christian men; insomuch that the whole city of Mitylene was destroyed almost to the ground. The isles also of Lemnus and Lesbos he won from the Venetians; in which island of Lesbos is the city of Mitylene.

Not far from this isle of Lesbos and Mitylene, there is a country in Asia toward the sea-side, bordering next to Europe, called Mysia, or of some called Mæsia, wherein stood the city of Troy. This country Mahomet coveting to win rather by policy and falsehood, than by doubtful danger of war, secretly sent for the prince to come to speak with him for certain causes (as he pretended) which would concern the profit and commodity of them both. When the king of Mysia, either for shame would not, or for fear durst not deny, he came to him as to confer upon necessary affairs in common to them appertaining. Mahomet caused the king to be apprehended, and cruelly slain, or rather torn in pieces; and so invading the land of Mysia, he exercised the like tyranny upon his kindred and affinity.

This Mysia by fraud being taken and lost, Mahomet flies again towards Europe, where he assailed the island Euboia, otherwise called Nigropont, making a bridge of marvellous fame over the sea Euripus, to convey over his army out of Greece, and there laid his siege to the city Chalcis, which at length in thirty days he overcame,

not without a great slaughter of his army, who in the siege is said to have lost forty thousand of the Turks. But the slaughter of the christians was greater, for when the city was won, the tyrant commanded, most cruelly, none to be spared within the whole city, but to be put to the sword, whoever was above the age of twenty years. This cruelty was shewed of the barbarous tyrant for anger and fury, because such a number of his Turks were slain at the siege thereof, being reckoned (as is said) to forty thousand. In the fierce siege of this city it is memorable that is in histories recorded, how that the women of that city, seeing the men begin to faint, and the city to lie in present danger, took the matter themselves in hand, and playing the men, went to the walls, and there defended the city with no less trouble to the enemy than the men had before done, and so for a space continued, so long as any man's strength and diligence could do any good. A great cause of the loss of this city and island, is imputed to the cowardly timidity of the Venetian navy; who being there present, and having prosperous wind, yet durst not, or would not adventure upon the Turks' bridge, which if they had done, the island of Euboia and Chalcis had not so soon been overmatched of the Turks.

Thus all the east parts of Greece being subdued to the Turkish tyrant, with all Achaia, Attica, Acarnania, and Euboia, shortly after followed also Peloponnesus, brought in like subjection to the Turk. Within Peloponnesus were these provinces contained, Achaia, Messenia, Laconia, Argolica and Archadia, &c. The Venetians in this Peloponnesus had great possessions, and had made up the wall again toward the sea-side, near to the straits of Corinth, where for the more speed of the work, they had thirty thousand workmen in the building; which, when it came to the knowledge of the Turk, he broke into the country of Peleponnesus, with an army of eight thousand, and first wasted the regions of the Coroneans and Methoneans, and making a great slaughter of the Venetians, in short time he brought the whole dominion of Peloponnesus under his yoke and tribute.

It is long and more lamentable to recite all the victories of Mahomet against the christians, both by land and sea. Before was declared how truce was taken between Georgius Scanderbeg, and the Turk for ten years; which truce being expired, Mahomet leaves no time unspent, no diligence unsought, but makes with all his power to Epirus and Albania, which he, after long siege, at length overcame and subdued. When Scanderbeg the valiant captain had done against the Turk what in man's strength did lie, yet being overmatched with power and multitude, seeing no possibility to make his party good, he was forced to depart his country as an exile, and went to Italy, and there being sent for by the pope's letters, openly declared that it was not possible otherwise to resist the furious rage of the barbarous Turks by the strength of any one king or prince, unless all Europe with one consent should join their power and force together. And thus, Scanderbeg, a man of puissant courage, being driven out of his country, continued his life in exile. His courage and vehemency is reported to have been such, that in fighting against the barbarous enemy, for very eagerness of spirit, his blood was seen to burst out of his lips. It is testified also of him, that being challenged he never refused to fight, and in fighting, never turned his back, neither yet was he ever wounded but only once with a light shaft in his foot, neither did he ever set against the Turk with more than six thousand horsemen and three thousand footmen. He is said with his own hand to have slain above two thousand Turks, whom with such violence he did strike, that many of them he did cleave asunder, from the head to the middle.

Neither yet was the insatiable greediness of this Turkish hell-hound satisfied with all this, but still he conceived greater things in his mind, thinking to conquer the whole world; and so passing forward towards Europe, he subdued all Illyria. Then passing into Wallachia, set upon Dracula, the prince thereof. Dracula, although he had no great power of soldiers, yet so enclosed and environed the Turk, that he had almost lost his whole army, of whom a great part was destroyed, and many of his ensigns taken. Shortly afterwards he sent Ahmet with one hundred ships into Italy, and he, passing along by the coast, spoiled and wasted several places, till at length he came to Hydruntium (Otranto) a city in Calabria in Italy, which after a long siege he overcame and subdued, and brought such a terror into all Italy, that the pope, forgetting all other things, yet mindful of himself, with all haste fled out of Rome. After the city of Hydruntium was taken, which was A. D. 1481, Matthias Corvinus, Huniades's son, was sent for by the Italians, to set upon the city, for its rescue, when Ahmet was about to make his return with five-and-twenty thousand Turks, in the meantime news came that Mahomet the great Turk was dead; the siege brake up, and the city was delivered to the Italians again, and so Italy was delivered at that time out of peril and danger. This Mahomet won from the christians two hundred cities, and twelve kingdoms, and two empires, which he joined both together. He died A. D. 1481, after having reigned fifty years.

X. BAJAZET the Second.—Mahomet had three sons; of which Mustapha, the eldest, through voluptuousness, died before his father. The other two were Bajazet and Demes; about whom great controversy arose amongst the Turks, which of them should succeed in their father's kingdom. For neither of them was present at Constantinople when Mahomet died; Bajazet being in Cappadocia, and Demes, in Lycaonia, when great dissension was among the nobles for the succession, and great strife and bloodshed for the matter, the janizaries, who were the Turk's guard, proclaimed Bajazet emperor. Bajazet coming at length from Cappadocia, partly through yielding, partly by corrupting with money, got the wills of the janizaries, and was made emperor. Demes, the other brother, being in Lycaonia more near, although he made no less speed in his coming, yet was prevented by Bajazet, and excluded out of Constantinople. Wherefore, he being put back from all hope of his kingdom, incited by some of his friends, moved war against his brother; but being overcome in three battles by Ahmet, Bajazet's captain, fled to the great master of Rhodes, leaving in a place called Carræ, his mother and two young children, whom Bajazet slew.

This Demes being with the master of the knights of Rhodes, was sent to the bishop of Rome, where being kept, and afterwards sent to Charles VIII., for an hostage of Pope Alexander VI. was poisoned by the way by Pope Alexander, as is before declared. After whose death, Bajazet, to requite Ahmet for his good service, put him to the halter, partly suspecting his power, partly for lucre sake, to have his treasure: his death was of great profit to the christians, as he was ever an utter enemy to the religion and name of Christ.

Bajazet thus being confirmed in his tyranny, made his expedition against Wallachia, where he subdued two great forts. From thence he removed his power, taking his voyage into Asia, thinking to be revenged of the sultan of Egypt, where he lost two great battles, the one fought at Adena, the other at Tarsus; but especially at Tarsus, the army of the Turk was so overthrown, that of an hundred thousand brought into the field, scarce the third part remained unslain.

Thus Bajazet being overthrown and terrified with evil luck, fighting against the sultan of Egypt, removed from Asia, and directed his army into Europe. Leading his army against the Venetians, he had with them many and doubtful conflicts, where the Turk was sometimes put to the worse, and sometimes again prevailed; out of Jadra and other cities about Dalmatia, he carried away great multitudes of christians into captivity, about A. D. 1498.

Two years after this, which was A. D. 1500, Bajazet with one hundred and fifty thousand armed men, entered into Peloponnesus; which although Mahomet had overrun before, yet the Venetians had defended Methone, or Modon, all this while against the Turks. The Turk besieged this city with three armies, having about the walls five hundred great brazen cannons, wherewith he bat-

tered the city both day and night: but the citizens, who were within the city committing themselves to God, defended their city as well as they could, rather choosing to die than to yield unto the Turk's tyranny. But the Turk prevailing, and they not able to withstand the siege, the christians assembled together into a certain house prepared for the purpose, both men, women, and children; where they setting the house on fire, gave themselves rather to be burned than to come into the tyrant's hands. Certain women also, with their children, cast themselves headlong into the sea, by that means to avoid the Turkish captivity. Some writers affirm that the Methonians, seeing five great ships of the Venetians coming with men and provisions toward them, issued down from the walls to the sea side to receive them; but were all taken captives, being above the number of a thousand: and all being tied with long ropes, were brought before the tyrant, and in his sight were cruelly slain, except certain nobles, whom Cherseogles, son-in-law to Bajazet, got pardoned, amongst whom was Andreas Gritto.

The Turk had to maintain war in Asia against Ismail Sophi or king of Persia. Which Sophi was stirred up by God's providence to war with this Bajazet, whereby the christian churches in Europe might have some breathing time, and freedom from the Turk's cruel tyranny and bloodshed. This Sophi was a valiant Turk, who with great power and victories had overrun a great compass of the eastern parts of Asia; and defeated many of the generals of Bajazet.

Thus, through the admirable example of God's justice and providence, were these Turks kept occupied, and so came it to pass, that these barbarians being blasphemous against the Son of God, should thus horribly run on to the destruction one of another, being worthily punished with mutual slaughter and bloodshed for their impiety and blasphemy against Christ and his religion, whereby in the meantime some rest was given to the christians.

Bajazet, partly by these victories discouraged, partly diseased and languishing of the gout, and partly also broken with age, finding himself unequal to the government of that tumultuous kingdom, began to talk with his nobles about the choosing of one to succeed him. The occasion whereof ministered much matter of inward wars among the Turks. This Bajazet had in all six sons, whereof three died before him, and three were yet left alive; to wit, Ahmet, Korkud, and Selim. Bajazet himself had most mind to Ahmet, but the chief of his nobles rather favoured Selim; and provoked him to stir up war against his father: and though that he was overcome in war, yet through intercession he was reconciled to his father, and is afterwards proclaimed emperor again against his father's will, through the help and favour of the soldiers, entering the first beginning of his kingdom, with the murdering of his own father. The story in some authors is thus declared.

After the janizaries had persuaded Bajazet that as he himself was unwieldly, he should therefore do well to constitute some successor, and having assigned Ahmet to succeed him; the janizaries being offended with Ahmet, because he would not enlarge their stipends, and bribe them, compassing about the king's palace with their privy swords which they had under their garments, with a mighty cry, required Selim to be appointed for their emperor. When Bajazet had answered, that he had assigned Ahmet, they refused him, because he was fat, gross, and unable thereto; but needs would have Selim, who was stout and warlike, as their emperor: and withal they drew out their swords, crying Selim, Selim! Then Bajazet, giving place to their fury, shewed himself content to give them Selim; whom the janizaries receiving, brought into the palace: Bajazet his father giving place to him, desires him not to be so hasty and furious in his doings, but to be modest and take heed what he did, and not to follow his fury, but to give place to time, which reveals all things, and think himself to be a man subject to dangers and jeopardies as other men are: and thus speaking, he resigned his imperial throne and seat to him, and went away all heavy, entering into a certain order of their religion. Whereupon followed great acclamations of the people, saluting Selim as emperor. Who then taking the rule upon him, began to govern with great cruelty, destroying many of his nobles, such as had stood against him, some with poison, some by other cruel means, and advancing his own side, with great honours and promotions.

Not long after Selim was thus settled in his kingdom, Bajazet his father, intending to see and prove how he behaved himself in his government, first entered into his treasure-house, where he found all his riches to be scattered and gone. Afterward he came into his armory, where all the spoils gotten by war were likewise wasted; then he entered into the jewel-house, where all his plate and gifts sent from kings and princes were kept, which likewise were dispersed and given away. At length he came into the stable, where also he seeing his principal horses to be wanting, sighing with himself, and crying vengeance upon him, he prepared himself, with the rest of the treasure which was remaining, to sail over into Natolia to his eldest son; and passing by an orchard near the sea-side, where he had appointed to take ship, he sat down under a tree, and began to curse his son, and to ask vengeance upon him, for that he had so despised his father, and was become so impious a wretch.

Selim hearing of his father's departure came into the orchard where he was, and seeming to be very heavy, and much lamenting that his father would so depart and go away, seeing that he desired not the government of the empire, but was contented only with the title thereof. "O father, (said he) do not thus privily depart away; do not procure this shame to your son, who so tenderly loves you. Let me have but the name only, and be you the emperor indeed. The end of your natural life most patiently I shall expect, which I pray God may long continue." And thus using many fair and flattering words to his father, he commanded a banquet with many dainty delicacies to be brought to him, but tempered and infected with poison. Which as soon as Bajazet had begun to taste, and felt the strength of the poison working in his body, he took his last farewell of his son, and going out of the city accompanied with a great retinue of men, yelling and crying out in the streets, in the middle of his journey he fell down and miserably died, (A. D. 1512.) Here mayest thou see, good reader, a cursed brood of this Turkish generation, where the father dies in cursing the son, and the son reigns by poisoning his father.

XI. SELIM I.— After this wretched Selim had exercised his barbarous cruelty upon his father, with like impiety he seeks the destruction of his brethren and their children, first beginning his murder with the five children his nephews, which were the sons of his three brethren who had previously died, then remained his other two brethren yet alive, Ahmet and Korkud with their children, likewise to be destroyed. Of whom the one had three sons, whom the father sent to Selim his brother, and their uncle, with fair and gentle words, to entreat him to be good to their father, offering to him their duty and service in all things, honouring him also as emperor. But cruel Selim commanded forthwith his nephews to be strangled. The father hearing of the cruel murder of his sons, leaving house and home, went and hid himself in the mountains, where he lived for a space with herbs and wild honey; but being betrayed by one of his men, he was brought to Selim, and so was strangled.

The wars and conquests of this Selim were very many in various parts of Asia. From thence triumphing he departed to Constantinople, intending to spend the rest of his time in persecuting the christians; but in that mean space he was stricken with a cankered sore inwardly, and died after he had reigned about eight years (A.D. 1520.)

The reign of this Turk was but short in number of years; but in number of his murders and cruel blood-

shed it might seem exceedingly long, which lived more like a beast than a man, for he never spared any of his friends or kindred. His father first he poisoned, his brethren and all his cousins he quelled, leaving none of all his kindred alive. Moreover, his chief and principal captains for small occasions he put to death, as Mustapha, Calogere, Chendeme, Bostang his son-in-law, and Juno Bassa.

It is said that he intended the poisoning of his own son Solyman, sending to him a shirt infected with a poison, because he seemed something freely to speak against the cruel demeanour of his father; but by means of his mother, the gift being suspected, was given to another who was his chamberlain, who putting on the shirt was struck with the poison, and died.

As to this Turk Selim, by the way here may be noted how the secret providence of the Lord kept him occupied with his Turkish wars at home, while the reformation of christian religion here in Europe, begun by Martin Luther, might the more quietly take some root without disturbance or interruption. For so it appears, that in the days of this Selim, Martin Luther first began to write against the pope's indulgences, which was A.D. 1516.

XII. SOLYMAN—the only son of Selim, succeeded after his father's death. In the beginning he seemed to some to be simple and sheepish, and not meet for the Turkish government. Wherefore certain of his nobles, consulting how to depose him, intended to set up another emperor. In which conspiracy especially are named Cajerbeius and Gazelli. This Cajerbeius was he that betrayed Campson the sultan of Egypt to Selim, who now also being in consultation with Gazelli and others about this matter, detected them also to Solyman. Wherefore Gazelli and his fellows being thus detected, were put to death by Solyman, proving that he was not so sheepish as he was thought of them to be, and as by his acts afterwards more fully appeared.

Solyman, after this execution of the conspirators, taking his voyage into Europe, first besieged Belgrade, which being a city in Hungary, was the strongest fort of all the Roman empire, and the chief defence at that time of all Christendom. The kingdom of Hungary at that time was under the government of Lewis, a young king without experience or knowledge. Whom other princes, and especially the covetous churchmen, so plundered, that they left him nothing but the bare name and title of his kingdom, by which, he being unsupplied both with men and money, was unable to match with such an enemy.

Another advantage also which the Turks had in besieging Belgrade, was that the christian princes at that time were in civil dissension and variance among themselves, and the pope with his churchmen also were so busy in suppressing Luther, and the gospel then newly springing, that they minded nothing else, except it were to maintain their wealth: which pope if he had set his care (as his duty was) so much in stirring up princes against the common enemy, as he was bent to deface the gospel, and to persecute the true professors thereof, it might have brought to pass that Belgrade might have been defended against the Turk.

Certainly whatever the pope then did, this had been his duty, setting all other things aside, to have had an earnest compassion of so many miserable and lost captives, who were fallen from their faith and religion into the misery and slavery of the Turk, and thraldom of the devil, and to have sought all means possible to have brought them, as lost sheep, into the fold again; which might have been done, if prelates and princes, joining together in christian concord, had loved so well the public glory of Christ, and souls of christians, as they regarded their own private, worldly, and frivolous quarrels. And even supposing that the pope had conceived never so much malice against Luther, and supposing his quarrel also to be good, yet the public church standing in such danger, as it then did by the invasion of the Turk, reason would, nature led, religion taught, time required, that a good prelate, forgetting lighter matters, should rather have laid his shoulder to the excluding of so great a danger, as was then imminent to himself and the universal church of Christ; but now his quarrel being unjust, and the cause of Luther being most just and godly, what is to be said or thought of such a prelate, who forbearing the Turk, whom in a time so dangerous he ought chiefly to have resisted, persecuted the truth which he should specially have maintained?

Solyman therefore taking this occasion, while our princes were thus at variance, without any resistance or interruption brought his army to Belgrade (A.D. 1521); which city being but slenderly defended, the Turk through his underminers, guns, and other engines of war, without great difficulty, and with little loss of his soldiers, soon subdued and overcame it.

After this victory Solyman resting himself a whole year, and casting in his mind how to make all sure behind him, thought it expedient for his purpose if he might obtain the island of Rhodes, for that was the only christian place that remained between him and Asia; wherefore the next year he brought his army of four hundred and fifty ships, and three hundred thousand men, to the besieging thereof. This Rhodes was a mighty and strong island. The inhabitants at the first manfully resisted the Turk, sparing no labour nor pains for the defence of themselves and of all Christendom; but afterwards being brought to extremity, and pinched with penury, seeing also no aid come from the christians, they began to languish in themselves. The Turks in the meantime casting up two great mountains with strength of hand, two miles off from the city, like rolling trenches carried them before them near to the city, in the tops whereof they planted their ordnance and artillery to batter the city. The master of the knights of Rhodes was then one Philip Villadamus, a Frenchman, in whom no diligence was wanted requisite to the defence of the city. The Rhodians likewise so valiantly behaved themselves upon the walls, that with their shot all the ditches about the city were filled with the carcases of dead Turks. Besides this, such a disease reigned in the Turk's camp, that thirty thousand of them died; and yet for all this Solyman would not cease from his siege. At length, by underminers casting down the ramparts, and outermost parts of the city, he won ground still more and more upon the Rhodians, and with mortar-pieces so battered the houses, that there was scarcely a free place standing in all the city. And thus the siege continued for the space of five or six months, and yet all this while no help came to them from the christians. Wherefore they being out of all hope, through the advice of Villadamus, yielded themselves to the Turk, upon condition that he would spare them with life and goods, which convention the Turk kept with them faithfully and truly.

Thus Solyman to his great glory, and to the utter shame of all christian princes, and to the ruin of all Christendom, got the noble Isle of Rhodes, although not without great loss of his army, so that at one assault twenty thousand Turks about the walls were slain with fire, sword, stones, and other engines. Whereby it may be conjectured what these Rhodians might or would have done, if succour had come to them from other christian princes as they looked for. This city was won upon Christmas-day, A.D. 1522.

This conquest of Rhodes being secured, Solyman the fourth year after brings back his army into Hungary, where he found none to resist him but Lewis the young king, who being accompanied with a small army, and not able to match with the Turk, yet of a hasty rashness and vain hope of victory, would needs set upon him, who if he had staid but a little had prospered the better. For John Vaivoda, a captain well exercised in Turkish wars before, was not far off, coming with a sufficient force of able soldiers; but Paulus the archbishop of Colosse, a Franciscan friar, a man more bold than wise, with his temerity and rashness troubled all their doings. For the whole sum of the army of the Hungarians contained in all but only twenty-four thousand horsemen and footmen, who at length coming to the battle, and being compassed about with a great multitude of the Turk's army, were brought into great distress. The Turks twice shot off their pieces against the christian army, yet scarce was any christian touched, which was thought to be done on purpose, because they were christians who had the ordering of the guns, for then the special gunners of the Turks were christians, whom for the sake of their gunnery they spared. Then the Turk's horsemen, coming upon the rear of the christian army, compassed them about, and by reason of their multitude overcharged their horsemen. Among whom was slain at the same time the archbishop of Colosse, with the bishops of Strygone and Varadine, and many other nobles beside. Also the king himself was compelled to fly into a marsh, where falling from his horse, being heavy laden with the harness, he was not able to rise again, but there miserably perished.

Solyman the Turk marvelled at the foolishness of Lewis, who with so small an army would presume to encounter with such a great host of two hundred thousand. This battle in Hungary was fought A.D. 1526.

After the decease of Lewis, Ferdinand succeeded in the kingdom, being duke of Austria and king of Hungary. Then Solyman, setting contention between John Vaivoda and Ferdinand for the kingdom of Hungary, marched to the city of Buda, which also in short time he made to surrender upon condition that they should escape with their lives and goods.

In the year 1529, Ferdinand, king of Hungary, recovered several holds, and warring against John Vaivoda his enemy, expelled him out of his kingdom. Whereupon Vaivoda, flying to the Turk, desired his aid. The Turk, glad to take that occasion, with great preparation addressed himself to return into Hungary, where recovering again the city of Buda, which Ferdinand had got from him a little before, he removed his army into Austria, spoiling and destroying by the way all that came to his hands, shewing many examples of great cruelty and tyranny most lamentable to hear and understand. For of some he put out their eyes, of some he cut off their hands, of some their ears and noses. And these examples of horrible and barbarous tyranny this wretched Turk perpetrated by the way coming toward Vienna, a noble city in Austria, besides the captives which he took by the way and led into most miserable slavery, amounting to the number of thirty thousand.

Among other holds by the way as the Turks came, there was a castle called Altenburch, strongly situated by nature, and defended by art; which castle the Turk intending not to pass, because he would make all things sure behind him, began to make his assault, and lay his ordnance against it. The warders and keepers of the castle, so soon as the Turk began to lay siege against them, making no resistance, of a womanly cowardliness sent their messengers to the Turk, to yield themselves ready to do his commandment, and further him with their supplies. Among whom were three hundred Bohemians, who were commanded to follow the army, that the Turk by them might learn what strength was in the city of Vienna; also where the king was, and what was to be done for the winning thereof.

Of whom when the Turk had understanding how all things stood, and how there were but twenty thousand men in Vienna able to bear armour, and that other cities of Austria would soon yield if that were taken, and that Vienna was victualled but for two months, and that the king was of late in Bohemia; the Turk being certified of all things, having no doubt in his mind of victory, made speed toward Vienna; and first coming to Neapolis, a city but eight miles distant from Vienna, he required them to yield themselves; who notwithstanding withstood, and repulsed him valiantly. Then the Turks assigned a place for the pitching of their tents and because it seemed somewhat too little for such a great multitude, they took in more ground to the compass of seven miles circuit. The multitude of his army, which he there planted, is accounted of some to extend to two hundred and fifty thousand soldiers. The Turk thus being planted, made daily excursions over all the country of Austria, especially about the city of Vienna, wasting and spoiling with great cruelty and murder among the poor christians.

Moreover, to make all things more sure toward the preparation of the siege, scouts were sent abroad and ambushments were laid about the side of the river Danube, to provide that no aid nor provisions should be brought to Vienna. It so pleased the Providence of the Lord (who disposes all things) that three days before the coming of the Turk, Frederick the earl palatine, who was then assigned by the empire to take the charge of Vienna, was come down by the river Danube, with fourteen thousand men, and with a certain troop of horsemen, well appointed and picked for the purpose. After the coming of this Frederick, provision also was appointed to follow shortly after by the river.

In the mean time, they who had the carriage and transport, hearing how the ways were laid, and all the passages ten miles about Vienna stopped by the Turks, although they knew the city to stand in great need of provisions, yet seeing there was no other remedy, rather than it should come to the enemy's hand, thought it best to sink their boats with their carriage, and so they did. Whereby although the christians wanted their relief, yet were the Turks disappointed of their prey and purpose.

The captains who had the keeping of the city, were chiefly Frederick the earl palatine, William Rogendorf, and Nicolas earl of Salme, they seeing themselves so straightened contrary to their expectation, although they had great causes to be discouraged, yet calling their courage to them, they consulted together for the best way to be taken ; and seeing that the little city of Neapolis (above mentioned) being eight miles distant from them, so valiantly withstood the Turks, that in one day they sustained seven assaults against all the main force of the Turkish army ; by their example and manful standing being the more animated and encouraged, they determined to abide the utmost before they would give over ; and first plucking down all the suburbs and buildings without the walls whereby the enemy might have any succour, they commanded all the farmers and inhabitants about the city to save themselves, and to bring in their goods within the walls. Such places as were weak within the walls, they made strong. About the towers and munition of the walls they provided ramparts and bulwarks distant eighty feet one from another, to keep off the shot ; and every man had his place and standing awarded to him upon the wall, and his office appointed what to do ; but especially that side of the city which lies to the river Danube, they fortified after the best manner ; for that way only now remained for victuals to be transported from the Bohemians to them. Wherefore eight ensigns were assigned to the keeping of the bridge, and in the plain, which was like an island enclosed within the river, a sufficient garrison of horsemen were placed, lying within the gunshot of the city, that if any grain or victuals were sent from the Bohemians, they might provide the same safely to be brought into the city.

These things thus being disposed and set in order, Lord William Rogendorff, to try the strength of the Turks, made divers sallies out with his horsemen, although much against the minds of the Austrians ; who, knowing the manner of the Turks, thought it better to suffer them, while either they might be wearied with time, or consumed for lack of victuals. Among many skirmishes which the christians had with the Turks, one especially was unfortunate to our men ; in which certain of the horsemen spying a small troop of the Turks scattering abroad from their company, made out after them, who suddenly and guilefully were enclosed by the Turks, before they could recover the gates of the city, and so were all taken alive ; of whom three were sent from the Turks into the city, to declare to the Viennians what strength they had seen in the camp of their adversaries, and to solicit them to yield their city for fear of punishment which would follow. The rest they reserved to torments and punishment, whom in the sight of the whole army, and of the christians (who should tell the same to the citizens) they caused every man to be drawn with four horses a-pieces, and so to be dismembered and plucked asunder.

After this was done, the barbarous Turk immediately sent his herald to talk with the captains of the city, whether they would yield the city upon honest conditions, or else would abide the arbitrement of war. If they would gently submit themselves, they should have all gentleness shewed to them. If they would be stubborn, and stand to their defence, he would also stand to his siege, so that he would spare neither man, woman, or child. To this the captains answered again, that they were contented that Solyman should stand to his siege, and do his utmost, what he would, or what he could. As for them, they were resolved to defend themselves and their city so long as they could ; the event and issue of victory, they said, was doubtful, and many times it happens, that they who begin the war, are wearied sooner than they who are challenged.

Solyman, disdaining this answer, first burning and consuming all the villages, houses and places round about the city, poisoning the springs and fountains which gave water to the city, and so stopping all passages that no relief should have way to them, began to approach the city, with three great camps ; sending word in scorn and contumely by one of his captains, that if they stood in need of soldiers, he would send to them the three hundred Bohemians (mentioned a little before) to aid them in their defence. To whom the palatine directed answer again, that they had more soldiers in the city than they needed. As for the Bohemians who had yielded, he might do with them what he would, for Vienna stood in no great need of them.

In the mean time a messenger coming from Ferdinand was privately let in by night into the city, he brought word that they should occupy the men in keeping out the enemy awhile ; for it would not be long, but both Ferdinand and Charles his brother, with the strength of all Germany, would be ready to rescue them. At this message the hearts of the soldiers began somewhat to be cheered, and to contemn the multitude of the adversaries, whose army extended in compass seven miles round the city walls.

In the meantime Solyman beat down to the ground the ramparts, with all the suburbs of the city, and in such a short time, that the hearts of the inhabitants were appalled with fear, lest the Turk with celerity and violence should prevail against the walls, as he did in beating down the ramparts. And no doubt the Turk had put the city in great hazard, had not night coming on broken off the siege for that day.

In the mean time the citizens laboured all night in repairing and refreshing the walls, to make all things sure against the next assault. The next day early in the morning, the Turks approaching the city again for a new assault, thinking to scale the walls, were so repulsed and manfully resisted by the Germans, that the ditches about the walls could not be seen for the bodies of the dead Turks that filled them ; so that the Turks were obliged to fight standing upon the bodies of the slain.

It happened at the same time, that a company of the Turks being seen wandering out of order, the Captain Rogendorff with two legions of horsemen issuing out of the city gate called Salmaria, and passing closely under the hill's side, so set upon them, that they slew a great number of them ; the rest driven to take the river, they destroyed, and so retired back to the city again. By this victory the Captain Rogendorff began to be terrible to the Turks. For in the skirmish (as afterwards was known) were slain so many, that of five thousand and three hundred horsemen and footmen, scarce one hundred and forty escaped alive.

Solyman thought to try this matter another way, and so bringing his forces toward the gate called the King's Gate, there making his trenches and bulwarks, planted his ordnance, with the violence whereof the walls were so battered and shaken, that no man was able to stand there. The Turk, seeing two great breaches made in the wall, commanded his soldiers in the dark smoke of the gunpowder, to press into the city. The same also was done at the Scottish Tower, by which the city was invaded in two places at one time. The inhabitants at first began to withstand them, new soldiers still coming in the place of them that were slain ; and so this assault continuing more than six hours together, our men began at length to languish and faint, not only in strength but also in courage, by which the city was in great danger, had not the two captains, Rogendorff in one place, and the earl of Salme in the other, manfully encouraged the soldiers to abide the brunt, and to bear out awhile the violence of the Turks, promising that immediately they should have aid from Ferdinand.

In the mean time the Turks came so thick for greediness of victory, scaling, climbing, and fighting upon the walls, that had it not been for the press and throng of the great multitude of the Turks, coming so thick that one of them could not fight for another, Vienna had been taken and utterly lost. But by the policy of the captains giving a sign within the city, as though new soldiers were called for, our men began to be encouraged, and the Turks' hearts to be discomfited.

When Solyman saw his army the second time repulsed, he began to attempt a new way, purposing by undermining to overthrow the city ; in which work especially, he used the help of the Illyrians, of whom he had a great number in his camp, expert in that kind of feat. These Illyrians beginning to break the earth at the gate Carinthia, and coming near the foundations of the tower, which they had attempted to burst into, could not work so closely under the ground, but that they were perceived by certain men above ; who, countermining against them, and filling their trenches as they went with gunpowder, so conveyed their train, that when fire should be set to it, the violence should burst out by the trenches of the enemies ; which done, suddenly the ground beneath made a great shaking, so that the tower did cleave asunder, and all the underminers of the Turks, working in their trenches, were smothered and destroyed, which came to the number (as it was supposed afterward) of eight thousand persons.

When Solyman saw that this way also would not serve, and had private intelligence that the walls about the gates of Stubarium were negligently kept, and that he might have there more easy entrance ; he secretly moved about ten garrisons of fresh soldiers, so as the townsmen should not perceive them : who came so suddenly upon them, that they had filled their ditches, and were upon the top of the fortresses, before our men were aware of them, or could make themselves ready to resist them. For although there was no lack of soldiers within the city, yet the whole brunt of the siege lay especially at the two gates, from whence the soldiers could not be well removed ; men however were sent to the spot now attacked. And thus the assault continued terrible and doubtful until (the dark night coming upon them) they could not well know the one from the other. In this affair there were counted of the Turks to be slain more than five thousand.

Then the Captain Rogendorff, commending the valiant standing of his soldiers, providing with all diligence against another assault, made up the breaches of the walls, and prepared all things necessary for resistance. The next morning, which was dark and misty, the Turks thinking to anticipate our men with their sudden coming, began again busily to mount upon the top of the walls.

It would require a long treatise here to describe the great distress and danger that the city was in those three days following. During all which time there was no rest, no intermission, nor diligence wanting either in the enemy's fighting against the city, or in our men in defending the same. For the Turks, besides the great ordnance, wherewith (as with a great tempest of gunshot) they never ceased battering the walls, and beating the fortifications of the city, sent also such heaps and multitudes of the Turks, to the scaling and climbing of the walls, that notwithstanding all the defeats, the number of them never seemed diminished ; till at last the soldiers of the Turks, perceiving themselves able by no means to prevail, but only run in danger of life, and to do no good, began to wrangle amongst themselves, repining against their dukes and captains, imputing the whole cause to them, that the city was yet untaken, and so the siege ceased for that time.

After this, when Solyman had purposed with his last and strongest siege to try the city the utmost that he was able to do, and had encouraged his soldiers to prepare themselves : the soldiers shewed themselves very unwilling to return again from whence they were so often repulsed before ; so that a great commotion began to rise in the Turk's camp. When the rumor came to Solyman's ears, he sends his grand captain to keep all the soldiers in order and obedience, or if they would be stubborn, to compel them, whether they would or not, to accomplish his commandment, who coming to the soldiers shewed to them the great Turk's message, and to animate and encourage them, declared that the opportunity was not to be neglected, neither could they now without great shame give over, after so many assaults, who, if they would sustain but one brunt more, the victory were in their own hands. The townsmen, he said, were wasted, and their victuals spent ; and the more to inflame their minds, he promised them not only great thanks and reward of their emperor, but also the whole spoil of the city.

But when all this could not stir up the tired Turks, using compulsion where persuasion would not serve, he appointed a number of horsemen to be set at their backs to force them either to go forward, or if they refused to destroy them with guns and spears. The Turks seeing themselves in such a straight, that whether they went or tarried it was to them the same peril, yet they would not set forward except the captain would take the lead before them, who thus spake : " Forsake your faith and allegiance, and betray the emperor of Constantinople to the christians if you will ; but I will discharge my duty towards the commonwealth and my emperor ;" and with that word advanced his ensign, making toward the city walls. When others followed him, and still more and more pressed after him, it came to pass that whole bodies of them were overthrown and slain by our men upon the walls, before it was known what they meant. Others terrified by their example gave back and left their array, and winding themselves by by-ways and under covert of the hills, returned again to their tents, and so came it to pass, that the strength of the enemies daily more and more decreasing, they had less hope every day of obtaining the city. For besides the innumerable slaughter of Turks upon the walls, the townsmen also watching the forages and purveyors of the Turks, as they ranged about for victuals for the camp, as occasion served them encompassed them, and encountered with them, so that of a whole legion scarcely the tenth part returned alive, by which the courage of the enemy began greatly to faint. As our men began to receive more hope and courage, so the Turks began still more to droop and to languish with despair, so that at length they scarce durst appear without the bounds where they were entrenched, but only in light skirmishes, when they were challenged by our men to come out and to shew themselves.

Solyman perceiving his soldiers thus daily to go to wreck, of whom he had lost already more than eighty thousand, and that with long tarrying he could do no good, being also in lack of forage, for the country about him was wasted, he began to consult with his captains and counsellors, what remained best to be done. The most part advised him to raise his siege, and provide for himself. The chief motive was, that he heard Frederick, the Palatine, was coming with a great army at Ratisbon towards Vienna. When Solyman had intelligence of this, thinking it not best to wait the coming of the Palatine, made haste with bag and baggage to remove his camp, and to retire ; and first sending his carriage before him, he made speed himself with his army to follow shortly after.

The Viennians, when they heard of the departure of the Turks, although at the first they scarcely believed it to be true, being afterward certified of their removing, and how it was in a manner of a flight, were greatly desirous to make out of the city after them. In which, although the presence of the Palatine with his army, if he had been there, might have stood them in great stead, yet they took the opportunity, and issuing out of the city, set after them with their horsemen, and first passing the tents (where the Turks had pitched their pavilions) they made such pursuit after them, that within a little time they overtook the rearward of the army; they made such havoc and destruction, that, as the author reports, there was not a shot discharged, nor weapon drawn, nor stroke struck, by the pursuers, which did not tell on the enemy.

Thus through the merciful protection of Amighty God, Austria was delivered from the fierce and barbarous hostility of the cruel Turks. Notwithstanding, that neither Ferdinand, the king, nor the emperor his brother, were present, but only the power of God, through the valiantness of the worthy Germans, defended that city; in defence of which consisted the safety and deliverance of all these west parts of Christendom. For the which immortal praise and thanks be unto our immortal God in Christ our Lord, according as he hath most graciously and worthily deserved of us. Wherein by the way take notice, gentle reader, how and after what manner God's blessing goes with the true followers of his religion; for the Turks in so many battles and sieges heretofore were never so repelled and foiled, as at this time in encountering with the protestants and defenders of sincere religion. This city of Vienna was besieged and delivered, A.D. 1529. The assaults of the Turk against the city are numbered to be twenty, and his repulses as many. The number of his army which he first brought, was two hundred and fifty thousand, whereof were slain eighty thousand and above.

In the year 1537, Solyman, who could not be quiet at home, nor rest in peace, returning out of Asia from his wars there into Europe with two hundred and seventy ships, great and little, set upon Corcyra, another island belonging to the Venetians, which he besieged ten days, wasting and burning the towns and fields as he went, beside the destruction of much people therein, whom partly he slew, partly led away captives. From thence he sailed to Zacinthus and Cythera, another island not far from Corcyra, bordering near to the coasts of Epirus and Greece. Where he suddenly by night invading the husbandmen in villages and fields, sleeping and mistrusting no harm, drew them out of their houses and possessions, men and women, besides children, to the number of nine hundred, whom he made his bondslaves; burning moreover their houses, and carrying away all the goods and cattle being without the said city of Zacinthus and Cythera.

From thence they turned their course to the siege of Egina, a rich and populous island, lying between Greece and Asia. Where at first the Eginians did manfully resist them in battle, and were likely to have prevailed; but wearied at length, and oppressed with innumerable thousands of fresh Turks, who still were sent in, to rescue the others who were overcome before, they were compelled to fly to the city of Egina. Which city the cruel Turks, with much labour, and violence of their great ordnance brought out of their ships, subdued and cast down to the ground; the citizens and inhabitants which the Turk after he had burned their houses, and ransacked their goods, commanded to be slain and killed every one. The women both noble and unnoble, with their infants, were shipped to Constantinople, and led away to perpetual misery and slavery, which was A.D. 1537.

In the year 1540, the restless Turk making his return toward Hungary, by the way passing by Dalmatia, laid siege to the town called Novum Castellum, defended by the Spaniards. In which town, because they refused to yield themselves, all the inhabitants and soldiers were put to the sword, and slain every one. This Novum Castellum, or Newcastle, was a strong fort of the christians, which being now in the Turk's power, he had great advantage over all those quarters of Dalmatia, Stiria, Carinthia, and Hungaria. From thence he proceeded further, keeping his course into Hungary, where he planted his forces against the city of Buda.

This Buda was a principal city in Hungary, under the government of George Monachus, who quarrelled with Ferdinand, and said that he would never any more trust the promises of christians, and immediately upon the same, sent to Solyman the Turk, for aid against the christians, promising that he would surrender to him free possession of Hungary, if he would come and vanquish the army of Ferdinand lying about the siege of Buda. The Turk made no long tarrying, but glad of the occasion, with a mighty army came into Hungary, and soon overpowering the host of Ferdinand, he got the city into his own hands, commanding George Monachus with his mother, to follow after his camp.

In the history of Joannes Ramus, it follows, that when Solyman the Turk had thus prevailed against the city of Buda, and against other parts of Hungary; by the assent of the empire, one Joachim, duke of Brandenburg, prince elector, was appointed with a puissant army of chosen soldiers of all nations, to recover the city of Buda from the Turk, and to deliver the other parts of Christendom from the fear of the Turk, A.D. 1542. Which Joachim, at his first setting forth, appeared so courageous and valiant, as if he would have conquered the whole world: but this great heat was so cooled in a short time by the Turk, that before any great danger was offered to him, he was glad to be discharged of the voyage, and with shame enough returned home again. And would God he had left behind him in the fields no more but his own shame. For the enemies having intelligence of his cowardly departure, thinking to work some point of mastery or victory before his going, set upon the right wing of his army, out of which they took away with them above five hundred strong and valiant soldiers, not killing them, but carrying them away alive. For whom it had been much better to have stood to their weapon, and to have died manfully upon the Turks, than by yielding themselves to be deprived of weapons and armour, and so to be left to the cursed courtesy of the foul Turks. What courtesy was shewed in the sequel, soon appeared. For after the Turks had led them out of Hungary into their own dominions, after a most horrible sort they disfigured and mangled them, and so sent them abroad through all Greece, to be witnesses of the Turkish victory. Their kind of punishment was thus: first, they had their right arm thrust through with an iron red hot, by which they would be unable and unmeet to all labour and warfare; secondly, their heads were shaven to the very sculls, after the manner of our friars and monks, when they are newly shaven; thirdly, they had all their limbs cruelly and shamefully mangled and mutilated.

But to return again to the city of Buda, from whence we have digressed, here we must not omit what falsehood and what cruelty the Turks used towards the christians there after their victory. For after Solyman the Turk, upon the yielding and submission of the men of Buda, had given to them his promise of safety and life, within a short time, he picking a quarrel with him for selling oxen to the christians, and for bargaining with them, slew all the magistrates of the city of Buda; as in all other cities wherever the christians yielded to him, he never, or very rarely kept his promise with them, nor did ever any christians speed better with the Turk, than they who most valiantly resisted him.

And as his promise with the magistrates of Buda was false and wretched; so his cruelty with the soldiers was much more notorious and abominable; for two cohorts or bands of christian soldiers came alive to his hands; to whom, when he seemed at first to grant pardon of life, he commanded that they should put on their armour again, and to dispose themselves in order and battle array, after the warlike manner of the christians; which, when they had accomplished readily, according to his commandment, and when he, riding about the ranks, had diligently viewed and beheld them a certain space, at length he commanded them to put off their armour again; which done, certain of the tallest and strongest of them he picked out, the rest he commanded by his soldiers coming behind them with swords, to be cut in pieces and slain. Of the others, whom he had elected and chosen, some he set for marks and buts to be shot at; some he appointed to his two sons, for them to slash with their swords and try their strength, which of them could give the deeper wound, and (as they termed it) the fairer blow, by which the most blood might flow out of their christian bodies.

After the winning of Buda, the Turk, purposing not to cease till he had subdued and brought under his obedience all Hungary, proceeding further with his army, first brought under a strong hold of the christians, named Pestum or Pesta, where a great number of christian soldiers were slain, and many were led away to more cruel affliction.

Then he came to another castle called Walpo, situate in the confines of Bosnia, Croatia, and Hungary; which fort or castle he besieged three months; no rescue or aid was sent to them, either from Ferdinand, king of Hungary, or from any other christian prince or princess. At length the fort was given up to the Turk; but more through the false treachery or cowardly heart of the soldiers than of the captain. Wherein is to be noted an example not unworthy of memory. For when the cowardly soldiers, either for fear or flattery, would needs surrender themselves and the place to the Turk, contrary to the mind of the captain, who in no case would agree to their yielding: they, thinking to find favour with the Turk, apprehended their captain, and gave him to Solyman. But see how the justice of God, sometimes by the hand of the enemy, disposes the end of things to the rewarding of virtue, and punishing of vice. For where they thought to save themselves by the danger of the faithful captain, the event turned clean contrary; so that the Turk was bountiful and very liberal to the captain, and the soldiers, notwithstanding that they had all yielded themselves, yet were all commanded to be slain.

The Turk proceeding from one fortified town to another, took them, and greatly and cruelly extended his conquests through all Hungary till he came to Alba; there, the Turks, using the occasion of a misty darkness, approached the walls, and got up to a certain fortress where the Germans were, before our men could well perceive them: where they pressed in so thick, and in such number, that although the christian soldiers, standing strongly to the defence of their lives, did what valiant men in cases of such extremity were able to do; yet being over-matched by the multitude of the Turks, and the suddenness of their coming, gave back, seeking to retire unto the inward walls. There was between the outward walls and inward gate of the city, a strait, or narrow passage, cast up in the manner of a bank or causeway, which passage happened to be barred and stopped. By reason of which the poor soldiers were forced to cast themselves into the ditch, thinking to swim as well as they could into the city: many of them sticking in the mud were drowned, one pressing upon another; many were slain by their enemies coming behind them. A few who could swim out were received into the city, but the chief captains and warders of the town were slain there.

The citizens being destitute of their principal captains and warriors, were in great perplexity and doubt among themselves what to do, some thinking good to yield, some counselling the contrary. Thus, while the citizens were distracted, the magistrates thinking to depend on the Turk's gentleness, sent out one of their heads to the Turk, who in the name of them all should surrender to him the city, and become to him tributaries, upon condition they might enjoy liberty of life and goods; which being granted, after the Turkish faith and assurance: the soldiers who were within the city, putting off their armour, were discharged and sent away.

Now see what happened to the yielding citizens. When the Turk had entered the town, and had visited the sepulchre of the kings, for three or four days he pretended much clemency toward the citizens, as though he came not to oppress them, but to be revenged of Ferdinand their king, and to deliver them from the servitude of the Germans. On the fourth day, all the chief and head men of the city were commanded to appear before the Turk, in a plain not far from the city where the con-

demned persons before were wont to be executed, as though they should come to swear to the Turk. At this command of the Turk, when the citizens in great number, and in their best attire were assembled, the Turk, contrary to his faith and promise, commanded suddenly a general slaughter to be made of them all. And this was the end of the citizens of Alba.

As the false and cruel Turk was thus raging in Hungary, and intended further to rage without all mercy and pity of the christians, and might easily then have prevailed and gone whither he would, for Charles the emperor, and Francis the French king, were at the same time in war and hostility, and also other christian princes, as Henry, duke of Brunswick against John Frederick, duke of Saxony; also princes and rulers were contending among themselves: behold the gracious providence of our Lord and God towards us, who seeing the misery, and having pity of his poor christians, suddenly reined this raging beast, and brought him out of Europe into his own country again, by occasion of the Persians, who were then in great preparation of war against the Turks, and had invaded his dominion. By which the Turks were kept there occupied, fighting with the Persians for a long time. Which wars at length being achieved and finished, (wherein the said Turk lost great victories, with slaughter of many thousands of his Turks) he was not only provoked by the instigation of certain evil-disposed Hungarians, but also induced by the discord of christian princes to return again into Europe, in hopes to subdue all parts to his dominion. When he had levied an army, incredible in multitude, see again the merciful providence and protection of our God toward his people. As the Turk was thus intending to set forward with his innumerable multitude against the christians, the hand of the Lord sent such a pestilence through all the Turk's army and dominions, reaching from Bithynia, and from Thrace to Macedonia, and also to Hungary, that all the Turk's possessions seemed almost nothing else but as an heap of dead corpses, whereby his voyage for that time was stopped, and he almost compelled to seek a new army.

Besides this plague, which was worse to them than any war, other domestic calamities, through God's providence, happened to Solyman, the great rover and robber of the world, which kept him at home from vexing the christians, especially concerning his eldest son Mustapha. This Mustapha being hated, and feared by Rustanus, the chief counsellor about the Turk, and by Rosa, the Turk's concubine, and afterwards his wife, was complained of to his father, accused, and at length so brought into suspicion and displeasure of the Turks, that his father caused him to be sent for to his pavilion, where six Turks with masks were appointed to put him to death: they put (after their manner) a small cord or bow-string full of knots about his neck, and so throwing him down upon the ground, not suffering him to speak one word to his father, with the twitch thereof strangled him to death, his father standing in a secret corner by, and beholding the same. Which fact being perpetrated, afterwards when the Turk would have given to another son, called Gianger, the treasures, horse, armour, ornaments, and the province of Mustapha his brother; Gianger crying out for sorrow at his brother's death, said he to his father, " Shame on thee, thou impious and wretched dog, traitor, murderer, I cannot call thee father, take the treasures, the horse and armour of Mustapha to thyself:" and with that, taking out his dagger, thrust it through his own body. And thus was Solyman murderer and parricide of his own sons; which was A. D. 1552.

Wherein is to be noted the singular providence and love of the Lord towards his afflicted christians. For this Mustapha, as he was courageous and greatly expert and exercised in all practise of war, so had he a cruel heart, maliciously set to shed the blood of the christians: wherefore, we have great cause to congratulate, and to give thanks to God, for the happy taking away of this Mustapha. And no less hope also and good comfort we may conceive of our loving Lord, to think that our merciful God, after these sore afflictions of his christians under these twelve Turks afore recited, now, after this Solyman, intends some gracious good work to Christendom, to reduce and release us out of this long and miserable Turkish captivity, as may be hoped now, by taking away of these young imps of this impious generation, before they should come to work their conceived malice against us : the Lord, therefore, be glorified and praised.   Amen.

Moreover, as I was in writing hereof, opportunely came to my hands a certain writing out of Germany, certifying us of such news and victory of late achieved against the Turk, as may not a little increase our hope and comfort us, touching the decay and ruin of the Turk's power and tyranny against us.   Which news are these : that after the Turkish tyrant had besieged, with an army of thirty thousand men, the famous and strong town and castle of Jula in Hungary, lying forty Dutch miles beyond the river Danube, which city had by the space of six weeks sustained many grievous assaults : God, through his great mercy and goodness so comforted the said town of Jula, and the poor christians therein, at their earnest prayers, that the Turk, with all his host was driven back by the hands of the general, called Karetshim Laslaw, and his valiant company : who not only defended the town, but also constrained the Turks to retire, to their great shame and confusion, with a great slaughter of the Turkish rabble ; for which, the everlasting God be praised for ever.

The manner of the overthrow was this.   As the general saw his advantage, with Captain George, and other horsemen of the Silesians and Hungarians, they set on the rearward of the Turks and killed about eight thousand of them, and took also some of their artillery, and followed them so fast, that the Turks were constrained to fly into a marshy ground, and to break the wheels of the rest of their artillery to save themselves, and therewith they got a very rich booty, rescuing besides, and taking from the Turks, a great number of christian prisoners.

This Solyman reigned forty-six years ; he began the same year in the which the Emperor Charles V. was crowned, which was A. D. 1520, and so has continued by God's permission, for a scourge to the christians, to the year 1566.   This Solyman, by one of his concubines, had his eldest son called Mustapha.   By another concubine called Rosa, he had four sons, Mahumet, Bajazet, Zelymus, and Gianger.   Of which sons, Mustapha and Gianger were slain (as ye heard before) by means of their own father.   And thus much concerning the wretched tyranny of the Turks.

Thus from time to time the church of Christ has had little or no rest in this earth ; what for the heathen emperors on the one side ; what for the proud pope on the other side ; on the third side, what for the barbarous Turk : for these are and have been from the beginning, the three principal and capital enemies of the church of Christ.   The cruelty and malice of these enemies against Christ's people has been such, that to judge which of them did most exceed in cruelty of persecution, it is hard to say ; but it may be thought that the bloody and beastly tyranny of the Turks, incomparably surmounts all the afflictions and cruel slaughters that ever were seen in any age, or read of in any history ; so that there is neither history so perfect, nor writer so diligent, who writing of the miserable tyranny of the Turks, is able to express or comprehend the horrible examples of the unspeakable cruelty and slaughter, exercised by these twelve Turkish tyrants upon poor christian men's bodies, within the compass of these later three hundred years.   Whereof although no sufficient relation can be made, nor number expressed ; yet to give to the reader some general guess or view thereof, let us first consider what dominions and empires, how many countries, kingdoms, provinces, cities, towns, strong holds, and forts, these Turks have surprised and won from the christians.   In all which victories, that there is almost no place which the Turks ever came to and subdued, where they did not either slay all the inhabitants, or lead away the most part into such captivity and slavery, that they continued not long after alive, or else so lived, that death almost had been more tolerable.

As in the time of the first persecutions of the Roman emperors, the saying was, That no man could step with his feet in all Rome, but he would tread upon a martyr : so here may be said, That almost there is not a town, city, or village in all Asia, Greece, also in a great part of Europe and Africa, whose streets have not flowed with the blood of the christians, whom the cruel Turks have murdered.   Of whom are to be seen in histories, heaps of soldiers slain, of men and women cut in pieces, of children stuck upon poles and stakes, whom those detestable Turks most spitefully (and that in the sight of their parents) use to gore to death : some they drag at their horse tails, and famish to death ; some they tear in pieces, tying their arms and legs to four horses ; others they make marks to shoot at ; upon some they try their swords how deep they can cut and slash.   The aged and feeble they tread under their horses : sex is not regarded, but women and children are barbarously murdered.   Whether the christians yield to them, or yield not, it is all the same.   As in their promises there is no truth, so in their victories there is no sense of manhood or mercy, but they make havoc of all.

So the citizens of Croja, after they had yielded and were promised their lives, were all destroyed, and that horribly.   In Mysia, after the king had given himself to the Turks, having promise of life, Mahomet the Turk slew him with his own hands.   The princes of Rasia had both their eyes put out, with basons red hot set before them.   Theodosia, otherwise called Capha, was also surrendered to the Turk, having the like assurance of life and safety ; and yet, contrary to the league, the citizens were put to the sword and slain.   At the winning and yielding of Lesbos, what a number of young men and children were put upon sharp stakes and poles, and so thrust through !   At the winning of the city of Buda, what tyranny was shewed and exercised against the poor christians who had yielded themselves, and against the two dukes, Christopher Bisserer and John Tranbinger, contrary to the promise and hand-writing of the Turk, is to be seen in the history of Melchior Soiterus.

The like also is to be read in the history of Bernard de Breydenbach, who, writing of the taking of Hydruntum, a city in Apulia, testifies of the miserable slaughter of the young men there slain ; of old men trodden under the horses' feet ; of matrons and maidens horribly outraged and murdered ; of women with child cut and rent in pieces ; of the priests in the churches slain ; and of the archbishop of that city, who, being an aged man, and holding the cross in his hands, was cut asunder with a wooden saw, &c.   The same Bernard, also writing of the overthrow of Nigropontus, otherwise called Chalcides, (A. D. 1471,) describes the like terrible slaughter which was exercised there, where the Turk, after his promise given to the contrary, most cruelly caused all the youth of Italy to be pricked upon sharp stakes ; some to be dashed against the hard stones, others to be cut asunder in the midst, and others with various kinds of torments to be put to death : insomuch, that all the streets and ways of Chalcides did flow with the blood of them which were there slain.   In which history the writer records one memorable example of maidenly courage, worthy of all christians to be noted and commended.   The history is told of the pretor's daughter of that city, who, being the only daughter of her father, and noted to be of an exceeding singular beauty, was saved out of the slaughter, and brought to Mahomet the Turk.   But she refusing to join the Turk's seraglio, or to embrace the Mahometan faith, was commanded to be slain and murdered, and so died she a martyr.

The like cruelty also was shewed upon them who kept the castle and afterwards yielding themselves upon hope of the Turk's promise, were slain every one.   What should I speak of the miserable slaughter of Methone, and the citizens thereof dwelling in Peloponnesus ? who, seeing no remedy, but that they must needs come into the Turks' hands, set the barn on fire where they were gathered together, men, women, and children; some women also voluntarily cast themselves into the sea, rather than they would sustain the Turks' captivity.

It is miserable to behold, long to recite, incredible to believe, all the cruel acts and horrible slaughters wrought by these miscreants against the christians through all places of the world, both in Asia, in Africa, but especially in Europe. Who is able to recite the innumerable societies and companies of the Grecians martyred by the Turks' sword in Achaia, Attica, Thessaly, Macedonia, Epirus, and all Peloponnesus? besides the island of Rhodes, and other islands, in the adjacent sea numbered to about two-and-fifty; of which also Patmos was one, where St. John wrote his Revelations. Where did ever the Turks set any foot, but the blood of christians was shed there, without pity or measure? and what place or province is there almost through the world, where the Turks either have not pierced, or are not likely shortly to enter? In Thrace, and through all the coasts of the Danube, in Bulgaria, Dalmatia, in Servia, Transylvania, Bosnia in Hungaria, also in Austria, what havoc has been made by them of christian men's bodies, it will pain any christian heart to remember. At the siege of Moldavia and many other places; also at the battle of Varna, where Ladislaus, king of Poland, with almost all his army, through the rashness of the pope's cardinal, were slain; at Xabiacchus, Lyssus, Dynastrum; at the siege of Gunza, and of the faithful town Scorad, where the number of the shot against their walls, at the siege, were reckoned to two thousand five hundred and thirty-nine. Likewise at the siege of Vienna, where all the christian captives were brought before the whole army and slain, and many drawn in pieces with horses; but especially at the winning of Constantinople, above mentioned: also at Croja and Methone, what beastly cruelty was shewed, it is unspeakable. For as in Constantinople, Mahomet, the drunken Turk, never rose from dinner, but he caused every day, for his sport, three hundred christian captives of the nobles of that city to be slain before his face; so in Methone, after his captain Omar had sent to him at Constantinople five hundred prisoners of the christians, the cruel tyrant commanded them all to be cut and divided in sunder by the middle, and so being slain, to be thrown out into the fields.

What christian heart will not pity the incredible slaughter done by the Turks in Euboia, where Faber testifies, "That innumerable people were stuck and gored upon stakes; divers were thrust through with a hot iron; children and infants, not yet weaned from the mother, were dashed against the stones, and many cut asunder in the midst?"

But never did country taste and feel more the bitter and deadly tyranny of the Turks, than did Rasia, called Mysia Inferior, and now Servia. Where (as writes Wolfgang Drechsterus) the prince of the same country being sent for, under fair pretence of words and promises, to come and speak with the Turk, after he was come of his own gentleness, thinking no harm, was apprehended, and wretchedly and falsely put to death, and his skin flayed off, his brother and sister brought to Constantinople for a triumph, and all the nobles of his country had their eyes put out.

Briefly to conclude, by the vehement and furious rage of these cursed caitiffs, it may seem that Satan the old dragon, for the great hatred he bears to Christ, has stirred them up to be the butchers of all christian people, inflaming their beastly hearts with such malice and cruelty against the name and religion of Christ, that they degenerating from the nature of men to devils, will neither by reason be ruled, nor by any blood or slaughter satisfied. Like as in the primitive age of the church, and in the time of Dioclesian and Maximilian, when the devil saw that he could not prevail against the person of Christ who was risen again, he turned all his fury upon his servants, thinking by the Roman emperors utterly to extinguish the name and profession of Christ out from the earth: so in this later age of the world, Satan being let loose again, rages by the Turks, thinking to make no end of murdering and killing, till he have brought (as he intends) the whole church of Christ, with all the professors thereof, under foot. But the Lord (I trust) will once send a Constantine to vanquish proud Maxentius, a Moses to drown indurate Pharaoh, a Cyrus to subdue the stout Babylonian.

And thus much, touching our christian brethren who were slain and destroyed by these blasphemous Turks. Now, many others were torn away violently from their country, from their wives and children, from liberty, and from all their possessions, into wretched captivity and extreme penury: it remains likewise to treat somewhat also concerning the cruel manner of the Turks' handling of the said christian captives. And first, here is to be noted, that the Turk never comes into Europe to war against the christians, but there follow after his army a great number of brokers or merchants, such as buy men and children to sell again, bringing with them long chains in hope of great bargains. In which chains they link by fifty and sixty together, such as remain undestroyed by the sword, whom they buy of the soldiers as part of the spoils of them that rob and spoil the christian countries.

Such as belong to the Sultan's share, i. e. a tenth of the whole, are sold to the use of husbandry or keeping of beasts. If they are young men or women, they are sent to certain places, there to be instructed in their language and arts, as shall be most for their advantage; and the first care of the Turks is this, to make them deny the christian religion; and after that they are appointed, every one as he seems most apt, either to the learning of their laws, or else to learn the feats of war. Their first rudiment of war is to handle the bow; first beginning with a weak bow, and, as they grow in strength, coming to a stronger bow; and, if they miss the mark, they are sharply beaten; and their allowance is twopence or threepence a-day, till they come and take wages to serve in war. Some are brought up for the purpose to be placed in the number of the wicked Janizaries.

Such as are young maidens and beautiful, are deputed for seraglios. They who are of little beauty, serve for matrons to do the drudgery work in their houses and chambers, or else are put to spinning, and such other labours; but so, that it is not lawful for them either to profess their christian religion, or ever to hope for any liberty.

The others who are bought and sold among private subjects, first are allured with fair words and promises to embrace Mahometanism, which, if they do, they are more favourably treated, but all hope is taken from them of returning again into their country; if they attempt that, the penalty is burning. And if such coming at length to liberty will marry, they may; but then their children remain bond to the master for him to sell at his pleasure; and, therefore, such as are wise amongst them will not marry. They who refuse to become Mahometans are miserably handled; for example whereof, the author who gives testimony hereof adduces his own experience. Such captives as are expert in any manual art or occupation, can better shift for themselves; but they who have no handicraft to live upon, are in worse case. And, therefore, such as have been brought up in learning, or be priests or noblemen, and such others whose tender education can abide no hardness, are the least reputed, and most of all others neglected by him that has the sale or keeping of them, because he sees less profit to rise of them than of the other; and therefore no cost of raiment is bestowed upon them, but they are carried about barehead and barefoot, both summer and winter, in frost and snow. And if any faint and be sick in the way, there is no resting for him in any inn, but first he is driven forward with whips, and if that will not serve, he is set peradventure upon some horse; or, if his weakness be such that he cannot sit, then is he laid overthwart the horse upon his belly like a calf; and if he chance to die, they take off his garment, such as he has, and throw him in a ditch.

They are brought forth to the market for sale, where the buyer, if he be disposed, plucking off their garments, vieweth all the bones and joints of their body: and if he like them he gives his price, and carries them away into miserable servitude, either to tilling of their ground, or to pasture their cattle, or to some other strange kind of misery incredible to speak of; insomuch that the author reports that he hath seen himself certain of such christian captives yoked together like horse and oxen, and to draw the plough. The maid servants likewise are kept in perpetual toil and work in close places, where neither they come in sight of any man, neither are they permitted to have any talk with their fellow-servants, &c. Such as are committed to keep beasts, lie abroad day and night in the wild fields, without house and harbour, and so changing their pasture go from mountain to mountain, of whom, also beside the office of keeping the beasts, other handy labour is exacted at spare hours, such as pleases their masters to put unto them.

Out of this misery there is no way for them to fly, especially for them that are carried into Asia beyond the seas, or if any do attempt so to do, he taketh his time chiefly about harvest, when he may hide himself all the day-time in the corn, or in woods or marshes, and find food, and in the night only he flies, and had rather be devoured of wolves and other wild beasts, than to return again to his master. In their flying they use to take with them an hatchet and cords, that when they come to the sea-side, they may cut down trees, and bind together the ends of them, and so where the sea of Hellespont is narrowest, about the Sestos and Abydos, they take the sea, sitting upon trees, where, if the wind and tide do serve luckily, they may run over in four or five hours. But the most part either perish in the floods, or are driven back again upon the coasts of Asia, or else are devoured of wild beasts in woods, or perish with hunger and famine. If any escape over the sea alive into Europe, they enter into no town by the way, but wander upon the mountains, following only the North Star for their guide.

As touching such towns and provinces which are won by the Turk, and wherein the christians are suffered to live under tribute: first, all the nobility there they kill and make away, the churchmen and clergy hardly they spare. The churches, with the bells and all the furniture, either they cast down, or else they convert to the use of their own blasphemous religion, leaving to the christians certain old blind chapels, which when they decay, it is permitted to our men to repair them again for a great sum of money given to the Turk. Neither are they permitted to use any open preaching or ministration, but only in silence and by stealth to frequent together. Neither is it lawful for any christian to bear office within the city province, nor to bear weapon, nor to wear any garment like to the Turks. And if any contumely or blasphemy, be it never so great, be spoken against them, or against Christ, yet must thou bear it, and hold thy peace. And then if thou speak one word against Mahomet, thy punishment is fire and burning. And if it chance a Christian being on horseback meet, or pass by a Mussulman, that is, a Turkish priest, he must light from his horse, and with a lowly look devoutly reverence and adore the Mussulman, or if he do not he is beaten down from his horse with clubs and staves.

Furthermore, for their tribute they pay the fourth part of their substance and gain to the Turk, beside the ordinary tribute of the christians, which is to pay for every poll within his family a ducat unto the Turk, which if the parents cannot do, they are compelled to sell their children into bondage. Other being not able to pay, go chained in fetters from door to door begging, to make up their payment, or else must lie in perpetual prison.

And thus have ye heard the lamentable afflictions of our christian brethren under the cruel tyranny and captivity of the Turks, passing all other captivities that ever have been to God's people, either under Pharaoh in Egypt, or under Nebuchadnezzar in Babylon, or under Antiochus in the time of the Maccabees. Under which captivity, if it so please the Lord to have his spouse the church to be nurtured, his good will be done and obeyed. But if this misery come by the negligence and discord of our christian guides and leaders, then have we to pray and cry to our Lord God, either to give better hearts to our guides and rulers, or else better guides and rulers to his flocks.

And these troubles and afflictions of our christian brethren suffered by the Turks, I thought good and profitable for our country people here in England to know, for so much as by the ignorance of these, and such like histories worthy of consideration, I see much inconvenience follows. Whereby it cometh to pass, that because we Englishmen being far off from these countries, and little knowing what misery is abroad, are the less moved with zeal and compassion to tender their grievances, and to pray for them whose troubles we know not. Whereupon also it follows that we not considering the miserable state of other, are the less grateful to God, when any tranquillity is granted to us. And if any little cloud arise upon us, be it never so little, as poverty, loss of living, or a little banishment out of our country for the Lord's cause, we make a greater matter of it, and all because we go no further than our own country, and only feeling our own cross, do not compare that which we feel with the great crosses to which the churches of Christ commonly in other places abroad are subject. Which if we rightly understood, and earnestly considered and pondered in our minds, neither would we so excessively forget ourselves in the time of our prosperity, nor yet so impatiently be troubled, as we are in time of our adversity, and all because either we hear not, or else we ponder not the terrible crosses which the Lord layeth upon our other brethren in other nations.

The Prophecies of the Holy Scriptures considered, touching the coming up and final ruin and destruction of this wicked kingdom of the Turk, with the revelations and foreshewings also of other authors concerning the same.

As you have sufficiently heard to what largeness the dominion of the Turks has increased, and understand what cruel tyranny these wretched miscreants have and do daily practise most heinously, wherever they come against the servants and professors, it shall not be unprofitable, but rather necessary, and to our great comfort, to consider and examine in the scriptures, with what prophecies the Holy Spirit of the Lord has forewarned us before of these heavy persecutions to come upon his people by this horrible antichrist. For as the government and constitution of times and states of monarchies and policies fall not to us by blind chance, but are administered and allotted to us from above, so it is not to be supposed, that such a great alteration of kingdoms, such a terrible and general persecution of God's people almost through all Christendom, and such a terror of the whole earth as is now moved and gendered by these Turks, comes without the knowledge, sufferance, and determination of the Lord, for such ends and purposes as his divine wisdom doth best know. For the better evidence and testimony of which he has left in his scriptures sufficient instruction and declaration, by which we may plainly see to our great comfort how these grievous afflictions and troubles of the church, though they are sharp and heavy to us, yet they come not by chance or by man's working only, but even as the Lord himself has appointed it.

In the later years of the Jewish kingdom, what troubles and afflictions that people sustained three hundred years together, but chiefly the last one hundred and sixty-six years before the coming of Christ, by Antiochus and his fellows, the history of the Maccabees can report. Wherein we have also notoriously to understand the miserable vexations and persecutions of christian churches in these later ends of the world by antichrist.

We read that this Antiochus, in the eighth year of his reign, in his second coming to Jerusalem, first gave forth in commandment, that all the Jews should relinquish the law of Moses, and worship the idol of Jupiter Olympius which he set up in the temple of Jerusalem.

The books of Moses and of the Prophets he burned. He set garrisons of soldiers to ward the idol. In the city of Jerusalem he caused the feasts and revels of Bacchus to be kept, full of all filth and wickedness. Old men, women, and virgins, such as would not leave the law of Moses, he murdered with cruel torments. The mothers that would not circumcise their children he slew. The children that were circumcised he hanged up by the necks. The temple he spoiled and wasted. The altar of God, and candlestick of God, with the other ornaments and furniture of the temple, partly he cast out, partly he carried away. Contrary to the law of God he caused them to offer and to eat swine's flesh. Great murder and slaughter he made of the people, causing them either to leave their law, or to lose their lives. Among whom, besides many others, with cruel torments, he put to death a godly mother with her seven sons, sending his cruel proclamations through the whole land, that whoever kept the observances of the Sabbath, and other rites of the law, and refused to condescend to his abominations, should be executed. No kind of calamity, nor face of misery could be shewed in any place, which was not there seen. Of the tyranny of this Antiochus it is historied at large in the book of Maccabees; and Daniel prophesying before of the same, declares that the people of the Jews deserved no less for their sins and transgressions.

By consent of all writers, this Antiochus bears a figure of the great antichrist, which was to follow in the latter end of the world, and is already come, and worketh what he can against us. Although, as St. John saith, there have been, and be many antichrists, as parts and members of the body of antichrist, which are forerunners, yet to speak of the head and principal antichrist, and great enemy of Christ's church, he is come in the latter end of the world, at what time shall be such tribulation as never was seen before; whereby is meant (no doubt) the Turk, prefigured by this Antiochus. By this antichrist I do also mean all such, as following the same doctrine of the Turks, think to be saved by their works, and not by their faith only in the Son of God, of what title and profession soever they be; especially if they use the like force and violence for the same as he doth, &c.

Of the tyranny of this Antiochus, and of the tribulations of the church in the latter times, both of the Jews' church, and also of the Christian church to come, let us hear and consider the words of Daniel in the eleventh chapter, and also in his seventh chapter, prophesying of the same as follows:—

"For the ships of Chittim shall come against him: therefore he shall be grieved, and return, and have indignation against the holy covenant: so shall he do; he shall even return, and have intelligence with them that forsake the holy covenant. And arms shall stand on his part, and they shall pollute the sanctuary of strength, and shall take away the daily sacrifice, and they shall place the abomination that maketh desolate. And such as do wickedly against the covenant shall he corrupt by flatteries: but the people that do know their God shall be strong, and do exploits. And they that understand among the people shall instruct many: yet they shall fall by the sword, and by flame, by captivity, and by spoil, many days. Now when they shall fall, they shall be holpen with a little help: but many shall cleave to them with flatteries. And some of them of understanding shall fall, to try them, and to purge, and to make them white, even to the time of the end: because it is yet for a time appointed. And the king shall do according to his will; and he shall exalt himself, and magnify himself above every god, and shall speak marvellous things against the God of gods, and shall prosper till the indignation be accomplished: for that that is determined shall be done. Neither shall he regard the God of his fathers, nor the desire of women, nor regard any god: for he shall magnify himself above all. But in his estate shall he honour the God of forces: and a God whom his fathers knew not shall he honour with gold, and silver, and with precious stones, and pleasant things. Thus shall he do in the most strong holds with

a strange god, whom he shall acknowledge and increase with glory: and he shall cause them to rule over many, and shall divide the land for gain. And at the time of the end shall the king of the south push at him: and the king of the north shall come against him like a whirlwind, with chariots, and with horsemen, and with many ships; and he shall enter into the countries, and shall overflow and pass over. He shall enter also into the glorious land, and many countries shall be overthrown: but these shall escape out of his hand, even Edom, and Moab, and the chief of the children of Ammon. He shall stretch forth his hand also upon the countries: and the land of Egypt shall not escape. But he shall have power over the treasures of gold and of silver, and over all the precious things of Egypt: and the Libyans and the Ethiopians shall be at his steps. But tidings out of the east and out of the north shall trouble him: therefore he shall go forth with great fury to destroy, and utterly to make away many. And he shall plant the tabernacles of his palaces between the seas in the glorious holy mountain; yet he shall come to his end, and none shall help him." (Dan. xi. 30—45.)

To this place of Daniel, might also be added the prophecy written in the seventh chapter, and tending to the like effect; where he treating of his vision of four beasts (which signify the four monarchies), and speaking now of the fourth monarchy, has these words:—

"After this I saw in the night visions, and behold a fourth beast, dreadful and terrible, and strong exceedingly; and it had great iron teeth: it devoured and brake in pieces, and stamped the residue with the feet of it: and it was diverse from all the beasts that were before it; and it had ten horns. I considered the horns, and, behold, there came up among them another little horn, before whom there were three of the first horns plucked up by the roots: and, behold, in this horn were eyes like the eyes of man, and a mouth speaking great things,—whose look was more stout than his fellows. I beheld, and the same horn made war with the saints, and prevailed against them; until the Ancient of days came, and judgment was given to the saints of the Most High; and the time came that the saints possessed the kingdom." (Dan. vii. 7, 8; 20—22.)

Thus have you the plain words of Daniel; in which as he manifestly describes the coming of Antiochus the great adversary, towards the latter end of the Jews, so by Antiochus is figured also to us the great adversary of Christ, which is the Turk.

Although some there are, who with great learning and judgment apply this place of Daniel not to the Turk, but to the pope, and that for six or seven special causes herein touched and noted.

The first is this, that the wicked transgressors of the covenant shall join with him deceitfully and hypocritically, who shall pollute the tabernacle of strength, and take away the perpetual sacrifice, and bring in the abomination of desolation.

The second note is, that the prophet declares, how the learned among the people shall teach many, and that they shall fall upon the sword, into fire and captivity, and shall be banished, whereby they shall be tried, chosen, and made bright and pure, &c. All which (say they) is not among the Turks, but only in the pope's church, where the faithful preachers and teachers of the people are slain and burned, &c. Where likewise it follows, that they shall be helped against antichrist, and that many false brethren should join them dissemblingly, &c. To this they allege, that the christians have no such help against the Turk, whereto such false brethren should join themselves, as is and has been commonly seen among the Christians against the pope, from time to time, almost in all countries.

Thirdly, that the king shall exalt himself above all that has the name of God, and shall lift up his mouth to speak presumptuously against God.

Fourthly, that he cares not for the desires of women, which may seem to note how the pope's doctrine shall forbid the honest and lawful marriage in churchmen.

The fifth specialty which they apply to the pope, is that which follows in the prophet, saying, "Neither shall he regard the God of his fathers, nor any god; but instead of him shall set up his god Muhuzzim, and shall worship him with silver and gold, and precious stones," &c. which they apply to the pope, setting up his god of bread, and worshipping him with glistering golden ornaments, and most solemn service.

Sixthly, it follows, "And he shall increase them with much glory and riches, and shall divide unto them lands and possessions," &c.; meaning that the pope, having dominion over treasures of gold and silver, and all precious things of the land, shall endue his cardinals, prelates, his flattering doctors, with friars, monks, and priests, and all such as shall take his part, with great privileges, liberties, revenues, and possessions. And thus I say, some there are who apply this prophecy of the seventh and eleventh chapters of Daniel to the bishop of Rome. Whom although I take to be an extreme persecutor of Christ's church, yet I judge rather those two chapters of Daniel concerning the little horn in the middle of the ten horns, and the great destroyer of the pleasant land and glorious holy mountain, to mean first Antiochus; and by him, secondly, to mean the great antichrist the Turk, who has now set already the tabernacles of his palace between the seas, according to the prophecies of Daniel.

Let us come now to the prophecies of the New Testament, and mark the words of St. Paul, writing to the Thessalonians, who then were christian, and now either are Turkish, or under the Turk, whose words are these: "That ye be not soon shaken in mind, or be troubled, neither by spirit, nor by word, nor by letter as from us, as that the day of Christ is at hand. Let no man deceive you by any means: for that day shall not come, except there come a falling away first, and that man of sin be revealed, the son of perdition; who opposeth and exalteth himself above all that is called God, or that is worshipped; so that he as God sitteth in the temple of God, shewing himself that he is God." (2 Thess. ii. 2—4.) Although this falling away and departing may have a double understanding, as well of the pope's sect (which is gone and departed from the free justification by faith only in Christ through the promise of grace) as of the Turks; yet leaving a while to speak of the pope, because it appears more notoriously in the Turk, we will chiefly apply it to him, in whom so aptly it agrees, that unless this great apostasy from the faith in so many churches had happened by the Turk, it had been hard to understand the apostle's mind, which now by the history of the Turks is easy and evident to be known, considering what a ruin has happened to the church of Christ by these miserable Turks, what empires, nations, kingdoms, countries, towns, and cities, he has removed from the name and profession of Christ, how many thousands, and infinite multitudes of christian men and children, in Asia, in Africa, and in Europe, are carried away from Christ's church to Mahomet's religion, some to serve for the Turk's guard among the janisaries, some for soldiers, some for miners, some for gunners, to fight and war against the christians; so that the most part of all the churches, planted once by the apostles, are now degenerated into Turks, only a small handful of christians reserved yet in these western parts of Europe, of which small remnant, what shall also become shortly, except Christ himself do help, Christ only himself knows.

Notwithstanding this text of the holy apostle may be verified also with no less reason upon the bishop of Rome, than upon the Turk, because he is a man of sin, that is, his seat and city is a great maintainer of wickedness, and also for that he is an adversary, that is, contrary in all his doings and proceedings to Christ.

Thirdly, for he sits in the temple of God, and so did not Mahomet.

Fourthly, because he is an exalter of himself, and sitteth more like a god than a man in Rome.

Fifthly, because he seduces, and has seduced by his apostasy, the most part of all Christendom from the doctrine and free promises of God, into a wrong and strange way of salvation, which is not to be justified freely before God but only by our faith in Christ his

well-beloved Son (to which faith the promise of God freely and graciously has annexed all our salvation only, and to no other thing); but the pope has taught us to work out our salvation by an infinite number of other things; so that he binds the necessity of our salvation also to this, that we must believe (if we will be saved) and receive him to be the vicar of Christ in earth, &c.

But to return again to the Turks. Among all the prophecies, both of the Old Testament and of the New, there is none that points out the antichristian kingdom of the Turks better than doth the Revelation of St. John, whose words let us weigh and consider. Who speaking of opening the seventh and last seal (which signifieth the last age of the world), and there writing of the seven trumpets of the seven angels, at the sounding of the sixth angel, he saith, "Loose the four angels which are bound in the great river Euphrates. And the four angels were loosed, which were prepared for an hour, and a day, and a month, and a year, for to slay the third part of men. And the number of the army of the horsemen were two hundred thousand thousand: and I heard the number of them. And thus I saw the horses in the vision, and them that sat on them, having breastplates of fire, and of jacinth, and brimstone: and the heads of the horses were as the heads of lions; and out of their mouths issued fire, and smoke, and brimstone. By these three was the third part of men killed, by the fire, and by the smoke, and by the brimstone, which issued out of their mouths." (Rev. ix. 14—18.)

By the seventh seal is meant the seventh and last age of the world, which last age of the world is from Christ to the judgment and resurrection of the dead.

By the seven angels with their seven trumpets is signified the seven plagues that come in this seventh and last age of the world.

By the sixth trumpet of the sixth angel is meant the sixth plague coming last and next before the plague of the great judgment-day, which sixth plague is here described to come by the eastern kings, that is, by the Turks.

By loosing the angels who had rule of the great river Euphrates, is signified the letting out of the east kings, that is, the Turks out of Scythia, Tartary, Persia, and Arabia, by whom the third part of Christendom shall be destroyed, as we see it this day has come to pass.

It follows in the prophesy, "For their power is in their mouth, and in their tails: for their tails were like unto serpents, and had heads, and with them they do hurt." (Rev. ix. 19.) Meaning that these Turks with the words of their mouths shall threaten great destruction of fire and sword, to them that will not yield to them, and in the end, when the Christians shall yield to them, trusting to their promises, they, like serpents, shall deceive them in the end, and kill them.

The like prophecy also, after the like words and sense, is to be seen and read in the sixteenth chapter of the Revelations, where St. John, treating of seven cups filled with the wrath of the living God, given to the hands of seven angels by one of the four beasts (that is, in the time of one of the four monarchies, which was the monarchy of Rome), speaks likewise of the sixth angel, "And the sixth angel poured out his vial upon the great river Euphrates; and the water thereof was dried up, that the way of the kings of the east might be prepared." (Rev. xvi. 12.)

By the sixth angel with the sixth vial is meant, as before the last plague save one that shall come upon the christians. By the kings of the east are meant the Saracens, and twelve Ottoman Turks. By drying up the river Euphrates, is signified the way of these Turks to be prepared by the Lord's appointment, to come out of the eastern to the western parts of the world, to molest and afflict the christians. It follows more in the text:—"And I saw three unclean spirits like frogs come out of the mouth of the dragon, and out of the mouth of the beast, and out of the mouth of the false prophet. For they are the spirits of devils, working miracles, which go forth unto the kings of the earth and of the whole world, to gather them to the battle of that great day of God Almighty." And it follows shortly after, "And he gathered them together into a place called iu the Hebrew tongue Armageddon." And immediately it followeth in the same place, " And the seventh angel poured out his vial into the air, ; and there came a great voice out of the temple of heaven, from the throne, saying, It is done." (Rev. xvi. 13. 16, 17.) Whereby it is to be understood, that towards the last consummation of the world great force shall be seen, and a mighty army of the enemies shall be collected and gathered against the people and saints of the Highest, and then comes the consummation.

Wherefore, it is not for nought that the Holy Spirit of God, in the same place, a little before the sixth angel pours out his vial, exhorts all the faithful, saying, " Behold, I come like a thief in the night ; blessed is he that watcheth and keepeth his garments, lest he walk naked, and men see his filthiness," &c.

Nicholas de Lyra ; and Paul, bishop of Burdens ; and Matthias Dorinke, writing upon the thirteenth chapter of the Apocalypse, and expounding the mystery of the second beast rising out of the earth, having the horns of a lamb, &c. apply it to Mahomet and the Turks, with a solemn declaration made upon the same. Which interpretation of theirs, although in some points it may seem to have some appearance of probability, yet, as touching the proper and natural meaning of the apostle in that place, speaking of the false Lamb, &c. if we consider well all the circumstances of that beast, and mark the consequence of the text, both of that which goes before and follows after, we must grant, that the description and interpretation of that false horned lamb must necessarily be applied only to the bishop of Rome, and none other, which is to be proved by six principal causes or arguments.

The first is, for that this beast is described to bear the horns of a Lamb ; by which Lamb, no doubt, is meant Christ. By the horns of the Lamb is signified the outward shew or resemblance of Christ our Saviour ; which shew or resemblance can have no relation to Mahomet, for he takes himself to be above Christ, and Christ as an excellent prophet of God sitting at his feet. Wherefore, seeing Mahomet comes neither as equal to Christ, nor as vicar under Christ, this prophecy cannot agree to him, but only to him who openly in plain words protests, that all Christ's lambs and sheep, not singularly, but universally, through the whole world, are committed to him as vicar of Christ, and successor of Peter, and that all men must confess the same of necessity, or else they are none of Christ's sheep, &c. Wherein it is easy to see where the pretended horns of the lamb grow.

The second argument, " And he spake like a dragon," &c. A lamb's horns and the mouth of a dragon do not agree together. And as they do not agree together in nature, so neither can they be found in any person, either Turk or other, so lively, as in the bishop of Rome. When thou hearest him call himself " The apostolical bishop, the vicar of Christ, the successor of Peter, the servant of God's servants," &c. thou seest in him the two horns of a lamb, and wouldst think him to be a lamb indeed, and such a one as would wash your feet for humility ; but hear him speak, and you shall find him a dragon. See and read the epistle of Pope Martin V., charging, commanding, and threatening emperors, kings, dukes, princes, marquises, earls, barons, knights, rectors, consuls, proconsuls, with their shires, counties, and universities, of their kingdoms, provinces, cities, towns, castles, villages, and other places. See the answer of Pope Urban II., and his message to King William Rufus. Behold the works and doings of Pope Innocent III. against King John.

Note also the answer of another pope to the king of England, which, for the price of the king's head, would not grant to him the investing of his bishops. Mark well the words and doings of Pope Hildebrand against the Emperor Henry IV.; also of Pope Alexander II. treading upon the neck of Frederick Barbarossa, not like a lamb treading upon a dragon, but like a dragon treading upon a lamb.

It follows, moreover. in the same prophecy, Rev.

xiii. 12, for the third argument, " And he exerciseth all the power of the first beast before him, and causeth the earth and them which dwell therein to worship the first beast, whose deadly wound was healed," &c.

In this prophecy two things are to be noted ; first, what the first beast is, whose power the second beast executes. Secondly, what this second beast is which so exercises his power in his sight. The first of these beasts having seven heads and ten horns, must needs signify the city of Rome, which may easily be proved by two demonstrations. First, by the exposition of the seventeenth chapter of Revelation, where is declared and described the beast to stand on seven hills, and to contain ten kings, having the whole power of the dragon given ; and also the same city to be named " The whore of Babylon, drunken with the blood of the saints." All which properties joined together, can agree in nowise to any kingdom but the heathen empire of Rome, which city, at that time of writing these prophecies, had the government of the whole world. The second demonstration or evidence may be reduced out of the number of the months assigned to this beast. For so it is written, that this beast had power to make, that is, to work his malice against Christ's people forty-two months, which months counted by Sabbaths of years, (that is, every month for seven years) makes up the just number of those years, in which the primitive church was under the terrible persecutions of the heathen emperors of Rome, as is before specified.

Which thing thus proved that the first beast must needs signify the empire and city of Rome, then must it necessarily follow that the second beast with the lamb's horns, must signify the bishop and pope of the same city of Rome. The reason whereof is evident by that which follows in the prophecy, where it is declared, that the second beast, having two horns of a lamb, received and exercised all the power of the first beast, before or in the sight of the said beast, which cannot be verified either in the Turks or in any other, but only in the pope of Rome, who (as you see) receives, usurps, and derives to himself all the power of that city and monarchy of Rome ; so that he saith, that when Constantine or Ludovicus yielded unto him the rule and kingdom of that city, he gave him but his own, and that which of right and duty belonged to him before.

And this authority or power over all the empire of Rome he works not in Asia, or in Constantinople, as the Turk does, but in the sight of the beast which gave him the power, that is, in the city of Rome itself, which is the first beast here in this prophecy of the Revelation described.

Fourthly, It follows further, " And he causeth the earth and them which dwell therein to worship the first beast, whose deadly wound was healed," &c. The interpretation of this part, as also of all the other parts of the same chapter, stands upon the definition of the first beast ; for it being granted, as cannot be denied, that the first beast signifies the city and empire of Rome ; it must consequently follow, that the bishop (whom we call the pope) of the city of Rome, must be understood by the second beast ; as neither Turk nor any other, but only the bishop of Rome has held up the estimation and dignity of that city, which began to be in ruin and decay by the Vandals, Goths, Herulians, and Lombards, about A.D. 456 ; but afterward, by the bishop of Rome, the pristine state and honour of that city revived again, and flourished in as great veneration as ever it did before. And that is it which the Holy Ghost seems here to mean of the first beast, saying, " That he had a wound of the beast, and was cured." For so it follows :

Fifthly, " Saying to them that dwell on the earth, that they should make an image to the beast, which had the wound by a sword, and did live. And he had power to give life unto the image of the beast, that the image of the beast should both speak, and cause that as many as would not worship the image of the beast should be killed. And he caused all, both small and great, rich and poor, free and bond, to receive a mark in their right hand, or in their foreheads : and that no man might buy or sell, save he that had the mark, or the name of the beast, or the number of his name," &c. (Rev. xiii. 14—17.)

By giving life to the image of the beast, and making it speak, it is presupposed that the beast was at the point of death, and lay speechless; inasmuch as the city of Rome began to lose and change name, and was called for a while Odacria, from Odoacer king of the Herulians, who by dint of sword surprised the Romans; and yet, notwithstanding, by the means of its prelates, the city of Rome, which was then ready to give up the ghost, recovered its majesty and strength again. It is even hard to say, whether Rome did ever ruffle and rage in tyranny, more tragically in the time of Nero, Domitian, Dioclesian, and other emperors, than it has done under the pope; or whether that Rome had all kings, queens, princes, dukes, lords, and all subjects more under obedience and subjection, when the emperors reigned, or now in the reign of the pope. And therefore it is said not without cause by the Holy Ghost, That it is given to him, to give life and speech to the image of the beast, causing all them to be slain which will not worship the image of the beast, &c. As for example, who sees not what multitudes of christian men, women, and children in all countries have been put to fire and sword? histories of all times will declare what havock has been made of christian blood about the pre-eminence and majority of the see of Rome; what churches and countries, both Greeks and Latins, have been excommunicated; what kings have been deposed, and emperors stripped from their imperial seat, and all because they would not stoop and bend to the image of the beast, that is, to the majesty and title of Rome, advanced so highly now by its bishop, as it was never higher before in the reign of Nero or Dioclesian. Wherefore, taking the first beast to signify the empire of Rome, which cannot be denied, it is plain, that the second beast must necessarily be applied to the pope and not to the Turk, as the Turk seeks nothing so little as the advancement of that empire, but rather strives against it to pluck it down.

The sixth and last argument is grounded upon the number of the name of the beast, expressed by the Holy Ghost in the same prophecy, by the letters χ ξ ς. In which letters, although there lies great darkness and difficulty to be understood, yet certain ancient fathers which were disciples and hearers of them which heard St. John himself, as Irenæus and others, expound the letters conjecturally, to contain the name of the beast, and to be the name of a man under this word λατεινος:[1] Whereas no other name lightly of any person, either in Greek or Latin, will agree to the same, save only the foresaid named λατεινος. There are some other solutions of these numbers, but of all names properly signifying any man, none comes so near to the number of this mystery, (if it go by order of letters) as the word λατεινος.

Let us come to the twentieth chapter of the Revelation, wherein the holy scripture seems plainly and directly to notify the Turks. The words of the prophecy are these:—

"And I saw an angel come down from heaven, having the key of the bottomless pit and a great chain in his hand. And he laid hold on the dragon, that old serpent, which is the devil, and Satan, and bound him a thousand years, and cast him into the bottomless pit, and shut him up, and set a seal upon him, that he should deceive the nations no more, till the thousand years should be fulfilled: and after that he must be loosed a little season."

And it follows after, "And when the thousand years are expired, Satan shall be loosed out of his prison, and shall go out to deceive the nations which are in the four quarters of the earth, Gog and Magog, to gather them together to battle: the number of whom is as the sand of the sea. And they went up on the breadth of the earth, and compassed the camp of the saints about, and the beloved city," &c. (ver. 7, 8, 9.)

To the perfect understanding of this prophecy, three things are necessary to be known. First, what is meant by binding up, and loosing out of Satan as the old dragon. Secondly, at what time and year first he was chained up and sealed for a thousand years. Thirdly, at what year and time these thousand years did end, when he should be loosed out again for a little season. Which three points being well examined and marked, the prophecy may easily be understood directly to be meant of the Turk.

First, by binding and loosing of Satan seems to be meant the ceasing and staying of the cruel and horrible persecution of the heathen emperors of Rome against the true christians, as is to be seen in 'The Ten first Persecutions in the Primitive Church,' in which most bloody persecutions, Satan then raged without all measure, till the time it pleased Almighty God to stop this old serpent, and to tie him shorter. And thus have you to understand what is meant by the binding up of Satan for a thousand years; whereby is signified, that the persecution against the christians stirred up by the beast (that is, in the empire of Rome, through the instigation of Satan) shall not always continue, but shall break up after a certain time, and shall cease for a thousand years, &c.

Now at what time and year this persecution, that is, the fury and rage of Satan should cease, is also declared in the Revelation before; where in the eleventh and thirteenth chapters we read, that the beast before mentioned shall have power to work his malice and mischief for the space of forty-two months, and no more, and then that Satan should be locked up for a thousand years. The computation of which months, being counted by Sabbaths of years (after the example of the sixty-nine weeks of Daniel, chapter xi.) it brings us to the just year and time, when that terrible persecution in the primitive church should end, and so it did. For, if we allow to every month a Sabbath of years, that is, reckon every month for seven years, and that makes two hundred and ninety-four years, which embraces the period between the eighteenth year of Tiberius, (under whom Christ suffered) and the death of Maxentius the last persecutor of the primitive church in Europe, subdued by Constantine, as may appear by calculating the years, months, and days, between the year of the reign of Tiberius, and the death of Maxentius; and so you have the account of the period when Satan was first bound up, after he had raged in the primitive church two-and-forty months. Which months, as is said, being counted by Sabbaths of years, after the usual manner of scripture, amount to two hundred and ninety-four years; and so much was the full time between the passion of our Lord, which was in the eighteenth year of Tiberius, to the last year of Maxentius.[2]

And here by the way comes a note to be observed, that as by the number of these forty-two months specified in the Revelations, the empire of Rome must necessarily be confessed to be the first beast, therefore it must by like necessity follow, the bishop of Rome is the second beast, with the two horns of the lamb, because he only has and does cause the empire of Rome to revive and to be magnified, which the Turk does not, but rather labours to the contrary. Wherefore let every christian man be wise, and beware in time how he takes the mark of the beast, lest peradventure it follow upon him, that he drink of that terrible cup of wrath mentioned. (Rev. xiv.)

Thirdly, it remains to be discussed touching the third point in this prophecy, that as we have found out (through the help of Christ) the year and time of Satan's binding, so we search out likewise the time and season of his loosing out, which by the testimony of scripture was approved to be a thousand years after his binding up, and rightly according to the time appointed it came to pass. For if we number well by the scripture the year of his binding up, which was from the passion of our Lord two hundred and ninety-four years,

---

(2) See note p. 69. [Ed].

and add thereto a thousand years, it mounts to one thousand two hundred ninety-four, which was about the time when Ottoman the first Turk began his conquests, which was the first spring and well-head of all these woful calamities that the church of Christ hath felt both in Asia, Africa, and Europe, almost these three hundred years past. For so we find in chronicles, that the kingdom of the Turks being first divided into four families, at length the family of Ottoman prevailed, and thereupon came those whom we now call Turks, which was about the same time when Pope Boniface VIII. was bishop of Rome.

In this long digression, wherein sufficiently has been described the grievous and tedious persecution of the Saracens and Turks against the christians, thou hast to understand, good reader, and to behold the image of a terrible antichrist evidently appearing both by his own doings, and also by the scriptures, prophesied and declared to us before. Now in comparing the Turk with the pope, if a question be asked, which of them is the truer or greater antichrist, it were easy to see and judge, that the Turk is the more open and manifest enemy against Christ and his church. But if it be asked which of the two has been the more bloody and pernicious adversary to Christ and his members, or which of them has consumed and spilt more christian blood, he with sword, or this with fire and sword together, neither is it a light matter to discern, neither is it my part here to discuss, who only write the history, and the acts of them both. Wherefore after the history of the Turks thus finished, we will now return to where we left off, in describing the domestic troubles and persecutions here at home under the bishop of Rome, after the burning of Babram in Norfolk.

In the days of King Henry VII. (A.D. 1506), in the diocese of Lincoln, in Buckinghamshire, one William Tylsworth was burned in Amersham, in a close, called Stanley, about sixty years ago. At which time one Joan Clerk, a married woman, who was the only daughter of William Tylsworth, and a faithful woman, was compelled with her own hands to set fire to her dear father; and at the same time her husband John Clerk did penance at her father's burning, and bear a fagot, as did also twenty-three other persons; and who afterwards were compelled to wear certain badges, and went abroad to certain towns to do penance, as to Buckingham, Aylesbury, and other towns. And also several of these men were afterwards burned in the cheek, as William Page, who at this present day is alive, and likewise carried a fagot with the others. Agnes Wetherly, who is still alive, testifies that at the burning of this William Tylsworth, were above sixty others who were obliged to carry fagots for their penance, of whom some were enjoined to bear and wear fagots at Lincoln the space of seven years, some at one time, some at another, &c. In which number was also one Robert Bartlet, a rich man, who for his professions' sake was put out of his farm and goods, and was condemned to be kept in the monastery of Ashryge, where he wore on his right sleeve a square piece of cloth, the space of seven years together.

About the same time of the burning of William Tylsworth, was one Father Roberts burned at Buckingham. He was a miller, and dwelt at Missenden. At his burning there were about twenty persons that were compelled to carry fagots, and to do such penance as the wicked Pharisees compelled them to. After that, by the space of two or three years, was burned at Amersham, Thomas Bernard, a husbandman, and James Mordon, a labourer, they were both burned at one fire; and there was William Littlepage (who is yet alive) compelled to be burned in the right cheek, and Father Rogers, and Father Reive, who afterwards were burned. This Father Rogers was in the bishop's prison fourteen weeks together, night and day, where he was so cruelly handled with cold, hunger and irons, that after his coming out of the prison, he was so lame in his back, that he could never go upright as long as he lived, as several honest men that are now living can testify. Also there were

thirty more burned in the right cheek, and obliged to carry fagots the same time. The cause was that they would talk against superstition and idolatry, and were desirous to hear and read the holy scriptures. The manner of their burning in the cheek was this; their necks were tied fast to a post, and their hands holden fast that they might not stir, and so the iron being hot, was put to their cheeks, and thus they bore about them the prints and marks of the Lord Jesus.

The cruel handling of Thomas Chase of Amersham, who was wickedly strangled and martyred in the Bishops' Prison at Woburn.

Among those who were so cruelly persecuted for the gospel and word of Christ, was one Thomas Chase of Amersham. This man by the report of such as knew him, was a man of a godly sober and honest behaviour (whose virtuous doings yet remain in memory) and could not abide idolatry and superstition, but many times would speak against it. Wherefore the ungodly and wicked did the more hate and despise him, and took him and brought him before the blind bishop, being at that time at Woburn in the county of Buckingham, and as it is written in the Acts that wicked Herod vexed certain of the church, and killed James, the brother of John, with the sword; and because he saw that it pleased the Jews, he proceeded farther, so this bishop had Thomas Chase before him, asking him many questions touching the Romish religion, with many taunts, checks, and rebukes, but what answer this godly man, Thomas Chase, made them is unknown. However it is to be supposed, that his answer was most zealous and godly in professing Christ's true religion and gospel, and to the extirpation of idolatry, and superstition, and hypocrisy, for that he was commanded to be put in the prison, in the bishop's house at Woburn, which had not been done to him, had not his answers been sound and upright. There Thomas Chase lay bound most painfully with chains, manacles, and irons, often pining with hunger, where the bishop's alms was daily brought to him by his chaplains, which alms were nothing else but checks, taunts, rebukes, and threatenings and mockings. All which cruelty the godly martyr took most quietly and patiently, remembering and having respect to Christ's promises: "Blessed are they which suffer for righteousness sake, for theirs is the kingdom of heaven," Matt. v. And as follows: "Blessed are ye when men revile you and persecute you," &c. When the bishop, with his band of shavelings, perceived that by their daily practices of cruelty they could not prevail against him, but rather that he was the more fervent and earnest in professing Christ's true religion, and that he did bear most patiently all their wickedness and cruelty to him, they imagined how and which way they might put him to death, lest there should be a tumult or an uproar among the people. And as Richard Hunne shortly after was hanged or strangled in Lollards' Tower, about A.D. 1514, even so these blood-suckers most cruelly strangled and put to death this Thomas Chase in prison, who most heartily called upon God to receive his spirit, as witnesses a certain woman that kept him in prison.

After these vipers of the wicked brood of antichrist had thus most cruelly and impiously murdered this faithful christian, they were at their wits' end, and could not tell what shift to make, to cloak their shameful murder; at last, to blind the ignorant silly people, these bloody butchers most slanderously caused it to be rumoured abroad by their dependents, that Thomas Chase had hanged himself in prison, which was a most shameful and abominable lie, for the prison was such, that a man could not stand upright, nor lie at ease. And besides, this man had so many manacles and irons upon him, that he could not well move either hand or foot, as the woman declares that saw him dead. And yet these holy catholics had not made an end of their wicked act in this both killing and slandering of this godly martyr; but to put out the remembrance of him, they caused him to be buried in the wood, called Norland-wood, in the highway betwixt Woburn and little Marlow, to the intent he should not be taken up again to be seen; and thus commonly are innocent men laid up by these unworthy clergymen. But he that is true hath promised at one time or another, to clear his true servants, not with lies and fables, but by his own true word. No secret, saith he, is so close but it shall be opened; neither is any thing so hid, that shall not at the last be known clearly. Such a sweet Lord is God always to those that are his true servants. Blessed be his holy name for ever and ever. Amen.

Thomas Harding being one of this company, thus molested and troubled in the town of Amersham, for the truth of the gospel, after his abjuration and penance was again sought for, and brought to the fire in the days of King Henry VIII.

After the martyrdom of these two, I read also of one Thomas Noris, who for the same cause, that is, for the profession of Christ's gospel, was condemned by the bishop, and burnt at Norwich the last day of March, (A. D. 1507.)

In the next year following, which was A.D. 1508, in the consistory of London, was Elizabeth Sampson of the parish of Aldermanbury, upon certain articles, and especially for speaking against pilgrimage and adoration of images, especially the images of our lady at Wilsdon, at Stanings, at Crome, at Walsingham, and against the sacrament of the altar. For these and certain other articles, she was compelled to abjure before Master William Horsey, chancellor, the day and year above written.

Laurence Ghest.

It is lamentable to remember, and almost impossible to comprehend the names, times, and persons of all who have been slain by the pope's clergy, for the true maintaining of Christ's cause, and his sacraments. Whose memory being registered in the book of life, although it need not our commemoration, yet for the more confirmation of the church, I thought it not unprofitable to relate the suffering and martyrdom of them who innocently have given their blood to be shed in Christ's cause.

In the catalogue of whom, next in order comes the memorial of Laurence Ghest, who was burned in Salisbury for the matter of the sacrament, in the days of King Henry VII. He was of a comely and tall personage, and otherwise not unfriended, for which the bishop and the clergy were the more loath to burn him, but kept him in prison for the space of two years. This Laurence had a wife and seven children. Wherefore they thinking to influence and persuade his mind, by awakening his fatherly affection toward his children, when the time came which they appointed for his burning, as he was at the stake, they brought before him his wife and his seven children. At the sight of them, although nature is commonly wont to work in other men, yet in him religion overcoming nature, made his constancy remain unmoveable, so that when his wife exhorted and desired him to save himself, he again began to desire her to be content, and not to be a stumbling block in his way, for he was in a good course, running toward the mark of his salvation; and so fire being put to him, he finished his life, renouncing not only wife and children, but also himself to follow Christ. As he was burning one of the bishop's men threw a firebrand at his face. At this the brother of Laurence, who was standing by, ran at him with his dagger, and would have slain him, had he not been otherwise prevented.

But among all the examples of God, of whom so many have suffered from time to time for Christ and his truth, I cannot tell if ever there were any martyrdom more notable and admirable, or wherein the plain demonstration of God's mighty power and judgment has at any time been more evident against the persecutors of his flock, than at the burning of a certain godly woman put to death in Chipping Sodbury, about the same time, under the reign of King Henry VII.

The constancy of which blessed woman, as it is glorious for all true godly christians to behold, so the example of the bishop's chancellor, which cruelly condemned the innocent, may offer a terrible spectacle to the eyes of all papistical persecutors to consider, and to take example, which the living God grant they may. Amen. The name of the town where she was martyred, was, as is said, Chipping Sodbury. The chancellor who condemned, was Doctor Whittington. The time of her burning was in the reign of Henry VII.

After this godly woman, and manly martyr of Christ, was condemned by the wretched chancellor, for the faithful profession of the truth, which the papists then called heresy, and the time now come when she should be brought to the place and pains of her martyrdom, a great concourse of all the multitude, both in the town and country about was gathered to behold her end. Among whom was also Doctor Whittington, the chancellor, there present to see the execution. Thus this faithful woman, and true servant of God, constantly persisting in the testimony of the truth, committing her cause to the Lord, gave over her life to the fire, refusing no pains nor torments to keep her conscience clear and unreproveable in the day of the Lord. The sacrifice being ended, the people began to return homeward, coming from the burning of this blessed martyr. It happened in the meantime, that as the popish executioners were busy in slaying this Lamb at the town's side, a certain butcher was as busy within the town slaying a bull, which bull he had fast bound in ropes ready to knock him on the head. But the butcher (belike not so skilful in his art of killing beasts, as the papists are in murdering christians) as he was lifting his axe to strike the bull, failed in his stroke, and smote a little too low, or else how he smit, I know not: this was certain that the bull, although somewhat grieved at the stroke, but yet not stricken down, put his strength to the ropes, and broke loose from the butcher into the street, at the very time when the people were coming in great crowd from the burning, who seeing the bull coming towards them, and supping him to be wild, gave way for the beast, every man shifting for himself as well as he might. Thus the people giving back, and making a lane for the bull, he passed through the throng of them, touching neither man nor child, till he came where the chancellor was. Against whom the bull, with a sudden vehemency, ran full butt with his horns, and gored him through and through, and so killed him immediately, to the great wonder of all that saw it.

Although the carnal sense of man be blind in considering the works of the Lord, imputing many times to blind chance the things which properly pertain to God's only praise and providence; yet in this so strange and so evident example, what man can be so dull or ignorant as not to see a plain interposition of God's mighty power and judgment, both in the punishing of this wretched chancellor, and also in admonishing all other persecutors, by his example, to fear the Lord, and to abstain from the like cruelty?

And thus much concerning the state of the church. Wherein is to be understood, what storms and persecutions have been raised up in all quarters against the flock and congregation of Christ, not only by the Turks, but also at home within ourselves, by the bishop of Rome and his retinue. Where also is to be noted in the days and reign of this King Henry VII. how mightily the working of God's gospel has multiplied and increased, and what great numbers of men and women have suffered for the same with us in England.

Now these things declared relating to the church, it remains to treat likewise of the commonwealth, which commonly follows the state of the church. Where the church is quietly and modestly governed, and the flock of Christ defended by godly princes in peace and safety, from devouring and violence of bloody wolves; the success of the civil estate, there and then for the most part, flourishes, and the princes long continue through God's preservation, in prosperity and tranquillity. Contrary-wise, where either the church of Christ through the negligence of princes, or through their instigation, the poor members of Christ are persecuted and devoured; shortly after comes some just recompence of the Lord upon those princes, that either their lives do not long continue, or else they find not that quiet in the common-wealth which they look for. Examples of this, as in all other ages, they are abundant, so in this present time are not lacking, whether we consider the state and condition of other countries far off, or else of our country near at home.

Not that I here affirm or define, as a general rule, that worldly success and prosperity of life always follow the godly, whom we see rather given over often to the wicked: yet, speaking of the duty of princes, I observe by examples of histories, that such princes as have most defended the church of Christ committed to their government, from injury and violence of the bishop of Rome, have not lacked at God's hand great blessing and felicity. Whereas contrarywise, they who either themselves have been persecutors of Christ's members, or have not shielded them by their protection from foreign tyranny and injuries, have lacked at God's hand that protection which the other had, as may appear by King Edward II., Richard III., King Henry IV., King Henry V., King Henry VI., &c., who, because either negligently they have suffered, or cruelly caused such persecuting laws to be made, and so much christian blood injuriously devoured, therefore have they been the less prospered of the Lord ; so that either they were deposed, or if they flourished for a while, yet they did not long continue, almost not half the time of the other kings before named.

And therefore, as the state of the commonwealth commonly follows the state of the church, so it had been to be wished that this King Henry VII., being otherwise a prudent and temperate prince, had not permitted the intemperate rage of the pope's clergy so much to have their wills over the poor flock of Christ as they had. Although he reigned nearly twenty-four years, yet, notwithstanding, here comes the same thing to be noted of which I spake : that when the church of Christ begins to be injured with violence, and to go to wreck through disorder and negligence, the state of the commonwealth cannot long endure without some alteration and strokes of God's correction. But however this mark is to be taken, thus lies the history : that after the burning and vexing of these poor servants of Christ above recited, when the persecution began now in the church to be hot, God calls away the king the same year, which was 1509, after he had reigned nearly the term of twenty-four years ; who if he had adjoined a little more compassionate respect, in protecting Christ's poor members from the fire of the pope's tyranny, to his other great virtues of singular wisdom, excellent temperance, and moderate frugality, so much had he been comparable with the best of those princes, as he had been inferior but to a few : but this defect which was wanted in him, was supplied most luckily (blessed be the Lord), by his posterity succeeding after him.

Among many other things incident in the reign of this King Henry VII., I have passed over the history of certain godly persons persecuted in the diocese of Coventry and Lichfield, as we find them in the registers of the diocese recorded, here following.

The year of our Lord, 1485, March 9, among other good men in Coventry, these nine here under-named, were examined before John bishop of Coventry and Litchfield in Saint Michael's church, upon the following articles :—

First, John Blomston was openly and publicly accused, reported and appeached, that he was a very heretic, because he had preached, taught, holden, and affirmed, that the power attributed to St. Peter in the church of God, by our Saviour Jesus Christ immediately, did not flit or pass from him, to remain with his successors.

That there was as much virtue in an herb, as in the image of the Virgin Mary.

That prayer and alms avail not the dead ; for immediately after death, he goes either to heaven or hell, whereupon he concludes there is no purgatory.

That it was foolishness to go on pilgrimage to the image of our lady of Doncaster, Walsingham, or the tower of the city of Coventry ; for a man might as well worship the blessed Virgin by fire-side in the kitchen, as in the aforesaid places, and as well might a man worship

the blessed Virgin, when he sees his mother and sister, as in visiting the images, because they are no more but dead stocks and stones.

Richard Hegham of the same city was accused, &c., to be a very heretic, because he held that a christian man being at the point of death, should renounce all his own works, good and ill, and submit him to the mercy of God.

That it was foolishness to worship the images of our lady of Tower in the city, or of other saints, for they are but stocks and stones.

That if the image of our lady of Tower were put into the fire, it would make a good fire.

That it were better to deal money to poor folks, than to offer to the images of Christ and other saints, which are but dead stocks and stones.

Robert Crowther of the same city, was accused that he was a heretic, because he held, that whoso receives the sacrament of the altar in deadly sin, or out of charity, receives nothing but bread and wine.

That neither bishop, nor priests, nor curates of churches, have power in the market of penance to bind or loose.

That pilgrimage to our lady of Tower is foolishness ; for it is but a stock on a stone.

John Smith was accused to be a very heretic, because he held, that every man is bound to know the Lord's prayer, and the creed in English.

That whoso believed as the churchmen believed, believes ill : and that a man had need to frequent the schools a good while, ere he can attain to the knowledge of the true and right faith.

That no priest has power to absolve a man in the market of penance from his sins.

Roger Brown of the same city, was also accused to be an heretic, because he held that no man ought to worship the image of our lady of Walsingham, nor the blood of Christ at Halies, but rather God Almighty, who would give him whatever he would ask.

That he held not up his hand, nor looked up, at the elevation of the Eucharist.

That he promised one to show him certain books of heresy, if he would swear that he would not utter them, and if he would credit them.

That he did eat flesh in Lent, and was taken in the act.

If any man were not confessed and absolved in his whole life long, and in the point of death would be confessed, and could not, if he had no more but contrition only, he should pass to joy without purgatory : and if he were confessed of any sin, and were enjoined only to say for penance one paternoster, if he thought he should have any punishment in purgatory for that sin, he would never be confessed for any sin.

Because he said all is lost that is given to priests.

That there was no purgatory, that would pardon all sins, without confession and satisfaction.

Thomas Butler of the same city was likewise openly accused as a very heretic, because he held that there were but two ways, that is to say, to heaven and to hell. That no faithful man should suffer any pain after the death of Christ, for any sin, because Christ died for our sins.

That there was no purgatory ; for every man immediately after death passes either to heaven or hell.

That whoever departs in the faith of Christ and the Church, however he has lived, shall be saved.

That prayers and pilgrimages are nothing worth, and avail not to purchase heaven.

John Falks was accused as a very heretic, because he did affirm, that it was a foolish thing to offer to the image of our lady, saying, what is it but a block ? If it could speak to me, I would give it a halfpenny-worth of ale.

That when the priest carries to the sick the body of Christ, why carries he not also the blood of Christ ?

That he did eat cow-milk upon the first Sunday of Lent.

That as concerning the sacrament of penance and absolution, no priest has power to absolve any man from his sins, inasmuch as he cannot make one hair of his head.

That the image of our lady was but a stone or a block.

Richard Hilmin was accused that he was a very heretic, because he did say and maintain, that it was better to part with money to the poor, than to give tithes to priests, or to offer to the images of our lady; and that it were better to offer to images made by God, than to images of God painted.

That he had the Lord's prayer and the salutation of the angel and the creed in English, and another book he saw and had, which contained the epistles and gospels in English, and according to them he would live, and thereby believed he would be saved.

That no priest speaks better in the pulpit than that book.

That the sacrament of the altar is but bread, and that the priests make it to blind the people.

That a priest while he is at mass, is a priest; and after one mass done, till the beginning of another mass, he is no more than a layman, and has no more power than a mere layman.

After they were forced to recant, they were absolved, and obliged to do penance.

In A. D. 1488, the third of April, Margery Coyt, wife of James Coyt of Ashburn, was brought before the foresaid John Bishop of Coventry and Lichfield, who was there accused that she said, that that which the priests lifted over their heads at mass, was not the true and very body of Christ; for if it was so, the priests could not break it so lightly into four parts, and swallow it as they do; for the Lord's body has flesh and bones, which that which the priests receive has not.

That priests buying forty cakes for a halfpenny, and shewing them to the people, and saying, that of every one of them they make the body of Christ, do nothing but deceive the people and enrich themselves.

Seeing God in the beginning created and made man, how can it be that man should be able to make God?

This woman also was constrained to recant, and so was she absolved and did penance.

Thus much I thought good to insert here, touching these men of Coventry, especially for this purpose, because our cavilling adversaries are wont to object against us the newness of Christ's old and ancient religion. To the intent therefore they may see this doctrine, not to be so new as they report, I wish they would consider both the time and articles here objected against these persons.

I should also in the same reign of King Henry VII., have induced that story of Johannes Picus Earl of Mirandula, the mention of whose name partly is touched before. This Picus Earl of Mirandula, being but a young man, was so excellently witted, and so singularly learned in all sciences and in all tongues, both Latin, Greek, and Hebrew, Chaldee, and Arabic, that coming to Rome booted and spurred, he set up ninety conclusions, to dispute with any in all Christendom, whoever would come against him. Of which conclusions several were on the matter of the sacrament, &c. And when none was found in all Rome, nor in Europe, that openly would dispute with him, privately and in corners certain of the pope's clergy, prelates, lawyers, and friars, appointed by the pope, consulted together to inquire upon his conclusions, whereupon they articulated against him for suspicion of heresy. And thus the unlearned clergy of Rome privately circumvented and entangled this learned earl in their snares of heresy, against whom they durst never openly dispute. He died at the age of thirty-two years, of such wit and forwardness, as is hard to say whether ever Italy bred up a better. In his sickness Charles VIII., then French king, moved with the fame of his learning, came to visit him.

The names of the Archbishops of Canterbury in this Sixth Book contained.

62. John Stratford.
63. John Kempe.
64. Thomas Bouchier.
65. John Morton.
66. Thomas Langhton.
67. Henry Dene.
    William Warham.

THE END OF THE SIXTH BOOK.

THE PROUD PRIMACY OF POPES DESCRIBED,

IN ORDER OF THEIR RISING UP BY LITTLE AND LITTLE, FROM FAITHFUL BISHOPS AND
MARTYRS, TO BECOME LORDS AND GOVERNORS OVER KINGS AND KINGDOMS,
EXALTING THEMSELVES IN THE TEMPLE OF GOD, ABOVE ALL
THAT IS CALLED GOD, ETC. II Thessalonians, ii. 4.

In the description of the primitive church, the reader has had set forth and exhibited before his eyes the grievous afflictions and torment, which, through God's secret sufferance, fell upon the true saints and members of Christ's church in that time, especially upon the good bishops, ministers, and teachers of the flock, of whom some were scourged, some beheaded, some crucified, some burned, some had their eyes put out, some one way, some another, miserably consumed ; which days of woeful calamity continued for nearly three hundred years. During which time the spouse and elect church of God, being sharply assaulted on every side, had no rest, nor joy, nor outward safety in this world, but passed all their days in much bitterness of heart, in continual tears and mourning under the cross, being spoiled, imprisoned, contemned, reviled, famished, tormented, and martyred everywhere ; they durst not tarry at home for fear and dread, and much less durst come abroad for the enemies, but only by night, when they assembled sometimes to sing psalms and hymns together. But notwithstanding, in all their dreadful dangers, and sorrowful afflictions, the goodness of the Lord left them not desolate ; but the more their outward tribulations increased, the more their inward consolations abounded ; and the farther off they seemed from the joys of this life, the more present was the Lord with them with grace and fortitude to confirm and rejoice their souls. And though their possessions and riches in this world were lost and spoiled, yet were they enriched with heavenly gifts above an hundred fold. Then was true religion really felt in heart. Then christianity was not merely shown in outward appearance, but was received in inward affection, and in the true image of the church, not in pretended outward shew, but in her effectual perfect state. Then was the name and fear of God engrafted in the heart, not only dwelling on the lips. Then faith was fervent, zeal ardent ; prayer was not merely on the lips, but groaned out to God from the bottom of the spirit. Then there was no pride in the church, nor leisure to seek riches, nor time to keep them. Contention for trifles was then so far from christians, that they were happy when they could meet to pray together against the devil, the author of all dissension. Briefly, the whole church of Christ Jesus, with all its members, the farther it was from the type and shape of this world, the nearer it was to God's favour and support.

The first rising of the Bishops of Rome.

After this long time of trouble it pleased the Lord at length mercifully to look upon the saints and servants of his Son, to release their captivity, to relieve their misery, and to bind up the old dragon the devil, who so long vexed them, whereby the church began to aspire to some more liberty ; and the bishops who before were as abjects utterly contemned by emperors, through the providence of God (who disposeth all things in his time after his own will) began now to be esteemed by emperors and had in honour ; and, further, as emperors grew more in devotion, so the bishops were more and more exalted, not only in favour, but also preferred to honour, so that in a short space they became not quarter-masters, but rather half emperors with emperors.

After this, as riches and worldly wealth crept into the clergy, and the devil had poured his venom into the church, so true humility began to decay, and pride to step in, till at last they played as the ivy does with the oak-tree, which first beginning with a goodly green show, embraces it so long that at length it overgrows it, and so sucks all his moisture from him, setting its root fast in his bark, till at last it both stifles the stock, and kills the branches, and so comes to be a nest for owls and all unclean birds. Not untruly, therefore, it was said by Augustine, " Religion begat riches, and the daughter has devoured the mother." The truth of which may appear in the history of the church of Rome and her bishops. For after the church of Rome, through the favour of emperors, was endowed with lands, donations, possessions, and patrimonies, so that the bishops feeling the pleasure of wealth, ease, and prosperity, began to increase in pomp and pride. The more they flourished in this world, the more God's Holy Spirit forsook them, till at last the bishops, who at the first were poor, creeping upon the ground, and persecuted, every man treading upon them in this world, now, instead of being persecuted people, began to be the persecutors of others, and to tread upon the necks even of emperors, and to bring the heads of kings and princes under their girdle. And not only that, but through pride and riches, they were so far gone from all true religion, that in the end they became the great adversary of God (whom we call antichrist) prophesied of so long before by the Spirit of God to come, sitting in the temple of God, &c. Of whom we thus read in the epistle of St. Paul, where he saith, " Now we beseech you, brethren, by the coming of our Lord Jesus Christ, and by our gathering together unto him, that ye be not soon shaken in mind, or be troubled, neither by spirit, nor by word, nor by letter as from us, as that the day of Christ is at hand. Let no man deceive you by any means : for that day shall not come, except there come a falling away first, and that man of sin be revealed, the son of perdition ; who opposeth and exalteth himself above all that is called God, or that is worshipped ; so that he as God sitteth in the temple of God, shewing himself that he is God." (2 Thess. ii. 1—4.)

By which words of St. Paul, we have several things to note : First, that the day of the Lord's coming was not then near at hand. Secondly, the apostle giving us a token before, to know when that day shall approach, bids us to look for an adversary first to be revealed. Thirdly, to shew what adversary this shall be, he expresses him not to be as a common adversary, such as were then in his time. For although Herod, Annas, and Caiaphas, the high priests and pharisees, Tertullus, Alexander the coppersmith, Elymas and Simon Magus, and Nero the emperor, in St. Paul's time, were great adversaries: yet here he means another besides these, greater than all the rest, not such a one as should be like to priest, king, or emperor, but such as far exceeding the state of all kings, priests, and emperors, should be the prince of priests, should make kings stoop, and should tread upon the neck of emperors, and make them to kiss his feet. Moreover, where the apostle saith, that he shall sit in the temple of God, thereby is meant, not merely the personal sitting of the pope in the city of Rome, but the authority and jurisdiction of his see exalted in the whole universal church, equal with God himself. For let men give to the pope that which he requires in his pontifical laws and decrees, and what difference is there between God and the pope? If God sets laws and ordinances, so does he. If God have his creatures, so has he. If God require obedience, so does he. If the breach of God's commandments are punished, much more are his. God has his religion, the pope also has his: yea, for God's one religion he has an hundred. God has set up an advocate, he has an hundred. God has instituted but a few holy-days, for God's one he hath instituted forty. Christ is the head of the church, so is the pope. Christ gives influence to his body, so does the pope. Christ forgives sin, the pope does no less. Christ expels evil spirits by his power, so the pope pretends to do by his holy water. Furthermore, where Christ went barefoot upon the bare ground, he with his golden shoes is carried upon men's shoulders. Christ never used any but the spiritual sword, he claims both spiritual and temporal. Christ bought the church, he both buys and sells the church. And if it be necessary to believe Christ to be the Saviour of the world, so it is necessary to believe the pope to be the head of the church. Christ paid tribute to Cæsar, he makes Cæsar pay tribute to him. Finally, the crown of Christ was of sharp thorns, the pope has three crowns of gold upon his head, so far exceeding Christ the Son of God in glory of this world, as Christ exceedeth him in the glory of heaven; whose intolerable pride and exaltation, according as St. Paul describes him in his epistle, we have here set forth, not only in these tables, and by his own facts to be noted, but also declared in his own words and registers, clementines, extravagants, and pontificals, as (the Lord willing) shall follow in order.

The exaltation of Popes above Kings and Emperors, out of History.

First, after Italy and the city of Rome were over-run by the Goths and Vandals, so that the seat of the empire was removed to Constantinople, then began John, patriarch of Constantinople, to put himself forth, and would needs be called universal bishop of the world; but the bishop of Rome in no case would suffer that, and stopped it. After this came the emperor's deputy, and exarch of Ravenna to rule Italy, but the bishop of Rome, through the aid of the king of the Lombards, soon mastered him.

Not long after (A.D. 600,) came Phocas the murderer, who slew the emperor of Constantinople, his master Mauricius, and his children. By which Phocas the bishops of old Rome aspired first to their pre-eminence to be counted the head bishops over the whole church, and so together with the Lombards began to rule the city of Rome. Afterwards, when the Lombards would not yield to him, in accomplishing his ambitious desire, but would needs require of the bishop the city of Rome, he stirred up Pepin, but first deposed Childeric the king of France, (A.D. 1751,) and so thrusting him into an abbey set up in his place Pepin and his son Charlemagne, to put down the king of the Lombards called Astulphus. And so he transferred the empire from Constantinople to France, dividing the spoil between him and them, so that the kings of France had all the possessions and lands which be-

fore belonged to the empire, and he received of them the quiet possession of the city of Rome, with such donations and lordships, which now they challenge to them under the name of St. Peter's patrimony, which they falsely ascribe to a donation of Constantine the Great.

It follows then in process of time, after the days of Pepin, Charlemagne, and Lewis (who had endowed these bishops of Rome, called now popes, with large possessions), that the kings of France were not so pliable to their beck, to aid and maintain them against the princes of Italy, who began then to pinch the bishops for their wrongfully usurped goods. The pope, therefore, practised with the Germans to reduce the empire to Otho, the first of that name, duke of Spain, referring the election to seven princes, electors of Germany, (A.D. 938,) notwithstanding, reserving still in his hands the negative voice, thinking thereby to enjoy what they had in quietness and security, and so he did for a good space.

At length, when some of these German emperors also, after Otho, began a little to spurn against the bishops and popes of Rome, some of them they accursed, some they subdued and brought to the kissing of their feet, some they deposed, and placed other in their possessions.

Henry IV. was so accursed by these bishops, that he was forced with his wife and child to wait attendance upon the pope's pleasure three days and three nights in winter, at the gates of Canosa, (A.D. 1077.) Besides all this, the pope raised up Rodolph to be emperor against him, who being slain in war, then Pope Gregory VII. stirred up his own son, Henry V. to fight against his own father, and to depose him; which Henry V. was also himself afterwards accursed and excommunicated, and the Saxons at last set up by the bishops to fight against him.

After this the emperors began to be somewhat calmed and more quiet, suffering the bishops to reign as they liked, till Frederick I., called Barbarossa, came and began to stir contention against them. However, they hampered both him and his son Henry in such a way, that they obliged Frederick to submit to be trod upon, (A.D. 1177), in the church of Venice; and afterwards the said bishops, crowning Henry VI. his son in the church of St. Peter, set his crown on his head with their feet, and with their feet spurned it off again, to make him know that the popes of Rome had power both to crown emperors and depose them again, (A.D. 1190.)

Then followed, (A.D. 1198,) Philip, brother to Henry, whom also the popes accursed, and set up in opposition to him, Otho duke of Saxony. Upon the death of Philip, (A.D. 1209), the pope conferred the imperial crown upon Otho IV., but this emperor, like his predecessors, was unwilling to submit to the pontiff's nod, and began to dispossess the bishops of their cities and lands which they had engrossed into their hands. This they could not bear, and immediately excommunicated him and put him aside; so that he was only suffered to reign four years, (A.D. 1212.)

At this time Frederick II., the son of Henry VI., was but young, whom the bishops of Rome supposing to find more mortified and tamed to their hand, advanced to be emperor. But that fell out much contrary to their expectation. For he perceiving the immoderate pomp and pride of the Roman bishops, which he could in no case abide, so nettled them and cut their combs, and waxed so stout against them, intending to extirpate their tyranny, and to reduce their pompous riches to the state and condition of the primitive church again, putting some of them to flight, and imprisoning some of their cardinals, that of three popes, one after another, he was accursed, circumvented by treason, at last deposed, and after that poisoned, and at last forsaken and died, (A.D. 1250.)

After this Frederick followed his son Conrad, whom the bishops for his disobedience soon despatched, exciting against him in mortal war the landgrave of Turin, by which he was at length driven into his kingdom of Naples, and there died.

This Conrad had a son called Conradine, duke and prince of Suevia. When this Conradine, after the decease of his father, came to enjoy his kingdom of Naples, these bishops stirred up against him Charles the French king's brother, so, that through crafty conveyance, both Conradine, who descended from the blood of so many emperors, and also Frederick duke of Austria, were both taken, and after much wretched handling in their miserable endurance, unseeming to their state, at length were both brought under the axe by the pope's procurement, and so both beheaded. And thus ended the imperial stock of Frederick I. surnamed Barbarossa.

The same that happened to Frederick the emperor, had almost also fallen upon Philip IV., the French king, by Pope Boniface VIII., who, because he could not have his commodities and revenues out of France after his will, sent out his bulls and letters patent to displace King Philip, and to place Albert king of the Romans in his room.

And thus hitherto in foreign histories. Now touching our own country princes here in England, to speak somewhat likewise of them : did not Pope Alexander III. presumptuously take upon him where he had nothing to do, to intermeddle with the king's subjects? for the death of Becket the rebel, although the king sufficiently cleared himself thereof, yet, notwithstanding, did he not wrongfully bring King Henry II. to such penance as it pleased him to enjoin, and also violently constrained him to swear obedience to the see of Rome? The like also was shewed before in this history to have happened to King John his son. For when the king like a valiant prince had held out against the tyranny of those bishops seven years together, were not all the churches in England barred up, and his inheritance with all his dominions given away by Pope Innocent III. to Lewis the French king, and he afterwards compelled to submit himself, and to make his whole realm feudatory to the bishops of Rome, and moreover the king himself driven also to surrender his crown to Pandulph the pope's legate, and so continued as a private person five days, standing at the pope's courtesy, whether to receive it again at his hands or no? And when the nobles of the realm rose afterwards against the king for the same, was he not then fain to seek and sue to the pope for succour ?

And yet notwithstanding all this that King John so yielded to the pope, he was both pursued by the nobles, and also in the end was poisoned by a subject of the popes's own religion, a monk of Swinsted.

Besides this King Henry II. and King John his son, see what kings have here reigned in England since their time, until the reign of King Henry VIII, who although there were prudent princes, and did what they could in providing against the proud domination of these bishops, yet were forced at length sore against their wills, for fear, to subject themselves, together with their subjects under usurped authority, insomuch as King Henry III. was fain to stoop and kiss the legate's knee.

The Image of Antichrist exalting himself in the Temple of God, above all that is named God, out of his own decrees, decretals, extravagants, pontificals, &c. word for word, as it is out of the said books here alleged and quoted.

(1) Forasmuch as it stands upon necessity of salvation, for every human creature to be subject to me the pope of Rome, it shall be therefore requisite and necessary for all men that will be saved, to learn and know the dignity of my see and excellency of my domination, as here is set forth according to the truth and very words of mine own laws, in style as follow : (2) First, my institution began in the Old Testament, and was consummated and finished in the New, in that my priesthood was prefigured by Aaron ; and other bishops under me were prefigured by the sons of Aaron, that were under him.

(3) Neither is it to be thought that my church of Rome has been preferred by any general council, but obtained the primacy only by the voice of the gospel, and the mouth of the Saviour. (4) And has in it neither spot nor wrinkle, nor any such thing. (5) Wherefore as other seats are all inferior to me, and as they cannot absolve me ; so have they no power to bind me or to stand against me, no more than the axe has power to stand or presume above him that hews with it, or the saw to presume above him that rules it. (6) This is the holy and apostolic mother church of all other churches of Christ ; (7) from whose rules it is not meet that any person or persons should decline ; but like as the Son of God came to do the will of his Father, so must you do the will of your mother, the church, the head of which is the church of Rome. (8) And if any other person or persons shall err from the said church, either let them be admonished, or else their names taken, to be known who they be that swerve from the customs of Rome. (9) Thus then as the holy church of Rome, of which I am governor, is set up to the whole world for a glass or example, reason would that whatever the church determines, or ordains, should be received by all men for a general and a perpetual rule for ever. (10) Whereupon we see it now verified in this church, that was prophesied by Jeremiah, saying, "Behold, I have set thee up over nations and kingdoms, to pluck up and to break down, to build and to plant," &c. (11) Whoso understands not the prerogative of this my priesthood, let him look up to the firmament, where he may see two great lights, the sun and the moon, one ruling over the day, the other over the night ; so in the firmament of the universal church, (12) God hath set two great dignities, the authority of the pope, and of the emperor. Of which two, this our dignity is so much weightier, as we have the greater charge to give account to God for kings of the earth, and the laws of men. (13) Wherefore be it known to you emperors, who know it also right well, that you depend upon the judgment of us ; we must not be brought and reduced to your will. (14) For, as I said, look what difference there is betwixt the sun and the moon, so great is the power of the pope ruling over the day, that is, over the spiritualty, above emperors and kings ruling over the night, that is, over the laity. (15) Now seeing then the earth is seven times bigger than the moon, and the sun eight times greater than the earth, it follows that the pope's dignity fifty-six times doth surmount the estate of the emperors. (16) Upon consideration of which, I say and pronounce, that Constantine the emperor did naughtily in setting the patriarch of Constantinople at his feet on his left hand. (17) And although the emperor wrote to me, alleging the word of St. Peter, commanding us to submit ourselves to every human creature, as to kings, dukes, and others for the cause of God, &c. 1 Pet. ii. Yet in answering again my decretal, I expounded the mind and the words of St. Peter to pertain to his subjects, and not to his successors, commanding the emperor to consider the person of the speaker, and to whom it was spoken. For if the mind of Peter had been there to debase the order of priesthood, and to make us underlings to every human creature, then every aspirant might have dominion over prelates, which makes against the example of Christ, setting up the order of priesthood to bear dominion over kings, according to the saying of Jeremiah : "Behold, I have set thee up over kings and nations," &c. (18) And as I feared not then to write this boldly to Constantine, so now I say to all other emperors, that they receiving of me their approbation, unction, consecration, and crown imperial, must not disdain to submit their heads under me, and swear to me their allegiance. (19) For so you read in the decree of Pope John, how that princes

---

(1) Pope Boniface VIII. Extravag. de majorit. & obed. cap. *Unam.*
(2) Distinct. 12. cap. *Decretis.*
(3) Pope Pelagius, Distinct. 21, cap. *Quamvis.*
(4) Pelagius, ibid.
(5) Pope Nicolas. Distinct. 21. cap. *Inferior.*
(6) Pope Lucius, 24, q. 1. cap. ii. *Recta.*
(7) Pope Calixtus, Dist. 12. cap. *Non decet.*
(8) Pope Innocentius. 11. cap. *Quis.*
(9) Pope Stephan. Distinct. 19. cap. *Enim vero.*

(10) Pope Boniface VIII. Extravag. cap. *Unam sanctam.* Item. Pope Joannes XXII. Extravag. cap. *Super gentes.*
(11) Pope Innocent III. art. de major. & obed. cap. *Solitæ.*
(12) Pope Gelasius, Dist. 96. cap. *Duo.*   (13) Ibidem.
(14) Innocentius de major. & obed. cap. *Solitæ.*
(15) Glossa. Ibidem.   (16) Ibidem.
(17) Innocentius. Ibid.
(18) Pope Clement V. Clement de jure jurando. cap. *Romani.*
(19) Pope Joannes, Dist. 96. cap. *Nunquam.*

heretofore have been wont to bow and submit their heads unto bishops, and not to proceed in judgment against the heads of bishops. (20) If this reverence and submission was wont to be given to bishops, how much more ought they to submit their heads to me being superior, not only to kings, but emperors? and that for two causes: first, for my title of succession, that I, pope of Rome, have to the empire, the room standing vacant; also for the fulness of power that Christ, the king of kings, and lord of lords, has given to me, though unworthy, in the person of Peter: (21) by reason of which, seeing my power is not of man but of God, who by his celestial Providence has set me over his whole universal church, master and governor, it belongeth therefore to my office to look upon every mortal sin of every christian man: (22) whereby all criminal offences, as well of kings as all others be subject to my censure, (23) in such sort, that in all manner of pleading, if any manner of person at any time, either before the sentence given, or after shall appeal to me, it shall be lawful for him so to do. (24) Neither must kings and princes think it much to submit themselves to my judgment, for so did Valentinian, the worthy emperor; so did Theodosius, and also Charles. (25) Thus you see all must be judged by me, and I of no man. Yea, and though I pope of Rome, by my negligence or evil demeanor, be found unprofitable, or hurtful, either to myself or others; yea, if I should draw with me innumerable souls by heaps to hell, yet may no mortal man be so hardy, so bold, or so presumptuous to reprove me, (26) or to say to me, Sir, why do you so? (27) For although you read that Balaam was rebuked of his ass, by which ass our subjects, by Balaam, we prelates are signified; yet that ought to be no example to our subjects to rebuke us. (28) And though we read in the scripture that Peter, who received power of the kingdom, and being chief of the apostles might by virtue of his office control all other, was content to come and give answer before his inferiors, objecting to him his going to the Gentiles; yet other inferiors must not learn by this example to be checkmate with their prelates, because that Peter so took it at their hands, shewing thereby rather a dispensation of humility, than the power of his office, by which power he might have said to them again in this wise, it becomes not sheep, nor belongs to their office to accuse their shepherd; (29) for else why was Dioscorus, patriarch of Alexandria, condemned and excommunicated at Chalcedon? Not for any cause of his faith, but only for that he durst stand against Pope Leo, and durst excommunicate the bishop of Rome; for who is he that has authority to accuse the seat of St. Peter? (30) Although I am not ignorant what St. Jerome writes, that St. Paul would not have reprehended St. Peter, unless he had thought himself equal to him. (31) Yet St. Jerome must thus be expounded by my interpretation, that this equality betwixt St. Peter and St. Paul consist not in like office of dignity, but in pureness of conversation. (32) For who gave St. Paul his licence to preach but St. Peter?

and that by the authority of God, saying, "Separate to me Paul and Barnabas," &c. (33) Wherefore be it known to all men, that my church of Rome is prince and head of all nations, (34) the mother of the faith, (35) the foundation cardinal, whereupon all churches do depend, as the door depends by the hinges, (36) the first of all other seats, without all spot or blemish. (37) Lady, mistress, and instructor of all churches, (38) a glass and a spectacle to all men, to be followed in all whatsoever she observes. (39) Which was never found yet to slide or decline from the path of apostolic tradition, or to be entangled with any newness of heresy; (40) against which church of Rome whoever speaks any evil, is forthwith an heretic, (41) yea, a very pagan, a witch, and an idolater or infidel, (42) having fulness of power only in her own hands in ruling, (43) deciding, absolving, condemning, casting out, or receiving in. (44) Although I deny not but other churches are partakers with her in labouring and carrying. (45) To which church of Rome it is lawful to appeal for remedy, from all other churches. Although it was otherwise concluded in the general council of Milevitane, that no man should appeal over the sea under pain of excommunication, yet my gloss comes in here with an exception: "Except the appeal be to the see of Rome," &c. (46) By the authority of which church of Rome all synods and decrees of councils stand confirmed. (47) And hath always full authority in her hands to make new laws and decreements, and to alter statutes, privileges, rights, or documents of churches; to separate things joined, and to join things separated upon right consideration, either in whole or in part, either personally or generally. (48) Of which church of Rome I am head as a king is over his judges, (49) the vicar of St. Peter, (50) yea, not the vicar of St. Peter properly, but the vicar of Christ properly, and successor of Peter, (51) vicar of Jesus Christ, (52) rector of the universal church, director of the Lord's flock, (53) chief magistrate of the whole world, (54) the head and chief of the apostolic church, (55) universal pope, and diocesan in all places exempt, as well as every bishop is in places not exempt, (56) most mighty priest, (57) a living law in the earth, (58) judged to have all laws in the chest of my breast, (59) bearing the room of no pure man, (60) being neither God nor man, but the admiration of the world, and a middle thing betwixt both. (61) Having both swords in my power, both of the Spiritual and Temporal jurisdiction, (62) so far surmounting the authority of the emperor, that I of mine own power alone without a council, have authority to depose him, or to transfer his kingdom, and to give a new election, as I did to Frederick and divers other. (63) What power then or potentate in all the world is comparable to me, who have authority to bind and loose both in heaven and in earth? (64) That is, who have power both of heavenly things, and also of temporal things. (65) To whom emperors and kings are more inferior, than lead is inferior to gold. (66) For do you not see the necks of great kings and princes bend under

---

(20) Pope Clement V. Clement de Sentent. & de rejudi pastoralis.
(21) Pope Innocent III. De judiciis, cap. *Novit.* (22) Ibidem.
(23) Pope Marcellus, caus. 2. q. 6. cap. *ad Romanam.*
(24) Innocent. Novteille.
(25) Bonifacius Martyr. dict. 40. cap. *Si Papa.*
(26) Glossa Extr. de sede vacant. ad Apostolatus.
(27) Pope Leo, caus. 2. q. 7. cap. *Nos.*
(28) Greg. 2. q. 7. cap. *Petrus.*
(29) Pope Nicolaus, Dist. cap. 21. *In cantum.*
(30) Jer. caus. 2. q. 7. cap. *Paulus.*
(31) Glossa Gratiani. Ib.
(32) Glossa in Diss. 11. cap. *Quis.*
(33) Caus. 2. q. 7. cap. *Beati.*
(34) Pope Nicolaus, Dist. 22. *Omnes.*
(35) Pope Anaclet, Dist. 22. cap. *Sacrosancta.*
(36) Pope Pelagius, Dist. 21. cap. *Quamvis.*
(37) Pope Nicolaus, Dist. 21. cap. *Denique.*
(38) Pope Stephen, Di. 29. *Enim vero.*
(39) Pope Lucius, 24. q. 1. *Arect.*
(40) Pope Nicolaus, Dist. 22. cap. *Omnes.*
(41) Pope Gregory, Dist. 81. cap. *Si qui.*
(42) Pope Leo, caus. 3. q. 62. cap. *Multum.*
(43) Dist. 20. cap. *Decretalis.*
(44) Pope Julius. caus. 2. q. 6. *qui se.*
(45) Causa. 2. q. 6. Arguta. Item. cap. *Ad Romanam.* caus. 2. q. 6. cap. *Placuit.* Glossa. Gratiani. Nisi.

(46) Pope Gelasi. 25. q. 1. cap. *Confidimus.*
(47) Pope Urbanus, 25. q. 1. cap. *Sunt.* P. Pelagius, 25. q. 2. cap. *Posteaquam.*
(48) Bulla Donationis, Dist. 96. cap. *Constant.*
(49) Pope Paschalis, Dist. 68. cap. *Ego.*
(50) Pope Clement V. Clement. cap. *Romani Glossa.*
(51) Pope Boniface VIII. Sext. Decret. cap. *Ubi.*
(52) Ibidem.
(53) Pope Boniface, prohem. Sext. Decret. 1. *Sacrosancta.*
(54) Anacletus, D. 22. cap. *Sacrosancta.*
(55) Pope Boniface IV. Sext. Decret. de pœnit. et remh. cap. 5. *Glossa.* Item Alexander IV. Sext. decret. cap. 4. in *Glossa.*
(56) Pope Hilarius, 25. q. 1. *Null.*
(57) Sixt. Decret. cap. *Ad Arbitris,* Glossa.
(58) Pope Boniface Sext. decret. de const. cap. *Licet.*
(59) Pope Innocent III., de trans. cap. *Quanto.*
(60) Prohem. Clement. Gloss. Papa Stupor mundi, &c. Nec Deus es nec homo, quasi neuter es inter utrumque.
(61) Pope Boniface Extravag. de Majorit et obed. cap. *Unam.* Item Dist. 22. cap. *Omnes.*
(62) Sext. Decr. de Sentent. et re. ca. ad. Apostoll. Item in Glossa, Ibidem.
(63) Pope Nicolaus, Dist. 22. cap. *Omnes.*
(64) Gloss. Ibidem.
(65) Pope Gelasius, Dist. 96. cap. *Duo.*
(66) Pope Gelasius, Ibidem.

our knees, yea and think themselves happy and well defenced, if they may kiss our hands? (67) Wherefore the sauciness of Honorius the emperor is to be reprehended, and his constitution abolished, who, with his laity would take upon him to intermeddle, not only with the temporal order, but also with matters ecclesiastical, and the election of the pope. (68) But here perchance some will object, the examples and words of Christ, saying, " That his kingdom is not of this world," and where he being required to divide betwixt two brethren their heritage, did refuse it. But that ought to be no prejudice to my power. (69) For if Peter, and I in Peter, if we, I say, have power to bind and loose in heaven, how much more then is it to be thought, that we have power in earth to loose and to take away empires, kingdoms, dukedoms, and what else soever mortal men may have, and to give them where we will? (70) And if we have authority over angels, which be the governors of princes, what then may we do upon their inferiors and servants? (71) And that you may not marvel when I say angels are subject to us, you shall hear what my blessed clerk Antoninus writes of the matter, saying, " That our power is greater than the angels in four things ;—1. In jurisdiction, 2. In administration of sacraments, 3. In knowledge, 4. In reward," &c. (72) And again in Bulla Clementis, do I not there command in my bull the angels of paradise, to absolve the soul of man out of purgatory, and to bring it into the glory of paradise? (73) And now besides my heavenly power, to speak of mine earthly jurisdiction, who did first transfer the empire from the Greeks to the Germans, but I? (74) And not only in the empire am I emperor, the place being empty, but in all ecclesiastical benefices have full right and power to give, to translate, and to dispose after my arbitrement. (75) Did not I, Zacharias, put down Childerick the old king of France, and set up Pepin? (76) Did not I, Gregory VII. set up Robert Wysard, and make him king of Sicily, and duke of Capua? &c. (77) Did not I the same Gregory also set up Rodolph against Henry IV. emperor? (78) And though this Henry was an emperor of most stout courage, who stood sixty-two times in open field against his enemies, (79) yet did not I, Gregory, bring him before us, and make him stand at my gate three days and three nights bare-footed and bare-legged, with his wife and child, in the depth of winter, both in frost and snow, intreating for his absolution, and afterwards excommunicated him again, so that he was twice excommunicated in my days? (80) Again, did not I, Pascal, after Gregory, set up the son of Henry against his father in war, to possess the empire, and to put down his father, and so he did? (81) Did not I, Pope Alexander, bring under Henry II. king of England, for the death of Thomas Becket, and cause him to go bare-foot to his tomb at Canterbury with bleeding feet? (82) Did not I, Innocent III. cause King John to kneel down at the feet of Pandulph my legate, and offer up his crown with his own hands; also to kiss the feet of Stephen Langton, a bishop of Canterbury: and besides, fine him in a thousand marks by the year? (83) Did not I, Urban II., put down Hugo, earl in Italy, discharging his subjects from their oath and obedience to him? (84) Did not I, Pascal II., excommunicate also his son Henry V., and get out of his hands

all his right and title of elections and donations of spiritual promotions? Did not I, Gelasius II., bring the captain of Cintius under, to the kissing of my feet? And after Gelasius, did not I, Calixtus II., quail the Emperor Henry V., and also bring in subjection Gregory, whom the emperor had set up against me as pope, bringing him into Rome upon a camel, his face to the horse tail, making him to hold the horse tail in his hand instead of a bridle? (85) Further, did not I, Innocent II., set up and make Lothaire to be emperor for driving out Pope Anacletus out of Rome? (86) Did not I, the said Innocent, take the dukedom of Sicily from the empire, and make Roger king thereof, whereby afterward the kingdom became the patrimony of St. Peter? (87) Did not I, Alexander III., suspend all the realm and churches of England for the king's marriage, (A. D. 1159?) (88) But what do I speak of kings? Did not Alexander bring the valiant emperor, Frederick I., to Venice, by reason of his son Otho there taken prisoner, and there in St. Mark's church made him fall down flat upon the ground while I set my foot upon his neck, saying the verse of the Psalm, " Thou shalt tread on the adder and the serpent," &c. (89) Did not I, Adrian IV., pope, an Englishman born, excommunicate the king of Sicily, and refuse his peace, which he offered? And had not he overcome me in plain field, I would have shaken him out of his kingdom of Sicily, and dukedom of Apulia. (90) Also, did not I, Adrian, control and correct the foresaid Frederic, emperor, for holding the left stirrup of my horse, when he should have holden the right? (91) And afterward did not I excommunicate and curse him, for he was so saucy to set his own name in writing before mine? (92) And although a poor fly afterward overcame and strangled me, yet I made kings and emperors to stoop. (93) Did not I, Innocent III., cast down Philip, brother to Frederic, from the imperial crown, being elected without my leave, and afterwards set him up again? And also set up Otho of Brunswick, and afterwards excommunicated and also deposed the same after four years, setting up the French king to war against him? (94) Then was Frederic II. set up by me, and reigned thirty-seven years; and yet five years before he died he was deposed. (95) Did not I, Honorius III., interdict him, for not restoring certain to their possessions at my request? (96) Whom also Gregory IX. excommunicated twice together, and raised up the Venetians against him. (97) And at length Innocent IV. spoiled him of his empire; after that he caused him to be poisoned, and at length to be strangled by one Manfred, and excommunicated his son Conrad after him, not only depriving him of his right inheritance, but also caused him, with Frederic, duke of Austria, to be beheaded. (98) Thus then, did not I excommunicate and depose all these emperors in order? Henry IV., Henry V., Frederic I., Philip, Otho IV., Frederic II., and Conrad his son? (99) Did not I interdict King Henry VIII. ? (100) And all his kingdom of England? (101) And had not his prudence and power prevented my practice, I had displaced him from his kingdom also. Briefly, who is able to comprehend the greatness of my power and of my seat? (102) For by me only general councils take their force and confirmation, (103) and the interpretation of the councils, and of all other causes

(67) Di. 96. cap. Illud.
(68) Ex citatione Hiero. Marii.
(69) Pope Hildebrandus, alias Gregorius 7. Ex. Platina, in vita Gregorii.
(70) Hildebrandus, Ibidem.
(71) Antoninus in tertia parte Summæ majoris.
(72) Bulla Clementis.
(73) Pope Innocent. de electione. cap. Venerabilem.
(74) Extrav. de præbend. & dig. cap. Execrabilis.
(75) Pope Zacharias, Caus. 15. q. 6. cap. Alius.
(76) Pope Hildebrand, alias Gregor. 7. Clement. cap. Pastoralis.
(77) Ex Gestis Hildebrandi.
(78) Baptista Egnatius.
(79) Platina, Benno Nauclerus.
(80) Platina, Egnatius Benno.
(81) Polydore Virgil. Historia ornalensis de rebus Anglorum.
(82) Chronica vernacula.
(83) Pope Urbanus, Caus. 15. q. 6. cap. Juratos.
(84) Pope Paschalis Cursulanus. Platina, Vincentius, Stella, Antoninus, Matthæus Parisiensis. Pope. Gelasius 2. Pope.

(85) Pope Innocentius 2.
(86) Nauclerus.
(87) Pope Alexander 3. de sponsal. & matr. cap. Non est.
(88) Nauclerus acta Rom. pontificum.
(89) Pope Adrian. vit. Rom. pontificum.
(90) Ex Aventino.
(91) Bulla Adriani contra Cæsarem.
(92) Acta Rom. Pont.
(93) Pope Innocentius 3. Ex Vitis & Actis Rom. pontificum. Ex ab Ursperg.
(94) Ex eodem.
(95) Pope Honor. 3. Ex. Mario.
(96) Pope Greg. 9. Ex eodem.
(97) Pope Innocent 4. Hieronymus Marius. Petrus de Vineis.
(98) Ex Chronic. Carionis.
(99) Hist. Anglor.
(100) Ibidem.
(101) Ibidem.
(102) Pope Marcellus, Dist. 17. cap. Synodum.
(103) Dist. 20. Decretales.

hard and doubtful, ought to be referred and stand to my determination. (104) By me the works of all writers, whatsoever they be, are either reproved or allowed. (105) Then how much more ought my writings and decrees to be preferred before all others? (106) So that my letters and epistles decretal be equivalent with the general councils. (107) And, whereas, God has ordained all causes of men to be judged by men, he has only reserved me, that is, the pope of Rome, without all question of men, unto his own judgment. (108) And, therefore, where all other creatures are under their judge, only I, who in earth am the judge of all, can be judged of none, either of emperor, nor the whole clergy, nor of kings, nor of the people. (109) For who has power to judge upon his judge? (110) This judge am I, and that alone, without any other resistance of any council joined to me. For I have power upon councils; councils have no power upon me. But if the council determine amiss, it is in my authority alone to infringe it, or to condemn whom I list without any council. (111) And all for the pre-eminence of my predecessor blessed St. Peter, which, by the voice of the Lord, he received, and ever shall retain. (112) Furthermore, and whereas all other sentences and judgments, both of councils, person or persons, may and ought to be examined, (113) for that they may be corrupted four ways, by fear, by gifts, by hatred, by favour, only my sentence and judgment must stand, (114) as given out of heaven by the mouth of Peter himself, which no man must (115) break or retract, (116) no man must dispute or doubt of. (117) Yea, if my judgment, statute, or yoke seem scarcely tolerable, yet for remembrance of St. Peter it must be humbly obeyed. (118) Yea, and moreover, obedience is to be given, not only to such decrees set forth by me in time of my popedom, but also to such as I do foresee and commit to writing before I be pope. (119) And although it be thought by some writers, to be given to all men to err, and to be deceived, (120) yet neither am I a pure man. (121) And again, the sentence of my apostolic seat is always conceived with such moderation, is concocted and digested with such patience and ripeness, and delivered out with such gravity and deliberation, that nothing is thought in it necessary to be altered or detracted. (122) Wherefore, it is manifest, and testified by the voice of holy bishops, that the dignity of this my seat is to be reverenced through the whole world, in that all the faithful submit themselves to it as to the head of the whole body; (123) whereof it is spoken to me by the prophet, speaking of the ark; if this be humbled, whither shall you run for succour, and where shall your glory become? Seeing then this is so, that so holy bishops and scriptures do witness with me, what shall we say then to such as will take upon them to judge of my doings, to reprehend my proceedings, or to require homage and tribute of me to whom all other are subject? (124) Against the first sort the scripture speaks, "Thou shalt not move a sickle unto thy neighbour's standing corn." Which thing to attempt against me, what is it but plain sacrilege? (125) According to my canonists, who thus define sacrilege to consist in three things; either when a man judges of his princes' judgment; or when the holy-day is profaned; or when reverence is not given to laws and canons. (126)

Against the second sort makes the place of the book of Kings, where we read the ark of God was brought from Gaza to Jerusalem, and in the way the ark inclining by reason of the unruly oxen, Ussah the Levite put forth his hand to help, and therefore was stricken of the Lord. By this ark is signified the prelates; by the inclination thereof, the fall of prelates, (127) who also are signified by the angels that Jacob saw going up and coming down the ladder: (128) also, by the prophet where he saith, "He bowed down the heavens and came down," &c. By Ussah and by the unruly oxen are meant our subjects. (119) Then, like as Ussah was stricken for putting his hand to the ark inclining, no more must subjects rebuke their prelates going awry. (130) Although here it may be answered again, that all are not prelates who are so called; for it is not the name that makes a bishop, but his life. (131) Against the third sort of such as would bring us under the tribute and exactions of secular men, makes the New Testament, where Peter was bid to give the groat in the fish's mouth, but not the head nor the body of the fish; no more is the head or body of the church subdued to kings, but only that which is in the mouth, that is, the external things of the church. And yet not they neither. (132) For so we read in the book of Genesis, that Pharaoh, in time of dearth, subdued all the land of the Egyptians, but yet he ministered to the priests, so that he took neither their possessions from them, nor their liberty. If then prelates of the church must be neither judged, nor reprehended, nor exacted, how much more ought I to be free from the same, (133) who am the bishop of bishops, and head of prelates? (134) For it is not to be thought that the case between me and other prelates; between my see and other churches, be like, (135) although the whole catholic and apostolic church make one bride-chamber of Christ; yet the catholic and apostolic church of Rome had the pre-eminence given over all other by the mouth of the Lord himself, saying to Peter, "Thou art Peter," &c. (136) Thus a discrepance and difference must be had in the church as it was betwixt Aaron and his children; (137) betwixt the seventy-two disciples, and the twelve apostles; betwixt the other apostles and Peter. (138) Wherefore it is to be concluded, that there must be an order and difference of degrees in the church between power, superior and inferior; without which order the universality of the whole cannot consist. (139) For, as among the angelical creatures above in heaven, there is set a difference and inequality of powers and orders, some be angels, some archangels, some cherubims, and seraphims: (140) so in the ecclesiastical hierarchy of the church militant in the earth, priests must not be equal with bishops, bishops must not be like in order with archbishops, with patriarchs or primates, (141) who contain under them three archbishops, as a king contains three dukes under him. In which number of patriarchs comes in the state of (142) cardinals or principals, so called, because as the door turneth by his hinges, so the universal church ought to be ruled by them. (143) The next and highest order above these is mine, who am pope, differing in power and majority, and honour reverential, from these and all other degrees of men. (144) For the better declaration of

(104) Pope Nicolaus, Dist. 19. cap. Si Romanorum.
(105) Ibidem.
(106) Dist. 20. Decretales.
(107) Symmachus Pope, 9. q. 3. cap. Aliorum.
(108) Pope Innocentium 6. q. 3. cap. Nemo.
(109) Ibidem.
(110) Pope Gelasius, 9. q. 3. cap. Cuncta.
(111) Ibidem.
(112) Anastasius Patriarch. Dist. q. 3. cap. Antiquis.
(113) Pope Greg. a. q. 3. cap. Quat.
(114) Pope Agatho, Dist. 19. cap. Sic omnes.
(115) Pope Nicholas, 9. q. 3. Putet.
(116) Pope Innocent. 2. Art. 17. q. 4. cap. Si quis.
(117) Dist. 19. cap. In memoriam.
(118) Sext. Decret. T. 7. De renunc. Quoniam Glossa.
(119) Offic. lib. 1.
(120) Glossa Extra. De verb. signif. cap. Ad.
(121) Pope Greg. Caus. 35. q. 9. cap. Apostolicæ.
(122) Pope Symmuchus. Caus. 9. q. 3. cap. Aliorum.
(123) Ibidem.

(124) Pope Greg. 6. p. 3. cap. Scriptum est.
(125) Caus. 17. q. 4. Sacrileg. Glossa.
(126) 2. q. 7. cap. Plærumque. Glossema Gratiani. Item.
(127) Ibidem.
(128) Ibidem.
(129) Ibidem.
(130) Ibidem. His ita.
(131) Pope Urbanus 23. q. cap. Tributum.
(132) Ibidem. Quamvis.
(133) Pope Benedict. Extr. De aut. & usupallli. cap. Sanct. 1.
(134) Pope Stephanus. Dist. 19. Enimvero.
(135) Pope Pelagus, Dist. 21. cap. Quamvis.
(136) Dist. 21. cap. Decretis.
(137) Pope Anaclet. Dist. 22. cap. In novo.
(138) Pope Bonifacius et Greg. Dist. 89. cap. Ad hoc.
(139) Ibidem.
(140) Dist. 89. cap. Singula.
(141) Ex citatione Buldecre. 5. scr. 3.
(142) De officio Archipresbyt. in Glossa.   (143)
(144) Ex. 3. parte Summæ majoris b. Antonini.

which, my canonists make three kinds of power in earth; *immediate*, which is mine immediately from God; *derived*, which belongeth to other inferior prelates from me; (145) *ministerial*, belonging to emperors and princes to minister for me. For which cause the anointing of princes, and my consecration differ; for they are anointed only in the arms or shoulders, and I in the head, to signify the difference of power betwixt princes and me. (146) This order, therefore, of priests, bishops, archbishops, patriarchs, and others, as a thing most convenient, my church of Rome has set and instituted through all churches, following therein, not only the example of the angelical army in heaven, but also of the apostles. (147) For among them also there was not an uniform equality or institution of one degree, (148) but a diversity or distinction of authority and power. Although they were all apostles together, yet it was granted notwithstanding to Peter (themselves also agreeing to the same) that he should bear dominion and superiority over all the other apostles. (149) And therefore he had his name given him Cephas, that is, head or beginning of the apostleship. (150) Whereupon the order of priesthood first in the New Testament began in Peter, to whom it was said, Thou art Peter, and upon thee I will build my church. (151) And I will give thee the keys of the kingdom of heaven; and thou being converted confirm thy brethren. (152) I have prayed for thee that thy faith shall not fail. Wherefore seeing such power is given to Peter, (153) and to me in Peter, being his successor; (154) who is he then in all the world that ought not to be subject to my decrees who have such power in heaven, in hell, in earth, with the quick and also the dead? (155) Commanding and granting in my bull sent to Vienna, to all such as died in their pilgrimage to Rome, that the pain of hell should not touch them; and also that all such as took the holy cross upon them should every one at his request, not only be delivered himself, but also deliver three or four souls, whoever he would, out of purgatory. (156) Again, having such promise and assurance that my faith shall not fail, who then will not believe my doctrine? For did not Christ himself first pray for Peter that his faith should not fail? (157) Also have I not a sure promise of Paul's own mouth, writing to my church by these words, "God is my witness whom I serve with my spirit, in the gospel of his Son, that without ceasing I make mention of you always in my prayers? Rom. i. 9. (158) Wherefore as I condemn worthily all who will not obey my decrees, to be dispossessed of all their honour without restitution, (159) so all they that believe not my doctrine, or stand against the privilege of the church, especially the church of Rome, I pronounce them heretics. (160) And as the other before is to be called unjust, so this man is to be called a heretic. (161) For why? he goes against the faith who goes against her who is the mother of faith. (162) But here may rise perhaps a doubt or scruple, that if my faith and knowledge stand so sure by the promise of Christ, and by the continual prayer of Saint Paul, whether is it true, or is it to be granted, that any other should excel me in knowlege, or interpretation of holy scripture? (163) For see whose knowledge is grounded on most reason, his words should seem to be of more authority. (164) Whereto I answer and grant, that many there are who have been more abundantly indowed with fuller grace of the Holy Ghost and greater excellency of knowledge; and therefore that the writings of Augustine, Jerome, and others ought to be preferred before the constitutions of some popes; yet I say in determination of causes, because they have not the virtue and height of that authority which is given to me, therefore in expounding of scriptures they are to be preferred, but in deciding of matters, they stand inferior to my authority. By virtue of which authority, (165) they themselves are allowed for doctors, and their works approved, but all other matters are ruled, through the power of the keys which were given to me immediately by Christ. Although I deny not but the same keys are also committed to other prelates, as they were to other apostles besides Peter. (166) Yet it is one thing to have the keys, and another thing to have the use of the keys. (167) Wherefore here is to be noted a distinction of keys, after the mind of my school doctors; one key which is called the key of order, having authority to bind and loose, but not over the persons whom they bind and loose, and this authority they take not immediately of Christ, but mediately by me the vicar of Christ. The other key is called the key of jurisdiction, which I the vicar of Christ take immediately of him, having not only authority to bind and loose, but also dominion over them on whom this key is exercised. By the jurisdiction of which key the fullness of my power is so great, that whereas all other are subjects; (168) yea and emperors themselves ought to subdue their executions to me; only I am subject to no creature, (169) no not to myself except I list, *in foro pœnitentiæ*, to my ghostly father submitting myself as a sinner, but not as pope. So that my papal majesty ever remains unpunished. Superior to all men, (170) whom all persons ought to obey, (171) and follow, (172) whom no man must judge nor accuse of any crime, either of murder, adultery, simony, or such like. (173) No man depose, but I myself; (174) No man can excommunicate me, yea though I communicate with the excommunicate, for no canon bindeth me. Whom no man must lie to, (175) for he that lies to me is a church robber, (176) and who obeys not me is an heretic, and an excommunicated person. (177) For as all the Jews were commanded to obey the high priest of the Levitical order, of what state and condition soever they were, so are all christian men more and less bound to obey me Christ's lieutenant on earth. Concerning the obedience or disobedience of whom ye have in Deut. xvii. (178) Where the common Gloss saith, that he who denieth to the high priest obedience, lies under the sentence and condemnation, as much as he that denies to God his omnipotence. Thus then it appears, that the greatness of my priesthood (179) began in Melchisedeck, was solemnized in Aaron, continued in the children of Aaron, perfected in Christ, represented in Peter, exalted in the universal jurisdiction, and manifested in Silvester, &c. So that through this pre-eminence of my priesthood, having all things subject to me, (180) it may seem well verified in me that which was spoken of Christ, Psalm viii. "Thou hast put all things under his feet; all sheep and

---

(145) Pope Innocent 3. De sacra unctione, Qui venisset.
(146) Pope Nicholaus, Dist. 22. cap. *Omnes*.
(147) Pope Clement, Dist. 80. cap. *In illis*.
(148) Pope Anacletus, Dist. 22. cap. *Sacrosancta*.
(149) Ibidem. Quasi vero Petrus non a Petra sed κέφας ἀπο τῆς κεφάλης. ducatur.
(150) Dist. 21. cap. *In novo*.
(151) Ibidem.
(152) Dict. 21. cap. *Decretis*.
(153) Pope Leo, dist. 19. cap. *Ita Dominus*.
(154) Pope Nicholaus in tantum, dist. 22.
(155) Pope Clemens in Bulla Viennæ in scriniis privilegiorum.
(156) Dist. 21. cap. *Decretis*.
(157) Pope Anacletus, dist. 22. cap. *Sacrosancto*. Scripture well applied, and like a clerk.
(158) Pope Damasus, 25. q. cap. *Omnia*. Item Pope Greg. Dist. 19. cap. *Null*.
(159) Pope Nicholaus Dist. 22. cap. *Omnes*.
(160) Ibidem.
(161) Ibidem.

(162) Dist. 20 cap. *Decretales*.
(163) Ibidem.
(164) Ibidem.
(165) Dist. 19. cap. *Si Romanorum*.
(166) Gabriel Biel, lib. 4. Dist. 19.
(167) Petrus de Palude.
(168) Dist. 95. cap. *Imperator*.
(169) Gabriel. lib. 4. Dist. 19.
(170) Pope Nicholaus, Dist. cap. *Si Romanorum*, in Glossa.
(171) Item 24. q. 1. Hæc est.
(172) Dist. 40. cap. *Si Papæ*.
(173) 2 q. 7. Nos si in Glossa.
(174) Extravag. de elect. Innotuit.
(175) De Pœnitentia, Dist. 1. cap. *Serpens*, in Glossa.
(176) Dist. 19. cad. *Nulli*.
(177) August. de. Ancho.
(178) Glossa Ordinar.
(179) Antoninus.
(180) Antoninus, Summa majoris, 3. part. Dist. 22.

and oxen, yea, and the beasts of the field, the fowls of the air, and the fish of the sea, &c. (181) Where is to be noted, that by oxen, Jews, and heretics, by beasts of the field, Pagans be signified. For although as yet they be out of the use of my keys of binding and loosing, yet they be not out of the jurisdiction of my keys, but if they return I may absolve them. (182) By sheep and all cattle are meant all christian men both great and less, whether they be emperors, princes, prelates, or others. By fowls of the air you may understand the angels and potentates of heaven, who will be all subject to me, in that I am greater than the angels ; and that in four things, as is before declared ; and in having power to bind and loose in heaven, (183) and to give heaven to them that fight in my wars. (184) Lastly, by the fishes of the sea, are signified the souls departed in pain or in purgatory, as Gregory by his prayer delivered the soul of Trajan out of hell, and I have power to deliver out of purgatory whom I please. (185) Lastly, by the fishes of the sea are signified such as are in purgatory ; so that they stand in need and necessity of other men's help, and yet are in their journey. Passengers belonging to the court of the pope, therefore they may be relieved out of the storehouse of the church, by the participation of indulgence. And forasmuch as some object that my pardons cannot extend to them that are departed, for that it was said to Peter, "Whatsoever thou shalt loose upon earth ;" and therefore seeing they are not upon earth, they cannot be loosed by me. Here I answer again by my doctors, that this word, " Upon the earth," may be explained in two manner of ways ; first, to him that is the looser, so that he who shall loose shall be upon the earth ; and so I grant that the pope being dead, can loose no man. Also it may be referred to him that is loosed, so that whoever is loosed must be upon the earth, or about the earth ; and so the souls in purgatory may be loosed, who, although they are not upon the earth, yet they are about the earth, at least they are not in heaven. And because oftentimes one question may rise upon another, and the heads of men now-a-days are curious, a man hearing now that I can deliver out of purgatory, will ask here a question, whether I am able also to empty all purgatory at once, or not ? to whom my canonist answers by a triple distinction : Touching my absolute jurisdiction, he saith, I am able to rid out all purgatory together, for as many as be under my jurisdiction, as all be, except only infants unbaptized, in limbo, and men departed only with the baptism of the Spirit, and such as have no friends to do for them that for which my pardons are given ; these only excepted. For all other besides, the pope, he saith, has power to release all purgatory at once, as touching his absolute jurisdiction. Although Thomas Aquinas (part 4), denies the same, forsomuch as Christ himself, he saith, when he came down, did not utterly at once release all purgatory. As touching my ordinary execution they hold, that I may if I will, but I ought not to do it. Thirdly, as concerning the divine acceptation, that is, how God would accept it if I did it, that, they say, is unknown to them, and to every creature, yea, and to the pope himself.

And to the intent I would all men to see and understand that I lack not witnesses more besides these, if I list to bring them out, you shall hear the whole quire of my divine clergy brought out, with a full voice testifying in my behalf in their books, transactions, distinctions, titles, glosses, and summaries, as by their own words here follows. The pope, say they, being the vicar of Jesus Christ through the whole world, is in the stead of the living God, has that dominion and lordship which Christ here in earth would not have, although he had it in habit, but gave it to Peter in act, that is, the universal jurisdiction both of spiritual things and also of temporal, which double jurisdiction was signified by the two swords in the gospel, and also by the offering of the wise men, who offered not only incense, but also gold, to signify not only

the spiritual dominion, but also the temporal, to belong to Christ and to his vicar. For as we read, " The earth is the Lord's, and the fulness thereof ;" as Christ saith, " All power is given to him both in heaven and earth :" so it is to be affirmed inclusive, that the vicar of Christ hath power of things celestial, terrestrial, and infernal. Which he took immediately of Christ ; all others take it immediately by Peter and the pope. Wherefore such as say that the pope has dominion only in spiritual things in the world, and not of temporal, may be likened to the councillors of the kings of Syria, (3 Reg. 20), which said " That the gods of the mountains be their gods, and therefore they have overcome us ; but let us fight against them in the low meadows, and in valleys where they have no power, and so we shall prevail over them." So evil councillors now-a-days, through their pestiferous flattery, deceive kings and princes of the earth, saying popes and prelates are gods of mountains, that is, of spiritual things only ; but they are not gods of valleys, that is, they have no dominion over temporal things, and therefore let us fight with them in the valleys, that is, in the power of the temporal possessions, and so we shall prevail over them. But what saith the sentence of God to them, let us hear. Because, saith he, " the Syrians say that the god of mountains is their god, and not the god of valleys, therefore I will give all this multitude into your hand, and ye shall know that I am the Lord." What can be more effectually spoken to set forth the majesty of my jurisdiction, which I received immediately of the Lord ; of the Lord, I say, and of no man. For whereas Constantine the emperor gave to Silvester this possession and patrimony ; that is so to be expounded and taken not so much for a donation, as to be counted for a restitution made of that which tyrannously was taken from him before. And again, whereas I have given at sundry times to Lewis the other emperors, of my temporal lands and possessions, yet that was done not so much for any recognising of homage to them, as for keeping peace with them. For I owe to emperors no due obedience that they can claim, but they owe to me as to their superior. And therefore for a diversity betwixt their degree and mine, in their consecration they take the unction on their arm, and I on the head. And as I am superior to them, so I am superior to all laws, and free from all constitutions. Who am able of myself, and by my interpretation, to prefer equity not being written before the law written ; having all laws within the chest of my breast, as is aforesaid. And whatsoever this my see shall enact, approve, or disapprove, all men ought to approve or reprove the same, without either judging, disputing, doubting, or retracting. Such is the privilege given of Christ, in the behalf of Peter, to the church of Rome, (186) that what country soever, kingdom or province, choosing to themselves bishops and ministers, although they agree with all other Christ's faithful people in the name of Jesus, that is, in faith and charity, believing in the same God, and in Christ his true Son, and in the Holy Ghost, having also the same creed ; the same evangelists and scriptures of the apostles : yet unless their bishops and ministers take their origin and ordination from this apostolic seat, they are to be counted not of the church. So that succession of faith only is not sufficient to make a church, except their ministers take their ordination by them who have their succession from the apostles. So their faith, supremacy, the chair of Peter, keys of heaven, power to bind and loose, all these are inseparable from the church of Rome : so that it is to be presumed, that God always providing, and St. Peter helping the bishoprick and diocese of Rome, it shall never fall from the faith. And likewise it is to be presumed and presupposed that the bishop of that church is good and always holy. Yea, and though he be not always good, or be destitute of his own merits, yet the merits of St. Peter, predecessor of that place, are sufficient for him, who has bequeathed and left a

---

(181) Antoninus, Summa majoris 3. part. Dist. 22.
(182) Ibidem.
(183) 23. q. cap. *Omnium.*

(184) Idem, Antoninus, ibid.
(185) Ibidem.
(186) Joan Driedo. De dogmatibus variis, l. 4.

perpetual dowry of merits, with inheritance of innocency, to his posterity, (187) yea, though he fall into homicide or adultery, he may sin, but yet he cannot be accused, but rather is excused by the murders of Samson, the thefts of the Hebrews, the adultery of Jacob. (188) Furthermore, the pope, say they, has all the dignities, and all power of all patriarchs. In his primacy, he is Abel; in government, the ark of Noah; in patriarchdom, Abraham; in order, Melchisedec; in dignity, Aaron; in authority, Moses; in seat judicial, Samuel; in zeal, Elias; in meekness, David; in power. Peter; in unction, Christ. My power, they say, is greater than all the saints. For whom I confirm, no man may infirm: I may favour and spare whom I please, (189) to take from one and to give to another. And if I am an enemy to any man, all men ought to eschew that person forthwith, and not tarry and look while I bid them so to do. All the earth is my diocese, and I the ordinary of all men, having the authority of the king of all kings upon subjects. I am all in all, and above all, (190) so that God himself, and I the vicar of God, have both one consistory, (191) and I am able to do almost all that God can do. (192) It is said of me, that have an heavenly arbitrator, and therefore am able to change the nature of things, and of nothing to make things to be, and of a sentence that is nothing to make it stand in effect; in all things that I list my will is to stand for reason. For I am able by the law to dispense above the law, and of wrong to make justice, in correcting laws and changing them. You have heard hitherto sufficiently out of my doctors. Now you shall hear greater things out of mine own decrees. (193) Read there *Dist. 96. Satis.* (194) Also 12 *Caus.* 11. q. 1. cap. *Sacerdotibus.* (195) Also 12. q. 1. cap. *Futuram.* Do you not find there expressed how Constantine the emperor sitting in the general council of Nice, called us prelates of the church, all gods? (196) Again, read my canon, *Decretal. De transl. Episc.* cap. *Quanto.* Do you not see there manifestly expressed, how not man, but God alone separates that which the bishop of Rome dissolves and separates? Wherefore if those things that I do be said to be done not of man, but of God; what can you make me but God? Again, if prelates of the church be called and counted of Constantine for gods, I then being above all prelates seem by this reason to be above all gods. Wherefore no marvel, if it be in my power to change time and times, to alter and abrogate laws, to dispense with all things, yea, with the precepts of Christ. For where Christ bids St. Peter put up his sword, admonishing his disciples not to use any outward force in revenging themselves; (197) do not I, Pope Nicolas, writing to the bishops of France, exhort them to draw out their material swords in pursuing their enemies, and recovering their possessions. Where Christ was present himself at the marriage in Cana of Galilee, (198) do not I, Pope Martin, in my distinction inhibit the spiritual clergy to be present at marriage feasts, and also to marry themselves? Where matrimony by Christ cannot be loosed but only for adultery, (199) do not I, Pope Gregory, writing to Boniface, permit the same to be broken for infirmity of body? (200) Against the express caution of the gospel, does not Innocent IV. permit to repel force by force? (201) Likewise against the Old Testament I do dispense in not giving tithes. (202) Against the New Testament in swearing. (203) Wherein two kinds of oaths are to be noted. Whereof some promissory, some be assertions, &c. (204) In vows, and that *ex toto voto,* whereas other prelates cannot dispense *ex toto a voto,* I can deliver *ex toto a voto,* like God himself. (205) In perjury if I absolve my absolution stands. (206) Where also note, that in all swearing always the authority of the superior is excepted. (207) Moreover, where Christ bids us to lend without hope of gain, do not I, Pope Martin, give dispensation for the same? and notwithstanding the council of Turin enacted the contrary, yet with two bulls I disannulled that decree. (208) What should I speak of murder, making it no murder nor homicide to slay them that are excommunicated. (209) Likewise against the law of nature. (210) Against the apostle. (211) Also against the canons of the apostles I can and do dispense. For where they in their canon command a priest for fornication to be deposed, I through the authority of Silvester do alter the rigour of that constitution, (212) considering the minds and bodies also of men now to be weaker than they were then. (213) Briefly, against the universal state of the church I have dispensation. And for marriage in the second degree of consanguinity and affinity between the brother's children, so that the uncle may not marry his niece, unless for an urgent and weighty cause. As for all such contracts betwixt party and party, where matrimony is not yet consummated, it is but a small matter for me to dispense withall. In short, if ye list briefly to hear the whole number of all such cases as properly appertain to my papal dispensation, which come to the number of one and fifty points, that no man may meddle withal but only I myself alone, I will recite them in English, as they be set forth in my canonical doctors.

Cases papal, to the number of one and fifty, wherein the Pope hath power only to dispense, and none else besides, except by special licence from him.

Determination of doubts and questions belonging to faith.

Translation of a bishop, elected or confirmed; likewise of abbots exempted.

Deposition of bishops.

The taking of resignation of bishops.

Exemptions of bishops, not to be under archbishops.

Restitution of such as are deposed from their order.

The judicial definition or interpretation of his own privileges.

Changing of bishoprics, or dismissal of convents, &c.

New correction of bishops' seats, or institution of new religions.

Subjection or division of one bishopric under another.

Dispensation for vowing to go to the Holy Land.

Dispensation for the vow of chastity, or of religion, or of holy orders.

Dispensation against a lawful oath, or vow made.

Dispensation against divers irregularities, as in crimes greater than adultery, and in such as are suspended for simony.

Dispensation in receiving into orders him that had two wives.

Dispensing with such as being within orders do that which is above their order, as if a deacon should say mass, being not yet priest.

To receive into order such as are blemished or maimed in body.

Dispensation with murder, or with such as willingly cut off any member of man's body.

---

(187) Hugo, in glossa, dist. 40. cap. *Non Not.*
(188) Gloss. in caus. 12. q. 3. cap. *Absis.*
(189) Gloss. in c. 11. q. 3. cap. *Si inimicus.*
(190) Hostiensis in cap. *Quanto de transl. præb.*
(191) Ex summa casuum fratris Baptistæ.
(192) Ex Citatione Henr. Bulling. de fine Seculi, Orat. Prima.
(193) Pope Nicolaus, Dist. 96. cap. *Satis.*
(194) 11 q. 11. cap. *Sacerdotibus.*
(195) 12 q. 1. cap. *Futuram.*
(196) Decretal. De transl. Episc. cap. *Quanto.*
(197) Pope Nicolaus, Causa 15. q. 6. cap. *Authoritatem.*
(198) Pope Martin, Dist. 14. cap. *Lector.*
(199) Pope Greg. Junior, 32. q. 7. cap. *Quod proposuisti.*
(200) Pope Innocent 4. Sext. Decret. de sententia excom. cap. *Dilecto.*

(201) Pope Alexander 3. De decimis, cap. *Ex parte.*
(202) Pope Nicolaus, 15. q. 6. cap. *Autoritatem.*
(203) De elect. & elect. potestate. Significasti, in Glossa.
(204) Baptista de Salis in Summa casuum ex Panormitano.
(205) Pope Innocent 4. De elect. Venerabilem.
(206) Ext. De Jurajurando cap. *Venientes.* Item Dist. de Elect. Significasti in Glossa.
(207) Pope Martinus 5. Extra, cap. *Regimini Universalis Ecclesiæ.*
(208) Pope Urbanus 2. Caus. 23. q. 3. cap. *Excommunicatorum.*
(209) Pope Nicolaus, caus. 15. q. 6. cap. *Autoritatem.*
(210) Ibidem.
(211) Dist. 82. 1. cap. *Presbyter.*
(212) Pope Pelagius Dist. 34. cap. *Fraternitatis.*
(213) Baptista de Salis, fol. 114 Ibidem.

Dispensation to give orders to such as have been under the sentence of the greater curse or excommunication.

Dispensation with such as being suspended with the greater curse do minister in any holy order.

Dispensation with such as be unlawfully born to receive orders or benefices.

Dispensation for pluralities of benefices.

Dispensation to make a man bishop before he be thirty years old.

Dispensation to give orders under age.

The pope only hath power to make and call a general council.

The pope alone has power to deprive an ecclesiastical person, and give away his benefice being not vacant.

The pope alone is able to absolve him that is excommunicated by name.

The pope only is able to absolve him whom his legate excommunicates.

The pope both judges in the causes of them that appeal unto him, and where he judges, none may appeal from him.

He only has authority to make deacon and priest, whom he made subdeacon, either upon Sundays, or upon other feasts.

Only the pope, and none else, at all times, and in all places, wears the pall.

The pope only dispenses with a man, either being not within orders, or being unworthy to be made bishop.

He only either confirms or deposes the emperor when he is chosen.

A man being excommunicated, and his absolution referred to the pope, none may absolve that man but the pope alone.

The same hath authority in any election, before it be made, to pronounce it one, when it is made.

He canonizes saints, and none else but he.

Dispensation to have many dignities and personages in one church, and without charge and cure of soul, belongs only to the pope.

To make that effectual which is of no effect, and contrarywise, belongs only to the pope.

To pluck a monk out of his cloister both against his own will and the abbot's, pertains only to the pope.

His sentence makes a law.

The same day in which the pope is consecrated, he may give orders.

He dispenses in degrees in consanguinity and affinity.

He is able to abolish laws, *quoad utrumque forum*, that is, both civil and canon, where danger is of the soul.

It is in his dispensation to give general indulgences to certain places or persons.

To legitimate what persons soever he please, as touching spiritualties, in all places, as touching temporalties, as honors, inheritance, &c.

To erect new religions, to approve or reprove rules or ordinances, and ceremonies in the church.

He is able to dispense with all the precepts and statutes of the church.

To dispense and to discharge any subject from the bond of allegiance, or oath made to any manner of person.

No man may accuse him of any crime, except of heresy, and not even that, except he be incorrigible.

The same is also free from all laws, so that he cannot incur into any sentence of excommunication, suspension, irregularity, or into the penalty of any crime, but in the note of crime he may well.

Finally, he by his dispensation may grant, yea, to a simple priest, to minister the sacrament of confirmation to infants, also to give lower orders, and to hallow churches and virgins, &c.

These be the cases wherein I only have power to dispense, and no man else, neither bishop, nor metropolitan, nor legate, without a licence from me.

After that I have now sufficiently declared my power in earth, in heaven, and in purgatory, how great it is, and what is the fulness thereof, in binding, loosing, commanding, permitting, electing, confirming, deposing, dispensing, doing and undoing, &c. I will treat now a little of my riches likewise, and great possessions, that every man may see by my wealth and abundance of all things, rents, tithes, tributes, my silks, my purple mitres, crowns, gold, silver, pearls and gems, lands and lordships, how God here prospers and magnifies his vicar on the earth. For to me pertains first the imperial city of Rome, the palace of Lateran, the kingdom of Sicily is proper to me, Apulia and Capua be mine. Also the kingdom of England and Ireland, are they not, or ought they not to be tributaries to me? (214) To these I adjoin also, besides other provinces and countries, both in the west and the east, from the north to the south, these dominions by name ; (215) as Ravenna, Corsica, Naples, &c. &c. &c. with divers other more, (216) which Constantine the emperor gave unto me, not that they were not mine before he gave them. (217) For in that I took them of him, I took them not as a gift but as a restitution. And that I rendered them again to Otho, I did it not for any duty to him, but only for peace sake. What should I speak here of my daily revenues of my first fruits, annats, palls, indulgences, bulls, confessionals, indults and rescripts, testaments, dispensations, privileges, elections, prebends, religious houses, and such like, which come to no small mass of money? Insomuch, that for one pall to the archbishop of Mentz, which was wont to be given for ten thousand (218) florins, now it is grown to twenty seven thousand florins, which I received of James, the archbishop, not long before Basil council ; besides the fruits of other bishoprics in Germany, coming to the number of fifty, whereby what advantage comes to my coffers, may partly be conjectured. But what should I speak of Germany, (219) when the whole world is my diocese, as my canonists do say, and all men are bound to believe, (220) except they will imagine (as the Manichæans do) two beginnings, which is false and heretical? For Moses saith, " In the beginning God made heaven and earth," and not in the beginnings. (221) Wherefore as I begun, so I conclude, commanding, declaring, and pronouncing, to stand upon necessity of salvation, for every human creature to be subject to me.

---

(214) Dist. 90. Constantinus.
(215) Ex Commentariis Theoderici Niemi, quem citat Illyricus in Catalogo testium, fol. 228.
(216) Dist. 96. Constantinus.
(217) Antoninus. In Summa majore, 3 part.

(218) Ex lib. Gra. nominum nationis Germanicæ.—Above fifty bishoprics in Germany. Æneas Sylvius.
(219) Sent. Decret. De denis, cap. *Felicis*, in Glossa. Item de privilegiis, cap. *Autoritatem*, in Glossa.
(220) Pope Bonifacius 8. Extr. de Majo. & obed. cap. *Unam-sanctam.*
(221) Ibidem.

ACTS AND MONUMENTS.

BOOK VII.

BEGINNING WITH

THE REIGN OF KING HENRY THE EIGHTH.

KING HENRY VII. died in the year 1509, and had by Elizabeth his wife four sons, and as many daughters. Three only survived, to wit, Prince Henry, Lady Margaret, and Lady Mary: of whom King Henry the Eighth succeeded his father; Lady Margaret was married to James IV., king of Scotland; and Lady Mary was affianced to Charles king of Castile.

Not long before the death of King Henry VII., Prince Arthur his eldest son espoused Lady Catherine daughter to Ferdinand, when fifteen years of age, and she was about the age of seventeen; shortly after this marriage, within five months he died at Ludlow, and was buried at Worcester. After his decease, the succession to the crown fell to King Henry VIII., who at the age of eighteen years, commenced his reign A.D. 1509, and shortly after married Catherine, the widow of his late brother Prince Arthur, in order that her dowry which was great, should not be transported out of the land. For this marriage, which was more politic than scriptural, he received a dispensation from Pope Julius, at the request of Ferdinand her father. The reign of this king continued with great nobleness and fame the space of thirty-eight years. During his time there was great alteration of things, in the civil state of the realm, and especially in the ecclesiastical state, and in matters appertaining to the church. For by him the usurped power of the bishop of Rome was exiled and abolished out of the realm, idolatry and superstition somewhat repressed, images defaced, pilgrimages abolished, abbeys and monasteries pulled down, monkish orders rooted out, the scriptures translated into the vernacular tongue, and the state of the church and religion redressed. Concerning all which things, we will endeavour (Christ willing) to discourse particularly and in order, after we first touch on a few matters, which are to be noted in the beginning of his reign.

Then first comes to our hands a turbulent tragedy, and a fierce contention which had long before troubled the church, and now was renewed afresh in this present year 1509, between two orders of begging-friars, to wit, the Dominican and the Franciscan friars, about the conception of the Virgin Mary the mother of Christ.

The Franciscans held of St. Francis, and followed the rule of his testament, commonly called *gray-friars* or *minorites*. Their opinion was this, that the Virgin Mary, prevented by the grace of the Holy Ghost, was so sanctified, that she was never subject one moment in her conception to original sin. The Dominican friars hold-ing of Dominick, were commonly called *black-friars*, or *preaching-friars*. Their opinion was this, that the Virgin Mary was conceived as all other children of Adam; so that this privilege only belongs to Christ, to be conceived without original sin: notwithstanding, the blessed Virgin was sanctified in her mother's womb, and purged from her original sin, as was also John the Baptist, Jeremiah, or any other privileged person. This frivolous question kindling and engendering between these two orders of friars, burst out into such a flame, that it occupied the heads and wits, schools and universities, almost through the whole church; some holding one part with Scotus, some the other part with Thomas Aquinas. The Minorites holding with Scotus their master, disputed and concluded, that she was conceived without all spot or stain of original sin; and thereupon caused the feast and service of the Conception of St. Mary the Virgin to be celebrated and solemnized in the church. On the other hand the Dominican friars taking part with Aquinas, preached, that it was heresy to affirm that the blessed Virgin was conceived without the guilt of original sin; and that they who celebrated the feast of her conception, or said any masses in honour of it, did sin grievously and mortally.

At the time when this fantasy waxed hot in the church, one side preaching against the other, Pope Sixtus the Fourth, A.D. 1476, who joining side with the Minorites or Franciscans, first sent forth his decree by authority apostolic, willing, ordaining, and commanding all men in holy church for evermore to solemnize this new-found feast of the Conception: offering to all men and women, who devoutly frequenting the church, would hear mass and service from the first evensong of the feast, to the octaves of the same, as many days of pardon, as Pope Urban IV. and Pope Martin V. granted for hearing the service of Corpus Christi day. And this decree was given and dated at Rome, A.D. 1476.

Moreover, the pope, in order that the devotion of the people might be the more encouraged in the celebration of this feast of the conception, added a new clause to the Ave Maria, granting great indulgence and release of sins to all such as would invocate the blessed Virgin with the addition, saying thus: "Hail, Mary, full of grace, the Lord is with thee, blessed art thou among women, and blessed is the fruit of thy womb, Jesus Christ; and blessed is Anna thy mother, of whom thy virgin's flesh hath proceeded without blot of original sin. Amen."

Wherein the reader many note for his learning three things: first, how the pope turns that improperly into a prayer, which was sent by God for a message or tidings. Secondly, how the pope adds to the words of the scripture, contrary to the express precept of the Lord. Thirdly, how the pope exempts Mary the blessed Virgin, not only from the seed of Abraham and Adam, but also from the condition of a mortal creature. For if there be in her no original sin, then she bears not the image of Adam, neither does she descend of that seed, of whose seed evil proceeds upon all men and women to condemnation, as St. Paul teaches, Rom. v. 14—16. Wherefore if she descend of that seed, then the infection of original evil must necessarily proceed to her. If she descend not thereof, then she comes not of the seed of Abraham, nor of the seed of David, &c. Again, seeing that death is the effect and wages of sin, by the doctrine of St. Paul, Rom. vi. 23. then she would not have had to suffer the curse and punishment of death, and so should never have died, if original sin had no place in her. But to return to our history: this constitution of the pope being set forth for the feast of the Conception of the blessed Virgin, A. D. 1476, it was not long after that Pope Sixtus, perceiving that the Dominican friars with their accomplices would not conform thereto, directed forth, by the authority apostolical, a bull in effect as follows:

"Whereas, the holy church of Rome hath ordained a special and proper service for the public solemnization of the feast of the Conception of the blessed Virgin Mary; certain orders of the Black Friars in their public sermons to the people in divers places, have not ceased hitherto to preach, and yet daily do, that all they who hold or affirm the glorious Virgin to have been conceived without original sin, be heretics; and they who celebrate the service of her conception, or do hear the sermons of them who so affirm, do sin grievously: also not contented herewith, do write and set forth books, maintaining their assertions to the great offence and ruin of godly minds. We, therefore, to prevent and withstand such presumptuous and perverse assertions which have risen, and more hereafter may arise, by such opinions and preachings, in the minds of the faithful; by the authority apostolical, do condemn and reprove the same; and by the motion, knowledge, and authority aforesaid, decree and ordain, That the preachers of God's word, and all other persons, of what state, degree, order, or condition soever they be, who shall presume to dare affirm or preach to the people these opinions and assertions to be true, or shall read, hold, or maintain any such books for true, having before intelligence hereof, shall incur thereby the sentence of excommunication, from which they shall not be absolved otherwise than by the bishop of Rome, except only in the time of death."

This bull, being dated A. D. 1483, gave no little heart and encouragement to the Gray-Friars Franciscans, who defended the immaculate conception of the holy Virgin against the Black Dominican Friars, holding the contrary side. By the authority of this bull, the Gray Order had got such a conquest over the Black Order of the Dominicans, that the Dominicans were compelled at length, for a perpetual memorial of the triumph, both to give to the glorious Virgin every night an anthem in praise of her conception, and also to subscribe to their doctrine; in which doctrine these, with other points, are contained.

1. That the blessed Virgin Mary suffered the griefs and adversities in this life, not for any necessity inflicted for punishment of original sin, but only because she would conform herself to the imitation of Christ.

2. That the Virgin, as she was not obliged to any punishment due for sin, as neither was Christ her son; so she had no need of remission of sins, but instead thereof had the divine preservation of God's help, keeping her from all sin, which was the only good she needed, and she had it.

3. That though the body of the Virgin Mary was subject to death, and died; this is to be understood to come not for any penalty due for sin, but either for imitation of and conformity to Christ, or else for the natural constitution of her body, being elemental, as were the bodies of our first parents: who, if they had not tasted of the forbidden fruit, would have been preserved from death, not by nature, but by grace, and the strength of other fruits and meats in paradise: which meats, because Mary had not, but did eat our common meats, therefore she died, and not for any necessity of original sin.

4. The universal proposition of St. Paul, who saith, "That the scripture hath concluded all men under sin," is to be understood thus, as speaking of all them who are not exempted by the special privilege of God, as is the blessed Virgin Mary.

5. If justification be taken for reconciliation of him that was unrighteous before, and now is made righteous: then the blessed Virgin is to be taken, not as justified by Christ, but just from her beginning by preservation.

6. If a Saviour be taken for him which saves men fallen into perdition and condemnation; then Christ is not the Saviour of Mary, but is her Saviour only in this respect, as saving her from not falling into condemnation, &c.

7. Neither did the Virgin Mary give thanks to God, nor ought to do so, for expiation of her sins, but for her preservation from sinning.

8. Neither did she pray to God at any time for remission of her sins, but only for the remission of other men's sins she prayed many times, and counted their sins for hers.

9. If the blessed Virgin had died before the passion of her Son, God would have reposed her soul not in the place among the patriarchs, or among the just, but in the same most pleasant place of paradise where Adam and Eve were before they transgressed.

These were the doting dreams and fantasies of the Franciscans, and of other papists, then commonly held in the schools, written in their books, preached in their sermons, taught in their churches, and set forth in pictures. So that the people was taught nothing else almost in the pulpits all this while, but how the Virgin Mary was conceived immaculate and holy, without original sin, and how they ought to call to her for help, addressing her with special titles as "The way of mercy,—The mother of grace,—The lover of piety,—The comforter of mankind,—The continual intercessor for the salvation of the faithful, and an advocate to the King her Son, who never ceases," &c. And although the greatest number of the school-doctors were of the contrary faction, as Peter Lombard, Thomas Aquinas, Bernard, Bonaventure, and others: yet these new papists shifted off their objections with frivolous distinctions and blind evasions.

The Dominican Friars, for their part, were not all silent, having great authorities, and also the scripture on their side. But yet the others having the apostolical see with them, had the better hand, and got the victory triumphantly, to the high exaltation of their order. For Pope Sixtus, by the authority apostolic, after he had decreed the conception-day of the Virgin to be sanctified perpetually, and also with his terrible bull had condemned for heretics all who withstood the same; the Dominican friars were driven to two inconveniences: the one was, to keep silence; the other was, to give place to their adversaries the Franciscans. Although, where the mouth durst not speak, yet the heart would work; and though their tongues were tied, yet their good-will was ready by all means possible to maintain their quarrel and their estimation.

It happened in this year, 1509, after this dissension between the Dominican and the Franciscan Friars, that certain of the Dominicans, thinking, by subtle sleight, to work in the people's heads that which they durst not attempt by open preaching, devised a certain image of the Virgin made so artificially, that the friars by private springs made it move, make gestures, lament, complain, weep, groan, and give answers to those that asked it;

so that the people were brought into a marvellous persuasion, till at length the fraud being detected, the friars were taken, condemned, and burnt at Berne in the year above-mentioned, 1509.

In the history of John Stumsius, this story partly appears: but in the registers and records of the city of Berne, the order and circumstance is more fully expressed and set forth, and is thus declared.

In the city of Berne there were certain Dominican friars, to the number chiefly of four principal actors and chiefs of that order, who had inveigled a certain simple poor friar, who had newly planted himself in the cloister: when the friars had so infatuated him with sundry superstitions, and feigned apparitions of St. Mary, St. Barbara, and St. Katherine, and imprinted, moreover, in him the wounds of St. Francis, he believed fully, that the Virgin Mary had appeared to him, and had offered him a red host consecrated with the blood also of Christ miraculously, that the blessed Virgin also had sent him to the senators of Berne, with instructions, declaring to them from the mouth of the virgin, "That she was conceived in sin; and that the Franciscan Friars were not to be credited nor suffered in the city, who were not yet reformed from that erroneous opinion of her conception." He added, moreover, "That they should resort to a certain image there of the Virgin Mary, (which image the friars by engines had made to weep) and should do their worship, and make their oblations to the same."

This feigned device was no sooner forged by the friars, but it was believed by the people; so that a great while the red-coloured host was undoubtedly taken for the true body and blood of Christ, and certain coloured drops of it sent abroad to noble personages and states for a great relic, and that too not without considerable cost in return. Thus the deceived people came flocking in great numbers to the image, and to the red host, and coloured blood, with many gifts and oblations. In short, the Dominican friars so had managed the matter, and had so swept all offerings to their own order from the order of the Franciscans, that all the alms came to their box. The Franciscans seeing their reputation decaying, and their kitchen waxing cold, and their coffers becoming empty, not able to abide that misery, and being not ignorant or unacquainted with such counterfeited doings, (for, as the proverb saith, "It is all halting before a cripple,") soon discovered the crafty juggling, and detected the fraudulent miracles of the Dominicans. Whereupon the four chief leaders above-named were apprehended and burned, of whom the provincial of the order was one.

And thus much touching the beginning and end of this tumultuous and popish tragedy, wherein it may evidently appear to the reader, how these turbulent friars could not agree among themselves, and in what frivolous trifles they wrangled together. But to let these ridiculous friars pass with their trifling phantasies, which deserve to be derided by all wise men: this is, in the mean time, to be lamented, to behold the miserable times of the church, in which the devil kept the minds of Christ's people so attentive and occupied in such friarly toys, that scarcely any thing was taught or heard in the church, but the commendation and exaltation of the Virgin Mary: but of our justification by faith, of grace, and of the promises of God in Christ, of the strength of the law, of the horror of sin, of the difference between the law and the gospel, of the true liberty of conscience, &c. little mention was made. Wherefore, in so blind a time of darkness it was very needful and requisite, that the Lord of his mercy should look upon his church, and send down his gracious reformation, which he did. For shortly after, through God's gracious raising him up, came Martin Luther, of whom the order of history now requires that we should treat, and we will do so (Christ willing) after the history of Richard Hunne, and a few other things premised, for the better opening of the history to follow.

Mention was made before of the doings of Pope Julius II., and of his warlike affairs, for which he was condemned, and not unjustly, in the council of Tours in France, (A. D. 1510,) and yet all this could not assuage the furious spirit of this pope, but the same year he invaded the city of Mutina and Mirandula, in Italy, and took them by force of war. Pope Julius, not long after, in the year 1512, refusing the peace offered by Maximilian the emperor, was encountered by Lewis the French king about Ravenna, upon Easter-day, where he was vanquished, and had of his army slain to the number of sixteen thousand. And the year following, (A. D. 1513,) this apostolic warrior, who had resigned his keys to the river Tiber before, made an end together both of his fighting and living, after he had reigned and fought ten years. After him succeeded next in the see of Rome, Pope Leo X.; about this time great changes began to work, as well in the temporal states, as in the state of the church. At which time the following potentates were reigning in their several kingdoms:—

	Began to reign.	Reigned.
Pope Leo X. in Rome, — —	A. D. 1513,	9 years.
Charles V., emperor of Germany,	A. D. 1519,	39 ——
Francis I., king of France, —	A. D. 1515,	32 ——
Henry VIII., king of England,	A. D. 1509,	38 ——
James V., king of Scotland, —	A. D. 1513,	29 ——

In the time of the above mentioned potentates, great alterations, troubles, and changes of religion were wrought in the church, by the mighty operation of God's hand, in Italy, France, Germany, England, and all Europe; such as have not been seen (although much groaned for) many hundred years before: as in the course of this history shall more manifestly appear.

But before we come to these alterations, taking the time as it lies before us, we will first speak of Richard Hunne, and certain other godly-minded persons here in England, who were afflicted for the word of Christ's gospel in great multitudes, as they be found and taken out of the registers of Fitzjames, bishop of London.

The History of some good Men and Women, who were persecuted for Religion in the City and Diocese of the Bishop of London; briefly extracted out of the Registers of Richard Fitzjames.

Beside the great number of the faithful martyrs and professors of Christ, that constantly, in the strength of the Holy Ghost, gave their lives for the testimony of his truth, I find recorded in the register of London, between the years 1509 and 1517, the names of many persons, both men and women, who, in the fulness of that dark and misty time of ignorance had also some portion of God's good Spirit, which induced them to the knowledge of his truth and gospel, and were troubled, persecuted, and imprisoned for the same: notwithstanding, by the proud, cruel, and bloody rage of the Romish see, and through the weakness and frailty of their own nature, (not then fully strengthened in God) they were for the time suppressed and kept under, as appears by their several abjurations made before Richard Fitzjames, then bishop of London, who was a most cruel persecutor of Christ's church, or else before his vicar-general deputed for that purpose. And, as many of the adversaries of God's truth have of late days disdainfully and braggingly cried out, and demanded in their public assemblies, asking, "Where was this your church and religion fifty or sixty years ago?" I have thought it not altogether vain, somewhat to stop such questioners, both by mentioning the names of those who suffered for the truth of this religion, and likewise opening some of the chief and principal matters for which they were so unmercifully afflicted: thereby to make known the continuance and consent of the true church of Christ in that age, touching the chief points of our faith, and also to shew what fond and frivolous matters the ignorant prelates in that time of blindness, were not ashamed to object against the poor and simple people, accounting them as heinous and great offences, yea, such as deserved death both of body and soul.

They were forty in number who were persecuted in

the time between the years 1510 and 1527; and here follows the particular examination of them all.

There were several particular articles (besides the common and general sort used in such cases) privately objected, such as they were accused of either by their curate, or their neighbours. And as I think it superfluous to make any large recital of all and every part of their several processes, I purpose therefore only to touch briefly on so many of the articles as may be sufficient to induce the christian reader to judge the sooner of the rest.

The chief objection against Joan Baker was, that she would not only herself not reverence the crucifix, but had also persuaded a friend of hers lying at the point of death, not to put any trust or confidence in the crucifix, but in God who is in heaven, and not in the dead images, which are but stocks and stones, and therefore she was sorry that ever she had gone so often on pilgrimage to St. Saviour and other idols. Also, that she held that the pope had no power to give pardons, and that the Lady Young (who was not long before that time burned) died a true martyr of God, and therefore she wished of God that she herself might do no worse than the Lady Young had done.

Against William Pottier, besides other false and slanderous articles (as that he denied the benefit and effect of Christ's passion) it was alleged, that he affirmed there were six Gods: the first three were the holy Trinity, the Father, the Son, and the Holy Ghost; the fourth was a priest's concubine being kept in his chamber; the fifth was the devil; and the sixth, that thing that a man sets his mind most upon.

The first part of this article he utterly denied, confessing most firmly and truly, the blessed Trinity to be only one God in one unity of deity. As to the other three he answered, that a priest delighting in his concubine made her as his god; likewise a wicked person, persisting in his sin without repentance, made the devil his god; and lastly, he granted, that he once heard of certain men, who by the singing and chattering of birds superstitiously sought to know what things were to happen either to themselves or others, said, that those men esteemed their birds as gods.

Among the articles objected against Thomas Goodred, Thomas Walker, Thomas Forge, Alice Forge, John Forge, John Calverton, John Woodrof, Richard Woolman, and Roger Hilliar, (as that they spoke against pilgrimages, praying to saints, and such like) this was principally charged against them, that they all denied the carnal and corporal presence of Christ's body and blood in the sacrament of the altar; and further, had concealed and consented to their teachers and instructors in that doctrine, and had not, according to the laws of the church, accused and presented them to the bishop or his ordinary. Also great and heinous displeasure was conceived against Richard Woolman, because he called the church of St. Paul a house of thieves, affirming, that the priests and other ecclesiastical persons there were not liberal givers to the poor (as they ought) but rather were takers away from them what they could get.

Likewise as Thomas Austy, Joan Austy, Thomas Grant, John Garter, Christopher Ravins, Dyonise Ravins, Thomas Vincent, Lewis John, Joan John, and John Web, were of one fellowship and profession of faith with those before recited, so they were almost all apprehended about one time, and chiefly charged with one opinion of the sacrament. Which declares evidently, that notwithstanding the dark ignorance of those corrupted times, yet God did ever in mercy open the eyes of some to behold the manifest truth, even in those things of which the papists now make the greatest vaunt, and boast of long continuance. Many of them were charged with having spoken against pilgrimages, and having read and used certain English books opposing the faith of the Romish church, as the four Gospels, Wickliff's Wicket, a Book of the Ten Commandments of Almighty God, the Revelation of St. John, the Epistles

of St. Paul and St. James, with others, which those Romish divines could never abide: and good cause why, for as darkness could never agree with light, no more can ignorance, the maintainer of that kingdom, with the true knowledge of Christ and his gospel.

It was further objected against Joan John, the wife of Lewis John, that she learned and maintained, that God commanded no holy-days to be kept, but only the sabbath-day, and therefore she would keep none but it; nor any fasting-days, affirming, that to abstain from sin was the true fast. That she had despised the pope, his pardons and pilgrimages, so that when any poor body asked an alms of her in the name and for the sake of the lady of Walsingham, (i. e. the image of the Virgin Mary at Walsingham,) she would answer in contempt of the pilgrimage, "The lady of Walsingham help thee!" and if she gave anything to him, she would then say, "Take this in the name of our lady in heaven, and let the other go." Which shews, that for lack of better instruction and knowledge, she yet ignorantly attributed too much honour to the true saints of God departed, though otherwise she abhorred the idolatrous worshipping of the dead images. By which example, as also by many others, I have just occasion to condemn the wilful subtlety of those, that in this bright shining light of God's truth, would yet, under colour of godly remembrance, still maintain the having of images in the church, craftily excusing their idolatrous kneeling and praying to them, by affirming, that they never worshipped the dead images, but the things that the images represented. But if that were their only doctrine and cause of having those images, why then would their predecessors so cruelly compel these poor simple people thus openly in their recantations to abjure and revoke their speaking against the gross adoration of the outward images only, and not against the thing represented, which many of them (as appears partly by this example) in their ignorant simplicity confessed might be worshipped? However, God be thanked, their hypocritical excuses cannot now have such place in the hearts of the elect of God as they have done heretofore, especially seeing the word of God so manifestly forbids as well the worshipping of them, as the making or having them for purposes of religion.

It was alleged against William Cowper, and Alice Cowper his wife, that they had spoken against pilgrimages, and worshipping of images; but chiefly the woman, who having her child hurt by falling into a pit or ditch, and earnestly persuaded by some of her ignorant neighbours to go on pilgrimage to St. Lawrence for help to her child, said, that neither St. Lawrence, nor any other saint could help her child, and therefore none ought to go on pilgrimage to any image made with man's hands, but only to Almighty God; for pilgrimages were worth nothing worth, except to make the priests rich.

To John Houshold, Robert Rascal, and Elizabeth Stamford, the article against the sacrament of the altar was objected, as also that they had spoken against praying to saints, and had despised the authority of the bishop of Rome, and of his clergy; but especially John Houshold was charged with having called them antichrists, and the pope himself "the great whore," who with his pardons had drowned in blindness all christian realms for money.

Also among other articles against George Browne, these were counted very heinous and heretical. First, that he had said, that he knew no cause why the cross should be worshipped, seeing that the same was the cause of pain to our Saviour Christ in the time of his passion, and not any ease or pleasure to him; alleging for example, that if he had had a friend hanged or drowned he would never after have loved that gallows or water by which his friend died. Another objection was, that he had erroneously, obstinately, and maliciously said (for so are their words), that the church was too rich. This matter, I may tell you, touched somewhat the quick, and therefore no marvel that they counted it erroneous and malicious; for take away their gain, and farewell to their religion. They also charged him with having refused holy water to be cast about his chamber, and likewise with having spoken against priests.

The greatest matter with which they charged John Wikes, was, that he had often and for a long time kept company with persons suspected of heresy, and had received them into his house, and there did hear them read erroneous and heretical books, contrary to the faith of the Romish church; and did also himself consent to their doctrine, and had many times secretly conveyed them away from such as were appointed to apprehend them.

John Southake, Richard Butler, John Sam, William King, Robert Durdant, and Henry Woolman, were charged with speaking words against the literal and carnal presence of Christ's body in the sacrament of the altar, and also against images, and the rest of the seven sacraments. They charged them with the reading of certain English heretical books, naming most blasphemously the gospel of Jesus Christ, by the four evangelists, to be of that number, as appears evidently by the eighth article objected by Thomas Bennet, doctor of law, chancellor and vicar-general to Richard Fitzjames, then bishop of London, against Richard Butler, the very words of which article, for a more declaration of truth, I have thought good here to insert, which are these:—" Also we object to you, that divers times, and especially upon a certain night, about the space of three years last past, in Robert Durdant's house of Iver Court, near unto Staines, you erroneously and damnably read in a great book of heresy of the said Robert Durdant's, all that same night, certain chapters of the gospels in English, containing in them divers erroneous and damnable opinions and conclusions of heresy, in the presence of the said Robert Durdant, John Butler, Robert Carder, Jenkin Butler, William King, and divers other suspected persons of heresy, then being present, and hearing your said erroneous lectures and opinions.'' To the same effect and purpose tended some of the articles propounded against the other four; whereby we may easily judge what reverence they, who yet desire to be counted the true and only church of Christ, bow to the word and gospel of Christ, when they are not ashamed to blaspheme it with most horrible titles of erroneous and damnable opinions and conclusions of heresy. But why should we marvel at this, when the Holy Ghost in several places of the scripture declares, that in the latter days there should come such proud and cursed talkers, who shall speak lies through hypocrisy, and have their consciences seared with an hot iron? Let us, therefore, now thank our heavenly Father for revealing them to us; and let us also pray him, that of his free mercy in his Son Christ Jesus, he would, if it be to his glory, either turn and soften all their hearts, or else, for the peace and quietness of his church he would in his righteous judgment take them from us.

About this time Richard Fitzjames ended his life, after whose death Cuthbert Tonstall (afterwards bishop of Durham), succeeded in the see and bishopric of London, who soon upon his first entry into the room, minding to follow rightly the footsteps of his predecessor, caused Edmund Spilman, priest, Henry Chambers, John Higgins, and Thomas Eglestone to be apprehended, and so to be examined upon articles; and in the end, either for fear of his cruelty, and the rigour of death, or else through hope of his flattering promises (such was their weakness), he compelled them to abjure and renounce their true professed faith touching the holy sacrament of Christ's body and blood, which was, that Christ's corporal body was not in the sacrament, but in heaven; and that the sacrament was a figure of his body, and not the body itself.

Moreover, about the same time there were certain articles objected against John Higges, alias Noke, alias Johnson, by the bishop's vicar-general, among which were these:—First, that he had affirmed, that it was as lawful for a temporal man to have two wives at once, as for a priest to have two benefices. Also, that he had in his custody a book of the four evangelists in English, and often read therein; and that he favoured the doctrines and opinions of Martin Luther, openly pronouncing, that Luther had more learning in his little finger than all the doctors in England in their whole bodies; and that all the priests in the church were blind, and had led the people the wrong way. Likewise it was alleged against him, that he had denied purgatory, and had said, that while he was alive he would do as much for himself as he could, for after his death he thought that prayers and almsdeeds could little help him.

With these and such like matters these poor and simple men and women were chiefly charged, and were excommunicated and imprisoned as heinous heretics, and at last compelled to recant; and some of them in utter shame and reproach, besides the ordinary bearing of fagots before the cross in procession, or else at a sermon, were enjoined for a penance (as they termed it) to appear once every year before their ordinary, as also to wear the sign of a fagot painted upon their sleeves, or other part of their outward garment, during all their lives, or so often and long as it pleased their ordinary to appoint. By which long, rigorous, and open punishing of them, they meant utterly to terrify and keep back all others from the true knowledge of Jesus Christ and his gospel. But the Lord be evermore praised, what little effect their wicked purposes had, these our most lightsome days of God's glorious gospel most joyfully declare.

Besides these, others more simple and ignorant were also troubled, who having but a very small taste of the truth, did yet at first gladly consent to the same; but being apprehended, they quickly again yielded, and therefore had only assigned them for their penance, the bearing of a little candle before the cross, without any further open abjuring or recanting. Among whom I find two especially; the one a woman, called Ellen Heyer, to whom it was objected, that she had neither confessed herself to the priest, nor yet received the sacrament of the altar for the space of four years, and had every year eaten flesh at Easter.

The other was a man named Robert Berkeway, who (besides most wicked blasphemies against God, which he utterly denied) was charged to have spoken heinous words against the pope's holy and blessed martyr, Thomas Becket, calling him thief, for that he wrought by crafts and imaginations.

Thus have I, as briefly as I could, summarily collected the principal articles objected against these weak and infirm earthly vessels; not meaning hereby either to excuse or condemn them in these their fearful falls and dangerous defections, but leaving them to the immeasurable rich mercies of the Lord, I wish only to make manifest the insatiable bloody cruelty of the pope's kingdom against the gospel and true church of Christ, for nothing would mitigate their envious rage, which they showed even against the very simple idiots, and that sometimes in most frivolous and irreligious cases. But now leaving them, I will (by God's grace) go forward with other more serious matters.

The Death and Martyrdom of William Sweeting and John Brewster.

In searching and perusing the register, for the collection of the names and articles before recited, I find that within the compass of the same years there were also some others, who after they had once shewed themselves as frail and inconstant as the rest, (being either pricked in conscience, or otherwise overcome with the manifest truth of God's most sacred word) became yet again as earnest professors of Christ as they were before, and for the same profession were the second time apprehended, examined, condemned, and in the end were most cruelly burned. Of which number were William Sweeting and John Brewster, who were both burned together in Smithfield the eighteenth day of October, A.D. 1511. The chief case alleged against them in their articles, was their faith concerning the sacrament of Christ's body and blood, which because it differed from the absurd and gross opinion of the new schoolmen, was counted as the most heinous heresy. There were other things besides objected against them, as the reading of certain forbidden books, and accompanying with such persons as were suspected of heresy. But one great and heinous offence counted amongst the rest, was their putting and leaving off the painted fagots, which they were at their first abjuring enjoined to wear as badges during their lives, or so long as it should please their ordinary to appoint, and not to leave them off upon pain of relapse, until they were dispensed with for the same. The breach of this injunction was esteemed to be of no small weight, and yet, the matter well and thoroughly considered, it seems by their confessions, that they were by necessity forced to it. For Sweeting being, for fear of the bishop's cruelty constrained to wander about the country to get his living, came at length to Colchester, where he was appointed by the parson of the parish of Magdalen to be the holy water clerk, and in that consideration had that infamous badge taken away from him. Brewster left off his at the command of the controller of the Earl of Oxford's house, who hiring the poor man to labour in the earl's household business, would not suffer him to wear that badge any longer. So that necessity of living compelled both of them to break that injunction : and therefore if charity had borne as great sway in the hearts of the pope's clergy as did cruelty, this trifle would not have been so heinously taken as to be brought against them for an article and a cause of condemnation to death. But where tyranny once takes place, all godly love, and all human reason and duties are quite forgotten. But to be brief, for these causes, as also because they had already once abjured, and yet as they termed it fallen again into relapse, they were both together burned in Smithfield ; although, as the register records, they again, before their death fearfully forsook their revived constancy, and submitting themselves to the discipline of the Romish church, craved absolution. However, as many of the registers' notes and records in such cases may well be doubted, I refer the knowledge thereof to the Lord, who is the trier of all truths. Not forgetting, however, if the report be true, to charge that priesthood and their wicked laws, with a more shameless tyranny and uncharitable cruelty than before ; for if they cease, their bloody malice towards such as so willingly submit themselves to their mercies ; what favour may the faithful and constant professors of Christ look for at their hands ? I might here also ask of them, how they follow the pitiful and loving admonition, or rather precept, of our Saviour Christ (whose true and only church they so stoutly boast to be), who says, " If thy brother trespass against thee seven times in a day, and seven times in a day turn again to thee, saying, I repent, thou shalt forgive him." (Luke xvii. 4.)

John Browne, father to Richard Browne, which Richard was in prison in Canterbury, and would have been burned, with two more, the day after the death of Queen Mary, but by the proclaiming of Queen Elizabeth they escaped.

The occasion of the first trouble of this John Browne, was by a priest sitting in a Gravesend barge. John Browne, being at the same time in the barge, came and sate hard by him ; after some communication, the priest asked him, " Dost thou know," said he, " who I am ? thou sittest too near me, thou sittest on my clothes ;" " No, Sir," said he, " I know not what you are." " I tell thee I am a priest." " What, sir, are you a parson, or vicar, or a lady's chaplain ?" " No," quoth he again, " I am a soul-priest, I sing for a soul," saith he. " Do you so, sir," quoth the other, " that is well done ; I pray you sir," quoth he, " where find you the soul when you go to mass ?" " I cannot tell thee," said the priest. " I pray you, where do you leave it, Sir, when the mass is done ?" " I cannot tell thee," said the priest. " Neither can you tell where you find it when you go to mass

nor where you leave it when the mass is done, how can you then save the soul ?" said he. " Go thy ways," said he, " thou art an heretic, and I will be even with thee." So at the landing, the priest taking with him Walter More, and William More, rode straightways to the Archbishop Warham, whereupon John Browne, within three days after, his wife being churched the same day, and he bringing in a mess of pottage to the table to his guests, was sent for, and his feet bound under his own horse, and so brought to Canterbury, neither his wife nor he, nor any of his, knowing where he was taken ; and there continuing from Low-sunday till the Friday before Whitsunday, his wife not knowing all this while where he was. He was set in the stocks overnight, and on the morrow went to death, and was burned at Ashford, A.D. 1517. The same night, as he was in the stocks at Ashford, where he and his wife dwelt, his wife then hearing of him, came and sat by him all the night before he was burned : to whom he declaring the whole story of how he was handled, shewed and told, how that he could not set his feet to the ground, for they were burnt to the bones, and told her how, by the two bishops Warham and Fisher, his feet were heated upon the hot coals, and burned to the bones " to make me," said he, " to deny my Lord, which I will never do ; for if I should deny my Lord in this world, he should hereafter deny me. I pray thee, therefore, good Elizabeth, continue as thou hast begun, and bring up thy children virtuously in the fear of God." And so the next day, on Whitsunday even, this godly martyr was burned. Standing at the stake, this prayer he made, holding up his hands :

" O Lord, I yield me to thy grace,
Grant me mercy for my trespass ;
Let never the fiend my soul chace.
Lord, I will bow, and thou shalt beat,
Let never my soul come in hell heat.

" Into thy hands I commend my spirit ; thou hast redeemed me, O Lord of truth."
And so he ended.

The History of Richard Hunne.

There was in the year 1514, one Richard Hunne, merchant-taylor, and freeman in the city of London, who was esteemed during his life, and taken not only for a man of true dealing and good substance, but also for a good catholic man. This Richard Hunne had a child at nurse in Middlesex, which died. Thomas Dryfield, the priest of the parish, sued Richard Hunne in the spiritual court for a bearing-sheet, for a mortuary for the son of Richard Hunne, who died at the age of five weeks. Hunne answered, " That as the child had no property in the sheet, he therefore would not pay it, nor ought the other to have it. The priest, moved with a covetous desire, and loth to lose his pretended right, cited him to appear in the spiritual court. Richard Hunne being troubled in the spiritual court, was forced to seek counsel of the learned in the law, and pursued a writ of *præmunire* against Thomas Dryfield, which when the rest of the priestly order heard of, indignant that any layman should attempt such a matter against any of them, and fearing that if they should now suffer this priest to be condemned, there would be ever after a liberty to all of the laity to do the like with the rest of the clergy in such cases ; they straightways, both to stop this matter, and also to be revenged of him, sought all the means they possibly could to intrap and bring him within the danger of their own cruel laws. And so making secret and diligent inquisition, and seeking all they could against him, at length they found means to accuse him of heresy to Richard Fitzjames, then bishop of London, who (desirous to satisfy the revenging and bloody affection of his chaplains) caused him to be apprehended and committed to prison in the Lollards' Tower at Paul's, so that none of his friends might be suffered to come to him. This Richard Hunne being clapt in the Lollards' Tower shortly after, at the earnest instigation of Dr. Horsey, the bishop's chancellor (a man more ready to prefer the clergy's cruel tyranny, than the truth of Christ s gospel) was brought before the bishop, at his manor of Fulham, the 2d day of December, where in his chapel he examined him upon these articles, collected against him by Horsey and his accomplices :—

1. That he had read, taught, preached, published, and obstinately defended, against the laws of Almighty God, that tithes, or paying tithes, was never ordained to be due, saving only by the covetousness of priests.

2. That he had read, taught, preached, published, and obstinately defended, that bishops and priests are the scribes and pharisees that crucified Christ and condemned him to death.

3. That he had read, taught, preached, &c., that bishops and priests are teachers and preachers, but no doers nor fulfillers of the law of God ; but catching, ravening and taking all things, and ministering and giving nothing.

4. Where and when one Joan Baker was detected and abjured of many great heresies, as appears by her abjuration, the said Richard Hunne said, published, taught, preached, and obstinately took upon him to say, that he would defend her and her opinions, if it cost him five hundred marks.

5. Afterwards, when Joan Baker, after her abjuration, was enjoined open penance, according to her demerits, the said Richard Hunne said, published, taught, and obstinately defended her, saying, the bishop of London and his officers have done open wrong to Joan Baker in punishing her for heresy ; for her sayings and opinions are according to the laws of God : wherefore the bishop and his officers are more worthy to be punished for heresy than she.

6. That the said Richard Hunne has in his keeping divers English Books, prohibited and condemned by the law ; as the apocalypse in English, epistles and gospels in English, Wickliff's damnable works, and other books containing infinite errors, in which he has been for a long time accustomed to read, teach, and study daily.

Particular answer to these several objections in the register I find none, saving that under them there is written in his name, with a different hand, these words: "As to these articles, I have not spoken them as they are here laid ; however I have unadvisedly spoken words somewhat sounding to the same effect, for which I am sorry, and ask God's mercy, and submit me to my Lord's charitable and favourable correction.'' Which they affirm to be written with Hunne's own hand : but how likely to truth that is, let the discreet wisdom of the reader judge by the whole sequel of this process. And further, if it were his own act, what occasion then had they so cruelly to murder him as they did, seeing he had already so willingly confessed his fault, and submitted himself to the charitable and favourable correction of the bishop ?

This examination being ended, the bishop sent him back again the same day unto the Lollards' Tower ; and then, by the appointment of Dr. Horsey his chancellor, he was committed from the custody of Charles Joseph the somner, to John Spalding the bell-ringer, a man by whose simpleness the subtle chancellor thought to bring his devilish homicide the easier to pass ; which he most cruelly did, by his suborned ministers, within two nights after, as is proved, by the inquiry, and final verdict of the coroner of London and his inquest. But when this usual practice of the papists was once accomplished, there were wanted no secret shifts nor worldly-wiles for the crafty colouring of this mischief: and therefore the next morning after they had, in the night, committed this murder, Spalding got himself out of the way into the city, and leaving the keys of the prison with one of his fellows, desired him to deliver them to the somner's boy who used to carry to Hunne his meat and other necessaries ; thinking that the boy, first finding the prisoner dead, and hanged as they left him, they might by his relation be thought free from having any hand in this matter. Which happened in the beginning almost as they wished. For the boy the same morning, accompanied with two of the bishop's somners, went about ten o'clock into the prison, to serve the prisoner as he was wont to do ; and when they came up, they found him hanged with his face towards the wall. They, astonished at this sight, immediately told the chancellor, who was then in the church, and watching, I suppose, for such news ; he forthwith got certain of his colleagues, and went with them into the prison, to see that which his own wicked conscience knew full well before, as was afterwards plainly proved, although he then made a fair face to the contrary, blazing abroad among the people by their officers and servants, that Hunne had hanged himself. However the people having good experience of the honest life and godly conversation of the man, and also of the devilish malice of his adversaries the priests, judged rather, that he was secretly murdered by their procurement. On this there arose great contention ; for the bishop of London on one side, taking his clergy's part, affirmed stoutly that Hunne had hanged himself : the citizens again on the other side, suspecting some secret murder, caused the coroner of London, according to law, to choose an inquest, and to take view of the dead body, and so to try the truth of the matter. As the bishop and his chaplains were then driven to extremity of shifts : and therefore wishing by some subtle show of justice to stop the mouths of the people, they determined, that while the inquest was occupied about their charge, the bishop should for his part proceed ex officio, in case of heresy against the dead person ; supposing, that if the party were once condemned of heresy, the inquest durst not then but find him guilty of his own death, and so clearly acquit them from all suspicion of murder. This determination of theirs they immediately put in practice, in order as follows :

Besides the articles before mentioned, which they affirm were objected against him in his life-time, Dr. Horsey, the bishop of London's vicar general, now after his death collected others out of the prologue of his English Bible, which he diligently perused, not to learn any good thing, but to get thereout such matter as he thought might best serve their cursed purpose, as appears by the tenor of the articles, which are these :

1. The book condemns all holy canons, calling them ceremonies and statutes of sinful men, and calls the pope, Satan and antichrist.

2. It condemns the pope's pardons, saying they are but impositions.

3. The said book of Hunne saith, that kings and lords called christian in name, and heathen in conditions, defile the sanctuary of God, bringing clerks full of covetousness, heresy and malice, to stop God's law, that it cannot be known, kept, and freely preached.

4. The book saith, that lords and prelates pursue fully and cruelly them that would teach truly and freely the law of God, and cherish them that preach sinful men's traditions and statutes, by which he means the holy canons of Christ's church.

5. That poor and simple men have the truth of the holy scriptures, more than a thousand prelates, and religious men, and clerks of the school.

6. That christian kings and lords set idols in God's house, and excite the people to idolatry.

7. That princes, lords, and prelates so doing, are worse than Herod that pursued Christ, and worse than the Jews and heathen men that crucified Christ.

8. That every man, swearing by our lady, or any other saint or creature, gives more honour to the saints than to the Holy Trinity, and so they are idolaters.

9. He saith that saints ought not to be honoured.

10. He condemns adoration, prayer, kneeling, and offering to images, which he calls stocks and stones.

11. He saith, that the very body of the Lord is not contained in the sacrament of the altar, but that men receiving it shall thereby keep in mind that Christ's flesh was wounded and crucified for us.

12. He condemns the university of Oxford, with all degrees and faculties in it, as arts, civil and canon laws, and divinity ; saying, that they hinder the true way to come to the knowledge of the laws of God and holy scripture.

13. He defends the translation of the Bible and holy scripture into the English tongue, which is prohibited by the laws of our holy mother church.

These articles thus collected, as also the others before specified, they caused, for a shew of their pretended justice and innocency, to be openly read the next Sunday, by the preacher at Paul's-Cross, and having now, as they thought, sufficient matter against him, they purposed to proceed to his condemnation.

Accordingly, the bishop of London, accompanied by the bishops of Durham and Lincoln, sat in judgment on Richard Hunne, the sixteenth day of December, taking as witnesses of their proceedings, six public notaries, his own register, and about twenty-five doctors, abbots, priors, and priests, with a great rabble of other common anointed catholics. Where after a solemn proclamation, that if there were any that would defend the opinions and books of Richard Hunne, they should presently appear and be heard according to law, he commanded all the articles and objections against Hunne openly to be read before the assembly : and then perceiving that none durst appear in his defence, by the advice of his assistants, he pronounced the sentence definitive against the dead carcase, condemning it of heresy, and therewith committed the same to the secular power, to be by them burned accordingly. Which ridiculous decree was accomplished in Smithfield the twentieth day of December, sixteen days after they had barbarously murdered him, to the great grief and indignation of all the people.

Notwithstanding after all this tragical and cruel handling of the dead body, and their fair show of justice, yet the inquest never stayed their diligent searching out of the true cause and means of his death. So that when they had been several times called before the king's privy council, (his majesty himself being sometimes present) and also before the chief judges and justices of the realm, and that the matter being thoroughly examined and perceived to be much bolstered up by the clergy, was wholly committed to their determination, they found by good proof and sufficient evidence, that Doctor Horsey, the chancellor; Charles Joseph, the somner; and John Spalding, the bell ringer, had privily and maliciously committed this murder, and therefore indicted them all three as wilful murderers. However, through the earnest suit of the bishop of London to Cardinal Wolsey, means were found that at the next sessions of gaol delivery, the king's attorney pronounced the indictment against Doctor Horsey to be false and untrue, and him not guilty of the murder, who, having yet a guilty conscience, durst never after for shame come again to London. But now that the truth of all this may seem more manifest and plain to all men's eyes, here shall follow word by word, the whole enquiry and verdict of the inquest, exhibited by them to the coroner of London, and so given up and signed with his own hand.

The Minutes of the Inquest.

The fifth and the sixth day of December, in the sixth year of the reign of our sovereign lord King Henry VIII. William Barnwell, coroner of London, the day and year above said, within the ward of Castle Baynard of London, assembled an inquest, whose names afterwards appear, and hath sworn them truly to enquire concerning the death of one Richard Hunne, who lately was found dead in the Lollards' Tower within St. Paul's church of London : whereupon all we of the inquest together went up into the said tower, where we found the body of the said Hunne hanging upon a staple of iron, in a girdle of silk, with a fair countenance, his head fair combed, and his bonnet sitting right upon his head, with his eyes and mouth fair closed, without any staring, gaping, or frowning, also without any drivelling in any place of his body ; whereupon by one assent we all agreed to take down the body of the said Hunne, and as soon as we began to heave the body it was loose, whereby we perceived that the girdle had no knot about the staple, but it was double cast, and the links of an iron chain, which did hang on the staple, were laid upon the girdle whereby he did hang : also the knot of the girdle that went about his neck, stood under his left ear, which caused his head to lean towards his right shoulder. Notwithstanding there

came out of his nostrils two small streams of blood to the quantity of four drops, save only these four drops of blood, the face, lips, chin, doublet, collar, and shirt of the said Hunne was clean from any blood. Also we found that the skin both of his neck and throat, beneath the girdle of silk, was fretted away, with that thing which the murderers had broken his neck with. Also the hands of the said Hunne were marked in the wrists, whereby we perceived that his hands had been bound. Moreover, we found that within the said prison there was no means whereby a man might hang himself, but only a stool, which stool stood upon a bolster of a bed, so unsteady that any man or beast might not touch it so little, but it was ready to fall, whereby we perceived, that it was not possible that Hunne could have hanged himself, the stool so standing. Also all the girdle from the staple to his neck, as well as the part which went about his neck, was too little for his head to come out thereat. Also it was not possible that the soft silken girdle should break his neck or skin beneath the girdle. Also we found in a corner, somewhat beyond the place where he did hang, a great parcel of blood. Also we found upon the left side of Hunne's jacket, from the breast downward, two great streams of blood. Also within the flap of the left side of his jacket we found a great cluster of blood, and the jacket folden down thereupon, which thing the said Hunne could never fold nor do after he was hanged. Whereby it appeareth plainly to us all, that the neck of Hunne was broken, and the great plenty of blood was shed before he was hanged. Wherefore we all find, by God and our consciences, that Richard Hunne was murdered. Also we acquit the said Richard Hunne of his own death.

"Also there was an end of a wax candle, which, as John, the bell-ringer, saith he left in the prison burning with Hunne that same Sunday at night that Hunne was murdered, which wax candle we found sticking upon the stocks, fair put out, about seven or eight foot from the place where Hunne was hanged, which candle in our opinion was never put out by him, for many likelihoods which we have perceived. Also at the going up of Master Chancellor into the Lollards' Tower, we have good proof that there lay on the stocks a gown, either of murrey, or crimson in grain, furred with shanks, whose gown it was we never could prove, neither who carried it away. All we find, that Master William Horsey, chancellor to my lord of London, hath had at his commandment both the rule and guiding of the said prisoner. Moreover, we all find that the said Master Horsey, chancellor, hath put Charles Joseph out of his office, as the said Charles hath confessed, because he would not deal and use the said prisoner so cruelly, and do to him as the chancellor would have had him to do. Notwithstanding the deliverance of the keys to the chancellor by Charles on the Saturday at night before Hunne's death, and Charles riding out of the town on that Sunday in the morning ensuing, was but a convention made betwixt Charles and the chancellor to colour the murder. For the same Sunday that Charles rode forth, he came again to the town at night, and killed Richard Hunne, as in the depositions of Julian Little, Thomas Chicheley, Thomas Simonds, and Peter Turner, doth appear.

"After colouring of the murder betwixt Charles and the chancellor conspired, the chancellor called to him one John Spalding, the bell-ringer of St. Paul's, and delivered to the same bell-ringer the keys of the Lollards' Tower, giving to the said bell-ringer a great charge, saying, ' I charge thee to keep Hunne more straightly than he hath been kept, and let him have but one meal a day; moreover, I charge thee let no body come to him without my licence, neither to bring him shirt, cap, kerchief, or any other thing, but that I see it before it come to him.' Also before Hunne was carried to Fulham, the chancellor commanded to be put upon Hunne's neck a great collar of iron, with a great chain, which is too heavy for any man or beast to wear, and long to endure.

"Moreover, it is well proved, that before Hunne's death the said chancellor came up into the said Lollards'

Tower, and kneeled down before Hunne, holding up his hands to him, praying of him forgiveness of all that he had done to him, and must do to him. And on Sunday following the chancellor commanded the penitentiary of St. Paul's to go up to him, and say a gospel, and make for him holy water, and holy bread, and give it to him, which he did; and also the chancellor commanded that Hunne should have his dinner. And at the same dinner-time Charles' boy was shut up in prison with Hunne, which was never done so before; and after dinner, when the bell-ringer let out the boy, the bell-ringer said to the same boy, "Come no more hither with meat for him till to-morrow, for my master chancellor hath commanded that he should have but one meal a day;" and the same night following Richard Hunne was murdered, which murder could not have been done without consent and licence of the chancellor, and also by the witting and knowledge of John Spalding, the bell-ringer; for there could no man come into the prison but by the keys which were in John, the bell-ringer's keeping. Also, as by my lord of London's book appears, John, the bell-ringer, is a poor innocent man. Wherefore we all perceive, that this murder could not be done but by the commandment of the chancellor, and by the witting and knowing of John, the bell-ringer.

Then follows certain minutes of the evidence, and at last the following verdict:—

The Sentence of the Inquest subscribed by the Coroner.

^z The inquisition intended and taken in the city of London, in the parish of St. Gregory, in the ward of Baynard Castle, in London, the sixth day of December, in the sixth year of the reign of King Henry VIII., before Thomas Barnwell, coroner of our sovereign lord the king, within the city of London aforesaid. Also before James Yarford and John Mundey, sheriffs of the said city, upon the sight of the body of Richard Hunne, late of London, tailor, who was found hanged in the Lollards' Tower, and by the oath and proof of lawful men of the same ward, and of other three wards next adjoining, as it ought to be, after the custom of the city aforesaid, to enquire how, and in what manner the said Richard Hunne came by his death: and upon the oath of John Barnard, Thomas Stert, William Warren, Henry Abraham, John Aborow, John Turner, Robert Allen, William Marlet, John Burton, James Page, Thomas Pickhill, William Burton, Robert Bridgwater, Thomas Busted, Gilbert Howell, Richard Gibson, Christopher Crafton, John God, Richard Holt, John Palmere, Edmund Hudson, John Arunsell, Richard Cooper, John Tim: The which said upon their oaths, that whereas the said Richard Hunne by the commandment of Richard, bishop of London, was imprisoned and brought to hold, in a prison of the said bishops, called the Lollards' Tower, lying in the cathedral church of St. Paul, in London, in the parish of St. Gregory, in the ward of Baynard Castle aforesaid; William Horsey, of London, clerk, otherwise called William Heresie, chancellor to Richard, bishop of London; and one Charles Joseph, late of London, somner, and John Spalding of London, otherwise called John the bellringer, did feloniously, as felons to our lord the king, with force and arms against the peace of our sovereign lord the king, and dignity of his crown, on the fourth day of December, in the sixth year of the reign of our sovereign lord aforesaid, of their great malice, at the parish of St. Gregory aforesaid, upon the said Richard Hunne they made a fray, and the same Richard Hunne they feloniously strangled and smothered, and also the neck they did break of the said Richard Hunne, and there feloniously slew him and murdered him; and also the body of the said Richard Hunne, afterward the same fourth day, year, place, parish, and ward aforesaid, with the proper girdle of the same Richard Hunne, of silk, black of colour, of the value of twelve pence, after his death, upon a hook driven into a piece of timber in the wall of the prison aforesaid, made fast, and so hanged him, against the peace of our sovereign lord the king, and the dignity of his crown: and so the said jury hath

sworn on the holy evangelists, that the said William Horsey, clerk, Charles Joseph, and John Spalding, of their set malice, then and there feloniously killed and murdered the said Richard Hunne in manner and form above said, against the peace of our sovereign lord the king, his crown and dignity.

Subscribed in this manner:

Thomas Barnwell, Coroner of the city of London.

After the twenty four had given up their verdict, sealed and signed with the coroner's seal, the cause was then brought into the parliament house, where the truth was laid so plain before all men's faces, and the fact so notorious, that immediately certain of the bloody murderers were committed to prison, and should no doubt have suffered what they deserved, had not the cardinal by his authority, practised for his popish children, at the suit of the bishop of London. Whereupon the chancellor, by the king's pardon, and secret shifting, rather than by God's pardon and his deserving, escaped, and went, as is said, to Exeter, &c.

But I will trouble the reader no further in this matter of Richard Hunne, being of itself so clear, that no impartial judge can doubt thereof. Wherefore to return to the purpose of our history; among the number of those which about this time of Richard Hunne were forced to deny and abjure their professed opinions, were Elizabeth Stamford, John Household, and others, who abjured about the year of our Lord, 1517. It is painful to see their weakness, yet to consider the confession of their doctrine in those days, is not unprofitable. We can see the same doctrine then taught and planted in the hearts of our forefathers, which is now publicly received, as well touching the Lord's sacrament of his body, as also other specialties. And although they had not then public authority to maintain the open preaching and teaching of the gospel, which the Lord's merciful grace has given us now; yet in secret knowledge and understanding they seemed then little or nothing inferior to these our times of public reformation, as may appear by this confession of Elizabeth Stamford; which may suffice for example, to understand what ripe knowledge of God's word was then abroad, although not publicly preached in churches, for fear of the bishops, yet in secret taught and received by many.

Among the number of whom was this Elizabeth Stamford, who being brought and examined before Fitzjames, bishop of London, (A.D. 1517,) confessed that she was taught by one Thomas Beele, these words, eleven years before: that Christ feeds, and nourishes his church with his own precious body, that is, the bread of life coming down from heaven: this is the worthy word that is worthily received, and joined to man to be in one body with him. This is not received by chewing of teeth, but by hearing with ears, and understanding with your soul, and wisely working thereafter. Therefore, saith St. Paul, I fear, brethren, that many of us be feeble and sick; therefore I counsel you, brethren, to rise and watch, that the great day of doom come not suddenly upon us, as the thief doth upon the merchant. Also this Thomas Beele taught and shewed her, that the sacrament of the altar was not the very body of Christ, but very bread: and that the sacrament was the very body of Christ put upon the cross after a divine and mystical manner. And moreover he taught her this lesson, that she should confess her sins to God, and that the pope's pardons and indulgences were nothing worth, and that worshipping of images and pilgrimages ought not to be done.

To this confession of Elizabeth Stamford, may also be added, the doctrine and confession of Joan Sampson, wife of John Sampson, carpenter, of Aldermanbury, in London: who being cited and examined before the bishop of London, certain witnesses were produced against her, who, being sworn, denounced Joan Sampson in these articles and opinions following:

1. That she being in labour, and Joan Sampson the elder, who was alive, being with her, she, after the usual manner of women, called for the help of the virgin Mary; but Joan spake against it, and was so grieved at

it that the other party was compelled to forsake the house.

2. Also, that she spake against pilgrimages, and the worshipping of the blessed Virgin, and of all saints, affirming that there is none holy but one.

3. Also, at another time, in the hearing of one Margaret Anworth, when she and other women were invoking the blessed Virgin, she stood against them, and spake against such invocations.

4. Also, that she speaking against the pilgrimage of our lady of Wilsden (as she was then called) and of St. Saviour at Barmsey, called the said St. Saviour, Sym Sawyer.

5. She was also accused of having two books in English, one bigger, and another lesser, which she committed to one John Anstead, a cook; which books are not named in the register.

6. She was also accused, that once, at a supper, in the hearing of certain men, and of a certain widow, named Joan White, she spake openly in contempt of the sacrament of the altar, saying, that the priests were idolaters, who did lift up the bread over their heads, making the people to worship it, and making the people to believe that it was the Lord's body; and that it was better to eat the altar cloth, if it might be eaten and digested as easily as the other.

Then follow, in the registers, the names of thirty-five persons who were compelled to abjure.

It was objected against one John Southwick, that when a man, named William Rivelay, coming from the church of the Gray-Friars, in London, had said to his wife that he had heard mass, and had seen his Lord God in form of bread and wine over the priest's head; John Southwick answered, "Nay, William, thou sawest not thy Lord God, thou sawest but bread and wine and the chalice." And when Rivelay answered again in the same words as before, saying, "I trust verily that I saw my Lord God in form of bread and wine, and this I doubt not." The other replying again, answered and said as before; "Nay, I tell thee thou sawest but only a figure or sacrament of him, which is in substance bread and wine," &c. This was A.D. 1520 In which year he was compelled to abjure.

All these persons above-named, held and agreed together in one doctrine and religion, against whom five or six special matters were objected, namely, for speaking against worshipping of saints, against pilgrimage, against invocation of the blessed Virgin, against the sacrament of the Lord's body, and for having scripture books in English: which books especially I find to be named, as these, the book of the four evangelists, a book of the epistles of Paul and Peter, the epistle of St. James, the book of the Revelation, and of antichrist, of the ten commandments, and ' Wickliff's Wicket,' with such like.

John Stilman, Martyr.

It would be tedious to recite the great multitude and number of good men and women who, in those days, recanted and abjured about the beginning of King Henry's reign and before: among whom there were some whom the Lord brought back again, and made strong in the profession of his truth. and constant to death; of which number John Stilman was one, who, about the twenty-fourth of September, A.D. 1518, was apprehended and brought before Richard Fitzjames, then bishop of London, at his manor of Fulham, (notwithstanding his former recantation, oath, and abjuration, made about eleven years then past, before Edmund, then bishop of Salisbury,) and was there examined and charged, as well for speaking against the worshipping, praying, and offering unto images: as also for denying the carnal and corporal presence in the sacrament of Christ's memorial: also, that since his former abjuration he had fallen into the same opinions again, and so into the danger of relapse: and further had highly commended and praised John Wickliffe, affirming that he was a saint in heaven, and that his book, called the

Wicket, was good and holy. Soon after his examination, he was sent from thence unto Lollards' Tower, at London, and on the twenty-second of October next ensuing, was brought openly into the consistory of Paul's, and was there judicially examined by Thomas Hed, the bishop's vicar-general, upon the contents of these articles following:—

" I. I object unto you, that you have confessed before my lord of London and me, Dr. Hed, his vicar-general, that about twenty years, past, one Stephen Moone, of the diocese of Winchester, (with whom you abode six or seven years after) did teach you to believe that the going on pilgrimage and the worshipping of images, as that of the lady of Walsingham and others, were not to be used. And also that afterwards one Richard Smart, who was burned at Salisbury about fourteen years past, did read unto you ' Wickliff's Wicket,' and likewise instructed you to believe that the sacrament of the altar was not the body of Christ: all which things you have erroneously believed.

" II. You have often read the said book, called ' Wickliff's Wicket,' and another book of the ten commandments, which Richard Smart did give you, and at the time of your first apprehension you did hide them in an old oak, and did not reveal them unto the bishop of Salisbury, before whom you were abjured of heresy about eleven years since; where you promised, by oath upon the evangelists, ever after to believe and hold as the Christian faith taught and preached, and never to offend again in the said heresies, or any other, upon pain of relapse. And further, you there promised to perform all such penance as the bishop of Salisbury did enjoin you: who then enjoined you upon the like pain, not to depart out of his diocese without his special licence.

" III. It is evident that you are relapsed, as well by your own confession, as also by your deeds, in that about two years after your abjuration you went into the said place where you had hidden your books; and then taking them away with you, you departed from the diocese of Salisbury, without the licence of the bishop, and brought them with you to London, where now being attached and taken with them upon great suspicion of heresy, you are brought to the bishop of London: by reason of your demeanour, you have shewed both your impenitent and dissembled conversion from your errors, and also your unfaithful abjuration and disobedience to the authority of our mother holy church, in that you performed not the penance; in which behalf you are voluntarily perjured, and also relapsed, in that you departed the same diocese without licence.

" IV. You are not only impenitent, disobedient, voluntarily perjured and relapsed by this your heretical demeanour, but also since your last attachment upon suspicion of heresy, you have maliciously spoken erroneous and damnable words, affirming before my lord of London, your ordinary, and me, judicially sitting at Fulham, that you were sorry that you ever abjured your opinions, and had not at first suffered manfully for them, for they were, and are are good and true; and therefore you will now abide by them to die for it. And furthermore, you have spoken against our holy father the pope, and his authority, damnably saying that he is antichrist, and not the true successor of Peter, or Christ's vicar on earth; and that his pardons and indulgences, which he grants in the sacrament of penance, are taught, and that you will have none of them. And likewise that the college of cardinals are limbs of antichrist: and that all other inferior prelates and priests are the synagogue of Satan. And moreover you said, that the doctors of the church have subverted the truth of holy scripture, expounding it after their own minds, and therefore their works be naught, and they in hell; but that Wickliff is a saint in heaven, and that the book called his Wicket is good, for therein he shews the truth. Also you did wish that there were twenty thousand of your opinion, against us scribes and pharisees, to see what you would do for the defence of your faith. All which heresies you did afterwards erroneously affirm before the archbishop of Canterbury, and then said that you would abide by them to die for it, notwithstanding his earnest persuasions to the contrary; and therefore for these premises you be evidently relapsed, and ought to be committed to the secular power."

After these articles thus propounded, and his constant persevering in the truth perceived, Dr. Hed, vicar-general, by his sentence definitive, did condemn him a relapsed heretic, on the twenty-fifth of October, and delivered him the same day to the sheriffs of London, to be openly burned in Smithfield.

Thomas Man, Martyr.

Next follows in this order of blessed martyrs, the persecution and condemnation of Thomas Man: who, March 29, A.D. 1518, was burned in Smithfield. This Thomas Man had been apprehended for the profession of Christ's gospel about six years before, (August 14, A.D. 1511,) and was examined upon these articles:—

1. That he had spoken against Auricular confession, and denied the corporeal presence of Christ's body in the sacrament of the altar.

2. That he believed that all holy men were priests.

3. That he had affirmed that the Father of heaven was the altar, and the Second Person the sacrament; and that upon Ascension-day the sacrament ascended to the altar, and there abides.

4. That he believed not aright in the sacrament of extreme unction.

5. That he had called certain priests, meanly arrayed knaves.

6. That he had said that pulpits were priest's lying stools.

7. That he had believed that images ought not to be worshipped, and that he neither believed in the crucifix, nor would worship it.

8. That he had affirmed that the word of God and God were all one, and that he that worthily receives the word of God, receives God.

9. That he had said that the popish church was not the church of God, but a synagogue: and that holy men were the true church of God.

For these matters he was a long time imprisoned, and at last, through frailty and fear of death, was content to abjure and yield himself to the judgment of the Romish church, and thereupon was enjoined, not only to make his open recantation, but also to remain as a prisoner within the monastery of Osney, and to bear a fagot before the first cross, at the next general procession in the university. All which, notwithstanding, he (being perhaps sorry for his offence in denying the truth, and also weary of his prison-like bondage) bethought himself how he might best escape; and therefore seeing a good opportunity, he fled, and seeking abroad in other counties for work, to sustain his life, he abode sometimes in Essex, sometimes in Suffolk; where he associated himself with such godly professors of Christ's gospel as he there could hear of. But within a few years after (such is the cruel rage of Satan and his wicked members, who never suffer the godly long to continue untroubled) he was again accused of relapse by the inquisition of London, and thereupon was apprehended and brought before Richard Fitzjames, the bishop of London, February 9, 1518.

And although as the register notes (but how truly God only knoweth) he again forsook his profession of Christ's gospel, and yielded himself to the bishop of Rome, requiring to be absolved from his curse of excommunication, and consented to do such penance as they should enjoin him, he was yet delivered to the sheriff of London, to be burned. The bishop's chancellor who condemned him desired the sheriff that he would receive this person as relapsed and condemned, and yet not punish him by rigorous rigour. The words in the sentence are: "We desire, in the bowels of our Lord Jesus Christ, that the punishment and execution of due severity, on thee, and against thee, may be so moderate, that there be no rigid rigour, nor yet loose mildness, but to the health and safety of thy soul," &c.

Wherein these Romish churchmen do well shew, that the laws of their church are grounded upon Pilate and Caiaphas. For as Caiaphas with his court of Pharisees cried against Christ to Pilate: "It is not lawful for us to put any man to death; but if thou let him go, thou art not Cæsar's friend." Even so they, first condemning the saints of God to death, and then delivering them to the secular magistrate to be executed, would yet cover their malignant hearts with the cloak of hypocritical holiness and unwillingness to shed blood. But God be thanked, who bringeth all things to light in his due time, and uncovereth hypocrisy at last, that she may be seen and known in her right colours.

Thus Thomas Man, the manly martyr of Jesus Christ, being condemned by an unjust sentence, was delivered to the sheriff of London sitting on horseback in Paternoster-row, before the bishop's door, A.D. 1518, he protesting to the said sheriff, that he had no power to put him to death, and therefore desired the sheriff to take him as a relapser and condemned, to see him punished. The sheriff immediately carried him to Smithfield, and there the same day in the forenoon caused him to become an angel in heaven.

In the deposition of one Thomas Risby, against this martyr it appears by the registers, that he had been in many places and counties in England, and had instructed many persons at Amersham, at London, at Chelmsford, at Stratford-Langthorn, at Uxbridge, at Burnham, at Henley upon Thames, in Suffolk and Norfolk, at Newbury, and many other places: where he testifies, that as he went westward, he found a great company of well-disposed persons, being of the same judgment touching the sacrament of the Lord's Supper that he was of, and especially at Newbury, where there was (as he confessed) a glorious and sweet society of faithful favourers, who had continued for the space of fifteen years together, till at last they were betrayed by a person, whom they trusted and made of their counsel, and then many of them, to the number of six or seven score, abjured, and three or four of them were burnt. From thence he came to the forest of Windsor, where he, hearing of the brethren who were at Amersham, removed there, where he found a godly and a great company, who had continued in that doctrine and teaching twenty-three years. Against these faithful christians of Amersham, there was great trouble and persecution in the time of William Smith bishop of Lincoln, about the year 1507, at which time so many were abjured, that it was called, "the great abjuration." In this congregation of faithful brethren, were four principal instructors. One was Tilesworth, who was burned at Amersham. Another was Thomas Chase, who was murdered and hanged in the bishop of Lincoln's prison at Woburn. The third was this Thomas Man, burned as is here mentioned in Smithfield, A.D. 1518, who, as appears, by his own confession, and no less also by his labours, was God's champion, and suffered much trouble by the priests for the cause of God. He confesses himself in the same register, that he had turned seven hundred people to his religion and doctrine, for which he thanked God. He conveyed also five couples of men and women from Amersham, Uxbridge, Burnham, and Henley upon Thames, where they dwelt, to Suffolk and Norfolk, that they might be brought (as he then termed it) out of the devil's mouth.

Robert Cosin, Martyr.

This Robert Cosin seems to be the same who in the former part of this history is mentioned, as called by the name of Father Robert, and was burnt in Buckingham. Of this Robert Cosin, I find in the registers of Lincoln, that he, with Thomas Man, had instructed and persuaded one Joan Norman, about Amersham, not to go on pilgrimage, nor to worship any images of saints. Also when she had vowed a piece of silver to a saint for the health of her child, they dissuaded her from the same, and said, that she needed not to confess to a priest, but that it was sufficient to lift up her hands to Heaven. Moreover, they were charged by the bishop, for teaching Joan, that she might as well drink upon Sunday before mass, as any other day, &c. And thus you see the doctrine of these good men, for which they were in those days abjured or condemned to death.

Christopher Shoomaker, Martyr.

To these blessed saints we will add Christopher Shoomaker, of whom I find this briefly recorded in the register of Sir John Longland, that the said Christopher Shoomaker, a parishioner of great Missenden, came to the house of John Say, and after other matters, read to him out of a little book the words which Christ spake to his disciples. And thus coming to his house about four times, at every time he read something out of the same book to him teaching him not to be deceived in the priest's celebration of the mass, and declaring that it was not the same very present body of Christ, as the priests did fancy, but in substance bread in remembrance of Christ; and taught him moreover, that pilgrimage, worshipping, and setting up candles to saints, were all unprofitable. And thus the said John Say being taught by this Christopher, and also confirmed by John Okenden and Robert Pope, was brought to the knowledge of the same doctrine. Thus much briefly I find in that register concerning Christopher Shoomaker; declaring further, that he was burned at Newbury about this time, which was A. D. 1518. And thus much out of the registers of London.

Doctor Colet.

About this time, died Doctor John Colet, A.D 1519 To whose sermons these men, about Buckinghamshire, had a great mind to resort. After he came from Italy and Paris, he first began to read the epistles of St. Paul openly in Oxford, instead of reading the works of Scotus and Thomas Aquinas. From whence he was called by the king, and made dean of St. Paul's: where he used to preach much with a great auditory, as well of the king's court, as of the citizens and others. His diet was frugal, his life upright, in discipline he was severe: so that his canons, because of their stricter rule, complained that they were made like monks. The honest and honourable state of matrimony he ever preferred before the unchaste singleness of priests. At his dinner commonly was read either some chapter of St. Paul, or of Solomon's proverbs. And although the blindness of that time carried him away after the common error of popery, yet in ripeness of judgment he seemed to incline from the common opinions of that age. The order of monks and friars he fancied not; neither could he favour the barbarous divinity of the school-doctors, so that, when Erasmus, speaking in the praise of Thomas Aquinas, commended him: Colet first supposing that Erasmus had spoken in jest, but afterwards finding that he was in earnest, burst out, saying, " Why tell you me of the commendation of that man, who unless he had been of an arrogant and presumptuous spirit, would not define and discuss things so boldly and rashly : and also, except he had been more worldly-minded than heavenly, would never have so polluted Christ's holy doctrine with man's profane doctrine, as he has done ?

The bishop of London at that time was Fitzjames. Who (bearing an old grudge and displeasure against Colet) with other two bishops, entered complaint against Colet to the archbishop of Canterbury, then William Warham. His complaint was divided into three articles : The *first* was for speaking against worshipping images : the *second* was about hospitality, that in treating of the words of the Gospel, " Feed, — feed, — feed :" John xxi. 15. when he had expounded the first two, as feeding with example of life, and with doctrine ; in the third, which the schoolmen expound for feeding with hospitality, he left out the outward feeding of the belly, and applied it another way. The *third* crime with which they charged him, was for speaking against such as used to preach only by written sermons, preaching nothing to the people, but what they brought in their papers with them. And, because the bishop of London used much to do

this, he took it as spoken against himself, and therefore bare this displeasure against Dr. Colet. The archbishop weighing the matter more wisely, and being well acquainted with Colet, took his part against his accusers, and at that time he was got out of trouble.

William Tindal, in his book in answer to Master More, testifies, that the bishop of London would have pronounced Colet, the dean of St. Paul's, an heretic, for translating the Lord's Prayer into English, had not the archbishop of Canterbury helped the dean.

But yet the malice of the bishop ceased not: being thus repulsed by the archbishop, he laid by another train how to accuse him to the king. It happened at the time, that the king was making preparation for war against France : so the bishop with his co-adjutors taking occasion upon certain words of Colet, in which he seemed to prefer peace before war, were it never so just ; accused him of it in their sermons, and also in the presence of the king.

It so happened at this time, that on Good Friday Doctor Colet, preaching before the king, treated of the victory of Christ ; exhorting all christians to fight under the standard of Christ, against the devil : adding moreover, what an hard thing it was to fight under Christ's banner, and that all they who upon private hatred or ambition took weapons against their enemy (one christian to slay another) did not fight under the banner of Christ, but rather of Satan : and therefore, he exhorted that christian men in their wars would follow Christ their prince and captain, in fighting against their enemies, rather than the example of Cæsar, or Alexander, &c. The king hearing Colet thus speak, and fearing lest the hearts of his soldiers might be withdrawn from his wars, which he had then in hand, took him aside and talked with him in secret conference, walking in his garden. Bishop Fitzjames, Bricot, and Standish, who were his enemies, thought now that Colet must needs be committed to the Tower, and waited for his coming out. But the king treating Doctor Colet with great gentleness, and bidding him familiarly to put on his cap, much commended him for his learning and integrity of life ; agreeing with him in all points, only he required him (that the soldiers should not rashly mistake what he had said) more plainly to explain his words ; which he did : and so after long communication and great promises, the king dismissed Colet with these words, saying, " Let every man choose what doctor he pleases, Colet shall be my doctor ;" and so he departed. So that none of his adversaries durst ever trouble him after that time.

Among many other memorable acts left behind him, Colet erected a foundation of the school of St. Paul's (I pray God the fruits of the school may answer the foundation) for the cherishing of youth in good letters, providing a sufficient stipend as well for the master, as for the usher: whom he wished rather to be appointed out of the number of married men, than of single priests. The first moderator of this school, was William Lily, a man no less notable for his learning, than was Colet for his foundation.

In turning over the registers and records of Lincoln likewise, and coming to A. D. 1520, and 1521, I find that as the light of the gospel began the more to appear, and the number of professors to increase, so the vehemency of persecution, and stir of the bishops began also to increase. Upon which then ensued great trouble and grievous affliction in many quarters of this realm, especially about Buckinghamshire and Amersham, Uxbridge, Henley, Newbury, in the diocese of London, in Essex, Colchester, Suffolk, and Norfolk, and other places. And this was before the name of Luther was heard of in these countries among the people ; so that they are much deceived and misinformed who condemn this kind of doctrine of novelty, asking where was this church and religion before Luther's time ? To whom it may be answered, that this religion and form of doctrine was planted by the apostles, and taught by true bishops ; it afterwards decayed, and is now reformed again ; and although it was not received nor admitted by the pope' clergy before Luther's time, neither is now, yet it was received by others, in whose hearts it pleased the Lord secretly to work, and they a great number, who both professed and suffered for the same. And if they think this doctrine so new that it was not heard of before Luther's time, how then came such great persecution before Luther's time here in England? If these were of the same profession which the pope's clergy were of, then was their cruelty unreasonable, so to persecute their own fraternity. And if they were otherwise, how then is this doctrine of the gospel so new, or the professors of it so lately sprung up as they pretend to be? But this comes only of ignorance, and through not knowing and well considering the times and antiquities of the church which have been before us; which if they did, they would see and confess that the church of England has not wanted great multitudes who tasted and followed the sweetness of God's holy word almost in as ample a manner, for the number of well-disposed hearts as now. Although public authority then was wanting to maintain the open preaching of the gospel, yet the secret multitude of true professors was not much unequal: certainly the fervent zeal of those christian days seemed much superior to these our days and times, as may appear by their sitting up all night in reading and hearing, also by the expenses and charges they incurred in buying books in English, some of whom gave five marks, some more, some less, for a book; some gave a load of hay for a few chapters of St. James, or of St. Paul in English. In which time of scarcity of books, and want of teachers, this one thing I greatly marvel at, to note in the registers, and to consider how notwithstanding the word of truth multiplied so exceedingly as it did amongst them. Wherein is to be seen no doubt the marvellous working of God's mighty power; for I find and observe in considering the registers, how one neighbour resorting and conferring with another, soon with a few words, did win and turn their minds to the truth of God's word and his sacraments. To see their labours, their earnest seeking, their burning zeals, their readings, their watchings, their sweet assemblies, their love and concord, their godly living, their faithful marrying with the faithful, may make us now in these our days of free profession, to blush for shame.

There were four principal points in which they stood against the church of Rome; in pilgrimage, in adoration of saints, in reading scripture books in English, and in the carnal presence of Christ's body in the sacrament.

As they were simple, and yet not uncircumspect in their doings, so the crafty serpent, being more wily than they by fraudulent subtlety so circumvented them, that the popish clergy caused the wife to detect the husband, the husband the wife; the father the daughter, the daughter the father; the brother to disclose his brother, and the neighbour the neighbour. Neither were any assemblies nor readings kept, but both the persons and also the books were known, neither was any word so closely spoken, nor article mentioned, but it was discovered. So subtlely did these prelates use their inquisitions and examinations, that nothing was done or said among these men, fifteen or twenty years before, so covertly, but it was brought at length to their intelligence. They had such captious interrogatories, and so many articles and suspicions; such spies and privy scouts were sent abroad by them; such authority and credit had they with the king, and in the king's name; such diligence they shewed; so violently and impudently they abused the book of the peaceable evangelists, wresting men's consciences upon their oath, swearing them upon the same to detect themselves, their fathers and mothers, and others of their kindred, with their friends and neighbours, and that to death.

For the better declaration of all which here first is to be noted touching the see of Lincoln, that after William Smith succeeded John Longland. Smith was not so bloody and cruel as Longland, who, for I find that in the time of "the great abjuration" and affliction of the Buckinghamshire men, where many were abjured, and some burned, yet he sent several quietly home without punishment and penance, bidding them go home and live as

good christian men should do. And many who were enjoined penance he released. This Smith died about the year 1515. The college of Brazen Nose in Oxford was built by him.

After him followed John Longland, a fierce and cruel vexer of the faithful servants of Christ. He to renew again the old persecution, which were not yet utterly quenched, began with one or two of those who had abjured, and caused them by oath to detect and betray not only their own opinions, but also to discover all others who were suspected. By which an incredible multitude of men, women, and maidens, were brought to examination, and strictly handled. And such were found in relapse were burned.

The rest were so burdened with superstitions and idolatrous penance and injunction, that either through grief of conscience they shortly afterwards died, or else lived with shame.

One Robert Bartlet, and Richard his brother, were detected as having abjured before in the time of William Smith bishop of Lincoln.

They being sworn, and confessing nothing before the bishop, at last were convicted by witness. Wherefore they were constrained at their next examination to utter themselves, and confess what they had both done and said; that is, that Robert had read to Richard his brother a parcel of scripture beginning thus: "James the servant of God, to the twelve tribes," &c. That he heard Tilseworth say, that images of saints were but stocks and stones, and dead things; and that he taught the same to his brother Richard, and concealed the words of Tilseworth. That he partly believed Thomas Mastal, teaching him that the true presence of Christ was not in the sacrament; and likewise of images and pilgrimages: for receiving the communion at Easter without confession, &c.

Robert Bartlet was obliged to prove against Agnes Wellis, his own sister, that he had twice instructed her not to worship images, and also had taught her in the epistle of St. James.

The following interrogatories were put to this Agnes Wellis:—

1. Whether she knew that some of the parish of Amersham were brought before William Smith, late bishop of Lincoln, for heresy?

2. Whether she knew that some of them erred in the sacrament of the altar, or in other sacraments, and what errors they were, and wherein?

3. Whether she knew any others to be suspected of the same heresy besides those of Amersham, who they were, and how many?

4. Whether she had been in the same company, or held the same opinions with them.

5. Whether she at any time had any conversation with Thurstan Littlepage? and if she had, how often she had been in his company, how, what time, in what place, who else were present, for what causes, and whether she knew him to be suspected for heresy?

6. Whether she knew and at any time had any conversation with Alexander Mastal? and if she had, how, when, in what place, who were present, for what causes, and whether she knew him to be suspected for heresy?

7. Whether she was ever detected to the office of William Smith, late bishop of Lincoln, at what time? and whether she was then called before the bishop for heresy or not?

8. Whether she had been reputed to be of the same sect with Thurstan Littlepage?

9. Whether she had been present at any time at the readings or conferrings between Thurstan Littlepage and other convicts?

10. Whether Thurstan Littlepage did ever teach her the epistle of St. James, or the epistles of St. Peter or Paul in English? and whether she had repeated the epistle of St. James to Thurstan, in the presence of Richard Bartlet her brother?

11. Whether Richard Bartlet her brother did teach her at any time the epistle of St. James? and if he did, how often, and in what place?

12. Whether she had been instructed by Thurstan Littlepage, or by any other, that in the sacrament of the altar was not the true body of Christ, but only the substance of bread?

13. Whether she had been instructed by Thurstan Littlepage, or any other, that pilgrimage was not to be used, nor the images of saints to be adored?

14. Whether she credited Thurstan Littlepage, or any other, teaching her in the premises? and whether she believed or expressly agreed with them in these articles?

15. Whether Robert Bartlet her brother did ever teach her the epistle of St. James; and if he did, how often, and where?

16. Whether Robert Bartlet had taught her, that pilgrimage was not to be used, and that images were not to be adored?

17. Whether she knew such a law or custom among them, that such as were of that sort contracted matrimony only with themselves, and not with other christians?

18. Whether she ever heard Thurstan or any other say, that they only who were of their doctrine were true christians?

19. When she came to receive, and was confessed, whether she uttered and confessed her heresies to the priest?

These captious and cruel interrogatories Agnes Wellis answered negatively to almost all of them, refusing to name any person to the bishop. But soon after, being otherwise schooled, I cannot tell how, she was compelled to detect both herself, her brother Robert Bartlet, Thurstan Littlepage, and also Isabel Morwin, wife of John Morwin, and others.

By this system of examination, brother was compelled to inform against brother, sister, or neighbour, until evidence was thus craftily obtained against several hundred of godly men and women, that they used to assemble together and read portions of the holy scriptures in the English tongue.

The reader may thus learn the number of the good men and women, who were troubled and molested by the church of Rome, and all in one year; of whom few or none were learned, being simple labourers and artificers, but it pleased the Lord to work in them knowledge and understanding, by reading a few English books, such as they could get. And here is to be noted the blind ignorance and uncourteous dealing of the bishops against them, not only by their violent oath and captious interrogatories, constraining the children to accuse their parents, and parents the children, the husband the wife, and the wife the husband, &c. But especially in most wrongfully afflicting them, only for believing God's word, and the reading of the holy scriptures.

Now it remains that we show the reasons and scriptures whereupon they grounded their views. And first, against pilgrimage, and against worshipping of images, they used this text of the Revelation, chap. ix., "I saw the horses in the vision, and them that sat on them, having breastplates of fire, and of jacinth, and brimstone: and the heads of the horses were as the heads of lions; and out of their mouths issued fire and smoke and brimstone. By these three was the third part of men killed, by the fire, and by the smoke, and by the brimstone, which issued out of their mouths. For their power is in their mouth, and in their tails: for their tails were like unto serpents, and had heads, and with them they do hurt. And the rest of the men which were not killed by these plagues yet repented not of the works of their hands, that they should not worship devils, and idols of gold, and silver, and brass, and stone, and of wood," &c. (Ex Regist. Longland. fol. 72.) Also they alleged the first commandment, that there is but one God, and that they ought not to worship more gods than one.

And as to the sacrament, they had their instruction partly out of "Wickliff's Wicket," partly out of the "Shepherd's Calendar;" where they read that the sacrament was made in remembrance of Christ, and ought to be received in remembrance of his body, &c. They also alleged the words of Christ spoken at the supper, when sitting with his disciples, he took bread, and blessed it, and brake it, and gave to his disciples, and said, "Eat: this (reaching out his arm, and showing the bread in his hand, and then noting his own natural body, and touching the same, and not the bread consecrated) is my body which is broken for you; this do in remembrance of me." And he likewise took the wine cup and bade them drink, saying, "This cup is the new testament in my blood: this do ye, as often as ye drink it, in remembrance of me." (1 Cor. xi. 24, &c.)

That Christ our Saviour sitteth on the right hand of the Father, and there shall be unto the day of judgment. Wherefore, they believed that in the sacrament of the altar the very body of Christ was not there.

Such reasons as these, taken out of the scripture, and out of the "Shepherd's Calendar," "Wickliff's Wicket," and out of other books they had among them. And although there was no learned man with them to ground them in their doctrine, yet they, communing and conferring together among themselves, converted one another, the Lord's hand working with them: so that in a short space the number of these men exceedingly increased; so that the bishop, seeing the matter almost past his power, was driven to make his complaint to the king, and require his aid for suppression of these men. Whereupon, King Henry, being then young, and inexpert in the bloody practices and blind leadings of these apostolical prelates, directed down the following letter to the sheriffs, bailiffs, officers, and others, for the aid of the bishop in this behalf.

The Copy of the King's Letter for the aid of John Longland, bishop of Lincoln, against the Servants of Christ, then falsely called Heretics.

"Henry VIII., by the grace of God, king of England and of France, lord of Ireland, defender of the faith: to all mayors, sheriffs, bailiffs, and constables, and to all other our officers, ministers, and subjects, hearing or seeing these our letters, and to every of them, greeting. Forasmuch as the right reverend father in God, our trusty and right well-beloved counsellor, the bishop of Lincoln, hath now within his diocese no small number of heretics, as it is thought, to his no little discomfort and heaviness: We, therefore, being in will and mind safely to provide for the said right reverend father in God and his officers, that they, or none of them, shall bodily be hurt or damaged by any of the said heretics or their favourers, in executing and ministering justice to the said heretics, according to the laws of holy church; do straightly charge and command you, and every of you, as ye regard our high displeasure, to be aiding, helping, and assisting to the said right reverend father in God, and his said officers, in the executing of justice in the premises, as they or any of them shall require you so to do; not failing to accomplish our commandment and pleasure in the premises, as ye intend to please us, and will answer to the contrary at your uttermost perils. Given under our signet at our castle at Windsor, the twentieth day of October, the thirteenth year of our reign."

The bishop thus being armed with the authority of the king's letter, and incited by his own fierceness, lost no time, but, to accomplish his violence upon the poor flock of Christ, he called before him all those in his diocese, who were suspected to incline toward those opinions: to such as had but newly been taken, and had not before abjured, he enjoined most rigorous penance. The others in whom he could find any relapse, yea, although they submitted themselves never so humbly to his favourable courtesy; and though also at his request, and for hope of pardon, they had shewed themselves great detecters of their brethren; yet, contrary to his fair words, and their expectation, he spared not, but read sentence of relapse against them, committing them to the secular arm to be burnt.

The books and opinions which these persons were charged with, and for the which they were abjured, are partly before expressed, partly here follow in a brief summary to be seen.

A brief Summary of their Opinions.

The opinions of many of these persons were, That he or she never believed in the sacrament of the altar, nor ever would.

That he was known of his neighbours to be a good fellow, meaning, that he was one of this sect or company.

For saying, that he would give forty pence on condition that such a one knew so much as he knew.

Some for saying, that they of Amersham, who had abjured before by Bishop Smith, were good men, and perfect christians, and simple folk who could not answer for themselves, and therefore were oppressed by the power of the bishop.

Some, for hiding others in their barns.

Some, for reading the scriptures, or treatises of scripture, in English: some, for hearing the same read.

Some, for defending; some, for marrying with them who had abjured.

Some, for saying that matrimony was not a sacrament.

Some, for saying that worshipping of images was mummery; some, for calling images carpenters' chips; some, for calling them stocks and stones; some, for calling them dead things.

Some, for saying that money spent upon pilgrimage, served but to maintain thieves and harlots.

Others, for saying, that nothing graven with man's hand was to be worshipped.

Another, for calling his vicar a poll-shorn priest.

Another, for calling a certain blind chapel in ruin, an old fair milk-house.

Another, for saying, that alms should not be given before it did sweat in a man's hand.

Some, for saying, that they who die, pass straight either to heaven or hell.

Isobel Bartlet was brought before the bishop and abjured, for lamenting her husband when the bishop's man came for him, and saying, that he was an undone man, and she a dead woman.

For saying that Christ, departing from his disciples into heaven, said, That once he was in sinners' hands, and would come there no more.

Some were condemned for receiving the sacrament at Easter, and doubting whether it was the very body of Christ, and not confessing their doubt to their ghostly Father.

Some, for reading the gospels—the epistles—and Revelation. Some, for having the creed and Lord's prayer in English.

Some for saying, that the pope had no authority to give pardon, or to release man's soul from sin; and that it was nothing but blinding of the people to get their money.

The penance enjoined to these parties, by this John Longland, bishop of Lincoln, was almost uniform, save that they were severally committed to several monasteries, there to be kept all their life, except they were otherwise dispensed with by the bishop.

And they were all at the same time compelled to abjure; by which word, "abjure," is meant, that they were constrained by their oath, swearing upon the evangelists, and subscribing with their hand, and a cross to the same, to say that they utterly and voluntarily renounced, detested, and forsook, and never should hold hereafter these opinions, contrary to the determination of the holy mother church of Rome: and, further, that they should detect to their ordinary, whomever they should see or suspect hereafter to teach, hold, or maintain the same.

Among the forenamed persons who thus submitted themselves, and were put to penance, there were some, who, because they had been abjured before, were now condemned for relapse, and had sentence read against them, and so were committed to the secular arm to be burned: whose names here follow :—Thomas Bernard,

James Morden, Robert Rave, John Scrivener, martyrs. (A. D. 1521.)

Of these, mention is made before, both touching their abjuration, and also their martyrdom. To whom we may add, Joan Norman, Thomas Holmes.

This Thomas Holmes, although he had disclosed and detected many of his brethren; thinking thereby to please the bishop, and to save himself, and was thought to be a man paid by the bishop for that purpose: yet, in the bishop's register appears the sentence of relapse and condemnation, written and drawn out against him; and most probable it is that he was also adjudged and executed with the others.

As touching the burning of John Scrivenes, here it is to be observed, that his children were compelled to set fire to their father; and, in like manner, Joan Clerke also, daughter of William Tilseworth, was constrained to apply the fire to the burning of her own father.

The example of which cruelty, is not only contrary both to God and nature, but it has not even been seen or heard of in the memory of the heathen.

THE REFORMATION.

Although it cannot be sufficiently expressed with the tongue, or pen of man, into what miserable ruin and desolation the church of Christ was brought in those later days: yet partly, by the reading of these histories, some intelligence may be given to those who have judgment to mark, or eyes to see in what blindness and darkness the world was drowned during the space of upwards of four hundred years. By the viewing and considering of which times and histories, thou mayst understand (gentle reader) how the religion of Christ, which only consists in spirit and truth, was wholly turned into outward observances, ceremonies, and idolatry. We had so many saints, so many gods, so many monasteries, so many pilgrimages. We had as many churches, as many reliques forged and feigned. Again, we believed so many reliques, so many lying miracles. Instead of the only living Lord, we worshipped dead stocks and stones. In place of immortal Christ, we adored mortal bread. How the people were led, so that the priests were fed, no care was taken. Instead of God's word, man's word was set up. Instead of Christ's testament, the pope's testament, that is the cannon-law. Instead of St. Paul, Aquinas took place, and almost full possession. The law of God was little read, the use and end of it was less known; and as the end of the law was unknown, so the difference between the gospel and the law was not understood, the benefit of Christ not considered, the effect of faith not examined. Through this ignorance it cannot be told what infinite errors, sects, and religions crept into the church, overwhelming the world, as with a flood of ignorance and seduction. And no marvel; for where the foundation is not well laid, what building can stand or prosper ? The foundation of all our christianity is only this; the promise of God in the blood of Christ his Son, giving and promising life to all that believe in him: Giving (saith the scripture) *to* us, and not bargaining or indenting *with* us. And that freely for Christ's sake, and not conditionally for our merits' sake.

Furthermore, freely (saith the scripture) by grace, that the promise might be firm and sure, and not by the works that we do, which always are doubtful. By grace (saith the scripture) through promise, to all and upon all them that believe, and not by the law upon those that deserve. For if it come by deserving, then it is not of grace: if it be not of grace, then it is not of promise; and contrariwise, if it be of grace and promise, then it is not of works, saith St. Paul. Upon the foundation of God's free promises and grace, first builded the patriarchs, kings, and prophets. Upon this same foundation also Christ the Lord builded his church. Upon which foundation the apostles likewise builded the apostolic or catholic church.

So long as the church retained this apostolical and catholic foundation, so long it continued pure and sound, which endured a long time after the apostles' time. But afterwards in process of years, through wealth and negligence, so soon as this foundation began to be lost, there came in new builders, who would build upon a new foundation a new church, which we call now the church of Rome; who being not content with the old foundation, and the head corner-stone, which the Lord by his word had laid, laid the groundwork upon the condition and strength of the law and works. Although it is not to be denied, but that the doctrine of God's holy law, and of good works according to the same, is a thing most necessary to be learned and followed by all men: yet it is not that foundation whereupon our salvation consists, neither is that foundation able to bear up the weight of the kingdom of heaven, but is rather the thing which is builded on the foundation, which foundation is Jesus Christ; according as we are taught by St. Paul, saying, "Other foundation can no man lay than that is laid, which is Jesus Christ," &c.

But this ancient foundation, which the old ancient church of Christ laid, has been now long forsaken, and instead of it a new church, with a new foundation, has been erected, not upon God's promise, and his free grace in Christ Jesus, nor upon free justification by faith, but upon merits and deserts of men's working. And here they have planted all their new devices, so infinite, that they cannot well be numbered; as masses-trecenaries, dirges, obsequies, matins, and hours-singing-service, vigils, midnight-rising, barefoot-going, fish-tasting, Lent-fast, Ember-fast, stations, rogations, jubilees, advocation of saints, praying to images, pilgrimage-walking, works of supererogation, application of merits, orders, rules, sects of religion, vows of celibacy, wilful poverty, pardons, relations, indulgences, penance, and satisfaction, with auricular confession, founding of abbeys, &c. And who is able to recite all their laborious buildings, falsely framed upon a wrong ground, and all for ignorance of the true foundation, which is the free justification by faith in Christ Jesus the Son of God.

Moreover note, that as this new-found church of Rome was thus deformed in doctrine, so was it corrupt in order of life and deep hypocrisy, doing all things only under pretences and dissembled titles; so under the pretence of Peter's chair, they exercised a majesty above emperors and kings. Under the visor of their vowed celibacy, reigned adultery; under the cloak of professed poverty, they possessed the goods of the temporalty; under the title of being dead to the world, they not only reigned in the world, but also ruled the world; under the colour of the keys of heaven to hang under their girdle, they brought all the states of the world under their girdle, and crept not only into the purses of men, but also into their consciences: they heard their confessions; they knew their secrets; they dispensed as they were disposed, and absolved what they chose; and finally, when they had brought the whole world under their subjection, their pride neither ceased, nor could their avarice be ever satisfied.

In these so blind and miserably corrupt days of darkness and ignorance, thou seest, good reader, how necessary it was, and high time, that the reformation of the church should come, which now most happily and graciously began to work, through the merciful providence of Almighty God; although he suffered his church to wander and start aside, through the seduction of pride and prosperity, for a long time, yet at length it pleased his goodness to have respect to his people, and to reduce his church to its pristine foundation and frame again, from whence it was piteously decayed. Of this I have now to treat, intending by the grace of Christ to declare how, and by what means first this reformation of the church began, and how it proceeded, increasing by little and little to this perfection which we now see.

And here we have first to behold the admirable work of God's wisdom. For as the first decay and ruin of the church began by rude ignorance, and lack of knowledge in teachers; so, to restore the church again by doctrine and learning, it pleased God to open to man the art of printing shortly after the burning of John Huss and Jerome. Printing opened to the church the instru-ments and tools of learning and knowledge, which were good books and authors who before lay hid and unknown. The science of printing being found, immediately followed the grace of God, which stirred up good understandings to conceive the light of knowledge and of judgment: by which light darkness began to be seen, and ignorance to be detected; truth to be discerned from error; and religion from superstition.

After these men, stirred up by God, there followed others, increasing daily more and more in science, in languages, and perfection of knowledge, who being so armed and furnished with the help of good letters, that they encountered the adversary, sustaining the cause and defence of learning against barbarity; of truth against error; of true religion against superstition. Here began the first assault against the ignorant and barbarous faction of the pope's church. After these men, by their learned writings and laborious travel, had opened a window of light to the world, and had made (as it were) a way more ready for others to come after them, immediately, according to God's gracious appointment, followed Martin Luther, with others after him, by whose ministry it pleased the Lord to work a more full reformation of his church.

The History of Dr. Martin Luther, with his Life and Doctrine described.

Martin Luther, born at Isleben in Saxony, A.D. 1483, was sent to the university, first of Magdeburg, then of Erfurth. In this university of Erfurth there was an aged man in the convent of the Augustinians, with whom Luther, being of the same order, an Augustinian friar, had conference upon many things, especially touching the article of remission of sins; which article the aged father opened to Luther after this sort, declaring, that we must not generally believe only forgiveness of sins to be, or to belong, to St. Peter, to St. Paul, to David, or such good men alone; but that God's express commandment is, that every man should believe his sins individually to be forgiven him in Christ; and further said, that this interpretation was confirmed by the testimony of St. Bernard, and shewed him the place, in the Sermon of the Annunciation, where it is thus set forth:—"But add thou that thou believest this, that by him thy sins are forgiven thee. This is the testimony that the Holy Ghost gives thee in thy heart, saying, thy sins are forgiven thee. For this is the opinion of the apostle, that man is freely justified by faith."

By these words Luther was not only strengthened, but was also instructed in the full meaning of St. Paul, who repeats so many times this sentence, "We are justified by faith." And having read the expositions of many upon this place, he perceived, as well by the purpose of the old man, as by the comfort he received in his spirit, the vanity of those interpretations, which he had read before by the schoolmen. And so reading by little and little, comparing the sayings and examples of the prophets and apostles, and continual invocation of God, and exercise of faith and prayer, he perceived that doctrine most evidently. Then he began to read St. Augustine's books, where he found many comfortable things: among others, in the Exposition of the Psalms, and especially the Book of the Spirit and Letter, which confirmed this doctrine of faith and consolation in his heart not a little. And yet he laid not aside the Sententiaries, as Gabriel and Cameracensis. Also he read the books of Occam, whose subtlety he preferred above Thomas Aquinas and Scotus. He read also Gerson; but, above all the rest, he perused St. Augustine's works all over, with attentive meditation; and thus he continued his study at Erfurth for the space of four years in the convent of the Augustines.

About this time one Staupitius, a famous man, was promoting the erection of an university in Wittenburg, and endeavouring to have schools of divinity founded in this new university: when he had considered the spirit and learning of Luther, he invited him from Erfurth, to place him in Wittenburg, (A.D. 1508,) at the age of twenty-six. There his learning appeared in the ordinary exercise, both of his disputations in the schools, and in preaching in churches, where many wise and learned men attentively heard Luther.

Dr. Mellarstad would often say, that Luther was of such a wonderful spirit, and so ingenious, that he was sure that he would introduce a more compendious, easy, and familiar manner of teaching.

There he expounded the logic and philosophy of Aristotle, and in the meanwhile omitted not his study in theology. Three years afterwards he went to Rome, about some contentions of the monks, and returning the same year he was graduated as a doctor, at the expense of the elector Frederick duke of Saxony, according to the solemn manner of the schools; for he had heard him preach, well understood the quietness of his spirit, diligently considered the force of his words, and held in high admiration those profound matters which he so exactly explained in his sermons.

After this he began to expound the Epistle to the Romans, and then the Psalms, where he shewed the difference betwixt the law and the gospel. He also overthrew the error that then reigned in schools and sermons, that men may merit remission of sins by their own works, and that they are just before God by outward discipline, as the pharisees taught. Luther diligently led the minds of men to the Son of God; and as John the Baptist pointed to the Lamb of God which took away the sins of the world, even so Luther shining in the church as a bright star after a long, cloudy, and obscure sky, clearly shewed, that sins are freely remitted for the love of the Son of God, and that we ought faithfully to embrace this bountiful gift.

These happy beginnings got him great authority, especially as his life corresponded to his profession. The consideration of which allured to him wonderfully the hearts of his auditors, and also many notable personages.

All this while Luther yet altered nothing in the ceremonies, but precisely observed his rule among his fellows; he meddled in no doubtful opinions, but taught this only doctrine as the principal of all others to men, opening and declaring the doctrine of repentance, of remission of sins, of faith, as the only true comfort in times of adversity. Every man received good taste of this sweet doctrine, and the learned conceived high pleasure to behold Jesus Christ, the prophets, and apostles, come forth into light out of darkness, by which they began to understand the difference between the law and the gospel; between the promises of the law and the promise of the gospel; between spiritual righteousness and civil things; which certainly could not have been found in Thomas Aquinas, Scotus, and such like authors, who were studied at that time.

It happened about this time, that many were induced by Erasmus's learned works, to study the Greek and Latin tongues; who perceiving a more gentle and ready order of teaching than before, began to have in contempt the monks' barbarous and sophistical doctrine; and especially such as were of a liberal nature and good disposition. Luther began to study the Greek and Hebrew tongue, that after he had learned the phrase and propriety of the language, and drawn the doctrine from the very fountains, he might give more sound judgment.

As Luther was thus occupied in Germany (A.D. 1516,) Leo X. having succeeded Julius II. was pope of Rome, who, under a pretence of war against the Turk, sent a jubilee with his pardons abroad through all christian realms and dominions, by which he gathered together innumerable riches and treasure. The gatherers and collectors persuaded the people, that whoever would give ten shillings, should at his pleasure deliver one soul from the pains of purgatory. For this they held as a general rule, that God would do whatever they would have him, according to the saying, "Whatsoever you shall loose upon earth, shall be loosed in heaven." But if it were but one jot less than ten shillings, they preached that it would profit them nothing.

This filthy kind of pope's merchandize, as it spread through all quarters of christian regions, so came also to Germany, through means of a certain Dominican friar named Tetzel, who most impudently caused the pope's indulgences or pardons to be carried and sold about the country. Luther, much moved with the blasphemous sermons of this shameless friar, and having his heart earnestly bent to maintain true religion, published certain propositions concerning indulgences, and set them openly on the temple that joins the castle of Wittenberg, on the 30th of September, A.D. 1517.

This friar, hoping to obtain the pope's blessing, assembled certain monks and divines of his convent, and forthwith commanded them to write something against Luther. And while he would not himself seem to be dumb he began not only to inveigh in his sermons, but to thunder against Luther crying, "Luther is an heretic, and worthy to be persecuted with fire." And besides this, he burned openly Luther's propositions, and the sermons which he wrote on indulgences. The rage and fury of this friar forced Luther to treat more amply of the cause, and to maintain his argument.

And thus arose the beginning of this controversy, wherein Luther, neither suspecting nor dreaming of any change that might happen, did not utterly reject the indulgences, but only required a moderation in them; and therefore they falsely accuse him, who blaze that he began with plausible matter, by which he might get praise, to the end that in process of time he might change the state of the commonweal, and purchase authority either for himself or others.

And certainly he was not stirred up by the court, for the Duke Frederick was offended that such contention and controversy should arise.

And as this Duke Frederick was one of all the princes of the time that most loved quietness and tranquillity, so he neither encouraged nor supported Luther, but often shewed the heaviness and sorrow which he bore in his heart, fearing still greater dissensions. But being a wise prince, and following the counsel of God, and well deliberating thereon, he thought with himself that the glory of God was to be preferred above all things. Nor was he ignorant what blasphemy it was, horribly condemned by God, obstinately to oppose the truth. Wherefore he did as a godly prince should do; he obeyed God, committing himself to his holy grace, and omnipotent protection. And although Maximilian the emperor, Charles king of Spain, and pope Julius, had given commandment to the Duke Frederick that he should prohibit Luther from all place and liberty of preaching; yet the Duke, considering with himself the preaching and writing of Luther, and weighing diligently the testimonies and places of scripture which he alleged, would not withstand the thing which he judged to be true and sincere. And yet he did not do this, trusting to his own judgment, but was very anxious to hear the judgment of others, who were both aged and learned. In the number of whom was Erasmus, whom the duke desired to declare to him his opinion touching the matter of Martin Luther; saying and protesting, that he would rather the ground should open and swallow him, than he would bear with any opinions which he knew to be contrary to manifest truth; and therefore he desired him to declare his judgment in the matter to him freely and friendly.

Erasmus, thus being intreated by the duke, began thus jestingly and merrily to answer the duke's request, saying, that, in Luther were two great faults; first, that he would touch the bellies of monks: the second, that he would touch the pope's crown; which two matters are in no case to be tampered with. Then, opening his mind plainly to the duke, he said, that Luther was occupied in detecting errors, and that a reformation was to be wished, and very necessary in the church: and he added, that the effect of his doctrine was true; but only he wished in him a more temperate moderation and manner of writing. Duke Frederick shortly after wrote to Luther seriously, exhorting him to temper the vehemence of his style. This was at the city of Cologne, shortly after the coronation of the new emperor.

Erasmus the next year wrote to the archbishop of Mentz an epistle touching the cause of Luther. In which epistle he signifies to the bishop "That many things were in the books of Luther condemned by monks and divines for heretical, which in the books of Bernard and Austin are read as sound and godly."

Also "That the world is burdened with men's institutions, with school-doctrines and opinions, and with the tyranny of begging friars; which friars, being nothing but the pope's servants and underlings, yet have they so grown in power and multitude, that they are now terrible both to the pope himself, and to all princes. Who so long as the pope makes with them, so long they make him more than God; but if he make any thing against their purpose or advantage, then they weigh his authority no more than a dream or phantasy."

"Once," said he, "it was counted an heresy when a man opposed the gospel or articles of the faith; now he that dissents from Thomas Aquinas is an heretic; whatever they like not, whatever they understand not, that is heresy. To speak Greek is heresy; or to speak more finely than they do, that is with them heresy." And thus much by the way concerning the judgment of Erasmus.

Now to return, and to treat of the acts and conflicts of Luther with his adversaries. After Tetzel, with his fellow-monks and friars, had cried out with open mouth against Luther, in maintaining the pope's indulgences; and after Luther, in defence of his cause, had set up propositions against the open abuses of indulgences, it was wonderful to see how soon those propositions were spread abroad in far places, and how greedily they were caught up in the hands of persons both far and near. And thus the contention increasing between them, Luther was compelled to write more largely and fully than otherwise he thought, which was in A.D. 1517.

Yet all this while Luther never thought of any alteration, much less such a reformation of doctrine and ceremonies as afterwards followed. But hearing that he was accused to the bishop of Rome, he wrote humbly to him, in which writing he declares the outrage of those pardon-mongers who so excessively cheated the simple people, to the great slander of the church, and shame to his holiness; and so proceeding, in the end of his writing thus submits himself.

"Wherefore," saith he, "most holy father, I offer myself prostrate under the feet of your holiness, with all that I am, and all that I have. Save me, kill me, call me, recall me, approve me, reprove me as you shall please. Your voice, the voice of Christ in your speaking, I will acknowledge. If I have deserved death, I shall be contented to die; for the earth is the Lord's, and all the fulness thereof, who is blessed for ever. Amen." This was in A.D. 1518.

After Martin Luther, provoked by Tetzel, had declared his mind in writing, lowly and humbly, and had set up certain propositions to be disputed; not long after, among other monks and friars, steps up Silvester de Prierio, a Dominican friar, who began to publish abroad an impudent and railing dialogue against him.

Next after this Sylvester stept forth Eckius, and opposed the conclusions of Luther. Against whom D. Andrew Bedenstein, archbishop of Wittenberg, came forth, making his apology in defence of Luther.

Then was Martin Luther cited the 7th of August, by Jerome bishop of Ascalon, to appear at Rome. About which time Thomas Cajetan, cardinal, the pope's legate, was then at the city of Augsburgh, having before been sent down with certain mandates of Pope Leo to that city. The University of Wittenberg hearing of Luther's citation, soon directed their letters, with their public seal, to the pope in Luther's behalf. Also another letter they sent to Charles Militz, the pope's chamberlain; also good Frederick ceased not for his part to solicit the matter with his letters and earnest suit with Cardinal Cajetan, that the cause of Luther might be removed from Rome to Augsburgh, in the hearing of the cardinal. Cajetan, at the suit of the Duke, wrote to the pope, from whom he received this answer, 23d August: "That he had cited Luther to appear personally before him at Rome, by Jerome bishop of Ascalon, auditor of the chamber, which bishop had diligently done what was commanded him; but Luther, abusing and contemning the gentleness offered, not only refused to come, but also became more bold and stubborn, continuing, or rather increasing in his former heresy. Wherefore he desired that the cardinal should cite and call up the said Luther, to appear at the city of Augsburgh before him, adjoining withal the aid of the princes of Germany, and of the emperor, if need required; so that when the said Luther should appear, he should lay hands upon him, and commit him to safe custody, and then he should be brought up to Rome; and if he perceived him to come to any knowledge or amendment of his fault, he should release him and restore him to the church again, or else he should be interdicted, with all his adherents, abettors, and maintainers, of whatever state or condition they were, whether they were dukes, marquises, earls, barons, &c. Against all which persons and degrees, he desired him to extend the same curse and malediction (only the person of the emperor excepted) interdicting, by the censure of the church, all such lands, lordships, towns, tenements, and villages, as should minister any harbour to Luther, and were not obedient to the see of Rome. Contrariwise, to all such as shewed themselves obedient, he should promise full remission of all their sins."

The pope directs other letters also at the same time to Duke Frederick, complaining with many grievous words against Luther.

The cardinal being thus charged with injunctions from Rome, according to his commission, sends with all speed for Luther, to appear at Augsburgh, before him.

About the beginning of October, Martin Luther yielding his obedience to the church of Rome, came to Augsburgh at the cardinal's message (at the charges of the noble prince elector, and also with his letters of commendation) where he remained three days before he came to his presence, for it was provided by his friends that he should not confer with the cardinal till a sufficient warrant or safe-conduct was obtained of the emperor Maximilian. Which being obtained, he soon entered, offering himself to the presence of the cardinal, and was there received by the cardinal very gently; who, according to the pope's command, propounded to Martin Luther three things, to wit:—

1. That he should repent and revoke his errors.

2. That he should promise, from that time forward, to refrain from the same.

3. That he should refrain from all things that might by any means trouble the church.

When Martin Luther required to be informed wherein he had erred, the legate brought forth a papal bull, called the Extravagant of Clement, which begins, "Unigenitus," &c., because that he, contrary to that canon, had held and taught in his fifty-eight propositions, "That the merits of Christ, are not the treasure of indulgences or pardons." Secondly, the cardinal, contrary to the seventh proposition of Luther, affirmed, that faith is not necessary to him that receives the sacrament.

Another day, in the presence of four of the emperor's council, having a notary and witnesses present, Luther protested for himself, in this manner following:—

"I Martin Luther, an Augustinian friar, protest, that I do reverence and follow the church of Rome in all my sayings and doings, present, past, and to come; and if any thing has been, or shall be said by me to the contrary, I count it, and am willing that it be counted and taken as though it had never been spoken. But because the cardinal has required at the command of the pope three things of me,

1. That I should return again to the knowledge of myself.

2. That I should beware of falling into the same again hereafter.

3. That I should promise to abstain from all things which might disquiet the church of God;

"I protest here this day, that whatever I have said, seems to me to be sound, true, and catholic; yet for the further proof of it, I offer myself personally, either here or elsewhere, publicly to give a reason of my sayings. And if this please not the legate, I am ready also in writing to answer his objections, if he have any against me; and to hear the sentence and judgment of the universities of the empire, Basil, Friburg, and Louvaine."

After this, Luther prepares an answer to the legate, teaching that the merits of Christ are not committed to men; that the pope's voice is to be heard when he speaks agreeably to the scriptures; that the pope may err, and that he ought to be reprehended. Moreover he shewed, that in matters of faith, not only the general council, but also every faithful christian is above the pope, if he depend on better authority and better reason: that the extravagant bull contains untruths: that it is an infallible truth that none is righteous: that it is necessary for him that comes to the receiving of the sacrament to believe: that faith in the remission of sins is necessary; that he ought not to decline from the truth of the scripture: that he sought nothing but the light of the truth, &c.

But the cardinal would hear no scriptures; he disputed without scriptures; he devised glosses and expositions out of his own head; and by subtle distinctions like a very Proteus he avoided all things. After this, Luther being commanded to come no more into the presence of the legate, except he would recant, abode there still, and would not depart. Then the cardinal sent for John Stupitius, vicar of the Augustinians, and moved him earnestly to bring Luther to recant. Luther tarried the next day also, and nothing was said to him. The third day also he tarried, and delivered his mind in writing; in which, first, "he thanked him for his courtesy and great kindness, which he perceived by the words of Stupitius, toward him, and therefore was the more ready to gratify him in whatever kind of office he could do him service, confessing that where he had been somewhat sharp and eager against the pope's dignity, that was not so much of his own mind, as it was to be ascribed to the importunity of some who gave him occasion. Notwithstanding as he acknowledged his excess, so he was ready to shew more moderation hereafter, and also promised to make amends to the bishop, and that in the pulpit, if he pleased. And as to the matter of pardons, he promised also to proceed no further, if his adversaries likewise were bound to keep silence. But as he was pressed to retract his sentence which he had previously defended, as he had said nothing but with a good conscience, and which was agreeable to the firm testimonies of the scripture, therefore he humbly desired the determination of it to be referred to the bishop of Rome; for nothing could be more grateful to him, than to hear the voice of the church speaking." &c.

Who does not see by this humble submission of Luther, that if the bishop of Rome would have been satisfied or contented with any reason, he had never been troubled any further by Luther? But the secret purpose of God had a further work to do; for the time was now come when God thought good that pride should have a fall. Thus while the unmeasurable desire of that bishop sought more than enough (like Esop's dog coveting to have both flesh and shadow) he not only missed what he gaped for, but also lost what he had.

This writing Luther delivered to the cardinal, the third day after he was commanded out of his sight. Which letter or writing the cardinal little regarded. When Luther saw that he would give no answer to the letter, he yet remained after the fourth day, and still nothing was answered; the fifth day likewise was passed with silence, and nothing done. At length, by the counsel of his friends, and especially because the cardinal had said before that he had a commandment to imprison Luther and John Stupitius; after he had made and set up his appeal where it might be seen and read, he departed, thinking that he had shewed obedience long enough. Luther himself records all this, and shews why he submitted himself to the church of Rome; declaring that even those things which are most truly spoken, yet ought to be maintained and defended with humility and fear; and he protests that he reverences and follows the church of Rome in all things, and that he sets himself only against those which, under the name of the church of Rome, go about to set forth and commend Babylon to us.

Thus Luther, being rejected from the presence of the cardinal Cajetan after six days' waiting, departed by the advice of his friends, and returned into Wittenberg, leaving a letter in writing to be given to the cardinal, wherein he declared sufficiently,—his obedience in his coming,—the reasons of his doctrine,—his reasonable submission to the see of Rome,—his long waiting after he was repelled from the cardinal's presence,—the charges of the duke,—and finally, the cause of his departing. Besides this letter to the cardinal, he left also an appeal to the bishop of Rome, from the cardinal, which he caused to be published before his departure.

After Luther had departed and returned again into his own country, Cajetan writes to Duke Frederick a sharp and biting letter, in which first he notices his gentle entreating and good will shewn to reduce Luther from his error. Secondly, he complains of the sudden departing of him, and of Stupitius. Thirdly, he declares the danger of Luther's doctrine against the church of Rome. Fourthly, he exhorts the duke, that as he tenders his own honour and safety, and regards the favour of the high bishop, he will send him to Rome, or expel him out of his dominions, forasmuch as such a pestilence could not, and ought not by any means to be suffered.

To this letter of the cardinal the duke answers at large, clearing both Luther and himself; Luther, in that he following his conscience, grounded upon the word of God, would not revoke that for an error, which could be proved to be no error; and himself he excuses thus, that where it is required of him to banish him his country, or to send him up to Rome, it would be little becoming him to do so, and less conscientious, unless he knew just cause why he should do so, which if the cardinal would or could declare to him, there should lack nothing in him which was the duty of a christian prince to do. And therefore he desired him to endeavour with the bishop of Rome, that innocency and truth be not oppressed before the crime or error be lawfully convicted.

This done, the duke sends the letter of the cardinal to Martin Luther, who answered again to the prince, shewing first how he came obediently to Cajetan with the emperor's warrant, and what talk there was between them; how Cajetan pressed him, against his conscience and manifest truth, to revoke these errors. First, that the merits of Christ's passion were not the treasure of the pope's pardons. Secondly, that faith was necessary in receiving the sacraments. Although in the first he was content to yield to the cardinal; yet in the second, because it touched a great part of our salvation, he could not with a safe conscience retract, but desired to be taught by the scriptures, or at least, that the matter might be brought into open disputation in some free place of Germany, where the truth might be discussed and judged by learned men. The cardinal, not pleased with this, in great anger cast out many menacing words, and would not admit him any more to his presence; and yet he persisting in his obedience to the church of Rome, gave attendance, waiting upon the cardinal's pleasure a sufficient time.

At last, when no answer would come, after he had waited the space of five or six days, to his great loss and greater danger, by the persuasion of his friends he departed. At which, if the cardinal was displeased, he had most cause to blame himself. "And now, as the cardinal threatens me," saith he, " not to let the matter fall, but that the process shall be pursued at Rome, unless I either come and present myself, or else be banished your dominions, I am not so much grieved for mine own sake as that you should sustain on my account any danger or peril. And therefore seeing there is no place nor country, which can keep me from the malice of my adversaries, I am willing to depart hence, and to forsake my country, whithersoever it shall please the Lord to lead me, thanking God who has counted me worthy to suffer thus much for the glory of Christ's name."

At this time the cause of Luther was in great danger, and he himself was ready to fly the country, and the duke again was as much afraid to keep him, had not the marvellous providence of God provided a remedy where the power of man failed, by stirring up the whole university of Wittenberg, who seeing the cause of truth thus declining, with a full and general consent addressed their letters to the prince, in defence of Luther and of his cause, making their humble suit to him, that he of his princely honour would not suffer innocency and the simplicity of truth, so clearly exposed in the scriptures, to be foiled and oppressed by mere violence of certain malignant flatterers about the pope, but that the error may first be shewn and convicted, before the party be pronounced guilty.

By these letters the duke began more seriously to consider in his mind the cause of Luther, and to read his works, and also to hearken to his sermons. By which (through God's holy working) he grew to knowledge and strength, perceiving in Luther's quarrel more than he did before. This was about the beginning of December, A.D. 1518.

As this passed on, Pope Leo, playing the lion at Rome, in the month of November, to establish his seat against the defection which he feared was coming, had sent forth new indulgences into Germany, and all quarters abroad, with a new edict, wherein he declared this to be the catholic doctrine of the holy mother church of Rome, prince of all other churches, that bishops of Rome, who are successors of Peter, and vicars of Christ, have this power and authority given to release and dispense, also to grant indulgences available both for the living, and for the dead lying in the pains of purgatory; and this doctrine he charged to be received of all faithful christian men, under pain of the great curse, and utter separation from all holy church.

This popish decree and indulgence, as a new merchandise to get money, having been sent into all quarters of Christendom for the holy father's advantage, came also to be received in Germany about the month of December. Luther in the meantime, hearing that at Rome they were about to proceed and pronounce against him, provided a certain appeal in due form of law, wherein he appeals from the pope to the general council.

When Pope Leo perceived that his pardons would not prosper to his mind, and that Luther could not be brought to Rome, he sent his chamberlain, Charles Miltitz, who was a German, into Saxony to Duke Frederick, with a golden rose, after the usual ceremony, with secret letters also to certain noblemen of the duke's council, to solicit in favour of the pope's cause, and to remove the duke's mind, if it might be, from Luther.

But before Miltitz approached Germany, the Emperor Maximilian died in Jan. 1519. Then two candidates stood for the election, to wit, Francis the French king, and Charles king of Spain, who was also duke of Austria, and duke of Burgundy. To make this matter short, through the means of Frederick prince elector (who having the offer of the preferment, refused it) the election fell to Charles, called Charles V., about the end of August.

In the month of June previously, there was a public disputation at Leipsic, a city under the dominion of George duke of Saxony, uncle to Duke Frederick. This disputation first began through the occasion of John Eckius, a friar, and Andrew Carolostad, a doctor of Wittenberg. This Eckius had impugned certain propositions or conclusions of Martin Luther, which he had written the year before against the pope's pardons. Against him Carolostad wrote in defence of Luther. Eckius, to answer Carolostad, set forth an apology; which apology Carolostad confuted in writing. To this disputation Martin Luther came with Philip Melancthon, who not a year before had come to Wittenberg; Luther not thinking then of disputing any thing because of his appeal already mentioned, but only to hear what was said and done.

Before the entering into the disputation it was agreed that every thing should be penned by notaries, and afterwards published. But Eckius afterwards went back from that, pretending that the penning of the notaries would be an hinderance to them, by which their reasoning would be the more languid. But Carolostad would not dispute without notaries. The sum of their disputation was reduced to certain conclusions. Among which, first came in question to dispute of free will, that

is, whether a man have of himself any election or purpose to do that which is good. When the question was to be discussed, what the will of man may do of itself, without grace; they, through heat of contention, fell into other matters little or nothing appertaining to that Carolostad proposed. Eckius affirmed that the pure strength to do good is not in man's will, but is given of God to man, to take interest and increase of man again, which at first he seemed to deny. Then being asked by Carolostad whether the whole and full good work that is in man proceeds of God? He answered, the whole good work, but not wholly, granting that the will is moved by God, but that to consent is in man's power. Against this Carolostad reasoned, alleging certain places of Augustine, and of St. Paul, who saith, "That God worketh in us both to will, and to do." And this opinion of Carolostad seemed to prevail. And thus a whole week was lost about this contentious and sophistical altercation between Eckius and Carolostad.

Luther, as was said, came not thinking at all to dispute, but having liberty granted by the duke, and under the pope's authority, was challenged, and forced against his will, to dispute with Eckius. The matter of their controversy was about the authority of the bishop of Rome. Luther had previously set forth in writing, that they who attribute the pre-eminency to the church of Rome, have no other foundation for it than the pope's decrees, which had been set forth not much more than four hundred years before; and these decrees he affirmed to be quite contrary to all ancient histories, for above a thousand years past, and also contrary to the holy scriptures, and to the Nicene council.

Against this assertion Eckius set up a contrary conclusion, saying, "That they who hold that the supremacy and pre-eminence of the church of Rome above all other churches was not before the time of pope Silvester I. do err, forasmuch as they who succeed in the see and faith of Peter, were always received for the successors of Peter, and vicars of Christ on earth."

Though this was the last of all the other points of Eckius, yet he thought to begin with this against Luther, in order to bring him into more displeasure with the bishop of Rome; but Luther refused to dispute, alleging that the subject was more unpleasant than necessary for that time, and also that for the bishop of Rome's sake, he had much rather keep silence on the point. But if he must needs be forced to it, he wished the fault should be understood to be where it really was, namely, in his adversaries who challenged him to it. Eckius again clearing himself, transfers all the fault to Luther, who first in his treatise on indulgences, asserted that before Pope Silvester's time the church of Rome had no pre-eminence above other churches.

Thus Luther being constrained to dispute, whether he would or no, the question began to be propounded as to the supremacy of the bishop of Rome, which supremacy, Eckius contended was found and grounded upon God's law. Luther on the other side denied not the supremacy of the bishop of Rome above other churches, neither did he deny it to be universal over all churches, but he only affirmed it not be instituted by God's law. Upon this question the disputation continued for the space of five days. During all which time Eckius very dishonestly and discourteously demeaned himself, studying by all means how to bring his adversary into hatred with the auditors, and into danger with the pope. The reasons of Eckius were these: "Forasmuch as the church, being a civil body, cannot be without a head, therefore as it stands with God's law, that other civil governments should not be destitute of a head; so it is requisite by God's law, that the pope should be the head of the universal church of Christ." To this Martin Luther answered, "That he confesses and grants the church not to be headless so long as Christ is alive, who is the only head of the church; neither does the church require any other head beside him, forasmuch as it is a spiritual kingdom, and not earthly." And he alleged for him the place of Coloss. i. 18. Eckius again produces certain places out of Jerome and Cyprian, which made very little way to prove the primacy of the pope to exist by the law of God. As to the testimony of Bernard, the authority of that author was not of any great force in this question.

Then he came to the place of St. Matthew, "Thou art Peter, and upon this rock will I build my church," &c. To this was answered, "That this was a confession of faith; and that Peter there represents the person of the whole universal church, as Augustine expounds it. Also, that Christ in that place means himself to be the rock, as is manifest both by his words, and the structure of the sentence, and many other conjectures. Also to the place of St. John, (xxi. 16.) "Feed my sheep" (Which words Eckius alleged were spoken, peculiarly to Peter alone). Luther answered, "That after these words were spoken, an equal authority was given to all the apostles, where Christ saith to them, "Receive ye the Holy Ghost: whose soever sins ye remit, they are remitted," &c. By these words (saith he) Christ, assigning to them their office, teaches what it is to feed, and what he ought to be who feeds." After this, Eckius came to the authority of the council of Constance; alleging this among others,—"That it stands upon necessity of our salvation, to believe the bishop of Rome to be supreme head of the church: alleging, moreover, that in that council it was debated and discussed, that a general council could not err. To this Martin Luther answered discreetly, saying, "That all the articles which John Huss held were not condemned in that council for heretical. Again, of what authority that council of Constance is to be esteemed, he left to other men's judgments. This is most certain (said he) that no council has authority to make new articles of faith." Here Martin Luther was exclaimed against by Eckius and his accomplices, for diminishing the authority of general councils; although he meant to confirm their authority. Yet he was called a heretic and a schismatic, and one of the Bohemian faction, with many other terms of reproachful insult. Eckius then granted the authority of the apostles to be equal: and yet that it did not follow thence, that the authority of all bishops was equal. In conclusion, Eckius could not bear that any one should decline from any word or sentence of the pope's decrees, or the constitutions of the fathers. To this Luther answered, grounding himself upon the place in Gal. ii. 6, where St. Paul, speaking of the principal apostles, saith, "And of them who seemed to be somewhat, whatever they were, it maketh no matter to me, for God accepteth no man's person: nevertheless, that they seemed to be somewhat added nothing to me," &c. Eckius said to this "That as to the authority of the apostles, they were all chosen by Christ, but were ordained bishops by St. Peter." And when Luther brought forth the constitution of the decree, which saith, "Let not the bishop of Rome be called universal bishop," &c. Eckius answered, "That the bishop of Rome ought not to be called universal bishop; yet he may be called bishop of the universal church." And thus much touching the question of the pope's supremacy.

From this matter they entered next upon purgatory, where Eckius kept no order; for when they should have disputed what power the pope has in purgatory; Eckius turns the scope of the question, and endeavours to prove that there is purgatory; and alleges the place of Maccabees. Luther, leaning upon the judgment of Jerome, affirms the book of Maccabees to be not canonical. Eckius again replies, that the book of Maccabees was of no less authority than the gospels. Also, he alleges the place, 1 Cor. iii. 15, "He himself shall be saved; yet so as by fire." Also, the place of Matthew v. 25, "Agree with thine adversary quickly whiles thou art in the way with him, lest he deliver thee to prison,—thou shalt not come out thence till thou hast paid the uttermost farthing," &c. To this he added also, Psal. lxvi. 12, "We went through fire and water," &c. How these places are wrested to purgatory, let the reader discern and judge. Then was brought on the question of indulgences, of which Eckius seemed to make but a trifle, and a matter of nothing, and so passed it over.

At last they came to the question of penance: touching which, the reasons of Eckius digressed much from the purpose, and went to prove, that there are some pains of satisfaction, which Luther never denied; but that for every particular offence such particular penance is exacted of God's justice upon the repentant sinner, as is in man's power to remit or release; such penance neither Luther, nor any true christian would admit.

And thus ye have the chief effect of this disputation between Luther and Eckius at Leipsic, in the month of July, 1519.

About the beginning of the same year, 1519, Ulric Zuinglius came first to Zurich, and there began to teach. In the sixteenth article in his book of articles, he records, that Luther and he at the same time, one not knowing or hearing of the other, began to write against the pope's pardons and indulgences. Yet, if the time be rightly counted, I suppose we shall find that Luther began a year or two before Zuinglius. Notwithstanding, Sleidan testifies, that in this year, when Sampson, a Franciscan, came with the pope's pardons to Zurich, Ulric Zuinglius withstood him, and declared his pardons to be but a vain seducing of the people, to inveigle away their money.

In the next year, which was 1520, the friars and doctors of Louvaine, and of Cologne, condemned the books of Luther as heretical. Luther again effectually defended himself, and charged them with obstinate violence and malicious impiety. About this same time flashed out from Rome the thunderbolt of Pope Leo against Luther, although he had so humbly and obediently reverenced both the person of the pope, and the authority of his see, and had also dedicated to him the book intituled, "Of Christian Liberty." In which book he discusses and proves these two points principally.

1. That a christian man is free, and Lord over all things, and subject to none.

2. That a christian man is a diligent underling and servant of all men, and to every man subject.

Also, in the same year he set out a defence of all his articles, which the pope's bull had before condemned.

Another book also he wrote to the nobility of Germany, in which he impugns and shakes the three principal walls of the papists; the first whereof is this:—

1. Whereas the papists say, that no temporal or profane magistrate has any power over the spirituality, but that the spirituality have power over the other.

2. Where any place of scripture, being in controversy, it is to be decided, they say, "No man may expound the scripture, or be judge of it, but only the pope."

3. When any council is brought against them, they say, "That no man has authority to call a council, but only the pope."

Moreover, in this book he handles and discourses on other matters: That the pope can stop no free council; also what things ought to be handled in councils: That the pride of the pope is not to be suffered. What money goes out of Germany yearly to the pope, amounts to the sum of three millions of florins. Furthermore, in this book he proves and discusses, that the emperor is not under the pope; and that the donation of Constantine is not true, but forged: That priests may have wives: That the voices of the people ought not to be separated from the election of ecclesiastical persons: That interdicting and suspending of matrimony at certain times was introduced from avarice: what is the right use of excommunication: That there ought to be fewer holy-days: That liberty ought not to be restrained in meats: That wilful poverty and begging ought to be abolished: What damage and inconvenience have grown up by the council of Constance: and what misfortunes Sigismund the emperor sustained, for not keeping faith and promise with John Huss and Jerome of Prague: That heretics should be convinced not by fire and faggot, but by evidence of scripture, and God's word: How schools and universities ought to be reformed:

What is to be said and judged of the pope's decretals : That the first teaching of children ought to begin with the gospel.

In the month of October this year, the new emperor, Charles V. was crowned at Aix-la-Chapelle; and about the month of November, Pope Leo sent again to Duke Frederick two cardinals, of whom the one was Jerome Leander, who, after a few words of high commendation, premised to the duke, touching his noble progeny and his other famous virtues, then they made two requests to him in the pope's name; first, That he would cause all the books of Luther to be burned. Secondly, That he would either cause Luther to be executed, or else would send him up to Rome to the pope.

These two requests seemed very strange to the duke: who, answering the cardinals, said, "That he having been long absent from thence, on other public affairs, could not tell what had been done, neither had he communicated on the doings of Luther. However, this he had heard, that Eckius was a great disturber not only of Luther, but of other learned and good men of his university. As for himself, he was always ready to do his duty; first, in sending Luther to Cajetan the cardinal at the city of Augsburgh, and afterwards, at the pope's command, would have sent him out of his dominions, had not Meltitz, the pope's own chamberlain, given contrary counsel to retain him still in his own country, fearing lest he might do more harm in other countries than where he was better known: and so now also he was as ready to do his duty, wherever right and equity required. But as in this cause he sees much hatred and violence shewn on one side, and no error yet convicted on the other side, but that it had rather the approbation of many well learned and sound men of judgment; and as also the cause of Luther was not yet heard before the emperor, therefore he desired the legates to arrange with the pope's holiness, that certain learned persons of gravity and upright judgment might be assigned to have the hearing and determination of this matter, and that his error might first be known and proved, before he was made a heretic, or his books burned. And then when he should see his error by manifest and sound testimonies of scripture, Luther should find no favour at his hands; otherwise he trusted that the pope's holiness would exact nothing of him, which he might not with equity and honour of his place and estate, reasonably perform, &c.

Then the cardinals, declaring to the duke again, that they could do no otherwise, than according to the form of their commission, and so they took the books of Luther, and shortly after set fire upon them, and openly burnt them. Luther hearing this, in like manner called together all the students and learned men in Wittenberg, and there taking the pope's decrees, and the bull lately sent down against himself, openly and solemnly, accompanied with a great number of people following him, he set them likewise on fire, and burnt them, on the 10th of December.

A little before these things passed between the pope and Martin Luther, the emperor had commanded and ordained a sitting or assembly of the states of all the empire to be held at the city of Worms, on the sixth day of January next ensuing. In which assembly, through the means of Duke Frederick, the emperor gave forth, That he would have the cause of Luther there brought before him, and so it was. For when the assembly was commenced in the city of Worms, afterwards, upon the sixth day of March following, the emperor, through the advice of Duke Frederick, directed his letters to Luther; signifying, that for so much as he had set forth certain books, he therefore, by the advice of his peers and princes about him, had ordained to have the cause brought before him in his own hearing, and therefore he granted him licence to come, and return home again. And that he might safely and quietly do so, he promised to him by public faith and credit, in the name of the whole empire, his passport and safe conduct; as by the instrument which he sent to him, he might the more fully be assured. Wherefore, without all doubt or distrust, he desired him to repair to him, and

to be there present the one-and-twentieth day after the receipt thereof.

Martin Luther being thus provided with his safe conduct by the emperor, and after having been accursed at Rome upon Maunday Thursday, by the pope; he, shortly after Easter, speeds his journey to Worms; where he appeared before the emperor and all the states of Germany; how constantly he stuck to the truth, and defended himself, and answered his adversaries, shall now be detailed.

The Acts and Doings of Martin Luther before the Emperor at the City of Worms.

In the year 1521, about seventeen days after Easter, Martin Luther entered Worms, having been sent for by the Emperor Charles V., &c. And whereas Luther having published three years before certain propositions to be disputed in the town of Wittenberg in Saxony, against the tyranny of the pope—which, notwithstanding, were torn in pieces, condemned and burned by the papists, and yet convinced by no manifest scriptures, or probable reason—the matter began to grow to a tumult and agitation; and yet Luther maintained all the while openly his cause against the clergy. Upon this it seemed good to some, that Luther should be summoned, assigning to him a herald-at-arms, with a letter of safe conduct by the emperor and princes. Being sent for, he came, and was brought to the house of the knights of Rhodes, where he was lodged, well treated, and visited by many earls, barons, knights of the order, gentlemen, priests, and the commonalty, who frequented his lodging until night.

To conclude, he came, contrary to the expectation of many; for although he was sent for by the emperor's messenger, and had letters of safe conduct, yet, as a few days before his books had been condemned by public proclamation, it was much doubted by many whether he would come: especially as his friends deliberated together in a village nigh at hand, (where Luther was first advertised of these occurrences) and many persuaded him not to venture himself into such danger. When he had heard their whole persuasion and advice, he answered in this wise :—" As, since I am sent for, I am resolved and certainly determined to enter Worms, in the name of our Lord Jesus Christ; yea, although there were so many devils to resist me, as there are tiles to cover the houses in Worms."

The fourth day after his arrival, a gentleman, named Ulrick of Pappenheim, lieutenant-general of the men at arms of the empire, was commanded by the emperor, before dinner, to go to Luther, and to enjoin him to appear before his imperial majesty, the princes electors, dukes, and other estates of the empire, at four o'clock in the afternoon, to be informed of the cause of his being sent for; to which he willingly assented, as was his duty.

Therefore, at four o'clock, Ulrick of Pappenheim, and Caspar Sturm the emperor's herald, (who conducted Luther from Wittenberg to Worms,) came for Luther, and accompanied him through the garden of the knights of Rhodes, to the earl palatine's palace: and lest the people that thronged in should molest him, he was led by secret stairs to the place where he was appointed to have the audience. Yet, many who perceived this stratagem, violently rushed in, and were resisted, but in vain, and many ascended the galleries, because they desired to see Luther.

Thus standing before the emperor, the electors, dukes, earls, and all the estates of the empire assembled there, he was first advertised by Ulric of Pappenheim to keep silence, until such time as he was required to speak. Then John Eckius, above-mentioned, who was the bishop of Triers' general official, with a loud and intelligible voice, first in Latin, then in Dutch, according to the emperor's command, said and proposed this sentence :—

" Martin Luther, his sacred and invincible imperial majesty hath enjoined, by the consent of all the estates of the holy empire, that thou shouldst be appealed before the throne of his majesty, to the end, that I might demand of thee these two points.

"First, whether thou confess these books here, (for he shewed a heap of Luther's books, written in the Latin and Dutch tongues), and which are in all places dispersed, entitled with thy name, be thine, and that thou dost affirm them to be thine, or not?

"Secondly, whether thou wilt recant and revoke them, and all that is contained in them, or rather meanest to stand to what thou hast written?"

Then, before Luther prepared to answer, Jerome Scurffus, a lawyer of Wittenberg, required that the titles of the books should be read. Forthwith Eckius named some of the books, and those principally which were printed at Basil, among which he named his Commentaries upon the Psalms, his book on Good Works, his Commentary upon the Lord's Prayer, and others which were not controversial.

After this, Luther answered in Latin and in Dutch :—

"Two things are proposed to me by his imperial majesty: First, whether I will avow all those books that bear my name. Secondly, whether I will maintain or revoke anything that I have devised or published. I will answer as briefly as I can.

"In the first place, I can do no otherwise than recognise those books to be mine, which were named; and, certainly, I will never recant any clause of them. In the second place, to declare whether I will wholly defend, or call back any thing contained in them; as there are questions of faith and the salvation of the soul, (and this concerns the word of God, which is the greatest and most excellent matter that can be in heaven or earth, and which we ought duly and evermore to reverence,) this might be accounted a rashness of judgment in me, and even a most dangerous attempt, if I should pronounce any thing before I were better advised, considering I might recite something less than the matter imports, and more than the truth requires, if I did not premeditate what I would speak. These two things being well considered, doth bring to my mind this sentence of our Lord Jesus Christ, where it is said, 'Whosoever shall deny me before men, him will I also deny before my Father, who is in heaven.' I require then for this cause, and humbly beseech his imperial majesty to grant me liberty and leisure to deliberate, so that I may satisfy the interrogation made to me, without prejudice of the word of God, and peril of mine own soul."

Whereupon the princes began to deliberate. Then Eckius, the prolocutor, pronounced their resolution, saying, "Although, master Luther, thou hast sufficiently understood, by the emperor's command, the cause of thy appearance here, and therefore dost not deserve to have any further respite given thee to determine; yet the emperor's majesty, of his mere clemency, grants to thee one day to meditate thy answer, so that to-morrow, at this hour, thou shalt exhibit thine opinion, not in writing, but pronounce the same with thy voice."

Then Luther was led to his lodging by the herald. But here I must not forget, that in the way as he was going to the emperor, and when he was in the assembly of the princes, he was exhorted by others to be courageous, and manly to demean himself, and not to fear them that can kill the body, but not the soul, but rather to dread him that is able to send both body and soul to everlasting fire.

He was encouraged too by the words of our Lord, that "When thou art before kings, think not what thou shalt speak, for it shall be given to thee in that hour what thou shalt say."

The next day, at four o'clock, the herald again came, and brought Luther from his lodging to the emperor's court, where he staid till six o'clock, for the princes were occupied in grave consultations; there he was surrounded with a great number of people, and almost smothered for the press that was there. Then, afterwards, when the princes were set, and Luther entered, Eckius, the official, began to speak in this manner :—

"Yesterday, at this hour, the emperor's majesty assigned thee to be here master Luther, for thou didst affirm those books that we named yesterday were thine. Further, to the interrogation made by us, whether thou wouldest approve of all that is contained in them, or retract and make void any part of them, thou didst require time for deliberation, which was granted, and is now expired. Although thou oughtest not to have had opportunity granted to deliberate, considering it was not unknown to thee wherefore we cited thee. And as concerning the matter of faith, every man ought to be so prepared, that at all times, whenever he shall be required, he may give certain and constant reason thereof; and thou, especially, being counted a man of such learning, and so long time exercised in theology. Then, go to, answer even now to the emperor's demand, whose clemency thou hast experienced in giving thee leisure to deliberate. Wilt thou now maintain all thy books which thou hast acknowledged, or revoke any part of them, and submit thyself?"

The official made this interrogation in Latin and in Dutch. Martin Luther answered in Latin and in Dutch, in this wise, modestly and lowly, and yet not without some stoutness of spirit, and christian constancy, so that his adversaries would gladly have had his courage more humbled and abased, but yet more earnestly they desired his recantation, of which they were in some hopes, when they heard him desire respite to make his answer.

His Answer was this :—

"Most magnificent emperor, and you most noble princes, and my most gentle lords, I appear before you here at the hour prescribed to me yesterday, yielding the obedience which I owe; humbly beseeching, for God's mercy, your most renowned majesty, and your graces and honours, that ye will minister to me this courtesy, to attend to this cause benignly, which is the cause, (as I trust,) of justice and truth. And if, by ignorance, I have not given to every one of you your just titles, or if I have not observed the ceremonies and countenance of the court, offending against them, it may please you to pardon me of your benignities, as one that hath frequented cloisters, and not courtly civilities. And first, as touching myself, I can affirm or promise no other thing, but only this; that I have taught hitherto in simplicity of mind, that which I have thought to tend to God's glory, and to the salvation of men's souls.

"Now, as concerning the two articles objected by your most excellent majesty, whether I would acknowledge those books which were named, and are published in my name, and whether I would maintain or revoke them, I have given a resolved answer to the first, in which I persist, and shall persevere for evermore, that these books are mine, and published by me in my name; unless it has since happened, by some fraudulent dealing of mine enemies, that there be any thing foisted into them, or corruptly altered. For I will acknowledge nothing but what I have written, and that which I have written I will not deny.

"Now, to answer the second article. I beseech your most excellent majesty, and your graces, to vouchsafe to give ear. All my books are not of one sort. There are some in which I have so simply and soundly declared, and opened the religion of, christian faith, and of good works, that my very enemies are compelled to confess them to be profitable, and worthy to be read of all christians. And truly, the pope's bull, (how cruel and tyrannous soever it be,) judges some of my books to be blameless; although, with severe sentence he thunders against me, and with monstrous cruelty condemns my books; which books if I should revoke, I might worthily be thought to transgress the office of a true christian, and to be one that opposes the public confession of all people. There is another sort of my books, which contain invectives against the papacy, and others of the pope's retinue, who have, with their pestiferous doctrine, and pernicious examples, corrupted the whole state of our christianity. Nor can any deny or dissemble this, for universal experience, and common complaint of all bear witness to it, that the consciences of all faithful men are most miserably entrapped, vexed, and cruelly tormented by the pope's laws and doctrines of men. Also, that the goods and substance of christian people are devoured, especially in this noble and famous country of Germany, and even yet, in a most detestable manner, are suffered still to be devoured, without measure, by incredible tyranny; notwithstanding that they themselves have ordained to the contrary in their own proper laws, wherein they themselves have decreed, 'That all such laws of popes, as are repugnant to the doctrine of the gospel, and the opinions of the ancient fathers, are to be judged erroneous, and reproved.'

"If, then, I should revoke these, I do nothing but add more force to their tyranny, and open not only windows but wide gates to their impiety, which is likely to extend more wide and more licentiously than ever; and by my retracting, their insolent assumptions shall be made more licentious, and less subject to punishment, intolerable to the common people, and more confirmed and established, especially if it be known that I have done this by the authority of your most excellent majesty, and the sacred Roman empire. O, Lord! what a cover or shadow shall I be then to cloak their naughtiness and tyranny!

"The rest, or third sort of my books, are such as I have written against some persons, to wit, against such as with tooth and nail labour to maintain the Romish tyranny, and to deface the true doctrine and religion which I have taught and professed. As to these, I plainly confess, I have been more vehement than my religion and profession required; for I make myself no saint, and I dispute not of my life, but of the doctrine of Christ.

"And these I cannot without prejudice call back; for, by this recantation it will come to pass, that tyranny and impiety shall reign, supported by my means, and so they shall exercise cruelty against God's people more violently and ragingly than before.

"Nevertheless, as I am a man, and not God, I can no otherwise defend my books, than did my very Lord Jesus Christ defend his doctrine; who being examined before Annas, and having received a buffet of the officials, said, 'If I have spoken evil, bear witness of the evil.'

"If the Lord, (who was perfect, and could not err,) refused not to have testimony given against his doctrine, yea of a most vile servant, how much the more ought I, who am but vile corruption, and can of myself do nothing but err, earnestly seek and require if any will bear witness against my doctrine.

"Therefore, I require, for God's mercy, your most excellent majesty, your graces and right honourable lordships, or whatsoever he be of high or low degree, here to give his testimony to convict my errors, and confute me by the scriptures, either out of the prophets, or the apostles, and I will be most ready, if so instructed, to revoke any manner of error; yea, and I will be the first that shall consume mine own books, and burn them.

"I suppose it may seem, that I have well weighed beforehand the perils and dangers, the divisions and dissensions which have arisen throughout the whole world, by reason of my doctrine, whereof I was vehemently and sharply yesterday admonished. Concerning which divisions of men's minds, what other men judge I know not. As to myself, I conceive no greater delight in any thing, than when I behold discords and dissensions stirred up for the word of God; for such is the course and proceedings of the Gospel. Jesus Christ saith, 'I came not to send peace, but a sword; I came to set a man at variance with his father,' &c. (Matt. x. 34.)

"And, further, we must think, that our God is marvellous and terrible in his counsels; lest perhaps that which we endeavour with earnest study to achieve and bring to pass, (if we begin first with condemning his word,) may redound again to a sea of evil; and lest the new reign of this young and bounteous prince Charles, (in whom, next after God, we all conceive singular hope,) be lamentable, unfortunate, and miserably begun.

"I could exemplify this with authorities of the scriptures more effectually, as by Pharaoh, the king of Egypt, and the kings of Israel, who then most obscured the bright sun of their glory, and procured their own ruin, when by their counsels, and not by God's counsels, they attempted to pacify and establish their governments and realms; for it is he that entraps the wily in their wiliness, and subverts mountains before they be aware. Wherefore, it is good to dread the Lord.

"I speak not this, supposing that so politic and prudent heads have need of my doctrine and admonition, but because I would not omit to profit my country, and offer my duty or service. And thus I humbly commend myself to your most excellent majesty, and your honourable lordships, beseeching you that I may not incur your displeasure, or be contemned of you through the persecution of my adversaries. I have spoken."

Then Eckius, the emperor's prolocutor, with a stern countenance began, and said, "That Luther had not answered to any purpose. Neither behoved it him to call in question things concluded and defined by general councils; and, therefore, required of him a plain and direct answer, whether he would revoke or no?"

Then Luther.—"Considering, (said he,) your sovereign majesty and your honours require a plain answer, this I say and profess as resolutely as I may, without doubtfulness or sophistication, that if I be not convinced by testimonies of the scriptures, and by probable reasons, (for I believe not the pope, neither his general councils, which have erred many times, and have been contrary to themselves,) my conscience is so bound in these scriptures, and the word of God, which I have alleged, that I will not, and may not revoke any thing, considering it is not godly or lawful to do any thing against conscience. Hereupon I stand and rest. God have mercy upon me."

The princes consulted together upon this answer; and when they had diligently examined the same, the prolocutor began thus:—

"Martin," said he, "thou hast more immodestly answered than beseemed thy person, and also little to the purpose. Thou dividest thy books into three sorts, in such a way as that all that thou hast said, makes nothing to the interrogation proposed; and, therefore, if thou hadst revoked those wherein the greatest part of thine errors is contained, the emperor's majesty, and the noble clemency of others, would have suffered the rest to sustain no injury. But thou dost revive, and bring to light again, all that the general council of Constance has condemned, which was assembled of all the nation of Germany, and now requirest to be convinced by the scriptures, wherein thou greatly errest. For what availeth it to renew disputation of things so long time condemned by the church and councils, unless it should be necessary to give a reason to every man of every thing that is concluded? Now if it should be permitted to every one that opposes the determination of the church and councils, that he must be convinced by the scriptures, we shall have nothing certain and established in Christendom.

"And this is the cause that the emperor's majesty requires of thee a simple answer, either negative or affirmative, whether thou mindest to defend all thy works as christian, or no?"

Then Luther turning to the emperor and the nobles, besought them not to force or compel him to yield against his conscience, confirmed with the holy scriptures, without manifest arguments alleged to the contrary by his adversaries.

"I have declared and rendered," said he, "mine answer simply and directly, neither have I any more to say, unless mine adversaries, with true and sufficient proofs, grounded upon the scripture, can reduce and resolve my mind, and refute mine errors which they lay to my charge. I am tied, as I said, by the scriptures; neither may I, or can I, with a safe conscience, assent to them. For as to general councils, with whose authority only they press me, I am able to prove, that they have both erred, and have defined many things contrary to themselves; and therefore the authority of them is not sufficient, for the which I should retract those things, the verity of which stands so firm and manifest in the holy scripture, that neither of me ought it to be required, nor could I do so without impiety."

The official again answered denying that any man

could prove the councils could have erred. But Luther alleged that he could, and promised to prove it; and now night approaching, the lords rose and departed. And after Luther had taken his leave of the emperor, many Spaniards scorned and scoffed the good man in the way going to his lodging, hollowing and whooping after him a long while.

Upon the following Friday, when the princes electors, dukes, and other estates were assembled, the emperor sent to the whole body of the council a letter, containing in effect as follows:—

The Emperor's Letter.

" Our predecessors, who truly were christian princes, were obedient to the Romish church, which Martin Luther now opposes. And therefore inasmuch as he is not determined to retract his errors in any one point, we cannot, without great infamy and stain of honour, degenerate from the examples of our elders, but will maintain the ancient faith, and give aid to the see of Rome. And further, we are resolved to pursue Martin Luther and his adherents, by excommunication, and by other means that may be devised, to extinguish his doctrine. Nevertheless we will not violate our faith, which we have promised him, but mean to give order for his safe return to the place from whence he came."

The princes electors, dukes, and other estates of the empire, sat and consulted about this sentence, on Friday all the afternoon, and on Saturday the whole day, so that Luther had yet no answer from the emperor.

During this time, many princes, earls, barons, knights of the order, gentlemen, priests, monks, with others of the laity and common sort visited him. All these were present at all hours in the emperor's court, and could not be satisfied with the sight of him. Also there were bills set up, some against Luther, and some, as it seemed, with him. Notwithstanding many supposed, and especially such as well conceived the matter, that this was subtlely done by his enemies, that thereby occasion might be offered to violate the safe conduct given to him. Which the Romish ambassadors with all diligence endeavoured to bring to pass.

The Monday following, the archbishop of Triers advertised Luther, that on Wednesday next he should appear before him, at nine of the clock, and assigned him the place. On St. George's day, a chaplain of the archbishop of Triers came to Luther, by the commandment of the bishop, signifying, that at that hour and place prescribed, he must on the morrow after appear before him.

The morrow after St. George's day, Luther obeying the archbishop's commandment, entered his palace, accompanied thither with his chaplain, and one of the emperor's heralds, and such as came in his company out of Saxony to Worms, with his chief friends. Then Dr. Vœus, the Marquess of Baden's chaplain, began to declare and protest in the presence of the archbishop of Triers, Joachin Marquess of Brandenburgh, George Duke of Saxony, the bishops of Augsburgh and Brandenburgh, and others, that Luther was not called there to be conferred with, or to a disputation, but only that the princes had procured licence of the emperor's majesty, through christian charity, to have liberty granted to them to exhort Luther benignly and brotherly.

He said further, that although the councils had ordained many things, yet that they had not determined contrary matters. And even though they had greatly erred, yet their authority was not therefore abased, or at the least they did not err so that it was lawful for every man to impugn their opinions.

He said moreover, that Luther's book would breed great tumult and incredible troubles; and that he abused the common sort with his book of christian liberty, encouraging them to shake off their yoke, and to confirm in them disobedience. The believers were all of one heart and soul, and therefore it was requisite and necessary to have laws. It was to be considered, said he, although he had written many good things, and, no doubt, of a good mind, as *de triplice justicia*, and other matters, yet how the devil now by crafty means goeth

about to bring to pass, that all his works for ever should be condemned. For by these books which he wrote last, men, said he, would judge and esteem him, as the tree is known, not by the blossom, but by the fruit.

Here he added something of the noon devil, and of the spirit coming in the dark, and of the flying arrow. All his oration was exhortatory, full of rhetorical figures about honesty, the utility of laws, the dangers of conscience, of the commonwealth, repeating often, in his oration, that this admonition was given from a singular good will and great clemency. In concluding his oration, he added menaces, saying, that if Luther would abide in his intention, the emperor would proceed further, and banish him from the empire.

Martin Luther answered: " Most noble princes, and my most gracious lords, I render most humble thanks for your benignities and singular good wills, whence proceedeth this admonition; for I know myself to be safe, as by no means I can deserve to be admonished of so mighty estates."

Then he frankly pronounced, that he had not reproved all councils, but only the council of Constance; and for this principal cause, that it had condemned the word of God, which appeared in the condemnation of this article propounded by John Huss:—"The church of Christ is the communion of the predestinate." It is evident, said he, that the council of Constance abolished this article, and consequently the article of our faith; " I believe in the holy church universal;" and said, that he was ready to spend life and blood, if he were not compelled to revoke the manifest word of God; for in defence of it we ought rather to obey God than men. If Christ's sheep were fed with the pure pasture of the gospel: if the faith of Christ was sincerely preached, and if there were good ecclesiastical magistrates who duly would execute their office, we should not need, saith he, to charge the church with men's traditions. Further, he knew well we ought to obey the magistrates and higher powers, how unjustly and perversely soever they lived. We ought also to be obedient to their laws and judgment: all which he had taught, said he, in all his works; adding further, that he was ready to obey them in all points, so that they enforced him not to deny the word of God.

Then Luther was desired to stand aside, and the princes consulted what answer they might give him. This done, they called him into a parlour, where the aforesaid Dr. Vœus repeated his former matters, admonishing Luther to submit his writings to the emperor, and to the princes' judgment.

Luther answered humbly and modestly, that he could not permit that men should say he would shun the judgment of the emperor, princes, and superior powers of the empire; he would not refuse to stand to their trial, and that he was contented to suffer his writings to be discussed, considered, and judged by the simplest, provided it were done by the authority of the word of God and the holy scriptures; and that the word of God made so much for him, and was so manifest to him, that he could not give place, unless they could confute his doctrine by the word of God. This lesson, said he, he learnt of St. Augustine, who writes, " That he gave this honour only to those books which are called canonical, that he believed the same only to be true. As touching other doctors, although in holiness and excellency of learning they surpassed, yet he would not credit them further than they agreed with the touchstone of God's word. Further, said he, " St. Paul gives us a lesson, writing to the Thessalonians, ' Prove all things, hold fast that which is good;' and to the Galatians, ' Though an angel from heaven preach any other doctrine, let him be accursed.' "

Finally, he meekly besought them not to urge his conscience, which was bound by the word of God and holy scripture, to deny the same excellent word. And thus he commended his cause and himself to them, and especially to the emperor's majesty, requiring their favour that he might not be compelled to do any thing in this matter against his conscience: in all other causes he would submit himself with all kind of obedience and due subjection.

As Luther had thus ended his talk, Joachim the elector, Marquis of Brandenburgh, demanded if his meaning was this, that he would not yield, unless he were convinced by the scripture. "Yea truly, right noble lord," quoth Luther, "or else by ancient and evident reasons." And so the assembly broke up, and the princes repaired to the emperor's court.

After their departure, the archbishop of Triers, accompanied with a few of his familiars, namely, John Eckius his official, and Cochleus, commanded Luther to repair into his parlour. With Luther was Jerome Scurfe and Nicholas Ambsdorff for his assistants.

They prayed him that he would submit his writing to the judgment of the next general council. Luther agreed to this, but with this condition, that they themselves should present the articles collected out of his books to be submitted to the council in such sort, as should be authorized by the scripture, and confirmed with the testimonies of the same.

They then leaving Luther, departed, and reported to the archbishop of Triers, that he had promised to submit his writings in certain articles, to the next council, and in the mean space that he would keep silence; which Luther never thought; who neither with admonitions, nor yet with menaces, could be induced to deny or submit his books to the judgment of men (he had so fortified his cause with clear and manifest authorities of scripture) unless they could prove by sacred scripture, and apparent reasons to the contrary.

It chanced then by the special grace of God, that the archbishop of Triers sent for Luther, thinking presently to hear him.

Then the archbishop intreated Luther, and conferred with him very gently, first removing such as were present. In this conference Luther concealed nothing from the archbishop; affirming that it was dangerous to submit a matter of so great importance to those who had already condemned his opinion, and approved the pope's bull.

Then the archbishop, bidding a friend of his draw nigh, required Luther to declare what remedy might be ministered to help this difficulty. Luther answered, "That there was no better remedy than such as Gamaliel alleged in the fifth chapter of the Acts of the Apostles, saying, If this council, or this work, proceed of men it shall come to nought: but if it be of God, ye cannot destroy it. And so he desired that the emperor might be advertised to write to the pope, that he knew certainly that if this enterprise proceeded not of God, it would be abolished within three, yea within two years.

The archbishop inquired of him what he would do, if certain articles were taken out of his books to be submitted to the general council. Luther answered, "Provided that they be not those which the council of Constance condemned." The archbishop said, "I fear they will be the very same; but what then?" Luther replied, "I will not, and I cannot hold my peace on such matters, for I am sure by their decrees the word of God was condemned; therefore I will rather lose head and life, than abandon the manifest word of my Lord God."

Then the archbishop, seeing Luther would in nowise give over the word of God to the judgment of men, gently bad Luther farewell; who then prayed the archbishop to intreat the emperor's majesty to grant to him gracious leave to depart. He answered he would take order for him, and speedily advertise him of the emperor's pleasure.

Within a small while after, John Eckius the archbishop's official, in the presence of the emperor's secretary, said to Luther, by the command of the emperor, that since he had been admonished by his imperial majesty, the electors, princes, and estates of the empire, and notwithstanding would not return to unity and concord, it remained that the emperor, as advocate of the catholic faith, should proceed further; and it was the emperor's ordinance, that he should within twenty-one days return boldly under safe-conduct, and be safely guarded to the place from whence he came; provided that he raised no commotion among the people in his journey, either in conference or by preaching.

Luther hearing this, answered very modestly, and christianly; "Even as it hath pleased God, so is it come to pass, the name of the Lord be blessed." He said further, he thanked most humbly the emperor's majesty, and all the princes and estates of the empire, that they had given to him benign and gracious audience, and granted him safe-conduct to come and return. Finally he said, he desired none other of them, than a reformation according to the sacred word of God, and consonancy of holy scripture, which he desired in his heart: otherwise he was prepared to suffer all chances from his imperial majesty, as life, and death, goods, fame, and reproach; reserving nothing to himself, but the only word of God, which he would constantly confess to the end: humbly recommending himself to the emperor's majesty, and to all the princes and other estates of the sacred empire.

The morrow after, which was April 26, after he had taken his leave of such as supported him, and his benevolent friends that often visited him, he departed from Worms. The emperor's herald Casper Sturm followed and overtook him at Oppenheim, being commanded by the emperor to conduct him safely home.

The usual prayer of Martin Luther.

"Confirm in us, O God, what thou hast wrought, and perfect the work that thou hast begun in us, to thy glory. Amen."

Martin Luther thus being dismissed by the emperor, departed from Worms towards his country, accompanied with the emperor's herald, and the rest of his company, having only one-and-twenty days granted to him for his return. In the meantime he writes to the emperor, and to other nobles of the empire, repeating briefly to them the whole action and order of things there done, desiring of them their lawful good will and favour, which as he hath always stood in need of, so now he most earnestly craves, especially in this, that his cause, which is not his, but the cause of the whole church universal, may be heard with equity, and decided by the rule and authority of holy scripture: signifying moreover, that whenever they shall please to send for him, he shall be ready at their command, at any time or place, upon their promise of safety, to appear, &c.

During the time of these doings, the doctors and school-men of Paris were not behind hand, but to shew their cunning, condemned the books of Luther, extracting out of them certain articles as touching the sacraments, laws, and decrees of the church, equality of works, vows, contrition, absolution, satisfaction, purgatory, free-will, privileges of the holy church, councils, punishment of heretics, philosophy, school divinity, and other matters. Unto whom Philip Melancthon wrote an answer, and also Luther himself, though pleasantly and jestingly.

It was not long after this, that Charles the new emperor, to purchase favour with the pope (because he was not yet confirmed in his empire) provides and directs a solemn writ of outlawry against Luther, and all those that take his part; commanding Luther, wherever he might be got, to be apprehended, and his books burned. By which decree, proclaimed against Luther, the emperor procured no small thanks with the pope; so that the pope, ceasing to take part with the French King, joined himself wholly to the emperor. In the mean time Duke Frederick, to give some place to the emperor's proclamation, conveyed Luther a little out of sight secretly, by the help of certain noblemen whom he well knew to be faithful and trusty to him in that particular. There Luther being kept close and out of company, wrote several letters, and books to his friends; among which he dedicated one to his order of Augustinian friars, entitled, "The mass abolished:" the friars being encouraged by him, began at first to lay aside their private masses. Duke Frederick fearing lest it would breed some great stir or tumult, caused the judgment of the whole university of Wittenberg to be asked in the matter.

The opinion of the whole university being ascertained, it was shewn to the duke, that he would do well and godly, by the whole advice of the learned there, to command the use of the mass to be abolished through his dominions: and though it could not be done without tumult, yet that was no reason why true doctrine should be checked. Neither ought such disturbance to be imputed to the doctrine taught, but to the adversaries, who willingly and wickedly kick against the truth. For fear of such tumults therefore, we ought not to cease from that which we know should be done, but must go constantly forward in defence of God's truth however the world may esteem us, or rage against it. Thus they shewed their judgment to Duke Frederick.

It happened moreover about the same year and time, (A.D. 1521,) that King Henry VIII., pretending an occasion to impugn the book "On the Babylonish captivity," wrote against Luther. In which book,

1. He reproves Luther's opinion about the pope's pardons.

2. He defends the supremacy of the bishop of Rome.

3. He labours to refute all his doctrine of the sacraments.

This book, although it bore the king's name in the title, yet it was another that planned it, and another again who formed the style of it. But whoever had the labour of this book, the king had the thanks and also the reward. For the bishop of Rome gave to King Henry VIII., for the book against Luther, the style and title of "Defender of the Faith," and to his successors for ever.

Shortly after this, within the compass of the same year, Pope Leo, after he had warred against the French, and had got from them, through the emperor's aid, the cities of Parma, Placentia, and Milan, sitting at supper, and rejoicing at three great gifts that God had bestowed upon him: said, 1. That he, being banished out of his country, was restored to Florence again with glory. 2. That he had deserved to be called apostolic. 3. That he had driven the Frenchmen out of Italy. After he had spoken these words, he was seized with a sudden fever, and died shortly after, being of the age of forty-seven years: some suspect that he died of poison. Adrian VI., schoolmaster to Charles the emperor, succeeded and lived not much above one year and a half in his papacy. This Adrian was a German, brought up at Louvaine; and as in learning he exceeded the common sort of popes, so in moderation of life and manners he seemed not so intemperate as some other popes. And yet like a right pope, nothing degenerating from his see, he was a mortal enemy to Martin Luther. In his time, shortly after the council of Worms was broken up, another meeting or assembly was appointed by the emperor at Nuremberg, of the princes, nobles, and states of Germany, A.D. 1522.

To this assembly Adrian sent his letters in manner of a brief, with an instruction also to his legate Cheregata, to inform him how to proceed, and what to allege against Luther, before the assembled princes. In this letter of instruction, among other matters, is the following admission by the pope himself, of the necessity of the reformation: he thus writes to his legate.

"This you shall say to them, that we confess ourselves, and deny not, but that God suffereth this persecution to be inflicted upon his church for the sins of men, especially of priests and prelates of the clergy. For certain it is, that the hand of the Lord is not shortened, that he cannot save; but our sins have divided between God and us, and therefore he hideth his face from us that he will not hear us. The scripture testifieth, that the sins of the people do issue out from the sins of the priests; and therefore, (saith St. Chrysostom) Christ, going about to cure the sick city of Jerusalem, first entered into the temple, to correct the sins of the priests like a good physician, who first begins to cure the disease from the very root. We know that in this holy see there have been many abominable things for a long time wrought and practised: as abuses in matters spiritual, and also excesses in life and manners, and all things turned clean contrary. And no marvel, if the sickness first beginning at the head, that is, at the high bishops, have descended afterward to inferior prelates. All have declined, every one after his own way; neither hath there been one that hath done good, no not one. Wherefore there is need that we all give glory to God, and that we humble our souls to him, considering every one of us from whence he hath fallen; and that every one do judge himself before he be judged of God in the rod of his fury. For the redress whereof you shall insinuate to them, and promise in our behalf, that in us shall be lacking no diligence of a better reformation, first beginning with our own court; that like as the contagion first from thence descended into all the inferior parts; so reformation and amendment of all that is amiss, from the same place again, shall take its beginning. To that they shall find us so much the more ready, because we see the whole world so desirous of the same. We ourselves, (as you know) never sought this dignity, but rather desired, if we otherwise might, to have led a private life, and in a quiet state to serve God: and also would utterly have refused the same, had not the fear of God, and the manner of our election, and misdoubting of some schism to follow after, urged us to take it. And thus took we the burthen upon us, not for any ambition of dignity, or to enrich our friends and kinsfolks, but only to be obedient to the will of God, and FOR REFORMATION OF THE CATHOLIC CHURCH, and for relief of the poor, and especially for the advancement of learning and learned men, with such other things more as appertains to the charge of a good bishop and lawful heir of St. Peter. And though all errors, corruptions, and abuses be not straightways amended by us, men ought not thereat to marvel. The sore is great, and far grown, and is not single, but of manifold maladies together compacted, and therefore to the curing of it we must proceed by little and little, first beginning to cure the greater and the most dangerous, lest while we intend to amend all, we destroy all. All sudden mutations in a commonweath, (saith Aristotle) are perilous: and he that wringeth too hard, straineth out blood."

The Answer of the noble and reverend Princes, and States of the sacred Roman Empire, exhibited to the Pope's Ambassador.

"The noble and renowned prince Lord Ferdinand, lieutenant to the emperor's majesty, with other reverend peers in Christ, and mighty princes electors, and other states and orders of this present assembly of the Roman empire in Nuremberg convented, have gratefully received, and diligently perused the letters sent in form of a brief, with the instructions also of the most holy father in Christ and Lord, Lord Adrian, the high bishop of the holy and universal church of Rome, presented unto them in the cause of Luther's faction.

"By the aforesaid letters and writings, they first understand his holiness to have been born, and to have had his native origin and parentage out of this noble nation of Germany, at which they do not a little rejoice. Of whose great virtues and ornaments, both in mind and body, they have heard great fame and commendation, even from his tender years: by reason whereof they are so much the more joyous of his advancement and preferment, by such consent of election, to the height of the apostolical dignity, and yield to God most hearty thanks for the same: praying also, from the bottom of their hearts, for his excellent clemency, and the perpetual glory of his name, and for health of souls, and the safety of the universal church, that God will give his holiness long continuance of felicity: having no misdoubt, but that, by such a full and consenting election of such a pastor of the universal catholic church, great profit and advantage will ensue. Which thing to hope and look for, his holiness openeth to them an evident declaration in his own letters, testifying and protesting what a care it is to him both day and night, how to discharge his pastoral function, in studying for the health of the flock to him committed: and especially in converting the minds of christian princes from war to peace. Declaring moreover, what subsidy and relief his holiness hath sent to the soldiers of Rhodes, &c. All which things they having considered with themselves, conceive exceeding hope and comfort in their minds, thus reputing and trusting that this concord of christian princes will be a great help and stay to the better quieting of things now out of frame; without which neither the state of the commonwealth, nor of the christian religion, can be rightly redressed, and much less the tyranny of the barbarous Turks repressed.

" Wherefore the excellent prince, lord lieutenant to the emperor's majesty, with the other princes electors, and orders of this present assembly, most heartily do pray, that his holiness will persist in this his purpose and diligence, as he hath virtuously begun, leaving no stone unremoved; so that the disagreeing hearts of christian princes may be reduced to quiet and peace; or if that will not be, yet at least some truce and intermission of domestic dissensions may be obtained for the necessity of the time now present, whereby all christians may join their powers together, with the help of God, to go against the Turk, and to deliver the people of Christ from his barbarous tyranny and bondage. Whereunto both the noble prince lord lieutenant, and other princes of Germany, will put to their helping hands, to the best of their ability.

" And whereas by the letters of his holiness, with his instruction also exhibited unto them by his legate, they understand that his holiness is afflicted with great sorrow for the prospering of Luther's sect, whereby innumerable souls, committed to his charge, are in danger of perdition, and therefore his holiness vehemently desireth some speedy remedy against the same to be provided, with an explication of certain necessary reasons and causes, whereby to move the German princes thereunto; and that they will tender the execution of the apostolic sentence, and also of the emperor's edict set forth touching the suppressing of Luther. To these the lord lieutenant, and other princes and states do answer, that it is to them no less grief and sorrow than to his holiness; and also they do lament as much for these impieties and perils of souls, and inconveniences which grow in the religion of Christ, either by the sect of Luther, or any otherwise. Further, what help or counsel shall lie in them for the extirpating of errors, and decay of souls' health, what their moderation can do, they are willing and ready to perform; considering how they stand bound and subject, as well to the pope's holiness, as also to the emperor's majesty. But why the sentence of the apostolic see, and the emperor's edict against Luther, hath not been put in execution hitherto, there hath been (said they) causes great and urgent, which have led them thereto; as first, in weighing and considering with themselves, that great evils and inconveniences would thereupon ensue. For the greatest part of the people of Germany have always had this persuasion, and now by reading Luther's books, are more therein confirmed that great grievances and inconveniences have come to this nation of Germany by the court of Rome; and therefore if they should have proceeded with any rigor in executing the pope's sentence, and the emperor's edict, the multitude would conceive and suspect in their minds, this to be done for subverting the verity of the gospel, and for supporting and confirming the former abuses and grievances, whereupon great wars and tumults, no doubt, would have ensued: which thing of the princes and states there hath been well perceived by many arguments. For the avoiding whereof, they thought to use more gentle remedies, serving more opportunely for the time.

" Again, whereas the reverend lord legate (said they) in the name of the pope's holiness, hath been instructed, to declare unto them, that God suffereth this persecution to rise in the church for the sins of men, and that his holiness doth promise therefore to begin the reformation with his own court, that as the corruption first sprang from thence to the inferior parts, so the redress of all again should first begin with the same: also, whereas his holiness, of a good and fatherly heart, doth testify in his letters that he himself did always dislike that the court of Rome should intermeddle so much,

and derogate from the concordates of the princes, and that his holiness doth fully purpose in that behalf, during his papacy, never to practice the like, but so to endeavour, that every one, and especially the nation of the Germans, may have their proper due and right, granting especially to the said nation his peculiar favour: who seeth not by these premises, but that this most holy bishop omitteth nothing which a good father, or a devout pastor may or ought to do to his sheep? Or who will not be moved hereby to a loving reverence, and to amendment of his defaults; namely, seeing his holiness so intendeth to accomplish the same in deed, which in word he promiseth, according as he hath begun?

" And thus undoubtedly, both the noble lord lieutenant, and all other princes and states of the empire, well hope that he will, and pray most heartily that he may do, to the glory of our eternal God, to the health of souls, and to the tranquillity of the public state. For unless such abuses and grievances, with certain other articles also, which the secular princes (assigned purposely for the same) shall draw out in writing, shall be faithfully reformed, there can be no true peace and concord between the ecclesiastical and secular estates, nor can any true extirpation of this tumult and errors in Germany be expected; for partly by long wars, and partly by reason of other grievances and hindrances, this nation of Germany hath been so wasted and consumed in money, that it is scarcely able to sustain itself in private affairs, and necessary upholding of justice within itself; much less than to minister aid and succour to the kingdom of Hungary, and to the Croatians, against the Turk. And whereas all the states of the sacred Roman empire do not doubt, but the pope's holiness doth right well understand how the German princes did grant and condescend for the money of annates to be levied to the see of Rome for a certain term of years, upon condition that the said money should be converted to maintain war against the Turkish infidels, and for the defence of the catholic faith: and whereas the term of these years having now long since expired, when the said annates should have been gathered, and yet that money hath not been so bestowed to that use for which it was first granted. Wherefore if any such necessity should now come, that any public contributions should be demanded of the German people against the Turk, they would answer again, Why has not that money of annates, which was reserved many years before, not been bestowed and applied to that use; and so they would refuse to allow any more such burthens to be laid upon them for that cause.

" Wherefore the said lord lieutenant, and other princes and degrees of the empire, make earnest petition, that the pope's holiness will with a fatherly consideration expend what had been collected, and cease hereafter to require such annates[1] which are accustomed to be paid to the court of Rome, on the death of bishops, and other prelates or ecclesiastical persons, and suffer them to remain to the chamber of the empire, whereby justice and peace may be more commodiously administered, the tranquillity of the public state of Germany maintained, and also that by the same, due helps may be ordained and disposed to other christian potentates in Germany against the Turk, which otherwise without the same is not to be hoped for.

" I. Whereas the pope's holiness desireth to be informed in what way it may be best to take in resisting those errors of the Lutherans. To this the lord lieutenant, with other princes and nobles, did answer, that whatsoever help or counsel they can devise, with willing hearts they will be ready to give. Seeing therefore that the state, as well ecclesiastical as temporal, is far out of frame, and have so much corrupted their ways; and seeing not only of Luther's part, and of his sect, but also by divers other occasions besides, so many errors, abuses, and corruptions have crept in; it is requisite and necessary that some effectual remedy be provided,

(1) Annates was a certain portion of money wont to be paid to the court of Rome, out of the first year's fruits at the vacation of an ecclesiastical living.

as well for redress of the church, as also for repressing the Turk's tyranny. Now the lord lieutenant and other estates and princes do not see that any more present or effectual remedy can be had than this, that the pope's holiness, by the consent of the emperor's majesty, do summon a free christian council in some convenient place of Germany, as at Strasburg, or at Mentz, or at Coblentz, and that it may be with as much speed as convenient, so that the congregation of the said council be not deferred above one year: and that in this council it may be lawful for every person that there shall have interest, either temporal or ecclesiastical, freely to speak and consult, to the glory of God, and health of souls, and the public wealth of Christendom, without impeachment or restraint, whatsoever oath or other bond to the contrary notwithstanding: yea, and it shall be every good man's part there to speak, not only freely, but to speak that which is true, to the purpose, and to edifying, and not to pleasing or flattering, but simply and uprightly to declare his judgment, without all fraud or guile. And as touching by what ways these errors and tumults of the German people may best be stayed and pacified in the meantime, until the council be set, the foresaid lord-lieutenant, with the other princes, thereupon have consulted and deliberated, that forasmuch as Luther, and certain of his fellows, be within the territory and dominions of the noble Duke Frederick, the said lord-lieutenant, and other states of the empire, shall so labour the matter with the afore-named prince, duke of Saxony, that Luther and his followers, shall not write, set forth, or print anything during the said mean space: neither do they doubt but that the said noble prince of Saxony, for his christian piety, and obedience to the Roman empire, as becometh a prince of such excellent virtue, will effectually condescend to the same.

" II. The said lord-lieutenant and princes shall labour so with the preachers of Germany, that they shall not in their sermons teach or blow into the people's ears such matter whereby the multitude may be moved to rebellion or uproar, or to be induced into error; and that they shall preach and teach nothing but the true, pure, sincere, and holy gospel, and approved scripture, godly, mildly, and christianly, according to the doctrine and exposition of the scripture, being approved and received of Christ's church, abstaining from all such things which are better unknown than learned of the people, and which to be subtely searched, or deeply discussed, is not expedient. Also, that they shall move no contention of disputation among the vulgar sort; but whatsoever hangeth in controversy, the same they shall reserve to the determination of the council to come.

" III. The archbishops, bishops, and other prelates within their diocese, shall assign godly and learned men, having good judgment in the scripture, which shall diligently and faithfully attend upon such preachers; and if they shall perceive the said preachers either to have erred, or to have uttered anything inconveniently, they shall godly, mildly, and modestly advertise and inform them thereof, in such sort as that no man shall justly complain of the truth of the gospel being impeached. But if the preachers, continuing still in their stubbornness, shall refuse to be admonished, and will not desist from their lewdness, then shall they be restrained and punished by the ordinaries of the place.

" Besides, the said princes and nobles shall provide and undertake, so much as shall be possible, that, from henceforth during the aforesaid time, no new book shall be printed, especially none of these famous libels, neither shall they be privily or openly sold. Also order shall be taken amongst all potentates, that if any shall set out, sell, or print any new work, it shall first be seen and perused of certain godly, learned, and discreet men appointed for that purpose; so that if it be not admitted and approved by them, it shall not be permitted to be published in print, or to come abroad. Thus by these means they hope, that the tumults, errors, and offences among the people, shall cease; especially if the pope's holiness himself shall begin with an orderly and due reformation, in the above-mentioned grievances,

and will procure such a free and christian council as hath been said, and if so, then the people will be well contented and satisfied. Or if the tumult shall not so fully be calmed as they desire, yet the greater part will thus be quieted; for all such as are honest and good men, no doubt, will be in great expectation of that general council which will shortly be assembled. Finally, as concerning priests which contract matrimony, and religious men leaving their cloisters, whereof intimation was also made by the apostolical legate, the aforesaid princes do consider, that forasmuch as in the civil law there is no penalty for those that are ordained, they shall be referred to the canonical constitutions, to be punished thereafter accordingly, that is, by the loss of their benefices and privileges, or other condign censures, and that the said ordinaries shall in no case be stopped or inhibited by the secular powers from the correction of such; but that they shall add their help and favour to the maintenance of ecclesiastical jurisdiction, and shall direct in their public edicts and precepts, that none shall impeach or prohibit the said ordinaries in their ecclesiastical castigation upon transgressors.

" To conclude, the redoubted prince lord-lieutenant, and other princes, estates, and orders of the empire, vehemently and most heartily do pray and beseech, that the pope's holiness, and the reverend lord his legate will accept and take all the premises to be no otherwise spoken and meant, than of a good, free, sincere, and a christian mind. Neither is there anything that all the aforesaid princes, estates, and nobles, do more wish and desire, than the furtherance and prosperous estate of the holy catholic church of Rome, and of his holiness. To whose wishes, desires, and obedience, they offer and commend themselves most ready and obsequious, as faithful children."

Thus hast thou, loving reader, the full discourse, both of the pope's letter, and of his legate's instructions, with the answer also of the states of Germany to the said letter and instructions, to them exhibited in the diet of Nuremburg. Also, what was concluded at the said diet, and what order and consultation was taken, first touching the grievances of Germany, which they exhibited to the pope, then concerning a general council to be called in Germany, also for printing, preaching, and for priests' marriage, hath been likewise declared, &c.

The disturbance about priests' marriage, was occasioned first by the ministers of Strasburg, who about this time began to take wives, and they therefore were cited by the bishop of Strasburg to appear before him on a certain day, as violaters of the laws of holy church, of the holy fathers, the bishops of Rome, and of the emperor's majesty, to the prejudice both of their own order of priesthood, and of the majesty of Almighty God; but they referred their cause to the hearing of the magistrates of the same city, who, being suitors for them unto the bishops, laboured to have the matter either released, or at least to be delayed for a time.

It would be tedious to recite all the circumstances following upon this diet or assembly of Nuremburg; how their decree was received of some, of some neglected, of divers diversely wrested and expounded. It may be enough to say that the states address the pope to convene a general council to settle and determine these matters, and they enact the *Interim*, which required that all persons should be silent, and all publications cease, and all changes of religion be unlawful until such general council should assemble and decide.

In the same session of Nuremburg mention was made of certain grievances to the number of an hundred, exhibited to the bishop of Rome. From these one hundred grievances, thus publicly complained of in the diet by the princes of Germany, the world may see and judge not only what abuses and corruptions, monstrous and incredible, lay hid under the glorious title of the holy church of Rome, but may also understand with what hypocrisy and impudence the pope takes upon him so grievously to complain against Luther and others, when in all the universal church of Christ there is none so much to be blamed in every way as he himself appears by these complaints of the German princes against the pope's intolerable oppressions and grievances. It would be too long to insert all these one hundred grievances thus solemnly objected to in the diet; but the few which follow will illustrate the then corrupt state of the church of Rome.

A Complaint for selling Remission of Sins for Money.

The burden and grievance of the pope's indulgences and pardons is most insupportable. The bishops of Rome, under pretence of building some church in Rome, or to war against the Turks, do make out their indulgences with their bulls, persuading and promising to the simple people strange and wonderful benefits of remission à pœna et culpa, that is, from all their sins and punishment due for the same, and that not in this life only, but also after this life, to them that are burning in the fire of purgatory. Through the hope, of which true piety is almost extinct in all Germany, while every evil-disposed person promises to himself, for a little money, license and impunity to do what he pleaseth: whereupon followeth fornication, adultery, perjury, homicide, robbing, and spoiling, rapine, usury, with a whole flood of all mischiefs, &c.

A Complaint against the Immunities of Clergymen.

Whoever that hath received any ecclesiastical orders, great or small, thereby contends to be freed from all punishment of the secular magistrate, how great soever his offence may be: neither doth he unadvisedly presume thereupon, but is maintained in that liberty to sin, by the principal estates of the clergy. For it hath often been seen, that whereas by the canonical laws priests are forbidden to marry, they afterwards diligently labour and go about day and night to tempt matrons, virgins, and the wives, daughters, and sisters of the laymen; and through their continual importunity and labour, partly with gifts and rewards, and flattering words, partly by their secret confessions (as they call them) as it has been found by experience, they bring to pass that many virgins and matrons, which otherwise would be honest, have been overcome and moved to sin and wickedness: and it happeneth oftentimes, that they do detain and keep away the wives and daughters from their husbands and fathers, threatening them with fire and sword that do require them again. Thus, through their raging immorality, they heap and gather together innumerable mischiefs and offences. It is to be marvelled at, how licentiously, without punishment they daily offend in robberies, murder, accusing of innocents, burning, rapine, theft, and counterfeiting of false coin, besides a thousand other kinds of mischiefs, contrary and against all laws both of God and man, not without great offence of others, trusting only upon the freedom and liberty of sin, which they usurp to themselves by the privilege of their canons.

Wherefore necessity and justice doth require, that the privileges of the clergy should be abrogated and taken away, and in their place it be provided, ordained, and decreed, that the clergy, of what order or degree soever they be, shall have like laws, like judgment and punishment as the laity have; so that they pretend no prerogative or freedom in like offence, more than the laymen; but that every one of the clergy offending, under the judge where the offence is committed, shall be punished for his act, according to the measure and quality of his offence, in such manner as other malefactors are, with the punishment appointed by the common laws of the empire.

The Church burdened with a number of Holy-days.

Moreover, the common people are not a little oppressed with the great number of holy-days, for there are now so many holy-days, that the husbandmen have scarcely time to gather the fruits of the earth, which they have brought forth with so great labour and travel, being often in danger of hail, rain, and other storms, which fruits notwithstanding, if they were not prevented with so many holy-days, they would gather and bring home without any loss. Besides, upon these holy-days innumerable offences are committed and done, rather than God honoured or worshipped. Which thing is so manifest, that it needeth no witness. For that cause the estates of the sacred empire think it best and most profitable for the christian commonwealth, that this great number of holy-days should be diminished, which ought rather to be celebrated in spirit and truth, than with the external worship, and be better kept with abstinence from sin.

Baptizing of Bells.

Also the bishops have invented, that no other but themselves may baptize bells for the lay people, whereby the simple people upon the affirmation of the suffragans do believe that such bells so baptized will drive away evil spirits and tempests. Whereupon a great number of godfathers are appointed, especially such as are rich, which at the time of baptizing, holding the rope wherewithal the bell is tied, the suffragan speaking before them, as is accustomed in the baptizing of young children, they altogether do answer, and give the name to the bell. The bell having a new garment put upon it, as is accustomed to be done unto the christians; after this they go unto sumptuous banquets, whereunto also the gossips are bidden, that thereby they might give the greater reward; and the suffragans, with their chaplains and other ministers, are sumptuously fed. Yet doth not this suffice, but that the suffragan also must have a reward, which they do call a small gift or present; whereby it happeneth oftentimes, that even in small villages a hundred florins are consumed and spent in such christenings. Which is not only superstitious, but also contrary unto the christian religion, a seducing of the simple people, and mere extortion. Notwithstanding the bishops, to enrich their suffragans, do suffer these things, and others far worse. Wherefore such wicked and unlawful things ought to be abolished.

Complaint of Officials for maintaining unlawful Usury.

Furthermore, the officials being allured through the greedy and insatiable desire of money, do not only not forbid unlawful usuries and gains of money, but also suffer and maintain the same. Moreover, they taking a yearly stipend and pension, do suffer the clergy and other religious persons unlawfully to dwell with their concubines and harlots, and to beget children by them. Both which things how great peril, offence, and detriment they do bring both unto body and soul, every man may plainly see (so that it need not to be rehearsed) except he will make himself as blind as a mole.

Complaint of Officials permitting unlawful cohabitation with others, when the Husband or Wife are long absent.

Furthermore, where it so happeneth (as it doth oftentimes) that either the good man, or the good wife, by means of war, or some other vow, hath taken in hand some long journey, and so tarrieth longer than serveth the appetite of the other, the official, taking a reward of the other, giveth licence to the party to dwell with any other person, not having first regard, or making inquiry whether the husband or wife, being absent, be in health or dead. And because these their doings should not be evil spoken of, they name it a toleration of sufferance, not without a great offence to all men, and to the great contempt of holy matrimony.

Complaint against Incorporations or Impropriations, and other plundering of the People by Churchmen.

Many parish churches are subject unto monasteries, and to the parsons of other churches, by means of incorporations, as they call them, or otherwise, which they are bound also, according to the canon laws, to foresee and look unto by themselves, when as they do put them forth unto others to be governed, reserving for the most part unto themselves the whole stipend of the benefits and tithes; and moreover aggravate and charge the same with so great pensions, that the hireling priests, and other ministers of the church, cannot have thereupon a decent and competent living. Whereby it cometh to pass, that these hireling priests (for they must needs have whereupon to live) do with unlawful exactions miserably spoil and devour the poor sheep committed unto them, and consume all their substance. For when the sacraments of the altar and of baptism are to be administered, or when the first, the seventh, the thirteenth, and the year-day must be kept; when auricular confession cometh to be heard, the dead to be buried, or any other ceremony whatsoever about the funeral is to be done, they will not do it freely, but extort and exact so much money, as the miserable commonalty is scarce able to disburse; and daily they do increase and augment these their exactions, driving the simple poor people to the payment thereof, by threatening them with excommunication, or by other ways compelling them to be at such charge: which otherwise through poverty are not able to maintain obsequies, year-minds, and such other like ceremonies, as to the funerals of the dead be appertaining.

Priests compelled to pay Tribute for Concubines.

Also in many places the bishops and their officials do not only suffer priests to have concubines, so that they pay certain sums of money, but also compel continent and chaste priests, which live without concubines, to pay tribute for concubines, affirming that the bishop hath need of money, which being paid, it shall be lawful for them either to live chaste, or to keep concubines. How wicked a thing this is, every man doth well understand and know.

These, with many other burthens and grievances to the number of an hundred, the secular states of Germany delivered to the pope's legate, having, as they said, many more grievous grievances besides these, which had likewise much need of redress; but because they would not exceed the limits of reasonable brevity, they would content themselves, they said, with these hundred, reserving the rest to a more apt and more convenient opportunity, steadfastly trusting and hoping that when those hundred grievances should be abolished, the other would also decay and fall with them. This was about A. D. 1523. Which being done, the assembly of Nuremburg broke up for a time, and was prorogued to the next year.

In the meantime Pope Adrian died. After him succeeded Pope Clement VII., who, A. D. 1524, sent down his legate, Cardinal Campejius, to the council of the German princes assembled again at Nuremburg, with letters also to Duke Frederick, full of many fair petitions and sharp complaints, &c. But as to the grievances above-mentioned, no word nor message at all was sent, neither by Campejius, nor by any other. Thus, when any thing was to be complained of against Luther, either for suppression of the liberty of the gospel, or for upholding of the pope's dignity, the pope was ever ready with all diligence to call upon the princes; but when any redress was to be required for the public weal of christian people, or touching the necessary reformation of the church, the pope gives neither ear nor answer.

And having thus discoursed of what passed between the pope and princes of Germany, at the diet of Nuremburg, let us now proceed again to the history of Luther, of which you have heard before, how he was kept secret and solitary for a time, by certain nobles in Saxony, because of the emperor's edict. In the meantime, while Luther had thus absented himself from Wittenberg, Andrew Carolostad, proceeding more roughly and eagerly in matters of religion, had excited the people to throw down images in the temples. Luther, returning again to the city, greatly reproved the rashness of Carolostad, declaring that such proceedings were not orderly, but that pictures and images ought first to be thrown out of the hearts and consciences of men, and that the people ought first to be taught, that we are saved before God, and please him only by faith, and that images serve to

to no good purpose. This being done, and the people being well instructed, there would be no danger in images, but they would fall of their own accord. Not that he would maintain images, or suffer them; but that their removal ought to be done by the magistrate, and not by every private man without order and authority.

The cause why Luther opposed that violent throwing down of images, and against Carolostad, seems partly to arise because Pope Adrian, in his letters to the princes and states of Germany, grievously complains and charges the followers of Luther with sedition and tumults, and rebellion against magistrates, as subverters and destroyers of all order and obedience. Therefore Luther, to stop the mouth of such slanderers, and to prevent such sinister suspicions, was forced to proceed as much as was possible, with order and authority.

But while Luther, for these causes differed from the more vehement proceedings of Carolostad, he also differed somewhat from Zuinglius. Now though Luther went a little astray, and dissented from Zuinglius in this one matter of sacrament; yet in all other doctrines they accorded, as appeared in the synod at Marpurg, which was A. D. 1529, where both Luther and Zuinglius were present, and conferring together, agreed in these articles:

1. On the unity and trinity of God. 2. In the incarnation of the Word. 3. In the passion and resurrection of Christ. 4. In the article of original sin. 5. In the article of faith in Christ Jesus. 6. That this faith cometh not of merits, but by the gift of God. 7. That this faith is our righteousness. 8. Touching the external word. 9. Likewise they agreed in the articles of baptism. 10. Of good works. 11. Of confession. 12. Of magistrates. 13. Of men's traditions. 14. Of baptism of infants. 15. Lastly, concerning the doctrine of the Lord's Supper: this they did believe and hold; first, that both the kinds thereof are to be ministered to the people according to Christ's institution, and that the mass is not the means by which a man may obtain grace both for the quick and the dead. Also that the sacrament (which they call of the altar) is a true sacrament of the body and blood of the Lord. And that the spiritual eating of his body and blood is necessary for every christian man. And furthermore, that the use of the sacrament tends to the same effect as the word, given and ordained by Almighty God, that thereby infirm consciences may be stirred to belief by the Holy Ghost, &c.

In all these sums of doctrine Luther and Zuinglius consented and agreed, nor were their opinions so different in the matter of the Lord's Supper, but that in the principal points they accorded. For if the question be asked of them both, what is the material substance of the sacrament, which our outward senses behold and feel? they will both confess bread, and not the accidents only of bread. Further, if the question be asked, whether Christ be there present? they will both confess his true presence to be there, only in the manner of presence they differ. Again, ask whether the material substance laid before our eyes in the sacrament, is to be worshipped? they will both deny it, and judge it idolatry. And likewise for transubstantiation, and the sacrifice of the mass, they both do abhor, and do deny them; as also they agree that the communion in both kinds should be administered.

Only their difference is in this, concerning the sense and meaning of the words of Christ, *Hoc est corpus meum,* This is my body, &c. which words Luther expoundeth to be taken nakedly and simply as the letter standeth, without trope or figure, and therefore holdeth the body and blood of Christ truly to be in the bread and wine, and so also to be received with the mouth. Uldric Zuinglius, with John Oecolampadius, and others, do interpret these words otherwise, as to be taken not literally, but with a spiritual meaning, and to be expounded by a trope or figure, so that the sense of these words: "This is my body," is thus to be expounded: this signifieth my body and blood. With Luther the Saxons consented. The Helvetians coincided with Zuinglius. And as time went on, so the division of these opinions increased and spread farther ; the one part being called from Luther, Lutherans ; the other having the name of Sacramentaries. Notwithstanding, in this one unity of opinion, both the Lutherans and Sacramentaries accorded and agreed, that the bread and wine there present is not transubstantiated into the body and blood of Christ, but is a true sacrament of the body and blood.

Luther lived until the age of sixty-three, and had continued writing and preaching about twenty-nine years. As to his death, the words of Melancthon are these :

" In the year of our Lord 1546, and on the 17th of February, Dr. Martin Luther sickened a little before supper of his accustomed malady, the oppression of humours in the orifice or opening of the stomach, of which I remember I have seen him often diseased in this place. This sickness became violent after supper, he struggling against it, and retired into his chamber, and there rested on his bed two hours, during all which time his pains increased. And as Dr. Jonas was lying in his chamber, Luther awakened, and prayed him to rise, and to call up Ambrose his children's schoolmaster, to make fire in another chamber. When he entered it, Albert earl of Mansfield, with his wife, and others, at that instant came into his chamber. Finally, feeling his fatal hour approach, before nine o'clock in the morning, February 18th, he commended himself to God with this devout prayer.

The Prayer of Luther at his death.

" My heavenly Father, eternal and merciful God, thou hast manifested unto me thy dear Son, our Lord Jesus Christ ; I have taught him, I have known him, I love him as my life, my health, my redemption ; whom the wicked have persecuted, maligned, and with injury afflicted. Draw my soul to thee."

" After this he said, thrice : ' I commend my spirit into thy hands, thou hast redeemed me, O God of truth. God so loved the world, that he gave his only begotten Son, that whosoever believeth in him should not perish but have everlasting life.' John iii. 16.

" Having repeated oftentimes his prayers, he was called to God, to whom he so faithfully commended his spirit, to enjoy, no doubt, the blessed society of the patriarchs, prophets, and apostles in the kingdom of God, the Father, Son, and the Holy Ghost. Let us now love the memory of this man, and the doctrine that he taught. Let us learn to be modest and meek : let us consider the wretched calamities and marvellous changes, that shall follow this sorrowful event. I beseech thee, O Son of God, crucified for us, the risen Emmanuel, govern, preserve, and defend thy church."

Frederick Prince Elector died long before Luther, in the year of our Lord 1525, leaving no issue behind him, for he lived a single life, and was never married ; and was succeeded by John Frederick duke of Saxony.

After this council of Nuremburg, immediately followed another sitting at Ratisbone, where were present Ferdinand, Campejius, the cardinal of Salisburg, the two dukes of Bavaria, the bishops of Trent and Ratisbone ; also the legates of the bishops of Bamberg, Spires, Strasburgh, Augsburgh, Constance, Basil, Frising, Passame, and Brixime. By whom in the said assembly it was concluded :

That forasmuch as the emperor, at the request of Pope Leo, had condemned, by his public edict set forth at Worms, the doctrine of Luther as erroneous and wicked ; and also as it was agreed upon in both the assemblies of Nuremburg, that the said edict should be obeyed of all men ; they likewise, at the request of Cardinal Campejius, do will and command the aforesaid edict to be observed through all their fines and precincts : that the gospel, and all other holy scriptures, should be taught in churches according to the interpretation of the ancient fathers : that all they who revive any old heresies before condemned, or teach any new thing contumeliously, either against Christ, his blessed

mother and holy saints, or which may breed any occasion of sedition, are to be punished according to the tenor of the edict abovesaid : that none be admitted to preach without the licence of his ordinary : that they who are already admitted, shall be examined how, and what they preach : that the laws which Campejius is about to set forth for reformation of manners, shall be observed : that in the sacraments, in the mass, and all other things, there shall be no innovation, but all things to stand as in before time they did : that all they which approach to the Lord's Supper without confession and absolution, or do eat flesh on days forbidden, or which do run out of their order ; also priests, deacons, and sub-deacons, that be married, shall be punished : that nothing shall be printed without consent of the magistrate : that no book of Luther, or any Lutheran shall be printed or sold, &c. And lest it might be said, that this faction of Luther takes its origin in the corrupt life of priests, Campejius, with his assistants in the convocation of Ratisbone, charges and commands, that priests should live honestly, go in decent apparel, play not the merchants, haunt not the taverns, be not covetous, nor take money for their ministration ; and that such as keep concubines should be removed ; the number also of holy-days was to be diminished, &c.

These things Campejius wished to have had enacted in a full council, and with the consent of all the empire : but when he could not accomplish it, because the minds of many were gone from the pope ; he was fain there to get it ratified in this conference, with the assents of the bishops above named.

The matters which have been discoursed upon may more fully be seen in the commentaries of John Sleidan ; it now remains for us, after having finished the history of Martin Luther, to touch upon the history of Zuinglius, and the Helvetians.

The Acts and Life of Zuinglius ; and of the receiving the Gospel in Switzerland.

In the treating of Luther's history, mention was made of Ulric Zuinglius, who first lived at Glarona, in a place then called our Lord's hermitage, from thence he removed to Zurich, about A. D. 1519, and there began to teach, dwelling in the Minster, among the canons or priests of that close, using with them the same rites and ceremonies during the space of two or three years, where he continued reading and explaining the scriptures to the people, with great pains and no less dexterity. And as Pope Leo the same year had renewed his pardons again through all countries, Zuinglius zealously withstood them, detecting such abuses by the scriptures, and such other corruptions as reigned then in the church, and so he continued for the space of two years and more, till at length Hugo, bishop of Constance, wrote his letter to the senate of the said city of Zurich, complaining grievously of Zuinglius. He also wrote another letter to the college of canons, where Zuinglius was dwelling, complaining of those new teachers who troubled the church, and exhorted them earnestly to beware, and to take diligent heed to themselves. And as both the pope and the imperial majesty had condemned all such new doctrine, by their decrees and edicts, he willed them therefore to admit no such new innovations of doctrine, without the common consent of those to whom they appertained. Zuinglius hearing of this, refers his cause to the judgment and hearing of the senate, not refusing to render to them an account of his faith. And as the bishop's letter was read openly in the college, Zuinglius directs another letter to the bishop, declaring that the said letter proceeded not from the bishop, and that he was not ignorant who were the authors thereof, desiring him not to follow their sinister counsels ; because truth, said he, is a thing invincible, and cannot be resisted. After the same tenor, certain other persons of the city likewise wrote to the bishop, desiring him that he would attempt nothing that should be prejudicial to the liberty and free course of the gospel ; requiring, moreover, that he would restrain the filthy and infamous lives of the priests, and that he should permit them to have their lawful wives, &c. This was A.D. 1522.

Besides this, Zuinglius wrote also another letter to the whole nation of the Swiss, admonishing them in no case to hinder the course of pure doctrine, nor to bring any trouble upon the priests that were married. For as for the vow of their single life, it came, saith he, from the devil, and a devilish thing it is. And, therefore, as the Swiss had a right and custom in their towns, that when they received a new priest into their churches, they used to advise him to take his concubine, Zuinglius exhorted them to grant permission to them to take their wives in honest matrimony, rather than to take concubines, against the precept of God.

Thus, as Zuinglius continued some years, labouring in the word of the Lord, offence began to rise at this doctrine, and the Dominican friars began to preach against him. But he, ever keeping himself within the scriptures, protested that he would make good by the word of God, what he taught. Upon this, the magistrates and senate of Zurich, sent forth a command to all priests and ministers within their dominions, to repair to the city of Zurich, against the nine-and-twentieth day of January next ensuing, (A.D. 1523,) and there every one to speak freely, and to be heard quietly, touching these controversies of religion, directing also their letters to the bishop of Constance, that he would either repair there himself, or else send his deputy. When the appointed day came, the bishop's vice-gerent, John Faber, was present. The consul first stating the object of this assembly, required that if any one had to object against the doctrine of Zuinglius, he should freely and quietly declare his mind.

Zuinglius had set forth all his doctrine in order, to the number of sixty-seven articles, which articles he published, that they who were so disposed, might be the better prepared for the disputation. Faber began to state the cause of his being sent there, and argued that neither the time nor the place were fit for discussing such matters, but that the matter belonged to a general council. Zuinglius, however, still continued requiring him, that if he had any thing to say, he would openly and freely say it. To this he answered, that he would confute his doctrine by writing. After this, when no man appeared to dispute, the assembly broke up. Upon which the senate of Zurich caused it to be proclaimed through all their dominion, that the traditions of men should be abandoned, and that the gospel of Christ should be purely taught out of the Old and New Testament.

After these things the cantons of Switzerland direct their public letters to the men of Zurich, wherein they made much lament, and complain of this new broached doctrine, which had set all men together by the ears, through the occasion of certain rash and new fangled heads, who have greatly disturbed both the state of the church and of the commonwealth, and have scattered the seeds of discord. For now all fasting was laid down, and all days are alike to eat both flesh and eggs, as well one as another. Priests and religious persons, both men and women, broke their vows, ran out of their order, and fell to marrying. God's service was decayed, singing in the church left, and prayer ceased. Priests grew in contempt. Religious men were thrust out of their cloisters. Confession and penance was neglected, so that men would not stick to presume to receive at the holy altar, without any confession previously made to the priest. The holy mass derided and scorned. Our blessed lady, and other saints, blasphemed. Images cast down and broken in pieces. Neither was there any honour given to the sacrament. To make short, men had now assumed such a licence and liberty, that even the Holy Ghost could not be safe in the priest's hands, &c.

All this disorder, as it is of no small importance, so it

was, said they, so grievous and lamentable, that they thought it their duty to suffer it no longer. They sent unto them before the like admonition, and also wrote to them by certain of the clergy, and craving their aid in the same; which seeing it is so, they did now again earnestly call upon them touching the premises, desiring them to put an end to such doings, and to take a better way, continuing in the religion of their ancestors which were before them. And if there were any such thing, wherein they were grieved and offended against the bishop of Rome, the cardinal, bishops, or other prelates, either for their ambition in heaping, exchanging and selling the dignities of the church, or for their oppression in emptying men's purses by their indulgences, or else for their usurped jurisdiction and power, which they extend too far, and corruptly apply it to matters external and political, which only ought to serve in such cases as be spiritual. If these, and such other abuses, were the causes wherewith they were so grievously offended, they promised that for the correction and reformation thereof, they would also themselves join their diligence and good will thereto; for so much therefore they would confer with them, how and by what way such grievances might best be removed.

To this effect were the letters of the Helvetians written to the senate and citizens of Zurich. To which, their answer was as follows:—

An Answer again of the Men of Zurich.

"First, declaring, how their ministers had laboured and travelled among them, teaching and preaching the word of God for the space of five years; whose doctrine at first seemed to them very strange and novel, because they never heard it before. But after they understood and perceived the scope[1] of that doctrine only to tend to this, to set forth Christ Jesus to us, as the pillar and refuge of our salvation, who gave his life and blood for our redemption, and who only delivers us from eternal death, and who is the only advocate of mankind before God; they could not do otherwise, but receive with ardent affection so wholesome and joyful a message.

"The holy apostles and faithful christians, after they had received the gospel of Christ, did not fall out in debate and variance, but lovingly agreed and consented together: and so they trusted (said they) that they should do, if they would likewise receive the word of God, setting aside men's doctrines and traditions different from it.

"Whatever Luther or any other man teaches, whether it be right or wrong, is not such for the names of the persons, but only because it agrees or disagrees with the word of God.

"And if Christ only is worshipped, and men are taught to repose their confidence solely in him, neither the blessed Virgin, nor any saint, receives any injury.

"And whereas they charge their ministers with wresting the scriptures after their own interpretation, God had stirred up such a light now in the hearts of men, that the most part of their city have the bible in their hand, and diligently peruse it: so that their preachers cannot so wrest the scriptures, but it would quickly be perceived.

"And whereas they have accused them of error, yet there was never any man who could prove any error in them : although the bishops of Constance, of Basil, of Curiake, with others of the universities, and themselves also had desired to do so; yet to this day neither they nor any other did so.

"And if the bishops object and say that the word of God ought not to be handled by vulgar people, they answered that it was not consistent with equity and reason. For although it belonged to the bishop's office

<hr>

(1) If the scope of doctrine be well marked between the papists and the protestants, it will not be hard for any man to judge which is the true doctrine. For the whole end and scope of the pope's doctrine tendeth to set up the honour and wealth of man, as may appear by the doctrine of supremacy, of confession, of the mass of the sacrament of the altar, &c. All which do tend to the

magnifying of priests; like as purgatory, obsequies, pardons, and such others as serve for their profit. Contrariwise, the teaching of the protestants, as well touching justification, original sin, as also the sacraments and invocation, and all other such like, tend only to the setting up of Christ alone, and casting down of man. —FOXE.

to provide that the sheep should not go astray; yet because they will not see to their charge, but leave it undone, referring every thing to the fathers and to councils; therefore it was right that they should hear and learn, not what man determines, but what Christ himself commands in the scripture. Neither have their ministers given any occasion for this division; but rather they, who for their own private lucre and preferments, contrary to the word of the Lord, seduce the people into error, and grievously offending God, provoke him to plague them with manifold calamities.

"As for the eating of flesh and eggs, it was free to all men, and forbidden to none by Christ.[1]

"And as to matrimony, God himself was the author of it, and he hath left it free for all men. Also St. Paul desires a minister of the church to be the husband of one wife.

"And seeing that bishops for money permit their priests to have concubines, which is contrary to God's law, and to good example, why then might they not as well obey God in permitting lawful matrimony, which he has ordained, as resist God in forbidding it? The same is to be said also of women vowing celibacy.

"And as for monasteries, and other houses of canons, they were first given for relief only of the poor and needy; whereas now those who inhabit them are wealthy, and able to live on their own patrimony. Yet nevertheless the men of Zurich have used such moderation, that they have permitted the inhabitants of those monasteries to enjoy their possessions during the term of their natural life, lest any one should have cause of just complaint.

"Ornaments of churches serve nothing towards God's service; but it agrees well with the service of God that the poor should be relieved. Christ commanded the young man in the gospel not to hang up his riches in the temple, but to sell them, and distribute them to the needy.

"The order of priesthood they do not condemn; such priests as will discharge their duty, and teach soundly, they prize and magnify. As for the other rabble, who serve to no public good, but rather damnify the commonwealth, if the number were diminished by little and little, and their livings put to better use, they doubted not but it would be a service well done to God.

"As for secret confession, in which men tell their sins in the priest's ear, of what virtue this confession is they leave it in suspense. But that confession, whereby repenting sinners fly to Christ, our only intercessor, they account not only as profitable, but also necessary to all troubled consciences. As for satisfaction, which priests use, they reckon it but a practice to get money, and not only erroneous, but also full of impiety. True penance and satisfaction is, for a man to amend his life.

"The orders of monks come only by the invention of man, and not by the institution of God.

"And as to the sacraments, such as are of the Lord's institution, they do not despise, but receive with all reverence. And so with reverence they use the sacrament of the Lord's supper, according as the word of God prescribes, not as many abuse it, making it an oblation and a sacrifice.

"Wherefore, as before, so now again they desire that if they think this their doctrine repugnant to the holy scripture, they would gently shew and teach them their error." And thus much was contained in the answer of the men of Zurich unto the letter of their colleagues of Helvetia.

In the meantime the bishop of Constance, with the advice of his council, answered them as he was requested to do, in a book, wherein he declares what images and pictures those were which the profane Jews and Gentiles adored, and what images these are which the church has received and admitted; and what difference there is between those idols of the Jews and Gentiles,

and these images of the christians. The conclusion was, that whereas the scripture speaks against images, and permits them not to be suffered, that, said he, is to be understood of such images and idols, as the Jews and idolatrous Gentiles used; and not such images and pictures as the church has received.

From this he enters into the discourse of the mass, where he endeavours to prove by the pope's canons and councils, that the mass is a sacrifice and oblation.

This book he sent to the senate of Zurich, about the beginning of June, exhorting them not to suffer their images, or the mass to be abrogated; and shortly afterwards he published the book in print, and sent it to the priests and canons of the Minster of Zurich, requiring them to follow the custom of the church.

The senate, in answer to the bishop's book, about the middle of August wrote to him; declaring that they had read over and over again his book with all diligence: and that they were glad that he had sent it abroad in print, because the whole world thereby would the better judge between them. After this, they explained to him the judgment and doctrine of their ministers and preachers: and finally, by the authority and testimonies of the scriptures, proved the doctrine of his book to be false. But before they sent their answers to him, about the thirteenth day of June, they commanded all the images within the city, and through all their dominions, to be taken down and burned quietly, and without any tumult.

And in the month of April following, the magistrates and senate of the city of Zurich, commanded the mass, with all its ceremonies, to be suppressed, both within the city, and throughout all their jurisdiction: and instead thereof was placed the Lord's supper, the reading of the prophets, prayer, and preaching.

All this while the gospel was not as yet received in any other part of Helvetia, but only in Zurich. Wherefore the other twelve towns appointed a meeting at Baden: where were present among the divines, John Faber, Eckius, and Murnerus. The bishops also of Lucerne, Basil, Coire, and Lausanne, sent their deputies there. The questions there propounded were these.

That the true body and blood of Christ is in the sacrament.

That the mass is a sacrifice for the quick and dead.

That the blessed Virgin, and other saints, are to be invoked as mediators and intercessors.

That images ought not to be abolished.

That there is a purgatory

Which conclusions or assertions, Eckius took upon him to defend. Against him reasoned Oecolampadius, (who was then chief preacher at Basil) with others. Zuinglius at that time was not present, but by writing confuted the doctrine of Eckius; declaring the causes of his absence: which were, that he durst not, for fear of his life, commit himself to the hands of his enemies: and that he refused not to dispute, but only the place of the disputation; and that if they would assign the place of disputation, either at Zurich, or at Berne, or at Saintgallum, he would not refuse to come. The conclusion of the disputation was this, that all should remain in that religion which they had hitherto kept, and should follow the authority of the council, and should not admit any new doctrine within their dominions, &c.

As the time proceeded, and dissension about religion increased, it followed the next year after, (A.D. 1527,) in the month of December, that the senate and people of Berne assigned another disputation within their city, and called to it all the bishops near them; warning them both to come themselves, and to bring their divines with them, or else to lose all such possessions as they had within the bounds of their precinct. After this they appointed certain ecclesiastical persons to dispute, prescribing and determining the whole disputation to be decided only by the authority of the old and new testament. To all that would come, they granted a safe conduct. Also, they

---

(1) It was the pope's law then, that in Lent no man should eat flesh, or eggs, nor any other white meat; wherein it may seem to be verified what St. Paul had prophesied, 1 Tim. iv. "In the latter times some shall depart from the faith, giving heed to seducing spirits, and doctrines of devils, forbidding to marry, and commanding to abstain from meats," &c.

appointed, that all things should be done modestly, without injury and brawling words; and that every one should have leave to speak his mind freely, and with such deliberation, that every man's saying might be received by the notary, and penned: with this proviso previously arranged, that whatever should be agreed upon, should be ratified and observed through all their dominions: and that men might come there better prepared, they propounded in public writing, ten questions to be defended of their ministers by the scriptures; the ministers were, Francis Colbus, and Berthold Halletus. The questions were these.

1. That the true church, whereof Christ is the head, rises out of God's word, and continues in the same, and hears the voice of no other.

2. That the same church makes no laws without the word of God.

3. That the traditions, ordained in the name of the church, do not bind, but so far as they are consonant to God's word.

4. That Christ only has made satisfaction for the sins of the world: and therefore if any man say that there is any other way of salvation, or any other means to put away sin, he denies Christ.

5. That the body and blood of Christ cannot be received really and corporally, by the testimony of the scripture.

6. That the use of the mass, in which Christ is said to be present and offered up to his heavenly Father, for the quick and the dead, is against the scripture, and injurious to the sacrifice which Christ made for us.

7. That Christ only is to be invoked, as the mediator and advocate of mankind with God the Father.

8. That there is no place to be found in the holy scripture, wherein souls are purged after this life; and, therefore, all those prayers and ceremonies, yearly dirges, and obits, which are bestowed upon the dead; also lamps, tapers, and such other things, profit nothing at all.

9. That to set up any picture or image to be worshipped, is repugnant to the holy scripture; and, therefore, if any such are erected in churches for that intent, they ought to be taken down.

10. That matrimony is prohibited to no state or order of men, but for avoiding fornication generally is commanded and permitted to all men by the word of God. And as all immoral persons are excluded from the communion of the church, therefore this unchaste and filthy single life of priests, is most of all inconvenient for the order of priesthood.

When the senate and people of Berne had sent abroad their letters with these questions to all the Helvetians, exhorting them both to send their learned men, and to suffer all others to pass safely through their countries: several of the cantons refused to take any part, or suffer their divines to take any part, in the proposed discussion, saying, that it was not lawful for any nation or province to alter the state of religion, but that it belonged to a general council: wherefore, they desired them that they would not attempt any such wicked act, but continue in the religion which their parents and elders had observed: and in fine, they concluded, that they would neither send, nor suffer any of their learned men to come, nor yet grant safe conduct to any others to pass through their country.

Notwithstanding this, the lords of Berne proceeding in their purpose, upon the day prescribed (which was January 7) began their disputation. Of all the bishops there was not one present; but the city of Basil, Zurich, Strasburg, Augsburg, Constance, and others, sent their ambassadors to it.

The doctors of the city of Berne began the disputation. There were present Zuinglius, Oecolampadius, Bucer, Capito, Blaurerus, with others,—all of whom defended the affirmative of the conclusions propounded. On the other side, the chief was Conrad Tregerus an Augustinian friar, who, when he, to prove his assertion, was driven out of the scriptures, sought help of other authority, but the moderators of the disputation would

not permit it, (as being contrary to the order before arranged) so he departed, and would dispute no more.

The disputation continued nineteen days; in the end it was agreed by the assent of the most part, that the conclusions were consonant to the truth of God's word, and should be ratified not only in the city of Berne, but also proclaimed by the magistrates in other cities adjoining; and that masses, altars, and images, in all places, should be abolished.

At the city of Constance, some things began to be altered a little before. And now, after this disputation at Berne, the images and altars, with ceremonies and masses, were abolished at Constance.

They of Geneva also, were not behind in following the example of the city of Berne, in extirpating images and ceremonies. By reason of which the bishop and clergy left the city in no small anger.

To commemorate this event, they caused a pillar to be erected, and thereupon to be placed in golden letters, the day and year when this reformation from popery to true christianity began among them, as a perpetual memorial to all posterity to come. This was A. D. 1528.

After the account of this disputation at Berne had reached other cities, the ministers of Strasburg began likewise to affirm and teach, that the mass was wicked, and a great blasphemy against God's holy name, and therefore should be abolished, and the right use of the Lord's supper restored. On the other hand, the bishop of Rome's clergy held that the mass was good and holy; which kindled great contention on both sides: when the senate and magistrates of that city would have brought the matter to a discussion, but they could not, because the priests would not consent; they therefore commanded them to silence.

For a long time the bishop of Strasburg succeeded in putting off the change of religion, till at last the senate of Strasburg, seeing the matter hang in controversy for the space of two years, and the preachers daily calling upon them for a reformation; and petition also having been made to them by the citizens, assembled in their great council to the number of three hundred, as they are accustomed to do on great matters of importance. And there debating the case with themselves, some declaring on one side, if they abolished the mass, what danger they should incur from the emperor. On the other side, if they did not, how much they should offend God; and, therefore, giving time to consult, required them, at the next meeting, to declare their sentence in the matter. When the day came the voices and judgments of those who went against the mass, prevailed. Upon which immediately a decree was made, the twentieth of February, A. D. 1529, that the mass should be suspended till the Romanists could prove by good scripture, the mass to be a service available and acceptable before God.

This decree being established by the consent of the whole city, the senate soon commanded it to be proclaimed, and to take full effect, so far as their limits and dominion extended; and afterward by letters certified their bishop touching the matter.

Thus the mass was overthrown in Zurich, in Berne, and Geneva, and in Strasburg, you have heard. Now, what followed in Basil, remains to be stated. In Basil was Oecolampadius, a preacher, by whose diligent labour and travel, the gospel began to take such effect, that there arose great dissension among the citizens about religion, and especially about the mass. Upon this the senate of Basil appointed, That after an open discussion it should be determined by voices, what was to be done.

Owing to the intrigues of some of the senate, this discussion was delayed, and the reformation retarded. The citizens proceeded to violent measures, armed themselves, and proceeded to coerce the senate. It happened the very same day, that certain of the citizens, such as were appointed to go about the city to see things in order, came into the church, where one of them thrusting at a certain image with his staff, it fell down and broke. Other images also were served after the same sort of devotion. When the priests came running to them, as they would not go beyond their commission, departed.

When word was brought to the citizens in the market-place, the matter seemed worse to them than it really was, so they sent three hundred armed men to rescue their fellows in the church, supposing them to be in danger. On coming to the church, and not finding their fellows there, and all things quiet, save only a few images broken down, they, likewise, lest they should have lost all their labour, threw down all the other idols and images which they found standing there; and so passing through all the churches in the city, did the same. And when some of the senate came forth to appease the tumult, the citizens said, "What you have been consulting and advising about for these three years, whether it were best to be done or not, we have despatched in one hour, that from henceforth no more contentions may arise between us for images;" and so the senate permitted them free leave, without any more resistance. A decree at the same time was made, that as well within the city of Basil as without, throughout their whole jurisdiction, the mass, with all idols, should be abandoned; and, further, that in all such matters and cases as concerned the glory of God and the affairs of the public weal, besides the number of the other senators, two hundred and sixty of the burghers or citizens should be appointed out of every ward in the city to sit with them in council. These decrees being established, after they had kept watch and ward about the city three days and nights, every one returned again to his house, quiet and joyful, without any blood or stroke given, or anger wreaked, but only upon the images.

On the third day, which was Ash Wednesday, all the wooden images were distributed among the poor of the city, to serve them for firewood. But when they could not well agree in dividing the prey, but fell to brawling among themselves, it was agreed that the images should be burned all together; so that, in nine great heaps, all the stocks and idols were the same day burned to ashes before the great church door. And thus, by God's ordinance, it came to pass, that the day in which the pope's priests shew forth all their mourning, and mark men's foreheads with ashes, in remembrance that they are but ashes, was to the whole city a festival, and joyful day, for turning their images to ashes; and so the day is observed and celebrated every year still, to this present time, with all mirth, plays, and pastimes, in remembrance of the ashes, which day may there be called rightly, Ash Wednesday of God's own making.

All this time the emperor and the French king were together occupied in wars and strife; which, as it turned to the great damage and detriment of the French king, who was taken prisoner by the emperor, so it happened most opportunely for the success of the Gospel; for otherwise, these Helvetians, and other Germans, should not have had that leisure and rest to reform religion, and to link themselves in league together, as they did. But thus Almighty God, of his secret wisdom, disposes times and occasions to serve his will and purpose in all things. Although Ferdinand, the emperor's brother, and deputy in Germany, lost no time nor diligence to do what he could in resisting the proceedings of the Protestants, as appeared both by the decree set forth at Ratisbone, and also at Spires, in which council of Spires, Ferdinand, at the same time, (A.D. 1529,) had decreed against the Protestants in effect, as follows:—

"First, That the edict of the emperor made at Worms, should be in force through all Germany, till the general council, which should shortly follow. Also, that they who had already altered their religion, and now could not revoke the same for fear of sedition, should attempt no more innovations till the time of the general council.

"Also, That the doctrine of those who hold the Lord's supper otherwise than the church teaches, should not be received, nor the mass altered. And that all ministers of the church should be enjoined to use no interpretation of holy scripture, but the exposition of the church doctors; while other matters that were disputable, were not to be touched. Also, that all persons and states should keep peace, so that for religion neither party should molest the other. All who should transgress these decrees, were to be outlawed and exiled."

To this session at Spires the ambassadors of Strasburg were not admitted, but refused by Ferdinand, because they had rejected the mass. And, therefore, the city of Strasburg refused to pay any contribution against the Turk, unless they, with the other German states, were admitted to the councils. The other princes which were received, and who opposed the decree, and shewed their case in an elaborate protestation, written for that purpose, were:—John, duke of Saxony; George, elector of Brandenburg; Ernest and Francis, earls of Lunenburg; the Landgrave of Hesse; and the prince of Anhalt. All such cities as subscribed and consented to the protestation of these princes, soon joined themselves in a common league with them, upon which they received the name, and were therefore called PROTESTANTS. The names of the cities were these,—Strasburg, Nuremberg, Ulm, Constance, Rottigen, Windseim, Memmingen, Lindaw, Kempten, Heilbron, Wissemburg, Nortlingen, Saint Gall.

As to the council of Augsburg, which followed the year after the assembly of Spires, (A.D. 1530,) how the princes and protestants of Germany exhibited their confession in the council, and what labour was sought to confute it, and how constantly duke Frederick persisted in defence of his conscience, against the threatening words and replies of the emperor; also, in what danger the princes had been, had not the Landgrave privately, by night, slipped out of the city, need not, as yet, be detailed.

To return, therefore, to Zuinglius and the Helvetians. The two cantons of Zurich and Berne, who had reformed their religion, were grossly insulted by the five other cantons, who insultingly hanged the arms of those two cities on a gallows, which led to a war between them, (A.D. 1531.)

The French king, with other townships of Switzerland, laboured to bring them to agreement, drawing out certain conditions of peace between them, which conditions were:—That all contumelies and injuries should be forgotten. That, hereafter, neither part should molest the other. That they who were banished for religion, should again be restored. That the five cantons might remain without disturbance in their religion, so that none should be restrained among them from the reading of the Old and New Testament. That no kind of disturbance should be raised against those of Berne and Zurich; and that all should confer mutual helps together, one to succour the other, as in times past. But the five cantons would not observe these covenants. Wherefore the men of Zurich and Berne, declaring, first, their cause in public writing, to excuse the necessity of their war, being pressed with so many wrongs, and constrained to take the sword in hand, beset the high-ways and passages, that no victuals or other forage should come to the other cantons. When they of the five towns began to be pinched with want and penury, they armed themselves secretly, and set forward in warlike array towards the borders of Zurich. There was a garrison of the Zurich men there, to the number of a thousand and more. And word was sent to the city of Zurich to succour their men with speed; but their enemies approached so fast that they could hardly come to rescue them: for, when they were come to the top of the hill, they saw their fellows in great distress in the valley under them. Upon which, they encouraging themselves, made down the hill with more haste than order, striving who might go fastest; but the nature of the hill was such, that there could but one go down at once, and so were discomfited and overmatched by the multitude. Among the slain was Ulric Zuinglius, the blessed servant and saint of God.

As to the cause which moved Zuinglius to go out with his citizens to the war, it is sufficiently declared and excused by Sleidan, and especially by Oecolampadius. It was an old received custom among the Zurich men, that when they went forth in warfare, the chief minister of the church went with them. Zuinglius, also, being a man of courage, considering if he should remain at home when war was attempted against his citizens, and if he, who in his sermons so encouraged others, should now faint so cowardly, and tarry behind when the time of danger came, thought that he ought not to refuse to take part with his brethren.

Oecolampadius adds, that he went out, not as a captain of the field, but as a good citizen with his citizens, and a good shepherd ready to die with his flock. And which of them all, saith he, that most cry out against Zuinglius, can shew any such noble heart to do the like? Again, neither did he go out of his own accord, but rather desired not to go, foreseeing, belike, what danger thereof would ensue. But the senate being importunate upon him, would have no refusal, urging him to go ; among whom were thought to have been some false betrayers, objecting to him, that he was a dastard if he refused to accompany his brethren, as well in time of danger as in peace. When he was slain, great cruelty was shewn upon the dead corpse by his popish enemies ; such was their hatred to him, that their malice could not be satisfied, unless also they should burn his dead body.

The report goes, that after his body was cut, first in four pieces, and then consumed with fire, three days after his death his friends came to see whether any part of him was remaining, and they found his heart in the ashes, whole and unburned, in much the same way as was also the heart of Cranmer, archbishop of Canterbury, which, as it is reported, was found unconsumed in the ashes.

Such, too, was the rage of these five popish cantons, against the abbot Cappello, who was also killed, that they took his dead body, and putting out both its eyes, clothed it in a monk's cowl, and set it in the pulpit to preach, railing and jesting upon him in a most despiteful manner. Ulric Zuinglius was, when he died, forty-four years of age—younger than Martin Luther by four years.

Oecolampadius the preacher of the city of Strasburg, hearing of the death of Zuinglius his dear friend, took thereat inward grief and sorrow, so that it is thought to have increased his disease, and so he also departed this life, Nov. A.D. 1531, being of the age of forty-nine years, elder than Martin Luther by one year. Although this Oecolampadius then died, yet his learned and famous commentaries upon the prophets, with other works which he left behind him, live still, and shall never die.

The year following, which was A.D. 1532, in the month of August, died also the worthy and memorable prince John Frederick Duke of Saxony, who for testimony of Christ and of his gospel, sustained such trials and so vehement conflicts with the emperor, and that especially at the council assembled at Augsburgh, that unless the almighty hand of the Lord had sustained him, it had not been possible for him, or any prince, to have endured so constant and unmoveable against so many persuasions and assaults, as he did to the end. After him succeeded John Frederick his son, &c.

And thus have you the history of Zuinglius, and of the church of Switzerland, with their proceedings and troubles, from the first beginning of their reformation of religion.

From the beginning of this book, good reader, thou hast heard of many troubles in the church of Christ, concerning the reformation of various abuses and great errors that had crept into the church of Rome. What godly man has there been, within the space of these five hundred years, either virtuously disposed, or excellently learned, who has not disapproved the disorderly doings and corrupt examples of the see and bishop of Rome from time to time, to the coming of Luther? It may well be wondered at, that as this Romish bishop had great enemies from time to time, speaking and working, preaching and writing against him, yet no one could ever succeed till the coming of Luther. The cause of this seems to be, that while others before him, when speaking against the pomp, pride, and avarice of the bishop of Rome, charged him only, or chiefly, with the manner of life. Luther went further, charging him not only with evil life, but also with evil learning ; not with his doings, but with his doctrine ; not picking at the rind, but plucking up the root ; not seeking the man, but shaking his seat ; yea and charging him with plain heresy, as prejudicial and injurious to the blood of Christ, contrary to the true understanding of the sacred testament of God's holy word. For while the foundation of our faith, grounded upon the holy scripture, teaches and leads us to be justified only by the merits of Christ, and the price of his blood ; the pope, with a con-

trary doctrine, teaches us to seek our salvation not by Christ alone, but by the way of men's meriting and deserving by works. Whereupon rose divers sorts of orders and religious sects among men, some professing one thing and some another, and every man seeking his own righteousness, but few seeking the righteousness of him who is appointed by God to be our wisdom, righteousness, sanctification, and redemption.

Martin Luther, therefore, reducing all things to the foundation and touchstone of the scripture, opened the eyes of many who before were drowned in darkness. It cannot be expressed what joy, comfort, and consolation came to the hearts of men, some lying in darkness and ignorance, some wallowing in sin, some in despair, some macerating themselves by works, and some presuming upon their own righteousness, to behold that glorious privilege of the great liberty and free justification in Christ Jesus. And to speak briefly, the more glorious did the benefit of this doctrine appear to the world after long ignorance, so the greater was the persecution that followed. And where the elect of God took most occasion of comfort and of salvation, there the adversaries found most matter for vexation and disturbance, as we commonly see the word of God bring with it dissension and trouble ; and therefore truly it was said of Christ, that he came not to send peace on earth but the sword. And this was the cause why, after the doctrine and preaching of Luther, so great troubles and persecutions followed in all quarters of the world : thence there arose great disquiet among the prelates, and many laws and decrees were made to overthrow the truth, by the cruel handling of many good and christian men. Thus while authority, armed with laws and rigour, strove against the truth, it was lamentable to hear how many christian men were troubled, and went to wreck, some tost from place to place, some exiled out of the land for fear, some forced to abjure, some driven to caves in woods, some wracked with torment, and some pursued to death with fire and fagot. Of whom we have now to treat, beginning with some that suffered in Germany, and then returning to our own histories and martyrs in England.

Henry Voes and John Esch, Augustinian Friars.

In A.D. 1523, two young men were burnt at Brussels, the one named Henry Voes, at the age of 24 years ; and the other John Esch, who formerly had been of the order of the Augustinian friars. They were degraded the first day of July, and spoiled of their friars' weeds, at the suit of the pope's inquisitor ; and the divines of Louvaine, because they would not retract the doctrine of the gospel, which the papists called Lutheranism. Their examiners were Hochestratus and others, who demanded of them, what they believed? They said, the books of the Old Testament and the New, wherein were contained the articles of the creed. Then were they asked, whether they believed the decrees of the councils, and of the fathers? They said, such as were agreeing to the scripture they believed. After this they proceeded further, asking, whether they thought it any deadly sin to transgress the decrees of the fathers, and of the bishop of Rome? That, said they, belongs only to the commandment of God, to bind the conscience of man ; when they constantly persisted and would not retract, they were condemned to be burned. Then they began to give thanks to God their heavenly Father, who had delivered them through his great goodness, from that false and abominable priesthood, and made them priests of his holy order, receiving them to himself as a sacrifice of sweet odour. Then there was a bill written, which was delivered unto them to read openly before the people, to declare what faith and doctrine they held. The greatest error that they were accused of was, that men ought to trust only in God, as men are liars and deceitful in all their words and deeds, and therefore there ought no trust or confidence to be put in them.

As they were led to the place of execution, on the first of July, they went joyfully and cheerfully, making continual protestation that they died for the glory of God, and the doctrine of the gospel, as true christians, believing and following the holy church of the Son of God, saying also that it was the day which they had long desired. After they were come to the place where they were to be burned, and were despoiled of their garments, they tarried a long time in their shirts, and joyfully embraced the stake they were to be bound to, patiently and joyfully enduring whatever was done to them, praising God with "We praise thee, O God," &c., and singing psalms, and rehearsing the creed, in testimony of their faith. A certain doctor, beholding their cheerfulness, said to Henry, that he should not so foolishly glorify himself: he answered, "God forbid that I should glory in anything, but only in the cross of my Lord Jesus Christ." Another counselled him to have God before his eyes: he answered, "I trust that I carry him truly in my heart." One of them seeing that fire was kindled at his feet, said, "Methinks ye do strew roses under my feet." Finally, the smoke and the flame mounting up to their faces, choked them.

Henry being demanded among other things, whether Luther had seduced him or no? "Yea," said he, "even as Christ seduced his apostles." He said also, that it was contrary to God's law, that the clergy should be exempted from the power and jurisdiction of the magistrate ordained of God; for such as were ordained in office by the bishops have no power, but only to preach the word of God, and to feed their flock. After their death, their monastery was dissolved at Antwerp.

Henry Sutphen, monk, put to death in Diethmar.

The next year after the burning of those two christian martyrs at Brussels, above mentioned, with like tyranny also was martyred and burned, without all order of judgment or just condemnation, about the city of Diethmar, on the borders of Germany, one Henry Sutphen, monk, A.D. 1524. This Sutphen had been with Martin Luther, and coming to Antwerp was excluded from thence for the gospel's sake, and came to Bremen, not to preach, but to go to Wittenburg, being driven from Antwerp. Whilst at Bremen, he was there asked by certain godly citizens to make one or two brief exhortations upon the gospel. Through the earnest love and zeal that was in him, he was easily assured and persuaded to do this. He preached his first sermon to the people on the Sunday before St. Martin's day. When the people heard him preach the word of God so sincerely, they desired him to preach again the second time, and were so in love with his doctrine, that the whole parish required him to tarry among them to preach the gospel; but being afraid of danger he refused for a time. When the religious orders learned this, especially the canons, monks, and priests, they sought to oppress him, and to thrust him, and also the gospel of Christ out of the city, which was their chief seeking. They went to the senate, desiring that such an heretic might be banished from the town, as in his doctrine he preached against the catholic church. Upon the complaint of the canons, the senate sent for the wardens and head men of the parish where Henry had preached, who being come together, the senate declared to them the complaint of the canons, and all the other religious men. The citizens of Bremen, taking their preacher's part, answered, that they had hired a learned and honest man to preach to them, and to teach them sincerely and truly the word of God; however, if the chapter-house, or any other, could bring testimonial or witness, that the preacher had taught anything which either savoured of heresy, or was repugnant to the word of God, that then they were ready with the chapter-house to persecute him, for God forbid that they should maintain an heretic. But if the canons of the chapter-house, and the other religious orders will not declare and shew that the preacher, whom they had hired, had taught any error or heresy, but if they were set on only through malice to drive him away, they ought not therefore by any means to suffer it. So they petitioned the senate, with all humble obedience, that they would

not require it of them, but grant them equity and justice, saying, that they were disposed to assist their preacher always, and to plead his cause.

When the monastic orders learned that they could not prevail, they burst out into a fury, and began to threaten, and went to the archbishop to certify that the citizens of Bremen were become heretics.

When the bishop heard of these things, he sent two of his council to Bremen, requiring that Henry should be sent to him without delay. When they were asked why they should send him, they answered, Because he preached against the holy church. Being again demanded in what articles, they had nothing to say. One of these counsellors was the bishop's suffragan, a naughty pernicious hypocrite, who sought by all possible means to carry away Henry a captive. The answer of the senators was, that as the preacher had not been convicted for any heresy, they could by no means consent that Henry should be carried away; so they earnestly pressed the bishop that he would speedily send his learned men to Bremen to dispute with him, and if he were convinced, they promised without any delay that he should be punished and sent away, if not, they would in no wise let him depart. The suffragan answered, by requiring that he might be delivered into his hands for the quietness of the whole country; but the senate continued still in their former mind. The suffragan being moved with anger at this, departed from Bremen, and would not confirm their children.

When thus the popish prelates were disappointed, they held a provincial council at Buckstade. To this council were called the prelates and learned men of the diocese, to determine what was to be believed.

Henry also was called to the council, although they had already decreed to proceed against him, as against a heretic; wherefore the rulers of the city, together with the commonalty, detained him at home, foreseeing and suspecting the malice of the council. Then Henry gathered his doctrine into a few articles, and sent it with his letters to the archbishop; excusing his innocency, offering himself as ready, if he were convicted of any error by the testimony of the holy scripture, to recant it, earnestly requiring that his errors might be convicted by the holy scriptures, by the testimony of which he had hitherto proved his doctrines, and doubted not hereafter to confirm them. Henry contemning their madness, proceeded daily in preaching the gospel, adding always this protestation, that he was ready willingly to give account touching his faith and doctrine to every man that would require it. In the meantime the holy Romans could not be idle, but sent their chaplains to every sermon to entrap him in his words. But God, whose footpaths are in the midst of the floods, would have his marvellous power to be seen in them, for he converted many of them, so that the greater part of those who were sent to hearken, openly acknowledged his doctrine to be God's truth, against which no man should contend, and such as in all their lives before they had not heard. But the chief priests, canons, and monks were so hardened and blinded with Pharaoh, that they became worse for these admonitions. When God saw fit that Henry should confirm the truth that he had preached, he sent him among the cruel murderers appointed for that slaughter, on the occasion that follows.

It happened in the year 1524, that this Henry was sent for by letters, by Nicholas Boy, parish priest, and other faithful christians of the parish of Meldorph, which is a town in Diethmar, to preach the gospel to them, and deliver them out of the bondage of antichrist.

These letters being received upon St. Catherine's evening, he called together six brethren, honest citizens, and opened to them how he was sent for by them of Diethmar to preach the gospel; adding, that he was not only a debtor to them, but to all others who required his aid. Wherefore he thought good to go to Diethmar, to see what God would work by him, requiring also that they would help him with their advice by what means he might best take his journey.

Having prepared all things for his journey, on the twenty-second of October he departed and came to Meldorph, where he was joyfully received by the parish priest and others. Although he had not yet preached, the devil with his members began to fret and fume for anger. Above all other, one Augustine Tornborch, prior of the Black Friars, began to take counsel with others what was to be done. It was agreed by them, above all things, to withstand the beginnings, and that he should not have licence to preach: for if he preached, and the people should hear him, it was to be feared that the wickedness and craft of the priests and monks should be exposed, which being manifest, they knew plainly that it would be but a folly to resist, remembering what had happened so lately before in Bremen. The prior early on the following morning (for he had not slept well all night for care) went with great speed unto Heida, to speak with the forty-eight presidents of the country, to whom with great complaints he shewed how that a seditious fellow, a monk was come from Bremen, who would seduce all the people of Diethmar as he had done those of Bremen. There were others that assisted this prior in persuading the forty-six, who were simple and unlearned men, that they would obtain great favour and good-will of the bishop of Bremen, if they would put this heretical monk to death. When these men heard these words, they decreed that the monk should be put to death, without being heard or seen, much less convicted.

When this was notified to him he said that he ought to obey the word of God, rather than man. And that if it pleased God that he should lose his life there, it was as near a way to heaven, as in any other place. The next day Henry went up into the pulpit, and preached a sermon, expounding the place of Paul, Rom. i. 9. "God is my witness," &c. After the sermon, the whole congregation being called together, the prior Augustine delivered the letters that were sent by the forty-eight presidents, the tenor whereof was this: that they of Meldorph should be fined with a fine of a thousand gilders, if they suffered the monk to preach. When they heard these letters read, they were much moved. And they all determined with one voice, to keep Henry as their preacher, and to defend him: for when they heard the sermon, they were greatly offended with the prior.

After dinner Henry preached again, expounding the place of St. Paul, Rom. xv. 1. "We who are strong ought," &c. The next day the citizens of Meldorph sent messengers to Heida, offering to answer in all cases before all men, for their preacher, whom they had received. Besides that, the messengers declared what christian and godly sermons they had heard him preach. The parish priest also wrote letters by the messengers to the forty-eight rulers, in which he excused himself, that it was never his wish, nor the intention of Henry to move sedition, but only to preach sincerely the word of God, and he offers himself as ready to answer for Henry to all men, whenever he should be called on; and earnestly desiring them not to give credit to the monks, who being blinded with hatred and avarice, had determined to oppress the truth: adding also, that it was against all reason, that a man should be condemned, before the truth was tried, and his cause declared; and that if, after due inquisition, he should be convicted, then he should suffer punishment. This submission with the public testimonial was not regarded; but in the end one of the council, Peter Dethleve recommended the whole matter should be referred to the next general council. With this answer they were all very well contented; and the messengers returned to Meldorph with great joy and gladness, declaring to the whole congregation the answer that was made.

Upon St. Nicholas day, Henry preached twice, with such a spirit and grace, that all men held him in admiration, praying God most earnestly, that they might long have such a preacher. Upon the day of "the Conception of our Lady," he also preached two sermons upon the first chapter of Matthew; wherein he rehearsed the promises made by God to our forefathers, and under what faith our fathers had lived; adding also, that all reference to works being set apart, we must be justified by the same faith. All these things were spoken with such boldness of spirit, that all men greatly marvelled at him, giving thanks to God for his great mercy, in having sent them such a preacher, desiring him moreover, that he would tarry with them all Christmas to preach.

In the meantime, the prior Augustine Tornborch and Master John Schink were not idle: for the prior went to the Franciscan monks, and minors, for help and council. For those kinds of friars above all others are best instructed by their hypocrisy to deceive the poor and simple people. These friars straightway sent for those persons, who had all the rule and authority, and especially Peter Hannus, Peter Swine, and Nicholas Roden; to whom they declared, with great complaints, what an heretical monk had preached, and how he had obtained the favour of all the simple people; which if they did not speedily provide for, and withstand in the first beginnings, and put the heretic to death, it would come to pass, that soon the honour of the Virgin Mary, and all saints, together with the two abbeys, would come to utter ruin and decay.

When these men heard these words, they were greatly moved. Peter Swine answered, that they had before written to the parish priest and to Henry what was best to be done; but if they thought good, they would write again. "No," said the prior, "this matter must be attempted another way: for if you write to the heretic, he will by and by answer you again. And it is to be feared, that the contagion of his heresy may infect some of you, being unlearned men: for if you give him leave to speak, and to answer, there is no hope that you shall overcome him." So they finally determined to take Henry by night, and burn him before the people should know it. This device pleased them all, but especially the Franciscan friars. Peter Hannus, who was the prior's chief friend, wishing to get the chief praise and thanks in the matter, associated with him other rulers of the neighbouring towns. And all these being assembled together in the parish of the new church, in the house of Mr. Gunter, where the chancellor consulted with them how they might burn Henry secretly. They concluded that on the day after "the Conception of our Lady," they would meet at Henning, which is five miles from Meldorph, with a great band of husbandmen. There assembled above five hundred men, unto whom was declared the cause of their assembling, and also instructed them in what was to be done; for before that no man knew the cause of the assembly; but only the presidents. When the husbandmen understood it, they would have returned back again, refusing such a detestable and horrible deed. But the presidents with most bitter threats kept them in obedience; and in order that they should be the more courageous, they gave them three barrels of Hamburgh beer to drink.

About midnight they came in arms to Meldorph; the monks having prepared torches for them, that Henry should not slip away in the dark. They had also with them a traitor, named Hennegus, by whose treason they had perfect knowledge of every thing. With great violence they burst into the house of the parish priest, breaking and spoiling every thing, as is the manner of drunken people. If they found either gold or silver they took it away. When they had spoiled all things, they violently fell upon the parish priest, and with great noise cried out, "Kill the thief, kill the thief!" Some of them took him by the hair of the head, and pulled him out into the dirt, forcing him to go with them as a prisoner: others cried out, saying, that the parish priest was not to be meddled with, for they had no commission to take him. After they had satisfied their violence upon the parish priest, with great rage and fury they ran upon Henry, and drawing him naked out of his bed, bound his hands behind him: being so bound, they drew him to and fro so long, that Peter Hannus, who otherwise was unmerciful and a cruel persecutor of the word of God, desired them that they should let him alone; for that he would follow of his own accord. When he was brought to Hemmingsted, they asked him how and for what intent he came to Diethmar? He gently declared the whole cause of his coming : but they all in a rage cried out, " Away with him, Away with him! for if we hear him talk any longer, it is to be feared that he will make us also heretics." Then being very weary and faint, he asked to be set on horse-back, for his feet were all cut and hurt with the ice, for he was led all night barefoot. When they heard him say so, they mocked and laughed at him, saying, " Must we hire a horse for a heretic ? he shall go on foot whether he will or no." Because it was night they carried him naked to Heida. Afterwards they brought him to a certain man's house named Calden, and bound him there with chains in the stocks. The master of the house seeing the cruel deed, taking compassion upon Henry, would not suffer it. So he was carried away to a priest's house, and shut up in a cupboard, and was kept there by the rude people, who all the night mocked and scorned him. Amongst others that came to him, were Simon in Altennord, and Christian, parish priest of the new church, both alike ignorant and wicked persecutors of the word of God, demanding why he had forsaken his holy habit? He answered by the scriptures; but those ignorant persons understood nothing about what he said. Gunter also came to him, inquiring whether he had rather be sent to the bishop of Bremen, or receive his punishment in Diethmar? Henry answered, " If I have preached any thing contrary to God's word, or done any wicked act, it is in their hands to punish me." Gunter answered, " Hark, I pray you, good friends, hark, he desires to suffer in Diethmar." The common people continued all that night in immoderate drinking.

In the morning about eight o'clock, they gathered together in the market-place to consult what they should do : where the rustic people boiling with drink, cried out, " Burn him! burn him!—to the fire with the heretic! Without doubt, if we do it, we shall this day obtain great glory and praise both of God and man ; for the longer he lives, the more he will seduce with his heresy." Why need many words ? Sure he was to die ; for they had condemned this good Henry without any judgment, without hearing his cause, to be burned. At last they commanded the crier to proclaim, that every man who was at the taking of him, should be ready in arms to bring him forth to the fire. Among the others the Franciscan friars were present, encouraging the drunken rude people, saying, " Now you go the right way to work." Then they bound Henry, hands, feet, and neck, and with great noise brought him forth to the fire. As he passed by, a woman standing at her door, who wept abundantly at seeing this pitiful sight, Henry turned to her and said, " I pray you, weep not for me." When he came to the fire, he sate down for very weakness upon the ground. There was present one of the presidents named May, who condemned Henry to be burned, pronouncing this sentence upon him :

" Forasmuch as this thief hath wickedly preached against the worship of our blessed Lady, by the commandment and sufferance of our reverend father in Christ, the bishop of Bremen, and my lord, I condemn him here to be burned and consumed with fire." Henry answered, " I have done no such thing:" and, lifting up his hands towards Heaven, he said, " O Lord, forgive them, for they offend ignorantly, not knowing what they do : thy name, O Almighty God, is holy."

In the mean time a woman, the wife of Jungar, and sister of Peter Hannus, offered herself to suffer a thousand stripes, and to give them much money, if they would stay the process, and keep him in prison, until that he could plead his cause before the whole convocation of the country. When they had heard these words, they waxed more mad, and threw the woman down under their feet, and trod upon her, and beat Henry unmercifully. One of them struck him behind on the head with a sharp dagger. John Holmes, of the new church, struck him with a mace. Others thrust him in the back, and in the arms. And this was not done only once or twice, but as often as he began to speak. Master Gunter cried out, encouraging them, saying, " Go to, boldly, good fellows, truly God is present with us."

After this, he brought a Franciscan friar to Henry,

that he should confess to him. Henry asked him in this manner ; " Brother, when have I done you an injury, either by word or deed, or when did I ever provoke you to anger ?" " Never," said the friar. " What then should I confess to you," said he, " that you think you might forgive me ?" The friar, being affected at these words, departed. The fire as often as it was kindled, would not burn. However they satisfied their minds upon him, by striking and pricking him with all kinds of weapons. Henry standing in the meantime in his shirt before all this rude people ; at last, having got a ladder, they bound him to it. And when he began to pray, and to repeat his creed, one struck him upon the face with his fist, saying, " Thou shalt first be burnt, and afterwards pray and prate as much as thou wilt." Then another treading upon his breast, bound his neck so hard to a step of the ladder, that the blood gushed out of his mouth and nose.

After he was bound to the ladder, he was set upright. Then one running to him, set his halbert for the ladder to lean against, but the ladder, slipping away from the point of the halbert, caused that the halbert struck him through the body. Then they cast this good man, ladder and all upon the wood. Then John Holmes ran to him, and struck him with a mace upon the breast, till he was dead and stirred no more. Afterwards they roasted him upon the coals ; for the wood, as often as it was set on fire, would not burn out. And thus this godly preacher finished his martyrdom, A.D. 1524.

About the same time many other godly persons, and such as feared God, for the testimony of the gospel, were thrown into the Rhine, and into other rivers, where their bodies were afterwards found, and taken up. Also in the town of Diethmar another faithful saint of God, named John, suffered the like martyrdom. Thus these two blessed and constant martyrs, as two shining lights set up by God, in testimony of his truth, offered up the sacrifice of their confession sealed with their blood, in a sweet savour unto God.

At the town of Hala likewise, another preacher named George, for ministering the sacrament of the Lord's Supper in both kinds, i. e. in both bread and wine, was martyred by the monks and friars.

At Prague also, in Bohemia, another, for changing his monkery into matrimony, did suffer in like manner. Ex Lud. Rab.

In the same year, 1524, Oct. 22, the town of Miltenberg in Germany was taken and ransacked, and several of the inhabitants slain, and many imprisoned for maintaining and keeping with them Carolostad as their preacher.

In the same catalogue of holy martyrs is to be placed Gasper Tamber, and also another named George, who were both burned at Vienna.

The lamentable Martyrdom of John Clerk, of Melden in France.

Melden is a city in France, ten miles from Paris, where John Clerk was apprehended, A.D. 1523, for setting up upon the church door a writing against the pope's pardons lately sent there from Rome, in which he named the pope to be antichrist, for which his punishment was this, that three several days he should be whipped and afterwards have a mark branded on his forehead, as a note of infamy. His mother being a christian woman, although her husband was an adversary, when she beheld her son thus piteously scourged, and ignominiously deformed in the face, constantly and boldly encouraged her son, crying with a loud voice, " Blessed be Christ, and welcome be these prints and marks."

After this punishment, John went to Metz, where he remained at his trade, being a wool-carder. The people of that city used to go, on a certain day to the suburbs to worship certain blind idols near by, after an old custom amongst them ; so he, being inflamed with zeal, went out of the city on the preceding day, to the place where the images were, and broke them all in pieces. The next day, when the canons, priests, and monks, keeping their old custom, had brought with them the people out of the city to the place of idolatry, to worship as they were wont, they found all their blocks and stocks broken upon the ground. They were enraged at this, and seized John Clarke, who confessed the act. The people, being not yet acquainted with that kind of doctrine, were wonderfully moved against him, crying out upon him in a great rage. He was soon tried and condemned, and led to the place of execution, where he sustained extreme torments. For first his hand was cut off from his right arm, then his nose with sharp pincers was violently plucked from his face; after that both his arms and his paps were likewise plucked and drawn with the same instrument. To all those who stood by it was an horror to behold the grievous and doleful sight of his pains: again to behold his patience, or rather the grace of God giving him the gift to suffer, it was a wonder. Thus quietly and constantly he endured in his torments, pronouncing, or in a manner singing the verses of the hundred and fifteenth Psalm: "Their idols are silver and gold, the work of man's hand," &c. His rent body was committed to the fire and consumed. This was about A.D. 1524.

John Castellane.

In A.D. 1524, Master John Castellane, born at Tournay, a doctor of divinity, after he was called to the knowledge of God, and had become a true preacher of his word, and had preached in France, and had laid some foundation of the doctrine of the gospel in the town of Metz, in returning from thence was taken prisoner by the cardinal of Lorraine's servants, by whom he was carried to the castle of Nommenie; at this the citizens of Metz took great displeasure, and were grievously offended to have their preacher apprehended and imprisoned, so they took some of the cardinal's subjects and kept them prisoners. John Castellane was most cruelly handled from the fourth day of May until the twelfth day of January; during all which time he persevered constantly in the doctrine of the Son of God. Thence he was carried to the castle of Vike, persevering constantly in the profession of the same doctrine; so that they proceeded to the sentence of his degradation, that he might be delivered over to the secular power. And as the form of the sentence and process of degrading is remarkable, we have thought good to annex it here to shew the horrible blasphemies joined with gross and brutish subtlety in those high mysteries which the enemies of the truth use in their processes against the children of God, whereby every man, even the most ignorant, may perceive the horrible blindness that these papists are blinded with.

The Sentence of Degradation.

"Concerning the process inquisitory, formed and given in form of an accusation against thee John Castellane, priest and religious man of the friars Eremites of the order of St. Augustine, and understanding likewise thy confession, which thou hast made of thine own good will, of maintaining false and erroneous doctrine; and marking also besides this, the godly admonitions, and charitable exhortations which we made unto thee in the town of Metz, which thou like unto the adder hast refused and given no ear unto; also considering thine answers made and reiterated to interrogatories, by means of thine oath, in which thou hast devilishly hidden and kept back not only the truth, but also, following the example of Cain, hast refused to confess thy sins and mischievous offences. And finally, hearing the great number of witnesses sworn and examined against thee, their persons and depositions diligently considered, and all other things worthy of consideration being justly examined, the Reverend Master Nicholas Savin, doctor of divinity, and inquisitor of the faith, assistant unto us, hath entered process against thee, and given full information thereof; this our purpose and intent being also communicated unto divers masters and doctors both of the civil and canon laws here present, which have subscribed and signed thereto, whereby it appeareth, that

thou John Castellane hast oftentimes, and in divers places, openly and manifestly spread abroad and taught many erroneous propositions, full of the heresy of Luther, contrary and against the catholic faith, and the verity of the gospel, and the holy apostolic see, and so accursedly looked back and turned thy face, that thou art found to be a liar before almighty God. It is ordained by the sacred rules of the canon law, that such as through the sharp darts of their venomous tongue do pervert the scriptures, and go about with all their power to corrupt and infect the souls of the faithful, should be punished and corrected with most sharp correction, to the end that others should be afraid to attempt the like, and apply themselves the better to the study of christian concord, through the example set before their eyes, as well of severity as of clemency. For these causes, and others rising upon the said process, by the apostolic authority, and also the authority of our said reverend lord the cardinal, which we do use in this our sentence definitive, which we sitting in our judgment-seat declare in these writings, having God only before our eyes, and surely considering, that what measures we mete unto others, the same shall be measured to us again. We pronounce and declare sententially and definitively thee John Castellane, being here present before us, and judge thee because of thy deserts, to be excommunicated with the greatest excommunication, and therewithal to be culpable of treason against the divine majesty, and a mortal enemy of the catholic faith and truth of the gospel; also to be a manifest heretic, and a follower and partaker of the execrable ¹cruelty of Martin Luther, a stirrer up of old heresies already condemned; and therefore as thou oughtest to be deposed and deprived of all priestly honour and dignity, of all thy orders, of thy shaving and religious habit, also of thy ecclesiastical benefices, if thou hast any, and from all privilege of the clergy. So we here presently do depose, deprive, and separate thee, as a rotten member, from the communion and company of all the faithful; and being so deprived, we judge that thou oughtest to be actually degraded; that done, we leave thee unto the secular powers, committing the degradation and actual execution of this our sentence unto the reverend lord and bishop here present, with the authority and commandment aforesaid."

This sentence being thus ended with their sermon also, the bishop of Nicopolis sitting in pontificalibus in the judgment-seat, being a suffragan of Metz, with the clergy, nobles, and people about him, proceeded to the degrading (as they called it) of John Castellane. Thus John Castellane being prepared and made ready for his degradation by the officers of the bishop, was apparelled in his priestly attire, and afterwards brought forth from the chapel by the priests, with all his priestly ornaments upon him, and holding his hands together, he knelt down before the bishop. Then the officers gave him the chalice in his hand, with wine and water, the patine and the host; all which things the bishop who degraded him, took from him, saying, "We take away from thee, or command to be taken from thee, all power to offer sacrifice unto God, and to say mass, as well for the quick as the dead."

Moreover, the bishop scraped the nails of both his hands with a piece of glass, saying, "By this scraping we take away from thee all power to sacrifice, to consecrate, and to bless, which thou hast received by the anointing of thy hands." Then he took away from him the chesile, saying, "We do deprive thee of this priestly ornament, which signifies charity; for certainly thou hast forsaken the same, and all innocency." Then taking away the stole, he said, "Thou hast villanously rejected and despised the sign of our Lord, which is represented by this stole; wherefore we take it away from thee, and make thee unable to exercise and use the office of priesthood, and all other things appertaining to priesthood." The degradation of the order of priest-

---

(1) If Luther be to be noted of cruelty, who teacheth all men, and killeth no man, what then is to be noted in the pope, who killeth all God's children and teacheth none?—Foxe.

hood being thus ended, they proceeded to the order of deacon. Then the ministers gave him the book of the gospels, which the bishop took away, saying, "We take away from thee all power to read the gospels in the church of God, for it appertains only to such as are worthy." After this he spoiled him of the dalmatike, which is the vesture that the deacons use, saying, "We deprive thee of this Levitical order; for thou hast not fulfilled thy ministry and office." After this the bishop took away the stole from behind his back, saying, "We justly take away from thee the white stole which thou didst receive undefiled, which also thou oughtest to have carried in the presence of our Lord; and to the end that the people dedicated unto the name of Christ, may take example by thee, we prohibit thee any more to exercise or use the office of deaconship. Then they proceeded to degrade him from the subdeaconship, and taking away from him the book of the epistles, and his subdeacon's vesture, deposed him from reading of the epistles in the church of God: and so proceeding to all the other orders, degraded him from the order of Benet and Bollet, from the order of exorcist, from the lectorship, and last of all, from the office of door-keeper, taking from him the keys, and commanding him hereafter not to open or shut the vestry, nor to ring any more bells in the church. That done, the bishop went forward to degrade him from his first shaving, and taking away his surplice, said, "By the authority of God Almighty, the Father, the Son, and the Holy Ghost, and by our authority we take away from thee all clerical habit, and despoil thee of all ornament of religion: also, we depose and degrade thee of all order, benefit, and privilege of the clergy, and as one unworthy of that profession, we commit thee to the servitude and ignominy of the secular state." Then the bishop took the shears and began to clip his head, saying in this manner, "We cast thee out as an unthankful child of the Lord's heritage, whereunto thou wast called, and take away from thy head the crown, which is the royal sign of priesthood, through thine own wickedness and malice." The bishop also added these words: "That which thou hast sung with thy mouth, thou hast not believed with thy heart, nor accomplished in work, wherefore we take from thee the office of singing in the church of God."

The degrading being thus ended, the procurator fiscal of the court and city of Metz, required of the notary an instrument or copy of the degrading; then the ministers of the bishop stripped him of his clerical habit, and put upon him the apparel of a secular man. That done, the bishop that degraded him proceeded no further, but said, "We pronounce that the secular court shall receive thee into their charge, being thus degraded of all clerical honour and privilege."

Then the bishop, after a manner, intreated the secular judge for him, saying "My lord judge, we pray you as heartily as we can, for the love of God, and from tender pity and mercy, and for respect of our prayers, that you will not in any point do any thing that shall be hurtful to this miserable man, or tending to his death, or maiming of his body." These things being thus done, the secular judge of the town of Vike, confirming the sentence, condemned Mr. John Castellane to be burned, which death he suffered on the twelfth day of January, 1525, with such a constancy, that not only a great company of ignorant people were thereby drawn to the knowledge of the truth, but also a great number who had already some knowledge of it, were greatly confirmed by his constant valiant death.

John Diazius, a Spaniard, martyred, A.D. 1546.

John Diazius, a Spaniard, having been at Paris thirteen years, returned from thence to Geneva, then to Basil, and afterwards to Strasburg; from whence he was sent ambassador with Bucer and others, to the council at Ratisbon, where, talking with Peter Malvenda, the pope's factor, he stated his views of religion to him, so that Malvenda wrote to the friar, who was the emperor's confessor, about him; at the reading of which letters, Marquina was present. And so Alphonso Diazius,

brother to John Diazius, one of the pope's lawyers in Rome, learned the opinion of his brother John.

After the council of Ratisbon, John Diazius was occupied in Germany in the printing of Bucer's book, and his brother Alphonso having come from Rome to Ratisbon, where Malvenda was, and having brought with him a notorious ruffian or assassin belonging to the city of Rome, Malvenda and Alphonso consulting about their devilish purpose, laboured to ascertain from the friends of Diazius where he was to be found; hereof Alphonso and the homicide having knowledge by certain of his secret friends, pretending great matters of importance, came to Newburgh, where Diazius was printing of Bucer's book. Having succeeded in this they came to him, and after long debating on religion between the two brothers, Alphonso seeing the heart of his brother John, planted so constantly on the sure rock of God's truth, that he could not be moved from his opinion, or persuaded to ride in his company (being so advised by Bucer and his friends), pretended to take his leave of his brother in a friendly spirit, and to depart; but shortly afterwards, he returned secretly with his assassin, and on the way they purchased a hatchet.

When this was done, Alphonso sends his man in disguise with letters to his brother, he himself following afterwards. And as John Diazius in the morning was rising out of his bed to read the letters, the man with his hatchet clove his head to the brains, leaving the hatchet in his head; and so he and Alphonso took to their horses, which stood without the city gate, with as much speed as they could. The people of Newburgh hearing of the horrible act, sent out horsemen after them, who, coming to Augsburgh, and hearing that the murderers had passed through, gave up the pursuit, and returned. One in the company, however, more zealous than the rest, would not return, but pursued them still, and in the city of Oenipont, caused them to be arrested and put into prison. Otto, the elector Palatine, hearing of their arrest, writes to the magistrates of Oenipont for judgment; but through the intrigues of the papists, and the crafty lawyers, the judicial sentence was so delayed, from day to day, then from hour to hour, that the emperor's letters came at last, requiring the matter to be reserved to his hearing. And thus the terrible murder of Cain and his fellow, was bolstered up by the papists. The like of which, from the memory of man, was never heard of since the first example of Cain, who slew his own brother Abel. But although true judgment in this world be perverted, yet such bloody Cains, with their wilful murder, shall not escape the hands of Him who shall judge truly both the committers, and the bolsterers up of all mischievous wickedness.

In 1546, Charles, the emperor, held an armed council at Augsburgh, after his victory in Germany. Where some endeavoured to make concord between the gospel of Christ, and the traditions of the pope, that is, to make a medley of them both, and so framed a new form of religion, called the Interim. Upon this began a new form of persecution in Germany. For the emperor proceeded strictly against those who would not receive the Interim, intending to have overcome the reformers, but the Lord disappointed his purpose.

Among those who withstood this Interim, besides others, were the citizens of Constance. For which three thousand Spaniards came by night against the town of Constance, where they killed three of the watchmen, who watching in the suburbs, went to ascertain the noise which they heard in the woods. The device of the Spaniards was, that when the citizens were at the sermon, suddenly to set upon the city and take it. But, as the Lord would, some began to suspect it in the night, so that the citizens had intelligence and were in readiness. When the morning came, the Spaniards were at the gate to break into the city. But being driven from thence, and their captain Alphonso slain, they went to the bridge over the Rhine. But being beat also from thence, and a great number of them drowned in the river, the Spaniards broke down the bridge to prevent pursuit.

At the same time many godly ministers of the churches in Germany, were in great danger, especially such as refused to receive the Interim ; of whom some were cast into prison. In which number of prisoners was Martin Frectius, with four other preachers, also his brother George, for coming to his house to comfort him. Musculus at the same time, with other preachers, went from Augsburgh, Brentius from Halle, Blaurerus from Constance, Bucer from Strasburg.

It would fill another volume, to include the acts and histories of all who in other countries suffered for the gospel. But praised be the Lord, every region almost has its own historian, who has sufficiently discharged that duty ; so that I shall the less need to overcharge this volume : it shall suffice to collect three or four histories, recorded by Oecolampadius and the rest, to bring it into a brief table, and so I shall return to occupy myself with our own matters at home.

Wolfgang Schuch, a German in Lotharing, Martyr.

Wolfgang Schuch, coming to St. Hyppolite, a town in Lotharing, and being received as their pastor, laboured to extirpate out of the hearts of the people idolatry and superstition ; which, through the grace of Christ working with him, he in a short time brought to pass ; so that the observance of Lent, images, and all idols, with the abomination also of the mass, was utterly abolished. It was not long before rumour of this came to the duke Anthony, prince of Lorraine, (under whose dominion they were,) through the report of the adversaries misrepresenting these people ; as, though they, in relinquishing the doctrine and faction of the pope, went about to reject and shake off the authority of princes and all governors. By means of which sinister report they incensed the prince so, that he threatened to destroy the town with sword and fire. Wolfgang being informed of this, wrote to the duke's uncle, in a most humble and obedient way, in defence both of his ministry, of his doctrine, and of the whole cause of the Gospel.

In which epistle he excused the people, and said, that those slanderous reporters were more worthy to be punished for their false rumours and forged slanders. And he also opened and explained the cause of the Gospel, and of our salvation, as consisting only in the free grace of God, through faith in Christ his Son, comparing also the same doctrine of the gospel, with the doctrine of the church of Rome.

That done, he touched upon our obedience, honour, and worship, which first we owe to God and to Christ, next under him to the princes, whom God hath raised up and endued with authority, and to whom they offered themselves now, and at all times, most ready with all service and duty, &c.

But with this epistle Wolfgang availed nothing ; so, when he saw no other remedy, rather than the town should come into any danger on his account, the good man, of his own accord, rendered a confession of his doctrine, and delivered the town from danger, by taking all the danger upon himself.

As soon as he was come to Nantz, hands were immediately laid on him, and he was cast into a stinking prison, where he was sharply and bitterly handled. In that prison he continued for the space of a whole year, yet would not be moved from his constancy, neither with the straightness of the prison, nor with the harshness of his keepers, nor yet with the compassion of his wife and children, of which he had about six or seven. Then was he removed to the house of the Gray Friars, where he learnedly confuted all that stood against him.

There was a friar named Bonaventure, provincial of that order, whose person was monstrously overgrown, but much more gross in blind ignorance, and a man utterly rude, a contemner of all civility and honesty ; who, being long confessor to the duke, and of great authority in Lorraine, as he was an enemy to virtue and learning, so was he ever persuading the duke, to banish out of the court and country, all learned men. The sum of all his divinity was this, that it was sufficient to salvation only, to know the Pater Noster, (Our Father,) and Ave Maria, (Hail, Mary !) And thus was the duke brought up and trained, and in nothing else, as the duke himself ofttimes confessed. This Bonaventure being judge, where

Wolfgang disputed, or was examined, had nothing else in his mouth, but "Thou heretic, Judas, Beelzebub, &c." Wolfgang bearing patiently those injuries which referred to himself, proceeded mightily in his disputation by the scriptures, confuting or rather confounding his adversaries ; who, being no otherwise able to make their party good, took his bible, with his notes in the margin, into their monastery, and burned it ! At the last disputation duke Anthony himself was present, altering his apparel, so that he might not be known, who, although he understood not Wolfgang, who spoke in Latin, yet, perceiving him to be bold and constant in his doctrine, gave sentence that he should be burned, because he denied the church and sacrifice of the mass. Wolfgang hearing the sentence of his condemnation, began to sing the hundred and twenty-second psalm.

As he was led to the place of execution, and when passing by the house of the Gray Friars, Bonaventure, who was sitting at the door, cried out to him, "Thou heretic, do thy reverence here to God, and to our lady, and to his holy saints," shewing to him the idols standing at the Friars' gate. To whom Wolfgang answered, "Thou hypocrite, thou painted wall, the Lord shall destroy thee, and bring all thy false dissimulation to light." When they were come to the place of his martyrdom, first his books were thrown into the fire ; then they asked him, "Whether he would have his pain diminished and shortened ?" He said, "No," bidding them to do their will, "for," said he, "as God has been with me hitherto, so I trust now he will not leave me, when I shall have most need of him ;" concluding his words thus, "that they should put the sentence in execution." And so, beginning to sing the fifty-first psalm, he entered into the place, heaped up with fagots and wood, continuing to sing his psalm, till the smoke and flame took from him both his voice and life.

The singular virtue, constancy, and learning of this blessed man, as it refreshed and greatly edified the hearts of many good men, so it astonished the minds of his adversaries, and wrought to their confusion.

John Huglein, Martyr.

John Huglein, a priest, was burned at Merspurg, (A.D. 1526,) by the bishop of Constance, because he did not hold the bishop of Rome's doctrine in all points.

George Carpenter, Martyr.

On the 8th of February, (A.D. 1527,) George Carpenter of Emering, was burned in Munchen, in Bavaria. When he came before the council his offences were read, contained in four articles :—

First, That he did not believe that a priest could forgive a man's sins.

Secondly, That he did not believe that a man could call God out of heaven.

Thirdly, That he did not believe that God was in the bread, which the priest hangs over the altar, but that it was the bread of the Lord.

Fourthly, That he did not believe that the very element of the water itself in baptism gives grace.

Which four articles he refused to recant. Then came to him a certain schoolmaster, saying, "My friend George, dost thou not fear the death and punishment which thou must suffer ? If thou wert let go, wouldst thou return to thy wife and children ?" He answered ; "If I were at liberty, whither should I rather go, than to my wife and beloved children ?" Then said the schoolmaster, "Revoke your former opinion, and you shall be set at liberty." George answered, "My wife and my children are so dearly loved by me, that they cannot be bought from me for all the riches and possessions of the duke of Bavaria ; but for the love of the Lord God I will willingly forsake them." When he was led to the place of execution, the schoolmaster spake to him again, saying, "Good George, believe in the sacrament of the altar ; do not affirm it to be only a *sign*." He answered, "I believe this sacrament to be *a sign* of the body of Jesus Christ offered upon the cross for us." Then said the schoolmaster, "What dost thou mean, that thou dost so little esteem baptism, knowing that Christ suffered himself to be baptised in Jordan?" He answered, and shewed the true use of baptism, and the end why Christ was baptised in Jordan, and how necessary it was that Christ should die and suffer upon the cross. "The same Christ," said he, "will I confess this day before the whole world; for he is my Saviour, and in him I believe."

After this came one Master Conrade Scheter, the vicar of the Cathedral church, saying, "George, if thou wilt not believe the sacrament, yet put all thy trust in God, and say, ' I trust my cause to be good and true, but if I should err, truly I would be sorry and repent.' " George Carpenter answered, "God, suffer me not to err, I beseech thee." Then Master Conrade began the Lord's prayer :—" Our Father which art in heaven." When Carpenter answered, " Truly thou art our Father, and no other, this day I trust to be with thee." Then Master Conrade went forward with the prayer, saying, " Hallowed be thy name." Carpenter answered, " O, my God, how little is thy name hallowed in this world !" Then said Conrade, " Thy kingdom come." Carpenter answered, " Let thy kingdom come this day to me, that I also may come to thy kingdom." Then said Conrade, " Thy will be done in earth, as it is in heaven." Carpenter answered, "For this cause, O Father ! am I now here, that thy will might be fulfilled, and not mine." Then said Conrade, "Give us this day our daily bread." Carpenter answered, " The only living bread, Jesus Christ, shall be my food." Then said Conrade, " And forgive us our trespasses, as we forgive them that trespass against us." Carpenter answered, "With a willing mind do I forgive all men, both my friends and adversaries." Then said Master Conrade, " And lead us not into temptation, but deliver us from all evil." Carpenter answered, " O, my Lord ! without doubt thou shalt deliver me, for upon thee only have I laid all my hope." Then he began to rehearse the creed, saying, " I believe in God the Father Almighty." Carpenter answered, "O, my God ! in thee alone do I trust; in thee, only, is all my confidence, and upon no other creature." In this manner he answered to every word. His answers, if they should be described at length, would be too long. The schoolmaster said, " Dost thou believe so truly and constantly in thy Lord and God with thy heart, as thou dost cheerfully seem to confess him with thy mouth ?" He answered, " It were a very hard matter for me, if I, who am ready here to suffer death, should not believe that with my heart, which I openly profess with my mouth ; for I knew before that I must suffer persecution if I would cleave unto Christ, who saith, 'Where thy treasure is, there will thy heart be also.' " Then said Master Conrade to him, " Dost thou think it necessary after thy death, that any man should pray for thee, or say mass for thee ?" He answered, " So long as the soul is joined to the body, pray God for me, that he will give me grace and patience, with all humility, to suffer the pains of death with a true christian faith ; but when the soul is separate from the body, then I have no more need of your prayers." Then he was desired by certain christian brethren, that, as soon as he was cast into the fire, he should give some sign or token what his faith was. He answered, " This shall be my sign and token, that so long as I can open my mouth, I will not cease to call upon the name of Jesus."

Behold what an incredible constancy was in this godly man. His face and countenance never changed colour, but he went cheerfully to the fire. " In the midst of the town this day," said he, "will I confess my God before the whole world." When he was laid upon the ladder, and after the executioner had put a bag of gunpowder about his neck, he said, " Let it be so, in the name of the Father, and of the Son, and of the Holy Ghost." When they thrust him into the fire, he with a loud voice cried out, " Jesus ! Jesus !" Then the executioner turned him over, and again he cried, " Jesus ! Jesus !" and joyfully yielded up his spirit.

Leonard Keyser.

Here also is not to be passed over the wonderful constancy of Mr. Leonard Keyser, of Bavaria, who was burned for the gospel. This man, being at his study in Wittenburg, was sent for by his brethren, who certified to him, that if he ever wished to see his father alive, he should come with speed, which he did. He was scarcely come thither, when, by the command of the bishop of Passaw, he was taken. The articles upon which he was accused, and for which he was most cruelly put to death, and shed his blood for the testimony of the truth, were these :—

That faith only justifies.

That works are the fruits of faith.

That the mass is no sacrifice or oblation.

That he rejected confession, satisfaction, the vow of chastity, purgatory, difference of days, and affirmed only two sacraments, and denied invocation of saints.

Sentence was given against him, that he should be degraded, and put into the hands of the secular power. The good and blessed martyr, early in the morning, being rounded and shaven, and clothed in a short gown, and a black cap set upon his head, all cut and jagged, was delivered to the officer. As he was led out of the town to the place where he was to suffer, he boldly spake, turning his head first on the one side, and then on the other, saying, " O Lord Jesus, remain with me, sustain, and help me, and give me force and power."

Then the wood was made ready, and he began to cry with a loud voice, " O Jesus, I am thine, have mercy upon me, and save me ;" and then he felt the fire begin sharply under his feet, his hands, and about his head : and because the fire was not great enough, the executioner plucked the body, half burnt, with a long hook from under the wood. Then he made a great hole in the body, through which he thrust a stake, and cast him again into the fire. This was August 16, A.D. 1526.

Wendelmuta, Martyr.

In Holland also, in the year 1527, was martyred and burned a good and virtuous widow, named Wendelmuta. This widow receiving to her heart the brightness of God's grace, by the appearing of the gospel, was apprehended and committed to the castle of Werden, and shortly after was brought to appear at the general sessions of that country. Several monks were appointed to talk with her, that they might convince her, and win her to recant ; but she constantly persisting in the truth would not be removed. Many also of her kindred were suffered to persuade with her. Among whom there was a noble matron, who loved and favoured dearly the widow in prison. This matron coming, and communing with her, said, " My Wendelmuta, why dost thou not keep silence, and think secretly in thine heart these things which thou believest, that thou mayest prolong here thy days and life ?" She answered, " Ah, you know not what you say. It is written, ' With the heart man believeth unto righteousness ; and with the mouth confession is made unto salvation.' " (Rom. x. 10.) And thus remaining firm and steadfast in her belief and confession, the twentieth day of November she was condemned by sentence as an heretic, to be burned to ashes, and her goods to be confiscated, she taking the sentence of her condemnation mildly and quietly.

After she came to the place where she was to be executed, a monk had brought out a cross, desiring her to kiss and worship her God. " I worship," said she, " no wooden god, but only that God who is in heaven :" and so with a joyful countenance she went to the stake. Then taking the powder, and laying it to her breast, she gave her neck willingly to be bound, and with an ardent prayer commending herself to the hands of God. When the time came that she should be strangled, she modestly closed her eyes, and bowed down her head as one that would take a sleep. The fire then was put to the wood, and she, being strangled, was burned afterwards to ashes, instead of this life, to get the immortal crown in heaven, (A.D. 1527.)

Peter Flistedin, and Adolphus Clarebach.

In the number of these German martyrs, are also Peter Flistedin and Adolphus Clarebach, two men of singular learning, and knowledge of God's holy word. In the year 1529, because they dissented from the papists in divers points, and especially on the supper of the Lord, and the pope's other traditions and ceremonies, after they had endured imprisonment a year and a half by the command of the archbishop and senate, they were put to death and burned in Cologne, not without the great grief and lamentation of many good christians; all the fault being put upon certain divines, who at that time preached that the punishment and death of certain wicked persons should pacify the wrath of God, which then plagued Germany with a strange disease, for at that season the sweating sickness mortally raged throughout all Germany.

A LIST OF THE NAMES AND CAUSES OF THE MARTYRS,

WHO GAVE THEIR LIVES FOR THE TESTIMONY OF THE GOSPEL, IN GERMANY, FRANCE, SPAIN, ITALY, AND OTHER FOREIGN COUNTRIES, SINCE LUTHER'S TIME.

THE MARTYRS OF GERMANY.

One Nicholas of Antwerp.

The curate of Melza, by Antwerp, used to preach to a great number of people without that town ; and the emperor hearing of it, gave leave to take the uppermost garment of all who came to hear, and offered thirty guilders to whoever would take the priest. Afterwards, when the people were gathered, and the curate not there, this Nicholas stepped up in his place and preached. Wherefore he, being apprehended, was put in a sack, and drowned at Antwerp, 1524.

Joan Pistorius, a learned man of Holland.

Pistorius was a priest ; then he married, and after that he preached against the mass and pardons, and against the subtle abuses of priests. He was committed to prison with ten malefactors, whom he comforted; and to one, being half naked, and in danger of cold, he gave his gown. His father visiting him in prison, did not dissuade him, but bade him be constant. At last he was condemned, and degraded, having a fool's coat put upon him. His fellow-prisoners at his death sung, "We praise thee," &c. Coming to the stake, he was first strangled, and then burned, saying at his death, " O death, where is thy sting? O grave, where is thy victory ?" (1 Cor. xv. 55.)

Matthias Weibell, Schoolmaster.

For saying somewhat against the abbott's first mass, and against the carrying about relics, he was hanged in Suevia.

A certain godly Priest.

This priest being commanded to come and give good advice to sixteen countrymen that were about to be beheaded, was afterwards bid himself to kneel down to have his head cut off, no cause nor condemnation further being laid against him, but only of mere hatred against the gospel.

George Scherter.

After this George had instructed the people in knowledge of the gospel in Rastadt, he was accused and put in prison, where he wrote a confession of his faith. He was condemned to be burned alive; but means were made that first his head should be cut off, and his body afterwards cast into the fire.

Henry Fleming, A.D. 1535.

This Henry, a friar, of Flanders, forsook his habit, and married a wife. Being offered life if he would confess his wife to be a harlot, refused to do so, and was burnt at Tournay.

Twenty-eight Christian Men and Women of Louvaine; Paul a Priest; two aged Women, at Antonia. Two Men at Louvaine. A.D. 1543.

When some of the city of Louvaine were suspected of Lutheranism, the emperor's procurator came from Brussels to make inquisition. After inquisition, bands of armed men came and beset their houses in the night, many were taken in their beds, plucked from their wives and children, and divided into different prisons. Through terror many citizens returned again to idolatry. But there were twenty-eight who remained constant in that persecution. The doctors of Louvaine, especially the inquisitor, came and disputed with them, thinking either to confound them, or to convert them. But the Spirit of the Lord wrought so strongly with his saints, that they went away rather confounded themselves.

Among them there was one Paul, a priest, about the age of sixty years ; the rectors, with their colleagues, brought him out of prison to the Austin friars, where he was degraded. But at length for fear of death he began to stagger in his confession, and so was condemned to perpetual prison, in a dark and stinking dungeon, where he was suffered neither to read nor write, nor any man to come to him, and only to be fed with bread and water. There were two others who were put to the fire and burnt.

Then was an old man and two aged women condemned, the man to be beheaded, the two women to be buried alive, which death they suffered very cheerfully. Other prisoners, who were not condemned to death, were deprived of their goods, and commanded to come to the church in a white sheet, and there kneeling with a taper in their hand, to ask forgiveness ; and they who refused to do so, and to abjure the doctrine of Luther, were put to the fire.

Master Perseval at Louvaine, A.D. 1544.

Not long after this, one Master Perseval of the university of Louvaine, was thrown into prison for condemning certain popish superstitions, and speaking in commendation of the gospel. Then being accused of Lutheranism, he was adjudged to perpetual prison, there to be fed only with bread and water, which punishment he took patiently for Christ's sake. But what became of him no man could learn nor understand. Some think that he was starved to death, or that he was secretly drowned.

Justus Jusburg, at Brussels, A.D. 1544.

Justus Jusburg, a skinner of Louvaine, being suspected of Lutheranism, was found to have the New Testament in his house, and certain sermons of Luther, for which he was committed. There were at the same time in the prison, Egidius, and Francis Encenas, a Spaniard, who secretly came to him, and confirmed him in the cause of righteousness. Thus is the providence of the Lord never wanting to his saints in time of necessity. Shortly after the doctors and masters of Louvaine came to examine him touching religion, on the pope's supremacy, sacrifice of the mass, purgatory, and the sacrament. When he had answered plainly and boldly according to the scriptures, he was condemned to the fire ; but through intercession made to the queen, his burning was pardoned, and he was only beheaded.

Giles Tilleman, at Brussels, A.D. 1544.

This Giles was born in Brussels of honest parents. He began to receive the light of the gospel through the reading of the holy scriptures, and increased therein exceedingly. And as he was fervent in zeal, so he was humane, mild, and pitiful. Whatever he had, that necessity could spare, he gave away to the poor, and only lived by his trade. Some he refreshed with his meat; some with clothing; to some he gave his shoes; some he helped with household stuff; to others he ministered wholesome exhortation of good doctrine. One poor woman was brought to bed, and had no bed to lie upon, whereupon he brought his own bed to her, and was contented himself to lie upon straw.

Egidius, being detected by a priest, was taken at Louvaine for that religion which the pope calls heresy. And after having being detained eight months in prison, he was sent to Brussels to be judge, where he comforted some who were in prison, and exhorted them to the constancy of the truth and to the crown which was prepared for them.

Certain of the Gray friars sometimes were sent to him, but he would always desire them to depart from him: and when the friars at any time called him names, he held his peace at such personal injuries, that those blasphemers would say abroad, that he had a dumb devil in him. But when they talked of religion, there he spared not, but answered them fully by evidences of the scripture, so that many times they would depart wondering. At various times he might have escaped from the doors having been set open, but he would not bring his keeper into peril.

He was condemned to the fire, privately, contrary to the use of the country; for they durst not openly condemn him for fear of the people, so well was he beloved. When tidings of the sentence came to him, he gave hearty thanks unto God, that the hour was come when he might glorify the Lord.

Standing at the stake the blessed martyr, lifting up his eyes to heaven in the middle of the flame, died, to the great lamentation of all. So that after that time, when the friars would go about for their alms, the people would say, "It was not meet for them to receive alms with bloody hands."

Persecution at Ghent and Brussels, A.D. 1543, 1544.

When the Emperor Charles was in Ghent, the friars and doctors obtained, that the edict made against the Lutherans, might be read openly twice a-year. Which being obtained, great persecution followed; so that there was no city nor town in all Flanders, where some were not banished, or beheaded, or condemned to perpetual prison, or had not their goods confiscated: neither was there any respect of age or sex.

Afterwards the emperor coming to Brussels, there was terrible slaughter, and persecution of God's people, in Brabant, Hennegow, and Artoise; the horror and cruelty of which is almost incredible; so that at one time as good as two hundred men and women together were brought out of the country into the city, of whom some were drowned, some buried alive, some privately made away with, others sent to perpetual prison.

Martin Hœrblock, Fishmonger at Ghent, A.D. 1545.

This Martin, through a sermon of his parish priest, beginning to taste some workings of grace and repentance, went out of Ghent for the space of three months, seeking the company of godly christians, who used the reading of the scriptures: and being more instructed he returned again to the city of Ghent, where all his neighbours first began to marvel at the sudden change of this man. The Franciscans who knew him before, now seeing him so altered from their ways and superstition, and seeing him visit the captives in prison, to comfort them in persecution, and to confirm them in the word of God, they conspired against him, and seized and imprisoned him. The friars examined him in the sacrament, asking him why he was so earnest to have it in both kinds, seeing (said they) that it is but a naked sacrament, as you say? He answered, that the elements were naked, but the sacrament was not naked, as the elements of bread and wine being received after the institution of Christ, do now make a sacrament and a mystical representation of the Lord's body, communicating himself with our souls. And as touching the receiving in both kinds, because it is the institution of the Lord, Who is he (said Martin) that dare alter the same? Then was he brought before the council of Flanders. The causes laid against him were the sacrament, purgatory, and praying for the dead: and for these he was condemned and burned at Ghent, and all his goods confiscated. As he stood at the stake, a Franciscan friar said to him, "Martin, unless thou dost turn, thou shalt go from this fire to everlasting fire." "It is not in you," said Martin, "to judge." For this the friars were afterwards so hated, that many rhymes were written against them.

Nicholas Vanpoule, John de Buck and his wife, at Ghent, A.D. 1545.

The day after the burning of Martin, which was the ninth of May, these three also were burned for the same cause, for which the other was condemned and burned the day before; but only that the woman was buried alive. All of whom took their martyrdom with much cheerfulness.

Ursula, and Maria, at Delden, A.D. 1545.

Delden is a town in Lower Germany, three miles from Daventry, where these two virgins of noble parentage were burned. After diligently frequenting churches and sermons, and being instructed in the word of the Lord, they believed, that as the benefit of salvation comes only by our faith in Christ, all the other merchandise of the pope, which he sells to the people for money, was needless. Mary, being the younger, was put first into the fire; where she prayed ardently for her enemies, commending her soul to God. The judges greatly marvelled at her constancy.

Then they exhorted Ursula to turn, or if she would not, at least that she should require to be beheaded. She said, that she was guilty of no error, nor defended any thing, but what was consonant to the scripture, in which she trusted to persevere to the end. And as to the kind of punishment, she said, she feared not the fire, but rather would follow the example of her dear sister that went before.

Andrew Thiessen, Katharine his wife, Nicholas Thiessen, Francis Thiessen, brethren, at Mechlin, A.D. 1545.

Andrew Thiessen, citizen of Mechlin, had three sons and a daughter, whom he instructed diligently in the doctrine of the gospel, and despised the doings of popery. Being hated and persecuted of the friars and priest there, he went to England and there died. Francis and Nicholas his two sons went to Germany to study; and returning again to their mother, and sister, and younger brother, by diligent instruction brought them to the right knowledge of God's gospel: the parson there taking counsel together with William de Clerk, the head magistrate of the town of Mechlin, and others, agreed, that the mother with her four children should be sent to prison: where great labour was employed to reclaim them to their church. The two younger, being not yet settled either in years or doctrine, inclined to them, and were delivered. The mother, who would not consent, was condemned to perpetual prison. The other two, Francis and Nicholas, standing firmly to their confession, defended, that the catholic church was not the church of Rome; that the sacrament was to be ministered in both kinds; that auricular confession was to no purpose; that invocation of saints was to be left; that there was no purgatory. The friars they called hypocrites, and contemned their threatenings. The magistrates, after disputations, tried torments, to learn of them who was their master, and what companions they had. "Their master," they said, "was Christ which bare his cross before. Friends they had innumerable, and dispersed in all places." At last they were brought to the judges: their articles was read, and they were condemned to be burned. Coming to the place of execution, as they began to exhort the people, gags were thrust into their mouths, which they through vehemency in speaking thrust out again, desiring for the Lord's sake that they might have leave to speak. And so singing with a loud voice, "I believe in one God," &c. they were fastened to the stake, praying for their persecutors, and exhorting one another, to bear the fire patiently. The one feeling the flame to come to his beard, "Ah!" said he, "what a small pain is this, to be compared to the glory to come!" Thus the patient martyrs committed their spirit to the hands of God.

Marion, Wife of Adrian Taylor, Tournay, A.D. 1545.

In the same persecution was apprehended also one Adrian and Marion his wife. The cause of their trouble, as also of the others, was the emperor's decree made in the council of Worms against the Lutherans. Adrian, being not so strong a man, gave back from the truth, and was only beheaded; but his wife being stronger than a woman, withstood their threats, and therefore was enclosed in an iron grate and laid in the earth and buried alive, according to the usual punishment of that country for women.

Master Peter Bruley, Preacher, A.D. 1545.

Master Peter Bruley was preacher in the French church at Strasburg. At the earnest request of faithful brethren he came down to visit the lower countries about Artois and Tournay in Flanders; where he most diligently preached the word of God to the people in houses, the doors standing open.

When the magistrates of Tournay had shut the gates of the town, and had made search for him three days, he was privately let down the wall in a basket during the night; and, as he was let down to the ditch ready to take his way, one of them who let him down, leaning over the wall to bid him farewell, caused unawares a stone to slip out of the wall, which, falling upon him, broke his leg, by which he was heard by the watchmen complaining of his wound, and so was taken, giving thanks to God, by whose Providence he was there staid to serve the Lord in that place. So long as he remained in prison, he ceased not to fulfil the part of a diligent preacher, teaching, and confirming all that came to him in the word of grace. Being in prison he wrote his own confession and examination, and sent it to the brethren. He remained in prison four months. His sentence was given by the emperor's commissioners at Brussels, That he should be burned to ashes, and his ashes thrown into the river. He cheerfully and constantly took his martyrdom, and suffered it.

Peter Miocius, Bergiban, Tournay, A.D. 1545.

The coming of Master Peter Bruley into the country of Flanders, did much good among the brethren. This Peter, before he was called to the gospel, had led a wicked life, but after the gospel began to work in him, it altered his character so much, that he excelled all other men in godly zeal and virtue. In his first examination he was asked, "Whether he was one of the scholars of Peter Bruley?" He said he was, and that he had received much fruit by his doctrine. "Wilt thou then defend his doctrine?" said they. "Yea," said he, "for it is consonant both to the Old Testament and to the New." And for this he was let down into a deep dungeon under the castle-ditch, full of toads and filthy vermin. Shortly afterwards the senate, with certain friars, came to examine him, to see whether they could convert him. He answered and said, "That when he had lived such an ungodly life, they never spake a word against him: but now, for favouring the word of God, they sought his blood."

There was also one Bergiban in the prison at the same time, who had been an active man in the gospel, before the coming of Bruley; but the commissioners having threatened him with cruel torments, and horror of death, he began by little and little to waver and shrink from the truth, at the fair words of the false friars and priests, who promised to have his punishment changed into being beheaded, and at this he was fain to grant their requests: upon which the adversaries taking their advantage, came to Miocius, and told them of Bergiban's retractation, wishing him to do the like. But he stoutly persisting in the truth, endured to the fire, where, having powder put to his breast, he was dispatched. The friars, hearing the crack of the powder upon his breast, told the people, that the devil came out of him and carried away his soul!

A Priest of Germany.

John Gastius writes of a certain prince, but does not name him, who put out the eyes of a priest in Germany for no other cause than that he said the mass was no sacrifice, in the sense in which many priests take it. Neither did the cruel prince immediately put him to death, but first kept him in prison for a long time, afflicting him with torments. Then he was brought forth to be degraded, after a barbarous manner. First, they shaved the crown of his head, then rubbed it hard with salt, so that the blood came running down his shoulders. After that they raised and paired the tops of his fingers with cruel pain, that no savour of the holy oil might remain. At last the patient and godly martyr, four days after, yielded up his life and spirit.

A godly Priest in Hungary.

In Hungary a godly priest preached, that the eating of flesh is not prohibited in the scripture: for which the cruel bishop, after he had imprisoned him some weeks, caused him to be brought out, and his body to be tied over with hares, geese, and hens hanging round about him: and so the beastly bishop made dogs be set upon him, which cruelly rent and tore whatever they could catch: and thus the good minister of Christ, being driven about the city with the barking of dogs, died, and was martyred. But within a few days after, the impious bishop, by the stroke of God's just hand, fell sick and became mad, and so raving without sense or wit, died miserably.

Master Nicholas Finchman. Marion, Wife of Augustine, A.D. 1549.

Master Nicholas, and Barbara his wife; also Augustine a barber, and Marion his wife, after they had been at Geneva, came into Germany, to pass over into England. By the way coming to Hainault, Augustine desired Master Nicholas to come to Bruges to visit and comfort certain brethren there; which he willingly did. From thence they continued their journey toward England. But in the way Augustine and his wife, being known, were detected. Augustine escaped that time out of their hands, and could not be found. The soldiers then laying hands upon Nicholas and the two women, brought them back again to Tournay. In returning by the way, when Master Nicholas at the table gave thanks (as the manner is of the faithful) the wicked ruler scorning them, and swearing like a tyrant, said, "Now let us see, thou lewd heretic, whether thy God can deliver thee out of my hand." Nicholas answering again modestly, asked, "What had Christ ever offended him, that he with his blasphemous swearing did so tear him in pieces?" desiring him, "that if he had any thing to say against Christ, that he would rather wreak his anger upon his poor body, and let the Lord alone." After this, they bound their hands and feet, and laid them in the dungeon.

Nicholas shortly after was brought before the judges, and condemned to be burned to ashes. On which sentence Nicholas blessed the Lord, who had counted him worthy to be a witness in the cause of his dear and well-beloved Son, and then patiently taking his death, commended up his spirit unto God in the midst of the fire.

Marion, Wife of Augustine. A.D. 1549.

After the martyrdom of this Master Nicholas, Marion the wife of Augustine was called for. With her they had much talk about the manner and state of Geneva, asking her how the sacraments were administered there, and whether she had celebrated there the Lord's supper? She answered, that the sacraments there were celebrated after the Lord's institution, of which she was no celebrater, but a partaker. The sentence of her condemnation was, that she should be interred alive. When she was let down to the grave, kneeling, she desired the Lord to help her; and before she should be thrown down, she desired her face might be covered with a napkin or some linen cloth; being so covered, and the earth thrown upon her face and body, the executioner stamped upon her with his feet, till her breath was past.

Augustine the Husband of Marion, A.D. 1549.

We heard before how Augustine escaped at the taking of Nicholas and the two women, but having returned to the town of Beaumont in Hainault, he was known and detected to the magistrate. Being taken, he was examined, and valiantly standing to the defence of his doctrine, he answered his adversaries with great boldness.

Among others who came to him was the warden of the Gray friars, who persuaded him to relent, or he should be damned in hell-fire perpetually. Augustine answering said, "Prove that which you said by the authority of God's word, that a man may believe you. You say much, but you prove nothing, rather like a doctor of lies, than of truth," &c. At last, being condemned to be burnt, he was brought to the inn where he was to take horse; where was a certain gentleman, a stranger, who, drinking to him in a cup of wine, desired him to have pity upon himself; and if he would not favour his life, yet that he would favour his own soul. Augustine said, after he had thanked him for his good will, "What care I have," said he, "of my soul, you may see by this, that I had rather give my body to be burned, than to do that which was against my conscience." When the day of his martyrdom came, the people being offended at his constancy, cried out to have him drawn at a horse's tail in place of burning; but the Lord would not suffer that. In fine, being tied to the stake, and fire set to him, he prayed to the Lord, and so in the fire patiently departed.

A certain Woman at Augsburgh, A.D. 1550.

At Augsburgh a woman dwelling there, seeing a priest carry the host to a sick person with taper-light, as the manner is, asked him what he meant by going with candle-light at noon-day. For this she was apprehended, and in great danger, had it not been for the earnest suit and prayers of the women of that city, and at the intercession of Mary the emperor's sister.

Two Virgins in the Diocese of Bamberge. A.D. 1551.

In the diocese of Bamberge, two virgins were led out to slaughter, which they sustained with patient hearts and cheerful countenances. They had garlands of straw put on their heads on going to their martyrdom, on which one comforting the other said, "Seeing Christ for us bare a crown of thorns, why should we stick to bear a crown of straw? no doubt but the Lord will render us better than crowns of gold." Some said that they were anabaptists; and it might be, said Melancthon, that they had some fond opinion; yet they held, saith he, the foundation of the articles of our faith, and they died blessedly, in a good conscience, and knowledge of the Son of God. Few live without errors. Flatter not yourselves, thinking yourselves so clear that you cannot err.

Hostius, otherwise called George, at Ghent, A.D. 1555.

This Hostius had been in the French church in England, during the reign of King Edward. After the coming of Queen Mary, he went to Friesland, with his wife and children. From thence he came to Ghent, where he heard that there was a Black friar who used to preach good doctrine, and being desirous to hear him, he came to his sermon. The friar, contrary to his expectation, preached in defence of transubstantiation, at which his heart was so full that he could scarcely refrain from speaking until the sermon was finished. As soon as the friar had come down from the pulpit, he burst out and charged him with false doctrine, persuading the people as well as he could be heard, by the scriptures, that the bread was but a sacrament only of the Lord's body. He had not gone far, when Hesselius the chamberlain overtook him, and carried him to prison. Then were doctors and friars brought to reason with him, of the sacrament, of the invocation of saints, and purgatory. He ever stood to the trial only of the scripture, which they refused. When he was condemned, he was commanded not to speak to the people. The officer made great haste to have him dispatched. Wherefore he, mildly like a lamb, praying for his enemies, gave himself to be bound; first they strangled him, and then consumed his body with fire.

Bertrand de Blas, at Tournay, A.D. 1555.

The story of Bertrand is lamentable, his torments incredible, the tyranny shewed to him horrible, the constancy of the martyr admirable. This Bertrand, being a silk weaver, went to Wesell for the cause of religion, and being desirous to draw his wife and children from Tournay to Wesell, he came thrice to persuade her to go with him. When she could not be entreated, he, remaining a few days at home, set his house in order, and desired his wife and brother to pray that God would establish him in the enterprise which he went about. He went upon Christmas day to the high church of Tournay, where he took the cake out of the priest's hand, as he would have lifted it over his head at mass, and stamped it under his feet, saying, that he did it to shew the glory of that god, and what little power he had; with other words more to the people, to persuade them that the cake or fragment of bread was not Jesus their Saviour.

At the sight of this the people stood all amazed. At length such a stir followed, that Bertrand could hardly escape with life. The noise of this was soon carried to the bailiff of Hainault, and governor of the castle of Tournay, who lay sick of the gout at Biesie. He like a madman cried out, that God would ever be so patient as to suffer that contumely to be trodden underfoot; adding, that he would revenge his cause, so that it should be an example for ever to all posterity; and forthwith the furious tyrant commanded himself to be carried to the castle of Tournay. Bertrand being brought before him, was asked, whether he repented of his act, or whether he would so do, if it were to be done again? Who answered, that if it were an hundred times to be done, he would do it; and if he had an hundred lives, he would give them in that quarrel. Then was he thrice tormented most miserably. They then proceeded to the sentence, more like tyrants than christian men. By the tenor of which sentence, this was his punishment:—

First, he was drawn from the castle of Tournay to the market-place, having a ball of iron put into his mouth. Then he was set upon a stage, where his right hand, wherewith he took the host, was crushed and pressed between two hot irons, with sharp iron edges fiery red, till the form and fashion of his hand was misshapen. In like manner they brought irons for his right foot, made fire-hot, which of his own accord he put to his foot, to suffer as his hand had done, with wonderful constancy and firmness of mind. That done they took the ball of iron out of his mouth, and cut off his tongue, who notwithstanding, with continual crying, ceased not to call upon God; whereby the hearts of the people were greatly moved. Upon this the tormentors thrust the iron ball into his mouth again. Then his legs and his arms were bound behind him with an iron chain going about his body, and so he was let down flat upon the fire. The aforesaid governor standing by and looking on, caused him to be let up again, and so down and up again, till at last the whole body was spent to ashes, which he commanded to be cast into the river; when this was done, the chapel where this mass-god was so treated was locked up, and the board whereupon the priest stood was burnt, and the marble stone upon which the host fell was broken in pieces.

In the same year, 1555, two hundred ministers and preachers of the gospel were banished out of Bohemia for preaching against the superstition of the bishop of Rome, and extolling the glory of Christ.

The Preachers of Locrane exiled.

Locrane is a place between the Alps, yet subject to the Helvetians. When these had received the gospel, and the five cantons of the Helvetians were not well pleased, but would have them punished, and great contention was among the Helvetians about it, it was concluded at length, that the ministers should be exiled.

Francis Warlut, Alexander Dayken, at Tournay, A.D. 1562.

After these two good men had been conversant in the reformed churches in other countries, at last, for conscience sake, they returned home to do good in their own country of Tournay.

So, as the people there resorted to a field or wood without the city, with a preacher, to hear the word of God, and to pray ; the adversaries so pursued them, that they took above thirty, of whom these two among the rest were apprehended ; and thinking no less but that they should be burned, they began to sing psalms. At length being brought forth, first one, then the other, they were both beheaded. And where the judges had intended to quarter their bodies, and to set them up by the high ways, yet was it so provided, God working in the hearts of the people, that they were both committed to sepulture.

Gillotus Viver, James Faber his father-in-law, Michael Faber son of James, Anna, wife of Gillotus, and daughter of James Faber, suffered in the cause of the gospel at Valence. James Faber, being an old man, said that although he could not answer or fortify them in reasoning, yet he would constantly abide in the truth of the gospel. Anna, his daughter, being with child, was respited ; after she was delivered she followed her husband and father in the like martyrdom.

Michella Caignoucle, at Valence, A.D. 1550.

Michella, wife of James Clerk, who was before burned when she was offered to be married, and to be carried out of the country to some reformed church, refused so to do, but would abide her vocation, and so was condemned with Gillotus to be burned.

Godfrid Hamelle, at Tournay, A.D. 1552.

This Godfrid, a tailor, was taken and condemned at Tournay. When they had condemned him by the name of an heretic : "Nay," said he, "not an heretic, but an unprofitable servant of Jesus Christ." When the executioner went about to strangle him to diminish his punishment, he refused it, saying, "That he would abide the sentence that the judges had given."

Beside these Germans there were a great number both in the higher and lower countries of Germany, who were secretly drowned, or buried, or otherwise made away with in prison, whose names although they are not known to us, yet they are registered in the book of life. In the Dutch book of Adrian, others are numbered in the catalogue of these German martyrs, who suffered in several places of the low country : the names of some of these are :—

John Malo, Damian Witrocke, Waldrew Calier, John Porceau, Julian, Vanden Swerde, Adrian Lopphen, Bawdwine. At Bergen, were burnt, in the year 1555, John Malo, Damian Witrocke, Waldrew Calier ; buried alive, John Porceau. At Aste also suffered one Julian, 1541, and Adrian Lopphen, 1555, At Brussels, 1559, one Bawdwine, beheaded. Another called Gilleken Tilleman burnt, 1551.

Add moreover to the catalogue of Dutch martyrs burnt in the Low Countries under the emperor's dominion, the names of these following : William Swole burnt at Mechlin, 1529. Nicholas Van Pole, at Ghent, beheaded. Robert Ogvier, and Joan his wife, with Baudicon, and

Martin Ogvier, their children, who suffered at Lisle, 1556. Master Nicholas burnt at Mons in Hainault : Lawrence, of Brussels, at Mons ; John Fasseau at Mons; Cornelius Volcart at Bruges, 1553. Hubert, the printer, and Philebert Joyner, at Bruges, 1553. A woman buried with thorns under her ; Peter le Roux at Bruges, 1552. At Mechlin suffered Francis and Nicholas, two brethren, 1555. At Antwerp were burnt Adrian, a painter, and Henry, a tailor, 1555. Also Cornelius Halewine, locksmith, and Herman Janson the same year. John du Camp, schoolmaster, 1557, with a number of others, who in the book are to be seen and read.

In 1525, we read also in the French history, of a certain monk, who, because he forsook his abominable order, and was married, was burned at Prague.

A Preacher poisoned at Erfurt.

In the collections of Henry Patalion, we read also of a certain godly preacher who was poisoned for preaching the word of truth, by the priests of Erfurt.

And here ceasing with these persecutions in Germany, we will now, Christ willing, proceed further to the French martyrs, comprehending in a like manner the names and causes of such as in that kingdom suffered for the word of God, and the cause of righteousness.

THE FRENCH MARTYRS.

James Pavane, Schoolmaster, at Paris, A.D. 1524.

This James, being taken by the bishop of Meux, was compelled to recant. Afterward returning again to his confession, he was burned at Paris, in the year 1525.

Dionysius de Rieux, at Meux, A.D. 1528.

This Denis was one of them who was burned for saying that the mass is a plain denial of the death and passion of Christ. He was always wont to have in his mouth the words of Christ : "He that denieth me before men, him I will also deny before my Father ;" and to muse upon the same earnestly. He was burnt with a slow fire.

John de Cadurco, Bachelor of the Civil Law, A.D. 1533.

This John, for making an exhortation to his countrymen upon Allhallows-day, and after sitting at a feast where it was propounded that every one should bring forth some sentence, because he brought forth this ; "Christ reigns in our hearts," and prosecuted it by the scriptures, he was accused, taken, and degraded, and afterwards burned. At his degradation, one of the Black friars of Paris preached, taking for his text the words of St. Paul, 1 Tim. iv. 1. "The Spirit speaketh expressly that in the later times, men shall depart from the faith, giving heed to seducing spirits and doctrines of devils," &c. And in handling that place, either he could not, or would not proceed further in the text. Cadurco cried out to him to proceed, and read further. The friar stood dumb and could not speak a word.

Then Cadurco, taking the text, continued it : "Teaching lies in hypocrisy, having their conscience seared with a hot iron, forbidding to marry, and commanding to abstain from meats which God hath created to be received with thanksgiving," &c.

Bartholomew Myler, a lame cripple : John Burges, merchant, the receiver of Nantz ; Henry Hoille of Couberon ; Catella, a schoolmistress ; Stephen de la Forge, merchant, 1533. These five here specified, for certain papers circulated abroad against the abomination of the mass, and other superstitious absurdities of the pope, were condemned and burned in the city of Paris. Henry of Couberon had his tongue bored through, and tied fast to one of his cheeks with an iron wire ; he likewise with the others was burned.

Alexander Canus, Priest, otherwise called Laurentius Cruceus, at Paris, A.D. 1533.

For the sincere doctrine and confession of Christ's

true religion, he was burned in Paris ; having but a small fire he suffered much torment.

John Pointer, Surgeon, at Paris, A.D. 1533.

This surgeon being detected and accused by the friars, was first condemned to be strangled, and then burned ; but afterwards, because he would not do homage to a certain idol at the command of a friar that came to confess him, his sentence was changed to have his tongue cut out, and so to be burned.

Peter Gaudet, Knight of Rhodes, A.D. 1533.

This Peter, being at Geneva with his wife, was put in prison for defence of the gospel ; and, after long torments, was burned.

Quoquillard, A.D. 1534.

At Bezançon, in Burgundy, this Quoquillard was burned for the confession and testimony of Christ's gospel.

Nicholas, a scrivener; John de Poix; Stephen Burlet, 1534.

These three were executed and burned for the cause of the gospel, in the city of Arras.

Mary Becaudella, at Fountaigne, A.D. 1534.

This Mary being virtuously instructed by her master where she lived ; and being afterwards at a sermon where a friar preached, she found fault with his doctrine, and refuted the same by the scriptures. He procured her to be burned at Fountaigne.

John Cornon, 1535.

John Cornon was a husbandman of Mascon, and unlettered ; but one to whom God gave such wisdom, that his judges were amazed, when he was condemned by their sentence and burned.

Martin Gonin, in Dauphine, A.D. 1536.

This Martin being taken for a spy on the borders of France, towards the Alps, was committed to prison. In his going out, his jailor espied about him the letters of Farrell, and of Peter Viret. Therefore being examined by the king's procurator, and of the inquisitor, touching his faith, he was cast into the river and drowned.

Claudius Painter, a Goldsmith, at Paris, A.D. 1540.

Claudius going about to convert his friends and kinsfolks in his doctrine, was committed and condemned to be burned : but the high parliament of Paris, correcting that sentence, added, that he should have his tongue cut out before, and so be burned.

Stephen Brune, a Husbandman, at Rutiers, A.D. 1540.

Stephen Brune after confession of his faith, was adjudged to be burned. Which punishment he took so constantly, that it was a wonder to them. His adversaries commanded after his death, that none should make any more mention of him, under pain of heresy.

Constantius of Rouen, with three others, A.D. 1542.

These four, for the defence of the gospel being condemned to be burned, were put in a cart. They said, that they were reputed here as the offscouring of the world, but yet their death was a sweet odour unto God.

John du Becke, Priest, A.D. 1543.

For the doctrine of the gospel he was degraded, and constantly abode the torment of fire in the city of Troyes in Champagne.

Aymond de Lauoy, at Bourdeaux, A.D. 1543.

Aymond preached the gospel at Saint Faith's in Anjou, where he was accused by the parish priest, and by other priests, as having taught false doctrine. When the magistrates of Bourdeaux had given command to apprehend him, he was desired by his friends to fly : but he would not, saying, he had rather never have

been born, than to do so. It was the office of a good shepherd, he said, not to fly in time of peril, but rather to abide the danger, lest the flock should be scattered : or lest in so doing, he should leave some scruple in their minds, to think, that he fed them with dreams and fables, contrary to the word of God. Wherefore he told them, that he feared not to yield both body and soul for the truth which he had taught ; saying, with St. Paul, " That he was ready, not to be bound only, but also to die for the Lord Jesus."

When the somner came to arrest him, the people rose, in defence of their preacher, and flew upon the somner, to deliver him out of his hands. But Aymond desired them not to prevent his martyrdom, for as it was the will of God that he should suffer, he would not resist. So Aymond was carried to Bourdeaux. Many witnesses, chiefly priests, came against him, with Mr. Riverack : who had said often before, that if it should cost him a thousand crowns, he would have him burned. He made many exceptions against the false witnesses, but they would not be taken. The amount of their accusation was only that he had denied purgatory.

He continued about nine months in prison, bewailing exceedingly his former life, though no man could charge him outwardly with any crime. After that, he was examined with torments. One of the head presidents came to him, and shaking him by the beard, bade him tell what fellows he had of his religion. To whom he answered, that he had no other fellows, but such as knew and did the will of God his Father. In these torments he continued two or three hours, comforting himself with these words ; " This body," said he, " once must die, but the spirit shall live : the kingdom of God abideth for ever." In the time of his tormenting, he fainted, but afterwards on coming to himself again, he said, " O Lord, Lord, why hast thou forsaken me ?" To whom the president, " Nay, wicked Lutheran, thou hast forsaken God." Then said Aymond, " Alas, good masters, why do you thus miserably torment me ? O Lord, I beseech thee forgive them, they know not what they do." So constant was he, that they could not force him to utter one man's name.

On the next Saturday following, sentence of condemnation was given against him. Then certain friars were appointed to hear his confession ; he refused them, choosing some of his own order, the parish priest of St. Christopher's, bidding the friars depart, for he would confess his sins to the Lord. " Do you not see," said he, " how I am troubled enough with men, will ye yet trouble me more ? Others have had my body, will ye also take from me my soul ? Away from me, I pray you." At last, when they refused to let him have the parish priest, he took a Carmelite ; with whom he had long converse, and at last converted him to the truth. Shortly after, the judges, Cassanges, and Longa, with others, came to him ; Aymond began to preach to them and declare his mind touching the Lord's Supper : but Longa, interrupting him, demanded of him thus.

Judge.—First declare to us your mind, what you think of purgatory ?

Martyr.—In scripture all these are one, to purge, to cleanse, and to wash. Whereof we read in Isaiah, in the epistles of St. Paul, and of St. Peter ; " He hath washed you in his blood. Ye are redeemed, not with gold, but with the blood of Christ," &c. Heb. ix. 12. 1 Peter i. 18. And how often do we read, in the epistles of St. Paul, that we are cleansed by the blood of Christ from our sins, &c.

Judge.—These epistles are known to every child.

Martyr.—To every child ? Nay, I fear you have scarce read them yourself.

A friar.—With one word you may satisfy them, if you will say, that there is a place where the souls are purged after this life.

Martyr.—That I leave for you to say, if you please. What, would ye have me damn my own soul, and say that which I know not ?

Judge.—Dost not thou think, that when thou art dead, thou shalt go to purgatory ? And that he that died in venial sin, shall pass straight into paradise ?

Martyr.—Such trust I have in my God, that the same day when I shall die, I shall enter into paradise.

Another judge.—Where is paradise?

Martyr.—There where the majesty and glory of God is.

Judge.—The canons make mention of purgatory, and you in your sermons have used always much to pray for the poor.

Martyr.—I have preached the word of God, and not the canons.

Judge.—Dost thou believe in the church?

Martyr.—I believe as the church regenerated by the blood of Christ, and founded in his word, hath appointed.

Judge.—What church is that?

Martyr.—The church is a Greek word, signifying as much as a congregation or assembly : and so I say, that whensoever the faithful do congregate together, to the honour of God, and the extending of christian religion, the Holy Ghost is verily with them.

Judge.—By this it should follow, that there are many churches : and where any rustic clowns assemble together, there must be a church.

Martyr.—It is no absurd thing to say that there are many churches or congregations among christians : and so speaks St. Paul, to all the churches which are in Galatia, &c. And yet all these congregations make but one church.

Judges.—The church wherein thou believest, is not the same church which our creed calls the holy church?

Martyr.—I believe the same.

Judge.—And who should be head of that church?

Martyr.—Jesus Christ.

Judge.—And not the pope?

Martyr.—No.

Judge.—And what is he then?

Martyr.—A minister, if he be a good man, as other bishops : of whom St. Paul thus writes ; " Let a man so account of us, as ministers of Christ, and stewards of the mysteries of God," &c. 1 Cor. iv. 1.

Then the judges leaving him with the friars, departed, counting him as a damned creature. Aymond, however, putting his trust in God, was full of comfort, saying with St. Paul, " Who shall separate me from the love of God? Shall the sword, hunger, or nakedness? No, nothing shall pluck me from him. But rather I have pity on you," said he, and so they departed. Not long after, he was brought to the place of execution, singing by the way the hundred and fourteenth Psalm. He thanked moreover the keeper, and desired him to be good to his poor prisoners. And so taking his leave of them, and desiring them to pray for him ; also giving thanks to the mistress-keeper for her gentleness to him, he proceeded to his execution. As he came near the church of St. Andrew, they desired him to ask mercy of God, and of blessed St. Mary, and of St. Justice. " I ask mercy," said he, " of God, and his justice, but the Virgin, blessed St. Mary, I never offended, nor did any thing for which I should ask her mercy. In passing a certain image of the Virgin Mary, great offence was taken against him, because he called upon Christ Jesus only, and made no mention of her. So he lifted up his voice to God, praying that he would never suffer him to invocate any other. Coming to the place where he was to suffer, he was tumbled out of the cart upon the ground, testifying to magistrates and to the people standing by, that he died for the gospel of Jesus Christ. He would have spoken more, but he was not suffered, by the officers, crying, " Dispatch him! dispatch him! let him not speak." Then speaking a few words softly in the ear of the Carmelite whom he had converted, he was bid to step up to the stage. There the people beginning to listen to him, he said thus ; " O Lord, make haste to help me, tarry not, do not despise the works of thy hands : and you, my brethren, that are students and scholars, I exhort you to study and learn the gospel : for the word of God abideth for ever : labour to know the will of God, and fear not them that kill the body, but have no power upon your souls: my flesh," said he, " striveth against the spirit, but I shall shortly cast it away. My good masters, I beseech you pray for me.

O Lord my God, into thy hands I commend my soul." As he was often repeating the same words, the executioner took and strangled him. And thus that blessed saint gave up his life; his body afterwards was consumed with fire.

Francis Bribard, A.D. 1544, was said to be the secretary of the cardinal of Ballaie. Being condemned for the gospel, his tongue was cut off, and with great constancy he suffered martyrdom by burning.

William Husson, an apothecary at Rouen, in 1544, went to the palace, and there scattered certain books concerning christian doctrine, and the abuse of human tradition.

The council was so moved at this, that they commanded all the gates of the city to be locked, and diligent search to be made to find out the author, so that William Husson was taken by the way riding to Dieppe, and brought again to Rouen. Being there examined, he declared his faith boldly, and how he came purposely to disperse those books in Rouen, and went to do the like at Dieppe.

The week ensuing he was condemned to be burnt alive. After the sentence he was brought in a cart, accompanied with a doctor, a Carmelite friar ; and when before the great church they put a torch into his hand, and required him to do homage to the image of the Virgin Mary, and because he refused to do this they cut out his tongue. The friar then preached a sermon, and when he spoke anything of the mercies of God, the said William hearkened to him ; but when he spoke of the merits of saints, and other dreams, he turned away his head. The friar looking upon the countenance of Husson, lifted up his hand to heaven, saying, with great exclamation, that he was damned, and was possessed with a devil. When the friar had ceased his sermon, this godly Husson had his hands and feet bound behind his back, and with a pully was lifted up into the air ; and when the fire was kindled he was let down into the flame, where the blessed martyr with a smiling and cheerful countenance looked up to heaven, never moving or stirring till he let down his head, and gave up his spirit. All the people there present were not a little astonished, some saying that he had a devil ; others maintained the contrary, saying, if he had a devil, he would have fallen into despair.

This Carmelite friar was called Delanda, who afterwards was converted, and preached the gospel.

James Cobard, a schoolmaster, and many others taken at the same time, 1545.—This James, schoolmaster in the dukedom of Barens in Lorraine, disputed with three priests, that the sacrament of baptism, and of the supper did not avail, unless they were received with faith ; which was as much as to say, that the mass profited neither the quick nor the dead. For which, and also for his confession, which he sent while in prison by his mother to the judge, he was burned, and most quietly suffered.

Also in 1546, at Meaux a city, in France, near to Paris, where William Briconatus was bishop, this bishop did much good, and brought to them the light of the gospel, and reformed the church ; but afterwards, though he apostatised, yet there were many who remained constant. Then came the burning of James Pavane ; and as superstition began to grow more and more, those who had continued steadfast began to assemble in Mangin's house, and to set up a church for themselves, after the example of the French church in Strasburg. They began with twenty or thirty, and increased in a short time to three or four hundred. On the matter being known to the senate of Paris, the chamber was beset where those persons were, and they were taken. Sixty-two men and women were bound and brought to Paris, singing psalms, especially the seventy-ninth Psalm. To these it was chiefly objected, that they being laymen, ministered the sacrament of the body and blood of the Lord.

Of these sixty-two, fourteen were specially steadfast, and were condemned, and racked to compel them to confess more of their fellows, but would not do so; the rest were scourged and banished the country. These fourteen were sent to sundry monasteries to be converted; but that would not answer; they then were sent in a cart to Meaux to be burned; and when on the way, about three miles from Paris, they met by chance a weaver of Couberon, who cried to them aloud, bidding them to be of good cheer, and to cleave fast to the Lord. This man was also taken, and bound and put in the cart with them. On coming to the place of execution, which was before Mangin's house, they were told, that those who would be confessed should not have their tongues cut out, but that the others should. Of the fourteen there were seven who to save their tongues confessed; the other seven refused. As they were burning, the people sung psalms. The priests would also sing their songs: "O saving Host," &c. and "Hail, O Queen of heaven," &c. while the sacrifice of these holy martyrs was finished. Their wives being compelled to see their husbands in torments, were afterwards put in prison, whence they promised to be freed if they would only say that their husbands were damned, but they refused.

At Paris, in 1546, *Peter Chapot,* a printer, after having been at Geneva, came into France, and brought with him some books of the holy scripture, which he dispersed abroad among the faithful, when his great zeal caused him to be apprehended.

On being brought before the commissaries, he rendered an account of his faith, and exhibited a supplication, or writing, in which he learnedly informed the judges to do their office uprightly. Then were three doctors of the Sorbonne assigned to dispute with him, who when they could find no advantage, but rather shame at his hands, were angry with the judges for making them dispute with heretics.

This done, the judges consulting on his condemnation, could not agree, so that Chapot might have escaped, had not a wicked person wrought his condemnation, that he should be burned. At his execution, friar Maillard called upon him not to speak to the people, but he desired him to pray. Then he bade him pray to our Lady, and confess her to be his advocate. He confessed that she was a blessed Virgin, and recited the Lord's Prayer and the Creed, and was about to speak of the mass, but Maillard would not let him, making haste to his execution, and said, unless he would say the "Hail Mary," he should be burnt. Then Chapot prayed, "O Jesus Son of David, have mercy upon me." Maillard then bade him say, "Jesus, Maria," and that he should be only strangled. Chapot was so weak that he could not speak. "Say," said Maillard, "Jesus Maria, or else thou shalt be burned." As Chapot was thus striving with the friar, suddenly, as it happened, that Jesus Maria, slipped from his mouth; but he instantly repressing himself, "O God," said he, "what have I done! pardon me, O Lord, to thee only have I sinned." Then Maillard commanded the cord to be put about his neck to strangle him. After all things were done, Maillard, full of anger, went to the council-house, declaring what an uproar had almost happened among the people; saying, that he would complain of the judges for suffering those heretics to have their tongues. Immediately a decree was made, that all who were to be burned, unless they recanted at the fire, should have their tongues cut off; which law was afterwards diligently observed.

Saintinus Nivet at Paris, in 1546.—After the burning of the fourteen, described before, this Saintinus, who was a cripple, had removed away from Meaux, but after a time he returned, and, as he was selling certain small wares in the fair, he was known again and apprehended. Information having been given. he was examined, and at first he confessed all, and more than they were willing to hear. But as they were examining him on certain points of religion, and asked him whether he would stand to what he said, or not, he gave this answer, which is worthy to be registered in all men's hearts, saying, " And I ask you again, lord judges,

dare you be so bold as to deny what is so plain and manifest by the open words of the scripture?" So little regard had he to saving his own life, that he desired the judges, for God's sake, that they would rather take care of their own lives and souls, and consider how much innocent blood they spilled daily in fighting against Christ Jesus and his gospel.

At last, being brought to Paris, he there suffered martyrdom: no kind of cruelty was wanting, which the innocent martyrs of Christ Jesus were wont to undergo.

Stephen Polliot, in 1546, on coming out of Normandy, where he was born, to Meaux, was compelled to fly, but was apprehended and brought to Paris, and there cast into a foul and dark prison. In which prison he was kept in bands and fetters a long time, where he saw almost no light. At length being called before the senate, and his sentence being given to have his tongue cut out, and to be burned alive, his books hanging about his neck in a bag, "O Lord," said he, "is the world in blindness and darkness still?" At last the worthy martyr of Jesus Christ was put into the fire, where with much patience he ended this transitory life.

John English, in 1547, was executed and burned at Sens in Burgundy, being condemned by the high court of Paris, for confessing the true word of God.

Michael Michelote, a tailor, in 1547, was apprehended for the gospel's sake, and sentenced if he would turn, to be beheaded; and if he would not turn, then to be burned alive. On being asked, which of these two he would choose? answered, that he trusted, that he who had given him grace not to deny the truth, would also give him patience to endure the fire. He was burned.

Leonard de Prato, in 1547, when going from Dijon to Bar, a town in Burgundy, with two false brethren, and talking with them about religion, was betrayed by them, and afterwards burned.

Seven Martyrs, A. D. 1457.

John Taffington, and *Joan* his wife, *Simon Mareschal,* and *Joan* his wife, *William Michaut, James Boulerau,* and *James Bretany.*—All these seven being of the city of Langres, were committed to the fire for the word and truth of Jesus Christ, in which they died with much strength and comfort; but especially Joan, who was Simon's wife, being reserved to the last, because she was the youngest, confirmed her husband, and all the others with words of singular consolation; declaring to her husband, that they should the same day be married to the Lord Jesus, to live with him for ever.

Michael Mareschall, John Camus, Great *John Camus,* and *John Serarphin,* in the same year, and about the same time, for the like confession of Christ's gospel, were condemned by the senate of Paris, and in the same city also with the like cruelty were burned.

Octovien Blondel, a merchant of precious stones at Paris, 1548.—This Octovien was well known both at court and elsewhere; he was a singularly honest man of great integrity, and also a favourer of God's word. Being at his host's house at Lyons, he rebuked the filthy talk, and superstitious behaviour, which he heard and saw there. The host, bearing to him a grudge, had some talk with one Gabriel, concerning the riches, and a sumptuous collar set with rich jewels belonging to this Octovien.

Thus these two consulting together, suborned a person to borrow of him a sum of crowns; which, because Octovien refused to lend, the other caused him to be apprehended for heresy, thinking thereby to make attachment of his goods. But such order was taken by Blondel's friends, that they were frustrated in their purpose. Then Blondel being examined as to his faith, gave a plain and full confession of that doctrine, which he had learned: for which he was committed to prison, where he did much good to the prisoners.

For some that were in debt, he paid their creditors and loosed them out. To some he gave meat, to others raiment. At length, through the importune persuasions of his parents and friends, he gave over and changed his confession. However, the Presenteur Gabriel appealed up to the high court of Paris. There Octovien being asked again, touching his faith, which of his two confessions he would stick to? he being before admonished of his fall, and of the offence given by it to the faithful, said he would live and die in his first confession, which he defended as consonant to the truth of God's word. He was therefore condemned to be burned, and his execution was hastened lest his friends at court might save his life.

Hubert Cheriet, alias *Burre*, tailor, at Dijon, 1549. —Hubert, being a young man of the age of nineteen years, was burned for the gospel at Dijon; who neither, by any terrors of death, nor allurements of his parents, could be otherwise persuaded, but constantly to remain in the truth unto death.

Master *Florent Venote*, priest at Paris, 1549.—This Florent remained in prison in Paris, about four years. During which time there was no torment which he did not overcome. Besides other torments, he was put in a narrow prison so straight, that he could neither stand nor lie, which they call the hose or boot, because it is straight beneath, and wider above. In this he remained seven weeks, where the tormentors affirm, that no thief or murderer could ever endure fifteen days, but was in danger of life or madness. At last, when there was a great shew in Paris at the king's coming to the city, Florent and other martyrs were put to death. He had his tongue cut off, and was brought to see the execution of them all; then, last of all, he was put in the fire and burned the ninth of July, in the place called Maulbert.

Ann Audebert, an apothecary's wife and widow at Orleans, 1549.—Going to Geneva, she was taken and brought to Paris, and by the council adjudged to be burned at Orleans. When the rope was put about her, she called it her wedding-girdle wherewith she should be married to Christ. And as she was to be burned upon a Saturday, upon Michaelmas-even: "Upon a Saturday," said she, "I was first married, and upon a Saturday I shall be married again." And seeing the cart brought in which she was to be carried, she rejoiced thereat, shewing such constancy in her martyrdom as made all the beholders to marvel.

A poor Tailor of Paris, 1549.

Among many other godly martyrs that suffered in France, the history of this poor tailor is not the least nor worst to be remembered. His name is not yet sought out in the French histories through want of diligence in those writers. The history is this: Not long after the coronation of Henry II., the French king, at whose coming into Paris several good martyrs were brought out and burned for a spectacle: a certain poor tailor, who then dwelt not far from the king's palace, was apprehended, because upon a certain holy-day he followed his occupation, and worked for his living. Before he was led to prison, the officer asked him, "Why he laboured giving no observance to the holy-day?" he answered, "That he was a poor man, living only upon his labour: and as for the day, he knew no other but only the Sunday, wherein he might not lawfully work for his living." Then the officer began to ask of him many questions: which the poor tailor so answered, that he was soon clapt in prison. After that, the officer coming into court to shew what good service he had done for holy church, declared how he had taken a Lutheran working upon a holy-day. When the rumour was noised in the king's chamber, the poor man was sent to appear, that the king might hear him.

Only a few of the chief peers remained about the king when the simple tailor was brought. The king sitting in his chair, commanded Peter Castellan, bishop of Mascon, (a man very fit for such inquisitions) to question him. The tailor being entered, and nothing appalled at the king's majesty, after his reverence done to the prince, gave thanks to God, that he had so greatly dignified him, as to bring him where he might testify his truth before such a mighty prince. Then Castellan, began to reason with him touching the great and chief matters of religion. The tailor, without fear, or any halting in his speech, with wit and memory, answered excellently in behalf of the sincere doctrine and simple truth of God's gospel.

The nobles who were present, with cruel taunts and rebukes, did what they could to dash him out of countenance. Yet all this terrified him not, but with boldness of heart and free liberty of speech, he defended his cause, or rather the cause of Christ the Lord, neither flattering their persons, nor fearing their threats; which was to them a matter of astonishment to behold that simple poor artificer stand so firm and bold, answering before a king, to the questions propounded against him. When the king seemed to muse with himself, as one who might have been led to further knowledge, the bishop and other courtiers seeing the king in such a muse, said, he was an obstinate and stubborn person, and therefore should be sent to the judges, and punished: and so, within a few days after, he was condemned to be burned alive.

Claudius Thierry, at Orleans, 1549.—The same year, and for the same doctrine of the gospel, one Claudius also was burned at the town of Orleans, being apprehended by the way coming from Geneva to his country.

Leonard Galimard, at Paris, 1549.—This Leonard, for the confession likewise of Christ and his gospel, was taken and brought to Paris, and there, by the sentence of the council, was judged to be burned the same time that Florent Venote, above-mentioned, suffered at Paris.

Macæus Moreou, at Troyes, 1549.—He was burned in Troyes in Champaine, remaining constant to the end in the gospel, for which he was apprehended.

Joannes Godeau, Gabriel Beraudinus, A. D. 1550.— These two were of the church of Geneva. Godeau, standing to his confession, was burned. Gabriel, though he began a little to shrink for fear of the torments, yet, being confirmed by the constant death of Godeau, recovered again, and standing likewise to his confession, first had his tongue cut out. And so these two, after they had confirmed many in God's truth, gave their life for Christ's gospel.

Thomas Sanpaulinus at Paris, 1551.—This young man, of the age of eighteen years, coming from Geneva to Paris, rebuked there a man for swearing. For which cause, being suspected for a Lutheran, he was watched and brought before the council of Paris, and put in prison, where he was racked and miserably tormented, so that he might either change his opinion, or confess others of his profession. His torments and rackings were so sore that the sight of them made Aubert, one of the council, a cruel and vehement enemy against the gospel, to turn his back and weep. The young man, when he had made the tormentors weary with racking, and yet would utter none, at last was brought to Maulbert place, in Paris, to be burned; being in the fire, he was plucked up again upon the gibbet, and asked whether he would turn? he said, "That he was in his way towards God, and therefore desired them to let him go." Thus this glorious martyr glorified the Lord with constant confession of his truth.

Mauricius Secenate in Provence, 1551.—Being interrogated by the lieutenant of that place, this martyr made his answers so that no great advantage could be taken of them. But he being greatly troubled in his conscience for dissembling with the truth, and being called afterwards before the chief judge, he answered so directly, that he was condemned and burned in Provence.

John Putte, or *de Puteo*, sirnamed *Medicus*, at Uzez in Languedoc, 1551.—This Medicus had a controversy about a certain pit with a citizen of the town of Uzez, where he dwelt. He, to cast Medicus in the law, accused him of heresy, bringing for his witnesses those labourers whom Medicus had hired to work in his vineyard: being examined on the sacrament of the Lord's Supper, he was condemned and burned at Uzez in Languedoc.

Claudius Monerius at Lyons, 1551.

This man being well instructed in the knowledge of God's word, came to Lyons, and there taught children. Hearing of the lord president's coming to the city, he went to give warning to a certain friend of his, and conducted him out of the town. In returning again to comfort the man's wife and children, he was taken in his house: and so he confessing that which he knew to be true, and standing to that which he confessed, after much afflictions in prisons and dungeons, was condemned and burned at Lyons. Certain of the judges could not forbear weeping at his death.

In prison he wrote some letters, but one especially very comfortable to all the faithful. He wrote also the questions of the official, with his answers, which we have here contracted as follows :—

Official.—What believe you of the sacrament? Is the body of Christ in the bread, or no?

Martyr.—I worship Jesus Christ in heaven, sitting at the right hand of God the Father.

Official.—What say you about purgatory?

Martyr.—Forsomuch as there is no place of mercy after this life, therefore there is no need of any purgation; but it is necessary that we be purged before we go hence.

Official.—What think you of the pope?

Martyr.—I say he is a bishop as other bishops are, if he be a true follower of St. Peter.

Official.—What say you of vows?

Martyr.—No man can vow to God so much, but the law requires much more than he can vow.

Official.—Are not saints to be invoked?

Martyr.—They cannot pray without faith, and therefore it is in vain to call upon them. And again, God has appointed his angels about us, to minister in our necessities.

Official.—Is it not good to salute the blessed Virgin with the "Hail Mary!"

Martyr.—When she was on earth she had need of the angel's greeting; for then she had need of salvation, as well as others; but now she is so blessed, that no more blessing can be wished to her.

Official.—Are not images to be had?

Martyr.—The nature of man is so prone to idolatry, ever occupied in those things which lie before his eyes, rather than upon those which are not seen; images therefore are not to be set before christians. You know nothing is to be adored, but that which is not seen with eyes, that is, God alone, who is a Spirit, and him we must worship only in spirit and in truth.

In 1552, *Renat Poyet*, the son of William Poyet, who was chancellor of France, for the true and sincere profession of the word of God, constantly suffered martyrdom, and was burned in the city of Salmure.

John Joyer, and his servant at Toulouse, 1552.—These two coming from Geneva to their country with certain books, were apprehended and brought to Toulouse, where the master was first condemned. The servant being young, was not so prompt to answer them, but sent them to his master, saying, that he should answer them. When they were brought to the stake, the young man first going up, began to weep. The master fearing lest he would give over, ran to him, and he was comforted, and they began to sing. As they were in the fire, the master standing upright to the stake, shifted the fire from him to his servant, being more careful for him than for himself; and when he saw him dead, he bowed down into the flame, and so expired.

Hugonius Gravier, a schoolmaster and minister after of Cortillon, in the country of Newcastle. At Burg in Bresse, a day's journey from Lyons, in 1552, this Gravier was burnt. He coming from Geneva to Newcastle was there elected to be minister. On going to see his wife's friends at Mascon, he was taken, with all his company; and desiring the women and the rest of the company to lay the fault on him for bringing them out, he was sentenced to be burned, although the lords of Berne sent their heralds to save his life, and the official declared him to be an honest man, and to hold nothing but agreeing with the scriptures.

Martial Alba, Petrus Scriba, Bernard Seguine, Charles Faber, Peter Navihere, at Lyons, 1553.

These five students, after they had remained in the university of Lausanne a certain time, agreed amongst themselves, being all Frenchmen, to return home every one to his country, that they might instruct their parents and friends in such knowledge as the Lord had given them. So taking their journey they came to Geneva, where they remained a while. From thence they went to Lyons, where they were apprehended and led to prison, and where they continued a whole year. As they were learned in the scriptures, every one of them exhibited severally a learned confession of his faith; and, through the power of the Lord's Spirit, confounded the friars, with whom they disputed.

They were examined as to the sacrament of the Lord's body, of purgatory, confession and invocation, free will, and the supremacy, &c. Although they proved their cause by scripture, and refuted their adversaries in reasoning, yet right being overcome by might, sentence was given, and they were burnt at Lyons. When set upon the cart, they began to sing psalms. As they passed by the market-place, one of them with a loud voice saluted the people with the words of the last chapter to the Hebrews, "The God of peace which brought again from the dead the great Shepherd of the sheep by the blood of the everlasting covenant," &c. Coming to the place, the two youngest went up upon the heap of wood to the stake, and there were fastened, and so after them the rest. Martial Alba being the eldest, was the last; being stripped of his clothes, and brought to the stake, he desired this petition of the governor—that he might go about to his companions tied at the stake, and kiss them: which being granted, he went and kissed every one, saying, "Farewell, my brother." The other four, following the example, bad each one, "Farewell, my brother." With that, fire was commanded to be put to them. So the blessed martyrs, in the midst of the fire, spake one to another to be of good cheer, and so departed.

The Examinations briefly touched.

Friar.—Thou sayest, friend, in thy confession, that the pope is not supreme head of the church. I will prove to the contrary. The pope is successor of Peter, and therefore he is supreme head of the church.

Martyr.—I deny that he is successor to Peter.

Then another friar.—Thou sayest St. Peter is not the head of the church, I will prove he is; for our Lord said to Peter, "Thou shalt be called Cephas;" which Cephas is as much as to say in Latin, a head; and therefore Peter is head of the church.

Martyr.—Where find you that interpretation? St. John in his first chapter doth expound it otherwise: "Thou shalt be called Cephas, which is by interpretation a stone."

Then the judge Villard, calling for a New Testament, turned to the place, and found it to be so. Upon which the friar was utterly dashed and stood mute.

Friar.—Thou sayest in thy confession, that a man hath no free will, I will prove it. It is written in the gospel, how a man going from Jerusalem to Jericho fell among thieves, and was spoiled, maimed, and left half dead, &c. Thomas Aquinas expounds this parable to mean free-will, which he saith is maimed; yet not so but that some power remains in man to work.

Martyr.—This interpretation I refuse and deny.

Friar.—What! thinkest thou thyself better learned than St. Thomas?

Martyr.—I arrogate no such learning to myself. But I say this parable is not to be so expounded, but is set forth by the Lord to commend charity towards our neighbour, how one should help another.

Friar.—Thou sayest in thy confession, that we are justified only by faith, I will prove that we are justified by works. St. Paul, Hebrews xiii. 16, saith, " To do good and to distribute forget not; for with such sacrifices God is merited." Now as we merit God by our works, so we are justified by our works.

Martyr.—The words of St. Paul in that place are to be translated thus :—" With such sacrifices God is well pleased."

Vilard the judge turned to the book, and found the place even as the prisoner said. Here the friars were marvellously appalled and troubled in their minds. One asked then, what he thought of confession?

To whom the martyr answered, That confession is to be made to God only; and that those places which they allege for auricular confession, out of St. James and others, are to be expounded of brotherly reconciliation between one another, and not of confession in the priest's ear. And here again the friars had nothing to say against it.

A Black friar.—Dost thou not believe the body of Christ to be locally and corporally in the sacrament? I will prove the same: Jesus Christ taking bread said, " This is my body."

Martyr.—The verb " is" is not to be taken here substantively in its own proper signification, as shewing the nature of a thing in substance, but as noting the property of a thing, signifying, after the manner and phrase of the scripture; where one thing is wont to be called by the name of another, so as the sign is called by the name of the thing signified, &c. So is circumcision called by the name of the covenant, and yet it is not the covenant. So the lamb has the name of the passover, yet it is not the same. In which two sacraments of the old law you see the verb "is," must be taken, not as shewing the substance of being, but the property of being in the thing that is spoken of. And so likewise in the sacrament of the new law.

Friar.—I will prove that they of the Old Testament were not partakers of the same grace with us. " The law," saith St. Paul, " worketh wrath ;" and they that are under the law are under a curse ; therefore they of the old law and testament were not partakers of the same grace with us.

Martyr.—St. Paul here proves that no man can be justified by the law, but that all men are under the anger and curse of God thereby, forasmuch as no man performs that which is comprehended in the law, so therefore we have need every man to run to Christ, to be saved by faith, seeing that no man can be saved by the law. For whoever trusts to the law, hoping to find justification thereby, and not in Christ only, the same remains still under the curse ; not because the law is cursed, or that any particular time is under the curse, but because of the weakness of our natures, which are not able to perform the law.

The official, seeing the friar here at a point, said, Thou heretic! dost thou deny the blessed sacrament?

Martyr.—No, sir, but I embrace and reverence the sacrament, as it was instituted of the Lord, and left by his apostles.

Official.—Thou deniest the body of Christ to be in the sacrament, and thou callest the sacrament bread.

Martyr.—The scripture teaches us to seek the body of Christ in heaven, and not in earth, where we read, Coloss. iii. 1. " If ye be risen with Christ, seek those things which are above, where Christ sitteth at the right hand of God," &c. And whereas I affirm the sacrament not to be the body, but bread, speaking of bread remaining in its own substance, I do no other than St. Paul does, who (1 Cor. xi. 26.) calls it bread likewise four or five times together.

Official.—Thou naughty heretic! Jesus Christ said that he was a vine, and a door, &c.. where he speaks

figuratively. But the words of the sacrament are not to be so expounded.

Martyr.—Those testimonies which you alleged make more for me than for you.

Official.—What sayest thou, heretic! is the bread of the Lord's Supper, and the bread that we eat at home, all one, and is there no difference between them?

Martyr.—In nature and substance there is no difference ; in quality and in use there is much difference. For the bread of the Lord's table, though it be of the same nature and substance as the bread that we eat at home, yet when it is applied to be a sacrament, it takes another quality, and is set before us to seal the promise of our spiritual and eternal life.

About the same time, when these five students above specified were apprehended, *Peter Bergerius* also was taken at Lyons, and examined, and made the like confession with them, and shortly after them suffered the same martyrdom. He had a wife and children at Geneva, to whom he wrote sweet and comfortable letters. In the dungeon with him there was a certain thief and malefactor who had lain there seven or eight months. · This thief, for pain and torment, cried out to God and cursed his parents that begat him, being almost eaten up with lice, miserably handled, and fed with such bread as dogs and horses had refused to eat. So it pleased the goodness of Almighty God, that through the teaching and prayer of Bergerius, he was brought to repentance of himself, and knowledge of God, learning much comfort and patience by the word of the gospel preached to him.

Stephen Peloquine, Dionysius Peloquine, at Lyons, 1553.—Stephen Peloquine, brother to Dionysius, was taken, with Ann Audebert, and martyred for the gospel at the same time, with a small fire. After whom followed Dionysius Peloquine, in the same martyrdom. The articles for which he was condemned, were the mass, the sacrament, auricular confession, purgatory, the Virgin Mary, and the pope's supremacy. He suffered in the year 1553. In his martyrdom, such patience and fortitude God gave him that when he was half burned, yet he never ceased holding up his hands to heaven, and calling upon the Lord, to the great admiration of them that looked on.

Lewis Marsacus, Michael Gerard, Stephen Gravot, at Lyons, 1553.—At Lyons, in the same year, these three also were apprehended and sacrificed. Lewis had served the king in his wars. He was trained up in the knowledge and doctrine of the Lord. He was examined upon several articles, as invocation of saints, and of the Virgin Mary, free will, merits, and good works, auricular confession, fasting, the Lord's Supper. In his second examination, they inquired of him, and also of the other two touching vows, the sacraments, the mass, and the vicar of Christ. In all which articles, because their judgment dissented from the doctrine of the pope's church, they were condemned.

When the sentence of condemnation was given against these three, they were so glad that they went out praising God, and singing psalms.

When brought out of prison to the stake, the executioner tied a rope about the necks of the other two. Marsac seeing himself spared because of his order and degree, asked that he also might have one of the precious chains about his neck, in honour of his Lord, which, being granted, these three blessed martyrs were committed to the fire, where, with meek patience, they yielded up their lives into the hands of the Lord, in testimony of his gospel.

Matthew Dimonetus, at Lyons, A.D. 1553.

This merchant first lived a vicious and detestable life, but being called notwithstanding by the grace of God, to the knowledge and favour of his word; he was shortly afterwards taken by the lieutenant, and the official, and after a little examination was sent to prison. Being examined by the inquisitor and the official, he refused to yield any answer, knowing no authority they had over him, except to the lieutenant.

His answers were, that he believed all that the holy universal church of Christ did truly believe, and all the articles of the creed. To the article of the holy catholic church, being bid to add also Roman, that is, the church of Rome, he refused. Advocates he knew none, but Christ alone. Purgatory he knew none, but the cross and passion of the Lamb, which purgeth the sins of all the world. True confession, he said, ought to be made not to the priest once a year, but every day to God, and to such whom we have offended. The eating of the flesh and blood of Christ he took to be spiritual; and the sacrament of the flesh and blood of Christ to be eaten with the mouth, and that sacrament to be bread and wine under the name and signification of the body and blood of Christ; the mass not to be instituted by Christ, being a thing contrary to his word and will. For the head of the church, he knew none but only Christ. Being in prison, he had great conflicts with the infirmity of his flesh, but especially with the temptation of his parents, brethren, and kinsfolks, and the sorrow of his mother; nevertheless, the Lord so assisted him, that he endured to the end. At his burning he spake much to the people, and was heard with great attention. He suffered July 15th, 1553.

William Neel, a friar, suffered in the same year, and was burned at Eureux in France. His trouble arose first for rebuking of the vicious demeanor of the priests there, and of the dean; for which the dean caused him to be sent to Eureux to the prison of the bishop.

Simon Laloe, a spectacle-maker at Dijon, in 1553, coming from Geneva into France, was arrested by the bailiff of Dijon. Three things were demanded of him. First, where he dwelt. Secondly, what was his faith. Thirdly, what fellows he knew of his religion. His dwelling, he said, was at Geneva. His religion was such as was then used at Geneva. As for his fellows, he said, he knew none, but only those of the same city of Geneva, where his dwelling was. When they could get no other answer but this, with all their racking and torments, they proceeded to his sentence, and pursued the execution of it, which was November 21, 1553.

The executioner, who was named James Silvester, seeing the great faith and constancy of that heavenly martyr, was so touched with repentance, and fell into such despair of himself, that they had much ado, with all the promises of the gospel, to recover any comfort. At last, through the mercy of Christ, he was comforted and converted, and so he with all his family removed to the church at Geneva.

Nicholas Nayle, a shoemaker, at Paris, in 1553, was apprehended, and stoutly persisting in confessing the truth, was tried with so cruel torments, to induce him to inform what companions he had of his profession, that his body was almost separated one joint from another; but so constant was he in his silence that he would reveal none. As they brought him to the stake, they first put a gag or piece of wood in his mouth, which they bound with cords to the hinder part of his head, so hard that his mouth on both sides gushed out with blood. By the way they passed by an hospital, where they desired him to worship the picture of St. Mary standing at the gate; but he turned his back as well as he could, and would not; for which the blind people were so enraged that they would have fallen upon him. After he was brought to the fire they so smeared his body with fat and brimstone, that at the first taking of the fire, all his skin was burned, and the inward parts not touched. With that the cords burst which were about his mouth, whereby his voice was heard in the midst of the flame, praising the Lord, and so the blessed martyr departed.

At Toulouse, in 1553, *Peter Serre*, was first a priest, then changing his religion he went to Geneva and learned the trade of a shoemaker. Afterwards he came to his brother at Toulouse, to do him good. His brother had

a wife, who was not well pleased with his religion and coming. She told another woman, one of her neighbours of this. What does she, but goes to the official and makes him privy of all. The official laid hands upon Peter, and brought him before the inquisitor; to whom he made such declarations of his faith, that he seemed to reduce the inquisitor to some feeling of conscience, and began to instruct him in the principles of true religion. Notwithstanding, he was condemned by the chancellor to be degraded, and committed to the secular judge. The judge inquiring of what occupation he was, he said, that of late he was a shoemaker. Whereby the judge, understanding that he had been of some other faculty before, required what it was. He said he had been of another faculty before, but he was ashamed to utter it, or to remember it, being the worst and vilest science of all others in the world besides. The judge and the people, supposing that he had been some thief, inquired to know what it was; but he for shame and sorrow stopped his mouth, and would not declare it. At last, through their importunate clamour, he was constrained to declare the truth, and said, that he had been a priest. The judge thereupon was so moved, that he condemned him; first, enjoining him in his condemnation to ask the king forgiveness, then judged him to have his tongue cut out, and so to be burned.

As he went to burning, he passed by the college of St. Martial, where he was bid to honour the picture of the Virgin standing at the gate. On refusing so to do, the judge commanded his tongue to be cut off; and so being put into the fire, he stood so quiet, looking up to heaven all the time of the burning, as though he had felt nothing, bringing such admiration to the people, that one of the parliament said, that to bring the Lutherans to the fire would do more hurt than good.

Stephen King, *Peter Denocheus*, at Chartres, in 1553. These two were suspected of Lutheranism, and so were apprehended by the marshal, and carried to Chartres, where, after their constant confession, on their examination, they were committed to prison for a long time. During which time, Stephen King composed many hymns in the praise of the Lord, to refresh his spirit in that doleful captivity. At length they were condemned, and executed with the cruel punishment of fire.

Antony Magnus, at Paris, in 1554, was sent by those who were in prison at Lyons, and by others also who were in captivity at Paris, to Geneva, to commend them to their prayers to God for them. He returned again into France, and there within three hours of his coming was betrayed and taken by certain priests at Bourges, and delivered to the official; after a few days, the king's justices took him from the official, and sent him to Paris; where, after great rebukes and torments suffered in the prison, and firmly persisting in the profession of the truth, he was adjudged, by their capital sentence, to have his tongue cut out, and to be burned at Paris.

William Alencon, a bookseller, did much good in the provinces of France by carrying books. Coming to Montpellier, he was there ensnared by false brethren, detected, and laid in prison. In his faith he was firm and constant to the end of his martyrdom, being burnt in 1554.

There was at the same time at Montpellier a certain clothworker, who was enjoined by the judges to make public recantation, and to be present also at the burning of Alencon. At beholding his constancy and death, it pleased God to strike into this man such boldness, that he desired the judges, that either he might burn with this Alencon, or else be brought again into prison. Wherefore within three days after, he was likewise condemned to the fire and burned.

Paris Panier, in 1554.—At Dola was beheaded a good and godly lawyer, named Paris Panier, for constant standing to the gospel of Christ.

Peter du Val, shoe-maker, at Nismes, in 1554, sustained grievous rackings and torments; with which his body being broken, dislocated, and maimed, he yet manfully bore all their extremity, and would name and reveal no one. Then he was taken to the fire, and there consumed.

John Filieul, carpenter—*Julian le Ville*, point-maker, in 1554.—These two blessed and constant martyrs, as they were going toward Geneva, with one of their sons and a daughter, were apprehended by the marshal; who in the way overtaking them, and most wickedly and Judas-like pretending great favour to them, and to their religion, which he, as he said, supposed them to be of, with these and many other fair words allured them to confess what was their faith; whither they went with their children; and also that their wives were at Geneva. When they had declared this, the wretched traitor gave a sign to the horseman, and so these simple saints of Christ were entrapped and brought to the castle of Nivern. Being in prison, they were examined, and they answered uprightly according to their faith.

Touching the sacrament, they affirmed the transubstantiation of the bishop of Rome to be against the article of the Creed, which says, that Christ is gone up to heaven, and there sitteth on the right hand of God; and therefore the bread and wine must needs remain in their proper nature, being, however, a sacrament or a holy sign of the body and blood of the Lord. For as by bread and wine the heart of man is comforted, so the body of Christ crucified, and his blood shed spiritually, has the like operation in the souls of believers.

As for the mass, they said it was a most superstitious thing, and mere idolatry. And if we put any salvation therein, it was utterly robbing the passion of Christ the Son of God, and that it was not once to be named in a christian's mouth. Also, that they who say that Peter either was pope, or author of the mass, are far deceived. And as for turning bread into the body of Christ, by the words of consecration, it was an error, they said, more of madmen than anything else; for God is neither subject to men, nor to the tongues or exorcisms of men. Purgatory they denied, save only through the blood of Jesus Christ.

As they would not deprive the saints of God of their due honour, so neither the saints themselves, said they, will be contented to rob God of the honour due only to him.

As to confession, their opinion was, that the wounds and cases of conscience belong to no man but only to God.

After these answers given and written, they were sent to the monastery of Sanpeter, there to be disputed with. Then the matter came to be debated among the judges, what was to be done with them. Some would have their goods to be taken by inventory, and themselves to be banished. But Bergeronius at last caused it to be determined, that they should be burned, and first to hear mass.

The officer, to cause them to recant, threatened them with torments. When all that would not turn them, he sent them to a friar to press them in disputation. But as he could do no hurt to them, so they could do no good to him. When their execution approached, the officer put into their hands, being tied, a wooden cross, which they took with their teeth and flung away; for which the officer commanded both their tongues to be cut off. At last when the tormentor came to smear them with brimstone and gunpowder, "Go to," they said, "salt on, salt on the stinking and rotten flesh." Finally, as the flame came bursting up to their faces, they persisting constant in the fire, gave up their lives, and finished their martyrdoms.

Denis Vayre, in this year 1554, suffered at Rouen; who, first leaving his popish priesthood, went to Geneva, where he learned the art of bookbinding, and brought many times books into France. After that, in the reign of King Edward VI. he came to Jersey, and there was minister, and preached. He came into Normandy with his books, into a town called Fueille: and when he went to hire a cart, William Langlois, with John Langlois, came and stopped his books, and him who had the custody of them. Denis, although he might have escaped, yet hearing the keeper of his books was in trouble, came, and presenting himself, was committed, and the other was delivered. After two months and a half imprisonment he was charged with being a spy, because he came out of England. Then he was removed to the bishop's prison, and then to Rouen, where sentence was given that he should be burned alive, and thrice lifted up and let down again into the fire. After the sentence given they threatened him with many terrible torments, unless he would disclose such as he knew of that side. He answered, that the sounder part of all France, and of the senate, was of that religion: notwithstanding he would reveal no man's name to them. And as for their torments, he said, he cared not; for if he were killed with racking, then he would not feel the burning of the fire. When they saw him care so little for their torments, they proceeded to his burning; and first, they put a cross in his hands, which he would not hold. Then because coming by the image of the Virgin Mary he would not adore it, they cried, "Cut out his tongue:" and so they cast him into the fire, where he should be thrice taken up; but the flame went so high that the executioner, being unable to come near him, cried to the people standing by to help, and the officers with their staves laid upon the people, to help their tormentors, but never a man would stir. And this was the end and martyrdom of that blessed Denis.

There was a rich merchant of Paris, who said in jest to the friars of St. Francis, "You wear a rope about your bodies, because St. Francis once should have been hanged, and the pope redeemed him upon this condition, that all his life after he should wear a rope." Upon this the Franciscan friars of Paris caused him to be apprehended, and laid in prison, and so judgment passed upon him that he should be hanged: but he, to save his life, was contented to recant, and did so. The friars hearing of his recantation, commended him, saying, if he continued so, he should be saved; and so calling upon the officers, caused them to make haste to the gallows, to hang him up while he was yet in a good way, said they, lest he should fall again! And so was this merchant, notwithstanding his recantation, hanged for jesting against the friars.

Thomas Calbergne, a coverlet-maker, 1554. — This Thomas had copied certain spiritual songs out of a book in Geneva, which he brought with him to Tournay, and lent to one of his friends. This book being seen, he was summoned before the justice, and examined about the book, which he said contained nothing but what was agreeing to the scripture, and that he would stand by it.

Then he was confined in the castle, and after nineteen days was brought to the town-house, and there adjudged to the fire; he went cheerfully to it, singing psalms. As he was in the flame, the warden of the friars stood crying, "Turn, Thomas, Thomas, it is yet time, remember him that came at the last hour." To whom he cried out of the flame with a loud voice, "And I trust to be one of that sort," and so calling upon the name of the Lord, gave up his spirit.

Richard Feurus, a goldsmith, when in England, in 1554, received there the knowledge of God's word. Then he went to Geneva, where he remained nine or ten years. From thence returning to Lyons, he was apprehended and condemned, but escaped.

After that, continuing at Geneva about the space of three years, he came upon business to the province of Dauphiny, and there as he found fault with the grace being said in Latin, he was detected, and taken in his inn in the night, by the under-marshal. The next day he was sent to the justice, and from him to the bishop; who ridding their hands of him, he was brought to the lieutenant who sent his advocate with a notary, to ex-

H H

amine him about his faith. The whole process of his examinations, with his adversaries and the friars, is long, the principal contents come to this effect.

Inquisitor.—Dost thou believe the church of Rome?

Martyr.—No, I do believe the catholic and universal church.

Inquisitor.—What catholic church is that?

Martyr.—The congregation or communion of christians.

Inquisitor.—What congregation is that, or of whom doth it consist?

Martyr.—It consisteth in the number of God's elect, whom God hath chosen to be the members of his Son Jesus Christ, of whom he is also the head.

Inquisitor.—Where is the congregation, or how is it known?

Martyr.—It is dispersed through the universal world, in divers regions, and is known by the spiritual direction wherewith it is governed, that is to say, both by the word of God, and by the right institution of Christ's sacraments.

Inquisitor.—Do you think the church that is at Geneva, Lausanne, Berne, and such other places, a more true church than the holy church of Rome?

Martyr.—Yea, verily, for these have the notes of the true church.

Inquisitor.—What difference then make you between those churches and the church of Rome.

Martyr.—Much; for the church of Rome is governed only by traditions of men, but those are ruled only by the word of God.

Inquisitor.—Dost thou not believe the Virgin Mary to be a mediatrix and advocate to God for sinners?

Martyr.—I believe, as in the word of God is testified, Jesus Christ to be the only mediator and advocate for all sinners; although the Virgin Mary be a blessed woman, yet the office of an advocate belongs not to her.

Inquisitor.—The saints that are in paradise, have they no power to pray for us?

Martyr.—No, but I judged them to be blessed, and to be contented with that grace and glory which they have.

Inquisitor.—And what then judge you of those who follow the religion of the church of Rome? Think you them to be christians?

Martyr.—No, because that church is not governed by the Spirit of God, but rather fights against the same.

Inquisitor.—Do you then esteem all them who separate themselves from the church of Rome to be christians?

Martyr.—I have not to answer for others, but only for myself. "Every man (saith St. Paul) shall bear his own burden."

At the next examination a Franciscan friar was brought to him, who, first touching the words that he spake in his inn, asked him, "why grace might not be said in Latin?" "Because," said he, "by the word of God christians are commanded to pray with heart and with spirit, and with that tongue which is most understood, and serves best to the edification of the hearers."

Friar.—God understands all tongues, and the church of Rome hath prescribed this form of praying, receiving the same from the ancient church and the fathers, who used then to pray in Latin. And if any tongue is to be observed in prayer, one more than another, why is it not as good to pray in the Latin tongue, as to pray in the French?

Martyr.—My meaning is not to exclude any kind of language from prayer, whether it be Latin, Greek, Hebrew, or any other, so that the same be understood, and may edify the hearers.

Inquisitor.—Dost thou believe in the holy host which the priest consecrates at the mass or no?

Martyr.—I believe neither in the host, nor in any such consecration.

Inquisitor.—Why? Dost thou not believe the holy sacrament of the altar, ordained of Christ Jesus himself?

Martyr.—Touching the sacrament of the Lord's Supper, I believe that whenever we use the same according to the prescription of St. Paul, we are refreshed spiritually with the body and blood of our Lord Jesus Christ, who is the true spiritual meat and drink of our souls.

Friar.—The friar then adduced the words of St. John's gospel, saying, "My flesh is meat indeed," &c., and said, that the doctors of the church had decided that matter already, and had approved the mass to be an holy memory of the death and passion of our Lord Jesus Christ.

Martyr.—The sacrament of the supper I believe to be ordained of the Lord for a memorial of his death, and for a stirring up of our thanksgiving to him. In which sacrament we have nothing to offer up to him, but do receive with all thanksgiving the benefits offered to us most abundantly in Christ Jesus his Son.

Inquisitor.—Dost thou believe in any purgatory?

Martyr.—I believe that Christ with his precious blood hath made an end of all purgatory, and purgation of our sins.

Inquisitor.—And dost thou think then there is no place after this life, where souls of men departed remain till they have made satisfaction for their sins?

Martyr.—No; but I acknowlege one satisfaction once made for the sins of all men, by the blood and sacrifice of Jesus Christ our Lord, which is the propitiation and purgation for the sins of the whole world.

Friar.—In the eighteenth chapter of Matthew, Christ speaking by way of a parable or similitude, of a certain cruel servant, who, because he would not forgive his fellow-servant, was cast into prison, saith, that he shall not come out from thence till he hath paid the uttermost farthing. By which similitude is signified unto us a certain middle place, which is left for satisfaction to be made after this life for sins.

Martyr.—First, the satisfaction for our sins by the death of Christ is plain and evident in the scriptures; as in these places: "Come unto me, all ye that labour and are heavy laden, and I will give you rest," Matt. xi. 28. "I am the door: by me if any man enter in, he shall be saved," John x. 9. "I am the way, the truth, and the life," John xiii. "Blessed are the dead that die in the Lord, for they rest from their labours," Rev. xiii. 13. Also to the thief who hanged with the Lord, it was said, "This day thou shalt be with me in paradise," &c. Secondly; as to this similitude, it has no other object but to admonish us of our duty, in shewing charity, and forgiving one another, which unless we do, there is no mercy to be looked for at the hands of God.

Friar.—Christ gave to St. Peter power to bind and loose, whose successor, and vicar of Christ, is the pope, for the government of the church, that it might have one head in the world, as it hath in heaven. And though the pastors do not live according to the word which they preach, yet their doctrine is not therefore to be refused, as Christ teaches.

Martyr.—If the pope and his adherents would preach the word purely and sincerely, mixing no inventions of their own, nor obtruding laws of their own devising, I would then embrace their doctrine, however their life were to the contrary: according as Christ tells us of the scribes and pharisees, admonishing us to follow their doctrine, and not their lives, Matt. xxiii. 3. But there is great difference, whether they sit in Moses's chair, or else in the chair of abomination, spoken of by Daniel, and also by St. Paul, where he saith, "That the man of sin, the son of perdition shall sit in the temple of God, exalting himself above all that is called God," 2 Thess. ii. 3.

And as touching the keys of binding and loosing, given to Peter, Christ therein assigned to Peter and the other apostles, the office of preaching the word of the gospel, which they well observed, in preaching nothing else but only the word, in which word is all the power contained of binding and loosing. Nor is it to be granted that the church has two heads, one in heaven, another in earth; the head is but one, even Jesus Christ, whom the Father hath appointed to be head alone both in heaven and earth.

The friar.—You have no understanding how to expound the scriptures, but the old doctors have expounded the scriptures, and holy councils, whose judgments are to be followed. But what say you to auricular confession?

The martyr.—I know no other confession but that which is to be made to God, and reconciliation towards our neighbour, which Christ and his apostles have commended to us.

Friar. — Have you not read in the gospel, how Christ doth bid us to confess to the priest, where he commanded the leper, being made whole, to shew himself to the priest?

Martyr. — The true church of the Lord Jesus Christ never observed this strange kind of confession, to carry our sins to the priest's ear. And though the church of Rome has intruded this manner of confessing, it follows not that it is to be received. And as to the leper whom the Lord sent to the priest, he was not sent to whisper his sins in the priest's ear, but only as a testimony of his health received, according to the law.

Of the other confession which is to be made to God, we have both the examples and testimonies of David in the Psalms, where he saith, that he confessed his sins unto the Lord, and received forgiveness of the same, (Psalm xxxii. 5.—li. 4.)

And thus was this godly Feurus remanded again by the deputy to the bishop's prison, and from thence shortly after removed to Lyons.

After he was come to Lyons, they proceeded at last to the sentence, condemning him first to have his tongue cut out, and then to be burned. All which he received willingly and quietly for righteousness sake, thus finishing his martyrdom, July 7, A.D. 1554.

Nicholas du Chesne, A.D. 1554.

The occasion why this Nicholas came into trouble, was, that going from Lausanne, to his sister, and her husband, and other of his friends, as he went from Besanson, toward the town of Gry, he did not pay homage to a cross in the way, where a monk, which was an inquisitor, overtook him, and thereby suspected him. He was guided by the monk, craftily dissembling his religion, to a lodging in Gry: where the justice of the place took him. Nicholas seeing how he was betrayed by the monk, "O false traitor," said he, "hast thou betrayed me?" Then after examination he was condemned. Being carried to the place of martyrdom, he was promised, that if he would kneel down and hear a mass, he should be let go. But Nicholas, armed with perseverance, said, he would rather die than commit such an act. Calling upon the name of the Lord, he took his death patiently.

John Bertrand, a Forester, A.D. 1556.

For the religion and gospel of Christ this John was apprehended, and led bound to Blois, where he was examined on divers points: as, whether he had spoken at any time against God, against the church, and the he-saints, and the she-saints of paradise? He said, No. Whether at any time he had called the mass abominable? Which he granted, because he, finding no mass in all the scripture, was commanded by St. Paul, that if an angel from heaven would preach any other gospel than that which was already received, he should be accursed. After his condemnation they would have him confess, and presented to him a cross to kiss. But he bade the friars with their cross depart; "That is not the cross," said he, "that I must carry." Entering into the cart before the multitude, he gave thanks to God, that he was not there for murder, theft, or blasphemy, but only for the cause of our Saviour. Being tied to the post, he sung the twenty-fifth Psalm. He was young, his countenance was exceeding cheerful and amiable, his eyes looked up to heaven. "O the happy journey," said he, seeing the place where he should suffer, "and the fair place that is prepared for me!" When the fire was kindled about him, "O Lord," cried he, "give thy hand to thy servant; I commend my soul unto thee;" and so meekly yielded up his spirit. His patient and joyful constancy astonished the people.

Peter Rousseau, being constant in his confession, was

put to the rack three times, which he suffered constantly with great torments. Afterwards he had his tongue cut off, and a ball of iron put in his mouth. Thus broken and maimed, he was drawn upon a hurdle to the fire, where he was lifted up into the air, and let down three times. When he was half-burned, the ball fell from his mouth, and he with a loud voice called on the name of God, saying, "Jesus Christ assist me." And so this blessed martyr gave up his life to God, A.D. 1556.

Arnold Moniere and *John de Cazes*, A. D. 1556.—After Arnold Moniere was taken and laid in prison, John de Cazes hearing of him, though warned that if he visited him he would be impeached of heresy, went to comfort him, and was imprisoned. After many examinations, sentence was given upon them to be burned. When the time of their martyrdom came, they were drawn through the dirt upon an hurdle to the place, accompanied with a number of bills, glaves, gunners, and trumpeters. When the blessed martyrs were bound to the post, they rejoicing that they were made worthy to suffer for Christ, made confession of their faith, and gave many exhortations to the people. But to prevent the people hearing these saints the trumpeters were commanded to sound, which never ceased during all the time of their suffering.

Bartholomew Hector, A.D. 1556.—This Hector came into Piedmont, to get his living by selling books, he was taken by a certain gentleman, and there arrested and sent to Turin, then examined, and at last condemned. Being condemned, he was threatened, that if he spake any thing to the people his tongue should be cut off; nevertheless he ceased not to speak. After his prayer, wherein he prayed for the judges, that God would forgive them and open their eyes, he was offered his pardon at the stake if he would recant, which he refused. Then he prepared himself for death, which he took patiently. Whereat many of the people wept, saying, "Why doth this man die, who speaks of nothing but of God?"

Philip Cene, and *James* his companion, A. D. 1557. —This Philip Cene was an apothecary at Geneva. He was taken at Dijon, imprisoned, and there burned with one James his companion. As Philip went to his death singing psalms, a friar stopped his mouth with his hand. Most of the people wept bitterly, saying, "Be of good courage, brethren, be not afraid of death." Which when one of the adversaries heard, he said to one of the magistrates, "Do you not see how almost half the people are on their side, and comfort them?"

Archambant Ceraphon, and *Matthew Nicholas du Russeau*, A.D. 1557.—These two were in prison also at Dijon. Archambant heard of certain prisoners at Dijon, to whom he wrote to comfort them with his letters. The next day he was searched, and letters were found about him. Then he was brought to Dijon, where he, with the other, called Master Nicholas du Russeau, suffered with great constancy.

Philbert Hamlin was first a priest, then he went to Geneva, where he exercised printing. After that he was made minister at the town of Allenart, where he did much good in edifying the people. At last he was apprehended, and with him his host, a priest, whom he had instructed in the gospel; and after confession of his faith, he was carried with the priest to Bourdeaux before the president. While he was in prison, a priest came in on a Sunday to say mass, when Philbert came and plucked his garments from his back with such zeal and vehemency, that the mass-garments, with the chalice and candlesticks, fell down and were broken, saying, "Is it not enough for you to blaspheme God in churches, but you must also pollute the prison with your idolatry?" The gaoler hearing this, in his fury laid upon him with his staff. He was removed to the common prison, and laid in a low pit, laden with great irons, so that his legs were swollen, and there he continued eight days.

At last Philbert was brought to the place of his martyrdom, and as he was exhorting the people the trumpets blew without ceasing, that his words might not be heard; and so being fastened to the post, this holy martyr, praying and exhorting the people, was strangled, and his body consumed with fire on Palm Sunday eve, 1557.

In 1557 *Nicholas Sartorius*, of the age of twenty-six years, came to Cambray, where a warden of the friars in the town of Ost had preached on Good Friday upon the Passion. The report of which sermon being recited to this Sartorius, he reprehended the error and blasphemies of it, which were against the holy Scriptures. Shortly after the party that told him went to a secretary named Ripet, who came to entrap Nicholas. " And did not our preacher," said he, " preach well?" —" No," said Nicholas, " but he lied falsely." Ripet asked, " And do you not believe the body of the Lord to be in the host?" Nicholas answered, " That would be against our Creed, which saith, ' That he ascended up, and sitteth,' &c." Ripet went forthwith to the friar to cause him to be apprehended. The friends of Nicholas perceiving the danger, wished him to fly and save himself, and accompanied him out of the town about three leagues. But he was taken at the town of St. Remy, at the foot of the mountain of Great St. Bernard. They brought him to the rack, and when the sergeant refused to draw the cord, the bailiff himself, and the receiver, with a canon, put him to the rack with their own hands. They pronounced sentence that he should be burned; which sentence he received with such constancy, that neither the king's receiver, nor all the other enemies, could divert him from the truth of the gospel, which he manfully maintained while any spirit remained in his body.

George Tardif, with one of Tours, an embroider, and *Nicholas*, a shoemaker of Joinville, A. D. 1558.— The historian of the French martyrs makes memorial of George Tardif, an embroiderer of Tours, and Nicholas of Joinville, declaring that these three were together in prison, and afterward suffered in sundry places one from the other. George Tardif was executed at Sens.

The embroiderer of Tours, as he was coming with five or six others out of a wood, being at prayer, was taken, and thereupon examined. Before he should be examined, he desired the judges that he might pray; which being granted, after his prayer made, wherein he prayed for the judges, for the king, and all estates, and for the necessity of all Christ's saints, he answered for himself with such grace and modesty, that the hearts of many were broken to the shedding of tears, seeking (as it seemed) nothing else but his deliverance. However he was sent at last to Tours, and there was crowned with martyrdom.

The third, which was Nicholas, was condemned and set in a cart, when his father, coming with a staff, would have beaten him, but the officers not suffering it would have struck the old man; but the son cried to the officers, and desired them to let his father alone, saying, that his father had power over him to do with him what he would. And so going to the place where he was to suffer, having a ball of iron put in his mouth, he was brought at length to the fire, in the town of Joinville, where he patiently received his death and martyrdom.

The Congregation of Paris persecuted, to the number of three or four hundred, at Paris, A. D. 1558.

On the fourth of September, 1558, a company of the faithful, to the number of three or four hundred, were assembled at Paris in a house to communicate together the Lord's Supper; but they were discovered by certain priests, who beset the house, and made an outcry, that the watch might come to take them, so that in a short time almost all the city was in arms, thinking some conspiracy to have been in the city. Then perceiving that they were Lutherans, a great part of them were in extreme rage, furiously seeking their blood, and stopped the streets and lanes with carts, and made fires to see that none should escape. The faithful seeing the suddenness of their fury, were in great fear; but being exhorted by the leaders of the congregation went to prayer. It was then resolved, that the men who had weapons should venture through the press: the women and children remained in the house, and a few men who were less bold than the others, to the number of six or seven score. Those that went out with weapons all escaped save only one, who was beaten down with stones, and so destroyed. The women, who were all gentlewomen, or of great wealth, only six or seven excepted, seeing no hope, and perceiving the fury of the people, went up to the windows, crying, " Mercy," and shewing their innocence, required ordinary justice. The king's attorney, with the commissaries and sergeants, with much ado appeased the people, and entered into the house, where viewing the women and children, and the other furniture prepared for that congregation, perceived sufficient testimonies of their innocence, so that for pity his eyes could not refrain from tears. However, proceeding in his office, he brought them all to prison. I omit here the furious usage of the people by the way, how despitefully they plucked and hailed the women, tore their garments, thrust off their hoods from their heads, and disfigured their faces with dust and dirt.

Besides these wrongs and oppressions done to these poor innocents, there followed the cruel and slanderous reports of the friars and priests, who, in their railing sermons uttered horrible falsehoods and calumnies against their morals. These rumours and defamations were no sooner given out, but they were received, and spread far, not only among the vulgar, but also among the court, and even to the king's ears.

Here the enemies began to triumph, thinking that the gospel was overthrown for ever. On the other side there was no less perplexity and lamentation among the brethren, sorrowing not so much for themselves, as for the imprisonment of their companions. However, they lost not their courage altogether, but they exhorted one another, considering the great favour and providence of God, in delivering them so wonderfully out of the danger. Some comfort they experienced, consulting together in this order, that first they should humble themselves to God in their own private families: secondly, to stop the slanders against their holy assemblies, they should write apologies, one to the king, another to the people. Thirdly, that letters of consolation should be written and sent to their brethren in prison.

The first apology was written to the king, and conveyed so secretly into his chamber, that it was found and read openly in the hearing of the king and all his nobles. The christians learnedly and discreetly cleared themselves of those reports, and shewed the malice of their enemies, especially of Satan, who ever from the beginning of the church has, and still goes about to overturn the right ways of the Lord. Nevertheless, this apology to the king served to little purpose. But the other apology to the people did inestimable good, in satisfying the rumours, and defending the true cause of the gospel.

As the faithful christians were thus occupied in writing their apologies, and in comforting their brethren in prison with their letters, the adversaries were not idle, but sought all possible means to hasten the execution, giving diligent attendance about the prison and other places, to satisfy their uncharitable desire with the death of those whose religion they hated.

Finally, a commission was directed out by the king, and presidents and councillors appointed to oversee the matter. Upon which many of the poor afflicted christians were brought forth to their judgment and martyrdom.

Of this godly company thus brought to judgment and to martyrdom, the first was Nicholas Clinet, of the age of sixty years. He was suspected by the judges to be a minister, and therefore was set to dispute against the chief of the Sorbonists, especially Maillard, whom he so confuted, both by the scriptures and also by their own sorbonical divinity, (wherein he had been well exercised and expert) in the presence of the lieutenant-civil, that the lieutenant confessed that he never heard a man better learned, and of more intelligence.

Another was named *Taurin Gravelle*, a lawyer. He was first a student of the law at Toulouse; after that he was made an advocate in the court of Paris: lastly, for his godliness he was ordained an elder to the congregation, with Clinet. This Taurin having a certain house, and seeing the congregation destitute of room, received them into his house. And when he perceived the house to be compassed with enemies, though he might have escaped, yet he would not, being prepared to answer for receiving the assembly into the house. The constancy of this man was invincible, in sustaining his conflicts with the sorbonists. In fine, these two godly elders finished their martyrdom in the cruel pains of the fire.

Next to Clinet and Gravelle was brought out *Mistress Philip*, gentlewoman, of the age of twenty-three years. She was a widow, who ceased not to serve the Lord in his church. She had many conflicts with the judges and the sorbonists, namely, Maillard. To the judges her answer was, " That she had learned the faith which she confessed in the word of God, and would live and die in the same." And being demanded whether the body of Christ was in the sacrament: " How is that possible," said she, " to be the body of Christ to whom all power is given, and which is exalted above all heavens, when we see the mice and rats, apes and monkeys, play with it, and tear it in pieces?" Her petition to them was, that as they had taken her sister from her, they yet would let her have a Bible or Testament to comfort herself. Her wicked neighbours, although they could touch her conversation with no part of dishonesty, yet they laid many things to her charge, as that there was much singing of psalms in her house, and twice or thrice an infinite number of persons were seen to come out of her house. Also, when her husband was dying, no priest was called for; neither was it known where he was buried; neither did they ever hear any word of their infant being baptized.

These three holy martyrs were condemned, September 27, and being put in a chapel, doctors were sent to them, but their constancy remained immoveable. After that they were sent in a dung-cart to the place of punishment. Clinet ever cried by the way, protesting, that he said or maintained nothing but the truth of God.

The gentlewoman, seeing a priest come to confess her, said, " That she had confessed unto God, and had received of him remission: other absolution she found none in scripture." And when certain councillors did urge her to take in her hands the wooden cross, alleging how Christ commanded every one to bear his cross: she answered, " My lords," said she, " you make me in very deed to bear my cross, condemning me unjustly, and putting me to death in the cause of my Lord Jesus Christ; who willeth us to bear our cross, but no such cross as you speak of."

Gravelle looked with a smiling countenance, and shewed a cheerful colour, declaring how little he regretted his condemnation: and being asked of his friends to what death he was condemned; " I see well (said he) that I am condemned to death, but to what death or torment I regard not." And coming from the chapel, when he perceived they went about to cut out his tongue, he offered his tongue willingly to be cut.

The gentlewoman also, being required to give her tongue, did so likewise, with these words :—" Seeing I do not refuse to give my body, shall I refuse to give my tongue? No, no." The constancy of Gravelle was admirable, casting up his sighs and groans to heaven, declaring thereby his ardent affection in praying to God. Clinet was somewhat more sad than the other, by reason of the feebleness of nature and his age. But the gentlewoman yet surmounted all the rest in constancy, changing neither countenance nor colour.

After the death of her husband, she used to go in a mourning weed, after the manner of the country. But the same day, going to her burning, she put on her French hood, and decked herself in her best array, as going to a new marriage, to be joined to her spouse Jesus Christ. And thus the three, with singular constancy, were burned; Gravelle and Clinet were burned alive. Philip the gentlewoman was strangled, after she had a little tasted the flame with her feet and visage; and so she ended her martyrdom.

Of the same company was also *Nicholas Cene*, a physician, and *Peter Gabart:* who, about five or six days after the other three, were brought forth to their death.

When the time of their execution was come, they perceived that the judges intended, that if they would relent, they should be strangled, if not, they should be burned alive, and their tongues be cut from them. Being content to suffer these torments for our Saviour Jesus Christ, they offered their tongues willingly to be cut. Gabart began to sigh because he could no more praise the Lord with his tongue. Then they were drawn out of prison in the dung-cart to the suburbs of St. Germain. The people, in rage and madness, followed with cruel injuries and blasphemies, as though they would have done the execution themselves upon them. The cruelty of their death was such as has seldom been seen: for they were held in the air over a small fire, and their lower parts burnt off, before the higher parts were much harmed with the fire. Nevertheless these blessed saints ceased not in all these torments to turn up their eyes to heaven, and to shew infinite testimonies of their faith and constancy.

In the same fire many Testaments and Bibles also were burnt.

Frederick Danvile, and *Francis Rebezies*, neither of them past twenty years of age, were among the company. How valiantly they behaved themselves in those tender years, sustaining the cause of our Lord Jesus Christ, what confession they made, what conflicts they had, disputing with the doctors of the Sorbonne, their own letters left in writing make record: the effect whereof briefly to touch is this; and first, concerning Frederick Danvil.

On the 12th of Sept. Frederick was brought before Benedict Jacobin, and his companion, a Sorbonist, who thus began to argue with him :—

Doctor.—Which think you to be the true church, the church of the Protestants, or the church of Paris?

Martyr.—I recognize that to be the true church where the gospel is truly preached, and the sacraments rightly ministered, as were left by Jesus Christ and his apostles.

Doctor.—And is the church of Geneva such a one as you speak of?

Martyr.—I so judge it to be.

Doctor.—And what if I prove the contrary, will you believe me?

Martyr.—Yea, if you shall prove it by the Scripture.

Doctor.—Or will you believe St. Augustine and other holy doctors innumerable?

Martyr.—Yea, so they dissent not from the scripture and the word of God.

Doctor.—By the authority of St. Augustine, the church is there, where is the succession of bishops. On this I frame this argument :—There is the church, where is the perpetual succession of bishops? In the church of Paris there is such succession of bishops, and therefore the church of Paris is the true church.

Martyr.—I answer, That if St. Augustine mean the succession of such as are true bishops indeed, which truly preach the gospel, and rightly administer the sacraments; such bishops I suppose to be at Geneva, where the gospel is truly preached, and the sacraments duly ministered, and not in the church of Paris. But if St. Augustine mean the succession of false bishops, such as neither preach nor minister according to God's word, it is in nowise to be granted.

Doctor.—What say you by auricular confession?

Martyr.—The same that I said before to monsieur lieutenant, that is, That I take it for a plantation, not planted by God in his word.

The Examination of Francis Rebezies.

Rebezies had three examinations: the first with the civil lieutenant; the second with the presidents and the councillors; the third with the friars. He was asked, whether he did not like to resort to the beautified temples to hear mass, or whether he did not take the mass to be an holy thing, and ordained of God? He answered that he believed it was a great blasphemy against God, and a service set up by the devil. Whether he did not acknowledge purgatory? Yea, that purgatory which is the death and passion of Christ, which takes away the sins of the world. "The death of Christ is the principal," said they, "but thou must also believe another." "Alas," said he, "can we never content ourselves with the simplicity of the gospel, but man always will be putting to something of his own brain. In so many places of the scripture we see the blood of Jesus Christ to be sufficient." When they objected and repeated the words of the parable, Mat. v., "Thou shalt not come out till thou hast paid the last farthing," he answered, "That the words of that parable had no relation but to civil matters; and that this word (until) means there, as much as never." The president asked, if he was not afraid to be burned, and bring his parents into such dishonour? He answered, that he knew well, "That all who would live godly in Christ Jesus, should suffer persecution." And that to him either to live or die was an advantage in the Lord. And as to his parents, "Christ," said he, "himself forewarns, 'That whosoever loveth father or mother more than him, is not worthy of him.'" —"Jesus Maria!" said the president, "what youth is this now-a-days, who cast themselves so headlong into the fire!"

He was brought before Benet, master of the doctors of the Sorbonne, and another called Jacobine, the 14th of October. The doctor began thus to object as follows:

Doctor.—I know well you hold the church to be, where the word is truly preached, and the sacraments sincerely ministered, according as they are left of Christ and his apostles.

Martyr.—That do I believe, and in that will I live and die.

Doctor.—Do you not believe, that whoever is without that church cannot obtain remission of his sins?

Martyr.—Whoever separates himself from that church, to make either sect, part, or division, cannot obtain remission of his sins.

Doctor.—Now let us consider two churches, the one wherein the word is rightly preached, and the sacraments administered; the other, wherein the word and sacraments be used otherwise. Which of these two ought we to believe?

Martyr.—The first.

Doctor.—Well said. Next is now to speak of the gifts given to the church: as the power of the keys, confession for the remission of sins, after we are confessed to a priest. Also we must believe the seven sacraments in the church truly administered, as they are here in the churches of Paris, where the sacrament of the altar is ministered, and the gospel truly preached.

Martyr.—Sir, now you begin to halt. As for my part, I do not receive in the church more than two sacraments, which were instituted for the whole community of christians. And as concerning the power of keys, and your confession, I believe that for remission of our sins, we ought to go to none other but only to God, as we read, 1 John i. 9, "If we confess our sins, God is faithful and just to forgive us our sins, and to cleanse us from all unrighteousness," &c.

Doctor.—Should I not believe that Christ, in the time of his apostles, gave to them power to remit sins?

Martyr.—The power that Christ gave to his apostles, if it will be well considered, is nothing disagreeing to my saying: and therefore I began to say, which here I confess, that the Lord gave to his apostles to preach the word, and so to remit sins by the same word.

Doctor.—Do you then deny auricular confession?

Martyr.—Yea, verily I do.

Doctor.—Ought we to pray to saints?

Martyr.—I believe not.

Doctor.—Jesus Christ being here upon the earth, was he not then as well sufficient to hear the whole world, and to be intercessor for all, as he is now?

Martyr.—Yes.

Doctor.—But we find that when he was here on earth, his apostles made intercession for the people: and why may they not also do the same as well now?

Martyr.—So long as they were in the world, they exercised their ministry, and prayed one for another; but now they being in paradise, all their prayer that they make is this, that they wish that they who are yet on earth may attain to their felicity: but to obtain any thing at the Father's hand, we must have recourse only to his Son.

Doctor.—If one man have such charge to pray for another, may not he then be called an intercessor?

Martyr.—I grant.

Doctor.—Well, then, you say there is but one intercessor. Whereupon I infer, that I, being bound to pray for another, need not now to go to Jesus Christ to have him an intercessor, but to God alone, setting Jesus Christ apart; and so ought we verily to believe.

Martyr.—You understand not, sir, that if God do not behold us in the face of his own well-beloved Son, then shall we never be able to stand in his sight. For if he shall look upon us, he can see nothing but sin. And if the heavens be not pure in his eyes, what shall be thought then of man, so abominable and unprofitable, "Who drinketh in iniquity like water," as Job says?

Then the other friar, seeing his fellow have nothing to answer to this, inferred as follows:

Doctor.—Nay, my friend, as touching the great mercy of God, let that stand, and now to speak of ourselves: this we know, that God is not displeased with them who have recourse to his saints.

Martyr.—Sir, we must not do after our own wills, but according to that which God wills and commands.

Doctor.—As no man comes into the presence of an earthly king or prince, without means made by some about him; so, or rather much more, to the heavenly king above, &c.

Martyr.—To this earthly example I will answer with another heavenly example of the prodigal son, who sought no other means to obtain his father's grace, but came to the father himself.

Doctor.—Touching the mass, what say you? believe you not that when the priest has consecrated the host, our Lord is there as well as he was hanging upon the cross?

Martyr.—No, verily; but I believe that Jesus Christ is sitting at the right hand of his Father; as appears from Heb. x., 1 Cor. xv., Col. iii.: and therefore to make short with you, I hold your mass for none other but a false and counterfeited service, set up by Satan, and retained by his ministers, by which you annihilate the precious blood of Christ, and his oblation once made of his own body; and you know right well that it is sufficient, and ought not to be reiterated.

Doctor.—You deceive yourselves in the word reiteration, for we do not reiterate it so as you think; as by example I will show you. You see me now in this religious garment; but if I should put on me a soldier's weed, then should I be disguised, and yet for all that I should remain the same still within my doublet, that I was before in my friar's weed. So is it with the sacrifice: we confess and grant that naturally he was once offered in sacrifice; but supernaturally, we sacrifice the same without reiteration.

Martyr.—Sir, this I say, that such a disguised sacrifice, is a diabolical sacrifice; and this you may take for a resolution.

Doctor.—And how is your belief touching the holy supper?

Martyr.—That if it be ministered to me by the minister, as it has been left by Christ and his apostles, preaching also the word purely withal, I believe that, in receiving the material bread and wine, I receive with lively faith the body and blood of Jesus Chist spiritually.

Doctor.—Say corporally.

Martyr.—No, sir, for his words are spirit and life ; and let this content you.

Doctor.—What say you, is it lawful for a priest to marry?

Martyr.—I believe it to be lawful for him, as the apostle saith, " Whoever has not the gift of continence, let him marry ; for it is better to marry than to burn." And if this do not content you, you may read what he writes of bishops and elders, 1 Tim. iii., and Tit. i.

And thus these doctors, affirming that he denied priesthood, gave him leave to depart, saying, " God have mercy on you." He said, " Amen."

After this, Rebezies and Frederick Danville were brought to be racked, that they might inform of the rest of the congregation. In the chamber they found three councillors, who thus began with them :—" Lift up thy hand. Thou shalt swear by the passion of Jesus Christ, whose image thou seest here," shewing him a great picture. Rebezies answered, " I swear to you by the passion of Christ, which is written in my heart." " Why dost thou not swear" said the councillors, " as we say to thee ?" " Because," said he, " it is a great blasphemy against the Lord." Then the councillors read the depositions, and beginning with Rebezies, said, " Wilt thou not tell us the truth, what companions thou knowest to be of this assembly ?" Rebezies named Gravelle, Clinet, who were already burned, and John Sansot. They said, that the court had ordered that if they would give no other answer but that, he should be put to the torture or rack ; and so he was commanded to be stripped to his shirt, having a cross put in his hand, being bid to commend himself to God and the Virgin Mary ; but he neither would receive the cross, nor commend himself to the Virgin Mary, saying, that God was able enough to guard him, and to save him out of the lion's mouth, and so, being drawn and stretched, he began to cry, " Come Lord, and shew thy strength, that man do not prevail," &c. But they cried, " Tell the truth, and thou shalt be let down." Nevertheless, he continued still in his calling and prayer to the Lord, so that they could get nothing from him. After they had long tormented him, the councillors said, " Wilt thou say nothing else ?" " I have nothing else," said he, " to say." And so they commanded him to be loosed, and be put by the fireside. Being loosed, he said to them, " Do you handle thus the poor servants of God ?" The like was done to Frederick Danvile also, of whom they could have no other answer. So mightily did God assist and strengthen his servants.

These constant and true martyrs of Christ, after they had returned from the torture unto their fellow prisoners, ceased not to thank and praise the Lord for his assistance. Frederick sighed often, and being asked why he did so? he said it was not for the evil that he had suffered, but for the evils that he knew they should suffer afterwards. " Notwithstanding," said he, " be strong, brethren, and be not afraid, assuring yourselves of the aid of God, who succoured us, and also will comfort you." Rebezies with the rack was so drawn and stretched, that one of his shoulders was higher than the other, and his neck drawn on one side, so that he could not move himself. When the night came they rejoiced together, and comforted themselves with meditation of the life to come, and contempt of this world, singing psalms together till it was day.

The next day they were again required to inform ; which when they refused, the sentence was read, that they should be brought in a dung-cart to Maulbert place, and there, having a ball in their mouths, be tied each one to his post, and afterward strangled, and so burned to ashes.

Being brought to the place of execution, a cross again was offered them, which they refused. Then a priest standing by, bade them believe in the Virgin Mary. " Let God," said they, " reign alone." The people standing by, " Ah, mischievous Lutheran !" said they : " Nay, a true christian I am," said he. When they were tied to their stakes, after their prayers, and they were ordered to be dispatched, one of them comforting the other, said ; " Be strong, my brother, be strong : Satan away from us !" One standing by, said, " These Lutherans do call upon Satan." One John Morel, who afterward died a martyr, answered, " I pray you let us hear what they say, and we shall hear them invoke the name of God." Upon this the people listened better to them, to hearken, as well as they could, what they said : they crying still as much as their mouths being stopped could utter ; " Assist us, O Lord." And so they, rendering up their spirits to the hands of the Lord, did consummate their martyrdom.

After the martyrdom of these two above said, the intention of the judges was to dispatch the rest one after another, and had procured process against twelve or thirteen. But a certain gentlewoman, then a prisoner among them, had presented causes of exceptions against them, by which the cruel rage of the enemies was staid to the month of July following. In the mean time, as this persecution was spread into other countries, the faithful cantons of Switzerland, perceiving these good men to be afflicted for the same doctrine which they preached in their churches, sent their ambassadors to the king to make supplication for them.

At the same time also came letters from the county palatine elector, to solicit the king for them. The king standing then in great need of the Germans for his wars, was contented at least, that they should proceed more gently with them ; and so the fire for that time ceased. Most of them were sent to abbeys, where they were kept at the charge of the priors, to be constrained to be present at the service of idolatry, especially the young scholars ; of whom some shrunk back, others being more loosely kept, escaped away.

Many of this godly company of French protestants were afterwards condemned, and suffered the rack, and were martyred, glorifying God by their faithfulness unto death. We have the account and history of above thirty martyrs in France, but it would occupy too much space to detail them all.

ACCOUNT OF THE SPANISH MARTYRS.

Franciscus San Romanus.

In the year 1540 this Francis was sent by certain Spanish merchants of Antwerp, to Breme, where, hearing the prior of the Austin friars preach, he was so touched through the marvellous working of God's Spirit, that he proceeded further, searching and conferring with learned men, so that in a short time he was grown ripe in knowledge in the word of life.

In the mean time the Spanish merchants of Antwerp understanding by his letters, his change of religion, sent him letters, pretending outwardly much good-will, but secretly practising his destruction. For at the day appointed for his coming, some friars were set ready to receive him, who took him coming down from his horse, rifled his books, brought him into a merchant's house near at hand, where they examined him ; when they found him not agreeing to their faith, they bound him hand and foot, and burnt his books before his face, threatening to burn himself also. At this disputation within the house divers Spaniards were present, which made the friars more bold. Being demanded of what faith and religion he was ; " My faith," said he, " is to confess and preach Christ Jesus only, and him crucified, which is the true faith of the universal church of Christ through the whole world ; but this faith and doctrine you have corrupted, taking another abominable kind of life, and by your impiety have brought the most part of the world into most miserable blindness." And to explain his faith to them more expressly, he recited all the articles of the creed.

Which done, then the friars asked, whether he believed the bishop of Rome to be Christ's vicar, and head of the church, having all the treasures of the church in his own power, being able to bind and loose ? Also to make new articles, and abolish the old, at his own will? Francis answered, "That he believed none of all this, but the contrary, namely, that the pope was antichrist, born of the devil, the enemy of Jesus Christ, transferring to himself God's honour, and being incited by the devil, turning all things upside down, and corrupting the purity of Christ's religion, partly by his false pretences beguiling, and partly by his extreme cruelty destroying the poor flock of Christ," &c. With the like boldness he uttered his mind against the mass and purgatory. The friars suffered him to speak, till he came to the pope, and began to speak against his dignity, and their profit; and then they could bear it no longer, but thundered against him words full of cruelty and terror. As they were burning of his books, and began also to cast the New Testament into the fire, Francis seeing that, began to thunder out against them again. The Spaniards supposing him not to be in his right senses, conveyed him to a tower six miles from Antwerp, where he was detained in a deep cave or dungeon, with much misery, for the space of eight months. In which time of his imprisonment many grave and discreet persons came to visit him, exhorting him that he would change his opinion, and speak more modestly. Francis answered again, that he maintained no opinion erroneous or heretical; and if he seemed to be somewhat vehement with the friars, that was not to be ascribed to him so much as to their own importunity; hereafter he would frame himself more temperately. Whereupon the Spaniards thinking him come to himself, discharged him out of prison, A.D. 1541.

San Romane being thus freed out of prison, came to a certain friend of his, named Franciscus Dryander (who afterward died a martyr) with whom he had much conference about religion: who gave him counsel. As to religion his counsel was, that he should say or do nothing for favour of men, whereby the glory of God should be diminished; but he required a sound and right judgment conformed to the rule of God's word, lest it might chance to him, as it did to many, who, being carried away with an inconsiderate zeal, leave their proper callings, and while they think to do good, and to edify, destroy and do harm, and cast themselves needlessly into danger. "It is God," said he, "that hath the care of his church, and will stir up faithful ministers for it; he cares not for such, as rashly intrude themselves into that function without any calling."

This advice, Francis willingly accepted, promising to moderate himself more considerately: but this promise was shortly broken, as you shall hear. For, passing from Dryander he went to Ratisbone, and there having opportunity to speak to the emperor, he stepped boldly to him, beseeching him to deliver his country and subjects of Spain from false religion, and to restore again the purity of Christ's doctrine, declaring and protesting, that the princes and protestants of Germany were in the truer part, and that the religion of Spain, drowned in ignorance and blindness, was greatly different from the true and perfect word of God. The emperor all this while gave him gentle hearing, signifying that he would consider upon the matter, and so act, as he trusted should be for the best. This quiet answer of the emperor ministered to him no little encouragement, he went the second, and also the third time, to the emperor, who quietly answered him as before. And yet Francis, not satisfied in his mind, sought the fourth time to speak to the emperor, but was repulsed by the Spaniards about the emperor, who would have thrown him headlong into the Danube, had not the emperor stopped them, and commanded him to be judged by the laws of the empire. Then Francis, with other captives, was delivered to the inquisitors; by whom he was laid in a dark prison under ground. Many times he was called for to be examined, and suffered great injuries and contumelies, but ever remained in his conscience firm and unmovable. The articles whereon he stood, and for which he was condemned, were these:

That life and salvation in the sight of God, comes to no man in his own strength, works or merits, but only by the free mercy of God, in the blood and sacrifice of his Son our Mediator.

That the sacrifice of the mass, which the papists do recount available, *ex opere operato*, for the remission of sin, both to the quick and the dead, is horrible blasphemy.

That auricular confession with numbering up of sins, that satisfaction, purgatory, pardons, invocation of saints, worshipping of images, are mere blasphemy against the living God.

That the blood of Christ is profaned and injured in these popish doctrines.

After the inquisitors perceived, that he could by no means be reclaimed from his assertions, they proceeded to the sentence, condemning him to be burned for an heretic. Many other malefactors were brought also with him to the place of execution, but they were all pardoned; he only, for the gospel, was taken and burned. As he was led to the place of suffering, they put upon him a mitre of paper, painted full of devils.

As he was brought out of the city-gate to be burned, there stood a wooden cross by the way: Francis was required to do homage to it; which he refused, answering, that "The manner of christians is not to worship wood, and he was a christian." Upon this arose great clamour among the vulgar people. But this was turned into a miracle. Such was the blind rudeness of the people, that they imputed this to the divine virtue, that it would not suffer itself to be worshipped by an heretic! and immediately, from the opinion of that miracle, the multitude with their swords hewed it in pieces, every man thinking himself happy that could carry away some chip or fragment of the cross!

As he was laid upon the wood, and the fire kindled about him, he lifted up his head toward heaven, which, when the inquisitors perceived, hoping that he would recant, they caused him to be taken from the fire. But when they perceived themselves frustrated in their expectation, they commanded him to be thrown in again, and so he was immediately dispatched.

After the martyrdom of this blessed man was thus consummated, the inquisitors proclaimed openly, that he was damned in hell, and that none should pray for him; yea, and that all were heretics whoever doubted of his damnation.

Rochus, 1545.—Rochus was a carver, or graver of images, who, as soon as he began to taste the gospel, ceased to make such images as used to serve for idolatry in the temples, and occupied himself in making seals, only he kept standing on his stall an image of the Virgin Mary, artificially graven, as a sign of his occupation. It happened that a certain inquisitor passing by, and beholding the carved image, asked of Rochus what was the price, which, when Rochus had set, the inquisitor offered him scarce half the money. The other answered, that he could not live at such a price. But still the inquisitor urged him to take his offer. Rochus said, "It shall be yours if you will give me what my labour and charges stand me in, but I cannot afford it at that price; I had rather break it in pieces." "Yea," saith the inquisitor; "break it; let me see thee." Rochus with that took up a chisel, and dashed it upon the face of the image, so that the nose, or some other part of the face was blemished. The inquisitor cried out as if he was mad, and commanded Rochus forthwith to prison. Rochus said that he might do what he liked with his own works. And if the workmanship of the image were not after his fancy, what was that to them? But all this could not help Rochus, and within three days after sentence was given that he should be burned, and so he was committed to the executioners.

I understand that there were many others in Spain whose hearts God had illuminated and stirred up both before and also after the establishment of the inquisition, to stand in defence of his gospel, and who were so persecuted, and died in prison. We will come now to this inquisition, speaking something of the ceremonial pomp, and also of the barbarous abuse and cruelty of it.

The execrable Inquisition of Spain.

The cruel and barbarous inquisition of Spain first began under King Ferdinand, and Elizabeth his wife, and was instituted against the Jews, who, after their baptism, maintained again their own ceremonies. But now it is employed against those who are ever so little suspected to favour the truth of the Lord. The Spaniards, and especially the great divines there, hold, that this holy and sacred inquisition cannot err, and that the holy fathers, the inquisitors, cannot be deceived.

Three sorts of men are principally in danger of these inquisitors. They that are rich, for the spoil of their goods. They that are learned, because they will not have their secret abuses detected. They that are in honour and dignity, lest they should work some shame or dishonour against them.

The abuse of this inquisition is most execrable. If any word shall pass out of the mouth of any, which may be taken in evil part; yea, though no word be spoken, yet if they bear any grudge or evil will against the party, they command him to be taken, and put in a horrible prison, and then find out crimes against him at their leisure, and in the meantime no man living is so hardy as once to open his mouth for him. If the father speak one word for his child, he is also taken and cast into prison as a favourer of heretics. Nor is it permitted to any person to go to the prisoner; but there he is alone where he cannot see so much as the ground where he is; and is not suffered either to read or write, but there continues in darkness palpable, in horrors infinite, in fear miserable, wrestling with the assaults of death.

By this it may be imagined what trouble and sorrow, what pensive sighs and thoughts they undergo, who are not thoroughly instructed in holy doctrine. We must add, moreover, to these distresses and horrors of the prison, the injuries, threats, whippings, scourgings, irons, tortures, and racks which they endure. Sometimes they are brought out, and shewed in some high place to the people, as a spectacle of rebuke and infamy. And thus they are detained there, some many years, and murdered by long torments, and whole days together treated much more cruelly out of all comparison than if they were in the hangman's hands to be slain at once. During all this time what is done in the process no person knows, but only the holy fathers and the tormentors who are sworn to execute the torments. All is done in secret. And after all these torments endured so many years in the prison, if any man is saved, it must be known only by guessing. For all the proceedings of the court of that execrable inquisition are open to no man, but all is done in close corners, by windings, by covertways, and secret counsels: the accuser is secret, the crime secret, the witness secret, whatever is done is secret, and the poor prisoner is never informed of any thing.

By this inquisition many good true servants of Jesus Christ have been brought to death, especially in these later years, since the royal and peaceable reign of this our Queen Elizabeth. The names and histories of whom we will here in part recite, as we have faithful records of such as have come to our hands by writing.

A.D. 1556, May 21st, in the town of Valladolid, where the council of the inquisition is wont to be kept, the inquisitors had brought together many prisoners, both of high and low estate, to the number of thirty; also the coffin of a certain noble woman, with her picture lying upon it, who had been dead long before, there to receive judgment and sentence. To the hearing of which sentence, they had ordained in the said town three mighty theatres or stages. Upon the first was placed Dame Jane, sister to King Philip, and chief regent of his realms; also Prince Charles, King Philip's son, with other princes and states of Spain. Upon the other scaffold was mounted the archbishop of Seville, prince of the synagogue of the inquisitors, with the council of the inquisition; also other bishops of the land, and the king's council with them.

After the princes and other spiritual judges and councillors were thus set in their places, with a great guard of archers and halberdiers, and armed soldiers, with four heralds-of-arms giving their attendance, and the earl marshal bearing the naked sword, all the market-place

where the stages were, being filled with an infinite multitude of all sorts standing there, and gazing out of windows and houses to hear and see the sentences and judgments of this inquisition; then after all were brought forth, as a spectacle and triumph, the poor servants and witnesses of Jesus Christ, to the number of thirty, clothed with their vesture of yellow cloth, coming both before them and behind them, spangled with red crosses, and having burning tapers in their hands; also before them was borne a crucifix covered with black linen cloth, in token of mourning. They who were to receive the sentence of death had mitres of paper upon their heads. Thus they were placed in their order, one under another.

Things being thus settled, there followed a sermon by a Dominican friar, which endured about an hour. After the sermon, the procurator general, with the archbishop went to the stage where the princes and nobles stood, to administer a solemn oath to them upon the crucifix; the tenor of which oath was this: "Your majesties shall swear, that you will favour the holy inquisition, and also give your consent unto the same; and not only that you shall by no manner of way hinder and impeach the same, but also you shall employ the utmost of your help and endeavour hereafter to see all them to be executed, who shall swerve from the church of Rome, and adjoin themselves to the sect of the Lutheran heretics, without all respect of any person or persons of what estate, degree, quality, or condition soever they be."

And thus much for the first article of the oath; the second was as follows:

"Your majesties shall swear, that you shall constrain all your subjects to submit themselves to the church of Rome, and to have in reverence all the laws and commandments of the same; and also to give your aid against all them whoever shall hold of the heresy of the Lutherans, or take any part with them."

In this sort and manner, when all the princes and states every one in their degree had received their oath, then the archbishop, lifting up his hand, gave them his benediction, saying, "God bless your highnesses, and give you long life." This solemn pageant thus finished, at last the poor captives and prisoners were called out, the procurator fiscal, or the pope's great collector, first beginning with Dr. Cacalla, and so proceeding to the other in order.

They then proceeded to the trial and condemnation of twenty-seven godly christians, including thirteen pious females, whose only sin was that they loved the gospel of Jesus Christ, as contained in his holy word, instead of the traditions of the papacy. It would be too tedious to mention all in detail. At last they came to the coffin and picture of the lady.

This poor coffin contained the corpse of dame Leonora de Bivero, already long dead. Above her coffin was her picture laid, which was also condemned with her dead corpse to be burned for an heretic; and yet I never heard of any opinion that this picture did hold, either with or against the church of Rome. This good mother, while she lived, was a worthy maintainer of Christ's gospel, with great integrity of life, and retained divers assemblies of the saints in her house for the preaching of the word of God. In fine, her corpse and image also, being brought before the fiscal, was condemned likewise to be burned for a Lutheran heretic, and all her goods to be seized, and her house to be cast down to the ground; and for a memorial of the same, a marble stone was appointed to be set up in the house, wherein the cause of her burning should be engraved.

After these sentences were thus pronounced, they, who were condemned to be burned, with the coffin of the dead lady and her picture upon it, were committed to the secular magistrate, and to their executioners. Then were they all taken, and every one set upon an ass, their faces turned backward, and led with a great garrison of armed soldiers to the place of punishment, which was without the gate of the town called Del Campo.

When they were come to the place, there were fourteen stakes set up of equal distance from one another, to which every one being fastened, they were all first strangled, and then burnt to ashes, save only Anthony Hucruello, who, because he had, both within and without the prison, vehemently detested the pope's spirituality, therefore was burned alive, and his mouth stopped from speaking. And thus these faithful christians, for the verity and pure word of God, were led to death as sheep to the shambles; who not only most christianly comforted one another, but did so exhort all them that were present, that all men marvelled greatly, both to hear their singular constancy, and to see their quiet and peaceable end.

THE ITALIAN MARTYRS.

Encenas, otherwise called Dryander, A.D. 1546.

This Encenas, or Dryander, a Spaniard, was sent by his superstitious parents, when young, to Rome; there growing up in age and knowledge, instructed by the Lord in the truth of his word, after he was known to dislike the pope's doctrine, and the impure doings at Rome, he was apprehended by some of his own countrymen at Rome. He was brought before the cardinals, and committed to prison. Afterwards he was brought forth to give testimony of his doctrine, which in the presence of the cardinals, and in the face of all the pope's retinue, he boldly and constantly defended. So that not only the cardinals, but especially the Spaniards being offended, cried out that he should be burned. The cardinals, before the sentence of death should be given, came to him, offering life if he would take the badge of reconciliation. But Encenas, still constant in the profession of truth, refused to receive any other condition or badge but the badge of the Lord, which was to seal the doctrine of his religion with the testimony of his blood. At last the faithful servant and witness of Christ was condemned to the fire; where he, in the sight of the cardinals, and in the face of the apostolic see, gave up his life for the testimony of the gospel.

And as mention has been made both in this history and others of Francis Encenas his brother, here is not to be omitted how Francis being a man of notable learning as ever was in Spain, being in the emperor's court at Brussels, offered the emperor, Charles V., the New Testament of Christ translated into Spanish. For which he was cast into prison, where he remained in sorrowful captivity and calamity the space of fifteen months, looking for nothing more than present death. At last, through the providence of Almighty God, the first day of February, A.D. 1545, he found the doors of the prison open; and so he, issuing out of the prison, escaped, and went to Germany.

Faninus, A.D. 1550.—Faninus, through the reading of godly books translated into the Italian tongue, was converted from great blindness to the wholesome knowledge of Christ and of his word. There was no diligence wanting in him to communicate to others that which he had received of the Lord; being persuaded that a man, receiving by the Spirit of God the knowledge and illumination of his truth, ought in no case to hide it in silence, as a candle under a bushel. And therefore, being occupied diligently in that, although he used not publicly to preach, but by private conference to teach, he was at length apprehended and committed to prison. He remained not long in prison, for by the earnest persuasions and prayers of his wife, his children, and other friends, he was so overcome that he gave over, and so was dismissed shortly out of prison. After this, it was not long until he fell into horrible distraction of mind; so that unless the great mercy of God had kept him up, he had fallen into utter desperation, for falling from the truth, and preferring the love of his friends and kindred before the service of Jesus Christ, whom he had professed so earnestly before. This wound went so deep into his heart, that he could in no case be quieted, before he had fully fixed and determined in his mind, to hazard his life more faithfully in the service of the Lord.

Being thus inflamed with zeal of spirit, he went about

all the country publicly preaching the pure doctrine of the gospel with great fruit and effect. As he was thus labouring, he was apprehended again, A.D. 1547, and condemned to be burned. But he said his hour was not yet come, and so it was not; for shortly after he was removed to Ferrara, where he was detained two years. At last the inquisitors of the pope's heresies condemned him to death, A.D. 1549; and yet his time being not come, he remained after that to the month of September, A.D. 1550. In the meantime many faithful and good men came to visit him; for which the pope commanded him to be inclosed in stricter custody; in which he suffered great torments for eighteen months, and yet he would have suffered greater, if the Dominican friars could have got him into their hands.

At length he was brought into a prison, where there were divers great lords, captains, and noble personages committed for stirring up commotions and factions (as the country of Italy is full of such) who at first hearing him speak began to set him at nought, and to deride him, supposing that it was but a melancholy humour that troubled his brain. Such as seemed more sage amongst them, began to exhort him to leave his opinion, and to live with men as other men do, and not to vex his mind, but to suspend his judgment till the matter was decided in the general council. Faninus, first giving them thanks for their friendly good will, modestly and quietly declared to them, how the doctrine which he professed was no humour nor opinion of man's brain, but the pure truth of God, founded in his word, and revealed to men in the gospel of Jesus Christ, and especially now in these days restored; which truth he had fully determined in his mind never to deny. And as in his soul, which was redeemed by the blood of the Son of God, he was free from all bondage; so likewise, as touching councils, he looked for no other sentence nor authority but that only which he knew to be declared to us by Christ Jesus in his gospel, which he both preached with his word, and confirmed with his blood, &c. With these and such other words, he so moved their minds, that they were wholly altered to a new life, having him now in admiration whom they before had in derision. He proceeded still to preach the word of grace, declaring and confessing himself to be a miserable sinner; but by the faith of the Lord Jesus, and through the grace only of him, he was fully persuaded and well assured his sins were forgiven; as all their sins also shall be remitted to them through their faith only in Christ, they believing his gospel.

There were others also besides these, who, having lived before a more delicate kind of life, could not well bear with the sharpness and the hardness of the prison. These also received such comfort from Faninus, that not only they were quietly contented, but also rejoiced in their captivity, by the occasion of which they had received and learned a better liberty than they ever knew before.

When the imprisonment of Faninus was known to his parents and kinsfolk, his wife and sister came to him with weeping persuasions, to move him to consider and have a care for his poor family. He answered, that his Lord and Master had commanded him not to deny him by looking to his family; and that it was enough for them that he had once for their sakes fallen into that cowardliness which they knew. Wherefore he desired them to depart in peace, and solicit him no more, for his end, he said, he knew drew near, and so he commended them unto the Lord.

About the same time died Pope Paul III., and after him succeeded Julius III., who sent letters and commandment that Faninus should be executed. When one of the magistrate's officers brought him word the next day, he rejoiced at it, and gave the messenger thanks, and began to preach a long sermon to them that were about him on the felicity and beatitude of the life to come. Then the messenger exhorted him that, in case he would change his opinion, he should save both his present life, and enjoy that which was to come. Another asked him how he should leave his little children and his wife? Faninus answered, that he had left them with an overseer, who would see to them sufficiently; and being asked who he was? "The Lord Jesus Christ," said he, "a faithful keeper and preserver of all that is committed to him." After the messenger was departed from Faninus, all full of tears and sorrow, the day following he was removed into the common prison, and delivered to the secular magistrate. In all his ways, his words, his gestures, and countenance, he shewed such constancy of faith, such modesty of manners, and tranquillity of mind, that they who previously were violent against him, thinking him to have a devil, began now favourably to hearken to him, and to commend him. With such grace and sweetness he talked, ever speaking of the word of God, that several of the magistrates' wives in hearing him could not abstain from weeping. The executioner himself also wept. One of the public scribes came to him and said, that if he would relent from his opinion, the pope's pleasure was that he should be saved: but that he refused. This was surprising, that he recited so many places of scripture without book, and that so truly and promptly, as though he had studied nothing else. One seeing him so cheerful and happy going to his death, asked, why he was so cheerful at his death, seeing Christ himself sweat blood and water before his passion? "Christ," said he, "sustained in his body all the sorrows and conflicts with hell and death due to us: by whose suffering we are delivered from sorrow and fear of them all." Early in the morning he was brought forth. After his prayers most earnestly made to the Lord, he meekly and patiently gave himself to the stake, where with a cord drawn about his neck he was strangled by the executioner in the city of Ferrara, three hours before day, that the people should not see him, nor hear him speak; and about noon his body was burned.

Dominick de Basana, at Placentia, A.D. 1550.

The same year Dominick also suffered in the city of Placentia. This Dominick was in Germany, when he received the first taste of Christ's gospel. Wherein he increased more and more, by conferring and reasoning with learned men, so that in a short time he was able to instruct many, and he did so, till in the year 1550, coming to the city of Naples, he there preached the word, and then proceeding to Placentia, preached there likewise to the people, of true confession, of purgatory, and of pardons. The next day he treated of true faith and good works, how far they are necessary to salvation, promising the day after to speak of antichrist, and to paint him out in his colours. When the hour came that he should begin his sermon, the magistrate of the city commanded him to come down from the chair in the market-place, and delivered him to the officers. Dominick was willing and ready to obey the commandment, saying, "That he much wondered that the devil could suffer him so long in that kind of exercise." He was led to the bishop's chancellor, and asked whether he was a priest, and how he was placed in that function. He answered, "That he was no priest of the pope, but of Jesus Christ, by whom he was lawfully called to that office." Then was he demanded, whether he would renounce his doctrine? He answered, "That he maintained no doctrine of his own, but only the doctrine of Christ, which also he was ready to seal with his blood, and also gave hearty thanks to God, who so accounted him worthy to glorify his name with his martyrdom." Upon this he was committed to a filthy and stinking prison, where, after he had remained a few months, he was exhorted to revoke, otherwise he should suffer; but still he remained constant in his doctrine. When the time came assigned for his punishment, he was brought to the market-place, where he had preached, and there was hanged; and most heartily praying for his enemies, he so finished his days in this miserable wretched world.

Galeazius Trecius, A.D. 1551.

In St. Angelo was a house of Augustinian friars, to whom a certain friar used to resort, named Maianard, a man expert in the study of scripture, and of a godly conversation. By this Maianard several, not only of friars, but also of other townsmen, were brought to the love and knowledge of God's word, and to the detestation of the pope's abuses. Among whom was this Galeazius, a gentleman of good calling, and wealthy in worldly substance, and very benevolent to the poor. In process of time, as this Galeazius increased in judgment and zeal, in setting forward the wholesome word of God's grace; as a light shining in darkness he could not so lie hid, but at last, in the year 1551, certain persons were sent to arrest and bring him to the bishop's palace, where he was kept in bonds.

When the time came that he should be examined, he was brought before the commissioners, where he rendered reasons of his faith, answering to their interrogatories with such evidence of scriptures, and constancy of mind, that he was an admiration to them that heard him. Not long after, through the importunate persuasion of his kinsfolk and friends, and other cold gospellers, laying many considerations before his eyes, he was brought at length to assent to certain points of the pope's doctrine. But yet the mercy of God, which thus began with him, left him not, but brought him again to such repentance, and bewailing of what he had done, that he became afterward still more valiant in defence of Christ; affirming that he never felt more joy of heart than at the time of his examinations, where he stood to the constant confession of the truth; and that he never tasted more sorrow in all his life, than when he slipped from the same by dissimulation. Declaring to his brethren, that death was much more sweet to him, with testimony of the truth, than life with the least denial of truth, and loss of a good conscience.

As Galeazius thus continued in the prison, looking for some occasion to recover from his fall, the inquisitors and priests again repaired to him, supposing that he would confirm now that which before he had granted to them. Galeazius returned again to the defence of his former doctrine, with much more boldness of spirit confessing Christ, and declaring his detestation of images, affirming and proving that God only is to be worshipped, and that in spirit and in truth; also that there are no mediators but Christ alone, and that he only and sufficiently by his suffering has taken away the sins of the whole world; and that all they who depart hence in this faith, are certain of everlasting life; they who do not, are under everlasting damnation; with such other matter as was utterly repugnant to the pope's proceedings. With this confession, as his mind was greatly refreshed, so the adversaries went away as much appalled, who, at last perceiving that he could not be revoked, caused him to be committed to the secular judge to be burned.

Thus Galeazius, early in the morning, being brought out of prison to the market-place, was there left standing bound to the stake till noon, as a gazing-stock for all men to look upon. In the meantime many came about him, exhorting him to recant, and not to cast away his life, whereas with ten words he might save it. But nothing could stir the mind of this valiant martyr. Fire was commanded at last to be put to the dry wood about him, and he was consumed, without any noise or crying, save only these words heard in the middle of the flame: "Lord Jesus!" This was A.D. 1551, November twenty-fourth.

Touching the story of this blessed martyr, this is to be given for a memorandum, that a little before Galeazius was burned, there was a controversy between the major of the city, and the bishop's clergy, for the expenses of the wood that should go to his burning. He, hearing of it, sent word to both the parties to agree, for that he himself of his own goods would see the cost of that matter discharged.

Doctor John Mollius, a Gray Friar, and a certain Weaver, A.D. 1553.

John Mollius Montilcinus, when but twelve years old, with his brother Augustinus, was placed by his parents in the house of the Gray Friars, where, in a short time, having a fresh wit, he far excelled his fellows in all languages and sciences. So growing up to the age of eighteen, he was ordained priest, and sang his first mass. After that he was sent to Ferrara to study, where he so profited in the space of six years, that he was assigned, by Vigerius, general of that order, to be doctor, and then reader in divinity; and he then, with his sophistry, opposed himself to the gospel. Afterwards he was connected with several universities with much distinction. In the meantime God wrought in his soul such light of his word, and of true religion, that he began secretly to expound the Epistle of St. Paul to the Romans to a few; which being known, his auditors increased so fast, that he was compelled to read openly in the temple. As the number of his audience daily augmented, so the eager fervency of their minds increased, so that every man almost came with his pen and ink to write: this was about the year 1538. There was at the same time, at Bononia, one Cornelius, an arrogant babbler, who, envying John, took upon him, at the request of Cardinal Campejus, to expound the same epistle of St. Paul, confuting and disproving the explanation of John, and extolling the pope with all his traditions. John extolled and commended only Christ and his merits to the people. But the purpose of Cornelius came to nothing. For the auditors who first came unto him, began by little to fall from him, while the concourse of the other man's auditors increased more and more.

When Cornelius perceived this, he persuaded Campejus, that unless he dispatched that man, the estimation of the church of Rome would greatly decay. But when they could not openly bring about their purpose, this secret way was devised, that Cornelius and John should come to open disputation; which disputation endured till three of the clock after midnight. At length, when neither party could agree, John was bid to return home to his house. As he was come down to the lower steps, where the place was most confined, so that his friends could not come to rescue him, (although by drawing their swords they declared their good wills,) he was taken and laid in prison. When the day came, such tumult and stir was in the whole city, that Cornelius was driven to hide himself. Also Campejus, the cardinal, with the bishop, were both contemned of the students. The next day the bishop of Bononia sent his chancellor to John in the prison, to signify to him, that either he must recant, or be burned. But he, being of a bold and cheerful spirit, would in nowise be brought to recant. This one thing grieved him, that he should be condemned without his cause being heard.

In the meantime, Laurentius Spatha, general of the order, posted up to Rome, and there so practised with the cardinal of the Holy Cross, the proctor in the court of Rome for the Gray friars, that the pope wrote down his letters to Campejus, that he should deliver John out of prison; so that he, within three months after, should personally appear at Rome. The friends of Mollius gave him counsel not to go to Rome, and offered him money to go to Germany; but he would not, saying, "That the gospel must also be preached at Rome." After he was come to Rome, and appeared before Pope Paul III., he humbly desired, that the cause might come in public hearing, but that could not be obtained. Then he was commanded to write his mind in articles, and to bring his proofs, which he diligently performed, treating of original sin, justification by faith, free will, purgatory, and such like; proving the said articles by the authority of the scripture, and of the ancient fathers, and exhibited them to the bishop of Rome. Upon this, certain cardinals and bishops were assigned to give the cause a hearing: they disputed with him three days, and could not feel that which he had proved. At last answer was made to him thus: that it was truth which he affirmed, nevertheless the same was not meet for this present time; for that it could not be taught or published without the detriment of the apostolic see; wherefore he should abstain hereafter from the epistles of St. Paul, and so return again safe to Bononia, and there profess philosophy. Thus as he was returned to Bononia, and all men there were desirous to know of his case, how he sped at Rome, openly in the pulpit he declared all things in order as they were done, and gave God thanks.

Herewith Campejus, being more offended than before, obtained of the pope, that the general of the order should remove the said John Mollius from Bononia, and place him somewhere else. So Mollius was sent to Naples, and there was appointed reader and preacher in the monastery of St. Laurence. But Peter, the viceroy there, not abiding his doctrine, so nearly sought his death, that he had much ado to escape with life, and so departing from thence, he went wandering in Italy, from place to place, preaching Christ wherever he came. Not long after this, when Cardinal Campejus was dead, he was called again to Bononia, by a good abbot named De Grassis, A.D. 1543, where he renewed again the reading of St. Paul's epistles after a secret sort, as he did before; but that could not be long undiscovered. By means of Cardinal de Capo, and by Bonaventura the general, he was apprehended the second time, and brought to Faventia, and laid there in a filthy and stinking prison, where he continued four years, no man having leave to come to him. At length, through the intercession of the Earl Petilian, and of the good Abbot De Grassis, he was again delivered, and sent to Ravenna, where he made his abode a few months, and there again taught the gospel of Christ as before; and whenever he spake of the name of Jesus, his eyes dropped tears, for he was fraught with a mighty fervency of God's Holy Spirit.

In process of time, when this abbot was dead, his sureties began to be weary of their bond, and so he was again now the third time reduced to prison by the pope's legates. There were then four men of great authority, who, being stirred up of God, had pity upon him, and bailed him out of prison. Of whom, one of the sureties took Mollius home, to instruct his children in the doctrine of religion and good letters. Furthermore, at the fame of this man, such a concourse of people came to see him, that the adversaries began to consult with themselves to kill him, lest his doctrine should disperse further abroad, to the detriment of the church of Rome.

Whereupon commandment was sent to the pope's legate to lay hands upon him, and to send him up fast bound to Rome. Where again, now the fourth time, he was imprisoned in the castle of Rome, and there continued eighteen months, being greatly assaulted, sometimes with flattering promises, sometimes with terrible threats, to give over his opinion: but his building could not be shaken, for it was grounded upon a sure rock. Thus Dr. Mollius, being constant in the defence of Christ's gospel, was brought, with other men (who were also apprehended for religion) into the temple of St. Mary (called De Minerva) the fifth day of September, 1553; either to revoke or to be burned. There sat six cardinals in high seats, besides the judge: before whom preached a Dominican friar, with cruelty inveighing against the poor prisoners, incensed the cardinals, with all the vehemency he might, to their condemnation. The poor men stood holding a burning taper in their hands: some for fear of death revolted. But this Doctor Mollius, with a weaver of Perusium, remained constant. Then Mollius began an earnest sermon in the Italian tongue, wherein he confirmed the articles of the faith by the sacred scriptures, declaring also that the pope was not the successor of Peter, but antichrist, and that his sectaries do figure the whore of Babylon. He cited them up to the tribunal seat of Christ, and threw away the burning taper from him. They condemned him with the weaver to the fire, and commanded them to be had away. So they were carried to the field, called Florianum, where they remained cheerful and constant. First, the weaver was hanged: Mollius then began to exhort the people to beware of idolatry, and to have no other saviours but Christ alone: for he only is the Mediator between God and man. And so he was also hanged, commending his soul to God, and afterwards laid in the fire and burned.

Two Monks. (A.D. 1554.)—In the same city of Rome, and about the same time, in the monastery of St. Austin, were found two monks in their cells, with their tongues and their heads cut off, only for rebuking the immoderate and outrageous excess of the cardinals.

In the same year, *Francis Gamba*, after he had received the knowledge of the gospel, went to Geneva, to confer with the wise and learned in that church, and there at the same time communicated with them. Afterward, in his returning home, as he was passing over the Lake of Como, he was taken and brought to Como, and committed to ward. During the time of his imprisonment, nobles and others, with doctors also, especially priests and monks, resorted to him, labouring by all manner of means, and most fair promises, to reduce him from his opinions: which seemed to some but fantasies coming of some humour: to some they seemed uncatholic or heretical. But he, constantly disputing with them by the manifest scriptures, declared the opinions which he defended not to be any vain speculations or imaginary fantasies of man's doting brain, but the pure truth of God, and the evident doctrine of Jesus Christ, expressed in his word, necessary for all men to believe, and also to maintain unto death: and, therefore, for his part, rather than he would be found false to Christ and his word, he was there ready not to deny, but to stand to Christ's gospel, to the shedding of his blood.

When he could in no wise be reclaimed from the doctrine of truth, letters came from the senate of Milan, that he should be executed; but through intercession of his friends, one week's respite was granted him, to prove whether he might be won again to the pope's church, that is to say, lost from God. Thus he being long and mightily, both assailed by friends, and terrified by enemies, yet by no persuasions would be overcome, but gave thanks to God, that he was made worthy to suffer the rebukes of this world, and cruel death, for the testimony of his Son; and so he went cheerfully to his death. Then came certain Franciscan friars to him to hear his confession, which he refused. They brought in their hands a cross for him to behold, to keep him from desperation at the feeling of the fire; but his mind, he said, was so filled with joy and comfort in Christ, that he needed neither their cross, nor them. After this, as he was declaring many comfortable things to the people, of the fruition of those heavenly joys above, which God hath prepared for his, that he should speak no more to the people, his tongue was bored through; and immediately being tied to the stake, he was strangled to death; every man there, who saw his constancy, giving testimony, that he died a good man.

Pomponius Algerius, at Rome, A. D. 1555.

Pomponius Algerius, a young man of great learning, was student in the university of Padua, where, not being able to conceal and keep close the truth of Christ's gospel, he ceased not both by doctrine and example of life, to inform as many as he could, and to bring them to Christ; for which he was accused of heresy to Pope Paul IV. Who, sending immediately to the magistrates of Venice, caused him to be apprehended at Padua, and carried to Venice, where he was long detained in prison, till at last the pope commanded the magistrates there to send him bound to Rome. After he was brought to Rome, manifold persuasions and allurements were tried to remove this virtuous and blessed young man from his opinions. But when no persuasions could prevail against the operation of God's Spirit in him, then was he judged to be burned alive; which death he sustained most constantly, to the great admiration of all that beheld him.

Being in prison at Venice, he wrote an epistle to the afflicted saints; which, for the notable sweetness and most wonderful consolation contained in it, in shewing forth the mighty operation of God's holy power working in his afflicted saints that suffer for his sake, I have thought good and expedient to communicate, as a principal monument amongst all other martyrs' letters, not only with the other letters which shall be inserted hereafter (the Lord willing) in the end of the book, but also in this present place to be read, to the intent that both they who are, or shall be hereafter in affliction, may take consolation; and also they that yet follow the trade of this present world, in comparing the joys and commodities thereof, with these joys here expressed, may learn and consider with themselves, what difference there is between them both, and thereby may learn to dispose themselves in such sort, as may be to their edification, and perpetual felicity of their souls. The copy of the letter, first written in Latin, we have translated into English, the tenor whereof here ensues.

A comfortable Letter of Pomponius Algerius, an Italian Martyr.

To his dearly beloved Brethren and fellow Servants of Christ, who are departed out of Babylon into Mount Sion; grace, peace and health, from God our Father, by Jesus Christ our Lord and Saviour.

"To mitigate your sorrow, which you take for me, I cannot but impart unto you some portion of my delight and joys, which I feel and find, that you may rejoice with me and sing before the Lord, giving thanks unto him, I shall utter that which no man will believe when I shall declare it. I have found a nest of honey and honey-comb in the entrails of a lion. Who will ever believe what I shall say, or what man will ever think in the deep dark dungeon to find a paradise of pleasure, in the place of sorrow and death,—to dwell in tranquillity and hope of life,—in an infernal cave to find joy of soul,—and where other men do weep, there to be rejoicing,—where others shake and tremble, there strength and boldness to be plenty? Who will ever think, or who will believe this? in such a woful state such delights? in a place so desolate, such society of good men? in strait bands and cold irons, such rest? All these things the sweet hand of the Lord, my brethren, doth minister unto me. Behold, he that was once far from me, now is present with me. Whom once I scarce could feel, now I see more apparently; whom once I saw afar off, now I behold near at hand; whom once I hungered for, the same now approacheth and reacheth his hand unto me. He doth comfort me, and filleth me with gladness; he driveth away all bitterness, he ministereth strength and courage, he healeth me, refresheth, advanceth, and comforteth me. O how good is the Lord, who suffereth not his servants to be tempted above their strength! O how easy and sweet is his yoke! Is there any like unto the Highest, who receiveth the afflicted, healeth the wounded, and nourisheth them? Is there any like unto him? Learn ye, wellbeloved, how amiable the Lord is, how meek and merciful he is, who visiteth his servants in temptations, neither disdaineth he to keep company with us in such vile and stinking caves. Will the blind and incredulous world, think you, believe this? Or rather will it not say thus? No, thou wilt never be able to abide long the burning heat, the cold snow, and the pinching hardness of that place, the manifold miseries, and other innumerable grievances; the rebukes and frowning faces of men how wilt thou suffer? Dost thou not consider and revolve in thy mind thy pleasant country, the riches of the world, thy kinsfolk, the delicate pleasures and honours of this life? Dost thou forget the solace of thy sciences, and fruit of all thy labours? Wilt thou thus lose all thy labours which thou hast hitherto sustained, —so many nights watched,—thy painful travels, and all thy laudable enterprizes, wherein thou hast been exercised continually even from thy childhood? Finally, fearest thou not death, which hangeth over thee, and that for no crime committed? O what a fool art thou, which for one word speaking mayest save all this, and wilt not? What a rude and unmannerly thing is this, not to be intreated at the instant petitions and desires of such, so many and so mighty, so just, so virtuous, so prudent and gracious senators, and such noble personages, &c.

"But now to answer; Let this blind world hearken to this again: What heat can there be more burning, than that fire which is prepared for thee hereafter? And likewise, what snow can be more cold than thy heart which is in darkness, and hath no light? What thing is more hard, and sharp, or crooked, than this present life which here we lead? What thing more odious and hateful than this world here present? and let these worldly men here answer me : What country can we have more sweet than the heavenly country above? What treasures more rich or precious than everlasting life? And who are our kinsmen, but they who hear the word of God? where are greater riches, or dignities more honourable, than in heaven? And as to the sciences, let this foolish world consider, are they not ordained to learn to know God, whom, unless we do know, all our labours, our night watchings, our studies, and all our enterprises serve to no use or purpose? all is but labour lost. Furthermore, let the miserable worldly man answer me ; What remedy or safe refuge can there be to him, if he lack God, who is the life and medicine of all men? And how can he be said to fly from death, when he himself is already dead in sin? If Christ be the way, the truth, and the life, how can there be any life without Christ? The heat of the prison to me is coldness ; the cold winter to me is a fresh spring-time in the Lord. He that fears not to be burned in the fire, how will he fear the heat of the weather? or what cares he for the pinching frost, who burns with the love of the Lord? The place is sharp and tedious to them that are guilty, but to the innocent and guiltless it is mellifluous. Here drops the delectable dew, here flows the pleasant nectar, here runs the sweet milk, here is plenty of all good things. And although the place itself is desert and barren, yet to me it seems a large walk, and a valley of pleasure ; here to me is the better and more noble part of the world. Let the miserable worldling say and confess, if there be any plot, pasture, or meadow, so delightful to the mind of man, as here. Here I see kings, princes, cities, and people ; here I see wars, where some are overthrown, some are victors, some thrust down, some lifted up. Here is the Mount Sion, here I am already in heaven itself. Here standeth first Christ Jesus in the front. About him stand the old fathers, prophets, and evangelists, apostles, and all the servants of God. Of whom some do embrace and cherish me, some exhort, some open the sacraments unto me, some comfort me, others are singing about me. And how then shall I be thought to be alone, among so many and such as these be, the beholding of whom to me is both solace and example? Here I see some crucified, some slain, some stoned, some cut asunder, and some quartered, some roasted, some broiled, some put in hot cauldrons, some having their eyes bored through, some their tongues cut out, some their skin plucked over their heads, some their hands and feet chopped off, some put in kilns and furnaces, some cast down headlong and given to the beasts and fowls of the air to feed upon ; it would ask a long time if I should recite all.

"To be short, I see many with many torments excruciated : yet, notwithstanding, all living, and all safe. One plaister, one salve cures all their wounds : which also gives to me strength and life, so that I sustain all these transitory anguishes and small afflictions, with a quiet mind, having a greater hope laid up in heaven. Neither do I fear mine adversaries who here persecute me and oppress me : for he that dwelleth in heaven shall laugh them to scorn, and the Lord shall have them in derision. I fear not thousands of people who compass me about. The Lord my God shall deliver me, my hope, my supporter, my comforter, who lifts up my head. He shall smite all them that stand up against me without cause, and shall dash the teeth and jaws of sinners asunder : for he only is all blessedness and majesty. The rebukes for Christ's cause makes us joyful ; for so it is written, " if ye be persecuted and reviled for Christ's sake, happy be you ; for the glory and Spirit of God rests upon you," 1 Pet. iv. 14. Be you therefore sure, that our rebukes which are laid upon us, redound to the shame and harm of the rebukers. In this world there is no abiding mansion ; and therefore I will travel up to the New Jerusalem which is in heaven, and which offers itself to me without paying any fine or income. Behold, I have entered already on my journey, where my house stands prepared for me, and where I shall have riches, kinsfolks, delights, and never failing honours. As for these earthly things here present, they are transitory shadows, vanishing vapours, and ruinous

walls. Briefly, all is but very vanity of vanities, whereas hope and the substance of eternity to come are wanting ; which the merciful goodness of the Lord has given as companions to accompany me, and to comfort me, and now do the same begin to work and to bring forth fruits in me. I have travelled hitherto, laboured and sweated early and late, watching day and night, and now my travels begin to come to effect. Days and hours have I bestowed upon my studies. Behold, the true countenance of God is sealed upon me, the Lord hath given mirth in my heart. And, therefore, in the same will I lay me down in peace and rest, Psalm iv. And who then shall dare to blame this our age consumed, or say that our years are cut off? What man can now cavil that these our labours are lost, who have followed and found out the Lord and Maker of the world, and who have changed death with life? My portion is the Lord (saith my soul) and therefore I will seek and wait for him. Now then, if to die in the Lord be not to die, but to live most joyfully, where is this wretched worldly rebel, who blames us of folly, for giving away our lives to death? O how delectable is this death to me, to taste the Lord's cup, which is an assured pledge of true salvation ! for so hath the Lord himself forewarned us, saying, ' The same that they have done to me, they will also do unto you.' Wherefore, let the doltish world, with its blind worldlings (who, in the bright sunshine yet go stumbling in darkness, being as blind as beetles) cease thus unwisely to carp against us for our rash suffering, as they count it. To whom we answer again with the holy apostle, That neither tribulation nor stripes, nor famine, nor nakedness, nor pearl, nor persecution, nor sword, shall be able ever to separate us from the love of Christ : we are slain all the day long, we are made like sheep appointed to the slaughter, Rom. viii. 35. 38. Thus we resemble Christ our Head, who said, ' That the disciple cannot be above his Master, nor the servant above his Lord.' The same Lord has also commanded, that every one shall take up his cross and follow him, Luke ix. Rejoice, rejoice, my dear brethren, and fellow-servants, and be of good comfort, when ye fall into sundry temptations. Let your patience be perfect in all parts. For so it has been foreshewn to us before, and is written, That they which shall kill you, shall think to do God good service. Therefore afflictions and death are as tokens and sacraments of our election and life to come. Let us then be glad and give thanks unto the Lord, when as we, being clear from all just accusation, are persecuted and given to death. For better is it, that we in doing well do suffer, if it so be the will of the Lord, than doing evil, 1 Pet. iii. 17. We have for our example Christ and the prophets, who spake in the name of the Lord, whom the children of iniquity did murder. And now we bless and magnify them that then suffered ; let us be glad and rejoice in our innocency and uprightness. The Lord shall reward them that persecute us ; let us refer all vengeance to him.

"I am accused of foolishness, for that I do not shrink from the true doctrine and knowledge of God, and do not rid myself out of these troubles, when with one word I may. O the blindness of man ! who sees not the sun shining, neither remembers the Lord's words ! consider therefore what he saith, ' Ye are the light of the world. A city built on a hill cannot be hid ; neither do men light a candle, and put it under a bushel, but upon a candlestick, that it may shine and give light to them in the house.' And in another place he saith, ' You shall be led before kings and rulers ; fear ye not them who kill the body, but him who killeth both body and soul : whosoever shall confess me before men, him will I also confess before my Father who is in heaven. And he that denieth me before men, him will I also deny before my Heavenly Father.' Wherefore seeing the words of the Lord are so plain, how, or by what authority will this wise councillor then approve this his counsel which he gives? God forbid that I should relinquish the commandments of God, and follow the counsels of men : for it is written ; ' Blessed is the man that walketh not in the counsel of the ungodly, nor standeth in the way of sinners, nor sitteth in the seat of the scornful,

Psalm i. 1. God forbid that I should deny Christ, where I ought to confess him. I will not set more by my life than by my soul: neither will I exchange the life to come, for this present world. O how foolishly speaks he who accuses me of foolishness.

"Neither do I take it to be a thing so uncomely, or unseeming for me, not to obey in this matter the requests of those so honourable, just, prudent, virtuous, and noble senators, whose desire (he saith) were enough to command me: for so are we taught of the apostles; 'That we ought to obey God, rather than men.' After that we have served and done our duty first unto God, then are we bound next to obey the powers of this world; whom I wish to be perfect before the Lord. They are honourable; but yet are they to be made more perfect in the Lord. They are just; but yet Christ, the seat of justice, is lacking in them. They are wise; but where is in them the beginning of wisdom, that is, the fear of the Lord? They are called virtuous, but yet I wish them more absolute in christian charity: they are good and gracious, but yet I miss in them the foundation of goodness, which is the Lord God, in whom dwelleth all goodness and grace. They are honourable; yet they have not received the Lord of glory, who is our Saviour, most honourable and glorious. Understand, you kings, and learn, you that judge the earth. Serve the Lord in fear, and rejoice in him with trembling. Hearken to doctrine, and get knowledge, lest you fall into God's displeasure, and so perish out of the way of righteousness. Why fret you, why rage you, O gentiles! O you people, why cast you in your heads the cogitations of vanity? You kings of the earth, and you princes, why conspire you together against Christ and against his only one? Psalm ii. How long will you seek after lies, and hate the truth? Turn you to the Lord, and harden not your heart. For this you must needs confess, that they who persecute the Lord's servants, do persecute the Lord himself. For so he saith himself; whatsoever men shall do to you, I will count it to be done not as unto you, but to myself.

"And now let these carnal counsellors and disputers of this world tell, wherein have they to blame me; if in my examinations I have not answered so after their mind and affection as they required of me? seeing it is not ourselves that speak, but the Lord that speaketh in us; as he himself doth forewitness, saying; 'when you shall be brought before rulers and magistrates, it is not ye that speak, but the Spirit of your Father which speaketh in you,' Matt. x. 18. 20. Wherefore if the Lord be true and faithful to his word, as it is most certain, then there is no blame in me: for he gave the words that I did speak; and who was I that could resist his will? If any man shall reprehend the things that I said, let him then quarrel with the Lord, whom it pleased to work so in me. And if the Lord be not to be blamed, neither am I herein to be accused, who did what I purposed not, and what I forethought not of. The things which there I uttered and expressed, if they were otherwise than well, let them shew it, and then will I say, that they were my words, and not the Lord's. But if they were good and approved, and such as cannot justly be accused, then must needs be granted, in spite of their teeth, that they proceeded of the Lord, and then who are they that shall accuse me? A people of prudence! or who shall condemn me? Just judges! and though they so do, yet nevertheless the word shall not be frustrated, neither shall the gospel be foolish, or therefore decay; but rather the kingdom of God shall the more prosper and flourish unto the Israelites, and shall pass the sooner unto the elect of Christ Jesus: and they who shall so do, shall prove the grievous judgment of God; neither shall they escape without punishment who are persecutors and murderers of the just. My well beloved, lift up your eyes, and consider the counsels of God. He showed unto us an image of his plague, which was for our correction: and if we shall not receive him, he will draw out his sword, and strike with sword, pestilence, and famine, the nation that shall rise against Christ.

"These have I written for your comfort, dear breth-ren. Pray for me. I kiss in my heart, with an holy kiss, my good masters, Sylvius, Pergula, Justus, also Fidel Rocke, and him that beareth the name of Lelia, whom I know, although being absent. Also the governor of the university, Syndicus, and all others, whose names are written in the book of life. Farewell all my fellow servants of God; fare you well in the Lord, and pray for me continually.

From the delectable orchard of Leonine prison, 12th August, A.D. 1555.

It is written of one Thebrotus, that when he had read the book of Plato, *De Immortalitate Animæ*, he was so moved and persuaded therewith, that he cast himself headlong down from an high wall, to be rid out of this present life. If those heathen philosophers, having no word of God, nor promise of any resurrection or life to come, could so soon be persuaded, by reading the works of Plato, to condemn this world and life here present; how much more is it to be required in christians, instructed with so many evidences and promises of God's most perfect word, that they should learn to cast off the carnal desires and affections of this miserable pilgrimage, and that for a double respect, not only in seeing, reading, and understanding so many examples of the miseries of this wretched world; but also much more in considering and pondering the heavenly joys and consolations of the other world remaining for us hereafter in the life to come. For a more full evidence thereof, I thought it good to give out the letter of Algerius above-prefixed, for an earnest of the same, and for a lively testimony for all true christians to read and consider. Now let us proceed further (the Lord willing) in our list of Italian martyrs.

Eighty-eight martyrs in one day, with one butcherly knife, slain like sheep.—A hundred and sixty others also condemned, at Calabria, A.D. 1560.

In Calabria likewise suffered a blessed number of Christ's well beloved saints, both old and young, put together in one house, even eighty-eight persons; all of whom, one after another, were taken out of the house, and so being laid upon the butcher's stall, like the sheep in the shambles, with one bloody knife were all killed in order. A spectacle most tragical for all posterity to remember, and almost incredible to believe. Wherefore for the more credit of the matter, lest we should seem either light of credit, to believe what is not true, or rashly to commit to pen things without due proof and authority; we have here annexed a piece of an epistle written by Master Simon Florius.

The end of a certain letter of Master Simon Florius, concerning a lamentable slaughter of eighty-eight Christian Saints in the parts of Calabria.

"As concerning news I have nothing to write, but only that I send you a copy of certain letters, printed either at Rome or at Venice, concerning the martyrdom or persecution in two several towns of Calabria, eighty Italian miles from the borders of Consentia; the one called St. Sixtus, within two miles of Montalto, under the seigniory of the duke of Montalto; the other called Guardia, situate upon the sea-coast, and twelve miles from St. Sixtus: which two towns are utterly destroyed, and eight hundred of the inhabitants there, or (as some write from the city of Rome) no less than a full thousand. He that wrote the letter, was servant to Ascanius Carracciolus. The country and people there I well knew to take the first original of their good doctrine and honest life from the Waldenses. For before my departure from Geneva, at their request, I sent them two schoolmasters, and two preachers. The last year the two preachers were martyred, the one at Rome, named Joannes Aloisius Pascalis, a citizen of Cunium: the other at Messina, named James Bovell, both of Piedmont: this year the residue of that godly fellowship were martyred in the same place. I trust this good seed sown in Italy, will bring forth good and plentiful fruit."

Now follows the copy of the letters sent from Montalto, a town in Calabria, eight miles distant from Consentia, bearing date the 11th of June, 1560. The writer of which letters, as ye may perceive, was one of them who call themselves catholics, and followers of the pope. The words of the letter are these.

Here followeth the copy of a letter sent from Montalto in Calabria, by a Romanist, to a certain friend of his in Rome, containing news of the persecution of Christ's people in Calabria, by the new Pope Pius the Fourth :—

"Hitherto, most noble lord, I have certified to you, what hath been done here daily about these heretics. Now I come next to certify to your lordship the horrible judgment begun this day, the eleventh of June, and executed very early in the morning against the Lutherans : which when I think upon, I verily quake and tremble. And truly the manner of their putting to death, was to be compared to the slaughter of calves and sheep. For they being all thrust up in one house together as in a sheepfold, the executioner comes in, and amongst them takes one and blindfolds him with a muffler about his eyes, and so leads him forth to a place near adjoining, where he commands him to kneel down ; which being done, he cuts his throat, and leaving him half dead, and taking his butcher's knife and muffler all full of blood comes again to the rest, and so leading them one after another, he dispatched them all to the number of eighty-eight. How doleful and horrible this spectacle was I leave to your lordship's judgment ; for to write of it, I myself cannot choose but weep. Neither was there any of the beholders there present who seeing one die, could abide to behold the death of another. But so humbly and patiently they went to death, as is almost incredible to believe. Some of them, as they were dying, affirmed, that they believed even as we do ; notwithstanding, the most part of them died in their obstinate opinions. All the aged persons went to death more cheerfully ; the younger were more timorous. I tremble and shake even to remember how the executioner held his bloody knife between his teeth, with the bloody muffler in his hand, and his arms all in clotted blood up to the elbows, going to the fold, and taking every one of them, one after another, by the hand, and so dispatching them all, no otherwise than a butcher kills his calves and sheep.

"It is moreover appointed, and the carts are come already, that those so put to death should be quartered, and conveyed in carts to parts of Calabria, where they shall be hanged upon poles in the highways and other places even to the confines of the same country. Unless the pope's holiness and the lord viceroy of Naples shall give in command to the lord marquis of Buccianus, governor of the said province, to stay his hand and go no further, he will proceed with the rack and torture, examining all others, and so increase the number, that he will nigh dispatch them all.

"This day it is also determined, that an hundred of the more ancient women should appear to be examined and racked, and after to be put to death, that the mixture may be perfect, for so many men so many women. And thus have you all that I can say of this justice. Now it is about two of the clock in the afternoon ; shortly we shall hear what some of them said when they went to execution. There are some of them so obstinate, that they will not look upon the crucifix, nor be confessed to the priest, and they will be burned alive.

"The heretics that are apprehended and condemned are to the number of one thousand six hundred, but as yet no more than these eighty-eight are already executed. This people have their original of the valley named Angrognia, near to Subaudia, and in Calabria are called Ultramontani. In the kingdom of Naples there are four other places of the same people, of whom whether they live well or no, as yet we know not ; for they are but simple people, without learning, wood-gatherers and husbandmen ; but, as I hear, very devout and religious, giving themselves to die for religion's sake.—From Montalto the 11th of June."

Marquess Buccianus above specified, had a son or bro-

ther, to whom the pope promised a cardinalship at Rome, if all the Lutherans were extirpated and rooted out in that province. That was probably the cause of his inhuman persecution and effusion of christian blood.

After this lamentable slaughter in Calabria, we must insert here the tragical persecution and horrible murder of the faithful flock of Christ, inhabiting Merindole in France, and the adjacent towns, in the time of Francis I. The furious cruelty of which persecution, although it cannot be set forth too much at large, we have contracted, omitting nothing which might seem worthy to be recorded. The history here follows :—

A notable history of the persecution and destruction of the people of Merindole and Cabriers in the country of Provence, where not a few persons, but whole villages and townships, with the most part of all the country, both men, women, and children, were put to all kind of cruelty, and suffered martyrdom for the profession of the gospel.

They that write of the beginning of this people say, that about two hundred years ago, they came out of the country of Piedmont to inhabit Provence, in certain villages destroyed by wars, and other places ; they used such labour and diligence, that they had abundance of corn, wine, oil, honey, almonds, with other fruits of the earth, and much cattle. Before they came there, Merindole was a barren desert, and not inhabited. But these good people, in whom God always had reserved some seed of piety, were compelled to dwell in that waste and wild desert, which, through the blessing of God, became exceeding fruitful. The world, in the meantime, so detested and abhorred them, and railed against them in such a manner, that it seemed as if they were not worthy that the earth should bear them. For they had long refused the bishop of Rome's authority, and observed a more perfect doctrine than others, ever since A.D. 1200.

For this cause they were often accused to the king, as despisers of the magistrates, and rebels. Wherefore they were called by divers names, according to the countries and places where they dwelt. For in the country about Lyons, they were called the " poor people of Lyons ;" in the borders of Sarmatia and Livonia, and other countries toward the north, they were called "Lollards ;" in Flanders and Artois, "Turelupins," from a desert where wolves haunt. In Dauphiny they were called " Chagnards," because they lived in places open to the sun. But most commonly they were called "Waldois," from Waldo, who first instructed them in the word of God ; which name continued until the name of Lutherans began.

Notwithstanding all this, the people dwelling at the foot of the Alps, and also in Merindole and Cabriers, and thereabout, always lived so godly, so uprightly, and justly, that in all their life and conversation, there appeared to be in them a great fear of God. That little light of true knowledge which God had given them, they laboured to kindle and increase daily more and more, sparing no charges to procure the holy scriptures, or to instruct the most intelligent in learning and godliness ; or else to send them into other countries, even to the farthest part of the earth, where they had heard that any light of the gospel had begun to shine.

For in the year 1530, understanding that the gospel was preached in Germany and Switzerland, they sent there two learned men, George Maurell and Peter Latom to confer with the wise and learned ministers of the churches there, in the doctrine of the gospel, and to know the whole form and manner which those churches used in the service and worshipping of God ; and particularly to have their advice upon certain points on which they were not agreed. These two, after long conference with the chiefest in the church of God, namely, Oecolampadius at Basil, and Bucer and Capito at Strasburg ; and at Berne, with Bathold Haller, as they were returning through Burgundy homeward, Peter Latom was taken at Dijon and cast into prison ; Maurell escaped, and returned alone to Merindole with the books and letters which he brought with him from the churches of

Germany; and declared to his brethren all his commission, and opened to them, how many and great errors they were in.

When the people heard these, they were moved with so much zeal to have their churches reformed, that they sent for the most ancient brethren, and the chiefest in knowledge and experience in all Calabria and Apulia to consult with them touching the reformation of the church. This matter was so handled, that it stirred up the bishops, priests, and monks in all Provence with great rage against them. Amongst others there was one cruel wretch called John de Roma, a monk, who obtaining a commission to examine those who were suspected to be of the Waldois or Lutheran profession, ceased not to afflict the faithful in all kind of cruelty that he could devise or imagine. Amongst other torments, this was one which he most delighted in, and most constantly practised; he filled boots with boiling grease, and put them upon their legs, tying them backward to a form, with their legs hanging down over a small fire, and so he examined them. Thus he tormented very many, and in the end most cruelly put them to death.

After the death of this cruel monster, the bishop of Aix, by his official, continued the persecution, and put a great number of them in prison; of whom some by force of torments turned from the truth; the others who continued constant, after he had condemned them of heresy, were put into the hands of the ordinary judge, who without any form of process or order of law, put them to death with most cruel torments.

After this, those of Merindole were cited personally to appear before the king's attorney. But they, hearing that the court had determined to burn them without any further process or order of law, durst not appear at the day appointed. For which the court awarded a cruel sentence against Merindole, and condemned all the inhabitants to be burned, both men and women, sparing none, no not even the little children and infants; the town to be razed, and their houses pulled to the ground; also the trees to be cut down, as well olive trees as all other, and nothing to be left, to the intent it should never be inhabited again, but remain as a desert or wilderness.

This bloody decree seemed so strange and wonderful, that in every place throughout all Provence there was great disputation concerning it, especially among the advocates and men of learning; so that many durst boldly and openly say, that they greatly marvelled how that court of parliament could be so mad, or so bewitched to give out such a decree, so manifestly injurious and unjust, and contrary to all right and reason, yea, to all sense of humanity; also contrary to the solemn oath which all such as are received to office in courts of parliament are accustomed to make, that is to say, to judge justly and uprightly, according to the law of God, and the just ordinances and laws of the realm, so that God thereby might be honoured, and every man's right regarded, without respect to persons.

Some of the advocates or lawyers, defending the decree said, that in case of Lutheranism, the judges are not bound to observe either right or reason, law or ordinance; and that the judges cannot fail or do amiss, whatever judgment they do give, so that it tend to the ruin and extirpation of all such as are suspected to be Lutherans.

To this the other lawyers and learned men answered, that in this way it would follow that the judges should now follow the same manner and form against the christians accused to be Lutherans, which the gospel witnesses that the priests, scribes, and pharisees followed in pursuing and persecuting, and finally condemning our Lord Jesus Christ.

The archbishop of Arles, the bishop of Aix, and divers abbots, priors, and others, assembled themselves together, to consult how this decree might be executed with all speed, intending to raise a new persecution; for otherwise, said they, our state and honour is likely to decay; we shall be reproved, contemned, and derided of all men. And if none should thus vaunt and set themselves against us, but these peasants, and such like, it were but a small matter; but many doctors of divinity, and men of the religious order, divers senators and advocates, many wise and well learned men, also a great part of the nobility, yea, even of the chiefest peers in all Europe, begin to contemn and despise us, counting us to be no true pastors of the church; so that except we see to this mischief, and provide a remedy in time, it is greatly to be feared, that we shall not only be compelled to forsake our dignities, possessions, and livings, which we now enjoy, but also the church being spoiled of her pastors and guides, shall hereafter come to miserable ruin, and utter desolation.

Then the archbishop of Arles gave his advice as follows: "Against the nobility," said he, "we must take heed that we attempt nothing rashly, but, rather we must seek all the means we can how to please them; for they are our shield,—our fortress and defence. And albeit we know that many of them do both speak and think evil of us, and that they are of these new gospellers, yet we must not reprove them, or exasperate them; we must rather seek how to win them, and to make them our friends again by gifts and presents; and by this policy we shall live in safety under their protection."

"It is well said," said the bishop of Aix; "but I can shew you a good remedy for this disease; we must go about with all our endeavour and power, and policy, and all the friends we can make, sparing no charges, but spending goods, wealth, and treasure, to make such a slaughter of the Merindolians and rustic peasants, that none shall be so bold hereafter, whatever they be, yea, although they be of the blood royal, once to open their mouths against us, or the ecclesiastical state. And to bring this matter to pass, we have no better way than to withdraw ourselves to Avignon, in which city we shall find many bishops, abbots, and other famous men, who will employ their whole endeavour to maintain and uphold the majesty of our holy mother, the church. This counsel was well liked by them all. Whereupon the said archbishop of Arles, and the bishop of Aix, went with all speed to Avignon, there to assemble out of hand the bishops, and other men of authority and credit, to consult of this matter. In this pestilent conspiracy, the bishop of Aix, a stout champion, and a great defender of the traditions of men, taking upon him to be the chief orator, began in a manner as follows:—

"O, ye fathers and brethren, ye are ignorant, that a great tempest is raised up against the little bark of Christ Jesus, now in great danger, and ready to perish. The storm cometh from the north, whereof all these troubles proceed. The seas rage, the waters rush in on every side, the winds blow and beat upon our house, and we without speedy remedy are like to sustain shipwreck and loss of all together. For oblations cease, pilgrimage and devotion waxeth cold, charity is clean gone, our estimation and authority is debased, our jurisdiction decayed, and the ordinances of the church despised. And wherefore are we set and ordained over nations and kingdoms, but to root out and destroy, to subvert and overthrow whatsoever is against our holy mother, the church? Wherefore let us now awake; let us stand stoutly in the right of our own profession, that we may root out from the memory of men for ever, the whole rout of the wicked Lutherans; those foxes, I say, which destroy the vineyard of the Lord; those great whales which go about to drown the little bark of the Son of God. We have already well begun, and have procured a terrible decree against these cursed heretics of Merindole. Let us therefore employ our whole endeavour, that nothing happen which may hinder that which we have so happily begun; and let us take good heed that our gold and silver do not witness against us at the day of judgment, if we refuse to bestow the same, that we may make so good a sacrifice unto God. And for my part I offer to wage and furnish of mine own costs and charges, a hundred men well horsed, with all other furniture to them belonging, and that so long, till the utter destruction and subversion of these wretched and cursed caitiffs is fully finished."

This oration pleased the whole multitude, saving one doctor of divinity, a friar jacobin, named Bassinet, who then answered again with this oration:—

"This is a weighty matter," said he, "and of great importance; we must therefore proceed wisely, and in the fear of God, and beware that we do nothing rashly. For if we seek the death and destruction of these poor and miserable people wrongfully, when the king and the nobility shall hear of such a horrible slaughter, we shall be in great danger, lest they do to us as we read in the scriptures was done to the priests of Baal. For my part I must say, and unfeignedly confess, that I have too rashly and lightly signed many processes against those who have been accused of heretical doctrine; but now I do protest before God, who seeth and knoweth the hearts of men, that, seeing the lamentable end and effect of mine assignments, I have had no quietness in my conscience, considering that the secular judges, at the report of the judgment and sentence given by me and other doctors my companions, have condemned all those to most cruel deaths, whom we have adjudged to be heretics. And the cause why in conscience I am thus disquieted, is this, that now of late, since I have given myself more diligently to the reading and contemplation of the holy scriptures, I have perceived that the most part of those articles, which they that are called Lutherans do maintain, are so conformable and agreeing to the scriptures, that for my part I can no longer gainsay them, except I should even wilfully and maliciously resist and strive against the holy ordinances of God. It seemeth to me, that we ought not any more to proceed in this matter as we have done in time past. It shall be sufficient to punish with fine, or to banish them, who shall speak against the constitutions of the church, and of the pope. And such as shall be plainly convicted by the holy scripture to be blasphemous or obstinate heretics, to be condemned to death according to the enormity of their crimes or errors, or else to perpetual prison. And this is my advice and counsel."

With this counsel of Bassinet all the company was offended, but especially the bishop of Aix, who, lifting up his voice above all the rest, said thus unto him: "O thou man of little faith! whereof art thou in doubt? Dost thou repent thee of that thou hast well done? Thou hast told here a tale that smelleth of fagots and brimstone. Is there any difference, thinkest thou, between heresies and blasphemies spoken and maintained against the holy scriptures, and opinions holden against our holy mother the church, and contrary to our holy father, the pope, a most undoubted and true God on earth? 'Art thou a master in Israel, and knowest thou not these things?'"

"It is true," said Bassinet again, "that my lord, the bishop of Aix, has well set out the manners and state of the clergy, and has aptly reproved the vices and heresies of this present time; and therefore so soon as mention was made of the ship of Christ Jesus, it came into my mind first of all of the high bishop of Jerusalem, the priests, the doctors of the law, the Scribes and Pharisees, who once had the government of this ship. But when they forsook the law of God, and served him with men's inventions and traditions, he destroyed those hypocrites in his great indignation; and having compassion and pity upon the people, who were like sheep without a shepherd, he sent diligent fishers to fish for men, faithful workmen into his harvest, and labourers into his vineyard, who shall all bring forth true fruits in their season. Secondly, considering the purpose and intent of the reverend lord bishop of Aix, I called to mind the saying of the apostle in his first epistle to Timothy, (chap. iv.), 'That in the latter days some shall depart from the faith, giving heed to seducing spirits, and doctrines of devils.' And the apostle gives a mark by which a man shall know them. Likewise our Lord Jesus Christ, in the seventh chapter of Matthew, saith, 'That the false prophets shall come clothed in sheepskins, but inwardly they are ravening wolves, and by their fruits they shall be known.' By these, and such other places, it is easy to understand who are they that go about to drown this little bark of Christ. Are they not those who fill the same with filthy and unclean things, with mire and dirt, with puddle and stinking

water? Are they not those who have forsaken Jesus Christ, the fountain of living water, and have digged unto themselves pits or cisterns which will hold no water? Truly, are they not those who vaunt themselves to be the salt of the earth, and yet have no savour at all; who call themselves pastors, and yet are not true pastors, for they minister not unto the sheep the true pasture and feeding, neither divide and distribute the true bread of the word of life. And, if I may be bold to speak it, would it not be at this present time as great a wonder to hear a bishop preach, as to see an ass fly? Are they not accursed of God who glory and boast that they themselves have the keys of the kingdom of heaven, and neither enter in themselves, nor suffer them that would enter, to come in? They may be known right well by their fruits; for they have forsaken faith, judgment, and mercy, and there is no honest, clean, or undefiled thing in them, but their habit, their rochet, and their surplice, and such other. Outwardly they are exceeding neat and trim, but within they are full of all abomination, rapine, gluttony, lust, and all manner of uncleanness; they are like painted sepulchres, which outwardly appear beautiful and fair, but within they are full of filth and corruption. A man shall know, I say, these ravening wolves by their fruits, who devour the quick and the dead under the pretence of long prayers; and as I am enforced to give place to the truth, and that you call me a master in Israel, I will not be afraid to prove by the holy scriptures, that your great pilot and patron the pope, and the bishops, the mariners, and such others who forsake the ship of Christ Jesus, to embark themselves in pinnaces and brigantines, are pirates and robbers of the sea, false prophets, deceivers, and not true pastors of the church of Jesus Christ."

When Doctor Bassinet had thus freely and boldly uttered his mind, the whole multitude began to gather about him, and spitefully railed at him. But the bishop of Aix, above others, raging and crying out as he had been mad: "Get thee out," said he, "from amongst us, thou wicked apostate; thou art not worthy to be in this company. We have burned daily a great many who have not so well deserved it, as thou hast; we may now perceive that there is none more steadfast and fervent in the faith than the doctors of the canon law. And therefore it were necessary to be decreed in the next general council, that none should have to do in matters of religion but they alone; for these knaves and beggarly monks and friars will bring all to naught." Then the other doctors of the same order boldly reproved the bishop of Aix for the injury he had done to them. After this there arose a great dissension among them, so that there was nothing at that time determined. After dinner all these reverend prelates assembled together again, but they suffered neither friar nor monk to be among them, except he were an abbot. In this assembly they made an agreement and confirmed it with an oath, that every man should himself endeavour that the decree of Merindole should be executed with all expedition, and that every man should furnish out men of war, according to his ability. The charge whereof was given to the bishop of Aix, and to the president of the canons, to solicit the matter, and to persuade by all possible means the presidents and councillors of the court of parliament, without fear or doubt, to execute the decree with drums, ensigns displayed, artillery, and all kind of furniture of war.

This conspiracy being concluded and determined, the bishop of Aix departed to Aix, to perform the charge which was given to him. They desired him to be, the next day after the council, at a banquet which should be made at the house of the bishop of Rieux. To this banquet such as were known to be the fairest and most beautiful women in all Avignon were called, to refresh and solace these good prelates, after the great pains and travel which they had taken for our holy mother, the church. After they had dined, they fell to dancing, playing at dice, and such other pastimes as are commonly wont to be used at the banquets and feasts of these holy prelates. After this they walked abroad to solace themselves, and to pass the time till supper.

As they passed through the streets, they saw a man who sold lewd images and pictures, with filthy rhymes and ballads. All these pictures were bought up by the bishops. In the same place, as they walked along, there was a bookseller who had set out to sell some bibles in French and Latin, with divers other books, which, when the prelates beheld, they were greatly moved thereat, and said unto him, " Darest thou be so hardy to set out such merchandise to sell here in this town ? Dost thou not know that such books are forbidden ?" The bookseller answered : " Is not the holy Bible as good as these goodly pictures which you have bought for these gentlewomen ?" He had scarce spoken these words, when the bishop of Aix said, " I renounce my part of Paradise, if this fellow be not a Lutheran." " Let him be taken," said he, " and examined what he is ;" and instantly the bookseller was taken and carried to prison, and spitefully handled ; for a company of knaves and ruffians, which waited upon the prelates, began to cry out : " A Lutheran, a Lutheran!—to the fire with him, to the fire with him !" and one gave him a blow with his fist, another pulled him by the hair, and others by the beard, in such sort that the poor man was all imbrued with blood before he came to prison.

The morrow after, he was brought before the judges, in the presence of the bishops, and was examined in the following manner : " Hast thou not set forth for sale the Bible and the New Testament in French ?" The prisoner answered, that he had done so. And being demanded, whether he understood or knew not, that it was forbidden throughout all Christendom to print or sell the Bible in any other language than in Latin ? He answered, that he knew the contrary, and that he had sold many Bibles in the French tongue, with the emperor's privilege, and many others printed at Lyons ; also New Testaments printed by the king's privilege. Furthermore, he said that he knew no nation throughout all Christendom, which had not the holy scriptures in their vulgar tongue; and afterwards with a bold courage thus he spake to them : " O you inhabitants of Avignon ! are you alone in all Christendom those men who despise and abhor the Testament of the Heavenly Father ? Will ye forbid and hide that which Jesus Christ hath commanded to be revealed and published ? Do you not know that our Lord Jesus Christ gave power unto his apostles to speak all manner of tongues, to this end, that his holy gospel should be taught unto all creatures in every language ? And why do you not forbid those books and pictures, which are full of filthiness and abomination, and provoke God's vengeance and great indignation upon you all ? What greater blasphemy can there be, than to forbid God's most holy books, which he ordained to instruct the ignorant, and to reduce and bring again into the way such as are gone astray ? What cruelty is this, to take away from the poor weak souls their nourishment and sustenance ? But, my lords, you shall give a heavy account, who call sweet bitter, and bitter sweet, who maintain abominable and detestable books and pictures, and reject that which is holy."

Then the bishop of Aix and the other bishops began to rage and gnash their teeth against this poor prisoner. " What need you," said they, " any more examination ? Let him be sent straight unto the fire without any more words." But the judge, Laberius, and certain others, were not of that mind, neither found they sufficient cause to put him to death, but went about to have him put to his fine, and to make him confess and acknowledge the bishop of Aix, and others, to be the true pastors of the church. But the bookseller answered, that he could not do it with a good conscience, forasmuch as he did see before his eyes, that these bishops maintained filthy books and abominable pictures, rejecting and refusing the holy books of God, and therefore he judged them rather to be the priests of Bacchus and Venus, than the true pastors of the church of Christ. Whereupon he was immediately condemned to be burned, and the sentence was executed the very same day. And for a sign or token of the cause of his condemnation, he carried two Bibles hanging about his neck, the one before, and the other behind him ; but this poor man had also the word of God in his heart, and in his mouth, and ceased not continually by the way, until that he came to the place of execution, to exhort and admonish the people to read the holy scriptures, so that several were thereby moved to seek after the truth.

The bishop of Aix returned to prosecute the execution of the decree against Merindole. The president answered him, that it was no small matter to put the decree of Merindole in execution ; also that the decree was given out more to keep the Lutherans in fear, than to execute it. Moreover, he said that the decree of Merindole was not definitive, and that the laws and statutes of the realm did not permit the execution thereof without further process. Then said the bishop, " If there be either law or statute which do hinder or let you, we carry in our sleeves to dispense therewithal." The president answered : " It were a great sin to shed the innocent blood." Then said the bishop : " The blood of them of Merindole be upon us, and upon our successors." Then said the president : " I am very well assured, that if the decree of Merindole be put in execution, the king will not be well pleased to have such destruction made of his subjects." Then said the bishop : " Although the king at the first do think it evil done, we will so bring it to pass, that within a short space he shall think it well done ; for we have the cardinals on our side, and especially the most reverend cardinal of Toulon, who will take upon him the defence of our cause, and we can do him no greater pleasure, than utterly to root out these Lutherans ; so that if we have any need of his counsel or aid, we shall be well assured of him ; and is not he the principal, the most excellent and prudent adversary of these Lutherans, which is in all Christendom ?"

By this and such other like talk the bishop of Aix persuaded the president and councillors of the court of parliament, to put the said decree in execution, and by this means, through the authority of the court, the drum was sounded throughout all Provence, the captains were prepared with their ensigns displayed, and a great number of footmen and horsemen began to set forward, and marched out of the town of Aix in order of battle, against Merindole, to execute the decree. The inhabitants of Merindole being advertised hereof, and seeing nothing but present death, with great lamentation commended themselves and their cause to God by prayer, making themselves ready to be murdered and slain, as sheep led unto slaughter.

Whilst they were in this grievous distress, piteously mourning and lamenting together, the father with the son, the daughter with the mother, the wife with the husband, suddenly there was news brought to them, that the army was retired, and no man knew at that time how, or by what means ; yet, notwithstanding, afterwards it was known that the lord of Alene, a wise man, and learned in the scriptures, and in the civil law, being moved with great zeal and love of justice, declared to the president Cassanes, that he ought not to proceed against the inhabitants of Merindole by way of force of arms, contrary to all form and order of justice, without judgment or condemnation, or without making any difference between the guilty and the innocent.

Then the Merindolians understanding that the army was retired, gave thanks to God, comforting one another with admonition and exhortation always to have the fear of God before their eyes, to be obedient to his holy commandments, subject to his most holy will, and every man to submit himself to his Providence, patiently attending and looking for the hope of the blessed, that is to say, the true life, and the everlasting riches, having always before their eyes for example our Lord Jesus Christ the very Son of God, who hath entered into his glory by many tribulations. Thus the Merindolians prepared themselves to endure and abide all the afflictions that it should please God to lay upon them : and such was their answer to all those that either pitied, or else sought their destruction. Whereupon the noise was so great, as well of the decree, as of the enterprise of the execution, and also of the patience and constancy of the Merindolians, that it was not hidden or kept secret from king Francis, a king of noble courage and great judgment; who gave command to the noble and virtuous lord Monsieur de Langeay, who then was his lieutenant in Turin, a city in Piedmont, that he should diligently inquire and search out the truth of all this matter. Whereupon the said Monsieur de Langeay sent unto Provence two men of fame and estimation, giving them in charge to bring unto him the copy of the decree, and diligently to inquire out all that followed and ensued thereupon; and likewise to make diligent inquiry as to the life and manners of the Merindolians, and others which were persecuted in the country of Provence.

These deputies brought the copy of a decree, and of all that happened thereupon, unto the said Monsieur de Langeay, declaring unto him the great injuries, pollings, extortions, exactions, tyrannies, and cruelties, which the judges, as well secular as ecclesiastical had used against them of Merindole, and others. As touching the behaviour and disposition of those which were persecuted, they reported that the inhabitants of Merindole, and the others that were persecuted, were peaceable and quiet people, beloved of all their neighbours, men of good behaviour, constant in keeping of their promise, and paying of their debts, without traversing or pleading at the law: that they were also charitable men, giving alms, relieving the poor, and suffered none amongst them to lack, or to be in necessity. Also they gave alms to strangers, and to the poor passengers, harbouring, nourishing, and helping them in all their necessities, according to their power. Moreover, that they were known by this, throughout all the country of Provence, that they would not swear, nor name the devil, or easily be brought to take an oath, except it were in judgment, or making some solemn covenant. They were also known by this, that they could never be moved nor provoked to talk of any dishonest matters, but in what company soever they came, where they heard any wanton talk, swearing or blasphemy to the dishonour of God, they straightway departed out of that company. Also they said, that they never saw them go to their business, but first they said their prayers. The said people of Provence furthermore affirmed, that when they came to any fairs or markets, or came to their cities on any occasion, they never in any manner were seen in their churches: and if they were, when they prayed they turned away their faces from the images, and neither offered candles to them, nor kissed their feet. Neither would they worship the relics of saints, nor once look upon them. And, moreover, if they passed by any cross or image of the crucifix, or any other saint by the way as they went, they would do no reverence unto them. Also the priests did testify, that they never caused them to say any masses, neither dirges, neither yet *de profundis*, neither would they take any holy water; and if it were carried home unto their houses, they would not say once, ' God have mercy;' yea, they seemed utterly to abhor it. To go on pilgrimage, to make any vows to saints, to buy pardons or remission of sins with money, yea, though it might be gotten for a halfpenny, they thought it not lawful. Likewise when it thundered or lightned, they would not cross themselves, but casting up their eyes unto heaven, fetch deep sighs. Some of them would kneel down and pray, without blessing themselves with the sign of the cross, or taking of holy water. Also they were never seen to offer, or cast into the bason any thing for the maintenance of lights, brotherhoods, churches, or to give any offering either for the quick or the dead. But if any were in affliction or poverty, those they relieved gladly, and thought nothing too much.

This was the whole tenor of the report made unto Monsieur de Langeay, touching the life and behaviour of the inhabitants of Merindole, and the others who were persecuted. Of all those things the said Monsieur de Langeay, according to the charge that was given him, advertised the king, who understanding these things, as a good prince moved with mercy and pity, sent letters of grace and pardon, not only for those who were condemned for lack of appearance, but also for all the rest of the country of Provence, who were accused and suspected in like cases.

On the other part, the bishops of Aix and Cavaillon pursued still the execution of the decree of Merindole. Then it was ordained by the court of parliament, that, according to the King's letters, John Durand, counsellor of the court of parliament, with a secretary, and the bishop of Cavaillon, with a doctor of divinity, should go unto Merindole, and there declare to the inhabitants the errors and heresies which they knew to be contained in their confession, and make them apparent by good and sufficient information; and having so convicted them by the Word of God, they should make them to renounce and abjure the heresies; and if the Merindolians did refuse to abjure, then they should make relation thereof, that the court might appoint how they should further proceed. After this decree was made, the bishop of Cavaillon would not tarry till the time which was appointed by the court for the execution of this matter; but he himself, with a doctor of Divinity, came to Merindole to make them abjure. The Merindolians answered, that he enterprised against the authority of the parliament, and that it was against his commission so to do. Notwithstanding he was very earnest with them that they should abjure, and promised them, if they would do so, to take them under his wings and protection, even as the hen doth her chickens, and that they should be no more robbed or spoiled. Then they required that he would declare to them what they should abjure. The bishop answered, that the matter needed no disputation, and that he required but only a general abjuration of all errors, which would be no damage or prejudice to them; for he himself would not hesitate to make the like abjuration. The Merindolians answered him again, that they would do nothing contrary to the decree and ordinance of the court, or the king's letters, wherein he commanded that first the errors should be declared to them, whereof they were accused: wherefore they were resolved to understand what those errors and heresies were, that being informed thereof by the Word of God, they might satisfy the king's letters; otherwise it were but hypocrisy and dissimulation to do as he required them. And if he could make it to appear to them by good and sufficient information, that they had held any errors and heresies, or should be convicted thereupon by the Word of God, they would willingly abjure; or if in their confession there were any word contrary to the scriptures, they would revoke the same. On the other hand, if it were not made manifest to them, that they had held any heresies, but that they had always lived according to the doctrine of the gospel, and that their confession was grounded upon the same, then they ought by no means to move or constrain them to abjure any errors which they held not, and that it were plainly against all equity and justice so to do.

Then the Bishop of Cavaillon was marvellously angry, and would hear no word spoken of any demonstration to be made by the word of God, but in a fury cursed and gave him to the devil that first invented that means. Then the doctor of divinity, whom the bishop brought thither, demanded what articles they were that were presented by the inhabitants of Merindole, for the bishop of Cavaillon had not yet shewn them to him. Then the bishop of Cavaillon delivered the doctor the confession, which after he had read, the bishop of Cavaillon said, " What! this is full of heresy." Then they of Merindole demanded, " In what point?" the bishop knew not what to answer. Then the doctor demanded to have time to look upon the articles of the confession, and to consider whether they were against the scriptures or no. Thus the bishop departed.

After eight days the bishop sent for this doctor, to understand how he might order himself to make their heresies appear which were in the said confession. Whereunto the doctor answered, that he was never so much abashed; for when he had beheld the articles of the confession, and the authorities of the Scriptures that were there alleged, he had found that those articles were wholly agreeable and according to the holy scriptures; and that he had not learned so much in the scriptures all the days of his life, as he had in those eight days, in looking upon those articles, and the authorities alleged.

Shortly after the Bishop of Cavaillon came to Merindole, and calling before him the children both great and small, gave them money, and commanded them with fair words to learn the Lord's prayer and the creed in Latin. The most part of them answered, that they knew the Lord's prayer and the creed already in Latin, but they could make no reason of that which they spake, but only in the vulgar tongue. The bishop answered that it was not necessary they should be so cunning, but that it was sufficient that they knew it in Latin; and that it was not requisite for their salvation, to understand or to expound the articles of their faith; for there were many bishops, curates, and doctors of divinity, whom it would trouble to expound the Lord's prayer and the creed. Here the bailiff of Merindole, named Andrew Maynard, asked, to what purpose it would serve to say the Lord's prayer and the creed, and not to understand the same? for in so doing they should but mock and deride God. Then said the bishop, " Do you understand what is signified by these words, ' I believe in God ?' " The bailiff answered, " I should think myself very miserable if I did not understand it ;" and then he began orderly to give an account of his faith. Then said the bishop, " I would not have thought there had been so great doctors in Merindole." The bailiff answered, " The least of the inhabitants of Merindole can do it yet more readily than I; but, I pray you, question but one or two of these young children, that you may understand whether they be well taught or no." But the bishop either knew not how to question them, or at the least would not.

Then one named Pieron Roy said, " Sir, one of these children may question one another, if you think it so good," and the bishop was contented. Then one of the children began to question with his fellows, with such grace and gravity as if he had been a schoolmaster; and the children one after another answered so to the purpose, that it was marvellous to hear; for it was done in the presence of many, among whom there were four religious men, that came lately out of Paris, of whom one said to the bishop, I must needs confess, that I have often been at the common schools of the Sorbonne in Paris, where I have heard the disputations of the divines; but yet I never learned so much as I have done by hearing these young children. Then said William Armant, " Did you never read that which is written in Matthew xi. 25, 26, where it is said, ' I thank thee, O Father, Lord of heaven and earth, because thou hast hid these things from the wise and prudent, and hast revealed them unto babes. Even so, Father; for so it seemed good in thy sight.' " Then every man marvelled at the ready answers of the children of Merindole.

When the bishop saw he could not thus prevail, he tried another way, and went about by fair and flattering words to bring his purpose to pass. Causing the strangers to go apart, he said, that he now perceived they were not so evil as many thought them to be; notwithstanding it was necessary that they should make some small abjuration, which only the bailiff, with two officers, might make generally in his presence, in the name of all the rest, without any notary to record the same in writing; and in so doing they should be loved and favoured of all men, and even of those who now persecuted them.

The bailiff, and the two officers, with divers other ancients of the town, answered, that they were fully resolved not to consent to any abjuration, however it were to be done, except that (which was always their exception) they could make it appear to them by the word of God, that they had held or maintained any heresy; marvelling much that he would go about to persuade them to lie to God and to the world.

After this, John Miniers, lord of Opide, near Merindole, forged a most impudent lie, giving the king to understand, that they of Merindole, and all the country near about, to the number of twelve or fifteen thousand, were in the field in armour with their ensigns displayed, intending to take the town of Marseilles, and to make it one of the cantons of the Switzers; and to stay this enterprise, he said, it was necessary to execute the decree: and by this means he obtained the king's letters patent, through the help of the cardinal of Tou-

lon, commanding the sentence to be executed against the Merindolians.

After this he gathered all the king's army, which was then in Provence ready to go against the Englishmen, and took up all besides, that were able to bear armour, in the chief towns of Provence, and joined them with the army which the pope's legate had levied for that purpose in Avignon, and all the country of Venice, and employed the same to the destruction of Merindole, Cabriers, and other towns and villages, to the number of twenty-two, giving commission to his soldiers to spoil, ransack, burn, and to destroy all together, and to kill man, woman, and child, without mercy.

But this arch-tyrant, before he came to Merindole, ransacked and burnt certain towns, namely, La Roche, St. Stephens, Ville Laure, Lormarin, La Motte, Cabriers, St. Martin, Pipin, and other places more, notwithstanding that the decree extended but only to Merindole, where the most of the poor inhabitants were slain and murdered without any resistance; women with child, and little infants born and to be born were most cruelly murdered; the paps of many women were cut off, which gave suck to their children, who looking for suck at their mother's breast, died for hunger. There never was any such cruelty and tyranny seen before. The Merindolians seeing all on a flaming fire round about them, left their houses, and fled into the woods.

Not long after it was shewn them how that Miniers was coming with all his power to give the charge upon them. This was in the evening, and that they might go through rough and cumbersome places, and hard to pass by, they all thought it most expedient for their safeguard to leave behind them all the women and children, with a few others, and among them also certain ministers of the church; the residue were appointed to go to the town of Mussi. And this they did upon the hope that the enemy would show mercy to the multitude of women and children who were destitute of all succour. No tongue could express what sorrow, what tears, what sighing, what lamentation there was at that woful departing, when they were compelled to be thus separated asunder, the husband from his dear wife, the father from his sweet babes and tender infants, the one never like to see the other again alive. Notwithstanding after the ministers had ended their ordinary sermons, with evening prayers and exhortations, the men departed that night, to avoid a greater inconvenience.

In the mean time Miniers came to Merindole, which was taken, ransacked, burnt, razed, and laid even with the ground.

When he had destroyed Merindole, he laid siege to Cabriers, and battered it with his ordinance; but when he could not win it by force, he, with the lord of the town, and Poulin, his chief captain, persuaded the inhabitants to open their gates, solemnly promising, that if they would so do, they would lay down their armour, and also that their cause should be heard in judgment with all equity and justice, and no violence or injury should be shewed against them. Upon this they opened their gates, and let in Miniers, with his captains, and all his army. But the tyrant when he was once entered, falsified his promise, and raged like a beast. For first of all he picked out about thirty men, causing them to be bound, and carried into a meadow near to the town, and there to be miserably cut and hewn in pieces.

Then he exercised his fury and outrage upon the women, and caused forty of them to be taken, of whom several were great with child, and put them into a barn full of straw and hay, and caused it to be set on fire; and when the women, running to the great window where the hay is wont to be cast into the barn, would have leaped out, but they were kept in with pikes and halberts. Then there was a soldier who, moved with pity at the crying out and lamentation of the women, opened a door to let them out; but as they were coming out, the tyrant caused them to be slain and cut in pieces. Many fled into the wine-cellar of the castle, and many hid themselves in caves, whereof some were carried into the meadow, and, after being stripped naked, were slain ;

others were bound two and two together, and carried into the hall of the castle, where they were slain by the captains, who rejoiced in their cruel and inhuman slaughter.

That done, this tyrant, more cruel than ever was Herod, commanded captain John de Gay with a band of ruffians to go into the church, where there was a great number of women, children, and young infants, and to kill all that he found there; which the captain refused at first to do, saying, that was a cruelty unusual among men of war. Whereat Miniers being displeased, charged him upon pain of rebellion and disobedience to the king, to do as he commanded him. The captain fearing what might ensue, entered with his men, and destroyed them all, sparing neither young nor old.

In the mean while certain soldiers went to ransack the houses for the spoil, where they found many poor men that had there hidden themselves in cellars, and other places, flying upon them, and crying out, " Kill, kill !" The other soldiers that were without the town, killed all that they could meet with. The number of those that were unmercifully murdered, were about a thousand persons of men, women, and children. The infants that escaped their fury, were baptized again by their enemies.

In token of this victory, the pope's officers caused a pillar to be erected in Cabriers, on which was engraven the year and the day of the taking and sacking of this town, by John Miniers, lord of Opide, and chief president of the parliament of Provence, for a memorial for ever of that barbarous cruelty, the like whereof was never before heard of. Whereupon we with all our posterity have to understand what are the reasons and arguments wherewith the antichrist of Rome is wont to uphold the impious seat of his abomination; who now is come to such excess and profundity of all kinds of iniquity, and all justice, equity, and verity being set aside, he seeketh the defence of his cause by no other thing but only by force and violence, terror, and oppression, and shedding of blood.

In the mean while the inhabitants of Merindole, and other places, were among the mountains and rocks, in great necessity of victuals, and in much affliction; they had procured some men who were in some favour and authority with Miniers, to make request to him, that they might depart safely whither it should please God to lead them, with their wives and children, although they had no more but their shirts to cover their nakedness. Miniers made this answer: " I know what I have to do; not one of them shall escape my hands; I will send them to dwell in hell among the devils."

Thus hast thou heard, loving reader, the terrible troubles and slaughters committed by the bishops and cardinals, against these faithful men of Merindole.

Now, touching the people of Merindole, is briefly to be noted, that this was not the first time that these men were vexed. For these inhabitants of Provence, and other coasts bordering about France and Piedmont, had their continuance from ancient times, and received their doctrine first from the Waldenses, or Albigenses, who were (as some say) about A. D. 1170; or (as others reckon) about A.D. 1216.

These Waldenses, otherwise called poor men of Lyons, beginning from Peter Waldo, being driven out of Lyons, were dispersed in divers countries, some fled to Massilia, some to Germany, some to Sarmatia, Livonia, Bohemia, Calabria, and Apulia; several strayed to France, especially about Provence and Piedmont, of whom came these Merindolians, and the Angrognians with others. They who were in the country of Toulouse, were called Albii, or Albigenses, from the place where they frequented. Against the Albigenses, Friar Dominic was a great actor, labouring and preaching against them ten years together; and caused many of them to be burned, for which he was highly accepted and rewarded in the apostolical court, and at length, by Pope Honorius III. was made patriarch of the Dominican friars.

These Albigenses, against the pope of Rome, had set up to themselves a bishop of their own, named Bartholomew. For which the see of Rome took great indignation against the Albigenses, and caused all the faithful catholics, and subjects of the church, to rise up in ar-

mour, and to take the sign of the holy cross upon them, and to fight against them, A.D. 1206; great multitudes of them were cruelly murdered, not only about Toulouse and Avignon, but also in all quarters, miserable slaughters and burnings long continued, from the reign of the emperor Frederick II., almost to this present time, through the instigation of the Roman popes.

Among other authors who write of those Waldenses, John Sleidan, treating of their continuance and doctrine, thus writes of them : " There are," saith he, " in the French Provence a people called Waldoi. These of an ancient custom among them do not acknowledge the bishop of Rome, and have ever used a manner of doctrine more pure than the rest, but especially since the coming of Luther, they have increased in more knowledge and perfection of judgment."

Concerning the confession and the doctrine of the Merindolians received of ancient time from their forefathers the Waldenses, thus it follows in the said book and place of John Sleidan.

" At last, after he had described what great cruelty was shewed against them, when the report hereof was spread in Germany, it offended the minds of many : and indeed the Switzers, who were then of a contrary religion to the pope, entreated the king that he would shew mercy to such as had fled. The year before he had received from his subjects of Merindole a confession of their faith and doctrine : the articles whereof were, that they, according to the Christian faith, confessed, first God the Father, Creator of all things : the Son, the only Mediator and Advocate of mankind : the Holy Spirit, the Comforter, and Instructor of all truth. They confessed also the church, which they acknowledged to be the fellowship of God's elect, whereof Jesus Christ is head. The ministers also of the church they allowed, wishing that such as did not their duty should be removed.

" And as touching magistrates, they granted likewise the same to be ordained of God to defend the good, and to punish the transgressors. And how they owe to him, not love only, but also tribute and custom, and no man herein to be excepted, even by the example of Christ, who paid tribute himself, &c.

" Likewise of baptism, they confessed the same to be a visible and an outward sign, but represents to us the renewing of the spirit, and mortification of the members.

" As touching the Lord's supper, they said and confessed the same to be a thanksgiving, and a memorial of the benefit received through Christ.

" Matrimony they affirmed to be holy, and instituted of God, and to be prohibited to no man.

" That good works are to be observed and exercised by all men, as the holy scripture teaches.

" That false doctrine, which leads men away from the true worship of God, ought to be eschewed.

" Finally, the order and rule of their faith they confessed to be the Old and New Testament ; protesting that they believed all such things as are contained in the apostolic creed : desiring moreover the king to give credit to this their declaration of their faith ; so that whatsoever was informed to him to the contrary was not true, and that they would well prove, if they might be heard."

The History of the Persecutions and Wars against the people called Waldenses or Waldois, in the Valleys of Angrogne, Lucerne, St. Martin, Perouse, and others, in the country of Piedmont, from the year 1555 to 1561.

To proceed now in the persecution of these Waldois, or Waldenses, you have heard how they, dividing themselves into various countries, fled to Provence, to Toulouse, of which sufficient hath been said. Some went to Piedmont, and the valley of Angrogne, of whom it follows now to treat.

Thus these good men, by long persecution, being driven from place to place, were in all places afflicted, but yet could never be utterly destroyed, nor yet compelled to yield to the superstitious and false religion of the church of Rome : but ever abstained from their corruption and idolatry, as much as was possible, and gave themselves to the word of God, as a rule both truly to serve him, and to direct their lives accordingly.

They had many books of the Old and New Testaments translated into their language. Their ministers instructed them secretly, to avoid the fury of their enemies who could not abide the light. They lived in great simplicity, and by the sweat of their brows. They were quiet and peaceable among their neighbours, abstaining from blasphemy, and the profaning of the name of God by oaths, and such other impiety: from games, dancing, songs, and other vices and dissolute life, and conformed their life wholly to the rule of God's word. Their principal care was always, that God might be rightly served, and his word truly preached: so that in our time, when it pleased God to set forth the light of his gospel more clearly, they never spared any thing to establish the true and pure ministry of the word of God and his sacraments. Which was the cause that Satan with his ministers so persecuted them of late more cruelly than he ever did before, as appears by the cruel and horrible persecutions which have been, not only in Provence, against those of Merindole and Cabriers; but also against those remaining in the valleys of Angrogne, and of Lucerne, and also in the valley of St. Martin and Perouse, in Piedmont. Which people of a long time were persecuted by the papists, and especially within these few years they have been vexed, so that it seems almost incredible: and yet God hath miraculously delivered them.

The people of Angrogne had before this time some to preach the word of God, and to minister the sacraments unto them privately; yet in the year 1555, in the beginning of the month of August, the gospel was openly preached in Angrogne. The ministers and the people intended at first to keep themselves still as secret as they might: but there was such concourse of people from all parts, that they were compelled to preach openly abroad. For this cause they built a church in the midst of Angrogne, where assemblies were made, and sermons preached.

At this time the French King held these valleys, and they were under the jurisdiction of the parliament of Turin. In the end of December following, news was brought, that it was ordained by the parliament, that certain horsemen and footmen should be sent to spoil and destroy Angrogne. Some who pretended great friendship to this people, counselled them not to go forward with their enterprise, but to forbear for a while, and to wait for better opportunity. But they, notwithstanding, calling upon God, determined with one accord constantly to persist in their religion, and in hope and silence to abide the good pleasure of God: so that this enterprise against Angrogne was soon dashed. The same time they began also openly to preach in Lucerne.

In the month of March 1556, the ministers of the valley of St. Martin preached openly. At that time certain gentlemen of the valley of St. Martin took a good man named Bartholomew, a bookbinder, prisoner, as he passed by the said valley, and sent him to Turin; and there, with a marvellous constancy, after he had made a good confession of his faith, he suffered death; so that several of the Parliament were astonished and appalled at his constancy.

From thence they went to the valley of St. Martin, and remained there a good while, tormenting the poor people, and threatening their utter ruin and destruction. After that they came to Lucerne, troubling and vexing the people there in like manner. From thence they went to Angrogne, accompanied with many gentlemen, and a great rabble of priests.

After they were come to Angrogne, the president having visited the two temples, caused a monk to preach in the one, the people being there assembled; who pretended nothing else, but only to exhort them to return to the obedience of the see of Rome. The aforesaid monk, with the president, and all his whole retinue, kneeled down twice, and called upon the Virgin Mary; but the ministers and all the people stood still, and would not kneel, making no sign or token of reverence. As soon as the monk had ended his sermon, the people

requested instantly that their minister might also be suffered to preach, affirming that the monk had spoken many things which were not according to the word of God. But the president would not grant their request. After that the president admonished them, in the name of the king and the parliament of Turin, that they should return to the obedience of the pope, upon pain of loss of goods and life, and utter destruction of their town. And he recited unto them the piteous discomfiture of their brethren and friends, which had been done before in Merindole and Cabriers, and other places in the country of Provence. The ministers and the people answered, that they were determined to live according to the word of God, and that they would obey the king and all their superiors in all things, so that God thereby were not displeased; and if it were shewn to them by the word of God, that they erred in any point of religion, they were ready to receive correction, and to be reformed. This talk endured about six hours together, even until night. In the end, the president said there should be a disputation appointed for those matters, to which the people gladly agreed.

Here he remained fourteen days, daily practising new devices to vex and torment them with new proclamations; now calling to him the syndics and head-officers, now severally, and now altogether, that so for fear he might make them relent; causing also assemblies to be made in every parish by such as he appointed, thinking thereby to divide the people. Notwithstanding he prevailed nothing with all that he could do; but still they continued constant. Insomuch that they with one accord presented a brief confession of their faith, with an answer to certain interrogatories propounded by the president, in which they confessed,—

That the religion wherein both they and their elders had been long instructed and brought up, was the same which is contained both in the Old and New Testament, and which is also briefly comprised in the twelve articles of the Christian belief.

Also, that they acknowledged the sacraments instituted by Christ, whereby he distributes abundantly his graces and great benefits, his heavenly riches and treasures to all those who receive the same with a true and lively faith.

Furthermore, that they received the creeds of the four general councils; that is to say, of Nice, Constantinople, Ephesus, and Chalcedon, and also the creed of Athanasius, wherein the mystery of the Christian faith and religion is plainly and largely set out.

Also, the ten commandments expressed in the 20th chapter of Exodus, and the 5th of Deut., in which the rule of a godly and holy life, and also the true service which God requires of us, is briefly comprised; and therefore following this article, they suffered not by any means (said they) any gross iniquities to reign amongst them; as unlawful swearing, perjury, blasphemy, cursing, slandering, dissension, deceit, wrong dealing, usury, gluttony, drunkenness, theft, murder, or such like; but wholly endeavoured themselves to live in the fear of God, and according to his holy will.

Moreover, they acknowledged the superior powers, as princes and magistrates, to be ordained of God; and that whosoever resisteth the same, resisteth the ordinance of God; and therefore humbly submitted themselves to their superiors with all obedience, so that they commanded nothing against God.

Finally, they protested, that they would in no point be stubborn, but if that their forefathers or they had erred in any one jot concerning true religion, the same being proved by the word of God, they would willingly yield and be reformed.

Their interrogatories were concerning the mass, auricular confession, baptism, marriage and burials, according to the institution of the church of Rome.

To the first they answered, that they received the Lord's supper as it was instituted by him and celebrated by his apostles; but as touching the mass, except the same might be proved by the word of God, they would not receive it.

To the second, touching auricular confession, they

said, that for their part they confessed themselves daily unto God, acknowledging themselves before him to be miserable sinners, desiring of him pardon and forgiveness of their sins, as Christ instructed his in the prayer which he taught them, "Lord forgive our sins;" and as St. John saith, "If we confess our sins to God, he is faithful and just to forgive us our sins, and to cleanse us from all unrighteousness;" and according to that which God himself saith by his prophet, "O Israel, if thou return, return unto me;" and again, "O Israel, it is I, it is I who forgiveth thee thy sins." So that, seeing they ought to return to God alone, and it is he only who forgives sins, therefore they were bound to confess themselves to God only, and to no other. Also it appears, that David in his Psalms, and the Prophets, and other faithful servants of God, have confessed themselves both generally and particularly unto God alone; yet if the contrary might be proved by the word of God, they would (said they) receive the same with all humbleness.

Thirdly, as touching baptism, they acknowledged and received that holy institution of Christ, and administered the same with all simplicity, as he ordained it in his holy gospel, without any changing, adding or diminishing in any point, and that all this they did in their mother-tongue, according to the rule of St. Paul, who directs that in the church every thing be done in the mother-tongue, for the edification of our neighbour, 1 Cor. xiv.; but as for their conjurations, oiling, and salting, except the same might be proved by the sacred scripture, they would not receive them.

Fourthly, as touching burials, they answered, that they knew there was a difference between the bodies of the true christians and the infidels, as the first are the members of Jesus Christ, temples of the Holy Ghost, and partakers of the glorious resurrection of the dead, and therefore they are accustomed to follow their dead to the grave reverently, with a sufficient company, and exhortation out of the word of God, as well to comfort the parents and friends of the dead, as also to admonish all men diligently to prepare themselves to die. But as for the using of candles or lights, praying for the dead, ringing of bells, except the same might be proved to be necessary by the word of God, and that God is not offended therewith, they would not receive them.

Fifthly, as touching obedience to men's traditions, they received and allowed all those ordinances which, as St. Paul says, serve for order, decency, and reverence of the ministry. But as for other ceremonies, which have been brought into the church of God, either as a part of divine service, or to merit remission of sins, or else to bind men's consciences, because they are repugnant to the word of God, they could by no means receive them.

And whereas the commissioners affirmed the said traditions to have been ordained by councils; first, they answered, that the greatest part of them were not ordained by councils. Secondly, that councils were not to be preferred above the word of God, which saith, "If any man, yea, or an angel from heaven, should preach unto you otherwise than that which hath been received of the Lord Jesus, let him be accursed." And therefore, said they, if councils have ordained any thing dissenting from the word of God they would not receive it.

Wherefore they required the commissioners, that a disputation might be had publicly, and in their presence, and then if it might be proved, by the word of God, that they erred, either in doctrine, or conversation, and manner of living, they were content with all humbleness to be corrected and reformed. Beseeching them to consider also that their religion had been observed and kept from their ancestors, until their time, many hundred years together; and yet, for their parts, being convicted by the infallible word of God, they would not obstinately stand to the defence thereof. Saying moreover, that they, together with the said lords' deputies, confessed all one God, one Saviour, one Holy Ghost, one law, one baptism, one hope in heaven; and, in sum, they affirmed that their faith and religion was firmly founded and grounded upon the pure word of God.

To be short, seeing it is permitted to the Turks, Saracens, and Jews (which are mortal enemies to our Saviour Christ,) to dwell peaceably in the fairest cities of Christendom, by good reason they should be suffered to live in the desolate mountains and valleys, having their whole religion founded upon the holy gospel, and worshipping the Lord Jesus, and therefore they most humbly besought them to have pity and compassion upon them, and to suffer them to live quietly in their deserts; protesting that they and theirs would live in all fear and reverence of God, with all due subjection and obedience to their lord and prince, and to his lieutenants and officers.

The president, and the rest of the commissions, perceiving that they laboured in vain, returned to Turin with the notes of their proceedings; which immediately were sent to the king's court, and there the matter remained one year before there was any answer made thereunto. During which time the Waldois lived in great quietness, as God of his infinite goodness is wont to give some comfort and refreshing to his poor servants, after long troubles and afflictions. The number of the faithful so augmented, that throughout the valleys God's word was purely preached, and his sacraments duly administered, and no mass was sung in Angrogne, nor in divers other places. The year after, the president of St. Julian, with his associates, returned to Pignerol, and sent for the chief rulers of Angrogne, and of the valley of Lucerne, that is, for six of Angrogne, and for two of every parish besides, and showed to them, how that the last year they had presented their confession, which was sent to the king's court, and there diligently examined by learned men, and condemned as heretical. Therefore the king willed and commanded them to return to the obedience of the church of Rome, upon pain of loss both of goods and life; enjoining them moreover to give him a direct answer within three days. From thence he went to Lucerne, and caused the householders, with great threatenings, to assemble themselves before certain by him appointed; but they with one assent persisted in their former confession. And lest they should seem stubborn in the defence of any erroneous doctrine, they desired that their confession might be sent to all the universities of Christendom, and if the same in any part were disproved by the word of God, it should immediately be amended; but contrariwise, if that were not done, then they to be no more disquieted.

The president, not contented with this, the next morning sent for six persons of Angrogne, and for two out of every other parish, whom he and the gentlemen of the country threatened very sorely, and warned twelve of the chief of Angrogne, and of the other parishes, to appear personally at the parliament of Turin, and to bring before the judges of the parliament their ministers and schoolmasters, thinking, if they were once banished the country, that then their enterprise might soon be brought to an end. To which it was answered, that they could not, nor ought not to obey such a commandment.

A little while after proclamation was made in every place, that no man should receive any preacher coming from Geneva, but only such as were appointed by the archbishop of Turin, and others his officers, upon pain of confiscation of their goods, and loss of their lives, and that every one should observe the ceremonies, rites, and religion used in the church of Rome. Furthermore, if any of the aforesaid preachers of Geneva came into those quarters, that they should immediately be apprehended, and that none of them should be concealed by any one.

Now after four years, viz., A.D. 1559, there was a peace concluded between the French king and the king of Spain; when the country of Piedmont (certain towns excepted) was restored to the Duke of Savoy; under whom the churches, and all other faithful people in Piedmont, continued in great quietness, and were not molested; and the duke himself was content to suffer them to live in their religion, knowing that he had no subjects more faithful and obedient than they were. But Satan hating all quietness, by his ministers stirred up the duke against the churches of Piedmont, and his own natural subjects. For the pope and the cardinals, seeing the good inclination of the duke towards this people, incensed him to do that which otherwise he would not. The pope's legate also, who then followed the court, and others that favoured the church of Rome, laboured by all means to persuade the duke that he ought to banish the Waldois; alleging that he could not suffer such a people to dwell within his dominion, without prejudice and dishonour to the apostolic see. Also that they were a rebellious people against the holy ordinances and decrees of their holy mother the church. And briefly, if he would indeed show himself a loving and obedient son, that he might no longer suffer the people, being so disobedient and stubborn against the holy father.

Such devilish instigations were the cause of these horrible and furious persecutions, wherewith these poor people of the valleys, and in the country of Piedmont, were so long vexed. And because they foresaw the great calamities which they were likely to suffer, to find some remedy for the same, if it were possible, all the churches of Piedmont with one common consent wrote to the duke, declaring in effect, that the only cause why they were so hated, and for which he was by their enemies so sore incensed against them, was their religion, which was no new or light opinion, but that wherein they and their ancestors had long continued, being wholly grounded upon the infallible word of God, contained in the Old and New Testament. Notwithstanding, if it might be proved by the same word that they held any false or erroneous doctrine, they would submit themselves to be reformed with all obedience.

But it is not certain whether this advertisement was delivered unto the duke; for it was said that he would not hear of that religion. But however, in the month of March following, there was a great persecution raised against the poor christians who were at Carignan. Amongst whom there were certain godly persons taken and burnt within four days after.

Shortly after, these churches of the Waldois, that is to say, Le Larch, Meronne, Meane, and Suse, were wonderfully assaulted. To recite all the outrage, cruelty, and villany that was there committed were too long; for brevity's sake we will recite only certain of the principal and best known. The churches of Meane and Suse suffered great affliction. Their minister was taken among others. Many fled away, and their houses and goods were ransacked and spoiled. The minister was a good and faithful servant of God, and endued with excellent gifts and graces, who in the end was put to a most cruel and shameful death. The great patience which he shewed in the midst of the fire, greatly astonished the adversaries. Likewise the churches of Larch and Meronne were marvellously tormented and afflicted. For some were taken and sent to the galleys, others consented and yielded to the adversaries, and a great number of them fled away. It is certainly known, that those who yielded to the adversaries were more cruelly handled than the others who continued constant in the truth. Whereby God declares how greatly he detests all such as play the apostate, and shrink from the truth.

But for the better understanding of the beginning of this horrible persecution against the Waldois, here note, that first of all the proclamations were made in every place, that none should resort to the sermons of the Lutherans, but should live after the customs of the church of Rome, upon pain of forfeiture of their goods, and to be condemned to the galleys for ever, or lose their lives. Three of the most cruel persons that could be found, were appointed to execute this commission.

At that time Charles de Comptes, of the valley of Lucerne, and one of the lords of Angrogne, wrote to the commissioners to use some lenity towards them of the valley of Lucerne. By reason whereof they were a while more gently treated than the rest. At that season the monks of Pignerol and their associates tormented grievously the churches near about them. They took the poor christians as they passed by the way, and kept them prisoners within their abbey. And having assembled a company of ruffians, they sent them to spoil those of the churches, and to take prisoners men, women, and children; and some they so tormented, that they were

compelled to swear to return to mass; others they sent to the galleys, and some they cruelly burnt. They who escaped were afterwards so sick, that they seemed to have been poisoned.

The gentlemen of the valley of St. Martin treated their tenants very cruelly, threatening them and commanding them to return to mass; also spoiling them of their goods, imprisoning them, and vexing them by all the means they could. But above all the others, there were two especially, that is to say, Charles Truchet, and Boniface his brother, who the second day of April, before day, with a company of Ruffians, spoiled a village of their own subjects named Renclaret; which as soon as the inhabitants of the village perceived, they fled to the mountains, then covered with snow, naked and without victuals, and there remained until the third night after. In the morning, his retinue took a minister of the valley prisoner, and led him to the abbey, where he was burnt soon after, with one other of the valley of St. Martin.

In the end of June next following, the lord of Raconig and the lord of la Trinite came to Angrogne, there to mitigate, as they said, the sore persecution, and caused the chief rulers and ministers to assemble together, propounding several points of religion concerning doctrine, the calling of ministers, the mass, and obedience towards princes and rulers; and declared to them, that their confession had been sent to Rome by the duke, and that they daily looked for an answer. To all these points the ministers answered. After this they demanded of the chief rulers, if the duke should cause mass to be sung in their parishes, whether they would submit to the same or not? They answered simply, that they would not. Then they demanded of them, if the duke would appoint them preachers, whether they would receive them? They answered, that if they preached the word of God purely, they would hear them. Thirdly, If that they were content that in the meantime their ministers should cease, and if they who should be sent preached not the word of God sincerely, then their ministers to preach again. If they would agree to this, they were promised that the persecution should cease, and the prisoners should be restored again. To this question, after they had conferred with the people, they answered, that they could by no means suffer that their ministers should forbear preaching.

The two lords, not contented with this answer, commanded, in the duke's name, that all the ministers who were strangers should instantly be banished the country, saying, that the duke would not suffer them to dwell within his dominions, for they were his enemies.

This done, immediately proclamations were made, and the persecution began to be more furious than before. Among others, the monks of Pignerol at that time were most cruel, for they sent out a company of hired ruffians, who daily spoiled and ransacked houses, and all that they could lay hands of; took men, women, and children, and led them captives to the abbey, where they were most spitefully afflicted and tormented. At the same time they sent also a band of ruffians by night to the minister's house of St. Germain, in the valley of Perouse, being led there by a traitor that knew the house, and had used to haunt there secretly; who knocking at the door, the minister knowing his voice, came forth immediately, and perceiving himself betrayed, fled; but he was soon taken and sore wounded, and yet they pricked him behind with their halberts to make him hasten his pace. At that time also they slew many, many they hurt, and others they brought to the abbey, where they kept them in prison, and cruelly handled them. The good minister endured sore imprisonment, and after that a most terrible kind of death with a wonderful constancy, for they roasted him by a small fire; and when half his body was burnt, he confessed and called upon the Lord Jesus with a loud voice.

The inquisitor, Jacomel, with his monks, and the collateral Corbis amongst others, shewed one practice of most barbarous cruelty against this poor man, who, when he should be burned, caused two poor women of St. Germain to carry fagots to the fire, and to speak these words to their pastor:—" Take this, thou wicked heretic, in recompence of thy naughty doctrine which thou hast taught us." To whom the good minister answered, " Ah, good woman ! I have taught you well, but you have learned ill." To be brief, they so afflicted and tormented those poor people of St. Germain, and the places thereabout, that after they were spoiled of their goods, and driven from their houses, they were compelled to fly into the mountains to save their lives. So great was the spoil of these poor people, that many who before had been men of great wealth, and with their riches had ministered succour and comfort to others, were now brought to such misery, that they were compelled to crave succour and relief of others.

Now forasmuch as the said monks, with their troops of ruffians (which were counted to be in number about three hundred), made such spoil and havoc in all the country, that no man could live there in safety, it was demanded of the ministers, whether it was lawful to defend themselves against the insolence and furious rage of the said ruffians ? The ministers answered, that it was lawful, warning them in any case to take heed of bloodshed. This question being once solved, they of the valley of Lucerne and of Angrogne, sent certain men to them of St. Germain to aid them against the supporters of these monks.

In the month of July they of Angrogne, being one morning at harvest upon the hill-side of St. Germain, perceived a company of soldiers spoiling them of St. Germain, and doubting lest they should go to Angrogne, made an outcry. Then the people of Angrogne assembled together upon the mountain, and some ran to St. Germain over the hill, and some by the valley. They who went by the valley met with the spoilers coming from St. Germain, loaded with spoil which they had gotten, and being but fifty, set upon them, amounting to the number of one hundred and twenty men, well-appointed, and gave them soon the overthrow. The passage over the bridge being stopped, the enemy was forced to take the river Chison, where many were sore hurt, others drowned, and some escaped with great difficulty ; and such a slaughter was made of them, that the river was dyed with the blood of those who were wounded and slain, but none of the Angronians were even hurt. If the river had been as great as it was wont commonly to be, there had not one man escaped alive. The noise of the harquebusses was great, and within less than one hour's space there were three or four hundred of the Waldois gathered together upon the river ; and at the same time they had purposed to fetch away their prisoners who were in the abbey, but they would not do it without the counsel of their ministers, and so deferred the matter until the next day. But their ministers counselled them not to venture any such thing, but to refrain themselves, and so they did. Yet they doubted not, but if they had gone immediately after that discomfiture to the abbey, they might have found all open, and easily have entered ; for the monks were so afraid, that they fled to save their relics and images.

The next day the commander of St. Anthony de Fossan came to Angrogne, accompanied with several gentlemen, saying, that he was sent by the duke ; and having assembled the chief rulers and ministers of Angrogne, and of the valley of Lucerne, after he had declared to them the cause of his coming, he read their supplication directed to the duke, which contained their confession, demanding of them, if it were the same which they had sent to the duke ? They answered, yea. Then he began to dispute, being sent, as he said, to inform them of their errors, not doubting but they would amend according to their promise. Then he entered into a disputation of the mass, in a great heat, deriving the same from the Hebrew word Massa, which signified (as he supposed) consecration, and shewed that this word Massa might be found in ancient writers. The ministers answered, that he ill applied the Hebrew word ; and further, that they disputed not of the word Massa, but of that which is signified by the same, which he ought first to prove by the word of God. Briefly, that he could not prove either by the word of God, or

the ancient fathers, their private mass, their sacrifice expiatory or propitiatory, their transubstantiation, their adoration, their application of the same for the quick and the dead, and such other matters which are principal parts of the said mass. The commander having here nothing to reply, fell into a marvellous choler, railing and raging as if he had been mad, and told them that he was not come to dispute, but to banish their ministers, and to place others in their stead, by the duke's commandment, which he could not, unless their ministers were first driven out of the country.

From thence he went to the abbey of Pignerol, where he and Jacomel caused a number of the poor inhabitants of Campillon, and of Fenil, to be taken prisoners, spoiling them of their goods, driving away their cattle, and forcing them to swear and forswear, and in the end ransomed them for great sums of money. About that time a gentleman of Campillon agreed with those who were fled, for thirty crowns to be paid into his hand, that he would warrant them from any further vexation or trouble, so that they remained quiet at home ; but when he had received the money, he caused the commander of Fossan with his men by night to come to his house, and then sent for the poor men, thinking traitorously to have delivered them into the hands of their mortal enemy, following therein the decree of the council of Constance, which is that no promise is to be kept with heretics. But God, knowing how to succour his people in their necessity, prevented this danger ; for one of them had intelligence of the commander's coming, and so they all fled.

After this, there were many commandments and injunctions given out through all the country, to banish these poor Waldois, with the doctrine of the gospel, if it were possible, out of the mountains and valleys of Piedmont ; but the poor people still desired, that according to that which they had so often before protested by word and writing, they might be suffered to serve God purely, according to the rule prescribed in his word, simply obeying their Lord and Prince always, and in all things.

In the end of October following, the rumour went that an army was levying to destroy them ; and in very deed there were certain bands levied, ready to march at an hour's warning. Those malefactors, who heretofore had fled or were banished for any offence or crime committed, were called home again, and pardoned of all together, if they would take them to their weapons, and go to destroy the Waldois. The ministers and chief rulers of the valleys of Lucerne and Angrogne, thereupon assembled together oftentimes to take advice what in such an extremity was best to be done. In the end they determined, that for certain days following there should be kept a general fast, and the Sunday after a communion ; also, that they should not defend themselves by force of arms, but that every one should withdraw himself to the high mountains, and every one to carry away such goods as they were able to bear ; and if their enemies pursued them thither, then to take such advice and counsel as it pleased God to give them. This article of not defending themselves seemed very strange to the people, being driven to such an extremity, and the cause being so just ; but yet every one began to carry their goods and victuals into the mountains, and for the space of eight days all the ways were filled with comers and goers to the mountains, like ants in summer, which provide for winter. All this they did in this great perplexity and danger, with a wonderful courage and cheerfulness, praising of God, and singing of psalms, and every one comforting another.

A few days after certain other ministers, hearing what they of Angrogne and Lucerne had concluded, wrote to them, that this resolution seemed very strange to some, that they ought not to defend themselves against the violence of their enemies, alleging many reasons, that in such extremity and necessity it was lawful for them so to do, especially the quarrel being just, that is, for the defence of true religion, and for the preservation of their own lives, and the lives of their wives and children, knowing that it was the pope and his ministers which were the cause of all these troubles and cruel wars, and not the duke, who was stirred up thereunto only by their instigations. Wherefore they might well and with good conscience withstand such furious and outrageous violence.

On the twenty-second of October the lord of Angrogne went from Lucerne to Mondevis, where he was then governor for the duke, and sent for the chief rulers of Angrogne at several times, declaring the great perils and dangers wherewith they were environed, the army being already at hand; yet promising them, if they would submit themselves, he would send immediately to stay the army. They of Angrogne answered, that they all determined to stand to that which they, two days before in their assembly, had put in writing. With this answer he seemed at that present to be content. The next day the rumour was, that they of Angrogne had submitted themselves to the duke. On the morrow, which was Sunday, there was nothing but weeping and mourning in Angrogne. The sermon being ended, the rulers were called before the ministers and the people, who affirmed that they wholly cleaved unto their former writing; and they sent secretly to the notary for the copy of that which was passed in the council-house at their last assembly before the Lord de Comptes, in which was comprised, that Angrogne had wholly submitted herself to the good pleasure of the duke. The people hearing that, were sore astonished, and protested rather to die than obey the same. And hereupon it was agreed, that at that very instant certain should be sent to the lord of Angrogne to signify to him, that the determination of the council was falsified, and that it might please him the next morning to come to Angrogne to hear the voice of the people, not only of the men, but also of the women and children. But he himself went not thither, having intelligence of the uproar, but sent thither the judge of that place. Then that which had been falsified was duly corrected; the judge laying all the blame upon the notary.

During this time the adversaries cried out through all the country of Piedmont: "To the fire with them, to the fire with them!" The Thursday after, Angrogne, by proclamations set up in every place, was exposed to the fire and sword. On Friday after, being the second of November, the army approached to the borders of the valley of Lucerne, and certain horsemen came to a place called St. John, a little beneath Angrogne. Then the people retired into the mountains. Certain of St. John perceiving that the horsemen not only spoiled their goods, but also took their fellows prisoners, set upon them. It is not certain what number of their enemies were there slain; but suddenly they retired to Bubiane, where their camp then was, and not one of them of St. John was slain or hurt. It happened at the same time, that two of the horsemen, being sore amazed, galloped before the rest towards the army, being ready to march towards Angrogne, crying, "They come, they come!" At whose cry the whole army was so astonished, that every man fled his way, and they were all so scattered, that the captains that day were not able to bring them in order again, and yet no creature followed them.

On the Saturday in the morning the army mustered near Angrogne. They of Angrogne had sent certain of their men to keep the passes, and stop the army that they should not enter, if it were possible. In the meantime the people retired into the meadow of Toure, and little thought of the coming of the army so soon, or that they would have made such a sudden assault; for they were yet carrying victuals and other stuff, so that few of them kept the passes. Now they who kept the straits, perceiving that their enemies prepared themselves to fight, fell down upon their knees, and made their prayers to God, that it would please him to take pity upon them, and not to look upon their sins, but to the cause which they maintained, and to turn the hearts of their enemies, and so to work, that there might be no effusion of blood; and if it were his will to take them, with their wives and infants out of this world, that he would then mercifully receive them into his kingdom. In this sort most fervent prayers were made by all those that kept the passes, with exhortation that they should all together cry unto God, and crave his succour and assistance in this great distress.

Their prayers thus ended, suddenly they perceived their enemies coming towards them through the vines to win the top of the mountain of Angrogne. In the mean time the prior of St. John and Jacomel were within the temple of Angrogne, and communed with the rulers touching an agreement. These were sent thither by the lord of la Trinite to keep the people occupied. To be short, the combat began in several places, and endured for a long space in the passes of Angrogne. The poor Waldois being but few in number, and some of them having but slings and cross-bows, were sore pressed by the multitude of their enemies. At length they retired to the top of the mountain, where they defended themselves until night.

When they had found a place where they might withstand their enemies who were still pursuing them, they turned themselves, and slew some of them, and wounded many. When the evening came, their enemies rested, and were about to encamp themselves, there to sup and lodge all night. Which thing when the Angrognians perceived, they went to prayer, desiring God to assist and succour them, but their enemies mocked them and laughed them to scorn. Then the poor people devised to send a drum into a little valley hard by; and as they were making their prayers unto God, and the drum sounded in the valley, the lord of la Trinite caused his soldiers, which were about to encamp themselves, to remove thence; which was a great advantage to the poor people, who now were sore wearied with travel, all wet with sweating, and very thirsty, and in great peril if God had not given them some little breathing time. Many of their enemies that day were slain, and many wounded, of which very few escaped; so they reported that the shot was poisoned, which this poor simple people never used to do in all these wars. Of the Angrognians that day there were but three slain, and one wounded, who afterwards was healed again. This combat gave great courage to the Waldois, and astonished their adversaries. At the same time when the army retired, they burnt many houses, and made great spoil as they went, destroying also the wines which were in the presses.

The lord of la Trinite with his army encamped in a village beyond Toure, at the foot of the hill, between Angrogne and the other towns of the valley of Lucerne, which professed the gospel. They of the said village were always sore against the Waldois, and haters of true religion, and were glad of this outrage and violence done against the possessors thereof: but they had their just plague, for they were all destroyed. After this the said lord of la Trinite caused the fortress to be built again, which the Frenchmen had raised, and placed there a garrison, and afterwards sent another to the fort of Villars, which is of the valley of Lucerne; and another he sent to the fortress of Perouse, and a fourth garrison he placed in the castle of St. Martin. They of Angrogne (seeing themselves to be now, as it were, in a sea of troubles) after they had recommended themselves unto God by prayer, and committed their cause unto him, sent to them of Perouse, St. Martin, and of Pragela, for aid and succour; who sent them all the help they were able.

The next day there came letters to Angrogne from the lord of la Trinite: the effect whereof was this; that he was sorry for what was done the day before, and that he came not thither to make war against them, but only to view if it were a place convenient to build a fort therein to serve the duke. Furthermore, that his soldiers seeing the people assembled, as it were to defy them, upon that occasion only were stirred up to give assault, and to set upon them. Also that he was sorry that such spoil was made of their goods, and such hurt done by fire. But if they would shew themselves obedient to the duke, he had good hope that all would be well, and trusted some good agreement would be made. The Angrognians answered, that they were marvellously grieved to be so assaulted, spoiled and tormented by the subjects of their liege and natural prince: and as they had oftentimes before offered themselves to be more obedient and faithful to their sovereign prince the duke, than any of all his subjects besides; so yet they still offered the same obedience. Also they most humbly besought him, not to think it strange if they, being constrained by such extreme necessity, defended themselves. Finally, as to their religion, they affirmed, that it was the pure word of God, even as it was preached by the prophets and apostles, and the same which their predecessors had observed for some hundred years past. Moreover, that the cause was not concerning the goods of this world, but the honour and glory of God, the salvation or destruction of the souls both of them and theirs. And therefore it were much better for them to die altogether, than to forsake their religion. And yet if it might be proved out of the word of God, that they were in error; not by force of arms, by blood and fire, they would then yield themselves with all obedience; most humbly beseeching him, and all others the lords of the country of Piedmont, to be their intercessors and advocates to the duke in this behalf.

Upon Monday, being the fourth day of November, the lord of la Trinite sent his army to Villars and Tailleret. The lesser company ascended towards Villars. The people seeing their enemies approaching, after they had called upon God with fervent prayer, strongly defended themselves, and slew many: many also were hurt, and the rest fled. The other company ascended towards Tailleret; and although they of that place were but few in number, and that part of the army the greater, yet making their prayers unto God, and commending their cause unto him, they defended themselves likewise valiantly.

In the meantime, they of Villars being emboldened by their late victory, came to assist their neighbours, and being assembled together, they courageously pursued their enemies, and put them to flight. In this pursuit it chanced that this poor people, by an ambush of their enemies who came another way, were suddenly enclosed on every side, and like to be destroyed; but yet they all escaped, and not one of them was slain, only three were hurt, who were soon cured again. On the enemy's side there were so many slain, that they were laid together by whole cart-loads. This was the reward of those who were desirous to shed innocent blood.

After the lord of la Trinite had received the letters of the Angrognians, he sent to them his secretary, accompanied with a gentleman of the valley; whose charge was to cause the chief rulers to send certain to commune with him, saying, that he had good tidings to declare to them; and, moreover, that he would deliver them a safe conduct to come and go. Whereupon they sent four to him, whom he intreated very courteously, and rehearsed to them, how the duke at his departure from the court, told him, that although the pope, the princes and cities of Italy, yea, his own council were fully resolved, that of necessity they of the said religion should be destroyed, yet notwithstanding, God otherwise put into his mind, and that he had taken counsel of God what he should do in this matter; that is, that he would use them gently. Furthermore, he declared to them, that the duchess bore them good affection, and favoured them very much, and that she had commended their cause to the duke, persuading him to have regard to that poor people, and that their religion was ancient and old, with many such other things. "Moreover, they had," said he, "great friends in the duke's court, not doubting but if they should send certain to the court with a supplication, they should obtain more than they themselves would require; and he for his part would employ himself in their affairs to the uttermost of his power: and so he promised that he would retire himself with his army. This he seemed to speak unfeignedly. The people desiring but to live peaceably in their religion, and under obedience to their lawful prince, were content to follow his counsel.

About this season they of Angrogne perceived that a part of the army ascended the hill of Tailleret, (which is the half way between Angrogne and those of the valley of Lucerne) and the other part had already gotten away, which led to the meadow of Toure, by which they of Angrogne might easily have been enclosed. Therefore they sent certain immediately to keep the way, who soon after encountered with their enemies and obtained the victory, pursuing and chasing them to their camp, not without great loss of their men. The number of their enemies slain, was not known; for their custom was immediately to carry away those who were slain. Not one of Angrogne perished that day, nor yet was hurt. It was feared that this combat would have hindered the agreement; but the lord of la Trinite could well dissemble the matter, and excused the day's journey, putting the fault upon them of Tailleret, whom he charged to have slain certain of his men in the highway, and amongst others his barber.

On Saturday following, being the ninth of November, the lord of la Trinite sent again for them of Angrogne, to consult with them touching the agreement, using the like communication as before; and added thereunto, that in token of true obedience they should carry their armour into two of the houses of the chief rulers, not fearing but that it should be safe; for it should remain in their own keeping, and if need were, they should receive it again. Also, that he upon Sunday (which was the next day) would cause a mass to be sung within the temple of St. Lawrence in Angrogne, accompanied with a very few, and thereby the duke's wrath would be assuaged.

The next morning he went into the temple (whereat they were sore aggrieved, however they could not withstand him) his army marching before him: and having caused a mass to be sung, he desired to see the meadow of Toure, so much spoken of, that thereof he might make a true report to the duke; and thither the rulers with a great troop of his own men went, the residue of his company remaining behind. The lord being entered into the meadow of Toure, the people began to make a commotion; whereof he having intelligence, returned immediately. All that day he shewed himself very courteous to all whom he met.

The people in the meantime perceived themselves to be in great danger, and were moved at the sight of the army, the spoil of the soldiers, the taking away of their armour, but especially because the lord of la Trinite had viewed the meadow of Toure, foreseeing his traitorous meaning and purpose. A few days after the lord of la Trinite sent his secretary Gastaut to Angrogne to talk with them concerning the agreement, which was read in the assembly by the secretary as follows.

To the most excellent and worthy Prince, the duke of Savoy, &c. our sovereign lord and natural Prince.

"Most noble and renowned prince, we have sent certain of our men unto your highness, to give testimony of our humble, hearty, and unfeigned obedience unto the same, and with all submission desire pardon touching the bearing of armour by certain of our people in their extreme necessity, and for all other our trespasses, for the which your sovereign grace might conceive any offence against us.

Secondly, to desire in most humble wise your said highness, in the name of our Lord Jesus Christ, that it would please the same, to suffer us to live with freedom of conscience in our religion, which also is the religion of our ancestors, observed for certain hundred years past. And we are persuaded, that it is the pure gospel of our Lord Jesus, the only truth, the word of life and salvation, which we profess. Also, that it may please your most gracious clemency not to take in ill part, if we, fearing to offend and displease God, cannot consent to certain traditions and ordinances of the church of Rome, and herein to have pity upon our poor souls, and the souls of our children, to the end that your highness be not in any wise charged in the just judgment of God for the same, where all men must appear to answer for their doings.

"On our part, we protest that we will seek nothing but to be the true servants of God, to serve him according to his holy word; and also to be true and loyal subjects to your highness, and more obedient than any others, being always ready to give our goods, our bodies, our lives, and the lives of our children, for your noble grace, as also our religion teaches us to do : only we desire that our souls may be left at liberty to serve God, according to his holy word.

"And we your poor humble subjects shall most heartily pray our God and Father for the good and long prosperity of your highness, for the most virtuous lady your wife, and for the noble house of Savoy."

To this supplication they of St. John, of Roccapiata, of St. Bartholomew, and of Perouse, with those of the valley of Lucerne, agreed. For it was concluded, that the agreement made should extend to all the confederates of the same religion. While they were treating of this agreement, the lord of la Trinite vexed cruelly them of Tailleret under this pretence, because they had not presented themselves to treat of this agreement: he tormented them after this sort; first he commanded that all their armour should be brought before him, and then they on their knees, should ask him pardon, because they came not to treat of the agreement with the rest ; which notwithstanding the most part of them did.

The next morning the chief of the householders went to the village named Bouvet, the appointed place, and when they had heard a sermon, and called upon God, they began to write their names. The enrolling of their names not being fully ended, word was brought that the soldiers had got the top of the mountain, and had taken all the passes; whereat they of Tailleret were sore amazed, and ran with all speed to defend their wives and children. Some they saved; the most part, with their goods, were in their enemies hands already. At this time with sacking, spoiling and burning, they did much mischief.

After this the lord of la Trinite sent word to them who were fled, that if they would return, he would receive them to mercy. The poor people for the most part, trusting on his promise, returned, and yet the next morning the soldiers came to apprehend them and their ministers, and beset the place on every side. Such as were swift of foot, and could shift best, escaped. The rest were all hurt or taken, and yet they all escaped by a marvellous means : for it happened that there was an old man who could not run fast, to whom one of the soldiers came with a naked sword in his hand to have slain him. The old man seeing the imminent danger, caught the soldier by the legs, overthrew him, and drew him by the heels down the hill.

The soldier cried out, "Help, help! this villain will kill me." His fellows hearing him cry, made haste to rescue him ; but in the mean time the old man escaped. The rest seeing what the old man had done, took courage, and though their armour and weapons were taken from them, yet with stones and slings they so beat and discomfited their enemies, that for that time they carried no prisoners away.

The day following the soldiers returning to the said Tailleret, robbed, spoiled, and carried away all that they could find, and so continued three days together ; which was very easy for them to do, because the poor men, fearing lest they should be charged with violating the agreement, made no resistance, but retired towards Villars.

The fourth day the lord of la Trinite, to torment the poor Taillerets yet more cruelly, sent his army again before day to the mountain, and into the same place, and because the people of the said village were retired towards Villars, and scattered in the high mountains, the soldiers not yet satisfied with spoiling and sacking the rest that they found in the said Tailleret, ranging about the confines thereof, sacked and made havoc on every side of whatsoever they could lay hands on, taking prisoners, both men and women.

The same day two women, the mother and the daughter, were found in a cave in the mountain, wounded to death by the soldiers, and died immediately after. So likewise a blind man, a hundred years of age, who had fled into a cave with his son's daughter, being eighteen years old, who fed him, was slain by the enemies, and as they pursued the maiden, she escaped from them, and fell from the top of the mountain, and died.

Shortly after, this lord sent his army to the temple of St. Lawrence in Angrogne, pretending to sing a mass there, and suddenly the soldiers besieged the minister's house. The minister being warned, assayed to escape. The soldiers attempted nothing by force. but used gentle persuasions to the contrary, for there were not yet many of them. But the minister pushed on further, and the soldiers followed him half a mile, but fearing the people, durst go no further. The minister withdrew himself into the rocks upon the mountain, accompanied with five others. The army was by and by at his heels, and sought a good while in the houses and cottages on every side, cruelly handling the people whom they took, to make them confess where their minister was, spoiling their houses, taking some prisoners, and beating others : but yet they could not learn of them where their minister was. At length they espied him among the rocks, where they thought to have enclosed him, and so they pursued him in the rocks, all covered with snow, until it was night, and could not take him. Then they returned and spoiled his house, and diligently searched out all his books and writings, and carried them to the lord of la Trinite in a sack, who caused them all to be burnt in his presence. That day they spoiled forty houses in Angrogne, broke their mills, and carried away all the corn and meal that they found.

About midnight the soldiers returned with torch-light to the minister's house to seek him, and searched every corner. The next morning commandment was given to the rulers of Angrogne, that within twenty-four hours they should deliver their minister, or else Angrogne should be put to fire and sword. The rulers answered, that they could not so do, for they knew not where he was, and that the soldiers had chased him over the mountains. After certain days, when the soldiers had burned houses, spoiled the people, broke. their mills, and did what mischief they could, the army retired.

The poor Waldois were in great captivity and distress, but especially because they had not the preaching of God's word among them as they were wont to have ; and therefore taking to them good courage, they determined to begin preaching again. The messengers which were sent to the duke were detained six weeks, and all that while were cruelly handled by the popish doctors, and were constrained by force and violence to promise to return to the mass. Now, when the messengers were returned, and the people understood that there was a new command that they should return to the mass : also that popish preachers were appointed, there was wonderful lamentation, weeping, and mourning, for this great calamity.

Hereupon, they of the valley of Lucerne and of Bouvet, being assembled together, by one assent sent two ministers, with others of the people, to the churches of Pragela, to signify to them the piteous estate of the poor churches of the valleys of Piedmont, to have their counsel and advice how to prevent the great dangers at hand if it were possible. For this cause they all went to prayer, and after they had long called upon God, desiring his grace, and the spirit of discretion and counsel, well to consider of those weighty and urgent affairs wherewith they were oppressed ; in the end it was concluded, that all the people dwelling in the valleys and mountains of Piedmont, and those of Dauphiny should join in a league together. They all promised by God's grace and assistance, to maintain the pure preaching of the gospel, and administration of the holy sacraments; the one to aid and assist the other, and to render all obedience to their superiors, so far as they were commanded by the word of God. Moreover, that it should be lawful for none of the valleys to promise or conclude any thing touching religion, without the consent of the rest of the valleys. And for confirmation of the league, certain of. the ministers and elders of the churches of Dauphiny were sent to the valley of Lucerne, to ascertain if they would give their consent.

These messengers, being arrived in the evening at the village of Bouvet, and the people being assembled, word was brought that the next day every householder should appear in the council-house, to know whether they would return to the mass or no; and that they who would receive the mass, should quietly enjoy their houses; and they who would not, should be delivered to the justices, and condemned to be burned, or sent to the galleys. The people were brought to this extremity, either to die or flee, or else to renounce God. To flee seemed to them best, if the great snow had not prevented them; therefore seeing themselves in such distress, they gladly consented to the league. After this, they exhorted one another, saying, "As we shall all be called upon to-morrow to renounce and forsake our God, and revolt again to idolatry, let us now make solemn protestation, that we will utterly forsake the false religion of the pope, and that we will live and die in the maintenance and confession of God's holy word. Let us all go to-morrow to the temple, to hear the word of God, and then let us cast down to the ground all the idols and altars." To this every man agreed, saying, "Let us do so. yea, and that too at the very same hour in which they have appointed us to be at the council-house."

The next day they assembled themselves in the church of Bouvet, and as soon as they came into the temple, without any further delay, they beat down the images and cast down the altars. After the sermon they went to Villars to do the like there. By the way they encountered a band of soldiers, who were going to spoil a village named Le Valle Guichard, and to take the poor inhabitants prisoners. The soldiers, seeing them so ill appointed, mocked them, and discharged their pistols at them, thinking to have put them to flight. But they valiantly defended themselves, and with stones chased them to the fortress. When they came to Villars, they beat down their images and altars, and afterwards besieged the fortress, and demanded the prisoners who were detained there.

The same day the judge of Lucerne, called Podesta, went to the council-house, to enroll the names of those who would return to the mass; but seeing what was done, he was afraid, and desired the people to suffer him to return quietly, which they willingly granted. Several gentlemen also of the valley came thither with the judge, to make their poor tenants forsake God; but seeing the tumult, they were glad to flee to the castle, where they and the garrison were besieged ten days together, not without great danger of their lives. The second day of the siege, the captain of Toure went with a company of soldiers to raise the siege; but they were either slain or discomfited. As much was done the third day. The fourth day he returned with three bands, and with the garrison of Toure, which caused a furious combat; many of their enemies were slain, and a great number wounded, and yet of those who besieged the fort there was not one man hurt.

In the time of this siege they attempted by various means to take the fortress, but without ordnance it was impossible to do so. The lord of la Trinite, returning with his army, came to the valley of Lucerne, and the next day might easily have raised the siege. Wherefore when the garrison, not knowing that the lord of la Trinite was so near, desired that they might depart with bag and baggage, which request was granted. In this siege half of the soldiers were slain, and many were wounded, as well with harquebusses as with stones, and the soldiers for lack of water were constrained to make their bread with wine, which tormented their stomachs, and caused great diseases. Here is not to be forgotten, that the soldiers who a while before so cruelly persecuted the poor ministers, seeking by all possible means to destroy them, now beseeched them to save their lives. The same night the fortress was razed.

The second day of February the lord of la Trinite encamped at Lucerne, and placed a garrison in the priory of St. John, a village of the Waldois between Lucerne and Angrogne. The next day in the morning the said lord of la Trinite sent word to them of Angrogne, that if they would not take part with the rest, they should be gently handled. All the week before they were solicited by him to consent to the same, but they would give no answer. The same day they of Angrogne, and the rest of the valleys, fully agreed and determined to defend their religion by force, and that the one should aid the other, and no agreement be made by any one without the consent of the rest. About noon the lord of la Trinite marched with his army by St. John, to enter into the borders of Angrogne by a place called La Sonnilette, where they had fought before. The people had made certain bulwarks of earth and stone, not more than three feet high, where they defended themselves valiantly against their enemies. When the enemy were so weary that they could fight no longer, they put fresh soldiers into their places, so that the combat endured till night, and all that day the army could not enter the borders of Angrogne. Many of the enemy were slain, and a great many hurt; and but two men of Angrogne were slain, of whom one was slain by his own folly, because he was too greedy upon the spoil. The army, being beaten and tired, rested awhile.

The following Friday, which was the seventh of February, at the break of day, the army marched towards Angrogne by five several places. The people of Angrogne were not yet assembled, and there were none to resist, but only a few who kept watch, who seeing their enemies coming upon them in so many places, and perceiving that they went about to enclose them, after they had valiantly fought for a space, recoiled by little and little to a high place where the combat was renewed with greater fierceness than before. But the lord of la Trinite seeing the loss of his men, and above all, that one of great credit and authority in the duke's court was wounded to death, blew a retreat, and descended to Angrogne, and there destroyed and burnt all the wines, victuals, and the rest of the goods that he could find; so that in a short space he had burnt about a thousand houses of Angrogne.

Toure is a little valley upon the borders of Angrogne, environed about with mountains two miles in length, but very narrow. On both sides, and in the midst thereof, there are about two hundred small houses and cottages; also meadows, pastures for cattle, ground for tillage, trees, and goodly fountains. On the south side and on the north the mountains are so high, that no man can that way approach the valley. On the other sides, a man may enter by seven or eight ways. This place is not more than two miles from Angrogne; the way is very narrow and hard to pass, because of the hills on both sides. There is also a river close by, but very small, and the banks are very high in many places. The people had carried there very few victuals, partly because the way was so difficult, and also through the sudden return of the army.

In the meantime the lord of la Trinite, after he had now twice assaulted Angrogne, sent to burn Rosa, and to discover the ways which led to the valley of Lucerne; but the soldiers were driven back four days together by those who kept the passes. Upon which he sent his whole army, whom they valiantly withstood from morning till night. Then they of Lucerne sent new aid. During this combat, an ambuscade of soldiers descended from the top of the mountain, by a place so hard to pass by, that no man would have suspected it. The poor people, seeing themselves so environed by their enemies, saved themselves, some running through the midst of their enemies, and others among the rocks.

The enemy being entered into Rosa, consumed all with fire and sword. The rest of the people fled by the secret way leading to the valley of Lucerne, and wandered all that night upon the mountains full of snow, laden with their stuff, carrying their little infants in their arms, and leading the others by the hands. When they of the valley saw them, they ran to them, praising God for their deliverance, for they thought they had all been slain. Although these poor people were here in such great extremity, yet they were joyful, and comforted themselves, without any lamentation or mourning, except the poor little infants who cried out for cold.

A few days after the lord of la Trinite entered into the valley of Lucerne by three ways, that is to say, by Rosa, by the plains, and by the sides of Tailleret. They who kept the passes, at first resisted their enemies valiantly, but perceiving that they were assailed on every side, they retired to Villars, and there defended themselves awhile.

But because they saw that their enemies had already passed the plain, and got above Villars towards Bouvet, they gave over, and left Villars, and fled to the mountains. The soldiers being entered, burned the houses, and slew all that they could find. The poor people who were fled into the mountains, seeing the village on fire, praised God, and gave him thanks, that he had made them worthy to suffer for his name, and for his cause; and also they were glad to see the village on fire, lest their enemies should encamp themselves there. Then the soldiers in great rage mounted the hills on every side, pursuing the poor people in great fury; but a few of them, after they had ardently called upon God, took courage, and beat back their enemies to Villars. This done, the army retired.

A few days after, the meadow of Toure was assaulted by three several ways on the east side. The combat endured a long time, many of the enemy were wounded, and many slain. But none of this poor people were slain on that day, only two were wounded, who were soon healed again. But to declare the conflicts, assaults, skirmishes, and alarms, which were at Angrogne and other places thereabouts, were too long; for brevity's sake it shall be sufficient to touch upon the most principal, and those which are most worthy of memory.

On Saturday, which was the 14th day of February, the people who were in the uppermost part of the meadow of Toure, perceived that a company of soldiers were ascended up the hill to Angrogne, and burning the rest of the houses there: they suspected that it was the policy of their enemies to draw them there, and in the meantime to set on them from behind, and so to win the meadow of Toure from them. Therefore they sent only six harquebusses against those soldiers; who having the higher ground, and not espied of their enemies, discharged all their guns together. Immediately the soldiers fled, although no man pursued them; whether they fled from policy, or for fear, it was not known.

Shortly after they of the meadow of Toure, who were on the watch on the top of the mountain, because every morning there was a sermon made, to which the people resorted, and they could see afar off round about them, espied a troop of soldiers marching on that side of the hill which is between the east and the north, and soon after that discovered another company, who marched on the north side towards the troop. The first were ascended an hour before the other, and fought on the top of the mountain called Melese, but they were soon discomfited; and because they could not run fast by means of the deep snow, and difficulty of the ways, in flying they fell down often upon the ground. Whilst they who pursued them were earnest in the chase, and had taken from them their drum, behold, there came to them some crying out, that the other troop was entered into the meadow of Toure, so they gave over the chase, or else not one of their enemies had escaped.

The other troop which came by the north side, took a high hill on the top of the mountain, which seemed to be almost inaccessible from the snow and ice which was there. When they were come to the top of the hill, they caused seven soldiers to go down the hill and to view the way, and to see whether the troop might descend that way or not. These seven went down almost to the houses. They sent also others to occupy the rest of the high places which were near to the foot of the hill and the rocks. In the meantime the ministers and the people, who were in the midst of the valley of the meadow, saw all this, and were much discouraged; so they went to prayer, and called upon God ardently, not without great sighs, lamentation and tears even until night.

The seven spies who came down to discover the way cried to their captain Truchet "Come down, come down, this day Angrogne shall be taken." The other cried to them again, "Ascend, ascend, and return, or else you shall be slain every one of you." Immediately issued out five against these spies, and took some and chased the rest. The first of the five who set upon them, cast two of them down upon the ground. Soon after, eight men of Angrogne issued out against the whole troop, and it was wonderful to see them go with such courage and boldness to assail such a multitude, and it seemed that they should have been all destroyed and hewn in pieces. The first of the eight went a good way before the others to discover the enemies, and carried a great staff somewhat bigger than an halbert; the other followed by two and two together, with harquebusses. These eight went from rock to rock, from hill to hill about the mountain, and chased their enemies valiantly. Then came twelve others, who, joining with the rest, fought with wonderful courage, and made great slaughter of their enemies. Soon after there came from the valley of Lucerne an hundred harquebusses, with one of their ministers, according to their manner, who were wont to send out a minister with them as well for prayer and exhortation as to keep the people in order, that they exceed not measure, as it came to pass that day.

At length they saw them also coming, who returned from the discomfiture of the former troop, making a great noise, and having a drum sounding before them, which they had taken from their enemies; they joined with them of the valley of Lucerne, and having made their earnest prayer to God, immediately came to succour the others that now were encountering valiantly the enemy. Then the enemy seeing such a company marching against them, with such courage and boldness, their hearts were so taken from them, that they suddenly fled. But as they could not well save themselves by running away, they turned back twice and fought, and some in the meantime fled.

He that carried the staff, and discovered the enemy, was but a very young and simple man, and was esteemed to be one that could do nothing but handle a hatchet, and keep cattle; and yet he, with those that followed, so discomfited the enemy, that it was wonderful to behold. He brake his great staff with laying upon them, and after that broke four of their own swords in pursuing them. There was a boy of eighteen years of age, and of small stature, who slew the lord of Monteil, master of the camp to the king; at which the enemy was astonished and discouraged. Another simple man, who one would have thought durst not once have looked Truchet in the face, for he was a very large man, strong and valiant, and one of the chief captains of the whole army, threw down Truchet with the stroke of a stone. Then a young man leaped upon him, and slew him with his own sword, and cleft his head in pieces.

This Truchet was one of the principal authors of the war, and one of the chief enemies of true religion, and of the poor Waldois, that could then be found. It was said also, that he vaunted and promised before hand to the lord of la Trinite, that he would deliver into his hands the meadow of Toure. But God soon brought his proud boasting to nought. And for his spoiling of the poor people, he lay spoiled and naked in the wild mountain of Angrogne. Two of the chief among them offered to pay a great sum of crowns for their ransom, but they could not be heard. They were pursued more than a mile, and were so discomfited, that they fled without any resistance, and if the night had not hindered them, they had pursued them further.

The minister, when he saw the great effusion of blood, and the enemy retreating, cried to the people, saying, that it was enough, and exhorted them to give thanks to God. They who heard him obeyed, and went to prayer; but they who were further off, and heard him not, chased the enemy till dark; insomuch, that if the rest had done the like, very few of their enemies had escaped. That day they had spoiled their enemies of a great part of their armour and ammunition. So God restored in this combat, and in others, to the poor Waldois the armour which the lord of la Trinite had taken from them before. Thanks were given to God in every place; and every man cried, "Who is he who sees not that God fighteth for us?" This victory gave great courage to the poor Waldois, and greatly astonished their enemies.

On the eighteenth of February, the lord of la Trinite, not satisfied with burning and destroying the greatest part of Villars, returned to burn all the little villages round about which appertain to the same, and especially to pursue the poor people who had fled to the mountains, and dividing his army into three parts, he entered by three several ways. The two first companies joined together between Villars and Bouvet, and having a great company of horsemen. From thence they went to seek the people who were in the mountain of Combe, by such a way as they did not expect, and where there were no warders to defend the place. Notwithstanding, the warders who were next, seeing their enemies ascending that way, speedily ran before them, and calling upon God for his aid and succour, they set themselves against their enemies; and although they were but thirty in number, yet they valiantly beat them back twice, coming out of their bulwarks, that is to say, certain houses which at that time served them for that purpose. Many of the enemies were slain at those two combats. The lord of la Trinite, seeing his men so fiercely driven back, sent out the greatest part of his army, who were esteemed to be fifteen hundred men. There came also about an hundred to succour the warders. The combat was very cruel and fierce. At length the poor people were assaulted so vehemently, that they were fain to forsake their bulwarks, losing two of their men. Then the enemy thought all to be theirs, and blew their trumpets, triumphing that they had put the people to flight. But the people retiring not farther than a stone's cast, took courage, and crying altogether to the Lord for succour, they turned themselves to the face of their enemies, and with great force and power they hurled stones at them with their slings.

After this their enemies rested themselves a while, and by and by they gave a furious assault, but yet they were again mightily resisted. Yet once again their enemies rested, and in the meantime the people went to prayer, calling upon God altogether, with their faces lifted up towards heaven, which terrified their enemies more than any thing else. After this they gave yet another great assault, but God by the hands of a few drove them back. Yea, God here shewed his great power, even in the little children also, who fervently called upon God, threw stones at their enemies, and gave courage to the men. So did also the women, and the vulgar sort, that is to say, those who were meet for no feats of war, remaining upon the mountain; and beholding these furious combats, kneeled upon the ground, and having their faces lifted up towards heaven, with tears and groanings they cried "Lord help us!" Who heard their prayers.

After these three assaults were given, there came one to them crying, "Be of good courage, God hath sent those of Angrogne to succour us." He meant, that they of Angrogne were fighting for them in another place, that is to say, towards Tailleret, where the third part of the army was. The people perceiving that they of Angrogne were come to that place to succour them, began to cry, "Blessed be God, who hath sent us succour: they of Angrogne are to succour us." Their enemies hearing this were astonished, and suddenly blew a retreat, and retired into the plain.

That troop which was gone towards Tailleret, divided themselves into three companies. The first marched by the side of the mountain, burning many houses, and joined with the main army. The second company, amounting to seven score, marched higher, thinking to take the people unawares. But they were strongly resisted by seven men and driven back. The third company attained the top of the mountain, thinking to inclose the people; but as God would, they of Angrogne, who came to succour them, encountered them, and put them to flight.

They of Villars, of whom mention is made before, after they had refreshed themselves with a little bread and wine (for the most part of them had eaten nothing all that day) chased their enemies till it was almost night, so fiercely, that the master of the camp was obliged to send to the lord of la Trinite, who was at Toure, for succour, or else all would have been lost. Which he did; and immediately he rode with all speed to Lucerne to save himself, hearing the alarm which was given at St. John by those of Angrogne, and fearing lest the way should have

been stopped. The army retired with great difficulty, notwithstanding the new aid which was sent them, and with great loss of men.

On Monday, being the 17th of March following, the lord of la Trinite, to be revenged of those of the meadow of Toure, assembled all the force that he could make with the gentlemen of the country. So that whereas before his army was commonly but four thousand, it was now between six and seven thousand: and secretly in the night he encamped with part of his army in the midst of Angrogne, from whence the poor inhabitants were fled. The next morning, after the sermon and prayers were ended, they perceived the other part of the army encamped at the foot of the mountain of Angrogne on the east side. Soon after they perceived how both parts of the army coasted the hill's side, one towards the other, being such a multitude, so glittering in their harness, and marching in such array, that the poor people at first were astonished. Notwithstanding, the assembly fell down upon their knees three or four times, crying, "Help us, O Lord," beseeching him to have regard to the glory of his holy name, to stay the effusion of blood, if it were his good pleasure, and to turn the hearts of their enemies to the truth of his holy gospel. These two parts of the army joined together near to the bulwarks of the meadow of Toure, and gave the assault in three several places. One of the bands mounted secretly by the rocks, thinking to have inclosed the people in their bulwarks. But as soon as they who kept the bulwark below had espied them, they forsook the place, and marched straight towards them; and as they marched, they met with the aid which was sent to them from the valley of Lucerne, very luckily, and coming as it were from heaven: who joining together, soon discomfited their enemies with stones and musketry. They pursued them fiercely in the rocks, and vexed them wonderfully, because the rocks are so steep that no man can ascend or descend without great pain and difficulty.

There was also another band which kept the top of the hill, to assault the bulwarks from thence. The middlemost bulwark was then assaulted, in which were very few to defend it: they, seeing the number of their enemies, retired, leaving only five to defend it. There was a huge rock not far from the bulwark; behind it a great number of the enemy were hid. And shortly there issued out two ensigns, assuring themselves to win the bulwark; but immediately one of their ensign-bearers was wounded to death. Whereupon many fell back: the other set up his ensign upon the bulwark. They who were within had neither halbert, nor any other long weapon, but only one pike, without any iron; which one of the five took, and threw down the ensign, and manfully beat back the scalers, and threw them down to the ground. Some of the enemy had entered into the bulwark by a door below, and slew one of the five who kept the middle part of the bulwark. The other four expected to be destroyed at once. Then one of the four chased away those who had entered below, with stones; and the other three leaving their pistols, defended themselves likewise with great stones: and perceiving the band who were on the rocks to flee, they took courage, and withstood their enemies valiantly till their companions were returned from the chase.

In the mean time the bulwark which was upon the side of the mountain, was furiously assailed by one-half of the army. Those that were within, suffered their enemies to approach near to the bulwark, without any gunshot or other defence: at which the enemy much marvelled: but when they were at hand, they fell upon them, some with throwing stones, others with rolling down mighty stones, and some with musketry. There was a huge stone rolled down, which passed throughout the whole army, and slew many. The soldiers at that time had won a little cottage near the bulwark, which did much hurt to the poor men. But among them one devised to roll down a great huge stone against the cottage, which so shook it, and amazed the soldiers, that they thought they had been all destroyed, and they fled, and never would enter it again.

Then the soldiers made fences of wood, five feet long,

three feet broad, and of the thickness of three boards : but they were so sore vexed with the shot of the musketry, that they were obliged to lay all those fences aside. The miners also made other defences of earth for the soldiers. But all the skill of the enemy availed them nothing : for the slaughter was so great, that in some places you might have seen three lying dead one upon another. The shot of a musket came so near the lord of la Trinite's head, that it broke a wand which he bore in his hand, and made him to retire six score paces ; and seeing his soldiers in such great numbers murdered and wounded on every side, he wept bitterly. Then he retired. That day he thought assuredly to have entered into the meadow of Toure. Moreover, he was determined, if that day's journey had not succeeded, to encamp thereby, and the next morning very early to renew the assault. Many gentlemen and others came there to see the discomfiture of the poor Waldois : and likewise those of the plain looked for nothing, but to hear the piteous ruin and desolation of this poor people. But God disposed it otherwise, for the lord of Trinity had much ado to save himself and his : and seeing the mischief which they intended to do to others was fallen now upon their own heads, they were wonderfully astonished. They of the plain also, when they saw the number of dead bodies and the wounded to be so great (for from noon until the evening they ceased not to carry them away) were likewise exceedingly dismayed.

Many marvelled why the people did not follow the army, but especially the soldiers, seeing the great discomfiture which they had done, and that they had gotten such advantage of them already ; but this was done for two causes. The one was, because they had already determined not to follow the army when once it retired, to avoid the effusion of blood, meaning only to defend themselves. The other cause was, that they were weary, and had spent all their ammunition : for many of them had shot off about thirty times, and none of them under twenty.

The next day one of the principal captains of the army surrendered his charge to the lord of la Trinite, saying to him, that he would never fight against this people any more ; and upon that he departed. It is a marvellous thing, and worthy of perpetual memory, that in that combat there were but two of the Waldois slain, and two wounded. Through the whole country of Piedmont, every man said, God fights for them. One of the captains confessed, that he had been at many fierce assaults and combats, and sundry well fought battles, but he had never seen soldiers so faint-hearted and amazed : yea, the soldiers themselves told him, they were so astonished, that they could not strike. They said, that this people never shot, but they wounded or killed some of the soldiers. Others said, that the ministers by their prayers conjured and bewitched them, that they could not fight : and indeed wonderful is it, marvellous are the judgments of God, that notwithstanding so many combats and conflicts, so great assaults and adventures, so much and so terrible shot, continually made against this poor people, yet all in a manner came to no effect : so mightily God's holy power wrought for his people. Insomuch that, for all the combats, skirmishes, and so many conflicts of the Angrognians there were but nine only that failed, and the whole number of those that were slain amounted only to fourteen persons.

The lord of la Trinite sent two gentlemen of the valley of Lucerne to them of Angrogne, to ask them if they would come to any agreement. To whom answer was made, that they would stand to their first answer. From that time he sent very often to treat of the agreement : but what his meaning was might well appear. For when the poor people hoped for some agreement, they were most furiously assaulted. Upon this there was a day assigned in the valley of Lucerne, to confer touching the agreement with certain men belonging to the lord of Raconig, and a safe conduct was promised and granted.

The night before the ministers and rulers of Angrogne were to take their journey, they perceived a company of soldiers going up a hill, by which the people of Angrogne should pass, and hid themselves in houses on the way side, thinking to take them of Angrogne unawares, who were sent to treat of the agreement. But they, having intelligence of this conspiracy, watched and guarded. It was an easy matter, as some thought, that night to have taken the lord of la Trinite, and to have spoiled his whole camp. But they of Angrogne and Lucerne would not execute this enterprise, lest thereby they should offend God, and pass the bounds of their vocation, taking upon them no more than to defend themselves.

At that time a pitiful case happened in the meadow of Toure. The lord of Raconig, seeming to be sorry for this war, sent into the meadow of Toure an honest man, Francis of Gilles, to consult what means were best to further the agreement, who, after conferring with the ministers and rulers, returned homeward that day according to his master's command, and having sent back one who conducted him, was murdered soon after at the foot of Angrogne, by two men of Angrogne, who otherwise seemed to be honest, and of good parentage. Soon after, one of the two who had committed this act, entered into the meadow of Toure, and was immediately apprehended and bound. He confessed the deed without any further delay. Immediately the other also was taken.

The Waldois were marvellously troubled and grieved with this act, and wrote to the lord of Raconig, declaring to him the whole circumstance, that they had the offenders in ward, and that if it would please him to send some to examine the matter, they for their part would so execute justice in the punishment of them, that their innocence to all men should appear. The lord of Raconig wrote to them that they should deliver to him the offenders, and that he would do such justice upon them as the case required. To which they of Angrogne answered, that upon three conditions they should be delivered according to his request. First, that the prisoners should be compelled to do nothing against their consciences ; and as touching religion, nothing should be spoken to them, but out of the word of God. Secondly, that speedy and sharp justice should be executed upon them ; and that hereafter this should be no prejudice to the liberties and privileges of the people of Angrogne. The third, that the execution of them should be upon the borders of Angrogne, for an example to all others. This being accorded with one assent (yea, without contradiction of their parents), they sent them prisoners, accompanied with sixty gunners, to the confines of Lucerne, and there delivered them into the hands of the lord of Raconig. This redounded to the great commendation of the people of Angrogne.

After this, the lord of la Trinite, having left garrisons about Angrogne, and the valley of Lucerne, went to Perouse, near the valley of St. Martin, to succour the garrison there, being in great danger, and remained there a month. During which time, they of Angrogne, and the valley of Lucerne, lived in more quietness than before ; but yet they were much afflicted, by reason of the scarcity of victuals which sore pressed them, and those of the meadow of Toure, for they were spoiled of their victuals. This poor people lived on milk and herbs, having very little bread. But afterwards, when they were like to be famished, God of his goodness sent them better succour, both of corn and bread than they had before. Their enemies thought to have taken the meadow of Toure by famine ; for they took away the victuals that were to be had in all places round about. Every household was suffered to have no more than should sustain them that day, and that also was very little, that they should not succour this poor people.

Afterwards, the lord of la Trinite, being returned from Perouse to Lucerne, sent some to treat of an agreement, and required to commune with some of the people. Then they began to consult and devise by all means how they might come to some good agreement. But on Monday, the 17th of April, by break of day, he sent certain bands of Spaniards, which he had there, with the garrison of Toure, to the mountain of Tailleret, by the way which leadeth to the meadow of Toure, on the south side. They murdered the men, women, and children of Tailleret whom they found in their beds. Then they marched on along

K K

upon the mountain, towards the meadow of Toure. Shortly after, the people perceived two other companies of soldiers, marching by Angrogne by two several ways, to assault the meadow of Toure. In the morning as soon as they rose, they blew their horns, for they saw them already entered. When they had offered their prayers, every man ran to meet the enemy, some on the east side, and others on the south. They who first resisted the enemy (who were already past the bulwarks), were in the beginning but twelve gunners, and a few others whom they caused to go up the hill, and roll down great stones. These twelve, having found a fit place for their purpose to stay the enemy, began to shoot at them. They, seeing themselves so assaulted both above and beneath, and the place so narrow and strait, turned back, and retired as fast as they could by the same way by which they came. If they had tarried a little longer, they had been enclosed between the two mountains, for the place was so narrow, that they could not have escaped. The people chased them to their camp, which was at Toure.

Within a few days after, the people of Angrogne were advertised by the lord of la Trinite's letters, that he fully determined to cut down their trees and vines, and destroy their corn on the ground: and that two forts should be built at Angrogne. The day was assigned, and horsemen appointed, with all speed to execute this mischievous enterprise. The poor people thought that they should be assailed as sore as ever, and have to fight as hard as ever they did before. But God prevented this cruel attempt; for the night before that this was intended to be executed, the lord of la Trinite received letters from the duke, which stopped this enterprise. They of the meadow of Toure being advertised that the lord of la Trinite now intended to send ordnance to beat down the bulwarks which were made of stones, they made a bulwark of earth, which was in compass about five hundred paces, which they might easily see from Lucerne. They in the meadow of Toure told the lord of la Trinite's men, that if they brought any artillery, they should not so soon carry it away again; and shortly after the ordnance was sent back.

About this time, the chief rulers and ministers of the Waldois earnestly requested the lord of Raconig to present a supplication which they had made to the duchess of Savoy, for they had intelligence that she was displeased that her subjects were so cruelly treated. In which supplication they declared the equity of their cause, protesting all due obedience to the duke, their sovereign lord, and if it might be proved by the pure word of God that they held any error, they would with all humble submission receive correction, and be reformed, humbly beseeching her grace to appease the displeasure which the duke had conceived against them, by the untrue surmises of their adversaries; and if there were any thing wherein they had offended him, they most humbly craved his gracious pardon.

About the same time the lord of la Trinite, by sickness, was in great danger of his life. Soon after the supplication was delivered the duchess sent an answer to the Waldois, by the lord of Raconig. The effect thereof was, that she had obtained of his grace, the duke, all that they demanded in their supplication, upon such conditions as the lord of Raconig would propose to them. But when they understood that the conditions were very rigorous, they sent another supplication to the duchess, in which they humbly besought her grace to interpose in their behalf, that the conditions and articles might be moderated. The articles here follow :—

1. That they should banish their ministers.

2. That they should receive the mass, and other ceremonies of the Romish church.

3. That they should pay a ransom to the soldiers for some of their men whom they had taken.

4. That they should assemble and preach no more as they were used to do.

5. That the duke would make fortresses at his pleasure in all that country, with other like things.

The people made humble request in this their last supplication, that it would please the duchess to give the duke, her husband, to understand how that these conditions were strange and rigorous. And as for their parts, although they had good trial of their ministers, that they were good men, and fearing God, of sound doctrine, of good life, and honest conversation ; yet, nevertheless, they were contented to do so, if he would give leave to some of them to remain ; requesting this, that it might be permitted to them to choose some other good ministers in their places, before they departed, lest their churches should remain without pastors.

Concerning the mass and other ceremonies of the church of Rome, if the duke should cause them to be ministered in their parishes, they neither would nor could withstand the same, and for their part, they would do no injury or violence to those that should minister them, or be present at them ; notwithstanding they besought him, that they might not be constrained to be present themselves at the ministration of them, or to pay any thing to the maintenance of them, or to yield either countenance or consent to them.

As to the ransom which was demanded of them for their prisoners, considering the extreme poverty that they were in, and the great calamities and damages which they had suffered, it was to them a thing impossible. Yea, if his highness were truly informed what loss they had sustained by burning, spoiling, and sacking of their houses and goods, without either mercy or pity, he would not only not require of them any such thing, but as a gracious and merciful prince, he would succour and support them, that they might be able to maintain their poor families, whom they nourished (as they were bound to do) to the service of God, and of their lord and prince; and therefore they desired that it might please him, that their poor brethren remaining in captivity and prison, and such as were sent to the galleys for the profession of their religion, might speedily be delivered and set at liberty.

As for their assemblies and preachings, they were contented that they should be kept only among themselves, in their accustomed places, and in other valleys where any assembly of the faithful might be, who were desirous to hear the preaching of the gospel.

Touching the fortresses, forasmuch as by those that were already made, they had suffered great molestation and trouble, as well as concerning their goods, as also their religion; they were assured that if he did build up new forts, they would never be able to bear the troubles, miseries, and calamities that would follow; and therefore they most humbly desired the duchess to be so good and gracious to them, as to obtain of the duke, that he would accept their persons in the stead of forts; and that, seeing those places were by nature and of themselves strong and well fortified, it might please their lord the duke to receive them into his protection and safeguard; and by the grace and assistance of God they would serve him themselves for such walls and forts, that he should not need to build any other. And because many of those who dwelt near about them had robbed and spoiled them, not only of their household goods and such other things, but also driven away their cattle; that it might please him to give them leave to recover the goods by way of justice, and to buy again that which the soldiers had sold, and that for the same price for which it was sold.

Briefly, they also besought their lord, that it might please him to be so gracious to them, as to grant them a confirmation of all their franchises, immunities, and privileges, as well general as particular, given to them as well by him as by his predecessors ; and likewise of those which as well they as their ancestors had bought of their lords, and to receive them, as his most humble and obedient subjects, into his protection and safeguard.

And because in time past, instead of good and speedy justice, all iniquity was committed by those that had the administration of justice in their valleys, and as their purses were emptied and punished rather than the malefactors, that it might please him to give order that such justice might be done among them ; whereby the wicked might be punished with all severity, and the innocent defended and maintained in their right.

Finally, forasmuch as divers of this poor people (being

astonished at the coming of the army, and fearing lest they should not only be spoiled of all their goods, but also that they with their wives and children should be utterly destroyed) had made promise against their consciences, to live according to the traditions of the church of Rome; they were troubled and tormented in spirit, and did nothing but languish in that distress. Wherefore they humbly besought the duchess to take pity upon them, and to obtain for them, that they might not be compelled to do any thing against their consciences, and that it might please the duke to permit them to live in liberty and freedom of conscience; also, that all their poor brethren banished for the cause of religion might return home to their houses; and that all confiscations and penalties made against them might be abolished. And for their part, they promised to give all due reverence and honour to God and his holy word, and to be true and faithful subjects to their lord and prince; yea, more than any others. Underneath the supplication there was written:

" Your faithful and humble subjects, the poor afflicted of the valleys of Lucerne, Angrogne, St. Martin, and Perouse, and generally all the people of the Waldois, who inhabit the country of Piedmont."

After this supplication was viewed and read of the duchess, she so persuaded the duke, that answer was made with these conditions, declared in these articles following:

Conclusions and Articles lastly agreed upon between the Right Honourable the Lord of Raconig on the part of his Highness the Duke, and them of the Valleys of Piedmont, called the Waldois.

That there shall shortly be made letters patent by his highness the duke, by which it may appear that he has forgiven and pardoned them of the valleys of Angrogne, Bouvet, Villars, Valquichard, Rova, Tailleret, La Rua de Bouvet (bordering upon Toure), St. Martin, Perouse, Roccapiata, St. Bartholomew, and all such as have aided them; of all such faults as they have committed as well as bearing arms against his highness, as against the lords and certain other gentlemen whom he retained and kept in his protection and safeguard.

That it shall be lawful for them of Angrogne, Bouvet, Villars, Valquichard, Rora, (members of the valley of Lucerne,) and for them of Rodoret, Marcele, Manaillon, and Salsa, members of the valley of St. Martin, to have their congregations, sermons, and other ministries of their religion in places accustomed.

That it shall be lawful for them of Villars (members of the valley of Lucerne) to have the same, but that only until the time that his highness doth build a fort in the same place. But while the said fort is in building, it shall not be lawful to have their preachings and assemblies within the precinct of the place, but it shall be lawful for them to build a place for that purpose near at hand, where they shall think good, on that side towards Bouvet. Nevertheless it shall be permitted to their ministers to come within the precinct aforesaid, to visit the sick, and exercise other things necessary to their religion, so that they preach not, nor make any assembly there.

It shall also be permitted to them of Tailleret, La Rua de Bouvet, bordering upon Toure, to have their sermons and assemblies in the accustomed places, so that they enter not for that purpose into the rest of the confines of Toure.

That it shall not be lawful for the said members of the valleys of Lucerne and St. Martin, to come to the rest of their borders, nor any other of his highness's dominions; nor to have their preachings, assemblies, or disputations, out of their own borders, they having liberty to have them therein. And if they be examined of their faith, it shall be lawful for them to answer without danger of punishment in body or goods.

The like shall be lawful for them of the parish of Perouse, who at this present time are fled because of their religion, and were wont to have their assemblies and preachings, and other ministries according to their

religion, at the place called Le Puis; so that they come not to other places and borders of the said parish.

It shall be permitted to them of the parish of Pinachia, of the valley of Perouse, who at this present time are fled because of their religion, and were wont to go to sermons and assemblies, and other ministries of their religion, to have the like, only at the place called Le Grandoubion.

It shall be permitted to them of the parish of St. Germain, of the valley of Perouse, and to them of Roccapiata, who at this present period are fled because of their religion, and continue in the same, to have only one minister, who may on one day preach at St. Germain, at the place called Le Adormilleux, and the other day at Roccapiata, at the place called Vandini only.

It shall be permitted to all them of the towns and villages of the valleys, who at this present time are fled, and continue in their religion, notwithstanding any promise or abjuration made before this war against the said religion, to repair and return to their houses with their households, and to live according to the same, going and coming to the sermons and assemblies which shall be made by their ministers in the places above specified, so that they obey that which is above-said.

And because that many of the said towns and villages dwell out of the precinct of the preaching, having need to be visited, and of other things according to their religion, their ministers, who dwell within the precinct, shall be suffered, without prejudice, to visit and duly aid them of such ministries as shall be necessary for them, so that they make no sermons or assemblies.

By especial grace it shall be permitted to all them of the valley of Meane, and them of St. Bartholomew, neighbours to Roccapiata, and are fled and continue in their religion, peaceably to enjoy the grace and liberties granted in the next article before, so that they observe all which they before promised to observe.

The goods already seized as forfeited, shall be restored to all the inhabitants of the said valleys, and to all that are fled and continue in their religion, as well of them of the said valleys, as of Roccapiata, St. Bartholomew, and of Meane, so that they be not seized for any other cause than for their religion, and for the war present and lately past.

It shall be lawful for them aforesaid to recover by way of justice, of their neighbours, their moveable goods and cattle, so it be not of soldiers; and that which hath been sold, they shall also recover by way of justice, so that they restore the price for which it hath been sold. Their neighbours shall have the like against them.

All the franchises, freedoms, and privileges, as well general as particular, granted as well by his highness' predecessors, as by himself, and obtained of other inferior lords, whereof they shall make proof by public writing, shall be confirmed unto them.

The said valleys shall be provided for, to have good justice ministered unto them, whereby they may know they are kept in safeguard by his highness, as well as all his other subjects.

The inhabitants of the said valleys shall make a roll of all the names and sirnames of all them of the valleys, who are fled for religion, as well such as have abjured as others, to the end that they may be restored and maintained in their goods and households, and enjoy such grace and benefits as their prince and lord hath bestowed on them.

And insomuch as it is known to every man, that the prince may build fortresses in his country, where it shall please him without contradiction, nevertheless to take all suspicion out of the minds of the aforesaid Waldois, it is declared, if at any time hereafter his highness will make a fort at Villars, the inhabitants of the said place shall not be constrained to bear the charges, but only as they shall think good, lovingly to aid their prince. Which fort being builded (by God's aid) a governor and captain shall therein be appointed, who shall attempt nothing but the service of his highness, without offence to the inhabitants, either in their goods or consciences.

It shall be lawful for them, before the discharging of such of their ministers, as it shall please his highness to have discharged, to choose and call others in their steads;

so that they choose not Master Martin de Pragela, nor change from one place to another of the said valleys, any of them who are discharged.

The mass, and other service after the usage of Rome, shall be kept in all the parishes of the said valleys, where the sermons, assemblies, and other ministries of their religion are made; but none shall be compelled to be present thereat, nor to support, aid, or favour such as shall use that service.

All the expenses and charges borne by his highness in this war, shall be forgiven and released to them for ever; also the 8000 crowns wherein the inhabitants of the said valleys were behind, as part of 16,000 crowns which they had promised in the war passed. And his highness will command that the writings for that cause made, shall be annulled and cancelled.

All the prisoners shall be rendered up and restored who shall be found to be in the hands of the soldiers, on paying a reasonable ransom, according to the goods which they may possess; and those who shall be adjudged to be wrongfully taken, shall be released without ransom.

Likewise all they of the said valleys, who for religion, and not for other causes, are detained in the galleys, shall be released without ransom.

Finally, it shall be lawful for all them of the said valleys, those of Meane, Roccapiata, and St. Bartholomew, of what degree, estate and condition soever they be (except ministers) to accompany and dwell, and to be in daily conversation with the rest of his highness's subjects, and to tarry, go, and come in all places of his highness's country, to sell and buy, and use all trades of merchandize, in all places in his highness's country, as before is said, so that they preach not, nor make any assemblies or disputations, as we have before said; and that they who be of the limits dwell not out of them; and they who be of the towns and villages of the said valleys dwell not out of them, nor of their borders; and in so doing they shall not be molested by any means, and shall not be offended or troubled in body or goods, but shall remain under the protection and safeguard of his highness.

Furthermore, his highness shall give orders to stay all troubles, inconveniencies, secret conspiracies of wicked persons, after such sort, that they shall remain quietly in their religion. For observation whereof, George Monastier, one of the elders of Angrogne; Constantion Dialestini, otherwise called Rembaldo, one of the elders of Villars; Pirrone Arduino, sent from the commonalty of Bouvet; Michael Ramondet, sent from the commonalty of Tailleret, and of La Rua de Bouvet, bordering upon Toure; John Malenote, sent from certain persons of St. John; Peter Paschall, sent from the commonalty of the valley of St. Martin; Thomas Romam of St. Germaine, sent from the commonalty of the same place, and of all the valley of Perouse, promise for them and their commonalties severally, that the contents of these conclusions aforesaid shall be inviolably kept, and for breach thereof do submit themselves to such punishment as shall please his highness; promising likewise to cause the chief of the families or the commonalties to allow and confirm the said promise.

The honourable lord of Raconig doth promise, that his highness the duke shall confirm and allow the aforesaid conclusions to them, both generally and particularly, at the intercession and special favour of the noble lady the princess.

In testimony whereof, the aforesaid lord of Raconig hath confirmed these present conclusions with his own hand; and the ministers have likewise subscribed in the name of all the said valleys; and they who can write, in the name of all their commonalties.

At Cavor, the 5th day of June, 1561.

Philip of Savoy, Francis Valla, Minister of Villars, Claudius Bergius, Minister of Tailleret, Georgius Monasterius, Michael Raymundet.

This accord being thus made and passed, by means of the duchess of Savoy, the poor Waldois have been in quiet to this present time; and God of his infinite goodness having delivered them out of so many troubles and conflicts, hath set them at liberty to serve him purely, and with quietness of conscience.

Wherefore there is not one at this present time but he sees and well perceives that God would make it known by experience to these poor Waldois, and all other faithful people, that all things turn to the best to them who love and fear him; for by all these afflictions which they suffered their heavenly Father hath brought them to repentance and amendment of life; he hath effectually taught them to have recourse to his fatherly mercy, and to embrace Jesus Christ for their only Saviour and Redeemer. He hath taught them to tame the desires and lusts of the flesh, to withdraw their hearts from the world, and lift them to heaven; and to be always in a readiness to come to him, as unto their most loving and gracious Father. To be short, he has sent them to the school of his children, to the end that they should profit in patience and hope; to make them to mourn, weep, and cry unto him. And above all, he has made them so often to prove his succours in time of need, to see them before their eyes, to know and touch them with their hands (as a man would say) after such sort, that they have had good occasion, and all the faithful with them, never to distrust so good a Father, and so careful for the health of his children, but to assure themselves they shall never be confounded, what thing soever happens.

And yet to see this more manifestly, and that every man may take profit therein, it shall be good to understand what this poor people did whilst they were in these combats and conflicts. So soon as they saw the army of their enemies approach, they cried all together for aid and succour to the Lord; and before they came to defend themselves, they went to prayer, and in fighting lifted up their hearts, and sighed to the Lord. As long as the enemy were at rest, every one of these poor people on their knees called upon God. When the combat was ended, they gave him thanks for the comfort and succour which they had felt. In the meantime the rest of the people, with their ministers, made their hearty prayer to God, with sighs and tears, and that from the morning until the evening. When night was come, they assembled again togther: they who had fought, rehearsed the wonderful aid and succour which God had sent them, and so altogether rendered thanks to him for his fatherly goodness. Always he changed their sorrow into joy. In the morning trouble and affliction appeared before them, with great terror on all sides: but by the evening they were delivered, and had great cause of rejoicing and comfort.

As for the monks and priests, who by such means thought to advance themselves, and to bring their trumpery in estimation, they have lost the little rule which they had over that people, and are confounded, and their religion brought to disdain. Thus God beateth down those who exalt themselves above measure, and maketh his adversaries to fall into the pits which they themselves have made. Let us pray to him therefore, that it would please him likewise to stretch out his mighty arm at this day to maintain his poor afflicted church, and to confound all the devices of Satan and his members, to the advancement of his glory and kingdom.

CONCLUSION.

Having thus comprehended the troubles and persecutions of such godly saints, and blessed martyrs, which have suffered in other foreign nations above mentioned: here now ending with them, and beginning the eighth book, we are, God willing, to return again to our own matters, and to prosecute such acts and records, as to our own country of England do appertain. In the process whereof, among many other things, may appear the marvellous work of God's power and mercy in suppressing and banishing out of this realm, the long usurped supremacy of the pope: also in subverting and overthrowing the houses of monks and friars, with divers other matters appertaining to the reformation of Christ's true church and religion. All which things as they have been long wished, and greatly prayed for in times past by many godly and learned men: so much more ought we now to rejoice and give God thanks, seeing these days of reformation which God hath given us. If John Husse, or good Jerome of Prague, or John Wickliff before them both, or William Brute, Thorpe, Swinderby, or the Lord Cobham; if Zisca with all the company of the Bohemians; if the Earl Raymund, with all the Toulousians; if the Waldois, or the Albigenses, with infinite. others, had been either in these our times now, or else had seen then this ruin of the pope, and revealing of antichrist, which the Lord now hath given unto us, what joy and triumph would they not have made! Wherefore now beholding that which they so long time have wished for, let us not think the benefit to be small, but render most humble thanks to the Lord our God; who by his mighty power, and the brightness of his word, has revealed this great enemy of his so manifestly to the eyes of all men, who before was so hid in the church, that few christians could discover him. For who would ever have judged or suspected in his mind, the bishop of Rome (commonly received and believed, almost of all men, to be the vicar and vicegerent of Christ here on earth) to be antichrist, and the great adversary of God, whom St. Paul so expressly prophesies of in these latter days to be revealed by the brightness of the Lord's coming, as all men now for the most part may see it is come to pass? Wherefore to the Lord, and Father of lights, who revealeth all things in his due time, be praise and glory for ever. Amen.

THE END OF THE SEVENTH BOOK.

ACTS AND MONUMENTS.

BOOK VIII.

THE HISTORY OF ENGLISH AFFAIRS APPERTAINING BOTH TO THE ECCLESIASTICAL AND CIVIL STATES.

Mistress Smith, widow; Robert Hatches, a shoemaker; Aacher, a shoemaker; Hawkins, a shoemaker; Thomas Bond,—a shoemaker; Wrigsham, a glover; Landsdale, a hosier, at Coventry, A.D. 1519.

THE principal cause of the apprehension of these persons was, their teaching their children and family the Lord's Prayer and ten commandments in English, for which they were upon Ash-Wednesday put in prison, till the Friday following.

Then they were sent to a monastery called Mackstock Abbey, six miles from Coventry. During which time their children were sent to the Gray Friars in Coventry, before the warden, called Friar Stafford: who examining them of their belief, and what heresies their fathers had taught them, charged them upon pain of suffering death, to meddle no more with the Lord's Prayer, the creed, and the ten commandments in English.

Upon Palm Sunday the fathers of these children were brought again to Coventry, and there the week before Easter they were condemned to be burned. Mistress Smith only was dismissed for the present. And because it was in the evening, being somewhat dark, Simon Mourton offered to go home with her. Now as he was leading her by the arm, and heard the ratling of a scroll within her sleeve, saith he, "What have ye here?" And so he took it from her, and saw that it was the Lord's Prayer, the articles of the creed, and the ten commandments in English; which when the wretched somner understood, he brought her back to the bishop, where she was immediately condemned, and burned with the six men beforenamed, on the 4th April, A.D. 1519.

When these were dispatched, the sheriffs went to their houses, and took all their goods and cattle for their own use, not leaving their wives and children any thing. And as the people began to complain of the cruelty, and the unjust death of these innocent martyrs, the bishop, with his officers and priests, caused it to be noised abroad by their tenants, servants, and farmers, that they were not burned for having the Lord's Prayer and the commandments in English, but because they ate flesh on Fridays and other fast days!

Robert Silkeb, 1521.—In the number of these men was Robert Silkeb, who fled, and for that time escaped.

But about two years after he was taken again, and brought to Coventry, where he was burned about the 13th day of January, 1521.

Patrick Hamilton, A.D. 1527.

Patrick Hamilton, a Scotchman, of an high and noble stock, and of the king's blood, young, and of flourishing age, called abbot of Fern, coming out of his country with three companions, to seek godly learning, went to the university of Marpurg in Germany; there, in conference and familiarity with learned men, like Francis Lambert, he so profited in knowledge, and mature judgment in matters of religion, that he was the first in all that university of Marpurg who publicly did set up conclusions there to be disputed of, concerning faith and works: arguing also no less learnedly than fervently upon the subject.

This learned Patrick increasing daily more and more in knowledge, and inflamed with godliness, at length began to revolve with himself his return to his country, being desirous to impart to his countrymen, some of the knowledge which he had received abroad. There not bearing the ignorance and blindness of that people, after he had valiantly taught and preached the truth, was accused of heresy, and afterwards constantly and stoutly sustaining the cause of God's gospel, against the high priest and archbishop of Saint Andrews, named James Beaton, was cited to appear before him and his college of priests, the first day of March, 1527. He being not only forward in knowledge, but also ardent in spirit, not tarrying for the appointed hour, came very early before he was looked for, and there mightily disputing against them, when he could not by the scriptures be convicted, he was oppressed by force: and the sentence of condemnation being given against him, the same day after dinner, he was led away to the fire, and there burned.

We think good to express here his articles, as we received them from Scotland, out of the registers.

The Articles and Opinions objected against Master Patrick Hamilton, by James Beaton, Archbishop of St. Andrews.

That man hath no free-will.

That there is no purgatory.

That the holy patriarchs were in heaven before Christ's passion.

That the pope hath no power to loose and bind; neither had any pope that power after St. Peter.

That the pope is Antichrist, and that every priest hath the power that the pope hath.

That Master Patrick Hamilton was a bishop.

That it is not necessary to obtain any bulls from any bishop.

That the vow of the pope's religion is a vow of wickedness.

That the popes' laws are of no strength.

That all christians, worthy to be called christians, do know that they are in the state of grace.

That none are saved, but those who are previously predestinate.

Whoever is in deadly sin, is unfaithful.

That God is the cause of sin in this sense, that is, that he withdraweth his grace from men, whereby they sin.

That it is devilish doctrine, to enjoin to any sinner actual penance for sin.

That the said Master Patrick himself doubteth whether all children, departing immediately after their baptism, are saved or condemned.

That auricular confession is not necessary to salvation.

These articles above written, were given in, and laid against Master Hamilton, and inserted in their registers, for which also he was condemned. But other learned men, who communed and reasoned with him, testify, that these articles following, were the very articles for which he suffered :—

1. Man hath no free-will.

2. A man is only justified by faith in Christ.

3. A man, so long as he liveth, is not without sin.

4. He is not worthy to be called a christian, who believeth not that he is in grace.

5. A good man doth good works. Good works do not make a good man.

6. An evil man bringeth forth evil works. Evil works being faithfully repented of, do not make an evil man.

7. Faith, hope, and charity, are so linked together, that one of them cannot be without another in any one man in this life.

Henry Forrest.—Within a few years after the martyrdom of Master Patrick Hamilton, one Henry Forrest, a young man, affirmed, that Master Patrick Hamilton died a martyr, and that his articles were true. For this he was apprehended, and put in prison by James Beaton, archbishop of St. Andrew's, who, shortly after, caused a friar, named Walter Lang, to hear his confession. To whom, when Henry Forrest, in secret confession, had declared his conscience, how he thought Master Patrick to be a good man, and wrongfully put to death, and that his articles were true and not heretical, the friar came and uttered to the bishop the confession that he had heard.

It followed, that his confession being brought as sufficient probation against him, he was summoned before the council of the clergy and doctors, and there concluded to be an heretic, equally with Master Patrick Hamilton, and there decreed to be given to the secular judges to suffer death.

When the day of his death came, and that he should first be degraded, and was brought before the clergy, as soon as he entered at the door, and saw the face of the clergy, he cried with a loud voice, saying, " Fie on falsehood! Fie on false friars! Revealers of confession! After this day, let no man ever trust any friars, contemners of God's word, and deceivers of men!" When they proceeded to degrade him, he said, with a loud voice, " Take from me not only your own orders, but also your own baptism," meaning, whatever is besides that which Christ himself instituted, whereto there are great additions in baptism. Then, after his degradation, they condemned him as an heretic. And so he suffered death for his faithful testimony of the truth of Christ and of his Gospel, at the north-church stile of the Abbey Church of St. Andrew.

James Hamilton, brother to Patrick; Catharine Hamilton; a wife of Leith; David Stratton; Master Norman Gurley.

Within a year after the martyrdom of Henry Forrest, all these five were called to the Abbey church of Holyroodhouse, in Edinburgh, in presence of King James V., who, upon the day of their accusation, was clad in red apparel. James Hamilton was accused as one that maintained the opinions of Master Patrick, his brother. To whom the king gave counsel to depart, and not to appear, for, in case he appeared, he could not help him; because, the bishops had persuaded him, that the cause of heresy did in no wise appertain to him. And so James fled, and was condemned as an heretic, and all his goods and lands were confiscated, and given unto others.

Catharine Hamilton, his sister, appeared upon the scaffold, and being accused of an horrible heresy, to wit, that her own works could not save her, she granted the same; and after long reasoning between her and Master John Speus, the lawyer, she concluded in this manner, " Work here, work there, what kind of working is all this? I know perfectly, that no kind of work can save me, but only the works of Christ my Lord and Saviour." The king hearing these words, turned himself about and laughed, and called her to him, and caused her to recant, because she was his aunt, and she escaped.

The woman of Leith was accused, that when the midwife in time of her labour, bade her say, " Our Lady help me," she cried, "Christ help me! Christ help me! in whose help I trust!" She also was caused to recant, and so escaped without confiscation of her goods, because she was married.

Master Norman Gurley, for that he said there was no such thing as purgatory, and that the pope was not a bishop, but Antichrist, and had no jurisdiction in Scotland.

David Stratton said, " There was no purgatory, but the passion of Christ, and the tribulations of this world;" and because that when Master Robert Lawson, vicar of Eglesrig, asked his tithe-fish of him, he cast them to him out of the boat, so that some of them fell into the sea. Therefore, he accused him as one that had said, that no tithes should be paid. These two, because after great solicitation made by the king, they refused to abjure and recant, were therefore condemned as heretics, and were burned between Leith and Edinburgh, that the inhabitants of Fife seeing the fire, might be struck with terror, so as not to fall into the like.

In 1553, *Thomas Harding*, dwelling at Chesham, in the county of Buckingham, with Alice, his wife, was first abjured by William Smith, bishop of Lincoln, (A.D. 1506), with others, who, at the same time, for speaking against idolatry and superstition, were taken and compelled, some to bear fagots, some burned in the cheeks with hot irons, some condemned to perpetual prison, some thrust into monasteries, and robbed of all their goods; some compelled to make pilgrimage to the great block, otherwise called our lady of Lincoln, some to Walsingham, some to St. Romuld of Buckingham, some to the Rood of Wendover, some to St. John Shorne, &c.; of whom we have made mention before.

At last Harding, (A.D. 1522), about the Easter holidays, when the other people went to the church to engage in their wonted idolatry, took his way into the woods, there solitarily to worship the true living God, in spirit and truth. As he was occupied with a book of English prayers, leaning or sitting upon a stile by the wood side, it chanced that one saw him, and came in great haste to the officers of the town, declaring, that he had seen Harding in the woods looking on a book. Upon this, immediately a rude rabble ran desperately to his house to search for books, and in searching under the boards of his floor, they found English books of the holy Scripture. Whereupon this godly father, with his books, was brought before John Longland, bishop of Lincoln, then lying at Woburn, who, with his chaplains, calling father Harding to examination, began to reason with him, proceeding rather with checks and rebukes, than with any sound arguments. Thomas Harding seeing their folly and rude behaviour, gave them but few words, but fixing his trust and care in the Lord, did let them say what they would. Thus at last they sent him to the bishop's prison, where he lay with hunger and pain enough for a certain space, till at length the bishop, sitting in his tribunal, condemned him for relapsing, to be burned to ashes, committing his martyrdom to Roland Messenger, vicar of Great Wickham, which Roland, at the day appointed, with a rabble of others like to himself, brought father Harding to Chesham again. The next day after his return, Roland made a sermon in Chesham church, causing Thomas Harding to stand before him all the time he was preaching; which sermon was nothing else but the maintaining of the jurisdiction of the bishop of Rome, and the state of the Apostolical See, with the idolatry, fancies, and traditions belonging unto the same. When the sermon was ended, Roland took him up to the high altar, and asked, whether he believed that in the bread, after the consecration, there remained any other substance than the substance of Christ's natural body born of the Virgin Mary. To this Thomas Harding answered, "The articles of our belief do teach us, that our Saviour Christ was born of the Virgin Mary, and that he suffered death under Pilate, and rose from death the third day; that he then ascended into heaven, and sitteth on the right hand of God, in the glory of his Father."

Then he was brought into a house in the town, where he remained all night in prayer and godly meditations. So, the next morning, came Roland again, with a company of bills and staves, to lead this godly father to his burning. A great number both of men and women followed him, of whom many bewailed his death, and the wicked rejoiced at it. He was brought forth, having thrust into his hands a little cross of wood, but no idol upon it. Then he was chained to the stake, and desiring the people to pray for him, and forgiving all his enemies and persecutors, he commended his spirit to God, and took his death most patiently and quietly, lifting up his hands to heaven, saying, "Jesus, receive my spirit!"

When they had set fire on him, there was one that threw a billet at him, and dashed out his brains; for what purpose he did so is not known, but it was supposed it was that he might have forty days of pardon; for proclamation was made, as at the burning of William Tilseworth, "That whosoever did bring a fagot or a stake to the burning of an heretic, should have forty days of pardon." Many ignorant people caused their children to bear billets and faggots to their burning.

Mistress Alice Doly. — Elizabeth Wighthill being brought before Dr. London, in the parsonage at Stanton Harcourt, and there put to her oath, deposed against Mistress Alice Doly, her mistress. That Mistress Doly, speaking of John Hacker, water-bearer, said, "That he was very expert in the gospels, and all other things belonging to divine service, and could express and declare it, and the Pater Noster, i. e., the Lord's prayer, in English, as well as any priest, and it would do one good to hear him." Saying, moreover, "That she wished in no case that this were known, lest it should hurt the poor man."

Over and besides, Elizabeth deposed, "That Mistress Doly, her mistress, shewed unto her that she had a book which held against pilgrimages; and, after that, she caused Sir John Booth, parson of Brittwell to read upon a book which he called the Golden Legends, and one saint's life he read, which did speak against pilgrimages. And after that was read, her mistress said unto her, 'Lo, daughter, now ye may hear as I told you, that this book speaks against pilgrimages.'

It was deposed against Mistress Doly, by this Elizabeth, that she being at Sir William Barenten's place, and seeing there in the closet, images new gilded, said to the said Elizabeth, "Look, here be my lady Barenten's gods." To whom the said Elizabeth answered again, "That they were set for remembrance of good saints." Then said she, "If I were in a house where no images were, I could remember to pray unto saints as well as if I did

see the images." "Nay," said the other, "images do provoke devotion." Then said her mistress, "Ye should not worship that thing that hath ears and cannot hear, and hath eyes and cannot see, and hath mouth and cannot speak, and hath hands and cannot feel."

Note here, good reader, in this time, which was above forty-six years ago, what good matter was there here to accuse and molest good women for!

Roger Hachman, A.D. 1525.—Against this Roger Hachman it was laid by deposition, that he sitting at the Church-aisle at Norfolk, said these words, "I will never look to be saved for any good deed that ever I did, neither for any that ever I will do, unless I may have my salvation by petition, as an outlaw shall have his pardon of the king"; and said, that if he might not have his salvation so, he thought he should be lost.

Robert West, A.D. 1529.—Against this Robert West, priest, it was objected, that he had commended Martin Luther, and thought that he had done well in many things, as in having wife and children, &c.

Also for saying, "That whereas the doctors of the church have commanded priests to say mattens and evensong, they had no authority to do so." For which he was abjured, and was enjoyned penance.

John Ryburn, A.D. 1530.—It was testified against John Ryburn, by his sister Elizabeth Ryburn, being put to her oath, that she coming to him upon the Assumption eve, found him at supper with butter and eggs, and being bid to sit down and eat with him, she answered, that it was not a convenient time then to eat. To whom he said again, "That God never made such fasting days; but you," quoth he, "are so far in Limbo Patrum, that you can never turn again." And in further communication, when she said that she would go on pilgrimage to the holy cross at Wendover; he said again, that she did wrong, "For there is never a step," said he, "that you take in going on pilgrimage, but you go to the devil; and you go to church to worship what the priest holds above his head, which is but bread; and if you cast it to the mouse he will eat it;" and said, that he would never believe that the priest has power to make his Lord.

Also, it was testified by another sister named Alice Ryburn, that she, being with her brother in a close called Brimer's-close, heard him say these words, "That a time shall come when no elevation shall be made." Whereunto she answering again, asked, "And what service shall we have then?" He said, "That service that we have now."

John Simonds.—It was laid against John Simonds, for saying that men walk all day in purgatory in this world, and when they depart out of this world, there are but two ways, either to hell or heaven.

He said, too, that priests should have wives.

It was reported by the confession of John Simonds, that he converted to his doctrine eight priests, and had helped two or three friars out of their orders.

William Wingrave, Thomas Hawks of Hichenden, Robert Hawks of Westwycomb, John Taylor, John Hawks, Thomas Hern of Cobshill, Nicholas Field, Richard Dean, Thomas Clerk the younger, William Hawks of Chesham, A.D. 1530.

These persons, with others, were examined, excommunicated and abjured, for being together in John Taylor's house at Hichenden, and there hearing Nicholas Field of London read a portion of scripture in English, and the expounding many things to them; for saying, that they who went on pilgrimage were accursed; that it booted not to pray to images, for they were but stocks made of wood, and could not help a man; that God Almighty biddeth us work, as well on one day as another, saving the Sunday, for six days he wrought, and the seventh day he rested; that they needed not to fast so many fasting days, except the embering days; for he had been beyond the seas in Germany, and there they used not so to fast, nor to make such holidays.

That offerings do no good, for they have them that have no need thereof. And when it was answered again by one, that they maintained God's service, "Nay," said Nicholas, "it maintained great houses, as abbeys and others."

That men should say their Paternoster and Ave Maria in English, with the creed, and declare the same in English.

That the sacrament of the altar was not, as it was pretended, the flesh, blood, and bone of Christ, but a sacrament, that is, a typical signification of his holy body.

To William Wingrave moreover it was objected, that he should say, that there was no purgatory; and if there were any purgatory, and every mass that is said should deliver a soul out of purgatory, there should be never a soul there; for that there were more masses said in a day than bodies buried in a month.

Simon Wisdom, of Burford was charged in judgment for having three books in English, one was the gospels in English, another was the psalter, the third was the sum of the holy scripture in English.

*James Algar of Aiger, A.D.*1530.—It was stated and objected to James Algar, first, that he speaking to a certain doctor of divinity named Aglionby, said, that every true christian man living after the laws of God, and observing his commandments, is a priest as well as he, &c.

That he would not have his executors to pay a penny for his soul after his death; for he would do it with his own hands while he was alive; and that his conscience told him, that the soul, so soon as it departs out of the body, goes straight either to heaven or hell.

When Dr. Aglionby had alleged to him the place of St. Matthew, chap. xvi., "Thou art Peter," &c., he answered him again with that which followeth in the gospel after, "Get thee behind me, Satan," &c.

The said James, hearing of a certain church to be robbed, said openly, it made no great force, for the church hath enough already.

Now, passing from the abjurations of those poor men, we will speak something of the life and doings of the other party who were their persecutors, and chief rulers then of the church, that it may be better discerned and judged what manner of church that was which then so persecuted the true doctrine of Christ, and the members of his church.

A brief Discourse concerning the history of Thomas Wolsey, cardinal of York; wherein is to be seen the express image of the proud, vain-glorious church of Rome, how far it differs from the true church of Christ Jesus.

Although it be not very pertinent to our history, nor very requisite in these weighty matters of Christ's holy martyrs to discourse much of Thomas Wolsey, cardinal of York; yet, as there are many who are carried away with a wrong opinion and estimation of that false glittering church of Rome, therefore, that the vain pomp and pride of that ambitious church, so far differing from all pure christianity and godliness, may appear to all men, I shall describe the ridiculous and pompous qualities, and demeanour of this Thomas Wolsey. For as the Lacedemonians, in times past, were accustomed to show drunken men to their children, to behold and look upon, that through the foulness of that vice, they might inflame them the more to the study and desire of sobriety; even so it shall not be hurtful sometimes to set forth examples which are not honest, that others might gather the instructions of better and more upright dealing.

And first to begin with the first coming of this cardinal, and his fellow-cardinal Campegio into England: it was about the time that Pope Leo, intending to make war against the Turks, sent three legates together from Rome; one went into Germany, another into France, Campegio into England. When he was come to Calais and the cardinal of York had knowledge of it, he sent certain bishops and doctors, with as much speed as he could, to meet the legate, and to shew him that if he

would have his embassy effectual, he should send to Rome to have the cardinal of York made legate, and joined with him in the commission. He much affected this, doubting, lest his own authority might perhaps be diminished through the coming of the legate; and therefore required to be joined with him in the embassy. Campegio being a man easy of belief, and suspecting nothing, sent to Rome with such speed, that within thirty days after, the bull was brought to Calais, in which they were both equally joined in commission.

When all things were ready, Campegio passed the seas and landed at Dover, and proceeded towards London. At every town he was received with procession, accompanied with all the lords and gentlemen of Kent. And when he came to Blackheath, the duke of Norfolk met him with a great number of prelates, knights, and gentlemen, all richly apparelled, and brought him into a rich tent of cloth of gold, where he put on a cardinal's robe furred with ermines, and so took his mule, and rode towards London. Now mark the great humility in this church of the pope, and compare the same with the other church of the martyrs, and see which of them is most gospel-like.

This Campegio had eight mules of his own, laden with goods and treasures; but the cardinal of York not thinking them sufficient for his state, he sent him, the night before he came to London, twelve mules more, with empty coffers covered with red. The next day these twenty mules were led through the city, as though they had been laden with treasures, apparel, and other necessaries, to the great admiration of all men, that they should receive a legate with so great a treasure and riches. For so the common people always judged and esteemed the majesty of the clergy, by nothing but by their outward shew and pomp; but in the midst of this great admiration, there happened a ridiculous spectacle, to the great derision of their pride and ambition. For as the mules passed through Cheapside, and the people were pressing about them to behold and gaze, it happened that one of the mules breaking his collar, ran upon the other mules, by which it happened, that they running so together, and their girths being loosed, overthrew their burthens, and there appeared the cardinal's gay treasure, not without great laughter and scorn of many, especially of boys and girls, some of whom gathered up pieces of meat, others some pieces of bread and roasted eggs, some found horse-shoes and old boots, with such other baggage, crying out, "Behold here is my lord Cardinal's treasure!" The muleteers being greatly ashamed, gathered together their treasure again as well as they could and went forward.

About three o'clock, the 29th day of July, the cardinal himself was brought through the city, with great pomp and solemnity, to St. Paul's church, where when he had blessed all men with the bishop's blessing, as the manner is, he was guided to the cardinal of York's house, where he was received by the cardinal, and by him on the next day, being Sunday, was conducted to the king, to fulfil his embassy against the Turk, who might have destroyed all Hungary, while they were studying with what solemnity to furnish out their embassy.

The cardinal of York being thus a legate, set up a court, and called it the court of the legate, and proved testaments, and heard causes, to the great hinderance of all the bishops of the realm. He visited bishops, and all the clergy, exempt and not exempt; and under colour of reformation, he got much treasure, and nothing was reformed, but came to more mischief; for by example of his pride, priests and all spiritual persons waxed so proud, that they wore velvet and silk both in gowns, jackets, doublets, and shoes, and bare themselves so highly that no man durst reprove anything in them, for fear of being called heretic, and then they would make him smoke or bear a faggot. And then the cardinal himself was so elated, that he thought himself equal to the king; and when he had said mass, he made dukes and earls to serve him with wine, and to hold the basin while he washed.

This glorious cardinal in his tragical doings exceeded all measure of a good subject, and became more like a prince than a priest. When he had well stored his own coffers, he fetched the greatest part of the king's treasure out of the realm, in twelve great barrels full of gold and silver, to serve the pope's wars; and as his avaricious mind was never satisfied with getting, so his restless head was so busy meddling in public matters, that he never ceased before he had set England, France, Flanders, Spain and Italy together by the ears.

Thus the legate, following the steps of his master the pope, and both of them well displaying the nature of their religion, under the pretence of the church practised great hypocrisy, and under the authority of the king used great extortion, with excessive taxes and loans. and valuation of every man's substance, so plundering the commons and merchants, that every man complained, but no redress was had. Nor yet were the churchmen altogether free from this cardinal, who under his legatine power gave by anticipation all benefices belonging to spiritual persons; by which it is hard to say whether he purchased to himself more riches or hatred of the clergy. So far his licence stretched, that he had power to suppress divers abbeys, priories, and monasteries; and he did so, taking from them all their goods, moveables, and immovables, except it were a little pension left to the heads of certain houses. By the legatine power, he held general visitations through the realm, sending Doctor John Alein, his chaplain, riding in his gown of velvet, and with a great train, to visit all religious houses, at which the friars observant much complained, and would not submit to it; so that they were publicly cursed at St. Paul's cross, by friar Forrest, one of the same order; so that the cardinal at length prevailed both against them and all others. Great hatred arose against him among the people, perceiving how, by visitations, making of abbots, probates of testaments, granting of faculties, licences, and other means, he had made his treasure equal with the king's, and every year sent great sums to Rome. And this was their daily talk against the cardinal.

Besides many other matters and grievances which stirred the hearts of the commons against the cardinal, there was this one which much incensed them; the cardinal had sent out commissions in the king's name that every man should pay the sixth part of his goods. Whereupon there followed great muttering among the commons, so that it had almost grown to some riotous commotion or tumult, especially in parts of Suffolk, had not the dukes of Norfolk and Suffolk with wisdom and gentleness stept in and appeased the same.

Another thing that caused the anger of many, or rather which moved them to laugh at the cardinal, was his insolent presumption to take upon him, as the king's chief counsellor, to set a reformation in the king's household, making and establishing new ordinances. He likewise made new officers in the house of the duke of Richmond. In like manner he ordained a council, and established another household for the Lady Mary, being then princess. All this, with much more, he took upon him, making the king believe that all should be at his honour, and that he needed not to take any pains, so that the charge of all things was committed to him.

And now to express some part of the practices and busy intermeddlings of this cardinal in princes' wars, first here is to be noted, that after long wars between England and France, in 1525, it happened that the French king, coming with his army towards Milan, at the siege of Pavia, was there taken by the duke of Bourbon, and viceroy of Naples, and so led prisoner into Spain. All this while the cardinal held with the emperor, hoping by him to be made pope; but when that could not be obtained, he went clean from the emperor to the French king.

After this victory, and the French king being taken prisoner, through great labour and solicitation, as well of others as of the cardinal and king Henry, conditions were proposed between the French king and the emperor; among which conditions it was agreed, that they should resist the Turks and oppress the Lutherans, and so the king was set at liberty, leaving behind him his two eldest sons for pledges. But shortly after he re-

voked his oath, being absolved by the bishop of Rome, and he said that he was forced to swear, or else he should never have been delivered. A. D. 1526. Pope Clement VII., seeing the French king restored to liberty, and doubting the power of the emperor in Italy, absolves the French king from his oath, joins together a confederacy of Venetians and other princes against the emperor, bearing great hatred against all them that favoured the emperor's part, especially the family of Colonna in Rome; and therefore to shew his hatred against them, Clement said to Pompey, cardinal of that family, in threatening words, "That he would take away his cardinal's hat." To whom the cardinal answered, "That if he did, he would put on a helmet to overthrow the pope's triple crown." Whereby it may appear what holiness and virtue lies in the pope and cardinals of that catholic see of Rome.

Thus the pope, under the lying title of holiness, was the father of much mischief and of great wars. For the duke of Bourbon, and others of the emperor's captains, having intelligence of the pope's purpose and confederacy, gathered their army together, and after much bloodshed and fighting, about Milan and Cremona, at length approached and laid siege to Rome, and after three sharp assaults obtained the city, with the whole spoil; they besieged the pope with his cardinals, in the castle of St. Angelo, and took him prisoner, A. D. 1527. The cause of the besieging of Rome you have heard; the manner of the taking of Rome and of the pope is thus described:

The sacking of Rome and taking of Pope Clement.

The emperor's army departing from Florence, took counsel to go to Rome, and they travelled by night and day, commonly travelling forty miles in a day and night, so that on the sixth day of May, with banners displayed, they came before the city of Rome, the Romans made bulwarks, ramparts, and other defences, and placed ordnance on the walls, and shot at them fiercely.

The duke of Bourbon determined that it was not best to lie still and be slain with ordnance, considering that they were all simple people, and without great ordnance; wherefore he determined to give the assault, and they manfully approached the walls. But the Romans valiantly defended them with guns, pikes, stones, and other weapons, so that their enemies were compelled to retreat. Then the Romans were glad and set many fair banners on their towers and bulwarks, and made great shouts; which the duke of Bourbon seeing, cried to a new assault. Then every man with a ladder mounted the walls; and at the first encounter, again the Romans drove them back, which the duke of Bourbon perceiving, cried, 'God and the emperor!' Then every man manfully set on. There was a sore fight; many an arrow shot, and many a man slain; but at last the emperor's men got the wall. At the three assaults were slain three hundred Switzers of the pope's guard. In this last assault the duke of Bourbon was wounded in the thigh with a gunshot, of which he shortly after died; and notwithstanding this, the army entered into Rome, and took the pope's palace, and set up the emperor's arms.

The same day that these three assaults were made, Pope Clement thought little of the emperor's army; for he had cursed them on the Saturday before; and when he was hearing mass, suddenly the Germans entered into the church, and slew his guard and others. He fled in all haste by a secret way to the castle of St. Angelo, and all that followed him and could not enter, were slain; and if he had been taken he had been slain. The cardinals and other prelates fled to the castle of St. Angelo, over the bridge, where many of the common people were trodden down as they gave way to the cardinals and other estates, that passed toward the castle for succour.

The pope was in the castle of St. Angelo, and with him were four-and-twenty cardinals, one thousand prelates and priests, five hundred gentlemen, and five hundred soldiers; immediately the captains determined to lay siege to the castle of St. Angelo. In the mean time the soldiers fell to spoil. Never was Rome so plundered either by the Goths or Vandals; for the soldiers were not content with the spoil of the citizens, but they robbed the churches, broke up the houses of close religious persons, and overthrew the cloisters.

The duke D'Urbino, with fifteen thousand men, came to aid the pope; but hearing that Rome was taken, he tarried forty miles from Rome, till he heard again. The marquis of Saluce, and Sir Frederico de Bodso, with fifteen thousand footmen, and a thousand horsemen, were at Virterbo, where, hearing that the city of Rome was taken, they also tarried. The cardinal of Colonna came with an army of Neapolitans to help the emperor's men, but when he saw the cruelty of the soldiers, he did little to help them, but he hated them much.

The bishop of Rome was thus besieged till the 8th of July; at which day he yielded; and then he was restored to give graces, and grant bulls as he did before; but he tarried still in the castle of St. Angelo, and had a great number of Germans and Spaniards to keep him; but the Spaniards bare most rule in the castle, for no man entered, nor came out of the castle but by them. When the month of July came, corn began to fail in Rome, and the pestilence began to wax strong; wherefore the great army removed to a place called Nervia, forty miles from Rome, leaving behind them such as kept the bishop of Rome.

When the cardinal here in England heard how his father of Rome was taken prisoner, he began to bestir himself, and he laboured with the king all that he might, to stir him up to fight with the pope against the emperor, and to be a defender of the church, which if he would do, the cardinal persuaded him that he should receive great reward at God's hand. The king answered and said, "My Lord, I more lament this evil chance than my tongue can tell; but when you say that I am the defender of the faith, I assure you, that this war between the emperor and the pope is not for the faith, but for temporal possessions and dominions; and now if Pope Clement is taken by men of war, what should I do? My person nor my people cannot rescue him; but if my treasure may help him, take that which seems to you most convenient."

Thus the cardinal, when he could not obtain at the king's hands what he wished, in stirring him up to mortal war, he made out of the king's treasure twelve score thousand pounds, which he carried over the sea with him. After this, the cardinal sent his commission as legate, to all the bishops, commanding fastings and solemn processions to be had.

The cardinal, passing the seas with these sums of money, departed from Calais, accompanied with Cuthbert Tonstal, bishop of London, the lord Sands, the king's chamberlain, the earl of Derby, Sir Henry Guildford, and Sir Thomas More, with many other knights and squires, to the number of twelve hundred horse, and having in his carriage fourscore wagons, and threescore mules and horses of burden.

It were long to discourse in this place of the manifold abuses and treasons which he practised when he came to the French court, in converting the great sums of money which he had obtained of the king for the relief and ransom of Pope Clement, who at that time was prisoner in the emperor's army, and in bestowing it in the hiring of soldiers, and furnishing out the French king's army; appointing also certain English captains, in the king of England's name, to go against the emperor, to rescue the pope; all which army was paid with the king of England's money.

Besides that, he privily by his letters caused Clarent, king-at-arms, to join with the French herald, and openly to defy the emperor; by which there began great displeasure between the emperor and the king.

When, as the Spanish ambassador complained to the cardinal, he laid all the fault upon Clarent; saying that Clarent had defied the emperor, without the king's knowledge, at the request of the herald of France: and therefore at his return he should lose his head at Calais. Clarent being informed of this, took shipping and came to England, into the king's presence before the cardinal knew of it. Where he shewed the king the cardinal's

letter of commission, and declared the whole circumstances. When the king heard the whole circumstances, and had a while mused upon it, he said, "O Lord Jesus! he that I trusted most, told me all these things differently. Well, Clarent, I will no more be so light of credence hereafter; for now I see well that I have been made believe the thing that was never done." And from that time forward the king never put any more confidence in the cardinal.

The cause why the cardinal bore the emperor all this malice appears to be this, that when Pope Clement was taken prisoner, he wrote to the emperor and requested that he should make him pope. But when he received an answer that did not please him, he waxed furious, and sought all means to displease the emperor, writing many menacing letters, that if he would not make him pope, he would make such a strife betwixt Christian princes as had not been for a hundred years before, so as to make the emperor repent it, even though it should cost the whole realm of England.

The emperor made answer in a little book to the many menacings of the cardinal, but especially to his threat, that if he would not make him pope, he would fetch such a strife betwixt Christian princes as had not been for a hundred years, though it should cost the whole realm of England. The emperor bid him look well about him, lest through his attempts he might bring the matter in that case, that it should cost him the realm of England indeed.

You have heard before, how that when Pope Clement was prisoner in the emperor's army, the cardinal required the king, because he bore the title of "Defender of the faith," that he would rescue the pope. Now, by what means, and upon what occasion this title of the "defender of the faith was given to the king, we think it good to say somewhat in this place. When Martin Luther had denounced and opposed the abomination of the pope and his clergy, and many books were come into England, the cardinal here thinking to find a remedy, sent immediately to Rome for this title of "defender of the faith."

When this glorious title was come from Rome, the cardinal brought it to the king at Greenwich; and though the king had had it already, and had read it, yet against the morning were all the lords and gentlemen sent for, that could in so short a space be gathered, to come and receive it with honour. In the morning the cardinal went through the back way into the friars observants, and part of the gentlemen went round about, and welcomed him from Rome: part met him half way, and some at the court-gate. The king himself met him in the hall, and brought him up into a great chamber, where was a seat prepared on high for the king and the cardinal to sit on, while the bull was read. Which pomp all men of wisdom and understanding laughed to scorn.

This done, the king went to his chapel to hear mass, accompanied with many nobles of his realm, and ambassadors of sundry princes. The cardinal being revested to sing mass, the earl of Essex brought the bason of water, the duke of Suffolk gave the assay, and the duke of Norfolk held the towel, and so he proceeded to mass. When mass was done, the bull was again published, the trumpets blew, the shawms and sackbuts played in honour of the king's new title. Then the king went to dinner; in the midst of which the king of heralds and his company began the largest, crying "*Henricus, Dei Gratia, Rex Angliæ et Franciæ, Defensor Fidei, et Dominicus Hiberniæ.*" Thus were all things ended with great solemnity.

All this while the cardinal was aspiring to be made pope, and with that view he had Stephen Gardiner shortly after sent ambassador to Rome, in the time of Pope Clement VII.; and that for two special causes, one was about the king's divorce, the other for promoting the cardinal to be pope. As touching the divorce we will speak hereafter. In the meantime as concerning the advancement of the cardinal, great labour was made, as may appear in the letters, sent from the cardinal to Stephen Gardener, in which letters he solicited Gardener, by all means to pursue the suit, desiring him to stick at no cost, so far as six or seven thousand pounds would stretch; for more, he said, he would not give for the triple crown. Mark here, christian reader, what an holy catholic church this is!

But we may here learn, how man purposes one thing and how God disposes another. For the king's purpose was to have the cardinal and legate of York placed in the papal see, thinking by that means, if this cardinal had been pope, his divorce might more easily be compassed, which otherwise he thought impossible to contrive. But God omnipotent, who only is the director of all affairs, brought it otherwise to pass, not as the king devised, but after his own wisdom; so that both the divorce was concluded, and yet neither Cardinal Wolsey was made pope, nor yet had Pope Clement died. Yea, he so ruled the matter, that notwithstanding Pope Clement was alive, yet both the divorce proceeded, and also the pope's authority was thereby utterly extinct and abolished out of this realm of England, to the singular admiration of God's wondrous works, and perpetual praise to his merciful goodness. Of which divorce, and suppressing of the pope's authority, we have to make declaration. But first, as we have begun with the cardinal of York, so we will make an end of him. That done, we will address ourselves to other matters of more importance.

As the ambassadors were travelling to Rome to promote the cardinal to be pope, although the pope was not yet dead, the cardinal in the meantime was playing the popish persecutor here at home. For first, he, sitting in his pontifical robes in the cathedral church of St. Paul's, under his cloth of state of rich cloth of gold, caused Friar Barnes, an Augustinian Friar, to bear a fagot, for some points which he called heresy. Also he caused two merchants to bear fagots for eating flesh on a Friday. At this time, the bishop of Rochester made a sermon against Martin Luther, who had written against the power of the bishop of Rome. This bishop in his sermon spake so much of the honour of the pope and his cardinals, and of their dignity and pre-eminency, that he forgot to speak of the gospel which he took in hand to declare.

After this, the cardinal, A.D. 1528, sitting at Westminster as legate, called before him the whole clergy, and there promised that all abuses of the church should be amended : but nothing else was done, save only he caused Thomas Arthur, Thomas Bilney, Geoffery Loni, and Thomas Gerrard, to abjure for speaking against the pope's authority, and his pompous pride.

The next year, (A.D. 1529,) the question of the king's marriage began to be revived. Upon which Cardinal Campegro was sent again into England from Rome, for the hearing and debating of the matter. He with Cardinal Wolsey, consulting with the king, although at first he seemed to incline to the king's wishes, yet afterwards perceiving the consequence of the case, that it might shake perhaps the chair of the pope's authority, if this case were thoroughly decided by the truth of God's word; he therefore, slipping his neck out of the collar, craftily betook himself out of the realm, before the appointed day came for determination. The king, thus seeing himself disappointed with false promises, and craftily deluded by the cardinals, and after so many delays and long expectation, and nothing concluded; he was grieved in his mind with them, but especially with Cardinal Wolsey, whom he had before so highly exalted, and promoted to so many great dignities; as to the archbishoprick of York, the bishoprick of Winchester, of Durham, the abbey of St. Alban's, besides the chancellorship of England, and many other high offices and preferments in the realm; this induced him to cast him out of favour, so that after that time he never came more into the king's presence.

Then followed a council of the nobles, which was summoned for the 1st of October. During which council all the lords and others of the king's council, resorted to Windsor to the king, and informed the king, that almost all things which Wolsey had done, by his legatine power, were in the case of præmunire : and that the cardinal had thereby forfeited all his lands, tenements, goods and chattels

to the king : so the king caused his attorney, Christopher Hales, to sue out a writ of præmunire against him.

And on the 17th of November, he sent the two dukes of Norfolk and Suffolk to his palace of Westminster, to bring the great seal of England ; which he was unwilling to deliver.

Besides this, the king sent Sir William Fitzwilliams, knight of the garter, and treasurer of his house, and Doctor Stephen Gardiner, newly-made secretary, to see that no goods should be embezzled out of his house : and further ordained, that the cardinal should remove to Esher, beside Kingston, there to wait the king's pleasure, and to have all things delivered to him, which were necessary for him, but not after his old pompous and superfluous fashion; for all his goods were seized to the king's use. When the seal was thus taken from the cardinal, the dukes of Norfolk and Suffolk, with many earls, bishops, and barons, came to the Starchamber on the 19th of October, when the duke of Norfolk declared, that the king's highness for many and various offences had taken from him his great seal and deposed him from all his offices : and lest men might complain for lack of justice, he had appointed him and the duke of Suffolk, with the assent of the other lords, to sit in the chamber, to hear and determine causes : and so that week they sate in the Star-chamber, and determined causes.

A few days after, in the same month, the cardinal removed out of his house called York place : and so he took his barge, and went to Putney by water, and there took his horse and rode to Esher, where he remained till after Lent.

During which time, being called for an answer in the king's bench to the præmunire, for giving benefices by pre-emption, in disturbance of men's inheritance, and other open causes in the præmunire, according to the king's license, he constituted John Scute and Edmond Jenney, apprentices of the law, his attorneys, who by his own warrant signed with his own hand, confessed all things concerning the siut, for they were too open to be cloaked or hidden ; and so judgment was given, that he should forfeit all his lands, tenements, goods, and chattles and should be out of the king's protection ; but for all that, the king sent him a sufficient protection, and of his gentleness left to him the bishoprics of York and Winchester, and gave him plate and stuff convenient for his degree; and the bishopric of Durham he gave to Doctor Tonstal bishop of London, and the abbey of St. Alban's he gave to the prior of Norwich : and to London he promoted Doctor John Stokesley, the ambassador to the universities, for the marriage, as you have heard before. For all this kindness shewed to the cardinal, yet still he maligned the king, as we shall hereafter relate. But first we will proceed in the course of these matters, as they passed in order.

The following year, A.D. 1530, in the month of November, was summoned a general parliament, to be held at Westminster. In which year, about the 23rd day of October, the king came to his manor of Greenwich, and there consulted with his council, for a meet man to be his chancellor, so that in no wise he were a man of the clergy : and so after long debate, the king resolved to appoint Sir Thomas More, knight, chancellor of the duchy of Lancaster, a man well learned in the languages, and also in the common law ; whose wit was fine, and full of imagination.

We stated before, how a council of the nobles was appointed by the king in October, to assemble in the Star-chamber about the cardinal's matter : and also how a parliament was summoned to begin in the month of November, in the following year, 1530. At the beginning of which parliament, after More the new chancellor had finished his oration, the commons were commanded to choose a speaker, who was Thomas Audley, Esquire, and attorney to the duchy of Lancaster. Thus the parliament being begun the sixth day of November, at Westminster, where the king with all the lords were set in the parliament chamber, the commons, after they had presented their speaker, assembled in the lower house, and began to debate upon their grievances, wherewith the clergy had grievously oppressed them, contrary both to all right, and to the law of the realm, and especially in these six great causes.

Grievances against the Clergy of England.

1. The first, for the excessive fines which the ordinaries took for probates of testaments, so that Sir Henry Guilford, knight of the garter, and controller of the king's house, declared in the open parliament, that he and others being executors to Sir William Compton, knight, paid for the probate of his will, to the cardinal and the archbishop of Canterbury, a thousand marks sterling.

2. The second cause was, the great taxing and extreme exaction which the spiritual men used, in taking of presents, or mortuaries.

3. The third cause was, that priests being surveyors, stewards, and officers to bishops, abbots, and other spiritual heads, held and occupied farms, granges, and grazing in every county, so that the poor husbandmen could have nothing but from them, and yet for that they paid dearly.

4. The fourth cause was, that abbots, priors, and spiritual men kept tan-houses, and bought and sold wool, cloth, and all manner of merchandise, as other temporal merchants did.

5. The fifth cause was, because the spiritual persons who were promoted to great benefices, and having their livings of their flock, were lying in the court in lords' houses, and took every thing from their parishioners, and spent nothing on them: so that for want of residence both the poor of the parish lacked refreshing, and universally all the parishioners lacked preaching and true instruction of God's word, to the great peril of their souls.

6. The sixth cause was, because one priest, being little learned, had ten or twelve benefices, and was resident on none, and many well learned scholars in the university, who were able to preach and teach, had neither benefice nor exhibition.

These things before this time might in no wise be touched, nor yet talked of by any man, except he would be made an heretic, or lose all that he had: for the bishops were chancellors, and had all the rule about the king, so that no man durst once presume to attempt any thing contrary to their profit or commodity.

But now, when God had illuminated the eyes of the king, and the time so served, that men dare more boldly express what they had long conceived in their heart against the clergy; the burgesses of the parliament appointed men learned in the law, to draw one bill of the probates of testaments, another for mortuaries, and the third for non-residence, pluralities, and taking farms by spiritual men.

Now to return to the cardinal again. During the time of the parliament, there was brought down to the commons the book of articles which the lords had put up to the king against the cardinal. The chief articles were these.

Articles objected against Cardinal Wolsey.

1. First, that he without the king's consent had procured himself to be appointed a legate, by which he took away the right of all bishops and spiritual persons.

2. In all writing that he wrote to Rome, or to any other prince, he wrote *Ego et Rex meus*, "I and my king," as one who would say, that the king was his servant.

3. That he slandered the church of England to the court of Rome: for his suggestion to be legate, was to reform the church of England.

4. He without the king's consent carried the king's great seal with him into Flanders, when he was sent ambassador to the emperor.

5. Without the king's consent he sent a commission to Sir Gregory de Cassali, knight, to conclude a league between the king and the duke of Ferrara.

6. That he caused the cardinal's hat to be put on the king's coin.

7. That he had sent innumerable substance to Rome, for the obtaining of his dignities, to the great impover-

ishment of the realm. With many other things which are touched more at large in chronicles.

These articles, with many more, being read in the commons' house, were confessed by the cardinal, and signed with his hand. Also there was shewn another writing sealed with his seal, by which he gave to the king all his possessions.

You have heard, how the cardinal was attainted in the præmunire, and how he was put out of the office of the chancellor, and lay at Esher: which was in 1530. The next year after, in the Lent season, the king by the advice of his council, licensed him to go into his diocese of York, and gave him command to keep within his diocese, and not to return southward, without the king's special license in writing.

So he made great provision to go northward, and newly apparelled his servants, and bought many costly things for his household. But some of his servants at this time departed from him to the king's service, and especially Thomas Cromwell, one of his chief council, and principal agent for him in the suppression of abbeys. After all things necessary for his journey were prepared, he took his journey northward, till he came to Southwell, which was in his diocese, and there he continued that year, but the lands he had given to his colleges in Oxford and Ipswich were now come to the king's hands, by his attainder in the præmunire: and yet the king of his gentleness, and for favour that he bore to good learning, erected again the college in Oxford, and where it was named the Cardinal's College, he called it the King's College, and endowed it with fair possessions, and ordained new statues and ordinances; and because the college of Ipswich was thought not to be profitable, he left that dissolved,

Notwithstanding that the cardinal of York was thus attainted in the præmunire, yet the king being good to him, had granted him the bishoprics of York and Winchester, with great substance, and had licensed him to abide in his diocese of York, where he so continued the space of a year. But in the year following, which was A.D. 1531, he wrote to the court of Rome, and to other princes, letters in reproach of the king, and, as much as in him lay, he stirred them to revenge his cause against the king and his realm, so that opprobrious words against the king were spoken to Doctor Edward Karne, the king's ambassador at Rome. And it was said to him, that on the cardinal's account the king should have the worse speed in the suit of his divorce and marriage. The cardinal also would speak fair to the people, to win their hearts, and declared ever that he was unjustly and untruly dealt with. Which fair speaking made many men believe that he spoke truly. And to gentlemen he gave great gifts to allure them to him; and to be had in more reputation among the people, he determined to be installed, or enthroned at York, with all the pomp that might be, and caused a throne to be erected in the cathedral church to such a height and fashion as was never seen, and sent to all the lords, abbots, priors, knights, esquires, and gentlemen of his diocese, to be at his manor of Cawood, on the sixth day of Nov., and so to bring him to York with all manner of pomp and solemnity.

The king, who knew of his doings, dissembled the matter, to see what he would do at length, till finding his proud heart so highly exalted, that he would be triumphantly installed without making the king privy, yea, and in a manner in disdain of the king, he thought it not meet nor convenient to suffer him any longer to continue in his malicious and proud purposes. Wherefore he directed his letters to the earl of Northumberland, commanding him with all diligence to arrest the cardinal, and to deliver him to the earl of Shrewsbury, great steward of the king's household. When the earl had seen the letters, he with a convenient number came to the manor of Cawood, on the 4th of Nov., and when he was brought to the cardinal in his chamber, he said to him: "My lord, I pray you be patient, for here I arrest you." "Arrest me!" said the cardinal. "Yea, said the earl; "I have a commandment so to do." "You have no such power," said the cardinal; "for I am both a cardinal, and a legate De Latere, and a peer of the college of Rome, and ought not to be arrested by any temporal power; for I am not subject to that power; wherefore, if you arrest me I will withstand it." "Well," said the earl, "here is the king's commission, and therefore I charge you to obey." The cardinal somewhat remembered himself, and said: "Well, my lord, I am content to obey; but although by negligence I fell into the punishment of the præmunire, and lost by the law all my lands and goods, yet my person was in the king's protection, and I was pardoned that offence; wherefore I marvel why I now should be arrested, and especially considering that I am a member of the see apostolic, on whom no temporal man ought to lay violent hands. I see the king lacketh good counsel." "Well," said the earl; "when I was sworn warden of the marshes, you yourself told me, I might with my staff arrest all men under the degree of a king; and now I am stronger, for I have a commission so to do, which you have seen." The cardinal at length obeyed, and was kept in a privy chamber, and his goods seized, and his officers discharged.

When the cardinal was thus arrested, the king sent Sir William Kingston, knight, captain of the guard, and constable of the Tower of London, with yeomen of the guard to Sheffield, to fetch the cardinal to the Tower. When the cardinal saw the captain of the guard, he was astonished, and shortly became sick; for he perceived some great trouble coming on him, and he took so much of a strong purgation, that his nature was not able to bear it. But Sir William Kingston comforted him, and by easy journeys brought him to the abbey of Leicester, on the 27th of Nov., where, for very feebleness of nature, caused by purgations and vomits, he died the second night following, and lies buried in the abbey.

By the ambitious pride and excessive worldly wealth of this one cardinal, all men may easily understand and judge what the state and condition of all the rest of the same order was in those days, as well in all other places of Christendom, as especially here in England, where the princely possessions and great pride of the clergy did not only far exceed the common measure and order of subjects, but also surmounted over kings and princes, and all other estates.

Among other acts of the cardinal, this is not to be forgotten, that he founded a new college in Oxford, for the supply of which he had gathered together all the best learned men he could, among which number were these: Clark, Tindal, Sommer, Frith, and Taverner, with others, who, holding an assembly together in the college, were accounted to be heretics, and were cast into a prison of the college where salt fish lay, and through the smell of which the most part of them were infected, and Clark being a tender young man, and the most singular in learning among them all, died in the prison.

And thus having detained the reader enough, or rather too much, with this vain-glorious cardinal, now we will bring back our history again to more fruitful matter, and, as the order of time requireth, we will first begin with Master Humphry Mummuth, a virtuous and a good alderman of London, who in the time of the cardinal was troubled, as in the history here followeth:

The trouble of Humphry Mummuth, Alderman of London.

Master Humphry Mummuth was a right godly and sincere alderman of London, who in the days of Cardinal Wolsey was troubled and put in the Tower, for the gospel of Christ, and for maintaining them that favoured it.

Stokesley, then bishop of London, objected articles to him, to the number of four-and-twenty; as for adhering to Luther and his opinions; for having and reading heretical books and treatises; for giving exhibition to William Tindal, Joy, and such others; for helping them over the sea to Luther; for ministering private help to translate, as well the Testament, as other books into English; for eating flesh in Lent; for affirming that faith only justifies; for derogating from men's constitutions;

for not praying to saints, not allowing pilgrimage, auricular confession, or the pope's pardons; briefly, for being an advancer of all Martin Luther's opinions, &c.

Being examined and cast into the Tower, he at last was compelled to make his suit or purgation, writing to the cardinal, then lord chancellor, and the whole council, out of the Tower. In which he answered to the accusation of those who charged him with certain books received from beyond the sea; also for his acquaintance with Master Tindall. He said, that he denied not, but that four years then past he had heard Tindall preach two or three sermons at St. Dunstan's in the West, and that afterwards meeting with Tindal, he had certain communication with him concerning his living, and was then told by him that he had none at all, but trusted to be in the bishop of London's service; for he then laboured to be his chaplain. But being refused by the bishop, he came again to Mummuth, and besought him to help him, who the same time took him into his house for half a year; where Tindal lived like a good priest, studying both night and day. He would eat but sodden meat by his good will, nor drink but small single beer. He was never seen in that house to wear linen about him, all the space of his being there. Whereupon Mummuth had the better liking to him, so that he promised him ten pounds, as he then said, for his father's and mother's souls, and all christian souls, with which money he afterwards sent him over to Hamburgh according to his promise. And yet not to him alone he gave this exhibition, but to others likewise who were not heretics; as to Doctor Royston, the bishop of London's chaplain, he exhibited forty or fifty pounds; to Doctor Wodiall, provincial of the Augustinian friars; as much or more to Doctor Watson, the king's chaplain; also to other scholars and priests; besides other charges bestowed upon religious houses, as upon the nunnery of Denney, above fifty pounds sterling.

And as touching his books, of which some were left with him by William Tindal, some he sent to him, and some were brought into his house, by whom he could not tell; these books, he said, did lie open in his house, for the space of two years together, he suspecting no harm to be in them. And moreover the same books being desired by different persons, as of the abbess of Denney, a friar of Greenwich, the father confessor of Sion, and many others, he let them have them, and yet never heard friar, priest, or laymen, find any fault with the books.

Thus he excusing himself, and moreover complaining of the loss of his credit by his imprisonment in the Tower, and of the injury to his trade, who was wont formerly to send abroad five hundred pieces of cloths, and set many clothiers to work in Suffolk, and in other places, of whom he bought all their cloths, who were now almost all undone; at length he was set at liberty, being forced to abjure, and after he was made knight by the king, and sheriff of London.

The History of Thomas Hitten.

Touching the memorial of Thomas Hitten, nothing remains in writing, but only his name, save that William Tindal in his apology against More, and also in another book intituled "The practice of prelates," once or twice makes mention of him. He was, says he, a preacher at Maidstone, whom the bishop of Canterbury, William Warham, and Fisher, bishop of Rochester, had long kept and tormented in prison with sundry torments, and notwithstanding that he continued constant; at last they burned him at Maidstone, for the constant and manifest testimony of Jesus Christ, and of his free grace and salvation, A.D. 1530.

Thomas Bilney, and Thomas Arthur, who abjured at Norwich, A. D. 1531.

In the history of Cardinal Wolsey, mention was made of some whom the Cardinal caused to abjure; as Bilney, Geoffery Loni, Garret, Barnes, and others, of whom we have now specially to treat. This Thomas Bilney was brought up in the University of Cambridge, even from a child, profiting in all kind of liberal sciences, even to the profession of both laws. But at last having got a better school-master, even the Holy Spirit of Christ, who endued his heart with the knowledge of better and more wholesome things, he came at last to this point, that, forsaking the knowledge of man's laws, he converted his study to those things which tended more unto godliness than profit.

As he was greatly inflamed with the love of true religion and godliness, even so there was in his heart an incredible desire to allure many to the same, desiring nothing more, than that he might stir up and encourage any to the love of Christ and sincere religion. Neither were his labours vain; for he converted many of his followers to the knowledge of the gospel, among which number was Thomas Arthur, and Master Hugh Latimer; Latimer at that time was cross-keeper at Cambridge, bringing it forth upon procession days. At last, Bilney, forsaking the University, went to many places, teaching and preaching, being associated with Arthur, who accompanied him from the University. The authority of Thomas Wolsey cardinal of York, of whom mention has been made before, at that time was great in England, but his pomp and pride much greater. Whereupon Bilney, with other good men, marvelling at the incredible insolence of the clergy, whom they could now no longer suffer or abide, began to shake and reprove this excessive pomp of the clergy, and also to question the authority of the bishop of Rome.

Then it was time for the cardinal to awake, and speedily to look about his business. Neither lacked he in this point any craft or subtlety of a serpent; for he understood well enough upon what slender a foundation their ambitious dignity was grounded, neither was he ignorant that their luciferous and proud kingdom could not long continue against the manifest word of God; especially if the light of the gospel should once open the eyes of men. For otherwise he did not greatly fear the power and displeasure of kings and princes. Only this he feared, the voice of Christ in his gospel, lest it should disclose and detect their hypocrisy and deceits, and force them to come into godly discipline: wherefore he thought good speedily in time to withstand these beginnings. So he caused Bilney and Arthur to be apprehended and cast into prison.

After this, on the 27th Nov. A.D. 1527, the cardinal accompanied with a great number of bishops, as the archbishop of Canterbury, Cuthbert of London, John of Rochester, Nicholas of Ely, John of Exeter, John of Lincoln, John of Bath and Wells, Henry of St. Asaph, with many other divines and lawyers, came into the chapter-house of Westminster, where master Thomas Bilney, and Thomas Arthur were brought before them, and the cardinal inquired of Master Bilney, whether he had, privately or publicly, preached or taught to the people the opinions of Luther or any other condemned by the church, contrary to the determination of the church. Bilney answered, that knowingly he had not preached or taught any of Luther's opinions, or any other, contrary to the catholic church. Then the cardinal asked him, whether he had not once made an oath before, That he should not preach, rehearse, or defend any of Luther's opinions, but should impugn the same every where? He answered, That he had made such an oath, but not lawfully. The cardinal then caused him to swear, to answer plainly to the articles and errors preached and set forth by him; as well in the city and diocese of London, as in the diocese of Norwich and other places, and that he should do it without any craft, qualifying or leaving out any part of the truth.

After he was thus sworn and examined, the cardinal proceeded to the examination of Master Thomas Arthur, causing him to take the like oath. Which done, he asked of him whether he had not once told Sir Thomas More, Kt., that in the sacrament of the altar there was not the very body of Christ? Which interrogatory he denied. Then the cardinal gave him time to deliberate till noon, and to bring in his answer in writing.

The second day of December, the bishops assembled again, and sware witnesses against Master Bilney. That

done they called for Master Arthur; to whose charge they laid these articles following.

Articles against Thomas Arthur.

1. That he exhorted the people in his prayers, to pray specially for those that are now in prison. Which article he denied.

2. That he said, Though men are restrained from preaching now-a-days, yet I may preach: First, By the authority of my lord cardinal; for I have his license. Secondly, By the authority of the University. Thirdly, By the pope. Fourthly, By the authority of God, where he saith, "Go preach the gospel to every creature." By which authority every man may preach, and there is neither bishop nor ordinary, nor yet the pope, that may make any law to prevent any man preaching the gospel. This article he confessed.

3. He said that when there were but a few holy and devout laws in the church, then men were afraid to offend them. Afterwards they made many laws for their advantage; and such as were pecuniary, those they observed; and such as are not pecuniary, those they regard not: and so now-a-days there are so many laws, that whether a man do ill or well, he shall be taken in the law. He confessed that he spake thus.

4. He said, Good people, if I should suffer persecution for the preaching of the gospel of God, yet there are seven thousand more that would preach the gospel of God as I do now. Therefore, good people, think not that if these tyrants and persecutors put a man to death, the preaching of the gospel is therefore to be forsaken. This article he confessed, except that he made no mention of tyrants.

5. That every man, yea, every layman, is a priest. He confessed that he spake such words, declaring in his sermon, that every christian man is a priest, offering up the sacrifice of prayer.

6. That men should not pray to saints in heaven, but only to God; and they should use no other mediator but Christ Jesus our only Redeemer. This article he denied.

7. He preached that they should not worship images of saints, which were nothing but stocks and stones. This he also denied.

8. He preached upon Whitsunday last, within the University of Cambridge, That a bachelor of divinity admitted of the University, or any other person having or knowing the gospel of God, should go forth and preach in every place: and if any bishop did accurse them for so doing, their curses would turn to the condemnation of themselves. He confessed this.

Which answers thus made and acknowledged, master Arthur did revoke and condemn the articles objected against him, and submitted himself to the punishment and judgment of the church.

The third day of December, the bishop of London with the other bishops assembling again, after Bilney had refused to return to the church of Rome, the bishop of London in discharge of his conscience (as he said) lest he should hide any thing that had come to his hands, exhibited to the notaries, in the presence of Master Bilney, certain letters, to wit, five letters or epistles, with one schedule in one of the epistles, containing his articles and answers folded therein, and another epistle folded in manner of a book, with six leaves; all which he commanded to be written out and registered, and the originals to be delivered to him again.

Here follows a Summary of certain Depositions, on the inquiry of Master Bilney's Doctrine and Preaching.

First, it was deposed, That in his sermon in Christ's church in Ipswich, he should preach and say, our Saviour Christ is our Mediator between us and the Father: what should we need then to seek any saint for a remedy? Wherefore, it is great injury to the blood of Christ, to make such petitions, and blasphemes our Saviour.

That man is so imperfect of himself, that he can in no wise merit by his own deeds.

Also, that the coming of Christ was long prophesied before, and desired by the prophets: but John Baptist, being more than a prophet, did not only prophesy, but with his finger shewed him: " Behold the Lamb of God which taketh away the sin of the world." Then if this were the very Lamb that taketh away the sins of the world, what an injury it is to our Saviour Christ, for any one to say that to be buried in St. Francis' Cowl should remit four parts of penance! what is then left to our Saviour Christ, who taketh away the sins of the world? This I will justify to be a great blasphemy to the blood of Christ.

Also, that it was a great folly to go on pilgrimage, and that preachers in times past have been antichrists; and now it hath pleased God somewhat to shew forth their falsehood and errors.

Also, that the miracles done at Walsingham, at Canterbury, and in Ipswich, were done by the devil, through the sufferance of God, to blind the poor people: and that the pope hath not the keys that Peter had, except he follow Peter in his living.

Moreover, it was deposed against him, That he was notoriously suspected as a heretic, and twice pulled out of the pulpit in the diocese of Norwich.

Also, it was deposed against him, That he, in the parish-church of Willesden, exhorted the people to put away their gods of silver and gold, and leave off their offerings to them. Also, that Jews and Saracens would have become christian men long ago, had it not been for the idolatry of christian men, in offering of candles, wax, and money to stocks and stones.

Over and besides these matters deposed against him, here follow other articles gathered out of his sermon, which he preached in the parish church of St. Magnus, in Whitsun week, (A.D. 1527.)

He said, pray only to God, and not to saints, in rehearsing the Litany; and when he came to " Holy Mary, pray for us," he said, Stop there.

He said, that christian men ought to worship God only, and not saints.

He said, that christian people should set up no lights before the images of saints: for saints in heaven need no light, and the images have no eyes to see.

He said, as Hezekiah destroyed the brazen serpent that Moses made by the commandment of God; even so should kings and princes now-a-days destroy and burn the images of saints set up in churches.

These five hundred years there has been no good pope, nor in all the times past can we find but fifty; for they have neither preached, nor lived well, or conformably to their dignity. Wherefore, till now they have born the keys of simony. Against whom, good people, we must preach to you. For we cannot come to them; it is a great pity: they have sore slandered the blood of Christ.

The people have foolishly of late gone upon pilgrimages, who had been better had they been at home.

Many have made vows, which are not possible for them to fulfil.

The preachers before this have been antichrists, and now it has pleased our Saviour Christ to shew their false errors, and to teach another way and manner of the holy gospel of Christ, to the comfort of your souls.

I trust that there shall and will come others besides me, who shall shew and preach to you the same faith and manner of living that I shew and preach to you, which is the very true gospel of our Saviour Christ, and the mind of the holy fathers, whereby you shall be brought from their errors, wherein you have been long seduced: for before this there have been many that have slandered you, and the gospel of our Saviour Christ.

These and many other such like charges were deposed against him by the deponents and witnesses. But now, before we return again to his examination, we here insert a dialogue between a friar named John Brusierd, and Master Thomas Bilney, as written down by the friar himself.

A Dialogue between Friar John Brusierd and Master Thomas Bilney, in Ipswich, concerning worshipping of Images.

Brusierd.—Although you have blasphemed most perniciously the immaculate flock of Christ with certain blasphemies, yet, being moved partly with our gentle petitions, partly pitying your case, I am come here to talk with you secretly. When you began to shoot the dart of your pestiferous error, more vehemently than you ought, against the breast of the ignorant multitude, you seem to pour upon the ground the precious blood of Christ, as with a certain vehement violence out of the miserable vessel of your heart. Where you said that none of the saints make intercession for us, nor obtain for us any thing, you have blasphemed the efficacy of the whole church, consecrated with the precious blood of Christ. Which thing you can not deny, especially as there is such incessant knocking at the gates of heaven, through the continual intercession of the saints, as appears in the sevenfold Litany.

Bilney.—I marvel at you, and cannot marvel enough, but that the vain custom of superstitious men, thinking themselves not heard but in much talking, doth put an end to my wonder. For our heavenly Father knoweth what we have need of before we ask. Also it is written, " There is one Mediator between God and men, the man Christ Jesus." If then there be but one Mediator between God and men, the man Christ Jesus, where is our blessed lady? Where is then St. Peter and other saints?

Brusierd.—I suppose that no man is ignorant, but that the divines of the primitive church have all affirmed that there is one Mediator between God and men. Neither could any at any time praise or pray to the saints, when yet they were living in the calamities of this body, and, wrestling with the winds of this world, were not yet come to the port of rest to which they were travelling. Paul (I grant) did rightly affirm that there was but one Mediator between God and men, for as yet there was no saint canonized or put into the Calendar. But now seeing the church knows, and certainly believes, through the undoubted revelations of God, that the blessed Virgin and other saints are placed in the bosom of Abraham, she, therefore, like a good mother, has taught, and that most diligently, her children, to praise the Omnipotent Jesus in his saints; and also to offer up by the same saints our petitions to God. It is that that the psalmist saith, " Praise ye the Lord in his saints." Rightly also do we say and affirm, That saints may pray for us. One man may pray for another, therefore, much more may saints that do enjoy the fruition of his High Majesty. For so it is written, " God is my witness, whom I serve in my spirit, in the gospel of his Son, that without ceasing I remember you in my prayer always for you," &c. Rom. i. 9.

Bilney.—I marvel that you, a learned man, are not yet delivered out of the dungeon of heresy through the help of the holy gospel: especially seeing that in the same gospel it is written, " Verily, verily, I say unto you, whatsoever you ask the Father in my name, he will give it you," John xvi. 23. He saith not, whatsoever ye ask the Father in the name of St. Peter, St. Paul, or other saints, but in *my* name. Let us ask therefore help in the name of Him, who is able to obtain for us whatever we ask, lest, peradventure, hereafter in the end of the world, at the judgment, we shall hear, " Hitherto in my name ye have asked nothing."

Brusierd.—Where ye marvel that I, a learned man, as you say, am not delivered yet from the dungeon of heresy through the help of the gospel: much more do you, who are far better learned than I, cause me to marvel at your foolish wonder. Nor can I choose but laugh at you, as one rapt to the third heaven of such high mysteries, and yet see not those things which are done here in the lower parts of philosophy: for what a ridiculous thing is it for a man to look so long upon the sun, that he can see nothing else but the sun? Moreover, what student is there in all Cambridge, be he never so young, that knows not, that the argument of authority, brought out negatively, has no force?

Bilney.—As the pharisees took Christ, so you take my words otherwise than I meant.

Brusierd.—Your words, which wander far from the scope of scripture, I do not like. What is in your meaning, and lies inwardly in your mind, I cannot tell.

Bilney.—Such as invoke the help either of Christ, or of any other saint, for any corporal infirmity, may be well resembled to delicate patients, who, being under the hand of physicians, and having medicines ministered for their diseases, not abiding the pain thereof, fling all away: therefore, I say, no man ought to implore the help of God, or of any saint, for corporal infirmity.

Brusierd.—O most pernicious and perilous heresy of all that ever I have heard! Thus you escaping from the smoke, fall into the fire, and, avoiding the danger of Scylla, you run upon Charybdis. O heart of man wrapped in palpable darkness! I wish, Master Bilney, that you would but once search out the first origin of these Rogation days: for so we read in the church history, that they were first ordained by Pope Gregory, with fasting, prayers, and holy processions, against the pestilence then reigning among the people. At which time, the people going in the procession, a certain image like to our blessed Lady, painted with the hands of St. Luke the evangelist, went before them, about which image, in the honour of the Virgin, angels sung this anthem: " O queen of heaven be glad," &c. To which anthem, the pope also adjoined this, " Pray to the Lord for us." Wherefore, seeing the angels worshipped the image of the glorious Virgin Mary, and seeing the holy father, Pope Gregory, with all the clergy, did pray for corporal infirmity, it appears manifestly that we ought to worship the saints, and also to give honour in a manner to their images: further, also, to pray to Almighty God and all saints for corporal infirmity, that we may be delivered from the same, so that they may say the like for us, which is said in the gospel, " Send them away, because they cry after us." And although there are infinite places in the holy scripture, wherewith we might easily resist your error, yet, standing herewith content, as sufficient, we will proceed to your second pestiferous error, wherein you, like an ungrateful child, go about to tear out the bowels of your mother. For whom you affirm blasphemously, the bishop of Rome to be the very antichrist, and that his privileges have no force against the gates of hell: in so saying, what do you but like a most unkind and unnatural child, spoil your loving mother of all her treasures, and wound her most miserably upon the earth? But as there is nothing so absurd, or so heretical, but shall be received by some itching ears: I would therefore now hear you declare, how he sits in the temple of God, as God, being exalted and worshipped above all that is named God, or how he sheweth himself as Lord in power and signs, and deceitful wonders.

Bilney.—Although incredulity does not suffer you to understand these things, yet I will help your incredulity, through the aid of the Lord, beseeching you, that setting all superstition apart, you will understand those things that are above. Do ye know the table of the ten commandments?

Brusierd.—According as the catholic doctors do expound them, I know them: but how you expound them I cannot tell.

Bilney.—And do you know also the constitutions of men, which are devised only by the dreams of men, to which men are so straightly bound, that under pain of death they are compelled to observe them?

Brusierd.—I know certain sanctions of the holy fathers, but such as you speak of as devised by men's dreams, I know none.

Bilney.—Now then let us set and compare these two together, and you shall easily understand that the bishop of Rome, whom they call the pope, sits in the temple of God, as God, to be extoled above all that is named God. It is written, " The temple of the Lord is holy, which temple ye are." Therefore the conscience of man is the temple of the Holy Ghost, in which temple, I will prove the pope to sit as God, and to be exalted above all that is called God. Whoso condemns the decalogue, or the table of the commandments of God, there is but a small punishment for him, neither is that punishment to death, but he that shall contemn or violate the constitutions, which you call the sanctions of men, is counted by all men's judgment guilty of death! What is this, but that the bishop of Rome sits and reigns in the temple of God; that is, in man's conscience, as God?

Brusierd.—Although this exposition seems unworthy for christian ears, yet I would hear you further how he shews himself in signs and deceitful wonders.

Bilney.—These wonders, which they call miracles, are wrought daily in the church, not by the power of God, as many think, but by the illusion of Satan, who, as the scripture witnesseth, has been loose five hundred years, according as it is written in the book of the Revelation, " After a thousand years Satan shall be loosed," &c. Neither are they to be called miracles of true christian men, but illusions rather, whereby to delude men's minds, to make them put their faith in our Lady, and in other saints, and not in God alone, to whom be honour and glory for ever.

Brusierd.—But that I believe and know that God and all his saints will take everlasting revenge upon thee, I would surely with these nails of mine be thy death, for this horrible and enormous injury against the precious blood of Christ. God saith, " I will not the death of a sinner, but rather that he be converted and live." And thou blasphemest him, as though he should lay secret snares of death for us that we should not know them. Which, if it were true, we might well say with Hugh de Saint Victore in this manner:—" If it be an error, it is of thee, O God, that we are deceived; for they be confirmed with such signs and wonders, as cannot be done but by Thee." But I am assured it is untrue and heretical: and therefore I will leave this matter, and will talk with you concerning the merits of saints. For once I remember, in a certain sermon of yours you said, " That no saint, though his suffering were never so great, and his life most pure, deserved any thing for us with God, either by his death or his life." Which is contrary to St. Augustine.

Bilney.—Christ saith one thing, St. Augustine another; Whether of these two shall we believe? For Christ, willing to deliver us out of this dark dungeon of ignorance, gave forth a certain parable of ten virgins, of which five were fools, and five were wise. By the five foolish virgins, wanting the oil of good works, he meant us all sinners. By the wise virgins he meant the company of all holy saints. Now let us hear what the five wise virgins answered to the five foolish, asking oil of them; " No," say they, " lest, peradventure, we have not sufficient for us, and for you. Go you rather to them that sell, and buy for yourselves." Wherefore, if they had not oil sufficient for themselves and also for the others, where then are the merits of saints wherewith they can deserve both for themselves and for us? I cannot see.

Brusierd.—You wrest the scriptures from the right understanding to a reprobate sense, that I am scarce able to hold mine eyes from tears, hearing with mine ears these words of you. Fare ye well.

The Submission of Master Thomas Bilney.

The fourth day of December, the bishop of London, with the other bishops his assistants, assembled again in the chapter-house of Westminster; where, also, Master Bilney was brought, and was exhorted and admonished to abjure and recant. Who answered, " That he would stand to his conscience." Then the bishop, after deliberation, putting off his cap, said, " In the name of the Father, and of the Son, and of the Holy Ghost, Amen. Let God arise and let his enemies be scattered:" and, making a cross on his forehead and his breast, by the counsel of the other bishops, he gave sentence against Master Bilney in this manner:—

I, by the consent and counsel of my brethren here

present, do pronounce thee, Thomas Bilney, who hast been accused of divers articles, to be convicted of heresy; and for the rest of the sentence we take deliberation till to-morrow.

The fifth day of December the bishops assembled there again; before whom Bilney was brought: whom the bishop asked if he would yet return to the unity of the church, and revoke his heresies which he had preached. Whereupon, Bilney answered, " That he would not be a slander to the gospel, trusting that he was not separate from the church; and that, if the multitude of witnesses might be credited, he might have thirty men of honest life on his part, against one to the contrary brought against him; which witnesses the bishop said came too late; for after publication they could not be received by the law.

In the afternoon, the bishop of London again asked him whether he would return to the church, and acknowledge his heresies. Bilney answered, that he trusted he was not separate from the church, and required time and place to bring in witnesses, which was refused. Then the bishop once again required of him, whether he would return to the Catholic church? He answered, that if they could teach and prove sufficiently that he was convicted, he would yield and submit himself, and desired again to have time and space to bring in again his refused witnesses, and other answer he would give none.

Being again asked whether he would return, or else the sentence must be read, he required the bishop to give him licence to deliberate until the morrow, whether he might abjure the heresies wherewith he was defamed, or no. The bishop granted him that he should have a little time to deliberate. But Bilney required space till the next morrow. But the bishop would not grant him his request, lest he should appeal. But at last the bishop granted him two nights respite to deliberate, that is to say, till Saturday, at nine o'clock, forenoon, and then to give a plain determinate answer.

The 7th day of December, the bishop of London, with the other bishops being assembled, Bilney also personally appeared. The bishop of London asked, whether he would now return to the unity of the church, and revoke the errors and heresies whereof he stood accused, detected, and convicted. Who answered, that now he was persuaded by his friends, he would submit himself, trusting that they would deal gently with him, both in his abjuration and penance. Then he desired that he might read his abjuration, which the bishop granted. When he had read the same secretly by himself, and was returned, being demanded what he would do in these premises, he answered, that he would abjure and submit himself, and there openly read his abjuration, and subscribed and delivered it to the bishop, who then absolved him, and for his penance enjoined him, that he should abide in prison appointed by the cardinal, till he were released by him; and, moreover, the next day he should go before the procession in the cathedral church of St. Paul's bare-headed, with a fagot on his shoulder, and should stand before the preacher at St. Paul's Cross, during the sermon.

After which abjuration, made about A.D. 1528, Bilney felt such repentance and sorrow, that he was near the point of utter despair, as is credibly testified by Master Latimer, whose words I here annex, written in his seventh sermon, preached before king Edward:—"I knew a man myself, Bilney, little Bilney, that blessed martyr of God, who what time he had borne his fagot, and was come again to Cambridge, had such conflicts within himself, (beholding this image of death,) that his friends were afraid to let him be alone. They were fain to be with him day and night, and comfort him as they could, but no comforts would serve. And as for the comfortable places of scripture, to bring them to him, it was as though a man should run him through the heart with a sword. Yet, for all this, he was revived, and took his death patiently, and died well against the tyrannical See of Rome."

Again, Master Latimer, speaking of Bilney in another of his sermons preached in Lincolnshire, has these words:—"That same Master Bilney, who was burned here

in England for the sake of God's word, was induced and persuaded by his friends to bear a fagot at the time when the cardinal was aloft, when bore the swinge. Now, when Bilney came to Cambridge again, a whole year after, he was in such an anguish and agony, that nothing did him good, neither eating nor drinking, nor any other communication of God's word, for he thought that all the whole scriptures were against him, and sounded to his condemnation. So that I many a time communed with him, (for I was familiarly acquainted with him), but all things whatever any man could allege to his comfort seemed to him to make against him. Yet, for all that, he afterwards came again. God endued him with such strength and perfectness of faith, that he not only confessed his faith in the gospel of our Saviour Jesus Christ, but also suffered his body to be burned for that same gospel's sake which we now preach in England,&c."

Furthermore, in the first sermon of Master Latimer, before the Duchess of Suffolk, he infers as follows:— "Here I have," said he, "occasion to tell you a story which happened at Cambridge. Master Bilney was the instrument whereby God called me to knowledge. For I may thank him, next to God, for that knowledge that I have in the word of God; for I was as obstinate a papist as any in England, insomuch, that when I should be made bachelor of divinity, my whole oration went against Philip Melancthon, and against his opinions. Bilney heard me at that time, and perceived that I was zealous without knowledge, came to me afterwards in my study, and desired me for God's sake to hear his confession. I did so, and, to say the truth, by his confession I learned more than before in many years. So, from that time forward, I began to inhale the word of God, and forsake the school-doctors and such fooleries, &c."

By this it appeareth how vehemently this good man was pierced with sorrow and remorse for his abjuration, for the space of nearly two years, that is, from the year 1529 to the year 1531. It followed then that he, by God's grace and good counsel, came at length to some quiet conscience, being fully resolved to give over his life for the confession of that truth which he had renounced. And thus being fully determined in his mind, he, in Trinity hall, at ten o'clock at night, took his leave of his friends, and said, that he would go to Jerusalem, alluding to the words and example of Christ in the gospel, going up to Jerusalem, when he was appointed to suffer his passion. And so Bilney, meaning to give over his life for the testimony of Christ's gospel, told his friends that he would go up to Jerusalem, and would see them no more: and immediately departed to Norfolk, and there preached, first privately in households, to confirm the brethren and sisters. Then he preached openly in the fields, confessing his sin, and preaching publicly the doctrine which he had abjured, to be the very truth, and desired all men to learn by him, and never to trust to their fleshly friends in causes of religion. And so setting forward in his journey toward the celestial Jerusalem, he departed from thence to Norwich, upon which he was apprehended and carried to prison.

Thomas Bilney, after his examination and condemnation before Doctor Pellas, doctor of law, and Chancellor, was first degraded by Suffragan Underwood, according to their popish manner, by the assistance of the friars and doctors. Which done, he was immediately committed to the lay power, and to the two sheriffs of the city, of whom Thomas Necton was one. This Thomas Necton was Bilney's especial friend, and sorry to receive him to such execution as followed. But such was the tyranny of that time, and dread of the chancellor and friars, that he could not do otherwise, but needs must receive him. Who notwithstanding, as he could not bear in his conscience himself to be present at his death; so, for the time that he was in his custody, he caused him to be more friendly looked to, and more wholesomely kept concerning his diet, than he was before.

After this, the Friday following, at night, which was before the day of his execution, Bilney had his friends resorting to him in the Guildhall, where he was kept. Some put him in mind, that though the fire, which he should suffer the next day, should be of great heat to his body, yet the comfort of God's Spirit should cool it to his everlasting refreshing. At this word Thomas Bilney putting his hand to the flame of the candle burning before them, and feeling the heat, O, said he, I feel by experience, and have known it long by philosophy, that fire by God's ordinance is naturally hot, but yet I am persuaded by God's holy word, and by the experience of some, mentioned in that word, that in the flame they felt no heat, and in the fire they felt no consumption: and I constantly believe, however the stubble of this my body shall be wasted by it, yet my soul and spirit shall be purged thereby; a pain for the time, whereon notwithstanding followeth joy unspeakable. And here he much treated of in this place of scripture. "Fear not, For I have redeemed thee, and called thee by thy name, thou art mine. When thou goest through the water I will be with thee, and the strong floods shall not overflow thee. When thou walkest in the fire, it shall not burn thee, and the flame shall not kindle upon thee, for I am the Lord thy God, the holy One of Israel."—Is. xliii. 1. Which he most comfortably treated of, as well in respect of himself, as applying it to the particular use of his friends. Of whom some took such sweet fruit that they caused the whole sentence to be fair written on tables, and some in their books. The comfort of which (on some of them) was never taken from them to their dying day.

The Saturday following, when the officers of execution with their gloves and halberts were ready to receive him, and to lead him to the place of execution without the city gate, called Bishop's Gate, in a low valley, commonly called The Lollards' Pit, under Saint Leonard's Hill, environed about with great hills, (which place was chosen for the people's quiet, sitting to see the execution) at the coming forth of Thomas Bilney out of the prison door one of his friends came to him, and with few words, spake to him, and prayed him in God's behalf to be constant, and to take his death as patiently as he could. Bilney answered, with a quiet and mild countenance, "Ye see when the mariner is entered his ship to sail on the troubled sea, how for a while he is tossed in the billows, but yet in hope, that he shall once come to the quiet haven, he bears in better comfort the perils which he feels: so am I now toward this sailing, and whatever storms I shall feel, yet shortly after shall my ship be in the haven, as I doubt not by the grace of God, desiring you to help me with your prayers to the same effect."

And so he going forth in the streets, giving much alms by the way by the hands of one of his friends, and accompanied with one doctor Warner, doctor of divinity, and parson of Winterton, whom he chose, as his old acquaintance, to be with him for his ghostly comfort; he came at last to the place of execution, and descended from the hill, apparelled in a layman's gown with his sleeves hanging down; and his arms out, his hair having been piteously mangled at his degradation, and drew near to the stake, and desired that he might speak some words to the people, and standing there, he said:—

"Good people, I am come hither to die, I was born to live under that condition, naturally to die again, and that ye might testify that I depart out of this present life, as a true christian man, in a right belief towards Almighty God, I will rehearse to you the articles of my creed:" and then he began to rehearse them in order, as they are in the common creed, with often elevating his eyes and hands to Almighty God, and at the article of Christ's Incarnation, having a little meditation in himself, and coming to the word crucified, he humbly bowed himself and made great reverence, and then proceeding in the articles, and coming to these words, " I believe the Catholic church," there he paused, and spake these words, " Good people, I must here confess to have offended the church, in preaching once contrary to her prohibition, at a poor cure belonging to Trinity Hall, in Cambridge, where I was a fellow, earnestly intreated to do so by the curate and other good people of the parish, shewing, that they had no sermon there for a long time before: and so moved in my conscience, I did make a poor

collation to them, and thereby ran into the disobedience of authority in the church;" however I trust at the general day, charity that moved me to this act, shall bear me out at the judgment seat of God;" and so he proceeded, without any words of recantation, or charging any man for procuring him his death.

This once done, he put off his gown, and went to the stake, and kneeling upon a little ledge coming out of the stake, on which he was afterwards to stand, to be better seen, he made his prayer with such earnest elevation of his eyes and hands to heaven, and in so good quiet behaviour, that he seemed not much to consider the terror of his death, and ended at the last his private prayers, with the 143rd Psalm, beginning, "Hear my prayer, O Lord, give ear to my supplications:" and the next verse, he repeated in deep meditation, thrice, "And enter not into judgment with thy servant, for in thy sight shall no man living be justified:" and so finishing that Psalm he ended his private prayers.

After that he turned himself to the officers, asking them if they were ready, and they answered, Yea. He then put off his jacket and doublet, and stood in his hose and shirt, and went to the stake, and the chain was cast about him; Doctor Warner came to him to bid him farewell, who spake but few words for weeping.

Thomas Bilney most gently smiled, and inclined his body to speak to him a few words of thanks, and the last were these, "Feed your flock, feed your flock, that when the Lord cometh, he may find you so doing: and farewell good master doctor, and pray for me;" and so he departed without any answer, sobbing and weeping. And while he thus stood upon the ledge at the stake, certain friars, doctors, and priors of their houses being present (as they were uncharitably and maliciously present at his examination and degradation, &c.) came to him and said, " O Master Bilney, the people are persuaded that we are the causers of your death, and that we have procured it, and it is likely that they will withdraw their charitable alms from us all, except you declare your charity towards us, and discharge us of the matter." Upon this Thomas Bilney spake with a loud voice to the people, " I pray you, good people, be never the worse to these men for my sake, as though they were the authors of my death; it was not they:" and so he ended.

Then the officers put reeds and fagots about his body, and set fire to them, which made a very great flame, and deformed his face, he holding up his hands, and knocking upon his breast, crying sometimes, "Jesus," sometimes " I believe." The flame was blown away from him by the violence of the wind, which was that day, and two or three days before very great: and so for a little pause he stood without flame, but soon the wood again took the flame, and then he gave up the ghost, and his body being withered, bowed downward upon the chain. Then one of the officers with his halbert smote out the staple in the stake behind him, and suffered his body to fall into the bottom of the fire, laying wood on it, and so he was consumed.

Thus have ye the true history, and martyrdom of this good man.

Master Stafford of Cambridge.

As the death of this godly Bilney did much good in Norfolk, where he was burned; so his diligent travel, in teaching and exhorting others, and example of life corresponding to his doctrine, left no small fruit behind him in Cambridge, being a great means of framing that University, and drawing many to Christ. Through him and partly also another called Master Stafford, the word of God began to spread there. Among them was Master Latimer, Doctor Barnes, Doctor Thistel of Pembroke Hall, Master Fooke, of Bennet College, and Master Soude of the same college, Doctor Warner above mentioned, with others.

This Master Stafford was then the public reader of the divinity lecture in that University: who, as he was a professor of Christ's gospel, so was he a diligent follower of that which he professed.

As the plague was then sore in Cambridge, and among

others a priest called Sir Henry Conjurer, lay sick of the plague, Master Stafford hearing of it, and seeing the horrible danger that his soul was in, was so moved in conscience to help the dangerous case of the priest, that, neglecting his own bodily health, to recover the other from eternal damnation, he came to him, exhorted, and so importuned him, that he would not leave him before he had converted him, and saw his conjuring books burned before his face. Which done, Mr. Stafford went home, and immediately sickened, and shortly after most christianly died.

Concerning this Master Stafford moreover it is to be noted, that Master Latimer, being yet a servant and a zealous papist, standing in the schools when Master Stafford read, persuaded the scholars not to hear him: and also preaching against him, exhorted the people not to believe him; and yet Latimer confessed himself, that he gave thanks to God, that he asked him forgiveness before he departed.

And thus much, by the way, of good Master Stafford, who, for his constant and godly perseverance in such a cause, may seem not unworthy to go with blessed Bilney in the fellowship of holy and blessed martyrs.

Account of Master Simon Fish.

Before the time of Bilney, and the fall of the cardinal, I should have placed the story of Simon Fish, with the book called The Supplication of Beggars, declaring how and by what means it came to the king's hand, and what effect followed, in the reformation of many things, especially of the clergy. But the missing of a few years in this matter breaks no great square in our history. The manner and circumstance of the matter is this.

After the light of the gospel, working mightily in Germany, began to spread its beams also in England, great stir and alteration followed in the hearts of many: so that coloured hypocrisy, and false doctrine, and painted holiness began to be discovered more and more by the reading of God's word. The authority of the bishop of Rome, and the glory of his cardinals was not so high, but such as had fresh wits, sparkled with God's grace, began to discern Christ from antichrist; that is, true sincerity from counterfeit religion. In the number of whom was Master Simon Fish, a gentleman of Gray's Inn. It happened the first year that this gentleman came to London, which was about A. D. 1525, that there was a play or interlude made by one Master Roo, of the same Inn, in which play was matter against the Cardinal Wolsey. And when none durst take upon them to play that part which touched the cardinal, this Master Fish took upon him to do it. Upon this, great displeasure ensued against him upon the cardinal's part, so that being pursued by the cardinal, the same night that this tragedy was played, he was compelled to leave his own house, and fled over the sea to Tindal. The year following this book was printed (being about the year 1527), and not long after, was sent over to the lady Anne Boleyn, who then lived at a place not far from the court. Which book her brother seeing in her hand, took it and read it, and gave it to her again, desiring her earnestly to give it to the king, which she did.

This was about A. D. 1528. The king, after he had received the book, demanded of her who wrote it. She answered, " A subject of his, one Fish, who was fled out of the realm for fear of the cardinal." After the king had kept the book in his bosom three or four days, information was given by the king's servants to the wife of Simon Fish, that she might send for her husband without danger. She, being encouraged, came first and made suit to the king for the safe return of her husband. Who, understanding whose wife she was, shewed a very gentle countenance towards her, asking where her husband was. She answered, " If it please your Grace not far off." " Then," saith he, " fetch him, and he shall come and go safe without peril, and no man shall do him harm." Saying, moreover, " that she had been much wronged, that he was absent from her so long ;" he had been absent now two years and a half. In the

mean time the cardinal was deposed, and More sat in the chancellorship.

Thus Fish's wife went immediately to her husband, who was lately come over, and lying privily within a mile of the court, and brought him to the king, about the year 1530. When the king saw him, and understood he was the author of the book, he received him with loving countenance. Who after a long talk for the space of three or four hours, as they were riding together a hunting, the king at length dismissed him, and bade him take home his wife, for she had taken great pains for him. He answered the king and said, he dare not do so, for fear of Sir Thomas More, the chancellor, and Stokesley, the bishop of London.

The king, taking the signet off his finger, desired him to have him recommended to the lord chancellor, charging him not to be so hard as to do him any harm. Master Fish, receiving the king's signet, went and declared his message to the lord chancellor, who took it as sufficient for his own discharge, but he asked him if he had any thing for the discharge of his wife; for she a little before had by chance displeased the friars, for not suffering them to say their gospels in Latin in her house, as they did in others, unless they would say it in English. Upon which the lord chancellor, though he had discharged the man, yet not ceasing his dislike to the wife, the next morning sent for her to appear before him, who, had it not been for her young daughter, who then lay sick of the plague, had probably suffered much trouble. Of which plague her husband, Master Fish, died within half a year, and she afterwards married Master James Bainham, who was burned not long after.

Now comes another statement of Edmund Moddis, the king's footman, on the same matter.

This Moddis being with the king, talking of religion, and of the new books that were come from beyond the seas, said, " If it might please his grace to pardon him, and such persons as he would bring to his grace, he should see such a book as was wonderful to hear of !" The king demanded who they were. He said, two of your merchants, George Elyot and George Robinson. The king appointed a time to speak with them. When they came before his presence in the privy chamber, he demanded what they had to say, or to shew him. One of them said, " That there was a book come to their hands, which they had there to shew his grace." When he saw it, he demanded if any of them could read it. " Yea," said George Elyot, " if it please your grace to hear it." " I think so," said the king, " for if need were, thou canst say it without book."

The whole book being read out, the king made a long pause, and then said, " If a man should pull down an old stone wall, and begin at the lower part, the upper part might chance to fall upon his head." And then he took the book and put it into his desk, and commanded them upon their allegiance that they should not tell to any man that he had seen the book, &c. The copy of the book here ensueth :

A certain book, intituled " The Supplication of Beggars," thrown and scattered at the Procession in Westminster, on Candlemas day, before King Henry the Eighth, for him to read, made by Master Fish.

To the King our Sovereign Lord,

Most lamentably complaineth their woful misery unto your highness, your poor daily beadmen, the wretched hideous monsters, on whom scarcely for honour any eye dare look, the foul unhappy sort of lepers, and other sore people, needy, impotent, blind, lame and sick, that live only by alms, how that their number is daily so sore increased, that all the alms of all the well disposed people of this your realm is not half enough for to sustain them, but that for very constraint they die for hunger. And this most pestilent mischief is come upon your said poor beadmen, by the reason that there is, in the times of your noble predecessors passed, craftily crept into this your realm, another sort, not of impotent, but of strong puissant and counterfeit holy and idle beggars and vagabonds, which since the time of their first entry, by all the craft and wilyness of Satan, are now increased under your sight, not only into a great number, but also into a kingdom.

These are not the herds, but the ravenous wolves going in herds' clothing, devouring the flock,—bishops, abbots, priors, deacons, archdeacons, suffragans, priests, monks, canons, friars, pardoners, and somners. And who is able to number this ravenous idle sort, who (setting all labour aside) have begged so importunately, that they have gotten into their hands, more than the third part of all your realm? The goodliest lordships, manors, lands, and territories are theirs; besides this, they have the tenth part of all the corn, meadow, pasture, grass, wood, colts, calves, lambs, pigs, geese and chickens. Over and besides, the tenth part of every servant's wages, the tenth part of wool, milk, honey, wax, cheese and butter; yea, and they look so narrowly upon their profits, that the poor wives must be accountable to them for every tenth egg, or else she getteth not her rights at Easter, and shall be taken as an heretic. Hereto have they their four offering days. What money do they pull in by probates of testaments, privy tithes, and by men's offerings to their pilgrimages, and at their first masses! every man and child that is buried must pay somewhat for masses and dirges, to be sung for him, or else they will accuse their friends and executors of heresy. What money get they by mortuaries, by hearing of confessions (and yet they keep thereof no counsel) by hallowing of churches, altars, superaltars, chapels and bells, by cursing of men, and absolving them again for money. What a multitude of money gather the pardoners in a year! How much money get the somners by extortion in a year, by citing the people to the commissaries' court, and afterwards releasing the apparents for money! Finally, the infinite number of begging friars, what get they in a year?

Here, if it please your grace to mark, you shall see a thing far out of joint. There are within your realm of England 52,000 parish churches. And this standing, that there be but ten households in every parish, yet are there 520,000 households. And of every of these households hath every of the five orders of friars, a penny a quarter for every order; that is, for all the five orders, five pence a quarter for every house; that is, for all the five orders, twenty pence a-year of every house; i. e., five hundred and twenty thousand quarters of angels; that is, 260,000 half angels, or 130,000 angels. Total, 430,333l. 6s. 8d. sterling! Whereof not 400 years past, they had not one penny.

Oh grievous and painful exaction, thus yearly to be paid! from which, the people of your noble predecessors the kings of the ancient Britons, ever stood free. And this will they have, or else they will procure him who will not give it to them to be taken as an heretic. What tyrant ever oppressed the people, like this cruel and vengeful generation? What subjects shall be able to help their prince; that is, after this fashion yearly polled? What good christian people can be able to succour us poor lepers, blind, sore, and lame, that are thus yearly oppressed? Is it any marvel that your people so complain of poverty? Is it any marvel that the taxes, fifteenths and subsidies that your grace most tenderly, of great compassion, hath taken among your people to defend them from the threatened ruin of their commonwealth, have been so slothfully, yea painfully, levied, seeing almost the uttermost penny, that might have been levied, hath been gathered before, yearly, by this ravenous insatiable generation? Neither the Danes nor the Saxons, in the time of the ancient Britons, should ever have been able to have brought their armies from so far hither into your land to have conquered it, if they had at that time such a sort of idle gluttons to feed at home. The noble king Arthur had never been able to have carried his army to the foot of the mountains, to resist the coming down of Lucius, the emperor, if such yearly exactions had been taken of his people. The Greeks had never been able to have so long continued at the siege of Troy, if they had had at home such an idle sort of cormorants to feed. The ancient Romans had never been able to have put all the whole world

under their obedience, if their people had been thus yearly oppressed. The Turk now in your time should never have been able to get so much ground of Christendom, if he had in his empire such a sort of locusts to devour his substance. Lay then these sums to the foresaid third part of the possessions of the realm, that ye may see whether it draw nigh unto the half of the whole substance of the realm or not; ye shall find that it draweth far above.

Now let us then compare the number of this unkind idle sort, to the number of the lay people, and we shall see whether it be indifferently shifted, or not, that they should have half. Compare them to the number of men, so are they not the hundredth person. Compare them to men, women and children, so are they not the four hundredth person in number. One part therefore, into four hundred parts divided, were too much for them, except they did labour. What an unequal burthen is it, that they have half with the multitude, and are not the four hundredth person of their number? What tongue is able to tell, that ever there was any commonwealth so sore oppressed since the world first began?

And what doth all this greedy sort of sturdy, idle, holy thieves, with these yearly exactions that they take of the people? Truly nothing, but exempt themselves from the obedience of your grace. Nothing but translate all rule, power, lordship, authority, obedience and dignity, from your grace to them. Nothing but that all your subjects should fall into disobedience and rebellion against your grace, and be under them, as they did to your noble predecessor king John; who because that he would have punished certain traitors that had conspired with the French king to have deposed him from his crown and dignity (among which a clerk called Stephen, whom afterwards against the king's will, the pope made bishop of Canterbury, was one) interdicted his land. For which matter your most noble realm wrongfully (alas for shame!) hath stood tributary not to any kind of temporal prince, but to a cruel devilish blood-sucker, drunken in the blood of the saints and martyrs of Christ ever since.

Here were an holy sort of prelates, that thus cruelly could punish such a righteous king, all his realm and succession, for doing right! Here were a charitable sort of holy men, that could thus interdict a whole realm, and pluck away the obedience of the people from their natural liege lord and king, for none other cause but for his righteousness! Here were a blessed sort, not of meek herds, but of blood-suckers, that could set the French king upon such a righteous prince, to cause him to lose his crown and dignity, to make effusion of the blood of his people, unless this good and blessed king of great compassion, more fearing and lamenting the shedding of the blood of his people, than the loss of his crown and dignity, against all right and concience, submitted himself unto them!

O case most horrible, that ever so noble a king, realm and succession, should thus be made to stoop to such a sort of blood-suckers! Where was his sword, power, crown and dignity become, whereby he might have done justice in this matter? Where was their obedience become that should have been subject under his high power in this matter? yea, where was the obedience of all his subjects become, that for maintenance of the commonwealth should have holden him manfully to have resisted these blood-suckers to the shedding of their blood? Was it not altogether by their policy translated from this good king unto them?

Yea, and what do they more? Truly nothing but apply themselves, by all the sleights they may, to have to do with every man's wife, every man's daughter, and every man's maid, that the worst vices should reign over all among your subjects, that no man should know his own child, to put right-begotten children clean beside their inheritance, in subversion of all estates and godly order. These be they, that by their abstaining from marriage to hinder the generation of the people, whereby all the realm at length, if it should be continued, shall be made desert and uninhabitable.

Where is your sword, power, crown, and dignity become, that should punish by punishment of death, even as other men are punished, the felonies, rapes, murders and treasons committed by this sinful generation? Where is their obedience become, that should be under your high power in this matter? Is it not altogether translated and exempt from your grace unto them? Yes truly, what an infinite number of people might have been increased to have peopled the realm, if this sort of folk had been married like other men? What breach of matrimony is there brought in by them? such truly as was never since the world began, among the whole multitude of the heathen. What a sort are there of them that marry priests' sovereign ladies, but to cloak the priests incontinency, and that they may have a living of the priests themselves for their labour? How many thousand doth such lubricity bring to beggary, theft and idleness, which should have kept their good name, and have set themselves to work, had not there been this excessive treasure of the spiritualty? What honest man dare take any man or woman into his service, that hath been at such a school with a spiritual man?

O the grievous shipwreck of the commonwealth, which in ancient time, before the coming of these ravenous wolves, was so prosperous that then there were but few thieves; yea, theft at that time was so rare, that Cæsar was not compelled to make penalty of death upon felony, as your grace may well perceive in his institutes. There was also at that time but few poor people, and yet they did not beg, but there was given them enough unasked; for there was at that time none of these ravenous wolves to ask it from them: as it appeareth in the Acts of the Apostles. Is it any marvel though there be now so many beggars, thieves, and idle people? Nay truly. What remedy? Make laws against them? I am in doubt whether ye be able. Are they not stronger in your own parliament-house than yourself? What a number of bishops, abbots, and priors are lords of your parliament? Are not all the learned men of your realm in fee with them, to speak in your parliament-house for them, against your crown, dignity, and commonwealth of your realm, a few of your own learned council only excepted? What law can be made against them that may be available? Who is he, though he be grieved very sore, that for the murder of his ancestor, ravishment of his wife, of his daughter, robbery, trespass, maim, debt, or any other offence, dare lay it to their charge by any way of action? And if he do, then is he by and by, by their wilyness, accused of heresy; yea, they will so handle him ere he pass, that except he will bear a fagot for their pleasure, he shall be excommunicated, and then by all his actions dashed.

So captive are your laws unto them, that no man whom they list to excommunicate, may be admitted to sue any action in any of your courts. If any man in your sessions dare be so hardy as to indict a priest of any such crime, he hath ere the year go out, such a yoke of heresy laid on his neck, that it makes him wish he had not done it. Your grace may see what a work there is in London; how the bishop rages for indicting of certain curates of extortion and incontinency, the last year in the Wardmote quest. Had not Richard Hunne commenced an action of *præmunire* against a priest, he had been yet alive, and no heretic at all, but an honest man. Did not divers of your noble progenitors, seeing their crown and dignity run into ruin, and to be thus craftily translated into the hands of this mischievous generation, make divers statutes for the reformation thereof, among which the statute of Mortmain was one, to the intent that after that time they should have no more given unto them? But what availed it? Have they not gotten into their hands more lands since then than any duke in England hath, the statute notwithstanding? Yea, have they not for all that translated into their hands, from your grace, half your kingdom through, only the name remaining to you for your ancestors' sake? So you have the name, and they the profit. Yea, I fear, if I should weigh all things to the utmost, they would also take the name to them, and of one kingdom make twain: the spiritual kingdom, as they call it, for they will be named first, and your temporal kingdom. And which of these two kingdoms,

suppose you, is like to overgrow the other, yea, to put the other clean out of memory? Truly the kingdom of the blood-suckers, for to them is given daily out of your kingdom; and that that is once given, never cometh from them again. Such laws have they, that none of them may either give or sell any thing. What law can be made so strong against them, that they, either with money, or else with other policy, will not break or set at naught? What kingdom can endure, that ever giveth thus from him, and receiveth nothing again? O how all the substance of your realm, your sword, power, crown, dignity, and obedience of your people, runneth headlong into the insatiable whirlpool of these greedy gulfs, to be swallowed and devoured!

Neither have they any other colour to gather these yearly exactions into their hands, but that they say they pray for us to God, to deliver our souls out of the pains of purgatory; without whose prayers, they say, or at least without the pope's pardon, we could never be delivered thence. Which, if it be true, then it is good reason that we give them all these things, although it were an hundred times as much. But there be many men of great literature and judgment, that for the love they have to the truth and to the commonwealth, have not feared to put themselves into the greatest infamy that may be, in abjection of all the world, yea, in peril of death, to declare their opinion in this matter; which is, that there is no purgatory, but that it is a thing invented by the covetousness of the spiritualty, only to translate all kingdoms from other princes unto them, and that there is not one word spoken of it in all the holy scripture. They say also, that if there were a purgatory, and also if that the pope with his pardons may for money deliver one soul from thence, he may deliver him as well without money; if he may deliver one, he may deliver a thousand: if he may deliver a thousand, he may deliver them all, and so destroy purgatory, and then he is a cruel tyrant, without all charity, if he keep them there in prison and in pain till men will give him money.

Likewise, say they, of all the whole sort of the spiritualty, that if they will pray for no man but for them that gave them money, they are tyrants, and lack charity, and suffer those souls to be punished and pained uncharitably for lack of their prayers. This sort of folks they call heretics; these they burn; these they rage against, put to open shame, and make them bear fagots; but whether they be heretics or no, well I know that this purgatory and the pope's pardons are all the cause of the transferring of your kingdom so fast into their hands. Wherefore it is manifest it cannot be of Christ; for he gave more to the temporal kingdom, he himself paid tribute to Cæsar; he took nothing from him, but taught that the high powers should be always obeyed; yea, himself, although he was most free lord of all, and innocent, was obedient to the high powers unto death. This is the great sore why they will not let the New Testament go abroad in your mother tongue, lest men should espy that they by their cloaked hypocrisy do translate thus fast your kingdom into their hands; that they are not obedient unto your high power; that they are cruel, unclean, unmerciful, and hypocrites; that they seek not the honour of Christ, but their own; that remission of sins is not given by the pope's pardon, but by Christ, for the sure faith and trust that we have in him.

Here may your grace well perceive, that except you suffer their hypocrisy to be disclosed, all is like to run into their hands; and as long as it is covered, so long shall it seem to every man to be a great impiety not to give them. For this I am sure, your grace thinketh, as the truth is, I am as good a man as my father; why may I not as well give them as much as my father did? And of this mind I am sure are all the lords, knights, squires, gentlemen, and yeomen in England; yea, and until it be disclosed, all your people will think that your statute of Mortmain was never made with any good conscience, seeing that it taketh away the liberty of your people, in that they may not as lawfully buy their souls out of purgatory by giving to the spiritualty, as their predecessors did in times past.

Wherefore if you will eschew the ruin of your crown and dignity, let their hypocrisy be uttered, and that shall be more speedful in this matter than all the laws that can be made, be they ever so strong; for to make a law to punish any offender, except it were more to give other men an example to beware how they commit such like offence, what would it avail? Did not Doctor Allen most presumptuously, now in your time, against his allegiance, do all that ever he could to pull from you the knowledge of such pleas as belong unto your high courts, unto another court, in derogation of your crown and dignity? Did not also Doctor Horsey and his accomplices, most heinously, as all the world knoweth, murder in prison that honest merchant Richard Hunne, for that he sued your writ of *præmunire* against a priest that wrongfully held him in plea in a spiritual court, for a matter whereof the knowledge belonged unto your high courts? And what punishment was there done that any man may take example of, to beware of like offence? Truly none, but that the one paid five hundred pounds, as it is said, to the building of your chamber; and when that payment was once made, the captains of his kingdom, because he fought so manfully against your crown and dignity, have heaped upon him benefice upon benefice, so that he is rewarded ten times as much. The other, as it is said, paid six hundred pounds for himself and his accomplices; which, because that he had likewise fought so manfully against your crown and dignity, was immediately, on having obtained your most gracious pardon, promoted by the captains of his kingdom, with benefice upon benefice, to the value of four times as much. Who can take example of punishment to beware of such like offence? Who is he of their kingdom that will not rather take courage to commit the like offence, seeing the promotions that fell to those men for their so offending? so weak and blunt is your sword to strike at one of the offenders of this crooked and perverse generation.

And this is by reason that the chief instrument of your law, yea, the chief of your council, and he who hath your sword in his hand, to whom also all the other instruments are obedient, is also a spiritual man, who hath ever such an inordinate love unto his own kingdom, that he will maintain that, though all the temporal kingdoms and commonwealths of the world should therefore utterly be undone. Here we leave out the greatest matter of all, lest that we declaring such an horrible carrion of evil against the ministers of iniquity, should seem to declare the one only fault, or rather the ignorance of our best beloved minister of righteousness, which is to be hid till he may have learned by these small enormities that which we have spoken of, to know it plainly himself.

But what remedy is there to relieve us your poor, sick, lame, and sore beadsmen? To make many hospitals for the relief of the poor people? Nay truly. The more the worse: for ever the fat of the whole foundation hangeth on the priests' beards. Divers of your noble predecessors, kings of this realm, have given lands to monasteries, to give a certain sum of money yearly to the poor people, whereof for the remoteness of the time, they give never one penny. They have likewise given to them, to have a certain number of masses said daily for them, whereof they never say one. If the abbot of Westminster should sing every day as many masses for his founders, as he is bound to do by his foundation, a thousand monks were too few. Wherefore if your grace will build a sure hospital that never shall fail, to relieve us all your poor beadsmen, then take from them all these things. Send these sturdy loobies abroad in the world to get them wives of their own, to get their living with their labour in the sweat of their faces, according to the commandment of God (Gen. iii. 19.) and to be an example to other idle people to go to labour. Tie these holy idle thieves to the carts, to be whipped naked about every market-town, till they fall to labour, that they by their importunate begging, take not away the alms that the good christian people would give to us sore, impotent, miserable people, your beadsmen. Then shall the number of the aforesaid monstrous sort, be reduced, as of whores, thieves, and idle people. Then shall

these great yearly exactions cease. Then shall not your sword, power, crown, dignity, and obedience of your people be transferred from you. Then shall you have full obedience of your people. Then shall the idle people be set to work. Then shall matrimony be much better kept. Then shall the generation of your people be increased. Then shall your commons increase in riches. Then shall the gospel be preached. Then shall none beg our alms from us. Then shall we have enough, and more than shall suffice us; which shall be the best hospital that ever was founded for us. Then shall we daily pray to God for your most noble estate long to endure."

Against this book of the beggars, Sir Thomas More shortly after wrote another book in answer to it, under the title of "The Poor Silly Souls Pewling out of Purgatory." In which, after More had first divided the whole world into four parts, that is, into heaven, hell, earth and purgatory; then he makes the dead men's souls, by a rhetorical *prosopopœia* to speak out of purgatory, sometimes lamentably complaining, sometimes pleasantly dallying and scoffing at the author of the beggars' book; sometimes scolding and railing at him, calling him fool, witless, frantic, an ass, a goose, a mad dog, an heretic, and all that. And no wonder, if these silly souls of purgatory seem so furnish and testy; for heat is testy, and soon inflames anger. But yet these purgatory souls must take good heed how they call a man a fool and heretic so often; for if the sentence of the gospel pronounce them guilty of hell fire, which say, "thou fool," it may be feared lest those poor, silly, melancholy souls of purgatory, calling this man fool so often, bring themselves thereby out of purgatory fire to the fire of hell; so that neither the five wounds of St. Francis, nor all the merits of St. Dominick, nor yet of all the friars, can release the poor wretches. But yet as I do not, nor cannot think that those departed souls either would so far overshoot themselves if they were in purgatory, or else that there is any such fourth place of purgatory, at all, unless it be in Master More's Utopia, I cease therefore to burden the souls departed, and lay all the wit on Master More, the author and contriver of this poetical book.

After the clergy of England, and especially the cardinal, understood these books of the Beggars' Supplication to be strewed abroad in the streets of London, and also before the king, the cardinal caused not only his servants diligently to gather them up, that they should not come into the king's hands, but also when he understood that the king had received one or two of them, he came to the king's majesty, saying, "If it shall please your grace, here are divers seditious persons who have scattered abroad books containing manifest errors and heresies; desiring his grace to beware of them." Whereupon the king, putting his hand in his bosom, took out one of the books, and delivered it to the cardinal. Then the cardinal, together with his bishops, consulted how they might provide a speedy remedy for this mischief, and determined to give out a commission to forbid the reading of all English books, and especially this book of "The Supplication of Beggars," and the New Testament of Tindal's Translation. This commission was done out of hand by Cuthbert Tonstal, bishop of London, who sent out his prohibition unto his archdeacons with all speed, for the forbidding of that book and others; the tenor of which prohibition is as follows:—[1]

A prohibition sent out by Cuthbert Tonstal, Bishop of London, to the Archdeacons of his Diocese, for the calling in of the New Testaments translated into English, with many other books.

"Cuthbert, by the permission of God, bishop of London, unto our well-beloved in Christ, the archdeacon of London, or to his official, health, grace, and benediction. By the duty of our pastoral office, we are bound diligently with all our power to foresee, provide

(1) The same prohibition was published by every bishop in his diocese.—BURNET.

for, root out, and put away all those things which seem to tend to the peril and danger of our subjects, and especially the destruction of their souls. Wherefore we having understanding by the report of several credible persons, and also by the evident appearance of the matter, that many children of iniquity, maintainers of Luther's sect, blinded through extreme wickedness, wandering from the way of truth, and the catholic faith, have craftily translated the New Tastament into our English tongue, intermixing therewith many heretical articles, and erroneous opinions, pernicious and offensive, seducing the simple people, attempting by their wicked and perverse interpretations, to profane the majesty of the scripture, which hitherto hath remained undefiled, and craftily to abuse the most holy word of God, and the true sense of the same, of which translation there are many books printed, some with glosses, and some without, containing in the English tongue that pestiferous and most pernicious poison dispersed throughout all our diocese of London in great number, which truly, without it be foreseen, without doubt will contaminate and infect the flock committed unto us, with most deadly poison and heresy, to the grievous peril and danger of the souls committed to our charge, and the offence of God's Divine Majesty; wherefore we, Cuthbert, the bishop aforesaid, grievously sorrowing for the premises, willing to withstand the craft and subtlety of the ancient enemy and his ministers, who seek the destruction of my flock, and with a diligent care to take heed unto the flock committed to my charge, desiring to provide speedy remedies for the premises, do charge you jointly and severally, and by virtue of your obedience straightly enjoin and command you, that by our authority you warn, or cause to be warned all and singular, as well exempt as not exempt, dwelling within your archdeaconries, that within thirty days' space, whereof ten days shall be for the first, ten for the second, and ten for the third and peremptory term, under pain of excommunication, and incurring the suspicion of heresy, they do bring in, and really deliver unto our vicar general, *all and singular such books as contain the translation of the New Testament in the English tongue;* and that you do certify to us, or our said commissary, within two months after the day of the date of these presents, duly, personally, or by your letters, together with these presents, under your seals, what you have done in the premises, under pain of contempt.

"Given under our seal, the three-and-twentieth day of October, in the fifth year of our consecration, A.D. 1526."

The like commission in like manner and form was sent to the other three archdeacons of Middlesex, Essex, and Colchester, for the execution of the same matter, under the bishop's seal.

Many other books were forbidden at this time, together with the New Testament. And among them were The Supplication of Beggars; The Revelation of Antichrist of Luther; The New Testament of Tindal; The Wicked Mammon; The Obedience of a Christian Man; An Introduction to St. Paul's Epistle to the Romans; A Dialogue betwixt the Father and the Son; and nearly one hundred other books besides written by the reformers.

The New Testament, above recited, began first to be translated by William Tindal, and was printed at Antwerp, and sent over into England in the year 1526. Cuthbert Tonstal, bishop of London, and Sir Thomas More, being aggrieved, devised how they could destroy that false erroneous translation, as they called it. It happened that there was one Augustine Packington, an English merchant, at Antwerp at that time, when the bishop was there in 1529. This man favoured Tindal, but pretended otherwise to the bishop. The bishop being desirous to bring his purpose to pass, said, that he would gladly buy the New Testaments. Packington hearing him say so, said, "My Lord, I can do more in this matter than most merchants can do, if it be your pleasure, for I know the Dutchmen and strangers that have bought them of Tindal, and have them here to sell; so, if it be your Lordship's pleasure to

obtain them, I must spend money to pay for them, or else I cannot have them, but if it is your pleasure to do so I will secure to you every book that is printed and unsold." The bishop said, "Do your diligence, gentle Master Packington; get them for me, and I will pay whatever is their cost, for I intend to burn and destroy them all at St. Paul's cross." This Augustine Packington went to William Tindal, and declared the whole matter, and so, upon compact made between them, the bishop of London had the books, Packington had the thanks, and Tindal had the money.[1] After this Tindal corrected the New Testament, and caused it again to be newly reprinted, so that they came thick and threefold over into England. When the bishop perceived that, he sent for Packington, who, by that time, had returned to England, and said to him, "How comes this, that there are so many New Testaments abroad? You promised me that you would buy them all." Then answered Packington, "Surely, I bought all that were to be had, but I perceive that they have reprinted more since. I see it will never be better so long as they have letters and stamps; wherefore, you had better buy the stamps too, and so then you shall be sure." At which answer the bishop smiled, and so the matter ended.

It happened, in the following year, that George Constantine was apprehended by Sir Thomas More, on suspicion of heresy; and after several examinations, among other things, More asked him, saying, "Constantine, I would have thee be plain with me in one thing that I will ask, and I promise thee, I will shew thee favour in all other things whereof thou art accused. There is beyond the sea Tindal, Joy, and a great many others; I know they cannot live without help. There are some that help and succour them with money, and thou being one of them, hadst thy part thereof, and therefore thou knowest from whence it came. I pray thee, tell me, who are they that help them thus?" "My Lord," quoth Constantine, "I will tell you truly; it is the bishop of London that hath helped us, for he hath bestowed among us a great deal of money to buy up the New Testaments to burn them, and that has been, and yet is, our only succour and comfort." "Now, by my troth," quoth More, "I think even the same, for so much I told the bishop before he went about it."

Of this George Constantine, it is reported by Sir Thomas More, that he being taken, seemed well contented to renounce his former doctrine, and not only to disclose others of his fellows, but also studied how these books, which he himself and others of his fellows had bought and shipped, might come to the bishop's hands to be burned, by whom the books were taken and burned. Constantine afterwards, by the help of some of his friends, escaped out of prison over the seas, and after that, in the time of king Edward, troubled the good bishop of St. David's, who was burned in Queen Mary's time.

On the return of Tonstal from Antwerp, he caused all the New Testaments which he had bought, to be publicly burned in St. Paul's church-yard, which gave great offence to many of the people; and to remove this feeling, the bishops gave out that they intended to set out a true translation of it. The bishops, by many complaints, and under the pretence that the translations of Tindal and Joy were not truly translated; and, besides, that in them were prologues and prefaces, that smelled of heresy, and railed against the bishops. They obtained a proclamation from the king, prohibiting the teaching or preaching of any thing against the dignity and ordinances of the church of Rome, and prohibiting the reading of any books contrary to the church of Rome. But the king commanded the bishops to call to them the best learned men of the universities, and that they should make a new translation, so that the people might not be

---

(1) Tindal was very glad of it; for, being convinced of some faults in his work, he was designing a new and correct edition, but he was poor, and the former impression not being sold off, he could not go about it; so he gave Packington all the copies that lay in his hands, for which the bishop paid the price, and brought them over to be burned.—BURNET.

ignorant in the law of God. Notwithstanding this command, the bishops did nothing at all to the setting forth of any new translation. But on the contrary, on the 24th of May, 1530, there was a paper drawn up, and agreed to by archbishop Warham, chancellor More, bishop Tonstal and others, which every incumbent was called upon to read to his parish, as a warning to prevent the contagion of heresy. In this paper it was declared that it was not necessary to set forth the scriptures in the vulgar tongue. Many of the people were so disappointed at this, that they only became the more eager to read Tindal's translation, by reason of which many things came to light. Soon after this time great trouble and persecution was raised up against the poor innocent flock of Christ.

Richard Byfield, Martyr.

This Richard Byfield, a monk of St. Edmundsbury, was converted by Dr. Barnes, and Master Maxwell, and Master Stacey, two godly men of London, brickmakers, and wardens of their company, who were grafted in the doctrine of Jesus Christ, and through their godly conversation of life, had converted many men and women, both in London and in the country; and once a year at their own cost, they went about to visit the brethren and sisters scattered abroad. Doctor Barnes at that time much resorted to the abbey of Bury, where Byfield was, to one Doctor Ruffam. At this time it happened that this Byfield the monk was chamberlain of the house to provide lodging for the strangers, and to see them well entertained; he delighted much in Doctor Barnes and in other laymen's conversation; and at last, Doctor Barnes gave him a New Testament in Latin, and the other two gave him Tindal's Testament in English, with a book called, "The Wicked Mammon," and "The Obedience of a Christian Man;" he had learned so much in two years, that he was cast into prison, sore whipped, and a gag put into his mouth, and then put into the stocks, and so continued three quarters of a year before Doctor Barnes could get him out; which he brought to pass, by the means of Doctor Ruffam, before-mentioned, and so he was committed to Doctor Barnes to go to Cambridge with him. By that time he had tasted so well of good letters, that he never returned home again to his abbey, but went to London to Maxwell and Stacey, where they kept him secretly a while, and then conveyed him beyond the sea. Doctor Barnes, himself, being by this time in the Fleet prison for God's word. This Byfield mightily prospered in the knowledge of God, and was serviceable to Master Tindal, and Master Frith; for he brought substance with him, and bought all their works, and the Germans' works, and sold them both in France and in England; and at last coming to London, he was there betrayed, and carried to the Lollards' Tower, and from thence to the Coalhouse.

This Richard Byfield being in the Coalhouse, was worse handled than he was before in the Lollards' Tower; for there he was tied by the neck, middle, and legs, standing upright by the walls, and manacled, to make him accuse others that had bought his books; but he accused none, but stood to his religion and confession of his faith, even to the very end, and was, in the consistory of St. Paul's, thrice put to his trial, whether he would abjure or not? He said he would dispute for his faith, and so he did to their great shame; Stokesley being his judge, with the assistance of Winchester, and other bishops.

The articles laid to Richard Byfield, by the aforesaid bishops, were these, (A.D. 1531, November 10.)

Articles laid to Richard Byfield.

First, that he had been many years a monk, professed of the order of St. Benedict, of St. Edmundsbury, in the diocese of Norwich.

2. That he was a priest, and had ministered and continued in the same order for the space of nine or ten years.

3. That since the feast of Easter last, he being beyond the sea, bought and procured divers and many books and treatises of sundry sorts, as well of Martin Luther's own works, as of others of his damnable sect, and of Oecolampadius the great heretic, and other heretics, both in Latin and English; the names of which books were contained in a little bill written with his own hand.

4. That in the year of our Lord 1528, he was detected and accused to Cuthbert, then bishop of London, for affirming and holding certain articles contrary to the holy church, and especially that all laud and praise should be given to God alone, and not to saints or creatures.

5. That every priest might preach the word of God by the authority of the gospel, and not to run to the pope or cardinals for license, as it appeared (said they) by his confession before the said bishop.

6. That he judicially abjured the said articles before the said bishop, and did renounce and forswear them and all other articles contrary to the determination of holy church, promising that from henceforth he would not fall into any of them, nor any other errors.

7. That he made a solemn oath upon a book, and the holy evangelists, to fulfil such penance as should be enjoined him by the bishop.

8. After his abjuration it was enjoined to him for penance, that he should go before the cross in procession, in the parish church of St. Botolph's, at Billingsgate, and bear a fagot of wood upon his shoulder.

9. It was enjoined him in penance, that he should provide an habit requisite and meet for his order and profession, as shortly as he might, and that he should come or go nowhere without such an habit; which he had not fulfilled.

10. That it was likewise enjoined him in penance, that he should, some time before the feast of the Ascension, then next ensuing his abjuration, go home unto the monastery of Bury, and there remain according to the vow of his profession; which he had not fulfilled.

11. That he was appointed by the bishop of London to appear before the said bishop, on the 25th day of April next after his abjuration, to receive the residue of his penance, and after his abjuration, he fled beyond the sea, and appeared not.

12. That on the 20th day of June next following his abjuration, he did appear before the said Bishop Tonstal, in the chapel of the bishop of Norwich's palace, and there it was newly enjoined him in part of penance, that he should provide him an habit convenient for his order and profession, within eight days then next following; which he had not done.

13. That it was there again enjoined him, that he should depart from the city, diocese, and jurisdiction of London, and no more to come within it, without the special license of the bishop of London, or his successor for the time being; which he had not fulfilled.

The sentence given against him.

In the name of God, Amen! We, John, by the sufferance of God, bishop of London, in a case of inquisition of heresy, and relapse of the same, &c.

Forsomuch as by the acts enacted, inquired, propounded, and alleged, and by thee judicially confessed, we do find that thou hast abjured certain errors and heresies, and damnable opinions by thee confessed, as well particularly as generally, before our reverend fellow and brother, then thy ordinary, according to the form and order of the church. And that one Martin Luther, together with his adherents and accomplices, receivers and favourers, whatsoever they be, was condemned as an heretic, by the authority of Pope Leo the Tenth, of most happy memory, and by the authority of the Apostolic See; and the books, and all writings, schedules and sermons of the said Martin Luther, his adherents and accomplices, whether they be found in Latin, or in any other languages, printed or translated, for the manifold heresies and errors, and damnable opinions that are in them, are condemned, reproved, and utterly rejected, and inhibition made by the authority of the said See, to all faithful Christians, under the pain of excommunication, and other punishments in that behalf, to be incurred by the law, that no man, by any means, presume to read, teach, hear, print, or publish, or by any means defend, directly, or indirectly, secretly or openly, in their houses, or in any other public or private places, any such manner of writings, books, errors, or articles, as are contained more at large in the apostolic letters, drawn out in form of a public instrument; whereunto, and to the contents thereof, we refer ourselves, as far as is expedient, and no otherwise. And forsomuch as we do perceive that thou didst understand the premises; and yet these things, notwithstanding after thy abjuration made, as is aforesaid, thou hast brought in divers and sundry times, many books of the said Martin Luther, and his adherents and accomplices, and of other heretics, the names, titles, and authors of which books here follow, and are these:—Martin Luther, Of the Abrogating of the Private Mass; The Declarations of Martin Luther upon the Epistles of St. Peter; Luther upon the Epistles of St. Paul and Jude; Luther upon Monastical Vowers; Luther's Commentary upon the Epistle of St. Paul to the Galatians; John Oecolampadius upon the exposition of these words, "This is my body;" the Annotations of Oecolampadius upon the Epistles of St. Paul unto the Romans, &c. &c.

Of all which kind of books, both in Latin and English, translated, set forth, and printed, containing not only Lutherian heresies, but also the damnable heresies of other condemned heretics; forasmuch as thou hast brought over from the parts beyond the sea, a great number into this realm of England, and especially to our city and diocese of London, and hast procured them to be brought and conveyed over; also, hast kept by thee, and studied those books, and hast published and read them unto divers Christian men, and many of those books also hast dispersed, and given to divers persons dwelling within our city and diocese of London, and hast confessed and affirmed before our official, that those books of Martin Luther, and other heretics, his accomplices and adherents, and all the contents in them, are good and agreeable to the true faith, saying, that they are good, and of the true faith; and by this means and pretence hast commended and praised Martin Luther, his adherents and accomplices, and hast favoured and believed their errors, heresies, and opinions. Therefore, we, John, the bishop, aforesaid, first calling upon the name of Christ, and setting God only before our eyes, by the counsel and consent of the divines and lawyers, with whom in this behalf we have conferred, do declare and decree thee, the aforesaid Richard Byfield, otherwise called Somersam, for the contempt of thy abjuration, as a favourer of the aforesaid Martin Luther, his adherents, accomplices, favourers, and other condemned heretics, and for commending and studying, reading, having, retaining, publishing, selling, giving, and dispersing the books and writings, as well of the said Martin Luther, his adherents and disciples, as of other heretics aforenamed, and also for crediting and maintaining the errors, heresies, and damnable opinions contained in the said books and writings, worthily to be, and have been an heretic; and that thou, by the pretence of the premises, art fallen again most damnably into heresy; and we pronounce that thou art, and hast been, a relapsed heretic, and hast incurred, and oughtest to incur, the pain and punishment of a relapse. And we so decree and declare, and also condemn thee thereunto, and that by the pretence of the premises, thou hast even, by the law, incurred the sentence of the greater excommunication; and, thereby, we pronounce and declare thee to have been and to be excommunicate; and clearly discharge, exonerate, and degrade thee from all privilege and prerogative of the ecclesiastical orders, and also deprive thee of all ecclesiastical office and benefice. Also, we pronounce and declare thee, by this our sentence or decree, the which we here promulgate and declare in these writings, that thou art actually to be degraded, deposed, and deprived, as followeth:—

In the name of God, Amen. We, John, by the permission of God, bishop of London, rightfully and lawfully proceeding in this behalf, do dismiss thee, Richard Byfield, alias Somersam, being pronounced by us a relapsed heretic, and degraded by us from all ecclesiastical privilege out of the ecclesiastical court, pronouncing that the secular power here present should receive thee under their jurisdiction; earnestly requiring and desiring in the bowels of Jesus Christ, that the execution of this worthy punishment to be done upon thee, and against thee in this behalf, may be so moderated, that there be neither overmuch cruelty, neither too much favourable gentleness, but that it may be to the health and salvation of thy soul, and to the extirpation, fear, terror, and conversion of all other heretics unto the unity of the Catholic faith. This, our final decree, by this our sentence definitive, we have caused to be published in form aforesaid.

On Monday the 20th day of November, (A.D. 1531.) in the Quire of the Cathedral church of St. Paul's, the bishop of London, called to him John, abbot of Westminster; Robert, abbot of Waltham; Nicholas, prior of Christ church of the city of London; Master J. Cox, auditor and vicar-general to the archbishop of Canterbury; Peter Ligham, official of the court of Canterbury; Thomas Bagh, chancellor of the church of St. Paul's; William Cliefe, archdeacon of London; John Inocent, canon residentiary of the same; William Briton, Robert Birch, and Hugh A-price, doctors of both laws, &c.; which religious persons, and other ecclesiastical men, thought it good that the bishop should pronounce, and give the sentence against him; and so he was delivered to the sheriffs to be taken to Newgate, they being commanded to bring him again upon Monday following into St. Paul's upper quire, there to give attendance upon the bishop of London; and by and bye the sheriffs were commanded to have him into the vestry, and then to bring him forth in Antichrist's apparel, to be degraded before them. When he had degraded him kneeling upon the highest step of the altar, he took his crosier staff, and smote him on the breast, so that he threw him down backwards, and brake his head that sounded it. When Byfield came to himself again, he thanked God that he was delivered from the malignant church of Antichrist, and that he was come into the true sincere church of Jesus Christ militant here in earth; "And I trust anon," said he, " to be in heaven with Jesus Christ, and the church triumphant for ever;" and he was then led forth through the quire to Newgate, and there rested about an hour in prayer; and afterwards went to the fire in his apparel, manfully and joyfully, and there, for lack of a speedy fire, was half an hour alive; and when the left arm was on fire and burned, he rubbed it with his right hand, and it fell from his body, and he continued in prayer to the end without moving. He was burned in Smithfield.

John Tewkesbury, Leather-seller of London, Martyr.

John Tewkesbury was converted by the reading of Tindal's Testament, and "The Wicked Mammon." He had the bible. In all points of religion he openly disputed in the bishop's chapel in his palace, and in the doctrine of justification, and all other articles of his faith, was very prompt in his answers, so that Tonstal, and all his learned men were ashamed that a leather-seller should dispute with them, with such power of the scriptures and heavenly wisdom, that they were not able to resist him. This disputation continued a week. The process of examinations and answers here follow, as they are extracted out of the bishop's register.

On Wednesday, 21st April, (A.D. 1529,) John Tewkesbury was brought into the Consistory at London, before Cuthbert, bishop of London, and his assistants, Henry, bishop of St. Asaph, and John, abbot of Westminster. The bishop of London then declared that he had often exhorted him to recant the errors and heresies which he held and defended, even as he did then again exhort him, not to trust too much to his own wit and learning, but unto the doctrine of the holy mother, the church. He made answer, that in his judgment he did not err from the doctrine of the holy mother the church. And, at the last, being examined upon errors, which, they said, were in the book called "The Wicked Mammon," he answered:—"Take ye the book and read it over, and I think, in my conscience, ye shall find no fault in it." And, being asked by the bishop, whether he had rather give credit to this book or to the gospel; he answered that the gospel is, and ever has been true.

The bishop said further to John Tewkesbury:—"I

tell thee, before God, and those here present, that the articles contained in the book are false, heretical, and condemned by the holy church—how thinkest thou?" He commanded him to answer determinately, under pain of the law, saying, that if he refused to answer, he must declare him an open and obstinate heretic, according to the order of the law.

He answered, "That he thought, in his conscience, there was nothing in the book but that which is true; and to this article objected, that is, that faith only justifies without works, he answers, "That is well said, and added, "I pray God, that the condemnation of the Gospel, and translation of the Testament be not to your shame, and that you be not in peril for it; for the condemnation of it and of the other is all one." He said, that he had studied the holy scriptures for the space of these seventeen years, and as he could see the spots of his face in the glass, so, in reading the New Testament, he knew the faults of his soul.

The bishop exhorted him to recant his errors. John Tewkesbury answered, "I pray you reform yourself, and if there be any error in the book, let it be reformed; I think it is good enough." The bishop appointed him to determine with himself against the morrow.

After some days, with advice of his friends, he submitted himself and abjured his opinions, and was enjoined penance, as follows.

That he should keep well his abjuration, under pain of relapse.

That the Sunday following, in St. Paul's Church in the open procession, he should carry a fagot, and stand at St. Paul's Cross with the same.

That on the Wednesday following he should carry the same fagot about Newgate-Market and Cheapside.

That on the Friday after, he should take the same fagot again at St. Peter's Church in Cornhill, and carry it about the market of Leaden-hall.

That he should have two signs of fagots embroidered, the one on his left sleeve, and the other on his right sleeve, and that he should wear them all his life time, unless he were otherwise dispensed with.

That on Whit-Sunday eve he should enter into the monastery of St. Bartholomew in Smithfield, and there abide, and not come out unless he were released by the bishop of London.

That he should not depart out of the city or diocese of London, without the special license of the bishop or his successors. Which penance he commenced the 8th day of May, 1529.

And thus much concerning his first examination, which was in the year 1529, when he was induced through infirmity, to retract and abjure his doctrine. Being afterwards confirmed by the grace of God, and moved by the example of Byfield, who was burned in Smithfield, he returned and constantly remained in the testimony of the truth, and suffered for it. Recovering more grace and better strength at the hand of the Lord, two years after being apprehended again, he was brought before Sir Thomas More, and the bishop of London; where certain articles were objected of him: the chief of which we briefly recite.

I. That he confessed that he was baptized, and intended to keep the catholic faith.

II. That he affirms, that the abjuration, oath, and subscription that he made before Cuthbert, late bishop of London, was done by compulsion.

III. That he had the books of "*the Obedience of a Christian Man,*" and of "*the Wicked Mammon,*" in his custody, and had read them since his abjuration.

IV. That he affirms that he suffered the two fagots that were embroidered on his sleeve, to be taken from him, for that he deserved not to wear them.

V. He saith, *that faith only justifies,* which has charity.

VI. He saith, that Christ is a sufficient mediator for us, and therefore no prayer is to be made to saints. Whereupon they laid unto him this verse of the anthem; "Hail queen of heaven, our *advocate.*" To which he answered, that he knew no other advocate but Christ alone.

VII. He affirms that there is no purgatory after this life, but that Christ our Saviour is a sufficient purgation for us.

VIII. He affirms, that the souls of the faithful, departing this life, rest with Christ.

IX. He affirms, that a priest, by receiving orders, receives more grace, if his faith be increased, but otherwise, not.

X. And last of all, he believes, that the sacrament of the flesh and blood of Christ, is not the very body of Christ, in flesh and blood, as it was born of the Virgin Mary.

Then the chancellor caused the articles to be read openly, with the answers unto the same; after which the bishop pronounced sentence against him and delivered him to the sheriffs of London; who burned him in Smithfield, 20th of December, 1531.

The apprehension of one Edward Freese, a painter.

Edward Freese was apprentice to a painter, and by working for his master in Bearsie Abbey, was known to the abbot, for he was a boy of talent and knowledge, and the abbot favoured him so much, that he would have made him a monk. The lad not liking that kind of living and not knowing how to get out because he was a novice, ran away, and came to Colchester in Essex, and remaining there according to his former vocation, was married and lived like an honest man. After he had been there a good time, he was hired to paint certain cloths for the new inn in Colchester, and in the upper boarder of the cloths he wrote certain sentences of scripture, and by that he was plainly known to be one of those whom they call heretics.

He was taken and brought to London, and so to Fulham, to the bishop's house, where he was cruelly imprisoned, with others of Essex; one Johnson and his wife, Wylie and his wife, and his son, and father Bate of Rowshedge. They were so straightly kept, that their wives and their friends could not come to them. After the painter had been there a long space, he was removed to the Lollard's Tower. While he was at Fulham, his wife being desirous to see her husband, and pressing to come in at the gate, being then with child, the porter lifted up his foot and kicked her on the belly, that at length she died of the same, but the child was destroyed immediately.

After that they were all put in the stocks for a long time, and then they were let loose in their prisons. Some had horselocks on their legs, and some had other irons. This painter would ever be writing on the walls with chalk or a coal; and because he would be writing many things, he was manacled by the wrists, so long, till the flesh of his arms was grown higher than his irons. By means of his manacles he could not comb his head, so that his hair was folded together.

After the death of his wife, his brother sued to the king for him, and he was brought out in the consistory at St. Paul's, and (as his brother reported) they kept him three days without meat before he came to his answer. Then, what by the long imprisonment and cruel treatment, and for lack of sustenance, the man could not say anything, but looked and gazed upon the people like a wild man, and if they asked him a question, he only answered, "My lord is a good man." And thus, when they had ruined his body, and destroyed his senses, they sent him back again to Bearsie Abbey; but he came away again from thence, and would not tarry amongst them: although he never came to his perfect mind, to his dying day.

His brother, whose name was Valentine Freese and his wife, gave their lives at one stake in York, for the testimony of Jesus Christ.

Also the wife of Father Bate, while he was at Fulham, made many supplications to the king without redress, and at the last she delivered one into his own hands, and he read it himself, whereupon she was appointed to go into Chancery Lane, to one, whose name (as it is thought) was Master Selyard, and at last she got a letter of Selyard to the bishop, and when she had it, she thought all her suit well bestowed, hoping that some good should come to her husband by it. And because the wicked officers in those days were crafty, and desirous of his blood, some of her friends desired to see the contents of her letter, and not suffer her to deliver it to the bishop: and as they thought, so they found indeed: for it was after this manner.

After commendations had, &c. "Look what you can gather against Father Bate, and send me word by your trusty friend, Sir William Saxie, that I may certify it to the king's majesty, &c." Thus the poor woman, when she thought her suit had been done, was in less hope of her husband's life than before. But it pleased God soon to deliver him: for he got out in a dark night, and was caught no more, but died within a short time after.

James Bainham, Lawyer and Martyr.

James Bainham, gentleman, was virtuously brought up by his parents, in the study of good letters, and had a knowledge both of the Latin and the Greek tongue. He gave himself to the study of the law, and was esteemed a man of virtuous disposition, and godly conversation, mightily addicted to prayer, an earnest reader of scripture, a great maintainer of the godly, a visitor of prisoners, liberal to scholars, very merciful to his clients, using equity and justice to the poor, very diligent in giving counsel to all the needy, widows, fatherless, and afflicted, without money or rewards; indeed a singular example to all lawyers.

This Master Bainham married the widow of Simon Fish, for which he was the more suspected, and at last was accused to Sir Thomas More, and arrested and carried out of the Middle Temple to the chancellor's house at Chelsea, where he continued in prison a while, till Sir Thomas More, finding he could not prevail on him to recant, cast him into prison in his own house, and whipping him at the tree in his garden, called the "Tree of Troth," and afterwards sent him to the Tower to be racked, and so he was, Sir Thomas More being present himself, till he had lamed him, because he would not accuse the gentlemen of the Temple of his acquaintance, nor shew where his books lay; and because his wife denied them to be at his house, she was sent to the Fleet, and their goods confiscated.

After they had thus practised against him what they could by tortures and torments, then was he brought before John Stokesley, bishop of London, the fifteenth day of December, A.D. 1531, in Chelsea, and there examined upon the following articles and interrogatories:—

1. Whether he believed there were any purgatory of souls hence departed?

He made answer as follows: "If we walk in the light, as he is in the light, we have fellowship one with another, and the blood of Jesus Christ his Son cleanseth us from all sin. If we say that we have no sin, we deceive ourselves, and the truth is not in us. If we confess our sins, he is faithful and just to forgive us our sins, and to cleanse us from all unrighteousness." 1 John i. 7—9.

2. Whether saints hence departed are to be honoured and prayed to, to pray for us?

He answered: "My little children, these things write I unto you, that ye sin not. And if any man sin, we have an advocate with the Father, Jesus Christ the righteous. And he is the propitiation for our sins: and not for ours only, but also for the sins of the whole world." 1 John ii. 1, 2. And further, upon occasion of these words, "All ye saints of God pray for us," being demanded what he meant by these words, "All ye saints," he answered, that he meant by them those that were alive, as St. Paul did by the Corinthians, and not by those that are dead: for he prayed not to them, he said, because he thought that they who are dead cannot pray for him. Also, when the whole church is gathered together, they pray one for another, or desire one to pray for another, with one heart; and that the will of the Lord may be fulfilled, and not ours. "And I pray," said he, "as our Saviour Christ prayed at his last hour: 'O my Father, if it be possible, let this cup pass from me: nevertheless not as I will, but as thou wilt.'" Matt. xxvi. 39.

3. He was demanded, whether he thought that any souls departed were yet in heaven or not?

He answered, that he believed that they are there where it pleased God to have them, that is to say, in the faith of Abraham, and that herein he would commit himself to the church.

4. It was demanded, whether he thought it necessary to salvation, for a man to confess his sins to a priest?

His answer was this, that it was lawful for one to confess and acknowledge his sins to another. As for any other confession he knew none. And further, he said, that if he came to the sermon, or any other place, where the word of God is preached, and there repented for his sin, he believed his sins forthwith forgiven of God, and that he needed not go to any confession.

5. That he should say and affirm, that the truth of the holy scriptures has been hid, and hath not appeared for these eight hundred years, neither was it known before now.

To this he said, that he meant no otherwise, but that the truth of holy scripture was never, these eight hundred years past, so plainly and expressly declared to the people as it has been within these six years.

6. He was demanded further, for what cause the holy scripture has been better declared within these six years, than it hath been these eight hundred years before?

He answered, to say plainly, he knew no man to have preached the word of God sincerely and purely, and after the true meaning of scripture, except Master Crome and Master Latimer, and that the New Testament, now translated into English, preaches and teaches the word of God; and that before that time men did only preach that folks should believe as the church believed, and then if the church erred men should err too. "However the church," said he, "of Christ cannot err: and that there were two churches, that is, the church of Christ militant, and the church of antichrist; and that this church of antichrist may and doth err, but the church of Christ doth not."

7. Whether he knew any person that died in the true faith of Christ, since the apostles' time?

He said, he knew Byfield, and thought that he died in the true faith of Christ.

8. He was asked what he thought of purgatory?

He answered, if any such thing had been mentioned to St. Paul about purgatory after this life, he thought St. Paul would have condemned it for an heresy. And when he heard Master Crome preach and say, that he thought there was a purgatory after this life, he thought in his mind that Master Crome lied, and spake against his conscience; and that there were an hundred more who thought the same as he did; saying, that he had seen the confession of Master Crome in print, a very foolish thing, as he judged.

And as concerning vows, he granted that there were lawful vows, as Ananias vowed (Acts v.); for it was in his own power, whether he would have sold his possession or not, and therefore he did offend. But vows of chastity, and all godliness, is given of God by his abundant grace, which no man of himself can keep, but it must be given him of God; and therefore a monk, friar, or nun, that hath vowed the vows of religion, if they think after their vows are made, that they cannot keep their promises that they made at baptism, they may go forth and marry, so that they keep, after their marriage, the promise that they made at baptism. And finally, he concluded, that he thought there were no other vows, but only the vow of baptism.

9. He was demanded, whether Luther being a friar, and taking a nun and marrying her, did well or no, and what he thought therein?

He answered, that he thought nothing. And when they asked him, whether it was immoral or not? he made answer, he could not say so.

As concerning the sacrament of extreme unction; he said, it was but a ceremony, neither did he know that a man should be the better for such oiling and anointing. The best of it was, that some good prayers were said at it.

Likewise, touching the sacrament of baptism, his words were these:—

" That as many as repent, and put on Christ, shall be saved: that is, as many as die concerning sin, shall live by faith with Christ. Therefore it is not we that live after that, but Christ in us. And so, whether we live or die, we are God's by adoption, and not by the water only, but by water and faith; that is, by keeping the promise made. ' For by grace are ye saved through faith,' saith St. Paul; ' and that not of yourselves: it is the gift of God.' " Eph. ii. 8.

He was asked moreover of matrimony, whether it was a sacrament or not, and whether it confers grace, being commanded in the old law, and not yet taken away?

His answer was, " That matrimony is an order or law, that the church of Christ hath made and ordained, by which men may take to themselves wives and not sin."

Lastly, for his books of scripture, and for his judgment of Tindal, because he was urged to confess the truth, he said, that he had the New Testament translated into the English tongue by Tindal within this month, and thought he offended not God in using and keeping the same, notwithstanding that he knew the king's proclamation to the contrary, and that it was prohibited in the name of the church at St. Paul's Cross. But for all that he thought the word of God had not forbid it; confessing, moreover, that he had in his keeping within this month these books:—" The Wicked Mammon," " The Obedience of a Christian Man," " The Practice of Prelates," " The Answer of Tindal to Thomas More's Dialogues," " The Book of Frith against Purgatory," " The Epistle of George Gee, alias George Clerk;" adding, that in all these books he never saw any errors. And if there were any such in them, then if they were corrected, it were good that the people had the books. And as concerning the New Testament in English, he thought it very good, and that the people should have it as it is. Neither did he ever know that Tindal was a naughty fellow. And to these answers he subscribed his name. This examination was the fifteenth day of December.

Now was the time either to save, or else utterly to cast himself away. Which of these ways he would take, the case present now required a present answer, for else the sentence definitive was ready there to be read, &c.

To conclude a long matter in few words: Bainham wavering in a doubtful perplexity, between life on the one hand, and death on the other, at length giving over to the adversaries, gave answer to them that he was contented to submit himself in those things wherein he had offended, excusing that he was deceived by ignorance. Then the bishop requiring him to state his mind plainly as to his answers above declared, and demanded what he thought thereof, whether they were true or not.

To this Bainham said, that it was too high for him to judge. And then being asked of the bishop, whether there was any purgatory? he answered and said, he could not believe that there was any purgatory after this life.

Upon other articles being examined and demanded, he granted as follows: that he could not judge whether Byfield died in the true faith of Christ or no; that a man making a vow, cannot break it without deadly sin; that a priest promising to live chaste, may not marry a wife; that he thinketh the apostles to be in heaven; that Luther did nought in marrying a nun; that a child is the better for confirmation; that it is an offence to God, if any man keep books prohibited by the church, the pope, the bishop, or the king; and said, that he pondered those points more now than he did before, &c.

The chancellor offering to him a bill of his abjuration, required him to read it, he did so.

After the reading of it, he burst out into these words, saying, that because there were many words in the abjuration, which he thought obscure, he protested that by his oath he intended not to go from such defence, which he might have had before his oath. The chancellor asked him why he made that protest. Bainham said, " For fear, lest any man of ill will accuse me hereafter." " Well, Master Bainham," said the chancellor, " take your oath, and kiss the book, or else I will do mine

office against you;" and so immediately he took the book in his hand and kissed it, and subscribed.

Which done, the chancellor receiving the abjuration at his hand put him to his fine, first to pay twenty pounds to the king. After that, he enjoined him penance, to go before the cross in procession at St. Paul's, and to stand before the preacher during the sermon at St. Paul's Cross, with a fagot upon his shoulder, on the next Sunday, and to return to the prison again, there to abide the bishop's determination; and so on the 17th day of Feb. he was released. It was scarce a month when he bewailed his abjuration, and was never quiet in his mind and conscience until he had acknowledged his fall to all his acquaintance, and asked God and all the world forgiveness before the congregation, in a warehouse in Bowlane; and immediately on the next Sunday after he came to St. Austin's, with the New Testament in his hand in English, and the " Obedience of a Christian Man" in his bosom, and stood up there before the people in his pew, there declaring openly with weeping tears, that he had denied God, and prayed all the people to forgive him, and to beware of his weakness, and not to do as he did; for," said he, " if I should not return again to the truth (having the New Testament in his hand) this word of God would damn me both body and soul at the day of judgment." And there he prayed every body rather to die than to do as he did; for he would not feel such an hell again as he did feel, for all the world's goods. Besides this, he wrote letters to the bishop, to his brother, and to others; so that shortly after he was apprehended, and committed to the Tower of London.

In due time he was tried as a relapsed heretic, and then the vicar-general, after he had taken deliberation and advice with his learned assistants, read the definitive sentence against him; whereby amongst other things, besides his abjuration, he pronounced and condemned him as a relapsed heretic, damnably fallen into sundry heresies, and so to be left unto the secular power; that is to say, to one of the sheriffs there present. After this sentence given, James Bainham was delivered into the hands of Sir Richard Gresham, sheriff, then being present, who caused him by his officers to be carried to Newgate, and he was burned in Smithfield the last day of April, A.D. 1532.

This Master Bainham, during his imprisonment, was very cruelly handled. For almost the space of a fortnight he lay in the bishop's coal-house in the stocks, with irons upon his legs. Then he was carried to the lord chancellor's, and there chained to a post two nights. Then he was carried to Fulham, where he was cruelly handled for the space of a fortnight. Then to the Tower, where he lay a fortnight, scourged with whips, to make him revoke his opinions. From thence he was carried to Barking, then to Chelsea, and there condemned, and so to Newgate from thence to be burned!

John Bent, a tailor, about this time, or not long before, was burned in the town of Devizes, in the county of Wiltshire, for denying of the sacrament of the altar, as they term it.

One Trapnel, Martyr.—Also about the same time was burned, in a town called Bradford, within the same county.

The History of three men hanged for the burning of the Rood of Dovercourt, collected out of a letter of Robert Gardiner, who was one of the doers of the same.

In the same year, 1532, there was an idol named the rood of Dover-court, to which there was a great resort of people. For at that time there was a rumour spread abroad amongst the ignorant sort, that the power of the idol of Dover-court was so great, that no man had power to shut the church-door where he stood, and therefore they let the church-door, both night and day, continually stand open, for the greater credit of their rumour. This seemed a great wonder to many ignorant men; but by others, whom God had blessed with his Spirit, it was greatly suspected, especially by those whose names follow:—Robert King of Dedham, Robert Debnam of Eastbergholt, Nicholas Marsh of Dedham, and

Robert Gardiner of Dedham, whose consciences were burthened to see the honour and power of the Almighty God so blasphemed by such an idol. Therefore they were resolved to travel out of Dedham in a goodly night, both hard frost and fair moonshine, although the night before and the night after were exceeding foul and rainy. It was, from the town of Dedham, to the place where the rood stood, ten miles. They went these ten miles, and found the church door open, which happened well for their purpose; for they found the idol, which had as much power to keep the door shut as to keep it open. They took the idol from his shrine, and carried him a quarter of a mile from the place where he stood, without any resistance of the idol. Then they struck fire with a flint-stone, and suddenly set him on fire, and he burned so brightly that he lighted them homeward one good mile out of the ten.

This done, there went a great talk abroad that they should have great riches in that place; but it was very untrue, for it was not their thought or enterprise, as they themselves afterwards confessed, for there was nothing taken away but his coat, his shoes, and tapers. The tapers helped to burn him, the shoes they had again, and the coat one Sir Thomas Rose burned, but they had neither penny, half-penny, groat, gold, nor jewel.

Three of them, however, were afterwards indicted of felony, and hanged in chains within half a year after, or thereabout; which three persons, at their death, through the Spirit of God, did more edify the people in godly learning, than all the sermons that had been preached there for a long time before.

The fourth man of this company, named Robert Gardiner, escaped their hands and fled; whom the Lord preserved, to whom be all honour and glory, world without end.

The same year, and the year before, there were many images cast down and destroyed in many places; as the image of the crucifix in the highway by Coggleshall, the image of St. Petronilla in the church of Great Horkesley, the image of St. Christopher by Sudbury, and another image of St. Petronilla in a chapel at Ipswich.

Also John Seward of Dedham overthrew the cross in Stoke-park, and took two images out of a chapel in the park, and cast them into the water.

The History, Examination, Death, and Martyrdom of John Frith.

Amongst all other evils there has been none for a long time which seemed to me more grievous than the lamentable death and cruel usage of John Frith, so learned and excellent a young man, who had so profited in all kind of learning and knowledge, that there was scarcely his equal among all his companions; and besides he had such a godliness of life joined with his doctrine, that it was hard to judge in which of them he excelled, being greatly praiseworthy in them both. But as to his doctrine, by the grace of Christ, we will speak hereafter. Notwithstanding his other singular gifts and ornaments of the mind by which he might have opened an easy way to honour and dignity, yet he chose rather to consecrate himself wholly to the church of Christ, shewing forth and practising the precept so highly commended of the philosophers, touching the life of man; which life, they say, is given to us in such sort, that how much better the man is, so much the less he should live to himself, but that we should think a great part of our birth due to our parents, a greater part to our country, and the greatest part of all bestowed upon the church, if we will be counted good men. First of all he began his study at Cambridge. Nature had planted in him, while a child, a great love of learning. He had also a wonderful promptness of wit, and a ready capacity to receive and understand any thing. Neither was there any diligence wanting in him, by which it came to pass, that he was not only a lover of learning, but also became a very learned man. When he had diligently laboured for certain years, with great profit to himself in the study of Latin and Greek, he at last became acquainted with William Tindal, through whose instructions he first received into his heart the seed of the gospel and sincere godliness.

At that time Thomas Wolsey, cardinal of York, prepared to build a college in Oxford, which had the name and title of Frideswide, but now named Christ's Church, not so much (as it is thought) for the love and zeal that he bore to learning, as for an ambitious desire of glory and renown, and to leave a perpetual name to posterity. This ambitious cardinal gathered together into that college whatever excellent things there were in the whole realm, either vestments, vessels, or other ornaments, besides provision of all kind of precious things. He also appointed to it all such men as were found to excel in any kind of learning and knowledge.

These men, conferring together upon the abuses of religion, at that time crept into the church, were therefore accused of heresy to the cardinal, and cast into a prison.

John Frith was dismissed from prison, upon condition that he would not pass above ten miles out of Oxford. Frith, after hearing of the examination of Dalaber and Garret, who bore fagots, went over the sea, and after two years he came over for exhibition of the prior of Reading (as was thought) and had the prior over with him.

Being at Reading, it happened that he was there taken for a vagabond, and brought to examination: where the simple man, who could not craftily enough colour himself, was set in the stocks. Where, after he had sate a long time, and was almost pined with hunger, and yet would not declare what he was, at last he desired that the schoolmaster of the town might be brought to him, who at that time was one Leonard Cox, a man very well learned. As soon as he came to him, Frith, by and by began in the Latin tongue to bewail his captivity.

The schoolmaster by and by, being overcome with his eloquence, did not only take pity and compassion upon him, but also began to love and embrace such an excellent wit and disposition, especially in such misery. Afterwards conferring more together upon many things, as touching the universities, schools, and tongues, they fell from the Latin into the Greek: in which Frith inflamed the love of that schoolmaster towards him, especially when the schoolmaster heard him so promptly by heart rehearse Homer's verses out of his first book of the Iliad. Upon this the schoolmaster went with all speed to the magistrates, grievously complaining of the injury which they shewed to so excellent and innocent a young man.

Thus Frith, through the help of the schoolmaster, was freely let out of the stocks, and set at liberty without further punishment. Yet his safety continued not long, owing to the great hatred and deadly pursuit of Sir Thomas More, who at that time being chancellor of England, persecuted him both by land and sea, besetting all the ways and havens, yea, and promising great rewards, if any man could bring him any news or tidings of him.

Thus Frith being on every side beset with troubles, and not knowing which way to turn, seeks for some place to hide himself in. Thus fleeing from one place to another, and often changing both his garments and his place, he yet could be in safety in no place; not long even among his friends: so that at last, being traitorously taken, he was sent to the Tower of London, where he had many conflicts with the bishops, but especially in writing with Sir Thomas More. The first occasion of his writing was this: he had a communication with a certain old familiar friend of his, about the sacrament of the body and blood of Christ. The whole disputation consisted especially in these four points:—

"1. That the matter of the sacrament is no necessary article of faith under pain of damnation.

"2. That forsomuch as Christ's natural body in like condition hath all properties of our body, sin only excepted, it cannot be, neither is it agreeable to reason, that he should be in two places or more at once, contrary to the nature of our body.

"3. Moreover, it shall not seem meet or necessary,

that we should in this place understand Christ's words according to the literal sense, but rather according to the order and phrase of speech, comparing phrase with phrase, according to the analogy of the scripture.

"4. Last of all, how that it ought to be received according to the true and right institution of Christ, although that the order which at this time is crept into the church, and is used now-a-days by the priests, do never so much differ from it."

And, as the treatise seemed somewhat long, his friend desired him that he would briefly commit it to writing, and give it to him for the help of his memory. Frith, although he was unwilling, and not ignorant how dangerous a thing it was to enter into such a matter, at the last, overcome by the entreaty of his friend, complied.

There was at that time in London, a tailor, named William Holt, who, feigning great friendship toward this party, urgently begged of him to let him read over that writing of Frith's; which, when he did, the other by and by carried it to More the chancellor. This was the occasion of great trouble, and also of death to Frith.

This was the whole sum of the reasons of Frith's book; first, to declare the pope's belief of the sacrament to be no necessary article of our faith; that is to say, that it is no article of our faith necessary to be believed under pain of damnation, that the sacrament should be the natural body of Christ; which he thus proveth. For many so believe, and yet in so believing the sacrament to be the natural body are not thereby saved, but receive it to their own damnation.

Again, in believing the sacrament to be the natural body, yet that natural presence of his body in the bread is not that which saves us, but his presence in our hearts by faith. And likewise, the not believing of his bodily presence in the sacrament, is not the thing that shall condemn us, but the absence of him out of our hearts, through unbelief. And if it be objected, that it is necessary to believe God's word under pain of damnation: to that he answers, "That the word taken in the right sense, as Christ meant, maintains no such bodily presence as the pope's church teaches, but rather a sacramental presence. And that," saith he, "may be further confirmed thus:—

"None of the old fathers, before Christ's incarnation, were bound, under pain of damnation, to believe this point.

"Now can we not be saved by the same faith that the old fathers were?

"And, therefore, none of us are bound to believe this point under pain of damnation.

"The first part," saith he, "is evident of itself. For how could they believe that which they never heard nor saw?

"The second part," saith he, "appears plainly by St. Augustine, writing ad Dardanum, and also by a hundred places more. Neither is there any thing that he doth more often inculcate than this, that the same faith that saved our fathers, saves us also; and, therefore, upon the truth of these two parts thus proved, must the conclusion needs follow."

Again, he argues thus:—

"None of the old fathers, before Christ's incarnation, did eat Christ corporally in their signs, but only mystically, and spiritually, and were saved.

"Now, we all eat Christ even as they did, and are saved as they were.

"And, therefore, none of us eat Christ corporally, but mystically, and spiritually, in our signs as they did.

For the proof of the first part, Frith declares how the ancient fathers, before Christ's incarnation, never believed any such point of this gross and carnal eating of Christ's body; and yet, notwithstanding, they did eat him spiritually and were saved: as Adam, Abraham, Moses, Aaron, Phinehas, and other godly Israelites besides. All which, saith he, did eat the body of Christ, and did drink his blood as we do. But this eating and drinking of theirs was spiritual, pertaining only to faith, and not to the teeth: "For they were under the cloud, and drank of that spiritual Rock that followed them:

and that Rock was Christ," which was promised them to come into the world. And this promise was first made to Adam, when, as it was said to the serpent; "I will put enmity between thee and the woman, and between thy seed and her seed," &c. And afterwards again, to Abraham: "In thy seed shall all nations be blessed," &c. Adding also the sacrament of circumcision, which was called the covenant; not because it was so, indeed, but because it was a sign and a token of the covenant made between God and Abraham, admonishing us thereby, how we should judge and think touching the sacrament of body and blood; to wit, that although it be called the body of Christ, yet we should properly understand thereby the fruit of our justification, which plentifully flows to all the faithful, by his most blessed body and blood. Likewise the same promise was made to Moses, the most meek and gentle captain of the Israelites, who did not only himself believe upon Christ, who was so often promised, but also prefigured him both by the manna which came down from heaven, and also by the water which issued out of the rock, for the refreshing of the bodies of his people.

Neither is it to be doubted, but that both the manna and the water had a prophetical mystery in them, declaring the very self-same thing then, which the bread and the wine do now declare unto us in the sacrament. They all did eat the same spiritual meat, and all did drink the same spiritual drink: all one spiritual thing, but not all one corporal matter (for they did eat manna, and we another thing) but the self-same spiritual thing that we do, and although they drank the same spiritual drink that we do, yet they drank one thing, and we another: which, nevertheless, signified all one thing in a spiritual sense. How did they drink all one thing? The apostle answers, "Of the spiritual Rock which followed them, for the Rock was Christ." The manna which came down from heaven, was the same unto them that our sacrament is unto us, and that by either of them is signified, that the body of Christ came down from heaven; and yet, notwithstanding, never any of them said, that the manna was the very body of the Messiah, as our sacramental bread is not indeed the body of Christ, but a mystical representation of the same. For, as the manna which came down from heaven, and the bread which is received in the supper, nourish the body, even so the body of Christ coming down from heaven, and being given for us, quickens the spirits of the believers unto life everlasting. Then, if the salvation of both people be alike, and their faith also one, there is no cause why we should add transubstantiation to our sacrament, more than they believed their manna to be altered and changed. Moreover, because they are named sacraments, even by the signification of the name they must needs be signs of things, or else of necessity they can be no sacraments.

When More had got a copy of this treatise, he sharpened his pen to make answer unto this young man (for so he calls him throughout his whole book) but when the book was once set forth, Frith got a copy, by means of his friends, and answered him out of the prison, omitting nothing that any man could desire to the perfect handling of the matter.

What knowledge and genius, and excellency of doctrine was in him may appear not only by his books which he wrote on the sacrament, but also in those which he wrote on purgatory. In which controversy he withstood the violence of three opponents, viz., Rochester, More, and Rastal, one by the help of the doctors, the other by wresting of the scriptures, and the third by the help of natural philosophy, had conspired against him. But he, as a Hercules, fighting not against two only, but even with all three at once, did so overthrow and confound them, that he converted Rastal.

Besides all these commendations of this young man, there was also in him a friendly and prudent moderation in uttering of the truth, joined with a learned godliness. Which has always so much prevailed in the church of Christ, that without it, all other good gifts of knowledge, be they ever so great, cannot greatly profit, but oftentimes do very much hurt.

And would to God that all things in all places were so free from all kinds of dissension, that there were no mention made amongst christians of Zuinglians and Lutherans, as neither Zuinglius nor Luther died for us, but that we might be all one in Christ. I do think that nothing could more grieve those worthy men, than that their names should be so abused to sects and factions, who so greatly withstood and strove against all factions.

But now, as we treat of the history of John Frith, I cannot choose, but must needs earnestly and heartily embrace the prudent and godly moderation which was in that man, who maintaining his controversy of the sacrament of the Lord's supper, no less godly than learnedly, yet did it so moderately, that he never seemed to strive against the papists, except he had been driven to it. In all other matters where necessity did not force him to contend, he was ready to grant all things for the sake of quietness.

When More brought against him the authority of Doctor Barnes, for the presence of the body and blood in the sacrament, he answered, that he would promise under this condition—that the sentence of Luther and Barnes might be held as ratified—he would never speak more of it: for they agreed with him, that the sacrament was not to be worshipped, and that idolatry being taken away, he was content to permit every man to judge of the sacrament, as God should put it into their hearts; for then there remained no more poison that any man ought or might be afraid of.

After he had now sufficiently contended in his writings with More, Rochester and Rastal, he was at last carried to Lambeth, before the archbishop of Canterbury, and afterwards to Croydon, before the bishop of Winchester, to plead his cause. Last of all, he was called before the bishops in a common assembly at London.

The order of his judgment, with the manner of his examination and articles which were objected against him, are comprised and set forth by himself in a letter written to his friends, whilst he was a prisoner in the Tower.

A Letter of John Frith to his Friends, concerning his troubles : wherein after he had first with a brief preface saluted them, entering then into the matter, he writes thus :—

" I doubt not, dear brethren, but that it doth greatly vex you to see the one part to have all the words, and freely to speak what they list, and the other to be put to silence, and not be heard. But refer your matters to God, who shortly shall judge after another fashion. In the meantime I have written to you as briefly as I may, what articles were objected against me, and what were the principal points of my condemnation, that you might understand the matter certainly.

" The whole matter of this my examination was comprehended in two special articles, that is to say, of purgatory, and of the substance of the sacrament.

" And first of all, as touching purgatory, they inquired of me whether I believed there was any place to purge the spots and filth of the soul after this life. But I said, that I thought there was no such place: for man, said I, consists and is made only of two parts, that is to say, of the body and the soul; the one is purged here in this world, by the cross of Christ, which he lays upon every child that he receives, as affliction, worldly oppression, persecution, imprisonment, &c. And last of all the reward of sin, which is death, is laid upon us ; but the soul is purged with the word of God, which we receive through faith, to the salvation both of body and soul. Now if you can shew me a third part of man besides the body and the soul, I will also grant to you the third place, which you call purgatory. But because you cannot do this, I must also of necessity deny to you the bishop of Rome's purgatory. Nevertheless, I count neither part a necessary article of our faith, to be believed under pain of damnation, whether there be such a purgatory or not.

" Secondly, they examined me touching the sacrament of the altar, whether it was the very body of Christ or not.

" I answered, that I thought it was both Christ's body and also our body, as St. Paul teaches us in the first epistle to the Corinthians, and tenth chapter. For in that it is made one bread of many grains of corn, it is called our body, which being divers and many members, are associated and gathered together into one fellowship or body. Likewise the wine, which is gathered of many clusters of grapes, and is made into one liquor. But the same bread again, in that it is broken, is the body of Christ, declaring his body to be broken and delivered to death, to redeem us from our iniquities.

" Furthermore, in that the sacrament is distributed, it is Christ's body, signifying that, as verily as the sacrament is distributed to us, so verily is Christ's body and the fruit of his passion distributed to all faithful people.

" In that it is received it is Christ's body, signifying that as verily as the outward man received the sacrament with his teeth and mouth, so verily doth the inward man, through faith, receive Christ's body and fruit of his passion, and is as sure of it as of the bread which he eateth.

" Well, said they, dost thou not think that his very natural body, flesh, blood, and bone, is really contained under the sacrament, and there present without all figure or similitude ? 'No,' said I, 'I do not think so : notwithstanding I would not that any should count, that I make my saying, which is the negative, any article of faith. For even as I say, that you ought not to make any article necessary of the faith on your part, which is an affirmative, so I say again, that we make no necessary article of the faith on our part, but leave it indifferent for all men to judge therein, as God shall open their hearts, and no side to condemn or despise the other, but to nourish in all things brotherly love, and one to bear another's infirmity.'

" After this they alleged the place of St. Augustine, where he saith, ' He was carried in his own hands.'

" I answered, that St. Augustine was a plain interpreter of himself ; for he says in another place, ' He was carried as it were in his own hands ;' which is a phrase of speech not of one that simply affirms, but only of one expressing a thing by a similitude. And although St. Augustine had not thus expounded himself, yet he writing unto Boniface plainly admonishes all men, that the sacraments represent and signify those things whereof they are sacraments, and many times even of the similitudes of the things themselves they take their names. And therefore, according to this rule it may be said, he was born in his own hands, when he bare in his hands the sacrament of his body and blood.

Then they alleged a place of Chrysostom, which at the first blush may seem to make much for them, who in a certain homily upon the supper writeth thus, ' Dost thou see bread and wine ? Do they depart from thee into the draught, as other meats do ? No, God forbid ; for as in wax, when it cometh to the fire, nothing of the substance remains nor abides : so likewise think that the mysteries are consumed by the substance of the body, &c.'

" These words I expounded by the words of the same doctor, which in another homily says on this manner, ' The inward eyes,' saith he, ' as soon as they see the bread, they flee over all creatures, and do not think of the bread that is baked of the baker, but of the bread of everlasting life, which is signified by the mystical bread.' Now compare these places together, and you shall perceive that the last expounds the first plainly. For he saith, dost thou see the bread and wine ? I answer by the second, Nay, for the inward eyes, as soon as they see the bread, do pass over all creatures, and do not any longer think upon the bread, but upon him which is signified by the bread. And after this manner he seeth it, and again he seeth it not : for as he seeth it with his outward and carnal eyes, so with his inward eyes he seeth it not, that is to say, regardeth not the bread, or thinketh not upon it, but is otherwise occupied. Even as when we play or do anything else negligently, we commonly are wont to say, we see not what we do ; but that indeed we do not see that which we go about, not because our mind is fixed on some other thing, and doth not attend unto that which the eyes do not see. In like manner may it be answered to that which follows, ' Do they depart from thee,' saith he, ' in the draught as other meats do ?' I will not so say, for other meats passing through the bowels, after they have of themselves given nourishment unto the body, be voided into the draft : but this is a spiritual meat, which is received by faith, and nourishes both body and soul unto everlasting life, neither is it at any time voided as other meats are.''

"Here peradventure many would marvel, that forsomuch as the matter touching the substance of the sacrament, being separate from the articles of the faith, and binding no man of necessity either to salvation or damnation, whether he believe it or not, but rather may be left indifferently unto all men, freely to judge either on the one part or on the other, according to his own mind, so that neither part do contemn or despise the other ; but that all love and charity be still holden and kept in this dissension of opinions : what then is the cause, why I would therefore so willingly suffer death ? The cause why I die is this, I cannot agree with the divines and other head prelates, that it should be necessarily determined to be an article of faith, and that we should believe under pain of damnation, the substance of the bread and wine to be changed into the body and blood of our Saviour JESUS CHRIST, the form and shape only not being changed. Which thing if it were most true (as they shall never be able to prove it by any authority of the scriptures or doctors) yet shall they not so bring to pass, that that doctrine, be it ever so true, should be held for a necessary article of faith. For there are many things both in the scriptures and other places, which we are not bound of necessity to believe as an article of faith.

"So it is true, that I was a prisoner and in bonds when I wrote these things, and yet for all that I will not hold it as an article of faith, but that you may without danger of damnation, either believe it, or think the contrary.

"But as touching the cause why I cannot affirm the doctrine of transubstantiation, various reasons lead me thereto.

First, I do plainly see it to be false and vain, and not to be grounded upon any reason, either of the scriptures or of approved doctors.

" Secondly, by my example I would not be an author to christians to admit anything as a matter of faith, more than their necessary points of the creed, wherein the whole sum of our salvation consists, especially such things, the belief of which have no certain argument of reason.

" I added, moreover, that their church, as they call it, hath no such power and authority, that it either ought or may bind us under the peril of our souls, to the believing of any such articles.

" Thirdly, Because I will not, for the favour of our divines or priests, be prejudicial in this point, to so many nations, of Germans, Helvetians, and others, who altogether rejecting the transubstantiation of the bread and wine into the body and blood of Christ, are all of the same opinion that I am, as well those that take Luther's part, as those that hold with Oecolampadius. Which things standing in this case, I suppose there is no man of any upright conscience, who will not allow the reason of my death, which I am put to for this only cause, that I do not think transubstantiation, although it were true indeed, should be established for an article of faith.''

But when no reason would prevail against the force and cruelty of these furious foes, on the 20th day of June, (A. D. 1533,) he was brought before the bishops of London, Winchester, and Lincoln. When he could not be persuaded to recant, or be brought to believe that the sacrament is an article of faith, he was condemned by the bishop of London to be burned, and sentence was given against him.

The sentence being read, the bishop of London directed his letter to Sir Stephen Peacock, mayor of London, and the sheriffs of the city, for receiving John Frith into their charge, who, being so delivered over to

them, on the 4th day of July, 1533, was carried to Smithfield to be burned, and when he was tied to the stake, it sufficiently appeared with what constancy and courage he suffered death ; for when the fagots and fire were put to him, he willingly embraced them, thereby declaring with what uprightness of mind he suffered his death for Christ's sake, and the true doctrine, whereof that day he gave with his blood a perfect and firm testimony. The wind made his death somewhat the longer, as it bore away the flame from him to his companion, who was tied to his back ; but he had established his mind with such patience, God giving him strength, that even as though he had felt no pain in that long torment, he seemed rather to rejoice for his companion, than to be careful for himself.

Thus truly is the power and strength of Christ, striving and vanquishing in his saints ; who sanctify us together with them, and direct us in all things to the glory of his most holy name. Amen.

Andrew Hewet.

Andrew Hewet, a young man of the age of four-and-twenty years, was apprentice with Master Warren, a tailor ; and as he went, upon a holiday, into Fleet-street, towards St. Dunstan's, he met with William Holt, and being suspected by Holt, who was a dissembling wretch, to be one that favoured the gospel, after a little talk with him, he went into a bookseller's house to avoid him. Then Holt sent for certain officers, and searched the house, and finding Andrew, apprehended him, and carried him to the bishop's house, where he was cast into irons. Being there a good while, he had a file conveyed to him, with which he filed off his irons, and got out of the gate. But being a man unskilful to hide himself, he met with one Withers, who was an hypocrite, as Holt was. Withers pretending a fair countenance to him, willed him to go with him, promising that he should be provided for ; and so he kept him in the country till Whitsuntide, and then brought him to London, to the house of one John Chapman, and there left him for the space of two days.

Then he came to Chapman's house again, and brought Holt with him ; and when they met Andrew they seemed as if they meant to do him much good, so they would needs sup there that night, and prepared meat at their own charges. They came at night and brought guests with them. When they had supped, they went their way, and Holt took out of his purse two groats, and gave them to Andrew, and embraced him in his arms. Within an hour after the bishop's chancellor, and serjeant Weaver came, and brought with them the watch, and searched the house, where they found John Chapman, and Andrew, and John Tibauld, whom they bound with ropes, and so carried them to the bishop's house. But Andrew Hewet they sent to the Lollard's Tower, and kept Chapman and Tibauld asunder. The next day bishop Stokesley came from Fulham, and after they were examined with a few threatening words, Chapman was committed to the stocks, with this threat, that he should tell another tale, or else he should sit there till his heels should drop from his body ; and Tibauld was shut up in a close chamber ; but Andrew Hewet, after a long and cruel imprisonment, was condemned to death, and burned with John Frith.

It was objected against Andrew Hewet, that he believed the sacrament of the altar, after the consecration, to be but a signification of the body of Christ, and that the host consecrated was not the very body of Christ. So, being demanded what he thought of the sacrament of the Lord's supper, he answered, " Even as John Frith thinks." Then one of the bishops asked, " Dost thou not believe that it is really the body of Christ, born of the Virgin Mary ?" " So," he said, " I do not believe." " Why not ?" said the bishop, " Because," said he, " Christ commanded me not to give credit rashly to all men, who say, ' Behold here is Christ, and there is Christ, for many false prophets shall arise.' ''

Then the bishops smiled at him ; and Stokesley, the bishop of London, said, " Why, Frith is an heretic, and

M M

already judged to be burned, and except thou revoke thine opinion, thou shalt be burned also with him." He saith, "I am content." Then the bishop asked him if he would forsake his opinions. He answered, "He would do as Frith did." He was sent to the prison to Frith, and afterwards they were carried together to the fire. The bishops used many persuasions to allure this good man from the truth, but he, manfully persisting in the truth, would not recant. Wherefore, on the 4th day of July, in the afternoon, he was carried into Smithfield with Frith, and there burned.

When they were at the stake, one Dr. Cook, a parson in London, openly admonished all the people that they should in no wise pray for them, no more than they would do for a dog. At which words, Frith smiling, desired the Lord to forgive them. These words not a little moved the people to anger. Thus, these two blessed martyrs committed their souls into the hands of God.

Thomas Benet, burned at Exeter.

This Thomas Benet was born in Cambridge, and made master of arts, a man very well learned, and of a godly disposition. This man, the more he grew and increased in the knowledge of God and his holy word, the more he disliked and abhorred the then corrupt state of religion; and, therefore, being desirous to live in more freedom of conscience, he forsook the university, and went into Devonshire, (A.D. 1524.) He came to the city of Exeter, and hiring a house, commenced teaching children, and by that means sustained his wife and family. He was of a quiet behaviour, of a godly conversation, and of a very courteous nature, humble to all men, and offensive to nobody. His greatest delight was to be at all sermons and preachings, of which he was a diligent and attentive hearer. The time which he had to spare from teaching, he gave wholly to his private study in the scriptures, having no dealings nor conferences with any body, saving with such as he could learn and understand to be favourers of the gospel, and zealous of God's true religion.

But as every tree and herb has his due time to bring forth his fruit, so did it appear by this man; for, daily seeing the glory of God blasphemed, idolatrous religion embraced and maintained, and that most false usurped power of the bishop of Rome extolled, he was so grieved in his conscience, and troubled in spirit, that he could not be quiet till he uttered his mind therein. He plainly opened and disclosed how blasphemously and abominably God was dishonoured, his word contemned, and his people, whom he so dearly bought, were by blind guides carried headlong to everlasting destruction; and, therefore, he could no longer endure, but must needs testify against their abominations; and, for his own part, for the testimony of his conscience, and for the defence of God's true religion, would yield himself most patiently, as God would give him grace, to die and to shed his blood therein, alleging that his death should be more profitable to the church of God, and for the edifying of his people, than his life should be. To whose persuasions, when his friends had yielded, they promised to pray to God for him, that he might be strong in the cause, and continue a faithful soldier to the end; which done, he gave order for the bestowing of such books as he had, and very shortly after, in the month of October, he wrote his mind on certain scrolls of paper, which he set upon the doors of the cathedral church; in which was written, "The pope is Antichrist, and we ought to worship God only, and no saints."

These bills being found, there was no small ado, and no little search made for the heretic that had set up these bills: and the mayor and his officers were not busy to find out this heretic; but to keep the people in their former blindness, order was taken that the doctors should resort to their pulpits every day, and confute this heresy. Nevertheless this Thomas Benet, keeping his own doings in secret, went the Sunday following to the cathedral church to the sermon, and by chance sate down by two men, who were the busiest in all the city in seeking and searching for heretics; and they behold-

ing Benet, said the one to the other; surely this fellow by all likelihood is the heretic that hath set up the bills, and it were good to examine him. Nevertheless when they had well beheld him, and saw the quiet and sober behaviour of the man, his attentiveness to the preacher, his godliness in the church, being always occupied in his book, which was a testament in the Latin tongue, were astonished, and had no power to speak to him, but departed and left him reading in his book.

In the meantime the canons and priests, the officers and commons of the city were very earnestly busied, how, or by what means such an enormous heretic, who had put up those bills might be espied and known; but it was long first. At last, the priests found out a way to curse him, whoever he was, with book, bell, and candle; which curse at that day, seemed most fearful and terrible. The manner of the curse was after this sort.

One of the priests apparelled all in white, ascended the pulpit. The other priests, with certain of the two orders of friars, and certain superstitious monks of St. Nicholas' house standing round about, and the cross (as the custom was) being holden up with holy candles of wax fixed to the same, he began his sermon, which was not so long, as tedious and superstitious: and concluded, "That that soul and abominable heretic who had put up such blasphemous bills, was for his blasphemy damnably cursed, and he besought God, our Lady, St. Peter, patron of that church, with all the holy company of martyrs, confessors, and virgins, that it might be known what heretic had put up such blasphemous bills, that God's people might escape the vengeance."

The manner of the cursing of Benet was extraordinary: the prelate said, "By the authority of God the Father Almighty, and of the blessed Virgin Mary, of St. Peter and St. Paul, and of the holy saints, we excommunicate, we utterly curse and ban, commit and deliver to the devil of hell, him or her, whosoever he or she be, that have in spite of God and of St. Peter, whose church this is, in spite of all holy saints, and in spite of our most holy father the pope, God's vicar here on earth, and in spite of the reverend father in God, John our diocesan, and the worshipful canons, masters, and priests, and clerks, who serve God daily in this cathedral church, fixed up with wax such cursed and heretical bills full of blasphemy, upon the doors of this and other holy churches within this city. Excommunicate plainly be he or she, or they, and delivered over to the devil, as perpetual malefactors and schismatics. Accursed may they be, and given body and soul to the devil. Cursed be they, he or she, in cities and towns, in fields, in ways, in paths, in houses, out of houses, and in all other places, standing, lying, or rising, walking, running, waking, sleeping, eating, drinking, and whatsoever thing they do besides. We separate them, him or her, from the threshold, and from all the good prayers of the church, from the participation of the holy mass, from all sacraments, chapels, and altars, from holy bread, and holy water, from all the merits of God's priests, and religious men, and from all their cloisters, from all their pardons, privileges, grants, and immunities, which all the holy fathers, popes of Rome, have granted to them; and we give them over utterly to the power of the fiend, and let us quench their souls, if they be dead, this night in the pains of hell fire, as this candle is now quenched and put out (and with that he put out one of the candles:) and let us pray to God (if they be alive) that their eyes may be put out, as this candle light is (so he put out the other candle:) and let us pray to God and to our Lady, and to St. Peter and St. Paul, and all holy saints, that all the senses of their bodies may fail them, and that they may have no feeling, as now the light of this candle is gone (and so he put out the third candle:) except they, he or she, come openly now and confess their blasphemy, and by repentance (as in them shall lie) make satisfaction unto God, our Lady, St. Peter, and the worshipful company of this cathedral church; and as this holy cross staff now falleth down, so might they, except they repent, and shew themselves;" and one first taking away the cross, the staff fell down. But oh, what a shout and noise was there, what terrible fear.

what holding up of hands to heaven, that curse was so terrible!

Now this fond foolish mockery being done and played off, Benet could no longer forbear, but fell to great laughter, but within himself, and for a long time could not cease, by which the poor man was observed. For those that were next to him, wondering at that great curse, and believing that it could not but light on one or other, asked good Benet, for what cause he did so laugh. "My friend," said he, "who can forbear, seeing such merry conceits and interludes played by the priests?" Straightway a noise was made, "Here is the heretic! here is the heretic! hold him fast, hold him fast! with that, there was a great confusion of voices, and much clapping of hands, and yet they were uncertain whether he were the heretic or not. Some say, that upon that he was taken and apprehended. Others report, that his enemies, being uncertain of him, departed, and so he went home to his house.

He was soon after apprehended, and on the morrow the canons and heads of the city examined him. When he confessed and said, "It was even I that put up those bills, and if it were to do, I would do it again; for in them I have written nothing but what is very truth." "Couldst not thou," said they, "as well have declared thy mind by mouth, as by putting up bills of blasphemy?" "No," said he, "I put up the bills, that many should read and hear what abominable blasphemers you are, and that they might the better know your antichrist, the pope, to be that boar out of the wood, who destroys and throws down the hedges of God's church; for if I had been heard to speak but one word, I should have been clapped fast in prison, and the matter of God hidden. But now I trust more of your blasphemous doings will thereby be opened and come to light; for God will so have it, and no longer will suffer you."

The next day he was sent to the bishop, who first committed him to the prison, called the bishop's prison, where he was kept in stocks and strong irons, with as much favour as if he were a dog. Then the bishop, and others of his clergy and friars, began to examine him and charge him, that contrary to the catholic faith he denied praying to saints, and also denied the supremacy of the pope. He answered in such sober manner, and so learnedly proved and defended his assertions, that he not only confounded and put to silence his adversaries, but also brought them into great admiration of him, the most part having pity and compassion on him. Among other priests and friars, Gregory Basset was most busy with him.

The principal point between Basset and him was concerning the supremacy of the bishop of Rome, whom he named antichrist, the thief, the mercenary, and murderer of Christ's flock: and these disputations lasted about eight days, where there repaired to him both the Black and Gray-Friars, with priests and monks of that city. They that had some learning persuaded him to believe the church, and shewed by what tokens she is known. The unlearned railed, and said, that the devil tempted him, and spit upon him, calling him heretic: but he only prayed God to give them a better mind, and to forgive them: "For," said he, "I will rather die, than worship such a beast, the very whore of Babylon, and a false usurper, as manifestly appears by his doings." They asked, "What he did, that he had not power and authority to do, being God's vicar?" "He doth," quoth he, "sell the sacraments of the church for money, he selleth remission of sins daily for money, and so do you likewise: for there is no day but you say masses for souls in feigned purgatory: yea, and you spare not to make lying sermons to the people, to maintain your false traditions, and foul gains. The whole world begins now to note your doings, to your utter confusion and shame." "The shame," say they, "shall be to thee, and such as thou art, thou foul heretic. Wilt thou allow nothing done in holy church? What a perverse heretic art thou!" "I am," said he, "no heretic, but a christian man; I thank Christ, and with all my heart will allow all things done and used in the church to the glory of God, and edifying of my soul: but I see nothing in your church, but what maintains the devil." "What is our church?" said they. "It is not my church," quoth Benet, "God give me grace to be of a better church, for verily your church is the plain church of antichrist, the malignant church, the second church, a den of thieves, and as far wide from the true universal and apostolic church, as heaven is distant from the earth." "Dost not thou think," said they, "that we pertain to the universal church?" "Yes," quoth he, "but as dead members, unto whom the church is not beneficial: for your works are the devices of man, and your church a weak foundation; for ye say and preach, that the pope's word is equal with God's word in every degree." "Why," said they, "did not Christ say to Peter, 'To thee I will give the keys of the kingdom of heaven?'" "He said that," quoth he, "to all the apostles as well as to Peter, and Peter had no more authority given him than they, or else the churches planted in every kingdom by their preaching are no churches. Doth not St. Paul say, ' Upon the foundation of the apostles and prophets?' Therefore I say plainly, that the church that is built upon a man, is the devils church or congregation, and not God's. And as every church this day is appointed to be ruled by a bishop or pastor, ordained by the word of God in preaching and administration of the sacraments under the prince the supreme governor under God: so to say, that all the churches with their princes and governors are subject to one bishop is detestable heresy, and the pope your God, challenging this power to himself, is the greatest schismatic that ever was in the church, and the most foul whore: of whom John in the revelation speaketh."

"O thou blind and unlearned fool," said they, "is not the confession and consent of all the world as we confess and consent; That the pope's holiness is the supreme head and vicar of Christ?" "That is," said Benet, "because they are blinded and know not the scriptures: but if God would of his mercy open the eyes of princes to know their office, his false supremacy would soon decay." "We think," said they, "thou art so malicious that thou wilt confess no church." "Look," said he, "where they are that confess the true name of Jesus Christ, and where only Christ is the head, and under him the prince of the realm, to order all bishops, ministers and preachers, and to see them do their duties in setting forth the only glory of God by preaching the word of God; and where it is preached, that Christ is our only advocate, mediator, and patron before God his Father, making intercession for us, and where the true faith and confidence in Christ's death and passion, and his only merits and deservings are extolled, and our own depressed; where the sacrament is duly without superstition or idolatry administered in remembrance of his blessed passion, and only sacrifice upon the cross once for all, and where no superstition reigneth, of that church will I be." "Doth not the pope," said they, "confess the true gospel? do not we all the same?" "Yes," said he, "but ye deny the fruits thereof in every point. Ye build upon the sands, not upon the rock." "And wilt thou not believe, indeed," said they, "that the pope is God's vicar?" "No," said he, "indeed." "And why?" said they. "Because," he answered, "he usurpeth a power not given him of Christ, no more than to other apostles; and also because he doth by force of that usurped supremacy blind the whole world, and doth contrary to all that ever Christ ordained or commanded." "What," said they, "if he do all things after God's ordinance and commandment, should he then be his vicar?" "Then," said he, "would I believe him to be a good bishop at Rome over his own diocese, and to have no further power. And if it pleased God, I would that every bishop did this in their diocese: then should we live a peaceable life in the church of Christ, and there should be no such seditions therein. If every bishop would seek no further power than over his own diocese, it were a goodly thing. Now because all are subject to one, all must do and consent to all wickedness as he doth, or be none of his. This is the cause of great superstition in every kingdom. And what bishop soever he be that preaches the gospel, and maintains the truth, is a true bishop of the church." "And doth not," said they, "our holy father the pope maintain the gospel?" "Yea," said he, "I think he doth read it, and peradventure believe it, and so do you also; but neither he nor you do fix the anchor of your salvation therein. Besides that, you bear such a good will to it, that you keep it close, that no man may read it but yourselves. And when you preach, God knows how you handle it: insomuch, that the people of Christ know no gospel, but the pope's gospel; and so the blind lead the blind, and both fall into the pit. In the true gospel of Christ confidence is none, but only in your popish traditions, and fantastical inventions." Then said a Black friar to him, "Do we not preach the gospel daily?" "Yes," said he, "but what preaching of the gospel is that, when with it, you extol superstitious things, and make us believe that we have redemptions through pardons and bulls from Rome, *a pœna et culpa*, as you term it: and by the merits of your orders you make many brethren and sisters, you take money yearly of them, you bury them in your coats, and in confession you beguile them: yea, and do a thousand superstitious things more; a man may be weary to speak of them." "I see," said the friar, "thou art a vile heretic, I will have no more talk with thee."

Then stepped to him a Gray friar, a doctor, and laid before him great and many dangers. "I take God to record;" said Benet, "my life is not dear to me, I am content to depart from it, for I am weary of it, seeing your detestable doings, to the utter destruction of God's flock; and for my part, I can no longer forbear: I had rather by death (which I know is not far off) depart this life, that I may no longer be partaker of your detestable idolatries and superstitions, or be subject unto antichrist your pope." "Our pope," said the friar, "is the vicar of God, and our ways are the ways of God." "I pray you," said Benet, "depart from me, and tell me not of your ways. He is only my way, which saith, 'I am the way, the truth, and the life.' In this way will I walk, his doings shall be my example, not yours, nor your false popes. His truth will I embrace, not the lies and falsehood of you and your pope. His everlasting life will I seek, the true reward of all faithful people. Away from me, I pray you. Vex my soul no longer, you shall not prevail. There is no good example in you, no truth in you, no life to be hoped for at your hands. You are all more vain than vanity itself. If I should hear and follow you thus, everlasting death should hang over me,—a just reward for all them that love the life of this world. Away from me, your company liketh me not."

When these canons and priests with the monks and friars, had done what they could, and had perceived that he would by no means recant; then they proceeded to judgment, and drew out their sentence against him, condemning him to be burned. This christian martyr, rejoicing that his end approached so near, yielded himself 'as a sheep before the shearer,' with all humbleness to abide and suffer the cross of persecution. And being brought to his execution, he made his most humble confession and prayer to Almighty God, and requested all the people to do the like for him, whom he exhorted with such gravity and sobriety, and with such a pithy oration to seek the true honouring of God, and the true knowledge of him, as also to leave the devises, fantasies, and imaginations of men's inventions, that all the beholders of him were astonished and in great admiration: insomuch that the most part of the people, as also the scribe who wrote the sentence of condemnation against him, did pronounce and confess that he was God's servant, and a good man.

Two esquires, namely, Thomas Carew, and John Barnehouse, standing at the stake by him, first with fair promises and good words, but at length, through threatenings, desired him to revoke his errors, and to call upon our Lady and the saints. To whom he with all meekness answered, "No, no, it is God only upon whose name we must call and we have no other advo-

cate with him, but only Jesus Christ, who died for us, and now sits at the right hand of the Father to be an advocate for us; and by him must we offer our prayers to God, if we will have them to take place and be heard." With which answer Barnehouse was so enraged, that he took a furze-bush upon a pike, and setting it on fire, thrust it into his face, saying, "Ah, heretic, pray to our Lady, or I will make thee do it."

To whom Thomas Benet, with an humble and a meek spirit, most patiently answered, "Alas, sir, trouble me not." And holding up his hands, he said, "Father, forgive them." After which the gentlemen caused the wood and furzes to be set on fire, and this godly man lifted up his eyes and hands to heaven, saying, "O Lord receive my spirit." And so continuing in prayer, he never stirred, but most patiently abode the torments of the fire, until his life was ended. For which let the Lord God be praised, and send us his grace and blessing, that at the latter day we may with him enjoy the bliss and joy provided and prepared for the elect children of God.

The Marriage between King Henry VIII. and Anne Boleyn; and Queen Catharine divorced.

After the death of prince Arthur, the lady Catharine, widow of prince Arthur, by the consent both of her father and his, and also by the advice of the nobles of this realm, that her dowry might remain still within the realm, was espoused after the decease of her husband, to his next brother, who was King Henry VIII.

This marriage seemed very strange for one brother to marry the wife of another. But what in this earth can be so hard or difficult, with which the pope, the omnipotent vicar of Christ, cannot dispense, if it please him? The pope who then ruled at Rome was Julius II., by whose dispensation this marriage, which neither nature would admit, nor God's law sanction, was concluded, approved, and ratified, and so continued as lawful, without any doubt or scruple for the space of near twenty years, till a doubt began first to be moved by the Spaniards, A. D. 1523, when the Emperor Charles promised to marry the lady Mary, daughter to the king of England. With this promise, the Spaniards were not contented, objecting, among other causes, that the lady Mary was begotten of the king of England by his brother's wife.

Upon this the emperor married the lady Isabella, daughter to Emanuel, the late king of Portugal, and the sister of John III., A.D. 1526. King Henry, being disappointed thus by the emperor, endeavoured through the French ambassadors, that lady Mary should be married to the French king's son, the duke of Orleans. After long debating, at length the matter was put off by the president of Paris raising a doubt, whether the marriage between the king and the mother of this lady Mary, who had been his brother's wife before, were good or not.

The king, upon this, began to consider the case more deeply, first with himself, afterwards with his nearest council; there were two things which chiefly troubled his mind, the one touched his conscience, the other concerned the state of his realm. For if that marriage with his brother's wife stood unlawful by the law of God, then neither was his conscience clear in retaining the mother, nor yet the state of the realm safe by succession of the daughter. It happened at the time that the cardinal, who was then nearest about the king, had fallen out with the emperor, for not assisting him to the papacy, for which cause he helped to set the matter forward. Thus the king, perplexed in his conscience, and careful for the commonwealth, and incited by the cardinal, could not rest, but inquired further to know what the word of God and learning would say to it. Nor was the case so hard, after it began once to become a public question, but that by the word of God, and the judgments of the best learned clerks, and also by the censure of the chief universities of all Christendom, to the number of ten and more, it was soon declared to be unlawful.

All these censures, books and writings of so many doctors, clerks, and universities, sent from all quarters of Christendom to the king, although they might suffice to have resolved, and did indeed resolve, the king's conscience, touching this scruple of his marriage ; yet he would not straightway use that advantage which learning gave him, unless he had the assent of the pope, and the emperor ; in which he perceived no little difficulty. For the pope, he thought, seeing the marriage was authorized before by the dispensation of his predecessor, would hardly turn his keys about to undo that which the pope before him had locked, and much less would he suffer those keys to be foiled, or come in any doubt, which was likely to come, if that marriage were proved incapable of dispensation by God's word, which his predecessor through his plenary power, had licensed. Again, the assent of the emperor he thought would be no less difficult, as the lady Catharine was the emperor's aunt, and a Spaniard. Nevertheless, his purpose was to ascertain what they would say to it, and therefore he sent Stephen Gardiner to Rome to treat with pope Clement. To the emperor he sent Sir Nicholas Harvey, knight, ambassador to the court of Ghent. First, pope Clement, not weighing the full importance of the matter, sent cardinal Campegio (as is said into England), joined with the cardinal of York.

At the coming of the legates, the king, first opening to them the grief of his conscience, seemed, with great reasons and persuasions to have sufficiently drawn the good will of those two legates to his side. Who also, of their own accord, pretended to shew a willing inclination to further the king's object. But yet the mouths of the common people, and especially of the women, and such others as favoured the queen, were not stopped. He, therefore, willing that all men should know his proceedings, caused all his nobility, judges, and counsellors, with divers other persons, to resort to his palace on the 8th of Nov. 1529, where he openly spoke in his council chamber as follows :—

The King's Oration to his Subjects.

" Our trusty and wellbeloved subjects, both you of the nobility, and you of the meaner sort, it is not unknown unto you, how that we both by God's provision, and true and lawful inheritance, have reigned over this realm of England almost the term of twenty years. During which time we have so ordered us (thanks be to God) that no outward enemy hath oppressed you, nor taken any thing from us, nor have we invaded any realm, but we have had victory and honour, so that we think that you nor none of your predecessors ever lived more quietly, more wealthy, nor in more estimation under any of our noble progenitors. But when we remember our mortality, and that we must die, then we think that all our doings in our lifetime are clearly defaced, and worthy of no memory, if we leave you in trouble at the time of our death ; for if our true heir be not known at the time of our death, see what mischief and trouble shall succeed to you and to your children. The experience thereof some of you have seen after the death of our noble grandfather, king Edward the Fourth, and some have heard what mischief and manslaughter continued in this realm between the houses of York and Lancaster, by which dissension this realm was like to have been nearly destroyed.

And although it hath pleased Almighty God to send us a fair daughter of a noble woman, and of me begotten, to our great comfort and joy, yet it hath been told us by divers great clerks, that neither she is our lawful daughter, nor her mother our lawful wife, but that we live together abominably and detestably in open adultery ; insomuch that when our ambassador was last in France, and motion was made that the duke of Orleans should marry our said daughter, one of the chief councillors to the French king, said, ' It were well done to know whether she be the king of England's lawful daughter or not for well known it is, that he begot her on his brother's wife, which is directly against God's law and his precepts.' Think you, my lords, that these words touch not my body and soul ? Think you that these things do not daily and hourly trouble my conscience, and vex my spirits ? Yes, we doubt not but if it were your

cause, every man would seek remedy, when the peril of your soul, and the loss of your inheritance is openly laid unto you. For this only cause I protest before God, and on the word of a prince, I have asked counsel of the greatest clerks in Christendom, and for this cause I have sent for this legate, as a man indifferent, only to know the truth, and so to settle my conscience, and for none other cause, as God can judge. And as touching the queen, if it be adjudged by the law of God that she is my lawful wife, there was never any thing more pleasant nor more acceptable to me in my life, both for the discharge and clearing of my conscience, and also for the good qualities and conditions which I know to be in her. For I assure you all, that beside her noble parentage of which she is descended (as you well know) she is a woman of most gentleness, of most humility and buxomness ; yea, and of all good qualities appertaining to nobility, she is without comparison, as I these twenty years almost have had the true experience ; so that, if I were to marry again, if the marriage might be good, I would surely choose her above all other women. But if it be determined by judgment, that our marriage was against God's law, and clearly void, then shall I not only sorrow the departing from so good a lady and loving companion, but much more lament and bewail my unfortunate chance, that I have so long lived in adultery to God's great displeasure, and have no true heir of my body to inherit this realm. These be the sores that vex my mind, these be the pangs that trouble my conscience, and for these griefs I seek remedy. Therefore I require you all, as our trust and confidence is in you, to declare to our subjects our mind and intent, according to our true meaning, and desire them to pray with us that the very truth may be known, for the discharge of our conscience and saving of our soul, and for the declaration hereof I have assembled you together, and now you may depart."

Shortly after this oration of the king, with which he stirred the hearts of a number, the two legates, being requested of the king, for the discharge of his conscience, to judge and determine upon the cause, went to the queen and declared to her how they were deputed as impartial judges between the king and her, to hear and determine whether the marriage between them stood with God's law or not. When she understood the cause of their coming, being somewhat astonished at first, after a little pausing with herself, she thus began :

"Alas, my lords," said she, "is it now a question whether I be the king's lawful wife or not, when I have been married to him almost twenty years, and never question was made before ? Many prelates yet alive, and lords also, and privy counsellors with the king at that time, then adjudged our marriage lawful and honest, and now to say it is detestable and abominable, I think very strange ; and especially when I consider what a wise prince the king's father was, and also the love and natural affection that king Ferdinand, my father, bore to me, I think that neither of our fathers were so uncircumspect, so unwise, and of so small imagination, but that they foresaw what might follow our marriage ; and the king, my father, sent to the court of Rome, and there, after long suit, with great cost and charge, obtained a licence and dispensation, that I being the one brother's wife, might, without scruple of conscience, marry with the other brother lawfully, which licence I have in my possession yet to shew ; which things make me to say and believe that our marriage was lawful, good and godly. But for all this trouble I have only to thank you, my lord cardinal of York, because I have wondered at your high pride and vain glory, and abhorred your voluptuous life and abominable immorality, and little regarded your presumptuous power and tyranny, therefore from malice you have kindled this fire, and set this matter abroad, and especially for the great malice you bear to my nephew the emperor, whom I perfectly know you hate worse than a scorpion; because he would not satisfy your ambition and make you pope ; and therefore you have said more than once, that you would trouble him and his friends, and you have kept your promise ; for all his wars and vexations he may thank you only. And as for me, his poor aunt and kinswoman, what trouble you have put me to by this new found doubt, God knoweth, to whom I commit my cause according to the truth."

The cardinal of York excused himself, saying, that he was not the beginner nor the mover of the doubt, and that it was much against his will that ever the marriage should come in question, but he said that by his superior, the bishop of Rome, he was deputed as a judge to hear the cause: which he swore on his profession to hear impartially; but whatever was said she believed him not; and so the legates took their leave of her and departed.

These words were spoken in French, and written by cardinal Campegio's secretary, who was present.

In the next year, 1530, at the Blackfriars of London, was prepared a solemn place for the two legates: who coming with their crosses, and all other Romish ceremonies, were set in two chairs covered with cloth of gold, and cushions of the same. When all things were ready, then the king and the queen were cited by Dr. Sampson to appear before the legates on the 31st of May; where (the commission of the cardinals being first read, wherein it was appointed by the court of Rome, that they should be the hearers and judges in the cause between them both) the king was called by name; who appeared by two proctors: then the queen was called, who being accompanied with four bishops, and others of her council, and a great company of ladies, came personally before the legates: who there, after her obeisance, with a sad gravity of countenance, uttering not many words, but appealed from the legates, as judges not competent, to the court of Rome, and so departed. Notwithstanding this appeal, the cardinals sat weekly, and every-day arguments on both sides were brought, but nothing definitive was determined.

As the time passed on, in the month of June, the king being desirous to see an end, came to the court, and the queen also, where he standing under his cloth of estate, uttered these or like words in effect as follows:

"My lords, legates of the see apostolic, who are deputed judges in this great and weighty matter, I most heartily beseech you to ponder my mind and intent, which only is to have a final end for the discharge of my conscience. For every good christian man knoweth what pain and what unquietness he suffereth who hath his conscience grieved. For I assure you on my honour, that this matter hath so vexed my mind, and troubled my spirits, that I can scarcely study any thing which should be profitable for my realm and people: and to have a quietness in body and soul is my desire and request, and not for any grudge that I bear to her that I have married; for I dare say, that for her womanhood, wisdom, nobility, and gentleness, never prince had such another: and therefore if I would willingly change I were not wise. Wherefore my suit is to you, my lords, at this time, to have a speedy end, according to right, for the quietness of my mind and conscience only, and for no other cause, as God knoweth."

When the king had spoken, the queen departed without saying any thing. Then she was called to know whether she would abide by her appeal, or answer there before the legates. Her proctor answered, that she would abide by her appeal. Notwithstanding, the councillors on both sides met almost every day and debated this matter, so that at last the divines were all of opinion that the marriage was against the law of God, if she were carnally known by the first brother; which she clearly denied. But to that it was answered, that prince Arthur, her husband, confessed the act. And at the time of the death of prince Arthur, she thought and judged that she was with child, and for that cause the king was deferred from the title and creation of the Prince of Wales almost half a year.

Thus when the divines on her side were beaten from the ground, then they fell to persuasions of natural reasons, how this should not be undone for three reasons: one was, because if it should be broken, the only child of the king would be illegitimised, which were a great mischief to the realm. Secondly, the separation would be a cause of great enmity between her kindred and this realm. And the third reason was, that the continuance for so long a time had made the marriage good. These persuasions, with many others, were set forth by the queen's counsel, and especially by the bishop of Rochester, who stood firm in her cause. But yet God's precept was not answered; so they left that ground, and fell to pleading, that the court of Rome had dispensed with this marriage. To this some lawyers said, that no earthly person is able to dispense with the positive law of God.

When the legates heard the opinions of the divines, and saw where the end of this question would tend, as men began to dispute the authority of the court of Rome, and especially because the cardinal of York perceived the king cast favour on the lady Anne, whom he knew to be a Lutheran, they thought best to rid themselves out of that difficulty in time; and so cardinal Campegio dissembling the matter, conveyed himself home to Rome again. The king seeing himself thus deluded by the cardinals, took no little grief:—the fall of the cardinal of York followed not long after.

This was in the year 1530. Shortly after it happened that the king by his ambassadors was advertised, that the emperor and the pope were both together at Bononia. So he directed Sir Thomas Bullen, created earl of Wiltshire, and doctor Stokesley (afterward bishop of London) and doctor Lee (afterwards archbishop of York) with his message to the pope's court, where the emperor was. Pope Clement fearing what might follow, if learning and scripture should here take place against the authority of their dispensations, and suspecting the emperor's displeasure, avoided the matter, answering the ambassadors, that he would not hastily decide in this case, but would hear the full matter disputed when he came to Rome, and would do justice according to right.

Although the king owed no such service to the pope, to stand to his arbitration either in this case, or in any other, having both the scripture to lead him, and his law in his own hands to warrant him, yet for quietness sake, and for that he might not rashly break order, he bare so long as conveniently he might. At length, after long delays and much dissembling, when he saw no hope of redress, he began somewhat to quicken and to look about him, what was best both for his own conscience, and the establishment of his realm.

No man here doubts, but that all this was wrought not by man's device, but by the secret purpose of the Lord himself, to bring to pass further things, which his Divine Providence was disposed to work. For as to the king's intent and purpose, he never meant nor minded any such thing as to seek the ruin of the pope, but rather sought all means contrary, how both to establish the see of Rome, and also to obtain the good will of the same see and court of Rome. And therefore intending to seek his divorce from Rome, at the beginning; his device was by Stephen Gardiner, his ambassador at Rome, to exalt the cardinal of York, as we before shewed, to be made pope and universal bishop, to the end that he ruling that apostolic see, the matter of his unlawful marriage, which so troubled his conscience, might come to a quiet conclusion without any further rumour of the world. Which purpose of his, if it had taken effect as he had devised it, and the English cardinal had once been made pope, no doubt but the authority of that see had never been exterminated out of England. But God being more merciful to us, took a better way. For both without, and contrary to the king's expectation, he so brought things to pass, that neither the cardinal of York was pope; and yet nevertheless the king succeeded in his purpose. For he was rid, by lawful divorce, not only from that unlawful marriage which troubled his conscience, but also from the miserable yoke of the pope's usurped dominion, which clogged the whole realm.

Thus God's holy Providence ruling the matter, as I said, when the king could get no favourable grant of the pope touching his cause, being so good and honest, he was enforced to take the redress of his right into his own hands, and seeing this Gordian knot would not be loosed at Rome, he was driven against his will, to play the noble Alexander himself, and with the sword of his princely authority cut the knot. For where the doctors and canonists had long disputed, and yet could never thoroughly discuss the largeness and fulness of the pope's two swords both temporal and spiritual, the king with one sword did so cut off both his swords, that he dispatched them both clean out of England. But first the king, like a prudent prince, following his own proverb, as one going about to cast down an old rotten wall, will not begin with the foundation first, but with the stones that lie on the top, so he, to prepare his way better to the pope, first began with the cardinal, casting him, by the law of præmunire, out of his goods and possessions. Shortly after this, about the year 1532, the king gave forth this proclamation:

"The king's highness straightly chargeth and commandeth, that no manner of person, what estate, degree, or condition soever he or they be of, do purchase, or attempt to purchase from the court of Rome, or elsewhere, nor use and put in execution, divulge, or publish any thing heretofore, within this year passed, purchased, or to be purchased hereafter, containing matter prejudicial to the high authority, jurisdiction, and prerogative royal of this his said realm, or to the let, hindrance, or impeachment of his grace's noble and virtuous intended purposes in the premises, upon pain of incurring his highness' indignation, and imprisonment, and further punishment of their bodies for their so doing, at his grace's pleasure, to the dreadful example of all others."

After this, the king, proceeding further, caused the rest of the spiritual lords to be called by process into the King's Bench, as the whole clergy of England, in supporting and maintaining the legantine power of the cardinal, were all entangled in the præmunire, and therefore were called into the King's Bench to answer. But the prelates in convocation at Canterbury concluded among themselves a humble submission in writing, and offered the king a subsidy or contribution, that he would be their good lord, and release them of the præmunire by act of parliament, first to be gathered in the province of Canterbury a hundred thousand pounds. And in the province of York eighteen thousand eight hundred and forty pound and ten pence. Which offer was accepted, and their pardon promised. In this submission the clergy called the king supreme head of the church of England, which thing they never confessed before.

Mention was made a little before of a parliament begun the 15th of January, A.D. 1533, in which the commons had put up a supplication, complaining of the straight dealing of the clergy in their proceeding ex officio. This complaint, although at the first it seemed not to be greatly tendered of the king, yet in prorogation of the parliament the time so wrought withal, that the king having more clear understanding of the abuses and enormities of the clergy, and especially of the corrupt authority of the see of Rome, provided certain acts against the same. First, as concerning the laws, decrees, ordinances, and constitutions made and established by the pretended authority of the bishops of Rome, to the advancement of their worldly glory, that who so did or spake any thing either against their usurped power, or against the said laws, decrees, or constitutions of theirs, not approved nor grounded upon holy scripture, or else being repugnant to the king's royal prerogative, should therefore stand in no danger, nor be impeachable of heresy. And likewise touching such constitutions, ordinances, and canons provincial or synodal, which were made in this realm in the convocation of bishops being either prejudicial to the king's prerogative, or not ratified before by the king's assent, or being otherwise onerous to the king and his subjects, or in any wise repugnant to the laws and statutes of this realm, they were committed to the judgment of two-and-thirty persons chosen by the king out of the higher and lower house, to be determined either to stand in strength, or to be abrogated at their discretion; and further, that all the clergy of this realm submitting themselves to the king, should and did promise in verbo Sacerdotii, never hereafter to presume to assemble in their convocations without the king's writ,

or to enact or execute such constitutions without his royal assent, &c.

Further, in the same parliament was enacted and decreed, that in causes and matters happening in contention, no person should appeal, provoke, or sue out of the king's dominions to the court of Rome, under pain of provisors, provision, or præmunire.

In the same parliament was defined and concluded, that all exportation of annates and first fruits of archbishoprics and bishoprics out of this realm to the see of Rome for any bulls, breves, or palls, or expedition of any such thing, should utterly cease.

Also for the investing of archbishops, bishops, or others of any ecclesiastical dignity, such order in the said parliament was taken that the king should send a license under the great seal, with a letter missive to the prior and convent, or to the dean and chapter of those cathedral churches where the see was vacant: by virtue of which license, or letters missive, they within twelve days should choose the person nominated by the king, and none other, and that election to stand effectual. Which election being done, then the party elect making first his oath and fealty to the king, if it were a bishop that was elect, then the king by his letters patent to signify the election to the archbishop of that province, and two other bishops, or else to four bishops within this realm to be assigned to that office, without any other suing, procuring, or obtaining any bulls, breves, or other things from the see of Rome.

Moreover, against all other exactions and great sums of money which used to be paid out of this realm to the bishop of Rome, in pensions, censures, Peter-pence, procurations, fruits, suits for provisions, and expeditions of bulls for archbishops and bishops, for delegacies and rescripts in causes of contentions and appeals, jurisdictions legative; also for dispensations, licenses, faculties, grants, relaxations, writs called Perinde valere, rehabilitations, abolitions, canonizations, and other infinite sorts of bulls, breves, and instruments of sundry natures, the number whereof were tedious to be recited; in the parliament it was ordained, that all such uncharitable usurpations, exactions, pensions, censures, portions, and Peter-pence which used to be paid to the see of Rome, should utterly cease, and never more be levied; so that the king with his honourable council should have power and authority from time to time, for the ordering, redress, and reformation of all manner of indulgences, privileges, &c., within this realm.

All these things being thus defined and determined in this parliament, and also being in the same parliament concluded, that no man of what estate, degree, or condition soever, hath any power to dispense with God's laws, it was therefore by the authority aforesaid, agreeing with the authority of God's word, assented, that the marriage aforetime solemnised between the king and the lady Catharine, being before wife to prince Arthur the king's brother, should be absolutely deemed and adjudged to be unlawful and against the law of God, and also reputed and taken to be of no value nor effect; and that the separation thereof by Thomas Cranmer Archbishop of Canterbury, should stand good and effectual to all intents; and also that the lawful matrimony between the king and the lady Anne his wife, should be established, approved, and ratified for good and consonant to the laws of Almighty God. And further also, for the establishing of the king's lawful succession, it was fully by the parliament adjudged, that the inheritance of the crown should remain to the heirs of their two bodies, that is, of the king and queen Anne his wife.

Not long after that, the king, perceiving the minds of the clergy not much favouring his cause, sent for the Speaker, and twelve of the commons-house, having with them eight lords, and said to them, "Well-beloved subjects, we had thought that the clergy of our realm had been our subjects wholly, but now we have well perceived that they are but half our subjects, yea, and scarce our subjects. For all the prelates at their consecration make an oath to the pope, contrary to the oath that they make to us, so that they seem to be his subjects, and not ours;" and so the king, delivering to them the copy of both the oaths, required them to invent some order that he might not thus be deluded of his spiritual subjects. The Speaker thus departed, and caused the oaths to be read in the commons-house.

The Oaths of the Clergy to the Pope.

" I, John, bishop or abbot of A., from this hour forward, shall be faithful and obedient to St. Peter, and to the holy church of Rome, and to my lord the pope, and his successors canonically elected. I shall not be of counsel nor consent, that they shall lose either life or member, or shall be taken or suffer any violence, or any wrong by any means. Their counsel confided to me by them, their messengers or letters, I shall not willingly discover to any person. The popedom of Rome, the rules of the holy fathers, and regalities of St. Peter, I shall help, and maintain, and defend against all men. The legate of the see apostolic going and coming, I shall honourably treat. The rights, honours, privileges, authorities of the church of Rome, and of the pope and his successors, I shall cause to be conserved, defended, augmented and promoted, I shall not be in counsel, treaty, or any act, in which any thing shall be imagined against him or the church of Rome, their rights, seats, honours, or powers ; and if I know any such to be moved or compassed, I shall resist it to my power, and as soon as I can, I shall advertise him, or such as may give him knowledge. The rules of the holy fathers, the decrees, ordinances, sentences, dispositions, reservations, provisions and commandments apostolic, to my power I shall keep, and cause to be kept, of others. Heretics, schismatics, and rebels to our holy father and his successors, I shall resist and persecute to my power. I shall come to the synod when I am called, except I be letted by a canonical impediment. The thresholds of the apostles I shall visit yearly personally, or by my deputy. I shall not alienate or sell my possessions without the pope's council. So God me help, and the holy evangelists."

This oath of the clergymen, which they were wont to make to the bishop of Rome, was abolished by statute, and a new oath ministered, wherein they acknowledged the king to be the supreme head under Christ in this church of England.

The Oath of the Clergy to the King.

" I, John B. of A. utterly renounce and clearly forsake all such clauses, words, sentences, and grants which I have or shall have hereafter of the pope's holiness, of and for the bishopric of A. that in any wise hath been, is, or hereafter may be hurtful or prejudicial to your highness, your heirs, successors, dignity, privilege, or estate royal : and also I do swear that I shall be faithful and true, and faith and truth I shall bear to you my sovereign lord, and to your heirs kings of the same, of life and limb, and earthly worship above all creatures, to live and die with you and yours against all people ; and diligently I shall be attendant to all your needs and business, after my wit and power ; and your counsel I shall keep and hold, acknowledging myself to hold my bishopric of you only ; beseeching you for restitution of the temporalties of the same ; promising (as before) that I shall be a faithful, true, and obedient subject unto your said highness, heirs, and successors during my life ; and the services and other things due to your highness, for the restitution of the temporalties of the same bishopric, I shall truly do, and obediently perform. So God me help and all saints."

These oaths being thus recited and opened to the people, were the cause that the pope lost all his jurisdiction here in England. The matter falling out more and more against the pope, Sir Thomas More, a great maintainer of the pope, and a heavy troubler of Christ's people, and now not liking well this oath, was forced to resign his chancellorship, and to deliver up the great seal of England into the king's hands. After whom succeeded Sir Thomas Audley, keeper of the great seal, a man incomparable in eloquence and

gifts of tongue, also with a godly disposed mind, and favourable inclination to Christ's religion.

These things being done in the parliament, the king within a short time after (November, A.D. 1532), privately married the lady Anne Boleyn, mother to our most noble queen (Elizabeth), who without all controversy was a special comforter and aider of all the professors of Christ's gospel, as well of the learned as the unlearned.

Queen Anne, shortly after her marriage had been publicly recognised, was crowned with high solemnity at Westminster ; and not long after her coronation, on the 7th of Sept., A. D. 1533, she was delivered of a fair lady ; for whose good deliverance *Te Deum* was sung in all places, and great preparation made for the christening.

The mayor and his brethren, with forty of the chief citizens were commanded to be present, with all the nobles and gentlemen. The king's palace, and all the walls between that and the Friars, and the Friars' church, was hung with tapestry ; also the font was of silver, and stood in the midst of the church, three steps high : it was covered with a fine cloth, and several gentlemen, with aprons and towels about their necks, gave attendance about it. Over the font hung a fair canopy of crimson satin fringed with gold. About it was a rail covered with say. Between the quoir and the body of the church was a close place with a pan of fire to make the child ready in. These things thus ordered, the child was brought into the hall, and then every man set forward, first the citizens, two and two ; then the gentlemen esquires, and chaplains. Next after followed the aldermen, and the mayor alone. Next the mayor, followed the king's council. Then the king's chaplains. Then barons, bishops, and earls. Then came the earl of Essex, bearing the covered gilt basons. After him the Marquis of Exeter, with the taper of virgin-wax. Next him the marquis of Dorset, bearing the salt. Behind him the lady Mary of Norfolk, bearing the chrysome, which was very rich of pearl and stone. The old duchess of Norfolk bare the child in a mantle of purple velvet, with a long train furred with ermine. The duke of Norfolk with his marshal's-rod, went on the right hand of the duchess, and the duke of Suffolk on the left hand. Before them went the officers of arms. The countess of Kent bare the long train of the child's mantle. Between the countess and the child, went the earl of Wiltshire on the right hand, and the earl of Derby on the left hand, supporting the train. In the midst over the child, was borne a canopy by the lord Rochford, the lord Hussey, the lord William Howard, and the lord Thomas Howard the elder. In this order they came to the church door, where the bishop of London met it, with divers abbots and bishops, and began the observances of the sacrament. The archbishop of Canterbury was godfather, and the old duchess of Norfolk, and the old marchioness of Dorset, widows, were godmothers, and the child's name was Elizabeth.

After all things were done at the church door, the child was brought to the font and christened. This done, garter the chief king-at-arms, cried aloud, " God of his infinite goodness, send prosperous life and long, to the high and mighty princess of England, Elizabeth." Then the trumpets blew, and the child was brought up to the altar, and immediately confirmed by the archbishop, the marchioness of Exeter being godmother. Then the archbishop of Canterbury gave the princess a standing cup of gold. The duchess of Norfolk gave her a standing cup of gold, fretted with pearl. The marchioness of Dorset, three gilt bowls pounced, with a cover. The marchioness of Exeter three standing bowls gilt and graven, with a cover. And so after a solemn banquet ended with hypocras, waters, and such like in great plenty, they returned in like order again to the court with the princess, and so departed.

At the birth of this noble lady, as there was no small joy to all good and godly men, and no less hope of prosperous success to God's true religion ; so on the other hand, the papists were not wanting in their malicious and secret attempts, and in their devilish devices, may sufficiently appear by the false hypocrisy and feigned holiness of a false hypocrite, who was this year found out. For certain monks, friars, and other evil-disposed persons, of a devilish intent, had put into the heads of many of the king's subjects, that they had a revelation of God and his saints, that he was highly displeased with king Henry for the divorce of the lady Catharine; and surmised amongst other things, that God had revealed to a nun, named Elizabeth Barton, whom they called the holy maid of Kent, that in case the king proceeded in the divorce, he should not be king of this realm one month after, and in the reputation of God not one day nor hour. This Elizabeth Barton, by false dissimulation practised and shewed to the people strange alterations of her visage, and other parts of her body, as if she had been wrapt or in a trance, and in these feigned trances, (as though she had been inspired of God,) she spake many words in rebuking sin, and reproving the gospel, which she called heresy; and uttered many things to the great reproach of the king and queen, and to the establishing of idolatry, pilgrimage, and the derogation of God's glory. Her naughtiness being espied out by the great labour and diligence of the archbishop of Canterbury, the Lord Cromwell, and Master Hugh Latimer, she was condemned and put to death, in April, 1533.

About the same time died also William Warham, archbishop of Canterbury, in whose place succeeded Thomas Cranmer, who was the king's chaplain, and a great disputer against the marriage of lady Catharine.

Ye heard before, how the parliament had enacted that no person after a certain day, should appeal to Rome for any cause. Notwithstanding which act, the queen, now called princess dowager, had appealed to the court of Rome before that act was made; so that it was doubted whether that appeal was good or not. This question was well handled in parliament, but much better in the convocation; and yet, in both houses it was alleged, yea, and by books shewed, that in the councils of Chalcedon, Africa, Toledo, and other famous councils in the primitive church; yea, in the time of St. Augustine, it was affirmed, declared, and determined, that a cause arising in one province, should be determined in the same, and that neither the patriarch of Constantinople should meddle in causes moved in the jurisdiction of the patriarch of Antioch, nor any bishop should intermeddle within another's province or country. Which things were so learnedly opened, and so ably set forth, that every man that had sense, and was determined to follow the truth, and not wilfully wedded to his own opinions, might plainly see, that all appeals made to Rome were clearly void, and of none effect; which doctrines and councils were shewn to the lady Catharine, who ever continued trusting more to the pope's partiality, than to the determination of Christ's truth.

Whereupon the archbishop of Canterbury (Cranmer), accompanied by the bishops of London, Winchester, Bath, Lincoln, and other dignitaries, in a great number, rode to Dunstable, which is six miles from Ampthill, where the princess dowager lay; and thereby she was cited to appear before the archbishop, in cause of matrimony, in the town of Dunstable. And, at the day appointed, she would not appear, but made default, and so was called peremptorily every day, fifteen days together, and at last, on the 23d of May, A.D. 1533, for lack of appearance, and for contumacy, by the assent of all learned men there present, she was divorced from the king, and their marriage declared to be void and of none effect; which sentence given, the archbishop, and all the others returned back again.

The Power of the Pope abolished in England.

These things thus finished and dispatched, concerning the marriage of queen Anne, and divorce of lady Catharine, next follows the year 1534, in which was assembled the high court of parliament, after many prorogations, upon the 3d day of February, wherein was made an act of succession for the greater security of the crown, to which every person, being of lawful age, was to be sworn. Every Sunday, during the sitting of parliament, a bishop preached at St. Paul's cross, who declared the pope not to be head of the church.

After this, commissions were sent over all England, to take the oath of all men and women to the act of succession; to which few objected, except Dr. John Fisher, bishop of Rochester; Sir Thomas More, late lord chancellor; and Dr. Nicholas Wilson, parson of St. Thomas the Apostle in London. Wherefore, these three persons, after long exhortation to them, made by the bishop of Canterbury at Lambeth, refusing to be sworn, were sent to the Tower, where they remained, and were often asked to be sworn; but the bishop and Sir Thomas More excused themselves by their writings, in which they said, that they had written before, that lady Catharine was queen, and therefore could not well go from that which they had written.

From the month of March, this parliament furthermore was prorogued to the 3d day of November abovesaid. At which time, amongst other statutes, most graciously, and by the blessed will of God it was enacted, that the pope, and all his college of cardinals, with his pardons and indulgences, which so long had clogged this realm of England, to the miserable slaughter of so many good men, and which never could be removed away before, was now abolished, eradicated, and expelled out of this land, and sent home again to their own country of Rome, from whence they came. God be everlastingly praised! Amen!

Act concerning the King's Highness to be the supreme head of the Church of England, and to have authority to reform and redress all errors, heresies, and abuses in the same. Cap. 1.

" Albeit the king's majesty justly and rightly is, and ought to be supreme head of the church of England, and so is recognised by the clergy of this realm in their convocations; yet, nevertheless, for corroboration and confirmation thereof, and for increase of virtue in Christ's religion within this realm of England, and to repress and extirpate all errors, heresies, and other enormities and abuses in the same, be it enacted, by authority of this present parliament, that the king, our sovereign lord, his heirs and successors, kings of this realm, shall be taken, accepted, and reputed the only supreme head in earth of the church of England, called Anglicana Ecclesia, and shall have and enjoy, annexed and united to the imperial crown of this realm, as well the title and stile thereof, as all honours, dignities, pre-eminences, jurisdictions, privileges, authorities, immunities, profits and commodities to the said dignity of supreme head of the same church, belonging and appertaining. And that our said sovereign lord, his heirs and successors, kings of this realm, shall have full power and authority, from time to time, to visit, repress, redress, reform, order, correct, restrain, and amend all such errors, abuses, offences, contempts, and enormities, whatsoever they be, which by any manner of spiritual authority or jurisdiction, ought, or may lawfully be reformed, repressed, ordered, redressed, corrected, restrained, or amended, most to the pleasure of Almighty God, the increase of virtue in Christ's religion, and for the conservation of the peace, unity, and tranquillity of this realm; any usage, custom, foreign laws, foreign authority, prescription, or any thing or things, to the contrary hereof notwithstanding."

That no man may cavil or surmise that this fatal fall and ruin of the pope came rashly upon the king's own partial affection, or by any temerity of a few; and not by the grave and advised judgment, approbation, and consent, generally and publicly, as well of the nobles and commons temporal, as also upon substantial grounds, and the very strength of truth, by the discussion and consultation of the spiritual and most learned persons in this realm, it shall be requisite to add, that the archbishops and bishops did solemnly and openly swear to the king, as supreme head of the church of England, to the exclusion of the usurped pretensions of the bishop of Rome, giving to the king alone the stile of supreme head, next under Christ, of the church of England, renouncing and abjuring, utterly and voluntarily, the pope's too long usurped jurisdiction in this realm, testifying moreover the same both with their own hand, and also with their seal.

Besides these confirmations and oaths of the bishops, you shall hear the decree and public sentence of the university of Cambridge, written and subscribed, and signed with the public seal of their university, the tenor of which their letter here followeth :—

A Letter of the University of Cambridge against the usurped power of the Bishop of Rome.

"To all and singular the children of the holy mother church, into whose hands these presents shall come, the whole society of regents, and not regents of the university of Cambridge, sendeth greeting in our Saviour Jesus Christ.

"Whereas of late a question having arisen among us, as to the power which the bishop of Rome claims to himself by the holy scriptures, over all provinces and nations in Christendom, and which he hath now exercised for a long time in England: and as our opinion concerning this question has been required, to wit, whether the bishop of Rome hath any power or authority in this kingdom of England, allotted to him by God in the scriptures, more than any other foreign bishop, or not : We thought it therefore good reason, and our duty for the searching out of the truth of the said question, that we should employ therein our whole endeavour and study, whereby we might render and publish to the world, what our reason and opinion is, touching the premises. For therefore we suppose, that universities were first provided and instituted of princes, to the end that both the people of Christ might in the law of God be instructed, and also that false errors, if any did rise, might through the vigilant care and industry of learned divines be discussed, extinguished, and utterly rooted out. For which cause we in our assemblies and convocations (after our accustomed manner) resorting and conferring together upon the question aforesaid, and studiously debating and deliberating with ourselves how and by what order we might best proceed for the finding out of the truth of the matter ; and at length choosing out certain of the best learned doctors and bachelors of divinity, and other masters, and having committed to them in charge, studiously to search and peruse the places of holy scripture; by the viewing and considering of which places together, they might certify to us what is to be said to the question propounded.

"Forasmuch therefore, as we having heard, and well advised, and thoroughly discussed in open disputations, what may be said on both sides of the question, those reasons and arguments do appear to us more probable, stronger, truer, and more certain, and agreeing much more near to the pure and native sense of scriptures, which do deny the bishop of Rome to have any such power given him of God in the scripture. By reason and force of which arguments we being persuaded, and joining together in one opinion, have with ourselves thus decreed to answer unto the question aforesaid, and in these writings thus resolutely do answer in the name of the whole University, and for an undoubted conclusion do affirm, approve, and pronounce, that the bishop of Rome hath no more state, authority, and jurisdiction given him of God in the scriptures, over this realm of England, than hath any other foreign bishop. And in testimony and credence of this our answer and affirmation, we have caused our common seal to be put to these our aforesaid letters accordingly. At Cambridge in our regent house: A.D. 1534."

Now, for a further declaration of their judgments and opinions, you shall hear what the bishops in their own books, prologues, and sermons, have written and published, touching the pope's supremacy; and we shall begin with Stephen Gardiner's book " on True Obedience," and briefly note out a few of his own words, wherein he not only confutes the pope's usurped authority, but also proves the marriage between the king and queen Catharine his brother's wife, was not lawful, in these words.

" And amongst these, if there is a commandment that a man shall not marry his brother's wife, what could the king's excellent majesty do otherwise, than that which he did by the whole consent of the people, and the judgment of his church, that is, to be divorced from unlawful marriage, and to use lawful and permitted marriage, and obeying (as meet it was) conformably to the commandment, to cast her off, whom neither law nor right permitted him to retain, and take himself to chaste and lawful marriage? Wherein, although the sentence of God's word (whereunto all things ought to stoop) might have sufficed ; yet his majesty was content to have the assisting consent of the most notable and grave men, and the censures of the most famous universities of the whole world ; and all to the intent that men should see that he did both what he might do, and ought to do uprightly, seeing that the best learned and most worthy men have subscribed to it, and shewing therein such obedience as God's word requireth of every good and godly man ; so as it may be said, that both he obeyed God, and obeyed him truly."

In his book, he also alleges the old distinction of the papists, wherein they give to the prince the government of things temporal, and to the church that of things spiritual, comparing the one to the greater light, the other to the lesser light, he confutes and derides the distinction, declaring that the sword of the church extends no further, than to teaching and excommunication, and refers all pre-eminence to the sword of the prince: alleging for this the second psalm ; " Be wise now therefore, O ye kings : be instructed ye judges of the earth."

Also the example of Solomon, who being a king, " appointed, according to the order of David his father, the course of the priests to their service, and the Levites to their charges, to praise and minister before the priests, as the duty of every day required: the porters also by their courses at every gate : for so had David the man of God commanded."—2 Chr. viii. 14.

Besides this, he alleges also the example of king Hezekiah, 2 Chron. xxix. He alleges moreover the example of Justinian, who made laws touching the faith, bishops, clerks, heretics and others.

Aaron obeyed Moses. Solomon gave sentence upon Abiathar the high priest.

Alexander the king, in the first of Maccabees writes to Jonathan ; " Now we have made thee this day the high priest of thy people, &c." So did Demetrius to Simon.

And where he reasons of the king's stile and title, being called king of England and of France, defender of the faith, lord of Ireland, and supreme head in earth of the church of England, immediately under Christ, &c. thus he adds his mind and censure, saying, that he sees no cause in this title, why any man should be offended, that the king is called head of the church of England, rather than of the realm of England; and adds his reason thereunto saying, If the prince and king of England be the head of his kingdom, that is, of all Englishmen his subjects, is there any cause why the same English subjects should not be subject to the same head likewise in this respect, because they are Christians, that is to say, for the title of godliness, as though that God, who is the cause of all obedience, should now be the cause of rebellion ?

At length he thus concludes with an exclamation saying, " To say that a king is the head of the kingdom, and not of the church, what an absurd and a foolish saying is this !"

" The light of the gospel," saith he, " so spreads its beams in all men's eyes, that the works of the gospel may be known, and the mysteries of Christ's doctrine opened ; both learned and unlearned, men and women, being in England, do see and perceive, that they have nothing to do with Rome, nor with the bishop of Rome, but that every prince in his own dominions is to be taken and accepted as a vicar of God, and vicegerent of Christ in his own bounds."

To these extracts from the books of Gardiner we

shall add a part of the preface to that book, which was written by Bonner, to shew how the judgments of men are changed by the vain glory and pomp of this world.

The Preface of Edmund Bonner, Archdeacon of Leicester, prefixed before Stephen Gardiner's Book, "On True Obedience."

"Forasmuch as there may be some who think that the controversy which is between the king's royal majesty, and the bishop of Rome, consists in this point, that his majesty hath taken the most excellent and most virtuous Lady Anne to wife, but which is far otherwise: we, to the intent, therefore, that all true hearty favourers of the gospel of Christ, who hate not, but love the truth, may the more fully understand the chief point of the controversy, and because they shall not be ignorant what is the unanimous opinion and resolute determination of the best and most learned bishops, with all the nobles and commons of England, not only in that case of matrimony, but also in defending the doctrine of the gospel: here shall be published the oration of the bishop of Winchester (a man excellently learned in all kind of learning) entitled 'On True Obedience.' But, as to this bishop's worthy praises, there shall be nothing spoken by me at this time, not only because they are infinite, but because they are far better known to all Christendom, than becomes me here to rehearse. And as for the oration itself (which, as it is most learned, so is it most elegant) to what purpose should I make any words of it, seeing it praises itself enough, and requires no recommendation? But yet, in this oration, whoever thou art, most gentle reader, thou shalt, beside other matters, see it notably and learnedly handled, of what importance, and how invincible the power and excellency of God's truth is, which, as it may now and then be pressed of the enemies, so it cannot possibly be oppressed and darkened after such sort, but it sheweth itself again at length more glorious and more welcome. Thou shalt see also, touching obedience, that it is subject to truth, and what is to be judged true obedience. Besides this, of men's traditions, which are for the most part most repugnant to the truth of God's law. And there, by the way, he speaks of the king's highness' marriage, which, by the ripe judgment, authority, and privilege of the most and principal universities of the world, and then, with the consent of the whole church of England, he contracted with the most excellent, and most noble lady, Queen Anne. After that, touching the king's majesty's title, as pertaining to the supreme head of the church of England. Last of all, of the false pretended supremacy of the bishop of Rome in the realm of England most justly abrogated: and how all other bishops being fellow-like to him in their function, yea, and in some points above him within their own provinces, were before-time bound to the king by their oath.

"But be thou most surely persuaded of this, good reader, that the bishop of Rome, if there were no other case but only this marriage, would easily content himself, and especially on his having some good morsel or other given to him to chew upon. But when he sees so mighty a king, being a right virtuous and learned prince, so sincerely and so heartily favour the gospel of Christ, and perceiving the yearly and great prey (yea, so large a prey, that it came to as much almost as all the king's revenues) snapped out of his hands, and that he can no longer exercise his tyranny in the king's majesty's realm (alas! heretofore, too cruel and bitter) nor make laws, as he hath done many, to the contumely and reproach of the Majesty of God, which is evident that he hath done in time past, under the title of the catholic church, and the authority of Peter and Paul (when, notwithstanding, he was a very ravening wolf, dressed in sheep's clothing, calling himself the servant of servants) to the great damage of the christian commonwealth."

In adding to these the judgment and arguments of Bishop Tonstal, we shall see how he agrees with them, or rather exceeds them, in his sermon preached before King Henry VIII. upon Palm Sunday: in this sermon he disputes against the supremacy of the bishop of Rome, and proves by manifest grounds, out of the scripture, ancient doctors, and councils, that the bishop of Rome has no such authority by the word of God; and he also reproves and condemns him with great zeal and ardent spirit, to be a proud Lucifer, disobedient to the ordinary powers of God set over him, contrary to Christ and Peter: and, finally, in raising up war against us for the same, he rebukes and defies him, as a most detestable sower of discord, and a murderer of christian men.

First, by the scripture he reasons, that all good men ought to obey the powers and governors of the world, as emperors, kings, and princes of all sorts; for so St. Peter plainly teaches us, 1 Pet. ii. saying, "Submit yourselves to every ordinance of man for the Lord's sake, whether it be to the king as supreme, or unto governors," &c. So that St. Peter, in his epistle, commands all princes in their office to be obeyed as the ministers of God, by all christian men: and St. Paul, Rom. xiii. saith, "Let every soul be subject to the higher powers; for the powers that be are ordained of God, and whosoever resisteth the powers, resisteth the ordinance of God, and shall receive unto himself damnation."

Also, another express commandment we have of Christ, Luke xxii. who, upon the occasion of his disciples striving for superiority, discusses the matter, saying, "The kings of the Gentiles exercise lordship over them; and they that exercise authority upon them are called benefactors. But ye shall not be so: but he that is greatest among you, let him be as the younger; and he that is chief, as he that doth serve," &c.

And again, Christ speaking to Pilate of his kingdom, declares that his kingdom is not of this world, and, therefore, saith Tonstal, those that go about to make of Christ's spiritual kingdom a worldly kingdom, do fall into the error of some heretics that expect that Christ, after the day of judgment, shall reign with all his saints here in the earth carnally in Jerusalem; the Jews believe that Messias is yet to come, and that when he shall come, he shall reign worldly in Jerusalem.

By these and such other places it may well appear, that Christ, neither before nor after his incarnation, (as Tonstal saith) did ever alter the authority of worldly kings and princes, but by his own word commanded them still to be obeyed by their subjects, as they had been in the ancient time, &c. and for example of the same he alleges, first, the example of Christ himself, Matt. xxii., who, being asked of the Jews, whether they should give tribute to Cæsar or not, he bade them give to Cæsar the things which are his, and to God the things that are his; signifying, that tribute was due to Cæsar, and that their souls were due to God, &c.

Also, it appeareth that Christ bade Peter pay tribute for him and his disciples, when it was demanded of him. And why? Because he would not change the order of obedience which was due by subjects to their princes.

Another example of Christ he cites out of the sixth of John, where, after Christ had fed five thousand and more, with a few loaves, and fewer fishes, and that the Jews would have taken him and made him their king, he fled from them, and would not consent to it: for the kingdom, saith he, that he came to set here in earth, was not a worldly and a temporal kingdom, but a heavenly and spiritual kingdom; that is, to reign spiritually by grace and faith in the hearts of all christian and faithful people, of what degree, or of what nature soever they may be, and to turn all people and nations, who, at his coming, were carnal, and lived after the lusts of the flesh, to be spiritual, and to live after the Spirit, that Christ, with his Father in heaven, might reign in the hearts of all men, &c.

And here, in these examples of Christ's humility, farther it is to be noted, how Christ the Son of God did submit himself not only to the rulers and powers of this world, but also humbled himself, and in a manner became servant to his own apostles: so far off was he from all ambitious and pompous seeking of worldly honour: for so it appeareth in him, not only by washing the feet of his apostles, but also, when the apostles, a little before his passion, fell out and contended among themselves, who among them should be superior, Christ sets before them the example of his own subjection, and asks this question: "Whether is greater, he that sitteth at meat, or he that serveth? is not he that sitteth at meat? but I am among you as he that serveth," &c.

Again, in Peter, what an example of reverent humility is seen in this, that notwithstanding he, with other apostles, having commission to go over all the world, yet, nevertheless, he being at Joppa, and sent for by Cornelius, durst not go to him, without the vision of a sheet let down from heaven, by which vision he was admonished not to refuse the Gentiles: or else he knew in himself no such primacy over all people and places, nor any such commission above the others, &c.

Peter, being rebuked by Paul his fellow brother, took no offence, but was content, submitting himself to due correction, Gal. ii.

But here, saith Tonstal, steps in the bishop of Rome and saith, "That Peter had authority given him above all the apostles, and alleges the words of Christ spoken to him, Matt. xvi. 'Thou art Peter, and upon this rock I will build my church, and to thee will I give the keys of the kingdom of heaven: and whatsoever thou shalt bind on earth, shall be bound in heaven,' &c. This, Christ said, saith the pope, and St. Peter is buried at Rome, whose successor I am, and I therefore ought to rule the church, as Peter did, and be the porter of the gates of heaven as Peter was, &c. And Christ said also to Peter, after his resurrection, 'Feed my sheep;' which he spake to him only, so that thereby he had authority over all Christ's flock; and I, as his successor, have the same. And, therefore, whoso will not obey me, king or prince, I will curse him, and deprive him of his kingdom; for all power is given to me that Christ has, and I am his vicar-general as Peter was here on earth over all, and none but I, as Christ is in heaven."

To open, therefore, the true sense of the scripture in the places aforesaid, and first to begin with the sixteenth chapter of Matthew. It is to be observed, that the question being put in general of Christ to all his apostles, what they thought or judged of him, Peter answering for them all (as he was always ready to answer) said, "Thou art the Christ, the Son of the living God. And Jesus answered and said unto him, Blessed art thou, Simon Barjona; for flesh and blood hath not revealed it unto thee, but my Father which is in heaven. And I say also unto thee, That thou art Peter, and upon this rock I will build my church; and the gates of hell shall not prevail against it." Matt. xvi. 16—18. That is to say, upon this rock of thy confession of me to be the Son of God I will build my church. For this faith contains the whole summary of our faith and salvation, as it is written, "The word is nigh thee, even in thy mouth, and in thy heart: that is, the word of faith, which we preach; that if thou shalt confess with thy mouth the Lord Jesus, and shalt believe in thine heart that God hath raised him from the dead, thou shalt be saved," &c. Rom. x. 8, 9. And this confession being uttered by the mouth of St. Peter, upon this confession of his, and not upon the person of St. Peter, Christ builds his church, as St. Chrysostom expounds that place in the twenty-sixth sermon of the Feast of Pentecost, saying, "Not upon the person of St. Peter, but upon his faith Christ hath builded his church. And what is this faith? This, 'Thou art the Christ, the Son of the living God.' What is it to say, 'Upon this rock?' That is, upon this confession of St. Peter," &c. And with this saying of Chrysostom ancient expositors (saith Tonstal) treating of that place, do agree; for if we should expound that place, that the church is builded upon the person of St. Peter, we should put another foundation of the church than Christ, which is directly against St. Paul, saying, "For other foundation can no man lay than that is laid, which is Jesus Christ," &c. 1 Cor. iii. 11.

And as St. Peter was the first of them that confessed Christ to be the Son of God, so was he most ardent in his faith, and bold, and hardy in Christ, as appears by his coming out of the ship in the great tempest, and also

in his being most vehement in his Master's cause, as appeared by his drawing out his sword; and after the Lord's resurrection, he is declared out of the second, third, and fourth chapters of the Acts, where the Jews withstanding the apostles' preaching the faith of Christ, St. Peter, as most ardent in faith, was ever most ready to defend the faith against the impugners thereof, and for speaking for all of them unto the people, &c., and therefore have these honourable names been given to him by the ancient interpreters; that sometimes he is called, the mouth of the apostles; the chief of the apostles; sometimes the prince of the apostles; sometimes the president of the whole church; and sometimes the name of primacy or priority has been attributed to him. And yet that St. Peter, notwithstanding these honourable names given to him, never had a rule or a judicial power given to him above all the other apostles, as is plain by St. Paul, and many others.

First, St. Paul, in writing to the Galatians, plainly declareth, "But contrariwise, when they saw that the gospel of the uncircumcision was committed unto me, as the gospel of the circumcision was unto Peter; for he that wrought effectually in Peter to the apostleship of the circumcision, the same was mighty in me towards the Gentiles." Gal. ii. 7, 8. Hereby it appeareth that St. Paul knew no primacy of St. Peter concerning people and places, except among the Jews. And St. Ambrose, expounding that place, saith thus: "The primacy of the Jews was given chiefly to St. Peter, although St. James and St. John were joined with him; as the primacy of the Gentiles was given to St. Paul, although St. Barnabas was joined with him, so that St. Peter had no rule over all."

That all the apostles had like dignity and authority, appears by St. Paul, where he saith, "Now therefore ye are no more strangers and foreigners, but fellow-citizens with the saints, and of the household of God; and are built upon the foundation of the apostles and prophets, Jesus Christ himself being the chief corner-stone." Eph. ii. 19, 20. Here he saith, that they are builded not upon the foundation of St. Peter only, but upon the foundation of the apostles, so that all they being in the foundation set upon Christ the very rock, whereupon standeth the whole church.

In Rev. xxi. 14, the new city, and the heavenly Jerusalem of Almighty God, is described of the Holy Ghost not with one foundation only of St. Peter, but with twelve foundations, after the number of the apostles.

St. Cyprian gives testimony likewise to the same effect, that the apostles had equal power and dignity given to them by Christ: and because all should preach one thing, therefore the beginning first came by one, who was St. Peter, who confessed for them all, that Christ was the Son of the living God. Saying further, that in the church there is one office of all the bishops, whereof every man hath a part allowed wholly to himself. Now, if the bishop of Rome may meddle over all, where he will, then every man has not wholly his part, for the bishop of Rome may also meddle in his part jointly with him; so that now he has it not wholly, which is against Cyprian.

St. Augustine likewise, expounding the gospel of John, in the fiftieth treatise, speaks of the keys of St. Peter, which he saith were given by Christ to St. Peter, not for himself alone, but for the whole church.

St. Cyril expounding the last chapter of St. John, and there speaking of the words of Christ spoken to St. Peter, "Feed my sheep," &c., thus understands them; that because St. Peter had thrice denied Christ, he thought that he had lost his apostleship, but Christ, to comfort him again, and to restore him to his office that he had lost, asked him thrice whether he loved him, and so restored him again to his office, which otherwise he durst not have presumed, saying to him, "Feed my sheep," &c. With which exposition the ancient holy expositors of that place agree. So that by these words of feeding Christ's sheep, the bishop of Rome can take no advantage to maintain his universal pastorality over all christian dominions.

Again, whereas the bishop of Rome saith, that Peter,

by these words of Christ spoken to him, hath a preeminence above the others, St. Paul, Acts xx. 28, proves the contrary; where he, speaking to the bishops assembled at Miletus, saith to them, " Take heed therefore unto yourselves, and to all the flock, over the which the Holy Ghost hath made you overseers, to feed the church of God, which he hath purchased with his own blood."

And Peter himself, likewise, (1 Peter v. 2.) saith, " feed the flock of God which is among you, taking the oversight thereof," &c.

So that by these scriptures conferred together, it may appear, that neither Matthew xvi. nor John xxi., proves that Peter had power, authority, or dignity given to him of Christ over all the other, nor that they should be under him: and yet, notwithstanding, his primacy still continues, in that he, first of all the apostles, confessed Christ to be the Son of the living God, in which confession all the other apostles, joined and preached with him. And thus the power of the bishops of Rome over all, which they would prove by those places wrongfully alleged for this purpose, utterly fails, and is not proved. And thus much for the scriptures and doctors.

Now, further proceeding in this matter, Tonstal cometh to councils and examples of the primitive church, as followeth :—

Faustinus, legate to the bishop of Rome, in the sixth council of Carthage, (A. D. 425,) alleged that the bishop of Rome ought to have the ordering of all great matters in all places by his supreme authority, bringing no scripture for him (for at that time no scripture was thought to make for it) but alleged for him, and that untruly, the first council of Nice, to make for his purpose. After this, when the book was brought forth, and no such article found in it, but the contrary, yet the council at that time sent to Constantinople, Alexandria, and Antioch, where the patriarchal sees were, to have the true copy of the council of Nice, which was sent to them. And another copy also was sent from Rome, whither also they sent for the same purpose.

After the copy was brought to them, and no such article being found in it, but, on the contrary, in the fifth chapter, that all causes ecclesiastical, should either be determined within the diocese, or else, if any were still aggrieved, then to appeal to the council provincial, and there the matter to take full end, so that for no such causes men should go out of their provinces; the whole council of Carthage wrote to Celestine, at that time bishop of Rome, That since the council of Nice had no such article in it, as was untruly alleged by Faustinus, but the contrary, they therefore desired him to abstain hereafter from making any such demand, denouncing to him that they would not suffer any cause, great or small, to be brought by appeal out of their country; and thereupon made a law, That no man should appeal out of the country of Africa, upon pain of being accursed. Wherewith the bishop of Rome ever after held himself content, and made no more business with them, seeing he had nought to say for himself to the contrary. And at this council St. Augustine was present, and subscribed his hand.

It was determined also in the sixth article of the said council of Nice, That in the East the bishop of Antioch should be chief; in Egypt the bishop of Alexandria; about Rome the bishop of Rome; and likewise in other countries the metropolitans should have their pre-eminence: so that the bishop of Rome never had meddling in those countries.

And, in the next article following, the bishop of Jerusalem (which city had been destroyed and lay desolate) was restored to his old prerogative, to be the chief in Palestine and in the country of Judea.

By this you see how the patriarch of Rome, during all this time of the primitive church, had no such primacy above other patriarchs, much less over kings and emperors, as may appear by Agatho, bishop of Rome, in whose time was the sixth council general, who, after his election, sent to the emperor at Constantinople, to have his election allowed, before he could be consecrated, as was the custom at that time so used, (A. D. 479.)

The like did St. Ambrose, and St. Gregory, and other popes before him. During all which time the bishops of Rome followed well the doctrine of St. Peter and St. Paul, left to them, to be subjects, and to obey their princes.

Thus, after that Bishop Tonstal, both by scriptures and ancient doctors, also by sufficient examples from the primitive church, proved and declared, how the bishops of Rome ought to submit themselves to the higher powers whom God has appointed over every creature in this world to be obeyed.

Now for the confirming this matter, and satisfying the reader, it shall not be much out of purpose to adduce also the public and general agreement of the whole clergy of England, confirmed and ratified in their own public book, made and set forth by them about the same time, called then "The bishop's book." In which, although many things were very imperfect, yet as touching the bishop of Rome's regality, we shall hear what was their whole opinion and provincial determination, as by their own words is to be seen as follows, subscribed also by their own names :—

" We think it convenient that all bishops and preachers shall instruct and teach the people committed unto their spiritual charge; that whereas certain men do imagine and affirm, that Christ should give unto the bishop of Rome power and authority, not only to be head and governor of all priests and bishops in Christ's church; but also to have and occupy the whole monarchy of the world in his hands; and that he may thereby lawfully depose kings and princes from their realms, dominions, and seigniories, and so transfer and give the same to such persons as he pleases; all which is utterly false and untrue; for Christ never gave to St. Peter, or unto any of the apostles, or their successors, any such authority. And the apostles, St. Peter and St. Paul, do teach and command, that all christian people, as well priests and bishops as others, should be obedient and subject unto the princes and potentates of the world, even although they were infidels.

And as for the bishop of Rome, it was many hundred years after Christ, before he could acquire or get any primacy or governance above any other bishops, out of his province in Italy; since which time he has ever usurped more and more. And although some part of his power was given to him by the consent of the emperors, kings, and princes, and by the consent also of the clergy in general councils assembled; yet surely he attained the most part thereof by marvellous subtlety and craft, and especially by conspiracy with great kings and princes; sometimes by training them into his devotion by pretence and colour of holiness and sanctity, and sometimes constraining them by force and tyranny. Whereby the said bishops of Rome aspired and rose at length unto such greatness in strength and authority, that they presumed and took upon them to be heads, and to enact laws by their own authority, not only unto all other bishops within Christendom; but also unto the emperors, kings, and others the princes and lords of the world; and that under the pretence of the authority committed unto them by the gospel. Wherein the said bishops of Rome do not only abuse and pervert the true sense and meaning of Christ's word; but they do also, clean contrary to the use and custom of the primitive church; and so do manifestly violate, as well the holy canons made in the church immediately after the time of the apostles, as also the decrees and constitutions made in that behalf by the holy fathers of the catholic church, assembled in the first general councils. And finally, they do transgress their own profession, made in their creation. For the bishops of Rome always, when they are consecrated and made bishops of that see, do make a solemn profession and vow, that they shall inviolably observe and keep all the ordinances made in the eight first general councils; among the which it is specially provided and enacted, that all causes shall be finished and determined within the province where the same began; and that by the bishops of the same province, and that no bishop shall exercise any jurisdiction out of his own diocese or province; and divers such other canons were then made and confirmed by the said councils to repress and take away out of the church all such primacy and jurisdiction over kings and bishops, as the bishops of Rome pretend now to have over the same. And we find that divers good fathers, bishops of Rome, did greatly reprove, yea, and abhor, as a thing clean contrary to the gospel, and the decrees of the church, that any bishop of Rome, or elsewhere, should presume, usurp, or take upon him the title and name of the universal bishop, or of the head of all priests, or of the highest priest, or any such like title. For confirmation whereof, it is out of all doubt, that there is no mention made either in the scriptures, or in the writings of any authentic doctor or author of the church, being within the time of the apostles, that Christ did ever make or institute any distinction or difference to be in the pre-eminence of power, order, or jurisdiction between the apostles themselves, or between the bishops themselves; but that they were all equal in power, order, authority, and jurisdiction. Whatever difference there is now among the bishops, since the time of the apostles, it was devised by the ancient fathers of the primitive church, not because it was according to scripture, but for the conservation of good order and unity of the catholic church, and that either by the consent and authority, or else at the least by the permission and sufferance of the princes and civil powers for the time ruling," &c.

Judge now for thyself, loving reader, if either Martin Luther himself, or any other Lutheran, could or did ever say more against the usurpation of the bishop of Rome, than these men have done. If they dissembled otherwise than they meant, who could ever dissemble so deeply? If they meant as they spake, who could ever turn head to tail so suddenly and so shortly as these men did? But as we write these things for edification, let us mark their reasons, and let the persons go.

And although the proofs and arguments heretofore alleged, might suffice to the full discussion of this matter against the pope's usurped primacy; yet we shall cite a certain epistle sent by bishop Tonstal, and by John Stokesley bishop of London, to Cardinal Pole, for a more ample confutation of the usurped power. About this time Cardinal Pole, brother to the Lord Montague, was attainted of high treason, and fled to Rome, where, within a short time after, he was made cardinal, (of whom more is to be spoken hereafter, the Lord so permitting, when we come to the time of Queen Mary.) While remaining at Rome, there was directed to him a certain epistle by Stokesley, bishop of London, and Tonstal, bishop of Durham, persuading him to relinquish and abandon the supremacy of the pope, and to conform himself to the religion of his king. It is as follows:—

"For the good will that we have borne to you in times past as long as you continued the king's true subject; we cannot a little lament and mourn, that you neither regarding the inestimable kindness of the king's highness heretofore shewed to you in your bringing up, nor the honour of the house that you be come of, nor the wealth of the country that you were born in, should so decline from your duty to your prince, that you should be seduced by fair words and vain promises of the bishop of Rome to wind with him, going about by all means possible, to pull down and put underfoot your natural prince and master; to the destruction of the country that hath brought you up, and for the vain-glory of a red hat to make yourself an instrument to set forth his malice, who hath stirred up, by all means that he could, all such christian princes as would give ear unto him, to depose the king's highness from his kingdom, and to offer it as a prey for them that should execute his malice, and to stir, if he could, his subjects against him, in stirring and nourishing rebellions in his realm, where the office and duty of all good christian men, and namely of us that be priests, should be to bring all commotion to tranquillity, all trouble to quietness, all discord to concord; and in doing contrary, we would shew ourselves to be but the ministers of Satan and not of Christ, who ordained all us that be priests to use in all places the legation of peace, and not of discord. But since that

cannot be undone that is done, second, it is to make amends, and follow the doing of the prodigal son spoken of in the gospel, who returned home to his father, and was well accepted; as no doubt you might be, if you will say as he said in acknowledging your folly, and do as he did in returning home again from your wandering abroad in service of them, who little care what come of you so that their purpose by you be served. And if you be moved by your conscience, that you cannot allow the king your master to be supreme head of the church of England, because the bishop of Rome hath heretofore for many years usurped that name universally over all the church, under pretence of the gospel of St. Matthew, saying, 'Thou art Peter, and on this rock I will build my church;' surely that text many of the most holy and ancient expositors take to be meant of the faith, then first confessed by the mouth of Peter; upon which faith, confessing Christ to be the Son of God, the church is builded, Christ being the very lowest foundation stone, whereupon both the apostles themselves, and also the whole faith of the church of Christ, by them preached through the world, is founded and built: and no other foundation can there be, but that only, as St. Paul saith, 'For other foundation can no man lay than that is laid, which is Jesus Christ,' 1 Cor. iii. 11.

"And where you think that Luke xxii. 32, proves the authority of the bishop of Rome, when Christ says, Peter, 'I have prayed for thee, that thy faith fail not: and when thou art converted, strengthen thy brethren;' surely that speaks only of the fall of Peter, known to Christ by his godly prescience, of which he gave an inkling, that after his fall Peter should not despair, but return again and confirm his brethren, as he ever, being most fervent was wont, to do. The place plainly opens itself that it cannot be otherwise taken but with this meaning, and not to be spoken but to Peter; for otherwise his successors must first fail in the faith, and then convert and so confirm their brethren. And whereas you think that this place of the gospel of John, 'Feed my sheep' was spoken only to Peter, and that those words make him shepherd over all, and above all; St. Peter himself testifies the contrary in his canonical epistle, where he saith to all priests, 'Feed the flock of Christ which is among you,' which he bad them do by the authority that Christ had put them in as follows: 'And when the chief shepherd shall appear, ye shall receive the incorruptible crown of eternal glory.' The same likewise St. Paul in the Acts testifies, saying, 'Take heed therefore unto yourselves and to all the flock, over the which the Holy Ghost hath made you overseers, to feed the church of God, which he hath purchased with his own blood,' Acts xx. 28. Where, in the original text, the word signifying to govern, or oversee, is the same that is spoken to Peter, feed, for it signifies both in the scripture. And that by these words he was not constituted a shepherd over all, is very plain by the fact that St. Peter durst not commence such intercourse among the Gentiles, but eschewed it as a thing unlawful, and much rather prohibited than commanded by God's law, until he was admonished by the revelation of the sheet, mentioned in Acts xi. 5—7; whereas, if Christ by these words, 'Feed my sheep,' had given such an universal government to Peter, then Peter, being more fervent than any other of the apostles to execute Christ's commandment, would of his own accord have gone before without any such new admonition, or having been sent for by Cornelius; except peradventure you would say, that Peter did not understand the words of Christ, for lack of the light which the later men have obtained, and thereby understand the words of Christ to Peter better than Peter himself did. And strange also it were to condemn Peter as a high traitor to his Master after his ascension; as if he indeed were worthy, if his Master had signified to him that the bishops of Rome, by his dying there, should be heads of all the church; and he knowing the same by these words 'Feed my sheep,' yet notwithstanding his Master's high legacy and commandment, would flee as he did from Rome, until his Master encountering him by the way, with terrible words, caused him to return."

After many references and arguments connected

with the ancient history of the church, the letter thus concludes :—

"Christian kings are sovereigns over the priests, as over all their subjects, and may command the priests to do their offices, as well as they do others ; and ought by their supreme office to see that all men of all degrees do their duties, whereunto they are called either by God or by the king ; and those kings that so do chiefly do execute well their office. So that the king's highness, taking upon him, as supreme head of the church of England, to see that as well spiritual as temporal men do their duties, doth neither make innovation in the church, nor yet trouble the order thereof ; but doth as the chief and best of the kings of Israel did, and as all good christian kings ought to do. Which office good christian emperors always took upon them, in calling the universal councils of all countries in one place and at one time to assemble together, to the intent that all heresies troubling the church might there be extirpated, calling and commanding as well the bishop of Rome as other patriarchs and all primates, as well of the East as of the West, of the South as of the North, to come to the said councils : as Marcian the emperor did in calling the great council of Chalcedon, A. D. 451, one of the four chief and first general councils, and in commanding Leo, then bishop of Rome, to come unto the same. And although Leo neither liked the time, and would have wished it deferred for a season, nor yet the place, for he would have had it in Italy ; yet the emperor by his own command summoned the council to meet at Chalcis, in Asia : yet Leo answered the emperor, that he would gladly obey his command, and sent thither his agents to appear there for him, as appears in the forty-first, forty-seventh, and forty-eighth epistles of Leo to Marcian, and in the forty-ninth epistle to Pulcheria the empress. Marcian likewise desires Theodosius, the emperor of the West, to summon a council of bishops to be called in Italy, for taking away such contentions and troubles, as at that time troubled the quietness of the churches. And in many epistles of Leo it manifestly appears, that the emperors always assembled general councils by their command : and in the sixth general council it appears very plainly, that at that time the bishops of Rome made no claim, nor used any title to call themselves heads universal over all the catholic church, as appears in the superscription or salutation of the aforesaid synodical preamble, which is in these words :

" ' To the most godly lords and most noble victors and conquerors, the well-beloved children of God and our Lord Jesus Christ, Constantine the great, emperor, and Heraclius and Tiberius, Cæsars : bishop Agatho, the servant of the servants of God, with all the convocations subject to the council of the see apostolic, sendeth greeting.'—And he expresses what countries he reckoned and comprehended in that superscription or salutation ; for it followeth, that those were under his assembly, which were in the North and East parts, so that at that time the bishop of Rome made no such pretence to be over and above all, as he now does by usurpation, vindicating to himself the spiritual kingdom of Christ, by which he remains in the hearts of all faithful people, and then changes it to a temporal kingdom over and above all kings, to depose them for his pleasure, preaching thereby the flesh for the spirit, and an earthly kingdom for an heavenly, to his own damnation, if he repent not : whereas he ought to obey his prince by the doctrine of St. Peter in his first epistle, saying, ' Submit yourselves to every ordinance of man for the Lord's sake, whether it be to the king as supreme, or unto governors, as unto them that are sent by him for the punishment of evil doers, and for the praise of them that do well.' 1 Pet. ii. 13, 14. Again, St. Paul, ' Let every soul be subject unto the higher powers.' Rom. xiii. 1. With other things before alleged. So that this his pretended usurpation as being above all kings is directly against the scriptures, given to the church by the apostles, whose doctrine whoever overturns, can be neither the head, nor yet the least member of the church.

"Wherefore, although ye have hitherto adhered to the wrongfully usurped power, moved as you write, by your conscience; yet since now that you see further, if you wish to regard the pure truth, and such ancient authors as have been written to you of in times past, we would exhort you, for the health of your soul, to surrender into the hands of the bishop of Rome your red hat, by which he seduced you, trusting so to make you, being come of a noble blood, an instrument to advance his own vain glory; whereof by the hat he made you participant, to allure you thereby the more to his purpose.

"In which doing you shall return to the truth from which you have erred; do your duty to your sovereign lord from whom you have declined, and please thereby Almighty God, whose laws you have transgressed : and in not doing so you shall remain in error, offending both Almighty God, and your natural sovereign lord, whom chiefly you ought to seek to please. Which thing, for the good that we heretofore have borne you, we pray Almighty God of his infinite mercy that you do not. Amen !"

When all the king's subjects and the learned of the realm had taken the oath of the king's supremacy, only Fisher, the bishop of Rochester, and Sir Thomas More, refused to be sworn : therefore they were committed to the Tower, and executed, A. D. 1535.

Among other acts of Fisher, he had been a great enemy and persecutor of John Frith, the godly and learned martyr of Jesus Christ, whom he and Sir Thomas More caused to be burned a year and a half before. For his learning and other virtues this bishop was well reputed and reported of by many, and also much lamented by some. But whatever his learning was, it was a pity that he, being endued with that knowledge, should be so far drowned in such superstition ; and the more pity that he was so obstinate in his ignorance ; but most pity of all, that he so abused the learning he had to such cruelty. But this we commonly see come to pass, as the Lord saith, " That whoso striketh with the sword, shall perish with the sword," and they that stain their hands with blood seldom bring their bodies unbloody to the grave ; as commonly appears by the end of bloody tyrants, and especially such as were persecutors of Christ's poor members ; in the number of whom was this bishop and Sir Thomas More, by whom good John Frith, Tewkesbury, Thomas Hitton, Byfield, with other saints of God were brought to their death. It was said, that the pope, to recompense bishop Fisher for his faithful service, had elected him cardinal, and sent him a cardinal's hat as far as Calais ; but the head that it should stand upon was cut off before the pope's hat could come to it.

Of Sir Thomas More something hath been said before. He was accounted a man both witty and learned ; but whatever he was beside, he was a bitter persecutor of good men, and a wretched enemy to the truth of the gospel, as by his books may appear, wherein he most slanderously and contumeliously writes against Luther, Zuinglius, Tindal, Frith, Barnes, Byfield, Bainham, Tewkesbury, and the articles and doctrines which they professed.

Briefly, as he was a sore persecutor of them that stood in the defence of the gospel, so on the other side he had such a blind devotion for the see of Rome, and so wilfully stood in the pope's quarrel against his own prince, that he would not give over until he brought himself to the scaffold.

The like also is to be said of the three monks of the charter-house, Ermew, Middlemore, and Nudigate, who the same year in the month of June were arraigned at Westminster for speaking traitorous words against the king's crown and dignity ; for which they were hanged, drawn, and quartered at Tyburn.

In the same year and for the same treason, with the like punishment, were executed John Houghton, prior of the Charter-house in London, Robert Laurence, prior of the charter-house of Belvail, Austen Webster, prior of the charter-house of Hexham.

Besides, and with these priors, suffered likewise two other priests, one called Reignold, brother of Sion, the other named John Haile, vicar of Thistleworth.

Shortly after the pope's supremacy was rejected, the

ruin of abbeys and religious houses in England began to follow in a right order and method, by God's divine providence. For the fall of the monasteries could not have followed, unless the suppression of the pope's supremacy had gone before; neither could any true reformation of the church have been attempted, unless the subversion of those superstitious houses had taken place.

Upon which, in the same year, in the month of October, the king having then Thomas Cromwell in his council, sent Dr. Lee to visit the abbeys, priories, and nunneries in all England, and to set at liberty all such religious persons as desired to be free, and all others that were under the age of four-and-twenty years; providing that such monks, canons, and friars as were dismissed, should have given to them by the abbot or prior, instead of their habit, a secular priest's gown, and forty shillings of money. And likewise the nuns to have given to them such apparel as secular women then commonly used, and also suffered to go where they would. At which time their chief jewels and reliques were taken from the abbeys and monasteries.

When the king had thus established his supremacy, and all things were quieted within the realm, he like a wise prince, and having wise counsel about him, forecasting with himself what foreign dangers might fall by other countries, which were all as yet in subjection to the bishop of Rome; save only a few German princes; and not doubting the malice of the pope, he thought it good to keep in by all possible means with other princes, and accordingly he sent ambassadors to the king of Scotland, the king of France, and to the emperor, to justify his proceedings respecting his marriage, and the suppression of the pope's supremacy.

But that we may be able to go forward with our history, we shall now relate the history of the good martyr of God, William Tindal, who was betrayed and put to death, (A.D. 1536.) Which William Tindal, as he was appointed a special organ of the Lord, to shake the inward roots, and foundation of the pope's proud prelacy, so the great prince of darkness, with his impious imps, having a special malice against him, left no way unsought to craftily entrap him, and falsely to betray him, and maliciously to take his life, as by the following process of his history here may appear.

The Life and History of the true Servant and Martyr of God, William Tindal, who, for his notable pains and travail may well be called the Apostle of England in this our later age.

William Tindal, the faithful minister and constant martyr of Christ, was born about the borders of Wales, and brought up from a child in the university of Oxford, where he grew up, and increased in the knowledge of tongues, and other liberal arts, but more especially in the knowledge of the scriptures, to which his mind was singularly addicted; so that in Magdalen-hall he read privately to certain students and fellows of Magdalen college some divinity, instructing them in the knowledge and truth of the scripture. His life and conversation were such, that all they that knew him, reputed and esteemed him to be a man of most virtuous disposition, and of life unspotted.

Thus he, in the university of Oxford, increasing more and more in learning, removed from thence to the university of Cambridge, where after he had likewise made his abode some time, and being now further ripened in the knowledge of God's word, he left that university also, and resorted to one Master Welch, a knight of Gloucestershire, and was there schoolmaster to his children. To this gentleman there resorted abbots, deans, archdeacons, with other doctors and great beneficed men, who, there together with Master Tindal, sitting at the same table, used often to enter into communication, and talk of learned men, as of Luther and Erasmus; also of other controversies and questions upon the scripture.

Then, Master Tindal, as he was learned and well practised in God's matters, so he spared not to shew simply and plainly his judgment; and when they, at any time, varied from Tindal in opinion and judgment, he would shew them in the book, and lay plainly before them the open and manifest places of the scriptures, to confute their errors, and confirm his sayings. And thus they continued for some time reasoning and contending together, until at length they entertained a secret dislike in their hearts against him.

Not long after this, it happened that some of these great doctors had invited Mr. Welch and his wife to a banquet, where they talked at will and pleasure, uttering their blindness and ignorance without any resistance. Then Master Welch and his wife coming home, and calling for Mr. Tindal, began to reason with him about those matters, which the priests had talked about at their banquet. Master Tindal, answering by scripture, maintained the truth, and reproved their false opinions. Then said the Lady Welch, a stout and a wise woman, "Well, there was such a doctor who could expend an hundred pounds, and another two hundred pounds, and another three hundred pounds; and what, is it reason, think you, that we should believe you before them?" Master Tindal gave her no answer at that time, and after that he talked but little in those matters. At that time he was about the translation of a book, written by Erasmus, called "The Manual of a Christian Soldier," which he delivered to his master and lady. After they had well perused it, the doctors and prelates were not so often invited to the house, neither had they the cheer and countenance when they came, as they had before.

As this grew on, the priests of the country clustering together, began to storm against Tindal, and railed against him in alehouses and other places. They raged and railed against him, affirming that his sayings were heresy; adding to his sayings more than ever he spake, and so accused him secretly to the chancellor, and others of the bishop's officers.

It followed not long after this, that there was a sitting of the bishop's chancellor, and warning was given to the priests to appear, amongst whom Master Tindal was also warned to be there. And whether he had any misdoubt by their threatenings, or knowledge given to him that they would lay some things to his charge, it is uncertain; but he prayed heartily to God, to give him strength to stand fast in the truth of his word.

Then when the time of his appearance before the chancellor came, he threatened him grievously, reviling and rating at him as though he had been a dog, and laid to his charge many things, though no accuser could be produced. Master Tindal, after this examination, escaping out of their hands, departed home.

There dwelt not far off a doctor, who had been chancellor to a bishop; he had been a familiar acquaintance with Master Tindal, and favoured him well. To him Tindal went and opened his mind upon some questions of the scripture, for to him he durst be bold to disclose his heart. To whom the doctor said, "Do you not know that the pope is very Antichrist, whom the scripture speaketh of? But beware what you say, for if you shall be perceived to be of that opinion, it will cost you your life;" and said moreover, "I have been an officer of his, but I have given it up, and defy him and all his works."

It was not long after, that Master Tindal happened to be in the company of a certain divine, and in disputing with him, the doctor burst out into these blasphemous words:—"We were better to be without God's laws than the pope's." Tindal hearing this, full of godly zeal, and not bearing that blasphemous saying, replied, "I defy the pope and all his laws," and added, "That if God spared him life, ere many years, he would cause a boy that drives the plough to know more of the scripture than he did."

After this, the dislike of the priests increasing still more and more against Tindal, they never ceased barking and rating at him, and laid many things to his charge, saying, that he was an heretic in sophistry, an heretic in logic, and an heretic in divinity.

To be short, Tindal being so molested and vexed, by the priests, was constrained to seek another place, and so coming to Master Welch, he requested that of his good will he would permit him to depart from him, saying, "Sir, I perceive that I shall not be suffered to tarry long in this country, neither shall you be able, though you would, to keep me out of the hands of the spiritualty; and, also, what displeasure might grow thereby to you by keeping me, God knoweth, for which I should be right sorry." So that, in fine, Tindal, with the good will of his master, departed, and soon after came up to London, and there preached a while, according as he had done in the country before, and especially about the city of Bristol. At length he bethinking himself of Cuthbert Tonstal, then bishop of London, especially for the great commendations of Erasmus, who, in his annotations, so extols him for his learning, that Tindal thought that if he could attain to his service, he would be a happy man. And so, coming to Sir Henry Guilford, the king's comptroller, and bringing with him an oration of Isocrates, which he had translated out of Greek into English; he desired him to speak to the bishop of London for him, which he did, and desired him to write an epistle to the bishop, and to go himself with it. But God, who secretly disposes the course of things, saw that this was not the best for Tindal's purpose, nor for the profit of his church, and therefore gave him to find little favour in the bishop's sight. And so he remained in London almost a year, marking the course of the world, and especially the demeanour of the preachers; how they boasted themselves, and set up their authority and kingdom; beholding also the pomp of the prelates, with other things which greatly displeased him. Insomuch, that he understood not only that there would not be room in the bishop's house for him to translate the New Testament, but also that there was no place to do it in all England; and, therefore, finding no place for his purpose within the realm, and having some aid and provision, by God's providence, given to him by Humphrey Mummuth, above recited, and other good men, he took his leave of the realm, and departed into Germany; where the good man, being inflamed with a tender care and zeal for his country, refused no travail nor diligence, so that by any possible means he could convey to his brethren and countrymen of England, the same understanding of God's holy word as the Lord had endued him with.

Whereupon considering in his mind, and partly also by conferring with John Frith, he thought no way more likely to conduce to this, than by translating the scriptures into the vernacular tongue, that the poor people might also read and see the plain simple word of God. He perceived, by experience, how it was not possible to establish the lay people in any truth, except the scriptures were so plainly laid before their eyes in their mother tongue, that they might see the meaning of the text; for otherwise, whatsoever truth should be taught them, these enemies of the truth would quench it again, either with apparent reasons of sophistry and traditions of their own making, founded without scripture; or else juggling with the text, and expounding it in such a sense, as would never be received, if the right order and meaning were seen.

Again, he perceived and considered that this only, or chiefly, was the cause of all the mischief in the church; that the scriptures of God were hid from the peoples' eyes; for then the abominable doings and idolatries maintained by the pharisaical clergy could not be seen, and therefore all their labour was with might and main to keep the scriptures down, so that it should not be read at all, or if it were, that they should darken the sense with the mist of their sophistry, and so entangle them, who rebuked or despised their abominations, with arguments of philosophy and with worldly similitudes, and apparent reasons of natural wisdom.

For these, and such other considerations, this good man was moved, (and no doubt stirred up by God,) to translate the scriptures into his mother tongue, for the public utility and profit of the simple common people of the country, first setting in hand with the New Testament, which he translated (A.D. 1526) After that he took in hand to translate the Old Testament, finishing the five books of Moses, to which he added most learned and godly prologues prefixed before each book worthy to be read again and again by all good christians, as he did also with the New Testament.

He wrote also other works under various titles, among which is that most worthy monument of his, entitled, "The Obedience of a Christian Man," by which, with singular dexterity, he instructs all men in the office and duty of Christian obedience; also other treatises, as "The Wicked Mammon," "The Practice of Prelates," with expositions upon certain parts of the scriptures, and other books, answering Sir Thomas More, and other adversaries.

The books of William Tindal having been published, and sent over into England, it cannot be described what a door of light they opened to the eyes of the whole English nation.

At his first departing out of the realm, he took his journey into the further parts of Germany, as also into Saxony, where he had a conference with Luther, and other learned men, where, after he had continued a certain season, he came into the Netherlands, and mostly lived in Antwerp, till the time of his apprehension.

When these godly books of Tindal, especially his translation of the New Testament, began to come into men's hands, they wrought great profit to the godly; so the ungodly, envying and disdaining that the poor people should be any thing wiser than they, and again, fearing lest by the shining beams of truth, their false hypocrisy and works of darkness should be discerned, began to bestir themselves. But especially Satan the prince of darkness, maligning the happy course and success of the gospel, set his might also, to impeach and hinder the blessed labours of that man. For when Tindal had translated the fifth book of Moses, intending to print it at Hamburgh, he sailed for that place; but by the way upon the coast of Holland, he suffered shipwreck, by which he lost all his books, writings and copies, and was compelled to begin all again. Thus having lost by that ship, his money, his copies and his time, he came in another ship to Hamburgh. There Master Coverdale waited for him, and helped him in the translating of the whole five books of Moses, from Easter to December, A.D. 1529.

When God's will was that the New Testament in the common tongue should come abroad, Tindal the translator added to the end a certain epistle, wherein he desired the learned to amend it, if ought were found amiss. Therefore if any such default had been in it, deserving correction, it had been the part of courtesy and gentleness, for men of knowledge and judgment to have shewed their learning therein, and to have corrected it. But the spiritual fathers then, being not willing to have that book to prosper, cried out upon it, that there were a thousand heresies in it, and that it was not to be corrected, but utterly suppressed! Some said it was not possible to translate the scriptures into English; some that it was not lawful for the lay people to have it in their mother-tongue; some that it would make them all heretics. And to induce the temporal rulers also to their purpose, they said that it would make the people rebel and rise against the king. All this Tindal himself, in his own prologue before the first book of Moses declares, shewing what great pains were taken by them in examining that translation, and comparing it with their own imaginations and terms, that with less labour, they might have translated themselves a great part of the bible: shewing that they examined every tittle and point in the said translation so narrowly, that there was not one (i) in it, but if it lacked a point over its head, they noted it, and numbered it to the ignorant people for an heresy! So great were the devices of the clergy (who should have been the guides of light to the people) to drive the people from the text and knowledge of the scripture, which they would neither translate themselves, nor yet suffer it to be translated by others; to the intent (as Tindal saith) that the world being kept still in darkness, they might live in the consciences of the people through vain superstition and false doctrine, to satisfy their wishes, their ambition, and insatiable covetousness, and to exalt their own honour, above king and emperor, yea and above God himself.

The bishops and prelates of the realm, thus incensed and inflamed in their minds, against the Old and New

Testament of the Lord as translated by Tindal, and conspiring together with all their heads and counsels, how to suppress it, never rested, till they had brought the king to consent. A proclamation in all haste was devised and set forth, that the testament of Tindal's translation, with other works of his and of other writers, were prohibited. This was about the year 1527. And yet not contented with this, they proceeded to entangle him in their nets, and to deprive him of his life.

William Tindal, when at Antwerp, lodged in the house of Thomas Pointz, an Englishman. And there came out of England, one whose name was Henry Phillips, having the appearance of a gentleman, and accompanied by a servant, but wherefore he came, or for what purpose he was sent, no man could tell.

Tindal was often invited to dinner and supper amongst the merchants; by means of which this Henry Phillips became acquainted with him, and in a short time Tindal had a great confidence in him, and brought him to his lodging to the house of Thomas Pointz, and had him also once or twice with him to dinner and supper. Through the means of this Henry Phillips was William Tindal betrayed. After dining together at the house of Thomas Pointz, as they were leaving it, Tindal was seized by two officers whom Phillips had brought there for that purpose, and then this traitor delivered him up to the emperor's partizans, his books were all seized and himself cast into prison. Tindal being brought to his answer, was offered to have an advocate and a proctor, but he refused, saying, that he would answer for himself; and so he did.

At last, after much reasoning, although he deserved no death, he was condemned by virtue of the emperor's decree, made in the assembly at Augsburgh, and brought forth to the place of execution; he was there tied to the stake, and then strangled by the hangman, and afterward consumed with fire in the town of Vilvorde, A.D. 1536, crying thus at the stake with a fervent zeal, and a loud voice, "Lord! open the king of England's eyes."

Such was the power of his doctrine, and sincerity of his life, that during the time of his imprisonment (which endured a year and a half) it is said, he converted his keeper, his daughter, and others of his household. Also the rest that were conversant with him in the castle reported of him, that if he were not a good christian, they could not tell whom to trust.

The procurator general, the emperor's attorney, being there, left his testimony of him, that he was "a learned, a good and a godly man."

As to his translation of the New Testament, at which his enemies carped so much, and pretended that it was full of heresies, thou shalt hear what faithful dealing, and sincere conscience he used in the work, by the testimony and allegation of his own words written in his epistle to John Frith.

The Testimony of John Frith in his Book of the Sacrament, concerning William Tindal.

"And Tindal, I trust, lives, well content with such a poor apostle's life, as God gave his Son Christ, and his faithful ministers in this world, who is not sure of so many mites, as ye are yearly of pounds, although I am sure that for his learning and judgment in scripture, he was more worthy to be promoted than all the bishops in England. I received a letter from him, which was written since Christmas, wherein among other matters he writes this:—

"'I call God to record against the day we shall appear before our Lord Jesus, to give a reckoning of our doings, that I never altered one syllable of God's word against my conscience, nor would do this day, if all that is in earth, whether it be honour, pleasure, or riches, might be given to me. Moreover I take God to witness to my conscience, that I desire of God to myself in this world, no more than that without which I cannot keep his laws,' &c.

"Judge, christian reader, whether these words be not spoken of a faithful clear innocent heart. And as for his behaviour, it is such, that, I am sure no man can reprove him of any sin; although no man is innocent before God, who beholdeth the heart."

And thus being about to conclude the life and history of William Tindal, it remaineth for us to present to the reader certain of his private letters, which he wrote to John Frith; one under his own name, and the other under the name of Jacob, written and delivered to John Frith, being then a prisoner in the Tower.

A Letter sent from Tindal, unto Master Frith, being then in the Tower.

"The grace and peace of God the Father, and of Jesus Christ our Lord be with you, Amen. Dearly beloved brother John, I have heard say, how the hypocrites now that they have overcome that great matter which prevented them, or at the least have stopped it, they return to their old nature again. The will of God be fulfilled, and that which he hath ordained to be ere the world was made, may that come, and his glory reign over all.

"Dearly beloved, however the matter be, commit yourself wholly and only unto your most loving Father, and most kind Lord: fear not men that threaten, nor trust men that speak fair; but trust him that is true of promise, and able to make his word good. Your cause is Christ's gospel, a light that must be fed with the blood of faith. The lamp must be dressed and snuffed daily, and oil poured in every evening and morning, that the light go not out. Though we be sinners, yet is the cause right. If when we be buffeted for well doing, we suffer patiently and endure, that is acceptable to God. For to that end we are called. For Christ also suffered for us, leaving us an example that we should follow his steps, who did no sin. Hereby have we perceived love, that he laid down his life for us; therefore we ought also to lay down our lives for the brethren. Rejoice and be glad, for great is your reward in heaven. For we suffer with him, that we may also be glorified with him: who shall change our vile body, that it may be fashioned like unto his glorious body, according to the working whereby he is able even to subject all things unto him.

"Dearly beloved, be of good courage, and comfort your soul with the hope of this high reward, and bear the image of Christ in your mortal body, that it may at his coming be made like to his immortal; and follow the example of all your other dear brethren, who choose to suffer in hope of a better resurrection. Keep your conscience pure and undefiled, and speak nothing against that. Stick at necessary things, and remember the blasphemies of the enemies of Christ, saying, they find none that will not abjure rather than suffer the extremity. Moreover, the death of them that come back again after they have once abjured, though it be accepted with God, yet it is not glorious: for the hypocrites say, he must needs die, and abjuring will not help. But if it might have helped, they would have abjured five hundred times, but seeing it would not help them, therefore of pure pride, and mere malice together, they spake with their mouths what their conscience knoweth to be false. If you give yourself, cast yourself, yield yourself, commit yourself wholly and only to your loving Father, then shall his power be in you and make you strong, and that so strong, that you shall feel no pain, in that which should be to another instant death; and his Spirit shall speak in you, and teach you what to answer, according to his promise: he shall set out his truth by you wonderfully, and work for you above all that your heart can imagine; yea, and you are not yet dead, though the hypocrites all, with all that they can make, have sworn your death. To look for no man's help, brings the help of God to them that seem to be overcome in the eyes of the hypocrites: yea, it shall make God to carry you through thick and thin for his truth's sake, in spite of all the enemies of his truth. There falleth not a hair till his hour be come; and when his hour is come, necessity carries us hence though we be not willing. But if we be willing, then have we a reward and thanks.

"Fear not the threatening, therefore, neither be overcome of sweet words; with which the hypocrites shall assail you. Neither let the persuasions of worldly wisdom bear rule in your heart, no, though they be your friends that counsel you. Let Bilney be a warning to you. Let not your body faint. He that endureth to the end shall be saved. If the pain be above your strength, remember, 'Whatsoever ye shall ask in my name, I will give it you.' And pray to your Father in that name, and he shall cease your pain, or shorten it. The Lord of peace, of hope, and of faith, be with you, Amen.

"WILLIAM TINDAL."

Another notable and worthy Letter of Master William Tindal, sent to the said John Frith, under the name of Jacob.

"The grace of our Saviour Jesus, his patience, meekness, humbleness, circumspection, and wisdom, be with your heart, Amen.

"Dearly beloved brother Jacob, mine heart's desire in our Saviour Jesus, is that you arm yourself with patience, and be bold, sober, wise and circumspect, and that you bow yourself to the ground, avoiding high questions, that pass the common capacity. But expound the law truly, and open the veil of Moses to condemn all flesh, and prove all men sinners; and all deeds under the law, before mercy have taken away the condemnation thereof, to be sin and damnable; and then as a faithful minister, set abroad the mercy of our Lord Jesus, and let the wounded consciences drink of the water of him. And then shall your preaching be with power, and not as the doctrine of the hypocrites; and the Spirit of God shall work with you, and all consciences shall bear record unto you, and feel that it is so. And all doctrine that casteth a mist on those two, to shadow and hide them, I mean the law of God, and mercy of Christ, that resist you with all your power. Sacraments without signification refuse. If they put significations to them, receive them, if you see it may help, though it be not necessary.

"Of the presence of Christ's body in the sacrament, meddle as little as you can, that there appear no division among us. Barnes will be hot against you. The Saxons be sore on the affirmative; whether constant or obstinate I remit it to God. Philip Melancthon is said to be with the French king. There are some in Antwerp that say, that they saw him come into Paris with an hundred and fifty horses, and that they spake with him. If the Frenchmen receive the word of God, he will plant the affirmative in them. George Joy would have put forth a treatise of that matter, but I have stopt him as yet: what he will do if he get money, I wot not. I believe he would make many reasons little serving to that purpose: My mind is that nothing be put forth till we hear how you shall have sped. I would have the right use preached, and the presence to be an indifferent thing, till the matter might be reasoned in peace at leisure of both parties. If you be required, shew the phrases of the scripture, and let them talk what they will. For to believe that God is every where, hurteth no man that worshippeth him nowhere but within the heart, in spirit and verity: even so to believe that the body of Christ is every where (though it cannot be proved) hurteth no man that worshippeth him nowhere save in the faith of his gospel. You perceive my mind: howbeit if God shew you otherwise, it is free for you to do as he moveth you.

"I guessed long ago, that God would send a madness into the head of the spiritualty, to catch themselves in their own subtlety, and I trust it is come to pass. And now me thinketh I smell a counsel to be taken, little for their profits in time to come. But you must understand, that it is not of a pure heart and for love of the truth, but to avenge themselves, and to eat the whore's flesh, and to suck the marrow of her bones. Wherefore cleave fast to the Rock of the help of God, and commit the end of all things unto him: and if God shall call you, that you may then use the wisdom of the worldly, as far as you perceive the glory of God may come there-

of, refuse it not; and ever thrust in, that the scripture may be in the mother tongue, and learning set up in the universities. But if aught be required contrary to the glory of God, and his Christ, then stand fast, and commit yourself to God, and be not overcome of men's persuasions; which haply shall say, We see no other way to bring in the truth.

"Brother Jacob, beloved in my heart, there liveth none in whom I have so good hope and trust, and in whom my heart rejoiceth, and my soul comforteth herself, as in you; not the thousandth part so much for your learning, and what other gifts else you have, as because you will creep slow by the ground, and walk in those things that the conscience may feel, and not in the imaginations of the brain: in fear, and not in boldness: in open necessary things, and not to pronounce or define of hid secrets, or things that neither help nor hinder, whether it be so or not, in unity, and not in seditious opinions: insomuch that if you be sure you know, yet in things that may abide leisure, you will defer, or say (till others agree with you) methinks the text requireth this sense or understanding. Yea, and if you be sure that your part be good, and another hold the contrary, yet if it be a thing that maketh no matter, you will laugh and let it pass, and refer the thing to other men, and stick you stiffly and stubbornly in earnest and necessary things. And I trust you will be persuaded even so of me: for I call God to record against the day we shall appear before our Lord Jesus, to give a reckoning of our doings, that I never altered one syllable of God's word against my conscience, nor would this day, if all that is in the earth, whether it be pleasure, honour, or riches, might be given me. Moreover, I take God to witness to my conscience, that I desire of God to myself in this world, no more than that without which I cannot keep his laws.

"Finally, if there were in me any gift at hand, that could help and aid you if need required, I promise you I would not be far off, and commit the end to God. My soul is not faint, though my body be weary. But God hath made me evil favoured in this world, and without grace in the sight of men, speechless and rude, dull and slow witted; your part shall be to supply what lacketh in me: remembering, that as lowliness of heart shall make you high with God, even so meekness of words shall make you sink into the hearts of men. Nature giveth age authority, but meekness is the glory of youth, and giveth them honour. Abundance of love maketh me exceed in babbling.

"Sir, as concerning purgatory and many other things, if you be demanded, you may say, if you err, the spiritualty hath so led you, and that they have taught you to believe as you do. For they preached to you all such things out of God's word, and alleged a thousand texts, by reason of which texts you believed as they taught you, but now you find them liars, and that the texts mean no such things, and therefore you can believe them no longer, but are as you were before they taught you, and believe no such thing: howbeit you are ready to believe, if they have any other way to prove it; for without proof you cannot believe them when you have found them with so many lies, &c. If you perceive wherein we may help, either in being still or doing somewhat, let us have word, and I will do mine uttermost.

"My lord of London hath a servant called John Tisen, with a red beard, and a black reddish head, and was once my scholar; he was seen in Antwerp, but came not among the Englishmen: whither he is gone as a secret ambassador I do not know.

"The mighty God of Jacob be with you, to supplant his enemies, and give you the favour of Joseph; and the wisdom and the spirit of Stephen be with your heart, and with your mouth, and teach your lips what they shall say, and how to answer to all things. He is our God, if we despair in ourselves, and trust in him: and his is the glory. Amen.

"WILLIAM TINDAL.

"I hope our redemption is nigh."

The Deaths of Lady Catharine, and of Queen Anne.

In the same year in which William Tindal was burned, died the lady Catharine, princess dowager, in the month of January, 1536.

After whom, in the same year, in the month of May, followed the death also of Queen Anne, who had been married to the king about three years. In certain records we find, that the king being in his justs at Greenwich, suddenly with a few persons departed to Westminster, and the next day after Queen Anne his wife was conveyed to the Tower, with the lord Rochford her brother and others; and on the ninteenth day after was beheaded. The words of this worthy and Christian lady at her death were these :—

"Good Christian people, I am come hither to die, for, according to the law, and by the law I am judged to death, and therefore I will speak nothing against it. I am come hither to accuse no man, nor to speak anything of that whereof I am accused and condemned to die, but I pray God to save the king, and send him long to reign over you, for a gentler or more merciful prince was there never; and to me he was a very good, a gentle, and a sovereign lord. And if any person will meddle with my cause, I require them to judge for the best. And thus I take my leave of the world, and of you all, and I heartily desire you all to pray for me. O Lord have mercy on me! To God I commend my soul." And so she kneeled down, saying, "To Christ I commend my soul; Jesus, receive my soul." Repeating the same several times, till at length the stroke was given, and her head was struck off.

And this was the end of that godly lady and queen. Godly I call her, whatever the cause was, or charge objected against her. Her last words spoken at her death declared no less her sincere faith and trust in Christ, than did her quiet modesty utter forth the goodness of the cause and matter, whatsoever it was. Certain this was, that for the rare and singular gifts of her mind so well instructed, and given toward God, with such a fervent desire unto the truth and setting forth of sincere religion, joined with like gentleness, modesty, and pity toward all men, there have not many such queens before her borne the crown of England. Principally this one commendation she left behind her, that during her life, the religion of Christ most happily flourished, and had a right prosperous course.

Many things might be written more of the manifold virtues, and the quiet moderation of her mild nature; how lowly she would bear, not only to be admonished, but also of her own accord would require her chaplains plainly and freely to tell whatever they saw in her amiss. Also how bountiful she was to the poor, passing not only the common example of other queens, but also the revenues almost of her estate; insomuch that the alms which she gave in three quarters of a year, in distribution, is summed up to have amounted to fourteen or fifteen thousand pounds. Besides the great sum of money which her grace intended to have sent into four sundry quarters of the realm, as for a stock there to be employed for the behoof of poor artificers and occupiers. Again, what a zealous defender she was of Christ's gospel, all the world knows, and her acts do and will declare to the end of the world.

This I cannot but marvel at, why the parliament held this year, that is, in the twenty-eighth year of the king (which parliament three years before had established and confirmed this marriage as most lawful) should now so suddenly, and contrary to their own doings, repeal and annul the marriage again as unlawful. But in this act of parliament lay (no doubt) some great mystery; which I will not pause to discuss, but only that it may be suspected that some secret practising of the papists was in it, considering what a mighty check she was to their purposes, and what a strong bulwark she was for the maintenance of Christ's gospel.

All this seems to be the drift of the wily papists, who seeing the pope repulsed out of England, by means chiefly of this queen, and fearing always the succession of this marriage, thought to prevent that peril by whispering in the king's ears.

Again, Stephen Gardiner (who was a secret worker against that marriage, and a perpetual enemy to the lady Elizabeth) being then abroad with the French king, and the great master of France, ceased not in his letters still to put the king in fear, that the foreign princes and powers of the world, with the pope, would never be reconciled to the king, neither should he ever be in security, unless he repealed the acts before passed, for the ratification of that succession. Which when they had now brought it to pass after their own desire and had got both now the queen beheaded, and Elizabeth the king's daughter disinherited, they thought all things were for ever sure. But yet God's providence still went beyond them, and deceived them; for after the suffering of queen Anne, the king within three days after married lady Jane Seymour, of whom came king Edward, as great an enemy to God's enemy the pope, as ever his father was, and greater too.

In the mean time, when these things were doing in England, Paul III., bishop of Rome, was not slow to help forward his own advantage. Who seeing his kingdom and seat darkened in Germany and in England, thought it high time to bestir himself; and therefore to provide some remedy against further dangers, appointed a general council at Mantua, in Italy, requiring all kings and princes either personally to be there, or else to send their ambassadors under fair pretences, so as to suppress heresies, and to restore the church, and to war against the Turk, &c. This bull was subscribed with the hands of six-and-twenty cardinals, and set up in the great cities, that it might be known and published to the whole world. To this bull the protestants of Germany answered; that as the council was to be convened at Mantua, in the pope's own country; that that alone would be a sufficient cause why they should refuse to resort to it. Our king also entered his protest against this council, and declined to attend it. This protest was as follows :—

A Protestation in the name of the King, and the whole Council and Clergy of England, why they refuse to come to the Pope's Council at his call.

"Seeing that the bishop of Rome is convening learned men from all parts, inducing them by great rewards, making as many of them cardinals as he thinks meet, and ready to defend frauds and untruths; we could not but with much anxiety cast with ourselves, what so great a preparation should mean. As chance was, we guessed even as it followed. We have been so long acquainted with Romish subtleties and popish deceits, that we well and easily judged the bishop of Rome to intend an assembly of his adherents, and men sworn to think all his wishes to be laws; we were not deceived. Paul, the bishop of Rome, has called a council, to which he knew well either few or none of the Christian princes could come. Both the time that he convened it, and also the place where he appointed it, might assure him of this. But whither wander not these popish bulls? whither go they not astray? what king is not cited and summoned by a proud minister and servant of kings, to come to bolster up errors, frauds, deceits, and untruths, and to set forth this feigned general council? For who will not perceive that Paul, the bishop of Rome, goes sooner about to make men believe that he pretends a general council, than that he desires one indeed? No, who can less desire it, than they that despair of their cause, except they are judges, and give sentence themselves against their adversaries? We who greatly against our will at any time leave off the procuring to the realm any advantage, need neither come ourselves, nor yet send our proctors there, nor yet make our excuse for either. For who can accuse us, that we come not at his call, who has no authority to call us?

"But for a moment let us grant that he may summon us, and that he has authority so to do, yet (we pray you) may not all men see, what avails it to come to this council, where you shall have no place, except you are known both willing to oppress truth, and also ready to confirm and establish errors? Do not all men perceive as well as we, with what integrity, fidelity, and religion, these men go about to discuss matters in controversy, that take them in hand in so troublesome a time as this is? Is it not plain what fruit Christendom may look for, when Mantua is chosen as the place to hold his council in? Is there any prince not being of Italy, yea, is there any of Italy, prince, or other differing from the pope, that dares come to this assembly, and to this place? If there come none that dare speak for truth, none that will venture his life; is it strange if the bishop of Rome being judge, and no man repining, no man gain-saying; the defenders of the papacy obtain that popish authority, now which is quailing and almost fallen, to be set up again?

" Is this the way to help things afflicted? to redress troubled religion? to lift up oppressed truth? Shall men in this way know, whether the Roman bishops (who in very deed are, if ye look upon either their doctrine or their life, far under other bishops) ought to be made like their fellows, that is, to be pastors in their own diocese, and so to use no other power; or else, whether they may make laws, not only for other bishops, but also for kings and emperors? O boldness, meet to be beaten down with force, and not to be convinced with arguments! Can either Paul, that now lords it, or any of his partizans go about in earnest to heal the sicknesses, to take away the errors, to pluck down the abuses that now are crept into the church, and are bolstered up in it, by such councils as now is likely to be at Mantua?

" Is it very likely, that those who prowl for nothing but profit, will right gladly pull down all such things as their forefathers made, only for the increase of money? Whereas their forefathers, when their honour, power, and primacy were called in question, would either in despite of God's law maintain their dignity, or to say better, their intolerable pride: is it likely that these will not tread in their steps, and make naughty new canons, whereby they may defend old evil decrees? Howbeit, what need we to care, either what they have done, or what they intend to do hereafter, forasmuch as England hath taken her leave of popish crafts for ever, never to be deluded with them hereafter? Roman bishops have nothing to do with English people; the one doth not traffick with the other; at the least, though they will have to do with us, yet we will have none of their merchandize, none of their stuff. We will receive them into our council no more. We have sought our hurt, and bought our loss a great while too long. Surely their decrees, either touching things set up or put down, shall have no other place with us, than all bishops' decrees have, that is, if we like them, we admit them; if we do not, we refuse them. But lest men shall think that we follow our own senses too much, and that we, moved by small or no just causes, forsake the authority, censures, decrees, and popish councils, we thought it best here to shew our mind to the whole world. Wherefore we protest before God and all men, that we embrace, profess, and will ever so do, the right and holy doctrine of Christ. All the articles of his faith, no jot omitted, are all so dear to us, that we should much sooner stand in jeopardy of our realm, than see any point of Christ's religion in jeopardy with us. We protest that we never went from the unity of his faith, neither will we depart an inch from it. No, we will much sooner lose our lives, than any article of our belief shall decay in England. We who, in all this cause, seek nothing but the glory of God, the profit and quietness of the world, protest that we can suffer deceivers no longer. We never refused to come to a general council; no, we promise all our labour, study, and fidelity, to the setting up of trampled truth, and troubled religion, in their place again; and to do all that shall lie in us, to finish such controversies as have too long vexed Christendom. Only we wish all Christian men to be admonished, that we can suffer no longer that they should be esteemed willing to take away errors, who, by all the ways their wits will serve them, go about that no man, under pain of death may speak against any error or abuse.

" We would have a council, we desire it, yea, and crave nothing so oft of God, as that we may have one. But yet we wish that it be such as christian men ought to have, that is, frank and free, where every man without fear may say his mind. We desire that it be an holy council, where every man may go about to set up godliness, and not apply all their study to oppressing the truth. We wish it to be general, that is to say, kept at such time, and in such place, that every man who seeks the glory of God may be present, and there frankly open his mind. For how can it seem general, when either every man that dissents from the bishop of Rome is compelled to be from it; or when they that are present are hindered by terror, from saying boldly what they truly think; for who would not gladly come to such a council, except it be the pope, his cardinals, and popish bishops? On the other side, who is so foolish, where the chief point that is to be handled in this council is the pope's own cause, power, and primacy, as to grant that the pope should reign, should be judge, should be president of this council? if he, who indeed can never think himself able to defend his cause before any other judge, be evermore made his own judge and so controversies not decided, but errors set up, what can be devised in the commonwealth of Christendom more hurtful to the truth than general councils?

" And here to touch somewhat their impudent arrogancy, by what law, power, or honest title take they upon them to call kings, to summon princes to appear, where their bulls command them? In time past all councils were appointed by the authority, consent and commandment of the emperor, kings and princes; why now takes the bishop of Rome this upon him? Some will say, it is more likely that bishops will more attend to the cause of religion, and be more glad to have errors taken away, than emperors, kings, and princes. The world hath good experience of them, and every man sees how faithfully they have handled religious matters! Is there any man that does not see how virtuously Paul now goes about by this occasion to set up his tyranny again? Is it likely that he who chooses such a time as this is to keep a council, much intends the redress of things that are amiss? that he seeks the restoring of religion who now calls a council, while the emperor and the French king, two princes of great power, are so bent on wars that neither they, nor any other christian prince can, in a manner, do any thing but look for the end of this long war? Go to, go to, bishop of Rome; the occasion long-wished-for offers herself to you; take her, she opens a window for your frauds to creep in at. Call your cardinals, your own creatures, shew them that this is a jolly time to deceive princes in."

And so the king, proceeding in his protestation, declared how the pope, after he had summoned his council first at Mantua, shortly after directed out another bull proroguing the same council to the month of November, pretending for his excuse that the Duke of Mantua would not suffer him to keep any council there, unless he maintained a number of warriors for defence of the town, and the king thus concludes:—

" No, we will the pope and his adherents to understand that which we have oft said, and now say, and ever will say, he nor his hath neither authority nor jurisdiction in England. We give him no more than he has, that is, none at all. That which he has usurped against God's law, and extorted by violence, we by good right take from him again. But he and his will say, we gave them a primacy. We hear them well: we gave it you indeed! If you have authority upon us as long as our consent gives it you, and you will make your plea upon our consent, then let it have even an end where it began; we consent no longer, your authority must needs be gone. If we being deceived by false pretence of evil-alleged scriptures, gave to you what we ought to have refused, why may we not, our error now perceived, and your deceit espied, take it again? We princes wrote ourselves to be inferior to popes. As long as we thought so, we obeyed them as our superiors. Now we write not as we did, and therefore they have no great cause to marvel, if we hereafter do not as we did; both the laws civil, and also the laws of God be on our side. For a freeman born does not lose his liberty, nor hurts the plea of his liberty, though he write himself a bondman.

" Again, if they lean to custom, we send them to Saint Cyprian, who saith, that custom, if truth be not joined with it, it is nothing, but ' An old error.' Christ said, ' I am the way, the truth, and the life.' He never said, ' I am the custom.' Wherefore, seeing custom serves you on one side, and scripture us on the other; are ye able to match us? In how many places does Christ admonish you to seek no primacy? No, but to be obedient to all creatures? Your old title, ' Servant of servants,' agrees badly with your new forged dignity. But we will not tarry in matters so plain : we only desire God, that Cæsar, and other christian princes, would agree upon some holy council, where truth may be tried, and religion set up, which has been hurt by nothing so sore, as by general not general councils; errors and abuses grow too fast. Get you learning, you that judge the earth, and invent some remedy for these so many diseases of the sick church. They that be wisest, do despair of a general council. Wherefore we think it now best, that every prince call a council provincial, and every prince redress his own realm. We make all men privy what we think best to be done, for the redress of religion. If they like it, we doubt not but they will follow it, or some other better. Our trust is, that all princes will so handle themselves in this behalf, that princes may enjoy their own, and priests of Rome content themselves with what they ought to have. Princes, as we trust, will no longer nourish wolves' whelps; they will subscribe no more to popish pride, to the papacy, &c.

" Favour our doings, O christian princes. Your honour and ancient majesty is restored. Remember there is nothing pertaining so much to a prince's honour, as to set forth truth, and to help religion. Take you heed that their deceits work not more mischief than your virtue can do good; and everlasting war we wish all princes had with this papacy. As for their decrees, so hearken to them, that if in this Mantuan assembly things be well done, you take them, but not as authorised by them; but that truth and things that maintain religion, are to be taken at all men's hands. And even as we will admit things well made, so if there be any thing determined in prejudice of truth, for the maintenance of their evil grounded primacy, or that may hurt the authority of kings, we protest to the whole world that we neither shall allow it, nor will at any time allow it.

" You have, christian readers, our mind concerning the general council. We think you all see, that Paul and his cardinals, bishops, abbots, monks, friars, with the rest of the rabblement, do nothing less intend, than the knowledge and search of truth. You see that this is not a proper time to meet, and that Mantua is no place for a general council. And though they were both meet, yet except some other authority call this council, we neither need to come, nor to send. You have now heard how every prince in his own realm may quiet such things as are amiss. If there be any of you that can show us a better way, we promise with all hearty desire, to do that which shall be thought best for the settling of religion, and that we will leave our own advices, if any man show us better. Which mind of ours, we most heartily pray God that gave it to us, not only to increase in us, but also to send it to all christian princes, all christian prelates, and all christian people."

A little before the death of Queen Anne, there was a parliament at Westminster, in which was given to the king by consent of the abbots, all such houses of religion, as were under three hundred marks. Which was a shrewd omen of the ruin of greater houses, which followed shortly after, as was and might easily be perceived by many, who then said, that the low bushes and brambles were cut down before, but great oaks would follow after.

Although the proceeding of these things did not well please the pope's friends in England, yet they began to take some comfort, when they saw Queen Anne dispatched. Nevertheless they were frustrated of their purpose. For the Lord raised up another queen, not greatly for their purpose, with her son King Edward. And also the Lord Cromwell at the same time began to grow in authority. Who, like a mighty pillar set up in the church of Christ, was enough alone to confound and overthrow all the malignant devices of the adversaries, so long as God gave him life.

Shortly after this marriage of the king with Queen Jane Seymour, in the month of June, during the continuation of the parliament, by the consent of the clergy holding then a solemn convocation in the church of St. Paul's, a book was set forth containing certain articles of religion necessary to be taught to the people; in which they treated specially of three sacraments, baptism, penance, and the Lord's supper. Other things were published concerning the alteration of certain points of religion, as that certain holydays were forbidden, and many abbeys suppressed. For which cause the rude multitude of Lincolnshire, fearing the utter subversion of their old religion, wherein they had been so long fostered, rose up in great commotion, to the number of near twenty thousand, having for their captain a monk called Doctor Mackerel, calling himself then Captain Cobler; but those rebels being repressed by the king's power, and desiring pardon, soon dispersed.

After this, followed a new insurrection in Yorkshire for the same causes, through the instigation of seditious persons, especially monks and priests, making them believe, that their silver chalices, crosses, jewels and other ornaments, should be taken out of their churches; and that no man should be allowed to be married, or to eat any good meat in his house, but should first give tribute there for to the king. But their especial malice was against Cromwell and certain other councillors. The number of these rebels was near forty thousand, having for their badges the five wounds, with the sign of the sacrament, and Jesus written in the midst.

This their devilish rebellion they termed by the name of a holy pilgrimage, but they served a wrong and a naughty saint. They had also in the field their streamers and banners, whereupon was painted Christ hanging upon the cross on the one side, and a chalice with a painted cake in it on the other side, with other such ensigns of like hypocrisy, pretending thereby to fight for the faith, and holy church.

As soon as the king was certified of this new seditious insurrection, he sent with all speed the duke of Norfolk, duke of Suffolk, marquis of Exeter, earl of Shrewsbury, and others with a great army, forthwith to encounter with the rebels.

These noble captains and councillors being well furnished with munition of war, approaching towards the rebels, and understanding both their number, and their intention to give battle, first with policy went about to appease all without bloodshed; then by the great wisdom and policy of the captains, a communication was had, and a pardon of the king's majesty obtained for all the captains, and chief doers of this insurrection, and they promised that in such things as they found themselves aggrieved with, they should gently be heard, and their reasonable petitions granted, and that their articles should be presented to the king, that by his highness' authority, and the wisdom of his council, all things should be brought into good order and conclusion; and with this order every man quietly departed.

In the time of this commotion in Yorkshire, and while the king was at Windsor, there was a butcher dwelling within five miles of Windsor, who caused a priest to preach that all they that took part with the Yorkshiremen, whom he called God's people, did fight in God's cause; for which both he and the priest were apprehended and executed.

Other priests also, with other persons, about the same time committing like treason against the king, suffered execution. Such a business had the king then to rid the realm from the servitude of the Romish yoke. But God's hand did still work in upholding his gospel and truth, against all seditious stirs, commotions, and rebellions.

In the following year, after the great execution had been done upon certain rebellious priests, and a few other laymen, with certain noble persons also and gentlemen; amongst whom was the lord Darcy, the lord Hussy, Sir Robert Constable, Sir Thomas Percy, Sir Francis Bygot, Sir Stephen Hamilton, Sir John Bulmer, and his wife, William Lomeley, Nicholas Tempest, with the Abbots of Gerney, and of Rivers, &c. In the month of October, 1537, was born prince Edward. His mother, queen Jane, died a few days after his birth, and left the king again a widower, in which estate he continued for the space of two years.

Here by the way it is to be understood, that during all this season, since the time that the king of England had rejected the pope out of the realm, both the emperors, the French king, and the king of Scots, with other foreign potentates (who were yet in subjection under the pope) bore him no great good favour inwardly, whatever they pretended outwardly.

Yet notwithstanding all this, the Lord defended his cause against them all. For although the French king was for a long time set on by the pope, yet hearing now of the birth of Prince Edward, the king's son by queen Jane, and understanding also by the death of queen Jane that the king was a widower, and perceiving that the king might join in marriage with the Germans, he began to give much more gentle words, and to demean himself more courteously, labouring to marry the queen of Navarre, his sister, to the king.

The ambassadors for the king, resident then in France, were Stephen Gardiner, with doctor Thirleby, &c. What Stephen Gardiner wrought secretly for the pope I have not expressly to charge him. Whether he did so, or what he did, the Lord knoweth all. But this is certain, that when doctor Bonner, then archdeacon of Leicester, was sent into France by the king to succeed Stephen Gardiner in the embassy, which was about the year of our Lord 1538, he found such dealing in the bishop of Winchester, as was not greatly to be trusted.

It is long to recite from the beginning, and few men peradventure would believe the brawling matters, the privy complaints, the contentious quarrels, and bitter dissensions between these two, and especially what despiteful contumelies doctor Bonner received at the hands of Winchester. For understand, good reader, that this doctor Bonner all this while remained yet, as he seemed, a good man, and was a great furtherer of the king's proceedings, and a favourer of Luther's doctrine, and was advanced only by the lord Cromwell. He was archdeacon of Leicester, parson of Bladon, of Dereham, Cheswick, and Cheriburton. Then he was made bishop of Hereford, and at last preferred to be bishop of London. The chief of which preferments and dignities were conferred upon him only by means of the lord Cromwell, who was then his chief and only patron; as Bonner himself in all his letters protests and declares.

This doctor Bonner, in the time of his first springing up, shewed himself a good man, and a steadfast friend to the gospel of Christ and to the king's proceedings: and on the other hand Stephen Gardiner halted then both with God and with the king. The contention between these two was very great, when the king sent Bonner to be his ambassador in France instead of Gardiner.

Which being so, we wonder greatly what should be the cause, that Bonner, seeing all his advancement was by the gospel, and by those of the gospel's side, and being then so hated by Stephen Gardiner, and being also at that time such a furtherer and defender of the gospel, could ever be so ungrateful and unkind as afterwards to join with Gardiner against the gospel, and now to persecute so vehemently that which he defended before so openly.

But to refer this to the book of His accounts, who shall judge one day all things uprightly, let us proceed in this Bonner's legation. Being now ambassador at the court of France, Bonner had given him in commission from the king to treat with the French king for the printing of the New Testament in English, and the Bible at Paris; also for slanderous preachers, and malicious speakers against the king; for goods of merchants taken and spoiled, and for the king's pension to be paid, &c. Bonner employed his diligence to the satisfaction of the king, and in discharge of his duty, save only that the

French king one time took some displeasure with him, for bearing himself somewhat more seriously and boldly before the king, in the cause of Grancetor the traitor.

So that the French king, sending a special messenger with his letters to the king of England, willed him to revoke and call this ambassador home, and to send him another.

The king of England sent answer again by other letters, in which he revoked and called home bishop Bonner, giving unto him about the same time the bishoprick of London, and sent in supply of his place Sir John Wallop, a great friend to Stephen Gardiner. Which was in February, about the beginning of the year 1540. Here now follows the oath of Bonner to the king, when he was made bishop of London.

The Oath of Doctor Edmund Bonner, when he was made Bishop of London, against the Pope of Rome.

" You shall never consent nor agree that the bishop of Rome shall practise, exercise, or have any manner of authority, jurisdiction, or power within this realm, or any other the king's dominion, but you shall resist the same at all times, to the uttermost of your power: and from henceforth you shall accept, repute, and take the king's majesty to be the only supreme head on earth of the church of England, and to your cunning, wit, and uttermost of your power, without guile, fraud, or other undue means, you shall observe, keep, maintain, and defend the whole effects and contents of all and singular acts and statutes made, and to be made, within this realm, in derogation, extirpation, and extinguishment of the bishop of Rome, and his authority, and other acts and statutes made, and to be made, in reformation and corroboration of the king's power of supreme head on earth of the church of England: and this you shall do against all manner of persons, of what estate, dignity, degree, or condition they be, and in nowise do nor attempt, nor to your power suffer to be done or attempted, directly or indirectly, any thing or things, privily or openly, to the let, hinderance, damage, or derogation thereof, or of any part thereof, by any manner of means, or for any manner of pretence: and in case any oath be made, or hath been made, by you, to any person or persons, in maintenance or favour of the bishop of Rome, or his authority, jurisdiction, or power, you repute the same as vain and annihilated: so help you God," &c.

Ecclesiastical Matters, A.D. 1538.

It will be judged, that I have lingered perhaps too much in these affairs of princes and ambassadors. Wherefore I purpose to put my history in order again, shewing such injunctions and articles as were devised and set forth by the king, for the benefit of his subjects. The king, when he had taken the title of supremacy from the bishop of Rome, and had transferred it to himself, then was a full prince in his own realm, (although he perceived, by the wisdom and advice of the Lord Cromwell and his council, that the corrupt state of the church had need of reformation in many things), yet because he saw how stubborn and untoward the hearts of many papists were to be brought from their old persuasions and customs, he durst not reform all at once, but proceeded by little and little, to bring greater purposes to perfection (which he no doubt would have done, if the Lord Cromwell had lived) and therefore he began with a book of articles bearing this title: " Articles devised by the King's Highness to establish Christian quietness and unity among the People," &c.

Articles devised by the King.

In the contents of this book, he first set forth the articles of our christian creed, which are necessarily and expressly to be believed by all men. Then, with the king's preface, follows the declaration of the three sacraments; of baptism, of penance, and of the sacrament of the altar. In drawing up which, he alters nothing from the old trade and system received from the church of Rome.

Then, proceeding to the cause of our justification, he declares, "That the mercy and grace of the Father promised freely to us for his Son Jesus Christ's sake, and for the merits of his passion and blood, are the only sufficient and meritorious causes of our justification : yet good works, with contrition, hope, and charity, and all other spiritual graces and motions, are necessarily required, and must needs concur also in remission of our sins ; that is, our justification ; and afterwards we being justified, must also have good works of charity, and obedience towards God, in the observing and fulfilling outwardly of his laws and commandments, &c.

As to images, he desires all bishops and preachers to teach the people how they may be safely used in churches, and not abuse them to idolatry, as thus : That they represent virtue and good example, and also may stir up men's minds and make them remember themselves, and lament their sins ; so far he permits them in churches. But otherwise, for avoiding idolatry, he charges all bishops and preachers diligently to instruct the people, that they commit no idolatry to them, in incensing of them, in kneeling and offering to them, with other similar worshippings, which ought not to be done, but only to God.

And, likewise, for honouring of saints, the bishops and preachers are commanded to inform the people how saints hence departed ought not to be reverenced or honoured. That is, that they are to be praised and honoured as the elect servants of Christ, or rather Christ is to be praised in them for their excellent virtues, and for their good example left to us, in teaching us to live in virtue and in goodness, and not to fear to die for Christ. And also as assistants of our prayers, but yet no confidence, nor any such honour was to be given to them, as is only due to God : and so charging the spiritual persons to teach their flock that all grace and remission of sins and salvation, can no otherwise be obtained but from God only, by the mediation of our Saviour Christ, who is a sufficient Mediator for our sins ; that all grace and remission of sin must proceed only by the mediation of Christ and no other.

From that he comes to speak of rites and ceremonies in Christ's church, as in having vestments used in God's service, sprinkling of holy water, giving of holy bread, bearing of candles on Candlemas-day, taking of ashes, bearing of palms, creeping to the cross, setting up the sepulchre, hallowing of the font, with other like customs, rites, and ceremonies ; all which old rites and customs the book doth not repeal, but admits them for good and laudable, so far as they put men in remembrance of spiritual things.

And so concluding with purgatory, he makes an end of those articles, thus saying : "That because the book of Maccabees allows praying for souls departed, he therefore disproves not so laudable a custom, which has so long continued in the church. But because there is no certain place expressed in scripture, he therefore thinks it necessary such abuses should be put away, which, under the name of purgatory, have been advanced : as to make men believe, that, by the pardons of the bishop of Rome, or by masses in any place, or before any image, souls might be delivered out of purgatory, and from the pains thereof, to be sent straight to heaven, and such other like abuses, &c.

These were the contents of that book of articles devised, and passed by the king's authority, a little before the stir of Lincolnshire and Yorkshire. In which book, although there were many and great imperfections and untruths not to be permitted in any truly reformed church, yet the king and his council, to bear with the weaklings which were newly weaned from their mother's milk of Rome, thought it might serve somewhat for the time, till better should come.

And so, not long after these articles, some other injunctions were given out about the year 1536, by which the number of holy-days were abrogated ; and especially such as fell in the harvest time : the keeping of which greatly hindered the gathering in of the corn, hay, fruit, and other such necessary commodities.

The King's Injunctions.

" Forasmuch as the number of holy-days is so excessively grown, and yet daily more and more by men's devotion, yea, rather superstition, was likely to increase further, that the same was and should be not only prejudicial to the commonweal, because it is an occasion as well of much sloth and idleness, the very nurse of thieves, vagabonds, and of divers other unthriftiness and inconveniences, as of decay of good trades and arts, profitable and necessary for the commonweal, and loss of man's food, being frequently destroyed through the superstitious observance of the holy-days, in not taking the opportunity of good and serene weather in time of harvest, but also pernicious to the souls of many men, who (being enticed by the licentious vacation and liberty of those holy-days) do commonly use and practise then more excess, riot, and superfluity, than upon any other days. And since the Sabbath-day was used and ordained but for man's use, and therefore ought to give place to the necessity of the same whenever the occasion shall occur, much rather ought any other holy-day instituted by man : it is therefore by the king's highness authority, as supreme head on earth of the church of England, with the common assent and consent of the prelates and clergy of this his realm, in convocation lawfully assembled and congregated, amongst other things, decreed, ordained, and established :

" First, That the feast of dedication of churches shall in all places throughout this realm, be celebrated and kept on the first Sunday of the month of October for ever, and upon none other day.

" Also, that the feast of the patron of every church within this realm, called commonly the church holy-day, shall not from henceforth be kept and observed as a holy-day, as heretofore have been used ; but that it shall be lawful to all and singular persons resident or dwelling within this realm, to go to their work, occupation, or mystery, and truly to exercise and occupy the same upon the said feast, as upon any other work-day, except the said feast of church-holy-day be such as must be for other causes universally observed and kept as a holy-day by this ordinance following.

" Also, that all those feasts or holy-days which shall happen to fall, or occur, either in the harvest time, which is to be accounted from the first day of July, unto the twenty-ninth day of September, or else in the term time at Westminster, shall not be kept or observed from henceforth as holy-days, but that it may be lawful for every man to go to his work or occupation upon the same, as upon any other work-day, except always the feasts of the Apostles, or of the blessed Virgin, and of St. George, and also such feasts as those wherein the king's judges at Westminster do not use to sit in judgment. All which shall be kept holy and solemn of every man, as in time past have been accustomed. Provided always, that it may be lawful to all priests and clerks, as well secular as regular, in the aforesaid holy-days, now abrogated, to sing or say their accustomed service for those holy-days, in their churches ; so as they do not the same solemnly, nor do ring to the same, after the manner used in high holy-days, nor command or indict the same to be kept or observed as holy-days.

" Finally, That the feasts of the nativity of our Lord, of Easter-day, of the nativity of St. John the Baptist, and of St. Michael the archangel, shall be from henceforth counted, accepted, and taken for the four general offering days.

" And for further declaration of the premises, be it known that Easter Term beginneth always the eighteenth day after Easter, reckoning Easter-day for one, and endeth the Monday next following the Ascension-day.

" Trinity Term beginneth always the Wednesday next after the octaves of Trinity Sunday, and endeth the eleventh or twelfth day of July.

" Michaelmas Term beginneth the ninth or tenth day of October, and endeth the 28th or 29th day of November.

" Hilary Term beginneth the twenty-third or twenty-fourth day of January, and endeth the twelfth or thirteenth day of February.

In Easter Term, upon the Ascension-day; in Trinity Term, upon the nativity of St. John Baptist; in Michaelmas Term, upon Allhallow-day; in Hilary Term, upon Candlemas-day; on which days the king's judges at Westminster do not use to sit in judgment, nor upon any Sunday."

After these articles and injunctions were thus given out by the king and his council, then follow as time served, other injunctions concerning images, relics, and miracles; and for abrogating pilgrimages, devised by superstition, and maintained for lucre's sake; also for the Lord's Prayer, the Creed, and the Ten Commandments, and the Bible to be translated into English, with other points necessary for religion: The words of which injunctions here ensue :—

Other Injunctions given by the authority of the King's Highness, to the Clergy of this Realm.

"In the name of God, Amen. In the year 1536, and of the most noble reign of our sovereign Lord Henry VIII. king of England and of France, defender of the faith, lord of Ireland, and in the earth supreme head of the church of England, the twenty-eighth, &c. I, Thomas Cromwell, knight, lord Cromwell, keeper of the privy seal of our said sovereign lord the king, and vicegerent to the same, for and concerning all his jurisdiction ecclesiastical within this realm, to the glory of Almighty God, to the king's highness' honour, the public weal of this realm, and increase of virtue in the same, have appointed and assigned these injunctions ensuing to be kept and observed of the dean, parsons, vicars, curates, and stipendiaries, resident or having cure of souls, or any other spiritual administration within this deanery, under the pains hereafter limited and appointed.

"The first is; that the dean, parsons, vicars, and others, having cure of souls any where within this deanery, shall faithfully keep and observe, and as far as in them may lie, shall cause to be kept and observed of all others, all and singular the laws and statutes of this realm, made for the abolishing and extirpation of the bishop of Rome's pretended and usurped power and jurisdiction within this realm. And for the establishment and confirmation of the king's authority, and jurisdiction within the same, as of the supreme head of the church of England; and shall to the uttermost of their wit, knowledge, and learning, purely, sincerely, and without any colour or dissimulation, declare, manifest, and open for the space of one quarter of a year now next ensuing, once every Sunday, and after that at the least twice every quarter of a year, in their sermons and other collations, that the bishop of Rome's usurped power and jurisdiction having no establishment nor ground by the law of God, was for most just causes taken away and abolished; and that therefore they owe to him no manner of obedience or subjection; and that the king's power is within his dominion the highest potentate and power under God, to whom all men within the same dominion, by God's commandment owe most loyalty and obedience before and above all other potentates in earth.

"Also, whereas certain articles were lately devised and set forth by the king's authority, and agreed to by the prelates and clergy of this his realm in convocation assembled, whereof part were necessary to be held and believed for our salvation, and the other part concerns and touches certain laudable ceremonies, rights, and usages of the church, which are meet and convenient to be kept and used for a decent and politic order in the same. It is ordered that the said dean, parsons, vicars, and other curates shall so open and declare, in their sermons and other collations, the said articles unto them that are under their cure, that they may plainly know and discern which of them are necessary to be believed and observed for their salvation; and what are not necessary, but only do concern the decent and politic order of the said church: according to such commandment and admonition as hath been given unto them heretofore, by the authority of the king in that behalf.

"Moreover, that they shall declare unto all such as are under their cure the articles likewise devised, set forth and authorised of late, for and concerning the abrogating of certain superfluous holydays, according to the effect and purport of the said articles : and persuade their parishioners to keep and observe the same inviolably, as things honestly provided, decreed, and established by the common consent and public authority for the benefit of this realm.

"Besides this, to the intent that all superstition and hypocrisy, which hath crept into divers men's hearts may vanish away, it is decreed that they shall not set forth or extol any images, relics, or miracles, for any superstition or lucre, nor allure the people by any encouragement to make pilgrimages to any saint otherwise than is permitted in the articles lately put forth by the authority of the king, and agreed to by the prelates and clergy of this realm in convocation assembled: as though it were proper or peculiar to that saint to give this or that commodity, seeing all goodness, health, and grace ought to be both looked and asked for only of God, as of the very author of the same, and of none other, for without him it cannot be given : But they shall exhort as well their parishioners, as other pilgrims, that they do rather apply themselves to the keeping of God's commandments, and the fulfilling of his works of charity; persuading them that they shall please God more by the true exercise of their bodily labour, travel, or occupation, and providing for their families, than if they went about to the said pilgrimages; and it shall profit more their souls' health, if they do bestow that on the poor and needy, which they would have bestowed upon the said images or relics.

"Also in their sermons and other collations, the parsons, vicars, and other curates, shall diligently admonish the fathers and mothers, masters, and governors of youth, being within their cure, to teach or cause to be taught their children and servants, even from their infancy, the Lord's Prayer, the articles of our faith, and the ten commandments in their mother tongue : And the same being taught, that they shall cause the said youth oft to repeat and understand. And to the intent that this may be more easily done, the said curates shall, in their sermons, deliberately and plainly recite the Lord's Prayer, articles, or commandments, one clause or article one day, and another another day, till the whole be taught and learned by little and little; and shall deliver the same in writing, or shew where printed books containing the same are to be sold to them that can read, or will desire the same ; and that the fathers and mothers, masters and governors, do bestow their children and servants, even from their childhood, either to learning, or to some honest exercise, occupation, or husbandry; exhorting, counselling, and by all the ways and means they may, as well in their sermons and collations, as otherwise, the said fathers, mothers, masters, and other governors being under their cure and charge, diligently to provide and foresee that the youth be in nowise kept or brought up in idleness, lest at any time afterward they be driven, for lack of some mystery or occupation to live by, to fall to begging, stealing, or some other unthriftiness; as we may daily see, through sloth and idleness, divers able-bodied men fall to—some to begging, some to theft and murder ; who after being brought to calamity and misery, impute a great part thereof to their friends and governors, who suffered them to be brought up so idly in their youth; when if they had been brought up and educated in some good literature, occupation, or mystery, they should, besides being rulers of their own families, have profited as well themselves as divers other persons, to the great benefit of the country.

"Also, that the said parsons, vicars, and other curates shall diligently provide that the sacraments and sacramentals be duly and reverently ministered in their parishes. And if at any time it happen either in any of the cases expressed in the statutes of this realm, or of special licence given by the king's majesty, that they are absent from their benefices, they shall leave their cure not to a rude or unlearned person, but to an honest well-learned and expert curate, that may teach the rude and unlearned of their cure wholesome doctrine, and reduce them to the right way, that they do not err; and always let them see, that neither they nor their vicars do seek more their own profit, promotion, or advantage, than the profit of the souls that they have under their cure, or the glory of God.

"Also, that every parson or proprietary of any parish church within this realm shall on this side the feast of St. Peter next coming, provide a book of the whole bible both in Latin and also in English, and lay the same in the quire, for every man that chooses to look and read therein, and shall discourage no man from the reading of any part of the bible, either in Latin or English; but rather comfort, exhort, and admonish every man to read the same, as the very word of God, and the spiritual food of man's soul, whereby they may the better know their duties to God, to their sovereign lord the king, and their neighbour; ever gently and charitably exhorting them, that using a sober and a modest behaviour in the reading and inquisition of the true sense of the same, they do in nowise stifly or eagerly contend or strive one with another about the same; but refer the declaration of those places that are in controversy to the judgment of them that are beter learned.

"Also the said dean, parsons, vicars, curates, and other priests shall in no wise, at any unlawful time, nor for any other cause than for their honest necessity, haunt or resort to any taverns or ale-houses; and after their dinner and supper they shall not give themselves to drinking or riot, spending their time idly by day or by night, at tables or card playing, or any other unlawful game; but at such times as they shall have such leisure, they shall read or hear somewhat of holy scripture, or shall occupy themselves with some other honest exercise; and that they always do those things which appertain to good behaviour and honesty, with profit of the commonweal, having always in mind, that they ought to excel all others in purity of life, and should be examples to all others to live well and christianly.

"Furthermore, because the goods of the church are called the goods of the poor, and in these days nothing is less seen than the poor to be sustained with the same; all parsons, vicars, prebendaries, and other beneficed men within this deanery, not being resident upon their benefices, who may expend yearly twenty pounds or above, either within this deanery or elsewhere, shall distribute hereafter yearly amongst their poor parishioners or other inhabitants there, in the presence of the churchwardens or some other honest men of the parish, the fortieth part of the fruits and revenues of their said benefices; lest they be worthily noted of ingratitude, who, reserving so many parts to themselves, cannot vouchsafe to impart the fortieth portion among the poor people of that parish, that is so fruitful and profitable to them.

"And to the intent that learned men may hereafter increase the more, for the executing of the said premises: Every parson, vicar, clerk, or beneficed man within this deanery, having yearly to expend in benefices or other promotions of the church, an hundred pounds, shall give competent exhibition to one scholar; and for as many hundred pounds more as he may have to expend, to so many scholars more, shall give like exhibition in the university of Oxford or Cambridge, or some grammar-school; which after they have profited in good learning, may be partners of their patron's cure and charge, as well in preaching as otherwise; in the execution of their offices, or may when need shall be otherwise, profit the commonwealth with their council and wisdom.

"Also that all parsons, vicars, and clerks, having churches, chapels, or mansions within this deanery, shall bestow yearly hereafter upon the same mansions or chancels of their churches being in decay, the fifth part of their benefices, till they shall be fully repaired; and the same so repaired they shall always keep and maintain in good state.

"All which and singular injunctions shall be inviol-

ably observed of the said deans, parsons, vicars, curates, stipendiaries, and other clerks and beneficed men, under pain of suspension, and sequestration of the fruits of their benefices, until they have done their duties according to these injunctions."

These injunctions and articles were given in the years 1536 and 1537; and in the following year other injunctions also were published for the further instruction of the people in the proceedings of religion, by which both the parsons of churches, and the parishes together, were enjoined to provide in every church a Bible in English: also for every parishioner to be taught by the minister, to understand and to say the Lord's prayer and creed, in their own vulgar tongue, with other necessary and most fruitful injunctions, as follows:

Injunctions exhibited, A.D. 1538.

"In the name of God, Amen. By the authority and commission of the most excellent Prince Henry, by the grace of God, king of England and of France, defender of the faith; lord of Ireland; and in earth supreme head, under Christ, of the church of England, I, Thomas Lord Cromwell, lord privy seal, vicegerent to the king, for all his jurisdiction ecclesiastical within this realm, do, for the advancement of the true honour of Almighty God, increase of virtue, and discharge of the king's majesty, give and exhibit unto you N. these injunctions following to be kept, observed and fulfilled upon the pains hereafter declared.

"First, that ye shall truly observe and keep all and singular the king's injunctions, given unto you heretofore in my name, by his grace's authority; not only upon the pains therein expressed, but also in your default after this second monition continued, upon further punishment to be straightly extended towards you by the king's arbitrament, or his vicegerent aforesaid.

"Also, that ye shall provide on this side the feast of N. next coming, one book of the whole Bible of the largest volume in English, and the same set up in some convenient place within the church, that you have cure of, where your parishioners may most conveniently resort to the same and read it. The charges of which book shall be rateably borne between you the parson and parishioners aforesaid, that is to say, the one half by you, and the other half by them.

"Also, that ye shall discourage no man privily, nor openly from the reading or hearing of the said Bible, but shall expressly provoke, stir, and exhort every person to read the same, as that which is the very lively word of God, that every christian person is bound to embrace, believe, and follow, if he look to be saved, admonishing them nevertheless to avoid all contention, and altercation therein, and to use an honest sobriety in the inquiry into the true sense of the same, and to refer the explanation of the obscure places, to men of higher judgment in scripture.

"Also, that you shall every Sunday and holy-day through the year openly and plainly recite to your parishioners, twice or thrice together, or oftener if need require, one article or sentence of the Lord's prayer or creed in English, to the intent that they may learn the same by heart, and so from day to day, to give them one like lesson or sentence of the same, till they have learned the whole Lord's prayer and creed in English by rote; and as they are taught every sentence of the same by rote, you shall expound and declare the understanding of the same unto them, exhorting all parents and householders to teach their children and servants the same, as they are bound in conscience to do; and that done, you shall declare unto them, the ten commandments, one by one, every Sunday and holy-day, till they be likewise perfect in the same.

"Also, that you shall in confessions, every Lent examine every person that cometh to confession to you, whether they can recite the articles of our faith, and the Lord's prayer in English, and hear them say the same particularly; wherein if they be not perfect, you shall declare to them, that every christian person ought to know the same before they should receive the blessed sacrament of the altar; and admonish them to learn the same more perfectly by the following year, or else, that they ought not to presume to come to God's Board without perfect knowledge of the same (and if they do, it is to the great peril of their souls),—so you shall declare unto them that you look for other injunctions from the king, by that time, to stay and repel all such from God's Board, as shall be found ignorant; wherefore do you thus admonish them, to the intent that they should avoid the peril of their souls, and also the worldly rebuke that they might incur hereafter by the same.

"Also, that you shall make, or cause to be made, in the church, and every other cure you have, one sermon every quarter of a year at the least, wherein you shall purely and sincerely declare the very gospel of Christ, and in the same exhort your hearers to the works of charity, mercy, and faith, especially prescribed and commanded in scripture, and not to repose their trust or affiance in other works devised by men's fancies besides the scriptures; as in wandering to pilgrimages, offering of money, candles, or tapers to feigned relics, or images, or kissing, or licking the same, saying over a number of beads, or such like superstition; for the doing of which you not only have no promise of reward in scripture, but contrariwise great threats and maledictions of God, as things tending to idolatry and superstition, which of all other offences, God Almighty doth most detest and abhor, for that the same diminisheth most his honour and glory.

"Also, that such feigned images as you know in any of your cures to be so abused with pilgrimages or offerings of any thing made thereunto, you shall, for avoiding of that most detestable offence of idolatry, forthwith take down, and without delay; and shall suffer from henceforth no candles, tapers, or images of wax, to be set before any image or picture, but only the light that commonly goeth across the church by the rood loft, the light before the sacrament of the altar, and the light about the sepulchre; which, for the adorning of the church and divine service, you shall suffer to remain still, admonishing your parishioners, that images serve for no other purpose, but as the books of unlearned men, that can read no letters, whereby they might be admonished of the lives and conversation of them, that the images represent. Which images if they abuse, for any other intent than for such remembrances, they commit idolatry in the same, to the great danger of their souls; and therefore the king's highness, graciously tending to the good of his subjects' souls, hath in part already, and more will hereafter travel for the abolishing of such images, as might be the occasion of so great an offence to God, and so great danger to the souls of his loving subjects.

"Also, that in all such benefices or cures as you have, whereupon you are not yourself resident, you shall appoint such curates in your stead, as both can by ability, and will also promptly execute these injunctions, and do their duty otherwise, that you are bound to do in every behalf accordingly, and profit their cure no less with good example of living, than with declaration of the word of God, or else their lack and defaults shall be imputed unto you, who shall straightly answer for the same, if they do otherwise.

"Also, that you shall admit no man to preach within any of your benefices or cures, but such as shall appear unto you to be sufficiently licensed thereunto by the king's highness, or his grace's authority, or the bishop of the diocese, and such as shall be so licensed, you shall gladly receive, to declare the word of God without any resistance or contradiction.

"Also, if you have heretofore declared to your parishioners any thing to the extolling or setting forth of pilgrimages to feigned relics or images, or any such superstition, you shall now openly before the same recant and reprove the same, shewing them, as the truth is, that you did the same upon no ground of scripture, but as being led and seduced by a common error and abuse which had crept into the church, through the sufferance and avarice of such as felt profit by the same.

"Also, if ye do or shall know any man within your pa-

rish, or elsewhere, that is an opposer of the word of God to be read in English, or sincerely preached, or of the execution of these injunctions; or a favourer of the pretended power of the bishop of Rome, now by the laws of this realm justly rejected and extirpated; you shall detect the same to the king, or to his honourable council, or to his vicegerent aforesaid, or to the justice of peace next adjoining.

"Also, that you and every parson, vicar, or curate, within this diocese, shall for every church keep one book of register, wherein you shall write the day and year of every wedding, christening, and burying, made within your parish for your time, and so for every man succeeding you likewise, and also therein set every person's name that shall be so wedded, christened, or buried; and for the safe keeping of the same book, the parish shall be bound to provide of their common charges one sure coffer with two locks and keys, whereof the one to remain with you, and the other with the wardens of every such parish wherein the said book shall be laid up; which book you shall every Sunday take forth, and in the presence of the said wardens, or one of them, write and record in the same, all the weddings, christenings, and buryings, made during the previous week; and that done, to lay up the said book in the said coffer as before, and for every time the same shall be omitted, the party that shall be in the fault thereof, shall forfeit to the said church three shillings and four pence, to be employed for the repair of the church.

"Also, that you shall once every quarter of a year, read these and the other former injunctions given unto you by authority of the king, openly and deliberately before all your parishioners, to the intent that both you may be the better admonished of your duty, and your said parishioners the more incited to ensue the same for their part.

"Also, forsomuch as by a law established, every man is bound to pay the tithes; no man shall by colour of duty omitted by their curates, detain their tithes, and so redouble one wrong with another, and be his own judge, but shall truly pay the same, as hath been accustomed, to their parsons and curates without any restraint or diminution; and such lack and default as they can justly find in their parsons and curates, to call for reformation thereof, at their ordinaries and other superiors' hands, who upon complaint and due proof thereof, shall reform the same accordingly.

"Also, that no parson shall from henceforth alter or change the order and manner of any fasting-day that is commanded, and indicted by the church, nor of any prayer, nor of divine service, otherwise than is specified in the said injunctions, until such time as the same shall be so ordered and transported by the king's authority: the evens of such saints, whose holy-days are abrogated, only excepted, which shall be declared henceforth to be no fasting days, except also the commemoration of Thomas à Becket, sometime archbishop of Canterbury, which shall be entirely omitted, and instead thereof, the Ferial service used.

"Also, that the knolling of the Aves after service, and certain other times, which hath been brought in and begun by the pretence of the bishop of Rome's pardon, henceforth be left and omitted, lest the people do hereafter trust to have pardon for the saying of their aves between the said knolling, as they have done in times past.

"Also, where in times past men have used in divers places in their processions, to sing *Ora pro nobis* to so many saints, that they had no time to sing the good suffrages following; as *Parce nobis Domine*, and *Libera nos Domine*, it must be taught and preached, that it would be better to omit it, and to sing the other suffrages, being more necessary and effectual. All which singular injunctions, I minister to you and to your parishioners, by the king's authority to be committed in this part, which I charge and command you by the same authority to observe and keep, upon pain of deprivation, sequestration of your fruits, or such other coercion as to the king or his vicegerent for the time being shall seem convenient."

By these articles and injunctions thus coming forth

one after another, for the necessary instruction of the people, it may appear, how well the king then deserved the title of his supreme government, given to him over the church of England; by which title and authority, he did more good for the redressing and advancing of Christ's church and religion in England, in these three years, than the pope, the great vicar of Christ, with all his bishops and prelates had done in the previous three hundred years. Such a vigilant care was then in the king and his council, that they were desirous by all ways and means to redress religion, to reform errors, to correct corrupt customs, to help ignorance, and to reduce the misleading of Christ's flock drowned in blind popery, superstition, customs, and idolatry, to some better form of more perfect reformation. He provided not only these articles, precepts, and injunctions above specified, to inform the rude people; but also procured the bishops to help forward the cause of decayed doctrine, with their diligent preaching and teaching of the people, according as you have before heard, that in the year 1534, during the whole time of parliament, there was appointed every Sunday a bishop to preach at St. Paul's Cross, against the supremacy of the bishop of Rome.

By the king's injunctions, A.D. 1538, all such images and pictures as were abused with pilgrimage or offerings of any idolatry were abolished: by virtue of which injunctions, several idols, and especially the most notable stocks of idolatry, were taken down in the same year; as the images of Walsingham, Ipswich, Worcester, the lady of Willesdon, Thomas à Becket, with many others, which had machinery to make their eyes open and roll about, and other parts of their body to stir, and many other false jugglings, with which the simple people had been a long time deceived. All which were detected, and destroyed.

Among these foul idols, there was also a certain old idolatrous image in Wales, named Darvel Gatheren: which in the month of May, in the year above mentioned, was brought up to London, and burned in Smithfield. With the idol also was burnt at the same time and hanged for treason, Friar Forrest, of whom some mention was partly made before in the history of Cardinal Wolsey.

Friar Forrest.

This Forrest was a friar, and had secretly in confessions declared to many of the king's subjects that the king was not supreme head of the church; and being apprehended, he was examined how he could say that the king was not the supreme head of the church, when he himself had sworn to the contrary? He answered, "That he took his oath with his outward man, but his inward man never consented thereto." And being accused of many damnable articles, and convicted; he submitted himself to the punishment of the church. Upon his submission, having more liberty than before to talk with whom he chose, he departed as far as ever from his submission. And when his abjuration was read to him, he refused it, and persevered in his errors: wherefore he was condemned, and fastened up in Smithfield, upon a gallows, by the middle and arms, and fire was put under him, and so he was consumed.

In the place of execution, there was a scaffold prepared for the king's most honourable council, and the nobles of the realm to sit upon, to grant him pardon, if he had any spark of repentance in him. There was also a pulpit prepared, where the right reverend father, Hugh Latimer, bishop of Worcester, declared his errors, and manifestly confuted them by scripture, with many godly exhortations to move him to repentance. But he neither would hear, nor speak. A little before, the image, called Darvell Gatheren, was brought to the gallows, and there also with the friar, was set on fire: the Welchmen much worshipped it, and had a prophecy among them, that this image should set a whole forest on fire. Which prophecy took effect; for he set this Friar Forrest on fire, and consumed him to nothing. The friar, when he saw the fire come, and that present death was at hand, caught hold of the ladder, and would

not let it go; he so impatiently took his death, as never any man that put his trust in God had done at any time. So in that manner he ungodly and unquietly ended his life.

In the month of October and November in the same year, shortly after the overthrow of these images and pilgrimages, followed also the ruin of the abbeys and religious houses, which, by the special motion of the Lord Cromwell (or rather and principally, by the singular blessing of Almighty God) were suppressed—they having been granted a little before by act of parliament unto the king's hand; whereupon not only the houses were razed, but their possessions also distributed among the nobility; so that all friars, monks, canons, nuns, and other sects of religion were then so rooted out of this realm from the very foundation, that there seemed, by God's grace, no possibility left for the generation of those strange weeds to grow any more; according to the true verdict of our Lord and Saviour Christ in his gospel, saying, "Every plant which my Father hath not planted, shall be rooted out," &c.

The History of the worthy Martyr of God, John Lambert, otherwise named Nicolson, with his Troubles, Examinations and Answers, as well before the archbishop of Canterbury, Warham, and other bishops: as also before King Henry VIII., by whom at length he was condemned to death, and burned in Smithfield, in A.D. 1538.

Immediately upon the ruin and destruction of the monasteries, followed the condemnation of John Lambert, the faithful servant of Jesus Christ, and martyr of blessed memory. This Lambert was first converted by Bilney, and studied in the university of Cambridge. Where after that he had sufficiently profited by the study of Latin and Greek, and had translated out of both tongues sundry things into English: being forced at last by violence of time, he departed beyond the seas to Tindal and Frith, and there remained for the space of a year and more, being preacher and chaplain to the English House at Antwerp; till he was disturbed by Sir Thomas More, and by the accusation of one Barlow. He was carried from Antwerp to London, and brought to examination first at Lambeth; then at the bishop's house at Oxford, before Warham, archbishop of Canterbury, and other adversaries, and had five-and-forty articles exhibited against him, to which he gave answers in writing. As the answers contain great learning, and give some light to the better understanding of the common questions of religion now in controversy, we shall here give them.

The Answer of John Lambert.

To your first article, wherein you ask whether I was suspected of heresy? I answer, that I am not certain what all persons at all seasons have deemed or suspected of me, perhaps some better, some worse; as the opinions of the people were never united, but thought variously of all the famous prophets, and of the apostles, yea, and of Christ himself: as appears in St. John, when Christ came into Jerusalem there arose a great noise, some saying, "That he was a very good man," others said, "nay," and called him a deceiver, because he led the people away from the law of Moses. Seeing therefore that all men could not speak well of Christ, who is the author of verity and truth, yea the very truth itself, and likewise of his best servants: why should I regard it, if at some time, some person for a like cause should suspect me amiss, and report evil of me. It is said in the gospel, "Woe be unto you, when all men speak well of you: for so did their fathers to the false prophets." If therefore at any season such infamy was put upon me, I am glad that I have so little regarded it, that I have forgotten it. And even though I did remember any such charge, yet I would be more than twice a fool to tell you of it: for it is written in your own law, "No man is bound to betray himself."

To your second article, where you inquire whether I

had any of Luther's books, since they were condemned; and how long I kept them, and whether I have spent any study in them? I say that I have indeed had them, and that both before they were condemned and also since, but I never will, nor can tell you, how long I have kept them; but the truth is, that I have studied them, and I thank God that I did so, for by them has God shewed to me, and also to a multitude of others, such light, as the darkness of those that call themselves the holy church, cannot abide. He covets above all things, as all his adversaries well know, that all his writings, and the writings of all his adversaries, might be translated into all languages; that all people might see and know, what is said on every side, by which men should the better judge what is the truth. And in this, I think, he requires nothing but equity; for the law would have no man condemned, or justified, until his cause were heard and known.

To your third article, wherein you ask whether I was constituted a priest, and in what diocese, and of what bishop; I say that I was made a priest in Norwich, and of the bishop's suffragan of the same diocese.

To the fourth, wherein you demand whether it be lawful for a priest to marry a wife, and whether a priest in some case be bound by the law of God to marry a wife? I say that it is lawful. yea, and necessary for all men that have not given to them of God the gift of chastity, to marry a wife, and that both Christ and St. Paul shew. In the nineteenth of Matthew, Christ speaking to the Pharisees that came to tempt him, saith, "Whosoever shall put away his wife, except it be for fornication, and shall marry another, committeth adultery: and whoso marrieth her which is put away, doth commit adultery." Matt. xix. 9. To that his disciples say unto him, if the case of the man be so with his wife, it shall be hurtful and not expedient to contract matrimony; Christ answers, "All men cannot receive this saying, save they to whom it is given," Matt. xix. 11.; meaning, that every man could not abide single or unmarried, but such only to whom it was given of God by a special grace so to continue.

To this St. Paul assents, when he had persuaded the Corinthians to single life; he concludes thus: "This I speak for your own profit; not that I may cast a snare upon you." 1 Cor. vii. 35. And a little before, "I would," says he, "that all men were even as I myself. But every man hath his proper gift of God, one after this manner, and another after that." 1 Cor. vii. 7.; shewing thereby, that unto some it is given of God to live continent, and to others to engender and procreate children. He proceeds further, and would have all men, none excepted, to marry, who want the gift of continency. "I say, therefore, to the unmarried and widows, it is good for them if they abide even as I. But if they cannot contain, let them marry: for it is better to marry than to burn." 1 Cor. vii. 8, 9. And again, "To avoid fornication, let every man have his own wife, and let every woman have her own husband." 1 Cor. vii. 2. He saith here, "every man and every woman," and not "some man or some woman;" he excepts neither priest nor nun, but every one both man and woman is bound, for avoiding of fornication, to marry, not having the gift of chastity.

Unto the fifth, where you do ask, whether I do believe that whatever is done by man, whether it be good or ill, comes of necessity; that is, whether man has free will, so that he may deserve joy or pain? I say, that to the first part of your riddle, I neither can, nor will give any definitive answer; as it surmounts my capacity, trusting that God shall send, hereafter, others that shall be of better learning and wit than I, to answer it. As concerning the second part, where you interpret; whether man has free will or not, so that he may deserve joy or pain; as for our deserving specially of joy, I think it very little or none, even when we do the very commandments and law of God; and that am I taught by our Saviour in St. Luke, where he saith thus: "But which of you, having a servant ploughing or feeding cattle, will say unto him by and by, when he is come from the field, Go and sit down to meat? And will not rather say unto him, Make ready wherewith I may sup, and gird thyself, and serve me, till I have eaten and drunken; and afterwards thou shalt eat and drink? Doth he thank that servant because he did the things that were commanded him? I trow not. So likewise ye, when ye shall have done all those things which are commanded you, say, We are unprofitable servants : we have done that which was our duty to do." Luke xvii. 7—10.

In which words you may clearly see, that he would not have us greatly esteem our merits, even when we have done what is commanded by God; but rather reckoning ourselves to be but servants unprofitable to God, for so much as he has no need of our well doing for his own advancement, but only that he loves to see us do well for our own sake: and moreover, that when we have done his bidding, we ought not so to magnify, either our self, or our own free will, but praise him with a meek heart, through whose benefit we have done (if at any time we do it) his will and pleasure; not regarding our merit, but his grace and benefit; whereby only is done all that in any wise is acceptable to him. And thus if we ought not to see merit in doing the commandments of God, much less should we look for merit, for observing our own inventions or traditions of men, to which there is no benefit promised in all scripture, which Paul calls the word of truth and of faith.

But here may be objected against me, that the reward is promised in many places to them that observe the precepts of God. Still such reward shall never be attained by us, except by the grace and benefit of him who worketh all things in all creatures.

Whereas in your sixth article, you inquire whether the sacrament of the altar be a sacrament necessary unto salvation; and whether after the consecration of the bread and wine by the priest, as by the minister of God, there is the very body and blood of Christ in likeness of bread and wine; I neither can nor will answer one word, otherwise than I have told since I was delivered into your hands. Neither would I have answered one whit then to this point, knowing so much as I do now, till you had brought forth some person that would have accused me to have erred in the question; which I am certain you cannot do, bringing any one that is honest and credible.

As concerning the other six sacraments, I make you the same answer that I have done to the sacrament of the altar, and none other. That is, I will say nothing until some men appear to accuse me in the same; unless I know a more reasonable cause than I have yet heard, why I ought to do so. But as to the form and fashion, I shall answer willingly so far as my rudeness will serve; I hold that such as are duly elected ministers in the church ought to baptize; except necessity require otherwise: and that the form used in the church is in mine opinion not uncommendable. Nevertheless it would edify much more, if it were uttered in the English instead of the Latin language; and it would cause people in the baptism of children more effectually to thank God for his institution of it, and for the high benefit represented in it.

In like manner, I also deem the same of the ministration in all the others; that it should be expedient to have them ministered openly in the English language, for the edifying of the people.

As touching private auricular confession, I say, that the common fashion now used was never ordained by Christ's law that is written in the Bible; neither can you prove by any authority from it, that we ought to confess all our offences particularly, with the circumstances of all to any man. I never said, nor will say, but that men seeing themselves aggrieved in conscience with some great temptation, may go to those whom they know and trust to be of steadfast credit, and to have good skill in the law of God, opening their grief to them, that they may have thorough advice, some ease, and remedy.

But in this, I mean not that they ought to go to their curate, or to any other priest, whose credit they deem not at all trusty, or their counsel sage, but to any person whom they know to be wise and discreet.

To the other part of your question, where you ask whether a priest may loose a sinner confessed and contrite for his sin, enjoining him wholesome penance? I say that Christ only looses a sinner who is contrite, by his word and promise; and the priest does nothing but shew and declare the word: Neither does declaration or ministry of the priest avail to loose any person, unless he that should be loosed give credence to the word ministered and shewed by the priest, which word or promise of Christ is called "The word of reconciliation," or atonement between God and man. And this testified St. Paul, where he saith, "God hath reconciled us to himself by Jesus Christ." 2 Cor. v. 18. See how it is God that looses us from sin, who is to make reconciliation or atonement betwixt us and him, and that through Christ whom he caused to die for that purpose. "And he hath given unto us the ministry of reconciliation." See how Christ's apostles called not themselves *the authors* of binding and loosing, but *ministers;* "For he (that is, God) reconciled the world unto himself, not imputing their trespasses unto them." Where you may know what reconciling is. "And hath committed (saith Paul) unto us the word of reconciliation," or tidings of atonement or reconciling.

Also that the power, by which men are loosed from sin, is not the priest's power, you may know by the vulgar saying, which is right true; yea, and with leisure, I doubt not, but that I can shew the same in the decrees, which is thus, "Only God forgiveth and pardoneth us of our sins."

Concerning enjoining of penance, I know of none that men need to admit, nor you to put or enjoin, except it be renovation of living in casting away old vice, and taking them to new virtue; which every true penitent intends, or ought to intend, verily by the grace and assistance of our Saviour Christ, to shew and perform.

Unto the eleventh article I say, that grace is given to them that duly receive the sacraments of Christ and his church, but whether by them or not, that I cannot define; for God sends his grace where he pleases, either with them, or without them, and when he pleases; so that it is at his will, and how and when. Moreover, many a person receives the sacrament that is destitute of grace to his confusion. So that I cannot affirm that the sacraments give grace; yet, in due receiving of the sacraments, I suppose and think that God gives grace to them that so take them, as he does to all good persons, even without them.

Whereas, in your twelfth article you ask, whether all things necessary to salvation are in holy scripture; and whether things there only are sufficient; and whether some things are to be believed and observed as necessary to salvation, which are not expressed in scripture. This is the question which is the head of all others objected against me. Yea, this is both the helm and stern of all together, and that which they contended to impugn.

But touching an answer unto this question, I suppose verily, that if I had Saint Cyril's works by me, I should not need to shew any other answer in this, than he hath shewed aforetime, writing upon this saying of St. John, "There are many things more which Jesus did." Notwithstanding, forsomuch as every man at all seasons cannot have what he would, and therefore must make other shifts; I hold that the first part of your question is very true, and therefore is to be affirmed, to wit, that all things needful for man's salvation, are mentioned in holy scripture; and that those things only which are there, are sufficient for the soul's health.

But why should I treat of this, except I would recite all scripture, which in every part is full of admonitions, exhorting and warning us to cleave fast to this way, which is the doctrine of the gospel? Which God, I beseech, grant us all both to know and love, taking heed that in no wise we be seduced therefrom by laws and doctrines of men. Look also to Colossians, chap. ii., and in the epistles to Timothy and Titus. So that I conclude, in holy scripture is contained sufficiently enough of doctrine, for the salvation of our souls; and this, because learned men call it the head article laid against me, I would that all men should well note it, and record my saying, whatever shall happen to me, for the truth is so, that hereon hangs the sum of all. Therefore, I shall recite it once again. I say, "That in holy scripture, and in it only, is contained the doctrine which is sufficient for the salvation of Christian men's souls." God give us grace that we may know it, to build our faith steadfastly upon it.

As to the latter part of your question, I say, that there are many things both to be observed and to be believed, that are not expressed in scripture; as the civil laws of princes and commonalties, ordained for civil government of the body, and all others; so that they are not hurtful to faith or charity, I reckon that we ought to keep them, not only for fear of punishment, but also for conscience sake, although such ordinances are not expressly and particularly required in scripture.

To the thirteenth article, where you ask whether I believe that there is a purgatory, and whether souls departed are there tormented and purged? I say that there is a purgatory in this world, which the scripture, and also the holy doctors call the fire of tribulation, through which all christians shall pass, as testifies St. Paul, in the second chapter of the second epistle to Timothy, whose testimony is notable and true, although few know it, and fewer, perhaps, will believe it. Mark you the words, good people, and know, that the words are his, and not mine: "All that will live godly in Jesus Christ shall suffer persecution." In this purgatory do I now reckon myself to stand. God enable me to persevere to his honour! Of this speaks also St. Peter, in these words, which pertain to the instruction of all Christian people;—"You," saith he, "who are kept by the power of God through faith unto salvation, ready to be revealed in the last time; wherein ye greatly rejoice, though now for a season, if need be, ye are in heaviness through manifold temptations: that the trial of your faith, being much more precious than of gold that perisheth, though it be tried with fire, might be found unto praise and honour and glory at the appearing of Jesus Christ," &c. 1 Pet. i. 5—7.

To the fourteenth article, where you ask whether holy martyrs, apostles and confessors departed from this world, ought to be honoured, called upon, and prayed to? I answer, with the words of St. Augustine, in his book "On True Religion," in his last leaf, where he says, "That we should worship no departed men, be they never so good and holy, for they seek no such honour, but would have us worship God alone; no, nor yet an angel, nor honour them, but only in the imitation of them; following their good acts in our living, as they followed our most merciful God while they were alive; not building churches in the name, or to the honour of them, for they would have no such honour done unto them; it is to them no pleasure, but contrariwise. No, the angels wish not that we should build any churches in reverence of them; but wish that we should honour the original maker and performer of all." Thus saith St. Augustine, "We shall follow their good acts, by helping the poor or helpless with alms and mercy, and dealing truly in word and deed, according to our state and calling, both towards God and man; which is no light matter to them that consider the thing well. But whoever shall truly and duly follow it, shall feel it as the burden of Christ's cross was to him, right weighty and grievous, when he bare it to Calvary; saving that we need not fear, for he hath promised to be with us in tribulation."

As to invocation, that is, calling upon them, we learn in scripture how we should call upon Almighty God in all necessities and tribulations. As in the Psalms every where, as in this, "Call upon me in the time of trouble, and I shall deliver you." Mark, how he saith here, "Call upon me," appointing neither one saint nor another. And also, in another place, "The Lord is nigh unto them that call upon him, that call upon him truly."

And thus used the holy prophets, patriarchs, apostles, and other good faithful people in old time, in all tribulation and anguish, to resort to the head Fountain, who is of grace infinite, as is shewn in many places in this wise. "In my trouble I called upon the Lord," saith David, "and he heard me graciously; when I was troubled, I cried unto the Lord, and he mercifully heard me;" also, I lift mine eyes unto the mountains, but from whence shall help come unto me? "Mine help," said he, "shall come from the Lord that made both heaven and earth."

Also, it is reported in the New Testament, by authority deduced out of the Old, where it is written, "Every one that calleth upon the name of the Lord shall be saved." And mark, it is said, "upon the name of the Lord," without sending us either to St. Christopher, or to St. Patrick's purgatory in Ireland, or to St. James in Galicia, or yet to any other saint; but he would have us that we should call upon Almighty God, and upon his name, for the love that he bears to Christ, who is always our advocate before our Father, to purchase mercy for our sins.

You argue that when one should desire to come to our sovereign to obtain some boon of him; he must first purchase the favour of his chamberlains or officers to bring him to the king's presence. In like manner it is betwixt God and us; of whom, if we would purchase any benefit, we must first go to the saints, making them our friends to go betwixt God and us, as mediators and intercessors. But I answer that I think such reasoners are deceived, in that they resemble God and the king together. For though the king be a full gracious prince, yet he is not in graciousness to be compared with God; and though he were as gracious as possible, yet hath he not the knowledge that is in God, for God knew of all things before the beginning of the world, and is every where, to see not only our outward dealing, but also all secret thoughts of all men's hearts; so that he needs no mediators to inform him of our desires, as the king needs. And he is full of infinite mercy, that I may as lightly, or as soon, obtain of him that which is for my good; as I should win by praying holy saints to be intercessors to him for me.

Therefore I take me to the sample of antiquity, I mean of the patriarchs, prophets, and apostles, and authority of scripture, which teach that we need not to fear, but may boldly resort to Christ himself, and his holy father, forasmuch as he bids us to do so, saying, "Come unto me all ye that labour and are heavy laden, and I will give you rest." Mat. xi. 28. Mark how he bids us resort to himself without fear. For he and his Father, who are all one, gives abundantly of all goodness to all men, and upbraideth no man for their unworthiness. But if we intend to obtain of him, we must lay all doubtfulness apart, and with a sure confidence in his mercy, ask of him that which we would have; so that I leave to others what they choose to do, praying Jesus that we all may wish for that which is most pleasing to him.

To the fifteenth article, you demand whether the saints in heaven, as mediators, pray for us? I say, that I believe saints in heaven do pray for us; for I suppose they know, generally, that all men living upon earth are wrapped in manifold miseries, like as they themselves also were. But I think they know not what particular miseries men upon earth are intangled with; therefore I believe that they pray for us as petitioners, but not as mediators, so far as I can see. For scripture speaks but of one Mediator, which I think signifies a maker of peace, or atonement betwixt God the Father and man. "There is one God, and one Mediator between God and men, the man Christ Jesus."

In the sixteenth article, you demand whether I believe that oblations and pilgrimages may be devoutly and meritoriously done to the sepulchres and relics of saints? I say that, what they may be, I cannot tell; for God can so work, that to those whom he hath chosen to be inheritors with him, all things shall turn to a good conclusion, as saith St. Paul, "All things shall work together for good to them that love God." Rom. viii. 28. Therefore, whether they may be done meritoriously or not, I will not define, God knoweth. But this I say, that God did never institute any such thing as pilgrimages in the New Testament, which is the truth and rule for all christian people to follow and believe.

As concerning the relics and tombs of saints, I have said before, what I think of the milk of our Lady, the blood which they say is at Norwich and other places, with such other things, with which I trust you do what ought to be done. And I beseech God you may do therein as your office requires, shewing example to other prelates to follow your lordship in good doing; as it is comely for a primate to do; remembering always, as St. Paul saith, "the time is short," and therefore it were good to set to hand in time.

Finally, holy Moses when he died would be so buried, that no man should know which was his grave, as it is witnessed in Deuteronomy; and, as the expositors testify, that the Jews, who were prone to new fangled worshipping, should not fall into idolatry, worshipping him as God, on account of the great and manifold miracles that were wrought by him while he was alive.

To conclude, I say, it is no point of my belief, to think that oblations and pilgrimages at saints' graves and relics are meritorious works, or that there is any devotion in so doing. That is godly which is instituted by scripture. If you think otherwise, I would desire to know for mine instruction, what part of scripture should make against me.

In the seventeenth article you ask, whether the fast in Lent, and others appointed by the common law, and received in the common usage, are to be observed? I say, that they are to be observed, and fasting discreetly is commendable.

Yet the breaking of these fasts shall not make a man a deadly sinner, except in his mind there be some other malicious affection, because no law of man, made without foundation of scripture, may bind any person, so that in breaking it, he shall therefore sin deadly. And of this sort made by man is the fast of Lent; and other days ordained in your laws without authority of scripture, which wills us to fast perpetually, eating and drinking only when need requires (not for any voluptuousness, as many, that recount themselves great fasters, I fear have done) yea, and that sparingly, foreseeing always that our stomachs be never cloyed "with drunkenness or surfeiting," as is commanded by our Saviour.

And (to tell the truth) I suppose the prelates should better have persuaded the people to pure fasting by instant preaching of the word of God; and fatherly exhortations, than by ordaining of so great a multitude of laws and constitutions.

To the eighteenth article you ask, whether it be laudable and profitable that worshipful images should be set up in churches for the remembrance of Christ and his saints? I say, that I know of no images that ought to be worshipped, such as are made by the hand of men; for, "Confounded be all they that serve graven images, that boast themselves of idols." Psalm xcvii. 7.

And as concerning the exciting of men's memory; I would suppose that if Christ's doctrine were so shewn and opened by preaching and teaching that people might clearly understand it, (and that is the principal office of prelates and curates) I think we should have little need of any other images, than that which should by wholesome doctrine be shewn to us by word of mouth and writing: Nothing is so effectual to exercise the remembrance of disciples, as the lively voice of good teachers.

So that I suppose if this lively doctrine of God has aforetime been diligently opened to the people, as curates ought to have done, we should not have needed to contend for setting up or taking down dumb stocks and lifeless stones, carved or made by men: and if prelates would begin to set up Christ's word (which, alas for pity! is not looked upon, but rather trodden down and despised; so that many are not ashamed to say, I will have no more learning in Christ's law than my predecessors; for they that magnify it must be sore punished, and taken for heretics, with such other grievous words) if this doctrine were yet set up in churches, I say, and truly opened, that all men might have their judgment thereby reformed and made clear; I think we should not greatly need the profit that comes by images made by men, to excite our remembrances to live to christianity.

For that word which came from the breast of Christ himself, and was written by them that wrote and spake by the suggestion of his Spirit, the Holy Ghost, shows perfectly his will, which is the true and certain image of his mind and device. If this, therefore, were diligently inculcated, I think we should be transformed anew, according to the mind of St. Paul, who, writing to the Colossians, says, "Lie not one to another, seeing that ye have put off the old man with his deeds; and have put on the new man, which is renewed in knowledge after the image of him that created him." Col. iii. 9, 10.

Unto the nineteenth article you ask, whether I believe that prayers of men living profit souls departed, and in purgatory? I made answer in the thirteenth article.

Unto the twentieth article you ask, whether men merit and deserve both by their fasting, and also by other deeds of devotion? I have shewn what I think thereof, in the fifth article.

In the twenty-first article you ask, whether I believe that men prohibited by bishops to preach, as suspected of heresy, ought to cease from preaching and teaching, until they have purged themselves of suspicion? I say, that men may be wrongfully suspected of heresy, either because they never believed such errors, as men by false suspicion deem them to believe; or else, when men, by sinister judgment think that to be an error, which is the very truth. And of this speaketh Isaiah, "Woe unto them that call evil good, and good evil; that put darkness for light, and light for darkness." Isaiah v. 20. As the bishops and the priests, with their orator Tertullus, called St. Paul, saying thus before Felix, we "pray thee that thou wouldest hear us of thy clemency a few words. For we have found this man a pestilent fellow, and a mover of sedition among all the Jews throughout the world, and a ringleader of the sect of the Nazarenes: who also hath gone about to profane the temple: whom we took, and would have judged according to our law. But the chief captain Lysias came upon us, and with great violence took him away out of our hands, commanding his accusers to come unto thee: by examining of whom thyself mayest take knowledge of all these things, whereof we accuse him." Acts xxiv. 4—8. This is to call, by perverse judgment, truth falsehood. And thus did their predecessors speak of the prophets, yea, and of Christ himself, calling him a seducer and preacher of heresy; men being thus suspected ought in no wise therefore to cease either from preaching or teaching.

We have another example of this in Acts, when Peter and John had done a miracle upon a man that had been lame from his nativity (whom, by the power of Christ they healed, and caused to go where he pleased,) the people hearing of this, came running about Peter and John. Peter seeing this, did exhort the people in a sermon, that they should not think that he or his companion St. John, had done this wonderful thing by their own power or holiness, but by the virtue of Christ, whom they and their head rulers had slain.

While they were thus speaking with the people, there came upon them the priests and officers of the temple, accompanied with the Sadducees; who being sore displeased that they should teach the people, and preach that men should arise from the dead by the name of Christ, whom they had caused to be crucified; and they therewith laid hands upon them, and put them in prison until the next day. On the following day they sent for the apostles, and demanded by what power, and in whose name they did this miracle? "Then Peter, filled with the Holy Ghost, said unto them, Ye rulers of the people, and elders of Israel, if we this day be examined of the good deed done to the impotent man, by what means he is made whole; be it known unto you all, and to all the people of Israel, that by the name of Jesus Christ of Nazareth, whom ye crucified, whom God raised from the dead, even by him doth this man stand here before you whole. This is the stone which was set at nought of you builders, which is become the head of the corner." Acts iv. 8—12.

These great men wondered that Peter should speak so freely, seeing that he and his fellow, John, were simple men, without any pompous apparel, or great guard of servants, and being unlearned men. At last they commanded them to depart out of their council-house, until they should commune more freely of the matter. Afterwards they called the apostles before them again, commanding them that they should no more preach or teach in the name of Jesus. "But Peter and John answered and said unto them, Whether it be right in the sight of God to hearken unto you more than unto God, judge ye. For we cannot but speak the things which we have seen and heard." Acts iv. 19, 20. Then the head priests threatening them sore gave them straight charge not to break their precept, and so let them go, not knowing any cause why they might punish them; for they feared lest the people would have taken part with the apostles, for the people gave glory to God for the miracle shewn by them.

Notwithstanding all these great threats, Peter wrought miracles still amongst the people; doing them to show that glory ought to be given to Jesus, by whose power and name they were done. Wherewith the hearts of the people melted for joy; so that they followed after the apostles whithersoever they went.

The primate of the priests, and all that were about him, on hearing of this, were filled with indignation, and laid hands upon the apostles, putting them into the common prison. But the angel of God in the night opened the prison doors, and brought them out, saying, "Go, stand and speak in the temple to the people all the words of this life." That is to say, Christ's doctrine; and so they did early in the morning. Then came forth the chief priest, and they whom they used to have about him, and called a council, in which were all the priests of Israel, or ancients of Israel. So they sent to the prison-house to have the apostles brought forth before them. When their servants came to the prison-house, and found the apostles gone from thence, they returned to their masters, saying, we found the prison fast shut round about in every part, and the keepers watching at the doors without fail diligently. But when we had opened the prison, we could find no body within.

Then as the high priests and officers of the temple heard this, they were in a great perplexity, doubting what would thereof come. Then came one unto them and showed them, saying, Behold the men that you put in prison are standing in the temple, preaching unto the people. Then went they thither, and brought the apostles with them without any violence; but they were afraid lest the people would have beaten them down with stones.

Then they caused the apostles to be brought into their council house, the high priest beginning his proposition against the apostles in this form: Have we not straightly commanded you (said he) that you should not preach in the name of Christ? And see, you have filled all Jerusalem with your doctrine. Will you bring this man's blood upon us? "Then Peter, and the other apostles answered and said, We ought to obey God rather than men. The God of our fathers raised up Jesus, whom ye slew and hanged on a tree. Him hath God exalted with his right hand to be a prince and a Saviour, for to give repentance to Israel, and forgiveness of sins." Acts v. 29—32.

These great rulers hearing this, were cut to the heart, and consulted together to slay the apostles. But one good man among their number advised them otherwise, whose advice they did approve. Then they called the apostles again before them, and causing them to be scourged, commanded them not to preach and teach in the name of Jesus, and so allowed them to depart.

Then went they away out of the council, rejoicing that God had made them worthy to suffer such rebukes for his name's sake. But yet they never ceased to teach and preach of Jesus Christ every day in the temple, and in all houses that they came into. This is written in the fourth, fifth, and sixth of the Acts of the Apostles, and for our instruction, doubt you not; for such practice is shewn in all ages. So that hereby you may see, when men be wrongfully suspected or accused of heresy, and so prohibited by bishops to preach the word of God, that they ought not for man's commandment to leave or stop, though they never purge themselves before them, for such will not admit any just purgation many times, but judge in their own causes, and that as they please.

In the twenty-second article you demand, whether I believe that it is lawful for all priests freely to preach the word of God or not; and that in all places, and to all persons to whom they shall please, although they are not sent? I say, that priests are called in scripture by two distinct words, that is to wit, *presbyteri* and *sacerdotes*. The first is to say, ancient men, seniors, or elders, or presbyters, and by that word the secular judges, or such like head-officers, are sometimes also called; as we read in Daniel, that they were so called who defamed and wrongfully accused Susanna; that this is seldom, and nothing so customable as those to be called *presbyteri*; but it is generally applied to those who are set in the church to guide the same by the word of God and his blessed doctrine.

The others are called priests in the New Testament, by this word, *sacerdotes*, that is to say, I think, sacrificers. And thus, as Christ was called king and priest, so all christian men in the New Testament are called kings and priests. The words in Rev. i. 5, 6. are, "Unto Jesus Christ that loved us, and washed us from our sins in his own blood, and hath made us kings and priests unto God and his Father, to him be glory and dominion for ever and ever, Amen." Thus saith St. John, speaking of all christian people. In like manner it is said, (1 Peter ii. 9.) where he writes unto all christian men, "Ye are a chosen generation, a royal priesthood, an holy nation, a peculiar people."

But this may seem a strange thing, that all persons should be called priests, and that in scripture, which cannot lie. Truth it is indeed, it may seem strange to some, as it did to me and many others, when we read it first, because we never read or heard of it before; and so did Christ's doctrine seem new to his apostles and to his audience, when he himself first preached it.

In the twenty-third article you ask, whether I believe that it is lawful for laymen of both kinds, that is to wit, both men and women, to sacrifice and preach the word of God? I say, that it is meet for none to preach openly the word of God, except they be chosen and elected to the same, either by God, or solemnly by men, or else by both; and therefore St. Paul calls himself in all his epistles, an apostle of God, that is to wit, a messenger of God. And to the Galatians he writes thus, "Paul, an apostle, not of men, neither by man, but by Jesus Christ, and God the Father who raised him from the dead." Also to the Romans, "How shall men preach, except they be sent?"

Notwithstanding, I say this, both by support of God's law, and also of laws written in the decrees, that in time of great necessity lay people may preach, both men and women.

As concerning sacrificing, I say that it is lawful for all men and women to sacrifice; but I mean not by sacrifice to say mass as priests do; but, as christian people who are *sacerdotes*, that is to say, sacrificers; so ought they to offer spiritual sacrifices, as writes St. Paul to the Romans, saying, "I beseech you, therefore, brethren, by the mercies of God, that ye present your bodies a living sacrifice, holy, acceptable unto God, which is your reasonable service. And be not conformed to this world; but be ye transformed by the renewing of your mind, that ye may prove what is that good, and acceptable, and perfect, will of God," Rom. xii. 1, 2.

Another manner of sacrifice which he requires is, that we should always offer to God the sacrifice of praise, that is, the "fruit of our lips giving thanks to his name;" or, as Hosea calls it, the sacrifice of "the calves of our lips," giving praise unto his name; and that we should not forget to do good, and to be serviceable to our neighbours; for in such sacrifices, saith he, God is well pleased.

In the twenty-fourth article you ask, whether excommunication, denounced by the pope against all heretics, obliges and binds them before God? I say, that it binds them before God, if it be lawfully denounced, that is, if they be in very deed, as they are named; and if he de-

nounces them with the consent of others, gathered with him in Christ's name, for the behalf of Christ's church.

The same declares the gospel, (Mat. xviii. 15—20,) "Moreover, if thy brother shall trespass against thee, go and tell him his fault between thee and him alone: if he shall hear thee, thou hast gained thy brother. But if he will not hear thee, then take with thee one or two more, that in the mouth of two or three witnesses every word may be established. And if he shall neglect to hear them, tell it unto the church: but if he neglect to hear the church, let him be unto thee as an heathen man and a publican. Verily I say unto you, Whatsoever ye shall bind on earth shall be bound in heaven; and whatsoever ye shall loose on earth shall be loosed in heaven. Again, I say unto you, That if two of you shall agree on earth as touching any thing that they shall ask, it shall be done for them of my Father which is in heaven. For where two or three are gathered together in my name, there am I in the midst of them." So that such excommunication ought to be done, as I think, by the congregation assembled together with their pastor, whose advice they ought principally to esteem and follow, if it be virtuous and godly.

And thus is it convenient to be done. For the pope is made of flesh, as well as other men, and therefore he may sometimes judge wrong; cursing the blessed, and blessing the cursed. And likewise may other prelates, judging the christian to be heretics, and the heretics christian.

In the twenty-fifth article you ask, whether every priest is bound to say daily his matins and evening-song, according as it is ordained by the church; or whether he may leave them unsaid, without offence or deadly sin? I say that prayer in scripture is much commended, and many great and unmeasurable benefits are shewed to ensue therefrom, that men should the more give themselves to it. With prayer doth St. Paul bid us fight in divers places, continuing in the same against our ghostly enemies. A figure of this we read in Exodus, when the Israelites fought in battle against a nation of infidels; I believe their captain was called Amalek. Moses stood upon a mountain to behold what should be the conclusion, and lifting up his hands prayed that it might well succeed with the Israelites; but in long holding them up, at last his fervour began to grow cold and faint, and his hands lagged downward; and as his hands grew heavy, which signifieth that his affection in praying abated and waxed cold, the infidels prevailed; but as he kept them upward (whereby was meant the intent prayer of a devout mind) he purchased victory to the Israelites. Aaron and Hur, who endited the law to the people, and were the interpreters, stood with Moses; who always, as they saw his arms to faint, did hold them up, so that finally the victory came unto Israel.

But no promise is made by God to them that daily say matins. Neither are we certain by the word of God, that we shall be blessed by him for saying matins; no more than we are certain that for repeating the fifteen O's once every day during the whole year, we shall see our Lady aid us before our death; as is testified in the scripture of the primer, but not by the scripture of the Bible; or that we shall have a like benefit for saying her psalter upon the ten beads, that comes from the crossed friars; or upon the five beads, hallowed at the charter-house; or fasting the ladies' fast, as men call it; or for fasting on the Wednesday; as is shewed by a book that is allowed to be printed and read, for it is neither the New Testament nor the Old.

In the twenty-sixth article you ask, whether I believe that the heads or rulers, by necessity of salvation, are bound to give to the people the holy scriptures in their mother language? I say that I think they are bound to see that the people may truly know holy scripture, and I do not know how that can be done so well, as by giving it to them truly translated into the mother tongue; that they may have it by them at all times to pass the time godly, whenever they have leisure.

I think it were profitable and expedient, that the holy scriptures were delivered by authority of the head rulers to the people, truly translated into the vernacular tongue. And whereas you add, whether they be bound by necessity of salvation to give them to the people? I will not so narrowly touch that point now; but I say that they are bound, by right and equity, to cause it to be delivered to the people in the vulgar tongue, for their edifying and consolation

In the twenty-seventh article you demand, whether it be lawful for the rulers, for some cause, upon their reasonable advice, to ordain that the scripture should not be delivered to the people in the vulgar language? All men may here see, that whoever devised these questions, thought that it is good for the people to have the scriptures in the vernacular tongue, and that I so saying could not be well reproved; and therefore they have laid out all these additions as it were to entrap me. " Whether the heads be bound, and that by necessity of salvation, to deliver it to the people ?" and " whether they may restrain it for some cause, and by some reasonable advice ?"

The scripture is the spiritual food and sustenance of man's soul. This is shewed to be true in many places of scripture; like as other meat is the food of the body. Then if he be an unkind father that keeps bodily meat away for the space of a week or a month from his children; it should seem that our bishops are not gentle pastors or fathers if they would keep away the food of men's souls from them, especially when others offer it, both for months, years, and ages. Neither do I see any opportunity of time or reasonable advice that should cause it to be withdrawn and taken away, but the contrary; for it is reasonable, convenient, and needful for men to eat their meat when they are hungry, and blessed are they that hunger and thirst after the word of God, which teaches to know him and do his pleasure at all times.

In the twenty-eighth article you ask, whether I believe the consecrations, hallowings, and blessings used in the church are to be praised? I say that I know not all of them, and therefore I will not dispraise them, neither can I speak very much for them, seeing I know them not; such as are the hallowing of bells, the hallowing of pilgrims when they go to Rome, the hallowing of beads, and such like. But those which I am advised of, and do remember, are in my opinion good; such as this—when the priest having consecrated the holy bread; he saith, " Lord bless this creature of bread, as thou didst bless the five loaves in the desert, that all persons tasting thereof may receive health," &c. Which I would wish every man might say in England, when he should go to meat, I like it so well.

Also this is a right good one, that is said over him that shall read the gospel : " The Lord be in your heart, and in your mind and mouth, to pronounce and show forth his blessed gospel." Which is also spoken over a preacher taking benediction when he shall go into a pulpit. And such good things I like very well, and think them commendable, wishing that all people might know what they mean, that they with joy of heart might pray joyfully with us, and delight in all goodness; which should be, if they were uttered in English, according to the mind of St. Paul, 1 Cor. xiv. 19, where he wisheth, in the church rather to speak five words with understanding that by his voice he might teach others, than ten thousand words in an unknown tongue.

In the twenty-ninth article you ask, whether I believe that the pope may make laws and statutes to bind all christian men, to the observance of the same, under the pain of deadly sin ; so that such laws and statutes be not contrary to the law of God? I say, if it be true that is written in the decrees, that laws are never confirmed, until they are approved by common consent of them that shall use them, then the pope's laws cannot bind all christian men, for the Greeks and the Bohemians never admitted them ; but refuse them utterly : so that I do not find that his laws may bind all christian men.

Finally, I cannot see that he hath authority to make laws ; which will bind men to the observance of them under pain of deadly sin, any more than has the king or the emperor. On the contrary, I think verily that the church was more full of virtue before the decrees or de-

cretals were made than it has been since. May God repair it, and restore it again to its ancient purity and perfection.

In the thirtieth article you ask, whether I believe that the pope and other prelates, and their deputies in spiritual things, have power to excommunicate priests, and lay-people, that are disobedient, from entering the church ; and to suspend them from the ministration of the sacraments ? I think that the pope and other prelates have power to excommunicate both priests and laymen, such as be rebellious against the ordinance of God, and disobedient to his law. For such are separated from God. And the prelates should pronounce of sinners as they find them ; that is to pronounce such to be excommunicated of God, and unworthy to administer any sacraments, or to be in communion with christian folk, who will not amend.

I am not certain that prelates generally have any such power. And though they had, I doubt whether charity should permit them to shew it forth and execute it without singular discretion. For in churches the word of God ought to be declared and preached ; that the sturdy who come thither and hearing it, may soon be smitten with compunction and repentance, and thereupon come to amendment.

Moreover, when you speak of prelates' deputies ; I think that such prelates are of little use to Christ's flock. It is necessary and right, that as the prelates themselves will have the revenues, tithes, and oblations of their benefices, that they themselves should labour and teach diligently the word of God, and not to shift the labour from one unto another till all be left undone.

In the thirty-first article you ask, whether faith only, without good works, may suffice to a man who has fallen into sin after his baptism, for his salvation and justifying ? I say, that it is the usage of scripture to say, faith only justifies and works salvation, before a man can do any other good works. And truly I do think in this matter, that a man fallen into sin after baptism shall be saved through faith, and have forgiveness by Christ's passion; although he does no more good deeds ; as when a man having a short life, lacks leisure to exercise other deeds of mercy. Notwithstanding true faith is of such virtue and nature, that when opportunity comes, it cannot but work plenteously deeds of charity ; which are a testimony and witness-bearer of man's true faith. This declares St. Augustine, " Good works make not a just or a righteous man, but a man once justified doth good works."

In the thirty-second article you ask, whether a priest marrying a wife, without the dispensation of the pope, sins deadly ? I say, that he doth not so much offend as those who give dispensations for money to priests to take concubines. Neither does he offend so much as the purchasers of such dispensations; for they clearly commit fornication and adultery, which is utterly forbidden by *God's* law ; and the priest of whom your demand speaks, offends only *man's* law.

In the thirty-third article you ask, whether a priest, being sore and oft troubled with incontinence, and therefore marrying a wife for a remedy, do sin deadly ? I cannot see but that a priest may marry. Therefore, following the law of God, I make the same answer that I made before of all priests ; that a priest, not having the gift of chastity, is bound to marry.

In the thirty-fourth article you ask, whether I ever prayed for John Wickliff, John Huss, and for Jerome of Prague, who were condemned of heresy at the council of Constance, or any one of them, since they have been dead; and whether I have openly or secretly done any such deeds of charity for them ; and affirming them to be in bliss and saved ? I say, that I never prayed for any of them, so far as I can remember. And though I had, it follows not, that in so doing I should be an heretic. For you know well, that there is a great country called Bohemia, where the people follow that same doctrine which their ancestors were taught by John Huss and Jerome of Prague ; whom (as I know) neither the pope nor you consider as heretics and infidels.

In the thirty-fifth article you ask, whether I have accounted them, or any of them to be saints; and worshipped them as saints? I say that in secret things, which I do not perfectly know, I follow the counsel of St. Paul, who desires that we should not judge too soon; but to abide to the coming of the Lord, who shall illuminate and shew forth clearly things that now lie hid in darkness. Therefore have I neither judged with them, nor against them; but have resigned such sentence to the knowledge and determination of God, whose judgment is infallible.

And whereas you say, they were condemned of heresy, at the council of Constance; if the council did right, God shall allow it. So that it is not need to ask of me, whether the acts of the same are commendable or not? Neither can I give any direct answer; for I do not know them. And although I did, yet am I not persuaded, because the council hath condemned them, that I must therefore believe them to be damned; for a council, as I believe, may sometimes decide erroneously.

In the thirty-sixth article you ask, whether I believe that every general council, and the council of Constance, represent the universal congregation or church? I say, that what such councils represent, I cannot certainly tell; and therefore believe neither yea nor nay. I know of no scripture to certify me of the same, nor yet any sufficient reason. The church I take to be all those that God hath chosen or predestinated to be inheritors of eternal bliss and salvation; whether they be temporal or spiritual, king or subject, bishop or deacon, father or child, Grecian or Roman. And this church spreads throughout the universal world, wherever any call upon the name of Christ; and there they most grow and assemble, where his blessed word is purely and openly preached and declared.

In the thirty-seventh article you ask, whether I believe that the same thing which the council of Constance, representing the universal church, hath approved, and doth approve for the maintenance of faith and souls' health, is to be approved and held of all christian people; and that that which the same council hath condemned and doth condemn, to be contrary to faith and good manners, ought of the same christian people to be believed and affirmed for a thing condemned? I say, that whatever the same council or any other have approved, being worthy of approbation, is of all christian people to be likewise approved. And again, whatever the same or any other has condemned, being worthy of condemnation, ought to be condemned by all christian people.

In the thirty-eighth article you demand, whether the condemnations of John Wickliff, John Huss, and Jerome of Prague, done upon their persons, books, and documents, by the holy general council of Constance, were duly and rightfully done? I answer, that it passes my knowledge, and I cannot tell; and I and all christian men may well suspend our sentence, being thereof ignorant, affirming neither the one nor the other, neither yea nor nay.

In the thirty-ninth article you ask, whether I believe that John Wickliff of England, John Huss of Bohemia, and Jerome of Prague; were heretics; and their books and doctrines to be perverse; for which they were condemned by the holy council of Constance as heretics? I say, that I know not whether they be heretics or not; nor whether their books be erroneous or not; nor whether they ought to be called heretics or not.

In the fortieth article you ask, whether I believe and affirm, that it is not lawful in any case to swear? I say, that I neither so believe, nor affirm, nor ever did.

In the forty-first article you ask, whether I believe that it is lawful at the command of a judge, to make an oath to say the truth; or any other oath, for purgation of infamy? I answer, that I never said to the contrary; but that I think and have thought it lawful to give an oath before a judge; to say the truth, if the judge so require it; and that by request lawful and convenient. As when a thing is in controversy betwixt two persons, upon which they sue unto a judge for sentence; when the judge cannot otherwise arrive at the truth; he may require an oath. As when the two women who contended before Solomon, to avoid the crime of murder; which the one had committed in pressing her child to death; and would have done the same upon the other, if Solomon had not by his wisdom otherwise discovered the truth. Solomon might, I suppose, to come by the more certain information of the thing, have caused one of them, or both, seeing it expedient for him, to swear. In this case the women would have been bound to obey him; but judges have need to be careful in requiring of oaths.

In the forty-second article you ask, whether a christian person despising the receiving of the sacraments of confirmation, extreme unction, or solemnising of matrimony, do sin deadly? I say, the same of the receiving of the sacraments themselves, as I have said before of the third article, and none otherwise.

In the forty-third article you ask, whether I believe that St. Peter was Christ's vicar, and having power on earth to bind and loose? I say, that I do not perceive clearly what you mean by this term "vicar;" for Christ never called St. Peter, nor any other so in scripture. If you mean, that after the departing hence of Christ, when he arose from the dead in his immortal body, and so went into heaven; that, he so being away, St. Peter occupied his room: then, I say, it is not true that St. Peter was his vicar, in any other manner than was St. Paul, or the other apostles. The one was no less a vicar than the other.

I think that St. Peter and all the rest of the apostles were Christ's vicars: if you mean by this word vicar, a deputy; or such like to preach his gospel, to minister sacraments, and to do divine service in God's church. And thus they were worthy to be called, as the scripture names them; Christ's true apostles, bishops, priests, &c.

In the forty-fourth article you ask, whether I believe that the pope is the successor of St. Peter? I say, that it seems to me a thing of no great value, whether a man believe so or not. I cannot see that it should be numbered amongst the articles of our faith; however, I will shew my rude thought on it, which is this:—

The pope may succeed in St. Peter's stead or office, and do the same duly in diligently feeding Christ's flock, and shewing virtuous example of living; and so in doing, he may and ought to be thought and named, a true successor of St. Peter. And thus is your lordship St. Peter's successor, performing the conditions, with other properties requisite to your order and duty: yea, and as many others as do truly their duty, and duly the office of a bishop. But otherwise the pope cannot be called the successor of St. Peter; merely because he is entered into St. Peter's office, not regarding what is requisite, nor following the track of virtue, but the contrary. Why should men call St. Peter's successors those that play the pagans, and follow Caiaphas, Simon Magus, or Judas? Such, verily, cannot rightly claim to be Peter's successors, no more than the night can claim to be the successor to the day. Yea, they ought rather to be called Peter's adversaries, forsomuch as they do not do his will, which is shewn by his own acts and writings, but work against the same.

So, the pope is the successor of St. Peter, if he follows St. Peter's godly living.

In the forty-fifth article you ask, whether I have promised at any time by my oath, or made any confederacy or league with any person or persons, that I would always hold and defend certain conclusions or articles, which seemed to you right and consonant to the faith? I say, that I do not remember that I ever made pact or confederacy with any person or persons; nor made any promise by oath, that I would always hold and defend any conclusions or articles, which seemed to me and others right and consonant to the faith; unless it hath chanced to me to say in this form, that I would never, with the aid of God, forsake or decline from the truth, neither for fear, nor yet for love of man or men.

And concerning opinions or conclusions, I can tell you of none other than I have shewed; the sum of which I reckon to be concluded in two propositions; which both are written in the New Testament.

The first in the Acts of the Apostles:—"This is the stone which was set at nought of you builders, which is become the head of the corner; neither is there salvation in any other, for there is none other name under heaven given among men, whereby we must be saved," Acts iv. 11, 12. This is one of the propositions wherein is comprehended my saying, which St. Paul thus expresses, " But of him are ye in Christ Jesus, who of God is made unto us wisdom, and righteousness, and sanctification, and redemption," 1 Cor. i. 30. And in another place, " For other foundation can no man lay than that is laid, which is Jesus Christ," 1 Cor. iii. 11.

The other proposition is written by the prophet Isaiah, and recited by our Saviour in the gospel of Mark, in these words : " Howbeit, in vain do they worship me, teaching for doctrines the commandments of men ; for, laying aside the commandment of God, ye hold the tradition of men, as the washing of pots and cups ; and many other such like things ye do. And he said unto them, full well ye reject the commandment of God, that ye may keep your own tradition," Mark vii. 7, 8, 9. Of this writes St. Paul very largely in divers places ; among others in the second chapter of Colossians, where he warneth the Colossians to take heed that no man do spoil them ; to steal them away by philosophy or vain deception, according to the constitutions of men, and ordinances of this world.

Thus I certify to all of you the opinions and conclusions which I intend, or have intended to sustain, being contained in the above two propositions. Other hold I none, but such as are mentioned in the creed ; both that which is sung at mass, and also in the other creed, that all people say every day. Finally, you require to know the names and surnames of them that were adherents to me. I say, that I know of none particularly that I remember, without I should note a great multitude, which you may know and hear of through all regions and realms of Christendom ; and though I did, I would not detect nor betray any one of them ; for I am bound to obey God rather than man. May God be with us, and grant the truth to be known ! Amen !

These answers of John Lambert to the forty-five articles, had been directed and delivered to Dr. Warham, archbishop of Canterbury, as it appeared, about A.D. 1532, when Lambert was in custody in the archbishop's house at Oxford. But so the providence of God wrought for Lambert, that within a short space after, (Aug. 1532,) the archbishop Warham died ; whereby, it seems, that Lambert for that time was delivered. In the meantime, Cranmer was sent over on an embassy with the earl of Wiltshire, Dr. Stokesley, Dr. Karne, Dr. Benett, and other learned men, to the bishop of Rome, to dispute the matter of the king's marriage openly ; first in the court of Rome, then in the court of the emperor. Where, after sundry promises and appointments made, yet when the time came, no man there appeared to dispute with them on these two propositions—first, that no man could or ought to marry his brother's wife ; secondly, that the bishop of Rome by no means ought to dispense to the contrary.

After the death of William Warham, Cranmer succeeded to that see. Lambert, in the meantime, being delivered, partly by the death of this archbishop, partly by the coming in of Queen Anne, returned to London, and there exercised himself in teaching children both in the Greek and Latin tongues.

Thus then after that John Lambert had continued in this vocation of teaching, with great commendation, it happened, (A.D. 1538) that he was present at a sermon which was preached in St. Peter's church, in London, by Dr. Tailor ; a man in those days not far from the gospel ; and afterwards, in the time of King Edward, made bishop of Lincoln, and at last in the time of Queen Mary deprived, and so ended his life among the confessors of Jesus Christ.

When the sermon was done, Lambert having gotten opportunity, went gently to the preacher to talk with him, and uttered divers arguments wherein he desired to be satisfied. All the matter or controversy was concerning the sacrament of the body and blood of Christ. Tailor excusing himself at that time for other business, desired him to write his mind ; and to come again when he had more leisure.

Lambert was contented, and so departed ; who, within a short time after, when he had written his mind, came again unto him. The sum of his arguments were ten. which he comprehended in writing ; partly by the scriptures, and partly by good reason, and by the doctors. The arguments men reported to be of great force and authority.

If, saith he, these words, " This cup is the New Testament," do not change either the cup or the wine corporally into the New Testament, it is not agreeable that the words spoken of the bread, should turn the bread corporally into the body of Christ.

Another reason was this,—that it is not agreeable to a natural body to be in two places or more at one time ; wherefore, it must follow of necessity, that either Christ had not a natural body ; or else truly, according to the common nature of a body, it cannot be present in two places at once ; and much less in many, that is to say in heaven and in earth, on the right hand of his Father, and in the sacrament.

Moreover, a natural body cannot be without its form and shape, conditions and accidents, like as the accidents and conditions also cannot be without their subject or substance. Then, forasmuch, as in the sacrament there is no quality, quantity, or condition of the body of Christ. and, finally, no appearance at all of flesh, who doth not very plainly perceive that there is no substantiated body of his in the sacrament ? And to reason by the contrary, all the proper conditions, signs, and accidents, whatever they be, pertaining to bread, we do see to be present in the sacrament, which cannot be there without the subject ; therefore, we must of necessity confess the bread to be there. He added also many other allegations out of the doctors. But to be short, this Tailor, the preacher, willing and desiring, as is supposed, to satisfy Lambert in this matter, conferred with Dr. Barnes. Barnes, although he did otherwise favour the gospel, and was an earnest preacher, notwithstanding seemed not greatly to favour this cause ; fearing it would breed some hinderance among the people to the preaching of the gospel, which was now in a good forwardness. He persuaded Tailer to put up the matter to archbishop Cranmer.

In this manner Lambert's affair first began, and was brought to this point, that it began of a private talk to be a public and common matter. For he was sent for by the archbishop, and brought into the open court, and forced to defend his cause openly ; for the archbishop had not yet favoured the doctrine of the sacrament, of which afterwards he was an earnest professor. In that disputation, it is said, that Lambert appealed from the bishops to the king ; but however the matter was, the rumour of that disputation was spread throughout the whole court.

I told you before, how king Henry, for two years past, shewing the part of an hard husband, had beheaded queen Anne, his wife (A.D. 1536) ; which not only greatly displeased the German princes, who, for that only cause had broken off the league with him, but also many good men in England.

Moreover, how that, after abbeys began to be subverted, and all their goods to be confiscated, the commons had conceived a very evil opinion of him, so that the seditious sort rebelled against him.

At that time, Stephen Gardiner, then bishop of Winchester, was in authority among the king's counsellors, who, as he was of a cruel nature, so was he no less of a subtle and crafty wit, ever gaping for some occasion how to hinder the gospel. He went to the king privately, admonishing him, and with fair flattering words giving him most pernicious counsel, declaring how great hatred and suspicion was raised upon him in all places.

First, for abolishing the bishop of Rome's authority, then for subversion of the monasteries, and also for the divorce of queen Catharine ; and now the time served, if he would take it, easily to remedy all these matters, and pacify the minds of them which were displeased and offended with him, if only in this matter of John Lambert he would manifest to the people how stoutly he would resist heretics ; and by this new rumour, he would extinguish all other former rumours, and also discharge himself of all suspicion, in that he now began to be reported to be a favourer of new sects and opinions.

The king, giving ear more willingly, than prudently or godly to this, immediately received the wicked counsel of the bishop, and sent out a general commission, commanding all the nobles and bishops of his realm, to come with all speed to London, to assist the king against heretics and heresies, upon which the king himself would sit in judgment.

These preparations being made, a day was set for Lambert to appear, and a great assembly of the nobles was gathered from all parts of the realm, not without much wonder and expectation in this so strange a case. All the seats and places were full of men round about the scaffold.

By and by the godly servant of Christ, John Lambert, was brought from the prison with a guard of armed men, even as a lamb to fight with many lions, and placed right over against where the king's royal seat was; so that now they tarried but for the king's coming.

At last the king himself did come as judge of that great controversy, with a great guard, clothed all in white, and covering by that colour all bloody judgment.

On his right hand sat the bishops, and behind them the famous lawyers, clothed all in purple, according to the manner. On the left hand sat the peers of the realm, justices, and other nobles in their order, behind whom sat the gentlemen of the king's privy chamber. And this was the manner and form of the judgment, which although it was terrible enough to abash any innocent man, yet the king's look, his cruel countenance, and his brows bent unto severity, did not a little augment this terror; plainly declaring a mind full of indignation, far unworthy such a prince; especially in such a matter, and against so humble and obedient a subject.

When the king was seated on his throne, he looked at Lambert with a stern countenance; and then turning himself to his counsellors, he called Dr. Day, bishop of Chichester, commanding him to declare unto the people the causes of this assembly and judgment.

The whole effect of his oration tended to this purpose, that the king would have all estates, degrees, bishops, and all others to be admonished of his will and pleasure; that no man should conceive such an opinion of him, as that the authority and name of the bishop of Rome being now utterly abolished, he would also extinguish all religion, or give liberty to heretics to trouble the churches of England without punishment; and, that they should not think that they were assembled to make any disputation upon the heretical doctrine; but only for this purpose, that the heresies of Lambert, and the heresies of all such, should be refuted, or openly condemned in the presence of them all.

When he had made an end of his oration, the king standing up, and leaning upon a cushion of white cloth of tissue, and turning himself towards Lambert, with his brows bent, as it were threatening some grievous thing to him, said these words; "Ho, good fellow, what is thy name?" Then the humble lamb of Christ, humbly kneeling down upon his knee, said, "My name is John Nicholson, although by many I am called Lambert." "What," said the king, "have you two names? I would not trust you, having two names, although you were my brother."

"O, most noble prince!" replied Lambert, "your bishops forced me to change my name." And after much talk in this manner, the king commanded him to go to the matter, and to declare his mind and opinion, what he thought as touching the sacrament of the altar.

Then Lambert beginning to speak for himself, gave God thanks who had so inclined the heart of the king, that he would not disdain to hear the controversies of religion, because it happened often through the cruelty of the bishops, that many good and innocent men were privily murdered and put to death, without the king's knowledge.

But now, forsomuch as that high and eternal king of kings, in whose hands are the hearts of all princes, hath inspired and stirred up the king's mind, that he himself will be present to understand the causes of his subjects, especially whom God of his divine goodness hath so abundantly endued with so great gifts of judgment and knowledge, he doth not mistrust but that God will

bring some great thing to pass through him, to the setting forth of the glory of his name.

Then the king, with an angry voice, interrupting his oration, "I came not hither," said he, "to hear mine own praises thus painted out in my presence, but briefly to go to the matter without any more circumstance." This he spake in Latin.

But Lambert being abashed at the king's angry words, contrary to all men's expectation, paused a while, considering.

But the king being hasty, with anger and vehemency said, "Why standest thou still? Answer as touching the sacrament of the altar, whether dost thou say, that it is the body of Christ, or wilt deny it?" And with that word the king lifted up his cap.

Lambert. "I answer with St. Augustine, that it is the body of Christ, after a certain manner."

The King. "Answer me neither out of St. Augustine, neither by the authority of any other, but tell me plainly, whether thou sayest it is the body of Christ or no?" These words the king spake again in Latin.

Lambert. "Then I do not deny it to be the body of Christ."

The King. "Mark well, for now thou shalt be condemned even by Christ's own words, 'This is my body.'"

Then he commanded Cranmer, archbishop of Canterbury to refute his assertion: who, first making a short preface to the hearers, began his disputation with Lambert, very modestly, saying, "Brother Lambert, let this matter be handled between us impartially, that if I shew your argument to be false by the scriptures, you will willingly refuse it; but if you shall prove it true by the manifest testimonies of the scripture, I promise that I will willingly embrace it."

The argument was taken out of the Acts of the Apostles, where Christ appeared to St. Paul: disputing that it is not disagreeable to the word of God, that the body of Christ may be in two places at once; who being in heaven was seen by St. Paul at the same time on earth; and if it may be in two places, why may it not be in places?

Lambert answered, saying, that it was not proved, that Christ's body was in two places, or more, but remained rather still in one place. For the scripture does not say, that Christ being upon the earth did speak to St. Paul: but that suddenly a light from heaven did shine round about him, and he falling to the ground, heard a voice, saying unto him, "Saul, Saul, why persecutest thou me? I am Jesus whom thou persecutest," &c. Here this place proves nothing but that Christ, sitting in heaven, might speak to St. Paul, and be heard upon earth.

The archbishop said, St. Paul himself witnesses, Acts xxvi. that Christ did appear to him in the vision.

But Lambert again said, that Christ witnessed in the same place, that he would again appear unto him, and deliver him out of the hands of the gentiles: yet we read in no place that Christ did corporally appear to him.

Thus, when they had contended about the conversion of St. Paul, and Lambert so answering for himself, that the king seemed greatly moved; and the bishop himself that disputed, seemed to be entangled, and all the audience amazed; then the bishop of Winchester alleged the twelfth chapter of the Corinthians, where St. Paul saith, Have I not seen Jesus? And again, in the fifteenth chapter: he appeared unto Cephas: and afterwards unto James, then to all the apostles, but last of all he appeared unto me as one born out of due time.

Lambert answered, he did not doubt but that Christ was seen, and did appear, but he did deny that he was in two or in divers places, according to the manner of his body.

Then Winchester again repeated the place out of 2 Cor. v. 16. "Wherefore henceforth know we no man after the flesh: yea, though we have known Christ after the flesh, yet now henceforth know we him no more."

Lambert answered, That this knowledge is not to be understood as a bodily knowledge, and that it so appeared sufficiently by St. Paul, who speaking of his own revelation, saith, "I knew a man, (whether in the body or out of the body, I cannot tell; God knoweth;) which was caught up into the third heaven; and whether in the body or out of the body, God knoweth." Whereby, a man shall easily gather, that in this revelation he was taken up in spirit into the heavens, and did see those things, rather than that Christ came down corporally from heaven, to shew them to him: especially, because it was said by the angel, That even as he ascended into heaven, so he should come again. And St. Peter saith, Whom the heavens must receive, it behoved to dwell in the heavens. And moreover appointing the measure of time, he addeth, " Until the times of the restitution of all things," &c.

After the bishop of Winchester had done, Tonstal bishop of Durham, spoke much of God's omnipotency, and saying, That if Christ could perform what he spake, touching the converting of the body into bread, without doubt he would speak nothing, but that he would perform.

Lambert answered, That there was no evident place of scripture, wherein Christ at any time says, That he would change the bread into his body: But this is a figurative speech, every where used in the scripture, when the name of the thing signified is attributed to the sign. By which figure of speech, circumcision is called the covenant, the lamb the passover, besides six hundred such other.

Now it remains to be settled, whether we shall judge all these, after the words pronounced, "to be straightway changed into another nature." Then they began to rage against Lambert; so that if he could not be overcome with arguments, he should be vanquished with rebukes and taunts.

Then again the king and the bishops raged against Lambert; so that he was not only forced to silence, but also might have been driven into a rage, if his ears had not been acquainted with such taunts before. After this the other bishops, every one in his order, as they were appointed, supplied their places of disputation.

There were appointed ten in number, for the performing of this tragedy, for his ten arguments, which were delivered to Tailor the preacher. It were too long in this place to repeat the reasons and arguments of every bishop; and no less superfluous were it to do so, especially as they were all but common reasons.

Lambert, compassed in with so many and great perplexities, vexed on one side with checks and taunts, and pressed on the other side with the authority and threats of the personages; and partly being amazed with the majesty of the place and the presence of the king, and especially being wearied with standing no less than five hours, from twelve of the clock, until five at night, chose rather to hold his peace.

Whereby it came to pass that these bishops, who last disputed with him, spoke what they chose without interruption, save only that Lambert would now and then allege somewhat out of St. Augustine for the defence of his cause; in which author he seemed to be very prompt and ready. But for the most part being overcome with weariness and other griefs, he remained silent.

At last, when the day was passed, and torches began to be lighted, the king said to Lambert, " What sayest thou now after all these great labours which thou hast taken upon thee, and all the reasons and instructions of these learned men: Art thou not yet satisfied? Wilt thou live or die? What sayest thou? Thou hast yet free choice."

Lambert answered; " I yield and submit myself wholly unto the will of your majesty." " Then," said the king, " commit thyself unto the hands of God, and not unto mine."

Lambert. " I commend my soul unto the hands of God, but my body I wholly yield and submit unto your clemency." Then said the king, " if you do commit yourself to my judgment, you must die; for I will not be a patron to heretics;" and by and by turning himself to Cromwell, he said, " Cromwell, read the sentence of condemnation against him." This Cromwell was at that time the chief friend of the gospellers. And here it is much to be marvelled at, to see how unfortunately it came to pass in this matter, that through the pestiferous and crafty counsel of this one bishop of Winchester, Satan did here perform the condemnation of this Lambert by no other ministers, than gospellers themselves, Tailor, Barnes, Cranmer, and Cromwell, who afterwards, in a manner, all suffered the same for the gospel's sake.

This undoubtedly was the malicious and crafty subtlety of the bishop of Winchester, who desired rather that the sentence might be read by Cromwell, than by any other; so that if he refused to do it, he should have incurred the like danger. But to be short, Cromwell, at the king's command, took up the schedule of condemnation, and read it.

Thus was John Lambert, in this bloody session, by the king judged and condemned to death; whose judgment now remaineth with the Lord against that day, when as before the tribunal seat of that great Judge both princes and subjects shall stand and appear, not to judge, but to be judged, according as they have done and deserved. *Ex testimonia cujusdam αυτηπτον*, A.G.

Upon the day that was appointed for this holy martyr of God to suffer, he was brought out of the prison at eight of the clock in the morning to the house of the Lord Cromwell, and so carried into his chamber; and it is reported by many, that Cromwell desired of him forgiveness, for what he had done. There Lambert, being admonished that the hour of his death was at hand, he was greatly comforted and cheered; and being brought out of the chamber into the hall, he saluted the gentlemen, and sate down to breakfast with them, shewing no manner of sadness or fear. When the breakfast was ended, he was carried straightway to the place of execution; where he should offer himself to the Lord a sacrifice of sweet savour, who is blessed in his saints, for ever and ever. Amen.

As to the terrible manner of the burning of this blessed martyr there is to be noted, that of all which have been burned and offered up at Smithfield, there was yet none so cruelly and piteously handled as he. For after his legs were consumed and burned up to the stumps, and the wretched tormentors and enemies of God had withdrawn the fire from him, so that but a small fire was left under him, then two that stood on each side of him with their halberts pitched him upon their pikes, as far as the chain would reach. Then he, lifting up such hands as he had, and his finger's ends flaming with fire, cried to the people in these words, " None but Christ, none but Christ!" and so being set down again from their halberts, fell into the fire, and there ended his life.

During the time that he was in the archbishop's ward at Lambeth, which was a little before the disputation before the king, he wrote an excellent confession or defence of his cause to king Henry.

In that treatise he confirmed his doctrine touching the sacrament by testimonies of the scriptures; by which he proves the body of Christ, whether it rises or ascends, or sits, or is conversant here, to be always in one place.

Then gathering the opinions of the ancient doctors, he proves and declares the sacrament to be a mystical matter. Yet he did not deny but that the holy sacrament was the very natural body of our Saviour, and the wine his natural blood; and that moreover his natural body and blood were in those mysteries, but after a certain manner, as all the ancient doctors interpret it. His argument is as follows:

" Christ is ascended bodily into heaven, and sits upon the right hand of the Father; that is to say, is with the Father in glory; that by the infallible promise of God, he shall not return before the general doom, which shall be at the end of the world. And as he is no more corporally in the world, so I cannot see how he can be corporally in the sacrament. And yet I acknowledge and confess, that the holy sacrament of Christ's body and blood is the very body and blood, in a certain manner, which shall be showed hereafter with your grace's favour and permission, according to the words of our Saviour, who when instituting the same holy sacrament, says,

'Take, eat; this is my body.' And again, 'This is my blood of the New Testament, which is shed for many for the remission of sins.' Matt. xxvi. 26—28.

"The scriptures for the confirmation of my opinion, are these: 'He was taken up; and a cloud received him out of their sight. And while they looked steadfastly toward heaven as he went up, behold, two men stood by them,' &c. Here it is evident that Christ departed and ascended in a visible and circumscribed body. That this departing was visible and in a visible body, these words do testify: 'Ye men of Galilee, why stand ye gazing up into heaven? This same Jesus, which is taken up from you into heaven, shall so come in like manner as ye have seen him go into heaven.' Acts i. 9—11. Here we see that Jesus is taken away into heaven. And then it must be from out of the world, according to that which we read, John xvi. 28. 'I came forth from the Father, and am come into the world: again, I leave the world, and go to the Father.'

"It is showed further, after what manner he shall come again, by these words, 'He shall so come in like manner as ye have seen him go into heaven.' Which is, as you did visibly see him ascend to heaven, a cloud embracing him and taking him from among you: even so shall you visibly see him come again in the clouds, as we read, Matt. xxvi. 64. 'Hereafter shall ye see the Son of man sitting on the right hand of power, and coming in the clouds of heaven.' And again, Matt. xxiv. 30. 'And they shall see the Son of man coming in the clouds of heaven with power and great glory.'

"My sentence is this: that Christ ascended into heaven, and so hath forsaken the world, and there shall abide, sitting on the right hand of his Father, without returning hither again, until the general doom; at which time he shall come from thence, to judge the dead and the living. All this I do believe is done in the natural body, which he took of the blessed Virgin Mary his mother, in which he also suffered passion for our safety and redemption upon a cross; which died for us, and was buried: in which he also did rise again to life immortal. That Christ is thus ascended in his manhood and natural body, and so taken up into heaven, we may soon prove; forsomuch as the godhead of him is never out of heaven, but ever replenishing both heaven and earth; and besides that, is infinite and interminable or uncircumscriptible, so that it neither can properly either ascend or descend, being without all alteration, and immutable, or immovable.

"So that now his natural body being taken up from among us, and departed out of the world, the same can no more return from thence to the end of the world. For as Peter witnesseth, Acts iii. 21. 'Whom the heaven must receive until the times of restitution of all things, which God hath spoken by the mouth of all his holy prophets since the world began.' And the same doth the article of our creed teach us, which is, from thence (i. e. from heaven) shall he come, to judge the quick and the dead. Which time St. Paul calls the appearing of our Lord Jesus Christ, (1 Tim. vi.)

"Seeing then that this natural body of our Saviour, which was born of his mother the Virgin Mary, is wholly taken up into heaven, and departed out of this world; and so saith St. Peter, he must remain in heaven until the end of the world, which he calleth the time when all things must be restored; this I say, seen and believed according to our creed and the scriptures, I cannot perceive how his natural body can be in this world, and in the sacrament. And yet notwithstanding is this true, that the holy sacrament is Christ's body, and blood, as after shall be declared."

The Death of Robert Packington.

Among other matters done this present year, (A.D. 1538,) was the lamentable death of Robert Packington, mercer of London, caused by the enemies of God's word. The story is this: Robert Packington, being a man of substance, and dwelling in Cheapside, used every day at five o'clock, winter and summer, to go to pray at a church then called St. Thomas of Acres, but now named Mercers' Chapel. When, one very misty morning, such as has seldom been seen, as he was crossing the street from his house to the church, he was suddenly shot with a gun, but the murderer was a great while unknown. Although many in the mean time were suspected, yet none could be found faulty therein; till at length by the confession of Doctor Incent, dean of St. Paul's, on his death-bed, it was made known, and by him confessed, that he himself was the author, by hiring an Italian, for forty crowns, to do the deed.

The cause why he was so little favoured with the clergy, was, that he was known to be a man of great courage, and one that could both speak, and also would be heard: for at the time he was one of the burgesses of the parliament for the city of London, and had talked somewhat against the covetousness and cruelty of the clergy, wherefore he was had in contempt with them; and it was thought that he also had had some talk with the king, for which he was the more had in disdain with them; and murdered by Doctor Incent, as has been declared.

And thus much of Robert Packington, who was the brother of Augustine Packington, who deceived Bishop Tonstal, in buying the new translated Testament of Tindal. This piteous murder, although it was privy and sudden, yet has it pleased the Lord not to keep it in darkness, but to bring it at length to light.

The burning of one Collins at London.

Neither is there here to be omitted the burning of one Collins, sometime a lawyer and a gentleman, who also suffered this year in Smithfield, (A.D. 1538.) Whom although I do not here recite as in the number of God's professed martyrs, yet neither do I think him to be clean sequestered from the company of the Lord's saved flock and family, notwithstanding that the church of Rome did condemn and burn him for an heretic: but rather do recount him as one belonging to the holy company of saints. At least this case of him and of his end, may well reprove and condemn their cruelty and madness, in burning without all discretion this man, being mad and deprived of his perfect wits, as the following will shew.

This gentleman had a wife of exceeding beauty and comeliness, but notwithstanding of so light behaviour and unchaste conduct (nothing corresponding to the grace of her beauty) that she forsook her husband; who loved her entirely, and betook herself to another. Which, when he understood, he took it very grievously and heavily to heart; and at last being overcome with exceeding grief and heaviness, he became mad, being at that time a student of the law in London. When he was thus deprived of his wits, by chance he came into a church, where the priest was saying mass; and when he came to the place where they use to hold up and show the sacrament, Collins seeing the priest holding up the host over his head, and showing it to the people; he, in like manner counterfeiting the priest, took up a little dog by the legs and held him over his head, showing him to the people. And for this he was by and by brought to examination, and condemned to the fire, and was burned, and the dog with him, in the same year in which John Lambert was burned.

The burning of Cowbridge at Oxford, A.D. 1538.

With this Collins may also be associated the burning of Cowbridge, who likewise being mad and beside his right senses, was either in the same or the next year following condemned by Longland bishop of Lincoln, and committed to the fire at Oxford. What the opinions and articles were wherewith he was charged, it is not necessary here to rehearse. For as he was then a man mad, and destitute of sense and reason, so his words and sayings could not be sound. Yea rather, what wise man would ever collect articles against him, who said he could not tell what. And if his articles were so horrible and mad as Cope in his dialogues declares them to have been, then was he in my judgment a man more fit to be sent to Bedlam than to have been sent to the fire in Smithfield to be burned. For what reason is it to require reason of a creature mad or unreasonable, or to make heresy of the words of a senseless man, not knowing what he affirmed?

William Leiton and Puttedew, Martyrs.

About the same time, one Puttedew also was condemned to the fire, for having gone into a church; and there merrily telling the priest, that after he had drunk up all the wine, he blessed the hungry people with the empty chalice. He was immediately apprehended and burned.

William Leiton, was a monk of Eye, in Suffolk, and was burned at Norwich, for speaking against a certain idol which was accustomed to be carried about in processions at Eye; and also for holding that the sacramental supper ought to be administered in both kinds.

In the burning of another man, named Peke, at Ipswich, I find it recorded, that when he was bound to a stake, and the furze set on fire about him: that one Doctor Reading who was standing there, with Doctor Heyre and Doctor Springwell, and having a long white wand in his hand, knocked him upon the shoulder, and said, "Peke, recant, and believe that the sacrament of the altar is the very body of Christ, flesh, blood, and bone, after the priest hath spoken the words of consecration over it, and here have I authority in my hand to absolve thee of thy unbelief;" and holding up a scroll of paper in his hand. When he had spoken these words, Peke answered, and said, "I reject it, and thee also;" and he spit blood, for his veins brake in his body for extreme anguish. And when Peke had so spoken, then Doctor Reading said, "To as many as shall cast a stick to the burning of this heretic, is granted forty days of pardon by my lord bishop of Norwich."

Then Baron Curson, Sir John Audley, knight, with many others there present, rose from their seats, and with their swords cut down boughs, and threw them into the fire, and so did all the multitude of the people.

In the year before this, which was 1537, it was stated how Pope Paul III. called a general council, to be held at Mantua. The king of England, among other princes, refused either to go or to send at the pope's call; and for defence of himself put out a public protestation, rendering just and sufficient reasons, why he would not, nor was bound to obey the pope's command. Which protestation is before to be read. This council, appointed to begin the 23d of May, was stopped by the duke of Mantua, pretending that he would suffer no council there, unless the pope would protect the city with a sufficient army, &c. For which cause the pope prorogued the council to the month of November following, appointing at the first no certain place. At length he named and determined the city of Trivirence, in the Venetian territory; to which, when the king was requested by the emperor and other states, to resort thither, either by himself, or to send; he again refused (as he had done before), and sent his protestation to the emperor and other christian princes.

"Henry VIII., by the Grace of God, King of England and France, &c. saluteth the Emperor, Christian Princes, and all true Christian men, desiring Peace and Concord amongst them.

"Whereas, not long since, a book came forth in our and all our council's names, which contained many causes why he refused the council, then, by the bishop of Rome's usurped power, first indicted at Mantua, to be kept the three-and-twentieth day of May, after prorogued to November, no place appointed where it should be kept: and, whereas, the same book doth sufficiently prove, that our cause could take no hurt; neither with any thing done or decreed in such a company of men addicted to one sect, nor in any other council called by his usurped power; we think it unnecessary, so oft to make new protestations, as the bishop of Rome and his courts, by subtlety and craft, do invent ways to mock the world by new pretended general councils. Yet, notwithstanding, because that some things now occurred, either upon occasion given us by change of the place, or

else through other considerations, which now being known to the world, may do much good, we thought we should do but even as that love enforceth us, which we owe unto Christ's faith and religion, to add this epistle. And yet we protest that we neither put forth that book, neither yet we would this epistle to be set before it, that thereby we should seem less to desire a general council than any other prince or potentate; but rather to be more desirous of it, so it were free for all parts, and universal. And further, we desire all good princes, potentates, and people, to esteem and think, that no prince would more willingly be present at such a council than we; such a one we mean, as we spoke of in our protestation made concerning the council of Mantua.

"Truly as our forefathers invented nothing more holy than general councils, used as they ought to be, so there is almost nothing that may do more hurt to the Christian commonwealth, to the faith, to our religion, than general councils, if they be abused to lucre, to gain, to the establishment of errors. They are called general, and even by their name admonish us, that all Christian men, who dissent in any opinion, may in them openly, frankly, and without fear of punishment or displeasure say their mind. For seeing such things as are decreed in general councils, touch equally all men that give assent to them, it is meet that every man may boldly say there what he thinks. And verily we suppose, that it ought not to be called a general council, where only those men are heard who are determined for ever, in all points, to defend the popish part, and to arm themselves to fight in the quarrel of the bishop of Rome, though it were against God and his scripture. It is no general council, neither ought it to be called general, where the same men are both advocates and adversaries, accusers and judges; no, it is against the law of nature, either that we should condescend to so unreasonable a law against ourselves, or that we should suffer ourselves to be left without all defence, and being oppressed with greatest injuries, to have no refuge to succour ourselves at. The bishop of Rome and his are our great enemies, as we and all the world may well perceive by his doings.

"He desireth nothing more than our hurt, and the destruction of our realm; do not we then violate the judgment of nature, if we give him power and authority to be our judge? His pretended honour, first gotten by superstition, after increased by violence, and other ways as evil as that; his power set up by pretence of religion, indeed both against religion, and also contrary to the word of God; his primacy, born by the ignorance of the world, nourished by the ambition of the bishops of Rome, defended by places of scripture falsely understood; these three things, we say, which are fallen with us, and are like to fall in other realms shortly, shall they not be established again, if he may decide our cause as it pleases him? If he may at his pleasure oppress a cause most righteous? Certainly he is very blind that sees not what end we may look for of our controversies, if such our enemy may give the sentence.

"We desire, if it were in any wise possible, a council, where there would be some hope that those things shall be restored, which now, being depraved, are likely (if not amended) to be the utter ruin of the Christian religion. And as we do desire such a council, and think it meet that all men in all their prayers should desire and crave it of God, even so we think it appertains to our office, to provide that these popish subtleties hurt none of our subjects, and also to admonish other christian princes, that the bishop of Rome may not by their consent abuse the authority of kings, either by the extinguishing of the true preaching of scripture, (that now beginneth to spring, to grow, and spread abroad) or to the troubling of princes' liberties, to the diminishing of kings' authorities, and to the great blemish of their princely majesty. We doubt not but an impartial reader will soon approve such things as we here write, not so much for our excuse, as that the world may perceive both the sundry deceits, crafts, and subtleties of the papists, and also how much we desire that controversies in matters of religion may once be taken away.

"What other princes will do we cannot tell; but we

will never leave our realm at this time; nor will we trust any proctor with our cause, wherein the whole stay and wealth of our realm stands, but rather we will be at the handling thereof ourself. For except another judge be agreed upon for those matters, and a more commodious place be provided for the debating of our causes; although all other things were as we would have them, yet we may lawfully refuse to come or send any to this pretended council. We will in no case make him our arbitrer, who, not many years past, (our cause not heard,) gave sentence against us. We require that such doctrine, as we, following the scripture, profess, be rightly examined, discussed, and brought to the scripture, as to the only touchstone of true learning.

"We will not suffer them to be abolished before they are discussed, or oppressed before they are known; much less will we suffer them to be trodden down, being so clearly true. No, as there is no jot in Scripture but we will defend, though it were with jeopardy of our life, and peril of this our realm; so there is nothing that oppresses this doctrine, or obscures it, but we will be at continual war with it. As we have abrogated all old popish traditions in this our realm, which either helped his tyranny, or increased his pride; so if the grace of God forsake us not, we will foresee that no new naughty traditions be made with our consent, to bind us or our health.

"If men will not be willingly blind, they shall easily see even by a due and evident proof in reason, though grace doth not yet by the word of Christ enter into them, how small the authority of the bishop of Rome is, by the lawful denial of the duke of Mantua for the place. For if the bishop of Rome did earnestly intend to keep a council at Mantua, and hath power of the law by God to call princes to what place he liketh: why hath he not also authority to choose what place he listeth? The bishop chose Mantua: the duke kept him out of it. If Paul the bishop of Rome's authority be so great as he pretendeth, why could he not compel Frederick the duke of Mantua, that the council might be kept there? The duke would not suffer it. No, he forbade him his town.

"How chanceth it, that here excommunications flee not abroad? Why doth he not punish this duke? Why is his power that was wont to be more than full, here empty? Wont to be more than all, here nothing? Doth he not call men in vain to a council, if they that come at his calling be excluded the place to the which he calleth them? May not kings justly refuse to come at his call, when the duke of Mantua may deny him the place that he chooseth? If other princes order him as the duke of Mantua had done, what place shall be left him, where he may keep his general council?

"Again, if princes have given him this authority to call a council, is it not necessary that they give him also all those things, without the which he cannot exercise that his power? Shall he call men, and will ye hinder him to find a place to call them unto? Truly he is not wont to appoint one of his own cities, a place to keep the council in. No, the good man is so faithful and friendly towards others, that seldom he desires princes to be his guests."

The protestation then concludes as follows:—

"Whether these our writings please all men or no, we think we ought not to pass much. No, if that which indifferently is written of us may please indifferent readers, our desire is accomplished. The false censure and mistaking of things by partial men shall not move us, or else very little. If we have said aught against the deceits of the bishop of Rome, that may seem spoken too sharply, we pray you impute it to the hatred we bear unto his vices, and not to any evil will that we bear him. No, that he and all his may perceive that we are rather at strife with his vices than with him and his; our prayer is, that it may please God at the last to open their eyes, to make soft their hard hearts, and that they once may with us (their own glory set apart) study to set forth the everlasting glory of the ever-living God.

"Thus, mighty emperor, fare you most heartily well, and you christian princes, the pillars and state of Chris-

tendom, fare you heartily well. Also all you, what people soever you are, who desire that the gospel and glory of Christ may flourish, fare you heartily well."

As the Lord of his goodness had raised up Thomas Cromwell to be a friend and patron to the gospel; so, on the contrary side, Satan had his organ also, which was Stephen Gardiner, by all wiles and subtle means to put back the same. Who, after he had brought his purpose to pass in burning good John Lambert, proceeding still in his crafts and wiles, and thinking under the name of heresies, sects, anabaptists, and sacramentaries, to exterminate all good books, and faithful professors of God's word out of England, so wrought upon the king, that the next year, which was A.D. 1539, he gave out these injunctions.

Certain other Injunctions set forth by the Authority of the King, against English Books, Sects, and Sacramentaries also, with putting down the Day of Thomas à Becket.

"First, that none, without special licence of the king, transport or bring from outward parts into England any manner of English books; neither yet sell, give, utter, or publish any such, upon pain to forfeit all their goods and chattels, and their bodies to be imprisoned, so long as it shall please the king's majesty.

"Also, that none shall print, or bring over any English books with annotations or prologues, unless such books be before examined by the king's privy-council, or others appointed by his highness: and yet not without these words be put thereto, *Cum Privilegio Regali*, and also, *Ad imprimendum solum*. Neither yet to imprint it, without the king's privilege be printed therewith in the English tongue, that all men may read it. Neither shall they print any translated book, without the plain name of the translator be to it, unless the printer is to be made the translator, and to suffer the fine and punishment thereof at the king's pleasure.

"Also, that none of the occupation of printing shall within the realm print, utter, sell, or cause to be published any English book of scripture, unless the same be first viewed, examined, and admitted by the king's highness, or one of his privy-council, or one bishop within the realm, whose name shall therein be expressed; upon pain of the king's most high displeasure, the loss of their goods and chattels, and imprisonment so long as it shall please the king.

"Also, those who are in any error, as sacramentaries, anabaptists, or others, shall not sell any books having such opinions in them; otherwise on being once known, both the books and such persons shall be detected and disclosed immediately unto the king's majesty, or one of his privy council; to the intent to have them punished without favour, even with the extremity of the law.

"Also, that none of the king's subjects shall reason, dispute, or argue upon the sacrament of the altar; upon pain of losing their lives, goods, and chattels, without any favour: only those excepted that be learned in divinity, and they to have such liberty only in their schools and other places appointed for such matters.

"Also, that the holy bread and holy water, procession, kneeling and creeping on Good Friday to the cross, and Easter-day, setting up of lights before the Corpus Christi, bearing of candles on Candlemas-day, purification of women delivered of child, offering of chrysomes, keeping of the four offering-days, paying their tithes, and such-like ceremonies, must be observed and kept till it shall please the king to change or abrogate any of them. (This article was made because many of the people were not satisfied or contented with the ceremonies then used.)

"Finally, that all those priests that are married, and such of them as are openly known to have wives, or that hereafter do intend to marry, shall be deprived of all spiritual promotion, and from doing any of the duties of a priest, and shall have no manner of office, dignity, cure, privilege, profit, or commodity, in anything appertaining to the clergy; but from thenceforth shall be taken, had, and reputed to be lay-persons, to all purposes and intents; and those that shall after this proclamation marry, shall expose themselves to his grace's indignation, and suffer punishment and imprisonment at his grace's will and pleasure.

"Also, he chargeth all archbishops, bishops, archdeacons, deacons, provosts, parsons, vicars, curates, and other ministers, and every of them in their own persons, within their cures diligently to preach, teach, open, and set forth to the people, the glory of God, and the truth of his word; and also considering the abuses and superstitions that have crept into the hearts and minds of many, by reason of their fond ceremonies, he chargeth them upon pain of imprisonment, at his grace's pleasure, not only to preach and teach the word of God accordingly; but also sincerely and purely declaring the difference between things commanded by God, and the rites and ceremonies in their church then used, lest the people thereby might grow into further suspicion.

"Also, forasmuch as it appears now clearly, that Thomas à Becket, formerly archbishop of Canterbury, stubbornly withstanding the wholesome laws established against the enormities of the clergy, by the king's noble progenitor King Henry II., for the well-being, rest, and tranquillity of this realm, did, of his froward mind, flee into France, and thence to the bishop of Rome, who was a maintainer of those enormities, to procure the abrogation of the said laws, whereby arose much trouble in this said realm. His death they untruly call a martyrdom; but that happened upon a rescue having been attempted, and on which occasion (as it is written) he gave opprobrious words to the gentlemen, who then counselled him to give up his stubbornness and to avoid the commotion of the people, who had risen up to attempt a rescue; and he not only called one of them by a bad name, but also took Tracey by the bosom, and violently shook him, and plucked him in such a manner, that he had almost thrown him down on the pavement of the church; so that in this affray, one of their company perceiving the same, struck him, and so in the throng Becket was slain: and further, that this canonization was made only by the bishop of Rome; because Becket had been a champion to maintain his usurped authority, and an encourager of the iniquity of the clergy.

"For these, and for other great and urgent causes, which it would be too tedious to recite, the king's majesty, by the advice of his council, had thought it expedient to declare to his loving subjects, that notwithstanding the said canonization, there appeareth nothing in his life and exterior conversation, whereby he should be called a saint, but rather esteemed to have been a rebel and traitor to his prince.

"Therefore his grace straightly chargeth and commandeth, that from henceforth the said Thomas à Becket shall not be esteemed, named, reputed, and called a saint, but Bishop Becket; and that his images and pictures through the whole realm shall be pulled down and thrown out of all churches, chapels, and other places; and that from henceforth the days which were used to be a festival in his name, shall not be observed; neither shall the service, office, antiphons, collects, and prayers, be read in his name, but razed and put out of all their books; and that all the festival days, already abrogated, shall be in nowise solemnized, but his grace's ordinances and injunctions thereupon observed; to the intent his grace's loving subjects shall be no longer blindly led and abused to commit idolatry, as they have done in times past; upon pain of his majesty's indignation, and imprisonment at his grace's pleasure.

Finally, his grace straightly charges and commands that his subjects keep and observe all and singular these injunctions made by his majesty, upon the pain therein contained."

Here followeth how Religion began to go backward.

To many who are yet alive, and who can testify to these things, it is not unknown, how variable the state of religion stood in these days; how hardly and with what difficulty it came forth, what chances and changes it suffered. Even as the king was ruled and gave ear sometime to one, sometime to another; so one while it went

forward, at another time as much backward again, and sometimes altered and changed for a season, according as those could prevail who were about the king. So long as Queen Anne lived, the gospel had success.

After, by sinister instigation of some about the king, she was made away with, the course of the gospel began again to decline; but the Lord then stirred up the lord Cromwell to help it, who no doubt would have done much for the increase of God's true religion, and had brought much more to perfection, if the pestilent adversaries had not craftily undermined him and supplanted his virtuous proceedings. By means of which adversaries it came to pass that lord Cromwell was accused of high treason by the duke of Norfolk, in the king's name, and arrested and sent to the Tower. He was hated by the popish party, for it was through him that many of the most important reforms were made. A bill of attainder was passed against him in June, and he was beheaded on Tower-hill, 28th July, 1540.

Among these adversaries, the chief was Stephen Gardiner, bishop of Winchester, who, with his confederates and adherents, dissatisfied with the state of the lord Cromwell, and at the late marriage of the lady Anne of Cleves, (who, in the beginning of the year 1540, was married to the king), as also grieved at the dissolution of the monasteries, and fearing the growing of the gospel, sought all occasions to interrupt these happy beginnings, and to train the king to their own purpose.

It happened that the lord Cromwell, for the better establishing of sincere religion, had devised a marriage for the king, to be concluded between him and the lady Anne of Cleves, whose other sister was already married to the duke of Saxony. By this marriage it was supposed that a perpetual league, amity, and alliance would be nourished between this realm and the princes of Germany; and so godly religion might be made more strong on both parts against the bishop of Rome, and his tyrannical religion. But the devil, ever envying the prosperity of the gospel, laid a stumbling-block in the way for the king to stumble upon. For when the parents of the noble lady were conferred with for the furtherance of the marriage, the duke of Saxony, her brother-in-law, disliked the marriage. The crafty bishop of Winchester, taking advantage of this, so alienated the king's mind from the duke, that he brought the king at length out of credit with that religion and doctrine which the duke had maintained for many years before.

This wily Winchester, with his crafty assistants, and also by other pestilent persuasions, ceased not to seek all means to overthrow religion. First, bringing the king, in hatred with the German princes, then putting him in fear of the emperor, of the French king, of the pope, of the king of Scotland, and other foreign powers; but especially of civil tumults and commotions within his own kingdom; which above all things he most dreaded, by reason of these innovations of religion, and the dissolving of abbeys, and the abolishing of rites, and other customs of the church, which had so fast a hold on the minds of the people, that it was to be feared that their hearts were or would be shortly stirred up against him, unless some speedy remedy were provided. The bishop exhorted the king for his own safeguard, and tranquillity of his realm, to see how and by what policy so manifold mischiefs might be prevented. He suggested that no other way or shift could be better devised, than to shew himself sharp and severe against the new sectaries, the anabaptists, and sacramentarians (as they called them); and that he should also set forth such articles, confirming the ancient catholic faith, as might recover his credit with christian princes, and that all the world might see and judge him to be a right and perfect catholic. By these and such suggestions the king was too much led away; and he then began to withdraw his defence from the reformation of true religion, supposing to procure to himself more safety in his own realm, and also to avoid such dangers as might happen by other princes. And therefore, although he had rejected the pope out of this realm, yet because he would declare himself nevertheless to be a good catholic son of the mother church, and a withstander of new innovations and heresies (as the blind opinion of the world then did esteem them) he stretched out his hand to the condemning and burning of Lambert; then he gave out those injunctions above prefixed, and now to increase this opinion with all men, in the year following, which was 1540, he summoned a parliament at Westminster, on the twenty-eighth day of April, of all the states and burgesses of the realm; also a synod or convocation of all the archbishops, bishops, and other learned of the clergy of this realm, to be in like manner assembled.

The Act of the Six Articles.

In this parliament, synod, or convocation, certain articles, matters, and questions, touching religion, were decreed by certain prelates, to the number of six, commonly called The Six Articles, to be received among the king's subjects for the purpose of unity. But what unity followed, the groaning hearts of a great number, and also the cruel death of many, both in the days of King Henry, and of Queen Mary, can so well declare, that as I pray God the like may never be felt hereafter.

The doctor of these wicked articles is worthy of no memory among christian men, but rather deserves to be buried in perpetual oblivion, yet the office of history compels us, for the light of posterity, faithfully and truly to comprise things done in the church, as well at one time as at another, this we shall do briefly, and recapitulate the sum of the six articles as they were given out

The First Article.

The first article agreed upon in this present parliament was this, that in the most blessed sacrament of the altar by the strength and efficacy of Christ's mighty word (it being spoken by the priest) is present really, under the form of bread and wine, the natural body and blood of our Saviour Jesus Christ, as conceived of the Virgin Mary, and after the consecration there remains no substance of bread or wine, or any other substance, but the substance of Christ, God and man.

The Second Article

Secondly, that the communion in both kinds is not necessary for salvation to all persons by the law of God, and that it is to be believed, and not doubted of, but that in the flesh, under form of bread, is the very blood, and with the blood, under form of wine, is the very flesh as well separate as they were both together.

The Third Article.

Thirdly, that priests, after the order of priesthood, may not marry by the law of God.

The Fourth Article.

Fourthly, that the vows of chastity or widowhood, by man or woman made to God advisedly, ought to be observed by the law of God; and that it exempteth them from other liberties of christian people, which otherwise they might enjoy.

The Fifth Article.

Fifthly, that it is meet and necessary that private masses be continued and admitted in this English church and congregation, and in them good christian people, ordering themselves accordingly, do receive both godly and goodly consolations and benefits, and it is agreeable also to God's law.

The Sixth Article

Sixthly, that auricular confession was expedient and necessary, and ought to be retained and continued in the church of God.

After these articles were concluded, the prelates perceiving that such a foul and violent act could not prevail, unless straight and bloody penalties were set upon them, caused to be ordained and enacted by the king and the lords spiritual and temporal, and the commons in the said parliament

"That if any person or persons within this realm of England, or any other the king's dominions, after the twelfth day of July next coming, by word, writing, im-

printing, cyphering, or any otherwise, should publish, preach, teach, say, affirm, declare, dispute, argue or hold any opinion, that in the blessed sacrament of the altar, under form of bread and wine (after the consecration thereof), there is not present really the natural body and blood of our Saviour Jesus Christ, as conceived of the Virgin Mary, or that after the said consecration there remaineth any substance of the bread or wine, or any other substance of Christ, God and man; or after the time abovesa d, publish, preach, teach, say, affirm, declare, dispute, argue, or hold opinion, That in the flesh, under the form of bread is not the very blood of Christ, or that with the blood of Christ, under the form of wine, is not the very flesh of Christ, as well apart, as though they were both together; or by any of the means abovesaid, or otherwise, preach, teach, declare, or affirm the said sacrament to be any other substance than is abovesaid, or by any means contemn, deprave, or despise the said blessed sacrament, that then every such person so offending, their aiders, comforters, counsellors, consenters, and abettors therein (being thereof convicted in form underwritten, by the authority abovesaid) should be deemed and adjudged heretics, and every such offence should be adjudged as manifest heresy, and that every such offender and offenders should therefore have and suffer judgment, execution, pain and pains of death by way of burning, without any abjuration, benefit of the clergy, or sanctuary, to be therefore permitted, had, allowed, or suffered; and also should forfeit and lose to the king's highness, his heirs and successors, all his or their honours, manors, castles, lands, tenements, rents, reversions, services, possessions, and all other his or their hereditaments, goods and chattels, farms and freeholds, whatever they were, through any such offence or offences committed or done, or at any time after, as in any case of high treason."

And as to the other five articles, the penalty devised for them was this· "That every such person or persons that preach, teach, obstinately affirm, uphold, maintain, or defend, after the twelfth of July of the said year, any thing contrary to the same; or if any being in-orders, or after a vow advisedly made, did marry, or make marriage, or contract matrimony, in so doing they should be adjudged as felons, and lose both life, and forfeit goods, as in the case of felony, without any benefit of the clergy, or privilege of the church or of the sanctuary," &c.

Also, "That every such person or persons, who after the day aforesaid, by word, writing, printing, cyphering, or otherwise, do publish, declare or hold opinion contrary to the five articles above expressed, being for any such offence duly convicted or attainted, for the first time, besides the forfeit of all his goods, and chattels, and possessions whatsoever, should suffer imprisonment of his body at the king's pleasure; and for the second time, being accused, presented, and thereof convicted, should suffer as in the case aforesaid of felony."

Also, "If any within the order of priesthood, before the time of the said parliament, had married or contracted matrimony, or vowed widowhood, the said matrimony should stand utterly void and be dissolved."

Also, "That the same danger that belonged to priests marrying wives, should also redound to women who are married to the priests"

Furthermore, for the more effectual execution of the premises, it was enacted by the said parliament, "That full authority of inquisition of all such heresies, felonies, and contempts, should be committed and directed down into every shire, to certain persons specially appointed; that such persons, three at the least (provided always the archbishop, or bishop, or his chancellor, or his commissary be one) should sit four times at least in the year, having full power to take information and accusation, by the depositions of any two lawful persons at the least, as well as by the oaths of twelve men, to examine and inquire of all and singular the heresies, felonies, and contempts above remembered; having also as ample power to make process against every person or persons indicted, presented, or accused before them; also to hear and determine the aforesaid heresies, felonies, contempts, and other offences, as well as if the matter had been presented before the justices of peace in their sessions. And also that the said justices in their sessions, and every steward or under-steward, or his deputy, in their law-days, should have power by the oaths of twelve lawful men to inquire likewise of all and singular the heresies, felonies, contempts, and other offences, and to hear and determine the same, to all effects of this present act," &c.

"Provided that no person or persons thereupon accused, indited or presented, should be admitted to challenge any that should be empanelled for the trial of any matter or cause, other than for malice or envy; which challenge should forthwith be tried in like manner, as in cases of felony, &c.

"Provided moreover, that every person that should be named commissioner in this inquisition, should first take oath, the tenor of which oath here ensueth.

The Oath of the Commissioners.

"You shall swear, that you to your cunning, wit and power, shall truly and indifferently execute the authority to you given by the king's commission, made for correction of heretics and other offenders mentioned in the same commission, without any favour, affection, corruption, dread, or malice, to be borne to any person or persons, as God you help and all saints."

And thus much is briefly collected out of the act and originals, which are to be seen in the *Stat. Anno* 31. *Reg. Hen.* 8. concerning the six articles, which otherwise for the bloody cruelty thereof, are called "The Whip with six strings," set forth after the death of queen Anne, and of good John Lambert, devised by the cruelty of the bishops, but especially of the bishop of Winchester, and at length also subscribed by king Henry.

These six articles above specified, although they contained manifest errors, heresies, and absurdities against all scripture and learning; yet such was the miserable and unhappy state of that time, and the power of darkness, that the simple cause of truth and of religion was utterly left desolate, and forsaken of all friends. For every man seeing that the king wished to have these articles passed, few in all that parliament would either appear to perceive what was to be defended, or durst defend what they understood to be true; save only Cranmer, archbishop of Canterbury, who then being married (as is supposed), like a constant patron of God's cause, took upon him the defence of that truth, which was so oppressed in the parliament, and for three days together continued disputing against these six wicked articles.

Cranmer behaved himself with such humble modesty, and with such obedience, towards his prince, and protesting that the cause was not his, but the cause of Almighty God, that his courage was not disliked of the king, and his reasons and allegations were so strong, that they could not well be refuted. The king, (who ever bare special favour to him) admired his zealous defence, and only desired him to depart out of the parliament house into the council chamber, for a time, (for safety of his conscience) till the act should pass; which Cranmer, notwithstanding, with humble protestation refused to do.

After the parliament was finished, and that matter concluded, the king considering the constant zeal of the archbishop, in defence of his cause, and partly also weighing the many authorities and reasons by which he had confirmed the same; sent the lord Cromwell, the dukes of Norfolk and Suffolk, and all the lords of the parliament, to dine with him at Lambeth: where they signified to him, that it was the king's pleasure, that they all should, in his highness' behalf, cherish, comfort, and animate him, as one that in that parliament had declared himself, both greatly learned, and also a man discreetly wise; and therefore they willed him not to be discouraged in any thing that was passed in that parliament contrary to his allegations.

Cranmer most humbly thanked, first the king's highness for his singular good affection towards him, and then all of them for their pains; adding, moreover, that

he hoped in God, that hereafter his allegations and authorities would be employed for the glory of God, and the advantage of the kingdom. Which allegations and authorities of his, I wish were extant to be seen and read. No doubt but they would stand, in time to come, in great good stead for the overthrow of the wicked and pernicious articles aforesaid.

Allegations against the six Articles.

In the meantime, forasmuch as these heretical articles are not so lightly to be passed over, whereby the rude and ignorant multitude hereafter may be deceived in the false and erroneous doctrine of them any more, as they have been in times past, for lack of right instruction, and experience of the ancient state and course of times in our forefathers' days; I thought, therefore, (the Lord thereunto assisting) so much as antiquity of histories may help to the restoring again of the truth and doctrine which is now decayed, to annex some allegations out of ancient records, which may throw some light for understanding of these new-fangled articles and heresies.

And first, as to the article of transubstantiation, wherein this parliament enacts, that the sacrament of the altar is the very natural body of Christ, the self same which was born of the Virgin Mary; and that there remains no substance of bread and wine, after the priest's consecration, but only the body and blood of Christ, under the outward forms of bread and wine: here it is to be noted, that this monstrous article of theirs was never obtruded, received, or held, either in the Greek church, or in the Latin church, for a catholic article of doctrine, until the time of the Lateran council at Rome, under Pope Innocent III., (A. D. 1215.)

And as it has been commonly understood by most people, that this article has ever been, since the time of Christ, a true catholic and general doctrine, commonly received and taught in the church, being approved by the scriptures and doctors, with the consent of all ages to this present time; therefore, that the contrary may appear, and that the people may see how far they have been beguiled, we will here make a little pause in our history, and examine this article.

This monstrous paradox of transubstantiation was never received publicly in the church before the time of the Lateran council, under Pope Innocent III., A. D. 1215, or at most before the time of Lanfranc, archbishop of Canterbury, 1070.

In the time of this Lanfranc, I deny not but that this question of transubstantiation began to come into controversy, and was reasoned upon, among certain learned of the clergy. But that this article of transubstantiation was publicly determined or authorized in the church for a general law or catholic doctrine of all men, necessarily to be believed, before the time of Innocent III., may be proved to be false.

And though our adversaries allege out of the old doctors certain speeches and phrases, which they wrest and wring to their purposes, as if this doctrine of transubstantiation stood upon the consent of the whole universal church, of all ages and times, of nations and people, and that the judgment of the church was never other than this: yet if the old doctors' sayings be well weighed and examined, it will be found that this prodigious opinion of transubstantiation had no such ground of consent and antiquity as they imagine; nor yet that any heresy or treason was made of denying of transubstantiation before the time of Innocent III., or at the farthest of Lanfranc.

But in our church of England it is most certain, that transubstantiation was unknown till a very late period, as is most evident from the epistles and homilies of Elfric. This Elfric was made archbishop of Canterbury about the year of our Lord 996, in the time of king Ethelred II., and of Wulfsine, bishop of Sherborne.

Elfric was of such estimation in those days amongst the most learned, for his learning, authority, and eloquence, that his writings were accepted and authorized amongst the canons and constitutions of the church in that time, as hereby may appear; for where the bishops and priests before the coming of William the Conqueror had collected a certain book of canons and ordinances to govern the clergy, gathered out of general and particular councils, out of the book of Gildas, out of the penitential books of Theodore, archbishop of Canterbury, out of the writings of Egbert, archbishop of York, out of the epistles of Alcuin, as also out of the writings of the old fathers of the primitive church, &c.—among the canons and constitutions are placed two epistles of Elfric.

Besides this he translated two books containing eighty sermons out of the Latin into the Saxon language, which used then generally to be read in churches on Sundays and other festival days of the year.

An Epistle of Elfric to Wulfstane, touching the Sacrament of the Lord's Supper.

"Christ himself blessed the eucharist before his suffering; he blessed the bread and brake it, thus speaking to his apostles, 'Take eat; this is my body.' And again, he blessed one chalice with wine, and also said unto them, 'Drink ye all of it, for this is my blood of the New Testament, which is shed for many for the remission of sins.' The Lord who hallowed the eucharist before his suffering, and said, that the bread was his own body, and that the wine was truly his blood, hallows daily by the hands of the priests, bread to be his body, and wine to be his blood, in spiritual mystery, as we read in books. Yet notwithstanding that lively bread is not bodily so, nor the self-same body that Christ suffered in; nor so that holy wine the Saviour's blood which was shed for us in bodily things; but in spiritual understanding. Both are truly; that bread is his body; and that wine also is his blood; as was the heavenly bread which we call manna, that fed for forty years God's people in the wilderness. And the clear water which did then run from the Rock in the wilderness was truly his blood, as St. Paul wrote in one of his epistles: All our fathers did eat in the wilderness the same spiritual meat, and drink the same spiritual drink; they drank of that spiritual Rock, and that Rock was Christ. The apostle hath said, as you have heard, that they all did eat the same spiritual meat; that they all did drink the same spritual drink. He saith not bodily, but spiritually; as Christ was not yet born, nor his blood shed, when the people of Israel did eat that meat, and drink of that Rock. The Rock was not bodily Christ, though he said so. It was the same mystery in the old law, and they did spiritually signify that spiritual eucharist of our Saviour's body which we consecrate now."

Besides the epistles of Elfric, which fight directly against transubstantiation, mention was also made of certain sermons, to the number of eighty, translated by Elfric out of the Latin into the Saxon, that is, into our English tongue. Of which eighty sermons, twenty-four were chiefly selected to be read, as homilies or treatises to the people.

There was one appointed to be read upon Easter day; which sermon being translated by Elfric, we have here exhibited it in English, that the christian reader may judge how the fantastical doctrine of transubstantiation, in those days of Elfric, and before his time, was not yet received nor known in the church of England.

The following are the words of this sermon for Easter-day, so far as relates to transubstantiation:—"He blessed bread before his suffering, and divided it to his disciples, thus saying, 'Take eat; this is my body: this do in remembrance of me.' Also he blessed the wine in a cup, and said, 'Drink ye all of it:' 'For this is my blood of the New Testament, which is shed for many for the remission of sins.' The apostles did as Christ commanded, that is, they blessed bread and wine for the eucharist, and gave it to be received in remembrance of him. Even so also their successors, and all priests by Christ's commandment, do bless bread and wine for the eucharist in his name with the apostolic blessing. Now men have often searched, and do yet often search, how bread that is gathered of corn, and through the heat of fire baked, may be turned to Christ's body; or how wine

that is pressed out of many grapes is turned through one blessing into the Lord's blood. Now say we to such men, some things are spoken of Christ by signification, and some are things certain. True this is, and certain, that Christ was born of a Virgin, and suffered of his own accord, and was buried, and on the third day arose from death. He is said to be bread by signification; and a lamb; and a lion, and a mountain. He is called bread, because he is our life, and angel's life. He is said to be a lamb for his innocency; and a lion for strength, wherewith he overcame the strong devil. But Christ is not so notwithstanding after true nature; neither bread, nor a lamb, nor a lion. Why is then the holy eucharist called Christ's body, or his blood, if it be not truly what it is called? Truly the bread and wine which in the supper by the priest is hallowed, show one thing without to human understanding, and another thing within to believing minds. Without, there is seen bread and wine both in figure and in taste; and they are truly after their hallowing Christ's body and blood, through spiritual mystery. An heathen child is christened, yet he altereth not his shape without, though he be changed within. He is brought to the font sinful through Adam's disobedience, howbeit he is washed from all sin within, though he hath not changed his shape without. Even so the holy font water, that is called the well-spring of life, is like in shape to other waters, and is subject to corruption; but the Holy Ghost's might cometh to the corruptible water through the priest's blessing, and it may after wash the body and soul from all sin, through spiritual might. Behold now we see two things in this one creature; after true nature, that water is corruptible moisture; and after spiritual mystery, hath wholesome virtue. So also if we behold the holy eucharist, after bodily understanding, then we see that it is a creature corruptible and mutable. If we acknowledge therein spiritual might, then understand we that life is therein, and that it giveth immortality to them that eat with belief. Much is betwixt the invisible might of the holy eucharist, and the visible shape of proper nature. It is naturally corruptible bread, and corruptible wine, and is by might of God's word truly Christ's body and blood; not so notwithstanding bodily, but spiritually. Much is betwixt the body of Christ which he suffered in, and the body which is hallowed for the eucharist. The body truly that Christ suffered in, was born of the flesh of Mary; with blood and with bone; with skin and with sinews; in human limbs; with a reasonable soul living; and his spiritual body, which we call the eucharist, is gathered of many corns, without blood and bone, without limb, without soul; and therefore nothing is to be understood therein bodily, but all is spiritually to be understood. Whatsoever is in that eucharist, which giveth substance of life, that is of the spiritual might, and invisible doing. Therefore is that holy eucharist called a mystery, because there is one thing in it seen, and another thing understood. That which is there seen, hath bodily shape; and that we do there understand hath spiritual might. Certainly Christ's body, which suffered death and rose from death, never dieth henceforth, but is eternal and incorruptible. That eucharist is temporal, not eternal, corruptible and divided into sundry parts, chewed between the teeth, and sent into the belly; howbeit nevertheless after spiritual might it is all in every part. Many receive that holy body, and yet notwithstanding it is whole in every part after spiritual mystery. Though some chew the less, yet is there no more might notwithstanding in the most part, than in the less; because it is whole in all men after the invisible might. This mystery is a pledge and a figure: Christ's body is truth itself. This pledge we do keep mystically, until we come to the truth itself, and then is this pledge ended. Truly it is, as we before have said, Christ's body, and his blood; not bodily, but spiritually. But now hear the apostle's word about this mystery. St. Paul the apostle speaketh of the old Israelites, thus writing in his epistle to faithful men, 'Moreover, brethren, I would not that ye should be ignorant, how that all our fathers were under the cloud, and all passed through the sea; and were all baptized unto Moses in the cloud and in the sea; and did all eat the same spiritual meat; and did all drink the same spiritual drink: (for they drank of that spiritual Rock that followed them; and that Rock was Christ.)' Neither was that stone, then, from which the water ran, bodily Christ, but it signified Christ, who called thus to all believing and faithful men: "If any man thirst, let him come unto me and drink;" and "out of his belly shall flow rivers of living water." This he said of the Holy Ghost, which they received who believed on him. The apostle Paul saith, that the Israelites did eat the same spiritual meat, and drink the same spiritual drink, because that heavenly meat that fed them forty years, and that water which from the rock did flow, had signification of Christ's body, and his blood that is now offered daily in God's church. It was the same which we now offer, not bodily, but spiritually."

After the time of Elfric, transubstantiation began first to be talked of among a few superstitious monks; so that as blindness and superstition began to increase, this gross opinion more and more prevailed; and about the year 1060, the denying of transubstantiation began to be accounted heresy.

Berenger, a Frenchman and archdeacon of Anjou, of all christian men was the first called and accounted an heretic for denying of transubstantiation.

This Berenger lived about the year 1060. The substance of his history is this; that when Berenger had professed the truth of the sacrament, and had stood in the open confession of it, according to the ancient doctrine received before in the church, he was so handled by superstitious monks, that, by evil entreaty, and for fear of death, he began to shrink and recant the truth. Of these malicious enemies against him, the chief troubler was Lanfranc, afterwards archbishop of Canterbury; and Hildebrand, afterwards bishop of Rome.

By these and other monks, the error and heresy of transubstantiation began first to be defended. The first that began to set up that faction in writing seems to be Paschasius, who lived a little before Berenger, about the time of Bertramn; and Lanfranc was the first that brought it into England.

On the other hand, the first that was openly troubled for denying transubstantiation, was this Berenger; with whom Lanfranc was supposed at first to hold and take part, but afterwards, to clear himself, he stood openly against him in the council, and wrote against him.

It follows in the act of the council, when the synod of archbishops, bishops, abbots, and other prelates were assembled together, the greater number held that the bread and wine were turned substantially into the body and blood of Christ. Others there were who held the contrary with Berenger, but at last were driven to give over. Berenger, among the rest, after he had long stood in the constant defence of the truth, at last submitted to their wills, and desired pardon of the council. And this was (as seems to William of Malmesbury) his first giving over. Afterwards, returning to himself again after the death of Pope Leo, and pricked with the sting of conscience, he was driven again to recognize the truth, which he had denied.

The pope, perceiving this, would not leave him so; but sent his cardinal chaplain, Hildebrand, into France, who so handled Berenger that he recanted again.

Again, Pope Nicholas II., congregating a council at Rome, (A. D. 1059,) sent for Berenger, who, being present, argued what he could for the justness of his cause; but all would not serve. Berenger being borne down on every side, when no remedy would serve, but he must needs recant again, desired to know what other confession of the sacrament the pope would have of him, besides that which he had confessed. Then Pope Nicholas committed that charge to Humbert, a monk of Lotharing, and afterwards a cardinal, that he should draw out in formal words the order of his recantation, which he should read and publicly profess before the people. The form of which words is registered in the decrees to the following effect:—" That he pretendeth with heart and mouth to profess, that he, ac-

knowledging the true, catholic, and apostolical faith, doth execrate all heresy, namely, that wherewith he hath lately been defamed, as holding that the bread and wine upon the altar, after the consecration of the priest, remain only a sacrament, and are not the very body and blood of our Lord Jesus Christ; neither can be handled or broken with the priest's hands, or chewed with the teeth of the faithful, otherwise than only by manner of a sacrament: consenting now to the holy and apostolical church of Rome, he professed with mouth and heart to hold the same faith touching the sacrament of the Lord's mass, which the lord Pope Nicholas, with his synod here present doth hold, and commandeth to be holden by his evangelical and apostolical authority; that is, that the bread and wine upon the altar, after consecration, are not only a sacrament, but also are the very true and self-same body and blood of our Lord Jesus Christ, and are sensibly felt and broken with hands, and chewed with teeth: swearing by the holy evangelists, that whosoever shall hold or say to the contrary, he shall hold them perpetually accursed, and if he himself shall hereafter presume to preach or teach against the same, he shall be content to abide the severity and rigour of the canons," &c.

This cowardly recantation of Berenger, as it offended a great number of the godly sort, so it gave to the other party no little triumph.

Some time after this, Pope Hildebrand summoned a new council at Rome in the church of Lateran, to revive again the affair of Berenger, about the year, as some hold, 1079.

Thus Berenger, being tossed by these monks and pharisees, was so confounded, and baited on every side; that partly for worldly fear, restraining him on the one side; partly for shame and grief of conscience that he had now twice denied the truth; he (as is reported) forsaking his goods, his studies, learning, and former state of life, became a labourer, and wrought with his hands for his living, all the residue of his life.

The opinion which Berenger maintained, touching the sacrament (as by his own words in Lanfranc's book may appear) was this:—" The sacrifice of the church consisteth of two things: the one visible, the other invisible, that is, of the sacrament, and of the thing or matter of the sacrament. Which thing (meaning the body of Christ) if it were here present before our eyes, it were a thing visible and to be seen: but being lifted up into heaven, and sitting on the right hand of his Father, until the time of restitution of all things (as St. Peter saith) it cannot be called down from thence. For the person of Christ consists of God and man; the sacrament of the Lord's table, consists of bread and wine; which, being consecrated, are not changed; but remain in their substances, having a certain resemblance or similitude of those things whereof they be sacraments," &c.

By these words of Berenger's doctrine, all indifferent readers may see and judge, that he affirmed nothing but what was agreeable to the holy scriptures, believing with St. Augustine, and all other ancient elders of the church; that in the holy supper all faithful believers are refreshed spiritually with the body and blood of the Lord, unto everlasting life.

The rude and mis-shapen doctrine of these monks concerning transubstantiation, as we have heard when and by whom it first began to be broached; so if we would now know by what learning and scripture they confirmed and established it, we must understand that their chief ground to persuade the people was at this time certain miracles forged by them and published both in their writings and preachings.

Many fabulous miracles are to be found in popish histories, counterfeited and forged under divers and sundry names; some referred to Gregory; some to Paschasius, and others; to recite which would fill a whole volume full of lies and fables. Among many, one is thus invented by Paschasius. There was a priest named Plegildus, who saw and handled with his hands visibly the shape of a child upon the altar, and after he had embraced and kissed him, it returned again to the likeness of bread

When this miracle was objected against Berenger, he merrily deriding the fable answered, "A godly piece of a varlet, that whom he kissed before with his mouth, by and by he goeth about to tear him with his teeth."

Another miracle is reported of a Jew-boy, who, upon entering the church with another lad who was his playfellow, saw upon the altar a little child broken and torn in pieces, and afterwards in portions distributed among the people. When the young Jew coming home told this to his father, he was condemned to be burned.

Being inclosed in a house, and the door fast where he was to be burned, he was found and taken out from thence by the christians, not only alive, but also not having one hair of his head hurt with the flames. Being asked by the christians how he was so preserved from the burning fire : "There appeared," said he, " to me a beautiful woman sitting in a chair, whose son the child was which was divided and distributed in the church among the people, who reached to me her hand in the burning flame, and with her gown kept the flame from me ; so that I was preserved from perishing," &c.

And these were then commonly the arguments of the monks, wherewith they persuaded the people to believe their transubstantiation. But to leave these monks' fictions, and to return to Berenger. Malmesbury reports of him, that after he had once or twice recanted, yet this doctrine of the sacrament remained still in the minds of his hearers.

Although in the time of Berenger, which was about A.D. 1060, this error of transubstantiation began to grow in strength, by the support of certain monks ; as Lanfranc, Guimund, Hugh bishop of Lincoln, Fulbert (of whom it is said in histories, that, when he was sick, our Lady gave him suck with her own breasts), and others ; yet all the while transubstantiation was not decreed for public law, or doctrine to be held by any general consent, either by the church of Rome, or any other council, before the council of Lateran, under Pope Innocent III., who, A.D. 1215, made the decree, as follows :—

" There is one universal church of the faithful, without which none can be saved ; in the which church the self-same Jesus Christ is both priest and also the sacrifice ; whose body and blood are truly contained in the sacrament of the altar, under the forms of bread and wine ; the bread being transubstantiated into the body, and the wine into the blood, by the power and working of God. So that to the accomplishing of this mystery of unity, we might take of his, the same which he hath taken of ours. And this sacrament none can make or consecrate, but he that is a priest lawfully ordained, according to the keys of the church, which Jesus Christ hath left to his apostles, and to their successors," &c.

And thus was the foundation laid for the building of transubstantiation, and the doctrine intruded for an article of faith into the church, necessarily to be believed of all men under pain of heresy !

But yet all the while, notwithstanding that the substance of bread and wine was now banished out of the sacrament, and utterly transcorporated into the substance of Christ's very body and blood ; yet this body was not elevated over the priest's head ; nor adored by the people till the days of Pope Honorius III., who, by his council, commanded adoration and elevation to be joined with transubstantiation, as one idolatry commonly brings forth another.

Again, the sacraments of the Lord's Supper being now consecrated, transubstantiated, elevated, and adored, yet it was not offered up for a sacrifice propitiatory for the sins of the quick and the dead ; nor for a remedy of the souls in purgatory ; nor for a merit *operis operati, sive bono motu utentis,* &c., before other popes, coming afterwards, added still new additions to the former inventions of their predecessors.

And thus we have the whole order and origin of these idolatrous parts of the mass, which first began with consecration. Then came transubstantiation by In-nocent ; and afterwards elevation and adoration by Honorius ; and last of all came the oblation meritorious and propitiatory for the quick and the dead in remission of sins, *ex opere operato !*

Which things being thus constituted by the usurped authority of the church of Rome, shortly after followed persecution, tyranny, and burning among the christians ; first beginning with the Albigenses, and the faithful congregation of Toulouse, about the time of Pope Innocent.

The second Article

As to the second article, which debars from the laypeople one-half of the sacrament, understanding that under one kind both parts are fully contained (as the world well knows that this article is but young invented, decreed, and concluded no longer since, than at the council of Constance, A.D. 1414,) I shall not need to dwell long upon the matter ; especially as sufficient has been said before in our discourse on the Bohemian history.

First, let us see the reasons of the adversaries in restraining the laity from the cup of this sacrament.

When they allege the place of St. Luke, where Christ was known in breaking of bread, &c. citing, moreover, many other places of scripture, wherein mention is made of breaking of bread ; we answer, although we do not utterly deny but that some of these places may be understood of the sacrament: yet that being granted, it follows not that only one part of the sacrament was ministered to the people without the other, when by the common use of speech under the naming of one part the whole action is meant. Neither does it follow that because that bread was broken among the brethren, therefore the cup was not distributed to them. For we find by the words of St. Paul, (1 Cor. xi. 26), that the use of the Corinthians was to communicate not only in breaking of bread, but in participating of the cup also.

It can be proved and demonstrated that this new-found custom differs from all antiquity and prescription of use and time ; and even although the custom were ancient, yet no custom may countermand the open and express commandment of God, which saith to all men, " Drink ye all of this," &c.

Again, seeing the cup is called the blood of the New Testament, who is he that dare or can alter the testament of the Lord, when none may be so hardy to alter the testament of a man, being once approved or ratified ?

Further, as concerning those places of scripture before alleged, of breaking of bread, whereupon they think themselves so sure that the sacrament was then administered but in one kind : in answer we say, first, it may be doubted whether all those places in scripture are to be referred to the sacrament. Secondly, admitting the same, yet they cannot infer, because one part is mentioned, that the full sacrament was not ministered. The common manner of the Hebrew phrase is, under breaking of bread to signify generally the whole feast or supper: as in the prophet Isaiah, these words, " Deal thy bread to the hungry," do signify as well giving drink as bread, &c. And thirdly, however these places be taken, yet it makes little for them, but rather against them. For if the sacrament were administered " in breaking of *bread,*" then they must needs grant, that if bread was there broken, there was *bread;* forasmuch as neither the accidents of bread without bread can be broken ; neither can the natural body of Christ be subject to any breaking by the scripture, which saith, " a bone of him shall not be broken." &c.

They object further and say, that the church, upon due consideration, may alter as they see cause, in rites, ceremonies, and sacraments.

Answer. The institution of this sacrament standeth upon the order, example, and commandment of Christ. He divided the bread severally from the cup, and afterwards the cup severally from the bread. This he did to give us example how to do the same after him, in remembrance of his death to the end of the world. And besides this example, he added an express commandment, "Do this," and "Drink ye all of this," &c. Against this order, example, and commandment of the gospel, no church nor council of men, nor angel in heaven has any power or authority to change or alter; according as we are warned, "If any preach unto you any other gospel besides that ye have received, let him be accursed," &c.

Among other objections, they allege certain perils as spilling, shedding, or shaking the blood out of the cup, or souring, or else sticking upon men's beards, &c. For which they say it is well provided that the half communion shall suffice.

To this it is soon answered, that as these causes were no hindrance to Christ, to the apostles, to the Corinthians, and to the brethren of the primitive church; but that in the public assemblies they received all the whole communion, as well in the one part as in the other; so neither are these causes so important now, to annul and make void the necessary commandment of the gospel; if we were as careful to obey the Lord, as we are curious to magnify our own devices; to strain at gnats; to stumble at straws; and to seek knots in rushes, which rather are growing in our own fantasies, than there where they are sought.

The Third Article.

Private masses, trental masses, and dirge masses, as they were never used before the time of Gregory, six hundred years after Christ, so they are against our christian doctrine. The mass is a work or action of the priest, applied to men for meriting of grace, *ex opere operato*, in which action the sacrament is first worshipped, and then offered up as a sacrifice for remission of sins (*à pœna et culpa*), for the quick and the dead. This definition agrees not with the rules of christian doctrine.

1. The first rule is, sacraments are instituted for some end and use, out of which use they are no sacraments. As the sacrament of baptism is a sacrament of regeneration and forgiveness of sins to the person that is baptized; but if it be carried about to be worshipped and shewed to others, as meritorious for their remission and regeneration, to them it is no sacrament.

2. A sacrament or ceremony profits them only who take and use them.

3. Only the death of Christ, and the work of his sacrifice upon the cross is to be applied to every man by faith, for salvation of his soul. Besides this, to apply any action or work of priest, or any other person, as meritorious of itself, and conducible to salvation, or to remission of sins, is derogatory to the covenant of God, and prejudicial to the blood of Christ.

4. To make idols of sacraments, and to worship dumb things for the living God, is idolatry.

5. Every good work that a man does profits only himself, and cannot be applied to other men.

6. No man can apply to another the sacrifice of Christ's death, but every man must apply it to himself by his own believing.

7. The passion of Christ once done, is a full and a perfect oblation and satisfaction for the sins of the whole world, both original and actual; by the virtue of which passion the wrath of God is pacified towards mankind for ever. Amen.

8. The passion of Christ once done, is the only object of that faith of ours which justifies us. And therefore whoever sets up any other object, beside that passion once done, for our faith to apprehend and behold the same, teaches damnable doctrine, and leads to idolatry.

Against all these rules private mass is directly opposed. For, beside that they transgress the order, example, and commandment of Christ (which divided the bread and cup to them all) they also bring the sacrament out of the right use to which it was ordained. For whereas that sacrament is instituted for a testimonial and remembrance of Christ's death, the private mass transfers it to another purpose; either to make of it a gazing idol;

or a work of application meritorious; or a sacrifice propitiatory for remission of sins; or a commemoration for souls departed in purgatory.

Furthermore, the institution of Christ is broken in this, that whereas the communion was given in common, the private mass suffers the priest alone to eat and drink up all, and when he has done, to bless the people with the empty cup.

2. Whereas sacraments properly profit none but them that use them; in the private mass the sacrament is received in the behalf not only of him that receives it, but of them also who are far off, or the dead in purgatory.

3. When nothing is to be applied for remission of sins, but only the death of Christ, the private mass comes in as a meritorious work done by the priest; which being applied to others, is available *ex opere operato*, both to him that does it, and to them for whom it is done.

4. Private masses and all other masses now used of the sacrament make an idol; of commemoration make adoration; instead of a receiving, make a deceiving; in place of shewing forth Christ's death make new oblations of his death, and of a communion make a single supping, &c.

5. Whereas in this general frailty of man's nature, no man can merit by any worthiness of working for himself, the priest in his private mass takes upon him to merit both for himself, and for many others.

6. It stands against scripture, that the sacrifice and death of Christ can be applied any otherwise to our benefit and justification, than by faith. Wherefore it is false that the action of the mass can apply the benefit of Christ's death unto us, by the mere act of its being offered.

7. Whereas the benefit of our salvation and justifying stands by the free gift and grace of God, through our faith in Christ; the application of these popish masses stops the freeness of God's grace, and makes that this benefit first comes through the priest's hands to us.

The eighth contrariety between private mass and God's word is in this; that where the scripture saith, *Unica oblatione consummavit eos, qui sanctificantur in perpetuum,* "With one offering he hath perfected for ever them that are sanctified;" the private mass proceeds in a contrary doctrine; makes of one oblation a daily oblation, and that which is perfectly done and finished now to be done again; and finally, that which was instituted only for eating and for a remembrance of that oblation of Christ once offered, the popish mass maketh an oblation and a new satisfaction daily to be offered for the quick and the dead.

To conclude, both the private and public masses of priests turn away the object of our faith from the body of Christ crucified, to the body of Christ in their masses. And where God annexes the promise of justification but only to our faith in the body of Christ crucified, they do annex promise of remission from both the guilt and punishment of sin, to their masses by their application; besides divers other horrible and intolerable corruptions, which spring of their private and public masses.

The Fourth and Fifth Articles,—of Vows and Priests' Marriage.

As we have discoursed before of the antiquity of transubstantiation, of the half communion, and of private masses; so now coming to the article of vows, and of priests' marriage, the reader will wish to be satisfied in this likewise, and to be certified from what time these vows and unmarried life of priests have continued. For the better establishing of the reader's mind against this wicked article of priests' marriage, it shall be no great labour lost, here briefly to recapitulate in the recitation of this matter, either what before hath been said, or what more is to be added. And that the world may see the law and decree of priests' single life, to be a doctrine of no ancient standing in this realm, but only since the time of Anselm, I will first allege the words of Henry Huntington, here following:

"The same year, at the feast of St. Michael, Anselm,

the archbishop of Canterbury, held a synod at London; in which synod he prohibited priests here in England to have wives, which they were not prohibited before to have. Which constitution seemed to some persons very pure and chaste. To others, again, it seemed very dangerous, lest, while men should seem to take upon them such celibacy more than they should be able to bear, by that occasion they might fall into horrible filthiness, which should redound to the exceeding slander of the christian profession," &c.

I deny not that before the time of Anselm, both Odo, and after him Dunstan archbishops of Canterbury, and Ethelwold bishop of Winchester, and Oswald bishop of Worcester, in the days of king Edgar, (A. D. 963,) as they were all monks themselves, so were they great opposers of the marriage of priests. Yet the priests who were then married, were not constrained to leave their wives, or their preferments, but only at their own choice. But yet this restraint of priests' lawful marriages, was never publicly established for a law here in the church of England, before the coming of Anselm, (in the days of William Rufus, and king Henry I.) who wrote in these words: "Boldly I command by the authority which I have by my archbishoprick, not only within my archbishoprick, but also throughout England, that all priests that keep women, shall be deprived of their churches, and all ecclesiastical benefices," &c. as ye may read more at large before. Which was about the same time, when Hildebrand, at Rome, began the same matter; and others, till Calistus II.; by whom the act against priests' marriage was brought to full perfection, and so has continued ever since.

It were tedious to number up the names of all such bishops and priests, who have been married since that time; but as to the time of this devilish prohibition for priests to have their wives, it is to be noted that in the year of our Saviour, 1076, when pope Hildebrand occupied the papal chair, this oath first began to be taken of archbishops and bishops, that they should suffer none to enter into the ministry, or into any ecclesiastical function, having a wife; and likewise the clergy to be bound to promise the same. This was, as I said, about the year 1076. Whereby the prophesy of St. Paul appears truly to be verified, speaking of these latter times, (1 Tim. iv. 1.) where he writes in these words: "Now the Spirit speaketh expressly, that in the latter times some shall depart from the faith, giving heed to seducing spirits, and doctrines of devils; speaking lies in hypocrisy; having their conscience seared with a hot iron; forbidding to marry, and commanding to abstain from meats, which God hath created to be received with thanksgiving of them which believe and know the truth."

In this prophecy of St. Paul two things are to be observed; First, the matter which he prophesieth of; that is, the forbidding of marriage; and forbidding of meats, which God generally has left free to all men. The second thing in this prophecy, is the time when this prophecy shall fall, that is, in the latter times of the world. So that this concurs right well with these years of pope Hildebrand, being a thousand years complete after the ascension of our Saviour; so that they may well be called the latter times.

This prophecy of St. Paul thus standing, as it does, firm and certain, that is, the forbidding of marriage must happen in the latter times of the world, then must it needs follow, that the married life of priests is more ancient in the church than is the single life,—than the law, I mean, commanding the single life of priests. Which may soon be proved to be true.

1. For, at the council of Nice, it is notorious that this devilish law for restraining marriage was stopped by Paphnutius.

2. Before this council of Nice, in the year 197, we read of Polycrates bishop of Ephesus, who dissenting from pope Victor about a certain controversy of Easterday, alleges for himself that his progenitors before him, seven together, one after another, succeeded in that seat, and he now, the eighth after them, was placed in the same; using this his descent from his parents not only as a defence of his cause, but also as a glory to himself.

3. Pope Sericius, about the year of our Lord 390, wrote to the priests of Spain about the matter of putting their wives from them, if his epistle be not counterfeit. These Spanish priests had then with them a bishop of Tarragona, who answering to Sericius, alleged the testimonies of St. Paul, that priests might lawfully retain their wives, &c. To this Sericius replied again, (if his writing is not forged) most arrogantly, and no less ignorantly, reproving the priests that were married; and for the defence of his cause, alleging this sentence of St. Paul, " If ye shall live after the flesh, ye shall die," &c. Whereby may appear not only how they in Spain then had wives, but also how blind these men were in the scriptures, who shewed themselves so great adversaries against priests' marriages.

4. To be short, the further we go, and the nearer we come to the ancient and primitive time of the church, the less ancient shall we find the deprivation of lawful matrimony amongst christian ministers; beginning even with the apostles, who, although they were not all married, yet many of them were, and the rest had power and liberty to have and keep their wives; witness St. Paul, where he writes of himself: " Have we not power to lead about a sister, a wife, as also the other apostles have?" Whereby it is to be seen, both what he might do, and what the other apostles did.

It can be sufficiently proved, and indeed is admitted, that the deprivation of priests' lawful marriage did not enter into the church, either Greek or Latin, at least it took no full possession, before pope Hildebrand's time, 1075; and especially pope Calistus' time, 1120; these were the first open objectors to priests' marriages.

Aventine, a faithful writer of his time, concerning the council of Hildebrand, has these words; " In those days priests commonly had wives, as other christian men had, and had children also; as may appear by ancient instruments and deeds of gift, which were then given to churches, to the clergy, and to religious houses: In which instruments both the priests, and their wives also with them, (which there be called Presbyterissæ), I find alleged as witnesses." It happened moreover at the same time, (saith Aventine,) " that the emperor had the investing of divers archbishopricks, bishopricks, abbeys, and nunneries within his dominions. Pope Hildebrand disdaining both these sorts, that is, both them that were invested by the emperor, and also all those priests that had wives, provided so in his council at Rome, that they who were promoted by the emperor to livings of the church, were accounted to come in by simony; the others, who were married priests, were counted for Nicholaitans. Whereupon pope Hildebrand, in writing to the emperor, to dukes, princes, and other great prelates and potentates, namely, to Berthold Zaringer, to Rodulph of Suevia, to Welphon of Bavaria, to Adalberon, and to their ladies, and to divers others to whom he thought good; also to bishops, namely, to Otto, bishop of Constance, with other priests and lay people,—willed them in his letters to refuse and to keep no company with those simoniacs, and those Nicholaitan priests (for so they were termed then), who had either any ecclesiastical living by the emperor, or who had wives; to avoid their masses; neither to talk; nor to eat or drink with them; nor once to speak to them; nor to salute them; but utterly to shun them, as men execrable and wicked, even as they would eschew the plague or pestilence.

" By this there ensued a mighty schism and affliction among the flock of Christ: For the priests went against their bishops, the people against the priests, the laity against the clergy. Briefly, all fell into confusion. Men and women, as every one was set upon mischief, wickedness, contention, and avarice, took thereby occasion, upon every light suspicion, to resist their minister, and to spoil the goods of the church. The vulgar people contemned the priests who had married wives, despised their religion, and all things that they did; yea, and in many places would purge the place where they had been with holy water. Also such was the mischief, that they would take the holy mysteries which those married priests had consecrated, and cast them in the dirt, and tread them under their feet: For so had Hildebrand taught them, that those were no priests, neither were they sacraments which they consecrated. So that by this occasion many false prophets arose, seducing the people from the truth of Christ by forged fables, and false miracles, and feigned glosses, wresting the scriptures as best served their own purposes."

To this testimony of Aventinus, above mentioned, we will also add the record of Gebuilerus, a writer of this our latter time, and one also of their own crew, who doth testify that in the time of the emperor Henry IV. (A. D. 1057,) the number of twenty-four bishops, both in Germany, Spain, and in France, were married, as well as the clergy also of their dioceses.

Of these Spanish bishops we read also in Isidore (who died about A.D. 636), in his book, *De Clericorum Vita*, that they ought either to lead an honest, chaste life; or else to have kept themselves within the bands of matrimony, &c. By this it is evident that the single life of priests was either then voluntary, or else that their marriage was not then restrained by any law.

Thus, if either the voice of scripture might have weight with these men; or if the examples of the apostles might move them (whom St. Ambrose witnesses to have been all married, except only St. Paul and St. John); or else if the multitude of married bishops and priests might prevail with them; it may be here stated:

That Tertullian was a married priest, as witnesses Jerome.

Spiridion, bishop of Cyprus, had a wife and children.

Hilary, bishop of Poictiers, was also married.

Gregory, bishop of Nyssa; Gregory, bishop of Nazianzem; Prosper, bishop of Rhegium; Cheremon, bishop of Nilus. All these were married bishops; and also Polycrates, and his seven ancestors, bishops.

Epiphanius, bishop of Constantiople in the time of Justinian, was the more commended, because his father and ancestors had been married priests and bishops.

Jerome saith, that in his time many priests were married men.

Pope Damasus recites a great number of bishops, or popes of Rome, who were priests' sons, during the first ten centuries after Christ: as, Felix III.; Gelasius I.; Boniface; Agapetus; Silverius; Theodorus, whose father was bishop of Jerusalem; Adrian II.; John X. John XV.

And besides these bishops of Rome, many other bishops and priests in other countries might be annexed to this catalogue, if our leisure was such as to admit our making a roll of them all.

The law forbidding priests to marry was never generally received in the church of Rome until the time of Gregory VII. (Hildebrand), that is, since A.D. 1073.

This pope Hildebrand was, of all others, the chief and principal enemy against the marriage of priests. For whereas all other approved canons and councils only enacted, that any clergyman, having a wife before his entering into his ministry, might enjoy the liberty of his marriage, so that he married not a widow, or a known harlot, or kept a concubine, or were twice married: now comes in pope Hildebrand, making the marriage of priests to be heresy, and further enacting, "That whatever clerk, deacon, or minister had a wife, either before his orders, or after, should utterly put her from him, or else forsake his ministry," &c.

And thus much for the antiquity and the bringing in of the celibacy of the priests. It first began, about the time of pope Nicholas 1058, and Alexander II. 1061, to be a custom; and afterwards it was made into a law by pope Hildebrand, and so spread from Italy into other countries, and at length also into England.

Whilst pope Nicholas and Hildebrand were busy at Rome, in introducing that practice, so Lanfranc, archbishop of Canterbury was likewise engaged in bringing about the same matter in England, although he did not begin altogether so roughly as pope Hildebrand did, as

it appears by his council held at Winchester: where, though he prohibited such as were prebendaries of cathedral churches to have wives, yet he did permit, in his decree, that such priests as dwelt in towns and villages, and had wives, should retain them still, and not be compelled to be separated from them; and that they who had none, should be prohibited from marrying; enjoining moreover the bishops to take care hereafter, that they presumed not to admit into order any priests or deacons, unless they should first make a solemn profession not to marry.

Then after Lanfranc succeeded Anselm in the see of Canterbury, who fiercely and eagerly laboured in this matter, abrogating utterly the marriage of priests, deacons, sub-deacons, and of the clergy generally; not permitting (as Lanfranc did) priests that had wives in villages and towns to keep them still, but utterly commanding, and that under great penalties, not only priests and deacons, but sub-deacons also, (which is against the council of Lateran,) who were already married, to be separated, and that none should be received into orders hereafter, without profession of perpetual celibacy.

And yet notwithstanding all this, the priests did not give much heed to these unlawful injunctions, but still kept their wives almost for two hundred years after, refusing and resisting for a long time the yoke of that servile bondage, to keep still their freedom from such vowing, professing, and promising; as may well appear by those priests of York, of whom Gerard, archbishop of York, speaks, in writing to Anselm, in these words:

"I much desire the purity of my clergymen: yet, except it be in a very few, I find in them the deafness of the adder, and the inconstancy of Proteus. With their stinging tongues they cast out sometimes threats, somewhile taunts and rebukes. But this grieveth me less in them that are further off. This grieveth me most of all, that they who are of mine own church, as in mine own bosom, and prebendaries of mine own see, contemn our canons, and argue like sophistical disputers, against the statutes of our council. The prebendaries, who irregularly have been taken into orders heretofore, without making vow or profession, refuse utterly to make profession to me. And they that are priests or deacons, having before openly married wives or concubines, will not be removed from them by any admonition from the altar. And when I call upon any to receive orders, they obstinately deny to profess celibacy in their ordering," &c.

Thus, for all this rigorous austerity, Anselm, was unable to enforce his decree made at London, against the marriage of priests; nor had the same monk greater success, either in his life time, or after his death. For although sundry priests, during his life-time, were compelled by his extremity to renounce their wives, yet many refused to obey him.

Many were contented rather to leave their benefices than their wives. A great number were permitted by king Henry VIII. for money to enjoy their wives; but this became so chargeable unto them, (saith Edmer, in his fourth book,) that at length two hundred priests, in their albes and priestly vestments, came barefoot to the king's palace, crying to him for mercy; and especially making their suit to the queen, who, though moved with compassion towards them, yet durst not make any intercession for them.

It is therefore evident, that this violent restraint of the lawful marriage of priests, within this realm of England, is of no such antiquity as hath been thought by many ignorant of the course of history. A brief summary will enable the reader to comprehend the whole matter.

First, about the year 946, the profession of single life, and displacing of marriage, began to come into practice in England by reason of St. Benet's monks, who then began to increase very much about the time of king Edgar, and especially by means of Oswald, bishop of York, Odo and Dunstan, archbishops of Canterbury, and Ethelwold, bishop of Winchester; so that in divers cathedral churches and bishops' sees, monks with their professed singleness of life crept in, and married ministers (who were then called secular priests) with their wives, were dispossessed out of sundry churches, not from their wives only, but from their places also ; and yet not in all churches, but only in those which have been mentioned.

Not long after that, about the time of pope Nicholas II., A.D. 1060, of Alexander II. and Hildebrand, there came into the see of Canterbury another monk called Lanfranc, who also, being a promoter of this professed celibacy, made the decree more general, that all prebendaries of any churches who were married should be displaced ; yet that the priests in towns and villages should not be compelled to leave their married wives, unless they wished to do so ; and last of all followed the monk Anselm, A.D. 1106, who made the laws which we have stated before.

I shall now conclude my observations on these articles with some remarks on the sixth article, touching auricular confession :—

Of confession three things we find expressed and approved in the scriptures. The first is our confession privately and publicly made to God alone ; and this confession is necessary for all men at all times. Wherefore St. John speaketh, " If we confess our sins, he is faithful and just to forgive," &c.

The second is the confession which is openly made in the face of the congregation. And this confession also has place when any thing is committed, which gives a public offence and slander to the church of God.

The third kind of confession is that which we make privately to our brother. And this confession is requisite, when we have injured our brother. Whereof the gospel speaks, " Go and reconcile thyself first to thy brother," &c. Also St. James says, " Confess your faults one to another," &c. Or else this confession may also have place, when any thing lies on our conscience, in which we need the counsel and comfort of some faithful brother. But we must use discretion in avoiding these points of blind superstition. First, that we put therein no necessity for remission of our sins, but that we use our own voluntary discretion, according as we see it expedient for the satisfying of our troubled mind. The second is, that we are not bound to any enumeration of our sins. The third, that we bind not ourselves to any one person more than to another, but that we use our free choice, whom we think can give us the best spiritual counsel in the Lord.

But as there is nothing in the church so good which through superstition may not be perverted ; so this confession also has not lacked abuses. First, the secret confession to God alone, as it has been counted insufficient ; so has it been but lightly esteemed by many. The public confession to the congregation has been turned to a standing in a sheet, or else has been bought off for money. The secret opening of a man's mind to some faithful or spiritual brother, in disclosing his infirmity or temptations, for counsel and godly comfort, has been turned into auricular confession in a priest's ear, for absolving of his sins.

Now, after having discussed these matters which refer to the six wicked articles, it follows next, in returning to the order of our history, to declare those events which ensued after the setting out of these articles. This brings us to the time and history of the lord Cromwell, a man whose great fame and deeds are worthy to live renowned in perpetual memory.

The History concerning the Life, Acts, and Death of Thomas Cromwell, Earl of Essex.

Thomas Cromwell, although born of a simple parentage, and of an obscure house, through the singular excellency of wisdom, united with industry of mind, and deserts of life, rose to high preferment and authority. By steps of office and honour, he ascended, at length, that not only he was made earl of Essex, but also secret counsellor to King Henry VIII., and vicegerent to his person.

In the simple estate and beginnings of this man, we may learn that the excellency of noble virtues and heroic prowess which advance to fame and honour, stand not merely upon birth and blood, but proceed from the gift of God, who " raiseth up the poor out of the dust, and lifteth the needy out of the dunghill ; that he may set him with princes, even with the princes of his people."

Although the humble condition and poverty of this man was, at the beginning, a great hindrance for virtue to shew herself, yet such was the activity and ripeness of nature in him ; so full and ready in wit ; in judgment, discreet ; in tongue, eloquent ; in service, faithful ; in spirit, courageous ; in his pen, active ; that being conversant in the sight of men, he could not be long neglected ; nor yet be unprovided of favour and help of friends to set him forward in place and office. Neither was there any place or office for which he was not qualified. Nothing was so hard which with wit and industry he could not compass ; neither was his capacity so good, but his memory was as great in retaining whatever he had attained ; which well appears in his repeating the whole text of the New Testament, as translated by Erasmus, without any book, in his journey in going and coming from Rome.

Thus in his growing years, as he increased in age and ripeness, he derived a delight in visiting foreign countries, that he might see the world, and to learn experience. In this manner he learned such tongues and languages as might the better serve for his use hereafter.

He spent his youth at Antwerp, in the situation of secretary, or in some such condition, to the English merchants.

It happened then that the town of Boston thought good to send to Rome, to renew their two pardons ; one called the great pardon, the other the lesser pardon ; which although it should stand them in great expenses of money, (for the pope's merchandise is always dear ware,) yet they had felt such sweetness thereof, that they like good catholic merchants, and the pope's good customers, thought to spare no cost, to have their pardons renewed. Yet all this was good religion then ; such was the lamentable blindness of that time !

It being thus determined and decreed among my countrymen of Boston, to have their pardons renewed from Rome, one Geoffrey Chambers, with another, was sent, well supplied with writings and money, and with all other things considered necessary for so chargeable and costly an exploit ; who, coming in his journey to Antwerp, conferred and persuaded with Thomas Cromwell to associate himself in that legation, and to assist in the contriving of it. Cromwell, having some skill of the Italian language, and as yet not grounded in religion in those his youthful days, was content to undertake the adventure, and took his journey to Rome. Cromwell, loth to spend much time, and more loth to spend his money, and perceiving that the pope must be served with some present or other, (for without rewards there is no doing at Rome,) began to think with himself, what to devise wherein he might best serve the pope's devotion.

At length having knowledge how that the pope greatly delighted in new fangled delicacies, and dainty dishes, it came into his mind to prepare certain fine dishes of jelly, after the best English fashion, which to them of Rome was not known nor seen before.

This done, Cromwell observing his time, as the pope had returned to his pavilion from hunting, approached with his English presents brought in with a song in the English tongue, and all after the English fashion. The pope suddenly marvelling at the strangeness of the song, and understanding that they were Englishmen, and that they came not empty handed, desired them to be called in. Cromwell there shewing his obedience, and offering his junkets, such as kings and princes only, said he, in the realm of England use to feed upon, desired the same to be accepted in benevolent part, which he and his companions, as poor suitors to his holiness, had there brought and presented, as novelties meet for his recreation, &c.

Pope Julius, seeing the strangeness of the dishes, commanded, by and by, his cardinal to try them, who in tasting liked it so well, and so likewise the pope after him, that knowing what their suits were, and requiring them to make known the way for making that meat, he, without any more ado, sealed both their pardons, as well the greater as the lesser.

And thus were the pardons of the town of Boston obtained. The copy of which pardons (which I have in my hands) comes to this effect: That all the brethren and sisters of the guild of our Lady in St. Botolph's church at Boston, should have free licence to choose for their confessor or spiritual father whom they would, either secular priest, or religious person, to assoil them plenarily from all their sins, except only in cases reserved to the pope.

Also that they should have licence to carry about with them an altar-stone, whereby they might have a priest to say mass, or other divine service where they would, without prejudice of any other church or chapel, though it were also before day; yea, and at three of the clock after midnight in the summer time.

Furthermore, that all such brethren and sisters of the said guild, which should resort to the chapel of our Lady in St. Botolph's church at the feast of Easter, Whitsuntide, Corpus Christi, the Nativity or Assumption of our Lady, or in the octaves of them; the feast of St. Michael; and first sunday in Lent; should have pardon no less than if they themselves personally had visited the stations of Rome.

Provided that every such person, man or woman, entering into the same guild, at his first entrance should give to the support of seven priests, twelve choristers, and thirteen beadsmen, and to the lights of the same brotherhood, and a grammar school, six shillings and eight-pence; and for every year after twelve-pence.

And these premises being before granted by pope Innocent, and pope Julius II., these pope Clement also confirmed; granting moreover, that whatever brother or sister of the same guild, through poverty, sickness, or any other hindrance, could not resort personally to the chapel, yet he should be dispensed with, as well for that as for all other vows, irregularities, censures canonical whatsoever; only the vow of going the stations of Rome, and going to St. James of Compostella excepted, &c.

He also granted unto them power to receive full remission a pœna et culpa, once in their life; or in the hour of death.

Also, that having their altar-stone, they might have mass said in any place, though it were unhallowed. And in the time of interdict, to have mass or any sacrament ministered: and also being departed, that they might be buried with christian burial, notwithstanding the interdict.

Extending moreover his grant to all such brethren and sisters, in resorting to the chapel of our Lady upon the Nativity, or Assumption of our Lady, and giving support to the chapel, at every such school festival day to have full remission of their sins. Or, if they could not be present at the chapel, yet if they came to their own parish church, and there said one Pater-noster, and an Ave Maria, they should enjoy the same remission; or whoever came every Friday to the same chapel, should have as much remission, as if he went to the chapel of our Lady, called, "the Ladder of Heaven."

Furthermore, that whatsoever christian people, of what estate or condition soever, either spiritual or temporal, would aid and support the chamberlains or substitutes of the guild, should have five hundred years of pardon.

Also, to all brothers and sisters of the guild was granted free liberty to eat in time of Lent, or other fasting days, eggs, milk, butter, cheese, and also flesh, by the counsel of their spiritual father and physician, without any scruple of conscience.

Also, that all partakers of the guild, who, once a quarter, or every Friday or Saturday, either in the chapel in St. Botolph's church, or in any other chapel, shall say a Pater-noster, Ave Maria, and Creed, or shall say or cause to be said masses for souls departed in purgatory,

shall not only have the full remission due to them who visit the chapel of "The Ladder of Heaven," or of St. John Lateran, but also the souls in purgatory shall enjoy full remission, and be released of all their pains.

Also, that all the souls departed of the brothers and sisters of the guild, also the souls of their fathers and mothers, shall be partakers of all the prayers, suffrages, almoses, fastings, masses, and matins, pilgrimages, and all other good deeds of all the holy church militant for ever, &c.

These indulgences, pardons, grants, and relaxations were given and granted by Nicholas V. Pius II. Sixtus IV. and Julius II.; of which Julius II. it seems that Cromwell obtained this pardon about the year 1510; which pardon afterwards, through the request of king Henry VIII. in 1526, was confirmed by pope Clement VII. And thus much concerning the pardon of Boston, renewed by the means of Thomas Cromwell.

All this while it appears, that Cromwell had yet no sound taste nor judgment of religion, but was wild and youthful, without sense or regard of God and his word, as he himself was wont ofttimes to declare to Cranmer archbishop of Canterbury, shewing what he was in his young days, and how he was in the wars of the Duke of Bourbon at the siege of Rome; also what a great doer he was with Geoffrey Chambers in publishing and setting forth the pardon of Boston every where in churches as he went; and so continued, till at length by learning the text of the New Testament translated by Erasmus in his going and returning from Rome, he began to be touched and called to a better understanding.

In the meantime cardinal Thomas Wolsey began to bear a great name in England, and to rule almost all under the king, or rather with the king.

In his establishment Thomas Cromwell was advanced, and there was about the same time in the household of the cardinal, Thomas More, afterwards knight and chancellor of England, and Stephen Gardiner, afterwards bishop of Winchester. All these three were brought up in one household, and all of the same standing; their ages were also not greatly discrepant; nor their wits much unequal; so neither was their fortune and advancement greatly different. And though in More and in Gardiner there was more skill of learning, yet there was in this man a more heavenly light of the mind, and more prompt and perfect judgment, equal eloquence, and more heroical and princely disposition.

It happened that Cromwell was solicitor to the cardinal, who had then in hand the building of certain colleges in Oxford now called Christ's church. By reason whereof certain small monasteries and priories were suppressed, and the lands seized into the cardinal's hands. The doing of this was committed to Thomas Cromwell, who shewed himself so very forward and industrious, that he procured to himself much grudge with the superstitious sort, and with some also of noble calling about the king. And thus was Cromwell first set to work by the cardinal to suppress religious houses; which was about the year 1525.

After the fall of Wolsey, Cromwell was for a time in disgrace with the king, but finding that none could so well serve him against the pope, he sent for him, willing to talk with him, to hear and know what he could say.

Cromwell being informed that the king wished to talk with him, and thereupon providing before hand for the interview, he had in readiness a copy of the oath, which the bishops use to make to the pope at their consecration; and so being called for, was brought to the king in his garden at Westminster, which was about A.D. 1530.

Cromwell, after most loyal obeisance to the king, made his declaration in all points; especially making manifest to his highness that his authority was abused in his own kingdom by the pope and his clergy, who being sworn to him, were afterwards dispensed from the same, and sworn anew to the pope; so that he was but half a king, and they but half his subjects, in his own land: which, said he, was derogatory to his crown, and utterly prejudicial to the common laws of his realm. Declaring thereupon in what manner his majesty might accumulate to himself great riches, so much as all the clergy in his realm was worth, if it so pleased him to take the occasion now offered. The king giving good ear to this, and liking right well his advice, required if he could give any evidence for that which he spake. All this, he said, he could establish; and that he had the copy of the oath to the pope there present to shew; and that no less also he could prove, if his highness would give him leave; and therewith shewed the bishops' oath to the king, and also their oath to the pope.

The king, following the spirit of his counsel, took his ring off his finger, and first admitting him his service, sent him to the convocation house among the bishops. Cromwell, having the authority of the king, boldly went into the clergy house; and there placing himself among the bishops (William Warham being then archbishop) began to make his oration; declaring to them the authority of a king, and the office of subjects, and especially the obedience of bishops and churchmen to the public laws, which were necessary to provide for the profit and quiet of the commonwealth. Which laws, notwithstanding they had all transgressed, and highly offended in derogation of the king's royal estate, and falling under the law of præmunire, in that they had not only consented to the power legatine of the cardinal, but also in that they had all sworn to the pope, contrary to the fealty of their sovereign lord the king; and therefore had forfeited to the king all their goods, chattels, lands, possessions, and whatever livings they had. The bishops hearing this were not a little amazed, and first began to excuse and deny the fact. But after Cromwell had shewed to them the very copy of the oath which they had made to the pope at their consecration; the matter was thus so plain that they could not deny it; and they began to shrink and to fall to entreaty, and desiring time to pause upon the matter. The end of it was, that to be quit of that præmunire by act of parliament, they had to pay to the king no less a sum than one hundred and eighteen thousand, eight hundred and forty pounds, (A.D. 1531.)

After this, A.D. 1532, Sir Thomas Cromwell growing in great favour with the king, was made knight and master of the king's jewel-house; and shortly after was admitted also into the king's council, which was about the coming in of queen Anne Boleyn. Within two years after the same, (A.D. 1534,) he was made master of the Rolls, Dr. Tailor being discharged.

Cromwell increasing in favour and honour, after this, in the year 1537, a little before the birth of king Edward, was made knight of the garter, and not long after was advanced to the earldom of Essex, and made great chamberlain of England. Besides all which honours, he was constituted also vicegerent to the king, representing his person. Which office, although it stands well by the law, yet seldom has there been seen in it any besides this Cromwell.

Now somewhat should be said of the noble acts, the memorable examples and worthy virtues that were in him. Among which his worthy acts and manifold virtues, in this one thing above all others rises his commendation for his singular zeal and labour in restoring the church of Christ, and subverting the synagogue of antichrist, the abbeys, I mean, and religious houses of the friars and monks. For so it pleased Almighty God, by means of Lord Cromwell, to induce the king to suppress first the chantries, then the friars' houses and small monasteries, till at length all the abbeys in England, both great and small were utterly overthrown and plucked up by the roots. These acts of his, as they may give a precedent of singular zeal to all christian realms, which no prince yet to this day dare follow; so to this realm of England, it wrought such benefit, as the fruit yet remains, and will remain still in the realm of England, though we seem little to feel it.

But here I must answer the complaint of certain of our countrymen. For so I hear of many who speak of the subversion of these monasteries, as evil and wicked. The buildings, say they, might have been converted into schools and houses of learning; the goods and possessions might have been bestowed to much better and more godly use of the poor, and maintaining of hospitality.

Neither do I deny but that these things are well spoken, and could willingly embrace their opinion with my whole heart, if I did not consider a more secret meaning of God's holy providence, than at the first blush appears to all men.

And first to omit the wicked and execrable life of these religious orders, full of all vice, which were found out by the king's visitors, and in their registers recorded, so horrible to be heard, so incredible to be believed, so stinking before the face of God and man, that it is no marvel if God's vengeance from heaven would not suffer any stone or monument of these abominable houses to be left.

Whosoever finds himself aggrieved with Cromwell's suppressing these monasteries of monks and friars, let him wisely consider, First, the doctrine, laws, and traditions of these men, whom we shall find in rebellion against the religion of Christ; pernicious to our salvation; derogatory to Christ's glory; and full of much blasphemy and damnable idolatry. Secondly, let him well consider the horrible and execrable lives of the cloisterers, as appears in the rolls and registers of matters found out by inquisition in the time of king Henry VIII.; which cannot here be spoken of, unless we speak as Matthew Paris speaks of the court of Rome, "Whose filthy stink," saith he, "did breathe up a most pestiferous fume, even to the clouds of heaven," &c.

Then all things being considered, what marvel is it, if God in his just judgment did set up lord Cromwell to destroy these sinful houses, whom their own corruptions could suffer no longer to stand? And as to the dispersing of their lands and possessions, if it was agreeable to the king, to bestow these abbey lands upon his nobles and gentlemen, or to restore them again to them from whom they came, or otherwise to gratify his nobility; what was that to Cromwell? But, you say, they might have been much better employed to other more useful purposes. To this I answer, that in such a kingdom as this, where laws and parliaments are very much subject to the disposition of the prince; and where it is not certain always what princes may come; the surest way to get rid of monkery and popery was to pack it out of the realm; or at once to do with their houses and possessions as king Henry then did. For otherwise, who cannot see that in queen Mary's time, if either the houses of monks had stood, or their lands had not been otherwise disposed of into the hands of such as they were, that then many of them had been restored and replenished again with monks and friars? And if dukes, barons, and the nobility were scarce able to retain the lands and possessions of abbeys, which had been distributed to them by king Henry, from the devotion of queen Mary,—who sought again to build the walls of Jericho,—what then should the meaner sort have done, let other men conjecture. Wherefore it is not unlikely, but that God's heavenly providence did foresee and dispose these things before, in the destruction of these abbeys. Or, otherwise we might have had such numerous swarms of friars and monks in their nests again before this day in England, as that ten Cromwells afterwards could not have unhoused them.

After the power and authority of the bishop of Rome was banished out of England, the bishops of his sect never ceased to seek all occasion either to restore it again, or at least to keep upright the things which remained. It happened, that after the abolishing of the authority of the pope that certain tumults began about religion; when it seemed good to king Henry that an assembly of learned men and bishops should be appointed, who should soberly and modestly consider and determine those things which pertained to religion. All the learned men, but especially the bishops, to whom this matter seemed chiefly to belong, having assembled, Cromwell purposed also to be present himself at this convocation, and meeting by chance with Alexander Alesse, a Scotchman, brought him with him to the convocation house, where all the bishops were assembled together, (A.D. 1537.) The bishops and prelates, who were waiting for the coming of Cromwell, as he came in, rose up and did obeisance to him as to their vicar-general;

and he again saluted every one in their degree, and sate down in the highest place at the table, according to his degree and office ; and after him every bishop in his order, and doctors. First over against him sate the archbishop of Canterbury; then the archbishop of York; the bishops of London, Lincoln, Salisbury, Bath, Ely, Hereford, Chichester, Norwich, Rochester, Worcester, &c. There Cromwell, in the name of the king, (whose secret councillor he was, and lord privy seal, and vicar-general of the realm) spake these words as follows :—

" Right reverend fathers in Christ : The king's majesty gives you high thanks that you have so diligently, without any excuse, assembled hither according to his commandment. And you are not ignorant that you are called hither to determine certain controversies, which at this time are moved concerning the christian religion and faith, not only in this realm, but also in all nations throughout the world. For the king studies day and night to promote quietness in the church ; and he cannot rest until all such controversies are fully debated and ended, through the determination of you and his whole parliament. For although his special desire is to set a stay for the unlearned people, whose consciences are in doubt what they may believe, and he himself by his excellent learning knows these controversies well enough ; yet he will suffer no common alteration but by the consent of you and his whole parliament. By which you may perceive his high wisdom, and also his great love towards you. And he desires you, for Christ's sake, that all malice, obstinacy, and carnal respect set apart, you will friendly and lovingly dispute among yourselves of the controversies moved in the church, and that you will conclude all things by the word of God, without any brawling or scolding ; neither will his majesty suffer the scriptures to be wrested and defaced by any glosses ; any papistical laws ; or by any authority of doctors or councils ; and much less will he admit any articles or doctrine not contained in the scriptures, but approved only by continuance of time and old custom, and by unwritten verities, as you were wont to do. You know well enough that you are bound to shew this service to Christ, and to his church, and yet his majesty will give you high thanks, if you will establish and conclude a godly and a perfect unity : whereunto this is the only way and means, if you will determine all things by the scriptures, as God commands you in Deuteronomy ; which thing his majesty exhorts and desires you to do.''

When Cromwell had finished his speech, the bishops rose up altogether, giving thanks to the king's majesty, not only for his great zeal towards the church of Christ, but also for his most godly exhortation, so worthy of a christian prince.

Then they immediately commenced the disputation ; when Stokesley, bishop of London, the first of all, being the most earnest champion and maintainer of the Romish decrees, (whom Cromwell a little before had checked by name, for defending unwritten verities,) endeavoured out of the old school glosses, to maintain the seven sacraments of the church ; the archbishop of York, the bishops of Lincoln, Bath, Chichester, and Norwich, also favoured his part. On the contrary part, was the archbishop of Canterbury, the bishops of Salisbury, Ely, Hereford, Worcester, with many others.

After much communication on both sides, and after a long controversy about the testimony of the doctors, who, as it seemed to them, dissented and disagreed among themselves, the archbishop of Canterbury, at last, spoke as follows :

" It becomes not men of learning and gravity to make much babbling and brawling about bare words, so that we agree in the very substance and effect of the matter. For to brawl about words is the property of sophisters, and such as mean deceit and subtlety, who delight in the debate and dissension of the world, and in the miserable state of the church ; and not of them who should seek the glory of Christ ; and should study for the unity and quietness of the church. There are weighty controversies now moved and put forth, not of ceremonies and light things, but of the true understanding, and of the right difference of the law and of the gospel ; of the manner and way how sins are forgiven ; of comforting doubtful and wavering consciences, by what means they may be certified that they please God ; seeing they feel the strength of the law accusing them of sin ; of the true use of the sacraments, whether the outward work of them doth justify man, or whether we receive our justification by faith. Also, which are the good works, and the true service and honour which please God ; and whether the choice of meats, the difference of garments, the vows of monks and priests, and other traditions which have not the word of God to confirm them ; whether these, I say, are right good works, and such as make a perfect christian man, or not ? Also, whether vain service and false honouring of God, and man's traditions, bind men's consciences, or not ? Finally, whether the ceremony of confirmation, of orders, and of annealing, and such others (which cannot be proved to be instituted of Christ, nor have any word in them to certify us of remission of sins) ought to be called sacraments, and to be compared with baptism and the supper of the Lord, or not?

" These are no light matters, but even the principal points of our christian religion. Wherefore we contend not about words and titles, but about high and earnest matters. Christ saith, ' Blessed are the peacemakers, for they shall be called the children of God.' And St. Paul, writing unto Timothy, commands bishops to avoid brawling and contention about words, which are profitable to nothing but unto the subversion and destruction of the hearers ; and admonishes him especially, that he should resist with the scriptures, when any man disputes with him of the faith ; and he adds a cause where he says, ' Doing this thou shalt save both thyself, and them who hear thee.' Now, if you will follow these counsellors, Christ and St. Paul, all contention and brawling about words must be set apart, and you must establish a godly and a perfect unity and concord out of the scriptures. Wherefore in this disputation we must first agree on the number of the sacraments, and what a sacrament signifies by the holy scriptures ; and when we call baptism and the supper of the Lord, sacraments of the gospel, we must decide what we mean thereby. I know right well that St. Ambrose and other authors call the washing of the disciples' feet and other things, sacraments, which I am sure you yourselves would not suffer to be numbered among the other sacraments.''

When he had ended his speech, Cromwell commanded Alesse, who stood by, to give his mind and opinion, declaring first to the bishops that he was the king's scholar, and therefore desired them to hear him.

Alesse. after he had first done his obeisance to the lord Cromwell, and to the other prelates of the church, then spoke as follows :

" Right honourable and noble lord ; and you most reverend fathers and prelates of the church ; although I come unprepared to this disputation, yet trusting in the aid of Christ, who promises to give both mouth and wisdom to us when we are questioned of our faith, I will utter my judgment of this disputation. And I think that my lord archbishop hath given you a profitable exhortation, that you should first agree on the signification of a sacrament, and whether you will call a sacrament a ceremony instituted of Christ in the gospel, or merely to signify a special or a singular virtue of the gospel, and of godliness (as St. Paul names remission of sins to be) ; or whether you mean every ceremony generally, which may be a token, or a signification of a holy thing, to be a sacrament ? For according to this latter signification, I will not object to grant to you that there are seven sacraments, and more too, if you will. But yet St. Paul seems to describe a sacrament after the just signification, where he saith, " That circumcision is a seal of the righteousness of faith.'' This definition of one particular sacrament must be understood to appertain to all sacraments generally; for the Jews had but one sacrament only. And he describes baptism after the same manner, in Ephesians v. 26, 'That Christ might sanctify the church, and cleanse it with the washing of water by the word.' For here also he adds the word and promise of God unto the ceremony. And Christ also requires faith where he says, 'Whosoever believeth and is baptized shall be saved.'

"And St. Augustine describes a sacrament thus:— 'The word of God coming into the element maketh the sacrament.' And in another place he says, 'A sacrament is a thing wherein the power of God, under the form of visible things, doth work secretly salvation.' And the 'Master of the Sentences' doth describe a sacrament no otherwise: 'A sacrament,' says he, 'is an invisible grace, and hath a visible form; and by this invisible grace I mean remission of sins.' Finally, St. Thomas denies that any man has authority to institute a sacrament. Now if you agree to this definition of a sacrament, it is an easy thing to judge of the number of those sacraments which have the manifest word of God, and are instituted by Christ, to signify unto us the remission of our sins."

When Alesse had concluded, after a learned account of the judgment of St. Augustine, the bishop of London, who could scarcely refrain himself all the while, broke out in this manner: "First of all," said he, "where you allege, that all the sacraments which are in the church were instituted by Christ himself, and have either some manifest ground in the scriptures, or ought to shew some signification of remission of sin, it is false, and not to be allowed."

Then said Alesse, that he would prove it, not only by manifest authorities of scripture, but also by evident testimonies of ancient doctors and school-writers.

But the bishop of Hereford (who had then lately returned from Germany, where he had been ambassador from the king to the protestants), being moved with the bishop of London's frowardness, turning himself first to Alesse, desired him not to contend with the bishop in such manner, by the testimonies of doctors and schoolmen; forasmuch as they do not all agree; neither are they steadfast among themselves in all points; but vary; and in many points are utterly repugnant. Wherefore if this disputation shall be decided by their minds and verdicts, there shall be nothing established. Furthermore, we are commanded by the king, that these controversies should be determined only by the rule and judgment of the scriptures. This he spoke to Alesse. Then turning himself to the bishops, he likewise admonished them in a grave speech, as follows:—

"Think you," said he, "that we can by any sophistical subtleties steal out of the world again the light which every man sees? Christ hath so lightened the world at this time, that the light of the gospel hath put to flight all misty darkness, and it will shortly have the higher hand of all clouds, though we resist in vain ever so much. The lay-people do now know the holy scriptures much better than many of us. And the Germans have made the text of the Bible so plain and easy by the Hebrew and Greek tongues, that now many things may be better understood without any glosses at all, than by all the commentaries of the doctors. And they have so opened these controversies by their writings, that women and children may wonder at the blindness and falsehood that has been hitherto. Wherefore you must consider earnestly what you will determine in these controversies, that you make not yourselves to be mocked and laughed to scorn of all the world; and that you bring them not to have this opinion of you, to think that you have neither one spark of learning, nor yet of godliness in you. And thus shall you lose all your estimation and authority with them, who before took you for learned men and profitable members to the commonwealth of Christendom. For that which you hope for, that there was never a heresy in the church so great, but that process of time with the power and authority of the pope, has quenched it, is nothing to the purpose. But you must change your opinion, and think, that there is nothing so feeble and weak, so that it be true; but it shall find place, and be able to stand against all falsehood. Truth is the daughter of Time, and Time is the mother of Truth. And whoever is besieged by truth cannot long continue; and upon whose side truth stands, that ought not to be thought transitory; or that it will ever fail. All things consist not in painted eloquence, and strength or authority. For the truth is of so great power, strength, and efficacy, that it can neither be defeated with words, nor be overcome by any strength; but after she has hidden herself for a long time, at length she puts up her head and appears, as it is written in Esdras, 'A king is strong; wine is strong; yet women are more strong; but truth excelleth all.'" 1 Esdras iv.

To this effect, and much more, did he speak and utter in that convocation, both copiously and discreetly. Through whose speech Alesse, being encouraged, proceeded further, to urge the bishop with arguments.

When he had spoken, the bishop of London interrupted him, and said, "Let us grant that the sacraments may be gathered out of the word of God; yet you are deceived if you think that there is no other word of God. And if you think that nothing pertains to the christian faith, but that only which is written in the Bible, then you err plainly with the Lutherans; for St. John saith, 'that Jesus did many things which are not written.' John xxi. 25. And St. Paul commands the Thessalonians to observe and keep certain unwritten traditions and ceremonies. Moreover, he himself did preach not the scriptures only, but even also the traditions of the elders. Finally, we have received many things of the doctors and councils, which, although they are not written in the Bible, yet we ought to grant that we received them of the apostles; and that they are of like authority with the scriptures; and finally, that they may worthily be called the unwritten word of God."

Now, when the lord Cromwell, the archbishop, with the other bishops, who defended the pure doctrine of the gospel, heard this, they smiled a little one to another, as they saw him fly off, even in the very beginning of the disputation, to his old rusty sophistry and unwritten verities. Then Alesse would have proceeded further to have confuted these sophistries, but the lord Cromwell bade him be content; and so he made an end with this protestation. "Right reverend bishop, you deny that our christian faith and religion leans only upon the word of God, which is written in the Bible: which, if I can prove and declare, then you will grant me that there are no sacraments but those that have the word of God to confirm them." To this he consented, and then immediately the assembly was dissolved for that day.

The next day, when the bishops had met, the archbishop of Canterbury sent his archdeacon, and commanded Alesse to abstain from any further disputation. Whereupon he wrote his mind, and delivered it to Cromwell, who afterwards shewed the same unto the bishops. Thus, through the industry of Cromwell, the discussions were brought to this end; that although religion could not then wholly be reformed, yet at that time there was some reformation throughout all England.

How desirous and studious this Cromwell was in the cause of Christ's religion, examples need not be brought. His whole life was nothing else but a continual care how to advance the right knowledge of the gospel, and to reform the house of God. He caused the people to be instructed in the Lord's prayer and in the apostles' creed in English. He also procured the scriptures to be translated and set forth in the same language, so that they might be read and understood by every Englishman: after that, to rescue the vulgar people from damnable idolatry, he caused certain of the grossest places of pilgrimage to be destroyed. And further, for the benefit of the poorer sort, who get their living by their daily labour, and by the work of their hands, he provided that various idle holydays should be abolished. He procured for them liberty to eat eggs and white meat in Lent. It was by him also provided, for the better instruction of the people, that beneficed men should be resident in their cures and parishes, to teach and to keep hospitality; as well as many other regulations for the reformation of religion: as by the proclamations, injunctions, and necessary articles of christian doctrine, which were set forth, by his means, in the king's name, may more abundantly appear.

It would require a long discourse to add his private benefits in helping good men and women out of troubles and great distresses; his whole life was full of such examples, being a man ordained of God to do many men good; and especially such as were in danger of persecution for religion's sake.

It were long to recite what innumerable benefits this worthy counsellor wrought and brought to pass in the realm, and especially in the church of England; what good orders he established; what wickedness he suppressed; what corruptions he reformed; what abuses he brought to light; what crafty jugglings; what idolatrous deceptions, and superstitious delusions he detected and abolished out of the church. What will posterity think of the church of the pope, which, for so many years, abused the people's eyes with an old rotten stock (called the Rood of Grace) in which were one hundred wires to make the image goggle with the eyes; to nod with the head; to hang the lip; to move and shake his jaws, according to the value of the gift which was offered? If it were a small piece of silver he would hang a frowning lip; if it were a piece of gold, then would his jaws go merrily! Thus miserably were the people of Christ abused; their souls seduced; their senses beguiled; and their purses spoiled; until this idolatrous forgery was disclosed by Cromwell's means, and the image, with all its machinery, openly exhibited at St. Paul's cross, and there torn in pieces by the people. The same was done with the blood of Hales, which, in the same way, was brought by Cromwell to St. Paul's cross, and there proved to be the blood of a duck!

What shall I speak of Darvel Gartheren; of the Rood of Chester, of Thomas Becket; our Lady of Walsingham; with an infinite multitude of the same kind? All which stocke and blocks of cursed idolatry Cromwell removed out of the way of the people, that they might walk more safely in the sincere service of Almighty God.

While the Lord Cromwell was thus occupied in profiting the commonwealth, and purging the church of Christ, it happened to him, as commonly it does to all good men, that where any virtue appears, there envy creeps in, and where true piety seeks most after Christ, there some persecution follows.

This, I say, as he was labouring in the commonwealth and doing good to the poor afflicted saints, and helping them out of trouble, the malice of his enemies was continually employed in hunting out for matter against him, and in this they never ceased, till in the end, by false trains and crafty surmises, they brought him out of the king's favour.

The chief and principal enemy against him was Stephen Gardiner bishop of Winchester; who, ever envying the state and felicity of the Lord Cromwell, and taking his occasion by the marriage of Lady Anne of Cleves being a stranger and foreigner, whispered in the king's ears what a perfect thing it would be to the quiet of the realm, and establishment of the king's succession, to have an English queen, and a prince purely English; so that the king's affection, the more it was diminished from Anne of Cleves, the less favour he bare to Cromwell.

After this, in the month of April 1540, was held a parliament, which after divers prorogations was continued till the month of July. In which month the Lord Cromwell being in the council-chamber, was suddenly apprehended and committed to the Tower. Many good men lamented and prayed heartily for him; so there were others on the contrary that rejoiced, especially of the religious sort, and of the clergy, such as had been of some dignity before in the church, and now by his means were put from it. For such was his nature, that in all his doings he could not abide any kind of popery, or false religion under the garb of hypocrisy, and less could

he abide the ambitious pride of popish prelacy, which while professing deep humility was so elated with pride, that kings could not rule in their own realms for them. These prelates he never could abide; so on the other hand they hated him as much, which was the cause of the shortening of his days; for he was afterwards attainted by parliament.

In the attainder many crimes, surmises, and accusations were brought against him; but chiefly and above all others he was charged and accused of heresy, as a supporter of them whom they accounted heretics; as Barnes, Clark, and others, whom, by his authority and letters written to sheriffs and justices, he had discharged out of prison. Also that he did disperse abroad among the king's subjects a great number of books, containing, as they said, manifest heresy; that he caused to be translated into our English tongue books comprising matter expressly against the sacrament of the altar; and that after the translation, he commended and maintained the same for good and christian doctrine. Over and besides all this, they brought in certain witnesses who especially charged him with having spoken words against the king in the church of St. Peter the Poor, in the month of March, in the thirtieth year of the king's reign (1539); which, if true, there are three things I have much to marvel at. First, if his adversaries had such sure matter against him, then what should move them to make such haste to have him dispatched out of the way, and not allow him to come to his purgation? Secondly, if the words had been so heinous against the king as his enemies pretend, why then did those witnesses who heard the words conceal such treason for the space of almost two years? Thirdly, if the king had known and believed these words to be true, and that Cromwell had indeed been such a traitor to his person, why then did the king so shortly afterwards lament his death, wishing to have Cromwell alive again? What prince will wish the life of him whom he undoubtedly suspects to have been a traitor to his life and person?

So long as Cromwell went with full sail of fortune, how moderately and how temperately he always bore himself, hath been declared before. So now the Lord Cromwell, being overthrown by the contrary wind of adversity, received the same with no less constancy and patience of a christian heart; nor yet was he so unprovided with counsel, but that he foresaw this tempest long before it fell, and prepared for it; for two years before, suspecting the conspiracy of his adversaries, and fearing what might happen, he called his servants, and there shewing to them in what a slippery state he stood, and also perceiving some stormy weather to gather already, required them to look diligently to their order and doings, lest through their fault any occasion might arise against him. And before the time of his apprehension, he introduced such order among his servants, that many of them, especially the younger, who had little else to take to, had left for them in their friends' hands means to relieve them, whatever should befal him. Cromwell was such a loving and kind master to his servants, that he provided beforehand almost for them all; insomuch that he gave to twelve children who were his musicians, twenty pounds a piece, and so committed them to their friends.

When a prisoner in the Tower, it is worthy noting how quietly he bare it; how valiantly he behaved himself; how gravely and discreetly he answered the commissioners sent to him. Whatever articles and interrogatories they propounded, they could put nothing to him, either concerning matters ecclesiastical or temporal, wherein he was not more ripened and more furnished in every condition than they themselves.

Among the rest of those commissioners who came to him, there was one whom the Lord Cromwell desired to carry for him a letter to the king, who, when he refused, by saying that he would carry no letter to the king from a traitor; then the Lord Cromwell desired him at least to convey from him a message to the king. To that the other was content, so that it were not against his allegiance. Then the Lord Cromwell taking witness of the other lords what he had promised, "You shall commend me," said he, " to the king, and tell him that when he has so well tried, and thoroughly proved you as I have done, he will find you as false a man as ever came about him."

Besides this, he wrote a letter from the Tower to the king; and when none durst take the carriage of it, Sir R. Sadler, whom he had preferred to the king before, being ever trusty and faithful to him, went to the king to understand his pleasure, whether he would permit him to bring the letter or not; which, when the king granted, Sadler presented the letter, which he commanded thrice to be read to him; so much did the king seem to be moved therewith.

Notwithstanding, by reason of the act of parliament before passed, the worthy and noble lord Cromwell, oppressed by his enemies, and condemned in the Tower, and not coming to his answer, was brought to the scaffold on Tower Hill, on the 28th day of July 1540, when he said these words:—

" I am come hither to die, and not to clear myself, as some think perhaps that I will. For if I should do so, I would be a very wretch. I am by the law condemned to die, and thank my Lord God that appointed me this death for mine offence. For since the time that I have had years of discretion, I have lived a sinner, and offended my Lord God, for which I ask him heartily forgiveness. And it is not unknown to many of you, that I have been a great traveller in this world, and being but of a base degree, was called to high estate; and since the time I came thereto, I have offended my prince, for which I ask him heartily forgiveness, and beseech you all to pray to God with me, that He will forgive me. And now I pray you that are here to bear me record, that I die in the catholic faith, not doubting in any article of my faith; no, nor doubting in any sacrament of the church. Many have slandered me, and reported that I have been a bearer of such as have maintained evil opinions, which is untrue. But I confess, that like as God by his Holy Spirit doth instruct us in the truth, so the devil is ready to seduce us, and I have been seduced; but bear me witness that I die in the catholic faith of the holy church: and I heartily desire you to pray for the king's grace, that he may long live with you in health and prosperity; and that after him, his son, prince Edward, that goodly child, may long reign over you. And once again I desire you to pray for me, that so long as life remains in this flesh, I may waver nothing in my faith." And so making his prayer, kneeling on his knees, he spake these words.

" O Lord Jesus, who art the only health of all men living, and the everlasting life of them who die in thee; I, a wretched sinner, do submit myself wholly unto thy most blessed will, and being sure that the thing cannot perish which is committed unto thy mercy, willingly now I leave this frail and wicked flesh, in sure hope that thou wilt in better wise restore it to me again at the last day in the resurrection of the just. I beseech thee most merciful Lord Jesus Christ, that thou wilt by thy grace make strong my soul against all temptation, and defend me with the buckler of thy mercy against all the assaults of the devil. I see and acknowledge that there is in myself no hope of salvation, but all my confidence, hope and trust is in thy most merciful goodness. I have no merits nor good works which I may allege before thee. Of sins and evil works, alas! I see a great heap; but yet, through thy mercy, I trust to be in the number of them to whom thou wilt not impute their sins; but wilt take and accept me for righteous and just, and to be the inheritor of everlasting life. Thou, merciful Lord, wast born for my sake; thou didst suffer both hunger and thirst for my sake; thou didst teach, pray, and fast for my sake; all thy holy actions and works thou wroughtest for my sake; thou sufferedst most grievous pains and torments for my sake; finally, thou gavest thy most precious body and thy blood to be shed on the cross for my sake. Now, most merciful Saviour, let all these things profit me, which thou hast thyself given for me. Let thy blood cleanse and wash away the spots and fulness of my sins. Let thy righteousness hide and

cover my unrighteousness. Let the merits of thy passion and blood-shedding be satisfaction for my sins. Give me, Lord, thy grace, that the faith of my salvation in thy blood waver not in me, but may ever be firm and constant. That the hope of thy mercy and life everlasting may never decay in me; that love wax not cold in me. Finally, that the weakness of my flesh be not overcome with the fear of death. Grant me, merciful Saviour, that when death hath shut up the eyes of my body, yet the eyes of my soul may still behold and look upon thee; and when death hath taken away the use of my tongue, yet may my heart cry and say unto thee, Lord, into thy hands I commend my soul; Lord Jesus, receive my spirit." Amen.

And thus, his prayer made, after he had godly and lovingly exhorted them that were about him on the scaffold, he quietly committed his soul into the hands of God, and so patiently suffered the stroke of the executioner.

Of the Bible in English, printed in the large volume; and of Edmund Bonner preferred to the bishoprick of London, by the means of the Lord Cromwell.

About the time when Edmund Bonner, bishop of Hereford, and ambassador to France, was first nominated and preferred by means of the lord Cromwell to the bishoprick of London, it happened, in November, 1539, that Cromwell procured of the king his gracious letters to the French king, to permit and license a subject of his to print the bible in English in the university of Paris, because paper was there more meet and apt to be had than in the realm of England, and also that there were more good workmen for the dispatch of the same. And the king wrote to his ambassador, who then was Edmund Bonner, in Paris, that he should aid and assist in the work. The bishop outwardly shewed great friendship to the printers; and he was so fervent, that he caused the Englishmen to put in print a New Testament in English and Latin, and himself took a great many of them, and paid for them, and gave them to his friends. And it chanced in the mean time, while the bible was printing, that king Henry VIII. preferred Bonner from the bishoprick of Hereford to be bishop of London; at which time Bonner, according to the statute law of England, took his oath to the king, acknowledging his supremacy, and called one of the Englishmen that printed the Bible, whom he then loved, although afterwards upon the change of the world he did hate him as much, whose name was Richard Grafton; to whom Bonner said, when he took his oath, " Master Grafton, so it is, that the king's most excellent majesty has by his gracious gift presented me to the bishoprick of London, for which I am sorry; for if it would have pleased his grace, I could have been well content to have kept mine old bishoprick of Hereford." Then said Grafton, " I am right glad to hear of it, and so I am sure will be a great number of the city of London; for though they do not know you, yet they have heard so much goodness of you, that they will be glad." Then said Bonner, " I pray God I may content them. And to tell you, Master Grafton, before God, (for that was commonly his oath,) the greatest fault that ever I found in Stokesley was, that he vexed and troubled poor men, as Lobeley the bookbinder and others, for having the scriptures in English; and, God willing, he did not so much hinder it as I will further it, and I will have set up in the church of St. Paul's at least six of the bibles, and I will pay you honestly for them, and give hearty thanks. But now I have especially called you to witness, that upon this translation of the bishops' sees, I must, according to the statute, take an oath to the king's majesty, acknowledging his supremacy, which, before God, I take with my heart, and so think him to be; and I beseech Almighty God to save him, and long to prosper his grace. Hold the book, Sir, and read you the oath," (said he to one of his chaplains,) and he laid his hand on the book, and so he took his oath: and after this he shewed great friendship to Grafton, and to his partner Edward Whitchurch, but especially to Miles Coverdale, who was the corrector of the great Bible.

After the king's letters were delivered, the French

king gave very good words, and was well contented to permit the work; and so the printer went forward and printed the book even to the last part, and then a quarrel was picked against the printer, and he was sent for to the inquisitors, and there charged with articles of heresy. Then the Englishmen were sent for that were at the cost and charge, and also such as had the correction of the same, who was Miles Coverdale; but having some warning what would follow, the Englishmen posted away as fast as they could to save themselves, leaving behind them all their Bibles, which were to the number of two thousand five hundred, called the Bibles of the great volume, and never recovered any of them, save that the lieutenant-criminal having them delivered to him to burn in Paris, sold some of them to a haberdasher to fold caps in, and those were bought again; but the rest were burned, to the great loss of those that bore the charge. But notwithstanding the loss, after they had recovered some of the books, and were comforted and encouraged by the lord Cromwell, the Englishmen went again to Paris, and there got the presses, letters, and servants of the printer, and brought them to London; and there they became printers themselves, (which before they never intended,) and printed out the Bible in London, and after that printed several impressions of them; but yet not without great trouble and loss, for the hatred of the bishops, namely, Gardiner and his fellows.

Here by the way, let me request the reader to note and understand, that in those days there were two Bibles in English, bearing different titles, and printed in different places: the first was called Thomas Mathews' bible, printed at Hamburgh, about A.D. 1532, the corrector of which was then John Rogers. The printers were Richard Grafton and Whitchurch. In the translation of this bible the greatest helper was William Tindal, who, with the help of Miles Coverdale had translated all the books, except the Apocrypha, and certain notes in the margin, which were added after. But as William Tindal was apprehended before this Bible was fully perfected, it was thought good to change the name of William Tindal, because that name was then odious, and to further it by a strange name of Thomas Mathews, John Rogers at the same time being corrector to the press, who had then translated the rest of the Apocrypha, and added also certain notes in the margin; and therefore it came to be called Thomas Mathews' Bible. Which Bible of Thomas Mathews, after it was printed and presented to the lord Cromwell, and the lord Cranmer archbishop of Canterbury, who both liked it very well, Cromwell presented it to the king; and obtained that it might be read freely by his majesty's subjects; so that there was printed upon the book one line in red letters, with these words, "Set forth with the King's most gracious Licence."

After the restraint of this Bible of Mathews, another Bible began to be printed at Paris, (A.D. 1540,) which was called "The Bible of the large Volume." The printers were Richard Grafton and Whitchurch, who bore the charges. The lord Cromwell was a great helper. The chief overseer was Miles Coverdale, who taking the translation of Tindal, compared it with the Hebrew, and amended many things.

After this the bishops, bringing their purpose to pass, brought the lord Cromwell out of favour, and shortly to death; and not long after, great complaint was made to the king against the translation of the Bible; and of the preface; and then was the sale of the Bible commanded to be stayed, the bishops promising to amend and correct it; but they never performed their promise. Then Grafton was called, and charged with the printing of Mathews' Bible; but he being fearful of trouble, made excuses for himself in all things. Then he was examined of the great Bible, and what notes he was to make. To which he answered, that he knew none. For his purpose was to have retained learned men to have made the notes; but when he perceived the king's majesty and his clergy not willing to have any, he proceeded no further. But for all these excuses Grafton was sent to the Fleet, and there remained six weeks; and before he came out was bound in three hundred pounds

that he should neither sell, nor print, nor cause to be printed, any more Bibles, until the king and the clergy should agree upon a translation. And thus was the Bible from that time stayed, during the remainder of the reign of King Henry VIII.

But yet one thing more is to be noted, that after the printers had lost their Bibles, they continued suitors to Bonner, to be a means to obtain of the French king their books again; but they continued suitors, and Bonner ever fed them with fair words, promising them much, but doing nothing for them, till at last Bonner was discharged of his embassay, and returned home, where he was welcomed by the lord Cromwell, who loved him dearly, and had a marvellous good opinion of him. And so long as Cromwell remained in authority, so long was Bonner at his beck, and friend to his friends, and enemy to his enemies: as he was at that time to Gardiner bishop of Winchester, who never favoured Cromwell, and therefore Bonner could not favour him; so he and Winchester were the greatest enemies that could be. But so soon as Cromwell fell, immediately Bonner and Winchester pretended to be the greatest friends that lived; and not a good word could Bonner speak of Cromwell, but used the vilest and bitterest that he could speak, calling him the rankest heretic that ever lived; and then such as Bonner knew to have been in good favour with Cromwell, he could never abide their sight. Insomuch, the very next day after Cromwell was apprehended, Grafton, who before had been very familiar with Bonner, met him suddenly, and said to him, That he was sorry to hear of the news that was abroad. "What is that?" said he. "Of the apprehension of lord Cromwell," replied Grafton. "Are you sorry for that?" said he; "it had been good that he had been dispatched long ago." With that Grafton knew not what to say; but came no more to Bonner. However, afterwards, Grafton being charged for the printing of a ballad made in favour of Cromwell, was called before the council, where Bonner was present; and there Bonner charged him with the words that he spake to him of Cromwell, and gave a long account of the matter. But lord Audley, who was then lord chancellor, discreetly and honourably cut off the matter, and entered into other talk.

The History of Doctor Robert Barnes, Thomas Gerrard, and William Jerome, Divines.

As in battles the chief point of victory consists in the safety of the general or captain: even so when the valiant standard-bearer and stay of the church of England, Thomas Cromwell, was taken out of the way, miserable slaughter of good men and good women ensued. For Winchester, having now got his full purpose, and free course to exercise his cruelty, it was wonderful to see what troubles he raised in the Lord's vineyard. And lest by delay he might lose the occasion offered, he straightway made his first assaults upon Robert Barnes, Thomas Gerrard, and William Jerome, whom, within two days after Cromwell's death, he caused to be executed. First of all we will speak of Dr. Barnes, whose particular history here follows:

This Barnes, after he came from the University of Louvain, went to Cambridge, where he was made prior and master of the house of the Augustines. At that time the knowledge of good letters was scarcely entered into the University. Barnes having a taste for good learning and authors, began to read Terence, Plautus, and Cicero; so that what with his industry, pains, and labour, he caused the university shortly to flourish with good letters, and made a great part of the students learned. After those foundations had been laid, then he read openly St. Paul's epistles, because he would have Christ and his holy word taught there; and thereby in a short time he made some good divines. The same order of disputation which he kept in his house, he observed likewise in the university abroad, where he disputed with any man in the common schools. The first man that answered Dr. Barnes in the scriptures, was Master Stafford, on being examined for his form to be a bachelor of divinity, which disputation was marvellous in the sight of the doctors, and joyful to the godly in spirit.

Thus Barnes, with his reading, disputation, and preaching, became famous and mighty in the scriptures, always preaching against bishops and hypocrites; and yet did not see his inward and outward idolatry, which he both taught and maintained, till that good Master Bilney with others, (as is related in the life of Master Bilney,) converted him wholly to Christ.

The first sermon that ever he preached of this truth was on the Sunday before Christmas day, at St. Edward's church, belonging to Trinity Hall in Cambridge. For that sermon he was immediately accused of heresy by two fellows of the King's Hall. Then the godly and learned in Christ, both of Pembroke Hall, St. John's, Peter's House, Queen's College, the King's College, Gunwel Hall, and Benet College, shewed themselves, and flocked together openly, both in the schools and at sermons in St. Mary's; and at the Austins; and at other disputations; and then they conferred continually together.

At this time much trouble began to ensue. The adversaries of Barnes accused him in the Regent-house before the vice-chancellor; and presented articles against him; to these he promised to make answer at the next convocation. Then Nottoris, a violent enemy to Christ, moved Barnes to recant; but he refused to do so, until within six days of Shrovetide. Then suddenly there was sent down to Cambridge a sergeant-at-arms, who arrested Dr. Barnes openly in the convocation-house, to make all others afraid.

But good Dr. Farman, of Queen's College, sent word to the chambers of those that were suspected of possessing Luther's books, who were in number thirty persons. But, God be praised, they were conveyed away by the time that the sergeant-at-arms, the vice-chancellor, and the proctors were at every man's chamber. In the morning he was carried by the sergeant-at-arms to cardinal Wolsey, at Westminster; and there-after waiting all day, he could not speak with him till night. Then by reason of Doctor Gardiner, secretary to the cardinal, and Master Fox, master of the Wards, he spake the same night with the cardinal in his chamber of estate, kneeling on his knees. Then said the cardinal to them, "Is this Dr. Barnes, your man that is accused of heresy?" "Yea, and please your grace, and we trust you shall find him reformable, for he is both well learned and wise." "What, Master Doctor," said the cardinal, "had you not a sufficient scope in the scriptures to teach the people; but that my golden shoes, my pillars, my golden cushions, my crosses did so offend you, that you must make us ridiculous amongst the people? We were that day laughed to scorn. Verily it was a sermon more fit to be preached on a stage than in a pulpit." And he answered, "I spake nothing but the truth out of the scriptures, according to my conscience, and according to the old doctors;" and then he delivered him six sheets of paper written, to confirm and corroborate his statements.

He received them smiling, saying, "We perceive, then, that you intend to stand to your articles, and to shew your learning."

"Yea," said Barnes, "that I do intend, by God's grace, with your lordship's favour." He answered, "I will ask you a question: Whether do you think it more necessary that I should have all this royalty, because I represent the king's majesty's person in all the high courts of this realm, to the terror and keeping down of all rebellious treasons, traitors, all the wicked and corrupt members of this commonwealth; or to be as simple as you would have us; to sell all these things, and to give it to the poor; and to throw away this majesty of a princely dignity, which is a terror to all the wicked?" He answered; "I think it necessary that it be sold and given to the poor. For this is not comely for your calling; nor is the king's majesty maintained by your pomp and poll-axes, but by God."

Then answered he: "Lo, master doctors, here is the learned wise man that you told me of." Then they

kneeling down, said, "We desire your grace to be good unto him, for he will be reformable."

Then said he; "Stand you up; for your sakes and the university we will be good unto him. How say you, master doctor, do you not know that I am a legate, and that I am able to dispense in all matters concerning religion within this realm, as much as the pope may?" He said; "I know it to be so." "Will you then be ruled by us, and we will do all things for your welfare, and for the welfare of the university?" He answered; "I thank your grace for your good will: I will abide by the holy scriptures, according to the simple talent that God has lent me." "Well," said he, "thou shalt have thy learning tried to the utmost, and thou shalt have the law."

Then he required him that he might have justice with equity; and forthwith he would have been sent to the Tower; but Gardiner and Fox became his sureties that night; and so he returned to Mr. Parnel's house, where he commenced writing again, and slept not; Master Coverdale, Master Goodwin, and Master Field, being his writers; and in the morning he came to Gardiner and Fox, and was committed to the sergeant-at-arms to bring him into the chapter-house at Westminster, before the bishops and the abbot of Westminster.

At the same time, when Doctor Barnes was to appear before the cardinal, there were five men to be examined for Luther's book and Lollardy; but after they saw Barnes they set the other aside, and asked the sergeant-at-arms what was his errand. He said he had brought one Doctor Barnes to be examined of heresy, and presented both his articles and his accusers. Then immediately after a little talk, they sware him, and laid his articles to him. Then they called the master of the Fleet, and he and five others were committed to the Fleet. Then they called Doctor Barnes again, and asked him whether he would subscribe to his articles or not; and he subscribed willingly; when they committed him and young Master Parnel to the Fleet also with the others. There they remained till Saturday morning, and the warden of the Fleet was commanded that no man should speak with Barnes.

On the Saturday he came again into the chapter-house, and there remained till five o'clock at night. And after long disputations, threatenings, and scornings, about five o'clock at night they called him, to know whether he would abjure or be burned. He was then in a great agony, and thought rather to burn than to abjure. But afterwards he was persuaded rather to abjure than to burn. Upon that, falling upon his knees, he consented to abjure, and the abjuration being put into his hand, he abjured as it was there written, and then he subscribed it with his own hand; and yet they would scarcely receive him into the bosom of the church as they termed it. Then they put him to his oath, and charged him to execute, do, and fulfil all that they commanded him; and he promised so to do.

They then commanded the warden of the Fleet to carry him and his fellows to the place from whence he came, to be kept close in prison, and in the morning to provide five fagots for Dr. Barnes, and the other men. The fifth man was commanded to have a taper of five pounds weight provided for him to offer to the rood of Northen in St. Paul's; and all these things to be ready by eight of the clock in the morning; and that he, with all that he could muster with bills and glaves, and the knight marshal, with all his tipstaffs that he could gather, should bring them to St. Paul's and conduct them home again. In the morning they were all ready by the hour appointed, in St. Paul's church, the church being so full that no man could get in. The cardinal had a scaffold made on the top of the stairs for himself, with thirty-six abbots, and mitred priors, and bishops; and he in his pomp sate there enthroned, with his chaplains and spiritual doctors in gowns of damask and satin, and he himself in purple, even like a bloody antichrist. And there was a new pulpit erected, on the top of the stairs also, for the bishop of Rochester to preach against Luther and Dr.

Barnes; and great baskets full of books were standing before them within the rails, which were commanded, after the great fire was made before the rood of Northen, to be burned there, and these heretics, after the sermon, to go thrice about the fire, and to cast in their fagots.

Now, during the sermon, Dr. Barnes and the others were commanded to kneel down and ask forgiveness of God, the catholic church, and the cardinal; and after that he was commanded at the end of the sermon to declare that he was more charitably handled than he deserved, his heresies were so horrible and so detestable; and he once again kneeled down, desiring the people to pray for him; and so the cardinal departed under a canopy, with all his mitred men with him, till he came to the second gate of St. Paul's, and then he took his mule, and the mitred men came back. Then these poor men being ordered to come down, the bishops commanded the knight marshal and the warden of the Fleet to carry them about the fire; and after this they were brought to the bishops, and there kneeled down for absolution. Rochester stood up and declared unto the people how many days of pardon and forgiveness of sins they had for being at that sermon, and there absolved Dr. Barnes with the others.

This done, the warden of the Fleet and the knight marshal were commanded to convey them to the Fleet again.

Barnes continued in the Fleet the space of half a year; and at length he was committed as a free prisoner to the Austin friars, in London, who complained of him to the lord cardinal; upon which he was removed to the Austin friars of Northampton, and there to be burned. At last, one Master Horne, who had brought him up, and who was his especial friend, having intelligence that a writ would shortly be sent down to burn him, gave him counsel to feign himself to be insane, and that he should write a letter to the cardinal and leave it on his table, to declare that he was gone to drown himself in a certain place, and then to leave his clothes in the place; and another letter to the mayor to search for him in the water, because he had a letter written in parchment about his neck, closed in wax for the cardinal. Upon this they were seven days in searching for him, but he, in the meantime was conveyed to London in a poor man's apparel, and took shipping and went to Antwerp, and so to Luther, and there fell to study till he had made an answer to all the bishops of the realm, and had written a book intituled, "*Acta Romanorum Pontificum*," and another book with a supplication to king Henry.

Dr. Barnes was made strong in Christ, and got favour both with the learned in Christ and with the foreign princes in Germany, and was intimate with Luther, Melancthon, and others, and with the duke of Saxony, and with the king of Denmark, who in the time of More and Stokesley sent him with the Lubecks as an ambassador to Henry VIII.

Sir Thomas More, then chancellor, would gladly have entrapped him, but the king would not let him, for Cromwell was his great friend. And ere he went, the Lubecks and he disputed with the bishops of this realm in defence of the truth, and so he departed again with the Lubecks. After his going again to Wittemberg to the duke of Saxony, and to Luther, he remained there to forward his works in print which he had begun, from whence he returned in the beginning of the reign of queen Anne Boleyn, and continued a faithful preacher in the city, being all her time well entertained and promoted. After that he was sent ambassador by king Henry VIII. to the duke of Cleves, to negociate a marriage between himself and the lady Anne of Cleves; he was well accepted in the embassy, and in all his doings, until the time that Stephen Gardiner came out of France; but after he came, neither religion prospered, nor the queen's majesty, nor Cromwell, nor the preachers; for, after the marriage of the lady Anne of Cleves, he never ceased until he had grafted the marriage on another stock.

Not long after, Dr. Barnes, with his brethren, were apprehended and carried before the king at Hampton Court, and there examined. Gardiner sought by all subtle means how to entangle and to entrap them into further danger, which not long after was brought to pass. They were enjoined to preach three sermons; at which Stephen Gardiner was present, with the mayor, either to bear record of their recantation, or else, as the Pharisees came to Christ, to entrap them in their words. When these three had thus preached their sermons, Barnes, preaching the first sermon, and seeing Stephen Gardiner there present, humbly desired him in the face of all the audience, if he forgave him, to hold up his hand; and Gardiner held up his finger; yet, shortly after, they were sent for to Hampton Court; and from thence were carried to the Tower, whence they never came out till they came to their death.

And thus hitherto concerning the history of Barnes. Now let us, likewise, consider the history and doings of Thomas Gerrard.

The History of Thomas Gerrard or Garret, as written by Anthony Dalaber.

"About A.D. 1526, Master Gerrard, curate in Honey Lane, in London, came to Oxford, and brought with him sundry books in Latin, treating of the scriptures, with the first part of '*Unio dissidentium*,' and Tindal's first translation of the New Testament in English, which books he sold to the scholars in Oxford.

"After he had been there a while, it was not unknown to cardinal Wolsey, and to the bishop of London, and to others, that Master Gerrard had a great number of those books, and that he was gone to Oxford to make sale of them there, to such as he knew to be lovers of the gospel. Wherefore they determined forthwith to make a search through all Oxford, to apprehend and imprison him, and to burn all and every his books, and himself too if they could. But at that time one of the proctors, Master Cole, of Magdalen College, was well acquainted with him, and therefore he gave secret warning to a friend of Master Gerrard, and advised that he should, as secretly as he could, depart out of Oxford; for if he were taken, he would be forthwith sent up to the cardinal, and be committed to the Tower.

"I, Anthony Dalaber, having books of Master Gerrard, had been in my county in Dorsetshire, where I had a brother, parson of the parish, who was very desirous to have a curate from Oxford; it seemed good that Master Gerrard, changing his name, should be sent, with my letters, into Dorsetshire to my brother, to serve him there for a time, until he might secretly from thence convey himself somewhere over the sea. Accordingly, I wrote letters to my brother, for Master Gerrard to be his curate, but not declaring what he was, for my brother was a rank papist, and afterwards was the most mortal enemy that ever I had for the gospel's sake.

"Accordingly, on the Wednesday, Mr. Gerrard departed out of Oxford toward Dorsetshire, with his letters. How far he went, and by what occasion he returned, I know not. But on the next Friday, in the night-time, he came back; and so, after mid-night, in the search which was then made for him, he was apprehended and taken in his bed by the two proctors, and in the morning was delivered to one Dr. Cottisford, master of Lincoln college, then being a commissary of the university, who kept him as a prisoner in his own chamber. There was great joy and rejoicing among all the papists at his apprehension. I was utterly ignorant of Mr. Gerrard's sudden return, and that he was taken, until he came into my chamber and said he was undone, for he was taken. Thus he spake unadvisedly in the presence of a young man that came with him. When the young man was departed, I asked him what he was, and what acquaintance he had with him. He said, he knew him not: but he had been to seek a monk of his acquaintance in that college, who was not in his chamber, and desired his servant to bring him to me: and so he declared how he was returned and taken that night, and that now, when the commissary and all his company were gone to even-song, and had locked him alone in his chamber, he hearing nobody stirring in the college, put back the bar of the lock with his finger, and so came away.

"Then said I to him, 'Alas, Mr. Gerrard, by this your uncircumspect coming to me, and speaking so before this young man, you have disclosed yourself, and utterly undone me.' I asked him, why he went not to my brother with my letters accordingly. He said, after that he was gone a day's journey and a half, he was so fearful, that he returned again to Oxford. But now with deep sighs and plenty of tears, he prayed me to help to convey him away, and so he cast off his hood and his gown, wherein he came unto me, and desired me to give him a coat with sleeves, if I had any, and told me that he would go into Wales, and thence convey himself into Germany, if he might. Then I put on him a sleeved coat of mine. He would also have had another manner of cap of me, but I had none but priest-like, such as his own was.

"Then we both kneeled down together upon our knees, and lifting up our hearts and hands to God our heavenly Father, we entreated him with plenty of tears so to conduct and prosper him in his journey, that he might well escape the danger of all his enemies, to the glory of his holy name, if it was his good pleasure and will so to do; and then we embraced and kissed each other, and the tears so abundantly flowed out from both our eyes, that our faces were all wet with them, and scarcely for sorrow could we speak one to another; and so he departed from me apparelled in my coat, being committed unto the guidance of our Almighty and Merciful Father.

"When he was gone down the stairs from my chamber, I straightways did shut my chamber-door, and went into my study, and took the New Testament in my hands, kneeled down on my knees, and with many a deep sigh and salt tear I did with much deliberation read over the tenth chapter of St. Matthew's gospel; and when I had so done, with prayer I did commit unto God our dearly beloved brother Gerrard, earnestly beseeching him, in and for Jesus Christ's sake, his only begotten Son, our Lord, that he would vouchsafe not only safely to conduct and keep our said dear brother from the hands of all his enemies; but also that he would endue his tender and lately born little flock in Oxford with heavenly strength by his Holy Spirit, that they might be well able thereby valiantly to withstand to his glory all their fierce enemies, and also might quietly, to their own salvation, with all godly patience, bear Christ's heavy cross, which I now saw was presently to be laid on their young and weak backs, unable to bear so great a burthen, without the help of his Holy Spirit.

"This done, I laid aside my book, folded up Master Gerrard's gown and hood, and laid them in my press among mine apparel, and so having put on my short gown, shut up my study and chamber-doors, and went toward Frideswides, to speak with that worthy martyr of God, Master Clark, and others, and to declare to them what had happened. But of purpose I went by St. Mary's church, to go first to Corpus Christi college, to speak with Diet and Udal, my faithful brethren and fellows in the Lord there. By chance I met by the way with a brother of ours, one Master Eden, fellow of Magdalene College, who, as soon as he saw me, came with a pitiful countenance, saying, that we were all undone, for Master Gerrard was returned again to Oxford, and was taken the previous night, and was in prison with the commissary. I said it was not so. He replied it was so. I told him it could not be so; for I was sure he was gone. He answered, "I know he went with your letters, but he came again yesterday evening, and was taken in his bed at Radleis this night. But I told him again, that I was well assured he was gone, for I spake with him later than either the proctor or the commissary did: and then I declared the whole matter to him; how and when he came to me; and how he went his way, desiring him to declare the same to our brethren whom he should meet with; and to give God hearty thanks for his wonderful deliverance, and to beseech him also that he would grant him safely to pass away from all his ene-mies, and I told him that I was going unto Master Clark of Frideswides, to declare unto him this matter; for I knew and thought verily that he and others there were in great sorrow for this matter.

"Then I went straight to Frideswides; and even-song was begun, and the dean and the other canons were there. As I stood there, in comes Dr. Cottisford the commissary, as fast as he could, bareheaded, and as pale as ashes, and he goes to the dean, where he was sitting in his stall, and talked with him very sorrowfully. I went aside from the choir-door, to hear and see more. The commissary and dean came out of the choir wonderfully troubled. About the middle of the church Dr. London met them, puffing, blustering, and blowing, like a hungry and greedy lion seeking his prey. They talked together awhile, but the commissary was much blamed for keeping his prisoner so negligently, so that he wept for sorrow: and it was known abroad that Master Gerrard had escaped; but whither no man could tell. The doctors departed, and sent their servants and spies every where. Master Clark, about the middle of *Compline*, came out of the choir: I followed him to his chamber, and declared what had happened. He was glad, and sent for one Master Sumner, and Master Betts, fellows and canons there. In the meanwhile he gave me a very good exhortation, praying God to give me, and all the rest of our brethren, 'the prudence of the serpent, and harmlessness of the dove,' for we should shortly have much need of it, as he thought.

"When we had ended our supper, and committed our whole cause with fervent sighs and hearty prayers unto God our heavenly Father, I went to Alborn Hall, and there lay that night. In the morning I was up very early, and as soon as I could get out of the door I went straight towards Gloucester College to my chamber. It had rained that morning, and I had sprinkled my hose and shoes with mire. When I was come to Gloucester College, which was about six o'clock, I found the gates fast shut; at which I much marvelled, for they were wont to be opened daily long before that time. Then I walked up and down a whole hour before the gates were opened. In the meanwhile my musing head being full of forecasting cares, and my sorrowful heart flowing with doleful sighs, I fully determined in my conscience before God, that if I should chance to be taken and examined, I would accuse no man, nor declare anything further than I did already perceive was manifestly known before. And so when the gate was opened, thinking to change myself, and to put on a longer gown, I went in towards my chamber, and going up the stairs, would have opened my door, but I could not do it; by which I perceived that my lock had been meddled with; and yet at last with much ado I opened the lock; but when I came in, I saw my bed all tossed and tumbled, my clothes in my press thrown down, and my study-door open. I was much amazed, and thought verily that some search was made there that night for Master Gerrard, and that it was known of his being with me, by the monk's man that brought him to my chamber.

"Now there was lying in the next chamber to me a monk, who, as soon as he had heard me in the chamber, came to me, and told how Master Gerrard was sought for in my chamber that night, and what ado there was made by the commissary and the two proctors, with bills and swords thrust through my straw bed, and how every corner of my chamber was searched for Master Gerrard. And although his gown and his hood lay there in my press with my clothes, yet they perceived them not. Then he told me he was commanded to bring me, as soon as I came in, to the prior of the students, named Anthony Dunstan, a monk of Westminster. This so troubled me, that I forgot to make clean my hose and shoes, and to put on another gown; and therefore all dirty as I was, and in my short gown, I went with him to the prior's chamber, where I found the prior standing and looking for my coming. He asked me where I had been that night: I told him I lay at Alborn Hall with my old fellow Fitzjames, but he would not believe me. He asked me if Master Gerrard were with me yesterday ? I told him, ‘Yea.’ Then he would know where he was, and wherefore he came to me. I told him ‘I knew not where he was, except he were at Woodstock. For so,’ I continued, ‘ he had shewed me that he would go thither, because one of the keepers there was his friend, and had promised him a piece of venison to make merry with at the Shrovetide ; and that he would have borrowed a hat and a pair of high shoes of me, but I had none to lend him.’ Then he observed on my finger a big ring of silver very well double gilt, with two letters A. D. engraved in it for my name ; I suppose he thought it to be gold. He required it. I took it to him. When he had it in his hand, he said it was his ring, for therein was his name : an A. for Anthony, and a D. for Dunstan. When I heard him say that, I wished in my heart to be as well delivered from and out of his company, as I was assured to be delivered from my ring for ever.

“ Then he called for pen, ink, and paper, and commanded me to write when and how Gerrard came to me, and where he was gone. I had scarcely written three words, when the chief beadle, with two or three of the commissary’s men were come to the prior, requiring him to bring me away to Lincoln College to the commissary, and to Dr. London. When I was brought into the chapel, there I found Dr. Cottisford, commissary, Dr. Higdon, then dean of the Cardinal’s College, and Dr. London, warden of the New College, standing together at the altar in the chapel. When I was brought to them, after salutations given and taken between them, they called for chairs and sat down, and then called for me to come to them. First they asked what my name was. I told them that my name was Anthony Dalaber. Then they also asked me how long I had been a student in the university ? and I told them almost three years. And they asked me what I studied. I told them I had read sophistry and logic in Alborn Hall, and now was removed to Gloucester College to study the civil law. Then they asked me whether I knew Master Gerrard, and how long I had known him ? I told them I knew him well, and had known him almost a twelvemonth. They asked me when he was with me ? I told them yesterday afternoon.

“ Now by this time, while they had me in this talk, one came to them, with pen, ink, and paper ; I think it was the clerk of the University. As soon as he was come, there was a board with a form for him to sit on, set between the doctors and me, and a great mass-book laid before me ; and I was commanded to lay my right hand on it, and to swear that I should truly answer such interrogatories as I should be by them examined upon. I hesitated at first ; but afterwards, being persuaded by them, partly by fair words, and partly by great threats, I promised to do as they would have me ; but in my heart meant not to do so. So I laid my hand on the book, and one of them gave me my oath ; and that done, commanded me to kiss the book. Then they made great courtesy between them who should examine me, and put interrogatories to me. At the last, the greatest papistical pharisee of them all, Doctor London took upon himself to do it.

“ Then he asked me by my oath, where Master Gerrard was, and whither I had conveyed him. I told him I had not conveyed him, nor yet knew where he was ; nor whither he was gone, except he were gone to Woodstock, as I had before said, as he told me he would. Then he asked me again when he came to me ; how he came to me ; what and how long he talked with me ; and whither he went from me. I told him he came to me about the time of even-song, and that one brought him to my chamber-door, whom I knew not ; and that he told me he would go to Woodstock for some venison to make merry with this Shrovetide ; and that he would have borrowed a hat, and a pair of high shoes of me ; but I had none to lend him ; and then he straight went his way from me, but whither I know not. All these my sayings the scribe wrote in a book.

“ Then they earnestly required me to tell them whither I had conveyed him ; for surely, they said, I brought him somewhere this morning, as they might perceive by my foul shoes and hose, I had travelled with him the most part of this night. I answered plainly that I lay at Alborn Hall, and that I had good witness thereof there. They asked me where I was at even-song. I told them at Frideswides, and that I saw first Master Commissary ; and then Dr. London come thither at that time to the dean of Frideswides ; and that I saw them talking together in the church there. Dr. London and the dean threatened me, that if I would not tell the truth where I had taken him, or whither he was gone, I should surely be sent to the Tower of London, and there be put to the torture. But Master Commissary entreated me with gentle words, to tell him where he was, that he might secure him again, and that he would be my very great friend, and deliver me out of trouble. I told him I could not tell where he was. Thus they did occupy and toss me almost two hours in the chapel ; sometimes with threatenings and foul words ; and then with fair words and fair promises. Then he that brought Mr. Gerrard to my chamber was brought before me, and caused to declare what Mr. Gerrard said to me at his coming to my chamber ; but I said plainly I heard him say no such thing ; for I thought my nay to be as good as his yea, seeing it was to rid and deliver my godly brother of trouble and peril of his life.

“ At last, when they could get nothing from me to hurt or accuse any man, or know any thing of that which they sought, they all three together brought me up into a great chamber over the commissary’s chamber, wherein stood a great pair of very high stocks. Then Master Commissary asked me for my purse and girdle ; took away my money and my knives, and then put both my legs into the stocks, and so locked me fast in them ; in which I sat, my feet being almost as high as my head ; and so, leaving me alone, after locking the chamber-door, they departed, (I think to their abominable mass). When they were all gone, then came to my remembrance the worthy forewarning and godly declaration of that most constant martyr of God, Master John Clark, my father in Christ, who well nigh two years before that, when I earnestly desired him to permit me to be his scholar, and that I might go with him continually when and wherever he should teach or preach, said to me much after this sort : Dalaber, you desire you know not what, and that which you are, I fear, unable to take upon you : for though now my preaching be sweet and pleasant to you, because there is yet no persecution laid on you for it, yet the time will come, and that peradventure shortly, if we continue to live godly therein, that God will lay on you the cross of persecution to try you, whether you can as pure gold abide the fire, or as stubble and dross be consumed. For the Holy Ghost plainly affirms by St. Paul, ‘If any man will live godly, he shall suffer persecution.’ 2 Tim. iii. 12. Yea, you shall be called and judged an heretic ; you shall be abhorred of the world ; your own friends and kinsfolk will forsake you, and also hate you ; and you shall be cast into prison ; and no man shall dare to help or comfort you ; and you shall be accused and brought before the bishops to your reproach and shame, to the great sorrow of all your faithful friends and kinsfolk. Then will you wish you had never known this doctrine ; then will you curse Clark, and wish that you had never known him ; because he had brought you into all these troubles.

“ At which words I was so grieved, that I fell down on my knees at his feet, and with abundance of tears and sighs, even from the very bottom of my heart I earnestly besought him, that for the tender mercy of God shewed to us in our Lord Jesus Christ, he would not refuse me, but receive me into his company, as I had desired, saying that I trusted verily, that he who had begun this in me would not forsake me, but give me grace to continue therein unto the end. When he heard me say this, he came to me and took me up in his arms and kissed me,—the tears trickling down from his eyes ;—and said to me, ‘ The Lord Almighty grant you so to do ; and from thenceforth for ever take me for your father, and I will take you for my son in Christ.’ Now there were at this time in Oxford several graduates and scholars at the colleges and halls, whom God had called to the knowledge of his holy word, who all resorted to Mr. Clark's disputations and lectures in divinity; and when they might not come conveniently, I was by Mr. Clark appointed to resort to every one of them weekly, and to know what doubts they had in any place of the scripture, that by me from him they might have the true understanding of the same. Which exercise did me much good and profit, to the understanding of the holy scriptures, which I most desired.

"This forewarning and godly declaration, (I say,) of this most godly martyr of God, Mr. Clark, coming to my remembrance, caused me with deep sighs to cry to God from my heart, to assist me with his Holy Spirit, that I might be able patiently and quietly to bear and suffer whatsoever it should please him of his Fatherly love to lay upon me, to his glory, and the comfort of my dearly beloved brethren, whom I thought now to be in great fear and anguish, lest I should be an accuser of them all; for to me they were all well known, and all their doings in that matter. But, God be praised, I was fully bent never to accuse any of them, whatever should happen to me. Before dinner Master Cottisford came up to me, and requested me earnestly to tell him where Master Gerrard was, and if I would do so, he promised me straightways to deliver me out of prison. But I told him I could not tell where he was; no more indeed I could. Then he departed to dinner, asking me if I could eat any meat; I told him, yea, right gladly. He said he would send me some. When he was gone, his servants asked me many questions, which I do not now remember; and some of them spake to me fair words, and some threatened me, calling me heretic, and so departed, locking the door fast upon me."

Thus far Anthony Dalaber has prosecuted this history, who, before finishing it, died in 1562, in the diocese of Salisbury.

After this, Gerrard was apprehended and taken by Master Cole, the proctor, as his men were going westward, at a place called Hinksey, a little beyond Oxford, and so being brought back again was committed to ward; he was brought before the commissary, Dr. London, and Dr. Higdon, dean of Frideswides, (now called Christ's College,) in St. Mary's church, where they, sitting in judgment, convicted him according to their law as a heretic, and afterwards compelled him to carry a faggot in open procession from St. Mary's church to Frideswides, and Dalaber likewise with him, Gerrard having his red hood on his shoulders like a master of arts. After that, they were sent to Osney, there to be kept in prison till further orders were taken.

Besides these, there were a great number also suspected to be infected with heresy, as they called it, for having such books of God's truth as Master Gerrard sold to them; and many were forced to forsake their colleges and return to their friends. Against the procession-time they made a great fire, into which all such as were in the procession, who had been convicted or suspected of heresy, were commanded every man to cast a book as they passed, in token of repentance and renouncing of their errors.

After this, Master Gerrard, flying from place to place, escaped their tyranny, till this present time, when he was again apprehended and burned in Smithfield with Doctor Barnes and William Jerome, vicar of Stephney. Thus, these three godly men, with great constancy, endured martyrdom in the fire.

The Life and History of William Jerome, Vicar of Stephney, and Martyr of Christ.

The third who suffered with Barnes and Gerrard, was Wm. Jerome, vicar of Stephney. This Jerome being a diligent preacher of God's word, for the comfort and edification of the people, had preached many sermons, in which he laboured to weed out the roots of men's traditions, doctrines, dreams, and fantasies. In so doing he could not otherwise but provoke much hatred against him amongst the adversaries of Christ's gospel.

It so happened, that on preaching one Sunday at St. Paul's, he made there a sermon, wherein he recited and

mentioned Hagar and Sarah, declaring what these two signified. He shewed how Sarah and her child Isaac and all they that were Isaac's, and born of the free woman Sarah, were freely justified: and they that were born of Hagar, the bond woman, were bound and under the law, and could not be freely justified. In these words, what was there said, but what St. Paul himself expounds in his epistle to the Galatians (fourth chapter), or what could here be gathered, but what was consonant to sound doctrine? The point was this; he was accused of preaching erroneously at St. Paul's cross, teaching the people that all that were born of Sarah were freely justified; speaking there absolutely without any condition, either of baptism or of penance, &c. Who doubts here, but if St. Paul himself had been at St. Paul's cross, and had preached the same words to Englishmen, which he wrote to the Galatians, he had been apprehended for an heretic for preaching against the sacrament of baptism and repentance?

And thus much concerning the several histories of these three good men. Now let us see the order of their martyrdom, joining them together; what was the cause of their condemnation; and what were their protestations and words at their suffering.

Barnes, Jerome, and Gerrard, being committed to the Tower after Easter, remained there till the 30th day of July, which was two days after the death of the Lord Cromwell. Then process was issued against them by the king's council in parliament; to which process Gardiner confessed himself that he was privy. Whereupon these three good saints of God, on the thirtieth day of July, not coming to any answer; nor yet knowing any cause of their condemnation, without any public hearing, were brought together from the Tower to Smithfield, where, while preparing themselves for the fire, gave there at the stake many and sundry exhortations, among whom Dr. Barnes first began with this protestation following:—

"I am come hither to be burned as an heretic, and you shall hear my belief; whereby you shall perceive what erroneous opinions I hold. I take God to record, I never, to my knowledge, taught any erroneous doctrine, but only those things which scripture led me to; and that in my sermons I never maintained any error, neither moved nor gave occasion of any insurrection. Although I have been slandered for preaching that our Lady was but a saffron-bag, which I utterly protest before God that I never meant it, nor preached it; but all my study and diligence hath been utterly to confound and confute all men of that doctrine, as are the anabaptists, who deny that our Saviour Christ did take any flesh of the blessed Virgin Mary, which sect I detest and abhor. And in this place there have been burned some of them, whom I never favoured nor maintained; but always with all diligence did I study to set forth the glory of God; the obedience to our sovereign lord the king; and the true and sincere religion of Christ: and now hearken to my faith:

"I believe in the holy and blessed Trinity, three Persons in one Godhead, that created and made all the world; and that this blessed Trinity sent down this second Person, Jesus Christ, into the womb of the most blessed and purest Virgin Mary. And here bear me record, that I do utterly condemn that abominable and detestable opinion of the anabaptists, who say that Christ took no flesh of the Virgin. For I believe that without man's will or power he was conceived by the Holy Ghost, and took flesh of her, and that he suffered hunger, thirst, cold, and other passions of our body, sin excepted, according to the saying of St. Paul, 'He was made in all things like unto his brethren,' except sin. And I believe that his death and passion was the sufficient ransom for the sin of all the world. And I believe that through his death he overcame sin, death, and hell, and that there is none other satisfaction unto the Father, but this his death and passion only, and that no work of man did deserve anything of God, but only his passion, as touching our justification, for I know the best work that ever I did is impure and imperfect." And with this he cast abroad his hands, and desired God to forgive him his trespasses. "For although perchance," said he, "you know nothing by me, yet do I confess, that my thoughts and cogitations be innumerable; wherefore I beseech thee, O Lord, not to enter into judgment with me, according to the saying of the prophet David, 'Enter not into judgment with thy servant, O Lord.' And in another place, 'If thou, Lord, shouldst mark iniquity, O Lord, who shall stand?' Wherefore I trust in no good work that ever I did, but only in the death of Christ. I do not doubt through him to inherit the kingdom of heaven. Take me not here that I speak against good works, for they are to be done; and verily they that do them not shall never come into the kingdom of God. We must do them, because they are commanded us of God, to show and set forth our profession, not to deserve or merit; for that is only the death of Christ.

"I believe that there is a holy church; and a company of all them that do profess Christ; and that all that have suffered and confessed his name are saints, and that they all do praise and bless God in heaven, more than I or any man's tongue can express; and that always I have spoken reverently, and praised them as much as scripture willed me to do. And that our Lady, I say, was a virgin immaculate and undefiled; and that she is the most pure virgin that ever God created, and a vessel elect of God, of whom Christ should be born." Then said Mr. Sheriff, "You have said well of her before." And being afraid that Mr. Sheriff had been or should be aggrieved with any thing that he should say, he said, 'Mr. Sheriff, if I speak any thing that you will me not, do no more than beckon me with your hand, and I will straightway hold my peace; for I will not be disobedient in any thing, but will obey.'

Then there was one that asked him his opinion of praying to saints. Then said he, "Now of saints you shall hear my opinion. I have said something before, I think, of them, how that I believe they are in heaven with God; and that they are worthy of all the honour that scripture willeth them to have. But I say, throughout scripture we are not commanded to pray to any saints. Therefore I neither can nor will preach to you that saints ought to be prayed to; for then should I preach to you a doctrine of my own head. Notwithstanding whether they pray for us or no, that I refer to God. And if saints do pray for us, then I trust to pray for you within this half hour, Mr. Sheriff, and for every christian man living in the faith of Christ, and dying in the same as a saint. Wherefore if the dead may pray for the quick, I will surely pray for you."

"Well have you anything more to say?" Then spake he to Mr. Sheriff, and said, "Have you any articles against me for which I am condemned?" And the sheriff answered "No." "Then," said he, "is there here any man else that knows why I must die, or that by my preaching has been led into error? Let them now speak, and I will give them an answer." And no man answered. Then said he, "Well, I am condemned by the law to die, and as I understand by an act of Parliament; but wherefore I cannot tell, but probably for heresy, for we are likely to burn. But they who have been the occasion of it, I pray God to forgive them, as I would be forgiven myself. And Stephen bishop of Winchester that now is, if he have sought or wrought this my death either by word or deed, I pray God to forgive him, as heartily, as freely, as charitably, and without feigning, as ever Christ forgave them that put him to death. And if any of the council, or any other have sought or wrought it through malice or ignorance, I pray God to forgive their ignorance, and illuminate their eyes that they may see and ask mercy for it. I beseech you all to pray for the king as I have done ever since I was in prison; and do now that God may give him prosperity, and that he may long reign among you; and after him that godly Prince Edward may so reign, that he may finish those things that his father has begun. I have been reported to be a preacher of sedition and disobedience to the king's majesty; but here I say to you that you are all bound by the commandment of God to obey your prince with all humility, and with all your heart; yea, not so much as in a look to show

yourselves disobedient to him, and that not only for fear of the sword, but also for conscience sake before God."

Then spake he to the sheriff, and said, "Mr. Sheriff, I require you on God's behalf to have me commended unto the king, and to shew him that I require of his grace these five requests: first, that where his grace hath received into his hands all the goods and substance of the abbeys—" Then the sheriff desired him to stop there. He answered Mr. Sheriff: "I warrant you I will speak no harm; for I know it is well done that all such superstition be clean taken away; and the king hath well done in taking it away. But his grace is made a whole king, and obeyed in his whole realm as a king (which neither his father nor grandfather, neither his ancestors that reigned before him ever had), and that through the preaching of us and such other wretches as we are, who always have applied our whole studies, and given ourselves for the setting forth of the same, and this is now our reward. Well, it makes no matter. Now he reigns among you; I pray God that he may long live and reign among you. Would to God it may please his grace to bestow the said goods, or some of them, to the comfort of his poor subjects, who surely have great need of them. The second that I desire his grace is, that he will see that matrimony be had in more reverence than it is; and that men for every light cause invented cast not off their wives, and live in adultery and fornication. The third, that abominable swearers may be punished; for the vengeance of God will come on them for their mischievous oaths. The fourth, that his grace would set forth Christ's true religion; and seeing he has begun, go forward and make an end; for many things have been done, but much more is to do; and that it would please his grace to look on God's word himself, for that it has been obscured with many traditions invented of our own brains." "Now," said he, "how many petitions have I spoken of?" And the people said, "four." "Well," said he, "even these four are sufficient, which I desire you, that the king's grace may be certified of, and say, that I most humbly desire him to look earnestly upon them; and that his grace take heed that he be not deceived with false preachers and teachers and evil counsel, for Christ saith, that such false prophets shall come in sheep's clothing."

Then he desired all men to forgive him, and if he had said any evil at any time unadvisedly, whereby he had offended any man; or given any occasion of evil that they would forgive it him, and amend that evil they took of him; and to bear him witness that he detested and abhorred all evil opinions and doctrines against the word of God; and that he died in the faith of Jesus Christ, by whom he doubted not but to be saved. And with these words he desired them all to pray for him; and then he turned him about, and put off his clothes, making ready for the fire, there patiently to take his death.

The like confession made also Jerome and Gerrard, professing in like manner their belief, reciting all the articles of the christian faith, briefly declaring their minds upon every article; whereby the people might understand that there was no cause nor error in their faith; protesting that they denied nothing that was either in the Old or New Testament, set forth by their sovereign lord the king, whom they prayed the Lord long to continue among them, with his most dear son, Prince Edward. Which done, Jerome added this exhortation in the few words, which follow:

"I say unto you, good brethren, that God has bought us all with no small price, neither with gold nor silver; or other such things of small value, but with his most precious blood. Be not unthankful therefore to him; but do as much as to christian men belongs, to fulfil his commandments, that is, 'Love your brethren.' Love hurteth no man, love fulfilleth all things. If God hath sent thee plenty, help thy neighbour that hath need. Give him good counsel. If he lack, consider, if you were in necessity, thou wouldst gladly be refreshed. And, again, bear your cross with Christ. Consider what reproof, slander, and reproach he suffered of his enemies, and how patiently he suffered all things. Consider that all that Christ did was of his own goodness, and not of our deserving. For if we could merit our own salvation, Christ would not have died for us. But for Adam's breaking of God's precepts we had been all lost, if Christ had not redeemed us again. And as Adam broke the precepts, and was driven out of Paradise ; so we, if we break God's commandments, shall have damnation, if we do not repent and ask mercy. Now, therefore, let all christians put no trust or confidence in their works, but in the blood of Christ ; to whom I commit my soul, beseeching you all to pray to God for me, and for my brethren here present with me, that our souls, leaving these wretched carcasses, may depart in the true faith of Christ."

In a similar manner Gerrard protested, and exhorted the people ; and ended his protestation as follows :

"I also detest, abhor, and refuse all heresies and errors ; and if, either by negligence or ignorance, I have taught or maintained any, I am sorry for it, and ask mercy of God ; or if I have been so vehement or rash in preaching, whereby any person has taken any offence, error, or evil opinion, I desire him, and all other persons whom I have in any way offended, forgiveness. Notwithstanding to my remembrance I never preached wittingly, or willingly, any thing against God's holy word, or contrary to the true faith ; to the maintenance of errors, heresies, or vicious living, but have always, for my little learning, set forth the honour of God, and the right obedience to his laws ; and also the king's. And if I could have done better, I would. Wherefore, Lord, if I have taken in hand to do that thing which I could not perfectly perform, I desire thy pardon for my bold presumption. And I pray God send the king's grace good and godly counsel, to his glory, to the king's honour, and the increase of virtue in this his realm. And thus now I yield my soul up unto Almighty God, trusting and believing that he of his infinite mercy, for his promise made in the bood of his Son, our most merciful Saviour, Jesus Christ, will take it, and pardon me of all my sins ; whereby I have most grievously from my youth offended his majesty ; wherefore I ask him mercy, desiring you all to pray with me and for me, that I may patiently suffer this pain, and die steadfastly in true faith, perfect hope and charity."

And so, after they had engaged in prayer, wherein they desired the Lord Jesus to be their comfort and consolation in this their affliction, and to establish them with perfect faith, constancy, and patience through the Holy Ghost, they taking each other by the hands, and kissing one another, quietly and humbly offered themselves to the hands of the tormentors ; and so took their death both christianly and constantly, with such patience as might well testify the goodness of their cause, and quiet of their conscience.

Wherein is to be noted how mightily the Lord works with his grace and fortitude in the hearts of his servants, especially in such as suffer with a guiltless conscience for religion's sake, above others who suffer for their deserts. For whereas they who suffer as malefactors, are commonly heavy and pensive in their death ; so the others with heavenly alacrity and cheerfulness, abide whatever it pleaseth the Lord to lay upon them.

A note of three Papists executed the same time with Barnes, Jerome, and Gerrard.

At the same time, and in the same place, three others also were executed, though not for the same cause, but rather the contrary, namely, for denying the king's supremacy, whose names were Powel, Fetherstone, and Abel. This spectacle happening on the same day, brought the people into a marvellous doubt of their religion, which part to follow, as might well happen among ignorant people, seeing two contrary parties suffering ; the one for popery ; the other against popery,—both at one time. This circumstance happened by reason of a certain division among the king's council, who were so

equally divided among themselves, that the one half seemed to hold with the one religion, and the other half with the contrary.

The names of those, although it is not necessary to express them, yet, for the setting forth of the truth, we have thought good here to annex :—

PROTESTANTS.	PAPISTS.
Canterbury.	Winchester.
Suffolk.	Durham.
Beauchamp.	Norfolk.
Lisle.	Southampton.
Russel, treasurer.	Anthony Brown.
Paget.	William Paulet.
Sadler.	John Baker.
Audley.	Richard, chancellor of the Augmentation.
	Wingfield, vice-chancellor.

This division and separation of the council among themselves, caused both these parties above mentioned to suffer, the one for one religion, and the other for another. For, as the one part of the council called for the execution of Barnes, Gerrard, and Jerome, so the other part likewise called for the execution of the law upon Powel, Fetherstone, and Abel.

Thus, having discussed the six articles, with other matters, in the parliament, concerning the condemnation of Lord Cromwell, of Dr. Barnes, and his companions, let us now consider what great vexations ensued after the setting forth of these articles, through the whole realm of England. First is to be mentioned the severe commissions sent forth by the king's authority, to the bishops, chancellors, officials, justices, mayors, and bailiffs, in every shire, and other commissioners ; and especially to Edmund Bonner, bishop of London, and to the mayor, sheriffs, and aldermen, to inquire diligently for all heretical books, and to burn them. Also to inquire for all such persons whatsoever, as were culpable or suspected of such felonies, heresies, contempts, or transgressions, or speaking any words contrary to the act of the six articles.

Upon this commission being given to Edmund Bonner, he came to the Guildhall with other commissioners, to sit upon the statute of the six articles. He began soon to put his authority in execution. And first he charged certain juries to take their oath upon the statute ; who, being sworn, had a day appointed to give their verdict. On which day they indicted sundry persons, who, shortly after, were apprehended ; and after remaining there a while, were, by the king and his council, discharged at the Star Chamber, without any further punishment.

Not long after this, Sir William Roch being mayor, Bonner, with other commissioners, sate at the Guildhall. When the juries were sworn, Bonner took upon him to give the charge, and began with a tale of Anacharsis, by which he admonished the juries to spare no persons, of what degree soever they were ; and at the end of his charge, he brought to the bar a boy, whose name was Mekins, declaring how grievously he had offended by speaking certain words against the state, and of the death of Dr. Barnes, and produced to the court two witnesses, who were there sworn in the face of the court.

So a day was assigned upon which the juries should give their verdict ; at which day both the commissioners and the juries met at Guildhall. Then the clerk of the peace called on the juries by their names, and when their appearance was taken, Bonner bade them put in their presentments. Then said the foreman of the jury, whose name was William Robins ; "My lord, we have found nothing." At which words he raged as one in an agony, and said, "Nothing! have you found nothing ? What, nothing ? By the faith I owe to God I would trust you upon your obligation, but by your oath I will trust you nothing." Then said some of the commissioners ; "My lord, give them a longer day." "No," said he, "in London they ever find nothing ; I pray you, what do you say to Mekins ?" "My lord," replied the foreman, "we can say nothing to him for we find the witnesses to disagree. One affirms that he said the sacrament was nothing but a ceremony; and the other, nothing but a signification." "Why," said Bonner, "did he not say that Barnes died holy?" Then pausing a while, he bade them call the other jury. "Put in your verdict," said he. "My lord," said one, "we have found nothing." "Jesus!" said he, "is not this a strange case?"

Then one of the jury, whose name was Ralph Foxley, said, "My lord, when you gave us charge, we desired to have the parsons and curates of every parish to give us instructions, and it was denied us." Then stood up the recorder, and said, "It was true, indeed, what he had spoken," and there withal said, "this last year were charged two juries, who did many things naughtily and foolishly, and did as much as in them lay to make an uproar among the king's people, and therefore it was thought not meet that they should give information to you." "Nay, nay," said Bonner, "this was the cause: If the parson or curate should give information according to his knowledge, then what will they say? I must tell my confession to knave-priest, and he shall go by and by and open it." "What," said my lord mayor, "there is no man, I trow, that will say so." "Yes, by my troth," answered Bonner, "knave priest, knave-priest." Then said my lord mayor somewhat smiling, "There be some of them slippery fellows; and as men find them, so will they oft-times report." Bonner, not well contented with those words, said to the jury, "My masters, what say you to Mekins?" They answered, "The witnesses do not agree, therefore we do not allow them." "Why," said Bonner, "this court hath allowed them." Then said one of the jury to the recorder, "Is it sufficient for our discharge, if this court do allow them?" "Yea," said the recorder, "it is sufficient;" and said, "go you aside together awhile, and bring in your verdict." After the jury had talked together a little while, they returned to the bar again with their indictment, which at Bonner's hand was friendly received; so both they and the other jury were discharged. Thus ended the court for that day. Shortly after they sate for life and death. Mekins being brought to the bar, and the indictment read, Bonner said to him; "Mekins, confess the truth, and submit thyself to the king's law, that thy death may be an example to all others."

This Richard Mekins being but a child, who had not passed the age of fifteen years, as he had heard some other folks talk, so he chanced to speak against the sacrament of the altar. Which coming to Bonner's ears, he never left him before he had brought him to the fire. During the time of his imprisonment, neither his poor father nor mother durst aid him with any relief, by which he endured great misery. When he was brought to the stake, he was taught to speak much good of the bishop of London, and of the great charity he shewed to him, and to defy and detest all heretics and heresies, but especially Doctor Barnes, to whom he imputed the learning of that heresy, which was the cause of his death. The poor lad would for his life have gladly said that the twelve apostles had taught it to him; such was his childish innocency and fear. But many spake and said, "It was a great shame for the bishop; whose part and duty it had been rather to have laboured to save his life, than to procure that terrible execution, seeing that he was such an ignorant soul, that he knew not what the affirming of heresy was."

Richard Spencer, Ramsey, and Hewet, who suffered at Salisbury.

About the same time also, a certain priest was burned at Salisbury, who, leaving his papistry, had married a wife, and became a player, with one Ramsey and Hewet, which three were all condemned and burned; against whom, and especially against Spencer, was laid matter concerning the sacrament of the altar. He suffered at Salisbury.

Although this inquisition was meant especially concerning the six articles, yet so it fell out, that doubts began to arise, and to be moved, whether they might inquire as well of all other opinions, articles, and causes, or for speaking against the holy bread, holy water, or for favouring the cause of Barnes, of Friar, of Ward, Sir Thomas Rose, &c. Whereupon great perturbation followed in almost all parishes throughout London, in the year 1541.

A brief account of the Troubles at London in the time of the Six Articles; and a list of the Names of some of the Persons who were persecuted for speaking against them.

John Dixe, was never observed to confess in Lent, nor to receive at Easter, and to be a sacramentary.

Richard Chepeman, for eating flesh in Lent, and for working on holy-days, and not coming to the church.

Mistress Cicely Marshall, for not bearing her palm, and despising holy bread and holy water.

Michael Haukes, for not coming to the church, and for receiving young men of the new learning.

John Browne, for bearing with Barnes.

Mistress Annes Bedikes, for despising our Lady, and not praying to saints.

Andrew Kempe, William Pahen, Richard Manerd, for disturbing the service of the church with babbling out of the New Testament.

William Wyders, denied, two years before, the sacrament to be Christ's body, and said that it was but only a sign.

William Stokesley, for rebuking his wife at the church for taking holy water.

Roger Davy, for speaking against worshipping of saints.

Master Blage, for not coming to his parish church, nor confessing, or receiving.

William Clinch, for saying, when he saw a priest preparing for the mass, "You shall see a priest now go to masking." Also, for calling the bishop of Winchester, "False flattering knave." Also, for burying his wife without a dirge.

William Plaine, seeing a priest going to mass, said, "Now you shall see one in masking." Also, when he came to the church, he disturbed the divine service by reading aloud the English Bible.

Herman Johnson, Jerome Akon, Giles Hosterman, Richard Bonfeld, Thomas Couper, Humphrey Skinner, John Sneudnam, Richard Phillips, and John Celos.— These nine persons were presented, because they were not confessed in Lent, nor had received at Easter.

John Jones, William Wright, Peter Butcher, and Roger Butcher.—These four were presented for not keeping the divine service in the holy-days.

Mistress Brisley, for reasoning on the new learning, and not attending the church.

Mistress Castle, for being a meddler and a reader of the scriptures in the church.

Master Galias of Bernard's Inn, for withstanding the curate in censing the altars on Corpus Christi even, and saying openly, that he did wrong.

Master Pates, of David's Inn, and Master Galias, for vexing the curate in the body of the church, in declaring the king's injunctions, and reading the bishop's book; so that he had much ado to make an end.

William Beckes and his wife, were suspected to be sacramentaries, and for not kneeling to the cross on Good Friday.

Thomas Langham, William Thomas, Richard Beckes, and William Beckes.—These four were presented for interrupting the divine service.

Ralph Symonds, for not keeping our Lady's mass, which he was bound to keep.

John Smith an apprentice, for saying, "that he had rather hear the crying of dogs, than priests singing matins or even-song.

Thomas Bele, John Sturgeon, John Wilshire, Thomas Simon, Ralph Clervis, and his wife, James Banaster, Nicholas Barker, John Sterky, Christopher Smith, and Thomas Net.—These eleven persons of St. Magnus parish, were presented and accused for maintaining certain preachers (as it was called) of the new learning.

Nicholas Philips, for maintaining heresies and scripture books, and for neither using fasting nor prayer.

Richard Bigges, for despising holy bread, putting it in the throat of a dog, and for not adoring at the elevation.

Mistress Elizabeth Statham, for maintaining in her house Latimer, Barnes, Gerrard, Jerome, and others.

John Duffet, for marrying a woman who was thought to be a nun.

Hilliard and Duffet, for maintaining Barnes, Jerome, and Gerrard, with others.

Grafton and Whitchurch, suspected not to have been confessed.

John Greene, Mother Palmer, Christopher Coots, William Selly, Alexander Frere, William Bredi, John Bush, William Somerton, George Durant, and Davids, an apprentice.—All these being of the parish of St. Martin's, were presented for contemning the ceremonies of the church. Also some for walking in the time of consecrating mass, with their caps on. Some for turning their heads away; some for sitting at their doors when sermons were in the church, &c.

Robert Andrew, for receiving heretics into his house, and keeping disputation of heresy there.

John Williamson, Thomas Buge, Thomas Gilbert, William Hickson, Robert Daniel, and Robert Smitton.—These six were suspected of being sacramentaries and rank heretics, and procurers of heretics to preach, and to be followers of their doctrine.

John Mayler, for being a sacramentary, and a railer against the mass.

Richard Bilby, draper, was presented for saying these words, "That Christ is not present in the blessed sacrament!"

Henry Patinson, and Anthony Barber.—These two were detected for permitting their boys to sing a song against the sacrament of the altar. Also Patinson came not to confession.

Robert Norman, also refused to come to confession, saying, "That none of his servants should be absolved by a knave-priest."

John Humfrey, for speaking against the sacraments, and ceremonies of the church.

William Smith and his wife, and John Cooke and his wife.—These two couples were presented for not coming to service in their parish church; and for saying it was lawful for priests to have wives.

William Gate or Cote, William Aston, John Humfrey, and John Cooke. — These four were presented, for saying, "That the mass was made of pieces and patches." Also for despising of matins, mass, and even-song.

John Miles and his wife, John Millen, John Robinson, Richard Millar, John Green and his wife, and Arnold Chest.—All these were put up for railing against the sacraments and ceremonies.

John Crosdall, John Clerke, and John Owel.—These three labouring men were presented for not coming to divine service on holy-days, and for labouring on the same.

Thomas Grangier, and John Dictier; noted for common singers against the sacraments and ceremonies.

John Sutton and his wife, and John Segar.—These three were noted to be despisers of auricular confession.

John Rawlins, John Shiler, William Chalinger, John Edmonds, and John Richmond and his wife, for despising holy bread and holy water, and not attending divine service.

Margaret Smith, for dressing flesh meat in Lent.

Thomas Trentham, for reasoning against the sacrament of the altar, and saying that the sacrament was a good thing, but it was not very God.

Robert Granger, William Petingale, William May and his wife, John Harrison and his wife, Robert Welch, John Benglosse, John Pitley, Henry Foster, Robert Causy, and William Pinchbeck and his wife.—All these thirteen were put up by the inquisition, for not observing proper reverence at the celebration of the mass.

The wife of Martyn Bishop was presented by her curate, for not going to confession in Lent, or receiving at Easter. Also she slighted the curate, when he told her of it.

Robert Plat and his wife.—These were great reasoners in scripture, saying, that confession avails nothing; and that he, though not able to read, would not use beads to say his prayers on.

Thomas Aduet, John Palmer, and Robert Cooke.—The charge laid to these three persons, was for reasoning about the scriptures and the sacraments.

The register says, that they denied all the sacraments. But this popish hyperbole will find little credit, where experience, acquainted with popish practices, sits as the judge.

John Cockes.—This man was noted for a great searcher out of new preachers, and a maintainer of Barnes's opinions.

John Boultes, for forbidding his wife to use beads in saying her prayers.

Thomas Kelde.—He refused to take penance and absolution; and did eat flesh upon a Friday before Lent.

Nicholas Newell, a Frenchman, presented as a man far gone in the new sect; and that he was a great jester at the saints and at our Lady.

John Hawkins and his servant, Thomas Chamberlaine and his wife, John Curteys, Mr. Dissel, his wife, and his servant.—These eight were great reasoners, and despisers of ceremonies.

The curate of St. Katherine Coleman.—He was noted for calling suspected persons to his sermons by a beadle, without ringing of any bell; and when he preached he left his matters doubtful.

Also, for preaching without the commandment of his parson.

Also, for that he was a Scottish friar, driven out of his country for heresy.

Tulle Bustre, his wife, and his son-in-law.—These were noted for seldom attending the church, and many times were seen to labour upon the holy-days.

William Ettis and his wife.—Ettis and his wife were noted for maintaining certain preachers; and for causing one Taverner, a priest, to preach against the king's injunctions.

Merifield and his son-in-law; Nicholas Russel, of the Saracen's Head in Friday-street, William Callaway, and Thomas Gardiner, with three apprentices.—Against this company presentation was made for assembling together in the evening; and for bringing ill preachers, that is to say, good preachers, amongst the people.

Thomas Plummer was presented for saying, "That the sacrament was blessed to him that doth take it; and not blessed to him that doth not."

Shermons, of the Carpenter's-hall in Christ's parish, was presented for procuring an interlude to be openly played, in which priests were railed at, and called knaves.

Lewis Morall, a servant, and James Ogule and his wife.—Noted not to have confessed certain years before.

Thomas Babam was accused not to have confessed in his parish church.

The parson and curate of St. Antholin's, for not using the ceremonies in making holy water; nor keeping their processions on Saturdays.

Lewis Bromfield, for not taking the sacrament; and for absenting himself from the church on holy-days.

John Sempe, and John Goffe, for dispraising a certain anthem of our Lady, beginning Te matrem, &c., saying, that there is heresy in the same.

Gilbert Godfrey, for absenting himself from the church on holy-days.

Thomas Cappes, for saying these words, "That the sacrament of the altar was but a memory and a remembrance of the Lord's death."

John Mailer, grocer, for calling the sacrament of the altar the baked God; and for saying that the mass was called beyond the sea, missa, for that all is amiss in it.

John Hardyman, a parson of St. Martin's in Ironmonger-lane, presented for preaching openly, that confession is confusion and deformation; and that the cere-

monies of the church were to be abhorred. Also for
saying, that it was a mischief to esteem the sacraments
to be of such virtue; for in so doing they take the glory
of God from him: and for saying, that faith in Christ
is sufficient, without any other sacraments, to justify.

Christopher Dray, plumber, for saying of the sacrament of the altar, that it was not offered up for remission of sins; and that the body of Christ was not there,
but only by representation and signification.

Robert Ward, shoemaker, presented by three witnesses for speaking against the sacrament of the altar:
he died in prison in Bread-street.

Nicholas Otes, for not coming to the sacrament at
Easter; he was sent to Newgate.

Herman Peterson, and James Gosson, for not coming
to absolution and the sacrament at the time of Easter.
These were committed to prison in Bread-street.

Richard White, haberdasher, for saying, that he did
not think that Christ was in the sacrament of the altar
within the sepulchre, but in heaven above.

Giles Harrison being in a place without Aldgate, and
merrily jesting in a certain company of neighbours,
where some of them said, "Let us go to mass;" "I
say, tarry," said he; and so taking a piece of bread in
his hands, lifted it up over his head: and likewise taking
a cup of wine, and bowing down his head, made therewith a cross over the cup, and so taking the cup in both
his hands, lifted it over his head; saying these words,
"Have ye not heard mass now?" For which he was
presented to Bonner, then bishop of London.

Richard Bostock, priest, for saying that auricular
confession killed more souls than all the bills, clubs,
and halters had done since King Henry was king of
England, &c. Also for saying, that the water in the
Thames has as much virtue as the water that the priests
hallow.

Margaret Ambsworth, for having no reverence for the
sacrament; and for instructing maids; and being a
great doctress.

John Leicester, William Raynold, Christopher Townes-
end, Thomas David Skinner, Thomas Mabs, Thomas
Starckey, Christopher Holybread, Martyn Donam, and
William Derby.—All these were noted and presented
for maintaining of Barnes, and such other preachers;
and many of their wives for not taking holy bread; nor
going in procession on Sundays.

Lawrence Maxwel, bricklayer, for speaking and reasoning against auricular confession.

John Coygnes, or Livelonde, for holding against the
sacrament of the altar, and not receiving at Easter.

Gerard Frise was presented by two witnesses, for affirming that a sermon preached is better than the sacrament of the altar; and that he had rather go to hear a
sermon than to hear a mass.

Dominic Williams, a Frenchman, for not receiving
the sacrament of the altar at Easter.

Thomas Lancaster, priest.—He lay in the Compter
in the Poultry, for compiling and bringing over prohibited books. Also, Gough, a stationer, was troubled
for resorting to him.

Friar Ward was put in the Compter in Bread-street,
for marrying after his vow of celibacy.

Friar Wilcock, a Scotch friar, was imprisoned in the
Fleet, for preaching against confession; holy water;
against praying to saints, and for souls departed; against
purgatory; and for holding that priests might have
wives, &c.

John Taylor, doctor in divinity, was presented for
preaching at St. Bride's in Fleet-street, that it is as
profitable for a man to hear mass and see the sacrament,
as to kiss Judas's mouth, which kissed Christ our
Saviour, &c.

W. Tolwine, parson of St. Antholin's, was presented
and examined before Edmund Bonner, for permitting
Alexander Seton to preach in his church, having no
license; and also for allowing the said Alexander Seton,
in his sermons, to preach against Dr. Smith.

It was also objected, that he used to make holy water,
leaving out the general exorcism.

Against this objection Tolwine defended himself, saying, "That he took occasion to do so by the king's injunctions, which say, 'That ceremonies should be used,
all ignorance and superstition set apart.'"

In the end, Tolwine was forced to stand at St. Paul's
Cross to recant.

At the same time Robert Wisedom, parish priest of
St. Margaret's, in Lothbury; and Thomas Becon, were
brought to St. Paul's Cross, to recant and to revoke
their doctrine, and to burn their books.

Sir George Parker, parson of St. Pancras, and curate
of Little Allhallows, was noted, suspected, and brought
before the ordinary, for having certain books.

Sir John Byrch, priest of St. Botolph's-lane, was
complained of for being a busy reasoner in certain
opinions, which agreed not with the pope's church.

Alexander Seton, a Scotchman, was denounced, detected, and presented, by three priests; of whom one
was fellow of Whittington College, called Richard Taylor;
another was John Smith; the third was John Hunting-
don, who afterwards was converted to the same doctrine
himself.

This Seton was chaplain to the duke of Suffolk; and
from his sermons his adversaries raised against him
fifteen objections, or rather cavils, which I shall here
exhibit to the reader; that men may see how consonant
the doctrine Seton then preached was with the scriptures.

*Certain Places or Articles gathered out of Seton's
Sermons by his Adversaries.*

"There is nothing in heaven or earth, creature or other,
that can be any means towards our justification; nor
can any man satisfy God the Father for our sins, save
only Christ, and the shedding of his blood.

"He that preaches that works have merit; or are any
means to our salvation; or are any part of our justification, preaches a doctrine of the devil.

"If any thing else, save only Christ, be a means towards our justification, then Christ only does not justify us.

"I say, that neither thy good works, nor any thing
that thou canst do, can be one jot or tittle towards thy
justification. For if they be, then is not Christ a full
justifier; and that I will prove by a familiar example:

"They that preach that works have merit, do make
works the tree; which are only the fruits of justification
wrought by him who is justified.

"I would ask a question, whether he that works is a
good man, or bad; for he must be one of them. If he
be a good man, he cannot but bring forth good fruits;
if he be a bad man, he cannot bring forth but ill fruit;
for a good tree cannot bring forth ill fruit.

"He that says that works do merit any thing towards
our salvation, makes works helpmate with Christ, and
plucks from Christ what is his, and gives it to works.
Some will ask, wherefore, then, should I do good works?
I answer, good works are to be done for no cause else,
but only for the glory of God, and not that they may
merit anything at all. And he that says that good works
are to be done for any other cause, than for the glory
of God only; and will have them to merit; or be any
means towards our justification, I say he lies, and I believe him not.

"He that can shew me from any part of scripture,
that works do merit, or are any means to our justification, for the first scripture I will lose both mine ears;
for the second, my tongue; and for the third, my neck.

"Men say that we deny good works, and fasting and
prayer. They lie on us; we deny nothing but popish
works, and popish fasting, and popish prayer; and he
that preacheth that works do merit, or fasting doth
merit, or prayer doth merit, preaches a popish doctrine.

"If you ask, if good works shall be rewarded, I say
yea, and with no less than eternal glory; but for no
merit that they deserve; for they deserve nothing; but
only because God hath promised, not for the merit of
the work, but for his promise sake, and he will not break
his promise."

To these and other objections he made answer in

writing; first denying many things presented, taking upon his conscience, that he never spake some of those words; and again, many things that he never meant to such an end or purpose. But notwithstanding all this, the ordinary proceeded in his judgment, ministering to him certain interrogatories (after the Popish course) to the number of ten articles. The greatest matter laid against him, was for preaching free justification by faith in Christ Jesus, against false confidence in good works, and man's free will. Also for affirming that private masses, dirges, and other prayers profited not the souls departed; so that in the end, he was caused to recant at St. Paul's cross, 1541.

Add to these, Doctor Tailor, parson of St. Peter's, Cornhill: South, parish priest of Allhallows, Lombard-street: Some, a priest: Giles, the king's brewer: Thomas Lancaster, priest. All of whom were imprisoned likewise for the six articles.

To be short, such a number in London and Calais, and other quarters, were then apprehended through the inquisition, that all the prisons in London were too small to hold them; so that they were obliged to lay them in the halls. At last, by means of the good lord Audley, such pardons were obtained of the king, that they were all discharged, being bound only to appear in the star-chamber the next day after All-souls, there to answer if they were called upon.

An Account of John Porter, cruelly martyred for reading the Bible.

John Porter, in the year 1541, was cruelly handled for reading the Bible in St. Paul's church. It was stated already that Edmund Bonner, bishop of London, being then ambassador at Paris, was a great actor in setting forward the printing of the Bible; promising that he would have six of those Bibles set up in the church of St. Paul in London; which also at his coming home he performed.

The Bibles thus standing in St. Paul's church by the command of the king, and the appointment of Bonner, many well-disposed people used to resort there, especially when they could get any that had an audible voice to read to them. After Cromwell was dead, it happened, amongst several godly persons, who frequented there the reading of the Bible, that John Porter used sometimes to be occupied in that godly exercise, to the edifying of himself as well as others. This Porter was a comely young man, and of high stature; who by diligent reading of the scriptures, and by hearing of such sermons as were then preached by those who were the setters forth of God's truth, became very expert. The Bible then being set up by Bonner's command upon several pillars in St. Paul's church, fixed to them with chains for all men to read them that wished, great multitudes would resort to hear this Porter, because he could read well, and had an audible voice. Bonner and his chaplains being grieved, (and the world beginning then to frown upon the gospellers,) sent for Porter, and rebuked him very sharply for his reading: but Porter answered him that he trusted he had done nothing contrary to the law; neither contrary to the advertisements which he had ordered to be fixed in print over every Bible.

Bonner then laid to his charge that he had made expositions upon the text, and had gathered great multitudes about him to make tumults. He answered, he trusted that that could not be proved. But Bonner sent him to Newgate, where he was cruelly fettered with irons about his legs and arms; and with a collar of iron about his neck fastened to the wall in the dungeon: being there so inhumanly handled, that he was compelled to send for a kinsman of his, whose name was also Porter, who, seeing his kinsman in this miserable case, entreated Jewet, then keeper of Newgate, that he might be released out of those cruel irons; and so through friendship and money, had him up among other prisoners, who lay there for felony and murder, where Porter being among them, hearing and seeing their wickedness and blasphemy, exhorted them to amendment of life, and gave to them such instructions as he had learned of the scriptures; for which he was complained against and so carried down, and laid in the lowest dungeon of all, oppressed with bolts and irons, where within six or eight days after he was found dead.

Thomas Sommers, imprisoned for the Gospel.

Amongst these Londoners thus troubled by the clergy, we will add also a note of a merchant called Thomas Sommers, who died in the Tower of London for the gospel. Being a very honest and wealthy merchant, he was sent for by the lord cardinal, and committed to the Tower, because he had Luther's books; and his judgment was, that he should ride from the Tower to Cheapside, carrying a new book in his hand, and with books hung round about him, with three or four other merchants. And when Master Sommers was to be set on a collier's nag, as the rest of his fellow-prisoners were, a friend of his brought him a very good horse, with bridle and saddle; and when the bishop's officers came to dress him with books, as they had trimmed the others, and would have made holes in his garment to have thrust the strings of the books in; "Nay," said Sommers, "I have always loved to go handsomely in my apparel," and taking the books and opening them, he bound them together by the strings, and cast them about his neck (the leaves being all open) like a collar; and being on horseback, rode foremost through the streets, till they came about the standard in Cheapside, where a great fire was made to burn their books in, and a pillory set up there for four persons.

When they came to the fire, every one of them having a book in his hand, they were commanded to cast their books into the fire. But when Master Sommers saw that his New Testament should be burned, he threw it over the fire; which was seen by some of God's enemies; and brought to him again commanding him to cast it into the fire; which he would not do, but cast it through the fire. Which was done three times. But at last a stander-by took it up, and saved it from burning.—But not long after, Master Sommers was cast again into the Tower by the cardinal, through the cruelty of the bishops and their adherents, and soon after died in the prison for the testimony of his faith.

What trouble and vexation happened among the godly brethren in London for the six articles, we have thus concisely detailed. But this rigorous inquisition was not confined to this city only, but extended to Salisbury, Norfolk, Lincoln, and through all shires and quarters of the realm.

About the same time, John Longland, bishop of Lincoln, burned two men upon one day; the one named Thomas Bernard, and the other James Morton: one for teaching the Lord's prayer in English, and the other for possessing the epistle of St. James translated into English.

In Oxford also, about the same time, recanted one Master Barber, master of arts of that university, a man excellently learned. Who being called up to Lambeth before the archbishop Thomas Cranmer, was so firm in the cause of the sacrament, and so learnedly defended himself that neither Cranmer himself, nor any other could answer his objections out of Augustine: in which he was so prompt, that the archbishop, with the rest of his company, greatly admired him. He, however, at last relented; and, returning again to Oxford, was there caused to recant.

A merry and pleasant Narration, touching a false report of Fire, raised among the Doctors and Masters of Oxford in St. Mary's Church, at the Recantation of Master Malary, Master of Arts of Cambridge.

This recantation of Master Barber, in the University of Oxford, brings to remembrance another recantation, happening not long before, which I thought I ought not to pass over, as a merry ridiculous spectacle, not unworthy to be remembered, and here inserted ; to recreate and refresh by the way the weary mind of the reader, after so many bloody and lamentable stories, executions, recantations, and tragedies. The story is this :—

There was one Master Malary, a Master of Arts of Cambridge, and scholar of Christ's College, who for holding opinions contrary to the determination of the holy mother church of Rome ; that is, for the right truth of Christ's Gospel, was brought before the bishops, and in the end sent to Oxford ; there openly to recant, and to bear his fagot, to the terror of the students of that University. The time and place was appointed when he should be brought solemnly into St. Mary's church upon a Sunday, where a great number of the head doctors and divines, and others of the university, were assembled ; besides a great multitude of citizens, who came to behold the sight. In order that solemnity might not pass without some effectual sermon for the mother church of Rome, doctor Smith, then reader of the divinity lecture, was appointed to preach the sermon at this recantation. There was assembled a mighty audience of all sorts of degrees, as well of students as others. Few were absent who loved to hear or see any news ; so that there was no place in the whole church which was not filled with the concourse of people.

All things being thus prepared and set in readiness, Malary comes forth with his fagot upon his shoulder. Not long after, the doctor proceeds into the pulpit, to deliver his sermon, the argument of which was wholly upon the sacrament. The doctor, for the more confirmation of his words, had provided the holy wafer, and the sacrament of the altar, to hang by a string before him in the pulpit. Thus the doctor, commencing his sermon, had scarcely proceeded into it, the people giving great reverence to his doctrine, when suddenly was heard in the church the voice of one crying in the street, " Fire ! fire !" The occasion was this : a man coming from Allhallows parish, saw a chimney on fire, and so passing in the street by St. Mary's church, cried " Fire ! fire !"

This sound of fire being heard in the church, went from one to another, that at length it came to the ears of the doctors, and at last to the preacher himself ; who, as soon as they heard it, being amazed with sudden fear and marvelling what the matter meant, began to look up to the top of the church, and to the walls. The others seeing them look up, looked up also. Then they began to cry out with a loud voice, " Fire ! fire." " Where ?" saith one ! " Where ?" saith another. " In the church," saith a third. The mention of the church was scarcely pronounced, when, as in one moment, there was a common cry among them, " The church is on fire ! the church is on fire by heretics !" &c. And although no man saw any fire at all, yet as all men cried out, so every man thought it true. Then there was such fear and tumult through the whole church, that it cannot be described in words.

Thus this strong imagination of fire being fixed in their heads, as nothing could move them to think but that the church was on fire, so every thing that they saw or heard increased this suspicion in them. The first and chief occasion that augmented this suspicion, was the heretic there bearing his fagot, which led them to imagine that all other heretics had conspired with him to set the church on fire.

After this, through the rage of the people, and running to and fro, the dust was so raised, that it seemed as if it had been smoke. Which, together with the outcry of the people, made them so afraid, that leaving the sermon, they began all to run away. But such was the press of the multitude, running together, that the more they laboured, the less they could get out. For whilst they ran all headlong to the doors, every man striving to get out first, they thrust one another, and stuck so fast, that they who were without, could not get into the church, and they that were within could not get out. So that one door being stopped, they ran to another on the north side. But there again was the like or greater throng. So the people clustering and thronging together, it put many in danger, and brought many to

their end, by bruising of their bones or sides. There was yet another door towards the west, which could not be opened for the press of people.

At last, when they were past all hope to get out, then they were exceedingly amazed, and ran up and down, crying out upon the heretics who had conspired their death. The more they ran about and cried out, the more smoke and dust rose in the church. I think some were howling and weeping, some were running up and down, and playing the madman, now hither, now thither, as being tossed to and fro with waves and tempests, trembling and quaking, raging and fearing, without any manifest cause ; the doctors laden with so many badges of wisdom, were seeking holes and corners to hide themselves in, gasping, breathing, and sweating, and for very horror almost beside themselves. Whilst one said that he plainly heard the noise of the fire ; another affirmed that he saw it with his eyes ; and another swore that he felt the molten lead dropping down upon his head and shoulders. Such is the force of imagination, when it is once grafted in men's hearts through fear. In all the whole company, there was none that behaved himself more modestly than the heretic that was there to do penance ; who casting his fagot off from his shoulders, kept himself quiet.

All the others never made an end of running up and down and crying out. None cried out more earnestly than the doctor that preached, who first of all cried out in the pulpit, saying, " These are the trains and subtilities of the heretics against me ! Lord have mercy upon me ! Lord have mercy upon me !" In all this there was nothing more feared than the melting of the lead, which many affirmed that they felt dropping upon their bodies. Now in this sudden terror and fear, which took from them all reason, none acted more ridiculously than such as seemed the greatest and wisest men, save that in one or two somewhat more quietness of mind appeared. Among whom was one Claymund, president of Corpus Christi College (whom for reverence and learning's sake I do here name) and a few other aged persons with him, who for their age and weakness durst not thrust themselves into the throng among the rest, but kneeled down quietly before the high altar, committing themselves and their lives to the sacrament. The others, who were younger and stronger, ran up and down through the press, marvelling at the uncivility of men, and angry with the unmannerly multitude that would give no room to the doctors, bachelors, masters, and other graduates and regent masters. But as the terror and fear was common to all, so was there no difference made of persons or degrees, every man scrambling for himself. The violet cap, or purple gown did there nothing avail the doctor ; neither the master's hood nor the monk's cowl was respected.

Yea, if the king or queen had been there at that present and in that perplexity, they had been no better than a common person. After they had long striven and assayed all manner of ways and saw no remedy, neither by force, neither authority to prevail, they fell to entreating and offering of rewards, one offering twenty pounds, another his scarlet gown, so that any man would pull him out.

Some stood close to the pillars, thinking themselves safe under the vaults of stone from the dropping of the lead. Others, being without money, knew not which way to turn themselves. One, a president of a college pulling a board from the pews, covered his head and shoulders with it against the scalding lead, which they feared much more than the fall of the church. Another, who had a grand paunch, a monk, seeing the doors stopped and every way closed up, thought to get out through a glass window ; but the iron grates prevented him ; however, he would make the attempt. When he had broken the glass, and was come to the space between the grates, he thrust in his head with one shoulder, and it went through easy enough. Then he laboured to get the other shoulder after ; but there was a great labour about that, for he stuck long by the shoulders, though at last he succeeded. For what does not labour overcome ? Thus far he was now got. But by what part of his body he afterwards stuck fast, I am not going to say; but this is most certain that he did stick fast between the grates, and could neither get out nor in.

After some time there was at last a way found for the crowd, so that some going over the heads of others got out.

Here also happened another incident to one of the monks: there was a young lad, who, seeing the doors fast stopped with the press or multitude, and that he had no way to get out, climbed up upon the door, and there staying upon the top of the door, was forced to remain quiet. For he durst not come down into the church again for fear of the fire, and he could not leap down toward the street without danger. By chance, among them that got out over men's heads, he saw a monk who had a great wide cowl hanging at his back. This the boy thought to be a good occasion for him to escape by. When the monk came near to him, the boy who was on the top of the door, slipped down into the monk's cowl, thinking that if the monk escaped, he should also get out with him. At last the monk got out, and feeling his cowl heavier than it was accustomed to be, and hearing the voice of one speaking behind, he was more afraid than before, thinking that the evil spirit which had set the church on fire had got into his cowl, so he began to play the exorcist: "In the name of God," said he, "and all saints, I command thee to declare what thou art, that art behind at my back." To whom the boy answered, "I am Bertram's boy." "But I," said the monk, "adjure thee in the name of the inseparable Trinity, that thou wicked spirit do tell me who thou art, and that thou get hence." With that his cowl began to crack upon his shoulders, and the boy took to his legs and ran away as fast as he could.

At length, after much delay, all were got out of the church, and discovered the folly of their false alarm.

The fourth and fifth Marriages of King Henry VIII.

In the same year, and immediately after the apprehension of Lord Cromwell, the king was divorced from Lady Anne of Cleves (July 1540). The cause of which separation being wholly committed to the clergy of the convocation, it was by them defined, concluded, and granted, that the king being freed from that pretended matrimony (as they called it) might marry whom he would, and so might she likewise; who, consenting to the divorce herself, by her letters, was no more called queen, but only Anne of Cleves. The king, in the same month, was married to his fifth wife, who was the lady Catharine Howard, niece to the duke of Norfolk, and daughter to the Lord Edmund Howard, the duke's brother. But this marriage, likewise, did not continue long.

In the month of August, and in the same year, I find in some records, besides the chapter-house monks above recited, whom Cope sanctifies for holy martyrs, for suffering in the denial of the king's supremacy, six others, who were also brought to Tyburn and there executed in the like charge of rebellion. Of whom the first was the prior of Doncaster; the second, a monk of the Charterhouse of London, called Giles Horn, some call him William Horn; the third, one Thomas Ipsam, a monk of Westminster, who had his monk's garment plucked from his back, being the last monk in King Henry's days that wore the monkish dress; the fourth, one Philpot; the fifth, one Carew; the sixth was a friar.

Now, as to the marriage between the king and the Lady Howard, it endured not long; for in the year following, the Lady Catharine was accused to the king for violation of the marriage vows, and was beheaded on Tower-hill on the 12th of February, 1542.

After the death of this lady, the king, calling to remembrance the words of the Lord Cromwell; and missing now more and more his old councillor; and partly also suspecting somewhat the ways of Winchester; began a little to set his foot again in the cause of religion. And although he ever bare a special favour to Thomas Cranmer, archbishop of Canterbury, yet now the more

he missed the Lord Cromwell, the more he inclined to the archbishop, and also to the right cause of religion. And therefore, in the month of October, after the execution of this queen, the king understanding that some abuses yet remained unreformed, namely, pilgrimages and idolatry, and other things, directed his letters to the archbishop of Canterbury, for the speedy reformation of the same.

The King's Letters to the Archbishop, for the abolishing of Idolatry.

"Right reverend father in God, right trusty and well-beloved, we greet you well, letting you know, that whereas, heretofore, upon the zeal and remembrance which we had to our bounden duty towards Almighty God, perceiving sundry superstitions and abuses to be used and embraced by our people, whereby they grievously offended him and his word, we not only caused the images and bones of such as they resorted and offered to, with the ornaments of the same, and all such writings and monuments of feigned miracles, wherewith they were deceived, to be taken away in all places of the realm, but also by our injunctions commanded that no offering or setting up of lights or candles should be suffered in any church, but only to the blessed sacraments of the altar: it is lately come to our knowledge, that, notwithstanding this our good intent and purpose, the shrines, coverings of shrines, and monuments of those things do yet remain in sundry places of this realm, much to the slander of our doings, and to the great displeasure of Almighty God, being means to allure our subjects to their former hypocrisy and superstition, and also that our injunctions be not kept. For the due and speedy reformation whereof, we have thought meet, by these our letters, expressly to will and command you, that immediately upon the receipt hereof, you shall not only cause due search to be made in the cathedral church for those things, and if any shrine, covering of shrine, table, monument of miracles, or other pilgrimages, do there continue, to cause it to be so taken away, as that there may remain no memory of it; but also that you shall take order with all the curates, and others having charge within your diocese to do the same, and to see that our injunctions be duly kept, without failing, as we trust you, and as you will answer to the contrary.

"Given under our signet, at our town of Hull, the fourth day of October, in the thirty-fourth year of our reign (1542)."

Another proclamation was given out, in the following year, by the king's authority, wherein the pope's law, forbidding white meats to be eaten in Lent, was repealed.

A Proclamation concerning eating of White Meats, made the ninth of February, in the thirty-fourth year of the Reign of the King's most Royal Majesty.

"Forasmuch as by divers and sundry occasions, as well herrings, lings, saltfish, salmon, stockfish, as other kinds of fish have been this year scant, and also enhanced in prices above the old rate and common estimation of their value, so that if the king's loving subjects should be enforced only to buy and provide herring, and other salt store of fish, for the necessary and sufficient sustentation and maintenance of their household and families all this holy time of Lent, according as they have been wont in times past to do, and should not be by some other convenient means relieved therein, the same might and should undoubtedly redound to their insupportable charge and detriment; and forasmuch as his highness considers how this kind and manner of fasting, that is to say, to abstain from milk, butter, eggs, cheese, and other white meats, is but a mere positive law of the church, and used by a custom within this realm, and of no other force or necessity; but the same may be upon considerations and grounds altered and dispensed with from time to time, by the public authority of kings and princes, whenever they shall perceive the same to tend to the hurt and damage of their people:

the king's highness, therefore, most graciously consider-ing and tendering the wealth and commodity of his people, has thought good, for the considerations above rehearsed, to release and dispense with the said law and custom of abstaining from white meats in this holy time of Lent, and of his special grace and mere motion giveth and granteth unto all and singular his subjects within this his realm, and in all his grace's dominions, free liberty, faculty, and licence, to eat all manner of white meats, as milk, eggs, butter, cheese, and such like, during the time of this Lent, without any scruple or grudge of conscience, any law, constitution, use, or custom to the contrary, notwithstanding.

" Wherein, nevertheless, his highness exhorts, and in the name of God requires all such his faithful subjects, as may, will, or shall enjoy this his grant or faculty, that they be in nowise scrupulous or doubtful thereof, nor abuse or turn the same into a fleshly or carnal liberty ; but rather endeavour themselves to their possible powers, with this liberty of eating of white meats, to observe also that fast which God most especially re-quireth of them, that is to say, to renounce the world and the devil, with all their pomps and works ; and also to subdue and repress their carnal affections and the corrupt works of the flesh, according to their vow and profession made at the font-stone ; for in these points especially consists the very true and perfect abstinence or fasting of a christian man ; thus to endure and con-tinue from year to year, till the king's highness' pleasure shall, by his majesty's proclamation, be published to the contrary."

The Trouble and Persecution of four Windsor-men, Robert Testwood, Henry Filmer, Anthony Pearson, and John Marbeck, persecuted for Righteousness' sake, and for the Gospel.

We come now to the history of the four Windsor-men, persecuted for the true testimony of God's word ; three were martyred and sacrificed in the fire ; the fourth (named Marbeck) had his pardon. First, I have to shew the origin of their troubles ; secondly, the manner and order of their death as they suffered together ; which was A. D. 1543.

The Origin of Testwood's Trouble.

In A.D. 1533 there was one Robert Testwood, in the city of London, who for his knowledge in music had so great a name that the musicians in Windsor college thought him a worthy man to have a room among them. Whereupon they informed Dr. Sampson their dean. But as some of the canons had at that time heard of Test-wood, that he smelled of the new learning, as they called it, it would not be consented to at the first. Notwith-standing on some entreaty on the part of the musicians, Testwood was sent for to be heard. And being there four or five days among the choirmen, he was so well liked both for his voice and skill, that he was admitted, and settled in Windsor, and held in good estimation with the dean and canons a great while ; but when they per-ceived, for he could not well dissemble his religion, that he leaned to Luther's sect, they began to dislike him. It was his chance one day to be at dinner with one of the canons, named Dr. Rawson ; at which dinner, among others, was one of King Edward's four chantry priests, named Ely. This Ely began to rail against laymen who took upon them to meddle with the scriptures, and to be better learned than they who had been students in the universities of Oxford and Cambridge all the days of their lives. Then Testwood, perceiving he meant him, said, " Master Ely, I think it no hurt for a layman, as I am, to read and to know the scriptures."

" Which of you," said Ely, " that are unlearned knows them or understands them ? St. Paul saith, ' If thine enemy hunger, feed him ; if he thirst, give him drink, for in so doing thou shalt heap coals of fire on his head.' Now, Sir, what means St. Paul by those coals of fire ?" " Marry, Sir," said Testwood, " he means nothing, as I have learned, but burning love and kind-

ness ; that by doing good to our enemies we should thereby win them." " Ah, sir," quoth he, " you are an old scholar, indeed."

After this they fell into further communication about the pope, whose supremacy was much spoken of at that time, but not known to be so far in question in the Par-liament house as it was. And in their talk Ely demand-ed of Testwood, whether the pope ought to be head of their church, or not ? Against which Testwood durst not say his full mind, but reasoned within bounds a great while. But when Testwood, forgetting himself, chanced to say, That every king, in his own realm and dominion, ought to be the head of the church under Christ, Ely was so chafed, that he rose from the table in great fume, calling him " heretic," and all that was bad, and so went brawling and scolding away, to the great disquieting of the company.

Then was Testwood very sorry to see the old man take it so grievously. Whereupon after dinner he went and sought Master Ely, and found him walking in the body of the church, thinking to talk with him charitably, and so to be friends again ; but as Testwood pressed towards him, the other shunned him, and would not come nigh him, but spit at him ; saying to others that walked by, " Beware of this fellow, for he is the greatest heretic and schismatic that ever came into Windsor."

After Ely had made his complaint to the dean's de-puty, and others of the canons, they were all against Testwood, purposing at the dean's coming home to have punished Testwood. But it was not ten days after that the king's supremacy passed in the parliament-house ; upon which the dean (Dr. Sampson) came home suddenly in the night, and sent his verger to all the canons and ministers of the college, from the highest to the lowest, commanding them to be in the charter-house by eight of the clock in the morning. Then Ely consulted with the canons overnight, and thought on the next day to have put Testwood to a great plunge. " But he that layeth a snare for another man," saith Solomon, " shall be taken in it himself." And so was Ely. For when the dean and every man were come and placed in the chapter-house, and the dean had commended the ministers of the church for their diligence in attending the choir, he began, contrary to every man's expectation, to inveigh against the bishop of Rome's supremacy and usurped authority, confuting it by manifest scriptures and proba-ble reasons, so earnestly, that it was a wonder to hear ; and at length declared openly, that by the whole consent of the parliament-house, the pope's supremacy was utterly abolished out of this realm of England for ever, and so commanded every man there, upon his allegiance, to call him pope no more, but bishop of Rome ; and what-ever he were that would not do so, or did from that day forth maintain or favour his cause by any means, he should not only lose the benefit of that house, but be re-puted as an utter enemy to God, and to the king. The canons hearing this, were all struck dumb. Yet Ely's heart was so full, that he would utter his spite against Testwood ; but the dean called him old fool, and took him up so sharply, that he was glad to hold his peace. Then the dean commanded all the pope's pardons which hung about the church to be brought into the chapter-house, and cast into the fire, and burnt before their faces, and so departed.

Testwood was one day walking in the church, and be-held the pilgrims, especially of Devonshire and Corn-wall, how they came in with candles and images of wax in their hands, to offer to good King Henry of Windsor, as they called him. It grieved him to see such great idolatry committed, and how vainly the peo-ple had spent their goods in coming so far to kiss a spur, and to have an old hat set upon their heads ; so that he could not refrain, but, seeing a company who had made their offerings stand gazing about the church, went to them, and with all gentleness began to exhort them to leave such false worshipping of dumb creatures, and to learn to worship the true living God aright, putting them in remembrance what those things were which they wor-shipped, and how God many times had plagued his peo-ple for running to worship such stocks and stones, and would plague them and their posterity, if they would not leave it.

After this way he admonished them till at last his words took such place in some of them, that they said they never would go on a pilgrimage any more. Then he went further, and found another set licking and kissing a white lady made of alabaster, which image was carved in a wall behind the high altar, and bordered about with a pretty border, which was made like branches with hanging apples and flowers. And when he saw them so superstitiously use the image as to wipe their hands upon it, and then to stroke them over their heads and faces as though there had been great virtue in touching the picture, he raised his hand, in the which he had a key, and struck a piece of the border about the image, and with the glance of the stroke chanced to break off the image's nose. "Lo, good people," cried he, "you see that it is nothing but earth and dust, and cannot help itself; and how then will you have it to help you? For God's sake, brethren, be no more deceived." And so he gat him home to his house, for the uproar was so great, that many came to see the image how it was defaced. And among others came one William Simons, a lawyer, who seeing the image without a nose, took the matter grievously, and looking down upon the pavement, he spied the nose where it lay, which he took up and put into his purse, saying it should be a dear nose to Testwood.

Many were offended with Testwood—the canons for speaking against their profit, the wax sellers for hindering their market, and Simons for the image's nose. And some of the canons threatened to kill him. So Testwood kept his house, and durst not come forth, but sent the whole matter in writing by his wife, to Cromwell, the king's secretary, who was his special friend. The canons hearing that Testwood was about to send to Cromwell, sent the verger to him to come to the church; who sent them word again that he was in fear of his life, and therefore would not come. Then they sent two of the eldest minor canons to entreat him, and to assure him that no man should do him harm. He made them a plain answer, that he had no trust in their promises, but would complain to his friends. Then they knew not what shift to make, for of all men they feared Cromwell, but sent in post-haste for old Master Ward, a justice of peace, dwelling three or four miles off, who being come, and hearing the matter, was very loth to meddle in it. But notwithstanding, through their entreaty, he went to Testwood, and after much persuasion and faithfully promising him, by the oath he had made to God and the king, to defend him from all danger and harm, Testwood was content to go with him.

And when Master Ward and Testwood were come to the church, and were going toward the chapter-house, one of the canons drew his dagger at Testwood, and would have been upon him, but Master Ward with his man resisted, and got Testwood into the chapter-house. Now Testwood, being alone in the chapter-house, with the canons and Master Ward, was gently treated, and the matter so pacified, that Testwood was allowed quietly to come and go to the church, and do his duty as he had done before.

Upon a relic Sunday, as they named it, when every minister, after their old custom, should have borne a relic in his hand in a procession, one was brought to Testwood. Which relic, as they said, was a rochet of Bishop Becket's. And as the sexton would have put the rochet in Testwood's hands, he pushed it from him, and so the rochet was given to another.

In the days of Master Franklen, who succeeded Doctor Sampson in the deanery of Windsor, there was set up at the choir door a foolish printed paper, all to the praise and commendation of our Lady, ascribing to her our justification, our salvation, our redemption, the forgiveness of sins, &c., to the great derogation of Christ. Which paper, one of the canons named Magnus, caused to be set up in despite of Testwood and his sect. When Testwood saw this paper, he plucked it down secretly. The next day another was set up in the same place. Then Testwood coming into the church, and seeing another paper

set up, and also the dean coming a little way off, made haste to be at the choir door, while the dean staid to take holy water, and reaching up his hand as he went, plucked away the paper with him. The dean being come to his stall, called Testwood to him, and said, that he marvelled greatly how he durst be so bold as to take down the paper in his presence? Testwood answered again, that he marvelled much more, that his mastership would suffer such a blasphemous paper to be set up, beseeching him not to be offended with what he had done, for he would stand to it. So the dean being a timorous man, made no more ado with him. After this no more papers were set up, but poor Testwood was abused among them at every meal, and denounced as an heretic, and would carry a fagot one day, &c.

A story is told of one Robert Philips, gentleman of the king's chapel, and Testwood; which, though it was but a merry prank of a singing man, yet it grieved his adversary wonderfully. The matter was this: Robert Philips was so notable a singing man, that wherever he came, the best and longest song, with most counterverses in it, were set up at his coming. And so he chancing to be at Windsor, a long song was set up, called *Lauda Vivi*. In which song there was one counterverse toward the end that began with "*O redemptrix et salvatrix;*" which verse, of all others, Robert Philips would sing, because he knew that Testwood could not abide it. Now, Testwood knowing his mind well enough, joined with him on the other part; and when he heard Robert Philips begin to fetch his flourish with, "*O redemptrix et salvatrix,*" Testwood was as quick to answer him again with "*Non redemptrix, nec salvatrix;*" and so striving there with "*O*" and "*Non,*" who should have the mastery, they made an end of the verse. At this there was good laughing in the sleeves to some; but Robert Philips, with others of Testwood's enemies, were much offended.

Within fourteen days after this, the lords of the garter (as their yearly custom is), came to Windsor to keep St. George's feast, at which feast the duke of Norfolk was president; to whom the dean and canons made a grievous complaint. Testwood being called before the duke, he took him up, and reviled him, as though he would have sent him to be hanged. Yet Testwood so behaved himself to the duke, that in the end he let him go, to the great discomfort of the dean and canons.

These are the causes which moved Testwood's enemies to seek his destruction.

The Origin of Henry Filmer's Troubles.

About A.D. 1540, after all the orders of superstitious and begging friars were suppressed, it happened that one Sir Thomas Melster, who had been a friar, and changed his friar's coat, but not his friar's heart, was appointed vicar of Windsor. This priest made a sermon to his parishioners, in which he declared many old friars' tales, as that our Lady held out her breasts to St. Bernard, and spouted her milk into his eyes, with such like tales, that many honest men were offended, and especially this Henry Filmer, who was then one of the churchwardens, who was so zealous for God's word, that he could not abide to hear the glory of Christ so defaced with superstitious fables. So he took an honest man or two with him, and went to the priest, with whom he talked so honestly and so charitably, that in the end the priest gave him hearty thanks, and was content to reform himself without any more ado, and they parted friends.

Now there was one in the town called William Simons, a lawyer, who hearing that Filmer had been with the priest, and reproved him for his sermon, got him to the vicar, and so excited him, that he slipped away from the promise he had made to Filmer. Then Simons meeting with Filmer, reviled him, saying he would bring him before the bishop. Filmer hearing the matter renewed, which he had thought had been suppressed, stood against Simons, and said that the vicar had preached false and unsound doctrine, and he would say as much to the bishop whenever he came before him.

Then Simons went to the mayor, and procured a letter in the priest's favour, and departed to go to the bishop, (whose name was Doctor Capon), and took the priest with them.

Filmer consulted with his friends what was best to do, who drew out certain notes of the vicar's sermon, and prepared themselves to be at Salisbury as soon as Simons, or before him. Thus, both parties being in readiness, it chanced that they set forth from Windsor all in one day. But as the priest, being an impotent man, could not ride very fast, Filmer and his company got to the town before Simons, and went to the bishop, and delivered up their bill to him; which bill, when the bishop had seen and perused it well, he gave them great thanks for their pains, saying the priest had preached heresy, and should be punished.

Then Filmer declared to the bishop the form of the talk he had with the priest, and the end of it, and how the matter, being renewed again by Simons, forced him and his company to trouble his lordship with it. "Well," said the bishop, "you have done like honest men. Come to me soon again, and you shall know more;" and so they departed from the bishop to their inn. And while they were there reposing themselves, Simons, with his company, came to the town, and (not knowing the other to be come), got themselves up to the bishop in all haste, taking the priest with them.

The bishop, hearing of more Windsor men, demanded who they were, and being informed that it was the vicar of the town, with others, he caused the vicar to be brought in. To whom he said, "Are you the vicar of Windsor?" "Yea, my lord," said he. "How chances it," asked the bishop, "that you are complained of? for there have been with me certain honest men of your town who have delivered up a bill of erroneous doctrine against you. If it be so, I must needs punish you;" and opening the bill, he read it to him. "How say you," questioned the bishop; "is this true or not?" The vicar could not deny it; but humbly submitted himself to the bishop's correction. Then was his company called in, and when the bishop saw Simons, he knew him well; and said, "Wherefore come ye, Master Simons?" "Please your lordship," said he, "we are come to speak in our vicar's cause, who is a man of good conversation and honesty, and doth his duty so well in every point, that no man can find fault with him, except a fellow we have in our town, called Filmer, who is so corrupt with heresy, that he is able to poison a whole country; and truly, my lord, there is no man that can preach or teach any thing that is good and godly, but he is ready to control it; wherefore we beseech your lordship that he may be punished as an example to others, that our vicar may do his duty quietly, as he has done before this busy fellow troubled him. And that your lordship may the better credit my words, I have brought with me these honest men of the town; and a testimonial from the mayor and his brethren, to confirm the same;" and so he held the writing out in his hand.

Then said the bishop; "So God help me, Master Simons, you are greatly to blame, and most worthy to be punished of all men, that will so impudently go about to maintain your priest in his error, who has preached heresy, and has confessed it; wherefore I may not, nor will not let it go unpunished. And as for that honest man, Filmer, of whom you have complained, I tell you plainly that he hath in this point shewed himself to be a great deal more honest than you. But in hope you will no more bear out your vicar in his evil doings, I will remit all things this time, saving that he shall next Sunday recant his sermon openly before all his parishioners in Windsor church;" and so the bishop called in Filmer and his company, who waited without, and delivered the priest's recantation to them; with a great charge to see it truly observed in all points. Then Simons took his leave of the bishop, and departed, disappointed of his purpose, and sore ashamed. For this cause Simons could never brook Filmer; but when he met him at any time after, would hold up his finger, and say, "I will be even with you one day; trust me!"

The Origin of Anthony Pearson's Troubles.

There was a priest, named Anthony Pearson, who much frequented Windsor, about the year 1540, and using the talent that God had given him in preaching, was greatly esteemed among the people, who flocked so much to his sermons, that the great priests of the castle, with other papists in the town, especially Simons, were much offended; so that Simons at the last began to gather his sermons, and to mark his auditors: from which followed the death of several, and the troubles of many honest men. For, about a year after, a minister of Satan, called Doctor London, warden of the New College, in Oxford, was admitted one of the prebendaries of Windsor. At his first residence dinner which he gave to the clerks, his whole talk to two gentlemen strangers at his board, was nothing else but of heretics, and what a desolation they would bring the realm to, if they were suffered. "And by St. Mary, masters," says he, at last, "I cannot tell, but there goes a strange report abroad of this house." Some made answer; "It was undeserved." "I pray God it be so," says he. "I am but a stranger, and have but small experience among you; but I have heard it said before I came hither, that there are some in this house, that will neither have prayer nor fasting."

Then spake Testwood: "By my truth, sir," says he, "I think that was spoken of malice; for prayer, as your mastership knows better than I, is one of the first lessons that Christ taught us." "Yea marry, sir," replied he; "but the heretics will have no invocation to saints, which all the old fathers allow." "What the old fathers do allow," says Testwood, "I cannot tell; but Christ appoints us to go to his Father, and to ask our petitions of him in Christ's name." "Then you will have no mediator between you and God," said Doctor London. "Yes, sir," replied Testwood; "our mediator is Christ, as St. Paul saith, 'There is one mediator between God and man, even Jesus Christ.'" Upon this Doctor London said grace, and turned the conversation.

When Doctor London had been at Windsor a while, and learned what Testwood was, and also what heretics were in the town, and how they increased daily by reason of a priest, called Anthony Pearson, he was so bent against them, that he gave himself wholly to the devil to do mischief. And to bring his wicked purpose about, he conspired with Simons and others, how they might compass the matter: first, to have all the arch-heretics, as they termed them, in Windsor, indicted for heresy. They had a good ground to work upon, as they thought, which was the six articles; so they began to build and practice thus: First, they drew out certain notes of Anthony Pearson's sermons, which he had preached against the sacrament of the altar, and their popish mass. That done, they put in Sir William Hobby, with the good lady his wife; Sir Thomas Cardine; Mr. Edmund Harman; Mr. Thomas Weldon; with Snowbal and his wife, as chief aiders, helpers, and maintainers of Anthony Pearson. They also noted Doctor Haynes, dean of Exeter, and a prebendary of Windsor, to be a receiver of all suspected persons. They wrote also the names of all such as commonly attended Anthony Pearson's sermons, and of all such as had the Testament, and favoured the gospel.

Then they had spies to walk up and down the church, to hearken and hear what men said, and to mark who did not worship the sacrament, at the elevation. Some of these spies were chantry priests. When they had gathered as much as they could, Doctor London, with two of his brethren, gave them up to the bishop of Winchester, Stephen Gardiner, with a great complaint against the heretics that were in Windsor, declaring how the town was disquieted through their doctrine and evil example. Wherefore they besought his lordship's help, in purging the town and castle of such wicked persons. The bishop, hearing their complaint, praised their doings, and bade them go forward, and they should not lack his help. Then they plied the matter, sparing neither for money nor pains.

Bishop Gardiner, seizing a convenient time, went to the king, complaining what heretics his grace had in his realm, and how they had not only crept into every corner of his court, but even into his privy chamber, beseeching therefore his majesty that his laws might be prosecuted; the king, giving credit to these words, was content his laws should be executed on such as were offenders. Then the bishop forthwith procured a commission for a private search to be had in Windsor for books and letters; which commission the king granted to take place in the town of Windsor, but not in the castle.

At this time, the canons of Exeter had accused Doctor Haynes, their dean, to the council, for preaching against holy bread, and holy water; and for saying in one of his sermons, that marriage and hanging were destiny; upon which they gathered treason against him, because of the king's marriage. The bishop of Winchester had also informed the council of Master Hobby, how he was a great maintainer of heretics. Whereupon both he and Doctor Haynes were apprehended and sent to the Fleet. But it was not very long after, that, by the mediation of friends, they were both delivered.

Now, as to the commission for searching for books, Mr. Ward, and one Fachel of Reading, were appointed commissioners, who came to Windsor the Sunday before Palm Sunday, 1543, and began their search at night. In which search were apprehended Robert Benet, Henry Filmer, John Marbeck, and Robert Testwood, for certain books and writings found in their houses, against the six articles, and kept in ward till the Monday after, and then brought up to the council, all save Testwood, with whom the bailiffs of the town were charged, because he lay ill of the gout. The other three, being examined before the council, were committed to prison; Filmer and Benet to the bishop of London's gaol, and Marbeck to the Marshalsea; whose examination is here set out, to declare the great goodness of the council, and the cruelty of the bishop.

Examination of John Marbeck.

This Marbeck had begun a great work in English, called the Concordance of the Bible: which book, being not half finished, was, among his other books, taken to the council. And when he came before them to be examined, the work lay before the bishop of Winchester. Who beholding the poor man a while, said, "Marbeck, dost thou know wherefore thou art sent for?" "No, my lord," said he. "No!" said the bishop? "that is a marvellous thing." "Forsooth, my lord," said he, "unless it be for a certain search made of late in Windsor, I cannot tell wherefore it should be." "Then thou knowest the matter well enough," said the bishop, and taking up a quire of the Concordance in his hand, said, "understandest thou the Latin tongue?" "No, my lord," said he, "but simply." "No!" said the bishop. And with that spake Master Wrisley, (then secretary to the king) "he saith, but simply." "I cannot tell," said the bishop, "but the book is translated word for word out of the Latin Concordance," and so began to declare to the rest of the council, the nature of a Concordance, and how it was first compiled in Latin by the great diligence of the learned men for the ease of preachers; concluding with this reason, that if such a book should go forth in English, it would destroy the Latin tongue. And so casting down the quire again, he reached another book, which was the book of Isaiah the prophet, and turning to the last chapter, gave the book to Marbeck, and asked him who had written the note in the margin. The other looking upon it, said, "Forsooth, my lord, I wrote it." "Read it," said the bishop. Then he read it thus, "Heaven is my throne, and the earth is my footstool." "Nay," said the bishop, "read it as thou hast written it." "Then shall I read it wrong," said he, "for I had written it false." "How hadst thou written it," said the bishop. "I had written it," said he, "thus; Heaven is my throne, and the earth is not my footstool." "Yea," said the bishop, "that was thy meaning." "No, my lord, it was but an oversight in writing; for, as your lordship seeth, this word (not) is blotted out." At this time other matters came into the council, so that Marbeck was had out to the next chamber.

On the next day, one of the bishop of Winchester's gentlemen brought two great books under his arm, and finding Marbeck walking up and down in the chapel, demanded of the keeper why he was not in irons. "I had no such commandment," said he, "for the messenger who brought him from the council, said, "It was their pleasure he should be gently used;" and so he called for a room, to which he carried the prisoner, and said, "Marbeck, my lord favours thee well for certain good qualities that thou hast, and hast sent me to admonish thee to beware, and lest thou cast away thyself wilfully. If thou wilt be plain, thou shalt do thyself much good; if not, thou shalt do thyself much harm. I assure thee, my lord laments thy case, for he has always heard good report of thee; now see to thyself, and play the wise man. Thou art acquainted with a great many heretics, as Hobby and Haines, with others, and knowest much of their secrets; if thou wilt now tell of them, he will procure thy deliverance out of hand, and prefer thee to a better living."

"Alas, sir," said he, "what secrets do I know? I am but a poor man, and was never worthy to be conversant either with Master Hobby or Master Haines, to know their minds." "Well," said the gentleman, "make it not so strange, for my lord knows well enough in what estimation they had both thee and Anthony Pearson." "For Anthony Pearson," said he, "I can say nothing, for I never saw him with them. And as for myself, I cannot deny but that they have always taken me for an honest poor man, and shewed me much kindness; but as for their secrets, they were too wise to commit them to any such as I am."

"Peradventure," said the gentleman, "thou fearest to utter any thing of them, because they were thy friends, lest they, hearing thereof, might hereafter withdraw their friendship from thee: which thou needest not fear, I warrant thee, for they are sure enough, and never like to pleasure thee any more, nor any man else."

With that the water stood in Marbeck's eyes. "Why weepest thou," said the gentleman? "Oh, sir," said he, "I pray you pardon me; these men have done me good, wherefore I beseech the living God, to comfort them as I would be comforted myself."

"Well," said the gentleman, "I perceive thou wilt play the fool;" and then he opened one of the books, and asked him if he understood any Latin. "A little, sir," said he. "How is it then," said the gentleman, "that thou hast translated thy book out of the Latin Concordance, and yet understandest not the tongue?" "I will tell you," said he: "in my youth I learned the principles of my grammar, whereby I have some understanding, though it be very small." Then the gentleman began to try him in the Latin Concordance and English Bible which he had brought: and when he was satisfied, he departed, leaving Marbeck alone in the chamber.

About two hours after, the gentleman came again, with a sheet of paper folded in his hand, and set him down upon the bed's side, as before, and said. "By my troth, Marbeck, my lord sees so much wilfulness in thee, that he saith it is pity to do thee good." "Sir," said he, "there is nothing that I can do and say with a safe conscience, but I am ready to do it at his lordship's pleasure." "What tellest thou me," said the gentleman, "of thy conscience? Thou mayest with a safe conscience, reveal those that be heretics, and thou canst do God and the king no greater service." "If I knew, sir," said he, "who were an heretic, indeed, it were well; but if I should accuse him to be an heretic that is none, what a worm would that be in my conscience so long as I lived? Yea, it were a great deal better for me to be out of this life, than to live in such torment." "In faith," said the gentleman, "thou knowest as well who are heretics of thy fellows at home, and who are not, as I know this to be paper in my hand. Peradventure thy wits are troubled, so that thou canst not call things to remembrance; I have brought thee ink and paper, that thou mayest write such things as shall come to thy mind;" and so laid down the ink and paper, and went his way.

Now was Marbeck so full of heaviness and woe, that he knew not what to do, nor how to set a pen to the book to satisfy the bishop's mind, unless he accused men to the wounding of his own soul. And thus being compassed about with nothing but sorrow and care, he cried out to God in his heart, and fell down on his knees, with tears, and said,—

"O most merciful Father of heaven, thou that knowest the secret doings of all men, have mercy upon thy poor prisoner, who is destitute of all help and comfort. Assist me, O Lord, with thy special grace, that, to save this frail and vile body, which shall turn to corruption at his time, I may have no power to say or to write any thing that may be to the casting away of my christian brother; but rather, O Lord, let this vile flesh suffer at thy will and pleasure. Grant this, O most merciful Father, for thy dear Son Jesus Christ's sake."

Then he rose up and began to search his conscience what he might write, and at last framed out these words: "Whereas your lordship will have me to write such things as I know of my fellows at home; please it your lordship to understand, that I cannot call to remembrance any manner of thing whereby I might justly accuse any one of them, unless it be that the reading of the New Testament, which is common to all men, be an offence; more than this I know not."

Now the gentleman, about the hour appointed, came again, and found Marbeck walking up and down the chamber. "How now," said he, "hast thou written nothing?" "Yes, sir," said he, "as much as I know." "Well said," observed the gentleman; and took up the paper. Which when he had read, he cast it from him in a great rage, swearing by our Lord's body, that he would not for twenty pounds carry it to his lord and master. "Therefore," said he, "go to it again, and advise thyself better, or else thou wilt set my lord against thee, and then art thou utterly undone." "By my troth, sir," said Marbeck, "if his lordship shall keep me here these seven years, I can say no more than I have said." "Then thou wilt repent it," said the gentleman; and so departed.

The next day, the bishop sent for Marbeck to his house, and as he was entering into the bishop's hall, he saw the bishop himself coming out at a door at the upper end, with a roll in his hand, and going towards the great window, he called the poor man to him, and said, "Marbeck, wilt thou cast away thyself?" "No, my lord," said he, "I trust not." "Yes," said the bishop, "thou goest about it, for thou wilt utter nothing. What tempted thee to meddle with the scriptures?" And with that he went away from the window, out of the hall, and the poor man following him from place to place, till he had brought him into a long gallery; when there, the bishop began: "Ah, sir, the nest of you is broken." And unfolding his roll, he said, "Behold, here are your captains, both Hobby and Haynes, with all the whole pack of thy sect about Windsor, and yet thou wilt tell of none of them." "Alas, my lord, how should I accuse them, of whom I know nothing?" "Well," said the bishop, "if thou wilt needs cast away thyself, who can prevent thee?"

And in speaking these words, one of his chaplains, (called Master Medow) came up, to whom the bishop said, "Here is a marvellous thing; this fellow has taken upon him to set out the Concordance in English, which book, when it was set out in Latin, was not done without the help and diligence of a dozen learned men, at least, and yet he asserts that he has done it alone. But say what thou wilt," said the bishop, "except God himself would come down from heaven and tell me so, I will not believe it." And so going forth to a window where two great bibles lay upon a cushion, the one in Latin and the other in English, he called Marbeck to him, and pointing his finger to a place in the Latin Bible, said, "Canst thou English this sentence?" "Nay, my lord," said he, "but I can fetch out the English in an English Bible." Then Marbeck turning over the English Bible, found out the place, and read it to the bishop. So he tried him three or four times, till one of his men came up and told him the priest was ready to go to mass.

When the bishop was come from mass, he said, "This is a marvellous sect, for nothing can make one of them betray another." Then there was nothing said among the bishop's gentlemen, as they were making him ready to go to the court, but "Crucify him," upon the poor man. And when the bishop's white rochet was on him, "Well Marbeck," said he, "I am now going to the court, and had purposed, if I had found thee tractable, to have spoken to the king's majesty for thee, and to have given thee thy meat, drink, and lodging here in mine house; but seeing thou art so wilful and so stubborn, thou shalt go to the devil."

It was not half an hour after, until the bishop sent one of his gentlemen to the under-keeper, commanding him to put irons upon Marbeck, and to keep him fast shut up in a chamber alone, and when he should bring him down to dinner or supper, to see that he spoke to no man, and no man to him.

About three weeks before Whitsunday Marbeck was sent for to the bishop of London's house, where sat in commission Dr. Capon, bishop of Salisbury, Dr. Skip, bishop of Hereford, Dr. Goodrick, bishop of Ely, Dr. Oking, Dr. May, and the bishop of London's scribe, having before them all Marbeck's books. Then said the bishop of Salisbury, "Marbeck, we are here in commission, sent from the king's majesty to examine thee of certain things, whereof thou must be sworn to answer us faithfully and truly." Then the bishop of Salisbury laid forth before him his three books of notes, demanding whose hand they were. He answered, they were his own hand, and notes which he had gathered out of other men's works, six years ago. "For what cause," said the bishop of Salisbury, "didst thou gather them?"—"For none other cause, my lord, but to come by knowledge. For I being unlearned, and desirous to understand some parts of scripture, thought by reading of learned men's works to come the sooner thereby: and where I found any place of Scripture opened and expounded by them, that I noted, as you see, with a letter of his name in the margin, who was the author of the work." Then the bishop of Salisbury drew out a quire of the Concordance, and laid it before the bishop of Hereford, and asked, "Whose help hadst thou in setting forth this book?"—"My lord," said he, "no help at all."—"How couldst thou," said the bishop, "invent such a book, or know what a Concordance meant, without an instructor?"—"When," said I, "Thomas Mathews' Bible came out in print, I was desirous to have one of them: and being a poor man, and not able to buy one, determined to borrow one, and to write it out. And when I had written out the five books of Moses on fair great paper, and was entered into the book of Joshua, my friend Master Turner chanced to see me writing out the Bible, and asked me what I meant? And when I told him the cause, 'Tush,' said he, 'thou goest about a vain and tedious labour. But this were a profitable work for thee, to set out a Concordance in English.'—'A Concordance,' said I, 'what is that?' Then he told me it was a book to find out any word in the whole Bible by the letter, and that there was such a one in Latin already. And this, my lord, is all the instruction that ever I had before or after."—"A good wit with diligence," said the bishop of Hereford, "may bring hard things to pass."—"It is a great pity," said the bishop of Ely, "he had not the Latin tongue."—"I cannot believe," said the bishop of Salisbury, "that he hath done any more in this work, than written it out after some other that is learned."

"My lords," said Marbeck, "I shall beseech you all to pardon me what I shall say, and to grant my request if it shall seem good to you. I do marvel greatly wherefore I should be so examined for this book, and wherein I have committed offence in doing of it? If I have offended, then were I sorry that any other should be molested or punished for my fault. Therefore to clear all men in this matter, this is my request; that you will try me in the rest of the book that is undone. You see that I am yet but at the letter L; beginning now at M, and take out what word you will of that letter, and so in every letter following; and give me the words on a piece of paper, and set me in a place alone where it shall please you, with ink and paper, the English Bible, and the Latin Concordance: and if I bring you not these words written in the same order and form that the rest before is, then was it not I that did it, but some other."

"By my truth, Marbeck," replied the bishop of Ely, "that is honestly spoken; and then thou shalt bring many men out of suspicion."

When dinner was done, the bishop of Salisbury came down into the hall, commanding ink and paper to be given to Marbeck; and being now in his prison-chamber, he fell to his business so expertly, that by the next day when the bishop sent for him, he had written so much, in the same order and form as he had done the rest before, as filled three sheets of paper and more; which, when he had delivered to the bishop of Salisbury, he marvelled and said, "Well, Marbeck, thou hast now put me out of all doubt."

Upon Whitsunday Marbeck was sent for once again, where he found Dr. Oking with another gentleman, with a chain of gold about his neck, sitting together in one of the stalls, looking upon an epistle of John Calvin's, which Marbeck had written out; and when they saw the prisoner, they rose and had him up to a side altar, leaving his keeper in the body of the church. Now as soon as Marbeck saw the face of the gentleman, he saw it was the same person that first examined him in the Marshalsea, but never knew his name, till now he heard Dr. Oking call him Master Knight. This Master Knight held the paper to Marbeck, and said, "Look upon this, and tell me whose hand it is." When Marbeck had taken the paper, and seen what it was, he confessed it to be all his hand, saving the first leaf and the notes in the margin.

Here they wanted him to prove that it was the handwriting of Heines, and they threatened him with the torture to compel him. "By my truth, sir," said Marbeck, "if you do tear my whole body in pieces, I trust in God you shall never make me accuse any man wrongfully."—"If thou be so stubborn," said Dr. Oking, "thou wilt die for it."—"Die, Master Oking!" said he; "wherefore should I die? You told me the last day I was before the bishops, that as soon as I had made an end of the piece of the Concordance, I should be delivered; and shall I now die? But whenever you shall put me to death, I doubt not but I shall die God's true man and the king's."—"How so?" said Knight. "How canst thou die a true man to the king, when thou hast offended his laws? Is not this epistle, and most of the notes thou hast written, directly against the six articles?"—"No, sir," said Marbeck, "I have not offended the laws of the king; for since the first time I began with the Concordance, which is almost six years ago, I have been occupied in nothing else. So that both this epistle, and all the notes I have gathered, were written a great while before the Six Articles came forth; and are clearly remitted by the king's general pardon."—"Trust not to that," said Knight, "for it will not help thee." And so they committed him to his keeper, who conveyed him away again to prison.

The Manner of their Condemnations, and how they died.

Stephen Gardiner, bishop of Winchester, had so compassed his matters, that no man bore so great sway about the king as he did. The saying went abroad, that the bishop had bent his bow to shoot at some of the head deer. But in the meantime three or four of the poor were caught; namely, Anthony Pearson, Henry Filmer, and John Marbeck, who were sent to Windsor, and imprisoned in the town gaol; and Testwood (who had kept his bed) was brought out of his house upon crutches, and laid with them; but as for Benet (who should have been the fifth man) he happened to be sick of the pestilence, and he was left behind, whereby he escaped the fire.

Now these men being brought to Windsor, there was a sessions specially procured to be held; against which sessions all the farmers belonging to the college of Windsor were warned to appear, because they could not select papists enough in the town to go upon the jury when the trial came on.

The prisoners were separately indicted and convicted, and now being condemned, they prepared to die on the morrow, comforting one another in the death and passion of their Master, Christ, who had led the way before them, trusting that the same Lord, who had made them worthy to suffer so far for his sake, would not now withdraw his strength, but give them steadfast faith and power to overcome those fiery torments, and of his free mercy and goodness (without their deserts) for his promise sake, receive their souls. Thus they lay all the night, till sleep overpowered them, calling upon God for his aid and strength, and praying for their persecutors; that God of his merciful goodness would forgive them, and turn their hearts to the love and knowledge of his blessed and holy word: yea, such heavenly talk was among them that night, that the hearers who were watching the prison without, whereof the sheriff himself was one, with other gentlemen, were constrained to shed tears, as they themselves confessed.

On the morrow, which was Friday, as the prisoners were all preparing themselves to go to suffer, word was brought to them that they should not die that day. The cause was this: the bishop of Salisbury, and others among the commissioners, had sent a letter by one of the sheriff's gentlemen, called Mr. Frost, to the bishop of Winchester (the Court being then at Oking) in favour of Marbeck. At the sight of which letter, the bishop straightway went to the king, and obtained his pardon. Which being granted, he caused a warrant to be made out of hand for the sheriff's discharge, delivering the same to the messenger, who returned with speed and great joy (for the love he bare to the party), bringing good news to the town, of Marbeck's pardon.

On the Saturday morning, when the prisoners were to go to execution, they took their leave of Marbeck (their fellow-prisoner), and praised God for his deliverance; wishing to him the increase of godliness and virtue; and last of all besought him to help them heartily with his prayer unto God, to make them strong in their afflictions; and so kissing him one after another, they departed.

Now as the prisoners passed through the throng in the streets, they desired all the faithful people to pray for them, and to stand fast in the truth of the gospel, and not to be moved at their afflictions; for it was the happiest thing that ever came to them. And whenever Doctor Blithe and Arch (who rode on each side the prisoners) endeavoured to persuade them to turn to their mother church; "Away," would Anthony cry, "away with your Romish doctrine and all your trumpery, for we will no more of it." When Filmer was come to his brother's door, he staid and called for his brother; but he could not be seen, for Dr. London had kept him out of sight. And when he had called for three or four times, and saw he came not, he said, "And will he not come? then God forgive him, and make him a good man." And so going forth, they came to the place of execution, where Anthony Pearson, with a cheerful countenance, embraced the post in his arms, and kissing it, said, "Now, welcome mine own sweet wife; for this day shalt thou and I be married together in the love and peace of God."

When these three godly martyrs were bound to the post, a certain young man of Filmer's acquaintance brought him some drink, asking him if he would drink; "Yea," said Filmer, "I thank you. And now, my brother," said he, "I shall desire you in the name of the living Lord to stand fast in the truth of the gospel of Jesus Christ, which you have received;" and then he asked his brother Anthony, if he would drink. "Yea, brother Filmer," said he, "I pledge you in the Lord." And when he had drank, he gave it to Anthony, and he likewise gave it to Testwood. Of which drinking their adversaries made a jesting-stock, and reported abroad that they were all drunk, and knew not what they said; when they were no otherwise drunk then were the apostles when the people said they were full of new wine, as their deeds declared; for when Anthony and Testwood had both drank, Filmer rejoicing in the Lord, said, " Be merry, my brethren, and lift up your hands unto God; for after this sharp breakfast, I trust we shall have a good dinner in the kingdom of Christ our Lord and Redeemer." At these words, Testwood, lifting up his hands and eyes to heaven, desired the Lord above to receive his spirit. And Anthony Pearson, pulling the straw to him, laid a good deal of it upon the top of his head, saying, " Now am I dressed like a true soldier of Christ, by whose merits only I trust this day to enter into his joy." And so they yielded up their souls to the Father of heaven, in the faith of his dear Son Jesus Christ, with such humility and steadfastness, that many who saw their patient suffering, confessed that they could have found in their hearts to have died with them.

Soon after these martyrdoms, the whole conspiracy between Dr. London and Simons, for the putting these good men to death, was found out and exposed, for they conspired also to indite some of the council.

After this the king withdrew his favour from the bishop of Winchester, and being more and more informed of the conspiracy of Dr. London and Simons, he commanded certain of his council to search out the ground of it.

Whereupon, Dr. London and Simons were apprehended and brought before the council, and examined upon their oath of allegiance: and for denying their mischievous and traitorous purpose, which was manifestly proved to their faces, they were both perjured, and, in fine, adjudged as perjured persons, to wear papers in Windsor; and Ockam to stand upon the pillory in the town of Newbury where he was born.

The judgment of all these three was to ride about Windsor, Reading, and Newbury, with papers on their heads, and their faces turned to the horses' tails, and to stand upon the pillory in each of these towns, for false accusation of the forenamed martyrs, and for perjury.

And thus much touching the persecution of these good saints of Windsor, according to the copy of their own acts, received and written by John Marbeck, who is yet alive.

The Persecution in Calais, with the Martyrdom of Adam Damlip and others.

In the year 1539, there came to Calais one George Bucker, alias Adam Damlip, who had been in time past a great papist, and chaplain to Fisher, bishop of Rochester; and after the death of the bishop had travelled through France and Italy; and as he went, conferred with learned men concerning matters of controversy in religion; and so proceeding in his journey to Rome, where he thought to have found all godliness and sincere religion, in the end, he found there, (as he confessed) such blasphemy of God, contempt of Christ's true religion, looseness of life, and abundance of all abominations and filthiness, that his heart and conscience abhorred to remain there any longer; although he was greatly requested by Cardinal Pole to continue, and to read three lectures in the week in his house; for which he offered him great entertainment, which he refused; and so returning homeward, having a piece of money given him by the cardinal at his departure, came to Calais, who, as he was waiting there for a passage to England, was perceived by William Stevens and Thomas Lancaster, to be a learned man; and that he having been of late a zealous papist, was now turned to a more perfect knowledge of true religion; he was by them heartily entreated to stay at Calais for some time, and to read there a day or two, to the intent that he might do some good to the people after his painful travel. To this request Adam gladly consented. Stevens brought him to the lord Lisle, the king's deputy of the town and marches of Calais, and declared thoroughly what conference and talk had been between Adam Damlip and himself. The lord deputy desired Damlip to stay there, and to preach three or four days or more at his pleasure, saying, that he should have both his licence and the commissary's also. Where, after he had preached three

or four times, he was so well liked both for his learning, his utterance, and the truth of his doctrine, that not only the soldiers and commoners, but also the lord deputy and a great part of the council, gave him great praise and thanks for it; and the lord deputy offered him a chamber in his own house; to dine and sup every meal at his own mess; to have a man or two of his servants to wait upon him; and to have whatever he wanted, if it were to be had for money; yea, and what he might desire in his purse to buy books or otherwise; so that he would tarry there among them, and preach only so long as it should seem good to himself. Who, refusing his lordship's great offer, most heartily thanked him, and besought him to be only so good to him, as to appoint him some quiet and honest place in the town, where he might not be disturbed or molested, but have opportunity to give himself to his book, and he would daily, once in the forenoon, and again by one o'clock in the afternoon, by the grace of God, preach among them according to that talent which God had given him. At which answer the lord deputy greatly rejoiced, and thereupon sent for William Stevens, whom he earnestly required to receive and lodge Damlip in his house; promising to see paid to the utmost whatever he should demand.

This godly man, for the space of twenty days or more, once every day, at seven of the clock, preached very godly, learnedly, and plainly, the truth of the blessed sacrament of Christ's body and blood, mightily inveighing against all popery, and confuting the same; but especially those two most pernicious errors or heresies, transubstantiation and the propitiatory sacrifice of the Romish mass, by true conference of the scriptures, and applying of the ancient doctors: he earnestly exhorted the people to turn from popery, declaring how popish he himself had been; and how, by the detestable wickedness that he saw universally in Rome, he was returned so far homewards, and had now become an enemy, through God's grace, to all popery, shewing that if gain or ambition could have moved him to the contrary, he might have been entertained of Cardinal Pole; but for very conscience sake, joined with true knowledge, grounded on God's most holy word, he now utterly abhorred all popery, and wished them most earnestly to do the same.

And thus he continued for some time to read in the chapter-house of the White friars; but the place not being large enough, he was desired to read in the pulpit; and so proceeding in his lectures, (wherein he declared how the world was deceived by the Roman bishops, who had set forth the absurd doctrine of transubstantiation,) he came at length to speak against the pageant or picture of the resurrection, which was in St. Nicholas church, declaring it to be mere idolatry.

Upon which sermon, or lecture, there came a commission from the king to the lord deputy; Master Greenfield; Sir John Butler, commissary; the king's mason and smith; with others: that they should search whether there were three hosts lying upon a marble stone besprinkled with blood, as was set forth in the papal bull of indulgences to that altar; and if they found it not so, that immediately it should be plucked down. In searching, as they brake up a stone in a corner of the tomb, they, instead of three hosts, found soldered on the cross of marble lying under the sepulchre, *three plain white counters, which they had painted like hosts, and a bone that is in the tip of a sheep's tail!* All which trumpery Damlip shewed to the people on the next day, which was Sunday, out of the pulpit, and afterwards they were sent by the lord deputy to the king.

Envy soon stirred up the prior of the White friars, to bark against him. Yet, after Adam had confuted the friar's erroneous doctrine of transubstantiation, and of the propitiatory sacrifice of the mass; the friar outwardly seemed to give place, ceasing openly to inveigh, and secretly practised to impeach him by letters sent to the clergy in England: so that, within eight or ten days after, Damlip was sent for to appear before the archbishop of Canterbury, with whom was Gardiner bishop of Winchester, Sampson bishop of Chichester, and others; before whom he most constantly affirmed and defended the doctrine which he had taught, answering, confuting, and solving the objections of his adversaries.

Then the bishops began to threaten to confute him with their accustomed arguments,—fire and fagot,—if he would still stand to the defence of what he had spoken. Damlip answered, that he would on the next day deliver fully in writing what he had said. On the morrow they intended to have apprehended him, but he had secret intimation from the archbishop of Canterbury, that if he personally appeared, he would be committed to ward, and not likely then to escape death. He therefore sent four sheets of paper learnedly written in the Latin tongue, containing his faith and his arguments; proofs from the scriptures; and allegations from the doctors. Which done, he went into the west country, and there kept all the time, while great trouble kindled against God's people in Calais.

In the meantime, William Smith, a curate at Calais, continued to preach the gospel against popery, as did Champion and Garret, whom the king sent there to instruct the people, till at last God's enemies wrote to some in England, making grievous complaints to the lords of the privy council, against some of the town of Calais, affirming that they were horribly infected with heresies and pernicious opinions.

A great persecution against many persons followed this: and that the same may the better appear, we will give a brief account of Ralph Hare, a man so unlearned that he could scarce read; yet through God's grace was very zealous; and therewith led so godly and temperate a life, as not one of his enemies could accuse or blame his sober life and conversation. He was charged as one that had spoken against auricular confession, against holy bread and holy water; and that he was one who would not lightly swear an oath; nor engage in any manner of pastime; but was always in a corner by himself, looking on his book. This poor simple man being charged by the commissioners, that he was a naughty and erroneous man, was desired to take good heed to himself, lest through obstinacy he turned his erroneous opinions into plain heresy; for an error defended is heresy.

"My good lords," said the poor man, "I take God to record, I would not willingly maintain any error or heresy. Wherefore I beseech you let my accusers come face to face before me. For if they charge me with that which I have spoken, I will not deny it. Moreover, if it be truth, I will stand to it; and otherwise, if it be an error, I will with all my heart utterly forsake it; I mean if it be against God's holy word, for the Lord is my witness; I seek and daily pray to God, that I may know the truth, and flee from all errors; and I trust the Lord will save me and preserve me from them."

"Aha!" said the bishop of Winchester, "do you not hear what he saith, my lord? I perceive now that thou art a naughty fellow." "Alas, my lord," said Ralph Hare, "what evil said I?" "Marry sir, you said 'the Lord, the Lord,' and that is a sign of a heretic," replied Winchester. "What is that, my lord? for God's sake tell me," said Hare. "Thou art naught, thou art naught," said he. At which words the simple man began to tremble, and seemed much dismayed and driven into a great agony and fear. Which Winchester perceiving, said to him, "Ralph Hare, Ralph Hare, by my troth, I pity thee much. For in good faith, I think thee to be a good simple man, but thou hast had shrewd and subtle schoolmasters, who have seduced thee, good poor simple soul, and therefore I pity thee; and it were indeed a pity that thou shouldst be burnt; for thou art a good fellow, a tall man, and hast served the king right well in his wars. I have heard thee well commended, and thou art yet able to do the king as good service as ever thou wast; and we all will be a means to his grace to be a good gracious lord unto thee, if thou wilt take pity on thyself, and leave thy errors. For I dare say for us all that are commissioners, that we would be loath that thou shouldst be cast away. For, alas! poor simple man, we perceive thou hast been seduced by others."

"How sayest thou, therefore, thou knowest my lord of Canterbury is a good gentle lord, and would be loath thou shouldst be cast away? Tell me, canst thou be content to submit thyself unto him, and to stand to such order, as he and we shall take in this matter? how sayest thou, man? speak." The poor man falling upon his knees, and shedding tears, answered, speaking to the archbishop of Canterbury in this wise, "My good lord, for Christ's sake be good unto me; and I refer myself unto your grace's order, to do with me what you please."

The archbishop of Canterbury, considering what danger he was ready to fall into, and pitying the same (though the simplicity of the man was so great that he perceived it not) said, "Nay, Ralph Hares, stand up and advise thyself, and commit not thyself to me, for I am but one man, and in commission but as the others are; so that it lieth in me to do nothing. But if thou do commit thyself to all, then thou committest thyself to the laws; and the law is ordained to do every man right." "Go to, Ralph Hare," said Winchester, "submit thyself to my lord and us: it is best for thee to do so." Whereupon he fell upon his knees again, and said, "My lords and masters all, I submit myself wholly unto you." And therewith a book was held to him, and an oath given him to be obedient to them and to all ecclesiastical laws. And straightway he was enjoined to abjure, and to bear a fagot three several days: moreover, the poor man lost his whole living that he had at Calais.

This simple man, on hearing his penance, at the first earnestly refused to stand to it, and with piteous exclamation, said, "O my lord of Winchester! my lord of Winchester! have you made me a log ready to be laid upon the fire, whenever any wicked man of malice, by provocation of the devil, shall falsely lay any small trifle to my charge? Or shall I be thus handled, with nothing proved to my face against me? Alas, I have always hated errors and heresies." "Content thyself, Hare: there is now no remedy; thou must either do thy penance, or be burnt," said the commissioners.

The History of William Smith.

William Smith, curate of Our Lady parish, in Calais, was called before them, and charged with the same errors and opinions that were objected against Ralph Hare; and it was added, that he had spoken and preached against our blessed Lady; against praying to saints; against doing good works; and many other such things: and one Richard Long, a man-at-arms at Calais, proved against Smith, and Brooke, by an oath taken upon a book, that Smith and Brooke did eat flesh together in Lent in Brooke's house. "For a miller's boy," said he, "came into Brooke's kitchen and saw half a lamb lying roasting at the fire." Whereas the truth is, that William Smith, during all the time of Lent, never came once within Brooke's house.

After all these things had taken place, the minds of the adversaries were not yet satisfied; but still suggested new complaints to the king's ears against the town of Calais; making the king believe, that through new opinions the town was so divided, that it was in great danger. Whereupon, shortly after, commissioners were sent over by the king to Calais, with special instructions signed by the king's majesty's own hand. Upon their arrival, Doctor Curain preached a notable sermon, exhorting all men to charity, having nothing in his mouth but charity, charity. But as it seemed afterwards, such a burning charity was in him and the rest of the commissioners, that, had not God pitied his innocent servants, there had been an hundred burnt or hanged shortly after.

On the morrow, after the sermon, all the commissioners solemnly received the sacrament: and at afternoon the council assembled with the commissioners; and after their consultation, tipstaffs summoned above fourscore persons to appear on the morrow at eight of the clock before the council, who at their appearance, were commanded upon their allegiance to present all such heretics, schismatics, and seditious persons, as they did know, and in no wise to doubt or dread to do so; for they should have great advantage thereby; yea, they should either have their livings or their goods; and besides that, they should have great thanks at the king's majesty's hand, and his honourable council.

These things were not so secretly done but they were betrayed, and came to honest men's knowledge. Whereupon such fear and distrust overtook all men, that neighbour distrusted neighbour, the master the servant, the servant the master, the husband the wife, the wife the husband, and almost every one the other, that it was lamentable to see how mournful men and women went in the streets, hanging down their heads, shewing evident tokens of the anguish of their hearts.

On the Wednesday in Easter week, sundry inquests were charged on their oaths to make inquisition for all manner of heretics, erroneous opinions, and seditions: as, an inquest of aldermen; another of men-at-arms, and another of constables and vintners; another of common soldiers, and another of commoners. And shortly after their presentments, on Good Friday, there were brought before the commissioners, and straight were sent to close prison, Anthony Pickering, gent., Henry Turner, gent., Sir George Darby, priest, John Shepheard, William Pellam, William Keverdale, John Whitwood, John Boote, Robert Clodder, Coppen de Hane, and Matthew de Hound: concerning whom were sundry reports: some said they would be hanged; some said burnt; some said hanged, drawn and quartered; some said nailed to the pillory: so that it was pitiful to see the lamentation that their wives, their children, servants, and friends, made secretly where they durst; for they found every where words of discomfort, and no where of comfort.

William Stevens, after his return from London, besides many other articles laid to him for religion to the number of forty, was charged by the lord deputy, that he had supported Adam Damlip, hired him to preach, and had given him meat, drink, and lodging; and then Brooke was brought before the commissioners, and committed to close prison in the mayor's gaol.

This kind of handling of Brooke made all his friends, but especially his wife, greatly afraid of the malice of his enemies: moreover, all his goods and lands were seized, and his wife thrust into the meanest place in all his house, with her children and family; the keys of all the doors and chests also taken from her. She was rigorously treated at Sir Edward Kingley's hand, controller of the town, saying to her, that if she liked not the room, he would thrust her quite out of the doors. "Well, sir," said she, "well, the king's slaughter-house was wronged when you were made a gentleman;" and with all speed she wrote a letter to the lord Cromwell, therein discoursing how hardly those poor men were handled, that were committed to ward and close prison; and that all men feared (what through the malice of the papistical enemies, and the great rigour and ignorant zeal of those that were in authority) they should shortly for their faith and consciences be put to death; but chiefly her husband, who was yet more extremely handled than any other. So that unless his honour vouchsafed to be a means to the king's majesty, that they with their causes might be sent over to England, they were but dead men.

Lord Cromwell immediately wrote to the commissioners, declaring, that the king's majesty's pleasure and commandment was, that the traitor and heretic Brooke, with a dozen or twenty accomplices, should with their accusers be immediately sent over, that here in England they might receive their judgment, and there at Calais, to the great terror of like offenders hereafter, suffer according to their deserts.

Now by the time that the said commissioners had received these letters, they had made out precepts for eight or ninescore more honest men to be cast into prison. But these letters so appalled them, that they stayed and afterwards sent no more to prison; making, however, as diligent inquisition as was possible, to have found some matter against them. They sent the thirteen prisoners through the market, Brooke going before with irons on his legs, as the chief captain; the rest following him two and two without irons, till on shipboard, and then they were all coupled in irons two and two together.

When in the ship, because they were loath to go under the hatches, Sir John Gage with a staff smote some of them cruelly; whereupon Anthony Pickering said to him, "Sir, I beseech you be as good to us as you would be to your horses or dogs; let us have a little air that we may not be smothered." Yet that request could not be obtained, but the hatches were put down close, and they guarded and kept with a great company of men; and so sailing forward, by God's merciful providence, were within four-and-twenty hours at anchor before the Tower of London.

When the lord Cromwell understood they were come, he commanded their irons to be smitten off at the Tower wharf, and the prisoners to be brought unto him. When he saw them, he smiled upon them, steadfastly beholding each of them, and then said, " Sirs, you must take pains for a time, and go your way to the Fleet, and submit yourselves prisoners there, and shortly you shall know more." So indeed they did; and that evening he sent them word to be of good cheer, for if God continued him life, they should shortly go home with as much honour as they came with shame.

While these persecuted men lay in the Fleet, and William Stevens in the Tower, to wit the nineteenth day of July, A.D. 1541, the lord Cromwell, for treason laid against him, was beheaded at Tower-hill, as is before specified. Then had the poor Calais men great cause to fear, if they had not altogether depended on the merciful providence of their heavenly Father, whose blessed will they knew directed all things. But he in the midst of these troubles and miseries so comforted them, that even as their dangers and troubles increased, so likewise did their consolation and joy abound. Matthew de Hound, one of these thirteen, who was in trouble only because he heard Copen de Hall read a chapter of the New Testament, and was as deep in punishment, and in banishment from his wife, children, and country, as the rest, got in a short time such instruction, that having his mind fraught with godly zeal unto God's glory, and the true doctrine of Christ, within a few months after his deliverance out of the Fleet, was cruelly, in a most constant faith and patience, burned in Flanders, for inveighing constantly against the wicked honouring of images, and praying to departed saints.

Now when all hope in man was past, the right honourable Lord Audley, lord chancellor of England, without further examination, discharged the thirteen that were in the Fleet, and at length, two years after, he released William Stevens also, by the king's own motion, out of the Tower, saying at the discharging of those thirteen, " Sirs, pray for the king's majesty; his pleasure is that you shall all be presently discharged. And though your livings be taken from you, yet despair not, God will not see you lack. But for God's sake, sirs, beware how you deal with popish priests; for, so God save my soul, some of them be knaves. Sirs, I am commanded by the council to tell you, that you are discharged by virtue of the king's general pardon; but that pardon excepts and forbids all sacramentaries, and the most part, or all of you, are called sacramentaries: therefore I cannot see how that pardon does you any good. But pray for the king's highness, for his grace's pleasure is that I should dismiss you, and so I do, and pity you all. Farewell, Sirs."

So giving God most hearty thanks for his mighty and merciful delivering of them, they departed.

The Second Apprehension and Martyrdom of Adam Damlip.

Concerning Adam Damlip, otherwise called George Bucker, you heard before how he was called before the bishops, and being secretly warned not to appear again before the bishops, departed into the west country, and there continued teaching a school about a year or two. After that the good man was again apprehended by the inquisition of the six articles, and brought up to London, where he was sent to the Marshalsea, by Stephen Gardiner, and there lay two years or thereabout.

During the imprisonment of this George in the Marshalsea, John Marbeck also was committed to the same prison. The custom of that time required, that at Easter every person must needs come to confession. Whereupon Marbeck, with the rest of the prisoners there, was forced to come upon Easter-day to Adam Damlip, who was then confessor to the whole house, to be confessed. By this occasion John Marbeck, who had never seen him before, entering into conference with him, perceived who he was, what he had been, what troubles he sustained, and how long he had lain there in prison.

This Damlip, for honest and godly behaviour, was beloved of all the whole house; but especially by the keeper: and being suffered to go at liberty within the house, he did much good among the common sort of prisoners, in rebuking vice and sin; and kept them in such good order that the keeper thought himself to have a great treasure of him.

Now when he had drawn out an epistle to the bishop, earnestly desiring to be brought to his examination, he delivered it to the keeper, desiring him to deliver it at the court to the bishop of Winchester; and he did so.

The keeper came home at night very late, and when the prisoners, who had tarried supper for his coming, saw him so sad and heavy, they deemed something to be amiss. At last the keeper, casting up his eyes upon George, that is, Adam Damlip, said, "O George! I can tell thee tidings." "What is that, Master?" said he. "Upon Monday next thou and I must go to Calais." "To Calais, master! What to do?" "I know not," replied the keeper, and pulled out of his pocket a piece of wax with a little parchment hanging thereat, which seemed to be a precept. And when George saw it, he said, "Well, well, now I know what the matter is." "What?" said the keeper. "Truly I shall die in Calais." "Nay," said the keeper, "I trust it be not so." "Yes, yes, it is most true, and I praise God for his goodness therein." And so the keeper and they went together to supper, with heavy cheer for George, as they called him; who notwithstanding was merry himself, and did eat his meat as well as ever he did in all his life: so that some said to him, that they marvelled how he could eat his meat so well, knowing he was so near his death. "Ah, masters," said he, "do you think that I have been God's prisoner so long in the Marshalsea, and have not yet learned to die? Yes, yes, and I doubt not but God will strengthen me therein."

And so on Monday, early in the morning, before day, the keeper, with three of the knight marshal's servants, conveyed Adam Damlip to Calais, and there committed him to the mayor's prison. Upon which day John Butler, the commissary, and Daniel the curate of St. Peter's were also committed to the same prison, and commandment given for no man to speak with Butler.

Saturday next was the day of execution for Damlip. The crime which first they laid to his charge, was heresy. But because by an act of parliament all such offences, done before a certain day, were pardoned, yet for receiving the money of Cardinal Pole, as you heard before, he was condemned of treason, and in Calais cruelly put to death, being drawn, hanged, and quartered.

The day before his execution, there came to him Master Mote, then parson of Our Lady church in Calais, saying, "Your four quarters shall be hanged at four parts of the town." "And where shall my head be?" said Damlip. "Upon the lantern gate," said Mote. Damlip answered, "Then I shall not need to provide for my burial." At his death, Sir R. Ellerker, knight, then knight-marshal, would not suffer the innocent and godly man to declare either his faith, or the cause he died for; but said to the executioner "Despatch the knave; have done."

Dod, a Scotchman, burned in Calais.

There was about this time a Scotchman, named Dod, who, coming out of Germany, was taken with certain German books about him, and being examined. and standing constantly to the truth that he had learned, was condemned to death, and burned in Calais, within the space of a year, or thereabout, after the other godly martyr above mentioned.

During the time of these six articles, which brought many good men to death, it happened by another act for the king's supremacy, that the contrary sect of the papists was not undisturbed. For, besides the death of More, and the bishop of Rochester, and the Charterhouse monks, friars, and priests above specified, about this year also was condemned and executed two others, of whom one was a priest of Chelsea, named Lark, who was put to death at London for defending the bishop of Rome's supremacy above the king's authority: the other was Germaine Gardiner (near kinsman to Stephen Gardiner, and yet more near to his secret counsel, as is supposed), who likewise in intriguing for the pope against the king's jurisdiction, was taken and brought to the gibbet.

Upon the detection of Germaine Gardiner, being secretary to Gardiner, bishop of Winchester, his kinsman, it seemed to some, and it was so insinuated to the king, that Germaine neither would nor durst attempt any such matter of popery, without some setting on, or consent of the bishop, he being so near to him, and in all his secrets: the king began somewhat to doubt the bishop; but yet Gardiner so managed matters, that he kept in favour with the king, to the great troubling of the realm, and especially of Christ's church.

In the dreadful law of the six articles, a penalty was appointed for the breach of the same, as treason and felony, so that no recantation would serve. This severity was a little mitigated by another parliament, A.D. 1544, by which it was decreed, that such offenders as were convicted for the first time should recant and renounce their opinions; and if the party refused to recant in such form as should be laid by his ordinary, or after his recantation if he soon offended again, then for the second time he should abjure and bear a fagot. Which if he refused to do, or else, being abjured, if a third time he offended, then he was to sustain punishment according to the law, &c. Although the straightness and rigour of the former act was thus somewhat tempered, yet the venom and poison of the errors of those articles remained still. By the last-mentioned parliament, moreover, many things were provided for the advancement of popery, under the colour of religion; so that all manner of books of the Old and New Testament, bearing the name of William Tindal, or any others having prologues, or containing any matters, annotations, preambles, words or sentences, contrary to the six articles, were prohibited. In like manner all songs, plays and interludes, with all other books in English, containing matter of religion, tending any way against the six articles, were prohibited.

It was moreover provided, that the text of the New Testament, or of the Bible, being prohibited to all women, artificers, apprentices, journeymen, servingmen, yeomen, husbandmen, and labourers; yet was permitted to noblemen, and gentlemen, and gentlewomen, to read and peruse, to their edifying, provided they did it quietly without arguing, discussing, or expounding upon the scripture.

Besides this, where, before, the offender or defendant might not be suffered to bring in any witnesses to clear himself; in this parliament it was permitted to the party detected, or complained of, to try his cause by witnesses, as many, or more in number, as the others who deposed against him, &c.

By these and other qualifications of the six articles, it may appear that the king began to disfavour Gardiner, and to discountenance his doings, by which he was the more forward to further the desolate cause of religion, as may appear by other provisions of the parliament, A.D. 1545, wherein it was decreed by an act, that the king should have full power and authority to appoint thirty-two persons, to wit, sixteen of the clergy, and sixteen of the temporalty, to peruse, over-see, and examine the canons, constitutions, and ordinances of the canon law, as well provincial as synodal; and so, according to their discretions, to set and establish an order of the ecclesiastical laws, such as should be thought by the king and them convenient to be received and used within this realm. Which statute, as it is most needful for the government of the church of England, so, would God it had been brought to perfection!

Kerby, and Roger Clarke, of Suffolk, Martyrs.

Coming now to the year 1546, first noticing the priest. whose name was Saxy, who was hanged in the porter's lodge of Stephen Gardiner, bishop of Winchester, and that, as it is supposed, not without the consent of the bishop and the secret conspiracy of that bloody generation; also one Henry with his servant, burned at Colchester; I will proceed to the history of Kerby, and Roger Clarke of Mendelsham, who were apprehended at Ipswich, A.D. 1546, and brought before the lord Wentworth, with other commissioners, appointed there to sit upon their examinations.

In the meantime, Kerby and Rogers being in the gaoler's house, there came in Master Robert Wingfield with Master Bruess, of Wenneham; who having conference with Kerby, Master Wingfield said to Kerby, "Remember, the fire is hot; take heed of thine enterprise, that thou take no more upon thee than thou shalt be able to perform. The terror is great, the pain will be extreme, and life is sweet. Better it were to stick to mercy, while there is hope of life, than rashly to begin, and then to shrink," with such like words of persuasion. To whom he answered again, "Ah, Master Wingfield, be at my burning, and you shall say, there standeth a christian soldier in the fire: for I know that fire and water, sword, and all other things, are in the hands of God; and he will suffer no more to be laid upon us than he will give strength to bear."—"Ah, Kerby," said Master Wingfield, "if thou be at that point, I will bid thee farewell; for I promise thee I am not so strong that I am able to burn." And so both the gentlemen saying that they would pray for them, shook hands with them, and departed.

When Kerby and Clarke came to the judgment-seat, the lord Wentworth, with all the rest of the justices, were there already; the commissary also, by virtue of the statute, ex-officio, sitting next to the lord Wentworth, Kerby and Clarke lifted up their eyes and hands to heaven with great devotion, making their prayers secretly to God.

That done, their articles were declared to them with all circumstances of the law: and then it was demanded and required of them, whether they believed, that after the words spoken by a priest (as Christ spoke them to his apostles) there were not the very body and blood of Christ, flesh, blood, and bone, as he was born of the Virgin Mary, and no bread after.

To which words they answered and said, No, they did not so believe; but that they did believe the sacrament which Christ Jesus did institute at his last supper, was to put all men in remembrance of his precious death and blood-shedding for the remission of sins, and that there was neither flesh nor blood to be eaten with the teeth, but bread and wine, and yet more than bread and wine, for that it is consecrated to an holy use. Then with much persuasions, both with fair means and threats beside, were these two poor men hardly treated. But they continued both faithful and constant, choosing rather to die than to live, and so continued to the end.

Then sentence was given upon them both, Kerby to be burned in the town on the next Saturday, and Clarke to be burned at Bury the Monday after. Kerby, when his judgment was given by the lord Wentworth, with most humble reverence holding up his hands and bowing himself devoutly, said, "Praised be Almighty God!" and so stood still without any more words.

The next day, about ten of the clock, Kerby was brought to the market-place, where a stake was ready, and wood, broom, and straw, and put off his clothes to his shirt, having a night-cap upon his head, and so was fastened to the stake with irons; there being in the gallery the lord Wentworth. with the most of the jus-

tices of those parts, where they might see his execution, how everything should be done, and might hear what Kerby would say; and also a great number of people, about two thousand. There was also standing in the gallery by the lord Wentworth, Doctor Rugham, who was once a monk of Bury, and sexton of the house, having on a surplice and a stole about his neck.

All this while Kerby was being compassed with irons and faggots, broom and straw, nothing changing in countenance, but with a most meek spirit glorifying God. Then Doctor Rugham preached upon the sixth chapter of St. John; and in handling his text, as often as he alleged the scriptures, and applied them rightly, Kerby told the people that he said true, and bade the people believe him. But when he did otherwise, he said, "You say not true, believe him not, good people." Upon which the voice of the people judged Doctor Rugham to be a false prophet. So when he had ended, he said to Kerby, "Thou good man, dost not thou believe that the blessed sacrament of the altar is the very flesh and blood of Christ, and no bread, even as he was born of the Virgin Mary?" Kerby answering boldly, said, "I do not so believe." "How doest thou believe?" said the Doctor. Kerby said, "I do believe that in the sacrament that Jesus Christ instituted at his last supper, is his death, and passion, and bloodshedding for the redemption of the world, to be remembered, and (as I said before) yet bread, and more than bread, for it is consecrated to a holy use."

Then said the undersheriff to Kerby, "Hast thou anything more to say?" "Yea, Sir," said he, "if you will give me leave." "Say on," said the sheriff.

Then Kerby, taking his night-cap from his head, put it under his arm, as though it should have done him service again: but remembering himself, he cast it from him, and lifting up his hands, he said the hymn, "We praise thee, O God," &c., and the creed, with other prayers in the English tongue. The lord Wentworth, while Kerby was doing thus, concealed himself behind one of the posts of the gallery, and wept, and so did many others. Then said Kerby, "I have done: you may execute your office, good Mr. Sheriff." Then fire was set to the wood, and with a loud voice he called unto God, knocking on his breast, and holding up his hands so long as his remembrance would serve, and so ended his life, the people giving shouts, and praising God with great admiration of his constancy.

On Monday, about ten o'clock, Roger Clarke was brought out of prison, and went on foot to the gate, called Southgate, in Bury, and by the way the procession of the host met them; but he went on, and would not bow cap, nor knee, but with most vehement words rebuked that idolatry and superstition, the officers being much offended. Without the gate, where was the place of execution, the stake being ready, and the wood lying by, he came and kneeled down, and said, "My soul doth magnify the Lord," &c., in English, making as it were a paraphrase upon the same, wherein he declared how that the blessed Virgin Mary, who might as well rejoice in pureness, as any other, yet humbled herself to our Saviour. "And what sayest thou, John Baptist," said he, "the greatest of all men's children? Behold the Lamb of God which taketh away the sin of the world." And thus with a loud voice he cried to the people, while he was being fastened to the stake, and then the fire was set to him, where he suffered pains unmercifully; for the wood was green, and would not burn, so that he was choked with smoke; and moreover, being set in a pitch barrel, he was sorely pained, till he had got his feet out of the barrel. And at length one standing by, took a fagot-stick, and striking at the ring of iron about his neck, happened to hit him upon the head, so that he sunk down into the fire, and so was dispatched.

This year also it was ordained and decreed, and solemnly given out in proclamation by the king's name and authority, and his council, that the English procession should be used throughout all England, according as it was set forth by his council, and none other, to be used throughout the whole realm.

About the latter end of this year 1545, in the month of November, after the king had subdued the Scots, and joining together with the emperor, had invaded France, and got from them the town of Boulogne, he summoned his high court of parliament. In which was granted to him, besides other subsidies of money, all colleges, chantries, free chapels, hospitals, fraternities, brotherhoods, guilds and perpetuities of stipendiary priests, to be disposed of at his will and pleasure. Whereupon in December following, the king, after his wonted manner, came into the parliament-house to give his royal assent to such acts as were passed; where, after an eloquent oration made to him by the speaker, he answered again not by the lord chancellor (as the manner was) but by himself. In which oration, first eloquently and lovingly he declared his grateful heart to his loving subjects for their grants and supplies offered to him. In the second part, with no less vehemency he exhorts them to concord, peace, and unity. Whereto if he had also joined the third part, that is, as in words he exhorts to unity, so he had himself first begun to take away the occasion of division, disobedience, and disturbance from his subjects, that is, had removed the stumbling-block of the six articles out of the people's way, which set brother against brother, neighbour against neighbour, the superior against the subject, and the wolves to devour the poor flock of Christ; then he had not only spoken, but also done like a worthy prince.

When these chantries and colleges thus by act of parliament were given into the king's hands in December, 1545, the Lent following, Doctor Crome, preaching in the Mercer's chapel, among other reasons and persuasons to rouse the people from the vain opinion of purgatory, argued thus: that if trentals and chantry masses could avail souls in purgatory, then the parliament did not act well in giving away monasteries, colleges, and chantries, which served principally to that purpose. But if the parliament did well (as no man could deny) in dissolving them, and bestowing the same upon the king, then it is plain, that such chantries and private masses do nothing to relieve those in purgatory. This dilemma of Doctor Crome, no doubt, was unanswerable. But still the charitable prelates, notwithstanding the king's exhortation to charity, were so charitable to him, that on Easter they so handled him, that they made him recant. And if he had not, they would have dissolved him and his argument in burning fire, so burning hot was their charity, according as they did Anne Askew and her companions in the month of July the year following. Whose tragical history and cruel handling now, the Lord willing, you shall hear.

The first examination of Mrs. Anne Askew, before the Inquisitors, A.D. 1545.

"To satisfy your expectation, good people," said she, "this was my first examination in the year of our Lord, 1545, and in the month of March.

"1. Christopher Dare examined me at Sadler's Hall, and asked, if I did not believe that the sacrament hanging over the altar was the very body of Christ really. Then I asked this question of him in return: 'Wherefore was St. Stephen stoned to death?' and he said, 'He could not tell.' Then I answered, 'That no more would I answer his question.'

"2. He said that there was a woman who testified that I read how God was not in temples made with hands. Then I shewed him the seventh and seventeenth chapters of the acts of the apostles, what St. Stephen and St. Paul had said there. Upon which he asked me how I understood those sentences? I answered; 'I would not throw pearls amongst swine, for acorns were good enough.'

"3. He asked me why I said I had rather read five lines in the Bible, than hear five masses in the temple: I confessed that I said so; not for the dispraise of either the epistle or the gospel, but because the one did greatly edify me, and the other nothing at all. As St. Paul says in the fourteenth chapter of his first epistle to the Corinthians: 'If the trumpet give an uncertain sound, who will prepare himself to the battle?'

"4. He laid to my charge, that I said, 'If a bad priest ministered, it was the devil, and not God.' My answer was, that I never spake any such thing. But this was my saying; 'That whoever he were that ministered to me, his ill conditions could not hurt my faith, but in spirit I received nevertheless the body and blood of Christ.'

"5. He asked me what I said concerning confession: I answered him, that my meaning was as St. James saith, 'That every man ought to acknowledge his faults to others, and pray one for the other.'

"6. He asked me what I said about the king's book? And I answered him, that I could say nothing about it, because I never saw it.

"7. He asked me if I had the Spirit of God in me: I answered, I had not. I was but a reprobate or castaway. Then he said he had sent for a priest to examine me, who was here at hand.

"The priest asked me what I said to the sacrament of the altar, and required much to know my meaning. But I desired him again to hold me excused concerning that matter: no other answer would I make him, because I perceived him to be a papist.

"8. He asked me, if I did not think, that private masses helped the souls departed: I said, 'It was great idolatry to believe more in them, than in the death who Christ died for us.'

"Then they brought me to my lord mayor, and he examined me, as they had before, and I answered him directly in all things as I answered before. Besides this, my lord mayor laid one thing to my charge, which was never spoken by me, but by them; and that was, whether a mouse, eating the host, received God or not? This question I never asked, but they asked it of me; and I made them no answer, but smiled.

"Then the bishop's chancellor rebuked me, and said that I was much to blame for uttering the scriptures. 'For St. Paul,' he said, 'forbade women to speak or to talk of the word of God.' I answered him that I knew Paul's meaning as well as he, which is in the 1 Corinthians xiv., that a woman ought not to speak in the congregation in the way of teaching: and then I asked him how many women he had seen go into the pulpit and preach? He said he never saw any. Then I said, he ought to find no fault in poor women, except they had offended the law.

"Then the lord mayor commanded me to prison: I asked him if sureties would not serve me; and he made me a short answer, that he would take none. Then was I taken to the Compter, and there remained eleven days, no friend being admitted to speak with me. But in the meantime there was a priest sent to me, who said that he was commanded by the bishop to examine me, and to give me good counsel. He first asked me for what cause I was put in the Compter, and I told him I could not tell. Then he said, it was a great pity that I should be there without cause, and concluded that he was very sorry for me.

"2. He said it was told him that I denied the sacrament of the altar. And I answered again, 'That which I have said, I have said.'

"3. He asked me if I were content to be confessed and absolved. I told him, that if I might have one of these three, Doctor Crome, William Whitehead, or Huntington, I was contented, because I knew them to be men of wisdom.

"4. He asked, if the host should fall, and a beast did eat it, whether the beast received God or not? I answered; 'Seeing that you have taken the pains to ask the question, I desire you to answer it yourself; for I will not do it, because I perceive you come to tempt me.' And he said it was against the order of schools, that he who asked the question should answer it. I told him I was but a woman, and knew nothing of the order of schools.

"5. He asked me if I intended to receive the sacrament at Easter, or not? I answered, that otherwise I were no christian woman; and I rejoiced that the time was so near at hand. And then he departed with many fair words.

"The twenty-third day of March, my cousin Britain came to the Compter to me, and asked me whether I might be put to bail, or not? Then he went immediately to my lord mayor, desiring him that I might be bailed. My lord answered him, and said that he would be glad to do the best that in him lay. However he could not bail me, without the consent of a spiritual officer, requiring him to go and speak with the chancellor of London. For he said, that as he could not commit me to prison without the consent of a spiritual officer, no more could he bail me without the consent of the same.

"So he went to the chancellor. He answered him, that the matter was so heinous, that he durst not of himself do it without my lord of London were made privy thereunto. But he said he would speak unto my lord in it, and bade him repair to him on the morrow, and he should then know my lord's pleasure. And upon the morrow he came thither, and spake both with the chancellor, and with the bishop of London. The bishop declared to him that he was very well contented that I should come forth to communication, and appointed me to appear before him the next day at three of the o'clock at afternoon. Moreover, he said to him, that he wished there should be at the examination such learned men as I was partial to, that they might see, and report that I was handled with no rigor. He answered him, that he knew no man that I had more affection to than to another. Then said the bishop; 'Yes, as I understand, she is partial to Crome, Whitehead, and Huntington, that they might hear the matter, for she knew them to be learned, and of a godly judgment.' Also, he required my Cousin Britain, that he should persuade me to utter even the very bottom of my heart; and he sware by his fidelity, that no man should take any advantage of my words, neither yet would he lay aught to my charge for any thing that I should there speak.

"On the morrow, the bishop of London sent for me at one o'clock, his hour being appointed at three; and as I came before him, he said he was very sorry for my trouble, and desired to know my opinions in such matters as were laid against me. He required me also to utter the secrets of my heart, bidding me not to fear in any point, for whatever I did say in his house, no man should hurt me for it. I answered, 'As your lordship appointed three of the clock, and my friends will not come till that hour, I desire you to pardon me of giving answer till they come.' Then he said that he thought it meet to send for those men. Then I desired him not to put them to trouble, because the two gentlemen who were my friends, were able enough to testify what I should say. He commanded his archdeacon to commune with me, who said to me, 'Mistress, wherefore are you accused and thus troubled here before the bishop?' To whom I answered: 'Sir, ask, I pray you, my accusers, for I know not as yet.' Then he took my book out of my hand, and said, 'Such books as this have brought you to the trouble that you are in. 'Beware,' said he; 'beware, for he that wrote this book, was a heretic, I warrant you, and burned in Smithfield.' And then I asked him if he were certain and sure that that was true that he had spoken. And he said he knew well the book was by John Frith. Then I asked him if he were not ashamed to judge of the book before he saw it. I said also, that such unadvised hasty judgment is a token of a very slender knowledge. Then I opened the book and shewed it him. He said he thought it had been another, for he could find no fault therein. Then I desired him to be no more so unadvisedly rash and swift in judgment, till he thoroughly knew the truth, and so he departed from me. Immediately after came my Cousin Britain, with others, as Master Hall of Gray's Inn, and others. Then my lord bishop of London said to me, that he wished I should take the counsel of such as were my friends and well-wishers, which was, that I should utter all things that burdened my conscience; for he assured me, that I need not fear to say any thing. For, as he had promised then, he promised me, and would perform it; which was, that neither he, nor any man for him should take advantage of me for any word that I should

speak, and therefore he bade me say my mind without fear. I answered him, that I had nought to say, for my conscience, I thanked God, was burdened with nothing.

"Then he brought forth this unsavory similitude; that if a man had a wound, no surgeon would cure it before he had seen it. 'In like manner,' saith he, 'I can give you no good counsel, unless I know wherewith your conscience is burdened.' I answered, that my conscience was clear in all things, and to lay a plaster unto the whole skin, appeared much folly.

"'Then you drive me,' saith he, 'to lay to your charge your own report, which is this; you said, that he that receives the sacrament by the hands of an ill priest, or a sinner, receives the devil, and not God.' To that I answered, that 'I never spake such words. But, as I said before, both to the inquest and to my lord mayor, so say I now again, that the wickedness of the priest should not hurt me, but in spirit and faith I received no less than the body and blood of Christ.' Then said the bishop to me, 'What is this *in spirit*? I will not take you at the advantage.' Then I answered: 'My lord, without faith and spirit, I cannot receive him worthily.'

"Then he told me, that I had said that the sacrament remaining in the pix, was but bread. I answered, that I never said so, but that indeed the inquest asked me such a question, and I would not answer it, I said, till such a time as they had answered me this question of mine: wherefore was Stephen stoned to death? They said they knew not. Then said I again, no more would I tell them what it was.

"Then said my lord to me, that I alleged a certain text of the scriptures, and I answered that I alleged none other but St. Paul's own saying to the Athenians, in the eighteenth chapter of the Acts of the Apostles, 'That God dwelleth not in temples made with hands.' Then he asked me what my faith and belief was in that matter? I answered him, 'I believe as the scripture teaches me.'

"Then he inquired of me, 'What if the scripture says, that it is the body of Christ?' 'I believe,' said I, 'as the scripture teaches me.' Then he asked again, 'What if the scripture says that it is not the body of Christ?' My answer was still, 'I believe as the scripture informs me.' And upon this he tarried a great while, to drive me to make him an answer to his own mind. However, I would not, but concluded with him, that I believed therein and in all other things, as Christ and his apostles left them.

"Then he asked me why I had so few words? And I answered, 'God has given me the gift of knowledge, but not of utterance: and Solomon saith, That a woman of few words is the gift of God.'

"Fifthly, my lord laid to my charge, that I said that the mass was superstitious, wicked, and no better than idolatry. I answered him, 'No, I said not so. However I said the inquest did ask me whether private mass did relieve souls departed or not? To whom I answered, O Lord, what idolatry is this, that we should rather believe in private masses than in the healthsome death of the dear Son of God!' Then said my lord again, 'What an answer is that!' 'Though it be but mean,' said I, 'yet it is good enough for the question.'

"Then I told my lord, that there was a priest who heard what I said there before my lord mayor and them. With that the chancellor answered, 'Who was the same priest?' 'So she spake it in very deed,' saith the priest, 'before my lord mayor and me.'

"Then were there certain priests, as Dr. Standish and others, who tempted me much to know my mind. And I answered them always thus; 'What I said to my lord of London, I have said.' Then Dr. Standish desired my lord to bid me say my mind concerning the text of St. Paul, that I, being a woman, should interpret the scriptures, especially where there were so many wise and learned men.

"Then my lord of London said, he was informed that one asked of me, if I would receive the sacrament at Easter, and that I made a mock of it.

"Then I desired that mine accuser might come forth, which my lord would not. But he said again to me, 'I sent one to give you good counsel, and at the first word you called him papist.' That I denied not, for I perceived he was no less.

"Then he rebuked me, and said that I reported, that there were against me threescore priests at Lincoln. 'Indeed,' quoth I, 'I said so. For my friends told me, if I came to Lincoln, the priests would assault me and put me to great trouble: and when I heard it, I went there indeed, not being afraid, because I knew my cause to be good. Moreover I remained there nine days, to see what would be said to me. And as I was in the minster reading the Bible, they resorted to me by two and two, by five and by six, to have spoken to me, yet they went their ways again without speaking.'

"Then my lord asked if there were not one that did speak to me. I told him 'Yes, that there was one of them at last who did speak to me.' And my lord then asked me what he said? I told him his words were of small effect, so that I did not now remember them. Then said my lord 'There are many that read and know the scripture, and yet follow it not.' I said again, 'My lord, I would wish that all men knew my conversation and living in all points; for I am sure, myself, this hour, that there are none able to prove any dishonesty by me. If you know that any can do it, I pray you bring them forth.' Then my lord went away, and said he would write somewhat of my meaning, and so he wrote a great deal. But what it was I have not in my memory: for he would not suffer me to have the copy. Only I remember this small portion of it:

"'Be it known, of all men, that I, Anne Askew, do confess this to be my faith and belief, notwithstanding many reports made to the contrary. I believe that they who receive the sacrament at the hands of a priest, whether his conversation be good or not, do receive the body and blood of Christ in substance really. Also I do believe, that after the consecration, whether it be received or reserved, it is no less than the very body and blood of Christ in substance. Finally, I do believe in this and in all other sacraments of holy church in all points, according to the old catholic faith of the same. In witness whereof, I the said Anne have subscribed my name.'

"There was somewhat more in it, which, because I had not the copy, I cannot now remember. Then he read it to me, and asked me if I agreed to it. And I said again, 'I believe so much of it, as the holy scripture agrees to: wherefore I desire you, that you will add that to it.' Then he answered, that I should not teach him what he should write. With that he went into his great chamber and read it before the audience, who wished me to set my hand to it, saying, that I had favour shewed me. Then said the bishop, 'I might thank others, and not myself, for the favour that I found at his hand: for he considered, that I had good friends, and also that I came of a worshipful stock.'

"Then answered one Christopher, a servant to Master Denny: 'Rather ought you, my lord, to have done it for God's sake than for man's.' Then my lord sat down, and I wrote after this manner: 'I Anne Askew, do believe all manner of things contained in the faith of the catholic church.'

"Then because I added to it 'the catholic church,' he ran into his chamber in a great fury. With that, my cousin Britain followed, desiring him for God's sake to be a good lord to me. He answered, that I was a woman, and that he was nothing deceived in me. Then my cousin Britain desired him to take me as a woman, and not to set my weak woman's wit to his lordship's great wisdom.

"Then Dr. Weston went in to him, and said, that the cause why I wrote there 'the catholic church,' was, that I understood not the church written before. So with much ado they persuaded my lord to come out again, and to take my name, with the names of my sureties, which were my cousin Britain and Master Spilman of Gray's Inn.

"This being done, we thought that I should have been put to bail immediately, according to the order of the law. Howbeit he would not suffer it, but committed me from thence to prison again until the morrow, and then he desired me to appear in the guild hall, and so I did. Notwithstanding they would not put me to bail there neither, but read the bishop's writing to me, as before, and so commanded me again to prison. Then were my sureties appointed to come before them on the morrow, in St. Paul's church, who did so. Notwithstanding, they would once again have broken off with them, because they would not be bound also for another woman at their pleasure, whom they knew not, nor yet what matter was laid to her charge. Notwithstanding at last, after much ado and reasoning to and fro, they took a bond of them of recognizance for my forthcoming: and thus I was at the last delivered.

"Written by me, ANNE ASKEW."

The second Apprehension and Examination of the worthy Martyr of God, Mistress Anne Askew, A.D. 1546.

"'I do perceive, (dear friend in the Lord) that thou art not yet persuaded thoroughly in the truth, concerning the Lord's supper, because Christ said to his apostles; 'Take, eat, this is my body which is given for you.'

"In giving forth the bread as an outward sign or token received with the mouth, he wishes them in perfect belief to receive that body which should die for the people, and to think the death thereof to be the only health and salvation of their souls. The bread and wine were left us for a sacramental communion, or a mutual participation of the inestimable benefits of his most precious death and bloodshedding, and that we should be thankful together for that most necessary grace of our redemption. For he said, 'This is my body, which is given for you; this do in remembrance of me.' Luke xxii. 9. Again, 'As often as ye eat this bread, and drink this cup, ye do shew the Lord's death till he come.' 1 Cor. xi. 26. Otherwise we should have been forgetful of what we ought to have in daily remembrance, and also have been altogether unthankful for it; therefore it is meet that in our prayers we call unto God to graft in our hearts the true meaning of the Holy Ghost concerning this communion. For St. Paul saith, 'The letter killeth; but the spirit giveth life.' 2 Cor. iii. 6. Mark well the sixth chapter of John, where all is applied to faith: note also the fourth chapter of St. Paul's second Epistle to the Corinthians, and in the end you shall find, that the things which are seen are temporal, but they that are not seen are eternal. Yea, look in the third chapter to the Hebrews, and ye shall find that Christ as a Son (and no servant) ruleth over his house, whose house are we, and not the dead temple, if we hold fast the confidence and rejoicing of our hope to the end. Wherefore, as said the Holy Ghost, 'To-day, if ye will hear his voice, harden not your hearts,' &c. Ps. xcv.

"Your request as concerning my fellow-prisoners, I am not able to satisfy, because I heard not their examinations. But the effect of mine was this: Being asked before the council concerning Master Kyme, I answered, that my lord chancellor knew already my mind in that matter. They with that answer were not contented, but said it was the king's pleasure that I should open the matter to them. I answered them plainly, I would not do so; but if it were the king's pleasure to hear me, I would shew him the truth. Then they said it was not meet for the king to be troubled with me. I answered, that Solomon was reckoned the wisest king that ever lived, yet he refused not to hear two poor common women, much more his grace a simple woman and his faithful subject. So in conclusion, I made them no other answer in that matter. Then my lord chancellor asked me my opinion of the sacrament. My answer was this: 'I believe that as often as I in a christian congregation do receive the bread in remembrance of Christ's death, and with thanksgiving, according to his holy institution, I received therewith the fruits also of his most glorious passion.' The bishop of Winchester bade me make a direct answer. I said I would not sing a new song of the Lord in a strange land. Then the bishop said I spoke in parables. I answered, 'It is best for you, for if I shew you the open truth, you will not accept it.' Then he said I was a parrot. I told him again, I was ready to suffer all things at his hands, not only his rebukes, but all that should follow besides, yea, and all things gladly.

"Then I had rebukes from the council, because I would not express my mind in all things as they would have me. But they were not, in the mean time, unanswered for all that, which now to rehearse were too much, for I was with them there about five hours.

"The next day I was brought again before the council. Then they would needs know of me what I said to the sacrament. I answered, that I already had said what I could say. Then after many words they bade me go aside. Then came my lord Lisle, my lord of Essex, and the bishop of Winchester, requiring me earnestly that I should confess the sacrament to be flesh, blood, and bone. Then I said to my lord Parr, and my lord Lisle, that it was a great shame for them to give counsel contrary to their knowledge.

"Then the bishop said he would speak with me familiarly. I said, So did Judas, when he betrayed Christ. The bishop desired to speak with me alone; but I refused that. He asked me why? I said, that in the mouth of two or three witnesses every matter should be established, after Christ's and Paul's doctrine, Matt. xviii., 2 Cor. xiii.

"Then my lord chancellor began to examine me again of the sacrament. I asked him how long he would halt on both sides. Then he went his way. The bishop said I should be burnt. I answered, 'That I had searched all the scriptures, yet I never find that either Christ or his apostles put any creature to death. Well, well,' said I, 'God will laugh your threatenings to scorn.' Then was I commanded to stand aside, and Dr. Cox, and Dr. Robinson came to me. In conclusion, we could not agree.

"Then they made me a bill of the sacrament, desiring me to set my hand to it; but I would not. Then on the Sunday I was sick, thinking no less than to die. Then I desired to speak with Master Latimer, but it was not allowed. Then I was sent to Newgate in the extremity of sickness; for in all my life before I was never in such pain. Thus may the Lord strengthen us in the truth. Pray, pray, pray!

The Confession of me, Anne Askew, for the time I was in Newgate, concerning my Belief.

"I find in scripture that Christ took the bread and gave it to his disciples, saying, 'Take, eat, this is my body which is broken for you,' meaning in substance, his own very body, the bread being the sign or sacrament of it. For after like manner of speaking he said he would break down the temple, and in three days build it up again, signifying by the temple his own body, as St. John declares it, John ii. 21; and not the stony temple itself. So that the bread is but a remembrance of his death, or a sacrament of thanksgiving for it; whereby we are knit to him by a communion of christian love, although there are many that cannot perceive the true meaning of it; for the veil that Moses put over his face before the children of Israel, that they should not see the clearness thereof; (Exod. xxiv., and 2 Corinth. iii.); I perceive the same veil remaineth to this day. But when God shall take it away, then shall these blind men see. For it is plainly expressed in the history of Bel in the bible, that God dwells in no thing material. 'O king,' says Daniel, 'be not deceived, for God will be in nothing that is made with hands of men.' 'Ye stiffnecked and uncircumcised in heart and ears, ye do always resist the Holy Ghost: as your fathers did, so do ye.' Acts vii. 51.

"Written by me, Anne Askew, that neither wishes death, nor fears his might, and as joyful as one that is bound towards heaven."

"Truth is laid in prison, Luke xxi. The law is turned to wormwood, Amos vi. And there can no right judgment go forth, Isa. lix.

"Take away all iniquity, and receive us graciously: so will we render the calves of our lips. Neither will we say any more to the work of our hands, Ye are our gods: for in thee the fatherless findeth mercy." Hosea xiv. 2, 3.

"Oh if they will do this, saith the Lord, I will heal their backsliding; I will love them freely.' And 'Ephraim shall say, What have I to do any more with idols? I have heard him and observed him: I am like a green fir-tree; 'from me is thy fruit found. Who is wise, and he shall understand these things? prudent, and he shall know them? for the ways of the Lord are right, and the just shall walk in them: but the transgressors shall fall therein." Hosea xiv. 8, 9.

"'Solomon,' saith St. Stephen, 'built an house for the God of Jacob. Howbeit the Most High dwelleth not in temples made with hands; as saith the prophet, Heaven is my throne, and earth is my footstool: what house will ye build me? saith the Lord: or what is the place of my rest? Hath not my hand made all these things?' Acts vii. 48—50.

"'Woman believe me,' saith Christ to the Samaritan, "the hour cometh, when ye shall neither in this mountain, nor yet at Jerusalem, worship the Father. Ye worship ye know not what: we know what we worship: for salvation is of the Jews. But the hour cometh, and now is, when the true worshippers shall worship the Father in spirit and in truth: for the Father seeketh such to worship him. God is a Spirit: and they that worship him must worship him in spirit and in truth.' John iv. 21—24.

"'Labour not,' saith Christ, 'for the meat that perisheth, but for that meat which endureth unto everlasting life, which the Son of Man shall give unto you: for him hath God the Father sealed.' John vi. 27."

The sum of the Condemnation of me, Anne Askew, at the Guildhall.

"They said that I was an heretic, and condemned by the law, and demanded if I would stand in mine opinion? I answered, 'That I was not an heretic; neither yet deserved I any death by the law of God. But as concerning the faith which I uttered and wrote to the council, I would not,' I said, 'deny it, because I knew it to be true.' Then would they know if I denied the sacrament to be Christ's body and blood. I said 'Yea. For the same Son of God who was born of the Virgin Mary is now glorious in heaven, and will come again from thence at the latter day in like manner as he ascended, (Acts i. 11.) And as for what you call your God, it is a piece of bread. For a proof of it, mark it when you choose, let it lie in the box three months, and it will be mouldy and so turn to nothing that is good; so that I am persuaded it cannot be God.'

"After that, they wished me to have a priest. And then I smiled. Then they asked me if it were not good; I said I would confess my faults unto God, for I was sure that he would hear me with favour. And so we were condemned.

"My belief which I wrote to the council was this. That the sacramental bread was left us to be received with thanksgiving, in remembrance of Christ's death, the only remedy of our souls' recovery; and that thereby we also receive the whole benefits and fruits of his most glorious passion. Then would they know, whether the bread in the box were God or not. I said, 'God is a Spirit, and they that worship him must worship him in spirit and in truth,' (John iv.) Then they demanded, 'Will you plainly deny Christ to be in the sacrament?' I answered, that 'I believe faithfully the eternal Son of God not to dwell there;' in proof of which I recited again the history of Bell, and the nineteenth chapter of Daniel, the seventh and seventeenth of the Acts, and the twenty-fourth of Matthew: concluding thus; 'I neither wish death, nor yet fear his might, God have the praise with thanksgiving.'"

My Letter sent to the Lord Chancellor.

"The Lord God, by whom all creatures have their beginning, bless you with the light of his knowledge. Amen.

"My duty to your lordship remembered, &c. It might please you to accept this my bold suit, as the suit of one which upon due consideration is moved to the same, and hopes to obtain it. My request to your lordship is only that it may please you to be a mediator for me to the king's majesty, that his grace may be certified of these few lines which I have written concerning my belief, which, when it shall be truly compared with the hard judgment given against me for the same, I think his grace shall well perceive me to be weighed in an uneven pair of balances. But I remit my matter and cause to Almighty God, who rightly judges all secrets. And thus I commend your lordship to the governance of him, and fellowship of all saints, Amen.

"By your handmaid,   ANNE ASKEW."

My Faith briefly written to the King's grace.

"I Anne Askew, of good memory, although God has given me the bread of adversity, and the water of affliction, yet not so much as my sins have deserved, desire this to be known to your grace, that forasmuch as I am by the law condemned as an evil doer; here I take heaven and earth to record, that I shall die in my innocency. And according to what I have said first and will say last, I utterly abhor and detest all heresies. And as concerning the supper of the Lord, I believe so much as Christ has said, which he confirmed with his most blessed blood. I believe so much as he willed me to follow, and believe so much as his catholic church teaches. For I will not forsake the commandment of his holy lips. But look, what God has charged me with by his mouth, that have I shut up in my heart. And thus briefly for lack of learning. "ANNE ASKEW."

The effect of my Examination and handling since my Departure from Newgate.

"Then there came to me Nicholas Shaxton, and counselled me to recant as he had done. I said to him, That it would have been good for him never to have been born.

"Then Master Rich sent me to the Tower, where I remained till three o'clock.

"Then came Master Rich as one of the council, charging me upon my obedience to show if I knew any man or woman of my sect. My answer was that I knew none. Then they asked me of my lady of Suffolk, my lady of Sussex, my lady of Hertford, my lady Denny, and my lady Fitzwilliams. To whom I answered, 'If I pronounce anything against them, I am not able to prove it.'

"Then they said that there were gentlewomen who gave me money. I said I knew not their names.

"Then they put me on the rack, because I confessed no ladies or gentlewomen to be of my opinion; and there they kept me a long time, and because I lay still and did not cry, my lord chancellor and Master Rich took pains to rack me with their own hands till I was nigh dead.

"Then the lieutenant caused me to be loosed from the rack. Immediately I swooned away, and then they recovered me again. After that I sat two long hours reasoning with my lord chancellor upon the bare floor. But my Lord God, I thank his everlasting goodness, gave me grace to persevere, and will do, I hope, to the very end.

"Then was I brought to a house, and laid in a bed, with weary and painful bones, I thank my Lord God for it. Then my lord chancellor sent me word if I would leave my opinion, I should want nothing; but if I would not, I should forthwith be sent to Newgate, and so be burnt. I sent him word again, that I would rather die than break my faith.

"Thus the Lord open the eyes of their blind hearts, that the truth may take place. Farewell, dear friend, and pray, pray, pray!"

The manner of her racking in the Tower was thus; first, she was led down into a dungeon, where the lieutenant commanded the jailor to pinch her with the rack. Which being done so much as he thought sufficient, he went to take her down, supposing that he had done enough. But Wriothesley the chancellor, not contented that she was loosed so soon, and having confessed nothing, commanded the lieutenant to strain her on the rack again. Which because he refused to do, pitying the weakness of the woman, he was threatened by Wriothesley, saying, that he would signify his disobedience to the king: and so he and Master Rich, throwing off their gowns, played the tormentors themselves; first asking her if she were with child. To whom she answered again, "Ye shall not need to spare me for that, but do your will upon me;" and so quietly and patiently praying to the Lord, she bore their tyranny, till her bones and joints were almost pulled asunder, so that she was carried away in a chair. When the racking was over, Wriothesley and his fellow took their horses, and rode towards the court.

In the meantime, while they were making their way by land, the lieutenant taking boat, went to the court in all haste to speak with the king before the others, and did so. Who there making his humble suit to the king, desired his pardon, and showed him the whole matter, and of the racking of Mrs. Askew, and that he was threatened by the lord chancellor, because at his commandment, not knowing his highness's pleasure, he refused to rack her; which he for compassion could not find in his heart to do, and therefore humbly desired his highness's pardon. Which when the king had understood, he seemed not very well to like their extreme handling of the woman, and also granted to the lieutenant his pardon, desiring him to return and see to his charge.

Great expectation was in the mean season among the warders and officers of the Tower, waiting for his return. When they saw him come so cheerfully, declaring how he had sped with the king, they were not a little joyous, and gave thanks to God.

Anne Askew's Answer to John Lacel's Letter.

"O friend, most dearly beloved in God, I marvel not a little what should move you to judge in me so slender a faith as to fear death, which is the end of all misery In the Lord I desire you not to believe of me such weakness. For I doubt it not, but God will perform his work in me as he has begun. I understand the council is not a little displeased, that it should be reported abroad that I was racked in the Tower. They say now that what they did there was but to frighten me; whereby I perceive they are ashamed of their uncomely doings, and fear much lest the king's majesty should have information thereof, wherefore they would no man to noise it. Well, for their cruelty God forgive them!

"Your heart in Christ Jesus. Farewell, and pray."

The Purgation or Answer of Anne Askew, against the false surmises of her Recantation.

"I have read the process which is reported of them, that know not the truth, to be my Recantation. But, as the Lord liveth, I never meant to recant. Notwithstanding this, I confess, that in my first troubles I was examined by the bishop of London about the sacrament. Yet had they no confession of my mouth but this, That I believed therein as the word of God did bind me to believe. More they never had of me. Then he made a copy, which is now in print, and required me to set my hand thereto; but I refused it. Then my two sureties did wish me not to hesitate, for they said it was no great matter.

"Then, with much ado, at last I wrote thus: 'I, Anne Askew, do believe this, if God's word do agree to the same, and the true catholic church.' Then the bishop being in great displeasure with me, because I made doubts in my writing, commanded me to prison, but afterwards by the means of friends I came out again. Here is the truth of that matter. And as concerning the thing that ye covet most to know, resort to the sixth of John, and be ruled always thereby. Thus fare ye well.

"ANNE ASKEW."

The Confession of the Faith which Anne Askew made in Newgate before she suffered.

" I, Anne Askew, of good memory, although my merciful Father hath given me the bread of adversity, and the water of trouble, yet not so much as my sins have deserved,—do confess myself here a sinner before the throne of his heavenly majesty, desiring his forgiveness and mercy. And forasmuch as I am by the law unrighteously condemned for an evil doer concerning opinions, I take the same most merciful God of mine, who hath made both heaven and earth, to record, that I hold no opinions contrary to his most holy word. And I trust in my merciful Lord, who is the giver of all grace, that he will graciously assist me against all evil opinions which are contrary to his blessed truth. For I take him to witness, that I have, and will, unto my life's end, utterly abhor them to the uttermost of my power.

" But this is the heresy which they report me to hold, that after the priest hath spoken the words of consecration, there remaineth bread still. They both say, and also teach it for a necessary article of faith, that after these words are once spoken, there remaineth no bread, but even the self-same body that hung upon the cross on Good Friday, both flesh, blood, and bone. To this belief of theirs I say nay. For then were our common creed false, which saith, that he sitteth on the right hand of God the Father Almighty, and from thence shall come to judge the quick and the dead. Lo! this is the heresy that I hold, and for it must suffer death. But as touching the holy and blessed supper of the Lord, I believe it to be a most necessary remembrance of his glorious sufferings and death. Moreover, I believe as much therein as my eternal and only Redeemer Jesus Christ would I should believe.

" Finally, I believe all those scriptures to be true, which he hath confirmed with his most precious blood. Yea, and as St. Paul saith, Those scriptures are sufficient for our learning and salvation, that Christ hath left here with us; so that I believe we need no unwritten verities to rule his church with. Therefore look what he hath said unto me with his own mouth, in his holy gospel, that I have with God's grace closed up in my heart; and my full trust is, as David saith, ' That it shall be a lamp unto my feet, and a light unto my path.''

" There are some that do say I deny the eucharist or sacrament of thanksgiving; but those people do untruly report of me. For I both say and believe it, that if it were administered like as Christ instituted it and left it, a most singular comfort it were to us all. But as concerning your mass, as it is now used in our days, I do say and believe it to be the most abominable idol that is in the world. For my God will not be eaten with teeth, neither yet dieth he again. And upon these words that I have now spoken, will I suffer death.

" O Lord, I have more enemies now than there be hairs on my head: yet, Lord, let them never overcome me with vain words, but fight thou, Lord, in my stead; for on thee I cast my care. With all the spite they can imagine, they fall upon me, who am thy poor creature. Yet, sweet Lord, let me not sit by them who are against me; for in thee is my whole delight. And, Lord, I heartily desire of thee, that thou wilt of thy most merciful goodness forgive them that violence which they do and have done unto me. Open also thou their blind hearts, that they may hereafter do that thing in thy sight, which only is acceptable before thee, and to set forth thy truth aright, without all vain fantasy of sinful men. So be it, O Lord, so be it.

" By me, ANNE ASKEW."

A few words remain to be said concerning her end and martyrdom. After she, born as she was of such kindred, that she might have lived in great wealth and prosperity, if she would rather have followed the world than Christ, had now been so tormented, that she could neither live long in so great distress, neither yet be suffered to die in secret; the day of her execution being ap-

pointed, she was brought into Smithfield in a chair, because she could not go on her feet, on account of her great torments. When she was brought to the stake, she was tied by the middle with a chain that held up her body. When all things were thus prepared, Doctor Shaxton, who was appointed to preach, began his sermon, Anne Askew hearing, and answering him; where he said well, she confirmed the same; where he said amiss, " There," said she, " he misses, and speaks without the book."

The sermon being finished, the martyrs, standing there, tied at three several stakes, began their prayers. The concourse of the people was very great, the place where they stood being railed about to keep out the press. Upon the bench, under St. Bartholomew's church, sate Wriothesley, chancellor of England, the old duke of Norfolk, the old earl of Bedford, the lord mayor, with others.

Wriothesley, lord chancellor, sent to Anne Askew, offering to her the king's pardon if she would recant. Who, refusing once to look upon them, made answer, that she came not thither to deny her Lord and Master. Then were the letters likewise offered unto the others, who in like manner, following the constancy of the woman, refused not only to receive them, but also to look upon them. Whereupon the lord mayor, commanding fire to be put to the fagots, cried with a loud voice, " Let justice be done."

Thus the good Anne Askew, with these blessed martyrs, having passed through so many torments, now ended the long course of her agonies, being compassed in with flames of fire, as a blessed sacrifice unto God; she slept in the Lord, A.D. 1546, leaving behind her a singular example of christian constancy for all men to follow.

John Lassels, John Adams, and Nicholas Belenian, were the names of those burnt along with her. Belenian was a priest of Shropshire, Adams a tailor, and Lassels, a gentleman of the court and household of king Henry.

It happened well for them, that they died together with Anne Askew. For though they were strong and stout men, yet, through the example and exhortation of her, they received great comfort in that painful kind of death: and beholding her invincible constancy, and also stirred up through her persuasions, shewed no kind of fear.

Thus confirming one another with mutual exhortations, their bodies were consumed in the fire, about the month of June, 1546.

As Winchester and other bishops did set on king Henry against Anne Askew and her fellow-martyrs, so Doctor Repse, bishop of Norwich, incited no less the old duke of Norfolk against one Rogers; who about the same time was condemned and suffered martyrdom for the six articles, in Smithfield.

The History of Queen Catharine Parr.

After these stormy histories, we must now treat of the afflictions of the virtuous and excellent lady, queen Catharine Parr, the last wife of king Henry.

About a year after the king returned from Boulogne, he was informed that queen Catharine Parr was very much given to the reading of the holy scriptures, and that she had learned and godly persons to instruct her in them; with whom she used to have private conference touching spiritual matters; but especially that in Lent, every day in the afternoon for the space of an hour, one of her chaplains delivered a sermon in her privy chamber, to her and the ladies of her privy chamber, or others that were disposed to hear. Which things, as they were not secretly done, so neither were the preachings unknown to the king; who seemed to like it very well. This made her the more bold (being indeed very zealous towards the gospel) to debate with the king touching religion; oftentimes desiring, and even persuading the king, that as he had, to the glory of God, and his eternal fame, begun a good and a godly work in banishing that monstrous idol of Rome (the pope), so he would thoroughly perfect and finish the same, cleansing and purging his church of England, wherein as yet remained great superstition.

And although the king, towards his latter end, grew very stern and obstinate, so that it was only of few he could be content to be taught, but least of all to be contended with by argument; still to her he refrained himself, and treated her with great respect, either through reverence for the cause, or else for the singular affection which, till a very short time before his death, he always bore to her. For besides the virtues of her mind, she was endued with very rare gifts of nature, as singular beauty, favour, and a comely personage; things wherein the king was greatly delighted; and so she enjoyed the king's favour, and would have done great good, had not the malicious practice of certain professed enemies against the truth prevented her; even to the utter alienating of the king's mind from religion, and almost to the extreme ruin of the queen and others with her, if God had not succoured her in her distress. The conspirers and practisers of her death were Gardiner bishop of Winchester, Wriothesley then lord chancellor, and others. These men, for the furtherance of their ungodly purpose, sought to revive, stir up, and kindle evil and pernicious humours in their prince and sovereign lord, to the intent to deprive her of the great favour which she then stood in with the king, (which they not a little feared would turn to the utter ruin of their antichristian sect, if it should continue.) They made their wicked entry upon their mischievous enterprise, after this manner. They knew the king disliked to be contended with in any argument. This humour of his, although the queen would not cross in smaller matters, yet in cases of religion as occasion served, she would not confine herself to reverent terms and humble talk, entering with him into discourse, with sound reasons of scripture. This the king was so well accustomed to, that he took all in good part, which greatly appalled her adversaries; who perceiving her so thoroughly grounded in the king's favour, they durst not for their lives once open their lips to the king in any respect to touch her, either in her presence, or behind her back.

It happened, however, in the time of the king's sickness, that he had left off his accustomed manner of visiting the queen: and therefore she sometimes was sent for, and sometimes of herself would come to visit him. At which time she would not fail to use all occasions to move him, zealously to proceed in the reformation of the church. The sharpness of the disease had increased the king's accustomed impatience, so that he began to shew some tokens of dislike; and contrary to his manner, one day breaking off the conversation, he took occasion to enter into other talk, which somewhat amazed the queen. To whom, notwithstanding, in her presence he gave neither evil word nor countenance, but knit up all arguments with gentle words and loving countenance; and after other pleasant talk, she for that time took her leave of his majesty; who after his manner bid her farewell "Sweet heart;" for that was his usual term to the queen.

At this visit the bishop of Winchester chanced to be present, as also at the queen's taking her leave, (who did not fail to observe the king's sudden interrupting of the queen in her talk, and falling into other matter,) and thought that if the iron were struck whilst it was hot, and the king's humour were helped, such disliking might follow to the queen, as might overthrow both her and all her endeavours; and he only awaited some occasion to renew in the king's memory the former disliked argument. His expectation in that respect did nothing fail him; for the king even at that time shewed himself no less prompt and ready to receive information, than the bishop was maliciously bent to stir up the king's indignation against her. The king, immediately upon her departure from him, used these or like words, "A good hearing it is when women become such clerks, and a thing much to my comfort, to come in mine old days to be taught by my wife."

The bishop hearing this, seemed to dislike that the queen should so much forget herself, as to take upon her to stand in any argument with his majesty, whom he to his face extolled for his rare virtues, and especially for his learned judgment in matters of religion, above not only princes of that and other ages, but also above professed doctors in divinity; and said that it was an unseemly thing for any of his majesty's subjects to reason and argue with him so impudently; and grievous to him for his part, to hear of it, as well as others of his majesty's counsellors and servants; inferring, moreover, how dangerous and perilous a matter it is, and ever hath been, for a prince to suffer such insolent words at his subject's hands: who, as they take boldness to oppose their sovereign in words, so they want no will, but only power and strength, to overthrow them in deeds.

Besides this, that the religion so stiffly maintained by the queen did not only disallow and dissolve the policy and government of princes, but also taught the people that all things ought to be in common; so that what colour soever they pretended, their opinions were indeed so odious, and for the prince's estate so perilous, that (saving the reverence they bore unto her for his majesty's sake,) he durst be bold to affirm that the greatest subject in this land, speaking those words that she did speak, and defending likewise those arguments that she did defend, had with justice by law deserved death.

Howbeit for his part, he would not, nor durst not, without good warrant from his majesty, speak his knowledge in the queen's case, although very apparent reasons urged him, and such as his dutiful affection towards his majesty, and his zeal for the preservation of his state, would scarce give him leave to conceal, though the uttering of it might, through her and her faction, be the utter destruction of him, and of such as chiefly tended to the prince's safety, without his majesty would take upon him to be their protector. Which if he would do, he with other faithful counsellors could disclose such treason, cloaked with this cloak of heresy, that his majesty should easily perceive how perilous a matter it is to cherish a serpent in his own bosom.

These and such other phrases whetted the king to anger and displeasure towards the queen. Thus Winchester with his flattering words so far insinuated himself with the king at that time, and so filled the king's distrustful mind, that before they separated, the king had given command, with warrant to certain of them, to consult together about the drawing up of certain articles against the queen, wherein her life might be touched; which the king pretended he fully resolved not to spare. With this commission they departed, resolved to put their pernicious practice into as mischievous execution.

During the time of deliberation about this matter, they failed not to use all kind of mischievous practices, as well as to suborn accusers, as otherwise to betray her, in seeking to ascertain what books forbidden by law she had in her closet. And the better to bring their purpose to pass, because they would not upon the sudden but gradually deal with her, they thought it best, at the first, to begin with some of those ladies, whom they knew to be intimate with her, and of her blood. The chief, and most in estimation, and privy to all her doings, were these: the lady Herbert, afterwards countess of Pembroke, and sister to the queen, and chief of her privy chamber; the lady Lane, being of her privy chamber, and also her cousin-german; the lady Tyrwhitt, of her privy chamber, and for her virtuous disposition in very great favour and credit with her.

It was devised that these three should first of all have been accused and brought to answer to the six articles; and upon their apprehension in the court, their closets and coffers should have been searched, that somewhat might have been found by which the queen might be charged; which being found, the queen herself presently should have been taken, and likewise carried by night by barge to the Tower.

The king at that time lay at Whitehall, and used very seldom, being unwell, to stir out of his chamber or private gallery; and few of his council, but by especial command, resorted to him. This purpose was handled so secretly, that it grew now within a few days of the time for the execution of the matter, and the poor queen neither knew nor suspected anything at all; and therefore used after her accustomed manner, when she came to visit the king, still to deal with him touching religion as before. The king all this while gave her leave to utter her mind at the full without contradiction. Thus after her accustomed conference with the king, when she had taken her leave of him, it chanced that the king brake the whole matter to one of his physicians, pretending to him, as though he intended not any longer to be troubled with such a doctress as she was; and also declaring what trouble was in working against her by her enemies; but yet charging him withal, upon peril of his life, not to utter it to any creature living: and thereupon declared to him the parties above-named, with all circumstances, and when and what the final resolution of the matter should be.

The queen all this while, compassed about with enemies and persecutors, perceived nothing of all this, nor what was working against her, and what traps were laid for her by Winchester and his fellows. But see what the Lord God did for his poor handmaiden, in rescuing her from the pit of ruin, whereinto she was ready to fall unawares. For as the Lord would, so came it to pass, that the bill of articles drawn up against the queen, and subscribed with the king's own hand (although dissemblingly you must understand), falling from the bosom of one of the councillors, was found by some godly person, and brought immediately to the queen. Who reading there the articles against her, and perceiving the king's own hand to the same, fell immediately into a great agony, bewailing and talking on in such sort, as was lamentable to hear and see, as certain of her ladies and gentlewomen being yet alive, who were then present about her, can testify.

The king hearing what perplexity she was in, almost to the peril and danger of her life, sent his physicians to her; who seeing what extremity she was in, did what they could for her recovery. Then Wendy, the physician to whom the king had spoken, perceiving by her words what the matter was, for the comforting of her mind, began to break with her in secret, touching the articles against her, which he himself, he said, knew right well to be true; although he stood in danger of his life, if ever he were known to utter it to any living creature. Nevertheless, partly for the safety of her life, and partly for the discharge of his own conscience, having remorse to consent to the shedding of innocent blood, he could not but give her warning of that mischief that hung over her head, beseeching her to use all secresy, and exhorted her to frame and comport herself to the king's mind, saying, he did not doubt, but if she would do so, and shew her humble submission to him, she should find him gracious and favourable to her.

It was not long after this, that the king hearing of the dangerous state in which she still remained, came to her himself. To whom, after that she had uttered her grief, fearing lest his majesty, she said, had taken displeasure with her, and had utterly forsaken her, he, like a loving husband, with sweet and comfortable words, so refreshed and appeased her mind, that she began somewhat to recover; and so the king, after he had tarried there about the space of an hour, departed.

After this the queen, remembering with herself the words that Mr. Wendy had said to her, devised how by some good opportunity she might repair to the king's presence. And so first commanding her ladies to convey away their books which were against the law, the next night after supper, she, waited upon only by the lady Herbert her sister, and the lady Lane, who carried the candle before her, went to the king's bedchamber, whom she found sitting and talking with several gentlemen of his chamber. Whom when the king beheld, he very courteously welcomed her, and breaking off the talk, which before her coming he had with the gentlemen, began of himself, contrary to his manner, to enter into talk of religion, seeming, as it were, desirous to be resolved by the queen of certain doubts which he propounded.

The queen perceiving to what purpose this talk tended, not being unprovided in what sort to behave herself towards the king, resolved his questions as the time and opportunity required, mildly, and with reverent countenance, answering again after this manner:

"Your majesty," said she, "does right well know, neither am I myself ignorant, what great imperfection and weakness by our first creation is allotted to us women, to be ordained and appointed as inferior and subject to man as our head, from which head all our direction ought to proceed; and that as God made man to his own shape and likeness, whereby he, being indued with more special gifts of perfection, might rather be stirred to the contemplation of heavenly things, and to the earnest endeavour to obey his commandments, even so also made he woman of man, of whom and by whom she is to be governed, commanded, and directed. Thus womanly weaknesses and natural imperfection ought to be tolerated, aided, and borne withal, so that by wisdom such things as be lacking in her ought to be supplied.

"Since, therefore, that God has appointed such a natural difference between man and woman, and your majesty being so excellent in gifts and ornaments of wisdom, and I a silly poor woman, so much inferior in all respects of nature to you, how then comes it now to pass that your majesty, in such causes of religion, will seem to require my judgment? Which when I have uttered and said what I can, yet must I, and will I, refer my judgment in this, and in all other cases, to your majesty's wisdom, as my only anchor, supreme head and governor here in earth, next under God, to lean to."

"Not so, by St. Mary," replied the king, "you are become a doctor, Kate, to instruct us, as we take it, and not to be instructed or directed by us."

"If your majesty take it so," said the queen, "then has your majesty very much mistaken, who have ever been of the opinion, to think it very unseemly, and preposterous for the woman to take upon her the office of an instructor or teacher to her lord and husband, but rather learn of her husband, and to be taught by him. And where I have, with your majesty's leave, heretofore been bold to hold talk with your majesty, wherein sometimes in opinions there has seemed some difference, I have not done it so much to maintain opinion, as I did it rather to minister talk, not only to the end your majesty might with less grief pass over this painful time of your infirmity, being attentive to our talk, and hoping that your majesty should reap some ease by it; but also, that I hearing your majesty's learned discourse might receive to myself some profit. Wherein, I assure your majesty, I have not missed any part of my desire in that behalf, always referring myself in all such matters to your majesty, as by ordinance of nature it is convenient for me to do."

"And is it even so, sweetheart?" answered the king, "and tended your arguments to no worse end? Then perfect friends we are now again, as ever at any time heretofore." And as he sate in his chair, embracing her in his arms, and kissing her, he added this, saying, "That it did him more good at that time to hear those words out of her own mouth, than if he had been informed that an hundred thousand pounds in money had fallen to him." And with great signs and tokens of marvellous joy and affection, with promises and assurances never again in any sort more to mistake her, he entered into other very pleasant discourse with the queen and the lords, and the gentlemen standing by, and then in the end he gave her leave to depart.

Now then, God be thanked, the king's mind was quite altered, and he detested in his heart (as afterwards he plainly shewed) this tragical practice of those cruel Caiaphases; who not understanding the king's mind, and good disposition towards the queen, were busily occupied about thinking and providing for their next day's labour; which was the day on which they had determined to have carried the queen to the Tower.

The day, and almost the hour appointed, being come, the king being disposed in the afternoon to take the air, (waited upon by two gentlemen only of his bedchamber), went into the garden, whither the queen also came, having been sent for by the king himself, accompanied by the three ladies above named to wait upon her; with whom the king at that time disposed himself to be as pleasant as ever he was in all his life before. When suddenly, in the midst of their mirth, the hour determined being come, in comes the lord chancellor into the garden, with forty of the king's guards at his heels, to have taken the queen, together with the three ladies, whom they had before purposed to apprehend alone; the king sternly beholding them, broke off his mirth with the queen, and stepping a little aside, called the chancellor to him. Who upon his knees spake certain words to the king, but what they were (for they were softly spoken, and the king a good distance from the queen), is not well known; but it is most certain that the king's reply to him was, "Knave;" yea, "Arrant knave, beast, and fool;" and with that the king commanded him presently to begone out of his presence. Which words, although they were uttered somewhat low, yet they were so vehemently whispered out by the king, that the queen with her ladies overheard them; which had been not a little to her comfort, if she had known at that time the whole cause of his coming, so perfectly as afterwards she knew it. Thus departed the lord chancellor out of the king's presence as he came, with all his train, the whole device being utterly broken.

The king, after his departure, immediately returned to the queen; whom she perceiving to be very much chafed (albeit coming towards her, he forced himself to put on a cheerful countenance), with as sweet words as she could utter she endeavoured to qualify the king's displeasure, with a request to his majesty in behalf of the lord chancellor, whom he seemed to be offended with; saying, for his excuse, "That although she knew not what just cause his majesty had at that time to be offended with him, yet she thought that ignorance, not will, was the cause of his error, and so besought his majesty (if the cause were not very heinous) at her humble suit to take it."

"Ah, poor soul," said he, "thou little knowest how ill he deserves this grace at thy hands. Of my word, sweetheart, he has been towards thee an arrant knave, and so let him go." To this the queen in charitable manner replying in few words, ended that talk; having also by God's blessing happily, for that time and ever, escaped the dangerous snares of her bloody and cruel enemies for the gospel's sake.

The pestiferous purpose of this bishop, and of suchlike bloody adversaries practising thus against the queen, puts me in remembrance of such another story of his wicked working in like manner, a little before; but much more pernicious and pestilent to the public church of Jesus Christ, than this was dangerous to the private estate of the queen. Which story I thought here, as in a convenient place, to be notified to all posterity, according as I had it faithfully recorded to me by one who heard it from Archbishop Cranmer's own mouth.

A Discourse, touching a certain Policy used by Stephen Gardiner, Bishop of Winchester, in staying King Henry VIII. from redressing certain Abuses of Ceremonies in the Church, being Ambassador beyond the Seas.—Also the Communication of King Henry VIII. with the Ambassador of France, at Hampton-court, concerning the Reformation of Religion, as well in France as in England. August, A.D. 1546.

It chanced in the time of King Henry VIII., when his highness, not many years before his death, concluded a league between the emperor, the French king, and himself, that the bishop of Winchester, Stephen Gardiner by name, was sent as ambassador beyond the seas for that purpose. In whose absence Thomas Cranmer, archbishop of Canterbury, attending upon the king's court, sought occasion to further the reformation of religion. For as the archbishop was always diligent and forward to prefer and advance the sincere doctrine of the gospel; so was that other bishop a contrary instrument, continually spurning against it, in whatever

part of the world he remained. For even now he being beyond the seas, in the temporal affairs of the realm, forgot not, but found the means, as a most valiant champion of the bishop of Rome, to stop and hinder, as well the good diligence of the archbishop, as the godly disposition of the king's majesty, which thus happened:

Whilst the bishop of Winchester was now remaining beyond the seas, the king's majesty and the archbishop having conference together for reformation of some superstitious enormities in the church; among other things, the king determined forthwith to pull down the roods in every church, and to suppress the accustomed ringing on Allhallow's-night, with a few such-like vain ceremonies; and, therefore, when the archbishop took his leave of the king, to go into his diocese, his highness desired him to remember, that he should cause two letters to be devised: "By me," said the king, "to be signed; the one to be directed to you, my lord, and the other to the archbishop of York, wherein I will command you both to send forth your precepts to all other bishops within your provinces, to see those enormities and ceremonies reformed without delay, that we have communed of."

So upon this, the king's pleasure being known, when the archbishop of Canterbury was come into Kent, he caused his secretary to write these letters according to the king's mind; and being in readiness, he sent them to the court to Sir Anthony Denny, for him to get them signed by the king. When Master Denny had moved the king thereto, the king made answer, "I am now otherwise resolved; for you shall send my lord of Canterbury word, that since I spake with him about those matters, I have received letters from my lord of Winchester, now on the other side of the sea, about the conclusion of a league between us and the emperor, and the French king; and he writes plainly to us, that the league will not prosper, nor go forward, if we make any other innovation, change, or alteration, either in religion or ceremonies, than heretofore has been already commenced and done. Wherefore my lord of Canterbury must take patience herein, and forbear, until we may espy a more apt and convenient time for that purpose."

Which matter of reformation began to be revived again, when the great ambassador from the French king, came to the king's majesty at Hampton Court, not long before his death; where no gentleman was permitted to wait upon his lord and master, without a velvet coat and a chain of gold. And for the entertainment of the ambassador, there were built in the park three very great and sumptuous banqueting houses. At first it was purposed, that the ambassador should have been three nights very richly banqueted. But as it chanced, that the French king's great affairs became suddenly changed, so that this ambassador was sent for home in haste, before he had received half the noble entertainment that was prepared for him; and he had but the fruition of the first banqueting house.

Now, what prince-like order was there used in the furniture of the banquet, as well in places of the noble estates, namely, the king's majesty, and the French ambassador, with the noblemen both of England and France on the one part, and of the queen's highness and the lady Anne of Cleves, with other noble women and ladies of the other part, as also touching the great and sumptuous preparation of costly and fine dishes there displayed, it is not our purpose here to treat of; but only to consider and note the conference and communication had the first night after the banquet was finished, between the king's majesty, the ambassador, and the archbishop of Canterbury (the king's highness standing openly in the banqueting-house, in the open face of all the people, and leaning one arm upon the shoulder of the archbishop of Canterbury, and the other arm upon the shoulder of the ambassador) touching the establishing of godly religion between those two princes in both their realms: as by the report of the archbishop to his secretary, upon occasion of his service to be done in

King Edward's visitation, then being register in the visitation, relation was made on that behalf as follows:—

When the visitation was put in a readiness, before the commissioners should proceed in their voyage, the archbishop sent for the register to Hampton Court, and desired him to make notes of certain things in the visitation; he gave to him instruction, having then further talk with him touching the good effect and success of the visitation. Upon which occasion the register said to his master the archbishop; "I remember, that you not long ago caused me to write letters, which King Henry VIII. should have signed and directed to your grace and the archbishop of York, for the reformation of certain enormities in the churches, as taking down of the roods, and forbidding of ringing on Alhallow-night, and such like vain ceremonies. Which letters your grace sent to the court to be signed by the king's majesty, but as yet I think that there was never any thing done."

"Why," said the archbishop, "did you never hear that those letters were suppressed and stopped?" The archbishop's servant answered; "as it was," said he, "my duty to write those letters, so was it not my part to be inquisitive what became of them." "Indeed," replied the archbishop, "my lord of Winchester being then beyond the seas, about the conclusion of a league between the emperor, the French king, and the king our master, and fearing that some reformation should here pass in the realm, touching religion in his absence, wrote to the king's majesty, bearing him in hand, that the league would not prosper nor go forwards on his majesty's behalf if he made any other innovation, or alteration, in religion, or ceremonies in the church; which caused the king to stay the signing of those letters, as Sir Anthony Denny wrote to me by the king's command."

Then said his servant again to him; "Forsomuch as the king's good intent did not then take place, now your grace may go forward in those matters, as the opportunity of the time is much better serving than in King Henry's days."

"Not so," said the archbishop. "It was better to attempt such reformation in King Henry's day than at this time, the king being in his infancy. For if the king's father had set forth any thing for the reformation of abuses, who was he that durst gainsay it? Indeed, we are now in doubt how men will take the change, or alteration of abuses in the church; and, therefore, the council has forborne especially to speak of it, and of other things which gladly they would have reformed, referring all those, and such like matters, to the discretion of the visitors. But if King Henry VIII. had lived to this day with the French king, it had been past my lord of Winchester's power to have influenced the king's highness, as he did when he was about the same league."

"I am sure you were at Hampton Court," replied the archbishop, "when the French king's ambassador was entertained there at those solemn banqueting houses, not long before the king's death; namely, when after the banquet was done the first night, the king leaning upon the ambassador and me, if I should tell what communication passed between the king's highness and the ambassador, concerning the establishing of sincere religion, a man would hardly have believed it. Nor had I myself thought the king's highness had been so forward in those matters as he then appeared. I may tell you it concerned more than the pulling down of roods, and suppressing the ringing of bells: I take it, that few in England would have believed, that the king's majesty and the French king had been at this point, not only within half a year after to have changed the mass in both the realms into a communion as we now use it), but also utterly to have extirpated and banished the bishop of Rome, and his usurped power, out of both their realms and dominions. Yea, they were so thoroughly and firmly resolved in that behalf, that they meant also to exhort the emperor to do the like in Flanders and his other countries and seigniories, or else they would break off from him. And herein the king's highness commanded me (said the archbishop) to pen a form to be sent to the French king to consider of. But

the deep and most secret Providence of Almighty God, visiting this realm with a sharp scourge for our iniquities, prevented for a time this their most godly device and intent, by taking to his mercy both these princes."

A brief Narration of the Trouble of Sir George Blage.

Here may something be said of Sir George Blage, one of the king's privy chamber, who, being falsely accused by Sir Hugh Caverley, knight; and Master Littleton; was sent for by Lord Chancellor Wriothesley, and carried to Newgate, and thence to Guildhall, where he was condemned and appointed to be burned. The words which his accusers laid to him were these; "What if a mouse should eat the bread? Then, in my opinion, they should hang the mouse." Whereas, to the end of his life, he protested that he never spoke these words. But the truth, as he said, was this; that they, walking with him in St. Paul's church after a sermon of Doctor Crome's, asked if he were at the sermon. He said, "Yea." "I heard," saith Master Littleton, "that he said in his sermon, That the mass profits neither for the quick nor for the dead." "No," saith Master Blage, "wherefore then? perhaps for a gentleman when he rides in hunting, to keep his horse from stumbling!" And so they departed, and immediately after he was apprehended and condemned to be burned. When this was heard among those of the Privy Chamber, the king hearing them whispering (which he could never abide) commanded them to tell him the matter. Upon which the matter being told, and suit made to the king, especially by the good earl of Bedford, then lord privy seal, the king being very offended that they would come so near him, into his Privy Chamber, without his knowledge, sent for Wriothesley, commanding him immediately to draw out the pardon himself, and so he was set at liberty. Blage coming afterwards into the king's presence; "Ah, my pig," saith the king to him, for so he used to call him. "Yea," said he, "if your Majesty had not been better to me than your bishops were, your pig had been roasted ere this time."

Then the popish leaders, when they had martyred Mrs. Askew and the others, and being now in their triumph, like the pharisees when they had brought Christ to his grave, devised among themselves how to keep him down still, and to over-tread truth for ever. On consulting with certain of the council, they made out a hard proclamation, authorized by the king's name, for abolishing the scriptures, and all such English books as might set forth God's true word, and grace of the gospel.

A Proclamation for the abolishing of English Books, the eighth day of July, A. D. 1546.

"The king's most excellent majesty understanding how, under the pretence of expounding and declaring the truth of God's scripture, divers evil disposed persons have taken upon them to utter and sow abroad, by books printed in the English tongue, sundry pernicious and detestable errors and heresies, not only contrary to the laws of this realm, but also repugnant to the true sense of God's law and word, by reason whereof certain men of late, to the destruction of their own bodies and souls, and to the evil example of others, have attempted, arrogantly and maliciously, to impugn the truth, and therewith trouble the sober, quiet, and godly religion, united and established under the king's majesty in this his realm; his highness minding to foresee the dangers that might ensue of the said books, is enforced to use his general prohibition, commandment, and proclamation, as follows:—

"First, That from henceforth no man, woman, or person, of what estate, condition, or degree soever he or they be, shall, after the last day of August next ensuing, receive, have, take, or keep in his or their possession, the text of the New Testament of Tindal's or Coverdale's translation in English, nor any other than is permitted by the act of parliament made in the session of the parliament held at Westminster in the four-and-thirtieth and five-and-thirtieth year of his majesty's most noble reign; nor after the said day shall receive, have, take, or keep, in his or their possession, any manner of books printed or written in the English tongue, which be, or shall be set forth in the names of Frith, Tindal, Wickliff, Joy, Roy, Basil, Bale, Barnes, Coverdale, Turner, Tracy, or by any of them, or any other book or books, containing matter contrary to the said act made in the year thirty-four or thirty-five; but shall, before the last day of August next coming, deliver the same English book, or books, to his master in that household, if he be a servant, or dwell under any other, and the master or ruler of the house, and such other as dwell at large, shall deliver all such books of these sorts as they have, or shall come to their hands, delivered as before or otherwise, to the mayor, bailiff, or chief constable of the town where they dwell, to be by them delivered over openly, within forty days next following after the said delivery, to the sheriff of the shire, or to the bishop's chancellor, or commissary of the same diocese, to the intent the said bishop, chancellor, commissary, and sheriff, and every of them, may cause them immediately to be openly burned: which thing the king's majesty's pleasure is, that every of them shall see executed in most effectual sort, and of their doings thereof make certificate to the king's majesty's most honourable council, before the first day of October next coming.

" And to the intent that no man shall mistrust any danger of such penal statutes as are passed in this behalf, for the keeping of the said books, the king's majesty is most graciously contented by this proclamation to pardon that offence to the said time appointed by this proclamation for the delivery of the said books, and commands that no bishop, chancellor, commissary, mayor, bailiff, sheriff, or constable, shall be curious to mark who brings forth such books, but only order and burn them openly, as is in this proclamation ordered. And if any man, after the last day of August next coming, shall have any of the said books in his keeping, or be proved, and convicted by sufficient witness before four of the king's most honourable council, to have hidden them, or used them, or any copy of any of them, or any part of them, whereby it should appear that he willingly hath offended the true meaning of this proclamation, the same shall not only suffer imprisonment and punishment of his body at the king's majesty's will and pleasure, but also shall make such fine and ransom to his highness for the same, as by his majesty, or four of his grace's said council, shall be determined, &c.

" Finally, His majesty straightly charges and commands, that no person or persons, of what estate, degree, or condition, soever he or they be, from the day of this proclamation, presume to bring any manner of English book, concerning any manner of christian religion, printed in the parts beyond the seas, into this realm, to sell, give, or distribute, any English book printed in outward parts, or the copy of any such book, or any part thereof, to any person, dwelling within this his grace's realm, or any other his majesty's dominions, unless the same shall be specially licensed so to do by his highness' express grant to be obtained in writing for the same, upon the pains before limited, and therewithal to incur his majesty's extreme indignation."

Having procured this proclamation, they proceeded to prohibit all the books that taught the gospel of Christ, under pretence that they taught heresy and every evil thing; and thus they slandered, under names of heresy and blasphemy, the writings and doctrine, and persons, of the protestants: and while they thus prohibited all true doctrine, they themselves published many books against the protestants, in which they most falsely and untruly call them heretics, charging them as blasphemers of God, contemners of God and men, church robbers, cruel, false liars, crafty deceivers, unfaithful, promise-breakers, disturbers of the public peace and tranquillity, corrupters and subverters of the commonwealth, and all else that is bad.

In much like sort was Socrates accused by his countrymen for a corrupter of the youth, whom Plato notwithstanding defends. Aristides, the Just, lacked not his unjust accusers. Was it not objected to St. Paul, that he was a subverter of the law of Moses, and that we might do evil that good might come? How was it laid to the christian martyrs in the primitive church for worshipping of an ass's head, and for sacrificing of infants? And to come more near to these our latter days, you heard likewise how falsely the christian congregation of the Frenchmen gathered together in the night at Paris, to celebrate the holy communion, were accused of horrible wickedness, which we must not name, and were condemned to the fire, and burned. Finally, what innocency is so pure, or truth so perfect, which can be void of these slanders and criminations, when our Saviour Christ himself was noted for a wine-drinker, and a common haunter of the publicans, &c.

Even so likewise it pleases our Lord and Saviour Christ to keep and to exercise his church under the like kind of adversaries now reigning in the church, who under the name of the church will needs maintain a portly state and kingdom in this world; and because they cannot uphold their cause by plain scripture and the word of God, they bear it out with railing and slandering, making princes and the simple people believe, that all are heretics, schismatics, blasphemers, rebels, and subverters of all authority and government, whoever dare reply with any scripture against their doings.

It is written of Nero, that when he himself had caused the city of Rome to be set on fire, and it had burned seven nights, he made open proclamation that the innocent christians had set the city on fire, to stir the people against them, whereby he might burn and destroy them as rebels and traitors.

Not much unlike seems the dealing of these papists, who when they are the true heretics themselves, and have burnt and destroyed the church of Christ, make out their exclamations, bulls, briefs, articles, books, censures, letters, and edicts against the poor protestants, to make the people believe, that they are the heretics, schismatics, and disturbers of the whole world. Who if they could prove them, as they reprove them to be heretics, they were worthy to be heard. But now they cry out upon them "heretics!" and can prove no heresy; they accuse them of error, and can prove no error; they call them schismatics, and what church since the world stood hath been the mother of so many schisms as the mother church of Rome? They charge them with dissension and rebellion; and what dissension can be greater than to dissent from the scriptures and word of God? Or what rebellion is so great as to rebel against the Son of God, and against the will of his eternal Testament? They are disturbers, they say, of peace and public authority; which is as true, as that the christians set the city of Rome on fire. What doctrine did ever attribute so much to public authority of magistrates, as do the protestants? or who ever attributed less to magistrates, or deposed more dukes, kings, and emperors, than the papists? They, that say the bishop of Rome is no more but the bishop of Rome, and ought to wear no crown, is not a rebel against his king and magistrates, but rather a maintainer of their authority; which indeed the bishop of Rome cannot abide. Briefly, wilt thou see who are the greater heretics, the protestants or papists? Let us try it by a measure, and let this measure be the glory only of the Son of God, who cannot fail. Now judge, I beseech thee, whosoever knows the doctrine of them both, whether of these two do ascribe more or less to the majesty of Christ Jesus our King and Lord; the protestants, which admit none other head of the church, nor justifier of our souls, nor forgiver of our sins, nor advocate to his Father, but him alone; or else the papists, who can abide none of these articles, but condemn them for heresy. Which being so (as they themselves will not deny) now judge, good reader, who hath set the city of Rome on fire, Nero, or the christians.

But to return again to our former purpose, which was to shew the proclamation of the bishops for abolishing English books, as being corrupt and full of heresy, which notwithstanding we have declared to contain no heresy, but sound and wholesome doctrine, according to the perfect word and scripture of God.

Now, when the prelates of the pope's side had procured this proclamation for the condemnation of all such English books, printed or unprinted, as made against their advantage, they triumphed not a little, thinking they had overthrown the gospel for ever, and that they had firmly established their kingdom. Who would have thought, after so straight, so precise, and so solemn a proclamation, set forth and armed with the king's terrible authority; also after the cruel execution of Anne Askew, Lassels, and the rest, who would have thought, I say, but that the gospel must needs be overthrown? seeing what sure work the papists had made, in setting up their cause, and throwing down the cause of truth.

But it is not a new thing with the Lord, to shew his power against man, who, when he counts himself the most sure, is then furthest off; and when he supposes to have done all, is then to begin again. So was it in the primitive church before Constantine's time, that when Nero, Domitian, Maximin, Decius, and other emperors impugning the gospel and profession of Christ, did not only institute laws and make proclamations against the christians, but they also did engrave the same laws in tables of brass, minding to make all things firm for ever; yet we see, how with a little turning of God's hand all their mighty devices, and brazen laws were turned to wind and dust. So little does it avail for man to wrestle against the Lord and his proceedings. Man's building is mortal and ruinous, of brittle brick, and mouldering stones; yet that which the Lord takes in hand to build, neither can time waste, nor man pull down. What God sets up, there is neither power nor striving to the contrary. What he intends, stands; what he blesses, prevails. And yet man's presumption will not cease still to erect up towers of Babel against the Lord, which the higher they are built up, fall with the greater ruin. For what can stand, that stands not with the Lord?

The proclamation, though it was terrible for the time, yet not long after, by reason of the king's death (whom the Lord shortly afterwards took to his mercy) it became of no avail. So that where the prelates thought to make their jubilee, it turned to a day of lamentation. Such are the admirable workings of the Lord of Hosts, whose name be sanctified for ever.

This do I not infer for any other purpose, but only that the works of the Lord may be seen; admonishing thee, good reader, that as to the king, (who in this proclamation had nothing but the name only,) here is nothing spoken but to his honour and praise. Who, of his own nature and disposition, was so inclinable and forward in abolishing the almost invincible authority of the pope, in suppressing monasteries, in repressing idolatry and pilgrimage, &c., which enterprises as never king of England did accomplish (though some began to attempt them) before him; so yet to this day we see but few in other realms dare follow the same.

If princes have always their counsel about them, that is but a common thing. If sometimes they have evil counsel ministered, that I take to be the fault rather of such as are about them, than of princes themselves. So long as queen Anne, Thomas Cromwell, bishop Cranmer, Master Doctor Buts, with such like were about him, and could prevail with him, what organ of Christ's glory did more good in the church than he; as is apparent by such monuments, instruments, and acts set forth by him; in setting up the Bible in the church; in exploding the pope with his vile pardons: in removing divers superstitious ceremonies; in bringing into order the inordinate orders of friars and sects; in putting chantry priests to their pensions; in permitting white meat in Lent; in destroying pilgrimage worship; in abrogating idle and superfluous holydays, both by public acts, and also by private letters sent to Bonner tending to this effect. One of these letters we here subjoin:

By the King.

"Right reverend father in God, right trusty and well-beloved, we greet you well. And whereas considering the manifold inconveniences which have ensued, and daily do ensue to our subjects by the great superfluity of holydays, we have by the assent and consent of all you the bishops and other notable personages of the clergy of this our realm, in full congregation and assembly had for that purpose, abrogated and abolished such as be neither canonical, nor meet to be suffered in a commonwealth; for the manifold inconveniences which do ensue of the same, as is rehearsed, and to the intent our determination therein may be duly observed and accomplished, we have thought convenient to command you immediately upon the receipt hereof, to address your commandments in our name to all the curates, religious houses, and colleges within your diocese, with a copy of the act made for the abrogation of the holydays aforesaid, a transcript whereof ye shall receive herewith, commanding them and every of them, in no wise, either in the church or otherwise, to indict or speak of any of the said days and feasts abolished; whereby the people might take occasion either to murmur, or contemn the order taken therein, and to continue in their accustomed idleness, the same notwithstanding; but to pass over the same with such secret silence, as they may have like abrogation by disuse, as they have already by our authority in convocation. And forasmuch as the time of harvest now approaches, our pleasure is, you shall with such diligence and dexterity put this matter in execution, as it may immediately take place for the benefit of our subjects at this time accordingly without failing, as ye will answer unto us for the contrary.

"Given under our signet, at our monastery of Chertsey, the eleventh day of August."

Thus while good counsel was about him, and could be heard, he did much good. So again when sinister and wicked counsel, under subtle and crafty pretences, had the ascendancy over him, thrusting truth and charity out of the prince's ears; so much did religion and all good things go prosperously forward before, and so much on the contrary side all revolted backward again. Whereupon proceeded this proclamation above-mentioned, concerning the abolishing and burning of English books. Which proclamation bearing the name of the king's majesty, but being the very deed of the popish bishops, no doubt had done much hurt in the church among the godly sort, bringing them either into great danger, or else keeping them in much blindness, had not the shortness of the king's days stopped the malignant purposes of the prelates, causing the king to leave that by death to the people, which by his life he would not grant. For within four months after, the proclamation coming out in August, he died on the 27th day of January (A.D. 1547) after having reigned nearly thirty-eight years, leaving behind him three children, who succeeded him in his kingdom, king Edward, queen Mary, and queen Elizabeth; of whom it remains now to prosecute (by the permission and sufferance of Christ our high Lord and Prince) in the process of this history, according to the order of their succession, and the acts done by them in the church shall require: after I shall have first prosecuted certain other matters by the way.

The History touching the Persecution in Scotland.

Thus having finished the time and reign of king Henry VIII., it remains now, according to my promise made before, here to place and adjoin so much as doth come to our hands, touching the persecution of Scotland, and of the blessed martyrs of Christ, who in that country likewise suffered for the true religion of Christ, and testimony of their faith.

To proceed therefore in the history of the affairs of Scotland, next after the mention of David Stratton and Master Nicolas Gurlay, with whom we ended before, the order of time requires us to advert to the memory of Sir John Borthwick, knight, commonly called Captain Borthwick. Who being accused of heresy, as the papists call it, and cited to answer for the same, A.D. 1540, did not appear, but escaped into other countries: though absent, however, he was condemned by the sentence of

David Beaton, archbishop of St. Andrews, and other prelates of Scotland, and all his goods confiscated, and his picture at last burned in the open market-place.

The Sentence of Condemnation against Sir John Borthwick, knight, by the Cardinal, Bishops, and Abbots in Scotland, A.D. 1540.

[After reciting the articles with which he was charged, it thus concludes:]

" Of all which the premises, and many other errors by him holden, spoken, published, affirmed, preached, and taught, the common fame and report is, that the said Sir John Borthwick is holden, reputed, and accounted of very many as a heretic, and principal heretic, who holdeth evil opinions of the catholic faith.

Where we, David, by the title of St. Stephen, in Mount Celio, prelate and cardinal of the holy church of Rome, archbishop of St. Andrews, primate of the whole kingdom of Scotland, and born legate of the apostolic see, sitting after the manner of judges in our tribunal seat, the most holy gospels of God being laid before us, that our judgment might proceed from the face of God, and our eyes might behold and look upon equity and justice, having only God, and the verity and truth of the catholic faith before our eyes, his holy name being first called upon, having, as is before said, hereupon holden a council of wise men, as well divines as lawyers, we pronounce, declare, decree, determine, and give sentence, that the said Sir John Borthwick, called Captain Borthwick, being suspected, infamed, and accused of the errors and heresies before said, and wicked doctrines manifoldly condemned, as is aforesaid, and by lawful proofs against him in every of the premises had, being convicted and lawfully cited and called, not appearing, but as a fugitive, runaway, and absent, even as though he were present, to be a heretic; and is, and hath been convicted as a heretic; and as a convict heretic and heresiarch to be punished and chastened with due punishment, and afterwards to be delivered and left unto the secular power. Moreover, we confiscate and make forfeit, and by these presents declare and decree to be confiscated and made forfeit all and singular his goods, moveables, and unmoveables, howsoever and by whatsoever title they be gotten, and in what place or part soever they be, and all his offices whatsoever he hath hitherto had, reserving notwithstanding the dowry and such part and portion of his goods, as by the law, custom, and right of this realm unto persons confiscate ought to appertain. Also, we decree that the picture of the said John Borthwick being formed, made, and painted to his likeness, be carried through this our city, to our cathedral church; and afterwards to the market cross of the same city; and there in token of malediction and curse, and to the terror and example of others; and for a perpetual remembrance of his obstinacy and condemnation, to be burned. Likewise we declare and decree, that notwithstanding, if the said John Borthwick be hereafter apprehended and taken, he shall suffer such like punishment due by order of law unto heretics, without any hope of grace, or mercy to be obtained in that behalf. Also we plainly admonish and warn, by the tenour of these presents, all and singular faithful christians, both men and women, of what dignity, state, decree, order, condition, or pre-eminence soever they be, or with whatever dignity, or honour ecclesiastical, or temporal they be honoured, that from this day forward they do not receive or harbour the said Sir John Borthwick, commonly called Captain Borthwick, being accused, convicted, and declared a heretic, and arch-heretic, into their houses, hospitals, castles, cities, towns, villages, or other cottages, whatever they be, or by any manner of means admit him thereunto, either by helping him with meat, drink, or victuals, or any other thing whatever it be, they do shew unto him any manner of humanity, help, comfort, or solace, under the pain and penalty of greater and further excommunication, confiscation and forfeitures; and if it happen that they be found culpable or faulty in the premises, that they shall be accused therefore as the favourers, receivers, defenders, maintainers, and abettors of heretics,

and shall be punished therefore according to the order of law, and with such pain and punishment as shall be due unto men in such behalf."

And now to prosecute such others as followed, beginning first in order with Thomas Forrest and his fellows : their history is as follows :

Not long after the burning of David Straiton and Master Gourlay, in the days of David Beaton, cardinal, and archbishop of St. Andrews; and George Crichton, bishop of Dunkeld; a canon of St. Colme's Inche, and vicar of Dolone, called Dean Thomas Forrest, preached every Sunday to his parishioners out of the epistle or gospel, as it fell for the time; which, then, was a great novelty in Scotland, to see any man preach, except a Black friar, or a Gray friar; and therefore the friars envied him, and accused him to the bishop of Dunkeld (in whose diocese he remained) as a heretic, and one that shewed the mysteries of the scriptures, to the vulgar people, in English, to make the clergy detestable in the sight of the people. The bishop of Dunkeld, moved by the instigation of the friars, called Dean Thomas, and said to him; " Dean Thomas, I love you well, and therefore I must give you counsel, how you shall rule and guide yourself." To whom Thomas said : " I thank your lordship heartily." Then the bishop began his counsel after this manner.—

" Dean Thomas, I am informed that you preach the epistle, or gospel, every Sunday to your parishioners, and that you take not the cowl, nor the uppermost cloth from your parishioners, which thing is very prejudicial to the churchmen; and therefore, Dean Thomas, I would you took your cowl, and your uppermost cloth, as other churchmen do, or else it is too much to preach every Sunday; for in so doing you may make the people think that we should preach likewise. But it is enough for you, when you find any good epistle, or any good gospel, that sets forth the liberty of the holy church, to preach that, and let the rest alone."

Thomas answered; " My lord, I think that none of my parishioners will complain that I take not the cowl, nor the uppermost cloth, but will gladly give me the same, together with any other thing that they have, and I will give and communicate with them any thing that I have, and so, my lord, we agree right well, and there is no discord among us.

" And where your lordship saith, it is too much to preach every Sunday; indeed I think it is too little, and also would wish that your lordship did the like." " Nay, nay, Dean Thomas," said the bishop; " let that be; for we are not ordained to preach." Then said Thomas ; " Where your lordship bids me preach, when I find any good epistle, or a good gospel, truly, my lord, I have read the New Testament and the Old, and all the epistles and gospels, and among them all I could never find an evil epistle, or an evil gospel; but if your lordship will shew me the good epistle, and the good gospel, and the evil epistle, and the evil gospel, then I shall preach the good, and omit the evil." Then spake my lord stoutly, and said, " I thank God that I never knew what the New and Old Testament was" (and of these words rose a proverb which is common in Scotland : ' Ye are like the bishop of Dunkeld, that knew neither new nor old law'), "therefore, Dean Thomas, I will know nothing but my mass book, and my pontifical. Go your way, and leave off all these fantasies ; for if you persevere in these erroneous opinions, you will repent it when you may not mend it." Thomas said; " I trust my cause is just in the presence of God, and therefore I care not much what follows;" and so my lord and he separated at that time. And soon after a summons was directed from the cardinal of St. Andrews, and the bishop of Dunkeld, upon the Dean Thomas Forrest, upon two Black friars, called Friar John Kelore, and another called Beverage, and upon a priest of Stirling, called Duncan Simpson, and one gentleman called Robert Forster, in Stirling, with other three or four with them of the town of Stirling, who, at the day of their appearance, were condemned to death without any opportunity for recantation, because (as was alleged) they were heresiarch, or chief heretics and teachers of heresy; and especially because many of them were at the bridal and marriage of a priest, who was vicar of Twybody, beside Stirling; and did eat flesh in Lent, at the bridal, and so they were all together burnt upon the castle hill, Edinburgh, where they that were first bound to the stake godly and marvellously comforted them who came behind.

The persecution, by the Cardinal of Scotland, against certain persons in Perth.

There was a certain act of parliament made in the government of the lord Hamilton, earl of Arran, and governor of Scotland, giving privilege to all men of the realm of Scotland, to read the scriptures in their mother tongue; forbidding, nevertheless, all reasoning, conference, or convocation of people to hear the scriptures read or expounded. Which liberty of private reading, being granted by public proclamation, bore fruit; so that in several parts of Scotland there were opened the eyes of the servants of God to see the truth, and abhor the papistical abominations.

At this time there was a sermon made by Friar Spense, in Perth, affirming prayer made to saints to be so necessary, that without it there could be no hope of salvation to man. Which blasphemous doctrine, a burgess of the town, Robert Lamb, could not bear, but accused him publicly of erroneous doctrine, and adjured him in God's name to utter the truth. This the friar, being stricken with fear, promised to do; but the trouble, tumult, and stir of the people increased so, that the friar could have no audience, and yet Robert, with great danger of his life, escaped the hands of the multitude, especially of the women, who were proceeding to extreme cruelty against him.

At this time, (A.D. 1543,) the enemies of the truth procured John Charters, who favoured the truth, and was provost of the city and town of Perth, to be deposed from his office by the governor's authority, and a papist called Master Alexander Marbeck chosen in his room, that they might accomplish the more easily their wicked and ungodly purpose.

After deposing the former provost, and electing the other, in the month of January there came to Perth the governor, the cardinal, the earl of Argyle, justice Sir John Campbell, of Lundie, knight, and Justice Defort, the lord Borthwick, the bishops of Dunblane, and Orkney, with others of the nobility. And although there were many accused for the crime of heresy, as they called it, yet the following persons only were apprehended at that time; Robert Lamb, William Anderson, James Hunter, James Reveleson, James Founleson, and Hellen Stirke, his wife, and were cast that night into the Spay Tower of the city, on the morrow after, to receive judgment.

The next day when they appeared, and were brought forth to judgment, there was laid in general to all their charge the violating of the act of parliament before expressed, and their conference and assemblies in hearing and expounding of the scriptures against the tenor of the act. Robert Lamb was accused especially for interrupting the friar in the pulpit, which he not only confessed, but also confirmed constantly, that it was the duty of no man, who understood and knew the truth, to hear the same impugned without contradiction; and therefore many who were there present in judgment, who hid the knowledge of the truth, should bear the burden in God's presence for consenting. This Robert, also, with William Anderson, and James Raveleson, were accused for hanging up the image of St. Francis in a cord, nailing rams' horns to his head, and a cow's rump to his tail, and for eating of a goose on Allhallow even.

James Hunter, being a simple man and without learning, could be charged with no great knowledge in doctrine, yet because he often frequented that suspected company, he was accused.

The woman, Hellen Stirke, was accused because in her childbed she was not accustomed to call upon the name of the Virgin Mary, but only upon God for Jesus Christ's sake, and because she said, that if she herself had been in the time of the Virgin Mary, God might have looked to her humility and base estate, as he did to the virgin's, in making her the mother of Christ; thereby meaning, that there were no merits in the virgin, which procured her that honour to be made the mother of Christ, and to be preferred before other women, but only God's free mercy exalted her to that estate. Which words were counted most execrable in the face of all the clergy, and of the whole multitude.

James Raveleson, when building a house, set upon the top of his fourth stair the three crowned diadem of Peter, made of wood, which the cardinal took as done in mocking of his cardinal's hat, and this procured no favour to James at their hands.

These persons were condemned and judged to death, and that by an assize, for violating, as was alleged, the act of parliament, in reasoning and conferring upon the scriptures; for eating flesh upon days forbidden; for interrupting the holy friar in the pulpit; for dishonouring images, and blaspheming the Virgin Mary.

After their sentence was given, their hands were bound, and the men cruelly treated. Which the woman beholding, desired likewise to be bound by the sergeants with her husband for Christ's sake.

There was great intercession made by the people of the town for the life of these persons to the governor, who of himself was willing to have done so, that they might have been delivered. But the governor was so under subjection to the cruel priests, that he could not do what he would. Yea, they threatened to assist his enemies and to depose him, except he assisted their cruelty.

There were some priests in the city, who ate and drank before in these honest men's houses, to whom the priests were much bound. These priests were earnestly desired to intreat for them at the cardinal's hands; but they altogether refused, desiring rather their death than preservation. So cruel are these wicked men from the lowest to the highest.

Then they were carried by a great band of armed men, (for they feared rebellion in the town except they had their men of war) to the place of execution, which was common to all thieves, and that to make their cause appear more odious to the people.

Robert Lamb, at the foot of the gallows, made his exhortation to the people, desiring them to fear God, and leave the leaven of papistical abominations. So every one comforting another, and assuring themselves that they should sup together in the kingdom of heaven that night, they commended themselves to God, and died constantly in the Lord.

His wife desired earnestly to die with her husband, but she was not suffered; yet following him to the place of execution, she gave him comfort, exhorting him to perseverance and patience for Christ's sake, and parting from him with a kiss, said, "Husband, rejoice, for we have lived together many joyful days; but this day in which we must die, ought to be most joyful unto us both, because we must have joy for ever; therefore I will not bid you good night, for we shall suddenly meet with joy in the kingdom of heaven." After that she was taken to a place to be drowned, and although she had a child sucking at her breast, yet this moved not the unmerciful hearts of her enemies. So after she had commended her children to the neighbours of the town for God's sake, and the child was given to the nurse, she sealed the truth by her death.

The Condemnation of Master George Wishart, who suffered Martyrdom, A.D. 1546.

I will solicit the attention of the reader to the uncharitable manner of the accusation of Master George Wishart, by the bloody enemies of Christ's faith. Note also the articles of which he was accused, and his meek answers. Finally, ponder on the furious rage and tragical cruelty of the malignant church of Rome, in persecuting this blessed man of God; and his humble, patient, and most godly answers made to them at the moment, without regarding their menacings and threats, but not moving his countenance nor changing his visage.

But before I advert to his articles, I thought it not impertinent to touch somewhat concerning the life and conversation of this godly man, according as it came to my hands, certified in writing by a scholar of Wishart, named Emery Tylney, whose words, as he wrote them to me, here follow :—

"About the year 1543, there was in the University of Cambridge one Mr. George Wishart, commonly called Mr. George of Benet's college, a man of tall stature ; judged by his physiognomy to be of a melancholy disposition, black-haired, long-bearded, comely of person, well spoken after his country of Scotland, courteous, lowly, lovely, glad to teach, desirous to learn, and well-travelled ; never having on him for his habit or clothing but a mantle or frieze-gown to the shoes, a black millian fustian doublet, and plain black hose, coarse new canvass for his shirts, and white falling bands and cuffs at his hands. All which apparel he gave to the poor, some weekly, some monthly, some quarterly, as he liked, saving his French cap, which he kept the whole year of my being with him.

"He was a man modest, temperate, fearing God, hating covetousness ; for his charity had never end, night, noon, nor day ; he forbore one meal in three, one day in four for the most part, except something to comfort nature. He lay hard upon a puff of straw, and coarse new canvass sheets, which, when he changed, he gave away. He had commonly by his bedside a tub of water, in which (his people being in bed, the candle put out, and all quiet) he used to bathe himself, as I being very young, being assured, often heard him, and in one light night discerned him ; he loved me tenderly, and I him, for my age, as effectually. He taught with great modesty and gravity, so that some of his people thought him severe, and would have slain him ; but the Lord was his defence. And he, after due correction for their malice, by good exhortation, amended them and went his way. O that the Lord had left him to me his poor boy, that he might have finished what he had begun ! For in his religion he was as you see here in the rest of his life, when he went into Scotland, with some of the nobility, that came for a treaty to king Henry VIII. His learning was no less sufficient than his desire ; always pressed and ready to do good in that he was able, both in the house privately, and in the school publicly, professing and reading divers authors.

"If I should declare his love to me, and all men, his charity to the poor, in giving, relieving, caring, helping, providing, yea, infinitely studying how to do good unto all, and hurt to none, I should sooner want words than just cause to commend him.

"All this I testify with my whole heart, and truth of this godly man. He that made all, governeth all, and shall judge all, knoweth that I speak the truth, that the simple may be satisfied, the arrogant confounded, the hypocrite disclosed.

"EMERY TYLNEY."

Master George Wishart was in captivity in the castle of St. Andrews, where the dean of the town was sent by command of the cardinal to summon him, that he should upon the morning following appear before the judge, to give an account of his seditious and heretical doctrine.

To whom Master George answered, "What need my lord cardinal to summon me to answer for my doctrine before him, under whose power and dominion I am thus bound with irons ? May not my lord compel me to answer by his power ? Or believes he that I am unprepared to render account of my doctrine ?"

On the next morning, the cardinal caused his servants to dress themselves in their most warlike array, with all their arms, more prepared for war than for the preaching of the word of God. And when these armed champions, marching in warlike order, had conveyed the bishops into the abbey church, they sent for Master George, who was conveyed into the church by the captain of the castle, accompanied by a hundred men-at-arms ; like a lamb they led him to the sacrifice. As he entered into the abbey church door, there was a poor man lying there afflicted with great infirmities, who asked of him alms, to whom he flung his purse. And when he came before the lord cardinal, the subprior of the abbey, called dean John Winryme, stood up in the pulpit, and made a sermon to all the congregation, taking his matter out of Matthew xiii., whose sermon was divided into four principal parts.

The first part was a brief and short declaration of the evangelist.

The second part of the interpretation of the good seed. And because he called the word of God the good seed, and heresy the evil seed, he declared what heresy was, and how it may be known ; which he defined in this manner, "Heresy is a false opinion defended with pertinacity, clearly contrary to the word of God."

The third part of the sermon was, the cause of heresy within that and other realms. The cause of heresy is the ignorance of those who have the cure of souls ; to whom it necessarily belongs to have the true understanding of the word of God, that they may be able to win the false teachers of heresies, with the sword of the Spirit, which is the word of God ; and not only to win again, but also to overcome them, as says St. Paul : "For a bishop must be blameless, as the steward of God ; not selfwilled, not soon angry, not given to wine, no striker, not given to filthy lucre ; but a lover of hospitality, a lover of good men, sober, just, holy, temperate ; holding fast the faithful word as he hath been taught, that he may be able by sound doctrine both to exhort and to convince the gainsayers." Titus i. 7—9.

The fourth part of his sermon was how heresies should be known. Heresies (said he) are known after this manner : as the goldsmith knows the fine gold from the imperfect by the touchstone, so likewise may we know heresy by the undoubted touchstone, that is, the true, sincere, and undefiled word of God. At last he added, that heretics should be put down in this present life : which proposition the gospel appeared to contradict ; "Let them grow together till the harvest ;" the harvest is the end of the world. Nevertheless, he affirmed that they should be put down by the civil magistrate and the law. And when he ended his sermon, they caused Master George to ascend the pulpit, there to hear his accusation and articles. And right against them stood John Lauder, laden full of curses written on paper ; who took out a roll, both long and full of cursings, threats, maledictions, and words of devilish spite and malice, saying to the innocent Master George so many cruel and abominable words, and he hit him so spitefully with the pope's thunder, that the ignorant people dreaded lest the earth would have speedily swallowed him up. Notwithstanding he stood still with great patience, hearing their sayings, not once moving or changing his countenance.

When this well-fed priest had read through all his menacings, his face running down with sweat, and frothing at his mouth like a boar, he spit at Master George's face, saying, "What answerest thou to these sayings, thou runagate traitor, thief, which we have duly proved by sufficient witness against thee ?" Master George hearing this, kneeled down upon his knees in the pulpit, making his prayer to God. When he had ended his prayer, sweetly and christianly he answered to them all as follows :—

"Many horrible sayings and many abominable words ye have spoken here this day, which not only to teach, but also to think, I thought a great abomination. Wherefore I pray you quietly to hear me, that you may know what were my sayings and the manner of my doctrine. This my petition, my lord, I desire to be heard for three causes.

"The first is, because through preaching of the word of God, his glory is made manifest. It is reasonable, therefore, for the advancing of the glory of God, that you hear me, teaching truly the pure word of God, without any dissimulation.

"The second reason is, because that your salvation springs from the word of God ; for he works all things by his word. It were therefore an unrighteous thing if you should stop your ears from me, teaching truly the word of God.

"The third reason is, because your doctrine utters many blasphemous and abominable words, not coming from the inspiration of God, but of the devil, with no less peril than that of my life. It is just, therefore, and reasonable that you should know what my words and doctrine are, that I perish not unjustly, to the great peril of your souls. Wherefore, both for the glory and honour of God, your own salvation, and safety of my life, I beseech you to hear me, and I shall recite my doctrine without any colour.

"First and chiefly, since the time I came into this realm I taught nothing but the commandments of God, the twelve articles of the creed, and the Lord's prayer in the mother tongue. Moreover, in Dundee I taught the epistle of St. Paul to the Romans. And I shall show you faithfully what manner I used when I taught.

Then suddenly with a loud voice, the accuser cried, "Thou heretic, runnagate, traitor, and thief, it was not lawful for thee to preach. Thou hast taken the power into thine own hand, without any authority of the church. We forethink that thou has been a preacher so long." Then all the whole congregation of the prelates, with their accomplices, exclaimed, "If we give him license to preach, he is so crafty, and in the holy scripture so exercised, that he will persuade the people to his opinion, and raise them against us."

Master George seeing their malicious and wicked intention, appealed from the lord cardinal to the lord governor, as to an indifferent and equal judge. To whom the accuser, John Lauder, answered, "Is not my lord cardinal the second person within this realm, chancellor of Scotland, archbishop of St. Andrews, bishop of Meropois, commendator of Aberbrothwick, *legatus natus, legatus à latere?* And so reciting a long list of titles, he asked, "Is not my lord cardinal an equal judge? Whom other desirest thou to be thy judge?"

To whom this humble man answered, "I refuse not my lord cardinal; but I desire the word of God to be my judge, and the temporal estate; with some of your lordships mine auditors; because I am here my lord governor's prisoner." Whereupon the proud and scornful people that stood by mocked him, saying, "Such man, such judge! speaking seditious and reproachful words against the governor, and others the nobles, meaning them also to be heretics." And without delay they would have given sentence upon Master George, without further process, had not certain men counselled the cardinal to read the articles, and to hear his answers, that the people might not complain of his condemnation.

These were the articles following, with his answers, as far as they would give him leave to speak. For when he intended to answer their charges, and shew his doctrine, they stopped his mouth with another article.

1. "Thou false heretic, runnagate, traitor, and thief, deceiver of the people, thou despisest the holy church, and in it contemnest my lord governor's authority. And this we know for surety, that when thou preached in Dundee, and was charged by my lord governor's authority to desist, nevertheless thou wouldst not obey, but persevered in the same; and, therefore, the bishop of Brechin cursed thee, and delivered thee into the devil's hands, and gave thee in commandment that thou shouldst preach no more. That, notwithstanding, thou didst continue obstinately."

"My lords, I have read in the Acts of the Apostles, that it is not lawful to desist from the preaching of the gospel for the threats and menaces of men. Therefore it is written, 'We ought to obey God rather than men.' (Acts v. 29.) I have also read in the prophet Malachi, 'I will even send a curse upon you, and I will curse your blessings.' (Mal. ii. 2.) Believing firmly, that the Lord will turn your cursings into blessings."

2. "Thou false heretic didst say, that the priest standing at the altar saying mass, was like a fox wagging his tail."

"My lords, I said not so; these were my sayings:

The moving of the body outward, without the inward moving of the heart, is nought else but the playing of an ape, and not the true serving of God. For God is a searcher of men's hearts; therefore who will truly adore and honour God, he must in spirit and truth honour him."

3. "Thou false heretic didst preach against the sacraments, saying, that there were not seven sacraments."

"My lords, if it be your pleasures, I never taught of the number of the sacraments, whether they were seven or eleven. So many as are instituted by Christ are shewed to us by the gospel. I profess them openly; and except it be the word of God I dare affirm nothing."

4. "Thou false heretic hast openly taught, that auricular confession is not a blessed sacrament. And thou sayest that we should only confess to God, and to no priest."

"My lords, I say, that auricular confession, seeing that it has no promise of the gospel, cannot be a sacrament. Of the confession to be made to God, there are many testimonies in scripture, as when David saith, 'I acknowledged my sin unto thee, and mine iniquity have I not hid. I said, I will confess my transgressions unto the Lord; and thou forgavest the iniquity of my sin.' (Psalm xxxii. 5.) Here confession signifies the secret knowledge of our sins before God. When I exhorted the people in this manner, I reproved no manner of confession. And further, St. James saith, 'Confess your faults one to another, and pray one for another, that ye may be healed.'" (James iii. 16.)

When he had said these words, the bishops and their accomplices cried, and gnashed their teeth, saying, "See you not what colours he has in his speaking, that he may beguile us, and seduce us to his opinion?"

5. "Thou heretic didst openly say, that it was necessary to every man to know and understand his baptism, and what it was, contrary to general councils, and the estate of the holy church."

"My lords, I believe there are none so unwise here, that will make merchandise with a Frenchman, or any other unknown stranger, except he know and understand first the condition or promise made by the Frenchman, or stranger: so, likewise, I would that we understood what we promise to God, in the name of the infant in baptism. For this cause I believe you have confirmation."

Then said Master Bleiter, chaplain, that he had the devil within him, and the spirit of error. Then a child answered him, saying, "The devil cannot speak such words as yonder man speaks."

6. "Thou heretic, traitor, thief, thou saidst that the sacrament of the altar was but a piece of bread baked upon the ashes, and nothing else; and all that is there done, is but a superstitious rite against the commandment of God."

"Oh Lord God! so manifest lies and blasphemies the scripture does not teach you. As concerning the sacrament of the altar, my lords, I never taught anything against the scriptures, which I shall by God's grace make manifest this day; being ready to suffer death for it.

"The lawful use of the sacrament is most acceptable to God; but the great abuse of it is very detestable to him. But what occasion they have to say such words of me, I shall shew your lordships. I once chanced to meet with a Jew, when I was sailing on the Rhine. I inquired of him what was the cause of his pertinacity, that he did not believe that the true Messias was come, considering that they had seen all the prophecies which were spoken of him fulfilled? Moreover the prophecies taken away, and the sceptre of Judah, and by many other testimonies of the scripture I proved to him that Messias was come, whom they called Jesus of Nazareth. This Jew answered again, 'When Messias comes, he shall restore all things, and he shall not abrogate the law, which was given to our forefathers, as ye do. For why? we see the poor almost perish through hunger amongst you; yet you are not moved with pity toward them; but amongst us Jews (though we are poor) there are no beggars found.—Secondly: it is forbidden by the law to feign any kind of imagery of things in heaven above, or in the earth beneath, or in the sea under the earth, but one God only is to be honoured; but your sanctuaries and churches are full of idols.—Thirdly: a piece of bread baken upon the ashes you adore and worship, and say, that it is your God.' I have rehearsed here but the sayings of the Jew, which I never affirmed to be true."

Then the bishops shook their heads, and spit on the earth.

7. "Thou false heretic didst say, that extreme unction was not a sacrament."

"My lords, I never taught anything of extreme unction in my doctrine, whether it were a sacrament or not."

8. "Thou false heretic saidst, that holy water is not so good as wash, and such like. Thou didst condemn conjuring, and said, that holy church's cursings avail not."

"My lords, as for holy water, I taught nothing about it in my doctrine. Conjurings and exorcisms, if they were conformable to the word of God, I would commend them; but as they are not conformable to the commandment and word of God, I reprove them."

9. "Thou false heretic and runnagate hast said, that every layman is a priest, and such-like. Thou saidst, that the pope hath no more power than any other man."

"My lords, I taught nothing but the word of God. I remember that I have read in some places in St. John and St. Peter, of whom one says, ' And hath made us kings and priests.' (Rev. i. 6.) The other says, ' But ye are a chosen generation, a royal priesthood.' (1 Pet. ii. 9.) Wherefore I have affirmed, that any man being skilful in the word of God, and the true faith of Jesus Christ, has this power from God, and not by the power or violence of men, but by the virtue of the word of God, which word is called ' The power of God,' (Rom. i. 16.) as witnesses St. Paul evidently enough. And again I say, that any unlearned man, not exercised in the word of God, nor yet constant in his faith, whatever estate or order he be of, I say, he has no power to bind or loose, seeing he wants the instrument by which he binds or looses, that is to say, the word of God."

After that he had said these words, all the bishops laughed, and mocked him. When he beheld their laughing, "Laugh ye," said he, " my lords? Though these sayings appear scornful, and worthy of derision to your lordships, nevertheless they are very weighty to me, and of great value, because they concern not only myself, but also the honour and glory of God." In the meantime, many godly men beholding the great cruelty of the bishops, and the invincible patience of Master George, greatly mourned and lamented.

10. "Thou false heretic saidst, that a man hath no free will, but is like to the Stoics, who say, that it is not in man's will to do anything; but that all concupiscence and desire comes by God, whatever kind it be of."

"My lords, I said not so, truly; I say, that as many as believe in Christ firmly, to them is given liberty, conformable to the saying of St. John, ' If the Son, therefore, shall make you free, ye shall be free indeed.' (John viii. 36.) On the contrary, as many as believe not in Christ Jesus, they are bond-servants of sin. ' Whosoever committeth sin is the servant of sin.' " (John viii. 34.)

11. "Thou false heretic saidst, it is as lawful to eat flesh upon the Friday, as on Sundays."

"I have read in the epistles of St. Paul, that who is clean, unto him all things are clean. On the contrary, to the filthy man all things are unclean. A faithful man, clean and holy, sanctifies by the word, the creature of God. But the creature makes no man acceptable to God. So that a creature may not sanctify any impure and unfaithful man. But to the faithful man all things are ' sanctified by the word of God and prayer.' " (1 Tim. iii. 5.)

After these sayings of Master George, then said all the bishops with their accomplices, " What need we any witness against him? Has he not openly here spoken blasphemy?"

12. "Thou false heretic didst say, that we should not pray to saints, but to God only. Say whether thou hast said this, or not; speak shortly."

For the weakness and infirmity of the hearers he said, without doubt plainly, that saints should not be honoured. "My lord," said he, " there are two things worthy of note. The one is certain; the other uncertain. It is found plainly and certain in scripture, that we should worship and honour one God, according to the saying of the first commandment, ' Thou shalt worship the Lord thy God, and him only shalt thou serve.' (Matt. iv. 10.) But as for praying to and honouring of saints, there is great doubt among many whether they hear or not invocation made to them. Therefore I exhorted all men equally in my doctrine, that they should leave the unsure way, and follow that way which was taught us by our Master Christ. He is our only Mediator, and makes intercession for us to God his Father. He is the door by which we must enter in. He that entereth not in by this door, but climbeth up another way, is a thief and a murderer. He is the Truth and the Life. He that goeth out of this way, there is no doubt but he shall fall into the mire; yea, verily, is fallen into it already. This is my doctrine, which I have ever followed. Verily, that which I have heard and read in the word of God I taught openly, and in no corners. And now ye shall witness the same, if your lordships will hear me. Except it stand by the word of God, I dare not be so bold as to affirm anything."

13. "Thou false heretic hast preached plainly, saying, that there is no purgatory; and that it is a feigned thing, that any man after this life can be punished in purgatory."

"My lords, as I have oftentimes said heretofore, without witness and testimony of the scriptures I dare affirm nothing. I have oftentimes read over the Bible, and yet such a term I never found, nor yet any place of scripture applicable to it. Therefore I was ashamed to teach that which I could not find in the scriptures."

Then said he to Master John Lauder, his accuser, " If you have any testimony of the scriptures, by which you may prove any such place, shew it now before this auditory." But this accuser had not a word to say for himself, but was as dumb as a beetle in that matter.

14. "Thou false heretic hast taught plainly against the vows of monks, friars, nuns, and priests; saying, that whoever was bound to such vows, they vowed themselves to the estate of damnation. Moreover, that it was lawful for priests to marry wives, and not to live single."

"My lords, I have read in the gospel, that as many as have not the gift of chastity, nor yet have overcome the concupiscence of the flesh, nor have vowed chastity, should marry. You have experience, although I should hold my peace, to what inconvenience they have vowed themselves."

When he had said these words, they were all dumb, thinking it better to have ten concubines, than one married wife.

15. "Thou false heretic and runnagate saidst, thou wilt not obey our general nor provincial councils."

"My lords, what your general councils are I know not, I was never exercised in them; but to the pure word of God I gave my labours. Read here your general council, or else give me a book wherein they are contained, that I may read them. If they agree with the word of God, I will not disagree."

Then the ravening wolves said, " Wherefore let him speak any further? Read forth the rest of the articles, and stay not upon them."

Among these cruel tigers there was one false hypocrite, a seducer of the people, called John Graifind Scot, standing behind John Lauder, hastening him to read the rest of the articles, and not to tarry upon his godly answers. " For we may not listen to them," said he, " any more than the devil may abide the sign of the cross."

16. "Thou heretic saidst, that it is in vain to build to the honour of God costly churches, seeing that God re-

mains not in the churches made with men's hands, nor yet can God be in so little space as between the priest's hands."

"My lords, Solomon says, 'Behold, the heaven and heaven of heavens cannot contain thee; how much less this house that I have builded?' (1 Kings viii. 27.) And Job consents to the same sentence; 'Canst thou by searching find out God? canst thou find out the Almighty unto perfection? It is high as heaven; what canst thou do? deeper than hell; what canst thou know? The measure thereof is longer than the earth, and broader than the sea.' (Job xi. 7—9.) So that God cannot be comprehended in one place, because he is infinite. Notwithstanding these sayings, I never said that churches should be destroyed; but of the contrary I affirm ever, that churches should be sustained and upholden; that the people should be congregated into them, there to hear of God. And moreover, wheresoever is true preaching of the word of God, and the lawful use of the sacraments, undoubtedly there is God himself; so that both these sayings are true together; God cannot be comprehended in any place, and wheresoever two or three are gathered together in his name, there is he present in the midst of them."

Then said he to his accuser, "If you think any otherwise than I say, shew forth your reasons before this auditory." Then he without all reason being dumb, and not answering one word, proceeded forth in his articles.

17. "Thou false heretic contemnest fasting, and said thou should not fast."

"My lord, I find that fasting is commended in the scripture; therefore I were a slanderer of the gospel, if I contemned fasting. And not only so, but I have learned by experience, that fasting is good for the health of the body; but God knows who fasts the true fast."

18. "Thou false heretic hast preached openly, saying, that the soul of man shall sleep till the latter day of judgment, and shall not obtain life immortal until that day."

"God, full of mercy and goodness, forgive them that say such things of me: I know surely by the word of God, that he who has begun to have the faith of Jesus Christ, and believes firmly in him, I know surely that the soul of that man shall never sleep, but shall live an immortal life. Which life from day to day is renewed in grace and augmented; nor yet shall ever perish or have an end, but shall ever live immortal with Christ. To which life all that believe in him shall come, and rest in eternal glory, Amen."

When the bishops with their accomplices had accused this innocent man in this manner, they condemned him to be burnt as an heretic, having no respect to his godly answers and true reasons, nor yet to their own consciences, thinking verily they should do to God good sacrifice, conformable to the saying in St. John, "They shall put thee out of the synagogues: yea, the time cometh, that whosoever killeth you will think that he doeth God service." John xvi. 2.

The Prayer of Master George Wishart.

"O immortal God, how long shalt thou suffer the great cruelty of the ungodly to exercise their fury upon thy servants who further thy word in this world, seeing they desire to be contrary, that is, to choke and destroy the true doctrine and verity, by the which thou hast shewed thyself unto the world, which was all drowned in blindness and ignorance of thy name. O Lord, we know surely that thy true servants must needs suffer, for thy name's sake, persecution, affliction and troubles in this present life, which is but a shadow, as thou hast shewed to us, by thy prophets and apostles. But yet we desire thee heartily, that thou keep, defend and help thy congregation, which thou hast chosen before the beginning of the world, and give them thy grace to hear thy word, and to be thy true servants in this present life."

Then they caused the common people to depart, whose desire was always to hear that innocent man speak. Then the sons of darkness pronounced their sentence, not having respect to the judgment of God. And when all this was done, the cardinal caused his warders to pass again with the meek lamb into the castle, until such time as the fire was made ready. When he was come into the castle, then there came two gray fiends, friar Scot and his mate, saying, "Sir, you must make your confession to us." He answered and said, "I will make no confession to you. Go fetch me yonder man that preached this day, and I will make my confession to him." Then they sent for the sub-prior of the abbey, who came to him with all diligence. But what he said in this confession, I cannot shew.

When the fire was made ready, and the gallows erected, at the west part of the castle near to the priory, the lord cardinal dreading lest Master George should be taken away by his friends, commanded that all the ordnance of the castle should be turned against that part, and that all his gunners should be ready and stand by their guns, until such time as he was burned. All this being done, they bound Master George's hands behind his back, and led him forth with their soldiers from the castle, to the place of execution. As he came forth from the castle gate, there met him certain beggars asking him alms for God's sake. To whom he answered, "I want my hands wherewith I should give you alms, but the merciful Lord, of his benignity and abundance of grace, vouchsafe to give you necessaries both to your bodies and souls." Then afterward met him two false fiends, I should say, friars, saying, "Master George, pray to our Lady, that she may be mediatrix for you to her Son." To whom he answered meekly, "Cease, tempt me not, my brethren." After this he was led to the fire with a rope about his neck, and a chain of iron about his middle.

When he came to the fire, he went down upon his knees and rose again, and thrice he said these words, "O thou Saviour of the world, have mercy on me! Father of heaven, I commend my spirit into thy holy hands." When he had made this prayer, he turned him to the people and said these words:

"I beseech you, christian brethren and sisters, that you be not offended in the word of God for the affliction and torments, which ye see already prepared for me. But I exhort you that you love the word of God, and suffer patiently and with a comfortable heart for the word's sake, which is your undoubted salvation, and everlasting comfort.

"Moreover, I pray you shew my brethren and sisters, who have heard me often before, that they cease not, nor leave off the word of God which I taught to them, after the grace given to me, for any persecutions or troubles in this world, which last not; and shew to them that my doctrine was no old wife's fables after the constitutions made by men. And if I had taught men's doctrine, I had gotten great thanks by men. But for the world's sake and true gospel, which was given to me by the grace of God, I suffer this day by men, not sorrowfully, but with a glad heart and mind. For this cause I was sent, that I should suffer this fire for Christ's sake. Consider, and behold my visage, you shall not see me change my colour. This grim fire I fear not. And so I pray you to do, if any persecution come to you for the word's sake, and not to fear them that slay the body, and afterward have no power to slay the soul. Some have said of me, that I taught, that the soul of man did sleep until the last day. But I know surely, and my faith is such, that my soul shall sup with my Saviour Christ this night, ere it be six hours." Then he prayed for them who accused him, saying, "I beseech thee, Father of heaven, to forgive them that have, of any ignorance, or of any evil mind, forged any lies upon me; I forgive them with all my heart. I beseech Christ to forgive them that have condemned me to death this day ignorantly."

And last of all he spoke to the people in this manner; "I beseech you, brethren and sisters, to exhort your prelates to the learning of the word of God, that they at last may be ashamed to do evil, and learn to do good. And if they will not convert themselves from their wicked errors, there shall hastily come upon them the wrath of God, which they shall not escape." Many faithful words said he in the mean time, taking no heed or care of the cruel torments, which were then prepared for him.

And at last the hangman, that was his tormentor, sat down upon his knees, and said; "Sir, I pray you forgive me, for I am not guilty of your death." To whom he answered, "Come hither to me." When he was come to him, he kissed his cheek, and said, "Lo, here is a token that I forgive thee. Do thine office;" and by and by he was put upon the gibbet and hanged, and there burnt to powder. When the people beheld the great torment, they could not withhold from piteous mourning and complaining of this innocent lamb's slaughter.

The Martyrdom of Adam Wallace.

On a platform erected at the Black friars' church in Edinburgh, there was the lord governor: behind him sat Master Gawin Hamilton, dean of Glasgow, representing the metropolitan pastor. Upon a seat on his right hand sat the archbishop of St. Andrews. At his back stood the official of Lothian. Next to the archbishop of St. Andrews, sat the bishop of Dunblane, the bishop of Murray, the abbot of Dunfermline, the abbot of Glenluce, with other churchmen of that city: and at the other end of the seat sat Master Ouchiltrie: on his left hand sat the earl of Argyle, justice, with his deputy Sir John Campbell, of Lundie. Next him the earl of Huntley. Then the earl of Angus, the bishop of Galloway, the prior of St. Andrews, the bishop of Orkney, the lord Forbes, dean John Winryme, sub-prior of St. Andrews; and behind the seats stood the whole senate, the clerk of the register, &c.

At the further end of the chancel wall, in the pulpit, was placed Master John Lauder, parson of Marbottle the accuser, clad in a surplice and red hood, and a great congregation of the people in the body of the church, standing on the ground.

After that Adam Wallace was brought in, a simple poor man in appearance, and was commanded to look to the accuser; who asked him what was his name; he answered, "Adam Wallace." The accuser said he had another name, which he granted, and said he was commonly called Feane. Then he asked where he was born? "Within two miles of Fayle," said he, "in Kyle." Then said the accuser, "I am sorry that such a poor man as you should put these noble lords to so great inconvenience this day by your vain speaking." "And I must speak," said he, "as God gives me grace, and I believe I have said no evil to hurt any body." "Would God," said the accuser, "you had never spoken; but you are brought forth for such horrible crimes of heresies, as were never imagined nor heard of in this country before, and shall be sufficiently proved, that you cannot deny it."

"Adam Wallace, alias Feane: thou art openly accused for preaching, saying, and teaching of the blasphemies and abominable heresies under-written. First, thou hast said and taught that the bread and wine on the altar, after the words of consecration, are not the body and blood of Jesus Christ."

He turned to the lord governor, and lords aforesaid, saying; "I never said, nor taught any thing but what I found in this book (having there a Bible at his belt in French, Dutch, and English) which is the word of God, and if you will be content that the Lord God and his word be my judge, where I have said wrong, I shall take that punishment you shall put upon me; for I never said any thing concerning this that I am accused of, but that which I found in this book."

"What didst thou say?" said the accuser. "I said, answered he, "that after our Lord Jesus Christ had eaten the paschal lamb in his last supper with his apostles, and fulfilled the ceremonies of the old law, he instituted a new sacrament in remembrance of his death then to come. "And, as they were eating, Jesus took bread, and blessed it, and brake it, and gave it to his disciples, and said, Take, eat; this is my body. And he took the cup, and gave thanks, and gave it to them, saying, Drink ye all of it: for this is my blood of the New Testament, which is shed for many for the remission of sins." Matt. xxvi. 26—28. And in St. Luke it is added, "This do in remembrance of me." Luke xxii. 19.

Then said the bishop of St. Andrews and the official of Lothian, with the dean of Glasgow, and many other prelates, "We know this well enough." The Earl of Huntly said, "Thou answerest not to that which is laid to thee; say either nay or yea to it." He answered, "If you will admit God and his word spoken by the mouth of his blessed Son Jesus Christ our Lord and Saviour, you will admit that which I have said; for I have said and taught nothing but what the Word, which is the trial and touchstone says; which ought to be judge to me, and to all the world."

"Why," said the Earl of Huntly, "Hast thou not a judge good enough? and think you that we know not God and his word? Answer to that which is spoken to thee." And then they made the accuser speak the same thing over again. "Thou sayest," said the accuser, "and hast taught, that the bread and wine in the sacrament of the altar, after the words of the consecration, are not the body and blood of our Saviour Jesus Christ."

He answered, "I never said more than the written word says; for I know well by St. Paul when he saith, 'Wherefore, whosoever shall eat this bread and drink this cup of the Lord unworthily, shall be guilty of the body and blood of the Lord. For he that eateth and drinketh unworthily, eateth and drinketh damnation to himself, not discerning the Lord's body.' And therefore when I taught, which was but seldom, and to them only who required and desired me, I said, 'That if the sacrament of the altar were truly administered, and used as the Son of the living God did institute it, where that was done, there was God himself by his divine power.'"

The bishop of Orkney asked him, "Believest thou not that the bread and wine in the sacrament of the altar, after the words of consecration, is the very body of God, flesh, blood, and bone?"

He answered, "I know not what that word consecration means. I have not much Latin, but I believe that the Son of God was conceived of the Holy Ghost, and born of the Virgin Mary, and has a natural body, with hands, feet, and other members, and in the same body he walked up and down in the world, preached and taught; he suffered death under Pontius Pilate, was crucified, dead, and buried, and that by his godly power he raised that same body again the third day; and the same body ascended into heaven, and sitteth at the right hand of the Father, who shall come again to judge both the quick and the dead. And that this body is a natural body, with hands and feet, and cannot be in two places at once, he sheweth well himself; for which everlasting thanks be to him who makes this matter clear. When the woman brake that ointment on him, answering some of his disciples who grudged it, he said, 'The poor you have always with you, but me ye have not always:' meaning his natural body. And likewise at his ascension he said to the same disciples who were fleshly, and would ever have had him remaining with them corporally, 'It is needful for you that I go away, for if I go not away, the Comforter (the Holy Ghost) will not come unto you;' (meaning that his natural body must be taken away from them.) 'But be of good cheer; for I am with you always, until the end of the world.'

"And that the eating of his very flesh profits not, may be well known by his words which he spake in St. John; where, after he had said, 'Except ye eat the flesh of the Son of Man, and drink his blood, ye have no life in you;' they murmured thereat, and he reproved them for their gross and fleshly taking of his words, and said, 'What and if ye shall see the Son of Man ascend up where he was before? It is the Spirit that quickeneth; the flesh profiteth nothing;' to be eaten as they took it, and even so take you it." (vi. 53—63.)

"It is a horrible heresy," said the bishop of Orkney. Then he was bid to hear the accuser, who propounded the second article, and said, "Thou saidst likewise, and didst openly teach that the mass is very idolatry, and abominable in the sight of God."

"He answered and said, "I have read the word of God in three tongues, and have understood them so far as God gave me grace, and yet I never read that word mass in it all : but I found that the thing that was highest and most in estimation amongst men, and not in the word of God, was idolatry, and abominable in the sight of God. And I say that the mass is holden greatly in estimation amongst men and is not founded on the Word ; there I said it was idolatry, and abominable in the sight of God. But if any man will find it in the scripture, and prove it by God's word, I will acknowledge my error, and will submit to all lawful correction and punishment."

"Go to the third article," said the archbishop.

Then said the accuser, "Thou hast openly taught, that the God whom we worship is but bread, sown of corn, grown of the earth, baked of men's hands, and nothing else."

He answered, "I worship the Father, the Son, and the Holy Ghost, three Persons in one Godhead, who made and fashioned the heaven and earth, and all that is therein ; but I know not what God you worship ; and if you will show me whom you worship, I will show you what he is, as I can by my judgment."

"Believest thou not," said the accuser, "that the sacrament of the altar, after the words of consecration betwixt the priest's hands, is the very body and blood of the Son of God, and God himself?" "What the body of God is," said he, "and what kind of body he has, I have shewed you ; so far as I have found it declared in the scriptures."

Then said the accuser, "thou hast preached, and openly taught other great errors and abominable heresy against all the seven sacraments, which for shortness of time I omit and pass over. Dost thou admit the articles that thou art accused of or not?" And then the accuser repeated the above three articles, and asked him whether he granted or denied them?

He answered as he had before said, and that he had said nothing but what agreed with the holy word as he understood it, so God judge him, and his own conscience accuse him ; and by that would he abide till the time he were better instructed by the scriptures, even to the death : and he said to the lord governor and other lords, "If you condemn me for holding by God's word, my innocent blood shall be required at your hands, when ye shall be brought before the judgment-seat of Christ, who is mighty to defend my innocent cause, before whom you shall not deny it ; nor yet be able to resist his wrath ; to whom I refer the vengeance, as it is written, 'Vengeance is mine, I will repay, saith the Lord.'"

Then they passed sentence, and condemned him, and so left him to the secular power, in the hands of Sir John Campbell, justice deputy, who delivered him to the provost of Edinburgh to be burned on the Castle-hill. He was put in prison with irons about his legs and neck, and given in charge to Sir Hugh Terry, to keep the key, an ignorant minister, and a ready servant of Satan and of the bishops ; who, by direction, sent to the poor man two Gray friars to instruct him, with whom he would not enter into any communication. Soon after there was sent to him two Black friars, an English friar, and another subtle sophist. Wallace would have reasoned and declared his faith by the scriptures with the English friar; but he answered that he had no commission to enter into disputation with him, and so departed.

Then there was sent to him a worldly-wise man, though ungodly in the understanding of the truth, the dean of Roscalrige, who gave him christian consolation ; who exhorted him to believe the reality of the sacrament after the consecration ; but he would consent to nothing that had not evidence in the holy scriptures, and so passed over that night in singing and praising God to the tears of many hearers. having learned the psalter of David without book. For they had before spoiled him of his bible, which, till after he was condemned, was always with him wherever he went. After Sir Hugh knew that he had certain books to read and comfort his spirit, he came in a rage, and took the same from him, leaving him destitute of consolation, and gave ungodly and injurious provocations, in order to pervert the poor man from the patience and hope he had in Christ his Saviour ; but God suffered him not to be moved.

Thus this godly man abode in irons all night and all the next morning ; when provision was commanded to be made for his burning against the next day. Which day the lord governor, and all the principal, both spiritual and temporal lords, departed from Edinburgh to their other business.

After they were departed, came the dean of Roscalrige to him again, and reasoned with him ; but Wallace answered as before, that he would say nothing concerning his faith, but as the scripture testifies, yea, though an angel came from heaven to persuade him to the same ; saving that he confessed himself to have received good consolation of this dean in other respects as becomes a christian.

Then came in Sir Hugh Terry again, and examined him, and said he would make devils come out of him before evening. He answered, "You should rather be a godly man to give me consolation in my case. When I knew you were come, I prayed God I might resist your temptations ; which, I thank him, he has made me able to do ; therefore I pray you, let me alone in peace." Then he asked of one of the officers who stood by, "Is your fire making ready?" Who told him it was. He answered, "As it pleaseth God. I am ready sooner or later as it shall please him ;" and then he spake to a faithful one in that company, and bade him commend him to all the faithful, being sure to meet together with them in heaven. From that time to his coming to the fire, no man spake with him.

When he was brought out of prison, the provost, with great menacing words, forbade him to speak to any man, or any man to him. Coming from the town to the castle hill, the common people said, "God have mercy upon him." "And on you too," said he. Being beside the fire, he lifted up his eyes to heaven twice or thrice, and said to the people, "Let it not offend you that I suffer death this day for the truth's sake ; for the disciple is not greater than his master." Then was the provost angry that he spake. Then looked he to heaven again, and said, "They will not let me speak." The cord being about his neck, the fire was lighted, and so he departed to God with great constancy.

The Schism that arose in Scotland about the Pater-noster.

After Richard Marshall, doctor of divinity, and prior of the Black friars at Newcastle, in England, had declared in his preaching at St. Andrews, in Scotland, that the Lord's Prayer (commonly called the Pater-noster) should be said only to God, and not to saints, or to any other creature ; the doctors of the university of St. Andrews, together with the Gray friars, who had long ago taught the people to say the Pater-noster to saints, had great indignation that their old doctrine should be opposed, and stirred up a Gray friar, called Friar Toittis, to preach again to the people, that they should and might pray the Pater-noster or our Lord's Prayer to saints ; who, finding no part of the scriptures to found his purpose upon, yet came to the pulpit on the first of November, being the feast of Allhallows, (A.D. 1551), and took the text from the gospel that day read in their mass, in the fifth of Matthew, containing these words : "Blessed are the poor in spirit, for theirs is the kingdom of heaven."

This feeble foundation being laid, the friar began to reason most impertinently, that the Lord's Prayer might be offered to saints, because every petition appertains to them. "For if we meet an old man in the street," said he, "we will say to him, 'Good day, father,' and therefore much more may we call the saints our fathers ; and because we grant also that they are in heaven, so we may say to every one of them, 'Our Father which art in heaven.' Our Father, God, has made their names holy, and therefore ought we as followers of God, to hold their names holy, and so we may say to any of the saints, 'Our Father which art in heaven, hallowed be thy name.' And for the same cause," said the friar, "as they are in the kingdom of heaven, so that kingdom is theirs by possession; and so praying for the kingdom of heaven, we may say to them, and every one of them, 'Thy kingdom come.' And except their will had been the very will of God, they had never come to that kingdom. And therefore seeing their will is God's will, we may say to every one of them, 'Thy will be done.'"

But when the friar came to the fourth petition, touching our daily bread, he began to be astonished and ashamed, so that he did sweat abundantly; partly because his sophistry began to fail him, not finding such a colour for that part as for the other which went before, and partly because he spoke against his own knowledge and conscience; and so he was compelled to confess that it was not in the saints' power to give us our daily bread, but that they should pray to God for us, said he, that we may obtain our daily bread by their intercession; and so he commented on the rest of the prayer to the end. Not yet content with this detestable doctrine, he affirmed most blasphemously, that St. Paul's napkin, and St. Peter's shadow did miracles, and that the virtue of Elijah's cloak divided the waters, attributing nothing to the power of God; with many other errors of the papists, horrible to be heard.

Upon this, followed a dangerous schism in the church of Scotland, not only to the clergy, but the whole people were divided among themselves, one defending the truth, and another the papistry; so that there arose a proverb; "*To whom say you your* PATER-NOSTER?" And although the papists had the upper hand as then (so great was the blindness of that age), yet God so inspired the hearts of the common people, that so many as could understand the bare words of the Lord's Prayer in English (which was then said in Latin), utterly detested that opinion, holding that it should in nowise be said to saints; so that the tradesmen and others, when the friar came among them, put him to great shame, crying "Friar Pater-noster! Friar Pater-noster!" who, at last, being convicted in his own conscience, and ashamed of his former sermon, he was compelled to leave the town of St. Andrews.

At length the christians were so offended, and the papists, on the other side, so proud and wilful, that it was necessary that the clergy at last should be assembled to dispute and conclude the whole matter, that the lay-people might be put out of doubt. Which being done, and the university agreed, there ensued much subtle sophistry. For some of the popish doctors affirmed that it should be said to God *formaliter*, and to saints *materialiter*. Others, *ultimatè et non ultimatè*. Others said it should be said to God *principaliter*, and to saints *minus principaliter*. Others that it should be said to God *primariè*, and to saints *secundariè*. Others that it should be said to God *capiendo strictè*, and to saints *capiendo largè*. Which vain distinctions being heard and considered by the people, they that were simple remained in greater doubt than they were in before; so that a well aged man, and a servant to the subprior of St. Andrews, called the subprior's Thome, being asked to whom he said his Pater-noster; he answered, "To God only." Then they asked him again what should be said to the saints; he answered, "Give them plenty of aves and creeds, for that will suffice them well enough, although they spoil God of his right." Others said, that because Christ, who made the Pater-noster, never came into the isle of Britain, and so understood not the English tongue, therefore it was that the doctors concluded it should be said in Latin.

This trouble and open slander yet continuing, it was thought good to call a provincial council to decide the matter. Which, being assembled at Edinburgh, the papists, being destitute of reason, defended their parts with lies, alleging that the university of Paris had concluded that the Lord's Prayer should be said to the saints. But as that could not be proved, and they could not prevail by reason, they used their will instead. Friar Scot, being asked to whom he should say the Pater-noster, answered: "Say it to the devil." So the council, perceiving they could profit nothing by reasoning, were compelled to omit voting.

But then they that were called churchmen were found divided among themselves. For some bishops, with the doctors and friars, consented that the Pater-noster should be said to the saints; but the bishops of St. Andrews, Caithness, and Atheins, with other learned men, refused to subscribe to it. Finally, with consent of both parties, commission was given by the holy church to Dean John Winrame, then subprior of St. Andrews, to declare to the people how and after what manner they should pray the Lord's Prayer; who, accepting of the commission, declared that it should be said to God, with some other restrictions, which are not necessary to relate. And so, by little and little, the tumult ceased.

The Martyrdom of Walter Mille.

Among the rest of the martyrs of Scotland, the constancy of Walter Mille is not to be passed over with silence. Out of whose ashes sprang thousands of the same opinion and religion in Scotland, who altogether chose rather to die than to be any longer trodden upon by the tyranny of the cruel and ignorant bishops, abbots, monks and friars; and so the church of Scotland began to debate the true religion of Christ against the Frenchmen and papists; for the controversy ensued soon after the martyrdom of Walter Mille.

In the year 1558, in the time of Mary, queen regent of Scotland, and John Hamilton being bishop of St. Andrews, and primate of Scotland, this Walter Mille (who in his youth had been a papist) after he had been in Germany, and had heard the doctrine of the gospel, returned again into Scotland, and, setting aside all papistry and constrained celibacy, married a wife, which brought him under the suspicion of the bishops of Scotland for heresy; and after long watching for him he was taken by two popish priests, and brought to St. Andrews, and imprisoned in the castle. When in prison, the papists earnestly laboured to seduce him, and threatened him with death and torments, to cause him to recant and forsake the truth. But seeing that he remained still firm, and constant, they laboured to persuade him by fair promises; and offered to him a monk's portion for all the days of his life, in the abbey of Dunfermline, if he would deny the things he had taught, and grant that they were heresy; but he, continuing in the truth even to the end, despised their threatenings and fair promises.

Then assembled together the bishop of St. Andrews, Murray, Brechin, Caithness, and Atheins, the abbots of Dunfermline, Landors, Balindrinot, and Towpers, with the doctors of theology of St. Andrews, as John Greson, Black friar, and John Winrame, subprior of St. Andrews, William Cranston, provost of the Old College, with divers other friars, Black and Gray. These being assembled, and having consulted together, he was taken out of prison, and brought to the metropolitan church, where he was put in a pulpit before the bishops, on the 20th day of April. Being brought into the church, and climbing up into the pulpit, he appeared so weak and feeble of person, partly by age, and partly by ill treatment, that he could not climb up without help; then they gave up the hope of hearing him, for weakness of voice. But when he began to speak, he made the church ring and sound again, with so great courage and stoutness, that the christians who were present were no less rejoiced than the adversaries were confounded and ashamed. He being in the pulpit, and on his knees at prayer, Andrew Oliphant, one of the bishops' priests, commanded him to arise, and to answer to his articles, saying on this manner: "Walter Mille, arise and answer to the articles, for you delay my lord here too long." To whom Walter, after he had finished his prayer, answered, saying, "We ought to obey God rather than man; I serve one more mighty, even the Omnipotent Lord. Now say what thou hast to say."

Oliphant.—"What think you of priests' marriage?"

Mille.—"I hold it a blessed bond; for Christ himself maintained it, and approved the same, and also made it free to all men; but you think it not free to you; you abhor it, and in the meantime take other men's wives and daughters, and will not keep the bond that God has made. You vow chastity, and break it. St. Paul had rather marry than burn; which I have done, for God never forbade marriage to any man, of what state or degree soever he were."

Oliphant.—"Thou sayest there are not seven sacraments."

Mille.—"Give me the Lord's supper and baptism, and take you the rest, and part them among you. For if there be seven, why have you omitted one of them, to wit, marriage, and given yourselves to ungodly immoralities?"

Oliphant.—"Thou art against the blessed sacrament of the altar, and sayest that the mass is wrong, and is idolatry."

Mille.—"A lord or a king sends and calls many to a dinner, and when the dinner is in readiness, he causes a bell to be rung, and the men come to the hall, and sit down to be partakers of the dinner; but the lord, turning his back to them, eats all himself, and mocks them; so do ye."

Oliphant.—"Thou deniest the sacrament of the altar to be the very body of Christ really in flesh and blood."

Mille.—"The scripture of God is not to be taken carnally, but spiritually; and stands in faith only: and as for the mass, it is wrong, for Christ was once offered on the cross for man's trespass, and will never be offered again, for then he ended all sacrifice."

Oliphant.—"Thou deniest the office of a bishop."

Mille.—"I affirm that they, whom ye call bishops, do no bishops' works, nor use the office of bishops, (as St. Paul biddeth, writing to Timothy), but live after their own sensual pleasure, and take no care of the flock, nor yet regard they the word of God, but desire to be honoured and called 'My lords.'"

Oliphant.—"Thou spakest against pilgrimage."

Mille.—"I affirm and say, that it is not commanded in the scripture, and that there is no greater immorality committed in any place, than at your pilgrimages."

Oliphant.—"Thou preachedst secretly and privately in houses, and openly in the fields."

Mille.—"Yea, man, and on the sea also, sailing in a ship."

Oliphant.—"Wilt thou not recant thy erroneous opinions? And if thou wilt not, I will pronounce sentence against thee."

Mille.—"I am accused of my life; I know I must die once, and therefore as Christ said to Judas, what thou doest, do quickly. Ye shall know that I will not recant the truth, for I am corn, I am no chaff; I will not be blown away with the wind, nor burst with the flail; but I will abide both."

Then Andrew Oliphant pronounced sentence against him, that he should be delivered to the temporal judge, and punished as a heretic, which was to be burnt. His boldness and constancy so moved the hearts of many, that the bishop's steward of his regality, provost of the town, named Patrick Learmont, refused to be his temporal judge, to whom it properly appertained. Also the bishop's chamberlain, being charged therewith, would in nowise take upon him so ungodly an office. Yea, the whole town was so offended with his unjust condemnation, that the bishop's servants could not get, even for money, so much as a cord to tie him to the stake, or a tar barrel to burn him; but were constrained to cut the cords of their master's own pavilion to serve their turn.

Nevertheless, one servant of the bishop's, more ignorant and cruel than the rest, called Alexander Simmerwail, acting the office of a temporal judge, conveyed him to the fire, where his boldness and hardiness did more and more increase, so that the Spirit of God, working miraculously in him, made it manifest to the people, that his cause and articles were most just, and he innocently martyred.

When all things were ready for his death, and he brought with armed men to the fire, Oliphant bade him pass to the stake; and he said, "Nay, but wilt thou put me up with thy hand, and take part of my death? thou shalt see me pass up gladly; for by the law of God I am forbidden to put hands upon myself." Then Oliphant put him up with his hand, and he ascended gladly, and desired that he might have opportunity to speak to the people; but this Oliphant and other of the burners refused, saying that he had spoken too much, for the bishops were offended that the matter was so long continued. Then some of the young men committed both the burners, and the bishops, their masters, to the devil, saying that they believed they should lament that day, and desired Walter to speak what he pleased.

And so after he made his humble supplication to God on his knees, he arose, and standing upon the coals, said; "Dear friends, the cause why I suffer this day is not for any crime laid to my charge (although I be a miserable sinner before God), but only for the defence of the faith of Jesus Christ, set forth in the Old and New Testaments; for which, as the faithful martyrs have offered themselves gladly before, being assured after the death of their bodies of eternal felicity; so this day I praise God, that he has called me of his mercy among the rest of his servants to seal up his truth with my life; which, as I have received it of him, so I willingly offer it to his glory. Therefore, as you would escape the eternal death, be no more seduced with the lies of priests, monks, friars, priors, abbots, bishops, and the rest of the sect of antichrist, but depend only upon Jesus Christ and his mercy, that you may be delivered from condemnation." All the while there was great mourning and lamentation among the multitude; for they perceiving his patience, constancy, and hardiness, were not only moved and stirred up, but their hearts also were so inflamed, that he was the last martyr that died in Scotland for religion. After his prayer, he was hoisted up upon the stake, and being in the fire, he said, "Lord have mercy on me! Pray, people, while there is time;" and so he endured his cruel end with constancy.

In the same place where Walter Mille was burnt, the images of the great church of the abbey were burnt in the time of the Reformation.

And thus much concerning the martyrs who suffered in the realm of Scotland for the faith of Jesus Christ, and testimony of his truth.

Persecutions in Kent.

In looking through the registers of William Warham, archbishop of Canterbury, I find, besides those above comprehended, in the time and reign of King Henry, the names of others, of whom some suffered martyrdom for the testimony of God's word, and some recanted, who, although they here come a little out of order, and should have been placed before, in the beginning of King Henry's reign; yet, rather than they should entirely be omitted, I judged fit here to give them a place, being no less worthy to be registered and preserved from oblivion, than others before them, especially as they were martyred here in England, before the appearing and preaching of Martin Luther.

The martyrs alluded to are William Carder of Tenterden, weaver; Agnes Grebil of Tenterden; Robert Harrison of Halden; John Brown of Ashford; Edward Walker of Maidstone, cutler.

The Articles upon which the above five blessed Martyrs were accused and condemned.

1. For holding that the sacrament of the altar was not the very true body of Christ, but only material bread in substance.

2. That auricular confession was not to be made to a priest.

3. That no power is given by God to priests, of ministering sacraments, saying mass, or other Divine service, more than to laymen.

4. That the solemnization of matrimony is not necessary to salvation of souls, neither was it instituted of God, (as a sacrament, they meant.)

5. That the sacrament of extreme unction is not available or necessary to the soul's salvation.

6. That the images of the cross, of the crucifix, of the blessed Virgin, and other saints, are not to be worshipped; and that they who worship them commit idolatry.

7. That pilgrimages to holy places, and holy relics, are not necessary, nor meritorious to the soul's salvation.

8. That invocation is not to be made to saints, but only to God, and that He only heareth their prayers.

9. That holy bread and holy water have no more virtue after their consecration than before.

10. That they have believed, taught, and held all and every of the same damnable opinions before; as they did at that present time.

11. That though they now have confessed their errors, they would not have so done but only for fear of manifest proofs brought against them; neither would they ever have confessed the same of their own accord.

12. That they have communed and talked of the said damnable errors heretofore with divers other persons, and have possessed books concerning the same.

The order and form of Process used against these five Martyrs, A.D. 1511.

William Carder being brought before William Warham, archbishop, and his chancellor Cuthbert Tonstall, Doctor Sylvester, Doctor Welles, Clement, Brown, with others, the notaries being William Potking, and David Cowper, the articles and interrogatories above specified were laid to his charge. Which articles he denied, affirming that he never did; nor does hold any such opinion, otherwise than becomes what every christian man should do, who is ready to conform himself in all points to their doctrine; and therefore to clear himself the better against those interrogatories objected against him, he stood in denial of them. The other four martyrs after him did the same.

Notwithstanding all which, the uncharitable archbishop brought in against him such witnesses, as were abjured before, whom he knew, for fear of relapse, durst do no other but disclose whatever they knew; to wit, Christopher Grebil, William Rich, Agnes Ive, John Grebil, Robert Hills, and Steven Castelin. Whose depositions being taken, and Carder being asked what he could say for himself, he said he had nothing to produce against their attestations; but submitted himself to their mercy; adding, that if he had any disbelief of the sacraments of the church, contrary to the common holding of the catholics, he now was sorry and repented him. Which being done, the archbishop, notwithstanding his submission, and notwithstanding that the register makes no mention of any relapse contrary to law, at least contrary to all christian charity, proceeded to the reading of his sentence, and condemned him to be burnt.

Then, after him, Agnes Grebil was called and examined on the twelve articles, which she in like manner denied, as the other had done, putting her adversaries to their proof. Then the archbishop called for John Grebil, her husband, and Christopher and John Grebil her two sons, and caused them upon their oath to depose against their own natural mother!

First, John Grebil, her husband, being examined by virtue of his oath, to say how Agnes, his wife, believed of the sacrament of the altar, of going on pilgrimage, offerings, and worshipping of saints, images, &c. and how long she had held such opinion: deposed, that first, about the end of King Edward IV.'s days, in his house, by the teaching of John Ive, she was brought to that belief, and so from thence, daily, until the time of detection, she continued.

And besides that, said he, " when my children, Christopher and John, being about seven years of age, were then taught by me in my house, the error of the sacrament of the altar, and by Agnes, my wife, she was always

of one mind in the disbelief of the sacrament of the altar, that it was not Christ's body, flesh, and blood, but only bread." Further, being examined how he knew that she was steadfast in the said error; he said that she always, without contradiction, affirmed this teaching, and said the opinion was good, and that she was well contented that her children should be of the same opinions against the sacrament of the altar, &c.

The bishop, with his popish doctors, not contented with this, to set the husband against the wife, proceeding further in their popish zeal and caused her two children, Christopher and John, to be produced; one of the age of two-and-twenty, the other of nineteen, against their own mother; who, being pressed with their oath, witnessed, and said, that Agnes, their mother, held, believed, taught, and defended, that the sacrament of the altar was but bread, and not the very body of Christ's flesh and blood; that baptism was no better in the fount than out of the fount; that confirmation was of no effect; that the solemnization of matrimony was no sacrament; that confession to God alone was sufficient; also that going on pilgrimage, and worshipping of saints and images, was of none effect, &c. That their father, and Agnes, their mother, had held, taught, and communed of these errors within their house for three years past, as well on holy-days, as working days, affirming and teaching that these opinions were good and lawful, and to be held and maintained; and agreement was made among them, that none of them should discover of the other. Finally, that they never heard their father and mother holding or teaching any other opinions, than the said errors against the sacrament of the altar, and pilgrimages, offerings, worshipping of saints and images, as far as they could remember, &c.

Here hast thou, christian reader, before thine eyes, a horrible spectacle of impiety; first, of an unnatural husband, witnessing against his own wife; and of as unnatural children, accusing and witnessing against their own mother. Which although they had so done, the cause being of itself just and true, (as it was not,) yet it seems more than nature would have led them to do. Now the case being such, as by God's word standeth firm, sound, and perfect, what impiety was it for men to accuse a poor woman of heresy, which is no heresy? And yet the greatest impiety of all rests in these papists and popish priests, who were the authors of all this mischief. The cause why this good woman stood in the denial of these articles, was this, that she never thought that her husband and her own children, who alone were privy of her religion, would testify against her. And thus the archbishop, with his doctors, having now gained the end that they sought for, although she was ready to deny all errors, and to conform herself to their religion, yet they proceeded to their sentence, and condemned her to death.

After her condemnation, next was brought to examination Robert Harrison, who, because he stood in his denial, witnesses against him were produced. After the deposition of which witnesses, although he submitted himself to repentance and conformity, yet it would not be received, but sentence was read, and he was condemned with the other two to the fire.

Thus these three were condemned and burned, and certificate given up to the king, from Warham the archbishop, upon the same, (A. D. 1511.)

Besides these three godly martyrs, I find in the registers of William Warham two other godly martyrs also in the same year, and for the same twelve articles, condemned upon the depositions of certain witnesses. Their names were John Brown and Edward Walker.

Besides these five blessed saints of God, whom they so cruelly by their sentence condemned to death in the year 1511, we find also in the same registers of William Warham, a great number of others whom they for the same doctrine and like articles caused to be apprehended and put to open recantation; the names of which persons are given in the following list: .

John Grebil, the elder, of Benenden.

Christopher Grebil, his son.
John Grebil, son of John the Elder, of Benenden
W. Olbert, the elder, of Godmersham.
Agnes Ive, of Canterbury.
Agnes Chytenden, of Canterbury.
Thomas Manning, of Benenden.
Joan Colyn, of Tenderden.
Robert Hills, of Tenterden.
Alice Hills, his wife.
Thomas Harwood, of Rolvenden.
Joan Harwood, his wife.
Philip Harwood.
Stephen Castelyn, of Tenterden.
W. Baker, of Cranbrook.
Margaret Baker, his wife.
William Olbert, the younger, of Godmersham.
Agnes Reynold, of Cranbrook.
Thomas Field, of Boxley.
Joan Olbert, wife to W. Olbert, the elder, of Godmersham.
Elizabeth White, of Canterbury.
Thomas Church, of Great Charte
Vincent Lynch, of Halden.
John Rich, of Wittisham.
Joan Lynch, of Tenterden.
Thomas Browne, of Cranbrook.
John Franke, of Tenterden.
Joyce Bampton, wife of John Bampton, of Berstede.
Richard Bampton, of Boxley.
Robert Bright, of Maidstone.
William Lorkyn, of East Farley.
John Bannes, of Boxley, 1512.
John Buckherst, of Staplehurst
Joan Dodd, wife of John Dodd.
John Benet, of Staplehurst.
Rebecca Benet, his wife.
Joan Lowes, wife of Thomas Lowes, of Cranbrook.
Julian Hills, wife of Robert Hills, of Tenterden.
Robert Franke, of Tenterden.

The articles laid to these abjurers appear in the registers to be the same which were objected to the other five martyrs; by which articles and abjurations we may understand what doctrine of religion was most prevalent in England, *before the time that the name of Martin Luther was ever heard of here amongst us;* for all this is in the archbishop of Canterbury's Registers for A.D. 1511.

Three sorts of Judgments amongst the Papists against Heretics.

As to the penance and penalty enjoined to heretics as also to all others, the popish fathers, in their processes of heretical pravity, have three distinct kinds of judgments and proceedings.

Some they judge to be burned, that others being brought into terror by them, might more quietly maintain their kingdom, and reign supreme. And thus they condemned the five martyrs above-mentioned, although they were willing to submit themselves to the mother church; yet they could not be received, as by the words of the register, and by the tenor of their sentence appears.

And this sort of persons, thus condemned, consists either of such as have been before abjured, and fallen into relapse; or else such as stand constantly in their doctrine, and refuse to abjure; or else such as they intend to make a terror and example to others, notwithstanding, that they may be willing and ready to submit themselves, and yet cannot be received: and of the last sort were the five martyrs last named. So was also John Lambert, who, submitting himself to the king, could not be accepted. So was likewise Richard Mekins, and the three women of Guernsey, whose submission would not serve to save their lives, with many others. Against this sort of persons, the process which the papists use is this:—First, after they began once to be suspected, they were denounced and cited; then by virtue of inquisition they are taken and clapt fast in irons in prison; from thence they are brought forth at

last to examination, if they be not before killed by famine, cold, or strictness of imprisonment; then articles are drawn, or rather wrested, out of their writings or preachings; and they are put to their oath, to answer truly to every point and circumstance articulated against them. Which articles, if they seem to deny, or solve by true expounding, then witnesses are called in; and no matter what witnesses they are, be they ever so infamous in character. Or, if no other witnesses can be found, then is the husband brought in and forced to swear against the wife, or the wife against the husband, or the children against the mother, as in the example of Agnes Grebil. Or if no witness at all can be found, then are they strained upon the rack, or by other torments forced to confess their knowledge, and to impeach others. Neither might any be suffered to come to them, nor any public audience be given them to speak for themselves; till at last sentence is read against them, to give them up to the secular arm, or to degrade them, if they are priests, and then to burn them.

And yet the malignity of these adversaries does not here cease. For after the fire has consumed their bodies, they fall upon their books, and condemn them in like manner to be burned; and no man must be so hardy as to read their books, or keep them, under pain of heresy. But before they have destroyed these books, they first gather articles out of them, and so perversely wrest them to their own purposes, falsely, and contrary to the right meaning of the author, making them to appear to be the most heretical and execrable. Which being done, and the books destroyed, that no man may compare them with the articles, to discover their falsehood, they then set abroad these articles, that princes and people may see what heretics they were.

To the second order belongs that sort of heretics whom these papists do not condemn to death, but assign to monasteries, there to continue, and to fast all their life, with bread and sorrow, and water of affliction; and that they should not remove one mile out of the precinct of the monastery so long as they lived, without they were otherwise dispensed with by the archbishop or his successors.

The third kind of heretics were those whom these prelates judged not to perpetual prison, but only enjoined them penance, either to stand before the preacher, or else to bear a fagot about the market, or in procession; or to wear the picture of a fagot on their left sleeves, without any cloak or gown over it; or else to kneel at the saying of certain masses, or to say so many paternosters, aves, and creeds, to a certain saint; or to go in pilgrimage to a certain place; or to bear a fagot to the burning of some heretic; or to fast certain Fridays on bread and water; or, if it were a woman, to wear woollen alone on Fridays.

And thus much, out of the register of William Warham, archbishop of Canterbury. Many more examples might be collected out of other bishops' registers, if either leisure would serve me to search, or if the largeness of this volume would allow all to be inserted that might be found. Yet the history and martyrdom of Launcelot and his companions should not be forgotten.

The Martyrdom of Launcelot, one of the King's Guards; John, a Painter; and Giles German.

About the year 1539, one John, a painter, and Giles German, were accused of heresy, and while they were in examination at London before the bishop and other judges, by chance there came in one of the king's servants named Launcelot, a very strong and tall man, and of no less godly mind and disposition.

This man standing by, seemed by his countenance and gesture to favour both the cause and the poor men his friends. Whereupon, he being apprehended, was examined and condemned together with them. And the next day, at five o'clock in the morning, he was carried with them into St. Giles-in-the-fields, and there burned, there being but a small concourse of people at their death.

The Story of one Stile, a Martyr.

In the company and fellowship of the blessed saints and martyrs of Christ, who innocently suffered in king Henry's reign, for the testimony of God's word and truth, another good man, named Stile, also comes to my mind, who was with like cruelty oppressed and burned in Smithfield about the latter end of the time of Cuthbert Tonstall, bishop of London. With him there was burned also a book of the Apocalypse, which probably he was accustomed to read. When he saw this book fastened to the stake, to be burned with him, lifting up his voice, he said, "O blessed Apocalypse, how happy am I, that I shall be burned with thee?" And so this good man and the blessed Apocalypse were both together consumed in the fire.

And thus (through the gracious support of Christ our Lord) we have run over these thirty-seven laborious years of king Henry's reign. Under whose time and government, such acts and records, troubles, persecutions, recantations, practices, alterations, and reformations as then happened in the church, we have here discoursed, not omitting the statutes, injunctions, and proclamations, that were set forth by him in matters appertaining to the church. Although not comprehending all things so fully as might be, yet omitting as few things as we could.

Closing this eighth book with the death of king Henry VIII. we will next proceed to the time and reign of king Edward his son; first interposing a few words touching the death of king Henry.

After long languishing, infirmity growing more and more upon him, he lay from St. Steven's day to the latter end of January. His physicians at length perceiving that he was failing, and yet not daring to discourage him with thoughts of death, for fear of the act passed before in parliament, that none should speak any thing of the king's death (the act being made only for soothsayers, and talkers of prophesies) moved those that were about the king to put him in remembrance of his mortal state and fatal infirmity. Which when the rest were in dread to do, Master Denny, who was specially attendant upon him, boldly coming to the king, told him the state he was in, and that to man's judgment he was not likely to live, and therefore exhorted him to prepare himself for death, calling to remembrance his former life; and entreating him to call upon God in Christ for grace and mercy, as becomes every good christian man.

Although the king was loath to hear any mention of death, yet perceiving that it was the judgment of his physicians, and feeling his own weakness, he disposed himself to hearken to the words of Denny's exhortation, and to consider his past life. Which although he much accused, yet, said he, " is the mercy of Christ able to pardon me all my sins, even though they were greater than they are." Master Denny being glad to hear him speak thus, asked to know his pleasure, whether he would have any learned man sent for to confer with, and to open his mind to. The king answered again, that if he had any, he would have Doctor Cranmer, who was then at Croydon. And therefore, Master Denny asking the king whether he would have him sent for, " I will first," said the king, " take a little sleep, and then according as I feel myself I will advise upon the matter."

After an hour or two, the king awaking, and feeling feebleness increasing upon him, commanded Doctor Cranmer to be sent for; but before he could come, the king was speechless, and almost senseless. Notwithstanding, perceiving Doctor Cranmer, he reached his hand to him, held him fast; but could utter no words to him, and scarce was able to make any sign. Then the archbishop exhorting him to put his trust in Christ, and to call upon his mercy, desired him, though he could not speak, yet to give some token with his eyes, or with his hand, that he trusted in the Lord. Then the king, holding him with his hand, wrung his hand in his as hard as he could, and shortly after departed, after he had

reigned in this land the term of thirty-seven years and nine months, leaving behind him three children, Edward, Mary and Elizabeth.

We conclude this book with the following history of certain friars in France, A.D. 1534, as illustrative of the priestcraft of those times.

The wife of the mayor of the city of Orleans provided in her will, to be buried without any pomp or solemnity. For when any departs there, the bellmen are hired to go about the city, and in the places most frequented to assemble the people with the sound of the bell, and to declare the names and the titles of the parties deceased; also where and when they are to be buried, exhorting the people to pray for them. And when the corpse is carried forth, numbers of the begging friars go with it to the church, with many torches and tapers carried before them; and the more pomp and solemnity is used, the more is the concourse of people. But this woman would have none of all this pomp done for her. Wherefore her husband, who loved her well, followed her mind, and gave to these greedy cormorants, the friars, who waited for their prey, six crowns for a reward; yet they gaped for a great deal more. Afterwards when he cut down a wood and sold it, the friars craving to have part of it, freely without money, he refused them : this they took grievously, and as they loved him not before, they devised now a way to be revenged, saying, that his wife was damned everlastingly !

The workers of this tragedy were Colyman and Steven of Arras, both doctors of divinity; and the first indeed was a conjurer by profession, and had all his trinkets and his furniture concerning such matters in readiness, and they settled the matter thus :

They set a young man, who was a novice, above the vault of the church, and when they came to say their matins at midnight, after their accustomed manner, he made a wonderful noise and shrieking aloft. Then this Colyman went crossing and conjuring, but the other above would not speak. When charged to make a sign to declare if he were a dumb spirit, he rustled and made a noise again, and that was the sign.

When they had laid this foundation for their priestcraft, they went to certain of the chief men in all the city, and to such as favoured them the most, they related what a sad affair had happened; yet they did not say what it was, but entreated them to take the pains to come to their service at night. When they were come, and the service was begun, he that was aloft made a great noise. It was demanded what he wanted, and what he was, he signified that he could not speak : then he was commanded to answer to their interrogatories by signs and tokens. Now, there was a hole made for the purpose, and by laying his ear to it, he might hear and understand what the conjurer said. There was also a table at hand, and when any question was asked, he struck and beat upon the table, so that he might be heard beneath. Then the conjurer demanded whether he was any of those that had been buried in that church. After that, reckoning up many of their names in order, whose bodies had been buried there, he at last named the mayor's wife. Here the young man who was perched above in the roof, and who was playing the ghost, made a sign that he was the spirit of that woman. Then the friar asked whether she was damned, and for what offence? whether it were for covetousness, pride, or not doing the works of charity, or else for this new heresy and Lutheranism? What was the cause that he made such a noise, and was so unquiet? Whether it were that the body being buried within holy ground should be digged up again, and carried to some other place? To all these things this pretended ghost answered by signs as he was commanded; affirming or denying every thing by striking twice or thrice upon the table.

When he had thus signified that Luther's heresy was the cause of her damnation, and that her body must be taken up, the friars desired the citizens that were present, to bear witness of such things as they had seen and heard, and set their hands to it in writing. But they taking advice lest they should both offend the mayor, and bring themselves into trouble, refused to subscribe. Notwithstanding, the friars took the pix with the host, and the Lord's body (as they call it), and all their saints' relics, and carried them to another place, and there they said their mass; which they are wont to do by the pope's law, when a church is suspended and must be hallowed again: when the bishop's official heard of this, he came there to understand the matter better, and associating to him certain honest men he commanded the friar to conjure up the ghost in his presence, and he purposed to have appointed certain to go up to the vault, to see if any spirit appeared there. But Steven of Arras was against it, and exhorted them earnestly that they should not so do, saying, that the spirit ought not to be molested. And although the official earnestly urged them to conjure it up before him, yet he could not bring them to it. In the mean time the mayor, making his friends privy as to what he would do, went to the king, and informed him of the whole matter. And because the friars, trusting to their immunities and privileges, refused to come into judgment, the king chose certain out of the court of parliament at Paris, to examine the matter, and gave them full authority so to do. Whereupon they were carried to Paris, and constrained to make answer, but they would confess nothing.

Then they were sent again to prison, and kept apart, one from another; and the novice was kept in the house of Fumeus, a senator, and being often examined, he would confess nothing, fearing lest he should afterward be murdered by them for speaking against their order. But when the judges promised him that he should have no harm, and should come no more into the friars' hands, he declared to them the whole matter, and being brought before the others, he avouched the same. But they, although they were convicted, yet refused their judges, and relied on their privileges: but it was altogether in vain, for they were condemned in open judgment, that they should be carried again to Orleans, and committed to prison, and afterwards brought openly to the cathedral church, and so to the place of punishment, where malefactors are executed, and there they should make open confession of their wickedness.

THE END OF THE EIGHTH BOOK.

ACTS AND MONUMENTS.

BOOK IX.

CONTAINING

AN ACCOUNT OF THE ACTS AND EVENTS OF THE REIGN OF KING EDWARD VI.

AFTER the death of King Henry VIII., succeeded King Edward his son, of the age of nine years. He began his reign on the twenty-eighth day of January, A.D. 1547, and reigned six years and eight months, and eight days. He died on the sixth day of July, A.D. 1553. Of whose excellent virtues and singular graces wrought in him by the gift of God, although enough cannot be said to his commendation; yet because the renowned fame of such a worthy prince should not pass our history without some grateful remembrance, I propose briefly to touch some portion of his praise, taken out of the many things which might be described. For to stand upon all that might be said of him, would be too long: and yet to say nothing, were too unkind. If kings and princes, who have wisely and virtuously governed, have found in all ages writers to panegyrise and celebrate their acts and memory, such as never knew them, nor were subject to them, how much then are we Englishmen bound not to forget our duty to King Edward? A prince, though but of tender years, yet for his sage and mature ripeness in all princely ornaments, as I see but few to whom he may not be equal, so again I see not many to whom he may not justly be preferred.

And here to use the example of Plutarch in comparing kings and rulers, the Latins with the Greeks together, if I should seek with whom to match this noble King Edward, I find none with whom to make my comparison more aptly, than with good Josiah. For as one began his reign at eight years of age, so the other began at nine. Neither were their acts and zealous proceedings in God's cause very unlike. For as mild Josiah pulled down the high altars, cut down the groves, and destroyed all monuments of idolatry in the temple; so the like corruptions, dross, and deformities of popish idolatry, which had crept into the church of Christ, this King Edward removed, and purged the true temple of the Lord. Josiah restored the true worship and service of God in Jerusalem, and destroyed the idolatrous priests; King Edward, in England, likewise abolished idolatrous masses and false invocation, reduced again religion to a right sincerity, and would have brought it more to perfection if life and time had answered his godly purpose. And though he killed not, as Josiah did, the idolatrous sacrificers, yet he put them to silence, and removed them out of their places.

Moreover, in King Josiah's days the holy scriptures and book of God's word was utterly neglected and cast aside, which he most graciously repaired and restored again. And did not King Edward do the like, with the self-same book of God's blessed word, and with other wholesome books of christian doctrine, which before were decayed and extinguished in his father's days? Briefly, in all points and respects, no great difference is to be found between Josiah and this our godly king, but only in length of reign. Who, if he might have reached (by the sufferance of God) to the continuance of Josiah's reign, proceeding in those beginnings which in his youth appeared, no doubt but by his acts and doings some great perfection would have ensued to this church and realm. But the manifold iniquities of Englishmen deserved another plague, as in the sequel of this history shall be declared.

In the meantime, to proceed with the excellent virtues of this young christian Josiah, as we have begun, we will give a taste of the noble nature and princely qualities of this king, whereby the reader may judge for himself what is to be thought of the rest of his doings. And first to begin with that which is the chief property of all other external things in a prince, that is, to be loved of his subjects; such were the hearts of all English people towards this king, that there never was a prince in this realm more highly esteemed, or more dearly and tenderly beloved of all his subjects, but especially of the good and learned sort; and as he was beloved of his subjects, so he loved them again; of nature and disposition meek, and much inclined to clemency. He always spared and favoured the life of man, insomuch that when Joan was to be burned, all the council could not move him to put his hand to the warrant, but were obliged to get Dr. Cranmer to persuade him, and yet neither could he induce the king to do so, saying, "What, my lord, will you have me to send her quick to the devil in her error?" So that Dr. Cranmer himself confessed, that he had never so much to do in all his life, as to cause the king to sign his hand, saying, that he would lay all the charge thereof upon Cranmer before God. There wanted in him no promptness of wit, gravity of sentence, or ripeness of judgment. Favour and love of religion was in him from his childhood. And besides these notable excellences, and other great virtues in him, add moreover skill and knowledge of tongues and other sciences, wherein he excelled far beyond his years.

Of all his justices, magistrates, and gentlemen, that bare any authority within this realm, he knew their names, their housekeeping, their religion, and conversation what it was. There were few sermons in his court, especially in the lord protector's time, which he did not attend; and those he was present at, he noted them with his own hand.

But above all other examples of his commendation, and which is the chief point which ought most to concern all men, he was zealous in maintaining, promoting, preferring, embracing, and defending the true cause of Christ's holy gospel; and it was his study, his zealous fervency, and his admirable constancy therein, that, by his example, he promoted it in others.

In the days of this King Edward VI., the emperor Charles made a request to the king and his council, to permit the Lady Mary (who afterwards succeeded to the crown) to have mass in her house without prejudice of the law. And the council on a time, sitting upon matters of policy, and having that in question under consideration, sent Cranmer, then archbishop of Canterbury, and Ridley, then bishop of London, to intreat the king for it. Who coming to his grace, alleged their reasons and persuasions for the accomplishing of it. So the king hearing what they could say, replied out of the scriptures so gravely and wisely, that they were forced to give place to his reply, and acknowledge its truth. Then they, after long debating with his majesty, alleged what dangers the refusal might bring upon his grace; what breach of amity of the emperor's part; what troubles; what unkindness, and what occasions it would enforce, &c. To whom the king answered, desiring them to content themselves, for he would, he said, rather spend his life and all he had, than agree to and grant what he knew certainly to be against the truth. Which when the bishops heard, they urged him still to grant it. Then the good king seeing their importunate suit, his tender heart bursting out into bitter weeping, and sobbing, he desired them to be content. Then the bishops themselves, seeing the king's zeal and constancy, wept as fast as he, and took their leave of his grace; and on coming from him, the archbishop took Master Cheek, his schoolmaster, by the hand, and said, "Ah, Master Cheek, you may be glad all the days of your life that you have such a scholar, for he hath more divinity in his little finger, than all we have in all our bodies." Thus the Lady Mary's mass for that time was prevented.

Besides these heavenly graces and virtues, which are required in all faithful and Christian magistrates who have the government of Christ's flock, neither was he unprovided with such outward gifts and knowledge as appertain to the political government of his realm. So that he was not inexpert or ignorant of the exchange, and all the circumstances of the same touching doings beyond the sea, but was as skilful, and could say as much therein, as the chief doers in his affairs. Likewise in the entertaining of ambassadors, to whom he would give answer, and that to every part of their oration, to the great wonder of them that heard him, doing that in his tender years by himself, which many princes at their mature age seldom are wont to do but by others. And as he was a great noter of things that pertained to princely affairs, so he had a chest for every year, for the keeping of such records and matters as were passed and concluded by the council. He also would require from them a reason and cause for everything that passed their judgments. And of this chest he always kept the key about him. His notes also he cyphered in Greek letters, that those who waited on him should not read nor know what he had written. He had moreover great respect for justice, and to the despatch of poor men's suits, and would appoint hours and times with Master Cox, then Master of his requests, how and by what order they might be helped in their causes without long delay and attendance; and so also debate with him, that their matters might be heard and judged with equity.

Thus after the godly disposition of this king being declared, now we will describe the order and proceedings which he followed in his administration and government of both the states, as well political as ecclesiastical. Who, after the decease of his father, coming to the crown, because he was of young and tender age, was committed to sixteen governors. Among whom, especially, the Lord Edward Seymour, Duke of Somerset, his uncle, was appointed as protector and overseer of him and of the commonwealth; a man not so highly advanced for his consanguinity as for his noble virtues, and especially for his favour to God's word. Through the endeavour and industry of Seymour, first, that monstrous hydra with six heads, the six articles I mean, (which devoured up so many men before,) was abolished and taken away. Then he restored the holy scriptures in the mother tongue, and masses he extinguished and abolished. After small beginnings, by little and little, greater things followed in the reformation of the churches. Then such as were in banishment for the danger of the truth, were again received to their country. To be short, a new face of things began now to appear, as it were in a stage, new players coming in, the old ones being thrust out. For the most part the bishops of churches and dioceses were changed. Such as had been dumb prelates before, were compelled to give place to others who would preach and take pains.

Besides, men of learning and notable knowledge were sent for out of foreign countries, and cordially received and promoted in this country, among whom was Peter Martyr, Martin Bucer, and Paul Phagius. Of whom the first taught at Oxford; the other two professed at Cambridge, and with no small commendation of the whole university. Of the old bishops, some were committed to one ward, some to another. Bonner, bishop of London, was committed to the Marshalsea, and soon after, for his contempt and misdemeanour was deposed from his bishopric. Gardiner, bishop of Winchester, with Tonstal, bishop of Durham, was cast into the Tower for his disobedience, where he kept his Christmas three years together, more worthy of some other place without the Tower, if it had pleased God otherwise not to have meant a further plague to this realm by that man.

But these meek and gentle times of king Edward, under the government of this noble protector, have this one commendation, that among the whole number of the popish sort, of whom some stole privily out of the realm, many were crafty dissemblers, some were open and manifest adversaries, yet of all that multitude there was not one man that lost his life. In short, during the whole time of the six years of this king, much tranquillity, and as it were a breathing-time, was granted to the whole church of England: so that the rage of persecution ceasing, and the sword being taken out of the adversary's hand, there was now no danger to the godly, unless it were only by wealth and prosperity, which often brings more damage in corrupting men's minds, than any time of persecution or affliction.

Briefly, during all this time, neither in Smithfield nor in any other quarter of this realm, was any heard to suffer for any matter of religion, either papist or protestant, either for one opinion or another, except only two; one an Englishwoman, called Joan of Kent, and the other a Dutchman, named George.

Besides these two, there was none else in all king Edward's reign that died in any cause of religion; but one Thomas Dobbe, who in the beginning of this king's reign was apprehended and imprisoned for speaking against the idolatry of the mass, and died in the same prison.

This Thomas Dobbe, being a student and a master of arts in Cambridge, was brought up in the college called St. John's College, and was a fellow of the same, where he increased in the study of good letters; among his equals very forward; of nature and disposition simple and modest; of zeal towards God fervent; patient in injuries, and injurious to no man. At length this godly man, intending within himself to enter the Christian state of matrimony, resorted to a certain maiden not far off from where he dwelt. On which account he was greatly molested; and wickedly abused by three of that college, whose names were Hutchinson, Pindare, and Tayler.

who with their malicious handling, scornful dealing, rebukes, and contumelies, so much vexed the virtuous simplicity of the man, that they never left him; till at length they wearied him out of the college. Who there having no rest nor quietness, by the unreasonable and virulent handling of his adversaries, was compelled to seek some other place to settle himself. On coming up to London, he chanced to pass through St. Paul's church, where it happened that at the south side of the church there was a priest celebrating mass, being at the elevation as he passed by. The young man, replete with godly zeal, pitying the ignorance and idolatry of the people, in honouring so devoutly what the priest lifted up, was not able to forbear, but opening his mouth and turning to the people, he exhorted them not to honour the visible bread as God, which neither was God, nor yet ordained of God to be honoured, &c. For which he was apprehended by the Mayor, and accused to the archbishop of Canterbury, and committed to the Compter, where falling into a sickness, he died. Whose pardon notwithstanding was obtained of the lord Protector, and would have been brought him if he had lived. And thus much concerning Thomas Dobbe.

I find that in the first year of the reign of king Edward, there was one John Hume, servant to Master Lewnax, of Wresel, apprehended, accused, and sent up to the archbishop of Canterbury for these articles:

1. First for denying the sacrament (as it was then called of the altar) to be the real flesh and blood of Christ.

2. For saying that he never would take off his bonnet to it, even if he were to be burned for it.

3. For saying that if he should hear mass, he should be burned.

For this he was sent up by his master and mistress, aforesaid, with special letters to the archbishop, requiring him to be punished by law. But because I find no execution following, I therefore pass over this story.

These things premised, when this virtuous and godly young prince (endued as you have heard with special graces from God) was now peaceably established in his kingdom, and had a council about him, grave, wise, and zealous in God's cause, especially his uncle the duke of Somerset, he then most earnestly desired, as well the advancement of the true honour of Almighty God, and the planting of his sincere religion, as also the utter suppression and extirpation of all idolatry, superstition, hypocrisy, and other enormities and abuses, throughout his realms and dominions: and therefore following, as is before expressed, the good example of king Josiah, he determined forthwith to enter into some reformation of religion in the church of England.

And as at his first entry, (notwithstanding his father's good beginning in abolishing the usurped power of antichrist,) he yet found most of his laws greatly against this zealous enterprise; he therefore purposed by the advice of his wise and honourable council, and of his own regal power and authority, somewhat to prosecute his godly purpose, until such time as by the consent of the whole estate of parliament he might establish a more free, perfect, and uniform order therein.

Whereupon, intending first a general visitation over all bishoprics within his realm, to redress the abuses in the same, he chose out certain wise, learned, discreet, and worshipful personages to be his commissioners in that behalf, and so dividing them into several companies, assigned to them several dioceses to visit; appointing likewise to every company one or two godly learned preachers, who at every session should in their preaching both instruct the people in the true doctrine of the gospel of Christ, and in all love and obedience to it, and also earnestly warn them against their old superstition and wonted idolatry. And that they might be more orderly directed in this commission, there were delivered to them certain injunctions and ecclesiastical orders drawn out by the king's learned council, which they should both inquire of, and also command in his majesty's behalf to be thenceforth observed by every person, to whom they severally appertained within their circuits.

In which it was first enjoined, that all ecclesiastical persons should themselves observe, and cause to be observed by others, all such statutes as were made for the abolishing of the bishop of Rome's usurped power, and establishing of the king's supreme authority, and that they should every one, four times in the year at least, in their public sermons declare to the people, that the one, being most arrogantly usurped against the word of God, was now justly taken away, and the other was to be obeyed of all his grace's subjects.

And again, that every ecclesiastical person, having a cure, should preach, or cause to be preached within their several cures, one sermon every quarter of a year. In which they should sincerely set forth the word of God, and exhort the people to the works of faith and mercy prescribed in the scriptures, and not to works devised by man's imagination, as going on pilgrimages and otherlike idolatrous superstitions, which they should also to the utmost of their power reprove and speak against, declaring that all grace and goodness ought only to be sought for at God's hand, and not at any other creature's; and that they should not only forthwith take down and destroy all such images as had been heretofore abused by pilgrimage or offerings within their cures; but also should not thenceforth suffer any lights or other idolatrous oblation to be made or set up before any image that was yet suffered in the church.

Also that every holy-day (having no sermon in their church) they should immediately after the gospel distinctly read in the pulpit the Lord's Prayer, the Belief, and the Ten Commandments in the English tongue, exhorting the people not only to learn them, but also to teach them to their children and families, and also should charge all parents and governors of households, to bring up their youth in some good exercise or occupation, whereby they might afterwards serve the commonwealth, and not run about like vagabonds and idle loiterers, and thereby incur the danger of the laws.

And furthermore, that persons, having a cure, should see the holy sacraments of Christ reverently administered within their cures, and that if any of them (by special licence or other cases expressed in the statutes of this realm) should be at any time absent from their benefices, that then they should leave in their rooms some godly, learned, and discreet curate, that was able to instruct the people in all truth and godliness, not seeking themselves, but rather the profit of their flock.

And likewise, that they should see provided and set up in some most convenient and open place in every church, one great Bible in English, and one book of the paraphrases of Erasmus upon the gospels, both in English, that the people might reverently, without any argument or contention, read and hear the same at such times as they chose, and not to be prohibited by the parson and curate, but rather to be the more encouraged thereto.

And that the parsons and curates should not at any time (but for necessary causes) haunt any tavern or alehouse; neither should spend their time idly in unlawful games; but at every convenient leisure should give themselves to the reading or hearing of the holy scriptures.

Moreover, that in the time of confession, in every period of Lent, they should examine their parishioners, whether they could say the Lord's Prayer, the Ten Commandments, and the articles of the christian faith; and that if they could not, they should then reprove them, declaring further to them, that they ought not to presume to come to the Lord's table, without the true knowledge thereof, and earnest desire to fulfil them.

Also, that they should not admit any man to preach within their cures, but such as were lawfully licensed; and that those who had at any time before extolled and praised any idolatrous pilgrimage, or other superstition, should now openly recant before the people.

And if there were any open hinderer or disturber of the reading or preaching of the word of God within their parishes, that then they should forthwith bring the same unto the king's council, or to some justice of peace.

And further, that learning and knowledge might be

the better maintained, it was also ordained, that every beneficed person that could yearly spend twenty pounds or upwards, and was not resident upon their cures, should pay, towards the relief of the poor within their parish every year, the fortieth part of their fruits and profits; and likewise that every such as could spend one hundred pounds yearly, or more, should for every hundred pounds give a competent exhibition to some poor scholar within one of the universities of Oxford or Cambridge, or else in some other grammar-school of the realm.

And also that every priest, being under the degree of a bachelor of divinity, should have of his own one New Testament in English and Latin, with the paraphrases of Erasmus upon the same, and should diligently read and study it, and should collect and keep in memory all such comfortable places of the scriptures, as set forth the mercy, benefits, and goodness of Almighty God towards all penitent and believing persons, that they might comfort their flock in all danger of death, despair, or trouble of conscience; and that therefore every bishop in their visitations should from time to time try and examine them how they had profited in their studies.

And although the mass was then still by the law retained, yet was it enjoined, that at every high mass the sayer or singer should openly and distinctly read the gospel and the epistle in English, in the pulpit, or in some other convenient place that the people might hear. And in like place and manner should read every holy-day and Sunday, at matins, one chapter of the New Testament in English, omitting three of their nine Latin lessons, with their responds; and at even-song likewise, immediately after Magnificat, one chapter of the Old Testament instead of their wonted responds and memories.

Furthermore, because of the vain contentions that often fall among the people for going on procession, it was ordained, that thenceforth the priest and clerks should kneel in the midst of the church, and there distinctly sing or read the Litany in English, set forth by the authority of King Henry VIII., and that no person should depart out of the church in the time of reading the Scripture or the Litany, or during the time of any sermon, without just and urgent cause.

Likewise that the people should spend the holy-days in hearing the word of God; in private and public prayers; in acknowledging their offences unto God, and amendment of the same; in reconciling themselves charitably to their neighbours where displeasure has been given; in often receiving the communion of the body and blood of Christ; in visiting the poor and sick, and in all sober and godly conversation; and not in vanity, idleness, or drunkenness; neither yet in any bodily labour, otherwise than in the time of harvest, to save the fruits of the earth, if necessity so required; and that no curate should admit to the receiving of the holy communion any person who had maliciously and openly contended with his neighbours, unless he first openly reconciled himself again, and remitted all rancour and malice whatever.

Moreover, it was ordained that every dean, archdeacon, master of collegiate church, or hospital, and prebendary, being a priest, should himself personally preach twice every year at least, in some such place where he had jurisdiction and living; and that they and all other curates should teach the people, that no man of any private affection ought maliciously to violate any ceremony in the church, then not abrogated by the king's authority; so likewise they ought not on the other side to use them superstitiously or idolatrously, in attributing to them remission of sins, driving away of evil spirits, and other such like dreams and fancies of men, or else in putting any confidence of salvation in them. And further that they should utterly take away and destroy all shrines and monuments of feigned miracles, pilgrimages, and other idolatrous superstition, as well in their churches, as within their private houses.

Also that they should see provided within their churches a strong and fit chest for the safe keeping of the people's alms given towards the relief of the poor, and

that the curates should earnestly exhort and entreat their parishioners (especially at the making of their wills) that as they had been therefore willing to bestow much of their substance upon vain, superstitious, and blind devotions contrary to God's word, so now they would be much more ready to give some portion to their poor and needy brethren, knowing the same to be not only commanded in the word of God, but also promised to be rewarded. And for the better relief of the poor, it was also appointed that all money and profits arising upon fraternities, images, or given to the finding of idolatrous lights, should be converted to the same use. Last of all, for the want of learned curates, and other good preachers, it was enjoined that the curates (having no sermon) should every Sunday read to the people in their churches one of the homilies which should be shortly set forth for that purpose by the king's authority.

There were also other articles in the injunctions appointed for comeliness and due order in the churches; as for repairing of chancels, and priests' houses; for keeping of a register book of weddings, christenings, and burials; for reading of these injunctions every quarter; for due paying of tithes; for forbidding of any other alteration of service in the church, or fasting days; for making of comely pulpits for the preachers; for avoiding of simony in buying and selling of benefices; for the charitable using of priests; for praying only upon the English and Latin primers set forth by King Henry VIII.; for the teaching of grammar in the common schools; and lastly, that the chantry priests should teach young children either to write and read, or else some other good and profitable exercises.

Besides the general injunctions for the whole estate of the realm, there were also others particularly appointed for the bishops, which being delivered to the commissioners were likewise at their visitations committed to the bishops, with charge to be inviolably observed and kept upon pain of the king's majesty's displeasure; the effect whereof is as in manner following:

First, that they should to the uttermost of their wit and understanding see and cause all the king's injunctions in their diocese duly, faithfully, and truly to be kept and observed, and that they should personally preach within their diocese, at least once in every quarter of a year; that is to say, once in their cathedral churches, and thrice in several other places of their dioceses, as they should see it most convenient and necessary, except they had a reasonable excuse to the contrary. Likewise, that they should not retain in their service or household any chaplain, but such as were learned, or able to preach the word of God.

Moreover, that they should not give orders to any person, but such as were learned in the holy scriptures; neither should they refuse orders to them that were learned in the same, being of honest conversation and living. And lastly, that they should not at any time or place preach, or set forth to the people any doctrine contrary to the king's highness' homilies, neither yet should admit or give licence to any to preach within their diocese, but to such as they should know (or at least assuredly trust) would do the same. And if at any time by hearing, or by report reproved, they should perceive the contrary, they then should not only prohibit that person so offending, but also punish him and revoke his licence.

Now, during the time that the commissioners were occupied abroad in their circuits about the speedy and diligent execution of these godly and zealous orders and decrees of the king and his council, his majesty (with the advice of the same) yet still desiring a further reformation as well in religion, as also in his civil government, appointed a parliament of the three estates of his realm to be summoned to meet on the fourth day of November, in the first year of his reign, (A.D. 1547,) which continued to the twenty-fourth day of December. In which session, forasmuch as his highness desired the governance and order of his people to be in perfect unity and concord in all things, and especially in the true faith and religion of God, and therewith also duly weighed the great danger that his loving subjects were in for confessing the gospel of Christ, through many cruel statutes made by his predecessors against the same, (which, being still left in force, might both cause the obstinate to contemn his grace's godly proceedings, and also the weak to be fearful of their christian-like profession,) he therefore caused it, among other things, by the authority of the same parliament to be enacted, That all acts of parliament and statutes touching, mentioning, or in any wise concerning religion or opinions, that is to say, as well the statute made in the first year of the reign of King Richard II.; and the statute made in the second year of the reign of King Henry V.; and the statute made in the five-and-twentieth year of the reign of King Henry VIII., concerning punishment and reformation of heretics and Lollards, and every provision therein contained; and the statutes made for the abolishing of diversity of opinions in certain articles concerning christian religion, commonly called the Six Articles, made in the one-and-thirtieth year of the reign of King Henry VIII.; and also the statute made in the parliament begun the sixteenth day of January in the three-and-thirtieth year of the reign of the said King Henry VIII., and afterwards prorogued unto the one-and-twentieth day of January in the four-and-thirtieth year of his said reign, touching, mentioning, or in any wise concerning books of the Old and New Testament in English, and the printing, uttering, selling, giving, or delivering of books or writings, and retaining of English books or writings, and reading, preaching, teaching, or expounding the scriptures, or in anywise touching, mentioning, or concerning any of the said matters; and also one other statute made in the five-and-thirtieth year of the reign of the said king Henry the Eighth, concerning the qualification of the statute of the six articles; and all and every other act or acts of parliament, concerning doctrine or matters of religion, and all and every branch, article, sentence, matter, pains, or forfeitures contained, mentioned, or in anywise declared in any of the same acts and statutes, should from thenceforth be utterly repealed, made void, and of none effect.

By occasion of this, all his godly subjects, then abiding within the realm, had free liberty publicly to profess the gospel; and many learned and zealous preachers, before banished, were now not only licensed freely to return home again, but also encouraged boldly and faithfully to travel in their function and calling; so that God was much glorified, and the people in many places greatly edified.

Moreover, in the same session his majesty, with the lords spiritual and temporal, and the commons in the same parliament assembled, thoroughly understanding by the judgment of the best learned, that it was more agreeable to the first institution of the sacrament of the most precious body and blood of our Saviour Christ, and also more conformable to the common use and practice, both of the apostles and of the primitive church, for the space of five hundred years and more after Christ's ascension, that the holy sacrament should be administered to all christian people under both kinds, of bread and wine, than under the form of bread only; and also that it was more agreeable to the first institution of Christ, and the usage of the apostles and primitive church, that the people being present should receive the same with the priest, than that the priest should receive it alone; did, by their authority, enact, that the holy sacrament should be from thenceforth commonly delivered and administered to the people, throughout the churches of England and Ireland, and other the king's dominions, under both kinds of bread and wine, except necessity otherwise required: and also the priest, who should administer the same, should, at least one day before, exhort all persons who should be present, to prepare themselves to receive the same. And at the day prefixed, after some godly exhortation made by the minister, wherein should be further expressed the benefit and comfort promised to them who worthily receive this holy sacrament, and the danger and indignation of God threatened to them which presume to receive the same unworthily to the end that every man might try and examine his own conscience before he should

come to it; the minister should not, without a lawful cause, refuse it to any one person that would devoutly and humbly desire it.

After this consent of the parliament, the king being no less desirous to have the form of administration of the sacrament truly reduced to the right rule of the scriptures and the first use of the primitive church, than he was to establish the same by the authority of his own regal laws; he appointed certain of the most grave and best learned bishops, and others of his realm, to assemble together at his castle of Windsor, and there to argue and treat upon this matter, and to conclude and set forth one perfect uniform order according to the rule and use aforesaid.

And in the meantime, while the learned were thus occupied about their conferences, the lord protector and the rest of the king's council, further remembering that the time of the year then approached, wherein were practised many superstitious abuses and blasphemous ceremonies against the glory of God, and the truth of his word; they determined the utter abolishing thereof, and directed their letters to Cranmer, then archbishop of Canterbury, and metropolitan of England, requiring him that he should command every bishop within his province, forthwith to charge all the curates of their dioceses, that neither candles should be any more borne upon Candlemas day, nor yet ashes used in Lent, nor palms upon Palm Sunday.

Whereupon the archbishop, zealously favouring the good and christian-like purpose of the king and his council, immediately wrote to all the rest of the bishops of that province, and among them to Edmund Bonner, then bishop of London. Of whose rebellious and obstinate contumacy as we have hereafter more to say, I shall not now speak, but only by the way note his former dissimulation and cloaked hypocrisy, in outwardly consenting as well to this, as also to all the king's proceedings; but whether for fear or for any other subtle pretence I know not.

About the same period report was made to the lords of the council, that great contention and strife daily arose among the common people in various parts of this realm, for the pulling down and taking away of such images out of the churches, as had been idolatrously abused by pilgrimages, offerings, or otherwise, some affirming that one image was abused, others another, and most that neither of them was abused; so that if speedy remedy were not had, it might turn to further inconvenience. Wherefore, thinking it best, for avoiding of discord and tumult, that all manner of images should be clean taken out of all churches, and none suffered to remain, they again wrote their letters to the archbishop of Canterbury, requiring his ready aid in manner following:—

Letter of the Council sent to the Archbishop of Canterbury, for the abolishing of Images.

" After our right hearty commendations to your good lordship: whereas now of late in the king's majesty's visitations, among other godly injunctions commanded to be generally observed through all parts of this his highness's realm, one was set forth for the taking down of all such images as had at any time been abused with pilgrimages, offerings, or censings; albeit that this said injunction hath in many parts of this realm been quietly obeyed and executed, yet in many other places much strife and contention hath arisen and daily ariseth, and more and more increaseth about the execution of the same; some men being so superstitious, or rather wilful, as they would by their good will retain all such images still, although they have been most manifestly abused. And in some places also the images which by the said injunctions were taken down, are now restored and set up again; and almost in every place is contention for images, whether they have been abused or not. And while these men go on both sides, contending whether this or that image hath been offered unto, kissed, censed, or otherwise abused, proceedings have in some places taken place in such sort, as further inconveniences are like to ensue, if remedy be not found in time. Considering therefore, that almost in no place of this realm is any sure quietness, but where all images are clean taken away and pulled down already, to the intent that all contention in every part of the realm for this matter, may be put down, and that the lively image of Christ should not contend for the dead images, which are things not necessary, and without which the churches of Christ continued most godly for many years; we have thought good to signify unto you, that his highness's pleasure, with the advice and consent of us the lord protector, and the rest of the council, is, that immediately upon the sight hereof, with as convenient diligence as you may, you shall not only give orders that all the images remaining in any church or chapel within your diocese, be removed and taken away, but also by your letters signify unto the rest of the bishops within your province, his highness's pleasure, for the like order to be given by them and every one of them within their several dioceses. And in the execution hereof, we require both you and the rest of the said bishops to use such foresight as that the same may be quietly done, with as good satisfaction of the people as may be. Thus fare your good lordship heartily well.

"From Somerset-place, the 11th February, 1548."

When the archbishop had received these letters, he forthwith directed his precept to Bonner, bishop of London, requiring, and in the king's name commanding him, that with all speed he should as well give in charge unto the rest of the bishops within the province of Canterbury, to look immediately without delay to the diligent and careful execution of the contents of the letter through all parts of the diocese; as also that he himself should do the like within his own city and diocese of London. Whereupon he seeming then, with like outward consent as before, to allow these doings, presently (by virtue of the precept) did send out his mandate as well to the rest of the bishops, as also again to the bishop of Westminster.

By the time that these things were thus determined, the learned men whom the king had appointed to assemble together for the true and right manner of administering the sacrament of the body and blood of Christ according to the rule of the scriptures of God, and the first usage of the primitive church; they after their long, learned, wise, and deliberate counsels, finally concluded and agreed upon one godly and uniform order, not much differing from the manner at present used and authorized within this realm and church of England, commonly called The Communion. Which agreement being exhibited to the king, and most gladly accepted, was publicly printed, and by his majesty's council sent to every bishop of the realm; requiring and commanding them by letters on the king's majesty's behalf, that both they in their own persons should forthwith pay diligent and careful respect to the due execution thereof, and also should with all diligence cause the books which they then sent them, to be delivered to every parson, vicar, and curate within their diocese, that they likewise might well and sufficiently qualify themselves for the better distribution of the communion (according to the tenor of the book) against the feast of Easter then next ensuing, as more fully appears by their letters here following:—

Letters missive from the Council to the Bishops of the Realm, concerning the Communion to be administered in both kinds.

"After our most hearty commendations unto your lordship, whereas in the parliament lately holden at Westminster, it was amongst other things most godly established, that according to the first institution and use of the primitive church, the most holy sacrament of the body and blood of our Saviour Jesus Christ should be distributed to the people under the kinds of bread and wine; according to the effect whereof the king's majesty, minding, with the advice and consent of the lord protector's grace, and the rest of the council, to have the said statute well executed in such sort, or like as is agreeable with the word of God (so the same may be also faithfully and reverently received of his most loving

subjects, to their comfort and well-doing) hath caused sundry of his majesty's most grave and well-learned prelates, and other learned men in the scriptures, to assemble themselves for this matter: who, after long conference together, have, with deliberate advice, finally agreed upon such an order to be used in all places of the king's majesty's dominions in the distribution of the said most holy sacrament, as may appear to you by the book thereof, which we send herewith unto you. Knowing your lordship's knowledge in the scriptures, and earnest good will and zeal to the setting forth of all things according to the truth thereof, we are well-assured, you will of your own good will, and out of respect to your duty, diligently set forth this most godly order here agreed upon, and commanded to be used by the authority of the king's majesty: yet remembering the crafty practice of the devil, who ceases not to work, by all ways and means, the hindrance of all godliness; and considering furthermore, that a great number of the curates of the realm, either for lack of knowledge cannot, or for want of good mind will not, be so ready to set forth the same, as we would wish, and as the importance of the matter and their own bounden duties requires, we have thought good to pray and require your lordship, and nevertheless, in the king's majesty's our most dread Lord's name, to command you to have an earnest diligence and careful respect both in your own person, and by all your officers and ministers also, to cause these books to be delivered to every parson, vicar, and curate within your diocese, with such diligence as that they may have sufficient time well to instruct and advise themselves, for the distribution of the most holy communion, according to the order of this book, before this Easter time, and that they may, by your good means, be well directed to use such good, gentle, and charitable instruction of their simple and unlearned parishioners, as may be to all their good satisfaction as much as may be; praying you to consider, that this order is set forth to the intent there should be in all parts of the realm, and among all men, one uniform manner quietly used. The execution whereof, like as it shall stand very much in the diligence of you and others of your vocation; so do we forthwith require you to have a diligent respect thereunto, as ye tender the king's majesty's pleasure, and will answer for the contrary. And thus we bid your lordship right heartily farewell. From Westminster, the thirteenth of March, 1548."

By means of this letter, and the godly order of the learned, and also of the statute and act of parliament before mentioned, all private blasphemous masses were now by just authority fully abolished throughout this realm of England, and the right use of the sacrament of the most precious body and blood of our Saviour Jesus Christ truly restored instead of them. But, nevertheless, as at no time can any thing be so well done by the godly, but that the wicked will find some means subtlely to deface it; so at this time, through the perverse obstinacy and dissembling frowardness of many of the inferior priests and ministers of the cathedral, and other churches of this realm, there arose a marvellous schism and variety of fashions in celebrating the common service and administration of the sacraments, and other rites and ceremonies of the church. For some, zealously allowing the king's proceedings, gladly followed the order; and others, though not so willingly admitting them, yet dissembling, used some part of them; but many, carelessly contemning all, would still exercise their old accustomed popery.

Whereof the king and his council having good intelligence, and fearing the great inconveniences and dangers that might happen through this division, and being loath to use any great severity towards his subjects, but rather desirous, by some quiet and godly order to bring them to some conformity, did, by their prudent counsel again appoint the archbishop of Canterbury, with certain of the best learned and discreet bishops and other learned men, diligently to consider and ponder the premises: and thereupon, having as well an eye and respect to the most sincere and pure christian religion taught by the holy scriptures, as also to the usages of the primitive church, to draw and make one convenient and meet order, rite, and fashion of Common Prayer, and administration of the sacraments, to be had and used within this realm of England, and the dominions of the same. Who, after most godly and learned conferences, through the aid of the Holy Ghost, with one uniform agreement concluded, set forth, and delivered to the king's highness, a book in English, entitled, "A Book of the Common Prayer and Administration of the Sacraments, and other Rites and Ceremonies of the Church, after the use of the Church of England." Which his highness receiving, with great comfort and quietness of mind, forthwith exhibited to the lords and commons of the parliament then assembled at Westminster, about the fourth of November, in the second year of his reign, and in the year 1548, and continuing to the fourteenth day of March, then next ensuing.

Whereupon, the lords spiritual and temporal, and the commons of the parliament assembled, well and thoroughly considering, as well the most godly concern of the king's highness, of the lord protector, and other of his majesty's council, in gathering together the archbishops, bishops, and other learned men, as the godly prayers, orders, rites, and ceremonies in the said book mentioned, with the consideration of altering those things which were altered, and retaining those things which were retained in the book; as also the honour of God, and great quietness, which, by the grace of God, should ensue upon that one and uniform rite and order in such common prayer, rites, and ceremonies to be used throughout England, Wales, Calais, and the Marches of the same: they first gave to his highness most lowly and hearty thanks for the same, and then most humbly prayed him that it might be ordained and enacted by his majesty with the assent of the lords and commons in that parliament assembled, and by the authority of the same, That not only every person and persons who had offended concerning the premises (other than such as were then remaining in ward in the Tower of London, or in the Fleet) might be pardoned, but also that all and singular the ministers in any cathedral, or parish churches, or other places within the realm of England, Wales, Calais, and the Marches of the same, or other the king's dominions, should from and after the feast of Pentecost next coming, be bound to say and use each of the matins, evensong, celebration of the Lord's Supper, and administration of the sacraments, and all other common and public prayers, in such order and form as was mentioned in the book, and none otherwise. And although they were so godly and good, that they gave occasion to every honest and conformable man most willingly to embrace them; yet, lest any obstinate persons, who willingly would disturb so godly an order and quiet in this realm, should go unpunished; they further requested, That it might be ordained and enacted by the authority aforesaid, that if any manner of parson, vicar, or other minister whatever, that ought or should say or sing Common Prayer, mentioned in the book, or administer the sacraments, should, after the feast of Pentecost, then next coming, refuse to use the Common Prayer, or to administer the sacraments in such cathedral or parish churches, or other places, as he should use or minister the same, in such order and form as they were mentioned, and set forth in the book; or should use wilfully, and obstinately standing in the same, any other rite, ceremony, order, form, or manner of mass, openly or privily, or matins, evensong, administration of the sacraments, or other public prayer than was mentioned and set forth in the said book; or should preach, declare, or speak any thing in derogation or discredit of the said book, or any thing therein contained, or of any part thereof, and should be thereof lawfully convicted according to the laws of this realm by verdict of twelve men, or by his own confession, or by the notorious evidence of the fact, should lose and forfeit, unto the king's highness, his heirs and successors, for his first offence one whole year's profit of such one of his benefices or spiritual promotions, as it should please the king's highness to assign and appoint; and also for the

same offence should suffer imprisonment for six months without bail or mainprize. But if any such person, after his first conviction, should soon offend again, and be lawfully convicted, then he should, for his second offence, suffer imprisonment for one whole year, and should also be deprived, ipso facto, of all his spiritual promotions for ever, so that it should be lawful for the patrons and donors to give the same again unto any other learned man, in like manner as if the party so offending were dead. And if any person or persons should offend a third time, and be lawfully convicted, then he should, for the same third offence, suffer imprisonment during his life. If any such person or persons aforesaid, so offending, had not any benefice or spiritual promotion, that then he should for his first offence suffer imprisonment for six months without bail or mainprize; and for his second offence, imprisonment during life. Which request, or rather actual agreement of the lords and commons of the parliament, being once understood of the king, was also soon ratified and confirmed by his regal consent and authority, and thereupon the book of Common Prayer was presently printed, and commanded to be used throughout the whole realm and dominion, according to the tenor and effect of the statute.

Moreover, in the same session of the said parliament, it was enacted and established by the authority thereof, That, for as much as great, horrible, and unspeakable inconveniences had, from time to time, arisen amongst the priests, ministers, and other officers of the clergy, through their compelled chastity, and by such laws as prohibited them the godly and lawful use of marriage, that therefore all and every law and laws positive, canons, constitutions, and ordinances heretofore made by the authority of man only, which did prohibit or forbid marriage to any ecclesiastical or spiritual person or persons, of what estate, condition, or degree soever they were, or by what name or names they were called, which by God's law may lawfully marry, in all and every article, branch, and sentence concerning only the prohibition of the marriage of the persons aforesaid, should be utterly void and of none effect. And that all manner of forfeitures, pains, penalties, crimes, or actions, which were in the laws contained, and of the same did follow, concerning the prohibition of the marriage of the ecclesiastical persons, should be thenceforth also clearly and utterly void. By occasion of which, it was thence after lawful for any ecclesiastical person most godly to live in the pure and holy estate of matrimony according to the laws and word of God.

But if the first injunctions, statutes, and decrees of the prince were by many but slenderly regarded, with much less good affection were these (especially the book of Common Prayer) now received by several; yea, and that by some who had always before in outward show willingly allowed the former doings, as appears plainly by Bonner the bishop of London. Who although, by his former letters, and other mandates, he seemed to favour all the king's proceedings; yet did he (notwithstanding both the statute for the establishing of the communion, and the abolishing of all private masses, and also this statute of the ratifying and confirming of the book of Common Prayer) still suffer sundry idolatrous private masses of peculiar names (as the Apostles' mass, the Lady mass, and such like) to be daily solemnly sung within certain peculiar chapels of the cathedral church of St. Paul's, cloaking them with the names of the Apostles' communion, and our Lady's communion, not once finding any fault with them, until such time as the lords of the council were obliged by their letters to command and charge him to look better thereunto.

Over and besides all this, the lord protector, with the rest of the king's privy and learned council assembling together in the Star Chamber; for the advancement of the king's godly proceedings, called before them all the justices of peace, where was pronounced to them, by the lord Rich, then lord chancellor, an eloquent and learned admonition, requiring them to see to the due execution of the king's laws.

It is apparent from these acts what zealous care was in this young king, and in the lord protector, concerning the reformation of Christ's church, by these injunctions, letters, precepts, and exhortations. By which we have to note, not so much the careful diligence of the king and his learned council; as the lingering slackness of justices and lawyers, but especially of bishops, and old popish curates, by whose cloaked contempt, wilful connivance, and stubborn disobedience, the book of the common prayer, long after its publication, was either not known at all, or else very irreverently used through many places of the realm. When the king, by the complaint of several persons, perfectly understood this, he was not a little grieved to see the godly agreement of the learned, and the willing consent of the parliament, and his grace's own zealous desire having so little effect among his subjects; he therefore decreed, with the advice of his whole council, to write again to all the bishops of his realm, for speedy and diligent redress in this matter: commanding them that they themselves should have a more special regard to the execution of his wishes, and also that all others, within their several precincts and jurisdictions, should by their good instructions and example be the more frequently and with the better devotion, moved to use and frequent the same; as further appears by the ensuing letter:—

A Letter directed by the King, and his Council, to Bonner, Bishop of London.

"Right reverend father in God, right trusty and well-beloved, we greet you well: and whereas after great and serious debating and long conference of the bishops and other grave and well-learned men in the holy scriptures, one uniform order for common prayers and administration of the sacraments hath been, and is most godly set forth, not only by the common agreement and full assent of the nobility and commons of the late session of our late parliament, but also by the like assent of the bishops in the same parliament, and of all other the learned men of this our realm in their synods and convocations provincial: as it was much to our comfort, to understand the godly labour then taken diligently and willingly for the true opening of things mentioned in the said book, whereby the true service and honour of Almighty God, and the right ministration of the sacraments being well and sincerely set forth, according to the scriptures and use of the primitive church, much idolatry, vain superstition, and great and slanderous abuses were taken away: so it is no small occasion of sorrow to us, to understand by the complaints of many, that our said book, so much laboured for, and also sincerely set forth, remaineth in many places of this our realm, either not known at all, or not used, or at the least if it be used, very seldom, and that in such light and irreverent sort, as the people in many places either have heard nothing, or if they hear, they neither understand, nor have that spiritual delight in the same, that to good Christians appertaineth. The fault whereof, as we must of reason impute to you and other of your vocation, called by God, through our appointment, to due respect to this and such like matters; so considering that by these and such like occasions, our loving subjects remain yet still in their blindness and superstitious errors, and in some places in as irreligious forgetfulness of God, whereby his wrath may be provoked upon us and them; and remembering withal, that amongst other cures committed to our princely charge, we think this the greatest, to see the glory and true service of Him maintained and extolled, by whose clemency we acknowledge ourselves to have all that we have, we could not but, by advice and consent of our dearest uncle, Edward Duke of Somerset, governor of our person, and protector of our realm, dominions, and subjects, and the rest of our privy council, admonish you of the premises. Wherein, as it had been your office to have used an earnest diligence, and to have preferred the same in all places within your diocese, as the case required; so have we thought good to pray and require you, and nevertheless straightly to charge and command you, that from henceforth ye have an earnest and special regard to reduce these things, so as the curates may do their duties

more often and in more reverent sort, and the people be occasioned, by the good advices and examples of yourself, your chancellor, archdeacons, and other inferior ministers, to come oftener and with more devotion to their said common prayers, to give thanks to God, and to be partakers of the most holy communion. Wherein by showing yourself diligent, and giving good example in your own person, you shall both discharge your duty to the great Pastor, to whom we all have to account, and also do us good service: and on the other side, if we shall hereafter (these our letters and commandments notwithstanding) hear complaint, and find the like fault in your diocese, we shall have just cause to impute the fault thereof, and of all that ensueth thereof, to you, and consequently be occasioned thereby to see otherwise to the redress of these things; whereof we would be sorry. And therefore we do charge and command you, upon your allegiance, to look well upon your duty herein, as you respect our pleasure.

"Given under our signet at our manor of Richmond, the three and twentieth day of July, the third year of our reign, 1549."

The bishop of London, among the rest of the bishops, receiving these letters, did (as before) in outward shew willingly accept them; and therefore immediately with the said letters directed the following precept unto the dean and chapter of his cathedral church of St. Paul's, commanding them to look to the due accomplishing thereof accordingly.

A Letter of Bonner, to the Dean and Chapter of St. Paul's.

"Edmund by the grace of God, &c. To my well beloved brethren the dean and chapter of the cathedral church of St. Paul in London, and to the other ministers there and every of them, do send greeting. And whereas of late I have received letters of our sovereign lord the king, of such tenor as is hereunto annexed, and according to my most bounden duty am right well willing, and desiring that the said letters should be in all points duly executed and observed according to the tenor and purport of the same, as appertaineth: These, therefore, are to require, and also straightly to charge you and every of you on his majesty's behalf, &c., that you do admonish and command, or cause to be admonished or commanded, all and singular parsons, vicars, and curates, of your jurisdiction, to observe and accomplish the same from time to time accordingly; furthermore requiring and likewise charging you, and every of you, to make certificate herein to me, my chancellor or other my officers in this behalf, with such convenient celerity as appertaineth, both of your proceedings in the execution hereof, and also the persons and names of all such as from henceforth shall be found negligent in doing their duties in the premises, or any of them.

"Given at my house at Fulham, the 26th day of July, in the year of our Lord, 1549, and in the third year of his majesty's reign."

Moreover, as the king at this time hearing the muttering of rebellion then stirring, (whereof more shall hereafter be said,) and also being credibly informed that, through the evil example, slackness of preaching, and administering the sacraments, and careless contempt of bishop Bonner, not only many of the people within the city of London, and other places of his diocese, were very negligent and forgetful of their duties to God, in frequenting the divine service then established and set forth by the authority of parliament; but also that others, utterly despising it, did in secret places of his diocese often frequent the popish mass, and other foreign rites not allowed by the laws of this realm, therefore the king thought it good to appoint the lord protector and the rest of his privy council to call the bishop before them, and to deal with him according to their wise and discreet judgment.

Upon the 11th of August, 1549, they sent a messenger for him, and upon his appearance made declaration of such informations and complaints as had been brought against him. And then, after sharp admonitions and reproofs for his evil demeanours, they delivered to him, from the king, (for his better reformation and amendment), certain private injunctions to be followed and observed by himself. And as, in the first branch of the injunctions, he was personally assigned to preach at St. Paul's Cross on Sunday come three weeks then next ensuing, (because both the dangerous and fickle state of the times, and also partly his own suspicious behaviour so required,) they further delivered to him in writing such articles to treat upon in his sermon, as they thought then most meet and necessary for the time. All which injunctions and articles I here insert :—

Certain private Injunctions and Articles given to Bonner by the Council.

" Forasmuch as we are advertised, that among other disorders of our subjects at this present time, there are several in our city of London, and other places within your diocese, who being very negligent and forgetful of their duty to Almighty God, from whom all good things are to be looked for, do assemble themselves very seldom, and fewer times than they were heretofore accustomed, to common prayer, and to the holy communion (being now a time when it is more needful with heart and mind to pray to our heavenly Father for his aid and succour,) and for which we are right sorry: so we understand that through your evil example, and the slackness of your preaching and instructing of our people to do their duties, this offence to God is most generally committed. For where heretofore upon all principal feasts, and such as were called *majus duplex*, you yourself were wont to execute in person, now since the time that we by the advice of our whole parliament have set a most godly and devout order in our church of England and Ireland, ye have very seldom or never executed upon such other days, to the contempt of our proceedings, and evil example of others. And forasmuch as it is also brought to our knowledge, that many, as well in London as in other places of your diocese, frequent and haunt foreign rites of masses, and such as are not allowed by the orders of our realm, and contemn and forbear to praise and laud God, and pray after such rites and ceremonies, as in this realm are approved and set out by our authority; and further, that adultery and fornication is maintained and kept openly and commonly in the city of London, and other places of your diocese, whereby the wrath of God is provoked against our people; of which things you being heretofore admonished, yet hitherto have made no redress, as to the pastoral office, authority and cure of a bishop appertains. We, therefore, to whom the supreme cure and charge of this church appertains, to avert from us the high indignation of Almighty God, by the advice of our most entirely beloved uncle the lord protector, and the rest of our privy council, have thought it no less than our most bounden duty, peremptorily to admonish, charge, and warn you, that you most strictly look upon the premises, and see them so reformed that there may appear no negligence on your behalf, upon such pain as by our laws ecclesiastical and temporal we may inflict upon you, to deprivation or otherwise, as shall seem to us reasonable, according to the offence. And to the intent you should the better see to the reformation of the said abuses, we have thought good to give you these injunctions following :—

" 1. Ye shall preach at St. Paul's Cross, in London, in proper person, on Sunday come three weeks from the date hereof, and in the same sermon declare and set forth the articles hereunto annexed; and ye shall preach hereafter once every quarter of the year there, exhorting in your sermon the people to obedience, prayer, and godly living; and ye shall be present at every sermon hereafter made at St. Paul's cross, if sickness or some other reasonable cause do not hinder you.

" 2. You yourself in person shall from henceforth on every day which heretofore was accounted in this church of England a principal feast, or *Majus duplex*, and at all

such times as the bishops of London your predecessors were wont to celebrate and sing high mass, now celebrate and execute the communion at the high altar in St. Paul's, for the better example of all others, except sickness hinder you.

" 3. Ye shall yourself, according to your duty, and the office of a bishop, call before you all such as do not come and frequent the common prayer, and service in the church, or do not come to God's table, and receive the communion at the least once a year, or whoever do frequent or go to any other rite or service than is appointed by our book, either of matins, even-song, or mass, in any church, chapel, or other private places within your diocese; and ye shall see all such offenders brought before you and punished, according to the ecclesiastical laws, with severe and strict punishment. Likewise ye shall see one only order used in your diocese, according to our said book, and none other.

" 4. Ye shall both by yourself, and all your officers under you, search out and bring before you, more diligently than heretofore, (as appertaineth to your office) all adulterers, and see them punished according to the ecclesiastical laws, and the authority given you in that behalf.

" 5. We have heard also complaints, that the church of St. Paul's, and other churches in London are of late more neglected, as well in reparation of the glass, as other buildings and ornaments, than they were heretofore in the city of malice deny the payment of their due tithe to their curates, whereby the curates are both injured and made not so well able, and in a manner discouraged to do their duties. Which thing also our will and commandment is, ye shall diligently look to, and see redressed as appertaineth.

" 6. And for so much as all these complaints are made as most done and committed in London, to the intent you may look more earnestly, better, and more diligently to the reformation of them, our pleasure is that you shall abide and keep residence in your house there, as in the city, see, and principal place of your diocese, and no where else, for a certain time, until you shall be otherwise licensed by us.''

And thus having brought Bishop Bonner home to his own house, we shall there leave him a while to take his ease in his own lodging, till we return to him again, we will in the mean time make a little digression into Cornwall and Devonshire, to relate some part of the disloyal doings of those men against their meek and excellent prince. They were not contented with him, but contrary to all order, reason, nature and loyalty, advanced themselves in a rebellious conspiracy against him, and against his proceedings, through the pernicious instigation of popish priests, who hating the injunctions and godly order of reformation set forward by the king, and especially mourning to see their old popish church of Rome decaying, ceased not by all sinister and subtle means, under God's name and the king's, and under colour of religion, to persuade the people, and to assemble in companies, to gather captains, and at last to burst out in rank rebellion. Neither were there wanting among the lay sort, some as seditiously disposed to rebellion as they to mischief and madness.

Of whom the chief captains were, Humfrey Arundel, governor of St. Michael's Mount, James Rosogan, John Rosogan, John Pain, Thomas Underhill, John Soleman, William Segar. Of priests who were principal stirrers, and some of them governors of the camps, and afterwards executed, there were to the number of eight, whose names were Robert Bochim, John Temson, Roger Baratt, John Wolcock, William Asa, James Mourton, John Barow, Richard Bennet, besides a multitude of other popish priests. The number of those concerned in rebellion, amounted to little less than ten thousand stout traitors.

Their first intent was, after they had spoiled their own districts most miserably, to invade the city of Exeter, and so all other parts of the realm. But they were repulsed from Exeter, and then fell on spoiling and robbing where or whatever they might catch. At length laying their traitorous heads together, they consulted upon certain articles to be sent up. But such difference of opinion prevailed among them, that their plans utterly failed. Some seemed more tolerable. Others altogether unreasonable. Some would have no justice. Some would have no state of gentlemen. The priests ever harped upon one string, namely, to bring in the bishop of Rome into England again.

After much ado, at last, a few articles were agreed upon, to be forwarded to the king.

The Articles of the Commons of Devonshire, and Cornwall, sent to the King.

" 1. Forasmuch as man, except he be born of water and the Holy Ghost, cannot enter into the kingdom of God, and forasmuch as the gates of heaven be not opened without his blessed sacrament and baptism, therefore, we will that our curates shall minister this sacrament at all times of need, as well in the week-days, as on the holydays.

" 2. We will have our children confirmed of the bishop, whenever we shall, within the diocese, resort to him.

" 3. Forasmuch as we constantly believe, that after the priest has spoken the words of consecration being at mass, there celebrating and consecrating the same, there is very really the body and blood of our Saviour Jesus Christ, God and man, and that no substance of bread and wine remaineth after, but the very self same body that was born of the Virgin Mary, and was given upon the cross for our redemption ; therefore we will have mass celebrated as it has been in times past, without any man communicating with the priest ; as many, rudely presuming unworthily to receive the same, put no difference between the Lord's body and other kind of meat ; some saying that it is bread before and after, some saying that it is profitable to no man except he receive it, with many other abusive terms.

" 4. We will have the consecrated host reserved in our churches.

" We will have holy bread and holy water in remembrance of Christ his precious body and blood.

" 5. We will that our priests shall sing, or say with an audible voice God's service in the choir of the parish churches, and not God's service to be set forth like a Christmas play.

" 6. Forsomuch as priests be men dedicated to God, for ministering and celebrating the blessed sacraments and preaching God's word, we will that they shall live chaste without marriage, as St. Paul did, being the elect and chosen vessel of God, saying unto all honest priests, ' Be ye followers of me.'

" We will that the six articles which our sovereign lord king Henry the eighth set forth in his latter days, shall be used and so taken as they were at that time.

" We pray God save king Edward, for we be his, both body and goods."

The Answer sent by the King's Majesty, to certain of his people assembled in Devonshire.

" Although knowledge hath been given to us and our dearest uncle Edward duke of Somerset, governor of our person, and protector of all our realms, dominions and subjects, and to the rest of our privy council, of some assemblies made by you, who ought to be our loving subjects, against all order, law, and otherwise than ever any loving and kind subjects have attempted against their natural and liege sovereign lord ; yet we have thought it meet at this time, not to condemn or reject you, as we might justly do, but to use you as our subjects, thinking that the devil has not that power in you, to make you, of natural born Englishmen, so suddenly become enemies to your own native country ; or, of our subjects to make you traitors ; or under pretence to relieve yourselves, to destroy yourselves, your wives, children, lands, houses, and all other commodities of this your life. This we say, we trust that although ye be seduced by ignorance, ye will not be obstinate upon

knowledge. And though some among you (as ever there will be some tares amongst good wheat) forget God, neglect their prince, esteem not the state of the realm, but as careless, desperate men delight in sedition, tumult and wars ; yet nevertheless, the greater part of you will hear the voice of us your natural prince, and will by wisdom and counsel be warned, and cease your evils in the beginning, whose ends will be, even by Almighty God's order, your own destruction. Wherefore, as to you our subjects, seduced by ignorance, we speak, and are content to use our princely authority, like a father to his children, to admonish you of your faults, not to punish them, to put you in remembrance of your duties, not to avenge your forgetfulness.

" First, As to your disorderly rising in multitudes, and assembling yourselves against other our loving subjects, to array yourselves to war, who amongst you all can answer the same to Almighty God, charging you to obey us in all things ? Or how can any English good heart answer us, our laws, and the rest of our very loving and faithful subjects, who indeed by their obedience make our honour, estate, and degree ?

" Ye use our name in your writings, and abuse the same against ourself. What injury you do us, to call those who love us, to your evil purposes by the authority of our name ! God hath made us your king by his ordinance and providence, by our blood and inheritance, by lawful succession and our coronation ; but not to this end, as you use our name. We are your most natural sovereign lord and king, Edward the Sixth, to rule you, to preserve you, to save you from all your outward enemies, to see our laws well ministered, every man to have his own ; to suppress disorderly people, to punish traitors, thieves, pirates, robbers, and such like, yea, to keep our realms from foreign princes, from the malice of the Scots, of Frenchmen, and of the bishop of Rome. Thus, good subjects, our name is written ; thus it is honoured and obeyed ; this majesty it hath by God's ordinance, and not by man's. So that of this your offence we cannot write too much ; and yet doubt not but this is enough from a prince to all reasonable people, from a king to all kind-hearted and loving subjects, from a puissant king of England to every natural Englishman.

" Your pretences, which you say move you to do these things, and wherewith you seek to excuse this disorder, we assure you, are either all false, or so vain, that we doubt not but, after ye shall understand the truth, ye will all with one voice acknowledge yourselves ignorantly led, and seduced by error ; and if there are any that will not, they are rank traitors, enemies of our crown, seditious people, heretics, papists, or such as care not how they seek to provoke an insurrection, and who cannot become so rich with their own labours, and with peace, as they can do with spoils, with wars, with robberies, and such like ; yea, with the spoil of your own goods, with the living of your labours, the sweat of your bodies, the food of your own households, wives and children. Such they are, for a time, using pleasant persuasions to you, and in the end will cut your throats for your own goods.

You are persuaded that your children, even when necessity requires it, shall not be christened but upon the holydays. How false this is, learn of us. Our book which we have set forth by the free consent of our parliament, in the English tongue, teaching you the contrary, even in the first leaf, yea, the first side of the leaf of that part which treats of baptism. Good subjects, for to others we speak not, look and be not deceived. They who have put this false opinion into your ears, mean not the christening of children, but the destruction of you our christened subjects. Be this known to you, our honour is so much, that we may not be found faulty of our word. Prove it, if by our laws ye may not christen your children upon necessity, every day or hour in the week, then might you be offended ; but seeing you may do it, how can you believe them who teach you the contrary ? What think you do they mean in other things, who move you to break your obedience against us your king and sovereign, upon these false tales and persuasions. Therefore you all who will acknowledge us your sovereign lord, and who will hear the voice of us your natural king, may easily perceive how ye are deceived, and how subtlely traitors and papists with their falsehood, seek to achieve, and bring their purpose to pass. Every traitor will be glad to dissemble his treason, and feed it secretly, every papist his popery, and nourish it inwardly; and in the end, make you, our subjects, partakers of treason and popery, under the pretence of a commonwealth and holiness.

"And how are you seduced by those who put in your heads, that the blessed sacrament of Christ's body does not differ from other common bread? If our laws, proclamations, and statutes, are all to the contrary, why shall any man persuade you against them? We do ourselves in our own heart, our council in all their profession, our laws and statutes in all purposes, our good subjects in all their doings, most highly esteem that sacrament, and use the communion to our comfort. We make so much difference between it and other common bread, that we think no profit of other bread but to maintain our bodies. But of this blessed bread we take it to be the very food of our souls to everlasting life. How think you, good subjects, shall not we being your prince, your lord, your king by God's appointment, more prevail with truth than certain evil persons with open falsehood? Shall any seditious person persuade you that the sacrament is despised, which is by our laws, by ourself, by our council, by all our good subjects, esteemed, used, participated, and daily received? If ever ye were seduced, if ever deceived, if ever traitors were believed, if ever papists poisoned good subjects, it is now. It is not the christening of children, not the reverence of the sacrament, not the health of your souls that they shoot at, good subjects. It is sedition, it is high treason, it is your destruction they seek, how craftily, how piteously, how cunningly soever they do it. With one rule judge ye the end, which must come upon your purposes. Almighty God forbids, upon pain of everlasting damnation, disobedience unto us your king. If we should be slow, would God err? If your offence be towards God, do you think it pardoned without repentance? Is God's judgment mutable? Your pain is damnation, your judge is incorruptible, your fault is most evident.

"Likewise are ye evil informed in other articles, as for confirmation of your children, for the mass, for the manner of your service of matins and even-song. Whatever is therein ordered, has been long debated and consulted by many learned bishops, doctors, and other men of great learning in this realm; in nothing was so much labour and time spent, nothing so fully ended.

"As for the service in the English tongue, it has manifest reason for it. And yet perchance it seems to you a new service, yet indeed it is nothing other but the old. The self same words are in English which were in Latin, saving a few things taken out, which were so childish that it had been a shame to have heard them in English, as all they can judge who choose to report the truth. The difference is, that you our subjects may understand in English, being our natural country tongue, that which was heretofore spoken in Latin, then serving only for those who understood Latin, and now for all you who are born English. How can it with reason offend any reasonable man, that he shall understand what any other saith, and consent with the speaker? If the service of the church was good in Latin, it remains good in English: for nothing is altered, but to speak with knowledge that which was spoken with ignorance, and to let you understand what is said to you, to the intent you may further it with your own devotion; an alteration to the better, except knowledge be worse than ignorance. So that whoever has moved you to dislike this order, can give you no reason, nor answer yours, if ye understood it.

"Wherefore, you our subjects, remember, we speak to you, being ordained your prince and king by Almighty God. If in anywise we could advance God's honour more than we do, we would do it: And see that ye become subject to God's ordinances, obeying us your prince, and learn of them who have authority to teach you, who have power to rule you, and will execute our

justice if we be provoked. Learn not of them whose fruits are nothing but wilfulness, disobedience, obstinacy, dissimulation, and destruction of the realm.

"For the mass, we assure you, no small study or pains has been spent by all the learned clergy therein, and to avoid all contention, it is brought even to the very use as Christ left it, as the apostles used it, as the holy fathers delivered it; but it is indeed somewhat altered from what the popes of Rome for their gain had made it. And although ye may hear the contrary of some evil popish men, yet our majesty, who for our honour may not be blemished, nor stained, assures you, that they deceive you, abuse you, and blow these opinions into your heads, to accomplish their own purpose.

"And so likewise judge you of confirmation of children; and let them answer you this one question: Do they think that a child christened is damned, because it dies before confirmation? They are confirmed when they have arrived at the years of discretion, to learn that which they professed by baptism; taught in age that which they received in infancy; and yet no doubt but they are saved by baptism, not by confirmation; and made Christ's by christening, and taught how to continue by confirmation. Wherefore in the whole, mark, good subjects, how our doctrine is founded upon true learning, and theirs upon shameless errors.

"To conclude, beside our gentle manner of information to you, whatever is contained in our book, either for baptism, sacrament, mass, confirmation, and service in the church, is by our parliament established, by the whole clergy agreed, yea, by the bishops of the realm devised, and further, by God's word confirmed. And how dare ye trust, yea, how dare ye give ear, without trembling, to any person—to disallow a parliament—a subject to persuade against our majesty—a man of his singular arrogancy against the determination of the bishops, and all the clergy—any invented argument against the word of God?

"But now we resort to you our subjects, and say of your blindness, of your unkindness and unnatural conduct, that if we thought it had not begun of ignorance, and been continued by persuasion of certain traitors among you, who we think few in number, but busy in their doings, we could not be persuaded but to use our sword, and do justice, and, as we are ordained by God, redress your errors by revenge. But though love and zeal overcomes our just anger; yet how long that will be God knoweth, in whose hand our heart is; or rather for your own sakes, being our christened subjects, we would ye were persuaded rather than vanquished, informed than forced, taught than overthrown, quietly pacified than rigorously prosecuted.

"Ye require to have the statute of six articles revived; and do ye know what ye require? or know ye what ease you have with the loss of them? They were laws made, but quickly repented; they were too bloody to be borne by our people, and yet at the first indeed made of some necessity. Oh subjects! how are ye entrapped by subtle persons? We, of pity, because they were bloody, took them away; and you now will ignorantly ask them again. You know full well, that they helped us to extend rigour, and gave us cause to draw our sword very often; they were as a whetstone to our sword, and for your sakes we ceased to use them. And since our mercy moved us to write our laws with mildness and equity, how are ye blinded to ask them in blood?

"But leaving this manner of reasoning and resorting to the truth of our authority, we let you know these have been annulled by our parliament, with great rejoicing of our subjects, and not now to be called in question by subjects. Dare then any of you with the name of a subject stand against an act of parliament—a law of the whole realm? What is our power, if laws should be thus neglected? yea, what is your surety, if laws be not kept? Assure yourselves, that we of no earthly power under heaven make such a reputation, as we do of our power, to have our laws obeyed, and this cause of God, which we have taken in hand, to be thoroughly maintained, from which we will never remove a hair's breadth, nor give place to any creature living, much less to any subject, but therein will spend our royal person, our crown, treasure, realm, and all our state; whereof we assure you by our high honour. For herein indeed rests our honour, herein stands our kingdom, herein do all kings acknowledge us a king. And shall any of you dare breathe or think against our honour, our kingdom, our crown?

"In the end of this your request (as we are given to understand) ye would have them stand in force until our full age. To this we think, if ye knew what ye spake, ye would never have uttered that notion, nor ever have given breath to such a thought. For what think you of our kingdom? Are we of less authority for our age? Are we not your king now, as we shall be? Or shall ye be subjects hereafter, and are ye not now? Have not we the right we shall have? If we would suspend and hang our doings in doubt until our full age, ye must first know, as a king, we have no difference of years nor time, but as a natural man and creature of God, we have youth, and by his sufferance shall have age: We are your rightful king, your liege lord, your king anointed, your king crowned, the sovereign king of England, not by our age, but by God's ordinance, not only when we shall be of twenty-one years, but when we are of ten years. We possess our crown, not by years, but by the blood and descent from our father King Henry VIII. You are our subjects, because we are your king; and rule we will, because God hath willed. It is as great a fault in us not to rule, as in a subject not to obey.

"In truth, they who move this matter, if they durst utter themselves, would deny our kingdom. But our good subjects know their prince, and will increase, not diminish his honour; enlarge, not abate his power; acknowledge, not defer his kingdom till certain years. All is one, to speak against our crown, and to deny our kingdom, as to require that our laws may be broken, until we attain twenty-one years. Are we not your crowned, anointed, and established king? Wherein then are we of less majesty, of less authority, or less state, than were our progenitors, kings of this realm, except your unkindness, your unnaturalness will diminish our estimation? We have hitherto, since the death of our father, by the good advice and counsel of our dear and entirely beloved uncle, kept our state, maintained our realm, preserved our honour, defended our people from our enemies; we have hitherto been feared and dreaded of our enemies; yea, of princes, kings, and nations; yea, herein we are nothing inferior to any of our progenitors, which grace we acknowledge to be given to us from God, and how else, but by good obedience of our people, good counsel of our magistrates, due execution of our laws? By authority of our kingdom, England hitherto hath gained honour; during our reign, it hath won of the enemy, and not lost.

"It has been marvelled, that we of so young years, should have reigned so nobly, so royally, so quietly. And how chances it, that you our subjects of that our county of Devonshire, will give the first occasion to slander this our realm of England, to give courage to the enemy, to brand our realm with the evil of rebellion, to make it a prey to our old enemies, to diminish our honour, which God hath given, our father left, our good uncle and council preserved unto us? What greater evil could ye commit than even now, when our foreign enemy in Scotland, and upon the sea, seeks to invade us, to rise in this manner against our law, to provoke so justly our wrath, to ask our vengeance, and to give us occasion to spend that force upon you, which we meant to bestow upon our enemies, to begin to slay you with that sword which we drew against the Scots and other enemies, to make a conquest of our own people, which otherwise should have been of the whole realm of Scotland?

"Thus far ye see we have descended from our high majesty for love, to consider you in your base and simple ignorance, and have been content to send you an instruction like a fatherly prince, who of justice might have sent you your destruction like a king to rebels; and now let you know, that as ye see our mercy abundant, so if you provoke us farther, we swear to you by the living God, by whom we reign, ye shall feel the power of the same God in our sword; which, how mighty it is, no subject knoweth; how puissant it is, no private man can judge; how mortal it is, no English heart dare think. But surely, surely, as your lord and prince, your only king and master, we say to you, repent yourselves, and take our mercy without delay, or else we will forthwith extend our princely power, and execute our sharp sword against you, as against very infidels and Turks, and rather endanger our own royal person, state and power, than the same shall not be executed.

"And if ye will prove the example of our mercy, learn of those who lately did arise, pretending some grievances, and yet acknowledging their offences, who have not only received most humbly their pardon, but feel also, by our order, to whom all public order only pertains, redress devised for their grievances. In the end we admonish you of your duties towards God, to whom ye shall answer in the day of the Lord, and of your duties towards us, to whom ye shall answer by our order, and take our mercy whilst God so inclines us, lest when ye shall be constrained to ask, we shall be too much hardened in our heart to grant it to you; and where ye shall now hear of mercy, mercy and life, ye shall then hear of justice, justice and death.

"Given at Richmond, the 8th day of July, the third year of our reign."

Besides the articles of these Devonshire men, the rebels sent up also, not long after, a supplication to the king, to which answer again was made by the king's learned council.

Besides, to behold the malicious working of those popish priests, to kindle more the spark of sedition in the people's hearts, what rumours did they raise up against the king and his council! making the vulgar multitude to believe, that they should be made to pay, first for their sheep, next for their geese and pigs also, and such other things; and whatever they had in store, or should put into their mouths, they must pay a tax for it to the king! Of all which a word was never either thought or meant. But this seemed fit matter for such priests, by which to set the prince and his subjects together by the ears.

Against this seditious company of rebels, was sent by the king and his council, Sir John Russel, knight, lord privy seal, as lieutenant-general of the king's army, on whom chiefly depended the charge and conduct of suppressing this insurrection. To him also were joined, as in part of ordinary council in those affairs put under him, Sir William Herbert, Sir J. Pawlet, Sir Hugh Pawlet, Sir Thomas Speck, with the lord Gray, and others.

Thus the lord privy seal, accompanied by the lord Gray, advancing his power against the rebels, although not equal in number of soldiers, yet through the Lord's help, about the latter end of July, 1549, he gave them the repulse. They, notwithstanding, recovering themselves again, encountered the second time with the lord privy seal, about the beginning of August, by whom they were utterly vanquished and overthrown; so that the popish rebels not only lost the field, but a great part of them also lost their lives; lying there slain miserably in the chase for the space of two miles.

These rebels, to make their party more sure by the help and presence of their consecrated god, brought with them into the battle the pix, with the host in it, under his canopy, and instead of an altar, set him riding in a cart. Neither was there any want of masses, crosses, banners, candlesticks, with holy bread also, and plenty of holy water, to defend them from devils and all adversaries; which in the end neither could help their friends, nor yet could save themselves from the hands of their enemies. The consecrated god, and all the trumpery about him, was very soon after taken in the cart, and there thrown into the dust, leaving a notable lesson not to put their confidence hereafter in such vain idols, but only in the true and living God, and immortal Maker, serving him according to his prescribed word, and that only in the faith of his Son, and not after their own dreaming fantasies.

This event brings to my remembrance another similar popish field of battle (called Musselburgh field) fought in Scotland in the year before this, where the Scots likewise encamping themselves against the lord protector, and the king's power, brought with them to the battle the consecrated gods of their altars, with masses, crosses, banners, and all their popish array, having full confidence by virtue of them, to have a great victory against the English army. The number of the Scots army so far exceeded ours, and they were so appointed with their pikes in the front ranks against our horsemen (who gave the first onset) that our men were fain to retreat, not without the loss of divers gentlemen. Notwithstanding, the mighty arm of the Lord so turned the victory, that the Scots, in the end, with all their masses, pixes, and idolatrous trinkets, were put to the rout. Of whom in that field were slain between thirteen and fourteen thousand, and not more than a hundred Englishmen. The original cause of this war was the promise of the Scots, made before to king Henry, for the marriage of the young Scottish queen to king Edward, which promise the Scots afterwards broke.

During this commotion amongst the popish rebels in Cornwall and Devonshire, another disturbance began to be engendered in Oxford and Buckinghamshire, but that was soon appeased by lord Gray, who chased the rebels to their houses. Of whom two hundred were taken, and a dozen of the ringleaders delivered to him, whereof some were executed.

In Norfolk and parts thereabout, although the origin of their tumultuous stirring was not for the like cause, yet the obstinate hearts of that unruly multitude seemed no less bent upon mischief, and to disturb the public peace.

The rude and confused rabble was overthrown and slain, to the number, as is supposed, at the least of four thousand. And the chief stirrers and authors of that commotion were taken and executed, and one of them (Ket) was hanged in chains.

Besides these insurrections, about the latter end of July, 1549, another commotion began in Yorkshire. The causes moving them to raise this rebellion were these: first and principally, their traitorous hearts, grudging at the king's proceedings, in advancing and reforming the true honour of God, and his religion. Another cause was, trusting to a blind and fantastical prophecy, wherewith they were seduced, thinking the prophecy would shortly come to pass. The tenor of which prophecy, and the purpose of the traitors, was, "That there should no king reign in England; that the noblemen and gentlemen should be destroyed; and that the realm should be ruled by four governors, to be elected and appointed by the commons holding a parliament, to begin at the south and north seas of England." &c. They imagined that this their rebellion in the North, and the other of the Devonshire men in the West, meeting (as they intended) at one place, should be the means to bring about their traitorous devilish device.

Plotting together how they might find out more company to join with them in their detestable designs, their plan was to rise at once in two places, the one distant seven miles from the other, and at the first rush to kill and destroy such gentlemen and men of substance about them, as were favourers of the king's proceedings, or who would resist them.

It would be tedious to recite what riot these rebels gave themselves to, ranging about the country from town to town, to enlarge their rebellious band, taking those with force who were not willing to go, and leaving in no town where they came any man above the age of sixteen years. Thus their numbers were so increased, that in a short time they had gathered three thousand to favour their wicked attempts, and were like to have gathered more, had not the Lord's goodness, through prudent circumspection, interrupted the course of their furious beginning.

For first came the king's gracious and free pardon,

discharging and pardoning them and the rest of the rebels of all treasons, murders, felonies, and other offences done to his majesty, before the one-and-twentieth of August, A.D. 1549. This pardon influenced many of the rebels, and though the leaders contemptuously refused it, yet they were soon taken and executed, and this rebellion suppressed.

Matters concerning Edmund Bonner, Bishop of London.

Let us now return to Bonner, bishop of London, where we left him before, that is, in his own house, where he was commanded by the council to remain.

For the better understanding of the circumstances relating to Bonner, it will be requisite to retrace matters from the beginning of King Edward's time. King Edward, in the first year of his reign, A.D. 1547, for the order of his visitation, directed certain commissioners, as Sir Anthony Cook, Sir John Godsalve, knights; Mr. John Godsalve, Christopher Nevinson, doctors of the law; and John Madew, doctor of divinity; who sat in St. Paul's church upon their commission, there being present at the same time, bishop Bonner, John Royston, Polydore Virgil, Peter Van, and others. After the sermon made, and the commission read, they administered an oath to the bishop of London, to renounce the bishop of Rome, with his usurped authority, and to swear obedience to the king, according to the form of the statute made in the thirty-first year of king Henry VIII. Also that he should present and redress all such things as were needful to be reformed within the church.

Whereupon the bishop humbly and instantly desired them that he might see their commission, only for this purpose (as he said) that he might the better fulfil and put in execution the things wherein he was charged by them or their commission. To whom the commissioners answering, said they would deliberate more upon the matter, and so they called the other ministers of the church before them, and administered the like oath unto them, as they did to the bishop. To whom, moreover, certain interrogatories and articles of inquisition were read by Peter Lilly the public notary. Which done, after their oaths taken, the commissioners delivered to the bishop certain injunctions, as well in print as written, and homilies set forth by the king. All which things the bishop received under the words of this protestation, as followeth:—

"I do receive these injunctions and homilies with this protestation, that I will observe them, if they be not contrary and repugnant to God's law, and the statutes and ordinances of the church." And immediately he added, with an oath, that he never read the homilies and injunctions.

This protestation being made, Bonner instantly desired Peter Lilly, the registrar, to register it. And so the commissioners delivering the injunctions and homilies to Master Bellassere, archdeacon of Colchester, and Gilbert Bourn, archdeacon of London, Essex, and Middlesex, and enjoining them to put them into speedy execution, and also reserving other injunctions to be administered afterwards, as well to the bishop as to the archdeacons, according as they should see cause, &c., so continued the visitation till three o'clock the same day. At which hour and place, the commissioners sitting, and the canons and priests of the church appearing before them, and being examined upon virtue of their oath, for their doctrine and conversation; first John Painter. one of the cathedral church, there and then openly confessed that he lived vitiously and immorally. In which crimes divers other canons and priests of the church confessed in like manner, and could not deny themselves to be culpable.

After the commissioners had delivered to Master Royston, prebendary, and to the proctor of the dean and chapter of the cathedral church of St. Paul, the king's injunctions, and the book of homilies, enjoining them to see them executed, they prorogued their visitation until seven o'clock the next day.

By this visitation, it appears how Bonner made his protestation after receiving the king's injunctions. And further, we may perceive the immoral life and conversation of these unmarried priests of popery. The bishop shortly after his protestation, whether for fear, or for conscience, repenting himself, went to the king, where he submitted himself, and recanting his former protestation, craved pardon of the king for his demeanour toward his grace's commissioners. Which pardon although it was granted to him by the king, for acknowledging his fault, yet, for example, it was thought good that he should be committed to the Fleet.

The Form of Bonner's Recantation.

"Whereas I, Edmund, bishop of London, have at such time as I received the king's majesty's injunctions and homilies of my most dread sovereign lord, at the hands of his highness's visitors, did unadvisedly make such protestation, as now upon better consideration of my duty of obedience, and of the evil example that might ensue unto others thereof, appeareth to me neither reasonable, nor such as might well stand with the duty of an humble subject: forsomuch as the same protestation, at my request, was then by the register of that visitation, enacted and put in record; I have thought it my duty not only to declare before your lordships, that I do now upon better consideration of my duty, renounce and revoke my said protestation, but also most humbly beseech your lordships, that this my revocation of the same may be likewise put in the same records for a perpetual memory of the truth, most humbly beseeching your good lordships, both to take order that it may take effect, and also that my former and unadvised doings may be, by your good mediations, pardoned by the king's majesty.

"EDMUND, London."

Thus we see how he, upon his humble submission, received his pardon of the king, and yet for example sake was commanded to the Fleet; where he did not long continue, but according to the king's pardon, was restored both to his house and living again, in the first year of the king, 1548.

It will be remembered how, in the second, and a great part of the third year of the king, he demeaned himself, not advancing the king's proceedings; and yet acting in such a way as that no advantage could be taken against him by law, both in swearing his obedience to the king, and in receiving his injunctions; also in confessing his assent and consent touching the state of religion then; and in directing out his letters, according to the archbishop of Canterbury's precepts, to Cloney his sumner, to the bishop of Westminster, and other bishops, for abolishing images, for abrogation of the mass, for bibles to be set up in the churches, and for administering the sacrament in both kinds, with such other matters of reformation; till at length hearing of the death of the lord admiral, the lord protector's brother, and afterwards of the insurrection of the king's subjects, he began somewhat to draw back and slack in his pastoral diligence, so that in many places of his diocese and in London, the people were not only negligent in resorting to divine service, but also frequented and haunted foreign rites of masses, and he also himself, contrary to his wonted manner, upon principal feasts refused in his own person to officiate. Whereupon being suspected and complained of, and brought before the king's council, (as was said before,) after sharp admonitions and reproofs, had certain private injunctions sent to him to compel him on certain days to preach at St. Paul's Cross.

The delivery of these injunctions and articles to the bishop (with the time of his preaching appointed) was soon after known among the citizens and commons within the city of London, so that every man expecting the the time, wished to hear the preaching. The time being come, the bishop, according to the injunctions, publicly preached at the cross of St. Paul's on the first day of September. However, as hypocrisy never lurks so secretly in the hearts of the wicked, but that at one time or another, God in his most righteous judgment makes it open to the world, so his long cloaked obstinacy, and hatred against the king's godly proceedings, was most plainly manifested in his sermon.

For whereas he was commanded to treat only upon such special points as were mentioned in his articles; he, in order to withdraw the minds of the people as much as in him lay, from the right and true understanding of the holy sacrament administered in the holy communion then set forth by the authority of the king's majesty, (according to the true sense of the holy scripture,) spent most part of his sermon about the gross, carnal, and papistical presence of Christ's body and blood in the sacrament of the altar, and also not only slenderly touched on the rest of his articles, but with a rebellious and wilful carelessness utterly omitted the whole last article, concerning the lawful authority of the king's highness during his non-age; although he was by special command chiefly appointed to treat upon this, because it was the traitorous opinion of the popish rebels.

This contemptuous and disobedient dealing, as it greatly offended most of the king's faithful and loving subjects there present, so did it much displease that faithful and godly preacher, John Hooper, afterwards bishop of Worcester and Gloucester, and lastly a most constant martyr for the gospel of Christ, and also William Latimer, bachelor of divinity: and, therefore, they well weighing the foulness of the act, and their bounden allegiances to their prince, did thereon exhibit to the king's highness, under both their names, a bill of complaint or denunciation against the bishop.

The king's majesty having thus, by the information of these two credible persons, perfect intelligence of the contemptuous and perverse negligence of this bishop, in not accomplishing his highness' command, thought it necessary with all convenient speed to look more severely to the punishment of such dangerous and rebellious obstinacy; and therefore, by the advice of the lord protector, and the rest of his honourable council, he directed his commission under his great seal to the archbishop of Canterbury, the bishop of Rochester, and to other grave and trusty personages and counsellors, appointing and authorising them to call before them, as well the bishop of London, as also the denouncers, and, upon due examination and proof, to proceed against him summarily, according to law, either to suspension, excommunication, committing to prison, or deprivation.

The commission being sealed with the king's great seal, was by his highness's council forthwith delivered at the court to Thomas Cranmer, archbishop of Canterbury, and the rest of the commissioners being there all together present; who, upon the receipt of it, determined to sit at the archbishop's house at Lambeth on the Wednesday next ensuing, which was the eleventh day of September, and they appointed the bishop of London to be summoned before them. The manner of his behaviour at his appearance, because it both declares the froward nature and stubborn condition of the person, and also what estimation and authority he thought the commissioners to be of, must be described.

At his first entry into the place within the archbishop's house at Lambeth, where the archbishop and the commissioners sat, he passed by them with his cap upon his head (as if he saw them not), until some one plucked him by the sleeve, desiring him to do reverence to the commissioners. He laughingly turned himself, and spoke to the archbishop on this wise: "What, my lord, are you here? by my troth I saw you not."—"No," said the archbishop, "you would not see."—"Well," said he, "you sent for me; have you anything to say to me?"—"Yes," said the commissioners, "we have here authority from the king's highness to call you to account for the sermon you made lately at St. Paul's Cross, because you did not there publish to the people the article which you were commanded to preach upon." At which words the bishop, either because he did not like to hear of this matter, or else because he wished to make his friends believe that he was called to account only for his opinions in religion, began to speak of other matters, and said to the archbishop, "In good faith, my lord, I wish one thing were had in more reverence than it is."—"What is it?"

said the archbishop.—" The blessed mass," said he.—
" You have written very well of the sacrament : I marvel you do not more honour it." The archbishop of
Canterbury perceiving his subtlety, said to him again,
" If you think it well, it is because you understand it
not." The other then, adding to his ignorance an obstinate impudency, answered, " I think I understand it
better than you that wrote it." To which the archbishop replied, " Truly I will easily make a child that
is but ten years old to understand therein as much as
you. But what is this to the matter ?"

When they began to enter the judicial prosecuting of
their commission, and had called upon the denouncers
to propose such matter as they had to object against
him, he hearing them speak, fell to scorning and taunting them, saying to the one, that he spake like a goose;
and to the other, that he spake like a woodcock, and utterly denying their accusations to be true. The archbishop
seeing his peevish malice against the denouncers, asked
him, whether, if he would not believe them, he would
credit the people there present? And then (because
many of those present were at the bishop's sermon at
St. Paul's Cross) he stood up and read the article of the
king's authority, saying to them, " How say you, my
masters, did my lord of London preach this article ?"
They answered, " No, no." At which the bishop, turning himself about, deriding said, " Will you believe
this foolish people ?"

Besides this, he used many irreverent, unbecoming,
obstinate, and froward words towards the commissioners
(in defacing their authority with the terms of pretended
commissioners, pretended witnesses, and unjust, unlawful, and pretended proceedings, terming some of
them daws, woodcocks, fools, and such like) which I
will here omit, for they appear in the sequel of the
history.

Upon Wednesday, the eleventh day of September,
1549, in the third year of the reign of King Edward VI.,
Thomas Cranmer, archbishop of Canterbury, metropolitan and primate of all England, with Nicholas Ridley then bishop of Rochester, Sir William Petre, knight,
one of the king's two principal secretaries, and Master
William May, doctor of the civil law, and dean of St.
Paul's, by virtue of the king's commission, sat judicially, upon the examination of Edmund Bonner, bishop
of London, within the archbishop's chamber of presence, at his house in Lambeth, before whom there then
also personally appeared the said bishop. At which
time the archbishop, in the name of the rest, declared
to the bishop, that a grievous complaint had been heretofore made and exhibited against him in writing, to
the king's majesty and his most honourable council,
and that therefore his highness, with their advice, had
committed the examination thereof to him, and his colleagues there present; and there shewed a bill of complaint, exhibited to the king by William Latimer, and
John Hooper, ministers, which they requested Sir William Petre to read.

These things ended, the bishop, like a subtle lawyer,
having secret intelligence before of these matters (whatever he pretended to the contrary) pulled out of his
bosom a solemn protestation ready written, which he
exhibited to the commissioners, requesting that the
same might be openly read.

The protestation being read, he requested the commissioners that he might have the bill of complaint delivered to him. Which when he had well perused, he
said, that the same was very general, and so general, as
that he could not directly answer it. The archbishop
answered, that the special cause of the complaint against
him was, that he had transgressed the king's command,
given to him by his council, in that he in his sermon made
at St. Paul's Cross, did not set forth to the people the
king's highness' royal power in his minority, according
to the tenour of the article delivered to him for that
purpose; and for proof thereof he called William Latimer and John Hooper, who had put up the bill of complaint to the king against him.

When the bishop had earnestly looked upon them, he
said, " As for this merchant, Latimer I know him very

well, and have borne with him, and winked at his doings
a great while, but I have more to say to him hereafter.
But as to this other merchant, Hooper, I have not seen
him before, however I have heard much of his naughty
preaching." And then turning himself to the archbishop (on purpose, most like, to make his friends
think that he was not called thither to answer for his
contemptuous disobedience, but for matters of religion),
said to him, " Ah, my lord, now I see that the cause of
my trouble is not for the matter that you pretend
against me, but it is because I preached and set forth in
my late sermon the true presence of the most blessed
body and blood of our Saviour Jesus Christ to be in the
sacrament of the altar. For as for these my accusers,
as they are evil, infamous, notorious, and criminal persons, so are they manifest and notable heretics and seducers of the people, especially touching the sacrament
of the altar : and most of all this Hooper. For whereas
in my late sermon at St. Paul's Cross, I preached, that
in the blessed sacrament of the altar, after the words of
consecration, there is the true body and blood of our
Saviour Jesus Christ, the self-same in substance that
was hanged and shed upon the cross ;—he, the same day
at afternoon, having a great rabble with him of his damnable sect, openly in the pulpit in my diocese, preached
erroneously to the people against it ; and maliciously
inveighing against my sermon, denied the verity and
presence of Christ's true body and blood to be in the
sacrament, and also falsely and untruly interpreted and
expounded my words. And especially, where I preached
and affirmed the very true body and blood of our Saviour
Jesus Christ to be in the sacrament, the self-same substance that was hanged and shed upon the cross, he,
like an ass—as he is an ass indeed—falsely changed and
turned the word that into as, like an ass, saying, that I
had said as it hanged, and as it was shed upon the cross."

The archbishop perceiving the bishop's drift, and
hearing him talk so much of the presence of Christ's
body and blood in the sacrament, said to him, " My
lord of London, you speak much of a presence in the
sacrament; what presence is there, and of what presence do you mean?" The bishop being somewhat
stirred and moved in mind, as appeared by his choleric
countenance, spake again to the archbishop very earnestly,
and said, " What presence, my lord? I say and believe
that there is the very true presence of the body and
blood of Christ. What believe you, and how do you
believe my Lord ?" The archbishop, minding to nip
the gross absurdities of the papists, asked him further,
" Whether he were there, face, nose, mouth, eyes, arms,
and lips, with other lineaments of his body." The
bishop shaking his head, said, " Oh, I am right sorry
to hear your grace speak these words," and boldly urged
the archbishop to shew his mind therein. Who wisely
weighing the presumption of the party, with the place
and occasion of their assembly, refused to do so, saying, that their being there at that time was not to
dispute of those matters, but to prosecute their commission committed to them by their prince, and therefore
desired him to answer to such things as were objected
against him.

Upon which Bonner required to have a copy both of
the commission, and also of the denunciation, with time
to answer. Which the commissioners willingly granted,
assigning him to appear again before them upon Friday
then next following, at eight o'clock before noon, and
then to answer the tenor of the denunciation.

On Friday, the thirteenth of September, four commissioners, with Sir Thomas Smith Knight, the other of
the king's two principal secretaries, and joint commissioner with them, sat judicially in the archbishop's
chapel in his house at Lambeth; before whom appeared
the bishop of London : to whom the archbishop, in the
name of the rest, first said, " My lord of London, the
last time you were before us, we laid certain articles and
matter to your charge touching your disobedience to the
king's majesty, and you have this day to make your answer : wherefore, now shew us what you have to say
for your defence."

The bishop first asking the archbishop if he had said

all, and he again saying, "Yea," made this answer; "My lord, the last day that I appeared before you, I remember there sat in the king's majesty's commission, your grace, you my lord of Rochester, you Master Secretary Petre, and you Master Dean of St. Paul's, but now I perceive there sits also Master Secretary Smith, who because he sat not at the beginning, nor took there the commission upon him, ought not to do so : for by the law, they who begin must continue the commission." The archbishop answered, that he was no lawyer, and therefore could not shew what the law wills in that case, but, said he, if the law be so indeed, surely I take it to be an unreasonable law.

"Well," said the bishop, "there are here those that know the law, and yet I say not this to stand or stick much in this point with you, but to tell it you, as it were, by the way; for I have here mine answer ready."

Then said Master Secretary Petre to the bishop, "My lord, in good sooth, I must say to you, that although I have professed the law, yet by discontinuance and disuse thereof, and having been occupied a long time in other matters, I have perhaps forgotten what the law will do precisely in this point : but admit the law were as you say, yet yourself knows, my lord, that this is our certain rule in law, *Quod consuetudo est juris interpres optimus*, and I am sure you will not, nor cannot deny, but that the custom is commonly in this realm in all judgments and commissions used to the contrary; and in very deed we all together at the court, having the commission presented to us, took it upon us; and therefore you to stick in such trifling matters you shall rather in my judgment hurt yourself and your matter than otherwise."

"Truly, Master Secretary," said the bishop, "I have also of long while been disused in the study of law, but having occasion, partly by reason of this matter to turn to my books, I find the law to be as I say, and yet, as I said, I tell you hereof by the way, not minding to stick much with you in that point."

At which words, Master Secretary Smith said also to the bishop, "Well, my lord of London, as cunning as you make yourself in the law, there are here that know the law as well as you: and for my part I have studied the law too, and I promise you these are but quirks invented to delay matters, but our commission is to proceed summarily, and to cut off such frivolous allegations."

"Well," said the bishop again, "look well on your commission, and you shall find therein these words, 'To proceed according to the law and justice:' and I ask both law and justice at your hands."

Then Master Secretary Petre desired him to stand no more thereupon, but to proceed to his answer. Whereupon he took forth a writing, wherein was contained his answer to the denunciation exhibited the day before by Latimer and Hooper, and delivering it to the archbishop, said, that it was of his own handwriting, and for lack of sufficient time written so hastily and cursorily, that it could scarcely be read by any other; and therefore he desired to read it himself; and so taking it again, read it openly.

The purport of his answer was, that Hooper and Latimer were heretics, and therefore infamous and not to be believed or admitted as witnesses; and, further, that the injunctions given to him were not sealed with the broad seal, or signed by the king, and that, notwithstanding, he did preach against rebellion and in behalf of the king's authority; alleging thus, that the witnesses were not to be believed, and that the charge was not true.

Whilst he was reading the answer, objecting against his denouncers such causes, for which he would have had the denouncers repelled by the commissioners; the archbishop of Canterbury replied: "That if there were any such law, he thought it not to be a good or godly law, but a law of the bishop of Rome."

"No, sir," said the bishop of London, "it is the king's law used in this realm."

"Well, my lord," said the archbishop, "ye are too full of your law: I would wish you had less knowledge in that law, and more knowledge in God's law, and of your duty."

With that, Secretary Petre desired the bishop to proceed in reading his answers; who did so, and when he had finished, Latimer delivered a writing to the archbishop and the rest of the commissioners; who then said to the bishop of London, "here are certain articles which we intend to administer unto you."

The commissioners assigned him Monday the sixteenth of September then next following, to appear before them, and to make his full answers to all the articles administered to him by them this day.

On Monday, the sixteenth of September, the archbishop, associated with the bishop of Rochester; Secretary Smith; and Dr. May, dean of St. Paul's,—sat judicially within his chapel at Lambeth : before whom there and then appeared the bishop of London, as assigned in the last session: at which time he exhibited to the commissioners, in writing, his answers to the articles.

But before the same were read, the archbishop said to him, that his late answers, made the thirteenth of September to the denunciation, were very obscure, and contained also much matter of slander against Latimer and Hooper, and much untruth, and therefore they desired to purge themselves. Whereupon Latimer, obtaining leave to speak, said, that the bishop of London had most falsely, untruly, and uncharitably accused him, laying to his charge many feigned and untrue matters, and such as he would never be able to prove. For, whereas, he alleged, that William Latimer and John Hooper, with other heretics conspiring against him, did, the first day of September, after the bishop's sermon, assemble themselves together unlawfully against the bishop; that saying was most untrue. For neither that day, nor yet before that day, nor until certain days after, did he ever know or speak with Hooper. And as to his preaching there, he never held, taught, or preached any thing concerning the blessed sacrament, otherwise than he ought to do, nor otherwise than according to the scriptures, and true catholic faith of Christ's church; and therefore offered himself to be tried by the archbishop, or other such learned men as it should please the king's majesty, or the commissioners to appoint; and further, to submit to be hanged, drawn, and quartered, if the bishop could justly prove true the things that he had there shamefully laid to his charge. Then Master Hooper, upon like licence obtained, said to this effect.

"This ungodly man," pointing to the bishop, "has most uncharitably and ungodly accused me before your grace and this audience, and has laid to my charge that I am an heretic. Whereas, I take God to record, I never spoke, read, taught, or preached any heresy, but only the most true and pure word of God. And whereas, he says, I frequent the company of heretics; I do much marvel of his so saying; for it has pleased my lord protector's grace, my singular good lord and my lady's grace, to have me with them, and I have preached before them, and much used their company, with divers other worshipful persons, and therefore I suppose this man means them. And further, whereas he saith that I have made heretical books against the blessed sacrament of the body and blood of Christ, calling it mathematical, I perceive that this man knows not what this word mathematical there means, and therefore understands not my book: which, I take God to be my judge, I have made truly and sincerely, and according to his holy word : and by the same his holy word and scriptures I am always and shall be ready to submit myself to your grace's judgment and the superior powers to be tried;" with many such more words of like importance. Which ended, the archbishop asked the bishop, how he could prove that Hooper and Latimer assembled together against him on the first of September, as he had alleged, seeing they now denied it, and therefore willed him to answer forthwith.

The bishop then answered that he would duly prove it, if he might be admitted to do it according to law; and with that he pulled out of his sleeve certain books, saying, " I have this varlet's books which he made against the blessed sacrament which you shall hear." Then as he was turning certain leaves thereof, Hooper began again to speak : but the bishop, turning himself towards him, tauntingly said, " Put up your pipes, you have spoken for your part, I will meddle no more with you," and therewith read a certain sentence from the book. Which done, he said, " Lo, here you may see his opinion, and what it is." At which words, the people standing behind, and seeing his irreverent and unseemly demeanour and railing, fell suddenly into great laughing. Whereat, the bishop being moved, and perceiving not the cause why they laughed, turned him towards them in a great rage, saying, " Ah, woodcocks, woodcocks !"

Then said one of the commissioners, " Why say you so, my lord ?" " Indeed," replied he, " I may well call them woodcocks, that thus will laugh, and know not what at, nor yet heard what I said or read.

" Well, my lord of London," said the archbishop, " then I perceive you would persuade this audience, that you were called here for preaching your belief in the sacrament of the altar, and therefore you lay to these men's charge (meaning Hooper and Latimer) that they have accused you of that. However, there was no such thing laid to your charge, and therefore this audience shall hear openly read the denunciation that is put up against you, to the intent that they may the better perceive your dealing herein." And therewithal he said unto the people, " My lord of London would make you believe, that he is called hither for declaring and preaching his opinion touching the sacrament of the altar : but to the intent you may perceive how he goes about to deceive you, you shall hear the denunciation that is laid in against him, read to you ;" and thereupon he delivered the denunciation unto Sir John Mason, knight, who read it openly. Which done, the archbishop said again unto the audience, " Lo, you hear how the bishop of London is called for no such matter as he would persuade you."

With this the bishop, being in a raging heat, as one void of all humanity, turned himself about unto the people, saying, " Well, now hear what the bishop of London saith for his part." But the commissioners, seeing his inordinate contumacy, forbid him to speak any more, saying, " That he used himself very disobediently."

Notwithstanding, he still persisting in his irreverent manner of dealing with the commissioners, pulled out of his sleeve another book, and said to the archbishop ; " My lord of Canterbury, I have here a note out of your books that you made touching the blessed sacrament, wherein you affirm the verity of the body and blood of Christ to be in the sacrament ; and I have another book also of yours of the contrary opinion ; which is a marvellous matter."

To which the archbishop answered, that he made no books contrary one to another, and that he would defend his books ; however, he thought the bishop understood them not ; " for I promise you," said he, " I will find a boy of ten years old, that shall be more apt to understand that matter than you, my lord of London."

Thus, after a great many words, the commissioners, thinking it not good to spend any more time with him, desired him to shew his answers to the articles objected, the last day, against him. He, having them ready, read the same to them. Wherein he laments that one of his vocation, at the malicious denunciation of vile heretics, should be used after such a strange manner, having nevertheless done the best he could to declare his obedience to the king's majesty for the discouraging of rebellion ; and also for the truth of Christ's true body, and his presence in the sacrament of the altar ; for which alone the malicious denouncers, with their accomplices, had studied to trouble him.

Then in reply to the charge of omitting to defend the authority of the king, during his minority, he said, for the better setting forth of the king's majesty's power and authority in his minority, he had collected as well out of histories, as also out of the scriptures, the names of several young kings, who, notwithstanding minority, were faithfully and obediently honoured, and reputed for very true and lawful kings ; as Henry III. being but nine

years old ; Edward III. being but thirteen years ; Richard II. being but eleven years ; Henry VI. being not fully one year ; Edward V. being but eleven years ; Henry VIII. being but eighteen years of age. And out of the Old Testament, Uzziah, who was but sixteen years old ; Solomon and Manasseh being but twelve years ; Josiah, Jehoiachim, and Joash being but eight years of age when they entered their reigns. All which notes, with many others, he had purposed to declare, if they had come to his memory, as indeed they did not, because he was disturbed ; partly for lack of use of preaching, and partly by reason of a bill that was delivered to him from the king's council, to declare the victory then had against the rebels in Norfolk and Devonshire, which being of some length, confounded his memory ; and partly also because his book in his sermon fell from him, wherein were his notes which he had collected for that purpose ; so that he could not remember what he intended, but yet in general he persuaded the people to obedience to the king's majesty, whose minority was manifestly known to them and to all others.

When he had ended the reading of his answers, the commissioners said unto him that he had in the same very obscurely answered to the article beginning thus : " You shall also set forth in your sermon that our authority," &c. He answered, that he had already made as full and sufficient an answer in writing, as he was bound to make by law.

The judges again demanded of him, whether he would otherwise answer, or not ? To the which he said, " No, unless the law did compel him." Then they asked him whether he thought the law did compel him to answer more fully, or not ? He answered, " No ;" adding further that he was not bound to make answer to such positions.

The commissioners then seeing his froward contumacy, told him plainly, that if he persisted thus, and would not otherwise answer, they would, according to the law, take him as if he had confessed it. He said, as before, that he had already fully answered them ; but when they requested to have the notes, which he had made of his sermon, he said they should have them if they would send for them. And as in his answer he had stated that he did not know what the opinion of the rebels was, the judges declared to him that their opinion was, " That the king's majesty, before his grace came to the age of one-and-twenty years, had not so full authority to make laws and statutes, as when he came to further years ; and that his subjects were not bound to obey the laws and statutes made in his young age." The bishop answered, that he was not of the opinion of the rebels mentioned in that article, as appeared by his answers, as well to the denunciation, as also to the fifth article objected against him.

Which ended, they admitted for witnesses upon the articles objected against him, Master John Cheek, Henry Markham, John Joseph, John Douglas, and Richard Chambers, whom they bound with an oath upon the holy evangelists, truly to answer and depose upon the same articles in the presence of the bishop, who, like a wily lawyer, protested against the receiving, admitting, and swearing those witnesses, demanding also a competent time to minister interrogatories against them, with a copy of all the acts of that day. With this the delegates were well pleased, and assigned him to administer his interrogatories against Master Cheek on that day, and against the rest on the next day.

After this the judges delegate assigned the bishop to appear again before them upon Wednesday then next ensuing, between the hours of seven and eight of the clock before noon, in the hall of the archbishop's manor of Lambeth, there to shew cause why he should not be declared *pro confesso*, upon all the articles whereto he had not answered, and to see further process done in the matter ; and so (he still protesting against the validity of all their proceedings) they departed.

In the meanwhile the commissioners certified to the king's majesty and his council, of the bishop's demeanour, and what objections he had made against their proceedings, making doubts whether by the tenor of his majesty's commission, the commissioners might proceed not only at the denunciation, but also at their mere office; and also whether they might as well determine or hear the cause. His majesty, for the better understanding thereof, did on the seventeenth of September send to the commissioners a full and perfect declaration of his will and pleasure in the commission, giving them full authority to proceed at their own discretion.

After this declaration had been sent down to, and received back from the king, the bishop of London appeared again before them upon Wednesday, the 18th of September, in the great hall at Lambeth. Where he declared, that although he had already sufficiently answered all things, yet further to satisfy the term assigned unto him, to shew cause why he ought not to be declared *pro confesso* upon the articles, to which he had not fully answered, he had then a writing to exhibit why he ought not to be so declared, which he read there openly. Wherein under his accustomed irreverent terms of pretended, unjust, and unlawful process and assignment, he said he was not bound by the law (for good and reasonable causes) to obey the same, especially their assignment.

When his frivolous objections were read, the archbishop seeing his inordinate and intolerable contempt of manner and language towards them, charged him very sharply, saying, "My Lord of London, if I had sat here only as archbishop of Canterbury, it had been your duty to have used yourself more lowly, obediently, and reverently towards me than you have; but seeing that I with my colleagues sit here now as delegates from the king's majesty, I must tell you plainly, you have behaved yourself too inordinately. For at every time that we have sat in commission, you have used such unseemly fashions, without all reverence and obedience, giving taunts and checks as well to us, with the servants and chaplains, as also to certain of the most ancient that are here, calling them fools and daws, with such like expressions, as that you have given to the multitude an intolerable example of disobedience. And I assure you, my lord, there is you and another bishop whom I could name, that have used yourselves so contemptuously and disobediently, as the like I think has not before been heard of, by which ye have done much harm."

At which words the bishop said scornfully to the archbishop, "You show yourself to be a meet judge."

The archbishop then reminded him how indiscreetly the last day in the chapel he had called all the people "woodcocks."

He answered, that William Latimer, one of the denouncers, had practised with the audience, that when he lifted up his hand to them, they should say as he said, and do as he did; as, one time, upon the lifting up of his hand, "Nay, nay;" and at another time, "Yea, yea," and laughed they could not tell at what.

To which words Latimer replied, saying, "That he lifted not up his hand at any time, but only to cause them to hold their peace."

Then secretary Smith said to the bishop, that in all his writings and answers he did not once acknowledge them as the king's commissioners, but used always protestations, calling them pretended commissioners, pretended delegates, pretended commission, pretended articles, pretended proceedings, so that all things were pretended with him. "Such terms," said he, "proctors use to delay matters for their clients, when they will not have the truth known. But you, my lord, to use us the king's majesty's commissioners, with such terms, do very naughtily. And I pray you what else did the rebels do but act in the same way? For when letters and pardons were brought them from the king and his council, they would not credit them, but said they were none of the king's or his council's, but gentlemen's doings, with such like terms. But now, my lord, because we cannot make you confess whether, in your sermon, you omitted the article touching the king's majesty's authority in his tender age or not; but still have said that you will not answer otherwise than you have done, and that you have already sufficiently answered, so that we can by no means induce you to confess plainly

what you did, yea or nay; therefore I say, to the intent we may come to the truth, we have dilated the matter more at large, and have drawn out other articles whereunto you shall be sworn, and then I trust, you will dally with us no more as you have done."

Then the delegates ministered to him certain new articles and injunctions, and did there bind him with an oath in form of law to make a full and true answer. The bishop notwithstanding still protested the nullity and invalidity of these articles, injunctions, and process, desiring also a copy with a competent time to answer.

The judges decreed a copy, commanding him to come to his examination the next day.

Then the commissioners received for witness Sir John Mason, Sir Thomas Chalenor, knights, Master William Cecil, Armigal Wade, and William Hunnings, clerks to the king's council, whom they bound with a corporal oath in the presence of the bishop.

These articles being thus administered to the bishop of London, the next day, being Thursday the 19th of September, the before-named commissioners sate in the archbishop's chamber of presence at Lambeth, attending the coming of the bishop of London. Before whom there appeared Robert Johnson the bishop's registrar, who declared to the commissioners that the bishop his master could not at that time personally appear before them without great danger of his bodily health, because he feared to fall into a fever by reason of a cold that he had taken by too much overwatching himself the night before, whereby he was compelled to keep his bed: nevertheless, if he could without danger of his bodily health, he would appear before them the same afternoon. This excuse the judges were content to take in good part. Master Smith remarked, that "if he were sick indeed, the excuse was reasonable, and to be allowed; but," said he, "I promise you, my lord has so dallied with us, and used hitherto such delays, that we may mistrust that this is but a feigned excuse. However, upon your faithful declaration, we are content to tarry until one o'clock this afternoon," and so they did, desiring Master Johnson to signify then to them whether the bishop could appear or not.

At which hour Robert Johnson and Richard Rogers, gentlemen of the bishop's chamber appeared again before the commissioners, declaring that, for the causes before alleged, their master could not appear at that time. Whereupon Master secretary Smith said to them, "My lord of London, your master, has used us very homely, and sought delays hitherto, and now, perhaps, perceiving these last articles to touch the quick, and therefore loth to come to his answer, he feigns himself sick. But because he shall not so deceive us any more, we will send the knight marshal to him, commanding him if he be sick, indeed, to let him alone; for that is a reasonable excuse; but if he be not sick, then to bring him forthwith to us; for I promise you he shall not use us as he has done; and therefore Master Johnson you do the part of a trusty servant as becomes you; but it is also your part to show my lord his stubborn heart and disobedience, which does him more harm than he is aware of. What, thinks he to stand with a king in his own realm? Is this the part of a subject? Nay, I suppose we shall have a new Thomas à Becket. Let him take heed, for if he play these parts, he may happen to be made shorter by the head. He may appeal if he think good; but whither? To the bishop of Rome? I say he cannot appeal but to the same king who has made us his judges, and to the bench of his council; and how they will take this matter when they hear of it, I doubt not. He would make men believe that he was called before us for preaching his opinion of the sacrament; wherein I assure you he did both falsely and wickedly, and more than became him, and more than he had in commandment to do, for he was not desired to speak of that matter; but yet we will lay no such thing to his charge, and therefore we will not have him delay us." Which ended, the delegates decreed to tarry for him until the next day at two o'clock, being Friday, the 20th of September.

At which day and time the bishop appeared himself

personally before them in the same chamber of presence; where he exhibited his answers to the last articles.

After this, perceiving that Master secretary Smith was more quick with him than others of the commissioners, and that he would not suffer him any longer to dally out the matter with his vain subtleties in law, but urged him to go directly to his matter, and sometimes sharply rebuking him for his ill and stubborn behaviour towards them; he, to destroy his authority, exhibited in writing a recusation of the secretary's judgment against him, in which he rejects the secretary as a prejudiced and hostile person, unfit to sit in judgment upon him.

When this was read by the bishop, the secretary told him plainly, that he would proceed in his commission, and would be still his judge; and said further, "My lord, you say, in your recusation, that I said 'That you were acting like thieves, murderers, and traitors,' indeed I said it, and will so say again, since we perceive it by your doings."

The bishop in a great rage replied, saying, "Well, sir, because you sit here by virtue of the king's commission, and are secretary to his majesty, and also one of his highness' council, I must and do honour and reverence you; but, as you are but Sir Thomas Smith, and say as ye have said, 'That I do like thieves, murderers, and traitors,' I say, ye lie, and I defy you; and do what you can to me, I fear you not, and therefore what thou doest do quickly."

The archbishop with the other commissioners said to him, that for such his irreverent behaviour he was worthy imprisonment.

Then the bishop, in more mad fury than before, said again, "In God's name ye may send me whither you will, and I must obey you, and so will, except you send me to the devil, for thither I will not go for you. Three things I have: a small portion of goods, a poor carcase, and mine own soul: the two first ye may take, but as for my soul, ye shall not get it."

"Well," said the secretary then, "ye shall know that there is a king."

"Yea, sir," said the bishop, "but that is not you, neither, I am sure, will you take it upon you."

"No sir," said the secretary, "but we will make you know who it is;" and with that the commissioners commanded the bishop and all the rest to depart the chamber, until they called for him again.

Now that the commissioners were in consultation, the bishop, with Gilbert Bourn, his chaplain, Robert Warnington his commissary, and Robert Johnson his registrar, were tarrying in a vacant place before the door of the chamber; the bishop leaning on a cupboard, and seeing his chaplains very sad, said, "Sirs, what mean you? Why show you yourselves to be sad and heavy in mind, as appears to me by your outward gestures and countenances? I would wish you, and I require you to be as merry as I am, (laying therewith his hand upon his breast) for before God I am, not sad nor heavy, but merry and of good comfort, and am right glad and joyful of this my trouble, which is for God's cause, and it grieves me nothing at all. But the great matter that grieves me and pierces my heart is, that this Hooper and such other vile heretics and beasts are suffered and licensed to preach at Paul's Cross, and in other places within my diocese, most detestably preaching and railing at the blessed sacrament of the altar, and denying the verity and presence of Christ his true body and blood to be there, and so infect and betray my flock. But I say it is there in very deed, and in that opinion I will live and die, and am ready to suffer death for the same. Wherefore, ye being christian men, I do require you, and also charge and command you in the name of God, and on his behalf, as ye will answer him for the contrary, that ye go to the mayor of London, and to his brethren the aldermen, praying and also requiring them earnestly in God's name and mine, and for mine own discharge on that behalf, that from henceforth, when any such detestable and abominable preachers (and especially those who hold opinions against the blessed sacrament of the altar) do come to preach to them, they forthwith depart out of their presence, and do not

hear them, lest that they, tarrying with such preachers, should not only hurt themselves in receiving their poisoned doctrine, but also give encouragement to others, who thereby might take an occasion to think and believe that their erroneous and damnable doctrine is true and good."

And then, turning himself about, and beholding two of the archbishop's gentlemen, who kept the chamber door where the commissioners were in consultation, and perceiving that they had heard all his talk, he spake to them also and said, "And, sirs, ye be my lord of Canterbury's gentlemen, I know ye very well; and therefore I also require and charge you in God's behalf, and in his name, that ye do the like, where you shall chance to see and hear such corrupt and erroneous preachers, and also advertise my lord your master of the same, and of these my sayings that I have now spoken here before you, as ye are christian men, and shall answer before God for the contrary."

With this the commissioners called for the bishop again, who read unto them an instrument, containing an appeal to the king.

Then the delegates proceeded to the examination of the last answers, and finding them imperfect, they demanded of him on what special day of August he was sent for by the lord protector? To whom he obstinately answered, that he was not bound to make any other answer than he had already made, neither would he otherwise answer as long as Master secretary Smith was present, whom he had before recused, and would not recede from his recusation.

The secretary, seeing him so wilful and perverse, said sharply to him, "My lord, come off and make a full and perfect answer to these articles, or else we will take other order with you."

"In faith, sir," then said the bishop, "I thought ye had been learned; but now before God I perceive well that either ye are not learned, or else ye have forgotten it: for I have so often answered lawfully and sufficiently and have shewed causes sufficient and reasonable, that I must needs judge that you are too ignorant herein."

"Well," said Master secretary, "ye will not then otherwise answer?"

"No," said the bishop, "except the law do compel me."

"Then," said the secretary, "call for the knight marshal, that he may be had to ward."

With that all the rest of the commissioners charged the bishop, that he had very outrageously and irreverently behaved himself towards them, sitting on the king's majesty's commission, and especially towards Sir Thomas Smith, his majesty's secretary, and for that and other contumelious words which he had spoken, they declared they would commit him to the Marshalsea.

By this time the marshal's deputy came before them, whom Master secretary commanded to take the bishop as prisoner, and so to keep him, that no man might come to him.

When the secretary had ended, the bishop said to him, "Well, sir, it might have become you right well, that his grace of Canterbury, here present, being first in commission, and your better, should have done it."

Then the commissioners assigning him to be brought before them on Monday, to make full answer to these articles, or else to shew cause why he should not be declared guilty by confession, concluded the session.

Now, as the bishop was departing with the undermarshal, he turned himself in a great fury toward the commissioners, and said to Sir Thomas Smith, "Sir, where ye have committed me to prison, ye shall understand, that I will require no favour at your hands, but shall willingly suffer what shall be put to me, as bolts on my heels; yea, and if ye will, iron about my middle, or where ye will."

Then departing again, he yet returned once more, and said to the archbishop; "Well, my lord, I am sorry that I, being a bishop, am thus handled at your grace's hand; but more sorry that ye suffer abominable heretics to practise as they do in London and elsewhere, infecting and disquieting the king's liege people: and therefore I do require you, as you will answer to God and the king, that ye will henceforth abstain from doing thus; for if you do not, I will accuse you before God and the king's majesty." And so he departed, using many reproachful words against the common people, who stood and spake to him by the way as he went.

The sixth action or process against Bonner, Bishop of London.

It was assigned, that upon Monday, the twenty-third of the same month, the bishop should again appear before the commissioners, to shew a final cause why he should not be declared *pro confesso*, upon all the articles whereto he had not fully answered.

Accordingly, the bishop was brought before them by the under-marshal, and there declared that his appearance at that time and place was not voluntary; for that he was against his will brought there by the keeper of the Marshalsea; and he then intimated a general recusation of all the commissioners, alleging that because the archbishop with all his colleagues had neither observed the order of their commission, nor proceeded against him after any laudable form of judgment, but attempted many things unlawfully against his person, dignity, and state, especially in committing him to prison; and he therefore did refuse and decline from the judgment of the archbishop and his colleagues, and except against their jurisdiction; and therefore, according to his appeal, he purposed to submit himself to the tuition, protection, and defence of the king's majesty; for whose honour and reverence sake, he said, they ought not to proceed any further against him.

The archbishop, however, with the others, told him plainly that they would be still his judges, and proceed against him according to the king's commission.

Then the bishop, seeing that they would still proceed against him, intimated an appeal to the king's majesty.

The commissioners, notwithstanding, stood to their commission, and urged him straightly to make a more full answer to his articles than he had done.

The bishop said, that he would stand to his recusations and appeal, and would not make any other answer.

Then the delegates demanded of him what cause he had to allege, why he ought not to be declared *pro confesso*, upon the articles whereto he had not fully answered; the bishop still answering (as before) that he would adhere to his appeal and recusation.

Whereupon the archbishop, with consent of the rest, seeing his pertinacity, pronounced him contumacious, and declared him guilty, upon all the articles which he had not answered.

This done, Master secretary Smith shewed a letter which the bishop of London had sent unto the lord mayor, and the aldermen of the city of London, as follows:—

To the right honourable and my very good Lord, the Lord Mayor of London, with all his worshipful Brethren, my very dear and worshipful Friends, with speed.

"Right honourable, with my very humble recommendations: whereas I have perceived of late, and heard with mine ears, what vile beasts and heretics have preached to you, or rather like themselves prated and railed against the most blessed sacrament of the altar, denying the truth, and presence of Christ's true body and blood to be there, giving you and the people liberty to believe what ye list, teaching you detestably, that faith in this behalf must not be constrained, but that every man may believe as he will; by reason whereof, lest my presence and silence might to some have been seen to have allowed their heretical doctrine, and given credit to them, betraying my flock of the catholic sort, ye know I departed yesterday from the heretic praters' uncharitable charity, and so could have wished that you and all others that are catholic should have done, leaving those there with him that are already cast away, and will not be recovered. For you tarrying with him still,

shall not only hurt yourselves in receiving his poisoned doctrine, but also shall give countenance that their doctrine is tolerable by reason that ye are content to hear it, and say nothing against it. And because I cannot tell when I shall speak with you to advertise you hereof, therefore I thought good for mine own discharge and yours, thus much to write to you, requiring and praying you again and again in God's behalf, and for mine own discharge, that ye suffer not yourselves to be abused with such wicked preachers and teachers, in hearing their evil doctrine that you shall perceive them go about to sow. And thus our blessed Lord long and well preserve you all with this noble city in all good rest, godliness, and prosperity. Written in haste, this Monday morning, the sixteenth of September, 1549.

"Your faithful beadsman and poor bishop,
"EDMUND BONNER."

This letter being read, the secretary demanded of him whether he wrote it or not. To whom he would not otherwise answer, but that he would still adhere and stand to his former recusations and appeals. Which the commissioners seeing, determined to continue this case until Friday then next following, assigning the bishop to be there, to hear a final decree of this matter.

On Friday the commissioners did not sit in commission according to their appointment, but deferred it till Tuesday, the first of October. Upon which day the bishop appearing before them, the archbishop declared to him, that although upon Friday last they had appointed to pronounce their final decree and sentence in this matter, yet as they thought that that sentence (although they had just cause to give it,) would be very severe against him, they had not only deferred it until this day, but desiring to be friendly to him, and to use more gentle reformation towards him, had made such suit for him, that although he had grievously offended the king's majesty, yet if he would have acknowledged his fault, and have made some amends in submitting himself, he should have found much favour; the sentence would not have been so extreme against him, as it was likely to be now.

The bishop not at all regarding this gentle and friendly admonition, but persisting still in his contumacy, made another protest against the commissioners, and then appealed from them to the king, refusing to make answer, on the plea that he was not free, but a prisoner.

He then handed in both his protests and his appeal in writing, after having publicly read them.

These things ended, the archbishop said to him, "My lord where you say that you come compelled, or else you would not have appeared, I much wonder. For you would thereby make us and this audience here believe, that because you are a prisoner, you ought not therefore to answer; which, if it were true, were enough to confound the whole state of this realm. For I dare say, that of the greatest prisoners and rebels that ever your keeper there (meaning the under marshal) had under him, he cannot show me one that has used such defence as you have done."

"Well," said the bishop, "if my keeper were learned in the laws, I could shew him my mind."

"Well," said the archbishop, "I have read over all the laws as well as you, but to another end and purpose than you did, and yet I can find no such privilege in this matter."

Then Master Secretary Smith charged him very severely how disobediently and rebelliously he had behaved himself towards the king's majesty and authority.

The bishop answered again, "That he was the king's majesty's lawful and true subject, and did acknowledge his highness to be his gracious sovereign lord, or else he would not have appealed to him as he did, yea, and would gladly lay his hands, and his neck also, under his grace's feet, and therefore he desired that his highness's laws and justice might be administered to him."

"Yea," replied Master Secretary, "you say well my lord, but I pray you what else have all these rebels in Norfolk, Devonshire, and Cornwall, and other places done? Have they not said the same thing? We are the king's true subjects, we acknowledge him for our king, and we will obey his laws, with such like phrases; and yet when either commandment, letter, or pardon was brought to them from his majesty, they did not believe it, but said it was forged and made under a hedge, and was gentlemen's doings, so that they neither would nor did obey anything."

"Ah, sir," said the bishop, "I perceive your meaning; you would say that the bishop of London is a rebel like them."

"Yea, by my troth," said the secretary. Whereat the people laughed.

Then the dean of St. Paul's said to him, "That he marvelled much, and was very sorry to see him so untractable, that he would not suffer the judges to speak."

To whom the bishop disdainfully answered; "Well, Master Dean, you must say somewhat." And likewise at another time as the dean was speaking, he interrupted him and said, "You may speak when your turn comes."

Then said the secretary Smith, "I would you knew your duty."

"I would," retorted he again, "you knew it as well;" with an infinite deal more of such stubborn and contemptuous behaviour. Which the commissioners weighing, determined that the archbishop, with their whole consent, should openly read and publish their final decree or sentence definitive against him. Which he did, pronouncing him thereby to be clean deprived from the bishopric of London.

The sentence specified that the bishop of London had neglected the king's injunctions in his diocese, and especially had not complied with his majesty's command to preach in behalf of the king's authority as impeached by the rebels; and the sentence embodied the words of the royal injunctions, which he thus neglected, and which are as follows:—

"Ye shall also set forth in your sermon, that our authority of our royal power is (as of truth it is) of no less authority and force in this our younger age, than is and was of any of our predecessors, though the same were much elder, as may appear by example of Josiah and other young kings in scripture. And therefore all our subjects to be no less bound to the obedience of our precepts, laws, and statutes, than if we were thirty or forty years of age."

When this sentence of deprivation was ended, the bishop immediately appealed by word of mouth:—

"I, Edmund, bishop of London, brought in and kept here as a prisoner against my consent and will, do under my former protestation, and to the intent it may also appear, that I have not consented nor agreed to any thing done against me and in my prejudice, allege and say that this sentence given here against me, is *lex nulla*; and so far forth as it shall appear to be *aliqua*, I do say it is *iniqua* and *injusta*; and that therefore I do appeal to the most excellent and noble king Edward VI., by the grace of God, king of England, France, and Ireland, defender of the faith, and of the church of England, and also Ireland, next and immediately under God here on earth, supreme head, and unto his court of chancery or parliament, as the law, statutes, and ordinances of this realm will suffer and bear in this behalf, desiring instantly first, second, and third, according to the laws, letters, reverential or dimissory, to be given and delivered unto me in this behalf, with all things expedient, requisite, or necessary in any wise."

The judges said, "that they will declare and signify to the king's majesty what is done in this matter."

The archbishop considering that most of the audience did not understand the meaning of the sentence which was read in the Latin tongue, said to them, "Because there may be many of you here that understand not the Latin tongue, and so cannot tell what judgment has been given, I shall therefore shew you its effect;" and therewith declared in English the causes expressed in the sentence, adding these words:—

"Because my lord of London is found guilty in these matters, therefore we have here by our sentence deprived him of our bishopric of London; and this we shew to you that from henceforth you shall not esteem him any more as bishop of London."

Then Bonner desired the archbishop to declare likewise how he had appealed. But the other, seeing his froward contempt, refused it, saying, "you may do it yourself." Whereupon very disdainfully again he said, "What will your grace do with me, touching my imprisonment? Will you keep me still in prison?"

To whom the commissioners answered that they perceived now more in the matter than they did before, and that his behaviour was greater rebellion than he was aware of, and therefore they would not discharge him, but committed him again to his keeper to be kept in prison. Where he most justly remained until the death of that most worthy and godly prince king Edward VI. After which time he wrought most horrible mischief and cruelties against the saints of God, as will appear hereafter, throughout the whole reign of queen Mary.

Immediately after his deprivation, he wrote out of the Marshalsea other letters supplicatory to the lord chancellor, and the rest of the king's council. Wherein he complained, that by reason of the great enmity that the duke of Somerset and Sir Thomas Smith bare to him, his earnest suits unto the king and his council could not be heard. He therefore most humbly desired their lordships to consider him, and to let him have liberty to prosecute this matter before them, and he would daily pray for the good preservation of their honours; and afterwards wrote in the same way to the king's majesty.

The king, on receiving his petition, gave in charge and commandment to certain men of honour and worship, and persons skilful in the law, as to the lord Rich, high chancellor, the lord treasurer, the marquis of Dorset, the bishop of Ely; Lord Wentworth, Sir Anthony Wingfield, Sir William Herbert, knights; doctor Rich, Wooton, Edward Montague, lord chief justices; Sir John Baker, knight; with judge Hale, John Gosnold, doctor Oliver, and also doctor Layson, that they perusing all such acts, matters, and muniments of Bonner by him exhibited, produced, propounded, and alleged, with all his protestations, recusations, and appeals, should upon mature consideration give their direct answer, whether the appeal of Bonner were to be deferred to, whether the sentence against him stood by the law sufficient and effectual or not. Who soon after diligent discussion, and considerate advice, gave their answer, that the appeal of Edmund Bonner was null and unreasonable, and in no wise to be deferred to; and that the sentence by the commissioners against him was rightly and justly pronounced. And this was the conclusion of Bonner's whole matter and deprivation.

Thus then leaving Doctor Bonner a while in the Marshalsea, we will proceed further in the course of our history, as the order of years and time requireth. And although the trouble of the lord protector falls here jointly with the deprivation of Doctor Bonner; yet as he was shortly again delivered, I will therefore delay to treat of it till his second trouble, which was two years after; and so in the meantime, intend to continue the matter, touching the king's godly proceedings for reformation of religion in the year 1549.

And here first a note should be made of Peter Martyr and of his learned labours, and disputation in the University of Oxford this year with Doctor Chedsey, and others about the sacrament; which was, that the substance of bread and wine was not changed in the sacrament, and that the body and blood of Christ was not carnally and bodily in the bread and wine, but united to the same sacramentally.

In like manner, some mention here also should be made of the ecclesiastical laws, for the compiling of which thirty-two persons were assigned by act of parliament, 1549. But because these are rather matters of treatise than historical, I mean to defer the further consideration of them to the end of the history of this king's days, and so to pass forward to other matters in the meanwhile.

Books of Latin service called in and abolished.

It follows in our history, that certain of the vulgar multitude, hearing of the apprehension of the lord protector, and supposing that the alteration of public service into English, and the administration of the sacrament and other rites lately appointed in the church, had been the act chiefly or only of the lord protector, began now to spread abroad the report that they should now have their old Latin service with holy bread and holy water, and their other superstitious ceremonies again: therefore the king, with the privy council, directed out his letters of request, and straight commandment to the bishops, in their diocese, to cause the deans and prebendaries of their cathedral churches, all parsons, vicars, and curates, with the church-wardens of every parish within their diocese, to bring in and deliver up all antiphoners, missals, grailes, processionales, manuals, legends, pies, porthoses, journals, and ordinals after the use of Sarum, Lincoln, York, Bangor, Hereford, or any other private use; and all other books of service, which might be any hindrance to the service now set forth in English, charging also and commanding that all such as shall be found disobedient in this behalf should be committed to ward.

And because the king was informed that there was among the people a refusal to pay toward the finding of bread and wine for the holy communion, by which the communion in many places was omitted, the bishops in like manner had given in charge to provide for redress of this, and to punish them who should refuse. By which it appears that no wafer cakes, but common bread was then by the king's appointment ordinarily received and used in churches. This was about the latter end of December, A.D. 1549.

Taking down of Altars, and setting up the Table instead thereof.

In the year next, 1550, other letters were sent for taking down altars in churches, and setting up the table instead, to Nicholas Ridley, who, being bishop of Rochester before, was now made bishop of London in Bonner's place. The copy and contents of the king's letters are these:

The King's Letters to Nicholas Ridley, Bishop of London, &c.

"Right reverend father in God; right trusty and well-beloved, we greet you well. And whereas it is come to our knowledge, that the altars within the most part of the churches of this realm being already upon good and godly considerations taken down, there do yet remain altars standing in other churches, by occasion whereof much variance and contention ariseth among sundry of our subjects, who, if good foresight were not had, might perchance engender great hurt and inconvenience; we admonish you, that minding to have all occasion of contention taken away, which many times groweth by these and such like diversities, and considering that amongst other things belonging to our royal office and cure, we do account the greatest to be, to maintain the common quiet of our realm; we have thought good by the advice of our council to require you, and nevertheless especially to charge and command you, for the avoiding of all matters of further contention and strife about the standing or taking away of the said altars, to give substantial order throughout all your diocese, that with all diligence all the altars in every church or chapel, as well in places exempted as not exempted within your diocese, be taken down, and instead thereof a table to be set up in some convenient part of the chancel, within every such church or chapel, to serve for the administration of the blessed communion. And to the intent that the same may be done without the offence of such of our loving subjects as are not yet so well persuaded in that behalf as we would wish, we send unto you herewith certain considerations gathered and collected, that make for the purpose; which and such others as you shall think

meet to be set forth to persuade the weak to embrace our proceedings in this part, we pray you to cause them to be declared to the people by some discreet preachers, in such places as you shall think meet, before the taking down of the said altars; so as both the weak consciences of others may be instructed and satisfied as much as may be, and this our pleasure the more quietly executed. For the better doing whereof, we require you to open the aforesaid considerations in our cathedral church in your own person, if you conveniently may, or otherwise by your chancellor, or some other grave preacher, both there and in such other market towns and most notable places of your diocese, as you may think most requisite.

"Given under our signet at our palace of Westminster, the 24th day of November, in the fourth year of our reign."

Reasons why the Lord's Board should rather be after the form of a Table, than of an Altar.

I. The form of a table shall more move the simple from the superstitious opinions of the popish mass to the right use of the Lord's Supper. For the use of an altar is to make sacrifice; the use of a table is to serve for men to eat upon. Now, when we come to the Lord's board, what do we come for? To sacrifice Christ again, and to crucify him again? or to feed upon him that was only once crucified and offered up for us? If we come to feed upon him, spiritually to eat his body, and spiritually to drink his blood, which is the true use of the Lord's Supper, then no man can deny but the form of a table is more meet for the Lord's board than the form of an altar.

II. Whereas it is said, that the Book of Common Prayer makes mention of an altar; therefore it is not lawful to abolish that which the book allows. To this it is thus answered, the Book of Common Prayer calls the thing whereupon the Lord's Supper is administered indifferently a table, an altar, or the Lord's board, without prescribing any form, either of a table, or of an altar; so that whether the Lord's board have the form of an altar, or of a table, the book of Common Prayer calls it both an altar and a table. For as it calls it an altar, whereupon the Lord's Supper is administered, a table and the Lord's board, so it calls the table, where the holy communion is distributed with praise and thanksgiving unto the Lord, an altar, for there is offered the same sacrifice of praise and thanksgiving. And thus it appears that here is nothing either said or meant contrary to the Book of Common Prayer.

III. The popish opinion of mass was, that it might not be celebrated but upon an altar, or, at least, upon a super altar, to supply the fault of the altar, which must have had its prints and characters, or else it was thought that the thing was not lawfully done. But this superstitious opinion is more holden in the minds of the simple and ignorant by the form of an altar, than of a table; therefore it is more meet for the abolishing of this superstitious opinion, to have the Lord's board after the form of a table than of an altar.

IV. The form of an altar was ordained for the sacrifices of the law, and the Greek word so implies. But now both the law and the sacrifices thereof cease; and therefore the form of the altar used in the altar ought to cease with it.

V. Christ instituted the sacrament of his body and blood at his last supper at a table, and not at an altar, as appears manifestly by the three Evangelists. And St. Paul calls the coming to the holy communion, the coming to the Lord's Supper. And also it is not read, that any of the apostles, or the primitive church, did ever use any altar in the ministration of the holy communion.

Wherefore seeing the form of a table is more agreeable to Christ's institution, and with the usage of the apostles, and of the primitive church, than the form of an altar, therefore the form of a table is rather to be used than the form of an altar in the administration of the holy communion.

VI. It is said in the preface to the Book of Common Prayer, that if any doubt arise in the use and practising of the same book; to appease all such diversity, the matter shall be referred to the bishop of the diocese, who by his discretion shall take order for the quieting and appeasing of the same, so that the same order be not contrary to any thing contained in that book.

After these letters and reasons were received, Nicholas Ridley, bishop of London, held his visitation; wherein, among other injunctions, the bishop exhorted those churches in his diocese, where the altars then remained, to conform themselves to those other churches which had taken them down, and had set up instead of the multitude of their altars, one decent table in every church.

There arose a great diversity about the form of the Lord's board, some using it after the form of a table, and some of an altar. Wherein when the bishop was required to determine what was most meet, he declared he could do no less of his bouden duty, for the appeasing of such diversity, and to procure one godly uniformity, but to exhort all his diocese to that which he thought best agreed with scripture, with the usage of the apostles, and with the primitive church, and to that which is not only not contrary to any thing contained in the Book of Common Prayer, but also might highly further the king's most godly proceedings in abolishing of vain and superstitious opinions of the popish mass out of the hearts of the simple, and to bring them to the right use taught by the holy scriptures of the Lord's Supper; and so he appointed the form of a table to be used in his diocese; and in the church of St. Paul he broke down the wall then standing by the high altar.

Now we will enter into those matters which happened between King Edward and his sister Mary, as by their letters here following are to be seen:

To my Lord Protector and the rest of the King's Majesty's Council.

"My lord, I perceive by the letters which I lately received from you, and others of the king's majesty's council, that ye are all sorry to find so little conformity in me touching the observation of his majesty's laws. I am well assured, that I have offended no law, unless it be a late law of your own making, for the altering of matters in religion, which in my conscience is not worthy to have the name of a law, both for the king's honour-sake, the welfare of the realm, and giving an occasion of an evil report through all Christendom, besides the partiality used in the same, and (as my conscience is very well persuaded) the offending of God, which passes all the rest; but I am well assured that the king's father's laws were all allowed and consented to without compulsion by the whole realm, both spiritual and temporal, and all you executors sworn upon a book to fulfil the same, so that it was an authorised law, and I have obeyed that, and will do so with the grace of God, till the king's majesty, my brother, shall have sufficient years to be a judge in these matters himself. Wherein, my lord, I was plain with you at my last being at the court, and declared to you at that time whereto I would stand, and now do assure you all, that the only occasion of my stay from altering mine opinion, is for two causes.

"One principally for my conscience sake; the other, that the king, my brother, shall not hereafter charge me to be one of those that were agreeable to such alterations in his tender years. And what fruits daily grow by such changes, since the death of the king, my father, to every indifferent person it well appears, both to the displeasure of God, and unquietness of the realm.

"Notwithstanding, I assure you all, I would be as loath to see his highness take hurt, or that any evil should come to this his realm, as the best of you all, and none of you have the like cause, considering how I am compelled by nature, being his majesty's poor and humble sister, most tenderly to love and pray for him, and to this his realm (being born within the same) wish all health and prosperity to God's honour.

"And if any judge of me the contrary for mine opinion's sake, as I trust none doth, I doubt not in the end, with God's help, to prove myself as true a natural and humble sister, as they of the contrary opinion, with all their devices and altering of laws, shall prove themselves true subjects; praying you, my lord, and the rest of the council, no more to trouble and unquiet me with matters touching my conscience, wherein I am at a full point, with God's help, whatever shall happen to me, intending, with his grace, to trouble you little with any worldly suits, but to bestow the short time I think to live in quietness, and pray for the king's majesty, and all of you, heartily wishing that your proceedings may be to God's honour, the safeguard of the king's person, and quietness to the realm.

"Moreover, where your desire is, that I shall send my controller, and Doctor Hopton, to you, by whom you would signify your minds more amply, to my content and honour; it is not unknown to you all, that the chief charge of my house rests only upon the labours of my controller, who has not been absent from my house three whole days since the setting up of the same, unless it were for my letters patent; so that if it were not for his continual diligence, I think my little portion would not have stretched so far. And my chaplain, by occasion of sickness has been long absent, and is not yet able to ride.

"Therefore as I cannot forbear my controller, and my priest is not able to journey, so shall I desire you, my lord, and all the rest of the council, that having any thing to be declared to me, except on matters of religion, you will either write your minds, or send some trusty person, with whom I shall be contented to talk, and make answer as the case shall require; assuring you that if any servant of mine, either man or woman, or chaplain, should move me to the contrary of my conscience, I would not give ear to them, nor suffer the like to be used within my house. And thus, my lord, with my hearty commendations, I wish to you and the rest as well to do as myself.

"From my house at Kenning Hall, the two-and-twentieth day of June, 1549.
          "Your assured friend to my power,
                    "MARY."

To this letter the council replied, giving instructions to Doctor Hopton, who should himself inform the princess of the mind of the council, after which the king wrote to her as follow:

The King's Letter to the Lady Mary, twenty-fourth of January, 1550.

"Right dear, &c. We have seen by letters of our council, sent to you of late, and by your answer touching your chaplains having offended our laws in saying mass, the good and convenient advices of our council, and your fruitless and indirect mistaking the same: which moves us to write at this time, that where good counsel from our council has not prevailed, yet the like from ourself may have due regard. The whole matter we perceive rests in this, that you being our next sister, in whom above all others our subjects, nature should place the most estimation of us, would wittingly and purposely, not only break our laws yourself, but also have others maintained to do the same. Truly, however, the matter may have other terms, other sense it has not: and although by your letter it seems you challenge a promise made to you, that you may do so, yet surely we know the promise had no such meaning, either to maintain, or to continue your fault. You must know this, sister, you were at first, when the law was made, borne with, not that you should disobey the law, but that by our lenity and love you might learn to obey it. We made a difference between you and our other subjects, not that all others should follow our laws, and you only oppose them, but that you might be brought as far by love, as others were by duty. The error in which you rest is double, and so great, that neither for the love of God can we suffer it unredressed, neither for the love of you can we but wish it amended. First, you retain a fashion in honouring of God, who indeed, is thereby dishonoured, and you err in zeal for lack of knowledge, and having knowledge offered to you, you refuse it, not because it is knowledge, we trust (for then should we despair of you), but because you think it is not. And surely in this we can best reprehend you, because we learn daily in our school, that therefore we may learn things, because we know them not, and we are not allowed to say we know not those things, or we think they are not good, and therefore we will not learn them. Sister, you must think nothing can commend you more than reason, according to which you have been hitherto used; and now for very love we will, ourself, offer you reason. If you are persuaded in conscience contrary to our laws, you or your persuaders shall freely be suffered to say what you or they can, so that you will hear what shall be said again.

"In this point you see I pretermit my estate, and talk with you as your brother, rather than your supreme lord and king. Thus should you, being as well content to hear of your opinions as you are content to hold them, in the end thank us as much for bringing you to light as now, before you learn, you are loath to see it. And if thus much reason with our natural love shall not move you, whereof we would be sorry, then we must consider the other part of your fault, which is the offence of our laws. For though hitherto it has been suffered, in hope of amendment, yet now, if there be no hope, how shall there be sufferance? Our charge is to have the same care over every man's estate, that every man ought to have over his own. And in your own house as you would be loath openly to suffer one of your servants, being next you, most manifestly to break your orders, so must you think in our state it shall miscontent us to permit you, so great a subject, not to keep our laws. Your nearness to us in blood, your greatness in estate, the condition of this time makes your fault the greater. The example is unnatural, that our sister should do less for us than our other subjects. The cause is slanderous for so great a personage to forsake our majesty.

"Finally, It is too dangerous in a troublesome commonwealth, to make the people to mistrust a faction. We are young, you think, in years to consider this. Truly sister, it troubles us the more; for it may be, this evil suffered in you is greater than we can discern, and so we are as much troubled because we doubt whether we see the whole peril, as we do for what we do see. Indeed we will presume no further than our years gives us; that is, in doubtful things not to trust our own judgment, but in evident things we think there is no difference. If you should not do as other subjects do, were it not evident that you would not be a good subject? Were it not plain in that case, that you would use us not as your sovereign lord? Again, if you should be suffered manifestly to break our laws, would it not be a covert for others to do so? And if our law be broken, and contemned, where is our estate? These things are so plain, as we could almost have judged them six years past. And indeed it grieves us not a little, that you, who should be our greatest comfort in our young years, should alone give us occasion of discomfort. Think you not but it must needs trouble us, and if you can so think, you ought, sister, to amend it. Our natural love towards you without doubt is great, and therefore diminish it not yourself. If you will be loved by us, shew some token of love towards us, that we say not with the Psalm, "They rendered me evil for good." If you will be believed when by writing you confess us to be your sovereign lord, hear that which in other things is often alleged, "Shew me thy faith by thy works." In the answer of your letter to our council, we remember you hold only upon one reason divided into two parts. The first is, that in matters of religion your faith is no other, than as all Christendom does confess. The next is, you will assent to no alteration, but wish things to stand as they did at our father's death. If you mean in the first to rule your faith by that which you call Christendom, and not by this church of England, wherein you are a member, you shall err in many points,

such as our father's would not have suffered, whatever you may say of the standing still of things as they were left by him. The matter is too plain to write, what may be gathered, and too perilous to be concluded against you. For the other part, if you like no alteration by our authority, of things not altered by our father, you should do us too great an injury. We take ourself, for the administration of this our commonwealth, to have the same authority which our father had, diminished in no part, neither by example of scripture, nor by universal laws. The histories in scripture are plenteous, which show us that almost the best ordered church of the Israelites was by kings younger than we are. Well, sister, we will not in these things interpret your writings to the worst; love and charity shall expound them. But yet you must not be bold to offend in that whereunto you see your writings might be wrested. To conclude, we exhort you to do your duty, and if there be any impediment, not of purpose, you shall find a brotherly affection in us to remedy the same. To teach and instruct you we will give order, and so procure you to do your duty willingly, that you shall perceive you are not used merely as a subject, and only commanded; but as a daughter, a scholar, and a sister, taught, instructed, and persuaded. For which cause, when you have considered this our letter, we pray you that we may shortly hear from you."

The Lady Mary's Answer to the King.

"My duty most humbly remembered to your majesty, please it the same to understand that I have received your letters by Master Throgmorton, this bearer. The contents whereof do more trouble me than any bodily sickness, though it were even to the death; and the rather for that your highness doth charge me to be both a breaker of your laws, and also an encourager of others to do the like. I most humbly beseech your majesty to think that I never intended towards you otherwise than my duty compelleth me unto; that is, to wish your highness all honour and prosperity, for which I do and daily shall pray. And where it pleaseth your majesty to write, that I make a challenge of a promise made otherwise than it was meant, the truth is, the promise could not be denied before your majesty's presence, at my last waiting upon you. And although, I confess, the ground of faith (whereunto I take reason to be but an handmaid) and my conscience also hath and do agree with the same: yet touching that promise, for so much as it hath pleased your majesty (God knoweth by whose persuasion) to write, it was not so meant. I shall most humbly desire your highness to examine the truth thereof indifferently, and either your majesty's ambassador, now being with the emperor, shall inquire of the same, if it be your pleasure to have him move it, or else to cause it to be demanded of the emperor's ambassador here, although he were not within this realm at that time. And thereby it shall appear that in this point I have not offended your majesty, if it may please you so to accept it. And albeit your majesty (God be praised) hath at these years as much understanding, and more, than is commonly seen in that age, yet considering you do hear but one part (your highness not offended) I would be a suiter to the same, that till you were grown to more perfect years, it might stand with your pleasure to stay in matters touching the soul. So undoubtedly should your majesty know more, and hear others, and nevertheless be at your liberty and do your will and pleasure. And whatsoever your majesty hath conceived of me, either by letters to your council, or by their report, I trust in the end to prove myself as true to you, as any subject within your realm, and will by no means stand in argument with your majesty, but in most humble wise beseech you, even for God's sake, to suffer me, as your highness hath done hitherto. It is for no worldly respect I desire it, God is my judge; but rather than to offend my conscience, I would desire of God to lose all that I have, and also my life; and nevertheless, live and die your humble sister and true subject. Thus, after pardon craved of your majesty for my rude and bold writing, I beseech Almighty God to preserve the same in honour with as long continuance of health and life, as ever had noble king.

"From Beaulieu, the third of February.

"Your majesty's most humble and
"unworthy sister, MARY."

After many other letters from the council to the princess Mary, and from her in reply, as also to his majesty, the king wrote the following :—

The King's Letter to the Lady Mary.

"Right dearly and right entirely beloved sister, we greet you well, and let you know that it grieves us much to perceive no amendment in you, of that, which we for God's cause, your soul's health, our conscience, and the common tranquillity of our realm, have so long desired ; assuring you that our sufferance hath much more demonstration of natural love, than contentment of our conscience, and foresight of our safety. Wherefore although you give us occasion, as much almost as in you is, to diminish our natural love ; yet we are loath to feel it decay, and mean not to be so careless of you as we are provoked to be.

"And therefore meaning your weal, and therewith joining a care not to be found guilty in our conscience to God, having cause to require forgiveness that we have so long, for respect of love toward you, omitted our bounden duty, we send at this present our right trusty and right well-beloved councillor, the lord Rich, chancellor of England, and our trusty and right well beloved councillors, Sir Anthony Wingfield, knight, controller of our household, and Sir William Paget, knight, one of our principal secretaries, in message to you, touching the order of your house, willing you to give them firm credit in those matters they shall say to you from us, and do there, in our name.

"Given under our signet, at our castle of Windsor, the 24th day of August, in the first year of our reign."

A Copy of the King's Instructions, given to the said Lord Chancellor, Sir Anthony Wingfield, and Sir William Paget, knights, &c., the 24th of August, 1551.

"You the said lord chancellor and your colleagues shall immediately repair to the lady Mary, giving to her his majesty's hearty commendations, and shew the cause of your coming to be as follows :—

"Although his majesty has a long time, as well by his majesty's own mouth and writing, as by his council, endeavoured that the lady being his sister, and a principal subject and member of his realm, should both be indeed, and also shew herself conformable to the laws and ordinances of the realm, in the profession and rites of religion, using all gentle means of exhortation and advice that the reformation of the fault might willingly come of herself, as was the expectation and desire of his majesty, and all good and wise men ; yet notwithstanding his majesty sees that hitherto no manner of amendment has followed ; but by the continuance of the error, and manifest breach of his laws no small peril may happen to the state of his realm, the sufferance of such a fault being directly to the dishonour of God, and the great offence of his majesty's conscience, and that of all other good men ; and therefore of late, even with the consent and advice of the whole state of his privy council, and divers others of the nobility of his realm, whose names you may repeat, if you think convenient, his majesty did resolutely determine it just, necessary, and expedient, that her grace should not in anywise use or maintain the private mass, or any other manner of service, than such as by the law of the realm is authorized and allowed : and to signify this his majesty's determination to her grace, it was thought in respect of a favourable proceeding with herself, to have the same not only to be manifested by her own officers and servants, being most esteemed with her, but also to be executed

with them in her house, as well for the quiet proceeding in the very matter, as for the less molesting of her grace with any message by strangers, in that time of her solitariness, wherein her grace was then by reason of the late sickness. For which purpose, her three servants, Rochester, Englefield, and Waldgrave were sent in message in this manner. First, to deliver his majesty's letter to her ; next to discharge the complaints of saying mass, and prohibiting all the household from hearing any. Wherein the king's majesty perceives upon their own report being returned to the court, how negligently, and indeed how falsely they have executed their commandment and charge, contrary to the duty of good subjects, and to the manifest contempt of his majesty. Insomuch as they have before his majesty's council refused to do that which pertains to every true faithful subject, to the offence so far of his majesty, and derogation of his authority, that the punishment of them could in nowise be forborne, and yet in the manner of the punishment of them, his majesty and his council hath such consideration and respect of her person, being his sister, that without doubt his majesty could not with honour have had the like consideration or favour in the punishment of the dearest councillor he has, if any of them had so offended ; and therefore his majesty has sent you three not only to declare to her grace the causes of his sending thither of late his officers in message, but also the causes of their absence now presently. And further, in the default of the officers, to take order, as well with her chaplains, as with the whole household, that his majesty's laws may be there observed. And in the communication with her, you shall take occasion to answer in his majesty's name certain points of her letter lately sent to his majesty. The copy of which letter is now also sent to you to peruse, for your better instruction how to proceed therein. First, her allegation of the promise made to the emperor must be so answered as the truth of the matter serves, whereof every one of you have often heard sufficient testimony in the council. For her offering of her body at the king's will, rather than to change her conscience, it grieves his majesty much that her conscience is so settled in error, and yet no such thing is meant of his majesty, nor of any of his council, once to hurt or will evil to her body ; but even to the bottom of their hearts they wish to her a sound mind in a sound body. And therefore you shall do well to persuade her grace, that this proceeding cometh only of the conscience, the king hath to avoid offence to God, and of necessary counsel and wisdom to see his laws in so weighty causes executed. Also, because it is thought that Rochester had the care and consideration of her grace's provision of her household, and by his absence the same might be disordered or disfurnished : his majesty hath sent a trusty skilful man of his own household, to serve her grace for the time. Who also is sufficiently instructed by Rochester of the state of things in her household. And if there shall be anything lacking in the same, his majesty's pleasure is, that his servant shall advertise his own chief officers of his household, to the intent that the same may be supplied from any store here, or otherwise conveniently helped, so that her grace shall not lack.

"Having thus proceeded with her grace, for the declaration of the causes of your coming, you shall then cause to be called before you the chaplains, and all the rest of the household there present, and in the king's majesty's name most straightly forbid the chaplains either to say or use any mass or kind of service other than by the law is authorised ; and likewise you shall forbid all the rest of the company to be present at any such prohibited service, upon pain of being most severely punished ; as deservedly falling into the danger of the king's indignation, and alike charge them all, that if any such offence shall be openly or secretly committed, they shall advertise some of his majesty's council. In which case you shall use the reasons of their natural duty and allegiance that they owe as subjects to their sovereign lord, which derogates all other earthly duties.

"Also, if you shall find any of the priests, or any other person disobedient to this order, then you shall commit them forthwith to prison, as ye shall think convenient

"Also, forasmuch as ye were privy to the determination at Richmond, and there understood how necessary it was to have reformation herein ; his majesty upon the great confidence he hath in your wisdom and uprightness, remits to your discretion the manner of proceeding herein ; and if any thing shall chance to arise there otherwise than according to these instructions, then to assist you in the execution of your charge, our instructions in one sum are, to avoid the use of the private mass, and other unlawful service in the house of the lady Mary.

"Also, you shall devise by some means as you think fit, to have understanding after your departure, how the order you give is observed, and, as you shall judge fit, to certify the same to me."

Some Account of Stephen Gardiner, Bishop of Winchester.

Although the first imprisonment of Stephen Gardiner, bishop of Winchester, was before the deprivation of bishop Bonner, yet as he was not deposed from his bishopric till the next or second year after, (A.D. 1551,) I have therefore put off his history to this present place.

When the king's injunctions for a visitation of the whole realm were sent forth, this bishop displayed a spirit of neglect and disobedience ; and warned, in his sermons, the people against the preachers of the gospel, and generally against the king's proceedings. Having disobeyed the king's injunctions, he was sent to the Fleet, and there so misconducted himself, as also before the council, that he was committed to the Tower.

Certain of the council, by the king's appointment, had many times access to him in the Tower, to persuade him ; the duke of Somerset, the lord treasurer, the lord privy seal, the lord great chamberlain, and Master Secretary Petre. Who repairing to him on the tenth day of June, A.D. 1550, he desired of them to see the king's book of proceedings ; upon the sight of which he would make a full answer, seeming to be willing in all things to conform himself to the king's proceedings, and promising that in case anything offended his conscience, he would open it to none but to the council. Upon which it was agreed, that the book should be sent to him to see his answer, that his case might be resolved upon, and that he should have the liberty of the gallery and garden in the Tower, when the duke of Norfolk should be absent.

The answer of the bishop being received, through the report of the lords which had been with him, declaration was made the eighth of July, 1550, that his answers were doubtful. Therefore it was determined, that he should be directly examined, whether he would sincerely conform himself to the king's proceedings or not.

The following articles were therefore sent to him for his subscription as a proof of his conformity.

"Whereas I, Stephen, bishop of Winchester, having been suspected as one too much favouring the bishop of Rome's authority, decrees, and ordinances, and as one that did not approve or allow the king's majesty's proceedings in alteration of certain rites in religion, was summoned before the king's highness's council, and admonished thereof ; and having certain things appointed for me to do and preach for my declaration, have not done that as I ought to do, although I promised to do the same ; whereby I have not only incurred the king's majesty's indignation, but also divers of his highness's subjects have by my example taken encouragement (as his grace's council is certainly informed) to repine at his majesty's most godly proceedings ; I am right sorry therefore, and acknowledge myself condignly to have been punished, and do most heartily thank his majesty, that of his great clemency it hath pleased his highness to deal with me, not according to rigour, but mercy. And to the intent it may appear to the world how little I do repine at his highness's doings, which be in religion most

godly, and to the commonwealth most profitable, I do affirm and say freely of mine own will, without any compulsion, as ensueth :—

"I. That by the law of God, and the authority of the scriptures, the king's majesty, and his successors, are the supreme heads of the churches of England and of Ireland.

"II. That the appointing of holy-days and fasting days ; as Lent, Ember days, or any such like, or to dispense therewith, is in the king's majesty's authority and power : and his highness as supreme head of the churches of England and Ireland, and governor thereof, may appoint the manner and time of the holy-days and fasting days, or dispense therewith, as to his wisdom shall seem most convenient for the honour of God and the wealth of this realm.

"III. That the king's majesty hath most christianly and godly set forth, by and with the consent of the whole parliament, a devout and christian book of service of the church, to be used by the church ; which book is to be accepted and allowed of all bishops, pastors, curates, and all ministers, ecclesiastical of the realm of England, and so of him to be declared and commended in all places where he shall happen to preach or speak to the people of it, that it is a godly and christian book and order, and to be allowed, accepted, and observed of all the king's majesty's true subjects.

"IV. I do acknowledge the king's majesty, that now is (whose life God long preserve), to be my sovereign lord and supreme head, under Christ, to me as a bishop of this real, and natural subject to his majesty, and now in this his young and tender age, to be my full and entire king ; and that I, and all other his highness's subjects, are bound to obey all his majesty's proclamations, statutes, laws, and commandments, made, promulgated, and set forth in his highness's young age, as well as though his highness were at this present thirty or forty years old.

"V. I confess and acknowledge, that the statute commonly called the Statute of the Six Articles, for just causes and grounds, is by authority of parliament repealed and disannulled.

"VI. That his majesty and his successors have authority in the churches of England, and also of Ireland, to alter, reform, correct, and amend all errors and abuses, and all rites and ceremonies ecclesiastical, as shall seem from time to time to his highness and his successors most convenient for the edification of his people, so that the same alteration be not contrary or repugnant to the scriptures and law of God.

"Subscribed by STEPHEN WINCHESTER, with the testimonial hands of the council to the same."

To these articles, although Winchester with his own hand subscribed, granting the supremacy of the king, yet, because he stuck so much in the first point touching his submission, and would in no case subscribe, but only made his answer in the margin, it was therefore thought good, that the master of the horse, and Master Secretary Petre should repair to him again, exhorting him to look better upon it, and at the same time his subscription or answers were required to the following articles :—

Copy of the last Articles sent to the Bishop of Winchester.

"Whereas I, Stephen, bishop of Winchester, have been suspected as one that did not approve or allow the king's majesty's proceedings in alteration of certain rites in religion, and was convented before the king's highness's council, and admonished thereof, and having certain things appointed for me to do and preach for my declaration, have not done therein as I ought to do, whereby I have deserved his majesty's displeasure ; I am right sorry therefore. And to the intent it may appear to the world how little I do repine at his highness's doings, which are in religion most godly, and to the commonwealth most profitable, I do affirm as follows :—

" I. That the late king, of most famous memory, king Henry the eighth, our late sovereign lord, justly and of good reason and ground hath taken away, and caused to be suppressed and defaced, all monasteries and religious houses, and all conventicles and convents of monks, friars, nuns, canons, bonhoms, and other persons called religious, and that the same being so dissolved, the persons therein bound and professed to obedience to a person, place, habit, and other superstitious rites and ceremonies, upon that dissolution and order appointed by the king's majesty's authority as supreme head of the church, are clearly released and acquitted of those vows and professions, and at their full liberty, as though those unwitty and superstitious vows had never been made.

" II. That any person may lawfully marry, without any dispensation from the bishop of Rome, or any other man, with any person whom it is not prohibited to contract matrimony with, by the Levitical law.

" III. That the vowing and going on pilgrimage to images, or the bones or relics of any saints, hath been superstitiously used, and the cause of much wickedness and idolatry, and therefore justly has been abolished by the late king, and the images and relics so abused have been (great and godly considerations) defaced and destroyed.

" IV. That the counterfeiting of St. Nicholas, St. Clement, St. Catharine, and St. Edmund, by children heretofore brought into the church, was a mere mockery and foolishness, and therefore justly abolished and taken away.

" V. It is convenient and godly, that the scriptures of the Old and New Testament, that is, the whole Bible, be had in English and published, to be read of every man, and that whosoever doth repel and discourage men from reading thereof, doeth evil.

" VI. That the said late king, of just ground and reason, did receive into his hands the authority and disposition of chantries, and such livings as were given for the maintenance of private masses, and did well change divers of them to other uses.

" VII. The king's majesty that now is, by the advice and consent of the parliament, did upon just ground and reason, suppress, abolish, and take away the said chantries, and such other livings as were used and occupied for maintenance of private masses, and masses satisfactory for the souls of them that are dead, or finding of obites, lights, or other like things : The mass that was wont to be said of priests was full of abuses, and had very few things of Christ's institution, besides the epistle, gospel, the Lord's prayer, and the words of the Lord's supper; the rest, for the greater part, were invented and devised by bishops of Rome, and by other men of the same sort, and therefore justly taken away by the statutes and laws of this realm ; and the communion which is placed instead thereof, is very godly, and agreeable to the scriptures.

" VIII. That it is most convenient and fit, and according to the first institution, that all christian men should receive the sacrament of the body and blood of Christ in both the kinds, that is, in bread and wine.

" IX. And the mass, wherein only the priest receiveth and others do but look on, is but the invention of man, and the ordinance of the bishop of Rome's church, but not agreeable to the scriptures.

" X. That upon good and godly considerations it is ordered in the said book and order, that the sacrament should not be lifted up, and shewed to the people to be adored, but to be with godly devotion received, as it was when first instituted.

" XI. That it is well, politically, and godly done, that the king's majesty by act of parliament, hath commanded all images which have stood in churches and chapels, to be abolished and defaced, lest hereafter at any time they should give occasion of idolatry, or be abused, as many of them heretofore have been, with pilgrimages, and such idolatrous worshipping.

" XII. That, by the same authority of parliament, all mass-books, and other books of the service in Latin, heretofore used, should be abolished and defaced, as well for certain superstitions contained in them, as also to avoid dissension : And that the said service in the church should be through the whole realm in one uniform conformity, and no occasion through those old books to the contrary.

" XIII. That bishops, priests, and deacons, have no commandment of the law of God, either to vow chastity, or to abstain continually from marriage.

" XIV. That all canons, constitutions, laws positive, and ordinances of man, which prohibit or forbid marriage to any bishop, priest, or deacon, be justly, and upon godly grounds and considerations taken away and abolished by authority of parliament.

" XV. The homilies lately commanded and set forth by the king's majesty, to be read in the congregation of England, are godly and wholesome, and do teach such doctrine as ought to be embraced of all men.

" XVI. The book set forth by the king's majesty, by authority of parliament, containing the form and manner of making and consecrating of archbishops, bishops, priests, and deacons, is godly, and in no point contrary to the wholesome doctrine of the gospel, and therefore ought to be received and approved of by all the faithful members of the church of England, and especially the ministers of God's word, and by them commanded to the people.

" XVII. That the orders of sub-deacon, Benet and Colet, and such others as were commonly called minores ordines, are not necessary by the word of God to be reckoned in the church, and are justly left out in the said book of orders.

" XVIII. That the holy scriptures contain sufficiently all doctrine required of necessity for eternal salvation through faith in Jesus Christ, and that nothing is to be taught as required of necessity to eternal salvation, but that which may be concluded and proved by the holy scriptures.

" XIX. That upon good and godly considerations it was and is commanded by the king's majesty's injunctions, that the paraphrases of Erasmus in English, should be set up in some convenient place in every parish church of this realm, that the parishioners may most commodiously resort to read the same.

" XX. And because these articles aforesaid, do contain only such matters as are already published, and openly set forth by the king's majesty's authority, by the advice of his highness' council, for many great and godly considerations; and amongst others, for the common tranquillity and unity of the realm : his majesty's pleasure, by the advice aforesaid, is, that you the bishop of Winchester, shall not only affirm these articles with subscription of your hand, but also declare and profess yourself well contented, willing, and ready, to publish and preach the same at such times and places, and before such audience, as to his majesty from time to time shall seem convenient and requisite, upon pain of incurring such penalties and punishments as for not doing the same, may by his majesty's laws be inflicted upon you.

" These articles were sent to him on the fifteenth of July.

The bishop of Winchester receiving and perusing these articles, made this answer again :—That first touching the article of submission, he would in no wise consent, affirming, as he had done before, that he had never offended the king's majesty in any such sort as should give him cause thus to submit himself; praying earnestly to be brought to his trial, wherein he refused the king's mercy, and desired nothing but justice. And for the rest of the articles, he answered, that after he was past his trial on the first point, and was at liberty, then it should appear what he would do ; if not being reasonable, as he said, that he should subscribe them in prison.

Of this answer, when the king and his council had intelligence, it was agreed that he should be sent for before the whole council, and peremptorily required to subscribe the articles which had been sent to him ; but this he refused to do. Upon this the fruits of his bishopric were sequestered, and he was required to conform himself to their orders, within three months, upon pain of deprivation.

After this sequestration, the bishop was brought to Lambeth before the king's commissioners, namely, the archbishop of Canterbury; Nicholas bishop of London, Thomas bishop of Ely, Henry bishop of Lincoln; Secretary Petre, judge; Sir James Hales, knight; Dr. Leyson, Dr. Oliver, Lawyers; and John Gosnold, esquire, &c., to be examined by them on nineteen articles which were objected against him, charging him with direct disobedience to the royal injunctions.

After the articles were exhibited to him, and he had leave to answer, he used all the wary shifts and remedies of the law, by way of protesting, recusing, and excepting against the commission, and requiring also the copies both of the articles and of his protestation, of the actuaries; yea, he so cavilled and dallied from day to day to answer directly, that at last he appealed from them, reputing them not to be competent and impartial judges to hear and determine his cause, to the king's royal person; and in the end the commissioners proceeded to the sentence definitive against him, deposing him from all the rights and emoluments of the see of Winchester.

This sentence being given, the bishop of Winchester excepted against it as unjust, and of no effect in law, and then and there, immediately after the pronouncing of the sentence, by word of mouth, appealed to the king's royal majesty.

And here we leave Winchester for a while, till we come to treat of his death hereafter. Whom as we number amongst good lawyers, so is he to be reckoned among ignorant and bad divines, proud prelates, and bloody persecutors, as both by his cruel life and pharisaical doctrine may appear.

The Tragical History of the worthy Lord Edward Duke of Somerset, Lord Protector.

After having recorded so many troublous matters, we come now to the lamentable and tragical history of the lord Edward, duke of Somerset, the king's uncle, and protector of his person, and of his realm; and purpose to relate in order the origin and whole occasion, even from the beginning.

King Edward, after both his father and mother were dead, had three uncles by his mother's side, Edward, Thomas, and Henry Seymour; of the two first, one was made protector of the realm and the other high admiral. These two others so long as they were joined together in amity and concord, preserved both themselves, the king their nephew, and the whole commonwealth, from the violence and fear of all danger. But the subtle old serpent always envying man's felicity, through slanderous tongues, sought to sow discord between them; then suspicion; and last of all extreme hatred; so that the protector suffered his brother to be condemned, and to lose his head. By which it came to pass by God's judgment upon him, or because he, after the death of his brother and the king, (being yet but young and tender of age, was the less able to shift for himself) that not long after, he was overthrown by his enemies, and imprisoned in the Tower, and at last lost his head also, to the great lamentation of many good men.

For the better introduction of this history, we will begin with the brother of the lord protector, Sir Thomas Seymour, high admiral of England, who had married queen Catharine, late wife to king Henry VIII. Now it happened (upon what occasion I know not) that a difference took place between the queen and the duchess of Somerset, and then also in behalf of their wives, displeasure began between the brothers. Which although through the persuasion of friends it was for a time appeased, yet in a short period after it broke out again, both to the trouble of the realm, and especially to the confusion of themselves. First, it was laid to the lord admiral's charge, that he purposed to destroy the young king, and to transfer the crown to himself, and being attainted and condemned, he suffered at Tower-hill on the

twentieth of March, 1549. As there were many who reported that the duchess of Somerset had wrought his death, so there were many who thought and affirmed that the fall of one brother would be the ruin of the other.

It was not long after the beheading of the lord admiral, that insurrections began in divers quarters of the realm. By occasion of which, the lord Russel, lord privy seal, was sent to the West parts, and the lord Dudley, earl of Warwick, was sent with an army into Norfolk; where both he and a great number of gentlemen that were with him, meeting with the rebels, were in great danger: notwithstanding, in the end the rebels were overthrown, which was about the beginning of September, 1549. After this victory, in the month following, at the return of the earl of Warwick, there was great working and consultation among the lords, who assembled themselves in the house of Mr. York, and at Baynard's Castle, and in the lord mayor's house at London, against the lord protector, who then remained with the king at Hampton Court. Of which business and trouble thus the lord protector writes in his letters to the lord Russel in the West country.

A Letter of the Lord Protector, to the Lord Russel, Lord Privy Seal, concerning troubles working against him.

"After our right hearty commendations to your good lordship, here hath of late risen such a conspiracy against the king's majesty and us, as never hath been seen, the which they cannot maintain but with such vain letters and false tales surmised, as was never meant nor intended of us. They pretend and say, that we have sold Boulogne to the French, and that we withhold wages from the soldiers, and such other tales and letters they spread abroad (of which, if any one thing be true, we would not wish to live); the matter now being brought to a marvellous extremity, such as we would never have thought it could have come unto, especially of those men towards the king's majesty and us, of whom we have deserved no such thing, but rather much favour and love. But the case being as it is, this is to require and pray you to hasten hither to the defence of the king's majesty, with such force and power as you may, to shew the part of a true gentleman, and of a sincere friend: which thing we trust God shall reward, and the king's majesty in time to come, and we shall never be unmindful of it too. We are sure you shall have other letters from them; but as you tender your duty to the king's majesty, we require you to make no stay, but immediately repair with such force as you have to his highness's Castle of Windsor, and cause the rest of such force as you may command to follow you. And so we bid you right heartily farewell.

"From Hampton Court, the sixth of October.

"Your Lordship's assured loving friend,
"EDWARD SOMERSET."

To this letter of the lord protector, sent the 6th of October, the lord Russel returning answer upon the 8th, first laments the heavy dissension between the nobility and him, which he takes for such a plague, as a greater could not be sent by Almighty God upon this realm, being the next way, saith he, "to make us conquerors, slaves, and like to induce upon the whole realm an universal calamity and thraldom, unless the merciful goodness of the Lord help, and some wise order be taken in staying these great extremities." And as to the duke's request in his letters, forasmuch as he heard before of this broil of the lords, and fearing lest some conspiracy had been meant against the king's person, he hastened forward with such force as he could command for the safety of the king.

But to return to the matter of the lords, who, together with the earl of Warwick, were assembled at London against the lord protector; when the king with his council at Hampton Court heard of this, secretary Petre, with the king's message, was sent to them; but the lords detained him with them, making no answer to the message. Then the lord protector wrote to them as follows:

"My lords, we commend us most heartily unto you; and whereas the king's majesty was informed that you were assembled in such sort as you do now also remain, and was advised by us and such other of his council as were then here about his person, to send Master Secretary Petre unto you, with such message as thereby might have ensued the surety of his majesty's person, with preservation of his realm and subjects, and the quiet both of us and yourselves, as Master Secretary can well declare to you: his majesty and we of his council here do not a little marvel that you detain with you the said Master Secretary, and have not vouchsafed to send answer to his majesty, neither by him nor any other. And for ourselves, we do much more marvel and are right sorry, as both we and you have good cause to be, to see the manner of your doings bent with violence, to bring the king's majesty and us to these extremities. Now we do intend, if you will take no other way but violence, to defend as nature and our allegiance doth bind us, to extremity of death, and to put all into God's hand, who giveth victory as it pleaseth him: so that if any reasonable conditions and offers would take place (as hitherto none have been signified unto us from you, nor do we understand what you do require or seek, or what you do mean), and that you do seek no hurt to the king's majesty's person; as touching all other private matters, to avoid the effusion of christian blood, and to preserve the king's majesty's person, his realm, and his subjects; you shall find us agreeable to any reasonable condition that you will require. For we do esteem the king's safety and the tranquillity of the realm more than all other worldly things; yea, more than our own life. Thus praying you to send your determinate answer herein by Master Secretary Petre, or if you will not let him go, by this bearer. We beseech God to give both you and us grace to determine this matter, as may be to God's honour, the preservation of the king, and the quiet of us all, which may be, if the fault be not in you. And so we bid you most heartily farewell.

From the king's majesty's Castle of Windsor, the seventh of October, 1549."

After these letters received, and the reasonable condition of the lord protector,—yet not much regarded of the lords,—they, persisting still in their purpose, took this advice; first to keep themselves in the city of London, as strong as they might; and therefore calling upon the mayor and aldermen, they commanded them in any case to provide a good and substantial watch by night, and a good ward by day, for the safeguard of their city, and the ports and gates; which was consented unto, and the companies of London in their turn kept watch and ward accordingly.

Then these lords and councillors demanded of the lord mayor and his brethren five hundred men to aid them to fetch the lord protector out of Windsor from the king; but the mayor answered, that he could grant no aid without the assent of the common council of the city. So the next day a common council was warned. But in the meantime the lords of the council assembled themselves at the lord mayor's house, who then was Sir Henry Amcottes, fishmonger; and William Lock, mercer, and Sir John Aileph, were sheriffs; and there the council did agree and publish a proclamation against the lord protector, charging him as follows:

First, that the lord protector, by his malicious and evil government, was the occasion of all the sedition that of late happened within the realm.

2. The loss of the king's pieces in France.

3. That he was ambitious and sought his own glory, as appears by building of most sumptuous and costly houses in the time of the king's wars.

4. That he esteemed not the grave counsel of the councillors.

5. That he sowed division between the nobles, the gentlemen, and commons.

6. That the nobles have assembled themselves together at London for no other purpose but to cause the

protector to live within limits, and to take such order for the surety of the king's majesty as was fit, whatever the protector's doings might be; which they said were unnatural, ungrateful, and traitorous.

7. That the protector slandered the council to the king, and did what in him lay, to cause variance between the king and the nobles.

8. That he was a great traitor, and therefore the lords desired the city and commons to aid them, to take him from the king.

And in witness and testimony of the contents of the proclamation, the lords subscribed their names.

After the proclamation, the lords, or the most part of them, continuing in London, came the next day to the Guildhall, during the time that the Lord Mayor and his brethren sat in their court or inner chamber, and communed a long while with the mayor: and at last the mayor and his brethren came forth to the common council, where was read the king's letter sent to the mayor and citizens, commanding them to aid him with a thousand well appointed men out of their city, and to send them with all speed to his castle at Windsor.

This letter was directed to Sir Henry Amcottes, knight, lord mayor, to Sir Rowland Hill, knight, mayor elect, and to the aldermen and common council of the city of London. The day and date of the letter was the sixth of October, in the third year of his reign, being signed with the hand of the king, and of the lord protector.

This letter of the king and of the lord protector was not so secretly devised, nor so speedily sent, but the lords still remaining in London had knowledge immediately of it (by the means, as some suppose, of the lord Paget, who was then with the king and the protector), being there ready furnished with their own bands of serving-men, and other soldiers and men-at-arms.

The lords forthwith addressed their letters to the said lord mayor and aldermen also, in the king's name, not only for a support of armed men to serve their purposes, and for a sufficient watch to fortify their city, but also that they should not obey any such letters, proclamations, or injunctions sent to them from the duke. These letters of the lords came to the lord mayor and his brethren, the sixth day of the month of October.

After the receipt of these two letters, the one from the king, the other from the lords, which came both at one time, with contrary commandment to the lord mayor and citizens of London, they were perplexed what measures to take. On one side the name and authority of the king was much; on the other side the power of the lords, lying then in London, was not little, and seemed then to be such as would have no refusal.

The case thus standing in doubt, the recorder requested, that the citizens would grant their aid rather to the lords, for that the protector had abused both the king's majesty and the whole realm, and that unless he were taken from the king, and made to understand his folly, this realm was in great hazard; he therefore required that the citizens would assent to aid the lords with five hundred men.

By a great part in the common council no other answer was made but silence. But the recorder (who at that time was Mr. Brook) still looked to them for an answer. At last stepped up a wise and good citizen, named George Stadlow, and said:—

"In this case it is good for us to think of things past, to avoid the danger of things to come. I remember," said he, "in a story written in Fabian's Chronicle, of the war between the king and his barons, which was in the time of King Henry III., and then the barons (as our lords do now) demanded aid of the mayor and city of London, and that in a rightful cause for the commonwealth, which was for the execution of divers good laws against the king, who would not suffer those laws to be put in execution; and the city did aid them, and it came to an open battle, and the lords prevailed against the king, and took the king and his son prisoners, and upon certain conditions the lords restored the king and his son again to their liberties; and among all other conditions this was one, that the king should not only grant his pardon to the lords, but also to the citizens of London; which was granted, yea, and the same was ratified by act of parliament. But what followed? Was it forgotten? No surely, nor forgiven neither, during the king's life. The liberties of the city were taken away, strangers appointed to be our heads and governors, the citizens given away, body and goods, and with one persecution or another were most miserably afflicted. Such a thing is it to enter into the wrath of a prince, as Solomon saith, ' The wrath and indignation of a prince is death.' Wherefore, as this aid is required of the king's majesty, whose voice we ought to hearken to (for he is our high shepherd) rather than to the lords, and yet I would not wish the lords to be clearly shaken off; my counsel is, that they with us, and we with them may join in suit, and make our most humble petition to the king's majesty, that it would please his highness to hear such complaint against the government of the lord protector, as may be justly alleged and proved, and I doubt not but this matter will be so pacified, that neither shall the king nor yet the lords have cause to seek for further aid, nor we to offend either of them."

After this the commons stayed, and the lord mayor and his brethren for that time brake up, till they had further communed with the lords. The conclusion was, that the lords (upon what occasion I know not) sat the next day in council in the star-chamber, and from thence sent Sir Philip Hobby with the letter of credence to the king's majesty, beseeching and requesting his majesty to give credit to that which Sir Philip should declare to his majesty in their names; and the king gave him liberty to speak, and most gently heard all that he had to say. Who so handled the matter, declaring his message in the name of the lords, that in the end the lord protector was commanded from the king's presence, and shortly was committed to ward in a tower within the castle of Windsor; and soon after were arrested Sir Thomas Smith, Mr. Whalley, Mr. Fisher, and many other gentlemen that attended upon the lord protector. The same day the lords of the council resorted to the king, and the next day they brought from thence the lord protector, and the others that were there arrested, and conveyed them through the city of London to the Tower, and there left them.

And thus much concerning the first trouble of the lord protector duke of Somerset. Though his enemies seemed to intend no less than the spilling of his blood, yet the Lord above, the only Disposer of all men's purposes, so ordered the matter by means of the intercession of the king, that the proclamation which had made him a traitor, within three days after was called in again; and the duke was restored to liberty, which lasted two years and two days.

After which time, the duke of Somerset was again apprehended and committed to the Tower, and with him also Sir Michael Stanhope, Sir Ralph Vane, Sir Myles Partridge, and others. At length the time of his arraignment being come, the duke being brought from the Tower, was conveyed through London with the axe of the Tower before him, and with great preparation of bills, halberds, pikes, &c. A watch also was set and appointed before every man's door through the High street of London, and thus he was brought into Westminster-hall, where the lords of the council sitting as his judges in the middle of the hall, he was arraigned and charged both with treason and felony.

I pass over the unseemly speeches, the vile taunts, and despiteful rebukes used by certain of the sergeants and justices, and some others sitting there; all which he patiently and quietly suffered, and like a lamb, following the true Lamb and example of all meekness, was contented to take all things at their hands; and with no less patience to bear now their ungentle and cruel railings, than he did before their fulsome words and flatterings in time of his high estate and prosperity. And as the patience of this good duke was marvellous towards his enemies, so also was his discretion and temperance no less displayed in answering the articles objected to him; to these he replied, putting himself in

the end to be tried by his peers. Who then framed their verdict thus: " That as concerning treason, wherewith he was charged, they discharged him, but they accounted him guilty of felony." When the people (who were present in great numbers) heard the lords say, " Not guilty," (meaning of the treason) supposing that he had been entirely acquitted by these words, and especially seeing the axe of the Tower carried away, for great joy and gladness made an outcry, declaring their loving affection and hearty favour to the duke, whose life they greatly desired. But the people were deceived, and the innocent duke condemned to die for felony. Which act of felony had been made a little before against the rebels and unlawful assemblies, such as should seek or procure the death of any counsellor, so that every such attempt and procurement, according to the act, should be adjudged felony. By virtue of which act the duke being accused, with others, to intend and purpose the death of the duke of Northumberland, and of others beside, was condemned of felony, and sent back to the Tower.

At whose passage through the city great exclamations and outcries were made by the people, some rejoicing that he was acquitted, some bewailing that he was condemned.

He continued in the Tower till the twenty-second of January; upon which day, at the coming down of the letter of execution from the king and the council, the duke and uncle to the king being found no traitor, only being cast by the act of felony, was delivered unto the sheriffs, and so brought to the place of execution.

The order and manner of the execution have been related to us by a certain noble personage, who was there present, and near to him on the scaffold, beholding all things with his eyes, and with his pen also reporting them:

" On the twenty-second of January, 1552, in the sixth year of Edward VI., the noble duke of Somerset, uncle to king Edward, was brought out of the Tower of London, and delivered to the sheriffs of the city; and, surrounded by a great number of armed men both of the guard and others, he was brought to the scaffold on Tower-hill, where he nothing changing either voice or countenance, as calmly as if at home, kneeling down, and lifting up his hands, commended himself to God.

" After he had ended a few short prayers, standing up again, and turning himself toward the east side of the scaffold, not at all abashed, neither with the sight of the axe, nor yet of the executioner, nor of present death; but with alacrity and cheerfulness of mind and countenance as before times he was accustomed to hear the causes and supplication of others, and especially the poor (towards whom, as it were with a certain fatherly love to his children, he always shewed himself most attentive) he uttered these words to the people:

" ' Dearly beloved friends, I am brought hither to suffer death, although I never offended against the king either by word or deed, and have been always as faithful and true to this realm as any man has been. But forasmuch as I am by a law condemned to die, I do acknowledge myself, as well as others, to be subject thereto. Wherefore, to testify my obedience, which I owe to the laws, I am come hither to suffer death; whereto I willingly offer myself, with most hearty thanks to God, that has given me this time of repentance, who might, through sudden death, have taken away my life, that neither I should have acknowledged him nor myself.

" ' Moreover, dearly beloved friends, there is yet somewhat that I must put you in mind of, as touching the christian religion; which, so long as I was in authority, I always diligently set forth and furthered to my power. Neither do I repent me of my doings, but rejoice therein, since now the state of the christian religion comes much nearer to the form and order of the primitive church. Which thing I esteem as a great benefit given of God both to you and me; most heartily exhorting you all, that this which is most purely set forth to you, you will with like thankfulness accept and embrace, and set out the same in your living. Which thing, if you do not, without doubt greater mischief and calamity will follow.'

"When he had spoken these words, suddenly there was a terrible noise; and there came a great fear upon all men. This noise was as if it had been the noise of some great storm; as if a great deal of gunpowder enclosed in a magazine had exploded. To some again it seemed as if it had been a great multitude of horsemen running together, or coming upon them. So great was the noise in the ears of all men, although they saw nothing, that all the people being amazed without any evident cause, or any man seen, ran away, some into the ditches and puddles, and some into the houses; others being afraid of the horror and noise, fell down grovelling to the ground, with their pole-axes and halberds; and most of them cried out, 'Jesus save us, Jesus save us!' Those who stood still knew not where they were; and I myself who was there present among the rest, being also afraid in this confusion, stood still altogether amazed, expecting that some one would knock me on the head.

"In the mean time, the people by chance spied Sir Anthony Brown riding under the scaffold; which was the occasion of a new noise; for when they saw him coming, they conjectured that which was not true, but notwithstanding which they all wished for,—that the king, by that messenger, had sent his uncle pardon; and therefore with great rejoicing and casting up their caps they cried out, 'Pardon, pardon is come; God save the king!' Thus this good duke, although he was destitute of man's help, yet he saw, before his departure, in how great love and favour he was with all men. And truly I do not think that in so many deaths of dukes as have been in England within these few years, there were so many weeping eyes at one time; and not without cause. For all men saw in the fall of this duke the public ruin of England.

"But now to return. The duke standing still in the same place, modestly, and with a grave countenance, made a sign to the people with his hand, that they would keep themselves quiet. Which being done, and silence obtained, he spake to them in this manner.

"'Dearly beloved friends, there is no such matter here in hand as you vainly hope or believe. It seems thus good to Almighty God, whose ordinance it is meet and necessary that we all be obedient to. Wherefore I pray you all to be quiet, and to be contented with my death, which I am most willing to suffer; and let us now join in prayer to the Lord for the preservation of the king's majesty, to whom hitherto I have always shewed myself a most faithful and true subject. I have always been most diligent about his majesty in his affairs both at home and abroad, and no less diligent in seeking the common commodity of the whole realm!'

At which words all the people cried out and said, 'It is most true!'

"Then the duke proceeding, said, 'To whose majesty I wish continual health, with all felicity and all prosperous success.'

The people again cried out, 'Amen!'

"'Moreover, I do wish to all his councillors the grace and favour of God, whereby they may rule in all things uprightly with justice. To whom I exhort you all in the Lord to shew yourselves obedient, as it is your bounden duty, under the pain of condemnation, and also most profitable for the preservation and safeguard of the king's majesty.

"'Moreover, forasmuch as heretofore I have had oftentimes affairs with divers men, and it is hard to please every man, therefore if there be any that has been offended and injured by me, I most humbly require and ask him forgiveness, but especially Almighty God, whom throughout all my life I have most grievously offended; and all others, whatever they be, that have offended me, I do with my whole heart forgive them. Now I once again require you, dearly beloved in the Lord, that you will keep yourselves quiet and still, lest through your tumult you might trouble me. For although the spirit be willing and ready, the flesh is frail and wavering, and through your quietness I shall be much more quiet. Moreover, I desire you all to bear

me witness that I die here in the faith of Jesus Christ; desiring you to help me with your prayers, that I may persevere constant in the same to my life's end.'

"After this he, turning himself again about like a meek lamb, kneeled down upon his knees. Then Doctor Cox, who was there present to counsel and advise him, delivered a scroll into his hand, wherein was contained a brief confession to God. Which being read, he stood up again upon his feet, without any trouble of mind (as it appeared) and first bade the sheriffs farewell; then the lieutenant of the Tower, and others, taking them all by the hands who were upon the scaffold with him. Then he gave the hangman certain money. Which done, he put off his gown, and kneeling down again in the straw, untied his shirt-strings. After that, the hangman coming to him, turned down his collar round about his neck, and all other things which hindered him. Then lifting up his eyes to heaven, where only is hope, and covering his face with his own handkerchief, he laid himself down, shewing no token of trouble or fear, neither did his countenance change; but before his eyes were covered there began to appear a red colour in the midst of his cheeks.

"Thus this most meek and gentle duke lying along, and looking for the stroke, because his doublet covered his neck, he was commanded to rise up and put it off; and then laying himself down again upon the block, and calling thrice upon the name of Jesus, saying, 'Lord Jesus save me!' as he was the third time repeating the same, even as the name of Jesus was in uttering, in a moment he was bereft both of head and life, and slept in the Lord Jesus, being taken away from all dangers and evils of this life, and resting now in the peace of God; in the promotion of whose truth and gospel he always shewed himself an excellent instrument and member, and therefore has received the reward of his labours."

As to the manners, disposition, life, and conversation of the duke, what shall we need to say, when he cannot be sufficiently commended according to the dignity of his virtues? There was always in him great humanity, and such meekness and gentleness, as is rare to be found in so high estate. He was prone and ready to give ear to the complaints and supplications of the poor, and no less attentive to the affairs of the commonwealth; and if he, together with King Edward, had lived, they were like to have done much good in reforming many disorders within this realm. He was utterly ignorant of all craft and deceit, and as far void of all pride and ambition, as he was from doing of injury. He was of a gentle disposition, not coveting to be revenged; more apt and ready to be deceived, than to deceive. He ever showed his nobility along with love and zeal for the gospel and for religion The proof of which was sufficiently seen in his constant standing to God's truth, and zealous defence of it, against the bishops of Chichester, Norwich, Lincoln, London, and others, in the consultation at Windsor, in the first year of the king's reign.

But as there is nothing in this world so perfect in all respects, which is not blotted or darkened with some spot of vice; so among the manifold commendations of this duke, there was one thing which both stained his honour and estimation much, and also more endangered his own life; which was, that he, in consenting to the death of his brother, followed too rashly the persuasion of others, and weakened his own power, and also provoked the chastisement of God's scourge.

Before we conclude the history of this good king, this place seems not unfit to mention a few other things concerning the church and religion. Religion began to grow well, and to come happily forward during this king's days, had not the unhappy troubles of the state, owing to the lords not agreeing among themselves, disquieted the good prospect. But the malice of the devil, how subtlely it works! So long as the lords agreed among themselves, Winchester and Bonner, with all that faction, were cut short, and began to yield to conformity. But afterwards perceiving the nobles to be divided, the lord protector displaced, his brother the admiral beheaded, and the young king now left to himself, they began to take more heart. And thus, though nothing else will lead us, yet experience may teach us what discord works in public weals; and contrarily, what a necessary thing concord is to the advancement especially of God's matters appertaining to his church. For, as to the success of the gospel of peace, while public peace and the gospel joined together, it was wonderful how error and popery were confounded, and ashamed to shew their faces. So that both Dr. Smith, Chadsey, Standish, Young, Oglethorpe, with many others, recanted their former ignorance. Bonner, with his own hand, subscribed to the king's supremacy, and promoted his injunctions. The same also did Stephen Gardiner, subscribing with his own hand the first book of the king's proceedings, and no doubt had done the same to the second book also, had not the unfortunate discord fallen among the nobles in so unfortunate a time.

I shewed before, how in these peaceable days Peter Martyr, Martin Bucer, Paul Phagius, with other learned men, were entertained and provided for in the two universities of this realm, Oxford and Cambridge; and how they there, with their diligent industry, did much good. The learned and fruitful disputations of whom I have likewise present in my hands here to insert, but that the largeness of this volume compels me to make short, especially seeing the length of their disputations.

First, Peter Martyr, being called by the king to the public reading of the divinity lecture in Oxford, amongst his other learned exercises set up in the public schools three conclusions of divinity to be disputed and tried by argument. At which disputations were present the king's visitors, to wit, Henry, bishop of Lincoln; Doctor Cox, chancellor of that university; Dr. Hains, dean of Exeter; Richard Morison, Esq.; and Christopher Nevinson, doctor of civil law. The conclusions propounded were these :—

" 1. In the sacrament of thanksgiving there is no transubstantiation of bread and wine into the body and blood of Christ.

" 2. The body and blood of Christ is not carnally or corporally in the bread and wine; nor, as others use to say, under the kinds of bread and wine.

" 3. The body and blood of Christ be united to bread and wine sacramentally."

They who were the chief disputers against him on the contrary side, were Doctor Tresham, Doctor Chadsey, and Morgan.

The like disputation also about the same time was appointed and commenced at Cambridge, concerning the matter of the sacrament, the king's visitors being directed down for the same purpose by the king. The names of which visitors were these, Nicholas Ridley, bishop of Rochester; Thomas, bishop of Ely; Master John Cheek, the king's schoolmaster; Doctor May, civilian; and Thomas Wendy, the king's physician. The conclusions in that disputation propounded were these :—

Transubstantiation cannot be proved by the plain and manifest words of scripture, nor can thereof be necessarily collected, nor yet confirmed by the consents of the ancient fathers for these thousand years past.

This disputation continued three days. In the first, Dr. Madew answered; against whom disputed Dr. Glin, Mr. Langdale, Mr. Segewick, Mr. Young. In the second disputation Dr. Glin answered; against whom disputed Mr. Grindal, Mr. Perne, Mr. Gest, Mr. Pilkington. In the third disputation Mr. Perne answered; against whom disputed one Mr. Parker (not Dr. Matthew Parker), Mr. Pollard, Mr. Vavisor, Mr. Young.

At length, the disputations being ended, the bishop of Rochester, Dr. Nicholas Ridley, after the manner of the schools, made the following determination upon the conclusions :—

There has been an ancient custom among you, that after disputations in your schools there should be some determination made of the matters so disputed and debated, especially touching the Christian religion. It has seemed good to these worshipful assistants joined with me in commission from the king's majesty, that I should perform the same at this time; I will by your favourable patience declare, both what I think and believe myself, and what also others ought to think of the same. Which I wish that afterwards ye would with diligence weigh and ponder, every man at home.

The principal grounds or rather head-springs of this matter are specially five :—

The first is the authority, majesty, and truth of holy scripture.

The second is the most certain testimonies of the ancient catholic fathers, who after my judgment do sufficiently declare this matter.

The third is the definition of a sacrament.

The fourth is the abominable heresy of Eutiches, that may follow out of transubstantiation.

The fifth is the most sure belief of the article of our faith, " he ascended into heaven."

I. This transubstantiation is clearly against the words of the scriptures, and consent of the ancient catholic fathers. The scripture saith, " I will not drink hereafter of this fruit of the vine," &c. Now the fruit of this vine is wine; and it is manifest that Christ spake these words after the supper was finished, as it appears both in Matthew, Mark, and also in Luke, if they be well understood. There are not many places of scripture that confirm this, neither is it very material : for it it is enough if there is any one plain testimony for it. Neither ought it to be measured by the number of scriptures, but by the authority, and by the truth of the scriptures. And the majesty of this truth is as ample in one short sentence of the scripture as in a thousand.

Christ took *bread*, he gave *bread*. In the Acts, St. Luke calls it *bread*. So St. Paul calls it *bread* after the sanctification. Both of them speak of breaking, which belongs to the substance of bread, and in no wise to Christ's body, for the scripture says, " A bone of him shall not be broken." Christ says, " Do ye this in remembrance of me." St. Paul also says, " Do ye this in remembrance of me." And again, " As often as ye shall drink of this cup, do it in remembrance of me." And our Saviour Christ, in the sixth of St. John, speaking against the Capernaums, saith, " Labour not for the meat which perisheth." And when they asked, " What shall we do that we might work the works of God ?" He answered them thus, " This is the work of God, that ye believe on him whom he hath sent." You see how he exhorts them to faith, " For faith is that work of God." Again, " This is the bread which came down from heaven." But Christ's body came not down from heaven. Moreover, " He that eateth my flesh, and drinketh my blood, dwelleth in me, and I in him. My flesh," saith he, " is meat indeed, and my blood is drink indeed." When they heard this they were offended; and whilst they were offended, he said to them, " What and if ye shall see the Son of man ascend up where he was before ?" Whereby he went about to draw them from the gross and carnal eating. This body, saith he, shall ascend up into heaven, meaning altogether, as St. Augustine saith, " It is the spirit that quickeneth ; the flesh profiteth nothing. The words that I speak unto you, they are spirit and they are life," and must be spiritually understood. These are the reasons which persuade me to incline to this sentence and judgment.

II. Now my second ground against this transubstantiation are the ancient fathers a thousand years past. And so far are they from confirming transubstantiation, that they seem plainly to me to think and speak the contrary.

Dionysius in many places calls it " bread." The places are so manifest and plain, that I need not recite them.

Ignatius to the Philadelphians says, " I beseech you, brethren, cleave fast to one faith, and to one kind of preaching, using together one kind of preaching, using together one kind of thanksgiving; for the flesh of the Lord Jesus is one, and his blood is one which was shed for us : there is also one bread broken for us, and one cup of the whole church."

Irenæus writes thus, " Even as the bread that comes of the earth receiving God's name is now no more common bread, but sacramental bread, consisting of two natures, earthly and heavenly, even so our bodies receiving the eucharist, are now no more corruptible, having hope of the resurrection.''

Tertullian is very plain, for he calls it a figure of his body, &c.

Chrysostom writes to Cæsarius the monk, although he is not received by some, yet will I read the place to impress it more deeply in your minds, for it seems to shew plainly the substance of bread to remain. The words are these :—'' Before the bread is sanctified, we name it bread: but by the grace of God sanctifying the same, through the ministry of the priest, it is delivered from the name of bread, and is counted worthy to bear the name of the Lord's body, although the very substance of bread notwithstanding still remains therein, and now is taken not to be two bodies, but one body of the Son,'' &c.

Cyprian saith, '' Bread is made of many grains. And is that natural bread, and made of wheat ? Yea, it is so indeed.''

The book of Theodoret in Greek was lately printed at Rome, which if it had not been his, it should not have been set forth there, especially seeing it is directly against transubstantiation ; for he saith plainly, that bread still remaineth after the sanctification.

Gelasius also is very plain in this manner, '' The sacrament,'' saith he, '' which we receive of the body and blood of Christ, is a divine matter ; by reason of which we are made partakers by the same of the divine nature, and yet it ceases not still to be the substance of bread and wine. And therefore the representation and similitude of the body and blood of Christ are celebrated in the action of the mysteries,'' &c.

After this he recited certain places out of Augustine and Cyril which were not noted.

Isichus also confesses that it is bread.

Also the judgment of Bertram in this matter is very plain and manifest. And thus much for the second ground.

III. The third ground is the nature of the sacrament, which consists of three things, that is unity, nutrition, and conversion.

As touching unity, Cyprian thus writes, '' Even as of many grains is made one bread, so are we one mystical body of Christ.'' Wherefore bread must still needs remain, or else we destroy the nature of a sacrament.

Also they that take away nutrition, which comes by bread, take away likewise the nature of a sacrament. For as the body of Christ nourishes the soul, even so does bread likewise nourish the body of man.

Therefore they that take away the grains or the union of the grains in the bread, and deny the nutrition or substance of it, in my judgment are sacramentaries ; for they take away the similitude between the bread and the body of Christ. For they who affirm transubstantiation are indeed sacramentaries and Capernaites.

As touching conversion, that as the bread which we receive is turned into our substance, so are we turned into Christ's body, Rabanus and Chrysostom are sufficient witnesses.

IV. They who say that Christ is carnally present in the eucharist, take from him the truth of man's nature. Eutyches granted the divine nature in Christ, but his human nature he denied. So they that defend transubstantiation ascribe that to the human nature which only belongs to the divine nature.

V. The fifth ground is the certain persuasion of this article of faith : '' He ascended into heaven, and sitteth at the right hand,'' &c.

Augustine says, '' The Lord is above, even to the end of the world ; but yet the truth of the Lord is here also. For his body wherein he rose again must needs be in one place, but his truth is spread abroad every where.''

Also in another place, he saith, '' Let the godly also receive (that sacrament, but let them not be anxious (speaking there of the presence of his body.) For as to his majesty, his providence, his invisible and unspeakable grace, these words are fulfilled which he spake, ' I am with you unto the end of the world.' But according

to the flesh which he took upon him, according to that which was born of the Virgin, was apprehended of the Jews, was fastened to a tree, taken down again from the cross, wrapped in linen clothes, was buried and arose again, and appeared after his resurrection, so ' you shall not have me always with you,' and why ? because as concerning his flesh he was conversant with his disciples forty days, and they accompanying him, seeing him, but not following him ; he went up into heaven, and is not here, for he sitteth at the right hand of his father, and yet he is here, because he is not departed hence, as concerning the presence of his Divine Majesty.''

Mark and consider well what St. Augustine says : '' He is ascended into heaven, and is not here,'' says he. Believe not them therefore who say that he is here still on the earth.

Moreover, '' Doubt not,'' saith the same Augustine ; '' but that Jesus Christ, as concerning the nature of his manhood, is there from whence he shall come. And remember well and believe the profession of a christian man, that he arose from death, ascended into heaven, and sitteth at the right hand of his Father, and from that place and none other (not from the altars) shall he come to judge the quick and the dead, and he shall come as the angel said, as he was seen to go into heaven ; that is to say, in the same form and substance, unto which he gave immortality, but changed not his nature. After this form (meaning his human nature) we may think that it is every where.''

And in the same epistle, he says, '' Take away from our bodies limitation of places, and they shall be nowhere ; and because they are nowhere, they shall not be at all.''

Virgilius says, '' If the word and the flesh be both of one nature, seeing that the word is every where, why then is not the flesh also every where ? For when it was in earth, then verily it was not in heaven ; and now when it is in heaven, it is not surely in earth. And it is so certain, that it is not in earth, that as concerning the same we look for him from heaven, whom as concerning the word, we believe to be with us on earth.''

Also the same Virgilius says, '' Which things seeing they be so, the course of the scriptures must be searched of us, and many testimonies must be gathered, to shew plainly what a wickedness and sacrilege it is to refer those things to the property of the divine nature, which do only belong to the nature of the flesh ; and contrarywise, to apply those things to the nature of the flesh, which do properly belong to the divine nature.'' Which thing the transubstantiators do, whilst they affirm Christ's body not to be contained in any one place, and ascribe that to his humanity, which properly belongs to his divinity, as they do who will have Christ's body to be limited in no one certain place.

Now, in the latter conclusion concerning the sacrifice, because it depends upon the first, I will in a few words declare what I think. For if we did once agree in that, the whole controversy in the other would soon be at an end. Two things there are which persuade me that this conclusion is true ; that is, certain places of the scriptures, and also certain testimonies of the fathers. St. Paul saith, (Hebrews ix. 11, 12.), '' Christ being become a high priest of good things to come, by a greater and more perfect tabernacle not made with hands, that is to say, not of this building ; neither by the blood of goats and calves, but by his own blood, he entered in once into the holy place, having obtained eternal redemption for us,'' &c. And '' now once in the end of the world hath he appeared to put away sin by the sacrifice of himself.''

And again, '' Christ was once offered to bear the sins of many.''

Moreover, he saith, '' For by one offering he hath perfected for ever them that are sanctified.''

These scriptures persuade me to believe that there is no other oblation of Christ (although I am not ignorant there are many sacrifices), but that which was once made upon the cross.

The testimonies of the ancient fathers, which confirm the same, are out of '' Augustine ad Bonif.'' epistle 23. Again in his Book of Forty-three Questions, in the

Forty-first Question. Also in his Twentieth Book against Faustus the Manichæan, cap. xxi. And in the same book against Faustus, cap. xxviii. thus he writes: "Now the christians keep a memorial of the sacrifice past, with a holy oblation and participation of the body and blood of Christ."

Fulgentius, in his Book "De Fide," calls the same oblation a commemoration. And these things are sufficient for this time for a scholastical determination of these matters.

Disputations of Martin Bucer.

Beside these disputations, others were also held at Cambridge shortly after, by Martin Bucer, upon these conclusions following .

1. The canonical books of holy scripture alone do sufficiently teach the regenerated all things necessarily belonging unto salvation.

2. There is no church in earth which errs not in manners as well as in faith.

3. We are so justified freely of God, that before our justification it is sin, and provokes God's wrath against us whatever good work we seem to do. Then being justified, we do good works.

In these three propositions against Bucer disputed Mr. Sedgewick, Young, and Pern. Which disputations, because they are long, I mind to reserve them to some other convenient place. In the meantime, because great controversy has been, and is yet among the learned, and much effusion of christian blood about the words and meaning of the sacrament; to the intent that the truth of it may more openly be explained, and all doubtful scruples discussed, it shall not be out of place to adjoin a certain learned treatise in form of a dialogue, as appertaining to the argument, compiled, as it seemed, out of the writings of Peter Martyr, and other authors, by a learned and reverend person of this realm, who, under the persons of Custom and Truth, lays before our eyes, and teaches all men not to measure religion by custom, but to try custom by truth and the word of God; for else custom may soon deceive, but the word of God abides for ever.

A Dialogue explaining the Words of Christ: "This is my Body."

Custom.—I marvel much what madness is creeping into those men's hearts, who now a-days are not ashamed so violently to tread down the lively word of God, yea, and impudently to deny God himself.

Truth.—God forbid there should be any such. Indeed I remember that the Romish bishop was wont to have the Bible for his footstool, and so to tread down God's word when he stood at his mass. But thanks be to God he is now detected, and his abominations opened and blown throughout all the world. And I hear of no others that oppress God's word.

Custom.—No more? Yes, doubtless there are an hundred thousand more, and it is your duty to withstand them.

Truth.—As to my duty, you know it agrees not with my nature to bear with falsehood. But what are they? Disclose them if you will have them reproved.

Custom.—What! are you so great a stranger in these quarters? Hear you not how men daily speak against the sacrament of the altar, denying it to be the real body of Christ?

Truth.—In good sooth I have been a great while abroad, and returned but lately into this country. So you must pardon me if my answer be to seek in such questions. But go on in your tale. You have been longer here, and are better acquainted than I. What say they more than this?

Custom.—Than this? Why what can they possibly say more?

Truth.—Yes, there are many things worse than this: for this seems in some respects to be tolerable.

Custom.—What! methinks you dally with me. Seems it tolerable to deny the sacrament?

Truth.—They do not deny it, so far as I can gather by your words.

Custom.—Nay, then fare you well: I perceive you will take their part.

Truth.—I am not partial, but indifferent to all parties: for I never go further than the truth.

Custom.—I can scarcely believe you. But what is more true than Christ, who is truth itself? Or who ever was so hardy before as to charge Christ with a lie for saying these words, "This is my body?" The words are evident and plain: there is not in them so much as one obscure or dark letter; there is no cause for any man to cavil. And yet, though Christ himself affirmed it to be his body, men now-a-days are not abashed to say, "Christ lied, it is not his body." The evangelists all agree, the old writers stand on our side, the universal and catholic church has been in this mind these fifteen hundred years and more. And shall we think that Christ himself, his evangelists, all the whole catholic church has been so long deceived, and the truth now at length begotten and born in these days?

Truth.—You have moved a matter of great force and weight, and to it, without many words, I can make no full answer. Notwithstanding, because you provoke me to it, I will take part with them of whom you have made false report, for none of them ever reproved Christ of any lie. But on the other hand, they say, that many men of late days, not understanding Christ's words, have built and set up many fond lies in his name. Therefore, first I will declare the meaning of these words, "This is my body;" and next in what sense the church and the old fathers have evermore taken them. First therefore you shall understand, that scripture is not to be taken always as the letter sounds, but as the intent and purpose of the Holy Ghost was, by whom the scripture was uttered. For if you follow the bare words, you will soon shake down and overthrow the greatest part of the christian faith. What is plainer than these words, "My Father is greater than I?" Of those plain words sprang up the heresy of the Arians, who denied Christ to be equal with his Father. What is more evident than this saying, "I and my Father are one?" Yet thence arose the heresy of them who denied three distinct persons. "They all had one soul and one heart," was spoken by the apostles: yet each of them had a soul and heart peculiar to himself. "They are now not two, but one flesh," is spoken of the man and his wife; yet hath both the man and his wife their own bodies. "He is our very flesh," said Reuben of his brother, who notwithstanding was not their real flesh. "I am bread," said Christ, yet was he flesh, and no bread. "Christ was the stone," says St. Paul, and yet was no material stone. "Melchizedeck had neither father nor mother," and yet indeed he had both. "Behold the Lamb of God," says John the Baptist of Christ, notwithstanding Christ was a man, and not a lamb. Circumcision was called the covenant, whereas it was but a token of the covenant. The lamb was named the passover, and yet was it eaten in remembrance only of the passover. Jacob raised up an altar, and called it "The mighty God of Israel." Moses, when he had conquered the Amalekites, set up an altar, and called it by the names of God, Jehovah, and Tetragramatum. "We are all one bread," says St. Paul, yet were they not thereby turned into a loaf of bread. Christ hanging upon the cross, pointed out St. John to his mother, saying, "Behold thy son," and yet was he not her son. "So many as are baptised into Christ," says St. Paul, "have put on Christ," and so many as are baptized into Christ, are washed with the blood of Christ. Notwithstanding no man took the font water to be the natural blood of Christ. "The cup is the new testament," says St. Paul, and yet is not the cup indeed the very new testament. You see, therefore, that it is not strange, nor a thing unusual in the scriptures, to call one thing by another's name. So that you can no more prove the changing of the bread into Christ's body in the sacrament, because of the words, "This is my body," than prove the change of the wife's flesh into the natural and real body and flesh of the husband. because it is written, "They are not two, but one flesh;" or the altar of stone to be very God, because Moses pronounced it to be the mighty God of Israel. However, if you will needs stick to the letter, you make for me, and hinder yourself. For I will reason thus, and use your own weapon against you. The scripture calls it "*bread.*" The evangelists agree in calling it "*bread.*" St. Paul nameth it "*bread*" five times in one passage; wherefore I conclude by your own argument, that we ought not only to say, but also to believe that in the sacrament there remains *bread.*

Custom.—Methinks your answer is reasonable, yet I cannot be satisfied. Declare you therefore more at large, what moves you to think this of the sacrament. For I think you would not withstand a doctrine so long held and taught, unless you were forced by some strong reasons.

Truth.—First, in examining the words of Christ, I look to the meaning and purpose for which they were spoken. I see that Christ meant to have his death and passion kept in remembrance. For men of themselves are forgetful of the benefits of God. And therefore it was necessary that they should be admonished and stirred up with some visible and outward tokens, as with the passover lamb, the brazen serpent, and the like. For the brazen serpent was a token, that when the Jews were stung and wounded with serpents, God restored them and made them whole. The passover lamb was a memory of the great benefit of God, which, when he destroyed the Egyptians, saved the Jews, whose doors were sprinkled with the blood of a lamb. So likewise Christ left us a memorial and remembrance of his death and passion in outward tokens, that when the child should demand of his father, what the breaking of the bread and drinking of the cup means, he might answer him, that like as the bread is broken, so Christ was broken and rent upon the cross, to redeem the soul of man. And likewise as wine restores and comforts the body, so doth the blood of Christ cherish and relieve the soul. And this do I gather by the words of Christ, and by the institution and order of the sacrament. For Christ charged the apostles to do this in remembrance of him. I therefore argue that as nothing is ever done in mere remembrance of itself; and as the sacrament is used in remembrance of Christ; therefore the sacrament is not Christ, or it would be a memorial of itself. And I again argue that Christ never devoured himself, and yet Christ did eat the sacrament with his apostles; and therefore we may conclude that the sacrament is not Christ himself.

Besides this, I see that Christ ordained not his body, but a sacrament of his body. A sacrament, as St. Augustine declares, is an outward sign of an invisible grace. His words are *Sacramentum est invisibilis gratiæ visibile signum.* Out of which words I gather two arguments. The first is this; the sign of the body of Christ is not the thing signified, therefore they are not one. And again, one thing cannot be both visible and invisible; but the sacrament we know is visible, and the body of Christ invisible; and we may therefore conclude that they are not one, and the same.

I remember that Christ ministered this sacrament not to great and deep philosophers, but to a sort of ignorant and unlearned fishermen, who notwithstanding understood Christ's meaning right well, and delivered it, even as they took it at Christ's hand, to the people, and fully declared to them the meaning. But neither they, nor scarcely the apostles themselves, could understand what is meant by transubstantiation, impanation, dimensions, accidents, without subjects, &c. This is no learning for the unlearned and rude people, wherefore it is likely that Christ meant some other thing than has been taught of late days. Further, Christ's body is food, not for the body, but for the soul; and therefore it must be received with the instrument of the soul, which is faith. For as you receive sustenance for your body by the mouth, so the food of your soul must be received by faith, which is the mouth of the soul. And for that St. Augustine sharply rebukes them that think to eat Christ with their mouth, saying, " Why makest thou ready thy tooth and thy belly? believe, and thou hast eaten

Christ." Likewise speaking of eating the same body, he saith to the Capernaites, who understood him grossly as men do now a-days: " The words that I speak are spirit and life. It is the spirit that quickeneth, the flesh profiteth nothing."

Custom.—What mean you by this spirit, and by spiritual eating? I pray you utter your mind more plainly. For I know well that Christ has a body, and therefore must be eaten, as I think, with the mouth of the body. For the spirit and the soul as it has no body and flesh, so it has no mouth.

Truth.—You must understand, that a man is shaped of two parts, of the body and of the soul. And each of them has his life and his death, his mouth, his teeth, his food, and abstinence. For as the body is nourished and fostered with bodily meats, or else cannot live; so must the soul have his cherishing, otherwise it will decay and pine away. And therefore we justly say that the Turks, Jews, and heathen are dead, because they lack the lively food of the soul. But how then, or by what means will you find the soul? Doubtless not by the instrument of the body, but of the soul. For that which is received into the body, has no passage from thence into the soul. For Christ saith, " That whatsoever entereth in at the mouth goeth into the belly, and is cast out into the draught." And whereas you say that the spirit has no mouth, as it has no body or bones; you are deceived. For the spirit has a mouth, or else how could a man eat and drink justice? For undoubtedly his bodily mouth is not a fit instrument for it. Yet Christ saith, that he is blessed that hungers and thirsts for righteousness. If he hunger and thirst for righteousness, he must both eat and drink it, for otherwise he neither abates his hunger, nor quenches his thirst. Now, if a man may eat and drink righteousness with his spirit, no doubt his spirit hath a mouth. Whereof I argue that as the mouth of the soul is spiritual, so must be the food.

And in like manner Christ, speaking of the eating of his body, names himself "The bread," not for the body, but "of life," for the soul; and saith, "He that cometh to me shall never hunger; and he that believeth on me shall never thirst." Wherefore, whoever will be relieved by the body of Christ, must receive him as he will be received, with the instrument of faith, and not with his teeth or mouth. And whereas I say that Christ's body must be received and taken with faith, I mean not that you shall pluck down Christ from heaven, and put him in your faith, as in a visible place; but that you must with your faith rise and spring up to him, and leaving this world dwell above in heaven, putting all your trust, comfort, and consolation in him, who suffered grievous bondage to set you at liberty, creeping into his wounds, which were so cruelly pierced and dented for your sake. So shall you feed on the body of Christ, so shall you suck the blood that was poured out and shed for you. This is the spiritual, the very true, the only eating of Christ's body. And, therefore, St. Gregory calls it " The food of the mind, and not of the stomach." And St. Cyprian saith likewise, "We sharpen not our tooth, nor prepare our stomach."

Now to return. Seeing it is plain that Christ's body is meat for our spirit, and has nothing to do with our body, I will say that the sacrament is bodily food and increases the body; and therefore the sacrament is not the very body of Christ. That it nourishes the body is evident; for Christ calleth it the fruit of the vine, whose duty is to nourish. And for a proof, if you consecrate a whole loaf, it will feed you as well as your table bread. And if a little mouse get a host, he will crave no more meat to his dinner. Wherefore, as I said before, seeing that Christ's body is spiritual meat, and the bread of the sacrament bodily meat, I may conclude that the sacrament is not Christ's body. Besides this, where it was forbidden in the old law that any man should eat or drink blood, the apostles notwithstanding took the cup at Christ's hands, and drank of it, and never staggered, or shrunk at the matter; whence it may be gathered, that they took it for a mystery, for a token, and a remembrance, far otherwise than it has of late been taken.

Again, when the sacrament was given, none of them all crouched down, and took it for his God, forgetting him that sate there present before their eyes; but took it, and eat it, knowing that it was a sacrament and remembrance of Christ's body. Yea, the old councils commanded that no man should kneel down at the time of the communion, fearing that it should be an occasion of idolatry. And long after the apostles' time, as Tertullian writeth, women were suffered to take it home with them, and lay it up in their chests. And the priests many times sent it to sick persons by a child, which no doubt would have given more reverence to it, if they had taken it for their God. But a great while after, about three hundred years ago, Honorius III., bishop of Rome, took him and hanged him up, and caused men to kneel and crouch down, and all to deify him.

If the bread be turned and altered into the body of Christ, doubtless it is the greatest miracle that God ever wrought. But the apostles saw no miracle in it. Nazianzen, an old writer, and St. Augustine, treating of all the miracles that are in the scripture, do not number the sacrament for one. As for the apostles, it appears that they took it for no marvel, for they never mused at it, neither demanded how it might be; whereas in other things they evermore were full of questions. As to St. Augustine, he not only skipped over it, as no wonder, but by plain and express words testifies that there is no marvel in it.

A little before the institution of the sacrament, Christ spake of his ascension, saying, "Yet a little while, and the world seeth me no more." "Let not your heart be troubled, neither let it be afraid," because I go from you: "I tell you the truth; it is expedient for you that I go away; for if I go not away, the Comforter will not come unto you; but if I depart, I will send Him unto you:" with many other like warnings of his departure. St. Stephen saw him sitting at the right hand of his Father, and thought it a special revelation of God; but he never said that he saw him at the communion, or that he made him every day himself. And in the Acts of the Apostles, St. Peter saith, "That the heaven must receive Christ until the times of restitution of all things." Isaiah, Solomon, and St. Stephen say, "That God dwelleth not in temples made with man's hand." St. Paul wisheth that he were dissolved and dead, and were with Christ; not in the altar, doubtless, where he might be daily, but in heaven. And to be brief, it is in our creed, and we do constantly believe, that Christ is ascended into heaven, and sitteth at his Father's right hand; and no promise have we that he will come down at every priest's calling.

Custom.—Fye, you be far deceived, I can in nowise brook these words. You shut up Christ too straightly, and imprison him in one corner of heaven, not suffering him to go at large. He has deserved more gentleness at your hand, than to be tied up so short.

Truth.—I do neither lock up, neither imprison Christ in heaven, but according to the scriptures declare that he has chosen a blessed place, and one most worthy to receive his majesty; in which place whoso is enclosed, thinks not to be a prisoner; but if you take it for so heinous a thing that Christ should sit in heaven in the glory of his Father, what think you of them that imprison him in a little box, yea, and keep him in captivity so long, until he be mouldy and over-grown with vermine, and when he is past men's feeding on, are not contented to hang him till he stink, but will have him to a new execution, and burn him too? This is wonderful and extremely cruel imprisoning. But to return to the matter, we are certainly persuaded by the word of God, that Christ, the very Son of God, vouchsafed to take upon him the body and shape of man, and that he walked and was conversant among men in that one, and not in many bodies; and that he suffered death, rose again, and ascended to heaven in the selfsame body; and that he sitteth at his Father's right hand in his manhood, in the nature and substance of that body. This is our belief; this is the very word of God. Where-

fore they are far deceived, who, leaving heaven, will grope for Christ's body upon the earth.

Custom.—Nay, sir, but I see now you are far out of the way. For Christ has not so gross and fleshly a body as you think, but a spiritual and ghostly body, and therefore without repugnance it may be in many places at once.

Truth.—You say right well, and grant that Christ's body is spiritual. But I pray you answer me by the way; can any other body than that which is spiritual be at one time in sundry places?

Custom.—No, truly.

Truth.—Have we that selfsame sacrament that Christ gave to his disciples, or not?

Custom.—Doubtless we have the same.

Truth.—When was Christ's body spiritual? was it so even from his birth?

Custom.—No; for doubtless before he arose from death his body was earthly, as other men's bodies are.

Truth.—Well, but when gave Christ the sacrament to his disciples? Before he rose from the dead or afterwards?

Custom.—You know yourself he gave it before his resurrection, the night before he suffered his passion.

Truth.—Why then, methinks, he gave the sacrament at that time when his body was not spiritual.

Custom.—Even so.

Truth.—And was every portion of the sacrament dealt to the apostles, and received they into their mouths the very real and substantial body of Christ?

Custom.—Yea, doubtless.

Truth.—Mark well, what ye have said, for you have granted me a great contradiction. First, you say, that no body being not spiritual can be in several places at once. Then you say, that Christ's body at the last supper was not spiritual; and yet you hold, that he was there present visibly before the apostles' eyes, and in each of their hands and mouths all at once.

Custom.—Indeed you have driven me into the straits before I was aware of you; and I know not how I may escape your hands honestly. But the best refuge that I have is this, that I will not believe you.

Truth.—I desire you not to give credit to me, believe the word of God, yea, believe your own creed; for they both witness against you, that Christ's body is taken up into heaven, and there shall remain until he come to judge.

Custom.—Tush, what speak you of the word of God? there are many dark sayings in it which every man cannot attain to.

Truth.—I grant you there are obscure places in the scripture, yet not so obscure but that a man with the grace of God may perceive them; for it was written not for angels, but for men. But, as I understand, custom meddles but very little with the scripture. How say you of St. Augustine, St. Jerome, St. Ambrose? what if they stand on our side?

Custom.—No, no, I know them well enough.

Truth.—Well, as you know them, if they be called to witness it, they will give evidence against you. For St. Augustine, in all his books declares that Christ's body is placed in one room. Dei, i. he says, "Do not doubt the man Jesus Christ to be there, from whence he shall come. And remember well, and faithfully believe the christian confession, that he is risen, ascended into heaven, sitteth at the right hand of God the Father, and from thence, he shall come and from no other place, to judge the quick and the dead. And shall come in the same substance of body, to which he gave immortality, and took not the nature from it. After this form he is to be thought not to be dispersed in all places; for we must beware so to defend his divinity that we destroy not his humanity." All the old fathers witness the same. Now, to return to the matter; seeing that the word of God in many and sundry places, the creed, seeing all the old fathers do agree, that the body of Christ is ascended into heaven, and there remains at the right hand of the father, and cannot be in more than in one place, I do conclude that the sacrament is not the body of Christ; first, because it is not in heaven, neither sitteth at the Father's right hand; moreover, because it is in an hundred thousand boxes, whereas Christ's body filleth but one place. Furthermore, if the bread were turned into the body of Christ, then would it necessarily follow that sinners and unpenitent persons receive the body of Christ.

Custom.—Marry, and so they do. For St. Paul saith plainly, that they receive the body of Christ to their own confusion.

Truth.—No, not so. These are not St. Paul's words, but he saith, "Wherefore whosoever shall eat this bread, and drink this cup of the Lord, unworthily, shall be guilty of the body and blood of the Lord. But let a man examine himself, and so let him eat of that bread, and drink of that cup. For he that eateth and drinketh unworthily, eateth and drinketh damnation to himself, not discerning the Lord's body." (1 Cor. xi. 27—29.) Here he calls it in plain words *bread*. And although the sacrament be very bread, yet the injury redounds to the body of Christ. As if a man break the king's mace, or tread the broad seal under his foot, although he have broken and defaced nothing but silver and wax; yet is the injury the king's, and the doer shall be taken as a traitor. He that reads the gospel, wherein is declared the passion and death of Christ, and lives contrary to the gospel, shall doubtless be the more guilty of the death of Christ, because he hears and reads the word of God, and regards it not. In a certain country the manner is, that when the gospel is read, the king shall stand up with a naked sword in his hand, declaring thereby that he bears his sword in defence of the gospel. But if he himself oppresses the gospel, he bears the sword against himself; for the gospel shall turn to his judgment and condemnation. So will Christ so much more extremely punish a man, who knowing himself to be wicked and without repentance, and therefore none of the flock of Christ, yet notwithstanding will impudently creep into the company of Christian men, and receive the sacraments with them, as though he were one of the number. And this St. Paul meant, by the unworthy receiving of the sacrament of Christ's body. Wherefore a man may unworthily take the sacrament, and be guilty of the death of Christ, although he receive not Christ's body into his mouth, and chew it with his teeth. But what if I prove that every massing priest is guilty of the body and blood of Christ?

Custom.—I dare say you cannot prove it.

Truth.—But if I do prove it, will you believe me?

Custom.—I may well enough, for it is impossible to do it. For priests commonly are confessed before they go to mass, and how can they then take the sacrament unworthily?

Truth.—Indeed confession, if it be discreetly used, is a laudable custom, and to the unlearned man and feeble conscience is as good as a sermon; but because it was never commanded by Christ, nor received by the apostles, nor much spoken of by the old doctors, it cannot make much for the due receiving of the sacrament. But how do you like these words of St. Ambrose, "He takes it unworthily, that takes it otherwise than Christ ordained it?"

Custom.—That I like very well. But what do you gather from it?

Truth.—This will I gather. The massing priest takes the sacrament otherwise than Christ either commanded or taught, and thus he takes it unworthily, and so consequently to his condemnation.

Custom.—That is not so, for he does altogether as Christ commanded him.

Truth.—That shall appear. For Christ commanded it to be done in remembrance of him; the priest does it in remembrance of dead men. Christ took bread, and left it bread; the priest takes bread and conjures it away. Christ took bread and gave thanks; the priest takes bread and breathes upon it. Christ took bread and brake it; the priest takes bread and hangs it up. Christ took bread and dealt it to his apostles; the priest, because he is an apostle himself, takes bread and eats it every whit alone. Christ in the sacrament gave his own body to be eaten in faith; the priest for lack of faith

receives accidents and dimensions. Christ gave a sacrament to strengthen men's faith; the priest gives a sacrifice to redeem men's souls. Christ gave it to be *eaten*; the priest gives it to be *worshipped*. And to conclude, Christ gave *bread*; the priest saith he gives *a God*. Here is difference enough between Christ and the priest. Yet, moreover, Christ at his supper spake his words out and in a plain tongue; the priest speaks nothing but Latin or Greek, which tongues he often perceives not, and he whispers lest any poor man should perhaps perceive him. So it comes to pass, that the priest often knows no more what he himself says, than what he does. Thus you may see that the massing priest receives the sacrament of Christ's body far otherwise than ever Christ minded, and so unworthily and to his condemnation. Now if you think yourself satisfied, I will return to my former question, and prove more at large, that Christ's body cannot be eaten by the wicked, which must necessarily ensue if the bread were turned into the body of Christ. Christ in the sixth of St. John, speaking of the eating of his body, says, "He that eateth of this bread shall live for ever." (verse 58.) But sinful men take the sacrament of their condemnation, and live not for ever, therefore in the sacrament they receive not the body of Christ.

The sacrament in holy scripture is named "the breaking of bread;" which, to say the truth, were but a cold breaking, if there remained no bread to break, but certain fantasies of white and round. Yet whereas they with words, crossings, blessings, breathings, leapings, and much ado, can scarcely make one God; but they have such virtue in their fingers, that at one cross they are able to make twenty gods; for if they break the sacrament, every portion, yea, every mite must needs be a God. After the apostles' time there arose up heretics, who said that Christ walking here among men bodily upon the earth, had no real body, but a thing like a body; and so therewith dimmed men's sight. Against whom the old fathers used these arguments: Christ increased in growing, fasted, hungered, ate, wept, sweat, was weary, and in conclusion died, and had all other properties of a very body; wherefore he had a body. I will use the same kind of reasoning: it feeds, it tastes like bread, it looks like bread, the little silly mouse takes it for bread, and to be short, it has all the properties and tokens of bread. The old fathers, when there remained any part of the sacrament more than was spent at the communion, they used to burn it, and of it there came ashes. But there is nothing in the sacrament that can turn to ashes but only bread (for I think they burned not Christ's body to ashes). The emperor Henry, the sixth of that name, was poisoned in the host, and Victor the bishop of Rome in the chalice. But poison cannot hang in God's body and blood. What needs many words in a matter so evident? If you demand either God's word, or the doctors and the ancient writers, or your reason, or your eyes, or nose, or tongue, or fingers, or the mouse, all these agree in one, and answer together, "There is *bread*." Wherefore, if you reject so many and so constant witnesses, and so well agreeing in their tale, especially being such as will lie for no man's pleasure, I will appeal from you, and take you as no indifferent judge. If all these witnesses suffice you not, I will call the sacrament itself to record: it cries to you, and plainly advertises you what you should think of it: "I am," it saith, "grated with the teeth; I am conveyed into the belly; I perish; I can live no time; I canker; I suffer green mould; blue mould, red mould; I breed worms; I am kept in a box for fear of rats; if you leave me out all night, I shall be devoured before morning, for if the mouse get at me I am gone; I am bread, I am no God; believe them not." Thus cries the sacrament daily, and bears witness itself.

Custom.—The devil on such reasons! and therefore I will never trouble my brains to make you answer: but if it be true what you have said, why is the sacrament by Christ himself, as by his apostles, and the old fathers, called the body of Christ?

Truth.—Because it is no strange thing in scripture so

to speak, as I have declared before. But will you stand to St. Augustine's arbitration in this matter?

Custom.—To no man sooner.

Truth.—St. Augustine, in an epistle to his friend Boniface, gives a good cause why the sacrament, although it be not the body of Christ, is, notwithstanding, called the body of Christ; his words are these: "If sacraments had not a certain similitude of those things whereof they may be sacraments, then were they no sacraments. Of which similitude many times they take their name. Wherefore, *after a certain manner* the sacrament of the body of Christ is the body of Christ, and the sacrament of the blood of Christ is the blood of Christ," &c. Now, I think you are satisfied concerning the meaning of these words, "This is my body."

Custom.—Yet one thing moves me very much.

Truth.—What is that?

Custom.—The doctors and old writers, men inspired with the Holy Ghost, have evermore been against your doctrine; yea, and in these days the wisest men and best learned call you heretics, and your learning heresy.

Truth.—As to the old writers, I remember well they speak reverently of the sacraments, as every man ought to do, but where they deliver their mind with their right hand, you, Custom, receive it with the left. For where they say, that it is the body of Christ, and that it must be truly eaten, meaning that it effectually lays before the eyes Christ's body, and that it is to the faithful man no less than if it were Christ himself, and that Christ must be eaten in faith, not torn nor rent with the teeth: you say that however it is taken, it is Christ's body, and that there is no other eating but with the mouth.

And that the fathers meant no other thing than I have said, shall appear by their words. But as touching the learned and wise men of these days, I cannot blame them if they call my doctrine heresy; for they would condemn all ancient writers of heresy, if they were now alive. But I will answer you as to them directly. In the meanwhile, mark you how well their learning agrees. They say you must follow the letter, you must stick to the letter. But Origin saith, "If ye follow after the letter that which is written (unless ye shall eat the flesh of the Son of Man, there shall be no life in you) this letter killeth." Augustine says, "If the commanding speech be such as commandeth a thing wicked and horrible to be done, or a charitable thing to be undone, then this is a figurative speech; unless ye shall eat the flesh of the Son of Man, and shall drink his blood, there shall be no life in you: because in this speech he seemeth to command a wicked thing, it is therefore a figurative speech, commanding that we should communicate with the passion of our Lord, and sweetly to retain it in our remembrance."

Athanasius says, on John vi., "The words that Christ here speaketh are not carnal, but spiritual. For what body might have sufficed for all that should eat, to be a nourishment of the whole world? But therefore he maketh mention of the ascension of the Son of Man into heaven, to the intent to pluck them away from that corporal cogitation." And it is in this way that all the ancient fathers explain these words.

But what need I speak of the old fathers? It is not long since the sacrament grew out of its right understanding. For this word transubstantiation, whereby they signify the turning of the bread into the body of Christ, was never either spoken or heard, or thought of among the ancient fathers, or in the old church. But about 500 years past, Pope Nicholas II. (about 1059) confirmed that opinion of the changing of bread, and would have it made an article of faith; but this was not done until it was so declared by the council of Lateran (A.D. 1215,) in Rome. After which time ensued *Corpus Christi* day, masses of *Corpus Christi* reservation of the sacrament, with honour, with canopies, with incensing, with kneeling, with worshipping and adoration, &c. For they thought they could not do too much to him after the bishop of Rome had allowed him for a God.

But not quite 200 years before that time, when this doctrine first began to bud, (and yet notwithstanding had not so prevailed, but that a great number of learned and good men could know the sacrament to be a sacrament, and not Christ himself), Charles the Great, king of France, and emperor of Germany, demanded of a learned man, whose name was Bertram, what he thought of that strange kind of calling down Christ from heaven, and turning a little bit of bread into his natural body. To whom Bertram made answer in this wise: "This we say, that there is a great difference betwixt the body in which Christ suffered, and the blood which he shed upon the cross, and this body which every day is celebrated in the mystery of the passion of Christ. For this body is a pledge and similitude, but the other is the very truth itself. It appeareth that these are separated asunder by no less difference than is between a pledge and the thing whereof the pledge is given; or than is betwixt an image of a thing and the thing itself, whereof the image is; or than is between the form of a thing, and the truth itself." Thus wrote Bertram, Druthmar, and many others, and yet in all their time they were never once reproved of heresy. Thus wrote John Scotus also, but in about 200 years after his death he was judged and condemned for an heretic, and his books burned. Since which time, even till this day, although idolatry had great increase, yet there never wanted some good men who boldly would profess and set forth the truth, although they were well assured that their worldly reward should be spite, malice, imprisoning, sword, fire, and all kinds of torments. Thus so shortly, and in so few words as I could, I have declared unto you what Christ meant by these words, "This is my body;" what the apostles taught therein, and in what sort they delivered them to their successors; in what sense and meaning the holy fathers and old writers, and the universal and catholic church hath evermore taken them.

The End and Death of King Edward the Sixth.

Thus having discoursed of events in the reign of king Edward, we will now draw to the end and death of this blessed king, our young Josiah. Who, about a year and a half after the death of the duke of Somerset, his uncle, in the year 1553, entering into the seventeenth year of his age, and the seventh year of his reign, in the month of June, was taken from us, for our sins. no doubt, whom if it had so pleased the good will of the Lord to have spared with longer life, it was not unlikely that he would have so reformed the commonwealth here in the realm of England, as by good cause it might have been said of him that was said in the old time of the noble emperor Augustus, in reforming and advancing the empire of Rome, which empire he received of brick, but he left it of fine marble. But the condition of this realm, and the behaviour of the English people deserved not the benefit of so blessed a reformation, but rather such a plague of deformation as happened after his reign, as will appear in the history of his successor.

The time having now approached when it pleased Almighty God to call this young king from us, we are told that about three hours before his death, this godly child, his eyes being closed, speaking to himself, and thinking none to have been near him, was heard to pray thus —

The Prayer of King Edward before his Death.

"Lord God, deliver me out of this miserable and wretched life, and take me among thy chosen: howbeit, not my will, but thy will be done : Lord, I commit my spirit to thee. O Lord, thou knowest how happy it were for me to be with thee · yet for thy chosen's sake send me life and health, that I may truly serve thee. O my Lord God, bless thy people, and save thine inheritance. O Lord God, save thy chosen people of England. Oh my Lord God, defend this realm from papistry, and maintain thy true religion, that I and my people may praise thy holy name, for thy Son Jesus Christ's sake."

Then he turned his face, and seeing who was by him, said to them, "Are you so nigh? I thought you had been further off" Then Dr. Owen said, "We heard you speak to yourself He then smilingly said, I was praying to God" The last words of his pangs were these, " I am faint, Lord have mercy upon me, and take my spirit" And thus he yielded up the ghost on the 6th of July, 1553, and left a woeful kingdom behind to his sister Although in his will he had excluded his sister Mary from the succession of the crown, because of her corrupt religion, yet the plague, which God had destined to this sinful realm, could not so be avoided, but that she, being the elder daughter to King Henry, succeeded in possession of the crown Of whose dreadful and bloody government it remains now to discourse

This briefly it may suffice to understand, that for all the writing, sending, and practising with the lady Mary, by the king and his council, and also by bishop Ridley, yet she would not be reclaimed from her own opinion to give any hearing to the word and voice of truth Which positive will of the lady Mary, both this young king and also his father king Henry before him, knew right well, and were both much displeased against her for it, so that not only her brother did utterly sequestrate her in his will, but also her own father, considering her inclination, conceived such heart against her, that for a great space he secluded her from the title of princess, yea, and seemed so eagerly incensed against her, that he was fully inclined to proceed further with her, had not the intercession of Thomas Cranmer, the archbishop, reconciled the king again to favour and pardon his own daughter.

As you have heard already of the stout courage of the lady Mary toward her father, and also by her letters to her brother King Edward and his council so now let us infer somewhat of the stout talk and demeanour of the lady Mary toward Doctor Ridley, bishop of London, who gently coming to her of mere good will, had this communication with her, and she with him, as here follows —

About the eighth of September, 1552, Dr. Ridley, then bishop of London, lying at his house at Hadham, in Hertfordshire, went to visit the lady Mary, then at Hunsden, two miles off; and was gently entertained of Sir Thomas Wharton, and other her officers, till it was almost eleven o'clock, about which time the lady Mary came forth into her chamber of presence, and then the bishop saluted her grace, and said, that he was come to do his duty to her grace. Then she thanked him for his pains, and for a quarter of an hour talked with him very pleasantly, and said, that she knew him in the court when he was chaplain to her father, and could well remember a sermon that he made before king Henry her father, at the marriage of my lady Clinton that now is, to Sir Anthony Brown, &c, and so dismissed him to dine with her officers.

After dinner was done, the bishop, being called for by Mary, resorted again to her grace, between whom this communication was; first the bishop begins in manner as follows —

Bishop.—" Madam, I came not only to do my duty to see your grace, but also to offer myself to preach before you on Sunday next, if it will please you to hear me " At this her countenance changed, and, after silence for a space, she answered thus

Mary. " My lord as for this last matter I pray you make the answer to it yourself "

Bishop " Madam, considering mine office and calling, I am bound in duty to make to your grace this offer, to preach before you."

Mary —" Well, I pray you make the answer (as I have said) to this matter yourself, for you know the answer well enough But if there be no remedy but I must make you answer, this shall be your answer, the door of the parish church adjoining shall be open for you if you come, and you may preach if you list, but neither I nor any of mine shall hear you."

Bishop —" Madam, I trust you will not refuse God's word "

Mary —" I cannot tell what you call God's word, that is not God's word now, that was God's word in my father's days "

Bishop —" God's word is all one in all times, but has been better understood and practised in some ages than in others "

Mary.—" You durst not for your ears have avouched that for God's word in my father's days that you now do. And as for your new books, I thank God I never read any of them; I never did, nor never will "

And after many bitter words against the form of religion then established, and against the government of the realm, and the laws made in the youth of her brother, which she said she was not bound to obey till her brother came to perfect age, when, she affirmed, she would obey them, she asked the bishop whether he were one of the council he answered, "No." "You might well enough," said she, "as the council goes now a-days "

And so she concluded with these words " My lord, for your gentleness to come and see me, I thank you; but for your offering to preach before me, I thank you never a whit."

Then the bishop was brought by Sir Thomas Wharton to the place where they dined, and was desired to drink And after he had drank, he paused a while, looking very sadly, and suddenly broke out into these words : " Surely I have done amiss " " Why so?" said Sir Thomas Wharton. " For I have drank," said he, " in that place where God's word, offered, has been refused. whereas, if I had remembered my duty, I ought to have departed immediately, and to have shaken off the dust of my shoes for a testimony against this house " These words were spoken by the bishop with such vehemence, that some of the hearers afterwards confessed their hair to stand upright on their heads This done, the bishop departed, and so returned to his own house.

THE END OF THE NINTH BOOK.

ACTS AND MONUMENTS.

BOOK X.

CONTAINING

THE FIRST ENTERING OF QUEEN MARY TO THE CROWN, WITH THE ALTERATION OF
RELIGION IN THE REALM.

DURING the time of his sickness, when King Edward began to appear more feeble, a marriage was solemnized in the month of May, between the lord Guilford, son to the duke of Northumberland, and the lady Jane, the duke of Suffolk's daughter; whose mother being then alive, was daughter to Mary, king Henry's second sister, who was first married to the French king, and afterwards to Charles duke of Suffolk. The marriage being concluded, and the king waxing every day more sick, and when there seemed to be no hope of recovery, it was brought to pass by the consent not only of the nobility, but also of the chief lawyers of the realm, that the king by his testament should appoint the lady Jane, daughter to the duke of Suffolk, to be inheretrix to the crown of England, passing over his two sisters, Mary and Elizabeth.

To this all the king's council subscribed, and the chief of the nobility, the mayor and city of London, and almost all the judges and chief lawyers of this realm, saving only justice Hales, of Kent, a man both favouring true religion, and also as upright a judge as any in this realm, who, giving his consent to lady Mary, would in no case subscribe to lady Jane. Of this man (God willing) you shall hear more in the sequel of this history.

The causes laid against lady Mary, were that it was feared she would marry a stranger, and thereby entangle the crown, and also that she would alter the religion, used both in the days of King Henry her father, and also in those of her brother King Edward, and so bring in the pope, to the utter destruction of the realm, which indeed afterwards came to pass, as by the sequel of this history will well appear.

When king Edward was dead, this lady Jane was established in the kingdom by the consent of the nobles, and was forthwith proclaimed queen at London, and in other cities. Between this young damsel and king Edward there was little difference in age, though in learning and knowledge of the tongues she was not only equal, but also superior to him, being instructed by a master right nobly learned.

In the mean time, while these things were working at London, lady Mary, who had knowledge of her brother's death, wrote to the lords of the council, as follows —

A letter of the Lady Mary, sent to the Lords of the Council, wherein she claims the crown after the decease of King Edward.

" My lords, we greet you well, and have received sure advertisement, that our dearest brother the king, our late sovereign lord, is departed to God's mercy, which news how woeful they be unto our heart, He only knoweth, to whose will and pleasure we must, and do humbly submit us and our wills. But in this so lamentable a case, that is to wit, now after his majesty's departure and death, concerning the crown and governance of this realm of England with the title of France, and all things thereto belonging, what hath been provided by act of parliament, and the testament and last will of our dearest father, besides other circumstances advancing our right, you know. the realm, and the whole world knoweth, the rolls and records appear by the authority of the king our said father, and the king our said brother, and the subjects of this realm; so that we verily trust that there is no good true subject, that is, can, or would pretend to be ignorant thereof· and of our part we have of ourselves caused, and, as God shall aid and strengthen us, shall cause our right and title in this behalf to be published and proclaimed accordingly. And albeit this so weighty a matter seemeth strange, that our said brother dying upon Thursday at night last past, we hitherto had no knowledge from you thereof, yet we consider your wisdom and prudence to be such, that having oftentimes amongst you debated, pondered, and well weighed this present case with our estate, with your own estate, the commonwealth, and all our honours, we shall and may conceive great hope and trust, with much assurance in your loyalty and service, and therefore for the time interpret and take things not for the worst; and that you will, like noblemen, work the best. Nevertheless, we are not ignorant of your consultations, to undo the provisions made for our preferment, nor of the great bands and provisions forcible, wherewith ye be assembled and prepared, by whom, and to what end, God and you know, and nature cannot but fear some evil. But be it that some political consideration, or whatsoever thing else hath moved you thereto, yet doubt you not, my lords, but we can take all these your doings in gracious part, being also right ready to remit and fully pardon the same, and that freely to eschew bloodshed and vengeance against all those that can or will intend the same, trusting also assuredly you will take and accept this grace and virtue in good part as appertaineth, and that we shall not be forced to use the service of others our true subjects and friends, which in this our just and right cause, God in whom our whole affiance is, shall send us. Wherefore, my lords, we require you, and charge you, and every of you, that of your allegiance which you owe to God and us, and to none other, for our honour and the safety of our person only employ yourselves, and forthwith upon receipt hereof, cause our right and title to the crown and government of this realm to be proclaimed in our city of London, and other places, as to your wisdom shall seem good, and as to this case appertaineth, not failing hereof as our very trust is in you. And this our letter, signed with our hand, shall be your sufficient warrant in this behalf.

"Given under our signet, at our Manor of Kenning Hall, the ninth of July, 1553."

To this letter of the lady Mary, the lords of the council made answer again, as follows —

Answer of the Lords to the Lady Mary's Letter.

" Madam, we have received your letter, dated the ninth of this instant, declaring your supposed title, which you judge yourself to have to the imperial crown of this realm, and all the dominions thereunto belonging. For answer whereof, this is to advertise you, that forasmuch as our sovereign lady queen Jane is, after the death of our sovereign lord Edward the Sixth, a prince of most noble memory, invested and possessed with the just and right title to the imperial crown of this realm, not only by good order of the ancient laws of this realm, but also by our late sovereign lord's letters patent, signed with his own hand, and sealed with the great seal of England in presence of the most part of the nobles, councillors, judges, with several others, grave and sage personages, assenting and subscribing to the same : We must therefore, as of the most bounden duty and allegiance, assent unto her said grace, and to none other, except we should (which faithful subjects cannot) fall into grievous and unspeakable enormities. Wherefore we can do no less, but for the quiet both of the realm and you also, to advertise you, that forasmuch as the divorce made between the king of famous memory, king Henry the Eighth, and the lady Catharine your mother, was necessary to be had both by the everlasting laws of God, and also by the ecclesiastical laws, and by the most part of the noble and learned universities of Christendom, and confirmed also by the sundry acts of parliaments remaining yet in their force, and thereby you were justly made illegitimate and unheritable to the crown imperial of this realm, and the rules, and dominions, and possessions of the same, you will upon just consideration hereof, and of divers other causes, lawful to be alleged for the same, and for the just inheritance of the right line and godly order taken by the late king our sovereign lord king Edward the Sixth, and agreed upon by the nobles and great personages aforesaid, cease by any pretence to vex and molest any of our sovereign lady queen Jane her subjects from their true faith and allegiance due unto her grace. Assuring you, that if you will for respect shew yourself quiet and obedient (as you ought) you shall find us all and several ready to do you any service that we with duty may, and glad with your quietness to preserve the common state of this realm wherein you may be otherwise grievous unto us, to yourself, and to them. And thus we bid you most heartily farewell.

" From the Tower of London, in this ninth of July, 1553.

"Your ladyship's friends, shewing yourself an obedient subject.

Thomas Canterbury.	R. Rich.
The marquis of Winchester.	Huntington.
	Darcy.
John Bedford.	Cheyney.
William Northampton.	R Cotton
Thomas Ely, chancellor.	John Gates.
Northumberland.	W. Petre.
Henry Suffolk.	W. Cecil.
Henry Arundel.	John Cheke
Shrewsbury.	John Mason.
Pembroke	Edward North.
Cobham.	R. Bowes.

After this answer the lady Mary stole secretly away from the city, resting chiefly upon the good will of the commons, and yet perchance not destitute altogether of the secret advice of some of the nobles. When the council heard of her sudden departure, they speedily gathered an army, and assigned that the duke of Suffolk should take that enterprise in hand. But afterwards altering their minds, they thought it best to send the duke of Northumberland, with other lords and gentlemen, and that the duke of Suffolk should keep the Tower, where the lord Guilford and the lady Jane were lodged.

Mary in the meanwhile withdrew into Norfolk and Suffolk, where she understood the duke's name was in much hatred, for the service he had done there under king Edward, in subduing the rebels, and there gathering to her aid such of the commons as she could, at the same time keeping herself close within Framlingham Castle. To her, first of all, there resorted the Suffolk men; who being always forward in promoting the gospel, promised her their aid and help, provided she would not attempt an alteration of the religion, which her brother king Edward had before established by law publicly enacted, and received by the consent of the whole realm.

To this condition she soon agreed, with such promises to them that no innovation should be made in the matter of religion, so that no man would or could then have doubted her. Which promise, if she had as constantly kept, as they willingly preserved her with their bodies and weapons, she had done a deed both worthy her blood, and had also made her reign more stable to herself. For though a man be never so mighty of power, yet breach of promise is an evil upholder of quietness, fear is worse, but cruelty is the worst of all.

Thus Mary being guarded by the power of the protestants of Suffolk, vanquished the duke, and all those that came with her. In return for which it was (methinks) an heavy word that she answered to the Suffolk men afterwards, who made supplication to her grace to perform her promise: " Forasmuch," saith she, " as you, being but members, desire to rule your head, you shall one day well perceive, that members must obey their head, and not look to bear rule over it." And not only that, but also to cause the more terror to others, a certain gentleman named Master Dobbe, for reminding her of her promise, was punished, being three times set on the pillory to be a gazing stock to all men. Others delivered to her books and supplications made out of the scriptures, to exhort her to continue in the true doctrine then established, and these were sent to prison. But such is the condition of man's nature that we are for the most part more ready always to seek friendship when we stand in need of help than ready to requite a benefit once past and received.

The greatest help that made for the cause of the lady Mary was the short journeys of the duke, which by commission were assigned to him before. For the longer the duke lingered in his voyage, the lady Mary the more increased in power ; the hearts of the people being mightly bent to her : which after the council at London perceived, and understood how the common multitude withdrew their hearts from them to stand with her, and that certain noblemen began to go over to her, they changed also, and proclaimed the lady Mary queen.

And thus the duke of Northumberland was left destitute and forsaken at Cambridge with some of his sons and a few others, among whom the earl of Huntington was one, where they were arrested and brought to the Tower of London, as traitors to the crown.

Thus Mary was made queen, and the sword of authority put into her hand. When she had been thus advanced by the Protestants of Suffolk, and saw all things quiet, as her enemies were conquered, and the duke sent to the Tower, she followed not long after, being brought on the third day of August to London, to the great rejoicing of many men, but with a greater fear of many

Thus coming up to London, she took her first lodging at the Tower, where the lady Jane, with her husband the lord Guilford, a little before her coming, were imprisoned, and where they remained waiting her pleasure for more than six months. But the duke of Northumberland, within a month after his coming to the Tower, being adjudged to death, was brought forth to the scaffold, and there beheaded, August 22. Having received a promise and hope of pardon that if he would recant and hear mass, he consented, and denied in words that true religion which before in king Henry VIII and in king Edward VI's days he had declared himself both to favour and promote; exhorting also the people to return to the Catholic faith, as he termed it

At the same time, the duke of Northumberland, with Sir John Gates, and Sir Thomas Palmer, were put to death. This Palmer on the other side, confessed his faith, which he had learned in the gospel, and lamented that he had not lived more gospel like. In the meantime queen Mary entering thus upon her reign with the blood of these men, besides hearing mass in the Tower, gave a sad sign, especially by the delivering of Stephen Gardiner out of the Tower, that she would not stand to that which she had promised so faithfully to the Suffolk men, concerning the not altering the state of religion

Other things also followed, which every day more and more discomforted the people, shewing that the queen bore no good will to the present state of religion she not only released Gardiner, but made him lord chancellor of England and bishop of Winchester (doctor Poynet being put out), and also Bonner was restored to his bishopric again, and Doctor Ridley displaced. Doctor Day was appointed to the bishopric of Chichester; J. Scory being put out. Doctor Tonstal to the bishopric of Durham; Doctor Heath to the bishopric of Worcester, (Hooper being committed to the Fleet.) Doctor Veysey was appointed to Exeter, and Miles Coverdale put out. These things being perceived, great heaviness and discomfort grew more and more among all good men, so that there was now to be seen a miserable face of things in the whole commonwealth of England. They that could dissemble took no great care how the matter went, but those whose consciences were joined with the truth, perceived already the coals to be kindled, which would be the destruction of many a true christian man. In the meanwhile, queen Mary removed from the Tower to Hampton Court, and caused a parliament to be summoned for the 10th of October.

You heard before how several bishops were removed, and others placed in their sees among whom was Doctor Ridley bishop of London, a worthy man both of fame and learning. This Doctor Ridley, in the time of queen Jane, had made a sermon at St. Paul's Cross, declaring his mind to the people as to the lady Mary, and dissuading them, alleging there the incommodities and inconveniencies which might arise by receiving her as their queen, prophesying as it were before that which afterwards came to pass, that she would bring in a foreign power to reign over them; besides the subverting also of the christian religion then established; showing too, that Mary being in his diocese, he, according to his duty, had laboured much with her to turn her to his religion, and notwithstanding in all other points of civility she shewed herself sensible and tractable, yet in matters that concerned true faith and doctrine, she showed herself so stiff and obstinate that there was no other hope of her, but that she would disturb and overturn all that had been confirmed and planted by her brother before. Shortly after this sermon, queen Mary was proclaimed, upon which he repaired to Fremingham to salute the queen, but had such cold welcome, that, being spoiled of all his dignity, he was sent back upon a lame halting horse to the Tower.

Queen Mary seeing things not yet going on after her mind as she desired, devised with her council to bring that to pass by other means which by open law she could not accomplish, setting forth a prohibition by proclamation, that no man should preach or read openly in churches the word of God, besides other things also in the same proclamation.

A Prohibition of the Queen for Preaching, Printing, &c

" The queen's highness well remembering what great inconveniencies and dangers have grown to this her highness' realm in times past, through the diversity of opinions in question of religion, and hearing also that now of late, since the beginning of her most gracious reign, the same contentions are again much revived, through certain false and untrue reports and rumours spread by some light and evil disposed persons, hath thought good to make known to all her highness' most loving subjects, her most gracious pleasure in manner following " First, her majesty, being now, by the alone goodness of God, settled in her just possession of the imperial crown of this realm, and other dominions thereunto belonging, cannot now hide that religion which God and the world knoweth she hath ever professed from her infancy Which as her majesty is minded to observe and maintain for herself by God's grace, during her time, so doth her highness much desire, and would be glad the same were by all her subjects quietly and charitably embraced.

" And yet she signifies to all her majesty's loving subjects, that of her most gracious disposition and clemency her highness mindeth not to compel any of her said subjects thereunto, until such time as further order by common assent may be taken therein forbidding nevertheless all her subjects of all degrees, at their perils, to move seditions, or stir unquietness in her people, by interpreting the laws of this realm after their brains and fancies, but quietly to continue for the time, till (as before is said,) further order may be taken, and therefore willeth and straightly chargeth and commandeth all her said good loving subjects to live together in quiet sort and christian charity, leaving those new found devilish terms of papist or heretic, and such like, and applying their whole care, study, and travel to live in the fear of God, exercising their conversations in such charitable and godly doing as their lives may indeed express that great hunger and thirst of God's glory and holy word, which by rash talk and words many have pretended · and in so doing they shall best please God, and live without danger of the laws, and maintain the tranquillity of the realm. Whereof as her highness shall be most glad, so if any man shall rashly presume to make any assemblies of people, or at any public assemblies, or otherwise shall go about to stir the people to disorder or disquiet, she mindeth according to her duty, to see the same most severely reformed and punished according to her highness' laws.

" And furthermore, forasmuch as it is also well known, that sedition and false rumours have been nourished and maintained in this realm, by the subtlety and malice of some evil-disposed persons, who take upon themselves without sufficient authority to preach and to interpret the word of God after their own heads in churches, and other places both public and private, and also by playing of interludes, and printing of false-found books, ballads, rhymes, and other improper treatises in the English tongue, concerning doctrine, in matters now in question and controversy, touching the high points and mysteries of christian religion, which books, ballads, rhymes, and treatises are chiefly by the printers and stationers set out to sale to her grace's subjects, of an evil zeal for lucre and covetousness of vile gain. Her highness therefore straightly chargeth and commandeth all and every of her said subjects, of whatever state, condition, or degree they be, that none of them presume from henceforth to preach, or by way of reading in churches, or other public or private places, except in schools of the university, to interpret or teach any scriptures, or any manner of points of doctrine concerning religion, neither also to print any books, matter, ballad, rhyme, interlude, process or treatise, nor to play any interlude, except they have her grace's special licence in writing for the same, upon pain to incur her highness' indignation and displeasure.

"And her highness also further chargeth and commandeth all and every her subjects; that none of them of their own authority do presume to punish, and to rise against any offender in the causes aforesaid, or any other offender in words or deeds in the late rebellion committed or done by the duke of Northumberland, or his accomplices, or to seize any of their goods, or violently to use any such offender by striking, imprisoning, or threatening the same, but wholly to refer the punishment of all such offenders unto her highness and the public authority, whereof her majesty mindeth to see due punishment according to the order of her highness' laws.

"Nevertheless, as her highness intendeth not hereby to restrain and discourage any of her loving subjects, to give from time to time true information against any such offenders in the causes aforesaid, unto her grace or her council, for the punishment of every such offender, according to the effect of her highness' laws provided in that part . so her said highness exhorteth and strictly chargeth her subjects to observe her commandment and pleasure in every part aforesaid, as they will avoid her highness' indignation and most grievous displeasure. The severity and vigour whereof, as her highness shall be most sorry to have cause to put in execution, so doth she utterly determine not to permit such unlawful and rebellious doings of her subjects, whereof may ensue the danger of her royal estate, to remain unpunished, but to see her said laws touching these points to be thoroughly executed: which extremities she trusteth all her said subjects will foresee, dread, and avoid accordingly her highness straightly charging and commanding all mayors, sheriffs, justices of peace, bailiffs, constables, and all other public officers and ministers, diligently to see to the observing and executing of her commandments and pleasure, and apprehend all such as shall wilfully offend in this part, committing the same to the next gaol, there to remain without bail or mainprize, till upon certificate made to her highness, or her privy council, of their names and doings, and upon examination had of their offences, some further order shall be taken for their punishment to the example of others, according to the effect and tenor of the laws aforesaid.

"Given at our manor of Richmond, the 18th day of August, in the first year of our most prosperous reign."

Master Bourne Preaching at St. Paul's Cross.

About this time, or not long before, Bonner, bishop of London, being restored, appointed Master Bourne, a canon of St. Paul's, to preach at the Cross; he afterwards was bishop of Bath and Wells. Bourne taking occasion of the gospel of that day to speak something largely in justifying Bonner who was then present, "which Bonner," said he, "had preached before upon the same text in that place, that day four years, and was for the same most cruelly and unjustly cast into the most vile dungeon of the Marshalsea, and there kept during the time of king Edward" His words sounded so ill in the ears of the hearers, that they could not keep silence, and began to murmur and stir so that the mayor and aldermen, who were then present, greatly feared an uproar One person hurled a dagger at the preacher, but who it was could not then be proved; though afterwards it became known

Indeed, the stir was such, that the preacher drew in his head, and durst appear no more in that place. The matter of his sermon tended much to the dispraise of king Edward, which the people could not bear Then Master Bradford, at the request of the preacher's brother and others, stood forth and spake so mildly, christianly, and effectually, that with a few words he appeased all · and afterwards he and Master Rogers conducted the preacher between them from the pulpit to the grammar school, where they left him safe. But for this they were shortly after both rewarded with long imprisonment, and last of all with fire in Smithfield !

By reason of this tumult at St. Paul's Cross, an order was made by the lords of the council, and sent to the mayor and aldermen of London, desiring that they should call the next day following a common council of the city, and should charge every householder to cause their children, apprentices, and other servants to keep their own parish churches upon the holydays, and not to suffer them to attempt to break the peace. Commanding them also to signify to the assembly the queen's determination, which was, that her grace meant not to compel other men's consciences otherwise than God shall put into their hearts a persuasion of the truth that she herself believed in.

It was also ordered, that every alderman in his ward should forthwith send for the curates of every parish, and warn them not only to forbear to preach themselves, but also not to suffer any others to preach; or make any open or solemn reading of the scriptures in their churches, unless the preachers were licensed by the queen

On the next day after this sermon at St Paul's Cross, the queen's guard was at the Cross with their weapons to guard the preacher. And when the people withdrew themselves from the sermon, an order was given by the mayor, that the elders of all companies should be present so as to make a congregation, least the preacher should be discouraged by his small auditory.

On the 15th of August, A.D 1553, one William Rutler was committed to the Marshalsea, for uttering words against Master Bourne, for his sermon at St Paul's Cross.

On the 16th of August, Humfrey Palden was committed to the Compter, for words against Bourne's sermon at St. Paul's Cross

A letter was sent to the sheriffs of Buckinghamshire and Bedfordshire, to apprehend Fisher, parson of Ammersham, a preacher.

Another letter was sent to the bishop of Norwich, not to suffer any preacher or other to preach or expound the scriptures openly without special license from the queen.

The same day Master Bradford, Master Vernon, and Master Beacon, preachers, were committed to the charge of the lieutenant of the Tower.

The same day also Master John Rogers, preacher, was commanded to keep himself prisoner in his own house at St. Paul's, without having any conference with any others than those of his own household.

On the 22nd of August there were two letters directed to Master Coverdale, bishop of Exeter, and Master Hooper, bishop of Gloucester, to repair forthwith to the court, and there to attend the council's pleasure.

The same day Fisher, parson of Ammersham, made his appearance before the council, according to their letter of the 16th of August, and was appointed the next day to bring in a note of his sermon.

On the 24th of August, one John Melvin, a Scotchman and preacher, was sent to Newgate, in London, by the council.

On the 28th of August there was a letter sent to the mayor of Coventry and his brethren, for the apprehension of one Sanders, then vicar of St. Michael's, in Coventry, and to send him up to the council, with his examinations and other matters they could charge him with; with a commission to punish all such as had by means of his preaching used any talk against the queen's proceedings

On the 26th of August, Master Hooper, bishop of Worcester, made his personal appearance before the council, according to their letters of the 22nd of August

On the 31st of August, Master Coverdale, bishop of Exeter, made his appearance before the council, according to their letters of the 22nd of August.

On the 1st of September, Master Hooper and Master Coverdale appeared again before the council, when Master Hooper was committed to the Fleet, and Master Coverdale commanded to attend the lords' pleasure.

On the 2nd of September, Master Hugh Sanders, vicar of St. Michael's, in Coventry, was before the council for a sermon, and was commanded to appear again upon the Monday following.

The 4th of September, a letter was directed from the council to Master Hugh Latimer for his appearance before them.

About the 5th of September, Peter Martyr came to London from Oxford, where for a time he had been commanded to keep his house, and found there the archbishop of Canterbury, who offered to defend the doctrine of the book of Common Prayer, both by the scriptures and the doctors, assisted by Peter Martyr and a few others, as hereafter ye shall hear. But while they were in hope to come to disputations, the archbishop and others were imprisoned, but Peter Martyr was suffered to return.

The same day there was a letter sent to the mayor of Coventry to set Hugh Symonds at liberty, if he would recant his sermon, or if not, to detain him in prison.

On the 13th September, Mr. Hugh Latimer appeared before the council, according to their letter of the 4th of September, and was committed as a close prisoner to the Tower

The same day the archbishop of Canterbury appeared before the council, and was commanded to appear on the next day before them in the star-chamber.

On the 14th of September, the archbishop of Canterbury made his appearance before the lords in the star-chamber ; where they, charging him with treason and spreading abroad seditious bills to the disquieting of the state, committed him to the Tower of London, there to remain till further sentence, or order, at the queen's pleasure.

On the 15th of September, there was a letter sent to Master Horn, dean of Durham, for his appearance before them, and another was sent to him on the 7th of October, for his speedy appearance.

On the 16th of September, there were letters sent to the mayors of Dover and Rye, to suffer all French protestants to pass out of this realm, except such as should be signified to them by the French ambassador.

On the first day of October, queen Mary was crowned at Westminster, and on the tenth day of the same month began the parliament with the solemn mass of the Holy Ghost, after the popish manner, which was celebrated with great pomp in the palace of Westminster. To which mass, among the other lords, according to the custom, the bishops should have come. Those bishops who yet remained undeposed were the archbishop of York ; Doctor Taylor, bishop of Lincoln ; John Harley, bishop of Hereford. Of these bishops, Taylor and Harley, presenting themselves according to their duty, took their places among the lords, but after they saw the mass begin, and not bearing the sight, they withdrew : for which the bishop of Lincoln being examined, and protesting his faith, was commanded to attend ; but not long afterwards died by sickness Harley, because he was married, was excluded both from the parliament and from his bishopric

Mass being done, the queen, accompanied by the estates of the realm, was brought into the parliament-house, to enter and begin the consultation at which consultation or parliament were repealed all statutes made in the time of king Henry VIII. for premunire, and statutes made by king Edward VI. for the administration of common prayer and the sacrament in the English tongue and further, the attainder of the duke of Northumberland was confirmed by this parliament. In the meanwhile many men were forward in erecting altars and masses in churches. And of such persons as would adhere to the laws made in king Edward's time, till others should be established, some were marked and some apprehended. Among whom Sir James Hales, a knight of Kent, and justice of the Common Pleas, was one, who, although he had ventured his life in queen Mary's cause, in that he would not subscribe to the disinheriting of her by the king's will yet because at a quarter sessions he charged upon the statutes made in the time of king Henry VIII and Edward VI for the supremacy and religion, he was imprisoned, and so cruelly handled and put in fear by the talk that the warden of the Fleet used to have in his hearing, of such torments as were prepar-

ing for heretics, (or for what other cause God knoweth,) that he sought to rid himself out of this life by wounding himself with a knife , and afterwards was contented to say as they desired him upon which he was discharged , but he never rested till he had drowned himself in a river, half a mile from his house in Kent

During the time of this parliament, the clergy likewise held a convocation, with a disputation also, appointed by the queen's command, at St Paul's church in London In the convocation, Master John Harpsfield, bachelor of divinity, made a sermon to the clergy. After the sermon, it was agreed by the bishops, that they of the clergy-house, for avoiding confusion of words, should choose a prolocutor. To which office, by common assent, was named Doctor Weston, dean of Westminster, and presented to the bishops with an oration by Master Pye, dean of Chichester, and Master Wimbisley, archdeacon of London. Which Doctor Weston being chosen and brought to the bishops, made his oration to the house, with an answer again by Bishop Bonner.

After these things arranged in the convocation-house, they proceeded next to the disputation appointed, by the queen's command, about the matter of the sacrament. Which disputation lasted six days. Wherein Doctor Weston was chief on the pope's part ; who behaved himself outrageously in taunting and checking. Such as disputed on the other side were compelled some to fly, some to deny, and some to die, though to most men's judgments that heard the disputation they had the advantage, as may appear by the report of the disputation, the copy of which we here annex .—

The true Report of the Disputation had and begun in the Convocation-house at London, the 18th of Oct. A.D. 1553, written by one who was present at it.

Act of the First Day.

First upon Wednesday, being the 18th of October, Doctor Weston the prolocutor certified the house, "that it was the queen's pleasure, that they, being learned men, should debate of matters of religion, and constitute laws, which her grace and the parliament would ratify. And as there is a book of late set forth, called the Catechism bearing the name of this honourable synod, and yet put forth without your consent as I have learned, being a very pestiferous book, and full of heresies, and likewise a book of common prayer very abominable, I thought it therefore best to begin with the articles of the catechism concerning the sacrament of the altar, to confirm the natural presence of Christ in the same, and also transubstantiation Wherefore, it shall be lawful on Friday next ensuing for all men freely to speak their conscience in these matters, that all doubts may be removed, and they fully satisfied therein "

Act of the Second Day.

On Friday, being the 20th of October, when men thought they should have entered on the disputation of the questions proposed, the prolocutor exhibited two bills to the house , one for the natural presence of Christ in the sacrament of the altar , the other concerning the catechism, that they did not agree thereto requiring all to subscribe to the same, as he himself had done. The whole house immediately assented, except six, who were Philips, dean of Rochester ; Haddon, dean of Exeter ; Philpot, archdeacon of Winchester, Cheyney, archdeacon of Hereford, Ailmer, archdeacon of Stow ; and Young, chanter of St. David's. And while the rest were about to subscribe these two articles, John Philpot stood up and spake concerning the articles of the catechism, that it beareth the title of the synod of London last before this, although many of them who then were present were never made privy thereof in setting it forth ; because this house had granted authority to make ecclesiastical laws to certain persons appointed by the king's majesty, therefore it might be well said to be done in the synod of London, although such as be of this house now had no notice of it before the promulgation.

And he said, concerning the article of the natural

presence in the sacrament, that it was against order, and also very prejudicial to the truth, that men should be moved to subscribe before the matter was thoroughly examined; he therefore made this request to the prolocutor; that as there were so many learned men present on that side, and as on the other side there were not past five or six that had not subscribed; therefore, that equality might be had in this disputation, he desired that the prolocutor would arrange that some of those that set forth the catechism, might be brought to the house to shew what moved them to set it forth; also that Doctor Ridley and Master Rogers, with two or three more, might have leave to be present at this disputation, and be associated with them. This request was thought reasonable, and was proposed to Bishop Bonner, but it was refused to be allowed by him.

The Act of the Third Day

On Monday the 23rd of October, at the time appointed, in the presence of many earls, lords, knights, gentlemen, and others of the court and of the city, the prolocutor made a protestation, that the house had appointed this disputation, not to call the truth into doubt, but that these gainsayers might be resolved of their argument.

Then he demanded of Master Haddon, whether he would reason against the questions proposed or not. He made answer, that he had certified him before in writing, that he would not, since the request of such learned men as were demanded to be assistant with them would not be granted. Master Ailmer likewise was asked, who made the prolocutor the same answer; adding, that they had done too much prejudice already to the truth, to subscribe before the matter was discussed and that it would avail little or nothing to reason for the truth, since they were now determined to the contrary. After this he demanded of Master Cheyney whether he would propose his doubts concerning transubstantiation or not, "Yea," said he, "I would gladly my doubts were resolved, which move me not to believe transubstantiation.

"The first is out of St Paul to the Corinthians, who, speaking of the sacrament of the body and blood of Christ, calls it often 'bread' after the consecration.

"The second is out of Origen, who, speaking of this sacrament, saith, 'That the material part goes down to the excrements'

"The third is out of Theodoret, who, making mention of the sacramental bread and wine after the consecration, saith, "That they go not out of their former substance, form, and shape.'"

Then the prolocutor assigned Doctor Moreman to answer him, who, to St Paul, answered thus; "That the sacrament is called by him bread indeed. but it is thus to be understood, That it is the sacrament of bread, that is, the form of bread."

Then Master Cheyney alleged, that Hesychius called the sacrament both bread and flesh.

"Yea," said Moreman, "Hesychius calls it bread, because it was bread, and not because it is so" And passing over Origen, he came to Theodoret, and said, "That men mistook his authority, by interpreting a general into a special, as Peter Martyr hath done, interpreting οὐσία, for substance, which is a special signification of the word; whereas οὐσία is a general word, as well to accidents as to substance, and therefore I answer thus to Theodoret, That the sacramental bread and wine do not go out of their former substance, form, and shape, that is to say, not out of their accidental substance and shape."

After this Master Cheyney sat down, and Master Ailmer stood up as one that could not bear to hear such an answer to so grave an authority; and reasoned upon the authority of Theodoret alleged before by Master Cheyney, and declared, "That Moreman's answer to Theodoret was no just nor sufficient answer, but an illusion and subtle evasion, contrary to Theodoret's meaning For, if οὐσία, 'substance,' should signify an accident in the place alleged, then were it a word superfluous there, as there follow two other words which sufficiently signify the accidents of the bread, which are, 'shape' and 'form.'"

After this John Philpot stood up and said, "That

Doctor Moreman's interpretation was incorrect, and that it could not be taken to signify an accidental substance, as he would interpret it. For the occasion of Theodoret's writing plainly shewed that was a vain cavil, for the dispute was with Eutyches, an heretic, whether the body and human nature of Christ had yet an existence distinct from the divine nature? Eutyches said, that Christ, in his human nature, having ascended into heaven, and being there joined to the divinity, was absorbed or swallowed up, so that Christ became of one divine substance only. Against which opinion Theodoret writes, and, by the similitude of the sacrament, proves the contrary against the heretic: That like as in the sacrament of the body of Christ, after the consecration, there is the substance of Christ's humanity, with the substance of bread remaining as it was before, not being absorbed by the humanity of Christ, but joined by the divine operation; even so in the person of Christ, being now in heaven, of whom this sacrament is a representation, there are two substances, that is, his divinity and humanity united in one person, which is Christ, the humanity not being absorbed by the conjunction of the divinity, but remaining in his former substance.

"And this similitude," said Philpot, "brought in by Theodoret to confound Eutyches, proved nothing at all, if the very substance of the sacramental bread did not remain as it did before. But if Doctor Moreman's interpretation might take place for transubstantiation, then should the heretic have made a strong argument, to maintain his heresy, and to prove himself a good christian man, and he might well say thus to Theodoret· That as after the consecration in the sacrament, the substance of the bread is transubstantiated into the human body of Christ, so in the sacrament it is now but one substance of the humanity, and not the substance of bread as it was before, even so, likewise, the humanity ascending up by the power of God into heaven, and joined to the Deity, was turned into one substance with the Deity; so that now there remains but one divine substance in Christ, which is no more than in the sacramental signs of the Lord's Supper, after the consecration, there remains but one substance, according to that construction"

In answering to this, Doctor Moreman staggered, whose defect Philpot perceiving, said, "Well, Master Moreman, if you have no answer at present ready, I pray you devise one, if you can conveniently, against our next meeting here again."

With that the prolocutor was grievously offended, telling him that he should not boast there; but that he would be fully answered. Then said Philpot, "It is the thing that I desire, to be answered directly in this behalf; and I desire of you, and of all the house, that I may be sufficiently answered, which I am sure you are not able to do" No other answer was then made to Philpot's argument, except that he was commanded to silence.

Then stood up the dean of Rochester, offering himself to argue against the natural presence, wishing that the scriptures, and the ancient doctors, in this point might be weighed and followed. And against this natural presence, he thought the saying of Christ, in St. Matthew, sufficient, who said of himself, That the poor you have always with you, but me you have not always "which," said he, "was spoken concerning the natural presence of Christ's body, therefore we ought to believe as he taught, That Christ is not naturally present on earth in the sacrament of the altar"

To this it was answered by the prolocutor, "That we should not have Christ always present to exercise alms deeds upon him, but upon the poor, which is all that was here intended to be meant."

But the dean prosecuted his argument, and shewed it out of St. Augustine further, That that interpretation of the scriptures was no sufficient answer, who writes in the fiftieth Treatise of St. John, on this wise, on the same sentence, "When, as he said," saith St Augustine, 'Me you have not always with you,' he spake of the presence of his body. For, by his majesty, by his providence, by his unspeakable and invisible grace, that is fulfilled which is said of him, Behold I am with you until the consummation of the world. But in the flesh which the Word took upon him, in that which was born of the Virgin, in that which was apprehended of the Jews which was crucified on the cross, which was let down from the cross, which was wrapped in grave clothes, which was hid in the sepulchre, which was manifested in the resurrection, You shall not have me always with you. And why? For, after a bodily presence he was conversant with his disciples forty days, and they accompanying him, seeing and not following him, he ascended, and is not here; for there he sitteth at the right hand of the Father, and yet here he is, because he is not departed in the presence of his majesty. After another manner we have Christ always by the presence of his majesty, but after the presence of his flesh it is rightly said, You shall not verily have me always with you. For the church had him in the presence of his flesh a few days, and now by faith it apprehendeth him, and seeth him not with eyes."

To this authority Doctor Watson took upon him to answer, and said, "He would answer St. Augustine by St. Augustine, and having a book of notes in his hand, he alleged out of the seventieth Treatise upon St. John, that after that mortal condition and manner we have not now Christ on earth, as he was before his passion."

Against whose answer John Philpot replied, and said, "That Master Watson had not fully answered St. Augustine by St Augustine, as he would seem to have done, for that in the place above mentioned by the Dean of Rochester, he doth not only teach the mortal state of Christ's body before his passion, but also the immortal condition of the same after his resurrection, in which mortal body St. Augustine seems plainly to affirm, That Christ is not present upon the earth, neither in form visibly, nor in corporal substance invisibly."

To this nothing else being answered, the dean of Rochester proceeded in his argument, and read out of a book of annotations sundry authorities for the confirmation of it. To which Moreman, who was appointed to answer him, made no direct answer, but bade him make an argument, saying, "That the Dean had recited many words of doctors, but he had not made one argument."

Then said the dean, "The authorities of the doctors by me rehearsed, are sufficient arguments to prove my intent, to which my desire is to be answered by you." But still Moreman cried, make an argument, to shift off the authority which he could not answer. After this the dean made this argument of the institution of the sacrament, "'This do ye in remembrance of me and thus ye shall shew forth the Lord's death until he come.' The sacrament is the remembrance of Christ, and therefore the sacrament is not very Christ, for he is not yet come. For these words, 'Until he come,' plainly signify the absence of Christ's body" Then the prolocutor went about to show that these words, "Until he come," did not import any absence of Christ on the earth; but he answered nothing directly to the purpose In conclusion, the dean fell to questioning with Moreman, whether Christ did eat the paschal lamb with his disciples or not? He answered, "Yea." Further, he demanded whether he did eat likewise the sacrament with them, as he did institute it? Moreman answered, "Yea." Then he asked what he did eat, and whether he did eat his own natural body, as they imagine it or not? Which when Moreman had affirmed, then said the dean, "It is a great absurdity," and so he sat down

Against this absurdity Philpot stood up and argued, saying, he could prove by good reason deduced out of the scriptures, that Christ ate not his own natural body at the institution of the sacrament; and the reason is this

The receiving of Christ's body has a promise of remission of sins annexed to it, but Christ's own eating the sacrament had no promise of remission of sin, and therefore Christ in the sacrament did not eat his own body.

To this reason Moreman answered, denying that the sacrament had a promise of remission of sins annexed to it.

Then Philpot shewed the promise in the sacrament, "Which is given for you, which is shed for you, for the remission of sins." But Moreman would not acknowledge that to be any promise, so that he drove Philpot to the sixth of St. John, to vouch his saying with these words "The bread which I will give is my flesh, which I will give for the life of the world."

Moreman answering nothing directly to this argument, Harpsfield started up to supply that which was wanted in his behalf, and thinking to answer Philpot, confirmed more strongly his argument, saying, "Ye mistake the promise which is annexed to the body of Christ in the sacrament for it pertained not to Christ, but to his disciples, to whom Christ said, 'This is my body which is broken for you,' and not for Christ himself"

"You have said well for me," replied Philpot, "for that is my argument The promise of the body of Christ took no effect in Christ · I conclude therefore Christ ate not his own body"

Then the prolocutor said the argument was naught. For by the like argument he might go about to prove, that Christ was not baptized, because the remission of sin, which is annexed to baptism, took no effect in Christ. To which Philpot replied, that as Christ was baptized, so he ate the sacrament, but he took on him baptism, not that he had any need of it, or that it took any effect in him, but as our Master to give the church an example to follow him in the administration of the sacrament, and thereby to exhibit himself *to us*, and not to give himself to *himself*.

No more was said in this. But afterwards the prolocutor demanded of Philpot, whether he would argue against the natural presence or not? He answered, "Yea, if he would hear his argument without interruption, and assign one to answer him, and not many, which is a confusion to the opponent, and especially for him that was of an ill memory." By this time the night was come on; wherefore the prolocutor broke up the disputation for that time, and appointed Philpot to be the first that should begin the disputation the next day, concerning the presence of the sacrament.

The Act of the Fourth Day.

On Wednesday, the 25th of October, John Philpot was ready for the disputation, intending first to have made a certain oration, and a true declaration in Latin, of the matter of Christ's presence, which was then in question. Which the prolocutor perceiving, forbade Philpot to make any oration or declaration of any matter, commanding him also that he should make no argument in Latin, but to conclude his argument in English.

Then said Philpot, "This is contrary to your order taken at the beginning of this disputation For then you appointed that all the arguments should be made in Latin, and thereupon I have drawn and devised all mine arguments in Latin" But the prolocutor bade him still form an argument in English, or else to hold his peace.

Then said Philpot; "You have sore disappointed me, thus suddenly to go from your former order; but I will comply with your command, leaving mine oration apart; and I will come to my arguments But before I submit any argument, I will in one word declare what manner of presence I disallow in the sacrament, that the hearers may the better understand to what end and effect my arguments shall tend; not to deny utterly the presence of Christ in his sacrament, truly ministered according to his institution; but only to deny that gross and carnal presence, which you of this house have already subscribed to, to be in the sacrament of the altar, contrary to the true and manifest meaning of the scriptures, that by transubstantiation of the sacramental bread and wine, Christ's natural body should, by virtue of the words pronounced by the priest, be contained and included under the forms or accidents of bread and wine. This kind of presence imagined by men I do deny," continued Philpot, "and against this I will reason." But before he could make an end of what he would have said, he was interrupted by the prolocutor, and commanded to come to his argument. Philpot, being offended, fell down upon his knees before the earls and lords who were there present, of whom some were of the queen's council, beseeching them that he might have liberty to prosecute his arguments, without interruption of any man, which was gently granted him of the lords. But the prolocutor would not permit him, but still cried, "Hold your peace, or else make a short argument" "I am about it," said Philpot, "if you will let me alone But first, I must needs ask a question of my respondent (who was Doctor Chedsey) concerning a word or two of your supposition, that is, of the sacrament of the altar, what he means thereby, and whether he takes it, as some of the ancient writers do, terming the Lord's Supper the sacrament of the altar, partly because it is a sacrament of that lively sacrifice which Christ offered for our sins upon the altar of the cross, and partly because that Christ's body, crucified for us, was that bloody sacrifice, which the blood-shedding of all the beasts offered upon the altar in the old law, did prefigure and signify to us; or whether you take it otherwise; as for the sacrament of the altar, which is made of lime and stone, over which the sacrament hangs, and to be all one with the sacrament of the mass, as it is at this present in many places. This done, I will direct my arguments according as your answer shall give me occasion.

Then Chedsey made this answer, that in their supposition they took the sacrament of the altar, and the sacrament of the mass, to be all one

"Then," said Philpot, "I will speak plain English, as Master Prolocutor wishes me, and make a short resolution of it, that the sacrament of the altar, which ye reckon to be all one with the mass, once justly abolished, and now put in full use again, is no sacrament at all, neither is Christ in any wise present in it," and this his saying he offered to prove before the whole house, if they chose to call him to it And likewise he offered to vouch the same before the queen's grace and her most honourable council, before the face of six of the best learned men of the house of the contrary opinion, and would except none. "And if I shall not be able," said he, "to maintain by God's word what I have said, and confound those six who shall take upon them to withstand me in this point, let me be burdened with as many fagots as are in London, before the court gates" This he uttered with great vehemency of spirit.

At this the prolocutor, with others, were very much offended, demanding of him whether he knew what he said, or not? "Yea," said Philpot, "I wot well what I say," desiring no man to be offended with his saying for that he spake no more than by God's word he was able to prove. "And praised be God," continued he, "that the queen's grace has granted us of this house (as our prolocutor has informed us) that we may freely utter our consciences in these matters of controversy in religion; and therefore I will speak here my conscience freely, grounded upon God's holy word, for the truth, although some of you here present dislike it."

Then several of the house, beside the prolocutor, taunted and reprehended him for speaking thus against the sacrament of the mass, and the prolocutor threatened him, that he would send him to prison, if he would not cease speaking in that manner.

Philpot seeing himself thus abused, and not permitted with free liberty to declare his mind, fell into an exclamation, casting his eyes up towards heaven, and said, "O Lord, what a world is this, that the truth of thy holy word may not be spoken and adhered to?" And for very sorrow and heaviness the tears trickled out of his eyes.

After this, the prolocutor being moved by some that were about him, was content that he should make an argument. provided he would be brief "I will be as brief," said Philpot, "as I may conveniently be in uttering all that I have to say. And I will begin to ground my arguments upon the authority of the scriptures, whereupon all the building of our faith ought to be grounded, and I shall confirm the same by ancient doctors of the church. And I take the first argument out of the twenty-eight chapter of St. Matthew, of the saying of the angel at the sepulchre, saying, 'He is risen, he is not here.' and in St. Luke, in the twenty-third chapter,

the angel asks why they sought the living among the dead? Likewise the scripture testifies, that Christ is risen, ascended into heaven, and sitteth on the right hand of the Father all which is spoken of his natural body; and therefore his natural body is not on earth included in the sacrament.

"I will confirm this yet more effectually, by the saying of Christ in the sixteenth chapter of St. John; 'I came forth from the Father, and am come into the world' 'Again, I leave the world, and go to the Father.' Which coming and going he meant of his natural body. Therefore we may affirm that it is not found in the world.

"But I expect here," continued he, "to be answered with a distinction of visibly and invisibly, that he is visibly departed in his humanity, but invisibly he remains notwithstanding in the sacrament. But I will prove that no such distinction ought to take away the force of that argument, by the answer which Christ's disciples gave to him, speaking these words, 'Now thou speakest plainly and utterest no proverb.' Which words St Cyril interpreting, saith, 'That Christ spake without any manner of ambiguity and obscure speech.' And therefore I conclude that if Christ spake plainly, and without parable, saying, 'Again, I leave the world and go to the Father,' then that obscure, dark and imperceptible presence of Christ's natural body in the sacrament upon earth invisibly, contrary to the plain words of Christ, ought not to be allowed. For nothing can be more uncertain or more parabolical and insensible, than to say so."

Then Doctor Chedsey took upon him to answer. First, to the saying of the angel, "That Christ is not here." "And, why seek ye the living among the dead?" He answered, that these sayings pertained nothing to the presence of Christ's natural body in the sacrament, but that they were spoken of Christ's body in the sepulchre, when they thought him to have been in the grave still. And therefore the angel said "Why do ye seek the living among the dead?" And to the authority of the sixteenth chapter of St John where Christ saith, 'Now I leave the world and go to the Father,' he meant that of his ascension. And so likewise did Cyril, interpreting the saying of the disciples, that knew plainly that Christ would visibly ascend into heaven, but that does not exclude the invisible presence of his natural body in the sacrament For St. Chrysostom, writing to the people of Antioch, affirms the same, comparing Elijah and Christ together, and Elijah's cloak and Christ's flesh. "Elijah," said he, "when he was taken up in the fiery chariot, left his cloak behind him unto his disciple Elisha. But Christ, ascending into heaven, took his flesh with him, and left also his flesh behind him." Whereby we may right well gather, that Christ's flesh is visibly ascended into heaven, and invisibly abideth still in the sacrament of the altar.

To this Philpot replied, "You have not directly answered the saying of the angel 'Christ is not here, but is risen,' because you have omitted that which was the chief point of all. For I proceed further, as thus: He is risen, ascended, and sitteth at the right hand of God the Father, and therefore he is not remaining on the earth. Neither is your answer to Cyril sufficient. But by and by I will return to your interpretation of Cyril, and more plainly declare the same, after I have first disposed of the authority of Chrysostom, which is one of the chief arguments that you allege, to make for your gross carnal presence in the sacrament, which being well weighed and understood pertains nothing to it "

At that the prolocutor startled, that one of the chief pillars in this point should be overthrown; and therefore recited the authority in Latin first, and afterwards Englished the same, willing that all who were present to note that saying of Chrysostom, which he thought invincible on their side "But I will make it appear," said Philpot, "that it makes little for your purpose." And as he was about to declare his mind, the prolocutor interrupted him, as he did almost continually. Philpot, not being content, said; "Mr. Prolocutor thinks that he is in a sophistry school, where he knows right well the manner is, that when the respondent perceives that he is likely to be forced with an argument, to which he is not able to answer, he does what he can with cavil and interruption to drive him from it." This saying of Philpot was ill taken by the prolocutor and his adherents; and the prolocutor said, that Philpot could bring nothing to avoid that authority, but his own vain imagination. "Hear," said Philpot, "and afterwards judge. For I will do in this as in all other authorities, wherewith you shall charge me in refuting any of my arguments, answering either by sufficient authorities of scripture, or else by some other testimony with yours, and not of mine own imagination. And concerning the saying of Chrysostom, I have two ways to beat him from your purpose, the one out of the scriptures, the other out of Chrysostom himself, in the place alleged by you.

"First, where he seemeth to say, that Christ ascending took his flesh with him, and left also his flesh behind him, it is truth; for we all confess and believe that Christ took on him our human nature in the womb of the Virgin Mary, and through his passion has united us to his flesh, and thereby are we become one flesh with him, so that Chrysostom might right well say, that Christ ascending took his flesh, which he received of the Virgin Mary, away with him; and also left his flesh behind him, which is we that are his elect in this world, who are the members of Christ, and flesh of his flesh; as St. Paul, in the fifth chapter to the Ephesians, testifies saying, 'We are members of his body, of his flesh, and of his bones.' And if any man will reply, that he treats there of the sacrament; so that this interpretation cannot so aptly be applied to him in that place, then will I yet interpret Chrysostom another way by himself. For in that place, a few lines before those words which were here now lately read, are these words; that Christ after he ascended into heaven, left to us, indued with his sacraments, his flesh in mysteries, that is, sacramentally. And that mystical flesh Christ leaves as well to his church in the sacrament of baptism, as in the sacramental bread and wine. And that St. Paul justly witnesses, saying, 'As many of us as are baptised into Christ have put on Christ.' And thus you may understand that St. Chrysostom makes nothing for your carnal and gross presence in the sacrament, as you wrongfully take him."

Now, in the meanwhile Master Pye whispered the prolocutor in the ear, to put Philpot to silence, and to appoint some other, distrusting lest he would shake their carnal presence, if he held on long, seeing in the beginning he gave one of their chief foundations such a blow. Then the prolocutor said to Philpot that he had reasoned enough, and that some other should now supply his room. But he was not well content, saying, "Why, sir, I have a dozen arguments concerning this matter to be proposed, and I have yet scarce gone over my first argument."

"Well," said the prolocutor, "you shall speak no more now; and I command you to hold your peace." "You perceive," replied Philpot, "that I have stuff enough for you, and am able to withstand your false supposition, and therefore you command me to silence." "If you will not give place," said the prolocutor, "I will send you to prison." "This is not," answered Philpot, "according to your promise made in this house; nor yet according to your boast made at St. Paul's Cross, that men should be answered in this disputation to whatever they can say, since you will not suffer me out of a dozen arguments to prosecute one."

Then Master Pye took upon him to promise that he should be answered another day. Philpot, seeing he might not proceed in his purpose, being justly offended, ended, saying thus: "A number of you here, who hitherto have lurked in corners, and dissembled with God and the world, are now gathered together to suppress the sincere truth of God's holy word, and to set forth every false device, which you are not able to maintain by the catholic doctrine of the scriptures."

Then stepped forth Master Ailmer, chaplain to the duke of Suffolk, whom Master Moreman took upon him to answer. Master Ailmer objected several authorities for the confirming of the argument he took in hand the day before, to prove that "substance" in the sentence of Theodoret, brought in by Master Cheyney, must needs signify 'substance,' and not 'accidents.' Whose reasons, because they were all grounded and brought out of the Greek, I pass over, because they want their grace in English, and also their proper understanding. But his allegations so incumbered Doctor Moreman, that he desired a day to reply to them, for at that instant he was without a convenient answer.

Then the prolocutor called Master Haddon, dean of Exeter, and chaplain to the duke of Suffolk, who prosecuted Theodoret's authority in confirming Master Ailmer's argument. To whom Doctor Watson took upon him to give an answer, who was confounded, that he was not able to answer to the word 'Mysterium.' But as he seemed to doubt therein, Master Haddon took out of his bosom a Latin author to confirm his saying, and shewed it to Master Watson, asking him whether he thought that translation true, or that the printer were in any fault. "There may be a fault in the printer," said Watson, "for I am not remembered of this word." Then Master Haddon took out of his bosom a Greek book, wherein he shewed with his finger the same words, which Master Watson could not deny.

Then stept forth Mr. Perne, and made declaration of his mind against transubstantiation, whom the prolocutor answered, saying, "I much marvel, Mr. Perne, that you will say thus; for on Friday last you subscribed to the contrary." Which Master Palmer disliked, saying to the prolocutor, "That he was to blame so to reprehend any man, partly because this house is an house of free liberty for every man to speak his conscience, and partly because you promised yesterday, that notwithstanding any man had subscribed, yet he should have free liberty to speak his mind."

The Act of the Fifth Day.

On Friday, the 27th of October, Dr. Weston, the prolocutor, first propounded the matter, shewing that the convocation had spent two days in disputation already about one only doctor, who was Theodoret, and about one only word, which was "substance." Yet were they come the third day to answer all things that could be objected, so that they would shortly put together their arguments. So Master Haddon, dean of Exeter, desired leave to oppose Master Watson, who, with two others more, that is, Morgan and Harpsfield, was appointed to answer. Master Haddon demanded this of him, whether any substance of bread or wine remained after the consecration? Then Master Watson asked of him again, whether he thought there was a real presence of Christ's body or not? Master Haddon said, "It was not meet nor order-like that he who was appointed to be respondent should be opponent, and he whose duty was to object should answer." Yet Master Watson a long while would not agree to answer, but that being granted, at last an order was set, and Master Haddon had leave to proceed with his argument.

Then he proved by Theodoret's words, that the substance of bread and wine remained. For these are his words, "The same they were before the sanctification, which they are after." Master Watson said, that Theodoret meant not the same substance, but the same essence. Whereupon they were driven again unto the discussing of the Greek word "substance." Then Master Watson answered that it had not that signification only. But Master Haddon proved that it must needs signify so in that place. Then he asked Master Watson, when the bread and wine became symbols? He answered, "after the consecration, and not before." Then Master Haddon argued that Theodoret says, that what the bread and wine were before they were symbols, the same they remain still in nature and substance, after they are symbols; and as thus they were bread and wine before, therefore bread and wine they are afterwards still.

Then Mr. Watson fell to the denial of the author, and said he was a Nestorian; and he desired that he might answer to Master Cheyney who stood by, because he was more meet to dispute in the matter, because he had granted and subscribed to the real presence. Master Cheyney desired patience of the honourable men to hear him, trusting that he should so open the matter, that the truth should appear, that he would be no author of schism, nor hold any thing contrary to the holy mother the church, which is Christ's spouse. Doctor Weston liked this well, and commended him highly, saying that he was a well-learned and sober man, and well exercised in all good learning and in the doctors; and finally, a man meet for his knowledge to dispute in that place. "I pray you hear him," said he. Then Master Cheyney desired such as were there present to pray two words with him to God, and to say, *vincat veritas*, "may truth prevail," and have the victory, and all that were present cried with a loud voice, "*Vincat veritas, vincat veritas!*"

Then said Doctor Weston to him, that it was hypocritical. Men may better say, replied he, *vicit veritas*, "truth hath got the victory." Master Cheyney said, if he would give him leave, he would bring it to that point, that he might well say so.

Then he began with Master Watson after this sort· "You said that Master Haddon was unmeet to dispute, because he grants not the natural and real presence, but I say you are much more unmeet to answer, because you take away the substance of the sacrament."

Master Watson said, "He had subscribed to the real presence, and should not go away from that." So said Weston also, and the rest of the priests; so that for a great while he could have no leave to say any more, till the lords spake, and desired that he should be heard.

Then he told them what he meant by his subscribing to the real presence, far otherwise than they supposed. So then he went forward, and prosecuted Master Haddon's argument, and said that when they could not answer, they went to deny the author, and therefore he proved the author to be a catholic doctor, and that being proved, he confirmed that which was said of the nature and substance further.

Then was Master Watson forced to say, that the substance of the body, in the former part of the similitude of Theodoret signified quantity, and other accidents of sacramental tokens, and not the very substance of the same, for according to philosophy, the accidents of things are seen, and not the substances.

Then Master Cheyney appealed to the honourable men, and desired that they would give no credit to them in so saying· for if they would think as they teach, after their lordships had rode forty miles on horseback, they would not be able to say at night, that they saw not their horses all the day, but only the *colour* of their horses; and by this reason Christ must go to school, and learn of Aristotle to speak. For when he saw Nathanael under the fig-tree, if Aristotle had stood by, he would have said, "No, Christ, thou sawest not him, but the *colour of him*."

Then it was said by Watson "Suppose that Theodoret is with you, who is one that we never heard of printed till two or three years ago; yet is he only but one, and what is one against the whole consent of the church?" After this, Master Cheyney inferred, that not only Theodoret was of that mind, that the substance of bread and wine do remain, but others also.

Then was Master Harpsfield called in to see what he could say in the matter; who told a fair tale of the omnipotency of God, and of the imbecility and weakness of man's reason, he said, "That it was convenient whatever we saw, felt, or tasted, not to trust our senses." And he told a tale out of St. Cyprian, how a woman saw the sacrament burning "And that which burned there," said Harpsfield, "burns here, and becomes ashes, but what that was that burnt he could not tell." But Master Cheyney continued and forced them with this question "What it was that was burnt? It was either the substance of bread, or else the substance of the body of Christ, which was too great an absurdity to grant." At length they answered, "That it was a *miracle*." Master Cheyney smiled and said, "That he could at that rate say no more."

Then Master Weston asked of the company present whether those men were sufficiently answered or not? Certain priests cried, "Yea;" but they were not heard at all for the great multitude, who cried "No, no" Which cry was heard almost to the end of St Paul's Doctor Weston being much moved, answered bitterly, "That he asked not the judgment of the rude multitude and unlearned people, but of them who are of the house. Then asked he of Master Haddon and his fellows, whether they would answer them three other days? Haddon, Cheyney, and Ailmer said, "No" But Philpot, archdeacon of Winchester, stood up and said, that they should not say so, for they should be answered; and though all others refused to answer them yet he would not; but offered to answer them all one after another with whose proffer the prolocutor was not content, but railed on him, and said, "That he should go to Bedlam" To whom the archdeacon soberly made this answer, "That he was more worthy to be sent thither, who used himself so ragingly in that disputation." Then rose Dr. Weston and said:

"All the company have subscribed to our article, saving only these men. What their reasons are you have heard. We have answered them three days, upon promise (as it pleased him to descant, without truth, for no such promise was made) that they should answer us again as long as the order of disputation requires, and if they are able to defend their doctrine, let them do so."

Then Master Ailmer stood up, and proved how vain a man Weston was; for he affirmed that they never promised to dispute, but only to open and testify to the world what they believed in their consciences. For when they were required to subscribe, they refused, and said that they would shew good reasons which moved them, that they could not in their consciences subscribe, as they had partly already done, and were still able to do more sufficiently. "Therefore," said he, "it hath been ill called a disputation, and they were worthy to be blamed that were the authors of that name. For we meant not to dispute, nor now mean to answer till our arguments, which we have to propound, be solved, according as was appointed. For by answering we should but incumber ourselves, and profit nothing, since the matter is already decreed upon and determined, whatever we shall prove to the contrary."

The Act of the Sixth Day.

On Monday following, being the 30th of October, the prolocutor demanded of John Philpot, archdeacon of Winchester, whether he would answer to the questions before propounded to their objections or not? To whom he made this answer, that he would willingly do so, if according to their former determination, they would first answer to some of his arguments, as they had promised to do, whereof he had a dozen, not half of the first being yet decided. And if they would answer fully and sufficiently to one of his arguments, he promised that he would answer to all the objections that they should bring forth.

Then the prolocutor bade him propound his argument, and it should be answered by one of them to which Master Morgan was appointed. "Upon Wednesday last," said he, "I was forced to silence before I had prosecuted half mine argument, the sum whereof was this as was gathered by the just context of the scripture) that the human body of Christ was ascended into heaven, and placed on the right hand of God the Father wherefore it could not be situated upon earth in the sacrament of the altar, invisible after the imagination of man" The argument was denied by Morgan Philpot said, that this was it wherewith he had to confirm his first argument, if they would have suffered him the other day, as now he trusted they would, it was to this effect that to be bodily present, and to be bodily absent, to be on earth, and to be in heaven, and all at one and the same time are things contrary to the nature of a human body. And therefore it cannot be said of the human body of Christ, that the self-same body is both in heaven and also on earth at one instant, either visibly or invisibly.

Morgan in answer denied the first part of the argument Philpot said, that as one of our bodies cannot receive in itself any thing contrary to the nature of a body, as to be in St. Paul's Church and at Westminster at one instant, or to be at London visibly, and at Lincoln invisibly, at one time; for that is contrary to the nature of a body; so he concluded that the body of Christ could not be in more places than one, it is in heaven, and therefore cannot be contained in the sacrament of the altar.

Philpots added that St Peter in the sermon that he made in the third of the Acts, making mention of Christ, used these words, "Whom the heavens must receive until the restitution of all things," &c. Which words are spoken of his humanity. If heaven must hold Christ, then he cannot be here on earth, in the sacrament, as is pretended.

Then Morgan laughing at this, and giving no answer, Harpsfield stood up, being one of the bishop of London's chaplains, and took it upon him to answer to the saying of St. Peter, and demanded of Philpot, whether he would of necessity force Christ to any place, or not?

Philpot said, that he would not otherwise force Christ of necessity to any place, than he is taught by the words of the Holy Ghost, which say, that Christ's human body must abide in heaven until the day of judgment.

"Why," said Harpsfield, "do you not know that God is omnipotent?" "Yes," said Philpot, "I know that right well, neither doubt I any thing at all of his omnipotency. But of Christ's omnipotency what he may do is not our question, but rather what he doth. I know he may make a stone in the wall a man, if he will, and also that he may make more worlds, but doth he therefore do so? It were no good consequent so to conclude; he may do this or that, therefore he does it."

"Why," said the prolocutor, "then you will put Christ in prison in heaven." To which Philpot answered, "Do you reckon heaven to be a prison? God grant us all to come to that prison."

After some further arguing, Morgan asked Philpot whether he would be ruled by the universal church, or not?

"Yes," said he, "if it be the true catholick church. And since you speak so much of the church, I would be glad if you would declare what the church is?"

"The church," replied Morgan, "is diffused and dispersed throughout the whole world." "That is a diffuse definition," said Philpot, "for I am yet as uncertain as I was before, what you mean by the church · but I acknowledge no church but that which is grounded and founded on God's word, as St. Paul saith, 'Upon the foundation of the apostles and prophets,' and upon the scriptures of God."

"What," answered Moreman, "was the scripture before the church?" "Yea," said Philpot. "But I will prove nay," replied Moreman. "The church of Christ was before any scripture was written"

Philpot said, "That all prophecy uttered by the Spirit of God, was counted to be scripture before it was written in paper and ink, because it was written in the hearts, and graven in the minds, yea, and inspired in the mouths of good men, and of Christ's apostles by the Spirit of Christ; as the salutation of the angel was the scripture of Christ, and the word of God, before it was written." At that Moreman cried, "Fie, fie!" wondering that the scripture of God should be counted scripture before it was written, and affirmed, that he had no knowledge who could speak so.

Philpot answered, "That concerning knowledge for the trial of the truth about the questions in controversy, he would wish himself no worse matched than with Moreman."

At which the prolocutor was grievously offended, saying, That it was arrogantly spoken by Philpot to compare himself with such a worshipful learned man as Moreman was, being himself a man unlearned, yea, a madman, meeter to be sent to Bedlam than to be among such learned and grave men as were there assembled, and a man that never would be answered, and one that troubled the whole house; and therefore he commanded him no more to come into the house, demanding of the house, whether they would agree to this. A great company answered, "Yea." Then said Philpot again, that

he might think himself a happy man that was out of this company.

After this Morgan rose up and whispered to the prolocutor in the ear And then again the prolocutor spake to Philpot, and said, "Lest thou shouldst slander the house, and say that we will not suffer you to declare your mind, we are content you should come into the house as you have done before, provided you be apparelled with a long gown and a tippet, as we are, and that you shall not speak but when I command you." "Then," said Philpot "I had rather be absent altogether." Weston concluded all by saying, "You have the word, but we have the sword," which shewed the opinion in which this disputation was carried on.

They carried on reasoning in this manner until at length, about the 13th of December, queen Mary sends her commands to Bonner bishop of London, that he should dissolve and break up the convocation

During the time of this disputation, on the 20th day of November, the mayor of Coventry sent up to the lords of the council, Baldwin Clarke, J. Carelesse, Thomas Wilcocks, and Richard Estelin, for their behaviour upon Alhallow-day Carelesse and Wilcocks were committed to the Gatehouse, and Clarke and Estelin to the Marshalsea.

On the same day there was a letter directed to Sir Christopher Heydon, and Sir William Farmer, knights, for the apprehension of John Huntington, preacher, for making a rhyme against Dr. Stokes and the sacrament Who appearing before the council on the third of December next, was, upon his humble submission and promise to amend as well in doctrine as in living, again suffered to depart.

In the days of king Henry VIII., and also king Edward VI. after him, some noblemen, bishops, and others, were cast into the Tower; some charged with treason, as Lord Courtney and the Duke of Norfolk, some for the pope's supremacy, and suspicious letters tending to sedition, as Tonstal bishop of Durham, and others for other things, all of whom continued prisoners till queen Mary ascended the throne. The queen granted their pardon, and restored them to their former dignities. Gardiner bishop of Winchester, she not only delivered out of captivity, but also advanced to be high chancellor of England. To the lord Courtney she shewed such favour, that she made him Earl of Devonshire, so that there was a suspicion that she would marry him, but that proved otherwise

At the same time Bonner also had been prisoner in the Marshalsea, whom likewise Queen Mary delivered, and restored to the bishopric of London again, displacing Dr. Ridley, with other good bishops, as is abovementioned, namely, Cranmer, from Canterbury, the archbishop of York, Poinet from Winchester, John Hooper from Worcester, Barlow from Bath, Harley from Hereford, Taylor from Lincoln, Ferrar from St. Davids, Coverdale from Exeter, Scory from Chichester, &c., with a great number of archdeacons, deans, and briefly all such beneficed men as were married, or adhered to their profession. All were removed from their livings, and others of the contrary sect placed in them; as Cardinal Pole, who was then sent for, Gardiner, Heath, White, Day Troublefield &c

As to Cranmer, as there was rumour spread of him in London, that he had recanted, and caused mass to be said at Canterbury; to clear himself he published a declaration of his constancy, protesting that he neither had done so, nor intended to do so. Adding, that if it would so please the queen, he, with Peter Martyr and others would in open disputation sustain the cause of the doctrine taught and set forth in the days of king Edward VI., against all persons But while he was in expectation to have this disputation, he, with other bishops, was laid fast in the Tower, and Peter Martyr permitted to depart the realm.

After this, in the month of November, archbishop Cranmer, though he had refused to subscribe to the king's will in disinheriting Mary, alleging many grave reasons for her legitimacy, was arraigned in the Guildhall of London, and attainted of treason, with the lady

Jane, and three of the duke of Northumberland's sons, who at the entreaty of certain persons, were had again to the Tower, and there kept. Cranmer being pardoned of the treason, stood only in the action of doctrine, which they called heresy, of which he was right glad.

This being done in November, the people, and especially the churchmen, perceiving the queen so eagerly set upon her old religion, they likewise began in their quires to set up the pageant of St. Catharine, and of St Nicholas, and of their processions in Latin, after all their old solemnity.

And when the month of December was come, the parliament broke up In which parliament also communication was moved of the queen's marriage with king Philip the emperor's son

In the meanwhile cardinal Pole being sent for by queen Mary, was requested by the emperor to stay with him, that his presence in England should not be a hindrance to the marriage which he intended between his son Philip and queen Mary For making of which he sent a most ample embassy, with full power to contract the marriage.

On the 13th of January, A D. 1554, Dr. Crome, for his preaching upon Christmas-day without license, was committed to the Fleet.

On the 21st of January, Master Thomas Wootton was for matters of religion committed a close prisoner to the Fleet.

The death of the lady Jane Gray having now been determined upon, the queen sent, two days before her death, Master Fecknam, afterwards abbot of Winchester, to commune with her, and to turn her from the doctrine of Christ to queen Mary's religion. The effect of which communication here follows —

The Communication had between the Lady Jane and Fecknam.

Fecknam —Madam, I lament your heavy case, and yet I doubt not, but that you bear out this sorrow of yours with a constant and patient mind.

Jane   You are welcome to me, sir, if your coming be to give christian exhortation And as for my heavy case, (I thank God) I do so little lament it, that I rather account it a more manifest declaration of God's favour to me, than ever he shewed me at any time before. And therefore there is no cause why either you, or others who bear me good will, should lament or be grieved with my case, being a thing so profitable for my soul's health.

Fecknam.—I am come to you, sent from the queen and her council, to instruct you in the true doctrine of the right faith : although I have so great confidence in you, that I shall have, I trust, little need to labour with you much therein.

Jane.—I heartily thank the queen's highness, which is not unmindful of her humble subject · and I hope likewise that you will no less do your duty both truly and faithfully, according to that you were sent for.

Fecknam —What is then required of a christian man ?

Jane.—That he should believe in God the Father, the Son, and the Holy Ghost, three persons in one Godhead.

Fecknam.—What ? Is there nothing else to be required or looked for in a christian, but to believe in him ?

Jane.—Yes, we must love him with all our heart, with all our soul, and with all our mind, and our neighbour as ourself.

Fecknam.—Why ? Then faith justifies not, nor saves not.

Jane.—Yes, verily, faith only (as St Paul saith) justifies.

Fecknam.—Why ? St. Paul saith, If we have all faith without charity, it is nothing

Jane —It is true, for how can I love him whom I trust not ? or, how can I trust him whom I love not ? Faith and love go together, and yet love is comprehended in faith.

Fecknam.—How shall we love our neighbour ?

Jane.—To love our neighbour is to feed the hungry, to clothe the naked, and give drink to the thirsty, and to do to him as we would do to ourselves.

Fecknam   Why ? then it is necessary to salvation to do good works also, and it is not sufficient only to believe.

Jane   I deny that, and I affirm that faith only saves but it is meet for a christian, in token that he follows his Master, Christ, to do good works, yet may we not say that they profit to our salvation. For " when we have done all, yet we are all unprofitable servants," and faith only in Christ's blood saves us.

Fecknam —How many sacraments are there ?

Jane. Two. The one the sacrament of baptism, and the other the sacrament of the Lord's supper.

Fecknam —No, there are seven.

Jane —By what scripture find you that?

Fecknam.—Well, we will talk of that hereafter. But what is signified by your two sacraments ?

Jane.—By the sacrament of baptism I am washed with water, and regenerated by the Spirit, and that washing is a token to me that I am the child of God. The sacrament of the Lord's supper offered to me, is a sure seal and testimony that I am, by the blood of Christ, which he shed for me on the cross, made partaker of the everlasting kingdom

Fecknam.—Why ? what do you receive in that sacrament ? Do you not receive the very body and blood of Christ ?

Jane.—No, surely, I do not so believe. I think that at the supper I neither receive flesh nor blood, but bread and wine which bread when it is broken, and the wine when it is drunk, puts me in remembrance how that for my sins the body of Christ was broken, and his blood shed on the cross, and with that bread and wine I receive the benefits that come by the breaking of his body, and shedding of his blood for our sins on the cross.

Fecknam —Why ? Doth not Christ speak these words, " Take, eat, this is my body ?" Require you any plainer words ? Doth he not say it is his body ?

Jane. I grant he saith so , and so he saith, " I am the vine," " I am the door " but he is never the more the door nor the vine. Doth not St Paul say, " He calleth things that are not as though they were ?" God forbid that I should say, that I eat the very natural body and blood of Christ for then either I should pluck away my redemption, or else there were two bodies, or two Christs. One body was tormented on the cross, and if they did eat another body, then had he two bodies· or if his body were eaten, then it was not broken upon the cross, or if it was broken upon the cross, it was not eaten by his disciples.

Fecknam —Why ? is it not as possible that Christ by his power could make his body both to be eaten and broken, and to be born of a woman without seed of man, as to walk upon the sea, and other such like miracles as he wrought by his power only?

Jane.—Yes, if God wished to have performed any miracle at his supper, he might have done so · but I say that then he intended no work nor miracle, but only to break his body, and shed his blood on the cross for our sins But I pray you to answer me to this one question Where was Christ, when he said, " Take, eat, this is my body ?" Was he not at the table when he said so ? he was at that time alive, and suffered not till the next day. What took he but *bread*, what brake he but *bread* ? And what gave he but *bread?* Look, what he took, he brake and look, what he brake, he gave · and look, what he gave, they did eat and yet all this while he himself was alive, and at supper before his disciples, or else they were deceived.

Fecknam.—You ground your faith upon such authors as say and unsay both in a breath, and not upon the church, to which you ought to give credit.

Jane.—No, I ground my faith on God's word, and not upon the church. For if the church be a good church, the faith of the church must be tried by God's word, and not God's word by the church, nor yet my faith. Shall I believe the church because of antiquity ? or shall I give credit to the church that takes away from me the half-part of the Lord's supper, and will not let any man receive it in both kinds? Which things, if they refuse to us, then they refuse to us part of our salvation And I say, that it is an evil church, and not the spouse of Christ, but the spouse of the devil, that alters the Lord's supper, and both takes from it, and adds to it. To that church, say I, God will add plagues, and from that church will he take their part out of the book of life (Rev xxii 18.) Do they learn that from St. Paul, when he administered to the Corinthians in both kinds? shall I believe this church? God forbid.

Fecknam.—That was done for a good intent of the church, to avoid a heresy that sprung up from it.

Jane.—Why? shall the church alter God's will and ordinance for good intent? How did king Saul? The Lord God forbids it.

With these and such like persuasions he would have had her lean to the church of Rome, but he could not prevail. There were many more things of which they reasoned, but these were the chief.

After this, Fecknam took his leave, saying, that he was sorry for her "For I am sure," said he, "that we two shall never meet"

"True it is," said she, "that we shall never meet, except God turn your heart. For I am assured, unless you repent and turn to God, you are in an evil case · and I pray God, in his infinite mercy, to send you his Holy Spirit for he hath given you his great gift of utterance, if it pleased him also to open the eyes of your understanding."

A Letter of the Lady Jane sent to her Father.

"Father, although it hath pleased God to hasten my death by you, by whom my life should rather have been lengthened; yet I can so patiently take it, as I yield God more hearty thanks for shortening my woeful days, than if all the world had been given to my possession with life lengthened at my own will. And although I am well assured of your impatient temper, redoubled manifold ways, both in bewailing your own woe, and especially (as I hear) my unfortunate state, yet, my dear father, (if I may, without offence, rejoice in my own misfortunes,) methinks in this I may account myself blessed, that washing my hands with the innocency of my fact, my guiltless blood may cry before the Lord, "Mercy to the innocent." And yet, though I must needs acknowledge, that being constrained, and, as you know well enough, continually assayed, in taking upon me I seemed to consent, and therein grievously offended the queen and her laws yet do I assuredly trust, that this my offence towards God is so much the less, in that, being in so royal estate as I was, my forced honour never blended with my innocent heart. And thus, good father, I have opened unto you the state wherein I at present stand. Though death is at hand, which to you, perhaps, it may seem right woeful, to me there is nothing that can be more welcome, than from this vale of misery to aspire to that heavenly throne of all joy and pleasure with Christ our Saviour. In whose steadfast faith (if it may be lawful for the daughter so to write to the father) the Lord that hitherto hath strengthened you, so continue you, that at the last we may meet in heaven with the Father, the Son, and the Holy Ghost."

A Letter written by the Lady Jane, in the end of the New Testament in Greek, which she sent to her sister the Lady Catharine the night before she suffered.

"I have here sent to you, good sister Catharine, a book, which although it be not outwardly trimmed with gold, yet inwardly it is more worth than precious stones. It is the book, dear sister, of the law of the Lord. It is his testament and last will which he bequeathed to us wretches· which shall lead you to the path of eternal joy, and if you with a good mind read it, and with an earnest mind do purpose to follow it, it shall bring you to an immortal and everlasting life. It shall teach you to live, and learn you to die It shall win you more than you should have gained by the possession of your woful father's lands. For as, if God had prospered him, you should have inherited his lands, so if you apply diligently this book, seeking to direct your life after it, you shall be an inheritor of such riches, as neither the covetous shall withdraw from you, neither thief shall steal, neither yet the moths corrupt Desire with David, good sister, to understand the law of the Lord God. Live still to die, that you by death may purchase eternal life And trust not that the tenderness of your age shall lengthen your life, for as soon, if God call goeth the young as the old, and labour also to learn to die. Defy the world, deny the devil, and despise the flesh, and delight yourself only in the Lord. Be penitent for your sins, and yet despair not; be strong in faith, and yet presume not; and desire with St Paul to depart, and to be with Christ, with whom even death is life. Be like the good servant, and even at midnight be waking, lest when death cometh and stealeth upon you as a thief in the night, you be, with the evil servant, found sleeping; and lest for lack of oil, you be found like the five foolish virgins; and like him that had not on the wedding-garment, and then you be cast out from the marriage. Rejoice in Christ, as I do Follow the steps of your Master, Christ, and take up your cross lay your sins on his back, and always embrace him And as to my death, rejoice as I do, good sister, that I shall be delivered of this corruption, and put on incorruption. For I am assured, that I shall for losing of a mortal life, win an immortal life, which I pray to God to grant to you, and to send you of his grace to live in his fear, and to die in the true christian faith, from which, in God's name, I exhort you, that you never swerve, neither for hope of life nor for fear of death. For if you will deny his truth for to lengthen your life, God will deny you, and yet shorten your days. But if you will cleave unto him, he will prolong your days to your comfort and his glory. To which glory God brings me now, and you hereafter, when it pleaseth him to call you. Fare you well, good sister, and put your only trust in God, who only must help you."

We here give a certain prayer, made by the lady Jane, in the time of her trouble ·

"O Lord, thou God and Father of my life, hear me, a poor and desolate woman, who flieth unto thee only, in all troubles and miseries Thou, O Lord, art the only defender and deliverer of those who put their trust in thee, and therefore, I being defiled with sin, encumbered with affliction, unquieted with troubles, wrapped in cares, overwhelmed with miseries, vexed with temptations, and grievously tormented with the long imprisonment of this vile mass of clay, my sinful body, do come unto thee, O merciful Saviour, craving thy mercy and help, without which so little hope of deliverance is left, that I may utterly despair of any liberty. Although it is expedient, that seeing our life standeth upon trying, we should be visited sometime with some adversity, whereby we might both be tried whether we be of thy flock or not, and also know thee and ourselves the better; yet thou that saidst thou wouldst not suffer us to be tempted above our power, be merciful unto me now, a miserable wretch, I beseech thee, who with Solomon does cry unto thee, humbly desiring thee, that I may neither be too much puffed up with prosperity, neither too much pressed down with adversity, lest I being too full, should deny thee my God, or being brought too low, should despair, and blaspheme thee my Lord and Saviour. O merciful God, consider my misery, best known unto thee; and be thou now unto me a strong tower of defence, I humbly require thee. Suffer me not to be tempted above my power, but either be thou a deliverer unto me out of this great misery, or else give me grace patiently to bear thy heavy hand and sharp correction. It was thy right hand that delivered the people of Israel out of the hands of Pharaoh, which for the space of four hundred years did oppress them, and keep them in bondage. Let it therefore likewise seem good to thy Fatherly goodness, to deliver me, a sorrowful wretch, for whom thy Son Christ shed his precious blood on the cross, out of this miserable captivity and bondage, wherein I am now. How long wilt thou be absent? for ever?

O Lord, hast thou forgotten to be gracious, and hast thou shut up thy loving-kindness in displeasure? Wilt thou be no more entreated? Is thy mercy clean gone for ever, and thy promise come utterly to an end for evermore? Why dost thou make so long tarrying? Shall I despair of thy mercy, O God? far be that from me. I am thy workmanship created in Christ Jesus; give me grace therefore to tarry thy time, and patiently to bear thy works, assuredly knowing, that as thou canst, so thou wilt deliver me when it shall please thee, nothing doubting or mistrusting thy goodness towards me, for thou knowest better what is good for me than I do therefore do with me in all things what thou wilt, and plague me what way thou wilt. Only in the meantime arm me, I beseech thee, with thine armour, that I may stand fast, my loins being girded about with truth, having on the breastplate of righteousness, and shod with the shoes prepared by the gospel of peace, above all things, taking to me the shield of faith, wherewith I shall be able to quench all the fiery darts of the wicked, and taking the helmet of salvation, and the sword of the Spirit, which is thy most holy word; praying always with all manner of prayer and supplication, that I may refer myself wholly to thy will, abiding thy pleasure, and comforting myself in those troubles that it shall please thee to send me. Seeing such troubles be profitable for me, and seeing I am assuredly persuaded that it cannot be but well all that thou doest. Hear me, O merciful Father, for his sake, whom thou wouldst should be a sacrifice for my sins. To whom with thee, and the Holy Ghost, be all honour and glory. Amen."

It remains now to describe the manner of her execution, with her words and behaviour at the time of her death.

When she ascended the scaffold, she said to the people standing thereabout, "Good people, I am come hither to die, and by a law I am condemned to the same. The fact against the queen's highness was unlawful, and the consenting thereunto by me but touching the procurement and desire thereof by me or on my behalf, I do wash my hands thereof in innocency before God, and the face of you, good christian people, this day." And therewith she wrung her hands, wherein she had her book. Then said she, "I pray you all, good christian people, to bear me witness that I die a true christian woman, and that I do look to be saved by no other means but only by the mercy of God in the blood of his only Son Jesus Christ. And I confess, that when I did know the word of God, I neglected the same, loved myself and the world, and therefore this plague and punishment is happily and worthily happened unto me for my sins. And yet I thank God, that of his goodness he hath thus given me a time and respite to repent. And now, good people, while I am alive, I pray you to assist me with your prayers." And then kneeling down, she turned her to Fecknam, saying, "Shall I say this psalm?" And he said, "Yea." Then she repeated the psalm "Have mercy on me, O God," &c., in English, in the most devout manner throughout to the end, and then she stood up, and gave her maiden Mistress Ellen her gloves and handkerchief, and her book to Master Bruges, after which she untied her gown, and the hangman pressed upon her to help her off with it; but she desiring him to let her alone, turned towards her two gentlewomen, who helped her off therewith; and also with her frowes, paaft, and neckerchief, giving to her a fair handkerchief to fold about her eyes

Then the hangman kneeled down and asked her forgiveness, whom she forgave most willingly. Then he desired her to stand upon the straw; which doing, she saw the block. Then she said, "I pray you dispatch me quickly." Then she kneeled down, saying, "Will you take it off before I lay me down?" And the hangman said, "No, madam." Then she tied the handkerchief about her eyes, and feeling for the block, she said, "What shall I do? Where is it? Where is it?" One of the standers bye guiding her, she laid her head down upon the block, and then stretched forth her body, and said,

"Lord, into thy hands I commend my spirit," and so finished her life, in the year 1554, on the 12th day of February.

Thus was beheaded the lady Jane, and with her also the lord Guilford her husband, one of the duke of Northumberland's sons, two innocents in comparison with them that sat upon them For they ignorantly accepted that which the others had willingly devised, and by open proclamation consented to take from others, and give to them.

And not long after the death of the lady Jane, upon the 21st of the same month, was Henry Duke of Suffolk also beheaded at Tower Hill, on the fourth day after his condemnation About which time also were condemned for this conspiracy many gentlemen and yeomen, whereof some were executed at London, and some in the country In the number of whom was also the lord Thomas Gray, brother to the duke. Sir Nicholas Throgmorton very hardly escaped

The 24th of the same month (A.D. 1554) Bonner, bishop of London sent down a commission, directed to all the curates and pastors of his diocese, for taking of the names of such as would not come during the following Lent to auricular confession, and to the receiving at Easter. The copy of which monition here follows:—

A Monition of Bonner Bishop of London, sent down to all and singular Curates of his Diocese, for the certifying of the Names of such as would not come in Lent to Confession, and receiving at Easter.

"Edmund by the permission of God, bishop of London, to all parsons, vicars, curates, and ministers of the church within the city and diocese of London, sendeth grace, peace, and mercy, in our Lord everlasting. Forasmuch as by the order of the ecclesiastical laws and constitutions of this realm, and the laudable usage and custom of the whole catholic church by many hundred years ago, duly and devoutly observed and kept, all faithful people being of lawful age and discretion, are bound once in a year at least, except reasonable cause excuse them, to be confessed to their own proper curate, and to receive the sacrament of the altar, with due preparation and devotion And forasmuch also as we are credibly informed, that sundry evil-disposed and undevout persons, given to sensual passions, and carnal appetites, following the lusts of their body, and neglecting utterly the health of their souls, do forbear to come to confession according to the said usage, and to receive the sacrament of the altar accordingly, giving thereby pernicious and evil example to the younger sort, to neglect and contemn the same We minding the reformation hereof for our own discharge, and desirous of good order to be kept, and good example to be given, do will and command you by virtue hereof, that immediately upon the receipt of this our commandment, you and every one of you within your cure and charge, do use all your diligence and dexterity to declare the same, straightly charging and commanding all your parishioners, being of lawful age and discretion, to come before Easter next coming, to confession, according to the said ordinance and usage, with due preparation and devotion to receive the said sacrament of the altar, and that you do note the names of all such as are not confessed unto you, and do not receive of you the said sacrament, certifying us or our chancellor or commissary thereof before the sixth day of April next ensuing from the date hereof, that so we knowing thereby who did not come to confession, and receiving the sacrament accordingly, may proceed against them, as being persons culpable, and transgressors of the said ecclesiastical law and usage. Further also certifying us, our said chancellor or commissary, before the day aforesaid, whether you have your altars set up, chalice book, vestments, and all things necessary for mass, and the administration of sacraments and sacramentals, with procession, and all other divine service prepared and in readiness, according to the order of the catholic church, and the virtuous and godly example of the queen's majesty. And if you so have not, you then with the churchwardens cause the same to be provided for signifying by whose fault and negligence the same want or fault hath proceeded, and generally of the not coming of your parishioners to church, undue walking, talking, or using of themselves there irreverently in the time of divine service, and of all other open faults and misdemeanours, not omitting thus to do, and certify as before, as you will answer upon your peril for the contrary.

"Given at London, 23d of February, in the year 1554."

The month following, which was the month of March, and the fourth day of the said month, there was a letter sent from the queen to Bonner bishop of London, with certain articles annexed, to be put in speedy execution, requiring among other things that all the clergy who had married should be removed from their parishes, unless they abandoned their wives and did penance for their marriage, as may appear by these articles.

"Every bishop, and all other persons aforesaid, proceeding summarily, and with all celerity and despatch, may and shall deprive, or declare deprived, and remove, according to their learning and discretion, all such persons from their benefices and ecclesiastical promotions, who, contrary to the state of their order, and the laudable custom of the church, have married and used women as their wives, or otherwise notably and slanderously disordered or abused themselves : sequestering also, during the said process, the fruits and profits of the said benefices and ecclesiastical promotions.

"The said bishop, and all other persons aforesaid, shall use more lenity and clemency with such as have married, whose wives are dead, than with others whose wives do yet remain alive. And likewise such priests, as with the consent of their wives or women openly in the presence of the bishop do profess to abstain, to be used more favourably. In which case, after the penance effectually done, the bishop, according to his discretion and wisdom, may upon just consideration receive and admit them again to their former administration, so it be not in the same place, appointing them such a portion to live upon, to be paid out of their benefice whereof they are deprived, by discretion of the said bishop or his officer, as he shall think may be spared of the said benefice.

"Every bishop, and all other persons aforesaid, shall foresee that they suffer not any religious man, having solemnly professed celibacy, to continue with his woman or wife, but that all such persons after deprivation o. their benefice or ecclesiastical promotion, be also divorced every one from his said woman, and due punishment otherwise taken for the offence therein."

The queen also sent her rescript to the lord mayor of London to the same effect, who issued the following letter accordingly to the aldermen, &c. :—

"On the queen our most gracious and most benign sovereign lady's behalf, we most straightly charge and command you, that you the said aldermen, fail not personally to call before your own person in such place within your said ward, as to you shall seem most convenient and meet, upon Wednesday next coming, which shall be the 7th day of this present month, at seven o'clock in the morning of the same day, all and every the householders both poor and rich of your said ward, and then and there openly and plainly for your own discharge, and for the eschewing the perils that to you might otherwise be justly imputed and laid, do not only straightly admonish, charge, and command, in the queen our said sovereign lady's name and behalf, all and every the said householders, that both in their own persons, and also their wives, children, and servants, being of the age of twelve years and upwards, and every of them, do at all and every time and times from henceforth, and namely at the holy time of Easter, now approaching, honestly, quietly, obediently, and catholicly, use and behave themselves like good and faithful Christian people, in all and every thing and things touching and concerning the true faith, profession and religion of his catholic church, both according to the laws and precepts of Almighty God, and also their bounden duty of obedience towards our sovereign lady the queen, her laws,

and statutes, and her highness' most good example and gracious proceeding according to the same, and according to the right, wholesome, charitable, and godly admonition, charge, and exhortation, late set forth and given by the right reverend father in God, the bishop of London, our diocesan and ordinary, to all the parsons, vicars, and curates, within his diocese, but also that they and every of them do truly, without delay, advertise you of the names and surnames of all and every person and persons, that they or any of them, can or may at any time hereafter know, perceive, or understand to transgress or offend in any point or article concerning the premises at their utmost perils. That ye immediately after such notice thereof to you given, do forthwith advertise us thereof. Fail you not thus to do with all circumspection and diligence, as you will answer to our said most dread sovereign lady the queen for the contrary at your peril.

"Given at the Guildhall of the city of London, the fifth day of March in the first year of the reign of our said sovereign lady and queen.

"And likewise do you give to every of the said householders straightly in commandment, that they or their wives depart not out of the said city, until this holy time of Easter be past.

"Blackwell."

About the same time, when Doctor Bonner set forth this prescript, there came from the queen another proclamation against strangers and foreigners within this realm.

Upon this proclamation not only the strangers in king Edward's time received into the realm for religion, among whom was Peter Martyr and John Alasco, uncle to the king of Poland ; but many Englishmen fled, some to Friezland, some to Cleveland, some to Germany, where they were scattered into companies and congregations, at Wesel, at Frankfort, Embden, Markpurgh, Transborough, Basil, Arow, Zurich, Geneva, and other places : where, by the providence of God, they were all sustained, and there entertained with greater favour among strangers abroad than they could be in their own country at home, amounting nearly to the number of eight hundred persons, students, and others together.

In the month of March, the lord Courtney, earl of Devonshire, whom the queen had delivered out of the Tower, and the lady Elizabeth also the queen's sister, were both apprehended and committed to the Tower, on suspicion of having consented to Wyat's conspiracy a short time before.

Touching the imprisonment of the lady Elizabeth and lord Courtney, thou shalt note here for thy learning, good reader, a politic point of practice in Steven Gardiner, bishop of Winchester, not unworthy to be considered. This Gardiner being always an enemy to the lady Elizabeth, and thinking now by the occasion of Master Wyat's disturbance in Kent, to pick out some matter against the lord Courtney, and so in the end to entangle the lady Elizabeth, devised a pestilent practice of conveyance, as in the history here following may appear.

The story is this. The same day that Sir Thomas Wyat died, he desired the lieutenant to bring him to the presence of the lord Courtney. Who there before the lieutenant and the sheriffs kneeling down upon his knees, besought the lord Courtney to forgive him, for that he had falsely accused both the lady Elizabeth and him, and so being brought from thence to the scaffold to suffer there openly in the hearing of all the people, he cleared the lady Elizabeth and the lord Courtney, to be free and innocent from all suspicion of that commotion. At which confession Doctor Weston, standing by, cried to the people, saying, "Believe him not, good people, for he confessed otherwise before unto the council."

Not long after this, queen Mary, partly fearing the Londoners on account of Wyat's conspiracy, and partly perceiving that most of the city, for religion's sake, did not greatly favour her proceedings, summoned a parliament to be held at Oxford, as if to gratify that city, where the university, town, and country had shewed themselves very obedient, especially in restoring the popish religion. For this purpose great provision was made, both by the queen's officers, as well as by the townsmen and inhabitants of Oxford, and the country about.

But the queen's mind soon changed, and the parliament was held at Westminster in the April following. Then the queen proposed her marriage with king Philip, and the restoring the pope's supremacy. Her marriage was agreed upon; but the other request could not then be obtained.

When this parliament was summoned, she also summoned a convocation of the bishops, and of the clergy, writing to Bonner (whom she had made vicegerent instead of Cranmer, who was then in the Tower) after the tenor and form of a new stile, differing from the old stile of king Henry and king Edward, in the omission of the title of "Supreme Head" of the church of England and Ireland.

In this convocation, Bonner, bishop of London, being vicegerent and president, made an oration to the clergy, in which he seems to shew a piece of profound and deep learning, in setting forth the most incomparable and super-angelical order of priesthood, as may appear by this parcel or fragment of his oration.

"Wherefore it is to be known," said Bonner, "that priests and elders are worthy to be worshipped by all men, for the dignity which they have from God; as in Matthew xvi. 'Whatsoever ye shall loose upon earth,' &c; and 'whatsoever ye shall bind,' &c. For a priest by some means is like the Virgin Mary, and this is shewed by three points. As the blessed Virgin by five words did conceive Christ, as it is said, *fiat mihi secundum verbum tuum*, that is, 'Be it unto me according to thy word,' (Luke i) so the priest by five words doth make the very body of Christ. Even as immediately after the consent of Mary, Christ was all whole in her womb; so immediately after the speaking of the words of consecration, the bread is transubstantiated into the very body of Christ. Secondly, as the Virgin carried Christ in her arms, and laid him in an ox-stall after his birth; even so the priest after the consecration lifts up the body of Christ, and places it, and carries it, and handles it with his hands. Thirdly, as the blessed Virgin was sanctified before she had conceived, so the priest, being ordained and anointed before he doth consecrate, because without orders he could consecrate nothing: therefore the layman cannot do that thing, although he be ever so holy, and do speak the self-same words of consecration. Therefore here may be seen, that the dignity of priests by some means passes the dignity of angels, because there is no power given to any of the angels to make the body of Christ. Whereby the least priest on earth may do, that which the greatest and highest angel in heaven cannot do, as St. Bernard saith, 'O worshipful dignity of priests, in whose hands the Son of God is, as in the womb of the Virgin he was incarnate.' St. Augustine saith, that angels in the consecration of the sacred host do serve him, and the Lord of heaven descendeth to him. Whereupon St. Ambrose upon Luke saith, 'Doubt thou not the angels to be where Christ is present upon the altar.' Wherefore priests are to be honoured before all kings of the earth, princes, and nobles. For a priest is higher than a king, happier than an angel, maker of his Creator," &c.

On the 10th of March a letter was sent to the lieutenant of the Tower to deliver the bodies of Cranmer, archbishop of Canterbury, and bishops Ridley and Latimer, to Sir John Williams, to be conveyed by him to Oxford.

On the 26th of March, there was a letter directed to Sir Henry Doell, and one Foster, to attach the bodies of Taylor, parson of Hadley, and of Henry Askew, and to send them up to the council.

About the 10th of April, Cranmer, archbishop of Canterbury; Ridley, bishop of London; and Hugh Latimer, sometime bishop of Worcester, were conveyed as prisoners from the Tower to Windsor; and thence to the University of Oxford, to dispute with the divines and learned men of both the Universities of Oxford and Cambridge, about the presence, substance, and sacrifice of the sacrament. The names of the doctors and graduates appointed to dispute against them, were these: of Oxford, Weston, prolocutor, Tresham, Cole, Oglethorpe, Pye, Harpsfield, and Fecknam; of Cambridge, Young, vice-chancellor, Glin, Seaton, Watson, Sedgewick, Atkinson, &c. The articles or questions upon which they should dispute were these:

1. Whether the natural body of Christ was really in the sacrament, after the words spoken by the priest, or not?

2. Whether in the sacrament, after the words of consecration, any other substance did remain than the substance of the body and blood of Christ?

3. Whether in the mass there was a propitiatory sacrifice for the sins of the living and the dead?

After those from Cambridge were incorporated into the University of Oxford, on the 12th, and after a convocation on the 14th, and a solemn mass, they signed the articles.

The mass being done, they went in procession: First, the choir in their surplices followed the cross; then the first-year regents and proctors; then the doctors of law, and their beadles before them; then the doctors of divinity of both universities intermingled, the divinity and arts-beadles going before them; the vice-chancellor and prolocutor going together. After them the bachelors of divinity, *regentes et non regentes*, in their array; and last of all, the bachelors of law and art. After whom followed a great company of scholars and students who had not graduated. And thus they proceeded through the street to Christ's church, and there the choir sung a psalm, and after that a collect was read. This done, the commissioners, doctors, and many others, departed to Lincoln college, where they dined with the mayor of the town, one alderman, four beadles, Master Say and the Cambridge notary. After dinner they went all again to St. Mary's church, and there, after a short consultation in a chapel, all the commissioners came into the choir, and sat all on seats before the altar, to the number of thirty-three persons: and they sent to the mayor, that he should bring in Cranmer, who was brought to them by a number of bill-men.

Thus the reverend archbishop, when he was brought before the commissioners, reverenced them with much humility, and stood with his staff in his hand, a stool was offered him, but he refused to sit. Then the prolocutor, sitting in the midst in a scarlet gown, began with a short oration in praise of unity, and especially in the church of Christ; he spoke of the bringing up of Cranmer and of his taking degrees in Cambridge, and also how he was promoted by king Henry VIII., and had been his counsellor and a catholic man, one of the same unity, and a member thereof in times past, but of late years had separated and cut himself off from it, by teaching and setting forth of erroneous doctrines, making every year a new faith: and therefore it pleased the queen's grace, to send them of the convocation and other learned men, to bring him to this unity again, if it might be. Then the prolocutor informed him how they of the convocation house had agreed upon certain articles to which they wished him to subscribe.

The archbishop answered to the preface very ably, modestly, and learnedly, shewing that he was very glad of an unity, forasmuch as it was "the preserver of all commonwealths, as well of the heathen as of the christians," and so he dilated the matter with one or two stories of the Roman commonwealth. Which when he had done, he said, that he was very glad to come to an unity, provided it were in Christ, and agreeable to his holy word.

When he had thus spoken, the prolocutor caused the articles to be read to him, and asked him, if he would subscribe to them. Then the archbishop of Canterbury after having read them over three or four times, and touching the first article, he asked what they meant by the term, "natural body." "Do you not mean," saith he, "a sensible body?" Some answered, "The same that was born of the Virgin," but very confusedly; some saying one thing, some another. Then the archbishop denied it utterly, and when he had looked upon the other two, he said they were false, and against God's holy word and therefore he could not agree in a unity with them. The prolocutor assigned him to answer the articles on Monday next (April 16th), and so committed him to the mayor again, permitting him to name what books he wished for, and he should have them brought to him. The archbishop was greatly commended by every body for his modesty so that some masters of art of the university were seen to weep for him, though in judgment they were contrary to him.

Then Dr. Ridley was brought in, who, hearing the articles read, answered without any delay, saying, "They were all false; and that they sprang out of a bitter and sour root." His answers were sharp, witty, and very earnest. Then they laid to his charge a sermon that he made when he was bishop of Rochester, in which, they said, he spoke in favour of transubstantiation He denied it utterly, and asked whether they could bring any that heard him, who would say and affirm it; but they could bring no proof of it all

Then he was asked, whether he would dispute or not. He answered, that as long as God gave him life, he should not only have his heart, but also his mouth and pen to defend his truth; but he required time and books. They said he should dispute on Tuesday, and till that time he should have books. He said it was not reasonable that he should not have his own books, and time also to look for his disputations. Then they gave him the articles, and bade him write his mind about them that night.

Last of all came in Latimer, with a handkerchief, and two or three caps on his head, his spectacles hanging by a string at his breast, and a staff in his hand, he was set in a chair. And, after his denial of the articles, Wednesday was appointed for his disputation, but he alleged age, sickness, disease, and lack of books, saying, That he was almost as fit to be a captain of Calais as to dispute, but he would, he said, declare his mind either by writing or by word of mouth, and would stand to all they could lay upon his back; complaining, that he was permitted to have neither pen nor ink, nor books, except the New Testament there in his hand, which he said he had read over seven times deliberately; and yet could not find the mass in it; neither the marrow-bones nor sinews of the same. At which words the commissioners were not a little offended; and Dr Weston said, that he would make him grant that the mass had both marrow-bones and sinews in the New Testament. Master Latimer said, "That you will never do, Master Doctor," and so forthwith they put him to silence; so that when he was desirous to tell what he meant by those terms, he could not be suffered.

On Monday, the 16th of April, 1554, Doctor Weston, with the visitors, censors, and opponents, repairing to the divinity school, enstalled themselves in their places. Doctor Cranmer was brought there, and set in the answerer's place, with the mayor and aldermen sitting by him. Doctor Weston, prolocutor, after the custom of the university, began the disputation with an oration. His words, as he spake them, were these · "Ye are assembled here, brethren, this day, to confound the detestable heresy of the truth of the body of Christ in the sacraments," &c. At which words thus pronounced by the prolocutor unawares, many of the learned men there present burst out into laughter, as, even in the entrance of the disputations, he had betrayed himself, and his religion, in calling the opinion of the truth of Christ's body in the sacrament a detestable heresy The rest of his oration tended all to this effect, that it was not lawful by God's word to call these questions into controversy. Doctor Cranmer answered in this wise: "We are assembled to discuss these doubtful controversies, and to lay them open before the eyes of the world, of what ye think it unlawful to dispute. It is, indeed, not reasonable, that we should dispute about that which is determined before the truth be tried And if these questions are not called into controversy, surely my answer is looked for in vain "

Then Chedsey, the first opponent, began in this wise to dispute

"Reverend Master doctor, these three conclusions are put forth to us at present to dispute upon

"1 In the sacrament of the altar is the natural body of Christ, conceived of the Virgin Mary, and also his blood present really under the forms of bread and wine, by virtue of God's word pronounced by the priest

"2. There remaineth no substance of bread and wine after the consecration, nor any other substance, but the substance of God and man

"3. The lively sacrifice of the church is in the mass propitiatory, as well for the living as the dead

"These are the conclusions propounded, upon which our controversy rests Now that we might not doubt how you take them, you have already given to us your opinion. I term it your opinion, because it disagrees from the catholic opinion. I argue that as your opinion differs from the scripture, therefore you are deceived."

Cranmer —"I deny that my opinion differs from scripture."

Chedsey.—"Christ, when he instituted his last supper, spake to his disciples, saying, 'Take, eat, this is my body which is broken for you.' This is his true body "

Cranmer —"His true body is truly present to them that truly receive him , but *spiritually*. And so it is taken after a *spiritual* sort. For when he said, 'This is my body, it is all one as if he had said, 'This is the breaking of my body, this is the shedding of my blood. As often as you shall do this, it shall put you in remembrance of the breaking of my body, and the shedding of my blood, that as truly as you receive this sacrament, so truly shall you receive the benefit promised by receiving the same worthily.'

Chedsey —"Your opinion differs from the church, which saith, that the true body is in the sacrament, and therefore your opinion is false "

Cranmer — 'I say and agree with the church, that the body of Christ is in the sacrament effectually, because the passion of Christ is effectual."

Chedsey "Christ, when he spake these words, 'This is my body,' spake of the substance, but not of the effect "

Cranmer.—"I grant he spake of the substance, and not of the effect after a sort and yet it is most true that the body of Christ is effectually in the sacrament But I deny that he is there truly present in bread, or that his organical body is under the bread. It is still that bread which is taken out of the fruit of the ground and by man's hand brought to that visible shape, being round in form and without sense or life, nourishing the body, and strengthening the heart of man , of this bread, and not of any uncertain and wandering substance, as you say, the old fathers say that Christ spake these words, 'Eat, this is my body' And likewise also of the wine, which is the fruit of the vine pressed out of grapes, and makes man's heart merry, of the very same wine, I say, Christ spake, 'Drink, this is my blood.' And so the old doctors call this speaking of Christ tropical, figurative, anagogical, allegorical, which they interpret thus : that although the substance of bread and wine remain, and are received by the faithful, yet notwithstanding Christ changed the name of it, and called the bread by the name of his flesh, and the wine by the name of his blood. 'Not that it is so in very deed, but signified in a mystery.' So that we should consider, not what they are in their own nature, but what they import to us and signify, and we should understand the sacrament not carnally, but spiritually, and should attend not to the visible nature of the sacraments, neither have respect only to the outward bread and cup. But that, lifting up our minds, we should look up to the blood of Christ with our faith, should touch him with our mind, and receive him with our inward man, and that being like eagles in this life, we should fly up into heaven in our hearts, where that Lamb is resident at the right hand of his Father, 'which taketh away the sin of the world,' 'by whose stripes we are healed,' by whose passion we are filled at his table, and whose blood we receiving out of his holy side, do live for ever, being made the guests of Christ, having him dwelling in us through the grace of his true nature, and through the virtue and efficacy of his whole passion, being no less assured and certified, that we are fed spiritually unto eternal life by Christ's flesh crucified, and by his blood shed, the true food of our minds, than that our bodies are fed with meat and drink in this life and of this the mystical bread on the table of Christ, and the mystical wine, being administered and received after the institution of Christ, are to us a memorial, a pledge, a token, a sacrament, and a seal

"And as for your third article, which declares the mass to be a propitiatory sacrifice or oblation, I do not hold it to be an oblation of Christ. He offered himself to God the Father once to death upon the altar of the cross for our redemption, which was of such efficacy, that there is no more need of any sacrifice for the redemption of the whole world, for all the sacrifices of the old law he took away, performing in himself that in very deed, which they signified and promised. Whoever, therefore, shall fix the hope of his salvation in any other sacrifice, he falls from the grace of Christ, and is contumelious against the blood of Christ. For 'He was wounded for our transgressions, he was bruised for our iniquities the chastisement of our peace was upon him; and with his stripes we are healed' 'Neither by the blood of goats and calves, but by his own blood, he entered in once into the holy place, having obtained eternal redemption for us' 'For Christ is not entered into the holy places made with hands, which are the figures of the true, but into heaven itself, now to appear in the presence of God for us Nor yet that he should offer himself often, as the high priest entereth into the holy place every year with blood of others, For then must he often have suffered since the foundation of the world, but now once, in the end of the world, hath he appeared, to put away sin by the sacrifice of himself And as it is appointed unto men once to die, but after this the judgment, so Christ was once offered to bear the sins of many; and unto them that look for him shall he appear the second time, without sin, unto salvation' 'Who, after he had offered one sacrifice for sins, for ever sat down on the right hand of God. For by one offering he hath perfected for ever them that are sanctified. Now, where remission of these is, there is no more offering for sin.' But this only sacrifice of Christ, whoever shall seek any other propitiatory sacrifice for sin, makes the sacrifice of Christ of no validity, force, or efficacy. For if it be sufficient to remit sins, what need is there of any other? For the necessity of another argues and declares this to be insufficient. Almighty God grant that we may truly trust in one sacrifice of Christ, and that we to him again may repay our sacrifices of thanksgiving, of praise, of confessing his name, of true amendment, of repentance, of mercifulness towards our neighbours, and of all other good works of charity For by such sacrifices we shall declare ourselves neither ungrateful to God, nor altogether unworthy of this holy sacrifice of Christ And thus you have the true and sincere use of the Lord's holy supper, and the fruit of the true sacrifice of Christ Which, however, through captious or wrested interpretations, or by men's traditions, shall go about, otherwise than Christ ordained them to alter or transubstantiate, he shall answer to Christ in the latter day, when he shall understand (but then too late) that he has no participation with the body and blood of Christ, but that out of the supper of eternal life he has eaten and drank eternal condemnation to himself"

Chedsey —"The Scriptures in many places affirm, that Christ gave his natural body, Matthew xxvi , Mark xiv , Luke xxii "

Cranmer.—"If you understand by the natural body, one that has such proportion and members as he had when living here, then I answer in the negative "

Chedsey. "The scripture makes against you, for the circumstance teaches us not only that there is the body, but also teaches us what manner of body it is, and saith,

'The body shall be given which was not bread, but that which was crucified "

Cranmer —"I grant he said it was his body, which should be given. 'The body,' saith he, 'that shall be given for you' As if he said, 'This bread is the breaking of my body and this cup is the shedding of my blood.' What will ye say then ? is the bread *the breaking of his body*, and the cup *the shedding of his blood* really '"

After some further disputation Chedsey withdrew, and Oglethorpe began in his stead to question Cranmer

Oglethorpe. — " Your judgment differs from all churches."

Cranmer.—" Nay, I disagree with the papistical church."

Oglethorpe —" This you do through ignorance of logic."

Cranmer.—" Nay, this you say through the ignorance of the doctors."

Weston —" I will go plainly to work by the scriptures. What took he?"

Cranmer.—" Bread."

Weston.—" What gave he '"

Cranmer.—" Bread."

Weston " What brake he '"

Cranmer.—" Bread."

Weston,—" What did he eat ?"

Cranmer. " Bread."

Weston.—" He gave bread, therefore he gave not his body."

Cranmer.—" I deny the argument."

Cole. " This argument holds good It is bread, therefore it is not the body."

Cranmer.—" The like argument may be made. He is a Rock, therefore he is not Christ."

There was much further disputation on this question, chiefly confined to the ascertaining the opinions of the primitive church, which would be too long to insert here.

This disorderly disputation, sometimes in Latin, sometimes in English, continued almost till two o'clock When it was finished, and the arguments written and delivered to Master Say, the prisoner was taken away by the mayor, and the doctors dined together at the university college.

Disputation at Oxford between Doctor Smith, with his other Colleagues and Doctors, and Bishop Ridley.

The following day (April 17) Doctor Ridley was brought forth to dispute, with Doctor Smith for his principal opponent.

Besides this Smith, there was Weston, Tresham, Oglethorpe, Glin, Seaton, Cole, Ward, Harpsfield, Watson, Pye, Harding, Curton, and Fecknam . to all these opponents Ridley answered very learnedly. He made a preface to the questions, but they would not let him go on with it, saying it was blasphemy; and they would not suffer him to speak his mind. Smith could get nothing at his hands, so that others took his arguments and prosecuted them He shewed himself to be learned, and a great divine They could bring nothing, but what he knew as well as they

Weston, prolocutor.—" Good christian people and brethren, we have begun this day our school, by God's good speed I trust, and are entering into a controversy, whereof no question ought to be moved concerning the truth of the body of our Lord Jesus Christ in the eucharist. Christ is true, who said the words. The words are true which he spake, yea, truth itself that cannot fail. Let us therefore pray unto God to send down unto us his Holy Spirit, which is the true interpreter of his word, which may purge away errors, and give light, that truth may appear."

Smith—"This day three questions are propounded, whereof no controversy among christians ought to be moved, to wit

"1 Whether the natural body of Christ our Saviour, which was conceived of the Virgin, and offered for man's redemption upon the cross, is verily and really in the sacrament by virtue of God's word spoken by the priests, &c.

"2. Whether, in the sacrament, after the words of consecration, there is any other substance, &c.

"3. Whether there is in the mass a sacrifice propitiatory, &c.

"Touching which questions, although you have publicly and partly professed your judgment. Yet being not satisfied with your answer, I will demand your opinion on the first question, whether the true body of Christ, after the words pronounced, be really in the eucharist, or only the figure."

The Answer of Ridley.

"In matters appertaining to God we may not speak according to the sense of man, nor of the world. This first proposition is framed after another manner of phrase or kind of speech than the scripture uses; and it is very obscure and dark, by means of words of doubtful signification.

"First, there is a double sense in these words: 'by virtue of God's word;' for it is doubtful what word of God this is.

"Again, there is a doubtfulness in these words: 'of the priest;' whether any man may be called a priest but he who has authority to make a propitiatory sacrifice for the living and the dead."

Weston.—"Let this be sufficient."

Ridley.—"If we lack time at present, there is time enough hereafter."

Weston.—"These are but evasions; you consume the time in vain."

Ridley.—"I cannot start far from you, I am captive and bound."

Weston.—"Fall to it, my masters."

Smith.—"That which you have spoken may suffice at present."

Ridley.—"Let me alone, I pray you, for I have not much to say."

Weston.—"Go forward."

Ridley.—"Moreover, there is ambiguity in this word 'really,' which may be variously interpreted, so that the whole proposition is formed of phrases that are not scriptural, but are of doubtful signification.

"Now the error and falseness of the proposition, in the sense in which the Romish church takes it, may appear, in that they affirm the bread to be transubstantiated and changed into the flesh assumed by the word of God, and that too by virtue of a phrase which they have themselves devised, and which cannot be found in any of the scriptures. Which position is the foundation of transubstantiation, a foundation monstrous, and against reason, and destroying the analogy of the sacraments and therefore this proposition also, which is built upon this rotten foundation, is false, erroneous, and a detestable heresy."

Weston.—"We lose time."

Ridley.—"You shall have time enough."

Weston.—"Fall to reasoning. You shall have some other day for this matter."

Ridley.—"I have no more to say concerning my explication. If you will give me leave and let me alone, I will only speak a word or two in confirmation of this."

Weston.—"Go to; say on."

Ridley.—"No doctrine ought to be established in the church of God, which dissents from the word of God, from the rule of faith, and draws with it many absurdities that cannot be avoided.

"Yet the doctrine of transubstantiation maintains a real, corporeal, and carnal presence of Christ's flesh, assumed and taken by the word, to be in the sacrament of the Lord's supper, and that not by virtue and grace only, but also by the whole essence and substance of the body and flesh of Christ. Now such a presence disagrees with God's word, from the rule of faith, and cannot but draw with it many absurdities."

Weston.—"You consume time, which might better bestowed on other matters. Master opponent, I pray you, to your argument."

Smith.—"I will here reason with you upon transubstantiation, which you say is contrary to the rule and analogy of faith. I prove the contrary by the scrip-

tures and the doctors. But before I enter into argument with you, I demand first, whether in the sixth chapter of St. John there is any mention made of the sacrament, or of the real presence of Christ in the sacrament?"

Ridley.—"It is against reason that I should be prevented prosecuting that which I have to speak in this assembly, being not so long but that it may be comprehended in a few words."

Weston.—"Let him go on."

Ridley.—"This carnal presence is *contrary to the word of God*, as, appears in John xvi. 7, 'I tell you the truth. It is expedient for you that I go away, for if I go not away, the Comforter will not come unto you.' Acts iii. 21. 'Whom the heaven must receive until the times of restitution of all things which God hath spoken by the mouth of all his holy prophets.' Mat. ix. 15. 'Can the children of the bridegroom mourn as long as the bridegroom is with them? but the days will come, when the bridegroom shall be taken away from them, and then shall they fast.' John xvi. 22. 'But I will see you again, and your heart shall rejoice.' Mat. xiv. 23. 28. 'If any man shall say unto you, Lo, here is Christ, or there; believe them not. For wheresoever the carcase is, there will the eagles be gathered together.'

"*It differs from the articles of faith:* 'He ascended into heaven, and sitteth on the right hand of God the Father, from whence he shall come to judge both the quick and the dead.'

"*It destroys the institution of the Lord's supper,* which was commanded only to be used and continued until the Lord himself should come. If therefore he be really present in the body of his flesh, then must the supper cease for a remembrance is not of a thing present, but of a thing absent. And there is a difference between remembrance and presence, and (as one of the fathers saith) a figure is in vain where the thing figured is present.

"*It makes precious things common to profane and ungodly persons, and constrains men to confess many absurdities.* For it affirms, that wicked and ungodly persons, yea, (and as some of them hold, the wicked and faithless mice, rats, and dogs, also may receive the very real and corporeal body of the Lord, wherein the fulness of the Spirit of light and grace dwells; contrary to the manifest words of Christ in six places and sentences of the sixth chapter of St. John.

"*It confirms also and maintains that beastly kind of cruelty of the Anthropophagi,* that is, the devourers of man's flesh. For it is a more cruel thing to devour a living man, than to slay him."

Pye.—"He requires time to speak blasphemies! Leave your blasphemies!"

Ridley.—"I had little thought to have had such reproachful words at your hands."

Weston.—"All is quiet. Go to your arguments."

Ridley.—"I have not many more words to say."

Weston.—"You utter blasphemies with a most impudent face: leave off, and get you to the argument."

Ridley.—"*It forces men to maintain many monstrous miracles, without any necessity and authority of God's word.* For at the coming of this presence of the body and flesh of Christ, they thrust away the substance of bread, and affirm that the accidents remain without any subject, and instead of it, they place Christ's body without his qualities and the true manner of a body. And if the sacrament be reserved so long until it mould, and worms breed in it, some say that the substance of bread miraculously returns again, and some deny it. Others affirm that the real body of Christ goes down into the stomach of the receivers, and there abides so long only as they shall continue to be good, but others hold, that the body of Christ is carried into heaven, so soon as the forms of bread are bruised with the teeth! O workers of miracles! Truly, and most truly I see that fulfilled in these men, whereof St. Paul prophesied: 2 Thes. ii. 10—12. 'Because they received not the truth, that they might be saved,' 'God shall send them strong delusion, that they should believe a lie, that they all might be damned who believed not the truth, but had pleasure in unrighteousness.' This gross presence has brought forth that foolish fantasy of concomitance, by which is broken at this day and abrogated the commandment of the Lord for distributing of the Lord's cup to the laity.

"*It gives occasion to heretics to maintain and defend their errors*; as to Marcion, who said that Christ had but a fantastical body; and to Eutyches, who wickedly confounded the two natures in Christ.

"Finally, *It falsifies the sayings of the godly fathers and the catholic faith of the church*, which Vigilius, a martyr, and grave writer saith, was taught of the apostles, confirmed with the blood of martyrs, and was continually maintained by the faithful until his time   By the saying of the fathers, I mean of Justin, Irenæus, Tertullian, Origen, Eusebius, Emisene, Athanasius, Cyril, Epiphanius, Jerome, Chrysostom, Augustine, Vigilius, Fulgentius, Bertram, and other most ancient fathers. All those places, as I am sure, I have read making for my purpose, so I am well assured that I could shew the same, if I might have the use of my own books, which I will undertake to do, even upon the peril of my life, and loss of all that I may lose in this world.

"But now, my brethren, think not, because I disallow that presence which the first proposition maintains, as a presence which I take to be forged, fantastical, and contrary to God's word, perniciously brought into the church by the Romanists, that I therefore go about to take away the true presence of Christ's body in his supper rightly and duly administered, which is grounded upon the word of God, and made more plain by the commentaries of the faithful fathers. They who think thus of me, the Lord knoweth how far they are deceived. And to make the same evident, I will in a few words declare what true presence of Christ's body in the sacrament of the Lord's supper I hold and affirm.

"I say and confess with the evangelist Luke, and with the apostle Paul, that the bread on which thanks are given, is the body of Christ in remembrance of him and his death, to be set forth perpetually by the faithful until his coming again.

"I say and confess that the bread which we break is the communion and partaking of Christ's body.

"I say and believe that there is not only a signification of Christ's body set forth in the sacrament, but also that there is given to the godly and faithful the grace of Christ's body, that is, the food of life and immortality.

"I say also, with St. Augustine, that we eat life and we drink life · with Emisene, that we feel the Lord to be present in grace;—with Athanasius, that we receive celestial food, which comes from above;—the propriety of natural communion, with Hilary;—the nature of flesh and benediction which gives life in bread and wine, with Cyril,—and with the same Cyril, the virtue of the very flesh of Christ, life and grace of his body, the property of the only begotten, that is to say, life, as he himself in plain words expounds it.

"I confess also with Basil, that we receive the mystical advent and coming of Christ, grace and virtue of his very nature—the sacrament of his very flesh, with Ambrose—the body by grace, with Epiphanius—spiritual flesh, but not that which was crucified, with Jerome—grace flowing into a sacrifice, and the grace of the spirit, with Chrysostom—grace and invisible verity, grace and communion of the members of Christ's body, with Augustine.

"Finally, with Bertram, who was the last of all these, I confess that Christ's body is in the sacrament in this respect; namely, as he writes, because there is in it the spirit of Christ, that is, the power of the word of God, which not only feeds the soul, but also cleanses it. But of these I suppose it may clearly appear to all men, how far we are from that opinion, of which some go about falsely to slander us, saying, we teach that the godly and faithful receive nothing else at the Lord's table, but a figure of the body of Christ.

"As to the second proposition, which asserts that 'After the consecration there remaineth no substance of bread and wine, neither any other substance, than the substance of God and man,' I answer, that it is mani-

festly false, directly against the word of God, the nature of the sacrament, and the most evident testimonies of the godly fathers; and it is the rotten foundation of the other two conclusions propounded by you both of the first, and also of the third   I will not therefore now tarry upon any further explanation, being contented with that which is already given to the answer of the first proposition

"The circumstances of the scripture, the analogy and proportion of the sacraments, and the testimony of the faithful fathers ought to rule us in taking the meaning of the holy scriptures touching the sacrament. Now the words of the Lord's supper, the circumstances of the scripture, the analogy of the sacraments, and the sayings of the fathers, do most effectually and plainly prove a figurative speech in the words of the Lord's supper.

"*The circumstances of the scriptures*, ' Do this in remembrance of me.' ' As often as ye eat this bread and drink this cup, ye do shew the Lord's death till he come.' ' Let a man examine himself, and so let him eat of that bread, and drink of that cup.' ' They came together to break bread,' and they 'continued in breaking of bread.' ' The bread which we break,' &c. ' For we being many, are one bread and one body,' &c. 1 Cor. x. 14—17.

"*The analogy of the sacraments* is necessary · for the sacraments must have some similitude or likeness of the things whereof they be sacraments.

"*The sayings of the fathers* declare it to be a figurative speech, as it appears in Origen, Tertullian, Chrysostom, Augustine, Ambrose, Basil, Gregory Nazianzen, Hilary, and most plainly of all in Bertram. The sayings and places of all the fathers, whose names I have before recited against the assertion of the first proposition, quite overthrow transubstantiation. But of all most evidently and plainly, Irenæus, Origen, Cyprian, Chrysostom to Cesarius the monk, Augustine against Adamantus, Gelasius, Cyril, Epiphanius, Chrysostom; again on Matthew xx., Rabanus, Damascene and Bertram.

"I have for the proof of what I have spoken whatever was written by Bertram, a learned man, of sound and upright judgment, and ever counted a catholic for these seven hundred years until this our age. Whosoever shall read and weigh his treatise, considering the time of the writer, his learning, godliness of life, the allegations of the ancient fathers, and his manifold and well-grounded arguments, I cannot but marvel, if he have any fear of God at all, how he can with good conscience speak against him in this matter of the sacrament. This Bertram was the first person that arrested my attention, and that first brought me from the common error of the Romish church, and caused me to search more diligently and exactly both the scriptures and the writings of the old ecclesiastical fathers in this matter. And this I protest before the face of God, who knows I lie not in the things I now speak.

"As to the third proposition, which is, that ' In the mass is the lively sacrifice of the church, propitiatory and available for the sins as well of the quick as of the dead.'

"I answer this third proposition as I did the first. And moreover I say, that being taken in such sense as the words seem to import, it is not only erroneous, but so much to the derogation and null fying of the death and passion of Christ, that I judge it may and ought most worthily to be counted wicked and blasphemous against the most precious blood of our Saviour Christ.

"Concerning the Romish mass which is used at this day, or the lively sacrifice, propitiatory and available for the sins of the living and the dead, the holy scripture hath not so much as one syllable.

"As to these words, ' The lively sacrifice of the church,' there is a doubt whether they are to be understood figuratively and sacramentally.

"Moreover, in these words ' as well as,' it may be doubted whether they be spoken in mockery, as men are wont to say in sport, of a foolish or ignorant person, that he is apt as well in conditions as in knowledge , being apt indeed in neither of them.

"There is also a doubt in the word ' propitiatory.' whether it signifies here that which takes away sin, or that which may be made available for the taking away of sin; that is to say, whether it is to be taken in the active or in the passive signification

"Now the falseness of the proposition, after the meaning of the Romish Church, and the impiety in that sense which the words seem to import, is this, that they, leaning to the foundation of their fond transubstantiation, would make the quick and lively body of Christ's flesh, united and knit to the Divinity, to lie hid under the accidents and outward shews of bread and wine, which is very false, as I have said before; and they, building upon this foundation, hold that the same body is offered unto God by the priest in his daily masses to put away the sins of the living and the dead, whereas by the words of the apostle to the Hebrews it is evident that there is but one oblation, and one true and lively sacrifice of the church offered upon the altar of the cross, which was, is, and shall be for ever the propitiation for the sins of the whole world; and where there is remission of the same, 'there is', saith the apostle, 'no more offering for sin.'

"No other priest but Christ can sacrifice for sin, and that no man is called to this degree of honour but Christ alone, is evident. For there are only but two orders of priesthood allowed in the word of God: namely, the order of Aaron, and the order of Melchisedec. But now the order of Aaron is come to an end, and of the order of Melchisedec there is but one priest alone, even Christ the Lord, who has a priesthood that cannot pass to any other.

"Again, after eternal redemption is obtained, there is need of no more daily offering for it. And Christ having obtained for us this eternal redemption by the offering of himself, there is needed no more daily oblation for the living and the dead.

"Again, all remission of sins comes only by shedding of blood; but in the mass, which they call an unbloody sacrifice, there is no shedding of blood; and therefore in the mass there is no remission of sins, and consequently there is no propitiatory sacrifice.

"Again, where Christ does not suffer, he is not truly offered, for the apostle saith, 'Not that he might offer up himself often for then must he often have suffered since beginning of the world),' now where Christ is not offered, there is no propitiatory sacrifice; and therefore, in the mass there is no propitiatory sacrifice, 'But now once, in the end of the world, hath he appeared, to put away sin by the sacrifice of himself And as it is appointed unto men once to die, but after this the judgment; so Christ was once offered to bear the sins of many; and unto them that look for him shall he appear the second time, without sin, unto salvation'

"'By the which will,' saith the apostle, 'we are sanctified, through the offering of the body of Jesus Christ once for all.' And in the same place, 'But this man, after he had offered one sacrifice for sins, for ever sat down on the right hand of God For by one offering he hath perfected for ever them that are sanctified, and 'when he had by himself purged our sins, sat down on the right hand of the Majesty on high' I beseech you to mark these words 'by himself,' which, if well weighed, will without doubt put an end to all controversy

"'He hath reconciled us in the body of his flesh.' Mark, I beseech you, he saith not, in the mystery of his body; but in the body of his flesh.

"'If any man sin, we have an advocate with the Father, Jesus Christ the righteous, and he is the propitiation of our sins, and not for ours only, but for the sins of the whole world.'

"I know that all these places of the scriptures are avoided by two manner of subtle shifts the one is by the distinction of the bloody and unbloody sacrifice; as if our unbloody sacrifice of the church were anything else than the sacrifice of praise and thanksgiving; a commemoration, shewing forth, and a sacramental representation of that one only bloody sacrifice, offered up once for all The other is by depraving and wresting the sayings of the ancient fathers to such a strange kind of sense, as the fathers themselves never meant. For the meaning of the fathers was evidently that the redemption once made for the salvation of man, continues

in full effect for ever, and works without ceasing to the end of the world, that the sacrifice once offered cannot be consumed, that the Lord's death and passion is as effectual, the virtue of that blood once shed, as fresh at this day for the washing away of sins, as it was even the same day that it flowed out of the blessed side of our Saviour and finally, that the whole substance of our sacrifice, which is frequented of the church in the Lord's supper, consists in prayers, praise, and giving of thanks, and in remembering and shewing forth of that sacrifice once offered upon the altar of the cross.

"These are the things which I could answer to your three propositions, though I am destitute of all help in this shortness of time, and want of books. And because ye have lately given most unjust and cruel sentence against me, I do here appeal to a more just judgment of some other competent and lawful judge, according to the approved state of the church of England. If this appeal may not be granted to me upon earth, then do I fly (even as to my only refuge and alone haven of health) to the sentence of the Eternal Judge, that is, of the Almighty God, to whose most merciful justice towards us, and most just mercifulness, I do wholly commit myself and all my cause, not at all despairing of the defence of mine advocate and alone Saviour Jesus Christ, to whom, with the everlasting Father, and the Holy Spirit, the Sanctifier of us all, be now and for ever all honour and glory, Amen."

Smith—"You have occasioned me to go otherwise to work with you than I had thought to have done. You abuse the testimonies of scripture concerning the ascension of Christ, in order to take away his presence in the sacrament, as if this were a strong argument to enforce your matter."

Ridley.—"If you take the real presence of Christ according to the real and corporeal substance which he took of the Virgin, that presence being in heaven, cannot be on the earth also But if you mean a real presence of some property or attribute of his body, the ascension and abiding in heaven are no hindrance to that presence."

Weston.—"I will cut off all equivocation and doubt. For whenever we speak of Christ's body, we mean that which he took of the Virgin."

Ridley.—"Christ's ascension and abiding in heaven cannot consist with such a presence"

Smith —"His ascension and abiding in heaven, was no hindrance to his having visited the earth corporeally, and therefore is now no hindrance to his real presence in the sacrament."

Ridley —"I do not so strictly tie Christ up in heaven, that he may not once come into the earth at his pleasure. For whenever he will, he may come down from heaven, and be on the earth; but I affirm, that it is not possible for him in that corporeal way to be both in heaven and on earth at one time"

Smith —"Mark, I pray you, my masters, what he answers. First he saith, that the sitting of Christ at the right hand of the Father, is a hindrance to the real presence of his body in the sacrament, and then afterwards he flies from it again."

Ridley.—"I would not have you think that I imagine or dream of any such manner of sitting, as these men here sit in the school."

Smith.—"It is lawful for Christ, then, to be here present on the earth, when he chooses himself."

Ridley.—"Yea, when he chooses."

Smith.—"Therefore, he, ascending into heaven, does not restrain his real presence in the sacrament."

Ridley.—"I do not gainsay but that it is lawful for him to appear on the earth when he chooses, but prove you that he chooses it"

Smith.—"Then your answer depends upon the will of Christ, I perceive therefore I will join with you in that argument. Christ, after his ascension, was seen really and corporeally upon the earth; and, therefore, notwithstanding his ascension and abiding with his Father, he may be corporeally in the sacrament."

Ridley.—"I grant that he was seen on earth, but I deny that he may therefore be in the sacrament. I grant this, because I know that there are certain ancient fathers of that opinion : so that I am content to let you use that proposition as true. But let us first agree about the continual sitting at the right hand of the Father."

Smith.—"Does he so sit at the right hand of his Father, that he never forsakes the same?"

Ridley.—"Nay, I do not bind Christ in heaven so strictly. If you mean by his sitting in heaven, *to reign with his Father*, he may be both in heaven and also in earth. But if you understand his sitting to be *after a corporeal manner of sitting*, then is he always in heaven. For Christ to be corporeally here on earth, when corporeally he is resident in heaven, is contrary to the holy scriptures."

Smith "In Acts iii. we read that Christ shall sit perpetually at the right hand of God, until the consummation of the world."

Weston.—"I perceive you are come here to this issue, whether the body of Christ may be together both in earth and in heaven. I tell you that Christ is both in earth and in heaven together, and at one time, both one and the same natural Christ, in the truth and substance of his very body."

Ridley—"I deny that."

Smith. "I will prove that he appeared here in earth after his ascension."

Ridley.—"He appeared, I grant; but *how* he appeared, whether being then *in heaven* or *in earth*, is uncertain He appeared to Stephen, being then corporeally sitting *in heaven*. For, speaking after the true manner of man's body, when he is in heaven, he is not at the same time in earth; and when he is in earth, he is not at the same time corporeally in heaven."

Smith.—"Christ has been both in heaven and in earth all at one time. He was seen of St. Paul, after his ascending to heaven " 1 Cor. xv. 8.

Ridley. "He was seen really and corporeally indeed but whether being *in heaven* or *earth*, is a doubt. And of doubtful things we must judge doubtfully. You should prove that he was in heaven at the same time, that he was corporeally on earth."

Tresham—"He was seen so, that he might be heard, and therefore, he was corporeally on the earth, or else how could he be heard?"

Ridley.—"He who enabled Stephen to behold him in heaven, even he could bring to pass that Paul might hear him out of heaven."

Smith.—"Others as well as Paul saw him visibly and corporeally."

Ridley.—"I grant he was seen visibly and corporeally· but you have not proved that he was seen *in earth*."

After this, Doctor Glin began to reason, who (notwithstanding Master Ridley had always taken him for his old friend) made a very contumelious preface against him. This preface Master Ridley therefore did the more take to heart, because it proceeded from him. However, he thought, that Doctor Glin's mind was to serve the time For afterwards he came to the house wherein Master Ridley was kept, and, as far as Master Ridley could call to remembrance, before Doctor Young and Doctor Oglethorpe, he desired him to pardon his words. Which Master Ridley did even from the very heart, and wished earnestly, that God would give not only to him, but to all others, the true and evident knowledge of God's evangelical sincerity, that all offences put apart, they being perfectly and fully reconciled, might agree and meet together in the house of the heavenly Father.

Glin "I see that you elude or shift away all scripture and the fathers I will go to work with you after another way. Christ has here his church known in earth, of which you were once a child, although now you speak contumeliously of the sacraments."

Ridley "This is a grievous contumely, that you call me a shifter away of the scripture, and of the doctors . As to the sacraments, I never yet spoke contumeliously of them. I grant that Christ has here his church in earth: but that church ever received and acknowledged the eucharist to be a sacrament of the body of Christ, yet not the body of Christ really, but the body of Christ by grace."

Glin — "Then I ask this question; whether the Catholic church has ever or at any time been idolatrous ?"

Ridley—"The church is the pillar and ground of truth, and never yet has been idolatrous in respect of *the whole church*, but perhaps in respect of *some part* of it, which sometimes may have been seduced by evil pastors, and through ignorance "

Glin. "That church has ever worshipped the flesh of Christ in the eucharist, and according to you, must therefore have been idolatrous "

Ridley—"And I also worship Christ in the sacrament, but not because he is included in the sacrament· As I worship Christ also in the scriptures, not because he is really included in them. Notwithstanding I say, that the body of Christ is present in the sacrament, but yet sacramentally and spiritually, according to his grace giving life, and in that respect really, that is, according to his benediction giving life.

"Furthermore, I acknowledge gladly the true body of Christ to be in the Lord's supper, in such sort as the church of Christ (which is the spouse of Christ, and is taught of the Holy Ghost, and guided by God's word), doth acknowledge. But the true church of Christ acknowledges a presence of Christ's body in the Lord's supper to be communicated to the godly by grace, and spiritually, as I have often shewed, and by a sacramental signification, but not by the corporeal presence of the body of his flesh."

Glin —"But all the church adores Christ, verily, and really in the sacrament."

Ridley —"You know yourself that the eastern church would not acknowledge transubstantiation, as appears in the council of Florence."

Cole.—"That is false. For they acknowledged transubstantiation, although they would not treat of the matter, for they had not in their commission so to do "

Ridley —"Nay, they would determine nothing of the matter when the article was propounded to them."

Cole.—"It was not because they did not acknowledge it, but because they had no commission to do so."

Watson —"Good sir, I have determined to have respect of the time, and therefore I ask this question; when Christ said in the sixth of John, ' He that eateth my flesh, &c.' doth he signify in those words the eating of his true and natural flesh, or else of the bread and symbol ?"

Ridley.—"I understand that place of the very flesh of Christ to be eaten, *spiritually*. And further I say, that the sacrament also pertains to the spiritual eating. For without the spirit to eat the sacrament, is to eat it unprofitably For whoso eateth not spiritually, he eateth his own condemnation."

Watson.—"I ask then whether the eucharist be a sacrament ?"

Ridley.—"The eucharist, taken for a sign or symbol, is a sacrament."

Watson —"Is it instituted of God ?"

Ridley.—"It is '

Watson.—"Where?"

Ridley.—"In the supper."

Watson —"With what words is it made a sacrament ?"

Ridley.—"By the words and deeds which Christ said and did, and commanded us to say and do."

Watson —"It is a thing commonly received, that the sacraments of the new law give grace to them that worthily receive.'

Ridley.—"It is true, that grace is given by the sacrament, as by an instrument. The inward virtue and Christ give the grace through the sacrament."

Watson.—' What is a sacrament ?"

Ridley.—"I remember there are many definitions of a sacrament in Augustine. but I will take that which seems most fit to our present purpose,—*A sacrament is a visible sign of invisible grace* "

Watson "Grace is given to the receivers."

Ridley —"The fellowship or communion with Christ through the Holy Ghost is grace, and by the sacrament we are made the members of the mystical body of Christ, for by the sacrament the part of the body is grafted in the head."

Watson.—"But there is a difference between the mystical body, and natural body."

Ridley.—"There is a difference, but the head of them both is one."

Watson.—"But no promise of grace is made to bread and wine."

Ridley.—" I grant that grace belongs to the eucharist, according to this saying, 'The bread which we break, is it not the communication or partaking of the body of Christ?' And as he that eateth, and he that drinketh unworthily the sacrament of the body and blood of the Lord, eateth and drinketh his own damnation; even so he that eateth and drinketh worthily, eateth life, and drinketh life. I grant also that there is no promise made to bread and wine. But inasmuch as they are sanctified, and made the sacraments of the body and blood of the Lord, they have a promise of grace annexed to them; namely, of spiritual partaking of the body of Christ to be communicated and given, not to the bread and wine, but to them who worthily receive the sacrament."

After much more disputation of this kind, Doctor Tresham began to speak with zeal, and desired that he might be in stead of John the Baptist, in converting the hearts of the fathers, and in reducing bishop Ridley again to the mother church. Now at first, not knowing the person, he thought he had been some good old man, who had the zeal of God, although not according to knowledge, and began to answer him with kindness and reverence. But afterwards he smelled a fox under sheep's clothing.

Tresham.—"God Almighty grant that it may be fulfilled in me, that which was spoken by the prophet Malachi of John Baptist, that I may turn the hearts of the fathers to the children, and the hearts of the children to their fathers, that you at length may be converted. The wise man saith, 'Son, honour thy father, and reverence thy mother.' But you dishonour your Father in heaven, and pollute your mother the holy church here on earth, while you sit not by it."

Ridley.—"These by-words pollute your school."

Tresham.—"If there were an Arian who had that subtle wit that you have, he might soon shift off the authority of the scriptures and fathers."

Weston.—"Either dispute, or else hold your peace, I pray you."

Tresham.—"I bring a place here out of the council of Lateran, which council represented the universal church, wherein were congregated three hundred bishops, and seventy metropolitans, besides a great multitude of others; they decreed that bread and wine, by the power of God's word, was transubstantiated into the body and blood of the Lord. Therefore whoever saith contrary, cannot be a child of the church, but an heretic."

Ridley.—"Good sir, I have heard what you have cited out of the council of Lateran, and remember that there was as a great multitude of bishops and metropolitans as you say. But yet you have not numbered how many abbots, priors, and friars, were in that council, who were to the number of eight hundred."

A notary here said, "What! will you deny then the authority of that council, on account of the multitude of those priors?"

Ridley.—"No, sir, not so much for that cause, as because the doctrine of that council agreed not with the word of God, as appears by the acts of that council, which was held under Innocent the Third, a man (if we believe the histories) most pernicious to the church and commonwealth of Christ."

Tresham.—"What do you not receive the council of Lateran?" Then he with others cried out, "Write, write that down!"

Ridley.—"No, sir, I receive not that council; so write, and write it again."

Smith.—"I bring a canon out of the council of Nice

'None of the apostles said, this is a figure of the body of Christ None of the reverend elders said, the unbloody sacrifice of the altar was a figure'"

Ridley.—"This canon is not in the council of Nice. For I have read over this council many times"

Then came in another, whom Master Ridley knew not, and said, "The universal church, both of the Greeks and Latins, of the East and the West, have agreed in the council of Florence, uniformly in the doctrine of the sacrament, that in the sacrament of the altar there is the true and real body."

Ridley.—"I deny the Greek and the Eastern church to have agreed either in the council at Florence, or at any other time, with the Romish church in the doctrine of transubstantiation of bread into the body of Christ. For there was nothing in the council of Florence, wherein the Greeks would agree with the Romanists, although hitherto it was left free for every church to use, as they were wont, leavened or unleavened bread."

Here Doctor Cole cried out, and said, "they agreed together concerning transubstantiation of bread into the body of Christ."

Master Ridley said that could not be.

Here started up another person, unknown to Master Ridley, who affirmed with him, that there was nothing decreed concerning transubstantiation; the council left that, as a matter not meet nor worthy to disturb the peace and concord of the church. To whom Master Ridley answered again, saying, that he said the truth.

After some further disputation, Weston as prolocutor, dissolved the meeting, saying, "Here you see the stubborn, the boasting, the crafty, the inconstant mind of this man. Here you see, this day that the strength of the truth is without foil Therefore I beseech you all most earnestly to blow the note," he began. and they followed, "Truth hath the victory truth hath the victory!"

The Disputation had at Oxford, on Wednesday the eighteenth day of April, 1554, between Master Hugh Latimer answerer, and Master Smith, and other opposers.

On the next day after these disputations with bishop Ridley, Master Hugh Latimer was brought out to dispute.

There replied to him Smith, Cartwright, and Harpsfield; some others had snatches at him, and gave him bitter taunts. He did not escape hissings and scornful laughings, any more than they that went before him. He was very faint. and desired that he might not be kept long. He could not drink for fear of vomiting

Weston.—"Men and brethren, we are come together this day, (by the help of God,) to vanquish the arguments and opinions of adversaries, against the truth of the real presence of the Lord's body in the sacrament. And therefore, you, father, if you have any thing to answer, I admonish that you answer in short and few words."

Latimer.—"I pray you, good Master Prolocutor, do not exact that of me, which is not in me, I have not these twenty years much used the Latin tongue."

Weston.—"Take your ease, father."

Latimer.—"I thank you, sir, I am well, let me here protest my faith, for I am not able to dispute, and afterwards do your pleasure with me."

The Protestation of Master Hugh Latimer, given up in writing to Doctor Weston.

"The conclusions whereunto I must answer, are these:—

"The first is, That in the sacrament of the altar by the virtue of God's word pronounced by the priest, there is really present the natural body of Christ, conceived of the Virgin Mary, under the kinds of the appearance of bread and wine, in the like manner his blood.

"The second is, That after consecration there remaineth no substance of bread and wine, nor any other substance, but the substance of God and man.

"The third is, That in the mass there is the lively sacrifice of the church, which is propitiatory, as well for the sins of the quick, as of the dead.

"Concerning the first conclusion, methinks it is set forth with new found terms that are obscure, and do not sound according to the words of the scripture. However, I answer plainly, that to the right celebration of the Lord's supper there is no other presence of Christ required, than a spiritual presence: and this presence is sufficient for a christian man, as a presence by which we abide in Christ, and Christ abideth in us, to the obtaining of eternal life, if we persevere. And this same presence may be called most fitly a real presence, that is, a presence not feigned, but a true and faithful presence. I here state this, lest some scorner should suppose me to make nothing else of the sacrament, but a naked and a bare sign.

"Concerning the second conclusion, I dare be bold to say, that it has no ground in God's word, but is a thing invented and found out by man; and therefore is to be regarded as foolish and false. and I had almost said, as the mother and nurse of the other errors. It were good for my lords and masters of transubstantiation, to take heed lest they conspire with the Nestorians, for I do not see how they can avoid it.

"The third conclusion seems to sow sedition against the offering which Christ himself offered for us in his own proper person, according to that pithy place of St. Paul, where he saith, 'That Christ when he had by himself purged our sins, sat down on the right hand of the Majesty on high.' (Heb. i. 3.) And afterwards 'Wherefore in all things it behoved him to be made like unto his brethren, that he might be a merciful and faithful high priest in things pertaining to God, to make reconciliation for the sins of the people.' (Heb. ii. 17.) So that the expiation or taking away of our sins may be thought rather to depend on this, that Christ was an offering bishop, than that he was offered, were it not that he was offered by himself; and therefore it is needless that he should be offered by any other. I will speak nothing of the wonderful presumption of man, to dare to attempt this without a manifest vocation, especially as it tends to the overthrowing and making fruitless (if not wholly, yet partly) the cross of Christ; for truly it is no base or mean thing to offer Christ. And therefore worthily a man may say to my lords and masters the offerers, 'By what authority do ye this? and who gave you this authority? Where? when?' A man cannot (saith John Baptist) take any thing except it be given him from above. much less then may any man presume to usurp any honour, before he be called thereto. Again, 'If any man sin,' (saith St. John,) 'we have'—not a master or offerer at home, who can sacrifice for us at mass, but 'we have an advocate, Jesus Christ,' who once offered up himself; of which offering the efficacy and effect is endurable for ever, so that it is needless to have such offerers.

"I have taken the more pains to write, because I refuse to dispute, in consideration of my debility: that all men may know, how I have done so, not without pain, though having no man to help me, as I have never before been debarred from having. O, sir, you may chance to live till you come to the age and weakness that I am of. I have spoken in my time before two kings more than once, two or three hours together, without interruption. But now, that I may speak the truth (by your leave), I could not be suffered to declare my mind before you, no, not by the space of a quarter of an hour, without snatches, revilings, checks, rebukes, taunts, such as I have not felt the like, in such an audience, all my life long. Surely it cannot be but an heinous offence that I have given. But what was it? Forsooth I had spoken of the four marrow-bones of the mass; which kind of speaking I never read to be a sin against the Holy Ghost.

"I could not be allowed to shew what I meant by my metaphor. But, sir, now by your favour I will tell your mastership what I mean.

"The first is the popish consecration, which had been called God's body-making.

"The second is transubstantiation.

"The third is massal oblation.

"The fourth, adoration.

"These chief and principal portions, parts, and points belonging to the mass, I call the marrow-bones of the mass; which you, by force, might, and violence, intrude as parts of the scriptures, with racking and cramping, injuring and wronging the same.

"There are some persons that speak many false things more probable, and more like to the truth, than the truth itself."

"But what mean you," saith one interrupting him, "by this talk, so far from the matter?"

"Well, I hope, good masters, you will suffer an old man a little to play the child, and to speak one thing twice. You have changed the most holy communion into a private action; and you deny to the laity the Lord's cup, contrary to Christ's commandment and you blemish the annunciation of the Lord's death till he come: For you have changed the common prayer, called the divine service, with the administration of the sacraments, from the vulgar and known language, into a strange tongue, contrary to the will of the Lord revealed in his word. God open the door of your hearts, to see the things you should see herein! I would as fain obey my sovereign as any in this realm: but in these things I can never do it with an upright conscience. God be merciful unto us. Amen!"

Weston.—"Then do you refuse to dispute? Will you subscribe?"

Latimer.—"No, good Master; I pray be good to an old man. You may, if it please God, be once old, as I am. you may come to this age, and to this debility."

Weston.—"You said, upon Saturday last, that you could not find the mass, nor the marrow-bones of it in your book but we will find a mass in that book."

Latimer.—"No, good Master doctor, you cannot."

Weston.—"What find you, then, there?"

Latimer.—"I find a communion there."

Weston.—"Which communion, the first or the last?"

Latimer.—"I find no great diversity in them; they are one supper of the Lord: but I like the last very well."

Weston.—"The first was naught, belike."

Latimer.—"I do not well remember wherein they differ."

Weston.—"Then cake bread, and loaf bread, are all one with you. You call it the supper of the Lord; but you are deceived in that: for they had done the supper before, and therefore the scripture saith, 'After they had supped.' For you know that St. Paul finds fault with the Corinthians, for that some of them were drunk at this supper; and you know no man can be drunk at your communion."

Latimer.—"The first was called The Jewish Supper, when they did eat the paschal lamb together; the other was called The Lord's Supper."

Weston.—"That is false."

Smith.—"I will propose three questions as they are put to me. And first I ask this question of you, although it ought not to be called in question; but such is the condition of the church, that it is always vexed by the wicked. I ask, I say, whether Christ's body be really in the sacrament?"

Latimer.—"I trust I have obtained of Master Prolocutor that no man shall exact of me that which is not in me. And I am sorry that this worshipful audience should be deceived of their expectation. I have given up my mind in writing to Master Prolocutor."

Smith.—"Whatever you have given up, it shall be registered among the acts."

Latimer.—"Disputation requires a good memory: my memory is clean gone, and marvellously weakened, and never the better for the prison."

Weston.—"How long have you been in prison?"

Latimer.—"Three quarters of a year."

Weston.—"And I was in prison six years."

Latimer.—"The more pity, sir."

Weston.—"How long have you been of this opinion?"

Latimer.—"It is not long, sir, that I have been of this opinion."

Weston.—"The time hath been when you said mass full devoutly."

Latimer.—"Yea, I cry God's mercy heartily for it."

Weston.—"Where learned you this new-fangledness?"

Latimer.—"I have long sought for the truth in this matter of the sacrament, and have not been of this mind past seven years and my lord of Canterbury's book has especially confirmed my judgment in it. If I could remember all contained in it, I would not fear to answer any man."

Tresham.—"There are in that book six hundred errors."

Weston.—"You were once a Lutheran."

Latimer.—"No; I was a papist, for I never could perceive how Luther could defend his opinion without transubstantiation."

Weston.—"Luther said that the devil reasoned with him, and persuaded him that the mass was not good, so that Luther said mass, and the devil dissuaded him from it."

Latimer.—"I do not take in hand here to defend Luther's sayings or doings. If he were here, he would defend himself well enough, I trow."

Weston.—"Do you believe this, as you have written?"

Latimer "Yea, sir."

Weston.—"Then you have no faith."

Latimer—"Then would I be sorry, sir."

Tresham.—"It is written (John vi. 53), 'Except ye eat the flesh of the Son of Man, and drink his blood, ye have no life in you.' Which when the Capernaites and many of Christ's disciples heard, they said, 'This is a hard saying,' &c. Now that the truth may better appear, here I ask of you, whether Christ, speaking these words, did mean of his flesh to be eaten with the mouth, or of the spiritual eating of the same?"

Latimer—"I answer (as St. Augustine understands) that Christ in that passage meant of the spiritual eating of his flesh."

Tresham.—"Of what flesh meant Christ; his true flesh, or not?"

Latimer—"Of his true flesh, spiritually to be eaten in the supper by faith, and not corporeally."

Tresham.—"Of what flesh mean the Capernaites?"

Latimer—'Of his true flesh also, but to be eaten with the mouth; not the bodily mouth, but of the mouth of the spirit, mind, and heart."

Weston.—"You shall see what worshipful men you hang upon, one that has been of your mind, shall dispute with you. Master Cartwright, I pray you dispute?"

Cartwright.—"Reverend father, because it is given me in command to dispute with you, I will do it gladly But first understand ere we go any further, that I was in the same error that you are in, but I am sorry for it, and do confess myself to have erred, I acknowledge mine offence, and I wish and desire God that you may also repent with me."

Latimer—"Will you give me leave to tell what has caused you to recant? It is the pain of the law, which has brought you back, and converted you, and many more, which hinders many from confessing God And this is a great argument, there are few here can solve it."

Cartwright.—"That is not my case; but I will make you this short argument, by which I was converted from mine errors, namely, that if the true body of Christ be not really in the sacrament, all the whole church hath erred from the apostles' time."

Latimer "The popish church has erred, and still errs I think for the space of six or seven hundred years, there was no mention made of any eating, but spiritually, for, before these five hundred years, the church ever confessed a spiritual eating. But the Romish church begat the error of transubstantiation My lord of Canterbury's book handles that very well, and by him I could answer you if I had it."

Cartwright.—"Linus, and all the rest, confess the body of Christ to be in the sacrament, and St. Augustine grants that it is to be worshipped"

Latimer.—"We worship Christ in the heavens, and we worship him in the sacrament, but the mass-worship is not to be used."

Cole.—"Is it not a shame for an old man to lie? You say you are of the old fathers' faith where they say well; and yet you are not"

Latimer.—'I am of their faith when they say well, I refer myself to my lord of Canterbury's book wholly herein"

Smith.—"Then you are not of Chrysostom's faith, nor of St. Augustine's faith'

Latimer—"I have said, when they say well, and bring scripture for them, I am of their faith, and further St. Augustine requires not to be believed. Where have you authority given you to offer sacrifice?"

Weston "Hoc facite, do this; for facite in that place is taken for offerte, that is, offer you."

Latimer—"Is facere nothing but sacrificare to sacrifice? Why, then, no man must receive the sacrament but priests only, for there no other may offer but priests."

Weston—"Your argument is to be denied"

Latimer.—"Did Christ then offer himself at his supper?"

Pye—"Yea, he offered himself for the whole world"

Latimer. "Then if this word facite, 'do ye,' signify sacrificate sacrifice, it follows, as I said, that none but priests only ought to receive the sacrament to whom it is only lawful to sacrifice; and where find you that, I pray you?"

Weston.—"Forty years ago, whither could you have gone to have found your doctrine?"

Latimer—"The more cause we have to thank God, that has now sent the light into the world"

Weston "The light nay light and wicked preachers; you altered and changed so often your communions and altars, and all for this one end, to spoil and rob the church."

Latimer.—"These things pertain nothing to me, I must not answer for other men's deeds, but only for mine own."

Weston.—"Well, Master, this is our intention, to wish you well, and to exhort you to come to yourself, and remember, that without Noah's Ark there is no health. Remember what they have been who were the beginners of your doctrine, none but a few flying apostates, running out of Germany for fear of the fagot. Remember what they have been who have set forth the same in this realm a sort of fling-brains and light heads, who were never constant in any one thing as it was to be seen in the turning of the table, where, like a sort of apes, they could not tell which way to turn their tails, looking one day west, and another day east, one that way, and another this way. They will be like, they say, to the apostles; they will have no churches A hovel is good enough for them. They come to the communion with no reverence They get them a tankard, and one saith, 'I drink, and I am thankful,' 'the more joy of thee,' saith another. And in them was it true that Hilary saith, 'We make, every year and every month, a faith' A renegade Scot took away the adoration or worshipping of Christ in the sacrament, by whose procurement that heresy was put into the last communion book, so much prevailed that one man's authority. Your stubbornness comes of vain glory, which is to no purpose, for it will do you no good when a fagot is in your beard And we see all, by your own confession, how little cause you have to be stubborn. The queen's grace is merciful, if you will turn."

Latimer. "You shall have no hope in me of turning. I pray for the queen daily, even from the bottom of my heart, that she may turn from this religion"

Weston—"Here you all see the weakness of heresy against the truth, he denies all truth, and all the old fathers."

And thus thou hast, reader, the whole action of this disputation against these three worthy confessors and martyrs of the Lord; wherein thou mayest behold the disordered usage of the university men, the unmannerly custom of the school, the rude tumult of the multitude, the fierceness and interruption of the doctors, the full ground of all their arguments, the censures of the judges, the railing language of the prolocutor, being both the actor, the moderator, and also judge himself.

Such disturbance and confusion, more like a conspiracy than any disputation, without all form and order, was in the schools during the time of their answering, that neither could the answerers utter their minds, neither would the opponents be satisfied with any reasons Concerning which misruled disputation, Ridley himself reports as follows —

The Report and Narration of Bishop Ridley, concerning the Disputation against him and his fellow-prisoners at Oxford.

" I never yet, since I was born, saw or heard anything done or handled more vainly or tumultuously, than the disputation held with me in the schools at Oxford. Yea, verily, I could never have thought that it had been possible to have found amongst men accounted to be men of knowledge and learning in this realm, any so brazen-faced and shameless, so disorderly and vainly to behave themselves, more like stage-players in interludes to set forth a pageant, than grave divines in school, to dispute about religion. The clamours of the Sorbonne, which at Paris I have seen in times past, when popery most reigned, might be worthily thought, in comparison with this thrasonical ostentation, to have had much modesty. And no great marvel, seeing they who should have been moderators and overseers of others, and who should have given good examples in words and gravity, themselves, above all others, gave worst example, and did, as it were, blow the trumpet to the rest, to rave, roar, rage, and cry out By reason whereof it manifestly appears that they never sought for any truth or verity, but only for the glory of the world, and their own bragging victory But lest by the innumerable railings and reproachful taunts, wherewith I was baited on every side, our cause—yea, rather God's cause and his church's—should be evil spoken of, and slandered to the world through false reports, given out concerning our disputation, and so the truth might sustain some damage, I thought it no less than my duty to write my answers, that whosoever is desirous to know the truth may by this perceive as well all those things which were chiefly objected, as summarily that which was answered by me to them. However I confess this to be most true, that it is impossible to set forth either all that was tumultuously and confusedly objected on their parts, there being so many speaking at one time, and so fast, that one could not very well hear another, neither could all that was answered on my behalf to so many opponents be heard.

" A great part of the time appointed for the disputations was vainly consumed in opprobrious checks and reviling taunts, with hissing and clapping of hands, using the English tongue, to procure the people's favour All which, when I with great grief of heart beheld, protesting openly that such excessive and outrageous disorder was unseemly for those schools, and men of such learning and gravity, and that they who were the doers and stirrers of such things, did nothing else but betray the slenderness of their cause, and their own vanities ; I was so far off by this my humble complaint, from doing any good, that I was forced to hear such rebukes, checks, and taunts for my labour, as no person of any honesty, without blushing, could abide to hear the like spoken by a most vile varlet, against a most wretched ruffian.

" At the beginning of the disputation, when I should have confirmed mine answer to the first proposition in a few words, and that, after the manner and law of schools, before I could make an end of my first proof, which was not very long, even the doctors themselves cried out, ' He speaketh blasphemies, he speaketh blasphemies !' And when on my knees I besought them that they would vouchsafe to hear me to the end, at which the prolocutor being moved, cried out, ' Let him read it, let him read it ' Yet, when I began to read, there followed immediately such shouting, such noise, and tumult, such confusion of voices, crying ' Blasphemies, blasphemies ' as I, to my remembrance, never heard or read the like, except it be that one which was, in the acts of the apostles, stirred up of Demetrius the silversmith, and other of his occupation, crying out against Paul, ' Great is Diana of the Ephesians ! great is Diana of the Ephesians !' And except it be a certain disputation which the Arians had against the orthodox, and such as were of godly judgment in Africa, where it is said (according to Victor) that such as the president and rulers of the disputation were, such was the end of the disputations All were in a hurly-burly, and so great were the slanders which the Arians cast out, that nothing could quietly be heard

" The cries and the tumults against me so prevailed, that I was forced to leave off reading my proofs, although they were short. If any man doubt of the truth of this, let him ask any one that was there, and not utterly perverted in popery, and, I am assured, he will say I fall far short of the facts in my statement. But I will cease to complain of these things further."

He concludes his report with these words · " And thus was ended this most glorious disputation of the most holy fathers, sacrificers, doctors, and masters, who fought most manfully, as ye may see, for their God and goods, for their faith and felicity, for their country and kitchen, for their beauty and belly, with triumphant applauses and favour of the whole university."

The disputation of Master Latimer being ended on the 18th April, the commissioners sat on the 20th, in St Mary's church, and Doctor Weston used dissuasions with every one of them, and would not suffer them to answer unless directly and peremptorily, as his words were to say whether they would subscribe or not. He said to the archbishop of Canterbury that he was overcome in disputation. The archbishop answered, " That where Doctor Weston said, he had answered and opposed, and could neither maintain his own errors, nor impugn the truth ; all that he thus said was false. For that he was not suffered to oppose as he wished, nor could he answer as he was required, unless he would have brawled like them. Four or five continually interrupted him, so that he could not speak." Master Ridley and Master Latimer were asked what they would do. They replied, " That they would stand to what they had said." Then they were all called together, and the sentence read over them, declaring they were no more members of the church. And also that their favourers and patrons were condemned as heretics. In reading the sentence, they were asked, whether they would turn or not and they bade them read on in the name of God, for they were not minded to turn So they were all three condemned.

After which sentence of condemnation being awarded against them, they answered again every one in his turn as follows , the archbishop first beginning thus —

The Archbishop of Canterbury.

" From this your judgment and sentence, I appeal to the just judgment of Almighty God, trusting to be present with him in heaven, for whose presence in the altar I am thus condemned."

Doctor Ridley.

" Although I be not of your company, yet doubt I not but my name is written in another place, whither this sentence will send us sooner than we should by the course of nature have come."

Master Latimer

" I thank God most heartily, that he has prolonged my life to this end, that I may in this cause glorify God by that kind of death."

Doctor Weston's Answer unto Latimer.

" If you go to heaven in this faith, then I will never come thither, as I am at present persuaded."

After the sentence pronounced, they were separated one from another. The archbishop was returned to Bocardo, Ridley was carried to the sheriff's house; Latimer to the bailiff's.

On the Saturday following, they had a mass, with a general procession and great solemnity. Doctor Cranmer was forced to behold the procession out of Bocardo; Doctor Ridley out of the sheriff's house. Latimer also, being brought to see it from the bailiff's house, thought that he was going to be burnt, and spoke to one Augustine Cooper, a catchpole, to make a quick fire But when he came to Carfox, and saw the matter, he ran as fast as his old bones would carry him, to one Spencer's shop, and would not look towards it. Last of all, Doctor Weston carried the sacrament, and four Doctors carried the canopy over him.

Immediately after the sentence was given, Doctor Ridley writes to the prolocutor as follows.—

Doctor Ridley to the Prolocutor.

" Master prolocutor, you remember, I am sure, how you promised me openly in the schools, after my protestation, that I should see how my answers were there taken and written of the notaries whom you appointed to write what should be said, that I should have leave to add to them, or to alter them, as upon more deliberation should have seemed best. You granted me also, at the delivery of my answer to your first proposition, a copy of the same. *These promises are not performed.* If your sudden departure be any part of the cause of this, yet I pray you remember that they may be performed; for performance of a promise is to be looked for at a righteous judge's hands. Now I send you here my answers, in writing, to your second and third propositions, and do desire and require earnestly a copy of the same, and I shall by God's grace procure the pains of the writer to be paid for, and satisfied accordingly. Master Prolocutor, in the time of my answer in the schools, when I would have confirmed my sayings with authorities and reasons, you said then openly, that I should have time and place, to say and bring whatsoever I could another time, and the same your saying was then and there confirmed of others of the commissioners: yea, and, I dare say, the audience also thought then that I should have had another day, to have brought and said what I could for the declaration and confirmation of mine assertions. Now, that this was not done, but sentence so suddenly given before the cause was perfectly heard, I cannot but marvel," &c.

On Monday, the 23d of April, Doctor Weston, prolocutor, took his journey to London with the letters certificatory from the university to the Queen, by whom the archbishop of Canterbury directed his letters supplicatory to the council Which letters, after the prolocutor had received, and had carried them well-near half-way to London, he opened, and seeing the contents, sent them back again, refusing to carry them, &c.

The Archbishop of Canterbury's Letter to the Council.

" In right humblewise shews unto your honourable lordships, Thomas Cranmer, late archbishop of Canterbury, beseeching the same to be a means for me to the queen's highness for her mercy and pardon. Some of you know by what means I was brought and trained to the will of our late sovereign lord king Edward VI., and what I spake against the same, wherein I refer me to the reports of your honours and worships. Furthermore, this is to signify to your lordships, that upon Monday, Tuesday, and Wednesday last past, were open disputations here in Oxford against me, Master Ridley, and Master Latimer, in three matters concerning the sacrament. First, of the real presence Secondly, of transubstantiation and Thirdly, of the sacrifice of the mass. Upon Monday, against me upon Tuesday, against doctor Ridley, and upon Wednesday, against Mr. Latimer. How the other two were ordered, I know not; for we were separated, so that none of us knew what the other said, nor how they were ordered. But as concerning myself, I can report. Doctor Chedsey was appointed to dispute against me, but the disputation was so confused that I never knew the like; every man bringing forth what he liked without order, and such haste was made, that no answer was suffered to be fully given to any argument, before another brought forward a new argument. And in such weighty matters the disputation must needs be ended in one day, which could scantly be ended in three months. And when we had answered them, they would not appoint us one day to bring forth our proofs, that they might answer us, being required by me to do so, whereas I myself have more to say than can be well discussed, as I suppose, in twenty days. The right means to resolve the truth had been to have suffered us to answer fully to all that they could say, and then they again to answer us fully to all that we can say. But why they would not answer us, what other cause can there be, but that either they feared their matter, that they were not able to answer us, or else for some consideration they made such haste not to seek the truth, but to condemn us, that it must be done in post haste before the matters could be thoroughly heard. For in haste we were all three condemned of heresy. Thus much I thought good to signify unto your lordships, that you may know the indifferent handling of matters, leaving the judgment thereof unto your wisdom. And I beseech your lordships to remember me, a poor prisoner, unto the queen's majesty; and I shall pray, as I do daily, unto God, for the long preservation of your lordships in all godliness and felicity." April 23.

Now let us return for a little to our history, as regards other things that happened in other parts of the realm, in this tumultuous time of queen Mary. As events in that time were so numerous, it is hard to keep a perfect order in reciting them. Therefore to insert things left out before, we have thought here a little to interrupt the order of time, returning again to the month of July the year before, viz. 1553, at which time I showed before how the duke of Northumberland was apprehended by the guard, and brought to London by the earl of Arundel and other lords and gentlemen who had been appointed for that purpose on the 25th July, being St. James' day. The duke was sent to the Tower, where he remained.

The earl of Warwick, his eldest son, lord Ambrose and lord Henry Dudley, two of his younger sons, the earl of Huntington, lord Hastings, sir John Gates, sir Henry Gates, sir Andrew Dudley, sir Thomas Palmer, and Dr. Sands, chancellor of Cambridge, were all sent to the Tower at the same time.

On the 26th, the lord marquis of Northampton, the bishop of London, lord Robert Dudley, and sir Richard Corbes were committed to the Tower.

On the 27th, the lord chief justice of England, and the lord Mountacute, chief justice of the common pleas, were committed to the Tower.

On Friday the 28th, the duke of Suffolk, and sir John Cheek were committed to the Tower.

On the 30th, the lord Russel was committed to the sheriff of London's custody.

On the 31st, the earl of Rutland was committed to the Fleet; and the same day the duke of Suffolk was delivered out of the Tower again.

On Thursday the 3d of August, the queen entered into the city of London at Aldersgate, and so to the Tower, where she remained seven days, and then removed to Richmond.

On Saturday the 5th the Lord Ferris was committed to the Tower, and on the same day Doctor Bonner was delivered out of the Marshalsea; and at night Doctor Cocks was committed to the Marshalsea, and one Master Edward Underhill to Newgate. Also the same day Doctor Tonstall and Stephen Gardiner were delivered out of the Tower, and Gardiner received into the queen's privy council, and made lord chancellor.

On Sunday the 6th, Henry Dudley, captain of the guard at Guisnes, who before had been sent to the French king, by his cousin the duke of Northumberland, after the despatch of his embassy to the French king, returned to Guisnes, and was taken, and this day brought to the Tower.

On Monday the 7th, a dirge in Latin was sung within the Tower by all the king's chapel, and the bishop of Winchester was chief minister; the queen was present, and most part of the council.

On Tuesday the 8th, the king's body was brought to Westminster, and there buried; doctor Day, bishop of Chichester, preached. The same day a mass of *requiem* was sung within the Tower by the bishop of Winchester, who had on his mitre, and did all things as in times past was done. The queen was present.

On Thursday the Duke of Norfolk came forth of the Tower, with whom the Duchess of Somerset was also delivered.

On Sunday the 13th, doctor Bourne preached at St. Paul's Cross.

In the week following command was given throughout the city that no apprentices should come to the sermon, nor bear any knife or dagger.

On Wednesday, being the 16th day of August, Master Bradford, Master Beacon, and Master Vernon, were committed to the Tower: with whom also Master Sampson should have been committed, and was sought for the same time at Master Elsing's house in Fleet-street, where Master Bradford was taken; and because he was not found, the bishop of Winchester fumed like a prelate with the messenger.

On Friday the 18th, the duke of Northumberland, the marquis of Northampton, and the earl of Warwick, were arraigned at Westminster, and there the same day condemned, the duke of Norfolk that day being the high judge.

On the Saturday the 19th, sir Andrew Dudley, sir John Gates, sir Henry Gates, and sir Thomas Palmer, were arraigned at Westminster, and condemned the same day, the marquis of Winchester being high judge.

The same day a letter was sent to sir Henry Tyrrell, Antony Brown, and Edmund Brown, esquires, praying them to commit to ward all such as shall contemn the queen's order of religion, or shall keep themselves from church, there to remain until they be conformable, and to signify their names to the council.

On Sunday the 20th, Dr. Watson, the bishop of Winchester's chaplain, preached at St. Paul's Cross, at whose sermon was present the marquis of Winchester, the earl of Bedford, the earl of Pembroke, the lord Rich, and two hundred of the guard with their halberds, lest the people should have made any stir against the preacher.

On Monday the 21st, the duke of Northumberland, the marquis of Northampton, sir Andrew Dudley, sir John Gates, and sir Thomas Palmer, heard a mass within the Tower, and after mass they all five received the sacrament in one kind only, as in the popish time was used. On which day also Queen Mary set forth a proclamation, signifying to the people, that she could not hide any longer the religion which she from her infancy had professed, &c. Inhibiting in the proclamation, printing and preaching.

On Tuesday the 22d, the duke of Northumberland, sir John Gates, and sir Thomas Palmer, were beheaded on Tower-hill. The same day certain noble personages heard mass within the Tower, and likewise after mass received the sacrament in one kind.

On Sunday the 27th, Doctor Chedsey preached at St. Paul's Cross, and on the same day the archbishop of Canterbury, Sir Thomas Smith, and the dean of St. Paul's, were cited to appear the week following before the queen's commissioners in the bishop's consistory within St. Paul's.

About this time it was noised abroad by rumours falsely and craftily devised, either to establish the credit of the mass, or else to bring Thomas Cranmer, archbishop of Canterbury into discredit, that he, to curry favour with Queen Mary, had promised to say dirge mass after the old custom for King Edward, and that he had already said mass at Canterbury, &c. Wherefore to stop these slanders, Cranmer, on the 7th of September, set forth the following letter, which was printed.

A Purgation of Thomas Archbishop of Canterbury, against certain Slanders falsely raised against him.

"As the devil, Christ's ancient adversary, is a liar, and the father of lies, even so hath he stirred up his servants and members to persecute Christ and his true word and religion with lying: which he ceaseth not to do most earnestly at this present time. For whereas the prince of famous memory King Henry VIII., seeing the great abuses of the Latin mass, reformed some things therein in his lifetime; and afterwards, our late sovereign lord, King Edward VI. took the same wholly away, for the manifold and great errors and abuses of the same, and restored in the place thereof Christ's holy supper, according to Christ's own institution, and as the apostles used the same in the primitive church: the devil goeth about now by lying to overthrow the Lord's Supper again, and to restore his Latin satisfactory mass, a thing of his own invention and device. And to bring the same more easily to pass, some have abused the name of me, Thomas archbishop of Canterbury, bruiting abroad, that I have set up the mass at Canterbury, and that I offered also to say mass at the burial of our late sovereign prince King Edward VI., and that I offered to say mass before the queen's highness, and at St. Paul's church, and elsewhere. And although I have been well exercised these twenty years to suffer and bear evil reports and lies, and have not been much grieved thereat, but have borne all things quietly; yet when untrue reports and lies turn to the hindrance of God's truth, they are in nowise to be suffered. Wherefore these be to signify unto the world, that it was not I that set up the mass at Canterbury, but it was a false, flattering, lying, and dissembling monk, which caused mass to be set up there without my advice or counsel; *Reddat illi Dominus in die illo.* And as for offering myself to say mass before the queen's highness, or in any other place, I never did it, as her grace well knoweth. But if her grace will give me leave, I shall be ready to prove, against all that will say the contrary, that all that is contained in the holy communion, set out by the most innocent and godly prince King Edward VI., in his high court of parliament, is conformable to that order which our Saviour Christ did both observe, and command to be observed, and which his apostles, and the primitive church used many years; whereas the mass, in many things, not only hath no foundation of Christ, his apostles, nor the primitive church, but is manifestly contrary to the same, and containeth many horrible abuses in it. And although many, either unlearned or malicious, do report, that Peter Martyr is unlearned, yet if the queen's highness will grant thereunto, I, with the said Peter Martyr, and other four or five, which I shall choose, will, by God's grace, take upon us to defend, not only the common prayers of the church, the ministration of the sacraments, and other rites and ceremonies, but also all the doctrine and religion set out by our sovereign lord King Edward VI., to be more pure, and according to God's word, than any other that hath been used in England these thousand years: so that God's word may be judge, and that the reasons and proofs of both parties may be set out in writing, to the intent, as well that all the world may examine and judge thereon, as that no man shall start back from his writing. And where they boast of the faith, that hath been in the church these fifteen hundred years, we will join with them in this point; and that the same doctrine and usage is to be followed, which was in the church fifteen hundred years past; and we shall prove that the order of the church, set out at this present time, in this realm by act of parliament, is the same that was used in the church fifteen hundred years past, and so shall they be never able to prove theirs."

On Thursday, the 7th of September, Lord Mountacute, chief justice, and the lord chief baron were delivered out of the Tower.

On the 13th of September, the reverend father, master Hugh Latimer was committed to the Tower.

On the 14th of September, the archbishop of Canterbury was committed to the Tower

On the 26th of September, one Master Gray, of Cambridge, called before him one Master Garth, for that he would not suffer a boy of Peter-house to help him to say mass in Pembroke-hall, which was before any law was established for that behalf

The queen came to the Tower of London on Thursday, being the 28th of September, and upon the Saturday following she rode from the Tower through the city of London, where were made many pageants to receive her, and so she was triumphantly brought to Whitehall, in Westminster.

On Sunday, the 1st day of October, the queen's highness went from Whitehall to Westminster-abbey, accompanied with the most part of the nobility of this realm, namely, these · the duke of Norfolk, the earl of Arundel, the earl of Shrewsbury, the marquis of Winchester, the earls of Derby, Bedford, Worcester, Cumberland, Westmorland, Oxford, Sussex, Devonshire, Pembroke, the lord Dacres of the north, lord Ferris, lord Cobham, lord Abergavenny, lord Wentworth, lord Scroop, lord Rich, lord Vaux, lord Howard, lord Conias, lord Morley, lord Paget, and the lord Willoughby; with other nobles, and all the ambassadors of divers countries, the mayor of London, with all the aldermen. Also out of the abbey, to receive her, there came three silver crosses, and to the number of fourscore, or nearly, of singing men, all in very rich and gorgeous copes Amongst whom was the dean of Westminster, and several of her chaplains, who bare every one some ensign in their hands, and after them followed ten bishops all mitred, and their crosier staves in their hands, and rich copes upon every one of them. And in this order they returned from Westminster-hall before the queen to the abbey, where she was crowned by Stephen Gardiner, bishop of Winchester and lord chancellor of England. At the time of the coronation, Doctor Day, bishop of Chichester, made a sermon to the queen's majesty, and to the rest of the nobility.

Also there was a general pardon proclaimed within the abbey at the time of her coronation, out of which proclamation all the prisoners of the Tower and of the Fleet were excepted, and sixty-two more.

On the Tuesday the vice-chancellor of Cambridge challenged one Mr. Pierson, because he ministered still the communion in his own parish, and received strangers of other parishes to the communion, and would not say mass Upon which, within two days after, he was dismissed from farther administering in his cure.

On the Wednesday following the archbishop of York was committed to the Tower.

On the Thursday, the queen rode to the parliament in her robes, and all the nobility with her; and when they were met in the parliament-house, the bishop of Winchester made a solemn oration, and sergeant Polhard was chosen speaker of the parliament. The same day the bishops of Lincoln, Hereford, and Westchester, were dismissed from the parliament and convocation.

Also on the 10th, the earl of Huntington was delivered out of the Tower.

On the Sunday after, being the 15th, Lawrence Saunders preached at Allhallows in Bread-street in the morning, where he declared the abomination of the mass, with divers other matters, very notably and godly; whereof more shall be said when we come to his history. As he shewed himself to be God's faithful minister, so is he sure not to be defrauded of God's faithful promise, who says, "Whosoever, therefore, shall confess me before men, him will I also confess before my Father which is in heaven." (Matt. x. 32.) But about noon of the same day he was sent for by the bishop of London, and then committed to the Marshalsea.

On the Sunday following, being the 22nd, Doctor Weston preached at St. Paul's Cross. In the beginning of his sermon he desired the people to pray for the souls departed "You shall pray for all them that are departed, that are neither in heaven, nor in hell, but in

another place, being not yet sufficiently purged to come to heaven, that they may be relieved by your devout prayers" He called the Lord's table, where we celebrate our communion, an oyster-board ' He said, that the catechism in Latin, lately set out, was abominable heresy, and likened the compilers of the catechism to Julian the Apostate, and the book to a dialogue set out by Julian, in which Christ and Pilate were the speakers; with many other things Master Coverdale, at the time, learnedly confuted this sermon by writing.

In the week following began the disputations in the convocation-house in St Paul's church, of which sufficient has been before declared.

On the 26th, the vice-chancellor of Cambridge went to Clare-hall, and in the presence of Doctor Walker displaced Doctor Madew, and placed Master Swyborne in the mastership there, by the lord chancellor's letters, because he was (as they termed it) *uxoratus*, that is, "married"

On the 28th, the papists in King's college, Cambridge, had their whole service again in the Latin tongue, contrary to the law then in force

On the 3d of November the vice-chancellor sent for the curate of the Round parish in Cambridge, commanding him not to officiate any more in the English tongue, saying, he would have one uniform order of service throughout the town, and that in Latin, with mass, which was established on the 12th of this month.

On the 28th of November the archdeacon's official visited Hinton, where he gave charge to present all such as disturbed the queen's proceedings, in hindering the Latin service, the setting up of their altars, and saying mass It was easy to see how these fellows meant to proceed, having the law once on their side, who thus against a manifest law, would attempt the punishment of any man.

On the 15th of December there were two proclamations at London the one for the repealing of certain acts made by King Edward, and for the setting up of the mass, on the 20th of December then next following, the other was, that no man should interrupt any of those that would say mass.

The parliament beginning about the 5th of October, continued till the 6th of December, 1553. In which parliament were repealed all the statutes of *præmunire*, passed in the time of King Henry VIII., &c Also other laws and statutes concerning religion and the administration of sacraments, decreed under King Edward VI. In this parliament was appointed, that on the 20th of December next ensuing, the same year 1553, all the old form and manner of church-service, used in the last year of King Henry, should again be restored.

About this time a priest of Canterbury said mass on the one day, and the next day after he came into the pulpit, and desired all the people to forgive him, for he said, he had betrayed Christ, not as Judas did, but as Peter did, and there made a long sermon against the mass.

About this time a great number of new bishops, deans, &c. were chosen, more than were made at one time since the Conquest. Their names are these :—

Holyman, bishop of Bristol.
Coates, bishop of Westchester.
Hopton, bishop of Norwich.
Bourne, bishop of Bath.
White, bishop of Lincoln.
Mores, bishop of Rochester.
Morgan, bishop of St. David's.
Poole, bishop of St Asaph
Brookes, bishop of Gloucester.
Moreman, coadjutor to the bishop of Exeter.
Glin, bishop of Bangor
Fecknam, dean of St Paul's
Rainolds, dean of Bristol ; with others.

On the 12th of January, the vice-chancellor of Cambridge called a general congregation, where, among other things, he shewed, that the queen would have there a mass of the Holy Ghost upon the 18th of February following, for it was her birth-day.

On Saturday, the 13th, Doctor Crome was committed to the Fleet. Also on the Sunday following Mr. Addington was committed to the Tower, and information was also given in the court publicly by the bishop of Winchester, that the marriage between the queen's majesty and the king of Spain was concluded. On the day following, being Monday, the mayor, with the aldermen and certain commons were at the court, and they were commanded by the lord chancellor to prepare the city to receive the king of Spain, declaring to them what a catholic, mighty, prudent, and wise prince, the said king was.

On the Saturday following, being the 20th of January, the court of the first fruits and tenths was dissolved.

On Thursday the 25th, the lord marquis of Northampton was again committed to the Tower, and Sir Edward Warner with him.

On Saturday the 27th, Justice Hales was committed to the Marshalsea, and on the same day Mr. Rogers was committed to the Newgate. Upon the Saturday, and on the Sunday, and Monday following, the Londoners prepared a number of soldiers, (by the queen's command) to go into Kent against the commons· which soldiers, when they came to Rochester-bridge, where they should have set upon their enemies, most of them left their own captains and came over to the Kentish men, and so the captains returned to the court without men or victory, leaving behind them six pieces of ordnance and treasure.

About the latter end of January, the duke of Suffolk departed into Leicestershire. The earl of Huntington was sent to take him and bring him to London, who proclaimed the duke traitor by the way.

On Friday the 23d of February, 1554, about nine o'clock in the forenoon, the lord Henry Gray, duke of Suffolk, was brought from the Tower to the scaffold on Tower Hill; Doctor Weston accompanied him as his ghostly father, against the will of the duke. When the duke went up to the scaffold, Weston being on the left hand, pressed to go up with him. The duke, with his hand, put him down again off the stairs: and Weston, taking hold of the duke, forced him down likewise. And as they ascended the second time, the duke again put him down.

Then Weston said, that it was the queen's pleasure he should do so. At this the duke casting his hands abroad, ascended the scaffold, and paused a while. And then said, "Masters, I have offended the queen and her laws, and thereby am justly condemned to die, and am willing to die, desiring all men to be obedient, and I pray God that this my death may be an example to all men, beseeching you all to bear me witness, that I die in the faith of Christ, trusting to be saved by his blood only, and by no trumpery ceremonials. He died for me, and for all them that truly repent, and stedfastly trust in him. And I do repent, desiring you all to pray to God for me; and that when you see my breath depart from me, you will pray to God that he may receive my soul." And then he desired all men to forgive him, saying, that the queen had forgiven him.

Then Dr. Weston declared with a loud voice, that the queen's majesty had forgiven him With that the standers-by said, with good and audible voice, "Such forgiveness God send thee!" meaning Dr. Weston. Then the duke kneeled down and said the psalm, "O God be merciful unto me," &c. to the end, holding up his hands, and looking up to heaven. And when he had ended the psalm, he said, "Into thy hands I commit my spirit," &c. Then he arose and stood up, and delivered his cap and his scarf to the executioner.

Then the executioner kneeled down, and asked the duke forgiveness. And the duke said, "God forgive thee, and I do: and when thou dost thine office, I pray thee do it well, and send me out of this world quickly, and God have mercy upon thee." Then there stood up a man and said, "My lord, what shall I do for the money that you do owe me?" And the duke said, "Alas! good fellow, I pray thee trouble me not now, but go thy way to my officers." Then he knit a handkerchief about his face, and kneeled down and said, "Our Father which art in heaven," &c. to the end. And then he said, "Christ

have mercy upon me,' and laid down his head on the block, and the executioner took the axe, and at the first chop struck off his head, and held it up to the people, &c.

On this same day a number of prisoners had their pardon, and came through the city with their halters about their necks. They were in number above two hundred.

In this week, all such priests within the diocese of London as were married, were divorced from their livings, and commanded to bring their wives within a fortnight, that they might be likewise divorced from them. This the bishop did of his own power.

On Tuesday, in the same week, being the 27th of February, certain gentlemen of Kent were sent into Kent, to be executed there. Their names were these, the two Mantels, two Knevets, and Bret; with these Mr. Rudston also and others were condemned, and should have been executed, but they had their pardon.

As to Mr. Mantel the elder, here is to be noted, that as he was led to execution, and at his first casting under the gallows, the rope broke. Then they wanted him to recant the truth, and receive the sacrament of the altar (as they term it), and then they said he should have the queen's pardon: but Mr. Mantel, like a worthy gentleman, refused their insidious counsel, and chose rather to die than to live to the dishonouring of God. As he was reported falsely to have fallen from the constancy of his profession, to clear himself, and to reprove the sinister surmise of his recantation, he wrote this brief apology.

The Apology of Master Mantel.

"Perceiving that already certain false reports are raised concerning my answer in the behalf of my belief, while I was prisoner in the Tower of London, and considering how sore a matter it is to be an occasion of offence to any of those little ones that believe in Christ· I have thought it the duty of a christian man, as near as I can (with the truth) to take away this offence. It pleased the queen's majesty to send me Doctor Bourne, to whom at the first meeting I acknowledged my faith in all points to agree with the four creeds, that is, the Apostle's Creed, the Nicene Creed, the Athanasian Creed, and the *Te Deum.*

"Further, as concerning confession and penance, I declare that I could be content to shew to any learned minister of Christ's church any thing that troubled my conscience, and of such a man I would most willingly hear absolution pronounced.

"Touching the sacrament of the altar (as he termed it), I said that I believed Christ to be there present as the Holy Ghost meant, when these words were written, "This is my body."

"Further, when this would not satisfy, I desired him to consider, that I was a condemned man to die by law, and that it was more meet for me to seek a readiness and preparation to death. And insomuch as I dissented not from him in any article of the christian faith necessary to salvation, I desired him, for God's sake, no more to trouble me with such matters, to believe which is neither salvation nor not to believe, damnation. He answered, that if I dissented but in the least matter from the chatholic church, my soul was in great danger; therefore much more in this great matter, alleging this text, 'He that offendeth in the least of these, is guilty of them all.' 'Yea,' said I, 'this is true of the commandments of God.' To this I desired him to consider it was not my matter, nor could I in these matters keep disputation, nor did I intend to do so, and therefore to take these few words for a full answer, that I, not only in the matter of the sacrament, but also in all other matters of religion, believe as the holy catholic church of Christ (grounded upon the prophets and apostles) believes. But upon this word 'church' we agreed not; for I took exception at the antichristian popish church.

"Then we fell into talk about the mass, wherein we agreed not for I, both for the occasion of idolatry, and also the clear subversion of Christ's institution, thought it naught; and he, upon certain considerations supposed it good. I found fault that it was accounted a propitiatory sacrifice for sin, and at certain other applications of it. But he said that it was not a propitiatory sacrifice for sin (for the death of Christ only was the sacrifice) and this but a commemoration of the same. 'Then,' I replied, 'if you think so, (certain blasphemous collects left out I could be content were it not for offending my poor brethren that believe in Christ, which know not so much) to hear your mass.' 'See,' said he, 'how vain glory touches you.' 'Not so, sir,' replied I, 'I am not now, I thank God, in a case to be vain glorious.'

"Then I found further fault with it, that it was not a communion. 'Yea,' saith he, 'one priest saying mass here, and another there, and the third in another place, &c. is a communion.' 'This agrees scarcely with these words of St. Paul,' said I, 'Ye come together not for the better, but for the worse.' 'Yea, and it is a communion too,' said he, 'when they come together. Now draws on the time' (continued he) 'that I must depart from you to the court, to say mass before the queen, and must signify unto her in what case I find you, and methinks I find you sore seduced.' Then I said, 'I pray you report the best for I trust you find me not obstinate.' 'What shall I say? are you content to hear mass, and to receive the sacrament of the mass?' 'I beseech you,' said I, 'signify unto her majesty, that I am neither obstinate nor stubborn; for time and persuasion may alter me, but as yet my conscience is such, that I can neither hear mass, nor receive the sacrament after that sort.' Thus, after certain requests made to the queen's majesty concerning other matters, he departed.

"On the next day he came to me again, and brought with him St. Cyprian's works; for so I had required him to do the day before, because I would see his sermon *De Mortalitate*. He had in this book turned and interlined certain places, both concerning the church and the sacrament, which he wished me to read. I read as much as my time would serve, and at his next coming I said, that I was wholly of Cyprian's mind in the matter of the sacrament. Doctor Weston and Doctor Mallet then came to me, whom I answered much after that sort as I did the other. Doctor Weston brought in the place of St. Cyprian, 'Panis iste non effigie, sed natura mutatus,' &c. I asked of him how *natura* was taken in the convocation-house, in the disputation upon the place of Theodoret.

"To be short, Dr. Bourne came often to me, and I always said to him, that I was not minded, nor able to dispute in matters of religion but I believed as the holy catholic church of Christ, grounded upon the prophets and apostles, believes: and in the matter of the sacrament, as the holy fathers, St. Cyprian and St. Augustine write, and believed; and this answer and none other had they from me in effect; what words soever have been spread abroad of me, that I should be conformable to all things, &c. The truth is, I never heard mass, nor received the sacrament during the time of my imprisonment.

"One time he wished me to be confessed. I said, 'I am content.' We kneeled down to pray together in a window. I began without the 'Benedicite,' desiring him not to look at my hand for any superstitious enumeration of my sins. Then he was called away to the council. Thus much I bear only for my life, as God knows. If in this I have offended any christian, from the bottom of my heart I ask them forgiveness. I trust Christ hath forgiven me, who knows that I durst never deny him before men, lest he should deny me before his Heavenly Father.

"Thus I have left behind me, written with mine own hand, the substance of all the talk, especially of the worst that ever I granted to, to the utmost I can remember, as God knoweth. All the whole communication I have not written; for it were both too long and too foolish so to do. Now I beseech the living God, who hath received me to his mercy, and brought to pass, that I die steadfast and undefiled in his truth, at utter defiance and detestation of all papistical and antichristian doctrine, I beseech him (I say) to keep and defend all his chosen for his name's sake, from the tyranny of the bishop of Rome—that antichrist, and from the assault of all his sa-

tellites. God's indignation is known he will try and prove who are his. Amend your lives Deny not Christ before men, lest he deny you before his heavenly Father. Fear not to lose your lives for him, for ye shall find them again. May God hold his merciful hand over this realm, and avert the impending plagues from the same May God save the queen, and send her knowledge in his truth, Amen Pray, pray, pray, ye christians, and comfort yourselves with the scriptures.

"Written the 2d of March, A.D. 1554, by me, Walter Mantel, prisoner, whom both God and the world hath forgiven his offences. Amen."

In London, on the 17th of March every householder was commanded to appear before the aldermen of their ward, and were enjoined that they, their wives and servants, should prepare themselves to go to confession, and receive the sacrament at Easter, and that neither they, nor any of them should depart out of the city, until Easter was past.

On the 18th, being Sunday, the lady Elizabeth, the queen's sister, was brought to the Tower.

On the 25th day (being Easter-day), in the morning, at St Pancras, in Cheapside, the crucifix, with the pix, were taken out of the sepulchre, before the priest rose to the resurrection . so that when, after his accustomed manner, he put his hand into the sepulchre, and said very devoutly, "He hath risen, he is not here," he found his words true, for he was not there indeed! Being dismayed, they consulted among themselves whom they thought to be likeliest to have done this thing. They remembered one Marsh, who a little before had been put from his parsonage because he was married, and to his charge they laid that But when they could not prove it, they charged him with having kept company with his wife since they were divorced. He answered, "That he thought the queen had done him wrong to take from him both his living and his life" These words were taken very grievously, and he and his wife were both committed to prison.

On the 8th of April there was a cat hanged upon a gallows at the cross in Cheapside apparelled like a priest ready to say mass, with a shaven crown. Her two forefeet were tied over her head, with a round paper like a wafer-cake put between them. The queen and the bishops were very angry; and therefore, in the same afternoon, there was a proclamation issued, that whoever could bring forth the party that hanged up the cat, should have twenty nobles, which reward was afterwards increased to twenty marks, but none could or would earn it.

As to the first setting up of this gallows in Cheapside, we may observe, that after the sermon of the bishop of Winchester before the queen, for the execution of Wyat's soldiers, immediately on the 13th of February, there were set up a great number of gallows in different places of the city, namely, two in Cheapside, one at Leaden-hall, one at Billingsgate, one at St. Magnus church, one in Smithfield, one in Fleet-street, four in Southwark, one at Aldgate, one at Bishopsgate, one at Aldersgate, one at Newgate, one at Ludgate, one at St. James's Park Corner, one at Cripplegate all which gibbets and gallows, to the number of twenty, remained there from the 13th of February till the 4th of June, and then at the coming in of King Philip were taken down.

On the 11th of April Sir Thomas Wyat was beheaded and quartered at the Tower-hill, where he uttered these words touching the lady Elizabeth and the earl of Devonshire "Concerning," said he, "what I have said of others in my examination, to charge any others as partakers of my doings, I accuse neither my lady Elizabeth's grace, nor my lord of Devonshire. I cannot accuse them, neither am I able to say, that to my knowledge they knew anything of my rising." And when Doctor Weston told him, that his confession was otherwise before the council, he answered, "That which I said then, I said; but that which I say now, is true."

Concerning the condemnation of Thomas, archbishop of Canterbury, of Doctor Ridley, and Master Latimer, which took place on the 20th of April, we have already said enough.

On Friday the 27th of April, Lord Thomas Gray, the late duke of Suffolk's brother, was beheaded at Tower-hill.

In the month of May it was given out that a solemn disputation should be held at Cambridge between Bradford, Sanders, Rogers, and others of that side, and the doctors of both the universities on the other side, as had been in Oxford before. Upon this the godly preachers who were in prison having word of it, although they were destitute of their books, neither were ignorant of the purpose of the adversaries, and how the cause was prejudiced, also how the disputations were confusedly handled at Oxford; nevertheless they resolved not to refuse the offer of disputation, provided they might be quietly heard, and therefore wisely pondering the matter with themselves, by a public consent directed out of prison a declaration of their mind by writing, on the 8th of May. First, as touching the disputation, although they knew that they should do no good, as all things were determined beforehand, yet they would not deny to dispute, provided the disputation might be either before the queen, or before the council, or before either houses of parliament, or else that they might dispute by writing · for if the matter were brought to the doctors, they had sufficient proof, they said, by the experience of Oxford, that little good would be done at Cambridge; and so declaring the faith and doctrine of their religion and exhorting the people to submit themselves with all patience and humility to the higher powers, they appealed from them as their judges.

A Copy of a Declaration drawn up and sent out of Prison by Bradford, Sanders, and other godly Preachers, concerning their Disputation, and the Doctrine of their Religion.

" Because we hear that it is determined of the magistrates, and such as are in authority, especially of the clergy, to send us speedily out of the prisons of the King's Bench, the Fleet, the Marshalsea, and Newgate, where we are at present, and some of us have been for a long time, not as rebels, traitors, seditious persons, thieves, or transgressors of any laws of this realm, inhibitions, proclamations, or commandments of the queen's highness, or of any of the council's (God's name be praised therefore), but only for the conscience we have to God, and his most holy word and truth, upon most certain knowledge · because, we say, we hear that it is determined, that we shall be sent to one of the universities of Cambridge or Oxford, there to dispute with such as are appointed : as we purpose not to dispute otherwise than by writing, except it may be before the queen's highness and her council, or before the parliament-houses; and therefore perchance it will be rumoured abroad, that we are not able to maintain, by the truth of God's word, and the consent of the true and catholic church of Christ, the doctrine we have generally and severally taught, and some of us have written and set forth, by which the godly and simple may be offended, and somewhat weakened, we have thought it our bounden duty now, whilst we may, by writing to publish and notify the causes why we will n t dispute otherwise than is above said, to prevent the offence which might come thereby

" 1 Because it is evidently known to the whole world, that the determinations of both the universities in matters of religion, especially wherein we should dispute, are directly against God's word yea, against their own determinations in the time of our late sovereign lord and most godly prince, King Edward and further it is known they are our open enemies, and have already condemned our causes, before any disputation had of the same.

" 2. Because the prelates and clergy do not seek either us or the truth, but our destruction and their glory. For if they had sought us (as charity requires then they would have called us forth before their laws were so made, that frankly and without peril we might have spoken our consciences. Again, if they had sought for the truth, they would not have concluded controversies before they had been disputed; so that it easily appears, that they seek their own glory and our destruction, and not us and the truth and therefore we have good cause to refuse disputation, as a thing which shall not further prevail than to the setting forth of their glory, and the suppression of the truth.

" 3 Because the censors and judges (as we hear who they be are manifest enemies to the truth, and what is worse, obstinate enemies, before whom pearls are not to be cast, by the commandment of our Saviour Jesus Christ, and by his own example. That they are such, their doings of late at Oxford, and in the convocation house in October last, most evidently prove

" 4. Because some of us have been in prison these eight or nine months, where we have had no books, no paper, no pen, no ink, or convenient place for study, we think we should do wrong, thus suddenly to descend into disputation with them, who may allege, as they chose, the fathers and their testimonies, because our memories have not that which we have read, so readily, as to reprove, when they shall report and wrest the authors to their purpose, or to bring forth what we may have there for our advantage.

" 5. Because in disputation we shall not be permitted to prosecute our arguments, but be stopt when we should speak, one saying this, another that, the third his mind, &c. As was done to the godly learned fathers, especially Doctor Ridley, at Oxford, who was not permitted to declare his mind and meaning of the propositions, and had oftentimes half a dozen at once speaking against him, always preventing him from prosecuting his argument, and answering accordingly we will not speak of the hissing scoffing and taunting, which notoriously then was used. If in this sort, and much worse, they handled these fathers, much m re will they be shamelessly bold with us, if we should enter into disputation with them

" 6 Because the notaries that shall receive and write the disputations will be of their appointment and such as either do not, or dare not, favour the truth, and therefore must write either to please them, or else they themselves the censors and judges we mean , at their pleasure will put to, and take from that which is written by the notaries; who cannot, or must not have in their custody that which they write, longer than the disputation endureth, as their doings at Oxford declare. No copy nor scroll could any man have by their good will. For the censors and judges will have all delivered into their hands. Yea, if any man was seen there to write, as the report is, the same man was sent for, and his writings taken from him so must the disputation serve only for the glory, not of God, but of the enemies of his truth.

" For these causes we all think it so necessary not to dispute with them ; as, if we did dispute, we should do that which they desire and purposely seek, to promote the kingdom of antichrist, and to suppress (as much as may be) the truth. We will not speak of the offence that might come to the godly, when they should hear, by the report of our enemies, our answers and arguments framed you may be sure) for their fantasies to the slandering of the truth.

" Therefore we publish, and by this writing notify to the whole congregation and church f England, that for these causes we will not dispute with them, otherwise than with the pen, unless it be before the queen s highness and her council, or before the houses of the parliament. If they will write we will answer, and by writing confirm and prove out of the infallible truth, even the very word of God, and by the testimony of the good and most ancient fathers in Christ's church this our faith and every piece thereof, which hereafter we, collectively, do write and send abroad purposely, that our good brethren and sisters in the Lord may know it · and to seal up the same, we are ready, through God's help and grace to give our lives to the halter or fire, or otherwise, as God shall appoint humbly requiring, and in the bowels of our Saviour Jesus Christ beseeching, all that fear God, to behave themselves as obedient subjects to the queen's highness and the superior powers, which are ordained of God under her, rather after our example to give their heads to the block, than in any point to rebel, or once to mutter against the Lord's anointed, we mean our sovereign lady Queen Mary, into whose heart we beseech the Lord of mercy plentifully to pour the wisdom and grace of his Holy Spirit, now and for ever, Amen.

" 1. We confess and believe all the canonical books of the Old Testament, and all the books of the New Testament, to be the very true word of God, and to be written by the inspiration of the Holy Ghost, and are therefore to be heard accordingly, as the judge in all controversies and matters of religion.

" 2. We confess and believe that the catholic church, which is the spouse of Christ, as a most obedient and loving wife, doth embrace and follow the doctrine of these books in all matters of religion, and therefore she is to be heard accordingly, so that those who will not hear this church thus following and obeying the word of her husband, we account as heretics and schismatics, according to this saying, ' If he will not hear the church, let him be to thee as a heathen.'

" 3. We believe and confess all the articles of faith and doctrine set forth in the symbol of the apostles, which we commonly call the creed and in the symbols of the councils of Nice, kept A.D. 325, of Constantinople, A.D 381, of Ephesus kept A.D 431 ; of Chalcedon, kept A.D. 451, of Toledo, first and fourth. Also in the symbols of Athanasius, Irenæus, Tertullian, and of Damascenus, who died about the year 760, we confess and believe we say) the doctrine of the symbols generally and particularly, so that whosoever doth otherwise, we hold the same to err from the truth.

" 4. We believe and confess concerning justification, that as it comes only from God's mercy through Christ, so it is perceived and had by none, who are of years of discretion, otherwise than by faith only : which faith is not an opinion, but a certain persuasion wrought by the Holy Ghost in the mind and heart of man, whereby as the mind is illuminated, so the heart is inclined to submit itself to the will of God unfeignedly, and so shews forth an inherent righteousness, which is to be discerned in the article of justification, from the righteousness which God endues us withal, justifying us, although inseparably they go together. And this we do not for curiosity or contention's sake, but for conscience's sake, that it might be quiet, which it can never be, if we confound without distinction forgiveness of sins, and Christ's righteousness imputed to us, with regeneration and inherent righteousness. By this we disallow the papistical doctrine of free will, of works of supererogation, of merits, of the necessity of auricular confession and satisfaction towards God.

" 5. We confess and believe concerning the exterior service of God, that it ought to be according to the word of God ; and therefore in the congregation, all things public ought to be done in such a tongue as may be most to edify, and not in Latin, where the people understand not the same.

" 6. We confess and believe that God only by Christ Jesus is to be prayed unto and called upon ; and therefore we disallow invocation or prayer to saints departed this life.

" 7. We confess and believe, that as a man departs this life, so shall he be judged in the last day generally, and in the meantime is entered either into the state of the blessed for ever, or damned for ever ; and therefore is either past all help, or else needs no help of any in this life. By reason whereof we affirm purgatory, masses of the ladder of heaven, trentals, and such suffrages as the popish church obtrudes as necessary, to be the doctrine of antichrist.

" 8. We confess and believe the sacraments of Christ, which are baptism and the Lord's supper, that they ought to be ministered according to the institution of Christ, concerning the substantial parts of them ; and that they are no longer sacraments, than they are had in use, and used to the end for which they were instituted.

" And here we plainly confess, that the mutilation of

the Lord's supper, and the subtraction of the one kind from the lay people, is antichristian ; and so is the doctrine of transubstantiation of the sacramental bread and wine after the words of consecration, as they are called, also the adoration of the sacrament with honour due to God, the reservation and carrying about of the same ; also the mass as a propitiatory sacrifice for the living and dead, or a work that pleases God.

" All these we believe and confess to be antichrist's doctrine, as is the inhibition of marriage, as unlawful to any state. And we doubt not, by God's grace, but we shall be able to prove all our confessions here to be most true by the truth of God s word, and consent of the catholic church, which follows and has followed the government of God's Spirit, and the judgment of his word.

" And this through the Lord's help we will do, in disputation by word before the queen's highness and her council, either before the parliament houses, of whom we doubt not but to be indifferently heard, or else with our pens, whenever we shall be by them that have authority, required and commanded.

" In the meantime, as obedient subjects, we shall humble ourselves towards all that are in authority, and not cease to pray to God for them, that he would govern them all, generally and particularly, with the spirit of wisdom and grace. And so we heartily desire and humbly pray all men to do, in no point consenting to any kind of rebellion or sedition against our sovereign lady the queen's highness · but where they cannot obey, without disobeying God, there to submit themselves with all patience and humility to suffer, as the will and pleasure of the higher powers shall adjudge as we are ready, through the goodness of the Lord, to suffer whatever they shall adjudge us to, rather than we will consent to any doctrine contrary to this which we here confess, unless we shall be justly convinced of it, either by writing or by word, before such judges as the queen's highness and her council, or the parliament houses shall appoint. For the universities and clergy have condemned our cause already by the greater, but now by the better part, without any disputation of the same ; and therefore we most justly may and do appeal from them as our judges in this behalf except it may be in writing, that the matter may appear to all men. The Lord of mercy endue us all with the Spirit of his truth and grace of perseverance therein unto the end. Amen.

" The 8th day of May, A.D. 1554.

Robert Menaven, alias	John Wigorne.
Robert Ferrar.	Edward Crome.
Rowland Taylor.	John Rogers.
John Philpot.	Lawrence Sanders.
John Bradford.	Edmund Lawrence.
Glouc. Episcopus, alias	J P.
John Hooper	T. M.

" To these things above said, do I, Miles Coverdale, late of Exon, consent and agree, with these mine afflicted brethren, being prisoners, signed with mine own hand."

On the 19th day of May, the lady Elizabeth, sister to the queen, was brought to the Tower, and committed to the custody of Sir John Williams, afterwards lord Williams, of Tame, of whom her highness was gently and courteously treated : she afterwards was taken to Woodstock, and there committed to the keeping of Sir Henry Benifield, knight, of Oxborough, in Norfolk ; who, on the other side, both forgetting her estate and his own duty, shewed himself more hard and strict to her, than right.

On the Friday following, being the 20th of July, and St. Margaret's day, the prince of Spain landed at Southampton. The prince himself was the first that landed ; who immediately as he set foot upon the land, drew out his sword, and carried it naked in his hand a good way.

Then met him, a little without the town, the mayor of Southampton, with certain commoners, who delivered the keys of the town to the prince, who removed his sword, (naked as it was) out of his right into his left hand, and received the keys of the mayor without speaking any word, or appearance of thankfulness, and after a while, delivered the keys to the mayor again. At the town gate, the earl of Arundel and the lord Williams met him, and so he was brought to his lodging.

On the Wednesday following, being St. James's day, and the 25th of July, Philip, prince of Spain, and Mary, queen of England, were married together solemnly in the cathedral church at Winchester, by the bishop of Winchester, in the presence of a great number of noble men of both the realms. At the time of this marriage the emperor's ambassador being present, openly pronounced, that in consideration of that marriage, the emperor had granted and given unto his son the kingdom of Naples, &c.

Whereupon, on the first day of August following, there was a proclamation, that from that time forth the stile of all manner of writings should be altered, and this following should be used·

"Philip and Mary, by the grace of God, king and queen of England, France, Naples, Jerusalem, and Ireland, defenders of the faith, princes of Spain and Sicily, archdukes of Austria, dukes of Milan, Burgundy, and Brabant, Counts of Hapsburgh, Flanders, and Tyrol."

After the marriage, they removed from Winchester to other places, and by easy journeys came to Windsor Castle, where he was installed in the order of the garter, on Sunday, the 12th of August. At which time a herald took down the arms of England at Windsor, and in the place of them would have set up the arms of Spain, but he was commanded by certain lords to set them up again. From thence they both removed to Richmond, and from thence by water to London, and landed at the bishop of Winchester's house, through which they passed into Southwark park, and so to Southwark house, called Suffolk place, where they lay that night, August 17th.

The next day, being Saturday. the 18th of August, the king and queen's majesties rode from Suffolk place (accompanied with a great number, as well of noblemen as gentlemen) through the city of London to Whitehall, and at London bridge, as he entered at the draw-bridge, there was a great spectacle set up , two images, presenting two giants, one named Corineus, and the other Gogmagog, holding between them certain Latin verses, which for their vain ostentation of flattery I pass over.

And as they rode over the bridge, there was a number of ordnance shot off at the Tower, such as by old men's report the like had not been heard or seen for a hundred years past.

From London Bridge they passed the Conduit in Gracechurch-street, which was finely painted, with among other things, the nine Worthies, whereof King Henry the Eighth was one. He was painted in armour, having in one hand a sword, and in the other a book, upon which was written *Verbum Dei*, i. e *The word of God*, delivering the book to his son King Edward, who was painted in a corner by him.

But upon this there was no small contention raised · for the bishop of Winchester, lord chancellor, sent for the painter, and not only called him knave for painting a book in King Henry's hand, and especially for writing on it *Verbum Dei*, but also rank traitor and villain, saying to him that he should rather have put the book into the queen's hand (who was also painted there), for she had reformed the church and religion, with other things according to the pure and sincere word of God.

The painter answered and said, that if he had known that was the matter for which his lordship had sent for him, he could have remedied it, and not have troubled his lordship.

The bishop answered and said, that it was the queen's majesty's will and command that he should send for him · and so commanding him to wipe out the book and *Verbum Dei* too, he sent him home. So the painter departed; but fearing lest he should leave some part either of the book, or of *Verbum Dei* in King Henry's hand; he wiped away a piece of his fingers with it !

I pass over other pageants and pastimes, displayed to him in passing through London, with the flattering

verses set up in Latin, in which were blazoned out in one place the five Philips, as the five worthies of the world Philip of Macedon, Philip the emperor, Philip the bold, Philip the good, Philip of Spain and king of England.

In another poesy, King Philip was represented by an image of Orpheus, and all English people likened to brute and savage beasts following Orpheus' harp, and dancing after King Philip's pipe !

But one thing I cannot pass over touching the young flourishing shrine, newly set up at this time to welcome King Philip into St Paul's church.

Bonner was there in his royalty, and all his prebendaries about him in St. Paul's choir, the shrine laid along upon the pavements, and also the doors of St. Paul's being shut, the bishop with others said and sung divers prayers by it· that being done, they anointed it with oil in several places, and after the anointing, crept unto it, and kissed it.

After that they took it, and set it in its old accustomed place, and all the while the whole choir sang *Te Deum*, and when that was ended, they rang the bells, not only for joy, but also for the notable and great feat they had done.

Not long after this, a merry fellow came into St. Paul's and spied the shrine with Mary and John newly set up; among a great assemblage of people, he made a low courtesy to it, and said, " Sir, your mastership is welcome to town. I had thought to have talked further with your mastership, but that ye are here clothed in the queen's colours. I hope that ye are but a summer's bird, as ye be dressed in white and green."

The prince being in the church of St Paul's, after Doctor Harpsfield had finished his oration in Latin, set forward through Fleet-street, and so came to Whitehall, where he with the queen remained four days, and from thence removed to Richmond.

After this, all the lords had leave to depart into their counties, with commandment to bring all their arms and artillery into the Tower of London. There remained no English lord at the court, but the bishop of Winchester. From Richmond they removed to Hampton Court, where the hall door within the court was continually shut, so that no man might enter, unless his errand was first known, which seemed strange to Englishmen, that had not been used thereto.

About the eighth day of September, Bishop Bonner began his visitation, who charged six men in every parish to enquire (according to their oath) and to present before him, the day after St. Matthew's day, being the twenty-third of September, all such persons as either had or should offend in any of his articles, which he had set forth to the number of thirty-seven.

On the seventeenth of September, there was a proclamation in London, that all vagabonds and masterless men, as well strangers as Englishmen, should depart the city within five days; and strictly charging all innholders, victuallers, taverners, and alehouse keepers, with all others that sell victuals, that they (after the said five days should not sell any meat, drink, or any kind of victual to any servingman what-ever, unless he brought a testimonial from his master to declare whose servant he was, and were in continual household with his master, upon pain to run in danger of the law, if they offended

Upon *Corpus Christi* day, the procession being made in Smithfield, where the priest with his box went under the canopy, by chance there came a simple man, named John Street, who having some haste in his business, and finding no other way to pass through, went under the canopy by the priest. The poor man, being forthwith apprehended, was had to prison, the priest accusing him to the council, as if he had come to slay him. Then he was taken to Newgate, where he was cast into a dungeon, chained to a post, cruelly and miserably handled, and so extremely dealt with, that being but simple before, he was now frightened out of his wits altogether, and so was taken to Bedlam.

The bishop passing through the county of Essex, on his visitation, and being attended with divers worshipful of the shire (for so they were commanded) arrived at Stertford in Hertfordshire, where he rested certain days, solacing himself after that painful peregrination with no small feasting and banqueting, with his attendants, at the house of one Parsons his nephew, whose wife he commonly called his fair niece, and fair she was indeed); he took there great pleasure to hear her play upon the virginals (wherein she excelled), insomuch that every dinner (sitting by his side) she arose and played three several times at his request, for his good and spiritual devotion towards her. He next proceeded in his popish visitation towards Hadham, his own house and parish, not more than two miles from Stertford, the bells being there most solemnly rung out, as in all other places where he passed. At length drawing near to Hadham, when he heard no stirring in honour of his holiness, he grew into some choler, and the nearer he approached, the hotter was his fit: and the quieter the bells were, the unquieter was his mood. Thus he rode on, chafing and fuming with himself. " What means," saith he, " that knave the clerk, that he rings not? and the parson that he meets me not?" with sundry other furious words There this patient prelate, coming to the town, alighted, calling for the key of the church, which was then all unready, because as they pretended) he had anticipated his time by two hours, upon this he grew from choler to melancholy, so that no man would willingly deal with him to qualify his humour. At last, the church door being opened, the bishop entered, and finding no sacrament hanging up, nor shrine-loft decked after the popish precept (which had commanded about the same time a well favoured shrine, and of tall stature, to be set up universally in all churches) curtailed his small devotions, and fell from all choler and melancholy to flat madness, swearing and raging with an oath or two, that in his own church, where he hoped to have seen best order, he found most disorder, to his honour's most heavy discomfort, as he said, calling the parson (whose name was Doctor Bricket, " Knave, and heretic" Who there humbled himself, and yielded, as it were, to his fault, saying, He was sorry his lordship was come before he and his parish looked for him, and therefore could not do their duties to receive him accordingly · and as for those things which were wanted, he trusted in a short time he should compass that, which hitherto he could not bring about. Therefore if it pleased his lordship to come to his poor house where dinner was prepared) he would satisfy him in those things which his lordship thought amiss. Yet this reasonable answer could not satisfy nor assuage his passion. For the prelate utterly defied him and his cheer, commanding him out of his sight, saying, " Before God, thou art a knave; avaunt, heretic!" and then thrusting or striking at him, his hand gave Sir Thomas Josselin, knight, (who stood next the bishop) a good blow full upon the ear: who was somewhat astonished, " What means your lordship? have you been trained in Will Sommers' school, to strike him that stands next you?"

Then Master Fecknam, dean of St. Paul's, seeing the bishop still in this bitter rage, said, " O Master Josselin, you must bear with my lord, for truly his long imprisonment in the Marshalsea, and the misusing of him there hath altered him, that in these passions he is not ruler of himself, nor boots it any man to give him counsel until his heat be past, and then assure yourself, Master Josselin, my lord will be sorry for those abuses that now he cannot see in himself." He merily replied and said, " So it seems, Master Fecknam, now that he is come forth out of the Marshalsea, he is ready to go to Bedlam." At which merry conceit some laughed, and more smiled, because the nail was so truly hit upon the head. The bishop, nothing abashed at his own folly, gave a deaf ear.

After this worthy combat thus finished and achieved, this martial prelate presently betook him to his horse again, although he had purposed to tarry at Hadham three or four days, and so had made provision in his own house, but leaving his dinner he rode that night with a small company to Ware, where he was not looked for till three days after, to the great wonder of all the country, why he so anticipated his day.

At this hasty posting away of this bishop his whole train of attendants left him Also his doctors and chaplains, a few excepted, tarried behind, and dined at Doctor Bricket's, as merrily, as he rode towards Ware all chaffingly.

A Story of a Shrine set up in Lancashire.

We have mentioned the precept which commanded in every parish a shrine or image to be erected, both well-favoured and of a tall stature. This brings to mind what happened in a town in Lancashire called Cockerham, where the parishioners and churchwardens, having a like charge for the erecting of an image in their parish church, had made their bargain and agreed upon a price with one that could cunningly carve and paint such idols, for the framing of their shrine; who, according to his promise, made them one, and set it up in their church This done, he demanded his money; but they, disliking his workmanship, refused to pay him; whereupon he arrested them, and the matter was brought before the mayor of Lancaster, who was a very meet man for such a purpose, and an old favourer of the gospel, which was rare in that country. Then the carver began to declare how they covenanted with him for the making of a shrine and image, ready carved and set up in their church, which he according to his promise had done, and now demanding his money, they refused to pay him. " Is this true," quoth the mayor to the wardens? " Yea, sir," said they. " And why do you not pay the poor man his due " said he. " And if it please you, master mayor," said they, " because the one we had before was a well-favoured man, and he promised to make us such another but this that he has set us up now is the worst-favoured thing that ever you set your eyes on, gaping and grinning in such sort, that none of our children dare once look him in the face, or come near him " The mayor, thinking that it was good enough for that purpose if it had been worse; " My masters," said he, " however it may please you, the poor man's labour hath been never the less, and it is a pity that he should have any hindrance or loss thereby. Therefore I will tell you what you shall do , pay him the money you promised him, and go your ways home and look on it, and if it will not serve for a god, make no more to do, but clap a pair of horns on his head, and so he will make an excellent devil." This the parishioners took well, the poor man had his money, and many laughed well at it, but so did not the Babylonish priests.

This mayor above-mentioned continued a protestant almost fifty years, and was the only reliever of March the martyr, whose history follows hereafter, with meat, drink, and lodging, while he lay in Lancaster castle, for the space of three quarters of a year, before he was had to Chester to be burned, &c.

About this time there came a precept or mandate from Bonner bishop of London, to all bishops and curates within his diocese, for the abolishing of such scriptures and writings as had been painted on church walls in king Edward's days. The copy of which precept or mandate here we thought good to express, that the world might see the wicked proceedings of their impious zeal, or rather their malicious rage against the Lord and his word, and against the edifying of christian people; by which it might appear, by this blotting out of scripture, not only how blasphemously they spoke against the holy scriptures of God, but also how studiously they sought by all manner of means to keep the people still in ignorance.

A Mandate of Bonner, Bishop of London, to abolish the Scriptures and Writings painted upon the Church Walls

" Edmund, by God's permission bishop of London, to all and every the parsons, vicars, clerks, and lettered within the parish of Hadham, or within the precinct of our diocese of London, wheresoever being, sendeth greeting, grace and benediction.

"Because some children of iniquity, given up to carnal desires and novelties, have by many ways enterprised to banish the ancient manners and orders of the church, and to bring in and establish sects and heresies; taking from thence the picture of Christ, and many things besides instituted and observed of ancient time laudably in the same, placing in the room thereof such things as in such a place it behoved them not to do, and also have procured as a stay to their heresies, as they thought, certain scriptures wrongly applied to be painted upon the church walls, all which persons tend chiefly to this end; that they might uphold the liberty of the flesh, and marriage of the priests, and destroy, as much as lay in them, the reverent sacrament of the altar, and might extinguish and enervate holydays, fasting days, and other laudable discipline of the catholic church, opening a window to all vices, and utterly closing up the way to virtue. Wherefore we being moved with a christian zeal, judging that the premises are not to be long suffered, do for the discharge of our duty, commit unto you jointly and severally, and by the tenor hereof do straightly charge and command you, that at the receipt hereof, with all speed convenient, you do warn, or cause to be warned, first, second, and third time, and peremptorily, all and singular churchwardens and parishioners whosoever within our foresaid diocese of London, wheresoever any such scriptures or paintings have been attempted, that they abolish and extinguish such manner of scriptures, so that by no means they be either read or seen, and therein to proceed moreover as they shall see good and laudable in this behalf. And if after the said monition, the said churchwardens and parishioners shall be found remiss or negligent, or culpable, then you jointly and severally shall see the aforesaid scriptures to be razed, abolished and extinguished forthwith citing all and singular those churchwardens and parishioners (whom we also for the same do cite here by the tenor hereof) that all and singular the churchwardens and parishioners being slack and negligent, culpable therein, shall appear before us, our vicar-general and principal official, or our commissary special in our cathedral church of St. Paul at London, in the consistory there, at the hour appointed for the same, the sixth day next after their citation, if it be a court-day, or else at the next court-day after ensuing, where either we or our official or commissary shall sit · there to say and allege for themselves some reasonable cause, if they have or can tell of any, why they ought not to be excommunicated, or otherwise punished for their such negligence, slackness, and fault, to say and to allege, and further to do and receive, as law and reason requireth. And what you have done in the premises, do you certify us, or our vicar, principal official, or our commissary, diligently and duly in all things, and through all things, or let him among you thus certify us, who hath taken upon him to execute this mandate. In witness whereof we have set our seals to these presents.—Dated in the bishop's palace at London, the 25th day of the month of October, A.D. 1554. and of our translation the 16th."

In the university of Cambridge, and also of Oxford, by reason of the bringing in of these things, and especially for the alteration of religion, many wise and learned men departed the universities : of whom, some of their own accord gave over, some were thrust out of their fellowships, some were miserably handled : insomuch that in Cambridge, in the college of St. John, there were four-and-twenty places void together, in whose rooms were taken in four-and-twenty others, who neither in virtue nor in religion seemed equal to their predecessors.

About the fifth of October, and within a fortnight following, several householders, and servants and apprentices were apprehended, and committed to prison, for having and selling certain books sent into England by the preachers that fled into Germany and other countries : within one fortnight there were little less than threescore imprisoned for this matter.

On Sunday the fourth of November, five priests did penance at St. Paul's Cross, who were content to put away their wives. Every one of them had a taper in his hand, and a rod, wherewith the preacher did strike them.

On Friday the ninth of November, Barlow late bishop of Bath, and Master Cardmaker, were brought before the council in the Star Chamber, and were committed to the Fleet.

Cardinal Pole landed at Dover upon the 21st of Nov., on which day one act passed in the parliament for his restitution in blood, utterly repealing as false and most slanderous that act made against him in Henry VIII 's time; and on the next day, the king and the queen came both to the parliament-house to give their royal assent, and to establish this act.

On Saturday the 24th of Nov., the cardinal came by water to London, and so to Lambeth-house

On the Wednesday following, there was a general procession in St. Paul's for joy that the queen was likely to become a mother, as it was declared in a letter sent from the council to the bishop of London.

The same day were present at this procession ten bishops, with all the prebendaries of St. Paul's, and also the lord mayor with the aldermen, and a great number of commons of the city in their best array. The copy of the council's letter here follows :

Copy of a Letter from the Council to Edmund Bonner, Bishop of London, concerning Queen Mary's pregnancy.

"After our hearty commendations unto your good lordship · whereas it hath pleased Almighty God amongst other his infinite benefits of late most graciously poured upon us and this whole realm, to extend his benediction upon the queen's majesty in such sort, as she is conceived and quick of child; whereby (her majesty being our natural liege lady, queen, and undoubted inheritor of this imperial crown) good hope of certain succession in the crown is given unto us, and consequently the great calamities, which for want of such succession might otherwise have fallen upon us and our posterity, shall by God's grace be well avoided, if we thankfully acknowledge this benefit of Almighty God, endeavouring ourselves with earnest repentance to thank, honour, and serve him as we are most bounden. These are not only to advertise you of these good news, to be by you published in all places within your diocese, but also to pray and require you, that both yourselves do give God thanks with us for this especial grace, and also give order that thanks may be openly given by singing of *Te Deum* in all the churches within your said diocese; and that likewise all priests and other ecclesiastical ministers, in their masses, and other divine services, may continually pray to Almighty God so to extend his holy hand over her majesty, the king's highness, and this whole realm, as that this thing, being by his omnipotent power graciously thus begun, may by the same be well continued, and brought to good effect, to the glory of his name. Whereunto, albeit we doubt not you would of yourself have had special regard without these our letters, yet for the earnest desire we have to have this thing done out of hand, and diligently continued, we have also written these our letters, to put you in remembrance; and so bid your lordship most heartily well to fare.

"From Westminster the 27th of November, 1554."

Consequent upon this, there were certain prayers commanded to be publicly offered up for the safe delivery of the queen, and for the child to be a male, comely and well-favoured—so general was the expectation of a child.

The same day cardinal Pole came to the parliament-house, which was then kept in the great chamber of the court at Whitehall, for the queen was then sick, and could not go abroad : where the king and the queen's majesty, sitting under the cloth of state, and the cardinal sitting on the right hand, with all the other estates of parliament being present, the bishop of Winchester being lord chancellor, began in this manner .

"My lords of the upper house, and you, my masters of the nether house, here is present the right reverend father in God my lord cardinal Pole, come from the apostolic see of Rome, as ambassador to the king and queen's majesties, upon one of the weightiest causes that ever happened in this realm, and which pertaineth to the glory of God, and your universal benefit. The which embassage their majesties' pleasure is to be signified unto you all by his own mouth, trusting that you will receive and accept it in as benevolent and thankfulwise as their highnesses have done, and that you will give an attentive and inclinable ear unto him."

When the lord chancellor had ended, the cardinal began his oration, wherein he declared the causes of his coming, and what were his desires and requests. Setting forth how he possessed power from the pope to absolve them all of their sins.

The next day the three estates assembled again in the great chamber of the court at Westminster; where the king and queen's majesties and the cardinal being present, they did exhibit (all kneeling on their knees) a supplication to their highnesses, the tenor whereof ensueth.

"We, the lords spiritual and temporal, and the commons in this present parliament assembled, representing the whole body of the realm of England and dominions of the same, in our own names particularly, and also of the said body universally, in this supplication directed to your majesties with most humble suit, that it may by your gracious intercession and means, be exhibited to the most reverend father in God, the lord cardinal Pole, legate, sent specially here by our most holy father pope Julius III. and the see apostolic of Rome, do declare ourselves very sorry and repentant for the schism and disobedience committed in this realm and dominions of the same, against the said see apostolic, either by making, agreeing, or executing any laws, ordinances, or commandments against the supremacy of the said see, or otherwise doing or speaking that might impugn the same; offering ourselves, and promising by this our supplication, that for a token and knowledge of our said repentance, we be, and shall be always ready, under and with the authority of your majesties, to the uttermost of our power, to do that which shall be in us for the abrogation and repealing of the said laws and ordinances in this present parliament; as well for ourselves, as for the whole body whom we represent.

"Whereupon we most humbly beseech your majesties, as persons undefiled in the offence of this body towards the said see, which nevertheless God by his providence hath made subject unto your majesties, so to set forth this our most humble suit, that we may obtain from the see apostolic, by the said most reverend father, as well particularly as universally, absolution, release, and discharge from all danger of such censures and sentences, as by the laws of the church we have fallen in, and that we may as children repentant, be received into the bosom and unity of Christ's church, so as this noble realm, with all the members thereof, may in unity and perfect obedience to the see apostolic, and pope for the time being, serve God and your majesties, to the furtherance and advancement of his honour and glory, Amen."

The supplication having been read, the king and queen delivered it to the cardinal, who received it most gladly from their majesties; and after he had in few words given thanks to God, and declared what great cause he had to rejoice that his coming from Rome into England had taken most happy success; he, by the pope's authority, then gave them this absolution.

An Absolution pronounced by Cardinal Pole to the whole Parliament of England, in the Presence of the King and Queen.

"Our Lord Jesus Christ, who, with his most precious blood has redeemed and washed us from all our sins and iniquities, that he might purchase to himself a glorious spouse without spot or wrinkle, and whom the Father hath appointed head over all his church, he by his mercy absolve you. And we, by apostolic authority given unto us (by the most holy lord Pope Julius the third, his vicegerent in earth) do absolve and deliver you, and every of you, with the whole realm and dominions thereof, from all heresy and schism, and from all and every judgment, censures, and pains, for that cause incurred; and also we do restore you again unto the unity of our mother the holy church, as in our letters more plainly it shall appear in the name of the Father, of the Son, and of the Holy Ghost."

When all this was done, they went into the chapel, and there singing *Te Deum*, with great solemnity, declared the joy and gladness that was pretended for this reconciliation.

The report of this was, with great speed, sent unto Rome; as well by the king's and the cardinal's letters, as otherwise. Whereupon the pope caused processions to be made at Rome, and thanks to be given to God with great joy for the conversion of England to his church; and praising the cardinal's diligence, and the devotion of the king and queen, on Christmas eve, by his bulls he set forth a general pardon to all such as did truly rejoice for the same.

About this time a messenger was sent from the parliament to the pope, to desire him to confirm and establish the sale of the abbey-lands and chantry-lands, for the lords and the parliament would grant nothing in favour of the pope till their purchases of those lands were fully confirmed.

On Thursday the 6th of December, the whole convocation, both bishops and others, were sent for to Lambeth to the cardinal, who forgave them all their perjuries, schisms, and heresies, and they all there kneeled down and received his absolution, and after an exhortation and gratulation for their conversion to the catholic church by the cardinal, they departed.

On new-year's day, A.D. 1555, in the evening, certain honest men and women of the city, to the number of thirty, and a minister with them named Master Rose, were taken as they were in a house in Bow-churchyard at the communion, and all committed to prison.

As to the taking of this Master Rose and his fellows, word was brought to Master Hooper, then in the Fleet. Upon which Master Hooper sent a letter of consolation to the prisoners.

A Letter of Consolation sent from Master Hooper to the Godly Brethren taken in Bow-Church-yard in Prayer.

"The grace, favour, consolation, and aid of the Holy Ghost, be with you now and ever. So be it

"Dearly beloved in the Lord, ever since your imprisonment I have been marvellously moved with great affections and passions, as well of mirth and gladness, as of heaviness and sorrow. Of gladness in this, that I perceived how ye be bent and given to prayer and invocation of God's help in these dark and wicked proceedings of men against God's glory. I have been sorry to perceive the malice and wickedness of men to be so cruel, devilish, and tyrannical to persecute the people of God for serving of God, saying and hearing of the holy psalms, and the word of eternal life. These cruel doings do declare, that the papists' church is more bloody and tyrannical than ever was the sword of the heathens and gentiles.

"When I heard of your arrest, and what ye were doing, wherefore, and by whom ye were taken, I remembered how the Christians in the primitive church were used by the cruelty of unchristened heathens, in the time of Trajan the emperor, about 77 years after Christ's ascension into heaven: and how the Christians were persecuted very sorely as though they had been traitors and movers of sedition. Whereupon the gentle emperor Trajan required to know the true cause of Christian men's trouble. A very learned man named Pliny wrote unto him, and said: ' It was because the Christians said certain psalms before day unto one called Christ, whom they worshipped for God.' When Trajan the emperor understood it was for nothing but for conscience and religion, he caused by his commandments everywhere, that no man should be persecuted for serving God. But the pope and his church have cast you into prison, being taken even doing the work of God, and one of the excellentest works that is required of christian men that is, to wit, whilst ye were in prayer, and not in such wicked and superstitious prayers as the papists use, but in the same prayer that Christ hath taught you to pray. And in his name only ye gave God thanks for that ye have received, and for his sake ye asked for such things as ye want. O, glad may ye be that ever ye were born, to be apprehended whilst ye were so virtuously occupied! Blessed be they that suffer for righteousness' sake. For if God had suffered them that took your bodies, then to have taken your life also, now had you been following the Lamb in perpetual joys, away from the company and assembly of wicked men. But the Lord would not have you suddenly so to depart, but reserveth you, gloriously to speak and maintain his truth to the world.

"Be ye not careful what ye shall say, for God will go out and in with you, and will be present in your hearts and in your mouths to speak his wisdom, although it seemeth foolishness to the world. He that hath begun this good work in you, continue you in the same unto the end; and pray unto him that ye may fear him only, who hath power to kill both body and soul, and to cast them into hell-fire. Be of good comfort. All the hairs of your head are numbered, and there is not one of them can perish, except your heavenly Father suffer it to perish. Now ye are in the field, and placed in the fore-front of Christ's battle. Doubtless it is a singular favour of God, and a special love of him towards you, to give you this forward station and pre-eminence, as a sign that he trusteth you before others of his people Wherefore, dear brethren and sisters, continually fight this fight of the Lord. Your cause is most just and godly, ye stand for the true Christ (who is after the flesh in heaven), and for this true religion and honour, which is amply, fully, sufficiently, and abundantly contained in the holy Testament, sealed with Christ's own blood. How much are ye bound to God who puts you in trust with so holy and just a cause!

"Remember what lookers-on you have to see and behold you in your fight,—God and all his angels, who are ready always to take you up into heaven, if ye be slain in his fight. Also you have standing at your backs all the multitude of the faithful, who shall take courage, strength, and desire to follow such noble and valiant christians as you are. Be not afraid of your adversaries · for he that is in you is stronger than he that is in them. Shrink not, although it be pain to you; your pains are not now so great as hereafter your joys shall be. Read the comfortable chapters to the Romans viii 10, 15, Hebrews xi. 12, and upon your knees thank God that ever ye were accounted worthy to suffer anything for his name's sake. Read the second chapter of St. Luke's gospel, and there you shall see how the shepherds that watched their sheep all night, as soon as they heard that Christ was born at Bethlehem, by and by went to see him. They did not reason nor debate with themselves, who should keep the wolf from the sheep in the mean time, but did as they were commanded, and committed their sheep unto him, whose pleasure they obeyed. So let us do now we are called; commit all other things to him that calleth us. He will take heed that all things shall be well. He will help the husband, he will comfort the wife, he will guide the servants, he will keep the house, he will preserve the goods; yea, rather than it should be undone, he will wash the dishes, and rock the cradle. Cast therefore all your care upon God, for he careth for you.

"Besides this, you may perceive by your imprisonment, that your adversaries' weapons against you are nothing but flesh, blood, and tyranny. For if they were able, they would maintain their wicked religion by God's word: but for lack of that, they would violently compel us as they cannot by holy scripture persuade, because the holy word of God, and all Christ's doings, are contrary unto them. I pray you, pray for me, and I will pray for you And although we be asunder after the world, yet in Christ, I trust, for ever joining in the spirit, and so shall meet in the palace of the heavenly joys, after this short and transitory life is ended. God's peace be with you. Amen. The 14th of January, 1555."

On the Tuesday following, the 22nd of January, all the preachers that were in prison were called before the bishop of Winchester, lord chancellor, and others; after being asked whether they would recant and enjoy the queen's pardon, or else stand to what they had taught; they all answered, that they would stand to what they had taught, and were committed to closer prison than before, with charge that none should be allowed to speak with them.

On the 25th there was a general and solemn procession through London, to give God thanks for their conversion to the Romish church. To set out their glorious pomp, there were ninety crosses, a hundred and sixty priests and clerks, who had every one of them copes upon their backs, singing very lustily. There followed also eight bishops, and last of all came Bonner, the bishop of London, carrying the popish pix, containing the host, under a canopy.

Besides, there were also present the mayor, aldermen, and all the livery, the king also, and the cardinal, came to St. Paul's Church on the same day. After the procession there was also commandment given to make bonfires at night.

On the Monday following, being the 28th of January, the bishop of Winchester, and the other bishops, had commission from the cardinal to sit upon, and order, according to the laws, all such preachers and heretics (as they termed them) as were in prison, and according to this commission on the same day the bishop of Winchester and the other bishops, with certain of the council, called before them these three, Master Hooper, Master Rogers, and Master Cardmaker, who were brought thither by the sheriffs; after some communication they were committed to prison till the next day, but Cardmaker submitted himself to them.

On the 29th, Hooper, Rogers, Taylor, and Bradford were brought before them, when sentence of excommunication and judgment ecclesiastical was pronounced upon Hooper and Rogers, by the bishop of Winchester, who sat as judge, who drove them out of the church, according to their law and order. Taylor and Bradford were committed to prison till the next day.

On the 30th, Taylor, Crome, Bradford, Sanders, and Ferrar, sometime bishop of St. David's, were brought before the bishops, and Taylor, Sanders, and Bradford were likewise excommunicated, and sentence pronounced upon them, and so committed to the sheriffs. Crome desired two months' respite, and it was granted him; and Ferrar was again committed to prison till another time. All these men shewed themselves to be learned, as indeed they were but what avails either learning, reason, or truth itself, where will bears rule?

After the examination and condemnation of these good men and preachers, commissioners and inquisitors were sent abroad into all parts of the realm by reason whereof, a great number of most godly and true christians (especially out of Kent, Essex, Norfolk, and Suffolk) were apprehended, brought up to London, cast into prison, and afterwards most of them either consumed cruelly by fire, or else died in the prisons, and were buried on the dung-hills abroad in the fields, or in the prison.

We will, in another book, relate the tragical proceedings against the blessed martyrs and witnesses of Jesus Christ, in the bloody persecution of this time. We shall first recite a general supplication, given up in the name of the preachers lying in prison, to the king and queen during the time of the parliament.

To the king and queen's most excellent majesties, and to their most honourable and high court of parliament :—

"In most humble and lamentable wise complain unto your majesties, and to your high court of parliament, your poor desolate, and obedient subjects, H.F., T.B. P.R.S, &c. That whereas your said subjects, living under the laws of God, and of this realm, in the days of the late most noble King Edward VI., did in all things shew themselves true, faithful, and diligent subjects, according to their vocation, as well in the sincere ministering of God's most holy word, as in due obedience to the higher power, and in the daily practice of such virtues and good demeanour, as the laws of God at all times, and the statutes of the realm did then allow Your said subjects, nevertheless, contrary to all laws of justice, equity, and right, are, in a very extreme manner, not only cast into prison (where they have remained now these fifteen or sixteen months) but their livings also, their houses and possessions, their goods and books are taken from them, and they are slandered to be most heinous heretics, their enemies themselves being both witnesses, accusers, and judges, belying, slandering, and misreporting your said subjects at their pleasure; whereas your said subjects, being strictly kept in prison, cannot yet be suffered to come forth, and make answer accordingly.

"In consideration whereof, it may please your most excellent majesties, and this your high court of parliament, graciously to tender the present calamity of your said poor subjects, and to call them before your presence, granting them liberty, either by mouth, or writing in the plain English tongue, to answer before you, or before indifferent arbiters to be appointed by your majesties, unto such articles of controversy in religion as their said adversaries have already condemned them of, as of heinous heresies : provided, that all things may be done with such moderation and quiet behaviour, as becometh subjects and children of peace, and that your said subjects may have the free use of all their own books, and conference together among themselves.

"Which thing being granted, your said subjects doubt not but it shall plainly appear, that your said subjects are true and faithful christians, and neither heretics nor teachers of heresy, nor cut off from the true catholic universal church of Christ ; yea, that rather their adversaries themselves be unto your majesties as were the charmers of Egypt to Pharoah, Zedechias, and his adherents unto the king of Israel, and Barjesu to the proconsul, Sergius Paulus. And if your said subjects be not able by the testimony of Christ, his prophets, apostles, and godly fathers of his church, to prove, that the doctrine of the church, homilies, and service taught and set forth in the time of our late most godly prince and king, Edward VI., is the true doctrine of Christ's catholic church, and most agreeable to the articles of the christian faith, your said subjects offer themselves then to the most heavy punishment that it shall please your majesties to appoint.

"Wherefore for the tender mercy of God in Christ (which you look for at the day of judgment) your said poor subjects in bonds most humbly beseech your most excellent majesties, and this your high court of parliament, benignly and graciously to hear and grant this their petition, tending so greatly to the glory of God, to the edifying of his church, to the honour of your majesties, to the commendation and maintenance of justice, right, and equity, both before God and man. And your said subjects, according to their bounden duty, shall not cease to pray unto Almighty God for the gracious preservation of your most excellent majesties long to endure."

THE END OF THE TENTH BOOK.